P9-CRZ-812

GRADUATE STUDY IN PSYCHOLOGY

2006

American Psychological Association

American Psychological Association
Washington, DC

Published by
American Psychological Association
750 First Street, NE
Washington, DC 20002
www.apa.org

ISBN: 1-59147-315-2
ISSN: 0742-7220
39th edition

To order
APA Order Department
P.O. Box 92984
Washington, DC 20090-2984
Tel: (800) 374-2721, Direct: (202) 336-5510
Fax: (202) 336-5502, TDD/TTY: (202) 336-6123
Online: www.apa.org/books/
E-mail: order@apa.org

Printed in the United States of America

Contents

Foreword

This is the 39th edition of a book prepared to assist individuals interested in graduate study in psychology. The current edition provides information for more than 600 graduate departments, programs, and schools of psychology in the United States and Canada. The information was obtained from questionnaires sent to graduate departments and schools of psychology and was provided voluntarily. The American Psychological Association (APA) is not responsible for the accuracy of the information reported.

The purpose of this publication is to provide an information service, offering in one book information about the majority of graduate programs in psychology. Inclusion in this publication does not signify APA approval or endorsement of a graduate program, nor should it be assumed that a listing of a program in *Graduate Study in Psychology* means that its graduates are automatically qualified to sit for licensure as psychologists or are eligible for positions requiring a psychology degree.

However, programs listed in this publication have agreed to the following quality assurance provisions:

1. They have agreed to honor April 15 as the date allowed for graduate applicants to accept or reject an offer of admission and financial assistance for fall matriculation. This date adheres to national policy guidelines as stated by the Council of Graduate Schools and the Council of Graduate Departments of Psychology.

2. They have satisfied the following criteria. The program offers a graduate degree and is sponsored by a public or private higher education institution accredited by one of six regional accrediting bodies recognized by the U.S. Secretary of Education or, in the case of Canadian programs, the institution is publicly recognized by the Association of Universities and Colleges of Canada as a member in good standing, or the program indicates that it meets *all* of the following criteria:

   A. The graduate program, wherever it may be administratively housed, is publicly labeled as a psychology program in pertinent institutional catalogs and brochures.
   B. The psychology program stands as a recognizable, coherent organizational entity within the institution.
   C. There is an identifiable core of full-time psychology faculty.
   D. Psychologists have clear authority and primary responsibility for the academic core and specialty preparation, whether or not the program involves multiple administrative lines.
   E. There is an identifiable body of graduate students who are enrolled in the program for the attainment of the graduate degree offered.
   F. The program is an organized, integrated sequence of study designed by the psychology faculty responsible for the program.
   G. Programs leading to a doctoral degree require at least the equivalent of three full-time academic years of graduate study.
   H. Doctoral programs ensure appropriate breadth and depth of education and training in psychology as follows:

1) Methodology and history, including systematic preparation in scientific standards and responsibilities, research design and methodology, quantitative methods (e.g., statistics, psychometric methods), and historical foundations in psychology.
2) Foundations in psychology, including
   a. biological bases of behavior (e.g., physiological psychology, comparative psychology, neuropsychology, psychopharmacology);
   b. cognitive–affective bases of behavior (e.g., learning, memory, perception, cognition, thinking, motivation, emotion);
   c. social bases of behavior (e.g., social psychology; cultural, ethnic, and group processes; sex roles; organizational behavior); and
   d. individual differences (e.g., personality theory, human development, individual differences, abnormal psychology, psychology of women, psychology of the handicapped, psychology of the minority experience).
3) Additional preparation in the program's area of specialization, to include
   a. knowledge and application of ethical principles and guidelines and standards as may apply to scientific and professional practice activities;
   b. supervised practicum and/or laboratory experiences appropriate to the area of practice, teaching, or research in psychology; and
   c. advanced preparation appropriate to the area of specialization.

This publication may not answer all questions you have about graduate education in psychology. Some questions you may want to direct to particular graduate departments, programs, or schools of psychology. *For more information about general policies and information related to graduate education, visit the following Web site: http://www.apa.org/ed.*

Producing this publication involved the cooperation of many. I wish to express appreciation to all graduate departments, programs, and schools that contributed information. Also, I wish to acknowledge the work and assistance of a number of my APA colleagues in the Education Directorate, Internet Services, Research Office, and the Books Department who have contributed greatly to the success of this publication. Especially due recognition are Joan Freund, Renee Lyles, and Miama Walter (Education Directorate) for coordinating the collecting and editing of information; Dave Leeds (Internet Services) for the design and preparation of the online questionnaire; Jessica Kohout, PhD, Marlene Wicherski and Marco Salazar (Research Office) for assistance in questionnaire development, data analysis, and graphics; and Dan Brachtesende (Books Department) for preparing the final document for publication.

Paul Nelson, PhD
Deputy Executive Director and
   Director, Office of Graduate Education and Training
Education Directorate
American Psychological Association

Considering Graduate Study

Psychology is a broad scientific discipline bridging the social and biological sciences, influenced also by such disciplines as philosophy and mathematics. Psychology's applications are similarly diverse and responsive to problem solving in areas such as education and human development, health, family and community relations, organizations and other work environments, engineering and technology, the arts and architecture, communications, and political and judiciary systems.

Just as the discipline of psychology is broad, there are many types of graduate programs available in psychology. Thus, selecting a graduate program that is best for you requires thoughtful consideration. Because of the diversity of graduate programs, the American Psychological Association (APA) does not rank them. Rather, APA encourages you to think about the best match for you. Some programs are intensely focused on preparing an individual for an academic research career, while other programs focus on preparing an individual for applied research outside the university. Other programs prepare students to provide psychological services as licensed professional psychologists. Some programs bridge these various goals. Also, some programs offer a breadth of scholarly professional development in addition to a substantive focus in psychology to prepare individuals for a college teaching career in psychology. Substantive program areas of recent doctoral graduates are illustrated in Figure 1. For each department, program, or school, you are advised to review the section entitled *Orientation, Objectives, and Emphasis of Departments* for more information about various program emphases.

in health service areas of psychology but not programs in other areas of professional practice (e.g. industrial/organizational psychology). It does not accredit master's degree programs. You should know also that accreditation applies to educational programs (i.e., doctoral programs in professional psychology) and institutions (i.e., colleges, universities, and freestanding professional schools), not to individuals. It is a system for recognizing educational quality as defined by the profession or other accrediting bodies. Graduation from an accredited institution or program does not guarantee employment or licensure for individuals, although being a graduate of an accredited program may facilitate such achievement. All programs in this publication are in regionally accredited institutions. The doctoral programs that are APA accredited are identified as such. *For more information and the most current lists of accredited programs, see the APA Office of Program Consultation and Accreditation Web site at http://www.apa.org/ed.*

Programs, Degrees, and Employment

Although employment in research, teaching, and human service positions is possible for those with a master's degree in psychology, the doctoral degree is generally considered the entry-level degree in psychology for the independent, licensed practice of psychology as a profession. Increasingly, it is the preferred degree for college and university faculty and has long been a requirement for faculty positions in research universities. For specific information about employment outcomes of a program's graduates, review the section entitled *Employment of Department Graduates* in each listing.

At a broader level, Figure 2 summarizes types of settings in which graduates of master's degree programs are employed. About one fourth of those awarded an associate's degree continue in graduate or professional education in psychology or other fields. Some students earn a master's degree, work for a few years, then return to study for a doctorate in psychology or

Figure 1. New Doctorates in Psychology by Subfield: 2003–2004

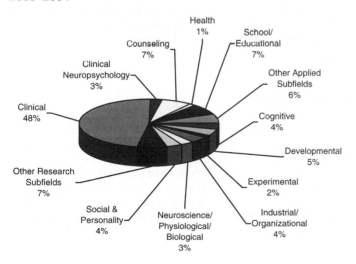

Source: 2005 *Graduate Study in Psychology.* Compiled by APA Research Office.

Figure 2. Psychology Master's Degree Recipients by Employment Setting: 1999

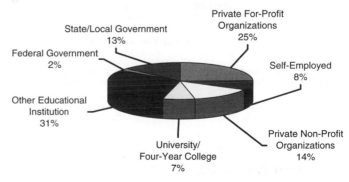

Source: National Science Foundation, Science Resources Statistics Division, 1999 SESTAT (Scientists and Engineers Statistical Data System).

Accreditation in Professional Psychology

Many students ask about a program's accreditation. The Committee on Accreditation of the APA accredits doctoral programs another field. Other students earn a master's degree as part of the doctoral program preparation. Still others bypass the master's degree and work directly on the doctorate. Doctoral programs vary in their practices and admission preferences in this regard. Thus, be sure to note this preference when reviewing the programs in which you are interested.

Doctoral programs also differ in terms of the type of doctoral degree awarded. The two most common doctoral degrees are the PhD and the PsyD. A few programs in Colleges of Education may offer the EdD. The PhD is the older doctorate and is generally regarded as the research degree. Although many professional psychology programs award it, especially those in university academic departments, they typically have an emphasis on research training and the integration of that with applied or practice training. The PsyD, first awarded in the late 1960s but increasing in popularity among professional school programs, is a professional degree in psychology (similar to the MD in medicine). Programs awarding the PsyD place major emphasis on preparing their graduates for professional practice as practitioner–scholars but typically with less extensive research training. Presently, about 75% of all doctoral degrees in psychology are PhDs; of the degrees awarded in clinical psychology, however, only 60% are PhDs, with the others being PsyDs. Figure 3 gives a profile of initial employment outcomes for PhD and PsyD program graduates. *For more information about degrees, employment, and salaries in psychology, you may wish to visit the Web site of the APA Research Office at http://research.apa.org/index.html.*

Figure 3. Primary Employment Settings of 2003 PhD and PsyD Recipients in Psychology

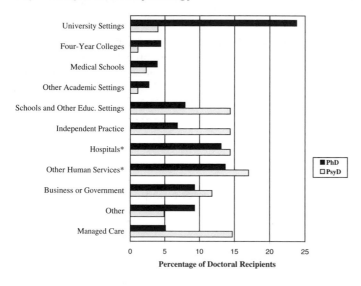

*Disproportionately high percentages are represented in these categories, as many recent graduates are still gaining experience in these organized settings prior to licensure.

Source: 2003 Doctorate Employment Survey, APA Research Office.

Admission Requirements

Requirements for admission vary from program to program. Many psychology programs prefer or require significant under-

graduate coursework in psychology, often the equivalent of a major or minor, whereas others do not. Evaluate your educational background and be realistic about your abilities and academic potential.

To assist in their evaluation of academic potential, many graduate departments require the Graduate Record Examination (GRE), and some require the Miller Analogies Test (MAT). If the programs in which you are interested require these standardized tests, you should take the GRE, GRE-Subject (Psychology), and the MAT in time for the scores to be included with your application materials.

Other criteria considered as admission factors may include previous research activity, work experience, clinically related public service, extracurricular activity, letters of recommendation, statement of goals and objectives, and an interview. Many programs rate letters of recommendation as high in importance, and an increasing number are requiring an interview. Of the departments and programs listed in this publication, 8% rated letters of recommendation as high in importance when considering students for admission. In addition, a clear statement of goals and objectives was rated as high in importance by 78% of departments and programs. Review the section entitled *Student Applications/Admissions* in this publication for information related to scores and other criteria considered.

Competition for Admission

Gaining entry into graduate school in psychology can be difficult. The number of applicants typically exceeds the number of student openings. The number of applications received by the department or school and the number of students accepted should provide a sense of the competition you can expect when applying to a particular department, program, or school. For more information, review the section entitled *Student Applications/Admissions*.

Time to Degree

Programs should be clear about the minimum number of years in full-time study (or part-time equivalent) required to complete the degree requirements. The reality of doctoral education and training is that students average 5 to 6 years after the bachelor's degree, some taking even longer to complete the degree. The time taken by students to complete their degrees is a result of many possible factors. One of those is the extent to which financial assistance is available.

Tuition and Financial Assistance

The cost of graduate education can be expensive. Tuition for out-of-state students in public institutions and for all students in private institutions will be higher. Many students require loans, even when working part time to pay for their graduate education. Indeed, the amount of debt incurred by graduate students can be significant, as illustrated by Figure 4.

Figure 4. Level of Cumulative Debt Related to Graduate Education: 2003 Doctorate Recipients

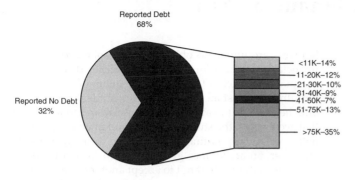

Reported Debt 68%

Reported No Debt 32%

<11K–14%
11-20K–12%
21-30K–10%
31-40K–9%
41-50K–7%
51-75K–13%

>75K–35%

Source: 2003 Doctorate Employment Survey, APA Research Office.

However, financial assistance in various forms is available to many students. Figure 4 indicates that about one third of those who earn their doctorate are debt free on graduation. Thus, you may wish to apply for a fellowship, scholarship, assistantship, or another type of financial assistance. Many fellowships and scholarships are outright grants or subsidies and require no service to the department or university. For departments and programs reporting in this publication, 62% indicated that they offer some form of fellowship or scholarship to first-year students, and 58% indicated they offered some form of fellowship or scholarship to advanced students.

Assistantships in teaching and research are also available in many programs. These are forms of employment for services in a department. Teaching assistantships may require teaching a class or assisting a professor by grading papers, acting as a laboratory assistant, and performing other such supporting work. Research assistants ordinarily work on research projects being conducted by program faculty. Among departments and programs reporting for this publication, more than one half offer teaching assistantships and research assistantships for first-year students. For advanced students, the availability of assistantships is similar.

The amount of work required for fellowships, assistantships, and traineeships is expressed in hours per week. The number of hours indicated should be considered an approximation. Stipends are expressed in terms of total stipend for an academic year of 9 months. Students should inquire, when receiving an offer of financial assistance, as to the amount to be given in terms of tuition remission (not requiring the student to pay tuition) versus a stipend (actual cash in hand).

For information about tuition costs and the types of assistance offered by departments and programs, review the section entitled *Financial Information/Assistance*.

Also, you may want to review information listed on the APA Education Web site at http://www.apa.org/ed for information about scholarships, fellowships, grants, and other funding opportunities.

Application Information

An application to a department or program of study is a very important document. Make sure it represents you in the best possible manner and that you confirm (a) the deadline for filing the application, (b) what documents are required, and (c) who should receive the application. In addition, do not forget the admission fee usually required when filing an application.

Most graduate programs in psychology accept students only for fall admission. However, if you are interested in winter, spring, or summer admission, check the application information listed in this publication for the program to which you are applying. Information about application deadlines in this publication are listed in the section entitled *Application Information*.

Rules for Acceptance of Offers for Admission and Financial Aid

The Council of Graduate Schools has adopted the following policy that provides guidance to students and graduate programs regarding offers of financial support. The policy was adopted by the Council of Graduate Schools in 1965 and reaffirmed in 1992. It was endorsed by the Council of Graduate Departments of Psychology in 1981 and reaffirmed in 2000. Graduate programs and schools currently listed in the book have agreed to honor the policy. The policy reads as follows:

Acceptance of an offer of financial support (such as graduate scholarship, fellowship, traineeship, or assistantship) for the next academic year by a prospective or enrolled graduate student completes an agreement that both student and graduate school expect to honor. In that context, the conditions affecting such offers and their acceptance must be defined carefully and understood by all parties.

Students are under no obligation to respond to offers of financial support prior to April 15; earlier deadlines for acceptance of such offers violate the intent of this Resolution. In those instances in which the student accepts the offer before April 15 and subsequently desires to withdraw that acceptance, the student may submit in writing a resignation of the appointment at any time through April 15. However, an acceptance given or left in force after April 15 commits the student not to accept another offer without first obtaining a written release from the institution to which a commitment has been made. Similarly, an offer by an institution after April 15 is conditional on presentation by the student of the written release from any previously accepted offer. It is further agreed by the institutions and organizations subscribing to the above Resolution that a copy of this Resolution should accompany every scholarship, fellowship, traineeship, and assistantship offer.

Explanation of Program Listings

The following summarizes the information solicited from each program:

Contact Information

The name of the university or school, address, telephone number, fax number, e-mail, and World Wide Web address are provided. There may be more than one department in an institution that offers degrees in psychology.

Department Information

The year the department was established, the name of the department chairperson, and the number of full-time and part-time faculty members in the department are provided.

Programs and Degrees Offered

This heading highlights the program areas in which degrees are offered by the department or school, the type of degree, and the number of degrees awarded.

APA Accreditation Status

Whether a program in clinical psychology, counseling psychology, school psychology, or combined professional scientific psychology is accredited when this publication went to press is noted. Because changes in accreditation status may occur after publication, please contact the APA Office of Program Consultation and Accreditation, or review the Web site at http://www.apa.org/ed.

Student Applications/Admissions

This section includes information about the number of applications received by the individual program areas of departments and schools. Also listed are the number of applicants accepted into the program and the number of openings anticipated in the next year. In addition, the information reflects the median number of years required for a degree and the number of students enrolled who were dismissed or voluntarily withdrew from the program before completing their degree requirements.

Standardized tests scores and other information are presented. Scores including the Graduate Record Exam Verbal (GRE-V), Quantitative (GRE-Q), and Analytical (GRE-A); the combined GRE-V + Q score; and the GRE-Subject (Psychology) score are listed.

Other criteria considered as admission factors are rated according to their importance for admission. These criteria include previous research activity, work experience, clinically related public service, extracurricular activity, letters of recommendation, statement of goals and objectives, and an interview. Characteristics of students enrolled in the department or programs psychology programs are also reported.

Financial Information/Assistance

Tuition figures per year and per academic unit are indicated. Note that some schools and institutions have different fee structures for doctoral and master's students. The words "non-state residents" are used by state universities that charge more for out-of-state residents than students who reside in the state. These fees should be used as rough guidelines and are subject to change.

Teaching assistantships, research assistantships, traineeships, or fellowships and scholarships are reported. The data for each type of assistance are listed for first year and advanced. The average amount awarded to each student and the average number of hours that must be worked each week are included in the listing. Contact information for financial assistance is also listed.

In addition, this section includes information related to internships, housing, and day care. The availability of housing and day care facilities, on and off campus, is indicated.

Employment of Department Graduates

This section provides information about employment activities of graduates. Data presented by departments or schools include information about master's and doctoral degree graduates, such as enrollment in psychology doctoral programs; enrollment by graduates in post-doctoral residency/fellowship programs; employment by graduates in academic teaching or research positions; and employment by graduates in business or industry, government agencies, hospitals, or other positions.

Additional Information

This section provides an opportunity to present the orientation, objectives, and emphasis of the department or school. Information is also presented about the special facilities or resources offered by the school or institution.

Also included in this section is information related to personal behavior and religious beliefs statements that are considered a condition for admission and retention with the program. All information in *Graduate Study in Psychology* is self-reported. In the interest of full disclosure to prospective students, therefore, departments, programs, or institutions by which they are governed that have a statement to this effect are requested to cite the statement or provide a Web site or address at which it can be found.

Application Information

This last section provides the addresses, deadlines, and fees for the submission of applications. There is not a common deadline for admission for programs of psychology.

2006

**Graduate
Study
in
Psychology**

Alabama, The University of
Department of Psychology
College of Arts and Sciences
P.O. Box 870348
Tuscaloosa, AL 35487-0348
Telephone: (205) 348-1919
Fax: (205) 348-8648
E-mail: *mbhubbard@as.ua.edu*
Web: *http://psychology.ua.edu*

Department Information:
1957. Chairperson: Kenneth L. Lichstein. Number of Faculty: total–full-time 24, part-time 2; women–full-time 10; minority–full-time 1.

Programs and Degrees Offered:
Listed in the following order: Program area, degree type (T if terminal Master's), number awarded 7/03–6/04. Clinical PhD (Doctor of Philosophy) 15, cognitive PhD (Doctor of Philosophy) 2.

APA Accreditation: Clinical PhD (Doctor of Philosophy).

Student Applications/Admissions:
Student Applications

Clinical PhD (Doctor of Philosophy)—Applications 2004–2005, 218. Total applicants accepted 2004–2005, 16. Number enrolled (new admits only) 2004–2005 full-time, 11. Openings 2005–2006, 12. The Median number of years required for completion of a degree are 6. The number of students enrolled full and part-time who were dismissed or voluntarily withdrew from this program area were 1. *Cognitive PhD (Doctor of Philosophy)*—Applications 2004–2005, 14. Total applicants accepted 2004–2005, 8. Number enrolled (new admits only) 2004–2005 full-time, 4. Openings 2005–2006, 4. The Median number of years required for completion of a degree are 6. The number of students enrolled full and part-time who were dismissed or voluntarily withdrew from this program area were 0.

Admissions Requirements:

Scores: Entries appear in this order: required test or GPA, minimum score (if required), median score of students entering in 2003–2004. Doctoral Programs: GRE-V 500, 540; GRE-Q 500, 680; overall undergraduate GPA 3.0, 3.7. GRE subject is preferred for the clinical program—500 minimum score.

Other Criteria: (importance of criteria rated low, medium, or high): GRE/MAT scores high, research experience high, work experience low, extracurricular activity low, clinically related public service low, GPA medium, letters of recommendation high, interview medium, statement of goals and objectives high, Interview not typical for cognitive program. For additional information on admission requirements, go to: http://psychology.ua.edu/admission.html.

Student Characteristics: The following represents characteristics of students in 2004–2005 in all graduate psychology programs in the department: Female–full-time 59, part-time 0; Male–full-time 20, part-time 0; African American/Black–full-time 4, part-time 0; Hispanic/Latino(a)–full-time 1, part-time 0; Asian/Pacific Islander–full-time 4, part-time 0; American Indian/Alaska Native–full-time 1, part-time 0; Caucasian–full-time 69, part-time 0; Multi-ethnic–full-time 0, part-time 0; students subject to the Americans With Disabilities Act–full-time 1, part-time 0.

Financial Information/Assistance:
Tuition for Full-Time Study: *Doctoral:* State residents: per academic year $4,630; Nonstate residents: per academic year $12,664. Tuition is subject to change.

Financial Assistance:
First Year Students: Teaching assistantships available for first-year. Average amount paid per academic year: $9,207. Average number of hours worked per week: 20. Tuition remission given: full. Research assistantships available for first-year. Average amount paid per academic year: $9,207. Average number of hours worked per week: 20. Tuition remission given: full. Fellowships and scholarships available for first-year. Average amount paid per academic year: $14,500. Tuition remission given: full.

Advanced Students: Teaching assistantships available for advanced students. Average amount paid per academic year: $9,207. Average number of hours worked per week: 20. Tuition remission given: full. Research assistantships available for advanced students. Average amount paid per academic year: $9,207. Average number of hours worked per week: 20. Tuition remission given: full. Traineeships available for advanced students. Average amount paid per academic year: $14,500. Average number of hours worked per week: 20. Fellowships and scholarships available for advanced students. Average amount paid per academic year: $14,500. Tuition remission given: full.

Contact Information: Of all students currently enrolled full-time, 100% benefitted from one or more of the listed financial assistance programs.

Internships/Practica: There are a number of practica available to graduate students. All doctoral students must take PY695/696, a teaching internship, in which the student teaches an introductory psychology class under the supervision of a faculty member. Two semesters of basic psychotherapy practicum are required of every doctoral student in clinical psychology. In this practicum, students conduct psychotherapy with four to six clients in the Department's Psychological Clinic. Students complete approximately 100 hours of direct client contact to fulfill this requirement. After basic psychotherapy practicum, doctoral clinical psychology students take either one or two (depending on specialty area) advanced practica in their area of specialization. Many of these practica are housed in community service agencies (e.g., state psychiatric hospital, community mental health center, University operated treatment center for disturbed children). In addition to these formal practica, most doctoral students in the clinical program are financially supported at some time during their graduate school years through field placements in various community agencies. These students are supervised by either licensed psychologists employed by these agencies or by Department of Psychology clinical faculty. In addition to the intervention practica discussed above, all clinical doctoral students must take two of the three graduate psychological assessment courses offered. These courses have a significant practicum component, requiring approximately 5 administrations of commonly used psychological assessment instruments with Psychological Clinic clients. In addition, students in the Adult Clinical specialization take advanced assessment and advanced intervention electives, which may have practicum components. For those doctoral students for whom a professional internship is required prior to graduation, 6 applied in 2003–2004. Of those who applied, 6 were placed in internships listed by the Association of Psychology Postdoctoral and Internship Programs (APPIC); 6 were placed in APA accredited internships.

Housing and Day Care: On-campus housing is available. See the following Web site for more information: http://catalogs.ua.edu/graduate/10440.html. On-campus day care facilities are available. See the following Web site for more information: http://www.ches.ua.edu/backup/children.

Employment of Department Graduates:
Master's Degree Graduates: Of those who graduated in the academic year 2003–2004, the following categories and numbers represent the post-graduate activities and employment of master's degree graduates: Enrolled in a post-doctoral residency/fellowship (n/a), employed in independent practice (n/a), total from the above (master's) (0).
Doctoral Degree Graduates: Of those who graduated in the academic year 2003–2004, the following categories and numbers represent the post-graduate activities and employment of doctoral degree graduates: Enrolled in a psychology doctoral program (n/a), enrolled in a post-doctoral residency/fellowship (6), employed in an academic position at a university (4), employed in an academic position at a 2-year/4-year college (1), employed in business or industry (management) (1), employed in a government agency (professional services) (2), employed in a hospital/medical center (1), not seeking employment (1), total from the above (doctoral) (16).

Additional Information:
Orientation, Objectives, and Emphasis of Department: The University of Alabama doctoral program in psychology was founded in 1957 and the clinical program has been continuously accredited by the American Psychological Association since 1959. The department trains scientists and scientist–practitioners for a variety of roles: research, teaching, and applied practice. Both the clinical and the experimental programs strongly emphasize furthering psychology as a science. The psychology department has awarded some 417 doctoral degrees, principally in the areas of clinical psychology, cognitive psychology, and intellectual disability. The department has also developed innovative subspecialty programs in areas such as individual differences/intellectual disability and, in the clinical program, psychology–law, health psychology, geropsychology, and clinical–child. The doctoral programs emphasize core knowledge in the social, cognitive, developmental, and biological aspects of behavior as well as methodological/statistical foundations. All students take additional courses designed to prepare them with the necessary knowledge and skills in their chosen specialty areas. A further objective of the department is to promote independent scholarship and professional development. Coursework is supplemented by the active collaboration of faculty and students in ongoing research projects and clinical activities. The department maintains access to a wide range of settings in which students can refine their research and applied skills.

Special Facilities or Resources: The department is housed in a three-story building that it shares with the Department of Mathematics. It is directly connected to the department's Psychological Clinic and the University's Computer Center. Facilities include student offices, excellent classroom and seminar space, and several research laboratories. Graduate students have access to microcomputers for research and word processing and videotaping capabilities for instruction and training. A major resource is the department's Psychological Clinic, which provides psychological assessment, referral, treatment planning, and direct intervention for a variety of clinical populations. The department's Child and Family Research Clinic serves as a specialized training and research laboratory. Both clinics include observation facilities. Also affiliated with the department is the Brewer-Porch Children's Center, a training and research facility for seriously disordered young children. The University of Alabama's Student Health Center also serves as a practicum site. Other research and clinical relationships are maintained with local psychiatric hospitals (Bryce Hospital and the Veterans Affairs Medical Center), the University Medical Center, DCH Regional Medical Center, Family Counseling Services, Institute for Social Science Research, city and county school systems, Indian Rivers Mental Health Center, and the Taylor Hardin Forensic Medical Facility. Paid advanced training or research positions are often available in these facilities. A number of faculty in the department have research grants that include student support. Some 30 adjunct faculty in diverse fields contribute to program enrichment.

Information for Students With Physical Disabilities: See the following Web site for more information: http://ods.ua.edu.

Application Information:
Send to: Office of the Graduate School, University of Alabama, Box 870118, Tuscaloosa, AL 35487-0118. Application available online. URL of online application: http://graduate.ua.edu/application/index.htm. Students are admitted in the Fall, application deadline December 15. Deadline for the applications to the clinical program is December 15; February 1 is the deadline for the cognitive program. *Fee:* $25.

Alabama, University of, at Birmingham
Department of Psychology
School of Social and Behavioral Sciences
415 Campbell Hall
Birmingham, AL 35294-1170
Telephone: (205) 934-3850
Fax: (205) 975-6110
E-mail: *cmcfarla@uab.edu*
Web: *http://www.psy.uab.edu*

Department Information:
1969. Chairperson: Carl E. McFarland Jr. Number of Faculty: total–full-time 28, part-time 58; women–full-time 9, part-time 16; minority–full-time 3, part-time 2.

Programs and Degrees Offered:

Listed in the following order: Program area, degree type (T if terminal Master's), number awarded 7/03–6/04. Behavioral neuroscience PhD (Doctor of Philosophy) 2, developmental PhD (Doctor of Philosophy) 0, medical/clincal PhD (Doctor of Philosophy) 5.

APA Accreditation: Clinical PhD (Doctor of Philosophy).

Student Applications/Admissions:

Student Applications

Behavioral neuroscience PhD (Doctor of Philosophy)—Applications 2004–2005, 16. Total applicants accepted 2004–2005, 3. Openings 2005–2006, 4. The Median number of years required for completion of a degree are 5. The number of students enrolled full and part-time who were dismissed or voluntarily withdrew from this program area were 1. *Developmental PhD (Doctor of Philosophy)*—Applications 2004–2005, 10. Total applicants accepted 2004–2005, 3. Openings 2005–2006, 5. The Median number of years required for completion of a degree are 5. The number of students enrolled full and part-time who were dismissed or voluntarily withdrew from this program area 0. *Medical/clinical PhD (Doctor of Philosophy)*—Applications 2004–2005, 80. Total applicants accepted 2004–2005, 8. Openings 2005–2006, 7. The Median number of years required for completion of a degree are 6. The number of students enrolled full and part-time who were dismissed or voluntarily withdrew from this program area were 0.

Admissions Requirements:

Scores: Entries appear in this order: required test or GPA, minimum score (if required), median score of students entering in 2003–2004. Doctoral Programs: GRE-V+Q 1150, 1240; GRE-Subject(Psych) no minimum stated; overall undergraduate GPA 3.00, 3.57; last 2 years GPA 3.20, 3.82.

Other Criteria: (importance of criteria rated low, medium, or high): GRE/MAT scores high, research experience high, work experience low, extracurricular activity low, clinically related public service medium, GPA high, letters of recommendation medium, interview medium, statement of goals and objectives medium.

Student Characteristics: The following represents characteristics of students in 2004–2005 in all graduate psychology programs in the department: Female–full-time 36, part-time 0; Male–full-time 19, part-time 0; African American/Black–full-time 6, part-time 0; Hispanic/Latino(a)–full-time 0, part-time 0; Asian/Pacific Islander–full-time 2, part-time 0; American Indian/Alaska Native–full-time 0, part-time 0; Caucasian–full-time 0, part-time 0; Multiethnic–full-time 0, part-time 0; students subject to the Americans With Disabilities Act–full-time 2, part-time 0.

Financial Information/Assistance:

Tuition for Full-Time Study: *Doctoral:* State residents: per academic year $2,300, $112 per credit hour; Nonstate residents: per academic year $7,168, $224 per credit hour. Tuition is subject to change.

Financial Assistance:

First Year Students: Fellowships and scholarships available for first-year. Average amount paid per academic year: $16,590.

Average number of hours worked per week: 15. Apply by January 15. Tuition remission given: full.

Advanced Students: Teaching assistantships available for advanced students. Average amount paid per academic year: $16,500. Average number of hours worked per week: 20. Tuition remission given: partial. Research assistantships available for advanced students. Average amount paid per academic year: $17,500. Average number of hours worked per week: 20. Tuition remission given: partial. Traineeships available for advanced students. Average amount paid per academic year: $18,000. Average number of hours worked per week: 20. Tuition remission given: partial. Fellowships and scholarships available for advanced students. Average amount paid per academic year: $17,500. Average number of hours worked per week: 20. Tuition remission given: partial.

Contact Information: Of all students currently enrolled full-time, 100% benefitted from one or more of the listed financial assistance programs. Application and information available online at: www.psy.uab.edu.

Internships/Practica: For those doctoral students for whom a professional internship is required prior to graduation, 6 applied in 2003–2004. Of those who applied, 6 were placed in internships listed by the Association of Psychology Postdoctoral and Internship Programs (APPIC); 6 were placed in APA accredited internships.

Housing and Day Care: On-campus housing is available. UAB Student Housing, 1604 9th Avenue South, DNMH 101G, Birmingham, AL 35294, Phone: (205) 934-2092. UAB Child Care Center, 1113 15th Street South, Birmingham, AL 35294-4553, Phone: (205) 934-7353. On-campus day care facilities are available.

Employment of Department Graduates:

Master's Degree Graduates: Of those who graduated in the academic year 2003–2004, the following categories and numbers represent the post-graduate activities and employment of master's degree graduates: Enrolled in a post-doctoral residency/fellowship (n/a), employed in independent practice (n/a), total from the above (master's) (0).

Doctoral Degree Graduates: Of those who graduated in the academic year 2003–2004, the following categories and numbers represent the post-graduate activities and employment of doctoral degree graduates: Enrolled in a psychology doctoral program (n/a), total from the above (doctoral) (0).

Additional Information:

Orientation, Objectives, and Emphasis of Department: The Department offers three doctoral programs: Clinical/Medical Psychology, Behavioral Neuroscience, and Developmental Psychology. Each program promotes rigorous scientific training for students pursuing basic or applied research careers. The programs are designed to produce scholars who will engage in independent research, practice, and teaching. Medical Psychology is a specialty within clinical psychology that focuses on psychological factors in health care. It is cosponsored by the UAB School of Medicine. The Behavioral Neuroscience Program provides individualized, interdisciplinary training for research on the biological bases of behavior. The Developmental Program trains students to conduct research to discover and apply basic principles of developmental psychology across the life span in an interdisciplinary context.

Students are exposed to the issues of development in its natural and social contexts, as well as in laboratories. Faculty research interests include: health psychology, substance abuse, clinical neuropsychology, psychopharmacology, human psychophysiology, brain imaging, sensation and perception, spinal cord injury, control of movement, aging, mental retardation/developmental disabilities, pediatric psychology, social ecology, cognitive development, developmental psychopathology, psychosocial influences on cancer, pain, and clinical outcomes evaluation.

Special Facilities or Resources: The University of Alabama at Birmingham is a comprehensive, urban research university, recently ranked by U.S. News and World Report as the number one up-and-coming university in the country. The UAB Psychology Department, in the School of Social and Behavioral Sciences, ranks among the top 10 psychology departments in the U.S. in federal/research funding. The UAB campus encompasses a 65-block area on Birmingham's Southside, offering all of the advantages of a university within a highly supportive city. Resources are available from the School of Medicine, Department of Physiological Optics, School of Public Health, Civitan International Research Center, Sparks Center for Developmental and Learning Disorders, Center for Aging, Department of Pediatrics, Department of Psychiatry and Behavioral Neurobiology, Neurobiology Research Center, School of Education, School of Nursing, Department of Computer and Information Sciences, Department of Biocommunications, University Hospital, a psychiatric hospital, and Children's Hospital.

Application Information:
Send to: The Graduate School, University of Alabama at Birmingham, Birmingham, AL 35294. Students are admitted in the Fall, application deadline February 1. Medical/Clinical—December 15. *Fee:* $25.

Alabama, University of, at Huntsville
Department of Psychology
Liberal Arts
Morton Hall 335, University of Alabama in Huntsville
Huntsville, AL 35899
Telephone: (256) 824-6191
Fax: (256) 824-6949
E-mail: *carpens@email.uah.edu*
Web: *http://www.uah.edu/colleges/liberal/psychology/*

Department Information:
1968. Chairperson: Sandra Carpenter. Number of Faculty: total–full-time 7; women–full-time 4; minority–full-time 1.

Programs and Degrees Offered:
Listed in the following order: Program area, degree type (T if terminal Master's), number awarded 7/03–6/04. Experimental–general MA/MS (Master of Arts/Science) (T) 5.

Student Applications/Admissions:
Student Applications
Experimental–general MA/MS (Master of Arts/Science)—Applications 2004–2005, 17. Total applicants accepted 2004–2005, 15. Number enrolled (new admits only) 2004–2005 full-time, 8. Number enrolled (new admits only) 2004–2005 part-time,

0. Openings 2005–2006, 12. The Median number of years required for completion of a degree are 2. The number of students enrolled full and part-time who were dismissed or voluntarily withdrew from this program area were 0.

Admissions Requirements:
Scores: Entries appear in this order: required test or GPA, minimum score (if required), median score of students entering in 2003–2004. Master's Programs: GRE-V+Q 1000, 1050.
Other Criteria: (importance of criteria rated low, medium, or high): GRE/MAT scores high, research experience high, work experience low, clinically related public service low, GPA high, letters of recommendation high, statement of goals and objectives high.

Student Characteristics: The following represents characteristics of students in 2004–2005 in all graduate psychology programs in the department: Female–full-time 13, part-time 0; Male–full-time 2, part-time 0; African American/Black–full-time 0, part-time 0; Hispanic/Latino(a)–full-time 0, part-time 0; Asian/Pacific Islander–full-time 0, part-time 0; American Indian/Alaska Native–full-time 0, part-time 0; Caucasian–full-time 15, part-time 0; Multi-ethnic–full-time 0, part-time 0; students subject to the Americans With Disabilities Act–full-time 0, part-time 0.

Financial Information/Assistance:
Tuition for Full-Time Study: *Master's:* State residents: per academic year $4,422, $314 per credit hour; Nonstate residents: per academic year $9,082, $633 per credit hour. Tuition is subject to change. See the following Web site for updates and changes in tuition costs: http://bursar.uah.edu/tuition.htm.

Financial Assistance:
First Year Students: Fellowships and scholarships available for first-year. Average number of hours worked per week: 0. Apply by May 1. Tuition remission given: full.
Advanced Students: Teaching assistantships available for advanced students. Average amount paid per academic year: $8,000. Average number of hours worked per week: 20. Apply by May 1. Tuition remission given: full. Research assistantships available for advanced students. Average amount paid per academic year: $8,000. Average number of hours worked per week: 20. Apply by May 1. Tuition remission given: full and partial. Fellowships and scholarships available for advanced students. Tuition remission given: full and partial.
Contact Information: Of all students currently enrolled full-time, 70% benefitted from one or more of the listed financial assistance programs.

Internships/Practica: No information provided.

Housing and Day Care: On-campus housing is available. On-campus day care facilities are available.

Employment of Department Graduates:
Master's Degree Graduates: Of those who graduated in the academic year 2003–2004, the following categories and numbers represent the post-graduate activities and employment of master's degree graduates: Enrolled in a psychology doctoral program (2), enrolled in another graduate/professional program (1), enrolled in a post-doctoral residency/fellowship (n/a), employed in independent practice (n/a), employed in an academic position at a 2-

year/4-year college (1), employed in business or industry (research/consulting) (1), employed in a community mental health/counseling center (2), total from the above (master's) (7).

Doctoral Degree Graduates: Of those who graduated in the academic year 2003–2004, the following categories and numbers represent the post-graduate activities and employment of doctoral degree graduates: Enrolled in a psychology doctoral program (n/a), total from the above (doctoral) (0).

Additional Information:

Orientation, Objectives, and Emphasis of Department: The content of our program is directed toward the study of psychology as an intellectual and scientific pursuit, as contrasted with training directly applicable to counselor or psychologist licensure and practice. Specialization areas include applied psychology, social/personality, cognitive, developmental, and biopsychological psychology. The program is designed for a small number of students who will work in close interaction with individual faculty members and with each other. Although there are a few structured courses that are required of all students, a substantial portion of the student's program focuses on individual readings, research, and thesis.

Special Facilities or Resources: Access to research facilities at NASA's Marshall Space Flight Center is available via an existing Space Act Agreement. Students also have access to archives at the National Children's Advocacy Center.

Application Information:

Send to: Department Chair, Department of Psychology, Morton Hall 335, University of Alabama in Huntsville, Huntsville, AL 35899. Students are admitted in the Fall, application deadline June 1; Spring, application deadline December 1; Summer, application deadline May 1. *Fee:* $35.

Auburn University

Counselor Education, Counseling Psychology, & School
  Psychology
College of Education
2084 Haley Center
Auburn University, AL 36849-5222
Telephone: (334) 844-5160
Fax: (334) 844-2860
E-mail: *coun@auburn.edu*
Web: *http://www.auburn.edu/coun*

Department Information:

1975. Professor & Head of Department: Holly A. Stadler. Number of Faculty: total–full-time 10, part-time 1; women–full-time 7, part-time 1; minority–full-time 2, part-time 1; faculty subject to the Americans With Disabilities Act 1.

Programs and Degrees Offered:

Listed in the following order: Program area, degree type (T if terminal Master's), number awarded 7/03–6/04. Education Specialist EdS (Education Specialist) 2, Counseling Psychology PhD (Doctor of Philosophy) 3, Counselor Education PhD (Doctor of Philosophy) 1, School Psychology PhD (Doctor of Philosophy) 0, School Psychometry MA/MS (Master of Arts/Science) (T) 2,

Counseling MA/MS (Master of Arts/Science) (T) 12, School Counseling MA/MS (Master of Arts/Science) (T) 9.

APA Accreditation: Counseling PhD (Doctor of Philosophy).

Student Applications/Admissions:

Student Applications

Education Specialist EdS (Education Specialist)—Applications 2004–2005, 1. Total applicants accepted 2004–2005, 1. Number enrolled (new admits only) 2004–2005 part-time, 2. Total enrolled 2004–2005 part-time, 2. Openings 2005–2006, 2. The Median number of years required for completion of a degree are 4. The number of students enrolled full and part-time who were dismissed or voluntarily withdrew from this program area were 0. *Counseling Psychology PhD (Doctor of Philosophy)*—Applications 2004–2005, 75. Total applicants accepted 2004–2005, 6. Number enrolled (new admits only) 2004–2005 full-time, 6. Openings 2005–2006, 6. The Median number of years required for completion of a degree are 6. The number of students enrolled full and part-time who were dismissed or voluntarily withdrew from this program area were 0. *Counselor Education PhD (Doctor of Philosophy)*—Applications 2004–2005, 20. Total applicants accepted 2004–2005, 9. Number enrolled (new admits only) 2004–2005 full-time, 5. Number enrolled (new admits only) 2004–2005 part-time, 2. Total enrolled 2004–2005 full-time, 23; part-time, 7. Openings 2005–2006, 5. The Median number of years required for completion of a degree are 4. The number of students enrolled full or part-time who were dismissed or voluntarily withdrew from this program area were 1. *School Psychology PhD (Doctor of Philosophy)*—Applications 2004–2005, 11. Total applicants accepted 2004–2005, 2. Number enrolled (new admits only) 2004–2005 full-time, 2. Total enrolled 2004–2005 full-time, 7; part-time, 6. Openings 2005–2006, 2. The Median number of years required for completion of a degree are 6. The number of students enrolled full and part-time who were dismissed or voluntarily withdrew from this program area was 2. *School Psychometry MA/MS (Master of Arts/Science)*—Applications 2004–2005, 1. Total applicants accepted 2004–2005, 1. Total enrolled 2004–2005 part-time, 4. Openings 2005–2006, 4. The Median number of years required for completion of a degree are 2. The number of students enrolled full and part-time who were dismissed or voluntarily withdrew from this program area were 1. *Counseling MA/MS (Master of Arts/Science)*—Applications 2004–2005, 43. Total applicants accepted 2004–2005, 27. Number enrolled (new admits only) 2004–2005 full-time, 19. Openings 2005–2006, 9. The Median number of years required for completion of a degree are 2. The number of students enrolled full and part-time who were dismissed or voluntarily withdrew from this program area were 1. *School Counseling MA/MS (Master of Arts/Science)*—Applications 2004–2005, 16. Total applicants accepted 2004–2005, 8. Number enrolled (new admits only) 2004–2005 full-time, 8. Total enrolled 2004–2005 full-time, 19; part-time, 2. Openings 2005–2006, 12. The Median number of years required for completion of a degree are 2. The number of students enrolled full and part-time who were dismissed or voluntarily withdrew from this program area were 2.

Admissions Requirements:

Scores: Entries appear in this order: required test or GPA, minimum score (if required), median score of students entering

in 2003–2004. Master's Programs: GRE-V no minimum stated; GRE-Q no minimum stated. Contact Director of particular Master's program in which you are interested for more specific data. Doctoral Programs: GRE-V no minimum stated, 480; GRE-Q no minimum stated, 570; GRE-V+Q no minimum stated, 1050; overall undergraduate GPA no minimum stated, 3.6; last 2 years GPA no minimum stated, 3.86; psychology GPA no minimum stated, 3.9. This information in item 12 is for the PhD program in Counseling Psychology—last two years of admissions.

Other Criteria: (importance of criteria rated low, medium, or high): GRE/MAT scores medium, research experience medium, work experience medium, extracurricular activity low, clinically related public service low, GPA high, letters of recommendation high, interview high, statement of goals and objectives high, This pattern of criteria is generally the same across program areas.

Student Characteristics: The following represents characteristics of students in 2004–2005 in all graduate psychology programs in the department: Female–full-time 82, part-time 20; Male–full-time 17, part-time 6; African American/Black–full-time 22, part-time 6; Hispanic/Latino(a)–full-time 2, part-time 0; Asian/Pacific Islander–full-time 4, part-time 0; American Indian/Alaska Native–full-time 1, part-time 0; Caucasian–full-time 70, part-time 20; Multi-ethnic–full-time 0, part-time 0; students subject to the Americans With Disabilities Act–full-time 1, part-time 0.

Financial Information/Assistance:

Tuition for Full-Time Study: *Master's:* State residents: per academic year $4,610; Nonstate residents: per academic year $13,830. Tuition is subject to change. Doctoral students on assistantantships typically receive full tuition remission-not guaranteed.

Financial Assistance:

First Year Students: Teaching assistantships available for first-year. Average amount paid per academic year: $5,500. Average number of hours worked per week: 13. Apply by April 1. Tuition remission given: full. Research assistantships available for first-year. Average amount paid per academic year: $4,300. Average number of hours worked per week: 10. Apply by April 1. Tuition remission given: full. Fellowships and scholarships available for first-year. Average amount paid per academic year: $15,000. Average number of hours worked per week: 10. Apply by varies. Tuition remission given: full.

Advanced Students: Teaching assistantships available for advanced students. Average amount paid per academic year: $5,500. Average number of hours worked per week: 13. Apply by April 1. Tuition remission given: full. Research assistantships available for advanced students. Average amount paid per academic year: $4,300. Average number of hours worked per week: 10. Apply by April 1. Tuition remission given: full. Fellowships and scholarships available for advanced students. Average amount paid per academic year: $15,000. Average number of hours worked per week: 10. Apply by varies. Tuition remission given: full.

Contact Information: Of all students currently enrolled full-time, 20% benefitted from one or more of the listed financial assistance programs.

Internships/Practica: University counseling centers; community mental health centers; community counseling agencies. For those doctoral students for whom a professional internship is required

prior to graduation, 5 applied in 2003–2004. Of those who applied, 5 were placed in internships listed by the Association of Psychology Postdoctoral and Internship Programs (APPIC); 5 were placed in APA accredited internships.

Housing and Day Care: On-campus housing is available. Typically the only graduate students living in university housing are those who work for university housing. These positions include both financial remuneration as well as free housing. Contact Departmental Administrative Assistant or University Housing. No on-campus day care facilities are available.

Employment of Department Graduates:

Master's Degree Graduates: Of those who graduated in the academic year 2003–2004, the following categories and numbers represent the post-graduate activities and employment of master's degree graduates: Enrolled in a post-doctoral residency/fellowship (n/a), employed in independent practice (n/a), total from the above (master's) (0).

Doctoral Degree Graduates: Of those who graduated in the academic year 2003–2004, the following categories and numbers represent the post-graduate activities and employment of doctoral degree graduates: Enrolled in a psychology doctoral program (n/a), employed in independent practice (1), employed in an academic position at a 2-year/4-year college (1), employed in other positions at a higher education institution (2), employed in a community mental health/counseling center (2), total from the above (doctoral) (6).

Additional Information:

Orientation, Objectives, and Emphasis of Department: The Department offers graduate education programs for counseling psychologists, school psychologists, counselors, and counselor educators. Graduates will develop the competencies to address psychological, social, and environmental barriers to educational achievement and personal development. In this process students will engage in rigorous and challenging educational experiences in order to fashion their own unique contributions to society. The department values teaching, research, and outreach that contributes to the missions of the College and University. Further, the department seeks to foster a culture in which individual creativity and scholarship is reinforced and nurtured. Diversity is considered a core value in all that we do.

Special Facilities or Resources: Interdisciplinary community. University partnership serving underserved, rural minority communities devoted to education, research and service. We also partner with University Student Affairs, Housing, and the Athletic Department.

Information for Students With Physical Disabilities: See the following Web site for more information: www.auburn.edu/academic/disabilities.

Application Information:
Send to: (Program Name), Counselor Education, Counseling Psychology, & School Psychology 2084 Haley Center, Auburn University, AL 36849-5222. Application available online. URL of online application: www.auburn.edu/coun. Students are admitted in the Fall, application deadline January 15. PhD in Counseling Psychology—January 15. PhD in School Psychology, Counselor Education—February 1. MA in Com-

munity Agency Counseling, School Counseling, School Psychometry, EdS in School Counseling, School Psychology—March 15. *Fee:* $25.

Auburn University

Department of Psychology
226 Thach Hall
Auburn University, AL 36849-5214
Telephone: (334) 844-4412
Fax: (334) 844-4447
E-mail: *bryangt@auburn.edu*
Web: *http://www.auburn.edu/psychology*

Department Information:

1948. Chairperson: Barry Burkhart. Number of Faculty: total–full-time 23, part-time 3; women–full-time 5, part-time 3; minority–full-time 3; faculty subject to the Americans With Disabilities Act 1.

Programs and Degrees Offered:

Listed in the following order: Program area, degree type (T if terminal Master's), number awarded 7/03–6/04. Clinical PhD (Doctor of Philosophy) 8, experimental PhD (Doctor of Philosophy) 1, industrial/organizational PhD (Doctor of Philosophy) 1, Applied Behavior Analysis in Developmental Disabilities MA/MS (Master of Arts/Science) (T) 0.

APA Accreditation: Clinical PhD (Doctor of Philosophy).

Student Applications/Admissions:

Student Applications

Clinical PhD (Doctor of Philosophy)—Applications 2004–2005, 160. Total applicants accepted 2004–2005, 7. Number enrolled (new admits only) 2004–2005 full-time, 7. Total enrolled 2004–2005 full-time, 47; part-time, 3. Openings 2005–2006, 8. The Median number of years required for completion of a degree are 6. The number of students enrolled full and part-time who were dismissed or voluntarily withdrew from this program area were 0. *Experimental PhD (Doctor of Philosophy)*—Applications 2004–2005, 10. Total applicants accepted 2004–2005, 2. Number enrolled (new admits only) 2004–2005 full-time, 2. Openings 2005–2006, 4. The Median number of years required for completion of a degree are 6. The number of students enrolled full and part-time who were dismissed or voluntarily withdrew from this program area were 0. *Industrial/Organizational PhD (Doctor of Philosophy)*—Applications 2004–2005, 51. Total applicants accepted 2004–2005, 4. Number enrolled (new admits only) 2004–2005 full-time, 4. Total enrolled 2004–2005 full-time, 9. Openings 2005–2006, 4. The Median number of years required for completion of a degree are 6. The number of students enrolled full and part-time who were dismissed or voluntarily withdrew from this program area were 0. *Applied Behavior Analysis in Developmental Disabilities MA/MS (Master of Arts/Science)*—Applications 2004–2005, 25. Total applicants accepted 2004–2005, 8. Number enrolled (new admits only) 2004–2005 full-time, 8. Number enrolled (new admits only) 2004–2005 part-time, 0. Openings 2005–2006, 10. The number of students enrolled full and part-time who were dismissed or voluntarily withdrew from this program area were 1.

Admissions Requirements:

Scores: Entries appear in this order: required test or GPA, minimum score (if required), median score of students entering in 2003–2004. Master's Programs: GRE-V no minimum stated, 410; GRE-Q no minimum stated, 570; GRE-V+Q no minimum stated, 970; GRE-Analytical no minimum stated, 620; overall undergraduate GPA no minimum stated, 3.35. The above data are for the Master's Concentration in Applied Behavior Analysis in Developmental Disabilities. Doctoral Programs: GRE-V no minimum stated, 540; GRE-Q no minimum stated, 700; GRE-Analytical no minimum stated, 5; overall undergraduate GPA no minimum stated, 3.6; psychology GPA no minimum stated, 3.8. The above data are for the clinical doctoral program.

Other Criteria: (importance of criteria rated low, medium, or high): GRE/MAT scores medium, research experience high, work experience medium, extracurricular activity low, clinically related public service medium, GPA high, letters of recommendation high, interview high, statement of goals and objectives medium, For I/O and EXP programs, clinically related public service has less significance. For additional information on admission requirements, go to: www.auburn.edu/psychology.

Student Characteristics: The following represents characteristics of students in 2004–2005 in all graduate psychology programs in the department: Female–full-time 58, part-time 3; Male–full-time 27, part-time 0; African American/Black–full-time 4, part-time 0; Hispanic/Latino(a)–full-time 2, part-time 0; Asian/Pacific Islander–full-time 3, part-time 0; American Indian/Alaska Native–full-time 0, part-time 1; Caucasian–full-time 76, part-time 2; Multi-ethnic–full-time 0, part-time 0; students subject to the Americans With Disabilities Act–full-time 0, part-time 0.

Financial Information/Assistance:

Tuition for Full-Time Study: *Master's:* State residents: per academic year $6,915, $191 per credit hour; Nonstate residents: per academic year $20,745, $573 per credit hour. *Doctoral:* State residents: per academic year $6,915, $191 per credit hour; Nonstate residents: per academic year $20,745, $573 per credit hour. Tuition is subject to change. See the following Web site for updates and changes in tuition costs: http://www.auburn.edu/administration/business_office/sfs/.

Financial Assistance:

First Year Students: Teaching assistantships available for first-year. Average amount paid per academic year: $12,000. Average number of hours worked per week: 13. Apply by January 14. Tuition remission given: full.

Advanced Students: Teaching assistantships available for advanced students. Average amount paid per academic year: $14,000. Average number of hours worked per week: 13. Tuition remission given: full. Research assistantships available for advanced students. Average amount paid per academic year: $14,000. Average number of hours worked per week: 13. Tuition remission given: partial.

Contact Information: Of all students currently enrolled full-time, 80% benefitted from one or more of the listed financial assistance programs. Application and information available online at: http://www.auburn.edu/psychology.

Internships/Practica: Current practicum sites that offer assistantships for clinical graduate students are Personal Assessment and Counseling Center (Auburn University, AL), Mt. Meigs Adolescent Correctional Facility (Mt. Meigs, AL), Lee County Youth Development Center (Opelika, AL), Head Start Program of Lee County (Auburn and Opelika, AL), the Auburn University School of Pharmacy, and the Auburn University College of Veterinary Medicine. Industrial/organizational psychology students receive paid practicum training at a number of area organizations, including Auburn University's Center for Governmental Services, Auburn University at Montgomery's Center for Business and Economic Development, and the Fort Benning Field Station of the Army Research Institute. Many I/O students participate in paid internships before completing their doctoral work. Experimental students have participated in practica at the Bancroft Center (NJ), Warm Springs Rehabilitation Center (GA), and the Army Research Institute (GA). Students in the Masters Program in Applied Behavior Analysis in Developmental Disabilities participate in a practicum program that involves various sites serving individuals with developmental disabilities at East Alabama Mental health and Mental Retardation Center in Opelika, as well as a program that trains them for consulting services in community settings. For those doctoral students for whom a professional internship is required prior to graduation, 1 applied in 2003–2004. Of those who applied, 1 were placed in an internship listed by the Association of Psychology Postdoctoral and Internship Programs (APPIC); 1 were placed in an APA accredited internship.

Housing and Day Care: On-campus housing is available. See the following Web site for more information: www.auburn.edu/housing/index.html. On-campus day care facilities are available.

Employment of Department Graduates:
   Master's Degree Graduates: Of those who graduated in the academic year 2003–2004, the following categories and numbers represent the post-graduate activities and employment of master's degree graduates: Enrolled in a post-doctoral residency/fellowship (n/a), employed in independent practice (n/a), employed in a government agency (professional services) (1), other employment position (6), total from the above (master's) (7).
   Doctoral Degree Graduates: Of those who graduated in the academic year 2003–2004, the following categories and numbers represent the post-graduate activities and employment of doctoral degree graduates: Enrolled in a psychology doctoral program (n/a), enrolled in a post-doctoral residency/fellowship (2), employed in an academic position at a 2-year/4-year college (1), employed in business or industry (research/consulting) (2), employed in a government agency (professional services) (1), not seeking employment (1), total from the above (doctoral) (7).

Additional Information:
   Orientation, Objectives, and Emphasis of Department: Graduate education in Auburn's psychology programs is intended to provide a balance between the skills and understanding required to generate new knowledge and the application of existing knowledge and theory to the solution of societal problems. The majority of the department's full-time faculty are in the applied specializations of clinical and industrial/organizational psychology. All faculty members are active scholars and are committed to the premise that psychology is a developing discipline in which inquiry, breadth, and flexibility are to be valued. Students are provided with direct experience, training, and supervision within community agencies and organizations, where the theory and techniques

of clinical psychology, experimental psychology, and industrial/organizational psychology can be practiced and refined. The clinical psychology training program emphasizes a scientist-practitioner approach that blends an empirical approach to knowledge within a clinical experiential context. The experimental program seeks to broadly inform its students about the issues and problems of psychology in general, and to provide the basic conceptual and technical skills needed to make original contributions to knowledge and theory in psychology. The industrial/organizational program focuses on understanding, predicting, and modifying behavior in organizational settings, typically but not limited to work environments. The Masters Program in Applied Behavior Analysis in Developmental Disabilities trains students to provide programmatic habilitative services to individuals with mental retardation and other developmental disorders with a need for training new skills and ameliorating behavioral problems. Degree requirements focus on integrating foundation and specialized coursework with practical experience.

Special Facilities or Resources: A substantial clinical psychology training grant from the State of Alabama, university teaching assistantships, a wide variety of contracts with community agencies, and faculty research contracts and grants have typically provided all doctoral psychology graduate students with financial support throughout their graduate careers. The department administers a multipurpose psychological services center. Relationships with extra-university agencies and organizations facilitate training in applied research.

Information for Students With Physical Disabilities: See the following Web site for more information: http://www.auburn.edu/academic/disabilities/.

Application Information:
Send to: Thane Bryant, Department of Psychology, 226 Thach Hall, Auburn University, AL 36849-5214. Application available online. URL of online application: www.auburn.edu/psychology. Students are admitted in the Fall, application deadline January 14. March 15 for Fall admission for Master's Concentration in Applied Behavior Analysis in Developmental Disabilities. *Fee:* $25.

Auburn University at Montgomery
Department of Psychology
School of Sciences
P.O. Box 244023
Montgomery, AL 36124-4023
Telephone: (334) 244-3306
Fax: (334) 244-3947
E-mail: *slobello@mail.aum.edu*
Web: *http://www.aum.edu/academics/sciences/index.cfm*

Department Information:
   1969. Chairperson: Peter Zachar, PhD Number of Faculty: total–full-time 10, part-time 12; women–full-time 3, part-time 6; minority–part-time 1.

Programs and Degrees Offered:
   Listed in the following order: Program area, degree type (T if terminal Master's), number awarded 7/03–6/04. Applied/clinical counseling MA/MS (Master of Arts/Science) (T) 7.

Student Applications/Admissions:

Student Applications

Applied/clinical counseling MA/MS (Master of Arts/Science)— Applications 2004–2005, 40. Total applicants accepted 2004–2005, 31. Total enrolled 2004–2005 full-time, 25, part-time, 5. Openings 2005–2006, 25. The Median number of years required for completion of a degree are 2. The number of students enrolled full and part-time who were dismissed or voluntarily withdrew from this program area were 3.

Admissions Requirements:

Scores: Entries appear in this order: required test or GPA, minimum score (if required), median score of students entering in 2003–2004. Master's Programs: GRE-V no minimum stated; GRE-Q no minimum stated; GRE-V+Q no minimum stated; MAT no minimum stated; overall undergraduate GPA 3.0. We require either the MAT or the GRE, plus undergraduate transcripts. We also require two letters of reference and a statement of interest.

Other Criteria: (importance of criteria rated low, medium, or high): GRE/MAT scores high, research experience low, work experience low, extracurricular activity low, clinically related public service medium, GPA high, letters of recommendation medium, interview low, statement of goals and objectives medium.

Student Characteristics: The following represents characteristics of students in 2004–2005 in all graduate psychology programs in the department: Female–full-time 15, part-time 2; Male–full-time 10, part-time 3; African American/Black–full-time 0, part-time 0; Hispanic/Latino(a)–full-time 0, part-time 0; Asian/Pacific Islander–full-time 0, part-time 0; American Indian/Alaska Native–full-time 0, part-time 0; Caucasian–full-time 0, part-time 0; students subject to the Americans With Disabilities Act–full-time 3, part-time 0.

Financial Information/Assistance:

Tuition for Full-Time Study: *Master's:* State residents: $120 per credit hour; Nonstate residents: $360 per credit hour. Tuition is subject to change. See the following Web site for updates and changes in tuition costs: http://www.aum.edu.

Financial Assistance:

First Year Students: Teaching assistantships available for first-year. Tuition remission given: partial. Fellowships and scholarships available for first-year. Tuition remission given: full.

Advanced Students: Teaching assistantships available for advanced students. Average number of hours worked per week: 15. Tuition remission given: partial. Fellowships and scholarships available for advanced students. Tuition remission given: full.

Contact Information: Of all students currently enrolled full-time, 50% benefitted from one or more of the listed financial assistance programs. Application and information available online at: See Dept. Chair for Information.

Internships/Practica: Internship and practica are available at several local agencies and organizations. Practica are often tailored to the interests and career objectives of the student.

Housing and Day Care: On-campus housing is available. See the following Web site for more information: http://www.aum.edu/home/about/studentaffairs/housing/. On-campus day care facilities

are available. See the following Web site for more information: http://www.aum.edu/home/services/childhood/. Jannett Baggett, Director (334) 244-3772; Kathy Glass, Secretary (334) 244-3441.

Employment of Department Graduates:

Master's Degree Graduates: Of those who graduated in the academic year 2003–2004, the following categories and numbers represent the post-graduate activities and employment of master's degree graduates: Enrolled in a psychology doctoral program (5), enrolled in another graduate/professional program (1), enrolled in a post-doctoral residency/fellowship (n/a), employed in independent practice (n/a), employed in an academic position at a university (0), employed in an academic position at a 2-year/4-year college (0), employed in other positions at a higher education institution (0), employed in a professional position in a school system (0), employed in business or industry (research/consulting) (0), employed in business or industry (management) (0), employed in a government agency (research) (0), employed in a government agency (professional services) (0), employed in a community mental health/counseling center (4), employed in a hospital/medical center (0), still seeking employment (0), other employment position (0), total from the above (master's) (10).

Doctoral Degree Graduates: Of those who graduated in the academic year 2003–2004, the following categories and numbers represent the post-graduate activities and employment of doctoral degree graduates: Enrolled in a psychology doctoral program (n/a), total from the above (doctoral) (0).

Additional Information:

Orientation, Objectives, and Emphasis of Department: Our MS program is designed to provide a core curriculum for those intending to pursue doctoral studies and to offer course and practicum experiences for those wishing to enter direct service positions.

Special Facilities or Resources: Computer facilities are available for student use.

Application Information:

Send to: Office of Enrollment Services, 130 Taylor Center, Auburn University Montgomery, P.O. Box 244023, Montgomery, AL 36124-4023. Application available online in Acrobat format (pdf) at http://www.aum.edu/Prospective_Students/Admissions/Application_Form/index.cfm?id=761. Application available online. Students are admitted in the Fall. Programs have rolling admissions. *Fee:* $25.

Jacksonville State University

Department of Psychology
College of Graduate Studies
700 Pelham Road, N.
Jacksonville, AL 36265-1602
Telephone: (256) 782-5402
Fax: (256) 782-5637
E-mail: *abeason@jsucc.jsu.edu*
Web: *http://www.jsu.edu/depart/psychology/welcome.html*

Department Information:

1971. Department Head: Allen Smith. Number of Faculty: total–full-time 8, part-time 5; women–full-time 3, part-time 3; minority–full-time 1.

Programs and Degrees Offered:
Listed in the following order: Program area, degree type (T if terminal Master's), number awarded 7/03–6/04. Applied MA/MS (Master of Arts/Science) (T) 10.

Student Applications/Admissions:
Student Applications
Applied MA/MS (*Master of Arts/Science*)—Number enrolled (new admits only) 2004–2005 full-time, 3. Number enrolled (new admits only) 2004–2005 part-time, 2. Total enrolled 2004–2005 full-time, 25; part-time, 12. Openings 2005–2006, 20. The Median number of years required for completion of a degree are 2. The number of students enrolled full and part-time who were dismissed or voluntarily withdrew from this program area were 1.

Admissions Requirements:
Scores: Entries appear in this order: required test or GPA, minimum score (if required), median score of students entering in 2003–2004. Master's Programs: GRE-V+Q no minimum stated; overall undergraduate GPA no minimum stated; psychology GPA no minimum stated. 450 times undergraduate GPA + GRE V + Q = 1600 or more OR 15 times undergraduate GPA + MAT = 60 or more.
Other Criteria: (importance of criteria rated low, medium, or high): GRE/MAT scores high, GPA high, letters of recommendation medium.

Student Characteristics: The following represents characteristics of students in 2004–2005 in all graduate psychology programs in the department: Female–full-time 20, part-time 8; Male–full-time 5, part-time 4; African American/Black–full-time 4, part-time 1; Hispanic/Latino(a)–full-time 1, part-time 0; Asian/Pacific Islander–full-time 2, part-time 0; American Indian/Alaska Native–full-time 0, part-time 0; Caucasian–full-time 9, part-time 10; Multi-ethnic–full-time 0, part-time 1; students subject to the Americans With Disabilities Act–full-time 0, part-time 0.

Financial Information/Assistance:
Tuition for Full-Time Study: *Master's:* State residents: per academic year $4,040, $202 per credit hour; Nonstate residents: per academic year $8,080, $404 per credit hour. Tuition is subject to change. See the following Web site for updates and changes in tuition costs: http://www.jsu.edu/depart/graduate/bulletin/index.html.

Financial Assistance:
First Year Students: Teaching assistantships available for first-year. Average amount paid per academic year: $5,000. Average number of hours worked per week: 20. Apply by August 28. Tuition remission given: partial. Research assistantships available for first-year. Average amount paid per academic year: $5,000. Average number of hours worked per week: 20. Apply by August 28. Tuition remission given: partial. Fellowships and scholarships available for first-year. Apply by August 28.
Advanced Students: No information provided.
Contact Information: Of all students currently enrolled full-time, 0% benefitted from one or more of the listed financial assistance programs. Application and information available online at: http://www.jsu.edu/depart/finaid/finaid.html.

Internships/Practica: Clinical and Behavior Analysis and Instructional Practica are offered. The Clinical Practicum includes super-vised clinical assessment, report writing, ethical principles, as well as the design and implementation of psychological treatment programs with a client population, in an on-campus clinic. The Behavior Analysis Practicum includes the application of psychological principles in areas such as developmental disabilities, organizational behavior management, remediation of academic behavior, and environmental psychology. The Instructional Practicum allows students to gain teaching experience assisting a professor.

Housing and Day Care: On-campus housing is available. See the following Web site for more information: http://www.jsu.edu/depart/rlmn/. On-campus day care facilities are available.

Employment of Department Graduates:
Master's Degree Graduates: Of those who graduated in the academic year 2003–2004, the following categories and numbers represent the post-graduate activities and employment of master's degree graduates: Enrolled in a post-doctoral residency/fellowship (n/a), employed in independent practice (n/a), total from the above (master's) (0).
Doctoral Degree Graduates: Of those who graduated in the academic year 2003–2004, the following categories and numbers represent the post-graduate activities and employment of doctoral degree graduates: Enrolled in a psychology doctoral program (n/a), total from the above (doctoral) (0).

Additional Information:
Orientation, Objectives, and Emphasis of Department: The objective of the program is to provide students with the requisite methodological skills as well as the theoretical and ethical background necessary for practice or research. Consistent with this objective is a 15 hour core sequence of courses covering biological, quantitative, methodological, and preprofessional areas. Students can then tailor the remaining coursework, research program, and practicum/internship experiences to fit their career objectives. Overall, the courses reflect a behavioral emphasis. Training is available to prepare students for state Master's level licensure or national certification as a behavior analyst. Student research and thesis is encouraged, especially for students preparing to pursue doctoral-level studies.

Special Facilities or Resources: The department has an on-campus clinic designed for psychological services and research in support of its teaching mission. The clinic affords opportunities for on-campus practica experiences. Practicum arrangements with a variety of agencies allow students to gain experience in a variety of applications of behavior analysis. Special facilities include an animal room, a running room with 15 chambers, student offices, and a seminar computer room. A network of control computers (which were developed at JSU and used in many other universities) runs experiments and provides interactive graphical analyses. Social Design: In the center for Social Design, students apply principles of environmental design to affect behavior. Precision Teaching: The Learning Skills department is affiliated with the Psychology Department and offers students opportunities to apply psychological principles in an instructional setting using computer assisted instruction.

Information for Students With Physical Disabilities: See the following Web site for more information: http://www.jsu.edu/depart/dss/index.html.

Application Information:
Send to: Jacksonville State University, College of Graduate Studies, 700 Pelham Road, N., Jacksonville, AL 36265-1602. Application available online. URL of online application: http://webhost.jsu.edu/Scripts/WebEncore.dll?Application-Graduate.html. Students are admitted in the Fall, application deadline August 27; Spring, application deadline January 2; Summer, application deadline April 28. *Fee:* $20.

South Alabama, University of
Department of Psychology
Arts and Sciences
LSCB Room 326
Mobile, AL 36688
Telephone: (251) 460-6371
Fax: (251) 460-6320
E-mail: *lchriste@usouthal.edu*
Web: *http://www.usouthal.edu/bulletin/artpsy.htm*

Department Information:
1964. Chairperson: Larry Christensen. Number of Faculty: total–full-time 14, part-time 8; women–full-time 6, part-time 3; minority–full-time 1, part-time 1.

Programs and Degrees Offered:
Listed in the following order: Program area, degree type (T if terminal Master's), number awarded 7/03–6/04. Clinical MA/MS (Master of Arts/Science) (T) 7, experimental MA/MS (Master of Arts/Science) (T) 1.

Student Applications/Admissions:
Student Applications
Clinical MA/MS (Master of Arts/Science)—Applications 2004–2005, 28. Total applicants accepted 2004–2005, 10. Number enrolled (new admits only) 2004–2005 full-time, 8. Openings 2005–2006, 12. The Median number of years required for completion of a degree are 2. The number of students enrolled full and part-time who were dismissed or voluntarily withdrew from this program area were 0. *Experimental MA/MS (Master of Arts/Science)*—Applications 2004–2005, 0. Total applicants accepted 2004–2005, 0. Openings 2005–2006, 3. The Median number of years required for completion of a degree are 2.

Admissions Requirements:
Scores: Entries appear in this order: required test or GPA, minimum score (if required), median score of students entering in 2003–2004. Master's Programs: GRE-V+Q 1000, 1050; overall undergraduate GPA 3.0, 3.44; psychology GPA 3.0, 3.84.
Other Criteria: (importance of criteria rated low, medium, or high): GRE/MAT scores high, research experience medium, work experience low, extracurricular activity low, clinically related public service medium, GPA high, letters of recommendation high, interview medium, statement of goals and objectives medium.

Student Characteristics: The following represents characteristics of students in 2004–2005 in all graduate psychology programs in the department: Female–full-time 13, part-time 0; Male–full-time 7, part-time 0; African American/Black–full-time 1, part-time 0; Hispanic/Latino(a)–part-time 0; Asian/Pacific Islander–part-time 0; American Indian/Alaska Native–full-time 0, part-time 0; Caucasian–full-time 20, part-time 0; Multi-ethnic–full-time 0, part-time 0; students subject to the Americans With Disabilities Act–full-time 0, part-time 0.

Financial Information/Assistance:
Tuition for Full-Time Study: *Master's:* State residents: per academic year $3,360, $149 per credit hour; Nonstate residents: per academic year $6,340, $298 per credit hour. Tuition is subject to change.

Financial Assistance:
First Year Students: Research assistantships available for first-year. Average amount paid per academic year: $6,000. Average number of hours worked per week: 20. Apply by March 1. Tuition remission given: full.
Advanced Students: Research assistantships available for advanced students. Average amount paid per academic year: $6,000. Apply by March 1. Tuition remission given: full.
Contact Information: Of all students currently enrolled full-time, 100% benefitted from one or more of the listed financial assistance programs.

Internships/Practica: Graduate students receive practical experience in the application of psychological assessment and treatment procedures in a variety of clinical settings. Emphasis is given to ethical and professional issues with intensive individual and group supervision. The Department of Psychology operates an outpatient teaching clinic where a variety of children and adults are seen for short-term assessment and treatment. External practicum placements are also available in a variety of community settings including a state mental hospital, a mental retardation facility and community substance abuse programs.

Housing and Day Care: On-campus housing is available. See the following Web site for more information: www.southalabama.edu/housing. No on-campus day care facilities are available.

Employment of Department Graduates:
Master's Degree Graduates: Of those who graduated in the academic year 2003–2004, the following categories and numbers represent the post-graduate activities and employment of master's degree graduates: Enrolled in a psychology doctoral program (3), enrolled in a post-doctoral residency/fellowship (n/a), employed in independent practice (n/a), do not know (5), total from the above (master's) (8).
Doctoral Degree Graduates: Of those who graduated in the academic year 2003–2004, the following categories and numbers represent the post-graduate activities and employment of doctoral degree graduates: Enrolled in a psychology doctoral program (n/a), total from the above (doctoral) (0).

Additional Information:
Orientation, Objectives, and Emphasis of Department: The University of South Alabama offers a master's program in general psychology that allows the student to choose either an applied or experimental focus. All students complete a core curriculum designed to provide them with knowledge of current theories, principles, and methods of experimental and applied psychology. This is followed by courses in either clinical or experimental areas. The clinical courses are designed to equip students with basic

psychological assessment and treatment skills that will enable them to function later in an applied employment setting under supervision of a licensed psychologist. Courses for the experimental student are designed to provide more extensive information in research design and experimental methods as well as theoretical background related to the student's thesis research. Both programs, as well as the core curriculum, are designed to provide students with the necessary theoretical and research background to pursue further graduate study, if they so choose. Graduate students in both areas receive individual attention and close supervision by departmental faculty.

Special Facilities or Resources: The Comparative Hearing Laboratory maintains exceptional sound room, computer, and animal facilities. Through the comparison of human, monkey, gerbil, and computer simulations of perception, the laboratory seeks to study how the brain has become specialized for language, and what has gone wrong with particular classes of communication and learning disorders. In addition to the Psychological Clinic and the Comparative Hearing Laboratory, the Department has laboratory facilities for neuropsychological and behavioral research, and has access to both mainframe and personal computer facilities. An EEG/ERP laboratory exists that is used for conducting research requiring the utilization of a dense array electrode cap. This laboratory is available for both faculty and graduate student research. A family interaction laboratory exists for studying parent–child interactions with the goal of enhancing parenting skills. Finally, a cognitive laboratory exists with the capability of studying linguistic enhancement. This laboratory also has an eye-tracking apparatus capable of being integrated into a variety of research projects.

Information for Students With Physical Disabilities: See the following Web site for more information: www.southalabama.edu/dss.

Application Information:
Send to: Director of Admission, Administration Bldg., Room 182, University of South Alabama, Mobile, AL 36688. Students are admitted in the Fall, application deadline March 1. *Fee:* $25.

Alaska Pacific University
Master of Science in Counseling Psychology (MSCP)
4101 University Drive
Anchorage, AK 99508
Telephone: (907) 564-8225
Fax: (907) 564-8396
E-mail: *rlane@alaskapacific.edu*
Web: *www.alaskapacific.edu*

Department Information:
1990. Director: Robert Lane, PhD Number of Faculty: total–full-time 4, part-time 4; women–full-time 2, part-time 2.

Programs and Degrees Offered:
Listed in the following order: Program area, degree type (T if terminal Master's), number awarded 7/03–6/04. Master of Science Counseling Psychology MA/MS (Master of Arts/Science) (T) 21.

Student Applications/Admissions:
Student Applications
Master of Science Counseling Psychology MA/MS (Master of Arts/Science)—Applications 2004–2005, 38. Total applicants accepted 2004–2005, 22. Total enrolled 2004–2005 full-time, 36; part-time, 6. Openings 2005–2006, 20. The Median number of years required for completion of a degree is 2. The number of students enrolled full or part-time who were dismissed or voluntarily withdrew from this program area was 1.

Admissions Requirements:
Scores: Entries appear in this order: required test or GPA, minimum score (if required), median score of students entering in 2003–2004. Master's Programs: MAT no minimum stated; overall undergraduate GPA 3.0, 3.2; psychology GPA 3.0, 3.0. *Other Criteria:* (importance of criteria rated low, medium, or high): GRE/MAT scores medium, work experience high, extracurricular activity medium, clinically related public service medium, GPA medium, letters of recommendation high, interview high, statement of goals and objectives high.

Student Characteristics: The following represents characteristics of students in 2004–2005 in all graduate psychology programs in the department: Female–full-time 27, part-time 4; Male–full-time 9, part-time 2; African American/Black–full-time 3, part-time 0; Hispanic/Latino(a)–full-time 0, part-time 1; Asian/Pacific Islander–full-time 0, part-time 1; American Indian/Alaska Native–full-time 1, part-time 0; Caucasian–full-time 0, part-time 0; students subject to the Americans With Disabilities Act–part-time 1.

Financial Information/Assistance:
Tuition for Full-Time Study: *Master's:* State residents: $450 per credit hour; Nonstate residents: $450 per credit hour.

Financial Assistance:
First Year Students: No information provided.
Advanced Students: Traineeships available for advanced students. Apply by March 15. Tuition remission given: partial.

Contact Information: Of all students currently enrolled full-time, 10% benefitted from one or more of the listed financial assistance programs.

Internships/Practica: A significant part of a counselor's education occurs outside the classroom through an internship experience. This is a two-semester opportunity for students to begin to apply theories and techniques of their classroom education as well as to focus their professional development in a specialized area of counseling. Internship opportunities are diverse in clientele and therapeutic context. In collaboration with the MSCP director and faculty, students identify internship sites consistent with their interests and needs. Examples of internship sites are Southcentral Foundation (Alaska Native services), Anchorage Center for Families, Alaska Children's Services, Southcentral Counseling Center (state mental health services), Alaska Human Services, Salvation Army Clitheroe Center, Alaska Native Hospital, McLaughlin Youth Center, Catholic Social Services, and private practitioners.

Housing and Day Care: On-campus housing is available. See the following Web site for more information: Housing available for graduate students. Web site is www.alaskapacific.edu. No on-campus day care facilities are available.

Employment of Department Graduates:
Master's Degree Graduates: Of those who graduated in the academic year 2003–2004, the following categories and numbers represent the post-graduate activities and employment of master's degree graduates: Enrolled in a post-doctoral residency/fellowship (n/a), employed in independent practice (n/a), total from the above (master's) (0).
Doctoral Degree Graduates: Of those who graduated in the academic year 2003–2004, the following categories and numbers represent the post-graduate activities and employment of doctoral degree graduates: Enrolled in a psychology doctoral program (n/a), total from the above (doctoral) (0).

Additional Information:
Orientation, Objectives, and Emphasis of Department: The master of science in counseling psychology (MSCP) program at Alaska Pacific University is a selective, rigorous program for the creative adult who plans to become a mental health practitioner or enter a doctoral program. Main objectives of the MSCP program are to foster the knowledge and skills needed to succeed as a professional counselor, to promote the integration of learning with practical "real life" issues in the field, and to encourage the development of leadership skills. To accomplish these educational objectives, the MSCP program is committed to providing individual attention to students, a personal and supportive atmosphere, and a mentorship approach to education. The curriculum is eclectic in theoretical orientation and celebrates diversity within the range of professional mental health approaches and techniques. A "hands on" approach to learning is emphasized along with an integration of theory and practice throughout the program. The program is committed to the centrality of multicultural awareness, ethical responsibility, and each student's personal growth and development. When students graduate from the MSCP program, they will have acquired a better understanding of themselves as human

beings, greater sensitivity for others, and professional competence in theory, research, practice, skills, and ethics.

Special Facilities or Resources: Our special resources lie in our unique blend of theoretical knowledge and practical experience that make up our counselor education program. This is enhanced by the diverse faculty and unique internship sites available in Alaska. Further, a cooperative rather than a competitive spirit is fostered. Because MSCP students progress through the program as an intact group, they develop a strong spirit of community. Class assignments and projects often are completed in a small-group format, with each member taking active responsibility for the final product of all. The MSCP curriculum includes a variety of course styles, with greatest emphasis given to seminar-style classroom interactions, experiential activities, and student-designed projects. Even in lecture-oriented courses, students engage in small-group learning activities and personal discovery. Practicing counselors and psychologists are regularly brought into the classroom as visitors and also serve on a regular basis as adjunct faculty. And faculty doors are open to students all of the time. Further, the curriculum is responsive to current factors that influence the profession, such as managed care and certification and licensure laws throughout the United States, and "cutting edge" therapies and techniques.

Information for Students With Physical Disabilities: See the following Web site for more information: http://www.alaskapacific.edu/.

Application Information:
Send to: Graduate Admissions Office, Alaska Pacific University, 4101 University Drive, Anchorage, AK 99508. *Fee:* $25.

Alaska, University of, Anchorage
Psychology/MS in Clinical Psychology
Arts and Sciences
3211 Providence Drive
Anchorage, AK 99508
Telephone: (907) 786-1795
Fax: (907) 786-4898
E-mail: *aypsych@uaa.alaska.edu*
Web: *psych.uaa.alaska.edu*

Department Information:
1967. Chairperson: Robert Madigan. Number of Faculty: total–full-time 18, part-time 4; women–full-time 10, part-time 2; minority–full-time 2.

Programs and Degrees Offered:
Listed in the following order: Program area, degree type (T if terminal Master's), number awarded 7/03–6/04. Clinical Psychology MA/MS (Master of Arts/Science) (T) 9.

Student Applications/Admissions:
Student Applications
Clinical Psychology MA/MS (Master of Arts/Science)—Applications 2004–2005, 50. Total applicants accepted 2004–2005, 15. Number enrolled (new admits only) 2004–2005 full-time, 12. Number enrolled (new admits only) 2004–2005 part-time, 0. Total enrolled 2004–2005 full-time, 24; part-time, 2. Openings 2005–2006, 12. The Median number of years required for completion of a degree are 2. The number of students enrolled full and part-time who were dismissed or voluntarily withdrew from this program area were 2.

Admissions Requirements:
Scores: Entries appear in this order: required test or GPA, minimum score (if required), median score of students entering in 2003–2004. Master's Programs: GRE-V no minimum stated, 510; GRE-Q no minimum stated, 540; GRE-V+Q no minimum stated, 1070; overall undergraduate GPA no minimum stated, 3.5; psychology GPA no minimum stated, 3.65. The GRE Psychology Subtest is not required if students have an undergraduate psychology major with a psychology GPA of 3.0 or greater.
Other Criteria: (importance of criteria rated low, medium, or high): GRE/MAT scores medium, research experience medium, work experience medium, extracurricular activity low, clinically related public service medium, GPA medium, letters of recommendation medium, statement of goals and objectives medium.

Student Characteristics: The following represents characteristics of students in 2004–2005 in all graduate psychology programs in the department: Female–full-time 18, part-time 0; Male–full-time 6, part-time 2; African American/Black–full-time 2, part-time 0; Hispanic/Latino(a)–full-time 0, part-time 0; Asian/Pacific Islander–full-time 1, part-time 0; American Indian/Alaska Native–full-time 7, part-time 0; Caucasian–full-time 12, part-time 2; Multi-ethnic–full-time 2, part-time 0; students subject to the Americans With Disabilities Act–full-time 1, part-time 1.

Financial Information/Assistance:
Tuition for Full-Time Study: Master's: State residents: $222 per credit hour; Nonstate residents: $453 per credit hour.

Financial Assistance:
First Year Students: Teaching assistantships available for first-year. Average amount paid per academic year: $3,000. Average number of hours worked per week: 12. Apply by June 1. Tuition remission given: full. Research assistantships available for first-year. Average amount paid per academic year: $3,000. Average number of hours worked per week: 20. Apply by June 1. Tuition remission given: full.
Advanced Students: Teaching assistantships available for advanced students. Average amount paid per academic year: $3,000. Average number of hours worked per week: 12. Apply by April 1. Tuition remission given: full. Research assistantships available for advanced students. Average amount paid per academic year: $3,000. Average number of hours worked per week: 20. Apply by April 1. Tuition remission given: full.
Contact Information: Of all students currently enrolled full-time, 70% benefitted from one or more of the listed financial assistance programs.

Internships/Practica: All students complete one semester of practicum in the Psychological Services Center, which is run by the Psychology Department. This closely supervised experience involves direct clinical contact with psychotherapy clients of all ages and backgrounds. Students spend an average of 20 hours per week on practicum and typically schedule five or six hours of face-to-face contact time with clients. All students also complete two semesters of internship at a community agency. Internship sites are selected on the basis of student preferences and their professional goals. Potential internship sites include private or public psychiatric inpatient facilities; private or public psychiatric outpatient facilities, including those that specialize in the treatment of Alaskan Natives, college students, or families; the school district; and residential homes for adolescents or the elderly. As with practicum, students typically spend 20 hours per week on internship and receive close supervision.

Housing and Day Care: On-campus housing is available. See the following Web site for more information: www.uaa.alaska.edu/housing/ (housing). On-campus day care facilities are available: tanaina@alaska.net (childcare).

Employment of Department Graduates:

Master's Degree Graduates: Of those who graduated in the academic year 2003–2004, the following categories and numbers represent the post-graduate activities and employment of master's degree graduates: Enrolled in a psychology doctoral program (1), enrolled in a post-doctoral residency/fellowship (n/a), employed in independent practice (n/a), employed in an academic position at a university (1), employed in a government agency (professional services) (1), employed in a community mental health/counseling center (6), total from the above (master's) (9).

Doctoral Degree Graduates: Of those who graduated in the academic year 2003–2004, the following categories and numbers represent the post-graduate activities and employment of doctoral degree graduates: Enrolled in a psychology doctoral program (n/a), total from the above (doctoral) (0).

Additional Information:

Orientation, Objectives, and Emphasis of Department: The MS degree in Clinical Psychology is designed to be responsive to the needs of a variety of Alaska mental health service settings and to meet prerequisites for licensing at the master's level in the state of Alaska. The MS degree allows graduates to pursue either the Licensed Professional Counselor (LPC) or the Licensed Psychological Associate (LPA) license. The goal of the program is to provide students with a well-rounded education that includes an evidence-based background in the best practices applicable to community mental health settings. The curriculum addresses local behavioral health needs in a context that is culturally sensitive and community focused. An important program goal is the recruitment and retention of non-traditional students.

Special Facilities or Resources: The Psychology Department runs an experimental research laboratory and a mental health clinic. Both settings have computer facilities for audio-visual recording or one-way observation. In addition, the department maintains close ties to the Center for Human Development: University Affiliated Program, which provides interdisciplinary training, research, and support for people with developmental disabilities by collaborating with a variety of state agencies and community providers. The Consortium Library is the major research library for Southcentral Alaska, with a collection of more than 694,000 volumes and subscriptions to more than 3,600 journals, including a well-maintained selection of psychology resources. The UAA

Information Technology Services provides microcomputer, mainframe, and Internet resources and it maintains four general access computer labs across the campus. The university also houses the Center for Alcohol and Addiction Studies, which addresses the problem of substance abuse in Alaska through educational, research, and public service programs; the Institute for Circumpolar Health Studies, which addresses health problems in Alaska and the Circumpolar North through instruction, information services, and basic and applied research in health and medicine; and the Institute of Social and Economic Research, which is devoted to studying economic and social conditions in Alaska.

Application Information:
Send to: Enrollment Services, University of Alaska Anchorage, 3211 Providence Drive, Anchorage, AK 99508. Students are admitted in the Fall, application deadline April 1. *Fee:* $45.

Alaska, University of, Fairbanks
Department of Psychology/MA Program in Community
  Psychology
College of Liberal Arts
P.O. Box 756480
Fairbanks, AK 99775-6480
Telephone: (907) 474-7007
Fax: (907) 474-5781
E-mail: *fypsych@uaf.edu*
Web: *http://www.uaf.edu/psych/*

Department Information:
  1984. Chairperson: Dr. Catherine Koverola. Number of Faculty: total–full-time 7, part-time 4; women–full-time 4, part-time 2; minority–full-time 2, part-time 1.

Programs and Degrees Offered:
  Listed in the following order: Program area, degree type (T if terminal Master's), number awarded 7/03–6/04. Community psychology MA/MS (Master of Arts/Science) (T) 9.

Student Applications/Admissions:
Student Applications
  Community psychology MA/MS (Master of Arts/Science)—Applications 2004–2005, 18. Total applicants accepted 2004–2005, 7. Number enrolled (new admits only) 2004–2005 full-time, 3. Number enrolled (new admits only) 2004–2005 part-time, 4. Total enrolled 2004–2005 full-time, 7; part-time, 16. The Median number of years required for completion of a degree are 3. The number of students enrolled full and part-time who were dismissed or voluntarily withdrew from this program area were 2.

Admissions Requirements:
  Scores: Entries appear in this order: required test or GPA, minimum score (if required), median score of students entering in 2003–2004. Master's Programs: overall undergraduate GPA no minimum stated. The UAF Graduate School requires the GRE for admission to graduate studies if an applicant's undergraduate GPA is lower than 3.0.
  Other Criteria: (importance of criteria rated low, medium, or high): GRE/MAT scores medium, research experience me-

dium, work experience high, extracurricular activity medium, clinically related public service high, GPA medium, letters of recommendation high, interview medium, statement of goals and objectives high.

Student Characteristics: The following represents characteristics of students in 2004–2005 in all graduate psychology programs in the department: Female–full-time 6, part-time 13; Male–full-time 1, part-time 3; African American/Black–full-time 0, part-time 0; Hispanic/Latino(a)–full-time 0, part-time 0; Asian/Pacific Islander–full-time 0, part-time 0; American Indian/Alaska Native–full-time 4, part-time 6; Caucasian–full-time 3, part-time 10.

Financial Information/Assistance:

Tuition for Full-Time Study: *Master's:* State residents: $202 per credit hour; Nonstate residents: $393 per credit hour.

Financial Assistance:

First Year Students: Teaching assistantships available for first-year. Average amount paid per academic year: $8,740. Average number of hours worked per week: 20. Apply by February 1. Tuition remission given: full. Research assistantships available for first-year. Average amount paid per academic year: $8,740. Average number of hours worked per week: 20. Apply by February 1. Tuition remission given: full. Fellowships and scholarships available for first-year. Average amount paid per academic year: $10,000. Average number of hours worked per week: 20. Apply by February 1. Tuition remission given: full.

Advanced Students: Teaching assistantships available for advanced students. Average amount paid per academic year: $9,120. Average number of hours worked per week: 20. Apply by February 1. Tuition remission given: full. Research assistantships available for advanced students. Average amount paid per academic year: $9,120. Average number of hours worked per week: 20. Apply by February 1. Tuition remission given: full. Fellowships and scholarships available for advanced students. Average amount paid per academic year: $10,000. Average number of hours worked per week: 20. Apply by February 1. Tuition remission given: full.

Contact Information: Of all students currently enrolled full-time, 85% benefitted from one or more of the listed financial assistance programs.

Internships/Practica: Several supervised internships are available to our Community Psychology graduate students. Chief Andrew Issacs Health Center and Yukon-Tanana Counseling Center, which are part of the mental health branch of Tanana Chiefs Conference, our local Athabaskan regional corporation, offers experience with this indigenous Alaskan population. Additional internships are available at Fort Wainwright Mental Health Center and the Fairbanks Mental Health Center, which offer services for adults, and the Farenkamp Youth Center, for child, adolescent, family, and adult services. Also available to the interested student are internships at the Fairbanks Vet Center, the University of Alaska Fairbanks Women's Center, and the Fairbanks National Alliance for the Mentally Ill. All our training sites offer exposure to work with Alaska Native populations. Students on internships engage in direct client contact as well as program development, evaluation research, and prevention work.

Housing and Day Care: On-campus housing is available. See the following Web site for more information: On-campus housing: www.uaf.edu/reslife/. On-campus day care facilities are available. See the following Web site for more information: Child care center: fnpm@uaf.edu.

Employment of Department Graduates:

Master's Degree Graduates: Of those who graduated in the academic year 2003–2004, the following categories and numbers represent the post-graduate activities and employment of master's degree graduates: Enrolled in a psychology doctoral program (1), enrolled in a post-doctoral residency/fellowship (n/a), employed in independent practice (n/a), employed in a community mental health/counseling center (4), other employment position (3), do not know (1), total from the above (master's) (9).

Doctoral Degree Graduates: Of those who graduated in the academic year 2003–2004, the following categories and numbers represent the post-graduate activities and employment of doctoral degree graduates: Enrolled in a psychology doctoral program (n/a), total from the above (doctoral) (0).

Additional Information:

Orientation, Objectives, and Emphasis of Department: The orientation of the MA program in Community Psychology is cross-cultural and rural. The program objective is to train community psychologists to meet the demand for mental health professionals in rural Alaska. This requires individuals who can work sensitively and effectively in urban and rural cross-cultural community contexts. Therefore, the program embodies a commitment to training in cross-cultural psychology that we believe is unique in terms of the extent of its emphasis. A special focus of the program is work with Alaska Native people. It includes courses devoted exclusively to cross-cultural applications in community psychology, counseling, psychological assessment, and psychopathology. These courses are in addition to basic coursework in these areas. Students also receive a strong grounding in the field of substance abuse and prevention psychology. Elective courses are available in prevention, consultation, and individual, group, and family therapy. Instruction is characterized by small class size and a high faculty-to-student ratio. In keeping with the social change orientation of community psychology, students receive training in program development, evaluation, and field-based research. Thesis work directed toward social change, cross-cultural issues in psychology, Native American issues, rural community psychology, rural service delivery, disabilities in rural areas, and psychological adjustment in extreme northern climates is encouraged. Finally, an internship requirement involving supervised training indicates our commitment to a skill-based, experimental component as an essential part of graduate psychology training.

Special Facilities or Resources: Community Psychology is housed in the Gruening Building on the UAF campus, a seven-story structure completed in 1970. Facilities available to graduate students include individual therapy rooms and a family/group therapy room, with computer video training equipment. Other computer facilities available to graduate students include a departmental lab and several university labs with PC's and Mac's. UAF is an international center for research in the Arctic and the North.

Information for Students With Physical Disabilities: See the following Web site for more information: www.uaf.edu/chc/Dis ability.htm.

Application Information:
Send to: Director, Community Psychology Program, University of Alaska Fairbanks, P.O. Box 756480, Fairbanks, AK 99775-6480. Students are admitted in the Fall, application deadline February 1. *Fee:* $50. If a student receives a teaching or research assistantship or a fellowship, he/she also receives a tuition waiver.

Argosy University/Phoenix, Arizona Professional School of Psychology

Clinical Psychology, Sport–Exercise Psychology, Professional Counseling
2233 W. Dunlap Avenue, Suite 150
Phoenix, AZ 85021
Telephone: (866) 216-2777 (toll-free)
Fax: (602) 216-2601
E-mail: *ahughes@argosyu.edu*
Web: *http://www.argosyu.edu*

Department Information:
1997. Chairperson: Philinda Smith Hutchings, PhD, ABPP. Number of Faculty: total–full-time 13; women–full-time 6; minority–full-time 6.

Programs and Degrees Offered:
Listed in the following order: Program area, degree type (T if terminal Master's), number awarded 7/03–6/04. Counseling MA/MS (Master of Arts/Science) (T) 9, Sport–Exercise Psychology MA/MS (Master of Arts/Science) (T) 8, Clinical Psychology PsyD (Doctor of Psychology) 22, Clinical Psychology MA/MS (Master of Arts/Science) (T) 24, School Psychology PsyD (Doctor of Psychology) 0, Forensic Psychology MA/MS (Master of Arts/Science) (T) 0, School Psychology MA/MS (Master of Arts/Science) (T) 0.

APA Accreditation: Clinical PsyD (Doctor of Psychology).

Student Applications/Admissions:
Student Applications
Counseling MA/MS (Master of Arts/Science)—Applications 2004–2005, 43. Total applicants accepted 2004–2005, 71. Number enrolled (new admits only) 2004–2005 full-time, 65. Number enrolled (new admits only) 2004–2005 part-time, 0. Openings 2005–2006, 40. The Median number of years required for completion of a degree are 2. The number of students enrolled full and part-time who were dismissed or voluntarily withdrew from this program area were 7. *Sport–Exercise Psychology MA/MS (Master of Arts/Science)*—Applications 2004–2005, 27. Total applicants accepted 2004–2005, 18. Number enrolled (new admits only) 2004–2005 full-time, 11. Total enrolled 2004–2005 full-time, 18; part-time, 2. Openings 2005–2006, 17. The Median number of years required for completion of a degree are 2. The number of students enrolled full and part-time who were dismissed or voluntarily withdrew from this program area were 1. *Clinical Psychology PsyD (Doctor of Psychology)*—Applications 2004–2005, 149. Total applicants accepted 2004–2005, 88. Number enrolled (new admits only) 2004–2005 full-time, 39. Number enrolled (new admits only) 2004–2005 part-time, 0. Total enrolled 2004–2005 full-time, 163. Openings 2005–2006, 45. The Median number of years required for completion of a degree are 5. The number of students enrolled full and part-time who were dismissed or voluntarily withdrew from this program area were 3. *Clinical Psychology MA/MS (Master of Arts/Science)*—Applications

2004–2005, 54. Total applicants accepted 2004–2005, 31. Number enrolled (new admits only) 2004–2005 full-time, 8. Number enrolled (new admits only) 2004–2005 part-time, 0. Openings 2005–2006, 15. The Median number of years required for completion of a degree is 2. The number of students enrolled full or part-time who were dismissed or voluntarily withdrew from this program area was 2. *School Psychology PsyD (Doctor of Psychology)*—Applications 2004–2005, 27. Total applicants accepted 2004–2005, 22. Number enrolled (new admits only) 2004–2005 full-time, 18. Number enrolled (new admits only) 2004–2005 part-time, 0. Openings 2005–2006, 15. The Median number of years required for completion of a degree is 5. The number of students enrolled full or part-time who were dismissed or voluntarily withdrew from this program area was 0. *Forensic Psychology MA/MS (Master of Arts/Science)*—Applications 2004–2005, 8. Total applicants accepted 2004–2005, 8. Number enrolled (new admits only) 2004–2005 full-time, 8. Total enrolled 2004–2005 full-time, 8. Openings 2005–2006, 40. The Median number of years required for completion of a degree are 2. The number of students enrolled full or part-time who were dismissed or voluntarily withdrew from this program area was 0. *School Psychology MA/MS (Master of Arts/Science)*—Applications 2004–2005, 11. Total applicants accepted 2004–2005, 11. Number enrolled (new admits only) 2004–2005 full-time, 6. Total enrolled 2004–2005 full-time, 6. Openings 2005–2006, 20. The Median number of years required for completion of a degree was 2. The number of students enrolled full or part-time who were dismissed or voluntarily withdrew from this program area was 0.
Other Criteria: (importance of criteria rated low, medium, or high): research experience low, work experience high, extracurricular activity medium, clinically related public service high, GPA high, letters of recommendation medium, interview high, statement of goals and objectives high, resume medium. For additional information on admission requirements, go to: www.argosyu.edu.

Student Characteristics: The following represents characteristics of students in 2004–2005 in all graduate psychology programs in the department: Female–full-time 192, part-time 38; Male–full-time 70, part-time 29; African American/Black–full-time 18, part-time 6; Hispanic/Latino(a)–full-time 28, part-time 2; Asian/Pacific Islander–full-time 7, part-time 4; American Indian/Alaska Native–full-time 10, part-time 0; Caucasian–full-time 185, part-time 49; Multi-ethnic–full-time 14, part-time 6; students subject to the Americans With Disabilities Act–full-time 9, part-time 0.

Financial Information/Assistance:
Tuition for Full-Time Study: *Master's:* State residents: per academic year $17,160, $750 per credit hour; Nonstate residents: per academic year $17,160, $750 per credit hour. *Doctoral:* State residents: per academic year $17,160, $750 per credit hour; Nonstate residents: per academic year $17,160, $750 per credit hour. Tuition is subject to change. See the following for updates and changes in tuition costs: Contact Department of Admissions toll free at (866) 216-2777.

Financial Assistance:
First Year Students: Fellowships and scholarships available for first-year. Average amount paid per academic year: $3,000. Apply by rolling.

Advanced Students: Teaching assistantships available for advanced students. Average number of hours worked per week: 40. Tuition remission given: partial.

Contact Information: Of all students currently enrolled full-time, 10% benefitted from one or more of the listed financial assistance programs. Application and information available online at: www.argosyu.edu.

Internships/Practica: The School maintains an extensive clinical training network including public and private hospitals, community mental health agencies, private practices, substance abuse and rehabilitation agencies, correctional facilities, and the Indian Health Service. For those doctoral students for whom a professional internship is required prior to graduation, 22 applied in 2003–2004. Of those who applied, 10 were placed in internships listed by the Association of Psychology Postdoctoral and Internship Programs (APPIC); 7 were placed in APA accredited internships.

Housing and Day Care: No on-campus housing is available. No on-campus day care facilities are available.

Employment of Department Graduates:
Master's Degree Graduates: Of those who graduated in the academic year 2003–2004, the following categories and numbers represent the post-graduate activities and employment of master's degree graduates: Enrolled in a post-doctoral residency/fellowship (n/a), employed in independent practice (n/a), total from the above (master's) (0).

Doctoral Degree Graduates: Of those who graduated in the academic year 2003–2004, the following categories and numbers represent the post-graduate activities and employment of doctoral degree graduates: Enrolled in a psychology doctoral program (n/a), enrolled in a post-doctoral residency/fellowship (11), employed in a government agency (professional services) (2), still seeking employment (2), total from the above (doctoral) (15).

Additional Information:
Orientation, Objectives, and Emphasis of Department: The mission of Argosy University/Phoenix is to educate and train students in the major areas of clinical psychology, sport–exercise psychology and professional counseling, and to prepare students for successful practitioner careers. The curriculum integrates theory, training, research and practice and prepares students to work with a wide range of populations in need of psychological services. Faculty are both scholars and practitioners and guide students through coursework and field experiences so that they might understand how formal knowledge and practice operate to inform and enrich each other. The School follows a generalist practitioner-scholar orientation exposing students to a broad array of clinical theories and interventions. Sensitivity to diverse populations, populations with specific needs, and multicultural awareness are important components of the school's training model.

Special Facilities or Resources: Concentration in Sport–Exercise Psychology within the clinical doctoral program.

Information for Students With Physical Disabilities: See the following Web site for more information: www.argosyu.edu.

Application Information:
Send to: Andy Hughes, Director of Admissions, Argosy University/ Phoenix, 2301 W. Dunlap Avenue, Suite 211, Phoenix, AZ 85021. Phone Number: toll free (866) 216-2777 ext. 227; e-mail: ahughes@argosyu.edu. Application available online. Students are admitted in the Fall, application deadline May 15; Spring, application deadline October 15. Programs have rolling admissions. Deadlines vary by program, contact the Department of Admissions toll free at (866) 216-2777 for more information. Priority deadline of January 15 for fall admission. *Fee:* $50.

Arizona State University
Department of Psychology
Box 871104
Tempe, AZ 85287-1104
Telephone: (480) 965-7598
Fax: (480) 965-8544
E-mail: *psygrad@asu.edu*
Web: *http://www.asu.edu/clas/psych*

Department Information:
1932. Chairperson: Keith Crnic. Number of Faculty: total–full-time 50, part-time 2; women–full-time 16; minority–full-time 8; faculty subject to the Americans With Disabilities Act 1.

Programs and Degrees Offered:
Listed in the following order: Program area, degree type (T if terminal Master's), number awarded 7/03–6/04. Clinical PhD (Doctor of Philosophy) 7, developmental PhD (Doctor of Philosophy) 0, quantitative PhD (Doctor of Philosophy) 1, social PhD (Doctor of Philosophy) 4, behavioral neuroscience PhD (Doctor of Philosophy) 0, Cognition and Behavior PhD (Doctor of Philosophy) 2.

APA Accreditation: Clinical PhD (Doctor of Philosophy).

Student Applications/Admissions:
Student Applications
Clinical PhD (Doctor of Philosophy)—Applications 2004–2005, 285. Total applicants accepted 2004–2005, 8. Number enrolled (new admits only) 2004–2005 full-time, 8. The Median number of years required for completion of a degree is 7. *Developmental PhD (Doctor of Philosophy)*—Applications 2004–2005, 20. Total applicants accepted 2004–2005, 2. Openings 2005–2006, 5. *Quantitative PhD (Doctor of Philosophy)*—Applications 2004–2005, 18. Total applicants accepted 2004–2005, 4. Number enrolled (new admits only) 2004–2005 full-time, 4. Openings 2005–2006, 2. The Median number of years required for completion of a degree is 5. *Social PhD (Doctor of Philosophy)*—Applications 2004–2005, 66. Total applicants accepted 2004–2005, 8. Openings 2005–2006, 5. *Behavioral neuroscience PhD (Doctor of Philosophy)*—Applications 2004–2005, 18. Total applicants accepted 2004–2005, 6. Total enrolled 2004–2005 full-time, 12. Openings 2005–2006, 2. The number of students enrolled full or part-time who were dismissed or voluntarily withdrew from this program area was 0. *Cognition and Behavior PhD (Doctor of Philosophy)*—Applications 2004–2005, 29. Total applicants accepted 2004–2005, 12. Number enrolled (new admits only) 2004–2005 full-time, 6. Total enrolled 2004–

2005 full-time, 18. Openings 2005–2006, 4. The Median number of years required for completion of a degree are 6. The number of students enrolled full and part-time who were dismissed or voluntarily withdrew from this program area were 1.

Admissions Requirements:

Scores: Entries appear in this order: required test or GPA, minimum score (if required), median score of students entering in 2003–2004. Master's Programs: GRE-V no minimum stated; GRE-Q no minimum stated; GRE-Analytical no minimum stated. GRE-Subject (Psychology) is strongly recommended for clinical applicants only. Doctoral Programs: GRE-V no minimum stated; GRE-Q no minimum stated; GRE-Subject(Psych) no minimum stated. Subject test is strongly recommended for clinical applicants only. Scores vary across programs.

Other Criteria: (importance of criteria rated low, medium, or high): GRE/MAT scores medium, research experience high, work experience low, extracurricular activity low, clinically related public service medium, GPA medium, letters of recommendation high, interview high, statement of goals and objectives high. Weightings vary across programs.

Student Characteristics: The following represents characteristics of students in 2004–2005 in all graduate psychology programs in the department: Female–full-time 86, part-time 0; Male–full-time 40, part-time 0; African American/Black–full-time 2, part-time 0; Hispanic/Latino(a)–full-time 16, part-time 0; Asian/Pacific Islander–full-time 16, part-time 0; American Indian/Alaska Native–full-time 3, part-time 0; Caucasian–full-time 89, part-time 0; Multi-ethnic–full-time 0, part-time 0; students subject to the Americans With Disabilities Act–full-time 0, part-time 0.

Financial Information/Assistance:

Tuition for Full-Time Study: *Master's:* State residents: per academic year $5,038; Nonstate residents: per academic year $13,358. *Doctoral:* State residents: per academic year $5,038; Nonstate residents: per academic year $13,358. Tuition is subject to change.

Financial Assistance:

First Year Students: Teaching assistantships available for first-year. Average amount paid per academic year: $12,285. Average number of hours worked per week: 20. Tuition remission given: full. Research assistantships available for first-year. Average amount paid per academic year: $12,285. Average number of hours worked per week: 20. Tuition remission given: full.

Advanced Students: Teaching assistantships available for advanced students. Average amount paid per academic year: $13,205. Average number of hours worked per week: 20. Tuition remission given: full. Research assistantships available for advanced students. Average amount paid per academic year: $13,205. Average number of hours worked per week: 20. Tuition remission given: full.

Contact Information: Of all students currently enrolled full-time, 91% benefitted from one or more of the listed financial assistance programs.

Internships/Practica: Doctoral clinical students complete practica in community agencies and in our in-house training clinic. For those doctoral students for whom a professional internship is required prior to graduation, 8 applied in 2003–2004. Of those who applied, 8 were placed in internships listed by the Association of Psychology Postdoctoral and Internship Programs (APPIC); 8 were placed in APA accredited internships.

Housing and Day Care: On-campus housing is available. On-campus day care facilities are available.

Employment of Department Graduates:

Master's Degree Graduates: Of those who graduated in the academic year 2003–2004, the following categories and numbers represent the post-graduate activities and employment of master's degree graduates: Enrolled in a post-doctoral residency/fellowship (n/a), employed in independent practice (n/a), total from the above (master's) (0).

Doctoral Degree Graduates: Of those who graduated in the academic year 2003–2004, the following categories and numbers represent the post-graduate activities and employment of doctoral degree graduates: Enrolled in a psychology doctoral program (n/a), total from the above (doctoral) (0).

Additional Information:

Orientation, Objectives, and Emphasis of Department: The department seeks to instill in students knowledge, skills, and an appreciation of psychology as a science and as a profession. To do so, it offers undergraduate and graduate programs emphasizing theory, research, and applied practice. The department encourages a multiplicity of theoretical viewpoints and research interests. The behavioral neuroscience area emphasizes the neural bases of motor disorders, drug abuse, and recovery of function following brain damage. The clinical program includes areas of emphasis in health psychology, child-clinical psychology, and community-prevention. Also offered are classes in psychopathology, prevention, assessment, and psychotherapy. The cognitive systems area includes cognitive psychology, adaptive systems, learning, sensation and perception, and cognitive development. The developmental area includes coursework and research experience in the core areas of cognitive and social development. The environmental area emphasizes the application of psychological research to environmental and population problems, including architectural design, urban planning, and human ecology. The quantitative area focuses on design, measurement, and statistical analysis issues that arise in diverse areas of psychological research. The social area emphasizes theoretical and laboratory skills combined with program evaluation and applied social psychology.

Special Facilities or Resources: The department has the Child Study Laboratory for training and research in developmental psychology, including both normal and clinical groups, particularly of preschool age; the Clinical Psychology Center, whose clients represent a wide range of psychological disorders and are not limited to the university community; and the experimental laboratories, with exceptional computer facilities for the study of speech perception, neural networks, categorization, memory, sensory processes, and learning. The clinical and social programs maintain continuing liaisons with a wide range of off-campus agencies for research applications of psychological theory and research. Our NIMH-funded Preventive Intervention Research Center provides a site for training in the design, implementation, and evaluation of preventative interventions. Quantitatively oriented students receive methodological experience in large-scale research programs and in our statistical laboratory.

Application Information:
Send to: Admissions Secretary, Department of Psychology, Arizona State University, P.O. Box 871104, Tempe, AZ 85287-1104. Application available online. URL of online application: http://www.asu.edu/clas/psych/gprogram/apply.htm. Students are admitted in the Fall, application deadlines are December 15 for Clinical, January 5 for all other programs. *Fee:* $50.

Arizona State University

Division of Psychology in Education
B-302, Payne Hall, P.O. Box 870611
Tempe, AZ 85287-0611
Telephone: (480) 965-3384
Fax: (480) 965-0300
E-mail: *dpe@asu.edu*
Web: *http://coe.asu.edu/psyched/*

Department Information:
1968. Division Director: Elsie G.J. Moore. Number of Faculty: total–full-time 34, part-time 6; women–full-time 19, part-time 3; minority–full-time 8.

Programs and Degrees Offered:
Listed in the following order: Program area, degree type (T if terminal Master's), number awarded 7/03–6/04. Educational: Learning PhD (Doctor of Philosophy) 1, Counseling Psychology PhD (Doctor of Philosophy) 9, Master of Counseling MA/MS (Master of Arts/Science) (T) 49, Master of Education in Counseling Other 0, Educational Psychology Other 7, Educational: Measurement, stat PhD (Doctor of Philosophy) 0, Educational: Life span development PhD (Doctor of Philosophy) 4, Educational Technology Other 16, Educational: School Psychology PhD (Doctor of Philosophy) 3, Educational Technology PhD (Doctor of Philosophy) 3.

APA Accreditation: Counseling PhD (Doctor of Philosophy). School PhD (Doctor of Philosophy).

Student Applications/Admissions:
Student Applications
Educational: Learning PhD (Doctor of Philosophy)—Applications 2004–2005, 10. Total applicants accepted 2004–2005, 4. Number enrolled (new admits only) 2004–2005 full-time, 0. Number enrolled (new admits only) 2004–2005 part-time, 0. Total enrolled 2004–2005 full-time, 8, part-time 5. Openings 2005–2006, 6. The Median number of years required for completion of a degree are 2. The number of students enrolled full and part-time who were dismissed or voluntarily withdrew from this program area were 1. *Counseling Psychology PhD (Doctor of Philosophy)*—Applications 2004–2005, 107. Total applicants accepted 2004–2005, 15. Number enrolled (new admits only) 2004–2005 full-time, 10. Number enrolled (new admits only) 2004–2005 part-time, 0. Total enrolled 2004–2005 full-time, 45; part-time, 15. Openings 2005–2006, 8. The Median number of years required for completion of a degree are 5. The number of students enrolled full and part-time who were dismissed or voluntarily withdrew from this program area were 5. *Master of Counseling MA/MS (Master of Arts/Science)*—Applications 2004–2005, 150. Total applicants accepted

2004–2005, 85. Number enrolled (new admits only) 2004–2005 full-time, 48. Number enrolled (new admits only) 2004–2005 part-time, 7. Total enrolled 2004–2005 full-time, 94; part-time, 68. Openings 2005–2006, 60. The Median number of years required for completion of a degree are 3. The number of students enrolled full and part-time who were dismissed or voluntarily withdrew from this program area were 7. *Master of Education in Counseling Other*—Applications 2004–2005, 2. Total applicants accepted 2004–2005, 1. Number enrolled (new admits only) 2004–2005 full-time, 0. Number enrolled (new admits only) 2004–2005 part-time, 1. Total enrolled 2004–2005 full-time, 4; part-time, 5. Openings 2005–2006, 5. The Median number of years required for completion of a degree are 2. The number of students enrolled full and part-time who were dismissed or voluntarily withdrew from this program area were 1. *Educational Psychology Other*—Applications 2004–2005, 14. Total applicants accepted 2004–2005, 9. Number enrolled (new admits only) 2004–2005 full-time, 6. Number enrolled (new admits only) 2004–2005 part-time, 4. Total enrolled 2004–2005 full-time, 20; part-time, 23. Openings 2005–2006, 10. The Median number of years required for completion of a degree are 2. The number of students enrolled full and part-time who were dismissed or voluntarily withdrew from this program area were 0. *Educational: Measurement, stat PhD (Doctor of Philosophy)*—Applications 2004–2005, 10. Total applicants accepted 2004–2005, 4. Number enrolled (new admits only) 2004–2005 full-time, 2. Number enrolled (new admits only) 2004–2005 part-time, 1. Total enrolled 2004–2005 full-time, 7; part-time, 9. Openings 2005–2006, 5. The number of students enrolled full and part-time who were dismissed or voluntarily withdrew from this program area were 0. *Educational: Life span development PhD (Doctor of Philosophy)*—Applications 2004–2005, 8. Total applicants accepted 2004–2005, 7. Number enrolled (new admits only) 2004–2005 full-time, 1. Number enrolled (new admits only) 2004–2005 part-time, 0. Total enrolled 2004–2005 full-time, 12; part-time, 17. Openings 2005–2006, 5. The Median number of years required for completion of a degree are 3. The number of students enrolled full and part-time who were dismissed or voluntarily withdrew from this program area were 5. *Educational Technology Other*—Applications 2004–2005, 22. Total applicants accepted 2004–2005, 16. Number enrolled (new admits only) 2004–2005 full-time, 3. Number enrolled (new admits only) 2004–2005 part-time, 8. Total enrolled 2004–2005 full-time, 10; part-time, 22. Openings 2005–2006, 20. The Median number of years required for completion of a degree are 2. The number of students enrolled full and part-time who were dismissed or voluntarily withdrew from this program area were 7. *Educational: School Psychology PhD (Doctor of Philosophy)*—Applications 2004–2005, 49. Total applicants accepted 2004–2005, 27. Number enrolled (new admits only) 2004–2005 full-time, 9. Number enrolled (new admits only) 2004–2005 part-time, 2. Total enrolled 2004–2005 full-time, 28; part-time, 13. Openings 2005–2006, 10. The Median number of years required for completion of a degree are 6. The number of students enrolled full and part-time who were dismissed or voluntarily withdrew from this program area were 5. *Educational Technology PhD (Doctor of Philosophy)*—Applications 2004–2005, 40. Total applicants accepted 2004–2005, 10. Number enrolled (new admits only) 2004–2005 full-time, 5. Number enrolled (new admits only) 2004–2005 part-time, 3. Total enrolled 2004–2005 full-time, 14; part-time, 12.

Openings 2005–2006, 9. The Median number of years required for completion of a degree are 5. The number of students enrolled full and part-time who were dismissed or voluntarily withdrew from this program area were 3.

Admissions Requirements:

Scores: Entries appear in this order: required test or GPA, minimum score (if required), median score of students entering in 2003–2004. Master's Programs: GRE-V no minimum stated, 500; GRE-Q no minimum stated, 570; MAT no minimum stated, 50; overall undergraduate GPA no minimum stated, 3.5; last 2 years GPA 3.00, 3.49. Counselor Education and Educational Technology will accept a MAT score in lieu of the GRE. Otherwise, the GRE is required by all programs. Doctoral Programs: GRE-V no minimum stated, 570; GRE-Q no minimum stated, 640; GRE-V+Q no minimum stated; overall undergraduate GPA no minimum stated, 3.49; last 2 years GPA 3.0, 3.62. Educational Technology PhD requires a 3.2 or above undergraduate GPA and 1200 GRE V+Q.

Other Criteria: (importance of criteria rated low, medium, or high): GRE/MAT scores medium, research experience high, work experience medium, extracurricular activity low, clinically related public service medium, GPA medium, letters of recommendation low, interview medium, statement of goals and objectives medium. Programs use the FRK index, which combines GRE V+Q with undergraduate GPA. Minimum FRKs are set by faculty admissions committees. For additional information on admission requirements, go to: http://coe.asu.edu/psyched; www.asu.edu/graduate.

Student Characteristics: The following represents characteristics of students in 2004–2005 in all graduate psychology programs in the department: Female–full-time 184, part-time 141; Male–full-time 58, part-time 48; African American/Black–full-time 12, part-time 4; Hispanic/Latino(a)–full-time 30, part-time 14; Asian/Pacific Islander–full-time 29, part-time 19; American Indian/Alaska Native–full-time 1, part-time 2; Caucasian–full-time 170, part-time 150; students subject to the Americans With Disabilities Act–full-time 0, part-time 1.

Financial Information/Assistance:

Tuition for Full-Time Study: *Master's:* State residents: per academic year $5,127; Nonstate residents: per academic year $13,647. *Doctoral:* State residents: per academic year $5,127; Nonstate residents: per academic year $13,647. Tuition is subject to change. See the following Web site for updates and changes in tuition costs: www.asu.edu/sbs/GraduateFees.html.

Financial Assistance:

First Year Students: Teaching assistantships available for first-year. Average amount paid per academic year: $5,813. Average number of hours worked per week: 10. Apply by April 15. Tuition remission given: partial. Research assistantships available for first-year. Average amount paid per academic year: $5,813. Average number of hours worked per week: 10. Apply by April 15. Tuition remission given: partial.

Advanced Students: Teaching assistantships available for advanced students. Average amount paid per academic year: $5,813. Average number of hours worked per week: 10. Apply by April 15. Tuition remission given: partial. Research assistantships available for advanced students. Average amount paid per aca-

demic year: $5,813. Average number of hours worked per week: 10. Apply by April 15. Tuition remission given: partial.

Contact Information: Of all students currently enrolled full-time, 27% benefitted from one or more of the listed financial assistance programs. Application and information available online at: http://www.asu.edu/graduate.

Internships/Practica: Our doctoral internships include APA-approved sites throughout the nation. Sites include university counseling centers, community mental health clinics, and hospitals. Practica for doctoral and master's students typically are local (the greater Phoenix area) and include university counseling centers, community mental health clinics, and hospitals. For those doctoral students for whom a professional internship is required prior to graduation, 9 applied in 2003–2004. Of those who applied, 6 were placed in internships listed by the Association of Psychology Postdoctoral and Internship Programs (APPIC); 6 were placed in APA accredited internships.

Housing and Day Care: No on-campus housing is available. No on-campus day care facilities are available.

Employment of Department Graduates:

Master's Degree Graduates: Of those who graduated in the academic year 2003–2004, the following categories and numbers represent the post-graduate activities and employment of master's degree graduates: Enrolled in a post-doctoral residency/fellowship (n/a), employed in independent practice (n/a), total from the above (master's) (0).

Doctoral Degree Graduates: Of those who graduated in the academic year 2003–2004, the following categories and numbers represent the post-graduate activities and employment of doctoral degree graduates: Enrolled in a psychology doctoral program (n/a), total from the above (doctoral) (0).

Additional Information:

Orientation, Objectives, and Emphasis of Department: The Division adheres to a scientist-practitioner model across all areas. The Counseling and School Psychology programs are APA accredited. Less than half of the doctoral graduates accept positions in colleges and universities; the remainder function in applied settings.

Special Facilities or Resources: The department staffs and operates a large-scale psychological assessment laboratory, and most students are currently assigned research and study space. Strong research relations exist with local schools, agencies, and private industry. The Counseling Training Center is a training facility for Master's and PhD level counseling students. The center serves clients from both the university and the general public.

Information for Students With Physical Disabilities: See the following Web site for more information: www.asu.edu/drs.

Application Information:
Send to: Admissions Secretary, Psychology in Education, Arizona State University, P.O. Box 870611, Tempe, AZ 85287-0611. Application available online. URL of online application: www.asu.edu/graduate/admissions. Students are admitted in the Fall. Counseling Psychology—December 1 for fall; School Psychology—January 1 for fall; Master of Counseling—January 15 for fall; Educational Psychology, Learning, Lifespan, and Measurement—February 15 for fall and October 15 for

spring; Educational Technology—rolling admissions. *Fee:* $50. The application fee cannot be waived.

Arizona, University of
Department of Psychology
Social and Behavioral Sciences
P.O. Box 210068
Tucson, AZ 85721
Telephone: (520) 621-7448
Fax: (520) 621-9306
E-mail: *kaszniak@u.arizona.edu*
Web: *http://psychology.arizona.edu/*

Department Information:
1914. Head: Alfred W. Kaszniak. Number of Faculty: total–full-time 33, part-time 9; women–full-time 14, part-time 6; minority–full-time 3.

Programs and Degrees Offered:
Listed in the following order: Program area, degree type (T if terminal Master's), number awarded 7/03–6/04. Clinical PhD (Doctor of Philosophy) 5, cognition and neural systems PhD (Doctor of Philosophy) 3, ethology and evolutionary PhD (Doctor of Philosophy) 1, psychology, policy, and law PhD (Doctor of Philosophy) 0, social PhD (Doctor of Philosophy) 0, program evaluation PhD (Doctor of Philosophy) 3.

APA Accreditation: Clinical PhD (Doctor of Philosophy).

Student Applications/Admissions:
Student Applications
Clinical PhD (Doctor of Philosophy)—Applications 2004–2005, 225. Total applicants accepted 2004–2005, 10. Number enrolled (new admits only) 2004–2005 full-time, 5. Openings 2005–2006, 6. The Median number of years required for completion of a degree are 7. The number of students enrolled full and part-time who were dismissed or voluntarily withdrew from this program area were 1. *Cognition and neural systems PhD (Doctor of Philosophy)*—Applications 2004–2005, 64. Total applicants accepted 2004–2005, 12. Number enrolled (new admits only) 2004–2005 full-time, 6. Openings 2005–2006, 8. The Median number of years required for completion of a degree are 6. The number of students enrolled full and part-time who were dismissed or voluntarily withdrew from this program area were 1. *Ethology and evolutionary PhD (Doctor of Philosophy)*—Applications 2004–2005, 19. Total applicants accepted 2004–2005, 1. Number enrolled (new admits only) 2004–2005 full-time, 1. Openings 2005–2006, 2. The Median number of years required for completion of a degree are 9. The number of students enrolled full and part-time who were dismissed or voluntarily withdrew from this program area were 0. *Psychology, policy, and law PhD (Doctor of Philosophy)*—Applications 2004–2005, 73. Total applicants accepted 2004–2005, 3. Number enrolled (new admits only) 2004–2005 full-time, 2. Openings 2005–2006, 2. The number of students enrolled full and part-time who were dismissed or voluntarily withdrew from this program area were 0. *Social PhD (Doctor of Philosophy)*—Applications 2004–2005, 40. Total applicants accepted 2004–2005, 2. Number enrolled (new admits only)

2004–2005 full-time, 2. Openings 2005–2006, 3. The number of students enrolled full and part-time who were dismissed or voluntarily withdrew from this program area were 0. *Program evaluation PhD (Doctor of Philosophy)*—Applications 2004–2005, 0. Total applicants accepted 2004–2005, 0. Number enrolled (new admits only) 2004–2005 full-time, 2. Openings 2005–2006, 1. The Median number of years required for completion of a degree are 7. The number of students enrolled full and part-time who were dismissed or voluntarily withdrew from this program area were 0.

Admissions Requirements:
Scores: Entries appear in this order: required test or GPA, minimum score (if required), median score of students entering in 2003–2004. Doctoral Programs: GRE-V no minimum stated, 543; GRE-Q no minimum stated, 618; GRE-Analytical no minimum stated, 750; GRE-Subject(Psych) no minimum stated, 683; overall undergraduate GPA 3.0, 3.71. The Clinical program requires the GRE subject score. For other programs, this score is recommended, but not required.
Other Criteria: (importance of criteria rated low, medium, or high): GRE/MAT scores medium, research experience high, work experience low, extracurricular activity low, clinically related public service low, GPA medium, letters of recommendation high, interview medium, statement of goals and objectives high. For additional information on admission requirements, go to: http://psychology.arizona.edu/.

Student Characteristics: The following represents characteristics of students in 2004–2005 in all graduate psychology programs in the department: Female–full-time 56, part-time 0; Male–full-time 36, part-time 0; African American/Black–full-time 1, part-time 0; Hispanic/Latino(a)–full-time 7, part-time 0; Asian/Pacific Islander–full-time 9, part-time 0; American Indian/Alaska Native–full-time 0, part-time 0; Caucasian–full-time 75, part-time 0; Multi-ethnic–full-time 0, part-time 0; students subject to the Americans With Disabilities Act–full-time 1, part-time 0.

Financial Information/Assistance:
Tuition for Full-Time Study: *Doctoral:* State residents: per academic year $2,174, $237 per credit hour; Nonstate residents: per academic year $6,664, $566 per credit hour. Tuition is subject to change.

Financial Assistance:
First Year Students: Teaching assistantships available for first-year. Average amount paid per academic year: $12,710. Average number of hours worked per week: 20. Tuition remission given: partial. Research assistantships available for first-year. Average amount paid per academic year: $12,710. Average number of hours worked per week: 20. Tuition remission given: partial. Traineeships available for first-year. Average amount paid per academic year: $12,710. Average number of hours worked per week: 20. Tuition remission given: partial. Fellowships and scholarships available for first-year. Average amount paid per academic year: $12,710. Average number of hours worked per week: 20. Tuition remission given: partial.
Advanced Students: Teaching assistantships available for advanced students. Average amount paid per academic year: $12,710. Average number of hours worked per week: 20. Tuition remission given: partial. Research assistantships available for advanced students. Average amount paid per academic year:

$12,710. Average number of hours worked per week: 20. Tuition remission given: partial. Traineeships available for advanced students. Average amount paid per academic year: $12,710. Average number of hours worked per week: 20. Tuition remission given: partial. Fellowships and scholarships available for advanced students. Average amount paid per academic year: $12,710. Average number of hours worked per week: 20. Tuition remission given: partial.

Contact Information: Of all students currently enrolled full-time, 88% benefitted from one or more of the listed financial assistance programs. Application and information available online at: http://psychology.arizona.edu/programs/g_each.php?option=3.

Internships/Practica: Clinical students are required to do a 1-year internship. UMC medical school does offer internship positions, although most of our students leave campus for the internship. All of the clinical students are placed in APA accredited internships. There are also various externships and practica available within the department as well as throughout the community. For those doctoral students for whom a professional internship is required prior to graduation, 3 applied in 2003–2004. Of those who applied, 3 were placed in internships listed by the Association of Psychology Postdoctoral and Internship Programs (APPIC); 3 were placed in APA accredited internships.

Housing and Day Care: On-campus housing is available. See the following Web site for more information: http://www.arizona.edu/prospective/graduate.shtml. On-campus day care facilities are available. See the following Web site for more information: http://www.arizona.edu/prospective/campus-services.shtml.

Employment of Department Graduates:

Master's Degree Graduates: Of those who graduated in the academic year 2003–2004, the following categories and numbers represent the post-graduate activities and employment of master's degree graduates: Enrolled in a post-doctoral residency/fellowship (n/a), employed in independent practice (n/a), total from the above (master's) (0).

Doctoral Degree Graduates: Of those who graduated in the academic year 2003–2004, the following categories and numbers represent the post-graduate activities and employment of doctoral degree graduates: Enrolled in a psychology doctoral program (n/a), enrolled in a post-doctoral residency/fellowship (6), employed in independent practice (1), employed in an academic position at a university (1), employed in other positions at a higher education institution (2), employed in a professional position in a school system (0), employed in a government agency (research) (1), employed in a hospital/medical center (0), still seeking employment (0), other employment position (0), do not know (1), total from the above (doctoral) (12).

Additional Information:

Orientation, Objectives, and Emphasis of Department: Our objectives as a department include contributing to the growth of knowledge about the mind and its workings, and the training of students to participate in this pursuit, as well as using this knowledge to benefit society. The department emphasizes research and training students headed toward both academic and applied careers. Required courses provide breadth of coverage, but emphasis is on research within the area of specialization, relying on independent work with individual faculty members. The interdisciplinary nature of the department fosters specialization in areas that cut across program boundaries and permits work with faculty members in various programs. The cognition and neural systems area emphasizes language, perception, attention, memory, aging, ensemble, recording of neural activity, and human neuroimaging; the clinical area emphasizes clinical neuropsychology, psychotherapy research, sleep disorders, psychophysiology, and assessment; the social area emphasizes prejudice and sterotyping, cognitive dissonance, self-esteem, and motivational factors in thought and behavior; the psychology, policy, and law area emphasizes the contributions of psychological science to legal and policy decisions; and the ethology and evolutionary area emphasizes quantitative ethology, invertebrate behavior, and human behavioral ecology. In addition to these formal programs, the department also offers specialization in evaluation and research methods. The department is the administrative home for the Center on Consciousness Studies and the Cognition and Neuroimaging Laboratory.

Special Facilities or Resources: The department has modern laboratories devoted to research in various areas of cognitive, clinical, neuroscientific, social, and comparative research. The department employs 5 technicians available for assistance with computers and other equipment. There are a number of clinics within the department, bringing in patients associated with research projects on aging, sleep disorders, memory disorders, depression, and others. The department has ties with a number of other programs on campus, including the departments of Anatomy, Family and Community Medicine, Neurology, Ophthalmology, Pediatrics, Pharmacology, Physiology, and Psychiatry in the College of Medicine, and the departments of Ecology and Evolutionary Biology, Family Studies, Linguistics, Management and Policy, Mathematics, Philosophy, Renewable and Natural Resources, Speech and Hearing Sciences, and Physics on the main campus. Ties also exist with various interdisciplinary programs, including Cognitive Science (many of whose laboratories are located in the Psychology Building), Applied Mathematics, and Neuroscience. Most of the department's faculty members are holders of research grants, permitting a significant proportion of the graduate students to serve as research assistants at various times during their training.

Information for Students With Physical Disabilities: See the following Web site for more information: http://drc.arizona.edu/.

Application Information:
Send to: Graduate Admissions, Department of Psychology, University of Arizona, 1503 E. University Blvd., Tucson, AZ 85721. Application available online. URL of online application: http://psychology.arizona.edu. Students are admitted in the Fall, application deadline December 15. *Fee*: $50.

Arizona, University of
Department of Special Education, Rehabilitation, and School Psychology
College of Education
Tucson, AZ 85721
E-mail: *Mishras@email.arizona.edu*

Department Information:
1966. Department Head: Lawrence Aleamoni, PhD.

Programs and Degrees Offered:
Listed in the following order: Program area, degree type (T if terminal Master's), number awarded 7/03–6/04. School Psychology PhD (Doctor of Philosophy), School Psychology EdS (Education Specialist).

APA Accreditation: School PhD (Doctor of Philosophy).

Student Applications/Admissions:
Student Applications
School Psychology PhD (Doctor of Philosophy)—School Psychology EdS (Education Specialist)

Student Characteristics: The following represents characteristics of students in 2004–2005 in all graduate psychology programs in the department: Caucasian–full-time 0, part-time 0.

Financial Information/Assistance:
Financial Assistance:
First Year Students: No information provided.
Advanced Students: No information provided.
Contact Information: No information provided.

Internships/Practica: No information provided.

Housing and Day Care: No on-campus housing is available. No on-campus day care facilities are available.

Employment of Department Graduates:
Master's Degree Graduates: Of those who graduated in the academic year 2003–2004, the following categories and numbers represent the post-graduate activities and employment of master's degree graduates: Enrolled in a post-doctoral residency/fellowship (n/a), employed in independent practice (n/a), total from the above (master's) (0).
Doctoral Degree Graduates: Of those who graduated in the academic year 2003–2004, the following categories and numbers represent the post-graduate activities and employment of doctoral degree graduates: Enrolled in a psychology doctoral program (n/a), total from the above (doctoral) (0).

Northcentral University
Psychology
Behavioral and Social Sciences
505 W. Whipple
Prescott, AZ 86301
Telephone: (888) 327-2877
Fax: (928) 541-7817
E-mail: *ccozby@ncu.edu*
Web: *http://www.ncu.edu*

Department Information:
1999. Chairperson: Chris Cozby. Number of Faculty: total–full-time 4, part-time 35; women–part-time 21; minority–part-time 2.

Programs and Degrees Offered:
Listed in the following order: Program area, degree type (T if terminal Master's), number awarded 7/03–6/04. General Psychology PhD (Doctor of Philosophy), Health Psychology PhD (Doctor of Philosophy), Industrial/Organizational Psychology PhD (Doctor of Philosophy), Marriage and Family Therapy MA/MS (Master of Arts/Science), Psychology MA MA/MS (Master of Arts/Science).

Student Applications/Admissions:
Student Applications
General Psychology PhD (Doctor of Philosophy)—Health Psychology PhD (Doctor of Philosophy)—Industrial/Organizational Psychology PhD (Doctor of Philosophy)—Marriage and Family Therapy MA/MS (Master of Arts/Science)—Psychology MA MA/MS (Master of Arts/Science)

Admissions Requirements:
Scores: Entries appear in this order: required test or GPA, minimum score (if required), median score of students entering in 2003–2004. Master's Programs: last 2 years GPA 2.0, 3.0. Doctoral Programs: last 2 years GPA 2.0, 3.0.
Other Criteria: (importance of criteria rated low, medium, or high): research experience low, work experience medium, extracurricular activity low, clinically related public service low, GPA low, letters of recommendation low, interview low, statement of goals and objectives medium. For additional information on admission requirements, go to: www.ncu.edu.

Student Characteristics: The following represents characteristics of students in 2004–2005 in all graduate psychology programs in the department: Caucasian–full-time 0, part-time 0.

Financial Information/Assistance:
Financial Assistance:
First Year Students: No information provided.
Advanced Students: No information provided.
Contact Information: Application and information available online at: www.ncu.edu.

Internships/Practica: No information provided.

Housing and Day Care: No on-campus housing is available. No on-campus day care facilities are available.

Employment of Department Graduates:
Master's Degree Graduates: Of those who graduated in the academic year 2003–2004, the following categories and numbers represent the post-graduate activities and employment of master's degree graduates: Enrolled in a post-doctoral residency/fellowship (n/a), employed in independent practice (n/a), total from the above (master's) (0).
Doctoral Degree Graduates: Of those who graduated in the academic year 2003–2004, the following categories and numbers represent the post-graduate activities and employment of doctoral degree graduates: Enrolled in a psychology doctoral program (n/a), total from the above (doctoral) (0).

Additional Information:
Orientation, Objectives, and Emphasis of Department: The department emphasizes applications of psychology. All instruction is carried out via distance learning in which learners and mentors work together in one-on-one relationship. Learners need to be highly motivated, independent, and conscientious.

Application Information:
Application available online. URL of online application: https://www.ncu.edu/applicant/. Students are admitted in the Programs have rolling admissions.

Northern Arizona University
Department of Psychology
Social and Behavioral Sciences
NAU Box 15106
Flagstaff, AZ 86011
Telephone: (520) 523-3063
Fax: (520) 523-6777
E-mail: *heidi.wayment@nau.edu*
Web: *http://www.nau.edu*

Department Information:
1967. Chairperson: Heidi Wayment. Number of Faculty: total–full-time 17, part-time 2; women–full-time 8, part-time 1.

Programs and Degrees Offered:
Listed in the following order: Program area, degree type (T if terminal Master's), number awarded 7/03–6/04. Applied Health MA/MS (Master of Arts/Science) (T) 5, General MA/MS (Master of Arts/Science) (T) 2.

Student Applications/Admissions:
Student Applications
Applied Health MA/MS (Master of Arts/Science)—Applications 2004–2005, 23. Total applicants accepted 2004–2005, 12. Number enrolled (new admits only) 2004–2005 full-time, 23. Openings 2005–2006, 10. *General MA/MS (Master of Arts/Science)*—Applications 2004–2005, 25. Total applicants accepted 2004–2005, 10. Number enrolled (new admits only) 2004–2005 full-time, 25. Openings 2005–2006, 10. The number of students enrolled full and part-time, who were dismissed or voluntarily withdrew from this program area were 0.

Admissions Requirements:
Scores: Entries appear in this order: required test or GPA, minimum score (if required), median score of students entering in 2003–2004. Master's Programs: GRE-V no minimum stated, 520; GRE-Q no minimum stated, 580; GRE-V+Q no minimum stated, 1100; overall undergraduate GPA no minimum stated, 3.5; last 2 years GPA no minimum stated, 3.6; psychology GPA no minimum stated, 3.5. Preference is for a combined GRE-V + GRE-Q of 1000 or more. An overall undergraduate GPA of 3.0 or above is preferred.
Other Criteria: (importance of criteria rated low, medium, or high): GRE/MAT scores high, research experience high, work experience low, extracurricular activity low, clinically related public service low, GPA high, letters of recommendation high, statement of goals and objectives high. Clinically related public service used only for applied health psychology program. Work experience and extracurricular activity given somewhat higher importance for applied health psychology program.

Student Characteristics: The following represents characteristics of students in 2004–2005 in all graduate psychology programs in the department: Female–full-time 20, part-time 16; Male–full-time 8, part-time 4; African American/Black–full-time 1, part-time 0; Hispanic/Latino(a)–full-time 2, part-time 1; Asian/Pacific Islander–full-time 0, part-time 0; American Indian/Alaska Native–full-time 0, part-time 2; Caucasian–full-time 25, part-time 17; Multi-ethnic–full-time 0, part-time 0; students subject to the Americans With Disabilities Act–full-time 0, part-time 0.

Financial Information/Assistance:
Tuition for Full-Time Study: *Master's:* State residents: per academic year $4,272, $219 per credit hour; Nonstate residents: per academic year $12,792, $552 per credit hour. Tuition is subject to change. See the following Web site for updates and changes in tuition costs: http://www4.nau.edu/bursar/fees_spring.htm.

Financial Assistance:
First Year Students: Teaching assistantships available for first-year. Average number of hours worked per week: 10. Apply by February 15. Tuition remission given: partial. Research assistantships available for first-year. Average number of hours worked per week: 10. Apply by February 15. Tuition remission given: partial.
Advanced Students: Teaching assistantships available for advanced students. Average number of hours worked per week: 10. Apply by n/a. Tuition remission given: partial. Research assistantships available for advanced students. Average number of hours worked per week: 10. Apply by n/a. Tuition remission given: partial.
Contact Information: Of all students currently enrolled full-time, 58% benefitted from one or more of the listed financial assistance programs.

Internships/Practica: Applied Health Psychology students are required to take two semesters of practicum in the department's Health Psychology Center. Our multipurpose training and service facility serves NAU students, faculty, and staff as well as community residents. In the Center, supervised graduate students in applied health psychology work to promote wellness and healthy lifestyles in adults and children through a variety of educational and treatment modalities. The Center offers programs on such topics as stress management, healthy eating and weight control, exercise, and smoking cessation, as well as group and individual interventions for these topics. The Center also provides psychological evaluation and behavioral management for health-related problems such as headaches, high blood pressure, cardiovascular disease, obesity, premenstrual syndrome, ulcers, diabetes, asthma, smoking, cancer, and chronic pain. Applied Health Psychology students also are encouraged to take one or more semesters of fieldwork placement at a variety of agencies in the surrounding communities (including ethnic and rural communities). General Psychology students also may enroll in fieldwork placement.

Housing and Day Care: On-campus housing is available. See the following Web site for more information: http://www4.nau.edu/reslife/reslife/. No on-campus day care facilities are available.

Employment of Department Graduates:
Master's Degree Graduates: Of those who graduated in the academic year 2003–2004, the following categories and numbers represent the post-graduate activities and employment of master's degree graduates: Enrolled in a post-doctoral residency/fellowship (n/a), employed in independent practice (n/a), employed in an

academic position at a 2-year/4-year college (1), other employment position (1), total from the above (master's) (2).

Doctoral Degree Graduates: Of those who graduated in the academic year 2003–2004, the following categories and numbers represent the post-graduate activities and employment of doctoral degree graduates: Enrolled in a psychology doctoral program (n/a), total from the above (doctoral) (0).

Additional Information:

Orientation, Objectives, and Emphasis of Department: The psychology department is committed to excellence in education at the graduate level, emphasizing teaching, scholarship, and service to the university and to the larger community. The nature of our discipline is such that it helps students understand the biological, social, and cultural influences on human thought, emotions, and behavior. The department's approach to these issues emphasizes the theoretical foundations, empirical research, innovative curriculum, and practical hands-on applications of psychological knowledge. In addition, the department strongly supports the university's mission of promoting opportunities for multicultural experiences and encouraging ethnic diversity of students and faculty. Throughout its curriculum, the department integrates research and scholarship with teaching. This includes the use of existing research to enhance course content and structure and also includes students' participation in faculty-directed research, student-initiated research, and collaborative faculty-student research. In addition to supporting research and scholarship within the university community, the department participates in the larger discipline of psychology by encouraging faculty and student attendance at professional conferences as well as publication in professional journals.

Special Facilities or Resources: The Department of Psychology has over 1,500 square feet of clinic space dedicated to training in Applied Health Psychology and a state-of-the-art psychophysiology/biofeedback laboratory. Other well-equipped research facilities are available in an adjunct building, and are assigned to faculty members engaged in research. A computer laboratory used for teaching purposes is also available for data collection. The department is housed in a modern building at the south end of the Flagstaff Mountain Campus. All teaching rooms are equipped with up-to-date technology. NAU is located in the city of Flagstaff, a four-season community of approximately 50,000 residents at the base of the majestic, 12,670-foot-high San Francisco Peaks. Flagstaff and the surrounding area offer excellent hiking and mountain-biking trails as well as cross-country and downhill skiing. Students enjoy the nearby diversity of Arizona's climate and attractions, from Grand Canyon National Park to metropolitan Phoenix in the Sonoran desert.

Information for Students With Physical Disabilities: See the following Web site for more information: http://www2.nau.edu/dss/.

Application Information:

Send to: Departmental Application: Department of Psychology, Graduate Programs, Northern Arizona University, Box 15106, Flagstaff, AZ 86011. Graduate Application: NAU Graduate College, P.O. Box 4125, Flagstaff, AZ 86011-4125. Application available online. URL of online application: http://www.nau.edu/gradcol/. Students are admitted in the Fall, application deadline February 15. *Fee:* $45.

Northern Arizona University
Educational Psychology
College of Education
COE 5774
Flagstaff, AZ 86011
Telephone: (928) 523-7103
Fax: (928) 523-9284
E-mail: *eps@nau.edu*
Web: *http://coe.nau.edu/academics/EPS*

Department Information:

1962. Chairperson: Ramona N. Mellott. Number of Faculty: total–full-time 21, part-time 9; women–full-time 11, part-time 2; minority–full-time 5, part-time 1.

Programs and Degrees Offered:

Listed in the following order: Program area, degree type (T if terminal Master's), number awarded 7/03–6/04. Community Counseling MA/MS (Master of Arts/Science) (T) 30, Certification in School Psychology MA/MS (Master of Arts/Science) (T) 7, School Counseling Other 46, Student Affairs MA/MS (Master of Arts/Science) (T) 6, Counseling Psychology PhD (Doctor of Philosophy) 2, School Psychology EdD (Doctor of Education) 0, Learning and Instruction PhD (Doctor of Philosophy) 0, Counseling–Human Relations Other 12.

Student Applications/Admissions:

Student Applications

Community Counseling MA/MS (Master of Arts/Science)—Applications 2004–2005, 89. Total applicants accepted 2004–2005, 57. Number enrolled (new admits only) 2004–2005 full-time, 45. Number enrolled (new admits only) 2004–2005 part-time, 7. Total enrolled 2004–2005 full-time, 56, part-time, 19. Openings 2005–2006, 40. The Median number of years required for completion of a degree are ? The number of students enrolled full and part-time who were dismissed or voluntarily withdrew from this program area were 0. *Certification in School Psychology MA/MS (Master of Arts/Science)*—Applications 2004–2005, 35. Total applicants accepted 2004–2005, 12. Number enrolled (new admits only) 2004–2005 full-time, 7. Number enrolled (new admits only) 2004–2005 part-time, 1. Total enrolled 2004–2005 full-time, 19, part-time, 7. Openings 2005–2006, 12. The Median number of years required for completion of a degree are 3. The number of students enrolled full and part-time who were dismissed or voluntarily withdrew from this program area were 0. *School Counseling Other*—Applications 2004–2005, 76. Total applicants accepted 2004–2005, 49. Number enrolled (new admits only) 2004–2005 full-time, 16. Number enrolled (new admits only) 2004–2005 part-time, 26. Total enrolled 2004–2005 full-time, 44, part-time, 79. Openings 2005–2006, 65. The Median number of years required for completion of a degree are 2. The number of students enrolled full and part-time who were dismissed or voluntarily withdrew from this program area were 0. *Student Affairs MA/MS (Master of Arts/Science)*—Applications 2004–2005, 16. Total applicants accepted 2004–2005, 8. Number enrolled (new admits only) 2004–2005 full-time 7. Number enrolled (new admits only) 2004–2005 part-time, 1. Total enrolled 2004–2005 full-time, 9, part-time, 3. Openings 2005–2006, 10. The Median number of years required for completion of a degree are 2. The number of students enrolled full and part-time who were dismissed or voluntarily withdrew from this program area were 0. *Counseling Psychology PhD (Doctor of Philosophy)*—Applications 2004–2005, 11. Total applicants accepted 2004–2005, 6. Number enrolled (new admits only) 2004–2005 full-time, 5. Number enrolled (new admits only) 2004–2005 part-time, 1. Total enrolled 2004–2005 full-time, 13, part-time, 15. Openings 2005–2006, 7. The Median number of years required for completion of a degree are 5. The number of students enrolled full and part-time who were dismissed or voluntarily withdrew from this program area were 1. *School Psychology EdD (Doctor of Education)*—Applications 2004–2005, 3. Total applicants accepted 2004–2005, 3. Number enrolled (new admits only) 2004–2005 full-time, 3. Number enrolled (new admits only) 2004–2005 part-time, 0. Total enrolled 2004–2005 full-time, 11, part-time, 13. Openings 2005–2006, 7. The Median number of years required for completion of a degree are 4. The number of students enrolled full and part-time who were dismissed or voluntarily withdrew from this program area were 1. *Learning and Instruction PhD (Doctor of Philosophy)*—Applications 2004–2005, 5. Total applicants accepted 2004–2005, 4. Number enrolled (new admits only) 2004–2005 full-time, 3. Number enrolled (new admits only) 2004–2005 part-time, 1. Total enrolled 2004–2005 full-time, 5, part-time, 3. Openings 2005–2006, 5. The Median number of years required for completion of a degree are 5. The number of students enrolled full and part-time who were dismissed or voluntarily withdrew from this program area were 0. *Counseling–Human Relations Other*—Applications 2004–2005, 15. Total applicants accepted 2004–2005, 15. Number enrolled (new admits only) 2004–2005 full-time, 8. Number enrolled (new admits only) 2004–2005 part-time, 3. Total enrolled 2004–2005 full-time, 21, part-time, 13. Openings 2005–2006, 10. The Median number of years required for completion of a degree are 2. The number of students enrolled full and part-time who were dismissed or voluntarily withdrew from this program area were 0.

Admissions Requirements:

Scores: Entries appear in this order: required test or GPA, minimum score (if required), median score of students entering in 2003–2004. Master's Programs: GRE-V no minimum stated, 520; GRE-Q no minimum stated, 500; overall undergraduate GPA no minimum stated; last 2 years GPA no minimum stated, 3.4. Doctoral Programs: GRE-V no minimum stated, 480; GRE-Q no minimum stated, 520.

Other Criteria: (importance of criteria rated low, medium, or high): GRE/MAT scores high, research experience low, work experience medium, extracurricular activity low, clinically related public service low, GPA high, letters of recommendation medium, statement of goals and objectives high.

Student Characteristics: The following represents characteristics of students in 2004–2005 in all graduate psychology programs in the department: Female–full-time 137, part-time 132; Male–full-time 45, part-time 16; African American/Black–full-time 8, part-time 5; Hispanic/Latino(a)–full-time 22, part-time 20; Asian/Pacific Islander–full-time 1, part-time 2; American Indian/Alaska Native–full-time 5, part-time 14; Caucasian–full-time 139, part-time 106; Multi-ethnic–full-time 6, part-time 2; students subject to the Americans With Disabilities Act–full-time 1, part-time 0.

Financial Information/Assistance:

Tuition for Full-Time Study: *Master's:* State residents: per academic year $4,736, $280 per credit hour; Nonstate residents: per academic year $13,384, $591 per credit hour. *Doctoral:* State residents: per academic year $4,736, $280 per credit hour; Nonstate residents: per academic year $13,384, $591 per credit hour. Tuition is subject to change. See the following Web site for updates and changes in tuition costs: http://www4.nau.edu/bursar/fees.htm.

Financial Assistance:

First Year Students: Teaching assistantships available for first-year. Average amount paid per academic year: $8,750. Average number of hours worked per week: 20. Apply by April 15. Tuition remission given: partial.

Advanced Students: Teaching assistantships available for advanced students. Average amount paid per academic year: $8,750. Average number of hours worked per week: 20. Apply by April 15. Tuition remission given: partial. Research assistantships available for advanced students. Average amount paid per academic year: $8,750. Average number of hours worked per week: 20. Apply by April 15. Tuition remission given: partial.

Contact Information: Of all students currently enrolled full-time, 25% benefitted from one or more of the listed financial assistance programs. Application and information available online at: http://www4.nau.edu/finaid/.

Internships/Practica: Our practitioner programs are built on competency-based models and include closely supervised experiential practica and internship components. Many of these experiences are offered in NAU's Counseling and Testing Center and the Institute for Human Development; student service facilities; public-school settings; reservation schools and communities; rural settings; and community agencies. In addition, the College of Education houses a Skills Lab Network that includes comprehensive testing and curriculum libraries and a practicum facility that uses both videotape and direct live feedback in the supervision of students working with clients. For those doctoral students for whom a professional internship is required prior to graduation, 11 applied in 2003–2004. Of those who applied, 5 were placed in internships listed by the Association of Psychology Postdoctoral and Internship Programs (APPIC).

Housing and Day Care: On-campus housing is available. See the following Web site for more information: Housing options: http://www.nau.edu/reslife/. These include family housing, fraternities/sororities, apartment-style halls, suite-style halls, graduate, over 21-year old floors, over 25-year old floor, non-smoking floor/halls, honors/scholars halls, 12-month contract option, 24-hour quiet floors, and Freshmen halls. On-campus day care facilities are available. See the following Web site for more information: http://www4.nau.edu/stulife/ChildCare/FAQ.htm. The NAU Child Care Voucher Program is a subsidy program designed to assist NAU students with child care expenses while they attend the University.

Employment of Department Graduates:

Master's Degree Graduates: Of those who graduated in the academic year 2003–2004, the following categories and numbers represent the post-graduate activities and employment of master's degree graduates: Enrolled in a psychology doctoral program (8), enrolled in another graduate/professional program (2), enrolled in a post-doctoral residency/fellowship (n/a), employed in independent practice (n/a), total from the above (master's) (10).

Doctoral Degree Graduates: Of those who graduated in the academic year 2003–2004, the following categories and numbers represent the post-graduate activities and employment of doctoral degree graduates: Enrolled in a psychology doctoral program (n/a), enrolled in a post-doctoral residency/fellowship (0), employed in independent practice (5), employed in an academic position at a university (0), employed in an academic position at a 2-year/4-year college (0), employed in a professional position in a school system (20), total from the above (doctoral) (25).

Additional Information:

Orientation, Objectives, and Emphasis of Department: Because of the barriers to learning and living in our society, there is an increasing need for professionally trained counseling and school psychology personnel. Our graduate programs are based on a developmental, experiential training model that includes understanding theory, learning assessment and intervention skills, practicing skills in a supervised clinical setting, and performing skills in vivo. Integrated throughout our programs is a scientist–practitioner orientation that prepares students to ascertain the efficacy of assessment and intervention techniques.

Special Facilities or Resources: Students in School Psychology programs complete portions of their practicum at sites located on the Indian reservations and work with children and schools affiliated with the Navajo, Hopi, and Supai tribes. The MA Community Counseling and the MEd School Counseling programs are also available at select sites in Arizona (i.e., Phoenix, Tucson and Yuma).

Information for Students With Physical Disabilities: See the following Web site for more information: www.nau.edu/dss.

Application Information:

Graduate College Application can be completed online or submitted to: Graduate College, Box 4125, NAU, Flagstaff, AZ 86011; Department Appication (paper only) should be submitted to: Educational Psychology, COE 5774, NAU, Flagstaff, AZ 86011. Application available online. URL of online application: http://www.applyweb.com/apply/northazg/. Students are admitted in the Fall, application deadline September 15; Spring, application deadline February 15. EdD—Counseling Psychology and School Psychology—January 15. EdD—Learning and Instruction—Rolling deadline. MA + Certification in School Psychology—February 15. MA Community Counseling, MEd School Counseling and Student Affairs—Dates above for Fall and Spring apply. For those program located at statewide sites (Phoenix, Tucson and Yuma), deadlines vary each year. Please call department office for more information. *Fee:* $45.

Arkansas, University of

Department of Psychology
J. William Fulbright College of Arts and Science
216 Memorial Hall
Fayetteville, AR 72701
Telephone: (479) 575-4256
Fax: (479) 575-3219
E-mail: *psycapp@comp.uark.edu*
Web: *http://www.uark.edu/depts/psyc*

Department Information:

1926. Chairperson: Douglas A. Behrend. Number of Faculty: total–full-time 16; women–full-time 3.

Programs and Degrees Offered:

Listed in the following order: Program area, degree type (T if terminal Master's), number awarded 7/03–6/04. Clinical PhD (Doctor of Philosophy) 6, Experimental PhD (Doctor of Philosophy) 2.

APA Accreditation: Clinical PhD (Doctor of Philosophy).

Student Applications/Admissions:

Student Applications

Clinical PhD (Doctor of Philosophy)—Applications 2004–2005, 160. Total applicants accepted 2004–2005, 5. Number enrolled (new admits only) 2004–2005 full-time, 5. Openings 2005–2006, 5. The Median number of years required for completion of a degree are 5. The number of students enrolled full and part-time who were dismissed or voluntarily withdrew from this program area were 1. *Experimental PhD (Doctor of Philosophy)*—Applications 2004–2005, 25. Total applicants accepted 2004–2005, 3. Number enrolled (new admits only) 2004–2005 full-time, 3. Openings 2005–2006, 3. The Median number of years required for completion of a degree are 5. The number of students enrolled full and part-time who were dismissed or voluntarily withdrew from this program area were 0.

Admissions Requirements:

Scores: Entries appear in this order: required test or GPA, minimum score (if required), median score of students entering in 2003–2004. Doctoral Programs: GRE-V 500, 600; GRE-Q 500, 645; GRE-Analytical 4.5, 5.0; overall undergraduate GPA 3.0, 3.81.

Other Criteria: (importance of criteria rated low, medium, or high): GRE/MAT scores high, research experience high, work experience low, extracurricular activity low, clinically related public service medium, GPA high, letters of recommendation high, interview high, statement of goals and objectives high. Clinically relevant service only considered for clinical applicants.

Student Characteristics: The following represents characteristics of students in 2004–2005 in all graduate psychology programs in the department: Female–full-time 28, part-time 0; Male–full-time 16, part-time 0; African American/Black–full-time 2, part-time 0; Hispanic/Latino(a)–full-time 2, part-time 0; Asian/Pacific Islander–full-time 0, part-time 0; American Indian/Alaska Native–full-time 0, part-time 0; Caucasian–full-time 39, part-time 0; Multi-ethnic–full-time 1, part-time 0; students subject to the Americans With Disabilities Act–full-time 0, part-time 0.

Financial Information/Assistance:

Tuition for Full-Time Study: *Doctoral:* State residents: per academic year $3,630, $242 per credit hour; Nonstate residents: per academic year $8,380, $572 per credit hour. Tuition is subject to change. See the following Web site for updates and changes in tuition costs: www.uark.edu/depts/gradinfo.

Financial Assistance:

First Year Students: Teaching assistantships available for first-year. Average amount paid per academic year: $13,300. Average number of hours worked per week: 20. Apply by January 1. Tuition remission given: full. Research assistantships available for first-year. Average amount paid per academic year: $13,300. Average number of hours worked per week: 20. Apply by January 1. Tuition remission given: full. Fellowships and scholarships available for first-year. Apply by January 1. Tuition remission given: full.

Advanced Students: Teaching assistantships available for advanced students. Average amount paid per academic year: $13,300. Average number of hours worked per week: 20. Tuition remission given: full. Research assistantships available for advanced students. Average amount paid per academic year: $13,300. Average number of hours worked per week: 20. Tuition remission given: full. Fellowships and scholarships available for advanced students. Tuition remission given: full.

Contact Information: Of all students currently enrolled full-time, 100% benefitted from one or more of the listed financial assistance programs. Application and information available online at: www.uark.edu/depts/psyc.

Internships/Practica: Doctoral students in the Clinical Training Program have always been able to obtain high-quality, APA-accredited predoctoral internships. Additionally, our students have numerous mental health agency placement opportunities throughout their tenure with us. These clerkship placements include local community mental health centers, the University Health Service, inpatient psychiatric hospitals, and several facilities dealing with disabilities, neuropsychology, and other clinical specialties. For those doctoral students for whom a professional internship is required prior to graduation, 4 applied in 2003–2004. Of those who applied, 4 were placed in internships listed by the Association of Psychology Postdoctoral and Internship Programs (APPIC); 4 were placed in APA accredited internships.

Housing and Day Care: On-campus housing is available. Additional housing information may be obtained from University Housing, 900 Hotz Hall, University of Arkansas, Fayetteville, AR 72701, by telephone at (479) 575-3951, or at housing.uark.edu. On-campus day care facilities are available. Limited on-campus child care is available.

Employment of Department Graduates:

Master's Degree Graduates: Of those who graduated in the academic year 2003–2004, the following categories and numbers represent the post-graduate activities and employment of master's degree graduates: Enrolled in a post-doctoral residency/fellowship (n/a), employed in independent practice (n/a), total from the above (master's) (0).

Doctoral Degree Graduates: Of those who graduated in the academic year 2003–2004, the following categories and numbers represent the post-graduate activities and employment of doctoral degree graduates: Enrolled in a psychology doctoral program (n/a), total from the above (doctoral) (0).

Additional Information:

Orientation, Objectives, and Emphasis of Department: The PhD program in clinical psychology follows the scientist-practitioner model of training. Our premise is that doctoral training in clinical psychology prepares individuals to be skilled mental health providers as well as competent researchers. Because many of our graduates will seek applied, direct service positions, we take seriously the role of training competent clinicians. We also actively recruit and intensively train students who aspire to be clinical scientists. Academic coursework, clinical practica, and research training are designed to promote the development of competency in both areas. Our goal is to train students who are capable of applying psychological theory, research methodology, and clinical skills to complex clinical problems and diverse populations. The PhD program in experimental psychology provides students with a broad knowledge of psychology via a core curriculum, with a specialized training emphasis in our Social and Cognitive Processes focus area via research team meetings, colloquia, and advanced seminars. Training in social, developmental and cognitive psychology within the focus area includes independent research experience and extensive and supervised classroom teaching experience. The program provides students with a thorough understanding of psychological principles and prepares them for careers as academicians and researchers.

Special Facilities or Resources: The Department of Psychology is housed in Memorial Hall, a multilevel building with 58,000 square feet of office and research space for faculty and students. The building contains modern facilities for both human and small animal research, including specialized space for use with individuals and small groups of children and adults. The on-site Psychological Clinic is a state-of-the-art training and research facility dedicated to providing practicum and applied research experiences for clinical students. The Clinic's treatment, testing, and research rooms are equipped with a closed-circuit videotaping system. Memorial Hall has comprehensive data analysis facilities, including personal computers networked to the University and internet. Finally, the Department is the beneficiary of a generous bequest that established the Marie Wilson Howells Fund, which provides funding for thesis and dissertation research, numerous research assistantships, student travel, and departmental colloquia. The department also nominates qualified students for supplemental Doctoral Fellowships available through the Graduate School.

Information for Students With Physical Disabilities: See the following Web site for more information: www.uark.edu/ua/csd/.

Application Information:
Send to: Admissions Coordinator, Department of Psychology, University of Arkansas, Memorial Hall 216, Fayetteville, AR 72701. Application available online. URL of online application: www.uark.edu/depts/psyc/application.html. Students are admitted in the Fall, application deadline January 1. Experimental Program will continue to consider applications received after January 1. *Fee:* $0. U.S. applicants should apply directly to the Department of Psychology and have all application materials (e.g., transcripts, GRE scores, letters of recommendation) for most efficient consideration; application materials of students accepted by the Department for admission will be submitted to the Graduate School for processing. The Department will pay the Graduate School application fees for admitted students. EXCEPTION: International applicants must apply to the Graduate School and pay a $50 application fee.

Arkansas, University of, Little Rock
Psychology Department/Masters of Applied Psychology
College of Arts, Humanities, and Social Sciences
2801 S. University
LIttle Rock, AR 72204
Telephone: (501) 569-3171
Fax: (501) 569-3047
E-mail: rjhines@ualr.edu
Web: www.ualr.edu

Department Information:
1969. Chairperson: Belinda Blevins-Knabe. Number of Faculty: total–full-time 12, part-time 31; women–full-time 2, part-time 16.

Programs and Degrees Offered:
Listed in the following order: Program area, degree type (T if terminal Master's), number awarded 7/03–6/04. Masters of Applied Psychology MA/MS (Master of Arts/Science) (T) 9.

Student Applications/Admissions:
Student Applications

Masters of Applied Psychology MA/MS (*Master of Arts/Science*)—Applications 2004–2005, 41. Total applicants accepted 2004–2005, 12. Number enrolled (new admits only) 2004–2005 full-time, 6. Number enrolled (new admits only) 2004–2005 part-time, 4. Total enrolled 2004–2005 full-time, 19, part-time, 15. Openings 2005–2006, 8. The Median number of years required for completion of a degree are 2. The number of students enrolled full and part-time who were dismissed or voluntarily withdrew from this program area were 0.

Admissions Requirements:
Scores: Entries appear in this order: required test or GPA, minimum score (if required), median score of students entering in 2003–2004. Master's Programs: GRE-V+Q 1000, 1000; overall undergraduate GPA 3.0, 3.35; last 2 years GPA 3.0; psychology GPA 3.0. GPA of 3.0 is required in statistic courses *Other Criteria:* (importance of criteria rated low, medium, or high): GRE/MAT scores high, research experience high, work experience high, extracurricular activity high, clinically related public service medium, GPA high, letters of recommendation high, interview high, statement of goals and objectives high. For additional information on admission requirements, go to: http://gradschool.ualr.edu/prospectivestudents.html.

31

Student Characteristics: The following represents characteristics of students in 2004–2005 in all graduate psychology programs in the department: Female–full-time 12, part-time 11; Male–full-time 7, part-time 4; African American/Black–full-time 3, part-time 1; Hispanic/Latino(a)–full-time 0, part-time 0; Asian/Pacific Islander–full-time 0, part-time 1; American Indian/Alaska Native–full-time 0, part-time 0; Caucasian–full-time 16, part-time 13; Multi-ethnic–full-time 0, part-time 0; students subject to the Americans With Disabilities Act–full-time 0, part-time 0.

Financial Information/Assistance:
Tuition for Full-Time Study: *Master's:* State residents: per academic year $3,384, $188 per credit hour; Nonstate residents: per academic year $7,380, $410 per credit hour. Tuition is subject to change. See the following Web site for updates and changes in tuition costs: http://gradschool.ualr.edu/tuition.html.

Financial Assistance:
First Year Students: Research assistantships available for first-year. Average amount paid per academic year: $3,225. Average number of hours worked per week: 10. Apply by March 15. Tuition remission given: partial.

Advanced Students: Teaching assistantships available for advanced students. Average amount paid per academic year: $3,225. Average number of hours worked per week: 10. Apply by March 15. Tuition remission given: partial. Research assistantships available for advanced students. Average amount paid per academic year: $3,225. Average number of hours worked per week: 10. Apply by March 15. Tuition remission given: partial.

Contact Information: Of all students currently enrolled full-time, 26% benefitted from one or more of the listed financial assistance programs. Application and information available online at: http://gradschool.ualr.edu/gainfo.html.

Internships/Practica: Internships for industrial/organization graduate students are available in the leading Human Relations departments in the region. Internships for students interested in developmental psychology are available in collaboration with Partners for Inclusive Communities in the areas of child care and Head Start.

Housing and Day Care: On-campus housing is available. See the following Web site for more information: http://housing.ualr.edu. No on-campus day care facilities are available.

Employment of Department Graduates:
Master's Degree Graduates: Of those who graduated in the academic year 2003–2004, the following categories and numbers represent the post-graduate activities and employment of master's degree graduates: Enrolled in a psychology doctoral program (3), enrolled in another graduate/professional program (3), enrolled in a post-doctoral residency/fellowship (n/a), employed in independent practice (n/a), employed in an academic position at a university (0), employed in an academic position at a 2-year/4-year college (2), employed in other positions at a higher education institution (0), employed in a professional position in a school system (0), employed in business or industry (research/consulting) (0), employed in business or industry (management) (7), employed in a government agency (research) (1), employed in a government agency (professional services) (0), employed in a community mental health/counseling center (3), employed in a hospital/medical center (0), still seeking employment (0), not seeking employment (0), other employment position (2), total from the above (master's) (21).

Doctoral Degree Graduates: Of those who graduated in the academic year 2003–2004, the following categories and numbers represent the post-graduate activities and employment of doctoral degree graduates: Enrolled in a psychology doctoral program (n/a), total from the above (doctoral) (0).

Additional Information:
Orientation, Objectives, and Emphasis of Department: The Master's of Applied Psychology (MAP) program offers preparation for careers in industrial/organizational and health psychology. The program also serves students seeking a master's degree as preparation for doctoral study in an area of experimental psychology (e.g., social, cognitive, or developmental psychology) at another university and students who wish to teach at the community college level. The Master of Applied Psychology is offered in three areas of concentration: (1) industrial/organizational psychology, (2) health psychology, and (3) general experimental psychology. The industrial/organizational track focuses on the application of psychological methods and theories in business and organizations. This track stresses personnel selection, personnel program evaluation, training, and organizational development. The health psychology track prepares individuals to pursue careers at the master's level in the field of health psychology or behavioral medicine. Health psychology is concerned with providing educational, scientific, and professional contributions of the dicipline of psychology to the promotion and maintenance of health, as well as the prevention and treatment of illness and related dysfunction. The pre-doctoral experimental track would prepare students who intend to apply to PhD programs in some area of experimental psychology (e.g. social, developmental, cognitive, physiological, sensation and perception). It is also intended for those who wish to teach psychology with a master's degree in a high school, junior college, or community college.

Special Facilities or Resources: The UALR psychology department offers students the opportunity to go beyond classroom learning and actually engage in activities similar to those of professionals in the field. The Biobehavioral Laboratory houses state-of-the-art equipment for faculty-student collaborations and classroom demonstrations. The Sleep Laboratory houses an incredible new Cadwell Dual-Purpose Polysomnograph with Synchronous Digital Video and EEG for night and day use. UALR also works very closely with the Arkansas State Police, Arkansas Department of Human Services Division of Mental Health Services, Arkansas State Hospital, Arkansas Department of Corrections, Rape Crisis, Inc., the University of Arkansas for Medical Sciences Department of Pediatrics, and Partners for Inclusive Communities. There are many other opportunities for research throughout Little Rock and surrounding communities. For additional information and contact information, please visit our website at http://www.ualr.edu/~psycinfo/labs.htm.

Information for Students With Physical Disabilities: See the following Web site for more information: http://www.ualr.edu/dssdept/index.html.

Application Information:
Send to: University of Arkansas at Little Rock Graduate Admissions Office, 2801 S. University Avenue, Little Rock, AR 72204-1099. Application available online. URL of online application: http://boss.

ualr.edu. Students are admitted in the Fall, application deadline March 15. *Fee:* $0. $30 application fee for international students only.

Central Arkansas, University of
Dept. of Psychology and Counseling
Education
201 Donaghey
Conway, AR 72035-0001
Telephone: (501) 450-3193
Fax: (501) 450-5424
E-mail: *DavidS@uca.edu*
Web: *http://www.coe.uca.edu*

Department Information:
1967. Chairperson: David Skotko. Number of Faculty: total–full-time 20, part-time 5; women–full-time 8, part-time 3; minority–full-time 1.

Programs and Degrees Offered:
Listed in the following order: Program area, degree type (T if terminal Master's), number awarded 7/03–6/04. School Psychology PhD (Doctor of Philosophy) 4, School Psychology MA/MS (Master of Arts/Science) 8, Counseling Psychology MA/MS (Master of Arts/Science).

Student Applications/Admissions:
Student Applications
School Psychology PhD (Doctor of Philosophy)—Applications 2004–2005, 10. Total applicants accepted 2004–2005, 5. Number enrolled (new admits only) 2004–2005 full-time, 5. Total enrolled 2004–2005 full-time, 13. Openings 2005–2006, 6. The Median number of years required for completion of a degree are 5. *School Psychology MA/MS (Master of Arts/Science)*—Applications 2004–2005, 14. Total applicants accepted 2004–2005, 6. Total enrolled 2004–2005 full-time, 17. Openings 2005–2006, 6. The Median number of years required for completion of a degree are 2. The number of students enrolled full and part-time who were dismissed or voluntarily withdrew from this program area were 0. *Counseling Psychology MA/MS (Master of Arts/Science)*—Total applicants accepted 2004–2005, 12. Total enrolled 2004–2005 full-time, 28. Openings 2005–2006, 15. The Median number of years required for completion of a degree are 2. The number of students enrolled full and part-time who were dismissed or voluntarily withdrew from this program area were 1.

Admissions Requirements:
Scores: Entries appear in this order: required test or GPA, minimum score (if required), median score of students entering in 2003–2004. Master's Programs: GRE-V 360, 495; GRE-Q 370, 470; GRE-V+Q 790, 955; overall undergraduate GPA 3.1, 3.5; last 2 years GPA no minimum stated; psychology GPA no minimum stated. Doctoral Programs: GRE-V 430, 500; GRE-Q 430, 500; overall undergraduate GPA 3.30, 3.55.
Other Criteria: (importance of criteria rated low, medium, or high): GRE/MAT scores medium, research experience medium, work experience medium, extracurricular activity medium, clinically related public service medium, GPA high, letters of recommendation medium, interview high, statement of goals and objectives high.

Student Characteristics: The following represents characteristics of students in 2004–2005 in all graduate psychology programs in the department: Female–full-time 49, part-time 0; Male–full-time 9, part-time 0; African American/Black–full-time 6, part-time 0; Hispanic/Latino(a)–full-time 1, part-time 0; Asian/Pacific Islander–full-time 2, part-time 0; American Indian/Alaska Native–full-time 1, part-time 0; Caucasian–full-time 0, part-time 0; students subject to the Americans With Disabilities Act–full-time 1, part-time 0.

Financial Information/Assistance:
Tuition for Full-Time Study: *Master's:* State residents: $200 per credit hour; Nonstate residents: $350 per credit hour. *Doctoral:* State residents: $200 per credit hour; Nonstate residents: $350 per credit hour. Tuition is subject to change. See the following Web site for updates and changes in tuition costs: www.uca.edu.

Financial Assistance:
First Year Students: Teaching assistantships available for first-year. Average amount paid per academic year: $5,700. Average number of hours worked per week: 20. Research assistantships available for first-year. Average number of hours worked per week: 20.
Advanced Students: Teaching assistantships available for advanced students. Average number of hours worked per week: 20. Research assistantships available for advanced students. Average amount paid per academic year: $8,000. Average number of hours worked per week: 20.
Contact Information: Of all students currently enrolled full-time, 50% benefitted from one or more of the listed financial assistance programs.

Internships/Practica: *Master's:* State residents: $200 per credit hour; Nonstate residents: $350 per credit hour. It is required prior to graduation, 4 applied in 2003–2004.

Housing and Day Care: On-campus housing is available. See the following Web site for more information: www.uca.edu/divisions/admin/housing. On-campus day care facilities are available.

Employment of Department Graduates:
Master's Degree Graduates: Of those who graduated in the academic year 2003–2004, the following categories and numbers represent the post-graduate activities and employment of master's degree graduates: Enrolled in a psychology doctoral program (6), enrolled in a post-doctoral residency/fellowship (n/a), employed in independent practice (n/a), employed in other positions at a higher education institution (0), employed in a professional position in a school system (6), employed in a community mental health/counseling center (11), employed in a hospital/medical center (2), other employment position (4), total from the above (master's) (29).
Doctoral Degree Graduates: Of those who graduated in the academic year 2003–2004, the following categories and numbers represent the post-graduate activities and employment of doctoral degree graduates: Enrolled in a psychology doctoral program (n/a), employed in independent practice (1), employed in an academic position at a university (1), employed in a professional position

in a school system (1), employed in a community mental health/ counseling center (1), total from the above (doctoral) (4).

Additional Information:

Orientation, Objectives, and Emphasis of Department: The MS degree in Counseling Psychology and School Psychology is designed so that it may serve either as terminal degree with professional employment opportunities or as a firm foundation for prospective doctoral candidates. Broad training is offered in understanding of psychological theories, assessment, and mental health interventions to enable graduates to function successfully in a variety of mental health and educational settings. The PhD in School Psychology is grounded in the scientist-practitioner model of training. Strong emphasis is placed on child mental health promotion, primary prevention, and intervention with a broad range of community related problems involving children, families, and schools. The program is responsive to ongoing soci-etal concerns and issues pertaining to children, families, and schools. It prepares its graduates to function in schools, clinics, community agencies, and hospitals.

Special Facilities or Resources: The department has (a) a fully operational computer instruction/research room that can be used for onsite research purposes; (b) human and animal research labs; (c) a multi-media computer system for research-related editing (e.g., self-modeling, therapy tapes).

Information for Students With Physical Disabilities: See the following Web site for more information: www.uca.edu.

Application Information:
Send to: Dept. Chair, Dept. of Psychology & Counseling, Box 4915, UCA, Conway, AR 72035. Students are admitted in the Fall, application deadline March 15; July 1; Summer, application deadline March 15. School Psychology PhD Program Deadline: February 10. *Fee:* $70.

STUDENT AFFILIATE APPLICATION

 AMERICAN PSYCHOLOGICAL ASSOCIATION

JOIN APA TODAY!

Send your completed application <u>with payment</u> to APA, Membership Department, 750 First Street, NE, Washington, DC, 20002-4242. Applications accompanied by credit card payments may be faxed to (202) 336-5568. Payments may be made by credit card, check, or money order (in U.S. dollars drawn on a U.S. bank) made payable to the American Psychological Association. Graduate student fee is just $43, undergraduate fee is just $27. Graduate students are automatically enrolled in the American Psychological Association of Graduate Students (APAGS) and receive *gradPSYCH*, the official magazine of APAGS. Undergraduates may become a member of APAGS and receive *gradPSYCH* for an additional $16. For more information, please call (202) 336-5580 (local), (800) 374-2721, or TDD/TTY (202) 336-6123; E-Mail: membership@apa.org.

Full Name_____
FIRST   MIDDLE   LAST

Mailing Address_____
STREET   CITY   STATE   ZIP

Phone (**)**_____   **Fax (**   **)**_____

E-Mail_____

Have you at any time been convicted of a felony, sanctioned by a professional ethics body, licensing board, or other regulatory body or by any professional or scientifc organization?   ❑ *Yes*   ❑ *No*

If yes, please provide an explanation on a separate sheet.

In making this application, I subscribe to and will support the objectives of the American Psychological Association as set forth in Article I of the Bylaws, and the Ethical Principles of Pyschologists and Code of Conduct, as adopted by the Association, and I affirm that the statements made in this application correctly represent my qualifications, and understand that if they do not, my affiliation may be voided. The Ethical Principles of Psychologists and Code of Conduct are available on APA's Web Site at ww.apa.org/ethics. The Bylaws are available at www.apa.org/governance. Copies of these documents are also available upon request.

Applicant Signature _____   **Date**_____

Please Provide the Following Information:

- Gender: ❑ Female   ❑ Male
- Please mark ONE alternative that best describes your status for the 2006 academic year:

    ❑ Freshman   ❑ Sophomore   ❑ Junior   ❑ Senior   ❑ Graduate Student   ❑ Intern   ❑ Other

- Mark the highest degree for which you are currently enrolled (only one).

    ❑ AA/AS/BA/BS/other undergraduate degree   ❑ MA (terminal - not part of work toward a doctorate degree)
    ❑ MS (terminal - not part of work toward a doctoral degree)   ❑ MEd   ❑ Education Specialist
    ❑ School Specialist   ❑ PhD   ❑ PsyD   ❑ EdD   ❑ Other (specify)_____

- I expect to receive my degree in (year) _____
- After receiving your degree, do you plan to pursue a license to practice as a psychologist?   ❑ Yes   ❑ No

Name on Card _____

Billing Address _____

_____

Credit Card Number _____

Signature of Cardholder _____

A. Student Affiliate Fee (check one)
☐ Graduate ($43) .... _____
(Includes APAGS Membership)
☐ Undergraduate ($27) .... _____

B. APAGS Membership and
   gradPYSCH (add $16) .... _____

C. TOTAL AMOUNT............................. _____

GSIP05

APA STUDENT E-Z APPLICATION
FOR MEMBERSHIP
(SEE OTHER SIDE FOR DETAILS)

- ◄ Fold and tape (do not staple) ► -

AMERICAN
PSYCHOLOGICAL
ASSOCIATION

Advancing psychology as a science, as a profession, and as a means of promoting education, health, and human welfare.

- ◄ Fold and tape (do not staple) ► -

Alliant International University: Fresno/Sacramento
Programs in Clinical Psychology
California School of Professional Psychology
5130 East Clinton Way
Fresno, CA 93727
Telephone: (559) 456-2777 x 2258
Fax: (559) 253-2267
E-mail: *lwitt@alliant.edu*
Web: *http://www.alliant.edu/cspp/*

Department Information:
1973. Systemwide Dean: Jean Lau Chin, EdD, ABPP. Number of Faculty: total–full-time 8, part-time 27; women–full-time 3, part-time 10; minority–full-time 1, part-time 2.

Programs and Degrees Offered:
Listed in the following order: Program area, degree type (T if terminal Master's), number awarded 7/03–6/04. Clinical Psychology PsyD (Doctor of Psychology) 17, Clinical Psychology PhD (Doctor of Philosophy) 24.

APA Accreditation: Clinical PsyD (Doctor of Psychology). Clinical PhD (Doctor of Philosophy).

Student Applications/Admissions:
Student Applications

Clinical Psychology PsyD (Doctor of Psychology)—Applications 2004–2005, 99. Total applicants accepted 2004–2005, 44. Number enrolled (new admits only) 2004–2005 full-time, 29. Number enrolled (new admits only) 2004–2005 part-time, 0. Total enrolled 2004–2005 full-time, 106, part-time, 8. Openings 2005–2006, 40. The Median number of years required for completion of a degree are 4. The number of students enrolled full and part-time who were dismissed or voluntarily withdrew from this program area were 5. *Clinical Psychology PhD (Doctor of Philosophy)*—Total enrolled 2004–2005 full-time, 44, part-time, 10. Openings 2005–2006, 20. The Median number of years required for completion of a degree are 5.5. The number of students enrolled full and part-time who were dismissed or voluntarily withdrew from this program area were 1.

Admissions Requirements:
Scores: Entries appear in this order: required test or GPA, minimum score (if required), median score of students entering in 2003–2004. Doctoral Programs: overall undergraduate GPA 3.00, 3.25; psychology GPA 3.00. A master's degree is not required for entry, but if a master's degree is held at the time of application, the minimum 3.0 GPA applies.
Other Criteria: (importance of criteria rated low, medium, or high): research experience medium, work experience medium, extracurricular activity low, clinically related public service medium, GPA high, letters of recommendation high, interview high, statement of goals and objectives high. For additional information on admission requirements, go to: www.alliant.edu/admissions/gradapply.htm.

Student Characteristics: The following represents characteristics of students in 2004–2005 in all graduate psychology programs in the department: Female–full-time 113, part-time 13; Male–full-time 37, part-time 5; African American/Black–full-time 10, part-time 0; Hispanic/Latino(a)–full-time 19, part-time 1; Asian/Pacific Islander–full-time 10, part-time 1; American Indian/Alaska Native–full-time 0, part-time 1; Caucasian–full-time 106, part-time 14; Multi-ethnic–full-time 5, part-time 1; students subject to the Americans With Disabilities Act–full-time 9, part-time 2.

Financial Information/Assistance:
Tuition for Full-Time Study: *Doctoral:* State residents: $795 per credit hour; Nonstate residents: $795 per credit hour. Tuition is subject to change. See the following Web site for updates and changes in tuition costs: www.alliant.edu/admissions/costs.htm.

Financial Assistance:
First Year Students: Research assistantships available for first-year. Average amount paid per academic year: $1,000. Average number of hours worked per week: 10. Apply by see dept. Fellowships and scholarships available for first-year. Average amount paid per academic year: $1,500. Apply by February 15.
Advanced Students: Teaching assistantships available for advanced students. Average amount paid per academic year: $3,000. Average number of hours worked per week: 10. Apply by see dept. Research assistantships available for advanced students. Average amount paid per academic year: $1,000. Average number of hours worked per week: 10. Apply by see dept. Fellowships and scholarships available for advanced students. Average amount paid per academic year: $1,500. Apply by April 15.
Contact Information: Of all students currently enrolled full-time, 50% benefitted from one or more of the listed financial assistance programs. Application and information available online at: www.alliant/edu/finaid/grad.htm.

Internships/Practica: The clinical psychology programs at Fresno and Sacramento emphasize the integration of academic coursework and research with clinical practice. In order to integrate appropriate skills with material learned in the classroom, students participate in a professional training placement experience beginning in the first year. The settings where students complete the professional training requirements include community mental health centers, clinics, inpatient mental health facilities, medical settings, specialized service centers, rehabilitation programs, residential/day care programs, forensic/correctional facilities, and educational programs. Third year students will spend fifteen hours per week in a practicum either at CSPP's Psychological Service Center or at some other CSPP-approved agency. During their final year, clinical students complete a full year internship at an appropriate APA or APPIC internship. CSPP also has formed the Central California Psychology Internship Consortium for students working to complete their internship in Central California. PhD students must also complete teaching practica. For those doctoral students for whom a professional internship is required prior to graduation, 28 applied in 2003–2004. Of those who applied, 7 were placed in internships listed by the Association of Psychology Postdoctoral and Internship Programs (APPIC); 17 were placed in APA accredited internships.

Housing and Day Care: No on-campus housing is available. No on-campus day care facilities are available.

Employment of Department Graduates:

Master's Degree Graduates: Of those who graduated in the academic year 2003–2004, the following categories and numbers represent the post-graduate activities and employment of master's degree graduates: Enrolled in a post-doctoral residency/fellowship (n/a), employed in independent practice (n/a), total from the above (master's) (0).

Doctoral Degree Graduates: Of those who graduated in the academic year 2003–2004, the following categories and numbers represent the post-graduate activities and employment of doctoral degree graduates: Enrolled in a psychology doctoral program (n/a), enrolled in a post-doctoral residency/fellowship (8), employed in other positions at a higher education institution (1), employed in a professional position in a school system (1), employed in a government agency (professional services) (1), employed in a community mental health/counseling center (1), employed in a hospital/medical center (4), still seeking employment (3), do not know (4), total from the above (doctoral) (23).

Additional Information:

Orientation, Objectives, and Emphasis of Department: The clinical psychology PsyD program emphasizes training in clinical skills and clinical application of research knowledge and is designed for students who are interested in careers as practitioners but it also includes a research component. The program is multisystemically or ecosystemically oriented and trains students to consider the role of diverse systems in creating and/or remedying individual and social problems. An empirical PsyD dissertation is required and may focus on program development and/or evaluation, test development, survey research, or therapeutic outcomes. The program in Sacramento is offered in an evening/weekend format for working professionals. The clinical psychology PhD program puts equal weight on training in clinical, research, and teaching skills. The program is for students whose goal is a teaching career in psychology. Emphasis areas are offered are: ecosystemic clinical child emphasis — trains students to work with infants, children, and adolescents, as well as with the adults in these clients' lives; health psychology emphasis — provides students with exposure to the expanding field of health psychology and behavioral medicine; forensic clinical psychology emphasis — prepares students to practice clinical psychology in a forensic environment. All courses required for an emphasis may not be available in Sacramento; students interested in an emphasis may need to travel to Fresno for courses.

Special Facilities or Resources: The Psychological Service Center serves the dual purpose of offering high quality psychological services to the community, particularly underserved segments, and continuing the tradition of education, training and service. The facility consists of eight therapy and two play therapy rooms, large conference room, student work room, TV/monitor, and staff offices. The campus is also home to the Association for Play Therapy.

Information for Students With Physical Disabilities: See the following Web site for more information: www.alliant.edu/about/ADA.htm.

Application Information:

Send to: Alliant International University Admissions Processing Center, 10455 Pomerado Road, San Diego, CA 92131-1799. Application available online. URL of online application: https://ais1.alliant.edu/apply/. Students are admitted in the Fall, application deadline January 15; Spring, application deadline November 15; Programs have rolling admissions. The programs have a January 15 priority deadline in order to provide a response by April 1 for applicants who need a decision by that date. Programs accept and admit appliants on a space available basis after any stated deadlines. For updated information on deadlines visit www.alliant.edu/admissions/gradtimelines.htm or contact the admissions office at 1-866-U-ALLIANT. *Fee:* $65. A limited number of application fee waivers are available for students with significant financial need.

Alliant International University: San Francisco Bay
Programs in Clinical Psychology and Clinical
  Psychopharmacology
California School of Professional Psychology
One Beach Street
San Francisco, CA 94133-1221
Telephone: (415) 955-2146
Fax: (415) 955-2179
E-mail: *jkulbeck@alliant.edu*
Web: *http://www.alliant.edu/cspp/*

Department Information:

1969. Systemwide Dean: Jean Lau Chin, EdD, ABPP. Number of Faculty: total–full-time 20, part-time 80; women–full-time 10, part-time 32; minority–full-time 5, part-time 11; faculty subject to the Americans With Disabilities Act 1.

Programs and Degrees Offered:

Listed in the following order: Program area, degree type (T if terminal Master's), number awarded 7/03–6/04. Clinical Psychology PsyD (Doctor of Psychology) 67, Clinical Psychology PhD (Doctor of Philosophy) 36, Clinical Psychology Respecialization Diploma 2, Clinical Psychopharmacology MA/MS (Master of Arts/Science) (T) 0.

APA Accreditation: Clinical PsyD (Doctor of Psychology). Clinical PhD (Doctor of Philosophy).

Student Applications/Admissions:

Student Applications

Clinical Psychology PsyD (Doctor of Psychology)—Applications 2004–2005, 189. Total applicants accepted 2004–2005, 133. Number enrolled (new admits only) 2004–2005 full-time, 75. Number enrolled (new admits only) 2004–2005 part-time, 1. Total enrolled 2004–2005 full-time, 270, part-time, 59. Openings 2005–2006, 70. The Median number of years required for completion of a degree are 4.9. The number of students enrolled full and part-time who were dismissed or voluntarily withdrew from this program area were 7. *Clinical Psychology PhD (Doctor of Philosophy)*—Applications 2004–2005, 99. Total applicants accepted 2004–2005, 48. Number enrolled (new admits only) 2004–2005 full-time, 28. Number enrolled (new admits only) 2004–2005 part-time, 1. Total enrolled 2004–2005 full-time, 120, part-time, 29. Openings

2005–2006, 25. The Median number of years required for completion of a degree are 5.9. The number of students enrolled full and part-time who were dismissed or voluntarily withdrew from this program area were 2. *Clinical Psychology Respecialization Diploma*—Applications 2004–2005, 2. Total applicants accepted 2004–2005, 2. Number enrolled (new admits only) 2004–2005 full-time, 1. Number enrolled (new admits only) 2004–2005 part-time, 1. Total enrolled 2004–2005 full-time, 1, part-time, 1. Openings 2005–2006, 2. The Median number of years required for completion of a degree are 2.2. The number of students enrolled full and part-time, who were dismissed or voluntarily withdrew from this program area were 0. *Clinical Psychopharmacology MA/MS (Master of Arts/Science)*—Applications 2004–2005, 91. Total applicants accepted 2004–2005, 89. Number enrolled (new admits only) 2004–2005 full-time, 0. Number enrolled (new admits only) 2004–2005 part-time, 52. Openings 2005–2006, 75. The number of students enrolled full and part-time who were dismissed or voluntarily withdrew from this program area were 3.

Admissions Requirements:

Scores: Entries appear in this order: required test or GPA, minimum score (if required), median score of students entering in 2003–2004. Master's Programs: Admission to the post-doctoral master's program in clinical psychopharmacology requires written proof from the State Board of Examiners that the applicant holds a current, valid license in good standing as a doctoral level psychologist. Doctoral Programs: overall undergraduate GPA 3.00, 3.30; psychology GPA 3.00.

Other Criteria: (importance of criteria rated low, medium, or high): GRE/MAT scores low, research experience high, work experience high, extracurricular activity low, clinically related public service high, GPA high, letters of recommendation high, interview high, statement of goals and objectives high, Admissions requirements vary by program. PhD programs place more emphasis on prior research experience; PsyD programs place more emphasis on clinical/work experience. For additional information on admission requirements, go to: www.alliant.edu/admissions/gradapply.htm.

Student Characteristics: The following represents characteristics of students in 2004–2005 in all graduate psychology programs in the department: Female–full-time 325, part-time 111; Male–full-time 66, part-time 50; African American/Black–full-time 21, part-time 6; Hispanic/Latino(a)–full-time 35, part-time 12; Asian/Pacific Islander–full-time 62, part-time 18; American Indian/Alaska Native–full-time 2, part-time 1; Caucasian–full-time 262, part-time 123; Multi-ethnic–full-time 9, part-time 1; students subject to the Americans With Disabilities Act–full-time 10, part-time 3.

Financial Information/Assistance:

Tuition for Full-Time Study: *Master's:* State residents: per academic year $4,900; Nonstate residents: per academic year $4,900. *Doctoral:* State residents: $795 per credit hour; Nonstate residents: $795 per credit hour. Tuition is subject to change. Tuition costs vary by program. See the following Web site for updates and changes in tuition costs: www.alliant.edu/admissions/costs.htm.

Financial Assistance:

First Year Students: Research assistantships available for first-year. Average amount paid per academic year: $1,500. Average number of hours worked per week: 10. Apply by see dept. Fellowships and scholarships available for first-year. Average amount paid per academic year: $1,500. Apply by Febraury 15.

Advanced Students: Teaching assistantships available for advanced students. Average amount paid per academic year: $3,000. Average number of hours worked per week: 10. Apply by see dept. Research assistantships available for advanced students. Average amount paid per academic year: $1,000. Average number of hours worked per week: 10. Apply by see dept. Fellowships and scholarships available for advanced students. Average amount paid per academic year: $1,500. Apply by April 15.

Contact Information: Of all students currently enrolled full-time, 75% benefitted from one or more of the listed financial assistance programs. Application and information available online at: www.alliant/edu/finaid/grad.htm.

Internships/Practica: During the first three years of the PsyD program and during the second and third years of the PhD program, students are engaged in field practica 8–16 hours per week. All students get experience working with adults, children/adolescents, and persons with severe mental illness as well as more moderate forms of dysfunction. The tremendous ethnic/racial diversity of the San Francisco Bay Area insures that all students get exposure to working with clients from a variety of cultural groups. Practica are selected and approved by CSPP based on the quality of training and supervision provided for the students. They include community mental health centers, neuropsychology clinics, hospitals, child guidance clinics, college counseling centers, forensic settings, couple and family therapy agencies, residential treatment centers, infant/toddler mental health programs, corporate settings, and school programs for children and adolescents. Students begin the required internship in the fourth year (PsyD program) or the fifth year (PhD program). Full-time internship options include APA-accredited or APPIC-member training programs pursued through the national selection process, or local internship programs approved by the California Psychology Internship Council (CAPIC). Students have the option of completing the internship requirement in two years of half-time experience. For those doctoral students for whom a professional internship is required prior to graduation, 93 applied in 2003–2004. Of those who applied, 11 were placed in internships listed by the Association of Psychology Postdoctoral and Internship Programs (APPIC); 19 were placed in APA accredited internships.

Housing and Day Care: No on-campus housing is available. No on-campus day care facilities are available.

Employment of Department Graduates:

Master's Degree Graduates: Of those who graduated in the academic year 2003–2004, the following categories and numbers represent the post-graduate activities and employment of master's degree graduates: Enrolled in a post-doctoral residency/fellowship (n/a), employed in independent practice (n/a), total from the above (master's) (0).

Doctoral Degree Graduates: Of those who graduated in the academic year 2003–2004, the following categories and numbers represent the post-graduate activities and employment of doctoral degree graduates: Enrolled in a psychology doctoral program (n/a), total from the above (doctoral) (0).

Additional Information:

Orientation, Objectives, and Emphasis of Department: CSPP's clinical psychology programs combine supervised field experiences with study of psychological theory, clinical techniques, and applied research. The PsyD is a practitioner-oriented program. The PhD provides a balance of clinical and research training and is intended for students who expect independent research, teaching, and scholarship to be a significant part of their professional careers in addition to clinical work. In addition to the usual offerings, special training opportunities are available in five areas: family-child-adolescent psychology, health psychology, multicultural-community psychology, psychodynamic psychology, and gender studies (which includes psychology of women, men, and gay/lesbian/bisexual issues). The PsyD program also offers an intensive Child and Family Track (which focuses on child assessment, child therapy, and family therapy) and a Forensic Family/Child Track (which focuses on child abuse, child custody, delinquency, and family court services). Students in the PsyD tracks are required to complete a specific sequence of courses, a dissertation, and an internship related to their track's focus. Other students in the PhD and PsyD programs can take many of these same training experiences on an elective basis. Multicultural/diversity issues are infused throughout the entire curriculum. Three major theoretical orientations are strongly represented in the program: cognitive-behavioral, family systems, and psychodynamic.

Special Facilities or Resources: Students can elect to receive supervised clinical experience through CSPP's Psychological Services Center (PSC)—a community mental health clinic that serves children, adults, couples, and families. The PSC enables faculty to model professional service delivery and to directly supervise and evaluate students' clinical work. Clinical services provided at the PSC include psychodiagnostic assessment and individual, couple, family, and group psychotherapy. The PSC has both Adult-Clinical and Child/Family-Clinical training programs. Computer labs are available to students and are fully equipped with SPSS and other statistical programs for research purposes. Designated space is available on campus for research activities (such as data collection), and the library is equipped with the major searchable databases for the research literature in psychology and related fields. The San Francisco clinical programs occupy approximately 31,000 square feet of space in a newly renovated historic building near the San Francisco waterfront across from Pier 39.

Information for Students With Physical Disabilities: See the following Web site for more information: www.alliant.edu/about/ADA.htm.

Application Information:
Send to: Alliant International University, Admissions Processing Center, 10455 Pomerado Road, San Diego, CA 92131. Application available online. URL of online application: https://ais1.alliant.edu/apply/. Students are admitted in the Fall, application deadline January 15; Spring, application deadline varies. Programs have rolling admissions. The priority deadline for doctoral programs is January 15; applicants who complete an application by that date are guaranteed notification by April 1. Applications submitted after that date will be reviewed on a space-available basis. Applications to the clinical psychopharmacology master's programs vary by location and cohort start date. For more information, visit www.alliant.edu/admissions/gradtimelines.htm or contact the admissions office at 1-866-U-ALLIANT. *Fee:* $65. A limited number of fee waivers are available for those with significant financial need.

Alliant International University: Fresno
Forensic Psychology Programs
College of Arts and Sciences
5130 East Clinton Way
Fresno, CA 93727-2014
Telephone: (559) 456-2777
Fax: (559) 253-2267
E-mail: *lwitt@alliant.edu*
Web: *www.alliant.edu/ssps/forensic/*

Department Information:
1996. Acting Program Director: Jana Price-Sharps, PhD. Number of Faculty: total–full-time 4, part-time 11; women–full-time 3, part-time 4; minority–part-time 2.

Programs and Degrees Offered:
Listed in the following order: Program area, degree type (T if terminal Master's), number awarded 7/03–6/04. Forensic Psychology PhD (Doctor of Philosophy) 6, Forensic Psychology PsyD (Doctor of Psychology) 9.

Student Applications/Admissions:
Student Applications
Forensic Psychology PhD (Doctor of Philosophy)—Applications 2004–2005, 47. Total applicants accepted 2004–2005, 22. Number enrolled (new admits only) 2004–2005 full-time, 9. Number enrolled (new admits only) 2004–2005 part-time, 0. Total enrolled 2004–2005 full-time, 31, part-time, 4. Openings 2005–2006, 12. The Median number of years required for completion of a degree are 4. The number of students enrolled full and part-time who were dismissed or voluntarily withdrew from this program area were 3. Forensic Psychology PsyD (Doctor of Psychology)—Applications 2004–2005, 40. Total applicants accepted 2004–2005, 16. Number enrolled (new admits only) 2004–2005 full-time, 12. Number enrolled (new admits only) 2004–2005 part-time, 0. Total enrolled 2004–2005 full-time, 41, part-time, 8. Openings 2005–2006, 20. The Median number of years required for completion of a degree are 4.1. The number of students enrolled full and part-time who were dismissed or voluntarily withdrew from this program area were 1.

Admissions Requirements:
Scores: Entries appear in this order: required test or GPA, minimum score (if required), median score of students entering in 2003–2004. Doctoral Programs: overall undergraduate GPA 3.0, 3.24; psychology GPA 3.0. The master's degree is not required for admission, but if held at the time of application, the minimum 3.0 GPA is required.
Other Criteria: (importance of criteria rated low, medium, or high): research experience high, work experience high, extracurricular activity low, clinically related public service medium, GPA high, letters of recommendation high, interview high, statement of goals and objectives high, Requirements vary by program. The PhD program puts more emphasis on prior research experience; the PsyD program on prior clinically-related experience. For additional information on admission requirements, go to: www.alliant.edu/admissions/gradapply.htm.

Student Characteristics: The following represents characteristics of students in 2004–2005 in all graduate psychology programs in the department: Female–full-time 61, part-time 10; Male–full-time 11, part-time 2; African American/Black–full-time 2, part-time 0; Hispanic/Latino(a)–full-time 2, part-time 1; Asian/Pacific Islander–full-time 4, part-time 1; American Indian/Alaska Native–full-time 1, part-time 0; Caucasian–full-time 57, part-time 10; Multi-ethnic–full-time 6, part-time 0; students subject to the Americans With Disabilities Act–full-time 2, part-time 0.

Financial Information/Assistance:

Tuition for Full-Time Study: *Doctoral:* State residents: $795 per credit hour; Nonstate residents: $795 per credit hour. Tuition is subject to change. Tuition costs vary by program. See the following Web site for updates and changes in tuition costs: www.alliant.edu/admissions/costs.htm.

Financial Assistance:

First Year Students: Research assistantships available for first-year. Average amount paid per academic year: $1,000. Average number of hours worked per week: 10. Apply by see dept. Fellowships and scholarships available for first-year. Average amount paid per academic year: $1,500. Apply by January 2.

Advanced Students: Teaching assistantships available for advanced students. Average amount paid per academic year: $3,000. Average number of hours worked per week: 20. Apply by see dept. Research assistantships available for advanced students. Average amount paid per academic year: $1,000. Average number of hours worked per week: 10. Apply by see dept. Fellowships and scholarships available for advanced students. Average amount paid per academic year: $1,500. Apply by April 15.

Contact Information: Of all students currently enrolled full-time, 83% benefitted from one or more of the listed financial assistance programs. Application and information available online at: www.alliant.edu/finaid/grad.htm.

Internships/Practica: Students in the PhD program complete a research internship in a law enforcement or other forensic setting. Students in the PsyD program complete a pre-doctoral internship. For full-time students, these internships typically occur in the fourth year and involve full-time or close to full-time activity. For those doctoral students for whom a professional internship is required prior to graduation, 5 applied in 2003–2004. Of those who applied, 1 were placed in internships listed by the Association of Psychology Postdoctoral and Internship Programs (APPIC); 2 were placed in APA accredited internships.

Housing and Day Care: No on-campus housing is available. No on-campus day care facilities are available.

Employment of Department Graduates:

Master's Degree Graduates: Of those who graduated in the academic year 2003–2004, the following categories and numbers represent the post-graduate activities and employment of master's degree graduates: Enrolled in a post-doctoral residency/fellowship (n/a), employed in independent practice (n/a), total from the above (master's) (0).

Doctoral Degree Graduates: Of those who graduated in the academic year 2003–2004, the following categories and numbers represent the post-graduate activities and employment of doctoral degree graduates: Enrolled in a psychology doctoral program (n/a), employed in a government agency (professional services) (1), employed in a community mental health/counseling center (1), employed in a hospital/medical center (6), still seeking employment (1), other employment position (1), do not know (10), total from the above (doctoral) (20).

Additional Information:

Orientation, Objectives, and Emphasis of Department: The forensic psychology PhD program prepares students for roles in administration in a variety of mental health agencies, correctional facilities and organizations, and law enforcement departments. Students are prepared to conduct research in both academic and government institutions; examine policy initiatives; and provide advocacy, lobbying, and mediation skills to agencies and organizations. The PsyD program has an applied psychology orientation. This curriculum prepares students to conduct assessments for the courts, to serve as expert witnesses, or to work as mental health treatment providers in a variety of forensic settings, including prisons, jails, offender treatment groups, youth facilities, among many others. Core areas in both programs include forensic psychology, theories of crime and justice, industrial and organizational psychology, legal research, psychopathology, research design and data analysis forensic mediation and dispute resolution, ethics, and substance abuse theory and treatment. While the programs are not specifically designed to train licensed psychologists, some students who enter the program may wish to seek clinical licensure after graduation. Arrangements can be made to take additional psychology courses required for licensing exams, and both PsyD and PhD students have become licensed.

Information for Students With Physical Disabilities: See the following Web site for more information: www.alliant.edu/about/ADA.htm.

Application Information:
Send to: Alliant International University, Admissions Processing Center, 10455 Pomerado Road, San Diego, CA 92131-1799. Application available online. URL of online application: https://ais1.alliant.edu/apply/. Students are admitted in the Fall, application deadline varies; Spring, application deadline varies. Programs have rolling admissions. The priority appliation deadline is January 2 for those wishing notification of early decision; however, applications are welcomed after that date from those who do not need an April 1 notification. *Fee:* $65. A limited number of fee waivers are available for those with significant financial need.

Alliant International University: Fresno/Sacramento
Program in Organizational Development
California School of Organizational Studies
5130 East Clinton Way
Fresno, CA 93727-2014
Telephone: (559) 456-2777
Fax: (559) 253-2267
E-mail: *tknott@alliant.edu*
Web: *www.alliant.edu/csos/*

Department Information:
1995. Program Director: Toni A. Knott, PhD. Number of Faculty: total–full-time 2, part-time 7; women–full-time 2, part-time 5; minority–part-time 1.

Programs and Degrees Offered:
Listed in the following order: Program area, degree type (T if terminal Master's), number awarded 7/03–6/04. Organization Development PsyD (Doctor of Psychology) 3, Organizational Behavior MA/MS (Master of Arts/Science) (T) 9.

Student Applications/Admissions:

Student Applications

Organization Development PsyD (Doctor of Psychology)—Applications 2004–2005, 8. Total applicants accepted 2004–2005, 6. Number enrolled (new admits only) 2004–2005 full-time, 1. Number enrolled (new admits only) 2004–2005 part-time, 3. Total enrolled 2004–2005 full-time, 12, part-time, 25. Openings 2005–2006, 20. The Median number of years required for completion of a degree are 7.5. The number of students enrolled full and part-time who were dismissed or voluntarily withdrew from this program area were 1. *Organizational Behavior MA/MS (Master of Arts/Science)*—Number enrolled (new admits only) 2004–2005 full-time, 0. Number enrolled (new admits only) 2004–2005 part-time, 0. Openings 2005–2006, 20. The Median number of years required for completion of a degree are 2.2. The number of students enrolled full and part-time who were dismissed or voluntarily withdrew from this program area were 0.

Admissions Requirements:

Scores: Entries appear in this order: required test or GPA, minimum score (if required), median score of students entering in 2003–2004. Master's Programs: overall undergraduate GPA 3.0; psychology GPA 3.0. Doctoral Programs: overall undergraduate GPA 3.0, 3.0; psychology GPA 3.0.

Other Criteria: (importance of criteria rated low, medium, or high): For additional information on admission requirements, go to: www.alliant.edu/admissions/gradapply.htm.

Student Characteristics: The following represents characteristics of students in 2004–2005 in all graduate psychology programs in the department: Female–full-time 10, part-time 14; Male–full-time 2, part-time 20; African American/Black–full-time 2, part-time 2; Hispanic/Latino(a)–full-time 3, part-time 2; Asian/Pacific Islander–full-time 1, part-time 2; American Indian/Alaska Native–full-time 0, part-time 0; Caucasian–full-time 6, part-time 28; Multi-ethnic–full-time 0, part-time 0; students subject to the Americans With Disabilities Act–full-time 0, part-time 1.

Financial Information/Assistance:
Tuition for Full-Time Study: *Doctoral:* State residents: $525 per credit hour; Nonstate residents: $795 per credit hour. Tuition is subject to change. Tuition costs vary by program. See the following Web site for updates and changes in tuition costs: www.alliant.edu/admissions/costs.htm.

Financial Assistance:

First Year Students: Research assistantships available for first-year. Average amount paid per academic year: $1,000. Average number of hours worked per week: 10. Apply by see dept. Fellowships and scholarships available for first-year. Average amount paid per academic year: $1,500. Apply by February 1.

Advanced Students: Teaching assistantships available for advanced students. Average amount paid per academic year: $3,000. Average number of hours worked per week: 10. Apply by see dept. Research assistantships available for advanced students.

Average amount paid per academic year: $1,000. Average number of hours worked per week: 10. Apply by see dept. Fellowships and scholarships available for advanced students. Average amount paid per academic year: $1,500. Apply by April 15.

Contact Information: Of all students currently enrolled full-time, 69% benefitted from one or more of the listed financial assistance programs. Application and information available online at: www.alliant/edu/finaid/grad.htm.

Internships/Practica: The second and third years of the doctoral program involve a professional placement in organizational studies.

Housing and Day Care: No on-campus housing is available. No on-campus day care facilities are available.

Employment of Department Graduates:
Master's Degree Graduates: Of those who graduated in the academic year 2003–2004, the following categories and numbers represent the post-graduate activities and employment of master's degree graduates: Enrolled in a psychology doctoral program (3), enrolled in another graduate/professional program (5), enrolled in a post-doctoral residency/fellowship (n/a), employed in independent practice (n/a), employed in an academic position at a university (0), employed in an academic position at a 2-year/4-year college (1), employed in other positions at a higher education institution (1), employed in a professional position in a school system (0), employed in business or industry (research/consulting) (1), employed in business or industry (management) (8), employed in a government agency (research) (0), employed in a government agency (professional services) (2), employed in a community mental health/counseling center (0), employed in a hospital/medical center (2), still seeking employment (0), not seeking employment (0), other employment position (3), do not know (0), total from the above (master's) (26).

Doctoral Degree Graduates: Of those who graduated in the academic year 2003–2004, the following categories and numbers represent the post-graduate activities and employment of doctoral degree graduates: Enrolled in a psychology doctoral program (n/a), enrolled in another graduate/professional program (0), enrolled in a post-doctoral residency/fellowship (0), employed in independent practice (2), employed in an academic position at a university (2), employed in an academic position at a 2-year/4-year college (1), employed in other positions at a higher education institution (0), employed in a professional position in a school system (0), employed in business or industry (research/consulting) (0), employed in business or industry (management) (1), employed in a government agency (research) (0), employed in a government agency (professional services) (1), employed in a community mental health/counseling center (0), employed in a hospital/medical center (1), still seeking employment (0), not seeking employment (0), other employment position (3), do not know (0), total from the above (doctoral) (11).

Additional Information:
Orientation, Objectives, and Emphasis of Department: The doctoral program prepares students for careers as consultants, leaders/managers, or faculty in community-college or other academic institutions. The program is three-years post-masters and accessible to working adults. Students focus on the individual as a scholar-practitioner, themes and cultures of organizations, and practice in the global community. During the program they learn

about managing change in complex organizations, examine and assess organizational procedures and processes, design interventions at the system/group/individual levels, and learn skills for OD consulting and conducting applied research. A PsyD project is a required part of the program. The master's program is a two year program for working professionals and may be taken jointly with another doctoral program at Alliant in Fresno. The program has a practical curriculum related to management issues involving people and organizational processes.

Special Facilities or Resources: California School of Organizational Studies operates the Organizational Consulting Center (OCC). Students may have opportunities to participate with faculty and OCC associates on consulting projects during their progams.

Information for Students With Physical Disabilities: See the following Web site for more information: www.alliant.edu/about/ADA.htm.

Application Information:

Send to: Alliant International University, Admissions Processing Center, 10455 Pomerado Road, San Diego, CA 92131-1799. Application available online. URL of online application: https://ais1.alliant.edu/apply/. Students are admitted in the Fall, application deadline February 1; Spring, application deadline varies. Programs have rolling admissions. Doctoral program has a February 1 deadline in order to provide a response by April 1 for applicants who need a decsion by that date. The program accepts applications and admits students on a space available basis after any stated deadlines. For complete information on deadlines, visit www.alliant.edu/admissions/gradtimelines.htm or contact the admissions office at 1-866-U-ALLIANT. *Fee:* $65. A limited number of fee waivers are available to those with significant financial need.

Alliant International University: Irvine
Marital and Family Therapy Program
California School of Professional Psychology
2500 Michelson Drive, Building 400
Irvine, CA 92612-1548
Telephone: (949) 833-2651
Fax: (949) 833-3507
E-mail: cbrewer@alliant.edu
Web: www.alliant.edu/cspp/mamft.htm

Department Information:

1973. Program Director: Scott Woolley, PhD. Number of Faculty: total–full-time 4, part-time 11; women–full-time 1, part-time 8; minority–full-time 1, part-time 3.

Programs and Degrees Offered:

Listed in the following order: Program area, degree type (T if terminal Master's), number awarded 7/03–6/04. Marital and Family Therapy MA/MS (Master of Arts/Science) (T) 4, Marital and Family Therapy PsyD (Doctor of Psychology) 0.

Student Applications/Admissions:
Student Applications

Marital and Family Therapy MA/MS (Master of Arts/Science)—Applications 2004–2005, 29. Total applicants accepted 2004–2005, 17. Number enrolled (new admits only) 2004–2005 full-time, 11. Number enrolled (new admits only) 2004–2005 part-time, 3. Total enrolled 2004–2005 full-time, 30, part-time, 10. Openings 2005–2006, 18. The Median number of years required for completion of a degree are 2. The number of students enrolled full and part-time who were dismissed or voluntarily withdrew from this program area were 1. *Marital and Family Therapy PsyD (Doctor of Psychology)*—Applications 2004–2005, 34. Total applicants accepted 2004–2005, 27. Number enrolled (new admits only) 2004–2005 full-time, 20. Number enrolled (new admits only) 2004–2005 part-time, 4. Total enrolled 2004–2005 full-time, 49, part-time, 26. Openings 2005–2006, 25. The number of students enrolled full and part-time who were dismissed or voluntarily withdrew from this program area were 2.

Admissions Requirements:
Scores: Entries appear in this order: required test or GPA, minimum score (if required), median score of students entering in 2003–2004. Master's Programs: overall undergraduate GPA 3.00, 3.01; psychology GPA 3.00. Doctoral Programs: overall undergraduate GPA 3.00, 3.0; psychology GPA 3.00.
Other Criteria: (importance of criteria rated low, medium, or high): GRE/MAT scores low, research experience medium, work experience medium, clinically related public service medium, GPA high, letters of recommendation medium, interview high, statement of goals and objectives high. For additional information on admission requirements, go to: www.alliant.edu/admissions/gradapply.htm.

Student Characteristics: The following represents characteristics of students in 2004–2005 in all graduate psychology programs in the department: Female–full-time 67, part-time 38; Male–full-time 13, part-time 16; African American/Black–full-time 6, part-time 2; Hispanic/Latino(a)–full-time 8, part-time 5; Asian/Pacific Islander–full-time 8, part-time 6; American Indian/Alaska Native–full-time 2, part-time 0; Caucasian–full-time 55, part-time 41; Multi-ethnic–full-time 1, part-time 0; students subject to the Americans With Disabilities Act–full-time 0, part-time 1.

Financial Information/Assistance:
Tuition for Full-Time Study: *Master's:* State residents: $795 per credit hour; Nonstate residents: $795 per credit hour. *Doctoral:* State residents: $795 per credit hour; Nonstate residents: $795 per credit hour. Tuition is subject to change. Tuition costs vary by program. See the following Web site for updates and changes in tuition costs: www.alliant.edu/admissions/costs.htm.

Financial Assistance:
First Year Students: Research assistantships available for first-year. Average amount paid per academic year: $1,000. Average number of hours worked per week: 10. Apply by see dept. Fellowships and scholarships available for first-year. Average amount paid per academic year: $750. Apply by varies.

Advanced Students: Teaching assistantships available for advanced students. Average amount paid per academic year: $3,000. Average number of hours worked per week: 10. Apply by see dept. Research assistantships available for advanced students. Average amount paid per academic year: $1,000. Average number of hours worked per week: 10. Apply by see dept. Fellowships and scholarships available for advanced students. Average amount paid per academic year: $750. Apply by varies.

Contact Information: Of all students currently enrolled full-time, 55% benefitted from one or more of the listed financial assistance programs. Application and information available online at: www.alliant.edu/finaid.grad.htm.

Internships/Practica: As part of the practicum experience, students complete 500 client contact hours, 250 of which must be with couples and families. Students receive at least 100 hours of individual and group supervision, 50 hours of which are based on direct observation, videotape, or audiotape. At least 25 of those hours must be videotape or direct observation. When students are ready to begin practicum, experienced faculty and staff assist students through each step in obtaining a field placement cite approved by AIU. While students are doing practicum training they are required to perform marriage and family therapy under a California state licensed, AAMFT approved supervisor or the equivalent.

Housing and Day Care: No on-campus housing is available. No on-campus day care facilities are available.

Employment of Department Graduates:
Master's Degree Graduates: Of those who graduated in the academic year 2003–2004, the following categories and numbers represent the post-graduate activities and employment of master's degree graduates: Enrolled in a post-doctoral residency/fellowship (n/a), employed in independent practice (n/a), total from the above (master's) (0).
Doctoral Degree Graduates: Of those who graduated in the academic year 2003–2004, the following categories and numbers represent the post-graduate activities and employment of doctoral degree graduates: Enrolled in a psychology doctoral program (n/a), total from the above (doctoral) (0).

Additional Information:
Orientation, Objectives, and Emphasis of Department: The mission of the Marital and Family Therapy Program is to prepare graduate students who are skilled in the theory, research, and clinical practice of the field of Marriage and Family Therapy and can integrate individual and systemic therapeutic models in an international, multicultural environment. The marital and family therapy (MFT) programs provide students with the essential training needed to pursue a career as a professional marriage and family therapist. The Master of Arts in MFT allows students to be licensed as a marital and family therapist (MFT) and the Doctor of Psychology in MFT allows a student to be licensed as a marital and family therapist and as a psychologist. Students who complete the MFT masters at Alliant can apply all of their masters degree coursework and practicum hours toward the doctoral program.

Information for Students With Physical Disabilities: See the following Web site for more information: www.alliant.edu/about/ADA.htm.

Application Information:
Send to: Alliant International University Admissions Processing Center, 10455 Pomerado Road, San Diego, CA 92131-1799. Application available online. URL of online application: https://ais1.alliant.edu/apply/. Students are admitted in the Fall, application deadline August 1; Spring, application deadline varies; Summer, application deadline varies; Programs have rolling admissions. For complete information on deadlines visit www.alliant.edu/admissions/gradtimelines.htm or contact the admissions office at 1-866-U-ALLIANT. *Fee:* $65. A limited number of fee waivers are available for those with significant financial need.

Alliant International University: Irvine
Programs in Educational and School Psychology
Graduate School of Education
2500 Michelson Drive, Building 400
Irvine, CA 92612-1548
Telephone: (949) 833-2651
Fax: (949) 833-3507
E-mail: *cbrewer@alliant.edu*
Web: *www.alliant.edu/gsoe/schpsych.htm*

Department Information:
2002. Systemwide Program Director: Rhonda Brinkley-Kennedy, PsyD. Number of Faculty: total–full-time 1, part-time 9; women–full-time 1, part-time 9; minority–full-time 1, part-time 3.

Programs and Degrees Offered:
Listed in the following order: Program area, degree type (T if terminal Master's), number awarded 7/03–6/04. Educational Psychology PsyD (Doctor of Psychology) 0, School Psychology MA/MS (Master of Arts/Science) (T) 7.

Student Applications/Admissions:
Student Applications
Educational Psychology PsyD (Doctor of Psychology)—Applications 2004–2005, 10. Total applicants accepted 2004–2005, 8. Number enrolled (new admits only) 2004–2005 full-time, 0. Number enrolled (new admits only) 2004–2005 part-time, 8. Openings 2005–2006, 10. The number of students enrolled full and part-time who were dismissed or voluntarily withdrew from this program area were 0. *School Psychology MA/MS (Master of Arts/Science)*—Applications 2004–2005, 44. Total applicants accepted 2004–2005, 37. Number enrolled (new admits only) 2004–2005 full-time, 12. Number enrolled (new admits only) 2004–2005 part-time, 3. Total enrolled 2004–2005 full-time, 24, part-time, 8. Openings 2005–2006, 18. The Median number of years required for completion of a degree are 1.7. The number of students enrolled full and part-time who were dismissed or voluntarily withdrew from this program area were 2.

Admissions Requirements:
Scores: Entries appear in this order: required test or GPA, minimum score (if required), median score of students entering in 2003–2004. Master's Programs: overall undergraduate GPA 2.5, 3.11; psychology GPA 2.5. Doctoral Programs: overall undergraduate GPA 3.0; psychology GPA 3.0. A master's degree is not required for the five year PsyD program, but if the degree is held at the time of application, the 3.0 minimum GPA applies.
Other Criteria: (importance of criteria rated low, medium, or high): research experience medium, work experience medium, extracurricular activity low, clinically related public service high, GPA high, letters of recommendation high, interview high, statement of goals and objectives high, Criteria differ by

program and level. For additional information on admission requirements, go to: www.alliant.edu/admissions/gradapply.htm.

Student Characteristics: The following represents characteristics of students in 2004–2005 in all graduate psychology programs in the department: Female–full-time 22, part-time 12; Male–full-time 2, part-time 5; African American/Black–full-time 0, part-time 1; Hispanic/Latino(a)–full-time 4, part-time 3; Asian/Pacific Islander–full-time 3, part-time 4; Caucasian–full-time 17, part-time 9; students subject to the Americans With Disabilities Act–full-time 1, part-time 0.

Financial Information/Assistance:

Tuition for Full-Time Study: *Master's:* State residents: $450 per credit hour; Nonstate residents: $450 per credit hour. *Doctoral:* State residents: $795 per credit hour; Nonstate residents: $795 per credit hour. Tuition is subject to change. Tuition costs vary by program. See the following Web site for updates and changes in tuition costs: www.alliant.edu/admissions/costs.htm.

Financial Assistance:

First Year Students: Research assistantships available for first-year. Average amount paid per academic year: $1,000. Average number of hours worked per week: 10. Apply by see dept. Fellowships and scholarships available for first-year. Average amount paid per academic year: $750. Apply by June 1.

Advanced Students: Teaching assistantships available for advanced students. Average amount paid per academic year: $3,000. Average number of hours worked per week: 10. Apply by see dept. Research assistantships available for advanced students. Average amount paid per academic year: $1,000. Average number of hours worked per week: 10. Apply by see dept. Fellowships and scholarships available for advanced students. Average amount paid per academic year: $750. Apply by April 1.

Contact Information: Of all students currently enrolled full-time, 50% benefitted from one or more of the listed financial assistance programs. Application and information available online at: www.alliant.edu/finaid/grad.htm.

Internships/Practica: Students in the master's program have practica tied to their coursework beginning in the first semester of their programs. Internships are required of students seeking a Pupil Personnel Services (PPS) credential post-masters or as part of the doctoral program in educational psychology. The 1200 required internship hours are completed at a public school district. Students interested in seeking clinical licensure must complete a separate internship.

Housing and Day Care: No on-campus housing is available. No on-campus day care facilities are available.

Employment of Department Graduates:

Master's Degree Graduates: Of those who graduated in the academic year 2003–2004, the following categories and numbers represent the post-graduate activities and employment of master's degree graduates: Enrolled in a post-doctoral residency/fellowship (n/a), employed in independent practice (n/a), total from the above (master's) (0).

Doctoral Degree Graduates: Of those who graduated in the academic year 2003–2004, the following categories and numbers represent the post-graduate activities and employment of doctoral degree graduates: Enrolled in a psychology doctoral program (n/a), total from the above (doctoral) (0).

Additional Information:

Orientation, Objectives, and Emphasis of Department: Programs train students with the skills necessary to work with students, teachers, parents, and other school professionals in today's school environments. Curriculum includes professional skills, professional roles courses, applied research, and professional concepts. The master's degree program prepares students to gain the PPS (Pupil Personnel Services) credential that allows them to practice in California's schools. Students take afternoon, evening, and weekend classes and engage in fieldwork. At the doctoral level, students complete special focus area courses, examples of which include adolescent stress and coping, school culture and administration, pediatric psychology, infant and preschool mental health, child neuropsychology, and provision of services for children in alternative placement. Students also complete a PsyD project.

Information for Students With Physical Disabilities: See the following Web site for more information: www.alliant.edu/about/ADA.htm.

Application Information:

Send to: Alliant International University, Admissions Processing Center, 10455 Pomerado Road, San Diego, CA 92131-1799. Application available online. URL of online application: https://ais1.alliant.edu/apply/. Students are admitted in the Fall, application deadline June 1; Spring, application deadline varies; Summer, application deadline varies. *Fee:* $50. A limited number of fee waivers are available to those with significant financial need.

Alliant International University: Los Angeles
Forensic Psychology Programs
College of Arts and Sciences
1000 South Fremont Avenue
Alhambra, CA 91803-1360
Telephone: (626) 284-2777
Fax: (626) 284-0550
E-mail: *sbyers-bell@alliant.edu*
Web: *www.alliant.edu/ssps/forensic/*

Department Information:
1999. Program Coordinator: Robert Leark, PhD. Number of Faculty: total–full-time 2, part-time 11; women–full-time 1, part-time 3; minority–part-time 2.

Programs and Degrees Offered:
Listed in the following order: Program area, degree type (T if terminal Master's), number awarded 7/03–6/04. Forensic Psychology PsyD (Doctor of Psychology) 1.

Student Applications/Admissions:
Student Applications
Forensic Psychology PsyD (Doctor of Psychology)—Applications 2004–2005, 62. Total applicants accepted 2004–2005, 29. Number enrolled (new admits only) 2004–2005 full-time, 14. Number enrolled (new admits only) 2004–2005 part-time, 0.

Total enrolled 2004–2005 full-time, 35, part-time, 4. Openings 2005–2006, 20. The Median number of years required for completion of a degree are 4.8. The number of students enrolled full and part-time who were dismissed or voluntarily withdrew from this program area were 1.

Admissions Requirements:
Scores: Entries appear in this order: required test or GPA, minimum score (if required), median score of students entering in 2003–2004. Doctoral Programs: overall undergraduate GPA 3.0, 3.29; psychology GPA 3.0. Master's degree is not required for entry, but if held at time entry, 3.0 minimum GPA applies.
Other Criteria: (importance of criteria rated low, medium, or high): research experience medium, work experience high, extracurricular activity low, clinically related public service high, GPA high, interview high, statement of goals and objectives high. For additional information on admission requirements, go to: www.alliant.edu/admissions/gradapply.htm.

Student Characteristics: The following represents characteristics of students in 2004–2005 in all graduate psychology programs in the department: Female–full-time 28, part-time 3; Male–full-time 7, part-time 1; African American/Black–full-time 3, part-time 1; Hispanic/Latino(a)–full-time 4, part-time 1; Asian/Pacific Islander–full-time 1, part-time 0; American Indian/Alaska Native–full-time 0, part-time 0; Caucasian–full-time 26, part-time 2; Multi-ethnic–full-time 1, part-time 0; students subject to the Americans With Disabilities Act–full-time 0, part-time 1.

Financial Information/Assistance:
Tuition for Full-Time Study: *Doctoral:* State residents: $795 per credit hour; Nonstate residents: $795 per credit hour. Tuition is subject to change. See the following Web site for updates and changes in tuition costs: www.alliant.edu/admissions/costs.htm.

Financial Assistance:
First Year Students: Research assistantships available for first-year. Average amount paid per academic year: $1,000. Average number of hours worked per week: 10. Apply by see dept. Fellowships and scholarships available for first-year. Average amount paid per academic year: $1,500. Apply by February 15.
Advanced Students: Teaching assistantships available for advanced students. Average amount paid per academic year: $3,000. Average number of hours worked per week: 20. Apply by see dept. Research assistantships available for advanced students. Average amount paid per academic year: $1,000. Average number of hours worked per week: 10. Apply by see dept. Fellowships and scholarships available for advanced students. Average amount paid per academic year: $1,500. Apply by February 15.
Contact Information: Of all students currently enrolled full-time, 80% benefitted from one or more of the listed financial assistance programs. Application and information available online at: www.alliant/edu/finaid/grad.htm.

Internships/Practica: A one year pre-doctoral internship is part of the program; this occurs in the fifth year of the program. For those doctoral students for whom a professional internship is required prior to graduation, 5 applied in 2003–2004. Of those who applied, 3 were placed in internships listed by the Association of Psychology Postdoctoral and Internship Programs (APPIC).

Housing and Day Care: No on-campus housing is available. No on-campus day care facilities are available.

Employment of Department Graduates:
Master's Degree Graduates: Of those who graduated in the academic year 2003–2004, the following categories and numbers represent the post-graduate activities and employment of master's degree graduates: Enrolled in a post-doctoral residency/fellowship (n/a), employed in independent practice (n/a), total from the above (master's) (0).
Doctoral Degree Graduates: Of those who graduated in the academic year 2003–2004, the following categories and numbers represent the post-graduate activities and employment of doctoral degree graduates: Enrolled in a psychology doctoral program (n/a), total from the above (doctoral) (0).

Additional Information:
Orientation, Objectives, and Emphasis of Department: The PsyD program has an applied psychology orientation and is offered in a part-time five-year curriculum. This format attracts students with prior work experience from a variety of fields. The curriculum prepares students to conduct assessments for the courts, to serve as expert witnesses, or to work as mental health treatment providers in a variety of forensic settings, including prisons, jails, offender treatment groups, youth facilities, among many others. Core areas include forensic psychology, theories of crime and justice, industrial and organizational psychology, legal research, psychopathology, research design and data analysis, forensic mediation and dispute resolution, ethics, and substance abuse theory and treatment. While licensure is not required for most forensic careers, some students who enter the program may choose to seek clinical licensure after graduating from the program. These students take additional courses in psychology that are required in order to be eligible to sit for the psychology licensing exam.

Information for Students With Physical Disabilities: See the following Web site for more information: www.alliant.edu/about/ADA.htm.

Application Information:
Send to: Alliant International University, Admissions Processing Center, 10455 Pomerado Road, San Diego, CA 92131-1799. Application available online. URL of online application: https://ais1.alliant.edu/apply/. Students are admitted in the Fall, application deadline varies. Programs have rolling admissions. The priority application deadline is January 2 for those wishing notification of early decision; however applications are welcomed after that date for those who do not need an April 1 notification. *Fee:* $65. A limited number of fee waivers are available for those with significant financial need.

Alliant International University: Los Angeles
Programs in Clinical Psychology
California School of Professional Psychology
1000 S. Fremont Avenue
Alhambra, CA 91803-1360
Telephone: (626) 284-2777
Fax: (626) 284-0550
E-mail: *sbyers-bell@alliant.edu*
Web: *http://www.alliant.edu/cspp/*

Department Information:
1970. Systemwide Dean: Jean Lau Chin, EdD, ABPP. Number of Faculty: total–full-time 23, part-time 41; women–full-time 13,

part-time 20; minority–full-time 9, part-time 7; faculty subject to the Americans With Disabilities Act 1.

Programs and Degrees Offered:

Listed in the following order: Program area, degree type (T if terminal Master's), number awarded 7/03–6/04. Clinical Psychology PhD (Doctor of Philosophy) 39, Clinical Psychology PsyD (Doctor of Psychology) 60.

APA Accreditation: Clinical PhD (Doctor of Philosophy). Clinical PsyD (Doctor of Psychology).

Student Applications/Admissions:

Student Applications

Clinical Psychology PhD (Doctor of Philosophy)—Applications 2004–2005, 101. Total applicants accepted 2004–2005, 55. Number enrolled (new admits only) 2004–2005 full-time, 30. Number enrolled (new admits only) 2004–2005 part-time, 0. Total enrolled 2004–2005 full-time, 168, part-time, 35. Openings 2005–2006, 25. The Median number of years required for completion of a degree are 5. The number of students enrolled full and part-time who were dismissed or voluntarily withdrew from this program area were 2. *Clinical Psychology PsyD (Doctor of Psychology)*—Applications 2004–2005, 184. Total applicants accepted 2004–2005, 115. Number enrolled (new admits only) 2004–2005 full-time, 82. Number enrolled (new admits only) 2004–2005 part-time, 0. Total enrolled 2004–2005 full-time, 269, part-time, 18. Openings 2005–2006, 75. The Median number of years required for completion of a degree are 3.9. The number of students enrolled full and part-time who were dismissed or voluntarily withdrew from this program area were 8.

Admissions Requirements:

Scores: Entries appear in this order: required test or GPA, minimum score (if required), median score of students entering in 2003–2004. Master's Programs: Admissions requirements vary by program. Doctoral Programs: overall undergraduate GPA 3.0, 3.11; psychology GPA 3.0. The master's degree is not required for entry, but if it is held at the time of application, the minimum 3.0 GPA applies.

Other Criteria: (importance of criteria rated low, medium, or high): research experience high, work experience medium, extracurricular activity low, clinically related public service medium, GPA medium, letters of recommendation medium, interview high, statement of goals and objectives high. Admissions requirements vary by program. PhD program places more emphasis on prior research experience; PsyD program places more emphasis on clinical/work experience. For additional information on admission requirements, go to: www.alliant.edu/admissions/gradapply.htm.

Student Characteristics: The following represents characteristics of students in 2004–2005 in all graduate psychology programs in the department: Female–full-time 355, part-time 43; Male–full-time 82, part-time 10; African American/Black–full-time 40, part-time 4; Hispanic/Latino(a)–full-time 58, part-time 4; Asian/Pacific Islander–full-time 60, part-time 3; American Indian/Alaska Native–full-time 3, part-time 1; Caucasian–full-time 268, part-time 40; Multi-ethnic–full-time 8, part-time 1; students subject to the Americans With Disabilities Act–full-time 7, part-time 2.

Financial Information/Assistance:

Tuition for Full-Time Study: *Doctoral:* State residents: $795 per credit hour; Nonstate residents: $795 per credit hour. Tuition is subject to change. See the following Web site for updates and changes in tuition costs: www.alliant.edu/admissions/costs.htm.

Financial Assistance:

First Year Students: Research assistantships available for first-year. Average amount paid per academic year: $1,000. Average number of hours worked per week: 10. Apply by see dept. Fellowships and scholarships available for first-year. Average amount paid per academic year: $1,500. Apply by April 15.

Advanced Students: Teaching assistantships available for advanced students. Average amount paid per academic year: $3,000. Average number of hours worked per week: 10. Apply by see dept. Research assistantships available for advanced students. Average amount paid per academic year: $1,000. Average number of hours worked per week: 10. Apply by see dept. Traineeships available for advanced students. Average number of hours worked per week: 25. Apply by variable. Fellowships and scholarships available for advanced students. Average amount paid per academic year: $1,500. Apply by April 15.

Contact Information: Of all students currently enrolled full-time, 85% benefitted from one or more of the listed financial assistance programs. Application and information available online at: www.alliant/edu/finaid/grad.htm.

Internships/Practica: All students engage in practica and internships. Students complete 2000 pre-doctoral internship hours as part of their programs. The majority of the professional training sites are within 40 miles of the campus. These agencies serve a diverse range of individuals across ethnicity, culture, religion, and sexual orientation. These sites provide excellent training, offering a variety of theoretical orientations related to children, adolescents, adults, families and the elderly. Students who wish to pursue full-time internships are encouraged to make applications throughout the country. For those doctoral students for whom a professional internship is required prior to graduation, 160 applied in 2003–2004. Of those who applied, 11 were placed in internships listed by the Association of Psychology Postdoctoral and Internship Programs (APPIC); 9 were placed in APA accredited internships.

Housing and Day Care: No on-campus housing is available. No on-campus day care facilities are available.

Employment of Department Graduates:

Master's Degree Graduates: Of those who graduated in the academic year 2003–2004, the following categories and numbers represent the post-graduate activities and employment of master's degree graduates: Enrolled in a post-doctoral residency/fellowship (n/a), employed in independent practice (n/a), total from the above (master's) (0).

Doctoral Degree Graduates: Of those who graduated in the academic year 2003–2004, the following categories and numbers represent the post-graduate activities and employment of doctoral degree graduates: Enrolled in a psychology doctoral program (n/a), enrolled in another graduate/professional program (0), enrolled in a post-doctoral residency/fellowship (35), employed in independent practice (17), employed in an academic position at a university (1), employed in an academic position at a 2-year/4-year college (3), employed in other positions at a higher education institution (4), employed in a professional position in a school system (13), employed in business or industry (research/consulting) (13), employed in business or industry (management) (3), employed in a government agency (research) (0), employed in a government agency (professional services) (1), employed in a community mental health/counseling center (16), employed in a hospital/medical center (1), still seeking employment (5), other employment position (3), do not know (5), total from the above (doctoral) (120).

Additional Information:

Orientation, Objectives, and Emphasis of Department: The clinical psychology PsyD and PhD programs at the California School of Professional Psychology prepare students to function as multi-faceted clinical psychologists through a curriculum based on an integration of psychological theory, research, and practice. Students develop competencies in seven areas: clinical health psychology; interpersonal/relationship; assessment; multifaceted multimodal intervention; research and evaluation; consultation/teaching; management/supervision/training; and quality assurance. The PsyD program is a practitioner program where candidates gain relatively greater mastery in assessment, intervention, and management/supervision. The PhD program is a based on a scholar-practitioner model where practice and scholarship receive equal emphasis and includes the following guiding principles: the generation and application of knowledge must occur with an awareness of the sociocultural and sociopolitical contexts of mental health and mental illness; scholarship and practice must not only build upon existing literature but also maintain relevance to the diverse elements in our society and assume the challenges of attending to the complex social issues associated with psychological functioning; and methods of research and intervention must be appropriate to the culture in which they are conducted. Practica and internship experiences are integrated throughout the programs. Students have the opportunity to choose a curricular emphasis in clinical health psychology, multicultural community clinical, or individual, family, and child clinical psychology. This last emphasis has a couple and family intervention sub-emphasis and a child intervention sub-emphasis.

Special Facilities or Resources: The Professional Services Center (PSC) is charged with the mission of developing professional training, research, and consultation opportunities for CSPP faculty and students, while providing services to a variety of public/private agencies. It is committed to developing effective and innovative service strategies and resources that address the needs of a wide range of clients with a particular focus on ethnically diverse, underserved populations. As a center "without walls," the PSC is the administrative umbrella for two major community-based programs: the Children, Youth, and Family Consortium and the School Court Accountability Project. These projects are designed to provide hands-on research, consulting, and clinical experience for students and to enhance the critically needed services to school-aged youth within the court system and school-aged populations. These programs enable participating CSPP faculty, staff, students, alumni/ae, and external consultant associates to provide services few other institutions can offer. Students also receive unique training and supervision that prepares them for critically needed roles as community advocates and leaders.

Information for Students With Physical Disabilities: See the following Web site for more information: www.alliant.edu/about/ADA.htm.

Application Information:
Send to: Alliant International University, Admissions Processing Center, 10455 Pomerado Road, San Diego, CA 92131-1799. Application available online. URL of online application: https://ais1.alliant.edu/apply/. Students are admitted in the Fall, application deadline January 15. Programs have rolling admissions. The programs have a January 15 priority deadline in order to provide a response by April 1 for applicants who need a decision by that date. Programs accept applications and admit students on a space-available basis after any stated deadlines. For complete information on deadlines visit www.alliant.edu/gradtimelines.htm or contact the admissions office at 1-866-U-ALLIANT. *Fee:* $65. A limited number of fee waivers are available for those with significant financial need.

Alliant International University: Los Angeles
Programs in Educational and School Psychology
Graduate School of Education
1000 South Fremont Avenue
Alameda, CA 91803-1360
Telephone: (626) 284-2777
Fax: (626) 284-0550
E-mail: *sbyers-bell@alliant.edu*
Web: *www.alliant.edu/gsoe/schpsych.htm*

Department Information:
1999. Systemwide Program Director: Rhonda Brinkley-Kennedy, PsyD. Number of Faculty: total–full-time 1, part-time 8; women–full-time 1, part-time 3; minority–full-time 1, part-time 5.

Programs and Degrees Offered:
Listed in the following order: Program area, degree type (T if terminal Master's), number awarded 7/03–6/04. School Psychology MA/MS (Master of Arts/Science) (T) 8, Educational Psychology PsyD (Doctor of Psychology) 3.

Student Applications/Admissions:
Student Applications
School Psychology MA/MS (Master of Arts/Science)—Applications 2004–2005, 33. Total applicants accepted 2004–2005, 19. Number enrolled (new admits only) 2004–2005 full-time, 14. Number enrolled (new admits only) 2004–2005 part-time, 2. Total enrolled 2004–2005 full-time, 23, part-time, 6. Openings 2005–2006, 20. The Median number of years required for completion of a degree are 2.2. The number of students enrolled full and part-time who were dismissed or voluntarily withdrew from this program area were 0. *Educational Psychology PsyD (Doctor of Psychology)*—Applications 2004–2005, 6. Total applicants accepted 2004–2005, 1. Number enrolled (new admits only) 2004–2005 part-time, 1. Total enrolled 2004–2005 full-time, 1, part-time, 7. Openings 2005–2006, 5. The Median number of years required for completion of a degree are 2.7. The number of students enrolled full and part-time who were dismissed or voluntarily withdrew from this program area were 3.

Admissions Requirements:
Scores: Entries appear in this order: required test or GPA, minimum score (if required), median score of students entering in 2003–2004. Master's Programs: overall undergraduate GPA

2.5, 2.84; psychology GPA 2.5. Doctoral Programs: overall undergraduate GPA 3.0; psychology GPA 3.0. Master's degree is not required for entry to the five year PsyD program, but if the degree is held at the time of application, the 3.0 minimum GPA applies.

Other Criteria: (importance of criteria rated low, medium, or high): research experience medium, work experience high, extracurricular activity low, clinically related public service high, GPA high, letters of recommendation high, interview high, statement of goals and objectives high. Criteria differ by program and level. For additional information on admission requirements, go to: www.alliant.edu/admissions/gradapply.htm.

Student Characteristics: The following represents characteristics of students in 2004–2005 in all graduate psychology programs in the department: Female–full-time 19, part-time 10; Male–full-time 5, part-time 3; African American/Black–full-time 5, part-time 0; Hispanic/Latino(a)–full-time 12, part-time 2; Asian/Pacific Islander–full-time 2, part-time 2; American Indian/Alaska Native–full-time 0, part-time 0; Caucasian–full-time 5, part-time 9; Multi-ethnic–full-time 0, part-time 0; students subject to the Americans With Disabilities Act–full-time 0, part-time 0.

Financial Information/Assistance:

Tuition for Full-Time Study: *Master's:* State residents: $450 per credit hour; Nonstate residents: $450 per credit hour. *Doctoral:* State residents: $795 per credit hour; Nonstate residents: $795 per credit hour. Tuition is subject to change. Tuition costs vary by program. See the following Web site for updates and changes in tuition costs: www.alliant.edu/admissions/costs.htm.

Financial Assistance:

First Year Students: Research assistantships available for first-year. Average amount paid per academic year: $1,000. Average number of hours worked per week: 10. Apply by see dept. Fellowships and scholarships available for first-year. Average amount paid per academic year: $1,500. Apply by June 1.

Advanced Students: Teaching assistantships available for advanced students. Average amount paid per academic year: $3,000. Average number of hours worked per week: 10. Apply by see dept. Research assistantships available for advanced students. Average amount paid per academic year: $1,000. Average number of hours worked per week: 10. Apply by see dept. Fellowships and scholarships available for advanced students. Average amount paid per academic year: $1,500. Apply by April 1.

Contact Information: Of all students currently enrolled full-time, 55% benefitted from one or more of the listed financial assistance programs. Application and information available online at: www.alliant/edu/finaid/grad.htm.

Internships/Practica: Students in the master's program have practica tied to their coursework beginning in the first semester of their programs. Internships are required of any students seeking the Pupil Personnel Services (PPS) credential post-masters or as part of the doctoral program in educational psychology. The 1200 internship hours are completed at a public school district. Those in the doctoral program who are interested in clinical licensure must complete a separate internship.

Housing and Day Care: No on-campus housing is available. No on-campus day care facilities are available.

Employment of Department Graduates:

Master's Degree Graduates: Of those who graduated in the academic year 2003–2004, the following categories and numbers represent the post-graduate activities and employment of master's degree graduates: Enrolled in a post-doctoral residency/fellowship (n/a), employed in independent practice (n/a), total from the above (master's) (0).

Doctoral Degree Graduates: Of those who graduated in the academic year 2003–2004, the following categories and numbers represent the post-graduate activities and employment of doctoral degree graduates: Enrolled in a psychology doctoral program (n/a), total from the above (doctoral) (0).

Additional Information:

Orientation, Objectives, and Emphasis of Department: Programs train students with the skills necesary to work with students, teachers, parents, and other school professionals in today's school environments. The curriculum includes professional skills, professional roles courses, applied research, and professional concepts. The master's degree program prepares students to gain the PPS (Pupil Personnel Services) credential that allow them to practice in California's schools. Students take afternoon, evening and weekend classes and engage in fieldwork. At the doctoral level students complete special focus area courses, examples of which include adolescent stress and coping, school culture and administration, pediatric psychology, infant and preschool mental health, child neuropsychology, and provision of services for children in alternative placement. Students also complete a PsyD project.

Information for Students With Physical Disabilities: See the following Web site for more information: www.alliant.edu/about/ADA.htm.

Application Information:
Send to: Alliant International University, Admissions Processing Center, 10455 Pomerado Road, San Diego, CA 93121-1799. Application available online. URL of online application: https://ais1.alliant.edu/apply/. Students are admitted in the Fall, application deadline June 1; Spring, application deadline varies. Programs have rolling admissions. *Fee:* $65. A limited number of fee waivers are available for those with significant financial need.

Alliant International University: Los Angeles
Programs in Organizational Studies
California School of Organizational Studies
1000 South Fremont Avenue
Alhambra, CA 91803-1360
Telephone: (626) 284-2777
Fax: (626) 284-0550
E-mail: *sbyers-bell@alliant.edu*
Web: *www.alliant.edu/csos/*

Department Information:
1981. Program Director: Jay M. Finkelman, PhD. Number of Faculty: total–full-time 4, part-time 5; women–part-time 5; minority–part-time 2.

Programs and Degrees Offered:
Listed in the following order: Program area, degree type (T if terminal Master's), number awarded 7/03–6/04. Industrial-Orga-

nizational PhD (Doctor of Philosophy) 2, Industrial-Organizational MA/MS (Master of Arts/Science) (T) 5, Organizational Behavior MA/MS (Master of Arts/Science) (T) 0, Industrial-Organizational Respecialization Diploma 0.

Student Applications/Admissions:

Student Applications

Industrial-Organizational PhD (Doctor of Philosophy)—Applications 2004–2005, 17. Total applicants accepted 2004–2005, 7. Number enrolled (new admits only) 2004–2005 full-time, 6. Number enrolled (new admits only) 2004–2005 part-time, 0. Total enrolled 2004–2005 full-time, 49, part-time, 11. Openings 2005–2006, 15. The Median number of years required for completion of a degree are 6. The number of students enrolled full and part-time who were dismissed or voluntarily withdrew from this program area were 0. *Industrial-Organizational MA/MS (Master of Arts/Science)*—Applications 2004–2005, 23. Total applicants accepted 2004–2005, 16. Number enrolled (new admits only) 2004–2005 full-time, 12. Number enrolled (new admits only) 2004–2005 part-time, 0. Openings 2005–2006, 15. The Median number of years required for completion of a degree are 2.2. The number of students enrolled full and part-time who were dismissed or voluntarily withdrew from this program area were 0. *Organizational Behavior MA/MS (Master of Arts/Science)*—Applications 2004–2005, 5. Total applicants accepted 2004–2005, 2. Number enrolled (new admits only) 2004–2005 full-time, 0. Number enrolled (new admits only) 2004–2005 part-time, 2. Openings 2005–2006, 5. The number of students enrolled full and part-time, who were dismissed or voluntarily withdrew from this program area were 0. *Industrial-Organizational Respecialization Diploma*—Applications 2004–2005, 1. Total applicants accepted 2004–2005, 0. Number enrolled (new admits only) 2004–2005 full-time, 0. Number enrolled (new admits only) 2004–2005 part-time, 0. Openings 2005–2006, 2. The number of students enrolled full and part-time who were dismissed or voluntarily withdrew from this program area were 0.

Admissions Requirements:

Scores: Entries appear in this order: required test or GPA, minimum score (if required), median score of students entering in 2003–2004. Master's Programs: overall undergraduate GPA 3.0, 3.0; psychology GPA 3.0. Doctoral Programs: overall undergraduate GPA 3.0, 3.29; psychology GPA 3.0. The master's degree is not required for doctoral program admission; however, if a master's is held at the time of application, the 3.0 minimum GPA applies.

Other Criteria: (importance of criteria rated low, medium, or high): research experience high, work experience high, extracurricular activity low, clinically related public service low, GPA high, letters of recommendation high, interview high, statement of goals and objectives high. Criteria vary by program. For additional information on admission requirements, go to: www.alliant.edu/admissions/gradapply.htm.

Student Characteristics: The following represents characteristics of students in 2004–2005 in all graduate psychology programs in the department: Female–full-time 43, part-time 7; Male–full-time 25, part-time 7; African American/Black–full-time 8, part-time 2; Hispanic/Latino(a)–full-time 7, part-time 2; Asian/Pacific Islander–full-time 8, part-time 2; American Indian/Alaska Native–full-time 0, part-time 0; Caucasian–full-time 41, part-time 8;

Multi-ethnic–full-time 4, part-time 0; students subject to the Americans With Disabilities Act–full-time 1, part-time 0.

Financial Information/Assistance:

Tuition for Full-Time Study: *Master's:* State residents: $795 per credit hour; Nonstate residents: $795 per credit hour. *Doctoral:* State residents: $795 per credit hour; Nonstate residents: $795 per credit hour. Tuition is subject to change. Tuition costs vary by program. See the following Web site for updates and changes in tuition costs: www.alliant.edu/admissions/costs.htm.

Financial Assistance:

First Year Students: Research assistantships available for first-year. Average amount paid per academic year: $1,000. Average number of hours worked per week: 10. Apply by see dept. Fellowships and scholarships available for first-year. Average amount paid per academic year: $1,500. Apply by varies.

Advanced Students: Teaching assistantships available for advanced students. Average amount paid per academic year: $3,000. Average number of hours worked per week: 10. Apply by see dept. Research assistantships available for advanced students. Average amount paid per academic year: $1,000. Average number of hours worked per week: 10. Apply by see dept. Fellowships and scholarships available for advanced students. Average amount paid per academic year: $1,500. Apply by April 15.

Contact Information: Of all students currently enrolled full-time, 71% benefitted from one or more of the listed financial assistance programs. Application and information available online at: www.alliant/edu/finaid/grad.htm.

Internships/Practica: Doctoral students may begin their practical training though the Center for Innovation and Change, working with faculty on pro bono consulting projects. A doctoral level field placement/internship is completed typically in the fourth year. Students spend 8–40 hours per week in a corporate, business, governmental, or non-profit setting. The majority of these are local to the student's campus; a few are outside the area, and are usually identified as part of a student's own career development interests. Students in the organizational psychology master's programs have a one semester practicum in organizational studies.

Housing and Day Care: No on-campus housing is available. No on-campus day care facilities are available.

Employment of Department Graduates:

Master's Degree Graduates: Of those who graduated in the academic year 2003–2004, the following categories and numbers represent the post-graduate activities and employment of master's degree graduates: Enrolled in a post-doctoral residency/fellowship (n/a), employed in independent practice (n/a), total from the above (master's) (0).

Doctoral Degree Graduates: Of those who graduated in the academic year 2003–2004, the following categories and numbers represent the post-graduate activities and employment of doctoral degree graduates: Enrolled in a psychology doctoral program (n/a), total from the above (doctoral) (0).

Additional Information:

Orientation, Objectives, and Emphasis of Department: The doctoral program is based on the philosophy that the foundations of effective organizational change are science-based, especially the science of human behavior in work settings. The program is designed to address both sides of the consultant/client relationship. The program integrates a strong foundation in the behavioral and organizational sciences; an understanding of intrapersonal and self-reflective approaches for examining human behavior; knowledge of interpersonal dynamics and political processes in professional practice, organizational interventions and consultant-clients relations; and professional experiential training. Graduates are prepared for careers in a wide variety of practice areas including management consulting, organizational assessment and design, human resources development, organizational development, diversity training, and change management. The master's degree programs are for those seeking preparation to begin or continue careers in organizational leadership and management. Some master's students are seeking an academic foundation for future doctoral work.

Special Facilities or Resources: At the California School of Organizational Studies Center for Innovation and Change in Los Angeles, graduate students apply what they are learning in the classroom by providing consulting services to non-profit organizations. Through the Center first and second year students form consulting teams that provide pro bono service to clients in the Los Angeles area. Each consulting team works with a faculty supervisor. Thus students get practical training beginning early on in their programs.

Information for Students With Physical Disabilities: See the following Web site for more information: www.alliant.edu/about/ADA.htm.

Application Information:

Send to: Alliant International University, Admissions Processing Center, 10455 Pomerado Road, San Diego, CA 92131-1799. Application available online. URL of online application: https://ais1.alliant.edu/apply/. Students are admitted in the Fall, application deadline February 1; Spring, application deadline varies; Programs have rolling admissions. The doctoral program has a February 1 priority deadline in order to provide a response by April 1 for applicants who need a decision by that date. Master's programs have later deadlines. Programs accept and admit applicants on a space available basis after any stated deadlines. For updates on deadlines and programs open, visit www.alliant.edu/admissions/gradtimelines.htm or contact the admission office at 1-866-U-ALLIANT. *Fee:* $65. A limited number of fee waivers are available to those with significant financial need.

Alliant International University: San Diego
Programs in Clinical Psychology and Marital and Family
 Therapy
California School of Professional Psychology
10455 Pomerado Road
San Diego, CA 92131-1799
Telephone: (858) 635-4772
Fax: (858) 635-4739
E-mail: *admissions@alliant.edu*
Web: *http://www.alliant.edu/cspp/*

Department Information:

1972. Systemwide Dean: Jean Lau Chin, EdD, ABPP. Number of Faculty: total–full-time 19, part-time 73; women–full-time 7, part-time 20; minority–full-time 2, part-time 5.

Programs and Degrees Offered:

Listed in the following order: Program area, degree type (T if terminal Master's), number awarded 7/03–6/04. Clinical Psychology PhD (Doctor of Philosophy) 22, Dual Clinical/Industrial-Organizational PhD (Doctor of Philosophy) 8, Clinical Psychology PsyD (Doctor of Psychology) 33, Marital and Family Therapy MA/MS (Master of Arts/Science) (T) 24, Marital and Family Therapy PsyD (Doctor of Psychology) 2, Clinical Psychology Respecialization Diploma 0.

APA Accreditation: Clinical PhD (Doctor of Philosophy). Clinical PsyD (Doctor of Psychology).

Student Applications/Admissions:

Student Applications

Clinical Psychology PhD (Doctor of Philosophy)—Applications 2004–2005, 120. Total applicants accepted 2004–2005, 61. Number enrolled (new admits only) 2004–2005 full-time, 31. Number enrolled (new admits only) 2004–2005 part-time, 0. Total enrolled 2004–2005 full-time, 189, part-time, 56. Openings 2005–2006, 40. The Median number of years required for completion of a degree are 5.5. The number of students enrolled full and part-time who were dismissed or voluntarily withdrew from this program area were 7. *Dual Clinical/Industrial-Organizational PhD (Doctor of Philosophy)*— Applications 2004–2005, 18. Total applicants accepted 2004–2005, 5. Number enrolled (new admits only) 2004–2005 full-time, 3. Number enrolled (new admits only) 2004–2005 part-time, 0. Total enrolled 2004–2005 full-time, 24, part-time, 5. Openings 2005–2006, 5. The Median number of years required for completion of a degree are 5.1. The number of students enrolled full and part-time who were dismissed or voluntarily withdrew from this program area were 1. *Clinical Psychology PsyD (Doctor of Psychology)*—Applications 2004–2005, 68. Total applicants accepted 2004–2005, 80. Number enrolled (new admits only) 2004–2005 full-time, 33. Number enrolled (new admits only) 2004–2005 part-time, 0. Total enrolled 2004–2005 full-time, 175, part-time, 25. Openings 2005–2006, 45. The Median number of years required for completion of a degree are 5.6. The number of students enrolled full and part-time who were dismissed or voluntarily withdrew from this program area were 3. *Marital and Family Therapy MA/MS (Master of Arts/Science)*—Applications 2004–2005, 93. Total applicants accepted 2004–2005, 48. Number enrolled (new admits only) 2004–2005 full-time, 31. Number enrolled (new admits only) 2004–2005 part-time, 0. Total enrolled 2004–2005 full-time, 54, part-time, 9. Openings 2005–2006, 30. The Median number of years required for completion of a degree are 1.7. The number of students enrolled full and part-time who were dismissed or voluntarily withdrew from this program area were 2. *Marital and Family Therapy PsyD (Doctor of Psychology)*—Applications 2004–2005, 44. Total applicants accepted 2004–2005, 27. Number enrolled (new admits only) 2004–2005 full-time, 15. Number enrolled (new admits only) 2004–2005 part-time, 1. Total enrolled 2004–2005 full-time, 40, part-time, 19. Openings 2005–2006, 20. The Median number of years required for completion of a degree are 8. The number of students enrolled full and part-time who were dismissed or voluntarily withdrew from this program area were 1. *Clinical Psychology Respecialization Diploma*—Applications 2004–2005, 0. Total applicants accepted 2004–2005, 0. Number enrolled (new admits only) 2004–2005 full-time, 0. Number enrolled (new admits only) 2004–2005 part-time, 0. Openings 2005–2006, 2. The number of students enrolled full and part-time who were dismissed or voluntarily withdrew from this program area were 0.

Admissions Requirements:

Scores: Entries appear in this order: required test or GPA, minimum score (if required), median score of students entering in 2003–2004. Master's Programs: overall undergraduate GPA 3.0, 3.32; psychology GPA 3.0. Doctoral Programs: overall undergraduate GPA 3.0, 3.35; psychology GPA 3.0. The master's degree is not required for admission to doctoral programs; however, if the master's degree is held at the time of application, the 3.0 minimum GPA applies.

Other Criteria: (importance of criteria rated low, medium, or high): GRE/MAT scores low, research experience medium, work experience medium, clinically related public service medium, GPA high, letters of recommendation medium, interview high, statement of goals and objectives high. Admissions criteria and their importance vary by program and degree level. PhD programs place more emphasis on prior research experience; PsyD programs place more emphasis on clinical/work experience. For additional information on admission requirements, go to: www.alliant.edu/admissions/gradapply.htm.

Student Characteristics: The following represents characteristics of students in 2004–2005 in all graduate psychology programs in the department: Female–full-time 405, part-time 107; Male–full-time 90, part-time 29; African American/Black–full-time 17, part-time 5; Hispanic/Latino(a)–full-time 41, part-time 13; Asian/Pacific Islander–full-time 39, part-time 9; American Indian/Alaska Native–full-time 9, part-time 1; Caucasian–full-time 384, part-time 108; Multi-ethnic–full-time 5, part-time 0; students subject to the Americans With Disabilities Act–full-time 12, part-time 1.

Financial Information/Assistance:

Tuition for Full-Time Study: *Master's:* State residents: $795 per credit hour; Nonstate residents: $795 per credit hour. *Doctoral:* State residents: $795 per credit hour; Nonstate residents: $795 per credit hour. Tuition is subject to change. Tuition costs vary by program. See the following Web site for updates and changes in tuition costs: www.alliant.edu/admissions/costs.htm.

Financial Assistance:

First Year Students: Research assistantships available for first-year. Average amount paid per academic year: $1,000. Average number of hours worked per week: 10. Apply by see dept. Fellowships and scholarships available for first-year. Average amount paid per academic year: $1,500. Apply by varies.

Advanced Students: Teaching assistantships available for advanced students. Average amount paid per academic year: $3,000. Average number of hours worked per week: 10. Apply by see dept. Research assistantships available for advanced students. Average amount paid per academic year: $1,000. Average number of hours worked per week: 10. Apply by see dept. Fellowships and scholarships available for advanced students. Average amount paid per academic year: $1,500. Apply by April 15.

Contact Information: Of all students currently enrolled full-time, 65% benefitted from one or more of the listed financial assistance programs. Application and information available online at: www.alliant/edu/finaid/grad.htm.

Internships/Practica: Clinical psychology doctoral students receive practicum and internship experience at more than 80 agencies which meet the requirements for licensure set by the California Board of Psychology. Assignments to these agencies result from an application process conducted by year level, with third, fourth, and fifth year students receiving priority for licensable placements. The option of doing an APA-accredited full-time internship in the fourth or fifth years (depending on the program and year level requirements) is available and encouraged. Marital and family therapy students complete a required practicum, and for doctoral students, a pre-doctoral internship. For those doctoral students for whom a professional internship is required prior to graduation, 147 applied in 2003–2004. Of those who applied, 5 were placed in APA accredited internships.

Housing and Day Care: On-campus housing is available. See the following Web site for more information: On-campus housing is available for graduate students at the San Diego campus. For more information visit www.alliant.edu/sandiego/housing/. No on-campus day care facilities are available.

Employment of Department Graduates:

Master's Degree Graduates: Of those who graduated in the academic year 2003–2004, the following categories and numbers represent the post-graduate activities and employment of master's degree graduates: Enrolled in a post-doctoral residency/fellowship (n/a), employed in independent practice (n/a), total from the above (master's) (0).

Doctoral Degree Graduates: Of those who graduated in the academic year 2003–2004, the following categories and numbers represent the post-graduate activities and employment of doctoral degree graduates: Enrolled in a psychology doctoral program (n/a), employed in independent practice (50), employed in an academic position at a university (1), employed in an academic position at a 2-year/4-year college (1), employed in a professional position in a school system (4), employed in a community mental health/counseling center (45), employed in a hospital/medical center (17), total from the above (doctoral) (118).

Additional Information:

Orientation, Objectives, and Emphasis of Department: Alliant International University's California School of Professional Psychology offers comprehensive PhD and PsyD programs of instruction in professional psychology with an emphasis on doctoral training in clinical psychology in which academic requirements are integrated with supervised field experience. Students are evaluated by instructors and field supervisors on the basis of their performance and participation throughout the year. Theory, personal growth, professional skill, humanities, investigatory skills courses, and field experience are designed to stimulate the graduate toward a scholarly as well as a professional contribution to society. Elective areas of emphasis in health psychology (PhD only), family and child psychology, clinical forensic psychology, psychodynamic, multicultural and international, and integrative psychology (PsyD only) are available within the clinical programs. Students in CSPP's Marital and Family Therapy MA and PsyD are trained to treat individuals, couples, and families with relational mental health issues from a systemic perspective. Skills are developed in mental health assessment, diagnosis, and treatment of individuals and relationship systems. The PsyD is based on the scholar-practitioner model; both degrees are offered in a format for working professionals. The dual clinical/industrial-organizational psychology PhD program is offered jointly with the California School of Organizational Studies; students fulfill the requirements of both specialties.

Special Facilities or Resources: The Center for Applied Behavioral Services (CABS) is a multi-service and training center. The Center incorporates the expertise of CSPP faculty in the delivery of direct services and in modeling specific techniques of treatment and service for practicum and interns. This is currently accomplished through an array of clinical and community services which are directed by faculty members.

Information for Students With Physical Disabilities: See the following Web site for more information: www.alliant.edu/about/ADA.htm.

Application Information:

Send to: Alliant International University Admissions Processing Center, 10455 Pomerado Road, San Diego, CA 92131-1799. Application available online. URL of online application: https://ais1.alliant.edu/apply/. Students are admitted in the Fall, application deadline varies; Spring, application deadline open. Programs have rolling admissions. Deadlines vary by program. Most doctoral programs have priority deadlines in January in order to provide a response by April 1 to applicants who need a decision by that date. Some doctoral programs and most master's programs have later deadlines. Programs accept applications and admit students on a space available basis after any stated deadlines. For complete information on deadlines visit www.alliant.edu/admissions/gradtimelines.htm or contact the admissions office at 1-866-U-ALLIANT. *Fee:* $65. A limited number of fee waivers are available for those with significant financial need.

Alliant International University: San Diego
Programs in Educational and School Psychology
Graduate School of Education
10455 Pomerado Road
San Diego, CA 92131-1799
Telephone: (858) 635-4772
Fax: (858) 635-4555
E-mail: *admissions@alliant.edu*
Web: *www.alliant.edu/gsoe/schpsych.htm*

Department Information:

2002. Systemwide Program Director: Rhonda Brinkley-Kennedy, PsyD. Number of Faculty: total–full-time 1, part-time 8; women–full-time 1, part-time 3; minority–full-time 1, part-time 1.

Programs and Degrees Offered:

Listed in the following order: Program area, degree type (T if terminal Master's), number awarded 7/03–6/04. Educational Psychology PsyD (Doctor of Psychology) 0, School Psychology MA/MS (Master of Arts/Science) (T) 0.

Student Applications/Admissions:

Student Applications

Educational Psychology PsyD (Doctor of Psychology)—Applications 2004–2005, 2. Total applicants accepted 2004–2005, 1. Number enrolled (new admits only) 2004–2005 full-time, 0.

Number enrolled (new admits only) 2004–2005 part-time, 1. Openings 2005–2006, 5. The number of students enrolled full and part-time who were dismissed or voluntarily withdrew from this program area were 0. *School Psychology MA/MS (Master of Arts/Science)*—Applications 2004–2005, 27. Total applicants accepted 2004–2005, 20. Number enrolled (new admits only) 2004–2005 full-time, 14. Number enrolled (new admits only) 2004–2005 part-time, 0. Total enrolled 2004–2005 full-time, 29, part-time, 6. Openings 2005–2006, 20. The number of students enrolled full and part-time who were dismissed or voluntarily withdrew from this program area were 2.

Admissions Requirements:

Scores: Entries appear in this order: required test or GPA, minimum score (if required), median score of students entering in 2003–2004. Master's Programs: overall undergraduate GPA 2.5, 3.05; psychology GPA 2.5. Doctoral Programs: overall undergraduate GPA 3.0; psychology GPA 3.0. Master's degree is not required for the five year PsyD program, but if the degree is held at the time of application, the 3.0 minimum GPA applies.

Other Criteria: (importance of criteria rated low, medium, or high): research experience medium, work experience medium, extracurricular activity low, clinically related public service high, GPA high, letters of recommendation high, interview high, statement of goals and objectives high, Criteria differ by program and level. For additional information on admission requirements, go to: www.alliant.edu/admissions/gradapply.htm.

Student Characteristics: The following represents characteristics of students in 2004–2005 in all graduate psychology programs in the department: Female–full-time 23, part-time 6; Male–full-time 6, part-time 3; African American/Black–full-time 1, part-time 1; Hispanic/Latino(a)–full-time 6, part-time 3; Asian/Pacific Islander–full-time 2, part-time 1; American Indian/Alaska Native–full-time 0, part-time 0; Caucasian–full-time 19, part-time 4; Multi-ethnic–full-time 1, part-time 0; students subject to the Americans With Disabilities Act–full-time 1, part-time 0.

Financial Information/Assistance:

Tuition for Full-Time Study: *Master's:* State residents: $450 per credit hour; Nonstate residents: $450 per credit hour. *Doctoral:* State residents: $795 per credit hour; Nonstate residents: $795 per credit hour. Tuition is subject to change. Tuition costs vary by program. See the following Web site for updates and changes in tuition costs: www.alliant.edu/admissions/costs.htm.

Financial Assistance:

First Year Students: Research assistantships available for first-year. Average amount paid per academic year: $1,000. Average number of hours worked per week: 10. Apply by see dept. Fellowships and scholarships available for first-year. Average amount paid per academic year: $750. Apply by June 1.

Advanced Students: Teaching assistantships available for advanced students. Average amount paid per academic year: $3,000. Average number of hours worked per week: 10. Apply by see dept. Research assistantships available for advanced students. Average amount paid per academic year: $1,000. Average number of hours worked per week: 10. Apply by see dept. Fellowships and scholarships available for advanced students. Average amount paid per academic year: $750. Apply by April 1.

Contact Information: Of all students currently enrolled full-time, 80% benefitted from one or more of the listed financial assistance programs. Application and information available online at: www.alliant/edu/finaid/grad.htm.

Internships/Practica: Students in the master's program have practica tied to their coursework beginning in the first semester of their programs. Internships are required of students seeking a Pupil Personnel Services (PPS) credential post-masters or as part of the doctoral program in educational psychology. The 1200 required internship hours are completed at a public school district. Students interested in seeking clinical licensure must complete a separate internship.

Housing and Day Care: On-campus housing is available. See the following Web site for more information: Housing is available for graduate students who are interested in living on the San Diego campus. For information, visit www.alliant.edu/sandiego/housing/. No on-campus day care facilities are available.

Employment of Department Graduates:

Master's Degree Graduates: Of those who graduated in the academic year 2003–2004, the following categories and numbers represent the post-graduate activities and employment of master's degree graduates: Enrolled in a post-doctoral residency/fellowship (n/a), employed in independent practice (n/a), total from the above (master's) (0).

Doctoral Degree Graduates: Of those who graduated in the academic year 2003–2004, the following categories and numbers represent the post-graduate activities and employment of doctoral degree graduates: Enrolled in a psychology doctoral program (n/a), total from the above (doctoral) (0).

Additional Information:

Orientation, Objectives, and Emphasis of Department: Programs train students with the skills necessary to work with students, teachers, parents, and other school professionals in today's school environments. Curriculum includes professional skills, professional roles courses, applied research, and professional concepts. The master's degree program prepares students to gain the PPS (Pupil Personnel Services) credential that allows them to practice in California's schools. Students take afternoon, evening, and weekend classes and engage in fieldwork. At the doctoral level, students complete special focus area courses, examples of which include adolescent stress and coping, school culture and administration, pediatric psychology, infant and preschool mental health, child neuropsychology, and provision of services for children in alternative placement. Students also complete a PsyD project.

Special Facilities or Resources: The Graduate School of Education at the San Diego campus houses the World Council of Curriculum and Instruction.

Information for Students With Physical Disabilities: See the following Web site for more information: www.alliant.edu/about/ADA.htm.

Application Information:

Send to: Alliant International University, Admissions Processing Center, 10455 Pomerado Road, San Diego, CA 92131-1799. Application available online. URL of online application: https://ais1.alliant.edu/apply/. Students are admitted in the Fall, application deadline June 1; Spring, application deadline varies; Summer, application deadline varies. Programs have rolling admissions. *Fee:* $50. A limited number of fee waivers are available for those with significant financial need.

Alliant International University: San Diego/Irvine
Programs in Organizational Studies
California School of Organizational Studies
6160 Cornerstone Court East
San Diego, CA 92121-3710
Telephone: (858) 635-4772
Fax: (858) 635-4739
E-mail: *hbucheli@alliant.edu*
Web: *www.alliant.edu/csos/*

Department Information:
1981. Program Director: Herbert George Baker, PhD. Number of Faculty: total–full-time 8, part-time 15; women–full-time 1, part-time 4; minority–full-time 2, part-time 2.

Programs and Degrees Offered:
Listed in the following order: Program area, degree type (T if terminal Master's), number awarded 7/03–6/04. Industrial-Organizational PhD (Doctor of Philosophy) 14, Consulting Psychology PhD (Doctor of Philosophy) 3, Industrial-Organizational MA/MS (Master of Arts/Science) (T) 11, Industrial-Organizational Respecialization Diploma 0, Organizational Behavior MA/MS (Master of Arts/Science) (T) 2, Dual Clinical/Industrial-Organizational PhD (Doctor of Philosophy) 8, Organizational Studies MA/MS (Master of Arts/Science) (T) 0.

Student Applications/Admissions:
Student Applications

Industrial-Organizational PhD (Doctor of Philosophy)—Applications 2004–2005, 33. Total applicants accepted 2004–2005, 16. Number enrolled (new admits only) 2004–2005 full-time, 5. Number enrolled (new admits only) 2004–2005 part-time, 0. Total enrolled 2004–2005 full-time, 45, part-time, 19. Openings 2005–2006, 15. The Median number of years required for completion of a degree are 6.3. The number of students enrolled full and part-time who were dismissed or voluntarily withdrew from this program area were 4. *Consulting Psychology PhD (Doctor of Philosophy)*—Applications 2004–2005, 7. Total applicants accepted 2004–2005, 5. Number enrolled (new admits only) 2004–2005 full-time, 5. Number enrolled (new admits only) 2004–2005 part-time, 0. Total enrolled 2004–2005 full-time, 24, part-time, 1. Openings 2005–2006, 12. The Median number of years required for completion of a degree are 4. The number of students enrolled full and part-time who were dismissed or voluntarily withdrew from this program area were 1. *Industrial-Organizational MA/MS (Master of Arts/Science)*—Applications 2004–2005, 19. Total applicants accepted 2004–2005, 10. Number enrolled (new admits only) 2004–2005 full-time, 4. Number enrolled (new admits only) 2004–2005 part-time, 1. Total enrolled 2004–2005 full-time, 19, part-time, 2. Openings 2005–2006, 15. The Median number of years required for completion of a degree are 1.7. The number of students enrolled full and part-time, who were dismissed or voluntarily withdrew from this program area were 1. *Industrial-Organizational Respecializa-*

tion Diploma—Applications 2004–2005, 1. Total applicants accepted 2004–2005, 0. Number enrolled (new admits only) 2004–2005 full-time, 0. Number enrolled (new admits only) 2004–2005 part-time, 0. Openings 2005–2006, 2. The number of students enrolled full and part-time who were dismissed or voluntarily withdrew from this program area were 0. *Organizational Behavior MA/MS (Master of Arts/Science)*—Applications 2004–2005, 8. Total applicants accepted 2004–2005, 3. Number enrolled (new admits only) 2004–2005 full-time, 0. Number enrolled (new admits only) 2004–2005 part-time, 1. Total enrolled 2004–2005 full-time, 1, part-time, 2. Openings 2005–2006, 10. The Median number of years required for completion of a degree are 2. The number of students enrolled full and part-time who were dismissed or voluntarily withdrew from this program area were 0. *Dual Clinical/Industrial-Organizational PhD (Doctor of Philosophy)*—Applications 2004–2005, 18. Total applicants accepted 2004–2005, 5. Number enrolled (new admits only) 2004–2005 full-time, 3. Number enrolled (new admits only) 2004–2005 part-time, 0. Total enrolled 2004–2005 full-time, 24, part-time, 5. Openings 2005–2006, 5. The Median number of years required for completion of a degree are 5.1. The number of students enrolled full and part-time who were dismissed or voluntarily withdrew from this program area were 1. *Organizational Studies MA/MS (Master of Arts/Science)*—Applications 2004–2005, 2. Total applicants accepted 2004–2005, 0. Openings 2005–2006, 5. The number of students enrolled full and part-time who were dismissed or voluntarily withdrew from this program area were 0.

Admissions Requirements:

Scores: Entries appear in this order: required test or GPA, minimum score (if required), median score of students entering in 2003–2004. Master's Programs: overall undergraduate GPA 3.0, 3.01; psychology GPA 3.0. Doctoral Programs: overall undergraduate GPA 3.0, 3.44; last 2 years GPA 3.0. A master's degree is not required for admission to the doctoral programs, but if held at the time of application, the minimum 3.0 GPA applies.

Other Criteria: (importance of criteria rated low, medium, or high): research experience high, work experience medium, extracurricular activity low, clinically related public service low, GPA high, letters of recommendation high, interview high, statement of goals and objectives high, Criteria vary by program. Research experience is more important for doctoral applicants; work experience is more important for some master's programs. For additional information on admission requirements, go to: www.alliant.edu/admissions/gradapply.htm.

Student Characteristics: The following represents characteristics of students in 2004–2005 in all graduate psychology programs in the department: Female–full-time 83, part-time 26; Male–full-time 31, part-time 8; African American/Black–full-time 14, part-time 3; Hispanic/Latino(a)–full-time 13, part-time 3; Asian/Pacific Islander–full-time 12, part-time 5; American Indian/Alaska Native–full-time 0, part-time 0; Caucasian–full-time 71, part-time 23; Multi-ethnic–full-time 4, part-time 0; students subject to the Americans With Disabilities Act–full-time 3, part-time 0.

Financial Information/Assistance:

Tuition for Full-Time Study: *Master's:* State residents: $795 per credit hour; Nonstate residents: $795 per credit hour. *Doctoral:* State residents: $795 per credit hour; Nonstate residents: $795 per credit hour. Tuition is subject to change. Tuition costs vary by program. See the following Web site for updates and changes in tuition costs: www.alliant.edu/admissions/costs.htm.

Financial Assistance:

First Year Students: Research assistantships available for first-year. Average amount paid per academic year: $1,000. Average number of hours worked per week: 10. Apply by see dept. Fellowships and scholarships available for first-year. Average amount paid per academic year: $1,500. Apply by April 1.

Advanced Students: Teaching assistantships available for advanced students. Average amount paid per academic year: $3,000. Average number of hours worked per week: 10. Apply by see dept. Research assistantships available for advanced students. Average amount paid per academic year: $1,000. Average number of hours worked per week: 10. Apply by see dept. Fellowships and scholarships available for advanced students. Average amount paid per academic year: $1,500. Apply by April 15.

Contact Information: Of all students currently enrolled full-time, 80% benefitted from one or more of the listed financial assistance programs. Application and information available online at: www.alliant/edu/finaid/grad.htm.

Internships/Practica: Doctoral students participate in two half-time internships in the third and fourth years of the program; this allows for the integration of professional training with courses, seminars and research. Consulting psychology doctoral students' internships have an individual/group focus in the third year and systemwide interventions focus in the fourth year. Master's students in IO psychology have a one-semester practicum in the last term of their programs. The majority of these internships are local to the students' campus.

Housing and Day Care: On-campus housing is available. See the following Web site for more information: Housing for graduate students is available on the San Diego campus for those interested. For more information visit www.alliant.edu/sandiego/housing/. No on-campus day care facilities are available.

Employment of Department Graduates:

Master's Degree Graduates: Of those who graduated in the academic year 2003–2004, the following categories and numbers represent the post-graduate activities and employment of master's degree graduates: Enrolled in a post-doctoral residency/fellowship (n/a), employed in independent practice (n/a), total from the above (master's) (0).

Doctoral Degree Graduates: Of those who graduated in the academic year 2003–2004, the following categories and numbers represent the post-graduate activities and employment of doctoral degree graduates: Enrolled in a psychology doctoral program (n/a), total from the above (doctoral) (0).

Additional Information:

Orientation, Objectives, and Emphasis of Department: The consulting psychology doctoral program combines individual, group, organization and systemic consultation skills to produce specialists in the psychological aspects of organizational consulting. The individual focus includes career assessment and executive coaching; the group focus includes team building and assisting dysfunctional work groups; the organizational/systemic focus includes the understanding, diagnosis and intervention with organizational systems. The industrial-organizational doctoral program is pattered after the doctoral level training guidelines prepared by the Educational and Training Committee of the Society for Industrial and Organizational Psychology (Division 14 of the APA). The programs emphasize personnel selections, work motivation, design of compensation systems, measurement and productivity. Master's programs lead to careers as internal consultants within organizations or other master's-level or entry-evel careers in organizations and provide foundations for further study if desired. These programs stress leadership, management, and organizational skills. Some master's programs are structured specifically for working professionals.

Special Facilities or Resources: The California School of Organizational Studies houses an Organizational Consulting Center (OCC). Some students may have opportunities to work with faculty or consultant associates from the center during their programs.

Information for Students With Physical Disabilities: See the following Web site for more information: www.alliant.edu/about/ADA.htm.

Application Information:

Send to: Alliant International University, Admissions Processing Center, 10455 Pomerado Road, San Diego, CA 92121-1799. Application available online. URL of online application: https://ais1.alliant.edu/apply/. Students are admitted in the Fall, application deadline February 1; Spring, application deadline varies; Summer, application deadline varies. Programs have rolling admissions. Doctoral programs have a February 1 priority deadline in order to provide a response by April 1 for applicants who need a decision by that date. Master's programs have later deadlines. Programs accept and admit applicants on a space available basis after any stated deadlines. For updated information on deadlines and programs open, visit www.alliant.edu/admissions/gradtimelines.htm or contact the local admissions office or application processing center at 1-866-U-ALLIANT. *Fee:* $65. A limited number of fee waivers are available to those with significant financial need.

Alliant International University: San Francisco Bay
Programs in Educational and School Psychology
Graduate School of Education
One Beach Street
San Francisco, CA 94133-1221
Telephone: (415) 955-2146
Fax: (415) 955-2179
E-mail: *jkulbeck@alliant.edu*
Web: *www.alliant.edu/gsoe/schpsych.htm*

Department Information:

2002. Systemwide Program Director: Rhonda Brinkley-Kennedy, PsyD. Number of Faculty: total– part-time 9; women–part-time 8; minority–part-time 3.

Programs and Degrees Offered:

Listed in the following order: Program area, degree type (T if terminal Master's), number awarded 7/03–6/04. School Psychology MA/MS (Master of Arts/Science) (T) 0, Educational Psychology PsyD (Doctor of Psychology) 0.

Student Applications/Admissions:
Student Applications

School Psychology MA/MS (Master of Arts/Science)—Applications 2004–2005, 10. Total applicants accepted 2004–2005, 4. Number enrolled (new admits only) 2004–2005 full-time, 3. Number enrolled (new admits only) 2004–2005 part-time, 0. Total enrolled 2004–2005 full-time, 12, part-time, 2. Openings 2005–2006, 12. The number of students enrolled full and part-time who were dismissed or voluntarily withdrew from this program area were 2. *Educational Psychology PsyD (Doctor of Psychology)*—Applications 2004–2005, 1. Total applicants accepted 2004–2005, 0. Number enrolled (new admits only) 2004–2005 full-time, 0. Number enrolled (new admits only) 2004–2005 part-time, 0. Openings 2005–2006, 5. The number of students enrolled full and part-time who were dismissed or voluntarily withdrew from this program area were 0.

Admissions Requirements:

Scores: Entries appear in this order: required test or GPA, minimum score (if required), median score of students entering in 2003–2004. Master's Programs: overall undergraduate GPA 2.5, 2.86; psychology GPA 2.5. Doctoral Programs: overall undergraduate GPA 3.0; psychology GPA 3.0. A master's degree is not required for entry into the five year PsyD program; however, if a master's degree is held at the time of application, the 3.0 minimum GPA applies.

Other Criteria: (importance of criteria rated low, medium, or high): research experience medium, work experience high, extracurricular activity low, clinically related public service high, GPA high, letters of recommendation high, interview high, statement of goals and objectives high. Criteria differ for master's and doctoral programs. For additional information on admission requirements, go to: www.alliant.edu/admissions/gradapply.htm.

Student Characteristics: The following represents characteristics of students in 2004–2005 in all graduate psychology programs in the department: Female–full-time 9, part-time 2; Male–full-time 3, part-time 0; African American/Black–full-time 1, part-time 1; Hispanic/Latino(a)–full-time 0, part-time 0; Asian/Pacific Islander–full-time 0, part-time 0; American Indian/Alaska Native–full-time 0, part-time 0; Caucasian–full-time 10, part-time 2; Multi-ethnic–full-time 0, part-time 0; students subject to the Americans With Disabilities Act–full-time 1, part-time 0.

Financial Information/Assistance:

Tuition for Full-Time Study: *Master's:* State residents: $450 per credit hour; Nonstate residents: $450 per credit hour. *Doctoral:* State residents: $795 per credit hour; Nonstate residents: $795 per credit hour. Tuition is subject to change. See the following Web site for updates and changes in tuition costs: www.alliant.edu/admissions/costs.htm.

Financial Assistance:

First Year Students: Research assistantships available for first-year. Average amount paid per academic year: $1,000. Average number of hours worked per week: 10. Apply by see dept. Fellowships and scholarships available for first-year. Average amount paid per academic year: $750. Apply by June 1.

Advanced Students: Teaching assistantships available for advanced students. Average amount paid per academic year: $3,000. Average number of hours worked per week: 10. Apply by see dept. Research assistantships available for advanced students. Average amount paid per academic year: $1,000. Average number of hours worked per week: 10. Apply by see dept. Fellowships and scholarships available for advanced students. Average amount paid per academic year: $750. Apply by April 1.

Contact Information: Of all students currently enrolled full-time, 78% benefitted from one or more of the listed financial assistance programs. Application and information available online at: www.alliant/edu/finaid/grad.htm.

Internships/Practica: Students in the master's program have practica tied to their coursework beginning in the first semester of their programs. Internships are required of any students seeking a Pupil Personnel Services (PPS) credential post-masters or as part of the doctoral program in educational psychology. The 1200 internships hours are completed at a public school district. Those in the doctoral program who are interested in clinical licensure must complete a separate internship.

Housing and Day Care: No on-campus housing is available. No on-campus day care facilities are available.

Employment of Department Graduates:

Master's Degree Graduates: Of those who graduated in the academic year 2003–2004, the following categories and numbers represent the post-graduate activities and employment of master's degree graduates: Enrolled in a post-doctoral residency/fellowship (n/a), employed in independent practice (n/a), total from the above (master's) (0).

Doctoral Degree Graduates: Of those who graduated in the academic year 2003–2004, the following categories and numbers represent the post-graduate activities and employment of doctoral degree graduates: Enrolled in a psychology doctoral program (n/a), total from the above (doctoral) (0).

Additional Information:

Orientation, Objectives, and Emphasis of Department: Programs train students with the skills necessary to work with students, teachers, parents, and other school professionals in today's school environments. The curriculum includes professional skills, professional roles courses, applied research, and professional concepts. The master's degree program prepares students to gain the PPS (Pupil Personnel Services) credential that allows them to practice in California's schools. Students take afternoon, evening and weekend classes and engage in fieldwork. At the doctoral level students complete special focus area courses, examples of which include adolescent stress and coping, school culture and administration, pediatric psychology, infant and preschool mental health, child neuropsychology, and provision of services for children in alternative placement. Students also complete a PsyD project.

Special Facilities or Resources: The San Francisco Bay campus of the Graduate School of Education houses the Cross Cultural Studies Institute.

Information for Students With Physical Disabilities: See the following Web site for more information: www.alliant.edu/about/ADA.htm.

Application Information:
Send to: Alliant International University, Admissions Processing Center, 10455 Pomerado Road, San Diego, CA 92131-1799. Application

available online. URL of online application: https://ais1.alliant.edu/apply/. Students are admitted in the Fall, application deadline June 1; Spring, application deadline varies; Summer, application deadline varies. Programs have rolling admissions. See information about timelines at www.alliant.edu/admissions/gradtimelines.htm or contact the admissions office at 1-866-U-ALLIANT. *Fee:* $50. A limited number of fee waivers are available for those with significant financial need.

Alliant International University: San Francisco Bay
Programs in Organizational Studies
California School of Organizational Studies
One Beach Street
San Francisco, CA 94133-1221
Telephone: (415) 955-2146
Fax: (415) 955-2179
E-mail: *jkulbeck@alliant.edu*
Web: *www.alliant.edu/csos/*

Department Information:
1983. Interim Program Director: Carl Mack, PhD. Number of Faculty: total–full-time 3, part-time 7; women–full-time 3, part-time 3; minority–full-time 1, part-time 3.

Programs and Degrees Offered:
Listed in the following order: Program area, degree type (T if terminal Master's), number awarded 7/03–6/04. Organizational Psychology PhD (Doctor of Philosophy) 9, Organizational Psychology MA/MS (Master of Arts/Science) (T) 1, Organizational Development MA/MS (Master of Arts/Science) (T) 0, Organizational Psychology Respecialization Diploma 0.

Student Applications/Admissions:

Student Applications
Organizational Psychology PhD (Doctor of Philosophy)—Applications 2004–2005, 16. Total applicants accepted 2004–2005, 11. Number enrolled (new admits only) 2004–2005 full-time, 2. Number enrolled (new admits only) 2004–2005 part-time, 1. Total enrolled 2004–2005 full-time, 39, part-time, 20. Openings 2005–2006, 15. The Median number of years required for completion of a degree are 6. The number of students enrolled full and part-time who were dismissed or voluntarily withdrew from this program area were 5. *Organizational Psychology MA/MS (Master of Arts/Science)*—Applications 2004–2005, 7. Total applicants accepted 2004–2005, 7. Number enrolled (new admits only) 2004–2005 full-time, 3. Number enrolled (new admits only) 2004–2005 part-time, 2. Total enrolled 2004–2005 full-time, 7, part-time, 3. Openings 2005–2006, 15. The Median number of years required for completion of a degree are 2. The number of students enrolled full and part-time who were dismissed or voluntarily withdrew from this program area were 1. *Organizational Development MA/MS (Master of Arts/Science)*—Applications 2004–2005, 4. Total applicants accepted 2004–2005, 0. Number enrolled (new admits only) 2004–2005 full-time, 0. Number enrolled (new admits only) 2004–2005 part-time, 0. Openings 2005–2006, 5. The number of students enrolled full and part-time who were dismissed or voluntarily withdrew from this program area were 0. *Organizational Psychology Respecialization Diploma*—Applications 2004–2005, 0. Total applicants accepted 2004–

2005, 0. Openings 2005–2006, 1. The number of students enrolled full and part-time who were dismissed or voluntarily withdrew from this program area were 0.

Admissions Requirements:

Scores: Entries appear in this order: required test or GPA, minimum score (if required), median score of students entering in 2003–2004. Master's Programs: overall undergraduate GPA 3.0, 3.18; psychology GPA 3.0. Doctoral Programs: overall undergraduate GPA 3.0, 3.18; psychology GPA 3.0. A master's degree is not required for entry to the doctoral program; however, if a master's degree is held at the time of admissions, the minimum 3.0 GPA applies.

Other Criteria: (importance of criteria rated low, medium, or high): research experience high, work experience high, extracurricular activity low, clinically related public service low, GPA high, letters of recommendation high, interview high, statement of goals and objectives high, Admission criteria vary by program and program level. For additional information on admission requirements, go to: www.alliant.edu/admissions/gradapply.htm.

Student Characteristics: The following represents characteristics of students in 2004–2005 in all graduate psychology programs in the department: Female–full-time 33, part-time 20; Male–full-time 16, part-time 10; African American/Black–full-time 7, part-time 2; Hispanic/Latino(a)–full-time 1, part-time 3; Asian/Pacific Islander–full-time 6, part-time 5; American Indian/Alaska Native–full-time 0, part-time 0; Caucasian–full-time 35, part-time 20; Multi-ethnic–full-time 0, part-time 0; students subject to the Americans With Disabilities Act–full-time 1, part-time 2.

Financial Information/Assistance:

Tuition for Full-Time Study: *Master's:* State residents: $795 per credit hour; Nonstate residents: $795 per credit hour. *Doctoral:* State residents: $795 per credit hour; Nonstate residents: $795 per credit hour. Tuition is subject to change. Tuition costs vary by program. See the following Web site for updates and changes in tuition costs: www.alliant.edu/admissions/costs.htm.

Financial Assistance:

First Year Students: Research assistantships available for first-year. Average amount paid per academic year: $1,000. Average number of hours worked per week: 10. Apply by see dept. Fellowships and scholarships available for first-year. Average amount paid per academic year: $1,500. Apply by February 15.

Advanced Students: Teaching assistantships available for advanced students. Average amount paid per academic year: $3,000. Average number of hours worked per week: 10. Apply by see dept. Research assistantships available for advanced students. Average amount paid per academic year: $1,000. Average number of hours worked per week: 10. Apply by see dept. Fellowships and scholarships available for advanced students. Average amount paid per academic year: $1,500. Apply by April 15.

Contact Information: Of all students currently enrolled full-time, 65% benefitted from one or more of the listed financial assistance programs. Application and information available online at: www.alliant/edu/finaid/grad.htm.

Internships/Practica: Organizational doctoral students develop skills through practical training experiences during the third and fourth years of the program. Students usually devote 8-40 hours per week to field placement assignments. Some training sites are local to the student's campus location; occasionally students find internships out-of-area or out-of-state sites that meet their professional training needs. Placements are available in a variety of settings including consulting firms, major corporations, government agencies, health care organizations, and non-profit agencies. Students in the master's programs have a one semester applied experience with supervision.

Housing and Day Care: No on-campus housing is available. No on-campus day care facilities are available.

Employment of Department Graduates:

Master's Degree Graduates: Of those who graduated in the academic year 2003–2004, the following categories and numbers represent the post-graduate activities and employment of master's degree graduates: Enrolled in a post-doctoral residency/fellowship (n/a), employed in independent practice (n/a), total from the above (master's) (0).

Doctoral Degree Graduates: Of those who graduated in the academic year 2003–2004, the following categories and numbers represent the post-graduate activities and employment of doctoral degree graduates: Enrolled in a psychology doctoral program (n/a), total from the above (doctoral) (0).

Additional Information:

Orientation, Objectives, and Emphasis of Department: Doctoral students gain exposure to three core areas of study: organizational theory, grounded in the behavioral sciences; quantitative and qualitative research methods; and professional practice skill development. The program focuses on research and practice in organizational consulting at the individual, team, and system levels; collaborative strategic change; organizational culture and leadership; multicultural competence; executive coaching and mentoring; organizational innovation, creativity and knowledge management. Programs are structured so students can attend at a moderated pace—this allows students to continue working while in their programs. Master's level programs provide solid education in organizational psychology and behavior; they are suitable for students who may wish to continue on to doctoral education. The master's in organization development is primarily for those who have backgrounds in other fields and wish to move into a managerial or OD position; three concentrations are offered in systemic change in a global context, building healthy organizations and applied research. The master's in organizational psychology provides a stronger research foundation.

Special Facilities or Resources: California School of Organizational Studies offers the Organizational Consulting Center (OCC). Students may have opportunities to participate with faculty and OCC associates on consulting projects during their programs.

Information for Students With Physical Disabilities: See the following Web site for more information: www.alliant.edu/about/ADA.htm.

Application Information:

Send to: Alliant International University, Admissions Processing Center, 10455 Pomerado Road, San Diego, CA 92131-1799. Application available online. URL of online application: https://ais1.alliant.edu/apply/. Students are admitted in the Fall, application deadline February

1; Spring, application deadline varies. Programs have rolling admissions. Doctoral program has a February 1 deadline in order to provide a response by April 1 for applicants who need a decision by that date. Master's programs have later deadlines. Programs accept applications and admit students on a space available basis after any stated deadlines. For complete information on deadlines visit www.alliant.edu/admissions/gradtimelines.htm or contact the admissions office at 1-866-U-ALLIANT. *Fee:* $65. A limited number of fee waivers are available for those with significant financial need.

Antioch University, Santa Barbara
Graduate Psychology Programs
801 Garden Street, Suite 101
Santa Barbara, CA 93101
Telephone: (805) 962-8179
Fax: (805) 962-4786
E-mail: *admissions@antiochsb.edu*
Web: *http://www.antiochsb.edu*

Department Information:
1977. Chairperson: Catherine Radecki-Bush, PhD Number of Faculty: total–full-time 4, part-time 40; women–full-time 4, part-time 22; minority–full-time 1, part-time 5.

Programs and Degrees Offered:
Listed in the following order: Program area, degree type (T if terminal Master's), number awarded 7/03–6/04. Clinical Psychology PsyD (Doctor of Psychology) 0, Clinical Psychology MA/MS (Master of Arts/Science) (T) 38.

Student Applications/Admissions:
Student Applications
Clinical Psychology PsyD (Doctor of Psychology)—Applications 2004–2005, 0. Total applicants accepted 2004–2005, 0. Number enrolled (new admits only) 2004–2005 full-time, 0. Number enrolled (new admits only) 2004–2005 part-time, 0. Openings 2005–2006, 20. The Median number of years required for completion of a degree are 3. *Clinical Psychology MA/MS (Master of Arts/Science)*—Total applicants accepted 2004–2005, 68. Number enrolled (new admits only) 2004–2005 full-time, 54. Number enrolled (new admits only) 2004–2005 part-time, 14. Total enrolled 2004–2005 full-time, 148, part-time, 33. The Median number of years required for completion of a degree are 2. The number of students enrolled full and part-time who were dismissed or voluntarily withdrew from this program area were 3.

Admissions Requirements:
Scores: Entries appear in this order: required test or GPA, minimum score (if required), median score of students entering in 2003–2004. Master's Programs: overall undergraduate GPA no minimum stated; last 2 years GPA no minimum stated; psychology GPA no minimum stated. No minimum GPA for MA Program but usually 3.0 Doctoral Programs: We also accept outstanding narrative evaluations from institutions like Antioch that do not calculate GPAs.
Other Criteria: (importance of criteria rated low, medium, or high): research experience low, work experience medium, extracurricular activity low, clinically related public service

medium, GPA low, letters of recommendation medium, interview high, statement of goals and objectives high, writing sample. The doctoral program requires two essays in lieu of GREs that are used to assess analytic and critical thinking. These are heavily weighted.

Student Characteristics: The following represents characteristics of students in 2004–2005 in all graduate psychology programs in the department: Female–full-time 117, part-time 30; Male–full-time 31, part-time 3; African American/Black–full-time 3, part-time 1; Hispanic/Latino(a)–full-time 16, part-time 1; Asian/Pacific Islander–full-time 4, part-time 1; American Indian/Alaska Native–full-time 1, part-time 0; Caucasian–full-time 123, part-time 30; Multi-ethnic–full-time 1, part-time 0; students subject to the Americans With Disabilities Act–full-time 2, part-time 0.

Financial Information/Assistance:
Tuition for Full-Time Study: *Master's:* State residents: per academic year $17,600, $475 per credit hour; Nonstate residents: per academic year $17,600, $475 per credit hour. *Doctoral:* State residents: per academic year $18,000, $500 per credit hour; Nonstate residents: per academic year $18,000, $500 per credit hour. Tuition is subject to change.

Financial Assistance:
First Year Students: No information provided.
Advanced Students: No information provided.
Contact Information: Of all students currently enrolled full-time, 0% benefitted from one or more of the listed financial assistance programs. Application and information available online at: Note: above are for the doctoral program which will seat its first class in fall 05.

Internships/Practica: Traineeships are available in community agencies, schools, and clinics, in Santa Barbara, San Luis Obispo, and Ventura Counties. Students may find placements working with children, adolescents, and seniors; with clients in recovery from chemical dependency; with survivors of sexual abuse, domestic violence, and child abuse; with mental, health clients; with court-referred clients; and with adults, couples, and families. Doctoral practica are being developed. No data yet available for doctoral practica or internship placement.

Housing and Day Care: No on-campus housing is available. No on-campus day care facilities are available.

Employment of Department Graduates:
Master's Degree Graduates: Of those who graduated in the academic year 2003–2004, the following categories and numbers represent the post-graduate activities and employment of master's degree graduates: Enrolled in a post-doctoral residency/fellowship (n/a), employed in independent practice (n/a), total from the above (master's) (0).
Doctoral Degree Graduates: Of those who graduated in the academic year 2003–2004, the following categories and numbers represent the post-graduate activities and employment of doctoral degree graduates: Enrolled in a psychology doctoral program (n/a), total from the above (doctoral) (0).

Additional Information:
Orientation, Objectives, and Emphasis of Department: The MA Clinical Psychology program is committed to the education and

training of students to develop: 1) critical thinking and reflective, learning in the acquisition of psychological knowledge; 2) basic skills in clinical psychology required to become ethical, professional therapists; 3) self-awareness, particularly as it pertains to professional clinical, practice; 4) awareness of self as an integral part of families, the mental health, community, and local communities; 5) understanding of diversity, including culture, ethnicity, gender, sexual orientation, age, and theoretical orientation. The MA Psychology-Individualized Concentration allows students to define and develop expertise in a particular area of interest. Past students have completed concentrations in Human Development, Feminist Psychology, and Interpersonal Relationships. For some areas of concentration, such as Organizational Psychology and Professional, Development and Career Counseling, a core curriculum has been developed. This nonclinical degree program is for students interested in pursuing professional careers in consulting, education, program development, business and government, as well as for students interested in applying to doctoral degree programs. The doctoral program is a new post MA PsyD degree in Clinical Psychology with a Family Psychology emphasis and a Family Forensic Concentration. Students will be enrolled in the first cohort in Fall 05.

Special Facilities or Resources: Faculty are all practicing professionals in their respective areas of expertise.

Application Information:
Send to: Admissions Office, Antioch University Santa Barbara, 801 Garden Street, Santa Barbara, CA 93101. Application available online. URL of online application: www.antiochsb.edu. Students are admitted in the Fall, application deadline August 17; Winter, application deadline November 16. Programs have rolling admissions. PsyD. Program Fall admit only. Priority application deadline is March 1. MA Psychology programs have rolling admissions. *Fee:* $60.

Argosy University/Orange County
Psychology
School of Psychology and Behavioral Sciences
3501 W. Sunflower Avenue
Santa Ana, CA 92704
Telephone: (714) 338-6200
Fax: (714) 437-1284
E-mail: *gbruss@argosyu.edu*
Web: *http://www.argosyu.edu*

Department Information:
2001. Dean, School of Psychology: Gary Bruss, PhD Number of Faculty: total–full-time 10, part-time 22; women–full-time 7, part-time 11; minority–full-time 2, part-time 3.

Programs and Degrees Offered:
Listed in the following order: Program area, degree type (T if terminal Master's), number awarded 7/03–6/04. PsyD (Doctor of Psychology) 0, Counseling Psychology EdD (Doctor of Education) 1, Counseling Psychology MA/MS (Master of Arts/Science) (T), Clinical Psychology MA/MS (Master of Arts/Science) (T) 0.

Student Applications/Admissions:
Student Applications
PsyD (Doctor of Psychology)—Applications 2004–2005, 159. Total applicants accepted 2004–2005, 53. Number enrolled (new admits only) 2004–2005 full-time, 27. Number enrolled (new admits only) 2004–2005 part-time, 3. Total enrolled 2004–2005 full-time, 68, part-time, 5. Openings 2005–2006, 38. The number of students enrolled full and part-time who were dismissed or voluntarily withdrew from this program area were 3. *Counseling Psychology EdD (Doctor of Education)—* Applications 2004–2005, 35. Total applicants accepted 2004–2005, 16. Number enrolled (new admits only) 2004–2005 full-time, 15. Number enrolled (new admits only) 2004–2005 part-time, 4. Total enrolled 2004–2005 full-time, 45, part-time, 10. Openings 2005–2006, 30. The Median number of years required for completion of a degree are 3. The number of students enrolled full and part-time who were dismissed or voluntarily withdrew from this program area were 14. *Counseling Psychology MA/MS (Master of Arts/Science)—*Applications 2004–2005, 89. Total applicants accepted 2004–2005, 48. Number enrolled (new admits only) 2004–2005 full-time, 25. Number enrolled (new admits only) 2004–2005 part-time, 7. Total enrolled 2004–2005 full-time, 46, part-time, 9. Openings 2005–2006, 35. The Median number of years required for completion of a degree are 2. The number of students enrolled full and part-time who were dismissed or voluntarily withdrew from this program area were 13. *Clinical Psychology MA/MS (Master of Arts/Science)—*Applications 2004–2005, 61. Total applicants accepted 2004–2005, 34. Number enrolled (new admits only) 2004–2005 full-time, 23. Number enrolled (new admits only) 2004–2005 part-time, 2. Total enrolled 2004–2005 full-time, 17, part-time, 2. Openings 2005–2006, 36. The number of students enrolled full and part-time who were dismissed or voluntarily withdrew from this program area were 5.

Admissions Requirements:
Scores: Entries appear in this order: required test or GPA, minimum score (if required), median score of students entering in 2003–2004. Master's Programs: overall undergraduate GPA 3.0, 3.1; last 2 years GPA 3.0, 3.1; psychology GPA 3.0, 3.1. Doctoral Programs: overall undergraduate GPA 3.25, 3.3; last 2 years GPA 3.25, 3.3; psychology GPA 3.25, 3.3. PsyD program requires a minimum GPA of 3.25 in total undergrad, last two years undergrad, and undergrad psychology courses. EdD CP program requires a minimum of 3.25 in Master's Programs (required for admission to the program). MA programs require 3.0 minimum in undergraduate psychology, and last two years of coursework.
Other Criteria: (importance of criteria rated low, medium, or high): research experience low, work experience medium, extracurricular activity medium, clinically related public service medium, GPA high, letters of recommendation high, interview high, statement of goals and objectives high. High emphasis on work experience for doctoral programs, although outstanding presentation in areas related to GPA, recommendation letters, interview, and personal statement can offset a deficit in work experience. Letters of recommendation from work, prior training, and/or academic references are expected for all programs. Emphasis on both clinical and academic references for doctoral applicants. For additional information on admission requirements, go to: www.argosyu.edu.

Student Characteristics: The following represents characteristics of students in 2004–2005 in all graduate psychology programs in the department: Female–full-time 145, part-time 22; Male–full-time 31, part-time 4; African American/Black–full-time 28, part-time 5; Hispanic/Latino(a)–full-time 27, part-time 4; Asian/Pacific Islander–full-time 20, part-time 5; American Indian/Alaska Native–full-time 1, part-time 0; Caucasian–full-time 100, part-time 12; students subject to the Americans With Disabilities Act–full-time 2, part-time 0.

Financial Information/Assistance:

Tuition for Full-Time Study: *Master's:* State residents: per academic year $11,400, $475 per credit hour; Nonstate residents: per academic year $11,400, $475 per credit hour. *Doctoral:* State residents: per academic year $22,500, $750 per credit hour; Nonstate residents: per academic year $22,500, $750 per credit hour. Tuition is subject to change. Tuition costs vary by program. See the following Web site for updates and changes in tuition costs: www.argosyu.edu.

Financial Assistance:

First Year Students: Fellowships and scholarships available for first-year. Average amount paid per academic year: $2,000. Average number of hours worked per week: 3. Apply by June 30. Tuition remission given: partial.

Advanced Students: Teaching assistantships available for advanced students. Average amount paid per academic year: $1,000. Average number of hours worked per week: 6. Apply by June 30. Tuition remission given: partial. Research assistantships available for advanced students. Average amount paid per academic year: $2,000. Average number of hours worked per week: 3. Apply by June 30. Tuition remission given: partial. Fellowships and scholarships available for advanced students. Average amount paid per academic year: $3,000. Average number of hours worked per week: 5. Apply by June 30. Tuition remission given: partial.

Contact Information: Of all students currently enrolled full-time, 3% benefitted from one or more of the listed financial assistance programs. Application and information available online at: argosyu.edu.

Internships/Practica: The specific clinical focus of the practicum varies according to the student's program, training needs, professional interests and goals, and the availability of practicum sites. MA Counseling and Clinical practica focus on training students in couples/family counseling and therapy skills. The PsyD Clinical Psychology practica provide one year of psychodiagnostic assessment training and one year of therapy training. The program is committed to finding a wide range of practicum sites to provide many options for student professional exposure and development. Our first wave of students shall be entering internships in the fall of 2005. Currently 10 of the 13 students have located APPIC sites, 1 an APA site, and 2 CAPIC sites (California based internships approved by CAPIC). For those doctoral students for whom a professional internship is required prior to graduation, 13 applied in 2003–2004. Of those who applied, 10 were placed in internships listed by the Association of Psychology Postdoctoral and Internship Programs (APPIC); 1 was placed in an APA accredited internship.

Housing and Day Care: No on-campus housing is available. No on-campus day care facilities are available.

Employment of Department Graduates:

Master's Degree Graduates: Of those who graduated in the academic year 2003–2004, the following categories and numbers represent the post-graduate activities and employment of master's degree graduates: Enrolled in a psychology doctoral program (0), enrolled in another graduate/professional program (0), enrolled in a post-doctoral residency/fellowship (n/a), employed in independent practice (n/a), employed in an academic position at a university (0), employed in an academic position at a 2-year/4-year college (0), employed in other positions at a higher education institution (0), employed in a professional position in a school system (0), employed in business or industry (research/consulting) (0), employed in business or industry (management) (0), employed in a government agency (research) (0), employed in a government agency (professional services) (0), employed in a community mental health/counseling center (0), employed in a hospital/medical center (0), still seeking employment (0), other employment position (0), total from the above (master's) (0).

Doctoral Degree Graduates: Of those who graduated in the academic year 2003–2004, the following categories and numbers represent the post-graduate activities and employment of doctoral degree graduates: Enrolled in a psychology doctoral program (n/a), enrolled in a post-doctoral residency/fellowship (0), employed in independent practice (0), employed in an academic position at a university (0), employed in an academic position at a 2-year/4-year college (0), employed in other positions at a higher education institution (0), employed in a professional position in a school system (0), employed in business or industry (research/consulting) (0), employed in business or industry (management) (0), employed in a government agency (research) (0), employed in a government agency (professional services) (0), employed in a community mental health/counseling center (0), employed in a hospital/medical center (0), still seeking employment (0), other employment position (0), total from the above (doctoral) (0).

Additional Information:

Orientation, Objectives, and Emphasis of Department: The graduate programs in psychology are designed to educate and train practitioners, with an additional emphasis on scholarly training in the doctoral programs. Courses and fieldwork experiences embrace multiple theoretical and intervention approaches, and a range of psychodiagnostic techniques (in the clinical programs), all of which are designed to serve a wide and diverse range of populations. Two concentrations are available, in Forensic Psychology and in Child/Adolescent Psychology. Students are taught by faculty with strong teaching and practitioner skills, with a strong focus on developing students with the fundamental clinical and counseling competencies required to pursue careers in psychology. Courses in applied and academic areas are considered to be critical in the development of practitioners with the skills to develop, innovate, implement, and assess delivery of services to clientele in clinical, counseling, and educational types of settings.

Information for Students With Physical Disabilities: See the following Web site for more information: www.argosyu.edu.

Application Information:

Send to: Director of Admissions, c/o Argosy University/Orange County, 3501 W. Sunflower Avenue, Santa Ana, CA 92704. Application available online. URL of online application: www.argosyu.edu. Students are admitted in the Fall, application deadline May 15; Spring, application deadline October 15; Summer, application deadline March

30. We offer a year around rolling admissions process for both the EdD-CP and MACP programs, with admissions points in the beginning and midterm for Fall, Spring, and Summer semesters. PsyD and MA Clinical applicant deadlines are January 15 for fall, with a May 15 deadline if spaces are available, and October 15 for spring term, with a November 15 deadline if spaces are still available. *Fee:* $50.

Argosy University/San Francisco Bay Area

999 A Canal Blvd.
Pt. Richmond, CA 94804
Telephone: (510) 215-0277
Fax: (510) 215-0299
E-mail: *amorrison@argosyu.edu*
Web: *www.argosyu.edu*

Department Information:
1999. Chairperson: Andrea Morrison, PhD Number of Faculty: total–full-time 8, part-time 9; women–full-time 5, part-time 5; minority–full-time 1, part-time 4.

Programs and Degrees Offered:
Listed in the following order: Program area, degree type (T if terminal Master's), number awarded 7/03–6/04. Counseling Psychology MA/MS (Master of Arts/Science) 0, Clinical Psychology MA MA/MS (Master of Arts/Science) (T) 2, Clinical Psychology PsyD (Doctor of Psychology) 9.

APA Accreditation: Clinical PsyD (Doctor of Psychology).

Student Applications/Admissions:
Student Applications
Counseling Psychology MA/MS (Master of Arts/Science)—Applications 2004–2005, 0. Total applicants accepted 2004–2005, 0. The number of students enrolled full and part-time who were dismissed or voluntarily withdrew from this program area were 0. *Clinical Psychology MA MA/MS (Master of Arts/Science)*—Applications 2004–2005, 40. Total applicants accepted 2004–2005, 10. Number enrolled (new admits only) 2004–2005 full-time, 10. Number enrolled (new admits only) 2004–2005 part-time, 0. Total enrolled 2004–2005 full-time, 15, part-time, 5. Openings 2005–2006, 20. The Median number of years required for completion of a degree are 2. The number of students enrolled full and part-time who were dismissed or voluntarily withdrew from this program area were 0. *Clinical Psychology PsyD (Doctor of Psychology)*—Applications 2004–2005, 275. Total applicants accepted 2004–2005, 125. Number enrolled (new admits only) 2004–2005 full-time, 58. Number enrolled (new admits only) 2004–2005 part-time, 4. Total enrolled 2004–2005 full-time, 132, part-time, 37. Openings 2005–2006, 65. The Median number of years required for completion of a degree are 4. The number of students enrolled full and part-time who were dismissed or voluntarily withdrew from this program area were 7.

Admissions Requirements:
Scores: Entries appear in this order: required test or GPA, minimum score (if required), median score of students entering in 2003–2004. Master's Programs: overall undergraduate GPA 3.0; last 2 years GPA 3.0; psychology GPA 3.0. Doctoral Programs: overall undergraduate GPA 3.25; last 2 years GPA 3.25; psychology GPA 3.25.
Other Criteria: (importance of criteria rated low, medium, or high): research experience low, work experience low, extracurricular activity medium, clinically related public service medium, GPA medium, letters of recommendation high, interview high, statement of goals and objectives high. For additional information on admission requirements, go to: www.argosyu.edu.

Student Characteristics: The following represents characteristics of students in 2004–2005 in all graduate psychology programs in the department: Female–full-time 111, part-time 33; Male–full-time 36, part-time 9; African American/Black–full-time 9, part-time 4; Hispanic/Latino(a)–full-time 9, part-time 3; Asian/Pacific Islander–full-time 11, part-time 9; American Indian/Alaska Native–full-time 1, part-time 2; Caucasian–full-time 117, part-time 24; students subject to the Americans With Disabilities Act–full-time 2, part-time 0.

Financial Information/Assistance:
Tuition for Full-Time Study: *Master's:* State residents: $750 per credit hour; Nonstate residents: $750 per credit hour. *Doctoral:* State residents: $750 per credit hour; Nonstate residents: $750 per credit hour. Tuition is subject to change. See the following Web site for updates and changes in tuition costs: www.argosyu.edu.

Financial Assistance:
First Year Students: Fellowships and scholarships available for first-year. Average amount paid per academic year: $16,500. Apply by Ongoing. Tuition remission given: full and partial.
Advanced Students: Teaching assistantships available for advanced students. Average amount paid per academic year: $400. Average number of hours worked per week: 12. Research assistantships available for advanced students. Traineeships available for advanced students.
Contact Information: Of all students currently enrolled full-time, 8% benefitted from one or more of the listed financial assistance programs. Application and information available online at: www.argosyu.edu.

Internships/Practica: Argosy University SFBA's database of approved San Francisco Bay Area sites includes community mental health centers; consortiums; state, community, and private psychiatric hospitals; medical and trauma centers; university counseling centers; schools; correctional facilities; residential treatment programs; independent and group practices; and corporate settings. Some sites serve the general population, while others service specific populations (e.g., children, adolescents, geriatrics, particular ethnic or racial groups, criminal offenders, etc.) or clinical problems (e.g., chemical dependency, eating disorders, medical and psychiatric rehabilitation, etc.). Argosy University SFBA is a member of the California Psychology Internship Council (CAPIC), which is a collaboration between Bay Area psychology graduate programs and internship programs in California. The Training Department works throughout the year to maintain positive relationships with existing sites and affiliate itself with new sites throughout the Bay area. Students are encouraged to review the database, CAPIC, APPIC and other site files kept in the training department and talk with the Training Director to identify placements that provide the type of experience desired.

Argosy University SFBA strongly encourages students to complete their training in settings that provide opportunities to work with diverse populations. It is essential that students learn to work with people who are different from themselves (e.g., race, ethnicity, disability, sexual orientation, etc.) in a supervised setting where they can learn the skills, knowledge and attitudes necessary to practice as a competent clinician. For those doctoral students for whom a professional internship is required prior to graduation, 28 applied in 2003–2004. Of those who applied, 4 were placed in internships listed by the Association of Psychology Postdoctoral and Internship Programs (APPIC); 7 were placed in APA accredited internships.

Housing and Day Care: No on-campus housing is available. No on-campus day care facilities are available.

Employment of Department Graduates:

Master's Degree Graduates: Of those who graduated in the academic year 2003–2004, the following categories and numbers represent the post-graduate activities and employment of master's degree graduates: Enrolled in a psychology doctoral program (0), enrolled in another graduate/professional program (0), enrolled in a post-doctoral residency/fellowship (n/a), employed in independent practice (n/a), employed in a professional position in a school system (1), do not know (1), total from the above (master's) (2).

Doctoral Degree Graduates: Of those who graduated in the academic year 2003–2004, the following categories and numbers represent the post-graduate activities and employment of doctoral degree graduates: Enrolled in a psychology doctoral program (n/a), enrolled in another graduate/professional program (0), enrolled in a post-doctoral residency/fellowship (9), employed in independent practice (0), total from the above (doctoral) (9).

Additional Information:

Orientation, Objectives, and Emphasis of Department: The clinical orientation of the program is integrative. All major theoretical orientations are presented, including psychodynamic, family systems, developmental, cognitive, and humanistic.

Special Facilities or Resources: Argosy University San Francisco Bay Area campus emphasizes specialized hands-on clinical training through our Intensive Clinical Training facility. Through the Intensive Clinical Training series, students work directly with clients referred from the community while being observed by a team through a one-way mirror. The team consists of the instructor and/or clinical assistant and fellow students who participate in pre and post-therapy sessions in which they provide input and feedback about the therapeutic process. Each client session is guided by the instructor/assistant who, through the use of a microphone, provides clinical guidance and interventions directly to the student therapist through an earpiece worn by the student. As the session progresses, the instructor/assistant educates the team about the dynamics of the therapist/client interaction and the treatment approach. Students may participate on three levels: 1) as a clinical observer and a member of the team; 2) as a student therapist working directly with clients, and 3) as a clinical assistant in concert with our Supervision/Consultation course.

Information for Students With Physical Disabilities: aheller@argosyu.edu.

Application Information:
Send to: Admissions Department, 999A Canal Blvd., Point Richmond, CA 94804. Application available online. URL of online application: www.argosyu.edu. Students are admitted in the Fall, application deadline January 15, 2005. Programs have rolling admissions. January 15th priority deadline for Fall. May 15th final deadllline depending on space availability. Rolling admissions depending on availability. *Fee:* $50.

Azusa Pacific University
Department of Graduate Psychology
901 E. Alosta, P.O. Box 7000
Azusa, CA 91702-7000
Telephone: (626) 815-5008
Fax: (626) 815-5015
E-mail: *mstanton@apu.edu*
Web: *http://www.apu.edu/* Search: *Clinical Psychology*

Department Information:
1976. Chairperson: Mark Stanton, PhD. Number of Faculty: total–full-time 12, part-time 16; women–full-time 5, part-time 15; minority–full-time 3, part-time 2.

Programs and Degrees Offered:
Listed in the following order: Program area, degree type (T if terminal Master's), number awarded 7/03–6/04. Clinical Psychology MA/MS (Master of Arts/Science) (T) 24, Clinical Psychology PsyD (Doctor of Psychology) 15, Clinical Psychology MA/MS (Master of Arts/Science) 14.

APA Accreditation: Clinical PsyD (Doctor of Psychology).

Student Applications/Admissions:

Student Applications

Clinical Psychology MA/MS (Master of Arts/Science)—Applications 2004–2005, 134. Total applicants accepted 2004–2005, 81. Number enrolled (new admits only) 2004–2005 full-time, 49. Number enrolled (new admits only) 2004–2005 part-time, 11. Total enrolled 2004–2005 full-time, 109, part-time, 42. Openings 2005–2006, 60. The Median number of years required for completion of a degree are 3. The number of students enrolled full and part-time who were dismissed or voluntarily withdrew from this program area were 4. *Clinical Psychology PsyD (Doctor of Psychology)*—Applications 2004–2005, 33. Total applicants accepted 2004–2005, 24. Number enrolled (new admits only) 2004–2005 full-time, 19. Number enrolled (new admits only) 2004–2005 part-time, 2. Total enrolled 2004–2005 full-time, 40, part-time, 22. Openings 2005–2006, 28. The Median number of years required for completion of a degree are 5. The number of students enrolled full and part-time who were dismissed or voluntarily withdrew from this program area were 1. *Clinical Psychology MA/MS (Master of Arts/Science)*—Applications 2004–2005, 59. Total applicants accepted 2004–2005, 31. Number enrolled (new admits only) 2004–2005 full-time, 14. Number enrolled (new admits only) 2004–2005 part-time, 2. Total enrolled 2004–2005 full-time, 14, part-time, 2. Openings 2005–2006, 20. The Median number of years required for completion of a degree are 2. The number of students enrolled full and part-time who were dismissed or voluntarily withdrew from this program area were 2.

Admissions Requirements:

Scores: Entries appear in this order: required test or GPA, minimum score (if required), median score of students entering in 2003–2004. Master's Programs: overall undergraduate GPA 3.0; psychology GPA 3.0. Doctoral Programs: GRE-V no minimum stated; GRE-Q no minimum stated; GRE-V+Q 1000; GRE-Analytical 4.5; overall undergraduate GPA 3.0; last 2 years GPA 3.0, 3.0; psychology GPA 3.0. Note: The GRE General exam, including verbal, quantitative, and analytical writing assessment is required. Scores are one consideration in the entire application. Verbal ability is important to success in the PsyD program. GRE Writing Assessment is required, so if applicant took GRE prior to inclusion of that section, s/he must take that section of the restructured exam.

Other Criteria: (importance of criteria rated low, medium, or high): GRE/MAT scores medium, research experience medium, work experience medium, extracurricular activity medium, clinically related public service medium, GPA high, letters of recommendation high, interview high, statement of goals and objectives high. No GRE/MAT scores required for MA; work experience of medium importance for MA; research experience of medium importance for MA; clinically related public service low for MA.

Student Characteristics: The following represents characteristics of students in 2004–2005 in all graduate psychology programs in the department: Female–full-time 130, part-time 44; Male–full-time 33, part-time 22; African American/Black–full-time 13, part-time 5; Hispanic/Latino(a)–full-time 32, part-time 12; Asian/Pacific Islander–full-time 14, part-time 6; American Indian/Alaska Native–full-time 0, part-time 0; Caucasian–full-time 95, part-time 40; Multi-ethnic–full-time 9, part-time 3; students subject to the Americans With Disabilities Act–full-time 0, part-time 0.

Financial Information/Assistance:

Tuition for Full-Time Study: *Master's:* State residents: $425 per credit hour; Nonstate residents: $425 per credit hour. *Doctoral:* State residents: $655 per credit hour; Nonstate residents: $655 per credit hour. Tuition is subject to change. See the following Web site for updates and changes in tuition costs: http://www.apu.edu/graduatecenter/services/sfs/costs/.

Financial Assistance:

First Year Students: Teaching assistantships available for first-year. Average amount paid per academic year: $6,250. Average number of hours worked per week: 15. Apply by April 15. Tuition remission given: partial. Research assistantships available for first-year. Average amount paid per academic year: $6,250. Average number of hours worked per week: 15. Apply by April 15. Tuition remission given: partial.

Advanced Students: No information provided.

Contact Information: Of all students currently enrolled full-time, 3% benefitted from one or more of the listed financial assistance programs.

Internships/Practica: PsyD students are required to complete 6 semesters of practicum experience. These experiences are gained in placements throughout Los Angeles, Orange, and San Bernardino Counties, which provide diverse clinical and multicultural experiences. A Counseling Center on the Azusa Pacific University campus also serves as a practicum site for doctoral students. A sequence of clinical practicum courses is offered simultaneously with the field placement experience. All doctoral students are required to complete one full year of psychology internship. APU places interns in a variety of sites (must be APA approved or those meeting APPIC standards) across the country. Students enrolled in the MA Program in Clinical Psychology complete a clinical training sequence that meets all requirements for future licensure as a Marital and Family Therapist (MFT) in the state of California. Students complete 250 hours of direct client contact in diverse, multi-cultural settings, such as community counseling centers, domestic violence clinics, and schools. Students receive training in individual, marital, and group therapy and exposure to treatments that have been demonstrated to be effective with specific problems. A sequence of clinical placement courses is offered simultaneously with the field placement experience. For those doctoral students for whom a professional internship is required prior to graduation, 11 applied in 2003–2004. Of those who applied, 9 were placed in APA accredited internships.

Housing and Day Care: No on-campus housing is available. No on-campus day care facilities are available.

Employment of Department Graduates:

Master's Degree Graduates: Of those who graduated in the academic year 2003–2004, the following categories and numbers represent the post-graduate activities and employment of master's degree graduates: Enrolled in a post-doctoral residency/fellowship (n/a), employed in independent practice (n/a), do not know (29), total from the above (master's) (29).

Doctoral Degree Graduates: Of those who graduated in the academic year 2003–2004, the following categories and numbers represent the post-graduate activities and employment of doctoral degree graduates: Enrolled in a psychology doctoral program (n/a), enrolled in a post-doctoral residency/fellowship (3), employed in other positions at a higher education institution (1), employed in a community mental health/counseling center (1), employed in a hospital/medical center (1), do not know (2), total from the above (doctoral) (8).

Additional Information:

Orientation, Objectives, and Emphasis of Department: The PsyD in Clinical Psychology with an emphasis in Family Psychology (APA accredited) prepares students for the practice of professional psychology. The program adheres to a practitioner-scholar model of training and emphasizes development of the core competencies in clinical psychology adopted by the National Council of Schools and Programs of Professional Psychology. The program requires completion of a rigorous sequence of courses in the science and practice of psychology. Requirements include three years of clinical training, successful demonstration of clinical competency through examination, completion of a clinical dissertation, and a predoctoral internship. Prespecialty education in family psychology and an emphasis in interdisciplinary studies, relating psychology to ethics, theology, and philosophy, is included. The program was designed to be consistent with the requirements of the Guidelines and Principles for Accreditation of Programs in Professional Psychology (APA, 1996). The MA in Clinical Psychology with an emphasis in Marriage and Family Therapy meets requirements for California MFT licensure. Concepts of individual psychology are integrated with interpersonal and ecological concepts of systems theory. Goals include cultivating the examined life, fostering theoretical mastery, developing practical clinical skills, encouraging clinically integrative strategies, and preparing psychotherapists to work in a culturally diverse world.

Special Facilities or Resources: All students have access to the APA PsycINFO database and all APA journals full-text online as part of their student library privileges. The new Darling Library provides an attractive and functional set of resources for the APU PsyD and MA. The library is technology-friendly and includes the Ahmanson Information Technology Center, an area with 75 computer desks. Each computer is wired into the university system for Internet and library catalog system searches. PsycINFO, as well as over 100 additional licensed databases, are available for student literature and subject searches. Eight "scholar rooms" were designed as a part of the Darling Graduate Library, to be used for conducting research and writing. Doctoral students in the dissertation phase of their program are given priority in the reservation of these rooms. There are also several conference rooms in the Darling Library that may be reserved for student study groups or research teams. The Department of Graduate Psychology runs the Child and Family Development Center (CFDC), which offers psychological services to the surrounding community as well as to faculty, staff and university students. The CFDC also contracts to provide services to the surrounding 12 schools in the Azusa Unified School District. The CFDC currently trains 25 MA and PsyD graduate students and has provided data for two doctoral dissertations.

Information for Students With Physical Disabilities: See the following Web site for more information: http://www.apu.edu/lec/language/.

Application Information:
Send to: Azusa Pacific University, Graduate Center, 901 E. Alosta, P.O. Box 7000, Azusa, CA 91702-7000. Application available online. URL of online application: http://www.apu.edu/apply/. Students are admitted in the Fall, application deadline February 15; Spring, application deadline October 31. PsyD Application deadline is February 15 (if space is available, extended case by case with a deadline of June 15). Application deadlines for MA are as follows: Spring deadline is October 31 and Fall deadline is June 15. *Fee:* $45 Domestic, $65 International.

California Institute of Integral Studies
School of Professional Psychology
1453 Mission Street
San Francisco, CA 94103
Telephone: (415) 575-6100
Fax: (415) 575-1264
E-mail: *info@ciis.edu*
Web: *http://www.ciis.edu*

Department Information:
1979. Chairperson: Harrison Voigt. Number of Faculty: total–full-time 18, part-time 35; women–full-time 10, part-time 20; minority–full-time 4, part-time 10.

Programs and Degrees Offered:
Listed in the following order: Program area, degree type (T if terminal Master's), number awarded 7/03–6/04. Clinical Psychol-

ogy PsyD (Doctor of Psychology) 18, Counseling Psychology MA/MS (Master of Arts/Science) (T) 45.

APA Accreditation: Clinical PsyD (Doctor of Psychology).

Student Applications/Admissions:
Student Applications
Clinical Psychology PsyD (Doctor of Psychology)—Applications 2004–2005, 125. Total applicants accepted 2004–2005, 44. Number enrolled (new admits only) 2004–2005 full-time, 32. Number enrolled (new admits only) 2004–2005 part-time, 0. Total enrolled 2004–2005 full-time, 140, part-time, 45. Openings 2005–2006, 32. The number of students enrolled full and part-time who were dismissed or voluntarily withdrew from this program area were 1. *Counseling Psychology MA/MS (Master of Arts/Science)*—Applications 2004–2005, 72. Total applicants accepted 2004–2005, 40. Number enrolled (new admits only) 2004–2005 full-time, 30. Number enrolled (new admits only) 2004–2005 part-time, 0. Total enrolled 2004–2005 full-time, 112, part-time, 31. Openings 2005–2006, 30. The Median number of years required for completion of a degree are 3. The number of students enrolled full and part-time who were dismissed or voluntarily withdrew from this program area were 6.

Admissions Requirements:
Scores: Entries appear in this order: required test or GPA, minimum score (if required), median score of students entering in 2003–2004. Master's Programs: overall undergraduate GPA 3.0, 3.3. Doctoral Programs: GRE-V no minimum stated, 556; GRE-Q no minimum stated, 584; overall undergraduate GPA 3.1, 3.5. GRE (verbal and quantitative) required but no minimum score is used to qualify.
Other Criteria: (importance of criteria rated low, medium, or high): GRE/MAT scores medium, research experience low, work experience medium, extracurricular activity medium, clinically related public service high, GPA high, letters of recommendation high, interview high, statement of goals and objectives high, written work sample high. Admissions criteria listed above apply to PsyD program. For the MA program, criteria are similar but may vary and GRE is not required. For additional information on admission requirements, go to: www.ciis.edu.

Student Characteristics: The following represents characteristics of students in 2004–2005 in all graduate psychology programs in the department: Female–full-time 193, part-time 62; Male–full-time 59, part-time 14; African American/Black–full-time 11, part-time 3; Hispanic/Latino(a)–full-time 19, part-time 7; Asian/Pacific Islander–full-time 16, part-time 5; American Indian/Alaska Native–full-time 1, part-time 0; Caucasian–full-time 203, part-time 58; Multi-ethnic–full-time 2, part-time 3; students subject to the Americans With Disabilities Act–full-time 2, part-time 0.

Financial Information/Assistance:
Tuition for Full-Time Study: *Master's:* State residents: per academic year $12,260, $635 per credit hour; Nonstate residents: per academic year $12,260, $635 per credit hour. *Doctoral:* State residents: per academic year $15,500, $795 per credit hour; Nonstate residents: per academic year $15,500, $795 per credit hour. Tuition is subject to change. See the following Web site for updates and changes in tuition costs: www.ciis.edu.

Financial Assistance:

First Year Students: Teaching assistantships available for first-year. Fellowships and scholarships available for first-year. Average amount paid per academic year: $5,000. Apply by May 1. Tuition remission given: partial.

Advanced Students: Teaching assistantships available for advanced students. Apply by varies. Fellowships and scholarships available for advanced students. Average amount paid per academic year: $5,000. Apply by May 1. Tuition remission given: partial.

Contact Information: Of all students currently enrolled full-time, 15% benefitted from one or more of the listed financial assistance programs. Application and information available online at: www.ciis.edu.

Internships/Practica: Internship and practicum placements are available throughout the greater San Francisco Bay Area at a broad variety of mental health service agencies. All doctoral internship sites are approved by APPIC or CAPIC. Not all internship positions are funded. For those doctoral students for whom a professional internship is required prior to graduation, 23 applied in 2003–2004. Of those who applied, 8 were placed in internships listed by the Association of Psychology Postdoctoral and Internship Programs (APPIC); 3 were placed in APA accredited internships.

Housing and Day Care: No on-campus housing is available. No on-campus day care facilities are available.

Employment of Department Graduates:

Master's Degree Graduates: Of those who graduated in the academic year 2003–2004, the following categories and numbers represent the post-graduate activities and employment of master's degree graduates: Enrolled in a post-doctoral residency/fellowship (n/a), employed in independent practice (n/a), total from the above (master's) (0).

Doctoral Degree Graduates: Of those who graduated in the academic year 2003–2004, the following categories and numbers represent the post-graduate activities and employment of doctoral degree graduates: Enrolled in a psychology doctoral program (n/a), total from the above (doctoral) (0).

Additional Information:

Orientation, Objectives, and Emphasis of Department: The Institute offers a unique program of education and training, broadening the usual conceptual framework for graduate training in psychology by including in the curriculum some exposure to Asian philosophical, humanistic, and transpersonal approaches to understanding human experience. The educational philosophy simultaneously values scholarly knowledge, inner development, applied research, and human service. Psychology programs at CIIS flourish within a fertile and broadening climate provided by other social science graduate programs in philosophy/religion, anthropology, and women's spirituality, along with online degree programs. Within the practitioner-scholar training model, the APA-accredited PsyD program provides knowledge of the foundations of scientific and professional psychology while emphasizing the understanding of consciousness, self-knowledge, and human evolution embodied in the philosophical and psychological traditions of both East and West. The clinical specialization prepares students for work with the broad range of clientele and systems found across the range of multidisciplinary service settings and the spectrum of populations served by the clinical psychologist. Experiential growth work is required in all programs. Several clinical concentrations are available. CIIS has a 28,000-volume library and a well-developed Placement Office to support academic studies.

Special Facilities or Resources: CIIS operates four separate community-based counseling centers: the on-campus Psychological Services Center operated by the PsyD Clinical Psychology program, and three counseling centers operated by the MA Counseling program. All counseling centers serve as primary training sites for the MA and PsyD programs.

Information for Students With Physical Disabilities: See the following Web site for more information: www.ciis.edu.

Application Information:
Send to: Office of Admissions. Students are admitted in the Fall, application deadline January 15. MA programs: April 15 for Fall, September 15 for Spring (not all programs). *Fee:* $65.

California Lutheran University
Psychology Department
60 W. Olsen Road
Thousand Oaks, CA 91360-2787
Telephone: (805) 493-3441
Fax: (805) 493-3479
E-mail: *saddler@clunet.edu*
Web: *http://www.clunet.edu*

Department Information:
1959. Director, Graduate Programs in Psychology: C. Douglas Saddler, PhD. Number of Faculty: total–full-time 5, part-time 14; women–full-time 3, part-time 8; minority–part-time 1.

Programs and Degrees Offered:
Listed in the following order: Program area, degree type (T if terminal Master's), number awarded 7/03–6/04. Clinical MA/MS (Master of Arts/Science) (T) 8, Marital and Family Therapy MA/MS (Master of Arts/Science) (T) 15.

Student Applications/Admissions:
Student Applications

Clinical MA/MS (Master of Arts/Science)—Applications 2004–2005, 20. Total applicants accepted 2004–2005, 14. Total enrolled 2004–2005 full-time, 7, part-time, 11. Openings 2005–2006, 15. The Median number of years required for completion of a degree are 2. The number of students enrolled full and part-time who were dismissed or voluntarily withdrew from this program area were 0. *Marital and Family Therapy MA/MS (Master of Arts/Science)*—Applications 2004–2005, 60. Total applicants accepted 2004–2005, 30. Total enrolled 2004–2005 full-time, 15, part-time, 19. Openings 2005–2006, 20. The Median number of years required for completion of a degree are 2. The number of students enrolled full and part-time who were dismissed or voluntarily withdrew from this program area were 1.

Admissions Requirements:

Scores: Entries appear in this order: required test or GPA, minimum score (if required), median score of students entering in 2003–2004. Master's Programs: last 2 years GPA 3.0. GRE is required only if upper division undergraduate GPA is below 3.0.

Other Criteria: (importance of criteria rated low, medium, or high): GRE/MAT scores low, research experience medium, work experience medium, extracurricular activity low, clinically related public service medium, GPA high, letters of recommendation high, interview high, statement of goals and objectives high.

Student Characteristics: The following represents characteristics of students in 2004–2005 in all graduate psychology programs in the department: Female–full-time 20, part-time 25; Male–full-time 2, part-time 5; African American/Black–full-time 2, part-time 1; Hispanic/Latino(a)–full-time 3, part-time 5; Asian/Pacific Islander–full-time 2, part-time 0; American Indian/Alaska Native–full-time 1, part-time 0; Caucasian–full-time 0, part-time 0; Multi-ethnic–full-time 1, part-time 0; students subject to the Americans With Disabilities Act–full-time 0, part-time 0.

Financial Information/Assistance:

Tuition for Full-Time Study: *Master's:* State residents: $410 per credit hour; Nonstate residents: $410 per credit hour. Tuition is subject to change.

Financial Assistance:

First Year Students: Teaching assistantships available for first-year. Average number of hours worked per week: 10. Apply by August 15. Tuition remission given: partial. Research assistantships available for first-year. Average number of hours worked per week: 10. Apply by August 15. Tuition remission given: partial.

Advanced Students: Teaching assistantships available for advanced students. Apply by August 15. Tuition remission given: partial. Research assistantships available for advanced students. Apply by August 15. Tuition remission given: partial.

Contact Information: Of all students currently enrolled full-time, 15% benefitted from one or more of the listed financial assistance programs.

Internships/Practica: A special feature of the Marital and Family Therapy Program is a 12-month practicum placement in the University's Marriage, Family, and Child Counseling Center. The Center is a low-cost community counseling facility, which provides an intensive on-site clinical training experience. Individual supervision, group supervision, staff training, peer support and sharing of learning experiences in an atmosphere designed to facilitate growth as a therapist create exceptional opportunities. Approximately 500 hours applicable to the California licensing requirement can be obtained through the MFT practicum experience.

Housing and Day Care: No on-campus housing is available. No on-campus day care facilities are available.

Employment of Department Graduates:

Master's Degree Graduates: Of those who graduated in the academic year 2003–2004, the following categories and numbers represent the post-graduate activities and employment of master's degree graduates: Enrolled in a post-doctoral residency/fellowship (n/a), employed in independent practice (n/a), total from the above (master's) (0).

Doctoral Degree Graduates: Of those who graduated in the academic year 2003–2004, the following categories and numbers represent the post-graduate activities and employment of doctoral degree graduates: Enrolled in a psychology doctoral program (n/a), total from the above (doctoral) (0).

Additional Information:

Orientation, Objectives, and Emphasis of Department: The Master of Science degree in Clinical Psychology provides both a scientific and practitioner foundation, with courses in research as well as clinical and assessment training. Students choose either a two-course sequence in Child & Adolescent Therapy or a two-course sequence in Psychiatric Rehabilitation, which focuses on clients who have serious mental illnesses. The Master of Science in Clinical Psychology provides excellent preparation for application to doctoral programs, provides skills leading toward careers in the mental health profession, and qualifies the graduate to teach in community colleges. The Master of Science Degree in Counseling Psychology prepares the student to become a professional Marital and Family Therapist. The program is designed to meet all academic requirements for the California state license in marital and family counseling. Over the years, graduates of this program have an outstanding record of successfully passing the state licensing examination. Graduates have built successful practices in both private and institutional fields. All of the Master's degree programs can be completed in two years, or three years on a part-time basis.

Application Information:
Send to: Marilyn Carpenter, Graduate Admission Counselor, 60 W. Olsen Road, Thousand Oaks, CA 91360. Students are admitted in the Fall, application deadline February 15; Spring, application deadline December 1; Summer, application deadline April 1. Master's program in Counseling Psychology (Marital & Family Therapy) generally only admits students in the fall semester. *Fee:* $50.

California Polytechnic State University
Psychology/Master of Science in Psychology
Liberal Arts
Cal Poly Psychology/Child Development Department
San Luis Obispo, CA 93407
Telephone: (805) 756-2456
Fax: (805) 756-1134
E-mail: *mbooker@calpoly.edu*
Web: *http://www.calpoly.edu/~psychhd*

Department Information:
1969. Chairperson: Basil A. Fiorito. Number of Faculty: total–full-time 20, part-time 15; women–full-time 11, part-time 9; minority–full-time 5, part-time 2.

Programs and Degrees Offered:
Listed in the following order: Program area, degree type (T if terminal Master's), number awarded 7/03–6/04. Counseling Marriage and Family MA/MS (Master of Arts/Science) (T) 11.

Student Applications/Admissions:

Student Applications

Counseling Marriage and Family MA/MS (Master of Arts/Science)—Applications 2004–2005, 83. Total applicants accepted 2004–2005, 26. Number enrolled (new admits only) 2004–2005 full-time, 14. Total enrolled 2004–2005 full-time, 31, part-time, 8. Openings 2005–2006, 20. The Median number of years required for completion of a degree are 3. The number of students enrolled full and part-time who were dismissed or voluntarily withdrew from this program area were 12.

Admissions Requirements:

Scores: Entries appear in this order: required test or GPA, minimum score (if required), median score of students entering in 2003–2004. Master's Programs: GRE-V+Q no minimum stated, 1125; GRE-Analytical no minimum stated, 5; last 2 years GPA 3.0, 3.74.

Other Criteria: (importance of criteria rated low, medium, or high): GRE/MAT scores high, research experience low, work experience medium, extracurricular activity medium, clinically related public service medium, GPA high, letters of recommendation high, statement of goals and objectives high.

Student Characteristics: The following represents characteristics of students in 2004–2005 in all graduate psychology programs in the department: Female–full-time 24, part-time 7; Male–full-time 7, part-time 1; African American/Black–full-time 0, part-time 0; Hispanic/Latino(a)–full-time 6, part-time 2; Asian/Pacific Islander–full-time 0, part-time 0; American Indian/Alaska Native–full-time 0, part-time 0; Caucasian–full-time 25, part-time 6; Multi-ethnic–full-time 0, part-time 0; students subject to the Americans With Disabilities Act–full-time 0, part-time 0.

Financial Information/Assistance:

Tuition for Full-Time Study: *Master's:* State residents: per academic year $4,218; Nonstate residents: per academic year $4,218, $226 per credit hour. Tuition is subject to change.

Financial Assistance:

First Year Students: No information provided.
Advanced Students: No information provided.
Contact Information: Of all students currently enrolled full-time, 0% benefitted from one or more of the listed financial assistance programs. Application and information available online at: http://www.ess.calpoly.edu/_finaid.

Internships/Practica: The Central Coast of California offers numerous well-supervised clinical internships in public and private non-profit agencies with a variety of client populations. Internships are selected based on their ability to provide: 1) quality supervision by a state-qualified licensed clinician; 2) clients with a wide variety of psychological disorders; 3) a variety of treatment modalities, i.e., individual, couple, family, and group therapy; 4) a wide variety of clients that represent the diversity of the community. Most internship students are placed at public agency sites which serve the country's entire range of ethnic and minority populations.

Housing and Day Care: On-campus housing is available. See the following Web site for more information: http://www.housing.calpoly.edu/. On-campus day care facilities are available. See the following Web site for more information: http://asi.calpoly.edu/children/.

Employment of Department Graduates:

Master's Degree Graduates: Of those who graduated in the academic year 2003–2004, the following categories and numbers represent the post-graduate activities and employment of master's degree graduates: Enrolled in a post-doctoral residency/fellowship (n/a), employed in independent practice (n/a), total from the above (master's) (0).

Doctoral Degree Graduates: Of those who graduated in the academic year 2003–2004, the following categories and numbers represent the post-graduate activities and employment of doctoral degree graduates: Enrolled in a psychology doctoral program (n/a), total from the above (doctoral) (0).

Additional Information:

Orientation, Objectives, and Emphasis of Department: The MS in Psychology is designed for persons who desire to practice in the field of clinical/counseling psychology. The MS in Psychology is accredited in the area of marriage and family counseling/therapy by the Council for Accreditation of Counseling and Related Educational Programs (CACREP), a specialized accrediting body recognized by the Council on Postsecondary Accreditation (COPA). The program's mission is to provide the state of California with highly competent master's-level clinicians who are academically prepared for the Marriage and Family therapist (MFT) license and counseling with individuals, couples, families, and groups in a multicultural society. The program fulfills the educational requirements for the state of California's Marriage and Family Therapist (MFT) license. Its mission is also to provide students who want to proceed on to doctoral programs in clinical or counseling psychology with sound research skills, thesis experience and clinical intervention training. Graduates find career opportunities in public social service agencies such as Mental Health and Departments of Social Services as well as in private non-profit and private practice counseling centers. Ten to twenty percent of graduates go on to doctoral programs in clinical or counseling psychology.

Special Facilities or Resources: Closely supervised on-campus practicum experiences leading to challenging internships in community agencies are the cornerstone of Cal Poly's preparation for the future clinician. The program runs a community counseling services clinic with three counseling offices and an observation room that provides direct viewing through one-way mirrors and remotely controlled video equipment. Closely supervised experience in Cal Poly's practicum clinic serving clients from the community provides trainees with the opportunity to develop skills and confidence before undertaking an internship.

Information for Students With Physical Disabilities: See the following Web site for more information: http://drc.calpoly.edu/.

Application Information:

Send to: Admissions Office, California Polytechnic State University, San Luis Obispo, CA 93407. Application available online. URL of online application: http://www.csumentor.edu/. Students are admitted in the Fall, application deadline February 15. *Fee:* $55.

California State University, Bakersfield

Department of Psychology
School of Humanities and Social Sciences
9001 Stockdale Highway
Bakersfield, CA 93311-1099
Telephone: (661) 664-2363
Fax: (661) 665-6955
E-mail: *kishida@csub.edu*
Web: *http://www.csub.edu/*

Department Information:

1970. Chairperson: Jess F. Deegan II. Number of Faculty: total–full-time 15, part-time 3; women–full-time 8, part-time 2; minority–full-time 8.

Programs and Degrees Offered:

Listed in the following order: Program area, degree type (T if terminal Master's), number awarded 7/03–6/04. General MA/MS (Master of Arts/Science) 1, marriage, family, and child MA/MS (Master of Arts/Science) (T) 13.

Student Applications/Admissions:

Student Applications

General MA/MS (Master of Arts/Science)—Applications 2004–2005, 4. Total applicants accepted 2004–2005, 3. Number enrolled (new admits only) 2004–2005 full-time, 2. Total enrolled 2004–2005 full-time, 4, part-time, 2. Openings 2005–2006, 10. The Median number of years required for completion of a degree are 2. The number of students enrolled full and part-time who were dismissed or voluntarily withdrew from this program area were 1. *Marriage, family, and child MA/MS (Master of Arts/Science)*—Applications 2004–2005, 40. Total applicants accepted 2004–2005, 26. Number enrolled (new admits only) 2004–2005 full-time, 9. Number enrolled (new admits only) 2004–2005 part-time, 15. Total enrolled 2004–2005 full-time, 9, part-time, 30. Openings 2005–2006, 20. The Median number of years required for completion of a degree are 3. The number of students enrolled full and part-time who were dismissed or voluntarily withdrew from this program area were 0.

Admissions Requirements:

Scores: Entries appear in this order: required test or GPA, minimum score (if required), median score of students entering in 2003–2004. Master's Programs: GRE-V no minimum stated, 500; GRE-Q no minimum stated, 500; GRE-V+Q no minimum stated, 1000; last 2 years GPA 3.00; psychology GPA 3.00. Those not meeting minima may petition for exceptional admission. For the MS in Counseling Psychology the GRE is NOT required.

Other Criteria: (importance of criteria rated low, medium, or high): work experience high, extracurricular activity low, clinically related public service high, GPA high, letters of recommendation high, interview low, statement of goals and objectives high. Above are admission criteria weightings for the MS in Counseling Psychology. Admission criteria weightings for the MA in Psychology: GRE Scores-high; research experience-high, work experience-medium, extracur. act-medium, clinical relations public service-low, GPA-high, letters of recommendations-high, invitations-none, statement of goals and objectives-high. For additional information on admission requirements, go to: MS in Couns. Psych see www.csub.edu/cpsy. MA in Psych see www.csub.edu/psychology/Grcourse.htm.

Student Characteristics: The following represents characteristics of students in 2004–2005 in all graduate psychology programs in the department: Female–full-time 10, part-time 34; Male–full-time 3, part-time 6; African American/Black–full-time 0, part-time 0; Hispanic/Latino(a)–full-time 5, part-time 7; Asian/Pacific Islander–full-time 2, part-time 2; American Indian/Alaska Native–full-time 0, part-time 0; Caucasian–full-time 10, part-time 10; students subject to the Americans With Disabilities Act–full-time 0, part-time 0.

Financial Information/Assistance:

Tuition for Full-Time Study: *Master's:* State residents: per academic year $3,190; Nonstate residents: per academic year $13,960. Tuition is subject to change. Tuition costs vary by program. See the following Web site for updates and changes in tuition costs: http://www.calstate.edu/PA/Info/fees.shtml.

Financial Assistance:

First Year Students: Fellowships and scholarships available for first-year. Apply by ASAP.

Advanced Students: Fellowships and scholarships available for advanced students.

Contact Information: Application and information available online at: http://www.csub.edu/FinAid/.

Internships/Practica: The MS program features practica in human communication, diagnostic interviewing, and individual, child, family, and group treatment in a university counselor training clinic. Two quarters of training in a modern, well-equipped on-campus training clinic is required. With approval, this is followed by two quarters of traineeship in one of a wide variety of community placements including substance abuse, dual diagnosis, perinatal intervention, child guidance, domestic violence, forensics, and college counseling.

Housing and Day Care: On-campus housing is available. See the following Web site for more information: Call (661) 664-3014. http://www.csub.edu/housing/ed_program.html. On-campus day care facilities are available. See the following Web site for more information: (661) 664-3165 http://www.csub.edu/childrens center/.

Employment of Department Graduates:

Master's Degree Graduates: Of those who graduated in the academic year 2003–2004, the following categories and numbers represent the post-graduate activities and employment of master's degree graduates: Enrolled in a psychology doctoral program (1),

enrolled in a post-doctoral residency/fellowship (n/a), employed in independent practice (n/a), employed in a professional position in a school system (1), employed in a government agency (professional services) (3), employed in a community mental health/counseling center (3), total from the above (master's) (8).

Doctoral Degree Graduates: Of those who graduated in the academic year 2003–2004, the following categories and numbers represent the post-graduate activities and employment of doctoral degree graduates: Enrolled in a psychology doctoral program (n/a), enrolled in a post-doctoral residency/fellowship (0), total from the above (doctoral) (0).

Additional Information:

Orientation, Objectives, and Emphasis of Department: We offer a 45-unit, 2 year MA program which offers training for either doctoral preparation or teaching psychology in community college settings. Students take courses in a broad range of areas of psychological research and participate in both research and teaching. Students must complete an empirical thesis at the end of their second year. The 90-unit MS is jointly sponsored by the Psychology Department and Advanced Educational Studies in the School of Education. Faculty teach principles and skills for the developing professional to work effectively and ethically with children, adolescents, adults, couples and families from diverse populations. The curriculum emphasizes a balance between content and application, theory and practice, and science and art. It is designed to meet the academic requirements established by the Board of Behavioral Sciences (BBS), Section 4980.37 of the Business and Professions Code for the California license in Marriage and Family Therapy (MFT). See website: www.csub.edu/cpsy.

Special Facilities or Resources: For MA students there are active programs in vision research, psycholinguistics, biopsychology, social psychology, and developmental psychology. On-site labs include a vision laboratory with extensive spatial frequency presentation and measuring equipment, an animal laboratory meeting stringent Federal standards, a speech and reading laboratory with recording equipment and computer stations for both voice activated and keypad responses, and observational labs. The department also maintains a file of psychological tests. For MS students three of the four full-time clinical faculty are licensed in the state of California. The university counselor training clinic is supervised by a licensed MFT.

Information for Students With Physical Disabilities: See the following Web site for more information: http://www.csub.edu/UnivServices/SSD/.

Application Information:

For MA: Send to Marianne Abramson, PhD, Psychology Graduate Coordinator, Psychology Department, California State University, Bakersfield, CA 93311-1099; for MS: Ms. Maria Delgado, Rm. 235, School of Education, California State University, Bakersfield, CA 93311-1099. URL of online application: http://www.csub.edu/Psychology/maapplication04.doc. Students are admitted in the Fall, application deadline April 15; Winter, application deadline October 15; Spring, application deadline February 15. For MA deadline is May 15 for subsequent Fall admission. *Fee:* $0. There is a separate application process for university admission. Contact: Admissions and Records, California State University Bakersfield, 9001 Stockdale Highway, Bakersfield, CA 93311-1099.

California State University, Chico
Psychology Department
College of Behavioral and Social Sciences
Chico, CA 95929-0234
Telephone: (530) 898-5147
Fax: (530) 898-4740
E-mail: *pspear@csuchico.edu/psy*
Web: *http://www.csuchico.edu*

Department Information:

1961. Chairperson: Paul Spear. Number of Faculty: total–full-time 17, part-time 19; women–full-time 7, part-time 7; minority–full-time 1, part-time 1.

Programs and Degrees Offered:

Listed in the following order: Program area, degree type (T if terminal Master's), number awarded 7/03–6/04. MA/PPS MA/MS (Master of Arts/Science) (T) 8, MA/Psychological Science MA/MS (Master of Arts/Science) (T), MS/MFT MA/MS (Master of Arts/Science) (T).

Student Applications/Admissions:

Student Applications

MA/PPS MA/MS *(Master of Arts/Science)*—Applications 2004–2005, 48. Total applicants accepted 2004–2005, 12. Total enrolled 2004–2005 full-time, 31. Openings 2005–2006, 12. The Median number of years required for completion of a degree are 3. MA/*Psychological Science MA/MS (Master of Arts/Science)*—Applications 2004–2005, 26. Total applicants accepted 2004–2005, 18. Total enrolled 2004–2005 full-time, 34. Openings 2005–2006, 15. MS/MFT MA/MS *(Master of Arts/Science)*—Applications 2004–2005, 48. Total applicants accepted 2004–2005, 26. Total enrolled 2004–2005 full-time, 45. Openings 2005–2006, 25.

Admissions Requirements:

Scores: Entries appear in this order: required test or GPA, minimum score (if required), median score of students entering in 2003–2004. Master's Programs: last 2 years GPA 2.75. Completion of either GRE V+Q+A or MAT. GRE-Subject (Psychology) not required but is considered if available. Last 60 units GPA - 2.75 minimum; Last 30 units GPA - 3.00 minimum

Other Criteria: (importance of criteria rated low, medium, or high): GRE/MAT scores medium, research experience low, work experience low, extracurricular activity low, clinically related public service medium, GPA high, letters of recommendation high, statement of goals and objectives high.

Student Characteristics: The following represents characteristics of students in 2004–2005 in all graduate psychology programs in the department: Female–full-time 71, part-time 0; Male–full-time 39, part-time 0; Caucasian–full-time 0, part-time 0.

Financial Information/Assistance:

Tuition for Full-Time Study: *Master's:* State residents: per academic year $2,454; Nonstate residents: per academic year $2,454.

Financial Assistance:

First Year Students: No information provided.
Advanced Students: No information provided.

Contact Information: No information provided.

Internships/Practica: For the MS degree: Individual and Child Counseling, Group Counseling, and Family Therapy practica are offered as well as post-practicum traineeships. School Psychology internships are required of all students seeking the School Psychology Credential.

Housing and Day Care: On-campus housing is available. See the following Web site for more information: www.csuchico.edu.hfs. Childcare: (530) 898-5865. On-campus day care facilities are available.

Employment of Department Graduates:

Master's Degree Graduates: Of those who graduated in the academic year 2003–2004, the following categories and numbers represent the post-graduate activities and employment of master's degree graduates: Enrolled in a post-doctoral residency/fellowship (n/a), employed in independent practice (n/a), employed in a professional position in a school system (14), employed in a community mental health/counseling center (15), total from the above (master's) (29).

Doctoral Degree Graduates: Of those who graduated in the academic year 2003–2004, the following categories and numbers represent the post-graduate activities and employment of doctoral degree graduates: Enrolled in a psychology doctoral program (n/a), total from the above (doctoral) (0).

Additional Information:

Orientation, Objectives, and Emphasis of Department: The Department offers three graduate programs. The Master of Science Degree prepares students to meet the educational requirements for Marriage and Family Therapy licensure in the State of California. It is designed to train competent professional counselors to work in mental health agencies and private practice. The curriculum is competency based and includes laboratory courses and practica, culminating in a family practicum and/or a post-practicum internship in a counseling agency. The Master of Arts Degree, Psychological Science Option, is designed to prepare students for doctoral work or teaching at the community college level. It offers extensive research experience, supervised teaching and advanced coursework in experimental psychology, and statistics. The Master of Arts Degree, Applied Psychology Option, is designed for students intending to enter our Pupil Personnel Services Credential program, which meets California requirements for a School Psychology Credential. The program has a prevention-oriented philosophy, is competency based, and provides practice in a variety of skills which enable school psychologists to serve all children. Trainees work in schools several days a week during 2 years of fieldwork.

Special Facilities or Resources: The Department of Psychology has modern, up-to-date laboratories, classrooms and seminar rooms, including laboratories in biopsychology, perception, learning, statistics, and a counseling training center.

Information for Students With Physical Disabilities: See the following Web site for more information: www.csuchico.edu/dss.

Application Information:
Send to: Graduate Coordinator California State University, Chico, Psychology Department, Chico, CA 95929-0234 www.csuchico.edu/

psy/. Application available online. Students are admitted in the Fall, application deadline March 1. *Fee:* $55.

California State University, Dominguez Hills
Department of Psychology/MA in Psychology Program - Clinical Emphasis
1000 East Victoria Street
Carson, CA 90747
Telephone: (310) 243-3427
Fax: (310) 516-3642
E-mail: *gradpsychology@csudh.edu*
Web: *http://www.csudh.edu*

Department Information:
1969. Coordinator, MA in Psychology Program: Karen I. Mason, PhD Number of Faculty: total–full-time 8, part-time 2; women–full-time 5; minority–full-time 4.

Programs and Degrees Offered:
Listed in the following order: Program area, degree type (T if terminal Master's), number awarded 7/03–6/04. Clinical MA/MS (Master of Arts/Science) (T) 18.

Student Applications/Admissions:

Student Applications

Clinical MA/MS (Master of Arts/Science)—Applications 2004–2005, 108. Total applicants accepted 2004–2005, 25. Total enrolled 2004–2005 full-time, 40, part-time, 10. Openings 2005–2006, 20. The Median number of years required for completion of a degree are 2. The number of students enrolled full and part-time who were dismissed or voluntarily withdrew from this program area were 0.

Admissions Requirements:

Scores: Entries appear in this order: required test or GPA, minimum score (if required), median score of students entering in 2003–2004. Master's Programs: last 2 years GPA 3.00, 3.5. *Other Criteria:* (importance of criteria rated low, medium, or high): GRE/MAT scores medium, research experience medium, work experience low, clinically related public service medium, GPA high, letters of recommendation high, interview low, statement of goals and objectives high. For additional information on admission requirements, go to: http://www.nbs.csudh.edu/psychology/maprogram.html.

Student Characteristics: The following represents characteristics of students in 2004–2005 in all graduate psychology programs in the department: Female–full-time 29, part-time 8; Male–full-time 11, part-time 2; African American/Black–full-time 5, part-time 3; Hispanic/Latino(a)–full-time 6, part-time 2; Asian/Pacific Islander–full-time 4, part-time 1; American Indian/Alaska Native–full-time 0, part-time 0; Caucasian–full-time 25, part-time 4.

Financial Information/Assistance:
Tuition for Full-Time Study: *Master's:* State residents: per academic year $3,257; Nonstate residents: $339 per credit hour. Tuition is subject to change.

Financial Assistance:

First Year Students: Fellowships and scholarships available for first-year. Average amount paid per academic year: $2,000. Apply by March/October.

Advanced Students: Teaching assistantships available for advanced students. Fellowships and scholarships available for advanced students. Average amount paid per academic year: $2,000. Apply by March/October.

Contact Information: Of all students currently enrolled full-time, 10% benefitted from one or more of the listed financial assistance programs.

Internships/Practica: The Master of Arts in Psychology offers you 550 supervised hours of practicum experience in a variety of settings.

Housing and Day Care: On-campus housing is available. See the following Web site for more information: http://www.csudh.edu. On-campus day care facilities are available.

Employment of Department Graduates:

Master's Degree Graduates: Of those who graduated in the academic year 2003–2004, the following categories and numbers represent the post-graduate activities and employment of master's degree graduates: Enrolled in a psychology doctoral program (5), enrolled in another graduate/professional program (0), enrolled in a post-doctoral residency/fellowship (n/a), employed in independent practice (n/a), employed in a government agency (professional services) (2), employed in a community mental health/counseling center (5), do not know (13), total from the above (master's) (25).

Doctoral Degree Graduates: Of those who graduated in the academic year 2003–2004, the following categories and numbers represent the post-graduate activities and employment of doctoral degree graduates: Enrolled in a psychology doctoral program (n/a), total from the above (doctoral) (0).

Additional Information:

Orientation, Objectives, and Emphasis of Department: The Clinical Psychology Master of Arts Program provides you with a solid academic background in clinical psychology as it is applied within a community mental health framework. This program prepares you for a career in counseling, teaching and research in community settings, which includes public or private agencies. Eighteen units of additional coursework prepare you for practice as a marriage and family therapist. Our graduates are successful in gaining admission to and graduating from the doctoral programs of their choice.

Special Facilities or Resources: Special resources include laboratory facilities, a course and experience in teaching psychology, computer facilities, and online PsychLIT retrieval system.

Application Information:

Send to: Department of Psychology, California State University, Dominguez Hills, 1000 E. Victoria Street, Carson, CA 90747. Application available online. URL of online application: http://www.nbs.csudh.edu/psychology/maapp.pdf. Students are admitted in the Fall, application deadline March 1. *Fee:* $55.

California State University, Fullerton

Department of Psychology
Humanities and Social Sciences
P.O. Box 6846
Fullerton, CA 92834-6846
Telephone: (714) 278-3589
Fax: (714) 278-7134
E-mail: *kkarlson@fullerton.edu*
Web: *http//Psych.fullerton.edu/*

Department Information:

1957. Chairperson: Daniel Kee. Number of Faculty: total–full-time 25, part-time 38; women–full-time 14, part-time 24; minority–full-time 5, part-time 9.

Programs and Degrees Offered:

Listed in the following order: Program area, degree type (T if terminal Master's), number awarded 7/03–6/04. Clinical Psychology MA/MS (Master of Arts/Science) (T) 6, Psychological Research MA/MS (Master of Arts/Science) (T) 9.

Student Applications/Admissions:

Student Applications

Clinical Psychology MA/MS (Master of Arts/Science)—Applications 2004–2005, 46. Total applicants accepted 2004–2005, 19. Total enrolled 2004–2005 full-time, 24, part-time, 8. Openings 2005–2006, 15. The Median number of years required for completion of a degree are 2. The number of students enrolled full and part-time who were dismissed or voluntarily withdrew from this program area were 2. *Psychological Research MA/MS (Master of Arts/Science)*—Applications 2004–2005, 35. Total applicants accepted 2004–2005, 14. Total enrolled 2004–2005 full-time, 21, part-time, 12. Openings 2005–2006, 13. The Median number of years required for completion of a degree are 3. The number of students enrolled full and part-time who were dismissed or voluntarily withdrew from this program area were 0.

Admissions Requirements:

Scores: Entries appear in this order: required test or GPA, minimum score (if required), median score of students entering in 2003–2004. Master's Programs: GRE-V 300, 506; GRE-Q 300, 616; GRE-Subject(Psych) 300, 620; overall undergraduate GPA 2.5, 3.2; last 2 years GPA 2.5, 3.4; psychology GPA 3.0, 3.4.

Other Criteria: (importance of criteria rated low, medium, or high): GRE/MAT scores high, research experience high, clinically related public service high, GPA high, letters of recommendation high, interview high, statement of goals and objectives high, There is not an interview required for the Master of Arts Program. For additional information on admission requirements, go to: http://psych.fullerton.edu.

Student Characteristics: The following represents characteristics of students in 2004–2005 in all graduate psychology programs in the department: Female–full-time 38, part-time 8; Male–full-time 17, part-time 3; African American/Black–full-time 2, part-time 0; Hispanic/Latino(a)–full-time 10, part-time 2; Asian/Pacific Islander–full-time 5, part-time 0; American Indian/Alaska Native–

full-time 0, part-time 0; Caucasian–full-time 36, part-time 9; Multi-ethnic–full-time 2, part-time 0.

Financial Information/Assistance:

Tuition for Full-Time Study: *Master's:* State residents: per academic year $1,600; Nonstate residents: per academic year $4,690. Tuition is subject to change. See the following Web site for updates and changes in tuition costs: http://www.fullerton.edu/.

Financial Assistance:

First Year Students: No information provided.

Advanced Students: No information provided.

Contact Information: Of all students currently enrolled full-time, 0% benefitted from one or more of the listed financial assistance programs.

Internships/Practica: A majority of the internships are done in agencies which do family therapy and substance abuse prevention and training. Most internships have live and videotape supervision. Students have done internships in policy psychology, county clinics, and inpatient settings as well. Most agencies combine clinical and community work and serve low income and minority populations.

Housing and Day Care: On-campus housing is available. Housing Office (714) 278-2168. On-campus day care facilities are available. Children's Center (714) 278-2961.

Employment of Department Graduates:

Master's Degree Graduates: Of those who graduated in the academic year 2003–2004, the following categories and numbers represent the post-graduate activities and employment of master's degree graduates: Enrolled in a psychology doctoral program (3), enrolled in a post-doctoral residency/fellowship (n/a), employed in independent practice (n/a), employed in an academic position at a university (4), employed in an academic position at a 2-year/4-year college (3), employed in other positions at a higher education institution (1), employed in business or industry (research/consulting) (1), employed in a community mental health/counseling center (11), total from the above (master's) (23).

Doctoral Degree Graduates: Of those who graduated in the academic year 2003–2004, the following categories and numbers represent the post-graduate activities and employment of doctoral degree graduates: Enrolled in a psychology doctoral program (n/a), total from the above (doctoral) (0).

Additional Information:

Orientation, Objectives, and Emphasis of Department: The MA program provides advanced coursework and research training in core areas of psychology. Completion of the MA can facilitate application to PhD programs in psychology and provides skills important to careers in education, the health professions, and industry. The MS program in clinical psychology is intended to prepare students for work in a variety of mental health settings, and the program contains coursework relevant for the MFT license in California. The program is also designed to prepare students for PhD work in both academic and professional schools of clinical psychology.

Special Facilities or Resources: The department has laboratories for research in cognitive psychology, conditioning, perception, biopsychology, social psychology, psychological testing, and de-velopmental psychology. The department also has extensive computer facilities.

Application Information:

Send to: Department Application: Graduate Office, Department of Psychology, California State Fullerton, P.O. Box 6846, Fullerton, CA 92834-6846. CSU, Fullerton application only available on line at: http://www.fullerton.edu. Students are admitted in the Fall, application deadline March 1. *Fee:* $55. Application Fee for University Application. There is no fee for the Department of Psychology Application. If you cannot afford the application fee, you may request a fee waiver. The fee waiver process is built in CSU Mentor (on line application), so you will not need to file a separate Request for an Application Fee Waiver. In some cases where the online application is unable to determine your eligibility to apply for a fee waiver, you will have to submit the request to the campus. The campus will inform you if you do not qualify for the waiver. Only California residents are eligible.

California State University, Long Beach

Department of Psychology
1250 Bellflower Boulevard
Long Beach, CA 90840-0901
Telephone: (562) 985-5000
E-mail: *psygrad@csulb.edu*
Web: *http://www.csulb.edu/~psych/*

Department Information:

1949. Chairperson: Kenneth F. Green. Number of Faculty: total–full-time 34, part-time 27; women full-time 14, part-time 15; minority–full-time 5.

Programs and Degrees Offered:

Listed in the following order: Program area, degree type (T if terminal Master's), number awarded 7/03–6/04. Research MA/MS (Master of Arts/Science) (T) 4, Industrial/Organizational MA/MS (Master of Arts/Science) (T) 4, Human Factors MA/MS (Master of Arts/Science) (T) 0.

Student Applications/Admissions:

Student Applications

Research MA/MS (Master of Arts/Science)—Applications 2004–2005, 74. Total applicants accepted 2004–2005, 42. Number enrolled (new admits only) 2004–2005 full-time, 25. Total enrolled 2004–2005 full-time, 28, part-time, 15. Openings 2005–2006, 45. The Median number of years required for completion of a degree are 5.5. *Industrial/Organizational MA/MS (Master of Arts/Science)*—Applications 2004–2005, 69. Total applicants accepted 2004–2005, 16. Number enrolled (new admits only) 2004–2005 full-time, 11. Total enrolled 2004–2005 full-time, 10, part-time, 13. Openings 2005–2006, 16. The Median number of years required for completion of a degree are 3.5. *Human Factors MA/MS (Master of Arts/Science)*—Total applicants accepted 2004–2005, 0. Number enrolled (new admits only) 2004–2005 full-time, 0. Total enrolled 2004–2005 full-time, 2. Openings 2005–2006, 10. The Median number of years required for completion of a degree are 2.

Admissions Requirements:

Scores: Entries appear in this order: required test or GPA, minimum score (if required), median score of students entering in 2003–2004. Master's Programs: GRE-V no minimum stated, 494; GRE-Q no minimum stated, 575; GRE-V+Q no minimum stated, 1069; last 2 years GPA no minimum stated, 3.55; psychology GPA no minimum stated, 3.50. GRE-Subject (Psychology) not required.

Other Criteria: (importance of criteria rated low, medium, or high): GRE/MAT scores high, research experience medium, work experience low, extracurricular activity low, GPA high, letters of recommendation high, statement of goals and objectives high. For additional information on admission requirements, go to: http://www.csulb.edu/~psych/gradprgm/prostud/gradapp.html.

Student Characteristics: The following represents characteristics of students in 2004–2005 in all graduate psychology programs in the department: Female–full-time 32, part-time 18; Male–full-time 8, part-time 10; African American/Black–full-time 2, part-time 3; Hispanic/Latino(a)–full-time 7, part-time 6; Asian/Pacific Islander–full-time 5, part-time 6; American Indian/Alaska Native–full-time 0, part-time 0; Caucasian–full-time 26, part-time 13; students subject to the Americans With Disabilities Act–full-time 2, part-time 0.

Financial Information/Assistance:

Tuition for Full-Time Study: *Master's:* State residents: per academic year $3,144; Nonstate residents: per academic year $3,144, $339 per credit hour. Tuition is subject to change. See the following Web site for updates and changes in tuition costs: http://www.csulb.edu/depts/enrollment/html/fees_and_charges.html.

Financial Assistance:

First Year Students: Research assistantships available for first-year. Average amount paid per academic year: $5,000. Average number of hours worked per week: 10. Apply by April 15. Fellowships and scholarships available for first-year. Average amount paid per academic year: $2,500. Apply by March 1.

Advanced Students: Research assistantships available for advanced students. Average amount paid per academic year: $5,000. Average number of hours worked per week: 10. Apply by April 15. Fellowships and scholarships available for advanced students. Average amount paid per academic year: $2,500. Apply by March 1.

Contact Information: Of all students currently enrolled full-time, 29% benefitted from one or more of the listed financial assistance programs. Application and information available online at: http://www.csulb.edu/depts/enrollment/html/financial_aid.html.

Internships/Practica: Graduate assistantship positions provide teaching, computer, and internship experiences to selected students in all the master's programs. Applications for graduate assistantships are available through the Graduate Office and are included in the application packet. Graduate assistantship assignments are based upon the pairing of each applicant's academic background, interests, and experience with current department needs. Specific assignments are geared toward providing educational experiences most appropriate for students in each program. Appointments are for ten hours per week. Available teaching assignments include assistance to the introductory and intermediate statistics, psychological assessment, critical thinking, program evaluation, computer applications, and research methods courses. In addition to the aforementioned paid departmental positions, volunteer and/or externally funded research positions can be arranged with individual faculty members. Such research opportunities are often available in the physiological, cognition, language, human factors, language acquisition, and social psychology laboratories. Various internships in outside industrial and organizational settings are options for second-year industrial/organizational MA students.

Housing and Day Care: On-campus housing is available. See the following Web site for more information: http://housing.csulb.edu/. On-campus day care facilities are available. See the following Web site for more information: http://www.csulb.edu/org/asi/cdc/index.html.

Employment of Department Graduates:

Master's Degree Graduates: Of those who graduated in the academic year 2003–2004, the following categories and numbers represent the post-graduate activities and employment of master's degree graduates: Enrolled in a post-doctoral residency/fellowship (n/a), employed in independent practice (n/a), total from the above (master's) (0).

Doctoral Degree Graduates: Of those who graduated in the academic year 2003–2004, the following categories and numbers represent the post-graduate activities and employment of doctoral degree graduates: Enrolled in a psychology doctoral program (n/a), total from the above (doctoral) (0).

Additional Information:

Orientation, Objectives, and Emphasis of Department: California State University Long Beach has three master's programs in psychology. The new Master of Science in Human Factors prepares students to apply knowledge of psychology to the design of jobs, information systems, consumer products, workplaces and equipment in order to improve user performance, safety and comfort. Students acquire a background in the core areas of experimental psychology, research design and methodology, human factors, computer applications and applied research methods. The Master of Arts, Research Option (MA-R) prepares students for doctoral work in any psychology field or for master's-level research or teaching positions. Core seminars include cognition, learning, physiological and sensory psychology, social, personality, and developmental psychology, and quantitative methods. MA-R graduates who apply to doctoral programs have high acceptance rates with financial support. The Master of Arts, Industrial and Organizational option (MAIO) offers preparation for careers for which a background in industrial/organizational psychology is essential. These fields include personnel, organizational development, industrial relations, employee training, and marketing research.

Special Facilities or Resources: The psychology building has extensive facilities available without charge. Computer facilities, with microcomputers and mainframe stations, include many current software packages. The physiological research lab, with a staffed animal compound, is used to study conditioned analgesia and neurotransmission. For research in stress and coping, interpersonal relations, social influence, gender psychology, and the biopsychology of mood, there are many research suites and a test materials center. These facilities, located in the psychology building, are for research and training in interviewing and case studies, forensic psychology, program and treatment evaluation, assessment of social support and family systems, self-management, and intervention strategies for hard-to-reach populations. Computer facilities are central to research in decision analysis, human-computer interface, statistical theory, assessment, and computer-aided instruction. Research in child temperament and hyperactivity, language acquisition, and cognition in older adults are done in special labs. A computerized human-factors lab is used to study audition and vision. Our diversified facilities also accommodate a large AIDS-education project, research in managing diversity in the workplace, and other topics in industrial/organizational psychology. Outstanding CSULB Library facilities are available.

Information for Students With Physical Disabilities: See the following Web site for more information: http://www.csulb.edu/depts/dss/.

Application Information:
Send to: Department application: Psychology Graduate Office, 1250 Bellflower Boulevard, Long Beach, CA 90840-0901. Must also apply to the university by March 1: www.csumentor.edu. Application available online. URL of online application: www.csulb.edu/~psych/gradprgm/prostud/gradapp.html. Students are admitted in the Fall, application deadline March 1; Spring, application deadline November 1. Spring 2006 admission deadline for MAR & MSHF: November 1, 2005 Fall 2006 admission deadline for MAIO: February 14, 2006, MAR & MSHF: March 1, 2006. Department application available online at: http://www.csulb.edu/~psych/gradprgm/prostud/gradapp.html or by writing or emailing request. *Fee:* $55. Fee for University application only.

California State University, Northridge
Department of Psychology
Social and Behavioral Sciences
18111 Nordhoff Street
Northridge, CA 91330-8255
Telephone: (818) 677-2827
Fax: (818) 677-2829
E-mail: *paul.skolnick@csun.edu*
Web: *http://www.csun.edu/psychology*

Department Information:
1958. Chair: Paul Skolnick. Number of Faculty: total–full-time 26, part-time 30; women–full-time 14, part-time 10; minority–full-time 5, part-time 10; faculty subject to the Americans With Disabilities Act 2.

Programs and Degrees Offered:
Listed in the following order: Program area, degree type (T if terminal Master's), number awarded 7/03–6/04. Clinical Psychology MA/MS (Master of Arts/Science) 7, General Psychology MA/MS (Master of Arts/Science) 4, Human Factors MA/MS (Master of Arts/Science) (T) 7.

Student Applications/Admissions:
Student Applications
Clinical Psychology MA/MS (Master of Arts/Science)—Applications 2004–2005, 65. Total applicants accepted 2004–2005, 15. Number enrolled (new admits only) 2004–2005 full-time, 14. Number enrolled (new admits only) 2004–2005 part-time,

0. Total enrolled 2004–2005 full-time, 28, part-time, 2. Openings 2005–2006, 12. The Median number of years required for completion of a degree are 2. The number of students enrolled full and part-time who were dismissed or voluntarily withdrew from this program area were 0. *General Psychology MA/MS (Master of Arts/Science)*—Applications 2004–2005, 25. Total applicants accepted 2004–2005, 13. Number enrolled (new admits only) 2004–2005 full-time, 8. Number enrolled (new admits only) 2004–2005 part-time, 0. Openings 2005–2006, 12. The Median number of years required for completion of a degree are 2. The number of students enrolled full and part-time who were dismissed or voluntarily withdrew from this program area were 0. *Human Factors MA/MS (Master of Arts/Science)*—Applications 2004–2005, 22. Total applicants accepted 2004–2005, 17. Number enrolled (new admits only) 2004–2005 full-time, 12. Number enrolled (new admits only) 2004–2005 part-time, 0. Openings 2005–2006, 12. The Median number of years required for completion of a degree are 2. The number of students enrolled full and part-time who were dismissed or voluntarily withdrew from this program area were 0.

Admissions Requirements:
Scores: Entries appear in this order: required test or GPA, minimum score (if required), median score of students entering in 2003–2004. Master's Programs: GRE-V 500, 500; GRE-Q 540, 540; GRE-V+Q no minimum stated; GRE-Analytical no minimum stated; GRE-Subject(Psych) 540, 540; overall undergraduate GPA 3.0, 3.5; last 2 years GPA 3.0, 3.5; psychology GPA 3.0, 3.5. GRE-Subject (Psychology) required for General Experimental Psychology and Clinical options.
Other Criteria: (importance of criteria rated low, medium, or high): GRE/MAT scores low, research experience high, work experience medium, extracurricular activity medium, clinically related public service high, GPA medium, letters of recommendation high, interview low, statement of goals and objectives high. For additional information on admission requirements, go to: www.csun.edu/psychology.

Student Characteristics: The following represents characteristics of students in 2004–2005 in all graduate psychology programs in the department: Female–full-time 41, part-time 0; Male–full-time 25, part-time 0; African American/Black–full-time 0, part-time 0; Hispanic/Latino(a)–full-time 0, part-time 0; Asian/Pacific Islander–full-time 0, part-time 0; American Indian/Alaska Native–full-time 0, part-time 0; Caucasian–full-time 0, part-time 0.

Financial Information/Assistance:
Tuition for Full-Time Study: *Master's:* State residents: per academic year $1,632; Nonstate residents: per academic year $1,632, $339 per credit hour. Tuition is subject to change. See the following Web site for updates and changes in tuition costs: http://www-admn.csun.edu/ucs/tuition.html.

Financial Assistance:
First Year Students: No information provided.
Advanced Students: No information provided.
Contact Information: Application and information available online at: www.csun.edu.

Internships/Practica: Graduate students in applied fields have available an array of practicum experiences in the area. Direct clinical practicum experience is required of the Clinical students, who receive supervised training in three campus clinics specializing in Parent Child Interaction Training, Child and Adolescent Diagnostic Assessment, and Cognitive–Behavioral Psychotherapy. In addition, clinical internships are available in many community sites including the University Counseling Services and local mental health care facilities. Human Factors students are connected with research and applications positions in the region. General Experimental students work with departmental faculty as well as with those at neighboring universities.

Housing and Day Care: On-campus housing is available. See the following Web site for more information: Contact the CSUN Housing Office at (818) 677-2160 or go to their Web site at http://housing.csun.edu. On-campus day care facilities are available.

Employment of Department Graduates:

Master's Degree Graduates: Of those who graduated in the academic year 2003–2004, the following categories and numbers represent the post-graduate activities and employment of master's degree graduates: Enrolled in a post-doctoral residency/fellowship (n/a), employed in independent practice (n/a), total from the above (master's) (0).

Doctoral Degree Graduates: Of those who graduated in the academic year 2003–2004, the following categories and numbers represent the post-graduate activities and employment of doctoral degree graduates: Enrolled in a psychology doctoral program (n/a), total from the above (doctoral) (0).

Additional Information:

Orientation, Objectives, and Emphasis of Department: The Department of Psychology has, as a primary goal, the assurance that students receive a strong theoretical foundation as well as rigorous methodological and statistical coursework. In addition, all students must complete a project or a thesis in order to display their knowledge of their content area and their methodological sophistication. The applied Human Factors program emphasizes both job-related skills and general skills should students desire to continue their education at the doctoral level (and many do). The General Experimental and Clinical programs emphasize the basic research and content knowledge required to enhance students' opportunities for entry into doctoral programs.

Special Facilities or Resources: Some professors have federal or private grants that employ graduate students as research assistants. In addition, we have laboratories in Physiological Psychology (Neuro Scan), computer applications for Cognitive and Human Factors Psychology, multiple child care sites for observation of children, and extensive research space.

Information for Students With Physical Disabilities: See the following Web site for more information: http://www.csun.edu/cod/index.htm.

Application Information:

Send to: Psychology Graduate Office, California State University Northridge, 18111 Nordhoff Street, Northridge, CA 91330-8255. Students are admitted in the Fall, application deadline February 15; Spring, application deadline November 1. The Clinical Psychology Program accepts Fall applications only. General-Experimental and Human Factors will accept Spring and Fall applications, space permitting. *Fee:* $55. Contact Admissions and Records Office for details (818) 677-3700.

California State University, Sacramento
Department of Psychology
6000 J Street
Sacramento, CA 95819-6007
Telephone: (916) 278-6254
Fax: (916) 278-6820
E-mail: *youngl@csus.edu*
Web: *http://www.csus.edu/psyc/programs/graduate*

Department Information:

1947. Chairperson: Arnold Golub. Number of Faculty: total–full-time 23, part-time 12; women–full-time 11, part-time 8; minority–full-time 3.

Programs and Degrees Offered:

Listed in the following order: Program area, degree type (T if terminal Master's), number awarded 7/03–6/04. Counseling-Psychology MA/MS (Master of Arts/Science) (T), doctoral preparation MA/MS (Master of Arts/Science) (T), industrial/organizational MA/MS (Master of Arts/Science) (T), behavior analysis MA/MS (Master of Arts/Science) (T), general master's MA/MS (Master of Arts/Science) (T).

Student Applications/Admissions:

Student Applications

Counseling-Psychology MA/MS (Master of Arts/Science)—Total applicants accepted 2004–2005, 15. The Median number of years required for completion of a degree are 4. *Doctoral preparation MA/MS (Master of Arts/Science)*—Total applicants accepted 2004–2005, 14. The Median number of years required for completion of a degree are 3. *Industrial/organizational MA/MS (Master of Arts/Science)*—Total applicants accepted 2004–2005, 8. The Median number of years required for completion of a degree are 3.

Admissions Requirements:

Scores: Entries appear in this order: required test or GPA, minimum score (if required), median score of students entering in 2003–2004. Master's Programs: GRE-V no minimum stated, 580; GRE-Q no minimum stated, 580; GRE-Subject(Psych) no minimum stated, 580.

Other Criteria: (importance of criteria rated low, medium, or high): GRE/MAT scores high, GPA high, letters of recommendation high. For additional information on admission requirements, go to: www.csus.edu/psyc/programs/graduate.

Student Characteristics: The following represents characteristics of students in 2004–2005 in all graduate psychology programs in the department: Female–full-time 9, part-time 21; Male–full-time 1, part-time 4; African American/Black–full-time 3, part-time 0; Hispanic/Latino(a)–full-time 3, part-time 0; Asian/Pacific Islander–full-time 10, part-time 0; American Indian/Alaska Native–full-time 0, part-time 0; Caucasian–full-time 0, part-time 0; students subject to the Americans With Disabilities Act–full-time 1, part-time 0.

Financial Information/Assistance:

Financial Assistance:

First Year Students: No information provided.

Advanced Students: Teaching assistantships available for advanced students. Fellowships and scholarships available for advanced students.

Contact Information: Of all students currently enrolled full-time, 10% benefitted from one or more of the listed financial assistance programs.

Internships/Practica: Students following either the Industrial-Organizational (I/O) or the Counseling Psychology programs will gain supervised on-site experience. I/O students typically enroll for several semesters of internship supervised by one of our faculty members. Opportunities are available in public sector organizations (e.g., state, county, and city personnel departments; public utilities) as well as private sector consulting firms, small businesses, and large corporations. Counseling Psychology students must also enroll for additional fieldwork in a community mental health setting with an on-site supervisor. Students may choose from more than a hundred sites in the Sacramento metropolitan area. These community sites must enter into a formal arrangement with the department, and the student's supervision hours must be officially logged.

Housing and Day Care: On-campus housing is available. See the following Web site for more information: www.csus.edu. On-campus day care facilities are available.

Employment of Department Graduates:

Master's Degree Graduates: Of those who graduated in the academic year 2003–2004, the following categories and numbers represent the post-graduate activities and employment of master's degree graduates: Enrolled in a psychology doctoral program (3), enrolled in a post-doctoral residency/fellowship (n/a), employed in independent practice (n/a), employed in business or industry (research/consulting) (2), employed in a government agency (research) (3), employed in a government agency (professional services) (4), employed in a community mental health/counseling center (3), total from the above (master's) (15).

Doctoral Degree Graduates: Of those who graduated in the academic year 2003–2004, the following categories and numbers represent the post-graduate activities and employment of doctoral degree graduates: Enrolled in a psychology doctoral program (n/a), total from the above (doctoral) (0).

Additional Information:

Orientation, Objectives, and Emphasis of Department: Our major programs are Doctoral Preparation, Industrial-Organizational (I/O), and Counseling Psychology. Doctoral preparation students take a strong research methods and quantitative course sequence in addition to content coursework in their interest area. They also engage in research during most of their program, and are encouraged to become teaching assistants. Our I/O program has been designed to meet the competencies specified by SIOP and involved both classroom and fieldwork experience. Students take both general survey and current literature I/O courses in addition to their research, statistics, and measurement/testing courses, and are also expected to gain job experience as an intern. The Counseling Psychology program meets the state licensing requirements for Marriage and Family Therapy; students are exposed to a variety of therapeutic orientations and must participate in multiple practicum courses. In addition, graduate students can supplement their program with a Teaching of Psychology mini-program in which they enroll in a formal teaching course and are then eligible to team teach an introductory psychology course in a subsequent semester. Those oriented toward a teaching career in a community college are advised to supplement their main course of study with this mini-program. We also have a program in Behavior Analysis which partially fulfills the requirements to become a Board Certified Behavior Analyst.

Special Facilities or Resources: The department occupies much of a relatively large building. Extensive facilities for human and animal research are available. We have a modern surgery room, animal colony, small group rooms with capabilities for audiovisual monitoring and recording, and a perception lab. A multi-room counseling suite within the building also has audiovisual capabilities; students enrolled in our practicum course provide services in this suite (under supervision) to clients from the community. One room in the building is maintained by the computer center; it contains thirty workstations.

Information for Students With Physical Disabilities: See the following Web site for more information: www.csus.edu.

Application Information:
Send to: Graduate Coordinator, Psychology Department, CSU, Sacramento, 6000 J Street, Sacramento, CA 95819-6007. Application available online: www.csus.edu/psyc/programs/graduate. Students are admitted in the Fall, application deadline March 1; Spring, application deadline November 1. *Fee:* $0.

California State University, San Bernardino
Department of Psychology
College of Social and Behavioral Sciences
5500 University Parkway
San Bernardino, CA 92407-2397
Telephone: (909) 880-5570
Fax: (909) 880-7003
E-mail: *lvanloon@csusb.edu*
Web: *http://psychology.csusb.edu//*

Department Information:
1967. Chairperson: Dr. Joanna Worthley. Number of Faculty: total–full-time 32, part-time 26; women–full-time 15, part-time 17; minority–full-time 7, part-time 5.

Programs and Degrees Offered:
Listed in the following order: Program area, degree type (T if terminal Master's), number awarded 7/03–6/04. Clinical/counseling MA/MS (Master of Arts/Science) (T) 7, general experimental MA/MS (Master of Arts/Science) (T) 3, industrial/organizational MA/MS (Master of Arts/Science) (T) 6, Child Development MA/MS (Master of Arts/Science) (T) 10.

Student Applications/Admissions:
Student Applications
Clinical/counseling MA/MS (Master of Arts/Science)—Applications 2004–2005, 38. Total applicants accepted 2004–2005, 8. Number enrolled (new admits only) 2004–2005 full-time, 11. Number enrolled (new admits only) 2004–2005 part-time, 0. Total enrolled 2004–2005 full-time, 18, part-time, 2. Open-

ings 2005–2006, 12. The Median number of years required for completion of a degree are 2. The number of students enrolled full and part-time who were dismissed or voluntarily withdrew from this program area were 0. *General experimental MA/MS (Master of Arts/Science)*—Applications 2004–2005, 47. Total applicants accepted 2004–2005, 28. Total enrolled 2004–2005 full-time, 19, part-time, 12. Openings 2005–2006, 15. The Median number of years required for completion of a degree are 3. The number of students enrolled full and part-time who were dismissed or voluntarily withdrew from this program area were 2. *Industrial/organizational MA/MS (Master of Arts/Science)*—Applications 2004–2005, 47. Total applicants accepted 2004–2005, 17. Total enrolled 2004–2005 full-time, 20, part-time, 5. Openings 2005–2006, 15. The Median number of years required for completion of a degree are 3. The number of students enrolled full and part-time who were dismissed or voluntarily withdrew from this program area were 1. *Child Development MA/MS (Master of Arts/Science)*—Applications 2004–2005, 22. Total applicants accepted 2004–2005, 10. Number enrolled (new admits only) 2004–2005 full-time, 10. Total enrolled 2004–2005 full-time, 14, part-time, 20. Openings 2005–2006, 15. The Median number of years required for completion of a degree are 3. The number of students enrolled full and part-time who were dismissed or voluntarily withdrew from this program area were 6.

Admissions Requirements:

Scores: Entries appear in this order: required test or GPA, minimum score (if required), median score of students entering in 2003–2004. Master's Programs: GRE-Subject(Psych) no minimum stated; overall undergraduate GPA 3.00; psychology GPA 3.00. Only the general experimental (GE) MA program requires GRE scores.

Other Criteria: (importance of criteria rated low, medium, or high): research experience high, work experience medium, extracurricular activity medium, clinically related public service medium, GPA high, letters of recommendation high, interview high, statement of goals and objectives high. Research experience is medium for clinical and I/O. Clinically related public service is high for clinical and medium for GE. There are no interviews for Child Development or GE. For additional information on admission requirements, go to: http://psychology.csusb.edu//.

Student Characteristics: The following represents characteristics of students in 2004–2005 in all graduate psychology programs in the department: Female–full-time 51, part-time 31; Male–full-time 20, part-time 8; African American/Black–full-time 4, part-time 0; Hispanic/Latino(a)–full-time 17, part-time 10; Asian/Pacific Islander–full-time 3, part-time 4; American Indian/Alaska Native–full-time 0, part-time 1; Caucasian–full-time 37, part-time 20; Multi-ethnic–full-time 0, part-time 0; students subject to the Americans With Disabilities Act–full-time 2, part-time 3.

Financial Information/Assistance:

Tuition for Full-Time Study: *Master's:* State residents: per academic year $3,490; Nonstate residents: $226 per credit hour. Tuition is subject to change. See the following Web site for updates and changes in tuition costs: www.csusb.edu.

Financial Assistance:

First Year Students: No information provided.

Advanced Students: Teaching assistantships available for advanced students. Average amount paid per academic year: $1,367. Average number of hours worked per week: 5. Apply by May 30.

Contact Information: Of all students currently enrolled full-time, 15% benefitted from one or more of the listed financial assistance programs.

Internships/Practica: Off campus internships are available for Clinical students during their second year and for Industrial/Organizational students at the end of their first year.

Housing and Day Care: On-campus housing is available. See the following Web site for more information: http://housing.csusb.edu/. On-campus day care facilities are available. See the following Web site for more information: Children's Center, Barbara Kirby Director, (909) 880-5928, http://www.csusb.edu/StdAff/ChldCtr/default.html Infant and Toddler Center Genevieve Arca, Site Director (909) 990-5661, garca@csusb.edu, (909) 880-5661.

Employment of Department Graduates:

Master's Degree Graduates: Of those who graduated in the academic year 2003–2004, the following categories and numbers represent the post-graduate activities and employment of master's degree graduates: Enrolled in a post-doctoral residency/fellowship (n/a), employed in independent practice (n/a), total from the above (master's) (0).

Doctoral Degree Graduates: Of those who graduated in the academic year 2003–2004, the following categories and numbers represent the post-graduate activities and employment of doctoral degree graduates: Enrolled in a psychology doctoral program (n/a), total from the above (doctoral) (0).

Additional Information:

Orientation, Objectives, and Emphasis of Department: The objective of the master of arts in psychology is to provide a program of study with courses selected from a variety of basic areas in psychology. The general-experimental psychology concentration provides a broad background suitable for entry into doctoral programs and employment requiring a master of arts in psychology. The Child Development program provides an in-depth background in child growth and development suitable for students planning on pursuing (or currently in) careers dealing with children or families or for pursuing a doctoral degree. The areas of concentration for the master of science degree program are clinical/counseling psychology or industrial/organizational psychology. The principal objective of the clinical/counseling program is to provide students with practical skills in counseling, through supervised training and experience and an understanding of relevant subject matter, knowledge, and research methodology. The program is designed to meet the basic requirements of California Assembly Bill 3657 (Section 4980.37), which specifies educational qualifications for licensure as marriage, family, and child counselors. The principal objective of the industrial/organizational program is to provide students with the skills to apply the principles and methods of psychology with organizations, public and private, and to settings where people are engaged in work. Although each of these concentrations differs in emphasis, both will prepare students for doctoral programs and career objectives such as teaching in a community college.

Special Facilities or Resources: Facilities include a community counseling center, physiological research laboratory, child development research institute and lab, infant and toddler center, small animal research laboratory, and perception laboratory. The department also has its own biofeedback laboratory, computerized cognitive laboratory, a well-equipped neuropharmacology laboratory, access to on-site child care center, and numerous agreements with community agencies.

Information for Students With Physical Disabilities: lflynn@c-susb.edu.

Application Information:
Send to: Luci Van Loon, Administrative Support Coordinator II, Department of Psychology, SBS-425, 5500 University Parkway, San Bernardino, CA 92407-2397. Application available online. Students are admitted in the Fall, application deadline, see below; Spring, application deadline March 1. Spring deadline: MA General Experimental March 1. Fall deadlines: MA General Experimental April 1; MS Clinical/Counseling February 1; MA Child Development March 1; MS Indus/Org March 1. *Fee:* $55.

California State University, San Marcos
Psychology
San Marcos, CA 92096
Telephone: (760) 750-4102
Fax: (760) 750-3418
E-mail: *mkidd@csusm.edu*
Web: *www.csusm.edu/psychology/*

Department Information:
1989. Chairperson: Marie Thomas. Number of Faculty: total–full-time 13, part-time 12; women–full-time 10, part-time 10; minority–full-time 1, part-time 1.

Programs and Degrees Offered:
Listed in the following order: Program area, degree type (T if terminal Master's), number awarded 7/03–6/04. General experimental MA/MS (Master of Arts/Science) (T) 9.

Student Applications/Admissions:
Student Applications

General experimental MA/MS (Master of Arts/Science)—Applications 2004–2005, 20. Total applicants accepted 2004–2005, 10. Total enrolled 2004–2005 full-time, 19, part-time, 8. Openings 2005–2006, 10. The Median number of years required for completion of a degree are 4. The number of students enrolled full and part-time who were dismissed or voluntarily withdrew from this program area were 4.

Admissions Requirements:
Scores: Entries appear in this order: required test or GPA, minimum score (if required), median score of students entering in 2003–2004. Master's Programs: GRE-V no minimum stated, 470; GRE-Q no minimum stated, 530; GRE-Analytical no minimum stated; overall undergraduate GPA 3.0, 3.5; last 2 years GPA 3.0; psychology GPA 3.0. GRE-Subject (Psychology) is recommended but not required.
Other Criteria: (importance of criteria rated low, medium, or high): GRE/MAT scores medium, research experience high,

work experience low, extracurricular activity low, clinically related public service low, GPA high, letters of recommendation high, statement of goals and objectives high. In the statement of goals and objectives, students must identify one or more faculty members in our department with whom they would like to work. We closely match students with faculty research interests. For additional information on admission requirements, go to: www.csusm.edu/psychology/.

Student Characteristics: The following represents characteristics of students in 2004–2005 in all graduate psychology programs in the department: Female–full-time 17, part-time 6; Male–full-time 2, part-time 2; African American/Black–full-time 0, part-time 0; Hispanic/Latino(a)–full-time 2, part-time 3; Asian/Pacific Islander–full-time 0, part-time 0; American Indian/Alaska Native–full-time 0, part-time 0; Caucasian–full-time 17, part-time 5; Multi-ethnic–full-time 0, part-time 0; students subject to the Americans With Disabilities Act–full-time 0, part-time 0.

Financial Information/Assistance:
Tuition for Full-Time Study: *Master's:* State residents: per academic year $2,624; Nonstate residents: per academic year $5,162. Tuition is subject to change. See the following Web site for updates and changes in tuition costs: www.csusm.edu.

Financial Assistance:
First Year Students: Teaching assistantships available for first-year. Average amount paid per academic year: $2,000. Average number of hours worked per week: 5. Apply by March 15. Research assistantships available for first-year. Apply by March 15. Fellowships and scholarships available for first-year. Apply by March 15. Tuition remission given: partial.
Advanced Students: Teaching assistantships available for advanced students. Average amount paid per academic year: $2,000. Apply by varies. Research assistantships available for advanced students. Apply by varies. Fellowships and scholarships available for advanced students. Apply by varies. Tuition remission given: partial.
Contact Information: Of all students currently enrolled full-time, 80% benefitted from one or more of the listed financial assistance programs. Application and information available online at: www.csusm.edu/psychology/ and www.csumentor.edu.

Internships/Practica: Teaching of Psychology (PSYC 680) is designed for students who hope someday to teach at either a community college or a 4-year institution. Students learn pedagogical techniques associated with the discipline of psychology and will become eligible for teaching assignments in the university.

Housing and Day Care: On-campus housing is available. See the following Web site for more information: www.csusm.edu/srl/ (note: on campus housing is very limited for graduate students). No on-campus day care facilities are available.

Employment of Department Graduates:
Master's Degree Graduates: Of those who graduated in the academic year 2003–2004, the following categories and numbers represent the post-graduate activities and employment of master's degree graduates: Enrolled in a psychology doctoral program (1), enrolled in a post-doctoral residency/fellowship (n/a), employed in independent practice (n/a), employed in an academic position at a university (1), employed in other positions at a higher educa-

tion institution (3), other employment position (1), do not know (3), total from the above (master's) (9).

Doctoral Degree Graduates: Of those who graduated in the academic year 2003–2004, the following categories and numbers represent the post-graduate activities and employment of doctoral degree graduates: Enrolled in a psychology doctoral program (n/a), total from the above (doctoral) (0).

Additional Information:

Orientation, Objectives, and Emphasis of Department: Our program is designed to accommodate students with different goals. The active research programs of our faculty, and our recognition of psychology as a scientific enterprise, provides students with the intensive research training and course work in primary content areas that are central to preparation for more advanced graduate work in any area of psychology. Likewise, students who have in mind careers in community college teaching, community service, mental health, or business and industry, will benefit from our program's emphasis on critical thinking, research methods, and advanced course work. It is our belief that excellent graduate education is best accomplished in an atmosphere in which graduate students are closely mentored by the faculty.

Special Facilities or Resources: Established in 1989, CSUSM is the 20th campus of the California State University system. Our facilities are new and are growing to meet the demands of our increasing student population. In Psychology, we offer excellent computer support, a specialized classroom for instruction in research methods, and shared research space for graduate students. Our faculty provide research opportunities for graduate students in a number of off-campus settings in the San Diego area.

Information for Students With Physical Disabilities: See the following Web site for more information: www. csusm.edu/dss/.

Application Information:

Send to: Ms. Margie Kidd, Administrative Coordinator, Department of Psychology, California State University San Marcos, San Marcos, CA 92096. Application available online. URL of online application: www.csusm.edu/psychology. Students are admitted in the Fall, application deadline March 15. *Fee:* $55. Fee may be waived for a limited number of low income applicants. Ask for a Request for Application Fee Waiver Form.

California, University of, Berkeley

Psychology Department
Letters and Sciences
3210 Tolman Hall MC 1650
Berkeley, CA 94720-1650
Telephone: (510) 642-1382
Fax: (510) 642-5293
E-mail: *psychapp@berkeley.edu*
Web: *http://psychology.berkeley.edu/*

Department Information:

1921. Chairperson: Stephen Hinshaw. Number of Faculty: total–full-time 42; women–full-time 15; minority–full-time 6; faculty subject to the Americans With Disabilities Act 1.

Programs and Degrees Offered:

Listed in the following order: Program area, degree type (T if terminal Master's), number awarded 7/03–6/04. Cognition, Brain, and Behavior PhD (Doctor of Philosophy) 2, Social/Personality PhD (Doctor of Philosophy) 3, Developmental PhD (Doctor of Philosophy) 1, Clinical Science PhD (Doctor of Philosophy) 11.

APA Accreditation: Clinical PhD (Doctor of Philosophy).

Student Applications/Admissions:

Student Applications

Cognition, Brain, and Behavior PhD (Doctor of Philosophy)—Applications 2004–2005, 90. Total applicants accepted 2004–2005, 11. Number enrolled (new admits only) 2004–2005 full-time, 7. Total enrolled 2004–2005 full-time, 36. Openings 2005–2006, 12. The Median number of years required for completion of a degree are 5. *Social/Personality PhD (Doctor of Philosophy)*—Applications 2004–2005, 155. Total applicants accepted 2004–2005, 11. Number enrolled (new admits only) 2004–2005 full-time, 5. Total enrolled 2004–2005 full-time, 26. Openings 2005–2006, 12. The Median number of years required for completion of a degree are 5. *Developmental PhD (Doctor of Philosophy)*—Applications 2004–2005, 48. Total applicants accepted 2004–2005, 10. Number enrolled (new admits only) 2004–2005 full-time, 4. Total enrolled 2004–2005 full-time, 12. Openings 2005–2006, 8. The Median number of years required for completion of a degree are 5. *Clinical Science PhD (Doctor of Philosophy)*—Applications 2004–2005, 268. Total applicants accepted 2004–2005, 4. Number enrolled (new admits only) 2004–2005 full-time, 4. Total enrolled 2004–2005 full-time, 35. Openings 2005–2006, 8. The Median number of years required for completion of a degree are 6.

Admissions Requirements:

Scores: Entries appear in this order: required test or GPA, minimum score (if required), median score of students entering in 2003–2004. Master's Programs: We do not have a Master's Program. Doctoral Programs: GRE-V no minimum stated; GRE-Q no minimum stated; GRE-V+Q no minimum stated; GRE-Analytical no minimum stated; overall undergraduate GPA 3.0; last 2 years GPA 3.0; psychology GPA 3.0.

Other Criteria: (importance of criteria rated low, medium, or high): GRE/MAT scores medium, research experience high, work experience high, extracurricular activity high, clinically related public service high, GPA medium, letters of recommendation high, interview high, statement of goals and objectives high.

Student Characteristics: The following represents characteristics of students in 2004–2005 in all graduate psychology programs in the department: Female–full-time 74, part-time 0; Male–full-time 36, part-time 0; African American/Black–full-time 2, part-time 0; Hispanic/Latino(a)–full-time 5, part-time 0; Asian/Pacific Islander–full-time 14, part-time 0; American Indian/Alaska Native–full-time 1, part-time 0; Caucasian–full-time 64, part-time 0; Multi-ethnic–full-time 4, part-time 0; students subject to the Americans With Disabilities Act–full-time 0, part-time 0.

Financial Information/Assistance:

Tuition for Full-Time Study: Doctoral: State residents: per academic year $6,818; Nonstate residents: per academic year $18,904.

Tuition is subject to change. See the following Web site for updates and changes in tuition costs: http://registrar.berkeley.edu/.

Financial Assistance:

First Year Students: Teaching assistantships available for first-year. Average amount paid per academic year: $14,445. Tuition remission given: partial. Research assistantships available for first-year. Average amount paid per academic year: $18,904. Tuition remission given: partial. Fellowships and scholarships available for first-year. Apply by December 15. Tuition remission given: full.

Advanced Students: Teaching assistantships available for advanced students. Average amount paid per academic year: $14,445. Tuition remission given: partial. Research assistantships available for advanced students. Average amount paid per academic year: $16,785. Tuition remission given: partial. Fellowships and scholarships available for advanced students.

Contact Information: Of all students currently enrolled full-time, 90% benefitted from one or more of the listed financial assistance programs.

Internships/Practica: The sole practicum experience on-site is the Psychology Clinic, a pre-internship site for 2nd and 3rd year students in the Clinical Science program. A community clinic, operating on a sliding scale basis, for individuals and families in the Bay Area, the Clinic offers assessment, individual therapy, couples therapy, child/family therapy, and consultations. For those doctoral students for whom a professional internship is required prior to graduation, 6 applied in 2003–2004. Of those who applied, 6 were placed in internships listed by the Association of Psychology Postdoctoral and Internship Programs (APPIC); 6 were placed in APA accredited internships.

Housing and Day Care: On-campus housing is available. housing.berkeley.edu. On-campus day care facilities are available. See the following Web site for more information: http://www.housing.berkeley.edu/child/families/.

Employment of Department Graduates:

Master's Degree Graduates: Of those who graduated in the academic year 2003–2004, the following categories and numbers represent the post-graduate activities and employment of master's degree graduates: Enrolled in a post-doctoral residency/fellowship (n/a), employed in independent practice (n/a), total from the above (master's) (0).

Doctoral Degree Graduates: Of those who graduated in the academic year 2003–2004, the following categories and numbers represent the post-graduate activities and employment of doctoral degree graduates: Enrolled in a psychology doctoral program (n/a), total from the above (doctoral) (0).

Additional Information:

Orientation, Objectives, and Emphasis of Department: The goal of the graduate program in Psychology at Berkeley is to produce scholar-researchers with sufficient breadth to retain perspective on the field of psychology and sufficient depth to permit successful independent and significant research. The members of the Department have organized themselves into four graduate training areas. These areas reflect a sense of intellectual community among the faculty and correspond, in general, with traditional designations in the field. However, each graduate training area has a distinctive stamp placed upon it by the faculty and students that make up the program. The majority of our students enter graduate training and fulfill the requirements established by the existent training areas listed below. These requirements vary from area to area but always involve a combination of courses, seminars, and supervised independent research. Students are also encouraged to take courses outside the Psychology Department, using the unique faculty strengths found on the Berkeley campus to enrich their graduate training.

Special Facilities or Resources: The Department of Psychology is housed in Tolman Hall, a building shared with the Graduate School of Education. A library devoted to books and journals in psychology and education is maintained on the second floor of this building. The main office of the Psychology Department, as well as faculty and teaching assistant offices are on the third floor of Tolman Hall. Research rooms for carrying out a variety of studies with human subjects are on the basement, ground, fourth, and fifth floors. The basement also houses a human audition laboratory, an electronics shop, and a machine and woodworking shop. A photographic darkroom is on the fifth floor. The Institute of Human Development is housed on the first floor of Tolman Hall, the Psychology Clinic on the second floor, and the Institute of Personality and Social Research on the fourth floor. The remaining research units—The Institute for Cognitive and Brain Sciences, the Field Station for the Study of Behavior, Ecology and Reproduction, the Institute of Industrial Relations, the Helen Wills Neuroscience Institute, the Henry H. Wheeler Center for Brain Imaging, and the Northwest Animal Facility are located elsewhere on campus and in the adjacent areas.

Information for Students With Physical Disabilities: See the following Web site for more information: http://dsp.berkeley.edu/.

Application Information:
Send to: Graduate Assistant, Department of Psychology, 3210 Tolman Hall, University of California at Berkeley, Berkeley, CA 94720-1652. Application available online. URL of online application: https://gradadm.berkeley.edu:7200/gapappl/grd_login_menu. Students are admitted in the Fall, application deadline December 15. Web applications strongly encouraged. Web application available October 1. *Fee:* $60.

California, University of, Berkeley
School Psychology Program, Graduate School of Education
Cognition and Development
Berkeley, CA 94720-1670
Telephone: (510) 642-7581
Fax: (510) 642-3555
E-mail: *frankc@berkeley.edu*
Web: *http://www-gse.berkeley.edu/program/sp/sp.html*

Department Information:
1966. Program Director: Frank C. Worrell. Number of Faculty: total–full-time 3, part-time 10; women–full-time 2, part-time 4; minority–full-time 1, part-time 1.

Programs and Degrees Offered:
Listed in the following order: Program area, degree type (T if terminal Master's), number awarded 7/03–6/04. School PhD (Doctor of Philosophy) 7.

APA Accreditation: School PhD (Doctor of Philosophy).

Student Applications/Admissions:

Student Applications

School PhD (Doctor of Philosophy)—Applications 2004–2005, 90. Total applicants accepted 2004–2005, 12. Number enrolled (new admits only) 2004–2005 full-time, 5. Openings 2005–2006, 10. The Median number of years required for completion of a degree are 7. The number of students enrolled full and part-time who were dismissed or voluntarily withdrew from this program area were 2.

Admissions Requirements:

Scores: Entries appear in this order: required test or GPA, minimum score (if required), median score of students entering in 2003–2004. Doctoral Programs: GRE-V no minimum stated, 600; GRE-Q no minimum stated, 640; GRE-V+Q no minimum stated, 1240; overall undergraduate GPA 3.00, 3.8.

Other Criteria: (importance of criteria rated low, medium, or high): GRE/MAT scores high, research experience high, work experience medium, extracurricular activity medium, clinically related public service medium, GPA high, letters of recommendation high, interview medium, statement of goals and objectives high.

Student Characteristics: The following represents characteristics of students in 2004–2005 in all graduate psychology programs in the department: Female–full-time 39, part-time 0; Male–full-time 2, part-time 0; African American/Black–full-time 4, part-time 0; Hispanic/Latino(a)–full-time 2, part-time 0; Asian/Pacific Islander–full-time 5, part-time 0; American Indian/Alaska Native–full-time 1, part-time 0; Caucasian–full-time 29, part-time 0; Multi-ethnic–full-time 0, part-time 0; students subject to the Americans With Disabilities Act–full-time 0, part-time 0.

Financial Information/Assistance:

Tuition for Full-Time Study: *Doctoral:* State residents: per academic year $7,457; Nonstate residents: per academic year $22,396.

Financial Assistance:

First Year Students: Teaching assistantships available for first-year. Average amount paid per academic year: $14,575. Average number of hours worked per week: 20. Apply by before F & S. Tuition remission given: partial. Research assistantships available for first-year. Average amount paid per academic year: $12,200. Average number of hours worked per week: 20. Apply by varies. Tuition remission given: partial. Fellowships and scholarships available for first-year. Average amount paid per academic year: $12,500. Apply by December 1.

Advanced Students: Teaching assistantships available for advanced students. Average amount paid per academic year: $14,575. Average number of hours worked per week: 20. Apply by before F & S. Tuition remission given: partial. Research assistantships available for advanced students. Average amount paid per academic year: $12,200. Average number of hours worked per week: 20. Apply by varies. Tuition remission given: partial. Fellowships and scholarships available for advanced students. Average amount paid per academic year: $10,000. Apply by March 1.

Contact Information: Of all students currently enrolled full-time, 80% benefitted from one or more of the listed financial assistance programs. Application and information available online at www.gse.berkeley.edu.

Internships/Practica: Required prior to graduation, 8 applied in 2003–2004.

Housing and Day Care: On-campus housing is available. See the following Web sites for more information: www.calrentals. housing.berkeley.edu, reshall@uclink.berkeley.edu, and apt@uclink.berkeley.edu. On-campus day care facilities are available. See the following Web site for more information: www.housing. berkeley.edu/child.

Employment of Department Graduates:

Master's Degree Graduates: Of those who graduated in the academic year 2003–2004, the following categories and numbers represent the post-graduate activities and employment of master's degree graduates: Enrolled in a post-doctoral residency/fellowship (n/a), employed in independent practice (n/a), total from the above (master's) (0).

Doctoral Degree Graduates: Of those who graduated in the academic year 2003–2004, the following categories and numbers represent the post-graduate activities and employment of doctoral degree graduates: Enrolled in a psychology doctoral program (n/a), employed in an academic position at a university (1), employed in an academic position at a 2-year/4-year college (1), employed in a professional position in a school system (4), not seeking employment (1), total from the above (doctoral) (7).

Additional Information:

Orientation, Objectives, and Emphasis of Department: The school psychology program is a doctoral program within the cognition and development area. The program emphasizes the scientist model of school psychological services, linking strong preparation in theory and research to applications in the professional context of schools and school systems. Through the thoughtful application of knowledge and skills, school psychologists work together with teachers and other school professionals to clarify and resolve problems regarding the educational and mental health needs of children in classrooms. Working as consultants and collaborators, school psychologists help others to accommodate the social systems of schools to the individual differences of students, with the ultimate goal of promoting academic and social development. Graduate work within the program is supervised by professors from the Departments of Education and Psychology. Students fulfill all requirements for the academic PhD in human development, with additional coursework representing professional preparation for the specialty practice of school psychology. The program is accredited by APA. A program brochure is available for anyone wishing further information.

Special Facilities or Resources: The school psychology program is based at the University of California, Berkeley, which is a major research university in a large metropolitan area of the country. Students have access to faculty research and university resources in countless topics and areas of specialization. The university and department sponsor numerous colloquia, speakers, and visiting lecturers from around the world throughout the year. Both intellectual and cultural resources abound. Ongoing research programs of faculty offer students opportunities to engage in applications of psychology to educational problems during their first three years of the program and in their dissertation research.

Information for Students With Physical Disabilities: See the following Web site for more information: http://dsp.berkeley.edu.

Application Information:

Send to: Admission Office, Graduate School of Education. Application available online. URL of online application: www.gse.berkeley.edu.

Students are admitted in the Fall, application deadline December 1. *Fee:* $60.

California, University of, Davis

Department of Psychology
College of Letters and Science
One Shields Avenue
Davis, CA 95616-8686
Telephone: (530) 752-9362
Fax: (530) 752-2087
E-mail: *wrantaramian@ucdavis.edu*
Web: *http://psychology.ucdavis.edu*

Department Information:
1957. Chairperson: Phillip R. Shaver. Number of Faculty: total–full-time 42, part-time 1; women–full-time 15, part-time 1; minority–full-time 3.

Programs and Degrees Offered:
Listed in the following order: Program area, degree type (T if terminal Master's), number awarded 7/03–6/04. Cognitive PhD (Doctor of Philosophy) 2, comparative PhD (Doctor of Philosophy) 1, developmental PhD (Doctor of Philosophy) 0, perception PhD (Doctor of Philosophy) 0, personality PhD (Doctor of Philosophy) 2, physiological PhD (Doctor of Philosophy) 0, social PhD (Doctor of Philosophy) 6, Quantitative PhD (Doctor of Philosophy) 2.

Student Applications/Admissions:
Student Applications
Cognitive PhD (Doctor of Philosophy)—Applications 2004–2005, 71. Total applicants accepted 2004–2005, 14. Number enrolled (new admits only) 2004–2005 full-time, 6. Number enrolled (new admits only) 2004–2005 part-time, 0. The Median number of years required for completion of a degree are 5. The number of students enrolled full and part-time who were dismissed or voluntarily withdrew from this program area were 1. *Comparative PhD (Doctor of Philosophy)*—Applications 2004–2005, 7. Total applicants accepted 2004–2005, 3. Number enrolled (new admits only) 2004–2005 full-time, 1. The Median number of years required for completion of a degree are 6. The number of students enrolled full and part-time who were dismissed or voluntarily withdrew from this program area were 0. *Developmental PhD (Doctor of Philosophy)*—Applications 2004–2005, 52. Total applicants accepted 2004–2005, 16. Number enrolled (new admits only) 2004–2005 full-time, 5. The number of students enrolled full and part-time who were dismissed or voluntarily withdrew from this program area were 0. *Perception PhD (Doctor of Philosophy)*—Applications 2004–2005, 4. Total applicants accepted 2004–2005, 1. Number enrolled (new admits only) 2004–2005 full-time, 0. *Personality PhD (Doctor of Philosophy)*—Applications 2004–2005, 21. Total applicants accepted 2004–2005, 4. Number enrolled (new admits only) 2004–2005 full-time, 2. The Median number of years required for completion of a degree are 3. *Physiological PhD (Doctor of Philosophy)*—Applications 2004–2005, 5. Total applicants accepted 2004–2005, 3. Number enrolled (new admits only) 2004–2005 full-time, 2. *Social PhD (Doctor of Philosophy)*—Applications 2004–2005, 80. Total applicants accepted 2004–2005, 11. Number enrolled (new admits only) 2004–2005 full-time, 4. The Median number of years required for completion of a degree are 5. *Quantitative PhD (Doctor of Philosophy)*—Applications 2004–2005, 9. Total applicants accepted 2004–2005, 5. Number enrolled (new admits only) 2004–2005 full-time, 3. Total enrolled 2004–2005 full-time, 4. The Median number of years required for completion of a degree are 5. The number of students enrolled full and part-time who were dismissed or voluntarily withdrew from this program area were 1.

Admissions Requirements:
Scores: Entries appear in this order: required test or GPA, minimum score (if required), median score of students entering in 2003–2004. Doctoral Programs: GRE-V no minimum stated, 640; GRE-Q no minimum stated, 720; GRE-Analytical no minimum stated, 5.5; overall undergraduate GPA 3.00, 3.58; psychology GPA no minimum stated, 3.82.
Other Criteria: (importance of criteria rated low, medium, or high): GRE/MAT scores high, research experience high, work experience low, extracurricular activity low, GPA high, letters of recommendation high, statement of goals and objectives high. For additional information on admission requirements, go to: http://psychology.ucdavis.edu.

Student Characteristics: The following represents characteristics of students in 2004–2005 in all graduate psychology programs in the department: Female–full-time 42, part-time 0; Male–full-time 27, part-time 0; African American/Black–full-time 1, part-time 0; Hispanic/Latino(a)–full-time 1, part-time 0; Asian/Pacific Islander–full-time 6, part-time 0; American Indian/Alaska Native–full-time 0, part-time 0; Caucasian–full-time 61, part-time 0; students subject to the Americans With Disabilities Act–full-time 1, part-time 0.

Financial Information/Assistance:
Tuition for Full-Time Study: *Doctoral:* State residents: per academic year $8,406; Nonstate residents: per academic year $23,100. Tuition is subject to change. See the following Web site for updates and changes in tuition costs: http://registrar.ucdavis.edu.

Financial Assistance:
First Year Students: Teaching assistantships available for first-year. Average amount paid per academic year: $14,600. Average number of hours worked per week: 20. Tuition remission given: full. Research assistantships available for first-year. Average amount paid per academic year: $13,100. Average number of hours worked per week: 20. Tuition remission given: full. Traineeships available for first-year. Average amount paid per academic year: $15,000. Tuition remission given: partial. Fellowships and scholarships available for first-year. Average amount paid per academic year: $5,000. Apply by January 15.
Advanced Students: Teaching assistantships available for advanced students. Average amount paid per academic year: $14,600. Average number of hours worked per week: 20. Tuition remission given: full. Research assistantships available for advanced students. Average amount paid per academic year: $14,200. Average number of hours worked per week: 20. Tuition remission given: full. Fellowships and scholarships available for advanced students. Average amount paid per academic year: $5,000. Apply by January 15.

Contact Information: Of all students currently enrolled full-time, 95% benefitted from one or more of the listed financial assistance programs. Application and information available online at: http://psychology.ucdavis.edu.

Internships/Practica: No information provided.

Housing and Day Care: On-campus housing is available. See the following Web site for more information: http://www.housing.ucdavis.edu. On-campus day care facilities are available. See the following Web site for more information: http://www.hr.ucdavis.edu/childcare.

Employment of Department Graduates:

Master's Degree Graduates: Of those who graduated in the academic year 2003–2004, the following categories and numbers represent the post-graduate activities and employment of master's degree graduates: Enrolled in a post-doctoral residency/fellowship (n/a), employed in independent practice (n/a), total from the above (master's) (0).

Doctoral Degree Graduates: Of those who graduated in the academic year 2003–2004, the following categories and numbers represent the post-graduate activities and employment of doctoral degree graduates: Enrolled in a psychology doctoral program (n/a), enrolled in a post-doctoral residency/fellowship (3), employed in an academic position at a university (4), employed in an academic position at a 2-year/4-year college (2), employed in business or industry (management) (1), employed in a government agency (research) (1), employed in a government agency (professional services) (1), total from the above (doctoral) (12).

Additional Information:

Orientation, Objectives, and Emphasis of Department: The department places strong emphasis on empirical research in five broad areas: (1) psychobiology (e.g., animal behavior, primatology, hormones and behavior, brain bases of social attachments, eating and obesity); (2) perception, cognition, and cognitive neuroscience (e.g., memory, attention, language, consciousness); (3) personality, social psychology, and social neuroscience (e.g., emotions, attitudes, prejudice, close relationships, cultural psychology, psychology of religion, brain bases of personality traits); (4) developmental psychology (cognitive, affective, and social development, personality development, effects of child abuse, brain bases of developmental disorders); and (5) quantitative psychology (e.g., psychometrics, multivariate statistics, hierarchical linear models, statistical models used in areas as diverse as neuroscience and longitudinal developmental research). Weekly colloquia in these five areas provide students with opportunities to hear about new research and present their own ideas and findings. Each student selects a three-person faculty advisory committee, which guides and evaluates the student's progress through the program. Major exams are tailored to each student by his or her advisory committee. Every faculty member has an active lab, permitting students to learn about anything from cellular recording and brain imaging to behavioral studies of development, perception, cognition, language, emotion, and both individual and social behavior, in both humans and nonhuman animals.

Special Facilities or Resources: The Psychology Department, which contains numerous state-of-the art laboratories, computer facilities, and a survey research facility, overlaps with several other major research centers on campus: a regional Primate Research Center, a Center for Neuroscience, a Center for Mind and Brain, and the M.I.N.D. Institute for research on developmental disorders. Departmental faculty members participate in campus-wide graduate groups in psychology, human development, animal behavior, neuroscience, and other fields, and in a cross-university Bay Area Affective Sciences Training Program. The university includes a medical school, a veterinary school, a business school, and a law school, as well as exceptionally strong programs in all of the biological and social sciences. The Department of Psychology offers graduate students an education that is intellectually exciting, personally challenging, and very forward-looking, one that prepares new teacher-scientist-scholars to advance the study of mind, brain, and behavior.

Information for Students With Physical Disabilities: See the following Web site for more information: http://sdc.ucdavis.edu.

Application Information:
Send to: Bill Antaramian, Graduate Program Coordinator, Psychology Department, University of California, One Shields Avenue, Davis, CA 95616-8686. Application available online. URL of online application: http://gradstudies.ucdavis.edu. Students are admitted in the Fall, application deadline December 15. Fellowship deadline is December 15. *Fee:* $60.

California, University of, Davis
Human Development
Agricultural and Environmental Sciences
One Shields Avenue
Davis, CA 95616-8523
Telephone: (530) 752-1926
Fax: (530) 752-5660
E-mail: *lcday@ucdavis.edu*
Web: *http://humandevelopment.ucdavis.edu*

Department Information:
1971. Chair, Human & Child Development Graduate Groups: Rand Conger. Number of Faculty: total–full-time 45; women–full-time 24; minority–full-time 5; faculty subject to the Americans With Disabilities Act 1.

Programs and Degrees Offered:
Listed in the following order: Program area, degree type (T if terminal Master's), number awarded 7/03–6/04. Child development MA/MS (Master of Arts/Science) (T) 2, Human Development PhD (Doctor of Philosophy) 2.

Student Applications/Admissions:
Student Applications

Child development MA/MS (Master of Arts/Science)—Applications 2004–2005, 14. Total applicants accepted 2004–2005, 7. Openings 2005–2006, 10. The Median number of years required for completion of a degree are 3. The number of students enrolled full and part-time who were dismissed or voluntarily withdrew from this program area were 1. *Human Development PhD (Doctor of Philosophy)*—Applications 2004–2005, 12. Total applicants accepted 2004–2005, 5. Total enrolled 2004–2005 full-time, 24, part-time, 2. Openings 2005–2006, 10. The Median number of years required for completion of a degree are 7. The number of students enrolled full and part-time who were dismissed or voluntarily withdrew from this program area were 1.

Admissions Requirements:

Scores: Entries appear in this order: required test or GPA, minimum score (if required), median score of students entering in 2003–2004. Master's Programs: GRE-V no minimum stated, 532; GRE-Q no minimum stated, 522; GRE-V+Q no minimum stated, 1054; GRE-Analytical no minimum stated, 4.5; overall undergraduate GPA 3.0, 3.54; last 2 years GPA 3.0; psychology GPA 3.0. Doctoral Programs: GRE-V no minimum stated, 465; GRE-Q no minimum stated, 627; GRE-V+Q no minimum stated, 1092; GRE-Analytical no minimum stated, 598; overall undergraduate GPA 3.0, 3.74; last 2 years GPA 3.0; psychology GPA 3.0. GRE subject test is recommended but not required.

Other Criteria: (importance of criteria rated low, medium, or high): GRE/MAT scores medium, research experience medium, work experience medium, extracurricular activity low, clinically related public service low, GPA high, letters of recommendation high, interview low, statement of goals and objectives high. For the Human Development PhD, we require a writing sample/paper.

Student Characteristics: The following represents characteristics of students in 2004–2005 in all graduate psychology programs in the department: Female–full-time 33, part-time 1; Male–full-time 5, part-time 1; African American/Black–full-time 4, part-time 0; Hispanic/Latino(a)–full-time 5, part-time 0; Asian/Pacific Islander–full-time 9, part-time 0; American Indian/Alaska Native–full-time 0, part-time 0; Caucasian–full-time 0, part-time 0; Multi-ethnic–full-time 1, part-time 0; students subject to the Americans With Disabilities Act–full-time 1, part-time 0.

Financial Information/Assistance:

Tuition for Full-Time Study: *Master's:* State residents: per academic year $8,408; Nonstate residents: per academic year $23,346. *Doctoral:* State residents: per academic year $8,408; Nonstate residents: per academic year $23,346. Tuition is subject to change. See the following Web site for updates and changes in tuition costs: http://www.ormp.ucdavis.edu/studentfees.

Financial Assistance:

First Year Students: Teaching assistantships available for first-year. Average amount paid per academic year: $14,144. Average number of hours worked per week: 20. Apply by Open. Tuition remission given: full. Research assistantships available for first-year. Average amount paid per academic year: $14,144. Average number of hours worked per week: 20. Apply by Open. Tuition remission given: full. Fellowships and scholarships available for first-year. Apply by December 1. Tuition remission given: full and partial.

Advanced Students: Teaching assistantships available for advanced students. Average amount paid per academic year: $14,144. Average number of hours worked per week: 20. Apply by Open. Tuition remission given: full. Research assistantships available for advanced students. Average amount paid per academic year: $14,144. Average number of hours worked per week: 20. Apply by Open. Tuition remission given: full. Fellowships and scholarships available for advanced students. Apply by December 1. Tuition remission given: full and partial.

Contact Information: Of all students currently enrolled full-time, 90% benefitted from one or more of the listed financial assistance programs.

Internships/Practica: For Child Development MS students, application of theories of learning and development to interaction with children six months to five years at the Center for Child and Family Studies and field studies with children and adolescents. Study of children's affective, cognitive and social development within the context of family/school environments, hospitals, and foster group homes. Child Life internships through the University of California Davis Medical Center. Internships through the 4-H Center for Youth Development, including 4-H and CE-sponsored out-of-school childcare, and the M.I.N.D. Institute, etc.

Housing and Day Care: No on-campus housing is available. On-campus day care facilities are available. See the following Web site for more information: http://www.hr.ucdavis.edu/childcare/.

Employment of Department Graduates:

Master's Degree Graduates: Of those who graduated in the academic year 2003–2004, the following categories and numbers represent the post-graduate activities and employment of master's degree graduates: Enrolled in a post-doctoral residency/fellowship (n/a), employed in independent practice (n/a), employed in a government agency (professional services) (1), do not know (1), total from the above (master's) (2).

Doctoral Degree Graduates: Of those who graduated in the academic year 2003–2004, the following categories and numbers represent the post-graduate activities and employment of doctoral degree graduates: Enrolled in a psychology doctoral program (n/a), employed in an academic position at a university (1), employed in a community mental health/counseling center (1), do not know (2), total from the above (doctoral) (4).

Additional Information:

Orientation, Objectives, and Emphasis of Department: Both the Child Development Master of Science and Human Development PhD are offered by a graduate group which is interdisciplinary in nature, with a core faculty housed in the Department of Human and Community Development, and other graduate group faculty housed in education, law, medicine, psychiatry, M.I.N.D. Institute and psychology. Child Development MS students will be prepared to teach at the community college level in developmental and to do applied/evaluation research, or pursue higher degrees. The Human Development PhD students will be prepared to teach at the University level to do basic or applied research in life span, cognitive, and social-emotional development from an interdisciplinary perspective with an appreciaton of the contexts of development (family, school, health, social-cultural, and social policy). There are extensive student research opportunities within all the departments from which faculty are drawn, as well as the Center for Child and Family Studies, the 4-H Extension Program's Center for Youth Development, the M.I.N.D. Institute, and the Center for Neuroscience.

Special Facilities or Resources: Center for Child and Family Studies, Infant Sleep Lab, Parent and Child Lab, Center for Neuroscience, Center for Youth Development, Cooperative Research and Extension Services for Schools, M.I.N.D. Institute. Extensive community placements in education, law enforcement, and social welfare.

Information for Students With Physical Disabilities: See the following Web site for more information: http://sdc.ucdavis.edu.

Application Information:
Send to: Lucy Day, Graduate Advisor, Human Development Dept., University of California, One Shields Avenue, Davis, CA 65616-8523. Application available online. URL of online application: http://sisweb. ucdavis.edu/. Students are admitted in the Fall, application deadline December 1. December 1 fellowship deadline. *Fee:* $60.

California, University of, Irvine
Cognitive Sciences Department
School of Social Sciences, UCI
Irvine, CA 92697-5100
Telephone: (949) 824-6692
Fax: (949) 824-2307
E-mail: *cogsci@uci.edu*
Web: *http://www.cogsci.uci.edu/*

Department Information:
1986. Chairperson: Charles E. Wright. Number of Faculty: total–full-time 21, part-time 12; women–full-time 5, part-time 7; minority–full-time 1, part-time 1.

Programs and Degrees Offered:
Listed in the following order: Program area, degree type (T if terminal Master's), number awarded 7/03–6/04. Cognitive PhD (Doctor of Philosophy) 3.

Student Applications/Admissions:
Student Applications
Cognitive PhD (Doctor of Philosophy)—Applications 2004–2005, 80. Total applicants accepted 2004–2005, 19. Number enrolled (new admits only) 2004–2005 full-time, 8. Openings 2005–2006, 15. The Median number of years required for completion of a degree are 6. The number of students enrolled full and part-time who were dismissed or voluntarily withdrew from this program area were 1.

Admissions Requirements:
Scores: Entries appear in this order: required test or GPA, minimum score (if required), median score of students entering in 2003–2004. Doctoral Programs: GRE-V no minimum stated, 578; GRE-Q no minimum stated, 713; GRE-Analytical no minimum stated, 711; overall undergraduate GPA 3.0; last 2 years GPA 3.5. All foreign students need to receive a score of 50 on the TSE.
Other Criteria: (importance of criteria rated low, medium, or high): GRE/MAT scores high, research experience high, work experience low, GPA medium, letters of recommendation high, interview high, statement of goals and objectives high.

Student Characteristics: The following represents characteristics of students in 2004–2005 in all graduate psychology programs in the department: Female–full-time 28, part-time 0; Male–full-time 18, part-time 0; African American/Black–full-time 0, part-time 0; Hispanic/Latino(a)–full-time 3, part-time 0; Asian/Pacific Islander–full-time 17, part-time 0; American Indian/Alaska Na-

tive–full-time 0, part-time 0; Caucasian–full-time 26, part-time 0; Multi-ethnic–full-time 0, part-time 0; students subject to the Americans With Disabilities Act–full-time 0, part-time 0.

Financial Information/Assistance:
Tuition for Full-Time Study: *Doctoral:* State residents: per academic year $8,565; Nonstate residents: per academic year $23,504. Tuition is subject to change. See the following Web site for updates and changes in tuition costs: http://www.rgs.uci.edu/grad/prospective/deadline.htm.

Financial Assistance:
First Year Students: Teaching assistantships available for first-year. Average amount paid per academic year: $14,300. Average number of hours worked per week: 20. Apply by April 15. Tuition remission given: partial. Research assistantships available for first-year. Average amount paid per academic year: $12,000. Average number of hours worked per week: 20. Apply by April 15. Tuition remission given: full. Fellowships and scholarships available for first-year. Apply by April 15. Tuition remission given: full and partial.
Advanced Students: Teaching assistantships available for advanced students. Average amount paid per academic year: $14,300. Average number of hours worked per week: 20. Apply by see Web site. Tuition remission given: partial. Research assistantships available for advanced students. Average amount paid per academic year: $14,000. Average number of hours worked per week: 20. Tuition remission given: full. Fellowships and scholarships available for advanced students. Apply by varies. Tuition remission given: full.
Contact Information: Of all students currently enrolled full-time, 99% benefitted from one or more of the listed financial assistance programs. Application and information available online at: http://www.fao.uci.edu.

Internships/Practica: None.

Housing and Day Care: On-campus housing is available. See the following Web site for more information: http://www.rgs.uci.edu/grad/prospective/index.htm. On-campus day care facilities are available.

Employment of Department Graduates:
Master's Degree Graduates: Of those who graduated in the academic year 2003–2004, the following categories and numbers represent the post-graduate activities and employment of master's degree graduates: Enrolled in a post-doctoral residency/fellowship (n/a), employed in independent practice (n/a), total from the above (master's) (0).
Doctoral Degree Graduates: Of those who graduated in the academic year 2003–2004, the following categories and numbers represent the post-graduate activities and employment of doctoral degree graduates: Enrolled in a psychology doctoral program (n/a), enrolled in a post-doctoral residency/fellowship (3), total from the above (doctoral) (3).

Additional Information:
Orientation, Objectives, and Emphasis of Department: The Department of Cognitive Sciences at the University of California, Irvine offers an undergraduate degree program in Psychology and a program of graduate study leading to a PhD degree in Psychology. The Department's graduate program provides research concentra-

tions in cognition and information processing, cognitive neuroscience, perception and action, and mathematical behavioral sciences. Modern cognitive science is a dynamic, interdisciplinary field, a fact that is reflected in the research programs carried out by faculty in UCI's Department of Cognitive Sciences. These programs span a broad spectrum ranging from perceptual mechanisms, to language, memory, and attention, through to higher cognitive abilities such as reasoning and decision making. The studies in these areas use several methodological approaches including collection of behavioral data, psychophysics, computational modeling, neuropsychology, and functional brain imaging. The faculty emphasize formal models as instrumental in understanding the nature of the human mind.

Special Facilities or Resources: The facilities of the Department of Cognitive Sciences are housed in three buildings with teaching labs, lecture rooms, and instructional computing equipment. Its research laboratories are on the technological forefront and highly computerized. A research-dedicated 4.0T whole body MR Imaging/Spectroscopy System supports research in cognitive neuroscience.

Information for Students With Physical Disabilities: See the following Web site for more information: http://www.disability. uci.edu/.

Application Information:

Send to: Graduate Advisor, Department of Cognitive Sciences, 3151 Social Science Plaza, University of California, Irvine, CA 92697. Application available online. URL of online application: https://www. rgs.uci.edu/grad/prospective/admission.htm. Students are admitted in the Fall, application deadline December 15. Application must be received before fall deadline of January 15 to ensure consideration for financial aid. *Fee:* $60.

California, University of, Irvine
Department of Psychology and Social Behavior
3340 Social Ecology II, University of California, Irvine
Irvine, CA 92697-7085
Telephone: (949) 824-5574
Fax: (949) 824-3002
E-mail: jnagaoka@uci.edu
Web: http://www.seweb.uci.edu/psb/

Department Information:

1992. Chairperson: Karen Rook, PhD Number of Faculty: total–full-time 24, part-time 9; women–full-time 17; minority–full-time 3.

Programs and Degrees Offered:

Listed in the following order: Program area, degree type (T if terminal Master's), number awarded 7/03–6/04. Psychology and Social Behavior PhD (Doctor of Philosophy) 1.

Student Applications/Admissions:
Student Applications

Psychology and Social Behavior PhD (Doctor of Philosophy)—Applications 2004–2005, 208. Total applicants accepted

2004–2005, 21. Number enrolled (new admits only) 2004–2005 full-time, 11. Total enrolled 2004–2005 full-time, 59. Openings 2005–2006, 12. The Median number of years required for completion of a degree are 6. The number of students enrolled full and part-time who were dismissed or voluntarily withdrew from this program area were 1.

Admissions Requirements:
Scores: Entries appear in this order: required test or GPA, minimum score (if required), median score of students entering in 2003–2004. Doctoral Programs: GRE-V no minimum stated, 670; GRE-Q no minimum stated, 680; GRE-V+Q no minimum stated, 1350; GRE-Analytical no minimum stated; overall undergraduate GPA 3.23, 3.72.
Other Criteria: (importance of criteria rated low, medium, or high): GRE/MAT scores medium, research experience high, work experience low, extracurricular activity low, GPA high, letters of recommendation high, interview high, statement of goals and objectives high. For additional information on admission requirements, go to: http://www.seweb.uci.edu/psb/gradprog.uci.

Student Characteristics: The following represents characteristics of students in 2004–2005 in all graduate psychology programs in the department: Female–full-time 44, part-time 0; Male–full-time 15, part-time 0; African American/Black–full-time 1, part-time 0; Hispanic/Latino(a)–full-time 4, part-time 0; Asian/Pacific Islander–full-time 9, part-time 0; American Indian/Alaska Native–full-time 0, part-time 0; Caucasian–full-time 44, part-time 0; Multi-ethnic full-time 1, part-time 0; students subject to the Americans With Disabilities Act–full-time 1, part-time 0.

Financial Information/Assistance:

Tuition for Full-Time Study: *Doctoral:* State residents: per academic year $8,567; Nonstate residents: per academic year $23,507. Tuition is subject to change. See the following Web site for updates and changes in tuition costs: http://www.reg.uci.edu/registrar/soc/fees.html.

Financial Assistance:

First Year Students: Teaching assistantships available for first-year. Average amount paid per academic year: $14,350. Average number of hours worked per week: 20. Tuition remission given: partial. Research assistantships available for first-year. Average amount paid per academic year: $13,500. Average number of hours worked per week: 20. Tuition remission given: full. Fellowships and scholarships available for first-year. Average amount paid per academic year: $14,350. Average number of hours worked per week: 0. Tuition remission given: full.

Advanced Students: Teaching assistantships available for advanced students. Average amount paid per academic year: $14,350. Average number of hours worked per week: 20. Tuition remission given: partial. Research assistantships available for advanced students. Average amount paid per academic year: $13,500. Average number of hours worked per week: 20. Tuition remission given: full. Fellowships and scholarships available for advanced students. Average amount paid per academic year: $14,350. Tuition remission given: full.

Contact Information: Of all students currently enrolled full-time, 95% benefitted from one or more of the listed financial assistance programs. Application and information available online at: http://www.rgs.uci.edu/grad/prospective/finance_edu.htm.

Internships/Practica: The school places a strong emphasis on field experiences as part of the education of students and maintains an extensive list of community agencies where students may seek various forms of research involvement. All students are required to take the course "Applied Psychological Research." An optional course "Applied Psychological Research in Community Settings" is available to students who would like to have field placement experience.

Housing and Day Care: On-campus housing is available. See the following Web site for more information: http://www.housing.uci. edu/gfh/. On-campus day care facilities are available. See the following Web site for more information: http://www.childcare. uci.edu/.

Employment of Department Graduates:

Master's Degree Graduates: Of those who graduated in the academic year 2003–2004, the following categories and numbers represent the post-graduate activities and employment of master's degree graduates: Enrolled in a post-doctoral residency/fellowship (n/a), employed in independent practice (n/a), total from the above (master's) (0).

Doctoral Degree Graduates: Of those who graduated in the academic year 2003–2004, the following categories and numbers represent the post-graduate activities and employment of doctoral degree graduates: Enrolled in a psychology doctoral program (n/a), employed in an academic position at a university (1), total from the above (doctoral) (1).

Additional Information:

Orientation, Objectives, and Emphasis of Department: The Department of Psychology and Social Behavior is united by an overarching interest in human adaptation in various sociocultural and developmental contexts. The department has emphases in four areas (Health Psychology, Developmental Psychology, Social and Personality Psychology, and Psychopathology and Behavioral Disorder). The multidisciplinary faculty, whose training is mainly in social, developmental, clinical, and community psychology, examines human health, well-being, and the ways in which individuals respond and adjust to changing circumstances over the life span. Faculty interests include stress and coping, cognitive and biobehavioral processes in health behavior, subjective well-being, cognition and emotion, social development and developmental transitions across the life span, cultural influences on cognition and behavior, psychology and law, aging and health, and societal problems such as violence and unemployment.

Special Facilities or Resources: In-house laboratories, including the Consortium for Integrative Health Studies, the Family Studies Lab, the Development in Cultural Contexts Lab, and the Health Psychology Lab, provide graduate students with direct access to state-of-the-art facilities and opportunities for research training. In addition, the department maintains strong ties with psychologists at other campuses in the area, including UC Los Angeles, UC Riverside, and UC San Diego (each approximately one hour away), and the UCI College of Medicine. For example, we participate in the Consortium on Families and Human Development, a joint undertaking of faculty members and graduate students at UCLA, UCR, UCI, and the University of Southern California. Selected students participate as predoctoral fellows in the Department's NIMH Training Program, and opportunities continually arise for all students to become involved in many ongoing faculty research projects.

Information for Students With Physical Disabilities: See the following Web site for more information: http://www.disability. uci.edu/.

Application Information:
Send to: Judy Nagaoka, Graduate Coordinator, 3340 Social Ecology II, Psychology and Social Behavior, School of Social Ecology UCI, Irvine, CA 92697-7085. Application available online. URL of online application: http://www.rgs.uci.edu/grad/prospective/admissions.htm. Students are admitted in the Fall, application deadline December 15. *Fee:* $60.

California, University of, Los Angeles
Department of Psychology
Letters and Science
405 Hilgard Avenue
Los Angeles, CA 90095-1563
Telephone: (310) 825-2617
Fax: (310) 206-5895
E-mail: *gradadm@psych.ucla.edu*
Web: *http://www.psych.ucla.edu*

Department Information:
1937. Chairperson: Robert A. Bjork. Number of Faculty: total–full-time 63, part-time 8; women–full-time 23; minority–full-time 10.

Programs and Degrees Offered:
Listed in the following order: Program area, degree type (T if terminal Master's), number awarded 7/03–6/04. Behavioral neuroscience PhD (Doctor of Philosophy) 3, clinical PhD (Doctor of Philosophy) 7, cognitive PhD (Doctor of Philosophy) 3, developmental PhD (Doctor of Philosophy) 1, learning and behavior PhD (Doctor of Philosophy) 1, measurement and psychometrics PhD (Doctor of Philosophy) 2, social PhD (Doctor of Philosophy) 3.

APA Accreditation: Clinical PhD (Doctor of Philosophy).

Student Applications/Admissions:
Student Applications
Behavioral neuroscience PhD (Doctor of Philosophy)—Applications 2004–2005, 35. Total applicants accepted 2004–2005, 5. Number enrolled (new admits only) 2004–2005 full-time, 2. Number enrolled (new admits only) 2004–2005 part-time, 0. Openings 2005–2006, 5. The Median number of years required for completion of a degree are 6. The number of students enrolled full and part-time who were dismissed or voluntarily withdrew from this program area were 0. *Clinical PhD (Doctor of Philosophy)*—Applications 2004–2005, 385. Total applicants accepted 2004–2005, 12. Number enrolled (new admits only) 2004–2005 full-time, 12. Openings 2005–2006, 12. The Median number of years required for completion of a degree are 6. The number of students enrolled full and part-time who were dismissed or voluntarily withdrew from this program area

were 0. *Cognitive PhD (Doctor of Philosophy)*—Applications 2004–2005, 55. Total applicants accepted 2004–2005, 8. Number enrolled (new admits only) 2004–2005 full-time, 9. Openings 2005–2006, 8. The Median number of years required for completion of a degree are 6. The number of students enrolled full and part-time who were dismissed or voluntarily withdrew from this program area were 0. *Developmental PhD (Doctor of Philosophy)*—Applications 2004–2005, 37. Total applicants accepted 2004–2005, 1. Number enrolled (new admits only) 2004–2005 full-time, 1. Openings 2005–2006, 3. The Median number of years required for completion of a degree are 6. The number of students enrolled full and part-time who were dismissed or voluntarily withdrew from this program area were 0. *Learning and behavior PhD (Doctor of Philosophy)*—Applications 2004–2005, 13. Total applicants accepted 2004–2005, 2. Number enrolled (new admits only) 2004–2005 full-time, 2. Openings 2005–2006, 2. The Median number of years required for completion of a degree are 6. The number of students enrolled full and part-time who were dismissed or voluntarily withdrew from this program area were 1. *Measurement and psychometrics PhD (Doctor of Philosophy)*—Applications 2004–2005, 7. Total applicants accepted 2004–2005, 0. Number enrolled (new admits only) 2004–2005 full-time, 1. Openings 2005–2006, 1. The Median number of years required for completion of a degree are 6. The number of students enrolled full and part-time who were dismissed or voluntarily withdrew from this program area were 0. *Social PhD (Doctor of Philosophy)*—Applications 2004–2005, 141. Total applicants accepted 2004–2005, 8. Number enrolled (new admits only) 2004–2005 full-time, 8. Openings 2005–2006, 8. The Median number of years required for completion of a degree are 6. The number of students enrolled full and part-time who were dismissed or voluntarily withdrew from this program area were 0.

Admissions Requirements:

Scores: Entries appear in this order: required test or GPA, minimum score (if required), median score of students entering in 2003–2004. Doctoral Programs: GRE-V no minimum stated, 653; GRE-Q no minimum stated, 734; GRE-Analytical no minimum stated, 5.55; GRE-Subject(Psych) no minimum stated, 737; overall undergraduate GPA no minimum stated, 3.69. Note: Analytical median score prior to October 2002 is 738.

Other Criteria: (importance of criteria rated low, medium, or high): GRE/MAT scores high, research experience high, work experience medium, extracurricular activity medium, clinically related public service medium, GPA high, letters of recommendation high, interview high, statement of goals and objectives high, The Clinical Area also requires an interview as part of the admissions process. After an initial screening of applications, the area invites select candidates to an on-campus interview. For additional information on admission requirements, go to: http://www.psych.ucla.edu/Grads/prospective.php.

Student Characteristics: The following represents characteristics of students in 2004–2005 in all graduate psychology programs in the department: Female–full-time 94, part-time 0; Male–full-time 62, part-time 0; African American/Black–full-time 2, part-time 0; Hispanic/Latino(a)–full-time 10, part-time 0; Asian/Pacific Islander–full-time 31, part-time 0; American Indian/Alaska Native–full-time 1, part-time 0; Caucasian–full-time 107, part-time

0; Multi-ethnic–full-time 1, part-time 0; students subject to the Americans With Disabilities Act–full-time 0, part-time 0.

Financial Information/Assistance:

Tuition for Full-Time Study: *Doctoral:* State residents: per academic year $7,468; Nonstate residents: per academic year $23,531. Tuition is subject to change. See the following Web site for updates and changes in tuition costs: http://www.registrar.ucla.edu/fees/grad.htm.

Financial Assistance:

First Year Students: Teaching assistantships available for first-year. Average amount paid per academic year: $14,572. Average number of hours worked per week: 20. Tuition remission given: partial. Research assistantships available for first-year. Average amount paid per academic year: $12,000. Average number of hours worked per week: 20. Tuition remission given: partial. Traineeships available for first-year. Average amount paid per academic year: $18,000. Average number of hours worked per week: 0. Fellowships and scholarships available for first-year. Average amount paid per academic year: $17,000. Average number of hours worked per week: 0. Apply by December 15.

Advanced Students: Teaching assistantships available for advanced students. Average amount paid per academic year: $16,500. Average number of hours worked per week: 20. Tuition remission given: partial. Research assistantships available for advanced students. Average amount paid per academic year: $15,100. Average number of hours worked per week: 20. Tuition remission given: partial. Traineeships available for advanced students. Average amount paid per academic year: $18,000. Average number of hours worked per week: 0. Fellowships and scholarships available for advanced students. Average amount paid per academic year: $17,000. Average number of hours worked per week: 0. Apply by varies.

Contact Information: Of all students currently enrolled full-time, 100% benefitted from one or more of the listed financial assistance programs. Application and information available online at: http://www.gdnet.ucla.edu/prospective.html.

Internships/Practica: VA Hospitals; San Fernando Valley Child Guidance Center; Street John's Child Development Center; Neuropsychiatric Institute/UCLA; UCLA Student Psych Services. For those doctoral students for whom a professional internship is required prior to graduation, 11 applied in 2003–2004. Of those who applied, 11 were placed in internships listed by the Association of Psychology Postdoctoral and Internship Programs (APPIC); 11 were placed in APA accredited internships.

Housing and Day Care: On-campus housing is available. See the following Web site for more information: http://www.housing.ucla.edu. On-campus day care facilities are available. Contact gmacdonald@be.ucla.edu.

Employment of Department Graduates:

Master's Degree Graduates: Of those who graduated in the academic year 2003–2004, the following categories and numbers represent the post-graduate activities and employment of master's degree graduates: Enrolled in a post-doctoral residency/fellowship (n/a), employed in independent practice (n/a), total from the above (master's) (0).

Doctoral Degree Graduates: Of those who graduated in the academic year 2003–2004, the following categories and numbers

represent the post-graduate activities and employment of doctoral degree graduates: Enrolled in a psychology doctoral program (n/a), enrolled in another graduate/professional program (0), enrolled in a post-doctoral residency/fellowship (9), employed in independent practice (0), employed in an academic position at a university (2), employed in an academic position at a 2-year/4-year college (1), employed in other positions at a higher education institution (3), employed in a professional position in a school system (0), employed in business or industry (research/consulting) (1), employed in business or industry (management) (0), employed in a government agency (research) (1), employed in a government agency (professional services) (0), employed in a community mental health/counseling center (0), employed in a hospital/medical center (1), still seeking employment (1), other employment position (1), do not know (0), total from the above (doctoral) (20).

Additional Information:

Orientation, Objectives, and Emphasis of Department: Rigorous scientific training is the foundation of the PhD program. The graduate curriculum focuses on the usage of systematic methods of investigation to understand and quantify general principles of human behavior, pathology, cognition and emotion. More specifically, the department includes such research clusters as psychobiology and the brain; child-clinical and developmental psychology; adult psychopathology and family dynamics; cognition and memory; health, community, and political psychology; minority mental health; social cognition and intergroup relations; measurement; and learning and behavior. In all these areas, the department's central aim is to train researchers dedicated to expanding the scientific knowledge upon which the discipline of psychology rests. This orientation also applies to the clinical program; while it offers excellent clinical training, its emphasis is on training researchers rather than private practitioners. In sum, the graduate training is designed to prepare research psychologists for careers in academic and applied settings—as college and university instructors; for leadership roles in community, government, and business organizations; and as professional research psychologists.

Special Facilities or Resources: The department is one of the largest on campus. Our three-connected buildings (known collectively as Franz Hall) provide ample space (over 120,000 square feet) for psychological research. Laboratory facilities are of the highest quality. Precision equipment is available for electro-physiological stimulation and recording, magnetic resonance imaging (MRI), and for all major areas of sensory study. Specially designed laboratories exist for studies of group behavior and naturalistic observation. An extensive vivarium contains facilities for physiological animal studies. Computing facilities are leading-edge at all levels, from microcomputers to supercomputer clusters. The department also houses the Psychology Clinic, a training and research center for psychotherapy and diagnostics. Other resources include the Fernald Child Study Center (a research facility committed to investigating childhood behavioral disorders); the National Research Center for Asian American Mental Health; the California Self-Help Center; and the Center for Computer-Based Behavioral Studies. Departmental affiliations with the Brain Research Institute, the University Elementary School, the Neuropsychiatric Institute, and the local Veterans Administration also provide year-round research opportunities.

Information for Students With Physical Disabilities: kmolini@saonet.ucla.edu.

Application Information:
Send to: Graduate Admissions Advisor, Psychology Department, 1285 Franz Hall, Box 951563, Los Angeles, CA 90095-1563. Application available online. URL of online application: http://www.psych.ucla.edu/Grads/instructions.php. Students are admitted in the Fall, application deadline December 15. Only clinical and social areas have a different deadline—December 15 for clinical and social; December 30 for other areas. *Fee:* $60.

California, University of, Riverside

Department of Psychology
Olmsted Hall
Riverside, CA 92521-0426
Telephone: (951) 827-6306
Fax: (951) 827-3985
E-mail: *psygrad@ucr.edu*
Web: *http://www.psych.ucr.edu*

Department Information:
1962. Chairperson: David Funder. Number of Faculty: total–full-time 26, part-time 1; women–full-time 11; minority–full-time 5.

Programs and Degrees Offered:
Listed in the following order: Program area, degree type (T if terminal Master's), number awarded 7/03–6/04. Cognitive PhD (Doctor of Philosophy) 0, Developmental PhD (Doctor of Philosophy) 1, Social/Personality PhD (Doctor of Philosophy) 2, Systems Neuroscience PhD (Doctor of Philosophy) 0.

Student Applications/Admissions:
Student Applications
Cognitive PhD (Doctor of Philosophy)—Applications 2004–2005, 24. Total applicants accepted 2004–2005, 12. Number enrolled (new admits only) 2004–2005 full-time, 6. Openings 2005–2006, 6. The Median number of years required for completion of a degree are 5. The number of students enrolled full and part-time who were dismissed or voluntarily withdrew from this program area were 1. *Developmental PhD (Doctor of Philosophy)*—Applications 2004–2005, 14. Total applicants accepted 2004–2005, 9. Number enrolled (new admits only) 2004–2005 full-time, 5. Openings 2005–2006, 5. The Median number of years required for completion of a degree are 5. The number of students enrolled full and part-time who were dismissed or voluntarily withdrew from this program area were 1. *Social/Personality PhD (Doctor of Philosophy)*—Applications 2004–2005, 46. Total applicants accepted 2004–2005, 9. Number enrolled (new admits only) 2004–2005 full-time, 6. Openings 2005–2006, 4. The Median number of years required for completion of a degree are 5. The number of students enrolled full and part-time who were dismissed or voluntarily withdrew from this program area were 0. *Systems Neuroscience PhD (Doctor of Philosophy)*—Applications 2004–2005, 2. Total applicants accepted 2004–2005, 2. Number enrolled (new admits only) 2004–2005 full-time, 0. Openings 2005–2006, 2. The number of students enrolled full and part-time who were dismissed or voluntarily withdrew from this program area were 0.

Admissions Requirements:
Scores: Entries appear in this order: required test or GPA, minimum score (if required), median score of students entering

in 2003–2004. Doctoral Programs: GRE-V no minimum stated; GRE-Q no minimum stated; GRE-V+Q 1100, 1210; overall undergraduate GPA no minimum stated; last 2 years GPA 3.4, 3.84. A strong GPA in science courses is recommended for applicants to the Systems Neuroscience area.

Other Criteria: (importance of criteria rated low, medium, or high): GRE/MAT scores medium, research experience high, work experience low, extracurricular activity low, GPA medium, letters of recommendation high, interview high, statement of goals and objectives high. For additional information on admission requirements, go to: http://www.psych.ucr.edu/grad/admissions.html.

Student Characteristics: The following represents characteristics of students in 2004–2005 in all graduate psychology programs in the department: Female–full-time 44, part-time 0; Male–full-time 20, part-time 0; African American/Black–full-time 0, part-time 0; Hispanic/Latino(a)–full-time 6, part-time 0; Asian/Pacific Islander–full-time 11, part-time 0; American Indian/Alaska Native–full-time 0, part-time 0; Caucasian–full-time 47, part-time 0; Multi-ethnic–full-time 0, part-time 0; students subject to the Americans With Disabilities Act–full-time 0, part-time 0.

Financial Information/Assistance:

Tuition for Full-Time Study: *Doctoral:* State residents: per academic year $6,574; Nonstate residents: per academic year $17,709. Tuition is subject to change. See the following Web site for updates and changes in tuition costs: http://www.graddiv.ucr.edu/FinSupport.html.

Financial Assistance:

First Year Students: Teaching assistantships available for first-year. Average amount paid per academic year: $13,400. Average number of hours worked per week: 20. Apply by January 3. Tuition remission given: full. Research assistantships available for first-year. Average amount paid per academic year: $13,400. Average number of hours worked per week: 20. Apply by January 3. Tuition remission given: full. Fellowships and scholarships available for first-year. Average amount paid per academic year: $15,000. Average number of hours worked per week: 0. Apply by January 3. Tuition remission given: full.

Advanced Students: Teaching assistantships available for advanced students. Average amount paid per academic year: $13,400. Average number of hours worked per week: 20. Apply by January 3. Tuition remission given: full. Research assistantships available for advanced students. Average amount paid per academic year: $13,400. Average number of hours worked per week: 20. Apply by January 3. Tuition remission given: full.

Contact Information: Of all students currently enrolled full-time, 95% benefitted from one or more of the listed financial assistance programs. Application and information available online at: http://www.psych.ucr.edu/grad/app.html.

Internships/Practica: No information provided.

Housing and Day Care: On-campus housing is available. See the following Web site for more information: www.housing.ucr.edu. On-campus day care facilities are available. See the following Web site for more information: http://138.23.50.239/childrenservices/DesktopDefault.aspx phone: (951) 827-5130 or -3854.

Employment of Department Graduates:

Master's Degree Graduates: Of those who graduated in the academic year 2003–2004, the following categories and numbers represent the post-graduate activities and employment of master's degree graduates: Enrolled in a post-doctoral residency/fellowship (n/a), employed in independent practice (n/a), total from the above (master's) (0).

Doctoral Degree Graduates: Of those who graduated in the academic year 2003–2004, the following categories and numbers represent the post-graduate activities and employment of doctoral degree graduates: Enrolled in a psychology doctoral program (n/a), enrolled in a post-doctoral residency/fellowship (0), employed in an academic position at a 2-year/4-year college (2), employed in business or industry (research/consulting) (1), do not know (0), total from the above (doctoral) (3).

Additional Information:

Orientation, Objectives, and Emphasis of Department: The orientation is toward theoretical and research training. Objectives are to provide the appropriate theoretical, quantitative, and methodological background to enable graduates of the program to engage in high-quality research. Additionally, training and experience in university-level teaching are provided. We also offer a minor in quantitative which may be completed by any student in the PhD program in Psychology regardless of main area of interest. A concentration in health psychology is also offered in the social and developmental areas. The cognitive area has a strong concentration in cognitive modeling.

Special Facilities or Resources: The department has just moved into new, expanded facilities. The department has equipment and support systems to help students conduct research in all aspects of behavior. The neuroscience laboratories are equipped with the latest instrumentation for hormonal assays, extracellular and intracellular electrophysiology, and microscopic analysis of neuronal morphology. Research in the cognitive area incorporates computer-assisted experimental control for most any kind of reaction time experiment and has facilities for video and speech digitization, and infrared eye-tracking. SGI and multi-processor Unix workstations are used for more graphics or data-intensive applications. The developmental faculty have laboratory facilities to study parents and children, have access to the campus daycare center for studies that involve toddlers and preschool children, and have been very successful in conducting research in a culturally diverse local school system. The developmental faculty all participate in the Center for Family Studies, an interdisciplinary center. The social/personality psychology labs support research in social perception, nonverbal communication, health psychology, emotional expression, and attribution processes using audiovisual laboratories and observation rooms. Direct, free, access is available to PsycInfo, PubMed, and many other online journals and databases.

Information for Students With Physical Disabilities: See the following Web site for more information: http://www.specialservices.ucr.edu/swd/default.html; TTY (951) 827-4538.

Application Information:

Send to: Graduate Admissions Psychology Department, University of California, Riverside, Riverside, CA 92521. Application available online. URL of online application: http://www.graddiv.ucr.edu/HowApply.html. Students are admitted in the Fall, application deadline

January 3. *Fee*: $60. No waivers possible for foreign applicants. Specific critieria apply for waiver of application fee. Contact Graduate Admissions in the Graduate Division, (951) 827-3313; grdadmis@pop.ucr.edu.

California, University of, San Diego

Department of Psychology
La Jolla, CA 92093-0109
Telephone: (858) 534-3002
Fax: (858) 534-7190
E-mail: *jwixted@ucsd.edu, rjwoods@ucsd.edu*
Web: *http://psy.ucsd.edu/*

Department Information:

1965. Chairperson: John T. Wixted. Number of Faculty: total–full-time 29, part-time 10; women–full-time 7, part-time 5; minority–full-time 2, part-time 1.

Programs and Degrees Offered:

Listed in the following order: Program area, degree type (T if terminal Master's), number awarded 7/03–6/04. Experimental PhD (Doctor of Philosophy) 11.

Student Applications/Admissions:

Student Applications

Experimental PhD (Doctor of Philosophy)—Applications 2004–2005, 229. Total applicants accepted 2004–2005, 26. Number enrolled (new admits only) 2004–2005 full-time, 15. Openings 2005–2006, 14. The Median number of years required for completion of a degree are 5.5. The number of students enrolled full and part-time, who were dismissed or voluntarily withdrew from this program area were 1.

Admissions Requirements:

Scores: Entries appear in this order: required test or GPA, minimum score (if required), median score of students entering in 2003–2004. Doctoral Programs: GRE-V 600, 650; GRE-Q 600, 660; GRE-V+Q 1200, 1310; overall undergraduate GPA 3.0, 3.8.

Other Criteria: (importance of criteria rated low, medium, or high): GRE/MAT scores high, research experience high, work experience medium, extracurricular activity low, clinically related public service low, GPA high, letters of recommendation high, interview high, statement of goals and objectives high.

Student Characteristics: The following represents characteristics of students in 2004–2005 in all graduate psychology programs in the department: Female–full-time 34, part-time 0; Male–full-time 21, part-time 0; African American/Black–full-time 0, part-time 0; Hispanic/Latino(a)–full-time 4, part-time 0; Asian/Pacific Islander–full-time 3, part-time 0; American Indian/Alaska Native–full-time 0, part-time 0; Caucasian–full-time 0, part-time 0.

Financial Information/Assistance:

Financial Assistance:

First Year Students: No information provided.
Advanced Students: No information provided.

Contact Information: Application and information available online at: http://psy.ucsd.edu/.

Internships/Practica: No information provided.

Housing and Day Care: On-campus housing is available. See the following Web site for more information: http://hds.ucsd.edu/hsgaffil/index.html. On-campus day care facilities are available. See the following Web site for more information: http://blink.ucsd.edu/Blink/External/Topics/Policy/1,1162,227,00.html?coming_from=Content.

Employment of Department Graduates:

Master's Degree Graduates: Of those who graduated in the academic year 2003–2004, the following categories and numbers represent the post-graduate activities and employment of master's degree graduates: Enrolled in a post-doctoral residency/fellowship (n/a), employed in independent practice (n/a), total from the above (master's) (0).

Doctoral Degree Graduates: Of those who graduated in the academic year 2003–2004, the following categories and numbers represent the post-graduate activities and employment of doctoral degree graduates: Enrolled in a psychology doctoral program (n/a), enrolled in a post-doctoral residency/fellowship (2), employed in an academic position at a university (3), employed in an academic position at a 2-year/4-year college (2), employed in business or industry (research/consulting) (1), not seeking employment (2), do not know (1), total from the above (doctoral) (11).

Additional Information:

Orientation, Objectives, and Emphasis of Department: The Department of Psychology at the University of California San Diego provides advanced training in research on most aspects of experimental psychology. Modern laboratories and an attractive physical setting combine with a distinguished faculty, both within the Department of Psychology and in supporting disciplines, to provide research opportunities and training at the frontiers of psychological science. The graduate training program emphasizes and supports individual research, starting with the first year of study. The Department offers the following emphases: behavior analysis, biopsychology, cognitive psychology, developmental psychology, sensation and perception, and social psychology.

Special Facilities or Resources: The Department shares research space and facilities with the Center for Brain and Cognition. Within the joint facilities, there are two computing facilities, a computational laboratory, visual and auditory laboratories, social psychology laboratories, cognitive laboratories, developmental laboratories, a clinic for autistic children, animal facilities, and extensive contacts with hospitals, industry, and the legal system. In addition to the numerous impressive libraries on campus, the Department also keeps a large selection of literature within our Mandler Library. Collaborative research is carried on with members of the Departments of Linguistics (who share our building), Cognitive Science, Computer Science and Engineering, Sociology, Music, Ophthalmology, Neurosciences, members of the UCSD School of Medicine, Scripps Clinic and Research Foundation, and with the Salk Institute for Biological Studies. The Scripps Institution of Oceanography, located on campus, provides facilities in neurosciences as does the School of Medicine. For a complete tour of the university and its facilities, visit: www.ucsd.edu/visit.

Information for Students With Physical Disabilities: See the following Web site for more information: http://orpheus.ucsd. edu/osd/.

Application Information:
Send to: Graduate Admission, Dept. of Psychology-0109, University of California-San Diego, La Jolla, CA 92093. Students are admitted in the Fall, application deadline January 6. *Fee:* $60.

California, University of, Santa Barbara
Counseling/Clinical/School Psychology
Graduate School of Education
Phelps Hall 1110
Santa Barbara, CA 93106-9490
Telephone: (805) 893-3375
Fax: (805) 893-3375
E-mail: *cosden@education.ucsb.edu*
Web: *www.education.ucsb.edu/ccsp/*

Department Information:
1965. Director of Training: Merith Cosden, PhD. Number of Faculty: total–full-time 11; women–full-time 4; minority–full-time 4.

Programs and Degrees Offered:
Listed in the following order: Program area, degree type (T if terminal Master's), number awarded 7/03–6/04. Counseling/Clinical/School PhD (Doctor of Philosophy) 12, School Other 3.

APA Accreditation: Combination PhD (Doctor of Philosophy).

Student Applications/Admissions:
Student Applications
Counseling/Clinical/School PhD (Doctor of Philosophy)—Applications 2004–2005, 294. Total applicants accepted 2004–2005, 20. Number enrolled (new admits only) 2004–2005 full-time, 11. Number enrolled (new admits only) 2004–2005 part-time, 0. Openings 2005–2006, 12. The Median number of years required for completion of a degree are 6. The number of students enrolled full and part-time who were dismissed or voluntarily withdrew from this program area were 2. *School Other*—Applications 2004–2005, 64. Total applicants accepted 2004–2005, 6. Number enrolled (new admits only) 2004–2005 full-time, 5. Number enrolled (new admits only) 2004–2005 part-time, 0. Openings 2005–2006, 4. The Median number of years required for completion of a degree are 3. The number of students enrolled full and part-time who were dismissed or voluntarily withdrew from this program area were 0.

Admissions Requirements:
Scores: Entries appear in this order: required test or GPA, minimum score (if required), median score of students entering in 2003–2004. Master's Programs: GRE-V no minimum stated, 590; GRE-Q no minimum stated, 655; GRE-V+Q no minimum stated, 1245; MAT no minimum stated; overall undergraduate GPA no minimum stated; last 2 years GPA 3.0, 3.66. GRE is preferred and MAT is accepted. Doctoral Programs:

GRE-V no minimum stated, 582; GRE-Q no minimum stated, 662; GRE-V+Q no minimum stated, 1244; MAT no minimum stated; overall undergraduate GPA no minimum stated; last 2 years GPA 3.0, 3.80. GRE-V+Q or V+A scores of 1200 is competitive. MAT is accepted and 65 score is competitive.
Other Criteria: (importance of criteria rated low, medium, or high): GRE/MAT scores medium, research experience high, work experience medium, extracurricular activity medium, clinically related public service medium, GPA high, letters of recommendation high, interview high, statement of goals and objectives high, Research experience less important for MEd. Match of interests with faculty important. For additional information on admission requirements, go to: www.education. ucsb.edu/CCSP/checklist.html.

Student Characteristics: The following represents characteristics of students in 2004–2005 in all graduate psychology programs in the department: Female–full-time 61, part-time 0; Male–full-time 13, part-time 0; African American/Black–full-time 2, part-time 0; Hispanic/Latino(a)–full-time 16, part-time 0; Asian/Pacific Islander–full-time 17, part-time 0; American Indian/Alaska Native–full-time 0, part-time 0; Caucasian–full-time 34, part-time 0; Multi-ethnic–full-time 5, part-time 0; students subject to the Americans With Disabilities Act–full-time 1, part-time 0.

Financial Information/Assistance:
Tuition for Full-Time Study: *Master's:* State residents: per academic year $8,377; Nonstate residents: per academic year $23,317. *Doctoral:* State residents: per academic year $8,377; Nonstate residents: per academic year $23,317. Tuition is subject to change. See the following Web site for updates and changes in tuition costs: www.graddiv.ucsb.edu.

Financial Assistance:
First Year Students: Teaching assistantships available for first-year. Average amount paid per academic year: $14,772. Average number of hours worked per week: 20. Apply by December 10. Tuition remission given: full and partial. Research assistantships available for first-year. Average amount paid per academic year: $14,772. Average number of hours worked per week: 20. Apply by December 10. Tuition remission given: full and partial. Fellowships and scholarships available for first-year. Average amount paid per academic year: $17,000. Average number of hours worked per week: 0. Apply by December 10. Tuition remission given: full.
Advanced Students: Teaching assistantships available for advanced students. Average amount paid per academic year: $14,772. Average number of hours worked per week: 20. Tuition remission given: full and partial. Research assistantships available for advanced students. Average amount paid per academic year: $14,772. Average number of hours worked per week: 20. Tuition remission given: full and partial. Fellowships and scholarships available for advanced students. Average amount paid per academic year: $17,000. Average number of hours worked per week: 20. Tuition remission given: full.
Contact Information: Of all students currently enrolled full-time, 90% benefitted from one or more of the listed financial assistance programs.

Internships/Practica: We provide supervised training in our Hosford Clinic, a sliding scale agency which serves clients from the community. Students in the clinical emphasis have external practica in community based agencies, students in the counseling emphasis have external practica at our Counseling and Career Services Center, and students in the school emphasis have external practica in the schools. For those doctoral students for whom a professional internship is required prior to graduation, 6 applied in 2003–2004. Of those who applied, 6 were placed in internships listed by the Association of Psychology Postdoctoral and Internship Programs (APPIC); 6 were placed in APA accredited internships.

Housing and Day Care: On-campus housing is available. See the following Web sites for more information: www.housing.ucsb. edu and www.graddiv.ucsb.edu. On-campus day care facilities are available.

Employment of Department Graduates:

Master's Degree Graduates: Of those who graduated in the academic year 2003–2004, the following categories and numbers represent the post-graduate activities and employment of master's degree graduates: Enrolled in a psychology doctoral program (0), enrolled in another graduate/professional program (2), enrolled in a post-doctoral residency/fellowship (n/a), employed in independent practice (n/a), total from the above (master's) (2).

Doctoral Degree Graduates: Of those who graduated in the academic year 2003–2004, the following categories and numbers represent the post-graduate activities and employment of doctoral degree graduates: Enrolled in a psychology doctoral program (n/a), enrolled in a post-doctoral residency/fellowship (7), employed in an academic position at a university (6), employed in a professional position in a school system (2), employed in a community mental health/counseling center (1), total from the above (doctoral) (16).

Additional Information:

Orientation, Objectives, and Emphasis of Department: The primary goal of the combined psychology program is to prepare graduates who will (a) conduct research and teach in university settings and (b) assume leadership roles in the academic community and in the helping professions. The program has a secondary goal of training students to provide psychological services in university, school, and community agency settings.

Special Facilities or Resources: The UCSB Combined Psychology Program has its own training clinic, the Hosford Clinic, which serves community clients, and which was completely renovated in 1987 and equipped with state-of-the-art video equipment for recording, reviewing, editing, and live monitoring of assessment and counseling sessions. Computer laboratories equipped with Macintosh and IBM personal computers are available for student use. Special computing facilities for statistical analyses are also easily accessible.

Application Information:

Send to: Student Affairs Office, Gevirtz Graduate School of Education, University of California, Santa Barbara, CA 93106-9490. Application available online. URL of online application: www.education.ucsb.edu/ CCSP/CCSPadm.html. Students are admitted in the Fall, application deadline December 10. *Fee:* $60.

California, University of, Santa Barbara
Department of Psychology
Santa Barbara, CA 93106-9660
Telephone: (805) 893-2793
Fax: (805) 893-4303
E-mail: *grad-info@psych.ucsb.edu*
Web: *http://www.psych.ucsb.edu*

Department Information:

1953. Chairperson: James Blascovich. Number of Faculty: total–full-time 28, part-time 1; women–full-time 8; minority–full-time 1.

Programs and Degrees Offered:

Listed in the following order: Program area, degree type (T if terminal Master's), number awarded 7/03–6/04. Cognitive and perception PhD (Doctor of Philosophy) 2, development and evolution PhD (Doctor of Philosophy) 1, neuroscience and behavior PhD (Doctor of Philosophy) 1, social PhD (Doctor of Philosophy) 5.

Student Applications/Admissions:

Student Applications

Cognitive and perception PhD (Doctor of Philosophy)—Applications 2004–2005, 41. Total applicants accepted 2004–2005, 12. Number enrolled (new admits only) 2004–2005 full-time, 5. The Median number of years required for completion of a degree are 5.5. The number of students enrolled full and part-time who were dismissed or voluntarily withdrew from this program area were 0. *Development and evolution PhD (Doctor of Philosophy)*—Applications 2004–2005, 43. Total applicants accepted 2004–2005, 3. Number enrolled (new admits only) 2004–2005 full-time, 1. Openings 2005–2006, 2. The Median number of years required for completion of a degree are 5.5. The number of students enrolled full and part-time who were dismissed or voluntarily withdrew from this program area were 0. *Neuroscience and behavior PhD (Doctor of Philosophy)*—Applications 2004–2005, 14. Total applicants accepted 2004–2005, 3. Number enrolled (new admits only) 2004–2005 full-time, 2. Openings 2005–2006, 2. The Median number of years required for completion of a degree are 6. The number of students enrolled full and part-time who were dismissed or voluntarily withdrew from this program area were 0. *Social PhD (Doctor of Philosophy)*—Applications 2004–2005, 89. Total applicants accepted 2004–2005, 8. Number enrolled (new admits only) 2004–2005 full-time, 5. Openings 2005–2006, 3. The Median number of years required for completion of a degree are 5.5. The number of students enrolled full and part-time who were dismissed or voluntarily withdrew from this program area were 0.

Admissions Requirements:

Scores: Entries appear in this order: required test or GPA, minimum score (if required), median score of students entering in 2003–2004. Master's Programs: GRE-V no minimum stated; GRE-Q no minimum stated; GRE-Analytical no minimum stated; last 2 years GPA no minimum stated; psychology GPA no minimum stated. There were no MA students admitted in 2004. Doctoral Programs: GRE-V no minimum stated, 595;

GRE-Q no minimum stated, 644; GRE-Analytical no minimum stated, 703; last 2 years GPA no minimum stated, 3.65. *Other Criteria:* (importance of criteria rated low, medium, or high): GRE/MAT scores medium, research experience high, work experience low, GPA medium, letters of recommendation high, statement of goals and objectives high. If applicant is interviewed (not required), this can be very important.

Student Characteristics: The following represents characteristics of students in 2004–2005 in all graduate psychology programs in the department: Female–full-time 39, part-time 0; Male–full-time 32, part-time 0; African American/Black–full-time 3, part-time 0; Hispanic/Latino(a)–full-time 4, part-time 0; Asian/Pacific Islander–full-time 3, part-time 0; American Indian/Alaska Native–full-time 0, part-time 0; Caucasian–full-time 61, part-time 0; students subject to the Americans With Disabilities Act–full-time 1, part-time 0.

Financial Information/Assistance:

Tuition for Full-Time Study: *Master's:* State residents: per academic year $6,861; Nonstate residents: per academic year $21,555. *Doctoral:* State residents: per academic year $6,861; Nonstate residents: per academic year $21,555. Tuition is subject to change.

Financial Assistance:

First Year Students: Teaching assistantships available for first-year. Average amount paid per academic year: $14,571. Average number of hours worked per week: 20. Apply by December 15. Tuition remission given: partial. Research assistantships available for first-year. Average amount paid per academic year: $14,571. Average number of hours worked per week: 20. Apply by December 15. Tuition remission given: full. Fellowships and scholarships available for first-year. Average amount paid per academic year: $18,000. Average number of hours worked per week: 0. Apply by December 15. Tuition remission given: full.

Advanced Students: Teaching assistantships available for advanced students. Average amount paid per academic year: $14,571. Average number of hours worked per week: 20. Tuition remission given: partial. Research assistantships available for advanced students. Average amount paid per academic year: $15,800. Average number of hours worked per week: 20. Tuition remission given: full. Fellowships and scholarships available for advanced students. Average amount paid per academic year: $18,000. Average number of hours worked per week: 0. Tuition remission given: full.

Contact Information: Of all students currently enrolled full-time, 97% benefitted from one or more of the listed financial assistance programs.

Internships/Practica: No information provided.

Housing and Day Care: On-campus housing is available. See the following Web site for more information: www.housing.ucsb.edu. On-campus day care facilities are available. See the following Web site for more information: http://www.sa.ucsb.edu/childcare/uchildcenter/index.asp.

Employment of Department Graduates:

Master's Degree Graduates: Of those who graduated in the academic year 2003–2004, the following categories and numbers represent the post-graduate activities and employment of master's degree graduates: Enrolled in a post-doctoral residency/fellowship (n/a), employed in independent practice (n/a), total from the above (master's) (0).

Doctoral Degree Graduates: Of those who graduated in the academic year 2003–2004, the following categories and numbers represent the post-graduate activities and employment of doctoral degree graduates: Enrolled in a psychology doctoral program (n/a), enrolled in a post-doctoral residency/fellowship (6), employed in an academic position at a university (2), employed in other positions at a higher education institution (1), total from the above (doctoral) (9).

Additional Information:

Orientation, Objectives, and Emphasis of Department: The major graduate program of the Department of Psychology consists of work leading to the PhD degree; however, the MA is also awarded. Specialized training is offered in neuroscience and behavior, cognitive and perceptual sciences, developmental and evolutionary psychology, and social psychology.

Information for Students With Physical Disabilities: See the following Web site for more information: http://www.sa.ucsb.edu/dsp/.

Application Information:

Send to: Graduate Admissions. Application available online. URL of online application: http://www.graddiv.ucsb.edu. Students are admitted in the Fall, application deadline December 15. *Fee:* $60.

California, University of, Santa Cruz
Psychology Department
273 Social Sciences 2
Santa Cruz, CA 95064
Telephone: (831) 459-4932
Fax: (831) 459-3519
E-mail: *jpcrutch@ucsc.edu*
Web: *http://psych.ucsc.edu/*

Department Information:

1965. Chairperson: Maureen Callanan. Number of Faculty: total–full-time 29, part-time 16; women–full-time 15, part-time 10; minority–full-time 8.

Programs and Degrees Offered:

Listed in the following order: Program area, degree type (T if terminal Master's), number awarded 7/03–6/04. Developmental PhD (Doctor of Philosophy) 3, social PhD (Doctor of Philosophy) 2, cognitive PhD (Doctor of Philosophy) 2.

Student Applications/Admissions:

Student Applications

Developmental PhD (Doctor of Philosophy)—Applications 2004–2005, 55. Total applicants accepted 2004–2005, 11. Number enrolled (new admits only) 2004–2005 full-time, 5. Total enrolled 2004–2005 full-time, 19, part-time, 1. Openings 2005–2006, 8. The Median number of years required for completion of a degree are 6. The number of students enrolled full and part-time who were dismissed or voluntarily withdrew from this program area were 0. *Social PhD (Doctor of Philosophy)*—

Applications 2004–2005, 63. Total applicants accepted 2004–2005, 6. Number enrolled (new admits only) 2004–2005 full-time, 4. Total enrolled 2004–2005 full-time, 14, part-time, 3. Openings 2005–2006, 7. The Median number of years required for completion of a degree are 6. The number of students enrolled full and part-time who were dismissed or voluntarily withdrew from this program area were 0. *Cognitive PhD (Doctor of Philosophy)*—Applications 2004–2005, 30. Total applicants accepted 2004–2005, 7. Number enrolled (new admits only) 2004–2005 full-time, 5. Total enrolled 2004–2005 full-time, 21, part-time, 1. Openings 2005–2006, 8. The Median number of years required for completion of a degree are 6. The number of students enrolled full and part-time who were dismissed or voluntarily withdrew from this program area were 0.

Admissions Requirements:

Scores: Entries appear in this order: required test or GPA, minimum score (if required), median score of students entering in 2003–2004. Doctoral Programs: GRE-V 50%, 570; GRE-Q 50%, 650; GRE-Analytical 50%, 665; overall undergraduate GPA 2.75, 3.5; last 2 years GPA 3.67, 3.7.

Other Criteria: (importance of criteria rated low, medium, or high): research experience high, work experience medium, extracurricular activity medium, GPA high, letters of recommendation high, statement of goals and objectives high.

Student Characteristics: The following represents characteristics of students in 2004–2005 in all graduate psychology programs in the department: Female–full-time 42, part-time 4; Male–full-time 12, part-time 1; African American/Black–full-time 0, part-time 0; Hispanic/Latino(a)–full-time 14, part-time 0; Asian/Pacific Islander–full-time 7, part-time 2; American Indian/Alaska Native–full-time 1, part-time 0; Caucasian–full-time 32, part-time 3; Multi-ethnic–full-time 0, part-time 0; students subject to the Americans With Disabilities Act–full-time 0, part-time 0.

Financial Information/Assistance:

Tuition for Full-Time Study: *Doctoral:* State residents: per academic year $9,390; Nonstate residents: per academic year $24,354. Tuition is subject to change. See the following Web site for updates and changes in tuition costs: http://www.graddiv.ucsc.edu/PSfeesandexpenses.html.

Financial Assistance:

First Year Students: Teaching assistantships available for first-year. Average number of hours worked per week: 20. Research assistantships available for first-year. Traineeships available for first-year. Fellowships and scholarships available for first-year. Apply by February 1.

Advanced Students: Teaching assistantships available for advanced students. Average number of hours worked per week: 20. Research assistantships available for advanced students.

Contact Information: Of all students currently enrolled full-time, 100% benefitted from one or more of the listed financial assistance programs.

Internships/Practica: None.

Housing and Day Care: On-campus housing is available. Graduate Student Housing, (831) 458-2462; Family Students Housing, (831) 459-2549; Off-campus Housing, (831) 459-4435. On-campus day care facilities are available.

Employment of Department Graduates:

Master's Degree Graduates: Of those who graduated in the academic year 2003–2004, the following categories and numbers represent the post-graduate activities and employment of master's degree graduates: Enrolled in a post-doctoral residency/fellowship (n/a), employed in independent practice (n/a), total from the above (master's) (0).

Doctoral Degree Graduates: Of those who graduated in the academic year 2003–2004, the following categories and numbers represent the post-graduate activities and employment of doctoral degree graduates: Enrolled in a psychology doctoral program (n/a), enrolled in another graduate/professional program (0), enrolled in a post-doctoral residency/fellowship (3), employed in independent practice (0), employed in an academic position at a university (3), employed in an academic position at a 2-year/4-year college (0), employed in other positions at a higher education institution (0), employed in a professional position in a school system (0), employed in business or industry (research/consulting) (0), employed in business or industry (management) (0), employed in a government agency (research) (1), employed in a government agency (professional services) (0), employed in a community mental health/counseling center (0), employed in a hospital/medical center (0), still seeking employment (0), not seeking employment (0), other employment position (0), do not know (0), total from the above (doctoral) (7).

Additional Information:

Orientation, Objectives, and Emphasis of Department: The Psychology Department at UC Santa Cruz offers a PhD degree with areas of specialization in cognitive, developmental, and social psychology. Students are prepared for research, teaching, and administrative positions in colleges and universities, as well as positions in schools, government, and other public and private organizations. The PhD is a research degree. Students are required to demonstrate the ability to carry through to completion rigorous empirical research and to be active in research throughout their graduate career. Course requirements establish a foundation for critical evaluation of research literature and the design of conceptually important empirical research. To support students in achieving these goals, each student must be associated with one of the faculty, who serves as academic advisor and research sponsor. The program requires full-time enrollment. Important Notes: The program does not offer courses, training, or supervision in counseling or clinical psychology. Students are not admitted to pursue only a Master's degree. However, students may be awarded a Master's degree as part of their studies for the PhD

Special Facilities or Resources: The department provides training to prepare the student for academic and applied settings. Graduate students have the use of a variety of research facilities, including a number of computer-controlled experimental laboratories. Electronic equipment is available to allow the generation of sophisticated written and pictorial vision displays, musical sequences, and synthesized and visual speech patterns. There are observational facilities for developmental psychological research, and a discourse analysis lab. A bilingual survey unit is under development which will utilize public opinion survey technology to study significant public policy, legal, and political issues that are critical to California's emerging majority population. Research opportunities exist with diverse sample groups in both laboratory and natural settings. The department has collaborative relationships with the National

Center for Research on Cultural Diversity, Second Language Learning, and the Bilingual Research Center.

Information for Students With Physical Disabilities: See the following Web site for more information: http://ucsc.edu/drc/.

Application Information:
Send to: Psychology Department, Graduate Program, 1156 High Street, University of California, Santa Cruz, CA 95064-1077, phone: (831) 459-4932. Paper application materials are no longer available, you will need to find access to the https://apply.embark.com/Grad/UCSantaCruz/74/ Web site. It is preferable that you submit your application online so that the information you submit can be imported into a database for all faculty to review. Application available online. URL of online application: https://apply.embark.com/Grad/UCSantaCruz/75/. Students are admitted in the Fall, application deadline December 15. *Fee:* $60.

Claremont Graduate University
Graduate Department of Psychology
School of Behavioral and Organizational Sciences
123 East Eighth Street
Claremont, CA 91711-3955
Telephone: (909) 621-8084
Fax: (909) 621-8905
E-mail: *psych@cgu.edu*
Web: *http://www.cgu.edu/sbos*

Department Information:
1926. Dean: Stewart I. Donaldson. Number of Faculty: total–full-time 11, part-time 58; women–full-time 6, part-time 26; minority–full-time 2, part-time 10.

Programs and Degrees Offered:
Listed in the following order: Program area, degree type (T if terminal Master's), number awarded 7/03–6/04. Applied Social Psych/Evaluation Co-Concentration MA/MS (Master of Arts/Science) (T) 1, Cognitive Psychology/Evaluation Co-Concentration MA/MS (Master of Arts/Science) (T) 0, Organizational/Evaluation Co-Concentration MA/MS (Master of Arts/Science) (T) 9, Developmental Psych/Evaluation Co-Concentration MA/MS (Master of Arts/Science) (T) 0, Human Resources Design MA/MS (Master of Arts/Science) (T) 12, Applied Cognitive Psychology PhD (Doctor of Philosophy) 6, Applied Developmental Psychology PhD (Doctor of Philosophy) 2, Applied Social Psychology PhD (Doctor of Philosophy) 4, Evaluation and Applied Research Methods PhD (Doctor of Philosophy) 0, Organizational Behavior, Industrial/Organizational PhD (Doctor of Philosophy) 2, Health Behavior Research (new in 2005) MA/MS (Master of Arts/Science) (T).

Student Applications/Admissions:
Student Applications
Applied Social Psych/Evaluation Co-Concentration MA/MS (Master of Arts/Science)—Applications 2004–2005, 57. Number enrolled (new admits only) 2004–2005 full-time, 8. Total enrolled 2004–2005 full-time, 11. Openings 2005–2006, 7. The Median number of years required for completion of a degree are 2. The number of students enrolled full and part-

time who were dismissed or voluntarily withdrew from this program area were 0. *Cognitive Psychology/Evaluation Co-Concentration MA/MS (Master of Arts/Science)*—Applications 2004–2005, 17. Number enrolled (new admits only) 2004–2005 full-time, 0. Openings 2005–2006, 3. The Median number of years required for completion of a degree are 2. The number of students enrolled full and part-time who were dismissed or voluntarily withdrew from this program area were 0. *Organizational/Evaluation Co-Concentration MA/MS (Master of Arts/Science)*—Applications 2004–2005, 50. Number enrolled (new admits only) 2004–2005 full-time, 10. Total enrolled 2004–2005 full-time, 27. Openings 2005–2006, 10. The Median number of years required for completion of a degree are 2. The number of students enrolled full and part-time who were dismissed or voluntarily withdrew from this program area were 1. *Developmental Psych/Evaluation Co-Concentration MA/MS (Master of Arts/Science)*—Applications 2004–2005, 33. Number enrolled (new admits only) 2004–2005 full-time, 1. Total enrolled 2004–2005 full-time, 2. Openings 2005–2006, 4. The Median number of years required for completion of a degree are 2. The number of students enrolled full and part-time who were dismissed or voluntarily withdrew from this program area were 0. *Human Resources Design MA/MS (Master of Arts/Science)*—Applications 2004–2005, 20. Number enrolled (new admits only) 2004–2005 full-time, 3. Number enrolled (new admits only) 2004–2005 part-time, 10. Total enrolled 2004–2005 full-time, 9, part-time, 23. Openings 2005–2006, 10. The Median number of years required for completion of a degree are 2. The number of students enrolled full and part-time who were dismissed or voluntarily withdrew from this program area were 3. *Applied Cognitive Psychology PhD (Doctor of Philosophy)*—Applications 2004–2005, 13. Number enrolled (new admits only) 2004–2005 full-time, 2. Total enrolled 2004–2005 full-time, 19. Openings 2005–2006, 7. The Median number of years required for completion of a degree are 5. The number of students enrolled full and part-time who were dismissed or voluntarily withdrew from this program area were 1. *Applied Developmental Psychology PhD (Doctor of Philosophy)*—Applications 2004–2005, 32. Number enrolled (new admits only) 2004–2005 full-time, 6. Total enrolled 2004–2005 full-time, 23. Openings 2005–2006, 7. The Median number of years required for completion of a degree are 5. The number of students enrolled full and part-time who were dismissed or voluntarily withdrew from this program area were 0. *Applied Social Psychology PhD (Doctor of Philosophy)*—Applications 2004–2005, 48. Number enrolled (new admits only) 2004–2005 full-time, 11. Total enrolled 2004–2005 full-time, 38. Openings 2005–2006, 8. The Median number of years required for completion of a degree are 6. The number of students enrolled full and part-time who were dismissed or voluntarily withdrew from this program area were 1. *Evaluation and Applied Research Methods PhD (Doctor of Philosophy)*—Applications 2004–2005, 8. Number enrolled (new admits only) 2004–2005 full-time, 6. Total enrolled 2004–2005 full-time, 11. Openings 2005–2006, 5. The Median number of years required for completion of a degree are 5. The number of students enrolled full and part-time who were dismissed or voluntarily withdrew from this program area were 0. *Organizational Behavior, Industrial/Organizational PhD (Doctor of Philosophy)*—Applications 2004–2005, 47. Number enrolled (new admits only) 2004–2005 full-time, 6. Total enrolled 2004–2005 full-time, 35. Openings 2005–2006, 7. The Median number of years required for completion of a degree are 5. The number of students enrolled full and part-time who were dismissed or voluntarily withdrew from this program area were 1. *Health Behavior Research (new in 2005) MA/MS (Master of Arts/Science)*—Openings 2005–2006, 5.

Admissions Requirements:

Scores: Entries appear in this order: required test or GPA, minimum score (if required), median score of students entering in 2003–2004. Master's Programs: GRE-V no minimum stated, 502; GRE-Q no minimum stated, 605; GRE-V+Q no minimum stated, 1107; GRE-Analytical no minimum stated, 4.80; overall undergraduate GPA 3.00, 3.34. HRD program requires either GRE or GMAT scores and weights work experience more heavily in admissions. Doctoral Programs: GRE-V no minimum stated, 553; GRE-Q no minimum stated, 650; GRE-V+Q no minimum stated, 1203; GRE-Analytical no minimum stated, 5.08; overall undergraduate GPA 3.00, 3.77.

Other Criteria: (importance of criteria rated low, medium, or high): GRE/MAT scores high, research experience medium, work experience medium, extracurricular activity medium, GPA high, letters of recommendation high, statement of goals and objectives high. HRD program does not require research experience but emphasizes work experience more strongly. For additional information on admission requirements, go to: www.cgu.edu/sbos.

Student Characteristics: The following represents characteristics of students in 2004–2005 in all graduate psychology programs in the department: Female–full-time 130, part-time 13; Male–full-time 45, part-time 10; African American/Black–full-time 12, part-time 1; Hispanic/Latino(a)–full-time 16, part-time 7; Asian/Pacific Islander–full-time 27, part-time 4; American Indian/Alaska Native–full-time 1, part-time 1; Caucasian–full-time 79, part-time 10; Multi-ethnic–full-time 39, part-time 3; students subject to the Americans With Disabilities Act–full-time 0, part-time 0.

Financial Information/Assistance:

Tuition for Full-Time Study: *Master's:* State residents: per academic year $27,902, $1,214 per credit hour; Nonstate residents: per academic year $27,902, $1,214 per credit hour. *Doctoral:* State residents: per academic year $27,902, $1,214 per credit hour; Nonstate residents: per academic year $27,902, $1,214 per credit hour.

Financial Assistance:

First Year Students: Teaching assistantships available for first-year. Average amount paid per academic year: $5,200. Average number of hours worked per week: 10. Research assistantships available for first-year. Average amount paid per academic year: $5,200. Average number of hours worked per week: 12. Fellowships and scholarships available for first-year. Average amount paid per academic year: $6,976. Tuition remission given: partial.

Advanced Students: Teaching assistantships available for advanced students. Average amount paid per academic year: $5,200. Average number of hours worked per week: 10. Research assistantships available for advanced students. Average amount paid per academic year: $5,200. Average number of hours worked per week: 12. Fellowships and scholarships available for advanced students. Average amount paid per academic year: $6,976. Apply by February 15. Tuition remission given: partial.

Contact Information: Of all students currently enrolled full-time, 100% benefitted from one or more of the listed financial assistance programs. Application and information available online at http://www.cgu.edu/pages/102.asp.

Internships/Practica: Research and consulting internships are available and encouraged for all students. Appropriate settings and roles are arranged according to the interests of individual students within the wide range of opportunities available in a large urban area. Typical settings include social service agencies; business and industrial organizations; hospitals, clinics, and mental health agencies; schools; governmental and regulatory agencies; and nonacademic research institutions, as well as numerous onsite research institutes.

Housing and Day Care: On-campus housing is available. See the following Web site for more information: http://www.cgu.edu/pages/1156.asp. On-campus day care facilities are available.

Employment of Department Graduates:

Master's Degree Graduates: Of those who graduated in the academic year 2003–2004, the following categories and numbers represent the post-graduate activities and employment of master's degree graduates: Enrolled in another graduate/professional program (1), enrolled in a post-doctoral residency/fellowship (n/a), employed in independent practice (n/a), employed in an academic position at a university (1), employed in an academic position at a 2-year/4-year college (1), employed in other positions at a higher education institution (4), employed in a professional position in a school system (2), employed in business or industry (research/consulting) (3), employed in business or industry (management) (5), employed in a hospital/medical center (2), other employment position (15), total from the above (master's) (34).

Doctoral Degree Graduates: Of those who graduated in the academic year 2003–2004, the following categories and numbers represent the post-graduate activities and employment of doctoral degree graduates: Enrolled in a psychology doctoral program (n/a), employed in other positions at a higher education institution (2), employed in business or industry (research/consulting) (1), employed in business or industry (management) (1), employed in a community mental health/counseling center (2), employed in a hospital/medical center (1), other employment position (3), total from the above (doctoral) (10).

Additional Information:

Orientation, Objectives, and Emphasis of Department: The program emphasizes contemporary human problems and social issues, and the organizations and systems involved in such issues, as well as basic substantive research in social, organizational, developmental, and cognitive psychology and health behavior. Unusual specialty opportunities are available in organizational behavior, applied cognitive psychology, applied social psychology, health psychology, program evaluation research. The program offers preparation for careers in public service and business and industry as well as teaching and research. Research, theory, and practice are stressed in such policy and program areas as organizations and work; human social and physical environments; social service systems; psychological effects of educational computer technology; health and mental health systems; crime, delinquency, and law; aging and life span education. Many opportunities are available for research, consulting, and field experiences in these and related areas. Strong emphasis is given to training in a broad range of research methodologics, from naturalistic observation to experimental design, with special attention to field research methods. Seminars, tutorials, independent research, individualized student program plans, practical field experience, and close advisory and collaborative relations with the faculty are designed to foster clarifications of individual goals, intellectual and professional growth, self-pacing, and attractive career opportunities.

Special Facilities or Resources: The school is equipped with labs for social, developmental, and cognitive research, supplies and equipment for field research, a student lounge, and a department library. The computer facilities are excellent, conveniently located, and include a wide variety of application programs. The department cooperates in overseeing research institutes for student-faculty grant or contract research, focusing on major problems of organizational and program evaluation research as well as research on social issues. Claremont Graduate University is a free-standing graduate institution within the context of the Claremont University Consortium of five colleges, the Graduate University, and the Keck Graduate Institute. This context allows the department to concentrate exclusively on graduate education in a relaxed, intimate context while enjoying the resources of a major university. In addition to the full-time graduate psychology faculty, there are more than 40 full-time faculty members from the undergraduate Claremont Colleges who participate in the graduate program and who are available to students for research, advising, and instruction. Resources from other programs within the Graduate University are also available to psychology students, in such areas as public policy, education, information sciences, business administration, executive management, economics, and government. The nearby Los Angeles basin is a major urban area that offers rich and varied opportunities for interesting research, field placements and internships, part-time employment, and career development.

Application Information:
Send to: Admissions Office, McManus Hall 131, Claremont Graduate University, Claremont, CA 91711. Application available online. URL of online application: www.cgu.edu/pages/102.asp. Students are admitted in the Fall, application deadline January 15; Spring, application deadline November 1. HRD program accepts applications throughout the year on a space-available basis. *Fee:* $55. Fee waived or deferred if need is certified.

Fielding Graduate University
School of Psychology
Clinical Psychology Doctoral Program
2112 Santa Barbara Street
Santa Barbara, CA 93105
Telephone: (805) 687-1099
Fax: (805) 687-4590
E-mail: *fuji@fielding.edu*
Web: *http://www.fielding.edu*

Department Information:
1974. Dean, Psychology: Ronald A. Giannetti. Number of Faculty: total–full-time 31, part-time 3; women–full-time 16, part-time 1; minority–full-time 4.

Programs and Degrees Offered:
Listed in the following order: Program area, degree type (T if terminal Master's), number awarded 7/03–6/04. Respecialization in Clin Psych Respecialization Diploma 1, Clinical PhD (Doctor of Philosophy) 23, Media Psychology PhD (Doctor of Philosophy) 0, Post Doctorate Neuropsychology Certificate Other.

APA Accreditation: Clinical PhD (Doctor of Philosophy).

Student Applications/Admissions:
Student Applications
 Respecialization in Clin Psych Respecialization Diploma—Applications 2004–2005, 8. Total applicants accepted 2004–2005, 6. Total enrolled 2004–2005 full-time, 19. The number of students enrolled full and part-time who were dismissed or voluntarily withdrew from this program area were 0. *Clinical PhD (Doctor of Philosophy)*—Applications 2004–2005, 433. Total applicants accepted 2004–2005, 95. Openings 2005–2006, 60. The Median number of years required for completion of a degree are 8. The number of students enrolled full and part-time who were dismissed or voluntarily withdrew from this program area were 22. *Media Psychology PhD (Doctor of Philosophy)*—Applications 2004–2005, 43. Total applicants accepted 2004–2005, 20. Total enrolled 2004–2005 full-time, 15. Openings 2005–2006, 10. The number of students enrolled full and part-time who were dismissed or voluntarily withdrew from this program area were 0.

Admissions Requirements:
 Scores: Entries appear in this order: required test or GPA, minimum score (if required), median score of students entering in 2003–2004. Doctoral Programs: overall undergraduate GPA 3.0. A minimum GPA of 3.0 for the highest degree earned is recommended.
 Other Criteria: (importance of criteria rated low, medium, or high): research experience high, work experience high, extracurricular activity medium, clinically related public service high, GPA medium, letters of recommendation medium, interview high, statement of goals and objectives high.

Student Characteristics: The following represents characteristics of students in 2004–2005 in all graduate psychology programs in the department: Female–full-time 523, part-time 0; Male–full-time 230, part-time 0; African American/Black–full-time 54, part-time 0; Hispanic/Latino(a)–full-time 47, part-time 0; Asian/Pacific Islander–full-time 23, part-time 0; American Indian/Alaska Native–full-time 8, part-time 0; Caucasian–full-time 577, part-time 0; Multi-ethnic–full-time 44, part-time 0; students subject to the Americans With Disabilities Act–full-time 7, part-time 0.

Financial Information/Assistance:
 Tuition for Full-Time Study: *Doctoral:* State residents: per academic year $16,980; Nonstate residents: per academic year $16,980. Tuition is subject to change.

Financial Assistance:
 First Year Students: Fellowships and scholarships available for first-year. Average amount paid per academic year: $2,000.
 Advanced Students: Fellowships and scholarships available for advanced students. Average amount paid per academic year: $2,000.

Contact Information: Of all students currently enrolled full-time, 5% benefitted from one or more of the listed financial assistance programs.

Internships/Practica: Students apply to APA or APPIC approved internships or comparable sites which offer an organized training program lasting one year full-time or two consecutive years half-time. Such internships provide a planned, integrated sequence of clinical and didactic experiences with the goal of providing sufficient training and supervision so that the intern can, upon completion, function responsibly as a postdoctoral psychologist. For those doctoral students for whom a professional internship is required prior to graduation, 34 applied in 2003–2004. Of those who applied, 19 were placed in internships listed by the Association of Psychology Postdoctoral and Internship Programs (APPIC); 9 were placed in APA accredited internships.

Housing and Day Care: No on-campus housing is available. No on-campus day care facilities are available.

Employment of Department Graduates:

Master's Degree Graduates: Of those who graduated in the academic year 2003–2004, the following categories and numbers represent the post-graduate activities and employment of master's degree graduates: Enrolled in a post-doctoral residency/fellowship (n/a), employed in independent practice (n/a), total from the above (master's) (0).

Doctoral Degree Graduates: Of those who graduated in the academic year 2003–2004, the following categories and numbers represent the post-graduate activities and employment of doctoral degree graduates: Enrolled in a psychology doctoral program (n/a), total from the above (doctoral) (0).

Additional Information:

Orientation, Objectives, and Emphasis of Department: The clinical psychology program of the Fielding Graduate University enables mid-career adults with mental health and human service experience to earn the PhD in clinical psychology. Our students bring a sense of autonomy, extensive personal and professional experience, and multiple adult responsibilities to their studies. The program's design accommodates these special characteristics of adult students. The program is based on the scholar/practitioner model. Progress is measured through explicit demonstrations of competence at a standard established by the faculty. Through seminars and guided study, the adult learner can pursue study at whatever location life circumstances permit. The program includes 3 components taken concurrently: academic, research, and clinical. The academic component consists of completing 12 core courses plus other required courses and their choice of electives courses to accumulate 84 units. Details of this process are contained in our catalog. The research component is designed to educate students in research methodology to ensure that students become critical consumers of research and scholars capable of contributing to research. It also trains students in the skills necessary to complete a theoretically based dissertation consisting of imaginative and scholarly inquiry. The clinical component consists of a practicum and internship as well as training and evaluation activities to help students learn and demonstrate their ability to function responsibly as practicing psychologists. Additionally, there is a respecialization in Clinical Psychology, which is a certificate program for postdoctoral psychologists who wish to respecialize as clinical psychologists.

Special Facilities or Resources: Students become members of a "cluster" or doctoral studies seminar in their geographical area consisting of a Regional Faculty and other students. Regular meetings are held and consist of a variety of learning activities including knowledge area and seminars, clinical and research training, faculty supervision consultation, as well as peer contact and support. Associate Deans are located in Santa Barbara. Each student is assigned to an Associate Dean who oversees the student's academic program. Our learning community is tied together by the Fielding Electronic Network, a rapid, cost-effective means of communication among faculty, students and administrative staff. The use of a personal computer enables contact with other members or groups of members. It is also used to offer electronic seminars. Two intensive week-long residential sessions are offered each year. These bring together all faculty and other scholars who offer seminars and other educational and training events. Two residential research sessions are held each year. These include research training, dissertation seminars, instruction in the use of research libraries and electronic databases, and lectures by invited research scholars. Psychological assessment laboratories are offered to provide training in conducting comprehensive psychodiagnostic evaluations.

Application Information:

Send to: Andrea Peeters, Psychology Admissions Counselor, Fielding Graduate University, 2112 Santa Barbara Street, Santa Barbara, CA 93105. Application available online. URL of online application: http://www.fielding.edu/admissions/index.htm. Students are admitted in the Fall, application deadline February 17; Spring, application deadline August 26. *Fee:* $75.

Fuller Theological Seminary
Graduate School of Psychology
180 N. Oakland Avenue
Pasadena, CA 91101
Telephone: (626) 584-5500
Fax: (626) 584-9630
E-mail: *sop-frontdesk@dept.fuller.edu*
Web: *http://www.fuller.edu/sop/main*

Department Information:
1965. Associate Dean: Linda Wagener, PhD Number of Faculty: total–full-time 15, part-time 2; women–full-time 5, part-time 1; minority–full-time 4, part-time 1.

Programs and Degrees Offered:
Listed in the following order: Program area, degree type (T if terminal Master's), number awarded 7/03–6/04. Clinical Psychology PhD (Doctor of Philosophy) 21, Clinical Psychology PsyD (Doctor of Psychology) 5.

APA Accreditation: Clinical PhD (Doctor of Philosophy). Clinical PsyD (Doctor of Psychology).

Student Applications/Admissions:
Student Applications
Clinical Psychology PhD (Doctor of Philosophy)—Applications 2004–2005, 86. Total applicants accepted 2004–2005, 48. Number enrolled (new admits only) 2004–2005 full-time, 27.

Number enrolled (new admits only) 2004–2005 part-time, 0. Total enrolled 2004–2005 full-time, 115, part-time, 35. Openings 2005–2006, 20. The Median number of years required for completion of a degree are 6. The number of students enrolled full and part-time who were dismissed or voluntarily withdrew from this program area were 0. *Clinical Psychology PsyD (Doctor of Psychology)*—Applications 2004–2005, 52. Total applicants accepted 2004–2005, 27. Number enrolled (new admits only) 2004–2005 full-time, 11. Number enrolled (new admits only) 2004–2005 part-time, 1. Total enrolled 2004–2005 full-time, 56, part-time, 18. Openings 2005–2006, 20. The Median number of years required for completion of a degree are 6. The number of students enrolled full and part-time who were dismissed or voluntarily withdrew from this program area were 1.

Admissions Requirements:

Scores: Entries appear in this order: required test or GPA, minimum score (if required), median score of students entering in 2003–2004. Doctoral Programs: GRE-V no minimum stated; GRE-Q no minimum stated; GRE-V+Q 1000, 1120; GRE-Subject(Psych) no minimum stated; overall undergraduate GPA 3.0, 3.76.

Other Criteria: (importance of criteria rated low, medium, or high): GRE/MAT scores high, research experience high, work experience medium, extracurricular activity medium, clinically related public service medium, GPA high, letters of recommendation high, interview high, statement of goals and objectives high. Research experience is less important for PsyD candidate than for PhD.

Student Characteristics: The following represents characteristics of students in 2004–2005 in all graduate psychology programs in the department: Female–full-time 117, part-time 32; Male–full-time 54, part-time 21; African American/Black–full-time 11, part-time 4; Hispanic/Latino(a)–full-time 10, part-time 3; Asian/Pacific Islander–full-time 30, part-time 8; American Indian/Alaska Native–full-time 0, part-time 1; Caucasian–full-time 120, part-time 36; Multi-ethnic–full-time 0, part-time 1; students subject to the Americans With Disabilities Act–full-time 1, part-time 2.

Financial Information/Assistance:

Tuition for Full-Time Study: *Master's:* State residents: per academic year $15,158, $249 per credit hour; Nonstate residents: per academic year $15,158, $249 per credit hour. *Doctoral:* State residents: per academic year $19,200, $430 per credit hour; Nonstate residents: per academic year $19,200, $430 per credit hour. Tuition is subject to change. See the following Web site for updates and changes in tuition costs: www.fuller.edu/registrar/tuition.asp.

Financial Assistance:

First Year Students: Research assistantships available for first-year. Average amount paid per academic year: $12,000. Average number of hours worked per week: 15. Apply by variable. Fellowships and scholarships available for first-year. Average amount paid per academic year: $2,045. Average number of hours worked per week: 0. Apply by application.

Advanced Students: Teaching assistantships available for advanced students. Average amount paid per academic year: $10,000. Average number of hours worked per week: 10. Apply by variable. Research assistantships available for advanced students.

Average amount paid per academic year: $12,000. Average number of hours worked per week: 15. Apply by variable. Traineeships available for advanced students. Average amount paid per academic year: $10,000. Average number of hours worked per week: 10. Apply by variable. Fellowships and scholarships available for advanced students. Average amount paid per academic year: $2,045. Average number of hours worked per week: 0. Apply by March 31.

Contact Information: Of all students currently enrolled full-time, 60% benefitted from one or more of the listed financial assistance programs. Application and information available online at: http://www.fuller.edu/finaid/.

Internships/Practica: Students are placed in field training sites throughout their program beginning in year one with clinical foundations, through 2 years of practicum, 1 year of assessment clerkships, 1 year of pre-internship (PhD only) and a full-time clinical internship. Students are placed at Fuller Psychological and Family Services clinic as well as in over 50 sites throughout the L.A. metropolitan area. Because of our location students are exposed to multiple methods of service delivery as well as to diverse ethnic, clinical, and age populations. Students obtain internships throughout the U.S. and Canada. For those doctoral students for whom a professional internship is required prior to graduation, 34 applied in 2003–2004. Of those who applied, 32 were placed in internships listed by the Association of Psychology Postdoctoral and Internship Programs (APPIC); 23 were placed in APA accredited internships.

Housing and Day Care: On-campus housing is available. See the following Web site for more information: www.fuller.edu/housing/. No on-campus day care facilities are available.

Employment of Department Graduates:

Master's Degree Graduates: Of those who graduated in the academic year 2003–2004, the following categories and numbers represent the post-graduate activities and employment of master's degree graduates: Enrolled in a post-doctoral residency/fellowship (n/a), employed in independent practice (n/a), total from the above (master's) (0).

Doctoral Degree Graduates: Of those who graduated in the academic year 2003–2004, the following categories and numbers represent the post-graduate activities and employment of doctoral degree graduates: Enrolled in a psychology doctoral program (n/a), enrolled in a post-doctoral residency/fellowship (12), employed in an academic position at a university (3), employed in other positions at a higher education institution (1), employed in a professional position in a school system (2), employed in a hospital/medical center (6), do not know (15), total from the above (doctoral) (39).

Additional Information:

Orientation, Objectives, and Emphasis of Department: The purpose of the Graduate School of Psychology is to prepare a distinctive kind of clinical psychologist: men and women whose understanding and action are deeply informed by both psychology and the Christian faith. It is based on the conviction that the coupling of Christian understanding with refined clinical and research skills will produce a psychologist with a special ability to help persons of faith on their journeys to wholeness. The school has adopted the scientist-practitioner model for its PhD program and the practitioner-evaluator model for its PsyD program.

Special Facilities or Resources: The Lee Edward Travis Research Institute (TRI) in the School of Psychology at Fuller Theological Seminary is committed to fostering interdisciplinary research into the relationships between social systems, environmental situations, personality, mental and affective states, biological processes, and spiritual and religious states and practices. Please go to our Web site at www.fuller.edu/sop/travis to learn more. Fuller Psychological & Family Services: This outpatient clinic provides assistance to individuals, couples, and families, including services to children and adolescents. Psychological interventions are offered for adjustment disorders, anxiety, depression, stress management, abuse and domestic violence, and physical conditions affected by psychological factors. Student trainees may be placed in the clinic for practicum, clerkship or pre-internship. Please see www.fuller.edu/sop/main/psychological_center.asp.

Information for Students With Physical Disabilities: oss-office@dept.fuller.edu.

Application Information:
Send to: Office of Admissions, Fuller Theological Seminary, 135 N. Oakland Avenue, Pasadena, CA 91182. Application available online. URL of online application: https://www.applyweb.com/apply/fuller/menu.html. Students are admitted in the Fall, application deadline January 1. Early admission deadline is November 30. *Fee:* $50. Fee is waived for early admission.

Humboldt State University
Department of Psychology
College of Natural Resources & Sciences
1 Harpst Street
Arcata, CA 95521
Telephone: (707) 826-3755
Fax: (707) 826-4993
E-mail: *wr9@humboldt.edu*
Web: *http://www.humboldt.edu/~psych*

Department Information:
1964. Professor: William Reynolds. Number of Faculty: total–full-time 15, part-time 15; women–full-time 6, part-time 11; minority–full-time 3, part-time 1.

Programs and Degrees Offered:
Listed in the following order: Program area, degree type (T if terminal Master's), number awarded 7/03–6/04. Academic research MA/MS (Master of Arts/Science) (T) 8, counseling MA/MS (Master of Arts/Science) (T) 9, school psychology MA/MS (Master of Arts/Science) (T) 9.

Student Applications/Admissions:
Student Applications
Academic research MA/MS (Master of Arts/Science)—Applications 2004–2005, 15. Total applicants accepted 2004–2005, 7. Number enrolled (new admits only) 2004–2005 full-time, 7. Number enrolled (new admits only) 2004–2005 part-time, 0. Total enrolled 2004–2005 full-time, 13, part-time, 8. Openings 2005–2006, 8. The Median number of years required for completion of a degree are 2. The number of students enrolled full and part-time who were dismissed or voluntarily withdrew

from this program area were 0. *Counseling MA/MS (Master of Arts/Science)*—Applications 2004–2005, 38. Total applicants accepted 2004–2005, 11. Number enrolled (new admits only) 2004–2005 full-time, 11. Total enrolled 2004–2005 full-time, 25, part-time, 4. Openings 2005–2006, 10. The Median number of years required for completion of a degree are 3. The number of students enrolled full and part-time who were dismissed or voluntarily withdrew from this program area were 0. *School psychology MA/MS (Master of Arts/Science)*—Applications 2004–2005, 42. Total applicants accepted 2004–2005, 10. Number enrolled (new admits only) 2004–2005 full-time, 8. Openings 2005–2006, 10. The Median number of years required for completion of a degree are 2. The number of students enrolled full and part-time who were dismissed or voluntarily withdrew from this program area were 0.

Admissions Requirements:
Scores: Entries appear in this order: required test or GPA, minimum score (if required), median score of students entering in 2003–2004. Master's Programs: overall undergraduate GPA 3.00. The Academic Research program requires a 3.25 GPA in Psychology courses.

Other Criteria: (importance of criteria rated low, medium, or high): GRE/MAT scores medium, research experience medium, work experience medium, extracurricular activity medium, clinically related public service medium, GPA high, letters of recommendation high, interview medium, statement of goals and objectives high, An interview is required for Counseling and School Psychology; research experience is important for Academic Research; clinically related public service or work experience is highly important for Counseling and School Psychology; school/child related work experience highly important for School Psychology. For additional information on admission requirements, go to: http://www.humboldt.edu/~psych/psych.html.

Student Characteristics: The following represents characteristics of students in 2004–2005 in all graduate psychology programs in the department: Female–full-time 42, part-time 6; Male–full-time 15, part-time 5; African American/Black–full-time 0, part-time 0; Hispanic/Latino(a)–full-time 6, part-time 1; Asian/Pacific Islander–full-time 2, part-time 2; American Indian/Alaska Native–full-time 0, part-time 0; Caucasian–full-time 53, part-time 10; Multi-ethnic–full-time 1, part-time 1; students subject to the Americans With Disabilities Act–full-time 0, part-time 0.

Financial Information/Assistance:
Tuition for Full-Time Study: Master's: State residents: per academic year $3,346; Nonstate residents: $339 per credit hour. Tuition is subject to change. See the following Web site for updates and changes in tuition costs: www.humboldt.edu.

Financial Assistance:
First Year Students: Fellowships and scholarships available for first-year. Average amount paid per academic year: $1,500. Apply by variable.

Advanced Students: Fellowships and scholarships available for advanced students. Average amount paid per academic year: $1,500. Apply by variable.

Contact Information: Of all students currently enrolled full-time, 10% benefitted from one or more of the listed financial assistance programs.

Internships/Practica: Humboldt's Future Faculty Training Program provides teaching internship opportunities (some paid) at the local community college. School Psychology internships (usually paid) are required of all students seeking the School Psychology credential. Counseling MA students are provided the opportunity to do fieldwork/practica in the department's Davis House Psychology Clinic, as well as in several local mental heath agencies.

Housing and Day Care: On-campus housing is available. Housing Office (707) 826-3451 (on campus); or (707) 826-3455 (off campus). On-campus day care facilities are available. Children's Center House (707) 826-3838.

Employment of Department Graduates:

Master's Degree Graduates: Of those who graduated in the academic year 2003–2004, the following categories and numbers represent the post-graduate activities and employment of master's degree graduates: Enrolled in another graduate/professional program (0), enrolled in a post-doctoral residency/fellowship (n/a), employed in independent practice (n/a), total from the above (master's) (0).

Doctoral Degree Graduates: Of those who graduated in the academic year 2003–2004, the following categories and numbers represent the post-graduate activities and employment of doctoral degree graduates: Enrolled in a psychology doctoral program (n/a), total from the above (doctoral) (0).

Additional Information:

Orientation, Objectives, and Emphasis of Department: The objectives of our department of psychology are to provide students with an understanding of principles and theories concerning human behavior and the processes by which such information is obtained; to provide a sound academic education for those working for degrees in psychology with a future goal of professional work in psychology; to offer a liberal arts major and minor in psychology for students seeking a quality liberal education; to provide quality professional graduate education for students working toward California School Psychologist credentials, Marriage and Family Therapist licenses and other specialized occupational fields; and to provide a flexibility in our offerings that responds to changing societal agenda and student needs. Our revised Academic Research Masters Program provides specializations in the following areas: Developmental Psychopathology, Biological Psychology, Social and Environmental Psychology, and Behavior Analysis. Students should select one of these areas when they apply to the AR program.

Special Facilities or Resources: The department has an on-campus clinic staffed by MA counseling students, an electronic equipment shop, a lab with biofeedback and EEG equipment, a lab equipped for research on motion sickness, observation and research access to an on-campus demonstration nursery school, a test library, and a computer laboratory. In 2006, the new Behavioral and Social Sciences Building will be completed providing exceptional research, instruction, faculty and student space for the Department of Psychology.

Information for Students With Physical Disabilities: Student Disability Resource Center (SDRC) (707) 826-4678.

Application Information:

Send to: 1. Office of Admissions, Humboldt State University, Arcata, CA 95521 - general admissions, 2. Department of Psychology, Humboldt State University, Arcata, CA 95521 - specific admissions requirements for each of the three programs - Contact Graduate Secretary - (707) 826-5264. Application available online. URL of online application: http://www.humboldt.edu/%7Egradst/new_student.html. Students are admitted in the Fall, application deadline February 15. Deadline for Academic Research MA program is March 1. *Fee:* $55. Partial out-of-state tuition waiver available.

Institute of Transpersonal Psychology
Department of Psychology
1069 East Meadow Circle
Palo Alto, CA 94303
Telephone: (650) 493-4430, ext. 216
Fax: (650) 493-6835
E-mail: *itpinfo@itp.edu*
Web: *http://www.itp.edu*

Department Information:

1975. Chairperson: Dr. Robert Morgan. Number of Faculty: total–full-time 13, part-time 8; women–full-time 6, part-time 5; minority–full-time 2, part-time 2.

Programs and Degrees Offered:

Listed in the following order: Program area, degree type (T if terminal Master's), number awarded 7/03–6/04. Transpersonal Clinical Psychology PhD (Doctor of Philosophy) 0, Counseling Psychology MA/MS (Master of Arts/Science) (T) 38, Psychology PhD (Doctor of Philosophy) 0, Distance Learning Master's MA/MS (Master of Arts/Science) 22, Distance Learning Certificates Other 30, Transpersonal Psychology PhD (Doctor of Philosophy) 17.

Student Applications/Admissions:

Student Applications

Transpersonal Clinical Psychology PhD (Doctor of Philosophy)— Applications 2004–2005, 0. Total applicants accepted 2004–2005, 0. Number enrolled (new admits only) 2004–2005 full-time, 0. Number enrolled (new admits only) 2004–2005 part-time, 0. Openings 2005–2006, 40. The number of students enrolled full and part-time who were dismissed or voluntarily withdrew from this program area were 0. *Counseling Psychology MA/MS (Master of Arts/Science)*—Applications 2004–2005, 58. Total applicants accepted 2004–2005, 45. Number enrolled (new admits only) 2004–2005 full-time, 32. Number enrolled (new admits only) 2004–2005 part-time, 0. Total enrolled 2004–2005 full-time, 78, part-time, 8. Openings 2005–2006, 30. The Median number of years required for completion of a degree are 3. The number of students enrolled full and part-time who were dismissed or voluntarily withdrew from this program area were 2. *Psychology PhD (Doctor of Philosophy)*— Applications 2004–2005, 59. Total applicants accepted 2004–2005, 48. Number enrolled (new admits only) 2004–2005 full-time, 36. Openings 2005–2006, 30. The number of students enrolled full and part-time who were dismissed or voluntarily withdrew from this program area were 9. *Distance Learning Master's MA/MS (Master of Arts/Science)*—Applications 2004–

2005, 22. Total applicants accepted 2004–2005, 21. Number enrolled (new admits only) 2004–2005 full-time, 18. Number enrolled (new admits only) 2004–2005 part-time, 0. Openings 2005–2006, 50. The Median number of years required for completion of a degree are 2. The number of students enrolled full and part-time who were dismissed or voluntarily withdrew from this program area were 3. *Distance Learning Certificates Other*—Applications 2004–2005, 31. Total applicants accepted 2004–2005, 30. Number enrolled (new admits only) 2004–2005 full-time, 26. Openings 2005–2006, 50. The Median number of years required for completion of a degree is 1. The number of students enrolled full and part-time who were dismissed or voluntarily withdrew from this program area were 9. *Transpersonal Psychology PhD (Doctor of Philosophy)*— Applications 2004–2005, 74. Total applicants accepted 2004–2005, 60. Number enrolled (new admits only) 2004–2005 full-time, 47. Total enrolled 2004–2005 full-time, 122, part-time, 8. Openings 2005–2006, 40. The Median number of years required for completion of a degree are 5. The number of students enrolled full and part-time who were dismissed or voluntarily withdrew from this program area were 8.

Admissions Requirements:

Scores: Entries appear in this order: required test or GPA, minimum score (if required), median score of students entering in 2003–2004. Master's Programs: overall undergraduate GPA 3.0. Doctoral Programs: overall undergraduate GPA 3.0.

Other Criteria: (importance of criteria rated low, medium, or high): research experience medium, work experience medium, extracurricular activity medium, clinically related public service medium, GPA medium, letters of recommendation high, interview high, statement of goals and objectives high, The Academic Writing Sample is required for applications to the Residential PhD and the Distance Learning PhD It is not required for any of the MA or Certificate programs. Research experience is not a criteria for admission to any of the MA programs. For additional information on admission requirements, go to: http://www.itp.edu/admissions/application2.cfm.

Student Characteristics: The following represents characteristics of students in 2004–2005 in all graduate psychology programs in the department: Female–full-time 269, part-time 4; Male–full-time 94, part-time 24; African American/Black–full-time 6, part-time 3; Hispanic/Latino(a)–full-time 6, part-time 0; Asian/Pacific Islander–full-time 12, part-time 1; American Indian/Alaska Native–full-time 3, part-time 0; Caucasian–full-time 211, part-time 14; Multi-ethnic–full-time 56, part-time 9; students subject to the Americans With Disabilities Act–full-time 0, part-time 0.

Financial Information/Assistance:

Tuition for Full-Time Study: *Master's:* State residents: per academic year $10,685, $442 per credit hour; Nonstate residents: per academic year $10,685, $442 per credit hour. *Doctoral:* State residents: per academic year $20,000, $533 per credit hour; Nonstate residents: per academic year $20,000, $533 per credit hour. Tuition is subject to change. Tuition costs vary by program. See the following Web site for updates and changes in tuition costs: http://www.itp.edu/admissions/tuition.cfm.

Financial Assistance:

First Year Students: Teaching assistantships available for first-year. Average amount paid per academic year: $1,368. Aver-

age number of hours worked per week: 6. Apply by August 1. Research assistantships available for first-year. Average amount paid per academic year: $1,368. Average number of hours worked per week: 6. Apply by August 1. Fellowships and scholarships available for first-year. Average amount paid per academic year: $875. Apply by August 1.

Advanced Students: Teaching assistantships available for advanced students. Average amount paid per academic year: $1,368. Average number of hours worked per week: 6. Apply by August 1. Research assistantships available for advanced students. Average amount paid per academic year: $1,368. Average number of hours worked per week: 6. Apply by August 1. Fellowships and scholarships available for advanced students. Average amount paid per academic year: $875. Apply by August 1.

Contact Information: Of all students currently enrolled full-time, 14% benefitted from one or more of the listed financial assistance programs. Application and information available online at: http://www.itp.edu/admissions/finAid.cfm.

Internships/Practica: The Transpersonal Counseling Center is a nonprofit community counseling center and training institute affiliated with the nation's leading institution of transpersonal studies. Clinical PhD students gain hands-on psychotherapy experience providing individual, couples, family and group psychotherapy to children, adolescents and adults. Traditional models of assessment and treatment are combined with transpersonal approaches. Applicants for internship must meet the criteria set out by the CAPIC uniform application process. Placement offers an opportunity to gain hours (SPE's) toward licensure as a Clinical Psychologist. The initial contract is for a one year half-time internship (20 hours/week) beginning in July and running to the next July, with renewal of contract possible. Each week at the Center comprises approximately 6-8 direct client therapy hours, one hour of individual supervision, and 2 and a half hours of group supervision and training. Two hours of service to the center and community outreach work is also expected weekly. Within an outpatient psychotherapy setting, interns are offered an opportunity to utilize any number of contemporary therapeutic modalities, while working from a transpersonal framework that includes attention to multiple layers of consciousness, spirituality, mind-body wellness and the relationship of the individual to the community in each of the aforementioned contexts. For those doctoral students for whom a professional internship is required prior to graduation, 22 applied in 2003–2004. Of those who applied, 9 were placed in internships listed by the Association of Psychology Postdoctoral and Internship Programs (APPIC).

Housing and Day Care: No on-campus housing is available. No on-campus day care facilities are available.

Employment of Department Graduates:

Master's Degree Graduates: Of those who graduated in the academic year 2003–2004, the following categories and numbers represent the post-graduate activities and employment of master's degree graduates: Enrolled in a post-doctoral residency/fellowship (n/a), employed in independent practice (n/a), total from the above (master's) (0).

Doctoral Degree Graduates: Of those who graduated in the academic year 2003–2004, the following categories and numbers represent the post-graduate activities and employment of doctoral degree graduates: Enrolled in a psychology doctoral program (n/a), total from the above (doctoral) (0).

Additional Information:

Orientation, Objectives, and Emphasis of Department: The mission of ITP's graduate programs is to produce skillful, well-rounded psychologists, counselors, teachers and educators through disciplined inquiry, scholarly research and self discovery in the context of a supportive community environment. Transpersonal Psychology applies the methods and tools of psychology to investigate experiences, developmental processes, and levels of identity that go beyond or transcend the ordinary personality. To adequately prepare students for this line of inquiry, ITP's curriculum is informed by a whole person learning model, which maintains that a student's education must attend to all aspects of his or her experience, including the mental, emotional, physical, spiritual, creative, and social dimensions. Besides integrating theory, research, and professional training, each degree program encourages students to cultivate transpersonal values, such as mindfulness, compassion, discernment, and an appreciation of differences, and to integrate these principles into their personal and professional lives. Collaborative learning is emphasized in order to understand the powerful role that others play in shaping one's education. Graduates are well prepared to follow traditional career paths while contributing an innovative transpersonal approach to their respective field. Students not only build a strong foundation of psychotherapeutic skills, but also learn how to communicate in a variety of complex relational circumstances.

Special Facilities or Resources: Named in honor of the illustrious American psychologist, philosopher, and writer, the William James Center for Consciousness Studies was established in 1994 as the research arm of the Institute of Transpersonal Psychology. The Center's projects emphasize exceptional human experiences, both psychic and mystical, psycho-spiritual transformation, and physical and psychological well-being and growth. These themes were of keen interest to William James throughout his life, and today, more than ever before, they provoke far-reaching questions for humanity. The aim of the Center is to foster and support studies that have clear implications for the field of transpersonal psychology. Researchers at the Center are encouraged to develop, initiate, and evaluate practical applications of the principles emerging from their work (for example, in education, business, wellness, counseling, therapy, and spiritual guidance). Research projects are designed and conducted primarily by Institute faculty, doctoral, and post-doctoral students; however, the Center is also designed to provide an umbrella for work by adjunct and visiting researchers and by outside investigators. Work at the William James Center for Consciousness Studies is carried out through narrative, empirical, and theoretical investigations, meetings and discussions, sponsorship of special projects, and funding applications.

Information for Students With Physical Disabilities: Please contact ITP's Dean of Students at pyue@itp.edu for assistance.

Application Information:

Send to: Institute of Transpersonal Psychology Admissions Office, 1069 East Meadow Circle, Palo Alto, CA 94303. Application available online. URL of online application: http://www.itp.edu/admissions/application2.cfm. Students are admitted in the Fall, application deadline May 1. Programs have rolling admissions. ITP's Distance Learning Master's and Certificate programs enroll students each quarter (Fall, Winter, Spring, and Summer), and applications are accepted up to three weeks prior to the start of the term. ITP's Distance Learning PhD program enrolls each July, and its application deadline is April 1. *Fee:* $55.

John F. Kennedy University (2004 data)

Graduate School of Professional Psychology
100 Ellinwood Way
Pleasant Hill, CA 94523
Telephone: (925) 969-3400
Fax: (925) 969-3401
E-mail: *mcconnell@jfku.edu*
Web: *http://www.jfku.edu*

Department Information:

1965. Dean: Keith McConnell. Number of Faculty: total–full-time 20, part-time 191; women–full-time 11, part-time 122; minority–full-time 3, part-time 28; faculty subject to the Americans With Disabilities Act 2.

Programs and Degrees Offered:

Listed in the following order: Program area, degree type (T if terminal Master's), number awarded 7/03–6/04. Counseling Psychology MA/MS (Master of Arts/Science) (T) 71, Organizational Psychology MA/MS (Master of Arts/Science) (T) 9, PsyD (Doctor of Psychology) 20, Sports Psychology MA/MS (Master of Arts/Science) (T) 12.

APA Accreditation: Clinical PsyD (Doctor of Psychology).

Student Applications/Admissions:

Student Applications

Counseling Psychology MA/MS (Master of Arts/Science)—Applications 2004–2005, 187. Total applicants accepted 2004–2005, 163. Total enrolled 2004–2005 full-time, 120, part-time, 154. Openings 2005–2006, 70. The Median number of years required for completion of a degree are 2. *Organizational Psychology MA/MS (Master of Arts/Science)*—Applications 2004–2005, 51. Total applicants accepted 2004–2005, 46. Total enrolled 2004–2005 full-time, 40, part-time, 10. Openings 2005–2006, 15. The Median number of years required for completion of a degree are 2. *PsyD (Doctor of Psychology)*—Applications 2004–2005, 86. Total applicants accepted 2004–2005, 39. Total enrolled 2004–2005 full-time, 70, part-time, 34. Openings 2005–2006, 30. The Median number of years required for completion of a degree are 5. The number of students enrolled full and part-time who were dismissed or voluntarily withdrew from this program area were 2. *Sports Psychology MA/MS (Master of Arts/Science)*—Applications 2004–2005, 41. Total applicants accepted 2004–2005, 41. Total enrolled 2004–2005 full-time, 30, part-time, 11. Openings 2005–2006, 20. The Median number of years required for completion of a degree are 2.

Admissions Requirements:

Scores: Entries appear in this order: required test or GPA, minimum score (if required), median score of students entering in 2003–2004. Master's Programs: overall undergraduate GPA 3.0, 3.0. Doctoral Programs: overall undergraduate GPA 3.0.
Other Criteria: (importance of criteria rated low, medium, or high): research experience medium, work experience high,

extracurricular activity high, clinically related public service high, GPA medium, letters of recommendation high, interview high, statement of goals and objectives high.

Student Characteristics: The following represents characteristics of students in 2004–2005 in all graduate psychology programs in the department: Female–full-time 189, part-time 153; Male–full-time 71, part-time 56; African American/Black–full-time 12, part-time 35; Hispanic/Latino(a)–full-time 13, part-time 18; Asian/Pacific Islander–full-time 12, part-time 16; American Indian/Alaska Native–full-time 2, part-time 3; Caucasian–full-time 0, part-time 0; Multi-ethnic–full-time 11, part-time 11; students subject to the Americans With Disabilities Act–full-time 4, part-time 2.

Financial Information/Assistance:

Tuition for Full-Time Study: *Master's:* State residents: $391 per credit hour; Nonstate residents: $391 per credit hour. *Doctoral:* State residents: $502 per credit hour; Nonstate residents: $502 per credit hour. Tuition is subject to change. See the following Web site for updates and changes in tuition costs: www.jfku.edu.

Financial Assistance:
   First Year Students: No information provided.
   Advanced Students: No information provided.
   Contact Information: Of all students currently enrolled full-time, 0% benefitted from one or more of the listed financial assistance programs.

Internships/Practica: *Master's:* State residents: $391 per credit hour; Nonstate residents: $391 per credit hour. 26 applied in 2003–2004.

Housing and Day Care: No on-campus housing is available. No on-campus day care facilities are available.

Employment of Department Graduates:

Master's Degree Graduates: Of those who graduated in the academic year 2003–2004, the following categories and numbers represent the post-graduate activities and employment of master's degree graduates: Enrolled in a post-doctoral residency/fellowship (n/a), employed in independent practice (n/a), total from the above (master's) (0).

Doctoral Degree Graduates: Of those who graduated in the academic year 2003–2004, the following categories and numbers represent the post-graduate activities and employment of doctoral degree graduates: Enrolled in a psychology doctoral program (n/a), enrolled in a post-doctoral residency/fellowship (10), employed in independent practice (2), employed in an academic position at a university (1), employed in a professional position in a school system (2), employed in a government agency (professional services) (2), employed in a community mental health/counseling center (4), employed in a hospital/medical center (3), still seeking employment (1), do not know (2), total from the above (doctoral) (27).

Additional Information:

Orientation, Objectives, and Emphasis of Department: The mission of the Graduate School of Professional Psychology is to create an innovative, diverse, and responsive environment for students that supports personal and professional learning. We are committed to active learning and community service, and are guided by

a commitment to traditionally underserved populations. Students acquire excellence in both traditional and emerging competencies and are taught by faculty who are practicing professionals in their field. The MA Counseling Psychology program offers specializations in Child and Adolescent Therapy, Addiction Studies, Cross-Cultural Issues, Expressive Arts, Couples and Families, and Sport Psychology. In addition to the MA degree, the Organizational Psychology program offers certificates in Coaching and Conflict Management. Students may also enroll in the Link Program and receive both the MA in Sports Psychology and the PsyD in Clinical Psychology.

Special Facilities or Resources: As noted, the Graduate School of Professional Psychology community counseling centers serve a broad-based clientele throughout the surrounding communities. The programs in the school are actively engaged in community service. For example, the Sports Psychology program is an active participant in the Life Enhancement Through Athletic and Academic Participation (LEAP) in numerous Bay Area schools. The Expressive Arts specialization in the Counseling Psychology MA program works with elementary school children from a variety of sites.

Information for Students With Physical Disabilities: accomm@jfku.edu.

Application Information:
Send to: Office of Admissions, John F. Kennedy University, 100 Ellinwood Way, Pleasant Hill, CA 94523. Students are admitted in the Fall, application deadline rolling; Winter, application deadline rolling; Spring, application deadline rolling; Summer, application deadline rolling. January 15 for PsyD (only have Fall admission). *Fee:* $50.

La Verne, University of
PsyD Program in Clinical-Community Psychology
Arts and Sciences
1950 Third Street
La Verne, CA 91750
Telephone: (909) 593-3511, ext. 4179
Fax: (909) 392-2745
E-mail: *bperlmutter@ulv.edu*
Web: *http://www.ulv.edu*

Department Information:
1997. Doctoral Program Chair: Barry F. Perlmutter, PhD Number of Faculty: total–full-time 12, part-time 14; women–full-time 5, part-time 7; minority–full-time 4, part-time 2.

Programs and Degrees Offered:
Listed in the following order: Program area, degree type (T if terminal Master's), number awarded 7/03–6/04. Clinical-community PsyD (Doctor of Psychology) 5.

APA Accreditation: Clinical PsyD (Doctor of Psychology).

Student Applications/Admissions:
Student Applications
   Clinical-community PsyD (Doctor of Psychology)—Applications 2004–2005, 80. Total applicants accepted 2004–2005, 30.

Number enrolled (new admits only) 2004–2005 full-time, 19. Openings 2005–2006, 20. The Median number of years required for completion of a degree are 5. The number of students enrolled full and part-time who were dismissed or voluntarily withdrew from this program area were 2.

Admissions Requirements:

Scores: Entries appear in this order: required test or GPA, minimum score (if required), median score of students entering in 2003–2004. Doctoral Programs: overall undergraduate GPA 3.25, 3.50; last 2 years GPA 3.25, 3.50; psychology GPA 3.25, 3.50.

Other Criteria: (importance of criteria rated low, medium, or high): research experience medium, work experience high, extracurricular activity low, clinically related public service high, GPA high, letters of recommendation high, interview high, statement of goals and objectives high. For additional information on admission requirements, go to: http://www.ulv.edu/psyd/admissions.phtml.

Student Characteristics: The following represents characteristics of students in 2004–2005 in all graduate psychology programs in the department: Female–full-time 56, part-time 0; Male–full-time 8, part-time 0; African American/Black–full-time 7, part-time 0; Hispanic/Latino(a)–full-time 22, part-time 0; Asian/Pacific Islander–full-time 5, part-time 0; American Indian/Alaska Native–full-time 0, part-time 0; Caucasian–full-time 28, part-time 0; Multi-ethnic–full-time 2, part-time 0; students subject to the Americans With Disabilities Act–full-time 0, part-time 0.

Financial Information/Assistance:

Tuition for Full-Time Study: *Doctoral:* State residents: $645 per credit hour; Nonstate residents: $645 per credit hour. Tuition is subject to change. See the following Web site for updates and changes in tuition costs: www.ulv.edu.

Financial Assistance:

First Year Students: Teaching assistantships available for first-year. Average amount paid per academic year: $2,000. Average number of hours worked per week: 6. Apply by June. Tuition remission given: partial. Research assistantships available for first-year. Average amount paid per academic year: $2,000. Average number of hours worked per week: 6. Apply by June. Tuition remission given: partial.

Advanced Students: Teaching assistantships available for advanced students. Average amount paid per academic year: $2,000. Average number of hours worked per week: 6. Apply by June. Tuition remission given: partial. Research assistantships available for advanced students. Average amount paid per academic year: $2,000. Average number of hours worked per week: 6. Apply by June. Tuition remission given: partial. Traineeships available for advanced students. Average amount paid per academic year: $4,000. Average number of hours worked per week: 20. Apply by March. Tuition remission given: partial.

Contact Information: Of all students currently enrolled full-time, 40% benefitted from one or more of the listed financial assistance programs.

Internships/Practica: The PsyD program includes supervised practica in the second and third years of the program, and consists of a minimum of 1500 hours of clinical-community activities. The culminating pre-doctoral internship in the fifth and final year of the program consists of an additional 1500 clinical hours, which is typically completed as a one-year full-time internship. While most students follow this track, a two-year half-time internship option is available. The Psychology department has an extensive network of practica and internship sites with mental health and educational settings throughout the San Gabriel and Pomona valleys, and the Inland Empire region. The on-campus Counseling Center is part of the Psychology department, is staffed by PsyD and Masters students, and is one of the largest practicum training sites. The PsyD program participates in a regional consortium of program and training site directors for doctoral programs, and is a graduate program member of CAPIC and NCSPP. For those doctoral students for whom a professional internship is required prior to graduation, 7 applied in 2003–2004. Of those who applied, 3 were placed in internships listed by the Association of Psychology Postdoctoral and Internship Programs (APPIC); 1 were placed in APA accredited internships.

Housing and Day Care: No on-campus housing is available. No on-campus day care facilities are available.

Employment of Department Graduates:

Master's Degree Graduates: Of those who graduated in the academic year 2003–2004, the following categories and numbers represent the post-graduate activities and employment of master's degree graduates: Enrolled in a post-doctoral residency/fellowship (n/a), employed in independent practice (n/a), total from the above (master's) (0).

Doctoral Degree Graduates: Of those who graduated in the academic year 2003–2004, the following categories and numbers represent the post-graduate activities and employment of doctoral degree graduates: Enrolled in a psychology doctoral program (n/a), total from the above (doctoral) (0).

Additional Information:

Orientation, Objectives, and Emphasis of Department: The clinical faculty consists of psychologists whose theoretical orientations include psychodynamic, humanist, behavioral, family systems, and community psychology, and who are clinically active in a range of clinical settings and populations. Faculty research interests include topics such as multi-culturalism, juvenile delinquency and adult forensic issues, substance abuse, psychotherapy outcome research, racial identity and acculturation, professional violations of mental health professionals, child and family development, moral development and decision making. The curriculum of the PsyD program in Clinical-Community psychology is anchored in an ecological and multi-cultural perspective, and involves a multi-disciplinary faculty who are actively involved in clinical and research activities. The PsyD program meets all pre-doctoral requirements for California psychology licensure. The program received APA accreditiation in April 2003. The MS (non-terminal) in Psychology is awarded to students at the end of the second year in the program. Students proceed through the program in a cohort model, taking all but elective courses together with their entering group. This fosters a high level of cooperation among students. Student-faculty ratios are relatively small, resulting in multiple opportunities for mentoring by faculty, and for student-faculty collaboration.

Special Facilities or Resources: Doctoral students have access to a wide network of local and regional clinical, research and library facilities in the metropolitan Los Angeles and Southern California area. The campus University Counseling Center is directed by the Psychology department and provides counseling services to university students and staff. The Center is equipped with videotape and biofeedback equipment. ULV's Wilson Library contains 200,000 volumes and over 2,000 current journal subscriptions. Access to library resources is available through reciprocal borrowing privileges at many academic libraries in the Southern California area, as well as through online catalogs and CD-ROM databases.

Information for Students With Physical Disabilities: See the following Web site for more information: http://www.ulv.edu/gaas/contact.phtml.

Application Information:
Send to: Graduate Student Services. Application available online. URL of online application: http://www.ulv.edu/psyd/admissions.phtml. Students are admitted in the Fall, application deadline January 15. Students will be considered after the deadline on a space available basis. *Fee:* $75. The application fee is waived for current ULV students.

Loma Linda University
Department of Psychology
11130 Anderson Street CB102
Loma Linda, CA 92350
Telephone: (909) 558-8577
Fax: (909) 558-0171
E-mail: *slane@psych.llu.edu*
Web: *http://www.llu.edu/llu/grad/psychology*

Department Information:
1994. Chairperson: Louis Jenkins. Number of Faculty: total–full-time 10, part-time 3; women–full-time 3, part-time 1; minority–full-time 3.

Programs and Degrees Offered:
Listed in the following order: Program area, degree type (T if terminal Master's), number awarded 7/03–6/04. Clinical Psychology PhD (Doctor of Philosophy) 6, Clinical Psychology PsyD (Doctor of Psychology) 7, Experimental Psychology PhD (Doctor of Philosophy) 2, Experimental Psychology MA/MS (Master of Arts/Science) (T) 0.

APA Accreditation: Clinical PhD (Doctor of Philosophy). Clinical PsyD (Doctor of Psychology).

Student Applications/Admissions:
Student Applications
Clinical Psychology PhD (Doctor of Philosophy)—Applications 2004–2005, 30. Total applicants accepted 2004–2005, 18. Openings 2005–2006, 8. The Median number of years required for completion of a degree are 7. The number of students enrolled full and part-time who were dismissed or voluntarily withdrew from this program area were 4. *Clinical Psychology PsyD (Doctor of Psychology)*—Applications 2004–2005, 24.

Total applicants accepted 2004–2005, 14. Total enrolled 2004–2005 full-time, 62. Openings 2005–2006, 11. The Median number of years required for completion of a degree are 5. The number of students enrolled full and part-time who were dismissed or voluntarily withdrew from this program area were 1. *Experimental Psychology PhD (Doctor of Philosophy)*—Applications 2004–2005, 3. Total applicants accepted 2004–2005, 3. Openings 2005–2006, 3. The Median number of years required for completion of a degree are 5. The number of students enrolled full and part-time who were dismissed or voluntarily withdrew from this program area were 1. *Experimental Psychology MA/MS (Master of Arts/Science)*—Applications 2004–2005, 5. Total applicants accepted 2004–2005, 1. Openings 2005–2006, 10. The Median number of years required for completion of a degree are 2. The number of students enrolled full and part-time who were dismissed or voluntarily withdrew from this program area were 2.

Admissions Requirements:
Scores: Entries appear in this order: required test or GPA, minimum score (if required), median score of students entering in 2003–2004. Master's Programs: GRE-V 500; GRE-Q 500; GRE-V+Q 1000; overall undergraduate GPA 3.0. Doctoral Programs: GRE-V 500; GRE-Q 610; GRE-V+Q 1110; GRE-Subject(Psych) 600; overall undergraduate GPA 3.5; psychology GPA 3.5.
Other Criteria: (importance of criteria rated low, medium, or high): GRE/MAT scores high, research experience high, work experience medium, extracurricular activity medium, clinically related public service high, GPA high, letters of recommendation high, interview high, statement of goals and objectives high. For PhD applicants, research experience is highly desirable. For PsyD applicants, clinical related experience is highly desirable.

Student Characteristics: The following represents characteristics of students in 2004–2005 in all graduate psychology programs in the department: Female–full-time 109, part-time 0; Male–full-time 36, part-time 0; African American/Black–full-time 11, part-time 0; Hispanic/Latino(a)–full-time 14, part-time 0; Asian/Pacific Islander–full-time 22, part-time 0; American Indian/Alaska Native–full-time 0, part-time 0; Caucasian–full-time 92, part-time 0; Multi-ethnic–full-time 6, part-time 0; students subject to the Americans With Disabilities Act–full-time 5, part-time 0.

Financial Information/Assistance:
Tuition for Full-Time Study: *Master's:* State residents: per academic year $11,500, $460 per credit hour; Nonstate residents: per academic year $11,500, $460 per credit hour. *Doctoral:* State residents: per academic year $16,560, $460 per credit hour; Nonstate residents: per academic year $16,560, $460 per credit hour. Tuition is subject to change.

Financial Assistance:
First Year Students: Research assistantships available for first-year. Average amount paid per academic year: $3,280. Average number of hours worked per week: 5. Fellowships and scholarships available for first-year. Average amount paid per academic year: $3,000. Apply by August 15. Tuition remission given: partial.

Advanced Students: Teaching assistantships available for advanced students. Average amount paid per academic year: $1,950. Average number of hours worked per week: 7. Research assistantships available for advanced students. Average amount paid per academic year: $6,560. Average number of hours worked per week: 10. Fellowships and scholarships available for advanced students. Average amount paid per academic year: $3,000. Apply by August 15. Tuition remission given: partial.

Contact Information: Of all students currently enrolled full-time, 35% benefitted from one or more of the listed financial assistance programs.

Internships/Practica: Second-year practicum experiences are obtained in the departmental clinic and in a satellite clinic which reaches a previously underserved area of the City of San Bernardino. Other department training experiences include the LLU Craniofacial Team Clinic & Growing Fit Multidisciplinary clinic for obese children. Second-year practicum students may also receive some supervised clinical training in area public and private school settings. The external practicum (20 hours per week, normally in the third year of the program) is entirely off the departmental campus. Students are expected to accumulate 950 to 1000 hours of supervised experience while on external practicum, with an absolute minimum of 250 hours being spent in direct service experiences with patients. External practicum students are presently placed in six settings: 1) The Rehabilitation Unit of the Loma Linda University Medical Center; 2) the California Institution for Women; 3) the California Youth Authority; 4) the Riverside County Department of Mental Health; 5) The San Bernardino County Department of Mental Health; and 6) the Casa Colina Hospital for Rehabilitative Medicine. A full-year (40 hours per week) of internship is required with sites available across the country. All acceptable internship sites must meet the criteria for membership in the Association of Psychology Postdoctoral and Internship Centers. For those doctoral students for whom a professional internship is required prior to graduation, 16 applied in 2003–2004. Of those who applied, 15 were placed in internships listed by the Association of Psychology Postdoctoral and Internship Programs (APPIC); 10 were placed in APA accredited internships.

Housing and Day Care: On-campus housing is available. See the following Web site for more information: http://www.llu.edu/student services. On-campus day care facilities are available.

Employment of Department Graduates:

Master's Degree Graduates: Of those who graduated in the academic year 2003–2004, the following categories and numbers represent the post-graduate activities and employment of master's degree graduates: Enrolled in a psychology doctoral program (11), enrolled in another graduate/professional program (3), enrolled in a post-doctoral residency/fellowship (n/a), employed in independent practice (n/a), employed in an academic position at a university (0), employed in an academic position at a 2-year/4-year college (0), employed in other positions at a higher education institution (0), employed in a professional position in a school system (0), employed in business or industry (research/consulting) (0), employed in business or industry (management) (0), employed in a government agency (research) (0), employed in a government agency (professional services) (0), employed in a community mental health/counseling center (0), employed in a hospital/medical center (0), still seeking employment (0), other employment position (0), total from the above (master's) (14).

Doctoral Degree Graduates: Of those who graduated in the academic year 2003–2004, the following categories and numbers represent the post-graduate activities and employment of doctoral degree graduates: Enrolled in a psychology doctoral program (n/a), enrolled in a post-doctoral residency/fellowship (9), employed in independent practice (0), employed in an academic position at a university (0), employed in an academic position at a 2-year/4-year college (0), employed in other positions at a higher education institution (1), employed in a professional position in a school system (0), employed in business or industry (research/consulting) (0), employed in business or industry (management) (0), employed in a government agency (research) (0), employed in a government agency (professional services) (0), employed in a community mental health/counseling center (12), employed in a hospital/medical center (4), still seeking employment (0), other employment position (1), total from the above (doctoral) (27).

Additional Information:

Orientation, Objectives, and Emphasis of Department: Doctoral training at Loma Linda University takes place within the context of a holistic approach to human health and welfare. The university motto to make man whole takes in every aspect of being human—the physical, psychological, spiritual, and social. Building on a university tradition of health sciences research, training, and service, the doctoral programs in the department offer a combination of traditional and innovative training opportunities. The PhD in clinical psychology follows the traditional scientist-practitioner model and emphasizes research and clinical training. The PsyD is oriented toward clinical practice with emphasis on the understanding and application of the principles and research of psychological science. The PsyD/DrPH dual degree program offers an innovative combination of education in psychology and the health sciences to train practitioners who are highly qualified in the application of psychology to health promotion, preventive medicine, and health care as well as clinical practice and research. The PhD in experimental psychology is designed to train a small number of individuals for careers in research and academia. Students in the experimental PhD program work closely with a research mentor; a current list of faculty and their research interests may be obtained from the department.

Special Facilities or Resources: As a health sciences university, Loma Linda provides an ideal environment with resources for research and clinical training in such areas as health psychology/behavioral medicine and the delivery of health services. LLU Medical Center has nearly 900 beds, is staffed by more than 5000 people, and is the "flagship" of a system including hundreds of health care institutions around the world. In addition, a number of institutions in the area, such as the LLU Behavioral Medicine Center, Jerry L. Pettis VA Hospital, Patton State Hospital, and the San Bernardino County Mental Health Department represent numerous opportunities for research and clinical training in psychology. In the area of teaching and research the department has a consortial agreement with the department of psychology at California State University, San Bernardino. By this agreement, students at a post-master's level have TA opportunities to get experience teaching undergraduate courses. At the same time, a select group of graduate faculty members at CSUSB have appointments at LLU significantly enhancing advanced seminar offerings and opportunities for research training in a number of areas, strengthening and complementing those available at LLU.

Information for Students With Physical Disabilities: See the following Web site for more information: http://www.llu.edu/graduate school/psychology.

Application Information:
Send to: Graduate School Admissions, Loma Linda, CA 92350. Application available online. Students are admitted in the Fall, application deadline December 31. Applicants to our dual-degree program, PsyD/DrPH must apply to our School of Public Health concurrently with their applicaiton to our PsyD program in the Department of Psychology. *Fee:* $60. Waivers must be approved by the Department of Psychology. It is necessary to have information about your GPA and GRE scores to make an adequate decision on fee waiver requests.

Mount Street Mary's College
Graduate Program in Counseling Psychology
Mount Street Mary's College
10 Chester Place
Los Angeles, CA 90007-2598
Telephone: (213) 477-2800
Fax: (213) 477-2797
E-mail: *gradadmission@msmc.la.edu*
Web: *http://www.msmc.la.edu*

Department Information:
Graduate Director: Dr. Corinne Mabry. Number of Faculty: total–full-time 5, part-time 6; women–full-time 5; minority–full-time 1.

Programs and Degrees Offered:
Listed in the following order: Program area, degree type (T if terminal Master's), number awarded 7/03–6/04. Graduate Program in Counseling Psychology MA/MS (Master of Arts/Science) (T).

Student Applications/Admissions:
Student Applications
Graduate Program in Counseling Psychology MA/MS (Master of Arts/Science)—Total enrolled 2004–2005 full-time, 54. Openings 2005–2006, 20. The Median number of years required for completion of a degree are 3. The number of students enrolled full and part-time who were dismissed or voluntarily withdrew from this program area were 1.

Admissions Requirements:
Scores: Entries appear in this order: required test or GPA, minimum score (if required), median score of students entering in 2003–2004. Master's Programs: overall undergraduate GPA 3.00.
Other Criteria: (importance of criteria rated low, medium, or high): GRE/MAT scores high, research experience medium, work experience medium, extracurricular activity medium, clinically related public service medium, GPA high, letters of recommendation high, interview high, statement of goals and objectives high. For additional information on admission requirements, go to http://www.msmc.la.edu.

Student Characteristics: The following represents characteristics of students in 2004–2005 in all graduate psychology programs in the department: Female–full-time 45, part-time 0; Male–full-time 9, part-time 0; African American/Black–full-time 10, part-time 0; Hispanic/Latino(a)–full-time 31, part-time 0; Asian/Pacific Islander–full-time 4, part-time 0; Caucasian–full-time 9, part-time 0.

Financial Information/Assistance:
Tuition for Full-Time Study: *Master's:* State residents: $557 per credit hour. Tuition is subject to change. See the following Web site for updates and changes in tuition costs: http://www.msmc.la.edu.

Financial Assistance:
First Year Students: No information provided.
Advanced Students: No information provided.
Contact Information: No information provided.

Internships/Practica: Field Experiences in Counseling Practicum relates counseling principles to a variety of clinical settings. Assessment, differential diagnosis, and short term and long term interventions are emphasized. For each course 120 hours of fieldwork are required, and 90 of those hours must be face-to-face with clients. Fieldwork must take place in a site approved by the instructor and department.

Housing and Day Care: No on-campus housing is available. No on-campus day care facilities are available.

Employment of Department Graduates:
Master's Degree Graduates: Of those who graduated in the academic year 2003–2004, the following categories and numbers represent the post-graduate activities and employment of master's degree graduates: Enrolled in a post-doctoral residency/fellowship (n/a), employed in independent practice (n/a), employed in a community mental health/counseling center (7), total from the above (master's) (7).
Doctoral Degree Graduates: Of those who graduated in the academic year 2003–2004, the following categories and numbers represent the post-graduate activities and employment of doctoral degree graduates: Enrolled in a psychology doctoral program (n/a), total from the above (doctoral) (0).

Additional Information:
Orientation, Objectives, and Emphasis of Department: Mount Street Mary's College offers a master of science in counseling psychology, with specializations in Marriage and Family Therapy (MFT) or Human Services Personnel Counseling (HSPC). The student-centered faculty emphasize leadership, service, and training geared toward preparing students for later professional practice.

Personal Behavior Statement: Students should refer to the Mount Street Mary's College Graduate Application to access the full text of the statement.

Special Facilities or Resources: The Doheny campus, where Psychology graduate students study, was originally an estate of private Victorian homes. To meet the growing needs of Doheny students, the new Sister Magdalen Coughlin Learning Complex, which houses a library, Cultural Fluency Center, Academic Building and Learning Resource Center, was built. Doheny affords easy access to neighboring USC and downtown Los Angeles, while housing classrooms and offices in a secure, park-like setting.

Information for Students With Physical Disabilities: See the following Web site for more information: http://www.msmc.la. edu.

Application Information:
Send to: The Graduate Division, Mount Street Mary's College, 10 Chester Place, Los Angeles, CA 90007-2598. Students are admitted in the Programs have rolling admissions. *Fee:* $50.

Pacific Graduate School of Psychology
Clinical Psychology Program
935 East Meadow Drive
Palo Alto, CA 94303
Telephone: (650) 843-3419 & (800) 818-6136
Fax: (650) 493-6147
E-mail: *ehilt@pgsp.edu*
Web: *http://www.pgsp.edu*

Department Information:
1975. Vice President of Enrollment Management: Elizabeth Hilt. Number of Faculty: total–full-time 13, part-time 25; women–full-time 7, part-time 15; minority–full-time 2, part-time 2.

Programs and Degrees Offered:
Listed in the following order: Program area, degree type (T if terminal Master's), number awarded 7/03–6/04. Clinical Psychology PhD (Doctor of Philosophy) 35, Psychology and Law Other 3, MBA/PhD Other 0, PsyD (Doctor of Psychology) 0, Distance Learning Master's Program MA/MS (Master of Arts/Science) (T) 6.

APA Accreditation: Clinical PhD (Doctor of Philosophy).

Student Applications/Admissions:
Student Applications
Clinical Psychology PhD (Doctor of Philosophy)—Applications 2004–2005, 147. Total applicants accepted 2004–2005, 135. Number enrolled (new admits only) 2004–2005 full-time, 41. Openings 2005–2006, 50. The Median number of years required for completion of a degree are 6. The number of students enrolled full and part-time who were dismissed or voluntarily withdrew from this program area were 4. *Psychology and Law Other*—Applications 2004–2005, 10. Total applicants accepted 2004–2005, 5. Number enrolled (new admits only) 2004–2005 full-time, 2. Openings 2005–2006, 5. The Median number of years required for completion of a degree are 7. The number of students enrolled full and part-time who were dismissed or voluntarily withdrew from this program area were 0. *MBA/PhD Other*—Applications 2004–2005, 4. Total applicants accepted 2004–2005, 2. Number enrolled (new admits

only) 2004–2005 full-time, 1. Total enrolled 2004–2005 full-time, 3. Openings 2005–2006, 5. The Median number of years required for completion of a degree are 6. The number of students enrolled full and part-time who were dismissed or voluntarily withdrew from this program area were 1. *PsyD (Doctor of Psychology)*—Applications 2004–2005, 70. Total applicants accepted 2004–2005, 46. Number enrolled (new admits only) 2004–2005 full-time, 22. Openings 2005–2006, 30. The number of students enrolled full and part-time who were dismissed or voluntarily withdrew from this program area were 1. *Distance Learning Master's Program MA/MS (Master of Arts/Science)*—Applications 2004–2005, 22. Total applicants accepted 2004–2005, 19. Number enrolled (new admits only) 2004–2005 part-time, 12. Total enrolled 2004–2005 part-time, 26. Openings 2005–2006, 30. The Median number of years required for completion of a degree are 2. The number of students enrolled full and part-time who were dismissed or voluntarily withdrew from this program area were 2.

Admissions Requirements:
Scores: Entries appear in this order: required test or GPA, minimum score (if required), median score of students entering in 2003–2004. Doctoral Programs: GRE-V+Q no minimum stated, 1150.

Other Criteria: (importance of criteria rated low, medium, or high): GRE/MAT scores high, research experience medium, work experience medium, extracurricular activity medium, clinically related public service medium, GPA high, letters of recommendation high, interview medium, statement of goals and objectives medium. Interview required for the following programs: PGSP–Stanford PsyD Consortium, JD/PhD Program, and MBA/PhD Programs. For additional information on admission requirements, go to: www.pgsp.edu.

Student Characteristics: The following represents characteristics of students in 2004–2005 in all graduate psychology programs in the department: Female–full-time 240, part-time 21; Male–full-time 68, part-time 3; African American/Black–full-time 16, part-time 1; Hispanic/Latino(a)–full-time 21, part-time 3; Asian/Pacific Islander–full-time 38, part-time 3; American Indian/Alaska Native–full-time 2, part-time 0; Caucasian–full-time 182, part-time 14; Multi-ethnic–full-time 38, part-time 0; students subject to the Americans With Disabilities Act–full-time 0, part-time 0.

Financial Information/Assistance:
Tuition for Full-Time Study: *Master's:* State residents: per academic year $15,000. *Doctoral:* State residents: per academic year $30,122. Tuition is subject to change. Tuition costs vary by program.

Financial Assistance:
First Year Students: No information provided.

Advanced Students: Teaching assistantships available for advanced students. Average amount paid per academic year: $3,000. Apply by N/A. Research assistantships available for advanced students. Average amount paid per academic year: $4,000. Apply by N/A.

Contact Information: Of all students currently enrolled full-time, 25% benefitted from one or more of the listed financial assistance programs.

Internships/Practica: All students take their second year of practicum in our Kurt and Barbara Gronowski Clinic and the third and fourth years in local agencies. All students are expected to complete an APA-accredited, APPIC or CAPIC-approved internship. For those doctoral students for whom a professional internship is required prior to graduation, 26 applied in 2003–2004. Of those who applied, 23 were placed in internships listed by the Association of Psychology Postdoctoral and Internship Programs (APPIC); 22 were placed in APA accredited internships.

Housing and Day Care: No on-campus housing is available. No on-campus day care facilities are available.

Employment of Department Graduates:

Master's Degree Graduates: Of those who graduated in the academic year 2003–2004, the following categories and numbers represent the post-graduate activities and employment of master's degree graduates: Enrolled in a post-doctoral residency/fellowship (n/a), employed in independent practice (n/a), total from the above (master's) (0).

Doctoral Degree Graduates: Of those who graduated in the academic year 2003–2004, the following categories and numbers represent the post-graduate activities and employment of doctoral degree graduates: Enrolled in a psychology doctoral program (n/a), enrolled in a post-doctoral residency/fellowship (25), employed in a professional position in a school system (1), employed in a community mental health/counseling center (1), employed in a hospital/medical center (1), other employment position (3), do not know (5), total from the above (doctoral) (36).

Additional Information:

Orientation, Objectives, and Emphasis of Department: Pacific Graduate School of Psychology (PGSP) is a freestanding graduate school offering doctoral degrees in clinical psychology to students from diverse backgrounds. The program is designed to integrate academic work, research, and clinical experiences at every level of the student's training. All students must develop a thorough understanding of a systematic body of knowledge that comprises the current field of psychology. They are expected to carry out an independent investigation that makes an original contribution to scientific knowledge in psychology and to demonstrate excellence in the application of specific clinical skills. PGSP considers this integration of scholarship, research, and practical experience the best training model for preparing psychologists to meet the highest standards of scholarly research and community service. Graduates are expected to enter the community at large prepared to do research, practice, and teach in culturally and professionally diverse settings.

Special Facilities or Resources: PGSP's setting as a free-standing graduate school of psychology is much enhanced by our San Francisco Bay Area location. We provide students with access to local university libraries (e.g., Stanford, UC Berkeley). The range of clinical experience available to students is inexhaustible. All faculty have active research programs in which students participate. Furthermore, PGSP has a close relationship with local VA medical centers.

Information for Students With Physical Disabilities: See the following Web site for more information: www.pgsp.edu.

Application Information:
Send to: Office of Admissions, Pacific Graduate School of Psychology, 935 East Meadow Drive, Palo Alto, CA 94303. Application available online. URL of online application: www.pgsp.edu. Students are admitted in the Fall, application deadline. Programs have rolling admissions; however, application is due January 15 for those who want to be considered for a PGSP fellowship. *Fee:* $100.

Pacific Graduate School of Psychology & Stanford University School of Medicine
Department of Psychiatry and Behavioral Sciences
PGSP–Stanford PsyD Consortium
935 East Meadow Drive
Palo Alto, CA 94303
Telephone: (800) 818-6136
Fax: (650) 493-6147
E-mail: *bongar@pgsp.edu*
Web: *http://www.pgsp.edu/consortium/*

Department Information:
2002. Chair and Co-Chair: Bruce Bongar, PhD & Bruce Arnow, PhD Number of Faculty: total–full-time 10, part-time 13; women–full-time 5, part-time 6; minority–full-time 2, part-time 1.

Programs and Degrees Offered:
Listed in the following order: Program area, degree type (T if terminal Master's), number awarded 7/03–6/04. PGSP–Stanford PsyD Consortium PsyD (Doctor of Psychology) 0.

Student Applications/Admissions:
Student Applications
PGSP–Stanford PsyD Consortium PsyD (Doctor of Psychology)— Applications 2004–2005, 89. Total applicants accepted 2004–2005, 22. Number enrolled (new admits only) 2004–2005 full-time, 20. Openings 2005–2006, 26. The number of students enrolled full and part-time, who were dismissed or voluntarily withdrew from this program area were 2.

Admissions Requirements:
Scores: Entries appear in this order: required test or GPA, minimum score (if required), median score of students entering in 2003–2004. Doctoral Programs: GRE-V no minimum stated; GRE-Q no minimum stated; overall undergraduate GPA no minimum stated; last 2 years GPA no minimum stated; psychology GPA no minimum stated. The PGSP institutional code for receipt of GRE scores is 4638.
Other Criteria: (importance of criteria rated low, medium, or high): GRE/MAT scores medium, research experience low, work experience low, extracurricular activity low, clinically related public service medium, GPA high, letters of recommendation high, interview high, statement of goals and objectives high.

Student Characteristics: The following represents characteristics of students in 2004–2005 in all graduate psychology programs in the department: Female–full-time 54, part-time 0; Male–full-time 14, part-time 0; African American/Black–full-time 3, part-time 0; Hispanic/Latino(a)–full-time 3, part-time 0; Asian/Pacific Islander–full-time 9, part-time 0; American Indian/Alaska Native–

full-time 0, part-time 0; Caucasian–full-time 51, part-time 0; Multi-ethnic–full-time 2, part-time 0; students subject to the Americans With Disabilities Act–full-time 0, part-time 0.

Financial Information/Assistance:

Tuition for Full-Time Study: *Doctoral:* State residents: per academic year $31,000; Nonstate residents: per academic year $31,000. Tuition is subject to change. See the following Web site for updates and changes in tuition costs: http://www.pgsp.edu/consortium/.

Financial Assistance:

First Year Students: Teaching assistantships available for first-year. Average amount paid per academic year: $750. Average number of hours worked per week: 6. Apply by rolling. Research assistantships available for first-year. Average amount paid per academic year: $1,500. Average number of hours worked per week: 5. Apply by rolling. Fellowships and scholarships available for first-year. Average amount paid per academic year: $5,000. Average number of hours worked per week: 8. Apply by April 1. Tuition remission given: partial.

Advanced Students: Teaching assistantships available for advanced students. Average amount paid per academic year: $750. Average number of hours worked per week: 6. Apply by rolling. Research assistantships available for advanced students. Average amount paid per academic year: $1,500. Average number of hours worked per week: 5. Apply by rolling. Fellowships and scholarships available for advanced students. Average amount paid per academic year: $5,000. Average number of hours worked per week: 8. Apply by March 31. Tuition remission given: partial.

Contact Information: Of all students currently enrolled full-time, 60% benefitted from one or more of the listed financial assistance programs.

Internships/Practica: The PGSP–Stanford Consortium training program provides students with experiences that are sequenced with increasing amounts of time spent in clinical work during each year of graduate training, with a total of approximately 2,000 clinical hours obtained prior to internship. Graduate students begin working in clinical settings as a volunteer during their first year; during their second and third years, students enroll in field practica that may take place in a variety of settings, such as Stanford and UCSF medical school hospitals and programs, community mental health centers, the Palo Alto V.A. Health Care System medical centers, county mental health systems, AIDS prevention project, and child/family psychiatric clinics. In the fourth year students will work on a clinical dissertation, and a fourth year practicum is optional but highly recommended. In the fifth year, following advancement to the candidacy for the Doctor of Psychology (PsyD) degree, the student is required to complete a 2,000-hour external pre-doctoral internship that provides high quality professional supervision and experience. No statistics are available for predoctoral internship placement because this is a new program and no students will be applying for internships until Fall 2005.

Housing and Day Care: No on-campus housing is available. No on-campus day care facilities are available.

Employment of Department Graduates:

Master's Degree Graduates: Of those who graduated in the academic year 2003–2004, the following categories and numbers represent the post-graduate activities and employment of master's degree graduates: Enrolled in a post-doctoral residency/fellowship (n/a), employed in independent practice (n/a), total from the above (master's) (0).

Doctoral Degree Graduates: Of those who graduated in the academic year 2003–2004, the following categories and numbers represent the post-graduate activities and employment of doctoral degree graduates: Enrolled in a psychology doctoral program (n/a), total from the above (doctoral) (0).

Additional Information:

Orientation, Objectives, and Emphasis of Department: This training program emphasizes a biopsychosocial understanding of psychological disorders (i.e., a model that conceptualizes psychological disorders and problems as having biological, psychological and social components). In addition, the program provides "cutting edge" training for student psychologist-practitioners in the use of empirically supported treatments for a wide variety of psychiatric illnesses and behavioral disorders. There are four primary training goals for the PGSP–Stanford Consortium: 1. To develop psychologists who can effectively evaluate sophisticated social research and apply empirically supported psychological interventions in their practice of psychology. 2. To educate highly trained psychologists who can contribute to the advancement of clinical psychology. 3. To produce clinical psychologists who are competent in psychological assessment, consultation, and supervision. 4. To provide theory, skills, and supervision necessary to enable students to confidentially and effectively engage in treatment interventions in response to our societal needs.

Special Facilities or Resources: The PGSP-Stanford Doctor of Psychology program draws upon nationally renowned faculty and resources from the Pacific Graduate School and the Stanford University School of Medicine's Department of Psychiatry and Behavioral Sciences. The five-year Doctor of Psychology degree program consists of three years of graduate coursework, a year spent working on a clinical dissertation, followed by a year-long internship in clinical psychology. As a practitioner-oriented graduate program, the focus is on intensive clinical training and will utilize the rich resources of the San Francisco Bay area mental health community for pre-internship basic and advanced supervised clinical experiences. The program strives for the earliest possible full recognition of the first year class (entering in 2002-2003) for licensure in all 50 states, as well as interstate mobility through the "Certificate of Professional Qualification in Psychology" from the Association of State and Provincial Psychology Boards. In addition, we will strive for full American Psychological Association accreditation of the PGSP-Stanford PsyD Consortium by academic year 2007-2008 - which will provide the entering class of 2002 with a fully APA accredited PsyD degree.

Application Information:
Send to: Office of Admissions PGSP–Stanford PsyD Consortium, 935 East Meadow Drive, Palo Alto, CA 94303. Application information available online: http://www.pgsp.edu/consortium/conapply.htm. Students are admitted in the Fall, application deadline March 31. *Fee:* $100.

Pacific, University of the

Department of Psychology
3601 Pacific Avenue
Stockton, CA 95211
Telephone: (209) 946-2133
Fax: (209) 946-2454
E-mail: *gradschool@uop.edu*
Web: *http://www.pacific.edu*

Department Information:

1960. Chairperson: Roseann Hannon, PhD Number of Faculty: total–full-time 7; women–full-time 2.

Programs and Degrees Offered:

Listed in the following order: Program area, degree type (T if terminal Master's), number awarded 7/03–6/04. Behavioral MA/MS (Master of Arts/Science) (T) 7.

Student Applications/Admissions:

Student Applications

Behavioral MA/MS (Master of Arts/Science)—Applications 2004–2005, 18. Total applicants accepted 2004–2005, 10. Number enrolled (new admits only) 2004–2005 full-time, 9. Total enrolled 2004–2005 full-time, 16. Openings 2005–2006, 10. The Median number of years required for completion of a degree are 3. The number of students enrolled full and part-time who were dismissed or voluntarily withdrew from this program area were 2.

Admissions Requirements:

Scores: Entries appear in this order: required test or GPA, minimum score (if required), median score of students entering in 2003–2004. Master's Programs: GRE-V no minimum stated, 480; GRE-Q no minimum stated, 600; GRE-V+Q no minimum stated, 1080; GRE-Analytical no minimum stated; overall undergraduate GPA 3.0, 3.67; last 2 years GPA 3.0, 3.71; psychology GPA 3.0, 3.79.

Other Criteria: (importance of criteria rated low, medium, or high): GRE/MAT scores low, research experience high, work experience medium, clinically related public service low, GPA high, letters of recommendation high, statement of goals and objectives high, applied experience high.

Student Characteristics: The following represents characteristics of students in 2004–2005 in all graduate psychology programs in the department: Female–full-time 13, part-time 0; Male–full-time 3, part-time 0; African American/Black–full-time 0, part-time 0; Hispanic/Latino(a)–full-time 2, part-time 0; Asian/Pacific Islander–full-time 3, part-time 0; American Indian/Alaska Native–full-time 0, part-time 0; Caucasian–full-time 11, part-time 0; Multi-ethnic–full-time 0, part-time 0; students subject to the Americans With Disabilities Act–full-time 0, part-time 0.

Financial Information/Assistance:

Tuition for Full-Time Study: *Master's:* State residents: per academic year $11,400, $760 per credit hour; Nonstate residents: per academic year $11,400, $760 per credit hour. See the following Web site for updates and changes in tuition costs: http://www.uop.edu/cop/psychology/programs.html#ma.

Financial Assistance:

First Year Students: Teaching assistantships available for first-year. Average amount paid per academic year: $7,675. Average number of hours worked per week: 20. Apply by February 1. Tuition remission given: partial. Traineeships available for first-year. Average amount paid per academic year: $8,500. Average number of hours worked per week: 20. Apply by February 1. Tuition remission given: partial.

Advanced Students: Teaching assistantships available for advanced students. Average amount paid per academic year: $7,675. Average number of hours worked per week: 20. Apply by February 1. Tuition remission given: partial. Traineeships available for advanced students. Average amount paid per academic year: $8,500. Average number of hours worked per week: 20. Apply by February 1. Tuition remission given: partial.

Contact Information: Of all students currently enrolled full-time, 100% benefitted from one or more of the listed financial assistance programs.

Internships/Practica:

Contained directly within the department is the Psychology Clinic, which provides services for families and children (e.g. behavioral interventions; evaluations for child custody, attention deficit disorder, etc.; parent training). All students are required to complete two years of experience working in the Clinic during their MA studies, or else to complete an appropriate alternative applied experience (e.g. business settings, educational settings). The department also directs the Community Re-entry Program (contracted directly with the local county), which provides a wide range of behaviorally-based programs to assist the mentally disabled/ill in becoming independent. This program provides half-time employment for eight graduate students per year. Students interested in developmental disabilities can work with the Behavioral Instructional Service (in cooperation with Valley Mountain Regional Center, which serves these clients), and part-time employment is available with this program. We also have contracts with several outside agencies at which students can obtain practica experience, including the Stockton Unified School District (ABA assessment and interventions for school problem behaviors) and BEST (early ABA interventions with children diagnosed with autism).

Housing and Day Care:

On-campus housing is available. See the following Web site for more information: http://www3.uop.edu/studentlife/housing/. No on-campus day care facilities are available.

Employment of Department Graduates:

Master's Degree Graduates: Of those who graduated in the academic year 2003–2004, the following categories and numbers represent the post-graduate activities and employment of master's degree graduates: Enrolled in a psychology doctoral program (1), enrolled in a post-doctoral residency/fellowship (n/a), employed in independent practice (n/a), other employment position (6), total from the above (master's) (7).

Doctoral Degree Graduates: Of those who graduated in the academic year 2003–2004, the following categories and numbers represent the post-graduate activities and employment of doctoral degree graduates: Enrolled in a psychology doctoral program (n/a), total from the above (doctoral) (0).

Additional Information:

Orientation, Objectives, and Emphasis of Department: The MA program emphasizes a behavioral approach. The coursework and academic training cover behavioral theories with emphases on applied behavior analysis and behavioral medicine/health psychology. Multiple settings are available for practicum work and research, and experience in relevant applied settings is required. The design and conduct of research are stressed throughout a student's graduate work and an empirical thesis is required. A coordinated program of courses, research, and applied experiences is developed for each student, and the faculty maintains an environment in which students achieve significant research accomplishments and applied interventions. Close contact between faculty and students is highly regarded and encouraged. Graduates are prepared for entrance into doctoral programs and for employment in a variety of applied settings including mental health, medicine/health care, and business. Graduates have qualified for and passed the behavior analysis certification examination of the Association for Applied Behavior Analysis.

Special Facilities or Resources: The department provides office space for faculty and graduate students, computing eqiupment, and video equipment for research projects. Applied research projects are also conducted in community settings (e.g. schools, medical settings). The Comunity Re-entry Program and Valley Mountain Regional Center (described above) also provide rich opportunities for research in community settings.

Information for Students With Physical Disabilities: See the following Web site for more information: http://www3.uop.edu/studentlife/housing/.

Application Information:
Send to: Dean of the Graduate School, University of the Pacific, 3601 Pacific Avenue, Stockton, CA 95211. Application available online. URL of online application: https://www.applyweb.com/apply/uopg/menu.html. Students are admitted in the Fall, application deadline February 15. Although the deadline for applications is February 15, we will accept late applications. However, applying after February 15 decreases an applicant's chances to receive funding. *Fee:* $75. Applicants can save $25 by applying online. The online application fee is $50.

Pepperdine University
Division of Psychology
Graduate School of Education and Psychology
6100 Center Drive - 5th Floor
Los Angeles, CA 90045
Telephone: (800) 888-4849
Fax: (310) 568-5755
E-mail: *csaunder@pepperdine.edu*
Web: *http://gsep.pepperdine.edu*

Department Information:
1951. Associate Dean: Robert A. deMayo. Number of Faculty: total–full-time 24, part-time 64; women–full-time 12, part-time 37; minority–full-time 6, part-time 8; faculty subject to the Americans With Disabilities Act 1.

Programs and Degrees Offered:
Listed in the following order: Program area, degree type (T if terminal Master's), number awarded 7/03–6/04. Clinical MA/MS (Master of Arts/Science) (T) 106, Clinical (Malibu Campus) MA/MS (Master of Arts/Science) (T) 24, General MA/MS (Master of Arts/Science) (T) 111, Clinical PsyD (Doctor of Psychology) 19.

APA Accreditation: Clinical PsyD (Doctor of Psychology).

Student Applications/Admissions:
Student Applications
Clinical MA/MS (*Master of Arts/Science*)—Applications 2004–2005, 270. Total applicants accepted 2004–2005, 219. Number enrolled (new admits only) 2004–2005 full-time, 154. Number enrolled (new admits only) 2004–2005 part-time, 19. Total enrolled 2004–2005 full-time, 371, part-time, 86. Openings 2005–2006, 100. The Median number of years required for completion of a degree are 2. *Clinical (Malibu Campus) MA/MS (Master of Arts/Science)*—Applications 2004–2005, 176. Total applicants accepted 2004–2005, 81. Number enrolled (new admits only) 2004–2005 full-time, 68. Number enrolled (new admits only) 2004–2005 part-time, 0. Openings 2005–2006, 40. The Median number of years required for completion of a degree are 2. The number of students enrolled full and part-time who were dismissed or voluntarily withdrew from this program area were 1. *General MA/MS (Master of Arts/Science)*—Applications 2004–2005, 105. Total applicants accepted 2004–2005, 91. Number enrolled (new admits only) 2004–2005 full-time, 61. Number enrolled (new admits only) 2004–2005 part-time, 4. Total enrolled 2004–2005 full-time, 144, part-time, 33. Openings 2005–2006, 50. The Median number of years required for completion of a degree are 2. *Clinical PsyD (Doctor of Psychology)*—Applications 2004–2005, 118. Total applicants accepted 2004–2005, 42. Number enrolled (new admits only) 2004–2005 full-time, 28. Number enrolled (new admits only) 2004–2005 part-time, 0. Openings 2005–2006, 26. The Median number of years required for completion of a degree are 5. The number of students enrolled full and part-time who were dismissed or voluntarily withdrew from this program area were 2.

Admissions Requirements:
Scores: Entries appear in this order: required test or GPA, minimum score (if required), median score of students entering in 2003–2004. Master's Programs: GRE-V no minimum stated, 470; GRE-Q no minimum stated, 500; MAT no minimum stated, 40; overall undergraduate GPA no minimum stated, 3.02. For the Evening Format MA programs, the GRE or MAT may be waived for applicants with seven or more years of qualified full-time work experience or a cumulative undergraduate GPA of 3.7 or higher. Doctoral Programs: GRE-V no minimum stated, 535; GRE-Q no minimum stated, 580; GRE-Subject(Psych) no minimum stated, 630; overall undergraduate GPA no minimum stated, 3.20.
Other Criteria: (importance of criteria rated low, medium, or high): GRE/MAT scores medium, research experience medium, work experience low, extracurricular activity low, clinically related public service low, GPA high, letters of recommendation high, interview high, statement of goals and objectives high, For the MA in Psychology and the MA in Clinical Psychology - work experience, letters of recommendation, and personal statements have medium importance, while previous research or clinical experience has low importance.

Student Characteristics: The following represents characteristics of students in 2004–2005 in all graduate psychology programs in

the department: Female–full-time 607, part-time 101; Male–full-time 110, part-time 18; African American/Black–full-time 61, part-time 13; Hispanic/Latino(a)–full-time 95, part-time 11; Asian/Pacific Islander–full-time 57, part-time 9; American Indian/Alaska Native–full-time 9, part-time 0; Caucasian–full-time 491, part-time 86; Multi-ethnic–full-time 4, part-time 0; students subject to the Americans With Disabilities Act–full-time 8, part-time 0.

Financial Information/Assistance:

Tuition for Full-Time Study: *Master's:* State residents: $705 per credit hour; Nonstate residents: $705 per credit hour. *Doctoral:* State residents: $890 per credit hour; Nonstate residents: $890 per credit hour. See the following Web site for updates and changes in tuition costs: http://gsep.pepperdine.edu/financialaid/costs.

Financial Assistance:

First Year Students: Teaching assistantships available for first-year. Average amount paid per academic year: $4,400. Average number of hours worked per week: 10. Apply by variable. Research assistantships available for first-year. Average amount paid per academic year: $4,400. Average number of hours worked per week: 10. Apply by variable. Traineeships available for first-year. Average amount paid per academic year: $4,400. Average number of hours worked per week: 10. Apply by variable. Fellowships and scholarships available for first-year. Average amount paid per academic year: $3,000. Average number of hours worked per week: 0. Apply by April 15. Tuition remission given: partial.

Advanced Students: Teaching assistantships available for advanced students. Average amount paid per academic year: $5,300. Average number of hours worked per week: 10. Apply by variable. Research assistantships available for advanced students. Average amount paid per academic year: $5,300. Average number of hours worked per week: 10. Apply by variable. Traineeships available for advanced students. Average amount paid per academic year: $5,300. Average number of hours worked per week: 10. Apply by variable. Fellowships and scholarships available for advanced students. Average amount paid per academic year: $6,675. Average number of hours worked per week: 0. Apply by April 15. Tuition remission given: partial.

Contact Information: Of all students currently enrolled full-time, 30% benefitted from one or more of the listed financial assistance programs. Application and information available online at: http://gsep.pepperdine.edu/af/finaid.

Internships/Practica: Students in the PsyD and MA in Clinical Psychology programs complete practicum requirements at Pepperdine clinics or affiliated agencies in the community. PsyD students complete predoctoral internships in approved agencies. Pepperdine clinical training staff assists students in locating training positions. For those doctoral students for whom a professional internship is required prior to graduation, 21 applied in 2003–2004. Of those who applied, 19 were placed in internships listed by the Association of Psychology Postdoctoral and Internship Programs (APPIC); 16 were placed in APA accredited internships.

Housing and Day Care: On-campus housing is available. See the following Web site for more information: http://www.pepperdine.edu/housing. No on-campus day care facilities are available.

Employment of Department Graduates:

Master's Degree Graduates: Of those who graduated in the academic year 2003–2004, the following categories and numbers represent the post-graduate activities and employment of master's degree graduates: Enrolled in a post-doctoral residency/fellowship (n/a), employed in independent practice (n/a), total from the above (master's) (0).

Doctoral Degree Graduates: Of those who graduated in the academic year 2003–2004, the following categories and numbers represent the post-graduate activities and employment of doctoral degree graduates: Enrolled in a psychology doctoral program (n/a), enrolled in another graduate/professional program (0), enrolled in a post-doctoral residency/fellowship (5), employed in independent practice (1), employed in an academic position at a university (0), employed in an academic position at a 2-year/4-year college (0), employed in other positions at a higher education institution (2), employed in a professional position in a school system (0), employed in business or industry (research/consulting) (0), employed in business or industry (management) (0), employed in a government agency (research) (0), employed in a government agency (professional services) (2), employed in a community mental health/counseling center (7), do not know (2), total from the above (doctoral) (19).

Additional Information:

Orientation, Objectives, and Emphasis of Department: The psychology degree programs are designed to provide the student with a theoretical and practical understanding of the principles of psychology within the framework of a strong clinical emphasis. Courses present various aspects of the art and science of psychology as it is applied to the understanding of human behavior, and to the prevention, diagnosis, and treatment of mental and emotional problems. The MA in psychology serves as the prerequisite for the PsyD degree, or for students seeking human services positions in community agencies and organizations. The MA in clinical psychology provides the academic preparation for the Marriage and Family Therapist license. The PsyD program ascribes to a practitioner-scholar model of training.

Special Facilities or Resources: The Master of Arts in Psychology and Clinical Psychology programs at Pepperdine University are offered at four campuses throughout Southern California. Computer laboratories and libraries are available at all four campuses offering the psychology program. Psychology clinics are located at Culver City, Irvine, and Encino.

Information for Students With Physical Disabilities: See the following Web site for more information: www.pepperdine.edu/studentaffairs/disabilityservices.

Application Information:

Send to: Pepperdine University, Graduate School of Education and Psychology, Office of Admissions, 6100 Center Drive, Los Angeles, CA 90045. Application available online. URL of online application: http://gsep.pepperdine.edu/admission/application. Students are admitted in the Fall, application deadline July 1; Spring, application deadline November 1; Summer, application deadline March 1. PsyD and MA Clinical (Malibu, daytime format) programs: Fall admission only: January 3 application deadline for PsyD; February 1 application deadline for MA Clinical (Malibu, daytime format). Evening format MA Clinical and General programs: Fall admission - July 1 application deadline; Spring admission - November 1 application deadline; Summer admission - March 1 application deadline. *Fee:* $55.

Phillips Graduate Institute
Clinical Psychology Doctoral Program
5445 Balboa Boulevard
Encino, CA 91316
Telephone: (818) 386-5600
Fax: (818) 386-5699
E-mail: *jrkussin@pgi.edu*
Web: *http://www.pgi.edu*

Department Information:
2001. Director, Clinical Psychology Doctoral Program: Jody Kussin, PhD. Number of Faculty: total–full-time 5, part-time 18; women–full-time 4, part-time 11; minority–full-time 1, part-time 5.

Programs and Degrees Offered:
Listed in the following order: Program area, degree type (T if terminal Master's), number awarded 7/03–6/04. Clinical Psychology PsyD (Doctor of Psychology).

Student Applications/Admissions:
Student Applications
Clinical Psychology PsyD (Doctor of Psychology)—Applications 2004–2005, 73. Total applicants accepted 2004–2005, 43. Number enrolled (new admits only) 2004–2005 full-time, 19. Number enrolled (new admits only) 2004–2005 part-time, 5. Openings 2005–2006, 32. The number of students enrolled full and part-time who were dismissed or voluntarily withdrew from this program area were 1.

Admissions Requirements:
Scores: Entries appear in this order: required test or GPA, minimum score (if required), median score of students entering in 2003–2004. Master's Programs: overall undergraduate GPA 3.00, N/A. Doctoral Programs: overall undergraduate GPA 3.00, N/A.

Other Criteria: (importance of criteria rated low, medium, or high): research experience low, work experience medium, extracurricular activity medium, clinically related public service high, GPA high, letters of recommendation medium, interview high, statement of goals and objectives medium.

Student Characteristics: The following represents characteristics of students in 2004–2005 in all graduate psychology programs in the department: Female–full-time 39, part-time 25; Male–full-time 9, part-time 10; African American/Black–full-time 3, part-time 3; Hispanic/Latino(a)–full-time 9, part-time 7; Asian/Pacific Islander–full-time 4, part-time 1; American Indian/Alaska Native–full-time 1, part-time 0; Caucasian–full-time 24, part-time 23; Multi-ethnic–full-time 7, part-time 1; students subject to the Americans With Disabilities Act–full-time 0, part-time 0.

Financial Information/Assistance:
Tuition for Full-Time Study: *Doctoral:* Nonstate residents: per academic year $15,840, $660 per credit hour. Tuition is subject to change. See the following Web site for updates and changes in tuition costs: www.pgi.edu.

Financial Assistance:
First Year Students: No information provided.

Advanced Students: Teaching assistantships available for advanced students. Average amount paid per academic year: $5,000. Average number of hours worked per week: 10. Apply by May 30.

Contact Information: Of all students currently enrolled full-time, 4% benefitted from one or more of the listed financial assistance programs.

Internships/Practica: The Clinical Placement Office provides students information and guidance in the choice of practica and internship experiences. For those doctoral students for whom a professional internship is required prior to graduation, 17 applied in 2003–2004. Of those who applied, 4 were placed in internships listed by the Association of Psychology Postdoctoral and Internship Programs (APPIC); 1 was placed in APA accredited internships.

Housing and Day Care: No on-campus housing is available. No on-campus day care facilities are available.

Employment of Department Graduates:
Master's Degree Graduates: Of those who graduated in the academic year 2003–2004, the following categories and numbers represent the post-graduate activities and employment of master's degree graduates: Enrolled in a post-doctoral residency/fellowship (n/a), employed in independent practice (n/a), total from the above (master's) (0).

Doctoral Degree Graduates: Of those who graduated in the academic year 2003–2004, the following categories and numbers represent the post-graduate activities and employment of doctoral degree graduates: Enrolled in a psychology doctoral program (n/a), total from the above (doctoral) (0).

Additional Information:
Orientation, Objectives, and Emphasis of Department: The Doctor of Psychology in Clinical Psychology provides the education and training to be eligible to apply for licensure in the state of California. The program integrates ecosystemic and family systems theory throughout the curriculum. In addition, students select advanced coursework in either diversity or forensic psychology to fulfill concentration area requirements.

Information for Students With Physical Disabilities: See the following Web site for more information: www.pgi.edu.

Application Information:
Send to: Office of Admissions, Phillips Graduate Institute, 5445 Balboa Boulevard, Encino, CA 91316. Students are admitted in the Fall, application deadline January 31. *Fee:* $75.

San Diego State University

Counseling and School Psychology
Education
5500 Campanille Drive
San Diego, CA 92182-1179
Telephone: (619) 594-6109
Fax: (619) 594-7025
E-mail: *csp@mail.sdsu.edu*
Web: *http://edweb.sdsu.edu/csp/*

Department Information:

1965. Chairperson: Carol Robinson-Zañartu, PhD. Number of Faculty: total–full-time 13, part-time 26; women–full-time 11, part-time 14; minority–full-time 5, part-time 13.

Programs and Degrees Offered:

Listed in the following order: Program area, degree type (T if terminal Master's), number awarded 7/03–6/04. School Psychology EdS (Education Specialist) 12, Marriage & Family Therapy MA/MS (Master of Arts/Science) (T) 25, School Counseling MA/MS (Master of Arts/Science) (T) 10, Community-Based Counseling MA/MS (Master of Arts/Science) (T) 24.

Student Applications/Admissions:

Student Applications

School Psychology EdS (Education Specialist)—Applications 2004–2005, 102. Total applicants accepted 2004–2005, 12. Number enrolled (new admits only) 2004–2005 full-time, 12. Openings 2005–2006, 12. The Median number of years required for completion of a degree are 4. The number of students enrolled full and part-time who were dismissed or voluntarily withdrew from this program area were 1. *Marriage & Family Therapy MA/MS (Master of Arts/Science)*—Applications 2004–2005, 130. Total applicants accepted 2004–2005, 18. Number enrolled (new admits only) 2004–2005 full-time, 12. Number enrolled (new admits only) 2004–2005 part-time, 12. Total enrolled 2004–2005 full-time, 69, part-time, 6. Openings 2005–2006, 24. The Median number of years required for completion of a degree are 3. The number of students enrolled full and part-time who were dismissed or voluntarily withdrew from this program area were 2. *School Counseling MA/MS (Master of Arts/Science)*—Applications 2004–2005, 86. Total applicants accepted 2004–2005, 14. Number enrolled (new admits only) 2004–2005 full-time, 10. Number enrolled (new admits only) 2004–2005 part-time, 2. Total enrolled 2004–2005 full-time, 23, part-time, 3. Openings 2005–2006, 12. The Median number of years required for completion of a degree are 2. The number of students enrolled full and part-time who were dismissed or voluntarily withdrew from this program area were 2. *Community-Based Counseling MA/MS (Master of Arts/Science)*—Applications 2004–2005, 118. Total applicants accepted 2004–2005, 24. Number enrolled (new admits only) 2004–2005 full-time, 24. Total enrolled 2004–2005 full-time, 24. Openings 2005–2006, 27. The Median number of years required for completion of a degree is 1. The number of students enrolled full and part-time who were dismissed or voluntarily withdrew from this program area were 0. *Culture and Community Trauma Studies Certificate Other*—

Admissions Requirements:

Scores: Entries appear in this order: required test or GPA, minimum score (if required), median score of students entering in 2003–2004. Master's Programs: GRE-V no minimum stated; GRE-Q no minimum stated; overall undergraduate GPA no minimum stated; last 2 years GPA no minimum stated.

Other Criteria: (importance of criteria rated low, medium, or high): GRE/MAT scores medium, research experience medium, work experience high, extracurricular activity medium, clinically related public service high, GPA high, letters of recommendation high, interview high, statement of goals and objectives high, portfolio applications high. Portfolio applications are assessed on multiple criteria, and include professional, personal and cross cultural readiness for graduate study. A percentage of applicants is selected from the portfolios for a day long interview, from which the cohort is selected annually. Criteria vary a bit by program (see Web sites). For additional information on admission requirements, go to: http://edweb.sdsu.edu/csp/.

Student Characteristics: The following represents characteristics of students in 2004–2005 in all graduate psychology programs in the department: Female–full-time 95, part-time 14; Male–full-time 50, part-time 2; African American/Black–full-time 22, part-time 1; Hispanic/Latino(a)–full-time 42, part-time 3; Asian/Pacific Islander–full-time 13, part-time 1; American Indian/Alaska Native–full-time 8, part-time 0; Caucasian–full-time 44, part-time 3; Multi-ethnic–full-time 22, part-time 1; students subject to the Americans With Disabilities Act–full-time 8, part-time 0.

Financial Information/Assistance:

Tuition for Full-Time Study: *Master's:* State residents: per academic year $2,014; Nonstate residents: $282 per credit hour. Tuition is subject to change. See the following Web site for updates and changes in tuition costs: http://www.sdsu.edu.

Financial Assistance:

First Year Students: Research assistantships available for first-year. Average amount paid per academic year: $4,000. Average number of hours worked per week: 10. Apply by Varies. Fellowships and scholarships available for first-year. Average amount paid per academic year: $7,000. Apply by Varies. Tuition remission given: partial.

Advanced Students: Research assistantships available for advanced students. Average amount paid per academic year: $4,000. Average number of hours worked per week: 10. Apply by Varies. Fellowships and scholarships available for advanced students. Average amount paid per academic year: $7,000. Apply by Varies. Tuition remission given: partial.

Contact Information: Of all students currently enrolled full-time, 18% benefitted from one or more of the listed financial assistance programs. Application and information available online at: contact each program office for detailed information about annual availability.

Internships/Practica: Internships in school psychology are consistent with the standards outlined by the National Association of School Psychologists (NASP) and are integrated into the final year of that program. Internships in School Counseling are consistent with the standards of the California Commission on Teacher Credentialing (CCTC) and occur in year two of that program. Traineeships in Marriage and Family Therapy are consistent with the standards of the American Association for Marriage and Family Therapy (AAMFT).

Housing and Day Care: On-campus housing is available. See the following Web site for more information: http://www.sa.sdsu.edu/hrlo/. On-campus day care facilities are available. See the following Web site for more information: http://www.sdsu.edu.

Employment of Department Graduates:

Master's Degree Graduates: Of those who graduated in the academic year 2003–2004, the following categories and numbers represent the post-graduate activities and employment of master's degree graduates: Enrolled in a psychology doctoral program (2), enrolled in another graduate/professional program (15), enrolled in a post-doctoral residency/fellowship (n/a), employed in independent practice (n/a), employed in an academic position at a 2-year/4-year college (2), employed in other positions at a higher education institution (3), employed in a professional position in a school system (16), employed in a community mental health/counseling center (16), employed in a hospital/medical center (2), other employment position (6), do not know (5), total from the above (master's) (67).

Doctoral Degree Graduates: Of those who graduated in the academic year 2003–2004, the following categories and numbers represent the post-graduate activities and employment of doctoral degree graduates: Enrolled in a psychology doctoral program (n/a), total from the above (doctoral) (0).

Additional Information:

Orientation, Objectives, and Emphasis of Department: The Department of Counseling and School Psychology is a graduate level professional preparation community which prepares school psychologists, family therapists, school and community counselors. We promote critical inquiry, reflection, self development and social action in its faculty and students, and are committed to work towards equity and economic and social justice. Our graduates are prepared to work in a multicultural and changing world in leadership roles in family, educational, and social systems.

Special Facilities or Resources: The department has a clinical training facility located in a highly diverse section of the urban community. Known as the Community Counseling Center, we serve the local community with students under faculty supervision, and sponsor continuing education activities. Students in the Marriage & Family Therapy Program are supervised by AAMFT-Approved supervisors; students in community counseling are supervised by university faculty members.

Information for Students With Physical Disabilities: See the following Web site for more information: http://www.sa.sdsu.edu/dss/dss_home.html.

Application Information:

Send to: Each program has its own admissions process in addition to the application to the university. Please visit the Web site for specific application information: http://edweb.sdsu.edu/csp/. Application available online. URL of online application: http://edweb.sdsu.edu/csp. Students are admitted in the Spring, application deadline February 1. Most programs currently list February 1 as the application deadline. Some begin review on that date. Check Web site for most current information. *Fee:* University application fee is $55. Departmental fee of $25 in 2005-06. Out of state tuition may occasionally be waived for one year should an applicant be selected as graduate assistant and be awarded the waiver.

San Diego State University
Department of Psychology
College of Sciences
5500 Campanile Drive
San Diego, CA 92182-4611
Telephone: (619) 594-5358
Fax: (619) 594-1332
E-mail: *judypric@sunstroke.sdsu.edu*
Web: *http://www.psychology.sdsu.edu*

Department Information:
1947. Chairperson: Claire Murphy. Number of Faculty: total–full-time 37, part-time 25; women–full-time 16, part-time 12; minority–full-time 5, part-time 1.

Programs and Degrees Offered:
Listed in the following order: Program area, degree type (T if terminal Master's), number awarded 7/03–6/04. Master of Arts MA/MS (Master of Arts/Science) 26, Master of Sciences MA/MS (Master of Arts/Science) (T) 8.

Student Applications/Admissions:
Student Applications
Master of Arts MA/MS (Master of Arts/Science)—Applications 2004–2005, 110. Total applicants accepted 2004–2005, 45. Number enrolled (new admits only) 2004–2005 full-time, 18. Number enrolled (new admits only) 2004–2005 part-time, 0. Openings 2005–2006, 18. The Median number of years required for completion of a degree are 2. The number of students enrolled full and part-time who were dismissed or voluntarily withdrew from this program area were 0. *Master of Sciences MA/MS (Master of Arts/Science)*—Applications 2004–2005, 39. Total applicants accepted 2004–2005, 12. Number enrolled (new admits only) 2004–2005 full-time, 10. Total enrolled 2004–2005 full-time, 31. Openings 2005–2006, 10. The Median number of years required for completion of a degree are 3. The number of students enrolled full and part-time who were dismissed or voluntarily withdrew from this program area were 0.

Admissions Requirements:
Scores: Entries appear in this order: required test or GPA, minimum score (if required), median score of students entering in 2003–2004. Master's Programs: GRE-V 500, 548; GRE-Q 500, 656; GRE-V+Q 1000, 1204; GRE-Subject(Psych) 500, 628; overall undergraduate GPA 2.85; last 2 years GPA 3.0; psychology GPA 3.0, 3.62.
Other Criteria: (importance of criteria rated low, medium, or high): GRE/MAT scores high, research experience high, work experience medium, extracurricular activity medium, clinically related public service low, GPA high, letters of recommendation high, statement of goals and objectives high.

Student Characteristics: The following represents characteristics of students in 2004–2005 in all graduate psychology programs in the department: Female–full-time 65, part-time 0; Male–full-time

38, part-time 0; African American/Black–full-time 2, part-time 0; Hispanic/Latino(a)–full-time 9, part-time 0; Asian/Pacific Islander–full-time 12, part-time 0; American Indian/Alaska Native–full-time 2, part-time 0; Caucasian–full-time 68, part-time 0; Multi-ethnic–full-time 10, part-time 0; students subject to the Americans With Disabilities Act–full-time 0, part-time 0.

Financial Information/Assistance:
Tuition for Full-Time Study: *Master's:* State residents: per academic year $3,243; Nonstate residents: per academic year $3,243, $339 per credit hour. Tuition is subject to change. See the following Web site for updates and changes in tuition costs: http://bfa.sdsu.edu/fm/co/cashiers/regfees.html.

Financial Assistance:
First Year Students: Teaching assistantships available for first-year. Average amount paid per academic year: $10,118. Average number of hours worked per week: 20. Apply by February 1. Research assistantships available for first-year. Average amount paid per academic year: $8,000. Average number of hours worked per week: 20. Apply by February 1.

Advanced Students: Teaching assistantships available for advanced students. Average amount paid per academic year: $10,118. Average number of hours worked per week: 20. Apply by February 1. Research assistantships available for advanced students. Average amount paid per academic year: $8,000. Average number of hours worked per week: 20. Apply by February 1.

Contact Information: Of all students currently enrolled full-time, 50% benefitted from one or more of the listed financial assistance programs. Application and information available online at: http://www.psychology.sdsu.edu/gradprograms.html.

Internships/Practica: An essential component of graduate training in Applied Psychology is an internship experience that provides students with an opportunity to apply their classroom training and acquire new skills in a field setting. Interns are placed in a variety of settings, such as community-based organizations, consulting firms, city and county organizations, education, hospitality, high tech and private industry. Through the internship experience students also develop close contacts with other psychologists and practitioners working in their field. Internships are normally undertaken during the summer following the first year in the program and during the fall semester of the second year.

Housing and Day Care: On-campus housing is available. See the following Web site for more information: www.sa.sdsu.edu/housing. On-campus day care facilities are available. See the following Web site for more information: http://www-rohan.sdsu.edu/dept/childfam/Childstudy.html#center.

Employment of Department Graduates:
Master's Degree Graduates: Of those who graduated in the academic year 2003–2004, the following categories and numbers represent the post-graduate activities and employment of master's degree graduates: Enrolled in a psychology doctoral program (7), enrolled in another graduate/professional program (3), enrolled in a post-doctoral residency/fellowship (n/a), employed in independent practice (n/a), employed in an academic position at a university (0), employed in an academic position at a 2-year/4-year college (1), employed in other positions at a higher education institution (4), employed in a professional position in a school system (0), employed in business or industry (research/consulting)

(5), employed in business or industry (management) (3), employed in a government agency (research) (0), employed in a government agency (professional services) (0), employed in a community mental health/counseling center (0), employed in a hospital/medical center (0), still seeking employment (1), not seeking employment (3), other employment position (4), do not know (3), total from the above (master's) (34).

Doctoral Degree Graduates: Of those who graduated in the academic year 2003–2004, the following categories and numbers represent the post-graduate activities and employment of doctoral degree graduates: Enrolled in a psychology doctoral program (n/a), total from the above (doctoral) (0).

Additional Information:
Orientation, Objectives, and Emphasis of Department: The MA degree program provides graduate level studies and preparation for PhD programs in several areas. It is particularly appropriate for students who need advanced work to strengthen their profiles for application to PhD programs, or for those wishing to explore graduate-level work before committing to PhD training. Our research-oriented program does not offer instruction in technical skills (e.g., intelligence testing) and does not have a counseling practicum or provide opportunities for development of clinical skills. Students gain valuable research experience, which may involve working with humans in non-clinical areas. Upon admission to the program, students are assigned a faculty research mentor who guides them through the research process leading to the thesis. Students take core classes in the major areas of psychology and electives in their areas of specialization. The MS Degree program in Applied Psychology has emphases in Program Evaluation and Industrial/Organizational Psychology. Students are prepared for professional careers in the public and private sectors or for doctoral-level training in Applied Psychology. All MS students take core courses in statistics and measurement and complete an internship.

Special Facilities or Resources: The following research labs welcome participation of master's students: Active Living and Healthy Eating; Alcohol Research; Behavioral Teratology; Brain Development Imaging; Categorical Distortions; Categorization; Child Language and Emotion; Cognitive Development; Intergroup Relations; Lifespan Human Senses; Measurement and Evaluation Research; Minority Community Health Intervention; Organizational Leadership and Citizenship; Organizational Research; Personality Assessment and Psychometrics; Personality Measurement; Motivational Intervention in Binge Drinking; Families Using Libraries for Improving Lifelong Learning; Effects of Social Support and Education on the Health and Well Being of People with Chronic Diseases; Psychosocial, Medical and Multicultural Aspects of Adjustment to Chronic Illness; Smoking Research; Social Development; Social Influence and Social Change; Stress and Coping; The Self and Social Psychology; Trial of Activity for Adolescent Girls. Students may also conduct research at Children's Hospital, where several faculty members have their offices. The department operates the Psychology Clinic, which serves the community at large. Other resources include the Center for Behavioral and Community Health Studies, Center for Behavioral Teratology, and the Center for Research in Mathematics and Science Education. SDSU has modern computer facilities and computer support services.

Information for Students With Physical Disabilities: See the following Web site for more information: http://www.sa.sdsu.edu/dss/dss_home.html.

Application Information:
Send to: Master's Programs Coordinator, Department of Psychology, San Diego State University, 5500 Campanile Drive, San Diego, CA 92182-4611. Application available online. URL of online application: http://www.psychology.sdsu.edu/MasApp2004-05.pdf. Students are admitted in the Fall, application deadline February 1. At this time departmental application is available online. Details about the program, as well as the departmental application, can be found at http://www.psychology.sdsu.edu/gradprograms.html. The completed application must be printed and a hard copy submitted to the Department of Psychology. Please include in the application packet 2 sets of original transcripts for every college-level institution ever attended, as well as 3 sealed and signed recommendations. A separate online application is required for the university, through www.CSUmentor.com). *Fee:* $55.

San Diego State University/University of California, San Diego Joint Doctoral Program in Clinical Psychology
SDSU Department of Psychology/UCSD Department of Psychiatry
SDSU: College of Sciences, UCSD: School of Medicine
San Diego State University, 6363 Alvarado Court, Suite #103
San Diego, CA 92120-4913
Telephone: (619) 594-2246
Fax: (619) 594-6780
E-mail: *psycjdp@sciences.sdsu.edu*
Web: *http://www.psychology.sdsu.edu/doctoral*

Department Information:
1985. Co-Directors: Elizabeth Klonoff, PhD, Robert Heaton, PhD Number of Faculty: total–full-time 8, part-time 94; women–full-time 4, part-time 32; minority–full-time 1, part-time 5.

Programs and Degrees Offered:
Listed in the following order: Program area, degree type (T if terminal Master's), number awarded 7/03–6/04. SDSU/UCSD Joint Doctoral Program (JDP) in Clinical Psych PhD (Doctor of Philosophy) 10.

Student Applications/Admissions:
Student Applications
SDSU/UCSD *Joint Doctoral Program in Clinical Psych PhD (Doctor of Philosophy)*—Applications 2004–2005, 342. Total applicants accepted 2004–2005, 14. Number enrolled (new admits only) 2004–2005 full-time, 13. Number enrolled (new admits only) 2004–2005 part-time, 0. Openings 2005–2006, 15. The Median number of years required for completion of a degree are 6. The number of students enrolled full and part-time who were dismissed or voluntarily withdrew from this program area were 0.

Admissions Requirements:
Scores: Entries appear in this order: required test or GPA, minimum score (if required), median score of students entering in 2003–2004. Doctoral Programs: GRE-V 550, 640; GRE-Q

550, 680; GRE-V+Q 1100, 1320; GRE-Subject(Psych) no minimum stated, 690; overall undergraduate GPA 3.0, 3.82; last 2 years GPA 3.25, 3.75. Master's not required for this program. JDP usually requires much higher scores and GPAs than the Graduate Admissions minimum.

Other Criteria: (importance of criteria rated low, medium, or high): GRE/MAT scores medium, research experience high, work experience low, clinically related public service medium, GPA high, letters of recommendation high, interview high, statement of goals and objectives high, These criteria are for the Joint Doctoral Program only. For additional information on admission requirements, go to: http://www.psychology.sdsu.edu/doctoral.

Student Characteristics: The following represents characteristics of students in 2004–2005 in all graduate psychology programs in the department: Female–full-time 57, part-time 0; Male–full-time 12, part-time 0; African American/Black–full-time 2, part-time 0; Hispanic/Latino(a)–full-time 9, part-time 0; Asian/Pacific Islander–full-time 7, part-time 0; American Indian/Alaska Native–full-time 0, part-time 0; Caucasian–full-time 47, part-time 0; Multi-ethnic–full-time 4, part-time 0; students subject to the Americans With Disabilities Act–full-time 0, part-time 0.

Financial Information/Assistance:
Tuition for Full-Time Study: *Doctoral:* State residents: per academic year $3,422; Nonstate residents: per academic year $3,422, $339 per credit hour. Tuition is subject to change. See the following Web site for updates and changes in tuition costs: Go to SDSU home page and click on Cashier's Office link.

Financial Assistance:
First Year Students: Research assistantships available for first-year. Average amount paid per academic year: $14,000. Average number of hours worked per week: 20. Apply by N/A. Tuition remission given: full. Fellowships and scholarships available for first-year. Average amount paid per academic year: $14,000. Average number of hours worked per week: 20. Apply by Varies. Tuition remission given: full.

Advanced Students: Teaching assistantships available for advanced students. Average amount paid per academic year: $15,000. Average number of hours worked per week: 20. Apply by N/A. Tuition remission given: full. Research assistantships available for advanced students. Average amount paid per academic year: $14,000. Average number of hours worked per week: 20. Apply by N/A. Tuition remission given: full.

Contact Information: Of all students currently enrolled full-time, 100% benefitted from one or more of the listed financial assistance programs. Application and information available online at: http://www.psychology.sdsu.edu/doctoral.

Internships/Practica: For doctoral students only- SDSU: Primary placement for all students in their second year is the Psychology Clinic. Students are taught general clinical skills. Therapy sessions are routinely videotaped for review in intensive weekly supervision session. UCSD: VA Outpatient Clinic: psychiatric outpatients—assessment and individual and group therapy. VA Medical Center: psychiatric inpatients—assessment, individual and group therapy. UCSD Outpatient Psychiatric Clinic: psychiatric outpatients—neuropsychological assessment and individual and group therapy. UCSD Medical Center: assessment and therapy of all types. All practicum placements are assigned for one full year beginning in the student's second year. For those doctoral students for whom a professional internship is required prior to graduation, 11 applied in 2003–2004. Of those who applied, 11 were placed in internships listed by the Association of Psychology Postdoctoral and Internship Programs (APPIC); 11 were placed in APA accredited internships.

Housing and Day Care: On-campus housing is available. Both universities provide housing and child care. Information will be available at interviews. On-campus day care facilities are available.

Employment of Department Graduates:

Master's Degree Graduates: Of those who graduated in the academic year 2003–2004, the following categories and numbers represent the post-graduate activities and employment of master's degree graduates: Enrolled in a post-doctoral residency/fellowship (n/a), employed in independent practice (n/a), total from the above (master's) (0).

Doctoral Degree Graduates: Of those who graduated in the academic year 2003–2004, the following categories and numbers represent the post-graduate activities and employment of doctoral degree graduates: Enrolled in a psychology doctoral program (n/a), enrolled in a post-doctoral residency/fellowship (10), total from the above (doctoral) (10).

Additional Information:

Orientation, Objectives, and Emphasis of Department: Our PhD program is a cooperative venture of an academic Department of Psychology (SDSU) and a medical school Department of Psychiatry (UCSD). This partnership between two different departments in two universities provides unusual opportunities for interdisciplinary research. We currently offer concentrations in behavioral medicine, neuropsychology, and experimental psychopathology. The scientist-practitioner model on which the program is based involves a strong commitment to research as well as clinical training. The program aims to prepare students for leadership roles in academic and research settings. Our program is designed as a 5-year curriculum with a core of classroom instruction followed by apprenticeship training in specialty areas with appropriate seminars and tutorials. Clinical experiences are integrated with formal instruction throughout. The program as a whole is designed to satisfy the criteria for APA accreditation.

Special Facilities or Resources: The UCSD Department of Psychiatry, through the medical school, UCSD hospitals, and the VA Medical Center, has available all of the modern research and clinical facilities consistent with the School of Medicine's ranking among the top ten in the country in biomedical research. These include specialty laboratories (e.g., sleep labs), access to clinical trials, supercomputing facilities, and state-of-the-art neurochemical and biochemical laboratory facilities. Qualified students interested in MRI studies have access to a number of fully-supported imagers. At SDSU, the Department of Psychology has a state-of-the-art video-equipped therapy training complex, as well as experiment rooms, equipment (e.g. computerized test administration capabilities), and supplies available for research, including computerized physiological assessment and biofeedback laboratories. Animal research can be conducted on campus, where small animals are housed in a modern vivarium staffed with a veterinarian. SDSU faculty also supervise research on more exotic species at Sea World and the San Diego Zoo. The College of Sciences maintains a completely equipped electronics shop, a wood shop,

a metal shop, and computer support facilities with several high end Unix servers, all staffed with full-time technicians. Collaborative relationships with faculty in the Graduate School of Public Health allow access to resources there as well.

Information for Students With Physical Disabilities: See the following Web site for more information: http://www.sdsu.edu/dss.

Application Information:
Send to: Student Selection Committee, 6363 Alvarado Ct. #103, San Diego, CA 92120-4913. Students must also apply to the SDSU Office of Admissions & Records, 5500 Campanile Dr., San Diego, CA 92182. The application for SDSU Admissions & Records can be submitted on line through www.csumentor.edu. JDP application Part I can be submitted on line, print out Part II, sign and mail copies of both parts to Selection Committee address. Application available online. URL of online application: http://www.psychology.sdsu.edu/doctoral. Students are admitted in the Fall, application deadline December 15. Please note that this information only applies to the SDSU/UCSD Joint Doctoral Program in Clinical Psychology. It does not include information about any other program. *Fee:* $55. Applicants must secure a waiver form from SDSU Admissions & Records. Must demonstrate financial need. The CSU Mentor application has space for requesting fee waiver at the end of the form.

San Francisco State University
Psychology
Behavioral and Social Science
1600 Holloway Avenue
San Francisco, CA 94132
Telephone: (415) 338-1275
Fax: (415) 338-2167
E-mail: *ljuang@sfsu.edu*
Web: *http://www.sfsu.edu/~psych/*

Department Information:
1923. Chairperson: Kathleen Mosier. Number of Faculty: total–full-time 25, part-time 21; women–full-time 13, part-time 12; minority–full-time 7, part-time 3.

Programs and Degrees Offered:
Listed in the following order: Program area, degree type (T if terminal Master's), number awarded 7/03–6/04. Clinical psychology MA/MS (Master of Arts/Science) (T) 11, developmental psychology MA/MS (Master of Arts/Science) (T) 6, I/O psychology MA/MS (Master of Arts/Science) (T) 8, research psychology MA/MS (Master of Arts/Science) (T) 4, school psychology MA/MS (Master of Arts/Science) (T) 9, social psychology MA/MS (Master of Arts/Science) (T) 3.

Student Applications/Admissions:

Student Applications

Clinical psychology MA/MS (Master of Arts/Science)—Applications 2004–2005, 162. Total applicants accepted 2004–2005, 10. Number enrolled (new admits only) 2004–2005 full-time, 10. Total enrolled 2004–2005 full-time, 22. Openings 2005–2006, 12. The Median number of years required for completion of a degree are 2. *Developmental psychology MA/MS (Master of Arts/Science)*—Applications 2004–2005, 31. Total applicants accepted 2004–2005, 11. Number enrolled (new admits only) 2004–2005 full-time, 11. Openings 2005–2006, 12. The Median number of years required for completion of a degree are 3. *I/O psychology MA/MS (Master of Arts/Science)*—Applications 2004–2005, 83. Total applicants accepted 2004–2005, 11. Number enrolled (new admits only) 2004–2005 full-time, 11. Openings 2005–2006, 12. The Median number of years required for completion of a degree are 3. *Research psychology MA/MS (Master of Arts/Science)*—Applications 2004–2005, 33. Total applicants accepted 2004–2005, 5. Number enrolled (new admits only) 2004–2005 full-time, 5. Total enrolled 2004–2005 full-time, 19. Openings 2005–2006, 12. The Median number of years required for completion of a degree are 3. *School psychology MA/MS (Master of Arts/Science)*— Applications 2004–2005, 109. Total applicants accepted 2004–2005, 10. Number enrolled (new admits only) 2004–2005 full-time, 10. Openings 2005–2006, 10. The Median number of years required for completion of a degree are 3. *Social psychology MA/MS (Master of Arts/Science)*—Applications 2004–2005, 32. Total applicants accepted 2004–2005, 7. Number enrolled (new admits only) 2004–2005 full-time, 7. Total enrolled 2004–2005 full-time, 14. Openings 2005–2006, 8. The Median number of years required for completion of a degree are 2.5.

Admissions Requirements:

Scores: Entries appear in this order: required test or GPA, minimum score (if required), median score of students entering in 2003–2004. Master's Programs: GRE-V no minimum stated; GRE-Q no minimum stated; GRE-Analytical no minimum stated; overall undergraduate GPA no minimum stated; last 2 years GPA no minimum stated; psychology GPA no minimum stated. Social requires the GRE-Subject test. Indus/Org requires the GRE-Writing test. None of the programs have a required minimum GPA; median GPAs vary by program areas.
Other Criteria: (importance of criteria rated low, medium, or high): GRE/MAT scores medium, research experience medium, work experience medium, extracurricular activity low, clinically related public service medium, GPA medium, letters of recommendation medium, interview medium, statement of goals and objectives medium, Clinical-clinical service; interview; statement. Developmental-goals & objectives statement. I/0-GRE; GPA; statement of experience. Research-research experience; letters of recommendation. School-statement of goals and objectives; interview; GPA; clinical service.

Student Characteristics: The following represents characteristics of students in 2004–2005 in all graduate psychology programs in the department: Female–full-time 105, part-time 0; Male–full-time 30, part-time 0; African American/Black–full-time 3, part-time 0; Hispanic/Latino(a)–full-time 12, part-time 0; Asian/Pacific Islander–full-time 15, part-time 0; American Indian/Alaska Native–full-time 1, part-time 0; Caucasian–full-time 65, part-time 0.

Financial Information/Assistance:

Tuition for Full-Time Study: *Master's:* State residents: per academic year $3,366; Nonstate residents: per academic year $11,502. Tuition is subject to change. Tuition costs vary by program. See the following Web site for updates and changes in tuition costs: http://www.sfsu.edu/prospect/costs.htm.

Financial Assistance:
   First Year Students: No information provided.
   Advanced Students: Teaching assistantships available for advanced students. Research assistantships available for advanced students.
   Contact Information: No information provided.

Internships/Practica: For clinical students, practica in the first year is provided in the Psychology Clinic. Second year internships are located throughout the San Francisco Bay area. For I/O students, an internship is required during the second year of study. Students are placed in various work organizations throughout the San Francisco Bay area. Students enrolled in the school Psychology program are required to complete a third year paid internship. The Social Psychology students have a year-long field placement.

Housing and Day Care: No on-campus housing is available. On-campus day care facilities are available. See the following Web site for more information: http://www.sfsu.edu/prospect/child.htm.

Employment of Department Graduates:
   Master's Degree Graduates: Of those who graduated in the academic year 2003–2004, the following categories and numbers represent the post-graduate activities and employment of master's degree graduates: Enrolled in a post-doctoral residency/fellowship (n/a), employed in independent practice (n/a), total from the above (master's) (0).
   Doctoral Degree Graduates: Of those who graduated in the academic year 2003–2004, the following categories and numbers represent the post-graduate activities and employment of doctoral degree graduates: Enrolled in a psychology doctoral program (n/a), total from the above (doctoral) (0).

Additional Information:
   Orientation, Objectives, and Emphasis of Department: Clinical: The theoretical orientation of the Clinical program is based on psychodynamic, developmental theory within a family and community systems framework. The Clinical program emphasizes training in psychotherapy and applied clinical experience. Developmental: The Developmental program takes a life span approach. Research and courses emphasize family systems, attachment, social, cognitive and emotional development, and the development of diverse populations. Training is provided on developmental research methods. Industrial/Organizational: The I/O MS program has a science/practice approach to workplace issues. The program prepares graduates for professional work in business, industry, and government and for continuing education in I/O psychology. School: The School Psychology program emphasizes, within a cultural context, developmental and psychodynamic theories with an applied interpersonal relations and family systems approach. Research: The Research program takes a basic scientific approach, including study of physiological issues. Social: The Social Psychology program, oriented toward research and applications in the public interest, prepares students for MA-level careers and doctoral study with training in both qualitative and quantitative methods.

   Special Facilities or Resources: The Child Study Center is a research and observation facility consisting of 32 pre-schoolers and their families. The Psychology Department Training Clinic is a full service clinic offering psychotherapy to the campus and the larger community. The Clinic is staffed by graduate students under the supervision of licensed clinicians. The Psychology Department Test Library is available to qualified users including students with faculty permission and supervision. Several faculty-led research laboratories are in operation.

Information for Students With Physical Disabilities: See the following Web site for more information: http://www.sfsu.edu/~dprc/welcome.html.

Application Information:

Send to: Graduate Secretary, Department of Psychology, San Francisco State University, 1600 Holloway Avenue, San Francisco, CA 94132. Application available online. URL of online application: http://www.sfsu.edu/~psych/psygrdap.htm. Students are admitted in the Fall, application deadline March 1; Spring, application deadline October 15. Only the Developmental Psychology program accepts students for the spring semester. The application deadline is October 15. *Fee:* $55. Processing fee applies to the University Application only. There is no fee for the Departmental Application.

San Jose State University
Department of Psychology
Social Sciences
One Washington Square
San Jose, CA 95192-0120
Telephone: (408) 924-5600
Fax: (408) 924-5605
E-mail: *nakamura@email.sjsu.edu*
Web: *www.psych.sjsu.edu*

Department Information:

Chairperson: Sheila Bienenfeld. Number of Faculty: total–full-time 21, part-time 11; women–full-time 12, part-time 5; minority–full-time 5, part-time 1; faculty subject to the Americans With Disabilities Act 1.

Programs and Degrees Offered:

Listed in the following order: Program area, degree type (T if terminal Master's), number awarded 7/03–6/04. Clinical MA/MS (Master of Arts/Science) (T) 10, Experimental MA/MS (Master of Arts/Science) (T) 5, Industrial/Organizational MA/MS (Master of Arts/Science) (T) 7.

Student Applications/Admissions:

Student Applications

Clinical MA/MS (Master of Arts/Science)—Applications 2004–2005, 65. Total applicants accepted 2004–2005, 21. Number enrolled (new admits only) 2004–2005 full-time, 12. Number enrolled (new admits only) 2004–2005 part-time, 5. Total enrolled 2004–2005 full-time, 13, part-time, 6. Openings 2005–2006, 15. The Median number of years required for completion of a degree are 2. The number of students enrolled full and part-time who were dismissed or voluntarily withdrew from this program area were 1. *Experimental MA/MS (Master of Arts/Science)*—Applications 2004–2005, 33. Total applicants accepted 2004–2005, 17. Number enrolled (new admits only) 2004–2005 full-time, 9. Openings 2005–2006, 14. The Median number of years required for completion of a degree are 2.

The number of students enrolled full and part-time who were dismissed or voluntarily withdrew from this program area were 3. *Industrial/Organizational MA/MS (Master of Arts/Science)*—Applications 2004–2005, 45. Total applicants accepted 2004–2005, 13. Number enrolled (new admits only) 2004–2005 full-time, 12. Number enrolled (new admits only) 2004–2005 part-time, 0. Openings 2005–2006, 15. The Median number of years required for completion of a degree are 3. The number of students enrolled full and part-time who were dismissed or voluntarily withdrew from this program area were 1.

Admissions Requirements:

Scores: Entries appear in this order: required test or GPA, minimum score (if required), median score of students entering in 2003–2004. Master's Programs: GRE-V no minimum stated; GRE-Q no minimum stated; GRE-Analytical no minimum stated; overall undergraduate GPA no minimum stated; last 2 years GPA 3.0; psychology GPA 3.0. GRE required for I/O & MA General only-No GRE for MS Clinical Program. MS Clinical GPA averages: 3.58 (Psychology GPA), 3.61 (Last 2 years GPA).

Other Criteria: (importance of criteria rated low, medium, or high): Clinical Program has specific course requirements for admission and requires minimum 1 year of applied clinical experience and 100 hours. For additional information on admission requirements, go to: psych.sjsu.edu/grad.

Student Characteristics: The following represents characteristics of students in 2004–2005 in all graduate psychology programs in the department: Female–full-time 35, part-time 7; Male–full-time 14, part-time 2; African American/Black–full-time 1, part-time 0; Hispanic/Latino(a)–full-time 3, part-time 0; Asian/Pacific Islander–full-time 5, part-time 0; American Indian/Alaska Native–full-time 0, part-time 0; Caucasian–full-time 0, part-time 0; Multi-ethnic–full-time 2, part-time 0; students subject to the Americans With Disabilities Act–full-time 0, part-time 0.

Financial Information/Assistance:

Tuition for Full-Time Study: *Master's:* State residents: per academic year $1,450; Nonstate residents: per academic year $2,000, $246 per credit hour. Tuition is subject to change. See the following Web site for updates and changes in tuition costs: http://www2.sjsu.edu/depts/bursar/.

Financial Assistance:

First Year Students: Teaching assistantships available for first-year. Research assistantships available for first-year. Fellowships and scholarships available for first-year.

Advanced Students: Teaching assistantships available for advanced students. Research assistantships available for advanced students. Fellowships and scholarships available for advanced students.

Contact Information: Of all students currently enrolled full-time, 50% benefitted from one or more of the listed financial assistance programs. Application and information available online at http://www2.sjsu.edu/depts/finaid/.

Internships/Practica: An internship is required for students in the Industrial/Organizational Psychology program. The program coordinator works with each student to determine the student's interests and helps find a placement site for each student.

Housing and Day Care: On-campus housing is available. See the following Web site for more information: http://housing.sjsu.edu/oncampus.stm. On-campus day care facilities are available. See the following Web site for more information: http://www.as.sjsu.edu/childcare/index.jsp.

Employment of Department Graduates:

Master's Degree Graduates: Of those who graduated in the academic year 2003–2004, the following categories and numbers represent the post-graduate activities and employment of master's degree graduates: Enrolled in a psychology doctoral program (4), enrolled in a post-doctoral residency/fellowship (n/a), employed in independent practice (n/a), employed in business or industry (research/consulting) (3), employed in business or industry (management) (5), employed in a government agency (research) (4), employed in a government agency (professional services) (2), employed in a community mental health/counseling center (10), total from the above (master's) (28).

Doctoral Degree Graduates: Of those who graduated in the academic year 2003–2004, the following categories and numbers represent the post-graduate activities and employment of doctoral degree graduates: Enrolled in a psychology doctoral program (n/a), total from the above (doctoral) (0).

Additional Information:

Special Facilities or Resources: The department maintains a variety of facilities and support staff to enhance instruction and research. For biological and cognitive research and instruction, the department has a number of laboratories and specialized laboratory equipment on campus, and lab technicians are available to construct additional equipment. For work in clinical and counseling psychology, the department has a Psychology Clinic consisting of therapy rooms and adjoining observation rooms equipped with audio and video equipment. These rooms are also available to individuals working in other areas, such as developmental, personality, and social psychology. In addition, students interested in counseling-related activities have access to a number of off-campus organizations. Three computer laboratories containing microcomputers and terminals hooked up to minicomputers and mainframes are available for students. These labs have extensive software, and computer consultants are on call to help with software and hardware problems, design and interpretation of statistical analyses, and computer exercises.

Information for Students With Physical Disabilities: See the following Web site for more information: www.drc.sjsu.edu.

Application Information:

Send to: Program coordinator (program name). All information and application materials are available online at psych.sjsu.edu/grad. A separate concurrent university application is also required. Application available online. URL of online application: www.psych.sjsu.edu/grad. Students are admitted in the Fall, application deadline 1/15; 2/1. Deadline for clinical/counseling is January 15; for the experimental psychology program and the industrial/organizational psychology program, it is February 1. *Fee:* $55. Deadline for clinical/counseling is January 15; for the experimental psychology program and the industrial/organizational psychology program, it is February 1.

Santa Clara University

Department of Counseling Psychology
Counseling Psychology, Education, and Pastoral Ministries
500 El Camino Real - Bannan Hall 226
Santa Clara, CA 95053
Telephone: (408) 551-1603
Fax: (408) 554-2392
E-mail: *sbabbel@scu.edu*
Web: *http://www.scu.edu/ecppm/*

Department Information:

1970. Chairperson: Jerrold Lee Shapiro, PhD. Number of Faculty: total–full-time 8, part-time 22; women–full-time 4, part-time 16; minority–full-time 1, part-time 5.

Programs and Degrees Offered:

Listed in the following order: Program area, degree type (T if terminal Master's), number awarded 7/03–6/04. Master of Arts in Counseling Psychology MA/MS (Master of Arts/Science) (T) 41, Counseling MA/MS (Master of Arts/Science) 13.

Student Applications/Admissions:

Student Applications

Master of Arts in Counseling Psychology MA/MS (Master of Arts/Science)—Applications 2004–2005, 74. Total applicants accepted 2004–2005, 60. Total enrolled 2004–2005 full-time, 25, part-time, 185. Openings 2005–2006, 60. The Median number of years required for completion of a degree are 3. The number of students enrolled full and part-time who were dismissed or voluntarily withdrew from this program area were 8. *Counseling MA/MS (Master of Arts/Science)*—Applications 2004–2005, 25. Total applicants accepted 2004–2005, 17. Total enrolled 2004–2005 full-time, 8, part-time, 31. Openings 2005–2006, 20. The Median number of years required for completion of a degree are 2. The number of students enrolled full and part-time who were dismissed or voluntarily withdrew from this program area were 4.

Admissions Requirements:

Scores: Entries appear in this order: required test or GPA, minimum score (if required), median score of students entering in 2003–2004. Master's Programs: GRE-V+Q no minimum stated; MAT no minimum stated. We require either the GRE V+Q or MAT. We do not have cut off or minimum scores.

Other Criteria: (importance of criteria rated low, medium, or high): GRE/MAT scores low, research experience low, work experience medium, extracurricular activity medium, clinically related public service high, GPA medium, letters of recommendation high, interview high, statement of goals and objectives high. For additional information on admission requirements, go to: http://www.scu.edu/cp/.

Student Characteristics: The following represents characteristics of students in 2004–2005 in all graduate psychology programs in the department: Female–full-time 29, part-time 185; Male–full-time 4, part-time 31; African American/Black–full-time 2, part-time 3; Hispanic/Latino(a)–full-time 6, part-time 35; Asian/Pacific Islander–full-time 4, part-time 38; American Indian/Alaska Native–full-time 0, part-time 1; Caucasian–full-time 21, part-time

77; Multi-ethnic–full-time 0, part-time 2; students subject to the Americans With Disabilities Act–full-time 2, part-time 3.

Financial Information/Assistance:
Tuition for Full-Time Study: *Master's:* State residents: $391 per credit hour. *Doctoral:* State residents: $391 per credit hour; Nonstate residents: $391 per credit hour. Tuition is subject to change. See the following Web site for updates and changes in tuition costs: http://www.scu.edu/cp/financial/index.htm.

Financial Assistance:
First Year Students: Teaching assistantships available for first-year. Average amount paid per academic year: $1,200. Average number of hours worked per week: 12. Apply by quarterly. Research assistantships available for first-year. Fellowships and scholarships available for first-year. Average amount paid per academic year: $2,500. Average number of hours worked per week: 0. Apply by quarterly.

Advanced Students: Teaching assistantships available for advanced students. Average amount paid per academic year: $1,200. Average number of hours worked per week: 12. Apply by quarterly. Research assistantships available for advanced students. Apply by varies. Fellowships and scholarships available for advanced students. Average amount paid per academic year: $2,500. Average number of hours worked per week: 0. Apply by quarterly.

Contact Information: Of all students currently enrolled full-time, 26% benefitted from one or more of the listed financial assistance programs. Application and information available online at: http://www.scu.edu/cp/financial/index.htm.

Internships/Practica: Counseling Practicum: Marriage and Family Therapy. Supervised counseling experience designed specifically to meet California MFT licensing requirements. Weekly seminars for consultation and discussion with a licensed supervisor on such topics as case management and evaluation, referral procedures, ethical practices, professional and client interaction, confidential communication, and interprofessional ethical considerations.

Housing and Day Care: On-campus housing is available. No on-campus housing for graduate students. On-campus day care facilities are available. See the following Web site for more information: Kids on Campus, Santa Clara University, 500 El Camino Real, Santa Clara, CA 95053-0858, Phone: (408) 554-4771, http://www.scu.edu/koc/info.cfm.

Employment of Department Graduates:
Master's Degree Graduates: Of those who graduated in the academic year 2003–2004, the following categories and numbers represent the post-graduate activities and employment of master's degree graduates: Enrolled in a psychology doctoral program (4), enrolled in another graduate/professional program (1), enrolled in a post-doctoral residency/fellowship (n/a), employed in independent practice (n/a), employed in an academic position at a 2-year/4-year college (2), employed in other positions at a higher education institution (4), employed in a professional position in a school system (4), employed in a government agency (professional services) (5), employed in a community mental health/counseling center (8), employed in a hospital/medical center (1), other employment position (6), do not know (19), total from the above (master's) (54).

Doctoral Degree Graduates: Of those who graduated in the academic year 2003–2004, the following categories and numbers represent the post-graduate activities and employment of doctoral degree graduates: Enrolled in a psychology doctoral program (n/a), total from the above (doctoral) (0).

Additional Information:
Orientation, Objectives, and Emphasis of Department: Santa Clara University's graduate programs in counseling and counseling psychology are offered through the Division of Counseling Psychology and Education. Programs lead to the Master of Arts in Counseling or the Master of Arts in Counseling Psychology, with the option of an emphasis in health psychology, career counseling, Latino Counseling or correctional psychology, with the possibility of preparing for the Marriage and Family Therapy license in California. Santa Clara is accredited by the Western Association of Schools and Colleges and is approved by the Board of Behavioral Science, Department of Consumer Affairs (California) to prepare students for MFT licensure. The faculty represent a diverse set of clinical theories and perspectives, and students gain a broad exposure to a range of theories and practical applications in counseling.

Special Facilities or Resources: Santa Clara University is located in the heart of Silicon Valley, with close connections to major business and academic resources in this area. The University has a complete complement of facilities including an excellent library, theatre, museum, and state of the art physical fitness center. The University has a dedication to educating the whole person and includes Centers of Distinction which explore diversity, ethics, and the interface of Technology and Society.

Information for Students With Physical Disabilities: See the following Web site for more information: http://www.scu.edu/cp.

Application Information:
Send to: Department of Counseling Psychology, Santa Clara University, 500 El Camino Real, Santa Clara, CA 95053-0201. Application available online. URL of online application: http://www.scu.edu/ecppm/about/admissions/counselingpsychology.cfm. Students are admitted in the Fall, application deadline April 1; Winter, application deadline November 1; Spring, application deadline February 1; Summer, application deadline April 1. *Fee:* $50.

Saybrook Graduate School and Research Center
Graduate School
747 Front Street, Third Floor
San Francisco, CA 94111-1920
Telephone: (415) 433-9200
Fax: (415) 433-9271
E-mail: *saybrook@saybrook.edu*
Web: *http://www.saybrook.edu*

Department Information:
1971. President: Maureen O'Hara. Number of Faculty: total–full-time 19, part-time 94; women–full-time 8, part-time 34; minority–full-time 3.

Programs and Degrees Offered:

Listed in the following order: Program area, degree type (T if terminal Master's), number awarded 7/03–6/04. Human Science MA/MS (Master of Arts/Science) 3, Human Science PhD (Doctor of Philosophy) 4, Organizational Systems MA/MS (Master of Arts/Science) 2, Psychology MA/MS (Master of Arts/Science) 15, Psychology PhD (Doctor of Philosophy) 22, Organizational Systems PhD (Doctor of Philosophy) 4, Psychology Licensure MA/MS (Master of Arts/Science) 1.

Student Applications/Admissions:

Student Applications

Human Science MA/MS (Master of Arts/Science)—Applications 2004–2005, 1. Total applicants accepted 2004–2005, 2. Number enrolled (new admits only) 2004–2005 full-time, 1. Total enrolled 2004–2005 full-time, 2. Openings 2005–2006, 10. The number of students enrolled full and part-time who were dismissed or voluntarily withdrew from this program area were 1. *Human Science PhD (Doctor of Philosophy)*—Applications 2004–2005, 17. Total applicants accepted 2004–2005, 9. Number enrolled (new admits only) 2004–2005 full-time, 4. Total enrolled 2004–2005 full-time, 32. Openings 2005–2006, 20. The Median number of years required for completion of a degree are 2. The number of students enrolled full and part-time who were dismissed or voluntarily withdrew from this program area were 4. *Organizational Systems MA/MS (Master of Arts/Science)*—Applications 2004–2005, 9. Total applicants accepted 2004–2005, 3. Number enrolled (new admits only) 2004–2005 full-time, 3. Total enrolled 2004–2005 full-time, 8. Openings 2005–2006, 20. The Median number of years required for completion of a degree are 1.5. The number of students enrolled full and part-time who were dismissed or voluntarily withdrew from this program area were 1. *Psychology MA/MS (Master of Arts/Science)*—Applications 2004–2005, 54. Total applicants accepted 2004–2005, 31. Number enrolled (new admits only) 2004–2005 full-time, 16. Total enrolled 2004–2005 full-time, 66. Openings 2005–2006, 30. The Median number of years required for completion of a degree are 2. The number of students enrolled full and part-time who were dismissed or voluntarily withdrew from this program area were 6. *Psychology PhD (Doctor of Philosophy)*—Applications 2004–2005, 158. Total applicants accepted 2004–2005, 81. Number enrolled (new admits only) 2004–2005 full-time, 42. Total enrolled 2004–2005 full-time, 305. Openings 2005–2006, 45. The Median number of years required for completion of a degree are 5. The number of students enrolled full and part-time who were dismissed or voluntarily withdrew from this program area were 32. *Organizational Systems PhD (Doctor of Philosophy)*—Applications 2004–2005, 38. Total applicants accepted 2004–2005, 26. Number enrolled (new admits only) 2004–2005 full-time, 11. Total enrolled 2004–2005 full-time, 57. Openings 2005–2006, 30. The Median number of years required for completion of a degree are 4. The number of students enrolled full and part-time who were dismissed or voluntarily withdrew from this program area were 3. *Psychology Licensure MA/MS (Master of Arts/Science)*—Applications 2004–2005, 54. Total applicants accepted 2004–2005, 31. Number enrolled (new admits only) 2004–2005 full-time, 21. Total enrolled 2004–2005 full-time, 36. Openings 2005–2006, 30. The Median number of years required for completion of a degree are 2. The number of students enrolled full and part-

time who were dismissed or voluntarily withdrew from this program area were 1.

Other Criteria: (importance of criteria rated low, medium, or high): research experience high, work experience medium, extracurricular activity low, clinically related public service medium, GPA medium, letters of recommendation medium, statement of goals and objectives high.

Student Characteristics: The following represents characteristics of students in 2004–2005 in all graduate psychology programs in the department: Female–full-time 359, part-time 0; Male–full-time 147, part-time 0; African American/Black–full-time 20, part-time 0; Hispanic/Latino(a)–full-time 10, part-time 0; Asian/Pacific Islander–full-time 13, part-time 0; American Indian/Alaska Native–full-time 2, part-time 0; Caucasian–full-time 217, part-time 0; Multi-ethnic–full-time 13, part-time 0.

Financial Information/Assistance:

Tuition for Full-Time Study: *Master's:* State residents: per academic year $15,800; Nonstate residents: per academic year $15,800. *Doctoral:* State residents: per academic year $15,800; Nonstate residents: per academic year $15,800. See the following Web site for updates and changes in tuition costs: http://www.saybrook.edu/student_resources/business_office/fees_costs.asp.

Financial Assistance:

First Year Students: Fellowships and scholarships available for first-year. Average amount paid per academic year: $2,000.

Advanced Students: Fellowships and scholarships available for advanced students. Average amount paid per academic year: $2,000.

Contact Information: Of all students currently enrolled full-time, 5% benefitted from one or more of the listed financial assistance programs. Application and information available online at: http://www.saybrook.edu/student_resources/financial_aid/how_to_apply.asp.

Internships/Practica: Saybrook graduate students are distributed throughout the United States and the world. Because of the distance learning format, it is impractical for Saybrook to offer internship and practica training based at Saybrook. Saybrook graduate students are often successful midlife professionals who are accomplished in their first careers. The Clinical Training Coordinator works with doctoral students to find training experiences that will provide solid clinical training while drawing upon the strengths and clinical interests of these mature students.

Housing and Day Care: No on-campus housing is available. No on-campus day care facilities are available.

Employment of Department Graduates:

Master's Degree Graduates: Of those who graduated in the academic year 2003–2004, the following categories and numbers represent the post-graduate activities and employment of master's degree graduates: Enrolled in a post-doctoral residency/fellowship (n/a), employed in independent practice (n/a), employed in an academic position at a university (1), employed in an academic position at a 2-year/4-year college (1), employed in other positions at a higher education institution (1), employed in business or industry (research/consulting) (2), employed in a government agency (professional services) (2), employed in a community mental health/counseling center (3), total from the above (master's) (10).

Doctoral Degree Graduates: Of those who graduated in the academic year 2003–2004, the following categories and numbers represent the post-graduate activities and employment of doctoral degree graduates: Enrolled in a psychology doctoral program (n/a), total from the above (doctoral) (0).

Additional Information:

Orientation, Objectives, and Emphasis of Department: The mission of Saybrook Graduate School and Research Center is to provide a unique and creative environment for graduate study, research, and communication in humanistic psychology, focused on understanding the human experience, in a distance learning format. Applying the highest standards of scholarship, Saybrook is dedicated to fostering the full expression of the human spirit and humanistic values in society.

Application Information:

Send to: Saybrook Graduate School, Admissions Department, 747 Front Street, 3rd floor, San Francisco, CA 94111-1920. Application available online. URL of online application: https://mars.saybrook.edu/SMS/MainAdmissionsLogin.jsp. Students are admitted in the Fall, application deadline June 1; Spring, application deadline December 16. *Fee:* $100.

Sonoma State University

Department of Counseling
1801 East Cotati Avenue
Rohnert Park, CA 94928
Telephone: (707) 664-2544
Fax: (707) 664-2038
E-mail: *maureen.buckley@sonoma.edu*
Web: *http://www.sonoma.edu/counseling*

Department Information:

1973. Chairperson: Maureen Buckley. Number of Faculty: total—full-time 6, part-time 7; women—full-time 3, part-time 4; minority—part-time 2.

Programs and Degrees Offered:

Listed in the following order: Program area, degree type (T if terminal Master's), number awarded 7/03–6/04. Marriage and Family Therapy MA/MS (Master of Arts/Science) (T) 27, School Counseling MA/MS (Master of Arts/Science) (T) 11.

Student Applications/Admissions:

Student Applications

Marriage and Family Therapy MA/MS (Master of Arts/Science)— Applications 2004–2005, 92. Total applicants accepted 2004–2005, 36. Number enrolled (new admits only) 2004–2005 full-time, 12. Number enrolled (new admits only) 2004–2005 part-time, 7. Total enrolled 2004–2005 full-time, 23, part-time, 32. Openings 2005–2006, 24. The Median number of years required for completion of a degree are 3. The number of students enrolled full and part-time who were dismissed or voluntarily withdrew from this program area were 3. *School Counseling MA/MS (Master of Arts/Science)—*Applications 2004–2005, 40. Total applicants accepted 2004–2005, 12.

Number enrolled (new admits only) 2004–2005 full-time, 5. Number enrolled (new admits only) 2004–2005 part-time, 7. Total enrolled 2004–2005 full-time, 12, part-time, 12. Openings 2005–2006, 12. The Median number of years required for completion of a degree are 2. The number of students enrolled full and part-time who were dismissed or voluntarily withdrew from this program area were 0.

Admissions Requirements:

Scores: Entries appear in this order: required test or GPA, minimum score (if required), median score of students entering in 2003–2004. Master's Programs: overall undergraduate GPA 3.0, 3.0; last 2 years GPA 3.0, 3.5.

Other Criteria: (importance of criteria rated low, medium, or high): research experience low, work experience medium, extracurricular activity medium, clinically related public service high, GPA medium, letters of recommendation high, interview high, statement of goals and objectives high. School counseling program looks for school-related service or clinical/social work with children or youth. For additional information on admission requirements, go to: www.sonoma.edu/counseling.

Student Characteristics: The following represents characteristics of students in 2004–2005 in all graduate psychology programs in the department: Female–full-time 27, part-time 31; Male–full-time 8, part-time 13; African American/Black–full-time 0, part-time 1; Hispanic/Latino(a)–full-time 5, part-time 8; Asian/Pacific Islander–full-time 1, part-time 0; American Indian/Alaska Native–full-time 1, part-time 0; Caucasian–full-time 25, part-time 33; Multi-ethnic–full-time 3, part-time 2; students subject to the Americans With Disabilities Act–full-time 1, part-time 1.

Financial Information/Assistance:

Tuition for Full-Time Study: *Master's:* State residents: per academic year $3,894; Nonstate residents: per academic year $3,894, $282 per credit hour. Tuition is subject to change. See the following Web site for updates and changes in tuition costs: http://www.sonoma.edu/ar/registration/fees.shtml.

Financial Assistance:

First Year Students: Fellowships and scholarships available for first-year. Average amount paid per academic year: $1,400. Apply by February 15.

Advanced Students: Fellowships and scholarships available for advanced students. Average amount paid per academic year: $1,400. Apply by February 15.

Contact Information: Of all students currently enrolled full-time, 40% benefitted from one or more of the listed financial assistance programs. Application and information available online at: http://www.sonoma.edu/FinAid/.

Internships/Practica: Our students generally have several internship options to choose from, and they are highly sought by agencies and schools as interns. We do limit the internship sites to Sonoma State University's service area, which is the North Bay/Tri-County region of the San Francisco Bay Area.

Housing and Day Care: On-campus housing is available. See the following Web site for more information: www.sonoma.edu/housing or (707) 664-2541. On-campus day care facilities are available. See the following Web site for more information: The

Children's School: (707) 664-2230 (look for link under www.sonoma.edu).

Employment of Department Graduates:

Master's Degree Graduates: Of those who graduated in the academic year 2003–2004, the following categories and numbers represent the post-graduate activities and employment of master's degree graduates: Enrolled in a post-doctoral residency/fellowship (n/a), employed in independent practice (n/a), total from the above (master's) (0).

Doctoral Degree Graduates: Of those who graduated in the academic year 2003–2004, the following categories and numbers represent the post-graduate activities and employment of doctoral degree graduates: Enrolled in a psychology doctoral program (n/a), total from the above (doctoral) (0).

Additional Information:

Orientation, Objectives, and Emphasis of Department: The 60-unit graduate program in counseling (nationally accredited through CACREP, affiliated with the American Counseling Association) prepares students for entry into the profession of counseling or student personnel services. The Marriage & Family Therapy (MFT) program prepares students for licensure as MFTs in California; the School Counseling students obtain a Pupil Personnel Services Credential. The program relies heavily on interpersonal skill training and field experience, beginning during the first semester and culminating with an intensive supervised internship in some aspect of counseling, permitting the integration of theoretical constructs and research appraisal with practical application during the second year. The department is prepared to assist students in obtaining field placements relevant to their projected professional goals. These placements include, but are not limited to, family service agencies, mental health clinics, counseling centers, public schools, community colleges, and college-level student counseling centers. Special characteristics of the program include the following: (1) early involvement in actual counseling settings, (2) development of a core of knowledge and experience in both individual and group counseling theory and practice, (3) encouragement in the maintenance and development of individual counseling styles, and (4) commitment to self-exploration and personal growth through participation in peer counseling, individual counseling, and group experiences. This aspect of the program is seen as crucial to the development of counseling skills and is given special consideration by the faculty as part of its evaluation of student readiness to undertake internship responsibilities.

Special Facilities or Resources: Center for Community Counseling (on campus).

Information for Students With Physical Disabilities: See the following Web site for more information: www.sonoma.edu/sas/drc/drc.html, (707) 664-2677 or (707) 664-2958 (text).

Application Information:

Send to: Counseling Department, Sonoma State University, 1801 E. Cotati Avenue, N220, Rohnert Park, CA 94928. Students are admitted in the Fall, application deadline January 31. *Fee:* $80. $25 fee for application to the Counseling Department, $55 fee for application to Sonoma State University, Total: $80.

Sonoma State University
Department of Psychology
1801 East Cotati Avenue
Rohnert Park, CA 94928
Telephone: (707) 664-2682
Fax: (707) 664-3113
E-mail: *charles.merrill@sonoma.edu*
Web: *http://www.sonoma.edu/exed/degrees/dindex.html*

Department Information:

1961. Chairperson: Arthur Warmoth, PhD Number of Faculty: total–full-time 14, part-time 9; women–full-time 8, part-time 7; minority–full-time 1.

Programs and Degrees Offered:

Listed in the following order: Program area, degree type (T if terminal Master's), number awarded 7/03–6/04. Art therapy MA/MS (Master of Arts/Science) (T) 7, Depth Psych. MA/MS (Master of Arts/Science) 8, organization development MA/MS (Master of Arts/Science) 10.

Student Applications/Admissions:

Student Applications

Art therapy MA/MS (Master of Arts/Science)—Applications 2004–2005, 25. Total applicants accepted 2004–2005, 10. Number enrolled (new admits only) 2004–2005 full-time, 0. Number enrolled (new admits only) 2004–2005 part-time, 0. Total enrolled 2004–2005 full-time, 20, part-time, 5. The Median number of years required for completion of a degree are 3. The number of students enrolled full and part-time who were dismissed or voluntarily withdrew from this program area were 0. *Depth Psych. MA/MS (Master of Arts/Science)*—Applications 2004–2005, 25. Total applicants accepted 2004–2005, 12. Number enrolled (new admits only) 2004–2005 full-time, 11. Number enrolled (new admits only) 2004–2005 part-time, 0. Total enrolled 2004–2005 full time, 22, part-time, 5. Openings 2005–2006, 14. The Median number of years required for completion of a degree are 2. The number of students enrolled full and part-time who were dismissed or voluntarily withdrew from this program area were 1. *Organization development MA/MS (Master of Arts/Science)*—Applications 2004–2005, 25. Total applicants accepted 2004–2005, 15. Number enrolled (new admits only) 2004–2005 full-time, 14. Total enrolled 2004–2005 full-time, 30, part-time, 5. Openings 2005–2006, 16. The Median number of years required for completion of a degree are 2. The number of students enrolled full and part-time who were dismissed or voluntarily withdrew from this program area was 1.

Admissions Requirements:

Scores: Entries appear in this order: required test or GPA, minimum score (if required), median score of students entering in 2003–2004. Master's Programs: last 2 years GPA 3.00, 3.45. *Other Criteria:* (importance of criteria rated low, medium, or high): research experience low, work experience high, extracurricular activity medium, clinically related public service medium, GPA high, letters of recommendation high, interview high, statement of goals and objectives high, Demonstrated graduate level writing ability in all programs.

Student Characteristics: The following represents characteristics of students in 2004–2005 in all graduate psychology programs in the department: Female–full-time 55, part-time 10; Male–full-time 17, part-time 5; African American/Black–full-time 2, part-time 0; Hispanic/Latino(a)–full-time 2, part-time 0; Asian/Pacific Islander–full-time 0, part-time 0; American Indian/Alaska Native–full-time 0, part-time 0; Caucasian–full-time 68, part-time 15; Multi-ethnic–full-time 0, part-time 0; students subject to the Americans With Disabilities Act–full-time 0, part-time 0.

Financial Information/Assistance:

Tuition for Full-Time Study: *Master's:* State residents: per academic year $8,100, $450 per credit hour; Nonstate residents: per academic year $8,100, $450 per credit hour. Tuition is subject to change. Tuition costs vary by program. See the following Web site for updates and changes in tuition costs: http://www.sonoma.edu/exed/degrees/dindex.html.

Financial Assistance:
First Year Students: Fellowships and scholarships available for first-year. Average amount paid per academic year: $700. Apply by January 15.
Advanced Students: No information provided.
Contact Information: Of all students currently enrolled full-time, 0% benefitted from one or more of the listed financial assistance programs.

Internships/Practica: Internships are optional for the Depth Psychology program. Internships are required as part of the Art Therapy program. Field projects working as a team of two or three students studying an organization are required in the Organization Development program.

Housing and Day Care: On-campus housing is available. Contact Housing Office at (707) 664-2541; The University mainly supports undergraduate housing, but it is possible for a single graduate student to share housing. Housing must be vacated in June. No married student housing. On-campus day care facilities are available. Child Care Center (707) 664-2230.

Employment of Department Graduates:
Master's Degree Graduates: Of those who graduated in the academic year 2003–2004, the following categories and numbers represent the post-graduate activities and employment of master's degree graduates: Enrolled in a psychology doctoral program (5), enrolled in another graduate/professional program (1), enrolled in a post-doctoral residency/fellowship (n/a), employed in independent practice (n/a), employed in an academic position at a university (0), employed in an academic position at a 2-year/4-year college (2), employed in other positions at a higher education institution (0), employed in a professional position in a school system (0), employed in business or industry (research/consulting) (20), employed in business or industry (management) (8), employed in a government agency (research) (0), employed in a government agency (professional services) (0), employed in a community mental health/counseling center (0), employed in a hospital/medical center (0), still seeking employment (15), not seeking employment (20), other employment position (10), total from the above (master's) (81).
Doctoral Degree Graduates: Of those who graduated in the academic year 2003–2004, the following categories and numbers represent the post-graduate activities and employment of doctoral degree graduates: Enrolled in a psychology doctoral program (n/a), total from the above (doctoral) (0).

Additional Information:
Orientation, Objectives, and Emphasis of Department: Art Therapy: Offers 36-units of coursework that meets both the educational standards of the American Art Therapy Association and continues the humanistic tradition of the SSU Psychology Department. To become professionally registered as an A.T.R., an additional 1500 post-master's supervised hours of work are required. Depth Psychology: An embodied 36-unit curriculum which integrates intensive personal process work in Jungian and archetypal psychology with conceptual learning and practical skills development. A small group environment enables students to develop skills in process work, group facilitation, arts expressions, dream work, personal growth facilitation and cross-cultural awareness. Organization Development: Provides professional preparation for mid-career individuals interested in learning how to develop more effective and humane organizations. A 36-unit program of seminar discussions, skill-building activities, and extensive field projects under faculty guidance. Participants gain the practical skills, conceptual knowledge, and field-tested experience to successfully lead organization improvement efforts.

Special Facilities or Resources: Facilities include a biofeedback lab and computer lab. The faculty are open to investigations in Depth psychology and organization development. The department has excellent interdisciplinary cooperation with sociology, gerontology, business and other related programs. Sonoma State University has a "state of the art" new library and information center.

Application Information:
Send to: MA Programs in Psychology, Department of Psychology, Sonoma State University, Rohnert Park, CA 94928. Students are admitted in the Fall, application deadline May 01. Programs have rolling admissions. Applications accepted on a rolling basis until quota reached. *Fee:* $55. No waiver or deferral of fees. Programs do qualify for low interest federal government loans.

Southern California, University of
Department of Psychology
College of Letters, Arts and Sciences
University Park - SGM 501
Los Angeles, CA 90089-1061
Telephone: (213) 740-2203
Fax: (213) 746-9082
E-mail: *itakarag@usc.edu*
Web: *http://psychology.usc.edu*

Department Information:
1929. Chairperson: Gerald C. Davison. Number of Faculty: total–full-time 34; women–full-time 8; minority–full-time 3.

Programs and Degrees Offered:
Listed in the following order: Program area, degree type (T if terminal Master's), number awarded 7/03–6/04. Neuroscience PhD (Doctor of Philosophy) 2, Clinical Science PhD (Doctor of Philosophy) 4, Developmental-Child PhD (Doctor of Philosophy)

1, quantitative PhD (Doctor of Philosophy) 0, Developmental-Aging PhD (Doctor of Philosophy) 1, social PhD (Doctor of Philosophy) 2.

APA Accreditation: Clinical PhD (Doctor of Philosophy).

Student Applications/Admissions:

Student Applications

Neuroscience PhD (Doctor of Philosophy)—Applications 2004–2005, 56. Total applicants accepted 2004–2005, 7. Number enrolled (new admits only) 2004–2005 full-time, 5. Openings 2005–2006, 6. The Median number of years required for completion of a degree are 5. The number of students enrolled full and part-time who were dismissed or voluntarily withdrew from this program area were 0. *Clinical Science PhD (Doctor of Philosophy)*—Applications 2004–2005, 329. Total applicants accepted 2004–2005, 9. Number enrolled (new admits only) 2004–2005 full-time, 7. Openings 2005–2006, 6. The Median number of years required for completion of a degree are 5. The number of students enrolled full and part-time who were dismissed or voluntarily withdrew from this program area were 0. *Developmental-Child PhD (Doctor of Philosophy)*—Applications 2004–2005, 28. Total applicants accepted 2004–2005, 1. Number enrolled (new admits only) 2004–2005 full-time, 0. Openings 2005–2006, 2. The Median number of years required for completion of a degree are 6. The number of students enrolled full and part-time who were dismissed or voluntarily withdrew from this program area were 0. *Quantitative PhD (Doctor of Philosophy)*—Applications 2004–2005, 8. Total applicants accepted 2004–2005, 1. Number enrolled (new admits only) 2004–2005 full-time, 1. Openings 2005–2006, 1. The number of students enrolled full and part-time who were dismissed or voluntarily withdrew from this program area were 0. *Developmental-Aging PhD (Doctor of Philosophy)*—Applications 2004–2005, 6. Total applicants accepted 2004–2005, 0. Total enrolled 2004–2005 full-time, 2. Openings 2005–2006, 1. The Median number of years required for completion of a degree are 5. The number of students enrolled full and part-time who were dismissed or voluntarily withdrew from this program area were 0. *Social PhD (Doctor of Philosophy)*—Applications 2004–2005, 57. Total applicants accepted 2004–2005, 5. Number enrolled (new admits only) 2004–2005 full-time, 4. Openings 2005–2006, 2. The Median number of years required for completion of a degree are 6. The number of students enrolled full and part-time who were dismissed or voluntarily withdrew from this program area were 0.

Admissions Requirements:

Scores: Entries appear in this order: required test or GPA, minimum score (if required), median score of students entering in 2003–2004. Doctoral Programs: GRE-V no minimum stated, 620; GRE-Q 560, 740; GRE-V+Q no minimum stated, 1360; overall undergraduate GPA no minimum stated, 3.62.

Other Criteria: (importance of criteria rated low, medium, or high): GRE/MAT scores high, research experience high, work experience medium, extracurricular activity low, clinically related public service medium, GPA high, letters of recommendation high, statement of goals and objectives high. Interview and clinically related public service are very important for the Clinical Science program but less so for other areas. For additional information on admission requirements, go to: http://psychology.usc.edu/grad_app.php.

Student Characteristics: The following represents characteristics of students in 2004–2005 in all graduate psychology programs in the department: Female- full-time 60, part-time 0; Male–full-time 37, part-time 0; African American/Black–full-time 5, part-time 0; Hispanic/Latino(a)–full-time 12, part-time 0; Asian/Pacific Islander–full-time 27, part-time 0; American Indian/Alaska Native–full-time 0, part-time 0; Caucasian–full-time 53, part-time 0; Multi-ethnic–full-time 0, part-time 0; students subject to the Americans With Disabilities Act–full-time 0, part-time 0.

Financial Information/Assistance:

Tuition for Full-Time Study: *Doctoral:* State residents: per academic year $25,704, $1,071 per credit hour; Nonstate residents: per academic year $25,704, $1,071 per credit hour. Tuition is subject to change. See the following Web site for updates and changes in tuition costs: http://www.usc.edu/students/enrollment/classes/.

Financial Assistance:

First Year Students: Teaching assistantships available for first-year. Average amount paid per academic year: $17,160. Average number of hours worked per week: 20. Tuition remission given: full. Research assistantships available for first-year. Average amount paid per academic year: $17,160. Average number of hours worked per week: 20. Tuition remission given: full. Traineeships available for first-year. Average amount paid per academic year: $20,772. Average number of hours worked per week: 0. Tuition remission given: full. Fellowships and scholarships available for first-year. Average amount paid per academic year: $23,000. Average number of hours worked per week: 0. Tuition remission given: full.

Advanced Students: Teaching assistantships available for advanced students. Average amount paid per academic year: $17,160. Average number of hours worked per week: 20. Tuition remission given: full. Research assistantships available for advanced students. Average amount paid per academic year: $17,169. Average number of hours worked per week: 20. Tuition remission given: full. Traineeships available for advanced students. Average amount paid per academic year: $20,772. Average number of hours worked per week: 0. Tuition remission given: full. Fellowships and scholarships available for advanced students. Average amount paid per academic year: $23,000. Average number of hours worked per week: 0. Tuition remission given: full.

Contact Information: Of all students currently enrolled full-time, 76% benefitted from one or more of the listed financial assistance programs. Application and information available online at: http://psychology.usc.edu/grad_app.php.

Internships/Practica: Students in the clinical psychology area take at least six semesters of clinical didactic-practica, each of which involves instruction and supervised clinical service provision. Students receive both group and individual supervision of their cases. The first year practica focus on clinical interviewing and formal assessment. In the second and third year, students take practica based on their interests and specialty track. Practica are offered in general adult psychotherapy, psychotherapy with older adults, and child/family psychotherapy. After admission to doctoral candidacy, all students must complete a one-year, APA approved, clinical internship for which students separately apply at the time. For those doctoral students for whom a professional internship is required prior to graduation, 4 applied in 2003–2004. Of those who applied, 4 were placed in internships listed by the Association of Psychology Postdoctoral and Internship Programs (APPIC); 4 were placed in APA accredited internships.

Housing and Day Care: On-campus housing is available. See the following Web site for more information: http://housing.usc.edu/. No on-campus day care facilities are available.

Employment of Department Graduates:

Master's Degree Graduates: Of those who graduated in the academic year 2003–2004, the following categories and numbers represent the post-graduate activities and employment of master's degree graduates: Enrolled in a post-doctoral residency/fellowship (n/a), employed in independent practice (n/a), total from the above (master's) (0).

Doctoral Degree Graduates: Of those who graduated in the academic year 2003–2004, the following categories and numbers represent the post-graduate activities and employment of doctoral degree graduates: Enrolled in a psychology doctoral program (n/a), enrolled in a post-doctoral residency/fellowship (2), employed in an academic position at a university (3), employed in business or industry (research/consulting) (2), employed in business or industry (management) (1), employed in a government agency (research) (1), still seeking employment (1), total from the above (doctoral) (10).

Additional Information:

Orientation, Objectives, and Emphasis of Department: Though oriented toward research and teaching, graduate training in psychology also shows concern for the applications of psychology. In addition to completing the required coursework, students in all specialty areas are expected to engage in empirical research throughout graduate study. Areas of specialization include clinical psychology, child development, adult development and aging, cognitive psychology, behavioral neuroscience, quantitative, and social psychology. Within the clinical science program, there are formal tracks in clinical-aging and child and family. The APA-approved clinical program incorporates the scientist-practitioner model and prepares students for careers in teaching and research, as well as in empirically oriented applied settings.

Special Facilities or Resources: We are housed in the upper six floors of a 10 story building. Ample laboratory and office space are supplemented by facilities in the Hedco Neurosciences building that is adjacent to the main Psychology building. A new FMRI Center attached to the Psychology building makes available state-of-the-art imaging facilities for faculty and student research.

Information for Students With Physical Disabilities: See the following Web site for more information: http://www.usc.edu/student-affairs/asn/DSP/.

Application Information:
Send to: Irene Takaragawa, Department of Psychology/SGM 508, University of Southern California, Los Angeles, CA 90089-1061. Application available online. URL of online application: http://psychology.usc.edu/grad_app.php. Students are admitted in the Fall, application deadline December 15. Extended deadline of December 31 for any unfilled slots in Developmental, Quantitative, or Social Psychology only. *Fee:* $65. Must send to the Office of Graduate Admissions, USC,

Los Angeles, CA, 90089-0911, the most current financial aid statement from current/last school of enrollment.

Southern California, University of, School of Medicine
Department of Preventive Medicine, Division of Health Behavior Research
USC/IPR, 1000 S. Fremont Avenue, Unit 8, Attn: Marny Barovich
Alhambra, CA 91803
Telephone: (626) 457-6648
Fax: (626) 457-4012
E-mail: *barovich@usc.edu*
Web: *http://www.usc.edu/medicine/hbrphd*

Department Information:
1984. Director: C. Anderson Johnson. Number of Faculty: total–full-time 21; women–full-time 11; minority–full-time 5.

Programs and Degrees Offered:
Listed in the following order: Program area, degree type (T if terminal Master's), number awarded 7/03–6/04. Health Behavior Research PhD (Doctor of Philosophy) 3.

Student Applications/Admissions:

Student Applications

Health Behavior Research PhD (Doctor of Philosophy)—Applications 2004–2005, 36. Total applicants accepted 2004–2005, 7. Number enrolled (new admits only) 2004–2005 full-time, 6. Openings 2005–2006, 5. The Median number of years required for completion of a degree are 7. The number of students enrolled full and part-time who were dismissed or voluntarily withdrew from this program area were 0.

Admissions Requirements:

Scores: Entries appear in this order: required test or GPA, minimum score (if required), median score of students entering in 2003–2004. Doctoral Programs: GRE-V 330, 615; GRE-Q 550, 665; GRE-V+Q 1120, 1270; overall undergraduate GPA 2.92, 3.45. A master's degree is not required.

Other Criteria: (importance of criteria rated low, medium, or high): GRE/MAT scores high, research experience medium, work experience low, GPA high, letters of recommendation high, interview low, statement of goals and objectives high. Students are invited to interview, but interviews are not required. For additional information on admission requirements, go to: www.usc.edu/medicine/hbrphd.

Student Characteristics: The following represents characteristics of students in 2004–2005 in all graduate psychology programs in the department: Female–full-time 20, part-time 0; Male–full-time 5, part-time 0; African American/Black–full-time 2, part-time 0; Hispanic/Latino(a)–full-time 3, part-time 0; Asian/Pacific Islander–full-time 8, part-time 0; American Indian/Alaska Native–full-time 0, part-time 0; Caucasian–full-time 10, part-time 0; Multi-ethnic–full-time 2, part-time 0; students subject to the Americans With Disabilities Act–full-time 0, part-time 0.

Financial Information/Assistance:

Tuition for Full-Time Study: *Doctoral:* State residents: per academic year $24,240, $1,010 per credit hour; Nonstate residents: per academic year $24,240, $1,010 per credit hour. Tuition is subject to change.

Financial Assistance:

First Year Students: Teaching assistantships available for first-year. Average amount paid per academic year: $25,457. Average number of hours worked per week: 20. Apply by February 1. Tuition remission given: full. Research assistantships available for first-year. Average amount paid per academic year: $25,457. Average number of hours worked per week: 20. Apply by February 1. Tuition remission given: full. Traineeships available for first-year. Average amount paid per academic year: $25,457. Average number of hours worked per week: 20. Apply by as available. Tuition remission given: full. Fellowships and scholarships available for first-year. Average amount paid per academic year: $25,457. Average number of hours worked per week: 20. Apply by February 1. Tuition remission given: full.

Advanced Students: Teaching assistantships available for advanced students. Average amount paid per academic year: $25,457. Average number of hours worked per week: 20. Apply by n/a. Tuition remission given: full. Research assistantships available for advanced students. Average amount paid per academic year: $25,457. Average number of hours worked per week: 20. Apply by n/a. Tuition remission given: full. Traineeships available for advanced students. Average amount paid per academic year: $25,457. Average number of hours worked per week: 20. Apply by as available. Tuition remission given: full. Fellowships and scholarships available for advanced students. Average amount paid per academic year: $25,457. Average number of hours worked per week: 20. Apply by February 1. Tuition remission given: full.

Contact Information: Of all students currently enrolled full-time, 84% benefitted from one or more of the listed financial assistance programs. Application and information available online at: http://www.usc.edu/dept/GRADSCHL/.

Internships/Practica: Three practica in health behavior are available to doctoral students: a) prevention, b) compliance, and c) health behavior topics. Through the practica, students gain practical experience in a variety of field settings to gain a certain type of skill such as curriculum development, media production, and patient education.

Housing and Day Care: On-campus housing is available. See the following Web site for more information: housing.usc.edu www.usc.edu/dept/childcare. On-campus day care facilities are available.

Employment of Department Graduates:

Master's Degree Graduates: Of those who graduated in the academic year 2003–2004, the following categories and numbers represent the post-graduate activities and employment of master's degree graduates: Enrolled in a post-doctoral residency/fellowship (n/a), employed in independent practice (n/a), total from the above (master's) (0).

Doctoral Degree Graduates: Of those who graduated in the academic year 2003–2004, the following categories and numbers represent the post-graduate activities and employment of doctoral degree graduates: Enrolled in a psychology doctoral program (n/a), employed in an academic position at a university (1), employed in business or industry (research/consulting) (1), other employment position (1), total from the above (doctoral) (3).

Additional Information:

Orientation, Objectives, and Emphasis of Department: The University of Southern California (USC) School of Medicine, Department of Preventive Medicine, Division of Health Behavior Research, offers a doctorate in preventive medicine, health behavior research (HBR), providing academic and research training for students interested in pursuing career opportunities in the field of health promotion and disease prevention research. The specific objective of the program is to train exceptional researchers and scholars in the multidisciplinary field of health behavior research who will apply this knowledge creatively to the goal of primary and secondary prevention of disease. Students receive well-rounded training that encompasses theory and methods from many allied fields, including communication, psychology, preventive medicine, statistics, public health, and epidemiology. Students receive research experience participating in projects conducted through the USC Institute for Health Promotion and Disease Prevention Research (IPR). Required core courses: foundations of health behavior, data analysis, behavioral epidemiology, biological basis of disease, basic theory and strategies in prevention, basic theories and strategies for compliance/adaptation, health behavior research methods, and research seminar in health behavior. In addition to core course requirements, the curriculum includes content courses from the Department of Preventive Medicine, Divisions of Biometry, Epidemiology, or Occupational Medicine.

Special Facilities or Resources: Faculty and other researchers at IPR are recognized leaders in community-based approaches to health promotion and disease prevention. The research at IPR integrates the scientific perspectives of epidemiology, the behavioral sciences, biology, communication, and policy research in disease etiology and prevention. IPR enjoys research collaborations in 10 schools and 35 departments within USC and with noted researchers and public health leaders in leading universities across the U.S., Europe, Latin America, and Asia. IPR's faculty and researchers are world leaders in school- and community-based prevention, cancer epidemiology, tobacco control, drug abuse, childhood obesity, nutrition, physical activity, cardiovascular disease, diabetes, health disparities, and health communication campaigns for chronic disease prevention. IPR has two National Institutes of Health (NIH) funded transdisciplinary research centers that integrate theories and methods across multiple disciplines to approach the complex problems of tobacco use and drug abuse. Supported by the NCI, the National Institute on Drug Abuse (NIDA), and the Robert Wood Johnson Foundation, the USC Transdisciplinary Tobacco Use Research Center studies tobacco use and prevention among ethnically diverse adolescents in California, Hawaii and China. The NIDA supported Transdisciplinary Drug Abuse Prevention Research Center translates basic research in memory and peer group dynamics into drug abuse prevention programs for adolescents. Both centers also train students and faculty in transdisciplinary approaches to research.

Application Information:
Send to: Doctoral Program Admissions (attn: Marny), USC/IPR, 1000 South Fremont Avenue, Unit 8 (suite #4203 if sending via express mail), Alhambra, CA 91803. Application available online. URL of online application: http://www.usc.edu/dept/admissions/grad/. Stu-

dents are admitted in the Fall, application deadline February 1. *Fee:* $65. $75 for international students.

Stanford University
Department of Psychology
Humanities & Sciences
Building 420
Stanford, CA 94305-2130
Telephone: (650) 725-2400
Fax: (650) 725-5699
E-mail: *admissions-info@psych.stanford.edu*
Web: *http://www-psych.stanford.edu*

Department Information:
1892. Chairperson: Laura Carstensen. Number of Faculty: total–full-time 32; women–full-time 13; minority–full-time 6.

Programs and Degrees Offered:
Listed in the following order: Program area, degree type (T if terminal Master's), number awarded 7/03–6/04. Concentration in Cognitive Psychology PhD (Doctor of Philosophy), Concentration in Social Psychology PhD (Doctor of Philosophy), Concentration in Area of Neuroscience PhD (Doctor of Philosophy), Concentration in Personality Psychology PhD (Doctor of Philosophy), Concentration in Developmental Psychology PhD (Doctor of Philosophy).

Student Applications/Admissions:
Student Applications
Concentration in Cognitive Psychology PhD (Doctor of Philosophy)—Concentration in Social Psychology PhD (Doctor of Philosophy)—Concentration in Area of Neuroscience PhD (Doctor of Philosophy)—Concentration in Personality Psychology PhD (Doctor of Philosophy)—Concentration in Developmental Psychology PhD (Doctor of Philosophy)

Admissions Requirements:
Scores: Entries appear in this order: required test or GPA, minimum score (if required), median score of students entering in 2003–2004. Doctoral Programs: GRE-V no minimum stated; GRE-Q no minimum stated; GRE-V+Q no minimum stated; GRE-Analytical no minimum stated; GRE-Subject(Psych) no minimum stated; overall undergraduate GPA no minimum stated; last 2 years GPA no minimum stated; psychology GPA no minimum stated.
Other Criteria: (importance of criteria rated low, medium, or high): GRE/MAT scores medium, research experience high, work experience low, extracurricular activity low, clinically related public service low, GPA high, letters of recommendation high, interview low, statement of goals and objectives high. For additional information on admission requirements, go to: http://www.gradadmissions.stanford.edu.

Student Characteristics: The following represents characteristics of students in 2004–2005 in all graduate psychology programs in the department: Female–full-time 53, part-time 0; Male–full-time 27, part-time 0; African American/Black–part-time 0; Hispanic/Latino(a)–part-time 0; Asian/Pacific Islander–part-time 0; Ameri-can Indian/Alaska Native–part-time 0; Caucasian–full-time 0, part-time 0; Multi-ethnic–part-time 0.

Financial Information/Assistance:
Financial Assistance:
First Year Students: Research assistantships available for first-year. Traineeships available for first-year. Fellowships and scholarships available for first-year.
Advanced Students: Teaching assistantships available for advanced students. Research assistantships available for advanced students. Traineeships available for advanced students. Fellowships and scholarships available for advanced students.
Contact Information: Of all students currently enrolled full-time, 75% benefitted from one or more of the listed financial assistance programs.

Internships/Practica: No information provided.

Housing and Day Care: On-campus housing is available. See the following Web site for more information: http://www.stanford.edu/dept/hds/has/. On-campus day care facilities are available.

Employment of Department Graduates:
Master's Degree Graduates: Of those who graduated in the academic year 2003–2004, the following categories and numbers represent the post-graduate activities and employment of master's degree graduates: Enrolled in a post-doctoral residency/fellowship (n/a), employed in independent practice (n/a), total from the above (master's) (0).
Doctoral Degree Graduates: Of those who graduated in the academic year 2003–2004, the following categories and numbers represent the post-graduate activities and employment of doctoral degree graduates: Enrolled in a psychology doctoral program (n/a), total from the above (doctoral) (0).

Additional Information:

Special Facilities or Resources: The department comprises facilities and personnel housed in Jordan Hall, where it maintains a psychology library and extensive laboratory and shop facilities, supervised by specialized technical assistants. Most of the laboratories are equipped with computer terminals linked directly to the university's computer center. Others are equipped with their own computers. In addition, the department has its own computer and a computer programmer on the psychology staff. The department maintains a nursery school close to the married students' housing area. This provides a laboratory for child observation, for training in nursery school practice, and for research.

Information for Students With Physical Disabilities: See the following Web site for more information: http://www.stanford.edu/group/DRC/.

Application Information:
Application will be accepted through our online application system, found at http://www.gradadmissions.stanford.edu. Paper applications can be requested through that website at an extra cost. The rest of our program information can be found at the department website at http://www-psych.stanford.edu. The department cannot provide any paper materials for admissions. Please contact http://www.gradadmissions.stanford.edu. Application available online. URL of online application: http://www.gradadmissions.stanford.edu. Students are admitted

in the Fall, application deadline December 15. GRE general and subject tests must be taken by the December 15 deadline. *Fee:* $100. Fee waiver from U.S. institutions only. Contact http://www.gradadmissions.stanford.edu for more information.

Vanguard University of Southern California

Graduate Program in Clinical Psychology
55 Fair Drive
Costa Mesa, CA 92626
Telephone: (714) 556-3610
Fax: (714) 662-5226
E-mail: *gradpsych@vanguard.edu*
Web: *http://www.vanguard.edu/gradpsych/*

Department Information:
1998. Director: Jerre White. Number of Faculty: total–full-time 3, part-time 6; women–full-time 2, part-time 2; minority–part-time 1.

Programs and Degrees Offered:
Listed in the following order: Program area, degree type (T if terminal Master's), number awarded 7/03–6/04. Clinical Psychology MA/MS (Master of Arts/Science) (T) 19.

Student Applications/Admissions:
Student Applications
Clinical Psychology MA/MS (Master of Arts/Science)—Applications 2004–2005, 95. Total applicants accepted 2004–2005, 43. Number enrolled (new admits only) 2004–2005 full-time, 22. Number enrolled (new admits only) 2004–2005 part-time, 3. Total enrolled 2004–2005 full-time, 49, part-time, 24. Openings 2005–2006, 25. The Median number of years required for completion of a degree are 2. The number of students enrolled full and part-time who were dismissed or voluntarily withdrew from this program area was 1.

Admissions Requirements:
Scores: Entries appear in this order: required test or GPA, minimum score (if required), median score of students entering in 2003–2004. Master's Programs: overall undergraduate GPA 2.5, 3.3; psychology GPA 3.0, 3.5.
Other Criteria: (importance of criteria rated low, medium, or high): research experience low, work experience medium, extracurricular activity low, clinically related public service medium, GPA high, letters of recommendation high, interview low, statement of goals and objectives high.

Student Characteristics: The following represents characteristics of students in 2004–2005 in all graduate psychology programs in the department: Female–full-time 38, part-time 15; Male–full-time 11, part-time 9; African American/Black–full-time 4, part-time 1; Hispanic/Latino(a)–full-time 8, part-time 5; Asian/Pacific Islander–full-time 2, part-time 1; American Indian/Alaska Native–full-time 0, part-time 0; Caucasian–full-time 34, part-time 17; Multi-ethnic–full-time 1, part-time 0; students subject to the Americans With Disabilities Act–full-time 0, part-time 0.

Financial Information/Assistance:
Tuition for Full-Time Study: *Master's:* State residents: per academic year $15,408, $642 per credit hour; Nonstate residents: per academic year $15,408, $642 per credit hour. Tuition is subject to change. See the following Web site for updates and changes in tuition costs: http://www.vanguard.edu/gradadmissions/detail.aspx?doc_id=2458.

Financial Assistance:
First Year Students: Fellowships and scholarships available for first-year. Average amount paid per academic year: $2,000.
Advanced Students: Teaching assistantships available for advanced students. Average amount paid per academic year: $3,000. Average number of hours worked per week: 8. Research assistantships available for advanced students. Average amount paid per academic year: $3,000. Average number of hours worked per week: 8. Fellowships and scholarships available for advanced students. Average amount paid per academic year: $3,000. Average number of hours worked per week: 8.
Contact Information: Of all students currently enrolled full-time, 90% benefitted from one or more of the listed financial assistance programs.

Internships/Practica: Each student is required to complete a minimum of 150 client contact hours at an approved practicum site. These sites currently include domestic violence shelters, county agencies, community clinics, and student counseling centers serving a variety of populations.

Housing and Day Care: No on-campus housing is available. No on-campus day care facilities are available.

Employment of Department Graduates:
Master's Degree Graduates: Of those who graduated in the academic year 2003–2004, the following categories and numbers represent the post-graduate activities and employment of master's degree graduates: Enrolled in a psychology doctoral program (0), enrolled in another graduate/professional program (0), enrolled in a post-doctoral residency/fellowship (n/a), employed in independent practice (n/a), employed in an academic position at a university (0), employed in an academic position at a 2-year/4-year college (0), employed in other positions at a higher education institution (2), employed in a professional position in a school system (0), employed in business or industry (research/consulting) (0), employed in business or industry (management) (0), employed in a government agency (research) (0), employed in a government agency (professional services) (0), employed in a community mental health/counseling center (12), employed in a hospital/medical center (1), still seeking employment (0), other employment position (4), do not know (0), total from the above (master's) (19).
Doctoral Degree Graduates: Of those who graduated in the academic year 2003–2004, the following categories and numbers represent the post-graduate activities and employment of doctoral degree graduates: Enrolled in a psychology doctoral program (n/a), total from the above (doctoral) (0).

Additional Information:
Orientation, Objectives, and Emphasis of Department: Vanguard University of Southern California is a university of Christian liberal arts and sciences. It is within this faith-based context that we offer a Master of Science in Clinical Psychology degree, which meets the educational requirements for licensure as a Marriage and Family Therapist in the state of California. The goal of the Graduate Program in Clinical Psychology is to equip its students

to serve with excellence as Christian mental health professionals. Our goal is met by providing the highest quality of rigorous academic training, guided professional development, and integrative faith based learning in a collaborative and supportive environment.

Special Facilities or Resources: None applicable.

Application Information:
Send to: Graduate Admissions, 55 Fair Drive, Costa Mesa, CA 92626. Application available online. URL of online application: http://www. vanguard.edu/gradpsych/application/. Students are admitted in the Fall, application deadline April 1. *Fee:* $45.

Wright Institute

Graduate School of Psychology
2728 Durant Avenue
Berkeley, CA 94704
Telephone: (510) 841-9230
Fax: (510) 841-0167
E-mail: *admissions@wrightinst.edu*
Web: *http://www.wrightinst.edu*

Department Information:
1969. Dean: Charles Alexander, PhD Number of Faculty: total–full-time 6, part-time 37; women–full-time 4, part-time 21; minority–full-time 3, part-time 16; faculty subject to the Americans With Disabilities Act 1.

Programs and Degrees Offered:
Listed in the following order: Program area, degree type (T if terminal Master's), number awarded 7/03–6/04. Clinical PsyD (Doctor of Psychology) 35.

APA Accreditation: Clinical PsyD (Doctor of Psychology).

Student Applications/Admissions:
Student Applications
Clinical PsyD (Doctor of Psychology)—Applications 2004–2005, 324. Total applicants accepted 2004–2005, 106. Number enrolled (new admits only) 2004–2005 full-time, 60. Number enrolled (new admits only) 2004–2005 part-time, 0. Openings 2005–2006, 55. The Median number of years required for completion of a degree are 5. The number of students enrolled full and part-time who were dismissed or voluntarily withdrew from this program area were 10.

Admissions Requirements:
Scores: Entries appear in this order: required test or GPA, minimum score (if required), median score of students entering in 2003–2004. Doctoral Programs: overall undergraduate GPA 3.0, 3.30. Because the Wright Institute seeks applicants with significant life accomplishment rather than those who simply test well, GRE scores are not factored into our admissions decision-making process. For research purposes, students are required to take the GRE General Test (which includes the analytic writing section) prior to matriculation.
Other Criteria: (importance of criteria rated low, medium, or high): research experience medium, work experience medium,

extracurricular activity medium, clinically related public service high, GPA medium, letters of recommendation high, interview high, statement of goals and objectives high. For additional information on admission requirements, go to: www. wrightinst.edu/ad/procedures.html.

Student Characteristics: The following represents characteristics of students in 2004–2005 in all graduate psychology programs in the department: Female–full-time 222, part-time 0; Male–full-time 67, part-time 0; African American/Black–full-time 20, part-time 0; Hispanic/Latino(a)–full-time 17, part-time 0; Asian/Pacific Islander–full-time 19, part-time 0; American Indian/Alaska Native–full-time 0, part-time 0; Caucasian–full-time 217, part-time 0; Multi-ethnic–full-time 16, part-time 0; students subject to the Americans With Disabilities Act–full-time 4, part-time 0.

Financial Information/Assistance:
Tuition for Full-Time Study: *Doctoral:* State residents: per academic year $20,800; Nonstate residents: per academic year $20,800. See the following Web site for updates and changes in tuition costs: www.wrightinst.edu/ad/tuition.html.

Financial Assistance:
First Year Students: Research assistantships available for first-year. Average amount paid per academic year: $1,600. Average number of hours worked per week: 4. Apply by open.
Advanced Students: Teaching assistantships available for advanced students. Average amount paid per academic year: $1,700. Average number of hours worked per week: 5. Apply by open. Research assistantships available for advanced students. Average amount paid per academic year: $1,600. Average number of hours worked per week: 4. Apply by open. Fellowships and scholarships available for advanced students. Average amount paid per academic year: $1,500. Apply by December 1.
Contact Information: Of all students currently enrolled full-time, 8% benefitted from one or more of the listed financial assistance programs.

Internships/Practica: The goal of the Wright Institute's field training program, which culminates with the clinical internship, is to enable students to integrate theoretical knowledge with professional clinical experience. Beginning with the first-year practicum, and in conjunction with the weekly case conference/professional development seminar, students learn how to work with a wide range of populations, treatment modalities, and professional roles. The Institute's Field Placement Office furnishes information and support to students in the practicum and internship application and selection processes. Students are encouraged to conduct their internships at APA-approved agencies. Wright Institute students are highly valued by the nation's most well-regarded internship sites, as they are by local Bay Area hospitals, clinics, and community mental health centers. The broad range of internship and practicum sites allows students to receive training in a variety of clinical settings serving the ethnically and culturally diverse populations of the greater Bay Area. The SF Bay Area has an established internship community, most of whom are members of the California Psychology Internship Council (CAPIC). The Board of Psychology in California recognizes a formal internship as a program accredited by the APA or which is a member of or meets the membership requirements of APPIC or CAPIC. Because many of our students are established residents of the SF Bay Area, we allow students to apply to APPIC and

CAPIC member programs. Our students who apply throughout the nation for APA internships are generally successful. For those doctoral students for whom a professional internship is required prior to graduation, 42 applied in 2003–2004. Of those who applied, 17 were placed in internships listed by the Association of Psychology Postdoctoral and Internship Programs (APPIC); 11 were placed in APA accredited internships.

Housing and Day Care: No on-campus housing is available. No on-campus day care facilities are available.

Employment of Department Graduates:

Master's Degree Graduates: Of those who graduated in the academic year 2003–2004, the following categories and numbers represent the post-graduate activities and employment of master's degree graduates: Enrolled in a post-doctoral residency/fellowship (n/a), employed in independent practice (n/a), total from the above (master's) (0).

Doctoral Degree Graduates: Of those who graduated in the academic year 2003–2004, the following categories and numbers represent the post-graduate activities and employment of doctoral degree graduates: Enrolled in a psychology doctoral program (n/a), enrolled in another graduate/professional program (0), enrolled in a post-doctoral residency/fellowship (12), employed in independent practice (2), employed in an academic position at a university (0), employed in an academic position at a 2-year/4-year college (1), employed in other positions at a higher education institution (1), employed in a professional position in a school system (1), employed in business or industry (research/consulting) (0), employed in business or industry (management) (0), employed in a government agency (research) (0), employed in a government agency (professional services) (1), employed in a community mental health/counseling center (11), employed in a hospital/medical center (6), still seeking employment (0), other employment position (0), do not know (0), total from the above (doctoral) (35).

Additional Information:

Orientation, Objectives, and Emphasis of Department: The Wright Institute teaches the scientific knowledge base of clinical psychology, and enriches that learning by exploring the meanings of students' experiences with clients. This unique learning method enables students to formulate and address clinical problems by examining the lenses through which they filter experience. The Institute promotes that educational endeavor by teaching students to think rigorously and critically. The program helps students apply critical thinking skills to three fundamental areas: clinical theory and research, understanding of the self in social context, and appreciation of the interaction between clinician and client. The curriculum at the Institute solidly grounds students in science and research methods, while challenging them to explore the conscious and unconscious ways in which they and their clients influence the creation and direction of therapy. Coursework is integrated with practical experience, providing for the systematic, progressive acquisition of skills and knowledge. Weekly case conferences/professional development seminars, begun in the first year, and continuing over the course of the full three years of residency, provide a rich forum for developing and integrating theory, technique, and reflective judgment. Practica and internship experiences consolidate the applied aspects of theoretical knowledge. Education about the multiple roles of the modern psychologist—clinician, supervisor, consultant and advocate—prepares students for working in fulfilling ways amid the changing realities of the health care field.

Special Facilities or Resources: The Wright Institute is located in a three-story English Tudor-style building which recently underwent a $3.5 million dollar renovation. The building now meets the highest seismic safety standards, is ADA compliant, and has completely new, environmentally sound electrical, plumbing, heating and air-conditioning systems. The Institute operates a well-respected, low-fee, on-site clinic that has been providing community mental health outpatient services for 30 years. Services include intake diagnostic reports, individual, couples and group psychotherapy. Second-year Wright Institute students who are supervised by highly experienced adjunct clinical faculty staff the Clinic. Students also participate in a weekly two-hour training conference. A database is maintained for research on the therapeutic process and related areas. The Institute's library provides free online access to major bibliographic databases including PsycINFO, MEDLINE, ERIC, Digital Dissertations, Lexis-Nexis, Mental Measurements Yearbook, EBSCO and ProQuest selected full-text journals. These online resources are also available to students from their home computers.

Application Information:

Send to: Admissions Director, The Wright Institute, 2728 Durant Avenue, Berkeley, CA 94704. Application available online. URL of online application: www.wrightinst.edu/ad/admissions.html. Students are admitted in the Fall, application deadline January 15. *Fee:* $50.

Colorado School of Professional Psychology

Professional School
555 E. Pikes Peak Avenue
Colorado Springs, CO 80903
Telephone: (719) 442-0505
Fax: (719) 389-0359
E-mail: *forrest@cospp.edu*
Web: *www.cospp.edu*

Department Information:
1998. President: Emory G. Cowan Jr. Number of Faculty: total–full-time 14, part-time 21; women–full-time 5, part-time 9; minority–full-time 1, part-time 1; faculty subject to the Americans With Disabilities Act 1.

Programs and Degrees Offered:
Listed in the following order: Program area, degree type (T if terminal Master's), number awarded 7/03–6/04. Doctor of Psychology PsyD (Doctor of Psychology) 1, Masters in Psychology (new program) MA/MS (Master of Arts/Science) (T) 20.

Student Applications/Admissions:
Student Applications
Doctor of Psychology PsyD (Doctor of Psychology)—Applications 2004–2005, 125. Total applicants accepted 2004–2005, 76. Number enrolled (new admits only) 2004–2005 full-time, 62. Number enrolled (new admits only) 2004–2005 part-time, 0. Openings 2005–2006, 40. The Median number of years required for completion of a degree are 4. The number of students enrolled full and part-time who were dismissed or voluntarily withdrew from this program area were 8. *Masters in Psychology (new program) MA/MS (Master of Arts/Science)*—Number enrolled (new admits only) 2004–2005 part-time 0. Openings 2005–2006, 30. The Median number of years required for completion of a degree are 2.

Admissions Requirements:
Scores: Entries appear in this order: required test or GPA, minimum score (if required), median score of students entering in 2003–2004. Master's Programs: MAT N/A, N/A; overall undergraduate GPA 3.0, N/A; last 2 years GPA 3.0, N/A; psychology GPA 3.0, N/A. Doctoral Programs: MAT N/A, N/A; overall undergraduate GPA 3.0, 3.5; last 2 years GPA 3.0, 3.5; psychology GPA 3.0, 3.5.
Other Criteria: (importance of criteria rated low, medium, or high): GRE/MAT scores low, research experience low, work experience low, extracurricular activity medium, clinically related public service low, GPA medium, letters of recommendation high, interview high, statement of goals and objectives high.

Student Characteristics: The following represents characteristics of students in 2004–2005 in all graduate psychology programs in the department: Female–full-time 116, part-time 0; Male–full-time 34, part-time 0; African American/Black–full-time 1, part-time 0; Hispanic/Latino(a)–full-time 15, part-time 0; Asian/Pa-cific Islander–full-time 5, part-time 0; American Indian/Alaska Native–full-time 0, part-time 0; Caucasian–full-time 129, part-time 0; Multi-ethnic–full-time 0, part-time 0; students subject to the Americans With Disabilities Act–full-time 0, part-time 0.

Financial Information/Assistance:
Tuition for Full-Time Study: *Master's:* State residents: $535 per credit hour; Nonstate residents: $535 per credit hour. *Doctoral:* State residents: $535 per credit hour; Nonstate residents: $535 per credit hour. Tuition is subject to change. See the following Web site for updates and changes in tuition costs: www.cospp.edu.

Financial Assistance:
First Year Students: No information provided.
Advanced Students: No information provided.
Contact Information: Of all students currently enrolled full-time, 0% benefitted from one or more of the listed financial assistance programs.

Internships/Practica: An essential component of graduate training for the clinical PsyD at the Colorado School of Professional Psychology is a 1200-hour-minimum supervised clinical practicum. The practicum provides students an opportunity to apply classroom training and acquire new skills in an outpatient mental health clinic. The practicum experience begins in coordination with the beginning of students' class work experience. An outpatient mental health clinic, the Switzer Counseling Center, is operated by COSPP. Students are provided a wide variety of clinical experiences working with individuals, couples, and families. The practicum experience focuses on assessment, diagnosis, treatment planning, and psychotherapy. Students may qualify to complete a portion of their practicum in other mental health settings. Other settings may provide specific training in areas of clinical concentration. Clinical concentrations include: Health Psychology, Trauma, Foresnsics, Marriage & Family Treatment, and Group Therapy. For those doctoral students for whom a professional internship is required prior to graduation, 13 applied in 2003–2004. Of those who applied, 2 were placed in internships listed by the Association of Psychology Postdoctoral and Internship Programs (APPIC); 2 were placed in APA accredited internships.

Housing and Day Care: No on-campus housing is available. No on-campus day care facilities are available.

Employment of Department Graduates:
Master's Degree Graduates: Of those who graduated in the academic year 2003–2004, the following categories and numbers represent the post-graduate activities and employment of master's degree graduates: Enrolled in a psychology doctoral program (20), enrolled in a post-doctoral residency/fellowship (n/a), employed in independent practice (n/a), other employment position (10), total from the above (master's) (30).
Doctoral Degree Graduates: Of those who graduated in the academic year 2003–2004, the following categories and numbers represent the post-graduate activities and employment of doctoral degree graduates: Enrolled in a psychology doctoral program (n/a),

employed in a government agency (professional services) (1), total from the above (doctoral) (1).

Additional Information:

Orientation, Objectives, and Emphasis of Department: The mission of the Colorado School of Professional Psychology is to provide an ethical, scholarly, and personalized graduate education that prepares individuals for practice in the profession of psychology. In addition to the Clinical Track (with concentrations in Marriage & Family Therapy, Organizational Consulting, Health Psychology, Group Therapy, Forensics, and Trauma), COSPP offers two additional Tracks within the PsyD program: Psychosocial Health (MSW required) and Business & Organizational Leadership.

Special Facilities or Resources: The Switzer Counseling Center is an agency of the Colorado School of Professional Psychology. It provides an on-site supervised training facility for COSPP doctoral students. The Switzer Counseling Center provides low-cost psychotherapy to individuals, couples, and families who have no third party insurance or have limited ability to pay. The Center fills two needs: the need of students to practice their psychotherapy skills and integrate their learning, and the need of the community for low-cost psychotherapy services.

Information for Students With Physical Disabilities: See the following Web site for more information: www.cospp.edu.

Application Information:
Send to: Jean Jones, Registrar, 555 E. Pikes Peak Avenue, Suite 108, Colorado Springs, CO 80903. Application available online. URL of online application: www.cospp.edu. Students are admitted in the Fall, application deadline March 1; Winter, application deadline August 1; Spring, application deadline January 15; Summer, application deadline March 30. There are two Winter terms, one begins in October (application deadline August 1) and one in January (application deadline October 15). Rolling enrollment. *Fee:* $50.

Colorado State University
Department of Psychology
Natural Sciences
200 W. Lake Street
Fort Collins, CO 80523-1876
Telephone: (970) 491-6363
Fax: (970) 491-1032
E-mail: *echavez@lamar.colostate.edu*
Web: *http://www.colostate.edu/Depts/Psychology/graduate*

Department Information:
1962. Chairperson: Ernest L. Chavez. Number of Faculty: total–full-time 28, part-time 9; women–full-time 11, part-time 5; minority–full-time 5, part-time 2.

Programs and Degrees Offered:
Listed in the following order: Program area, degree type (T if terminal Master's), number awarded 7/03–6/04. Counseling PhD (Doctor of Philosophy) 6, I/O PhD (Doctor of Philosophy) 0, Cognitive PhD (Doctor of Philosophy) 0, Applied Social PhD

(Doctor of Philosophy) 0, Behavioral Neuroscience PhD (Doctor of Philosophy) 0.

APA Accreditation: Counseling PhD (Doctor of Philosophy).

Student Applications/Admissions:
Student Applications
Counseling PhD (Doctor of Philosophy)—Applications 2004–2005, 214. Total applicants accepted 2004–2005, 17. Number enrolled (new admits only) 2004–2005 full-time, 8. Total enrolled 2004–2005 full-time, 25, part-time, 11. Openings 2005–2006, 7. The Median number of years required for completion of a degree are 6. The number of students enrolled full and part-time who were dismissed or voluntarily withdrew from this program area were 0. *I/O PhD (Doctor of Philosophy)*—Applications 2004–2005, 62. Total applicants accepted 2004–2005, 8. Number enrolled (new admits only) 2004–2005 full-time, 4. Total enrolled 2004–2005 full-time, 17, part-time, 6. Openings 2005–2006, 5. The Median number of years required for completion of a degree are 6. The number of students enrolled full and part-time who were dismissed or voluntarily withdrew from this program area were 0. *Cognitive PhD (Doctor of Philosophy)*—Applications 2004–2005, 15. Total applicants accepted 2004–2005, 3. Number enrolled (new admits only) 2004–2005 full-time, 0. Openings 2005–2006, 1. The Median number of years required for completion of a degree are 6. The number of students enrolled full and part-time who were dismissed or voluntarily withdrew from this program area were 0. *Applied Social PhD (Doctor of Philosophy)*—Applications 2004–2005, 42. Total applicants accepted 2004–2005, 3. Number enrolled (new admits only) 2004–2005 full-time, 1. Number enrolled (new admits only) 2004–2005 part-time, 0. Openings 2005–2006, 2. The Median number of years required for completion of a degree are 6. The number of students enrolled full and part-time who were dismissed or voluntarily withdrew from this program area were 0. *Behavioral Neuroscience PhD (Doctor of Philosophy)*—Applications 2004–2005, 14. Total applicants accepted 2004–2005, 4. Number enrolled (new admits only) 2004–2005 full-time, 1. Total enrolled 2004–2005 full-time, 4, part-time, 1. Openings 2005–2006, 1. The Median number of years required for completion of a degree are 6. The number of students enrolled full and part-time who were dismissed or voluntarily withdrew from this program area were 0.

Admissions Requirements:
Scores: Entries appear in this order: required test or GPA, minimum score (if required), median score of students entering in 2003–2004. Master's Programs: GRE-V no minimum stated; GRE-Q no minimum stated; GRE-V+Q no minimum stated; GRE-Analytical no minimum stated; overall undergraduate GPA no minimum stated; last 2 years GPA no minimum stated; psychology GPA no minimum stated. Doctoral Programs: GRE-V no minimum stated, 600; GRE-Q no minimum stated, 600; GRE-V+Q no minimum stated, 1200; GRE-Analytical no minimum stated, 600; GRE-Subject(Psych) no minimum stated, 650; overall undergraduate GPA 3.0, 3.7; last 2 years GPA no minimum stated, 3.5; psychology GPA no minimum stated, 3.8. GRE Subject required for Industrial/Organizational Program; optional for all others.
Other Criteria: (importance of criteria rated low, medium, or high): GRE/MAT scores medium, research experience high,

work experience medium, extracurricular activity medium, clinically related public service medium, GPA high, letters of recommendation high, statement of goals and objectives high.

Student Characteristics: The following represents characteristics of students in 2004–2005 in all graduate psychology programs in the department: Female–full-time 48, part-time 12; Male–full-time 19, part-time 6; African American/Black–full-time 1, part-time 0; Hispanic/Latino(a)–full-time 8, part-time 0; Asian/Pacific Islander–full-time 4, part-time 1; American Indian/Alaska Native–full-time 2, part-time 0; Caucasian–full-time 52, part-time 17; Multi-ethnic–full-time 0, part-time 0; students subject to the Americans With Disabilities Act–full-time 0, part-time 0.

Financial Information/Assistance:

Tuition for Full-Time Study: *Master's:* State residents: per academic year $3,386, $188 per credit hour; Nonstate residents: per academic year $14,109, $783 per credit hour. *Doctoral:* State residents: per academic year $3,386, $188 per credit hour; Nonstate residents: per academic year $14,109, $783 per credit hour. Tuition is subject to change. See the following Web site for updates and changes in tuition costs: www.colostate.edu.

Financial Assistance:

First Year Students: Teaching assistantships available for first-year. Average amount paid per academic year: $11,000. Average number of hours worked per week: 20. Apply by January 15. Tuition remission given: full. Research assistantships available for first-year. Average amount paid per academic year: $11,000. Average number of hours worked per week: 20. Apply by January 15. Tuition remission given: full. Fellowships and scholarships available for first-year. Average amount paid per academic year: $1,500. Average number of hours worked per week: 0. Apply by January 15. Tuition remission given: partial.

Advanced Students: Teaching assistantships available for advanced students. Average amount paid per academic year: $11,000. Average number of hours worked per week: 20. Apply by February 1. Tuition remission given: full. Research assistantships available for advanced students. Average amount paid per academic year: $11,000. Average number of hours worked per week: 20. Apply by February 1. Tuition remission given: full. Traineeships available for advanced students. Average amount paid per academic year: $11,000. Average number of hours worked per week: 20. Apply by February 1. Tuition remission given: full. Fellowships and scholarships available for advanced students. Average amount paid per academic year: $1,500. Average number of hours worked per week: 0. Apply by February 1. Tuition remission given: partial.

Contact Information: Of all students currently enrolled full-time, 100% benefitted from one or more of the listed financial assistance programs. Application and information available online at: www.colostate.edu/Depts/Psychology.

Internships/Practica: Completion of a five year excellence award (1998-2003) by the Colorado Commission on Higher Education allowed for the development of health related practica for Counseling students throughout Northern Colorado. The following are examples: oncology clinic, neuropsychology, local community college, primary health care, school districts, and cancer resource center. Industrial Organizational students consult with a variety of businesses throughout the state including: United Airlines, HP, Sun Systems, IBM, microbreweries and hospitals. The Tri

Ethnic Center for Prevention Research (TEC) and the Colorado Injury Control Research Center (CICRC) are a part of the department. TEC was designated a Center of Research and Scholarly Excellence by the University in 1991, 1998 and again in 2004. For those doctoral students for whom a professional internship is required prior to graduation, 11 applied in 2003–2004. Of those who applied, 11 were placed in internships listed by the Association of Psychology Postdoctoral and Internship Programs (APPIC); 11 were placed in APA accredited internships.

Housing and Day Care: On-campus housing is available. See the following Web site for more information: www.colostate.edu. On-campus day care facilities are available.

Employment of Department Graduates:

Master's Degree Graduates: Of those who graduated in the academic year 2003–2004, the following categories and numbers represent the post-graduate activities and employment of master's degree graduates: Enrolled in a post-doctoral residency/fellowship (n/a), employed in independent practice (n/a), total from the above (master's) (0).

Doctoral Degree Graduates: Of those who graduated in the academic year 2003–2004, the following categories and numbers represent the post-graduate activities and employment of doctoral degree graduates: Enrolled in a psychology doctoral program (n/a), enrolled in a post-doctoral residency/fellowship (2), employed in an academic position at a 2-year/4-year college (1), employed in other positions at a higher education institution (0), employed in a professional position in a school system (0), employed in business or industry (research/consulting) (1), employed in a government agency (professional services) (0), employed in a community mental health/counseling center (1), still seeking employment (1), total from the above (doctoral) (6).

Additional Information:

Orientation, Objectives, and Emphasis of Department: Colorado State University offers graduate training leading to the MS and PhD degrees in applied social, behavioral neuroscience, cognitive, counseling and industrial organizational psychology. A core program of study is required of all students in the first years of graduate work to insure a broad and thorough grounding in psychology. Graduate students in applied social, cognitive and behavioral neuroscience areas take positions in academic, research, or government agencies. Industrial/Organizational has opportunities for students to have experiences in selection techniques, occupational health psychology, assessment centers, organizational climate and structure, and consultation. Counseling students are trained in academic and applied skills with opportunities in behavior therapy, group techniques, assessment, outreach, consultation, and supervision. Emphasis is on diversity and breadth. In addition to the adult speciality, a program is available that will lead to a PhD in counseling psychology with advanced courses that deal with children and adolescents.

Special Facilities or Resources: Tri Ethnic Center for Prevention research, a NIDA, CDC and Justice Department funded research center, focuses on adolescent issues such as substance use, violence rural issues, and culturally appropriate prevention strategies. The CICR is currently in Year 4 of a 6 year funding cycle by the CDC, National Center for Injury Prevention and Control. CICR's focus is to address the prevention and control of injuries among rural and under-served populations.

Information for Students With Physical Disabilities: See the following Web site for more information: www.colostate.edu.

Application Information:
Send to: Graduate Admissions Committee, Department of Psychology, Colorado State University, Fort Collins, CO 80526-1876. Application available online. URL of online application: www.colostate.edu/Depts/Psychology. Students are admitted in the Fall, application deadline January 15. Industrial/Organizational - January 1 application deadline. Please note that deadlines are strictly adhered to. *Fee:* $50.

Colorado, University of, at Colorado Springs
Department of Psychology
Letters, Arts, and Sciences
1420 Austin Bluffs Parkway, P.O. Box 7150
Colorado Springs, CO 80933-7150
Telephone: (719) 262-4500
Fax: (719) 262-4166
E-mail: *ddubois@uccs.edu*
Web: *http://www.uccs.edu/psych*

Department Information:
1965. Chairperson: Dr. Robert L. Durham. Number of Faculty: total–full-time 14, part-time 6; women–full-time 7, part-time 3; minority–part-time 2.

Programs and Degrees Offered:
Listed in the following order: Program area, degree type (T if terminal Master's), number awarded 7/03–6/04. Clinical MA/MS (Master of Arts/Science) (T) 8, general experimental MA/MS (Master of Arts/Science) (T) 4, geropsychology PhD (Doctor of Philosophy) 0.

Student Applications/Admissions:
Student Applications
Clinical MA/MS *(Master of Arts/Science)*—Applications 2004–2005, 45. Total applicants accepted 2004–2005, 17. Number enrolled (new admits only) 2004–2005 full-time, 9. Openings 2005–2006, 12. The number of students enrolled full and part-time who were dismissed or voluntarily withdrew from this program area were 1. *General experimental MA/MS (Master of Arts/Science)*—Applications 2004–2005, 17. Total applicants accepted 2004–2005, 11. Number enrolled (new admits only) 2004–2005 full-time, 5. Total enrolled 2004–2005 full-time, 10. Openings 2005–2006, 5. *Geropsychology PhD (Doctor of Philosophy)*—Applications 2004–2005, 15. Total applicants accepted 2004–2005, 6. Number enrolled (new admits only) 2004–2005 full-time, 5. Openings 2005–2006, 3. The number of students enrolled full and part-time who were dismissed or voluntarily withdrew from this program area were 0.

Admissions Requirements:
Scores: Entries appear in this order: required test or GPA, minimum score (if required), median score of students entering in 2003–2004. Master's Programs: GRE-V no minimum stated, 485; GRE-Q no minimum stated, 565; GRE-V+Q no minimum stated, 1050; GRE-Analytical no minimum stated, 630; overall undergraduate GPA 2.75, 3.54. Doctoral Programs: GRE-V TBD, 485; GRE-Q TBD, 565; GRE-V+Q TBD, 1050;

GRE-Analytical TBD, 630; overall undergraduate GPA 2.75, 3.54.

Other Criteria: (importance of criteria rated low, medium, or high): GRE/MAT scores medium, research experience high, work experience low, extracurricular activity medium, clinically related public service high, GPA medium, letters of recommendation high, statement of goals and objectives high. Clinically related public service is not required for experimental.

Student Characteristics: The following represents characteristics of students in 2004–2005 in all graduate psychology programs in the department: Female–full-time 37, part-time 0; Male–full-time 7, part-time 0; African American/Black–full-time 0, part-time 0; Hispanic/Latino(a)–full-time 1, part-time 0; Asian/Pacific Islander–full-time 1, part-time 0; American Indian/Alaska Native–full-time 0, part-time 0; Caucasian–full-time 42, part-time 0; Multi-ethnic–full-time 0, part-time 0; students subject to the Americans With Disabilities Act–full-time 0, part-time 0.

Financial Information/Assistance:
Tuition for Full-Time Study: *Master's:* State residents: $232 per credit hour; Nonstate residents: $915 per credit hour. *Doctoral:* State residents: $232 per credit hour; Nonstate residents: $915 per credit hour. Tuition is subject to change. Tuition costs vary by program. See the following Web site for updates and changes in tuition costs: http://www.uccs.edu/%7Ebursar/site/tuition.htm.

Financial Assistance:
First Year Students: Teaching assistantships available for first-year. Research assistantships available for first-year. Fellowships and scholarships available for first-year.

Advanced Students: Teaching assistantships available for advanced students. Research assistantships available for advanced students. Fellowships and scholarships available for advanced students.

Contact Information: Of all students currently enrolled full-time, 65% benefitted from one or more of the listed financial assistance programs. Application and information available online at: http://www.uccs.edu/%7Efinaidse/index.html.

Internships/Practica: Practicum experiences are completed at the departmental CU Aging Center, the CU Counseling Center, or in community placements under licensed supervision (e.g., school settings, community health centers, state mental health facility, domestic violence center, impatient psychiatric hospital). The goal of these experiences is to expose students to clinical settings, to roles of clinical psychologists, and to begin the development of clinical skills.

Housing and Day Care: On-campus housing is available. See the following Web site for more information: http://web.uccs.edu/housing/. On-campus day care facilities are available. See the following Web site for more information: http://web.uccs.edu/fdc/default.htm.

Employment of Department Graduates:
Master's Degree Graduates: Of those who graduated in the academic year 2003–2004, the following categories and numbers represent the post-graduate activities and employment of master's degree graduates: Enrolled in a post-doctoral residency/fellowship

(n/a), employed in independent practice (n/a), total from the above (master's) (0).

Doctoral Degree Graduates: Of those who graduated in the academic year 2003–2004, the following categories and numbers represent the post-graduate activities and employment of doctoral degree graduates: Enrolled in a psychology doctoral program (n/a), total from the above (doctoral) (0).

Additional Information:

Orientation, Objectives, and Emphasis of Department: The program places special emphasis in general areas of applied clinical practice and general experimental psychology. The training will enable a student to prepare for a doctoral program, teach in community colleges, work under a licensed psychologist in private and public agencies, or work in university counseling centers. A research thesis is required of all students. There is a broad range of faculty research interests including: aging (e.g., psychopathology and psychological treatment of older adults, family dynamics, self-concept development, memory, cognition, and personality), social psychology, psychology and the law, personality, program evaluation, prevention of child abuse, and psychological trauma. Please see our Web site for additional information.

Special Facilities or Resources: Research facilities include clinical training laboratories with observational capabilities, laboratories for individual and small group research, a psychophysiological laboratory, and a computer laboratory. Columbine Hall houses a 50-station computer lab that is available for general use. The CU Aging Center, administered through the Psychology Department, is a community-based nonprofit mental health clinic designed to serve the mental health needs of older adults and their families. The mission of the Center is to provide state-of-the-art psychological assessment and treatment services to older persons and their families, to study psychological aging processes, and to train students in clinical psychology and related disciplines.

Application Information:

Send to: Dr. Hasker P. Davis, Director of Graduate Studies/Psychology Department. Application available online. URL of online application: http://web.uccs.edu/gradschl/app/. Students are admitted in the Fall, application deadline January 1. *Fee:* $60.

Colorado, University of, at Denver, and Health Sciences Center

Department of Psychology
College of Liberal Arts and Sciences
Campus Box 173, P.O. Box 173364
Denver, CO 80217-3364
Telephone: (303) 556-8565
Fax: (303) 556-3520
E-mail: *Allison.Bashe@cudenver.edu*
Web: *http://www.cudenver.edu/Academics/Colleges/CLAS/ Psychology/Degree+Programs/default.htm*

Department Information:

1960. Chairperson: Peter Kaplan, PhD. Number of Faculty: total–full-time 11, part-time 2; women–full-time 4, part-time 1; minority–full-time 2.

Programs and Degrees Offered:

Listed in the following order: Program area, degree type (T if terminal Master's), number awarded 7/03–6/04. Clinical Psychology MA/MS (Master of Arts/Science) (T) 7.

Student Applications/Admissions:

Student Applications

Clinical Psychology MA/MS (Master of Arts/Science)—Applications 2004–2005, 75. Total applicants accepted 2004–2005, 12. Number enrolled (new admits only) 2004–2005 full-time, 11. Number enrolled (new admits only) 2004–2005 part-time, 0. Total enrolled 2004–2005 full-time, 21, part-time, 3. Openings 2005–2006, 12. The Median number of years required for completion of a degree are 2. The number of students enrolled full and part-time who were dismissed or voluntarily withdrew from this program area was 0.

Admissions Requirements:

Scores: Entries appear in this order: required test or GPA, minimum score (if required), median score of students entering in 2003–2004. Master's Programs: GRE-V 500, 525; GRE-Q 500, 615; GRE-V+Q 1000, 1140; overall undergraduate GPA 3.0, 3.65.

Other Criteria: (importance of criteria rated low, medium, or high): GRE/MAT scores high, research experience high, work experience medium, extracurricular activity low, clinically related public service medium, GPA high, letters of recommendation high, interview high, statement of goals and objectives high. For additional information on admission requirements, go to: http://www.cudenver.edu/Academics/Colleges/CLAS/ Psychology/Degree+Programs/MA+Psychology.htm.

Student Characteristics: The following represents characteristics of students in 2004–2005 in all graduate psychology programs in the department: Female–full-time 16, part-time 3; Male–full-time 5, part-time 0; African American/Black–full-time 1, part-time 0; Hispanic/Latino(a)–full-time 1, part-time 0; Caucasian–full-time 18, part-time 3; Multi-ethnic–full-time 1, part-time 0.

Financial Information/Assistance:

Tuition for Full-Time Study: *Master's:* State residents: per academic year $5,032; Nonstate residents: per academic year $16,684. Tuition is subject to change. See the following Web site for updates and changes in tuition costs: www.cudenver.edu/Admissions/Bursar/Tuition/Graduate/Graduate+College+of+Liberal+Arts+and+Scie.

Financial Assistance:

First Year Students: Teaching assistantships available for first-year. Average amount paid per academic year: $5,238. Average number of hours worked per week: 10. Research assistantships available for first-year.

Advanced Students: Teaching assistantships available for advanced students. Average amount paid per academic year: $5,238. Average number of hours worked per week: 10. Research assistantships available for advanced students.

Contact Information: Of all students currently enrolled full-time, 75% benefitted from one or more of the listed financial assistance programs.

Internships/Practica: Internships in community agencies are available. Past students have completed internships at local mental health centers, residential treatment centers, hospitals, and Youth Services Centers (detentions). Funding (in the form of tuition vouchers) is available through the Americorps program. Students have the option of completing a thesis and/or pursuing an internship. Some students elect to complete both because that combination is in their best interests. Students electing the internship option may begin internships after completing the first year of courses. A total of 800 hours of supervised field experience is required for the internship. All field placements are subject to approval of the program director. It is sometimes possible to build the internship into a student's existing job, provided that the work performed is consistent with the objectives and emphasis of the program.

Housing and Day Care: No on-campus housing is available. On-campus day care facilities are available. See the following Web site for more information: http://www.tivoli.org/childcare/index.htm.

Employment of Department Graduates:

Master's Degree Graduates: Of those who graduated in the academic year 2003–2004, the following categories and numbers represent the post-graduate activities and employment of master's degree graduates: Enrolled in a post-doctoral residency/fellowship (n/a), employed in independent practice (n/a), total from the above (master's) (0).

Doctoral Degree Graduates: Of those who graduated in the academic year 2003–2004, the following categories and numbers represent the post-graduate activities and employment of doctoral degree graduates: Enrolled in a psychology doctoral program (n/a), total from the above (doctoral) (0).

Additional Information:

Orientation, Objectives, and Emphasis of Department: The principal objective of the program in clinical psychology is to prepare graduates for doctoral level work. Those graduates who have applied to doctoral programs have typically been admitted to one or more programs. For individuals not interested in pursuing further graduate work, the program offers rigorous training in applied skills such as diagnostic evaluation, psychological assessment of both adults and children, and empirically-based psychotherapy. Students have the option of completing a thesis and/or pursuing an internship. The thesis is an empirical research project culminating in a product suitable for publication or presentation at a professional meeting. Internships may be started following completion of all required course work. Clinical experience with a wide variety of populations in the Denver/Boulder area is available. Our intern applicants have been competitive in obtaining these placements.

Special Facilities or Resources: In July 2004, the University of Colorado, Denver Downtown Campus (our campus) merged with the University of Colorado Health Sciences Center. There are numerous possibilities for research collaborations with faculty at the Health Sciences Center in addition to the faculty members in our own department.

Information for Students With Physical Disabilities: See the following Web site for more information: www.cudenver.edu/Admissions/Registrar/Student+Resources/default.htm.

Application Information:

Send to: Dr. Allison Bashe, Program Director, Department of Psychology, University of Colorado at Denver and HSC, Campus Box 173, P.O. Box 173364, Denver, CO 80217-3364. Application available online. URL of online application: www.cudenver.edu/Admissions/Graduate+Admissions/default.htm. Students are admitted in the Fall, application deadline March 1. *Fee:* $50. International student application fee: $60.00.

Colorado, University of, Boulder
Department of Psychology
Arts and Sciences
Muenzinger D244, UCB 345
Boulder, CO 80309-0345
Telephone: (303) 492-1553
Fax: (303) 492-2967
E-mail: *admissions@psych.colorado.edu*
Web: *http://psych.colorado.edu*

Department Information:

1910. Chairperson: W. Edward Craighead. Number of Faculty: total–full-time 41, part-time 1; women–full-time 15, part-time 1; minority–full-time 7.

Programs and Degrees Offered:

Listed in the following order: Program area, degree type (T if terminal Master's), number awarded 7/03–6/04. Behavioral genetics PhD (Doctor of Philosophy) 1, behavior neuroscience PhD (Doctor of Philosophy) 2, clinical PhD (Doctor of Philosophy) 4, cognitive PhD (Doctor of Philosophy) 4, social PhD (Doctor of Philosophy) 3.

APA Accreditation: Clinical PhD (Doctor of Philosophy).

Student Applications/Admissions:

Student Applications

Behavioral genetics PhD (Doctor of Philosophy)—Applications 2004–2005, 8. Total applicants accepted 2004–2005, 3. Openings 2005–2006, 3. The Median number of years required for completion of a degree are 5. *Behavior neuroscience PhD (Doctor of Philosophy)*—Applications 2004–2005, 43. Total applicants accepted 2004–2005, 5. Number enrolled (new admits only) 2004–2005 full-time, 3. Openings 2005–2006, 3. The Median number of years required for completion of a degree are 6. The number of students enrolled full and part-time who were dismissed or voluntarily withdrew from this program area were 0. *Clinical PhD (Doctor of Philosophy)*—Applications 2004–2005, 145. Total applicants accepted 2004–2005, 6. Number enrolled (new admits only) 2004–2005 full-time, 5. Openings 2005–2006, 4. The Median number of years required for completion of a degree are 6. The number of students enrolled full and part-time who were dismissed or voluntarily withdrew from this program area were 0. *Cognitive PhD (Doctor of Philosophy)*—Applications 2004–2005, 55. Total applicants accepted 2004–2005, 8. Number enrolled (new admits only) 2004–2005 full-time, 4. Total enrolled 2004–2005 full-time, 23. Openings 2005–2006, 4. The Median number of years required for completion of a degree are 7. The number of students enrolled full and part-time who were dismissed or voluntarily withdrew from this program area were 0. *Social PhD (Doctor of Philosophy)*—Applications 2004–2005, 95. Total applicants accepted 2004–2005, 2. Number enrolled (new admits only) 2004–2005 full-time, 2. Openings 2005–2006, 2. The Median number of years required for completion of a degree are 5. The number of students enrolled full and part-time who were dismissed or voluntarily withdrew from this program area was 0.

Admissions Requirements:

Scores: Entries appear in this order: required test or GPA, minimum score (if required), median score of students entering in 2003–2004. Doctoral Programs: GRE-V no minimum stated, 640; GRE-Q no minimum stated, 690; GRE-V+Q no minimum stated, 1330; GRE-Analytical no minimum stated, 700; overall undergraduate GPA no minimum stated, 3.6. GRE Subject test is required for the clinical program, for the other programs it is recommended but not required.

Other Criteria: (importance of criteria rated low, medium, or high): GRE/MAT scores high, research experience high, work experience medium, extracurricular activity medium, clinically related public service medium, GPA high, letters of recommendation high, interview high, statement of goals and objectives high. Clinical work experience is only relevant in clinical program. Research experience is critical to admissions to all programs. For additional information on admission requirements, go to: http://psych.colorado.edu.

Student Characteristics: The following represents characteristics of students in 2004–2005 in all graduate psychology programs in the department: Female–full-time 60, part-time 0; Male–full-time 27, part-time 0; African American/Black–full-time 0, part-time 0; Hispanic/Latino(a)–full-time 5, part-time 0; Asian/Pacific Islander–full-time 5, part-time 0; American Indian/Alaska Native–full-time 2, part-time 0; Caucasian–full-time 74, part-time 0; Multi-ethnic–full-time 1, part-time 0; students subject to the Americans With Disabilities Act–full-time 1, part-time 0.

Financial Information/Assistance:

Tuition for Full-Time Study: *Doctoral:* State residents: $237 per credit hour; Nonstate residents: $1,083 per credit hour. Tuition is subject to change. See the following Web site for updates and changes in tuition costs: http://www.bursar.colorado.edu/.

Financial Assistance:

First Year Students: Teaching assistantships available for first-year. Average amount paid per academic year: $13,650. Average number of hours worked per week: 20. Tuition remission given: full. Research assistantships available for first-year. Average amount paid per academic year: $13,650. Average number of hours worked per week: 20. Tuition remission given: full. Traineeships available for first-year. Average amount paid per academic year: $19,500. Average number of hours worked per week: 20. Tuition remission given: full. Fellowships and scholarships available for first-year.

Advanced Students: Teaching assistantships available for advanced students. Average amount paid per academic year: $13,650. Average number of hours worked per week: 20. Tuition remission given: full. Research assistantships available for advanced students. Average amount paid per academic year: $13,650. Average number of hours worked per week: 20. Tuition remission given: full. Traineeships available for advanced students. Average amount paid per academic year: $19,500. Average number of hours worked per week: 20. Tuition remission given: full. Fellowships and scholarships available for advanced students.

Contact Information: Of all students currently enrolled full-time, 98% benefitted from one or more of the listed financial assistance programs. Application and information available online at: http://psych.colorado.edu.

Internships/Practica: For those doctoral students for whom a professional internship is required prior to graduation, 3 applied in 2003–2004. Of those who applied, 3 were placed in internships listed by the Association of Psychology Postdoctoral and Internship Programs (APPIC); 3 were placed in APA accredited internships.

Housing and Day Care: On-campus housing is available. See the following Web site for more information: http://www-housing.colorado.edu. On-campus day care facilities are available. See the following Web site for more information: http://www-housing.colorado.edu/children/index.html.

Employment of Department Graduates:

Master's Degree Graduates: Of those who graduated in the academic year 2003–2004, the following categories and numbers represent the post-graduate activities and employment of master's degree graduates: Enrolled in a post-doctoral residency/fellowship (n/a), employed in independent practice (n/a), total from the above (master's) (0).

Doctoral Degree Graduates: Of those who graduated in the academic year 2003–2004, the following categories and numbers represent the post-graduate activities and employment of doctoral degree graduates: Enrolled in a psychology doctoral program (n/a), enrolled in a post-doctoral residency/fellowship (17), employed in an academic position at a university (3), employed in other positions at a higher education institution (5), employed in a professional position in a school system (1), employed in business or industry (research/consulting) (2), total from the above (doctoral) (28).

Additional Information:

Orientation, Objectives, and Emphasis of Department: Our emphasis is on training graduate students who have the capability to advance knowledge in the field, and who are committed to applying their knowledge. We emphasize rigorous training in both the theory and methods of psychological research.

Special Facilities or Resources: The department is housed in a large and modern four-story building that contains ample space for offices, a clinic, and research laboratories. There are extensive research facilities available to students, both in individual laboratories and from the department generally. The department maintains its own network of VAX/VMS, Ultrix, Macintosh, and DOS computers used for data collection, data analysis, and manuscript preparation. There is also a departmental laboratory of Macintosh and DOS personal computers for "real-time" research. In addition, numerous laboratories in the department have their own computing capabilities. The facilities of the Institute of Behavioral Genetics, the Institute of Behavioral Science, the Institute of Cognitive Science and the Center for Neuroscience are available to students. Each of these institutes has its own laboratory space and specialized computer facilities. In addition, they attract a number of scholars from other disciplines on the campus.

Application Information:

Send to: Department of Psychology, Muenzinger Psychology Building, UCB 345, Boulder, CO 80309-0345. Application available online.

Students are admitted in the Fall, application deadline December 15. Clinical December 15; others January 1. *Fee:* $50. $60 Foreign Students.

Colorado, University of, Boulder

Educational Psychology Program
School of Education
Campus Box 249
Boulder, CO 80309-0249
Telephone: (303) 492-8399
Fax: (303) 492-7090
E-mail: *Hilda.Borko@Colorado.EDU*

Department Information:
Chairperson: Hilda Borko. Number of Faculty: total–full-time 4; women–full-time 1.

Programs and Degrees Offered:
Listed in the following order: Program area, degree type (T if terminal Master's), number awarded 7/03–6/04. Educational Psychological Studies MA/MS (Master of Arts/Science) 2, Educational Psychological Studies PhD (Doctor of Philosophy) 0.

Student Applications/Admissions:
Student Applications
Educational Psychological Studies MA/MS (Master of Arts/Science)—Applications 2004–2005, 13. Total applicants accepted 2004–2005, 3. Number enrolled (new admits only) 2004–2005 full-time, 2. Total enrolled 2004–2005 full-time, 4. Openings 2005–2006, 10. The Median number of years required for completion of a degree are 4. *Educational Psychological Studies PhD (Doctor of Philosophy)*—Applications 2004–2005, 12. Total applicants accepted 2004–2005, 1. Number enrolled (new admits only) 2004–2005 full-time, 1. Total enrolled 2004–2005 full-time, 10. Openings 2005–2006, 5.

Admissions Requirements:
Scores: Entries appear in this order: required test or GPA, minimum score (if required), median score of students entering in 2003–2004. Master's Programs: overall undergraduate GPA no minimum stated; last 2 years GPA no minimum stated; psychology GPA no minimum stated. Doctoral Programs: overall undergraduate GPA no minimum stated; last 2 years GPA no minimum stated; psychology GPA no minimum stated.
Other Criteria: (importance of criteria rated low, medium, or high): GRE/MAT scores high, research experience medium, work experience medium, extracurricular activity low, GPA high, letters of recommendation high, interview medium, statement of goals and objectives high. Interviews (in person or by phone) are not generally required; however, when scheduled, are helpful in the selection process.

Student Characteristics: The following represents characteristics of students in 2004–2005 in all graduate psychology programs in the department: Female–full-time 11, part-time 0; Male–full-time 3, part-time 0; African American/Black–full-time 0, part-time 0; Hispanic/Latino(a)–full-time 0, part-time 0; Asian/Pacific Islander–full-time 0, part-time 0; American Indian/Alaska Native–full-time 0, part-time 0; Caucasian–full-time 13, part-time 0; Multi-ethnic–full-time 0, part-time 0.

Financial Information/Assistance:
Tuition for Full-Time Study: *Master's:* State residents: per academic year $2,413, $263 per credit hour; Nonstate residents: per academic year $10,354, $1,144 per credit hour. *Doctoral:* State residents: per academic year $2,413, $263 per credit hour; Nonstate residents: per academic year $10,354, $1,144 per credit hour. Tuition is subject to change. See the following Web site for updates and changes in tuition costs: http://bursar.colorado.edu/now/grad.html.

Financial Assistance:
First Year Students: Teaching assistantships available for first-year. Average number of hours worked per week: 10. Apply by February 1. Tuition remission given: full and partial. Research assistantships available for first-year. Average number of hours worked per week: 10. Apply by February 1. Tuition remission given: full and partial. Fellowships and scholarships available for first-year. Average number of hours worked per week: 10. Apply by February 1. Tuition remission given: full and partial.
Advanced Students: Teaching assistantships available for advanced students. Tuition remission given: full and partial. Research assistantships available for advanced students. Tuition remission given: full and partial. Fellowships and scholarships available for advanced students. Tuition remission given: full and partial.
Contact Information: No information provided.

Internships/Practica: Because we do not offer a clinical program, we do not require internships or practica.

Housing and Day Care: On-campus housing is available. See the following Web site for more information: http://www.colorado.edu/GraduateSchool/living.html#housing. No on-campus day care facilities are available.

Employment of Department Graduates:
Master's Degree Graduates: Of those who graduated in the academic year 2003–2004, the following categories and numbers represent the post-graduate activities and employment of master's degree graduates: Enrolled in a post-doctoral residency/fellowship (n/a), employed in independent practice (n/a), total from the above (master's) (0).
Doctoral Degree Graduates: Of those who graduated in the academic year 2003–2004, the following categories and numbers represent the post-graduate activities and employment of doctoral degree graduates: Enrolled in a psychology doctoral program (n/a), total from the above (doctoral) (0).

Additional Information:
Orientation, Objectives, and Emphasis of Department: Within the Educational and Psychological Studies Program, faculty and students collaborate to facilitate the development of research, theory, and professional knowledge with an emphasis on learning and teaching in K–12 educational settings. The Educational and Psychological Studies Program is structured in accordance with a scientist-practitioner model with primary emphasis given to academic study and research. Whether students are preparing for university research and teaching, work in K–12 education, or employment in the private sector, all develop an academic founda-

tion in educational psychology. Onto that base, students and faculty advisors build programs of study that meet both the program goals and the student's interests. (Please note the School of Education does not offer programs in school psychology or counseling.).

Information for Students With Physical Disabilities: See the following Web site for more information: http://www.colorado.edu/disabilityservices/.

Application Information:

Send to: Office of Student Services, School of Education, Campus Box 249, University of Colorado, Boulder, CO 80309-0249. Application available online. URL of online application: http://www.colorado.edu/prospective/graduate/apply/application.html. Students are admitted in the Fall, application deadline February 1. *Fee:* $50.

Denver, University of
Counseling Psychology
College of Education
2450 South Vine Street
Denver, CO 80208
Telephone: (303) 871-2509
Fax: (303) 871-4456
E-mail: *cmcrae@du.edu*
Web: *http://www.du.edu*

Department Information:

1980. Director: Cynthia McRae. Number of Faculty: total–full-time 5, part-time 2; women–full-time 3, part-time 2; minority–full-time 1, part-time 1.

Programs and Degrees Offered:

Listed in the following order: Program area, degree type (T if terminal Master's), number awarded 7/03–6/04. Counseling MA/MS (Master of Arts/Science) (T) 20, counseling psychology PhD (Doctor of Philosophy) 3, educational psychology PhD (Doctor of Philosophy) 3, school psychology PhD (Doctor of Philosophy) 6.

APA Accreditation: Counseling PhD (Doctor of Philosophy).

Student Applications/Admissions:
Student Applications

Counseling MA/MS (Master of Arts/Science)—Applications 2004–2005, 90. Total applicants accepted 2004–2005, 40. Number enrolled (new admits only) 2004–2005 full-time, 23. Number enrolled (new admits only) 2004–2005 part-time, 0. Total enrolled 2004–2005 full-time, 41, part-time, 3. Openings 2005–2006, 22. The Median number of years required for completion of a degree are 2. The number of students enrolled full and part-time who were dismissed or voluntarily withdrew from this program area were 2. *Counseling psychology PhD (Doctor of Philosophy)*—Applications 2004–2005, 80. Total applicants accepted 2004–2005, 12. Number enrolled (new admits only) 2004–2005 full-time, 7. Number enrolled (new admits only) 2004–2005 part-time, 0. Total enrolled 2004–2005 full-time, 20, part-time, 23. Openings 2005–2006, 7. The Median number of years required for completion of a degree are 5.

The number of students enrolled full and part-time who were dismissed or voluntarily withdrew from this program area were 0. *Educational psychology PhD (Doctor of Philosophy)*—Applications 2004–2005, 10. Total enrolled 2004–2005 full-time, 2, part-time, 2. The Median number of years required for completion of a degree are 5. The number of students enrolled full and part-time who were dismissed or voluntarily withdrew from this program area were 0. *School psychology PhD (Doctor of Philosophy)*—Applications 2004–2005, 40. Total applicants accepted 2004–2005, 8. Number enrolled (new admits only) 2004–2005 full-time, 5. Number enrolled (new admits only) 2004–2005 part-time, 1. Total enrolled 2004–2005 full-time, 10, part-time, 2. Openings 2005–2006, 6. The Median number of years required for completion of a degree are 5. The number of students enrolled full and part-time who were dismissed or voluntarily withdrew from this program area was 1.

Admissions Requirements:

Scores: Entries appear in this order: required test or GPA, minimum score (if required), median score of students entering in 2003–2004. Master's Programs: GRE-V 500, 530; GRE-Q 500, 560; GRE-V+Q 1000, 1090; overall undergraduate GPA no minimum stated. Doctoral Programs: GRE-V 550, 575; GRE-Q 550, 617; GRE-V+Q 1100, 1192; overall undergraduate GPA no minimum stated.

Other Criteria: (importance of criteria rated low, medium, or high): GRE/MAT scores medium, research experience high, work experience high, extracurricular activity medium, clinically related public service high, GPA medium, letters of recommendation high, interview high, statement of goals and objectives high.

Student Characteristics: The following represents characteristics of students in 2004–2005 in all graduate psychology programs in the department: Female–full-time 30, part-time 2; Male–full-time 13, part-time 0; African American/Black–full-time 0, part-time 0; Hispanic/Latino(a)–full-time 5, part-time 0; Asian/Pacific Islander–full-time 6, part-time 0; American Indian/Alaska Native–full-time 3, part-time 0; Caucasian–full-time 0, part-time 0; Multi-ethnic–full-time 2, part-time 0; students subject to the Americans With Disabilities Act–full-time 0, part-time 0.

Financial Information/Assistance:

Tuition for Full-Time Study: *Master's:* State residents: $767 per credit hour; Nonstate residents: $767 per credit hour. *Doctoral:* State residents: $767 per credit hour; Nonstate residents: $767 per credit hour. See the following Web site for updates and changes in tuition costs: www.du.edu.

Financial Assistance:

First Year Students: Teaching assistantships available for first-year. Average amount paid per academic year: $4,750. Average number of hours worked per week: 10. Apply by April 1. Tuition remission given: partial. Research assistantships available for first-year. Average amount paid per academic year: $4,750. Average number of hours worked per week: 10. Apply by April 1. Tuition remission given: partial. Fellowships and scholarships available for first-year. Average amount paid per academic year: $3,000. Average number of hours worked per week: 0. Tuition remission given: partial.

Advanced Students: Teaching assistantships available for advanced students. Average amount paid per academic year:

$4,750. Average number of hours worked per week: 10. Apply by April 1. Tuition remission given: partial. Research assistantships available for advanced students. Average amount paid per academic year: $4,750. Average number of hours worked per week: 10. Apply by April 1. Tuition remission given: partial. Fellowships and scholarships available for advanced students. Average amount paid per academic year: $2,000. Average number of hours worked per week: 0. Apply by April 1. Tuition remission given: partial.

Contact Information: Of all students currently enrolled full-time, 75% benefitted from one or more of the listed financial assistance programs.

Internships/Practica: Both Doctoral and Master's students complete practica and internship as well as hours in a campus clinic. Most practica and internships are off campus. Doctoral students must complete APA approved internships (exceptions made in unusual circumstances). Doctoral students have opportunities to complete advanced practica in variety of settings including college counseling centers, hospitals and mental health agencies. MA students complete practica and internships in Denver area including adolescent treatment facilities, mental health centers, womens crisis centers, schools, etc. For those doctoral students for whom a professional internship is required prior to graduation, 9 applied in 2003–2004. Of those who applied, 9 were placed in internships listed by the Association of Psychology Postdoctoral and Internship Programs (APPIC); 9 were placed in APA accredited internships.

Housing and Day Care: On-campus housing is available. Department of Residence (303) 871-2246. On-campus day care facilities are available. Fisher Early Learning Center (303) 871-2723, Department of Residence (303) 871-2246.

Employment of Department Graduates:

Master's Degree Graduates: Of those who graduated in the academic year 2003–2004, the following categories and numbers represent the post-graduate activities and employment of master's degree graduates: Enrolled in a psychology doctoral program (6), enrolled in a post-doctoral residency/fellowship (n/a), employed in independent practice (n/a), employed in an academic position at a university (0), employed in an academic position at a 2-year/4-year college (0), employed in other positions at a higher education institution (2), employed in a professional position in a school system (2), employed in business or industry (research/consulting) (0), employed in business or industry (management) (0), employed in a government agency (research) (0), employed in a government agency (professional services) (0), employed in a community mental health/counseling center (10), total from the above (master's) (20).

Doctoral Degree Graduates: Of those who graduated in the academic year 2003–2004, the following categories and numbers represent the post-graduate activities and employment of doctoral degree graduates: Enrolled in a psychology doctoral program (n/a), employed in independent practice (1), employed in business or industry (research/consulting) (1), employed in a hospital/medical center (1), total from the above (doctoral) (3).

Additional Information:

Orientation, Objectives, and Emphasis of Department: The counseling psychology program at the University of Denver is designed to train counseling psychologists to work with normal populations of adolescents or adults who may be involved in life crises or who need help in making decisions. Counseling psychologists focus on encouraging individuals to understand themselves and their behavior, to develop necessary coping skills, and to solve life problems in light of this understanding and skill development. Life crises such as those that normally occur in the aging process, that is, developing an identity, midlife reevaluation, retirement, and grief or loss, are appropriate areas of concern for the counseling psychologists. They are equally concerned with helping individuals make vocational-educational decisions and take productive action in nuclear groups such as families or couples. They may teach communication or other interpersonal skills, time and stress management, and parenting. They may work in a remedial sense with individuals or groups in crisis or in a developmental, preventative role by providing information and training to prevent crises or more serious mental health problems. In these last two roles, they often function as educators, whether with individuals or with institutions. Although a counseling psychologist may employ some of the same techniques and study some of the same academic disciplines as do clinical psychologists and social workers, the emphasis on the developmental and educational aspects of mental health makes the discipline of counseling psychology unique.

Special Facilities or Resources: PhD students are required to complete a minor in one of two APA-approved clinical psychology programs on campus. Microcomputers and video equipment are available for use in conjunction with coursework. In-house clinic is available. Students are required to spend one evening a week for two quarters in clinic. Intensive supervision provided.

Information for Students With Physical Disabilities: Disability Services Program (303) 871-4333.

Application Information:
Send to: Graduate Studies, Office of Admission, 2199 South University Boulevard, Denver, CO 80208-0302. Application available online. URL of online application: www.du.edu. Students are admitted in the Fall, application deadline January 1. Master's Degree in Counseling applcation deadline is February 1. For the Doctorate in Counseling Psychology, the deadline is January 1. Fee: $50.

Denver, University of
Department of Psychology
Frontier Hall, 2155 South Race Street
Denver, CO 80208
Telephone: (303) 871-3803
Fax: (303) 871-4747
E-mail: info@nova.psy.du.edu
Web: http://www.du.edu/psychology

Department Information:
1952. Chairperson: Ralph J. Roberts. Number of Faculty: total–full-time 17, part-time 2; women–full-time 8, part-time 1; minority–full-time 1, part-time 2.

Programs and Degrees Offered:
Listed in the following order: Program area, degree type (T if terminal Master's), number awarded 7/03–6/04. Clinical Child PhD (Doctor of Philosophy) 4, Developmental PhD (Doctor of

Philosophy) 2, Psychology and the Law MA/MS (Master of Arts/Science) (T) 0, Social PhD (Doctor of Philosophy) 0, Cognitive PhD (Doctor of Philosophy) 2, Developmental Cognitive Neuroscience PhD (Doctor of Philosophy) 4.

APA Accreditation: Clinical PhD (Doctor of Philosophy).

Student Applications/Admissions:

Student Applications

Clinical Child PhD (Doctor of Philosophy)—Applications 2004–2005, 248. Total applicants accepted 2004–2005, 10. Number enrolled (new admits only) 2004–2005 full-time, 5. Openings 2005–2006, 6. The Median number of years required for completion of a degree are 6. The number of students enrolled full and part-time who were dismissed or voluntarily withdrew from this program area were 1. *Developmental PhD (Doctor of Philosophy)*—Applications 2004–2005, 18. Total applicants accepted 2004–2005, 2. Number enrolled (new admits only) 2004–2005 full-time, 0. Openings 2005–2006, 3. The Median number of years required for completion of a degree are 7. The number of students enrolled full and part-time who were dismissed or voluntarily withdrew from this program area were 2. *Psychology and the Law MA/MS (Master of Arts/Science)*—Applications 2004–2005, 4. Total applicants accepted 2004–2005, 1. Number enrolled (new admits only) 2004–2005 full-time, 1. Openings 2005–2006, 2. The Median number of years required for completion of a degree are 2. The number of students enrolled full and part-time who were dismissed or voluntarily withdrew from this program area were 0. *Social PhD (Doctor of Philosophy)*—Applications 2004–2005, 11. Total applicants accepted 2004–2005, 0. Number enrolled (new admits only) 2004–2005 full-time, 0. Total enrolled 2004–2005 full-time, 2. Openings 2005–2006, 3. The number of students enrolled full and part-time who were dismissed or voluntarily withdrew from this program area were 1. *Cognitive PhD (Doctor of Philosophy)*—Applications 2004–2005, 19. Total applicants accepted 2004–2005, 4. Number enrolled (new admits only) 2004–2005 full-time, 2. Total enrolled 2004–2005 full-time, 8. Openings 2005–2006, 4. The Median number of years required for completion of a degree are 6. The number of students enrolled full and part-time who were dismissed or voluntarily withdrew from this program area were 0. *Developmental Cognitive Neuroscience PhD (Doctor of Philosophy)*—Applications 2004–2005, 31. Total applicants accepted 2004–2005, 3. Number enrolled (new admits only) 2004–2005 full-time, 1. Total enrolled 2004–2005 full-time, 16. Openings 2005–2006, 6. The Median number of years required for completion of a degree are 6. The number of students enrolled full and part-time who were dismissed or voluntarily withdrew from this program area were 3.

Admissions Requirements:

Scores: Entries appear in this order: required test or GPA, minimum score (if required), median score of students entering in 2003–2004. Master's Programs: GRE-V 600, 580; GRE-Q 600, 660; GRE-V+Q 1200, 1240; overall undergraduate GPA 3.0, 3.71. Doctoral Programs: GRE-V 600, 580; GRE-Q 600, 650; GRE-V+Q 1200, 1240; overall undergraduate GPA 3.0, 3.71.

Other Criteria: (importance of criteria rated low, medium, or high): GRE/MAT scores high, research experience high, work experience medium, extracurricular activity medium, clinically

related public service high, GPA high, letters of recommendation high, interview high, statement of goals and objectives high. For additional information on admission requirements, go to: www.du.edu/psychology.

Student Characteristics: The following represents characteristics of students in 2004–2005 in all graduate psychology programs in the department: Female–full-time 43, part-time 0; Male–full-time 8, part-time 0; African American/Black–full-time 2, part-time 0; Hispanic/Latino(a)–full-time 4, part-time 0; Asian/Pacific Islander–full-time 5, part-time 0; American Indian/Alaska Native–full-time 0, part-time 0; Caucasian–full-time 39, part-time 0; Multi-ethnic–full-time 1, part-time 0; students subject to the Americans With Disabilities Act–full-time 0, part-time 0.

Financial Information/Assistance:

Tuition for Full-Time Study: *Master's:* State residents: per academic year $21,630, $721 per credit hour; Nonstate residents: per academic year $21,630, $721 per credit hour. *Doctoral:* State residents: per academic year $21,630, $721 per credit hour; Nonstate residents: per academic year $21,630, $721 per credit hour. See the following Web site for updates and changes in tuition costs: www.du.edu.

Financial Assistance:

First Year Students: Teaching assistantships available for first-year. Average amount paid per academic year: $12,000. Average number of hours worked per week: 20. Tuition remission given: full. Research assistantships available for first-year. Average amount paid per academic year: $12,000. Average number of hours worked per week: 20. Tuition remission given: full.

Advanced Students: Teaching assistantships available for advanced students. Average amount paid per academic year: $12,000. Average number of hours worked per week: 20. Tuition remission given: full. Research assistantships available for advanced students. Average amount paid per academic year: $12,000. Average number of hours worked per week: 20. Tuition remission given: full.

Contact Information: Of all students currently enrolled full-time, 100% benefitted from one or more of the listed financial assistance programs.

Internships/Practica: The department offers two clinical training facilities: the Child Study Center and the Neuropsychology Clinic. Both provide training in assessment and psychotherapy with children, families, and adults. Clinical students in their third or fourth year often do clinical placements in the community, such as local hospitals, day treatment programs, and other community agencies. Students in the Developmental Cognitive Neuroscience program attend neuropsychology rounds at a local rehab center and intern in the department's Neuropsychology Clinic. Practica in neuroimaging and research with abnormal populations are also provided. For those doctoral students for whom a professional internship is required prior to graduation, 5 applied in 2003–2004. Of those who applied, 5 were placed in internships listed by the Association of Psychology Postdoctoral and Internship Programs (APPIC); 5 were placed in APA accredited internships.

Housing and Day Care: On-campus housing is available. Contact Department of Residence (303) 871-2246. On-campus day care facilities are available. Contact Fisher Early Learning Center (303) 871-2723 for more information.

Employment of Department Graduates:

Master's Degree Graduates: Of those who graduated in the academic year 2003–2004, the following categories and numbers represent the post-graduate activities and employment of master's degree graduates: Enrolled in a post-doctoral residency/fellowship (n/a), employed in independent practice (n/a), total from the above (master's) (0).

Doctoral Degree Graduates: Of those who graduated in the academic year 2003–2004, the following categories and numbers represent the post-graduate activities and employment of doctoral degree graduates: Enrolled in a psychology doctoral program (n/a), enrolled in a post-doctoral residency/fellowship (2), employed in independent practice (1), employed in an academic position at a university (3), employed in business or industry (research/consulting) (1), employed in a government agency (research) (1), total from the above (doctoral) (8).

Additional Information:

Orientation, Objectives, and Emphasis of Department: Programs are oriented toward training students to pursue careers in research, teaching, and professional practice. They include Clinical Child, Cognitive, Developmental, and Social, as well as a Developmental Cognitive Neuroscience program that is open to students in any of the other programs and that fosters an interdisciplinary approach to cognitive neuroscience. The department was ranked 2nd in publication impact by the American Psychological Society, ranked 13th in the nation in Developmental Psychology by U.S. News and World Report, and is one of the few APA accredited child clinical programs. The department offers close collaborative relationships between faculty and students, with an emphasis on individualized tutorial relationships. The atmosphere encourages and offers students the freedom to seek out and work with multiple faculty members as fits the student's evolving interests. Our students are successful in publishing in prestigious journals, in winning predoctoral grants, and obtaining their first choice for clinical internships. Situated at the foot of the Rocky Mountains, Denver combines urban culture with readily accessible skiing, hiking, and biking in a climate that has over 300 days of sunshine.

Special Facilities or Resources: Our labs are custom-designed for the kinds of research conducted in our department, including the Center for Marital and Family Studies, the Relationship Center, the Developmental Neuropsychology Center, the Cognitive Psychology Lab, the Reading & Language Lab, the Social Neuroscience Lab, the Center for Infant Development, the Center for the Study of Self and Others, the Perception/Action Lab, The Emotion and Coping Lab, the Traumatic Stress Studies Lab, the Developmental Cognitive Neuroscience (DCN) Lab, and the Psychophysiology Lab. Labs are equipped with computers for controlling the presentation of stimuli and the collection of data. The psychophysiology labs include equipment to measure EDA, ECG, and EMG. The DCN lab includes a high-density electrophysiology system for measuring ERPs and EEGs in infants and young children. In addition, we have a host of conventional laboratory rooms with one-way observation windows and up-to-date audio and video recording equipment. Finally, we are closely partnered with the neuroimaging facilities at the University of Colorado Health Sciences Center, which allow us to conduct fMRI and MEG studies. In addition to research laboratories, the department also maintains its own clinical training facility, the Child Study Center, and it houses a Neuropsychology Clinic. The department enjoys excellent computer facilities. It maintains a local area computer network (LAN) that interconnects over 100 departmental PCs. Many graduate student offices are equipped with at least one PC, and there is a graduate student computer lab with 10 PCs, printers, and scanners. Research subjects are available from undergraduate classes, nearby schools and the university daycare center, and local hospitals and rehab centers for patients with neuropsychological disorders. Classrooms are smart-to-the-seat, allowing Internet access for students' laptops.

Information for Students With Physical Disabilities: See the following Web site for more information: www.du.edu/uds.

Application Information:
Send to: Graduate Studies Office, University of Denver, 2199 S. University Blvd., Denver, CO 80208 (self-addressed envelope is enclosed in application materials). Application available online. URL of online application: www.du.edu/grad. Students are admitted in the Fall, application deadline is December 15 for all programs. *Fee:* $50.

Denver, University of
Graduate School of Professional Psychology
2460 South Vine Street
Denver, CO 80208-3626
Telephone: (303) 871-3873
Fax: (303) 871-7656
E-mail: *gsppinfo@du.edu*
Web: *http://www.du.edu/gspp*

Department Information:
1976. Dean: Dr. Peter Buirski. Number of Faculty: total–full-time 16, part-time 32; women–full-time 8, part-time 19; minority–full-time 5, part-time 2.

Programs and Degrees Offered:
Listed in the following order: Program area, degree type (T if terminal Master's), number awarded 7/03–6/04. PsyD - Clinical Psychology PsyD (Doctor of Psychology) 35, Master of Arts - Forensic Psychology MA/MS (Master of Arts/Science) (T) 18, Master of Arts - International Disaster Psychology MA/MS (Master of Arts/Science) (T).

APA Accreditation: Clinical PsyD (Doctor of Psychology).

Student Applications/Admissions:
Student Applications
PsyD—Clinical Psychology PsyD (Doctor of Psychology)—Applications 2004–2005, 263. Total applicants accepted 2004–2005, 80. Number enrolled (new admits only) 2004–2005 full-time, 39. Openings 2005–2006, 35. The Median number of years required for completion of a degree are 4. The number of students enrolled full and part-time who were dismissed or voluntarily withdrew from this program area were 1. *Master of Arts - Forensic Psychology MA/MS (Master of Arts/Science)—* Applications 2004–2005, 104. Total applicants accepted 2004–2005, 51. Number enrolled (new admits only) 2004–2005 full-time, 27. Openings 2005–2006, 25. The Median number of years required for completion of a degree are 2. The number of students enrolled full and part-time who were

dismissed or voluntarily withdrew from this program area were 0.

Admissions Requirements:

Scores: Entries appear in this order: required test or GPA, minimum score (if required), median score of students entering in 2003–2004. Master's Programs: GRE-V no minimum stated, 550; GRE-Q no minimum stated, 550; GRE-Analytical no minimum stated, 4.5; overall undergraduate GPA no minimum stated, 3.5. GRE-Subject (Psychology) is optional for MA applicants. Doctoral Programs: GRE-V no minimum stated, 550; GRE-Q no minimum stated, 570; GRE-Analytical no minimum stated, 600; overall undergraduate GPA no minimum stated, 3.5. GRE Psychology subject test is optional for PsyD applicants.

Other Criteria: (importance of criteria rated low, medium, or high): GRE/MAT scores high, research experience medium, work experience high, extracurricular activity high, clinically related public service high, GPA high, letters of recommendation high, interview high, statement of goals and objectives high, required essay responses high. For additional information on admission requirements, go to: www.du.edu/gspp.

Student Characteristics: The following represents characteristics of students in 2004–2005 in all graduate psychology programs in the department: Female–full-time 126, part-time 0; Male–full-time 38, part-time 0; African American/Black–full-time 4, part-time 0; Hispanic/Latino(a)–full-time 5, part-time 0; Asian/Pacific Islander–full-time 6, part-time 0; American Indian/Alaska Native–full-time 1, part-time 0; Caucasian–full-time 148, part-time 0; Multi-ethnic–full-time 0, part-time 0.

Financial Information/Assistance:

Tuition for Full-Time Study: *Master's:* State residents: per academic year $27,036, $721 per credit hour; Nonstate residents: per academic year $27,036, $721 per credit hour. *Doctoral:* State residents: per academic year $34,608, $721 per credit hour; Nonstate residents: per academic year $34,608, $721 per credit hour. Tuition is subject to change. See the following Web site for updates and changes in tuition costs: www.du.edu.

Financial Assistance:

First Year Students: Research assistantships available for first-year. Average amount paid per academic year: $2,500. Tuition remission given: partial. Fellowships and scholarships available for first-year. Average amount paid per academic year: $2,500.

Advanced Students: Research assistantships available for advanced students. Average amount paid per academic year: $2,500. Tuition remission given: partial.

Contact Information: Of all students currently enrolled full-time, 45% benefitted from one or more of the listed financial assistance programs.

Internships/Practica: In addition to participation in the APPIC internship match, the GSPP offers an exclusive consortium of internship sites for which appropriate students may apply. For those doctoral students for whom a professional internship is required prior to graduation, 36 applied in 2003–2004. Of those who applied, 34 were placed in internships listed by the Association of Psychology Postdoctoral and Internship Programs (APPIC); 34 were placed in APA accredited internships.

Housing and Day Care: On-campus housing is available. See the following Web site for more information: http://www.du.edu/reslife/. On-campus day care facilities are available.

Employment of Department Graduates:

Master's Degree Graduates: Of those who graduated in the academic year 2003–2004, the following categories and numbers represent the post-graduate activities and employment of master's degree graduates: Enrolled in a post-doctoral residency/fellowship (n/a), employed in independent practice (n/a), total from the above (master's) (0).

Doctoral Degree Graduates: Of those who graduated in the academic year 2003–2004, the following categories and numbers represent the post-graduate activities and employment of doctoral degree graduates: Enrolled in a psychology doctoral program (n/a), total from the above (doctoral) (0).

Additional Information:

Orientation, Objectives, and Emphasis of Department: The Graduate School of Professional Psychology focuses on scientifically based training for applied professional work rather than on the more traditional academic-scientific approach to clinical training. In addition to the basic clinical curriculum, special emphases are available in several areas. Our students should have a probing, questioning stance toward human problems and, therefore, should be (1) knowledgeable about intra- and interpersonal theories, including assessment and intervention, (2) conversant with relevant issues and techniques in research, (3) sensitive to self and to interpersonal interactions as primary clinical tools, (4) skilled in assessing and effectively intervening in human problems, (5) able to assess effectiveness of outcomes, and (6) aware of current professional and ethical issues. To these ends the programs focus on major social and psychological theories; research training directed toward the consumer rather than the producer of research; technical knowledge of assessment; and intervention in problems involving individuals, families, groups, and institutional systems. Strong emphasis is placed on practicum training. There are no requirements for empirical research output. The Master's degree in Forensic Psychology supplements graduate-level clinical training with course work and practicum experiences in the legal, criminal justice, and law enforcement systems. The Master's degree in International Disaster psychology supplements graduate-level clinical training with coursework and practicum experiences in trauma, community building, and international field experience.

Special Facilities or Resources: The program offers its own in-house community psychological services center, and varied opportunities are available in many community facilities for the required practicum experiences.

Information for Students With Physical Disabilities: See the following Web site for more information: www.du.edu/gspp.

Application Information:

Send to: University of Denver, Graduate Admissions Office #216, 2197 S. University Blvd., Denver, CO 80208. Application available online. URL of online application: www.du.edu/gspp. Students are admitted in the Fall, application deadline January. *Fee:* $50.

Northern Colorado, University of
Division of Professional Psychology
College of Education
501 20th Street
Greeley, CO 80639
Telephone: (970) 351-2731
Fax: (970) 351-2625
E-mail: *david.gonzalez@unco.edu*
Web: *http://www.unco.edu/coe/ppsy*

Department Information:
1911. Division Director: David M. Gonzalez. Number of Faculty: total–full-time 14, part-time 5; women–full-time 8, part-time 3; minority–full-time 2.

Programs and Degrees Offered:
Listed in the following order: Program area, degree type (T if terminal Master's), number awarded 7/03–6/04. School Counseling MA/MS (Master of Arts/Science) (T) 18, Community Counseling MA/MS (Master of Arts/Science) (T) 70, Community Counseling Marriage MA/MS (Master of Arts/Science) 7, School Psychology EdS (Education Specialist) 31, Counseling Psychology PsyD (Doctor of Psychology) 6, School Psychology PhD (Doctor of Philosophy) 5, Counselor Education & Supervision PhD (Doctor of Philosophy) 0.

APA Accreditation: Counseling PsyD (Doctor of Psychology). School PhD (Doctor of Philosophy).

Student Applications/Admissions:
Student Applications
School Counseling MA/MS (Master of Arts/Science)—Applications 2004–2005, 73. Total applicants accepted 2004–2005, 32. Number enrolled (new admits only) 2004–2005 full-time, 19. Total enrolled 2004–2005 full-time, 65, part-time, 2. Openings 2005–2006, 25. The Median number of years required for completion of a degree are 2. The number of students enrolled full and part-time who were dismissed or voluntarily withdrew from this program area were 0. *Community Counseling MA/MS (Master of Arts/Science)*—Applications 2004–2005, 110. Total applicants accepted 2004–2005, 47. Number enrolled (new admits only) 2004–2005 full-time 45. Total enrolled 2004–2005 full-time, 104, part-time, 19. Openings 2005–2006, 45. The Median number of years required for completion of a degree are 2. The number of students enrolled full and part-time who were dismissed or voluntarily withdrew from this program area were 0. *Community Counseling Marriage MA/MS (Master of Arts/Science)*—Applications 2004–2005, 34. Total applicants accepted 2004–2005, 13. Number enrolled (new admits only) 2004–2005 full-time, 15. Total enrolled 2004–2005 full-time, 34, part-time, 5. Openings 2005–2006, 30. The Median number of years required for completion of a degree are 2. The number of students enrolled full and part-time who were dismissed or voluntarily withdrew from this program area were 0. *School Psychology EdS (Education Specialist)*—Applications 2004–2005, 35. Total applicants accepted 2004–2005, 22. Number enrolled (new admits only) 2004–2005 full-time, 15. Total enrolled 2004–2005 full-time, 58, part-time, 6. Openings 2005–2006, 15. The Median number of years required for completion of a degree are 3. The number

of students enrolled full and part-time who were dismissed or voluntarily withdrew from this program area were 0. *Counseling Psychology PsyD (Doctor of Psychology)*—Applications 2004–2005, 22. Total applicants accepted 2004–2005, 7. Number enrolled (new admits only) 2004–2005 full-time, 7. Total enrolled 2004–2005 full-time, 26, part-time, 3. Openings 2005–2006, 7. The Median number of years required for completion of a degree are 4.5. The number of students enrolled full and part-time who were dismissed or voluntarily withdrew from this program area were 1. *School Psychology PhD (Doctor of Philosophy)*—Applications 2004–2005, 31. Total applicants accepted 2004–2005, 9. Number enrolled (new admits only) 2004–2005 full-time, 9. Total enrolled 2004–2005 full-time, 27, part-time, 1. Openings 2005–2006, 8. The Median number of years required for completion of a degree are 6. The number of students enrolled full and part-time who were dismissed or voluntarily withdrew from this program area were 2. *Counselor Education & Supervision PhD (Doctor of Philosophy)*—Applications 2004–2005, 13. Total applicants accepted 2004–2005, 10. Number enrolled (new admits only) 2004–2005 full-time, 6. Number enrolled (new admits only) 2004–2005 part-time, 0. Openings 2005–2006, 8. The Median number of years required for completion of a degree are 5. The number of students enrolled full and part-time who were dismissed or voluntarily withdrew from this program area were 2.

Admissions Requirements:
Scores: Entries appear in this order: required test or GPA, minimum score (if required), median score of students entering in 2003–2004. Master's Programs: overall undergraduate GPA 3.0; last 2 years GPA 3.0. GRE's are required for master's degree applicants with a GPA lower than 3.0 (1000 GRE V & Q total) Doctoral Programs: GRE-V 500, 600; GRE-Q 500, 600; GRE-V+Q 1000, 1200; GRE-Analytical 3.5, 4.5; last 2 years GPA 3.5, 3.7.
Other Criteria: (importance of criteria rated low, medium, or high): GRE/MAT scores high, research experience medium, work experience high, extracurricular activity low, clinically related public service medium, GPA high, letters of recommendation high, interview high, statement of goals and objectives high, Research experience is of low importance for the master's degree programs, but of medium importance for the other programs.

Student Characteristics: The following represents characteristics of students in 2004–2005 in all graduate psychology programs in the department: Female–full-time 300, part-time 0; Male–full-time 67, part-time 0; African American/Black–full-time 1, part-time 0; Hispanic/Latino(a)–full-time 6, part-time 0; Asian/Pacific Islander–full-time 12, part-time 0; American Indian/Alaska Native–full-time 3, part-time 0; Caucasian–full-time 345, part-time 0; students subject to the Americans With Disabilities Act–full-time 2, part-time 0.

Financial Information/Assistance:
Tuition for Full-Time Study: *Master's:* State residents: per academic year $3,360, $168 per credit hour; Nonstate residents: per academic year $12,520, $689 per credit hour. *Doctoral:* State residents: per academic year $3,360, $168 per credit hour; Nonstate residents: per academic year $12,520, $689 per credit hour.

Financial Assistance:

First Year Students: Research assistantships available for first-year. Average amount paid per academic year: $6,000. Average number of hours worked per week: 8. Apply by April 15. Tuition remission given: partial. Fellowships and scholarships available for first-year. Average amount paid per academic year: $1,500. Apply by April 15. Tuition remission given: partial.

Advanced Students: Teaching assistantships available for advanced students. Average amount paid per academic year: $2,000. Apply by Variable. Research assistantships available for advanced students. Average amount paid per academic year: $6,000. Average number of hours worked per week: 8. Apply by April 15. Tuition remission given: partial. Fellowships and scholarships available for advanced students. Average amount paid per academic year: $1,500. Apply by Variable. Tuition remission given: partial.

Contact Information: Of all students currently enrolled full-time, 80% benefitted from one or more of the listed financial assistance programs.

Internships/Practica: Master's and doctoral practica take place within our in-house clinic. Master's internships are in mental health agencies or schools. Doctoral internships are APPIC and/or APA accredited. For those doctoral students for whom a professional internship is required prior to graduation, 5 applied in 2003–2004. Of those who applied, 5 were placed in internships listed by the Association of Psychology Postdoctoral and Internship Programs (APPIC); 4 were placed in APA accredited internships.

Housing and Day Care: On-campus housing is available. Go to UNC Web page, then type housing@unco.edu. No on-campus day care facilities are available.

Employment of Department Graduates:

Master's Degree Graduates: Of those who graduated in the academic year 2003–2004, the following categories and numbers represent the post-graduate activities and employment of master's degree graduates: Enrolled in a post-doctoral residency/fellowship (n/a), employed in independent practice (n/a), total from the above (master's) (0).

Doctoral Degree Graduates: Of those who graduated in the academic year 2003–2004, the following categories and numbers represent the post-graduate activities and employment of doctoral degree graduates: Enrolled in a psychology doctoral program (n/a), enrolled in a post-doctoral residency/fellowship (1), employed in independent practice (6), employed in an academic position at a university (2), employed in a professional position in a school system (12), employed in a community mental health/counseling center (4), total from the above (doctoral) (25).

Additional Information:

Orientation, Objectives, and Emphasis of Department: The Division of Professional Psychology offers graduate programs in the fields of counseling and school psychology that prepare students for careers in schools, community agencies, industry, higher education, and private practice. The division offers professional psychological services to the university and the local community through its clinic, a research and training facility. The school psychology program is based on the scientist-practitioner model of training (called a Data-Based Ecological Interventionist) and focuses on the interaction of content knowledge, process and assessment skills, the educational and community context, and research. The counseling psychology programs are based on the practitioner model of training and focus on content knowledge, the educational and community context, therapeutic skills, and their interaction. Students can be part of a cluster of outstanding psychology training programs. All programs are nestled within the Division of Professional Psychology with training in counseling psychology, school psychology, counselor education, school counseling, community counseling, and family therapy. Students have the opportunity to pursue elective coursework in any or all of these areas.

Special Facilities or Resources: The division maintains a laboratory facility for use by the counseling and school psychology programs. This facility is built around a central observation area, from which eight counseling rooms, five testing rooms, one neuropsychology lab, and three play therapy rooms can be observed and videotaped through one-way windows. All are furnished appropriately for the specific functions of each. All rooms are equipped with ceiling-mounted microphones with the observation area for each room supplied with an amplifier and earphone jacks. Several observation areas are also equipped with speakers. The main university library has provided excellent support for the professional psychology programs. Sufficient funding is provided annually for the purchase of relevant books, tapes, microforms, and microfiche. The journal collection is also updated annually, and facilities are available for several types of computer literature searches. Additionally, funding is available for purchasing tests listed in the Mental Measurements Yearbook.

Information for Students With Physical Disabilities: See the following Web site for more information: www.unco.edu/dac/dac.html.

Application Information:
Send to: Admissions Secretary, Division of Professional Psychology, University of Northern Colorado, Greeley, CO 80639. Application available online. URL of online application: www.unco.edu/coe/ppsy/. Students are admitted in the Fall, application deadline (see below). Counseling Psychology, PsyD December 15; School Psychology, EdS and PhD December 15; Counselor Education PhD January 1; Community Counseling and Marriage/Family, School Counseling, MA degrees February 1. *Fee:* $50. Fee is for the Graduate School Application Process.

Northern Colorado, University of (2004 data)
Educational Psychology
518 McKee
Greeley, CO 80639
Telephone: (970) 351-2807
Fax: (970) 351-1622
E-mail: *randy.lennon@unco.edu*

Department Information:
1982. Chairperson: Dr. Randy Lennon. Number of Faculty: total–full-time 7, part-time 4; women–full-time 3, part-time 4; faculty subject to the Americans With Disabilities Act 1.

Programs and Degrees Offered:

Listed in the following order: Program area, degree type (T if terminal Master's), number awarded 7/03–6/04. Educational PhD (Doctor of Philosophy) 7.

Student Applications/Admissions:

Student Applications

Educational PhD (Doctor of Philosophy)—Applications 2004–2005, 18. Total applicants accepted 2004–2005, 3. Total enrolled 2004–2005 full-time, 35. Openings 2005–2006, 8. The number of students enrolled full and part-time who were dismissed or voluntarily withdrew from this program area were 0.

Admissions Requirements:

Scores: Entries appear in this order: required test or GPA, minimum score (if required), median score of students entering in 2003–2004. Master's Programs: overall undergraduate GPA 3.0; last 2 years GPA 3.0. Doctoral Programs: GRE-V 550; GRE-Q 550; overall undergraduate GPA 3.0; last 2 years GPA 3.0.

Other Criteria: (importance of criteria rated low, medium, or high): GRE/MAT scores medium, research experience high, work experience low, GPA high, letters of recommendation high, statement of goals and objectives high.

Student Characteristics: The following represents characteristics of students in 2004–2005 in all graduate psychology programs in the department: Female–full-time 8, part-time 1; Male–full-time 8, part-time 12; African American/Black–full-time 1, part-time 0; Hispanic/Latino(a)–full-time 1, part-time 0; Asian/Pacific Islander–full-time 2, part-time 0; American Indian/Alaska Native–full-time 0, part-time 0; Caucasian–full-time 12, part-time 0.

Financial Information/Assistance:

Tuition for Full-Time Study: *Master's:* State residents: per academic year $3,180; Nonstate residents: per academic year $11,080. *Doctoral:* State residents: per academic year $3,180; Nonstate residents: per academic year $11,080.

Financial Assistance:

First Year Students: Teaching assistantships available for first-year. Average amount paid per academic year: $5,280. Average number of hours worked per week: 10. Tuition remission given: partial. Research assistantships available for first-year. Average amount paid per academic year: $5,280. Average number of hours worked per week: 10. Tuition remission given: partial.

Advanced Students: Teaching assistantships available for advanced students. Average amount paid per academic year: $5,280. Average number of hours worked per week: 10. Tuition remission given: partial. Research assistantships available for advanced students. Average amount paid per academic year: $5,280. Average number of hours worked per week: 10. Tuition remission given: partial.

Contact Information: Of all students currently enrolled full-time, 75% benefitted from one or more of the listed financial assistance programs.

Internships/Practica: Student practica are usually set up by the student in a school or related setting.

Housing and Day Care: On-campus housing is available. On-campus day care facilities are available.

Employment of Department Graduates:

Master's Degree Graduates: Of those who graduated in the academic year 2003–2004, the following categories and numbers represent the post-graduate activities and employment of master's degree graduates: Enrolled in a psychology doctoral program (3), enrolled in a post-doctoral residency/fellowship (n/a), employed in independent practice (n/a), total from the above (master's) (3).

Doctoral Degree Graduates: Of those who graduated in the academic year 2003–2004, the following categories and numbers represent the post-graduate activities and employment of doctoral degree graduates: Enrolled in a psychology doctoral program (n/a), enrolled in a post-doctoral residency/fellowship (2), employed in an academic position at a university (4), employed in a professional position in a school system (1), total from the above (doctoral) (7).

Additional Information:

Orientation, Objectives, and Emphasis of Department: The overall goal of both the master's and doctoral programs is to train scholars to undertake original basic and applied research in psychological processes as they apply to education. At the master's level, students take core of educational psychology courses and then concentrate in one of 4 areas: research, measurement and evaluation; human development; learning and cognitive processes; or an individually tailored domain. Master's level courses prepare students for a variety of careers depending on their area of concentration. Graduates may be prepared to design instructional materials in educational and business settings; to serve research, measurement, and evaluation functions in school districts, social agencies, or business organizations; or to serve as consultants in applied developmental settings such as day-care facilities, youth centers, or social agencies. At the doctoral level, students obtain a comprehensive general background in educational psychology and then specialize in one of three areas of emphasis: human development, learning and cognitive processes, or measurement and research. Graduates of the doctoral program are qualified to work as university professors, school consultants, and researchers in government and private agencies and business settings.

Special Facilities or Resources: UNC has been designated as the primary institution for graduate teacher education in the state. The College of Education includes more than 100 faculty members, and provides an excellent institutional environment for its master's and doctoral programs in educational psychology. In addition to the 7 full time educational psychology faculty, students may draw upon the varied expertise of faculty in educational technology, psychology, elementary and secondary education, special education, and applied statistics. The main campus library contains approximately 1.2 million units of hardbound volumes, periodicals, monographs, and government documents and houses the largest collection of educational literature in the state. The Colorado Alliance of Research Libraries provides access to other libraries in the region. The Interdisciplinary Center for Educational Technology provides media support, microcomputers, instructional design assistance, software, and consulting services for both students and faculty. Faculty and students also take advantage of the computer laboratories maintained by the university.

Application Information:

Send to: Graduate School, UNC. Students are admitted in the Fall, application deadline October; Spring, application deadline April.

Deadline for Master's Degree is March 1 and September 15. *Fee:* $35. Graduate School determines conditions for waiver or deferral of fee.

Northern Colorado, University of
Psychology
Arts & Sciences
501 20th Street
Greeley, CO 80639-0001
Telephone: (970) 351-2957
Fax: (970) 351-1103
E-mail: *Cherylynn.Tsikewa@unco.edu*
Web: *http://www.unco.edu/psychology/*

Department Information:
1982. Chairperson: Mark Alcorn. Number of Faculty: total–full-time 14, part-time 1; women–full-time 5.

Programs and Degrees Offered:
Listed in the following order: Program area, degree type (T if terminal Master's), number awarded 7/03–6/04. Human Neuropsychology MA/MS (Master of Arts/Science) (T) 5, General Psychology MA/MS (Master of Arts/Science) (T) 3.

Student Applications/Admissions:
Student Applications
Human Neuropsychology MA/MS (Master of Arts/Science)— Applications 2004–2005, 13. Total applicants accepted 2004–2005, 10. Openings 2005–2006, 5. The Median number of years required for completion of a degree are 2. The number of students enrolled full and part-time who were dismissed or voluntarily withdrew from this program area were 1. *General Psychology MA/MS (Master of Arts/Science)*—Applications 2004–2005, 13. Total applicants accepted 2004–2005, 10. Openings 2005–2006, 5. The Median number of years required for completion of a degree are 2. The number of students enrolled full and part-time who were dismissed or voluntarily withdrew from this program area were 0.

Admissions Requirements:
Scores: Entries appear in this order: required test or GPA, minimum score (if required), median score of students entering in 2003–2004. Master's Programs: overall undergraduate GPA 3.00.
Other Criteria: (importance of criteria rated low, medium, or high): research experience medium, work experience medium, extracurricular activity medium, clinically related public service low, GPA high, letters of recommendation high, statement of goals and objectives high.

Student Characteristics: The following represents characteristics of students in 2004–2005 in all graduate psychology programs in the department: Female–full-time 11, part-time 0; Male–full-time 7, part-time 0; African American/Black–full-time 1, part-time 0; Hispanic/Latino(a)–full-time 0, part-time 0; Asian/Pacific Islander–full-time 1, part-time 0; American Indian/Alaska Native–full-time 0, part-time 0; Caucasian–full-time 14, part-time 0; Multi-ethnic–full-time 0, part-time 0; students subject to the Americans With Disabilities Act–full-time 0, part-time 0.

Financial Information/Assistance:
Tuition for Full-Time Study: *Master's:* State residents: per academic year $3,702; Nonstate residents: per academic year $13,118. Tuition is subject to change. See the following Web site for updates and changes in tuition costs: http://www.unco.edu/acct services/budget/costs.htm.

Financial Assistance:
First Year Students: Research assistantships available for first-year. Average amount paid per academic year: $4,500. Average number of hours worked per week: 9. Apply by March 15. Tuition remission given: partial. Fellowships and scholarships available for first-year. Average amount paid per academic year: $1,200. Average number of hours worked per week: 0. Apply by March 1.
Advanced Students: Teaching assistantships available for advanced students. Average amount paid per academic year: $6,397. Average number of hours worked per week: 11. Apply by Spring. Tuition remission given: partial.
Contact Information: Of all students currently enrolled full-time, 56% benefitted from one or more of the listed financial assistance programs. Application and information available online at: http://www.unco.edu/grad/general/home.htm.

Internships/Practica: Teaching internship: Student learns how to teach at the college level and may conduct an Introductory Psychology class.

Housing and Day Care: On-campus housing is available. See the following Web site for more information: http://housing.unco.edu/. On-campus day care facilities are available. See the following Web site for more information: http://www.unco.edu/.

Employment of Department Graduates:
Master's Degree Graduates: Of those who graduated in the academic year 2003–2004, the following categories and numbers represent the post-graduate activities and employment of master's degree graduates: Enrolled in a psychology doctoral program (3), enrolled in another graduate/professional program (1), enrolled in a post-doctoral residency/fellowship (n/a), employed in independent practice (n/a), employed in an academic position at a university (0), employed in an academic position at a 2-year/4-year college (0), employed in other positions at a higher education institution (0), employed in a professional position in a school system (0), employed in business or industry (research/consulting) (2), employed in business or industry (management) (0), employed in a government agency (research) (0), employed in a government agency (professional services) (1), employed in a community mental health/counseling center (0), employed in a hospital/medical center (0), still seeking employment (0), other employment position (0), total from the above (master's) (7).
Doctoral Degree Graduates: Of those who graduated in the academic year 2003–2004, the following categories and numbers represent the post-graduate activities and employment of doctoral degree graduates: Enrolled in a psychology doctoral program (n/a), enrolled in a post-doctoral residency/fellowship (0), employed in independent practice (0), employed in an academic position at a university (0), employed in an academic position at a 2-year/4-year college (0), employed in other positions at a higher education institution (0), employed in a professional position in a school system (0), employed in business or industry (research/consulting) (0), employed in business or industry (management) (0), em-

ployed in a government agency (research) (0), employed in a government agency (professional services) (0), employed in a community mental health/counseling center (0), employed in a hospital/medical center (0), still seeking employment (0), other employment position (0), total from the above (doctoral) (0).

Additional Information:

Orientation, Objectives, and Emphasis of Department: The goal of psychology is to understand the processes involved in thoughts, actions, feelings, and experiences. To explain these processes, psychologists develop theories which guide hypotheses that are tested scientifically through qualitative and quantitative research methods. This scientific approach is applied by psychologists to the study of humans and other animals. The results of psychological research provide the basis for clinicians and counselors to help people overcome a variety of problems and assist people in achieving their full potential.

Special Facilities or Resources: Physiological Psychology Laboratory Animal Facility.

Information for Students With Physical Disabilities: See the following Web site for more information: http://www.unco.edu/.

Application Information:
Send to: Graduate School, University of Northern Colorado, Greeley, CO 80639. Application available online. Students are admitted in the Fall, application deadline February 15. March 15 for statement of intent to Psychology Department: Graduate Coordinator Psychology Dept., Campus Box 94 University of Northern Colorado, Greeley, CO 80639. *Fee:* $50.

Central Connecticut State University

Department of Psychology
1615 Stanley Street
New Britain, CT 06050-4010
Telephone: (860) 832-3100
Fax: (860) 832-3123
E-mail: *donis@ccsu.edu - waite@ccsu.edu as of 07/01/05*
Web: *http://www.psychology.ccsu.edu*

Department Information:
1967. Chairperson: Bradley Waite. Number of Faculty: total–full-time 19, part-time 22; women–full-time 9, part-time 11; minority–full-time 6, part-time 2.

Programs and Degrees Offered:
Listed in the following order: Program area, degree type (T if terminal Master's), number awarded 7/03–6/04. Community MA/MS (Master of Arts/Science) (T) 2, general MA/MS (Master of Arts/Science) (T) 4, Health MA/MS (Master of Arts/Science) 0.

Student Applications/Admissions:
Student Applications
Community MA/MS (Master of Arts/Science)—Applications 2004–2005, 4. Total applicants accepted 2004–2005, 3. Number enrolled (new admits only) 2004–2005 full-time, 0. Number enrolled (new admits only) 2004–2005 part-time, 0. Openings 2005–2006, 5. The Median number of years required for completion of a degree are 3. *General MA/MS (Master of Arts/Science)*—Applications 2004–2005, 26. Total applicants accepted 2004–2005, 18. Number enrolled (new admits only) 2004–2005 full-time, 9. Number enrolled (new admits only) 2004–2005 part-time, 9. Total enrolled 2004–2005 full-time, 15, part-time, 28. Openings 2005–2006, 10. The Median number of years required for completion of a degree are 5. *Health MA/MS (Master of Arts/Science)*—Applications 2004–2005, 8. Total applicants accepted 2004–2005, 3. Number enrolled (new admits only) 2004–2005 full-time, 1. Number enrolled (new admits only) 2004–2005 part-time, 2. Total enrolled 2004–2005 full-time, 2, part-time, 2. Openings 2005–2006, 7.

Admissions Requirements:
Scores: Entries appear in this order: required test or GPA, minimum score (if required), median score of students entering in 2003–2004. Master's Programs: overall undergraduate GPA 2.75.
Other Criteria: (importance of criteria rated low, medium, or high): research experience medium, work experience medium, extracurricular activity low, clinically related public service medium, GPA high, letters of recommendation high, statement of goals and objectives high.

Student Characteristics: The following represents characteristics of students in 2004–2005 in all graduate psychology programs in the department: Female–full-time 13, part-time 28; Male–full-time 4, part-time 4; African American/Black–full-time 1, part-time 3; Hispanic/Latino(a)–full-time 1, part-time 1; Asian/Pacific Islander–full-time 2, part-time 2; American Indian/Alaska Native–full-time 1, part-time 1; Caucasian–full-time 11, part-time 24; Multi-ethnic–full-time 1, part-time 1.

Financial Information/Assistance:
Tuition for Full-Time Study: *Master's:* State residents: per academic year $1,783, $345 per credit hour; Nonstate residents: per academic year $4,967, $345 per credit hour.

Financial Assistance:
First Year Students: Teaching assistantships available for first-year. Average amount paid per academic year: $2,700. Average number of hours worked per week: 10. Apply by April 25. Tuition remission given: partial.
Advanced Students: Teaching assistantships available for advanced students. Average amount paid per academic year: $2,700. Average number of hours worked per week: 10. Apply by April 25. Tuition remission given: partial.
Contact Information: Of all students currently enrolled full-time, 38% benefitted from one or more of the listed financial assistance programs.

Internships/Practica: We offer a variety of internships. For students in the community specialization, there are internships in prevention-oriented community programs dealing with substance abuse, teen pregnancy, etc. We also offer internships in developmental and counseling areas.

Housing and Day Care: On-campus housing is available. See the following Web site for more information: http://www.ccsu.edu/reslife/. On-campus day care facilities are available.

Employment of Department Graduates:
Master's Degree Graduates: Of those who graduated in the academic year 2003–2004, the following categories and numbers represent the post-graduate activities and employment of master's degree graduates: Enrolled in a post-doctoral residency/fellowship (n/a), employed in independent practice (n/a), total from the above (master's) (0).
Doctoral Degree Graduates: Of those who graduated in the academic year 2003–2004, the following categories and numbers represent the post-graduate activities and employment of doctoral degree graduates: Enrolled in a psychology doctoral program (n/a), total from the above (doctoral) (0).

Additional Information:
Orientation, Objectives, and Emphasis of Department: The psychology department contains 19 faculty members whose interests cover a wide range of psychological areas. Collectively, the orientation of the department is toward applied areas (clinical, community, health, applied, developmental), with generally little emphasis on animal learning/behavior. The specialization in community psychology focuses heavily on primary prevention. The general specialization is intended to expose students to a broad range of applied areas in psychology while the one in health psychology prepares students for careers in the field of health psychology. The three specializations have a strong research emphasis.

Special Facilities or Resources: The psychology department has limited space available for human experimental research. The department has a computer laboratory, and the university has very good computer facilities available for student use. Students may also work on applied research projects with faculty through the Center for Social Research at the University.

Application Information:
Send to: Office of Graduate Admissions, Central CT State University, 1615 Stanley Street, New Britian, CT 06050-4010. Application available online. URL of online application: www.ccsu.edu/grad/admissions. htm. Students are admitted in the Fall, application deadline April 25; Spring, application deadline December 1. *Fee:* $50.

Connecticut College
Department of Psychology
270 Mohegan Avenue
New London, CT 06320
Telephone: (860) 439-2330
Fax: (860) 439-5300
E-mail: *nmmac@conncoll.edu*
Web: *http://www.camel.conncoll.edu/ccacad/psycholgy/ind*

Department Information:
1960. Chairperson: Joan C. Chrisler, PhD. Number of Faculty: total–full-time 10, part-time 2; women–full-time 6, part-time 1.

Programs and Degrees Offered:
Listed in the following order: Program area, degree type (T if terminal Master's), number awarded 7/03–6/04. General MA/MS (Master of Arts/Science) (T) 7.

Student Applications/Admissions:
Student Applications
General MA/MS (Master of Arts/Science)—Applications 2004–2005, 20. Total applicants accepted 2004–2005, 10. Total enrolled 2004–2005 full-time, 4, part-time, 4. Openings 2005–2006, 7. The Median number of years required for completion of a degree are 2. The number of students enrolled full and part-time who were dismissed or voluntarily withdrew from this program area were 0.

Admissions Requirements:
Scores: Entries appear in this order: required test or GPA, minimum score (if required), median score of students entering in 2003–2004. Master's Programs: GRE-Subject(Psych) no minimum stated, 560; overall undergraduate GPA 3.60, 3.52; psychology GPA no minimum stated, 3.70.
Other Criteria: (importance of criteria rated low, medium, or high): GRE/MAT scores medium, research experience high, work experience low, extracurricular activity low, clinically related public service low, GPA high, letters of recommendation high, statement of goals and objectives high.

Student Characteristics: The following represents characteristics of students in 2004–2005 in all graduate psychology programs in the department: Female–full-time 4, part-time 2; Male–full-time 1, part-time 0; African American/Black–full-time 0, part-time 0; Hispanic/Latino(a)–full-time 0, part-time 0; Asian/Pacific Islander–full-time 0, part-time 0; American Indian/Alaska Native–full-time 0, part-time 0; Caucasian–full-time 5, part-time 2; Multiethnic–full-time 0, part-time 0; students subject to the Americans With Disabilities Act–full-time 0, part-time 0.

Financial Information/Assistance:
Tuition for Full-Time Study: *Master's:* State residents: per academic year $9,275, $331 per credit hour; Nonstate residents: per academic year $9,275, $331 per credit hour. Tuition is subject to change.

Financial Assistance:
First Year Students: Fellowships and scholarships available for first-year. Average amount paid per academic year: $3,975. Tuition remission given: partial.
Advanced Students: Fellowships and scholarships available for advanced students. Average amount paid per academic year: $3,975. Tuition remission given: partial.
Contact Information: Of all students currently enrolled full-time, 75% benefitted from one or more of the listed financial assistance programs.

Internships/Practica: The Master's Program offers two types of practicum courses - a research practicum or a clinical practicum. Each of these practicum courses lasts two semesters and requires a commitment of two 8-hour days a week. The research practicum is conducted under the supervision of an experienced scientist (typically a PhD or MD) in a setting outside the Psychology Department. This research is distinct from and in addition to both the student's Master's thesis and any involvement in Connecticut College faculty research. Past examples include research work at Yale University, University of Massachusetts Medical Center, Pfizer Pharmaceuticals Inc., the United States Naval Base in Groton, and Whiting Forensic Institute. The Clinical practicum consists of clinical experience in a variety of modalities and therapeutic settings. All clinical work is conducted under the supervision of experienced clinicians (typically a PhD or licensed MSW). Students perform evaluations, facilitate groups, engage in individual and family therapy, and conduct clinical research, depending upon the type of setting. Students also participate in case conferences, in-services, and research seminars at their settings, as well as a weekly seminar conducted in the Psychology Department. Examples of clinical settings include the West Haven VA Health Psychology Program, Street Francis Hospital, Child Guidance Clinic, Lawrence and Memorial Hospital Adolescent Partial Hospitalization program, University of Massachusetts Medical Center, University of Connecticut Medical Center, Waterford Country School, Rhode Island College Counseling Center, among many others.

Housing and Day Care: No on-campus housing is available. No on-campus day care facilities are available.

Employment of Department Graduates:
Master's Degree Graduates: Of those who graduated in the academic year 2003–2004, the following categories and numbers represent the post-graduate activities and employment of master's degree graduates: Enrolled in a psychology doctoral program (0), enrolled in another graduate/professional program (1), enrolled in a post-doctoral residency/fellowship (n/a), employed in inde-

pendent practice (n/a), employed in other positions at a higher education institution (1), total from the above (master's) (2).

Doctoral Degree Graduates: Of those who graduated in the academic year 2003–2004, the following categories and numbers represent the post-graduate activities and employment of doctoral degree graduates: Enrolled in a psychology doctoral program (n/a), total from the above (doctoral) (0).

Additional Information:

Orientation, Objectives, and Emphasis of Department: The department offers both clinical and research orientations. Concentrations are available in behavioral medicine, clinical, behavioral neuroscience, and personality-social. The faculty is diversified in their theoretical emphases. We provide training in traditional fields of experimental and clinical psychology and in special areas such as behavioral neuroscience, health psychology, environmental psychology, women and gender, behavior analysis, and personality research. The aim of most graduating students is to pursue the PhD, primarily in clinical psychology.

Special Facilities or Resources: In addition to shop and laboratory space for social, physiological, and conditioning and learning psychology, the Psychology Department has one-way observation suites and biofeedback and video equipment. The college's computer is housed in Bill Hall, the home of the Psychology Department, and graduate students have access to the building's computer terminals and microprocessors. Each graduate student is assigned desk space within Bill Hall.

Application Information:

Send to: Nancy M. MacLeod, Academic Assistant, Department of Psychology, Connecticut College #5516, 270 Mohegan Avenue, New London, CT 06320. Students are admitted in the Fall, application deadline February 15. *Fee:* $55.

Connecticut, University of

Department of Educational Psychology
NEAG School of Education
249 Glenbrook Road, Unit 2064
Storrs, CT 06269-2064
Telephone: (860) 486-4031
Fax: (860) 486-0180
E-mail: *reis@uconn.edu*
Web: *http://www.ucc.uconn.edu/~wwwepsy*

Department Information:

1960. Department Head: Sally M. Reis. Number of Faculty: total–full-time 17, part-time 3; women–full-time 7, part-time 1; minority–full-time 1.

Programs and Degrees Offered:

Listed in the following order: Program area, degree type (T if terminal Master's), number awarded 7/03–6/04. School Psychology PhD (Doctor of Philosophy) 9, Counseling Psychology PhD (Doctor of Philosophy) 4, School Psychology EdS (Education Specialist) 6, School Counseling MA/MS (Master of Arts/Science) 7.

APA Accreditation: School PhD (Doctor of Philosophy).

Student Applications/Admissions:

Student Applications

School Psychology PhD (Doctor of Philosophy)—Applications 2004–2005, 41. Total applicants accepted 2004–2005, 3. Number enrolled (new admits only) 2004–2005 full-time 3. Number enrolled (new admits only) 2004–2005 part-time, 0. Total enrolled 2004–2005 full-time, 18, part-time, 7. Openings 2005–2006, 4. The Median number of years required for completion of a degree are 4. The number of students enrolled full and part-time who were dismissed or voluntarily withdrew from this program area were 0. *Counseling Psychology PhD (Doctor of Philosophy)*—Applications 2004–2005, 18. Total applicants accepted 2004–2005, 4. Number enrolled (new admits only) 2004–2005 full-time, 0. Number enrolled (new admits only) 2004–2005 part-time, 2. Total enrolled 2004–2005 full-time, 8, part-time, 3. Openings 2005–2006, 5. The Median number of years required for completion of a degree are 6. The number of students enrolled full and part-time who were dismissed or voluntarily withdrew from this program area were 0. *School Psychology EdS (Education Specialist)*—Applications 2004–2005, 36. Total applicants accepted 2004–2005, 15. Number enrolled (new admits only) 2004–2005 full-time, 9. Number enrolled (new admits only) 2004–2005 part-time, 0. Openings 2005–2006, 6. The Median number of years required for completion of a degree are 3. The number of students enrolled full and part-time who were dismissed or voluntarily withdrew from this program area were 0. *School Counseling MA/MS (Master of Arts/Science)*—Applications 2004–2005, 39. Total applicants accepted 2004–2005, 21. Number enrolled (new admits only) 2004–2005 full-time, 19. Number enrolled (new admits only) 2004–2005 part-time, 2. Total enrolled 2004–2005 full-time, 35, part-time, 55. Openings 2005–2006, 15. The Median number of years required for completion of a degree are 3. The number of students enrolled full and part-time who were dismissed or voluntarily withdrew from this program area were 3.

Admissions Requirements:

Scores: Entries appear in this order: required test or GPA, minimum score (if required), median score of students entering in 2003–2004. Master's Programs: GRE-V no minimum stated; GRE-Q no minimum stated; GRE-V+Q no minimum stated; overall undergraduate GPA no minimum stated. GRE-V and Q required for School Psychology and Cognition & Instruction. Counseling Psychology requires MATs not GREs. Doctoral Programs: GRE-V 540, 573; GRE-Q 600, 630; GRE-V+Q 1150, 1203; overall undergraduate GPA 3.4, 3.5.

Other Criteria: (importance of criteria rated low, medium, or high): GRE/MAT scores high, research experience medium, work experience medium, extracurricular activity low, clinically related public service low, GPA medium, letters of recommendation high, interview high, statement of goals and objectives high. Counseling and School Psychology require interviews.

Student Characteristics: The following represents characteristics of students in 2004–2005 in all graduate psychology programs in the department: Female–full-time 61, part-time 49; Male–full-time 21, part-time 16; African American/Black–full-time 2, part-time 5; Hispanic/Latino(a)–full-time 2, part-time 1; Asian/Pacific Islander–full-time 1, part-time 0; American Indian/Alaska Native–full-time 1, part-time 0; Caucasian–full-time 76, part-time

59; Multi-ethnic–full-time 0, part-time 0; students subject to the Americans With Disabilities Act–full-time 0, part-time 0.

Financial Information/Assistance:

Tuition for Full-Time Study: *Master's:* State residents: per academic year $7,110, $395 per credit hour; Nonstate residents: per academic year $18,478, $1,027 per credit hour. *Doctoral:* State residents: per academic year $7,110, $395 per credit hour; Nonstate residents: per academic year $18,478, $1,027 per credit hour. See the following Web site for updates and changes in tuition costs: http://www.grad.uconn.edu/.

Financial Assistance:

First Year Students: Research assistantships available for first-year. Average amount paid per academic year: $17,220. Average number of hours worked per week: 20. Apply by September 1. Tuition remission given: full. Traineeships available for first-year. Average amount paid per academic year: $17,220. Average number of hours worked per week: 20. Apply by September 1. Tuition remission given: full.

Advanced Students: Research assistantships available for advanced students. Average amount paid per academic year: $18,123. Average number of hours worked per week: 20. Apply by September 1. Tuition remission given: full. Traineeships available for advanced students. Average amount paid per academic year: $18,123. Average number of hours worked per week: 20. Apply by September 1. Tuition remission given: full.

Contact Information: Of all students currently enrolled full-time, 70% benefitted from one or more of the listed financial assistance programs.

Internships/Practica: *Master's:* State residents: per academic year $7,110, $395 per credit hour; Nonstate residents: per academic year $18,478, $1,027 per credit hour is required prior to graduation, 4 applied in 2003–2004.

Housing and Day Care: On-campus housing is available. See the following Web site for more information: http://www.drl.uconn.edu. On-campus day care facilities are available. See the following Web site for more information: Child Development Center (phone: 860 486-2865, or http://www.childlabs.uconn.edu).

Employment of Department Graduates:

Master's Degree Graduates: Of those who graduated in the academic year 2003–2004, the following categories and numbers represent the post-graduate activities and employment of master's degree graduates: Enrolled in a psychology doctoral program (2), enrolled in another graduate/professional program (0), enrolled in a post-doctoral residency/fellowship (n/a), employed in independent practice (n/a), employed in an academic position at a university (0), employed in an academic position at a 2-year/4-year college (0), employed in other positions at a higher education institution (0), employed in a professional position in a school system (17), employed in business or industry (research/consulting) (0), employed in business or industry (management) (0), employed in a government agency (research) (0), employed in a government agency (professional services) (0), employed in a community mental health/counseling center (0), employed in a hospital/medical center (0), still seeking employment (0), other employment position (0), do not know (0), total from the above (master's) (19).

Doctoral Degree Graduates: Of those who graduated in the academic year 2003–2004, the following categories and numbers represent the post-graduate activities and employment of doctoral degree graduates: Enrolled in a psychology doctoral program (n/a), enrolled in another graduate/professional program (0), enrolled in a post-doctoral residency/fellowship (0), employed in independent practice (0), employed in an academic position at a university (1), employed in an academic position at a 2-year/4-year college (0), employed in other positions at a higher education institution (0), employed in a professional position in a school system (8), employed in business or industry (research/consulting) (0), employed in business or industry (management) (0), employed in a government agency (research) (0), employed in a government agency (professional services) (0), employed in a community mental health/counseling center (0), employed in a hospital/medical center (0), still seeking employment (0), other employment position (0), do not know (0), total from the above (doctoral) (9).

Additional Information:

Orientation, Objectives, and Emphasis of Department: The Department of Educational Psychology offers degree programs in the areas of counseling, cognition and instruction, evaluation and measurement, gifted and talented education, instructional media and technology, school psychology and special education at the graduate level and special education at the undergraduate level. The department also offers foundation or service courses for students who are pursuing majors in other disciplines. The department emphasizes the preparation of practitioners who are well grounded in theory to work in public education fields at all levels from elementary school through college and university settings. An equally important commitment has been made to advancing the science of education and expanding the body of knowledge that defines our discipline. To this end, a major portion of departmental activity is directed toward basic and applied research projects. Finally, the department is committed to the improvement of public education through participation in service activities of schools, institutions, agencies and professional organizations.

Special Facilities or Resources: Research space, equipment and/or opportunities exist in the following center/labs: The National Research Center for Gifted and Talented; The Pappanikou Special Education Center; and the University Program for Students with Learning Disabilities; The University of Connecticut Educational Microcomputing Laboratory; The Hartford Professional Development Academy.

Information for Students With Physical Disabilities: See the following Web site for more information: http://www.csd.uconn.edu/policies.html.

Application Information:

Send to: Graduate Admissions, Room 108, Whetten Center Box U-6A, 438 Whitney Road Ext, Storrs, CT 06269. Application available online. Students are admitted in the Winter, application deadline February 15. February 15 deadline for all admissions—Fall admits only. *Fee:* $55. $55.00 for electonic submission $75.00 for paper submission.

Connecticut, University of

Department of Psychology
College of Liberal Arts and Sciences
406 Babbidge Road, Unit 1020
Storrs, CT 06269-1020
Telephone: (860) 486-3515
Fax: (860) 486-2760
E-mail: *clowe@uconnvm.uconn.edu*
Web: *http://web.uconn.edu/psychology/*

Department Information:

1939. Head: Charles A. Lowe. Number of Faculty: total–full-time 53, part-time 4; women–full-time 24, part-time 4; minority–full-time 2, part-time 1.

Programs and Degrees Offered:

Listed in the following order: Program area, degree type (T if terminal Master's), number awarded 7/03–6/04. Behavioral Neuroscience PhD (Doctor of Philosophy) 5, Developmental PhD (Doctor of Philosophy) 1, Clinical PhD (Doctor of Philosophy) 6, Experimental PhD (Doctor of Philosophy) 5, Industrial/Organizational PhD (Doctor of Philosophy) 4, Social PhD (Doctor of Philosophy) 3.

APA Accreditation: Clinical PhD (Doctor of Philosophy).

Student Applications/Admissions:

Student Applications

Behavioral Neuroscience PhD (Doctor of Philosophy)—Applications 2004–2005, 32. Total applicants accepted 2004–2005, 4. Number enrolled (new admits only) 2004–2005 full-time, 1. Openings 2005–2006, 2. The Median number of years required for completion of a degree are 7. The number of students enrolled full and part-time who were dismissed or voluntarily withdrew from this program area were 0. *Developmental PhD (Doctor of Philosophy)*—Applications 2004–2005, 23. Total applicants accepted 2004–2005, 3. Number enrolled (new admits only) 2004–2005 full-time, 1. Number enrolled (new admits only) 2004–2005 part-time, 0. Openings 2005–2006, 4. The Median number of years required for completion of a degree are 8. The number of students enrolled full and part-time who were dismissed or voluntarily withdrew from this program area were 1. *Clinical PhD (Doctor of Philosophy)*—Applications 2004–2005, 233. Total applicants accepted 2004–2005, 13. Number enrolled (new admits only) 2004–2005 full-time, 9. Number enrolled (new admits only) 2004–2005 part-time, 0. Openings 2005–2006, 10. The Median number of years required for completion of a degree are 6. The number of students enrolled full and part-time who were dismissed or voluntarily withdrew from this program area were 0. *Experimental PhD (Doctor of Philosophy)*—Applications 2004–2005, 30. Total applicants accepted 2004–2005, 15. Number enrolled (new admits only) 2004–2005 full-time, 5. Number enrolled (new admits only) 2004–2005 part-time, 1. Total enrolled 2004–2005 full-time, 26, part-time, 1. Openings 2005–2006, 8. The Median number of years required for completion of a degree are 6. *Industrial/Organizational PhD (Doctor of Philosophy)*—Applications 2004–2005, 79. Total applicants accepted 2004–2005, 9. Number enrolled (new admits only) 2004–2005 full-time, 3. Number enrolled (new admits only)

2004–2005 part-time, 0. Openings 2005–2006, 3. The Median number of years required for completion of a degree are 7.25. The number of students enrolled full and part-time who were dismissed or voluntarily withdrew from this program area were 0. *Social PhD (Doctor of Philosophy)*—Applications 2004–2005, 73. Total applicants accepted 2004–2005, 12. Number enrolled (new admits only) 2004–2005 full-time, 6. Number enrolled (new admits only) 2004–2005 part-time, 0. Openings 2005–2006, 5. The Median number of years required for completion of a degree are 6. The number of students enrolled full and part-time who were dismissed or voluntarily withdrew from this program area were 1.

Admissions Requirements:

Scores: Entries appear in this order: required test or GPA, minimum score (if required), median score of students entering in 2003–2004. Doctoral Programs: GRE-V no minimum stated; GRE-Q no minimum stated; GRE-Analytical no minimum stated; overall undergraduate GPA 3.0.

Other Criteria: (importance of criteria rated low, medium, or high): GRE/MAT scores medium, research experience high, work experience low, clinically related public service low, GPA medium, letters of recommendation high, interview medium, statement of goals and objectives high. Check department admissions requirements for specific program areas on the Psychology Dept. Web site. The Clinical Division interviews applicants by invitation only. The clinical interviews are considered to be high in importance of criteria used for offering admission. The Behavioral Neuroscience Division may interview by invitation or by applicant request, however interviews are not required. The Developmental, Experimental, Industrial/Organizational, and Social divisions do not interview applicants as part of the admissions process. For additional information on admission requirements, go to: http://web.uconn.edu/psychology/.

Student Characteristics: The following represents characteristics of students in 2004–2005 in all graduate psychology programs in the department: Female–full-time 103, part-time 0; Male–full-time 56, part-time 1; African American/Black–full-time 7, part-time 0; Hispanic/Latino(a)–full-time 3, part-time 0; Asian/Pacific Islander–full-time 17, part-time 0; American Indian/Alaska Native–full-time 0, part-time 0; Caucasian–full-time 105, part-time 1.

Financial Information/Assistance:

Tuition for Full-Time Study: *Doctoral:* State residents: per academic year $7,524; Nonstate residents: per academic year $19,584. Tuition is subject to change. See the following Web site for updates and changes in tuition costs: http://www.bursar.uconn.edu/html/grad.html.

Financial Assistance:

First Year Students: Teaching assistantships available for first-year. Average amount paid per academic year: $8,278. Average number of hours worked per week: 10. Apply by January 1. Tuition remission given: full. Research assistantships available for first-year. Average amount paid per academic year: $8,278. Average number of hours worked per week: 10. Apply by January 1. Tuition remission given: full. Fellowships and scholarships available for first-year. Average amount paid per academic year:

$2,000. Average number of hours worked per week: 0. Apply by January 1.

Advanced Students: Teaching assistantships available for advanced students. Average amount paid per academic year: $8,668. Average number of hours worked per week: 10. Tuition remission given: full. Research assistantships available for advanced students. Average amount paid per academic year: $8,668. Average number of hours worked per week: 10. Tuition remission given: full. Fellowships and scholarships available for advanced students. Average amount paid per academic year: $2,000. Average number of hours worked per week: 0. Tuition remission given: full.

Contact Information: Of all students currently enrolled full-time, 90% benefitted from one or more of the listed financial assistance programs. Application and information available online at: http://www.financialaid.uconn.edu.

Internships/Practica: For those doctoral students for whom a professional internship is required prior to graduation, 3 applied in 2003–2004. Of those who applied, 3 were placed in internships listed by the Association of Psychology Postdoctoral and Internship Programs (APPIC); 3 were placed in APA accredited internships.

Housing and Day Care: On-campus housing is available. See the following Web site for more information: http://www.grad.uconn.edu/housing.html. On-campus day care facilities are available. See the following Web site for more information: The Child Development Laboratories, which are part of the School of Family Studies, offer full day and half day programs for children from six weeks to six years of age. For information, call the Child Development Labs at 860-486-2865, or check on their website: http://childlabs.uconn.edu/general.html.

Employment of Department Graduates:

Master's Degree Graduates: Of those who graduated in the academic year 2003–2004, the following categories and numbers represent the post-graduate activities and employment of master's degree graduates: Enrolled in a post-doctoral residency/fellowship (n/a), employed in independent practice (n/a), total from the above (master's) (0).

Doctoral Degree Graduates: Of those who graduated in the academic year 2003–2004, the following categories and numbers represent the post-graduate activities and employment of doctoral degree graduates: Enrolled in a psychology doctoral program (n/a), enrolled in a post-doctoral residency/fellowship (5), employed in an academic position at a university (1), employed in an academic position at a 2-year/4-year college (2), employed in business or industry (research/consulting) (4), employed in a community mental health/counseling center (1), not seeking employment (1), do not know (1), total from the above (doctoral) (15).

Additional Information:

Orientation, Objectives, and Emphasis of Department: All programs lead to the PhD in the fields of study of psychology. The areas within psychology are administered by six divisions, some of which have more than one area of concentration: (1) behavioral neuroscience (biopsychology, neuroscience); (2) developmental; (3) clinical; (4) experimental (cognition, ecological psychology, language); (5) industrial/organizational; and (6) social. Students must apply for admission to the psychology department and specify which area of concentration they want to be considered for. Areas of concentration are in close and friendly cooperation; however, they maintain semiautonomy in admission and program development. No single theoretical view dominates the department or any section thereof. While there is thorough training available in the application of psychology, the predominant orientation of the department is in the generation of new ideas through research.

Special Facilities or Resources: Resources include research rooms for individual experiments; computer-based laboratories for research in psycholinguistics, perception, and visual psychophysics. Graduate student computer laboratory; strong LAN and mainframe support with easy Internet access; on-site psychological services clinic; various types of electronic recording equipment; laboratories for comparative and physiological research with avian and mamalian species; laboratories in affiliated research institutions, including Haskins Laboratory in New Haven; psychological clinics/hospitals, mental hospital affiliates; child development laboratories, nursery school, day-care center in the School of Family Studies.

Information for Students With Physical Disabilities: See the following Web site for more information: http::/vm.uconn.edu/~wwwcap.

Application Information:
Send to: University of Connecticut, Graduate School, 438 Whitney Road, Ext., Unit 1006, Storrs, CT 06269-1006. Application available online. URL of online application: http://www.grad.uconn.edu/online.html. Students are admitted in the Fall, application deadline January 1. Clinical division: December 1; Social division and Industrial/Organizational division: December 15; all other divisions: January 1. *Fee:* $75. $55 fee for applications submitted using online application system.

Fairfield University (2004 data)
School and Applied Psychology & Special Education
Graduate School of Education and Allied Professions
Fairfield, CT 06430
Telephone: (203) 254-4000 ext. 2324
Fax: (203) 254-4047
E-mail: *dgeller@fair1.fairfield.edu*

Department Information:
1970. Professor and Chair, Programs in Psychology and Special Ed: Daniel Geller. Number of Faculty: total–full-time 5, part-time 10; women–full-time 3, part-time 5.

Programs and Degrees Offered:
Listed in the following order: Program area, degree type (T if terminal Master's), number awarded 7/03–6/04. School psychology MA/MS (Master of Arts/Science) 13, human services MA/MS (Master of Arts/Science) 24, foundations of advanced psychology MA/MS (Master of Arts/Science) 24, industrial/organizational psychology MA/MS (Master of Arts/Science) 24, personnel psychology MA/MS (Master of Arts/Science) 24.

Student Applications/Admissions:
Student Applications
School psychology MA/MS (Master of Arts/Science)—Applications 2004–2005, 47. Total applicants accepted 2004–2005,

21. Total enrolled 2004–2005 full-time, 21, part-time, 19. *Human services MA/MS (Master of Arts/Science)*—Applications 2004–2005, 51. Total applicants accepted 2004–2005, 36. Total enrolled 2004–2005 full-time, 17, part-time, 44. *Foundations of advanced psychology MA/MS (Master of Arts/Science)*—Applications 2004–2005, 51. Total applicants accepted 2004–2005, 36. Total enrolled 2004–2005 full-time, 17, part-time, 44. *Industrial/organizational psychology MA/MS (Master of Arts/Science)*—Applications 2004–2005, 51. Total applicants accepted 2004–2005, 36. Total enrolled 2004–2005 full-time, 17, part-time, 44. *Personnel psychology MA/MS (Master of Arts/Science)*—Applications 2004–2005, 51. Total applicants accepted 2004–2005, 36. Total enrolled 2004–2005 full-time, 17, part-time, 44.

Admissions Requirements:

Scores: Entries appear in this order: required test or GPA, minimum score (if required), median score of students entering in 2003–2004. Master's Programs: overall undergraduate GPA 2.67. 2.67 for School Psychology; 2.90 other grad psych-minimum

Other Criteria: (importance of criteria rated low, medium, or high): work experience medium, extracurricular activity medium, clinically related public service medium, GPA high, letters of recommendation high, interview high, statement of goals and objectives high.

Student Characteristics: The following represents characteristics of students in 2004–2005 in all graduate psychology programs in the department: Female–full-time 8, part-time 44; Male–full-time 6, part-time 16; African American/Black–full-time 0, part-time 4; Hispanic/Latino(a)–full-time 0, part-time 7; Asian/Pacific Islander–full-time 0, part-time 0; American Indian/Alaska Native–full-time 0, part-time 0; Caucasian–full-time 0, part-time 0.

Financial Information/Assistance:

Tuition for Full-Time Study: *Master's:* State residents: $390 per credit hour; Nonstate residents: $390 per credit hour.

Financial Assistance:

First Year Students: No information provided.
Advanced Students: No information provided.
Contact Information: No information provided.

Internships/Practica: A full year's internship in school psychology offers supervised experience in a school or clinical setting under joint supervision of the faculty and school or agency psychologist. This internship follows the "Field Work in Child Study" requirement, which is a more time-limited experience in school, agency, or mental health clinic settings. The field work in Applied Psychology is also a time limited experience in a psychologically oriented environment. The field work for the I/O program is a time limited experience in a corporate related organization.

Housing and Day Care: No on-campus housing is available. No on-campus day care facilities are available.

Employment of Department Graduates:

Master's Degree Graduates: Of those who graduated in the academic year 2003–2004, the following categories and numbers represent the post-graduate activities and employment of master's degree graduates: Enrolled in a psychology doctoral program (4), enrolled in another graduate/professional program (1), enrolled in a post-doctoral residency/fellowship (n/a), employed in independent practice (n/a), employed in a professional position in a school system (12), employed in business or industry (research/consulting) (15), employed in business or industry (management) (5), employed in a community mental health/counseling center (6), other employment position (6).

Doctoral Degree Graduates: Of those who graduated in the academic year 2003–2004, the following categories and numbers represent the post-graduate activities and employment of doctoral degree graduates: Enrolled in a psychology doctoral program (n/a).

Additional Information:

Orientation, Objectives, and Emphasis of Department: The school psychology program subscribes to the philosophy that students should be broadly educated and trained for a profession that serves people. In order to further the understanding of the complexities of human behavior, there must be an adequate grounding in concepts drawn from psychological science as well as a familiarity with the social and biological conditions that are basic to normal and deviant human development. The program covers a wide range of approaches, introduces students to them, and encourages students to evaluate their own responses from scholarly study and from an examination of themselves. Coursework encompasses the processes of healthy psychological development, interferences in such development, and interventive procedures intended to create a more favorable environment for learning and for improvement of the child's functioning. The Master of Arts program in applied psychology offers courses in psychology, combined with selected courses from other programs and schools of the university, to help prepare students to deal with a range of human problems in business, industry, and the public sector.

Special Facilities or Resources: The faculty have established close working relationships with various settings in which psychological services are provided. Included among these are schools, child guidance clinics, family agencies, and corporations having human resource development services. Research facilities, including an excellent computer center and excellent library, are available.

Application Information:

Students are admitted in the Fall, application deadline May 1; Spring, application deadline September 15; Summer, application deadline January 15. *Fee:* $50.

Hartford, University of
Department of Psychology
Arts & Sciences
200 Bloomfield Avenue
West Hartford, CT 06117
Telephone: (860) 768-4544
Fax: (860) 768-5292
E-mail: *psych@hartford.edu*

Department Information:
1953. Chair: Caryn Christensen, PhD Number of Faculty: total–full-time 12, part-time 25; women–full-time 6, part-time 10; minority–part-time 2.

Programs and Degrees Offered:

Listed in the following order: Program area, degree type (T if terminal Master's), number awarded 7/03–6/04. Clinical Practices in Psychology MA/MS (Master of Arts/Science) (T), General Experimental MA/MS (Master of Arts/Science) (T), School Psychology MA/MS (Master of Arts/Science), Organizational Behavior MA/MS (Master of Arts/Science) (T).

Student Applications/Admissions:

Student Applications

Clinical Practices in Psychology MA/MS (Master of Arts/Science)—Applications 2004–2005, 54. Total applicants accepted 2004–2005, 30. Number enrolled (new admits only) 2004–2005 full-time, 12. Total enrolled 2004–2005 full-time, 24. Openings 2005–2006, 14. The Median number of years required for completion of a degree are 2. *General Experimental MA/MS (Master of Arts/Science)*—Applications 2004–2005, 9. Total applicants accepted 2004–2005, 8. Number enrolled (new admits only) 2004–2005 full-time, 2. Total enrolled 2004–2005 full-time, 12, part-time, 6. Openings 2005–2006, 10. The Median number of years required for completion of a degree are 2. *School Psychology MA/MS (Master of Arts/Science)*—Applications 2004–2005, 31. Total applicants accepted 2004–2005, 16. Number enrolled (new admits only) 2004–2005 full-time, 13. Total enrolled 2004–2005 full-time, 34. Openings 2005–2006, 12. The Median number of years required for completion of a degree are 3. The number of students enrolled full and part-time who were dismissed or voluntarily withdrew from this program area were 0. *Organizational Behavior MA/MS (Master of Arts/Science)*—Applications 2004–2005, 28. Total applicants accepted 2004–2005, 22. Number enrolled (new admits only) 2004–2005 full-time, 19. Total enrolled 2004–2005 full-time, 4, part-time, 27. Openings 2005–2006, 15. The Median number of years required for completion of a degree are 2. The number of students enrolled full and part-time who were dismissed or voluntarily withdrew from this program area were 0.

Admissions Requirements:

Scores: Entries appear in this order: required test or GPA, minimum score (if required), median score of students entering in 2003–2004. Master's Programs: GRE-V no minimum stated, 440; GRE-Q no minimum stated, 500; GRE-V+Q no minimum stated; GRE-Analytical no minimum stated, 520; GRE-Subject(Psych) no minimum stated, 510; overall undergraduate GPA no minimum stated, 3.3; last 2 years GPA no minimum stated; psychology GPA no minimum stated, 3.2.

Other Criteria: (importance of criteria rated low, medium, or high): GRE/MAT scores medium, research experience medium, work experience medium, extracurricular activity low, clinically related public service medium, GPA medium, letters of recommendation high, statement of goals and objectives high.

Student Characteristics: The following represents characteristics of students in 2004–2005 in all graduate psychology programs in the department: Female–full-time 84, part-time 0; Male–full-time 23, part-time 0; African American/Black–full-time 0, part-time 0; Hispanic/Latino(a)–full-time 6, part-time 0; Asian/Pacific Islander–full-time 2, part-time 0; American Indian/Alaska Native–full-time 0, part-time 0; Caucasian–full-time 97, part-time 0; Multi-ethnic–full-time 2, part-time 0.

Financial Information/Assistance:

Tuition for Full-Time Study: Master's: State residents: $350 per credit hour; Nonstate residents: $350 per credit hour.

Financial Assistance:

First Year Students: Teaching assistantships available for first-year. Average amount paid per academic year: $2,550. Average number of hours worked per week: 15. Research assistantships available for first-year. Average amount paid per academic year: $2,000. Average number of hours worked per week: 10.

Advanced Students: Teaching assistantships available for advanced students. Average amount paid per academic year: $2,550. Average number of hours worked per week: 15. Research assistantships available for advanced students. Average amount paid per academic year: $2,000. Average number of hours worked per week: 10.

Contact Information: Of all students currently enrolled full-time, 25% benefitted from one or more of the listed financial assistance programs.

Internships/Practica: All Clinical Practices in Psychology students are assigned a half-time practicum throughout the second year of their academic program. The assignments for practica include mental health clinics, in- and outpatient services in hospitals, community centers, schools, and correctional institutions. Students are supervised both onsite by professional psychologists and at the University by the faculty. All School Psychology students are assigned a half-time practicum throughout their second year in a school setting and a full-time internship in their third year. Students are supervised by school psychologists on site and at the university by the faculty. General Experimental students have an option of a two semester, half-time practicum at a facility in the area of human resources.

Housing and Day Care: No on-campus housing is available. No on-campus day care facilities are available.

Employment of Department Graduates:

Master's Degree Graduates: Of those who graduated in the academic year 2003–2004, the following categories and numbers represent the post-graduate activities and employment of master's degree graduates: Enrolled in a post-doctoral residency/fellowship (n/a), employed in independent practice (n/a), total from the above (master's) (0).

Doctoral Degree Graduates: Of those who graduated in the academic year 2003–2004, the following categories and numbers represent the post-graduate activities and employment of doctoral degree graduates: Enrolled in a psychology doctoral program (n/a), total from the above (doctoral) (0).

Additional Information:

Orientation, Objectives, and Emphasis of Department: The primary orientation of the department in terms of undergraduate training might be best described as eclectic, and the goal is to provide a broadly based foundation in psychology for both the student who will graduate with an undergraduate major and the student who will use the major as a building block for further graduate training in the field. At the level of graduate training, the emphasis varies with the separate programs. The Clinical Practices in Psychology and School Psychology programs tend to be precisely focused in terms of professional preparation at the master's level of training, while the General Experimental program is more broadly based and is viewed as being preparatory to doctoral training.

Application Information:
Send to: Center for Graduate and Adult Academic Services, University of Hartford, 200 Bloomfield Avenue, West Hartford, CT 06117. Students are admitted in the Fall, application deadline February 15. All Programs: review begins February 15. Rolling admissions until filled. *Fee:* $40.

Hartford, University of
Graduate Institute of Professional Psychology
103 Woodland Street, 4th floor
Hartford, CT 06105
Telephone: (203) 520-1151
Fax: (203) 520-1156
E-mail: *viereck@hartford.edu or oppenheim@hartford.edu*
Web: *www.hartford.edu/gipp*

Department Information:
1993. Director: Otto Wahl. Number of Faculty: total–full-time 9, part-time 18; women–full-time 5, part-time 11; minority–full-time 1, part-time 2; faculty subject to the Americans With Disabilities Act 1.

Programs and Degrees Offered:
Listed in the following order: Program area, degree type (T if terminal Master's), number awarded 7/03–6/04. Doctorate in Clinical Psychology PsyD (Doctor of Psychology) 29.

APA Accreditation: Clinical PsyD (Doctor of Psychology).

Student Applications/Admissions:
Student Applications
Doctorate in Clinical Psychology PsyD (Doctor of Psychology)—Applications 2004–2005, 171. Total applicants accepted 2004–2005, 65. Total enrolled 2004–2005 full-time, 170. Openings 2005–2006, 28. The Median number of years required for completion of a degree are 6. The number of students enrolled full and part-time who were dismissed or voluntarily withdrew from this program area were 3.

Admissions Requirements:
Scores: Entries appear in this order: required test or GPA, minimum score (if required), median score of students entering in 2003–2004. Doctoral Programs: GRE-V no minimum stated, 510; GRE-Q no minimum stated, 580; GRE-Analytical no minimum stated, 590; GRE-Subject(Psych) no minimum stated, 610; overall undergraduate GPA no minimum stated, 3.55.
Other Criteria: (importance of criteria rated low, medium, or high): GRE/MAT scores medium, research experience medium, work experience medium, extracurricular activity low, clinically related public service medium, GPA high, letters of recommendation high, interview high, statement of goals and objectives high.

Student Characteristics: The following represents characteristics of students in 2004–2005 in all graduate psychology programs in

the department: Female–full-time 143, part-time 0; Male–full-time 31, part-time 0; African American/Black–full-time 15, part-time 0; Hispanic/Latino(a)–full-time 7, part-time 0; Asian/Pacific Islander–full-time 11, part-time 0; American Indian/Alaska Native–full-time 0, part-time 0; Caucasian–full-time 141, part-time 0; Multi-ethnic–full-time 0, part-time 0; students subject to the Americans With Disabilities Act–full-time 4, part-time 0.

Financial Information/Assistance:
Tuition for Full-Time Study: *Doctoral:* State residents: per academic year $20,500; Nonstate residents: per academic year $20,500. Tuition is subject to change. See the following Web site for updates and changes in tuition costs: uhaweb.hartford.edu/bursar.

Financial Assistance:
First Year Students: Research assistantships available for first-year. Average amount paid per academic year: $3,100. Average number of hours worked per week: 6. Apply by Varies. Fellowships and scholarships available for first-year. Average amount paid per academic year: $2,000. Apply by None.
Advanced Students: Teaching assistantships available for advanced students. Average amount paid per academic year: $5,200. Average number of hours worked per week: 10. Apply by Varies. Research assistantships available for advanced students. Average amount paid per academic year: $3,100. Average number of hours worked per week: 6. Apply by Varies. Fellowships and scholarships available for advanced students. Average amount paid per academic year: $2,000. Apply by None.
Contact Information: Of all students currently enrolled full-time, 61% benefitted from one or more of the listed financial assistance programs. Application and information available online at: www.hartford.edu.

Internships/Practica: Practica network is extensive (approximately 75 sites in 4 states), and includes child, adolescent, and adult placements. Students generally get their first or second choice of sites. Practica placement is coordinated with Professional Practice Seminar (2nd year) and Case Conference Seminar (3rd year) to insure student's clinical training needs are being met. Emphasis is placed upon the concept of "self-in-role" learning. For those doctoral students for whom a professional internship is required prior to graduation, 35 applied in 2003–2004. Of those who applied, 28 were placed in internships listed by the Association of Psychology Postdoctoral and Internship Programs (APPIC); 27 were placed in APA accredited internships.

Housing and Day Care: On-campus housing is available. Only for those who apply to become a resident fellow; generally only 2 positions available. No on-campus day care facilities are available.

Employment of Department Graduates:
Master's Degree Graduates: Of those who graduated in the academic year 2003–2004, the following categories and numbers represent the post-graduate activities and employment of master's degree graduates: Enrolled in a post-doctoral residency/fellowship (n/a), employed in independent practice (n/a), total from the above (master's) (0).
Doctoral Degree Graduates: Of those who graduated in the academic year 2003–2004, the following categories and numbers represent the post-graduate activities and employment of doctoral degree graduates: Enrolled in a psychology doctoral program (n/a),

enrolled in another graduate/professional program (0), enrolled in a post-doctoral residency/fellowship (6), employed in independent practice (1), employed in an academic position at a university (2), employed in an academic position at a 2-year/4-year college (1), employed in other positions at a higher education institution (1), employed in a professional position in a school system (2), employed in business or industry (research/consulting) (0), employed in business or industry (management) (0), employed in a government agency (research) (2), employed in a government agency (professional services) (0), employed in a community mental health/counseling center (4), employed in a hospital/medical center (4), still seeking employment (0), not seeking employment (4), other employment position (1), do not know (19), total from the above (doctoral) (47).

Additional Information:

Orientation, Objectives, and Emphasis of Department: The primary mission of the program is to prepare students for effective functioning in the multiple roles they will need to fill as practicing psychologists in these rapidly changing times. The program also espouses the principle of affirmative diversity, defined as upholding the fundamental values of human differences and the belief that respect for individual and cultural differences enhances and increases the quality of educational and interpersonal experiences.

Special Facilities or Resources: The Graduate Institute added a Child and Adolescent Proficiency Track in the Fall of 2003. The goal of the track is to allow students to develop not only broad clinical skills, but also strong therapeutic, assessment, and program development skills in working specifically with children, adolescents, and families.

Information for Students With Physical Disabilities: See the following Web site for more information: www.hartford.edu/support.

Application Information:
Send to: Center for Graduate and Adult Services, University of Hartford, 200 Bloomfield Avenue, Hartford, CT 06107. Application available online. Students are admitted in the Fall, application deadline January 15. *Fee:* $35.

Hartford, University of (2004 data)
Neuroscience Graduate Masters Program - Department of Biology
Arts & Sciences
200 Bloomfield Avenue
West Hartford, CT 06117
Telephone: (860) 768-5372
Fax: (860) 768-5002
E-mail: *harney@hartford.edu*
Web: *http://uhaweb.hartford.edu/biology/MNeuroscience.h*

Department Information:
1967. Director: Jacob P. Harney, PhD Number of Faculty: total–full-time 7, part-time 5; women–full-time 2, part-time 4; minority–part-time 2.

Programs and Degrees Offered:
Listed in the following order: Program area, degree type (T if terminal Master's), number awarded 7/03–6/04. Neuroscience MA/MS (Master of Arts/Science) (T) 5.

Student Applications/Admissions:
Student Applications
Neuroscience MA/MS (Master of Arts/Science)—Applications 2004–2005, 12. Total applicants accepted 2004–2005, 10. Total enrolled 2004–2005 full-time, 9, part-time, 7. Openings 2005–2006, 10. The Median number of years required for completion of a degree are 2.

Admissions Requirements:
Scores: Entries appear in this order: required test or GPA, minimum score (if required), median score of students entering in 2003–2004. Master's Programs: GRE-V no minimum stated, 530; GRE-Q no minimum stated, 540; GRE-V+Q no minimum stated; GRE-Analytical no minimum stated, 560; overall undergraduate GPA 2.5, 3.11.
Other Criteria: (importance of criteria rated low, medium, or high): GRE/MAT scores medium, research experience low, work experience medium, extracurricular activity medium, clinically related public service medium, GPA medium, letters of recommendation medium, interview medium, statement of goals and objectives high, GPA in science courses high.

Student Characteristics: The following represents characteristics of students in 2004–2005 in all graduate psychology programs in the department: Female–full-time 7, part-time 4; Male–full-time 2, part-time 3; African American/Black–full-time 0, part-time 0; Hispanic/Latino(a)–full-time 0, part-time 0; Asian/Pacific Islander–full-time 0, part-time 0; American Indian/Alaska Native–full-time 0, part-time 0; Caucasian–full-time 9, part-time 7; Multi-ethnic–full-time 0, part-time 0; students subject to the Americans With Disabilities Act–full-time 1, part-time 0.

Financial Information/Assistance:
Tuition for Full-Time Study: *Master's:* State residents: $325 per credit hour; Nonstate residents: $325 per credit hour. Tuition is subject to change. See the following Web site for updates and changes in tuition costs: http:www.hartford.edu/academics/g_bulletin/tuition.pdf.

Financial Assistance:
First Year Students: Teaching assistantships available for first-year. Average amount paid per academic year: $5,000. Average number of hours worked per week: 10. Apply by none. Tuition remission given: full. Research assistantships available for first-year. Average amount paid per academic year: $5,000. Average number of hours worked per week: 10. Apply by none. Tuition remission given: full.
Advanced Students: Teaching assistantships available for advanced students. Average amount paid per academic year: $5,000. Average number of hours worked per week: 10. Apply by none. Tuition remission given: full. Research assistantships available for advanced students. Average amount paid per academic year: $5,000. Average number of hours worked per week: 10. Apply by none. Tuition remission given: full.
Contact Information: Of all students currently enrolled full-time, 60% benefited from one or more of the listed financial assistance programs. Application and information available online

at: https://banweb1.hartford.edu/pls/prod/bwskalog.P_DispLogin Non.

Internships/Practica: No information provided.

Housing and Day Care: No on-campus housing is available. No on-campus day care facilities are available.

Employment of Department Graduates:
Master's Degree Graduates: Of those who graduated in the academic year 2003–2004, the following categories and numbers represent the post-graduate activities and employment of master's degree graduates: Enrolled in a post-doctoral residency/fellowship (n/a), employed in independent practice (n/a), total from the above (master's) (0).
Doctoral Degree Graduates: Of those who graduated in the academic year 2003–2004, the following categories and numbers represent the post-graduate activities and employment of doctoral degree graduates: Enrolled in a psychology doctoral program (n/a), total from the above (doctoral) (0).

Additional Information:
Orientation, Objectives, and Emphasis of Department: The objectives of the Neuroscience Master's Program is to give traditional and non-traditional students a foundation in the neurosciences both in the classroom and the laboratory that will allow them to successfully move on to doctoral programs, medical schools or to any number of science-related fields.

Special Facilities or Resources: The University of Hartford is breaking ground (Spring 2004) in the construction of a new Integrated Science, Engineering and Technology building which will house the Department of Biology and provide new classroom and laboratory space for the Neuroscience Master's Program.

Information for Students With Physical Disabilities: See the following Web site for more information: http://uhaweb.hartford.edu/reslife/students.htm.

Application Information:
Send to: Dr. Jacob P. Harney, Director, Neuroscience Graduate Program, University of Hartford, 200 Bloomfield Avenue, West Hartford, CT 06117. Application available online. Students are admitted in the Fall, application deadline none; Winter, application deadline none; Spring, application deadline none; Summer, application deadline none; Programs have rolling admissions. *Fee:* $40.

Southern Connecticut State University
Department of Psychology
501 Crescent Street
New Haven, CT 06515
Telephone: (203) 392-6868
Fax: (203) 392-6805
E-mail: *mazurj1@southernct.edu*
Web: *http://www.southernct.edu/departments/psychology/*

Department Information:
1893. Chairperson: Patricia Kahlbaugh. Number of Faculty: total–full-time 19, part-time 25.

Programs and Degrees Offered:
Listed in the following order: Program area, degree type (T if terminal Master's), number awarded 7/03–6/04. Psychology MA/MS (Master of Arts/Science) (T) 15.

Student Applications/Admissions:
Student Applications
Psychology MA/MS (*Master of Arts/Science*)—Applications 2004–2005, 76. Total applicants accepted 2004–2005, 44. Total enrolled 2004–2005 full-time, 16, part-time, 32. Openings 2005–2006, 25. The number of students enrolled full and part-time who were dismissed or voluntarily withdrew from this program area were 1.

Admissions Requirements:
Scores: Entries appear in this order: required test or GPA, minimum score (if required), median score of students entering in 2003–2004. Master's Programs: overall undergraduate GPA 2.5, 3.0; psychology GPA 3.0, 3.2.
Other Criteria: (importance of criteria rated low, medium, or high): research experience low, work experience low, GPA high, letters of recommendation low.

Student Characteristics: The following represents characteristics of students in 2004–2005 in all graduate psychology programs in the department: Female–full-time 13, part-time 27; Male–full-time 3, part-time 5; Caucasian–full-time 0, part-time 0.

Financial Information/Assistance:
Tuition for Full-Time Study: *Master's:* State residents: per academic year $2,880, $313 per credit hour; Nonstate residents: per academic year $8,028, $313 per credit hour. Tuition is subject to change.

Financial Assistance:
First Year Students: Teaching assistantships available for first-year. Average amount paid per academic year: $4,500. Average number of hours worked per week: 16. Apply by May 1. Tuition remission given: partial.
Advanced Students: Teaching assistantships available for advanced students. Average amount paid per academic year: $4,500. Average number of hours worked per week: 16. Apply by May 1. Tuition remission given: partial.
Contact Information: Of all students currently enrolled full-time, 20% benefitted from one or more of the listed financial assistance programs.

Internships/Practica: With departmental permission, MA students may arrange a one- or two-semester clinical internship (3 credits for one semester; 6 credits for two semesters).

Housing and Day Care: On-campus housing is available. See the following Web site for more information: www.southernct.edu/departments/graduatestudies/adreslife.php3. On-campus day care facilities are available. See the following Web site for more information: www.southernct.edu/services/?file=services.html.

Employment of Department Graduates:
Master's Degree Graduates: Of those who graduated in the academic year 2003–2004, the following categories and numbers represent the post-graduate activities and employment of master's degree graduates: Enrolled in a post-doctoral residency/fellowship

(n/a), employed in independent practice (n/a), total from the above (master's) (0).

Doctoral Degree Graduates: Of those who graduated in the academic year 2003–2004, the following categories and numbers represent the post-graduate activities and employment of doctoral degree graduates: Enrolled in a psychology doctoral program (n/a), total from the above (doctoral) (0).

Additional Information:

Orientation, Objectives, and Emphasis of Department: This rigorous, research-based program is designed to develop creative, problem-solving skills that graduates can apply to a variety of clinical, industrial, and educational settings. Leading to a master of arts degree, this program is flexible enough to be completed on either a full- or part-time basis, meeting the needs of a wide range of candidates. For potential doctoral candidates who can enter neither a PhD nor a PsyD program at the present time, this program provides the basis for later acceptance into a doctoral program. For those who are already working in clinical, educational, or industrial settings, it offers updating and credentials. In addition, this program provides ideal training for people who want to explore their personal interest in careers related to psychology. High school teachers may use the program to prepare themselves to teach psychology in addition to their current certification. In any case, this program emphasizes faculty advisement to help tailor the program to the needs of each individual student.

Information for Students With Physical Disabilities: See the following Web site for more information: http://www.southernct.edu/departments/dro/.

Application Information:
Send to: Graduate Studies, Southern Connecticut State University, New Haven, CT 06515. Students are admitted in the Fall, application deadline July 31; Spring, application deadline December 31; Summer, application deadline April 30. *Fee:* $40.

Wesleyan University
Psychology
207 High Street
Middletown, CT 06459-0408
Telephone: (860) 685-2342
Fax: (860) 685-2761
E-mail: jchiari@wesleyan.edu
Web: http://www.wesleyan.edu/psyc/

Department Information:
1913. Chairperson: Ruth Striegel-Moore. Number of Faculty: total–full-time 12, part-time 3; women–full-time 6, part-time 2; minority–full-time 2.

Programs and Degrees Offered:
Listed in the following order: Program area, degree type (T if terminal Master's), number awarded 7/03–6/04. General MA/MS (Master of Arts/Science) (T) 4.

Student Applications/Admissions:
Student Applications
General MA/MS (Master of Arts/Science)—Applications 2004–2005, 23. Total applicants accepted 2004–2005, 2. Number

enrolled (new admits only) 2004–2005 full-time, 2. Openings 2005–2006, 3. The Median number of years required for completion of a degree are 2. The number of students enrolled full and part-time who were dismissed or voluntarily withdrew from this program area were 0.

Admissions Requirements:
Scores: Entries appear in this order: required test or GPA, minimum score (if required), median score of students entering in 2003–2004. Master's Programs: overall undergraduate GPA no minimum stated.
Other Criteria: (importance of criteria rated low, medium, or high): GRE/MAT scores medium, research experience medium, GPA medium, letters of recommendation high, interview low, statement of goals and objectives high. For additional information on admission requirements, go to: http://www.wesleyan.edu/psyc/programs.htm#ma.

Student Characteristics: The following represents characteristics of students in 2004–2005 in all graduate psychology programs in the department: Female–full-time 3, part-time 0; Male–full-time 3, part-time 0; African American/Black–full-time 1, part-time 0; Hispanic/Latino(a)–full-time 0, part-time 0; Asian/Pacific Islander–full-time 0, part-time 0; American Indian/Alaska Native–full-time 0, part-time 0; Caucasian–full-time 4, part-time 0; Multiethnic–full-time 1, part-time 0; students subject to the Americans With Disabilities Act–full-time 0, part-time 0.

Financial Information/Assistance:
Financial Assistance:
First Year Students: Teaching assistantships available for first-year. Average amount paid per academic year: $14,000. Average number of hours worked per week: 10. Tuition remission given: full.
Advanced Students: Teaching assistantships available for advanced students. Average amount paid per academic year: $14,000. Average number of hours worked per week: 10.
Contact Information: Of all students currently enrolled full-time, 100% benefitted from one or more of the listed financial assistance programs. Application and information available online at: http://www.wesleyan.edu/grad/StudentServ/.

Internships/Practica: No information provided.

Housing and Day Care: On-campus housing is available. See the following Web site for more information: http://www.wesleyan.edu/grad/ mail to: gradoffice@wesleyan.edu Contact graduate office for this information. No on-campus day care facilities are available.

Employment of Department Graduates:
Master's Degree Graduates: Of those who graduated in the academic year 2003–2004, the following categories and numbers represent the post-graduate activities and employment of master's degree graduates: Enrolled in a post-doctoral residency/fellowship (n/a), employed in independent practice (n/a), employed in other positions at a higher education institution (1), employed in business or industry (research/consulting) (2), do not know (1), total from the above (master's) (4).
Doctoral Degree Graduates: Of those who graduated in the academic year 2003–2004, the following categories and numbers represent the post-graduate activities and employment of doctoral

degree graduates: Enrolled in a psychology doctoral program (n/a), total from the above (doctoral) (0).

Additional Information:

Orientation, Objectives, and Emphasis of Department: The department of Psychology at Wesleyan University offers a two-year program of study culminating in the master of arts degree. The hallmarks of the program are its selectivity, small size, and research orientation. Most students go on to pursue doctoral studies. Toward this end, the program is designed to provide a solid foundation of training in general psychology and additional experience in the fundamentals of research in a more specialized area of interest. Areas of expertise represented in the department include behavioral neuroscience, clinical, cognitive, developmental, personality, social psychology, and women's studies.

Special Facilities or Resources: 10 laboratories. All MA students who are between their first and second year of study have the option of receiving a summer research stipend of approximately $3000.

Application Information:

Send to: Graduate Coordinator, Psychology Department, Wesleyan University, 207 High Street, Middletown, CT 06459-0408. Application available online. URL of online application: http://www.wesleyan.edu/psyc/grad_MA.html. Students are admitted in the Spring, application deadline February 1. *Fee:* $0.

Yale University

Department of Psychology
P.O. Box 208205
New Haven, CT 06520-8205
Telephone: (203) 432-4518
Fax: (203) 432-7172
E-mail: *lauretta.olivi@yale.edu*
Web: *http://www.yale.edu/psychology*

Department Information:

1928. Chair: Kelly Brownell. Number of Faculty: total–full-time 30, part-time 1; women–full-time 11, part-time 1; minority–full-time 2.

Programs and Degrees Offered:

Listed in the following order: Program area, degree type (T if terminal Master's), number awarded 7/03–6/04. Behavioral Neuroscience PhD (Doctor of Philosophy) 2, Clinical PhD (Doctor of Philosophy) 2, Cognitive PhD (Doctor of Philosophy) 2, Developmental PhD (Doctor of Philosophy) 2, Social Personality PhD (Doctor of Philosophy) 2.

APA Accreditation: Clinical PhD (Doctor of Philosophy).

Student Applications/Admissions:

Student Applications

Behavioral Neuroscience PhD (Doctor of Philosophy)—Applications 2004–2005, 17. Total applicants accepted 2004–2005, 1. Number enrolled (new admits only) 2004–2005 full-time, 1. Number enrolled (new admits only) 2004–2005 part-time,

0. Openings 2005–2006, 2. The Median number of years required for completion of a degree are 6. The number of students enrolled full and part-time who were dismissed or voluntarily withdrew from this program area were 0. *Clinical PhD (Doctor of Philosophy)*—Applications 2004–2005, 347. Total applicants accepted 2004–2005, 5. Number enrolled (new admits only) 2004–2005 full-time, 2. Number enrolled (new admits only) 2004–2005 part-time, 0. Openings 2005–2006, 2. The Median number of years required for completion of a degree are 6. The number of students enrolled full and part-time who were dismissed or voluntarily withdrew from this program area were 0. *Cognitive PhD (Doctor of Philosophy)*—Applications 2004–2005, 87. Total applicants accepted 2004–2005, 5. Number enrolled (new admits only) 2004–2005 full-time, 3. Number enrolled (new admits only) 2004–2005 part-time, 0. Openings 2005–2006, 1. The Median number of years required for completion of a degree are 6. The number of students enrolled full and part-time who were dismissed or voluntarily withdrew from this program area were 0. *Developmental PhD (Doctor of Philosophy)*—Applications 2004–2005, 52. Total applicants accepted 2004–2005, 4. Number enrolled (new admits only) 2004–2005 full-time, 2. Number enrolled (new admits only) 2004–2005 part-time, 0. Openings 2005–2006, 3. The Median number of years required for completion of a degree are 6. The number of students enrolled full and part-time who were dismissed or voluntarily withdrew from this program area were 1. *Social Personality PhD (Doctor of Philosophy)*—Applications 2004–2005, 119. Total applicants accepted 2004–2005, 5. Number enrolled (new admits only) 2004–2005 full-time, 2. Number enrolled (new admits only) 2004–2005 part-time, 0. Openings 2005–2006, 4. The Median number of years required for completion of a degree are 6. The number of students enrolled full and part-time who were dismissed or voluntarily withdrew from this program area were 0.

Admissions Requirements:

Scores: Entries appear in this order: required test or GPA, minimum score (if required), median score of students entering in 2003–2004. Master's Programs: . We do not offer a terminal Master's Program. Doctoral Programs: GRE-V 600, 640; GRE-Q 600, 720; GRE-Analytical 5.0, 5.0; overall undergraduate GPA no minimum stated, 3.76.

Other Criteria: (importance of criteria rated low, medium, or high): GRE/MAT scores high, research experience high, work experience low, extracurricular activity low, clinically related public service medium, GPA medium, letters of recommendation high, statement of goals and objectives high. For additional information on admission requirements, go to: www.yale.edu/graduateschool/admissions.

Student Characteristics: The following represents characteristics of students in 2004–2005 in all graduate psychology programs in the department: Female–full-time 58, part-time 0; Male–full-time 28, part-time 0; African American/Black–full-time 3, part-time 0; Hispanic/Latino(a)–full-time 5, part-time 0; Asian/Pacific Islander–full-time 8, part-time 0; American Indian/Alaska Native–full-time 1, part-time 0; Caucasian–full-time 69, part-time 0; Multi-ethnic–full-time 0, part-time 0; students subject to the Americans With Disabilities Act–full-time 0, part-time 0.

Financial Information/Assistance:

Tuition for Full-Time Study: *Doctoral:* State residents: per academic year $0; Nonstate residents: per academic year $0.

Financial Assistance:

First Year Students: Fellowships and scholarships available for first-year.

Advanced Students: Teaching assistantships available for advanced students. Average amount paid per academic year: $14,000. Average number of hours worked per week: 15. Apply by June 30. Tuition remission given: full. Research assistantships available for advanced students. Average number of hours worked per week: 10. Tuition remission given: full. Traineeships available for advanced students. Tuition remission given: full. Fellowships and scholarships available for advanced students. Tuition remission given: full.

Contact Information: Of all students currently enrolled full-time, 100% benefitted from one or more of the listed financial assistance programs. Application and information available online at: http://www.yale.edu/graduateschool/financial/index.html.

Internships/Practica: Students are required to assist in teaching an average of 10–15 hours per week in their second, third, and fourth years as part of their educational program. Local facilities for predoctoral internships are the Veterans Administration Center in West Haven, Yale Psychological Services Clinic, the Yale Child Study Center, and Yale Department of Psychiatry, with placement in the Connecticut Mental Health Center, Yale-New Haven Hospital, or the Yale Psychiatric Institute. Also, internships are arranged in accredited facilities throughout the United States. For those doctoral students for whom a professional internship is required prior to graduation, 1 applied in 2003–2004. Of those who applied, 1 was placed in internships listed by the Association of Psychology Postdoctoral and Internship Programs (APPIC); 1 was placed in APA accredited internships.

Housing and Day Care: On-campus housing is available. See the following Web site for more information: www.yale.edu/hronline/gho/. Yale Daycare info Web site is: www.yale.edu/daycare. On-campus day care facilities are available.

Employment of Department Graduates:

Master's Degree Graduates: Of those who graduated in the academic year 2003–2004, the following categories and numbers represent the post-graduate activities and employment of master's degree graduates: Enrolled in another graduate/professional program (0), enrolled in a post-doctoral residency/fellowship (n/a), employed in independent practice (n/a), total from the above (master's) (0).

Doctoral Degree Graduates: Of those who graduated in the academic year 2003–2004, the following categories and numbers represent the post-graduate activities and employment of doctoral degree graduates: Enrolled in a psychology doctoral program (n/a), enrolled in a post-doctoral residency/fellowship (6), employed in independent practice (0), employed in an academic position at a university (6), employed in an academic position at a 2-year/4-year college (0), employed in other positions at a higher education institution (0), employed in a professional position in a school system (0), employed in business or industry (research/consulting) (1), employed in business or industry (management) (0), employed in a government agency (research) (0), employed in a government agency (professional services) (0), employed in a community mental health/counseling center (0), employed in a hospital/medical center (0), still seeking employment (2), other employment position (0), do not know (0), total from the above (doctoral) (15).

Additional Information:

Orientation, Objectives, and Emphasis of Department: The chief goal of graduate education in psychology at Yale University is the training of research workers in academic and other settings who will broaden the basic scientific knowledge on which the discipline of psychology rests. Major emphasis is given to preparation for research; a definite effort is made to give students a background for teaching. The concentration of doctoral training on research and teaching is consistent with a variety of career objectives in addition to traditional academics. The department believes that rigorous and balanced exposure to basic psychology is the best preparation for research careers. The first important aspect of graduate training is advanced study of general psychology, including method and psychological theory. The second is specialized training within a subfield. Third, the student is encouraged to take advantage of opportunities for wider training emphasizing research rather than practice. For the clinical area, research and practica are strongly integrated. Training is geared to the expectation that the majority of students will have research careers.

Special Facilities or Resources: Technical facilities available as adjuncts to research and teaching include university mechanical and electronics shops with full-time instrument-makers; animal colony, animal surgery, and histology laboratory; and special rooms equipped for observation, intercommunication, and recording as required for clinical supervision or testing or for interview training and research in experimental social psychology and also in child development. The department shares the use of the Yale Informational Technology Services. Training is available in a variety of programming languages and simulation techniques. Remote computer terminals are available, and individual microcomputers are commonly located in faculty laboratories. A networked computer laboratory for training students in research on intrapersonal and interpersonal processes is available. Computers are linked together in a local area network (LAN), and laboratory rooms share a common observation corridor equipped with one-way mirrors. The facility allows training in application of emerging research technologies to traditional and innovative research problems.

Information for Students With Physical Disabilities: See the following Web site for more information: www.yale.edu/rod/.

Application Information:

Send to: Graduate School, Yale University, Office of Admissions, P.O. Box 208323, New Haven, CT 06520-8323. Application available online. URL of online application: www.yale.edu/graduateschool/admissions. Students are admitted in the Fall, application deadline December 15. *Fee:* $85. Students who apply for fee waiver must first pay the fee, then, if waiver is approved, will get reimbursed.

Delaware, University of
Department of Psychology
College of Arts and Science
108 Wolf Hall
Newark, DE 19716
Telephone: (302) 831-2271
Fax: (302) 831-3645
E-mail: linnie@udel.edu
Web: http://www.psych.udel.edu/graduate/index.php

Department Information:
1946. Chairperson: Thomas DiLorenzo. Number of Faculty: total–full-time 29, part-time 2; women–full-time 8, part-time 1; minority–full-time 1.

Programs and Degrees Offered:
Listed in the following order: Program area, degree type (T if terminal Master's), number awarded 7/03–6/04. Clinical PhD (Doctor of Philosophy) 5, Behavioral Neuroscience PhD (Doctor of Philosophy) 2, Social PhD (Doctor of Philosophy) 2, Cognitive PhD (Doctor of Philosophy) 0.

APA Accreditation: Clinical PhD (Doctor of Philosophy).

Student Applications/Admissions:
Student Applications
Clinical PhD (Doctor of Philosophy)—Applications 2004–2005, 152. Total applicants accepted 2004–2005, 8. Number enrolled (new admits only) 2004–2005 full-time, 4. Number enrolled (new admits only) 2004–2005 part-time, 0. Openings 2005–2006, 8. The Median number of years required for completion of a degree are 6. The number of students enrolled full and part-time who were dismissed or voluntarily withdrew from this program area were 1. *Behavioral Neuroscience PhD (Doctor of Philosophy)*—Applications 2004–2005, 19. Total applicants accepted 2004–2005, 3. Number enrolled (new admits only) 2004–2005 full-time, 2. Number enrolled (new admits only) 2004–2005 part-time, 0. Openings 2005–2006, 3. The Median number of years required for completion of a degree are 7. The number of students enrolled full and part-time who were dismissed or voluntarily withdrew from this program area were 1. *Social PhD (Doctor of Philosophy)*—Applications 2004–2005, 36. Total applicants accepted 2004–2005, 5. Number enrolled (new admits only) 2004–2005 full-time, 3. Number enrolled (new admits only) 2004–2005 part-time, 0. Openings 2005–2006, 3. The Median number of years required for completion of a degree are 8. The number of students enrolled full and part-time who were dismissed or voluntarily withdrew from this program area were 1. *Cognitive PhD (Doctor of Philosophy)*—Applications 2004–2005, 13. Total applicants accepted 2004–2005, 1. Number enrolled (new admits only) 2004–2005 full-time, 0. Number enrolled (new admits only) 2004–2005 part-time, 0. Openings 2005–2006, 2. The number of students enrolled full and part-time who were dismissed or voluntarily withdrew from this program area were 1.

Admissions Requirements:
Scores: Entries appear in this order: required test or GPA, minimum score (if required), median score of students entering in 2003–2004. Master's Programs: Admission is for doctoral program only. Above information is not applicable. Doctoral Programs: GRE-V 410, 595; GRE-Q 380, 670; GRE-V+Q 790, 1265; overall undergraduate GPA 3.13, 3.88.
Other Criteria: (importance of criteria rated low, medium, or high): GRE/MAT scores high, research experience high, GPA high, letters of recommendation medium, interview medium, statement of goals and objectives medium.

Student Characteristics: The following represents characteristics of students in 2004–2005 in all graduate psychology programs in the department: Female–full-time 30, part-time 0; Male–full-time 16, part-time 0; African American/Black–full-time 4, part-time 0; Hispanic/Latino(a)–full-time 1, part-time 0; Asian/Pacific Islander–full-time 0, part-time 0; American Indian/Alaska Native–full-time 0, part-time 0; Caucasian–full-time 44, part-time 0; Multi-ethnic–full-time 1, part-time 0; students subject to the Americans With Disabilities Act–full-time 0, part-time 0.

Financial Information/Assistance:
Tuition for Full-Time Study: *Doctoral:* State residents: per academic year $3,152, $351 per credit hour; Nonstate residents: per academic year $7,995, $889 per credit hour.

Financial Assistance:
First Year Students: Teaching assistantships available for first-year. Average amount paid per academic year: $14,250. Average number of hours worked per week: 20. Apply by January 7. Tuition remission given: full. Research assistantships available for first-year. Average amount paid per academic year: $14,250. Average number of hours worked per week: 20. Apply by January 7. Tuition remission given: full. Fellowships and scholarships available for first-year. Average amount paid per academic year: $14,250. Apply by January 7. Tuition remission given: full.
Advanced Students: Teaching assistantships available for advanced students. Average amount paid per academic year: $15,000. Average number of hours worked per week: 20. Apply by N/A. Tuition remission given: full. Research assistantships available for advanced students. Average amount paid per academic year: $15,000. Average number of hours worked per week: 20. Apply by N/A. Tuition remission given: full. Fellowships and scholarships available for advanced students. Average amount paid per academic year: $15,000. Apply by February 29. Tuition remission given: full.
Contact Information: Of all students currently enrolled full-time, 100% benefitted from one or more of the listed financial assistance programs.

Internships/Practica: A wide range of practica experiences are available for clinical graduate students. For those doctoral students for whom a professional internship is required prior to graduation, 5 applied in 2003–2004. Of those who applied, 5 were placed in internships listed by the Association of Psychology Postdoctoral and Internship Programs (APPIC); 5 were placed in APA accredited internships.

Housing and Day Care: On-campus housing is available. See the following Web site for more information: http://www.udel.edu/housing/. On-campus day care facilities are available.

Employment of Department Graduates:

Master's Degree Graduates: Of those who graduated in the academic year 2003–2004, the following categories and numbers represent the post-graduate activities and employment of master's degree graduates: Enrolled in a post-doctoral residency/fellowship (n/a), employed in independent practice (n/a), total from the above (master's) (0).

Doctoral Degree Graduates: Of those who graduated in the academic year 2003–2004, the following categories and numbers represent the post-graduate activities and employment of doctoral degree graduates: Enrolled in a psychology doctoral program (n/a), total from the above (doctoral) (0).

Additional Information:

Orientation, Objectives, and Emphasis of Department: The department fosters a scientific approach to all areas of psychology. The training is organized around clinical, cognitive, behavioral neuroscience, and social areas, as well as an integrative developmental focus that cuts across area. All first-year students are required to complete first and second year research projects as well as take seminars in their program area of study. In the third and fourth year students take additional seminars, take a comprehensive qualifying exam or prepare a comprehensive paper and prepare dissertation proposals. Clinical students also participate in the training of practice skills. Beyond the first year, students work out their own research programs with faculty advice. The goal of this training is to prepare students to function as scientists and teachers in academic, applied, and clinical settings. Major current research interests in these areas are as follows: (1) clinical: evaluation of therapy, social development of children, community mental health, theory of emotions, communication of emotions, organic brain syndromes, family therapy, sex roles, sensation seeking, and sexuality; (2) cognitive: attention, pattern recognition, psycholinguistics, visual information processing, memory, and cognitive development; (3) behavioral neuroscience: neuroanatomy, developmental psychobiology, psychopharmacology, and neurobiology of learning; and (4) social: interpersonal conflict, racism, helping behavior, nonverbal communications, social power and influence, and decision-making. The program is flexible and encourages each student to develop his or her unique interests. The clinical program emphasizes empirically supported intervention and prevention techniques. A particular strength of the department and program is in child-clinical research, intervention and prevention, but students with interests in adult psychopathology and intervention would be equally at home and well served.

Special Facilities or Resources: The University's mainframe computing needs are met by several Unix timesharing systems. These systems are used primarily for administraive purposes, some special statistical analysis applications and for cognitive model simulations. The Department of Psychology is well equipped to handle department computing needs with a large assortment of Windows and MacIntosh microcomputers and several department servers that bear the brunt of department computing needs. Graduate students will find generous laboratory resources aimed to meet their computing needs individually. There is also a state-of-the-art computer classroom used for instructional purposes and available to graduate students around the clock for data reduction, statistical analysis and general word processing. The department laboratories are well equipped for the online control of experiments for human and animal subjects as well as for data analysis and modeling. Laboratories are generously equipped with videotape, acoustic, behavioral and physiological recording systems. The department also operates the Psychological Services Training Center for practicum training in clinical psychology.

Application Information:

Send to: The Office of Graduate Studies, 234 Hullihen Hall, University of Delaware, Newark, DE 19716. Application available online. Students are admitted in the Fall, application deadline January 7. *Fee:* $60. The fee may be waived or deferred by the Department of Psychology.

American University
Department of Psychology
College of Arts and Sciences
321 Asbury, 4400 Massachusetts Avenue, NW
Washington, DC 20016-8062
Telephone: (202) 885-1710
Fax: (202) 885-1023
E-mail: *psychology@american.edu*
Web: *http://www.american.edu/cas/psychology*

Department Information:

1929. Chairperson: Anthony L. Riley. Number of Faculty: total–full-time 17, part-time 4; women–full-time 6, part-time 2; minority–full-time 1.

Programs and Degrees Offered:

Listed in the following order: Program area, degree type (T if terminal Master's), number awarded 7/03–6/04. Behavior, Cognition and Neuroscience (BCAN) PhD (Doctor of Philosophy) 4, Clinical PhD (Doctor of Philosophy) 12, General MA/MS (Master of Arts/Science) (T) 12.

APA Accreditation: Clinical PhD (Doctor of Philosophy).

Student Applications/Admissions:

Student Applications

Behavior, Cognition and Neuroscience (BCAN) PhD (Doctor of Philosophy)—Applications 2004–2005, 25. Total applicants accepted 2004–2005, 10. Number enrolled (new admits only) 2004–2005 full-time, 6. Number enrolled (new admits only) 2004–2005 part-time, 0. Total enrolled 2004–2005 full-time, 20, part-time, 9. Openings 2005–2006, 6. The Median number of years required for completion of a degree are 7. The number of students enrolled full and part-time who were dismissed or voluntarily withdrew from this program area were 1. *Clinical PhD (Doctor of Philosophy)*—Applications 2004–2005, 284. Total applicants accepted 2004–2005, 11. Number enrolled (new admits only) 2004–2005 full-time, 6. Number enrolled (new admits only) 2004–2005 part-time, 0. Total enrolled 2004–2005 full-time, 44, part-time, 5. Openings 2005–2006, 7. The Median number of years required for completion of a degree are 7. The number of students enrolled full and part-time who were dismissed or voluntarily withdrew from this program area were 0. *General MA/MS (Master of Arts/Science)*—Applications 2004–2005, 158. Total applicants accepted 2004–2005, 59. Number enrolled (new admits only) 2004–2005 full-time, 16. Number enrolled (new admits only) 2004–2005 part-time, 0. Total enrolled 2004–2005 full-time, 24, part-time, 13. Openings 2005–2006, 20. The Median number of years required for completion of a degree are 2. The number of students enrolled full and part-time who were dismissed or voluntarily withdrew from this program area were 2.

Admissions Requirements:

Scores: Entries appear in this order: required test or GPA, minimum score (if required), median score of students entering in 2003–2004. Master's Programs: GRE-V no minimum stated, 550; GRE-Q no minimum stated, 610; GRE-Analytical no minimum stated, 5; overall undergraduate GPA no minimum stated, 3.51. Doctoral Programs: GRE-V no minimum stated, 620; GRE-Q no minimum stated, 690; GRE-Analytical no minimum stated, 5; GRE-Subject(Psych) no minimum stated, 720; overall undergraduate GPA no minimum stated, 3.73.

Other Criteria: (importance of criteria rated low, medium, or high): GRE/MAT scores high, research experience high, work experience medium, clinically related public service medium, GPA high, letters of recommendation high, interview high, statement of goals and objectives high. Interview, clinically related public service not required for Behavior, Cognition, and Neuroscience program. For additional information on admission requirements, go to: http://www.american.edu/cas/admissions/index.html.

Student Characteristics: The following represents characteristics of students in 2004–2005 in all graduate psychology programs in the department: Female–full-time 64, part-time 18; Male–full-time 14, part-time 5; African American/Black–full-time 5, part-time 0; Hispanic/Latino(a)–full-time 5, part-time 0; Asian/Pacific Islander–full-time 5, part-time 0; American Indian/Alaska Native–full-time 0, part-time 0; Caucasian–full-time 61, part-time 23; Multi-ethnic–full-time 2, part-time 0; students subject to the Americans With Disabilities Act–full-time 0, part-time 0.

Financial Information/Assistance:

Tuition for Full-Time Study: *Master's:* State residents: $989 per credit hour; Nonstate residents: $989 per credit hour. *Doctoral:* State residents: $989 per credit hour; Nonstate residents: $989 per credit hour. Tuition is subject to change. See the following Web site for updates and changes in tuition costs: http://admissions.american.edu/.

Financial Assistance:

First Year Students: Teaching assistantships available for first-year. Average amount paid per academic year: $17,802. Average number of hours worked per week: 20. Apply by January 1. Tuition remission given: full.

Advanced Students: Teaching assistantships available for advanced students. Average amount paid per academic year: $10,000. Average number of hours worked per week: 20. Apply by January 1. Tuition remission given: full.

Contact Information: Of all students currently enrolled full-time, 20% benefitted from one or more of the listed financial assistance programs. Application and information available online at: http://www.american.edu/cas/admissions/financialaid.htm.

Internships/Practica: The greater Washington, DC, metropolitan area provides a wealth of applied and research resources to complement our students' work in the classroom and faculty laboratories. These include the university's Counseling Center, local hospitals (Children's, Street Elizabeth's, Walter Reed, Georgetown University, National Rehabilitation), the Kennedy Institute, Gallaudet University, the NIH (NIMH, NINDS, NIA, NCI), the National Zoo, and the national offices of many agencies (e.g., APA, APS, NAMI). Field work and short-term internships are available in many city, county, and private organizations, such as the Alexandria, VA, Community Mental Health Center, the Montgomery County, MD, Department of Addiction, Victim, and Mental Health Services, the DC Rape Crisis Center, and Big Brothers. MA and PhD students can also earn degree credit while obtaining practical experience working in the private sector with autistic children, teaching self-management skills, volunteering at shelters for battered women or the homeless, or assisting at a psychologist's private practice. Many of these positions sometimes can provide funding. Externships offering practica in Rogerian, behavioral, and psychodynamic therapy are available for clinical PhD students either through the department or through clinical adjuncts or other local institutions. For those doctoral students for whom a professional internship is required prior to graduation, 6 applied in 2003–2004. Of those who applied, 6 were placed in internships listed by the Association of Psychology Postdoctoral and Internship Programs (APPIC); 6 were placed in APA accredited internships.

Housing and Day Care: On-campus housing is available. On-campus day care facilities are available.

Employment of Department Graduates:
Master's Degree Graduates: Of those who graduated in the academic year 2003–2004, the following categories and numbers represent the post-graduate activities and employment of master's degree graduates: Enrolled in a post-doctoral residency/fellowship (n/a), employed in independent practice (n/a), total from the above (master's) (0).
Doctoral Degree Graduates: Of those who graduated in the academic year 2003–2004, the following categories and numbers represent the post-graduate activities and employment of doctoral degree graduates: Enrolled in a psychology doctoral program (n/a), total from the above (doctoral) (0).

Additional Information:
Orientation, Objectives, and Emphasis of Department: The psychology department of American University offers two graduate programs. The PhD program has separate tracks in clinical psychology and behavior, cognition and neuroscience. The MA program has tracks in general, personality/social, and biological/experimental psychology. The doctoral program in clinical psychology trains psychologists to do therapy, assessment, research, university teaching, and consultation. The theoretical orientation is eclectic and follows the Boulder scientist-practitioner model. The doctoral program in behavioral neuroscience/experimental psychology involves intensive training in both pure and applied research settings. Students can work in laboratories exploring conditioning and learning, the experimental analysis of behavior, cognition and memory, physiological psychology, neuropsychology, and neuropharmacology. Study at the master's level provides the basis for further doctoral-level work and prepares students for immediate employment in a variety of careers including clinical-medical research, teaching, counseling and policy formulation, law enforcement, and government work. Our graduate students are expected to be professional, ethical, committed, full-time members of our psychology community. This concept of community implies an atmosphere of mutual support rather than competition, communication rather than isolation, and stimulation rather than disinterest.

Special Facilities or Resources: Nine well-equipped laboratories investigate conditioning and learning, clinical and experimental

neuropsychology, human cognition and memory, neuropharmacology, physiological psychology, rodent olfaction, social behavior, psychopathology, depression, anxiety disorders, emotion, eating disorders, parent–child interaction, addictive behavior, child development, and various other issues in applied and experimental psychology. In addition, students train in the Department's cognitive behavioral training clinic. Close working relationships with laboratories at the National Institutes of Health, the Walter Reed Army Institutes of Research, and Georgetown University's Hospital and School of Medicine allow additional training opportunities. The Washington Research Library Consortium (WRLC) provides access to six local college and university libraries in addition to AU's Bender Library, The National Library of Medicine, and the Library of Congress. AU's computing center supports IBM, Macintosh, and Unix systems, has dial-in access, and maintains fifteen computing labs. EagleNet, a campus-wide network service runs on Novell Netware 4.x and 5.0. Applications include WordPerfect, Quattro Pro, Presentations, Paradox, SAS, SPSS, Photoshop, Netscape, and e-mail as well as many Internet applications and services (Usenet newsgroups, electronic discussion lists-Listserv, file transfer, FTP, the ALADIN online catalog of the WRLC).

Information for Students With Physical Disabilities: See the following Web site for more information: http://www.american.edu/ocl/dss/index1.html.

Application Information:
Send to: College of Arts and Sciences Graduate Admissions, McKinley Building, 4400 Massachusetts Avenue, NW, Washington, DC 20016-8107. Application available online. URL of online application: https://my.american.edu/cgi/mvi.exe/A26.APPL.LOGIN?SCH=CAS. Students are admitted in the Fall. Deadlines—Clinical, January 1; Behavioral Neuroscience, January 1; MA, March 1. *Fee:* $50. Fall deadlines—Clinical, January 1; Behavioral Neuroscience, January 1; MA, March 1 The online application free is $50. The fee for paper mailed applications is $80.

Catholic University of America, The (2004 data)
Department of Psychology
4001 Harewood Road, NE, O'Boyle Hall, Room 314
Washington, DC 20064
Telephone: (202) 319-5750
Fax: (202) 319-6263
E-mail: *sebrechts@cua.edu*
Web: *http://psychology.cua.edu*

Department Information:
1891. Chairperson: Marc M. Sebrechts. Number of Faculty: total–full-time 13, part-time 4; women–full-time 6, part-time 1; minority–full-time 1.

Programs and Degrees Offered:
Listed in the following order: Program area, degree type (T if terminal Master's), number awarded 7/03–6/04. General MA/MS (Master of Arts/Science) (T) 9, Clinical PhD (Doctor of Philosophy) 7, Applied Experimental PhD (Doctor of Philosophy) 1, Human Development [Accepting for MA degree only] PhD (Doctor of Philosophy) 1, Psychology/Law MA/MS (Master of

Arts/Science) (T) 1, Human Factors MA/MS (Master of Arts/Science) (T) 0.

APA Accreditation: Clinical PhD (Doctor of Philosophy).

Student Applications/Admissions:

Student Applications

General MA/MS (Master of Arts/Science)—Applications 2004–2005, 49. Total applicants accepted 2004–2005, 25. Total enrolled 2004–2005 full-time, 23, part-time, 2. Openings 2005–2006, 16. The Median number of years required for completion of a degree are 3. *Clinical PhD (Doctor of Philosophy)*—Applications 2004–2005, 142. Total applicants accepted 2004–2005, 19. Openings 2005–2006, 6. The Median number of years required for completion of a degree are 6. The number of students enrolled full and part-time who were dismissed or voluntarily withdrew from this program area were 0. *Applied Experimental PhD (Doctor of Philosophy)*—Applications 2004–2005, 7. Total applicants accepted 2004–2005, 4. Openings 2005–2006, 3. The Median number of years required for completion of a degree are 6. The number of students enrolled full and part-time who were dismissed or voluntarily withdrew from this program area were 0. *Human Development [Accepting for MA degree only] PhD (Doctor of Philosophy)*—Applications 2004–2005, 6. Total applicants accepted 2004–2005, 0. *Psychology/Law MA/MS (Master of Arts/Science)*—Applications 2004–2005, 7. Total applicants accepted 2004–2005, 3. Openings 2005–2006, 2. The Median number of years required for completion of a degree are 3. *Human Factors MA/MS (Master of Arts/Science)*—Applications 2004–2005, 7. Total applicants accepted 2004–2005, 2. Openings 2005–2006, 2. The number of students enrolled full and part-time who were dismissed or voluntarily withdrew from this program area were 0.

Admissions Requirements:

Scores: Entries appear in this order: required test or GPA, minimum score (if required), median score of students entering in 2003–2004. Master's Programs: GRE-V no minimum stated, 510; GRE-Q no minimum stated, 570; GRE-V+Q no minimum stated, 1080; GRE-Analytical no minimum stated; overall undergraduate GPA no minimum stated, 3.4. Doctoral Programs: GRE-V no minimum stated, 590; GRE-Q no minimum stated, 630; GRE-V+Q no minimum stated, 1210; GRE-Analytical no minimum stated; GRE-Subject(Psych) no minimum stated; overall undergraduate GPA no minimum stated, 3.5. Psychology Subject Test is required for clinical program only.

Other Criteria: (importance of criteria rated low, medium, or high): GRE/MAT scores medium, research experience high, work experience medium, extracurricular activity low, clinically related public service medium, GPA high, letters of recommendation high, interview high, statement of goals and objectives high, Interview only for clinical PhD program. For additional information on admission requirements, go to: http://psychology.cua.edu/graduate/.

Student Characteristics: The following represents characteristics of students in 2004–2005 in all graduate psychology programs in the department: Female–full-time 66, part-time 1; Male–full-time 23, part-time 1; African American/Black–full-time 6, part-time 0; Hispanic/Latino(a)–full-time 4, part-time 0; Asian/Pacific Is-

lander–full-time 9, part-time 0; American Indian/Alaska Native–full-time 1, part-time 0; Caucasian–full-time 67, part-time 1; Multi-ethnic–full-time 2, part-time 1; students subject to the Americans With Disabilities Act–full-time 1, part-time 0.

Financial Information/Assistance:

Tuition for Full-Time Study: *Master's:* State residents: per academic year $23,600, $895 per credit hour; Nonstate residents: per academic year $23,600, $895 per credit hour. *Doctoral:* State residents: per academic year $23,600, $895 per credit hour; Nonstate residents: per academic year $23,600, $895 per credit hour.

Financial Assistance:

First Year Students: Research assistantships available for first-year. Average amount paid per academic year: $12,000. Average number of hours worked per week: 20. Apply by Rolling. Tuition remission given: full. Fellowships and scholarships available for first-year. Apply by January 15. Tuition remission given: full.

Advanced Students: Teaching assistantships available for advanced students. Average amount paid per academic year: $4,000. Average number of hours worked per week: 10. Apply by March 1. Tuition remission given: full. Research assistantships available for advanced students. Average amount paid per academic year: $12,000. Average number of hours worked per week: 20. Apply by Rolling. Tuition remission given: full. Fellowships and scholarships available for advanced students. Apply by March 1. Tuition remission given: full.

Contact Information: Of all students currently enrolled full-time, 90% benefitted from one or more of the listed financial assistance programs.

Internships/Practica: Students in the Clinical doctoral program begin practicum experience in their first year as a part of their courses in assessment and psychotherapy. Advanced courses are available in objective personality assessment and projective personality assessment. Both of these courses incorporate practicum experience. In their second year, clinical students do a practicum in individual psychotherapy in the university's counseling center, in which the clients are undergraduate and graduate students. The core clinical faculty supervises this year long practicum. An advanced psychotherapy practicum, supervised by a core clinical faculty member, is available in family therapy. All on-campus practica are supervised very closely. For example, in the second-year psychotherapy practicum, students are given 3.5 hours of supervision a week while they are seeing 2 or 3 clients. Additionally, in their third and fourth year, clinical students do 16-hour-a-week externships, supervised by licensed clinical psychologists, in one of many community settings in the area, such as community mental health centers, clinics, and hospitals. The clinical training culminates in a year long internship, preferably an APA-accredited internship. Applied Experimental and MA students have a number of research opportunities in the Washington DC area. Recent opportunities have included positions at the National Institutes of Health, the Army Research Institute, and National Defense University. For those doctoral students for whom a professional internship is required prior to graduation, 6 applied in 2003–2004. Of those who applied, 6 were placed in internships listed by the Association of Psychology Postdoctoral and Internship Programs (APPIC); 5 were placed in APA accredited internships.

Housing and Day Care: On-campus housing is available: housing.cua.edu. No on-campus day care facilities are available.

Employment of Department Graduates:

Master's Degree Graduates: Of those who graduated in the academic year 2003–2004, the following categories and numbers represent the post-graduate activities and employment of master's degree graduates: Enrolled in a psychology doctoral program (5), enrolled in a post-doctoral residency/fellowship (n/a), employed in independent practice (n/a), employed in a community mental health/counseling center (1), employed in a hospital/medical center (1), do not know (2), total from the above (master's) (9).

Doctoral Degree Graduates: Of those who graduated in the academic year 2003–2004, the following categories and numbers represent the post-graduate activities and employment of doctoral degree graduates: Enrolled in a psychology doctoral program (n/a), enrolled in a post-doctoral residency/fellowship (2), employed in independent practice (1), employed in other positions at a higher education institution (4), employed in a government agency (research) (1), employed in a community mental health/counseling center (1), total from the above (doctoral) (9).

Additional Information:

Orientation, Objectives, and Emphasis of Department: Two PhD programs, clinical and applied-experimental, are offered. Further specialization is offered in Children, Families, and Cultures and in the Cognitive, Affective and Neural Sciences. The objectives of the clinical program are to train according to the scientist-practitioner model in clinical and applied areas. The Children, Families, and Cultures specialization provides interdisciplinary training in both normal and abnormal developmental processes in the clinical program or in the MA human development program. The applied-experimental program emphasizes research in human cognition: current areas of interest include cognitive aging (serial pattern learning, Alzheimer's), spatial mental models (virtual reality, information visualization and memory applied to health issues). The Cognitive, Affective, and Neural Sciences track focuses on a range of cognitive deficits across the life span. Additional Master's programs are offered in Human Factors and General Psychology. A dual degree program MA Psychology/JD Law is available. Admission to CUA Columbus School of Law is a prerequisite.

Special Facilities or Resources: The department maintains several well-equipped laboratories for both cognitive science and clinical research. Capabilities exist for studies on auditory and visual perception, attention and memory, simulation, human computer interaction, virtual reality, and social interaction, including family interaction.

Information for Students With Physical Disabilities: See the following Web site for more information: http://disabilityservices.cua.edu/.

Application Information:
Send to: Office of Graduate Admissions, The Catholic University of America, 102 McMahon Hall, Washington, DC 20064. Application available online. Students are admitted in the Fall, application deadline January 15; Spring, application deadline October 1. Admission to clinical program available for Fall only. *Fee:* $55. We waive the application fee for those with serious financial difficulties that make it a hardship to pay the fee, and for others who would increase diversity in the student body, such as veterans and ethnic minorities. To request an application fee waiver, applicants must write a letter explaining the basis for their request and send it by U.S. Post to the Office of Graduate Admissions, 102 McMahon Hall, The Catholic University of America, Washington, DC 20064.

Gallaudet University
Department of Psychology
College of Liberal Arts, Sciences & Technologies
800 Florida Avenue, NE
Washington, DC 20002
Telephone: (202) 651-5540
Fax: (202) 651-5747
E-mail: *Virginia.Gutman@gallaudet.edu*
Web: *http://depts.gallaudet.edu/psychology/*

Department Information:
1955. Chairperson: Virginia Gutman, PhD Number of Faculty: total–full-time 16, part-time 2; women–full-time 12, part-time 1; minority–full-time 4; faculty subject to the Americans With Disabilities Act 3.

Programs and Degrees Offered:
Listed in the following order: Program area, degree type (T if terminal Master's), number awarded 7/03–6/04. Clinical PhD (Doctor of Philosophy) 1, School Psychology Other 6.

APA Accreditation: Clinical PhD (Doctor of Philosophy).

Student Applications/Admissions:

Student Applications

Clinical PhD (Doctor of Philosophy)—Applications 2004–2005, 24. Total applicants accepted 2004–2005, 8. Number enrolled (new admits only) 2004–2005 full-time, 6. Number enrolled (new admits only) 2004–2005 part-time, 0. Openings 2005–2006, 8. The Median number of years required for completion of a degree are 6. The number of students enrolled full and part-time who were dismissed or voluntarily withdrew from this program area were 1. *School Psychology Other*—Applications 2004–2005, 10. Total applicants accepted 2004–2005, 7. Number enrolled (new admits only) 2004–2005 full-time, 6. Number enrolled (new admits only) 2004–2005 part-time, 1. Total enrolled 2004–2005 full-time, 19, part-time, 1. Openings 2005–2006, 10. The Median number of years required for completion of a degree are 3. The number of students enrolled full and part-time who were dismissed or voluntarily withdrew from this program area were 0.

Admissions Requirements:

Scores: Entries appear in this order: required test or GPA, minimum score (if required), median score of students entering in 2003–2004. Master's Programs: GRE-V no minimum stated, 380; GRE-Q no minimum stated, 480; overall undergraduate GPA 3.0, 3.6. Occasionally, applicants with a GPA lower than 3.0 may be admitted conditionally. GRE-Writing median score is 4.5 Doctoral Programs: GRE-V no minimum stated, 430; GRE-Q no minimum stated, 460; overall undergraduate GPA 3.0, 3.4; psychology GPA no minimum stated, 3.60.

Occasionally, students with GPAs below this level may be admitted conditionally.

Other Criteria: (importance of criteria rated low, medium, or high): GRE/MAT scores medium, research experience medium, work experience high, extracurricular activity medium, clinically related public service high, GPA medium, letters of recommendation medium, interview high, statement of goals and objectives medium. Varies per program. Students with little experience in deafness or sign language may be required to take a summer immersion program prior to enrolling. For additional information on admission requirements, go to: http://gradschool.gallaudet.edu/gradschool/index.html.

Student Characteristics: The following represents characteristics of students in 2004–2005 in all graduate psychology programs in the department: Female–full-time 41, part-time 1; Male–full-time 9, part-time 0; African American/Black–full-time 5, part-time 0; Hispanic/Latino(a)–full-time 2, part-time 0; Asian/Pacific Islander–full-time 4, part-time 0; American Indian/Alaska Native–full-time 0, part-time 0; Caucasian–full-time 38, part-time 1; Multi-ethnic–full-time 1, part-time 0; students subject to the Americans With Disabilities Act–full-time 15, part-time 0.

Financial Information/Assistance:

Tuition for Full-Time Study: *Master's:* State residents: per academic year $10,600, $589 per credit hour; Nonstate residents: per academic year $10,600, $589 per credit hour. *Doctoral:* State residents: per academic year $10,600, $589 per credit hour; Nonstate residents: per academic year $10,600, $589 per credit hour. Tuition is subject to change. See the following Web site for updates and changes in tuition costs: http://gradschool.gallaudet.edu/.

Financial Assistance:

First Year Students: Research assistantships available for first-year. Average amount paid per academic year: $4,500. Average number of hours worked per week: 8. Fellowships and scholarships available for first-year. Average amount paid per academic year: $7,000. Average number of hours worked per week: 10. Tuition remission given: full.

Advanced Students: Teaching assistantships available for advanced students. Average amount paid per academic year: $4,500. Average number of hours worked per week: 8. Research assistantships available for advanced students. Average amount paid per academic year: $4,500. Average number of hours worked per week: 8. Fellowships and scholarships available for advanced students. Average amount paid per academic year: $7,000. Average number of hours worked per week: 10. Tuition remission given: full.

Contact Information: Of all students currently enrolled full-time, 90% benefitted from one or more of the listed financial assistance programs. Application and information available online at: http://financialaid.gallaudet.edu/.

Internships/Practica: Students in the School Psychology Psy Program (which includes the MA as a non-terminal degree), begin with a practicum experience in their first semester, visiting and observing school programs as part of their Introduction to School Psychology course. During their second semester they are involved in Practicum I (3 credit course), which involves closely supervised practicum doing cognitive assessments of deaf and hearing children (if appropriate) at laboratory schools on campus and a DC neighborhood school. Practicum II (3 credits) is taken the third semester and requires two full days per week for a minimum of 14 weeks in which they work with a school psychologist in the Washington Metropolitan area doing comprehensive assessments, and some counseling if opportunities are available, and observation on a limited basis during their fourth semester (an option). The third year (semesters 5 and 6) are spent in a full-time internship in a school program approved by the program. These internships are typically located in both residential schools for the deaf as well as public school systems serving mainstreamed deaf youngsters. Internship sites are located in all parts of the United States. Students in the clinical psychology doctoral program begin practicum in their second year, conducting psychological assessments and psychotherapy at the Gallaudet University Mental Health Center. Advanced students can apply for any of the more than 80 externships available in the Washington, DC area. These externships allow students to work with a wide variety of settings and populations in assessment, psychotherapy, and other psychological interventions. Experiences with both deaf and hearing clients are available. The pre-doctoral internship can be taken in any program approved by the faculty. For those doctoral students for whom a professional internship is required prior to graduation, 1 applied in 2003–2004. Of those who applied, 1 were placed in internships listed by the Association of Psychology Postdoctoral and Internship Programs (APPIC); 1 were placed in APA accredited internships.

Housing and Day Care: On-campus housing is available. See the following Web site for more information: http://gradschool.gallaudet.edu/gradschool/Comments/livingoncampus.html. On-campus day care facilities are available. See the following Web site for more information: http://clerccenter.gallaudet.edu/cdc/.

Employment of Department Graduates:

Master's Degree Graduates: Of those who graduated in the academic year 2003–2004, the following categories and numbers represent the post-graduate activities and employment of master's degree graduates: Enrolled in a post-doctoral residency/fellowship (n/a), employed in independent practice (n/a), other employment position (6), total from the above (master's) (6).

Doctoral Degree Graduates: Of those who graduated in the academic year 2003–2004, the following categories and numbers represent the post-graduate activities and employment of doctoral degree graduates: Enrolled in a psychology doctoral program (n/a), employed in independent practice (1), total from the above (doctoral) (1).

Additional Information:

Orientation, Objectives, and Emphasis of Department: The Psychology department at Gallaudet University offers graduate programs in school psychology and clinical psychology. The school psychology program awards a nonterminal Master of Arts degree in developmental psychology plus a Specialist in School Psychology degree with specialization in deafness. The clinical psychology program is a scholar-practitioner model PhD program, and trains generalist clinical psychologists to work with deaf, hard-of-hearing, and hearing populations. The school psychology program is both NCATE/NASP and NASDTEC-approved, and leads to certification as a school psychologist in the District of Columbia and approximately 24 states with reciprocity of certification. The full-time, 3-year program requires completion of at least 72 graduate semester hours, including a one-year internship. The APA accredited clinical psychology program is a five-year program providing balanced training in research and clinical skills with a variety of age groups, including deaf and hard-of-hearing children, adults, and older adults. The fifth year is designed as a full-time clinical psychology internship. A research-based dissertation is required.

Special Facilities or Resources: Gallaudet University is an internationally recognized center for research and training in areas related to deafness. With a student body of approximately 2100, the university trains deaf and hearing students in a variety of fields at the bachelor, master's, and doctoral levels. Gallaudet programs are located on historic Kendall Green, in northeast Washington, DC, near the U.S. Capitol, the Library of Congress, and the Smithsonian Institute. Also located on the campus are the Gallaudet University Mental Health Center, the Kendall Demonstration Elementary School, the Model Secondary School for the Deaf, the Gallaudet Research Institute, the Kellogg Conference Center, and the Merrill Learning Center, which contains the largest collection of references on deafness in the world. Gallaudet faculty, including both deaf and hearing individuals, possess a unique combination of scholarly activity in their respective disciplines and experience with deaf clients and research on deafness. The University is committed to a working model of a bilingual (American Sign Language and English), multicultural community, where deaf, hard of hearing, and hearing people can work together without communication barriers. Gallaudet University is accredited by the Middle States Association of Colleges and Secondary Schools and is a member of the Consortium of Universities of the Washington Metropolitan Area.

Information for Students With Physical Disabilities: See the following Web site for more information: http://depts.gallaudet.edu/oswd/.

Application Information:
Send to: Office of Graduate Admissions, Gallaudet University, 800 Florida Avenue, NE, Washington, DC 20002. Application available online. URL of online application: gradschool.gallaudet.edu. Students are admitted in the Fall, application deadline February 1. *Fee:* $50.

George Washington University
Department of Psychology
2125 G Street, NW
Washington, DC 20052
Telephone: (202) 994-6320
Fax: (202) 994-1602
E-mail: *psych@gwu.edu*
Web: *http://www.gwu.edu/~psycdept*

Department Information:
1922. Chairperson: Elliot Hirshman. Number of Faculty: total—full-time 19, part-time 3; women—full-time 9, part-time 3; minority—full-time 7.

Programs and Degrees Offered:
Listed in the following order: Program area, degree type (T if terminal Master's), number awarded 7/03–6/04. Applied Social Psychology PhD (Doctor of Philosophy) 6, Clinical PhD (Doctor of Philosophy) 11, Cognitive Neuroscience PhD (Doctor of Philosophy) 1.

APA Accreditation: Clinical PhD (Doctor of Philosophy).

Student Applications/Admissions:
Student Applications
Applied Social Psychology PhD (Doctor of Philosophy)—Applications 2004–2005, 121. Total applicants accepted 2004–2005, 5. Openings 2005–2006, 3. The Median number of years required for completion of a degree are 6. *Clinical PhD (Doctor of Philosophy)*—Applications 2004–2005, 300. Total applicants accepted 2004–2005, 12. Openings 2005–2006, 5. The Median number of years required for completion of a degree are 6. *Cognitive Neuroscience PhD (Doctor of Philosophy)*—Applications 2004–2005, 45. Total applicants accepted 2004–2005, 4. Openings 2005–2006, 2. The Median number of years required for completion of a degree are 6.

Admissions Requirements:
Scores: Entries appear in this order: required test or GPA, minimum score (if required), median score of students entering in 2003–2004. Doctoral Programs: GRE-V no minimum stated, 670; GRE-Q no minimum stated, 650; GRE-Analytical no minimum stated, 680; overall undergraduate GPA no minimum stated, 3.80.
Other Criteria: (importance of criteria rated low, medium, or high): GRE/MAT scores medium, research experience high, work experience medium, extracurricular activity medium, clinically related public service medium, GPA high, letters of recommendation medium, interview high, statement of goals and objectives high, Interview & Clinical Public Service Apply to Clinical program.

Student Characteristics: The following represents characteristics of students in 2004–2005 in all graduate psychology programs in the department: Female–full-time 66, part-time 0; Male–full-time 14, part-time 0; African American/Black–full-time 6, part-time 0; Hispanic/Latino(a)–full-time 6, part-time 0; Asian/Pacific Islander–full-time 8, part-time 0; American Indian/Alaska Native–full-time 0, part-time 0; Caucasian–full-time 0, part-time 0; students subject to the Americans With Disabilities Act–full-time 1, part-time 0.

Financial Information/Assistance:
Financial Assistance:
First Year Students: Teaching assistantships available for first-year. Tuition remission given: full. Research assistantships available for first-year. Tuition remission given: full. Fellowships and scholarships available for first-year. Tuition remission given: partial.
Advanced Students: Teaching assistantships available for advanced students. Tuition remission given: full. Research assistantships available for advanced students. Tuition remission given: full. Fellowships and scholarships available for advanced students. Tuition remission given: partial.
Contact Information: Of all students currently enrolled full-time, 100% benefitted from one or more of the listed financial assistance programs.

Internships/Practica: There is a wide variety of placements available in the DC Metro area. Placements are a required part of training in the clinical programs. For those doctoral students for whom a professional internship is required prior to graduation, 7 applied in 2003–2004. Of those who applied, 7 were placed in internships listed by the Association of Psychology Postdoctoral and Internship Programs (APPIC); 7 were placed in APA accredited internships.

Housing and Day Care: No on-campus housing is available. On-campus day care facilities are available.

Employment of Department Graduates:

Master's Degree Graduates: Of those who graduated in the academic year 2003–2004, the following categories and numbers represent the post-graduate activities and employment of master's degree graduates: Enrolled in a post-doctoral residency/fellowship (n/a), employed in independent practice (n/a), total from the above (master's) (0).

Doctoral Degree Graduates: Of those who graduated in the academic year 2003–2004, the following categories and numbers represent the post-graduate activities and employment of doctoral degree graduates: Enrolled in a psychology doctoral program (n/a), enrolled in a post-doctoral residency/fellowship (5), employed in independent practice (0), employed in an academic position at a university (1), employed in business or industry (research/consulting) (2), employed in a government agency (research) (1), total from the above (doctoral) (9).

Additional Information:

Orientation, Objectives, and Emphasis of Department: The department provides training in the basic science of psychology for each of its graduate programs. Specialized training is offered in three program areas: applied social, clinical, and cognitive neuropsychology. The applied social program focuses on theory and methods of addressing current social problems such as in health care, education, and the prevention of high risk social behaviors. The clinical program is an APA-approved program emphasizing both the basic science and applied aspects of clinical psychology. The focus of the program is Health Promotion and Disease Prevention in Diverse Urban Communities. The cognitive neuroscience program focuses on cognition, learning, and memory with emphasis on the psychobiological determinants of these functions. The training in each program addresses both scientific and professional objectives: Students are trained for careers in academic institutions, applied research, and professional practice.

Special Facilities or Resources: Excellent on-campus computer facilities; laboratories for child study, group studies, cognitive testing and small animal research. Convenient access to staff, libraries, and facilities at national health and mental health institutes (NIH), and Mental Health Training Centers for Clinical Students. See Home Page for information.

Application Information:
Send to: Graduate School, CSAS, George Washington University, Washington, DC 20052. Students are admitted in the Fall, application deadline December 15. Cognitive–Neuropscience and Applied Social–February 1. *Fee:* $65. Cognitive Neuropsychology and Applied Social–February 1.

George Washington University
Doctoral Program in Clinical Psychology
Columbian College of Arts and Sciences
2300 M Street, NW, Suite 910
Washington, DC 20037
Telephone: (202) 496-6260
Fax: (202) 496-6263
E-mail: *psyd@gwu.edu*
Web: *http://www.gwu.edu/~psyd*

Department Information:
1996. Director: Dorothy E. Holmes, PhD. Number of Faculty: total–full-time 2, part-time 7; women–part-time 4; minority–part-time 2.

Programs and Degrees Offered:
Listed in the following order: Program area, degree type (T if terminal Master's), number awarded 7/03–6/04. Clinical PsyD (Doctor of Psychology) 34.

APA Accreditation: Clinical PsyD (Doctor of Psychology).

Student Applications/Admissions:
Student Applications
Clinical PsyD (Doctor of Psychology)—Applications 2004–2005, 400. Total applicants accepted 2004–2005, 35. Number enrolled (new admits only) 2004–2005 full-time, 33. Openings 2005–2006, 30. The Median number of years required for completion of a degree are 4. The number of students enrolled full and part-time who were dismissed or voluntarily withdrew from this program area were 2.

Admissions Requirements:
Scores: Entries appear in this order: required test or GPA, minimum score (if required), median score of students entering in 2003–2004. Doctoral Programs: GRE-V no minimum stated, 548; GRE-Q no minimum stated, 588; GRE-V+Q 1000; GRE-Analytical no minimum stated, 592; overall undergraduate GPA 3.0, 3.26.
Other Criteria: (importance of criteria rated low, medium, or high): GRE/MAT scores medium, research experience medium, work experience medium, clinically related public service high, GPA medium, letters of recommendation high, interview high, statement of goals and objectives high. For additional information on admission requirements, go to: http://columbian.gwu.edu/grad/index.php/id/44.

Student Characteristics: The following represents characteristics of students in 2004–2005 in all graduate psychology programs in the department: Female–full-time 118, part-time 0; Male–full-time 32, part-time 0; African American/Black–full-time 8, part-time 0; Hispanic/Latino(a)–full-time 7, part-time 0; Asian/Pacific Islander–full-time 11, part-time 0; American Indian/Alaska Native–full-time 0, part-time 0; Caucasian–full-time 121, part-time 0; Multi-ethnic–full-time 3, part-time 0.

Financial Information/Assistance:
Tuition for Full-Time Study: *Doctoral:* State residents: $876 per credit hour; Nonstate residents: $876 per credit hour. Tuition is subject to change.

Financial Assistance:

First Year Students: Fellowships and scholarships available for first-year. Average amount paid per academic year: $7,200. Average number of hours worked per week: 0. Apply by none.

Advanced Students: Fellowships and scholarships available for advanced students. Average amount paid per academic year: $4,500. Average number of hours worked per week: 0. Apply by none.

Contact Information: Of all students currently enrolled full-time, 30% benefitted from one or more of the listed financial assistance programs.

Internships/Practica: The principal practicum setup is Center Clinic, our framing clinic run by faculty, clinical faculty and students under supervision. We have Clinic Affiliate Settings that provide patients and clinical opportunities under our supervision. Special interests and needs are served by independent externship settings. For those doctoral students for whom a professional internship is required prior to graduation, 44 applied in 2003–2004. Of those who applied, 34 were placed in internships listed by the Association of Psychology Postdoctoral and Internship Programs (APPIC); 16 were placed in APA accredited internships.

Housing and Day Care: No on-campus housing is available. No on-campus day care facilities are available.

Employment of Department Graduates:

Master's Degree Graduates: Of those who graduated in the academic year 2003–2004, the following categories and numbers represent the post-graduate activities and employment of master's degree graduates: Enrolled in a post-doctoral residency/fellowship (n/a), employed in independent practice (n/a), total from the above (master's) (0).

Doctoral Degree Graduates: Of those who graduated in the academic year 2003–2004, the following categories and numbers represent the post-graduate activities and employment of doctoral degree graduates: Enrolled in a psychology doctoral program (n/a), total from the above (doctoral) (0).

Additional Information:

Orientation, Objectives, and Emphasis of Department: The George Washington University PsyD program in Clinical Psychology has a broadly-based psychodynamic orientation. After completing the core curriculum in the first year, students choose from among four advanced tracks: (a) psychodynamic psychotherapy, (b) group and community intervention, (c) child and family therapy, and (d) diagnostic assessment. Students choose major and minor areas of concentration, with the goal of obtaining advanced, in-depth training in their specialties. The principal emphasis from the first semester of the program is on high-quality clinical training. For all three years of class work students participate in case seminars, practica and externships, culminating in a fourth-year internship. In the third year the student writes a major area paper on a clinical topic of interest. Additional emphases of the program include group and organizational dynamics, psychodynamic theory, psychodynamic child development and intervention, psychology and law, and comprehensive (biopsychosocial) diagnosis.

Special Facilities or Resources: In August 1997 our PsyD Program moved into a special facility designed for our needs, with all faculty and program offices, classrooms, training clinics, lounges and study areas in one location.

Information for Students With Physical Disabilities: See the following Web site for more information: www.gwu.edu/~dss.

Application Information:
Send to: Graduate Admissions, Columbian School of Arts and Sciences, The George Washington University, 801 22nd Street NW, Suite 107, Washington, DC 20052, (202) 994-6211, fax: (202) 994-6213, e-mail: askccas@gwu.edu. Application available online. URL of online application: http://columbian.gwu.edu/grad/index.php/id/44. Students are admitted in the Fall, application deadline January 15. Programs have rolling admissions. Prior to enrollment in the PsyD program, students are expected to have completed an introductory level statistics course. *Fee:* $55.

Georgetown University
Department of Psychology
Graduate School of Arts and Sciences
306 White Gravenor Hall, 3700 O Street, NW
Washington, DC 20057
Telephone: (202) 687-4042
Fax: (202) 687-6050
E-mail: *psychology@georgetown.edu*
Web: *http://www.georgetown.edu/departments/psychology/*

Department Information:
2003. Chairperson: Deborah A. Phillips, PhD Number of Faculty: total–full-time 15, part-time 2; women–full-time 7; minority–full-time 1.

Programs and Degrees Offered:
Listed in the following order: Program area, degree type (T if terminal Master's), number awarded 7/03–6/04. Lifespan Cognitive Neuroscience PhD (Doctor of Philosophy), Human Development and Public Policy PhD (Doctor of Philosophy) 0.

Student Applications/Admissions:
Student Applications
Lifespan Cognitive Neuroscience PhD (Doctor of Philosophy)— Applications 2004–2005, 13. Total applicants accepted 2004–2005, 4. Number enrolled (new admits only) 2004–2005 full-time, 3. Number enrolled (new admits only) 2004–2005 part-time, 0. Openings 2005–2006, 2. *Human Development and Public Policy PhD (Doctor of Philosophy)*—Applications 2004–2005, 37. Total applicants accepted 2004–2005, 5. Number enrolled (new admits only) 2004–2005 full-time, 2. Number enrolled (new admits only) 2004–2005 part-time, 0. Openings 2005–2006, 2. The number of students enrolled full and part-time who were dismissed or voluntarily withdrew from this program area were 0.

Admissions Requirements:
Scores: Entries appear in this order: required test or GPA, minimum score (if required), median score of students entering in 2003–2004. Doctoral Programs: GRE-V+Q 1300; GRE-Analytical 4.5; overall undergraduate GPA 3.50. A minimum score of 1300 is required on two sections of the GRE - Verbal and Quantitative. A minimum score of 4.5 is required on the Analytical Writing Exam. Applicants who took the GRE prior

to the new format should have scored at least at 1300 on two sections of the exam - Verbal, Quantitative or Analytical. *Other Criteria:* (importance of criteria rated low, medium, or high): GRE/MAT scores high, research experience high, work experience low, extracurricular activity low, clinically related public service low, GPA high, letters of recommendation high, interview high, statement of goals and objectives high. The 500-word statement of academic, professional, and personal goals should also (a) include a discussion of how graduate school in Developmental Science will help you to achieve these goals, (b) specify your interest in one of the two areas of concentration, and (c) indicate which faculty member/s you would want to work with and how you see their interests meshing with yours. This latter information is very important because the fit between student and faculty research interests is a key component in admissions decisions. Please identify your name, program to which you are applying, term of application, U.S. social security number (if applicable), and birthdate on your submitted statement. The Writing Sample, typically chosen from your undergraduate work, should best reflect your abilities and interests as they relate to your chosen concentration in the PhD program. For additional information on admission requirements, go to: http://www.georgetown.edu/departments/psychology/grad/gradnew.html.

Student Characteristics: The following represents characteristics of students in 2004–2005 in all graduate psychology programs in the department: Female–full-time 8, part-time 0; Male–full-time 0, part-time 0; African American/Black–full-time 0, part-time 0; Hispanic/Latino(a)–full-time 0, part-time 0; Asian/Pacific Islander–full-time 0, part-time 0; American Indian/Alaska Native–full-time 0, part-time 0; Caucasian–full-time 7, part-time 0; Multiethnic–full-time 1, part-time 0; students subject to the Americans With Disabilities Act–full-time 0, part-time 0.

Financial Information/Assistance:

Tuition for Full-Time Study: *Doctoral:* State residents: per academic year $27,528; Nonstate residents: per academic year $27,528. Tuition is subject to change. See the following Web site for updates and changes in tuition costs: http://finaid.georgetown.edu/coagrad.htm.

Financial Assistance:

First Year Students: Teaching assistantships available for first-year. Average amount paid per academic year: $16,400. Average number of hours worked per week: 15. Tuition remission given: full. Fellowships and scholarships available for first-year. Average amount paid per academic year: $19,400.

Advanced Students: Teaching assistantships available for advanced students. Average amount paid per academic year: $16,400. Average number of hours worked per week: 15. Tuition remission given: full. Fellowships and scholarships available for advanced students. Average amount paid per academic year: $19,400.

Contact Information: Of all students currently enrolled full-time, 100% benefitted from one or more of the listed financial assistance programs. Application and information available online at: http://www.georgetown.edu/students/student-aid/grmenu.htm.

Internships/Practica: No information provided.

Housing and Day Care: No on-campus housing is available. On-campus day care facilities are available. See the following Web

site for more information: Georgetown University has a campus child care center, Hoya Kids. http://www3.georgetown.edu/hr/hoya_kids/index.html.

Employment of Department Graduates:

Master's Degree Graduates: Of those who graduated in the academic year 2003–2004, the following categories and numbers represent the post-graduate activities and employment of master's degree graduates: Enrolled in a post-doctoral residency/fellowship (n/a), employed in independent practice (n/a), total from the above (master's) (0).

Doctoral Degree Graduates: Of those who graduated in the academic year 2003–2004, the following categories and numbers represent the post-graduate activities and employment of doctoral degree graduates: Enrolled in a psychology doctoral program (n/a), total from the above (doctoral) (0).

Additional Information:

Orientation, Objectives, and Emphasis of Department: This new program enrolled its first class in 2003. Its two concentrations provide an interdisciplinary education in the sciences concerned with the processes and contexts of development across the lifespan. It offers training in the theories and methods of the Developmental Sciences, enabling students to place the study of development into broader contexts - biological, familial, social, cultural, economic, historical, and political. The concentration in Human Development and Public Policy and the joint degree in Psychology and Public Policy link students to Georgetown's extensive network of policy scholars and programs, integrating a grounding in Developmental Science with instruction in quantitative and policy analysis skills, the policy process, and additional perspectives common to policy studies, notably economics and political science. The concentration in Lifespan Cognitive Neuroscience integrates grounding in Developmental Science with preparation for teaching and research on cognition and its neural bases. Students may focus their research on the behavioral/cognitive level, or may add neuro-imaging techniques to explore brain bases of cognition. This concentration maintains ties with Georgetown's Interdisciplinary Program in Neuroscience PhD program. Both concentrations prepare students for post-degree positions in institutions of higher education, research institutes, medical settings, nonprofit organizations, government agencies, and other policy settings.

Special Facilities or Resources: Graduate students have office space in a graduate student suite (first-years) or faculty laboratory space (later years). They enter a rich interdisciplinary community in which Psychology graduate students take courses with graduate students from public policy, neuroscience, linguistics, and other related disciplines. The Psychology Department contains an observational laboratory facility as well as faculty laboratories investigating a range of areas including children and the media, cognitive aging, social reasoning, developmental cognitive neuroscience, infant cognition, child care, animal models of developmental disorders, and research on adolescence, women, and the law. The Psychology Department also maintains the Georgetown Research Volunteer Project, a university-funded, web-based facility for recruiting research participants across the life span. The Medical Center, which is immediately adjacent to the Main Campus, contains the Center for Functional and Molecular Imaging, affording the opportunity to conduct research using fMRI and other state-of-the-art neuroimaging technology. Georgetown

University is situated in the nation's capital and has among its unique mix of resources a public policy institute, medical school, law school, and school of foreign policy, each of which is among the leading programs in the nation. The two graduate concentrations take full advantage of these resources.

Information for Students With Physical Disabilities: See the following Web site for more information: http://www.georgetown.edu/student-affairs/ldss/physical.html.

Application Information:
Send to: Office of Graduate Admissions, Graduate School of Arts and Sciences, Georgetown University, Attention: Credentials, Department of Psychology Graduate Program, Box 571004, 3700 O Street, NW, ICC-302, Washington, DC 20057-1004. Application available online. URL of online application: http://grad.georgetown.edu/pages/apply_online.cfm. Students are admitted in the Fall, application deadline December 1. Fee: $65. The application form must be submitted with a nonrefundable application fee. The paper application fee is $65, payable by check or money order only. The online application fee is $55, and may be paid by credit card, check or money order. The applicant's name, U.S. social security number (if applicable), program applying to, and term of application should be printed clearly on the check or money order if using that method of payment. Check or money orders should be made payable to Georgetown University. Requests for waiver of the application fee are not accepted. Students who are currently enrolled in a master's program at Georgetown University and are requesting PhD status in the same department are not required to pay an application fee.

Howard University (2004 data)
Department of Psychology
The Graduate School
525 Bryant Street, NW
Washington, DC 20059
Telephone: (202) 806-6805
Fax: (202) 806-4873
E-mail: *aroberts@howard.edu*
Web: *http://www.howard.edu*

Department Information:
1928. Chairperson: Albert Roberts. Number of Faculty: total–full-time 21, part-time 2; women–full-time 9, part-time 2; minority–full-time 13, part-time 2.

Programs and Degrees Offered:
Listed in the following order: Program area, degree type (T if terminal Master's), number awarded 7/03–6/04. Clinical PhD (Doctor of Philosophy) 4, developmental PhD (Doctor of Philosophy) 1, neuropsychology PhD (Doctor of Philosophy) 1, personality PhD (Doctor of Philosophy) 0, social PhD (Doctor of Philosophy) 1.

APA Accreditation: Clinical PhD (Doctor of Philosophy).

Student Applications/Admissions:
Student Applications
Clinical PhD (Doctor of Philosophy)—Applications 2004–2005, 135. Total applicants accepted 2004–2005, 10. Total enrolled 2004–2005 full-time, 26, part-time, 4. Openings 2005–2006, 6. The Median number of years required for completion of a degree are 6. The number of students enrolled full and part-time who were dismissed or voluntarily withdrew from this program area were 1. *Developmental PhD (Doctor of Philosophy)*—Applications 2004–2005, 36. Total applicants accepted 2004–2005, 7. Total enrolled 2004–2005 full-time, 18, part-time, 6. Openings 2005–2006, 4. The Median number of years required for completion of a degree are 5. The number of students enrolled full and part-time who were dismissed or voluntarily withdrew from this program area were 4. *Neuropsychology PhD (Doctor of Philosophy)*—Applications 2004–2005, 7. Total applicants accepted 2004–2005, 3. Total enrolled 2004–2005 full-time, 4, part-time, 2. Openings 2005–2006, 2. The Median number of years required for completion of a degree are 5. The number of students enrolled full and part-time who were dismissed or voluntarily withdrew from this program area were 0. *Personality PhD (Doctor of Philosophy)*—Applications 2004–2005, 15. Total applicants accepted 2004–2005, 5. Total enrolled 2004–2005 full-time, 6, part-time, 2. Openings 2005–2006, 2. The Median number of years required for completion of a degree are 6. The number of students enrolled full and part-time who were dismissed or voluntarily withdrew from this program area were 0. *Social PhD (Doctor of Philosophy)*—Applications 2004–2005, 16. Total applicants accepted 2004–2005, 6. Total enrolled 2004–2005 full-time, 6, part-time, 3. Openings 2005–2006, 3. The Median number of years required for completion of a degree are 6. The number of students enrolled full and part-time who were dismissed or voluntarily withdrew from this program area were 1.

Admissions Requirements:
Scores: Entries appear in this order: required test or GPA, minimum score (if required), median score of students entering in 2003–2004. Master's Programs: GRE-V no minimum stated; GRE-Q no minimum stated; overall undergraduate GPA 3.0, 3.4. You cannot receive an assistantship with a grade point average less than 3.26. Doctoral Programs: GRE-V no minimum stated; GRE-Q no minimum stated; overall undergraduate GPA 3.00, 3.5.
Other Criteria: (importance of criteria rated low, medium, or high): GRE/MAT scores low, research experience medium, GPA high, letters of recommendation high, interview high, statement of goals and objectives medium. Interview is of high importance for the clinical area only.

Student Characteristics: The following represents characteristics of students in 2004–2005 in all graduate psychology programs in the department: Female–full-time 48, part-time 12; Male–full-time 12, part-time 5; African American/Black–full-time 52, part-time 13; Hispanic/Latino(a)–full-time 1, part-time 0; Asian/Pacific Islander–full-time 1, part-time 0; American Indian/Alaska Native–full-time 0, part-time 0; Caucasian–full-time 6, part-time 0; students subject to the Americans With Disabilities Act–full-time 0, part-time 0.

Financial Information/Assistance:
Tuition for Full-Time Study: *Master's:* State residents: per academic year $11,195, $644 per credit hour; Nonstate residents: per academic year $11,195, $644 per credit hour. *Doctoral:* State residents: per academic year $11,195, $644 per credit hour; Nonstate residents: per academic year $11,195, $644 per credit hour.

Tuition is subject to change. See the following Web site for updates and changes in tuition costs: www.Howard.edu.

Financial Assistance:

First Year Students: Teaching assistantships available for first-year. Average amount paid per academic year: $10,000. Average number of hours worked per week: 20. Apply by May 1. Tuition remission given: full. Fellowships and scholarships available for first-year. Average amount paid per academic year: $13,500. Average number of hours worked per week: 0. Tuition remission given: full.

Advanced Students: Teaching assistantships available for advanced students. Average amount paid per academic year: $13,500. Apply by May 1. Fellowships and scholarships available for advanced students. Average amount paid per academic year: $15,000. Apply by May 1.

Contact Information: Of all students currently enrolled full-time, 45% benefitted from one or more of the listed financial assistance programs.

Internships/Practica: Internships and practica are available at various clinical sites in the District of Columbia, Maryland, and Virginia for students beginning in their first year of study. For those doctoral students for whom a professional internship is required prior to graduation, 8 applied in 2003–2004. Of those who applied, 8 were placed in internships listed by the Association of Psychology Postdoctoral and Internship Programs (APPIC); 6 were placed in APA accredited internships.

Housing and Day Care: On-campus housing is available. On-campus day care facilities are available. Howard University Early Learning Center, Howard Place, Washington, DC 20059.

Employment of Department Graduates:

Master's Degree Graduates: Of those who graduated in the academic year 2003–2004, the following categories and numbers represent the post-graduate activities and employment of master's degree graduates: Enrolled in a post-doctoral residency/fellowship (n/a), employed in independent practice (n/a), total from the above (master's) (0).

Doctoral Degree Graduates: Of those who graduated in the academic year 2003–2004, the following categories and numbers represent the post-graduate activities and employment of doctoral degree graduates: Enrolled in a psychology doctoral program (n/a), total from the above (doctoral) (0).

Additional Information:

Orientation, Objectives, and Emphasis of Department: The Graduate Program at Howard prepares students for careers in research, teaching and the practice of psychology. Advanced study in clinical, developmental, social, personality, and neuropsychology is offered. A major emphasis of the program is research training, and students are expected to conduct research throughout their graduate study.

Application Information:

Send to: Graduate Admissions, Graduate School of Arts and Sciences, Howard University, Washington, DC 20059. Students are admitted in the Fall, application deadline February 1. February 15 all other areas except clinical. *Fee:* $45.

Argosy University/Tampa

Florida School of Professional Psychology
School of Psychology and Behavioral Sciences
4410 North Himes Avenue Suite 150
Tampa, FL 33614
Telephone: (800) 850-6488
Fax: (813) 246-4045
E-mail: *tsheehan@argosyu.edu*
Web: *http://www.argosyu.edu*

Department Information:
1995. Interim Dean: Melanie Storms, PsyD Number of Faculty: total–full-time 6, part-time 4; women–full-time 3, part-time 2; minority–part-time 1; faculty subject to the Americans With Disabilities Act 1.

Programs and Degrees Offered:
Listed in the following order: Program area, degree type (T if terminal Master's), number awarded 7/03–6/04. Clinical Psychology PsyD (Doctor of Psychology).

APA Accreditation: Clinical PsyD (Doctor of Psychology).

Student Applications/Admissions:
Student Applications
Clinical Psychology PsyD (Doctor of Psychology)—Openings 2005–2006, 40.

Admissions Requirements:
Scores: Entries appear in this order: required test or GPA, minimum score (if required), median score of students entering in 2003–2004. Master's Programs: overall undergraduate GPA 3.0; last 2 years GPA 3.0; psychology GPA 3.0. Doctoral Programs: GRE-V 500; GRE-Q 500; GRE-V+Q 1000; MAT 50; overall undergraduate GPA 3.0, 3.53; last 2 years GPA 3.0; psychology GPA 3.0.
Other Criteria: (importance of criteria rated low, medium, or high): GRE/MAT scores low, research experience medium, work experience high, extracurricular activity medium, clinically related public service high, GPA high, letters of recommendation high, interview high, statement of goals and objectives high.

Student Characteristics: The following represents characteristics of students in 2004–2005 in all graduate psychology programs in the department: Caucasian–full-time 0, part-time 0.

Financial Information/Assistance:
Tuition for Full-Time Study: *Master's:* State residents: $715 per credit hour; Nonstate residents: $715 per credit hour. *Doctoral:* State residents: $715 per credit hour; Nonstate residents: $715 per credit hour. Tuition is subject to change. See the following Web site for updates and changes in tuition costs: www.argosyu.edu.

Financial Assistance:
First Year Students: Research assistantships available for first-year. Average amount paid per academic year: $3,000. Average number of hours worked per week: 5. Tuition remission given: partial. Fellowships and scholarships available for first-year. Tuition remission given: partial.
Advanced Students: Teaching assistantships available for advanced students. Average amount paid per academic year: $3,000. Average number of hours worked per week: 10. Tuition remission given: partial. Research assistantships available for advanced students. Average amount paid per academic year: $3,000. Average number of hours worked per week: 10. Tuition remission given: partial. Fellowships and scholarships available for advanced students.
Contact Information: Of all students currently enrolled full-time, 25% benefitted from one or more of the listed financial assistance programs.

Internships/Practica: All students are required to complete a 800-hour diagnostic practicum and a 800-hour therapy practicum. Opportunities for practicum experience are available at many sites throughout the community including community mental health centers, hospitals, schools, college counseling centers, private practices, forensic, geriatric and child treatment centers, medical centers and rehabilitation centers. Specialty practicum sites are developed based on student interest and availability.

Housing and Day Care: No on-campus housing is available. No on-campus day care facilities are available.

Employment of Department Graduates:
Master's Degree Graduates: Of those who graduated in the academic year 2003–2004, the following categories and numbers represent the post-graduate activities and employment of master's degree graduates: Enrolled in a post-doctoral residency/fellowship (n/a), employed in independent practice (n/a), total from the above (master's) (0).
Doctoral Degree Graduates: Of those who graduated in the academic year 2003–2004, the following categories and numbers represent the post-graduate activities and employment of doctoral degree graduates: Enrolled in a psychology doctoral program (n/a), total from the above (doctoral) (0).

Additional Information:
Orientation, Objectives, and Emphasis of Department: The Florida School of Professional Psychology is a practitioner-oriented program, based on the local clinical scientist model, established with the aim of training highly qualified clinical psychologists. In the belief that it is the responsibility of each clinician to determine his or her approach to therapy, the program strives to introduce students to a variety of clinical orientations. Emphasis is on clinical skills, particularly psychological assessment, diagnosis and psychotherapy. Students have the opportunity to focus on neuropsychology, geropsychology, child psychology, or marriage and family therapy.

Special Facilities or Resources: All faculty are experienced clinicians as well as educators. A number of general and specialized practicum sites are available to students. The departmental library houses a focused collection of monographs and journals and provides students access to electronic library resources throughout the Argosy University and state of Florida library systems. There is an observation room with one-way mirror and videotaping facilities on campus.

Information for Students With Physical Disabilities: contact: tsheehan@argosyu.edu.

Application Information:
Send to: Assistant Director of Admissions/FSPP, Argosy University-Tampa Campus, 4410 North Himes Avenue, Suite 150, Tampa, FL 33614. Application available online. URL of online application: http://www.argosyu.edu/content/?pg=19. Students are admitted in the Fall, application deadline March 15; Spring, application deadline November 15; Summer, application deadline March 30; Programs have rolling admissions. Applications are also accepted on a rolling admissions basis depending on the availability of seats for the next entering class. *Fee:* $50.

Barry University
Department of Psychology
School of Arts and Sciences
11300 NE 2nd Avenue
Miami Shores, FL 33161
Telephone: (305) 899-3270
Fax: (305) 899-3279
E-mail: *lszuchman@mail.barry.edu*
Web: *http://www.barry.edu*

Department Information:
1978. Chairperson: Lenore T. Szuchman. Number of Faculty: total–full-time 10, part-time 8; women–full-time 5, part-time 4; minority–full-time 1, part-time 1.

Programs and Degrees Offered:
Listed in the following order: Program area, degree type (T if terminal Master's), number awarded 7/03–6/04. Clinical Psychology MA/MS (Master of Arts/Science) (T) 11, School Psychology Other 3, Psychology MA/MS (Master of Arts/Science) 13.

Student Applications/Admissions:
Student Applications
Clinical Psychology MA/MS (Master of Arts/Science)—Applications 2004–2005, 50. Total applicants accepted 2004–2005, 35. Total enrolled 2004–2005 full-time, 15, part-time, 3. Openings 2005–2006, 15. The Median number of years required for completion of a degree are 3. *School Psychology Other*—Applications 2004–2005, 15. Total applicants accepted 2004–2005, 10. Number enrolled (new admits only) 2004–2005 part-time, 0. Total enrolled 2004–2005 full-time, 13, part-time, 5. Openings 2005–2006, 15. The Median number of years required for completion of a degree are 2. The

number of students enrolled full and part-time who were dismissed or voluntarily withdrew from this program area were 2. *Psychology MA/MS (Master of Arts/Science)*—Applications 2004–2005, 21. Total applicants accepted 2004–2005, 18. Total enrolled 2004–2005 full-time, 10, part-time, 8. Openings 2005–2006, 15. The Median number of years required for completion of a degree is 1.

Admissions Requirements:
Scores: Entries appear in this order: required test or GPA, minimum score (if required), median score of students entering in 2003–2004. Master's Programs: GRE-V no minimum stated; GRE-Q no minimum stated; GRE-V+Q 1000; overall undergraduate GPA 3.0. Master's GPA 3.4 required for admission to SSP
Other Criteria: (importance of criteria rated low, medium, or high): GRE/MAT scores medium, research experience medium, work experience medium, extracurricular activity low, clinically related public service medium, GPA high, letters of recommendation high, statement of goals and objectives medium.

Student Characteristics: The following represents characteristics of students in 2004–2005 in all graduate psychology programs in the department: Female–full-time 35, part-time 15; Male–full-time 3, part-time 1; African American/Black–full-time 7, part-time 4; Hispanic/Latino(a)–full-time 18, part-time 8; Asian/Pacific Islander–full-time 0, part-time 0; American Indian/Alaska Native–full-time 1, part-time 0; Caucasian–full-time 12, part-time 3; Multi-ethnic–full-time 0, part-time 1; students subject to the Americans With Disabilities Act–full-time 0, part-time 0.

Financial Information/Assistance:
Tuition for Full-Time Study: Master's: State residents: $685 per credit hour; Nonstate residents: $685 per credit hour. See the following Web site for updates and changes in tuition costs: http://www.barry.edu/admissionsFinancialAid/graduate/admissions/tuitionFees.htm.

Financial Assistance:
First Year Students: Teaching assistantships available for first-year. Average amount paid per academic year: $3,000. Average number of hours worked per week: 15. Apply by April 30. Tuition remission given: partial.
Advanced Students: Teaching assistantships available for advanced students. Average amount paid per academic year: $3,000. Average number of hours worked per week: 15. Apply by April 30. Tuition remission given: partial.
Contact Information: Of all students currently enrolled full-time, 15% benefitted from one or more of the listed financial assistance programs.

Internships/Practica: All students enrolled in the MS in Clinical Psychology Program must complete a one-semester practicum. Students in the 60-credit program must also complete a two-semester full-time clinical internship. Because Barry University is located in a large, multi-cultural metropolitan area, the program is able to offer more than the usual number and variety of settings for the internship experience. Sites include but are not limited to community mental health centers, assessment centers (primarily for the assessment of children), psychiatric hospitals, addiction treatment programs, nursing homes, and prison settings. Supervision is provided both at the site and by a clinical supervisor on campus. Students in the SSP program complete a practicum and an internship in the public schools. The internship is full-time for two semesters and can be done locally or at a distance from the campus.

Housing and Day Care: On-campus housing is available. See the following Web site for more information: http://www.barry.edu/studentServices/resLife/graduatehousing.htm. Contact Mr. Patrick Devine at (305) 899-3875 or pdevine@mail.barry.edu. No on-campus day care facilities are available.

Employment of Department Graduates:

Master's Degree Graduates: Of those who graduated in the academic year 2003–2004, the following categories and numbers represent the post-graduate activities and employment of master's degree graduates: Enrolled in a post-doctoral residency/fellowship (n/a), employed in independent practice (n/a), total from the above (master's) (0).

Doctoral Degree Graduates: Of those who graduated in the academic year 2003–2004, the following categories and numbers represent the post-graduate activities and employment of doctoral degree graduates: Enrolled in a psychology doctoral program (n/a), total from the above (doctoral) (0).

Additional Information:

Orientation, Objectives, and Emphasis of Department: In the MS Program in Clinical Psychology, students are expected to achieve competence in theory, assessment, therapy, and research. All clinical psychology students complete a thesis and a practicum. The 36-credit option, a 2-year program, is designed for students who want to go directly into a doctoral program. Students who complete the 3-year, 60-credit program meet licensure requirements for the Mental Health Counselor in Florida. The MS in Psychology is designed for the student who wishes to go on to the Specialist degree in School Psychology (SSP). The SSP program follows the scientist-practitioner model and integrates theoretical and practical training to prevent and remediate academic and emotional problems in the schools. Students gain expertise in evaluation, diagnosis, prescription, interventions, psychometric applications, research, consultation, and professional ethics and standards. Students who successfully complete the MS in Psychology and the SSP program will be prepared to meet licensure requirements for the private practice of school psychology in the state of Florida as well as certification requirements of the Florida State Board of Education. The School Psychology Program has been approved by the Department of Education of the State of Florida and the National Association of School Psychologists.

Special Facilities or Resources: The psychology department is composed of 11 full-time faculty members. Classes are small, and the students are given individual attention and supervision.

Information for Students With Physical Disabilities: See the following Web site for more information: http://www.barry.edu/StudentServices/disability/default.htm.

Application Information:
Send to: Office of Enrollment Services, Barry University, 11300 NE 2nd Avenue, Miami, FL 33161. Application available online. URL of online application: http://www.barry.edu/psychologyclinical/admissions/applyNow.asp. Students are admitted in the Fall. Rolling admissions for MS Psychology and SSP. MS Clinical deadline is February 15 with review continuing as long as space is available. Applicants may be admitted at other times but are urged to enroll in Fall term with undergraduate prerequisites completed in order to finish programs in timely fashion. *Fee:* $30. Waived for Barry University alumni.

Carlos Albizu University, Miami Campus (2004 data)
Doctoral Program, Non-Terminal Master's Program, Terminal Master's Programs
2173 NW 99th Avenue
Miami, FL 33172-2209
Telephone: (305) 593-1223
Fax: (305) 629-8052
E-mail: *grodriguez@albizu.edu*
Web: *http://www.albizu.edu*

Department Information:
1980. Chancellor: Gerardo Rodriguez-Menendez, PhD, MS Cl. Pharm. Number of Faculty: total–full-time 12, part-time 30; women–full-time 6, part-time 16; minority–full-time 9, part-time 19.

Programs and Degrees Offered:
Listed in the following order: Program area, degree type (T if terminal Master's), number awarded 7/03–6/04. Non-Terminal MA/MS (Master of Arts/Science) 38, Industrial/Organizational MA/MS (Master of Arts/Science) (T) 8, PsyD Program PsyD (Doctor of Psychology) 67, MA/MS (Master of Arts/Science) (T) 29.

APA Accreditation: Clinical PsyD (Doctor of Psychology).

Student Applications/Admissions:
Student Applications

Non-Terminal MA/MS (Master of Arts/Science)—Applications 2004–2005, 138. Total applicants accepted 2004–2005, 72. Total enrolled 2004–2005 full-time, 147, part-time, 14. Openings 2005–2006, 75. The Median number of years required for completion of a degree are 3. The number of students enrolled full and part-time who were dismissed or voluntarily withdrew from this program area were 19. *Industrial/Organizational MA/MS (Master of Arts/Science)*—Applications 2004–2005, 30. Total applicants accepted 2004–2005, 19. Total enrolled 2004–2005 full-time, 30, part-time, 8. Openings 2005–2006, 40. The Median number of years required for completion of a degree are 3. The number of students enrolled full and part-time who were dismissed or voluntarily withdrew from this program area were 0. *PsyD (Doctor of Psychology)*—Applications 2004–2005, 0. Total applicants accepted 2004–2005, 0. Total enrolled 2004–2005 full-time, 144, part-time, 19.

Openings 2005–2006, 33. The Median number of years required for completion of a degree are 7. The number of students enrolled full and part-time who were dismissed or voluntarily withdrew from this program area were 3. MA/MS (*Master of Arts/Science*)—Applications 2004–2005, 156. Total applicants accepted 2004–2005, 120. Total enrolled 2004–2005 full-time, 191, part-time, 36. Openings 2005–2006, 75. The Median number of years required for completion of a degree are 3. The number of students enrolled full and part-time who were dismissed or voluntarily withdrew from this program area were 9.

Admissions Requirements:

Scores: Entries appear in this order: required test or GPA, minimum score (if required), median score of students entering in 2003–2004. Master's Programs: overall undergraduate GPA 3.00, 3.04.

Other Criteria: (importance of criteria rated low, medium, or high): GRE/MAT scores low, research experience low, work experience medium, extracurricular activity low, clinically related public service medium, GPA high, letters of recommendation high, interview high, statement of goals and objectives high. For Terminal MS Programs Only: GRE/MAT Scores - None; Extracurricular Activity - Medium.

Student Characteristics: The following represents characteristics of students in 2004–2005 in all graduate psychology programs in the department: Female–full-time 405, part-time 50; Male–full-time 107, part-time 27; African American/Black–full-time 98, part-time 11; Hispanic/Latino(a)–full-time 391, part-time 61; Asian/Pacific Islander–full-time 3, part-time 0; American Indian/Alaska Native–full-time 0, part-time 0; Caucasian–full-time 18, part-time 3; Multi-ethnic–full-time 2, part-time 0; students subject to the Americans With Disabilities Act–full-time 2, part-time 1.

Financial Information/Assistance:

Tuition for Full-Time Study: *Master's:* State residents: per academic year $12,285, $455 per credit hour; Nonstate residents: per academic year $12,285, $455 per credit hour. *Doctoral:* State residents: per academic year $11,070, $615 per credit hour; Nonstate residents: per academic year $11,070, $615 per credit hour.

Financial Assistance:

First Year Students: No information provided.

Advanced Students: No information provided.

Contact Information: Of all students currently enrolled full-time, 0% benefitted from one or more of the listed financial assistance programs.

Internships/Practica: Carlos Albizu University, Miami Campus, operates the Goodman Psychological Services Center, which provides low-cost services to the community and functions as both a Practicum and internship site for doctoral students. All non-terminal master's students begin their Practicum work in the Center and later have the option of moving on to any of about thirty-five (35) Practicum sites in the community. The Goodman Center is also an APPIC member and offers a pre-doctoral internship which, in some instances, utilizes rotations with other clinical

providers in the community. The majority of internship candidates seek outside internships with the support and assistance of the Department of Field Placement. Terminal Master's students are placed during their senior year (8-12 months) at a variety of corporations, schools and human services settings with diverse client populations. Sixty Practicum sites are available in the tri-county area (Miami-Dade, Broward, Palm Beach). For those doctoral students for whom a professional internship is required prior to graduation, 47 applied in 2003–2004. Of those who applied, 43 were placed in internships listed by the Association of Psychology Postdoctoral and Internship Programs (APPIC); 14 were placed in APA accredited internships.

Housing and Day Care: No on-campus housing is available. No on-campus day care facilities are available.

Employment of Department Graduates:

Master's Degree Graduates: Of those who graduated in the academic year 2003–2004, the following categories and numbers represent the post-graduate activities and employment of master's degree graduates: Enrolled in a post-doctoral residency/fellowship (n/a), employed in independent practice (n/a), total from the above (master's) (0).

Doctoral Degree Graduates: Of those who graduated in the academic year 2003–2004, the following categories and numbers represent the post-graduate activities and employment of doctoral degree graduates: Enrolled in a psychology doctoral program (n/a), enrolled in a post-doctoral residency/fellowship (10), employed in independent practice (13), employed in an academic position at a university (1), employed in a professional position in a school system (2), employed in business or industry (management) (2), employed in a government agency (professional services) (12), employed in a community mental health/counseling center (14), employed in a hospital/medical center (11), other employment position (1), do not know (1), total from the above (doctoral) (67).

Additional Information:

Orientation, Objectives, and Emphasis of Department: Carlos Albizu University (CAU) has as its primary objective the training of psychologists, mental health counselors, marriage and family therapists, school counselors, and master's level industrial and organizational psychology practitioners at the highest level of professional competence with a special sensitivity to multicultural issues. The academic curriculum emphasizes a core of traditional courses, including training in theory and research methodology. Academic courses are sequenced to foster steady growth in conceptual mastery and technical skills within a multicultural context. Clinical training provides for the opportunity of applied practice in the areas of psychotherapy, psychodiagnostics, school counseling, and industrial and organizational services within settings serving a multicultural population. The PsyD Program curriculum offers three concentrations: General Practice, Neuropsychology, and Forensic Psychology. A Child Psychology concentration is slated to begin in the Fall 2004 academic session.

Special Facilities or Resources: The University has its own Psychological Services Center, which provides varied clinical services to the community while serving as a training site for Practicum and pre-doctoral interns. Throughout their internship and practica, students are supervised by licensed psychologists who monitor their work and evaluate their performance. Tools such as two-way mirrors and audiovisual equipment are used to provide supervision and feedback to the students.

Application Information:

Send to: Recruitment and Admissions Department, Carlos Albizu University, Miami Campus, 2173 NW 99th Avenue, Miami, FL 33172-2209. Students are admitted in the Fall. *Fee:* $50. Fee waived for on-site applications during select institutional events (i.e., Open House).

Central Florida, University of

Department of Psychology
Arts and Sciences
P.O. Box 161390
Orlando, FL 32816-1390
Telephone: (407) 823-2216
Fax: (407) 823-5862
E-mail: *psyinfo@mail.ucf.edu*
Web: *http://www.psych.ucf.edu/*

Department Information:

1968. Chairperson: Robert Dipboye. Number of Faculty: total–full-time 38, part-time 22; women–full-time 15, part-time 12; minority–full-time 5, part-time 6.

Programs and Degrees Offered:

Listed in the following order: Program area, degree type (T if terminal Master's), number awarded 7/03–6/04. Clinical MA/MS (Master of Arts/Science) (T) 8, Industrial/Organizational MA/MS (Master of Arts/Science) (T) 24, Applied Experimental and Human Factors PhD (Doctor of Philosophy) 6, Clinical PhD (Doctor of Philosophy) 2, Industrial-Organizational PhD (Doctor of Philosophy) 0.

APA Accreditation: Clinical PhD (Doctor of Philosophy).

Student Applications/Admissions:

Student Applications

Clinical MA/MS (Master of Arts/Science)—Applications 2004–2005, 80. Total applicants accepted 2004–2005, 16. Number enrolled (new admits only) 2004–2005 full-time, 16. Total enrolled 2004–2005 full-time, 23, part-time, 4. Openings 2005–2006, 15. The Median number of years required for completion of a degree are 2. The number of students enrolled full and part-time who were dismissed or voluntarily withdrew from this program area were 0. *Industrial/Organizational MA/MS (Master of Arts/Science)*—Applications 2004–2005, 85. Total applicants accepted 2004–2005, 20. Number enrolled (new admits only) 2004–2005 full-time, 16. Total enrolled 2004–2005 full-time, 24, part-time, 3. Openings 2005–2006, 12. The Median number of years required for completion of a degree are 2. The number of students enrolled full and part-time who were dismissed or voluntarily withdrew from this program area were 0. *Applied Experimental and Human Factors (AEHF) PhD (Doctor of Philosophy)*—Applications 2004–2005, 32. Total applicants accepted 2004–2005, 12. Number enrolled (new admits only) 2004–2005 full-time, 11. Number enrolled (new admits only) 2004–2005 part-time, 1. Total enrolled 2004–2005 full-time, 31, part-time, 27. Openings 2005–2006, 10. The Median number of years required for completion of a degree are 4. The number of students enrolled full and part-time who were dismissed or voluntarily withdrew from this program area were 0. *Clinical PhD (Doctor of Philosophy)*—Applications 2004–2005, 150. Total applicants accepted 2004–2005, 7. Number enrolled (new admits only) 2004–2005 full-time, 5. Total enrolled 2004–2005 full-time, 23, part-time, 8. Openings 2005–2006, 7. The Median number of years required for completion of a degree are 5. The number of students enrolled full and part-time who were dismissed or voluntarily withdrew from this program area were 0. *Industrial-Organizational PhD (Doctor of Philosophy)*—Applications 2004–2005, 62. Total applicants accepted 2004–2005, 15. Number enrolled (new admits only) 2004–2005 full-time, 4. Number enrolled (new admits only) 2004–2005 part-time, 0. Total enrolled 2004–2005 full-time, 28, part-time, 6. Openings 2005–2006, 5. The Median number of years required for completion of a degree are 5. The number of students enrolled full and part-time who were dismissed or voluntarily withdrew from this program area were 0.

Admissions Requirements:

Scores: Entries appear in this order: required test or GPA, minimum score (if required), median score of students entering in 2003–2004. Master's Programs: GRE-V+Q 1000, 1105; last 2 years GPA 3.0, 3.5; psychology GPA 3.0, 3.5. Doctoral Programs: GRE-V+Q 1000, 1197; last 2 years GPA 3.0, 3.7; psychology GPA 3.0, 3.7. GRE of 1000 or 3.0 GPA are minimum requirements to apply to Clinical PhD, Clinical MA, I/O MS and I/O PhD program. For AEHF the minimum GRE is 1100 and GPA 3.2.

Other Criteria: (importance of criteria rated low, medium, or high): GRE/MAT scores high, research experience high, work experience low, extracurricular activity medium, clinically related public service medium, GPA high, letters of recommendation high, interview high, statement of goals and objectives high. Criteria vary by program.

Student Characteristics: The following represents characteristics of students in 2004–2005 in all graduate psychology programs in the department: Female–full-time 91, part-time 26; Male–full-time 38, part-time 22; African American/Black–full-time 11, part-time 2; Hispanic/Latino(a)–full-time 7, part-time 7; Asian/Pacific Islander–full-time 6, part-time 1; American Indian/Alaska Native–full-time 0, part-time 0; Caucasian–full-time 97, part-time 37; Multi-ethnic–full-time 8, part-time 1; students subject to the Americans With Disabilities Act–full-time 0, part-time 0.

Financial Information/Assistance:

Tuition for Full-Time Study: *Master's:* State residents: per academic year $5,505, $229 per credit hour; Nonstate residents: per academic year $20,875, $869 per credit hour. *Doctoral:* State residents: per academic year $5,505, $229 per credit hour; Nonstate residents: per academic year $20,875, $869 per credit hour. Tuition is subject to change. See the following Web site for updates and changes in tuition costs: www.graduate.ucf.edu.

Financial Assistance:

First Year Students: Teaching assistantships available for first-year. Average amount paid per academic year: $7,000. Average number of hours worked per week: 20. Tuition remission given: full and partial. Research assistantships available for first-year. Average amount paid per academic year: $8,000. Average number of hours worked per week: 20. Tuition remission given: full and partial. Fellowships and scholarships available for first-year. Average amount paid per academic year: $12,000. Average number of hours worked per week: 20. Tuition remission given: full and partial.

Advanced Students: Teaching assistantships available for advanced students. Average amount paid per academic year: $7,000. Average number of hours worked per week: 20. Tuition remission given: full and partial. Research assistantships available for advanced students. Average amount paid per academic year: $10,000. Average number of hours worked per week: 20. Tuition remission given: full and partial. Fellowships and scholarships available for advanced students. Average amount paid per academic year: $15,000. Average number of hours worked per week: 20. Tuition remission given: full and partial.

Contact Information: Of all students currently enrolled full-time, 90% benefitted from one or more of the listed financial assistance programs. Application and information available online at: http://pegasus.cc.ucf.edu/~finaid.

Internships/Practica: Clinical: Internships for clinical masters students exist in community mental health centers and other agencies throughout Central Florida. Doctoral students complete their practica in our on-campus clinic as well as in a variety of community based clinical agencies. Human Factors: Human Factors students complete internships in a variety of government, business, and industry settings. Industrial/Organizational: I/O master's students complete practica placements in a variety of government, business and industry settings. Doctoral students complete an internship in a variety of business, industry and government settings. For those doctoral students for whom a professional internship is required prior to graduation, 3 applied in 2003–2004. Of those who applied, 3 were placed in internships listed by the Association of Psychology Postdoctoral and Internship Programs (APPIC); 3 were placed in APA accredited internships.

Housing and Day Care: On-campus housing is available. See the following Web site for more information: http://www.housing.ucf.edu/. On-campus day care facilities are available. See the following Web site for more information: http://www.csc.sdes.ucf.edu/.

Employment of Department Graduates:

Master's Degree Graduates: Of those who graduated in the academic year 2003–2004, the following categories and numbers represent the post-graduate activities and employment of master's degree graduates: Enrolled in a psychology doctoral program (5), enrolled in a post-doctoral residency/fellowship (n/a), employed in independent practice (n/a), employed in business or industry (research/consulting) (5), employed in a community mental health/counseling center (4), total from the above (master's) (14).

Doctoral Degree Graduates: Of those who graduated in the academic year 2003–2004, the following categories and numbers represent the post-graduate activities and employment of doctoral degree graduates: Enrolled in a psychology doctoral program (n/a), employed in an academic position at a university (2), employed in business or industry (research/consulting) (3), employed in a government agency (research) (2), total from the above (doctoral) (7).

Additional Information:

Orientation, Objectives, and Emphasis of Department: The PhD program in clinical psychology is designed for individuals seeking a research oriented career in the field of clinical psychology. The program also emphasizes training in consultation, teaching, supervision, and the design/evaluation of mental health programs. The MA program in clinical psychology has major emphases in assessment and evaluation skills; intervention, counseling, and psychotherapy skills; and an academic foundation in research methods. The program is designed to provide training and preparation for persons desiring to deliver clinical services at the master's level through community agencies. Graduates of this program meet the educational requirements for the mental health counselor state license. The MS program in industrial/organizational psychology has major emphases in selection and training of employees, applied theories of organizational behavior, job satisfaction, test theory and construction, assessment center technology, statistics and experimental design. As of Fall 2000 a PhD in Industrial/Organizational was approved and admitted an initial class of 10 students. I/O students receive training in the 21 competence areas detailed by Division 14 of the APA. The PhD program in human factors is patterned on the scientist-practitioner model of the APA. It adheres to the guidelines for education and training established by the committee for Education and Training of APA's Division 21 (Applied Experimental and Engineering Psychology). The Applied Experimental and Human Factors program is accredited by the Educational Committee of the Human Factors and Ergonomics Society. Concentration areas include human-computer interaction, human performance, and human factors in simulation and training.

Special Facilities or Resources: The department's facilities and resources include extensive videotape capability, an intelligence and personality testing library, a statistics library, computer facilities within the department and in the computer center, a counseling and testing center, a creative school for children, and a communicative disorders clinic. Doctoral students have use of specialized equipment in the department-based Human Visual Performance Laboratory and Team Performance Laboratory. The clinical program has extensive ties to a number of community agencies for practica and assistantship.

Information for Students With Physical Disabilities: See the following Web site for more information: http://www.sds.sdes.ucf.edu/.

Application Information:
On-line application should be sent to: University of Central Florida, The Office of Graduate Studies, P.O. Box 160112, Orlando, FL 32816-0112. Web address: www.graduate.ucf.edu Application materials should be sent to: University of Central Florida, Department of Psychology, ATTN: Graduate Admissions, P.O. Box 161390, Orlando, FL 32816-1390. Application available online. URL of online application: http://www.graduate.ucf.edu/gradonlineapp/. Students are admitted in the Fall, application deadline varies. Clinical PhD December 15, Clinical MA February 1, Industrial Organziational Psychology MS February 1, I/O PhD December 15, AEHF February 1. *Fee:* $30. None.

Embry-Riddle Aeronautical University
Human Factors and Systems
600 S. Clyde Morris Boulevard
Daytona Beach, FL 32114
Telephone: (386) 226-6790
Fax: (386) 226-7050
E-mail: *greenef@erau.edu*
Web: *http://www.humanfactorsandsystems.com*

Department Information:
1997. Chairperson: Fran Greene, PhD Number of Faculty: total–full-time 8, part-time 5; women–full-time 4, part-time 4; minority–full-time 1, part-time 1.

Programs and Degrees Offered:
Listed in the following order: Program area, degree type (T if terminal Master's), number awarded 7/03–6/04. Human Factors & Systems MA/MS (Master of Arts/Science) (T) 14.

Student Applications/Admissions:
Student Applications
Human Factors & Systems MA/MS (Master of Arts/Science)—Applications 2004–2005, 26. Total applicants accepted 2004–2005, 16. Number enrolled (new admits only) 2004–2005 full-time, 10. Number enrolled (new admits only) 2004–2005 part-time, 3. Total enrolled 2004–2005 full-time, 23, part-time, 11. Openings 2005–2006, 25. The Median number of years required for completion of a degree are 2. The number of students enrolled full and part-time who were dismissed or voluntarily withdrew from this program area were 1.

Admissions Requirements:
Scores: Entries appear in this order: required test or GPA, minimum score (if required), median score of students entering in 2003–2004. Master's Programs: GRE-V+Q 1000; overall undergraduate GPA 3.0.
Other Criteria: (importance of criteria rated low, medium, or high): GRE/MAT scores high, research experience high, work experience medium, extracurricular activity low, clinically related public service low, GPA high, letters of recommendation high, interview low, statement of goals and objectives high.

Student Characteristics: The following represents characteristics of students in 2004–2005 in all graduate psychology programs in the department: Female–full-time 18, part-time 6; Male–full-time 5, part-time 5; African American/Black–part-time 1; Hispanic/Latino(a)–full-time 3, part-time 0; Caucasian–full-time 15, part-time 6; students subject to the Americans With Disabilities Act–full-time 0, part-time 0.

Financial Information/Assistance:
Tuition for Full-Time Study: *Master's:* State residents: $930 per credit hour; Nonstate residents: $930 per credit hour.

Financial Assistance:
First Year Students: Teaching assistantships available for first-year. Average amount paid per academic year: $5,700. Average number of hours worked per week: 20. Tuition remission given: partial. Research assistantships available for first-year. Average amount paid per academic year: $5,700. Average number of hours

worked per week: 20. Tuition remission given: partial. Fellowships and scholarships available for first-year. Tuition remission given: partial.
Advanced Students: Teaching assistantships available for advanced students. Average amount paid per academic year: $6,300. Average number of hours worked per week: 20. Tuition remission given: partial. Research assistantships available for advanced students. Average amount paid per academic year: $6,300. Average number of hours worked per week: 20. Tuition remission given: partial. Fellowships and scholarships available for advanced students. Tuition remission given: partial.
Contact Information: Of all students currently enrolled full-time, 20% benefitted from one or more of the listed financial assistance programs.

Internships/Practica: The Master's Degree program at Embry-Riddle provides extensive opportunities for students to engage in paid and/or credit-based internship or co-op placements. Master's students are strongly encouraged, although not required, to take advantage of these placements. Previous placements of graduate students include premiere companies such as: Lockheed Martin, IBM, Veritas Software, Sikorsky Helicopter, the FAA, NTSB, and the United States Air Force. Placements typically range from 3-6 months and can be done at any time during the student's program.

Housing and Day Care: On-campus housing is available. See the following Web site for more information: On-campus housing is available. However, due to the limited amount of housing for graduate students, we recommend you also explore these web sites regarding off-campus housing: http://www.springstreet.com/apartments/home.jhtml?source=a1rnft2t117; http://www.rent.net/cgi-bin/chome/RentNet/scripts/home.jsp; http://www.rent-usa.com/rent-fl. No on-campus day care facilities are available.

Employment of Department Graduates:
Master's Degree Graduates: Of those who graduated in the academic year 2003–2004, the following categories and numbers represent the post-graduate activities and employment of master's degree graduates: Enrolled in a post-doctoral residency/fellowship (n/a), employed in independent practice (n/a), employed in other positions at a higher education institution (1), employed in business or industry (research/consulting) (1), employed in business or industry (management) (10), other employment position (2), total from the above (master's) (14).
Doctoral Degree Graduates: Of those who graduated in the academic year 2003–2004, the following categories and numbers represent the post-graduate activities and employment of doctoral degree graduates: Enrolled in a psychology doctoral program (n/a), total from the above (doctoral) (0).

Additional Information:
Orientation, Objectives, and Emphasis of Department: Embry-Riddle Aeronautical University prides itself on being the largest aviation and aerospace-based university in the world. As such, the focus of education is oriented to issues related to those domains and in other technologically advanced areas. The Human Factors and Systems Master's Degree program provides a fundamental, theoretical and applied education in the fields of human factors and systems. Electives in the program are then oriented toward exploring human factors and systems principles within aviation domains. Faculty interests and research opportunities for students

in the program are diverse. Current research interests range from personnel selection, to motivational issues, to design of cockpits. The diversity of faculty backgrounds adds to the eclectic nature of the research interests at Embry-Riddle. As such, students in the program can choose from a wide array of projects or thesis topics to pursue. Particular areas of faculty and student research currently include: development of heads-up displays, tunnel in the sky technology, pilot selection, pilot motivation, prediction of flight performance, virtual and augmented reality displays, security screening, human-computer interaction, and air traffic management systems. The university facilities include flight simulation laboratories, an air traffic management laboratory and other computer laboratories. The overall goal of the Embry-Riddle program is to train an individual to move directly into a career as a Human Factors or Systems Engineering specialist in industry, government or the military. In order to achieve this goal, the program provides training in research methodology and human factors applications. In addition, classes emphasize teamwork and development, as well as refinement of writing and oral communication skills.

Special Facilities or Resources: The university has a fleet of more than 100 single- and multiengine general aviation aircraft flying over 80.000 h/year on various levels of training missions and 20 dedicated procedural trainers and simulators ranging from FRASCA 141s through a Level D Boeing 737-300. The department has access to flight faculty/instructors with extensive background and experience and over 1500 students enrolled at various levels of flight training. The Human Performance Lab also contains equipment related to augmented reality, eye tracking, and flight performance meaurement. The laboratory contains a core set of PC-based flight simulation tools including an Elite flight simulation device for the investigation of a variety of information display issues, augmented by measurement tools such as the SeeingMachines FaceLab gaze monitoring tool. The department also has access to multiple air traffic control training and research laboratories on campus in coordination with faculty who have an extensive background and experience in civilian and military air traffic control both in the U.S. and internationally.

Application Information:
Send to: Graduate Programs, Embry-Riddle Aeronautical University, 600 S. Clyde Morris Blvd., Daytona Beach, FL 32114-3900. Application available online. URL of online application: https://www.erau.edu/db/gradadmissions/apply.html. Students are admitted in the Fall, application deadline August 3. *Fee:* $30. $50 for nonresidents.

Florida Atlantic University
Psychology
777 Glades Road, P.O. Box 3091
Boca Raton, FL 33431-0991
Telephone: (561) 297-3360
Fax: (561) 297-2160
E-mail: *psychology@fau.edu*
Web: *http://www.psy.fau.edu*

Department Information:
1965. Chairperson: David L. Wolgin. Number of Faculty: total–full-time 35; women–full-time 11; minority–full-time 3.

Programs and Degrees Offered:
Listed in the following order: Program area, degree type (T if terminal Master's), number awarded 7/03–6/04. Psychology MA/MS (Master of Arts/Science) 2, Psychology PhD (Doctor of Philosophy) 8.

Student Applications/Admissions:
Student Applications
Psychology MA/MS (*Master of Arts/Science*)—Applications 2004–2005, 40. Total applicants accepted 2004–2005, 12. Total enrolled 2004–2005 full-time, 16, part-time, 3. Openings 2005–2006, 12. The Median number of years required for completion of a degree are 2. The number of students enrolled full and part-time who were dismissed or voluntarily withdrew from this program area were 1. Psychology PhD (*Doctor of Philosophy*)—Applications 2004–2005, 60. Total applicants accepted 2004–2005, 9. Openings 2005–2006, 10. The Median number of years required for completion of a degree are 4. The number of students enrolled full and part-time who were dismissed or voluntarily withdrew from this program area were 0.

Admissions Requirements:
Scores: Entries appear in this order: required test or GPA, minimum score (if required), median score of students entering in 2003–2004. Master's Programs: GRE-V+Q 1100, 1100; last 2 years GPA 3.00, 3.80. GRE-Subject (Psychology) recommended but not required. Doctoral Programs: GRE-V+Q 1100, 1200; last 2 years GPA 3.00, 3.88. GRE-Subject (Psychology) recommended but not required.
Other Criteria: (importance of criteria rated low, medium, or high): GRE/MAT scores high, research experience high, work experience low, extracurricular activity low, clinically related public service low, GPA high, letters of recommendation high, statement of goals and objectives medium.

Student Characteristics: The following represents characteristics of students in 2004–2005 in all graduate psychology programs in the department: Female–full-time 23, part-time 3; Male–full-time 17, part-time 0; African American/Black–full-time 0, part-time 1; Hispanic/Latino(a)–full-time 2, part-time 0; Asian/Pacific Islander–full-time 5, part-time 0; American Indian/Alaska Native–full-time 1, part-time 0; Caucasian–full-time 0, part-time 0; students subject to the Americans With Disabilities Act–full-time 1, part-time 0.

Financial Information/Assistance:
Tuition for Full-Time Study: *Master's:* State residents: $186 per credit hour; Nonstate residents: $678 per credit hour. *Doctoral:* State residents: $186 per credit hour; Nonstate residents: $678 per credit hour. Tuition is subject to change. See the following Web site for updates and changes in tuition costs: http://www.fau.edu/gr-cat/tuition2.pdf.

Financial Assistance:
First Year Students: Teaching assistantships available for first-year. Average amount paid per academic year: $20,000. Average number of hours worked per week: 20. Apply by August 1. Tuition remission given: partial. Research assistantships available for first-year.

Advanced Students: Teaching assistantships available for advanced students. Average amount paid per academic year:

$20,000. Average number of hours worked per week: 20. Apply by August 1. Tuition remission given: partial. Research assistantships available for advanced students. Fellowships and scholarships available for advanced students.

Contact Information: Of all students currently enrolled full-time, 100% benefitted from one or more of the listed financial assistance programs.

Internships/Practica: No information provided.

Housing and Day Care: On-campus housing is available. See the following Web site for more information: http://www.fau.edu. On-campus day care facilities are available.

Employment of Department Graduates:
Master's Degree Graduates: Of those who graduated in the academic year 2003–2004, the following categories and numbers represent the post-graduate activities and employment of master's degree graduates: Enrolled in a post-doctoral residency/fellowship (n/a), employed in independent practice (n/a), total from the above (master's) (0).
Doctoral Degree Graduates: Of those who graduated in the academic year 2003–2004, the following categories and numbers represent the post-graduate activities and employment of doctoral degree graduates: Enrolled in a psychology doctoral program (n/a), total from the above (doctoral) (0).

Additional Information:
Orientation, Objectives, and Emphasis of Department: The PhD program emphasizes research in several areas of experimental psychology. Students may select courses and conduct research in five areas: cognitive psychology, developmental psychology, evolutionary psychology, psychobiology/neuroscience, and social/personality psychology. Current research by faculty includes psycholinguistics, sentence processing, visual perception, and speech production and perception; conflict in married couples; the relationship between tool use and style of play in preschool children; psychological adaptations to sperm competition in humans; mental synchronization in social interaction; neural mechanisms in recovery of function from brain damage, psychopharmacology, and nonlinear dynamics of brain and behavior; the use of traits to predict behavior, sex differences in mating, and domestic violence; and the dynamics of social influence. The MA program is designed to prepare students for entry into doctoral-level programs in all areas of psychology. Research in developmental psychology uses a campus laboratory school for children in kindergarten through the eighth grade. Research in social/personality psychology uses laboratories with video and online computer facilities. The cognitive psychology laboratories include testing rooms with a network of PCs for online control of experiments in perception, learning, language, and cognition. The EEG laboratory includes an acoustic isolation chamber and a variety of amplifying and recording systems.

Special Facilities or Resources: Additional information and online application forms are available at http://www.psy.fau.edu.

Information for Students With Physical Disabilities: See the following Web site for more information: http://www.psy.fau.edu.

Application Information:
Send to: (1) FAU Admissions Office, 777 Glades Road, Boca Raton, FL 33431; (2) Graduate Coordinator, Department of Psychology, FAU;

P.O. Box 3091, Boca Raton, FL 33431. Students are admitted in the Spring, application deadline January 15; Summer, application deadline June 1. PhD application deadline January 15. MA application deadline June 1. Fee: $20.

Florida Institute of Technology
School of Psychology
College of Psychology and Liberal Arts
150 West University Boulevard
Melbourne, FL 32901-6988
Telephone: (321) 674-8104
Fax: (321) 674-7105
E-mail: mkenkel@fit.edu
Web: http://www.fit.edu/acadres/psych

Department Information:
1978. Dean: Mary Beth Kenkel. Number of Faculty: total–full-time 17, part-time 24; women–full-time 5, part-time 8; minority–full-time 3, part-time 1.

Programs and Degrees Offered:
Listed in the following order: Program area, degree type (T if terminal Master's), number awarded 7/03–6/04. Applied Behavioral Analysis MA/MS (Master of Arts/Science) (T) 15, clinical PsyD (Doctor of Psychology) 19, I/O MA/MS (Master of Arts/Science) (T) 8, I/O PhD (Doctor of Philosophy) 2.

APA Accreditation: Clinical PsyD (Doctor of Psychology).

Student Applications/Admissions:
Student Applications
Applied Behavioral Analysis (ABA) MA/MS (Master of Arts/Science)—Applications 2004–2005, 72. Total applicants accepted 2004–2005, 54. Number enrolled (new admits only) 2004–2005 full-time, 32. Number enrolled (new admits only) 2004–2005 part-time, 0. Openings 2005–2006, 33. The Median number of years required for completion of a degree are 2. The number of students enrolled full and part-time who were dismissed or voluntarily withdrew from this program area were 1. Clinical PsyD (Doctor of Psychology)—Applications 2004–2005, 135. Total applicants accepted 2004–2005, 53. Number enrolled (new admits only) 2004–2005 full-time, 19. Number enrolled (new admits only) 2004–2005 part-time, 0. Total enrolled 2004–2005 full-time, 71, part-time, 6. Openings 2005–2006, 25. The Median number of years required for completion of a degree are 4. The number of students enrolled full and part-time who were dismissed or voluntarily withdrew from this program area were 3. I/O MA/MS (Master of Arts/Science)—Applications 2004–2005, 56. Total applicants accepted 2004–2005, 39. Number enrolled (new admits only) 2004–2005 full-time, 12. Number enrolled (new admits only) 2004–2005 part-time, 0. Openings 2005–2006, 20. The Median number of years required for completion of a degree are 2. The number of students enrolled full and part-time who were dismissed or voluntarily withdrew from this program area were 0. I/O PhD (Doctor of Philosophy)—Applications 2004–2005, 20. Total applicants accepted 2004–2005, 3. Number enrolled (new admits only) 2004–2005 full-time, 3. Number enrolled (new admits only) 2004–2005 part-time, 0. Total

enrolled 2004–2005 full-time, 9, part-time, 1. Openings 2005–2006, 6. The Median number of years required for completion of a degree are 4. The number of students enrolled full and part-time who were dismissed or voluntarily withdrew from this program area were 0.

Admissions Requirements:

Scores: Entries appear in this order: required test or GPA, minimum score (if required), median score of students entering in 2003–2004. Master's Programs: GRE-V no minimum stated, 450; GRE-Q no minimum stated, 560; GRE-V+Q no minimum stated, 980; overall undergraduate GPA no minimum stated, 3.43; last 2 years GPA no minimum stated, 3.68; psychology GPA no minimum stated, 3.66. Doctoral Programs: GRE-V no minimum stated, 490; GRE-Q no minimum stated, 580; GRE-V+Q no minimum stated, 1090; GRE-Subject(Psych) 600, 570; overall undergraduate GPA 3.0, 3.65. GRE subject test required for PsyD program only.

Other Criteria: (importance of criteria rated low, medium, or high): GRE/MAT scores medium, research experience medium, work experience high, extracurricular activity medium, clinically related public service high, GPA medium, letters of recommendation high, interview medium, statement of goals and objectives medium. For additional information on admission requirements, go to: www.fit.edu/admission/graduate/.

Student Characteristics: The following represents characteristics of students in 2004–2005 in all graduate psychology programs in the department: Female–full-time 123, part-time 4; Male–full-time 44, part-time 3; African American/Black–full-time 9, part-time 0; Hispanic/Latino(a)–full-time 12, part-time 0; Asian/Pacific Islander–full-time 7, part-time 1; American Indian/Alaska Native–full-time 0, part-time 0; Caucasian–full-time 139, part-time 6; Multi-ethnic–full-time 0, part-time 0; students subject to the Americans With Disabilities Act–full-time 0, part-time 0.

Financial Information/Assistance:

Tuition for Full-Time Study: *Master's:* State residents: per academic year $14,850, $825 per credit hour; Nonstate residents: per academic year $14,850, $825 per credit hour. *Doctoral:* State residents: per academic year $19,800, $825 per credit hour; Nonstate residents: per academic year $19,800, $825 per credit hour. Tuition is subject to change. Tuition costs vary by program.

Financial Assistance:

First Year Students: Research assistantships available for first-year. Average amount paid per academic year: $3,600. Average number of hours worked per week: 5. Apply by March 15. Fellowships and scholarships available for first-year. Average amount paid per academic year: $4,950. Average number of hours worked per week: 10. Apply by June 1.

Advanced Students: Teaching assistantships available for advanced students. Average amount paid per academic year: $7,200. Average number of hours worked per week: 10. Apply by March 15. Research assistantships available for advanced students. Average amount paid per academic year: $3,600. Average number of hours worked per week: 5. Apply by March 15. Fellowships and scholarships available for advanced students. Average amount paid per academic year: $4,950. Average number of hours worked per week: 10. Apply by June 1.

Contact Information: Of all students currently enrolled full-time, 29% benefitted from one or more of the listed financial assistance programs. Application and information available online at: www.fit.edu/admission/graduate/.

Internships/Practica: Students in the PsyD program complete a sequence of three or more separate practicum placements prior to internship. These include the Florida Tech's Community Psychological Services Center, and then options at other outpatient and inpatient facilities. Inpatient sites include adult psychiatric hospitals, rehabilitation hospitals, children and adolescent inpatient units, behavioral medicine practica within a medical hospital and a prison setting. Outpatient sites include mental health centers, private practice settings, VA outpatient clinics, and neuropsychological practices. Students gain experience in assessment and treatment of individuals, groups, couples and families, consultation and psychoeducational presentations. Treatment specialties include eating disorders, neuropsychology, aging, sexual abuse, domestic violence, PTSD, and drug and alcohol abuse. The I/O program has strong ties to local businesses in Brevard County. Students have been placed in a wide range of practicum sites including county and federal departments, aerospace and electronics industries, financial institutions, health care organizations, and management consulting firms. The Applied Behavior Analysis program has practicum sites with private and public agencies working with children with developmental disabilities, serious emotional and behavioral disorders and autism. For those doctoral students for whom a professional internship is required prior to graduation, 15 applied in 2003–2004. Of those who applied, 15 were placed in internships listed by the Association of Psychology Postdoctoral and Internship Programs (APPIC); 13 were placed in APA accredited internships.

Housing and Day Care: On-campus housing is available. auxservices.fit.edu/housing.html. No on-campus day care facilities are available.

Employment of Department Graduates:

Master's Degree Graduates: Of those who graduated in the academic year 2003–2004, the following categories and numbers represent the post-graduate activities and employment of master's degree graduates: Enrolled in a psychology doctoral program (4), enrolled in another graduate/professional program (0), enrolled in a post-doctoral residency/fellowship (n/a), employed in independent practice (n/a), employed in an academic position at a university (0), employed in an academic position at a 2-year/4-year college (0), employed in other positions at a higher education institution (3), employed in a professional position in a school system (2), employed in business or industry (research/consulting) (4), employed in business or industry (management) (0), employed in a government agency (research) (0), employed in a government agency (professional services) (2), employed in a community mental health/counseling center (2), employed in a hospital/medical center (2), still seeking employment (0), not seeking employment (1), other employment position (4), do not know (0), total from the above (master's) (24).

Doctoral Degree Graduates: Of those who graduated in the academic year 2003–2004, the following categories and numbers represent the post-graduate activities and employment of doctoral degree graduates: Enrolled in a psychology doctoral program (n/a), enrolled in another graduate/professional program (0), enrolled in a post-doctoral residency/fellowship (3), employed in independent practice (4), employed in an academic position at a university (1), employed in an academic position at a 2-year/4-year college

(0), employed in other positions at a higher education institution (0), employed in a professional position in a school system (0), employed in business or industry (research/consulting) (0), employed in business or industry (management) (0), employed in a government agency (research) (0), employed in a government agency (professional services) (6), employed in a community mental health/counseling center (2), employed in a hospital/medical center (3), still seeking employment (0), not seeking employment (1), other employment position (0), do not know (0), total from the above (doctoral) (20).

Additional Information:

Orientation, Objectives, and Emphasis of Department: The School of Psychology at Florida Institute of Technology offers the MS and PhD in Industrial/Organizational Psychology, the MS in Behavior Analysis, and the PsyD in Clinical Psychology. The clinical PsyD program trains students based on a practitioner/scientist model focused on development of clinical skills. The program incorporates multiple theoretical orientations and has emphases in neuropsychology, child psychology, marriage and family therapy, multi-cultural issues and forensic issues. In the Industrial/Organizational Psychology program, students are trained in advanced statistics, organizational research, industrial training and development, personnel selection, performance appraisal, group and team development and organizational research methodology. The program prepares graduates for a wide variety of careers in academics, management, human resources and consulting. The master's program in Applied Behavior Analysis offers two tracks: Clinical Behavior Analysis and Organizational Behavior Management. The program prepares graduates for employment as Board Certified Behavior Analysts and/or as internal or external consultants in business and industry.

Special Facilities or Resources: The facilities of the School of Psychology include the Psychology building, research labs in Grissom Hall, the University Counseling Center and the Community Psychological Services Center of Florida Tech. The academic building contains offices, classrooms, human research cubicles and rooms, computer facilities, and observation and treatment rooms. The University's Academic Computing Services-Microcenter provides computers and software, media conversion, digital graphic assistance, and professional editing of theses and papers for publication. The counseling centers include group and individual treatment rooms. Additionally students receive training and conduct research in several community service programs operated by the School of Psychology. These include: Center for Professional Services, a campus based consulting and research organization, and East Central Florida Memory Disorder Clinic, a joint project with Holmes Regional Medical Center that serves individuals with memory disorders by providing memory screenings, case management, education, wellness and support groups. The Family Learning Program offers psychological assessment and treatment to children who have suffered the trauma of sexual abuse and to all family members. Center for Traumatology Studies provides counseling services for combat veterans, and support groups for spouses and children.

Information for Students With Physical Disabilities: See the following Web site for more information: http://www.fit.edu/asc/handbook/Section_6.html.

Application Information:
Send to: School of Psychology Graduate Admissions, 150 W. University Blvd., Melbourne, FL 32901. Application available online. URL of online application: www.fit.edu/admission/graduate/. Students are admitted in the Fall. PsyD deadline is January 15. ABA deadline is March 1. Industrial/Organizational Psychology deadline is February 1. PsyD $60; PhD $60; MS $50.

Florida State University
Department of Psychology
Arts & Sciences
Tallahassee, FL 32306-1270
Telephone: (850) 644-2499
Fax: (850) 644-7739
E-mail: *grad-info@psy.fsu.edu*
Web: *http://www.psy.fsu.edu*

Department Information:
1918. Chairperson: Janet A. Kistner. Number of Faculty: total–full-time 38, part-time 1; women–full-time 14; minority–full-time 3, part-time 1.

Programs and Degrees Offered:
Listed in the following order: Program area, degree type (T if terminal Master's), number awarded 7/03–6/04. Cognitive Psychology PhD (Doctor of Philosophy) 2, Clinical Psychology PhD (Doctor of Philosophy) 6, Neuroscience PhD (Doctor of Philosophy) 1, Applied Behavior Analysis Specialty MA/MS (Master of Arts/Science) (T) 1, Social Psychology (began fall 2003) PhD (Doctor of Philosophy), Developmental Psychology (began fall 2004) PhD (Doctor of Philosophy).

APA Accreditation: Clinical PhD (Doctor of Philosophy).

Student Applications/Admissions:
Student Applications
Cognitive Psychology PhD (Doctor of Philosophy)—Applications 2004–2005, 28. Total applicants accepted 2004–2005, 11. Number enrolled (new admits only) 2004–2005 full-time, 7. Openings 2005–2006, 6. The Median number of years required for completion of a degree are 5. The number of students enrolled full and part-time who were dismissed or voluntarily withdrew from this program area were 1. *Clinical Psychology PhD (Doctor of Philosophy)*—Applications 2004–2005, 259. Total applicants accepted 2004–2005, 14. Number enrolled (new admits only) 2004–2005 full-time, 6. Openings 2005–2006, 10. The Median number of years required for completion of a degree are 7. The number of students enrolled full and part-time who were dismissed or voluntarily withdrew from this program area were 1. *Neuroscience PhD (Doctor of Philosophy)*—Applications 2004–2005, 28. Total applicants accepted 2004–2005, 5. Number enrolled (new admits only) 2004–2005 full-time, 3. Openings 2005–2006, 10. The Median number of years required for completion of a degree are 6. The number of students enrolled full and part-time who were dismissed or voluntarily withdrew from this program area were 0. *Applied Behavior Analysis Specialty MA/MS (Master of Arts/Science)*—Applications 2004–2005, 55. Total applicants accepted 2004–2005, 26. Number enrolled (new admits only) 2004–2005 full-

time, 19. Openings 2005–2006, 16. The Median number of years required for completion of a degree are 2. The number of students enrolled full and part-time who were dismissed or voluntarily withdrew from this program area were 0. *Social Psychology (began fall 2003) PhD (Doctor of Philosophy)*—Applications 2004–2005, 68. Total applicants accepted 2004–2005, 13. Number enrolled (new admits only) 2004–2005 full-time, 6. Total enrolled 2004–2005 full-time, 13. Openings 2005–2006, 4. The number of students enrolled full and part-time who were dismissed or voluntarily withdrew from this program area were 0. *Developmental Psychology (began fall 2004) PhD (Doctor of Philosophy)*—Applications 2004–2005, 16. Total applicants accepted 2004–2005, 5. Number enrolled (new admits only) 2004–2005 full-time, 4. Total enrolled 2004–2005 full-time, 4. Openings 2005–2006, 4. The number of students enrolled full and part-time who were dismissed or voluntarily withdrew from this program area were 0.

Admissions Requirements:

Scores: Entries appear in this order: required test or GPA, minimum score (if required), median score of students entering in 2003–2004. Master's Programs: GRE-V 500, 440; GRE-Q 500, 520; GRE-V+Q 1000, 980; last 2 years GPA 3.0, 3.69. Above GRE/GPA requirements are for the Applied Behavior Analysis master's specialty. Doctoral Programs: GRE-V 500, 580; GRE-Q 500, 700; GRE-V+Q 1000, 1260; last 2 years GPA 3.0, 3.74. The required minimum GRE & GPA vary slightly across the doctoral programs.

Other Criteria: (importance of criteria rated low, medium, or high): GRE/MAT scores high, research experience high, work experience low, extracurricular activity low, clinically related public service low, GPA high, letters of recommendation high, interview medium, statement of goals and objectives high, match with faculty research interest high. Research experience is not relevant for the Applied Behavior Analysis master's specialty. Relevant work or volunteer experience for this specialty is of medium to high importance. For additional information on admission requirements, go to: http://www.psy.fsu.edu.

Student Characteristics: The following represents characteristics of students in 2004–2005 in all graduate psychology programs in the department: Female–full-time 92, part-time 0; Male–full-time 40, part-time 0; African American/Black–full-time 12, part-time 0; Hispanic/Latino(a)–full-time 11, part-time 0; Asian/Pacific Islander–full-time 2, part-time 0; American Indian/Alaska Native–full-time 0, part-time 0; Caucasian–full-time 107, part-time 0; Multi-ethnic–full-time 0, part-time 0; students subject to the Americans With Disabilities Act–full-time 0, part-time 0.

Financial Information/Assistance:

Tuition for Full-Time Study: *Master's:* State residents: per academic year $3,924, $218 per credit hour; Nonstate residents: per academic year $14,760, $820 per credit hour. *Doctoral:* State residents: per academic year $3,924, $218 per credit hour; Nonstate residents: per academic year $14,760, $820 per credit hour. Tuition is subject to change. See the following Web site for updates and changes in tuition costs: http://www.sfs.fsu.edu/tuitrates.html.

Financial Assistance:

First Year Students: Teaching assistantships available for first-year. Average amount paid per academic year: $14,000. Aver-

age number of hours worked per week: 16. Tuition remission given: full. Research assistantships available for first-year. Average amount paid per academic year: $18,000. Average number of hours worked per week: 20. Tuition remission given: full. Traineeships available for first-year. Average amount paid per academic year: $20,000. Average number of hours worked per week: 20. Tuition remission given: full. Fellowships and scholarships available for first-year. Average amount paid per academic year: $18,000. Average number of hours worked per week: 0. Tuition remission given: full.

Advanced Students: Teaching assistantships available for advanced students. Average amount paid per academic year: $14,000. Average number of hours worked per week: 16. Tuition remission given: full. Research assistantships available for advanced students. Average amount paid per academic year: $18,000. Average number of hours worked per week: 20. Tuition remission given: full. Traineeships available for advanced students. Average amount paid per academic year: $20,000. Average number of hours worked per week: 20. Tuition remission given: full. Fellowships and scholarships available for advanced students. Average amount paid per academic year: $18,000. Average number of hours worked per week: 0. Tuition remission given: full.

Contact Information: Of all students currently enrolled full-time, 83% benefitted from one or more of the listed financial assistance programs. Application and information available online at: http://www.psy.fsu.edu/.

Internships/Practica: Community facilities provide a multitude of settings for practicum placements for clinical students and for master's students interested in applied behavior analysis. Students typically receive a stipend and tuition waivers for their practicum work in the community as well as excellent supervised experience and opportunities for research. Practicum settings for clinical students include an inpatient psychiatric hospital, a comprehensive evaluation center for children, a juvenile treatment program, forensic facilities, and other agencies in the community. Clinical psychology students complete a required unpaid practicum at our nationally recognized on-campus Psychology Clinic during the second year of study. The clinic provides empirically based assessment and therapy services to adults, children, and families in the north Florida region. Psychology faculty provides supervision. The clinical program culminates in a required one-year internship in an APA-approved facility. Clinical students from the FSU program have, over the years, been highly successful in obtaining excellent internships throughout the country. Applied Behavior Analysis master's students have diverse practicum sites from which to choose, including public schools, family homes, residential treatment facilities, businesses, consulting firms, and state agencies. For those doctoral students for whom a professional internship is required prior to graduation, 2 applied in 2003–2004. Of those who applied, 2 were placed in internships listed by the Association of Psychology Postdoctoral and Internship Programs (APPIC); 2 were placed in APA accredited internships.

Housing and Day Care: On-campus housing is available. See the following Web site for more information: http://www.housing.fsu.edu/. On-campus day care facilities are available. See the following Web site for more information: http://www.childcare.fsu.edu/.

Employment of Department Graduates:

Master's Degree Graduates: Of those who graduated in the academic year 2003–2004, the following categories and numbers

represent the post-graduate activities and employment of master's degree graduates: Enrolled in a psychology doctoral program (1), enrolled in a post-doctoral residency/fellowship (n/a), employed in independent practice (n/a), employed in a professional position in a school system (1), employed in a hospital/medical center (1), other employment position (11), total from the above (master's) (14).

Doctoral Degree Graduates: Of those who graduated in the academic year 2003–2004, the following categories and numbers represent the post-graduate activities and employment of doctoral degree graduates: Enrolled in a psychology doctoral program (n/a), enrolled in a post-doctoral residency/fellowship (3), employed in an academic position at a university (4), employed in other positions at a higher education institution (1), employed in a professional position in a school system (1), employed in a government agency (professional services) (1), employed in a community mental health/counseling center (1), total from the above (doctoral) (11).

Additional Information:

Orientation, Objectives, and Emphasis of Department: This is a scientifically-oriented department with almost $6 million in annual grant funding. The Clinical Psychology program promotes a scientifically based approach to understanding, assessing, and ameliorating cognitive, emotional, behavioral, and health problems. Integrative training in clinical science and clinical service delivery is provided. Cognitive Psychology students develop research and analytical skills while learning to coordinate basic research with theory development and application. Current research includes expert performance, skill acquisition, reading, memory, attention, language processing, and cognitive aging. Students in the Developmental Psychology program conduct basic and applied research. A developmental perspective is interdisciplinary; consequently members of the developmental faculty routinely hold appointments in one of our other doctoral programs. The Social Psychology program provides students with in-depth training in personality and social psychology, focusing on basic and applied research. Current research areas include the self, prejudice and stereotyping, and evolutionary perspectives on various topics. The interdisciplinary Neuroscience program offers students with broad training in brain and behavior research. Areas of emphasis include sensory processes, neural development and plasticity, behavioral and molecular genetics, regulation of energy balance and hormonal control of behavior. The terminal master's specialty in Applied Behavior Analysis focuses on analyzing and modifying behavior using well-established principles of learning.

Special Facilities or Resources: The department has a wide range of resources and technical support. Fully staffed and equipped electronic and machine shops support faculty and graduate student research. Highly trained staff provides assistance in graphic arts, photography, instrument and computer software design, and electronic communication services. A neurosurgical operating room, a neurohistological laboratory, and electrically or acoustically shielded rooms are available. Faculty and students have available to them online computers, a supercomputer, and workstations offering human eyetracking and brain wave and psychophysiological recording, among others. A molecular neuroscience laboratory provides equipment and training for studies of gene cloning and gene expression, as well as techniques to measure levels of hormones and neurotransmitters. The Clinical program administers an on-campus outpatient clinic that offers empirically based assess-

ment and therapy services to members of the Tallahassee and surrounding communities. The department was one of four in the U.S. recognized in 2003 by APA for innovative practices in graduate education in psychology. This recognition was for the on-campus clinic, which is a full-fledged clinical research laboratory. Based on research and case studies conducted at the clinic, faculty and students have published books and peer-reviewed articles. The department expects to move to a new, state-of-the-art building in 2006.

Information for Students With Physical Disabilities: See the following Web site for more information: www.fsu.edu/~staffair/dean/StudentDisability.

Application Information:
Send to: Graduate Program, Department of Psychology, Florida State University, Tallahassee, FL 32306-1270. Application available online. URL of online application: http://www.psy.fsu.edu. Students are admitted in the Fall, application deadline. The application deadline is December 1 for Clinical Psychology. The application deadline is December 15 for Developmental Psychology, Neuroscience, and Social Psychology and January 5 for Cognitive Psychology. The Applied Behavior Analysis MS Specialty application deadline is March 1. Applicants should confirm these dates on the department's website. *Fee:* $30. No waivers or deferrals of fee are available.

Florida State University
Psychological Services in Education
Education
307 Stone Building
Tallahassee, FL 32306-4453
Telephone: (850) 644-4592
Fax: (850) 644-8776
E-mail: *gpeterson@admin.fsu.edu*
Web: *http://www.fsu.edu/~coe/departments/epls/cpsp.html*

Department Information:
2002. Program Coordinator: Gary Peterson. Number of Faculty: total–full-time 8, part-time 2; women–full-time 2, part-time 1; minority–full-time 2.

Programs and Degrees Offered:
Listed in the following order: Program area, degree type (T if terminal Master's), number awarded 7/03–6/04. Combined Counseling and School PhD (Doctor of Philosophy) 10, Counseling EdS (Education Specialist) 60.

APA Accreditation: Combination PhD (Doctor of Philosophy).

Student Applications/Admissions:
Student Applications
Combined Counseling and School PhD (Doctor of Philosophy)—
Applications 2004–2005, 58. Total applicants accepted 2004–2005, 6. Total enrolled 2004–2005 full-time, 25, part-time, 11. Openings 2005–2006, 10. The Median number of years required for completion of a degree are 6. The number of students enrolled full and part-time who were dismissed or voluntarily withdrew from this program area were 0. *Counseling*

EdS (Education Specialist)—Applications 2004–2005, 129. Total applicants accepted 2004–2005, 54. Total enrolled 2004–2005 full-time, 59, part-time, 4. Openings 2005–2006, 40. The Median number of years required for completion of a degree are 2. The number of students enrolled full and part-time who were dismissed or voluntarily withdrew from this program area were 2.

Admissions Requirements:

Scores: Entries appear in this order: required test or GPA, minimum score (if required), median score of students entering in 2003–2004. Master's Programs: GRE-V+Q 1000, 1036; last 2 years GPA 3.0, 3.51. Doctoral Programs: GRE-V+Q 1000, 1142.

Other Criteria: (importance of criteria rated low, medium, or high): GRE/MAT scores medium, research experience medium, work experience medium, extracurricular activity low, clinically related public service medium, GPA high, letters of recommendation high, interview low, statement of goals and objectives high.

Student Characteristics: The following represents characteristics of students in 2004–2005 in all graduate psychology programs in the department: Female–full-time 77, part-time 14; Male–full-time 24, part-time 9; African American/Black–full-time 12, part-time 1; Hispanic/Latino(a)–full-time 8, part-time 1; Asian/Pacific Islander–full-time 4, part-time 0; American Indian/Alaska Native–full-time 0, part-time 0; Caucasian–full-time 82, part-time 16; students subject to the Americans With Disabilities Act–full-time 1, part-time 1.

Financial Information/Assistance:

Tuition for Full-Time Study: *Master's:* State residents: per academic year $5,550, $184 per credit hour; Nonstate residents: per academic year $17,190, $537 per credit hour. *Doctoral:* State residents: per academic year $5,550, $184 per credit hour; Nonstate residents: per academic year $17,190, $573 per credit hour.

Financial Assistance:

First Year Students: Teaching assistantships available for first-year. Average amount paid per academic year: $3,000. Average number of hours worked per week: 10. Apply by open. Research assistantships available for first-year. Average amount paid per academic year: $3,000. Average number of hours worked per week: 10. Apply by open. Fellowships and scholarships available for first-year. Average amount paid per academic year: $6,300. Average number of hours worked per week: 10. Apply by January 15.

Advanced Students: Teaching assistantships available for advanced students. Average amount paid per academic year: $3,000. Average number of hours worked per week: 10. Apply by open. Research assistantships available for advanced students. Average amount paid per academic year: $3,000. Average number of hours worked per week: 10. Apply by open. Fellowships and scholarships available for advanced students. Average amount paid per academic year: $5,000. Apply by January 15.

Contact Information: Of all students currently enrolled full-time, 60% benefitted from one or more of the listed financial assistance programs.

Internships/Practica: For those doctoral students for whom a professional internship is required prior to graduation, 7 applied in 2003–2004. Of those who applied, 6 were placed in internships listed by the Association of Psychology Postdoctoral and Internship Programs (APPIC); 4 were placed in APA accredited internships.

Housing and Day Care: On-campus housing is available. See the following Web site for more information: www.fsu.edu/housing. On-campus day care facilities are available. See the following Web site for more information: www.fsu.edu/child care Note: facilities are limited, so please apply early.

Employment of Department Graduates:

Master's Degree Graduates: Of those who graduated in the academic year 2003–2004, the following categories and numbers represent the post-graduate activities and employment of master's degree graduates: Enrolled in a post-doctoral residency/fellowship (n/a), employed in independent practice (n/a), total from the above (master's) (0).

Doctoral Degree Graduates: Of those who graduated in the academic year 2003–2004, the following categories and numbers represent the post-graduate activities and employment of doctoral degree graduates: Enrolled in a psychology doctoral program (n/a), enrolled in a post-doctoral residency/fellowship (1), employed in independent practice (1), employed in a hospital/medical center (2), other employment position (1), total from the above (doctoral) (5).

Additional Information:

Orientation, Objectives, and Emphasis of Department: The Combined Doctoral Program in Counseling Psychology and School Psychology allows students to acquire knowledge and skills necessary for the practice of counseling psychology and school psychology in a variety of applied settings, as well as enabling students to contribute to the advancement of the profession through research and service. Students are expected to acquire basic competency in counseling psychology or school psychology, leading to appropriate national certification and state licensure. Within this combined program, all students share a common core of experience in research and practice in counseling psychology and school psychology, while expressing a professional focus by selecting a concentration in counseling psychology or school psychology. The Combined Program reflects a scientist-practitioner model within the context of the mission of the College of Education. The faculty members in the program have work experience and research interests in the areas of career counseling, mental health counseling throughout the life span, and the delivery of psychological services in schools.

Special Facilities or Resources: The program uses three primary facilities for the development of counseling skills: (1) the Human Services Center and the Career Center. The Human Services Center is a service, research, and training facility that provides counseling services at a nominal cost to residents of Tallahassee and surrounding communities. This center offers individual counseling for anxiety or depression, relationship counseling, family counseling, and personal growth and development. The Human Services Center also serves as a referral source for public schools. (2) The Adult Learning and Evaluation Center is a referral source for FSU, FAMU, TCC and the community and is located in the College of Education. It serves to assist adults in identifying learning disabilities that may impede the attainment of educational and career progress. It offers students practica and assistantships in psychological assessment and consultation. (3) The Career Center is located in the Student Services Center and provides one of the most modern technologically-advanced career facilities in the nation. The Career Center provides opportunities for practica and internships as well as for student employment opportunities as career advisors. This Center serves as many as 6000 students per year with a variety of career concerns from choice of major to job placement. The overarching philosophy is one of a full-service career center that is able to treat not only the presenting career concern but related mental health issues as well.

Information for Students With Physical Disabilities: See the following Web site for more information: www.fsu.edu/StudentDisabilitiesResourceCenter.

Application Information:
Send to: Chair, Admissions Committee, Psychological Services in Education, Florida State University, 307 Stone Building, Tallahassee, FL 32306-4453. Application available online. URL of online application: http//www.epls.fsu.edu/psych__servoces/index.htm. Students are admitted in the Fall, application deadline February 1. *Fee:* $30.

Florida, University of
Department of Clinical and Health Psychology
Public Health and Health Professions
Box 100165 HSC
Gainesville, FL 32610-0165
Telephone: (352) 273-6455
Fax: (352) 273-6156
E-mail: *vcarter@phhp.ufl.edu*
Web: *www.phhp.ufl.edu/chp/*

Department Information:
1959. Chairperson: Ronald Rozensky. Number of Faculty: total–full-time 38; women–full-time 11; minority–full-time 2; faculty subject to the Americans With Disabilities Act 1.

Programs and Degrees Offered:
Listed in the following order: Program area, degree type (T if terminal Master's), number awarded 7/03–6/04. Clinical PhD (Doctor of Philosophy) 14.

APA Accreditation: Clinical PhD (Doctor of Philosophy).

Student Applications/Admissions:
Student Applications
Clinical PhD (Doctor of Philosophy)—Applications 2004–2005, 361. Total applicants accepted 2004–2005, 22. Number enrolled (new admits only) 2004–2005 full-time, 17. Number enrolled (new admits only) 2004–2005 part-time, 0. Total enrolled 2004–2005 full-time, 80, part-time, 7. Openings 2005–2006, 12. The Median number of years required for completion of a degree are 6. The number of students enrolled full and part-time who were dismissed or voluntarily withdrew from this program area were 3.

Admissions Requirements:
Scores: Entries appear in this order: required test or GPA, minimum score (if required), median score of students entering

in 2003–2004. Master's Programs: . We do not offer a terminal master's degree program. Doctoral Programs: GRE-V 500, 610; GRE-Q 500, 650; GRE-V+Q 1000, 1260; GRE-Analytical 3.0, 5.0; last 2 years GPA 3.00, 3.80.

Other Criteria: (importance of criteria rated low, medium, or high): GRE/MAT scores medium, research experience high, work experience medium, extracurricular activity medium, clinically related public service high, GPA medium, letters of recommendation high, interview high, statement of goals and objectives high. For additional information on admission requirements, go to: www.phhp.ufl.edu/chp/.

Student Characteristics: The following represents characteristics of students in 2004–2005 in all graduate psychology programs in the department: Female–full-time 62, part-time 6; Male–full-time 18, part-time 1; African American/Black–full-time 6, part-time 0; Hispanic/Latino(a)–full-time 4, part-time 0; Asian/Pacific Islander–full-time 7, part-time 0; American Indian/Alaska Native–full-time 0, part-time 0; Caucasian–full-time 62, part-time 7; Multi-ethnic–full-time 1, part-time 0; students subject to the Americans With Disabilities Act–full-time 0, part-time 0.

Financial Information/Assistance:
Tuition for Full-Time Study: *Doctoral:* State residents: per academic year $5,496, $229 per credit hour; Nonstate residents: per academic year $21,360, $890 per credit hour. Tuition is subject to change. See the following Web site for updates and changes in tuition costs: www.ufl.edu.

Financial Assistance:
First Year Students: Research assistantships available for first-year. Average amount paid per academic year: $12,000. Average number of hours worked per week: 20. Apply by December 1. Tuition remission given: full. Fellowships and scholarships available for first-year. Average amount paid per academic year: $15,000. Apply by December 1. Tuition remission given: full.

Advanced Students: Teaching assistantships available for advanced students. Average amount paid per academic year: $12,000. Average number of hours worked per week: 20. Tuition remission given: full and partial. Research assistantships available for advanced students. Average amount paid per academic year: $12,000. Average number of hours worked per week: 20. Tuition remission given: full and partial. Fellowships and scholarships available for advanced students. Average amount paid per academic year: $18,000. Tuition remission given: full.

Contact Information: Of all students currently enrolled full-time, 99% benefitted from one or more of the listed financial assistance programs. Application and information available online at: http://www.phhp.ufl.edu/chp.

Internships/Practica:
The Department of Clinical and Health Psychology runs a Psychology Clinic which is part of the Shands Hospital within the University of Florida Health Science Center. This clinic provides consultation, assessment, and intervention services to medical-surgical inpatients and outpatients, as well as community patients with emotional and behavioral problems. Major services include clinical health psychology, child/pediatric psychology and clinical neuropsychology. For those doctoral students for whom a professional internship is required prior to graduation, 9 applied in 2003–2004. Of those who applied, 9 were placed in internships listed by the Association of Psychology

Postdoctoral and Internship Programs (APPIC); 9 were placed in APA accredited internships.

Housing and Day Care: On-campus housing is available. See the following Web site for more information: http://www.housing.ufl.edu/housing/. On-campus day care facilities are available. See the following Web site for more information: http://www.coe.ufl.edu/Departments/BabyGator/.

Employment of Department Graduates:
Master's Degree Graduates: Of those who graduated in the academic year 2003–2004, the following categories and numbers represent the post-graduate activities and employment of master's degree graduates: Enrolled in a post-doctoral residency/fellowship (n/a), employed in independent practice (n/a), total from the above (master's) (0).
Doctoral Degree Graduates: Of those who graduated in the academic year 2003–2004, the following categories and numbers represent the post-graduate activities and employment of doctoral degree graduates: Enrolled in a psychology doctoral program (n/a), enrolled in a post-doctoral residency/fellowship (6), employed in independent practice (2), employed in an academic position at a university (2), employed in a government agency (research) (1), employed in a hospital/medical center (2), do not know (1), total from the above (doctoral) (14).

Additional Information:
Orientation, Objectives, and Emphasis of Department: The program is designed to develop doctoral-level professional psychologists in the scientist-practitioner model through development of broad clinical skills and competencies, through mastery of broad areas of knowledge in psychology and clinical psychology, and through demonstrated competencies in contributing to that knowledge by research. Within these program objectives particular emphases can be identified: clinical health psychology, clinical neuropsychology and clinical child/pediatric psychology. Courses, practica, conferences, committees, supervision, and settings are designed to augment each emphasis.

Special Facilities or Resources: The Department and its parent College, the College of Public Health and Health Professions, recently moved into a new building that houses faculty offices, student work spaces, and state-of-the-art classroom facilities. Department faculty currently occupy several thousand square feet of laboratory space for clinical and basic research. The Department is particularly strong in instrumentation and methodology for clinical research in pediatric psychology, health psychology, and neuropsychology. Psychophysiological and neuroimaging capabilities are present and utilized by many faculty. The clinical psychology program uses the extensive resources of the campus and community. The primary focus is in the Center for Clinical and Health Psychology of the University of Florida Health Science Center with its six colleges, and Shands Teaching Hospital and Clinics. Other sites utilized for clinical training include the university student health services; the university counseling center; and the VA Medical Center in Gainesville. Agencies and centers throughout the state and nation are also used, principally for intern training for students. The use of these varied resources is consonant with the program objectives. The trainee is directly involved with a broad scope of clinical and health problems, professionals, agencies, and settings.

Information for Students With Physical Disabilities: See the following Web site for more information: http://www.dso.ufl.edu/OSD/.

Application Information:
Send to: Graduate Admissions, Department of Clinical and Health Psychology, Box 100165 HSC, University of Florida, Gainesville, FL 32610-0165. Application available online. URL of online application: www.phhp.ufl.edu/chp/. Students are admitted in the Fall, application deadline December 1. *Fee:* $30. Application fee cannot be waived.

Florida, University of
Department of Psychology
Liberal Arts and Sciences
P.O. Box 112250
Gainesville, FL 32611-2250
Telephone: (352) 392-0601
Fax: (352) 392-7985
E-mail: *heesack@ufl.edu*
Web: *http://www.psych.ufl.edu*

Department Information:
1947. Professor and Chair: Martin Heesacker. Number of Faculty: total–full-time 52, part-time 4; women–full-time 11, part-time 1; minority–full-time 3.

Programs and Degrees Offered:
Listed in the following order: Program area, degree type (T if terminal Master's), number awarded 7/03–6/04. Behavior Analysis PhD (Doctor of Philosophy) 4, Cognitive PhD (Doctor of Philosophy) 2, Counseling PhD (Doctor of Philosophy) 7, Developmental PhD (Doctor of Philosophy) 5, Social PhD (Doctor of Philosophy) 2, Behavioral Neuroscience PhD (Doctor of Philosophy) 3.

APA Accreditation: Counseling PhD (Doctor of Philosophy).

Student Applications/Admissions:
Student Applications
Behavior Analysis PhD (Doctor of Philosophy)—Applications 2004–2005, 39. Total applicants accepted 2004–2005, 10. Number enrolled (new admits only) 2004–2005 full-time, 5. Number enrolled (new admits only) 2004–2005 part-time, 0. Total enrolled 2004–2005 full-time, 32, part-time, 8. Openings 2005–2006, 10. The Median number of years required for completion of a degree are 4. The number of students enrolled full and part-time who were dismissed or voluntarily withdrew from this program area were 1. *Cognitive PhD (Doctor of Philosophy)*—Applications 2004–2005, 31. Total applicants accepted 2004–2005, 5. Number enrolled (new admits only) 2004–2005 full-time, 1. Number enrolled (new admits only) 2004–2005 part-time, 0. Total enrolled 2004–2005 full-time, 11, part-time, 1. Openings 2005–2006, 4. The Median number of years required for completion of a degree are 4. The number of students enrolled full and part-time who were dismissed or voluntarily withdrew from this program area were 0. *Counseling PhD (Doctor of Philosophy)*—Applications 2004–2005, 136. Total applicants accepted 2004–2005, 11. Number enrolled (new admits only) 2004–2005 full-time, 10. Number enrolled (new admits only) 2004–2005 part-time, 0. Total enrolled

2004–2005 full-time, 36, part-time, 14. Openings 2005–2006, 8. The Median number of years required for completion of a degree are 4. The number of students enrolled full and part-time who were dismissed or voluntarily withdrew from this program area were 1. *Developmental PhD (Doctor of Philosophy)*—Applications 2004–2005, 25. Total applicants accepted 2004–2005, 2. Number enrolled (new admits only) 2004–2005 full-time, 2. Number enrolled (new admits only) 2004–2005 part-time, 0. Total enrolled 2004–2005 full-time, 13, part-time, 4. Openings 2005–2006, 5. The Median number of years required for completion of a degree are 4. The number of students enrolled full and part-time who were dismissed or voluntarily withdrew from this program area were 0. *Social PhD (Doctor of Philosophy)*—Applications 2004–2005, 52. Total applicants accepted 2004–2005, 2. Number enrolled (new admits only) 2004–2005 full-time, 2. Number enrolled (new admits only) 2004–2005 part-time, 0. Total enrolled 2004–2005 full-time, 10, part-time, 2. Openings 2005–2006, 1. The Median number of years required for completion of a degree are 4. The number of students enrolled full and part-time who were dismissed or voluntarily withdrew from this program area were 0. *Behavioral Neuroscience PhD (Doctor of Philosophy)* Applications 2004–2005, 20. Total applicants accepted 2004–2005, 7. Number enrolled (new admits only) 2004–2005 full-time, 5. Number enrolled (new admits only) 2004–2005 part-time, 0. Total enrolled 2004–2005 full-time, 18, part-time, 2. Openings 2005–2006, 4. The Median number of years required for completion of a degree are 4. The number of students enrolled full and part-time who were dismissed or voluntarily withdrew from this program area were 0.

Admissions Requirements:

Scores: Entries appear in this order: required test or GPA, minimum score (if required), median score of students entering in 2003–2004. Doctoral Programs: GRE-V+Q 1200, 1227.

Other Criteria: (importance of criteria rated low, medium, or high): GRE/MAT scores medium, research experience high, work experience medium, extracurricular activity medium, clinically related public service high, GPA medium, letters of recommendation high, interview medium, statement of goals and objectives high. Only the Counseling Psychology program requires clinically related experience.

Student Characteristics: The following represents characteristics of students in 2004–2005 in all graduate psychology programs in the department: Female–full-time 86, part-time 17; Male–full-time 34, part-time 14; African American/Black–full-time 10, part-time 2; Hispanic/Latino(a)–full-time 5, part-time 4; Asian/Pacific Islander–full-time 19, part-time 3; American Indian/Alaska Native–full-time 0, part-time 0; Caucasian–full-time 86, part-time 22; students subject to the Americans With Disabilities Act–full-time 0, part-time 0.

Financial Information/Assistance:

Tuition for Full-Time Study: *Master's:* State residents: per academic year $5,483, $228 per credit hour; Nonstate residents: per academic year $20,468, $889 per credit hour. *Doctoral:* State residents: per academic year $5,483, $228 per credit hour; Nonstate residents: per academic year $20,468, $889 per credit hour. Tuition is subject to change.

Financial Assistance:

First Year Students: Teaching assistantships available for first-year. Average amount paid per academic year: $10,500. Average number of hours worked per week: 14. Apply by January 15. Tuition remission given: full and partial. Research assistantships available for first-year. Average amount paid per academic year: $9,367. Average number of hours worked per week: 20. Apply by January 15. Tuition remission given: full and partial. Fellowships and scholarships available for first-year. Average amount paid per academic year: $15,000. Apply by January 15. Tuition remission given: full and partial.

Advanced Students: No information provided.

Contact Information: Of all students currently enrolled full-time, 95% benefitted from one or more of the listed financial assistance programs.

Internships/Practica: University Counseling Center, University of Florida Student Health Service, Family Practice Medical Group, Meridian Behavioral Healthcare, Alachua County Crisis Center, VA Medical Center, North Florida Treatment and Evaluation Center, and Northeast Florida State Hospital.

Housing and Day Care: On-campus housing is available. See the following Web site for more information: On-campus housing is available only for married graduate students. For more information, go to www.housing.ufl.edu. On-campus day care facilities are available. See the following Web site for more information: Baby Gator day care is located on campus and is available to all graduate students. Their website is http://www.coe.ufl.edu/BabyGator.

Employment of Department Graduates:

Master's Degree Graduates: Of those who graduated in the academic year 2003–2004, the following categories and numbers represent the post-graduate activities and employment of master's degree graduates: Enrolled in another graduate/professional program (1), enrolled in a post-doctoral residency/fellowship (n/a), employed in independent practice (n/a), other employment position (1), total from the above (master's) (2).

Doctoral Degree Graduates: Of those who graduated in the academic year 2003–2004, the following categories and numbers represent the post-graduate activities and employment of doctoral degree graduates: Enrolled in a psychology doctoral program (n/a), enrolled in another graduate/professional program (1), enrolled in a post-doctoral residency/fellowship (1), other employment position (9), total from the above (doctoral) (11).

Additional Information:

Orientation, Objectives, and Emphasis of Department: The graduate program in Psychology at the University of Florida is designed for those planning careers as researchers, teacher-scholars, and scientist–practitioners in Psychology. In addition to specialized training in one or more areas, a core program of theories, methods, and research in general psychology insures that each student will be well prepared in the basic areas of Psychology. The primary goal of the Department is educating scientists who will help advance psychology as a science through teaching, research, and professional practice. Because the University of Florida is a broad spectrum university, including almost all the major academic departments as well as professional schools on a single campus, a unique atmosphere exists for the evolution of the general program and the development of personal programs of study.

Each student also receives specialized training in at least one of the areas of specialization including cognition and sensory processes, counseling psychology, developmental, experimental analysis of behavior, psychobiology (comparative-physiological), and social. One of the fundamental goals of the doctoral program is to engage the student as early as possible in the area of interest while assuring a sound background of knowledge of theory, methodology, and major content areas so that maximum integration may be achieved. All students participate in various ongoing aspects of the academic community such as teaching, research, field experience, and professional activities. Seminars are offered in techniques of teaching accompanied by supervised undergraduate teaching. Continuous research experience is required. The Department participates in a number of interdisciplinary programs including sensory studies, neurobiological sciences, and gerontological studies.

Special Facilities or Resources: Special facilities in the department include laboratories in comparative, developmental, experimental analysis of behavior, cognitive and information processing, perception, personality, psychobiology, sensory, and social; an animal colony; a statistical computation laboratory; a laboratory in neuropsychology and developmental learning disabilities; the Communication Sciences Laboratory; and the Computing Center.

Application Information:

Send to: Graduate Studies Secretary, Psychology Department, University of Florida, Gainesville, FL 32611-2250. Application available online. URL of online application: www.psych.ufl.edu. Students are admitted in the Fall, application deadline January 15. *Fee:* $30.

Miami, University of
Department of Educational & Psychological Studies/Area of Counseling Psychology
Education
P.O. Box 248065
Coral Gables, FL 33124-2040
Telephone: (305) 284-3001
Fax: (305) 284-3003
E-mail: *bfowers@miami.edu*
Web: *http://www.education.miami.edu*

Department Information:

1967. Director of Training, Counseling Psychology Program: Blaine J. Fowers. Number of Faculty: total–full-time 7, part-time 4; women–full-time 2, part-time 2; minority–full-time 1, part-time 3.

Programs and Degrees Offered:

Listed in the following order: Program area, degree type (T if terminal Master's), number awarded 7/03–6/04. Counseling Psychology PhD (Doctor of Philosophy) 4, Marriage and Family Therapy MA/MS (Master of Arts/Science) (T) 10, Mental Health Counseling MA/MS (Master of Arts/Science) (T) 19.

Student Applications/Admissions:

Student Applications

Counseling Psychology PhD (Doctor of Philosophy)—Applications 2004–2005, 100. Total applicants accepted 2004–2005,

8. Number enrolled (new admits only) 2004–2005 full-time, 8. Total enrolled 2004–2005 full-time, 23, part-time, 12. Openings 2005–2006, 6. The Median number of years required for completion of a degree are 6. The number of students enrolled full and part-time who were dismissed or voluntarily withdrew from this program area were 2. *Marriage and Family Therapy MA/MS (Master of Arts/Science)*—Applications 2004–2005, 31. Total applicants accepted 2004–2005, 13. Total enrolled 2004–2005 full-time, 11, part-time, 12. Openings 2005–2006, 15. The Median number of years required for completion of a degree are 3. *Mental Health Counseling MA/MS (Master of Arts/Science)*—Applications 2004–2005, 43. Total applicants accepted 2004–2005, 35. Total enrolled 2004–2005 full-time, 22, part-time, 18. Openings 2005–2006, 15. The Median number of years required for completion of a degree are 3.

Admissions Requirements:

Scores: Entries appear in this order: required test or GPA, minimum score (if required), median score of students entering in 2003–2004. Master's Programs: GRE-V no minimum stated, 470; GRE-Q no minimum stated, 530; GRE-V+Q no minimum stated, 1000; overall undergraduate GPA no minimum stated, 3.28. Doctoral Programs: GRE-V no minimum stated, 592; GRE-Q no minimum stated, 625; GRE-V+Q no minimum stated, 1217; overall undergraduate GPA no minimum stated, 3.36.

Other Criteria: (importance of criteria rated low, medium, or high): GRE/MAT scores high, research experience medium, work experience medium, extracurricular activity low, clinically related public service medium, GPA high, letters of recommendation high, interview high, statement of goals and objectives high.

Student Characteristics: The following represents characteristics of students in 2004–2005 in all graduate psychology programs in the department: Female–full-time 18, part-time 7; Male–full-time 5, part-time 6; African American/Black–full-time 0, part-time 1; Hispanic/Latino(a)–full-time 7, part-time 2; Asian/Pacific Islander–full-time 0, part-time 0; American Indian/Alaska Native–full-time 0, part-time 0; Caucasian–full-time 14, part-time 10; Multi-ethnic–full-time 2, part-time 0; students subject to the Americans With Disabilities Act–full-time 1, part-time 0.

Financial Information/Assistance:

Tuition for Full-Time Study: *Master's:* State residents: $1,140 per credit hour; Nonstate residents: $1,140 per credit hour. *Doctoral:* State residents: $1,140 per credit hour; Nonstate residents: $1,140 per credit hour.

Financial Assistance:

First Year Students: Teaching assistantships available for first-year. Average amount paid per academic year: $13,000. Average number of hours worked per week: 20. Apply by January 2. Tuition remission given: partial. Research assistantships available for first-year. Average amount paid per academic year: $13,000. Average number of hours worked per week: 20. Apply by January 2. Tuition remission given: partial. Fellowships and scholarships available for first-year. Average amount paid per academic year: $18,000. Average number of hours worked per week: 0. Apply by January 2. Tuition remission given: partial.

Advanced Students: Teaching assistantships available for advanced students. Average amount paid per academic year: $13,000. Average number of hours worked per week: 20. Apply by April 15. Tuition remission given: partial. Research assistantships available for advanced students. Average amount paid per academic year: $13,000. Average number of hours worked per week: 20. Apply by April 15. Tuition remission given: partial. Fellowships and scholarships available for advanced students. Average amount paid per academic year: $18,000. Average number of hours worked per week: 0. Apply by February 1. Tuition remission given: partial.

Contact Information: Of all students currently enrolled full-time, 100% benefitted from one or more of the listed financial assistance programs.

Internships/Practica: Students complete one academic year practicum in our on-campus training clinic. Program faculty supervise the practicum through weekly one-to-one meetings and group supervision meetings. The practicum experience is supplemented by an off-campus placement. Therapeutic modalities in these placements include individual, couple, and group therapies. The off-campus placement is tailored to the student's career goals. Many students also complete an optional advanced practicum in their third year with placements tailored to their career goals. Placements include university counseling centers, psychiatric facilities, VA hospitals, behavioral medicine settings, correctional facilities, schools, among others. For those doctoral students for whom a professional internship is required prior to graduation, 5 applied in 2003–2004. Of those who applied, 5 were placed in internships listed by the Association of Psychology Postdoctoral and Internship Programs (APPIC); 5 were placed in APA accredited internships.

Housing and Day Care: On-campus housing is available. See the following Web site for more information: http://www.miami.edu/. On-campus day care facilities are available.

Employment of Department Graduates:

Master's Degree Graduates: Of those who graduated in the academic year 2003–2004, the following categories and numbers represent the post-graduate activities and employment of master's degree graduates: Enrolled in a post-doctoral residency/fellowship (n/a), employed in independent practice (n/a), total from the above (master's) (0).

Doctoral Degree Graduates: Of those who graduated in the academic year 2003–2004, the following categories and numbers represent the post-graduate activities and employment of doctoral degree graduates: Enrolled in a psychology doctoral program (n/a), employed in a community mental health/counseling center (3), employed in a hospital/medical center (1), other employment position (1), total from the above (doctoral) (5).

Additional Information:

Orientation, Objectives, and Emphasis of Department: The multicultural, health psychology, and family areas are foci in the doctoral program, which is designed to educate counseling psychologists following the scientist-practitioner model and to prepare individuals who will contribute to knowledge in psychology and who will be exemplary practitioners of psychological science. A sequence of research experiences is required as well as at least two semesters of supervised practicum and a full-year internship. In addition to coursework in the psychological founda-tions, requirements include the study of human development and personality (including career development), theories of therapy and the change process, therapeutic methodologies, and psychological assessment. We have begun to offer a 5 course sequence leading to a certificate in bilingual counseling (Spanish/English). The titles of the courses are: Professional Psychological Spanish, Hispanic and Latino Psychology, Community Interventions for Latino and Hispanic Populations, and Supervised Practice in Bilingual Counseling. Two of the five courses can be taken as required electives in the program.

Special Facilities or Resources: The Institute for Individual and Family Counseling, an on-campus clinic, is used as the primary practicum site. It is equipped with facilities for audio, video, and live supervision. The multi-cultural clientele of the Institute and the other agencies and schools in the Miami area are available for practica and fieldwork. Biofeedback and computer laboratories are available to students in the department. A biofeedback laboratory is available in the Institute for Individual and Family Counseling. A microcomputer laboratory is available to all students in the department. In addition, an assessment laboratory is an integral part of assessment training in the program.

Information for Students With Physical Disabilities: See the following Web site for more information: http://www.miami.edu/academic-development/addisab01.html.

Application Information:
Send to: Coordinator of Graduate Studies, School of Education (312 Merrick Building), University of Miami, P.O. Box 248065, Coral Gables, FL 33124. Students are admitted in the Fall, application deadline January 2; Winter, application deadline August 1. January 2 deadline is for Doctoral program applicants. August 1 deadline is for master's degree applicants. *Fee:* $50.

Miami, University of
Department of Psychology
College of Arts & Sciences
P.O. Box 248185
Coral Gables, FL 33124
Telephone: (305) 284-2814
Fax: (305) 284-3402
E-mail: *inquire@mail.psy.miami.edu*
Web: *http://www.psy.miami.edu*

Department Information:
1937. Chairperson: A. Rodney Wellens. Number of Faculty: total–full-time 41; women–full-time 20; minority–full-time 10.

Programs and Degrees Offered:
Listed in the following order: Program area, degree type (T if terminal Master's), number awarded 7/03–6/04. Applied Development PhD (Doctor of Philosophy) 0, Behavioral Neuroscience PhD (Doctor of Philosophy) 0, Adult Clinical PhD (Doctor of Philosophy) 3, Child Clinical PhD (Doctor of Philosophy) 5, Health Clinical PhD (Doctor of Philosophy) 1.

APA Accreditation: Clinical PhD (Doctor of Philosophy).

Student Applications/Admissions:

Student Applications

Applied Development PhD (Doctor of Philosophy)—Applications 2004–2005, 14. Total applicants accepted 2004–2005, 4. Number enrolled (new admits only) 2004–2005 full-time, 3. Number enrolled (new admits only) 2004–2005 part-time, 0. Openings 2005–2006, 6. The Median number of years required for completion of a degree are 6. The number of students enrolled full and part-time who were dismissed or voluntarily withdrew from this program area were 0. Behavioral Neuroscience PhD (Doctor of Philosophy)—Applications 2004–2005, 3. Total applicants accepted 2004–2005, 0. Number enrolled (new admits only) 2004–2005 full-time, 0. Number enrolled (new admits only) 2004–2005 part-time, 0. Openings 2005–2006, 1. The Median number of years required for completion of a degree are 6. The number of students enrolled full and part-time who were dismissed or voluntarily withdrew from this program area were 1. Adult Clinical PhD (Doctor of Philosophy)—Applications 2004–2005, 90. Total applicants accepted 2004–2005, 3. Number enrolled (new admits only) 2004–2005 full-time, 3. Number enrolled (new admits only) 2004–2005 part-time, 0. Openings 2005–2006, 3. The Median number of years required for completion of a degree are 6. The number of students enrolled full and part-time who were dismissed or voluntarily withdrew from this program area were 0. Child Clinical PhD (Doctor of Philosophy)—Applications 2004–2005, 153. Total applicants accepted 2004–2005, 8. Number enrolled (new admits only) 2004–2005 full-time, 6. Number enrolled (new admits only) 2004–2005 part-time, 0. Openings 2005–2006, 5. The Median number of years required for completion of a degree are 6. The number of students enrolled full and part-time who were dismissed or voluntarily withdrew from this program area were 0. Health Clinical PhD (Doctor of Philosophy)—Applications 2004–2005, 46. Total applicants accepted 2004–2005, 5. Number enrolled (new admits only) 2004–2005 full-time, 2. Number enrolled (new admits only) 2004–2005 part-time, 0. Openings 2005–2006, 5. The Median number of years required for completion of a degree are 5. The number of students enrolled full and part-time who were dismissed or voluntarily withdrew from this program area were 3.

Admissions Requirements:

Scores: Entries appear in this order: required test or GPA, minimum score (if required), median score of students entering in 2003–2004. Doctoral Programs: GRE-V 590, 630; GRE-Q 620, 650; GRE-V+Q 1210, 1300; overall undergraduate GPA 3.5, 3.5.

Other Criteria: (importance of criteria rated low, medium, or high): GRE/MAT scores high, research experience high, work experience medium, extracurricular activity medium, clinically related public service medium, GPA high, letters of recommendation high, interview high, statement of goals and objectives high. Clinically related public service not weighted for non-clinical programs. For additional information on admission requirements, go to: www.psy.miami.edu.

Student Characteristics: The following represents characteristics of students in 2004–2005 in all graduate psychology programs in the department: Female–full-time 62, part-time 0; Male–full-time 23, part-time 0; African American/Black–full-time 8, part-time 0; Hispanic/Latino(a)–full-time 16, part-time 0; Asian/Pacific Islander–full-time 4, part-time 0; American Indian/Alaska Native–

full-time 0, part-time 0; Caucasian–full-time 57, part-time 0; Multi-ethnic–full-time 0, part-time 0; students subject to the Americans With Disabilities Act–full-time 0, part-time 0.

Financial Information/Assistance:

Tuition for Full-Time Study: Doctoral: State residents: per academic year $21,744, $1,208 per credit hour; Nonstate residents: per academic year $21,744, $1,208 per credit hour.

Financial Assistance:

First Year Students: Teaching assistantships available for first-year. Average amount paid per academic year: $15,579. Average number of hours worked per week: 15. Apply by December 1. Tuition remission given: full. Research assistantships available for first-year. Average amount paid per academic year: $20,772. Average number of hours worked per week: 20. Apply by December 1. Tuition remission given: full. Traineeships available for first-year. Average amount paid per academic year: $20,772. Average number of hours worked per week: 15. Apply by December 1. Tuition remission given: full. Fellowships and scholarships available for first-year. Average amount paid per academic year: $20,772. Average number of hours worked per week: 0. Apply by December 1. Tuition remission given: full.

Advanced Students: Teaching assistantships available for advanced students. Average amount paid per academic year: $15,579. Average number of hours worked per week: 15. Tuition remission given: full. Research assistantships available for advanced students. Average amount paid per academic year: $20,772. Average number of hours worked per week: 20. Tuition remission given: full. Traineeships available for advanced students. Average amount paid per academic year: $20,772. Average number of hours worked per week: 15. Tuition remission given: full. Fellowships and scholarships available for advanced students. Average amount paid per academic year: $20,772. Average number of hours worked per week: 0. Tuition remission given: full.

Contact Information: Of all students currently enrolled full-time, 100% benefitted from one or more of the listed financial assistance programs. Application and information available online at: www.psy.miami.edu.

Internships/Practica: Practica sites are available for students enrolled in our APA-approved clinical program on the Coral Gables campus, Medical School campus and throughout Miami-Dade County. The department's Psychological Services Center and the University Counseling Center represent primary sites for students developing skills in psychological assessment and empirically-based interventions. Additional specialty practica are located in the Department of Pediatrics at Medical School, the Veterans Administration Medical Center and various clinics throughout Miami-Dade County. For those doctoral students for whom a professional internship is required prior to graduation, 9 applied in 2003–2004. Of those who applied, 9 were placed in internships listed by the Association of Psychology Postdoctoral and Internship Programs (APPIC); 9 were placed in APA accredited internships.

Housing and Day Care: No on-campus housing is available. On-campus day care facilities are available. UM/Canterbury Preschool, 1150 Stanford Drive, Coral Gables, FL 33124, (305) 284-5437.

Employment of Department Graduates:

Master's Degree Graduates: Of those who graduated in the academic year 2003–2004, the following categories and numbers represent the post-graduate activities and employment of master's degree graduates: Enrolled in a post-doctoral residency/fellowship (n/a), employed in independent practice (n/a), total from the above (master's) (0).

Doctoral Degree Graduates: Of those who graduated in the academic year 2003–2004, the following categories and numbers represent the post-graduate activities and employment of doctoral degree graduates: Enrolled in a psychology doctoral program (n/a), enrolled in a post-doctoral residency/fellowship (8), other employment position (1), total from the above (doctoral) (9).

Additional Information:

Orientation, Objectives, and Emphasis of Department: The mission of the Department of Psychology is to acquire, advance, and disseminate knowledge within the Psychological and Biobehavioral Sciences. In order to achieve these goals the Department seeks a balance among several academic endeavors including: basic scientific research, applied research, undergraduate teaching, graduate teaching, professional training and development, and service to the community. The department offers courses leading to the degree of Doctor of Philosophy. Prospective degree applicants are admitted to graduate study in psychology within one of three graduate Divisions: Adult, Child, or Health. The Adult Division offers students an integrated program in clinical psychology that includes a background in personality-social psychology as well as basic and applied aspects of adult psychopathology and treatment. Students admitted to the Child Division may choose from Clinical Child and Family, Pediatric Health, and Applied Developmental psychology. Students in the Health Division may choose between Health Clinical and Behavioral Neuroscience. All students receive experience teaching at least one undergraduate course as part of their graduate training. Students are supported by a variety of training grants, fellowships, teaching assistantships and research assistantships.

Special Facilities or Resources: The Psychological Services Center serves as a community-based mental health training clinic for clinical students. The Behavioral Medicine Research Building provides excellent research facilities for students in behavioral neuroscience and health psychology. The Behavioral Medicine Research Center located at the Veterans Administration Medical Center provides state-of-the-art facilities for research in psychoneuroimmunology. The Linda Ray Intervention Center and the Center for Autism and Related Disabilities provide excellent research opportunities for students in our child programs. Faculty research is supported by more than $14 million yearly in federal and state funding. The department recently moved to a new state-of-the-art research and teaching facility constructed for its use in 2003.

Application Information:

Send to: Graduate Admissions, Department of Psychology, P.O. Box 248185, Coral Gables, FL 33124. To access our online application go to https://www.applyweb.com/aw?mgrpsy/. Application available online. URL of online application: www.psy.miami.edu. Students are admitted in the Fall, application deadline December 1. *Fee:* $50.

North Florida, University of
Department of Psychology
4567 Street John's Bluff Road, South
Jacksonville, FL 32224-2673
Telephone: (904) 620-2807
Fax: (904) 620-3814
E-mail: *mchambli@unf.edu*
Web: *http://www.unf.edu*

Department Information:

1972. Chairperson: Minor H. Chamblin. Number of Faculty: total–full-time 20, part-time 12; women–full-time 9, part-time 7; minority–full-time 5; faculty subject to the Americans With Disabilities Act 2.

Programs and Degrees Offered:

Listed in the following order: Program area, degree type (T if terminal Master's), number awarded 7/03–6/04. General Psychology MA/MS (Master of Arts/Science) (T) 6, Counseling Psychology MA/MS (Master of Arts/Science) (T) 11.

Student Applications/Admissions:

Student Applications

General Psychology MA/MS (Master of Arts/Science)—Applications 2004–2005, 49. Total applicants accepted 2004–2005, 12. Openings 2005–2006, 15. The Median number of years required for completion of a degree are 2. The number of students enrolled full and part-time who were dismissed or voluntarily withdrew from this program area were 2. *Counseling Psychology MA/MS (Master of Arts/Science)*—Applications 2004–2005, 69. Total applicants accepted 2004–2005, 18. Total enrolled 2004–2005 full-time, 27, part-time, 3. Openings 2005–2006, 15. The Median number of years required for completion of a degree are 2. The number of students enrolled full and part-time who were dismissed or voluntarily withdrew from this program area were 2.

Admissions Requirements:

Scores: Entries appear in this order: required test or GPA, minimum score (if required), median score of students entering in 2003–2004. Master's Programs: GRE-V no minimum stated, 540; GRE-Q no minimum stated, 560; GRE-V+Q 1000; last 2 years GPA 3.0, 3.7; psychology GPA 3.0, 3.4.

Other Criteria: (importance of criteria rated low, medium, or high): GRE/MAT scores high, research experience medium, work experience medium, clinically related public service medium, GPA high, letters of recommendation medium, interview high, statement of goals and objectives medium. Research experience for general psychology and clinically related public service + interview for counseling psychology.

Student Characteristics: The following represents characteristics of students in 2004–2005 in all graduate psychology programs in the department: Female–full-time 41, part-time 3; Male–full-time 9, part-time 0; African American/Black–full-time 5, part-time 1; Hispanic/Latino(a)–full-time 3, part-time 0; Asian/Pacific Islander–full-time 1, part-time 0; American Indian/Alaska Native–full-time 0, part-time 0; Caucasian–full-time 41, part-time 2; students subject to the Americans With Disabilities Act–full-time 2, part-time 0.

Financial Information/Assistance:
Tuition for Full-Time Study: *Master's:* State residents: $248 per credit hour; Nonstate residents: $966 per credit hour.

Financial Assistance:
First Year Students: Teaching assistantships available for first-year. Research assistantships available for first-year. Traineeships available for first-year. Average amount paid per academic year: $5,000. Fellowships and scholarships available for first-year. Average amount paid per academic year: $850. Apply by June 1. Tuition remission given: partial.
Advanced Students: Teaching assistantships available for advanced students. Average amount paid per academic year: $1,600. Apply by June 1. Research assistantships available for advanced students. Traineeships available for advanced students. Average amount paid per academic year: $10,000. Apply by June 1. Fellowships and scholarships available for advanced students. Tuition remission given: partial.
Contact Information: Of all students currently enrolled full-time, 30% benefitted from one or more of the listed financial assistance programs.

Internships/Practica: No information provided.

Housing and Day Care: On-campus housing is available. See the following Web site for more information: www.unf.edu. On-campus day care facilities are available.

Employment of Department Graduates:
Master's Degree Graduates: Of those who graduated in the academic year 2003–2004, the following categories and numbers represent the post-graduate activities and employment of master's degree graduates: Enrolled in a post-doctoral residency/fellowship (n/a), employed in independent practice (n/a), total from the above (master's) (0).
Doctoral Degree Graduates: Of those who graduated in the academic year 2003–2004, the following categories and numbers represent the post-graduate activities and employment of doctoral degree graduates: Enrolled in a psychology doctoral program (n/a), total from the above (doctoral) (0).

Additional Information:
Orientation, Objectives, and Emphasis of Department: The Master of Arts in Counseling Psychology program is designed to prepare students for emerging professional roles as Florida licensed master's level practitioners. The program consists of 60 semester hours of coursework, including a two-semester practicum in a community mental health agency. The program balances theory and practice and is designed to provide the prospective practitioner with a firm theoretical foundation for developing counseling strategies as well as the ability to apply particular goal-oriented intervention tactics. The Master of Arts in General Psychology program is a broad-based, research-oriented program intended to equip students with the critical skills and knowledge necessary for continued occupation and educational advancement in fields related to psychology. The program consists of 37 semester hours of coursework designed around a core curriculum of statistics, research design, substantive areas of psychology, and a research-based thesis.

Special Facilities or Resources: Several teaching laboratories are housed within the psychology department. The counseling lab and the psychometric lab each consist of a large observation room, three small rooms for individual counseling/testing and one large seminar/classroom. The computer applications lab has 24 individual computer workstations and an instructor's server, with a local area network and connections to the university mainframe. New computers and printers were purchased during the 2004-2005 school year. The animal lab has six computerized stations for student research on rodents. In addition to these teaching laboratories, individual faculty research labs are also housed within the psychology department. These labs include a social cognition lab, social interaction lab, psychophysiology lab, human factors research lab, developmental lab, psychology and law lab, and human performance lab.

Application Information:
Send to: Michael Herkov, Coordinator, Master of Arts in Counseling Psychology; Randall Russac, Coordinator, Master of Arts in General Psychology. Application available online. URL of online application: https://csdweb.unf.edu/access/htdoes/onlineapp.htm. Students are admitted in the Fall, application deadline March 1. Application deadlines for MA Counseling Psychology March 1; MA General Psychology June 1. *Fee:* $20 online; $30 paper.

Nova Southeastern University
Center for Psychological Studies
3301 College Avenue
Fort Lauderdale, FL 33314
Telephone: (954) 262-5700
Fax: (954) 262-3859
E-mail: *cpsinfo@nova.edu*
Web: *http://www.cps.nova.edu*

Department Information:
1967. Interim Dean: Karen S. Grosby. Number of Faculty: total–full-time 32, part-time 50; women–full-time 8, part-time 9; minority–full-time 5, part-time 3; faculty subject to the Americans With Disabilities Act 1.

Programs and Degrees Offered:
Listed in the following order: Program area, degree type (T if terminal Master's), number awarded 7/03–6/04. Mental Health Counseling MA/MS (Master of Arts/Science) (T) 120, Clinical Psychology PhD (Doctor of Philosophy) 27, Clinical Psychology PsyD (Doctor of Psychology) 52, Clinical Psychopharmacology MA/MS (Master of Arts/Science) (T) 12, School Guidance Counseling MA/MS (Master of Arts/Science) (T) 60, School Psychology Other 0.

APA Accreditation: Clinical PhD (Doctor of Philosophy). Clinical PsyD (Doctor of Psychology).

Student Applications/Admissions:
Student Applications
Mental Health Counseling MA/MS (Master of Arts/Science)— Applications 2004–2005, 184. Total applicants accepted 2004–2005, 165. Total enrolled 2004–2005 full-time, 353, part-time, 50. Openings 2005–2006, 200. The number of students enrolled full and part-time, who were dismissed or voluntarily withdrew from this program area were 28. *Clinical Psy-*

chology PhD (Doctor of Philosophy)—Applications 2004–2005, 222. Total applicants accepted 2004–2005, 23. Number enrolled (new admits only) 2004–2005 full-time, 20. Total enrolled 2004–2005 full-time, 118. Openings 2005–2006, 18. The Median number of years required for completion of a degree are 6. The number of students enrolled full and part-time who were dismissed or voluntarily withdrew from this program area were 1. *Clinical Psychology PsyD (Doctor of Psychology)*—Applications 2004–2005, 344. Total applicants accepted 2004–2005, 102. Number enrolled (new admits only) 2004–2005 full-time, 92. Total enrolled 2004–2005 full-time, 358. Openings 2005–2006, 60. The Median number of years required for completion of a degree are 5. The number of students enrolled full and part-time who were dismissed or voluntarily withdrew from this program area were 2. *Clinical Psychopharmacology MA/MS (Master of Arts/Science)*—Applications 2004–2005, 31. Total applicants accepted 2004–2005, 29. Openings 2005–2006, 25. The number of students enrolled full and part-time who were dismissed or voluntarily withdrew from this program area were 0. *School Guidance Counseling MA/MS (Master of Arts/Science)*—Applications 2004–2005, 91. Total applicants accepted 2004–2005, 84. Total enrolled 2004–2005 full-time, 150, part-time, 42. Openings 2005–2006, 80. The Median number of years required for completion of a degree are 2. The number of students enrolled full and part-time who were dismissed or voluntarily withdrew from this program area were 2. *School Psychology Other*—Applications 2004–2005, 64. Total applicants accepted 2004–2005, 49. Number enrolled (new admits only) 2004–2005 full-time, 27. Number enrolled (new admits only) 2004–2005 part-time, 0. Openings 2005–2006, 55. The number of students enrolled full and part-time who were dismissed or voluntarily withdrew from this program area were 10.

Admissions Requirements:
Scores: Entries appear in this order: required test or GPA, minimum score (if required), median score of students entering in 2003–2004. Doctoral Programs: GRE-V no minimum stated, 483; GRE-Q no minimum stated, 555; GRE-V+Q 1000, 1038; GRE-Subject(Psych) no minimum stated, 620; overall undergraduate GPA 3.0, 3.55. GRE-V + Q > 1000 is preferred. GPA requirement may be satisfied by a Master's GPA> 3.5. GRE-P is recommended, but not required.
Other Criteria: (importance of criteria rated low, medium, or high): GRE/MAT scores high, work experience medium, extracurricular activity low, clinically related public service medium, GPA high, letters of recommendation high, interview high, statement of goals and objectives high, The importance of research is high for the PhD program.

Student Characteristics: The following represents characteristics of students in 2004–2005 in all graduate psychology programs in the department: Female–full-time 1045, part-time 0; Male–full-time 178, part-time 0; African American/Black–full-time 240, part-time 0; Hispanic/Latino(a)–full-time 228, part-time 0; Asian/Pacific Islander–full-time 24, part-time 0; American Indian/Alaska Native–full-time 4, part-time 0; Caucasian–full-time 685, part-time 0; Multi-ethnic–full-time 42, part-time 0; students subject to the Americans With Disabilities Act–full-time 8, part-time 0.

Financial Information/Assistance:
Tuition for Full-Time Study: *Master's:* State residents: $499 per credit hour; Nonstate residents: $499 per credit hour. *Doctoral:* State residents: $720 per credit hour; Nonstate residents: $720 per credit hour. Tuition is subject to change. See the following Web site for updates and changes in tuition costs: www.cps.nova.edu.

Financial Assistance:
First Year Students: Research assistantships available for first-year. Average amount paid per academic year: $5,600. Average number of hours worked per week: 15.
Advanced Students: Teaching assistantships available for advanced students. Average amount paid per academic year: $2,000. Average number of hours worked per week: 6. Research assistantships available for advanced students. Average amount paid per academic year: $5,600. Average number of hours worked per week: 15. Traineeships available for advanced students. Average amount paid per academic year: $5,400. Average number of hours worked per week: 15. Fellowships and scholarships available for advanced students. Apply by varies. Tuition remission given: partial.
Contact Information: Of all students currently enrolled full-time, 12% benefitted from one or more of the listed financial assistance programs. Application and information available online at: Assistantship & Scholarship information available at www.cps.nova.edu.

Internships/Practica: The Center for Psychological Studies (CPS) sponsors the Consortium Internship Program (APPIC member) that provides internship experiences in hospital and other settings within the South Florida Community. In addition to the extensive practicum placements available in the community, practicum opportunities for more than 100 students are provided through various CPS faculty supervised applied-research clinical programs located within the NSU Psychology Services Center. Areas of research include ADHD, alcohol and substance abuse, child and adolescent traumatic stress, clinical biofeedback, interpersonal violence, neuropsychological assessment, older adults, school psychology assessment and testing, the seriously emotionally disturbed, and trauma resolution integration. For those doctoral students for whom a professional internship is required prior to graduation, 76 applied in 2003–2004. Of those who applied, 77 were placed in internships listed by the Association of Psychology Postdoctoral and Internship Programs (APPIC); 61 were placed in APA accredited internships.

Housing and Day Care: On-campus housing is available. See the following Web site for more information: Visit www.nova.edu/cwis/studentaffairs/reslife for further information. On-campus day care facilities are available.

Employment of Department Graduates:
Master's Degree Graduates: Of those who graduated in the academic year 2003–2004, the following categories and numbers represent the post-graduate activities and employment of master's degree graduates: Enrolled in a post-doctoral residency/fellowship (n/a), employed in independent practice (n/a), employed in a professional position in a school system (11), employed in business or industry (management) (6), employed in a government agency (professional services) (1), employed in a community mental

health/counseling center (10), employed in a hospital/medical center (1), total from the above (master's) (29).

Doctoral Degree Graduates: Of those who graduated in the academic year 2003–2004, the following categories and numbers represent the post-graduate activities and employment of doctoral degree graduates: Enrolled in a psychology doctoral program (n/a), enrolled in a post-doctoral residency/fellowship (32), employed in independent practice (2), employed in an academic position at a university (1), employed in an academic position at a 2-year/ 4-year college (2), employed in a professional position in a school system (3), employed in a government agency (professional services) (1), employed in a community mental health/counseling center (6), employed in a hospital/medical center (17), other employment position (11), do not know (5), total from the above (doctoral) (80).

Additional Information:

Orientation, Objectives, and Emphasis of Department: The Center for Psychological Studies (CPS) is committed to providing the highest quality educational experience to future psychologists and counseling professionals. These training experiences provide individuals with a sophisticated understanding of psychological research and the delivery of the highest-quality mental health care. Through the intimate interplay between CPS academic programs and the Nova Southeastern University (NSU) Psychology Services Center, learning becomes rooted in real problems, and research activities attempt to find answers to extant concerns. The center offers master's programs in mental health counseling and school guidance and counseling, a specialist program (PsyS) in school psychology, two APA-accredited doctoral programs in clinical psychology, and a postdoctoral master's program in psychopharmacology. The doctor of psychology (PsyD) program provides emphasis on training professionals to do service while the doctor of philosophy (PhD) program provides greater emphasis on applied research. In response to changes in health care delivery and the profession of psychology, the center developed concentrations at the doctoral level. Concentrations/tracks based on the existing PsyD and PhD curriculum are available in the areas of Clinical Neuropsychology, Clinical Health Psychology, Forensic Psychology, Psychodynamic Psychology, Psychology of Long-Term Mental Illness, Child, Adolescent and Family, and School Psychology.

Special Facilities or Resources: The Center for Psychological Studies is housed in the Maltz Psychology Building, a 65,000 square-foot facility that includes classrooms with state-of-the-art computer technology, a microcomputer lab with 30 multimedia computers connected to major databases and the Internet, study carrels, lounges and meeting rooms, a fitness room, and the Psychology Services Center, where there are therapy rooms with audio and video monitoring capability, play-therapy rooms, and workstations for practicum students assigned to faculty specialty clinical programs. As a university-based professional school, CPS provides access to the NSU 325,000 square-foot Library, Research and Information Technology Center, as well as NSU's Schools of Law, Business and Systemic Studies, the colleges of its Health Professions Division (Medicine, Dentistry, Pharmacy, Allied Health, and Optometry), and its Family and School Center. Also included on NSU's 232-acre+ campus are five residence halls, recreation facilities, and the Miami Dolphins Training Center.

Application Information:
Send to: Enrollment Processing Services, Attn: Center for Psychological Studies, P.O. Box 299000, Ft. Lauderdale, FL 33329-9905. Students are admitted in the Fall, application deadline January 8. Applications for the doctoral programs are accepted only for the fall; the deadline is January 8. Application deadlines for master's and school psychology programs vary by site. Visit our web site at www.cps.nova.edu for further information. *Fee:* $50.

Saint Leo University
Department of Psychology, Counseling Psychology Program
Arts and Sciences
P.O. Box 6665
Saint Leo, FL 33574
Telephone: (352) 588-8285
Fax: (352) 588-8300
E-mail: *christopher.cronin@saintleo.edu*

Department Information:
1965. Chairperson: Christopher Cronin. Number of Faculty: total–full-time 5, part-time 2; women–full-time 1.

Programs and Degrees Offered:
Listed in the following order: Program area, degree type (T if terminal Master's), number awarded 7/03–6/04. Counseling Psychology MA/MS (Master of Arts/Science) (T).

Student Applications/Admissions:
Student Applications

Counseling Psychology MA/MS (Master of Arts/Science)—Applications 2004–2005, 25. Total applicants accepted 2004–2005, 14. Number enrolled (new admits only) 2004–2005 full-time, 5. Number enrolled (new admits only) 2004–2005 part-time, 9. Total enrolled 2004–2005 full-time, 5, part-time, 9. Openings 2005–2006, 25. The number of students enrolled full and part-time who were dismissed or voluntarily withdrew from this program area were 4.

Admissions Requirements:

Scores: Entries appear in this order: required test or GPA, minimum score (if required), median score of students entering in 2003–2004. Master's Programs: GRE-V no minimum stated; GRE-Q no minimum stated; GRE-V+Q no minimum stated; overall undergraduate GPA no minimum stated; last 2 years GPA no minimum stated; psychology GPA no minimum stated.

Other Criteria: (importance of criteria rated low, medium, or high): GRE/MAT scores medium, research experience medium, work experience medium, extracurricular activity low, clinically related public service medium, GPA high, letters of recommendation high, interview high, statement of goals and objectives high.

Student Characteristics: The following represents characteristics of students in 2004–2005 in all graduate psychology programs in the department: Female–full-time 4, part-time 4; Male–full-time 1, part-time 1; Hispanic/Latino(a)–full-time 1, part-time 0; Caucasian–full-time 4, part-time 5.

Financial Information/Assistance:

Tuition for Full-Time Study: *Master's:* State residents: per academic year $7,440, $310 per credit hour; Nonstate residents: per academic year $7,440, $310 per credit hour. Tuition is subject to change.

Financial Assistance:

First Year Students: No information provided.
Advanced Students: No information provided.
Contact Information: No information provided.

Internships/Practica: Students will complete a university-sanctioned internship in which they will accrue 1,000 hours of supervised experience in the local community. Internships are available at a variety of local mental health and psychiatric facilities.

Housing and Day Care: On-campus housing is available. Graduate students are eligible for housing in new apartment-style student housing buildings on the university campus grounds. Current housing costs are $1,910–$3,410 per semester for room and $1,720 for unlimited meal plan. No on-campus day care facilities are available.

Employment of Department Graduates:

Master's Degree Graduates: Of those who graduated in the academic year 2003–2004, the following categories and numbers represent the post-graduate activities and employment of master's degree graduates: Enrolled in a post-doctoral residency/fellowship (n/a), employed in independent practice (n/a), total from the above (master's) (0).
Doctoral Degree Graduates: Of those who graduated in the academic year 2003–2004, the following categories and numbers represent the post-graduate activities and employment of doctoral degree graduates: Enrolled in a psychology doctoral program (n/a), total from the above (doctoral) (0).

Additional Information:

Orientation, Objectives, and Emphasis of Department: Saint Leo University prepares graduate students to qualify as Licensed Mental Health Counselors (LMHC) in the State of Florida. The program has an applied professional emphasis which focuses on the preparation of Master's-level counselors for employment in various counseling settings. Students complete courses in counseling theories, therapy skills, and assessment in addition to learning how to administer and interpret select intellectual, neuropsychological, and personality instruments. The program of study allows both full-time and part-time enrollment. Full-time students are expected to enroll in 12 credit hours per semester for two academic years, including 12 credit hours during summer study. Part-time students are expected to enroll in 6 credit hours per semester for a total of three academic years, including 7–9 credit hours during summer study. Both part-time and full-time students take classes together in the evening to expose students to the other students in the program and various points of view, with full-time students also taking classes during the day. Students enrolled in the full-time program have the option of completing a Master's thesis. During the last two semesters, students complete a 1000 hour internship at a facility in the local community.

Special Facilities or Resources: The Saint Leo University library system includes the Cannon Memorial Library, which grants students access to books, periodicals, microforms, and other publications in the collections. The Cannon Memorial library facility has both group and individual study rooms available to meet students' research needs. Computerized search capabilities are available from within the library or via outside internet access and include PsycInfo with PsycArticles as well as a host of other scholarly search engines, most of which have links to full-text articles and eBooks. Students with a valid student ID also have library privileges at a large state university just 20 miles from the Saint Leo campus. In addition to the extensive library services available, students have access to individual and group therapy rooms and a psychology laboratory, all with audio/videotaping capabilities. Therapy rooms are equipped with one-way mirrors and intercom systems to allow live supervision.

Application Information:

Send to: Office of Admissions for Graduate Studies and Adult Enrollment MC 2248, Saint Leo University, P.O. Box 6665, Saint Leo, FL 33574-6665. Application available online. URL of online application: http://www.saintleo.edu/gradprograms. Students are admitted in the Fall, application deadline March 1. *Fee:* $45.

South Florida, University of
Department of Psychological and Social Foundations
College of Education
EDU 162
Tampa, FL 33620-7750
Telephone: (813) 974-3246
Fax: (813) 974-5814
E-mail: *kbradley@tempest.coedu.usf.edu*
Web: *www.coedu.usf.edu/schoolpsych*

Department Information:

1970. Chairperson: Harold Keller, PhD. Number of Faculty: total–full-time 29, part-time 1; women–full-time 15, part-time 1; minority–full-time 7, part-time 1.

Programs and Degrees Offered:

Listed in the following order: Program area, degree type (T if terminal Master's), number awarded 7/03–6/04. School Psychology PhD (Doctor of Philosophy) 4, School Psychology EdS (Education Specialist) 5.

APA Accreditation: School PhD (Doctor of Philosophy).

Student Applications/Admissions:

Student Applications

School Psychology PhD (Doctor of Philosophy)—Applications 2004–2005, 47. Total applicants accepted 2004–2005, 5. Number enrolled (new admits only) 2004–2005 full-time, 5. Number enrolled (new admits only) 2004–2005 part-time, 0. Total enrolled 2004–2005 full-time, 49, part-time, 1. Openings 2005–2006, 6. The Median number of years required for completion of a degree are 6. The number of students enrolled full and part-time who were dismissed or voluntarily withdrew from this program area were 1. *School Psychology EdS (Education Specialist)*—Applications 2004–2005, 67. Total applicants accepted 2004–2005, 3. Number enrolled (new admits only) 2004–2005 full-time, 3. Number enrolled (new admits only) 2004–2005 part-time, 0. Total enrolled 2004–2005 full-time,

18. Openings 2005–2006, 3. The Median number of years required for completion of a degree are 3. The number of students enrolled full and part-time who were dismissed or voluntarily withdrew from this program area were 1.

Admissions Requirements:

Scores: Entries appear in this order: required test or GPA, minimum score (if required), median score of students entering in 2003–2004. Master's Programs: GRE-V no minimum stated; GRE-Q no minimum stated; GRE-V+Q 800, 950; overall undergraduate GPA 3.0, 3.6; last 2 years GPA 3.0, 3.7. Doctoral Programs: GRE-V no minimum stated, 575; GRE-Q no minimum stated, 630; GRE-V+Q 1000, 1190; last 2 years GPA 3.00, 3.82.

Other Criteria: (importance of criteria rated low, medium, or high): GRE/MAT scores medium, research experience high, work experience medium, extracurricular activity medium, clinically related public service medium, GPA high, letters of recommendation high, interview high, statement of goals and objectives high, writing sample high. For additional information on admission requirements, go to: http://coedu.usf.edu/schoolpsych.

Student Characteristics: The following represents characteristics of students in 2004–2005 in all graduate psychology programs in the department: Female–full-time 56, part-time 0; Male–full-time 11, part-time 1; African American/Black–full-time 13, part-time 0; Hispanic/Latino(a)–full-time 6, part-time 0; Asian/Pacific Islander–full-time 2, part-time 0; American Indian/Alaska Native–full-time 0, part-time 0; Caucasian–full-time 46, part-time 0; Multi-ethnic–full-time 1, part-time 0; students subject to the Americans With Disabilities Act–full-time 1, part-time 0.

Financial Information/Assistance:

Tuition for Full-Time Study: *Master's:* State residents: per academic year $5,590, $232 per credit hour; Nonstate residents: per academic year $21,470, $895 per credit hour. *Doctoral:* State residents: per academic year $5,590, $232 per credit hour; Nonstate residents: per academic year $21,470, $895 per credit hour. Tuition is subject to change. See the following Web site for updates and changes in tuition costs: www.grad.usf.edu.

Financial Assistance:

First Year Students: Research assistantships available for first-year. Average amount paid per academic year: $10,200. Average number of hours worked per week: 16. Apply by May 1. Tuition remission given: partial. Fellowships and scholarships available for first-year. Average amount paid per academic year: $10,000. Average number of hours worked per week: 0. Apply by February 15. Tuition remission given: full.

Advanced Students: Teaching assistantships available for advanced students. Average amount paid per academic year: $10,200. Average number of hours worked per week: 16. Apply by May 1. Tuition remission given: partial. Research assistantships available for advanced students. Average amount paid per academic year: $10,200. Average number of hours worked per week: 16. Apply by May 1. Tuition remission given: partial. Fellowships and scholarships available for advanced students. Average amount paid per academic year: $10,000. Average number of hours worked per week: 0. Apply by February 15. Tuition remission given: partial.

Contact Information: Of all students currently enrolled full-time, 100% benefitted from one or more of the listed financial assistance programs. Application and information available online at: www.coedu.usf.edu/schoolpsych.

Internships/Practica: Our practica and internships integrate home, school, and community service programs for students at risk for educational failure and their families, including students with disabilities. We focus especially on the priorities of researching and promoting effective educational and mental health practices for all children, youth and their families. All doctoral students participate in practica during the first three years of the program. Practica settings include schools (public, charter, alternative), hospital settings, research settings, special agencies (e.g., Tampa Children's Cancer Center) and special programs (e.g., Early Intervention Program). Doctoral students participate in approximately 1000 hours of practicum prior to internship. All doctoral students complete a 2000-hour pre-doctoral internship in an APA-accredited/APPIC site or one that meets the APA/APPIC criteria.

Housing and Day Care: On-campus housing is available. See the following Web site for more information: www.reserv.usf.edu. On-campus day care facilities are available. See the following Web site for more information: www.isis2.admin.usf.edu/childcare/familycenter/top.htm.

Employment of Department Graduates:

Master's Degree Graduates: Of those who graduated in the academic year 2003–2004, the following categories and numbers represent the post-graduate activities and employment of master's degree graduates: Enrolled in a psychology doctoral program (5), enrolled in a post-doctoral residency/fellowship (n/a), employed in independent practice (n/a), employed in a professional position in a school system (2), total from the above (master's) (7).

Doctoral Degree Graduates: Of those who graduated in the academic year 2003–2004, the following categories and numbers represent the post-graduate activities and employment of doctoral degree graduates: Enrolled in a psychology doctoral program (n/a), employed in an academic position at a university (0), employed in a professional position in a school system (2), total from the above (doctoral) (2).

Additional Information:

Orientation, Objectives, and Emphasis of Department: Thorough admissions procedures result in the selection of outstanding students. This makes possible a faculty commitment to do everything possible to guide each student to a high level of professional competence. The curriculum is well organized and explicit such that students are always aware of program expectations and their progress in relation to these expectations. The student body is kept small, resulting in greater student-faculty contact than would otherwise be possible. Skills of practice are developed through non-threatening apprenticeship networks established with local school systems. This model encourages students to assist several professors and practicing school psychologists throughout their training. The notion here is to provide positive environments, containing rich feedback, in which competent psychological skills develop. We emphasize a scientist-practitioner model representing primarily a cognitive-behavioral orientation. Further, we support comprehensive school psychology, including consultation, prevention, intervention, and program evaluation.

Special Facilities or Resources: The University of South Florida is a comprehensive Research I (FL) and Doctoral/Research Universities-Extensive (Carnegie) university that has over 40,000 students on a 1,700 acre campus 10 miles northeast of downtown Tampa, a city of over 350,000 people. Amongst its faculty, the School Psychology Program has one APA Fellow, two past presidents of the National Association of School Psychologists, and faculty who have received over $18 million in federal and state grants over the past years. Students collaborate with professors and researchers in the program, the College of Education, Departments of Psychology and Psychiatry, the Florida Mental Health Institute, the Early Intervention Program, Shriner's Hospital, Tampa General and Street Joseph's hospitals, the Florida Department of Education and other settings. The program is housed in a new College of Education physical plant that has the latest fiber optic based technology, clinical and research observation areas, and strong technology support. Strong links exist with community schools and agencies.

Information for Students With Physical Disabilities: See the following Web site for more information: www.usf.edu/sds.

Application Information:
Send to: Linda Raffaele Mendez, Coordinator of Admissions, School Psychology Program, EDU 162, University of South Florida, Tampa, FL 33620-7750. Application available online. Students are admitted in the Fall, application deadline January 15. All application materials and fees should be submitted directly to the Coordinator of Admissions, School Psychology Program (address above). *Fee:* $30. Contact Program Director/Admissions Coordinator, School Psychology Program (raffaele @tempest.coedu.usf.edu).

South Florida, University of
Department of Psychology
Arts and Sciences
4202 E. Fowler Avenue, PCD 4118G
Tampa, FL 33620-7200
Telephone: (813) 974-2492
Fax: (813) 974-4617
E-mail: *donchin@shell.cas.usf.edu*
Web: *http://www.cas.usf.edu/psychology*

Department Information:
1964. Chairperson: Emanuel Donchin. Number of Faculty: total–full-time 33; women–full-time 10; minority–full-time 3.

Programs and Degrees Offered:
Listed in the following order: Program area, degree type (T if terminal Master's), number awarded 7/03–6/04. Clinical PhD (Doctor of Philosophy) 16, Cognitive and Neural Sciences PhD (Doctor of Philosophy) 2, Industrial/Organizational PhD (Doctor of Philosophy) 16.

APA Accreditation: Clinical PhD (Doctor of Philosophy).

Student Applications/Admissions:
Student Applications
Clinical PhD (Doctor of Philosophy)—Applications 2004–2005, 252. Total applicants accepted 2004–2005, 27. Number enrolled (new admits only) 2004–2005 full-time, 10. Openings 2005–2006, 9. The Median number of years required for completion of a degree are 8. The number of students enrolled full and part-time who were dismissed or voluntarily withdrew from this program area were 0. *Cognitive and Neural Sciences (CNS) PhD (Doctor of Philosophy)*—Applications 2004–2005, 39. Total applicants accepted 2004–2005, 8. Number enrolled (new admits only) 2004–2005 full-time, 5. Openings 2005–2006, 6. The Median number of years required for completion of a degree are 4. The number of students enrolled full and part-time who were dismissed or voluntarily withdrew from this program area were 1. *Industrial/Organizational PhD (Doctor of Philosophy)*—Applications 2004–2005, 132. Total applicants accepted 2004–2005, 22. Number enrolled (new admits only) 2004–2005 full-time, 12. Openings 2005–2006, 7. The Median number of years required for completion of a degree are 8. The number of students enrolled full and part-time who were dismissed or voluntarily withdrew from this program area were 1.

Admissions Requirements:
Scores: Entries appear in this order: required test or GPA, minimum score (if required), median score of students entering in 2003–2004. Doctoral Programs: GRE-V 500; GRE-Q 500; GRE-V+Q 1000, 1290, GRE-Analytical no minimum stated; last 2 years GPA 3.00, 3.6. Our Clinical Program recommends that GRE-Subject (Psychology) be taken.
Other Criteria: (importance of criteria rated low, medium, or high): GRE/MAT scores high, research experience high, work experience low, clinically related public service low, GPA high, letters of recommendation high, interview medium, statement of goals and objectives high. For additional information on admission requirements, go to: www.cas.usf.edu/psychology/gra_stud_application_index.htm.

Student Characteristics: The following represents characteristics of students in 2004–2005 in all graduate psychology programs in the department: Female–full-time 86, part-time 0; Male–full-time 41, part-time 0; African American/Black–full-time 13, part-time 0; Hispanic/Latino(a)–full-time 9, part-time 0; Asian/Pacific Islander–full-time 7, part-time 0; American Indian/Alaska Native–full-time 0, part-time 0; Caucasian–full-time 98, part-time 0; Multi-ethnic–part-time 0; students subject to the Americans With Disabilities Act–full-time 2, part-time 0.

Financial Information/Assistance:
Tuition for Full-Time Study: *Master's:* State residents: per academic year $5,592, $223 per credit hour; Nonstate residents: per academic year $21,456, $894 per credit hour. *Doctoral:* State residents: per academic year $4,194, $223 per credit hour; Nonstate residents: per academic year $16,092, $894 per credit hour. Tuition is subject to change. See the following Web site for

updates and changes in tuition costs: http://usfweb2.usf.edu/pfs/tuition_cost.htm.

Financial Assistance:

First Year Students: Teaching assistantships available for first-year. Average amount paid per academic year: $12,500. Average number of hours worked per week: 20. Tuition remission given: partial. Research assistantships available for first-year. Average amount paid per academic year: $12,500. Average number of hours worked per week: 20. Tuition remission given: partial. Fellowships and scholarships available for first-year. Average amount paid per academic year: $15,500. Tuition remission given: partial.

Advanced Students: Teaching assistantships available for advanced students. Average amount paid per academic year: $12,500. Average number of hours worked per week: 20. Tuition remission given: partial. Research assistantships available for advanced students. Average amount paid per academic year: $12,500. Average number of hours worked per week: 20. Tuition remission given: partial. Fellowships and scholarships available for advanced students. Average amount paid per academic year: $15,500. Tuition remission given: partial.

Contact Information: Of all students currently enrolled full-time, 73% benefitted from one or more of the listed financial assistance programs.

Internships/Practica: The Clinical Program operates its own Psychology Clinic within the Psychology Department, providing opportunities for practical training in clinical assessment and clinical psychological interventions. Students are active in the Psychology Clinic throughout their training. Clinical core-faculty provide most of the supervision of Clinic cases. The Clinical Psychology Program is fortunate to have a unique cluster of campus and community training facilities available for student placement. For example, we have student placements at or near such campus facilities as the USF Florida Mental Health Research Institute, the USF Counseling Center for Human Development, the Moffitt Cancer Center and Research Institute and the Tampa Veterans Administration Hospital as well as carefully selected community agencies. Students in the Industrial/Organizational Program are required to complete a predoctoral internship. Placements are made in numerous governmental, corporate and consulting firms both locally and nationally. Recent placements have included Cities of Tampa and Clearwater, GTE, Tampa Electric Company, Personnel Decisions Research Institute, Personnel Decisions, Inc., Florida Power and USF&G. For those doctoral students for whom a professional internship is required prior to graduation, 3 applied in 2003–2004. Of those who applied, 3 were placed in internships listed by the Association of Psychology Postdoctoral and Internship Programs (APPIC); 3 were placed in APA accredited internships.

Housing and Day Care: On-campus housing is available. See the following Web site for more information: www.reserv.usf.edu. On-campus day care facilities are available. See the following Web site for more information: www.coedu.usf.edu/clar/erccd.html; or email fleege@tempest.coedu.usf.edu; www.usfweb.usf.edu/childcare/familycenter/default.htm; or email usf@brighthorizons.com and moffitt@brighthorizons.com.

Employment of Department Graduates:

Master's Degree Graduates: Of those who graduated in the academic year 2003–2004, the following categories and numbers represent the post-graduate activities and employment of master's degree graduates: Enrolled in a post-doctoral residency/fellowship (n/a), employed in independent practice (n/a), total from the above (master's) (0).

Doctoral Degree Graduates: Of those who graduated in the academic year 2003–2004, the following categories and numbers represent the post-graduate activities and employment of doctoral degree graduates: Enrolled in a psychology doctoral program (n/a), enrolled in a post-doctoral residency/fellowship (4), employed in independent practice (2), employed in an academic position at a university (6), employed in an academic position at a 2-year/4-year college (1), employed in other positions at a higher education institution (3), employed in business or industry (research/consulting) (8), employed in a hospital/medical center (4), do not know (6), total from the above (doctoral) (34).

Additional Information:

Orientation, Objectives, and Emphasis of Department: The department attempts to educate graduate students to a high level of proficiency in research and in practice. The department expects its doctoral students to be of such quality as to take their place at major institutions of learning if they choose academic careers and to assume roles of responsibility and importance if they choose professional careers. The doctoral program in clinical psychology provides broad-based professional and research training to prepare students for careers in a variety of applied, research, and teaching settings. The doctoral program in cognitive and neural sciences prepares students for research careers in both applied and academic environments. This program also offers an interdisciplinary degree in Speech, Language, and Hearing Science in conjunction with the Department of Communication Sciences and Disorders. The doctoral program in industrial/organizational psychology provides professional and research training to prepare students for careers in industrial, governmental, academic, and related organizational settings.

Special Facilities or Resources: State-of-the-art facilities and equipment house the Psychology Department. There is ample research space for faculty, graduate, and advanced undergraduate students, including a large vivarium. An open-use lab has been equipped with computer terminals that access the mainframe computer on campus. The University Computer Center is available. The Psychological Services Center is operated as the department's facility for clinical practicum work. A state-of-the-art video system permits supervisory capabilities for clinical practica.

Information for Students With Physical Disabilities: See the following Web site for more information: http://www.sa.usf.edu/sds.

Application Information:

Send to: Graduate Admissions Coordinator, Psychology Department, University of South Florida, 4202 E. Fowler Avenue, PCD4118G, Tampa, FL 33620-7200. Application available online. URL of online application: www.usf.edu/forms.html. Students are admitted in the Fall, application deadline December 15/January 15. Clinical deadline for International and U.S. Residents is December 15. CNS and IO deadlines are January 2 for International and January 15 for U.S. Residents. *Fee:* $30. Proof of financial hardship, McNair Scholars.

West Florida, The University of (2004 data)
Department of Psychology
College of Arts and Sciences
11000 University Parkway
Pensacola, FL 32514-5751
Telephone: (850) 474-2363
Fax: (850) 857-6060
E-mail: psych@uwf.edu
Web: http://uwf.edu/psych

Department Information:
1967. Chairperson: Ronald W. Belter. Number of Faculty: total–full-time 13, part-time 4; women–full-time 6, part-time 3; minority–full-time 1.

Programs and Degrees Offered:
Listed in the following order: Program area, degree type (T if terminal Master's), number awarded 7/03–6/04. Counseling Psychology MA/MS (Master of Arts/Science) (T) 9, General Psychology MA/MS (Master of Arts/Science) (T) 7, Industrial/Organizational Psychology MA/MS (Master of Arts/Science) (T) 13.

Student Applications/Admissions:
Student Applications
Counseling Psychology MA/MS (Master of Arts/Science)—Applications 2004–2005, 63. Total applicants accepted 2004–2005, 28. Total enrolled 2004–2005 full-time, 47, part-time, 7. Openings 2005–2006, 18. The Median number of years required for completion of a degree are 2. The number of students enrolled full and part-time who were dismissed or voluntarily withdrew from this program area were 2. General Psychology MA/MS (Master of Arts/Science)—Applications 2004–2005, 18. Total applicants accepted 2004–2005, 12. Total enrolled 2004–2005 full-time, 21, part-time, 4. Openings 2005–2006, 15. The Median number of years required for completion of a degree are 2. The number of students enrolled full and part-time who were dismissed or voluntarily withdrew from this program area were 1. Industrial/Organizational Psychology MA/MS (Master of Arts/Science)—Applications 2004–2005, 58. Total applicants accepted 2004–2005, 27. Total enrolled 2004–2005 full-time, 19, part-time, 8. Openings 2005–2006, 15. The Median number of years required for completion of a degree are 2. The number of students enrolled full and part-time who were dismissed or voluntarily withdrew from this program area were 1.

Admissions Requirements:
Scores: Entries appear in this order: required test or GPA, minimum score (if required), median score of students entering in 2003–2004. Master's Programs: GRE-V no minimum stated, 459; GRE-Q no minimum stated, 540; GRE-V+Q 1000; overall undergraduate GPA 3.00.
Other Criteria: (importance of criteria rated low, medium, or high): GRE/MAT scores high, research experience medium, work experience medium, extracurricular activity medium, clinically related public service medium, GPA high, letters of recommendation high, statement of goals and objectives high, coursework high. Counseling applicants may be interviewed. For additional information on admission requirements, go to: http://uwf.edu/psych/graduate/.

Student Characteristics: The following represents characteristics of students in 2004–2005 in all graduate psychology programs in the department: Female–full-time 69, part-time 12; Male–full-time 18, part-time 7; African American/Black–full-time 6, part-time 3; Hispanic/Latino(a)–full-time 2, part-time 1; Asian/Pacific Islander–full-time 7, part-time 0; American Indian/Alaska Native–full-time 3, part-time 0; Caucasian–full-time 68, part-time 14; Multi-ethnic–full-time 1, part-time 1; students subject to the Americans With Disabilities Act–full-time 0, part-time 0.

Financial Information/Assistance:
Tuition for Full-Time Study: Master's: State residents: $208 per credit hour; Nonstate residents: $777 per credit hour. Tuition is subject to change. See the following Web site for updates and changes in tuition costs: http://uwf.edu/enrserv/fees.htm.

Financial Assistance:
First Year Students: Teaching assistantships available for first-year. Average amount paid per academic year: $2,000. Average number of hours worked per week: 10. Apply by April 15. Tuition remission given: partial. Fellowships and scholarships available for first-year. Average amount paid per academic year: $1,000. Apply by April 15.
Advanced Students: Teaching assistantships available for advanced students. Average amount paid per academic year: $2,000. Average number of hours worked per week: 10. Apply by April 15. Tuition remission given: partial. Fellowships and scholarships available for advanced students. Average amount paid per academic year: $750. Apply by April 15.
Contact Information: Of all students currently enrolled full-time, 59% benefitted from one or more of the listed financial assistance programs.

Internships/Practica: Master's students may elect either thesis or 600-hour internship (850-hour for mental health counseling licensure option). Faculty assist in finding suitable placements in field settings under qualified supervision. The student also prepares a portfolio demonstrating mastery of several specific competencies and includes an integrative paper reflecting on professional development. Practica (required for counseling students, optional for other students) are completed earlier in the program and involve more limited applied experience and closer supervision by faculty. Internship placements for Counseling students include a variety of local mental health agencies providing inpatient, outpatient and community outreach services. Internship placements for Industrial/Organizational students include a variety of business and healthcare settings.

Housing and Day Care: On-campus housing is available. See the following Web site for more information: http://uwf.edu/housing/. On-campus day care facilities are available. See the following Web site for more information: http://uwf.edu/childdev/.

Employment of Department Graduates:
Master's Degree Graduates: Of those who graduated in the academic year 2003–2004, the following categories and numbers represent the post-graduate activities and employment of master's degree graduates: Enrolled in a psychology doctoral program (6), enrolled in a post-doctoral residency/fellowship (n/a), employed in independent practice (n/a), employed in an academic position at a 2-year/4-year college (1), employed in other positions at a higher education institution (2), employed in business or industry

(management) (8), employed in a government agency (research) (2), employed in a community mental health/counseling center (6), other employment position (4), total from the above (master's) (29).

Doctoral Degree Graduates: Of those who graduated in the academic year 2003–2004, the following categories and numbers represent the post-graduate activities and employment of doctoral degree graduates: Enrolled in a psychology doctoral program (n/a), total from the above (doctoral) (0).

Additional Information:

Orientation, Objectives, and Emphasis of Department: The department is a member of the Council of Applied Master's Programs in Psychology and is committed to the philosophy of training with a foundation in general psychology (individual, social, biological, and learned bases of behavior) as the basis for training in application of psychology. Applied students receive significant supervised field experience. The departmental mission is preparation of master's level practitioners and preparation of students for doctoral work as well. The programs in Counseling Psychology and Industrial/Organizational Psychology are accredited by the Master's in Psychology Accreditation Council (MPAC). The department also offers a certificate in Health Psychology and Cognitive Psychology. The Counseling Psychology program offers a 60-hour option with coursework comparable to requirements for licensure as a Mental Health Counselor in Florida.

Special Facilities or Resources: The department is housed in a modern, 22,000 sq. ft. building with excellent research facilities, including a Neurocognition lab with a 128 channel Neuroscan ESI System. We also offer graduate courses at the Fort Walton Beach campus. Other University resources include the Institute for Business and Economic Research and the Institute for Human and Machine Cognition. We have links with CMHCs and local health/mental health professionals and organizations. Community resources include three major hospitals and a large Naval training facility. The department hosts student chapters of Psi Chi, Society for Human Resource Management (SHRM), and Student Psychological Association.

Information for Students With Physical Disabilities: See the following Web site for more information: http://uwf.edu/dss/.

Application Information:
Send to: Department of Psychology, Graduate Admissions, University of West Florida, 11000 University Parkway, Pensacola, FL 32514-5751. Application available online. Students are admitted in the Fall, application deadline February 1; Summer, application deadline February 1. GREQ, GREV required by February 1st. *Fee:* $20. Fee is waived for those students who received their bachelor's degree from the University of West Florida.

Argosy University/Atlanta

Clinical Psychology
Georgia School of Professional Psychology
980 Hammond Drive, Bldg 2, Suite 100
Atlanta, GA 30328
Telephone: (888) 671-4777
Fax: (770) 671-0476
E-mail: *jbinder@argosyu.edu*
Web: *http://www.argosyu.edu*

Department Information:

1990. Chairperson: Jeffrey Binder, PhD, ABPP. Number of Faculty: total–full-time 15, part-time 1; women–full-time 9; minority–full-time 3.

Programs and Degrees Offered:

Listed in the following order: Program area, degree type (T if terminal Master's), number awarded 7/03–6/04. Clinical Psychology MA/MS (Master of Arts/Science) (T) 0, Clinical Psychology PsyD (Doctor of Psychology) 34.

APA Accreditation: Clinical PsyD (Doctor of Psychology).

Student Applications/Admissions:

Student Applications

Clinical Psychology MA/MS (Master of Arts/Science)—Applications 2004–2005, 60. Total applicants accepted 2004–2005, 37. Number enrolled (new admits only) 2004–2005 full-time, 23. Number enrolled (new admits only) 2004–2005 part-time, 0. Openings 2005–2006, 25. The Median number of years required for completion of a degree are 2. The number of students enrolled full and part-time who were dismissed or voluntarily withdrew from this program area were 6. *Clinical Psychology PsyD (Doctor of Psychology)*—Applications 2004–2005, 178. Total applicants accepted 2004–2005, 94. Number enrolled (new admits only) 2004–2005 full-time, 65. Number enrolled (new admits only) 2004–2005 part-time, 0. Total enrolled 2004–2005 full-time, 222, part-time, 59. Openings 2005–2006, 65. The Median number of years required for completion of a degree are 5. The number of students enrolled full and part-time who were dismissed or voluntarily withdrew from this program area were 17.

Admissions Requirements:

Scores: Entries appear in this order: required test or GPA, minimum score (if required), median score of students entering in 2003–2004. Master's Programs: GRE-V no minimum stated; GRE-Q no minimum stated; GRE-V+Q no minimum stated; overall undergraduate GPA 3.0. Applicants may complete either the GRE or MAT. Doctoral Programs: GRE-V no minimum stated, 510; GRE-Q no minimum stated, 550; GRE-V+Q no minimum stated, 1060; overall undergraduate GPA 3.25, 3.35. Applicants may complete either the GRE or MAT.

Other Criteria: (importance of criteria rated low, medium, or high): GRE/MAT scores medium, research experience low, work experience high, extracurricular activity low, clinically related public service high, GPA high, letters of recommendation medium, interview high, statement of goals and objectives high, Applicants may complete either the GRE or MAT. For additional information on admission requirements, go to: http://www.argosyu.edu.

Student Characteristics: The following represents characteristics of students in 2004–2005 in all graduate psychology programs in the department: Female–full-time 207, part-time 42; Male–full-time 58, part-time 17; African American/Black–full-time 63, part-time 6; Hispanic/Latino(a)–full-time 7, part-time 1; Asian/Pacific Islander–full-time 6, part-time 2; American Indian/Alaska Native–full-time 2, part-time 0; Caucasian–full-time 172, part-time 45; Multi-ethnic–full-time 0, part-time 0; students subject to the Americans With Disabilities Act–full-time 12, part-time 0.

Financial Information/Assistance:

Tuition for Full-Time Study: *Master's:* State residents: $750 per credit hour; Nonstate residents: $750 per credit hour. *Doctoral:* State residents: $750 per credit hour; Nonstate residents: $750 per credit hour. Tuition is subject to change. See the following Web site for updates and changes in tuition costs: www.argosyu.edu.

Financial Assistance:

First Year Students: Research assistantships available for first-year. Average amount paid per academic year: $2,400. Average number of hours worked per week: 8. Apply anytime. Fellowships and scholarships available for first-year. Average amount paid per academic year: $3,000. Average number of hours worked per week: 0. Apply by April 1.

Advanced Students: Teaching assistantships available for advanced students. Average amount paid per academic year: $3,000. Average number of hours worked per week: 10. Apply by September 1. Research assistantships available for advanced students. Average amount paid per academic year: $2,400. Average number of hours worked per week: 8. Apply anytime. Fellowships and scholarships available for advanced students. Average amount paid per academic year: $3,000. Average number of hours worked per week: 0. Apply by April 1.

Contact Information: Of all students currently enrolled full-time, 25% benefitted from one or more of the listed financial assistance programs. Application and information available online at: http://www.argosyu.edu.

Internships/Practica: Practica and internship involve supervised clinical field training in which students work with clinical populations in health delivery settings. Practica offer opportunities to apply classroom knowledge, increase assessment and therapeutic skills, and develop professional and personal attitudes important to the identity of a professional psychologist. While all doctoral students complete a minimum of two years of practicum training, many elect to complete an additional one-year advanced practicum to gain further experience before internship. Students are placed at a diverse set of training sites formally affiliated with the MA and PsyD programs. The specific content and training vary according to the setting and expertise of supervisors. Training sites include state mental health facilities, outpatient clinics, private psychiatric hospitals, psychiatric units in community hospitals, university counseling centers, and private practice settings, as well as treatment facilities for developmentally disabled, behavior disordered and/or emotionally disturbed adults and children. In addition, a variety of specialized placements are available in facilities such as children's/pediatric hospitals, treatment centers for eating disorders, and neuropsychiatric rehabilitation programs. For those doctoral students for whom a professional internship is required prior to graduation, 52 applied in 2003–2004. Of those who applied, 49 were placed in internships listed by the Association of Psychology Postdoctoral and Internship Programs (APPIC); 46 were placed in APA accredited internships.

Housing and Day Care: No on-campus housing is available. No on-campus day care facilities are available.

Employment of Department Graduates:

Master's Degree Graduates: Of those who graduated in the academic year 2003–2004, the following categories and numbers represent the post-graduate activities and employment of master's degree graduates: Enrolled in a post-doctoral residency/fellowship (n/a), employed in independent practice (n/a), total from the above (master's) (0).

Doctoral Degree Graduates: Of those who graduated in the academic year 2003–2004, the following categories and numbers represent the post-graduate activities and employment of doctoral degree graduates: Enrolled in a psychology doctoral program (n/a), enrolled in a post-doctoral residency/fellowship (10), employed in independent practice (8), employed in an academic position at a 2-year/4-year college (1), employed in other positions at a higher education institution (1), employed in a hospital/medical center (1), not seeking employment (1), other employment position (1), do not know (12), total from the above (doctoral) (35).

Additional Information:

Orientation, Objectives, and Emphasis of Department: The primary purpose of the Clinical Psychology doctoral program is to educate and train students in the major aspects of clinical practice. The curriculum integrates theory, training, research, and practice, preparing graduates to work in a broad range of roles and to work with a wide range of populations in need of psychological services. Students who graduate from the doctoral program earn a Doctor of Psychology degree, indicating that the recipient has completed academic and training experiences essential to pursuing professional endeavors in the field of clinical psychology.

Special Facilities or Resources: See Internships/Practica.

Application Information:
Send to: Office of Admissions, Argosy University, 980 Hammond Drive, Bldg 2, Suite 100, Atlanta, GA 30328. Applications may be submitted online @www.argosyu.edu. Application available online. URL of online application: www.argosyu.edu. Students are admitted in the Fall, application deadline January 15; Programs have rolling admissions. *Fee:* $50.

Augusta State University

Department of Psychology
2500 Walton Way
Augusta, GA 30904-2200
Telephone: (706) 737-1694
Fax: (706) 737-1538
E-mail: *pboyd@aug.edu*
Web: *http://www.aug.edu/psychology/*

Department Information:
1963. Chairperson: Deborah S. Richardson. Number of Faculty: total–full-time 9, part-time 10; women–full-time 6, part-time 6; minority–full-time 1.

Programs and Degrees Offered:
Listed in the following order: Program area, degree type (T if terminal Master's), number awarded 7/03–6/04. Applied Psychology MA/MS (Master of Arts/Science) (T) 4, Experimental Psychology MA/MS (Master of Arts/Science) (T) 0.

Student Applications/Admissions:
Student Applications
Applied Psychology MA/MS (*Master of Arts/Science*)—Applications 2004–2005, 29. Total applicants accepted 2004–2005, 23. Number enrolled (new admits only) 2004–2005 full-time, 13. Number enrolled (new admits only) 2004–2005 part-time, 3. Total enrolled 2004–2005 full-time, 24, part-time, 12. Openings 2005–2006, 24. The Median number of years required for completion of a degree are 2. The number of students enrolled full and part-time who were dismissed or voluntarily withdrew from this program area were 3. *Experimental Psychology MA/MS (Master of Arts/Science)*—Applications 2004–2005, 4. Total applicants accepted 2004–2005, 4. Number enrolled (new admits only) 2004–2005 full-time, 3. Number enrolled (new admits only) 2004–2005 part-time, 0. Total enrolled 2004–2005 full-time, 3, part-time, 5. Openings 2005–2006, 5. The Median number of years required for completion of a degree are 2.

Admissions Requirements:
Scores: Entries appear in this order: required test or GPA, minimum score (if required), median score of students entering in 2003–2004. Master's Programs: GRE-V 400*, 420; GRE-Q 450*, 500; GRE-Analytical 3.5, 4.0; overall undergraduate GPA 2.5, 3.10. *Applicant must have taken the Graduate Record Examination (GRE) within the past five years with a minimum score of 400 on one of the subtests and at least 450 on the remaining two. If the GRE was taken after 10/01/02, the analytical score must be 3.5 or higher, one of the remaining scores must be 400 or better, and one score must reach 450 or better.

Other Criteria: (importance of criteria rated low, medium, or high): GRE/MAT scores high, research experience medium, work experience medium, extracurricular activity low, clinically related public service low, GPA high, letters of recommendation high, statement of goals and objectives medium.

Student Characteristics: The following represents characteristics of students in 2004–2005 in all graduate psychology programs in the department: Female–full-time 18, part-time 11; Male–full-

time 9, part-time 6; African American/Black–full-time 3, part-time 2; Hispanic/Latino(a)–full-time 1, part-time 0; Asian/Pacific Islander–full-time 2, part-time 0; American Indian/Alaska Native–full-time 0, part-time 0; Caucasian–full-time 21, part-time 15; students subject to the Americans With Disabilities Act–full-time 2, part-time 0.

Financial Information/Assistance:

Tuition for Full-Time Study: *Master's:* State residents: per academic year $3,725, $117 per credit hour; Nonstate residents: per academic year $13,166, $465 per credit hour. Tuition is subject to change. See the following Web site for updates and changes in tuition costs: www.aug.edu.

Financial Assistance:

First Year Students: Traineeships available for first-year. Average amount paid per academic year: $2,400. Average number of hours worked per week: 10. Tuition remission given: partial.

Advanced Students: Traineeships available for advanced students. Average amount paid per academic year: $2,400. Average number of hours worked per week: 10. Tuition remission given: partial.

Contact Information: Of all students currently enrolled full-time, 60% benefitted from one or more of the listed financial assistance programs. Application and information available online at: www.aug.edu/psychology.

Internships/Practica: Institutions that provide unique opportunities for fieldwork and internship experiences include two Veterans Administration hospitals, a regional psychiatric hospital, the Medical College of Georgia, Gracewood State School and Hospital, Dwight David Eisenhower Medical Center, and various other agencies. Internships are also available in business, education and private practice settings.

Housing and Day Care: No on-campus housing is available. No on-campus day care facilities are available.

Employment of Department Graduates:

Master's Degree Graduates: Of those who graduated in the academic year 2003–2004, the following categories and numbers represent the post-graduate activities and employment of master's degree graduates: Enrolled in a psychology doctoral program (0), enrolled in another graduate/professional program (0), enrolled in a post-doctoral residency/fellowship (n/a), employed in independent practice (n/a), employed in an academic position at a university (1), employed in an academic position at a 2-year/4-year college (0), employed in other positions at a higher education institution (0), employed in a professional position in a school system (0), employed in a government agency (research) (0), employed in a government agency (professional services) (0), employed in a community mental health/counseling center (0), employed in a hospital/medical center (0), still seeking employment (1), other employment position (2), total from the above (master's) (4).

Doctoral Degree Graduates: Of those who graduated in the academic year 2003–2004, the following categories and numbers represent the post-graduate activities and employment of doctoral degree graduates: Enrolled in a psychology doctoral program (n/a), total from the above (doctoral) (0).

Additional Information:

Orientation, Objectives, and Emphasis of Department: The graduate program in psychology at Augusta State University provides intensive training oriented toward the local and regional job markets. A secondary emphasis of the program is to provide an opportunity for graduate work in experimental psychology. The MS program is, for most students, a two-year program consisting of equal amounts of advanced experimental and theoretical coursework combined with courses relevant to professional psychology. Supervised internship experience in approved treatment or research facilities is also required.

Personal Behavior Statement: http://www.aug.edu/psychology/Plagiarism.html.

Special Facilities or Resources: The department maintains an active human and animal research laboratory and a clinical facility with videotaping and closed circuit television capabilities, and the university provides easy access to advanced computer resources. Students and faculty additionally engage in collaborative research at the Medical College of Georgia and Veterans Medical Center. Social and Developmental labs are available for teaching and research.

Information for Students With Physical Disabilities: See the following Web site for more information: www.aug.edu/counseling_and_testing_center.

Application Information:

Send to: Director of Graduate Studies, Department of Psychology, 2500 Walton Way, Augusta State University, Augusta, GA 30904-2200. Application available online. URL of online application: www.aug.edu/psychology/. Students are admitted in the Fall, application deadline June 1; Summer, application deadline rolling. *Fee:* $20.

Emory University
Department of Psychology
532 Kilgo Circle NE
Atlanta, GA 30322
Telephone: (404) 727-7438
Fax: (404) 727-0372
E-mail: *psych@emory.edu*
Web: *http://www.emory.edu/PSYCH/*

Department Information:

1945. Chairperson: Elaine Walker. Number of Faculty: total–full-time 35; women–full-time 15; minority–full-time 1.

Programs and Degrees Offered:

Listed in the following order: Program area, degree type (T if terminal Master's), number awarded 7/03–6/04. Clinical PhD (Doctor of Philosophy) 7, Cognition & Development PhD (Doctor of Philosophy) 1, Neuroscience & Animal Behavior PhD (Doctor of Philosophy) 3.

APA Accreditation: Clinical PhD (Doctor of Philosophy).

Student Applications/Admissions:

Student Applications

Clinical PhD (Doctor of Philosophy)—Applications 2004–2005, 237. Total applicants accepted 2004–2005, 6. Number enrolled (new admits only) 2004–2005 full-time, 6. Number enrolled (new admits only) 2004–2005 part-time, 0. Openings 2005–2006, 6. The Median number of years required for completion of a degree are 6. The number of students enrolled full and part-time who were dismissed or voluntarily withdrew from this program area were 2. *Cognition & Development PhD (Doctor of Philosophy)*—Applications 2004–2005, 37. Total applicants accepted 2004–2005, 4. Number enrolled (new admits only) 2004–2005 full-time, 5. Openings 2005–2006, 4. The Median number of years required for completion of a degree are 5. The number of students enrolled full and part-time who were dismissed or voluntarily withdrew from this program area were 0. *Neuroscience & Animal Behavior PhD (Doctor of Philosophy)*—Applications 2004–2005, 59. Total applicants accepted 2004–2005, 6. Number enrolled (new admits only) 2004–2005 full-time, 6. Number enrolled (new admits only) 2004–2005 part-time, 0. Openings 2005–2006, 4. The Median number of years required for completion of a degree are 7. The number of students enrolled full and part-time who were dismissed or voluntarily withdrew from this program area were 1.

Admissions Requirements:

Scores: Entries appear in this order: required test or GPA, minimum score (if required), median score of students entering in 2003–2004. Doctoral Programs: GRE-V 500, 560; GRE-Q 500, 670; GRE-V+Q 1000, 1230; GRE-Analytical 500, 780; overall undergraduate GPA 3.0, 3.62. The Clinical program requires the verbal and quantitative GRE scores. The Cognition and Development program and the Neuroscience and Animal Behavior program requires the verbal, quantitative, and analytical/written scores. For international students, the TOEFL score must be submitted as well.

Other Criteria: (importance of criteria rated low, medium, or high): GRE/MAT scores high, research experience high, work experience low, extracurricular activity low, clinically related public service medium, GPA high, letters of recommendation high, interview high, statement of goals and objectives high, fit with faculty interest high. Clinically related public service is less pertinent to the Cognition & Development and the Neuroscience & Animal Behavior programs.

Student Characteristics: The following represents characteristics of students in 2004–2005 in all graduate psychology programs in the department: Female–full-time 54, part-time 0; Male–full-time 18, part-time 0; African American/Black–full-time 7, part-time 0; Hispanic/Latino(a)–full-time 1, part-time 0; Asian/Pacific Islander–full-time 3, part-time 0; American Indian/Alaska Native–full-time 0, part-time 0; Caucasian–full-time 61, part-time 0.

Financial Information/Assistance:

Tuition for Full-Time Study: *Doctoral:* State residents: per academic year $28,192, $1,302 per credit hour; Nonstate residents: per academic year $28,192, $1,302 per credit hour. Tuition is subject to change. See the following Web site for updates and changes in tuition costs: http://www.emory.edu/GSOAS/PDF/2003_2005tuition_revised_.pdf.

Financial Assistance:

First Year Students: Fellowships and scholarships available for first-year. Average amount paid per academic year: $16,796. Average number of hours worked per week: 20. Apply by January 3. Tuition remission given: full.

Advanced Students: Teaching assistantships available for advanced students. Average amount paid per academic year: $19,500. Average number of hours worked per week: 20. Apply by January 25. Tuition remission given: full. Fellowships and scholarships available for advanced students. Average amount paid per academic year: $16,796. Average number of hours worked per week: 20. Apply by varies. Tuition remission given: full.

Contact Information: Of all students currently enrolled full-time, 100% benefitted from one or more of the listed financial assistance programs. Application and information available online at: http://www.emory.edu/GSOAS/funding.html#A.

Internships/Practica: For those doctoral students for whom a professional internship is required prior to graduation, 5 applied in 2003–2004. Of those who applied, 3 were placed in internships listed by the Association of Psychology Postdoctoral and Internship Programs (APPIC); 5 were placed in APA accredited internships.

Housing and Day Care: On-campus housing is available. See the following Web site for more information: http://www.emory.edu/RES_LIFE/GRAD/. On-campus day care facilities are available. See the following Web site for more information: http://www.emory.edu/FMD/web/kidcare.htm.

Employment of Department Graduates:

Master's Degree Graduates: Of those who graduated in the academic year 2003–2004, the following categories and numbers represent the post-graduate activities and employment of master's degree graduates: Enrolled in a post-doctoral residency/fellowship (n/a), employed in independent practice (n/a), total from the above (master's) (0).

Doctoral Degree Graduates: Of those who graduated in the academic year 2003–2004, the following categories and numbers represent the post-graduate activities and employment of doctoral degree graduates: Enrolled in a psychology doctoral program (n/a), enrolled in a post-doctoral residency/fellowship (6), employed in an academic position at a university (2), employed in business or industry (research/consulting) (1), employed in a community mental health/counseling center (1), total from the above (doctoral) (10).

Additional Information:

Orientation, Objectives, and Emphasis of Department: The primary emphasis of our clinical curriculum is to provide students with the knowledge and skills they need to function as productive clinical researchers in psychology. This requires a basic understanding of the determinants of human behavior, including biological, psychological, and social factors, and a strong background in research design and quantitative methods. The program in cognition and development at Emory is committed to the principle that cognition and its development are best studied together. The research interests of the faculty span a wide range, and are reflected in our graduate courses, which include memory, emotion, language, perception, and concepts and categories. The program in neuroscience and animal behavior approaches topics within the areas of neuroscience, physiological psychology, acquired behavior, and ethology as a unified entity. Research in neuroscience explores brain-behavior relationships; research on acquired behavior studies the on-going and evolutionary factors influencing individual adaptations; and ethological studies are concerned with understanding how animals function in their natural environment.

Special Facilities or Resources: The department has affiliations with the Emory Medical School, Yerkes National Primate Center, and the Center for Behavioral Neuroscience. In addition, faculty and students from many of the universities in the Atlanta area meet formally and informally to discuss common research interests.

Information for Students With Physical Disabilities: See the following Web site for more information: http://www.emory.edu/EEO/ODS/.

Application Information:
Send to: Ms. Terry Legge, Graduate Program Specialist, Department of Psychology, Emory University, Atlanta, GA 30322. Students are admitted in the Fall, application deadline January 3. Clinical: December 1; Cognition and Development: January 3; Neuroscience and Animal Behavior: January 1. *Fee:* $50.

Georgia Institute of Technology
School of Psychology
J.S. Coon Building
Atlanta, GA 30332-0170
Telephone: (404) 894-2680
Fax: (404) 894-8905
E-mail: *randall.engle@psych.gatech.edu*
Web: *http://www.psychology.gatech.edu*

Department Information:
1945. Chairperson: Randall W. Engle. Number of Faculty: total–full-time 25, part-time 2; women–full-time 6, part-time 1; minority–full-time 1.

Programs and Degrees Offered:
Listed in the following order: Program area, degree type (T if terminal Master's), number awarded 7/03–6/04. General experimental PhD (Doctor of Philosophy) 3, Engineering psychology PhD (Doctor of Philosophy) 3, Industrial/organization PhD (Doctor of Philosophy) 2, Human computer interaction MA/MS (Master of Arts/Science).

Student Applications/Admissions:
Student Applications
General experimental PhD (Doctor of Philosophy)—Applications 2004–2005, 36. Total applicants accepted 2004–2005, 5. Openings 2005–2006, 10. The number of students enrolled full and part-time who were dismissed or voluntarily withdrew from this program area were 0. *Engineering psychology PhD (Doctor of Philosophy)*—Applications 2004–2005, 17. Total applicants accepted 2004–2005, 7. Openings 2005–2006, 6. *Industrial/organization PhD (Doctor of Philosophy)*—Applications 2004–2005, 43. Total applicants accepted 2004–2005,

8. Openings 2005–2006, 6. *Human computer interaction MA/MS (Master of Arts/Science)*—Applications 2004–2005, 20. Total applicants accepted 2004–2005, 10. Openings 2005–2006, 15.

Admissions Requirements:
Scores: Entries appear in this order: required test or GPA, minimum score (if required), median score of students entering in 2003–2004. Doctoral Programs: GRE-V 550, 600; GRE-Q 550, 640; GRE-V+Q 1100, 1240; overall undergraduate GPA 3.0, 3.6.
Other Criteria: (importance of criteria rated low, medium, or high): GRE/MAT scores high, research experience high, work experience low, GPA high, letters of recommendation medium, statement of goals and objectives high.

Student Characteristics: The following represents characteristics of students in 2004–2005 in all graduate psychology programs in the department: Female–full-time 32, part-time 0; Male–full-time 25, part-time 0; African American/Black–full-time 2, part-time 0; Hispanic/Latino(a)–full-time 1, part-time 0; Asian/Pacific Islander–full-time 7, part-time 0; American Indian/Alaska Native–full-time 0, part-time 0; Caucasian–full-time 0, part-time 0; Multi-ethnic–full-time 2, part-time 0; students subject to the Americans With Disabilities Act–full-time 0, part-time 0.

Financial Information/Assistance:
Tuition for Full-Time Study: *Doctoral:* State residents: per academic year $1,578, $132 per credit hour; Nonstate residents: per academic year $6,312, $528 per credit hour. Tuition is subject to change. See the following Web site for updates and changes in tuition costs: http://www.oscarweb.gatech.edu/framers/bursars-fees.

Financial Assistance:
First Year Students: Teaching assistantships available for first-year. Average amount paid per academic year: $14,000. Average number of hours worked per week: 20. Apply by January 1. Tuition remission given: full. Research assistantships available for first-year. Average amount paid per academic year: $14,000. Average number of hours worked per week: 20. Apply by January 1. Tuition remission given: full. Traineeships available for first-year. Average amount paid per academic year: $16,500. Average number of hours worked per week: 20. Apply by January 1. Tuition remission given: full.
Advanced Students: Teaching assistantships available for advanced students. Average amount paid per academic year: $14,000. Apply by January 1. Tuition remission given: full. Research assistantships available for advanced students. Average amount paid per academic year: $14,000. Apply by January 1. Tuition remission given: full. Traineeships available for advanced students. Average amount paid per academic year: $16,500. Apply by January 1. Tuition remission given: full.
Contact Information: Of all students currently enrolled full-time, 100% benefitted from one or more of the listed financial assistance programs.

Internships/Practica: Internships are available for Industrial/Organizational and Engineering Psychology doctoral students in local corporations.

Housing and Day Care: On-campus housing is available. See the following Web site for more information: http://www.housing.gatech.edu/. On-campus day care facilities are available.

Employment of Department Graduates:

Master's Degree Graduates: Of those who graduated in the academic year 2003–2004, the following categories and numbers represent the post-graduate activities and employment of master's degree graduates: Enrolled in a post-doctoral residency/fellowship (n/a), employed in independent practice (n/a), total from the above (master's) (0).

Doctoral Degree Graduates: Of those who graduated in the academic year 2003–2004, the following categories and numbers represent the post-graduate activities and employment of doctoral degree graduates: Enrolled in a psychology doctoral program (n/a), employed in an academic position at a university (2), employed in other positions at a higher education institution (2), employed in business or industry (research/consulting) (4), total from the above (doctoral) (8).

Additional Information:

Orientation, Objectives, and Emphasis of Department: Programs are offered leading to the MS and PhD degrees with three areas of specialization: general-experimental (including cognitive psychology, cognitive aging, and animal behavior), industrial/organizational, and engineering psychology. Each program of study involves intensive exposure to the experimental and theoretical foundations of psychology with a strong emphasis on quantitative methods. It is the basic philosophy of the faculty that the student is trained as a psychologist first and a specialist second. Individual initiative in research and study is strongly encouraged and supported by close faculty-student contact.

Special Facilities or Resources: Special facilities or resources include affiliations with Southeast Center for Applied Cognitive Research on Aging, Georgia State Gerontology Center, Zoo Atlanta, close ties with College Computing (Graphics, Visualization and Usability Center) and the Georgia Tech Research Institute.

Application Information:

Send to: Graduate Coordinator, School of Psychology, Georgia Institute of Technology, Atlanta, GA 30332-0170. Students are admitted in the Fall, application deadline January 1 for all programs and degrees. *Fee:* $50. The Institute has a pre-application form without fee to determine the student's potential for acceptance into the program.

Georgia Southern University

Department of Psychology
College of Liberal Arts and Social Sciences
P.O. Box 8041
Statesboro, GA 30460-8041
Telephone: (912) 681-5539
Fax: (912) 681-0751
E-mail: *jmurray@georgiasouthern.edu*
Web: *http://class.georgiasouthern.edu/psychology/*

Department Information:

1967. Chairperson: Dr. John Murray. Number of Faculty: total–full-time 15; women–full-time 8.

Programs and Degrees Offered:

Listed in the following order: Program area, degree type (T if terminal Master's), number awarded 7/03–6/04. Master of Science in Psychology MA/MS (Master of Arts/Science) (T) 9.

Student Applications/Admissions:

Student Applications

Master of Science in Psychology MA/MS (Master of Arts/Science)—Applications 2004–2005, 27. Total applicants accepted 2004–2005, 21. Number enrolled (new admits only) 2004–2005 full-time, 13. Openings 2005–2006, 20. The Median number of years required for completion of a degree are 2. The number of students enrolled full and part-time who were dismissed or voluntarily withdrew from this program area were 0.

Admissions Requirements:

Scores: Entries appear in this order: required test or GPA, minimum score (if required), median score of students entering in 2003–2004. Master's Programs: GRE-V 450, 465; GRE-Q 450, 565; overall undergraduate GPA 3.00, 3.26. Applicants failing to meet one of the two requirements (GRE or GPA) but meeting the other may be admitted provisionally upon the recommendation of the graduate admissions committee.

Other Criteria: (importance of criteria rated low, medium, or high): GRE/MAT scores high, research experience medium, GPA high, letters of recommendation high, statement of goals and objectives high. For additional information on admission requirements, go to: http://cogs.georgiasouthern.edu/prospectivestudents.html.

Student Characteristics: The following represents characteristics of students in 2004–2005 in all graduate psychology programs in the department: Female–full-time 18, part-time 0; Male–full-time 7, part-time 0; African American/Black–full-time 2, part-time 0; Hispanic/Latino(a)–full-time 0, part-time 0; Asian/Pacific Islander–full-time 1, part-time 0; American Indian/Alaska Native–full-time 0, part-time 0; Caucasian–full-time 22, part-time 0; Multi-ethnic–full-time 0, part-time 0; students subject to the Americans With Disabilities Act–full-time 0, part-time 0.

Financial Information/Assistance:

Tuition for Full-Time Study: Master's: State residents: per academic year $2,106, $117 per credit hour; Nonstate residents: per academic year $8,370, $465 per credit hour. Tuition is subject to change. See the following Web site for updates and changes in tuition costs: http://cogs.georgiasouthern.edu/prospectivestudents.html.

Financial Assistance:

First Year Students: Research assistantships available for first-year. Average amount paid per academic year: $5,500. Average number of hours worked per week: 20. Apply by April 15. Tuition remission given: full.

Advanced Students: Research assistantships available for advanced students. Average amount paid per academic year: $5,500. Average number of hours worked per week: 20. Apply by April 15. Tuition remission given: full.

Contact Information: Of all students currently enrolled full-time, 28% benefitted from one or more of the listed financial assistance programs. Application and information available online at: http://cogs.georgiasouthern.edu/graduateassistantships.html.

Internships/Practica: 350 hours of practicum experience are required in the second year of the clinical track.

Housing and Day Care: On-campus housing is available. See the following Web site for more information: http://students.georgiasouthern.edu/housing/2005/. On-campus day care facilities are available. See the following Web site for more information: http://chhs.georgiasouthern.edu/flc/.

Employment of Department Graduates:

Master's Degree Graduates: Of those who graduated in the academic year 2003–2004, the following categories and numbers represent the post-graduate activities and employment of master's degree graduates: Enrolled in a post-doctoral residency/fellowship (n/a), employed in independent practice (n/a), total from the above (master's) (0).

Doctoral Degree Graduates: Of those who graduated in the academic year 2003–2004, the following categories and numbers represent the post-graduate activities and employment of doctoral degree graduates: Enrolled in a psychology doctoral program (n/a), total from the above (doctoral) (0).

Additional Information:

Orientation, Objectives, and Emphasis of Department: This two-year degree program has two tracks: the clinical track for those seeking immediate employment in the human services delivery settings and the experimental psychology track for those preparing to pursue immediately a PhD in psychology. The clinical track consists of coursework and practica in clinical assessment and therapy and has a thesis option. The experimental track consists of coursework and supervised research in traditional areas of interest such as social, developmental, personality, learning, cognitive, physiological, and sensation/perception and has a thesis requirement.

Information for Students With Physical Disabilities: See the following Web site for more information: http://students.georgiasouthern.edu/disability/.

Application Information:

Send to: Office of Graduate Admissions, Georgia Southern University, P.O. Box 8113, Statesboro, GA 30460-8113. Application available online. URL of online application: http://cogs.georgiasouthern.edu/prospectivestudents.html. Students are admitted in the Fall, application deadline July 1; Programs have rolling admissions. *Fee:* $30.

Georgia State University
Department of Psychology
College of Arts and Sciences
University Plaza
Atlanta, GA 30303-3083
Telephone: (404) 651-1622
Fax: (404) 651-1391
E-mail: *psyadvise-g@langate.gsu.edu*
Web: *http://www.gsu.edu/psychology*

Department Information:

1955. Chairperson: Mary K. Morris. Number of Faculty: total–full-time 38; women–full-time 21; minority–full-time 5.

Programs and Degrees Offered:

Listed in the following order: Program area, degree type (T if terminal Master's), number awarded 7/03–6/04. Clinical PhD (Doctor of Philosophy) 10, Community PhD (Doctor of Philosophy) 4, Developmental PhD (Doctor of Philosophy) 1, Neuropsychology and Behavioral Neurosciences PhD (Doctor of Philosophy) 3, Social/Cognitive PhD (Doctor of Philosophy) 3.

APA Accreditation: Clinical PhD (Doctor of Philosophy).

Student Applications/Admissions:

Student Applications

Clinical PhD (Doctor of Philosophy)—Applications 2004–2005, 399. Total applicants accepted 2004–2005, 12. Number enrolled (new admits only) 2004–2005 full-time, 9. Openings 2005–2006, 10. The Median number of years required for completion of a degree are 7. The number of students enrolled full and part-time who were dismissed or voluntarily withdrew from this program area were 0. *Community PhD (Doctor of Philosophy)*—Applications 2004–2005, 46. Total applicants accepted 2004–2005, 7. Number enrolled (new admits only) 2004–2005 full-time, 4. Openings 2005–2006, 5. The Median number of years required for completion of a degree are 7. The number of students enrolled full and part-time who were dismissed or voluntarily withdrew from this program area were 0. *Developmental PhD (Doctor of Philosophy)*—Applications 2004–2005, 20. Total applicants accepted 2004–2005, 4. Number enrolled (new admits only) 2004–2005 full-time, 3. Openings 2005–2006, 3. The Median number of years required for completion of a degree are 4. The number of students enrolled full and part-time who were dismissed or voluntarily withdrew from this program area were 0. *Neuropsychology and Behavioral Neurosciences PhD (Doctor of Philosophy)*—Applications 2004–2005, 31. Total applicants accepted 2004–2005, 6. Number enrolled (new admits only) 2004–2005 full-time, 2. Openings 2005–2006, 3. The Median number of years required for completion of a degree are 6. The number of students enrolled full and part-time who were dismissed or voluntarily withdrew from this program area were 0. *Social/Cognitive PhD (Doctor of Philosophy)*—Applications 2004–2005, 48. Total applicants accepted 2004–2005, 4. Number enrolled (new admits only) 2004–2005 full-time, 2. Openings 2005–2006, 3. The Median number of years required for completion of a degree are 7. The number of students enrolled full and part-time who were dismissed or voluntarily withdrew from this program area were 0.

Admissions Requirements:

Scores: Entries appear in this order: required test or GPA, minimum score (if required), median score of students entering in 2003–2004. Doctoral Programs: GRE-V no minimum stated, 564; GRE-Q no minimum stated, 651; GRE-V+Q no minimum stated, 1215; GRE-Analytical no minimum stated; overall undergraduate GPA no minimum stated, 3.62.

Other Criteria: (importance of criteria rated low, medium, or high): GRE/MAT scores high, research experience high, work experience medium, extracurricular activity low, clinically related public service medium, GPA high, letters of recommendation high, interview high, statement of goals and objectives high. For additional information on admission requirements, go to: http://www2.gsu.edu/~wwwpsy/HowToApply.htm.

Student Characteristics: The following represents characteristics of students in 2004–2005 in all graduate psychology programs in the department: Female–full-time 87, part-time 0; Male–full-time 25, part-time 0; African American/Black–full-time 18, part-time 0; Hispanic/Latino(a)–full-time 2, part-time 0; Asian/Pacific Islander–full-time 8, part-time 0; American Indian/Alaska Native–full-time 1, part-time 0; Caucasian–full-time 81, part-time 0; Multi-ethnic–full-time 2, part-time 0; students subject to the Americans With Disabilities Act–full-time 0, part-time 0.

Financial Information/Assistance:

Tuition for Full-Time Study: *Doctoral:* State residents: per academic year $4,044, $169 per credit hour; Nonstate residents: per academic year $16,170, $674 per credit hour. Tuition is subject to change. See the following Web site for updates and changes in tuition costs: http://www.gosolar.gsu.edu/webforstudent.htm.

Financial Assistance:

First Year Students: Teaching assistantships available for first-year. Average amount paid per academic year: $13,697. Average number of hours worked per week: 20. Tuition remission given: full. Research assistantships available for first-year. Average amount paid per academic year: $13,697. Average number of hours worked per week: 20. Tuition remission given: full.

Advanced Students: Teaching assistantships available for advanced students. Average amount paid per academic year: $16,376. Average number of hours worked per week: 20. Tuition remission given: full. Research assistantships available for advanced students. Average amount paid per academic year: $16,376. Average number of hours worked per week: 20. Tuition remission given: full.

Contact Information: Of all students currently enrolled full-time, 95% benefitted from one or more of the listed financial assistance programs. Application and information available online at: http://www2.gsu.edu/~wwwpsy/Financial.htm.

Internships/Practica: Practicum experiences are an important component of the clinical training program. Supervised therapy and assessment practica are available in a variety of settings. For clinical students, one source of training is the Psychology Clinic, which is located within the department. It provides services to students and members of the community in a variety of modalities, including assessment, individual therapy, group therapy, and family therapy. Another facility within the department is the Regent's Center for Learning Disorders, which offers comprehensive psychoeducational assessments to students and members of the community. Student clinicians are the primary providers of services in both of these clinics. In addition, there are numerous off-campus settings that offer supervised practicum experiences in a variety of areas including health psychology, neuropsychological assessment, personality assessment, psychiatric emergency room services, day treatment programs, etc. Many of these practica are available at Grady Memorial Hospital, a major metropolitan full-service facility located two blocks from the center of campus. Community students likewise do practica at various community based organizations. Often this research takes the form of needs assessment, program development, and program evaluation. For those doctoral students for whom a professional internship is required prior to graduation, 8 applied in 2003–2004. Of those who applied, 8 were placed in internships listed by the Association of Psychology Postdoctoral and Internship Programs (APPIC); 8 were placed in APA accredited internships.

Housing and Day Care: On-campus housing is available. See the following Web site for more information: Department of Housing's website http://www.gsu.edu/~wwwunh/. On-campus day care facilities are available.

Employment of Department Graduates:

Master's Degree Graduates: Of those who graduated in the academic year 2003–2004, the following categories and numbers represent the post-graduate activities and employment of master's degree graduates: Enrolled in a post-doctoral residency/fellowship (n/a), employed in independent practice (n/a), total from the above (master's) (0).

Doctoral Degree Graduates: Of those who graduated in the academic year 2003–2004, the following categories and numbers represent the post-graduate activities and employment of doctoral degree graduates: Enrolled in a psychology doctoral program (n/a), total from the above (doctoral) (0).

Additional Information:

Orientation, Objectives, and Emphasis of Department: The department is eclectic, and many philosophical perspectives and research interests are represented. The policy of the department is to promote the personal and professional development of students. This includes the discovery of individual interests and goals, the growth of independent scholarship and research skills, the mastery of fundamental psychological knowledge and methodology, and the development of various professional skills (e.g., clinical skills, community intervention).

Special Facilities or Resources: The facilities of the department permit work in cognition, development, neuropsychology, learning, infant behavior, sensation and perception, motivation, aging, social psychology, assessment, individual, group and family therapy, behavior therapy, and community psychology. Students may work with both human and nonhuman populations. Human populations include all age ranges and a variety of ethnic and socioeconomic backgrounds. Nonhuman populations include several species, such as hamsters and great apes.

Information for Students With Physical Disabilities: See the following Web site for more information: http://www.gsu.edu/%7Ewwwods/.

Application Information:

Send to: Applications sent via USPS should be sent to: Office of Graduate Studies, College of Arts and Sciences, Georgia State University, P.O. Box 3993, Atlanta, GA 30302-3993. If submitting application via UPS or FedEx, please send to: Office of Graduate Studies College of Arts and Sciences, Haas Howell Building, 75 Poplar Street, Suite 800, Atlanta, GA 30303. Application available online. URL of online application: https://www.applyweb.com/apply/gsucas/menu.html. Students are admitted in the Fall, application deadline January 5. Admission for graduate studies is for the Fall semester only. The January 5 deadline is uniform across the program. *Fee:* $50.

Georgia, University of

Department of Counseling and Human Development Services, Counseling Psychology Program
College of Education
402 Aderhold Hall
Athens, GA 30602
Telephone: (706) 542-1812
Fax: (706) 542-4130
E-mail: *bglaser@coe.uga.edu*
Web: *http://www.coe.uga.edu/echd*

Department Information:

1946. Department Head: Diane L. Cooper. Number of Faculty: total–full-time 19; women–full-time 12, part-time 1; minority–full-time 4.

Programs and Degrees Offered:

Listed in the following order: Program area, degree type (T if terminal Master's), number awarded 7/03–6/04. Community Counseling MA/MS (Master of Arts/Science) 11, Counseling Psychology PhD (Doctor of Philosophy) 12.

APA Accreditation: Counseling PhD (Doctor of Philosophy).

Student Applications/Admissions:

Student Applications

Community Counseling MA/MS (Master of Arts/Science)—Applications 2004–2005, 89. Total applicants accepted 2004–2005, 19. Number enrolled (new admits only) 2004–2005 full-time, 11. Number enrolled (new admits only) 2004–2005 part-time, 0. Openings 2005–2006, 12. The Median number of years required for completion of a degree are 2. *Counseling Psychology PhD (Doctor of Philosophy)*—Applications 2004–2005, 71. Total applicants accepted 2004–2005, 15. Number enrolled (new admits only) 2004–2005 full-time, 10. Number enrolled (new admits only) 2004–2005 part-time, 0. Total enrolled 2004–2005 full-time, 33, part-time, 2. Openings 2005–2006, 8. The Median number of years required for completion of a degree are 4. The number of students enrolled full and part-time who were dismissed or voluntarily withdrew from this program area were 1.

Admissions Requirements:

Scores: Entries appear in this order: required test or GPA, minimum score (if required), median score of students entering in 2003–2004. Master's Programs: GRE-V no minimum stated, 500; GRE-Q no minimum stated, 580; GRE-V+Q no minimum stated, 1080. MAT also accepted Doctoral Programs: GRE-V no minimum stated, 500; GRE-Q no minimum stated, 640; GRE-V+Q no minimum stated, 1140; overall undergraduate GPA no minimum stated, 3.17.

Other Criteria: (importance of criteria rated low, medium, or high): GRE/MAT scores medium, research experience high, work experience high, extracurricular activity low, clinically related public service medium, GPA medium, letters of recommendation high, interview high, statement of goals and objectives high. For additional information on admission requirements, go to: www.coe.uga.edu/echd.

Student Characteristics:

Student Characteristics: The following represents characteristics of students in 2004–2005 in all graduate psychology programs in the department: Female–full-time 38, part-time 1; Male–full-time 17, part-time 1; African American/Black–full-time 12, part-time 0; Hispanic/Latino(a)–full-time 0, part-time 0; Asian/Pacific Islander–full-time 2, part-time 0; American Indian/Alaska Native–full-time 0, part-time 0; Caucasian–full-time 20, part-time 2; Multi-ethnic–full-time 1, part-time 0; students subject to the Americans With Disabilities Act–full-time 2, part-time 0.

Financial Information/Assistance:

Tuition for Full-Time Study: *Master's:* State residents: per academic year $4,948, $169 per credit hour; Nonstate residents: per academic year $18,282, $725 per credit hour. *Doctoral:* State residents: per academic year $4,948, $169 per credit hour; Nonstate residents: per academic year $18,282, $690 per credit hour. Tuition is subject to change.

Financial Assistance:

First Year Students: Teaching assistantships available for first-year. Average amount paid per academic year: $10,232. Average number of hours worked per week: 13. Apply by December 15. Tuition remission given: full. Research assistantships available for first-year. Average amount paid per academic year: $10,232. Average number of hours worked per week: 13. Apply by December 15. Tuition remission given: full.

Advanced Students: Teaching assistantships available for advanced students. Average amount paid per academic year: $10,232. Average number of hours worked per week: 13. Apply by December 15. Tuition remission given: full. Research assistantships available for advanced students. Average amount paid per academic year: $10,232. Average number of hours worked per week: 13. Apply by December 15. Tuition remission given: full.

Contact Information: Of all students currently enrolled full-time, 100% benefitted from one or more of the listed financial assistance programs.

Internships/Practica: Practica opportunities are provided in two on-campus clinics: The Counseling and Personal Evaluation Center and the Counseling and Testing Center. For those doctoral students for whom a professional internship is required prior to graduation, 7 applied in 2003–2004. Of those who applied, 7 were placed in internships listed by the Association of Psychology Postdoctoral and Internship Programs (APPIC); 7 were placed in APA accredited internships.

Housing and Day Care: On-campus housing is available. See the following Web site for more information: http://ses.uga.edu. On-campus day care facilities are available.

Employment of Department Graduates:

Master's Degree Graduates: Of those who graduated in the academic year 2003–2004, the following categories and numbers represent the post-graduate activities and employment of master's degree graduates: Enrolled in a psychology doctoral program (3), enrolled in a post-doctoral residency/fellowship (n/a), employed in independent practice (n/a), employed in a community mental health/counseling center (5), total from the above (master's) (8).

Doctoral Degree Graduates: Of those who graduated in the academic year 2003–2004, the following categories and numbers represent the post-graduate activities and employment of doctoral degree graduates: Enrolled in a psychology doctoral program (n/a),

enrolled in a post-doctoral residency/fellowship (1), employed in independent practice (1), employed in other positions at a higher education institution (3), employed in a government agency (professional services) (1), employed in a community mental health/counseling center (1), total from the above (doctoral) (7).

Additional Information:

Orientation, Objectives, and Emphasis of Department: The goal of the program is to educate students in the scientist-practitioner model of training in professional counseling psychology. The program focuses on professional competency development in three areas: teaching, research, and clinical service. The theoretical orientations of faculty members vary widely, including representatives of most major schools of thought. The broad emphases of the program include developmental perspectives, cultural diversity perspectives, cognitive-behavioral approaches, and psychodynamic therapies.

Special Facilities or Resources: The University, the College, and the Department separately and collectively offer a number of services and fully-equipped facilities to assist students in conducting academic inquiry, including special computer labs, research assistance centers, and major libraries. Several members of the university's Counseling and Testing Center are adjunct faculty members, thereby offering consultation and instructional assistance.

Information for Students With Physical Disabilities: See the following Web site for more information: http://ses.uga.edu.

Application Information:

Send to: Admissions Committee, Department of Counseling and Human Development Services, 402 Aderhold Hall, The University of Georgia, Athens, GA 30602-7142. Students are admitted in the Fall, application deadline December 15. *Fee:* $50. Fee is for Graduate School Application only, subject to change.

Georgia, University of
Department of Psychology
Franklin College of Arts and Sciences
Athens, GA 30602-3013
Telephone: (706) 542-2174
Fax: (706) 542-3275
E-mail: *psydept@egon.psy.uga.edu*
Web: *http://www.uga.edu/psychology*

Department Information:

1921. Interim Department Head: Irwin Bernstein. Number of Faculty: total–full-time 43, part-time 4; women–full-time 16, part-time 3; minority–full-time 3.

Programs and Degrees Offered:

Listed in the following order: Program area, degree type (T if terminal Master's), number awarded 7/03–6/04. Applied PhD (Doctor of Philosophy) 8, Clinical PhD (Doctor of Philosophy) 5, Cognitive Experimental PhD (Doctor of Philosophy) 2, Lifespan Developmental PhD (Doctor of Philosophy) 2, Social PhD (Doc-

tor of Philosophy) 1, Neuroscience and Behavior PhD (Doctor of Philosophy) 0.

APA Accreditation: Clinical PhD (Doctor of Philosophy).

Student Applications/Admissions:
Student Applications

Applied PhD (Doctor of Philosophy)—Applications 2004–2005, 66. Total applicants accepted 2004–2005, 4. Number enrolled (new admits only) 2004–2005 full-time, 4. Total enrolled 2004–2005 full-time, 29. Openings 2005–2006, 5. *Clinical PhD (Doctor of Philosophy)*—Applications 2004–2005, 170. Total applicants accepted 2004–2005, 11. Number enrolled (new admits only) 2004–2005 full-time, 7. Total enrolled 2004–2005 full-time, 41. Openings 2005–2006, 8. The Median number of years required for completion of a degree are 5. *Cognitive Experimental PhD (Doctor of Philosophy)*—Applications 2004–2005, 16. Total applicants accepted 2004–2005, 5. Number enrolled (new admits only) 2004–2005 full-time, 3. Total enrolled 2004–2005 full-time, 16. Openings 2005–2006, 3. The Median number of years required for completion of a degree are 5.5. The number of students enrolled full and part-time who were dismissed or voluntarily withdrew from this program area were 0. *Lifespan Developmental PhD (Doctor of Philosophy)*—Applications 2004–2005, 14. Total applicants accepted 2004–2005, 4. Openings 2005–2006, 6. The Median number of years required for completion of a degree are 6.5. The number of students enrolled full and part-time who were dismissed or voluntarily withdrew from this program area were 0. *Social PhD (Doctor of Philosophy)*—Applications 2004–2005, 38. Total applicants accepted 2004–2005, 3. Number enrolled (new admits only) 2004–2005 full-time, 3. Openings 2005–2006, 2. The Median number of years required for completion of a degree are 5. The number of students enrolled full and part-time who were dismissed or voluntarily withdrew from this program area were 1. *Neuroscience and Behavior PhD (Doctor of Philosophy)*—Applications 2004–2005, 17. Total applicants accepted 2004–2005, 10. Number enrolled (new admits only) 2004–2005 full-time, 4. Total enrolled 2004–2005 full-time, 17.

Admissions Requirements:

Scores: Entries appear in this order: required test or GPA, minimum score (if required), median score of students entering in 2003–2004. Master's Programs: No MS program alone. Doctoral Programs: GRE-V+Q no minimum stated, 1225.
Other Criteria: (importance of criteria rated low, medium, or high): GRE/MAT scores medium, research experience high, work experience high, extracurricular activity medium, clinically related public service medium, GPA medium, letters of recommendation medium, interview medium, statement of goals and objectives high. Each program weighs according to its own criteria. Interviews are only required by Clinical. For additional information on admission requirements, go to: http://www.uga.edu/psychology/.

Student Characteristics: The following represents characteristics of students in 2004–2005 in all graduate psychology programs in the department: Female–full-time 73, part-time 16; Male–full-time 27, part-time 4; African American/Black–full-time 7, part-time 0; Hispanic/Latino(a)–full-time 2, part-time 0; Asian/Pacific Islander–full-time 0, part-time 0; American Indian/Alaska Native–full-time 1, part-time 0; Caucasian–full-time 53, part-time

9; Multi-ethnic–full-time 0, part-time 0; students subject to the Americans With Disabilities Act–full-time 2, part-time 1.

Financial Information/Assistance:

Tuition for Full-Time Study: *Master's:* State residents: per academic year $2,022, $169 per credit hour; Nonstate residents: per academic year $8,189, $684 per credit hour. *Doctoral:* State residents: per academic year $2,022, $169 per credit hour; Nonstate residents: per academic year $8,189, $684 per credit hour. Tuition is subject to change. See the following Web site for updates and changes in tuition costs: www.busfin.uga.edu/bursar/schedule.html.

Financial Assistance:

First Year Students: Teaching assistantships available for first-year. Average amount paid per academic year: $9,557. Average number of hours worked per week: 13. Tuition remission given: partial. Research assistantships available for first-year. Average amount paid per academic year: $9,557. Average number of hours worked per week: 13. Tuition remission given: partial. Fellowships and scholarships available for first-year. Average amount paid per academic year: $15,588. Average number of hours worked per week: 16. Tuition remission given: partial.

Advanced Students: Teaching assistantships available for advanced students. Average amount paid per academic year: $10,190. Average number of hours worked per week: 13. Tuition remission given: partial. Research assistantships available for advanced students. Average amount paid per academic year: $10,190. Average number of hours worked per week: 13. Tuition remission given: partial. Fellowships and scholarships available for advanced students. Average amount paid per academic year: $15,750. Average number of hours worked per week: 16. Tuition remission given: partial.

Contact Information: Of all students currently enrolled full-time, 80% benefitted from one or more of the listed financial assistance programs. Application and information available online at: http://www.gradsch.edu/.

Internships/Practica: For those doctoral students for whom a professional internship is required prior to graduation, 11 applied in 2003–2004. Of those who applied, 11 were placed in internships listed by the Association of Psychology Postdoctoral and Internship Programs (APPIC); 11 were placed in APA accredited internships.

Housing and Day Care: On-campus housing is available. See the following Web site for more information: www.uga.edu/housing. On-campus day care facilities are available. See the following Web site for more information: www.fcs.uga.edu/cfd/mcphaul.

Employment of Department Graduates:

Master's Degree Graduates: Of those who graduated in the academic year 2003–2004, the following categories and numbers represent the post-graduate activities and employment of master's degree graduates: Enrolled in a post-doctoral residency/fellowship (n/a), employed in independent practice (n/a), total from the above (master's) (0).

Doctoral Degree Graduates: Of those who graduated in the academic year 2003–2004, the following categories and numbers represent the post-graduate activities and employment of doctoral degree graduates: Enrolled in a psychology doctoral program (n/a), total from the above (doctoral) (0).

Additional Information:

Orientation, Objectives, and Emphasis of Department: Our emphasis is on research and the basic science aspects of psychology with a focus on doctoral education. A few state and private facilities provide internships. We have a cooperative liaison with several mental health facilties in the region as well as other universities.

Special Facilities or Resources: Facilities include a Research and Regents Center for Learning Disabilities, the Institute for Behavioral Research, and a Psychology Clinic.

Information for Students With Physical Disabilities: See the following Web site for more information: www.dissvcs.uga.edu.

Application Information:

Send to: Please send supplemental application and reference letters to: Department of Psychology, c/o Graduate Coordinator, University of Georgia, Athens, GA 30602-3013. Please send admission application to the attention of the Graduate Admissions office. Application available online. URL of online application: http://www.gradsch.uga.edu. Students are admitted in the Fall, application deadline December 1. The deadline for receipt of admission materials for Fall semester is December 1 for all programs. *Fee:* $50.

Georgia, University of
Program in School Psychology
Education
325 Aderhold Hall
Athens, GA 30602-7143
Telephone: (706) 542-4110
Fax: (706) 542-4240
E-mail: *mlease@uga.edu*
Web: *http://www.coe.uga.edu/edpsych/*

Department Information:
1968. Program Coordinator: Michele Lease. Number of Faculty: total–full-time 4; women–full-time 1.

Programs and Degrees Offered:
Listed in the following order: Program area, degree type (T if terminal Master's), number awarded 7/03–6/04. School PhD (Doctor of Philosophy) 7.

Student Applications/Admissions:
Student Applications
School PhD (Doctor of Philosophy)—Applications 2004–2005, 58. Total applicants accepted 2004–2005, 11. Number enrolled (new admits only) 2004–2005 full-time, 5. Openings 2005–2006, 6. The Median number of years required for completion of a degree are 5. The number of students enrolled full and part-time who were dismissed or voluntarily withdrew from this program area were 0.

Admissions Requirements:
Scores: Entries appear in this order: required test or GPA, minimum score (if required), median score of students entering in 2003–2004. Doctoral Programs: GRE-V 400, 579; GRE-Q

540, 618; GRE-V+Q 940, 1251; overall undergraduate GPA 2.86, 3.34.

Other Criteria: (importance of criteria rated low, medium, or high): GRE/MAT scores medium, research experience low, work experience low, extracurricular activity low, clinically related public service medium, GPA medium, letters of recommendation medium, interview low, statement of goals and objectives medium.

Student Characteristics: The following represents characteristics of students in 2004–2005 in all graduate psychology programs in the department: Female–full-time 33, part-time 0; Male–full-time 6, part-time 0; African American/Black–full-time 3, part-time 0; Hispanic/Latino(a)–full-time 1, part-time 0; Asian/Pacific Islander–full-time 2, part-time 0; American Indian/Alaska Native–full-time 0, part-time 0; Caucasian–full-time 33, part-time 0; students subject to the Americans With Disabilities Act–full-time 0, part-time 0.

Financial Information/Assistance:

Tuition for Full-Time Study: *Doctoral:* State residents: per academic year $4,358, $415 per credit hour; Nonstate residents: per academic year $16,058, $903 per credit hour. Tuition is subject to change.

Financial Assistance:

First Year Students: Teaching assistantships available for first-year. Average amount paid per academic year: $12,623. Average number of hours worked per week: 13. Apply by February 1. Tuition remission given: full. Research assistantships available for first-year. Average amount paid per academic year: $12,623. Average number of hours worked per week: 13. Apply by February 1. Tuition remission given: full.

Advanced Students: Teaching assistantships available for advanced students. Average amount paid per academic year: $13,643. Average number of hours worked per week: 13. Apply by February 1. Tuition remission given: full. Research assistantships available for advanced students. Average amount paid per academic year: $13,643. Average number of hours worked per week: 13. Apply by February 1. Tuition remission given: full.

Contact Information: Of all students currently enrolled full-time, 81% benefitted from one or more of the listed financial assistance programs.

Internships/Practica: For those doctoral students for whom a professional internship is required prior to graduation, 6 applied in 2003–2004. Of those who applied, 4 were placed in internships listed by the Association of Psychology Postdoctoral and Internship Programs (APPIC); 1 was placed in an APA accredited internship.

Housing and Day Care: On-campus housing is available. On-campus day care facilities are available.

Employment of Department Graduates:

Master's Degree Graduates: Of those who graduated in the academic year 2003–2004, the following categories and numbers represent the post-graduate activities and employment of master's degree graduates: Enrolled in a post-doctoral residency/fellowship (n/a), employed in independent practice (n/a), total from the above (master's) (0).

Doctoral Degree Graduates: Of those who graduated in the academic year 2003–2004, the following categories and numbers represent the post-graduate activities and employment of doctoral degree graduates: Enrolled in a psychology doctoral program (n/a), enrolled in a post-doctoral residency/fellowship (1), employed in independent practice (0), employed in an academic position at a university (0), employed in an academic position at a 2-year/4-year college (0), employed in other positions at a higher education institution (0), employed in a professional position in a school system (6), employed in business or industry (research/consulting) (0), employed in business or industry (management) (0), employed in a government agency (research) (0), employed in a government agency (professional services) (0), employed in a community mental health/counseling center (0), employed in a hospital/medical center (0), still seeking employment (0), other employment position (0), total from the above (doctoral) (7).

Additional Information:

Orientation, Objectives, and Emphasis of Department: The PhD program in school psychology supplies research-oriented school psychologists to educational settings, hospitals, clinics, and universities in which they can provide leadership in applied practice, research and teaching. The school psychology program follows the scientist-practitioner model, and emphasizes human development and developmental psychopathology and the central core elements of training.

Special Facilities or Resources: Special facilities and resources include access to a superior computer center, decentralized computational equipment, a major research library, and faculty members who are extraordinarily accessible to students. The department is strongly committed to affirmative action and fair treatment and is very proud that the majority of our students are women. Despite the suburban setting (a small urban area of 75,000 over an hour from Atlanta), we attract increasing numbers of Black, Asian, and out-of-state and out-of-region students and faculty. NASP and APA requirements and full accreditation from APA and NCATE form the foundation of our programs.

Application Information:
Send to: Graduate Admissions Office, Graduate Studies Building, The University of Georgia, Athens, GA 30602. Students are admitted in the Fall, application deadline February 1. Deadline dates are unrelated to degree; all applications are considered only for Fall admission. *Fee:* $30.

Valdosta State University
Psychology and Counseling
1500 North Patterson Street
Valdosta, GA 31698-0100
Telephone: (229) 333-5930
Fax: (229) 259-5576
E-mail: *PsycCoun@valdosta.edu*
Web: *http://coefaculty.valdosta.edu/psych/*

Department Information:
1965. Chairperson: Robert E. L. Bauer. Number of Faculty: total–full-time 19, part-time 2; women–full-time 4, part-time 1; minority–full-time 2.

Programs and Degrees Offered:
Listed in the following order: Program area, degree type (T if terminal Master's), number awarded 7/03–6/04. Clinical/Counseling MA/MS (Master of Arts/Science) (T) 6, Industrial/Organizational MA/MS (Master of Arts/Science) (T) 4, School Counseling EdS (Education Specialist) 0, School Psychology EdS (Education Specialist) 6, School Counseling Other 13.

Student Applications/Admissions:

Student Applications
Clinical/Counseling MA/MS (Master of Arts/Science)—Applications 2004–2005, 22. Total applicants accepted 2004–2005, 8. Number enrolled (new admits only) 2004–2005 full-time, 4. Number enrolled (new admits only) 2004–2005 part-time, 2. Total enrolled 2004–2005 full-time, 12, part-time, 8. Openings 2005–2006, 15. The Median number of years required for completion of a degree are 2. The number of students enrolled full and part-time who were dismissed or voluntarily withdrew from this program area were 0. *Industrial/Organizational MA/ MS (Master of Arts/Science)*—Applications 2004–2005, 18. Total applicants accepted 2004–2005, 8. Number enrolled (new admits only) 2004–2005 full-time, 4. Number enrolled (new admits only) 2004–2005 part-time, 2. Total enrolled 2004–2005 full-time, 14, part-time, 2. Openings 2005–2006, 14. The Median number of years required for completion of a degree are 2. The number of students enrolled full and part-time who were dismissed or voluntarily withdrew from this program area were 0. *School Counseling EdS (Education Specialist)*—Applications 2004–2005, 3. Total applicants accepted 2004–2005, 1. Number enrolled (new admits only) 2004–2005 full-time, 0. Number enrolled (new admits only) 2004–2005 part-time, 1. Openings 2005–2006, 5. The Median number of years required for completion of a degree are 2. The number of students enrolled full and part-time who were dismissed or voluntarily withdrew from this program area were 0. *School Psychology EdS (Education Specialist)*—Applications 2004–2005, 13. Total applicants accepted 2004–2005, 4. Number enrolled (new admits only) 2004–2005 full-time, 0. Number enrolled (new admits only) 2004–2005 part-time, 4. Total enrolled 2004–2005 full-time, 4, part-time, 13. Openings 2005–2006, 12. The Median number of years required for completion of a degree are 2. The number of students enrolled full and part-time who were dismissed or voluntarily withdrew from this program area were 1. *School Counseling Other*—Applications 2004–2005, 21. Total applicants accepted 2004–2005, 16. Number enrolled (new admits only) 2004–2005 full-time, 2. Number enrolled (new admits only) 2004–2005 part-time, 16. Total enrolled 2004–2005 full-time, 9, part-time, 33. Openings 2005–2006, 11. The Median number of years required for completion of a degree are 2. The number of students enrolled full and part-time who were dismissed or voluntarily withdrew from this program area were 0.

Admissions Requirements:
Scores: Entries appear in this order: required test or GPA, minimum score (if required), median score of students entering in 2003–2004. Master's Programs: GRE-V 400; GRE-Q 400; overall undergraduate GPA 3.00. MS in Psychology (reported here) differs from MEd and EdS in admissions criteria. Please write for details.
Other Criteria: (importance of criteria rated low, medium, or high): GRE/MAT scores high, research experience medium,

work experience medium, extracurricular activity low, clinically related public service low, GPA high, letters of recommendation medium, interview low, statement of goals and objectives low. Because criteria vary for different programs, please write for details by program. For additional information on admission requirements, go to: http://www.valdosta.edu/GRADSCHOOL/.

Student Characteristics: The following represents characteristics of students in 2004–2005 in all graduate psychology programs in the department: Female–full-time 26, part-time 48; Male–full-time 13, part-time 12; African American/Black–full-time 5, part-time 6; Hispanic/Latino(a)–full-time 0, part-time 2; Asian/Pacific Islander–full-time 0, part-time 0; American Indian/Alaska Native–full-time 0, part-time 0; Caucasian–full-time 34, part-time 52; Multi-ethnic–full-time 0, part-time 0; students subject to the Americans With Disabilities Act–full-time 0, part-time 0.

Financial Information/Assistance:
Tuition for Full-Time Study: *Master's:* State residents: per academic year $3,456, $117 per credit hour; Nonstate residents: per academic year $11,816, $465 per credit hour. Tuition is subject to change. See the following Web site for updates and changes in tuition costs: http://services.valdosta.edu/financial/gfeetable_Fall2.htm.

Financial Assistance:
First Year Students: Research assistantships available for first-year. Average amount paid per academic year: $2,452. Average number of hours worked per week: 15. Apply by July 15. Tuition remission given: full.
Advanced Students: Research assistantships available for advanced students. Average amount paid per academic year: $2,452. Average number of hours worked per week: 15. Apply by July 15. Tuition remission given: full.
Contact Information: Of all students currently enrolled full-time, 12% benefitted from one or more of the listed financial assistance programs. Application and information available online at: http://www.valdosta.edu/GRADSCHOOL/finaid.htm.

Internships/Practica: Master's Degree students are assigned to appropriate practica sites, related to their programs of study. Some sites offer stipends. All School Psychology EdS students work in schools during their internships and receive a stipend.

Housing and Day Care: On-campus housing is available. See the following Web site for more information: http://services.valdosta.edu/housing/. No on-campus day care facilities are available.

Employment of Department Graduates:
Master's Degree Graduates: Of those who graduated in the academic year 2003–2004, the following categories and numbers represent the post-graduate activities and employment of master's degree graduates: Enrolled in a psychology doctoral program (2), enrolled in another graduate/professional program (2), enrolled in a post-doctoral residency/fellowship (n/a), employed in independent practice (n/a), employed in an academic position at a university (0), employed in an academic position at a 2-year/4-year college (1), employed in other positions at a higher education institution (0), employed in a professional position in a school system (14), employed in business or industry (research/consulting) (0), employed in business or industry (management) (4),

employed in a government agency (research) (0), employed in a government agency (professional services) (0), employed in a community mental health/counseling center (5), employed in a hospital/medical center (1), still seeking employment (0), not seeking employment (0), other employment position (0), total from the above (master's) (29).

Doctoral Degree Graduates: Of those who graduated in the academic year 2003–2004, the following categories and numbers represent the post-graduate activities and employment of doctoral degree graduates: Enrolled in a psychology doctoral program (n/a), total from the above (doctoral) (0).

Additional Information:

Orientation, Objectives, and Emphasis of Department: The Department of Psychology and Counseling serves the citizens of the region and state by offering instruction, research, and services designed to advance the understanding of behavioral and cognitive processes and to improve the quality of life. The principal function of the department is to prepare students at the undergraduate and graduate levels to pursue careers within the discipline and affiliated areas. A related purpose is to provide courses for programs in education, nursing, and other disciplines. At the baccalaureate level, the students develop basic skills in scientific research, knowledge of psychological nomenclature and concepts, and are introduced to the diverse applications of psychology. The graduate programs prepare students to apply skills in schools, mental health agencies, government, industry, and other settings. Training at the graduate level is designed to prepare qualified, responsible professionals who may provide assessment, consulting, counseling, and other services to the citizenry of the region.

Information for Students With Physical Disabilities: See the following Web site for more information: http://www.valdosta.edu/ssp/.

Application Information:
Send to: Graduate School, Valdosta State University, 1500 North Patterson Street, Valdosta, GA 31698-0005. Application available online. URL of online application: http://www.valdosta.edu/gradschool/index_of_application_forms.htm. Students are admitted in the Fall, application deadline July 15; Spring, application deadline November 15; Summer, application deadline May 1. Programs have rolling admissions. Fee: $20. Filing application online- $25.00.

West Georgia, University of
Counseling & Educational Psychology
Education
237 Education Annex
Carrollton, GA 30118
Telephone: (638) 839-6554
Fax: (638) 839-6099
E-mail: *bsnow@westga.edu*
Web: *http://coe.westga.edu/cep/*

Department Information:
1969. Chairperson: Brent M. Snow, PhD. Number of Faculty: total–full-time 12; women–full-time 6; minority–full-time 2.

Programs and Degrees Offered:
Listed in the following order: Program area, degree type (T if terminal Master's), number awarded 7/03–6/04. Counseling EdS (Education Specialist), Counseling (MEd) Other.

Student Applications/Admissions:
Student Applications
Counseling EdS (Education Specialist)—Counseling (MEd) Other

Admissions Requirements:
Scores: Entries appear in this order: required test or GPA, minimum score (if required), median score of students entering in 2003–2004. Master's Programs: GRE-V 450; GRE-Q 450; GRE-V+Q 900; GRE-Analytical 3.5; overall undergraduate GPA 2.7.
Other Criteria: (importance of criteria rated low, medium, or high): GRE/MAT scores high, research experience low, work experience medium, extracurricular activity low, clinically related public service low, GPA high, letters of recommendation high, interview high, statement of goals and objectives high.

Student Characteristics: The following represents characteristics of students in 2004–2005 in all graduate psychology programs in the department: Caucasian–full-time 0, part-time 0.

Financial Information/Assistance:
Tuition for Full-Time Study: *Master's:* State residents: per academic year $1,480, $101 per credit hour; Nonstate residents: per academic year $5,098, $402 per credit hour. Tuition is subject to change. See the following Web site for updates and changes in tuition costs: www.westga.edu.

Financial Assistance:
First Year Students: Research assistantships available for first-year. Average amount paid per academic year: $6,000. Average number of hours worked per week: 13. Apply by July. Tuition remission given: full.
Advanced Students: Research assistantships available for advanced students. Average amount paid per academic year: $6,000. Average number of hours worked per week: 13. Apply by July. Tuition remission given: full.
Contact Information: Of all students currently enrolled full-time, 5% benefitted from one or more of the listed financial assistance programs.

Internships/Practica: Practicum (100 hours) and Internship (600 hours) are required of all graduate students in school and community counseling.

Housing and Day Care: On-campus housing is available. Residence Life Director, jclower@westga.edu. On-campus day care facilities are available.

Employment of Department Graduates:
Master's Degree Graduates: Of those who graduated in the academic year 2003–2004, the following categories and numbers represent the post-graduate activities and employment of master's degree graduates: Enrolled in a post-doctoral residency/fellowship (n/a), employed in independent practice (n/a), total from the above (master's) (0).
Doctoral Degree Graduates: Of those who graduated in the academic year 2003–2004, the following categories and numbers

represent the post-graduate activities and employment of doctoral degree graduates: Enrolled in a psychology doctoral program (n/a), total from the above (doctoral) (0).

Additional Information:

Orientation, Objectives, and Emphasis of Department: The Department's identity is in training professional counselors for schools and community agencies. Master's programs are accredited by the Council for Accreditation of Counseling and Related Educational Programs (CACREP)—the largest and most prestigious accreditation in the field of counseling. Professional identity of faculty and students is the American Counseling Association (ACA) and it's various divisions. Depending on the program emphasis, graduates qualify for the following credentials: licensed professional counselor, nationally certified counselor, and state certification in school counseling.

Special Facilities or Resources: The Department is nationally prominent and recognized as a leader in the transforming school counseling initiative. Excellent lab facilities.

Application Information:
Send to: Graduate School, University of West Georgia, Carrollton, GA 30118. Application available online. Students are admitted in the Fall, application deadline June 3; Spring, application deadline November 5; Summer, application deadline March 4.

West Georgia, University of
Department of Psychology
Arts and Sciences
1600 Maple Street
Carrollton, GA 30118
Telephone: (678) 839-6510
Fax: (678) 839-0611
E-mail: drice@westga.edu
Web: http://www.westga.edu~psydept

Department Information:
1967. Professor and Chair: Donadrian L. Rice. Number of Faculty: total–full-time 15, part-time 2; women–full-time 4, part-time 2; minority–full-time 1.

Programs and Degrees Offered:
Listed in the following order: Program area, degree type (T if terminal Master's), number awarded 7/03–6/04. Humanistic/Transpersonal MA/MS (Master of Arts/Science) (T) 13.

Student Applications/Admissions:
Student Applications
Humanistic/Transpersonal MA/MS (Master of Arts/Science)—Applications 2004–2005, 71. Total applicants accepted 2004–2005, 60. Number enrolled (new admits only) 2004–2005 full-time, 53. Number enrolled (new admits only) 2004–2005 part-time, 7. Total enrolled 2004–2005 full-time, 72, part-time, 11. Openings 2005–2006, 40. The Median number of years required for completion of a degree are 3. The number of students enrolled full and part-time who were dismissed or voluntarily withdrew from this program area were 1.

Admissions Requirements:
Scores: Entries appear in this order: required test or GPA, minimum score (if required), median score of students entering in 2003–2004. Master's Programs: GRE-V 400; GRE-Q 400; GRE-V+Q 800; overall undergraduate GPA 2.5.
Other Criteria: (importance of criteria rated low, medium, or high): GRE/MAT scores medium, research experience high, work experience high, clinically related public service medium, GPA high, letters of recommendation high, interview high, statement of goals and objectives high. For additional information on admission requirements, go to: http://www.westga.edu/~psydept/.

Student Characteristics: The following represents characteristics of students in 2004–2005 in all graduate psychology programs in the department: Female–full-time 42, part-time 6; Male–full-time 30, part-time 5; African American/Black–full-time 3, part-time 0; Hispanic/Latino(a)–full-time 2, part-time 0; Asian/Pacific Islander–full-time 0, part-time 0; American Indian/Alaska Native–full-time 0, part-time 0; Caucasian–full-time 67, part-time 11; students subject to the Americans With Disabilities Act–full-time 0, part-time 0.

Financial Information/Assistance:
Tuition for Full-Time Study: *Master's:* State residents: per academic year $3,370, $117 per credit hour; Nonstate residents: per academic year $11,730, $465 per credit hour. Tuition is subject to change. See the following Web site for updates and changes in tuition costs: http://www.westga.edu/policies/gradcat_2001.pdf.

Financial Assistance:
First Year Students: Research assistantships available for first-year. Average amount paid per academic year: $3,000. Average number of hours worked per week: 13. Tuition remission given: full.
Advanced Students: No information provided.
Contact Information: Of all students currently enrolled full-time, 25% benefitted from one or more of the listed financial assistance programs.

Internships/Practica: Internships are available at local facilities.

Housing and Day Care: On-campus housing is available. See the following Web site for more information: www.westga.edu/~psydept. No on-campus day care facilities are available.

Employment of Department Graduates:
Master's Degree Graduates: Of those who graduated in the academic year 2003–2004, the following categories and numbers represent the post-graduate activities and employment of master's degree graduates: Enrolled in a psychology doctoral program (6), enrolled in another graduate/professional program (7), enrolled in a post-doctoral residency/fellowship (n/a), employed in independent practice (n/a), employed in an academic position at a 2-year/4-year college (2), employed in other positions at a higher education institution (3), employed in a professional position in a school system (4), employed in a community mental health/counseling center (7), other employment position (5), total from the above (master's) (34).
Doctoral Degree Graduates: Of those who graduated in the academic year 2003–2004, the following categories and numbers represent the post-graduate activities and employment of doctoral

degree graduates: Enrolled in a psychology doctoral program (n/a), total from the above (doctoral) (0).

Additional Information:

Orientation, Objectives, and Emphasis of Department: The department is a pioneer of humanistic-transpersonal psychology. It differs from other programs in that it goes beyond conventional subjects and approaches a holistic and integrative understanding of human experience. Alongside demanding academic work, student growth and personal awareness are inherent to this venture since such reflection is considered an important factor in human understanding. Individual programs are designed according to personal needs and interests; the overall atmosphere is communal, encouraging personal and intellectual dialogue and encounter. Most conventional topic areas are taught. Beyond these are areas almost uniquely explorable in a program such as this: the horizons of consciousness through such vantages as Eastern and transpersonal psychologies, hermeneutics, existential and phenomenological psychologies, and critical psychology. Specific areas include women's studies; aesthetic and sacred experience; myths, dreams, and symbols; and creativity. Areas of applied interest are viewed as correlates of the learning process: skill courses related to human services, prevention and community psychology, counseling psychology, cross-cultural psychology, organizational development, and growth therapies. The department offers training in qualitative and traditional methodologies of research. Practicum and internship experience along with individual research and reading are highly encouraged for those who can profit from these. Interest areas include human science research; parapsychology; transpersonal and Eastern psychologies; counseling, clinical, community, and organizational development; and psychology in the classroom.

Special Facilities or Resources: Special resources include large library holdings in the areas of humanistic, parapsychology, transpersonal, philosophical, and Asian psychology. The library holds papers of Sidney M. Jourard, Edith Weiskoff-Joelsen and the Psychical Research Foundation Library. The department hosts major conferences, and faculty are associated with several journals and newsletters exploring orientation areas.

Information for Students With Physical Disabilities: See the following Web site for more information: http://www.westga.edu/~sdev.

Application Information:
Send to: Graduate Coordinator, Department of Psychology, State University of West Georgia, Carrollton, GA 30118. Application available online. URL of online application: www.westga.edu/~gradsch/. Students are admitted in the Fall, application deadline March 4; Spring, application deadline October 5. *Fee:* $20.

Argosy University/Hawaii
Clinical Psychology
American School of Professional Psychology
400 ASB Tower, 1001 Bishop Street
Honolulu, HI 96813
Telephone: (808) 536-5555
Fax: (808) 536-5505
E-mail: *hawaii@argosyu.edu*
Web: *http://www.argosyu.edu*

Department Information:
1994. Chair, Graduate Psychology Department: Richard P. Kappenberg, PhD Number of Faculty: total–full-time 9, part-time 2; women–full-time 5, part-time 1; minority–full-time 3, part-time 1.

Programs and Degrees Offered:
Listed in the following order: Program area, degree type (T if terminal Master's), number awarded 7/03–6/04. Clinical PsyD (Doctor of Psychology) 22, Marriage and Family MA/MS (Master of Arts/Science) (T) 41, Clinical Respecialization Diploma 0, Post Doctoral/ Clinical Psychopharmacology Other 0, Clinical PsyD School Psychology Concentration (Doctor of Psychology) 0, Clinical MA/MS (Master of Arts/Science) (T) 7, School Psychology MA/MS (Master of Arts/Science) (T) 0.

APA Accreditation: Clinical PsyD (Doctor of Psychology).

Student Applications/Admissions:
Student Applications
Clinical PsyD (Doctor of Psychology)—Applications 2004–2005, 155. Total applicants accepted 2004–2005, 45. Number enrolled (new admits only) 2004–2005 full-time, 46. Total enrolled 2004–2005 full-time, 137, part-time, 55. Openings 2005–2006, 40. The Median number of years required for completion of a degree are 6. The number of students enrolled full and part-time who were dismissed or voluntarily withdrew from this program area were 6. *Marriage and Family MA/MS (Master of Arts/Science)*—Applications 2004–2005, 79. Total applicants accepted 2004–2005, 60. Number enrolled (new admits only) 2004–2005 full-time, 60. Number enrolled (new admits only) 2004–2005 part-time, 0. Openings 2005–2006, 46. The Median number of years required for completion of a degree are 2. The number of students enrolled full and part-time who were dismissed or voluntarily withdrew from this program area were 12. *Clinical Respecialization Diploma*—Applications 2004–2005, 0. Total applicants accepted 2004–2005, 0. Number enrolled (new admits only) 2004–2005 full-time, 0. Number enrolled (new admits only) 2004–2005 part-time, 0. The Median number of years required for completion of a degree are 3. The number of students enrolled full and part-time who were dismissed or voluntarily withdrew from this

program area were 0. *Post Doctoral/ Clinical Psychopharmacology Other*—Applications 2004–2005, 5. Total applicants accepted 2004–2005, 6. Number enrolled (new admits only) 2004–2005 full-time, 5. Number enrolled (new admits only) 2004–2005 part-time, 0. Openings 2005–2006, 5. The Median number of years required for completion of a degree is 1. The number of students enrolled full and part-time who were dismissed or voluntarily withdrew from this program area were 0. *Clinical PsyD School Psychology Concentration (Doctor of Psychology)*—Applications 2004–2005, 9. Total applicants accepted 2004–2005, 7. Number enrolled (new admits only) 2004–2005 full-time, 0. Number enrolled (new admits only) 2004–2005 part-time, 8. Openings 2005–2006, 5. The number of students enrolled full and part-time who were dismissed or voluntarily withdrew from this program area were 0. *Clinical MA/MS (Master of Arts/Science)*—Applications 2004–2005, 22. Total applicants accepted 2004–2005, 12. Number enrolled (new admits only) 2004–2005 full-time, 12. Number enrolled (new admits only) 2004–2005 part-time, 0. Total enrolled 2004–2005 full-time, 10, part-time, 2. Openings 2005–2006, 7. The Median number of years required for completion of a degree are 2. The number of students enrolled full and part-time who were dismissed or voluntarily withdrew from this program area were 3. *School Psychology MA/MS (Master of Arts/Science)*—Applications 2004–2005, 19. Total applicants accepted 2004–2005, 6. Number enrolled (new admits only) 2004–2005 full-time, 0. Number enrolled (new admits only) 2004–2005 part-time, 6. Openings 2005–2006, 5. The number of students enrolled full and part-time who were dismissed or voluntarily withdrew from this program area were 4.

Admissions Requirements:
Scores: Entries appear in this order: required test or GPA, minimum score (if required), median score of students entering in 2003–2004. Master's Programs: overall undergraduate GPA 3.00, 3.12; last 2 years GPA 3.00, 3.41; psychology GPA 3.00, 3.36. No set GPA requirement for professional counseling program. Doctoral Programs: overall undergraduate GPA 3.25, 3.40; last 2 years GPA 3.25, 3.59; psychology GPA 3.25, 3.55. *Other Criteria:* (importance of criteria rated low, medium, or high): research experience low, work experience medium, extracurricular activity low, clinically related public service high, GPA medium, letters of recommendation medium, interview high, statement of goals and objectives high, diversity focus high.

Student Characteristics: The following represents characteristics of students in 2004–2005 in all graduate psychology programs in the department: Female–full-time 182, part-time 60; Male–full-time 65, part-time 14; African American/Black–full-time 6, part-time 8; Hispanic/Latino(a)–full-time 28, part-time 3; Asian/Pacific Islander–full-time 139, part-time 11; American Indian/ Alaska Native–full-time 6, part-time 4; Caucasian–full-time 47, part-time 36; Multi-ethnic–full-time 21, part-time 12; students subject to the Americans With Disabilities Act–full-time 0, part-time 2.

Financial Information/Assistance:

Financial Assistance:

First Year Students: Fellowships and scholarships available for first-year. Average amount paid per academic year: $10,000. Apply by April 30. Tuition remission given: partial.

Advanced Students: Teaching assistantships available for advanced students. Average amount paid per academic year: $600. Average number of hours worked per week: 15. Apply by n/a. Tuition remission given: partial. Fellowships and scholarships available for advanced students. Average amount paid per academic year: $10,000. Apply by April 30. Tuition remission given: partial.

Contact Information: Of all students currently enrolled full-time, 10% benefitted from one or more of the listed financial assistance programs.

Internships/Practica: Programs at Argosy University/Honolulu provide training in assessment and intervention through placement in community practica on O'ahu and throughout the Hawaiian Islands. Supervision is provided by licensed psychologists at these settings, and students are simultaneously enrolled in practicum seminars led by faculty with relevant expertise. These seminars combine teaching and case consultation to train students in specific clinical skills. Students are currently placed at settings that include university counseling centers, community mental health centers, outpatient treatment centers, residential adolescent treatment centers, day treatment and hospice programs, developmental evaluation clinics, substance abuse treatment centers, public and private schools, state courts, parole agencies, prisons, and psychiatric, medical, and veteran's hospitals. ASPP at AU/Hawaii maintains a predoctoral internship consortium for its Doctoral Program students that is listed with the Association of Psychology Postdoctoral and Internship Centers (APPIC). Both practicum and consortium internship sites serve client populations which are culturally diverse. For those doctoral students for whom a professional internship is required prior to graduation, 37 applied in 2003–2004. Of those who applied, 35 were placed in internships listed by the Association of Psychology Postdoctoral and Internship Programs (APPIC); 19 were placed in APA accredited internships.

Housing and Day Care: No on-campus housing is available. No on-campus day care facilities are available.

Employment of Department Graduates:

Master's Degree Graduates: Of those who graduated in the academic year 2003–2004, the following categories and numbers represent the post-graduate activities and employment of master's degree graduates: Enrolled in a psychology doctoral program (5), enrolled in another graduate/professional program (0), enrolled in a post-doctoral residency/fellowship (n/a), employed in independent practice (n/a), employed in an academic position at a university (0), employed in an academic position at a 2-year/4-year college (0), employed in other positions at a higher education institution (0), employed in a professional position in a school system (0), employed in business or industry (research/consulting) (0), employed in business or industry (management) (0), employed in a government agency (research) (0), employed in a government agency (professional services) (1), employed in a community mental health/counseling center (1), employed in a hospital/medical center (0), still seeking employment (0), other

employment position (0), do not know (0), total from the above (master's) (7).

Doctoral Degree Graduates: Of those who graduated in the academic year 2003–2004, the following categories and numbers represent the post-graduate activities and employment of doctoral degree graduates: Enrolled in a psychology doctoral program (n/a), enrolled in another graduate/professional program (0), enrolled in a post-doctoral residency/fellowship (3), employed in independent practice (1), employed in an academic position at a university (0), employed in an academic position at a 2-year/4-year college (0), employed in other positions at a higher education institution (1), employed in a professional position in a school system (2), employed in business or industry (research/consulting) (0), employed in business or industry (management) (0), employed in a government agency (research) (0), employed in a government agency (professional services) (2), employed in a community mental health/counseling center (1), employed in a hospital/medical center (2), still seeking employment (0), not seeking employment (0), other employment position (4), do not know (0), total from the above (doctoral) (16).

Additional Information:

Orientation, Objectives, and Emphasis of Department: The Argosy University/Honolulu Doctoral Program in Clinical Psychology (PsyD) prepares scholar-practitioners for both contemporary and emerging roles in professional psychology. The program supports the development of core competencies in psychological assessment, intervention, consultation/education, and management/supervision. Training emphasizes attention to human diversity and difference, self-reflexivity in clinical relationships, and critical evaluation and application of empirical literature to guide clinical decision making. Study programs may be selected in areas such as Diversity and Clinical Practice, Child and Family Clinical Practice, and Health Psychology. The Master of Arts in Clinical Psychology Program is designed to meet the needs of both those students seeking a terminal degree for work in the mental health field and those students who eventually plan to pursue a doctoral degree. The Clinical Respecialization Postdoctoral Program provides doctoral level psychologists with clinical courses and experiences. The Post-Doctoral Program in Clinical Psychopharmacology integrates relevant knowledge from medicine, pharmacology, nursing, and psychology. The Master of Arts in Professional Counseling - Marriage and Family Therapy Specialty Program is offered through weekend courses which are scheduled to allow concurrent employment; the format provides students an opportunity to continue professional development or to pursue a career change.

Information for Students With Physical Disabilities: See the following Web site for more information: http://www.argosyu.edu/.

Application Information:

Send to: Admissions Office, Argosy University / Honolulu, 400 ASB Tower, 1001 Bishop Street, Honolulu, HI 96813. Application available online. URL of online application: http://www.argosyu.edu/. Students are admitted in the Fall, application deadline January 15 and May; Spring, application deadline October 15. Professional Counseling: rolling admissions. *Fee:* $50.

Hawaii, University of
Department of Educational Psychology
College of Education
1776 University Avenue
Honolulu, HI 96822-2463
Telephone: (808) 956-7775
Fax: (808) 956-6615
E-mail: *edpsych@hawaii.edu*
Web: *http://www.hawaii.edu/edpsych/*

Department Information:
1965. Chairperson: Ann Bayer. Number of Faculty: total–full-time 7; women–full-time 5; minority–full-time 3.

Programs and Degrees Offered:
Listed in the following order: Program area, degree type (T if terminal Master's), number awarded 7/03–6/04. Educational Psychology (MEd) PhD (Doctor of Philosophy) 17, Educational Psychology PhD (Doctor of Philosophy) 0.

Student Applications/Admissions:
Student Applications
Educational Psychology (MEd) PhD (Doctor of Philosophy)—Applications 2004–2005, 44. Total applicants accepted 2004–2005, 19. Number enrolled (new admits only) 2004–2005 full-time, 7. Number enrolled (new admits only) 2004–2005 part-time, 12. Total enrolled 2004–2005 part-time, 48. The Median number of years required for completion of a degree are 2. The number of students enrolled full and part-time who were dismissed or voluntarily withdrew from this program area were 0. *Educational Psychology PhD (Doctor of Philosophy)*—Applications 2004–2005, 12. Total applicants accepted 2004–2005, 3. Total enrolled 2004–2005 part-time, 28. The Median number of years required for completion of a degree are 6. The number of students enrolled full and part-time who were dismissed or voluntarily withdrew from this program area were 0.

Admissions Requirements:
Scores: Entries appear in this order: required test or GPA, minimum score (if required), median score of students entering in 2003–2004. Master's Programs: last 2 years GPA 3.0, 3.23. Doctoral Programs: GRE-V no minimum stated, 640; GRE-Q no minimum stated, 630; GRE-V+Q no minimum stated; GRE-Analytical no minimum stated, 580; last 2 years GPA 3.0, 3.35.
Other Criteria: (importance of criteria rated low, medium, or high): GRE/MAT scores medium, research experience medium, work experience low, extracurricular activity medium, GPA medium, letters of recommendation medium, statement of goals and objectives medium. Criteria above pertain to the PhD program. The MEd program does not require the GRE or research experience.

Student Characteristics: The following represents characteristics of students in 2004–2005 in all graduate psychology programs in the department: Female–full-time 0, part-time 34; Male–full-time 0, part-time 14; African American/Black–full-time 0, part-time 0; Hispanic/Latino(a)–full-time 0, part-time 0; Asian/Pacific Islander–full-time 0, part-time 22; American Indian/Alaska Native–full-time 0, part-time 0; Caucasian–full-time 0, part-time 18;

Multi-ethnic–part-time 8; students subject to the Americans With Disabilities Act–full-time 0, part-time 0.

Financial Information/Assistance:
Tuition for Full-Time Study: *Master's:* State residents: per academic year $4,814, $193 per credit hour; Nonstate residents: per academic year $11,030, $452 per credit hour. *Doctoral:* State residents: per academic year $4,814, $193 per credit hour; Nonstate residents: per academic year $11,030, $452 per credit hour. See the following Web site for updates and changes in tuition costs: http://www.hawaii.edu/admrec/tuition.html.

Financial Assistance:
First Year Students: Teaching assistantships available for first-year. Average amount paid per academic year: $15,558. Average number of hours worked per week: 20. Apply by Auto w/ appl. Tuition remission given: full.
Advanced Students: No information provided.
Contact Information: Of all students currently enrolled full-time, 10% benefitted from one or more of the listed financial assistance programs. Application and information available online at: http://www.hawaii.edu/fas/.

Internships/Practica: Research and teaching internships are highly recommended for doctoral students; however, financial support continues to be very limited.

Housing and Day Care: On-campus housing is available. See the following Web site for more information: http://www.housing.hawaii.edu/. No on-campus day care facilities are available.

Employment of Department Graduates:
Master's Degree Graduates: Of those who graduated in the academic year 2003–2004, the following categories and numbers represent the post-graduate activities and employment of master's degree graduates: Enrolled in a post-doctoral residency/fellowship (n/a), employed in independent practice (n/a), total from the above (master's) (0).
Doctoral Degree Graduates: Of those who graduated in the academic year 2003–2004, the following categories and numbers represent the post-graduate activities and employment of doctoral degree graduates: Enrolled in a psychology doctoral program (n/a), total from the above (doctoral) (0).

Additional Information:
Orientation, Objectives, and Emphasis of Department: The primary objective of graduate training is the development of competent scholars in the discipline of educational psychology. Therefore, the faculty seeks students with research interests and abilities, independence of thought, and a willingness to actively participate in both formal and informal teaching and learning experiences. The students' efforts may be directed toward the attainment of the MEd or the PhD degree. Thesis (Plan A) and nonthesis (Plan B) options are available at the MEd level. Members of the faculty share a commitment to a model of graduate education that is humanistic and inquiry oriented. An extensive core of quantitative coursework—measurement, statistics, and research methodology—underlies most programs of study, especially at the doctoral level. In addition, core courses in human learning and development give the student a contextual framework within which inquiry methodologies are applied. The small size of the department ensures a high level of interaction among students and

faculty in and out of class. Working closely with the faculty, each student creates a degree plan uniquely suited to his or her academic goals. Interdisciplinary study is particularly encouraged.

Special Facilities or Resources: The college's Curriculum Research and Development Group affords opportunities for involvement in a wide variety of educational research and program evaluation activities, many of which are centered in the K-12 laboratory school on campus.

Information for Students With Physical Disabilities: See the following Web site for more information: http://www.catalog. hawaii.edu/general_information/student-life/support.htm.

Application Information:

Send to: Department of Educational Psychology, College of Education, 1776 University Avenue, Honolulu, HI 96822. Students are admitted in the Fall, application deadline February 1; Spring, application deadline September 1. PhD program has Fall admission only. Applications from foreign students have deadlines of January 15 and August 1 for Fall and Spring admission, respectively. *Fee:* $50. Application fee for non-U.S. Citizens is $50. Separate applications materials are submitted to the department and to the Graduate Division.

Hawaii, University of, Manoa
Department of Psychology
College of Social Sciences
2430 Campus Road
Honolulu, HI 96822-2294
Telephone: (808) 956-8414
Fax: (808) 956-4700
E-mail: *psych@hawaii.edu*
Web: *www.hawaii.edu/psychology*

Department Information:

1939. Chairperson: Stephen Haynes, PhD Number of Faculty: total–full-time 20, part-time 4; women–full-time 6, part-time 2; minority–full-time 3.

Programs and Degrees Offered:

Listed in the following order: Program area, degree type (T if terminal Master's), number awarded 7/03–6/04. Behavioral Neuroscience PhD (Doctor of Philosophy) 1, Clinical PhD (Doctor of Philosophy) 5, Community and Culture PhD (Doctor of Philosophy) 2, Developmental PhD (Doctor of Philosophy) 0, Experimental Psychopathology PhD (Doctor of Philosophy) 0, Marine Mammal Behavior & Biology PhD (Doctor of Philosophy) 1, Social-Personality PhD (Doctor of Philosophy) 2, Cognition PhD (Doctor of Philosophy) 1.

APA Accreditation: Clinical PhD (Doctor of Philosophy).

Student Applications/Admissions:

Student Applications

Behavioral Neuroscience PhD (Doctor of Philosophy)—Applications 2004–2005, 12. Total applicants accepted 2004–2005, 3. Number enrolled (new admits only) 2004–2005 full-time, 3. Openings 2005–2006, 3. The Median number of years required for completion of a degree are 6. The number of students enrolled full and part-time who were dismissed or voluntarily withdrew from this program area were 0. *Clinical PhD (Doctor of Philosophy)*—Applications 2004–2005, 155. Total applicants accepted 2004–2005, 8. Number enrolled (new admits only) 2004–2005 full-time, 8. Number enrolled (new admits only) 2004–2005 part-time, 0. Openings 2005–2006, 11. The Median number of years required for completion of a degree are 8. The number of students enrolled full and part-time who were dismissed or voluntarily withdrew from this program area were 0. *Community and Culture PhD (Doctor of Philosophy)*—Applications 2004–2005, 29. Total applicants accepted 2004–2005, 4. Number enrolled (new admits only) 2004–2005 full-time, 2. Openings 2005–2006, 4. The Median number of years required for completion of a degree are 5.75. The number of students enrolled full and part-time who were dismissed or voluntarily withdrew from this program area were 0. *Developmental PhD (Doctor of Philosophy)*—Applications 2004–2005, 13. Total applicants accepted 2004–2005, 1. Number enrolled (new admits only) 2004–2005 full-time, 1. Openings 2005–2006, 2. The number of students enrolled full and part-time who were dismissed or voluntarily withdrew from this program area were 0. *Experimental Psychopathology PhD (Doctor of Philosophy)*—Applications 2004–2005, 7. Total applicants accepted 2004–2005, 1. Number enrolled (new admits only) 2004–2005 full-time, 1. Openings 2005–2006, 2. The Median number of years required for completion of a degree are 6. The number of students enrolled full and part-time who were dismissed or voluntarily withdrew from this program area were 0. *Marine Mammal Behavior & Biology PhD (Doctor of Philosophy)*—Applications 2004–2005, 0. Total applicants accepted 2004–2005, 0. The Median number of years required for completion of a degree are 6. The number of students enrolled full and part-time who were dismissed or voluntarily withdrew from this program area were 0. *Social-Personality PhD (Doctor of Philosophy)*—Applications 2004–2005, 31. Total applicants accepted 2004–2005, 7. Number enrolled (new admits only) 2004–2005 full-time, 1. Openings 2005–2006, 6. The Median number of years required for completion of a degree are 6. The number of students enrolled full and part-time who were dismissed or voluntarily withdrew from this program area were 0. *Cognition PhD (Doctor of Philosophy)*—Applications 2004–2005, 8. Total applicants accepted 2004–2005, 1. Number enrolled (new admits only) 2004–2005 full-time, 1. Openings 2005–2006, 3. The number of students enrolled full and part-time who were dismissed or voluntarily withdrew from this program area were 0.

Admissions Requirements:

Scores: Entries appear in this order: required test or GPA, minimum score (if required), median score of students entering in 2003–2004. Master's Programs: GRE-V no minimum stated, 620; GRE-Q no minimum stated, 640; GRE-V+Q no minimum stated, 1260; GRE-Analytical no minimum stated, 5.5; overall undergraduate GPA 3.0, 3.5; last 2 years GPA 3.0. Doctoral Programs: GRE-V no minimum stated, 620; GRE-Q no minimum stated, 640; GRE-V+Q no minimum stated, 1260; GRE-Analytical no minimum stated, 5.5; overall undergraduate GPA 3.0, 3.5; last 2 years GPA 3.0. Numbers are same for MA and PhD. Most students are initially admitted into MA program and proceed to doctoral candidacy.

Other Criteria: (importance of criteria rated low, medium, or high): GRE/MAT scores high, research experience high, work experience low, extracurricular activity low, clinically related public service low, GPA high, letters of recommendation high, statement of goals and objectives high. For additional information on admission requirements, go to: www.hawaii.edu/psychology.

Student Characteristics: The following represents characteristics of students in 2004–2005 in all graduate psychology programs in the department: Female–full-time 70, part-time 0; Male–full-time 23, part-time 0; African American/Black–part-time 0; Hispanic/Latino(a)–part-time 0; Asian/Pacific Islander–part-time 0; American Indian/Alaska Native–part-time 0; Caucasian–full-time 0, part-time 0; students subject to the Americans With Disabilities Act–full-time 1, part-time 0.

Financial Information/Assistance:

Tuition for Full-Time Study: *Master's:* State residents: $193 per credit hour; Nonstate residents: $452 per credit hour. *Doctoral:* State residents: $193 per credit hour; Nonstate residents: $452 per credit hour. Tuition is subject to change. See the following Web site for updates and changes in tuition costs: http://www.hawaii.edu/admrec/tuition.html.

Financial Assistance:

First Year Students: Teaching assistantships available for first-year. Average amount paid per academic year: $13,296. Average number of hours worked per week: 20. Apply by January 1. Tuition remission given: full. Research assistantships available for first-year. Average amount paid per academic year: $13,296. Average number of hours worked per week: 20. Apply by January 1. Tuition remission given: full. Fellowships and scholarships available for first-year. Average amount paid per academic year: $0. Apply by January 1. Tuition remission given: full.

Advanced Students: Teaching assistantships available for advanced students. Average amount paid per academic year: $14,382. Average number of hours worked per week: 20. Apply by January 1. Tuition remission given: full. Research assistantships available for advanced students. Average amount paid per academic year: $14,382. Average number of hours worked per week: 20. Apply by January 1. Tuition remission given: full. Fellowships and scholarships available for advanced students. Average amount paid per academic year: $0. Apply by January 1. Tuition remission given: full.

Contact Information: Of all students currently enrolled full-time, 25% benefitted from one or more of the listed financial assistance programs. Application and information available online at: http://www.hawaii.edu/graduate/financial/html/assistantships.htm.

Internships/Practica: A minimum of 2 years of practica experience (18 to 20 hours per week) are required for all 2nd through 4th year graduate students in the clinical studies program. A variety of practica sites are available throughout the state and most include stipend support (average $14,000 per academic year). Sites include the department's Cognitive Behavior Therapy Clinic, community mental health outpatient centers, VA (including PTSD specialty clinics), mental health hospitals, child mental health institutions, UH counseling center, and state supported work with the seriously mentally disabled population. For those doctoral students for whom a professional internship is required

prior to graduation, 6 applied in 2003–2004. Of those who applied, 4 were placed in internships listed by the Association of Psychology Postdoctoral and Internship Programs (APPIC); 4 were placed in APA accredited internships.

Housing and Day Care: On-campus housing is available. See the following Web site for more information: http://www.housing.hawaii.edu/. On-campus day care facilities are available. See the following Web site for more information: http://www.hawaii.edu/osa/Childrens_Center.html.

Employment of Department Graduates:

Master's Degree Graduates: Of those who graduated in the academic year 2003–2004, the following categories and numbers represent the post-graduate activities and employment of master's degree graduates: Enrolled in a post-doctoral residency/fellowship (n/a), employed in independent practice (n/a), total from the above (master's) (0).

Doctoral Degree Graduates: Of those who graduated in the academic year 2003–2004, the following categories and numbers represent the post-graduate activities and employment of doctoral degree graduates: Enrolled in a psychology doctoral program (n/a), total from the above (doctoral) (0).

Additional Information:

Orientation, Objectives, and Emphasis of Department: The Department of Psychology's orientation is best characterized as a synthesis of biological, behavioral, and cognitive areas, with an overriding emphasis on empiricism (i.e., the study of psychological phenomena based on sound research findings). The graduate concentrations in clinical, developmental, community and culture, behavioral neuroscience, experimental psychopathology, social-personality, and cognition emphasize the development of research skills and knowledge that are applicable to a wide range of academic and applied settings. The clinical program adheres to the scientist-practitioner model of training, wherein research and clinical skills are equally emphasized. Research opportunities in all graduate concentrations are available. The faculty is particularly interested in admitting students who are interested in pursuing academically related careers.

Special Facilities or Resources: The Psychology Department is mainly housed in Gartley Hall, a historic campus building. Gartley Hall is devoted to facilities for office space, research, and teaching in psychology. Faculty members have specialized laboratories for research, including equipment to support cognitive, social and developmental work. Graduate students are assigned shared office space in Gartley Hall and have access to most departmental facilities. The computing facilities in the department and university are of a high standard, and the campus has good wireless internet coverage. Opportunities for study and research also exist elsewhere at the university and in the community. These include the Pacific Biosciences Research Center, the John A. Burns School of Medicine, the Center for Disability Studies, the Hawaii State Hospital at Kaneohe, Leahi Hospital, the State Departments of Health and Education, and the Osher Lifelong Learning Institute. Beyond the physical facilities available to the department is the unusual opportunity for research provided by the unique social and environmental structure of Hawaii. An important dimension is also provided by the East-West Center for Cultural Interchange, which provides fellowships for Asian and U.S. students and for senior scholars from mainland and foreign universities.

Information for Students With Physical Disabilities: See the following Web site for more information: http://www.hawaii.edu/osa/KOKUA.html.

Application Information:
Send to: Graduate Studies Chair, Department of Psychology, University of Hawaii at Manoa, 2430 Campus Road, Honolulu, HI 96822. Application available online. URL of online application: http://www.hawaii.edu/graduate/admissions/html/apply.htm. Students are admitted in the Fall, application deadline January 1. *Fee:* $50.

IDAHO

Idaho State University
Department of Psychology
Arts and Sciences
Box 8112
Pocatello, ID 83209
Telephone: (208) 282-2462
Fax: (208) 282-4832
E-mail: *turlkand@isu.edu*
Web: *http://www.isu.edu/departments/psych*

Department Information:
1968. Chairperson: Kandi Turley-Ames. Number of Faculty: total–full-time 11, part-time 7; women–full-time 6, part-time 2; minority–full-time 1, part-time 1; faculty subject to the Americans With Disabilities Act 1.

Programs and Degrees Offered:
Listed in the following order: Program area, degree type (T if terminal Master's), number awarded 7/03–6/04. Clinical PhD (Doctor of Philosophy) 2, Experimental-General MA/MS (Master of Arts/Science) (T) 2.

APA Accreditation: Clinical PhD (Doctor of Philosophy).

Student Applications/Admissions:
Student Applications
Clinical PhD (Doctor of Philosophy)—Applications 2004–2005, 53. Total applicants accepted 2004–2005, 14. Number enrolled (new admits only) 2004–2005 full-time, 7. Number enrolled (new admits only) 2004–2005 part-time, 0. Total enrolled 2004–2005 full-time, 23, part-time, 9. Openings 2005–2006, 6. The Median number of years required for completion of a degree are 6. The number of students enrolled full and part-time who were dismissed or voluntarily withdrew from this program area were 0. *Experimental-General MA/MS (Master of Arts/Science)*—Applications 2004–2005, 4. Total applicants accepted 2004–2005, 3. Number enrolled (new admits only) 2004–2005 full-time, 1. Number enrolled (new admits only) 2004–2005 part-time, 0. Total enrolled 2004–2005 full-time, 3, part-time, 4. Openings 2005–2006, 5. The Median number of years required for completion of a degree are 4. The number of students enrolled full and part-time who were dismissed or voluntarily withdrew from this program area were 0.

Admissions Requirements:
Scores: Entries appear in this order: required test or GPA, minimum score (if required), median score of students entering in 2003–2004. Master's Programs: GRE-V no minimum stated, 430; GRE-Q no minimum stated, 670; GRE-Analytical no minimum stated; GRE-Subject(Psych) no minimum stated, 550; last 2 years GPA 3.0, 3.9. GREs at the 50th percentile or higher are preferred on 2 of 3 aptitude tests and on the subject test in psychology. All applicants, however, must submit both the GRE aptitude test and the GRE Advanced Subject test in Psychology to be considered for admission. The GRE Analytical data are no longer available in the same

metric, and therefore, cannot be reported above. Doctoral Programs: GRE-V no minimum stated, 545; GRE-Q no minimum stated, 640; GRE-Analytical no minimum stated; GRE-Subject(Psych) no minimum stated, 625; last 2 years GPA 3.0, 3.9. GREs at the 50th percentile or higher are preferred on 2 of 3 aptitude tests and on the subject test in psychology. All applicants, however, must submit both the GRE aptitude test and the GRE Advanced Subject test in Psychology to be considered for admission. The GRE Analytical data are no longer reported in the same metric, and therefore, not reported above.
Other Criteria: (importance of criteria rated low, medium, or high): GRE/MAT scores medium, research experience medium, work experience low, extracurricular activity low, clinically related public service medium, GPA medium, letters of recommendation medium, interview medium, statement of goals and objectives medium, For the general-experimental MS program, clinically related public service is not relevant.

Student Characteristics: The following represents characteristics of students in 2004–2005 in all graduate psychology programs in the department: Female–full-time 20, part-time 9; Male–full-time 6, part-time 4; African American/Black–full-time 0, part-time 0; Hispanic/Latino(a)–full-time 0, part-time 1; Asian/Pacific Islander–full-time 1, part-time 0; American Indian/Alaska Native–full-time 0, part-time 0; Caucasian–full-time 25, part-time 12; Multi-ethnic–full-time 0, part-time 0; students subject to the Americans With Disabilities Act–full-time 0, part-time 0.

Financial Information/Assistance:
Tuition for Full-Time Study: *Master's:* State residents: per academic year $4,380, $219 per credit hour; Nonstate residents: per academic year $10,780, $321 per credit hour. *Doctoral:* State residents: per academic year $4,380, $219 per credit hour; Nonstate residents: per academic year $10,780, $321 per credit hour. Tuition is subject to change. See the following Web site for updates and changes in tuition costs: www.isu.edu/departments/areg/fees; mandatory $330 student health insurance premium per semester.

Financial Assistance:
First Year Students: Teaching assistantships available for first-year. Average amount paid per academic year: $10,807. Average number of hours worked per week: 15. Apply by March 1. Tuition remission given: full. Traineeships available for first-year. Average amount paid per academic year: $6,160. Average number of hours worked per week: 15. Apply by March 1. Tuition remission given: partial. Fellowships and scholarships available for first-year. Average amount paid per academic year: $1,800. Average number of hours worked per week: 0. Apply by March 1.
Advanced Students: Teaching assistantships available for advanced students. Average amount paid per academic year: $10,807. Average number of hours worked per week: 15. Apply by March 1. Tuition remission given: full. Traineeships available for advanced students. Average amount paid per academic year: $11,550. Average number of hours worked per week: 15. Apply by March 1. Tuition remission given: partial. Fellowships and scholarships available for advanced students. Average amount

paid per academic year: $1,800. Average number of hours worked per week: 0. Apply by March 1.

Contact Information: Of all students currently enrolled full-time, 100% benefitted from one or more of the listed financial assistance programs. Application and information available online at: Traineeships are on 11-month contracts.

Internships/Practica: Clinical practica are required for doctoral students admitted into the MS-PhD clinical program. First and second year students complete practica in the ISU Psychology Clinic under the supervision of clinical faculty. Third and fourth year students, however, often participate in community practica under the supervision of licensed psychologists employed by local mental health providers/agencies. One semester participation on an interdisciplinary evaluation team is also required. Seven clinical externships are also available for advanced students, providing stipends and supervised practice in applied settings. The average student entering APPIC internships from ISU has accumulated 1598 hours of supervised professional activities (median = 1482 hours). For those doctoral students for whom a professional internship is required prior to graduation, 1 applied in 2003–2004. Of those who applied, 1 was placed in an internship listed by the Association of Psychology Postdoctoral and Internship Programs (APPIC); 1 were placed in APA accredited internships.

Housing and Day Care: On-campus housing is available. See the following Web site for more information: www.isu.edu/housing/staff. University Housing Office (208) 282-2120. On-campus day care facilities are available. See the following Web site for more information: www.isu.edu/isutour/build-descrip/early-learning. Early Learning Center (208) 282-2769.

Employment of Department Graduates:
Master's Degree Graduates: Of those who graduated in the academic year 2003–2004, the following categories and numbers represent the post-graduate activities and employment of master's degree graduates: Enrolled in a psychology doctoral program (1), enrolled in a post-doctoral residency/fellowship (n/a), employed in independent practice (n/a), not seeking employment (1), total from the above (master's) (2).
Doctoral Degree Graduates: Of those who graduated in the academic year 2003–2004, the following categories and numbers represent the post-graduate activities and employment of doctoral degree graduates: Enrolled in a psychology doctoral program (n/a), employed in an academic position at a university (1), employed in a community mental health/counseling center (1), total from the above (doctoral) (2).

Additional Information:
Orientation, Objectives, and Emphasis of Department: The master of science program in general/experimental psychology provides students with an education in core areas of psychological science, such as personality/social, perception/cognitive, and sensory/physiological. This program of study, culminating in defense of a thesis, is designed to prepare students for doctoral work in psychology or careers in psychology or related fields that require mastery of the principles and methods of general/experimental psychology. The experimental MS in psychology is not intended to prepare students for careers in mental health. The mission of the ISU doctoral program is to train competent clinical psychologists who can apply and adapt general conceptual and technical skills in diverse regional and professional settings. An effective

clinical psychologist possesses a strong professional identity that includes: (a) a firm grounding in the science of psychology, and (b) knowledge of relevant theories and technical skills that aid in the amelioration of human suffering. Most importantly, a clinical psychologist understands the interactive relationship between science and practice. As such, the educational philosophy of the clinical training program at ISU is based on the traditional scientist-practitioner model of clinical training.

Special Facilities or Resources: The Psychology Department has office and laboratory space for all faculty. The ISU Psychology Clinic, housed in the same building, provides five individual therapy rooms, a child/family room, two testing rooms, and a group therapy room, all equipped with observation systems and videotape capabilities. Office space is provided to all graduate students. Computer access is available in offices, in the department, the clinic, and a university center located nearby. The university maintains an animal colony at which one psychology faculty member participates, an Office of Sponsored Programs (grant assistance), and an instructional technical resource center (Web site assistance).

Information for Students With Physical Disabilities: See the following Web site for more information: www.isu.edu/ada4isu/.

Application Information:
Send to: Admissions Committee, Psychology Dept., Box 8112, Idaho State University, Pocatello, ID 83209. Application available online. URL of online application: http://www.isu.edu/departments/graduate/graduate-application.html. Students are admitted in the Fall, application deadline January 15; Spring, application deadline November 1. For clinical students the deadline is January 15. Clinical students are only admitted to enter fall semester. For general MS students the fall admission deadline is March 1, and the spring admission deadline is November 1. Late applications will be considered for the general-experimental program. The online admission process is limited to the Graduate School application. All applicants must concurrently apply to the Psychology Department. *Fee:* $35.

Idaho, University of
Department of Psychology and Communication Studies
Letters, Arts, and Social Science
University of Idaho
Moscow, ID 83844-3043
Telephone: (208) 885-6324
Fax: (208) 885-7710
E-mail: cberreth@uidaho.edu
Web: http://www.class.uidaho.edu/psych/

Department Information:
Chairperson: Richard Reardon. Number of Faculty: total–full-time 12, part-time 2; women–full-time 2, part-time 1; minority–full-time 1.

Programs and Degrees Offered:
Listed in the following order: Program area, degree type (T if terminal Master's), number awarded 7/03–6/04. General Experimental MA/MS (Master of Arts/Science) (T) 0, Human Factors MA/MS (Master of Arts/Science) (T) 3, Industrial/Organizational

MA/MS (Master of Arts/Science) (T) 0, Neuroscience PhD (Doctor of Philosophy) 0.

Student Applications/Admissions:

Student Applications

General Experimental MA/MS (Master of Arts/Science)—Applications 2004–2005, 2. Total applicants accepted 2004–2005, 2. Number enrolled (new admits only) 2004–2005 full-time, 2. Total enrolled 2004–2005 full-time, 3. The Median number of years required for completion of a degree are 2. The number of students enrolled full and part-time who were dismissed or voluntarily withdrew from this program area were 0. *Human Factors MA/MS (Master of Arts/Science)*—Applications 2004–2005, 8. Total applicants accepted 2004–2005, 4. Number enrolled (new admits only) 2004–2005 full-time, 2. Number enrolled (new admits only) 2004–2005 part-time, 2. Total enrolled 2004–2005 full-time, 4, part-time, 20. Openings 2005–2006, 4. The Median number of years required for completion of a degree are 3. The number of students enrolled full and part-time who were dismissed or voluntarily withdrew from this program area were 0. *Industrial/Organizational MA/MS (Master of Arts/Science)*—Applications 2004–2005, 10. Total applicants accepted 2004–2005, 6. Number enrolled (new admits only) 2004–2005 full-time, 5. Openings 2005–2006, 4. The Median number of years required for completion of a degree are 2. The number of students enrolled full and part-time who were dismissed or voluntarily withdrew from this program area were 0. *Neuroscience PhD (Doctor of Philosophy)*—Applications 2004–2005, 2. Total applicants accepted 2004–2005, 1. Number enrolled (new admits only) 2004–2005 full-time, 1. Total enrolled 2004–2005 full-time, 1. Openings 2005–2006, 1. The Median number of years required for completion of a degree are 5. The number of students enrolled full and part-time who were dismissed or voluntarily withdrew from this program area were 0.

Admissions Requirements:

Scores: Entries appear in this order: required test or GPA, minimum score (if required), median score of students entering in 2003–2004. Master's Programs: GRE-V+Q 1000, 1120; overall undergraduate GPA 3.0, 3.5. Doctoral Programs: GRE-V+Q 1000.

Other Criteria: (importance of criteria rated low, medium, or high): GRE/MAT scores high, research experience high, work experience medium, extracurricular activity low, GPA high, letters of recommendation high, statement of goals and objectives high. Work experience more important for Human factors and I/O candidates than General Experimental candidates.

Student Characteristics: The following represents characteristics of students in 2004–2005 in all graduate psychology programs in the department: Female–full-time 7, part-time 10; Male–full-time 9, part-time 10; African American/Black–full-time 0, part-time 0; Hispanic/Latino(a)–full-time 1, part-time 0; Asian/Pacific Islander–full-time 1, part-time 0; American Indian/Alaska Native–full-time 0, part-time 0; Caucasian–full-time 14, part-time 20; Multi-ethnic–full-time 0, part-time 0; students subject to the Americans With Disabilities Act–full-time 0, part-time 0.

Financial Information/Assistance:

Tuition for Full-Time Study: *Master's:* State residents: per academic year $4,172, $205 per credit hour; Nonstate residents: per academic year $12,192, $328 per credit hour. Tuition is subject to change.

Financial Assistance:

First Year Students: Teaching assistantships available for first-year. Average amount paid per academic year: $4,875. Average number of hours worked per week: 10. Apply by March 1. Tuition remission given: partial. Research assistantships available for first-year. Average amount paid per academic year: $10,000. Average number of hours worked per week: 20. Apply by March 1. Tuition remission given: partial.

Advanced Students: Teaching assistantships available for advanced students. Average amount paid per academic year: $5,070. Average number of hours worked per week: 10. Apply by March 1. Tuition remission given: partial. Research assistantships available for advanced students. Average amount paid per academic year: $10,500. Average number of hours worked per week: 20. Apply by March 1. Tuition remission given: partial.

Contact Information: Of all students currently enrolled full-time, 100% benefitted from one or more of the listed financial assistance programs.

Internships/Practica: A few internships are available locally. Course credit is available in lieu of salary.

Housing and Day Care: On-campus housing is available. See the following Web site for more information: http://resnet.uidaho.edu/. On-campus day care facilities are available.

Employment of Department Graduates:

Master's Degree Graduates: Of those who graduated in the academic year 2003–2004, the following categories and numbers represent the post-graduate activities and employment of master's degree graduates: Enrolled in a psychology doctoral program (2), enrolled in another graduate/professional program (0), enrolled in a post-doctoral residency/fellowship (n/a), employed in independent practice (n/a), employed in an academic position at a university (0), employed in an academic position at a 2-year/4-year college (0), employed in other positions at a higher education institution (0), employed in a professional position in a school system (0), employed in business or industry (research/consulting) (3), employed in business or industry (management) (0), employed in a government agency (professional services) (1), employed in a community mental health/counseling center (0), employed in a hospital/medical center (0), other employment position (0), total from the above (master's) (6).

Doctoral Degree Graduates: Of those who graduated in the academic year 2003–2004, the following categories and numbers represent the post-graduate activities and employment of doctoral degree graduates: Enrolled in a psychology doctoral program (n/a), total from the above (doctoral) (0).

Additional Information:

Orientation, Objectives, and Emphasis of Department: In the Land Grant tradition of providing a "practical education," the Department of Psychology at the University of Idaho offers the MS degree in psychology with emphases in either Industrial/Organizational psychology (human resources, personnel, selection, organizational behavior) or Human Factors psychology (human technology interaction, ergonomics, human performance). The Department also provides off-campus and distance educational outreach by offering the MS in Psychology (human factors option only) through video and compressed video. The intent of both emphases is to develop knowledge and skills germane to a professional position. However, both programs also provide appropriate preparation for further graduate study. Thus, students are encouraged to develop analytical and problem solving skills that will serve them well in whatever they choose to do after graduation. Student placement figures show that most graduates have been very successful in obtaining positions in technical industries. The Department is small, but is able to address the broad needs of its students through working relationships with the College of Business and Economics, the College of Engineering, and the Department of Psychology at nearby (10 miles) Washington State University. The Department will consider, and has occasionally admitted, students for the general experimental MS. General experimental students typically use the program to prepare for admission to doctoral programs elsewhere. Starting in 2004, the Department began admitting students seeking a PhD degree in Neuroscience. This degree is interdisciplinary, and our primary partner is the Department of Biological Sciences.

Special Facilities or Resources: The Department is in temporary quarters, but is still able to provide approximately 2500 square feet of research space. Labs are equipped with up-to-date computers, graphics displays, and other apparatus. Research opportunities are available at remote sites, such as the Motion Analysis Lab at Shriners Hospital in Spokane, WA.

Application Information:
Send to: Graduate Admissions. Application available online. URL of online application: http://www.students.uidaho.edu/gradadmissions. Students are admitted in the Fall, application deadline March 1. Applications will be considered after the deadline, but availability of funding declines with passage of time. *Fee:* $30.

Adler School of Professional Psychology

Professional School
65 East Wacker Place - Suite 2100
Chicago, IL 60601-7203
Telephone: (312) 201-5900
Fax: (312) 201-5917
E-mail: *admissions@adler.edu*
Web: *http://www.adler.edu*

Department Information:
1952. Vice President of Academic Affairs: Frank Gruba-McCallister. Number of Faculty: total–full-time 19, part-time 5; women–full-time 7, part-time 1; minority–full-time 4, part-time 1; faculty subject to the Americans With Disabilities Act 3.

Programs and Degrees Offered:
Listed in the following order: Program area, degree type (T if terminal Master's), number awarded 7/03–6/04. Clinical Psychology PsyD (Doctor of Psychology) 29, Counseling Psychology MA/MS (Master of Arts/Science) (T) 81, Marriage and Family Counseling MA/MS (Master of Arts/Science) (T) 7, Substance Abuse Counseling Other 3, Art Therapy/Counseling MA/MS (Master of Arts/Science) (T) 6, Organizational MA/MS (Master of Arts/Science) (T) 3, Gerontological Psychology MA/MS (Master of Arts/Science) (T) 0, Police Psychology MA/MS (Master of Arts/Science) 0.

APA Accreditation: Clinical PsyD (Doctor of Psychology).

Student Applications/Admissions:
Student Applications
Clinical Psychology PsyD (Doctor of Psychology)—Applications 2004–2005, 194. Total applicants accepted 2004–2005, 70. Number enrolled (new admits only) 2004–2005 full-time, 64. Total enrolled 2004–2005 full-time, 140. Openings 2005–2006, 35. The Median number of years required for completion of a degree are 5. Counseling Psychology MA/MS (Master of Arts/Science)—Applications 2004–2005, 88. Total applicants accepted 2004–2005, 55. Total enrolled 2004–2005 full-time, 60. Openings 2005–2006, 45. The number of students enrolled full and part-time who were dismissed or voluntarily withdrew from this program area were 3. Marriage and Family Counseling MA/MS (Master of Arts/Science)—Applications 2004–2005, 10. Total applicants accepted 2004–2005, 10. Total enrolled 2004–2005 full-time, 26. Openings 2005–2006, 15. The number of students enrolled full and part-time, who were dismissed or voluntarily withdrew from this program area were 0. Substance Abuse Counseling Other—Applications 2004–2005, 5. Total applicants accepted 2004–2005, 4. Openings 2005–2006, 10. The Median number of years required for completion of a degree is 1. The number of students enrolled full and part-time who were dismissed or voluntarily withdrew from this program area were 0. Art Therapy/Counseling MA/MS (Master of Arts/Science)—Applications 2004–2005, 23. Total applicants accepted 2004–2005, 13. Number enrolled (new admits only) 2004–2005 full-time, 10. Total enrolled 2004–2005 full-time, 19, part-time, 15. Openings 2005–2006, 20. The number of students enrolled full and part-time who were dismissed or voluntarily withdrew from this program area were 0. Organizational MA/MS (Master of Arts/Science)—Applications 2004–2005, 4. Total applicants accepted 2004–2005, 4. Openings 2005–2006, 15. Gerontological Psychology MA/MS (Master of Arts/Science)—Applications 2004–2005, 3. Total applicants accepted 2004–2005, 3. Number enrolled (new admits only) 2004–2005 full-time, 2. Openings 2005–2006, 8. The number of students enrolled full and part-time who were dismissed or voluntarily withdrew from this program area were 0. Police Psychology MA/MS (Master of Arts/Science)—Applications 2004–2005, 32. Total applicants accepted 2004–2005, 32. Openings 2005–2006, 25. The Median number of years required for completion of a degree are 2.

Admissions Requirements:
Scores: Entries appear in this order: required test or GPA, minimum score (if required), median score of students entering in 2003–2004. Master's Programs: overall undergraduate GPA 3.00; last 2 years GPA 3.00; psychology GPA 3.00. Doctoral Programs: overall undergraduate GPA 3.25; last 2 years GPA 3.25; psychology GPA 3.25.

Other Criteria: (importance of criteria rated low, medium, or high): research experience low, work experience medium, extracurricular activity high, clinically related public service high, GPA high, letters of recommendation high, interview high, statement of goals and objectives high, mission consistant high. Masters in Art Therapy must also have 15 studio credits of art and present a portfolio at the time of interview. For additional information on admission requirements, go to: www.adler.edu.

Student Characteristics: The following represents characteristics of students in 2004–2005 in all graduate psychology programs in the department: Female–full-time 187, part-time 101; Male–full-time 63, part-time 29; African American/Black–full-time 30, part-time 12; Hispanic/Latino(a)–full-time 10, part-time 10; Asian/Pacific Islander–full-time 16, part-time 0; American Indian/Alaska Native–full-time 1, part-time 0; Caucasian–full-time 191, part-time 103; Multi-ethnic–full-time 7, part-time 0; students subject to the Americans With Disabilities Act–full-time 3, part-time 0.

Financial Information/Assistance:
Tuition for Full-Time Study: *Master's:* State residents: $456 per credit hour; Nonstate residents: $456 per credit hour. *Doctoral:* State residents: $456 per credit hour; Nonstate residents: $456 per credit hour. Tuition is subject to change. See the following Web site for updates and changes in tuition costs: www.adler.edu.

Financial Assistance:
First Year Students: Fellowships and scholarships available for first-year.
Advanced Students: Teaching assistantships available for advanced students. Average amount paid per academic year: $5,200. Average number of hours worked per week: 10. Apply by varies. Traineeships available for advanced students. Average

amount paid per academic year: $0. Average number of hours worked per week: 20. Fellowships and scholarships available for advanced students. Average amount paid per academic year: $5,000. Apply by June 1.

Contact Information: Of all students currently enrolled full-time, 6% benefitted from one or more of the listed financial assistance programs. Application and information available online at: www.adler.edu.

Internships/Practica: Practicum students, pre-doctoral interns, and post-doctoral interns have the opportunity to receive training at the school's licensed Psychological Services Center, which serves more than 250 clients weekly. Students under faculty supervision provide a wide range of services to the public including psychotherapy, psychological testing, art therapy, neurological assessments, forensic evaluations, support groups, and parenting classes. In addition to the counseling center on campus, students are placed in a number of satellite locations throughout the Chicago area in settings such as elementary and high schools, prisons, church counseling centers, transitional homes, and gerontological facilities. For those doctoral students for whom a professional internship is required prior to graduation, 35 applied in 2003–2004. Of those who applied, 15 were placed in internships listed by the Association of Psychology Postdoctoral and Internship Programs (APPIC); 9 were placed in APA accredited internships.

Housing and Day Care: No on-campus housing is available. No on-campus day care facilities are available.

Employment of Department Graduates:

Master's Degree Graduates: Of those who graduated in the academic year 2003–2004, the following categories and numbers represent the post-graduate activities and employment of master's degree graduates: Enrolled in a post-doctoral residency/fellowship (n/a), employed in independent practice (n/a), total from the above (master's) (0).

Doctoral Degree Graduates: Of those who graduated in the academic year 2003–2004, the following categories and numbers represent the post-graduate activities and employment of doctoral degree graduates: Enrolled in a psychology doctoral program (n/a), total from the above (doctoral) (0).

Additional Information:

Orientation, Objectives, and Emphasis of Department: The Adler School of Professional Psychology is a private, not-for-profit, institution of higher education. Founded in 1952, by Rudolf Dreikers, MD, The Adler School is the oldest psychology school in the country and the only accredited doctoral institution in the world having Alfred Adler's Individual Psychology as its major educational orientation. The reputation of the school has been built by an outstanding faculty who combine professional practice with their research, instructional, and clinical supervision responsibilities. Located in Chicago's Loop, the Adler School has an established reputation for providing educational programs, publications and clinical services. The student body comprises persons of diverse cultures, ages, educational backgrounds, and professional experiences. The Adler School continues to apply Adler's vision to today's social problems. The School's curricula prepare professionals to address social and global challenges as well as the needs of marginalized and underserved populations. Our on-campus, full service clinic offers an opportunity for students to train with faculty in a clinical setting. Degrees offered include

Masters of Arts in Counseling, Art Therapy, Marriage and Family Counseling, Organizational Psychology, Substance Abuse Counseling, Gerontological Psychology and a Doctor of Psychology (PsyD) as well as a number of specialization certificates such as clinical neuropsychology, substance abuse, clinical hypnosis and Adlerian psychology. The doctoral program is accredited by the American Psychological Association.

Special Facilities or Resources: An especially valuable asset to the programs offered is the school's licensed Psychological Services Center, which serves more than 250 clients weekly. Students under faculty supervision provide a wide range of services to the public including psychotherapy, psychological testing, art therapy, neuropsychological assessments, forensic evaluations, support groups, and parenting classes. Practicum students, pre-doctoral interns, and post-doctoral interns are involved at the counseling center on campus and at a number of satellite locations throughout the Chicago area in settings such as elementary and high schools, prisons, churches, transitional homes, and gerontological facilities. The Adler School of Professional Psychology is located in the center of downtown Chicago on the Chicago River. The School's location provides easy access to libraries and related facilities of some of the nation's best educational institutions, some with whom the library maintains cooperative lending agreements. The building is handicap accessible, available 365 days of the year, and has 24-hour security.

Information for Students With Physical Disabilities: See the following Web site for more information: www.adler.edu.

Application Information:
Send to: Office of Admissions, Adler School of Professional Psychology, 65 E. Wacker Place, Suite 2100, Chicago, IL 60601. Application available online. URL of online application: www.adler.edu. Students are admitted in the Fall, application deadline February 15; Winter, application deadline November 1. Programs have rolling admissions. PsyD deadline is February 15 for Fall and November 1 for Winter. All other programs are on rolling basis. *Fee:* $50. Documentation from social service agency documenting financial hardship. Fee is waived for McNair Scholars.

Argosy University/Illinois School of Professional Psychology, Chicago Campus
Clinical Psychology Department
20 South Clark Street, Third floor
Chicago, IL 60603
Telephone: (800) 626-4123
Fax: (312) 201-1907
E-mail: *adelaney@argosyu.edu*
Web: *http://www.argosyu.edu*

Department Information:
1976. Department Head of the Clinical Program: Annemarie Slobig. Number of Faculty: total–full-time 26, part-time 55; women–full-time 16, part-time 30; minority–full-time 8, part-time 6.

Programs and Degrees Offered:
Listed in the following order: Program area, degree type (T if terminal Master's), number awarded 7/03–6/04. Clinical MA/MS

(Master of Arts/Science) 46, Clinical Psychology Respecialization Diploma 1, Professional Counseling MA/MS (Master of Arts/ Science) 19, Clinical Psychology PsyD (Doctor of Psychology) 71.

APA Accreditation: Clinical PsyD (Doctor of Psychology).

Student Applications/Admissions:

Student Applications

Clinical MA/MS (Master of Arts/Science)—Applications 2004–2005, 165. Total applicants accepted 2004–2005, 97. Number enrolled (new admits only) 2004–2005 full-time, 50. Number enrolled (new admits only) 2004–2005 part-time, 4. Total enrolled 2004–2005 full-time, 95, part-time, 40. Openings 2005–2006, 45. The Median number of years required for completion of a degree are 2. The number of students enrolled full and part-time who were dismissed or voluntarily withdrew from this program area were 15. *Clinical Psychology Respecialization Diploma*—Applications 2004–2005, 0. Total applicants accepted 2004–2005, 0. Openings 2005–2006, 5. The Median number of years required for completion of a degree are 3. *Professional Counseling MA/MS (Master of Arts/Science)*—Applications 2004–2005, 60. Total applicants accepted 2004–2005, 41. Number enrolled (new admits only) 2004–2005 full-time, 38. Number enrolled (new admits only) 2004–2005 part-time, 3. Total enrolled 2004–2005 full-time, 81, part-time, 20. Openings 2005–2006, 40. The Median number of years required for completion of a degree are 2. The number of students enrolled full and part-time who were dismissed or voluntarily withdrew from this program area were 8. *Clinical Psychology PsyD (Doctor of Psychology)*—Applications 2004–2005, 275. Total applicants accepted 2004–2005, 174. Number enrolled (new admits only) 2004–2005 full-time, 62. Number enrolled (new admits only) 2004–2005 part-time, 23. Total enrolled 2004–2005 full-time, 280, part-time, 202. Openings 2005–2006, 80. The Median number of years required for completion of a degree are 5. The number of students enrolled full and part-time who were dismissed or voluntarily withdrew from this program area were 10.

Admissions Requirements:

Scores: Entries appear in this order: required test or GPA, minimum score (if required), median score of students entering in 2003–2004. Master's Programs: overall undergraduate GPA 3.0, 3.17; last 2 years GPA 3.0, 3.29; psychology GPA 3.0, 3.23. Doctoral Programs: overall undergraduate GPA 3.25, 3.38. For PsyD, require at least one of GPA categories to be 3.25 minimum.

Other Criteria: (importance of criteria rated low, medium, or high): research experience medium, work experience high, extracurricular activity medium, clinically related public service high, GPA high, letters of recommendation high, interview high, statement of goals and objectives high. MA Professional Counseling Program admits students after successful completion (including faculty review) of first four courses in program.

Student Characteristics: The following represents characteristics of students in 2004–2005 in all graduate psychology programs in the department: Female–full-time 395, part-time 129; Male–full-time 102, part-time 47; African American/Black–full-time 63, part-time 32; Hispanic/Latino(a)–full-time 28, part-time 9; Asian/Pacific Islander–full-time 29, part-time 9; American Indian/

Alaska Native–full-time 3, part-time 0; Caucasian–full-time 339, part-time 105; Multi-ethnic–full-time 35, part-time 21; students subject to the Americans With Disabilities Act–full-time 3, part-time 0.

Financial Information/Assistance:

Tuition for Full-Time Study: *Master's:* State residents: per academic year $18,981, $750 per credit hour. *Doctoral:* State residents: per academic year $22,500, $750 per credit hour. Tuition is subject to change.

Financial Assistance:

First Year Students: Fellowships and scholarships available for first-year. Average amount paid per academic year: $2,000. Average number of hours worked per week: 5. Apply by May 1. Tuition remission given: partial.

Advanced Students: Teaching assistantships available for advanced students. Average amount paid per academic year: $765. Average number of hours worked per week: 5. Apply by No Deadline. Tuition remission given: partial. Research assistantships available for advanced students. Average amount paid per academic year: $2,000. Average number of hours worked per week: 5. Apply by May 1. Tuition remission given: partial. Fellowships and scholarships available for advanced students. Average amount paid per academic year: $2,000. Average number of hours worked per week: 5. Apply by May 1. Tuition remission given: partial.

Contact Information: Of all students currently enrolled full-time, 7% benefitted from one or more of the listed financial assistance programs.

Internships/Practica: The School approves and monitors over 200 practica sites and assists students in locating and applying for internships across the country and in Canada. Both practica and internship sites offer a wide range of training populations and approaches to students in the school programs. For those doctoral students for whom a professional internship is required prior to graduation, 78 applied in 2003–2004. Of those who applied, 54 were placed in internships listed by the Association of Psychology Postdoctoral and Internship Programs (APPIC); 43 were placed in APA accredited internships.

Housing and Day Care: No on-campus housing is available. No on-campus day care facilities are available.

Employment of Department Graduates:

Master's Degree Graduates: Of those who graduated in the academic year 2003–2004, the following categories and numbers represent the post-graduate activities and employment of master's degree graduates: Enrolled in a post-doctoral residency/fellowship (n/a), employed in independent practice (n/a), total from the above (master's) (0).

Doctoral Degree Graduates: Of those who graduated in the academic year 2003–2004, the following categories and numbers represent the post-graduate activities and employment of doctoral degree graduates: Enrolled in a psychology doctoral program (n/a), total from the above (doctoral) (0).

Additional Information:

Orientation, Objectives, and Emphasis of Department: The ISPP/Chicago programs prepare students for contemporary practice through a clinically focused curriculum, taught by practitioner-scholar faculty, with a strong commitment to quality teaching and supervision. The current curricula have been structured to provide students with the fundamental knowledge and skills in psychological assessment and psychotherapy necessary to work with a wide range of traditional clinical populations. In addition, the required curricula include courses and perspectives designed to prepare students for emerging populations from diverse backgrounds and contemporary practice approaches now addressed by clinical psychology. PsyD students may satisfy basic requirements that address the learning of fundamental knowledge and competencies in intervention, assessment, population diversity, and professional practice areas through elective clusters that also provide choices that may conform to their individualized professional goals. As part of the commitment to providing both general and concentrated education and training for doctoral students, the PsyD program offers nine minors, or optional areas of electives choices for students wishing to focus their predoctoral studies in particular areas.

Special Facilities or Resources: The Illinois School of Professional Psychology offers pre-doctoral minors which support students' interests in the following areas: Child/Adolescent Psychology, Health Psychology, Family Psychology, Forensic Psychology, Psychoanalytic Psychology, Psychology of Maltreatment and Trauma, Client-Centered and Experiential Psychology and Psychology and Spirituality. The School has over 200 practicum sites available for student training in agencies, schools, clinics, hospitals, and practice organizations. Several faculty at the School have ongoing research projects in the following areas, in which students are invited to participate as they engage in their Clinical Research Projects: Effects of mindfulness meditation techniques on medical residents, intergenerational patterns related to sexual abuse, psychology of women, psychology in the schools, intergenerational cultural patterns in mother-daughter relationships, client-centered therapy with the severely mentally ill, personality disorders.

Application Information:
Send to: Admissions Department, Argosy University/Chicago Campus, (ISPP) 3rd Floor, 20 S. Clark Street, Chicago, IL 60603. Application available online. URL of online application: www.argosyu.edu. Students are admitted in the Fall, application deadline January 15; Spring, application deadline October 15; Summer, application deadline April 15. Professional Counseling, Spring deadline, October 15; Fall deadline, June 30; Summer deadline, February 28. *Fee:* $50.

Argosy University/Illinois School of Professional Psychology, Schaumburg Campus
Clinical Psychology
Illinois School of Professional Psychology
1000 Plaza Drive, Suite 100
Schaumburg, IL 60173
Telephone: (847) 290-7400
Fax: (574) 598-6158
E-mail: *jwasner@argosyu.edu*
Web: *http://www.argosyu.edu*

Department Information:
1994. Program Chair: Jim Wasner, PhD Number of Faculty: total–full-time 10, part-time 18; women–full-time 3, part-time 10; mi-nority–part-time 3; faculty subject to the Americans With Disabilities Act 1.

Programs and Degrees Offered:
Listed in the following order: Program area, degree type (T if terminal Master's), number awarded 7/03–6/04. Clinical Psychology MA/MS (Master of Arts/Science) (T) 12, Clinical Psychology PsyD (Doctor of Psychology) 23.

APA Accreditation: Clinical PsyD (Doctor of Psychology).

Student Applications/Admissions:
Student Applications
Clinical Psychology MA/MS (Master of Arts/Science)—Applications 2004–2005, 48. Total applicants accepted 2004–2005, 37. Number enrolled (new admits only) 2004–2005 full-time, 18. Number enrolled (new admits only) 2004–2005 part-time, 1. Total enrolled 2004–2005 full-time, 37, part-time, 3. Openings 2005–2006, 17. The Median number of years required for completion of a degree are 2. The number of students enrolled full and part-time who were dismissed or voluntarily withdrew from this program area were 3. *Clinical Psychology PsyD (Doctor of Psychology)*—Applications 2004–2005, 142. Total applicants accepted 2004–2005, 95. Number enrolled (new admits only) 2004–2005 full-time, 55. Number enrolled (new admits only) 2004–2005 part-time, 1. Total enrolled 2004–2005 full-time, 164, part-time, 5. Openings 2005–2006, 44. The Median number of years required for completion of a degree are 5. The number of students enrolled full and part-time who were dismissed or voluntarily withdrew from this program area were 8.

Admissions Requirements:
Scores: Entries appear in this order: required test or GPA, minimum score (if required), median score of students entering in 2003–2004. Master's Programs: overall undergraduate GPA 3.00, 3.18; last 2 years GPA 3.00, 3.36; psychology GPA 3.00, 3.26. Above requirements for the MA Clinical Program. Doctoral Programs: overall undergraduate GPA 3.25, 3.48; last 2 years GPA 3.25, 3.57; psychology GPA 3.25, 3.63. Students may be admitted into the doctoral program with only a BA/BS degree.
Other Criteria: (importance of criteria rated low, medium, or high): research experience low, work experience medium, extracurricular activity low, clinically related public service medium, GPA high, letters of recommendation high, interview high, statement of goals and objectives high. For additional information on admission requirements, go to: http://www.argosyu.edu.

Student Characteristics: The following represents characteristics of students in 2004–2005 in all graduate psychology programs in the department: Female–full-time 161, part-time 6; Male–full-time 40, part-time 2; African American/Black–full-time 19, part-time 2; Hispanic/Latino(a)–full-time 7, part-time 1; Asian/Pacific Islander–full-time 4, part-time 2; American Indian/Alaska Native–full-time 2, part-time 0; Caucasian–full-time 158, part-time 3; Multi-ethnic–full-time 11, part-time 0; students subject to the Americans With Disabilities Act–full-time 5, part-time 0.

Financial Information/Assistance:
Tuition for Full-Time Study: *Master's:* State residents: per academic year $18,000, $750 per credit hour; Nonstate residents: per

academic year $18,000, $750 per credit hour. *Doctoral:* State residents: per academic year $18,375, $750 per credit hour; Non-state residents: per academic year $18,375, $750 per credit hour. Tuition is subject to change.

Financial Assistance:

First Year Students: Teaching assistantships available for first-year. Average amount paid per academic year: $1,725. Average number of hours worked per week: 5. Apply by Varies. Traineeships available for first-year. Average amount paid per academic year: $2,000. Average number of hours worked per week: 7. Apply by Varies. Fellowships and scholarships available for first-year. Average amount paid per academic year: $2,000. Apply by Varies.

Advanced Students: Teaching assistantships available for advanced students. Average amount paid per academic year: $1,725. Average number of hours worked per week: 5. Apply by Varies. Traineeships available for advanced students. Average amount paid per academic year: $2,000. Average number of hours worked per week: 7. Apply by Varies. Fellowships and scholarships available for advanced students. Average amount paid per academic year: $2,000. Apply by Varies.

Contact Information: Of all students currently enrolled full-time, 25% benefitted from one or more of the listed financial assistance programs. Application and information available online at: http://www.argosyu.edu.

Internships/Practica: Clinical field training is a required component of all programs at the Argosy University-Illinois School of Professional Psychology/Schaumburg Campus and is a direct outgrowth of the practitioner emphasis of professional psychology. The school provides advisement and assistance in placing students in a wide variety of clinical sites, including hospitals, schools, mental health facilities, treatment centers, and social service agencies. The MA in clinical psychology requires a minimum of 750 hours of practicum experience. The PsyD program includes two years of practicum experience, including separate practica for diagnosis and assessment, and psychotherapy, with a minimum of 900 hours per year; plus an additional one-year full-time clinical internship. For those doctoral students for whom a professional internship is required prior to graduation, 22 applied in 2003–2004. Of those who applied, 18 were placed in internships listed by the Association of Psychology Postdoctoral and Internship Programs (APPIC); 9 were placed in APA accredited internships.

Housing and Day Care: No on-campus housing is available. No on-campus day care facilities are available.

Employment of Department Graduates:

Master's Degree Graduates: Of those who graduated in the academic year 2003–2004, the following categories and numbers represent the post-graduate activities and employment of master's degree graduates: Enrolled in a psychology doctoral program (9), enrolled in another graduate/professional program (0), enrolled in a post-doctoral residency/fellowship (n/a), employed in independent practice (n/a), employed in an academic position at a university (0), employed in an academic position at a 2-year/4-year college (0), employed in other positions at a higher education institution (0), employed in a professional position in a school system (0), employed in business or industry (research/consulting) (0), employed in business or industry (management) (0), employed in a government agency (research) (0), employed in a government agency (professional services) (0), employed in a

community mental health/counseling center (1), employed in a hospital/medical center (0), other employment position (1), do not know (1), total from the above (master's) (12).

Doctoral Degree Graduates: Of those who graduated in the academic year 2003–2004, the following categories and numbers represent the post-graduate activities and employment of doctoral degree graduates: Enrolled in a psychology doctoral program (n/a), enrolled in another graduate/professional program (0), enrolled in a post-doctoral residency/fellowship (5), employed in independent practice (3), employed in an academic position at a university (1), employed in an academic position at a 2-year/4-year college (1), employed in other positions at a higher education institution (1), employed in a professional position in a school system (2), employed in business or industry (research/consulting) (0), employed in business or industry (management) (0), employed in a government agency (research) (0), employed in a government agency (professional services) (0), employed in a community mental health/counseling center (4), employed in a hospital/medical center (3), other employment position (1), do not know (2), total from the above (doctoral) (23).

Additional Information:

Orientation, Objectives, and Emphasis of Department: The primary purpose of the Argosy University-Illinois School of Professional Psychology/Schaumburg Campus programs in Clinical Psychology is to educate and train students in the major aspects of clinical practice and prepare students for careers as practitioners. To ensure that students are prepared adequately, the curriculum integrates theory, training, research, and practice in preparing students to work with a wide range of populations in need of psychological services. Faculty are both scholars and practitioners and guide students through coursework and field experiences so that they might learn the work involved in professional psychology and understand how formal knowledge and practice operate to inform and enrich each other. The emphasis of the school is a scholar/practitioner orientation, with faculty skilled in all major theories of assessment and intervention. Working closely with faculty, students are provided with exposure to a variety of diagnostic and therapeutic approaches. Sensitivity to diverse populations, populations with specific needs, and multicultural issues are important components of all programs. The program also has emphasis areas in forensic psychology, clinical health psychology, child and family psychology, and multicultural psychology. A Forensic Certificate Program is available to both PsyD and post-graduate students.

Special Facilities or Resources: Faculty members actively encourage student involvement in research projects as a means of fostering mentoring relationships. The Argosy University-Illinois School of Professional Psychology/Schaumburg Campus has core faculty with extensive experience, enthusiasm, and expertise in the following areas: clinical research, forensic psychology, clinical health and rehabilitation psychology, brief therapy, cognitive-behavioral therapy, client-centered and experiential therapy, emotion focused therapy, severe psychopathology, substance abuse, addictive disorders, family and couples therapy, child development and therapy, psychodiagnostics, psychology of women, sexual orientation diversity, domestic violence, neuropsychology, clinical hypnosis, and psychoanalysis. In addition, the clinical training department has contracts with the Illinois Department of Correction at several correctional facilities to provide training in forensic psychology to practicum students, interns and post-doctoral fellows. These training contracts allow students to blend the knowledge attained in the classroom with professional on-site training in correctional and forensic psychology.

Information for Students With Physical Disabilities: See the following Web site for more information: http://www.argosyu.edu.

Application Information:
Send to: Jamal Scott, Director of Admissions, 1000 Plaza Drive, Suite 100, Schaumburg, IL 60173. Applicants may also email inquiries regarding admissions to: jscott@argosyu.edu. Application available online. URL of online application: www.argosyu.edu. Students are admitted in the Fall, application deadline May 15; Spring, application deadline November 15. Programs have rolling admissions. Deadlines may be extended dependent upon space availability. *Fee:* $50.

Benedictine University (2004 data)
Graduate Department of Clinical Psychology
College of Arts and Sciences
5700 College Road
Lisle, IL 60532
Telephone: (630) 829-6230
Fax: (630) 829-6231
E-mail: *esummers@ben.edu*
Web: *http://www.ben.edu*

Department Information:
1967. Chairperson: James F. Iaccino. Number of Faculty: total–full-time 4, part-time 2; women–full-time 3, part-time 2.

Programs and Degrees Offered:
Listed in the following order: Program area, degree type (T if terminal Master's), number awarded 7/03–6/04. MS in Clinical Psychology MA/MS (Master of Arts/Science) (T) 17.

Student Applications/Admissions:
Student Applications
MS in Clinical Psychology MA/MS *(Master of Arts/Science)*— Total applicants accepted 2004–2005, 16. Total enrolled 2004–2005 full-time, 14, part-time, 57. Openings 2005–2006, 25. The Median number of years required for completion of a degree are 3. The number of students enrolled full and part-time who were dismissed or voluntarily withdrew from this program area were 2.

Admissions Requirements:
Scores: Entries appear in this order: required test or GPA, minimum score (if required), median score of students entering in 2003–2004. Master's Programs: MAT no minimum stated; overall undergraduate GPA no minimum stated; last 2 years GPA no minimum stated.
Other Criteria: (importance of criteria rated low, medium, or high): GRE/MAT scores medium, research experience low, work experience medium, extracurricular activity medium, clinically related public service high, GPA medium, letters of recommendation high, interview high, statement of goals and objectives high. For additional information on admission requirements, go to: www.ben.edu/admissions/graduate.

Student Characteristics: The following represents characteristics of students in 2004–2005 in all graduate psychology programs in the department: Female–full-time 11, part-time 51; Male–full-time 3, part-time 6; African American/Black–full-time 1, part-time 4; Hispanic/Latino(a)–full-time 0, part-time 1; Asian/Pacific Islander–full-time 2, part-time 0; American Indian/Alaska Native–full-time 0, part-time 0; Caucasian–full-time 0, part-time 0; Multi-ethnic–full-time 0, part-time 0; students subject to the Americans With Disabilities Act–full-time 0, part-time 1.

Financial Information/Assistance:
Tuition for Full-Time Study: *Master's:* State residents: $410 per credit hour. See the following Web site for updates and changes in tuition costs: www.ben.edu/admissions/tuition_fees.asp.

Financial Assistance:
First Year Students: No information provided.
Advanced Students: No information provided.
Contact Information: Of all students currently enrolled full-time, 0% benefitted from one or more of the listed financial assistance programs. Application and information available online at: www.ben.edu/resources/financialaid/GradProgramTable03.htm.

Internships/Practica: The program has established relationships with over 100 mental health agencies, in-patient, out-patient, and social service agencies in the Chicago metropolitan area.

Housing and Day Care: On-campus housing is available. No child care facilities. We do have an apartment community on campus that has 1, 2, and 4 bedroom units. For further information contact (630) 829-6436, or visit the Web site for Founder's Woods: www.founderswoods.com. No on-campus day care facilities are available.

Employment of Department Graduates:
Master's Degree Graduates: Of those who graduated in the academic year 2003–2004, the following categories and numbers represent the post-graduate activities and employment of master's degree graduates: Enrolled in a post-doctoral residency/fellowship (n/a), employed in independent practice (n/a), total from the above (master's) (0).
Doctoral Degree Graduates: Of those who graduated in the academic year 2003–2004, the following categories and numbers represent the post-graduate activities and employment of doctoral degree graduates: Enrolled in a psychology doctoral program (n/a), total from the above (doctoral) (0).

Additional Information:
Orientation, Objectives, and Emphasis of Department: Our program is a rigorous one, offering two clinical internship experiences that more than meet the number of hours required for state licensure. Our program has a curriculum in place that satisfies all Licensed Clinical Professional Counselor (LCPC) licensure requirements. To date, more than 50% of our alumni have successfully passed the licensure exam. Our program is approved by the Illinois Department of Professional Regulation.

Special Facilities or Resources: The department has lab space provided for role play and audio and videotaping. The university opened the state-of-art Kindlon Hall of Learning in fall 2001. The building has a beautiful new library and teaching facilities.

Information for Students With Physical Disabilities: Contact tsonderby@ben.edu.

Application Information:
Send to: Graduate Admissions, Benedictine University, 5700 College Road, Lisle, IL 60532. Application available online. Students are admitted in the Fall, application deadline August; Winter, application deadline November; Spring, application deadline February; Summer, application deadline April. Programs have rolling admissions. *Fee:* $40. Application fee waived for Benedictine University, Illinois Benedictine College, or Street Procopius College alumni.

Chicago School of Professional Psychology
Professional School
325 N. Wells
Chicago, IL 60610
Telephone: (312) 329.6600
Fax: (312) 644.3333
E-mail: *admissions@csopp.edu*
Web: *http://www.csopp.edu*

Department Information:
1979. President: Michael Horowitz, PhD Number of Faculty: total–full-time 30, part-time 14; women–full-time 14, part-time 6; minority–full-time 7, part-time 1.

Programs and Degrees Offered:
Listed in the following order: Program area, degree type (T if terminal Master's), number awarded 7/03–6/04. Clinical PsyD (Doctor of Psychology) 53, Industrial & Organizational MA/MS (Master of Arts/Science) 18, Forensic Psychology MA/MS (Master of Arts/Science) (T) 9, Clinical, Counseling specialization MA/MS (Master of Arts/Science) (T) 73, Clinical, Applied Behavior Analysis specialization MA/MS (Master of Arts/Science) (T) 0, Business Psychology PsyD (Doctor of Psychology) 0.

APA Accreditation: Clinical PsyD (Doctor of Psychology).

Student Applications/Admissions:
Student Applications
Clinical PsyD (Doctor of Psychology)—Applications 2004–2005, 371. Total applicants accepted 2004–2005, 181. Number enrolled (new admits only) 2004–2005 full-time, 71. Number enrolled (new admits only) 2004–2005 part-time, 18. Total enrolled 2004–2005 full-time, 340, part-time, 85. Openings 2005–2006, 65. The Median number of years required for completion of a degree are 6. The number of students enrolled full and part-time who were dismissed or voluntarily withdrew from this program area were 3. *Industrial & Organizational MA/MS (Master of Arts/Science)*—Applications 2004–2005, 114. Total applicants accepted 2004–2005, 93. Number enrolled (new admits only) 2004–2005 full-time, 35. Number enrolled (new admits only) 2004–2005 part-time, 9. Total enrolled 2004–2005 full-time, 63, part-time, 16. Openings 2005–2006, 45. The Median number of years required for completion of a degree are 2. The number of students enrolled full and part-time who were dismissed or voluntarily withdrew from this program area were 2. *Forensic Psychology MA/MS (Master of Arts/Science)*—Applications 2004–2005, 245. Total applicants accepted 2004–2005, 176. Number enrolled (new admits only) 2004–2005 full-time, 68. Number enrolled (new admits only) 2004–2005 part-time, 17. Total enrolled 2004–2005 full-time, 131, part-time, 33. Openings 2005–2006, 75. The Median number of years required for completion of a degree are 2. The number of students enrolled full and part-time who were dismissed or voluntarily withdrew from this program area were 2. *Clinical, Counseling specialization MA/MS (Master of Arts/Science)*—Applications 2004–2005, 203. Total applicants accepted 2004–2005, 171. Number enrolled (new admits only) 2004–2005 full-time, 66. Number enrolled (new admits only) 2004–2005 part-time, 17. Total enrolled 2004–2005 full-time, 95, part-time, 24. Openings 2005–2006, 50. The Median number of years required for completion of a degree are 2. The number of students enrolled full and part-time who were dismissed or voluntarily withdrew from this program area were 0. *Clinical, Applied Behavior Analysis specialization MA/MS (Master of Arts/Science)*—Applications 2004–2005, 54. Total applicants accepted 2004–2005, 49. Number enrolled (new admits only) 2004–2005 full-time, 21. Number enrolled (new admits only) 2004–2005 part-time, 5. Total enrolled 2004–2005 full-time, 16, part-time, 4. Openings 2005–2006, 30. The Median number of years required for completion of a degree are 2. The number of students enrolled full and part-time who were dismissed or voluntarily withdrew from this program area were 6. *Business Psychology PsyD (Doctor of Psychology)*—Applications 2004–2005, 4. Total applicants accepted 2004–2005, 4. Number enrolled (new admits only) 2004–2005 full-time, 2. Number enrolled (new admits only) 2004–2005 part-time, 0. Openings 2005–2006, 30. The Median number of years required for completion of a degree are 5. The number of students enrolled full and part-time who were dismissed or voluntarily withdrew from this program area were 0.

Admissions Requirements:
Scores: Entries appear in this order: required test or GPA, minimum score (if required), median score of students entering in 2003–2004. Master's Programs: overall undergraduate GPA 3.0. Doctoral Programs: GRE-V no minimum stated; GRE-Q no minimum stated; GRE-V+Q no minimum stated; GRE-Analytical no minimum stated; overall undergraduate GPA 3.20.

Other Criteria: (importance of criteria rated low, medium, or high): GRE/MAT scores medium, research experience low, work experience high, extracurricular activity low, clinically related public service high, GPA high, letters of recommendation high, interview high, statement of goals and objectives medium. Clinical and Business PsyD Programs - Interviews are required and by invitation. For additional information on

243

admission requirements, go to: http://www.csopp.edu/admission.htm.

Student Characteristics: The following represents characteristics of students in 2004–2005 in all graduate psychology programs in the department: Female–full-time 518, part-time 130; Male–full-time 129, part-time 32; African American/Black–full-time 65, part-time 16; Hispanic/Latino(a)–full-time 39, part-time 10; Asian/Pacific Islander–full-time 26, part-time 6; American Indian/Alaska Native–full-time 0, part-time 0; Caucasian–full-time 517, part-time 130; students subject to the Americans With Disabilities Act–full-time 2, part-time 0.

Financial Information/Assistance:

Tuition for Full-Time Study: *Master's:* State residents: $615 per credit hour; Nonstate residents: $615 per credit hour. *Doctoral:* State residents: $730 per credit hour; Nonstate residents: $730 per credit hour. Tuition is subject to change. See the following Web site for updates and changes in tuition costs: http://www.csopp.edu/pages/finaid.html.

Financial Assistance:

First Year Students: Research assistantships available for first-year. Apply by March 1. Tuition remission given: partial. Fellowships and scholarships available for first-year. Apply by March 1. Tuition remission given: partial.

Advanced Students: Teaching assistantships available for advanced students. Apply by NA. Tuition remission given: partial. Research assistantships available for advanced students. Apply by NA. Tuition remission given: partial.

Contact Information: Of all students currently enrolled full-time, 30% benefitted from one or more of the listed financial assistance programs. Application and information available online at: http://www.csopp.edu/financialaid.htm.

Internships/Practica: Currently there are 240 Assessment and Therapy Practicum sites in the city and surrounding area at which our students train. For those doctoral students for whom a professional internship is required prior to graduation, 56 applied in 2003–2004. Of those who applied, 48 were placed in internships listed by the Association of Psychology Postdoctoral and Internship Programs (APPIC); 32 were placed in APA accredited internships.

Housing and Day Care: No on-campus housing is available. No on-campus day care facilities are available.

Employment of Department Graduates:

Master's Degree Graduates: Of those who graduated in the academic year 2003–2004, the following categories and numbers represent the post-graduate activities and employment of master's degree graduates: Enrolled in a post-doctoral residency/fellowship (n/a), employed in independent practice (n/a), total from the above (master's) (0).

Doctoral Degree Graduates: Of those who graduated in the academic year 2003–2004, the following categories and numbers represent the post-graduate activities and employment of doctoral degree graduates: Enrolled in a psychology doctoral program (n/a), total from the above (doctoral) (0).

Additional Information:

Orientation, Objectives, and Emphasis of Department: The Chicago School educates students to be competent practitioners by providing curricula that emphasize both a broad knowledge of the scientific and theoretical bases of psychology and the ability to apply that knowledge to specific employment situations. A student-centered environment, with personal advising and supervision provide opportunities for deepening awareness, knowledge, and skills. The programs are designed to integrate the study of cultural and individual differences and their impact in the clinical and work settings. The professional and ethical development of the student is of foremost concern throughout the educational program.

Special Facilities or Resources: The school has a Center for Multicultural and Diversity Studies that coordinates extracurricular learning activites and colloquia, sponsors a bi-annual Cultural Impact Conference and supports research opportunities with underserved populations in the community. The Center for Sustainable Solutions offers a variety of services ranging from leadership assessment and coaching to legal system advocacy. The Center provides precise support for organizations to leverage and enhance its resources from an operational, technological, and human asset perspective. The Centers provide hands-on experiences for students.

Application Information:

Send to: Magdalen Kellogg, Director of Admissions, Office of Admissions, Chicago School of Professional Psychology, 325 N. Wells, Chicago, IL 60610. Application available online. URL of online application: https://www.collegeapply.com/7885/index.html or https://www.collegeapply.com/7885M/index.html. Students are admitted in the Fall, application deadline March 1. Programs have rolling admissions. Early consideration deadline: PsyD programs January 15, MA programs February 15. General consideration deadline: PsyD programs March 1, MA programs April 1. *Fee:* $50.

Chicago, University of
Department of Psychology
5848 South University Avenue
Chicago, IL 60637
Telephone: (312) 702-8861
Fax: (312) 702-0886
E-mail: *marj@uchicago.edu*
Web: *http://psychology.uchicago.edu/*

Department Information:

1893. Chairperson: Howard Nusbaum. Number of Faculty: total–full-time 30; women–full-time 11.

Programs and Degrees Offered:

Listed in the following order: Program area, degree type (T if terminal Master's), number awarded 7/03–6/04. Language PhD (Doctor of Philosophy) 0, Social PhD (Doctor of Philosophy) 0, Perception PhD (Doctor of Philosophy), Cognition & Neuroscience Cogni PhD (Doctor of Philosophy) 1, Developmental PhD (Doctor of Philosophy) 4, Biopsychology PhD (Doctor of Philosophy) 0, Cogniton PhD (Doctor of Philosophy) 1.

Student Applications/Admissions:
Student Applications

Language PhD (Doctor of Philosophy)—Applications 2004–2005, 17. Total applicants accepted 2004–2005, 2. Number enrolled (new admits only) 2004–2005 full-time, 1. *Social PhD (Doctor of Philosophy)*—Applications 2004–2005, 99. Total applicants accepted 2004–2005, 9. Number enrolled (new admits only) 2004–2005 full-time, 2. Openings 2005–2006, 5. The number of students enrolled full and part-time who were dismissed or voluntarily withdrew from this program area were 0. *Perception PhD (Doctor of Philosophy)*—Applications 2004–2005, 5. Total applicants accepted 2004–2005, 2. Number enrolled (new admits only) 2004–2005 full-time, 1. Openings 2005–2006, 2. *Cognition & Neuroscience Cogni PhD (Doctor of Philosophy)*—The Median number of years required for completion of a degree are 4. The number of students enrolled full and part-time who were dismissed or voluntarily withdrew from this program area were 0. *Developmental PhD (Doctor of Philosophy)*—Applications 2004–2005, 24. Total applicants accepted 2004–2005, 6. Number enrolled (new admits only) 2004–2005 full-time, 3. Openings 2005–2006, 7. The Median number of years required for completion of a degree are 6. The number of students enrolled full and part-time who were dismissed or voluntarily withdrew from this program area were 0. *Biopsychology PhD (Doctor of Philosophy)*—Applications 2004–2005, 23. Total applicants accepted 2004–2005, 3. Number enrolled (new admits only) 2004–2005 full-time, 1. Total enrolled 2004–2005 full-time, 7. Openings 2005–2006, 2. The number of students enrolled full and part-time who were dismissed or voluntarily withdrew from this program area were 0. *Cogniton PhD (Doctor of Philosophy)*—Applications 2004–2005, 29. Total applicants accepted 2004–2005, 4. Number enrolled (new admits only) 2004–2005 full-time, 1. Total enrolled 2004–2005 full-time, 12. Openings 2005–2006, 10. The Median number of years required for completion of a degree are 6.

Admissions Requirements:

Scores: Entries appear in this order: required test or GPA, minimum score (if required), median score of students entering in 2003–2004. Doctoral Programs: GRE-V no minimum stated, 642; GRE-Q no minimum stated, 748; GRE-Analytical no minimum stated, 5; overall undergraduate GPA no minimum stated.

Other Criteria: (importance of criteria rated low, medium, or high): GRE/MAT scores high, research experience high, work experience low, extracurricular activity low, clinically related public service low, GPA high, letters of recommendation high, interview medium, statement of goals and objectives high.

Student Characteristics: The following represents characteristics of students in 2004–2005 in all graduate psychology programs in the department: Female–full-time 38, part-time 0; Male–full-time 20, part-time 0; African American/Black–full-time 3, part-time 0; Hispanic/Latino(a)–full-time 2, part-time 0; Asian/Pacific Islander–full-time 0, part-time 0; American Indian/Alaska Native–full-time 0, part-time 0; Caucasian–full-time 54, part-time 0; students subject to the Americans With Disabilities Act–full-time 0, part-time 0.

Financial Information/Assistance:

Tuition for Full-Time Study: *Doctoral:* State residents: per academic year $31,680; Nonstate residents: per academic year $31,680. Tuition is subject to change.

Financial Assistance:

First Year Students: Research assistantships available for first-year. Average number of hours worked per week: 15. Fellowships and scholarships available for first-year. Average amount paid per academic year: $15. Apply by December 28.

Advanced Students: Teaching assistantships available for advanced students. Average amount paid per academic year: $1,500. Average number of hours worked per week: 15. Tuition remission given: partial. Research assistantships available for advanced students. Average number of hours worked per week: 15. Tuition remission given: partial. Fellowships and scholarships available for advanced students. Average amount paid per academic year: $15. Apply by December 28. Tuition remission given: full.

Contact Information: Of all students currently enrolled full-time, 83% benefitted from one or more of the listed financial assistance programs.

Internships/Practica: No information provided.

Housing and Day Care: On-campus housing is available. No on-campus day care facilities are available.

Employment of Department Graduates:

Master's Degree Graduates: Of those who graduated in the academic year 2003–2004, the following categories and numbers represent the post-graduate activities and employment of master's degree graduates: Enrolled in a post-doctoral residency/fellowship (n/a), employed in independent practice (n/a), total from the above (master's) (0).

Doctoral Degree Graduates: Of those who graduated in the academic year 2003–2004, the following categories and numbers represent the post-graduate activities and employment of doctoral degree graduates: Enrolled in a psychology doctoral program (n/a), enrolled in a post-doctoral residency/fellowship (1), employed in an academic position at a university (1), employed in an academic position at a 2-year/4-year college (1), employed in business or industry (management) (2), total from the above (doctoral) (5).

Additional Information:

Orientation, Objectives, and Emphasis of Department: Our emphasis is on research. The department is made up of five different program areas. Consult our web page, http://psychology.uchicago.edu, for information on the Department and the five program areas. These programs are the Biopsychology Program, the Cognition Program, the Developmental Psychology Program, the Perception Program, and the Social Program.

Special Facilities or Resources: Facilities include a laboratory for conceptual psychology, an Audio Visual Laboratory, an Early Childhood Initiative, an Institute for Mind and Biology, and a wide range of laboratory facilities.

Application Information:

Send to: Social Science Division, Office of Admissions, Foster Hall 105, 1130 E. 59th Street, University of Chicago, Chicago, IL 60637. Students are admitted in the Fall, application deadline December 28. *Fee:* $55. In special circumstances, applicants may contact the Associate Dean of Students.

Concordia University

Department of Psychology
College of Arts and Sciences
7400 Augusta
River Forest, IL 60305
Telephone: (708) 771-8300
Fax: (708) 209-3167
E-mail: *grad.admission@curf.edu*
Web: *http://www.curf.edu*

Department Information:

Chairperson: Dr. Julia Rahn. Number of Faculty: total–full-time 9; women–full-time 4.

Programs and Degrees Offered:

Listed in the following order: Program area, degree type (T if terminal Master's), number awarded 7/03–6/04. Psychology MA/MS (Master of Arts/Science) 3, Community Counseling MA/MS (Master of Arts/Science) (T) 11, School Counseling MA/MS (Master of Arts/Science) 8.

Student Applications/Admissions:

Student Applications

Psychology MA/MS (*Master of Arts/Science*)—Applications 2004–2005, 4. Total applicants accepted 2004–2005, 4. The Median number of years required for completion of a degree are 2. *Community Counseling MA/MS* (*Master of Arts/Science*)—Applications 2004–2005, 28. Total applicants accepted 2004–2005, 22. The Median number of years required for completion of a degree are 3. *School Counseling MA/MS* (*Master of Arts/Science*)—Applications 2004–2005, 37. Total applicants accepted 2004–2005, 20. The Median number of years required for completion of a degree are 3.

Admissions Requirements:

Scores: Entries appear in this order: required test or GPA, minimum score (if required), median score of students entering in 2003–2004. Master's Programs: overall undergraduate GPA 2.85.

Other Criteria: (importance of criteria rated low, medium, or high): research experience medium, work experience medium, extracurricular activity low, clinically related public service medium, GPA high, letters of recommendation high, statement of goals and objectives high, counseling questions high.

Student Characteristics: The following represents characteristics of students in 2004–2005 in all graduate psychology programs in the department: Female–full-time 9, part-time 31; Male–full-time 1, part-time 9; Caucasian–full-time 0, part-time 0.

Financial Information/Assistance:

Tuition for Full-Time Study: *Master's:* State residents: $530 per credit hour; Nonstate residents: $530 per credit hour. Tuition is subject to change. See the following Web site for updates and changes in tuition costs: www.curf.edu.

Financial Assistance:

First Year Students: Research assistantships available for first-year. Average amount paid per academic year: $8,550. Average number of hours worked per week: 19. Apply by April 1.

Advanced Students: Research assistantships available for advanced students. Average amount paid per academic year: $8,550. Average number of hours worked per week: 19. Apply by April 1.

Contact Information: No information provided.

Internships/Practica: Internships and practica for the Community Counseling have been done in a variety of settings, including agencies, residential settings, social services agencies, hospitals, and religious organizations. School Counseling students have been placed in a variety of public and private, and urban and suburban schools. Our suburban location and solid relationships with many partners give our students choices from a wide variety of options.

Housing and Day Care: On-campus housing is available; 98% of housing facilities are undergraduate residence halls; 5–20 graduate students live on campus in residence halls. We have possible married housing but not family housing. Graduate students may apply for a private room and will be granted their request on a space-available basis. See our Web site at www.curf.edu/student_life/residence_halls/index.asp. On-campus day care facilities are available. Concordia offers on-campus child care for staff, students and faculty as well as community parents for full-time care. Students are encouraged to call the Early Childhood Center at (708) 209-3099 to see if space is available and to be put on a waiting list.

Employment of Department Graduates:

Master's Degree Graduates: Of those who graduated in the academic year 2003–2004, the following categories and numbers represent the post-graduate activities and employment of master's degree graduates: Enrolled in a post-doctoral residency/fellowship (n/a), employed in independent practice (n/a), total from the above (master's) (0).

Doctoral Degree Graduates: Of those who graduated in the academic year 2003–2004, the following categories and numbers represent the post-graduate activities and employment of doctoral degree graduates: Enrolled in a psychology doctoral program (n/a), total from the above (doctoral) (0).

Additional Information:

Orientation, Objectives, and Emphasis of Department: The Community Counseling program is designed to prepare graduates who are qualified to work as counselors in a variety of settings. Graduates from this program are trained to exhibit high standards of professional competence and ethical practice integrating theory, skills and values. The program requirements reflect current components of the Licensed Professional Counselor examination in the State of Illinois. Program objectives include 1) developing awareness and understanding of current and developing practice and professional issues relevant to the field of counseling, 2) developing awareness and understanding of multicultural issues and the current and evolving needs of our pluralistic society, and 3) demonstrating appropriate Christian values in their chosen profession.

Application Information:

Send to: Graduate Admission Office, Concordia University, 7400 Augusta, River Forest, IL 60305. An online application is also available at www.curf.edu. Students are admitted in the Fall, application deadline none; Spring, application deadline none; Summer, application deadline none. *Fee:* $0.

DePaul University

Department of Psychology
2219 North Kenmore - Room 420
Chicago, IL 60614
Telephone: (773) 325-7887
Fax: (773) 325-7888
E-mail: aknapp@depaul.edu
Web: http://www.depaul.edu/~psych/
dpupsy_graduatePrograms.html

Department Information:

1936. Chair: Christopher B. Keys, PhD. Number of Faculty: total–full-time 32, part-time 3; women–full-time 19, part-time 2; minority–full-time 7, part-time 1.

Programs and Degrees Offered:

Listed in the following order: Program area, degree type (T if terminal Master's), number awarded 7/03–6/04. Clinical PhD (Doctor of Philosophy) 7, Experimental PhD (Doctor of Philosophy) 0, Industrial/Organizational PhD (Doctor of Philosophy) 2, Community PhD (Doctor of Philosophy) 0, General Psychology MA/MS (Master of Arts/Science) (T) 6.

APA Accreditation: Clinical PhD (Doctor of Philosophy).

Student Applications/Admissions:

Student Applications

Clinical PhD (Doctor of Philosophy)—Applications 2004–2005, 256. Total applicants accepted 2004–2005, 10. Number enrolled (new admits only) 2004–2005 full-time, 8. Number enrolled (new admits only) 2004–2005 part-time, 0. Openings 2005–2006, 8. The Median number of years required for completion of a degree are 7. The number of students enrolled full and part-time who were dismissed or voluntarily withdrew from this program area were 2. *Experimental PhD (Doctor of Philosophy)*—Applications 2004–2005, 21. Total applicants accepted 2004–2005, 6. Number enrolled (new admits only) 2004–2005 full-time, 2. Number enrolled (new admits only) 2004–2005 part-time, 0. Openings 2005–2006, 3. The number of students enrolled full and part-time who were dismissed or voluntarily withdrew from this program area were 0. *Industrial/Organizational PhD (Doctor of Philosophy)*—Applications 2004–2005, 54. Total applicants accepted 2004–2005, 10. Number enrolled (new admits only) 2004–2005 full-time, 2. Number enrolled (new admits only) 2004–2005 part-time, 0. Openings 2005–2006, 4. The Median number of years required for completion of a degree are 5. The number of students enrolled full and part-time who were dismissed or voluntarily withdrew from this program area were 0. *Community PhD (Doctor of Philosophy)*—Applications 2004–2005, 24. Total applicants accepted 2004–2005, 4. Number enrolled (new admits only) 2004–2005 full-time, 2. Number enrolled (new admits only) 2004–2005 part-time, 0. Openings 2005–2006, 2. The number of students enrolled full and part-time who were dismissed or voluntarily withdrew from this program area were 1. *General Psychology MA/MS (Master of Arts/Science)*—Applications 2004–2005, 20. Total applicants accepted 2004–2005, 14.

Number enrolled (new admits only) 2004–2005 full-time, 9. Number enrolled (new admits only) 2004–2005 part-time, 0. Openings 2005–2006, 6. The Median number of years required for completion of a degree are 2. The number of students enrolled full and part-time who were dismissed or voluntarily withdrew from this program area were 0.

Admissions Requirements:

Scores: Entries appear in this order: required test or GPA, minimum score (if required), median score of students entering in 2003–2004. Master's Programs: GRE-V no minimum stated, 453; GRE-Q no minimum stated, 566; GRE-V+Q no minimum stated; GRE-Subject(Psych) no minimum stated, 556; overall undergraduate GPA no minimum stated, 3.44; psychology GPA no minimum stated. Doctoral Programs: GRE-V no minimum stated, 567; GRE-Q no minimum stated, 587; GRE-V+Q no minimum stated; GRE-Subject(Psych) no minimum stated, 624; overall undergraduate GPA no minimum stated, 3.76; psychology GPA no minimum stated.

Other Criteria: (importance of criteria rated low, medium, or high): GRE/MAT scores high, research experience high, work experience medium, extracurricular activity medium, clinically related public service medium, GPA high, letters of recommendation high, interview high, statement of goals and objectives high. Clinically related public service is not applicable for the Community, Experimental, I/O, or General MS programs. Only the Clinical and Community programs require interviews. For additional information on admission requirements, go to: www.depaul.edu/~psych/dpupsy_graduatePrograms.html.

Student Characteristics: The following represents characteristics of students in 2004–2005 in all graduate psychology programs in the department: Female–full-time 105, part-time 0; Male–full-time 51, part-time 0; African American/Black–full-time 22, part-time 0; Hispanic/Latino(a)–full-time 6, part-time 0; Asian/Pacific Islander–full-time 9, part-time 0; American Indian/Alaska Native–full-time 2, part-time 0; Caucasian–full-time 107, part-time 0; Multi-ethnic–full-time 10, part-time 0; students subject to the Americans With Disabilities Act–full-time 0, part-time 0.

Financial Information/Assistance:

Tuition for Full-Time Study: *Master's:* State residents: $407 per credit hour; Nonstate residents: $407 per credit hour. *Doctoral:* State residents: per academic year $14,652, $407 per credit hour; Nonstate residents: per academic year $14,652, $407 per credit hour. Tuition is subject to change. See the following Web site for updates and changes in tuition costs: www.depaul.edu/financial_aid/current/current_tuition.asp.

Financial Assistance:

First Year Students: Teaching assistantships available for first-year. Average amount paid per academic year: $7,660. Average number of hours worked per week: 16. Apply by January 10. Tuition remission given: full and partial. Research assistantships available for first-year. Average amount paid per academic year: $7,660. Average number of hours worked per week: 16. Apply by January 10. Tuition remission given: full and partial.

Advanced Students: Teaching assistantships available for advanced students. Average amount paid per academic year: $4,000. Average number of hours worked per week: 16. Apply by January 10. Tuition remission given: full and partial. Research assistantships available for advanced students. Average amount paid per academic year: $6,700. Average number of hours worked per week: 16. Apply by January 10. Tuition remission given: full and partial. Traineeships available for advanced students. Average amount paid per academic year: $8,000. Average number of hours worked per week: 16. Apply by March 1. Tuition remission given: full.

Contact Information: Of all students currently enrolled full-time, 73% benefitted from one or more of the listed financial assistance programs. Application and information available online at: www.depaul.edu/~psych/.

Internships/Practica: All of our clinical students are required to take a practicum course every quarter for the three years of their coursework. Though DePaul does not have an internship program, our students fulfill their internship requirement at top facilities in Chicago and across the nation. For those doctoral students for whom a professional internship is required prior to graduation, 4 applied in 2003–2004. Of those who applied, 4 were placed in internships listed by the Association of Psychology Postdoctoral and Internship Programs (APPIC); 4 were placed in APA accredited internships.

Housing and Day Care: On-campus housing is available. See the following Web site for more information: http://housing.depaul.edu/. No on-campus day care facilities are available.

Employment of Department Graduates:

Master's Degree Graduates: Of those who graduated in the academic year 2003–2004, the following categories and numbers represent the post-graduate activities and employment of master's degree graduates: Enrolled in a post-doctoral residency/fellowship (n/a), employed in independent practice (n/a), total from the above (master's) (0).

Doctoral Degree Graduates: Of those who graduated in the academic year 2003–2004, the following categories and numbers represent the post-graduate activities and employment of doctoral degree graduates: Enrolled in a psychology doctoral program (n/a), employed in an academic position at a university (1), employed in a professional position in a school system (1), employed in a community mental health/counseling center (1), employed in a hospital/medical center (1), total from the above (doctoral) (4).

Additional Information:

Orientation, Objectives, and Emphasis of Department: Our Clinical program has two separate tracks: Clinical-Child and Clinical-Community. When applying to the graduate program, students indicate their intent to focus on one track or the other. Students in the Clinical-Child track focus on treatment methods with children, family therapy, and behavior change. Research is developmental, systems-oriented, and applied in focus. Students in the Clinical-Community track are encouraged to be innovative designers of interventions, practitioners, and evaluators. Rather than emphasizing treatment, training focuses on health promotion, empowerment, and prevention within a range of populations. All students in the Clinical program do take some courses in both areas, and following admission into either track, students may combine elements of both areas of emphasis. The educational philosophy of the Department of Psychology is based upon a recognition of three components of modern psychology. The first of these is academic: the accumulated body of knowledge and theory relevant to the many areas of psychological study. The second is research: the methodologies and skills whereby the

science of psychology is advanced. The third is application: the use of psychology for individuals and society. A major function of the graduate curriculum in psychology is to bring to the student an awareness of the real unity of psychological study and practice, despite apparent diversity. The student must come to appreciate the fact that psychology is both a pure science and an applied science, and that these aspects are not mutually exclusive. This educational philosophy underlies all programs within the department. Each seeks to incorporate the three interrelated components of psychology at the graduate and professional levels; hence each program contains an academic, a research, and an applied component. It is the emphasis given to each component that is distinctive for each of our graduate programs. Students are strongly encouraged to work with faculty in research and tutorial settings. Doctoral candidates are given opportunities to gain teaching experience. Many students work in applied or research settings in the metropolitan Chicago area so that they can apply their graduate education to practical settings.

Special Facilities or Resources: Extensive facilities are available to support the graduate programs and research projects. We have state-of-the-art classrooms and computer facilities. The university also has a new library, recreation center, athletic facility, and student center. The community Mental Health Center, which is located in the same building as the psychology department, serves approximately 150,000 people. Our clinical students gain their initial practicum experiences in the Mental Health Center. In addition, the center serves as a venue for community and applied research. The university has prominent law and business colleges, which are well reputed in the midwestern business community and provide work opportunities for our experimental and industrial/organizational students. The department maintains an active network of our PhD graduates to help in obtaining jobs. There are many educational opportunities in this area, including colloquia, lectures, and regional and national organizations and conferences. We have an active graduate student organization that maintains contact with graduate students from other universities, providing opportunities to share educational experiences and recreational activities.

Information for Students With Physical Disabilities: See the following Web site for more information: http://studentaffairs.depaul.edu/studentdisabilities.html.

Application Information:
Send to: Department of Psychology, DePaul University, 2219 North Kenmore, Chicago, IL 60614-3504. Application available online. URL of online application: https://robin.depaul.edu/onlineapps/webapp/psychpass.asp. Students are admitted in the Fall, application deadline: Clinical Child and Clinical Community—December 15; Community—January 10; Industrial/Organizational—January 31; Experimental—February 15; General (MS)—May 15. *Fee:* $40. A student in need of financial aid may request a waiver of the application fee by submitting a personal letter requesting this consideration, a letter from the financial aid office of the institution attended outlining need, and official copies of financial aid transcripts. These materials must be sent with the application.

Eastern Illinois University

Department of Psychology
College of Sciences
Department of Psychology, Eastern Illinois University
Charleston, IL 61920
Telephone: (217) 581-2127
Fax: (217) 581-6764
E-mail: *cfjmh@eiu.edu*
Web: *http://psych.eiu.edu/*

Department Information:

1963. Chairperson: William A. Addison. Number of Faculty: total–full-time 22; women–full-time 7; minority–full-time 4.

Programs and Degrees Offered:

Listed in the following order: Program area, degree type (T if terminal Master's), number awarded 7/03–6/04. Clinical MA/MS (Master of Arts/Science) (T) 10, School Psychology Other 11.

Student Applications/Admissions:

Student Applications

Clinical MA/MS (Master of Arts/Science)—Applications 2004–2005, 35. Total applicants accepted 2004–2005, 15. Number enrolled (new admits only) 2004–2005 full-time, 8. Total enrolled 2004–2005 full-time, 18. Openings 2005–2006, 10. The Median number of years required for completion of a degree are 2. The number of students enrolled full and part-time who were dismissed or voluntarily withdrew from this program area were 1. *School Psychology Other*—Applications 2004–2005, 40. Total applicants accepted 2004–2005, 20. Number enrolled (new admits only) 2004–2005 full-time, 11. Openings 2005–2006, 10. The Median number of years required for completion of a degree are 3.

Admissions Requirements:

Scores: Entries appear in this order: required test or GPA, minimum score (if required), median score of students entering in 2003–2004. Master's Programs: overall undergraduate GPA 3.00, 3.44; last 2 years GPA no minimum stated; psychology GPA 3.25, 3.54.

Other Criteria: (importance of criteria rated low, medium, or high): GRE/MAT scores high, research experience medium, work experience medium, extracurricular activity medium, clinically related public service low, GPA high, letters of recommendation high, interview high, statement of goals and objectives high.

Student Characteristics: The following represents characteristics of students in 2004–2005 in all graduate psychology programs in the department: Female–full-time 38, part-time 0; Male–full-time 12, part-time 0; African American/Black–full-time 0, part-time 0; Hispanic/Latino(a)–full-time 2, part-time 0; Asian/Pacific Islander–full-time 3, part-time 0; American Indian/Alaska Native–full-time 0, part-time 0; Caucasian–full-time 44, part-time 0; Multi-ethnic–full-time 1, part-time 0.

Financial Information/Assistance:

Tuition for Full-Time Study: *Master's:* State residents: per academic year $3,520, $120 per credit hour; Nonstate residents: $342 per credit hour.

Financial Assistance:

First Year Students: Research assistantships available for first-year. Average amount paid per academic year: $6,600. Average number of hours worked per week: 16. Apply by March 1. Tuition remission given: full.

Advanced Students: Research assistantships available for advanced students. Average amount paid per academic year: $6,600. Average number of hours worked per week: 16. Apply by March 1.

Contact Information: Of all students currently enrolled full-time, 90% benefitted from one or more of the listed financial assistance programs.

Internships/Practica: A two-semester clinical internship in the second year of graduate study is required for the Master of Arts degree. The 12 semester hour internship includes a weekly seminar emphasizing treatment planning, ethical practice and case management, and requires 600 hours of supervised clinical practice in an approved community agency setting with regular on-campus clinical supervision coordinated with on-site supervision provided by an approved agency supervisor. Some internships carry a stipend and tuition waiver. During the two years of on-campus study required by the school psychology program, students participate in three practica. First-semester students complete a school-based practicum which is designed to orient them to the workings of the public education system. During the first semester of the second year students participate in an assessment practicum centered in the on-campus psychological assessment center. A field-based component of this practicum allows students to also complete assessment activities in a public school setting. During their last semester on campus, students participate in a field-based practicum devoted to enhancing counseling and consultation skills.

Housing and Day Care: On-campus housing is available. See the following Web site for more information: http://www.eiu.edu/~housing/. No on-campus day care facilities are available.

Employment of Department Graduates:

Master's Degree Graduates: Of those who graduated in the academic year 2003–2004, the following categories and numbers represent the post-graduate activities and employment of master's degree graduates: Enrolled in a post-doctoral residency/fellowship (n/a), employed in independent practice (n/a), employed in a professional position in a school system (10), employed in a community mental health/counseling center (10), total from the above (master's) (20).

Doctoral Degree Graduates: Of those who graduated in the academic year 2003–2004, the following categories and numbers represent the post-graduate activities and employment of doctoral degree graduates: Enrolled in a psychology doctoral program (n/a), total from the above (doctoral) (0).

Additional Information:

Orientation, Objectives, and Emphasis of Department: The Master of Arts degree in Clinical Psychology at Eastern Illinois University is designed to provide graduate training with a solid foundation in the art and science of clinical psychology. The program is a terminal master's degree training experience, which is approved by the Council of Applied Master's Programs in Psychology. The emphases highlight training and instruction in psychological interventions and therapy, assessment, and research. EIU graduates in Clinical Psychology possess a combination of skills in assessment, data management and analysis that uniquely position them amongst other master's level practitioners when it comes to assisting mental health organizations to meet the increasing demands of accurate evaluation, current, state-of-the-art programming, timely treatment protocols and accountability. The purpose of the school psychology program is to prepare students to deliver high quality services to students, parents, and professional personnel in public school settings. The program offers a generalist curriculum designed to allow students to develop the flexibility to practice in varied settings. Particular emphasis is placed on assessment, consultation, behavior management, and counseling. The importance of applied experiences is stressed.

Special Facilities or Resources: The Department of Psychology has a computer/statistics lab, an animal research lab as well as faculty directed research labs, one currently in use as setting for a NIH Grant. Training facilities include a three room suite used as a Psychology Assessment Center with one-way-mirror viewing for testing and interviews and videotaping facilities. A further Clinical/Observation research suite, with video and one-way mirror equipment is available for clinical training and supervised community services. Both applied programs enjoy viable cooperative agreements with a number of area educational, correctional and mental health agencies which serve as training and practica sites for graduate clinical experiences in addition to the internship sites.

Application Information:
Send to: Michael Havey, Coordinator, School Psychology Program; Anu Sharma, Coordinator, Graduate Program in Clinical Psychology, Department of Psychology, Eastern Illinois University, Charleston, IL 61920. Application available online. URL of online application: http://psych.eiu.edu/dept/grad.shtm. Students are admitted in the Fall, application deadline March 1. *Fee:* $30.

Governors State University
Division of Psychology and Counseling
College of Education
One University Parkway
University Park, IL 60466
Telephone: (708) 534-4991
Fax: (708) 534-8451
E-mail: *gsunow@govst.edu*
Web: *www.govst.edu*

Department Information:
1979. Interim Chairperson: Lonn Wolf. Number of Faculty: total–full-time 19, part-time 3; women–full-time 13, part-time 1; minority–full-time 7, part-time 1.

Programs and Degrees Offered:
Listed in the following order: Program area, degree type (T if terminal Master's), number awarded 7/03–6/04. Counseling MA/MS (Master of Arts/Science) (T) 32, school MA/MS (Master of Arts/Science) (T) 29, General MA/MS (Master of Arts/Science) (T) 29.

Student Applications/Admissions:
Student Applications
Counseling MA/MS (Master of Arts/Science)—Applications 2004–2005, 107. Total applicants accepted 2004–2005, 76. Number enrolled (new admits only) 2004–2005 full-time, 12. Number enrolled (new admits only) 2004–2005 part-time, 38. Total enrolled 2004–2005 full-time, 44, part-time, 137. Openings 2005–2006, 50. School MA/MS (Master of Arts/Science)—Total applicants accepted 2004–2005, 0. Number enrolled (new admits only) 2004–2005 full-time, 0. Number enrolled (new admits only) 2004–2005 part-time, 0. Total enrolled 2004–2005 full-time, 5, part-time, 23. General MA/MS (Master of Arts/Science)—Applications 2004–2005, 88. Total applicants accepted 2004–2005, 64. Number enrolled (new admits only) 2004–2005 full-time, 9. Number enrolled (new admits only) 2004–2005 part-time, 37. Total enrolled 2004–2005 full-time, 45, part-time, 82. Openings 2005–2006, 40. The Median number of years required for completion of a degree are 2.

Admissions Requirements:
Scores: Entries appear in this order: required test or GPA, minimum score (if required), median score of students entering in 2003–2004. Master's Programs: GRE-Subject(Psych) no minimum stated; overall undergraduate GPA 3.0; last 2 years GPA 3.0.
Other Criteria: (importance of criteria rated low, medium, or high): GRE/MAT scores low, work experience low, GPA medium, letters of recommendation medium, interview high, statement of goals and objectives high.

Student Characteristics: The following represents characteristics of students in 2004–2005 in all graduate psychology programs in the department: Female–full-time 87, part-time 192; Male–full-time 19, part-time 39; African American/Black–part-time 64; Hispanic/Latino(a)–part-time 22; Asian/Pacific Islander–part-time 4; American Indian/Alaska Native–part-time 2; Caucasian–full-time 0, part-time 217; Multi-ethnic–part-time 27.

Financial Information/Assistance:
Tuition for Full-Time Study: *Master's:* State residents: $143 per credit hour; Nonstate residents: $429 per credit hour. Tuition is subject to change.

Financial Assistance:
First Year Students: No information provided.
Advanced Students: Research assistantships available for advanced students. Tuition remission given: full.
Contact Information: Application and information available online at: http://www.govst.edu/financial/.

Internships/Practica: Counseling internships are readily available in a wide variety of community mental health and human service agencies.

Housing and Day Care: No on-campus housing is available. On-campus day care facilities are available. See the following Web site for more information: Child care only—http://www.govst.edu/users/gsas/child.htm.

Employment of Department Graduates:
Master's Degree Graduates: Of those who graduated in the academic year 2003–2004, the following categories and numbers

represent the post-graduate activities and employment of master's degree graduates: Enrolled in a post-doctoral residency/fellowship (n/a), employed in independent practice (n/a), total from the above (master's) (0).

Doctoral Degree Graduates: Of those who graduated in the academic year 2003–2004, the following categories and numbers represent the post-graduate activities and employment of doctoral degree graduates: Enrolled in a psychology doctoral program (n/a), total from the above (doctoral) (0).

Additional Information:

Orientation, Objectives, and Emphasis of Department: The graduate programs in the Division of Psychology and Counseling are appropriate for the returning adult student. Required classes are primarily offered during the early evening or evening hours. Most students work and are completing their program of studies on a part-time basis. Some classes are scheduled on the weekend.

Information for Students With Physical Disabilities: See the following Web site for more information: http://www.govst.edu/users/gsd/disability.htm.

Application Information:

Send to: The Office of Admissions, Governors State University, One University Parkway, University Park, IL 60466. Application available online. URL of online application: www.govst.edu. Students are admitted in the Fall, application deadline June 15; Winter, application deadline October 15; Spring, application deadline March 15. *Fee:* $25.

Illinois Institute of Technology
Institute of Psychology
3101 South Dearborn, LS-252
Chicago, IL 60616
Telephone: (312) 567-3500
Fax: (312) 567-3493
E-mail: *psychology@iit.edu*
Web: *http://www.iit.edu/colleges/psych/*

Department Information:

1929. Director: M. Ellen Mitchell. Number of Faculty: total–full-time 18, part-time 6; women–full-time 9, part-time 4; minority–full-time 3, part-time 1.

Programs and Degrees Offered:

Listed in the following order: Program area, degree type (T if terminal Master's), number awarded 7/03–6/04. Clinical PhD (Doctor of Philosophy) 15, Industrial/Organizational PhD (Doctor of Philosophy) 2, Personal and Human Resources Development MA/MS (Master of Arts/Science) (T) 5, Rehabilitation PhD (Doctor of Philosophy) 1, Rehabilitation Counseling MA/MS (Master of Arts/Science) (T) 6.

APA Accreditation: Clinical PhD (Doctor of Philosophy).

Student Applications/Admissions:

Student Applications

Clinical PhD (Doctor of Philosophy)—Applications 2004–2005, 76. Total applicants accepted 2004–2005, 22. Number enrolled (new admits only) 2004–2005 full-time, 13. Number enrolled (new admits only) 2004–2005 part-time, 0. Total enrolled 2004–2005 full-time, 55, part-time, 14. Openings 2005–2006, 13. *Industrial/Organizational PhD (Doctor of Philosophy)*—Applications 2004–2005, 72. Total applicants accepted 2004–2005, 35. Number enrolled (new admits only) 2004–2005 full-time, 8. Number enrolled (new admits only) 2004–2005 part-time, 0. Total enrolled 2004–2005 full-time, 37, part-time, 19. Openings 2005–2006, 12. *Personal and Human Resources Development (PHRD) MA/MS (Master of Arts/Science)*—Applications 2004–2005, 30. Total applicants accepted 2004–2005, 22. Number enrolled (new admits only) 2004–2005 full-time, 7. Number enrolled (new admits only) 2004–2005 part-time, 0. Openings 2005–2006, 20. The Median number of years required for completion of a degree are 2. *Rehabilitation PhD (Doctor of Philosophy)*—Applications 2004–2005, 0. Total applicants accepted 2004–2005, 0. Number enrolled (new admits only) 2004–2005 full-time, 0. Openings 2005–2006, 3. *Rehabilitation Counseling MA/MS (Master of Arts/Science)*—Applications 2004–2005, 27. Total applicants accepted 2004–2005, 22. Number enrolled (new admits only) 2004–2005 full-time, 13. Number enrolled (new admits only) 2004–2005 part-time, 0. Total enrolled 2004–2005 full-time, 25, part-time, 17. Openings 2005–2006, 30. The Median number of years required for completion of a degree are 2.

Admissions Requirements:

Scores: Entries appear in this order: required test or GPA, minimum score (if required), median score of students entering in 2003–2004. Master's Programs: GRE-V+Q 1000, 1200; overall undergraduate GPA 3.0, 3.6. The Master's in Rehabilitation does not require a GRE. Doctoral Programs: GRE-V+Q 1000, 1240; overall undergraduate GPA 3.0.

Other Criteria: (importance of criteria rated low, medium, or high): GRE/MAT scores high, research experience high, work experience high, extracurricular activity low, clinically related public service medium, GPA high, letters of recommendation high, interview high, statement of goals and objectives high, GPA and GRE are less important for MS programs; MS in rehabilitation does not require the GRE.

Student Characteristics: The following represents characteristics of students in 2004–2005 in all graduate psychology programs in the department: Female–full-time 100, part-time 35; Male–full-time 34, part-time 15; African American/Black–full-time 15, part-time 8; Hispanic/Latino(a)–full-time 5, part-time 3; Asian/Pacific Islander–full-time 14, part-time 0; American Indian/Alaska Native–full-time 0, part-time 0; Caucasian–full-time 95, part-time 38; Multi-ethnic–full-time 5, part-time 1; students subject to the Americans With Disabilities Act–full-time 4, part-time 1.

Financial Information/Assistance:

Tuition for Full-Time Study: *Master's:* State residents: $647 per credit hour; Nonstate residents: $647 per credit hour. *Doctoral:* State residents: $647 per credit hour; Nonstate residents: $647 per credit hour. Tuition is subject to change. See the following Web site for updates and changes in tuition costs: http://www.grad.iit.edu/admission/tuition.html.

Financial Assistance:

First Year Students: Fellowships and scholarships available for first-year. Tuition remission given: partial.

Advanced Students: Teaching assistantships available for advanced students. Average amount paid per academic year: $6,874. Average number of hours worked per week: 20. Apply by April 1. Tuition remission given: partial. Research assistantships available for advanced students. Average number of hours worked per week: 15. Apply by varies. Tuition remission given: partial. Fellowships and scholarships available for advanced students. Apply by varies. Tuition remission given: partial.

Contact Information: Of all students currently enrolled full-time, 30% benefitted from one or more of the listed financial assistance programs.

Internships/Practica: All students are required to complete field-work internships and practica. Experiences vary by program. As one of the largest cities in the United States, Chicago provides access to diverse practicum and internship sites. For those doctoral students for whom a professional internship is required prior to graduation, 9 applied in 2003–2004. Of those who applied, 9 were placed in internships listed by the Association of Psychology Postdoctoral and Internship Programs (APPIC); 9 were placed in APA accredited internships.

Housing and Day Care: There is on-campus housing but not child care; the housing office is accessible through the Web: www. iit.edu. No on-campus day care facilities are available.

Employment of Department Graduates:

Master's Degree Graduates: Of those who graduated in the academic year 2003–2004, the following categories and numbers represent the post-graduate activities and employment of master's degree graduates: Enrolled in a post-doctoral residency/fellowship (n/a), employed in independent practice (n/a), total from the above (master's) (0).

Doctoral Degree Graduates: Of those who graduated in the academic year 2003–2004, the following categories and numbers represent the post-graduate activities and employment of doctoral degree graduates: Enrolled in a psychology doctoral program (n/a), total from the above (doctoral) (0).

Additional Information:

Orientation, Objectives, and Emphasis of Department: The primary emphasis in the department is on a scientist-practitioner model of training. Our APA-approved clinical psychology program offers intensive clinical and research training with an emphasis on a cognitive theoretical framework, community involvement, and exposure to underserved populations. The MS in rehabilitation counseling prepares students to function as rehabilitation counselors for disabled persons. The PhD program in rehabilitation psychology prepares students for careers in rehabilitation education, research, and the practice of rehabilitation psychology. Our industrial/organizational program provides a solid scientific background as well as knowledge and expertise in personnel selection, evaluation, training and development, motivation, and organizational behavior.

Special Facilities or Resources: Facilities include laboratories for human behavior studies, psychophysiological research, infant and maternal attachment, and a testing and interviewing laboratory with attached one-way viewing rooms. Equipment includes programming apparatus for learning studies, specialized computer facilities, and videotaping and other audiovisual equipment. There are graduate student offices, a testing library of assessment equip-ment, and a student lounge. The Disabilities Resource Center is housed within psychology.

Information for Students With Physical Disabilities: Contact: kehr@iit.edu.

Application Information:
Send to: Admissions, Institute of Psychology. Application available online. URL of online application: http://www.grad.iit.edu/admission/apforms.html. Students are admitted in the Fall, application deadline January 15. Clinical deadline is January 15, I/O and PHRD deadline is February 15. Rehabilitation deadline is March 15. *Fee:* $40.

Illinois State University
Department of Psychology
College of Arts and Sciences
Campus Box 4620
Normal, IL 61790-4620
Telephone: (309) 438-8701
Fax: (309) 438-5789
E-mail: *psygrad@ilstu.edu*
Web: *http://www.psychology.ilstu.edu/*

Department Information:
1966. Chair: David Patton Barone. Number of Faculty: total–full-time 40, part-time 6; women–full-time 15, part-time 4; minority–full-time 4.

Programs and Degrees Offered:
Listed in the following order: Program area, degree type (T if terminal Master's), number awarded 7/03–6/04. Clinical-Counseling Psychology MA/MS (Master of Arts/Science) (T) 16, Developmental Psychology MA/MS (Master of Arts/Science) (T) 0, Cognitive & Behavioral Sciences MA/MS (Master of Arts/Science) (T) 4, School Psychology PhD (Doctor of Philosophy) 1, Quantitative MA/MS (Master of Arts/Science) (T) 1, Industrial/Organizational-Social MA/MS (Master of Arts/Science) (T) 6, School Psychology EdS (Education Specialist) 6.

APA Accreditation: School PhD (Doctor of Philosophy).

Student Applications/Admissions:
Student Applications
Clinical-Counseling Psychology MA/MS (Master of Arts/Science)—Applications 2004–2005, 69. Total applicants accepted 2004–2005, 17. Number enrolled (new admits only) 2004–2005 full-time, 12. Number enrolled (new admits only) 2004–2005 part-time, 0. Total enrolled 2004–2005 full-time, 23, part-time, 1. Openings 2005–2006, 12. The Median number of years required for completion of a degree are 2. The number of students enrolled full and part-time who were dismissed or voluntarily withdrew from this program area were 0. *Developmental Psychology MA/MS (Master of Arts/Science)*—Applications 2004–2005, 6. Total applicants accepted 2004–2005, 6. Number enrolled (new admits only) 2004–2005 full-time, 3. Number enrolled (new admits only) 2004–2005 part-time, 0. Total enrolled 2004–2005 full-time, 7, part-time, 4. Openings 2005–2006, 4. The Median number of years required for com-

pletion of a degree are 2. The number of students enrolled full and part-time who were dismissed or voluntarily withdrew from this program area were 1. *Cognitive & Behavioral Sciences MA/MS (Master of Arts/Science)*—Applications 2004–2005, 8. Total applicants accepted 2004–2005, 8. Number enrolled (new admits only) 2004–2005 full-time, 3. Number enrolled (new admits only) 2004–2005 part-time, 0. Total enrolled 2004–2005 full-time, 6, part-time, 4. Openings 2005–2006, 5. The Median number of years required for completion of a degree are 3. The number of students enrolled full and part-time who were dismissed or voluntarily withdrew from this program area were 0. *School Psychology PhD (Doctor of Philosophy)*—Applications 2004–2005, 18. Total applicants accepted 2004–2005, 13. Number enrolled (new admits only) 2004–2005 full-time, 5. Number enrolled (new admits only) 2004–2005 part-time, 0. Total enrolled 2004–2005 full-time, 27, part-time, 14. Openings 2005–2006, 7. The Median number of years required for completion of a degree are 6.6. The number of students enrolled full and part-time who were dismissed or voluntarily withdrew from this program area were 1. *Quantitative MA/MS (Master of Arts/Science)*—Applications 2004–2005, 4. Total applicants accepted 2004–2005, 4. Number enrolled (new admits only) 2004–2005 full-time, 4. Number enrolled (new admits only) 2004–2005 part-time, 0. Total enrolled 2004–2005 full-time, 8, part-time, 1. Openings 2005–2006, 2. The Median number of years required for completion of a degree are 2. The number of students enrolled full and part-time who were dismissed or voluntarily withdrew from this program area were 2. *Industrial/Organizational-Social MA/MS (Master of Arts/Science)*—Applications 2004–2005, 28. Total applicants accepted 2004–2005, 15. Number enrolled (new admits only) 2004–2005 full-time, 7. Number enrolled (new admits only) 2004–2005 part-time, 0. Total enrolled 2004–2005 full-time, 15, part-time, 8. Openings 2005–2006, 5. The Median number of years required for completion of a degree are 4. The number of students enrolled full and part-time who were dismissed or voluntarily withdrew from this program area were 0. *School Psychology EdS (Education Specialist)*—Applications 2004–2005, 56. Total applicants accepted 2004–2005, 10. Number enrolled (new admits only) 2004–2005 full-time, 8. Number enrolled (new admits only) 2004–2005 part-time, 0. Total enrolled 2004–2005 full-time, 21, part-time, 5. Openings 2005–2006, 7. The Median number of years required for completion of a degree are 3.2. The number of students enrolled full and part-time who were dismissed or voluntarily withdrew from this program area were 2.

Admissions Requirements:

Scores: Entries appear in this order: required test or GPA, minimum score (if required), median score of students entering in 2003–2004. Master's Programs: GRE-V no minimum stated, 500; GRE-Q no minimum stated, 570; GRE-V+Q no minimum stated; overall undergraduate GPA no minimum stated, 3.62; last 2 years GPA 3.0, 3.90; psychology GPA no minimum stated, 3.86. EdS/SSP degree figures have been included in the figures for the master's degree. Doctoral Programs: GRE-V no minimum stated, 510; GRE-Q no minimum stated, 630; GRE-V+Q no minimum stated; GRE-Subject(Psych) no minimum stated; overall undergraduate GPA no minimum stated, 3.76; last 2 years GPA 3.0, 3.66; psychology GPA no minimum stated, 3.82.

Other Criteria: (importance of criteria rated low, medium, or high): GRE/MAT scores medium, research experience medium, work experience medium, extracurricular activity low, clinically related public service medium, GPA high, letters of recommendation medium, interview medium, statement of goals and objectives medium. Interview required only for the PhD degree. For additional information on admission requirements, go to: www.psychology.ilstu.edu/grad/admreq.html.

Student Characteristics: The following represents characteristics of students in 2004–2005 in all graduate psychology programs in the department: Female–full-time 83, part-time 30; Male–full-time 24, part-time 10; African American/Black–full-time 2, part-time 2; Hispanic/Latino(a)–full-time 4, part-time 1; Asian/Pacific Islander–full-time 3, part-time 0; American Indian/Alaska Native–full-time 1, part-time 0; Caucasian–full-time 94, part-time 37; Multi-ethnic–full-time 0, part-time 0; students subject to the Americans With Disabilities Act–full-time 3, part-time 1.

Financial Information/Assistance:

Tuition for Full-Time Study: *Master's:* State residents: per academic year $3,480, $145 per credit hour; Nonstate residents: per academic year $7,272, $303 per credit hour. *Doctoral:* State residents: per academic year $3,770, $145 per credit hour; Nonstate residents: per academic year $7,878, $303 per credit hour. Tuition is subject to change. See the following Web site for updates and changes in tuition costs: http://www.comptroller.ilstu.edu/studentaccounts/tuitfees.stm.

Financial Assistance:

First Year Students: Teaching assistantships available for first-year. Average amount paid per academic year: $3,380. Average number of hours worked per week: 8. Apply by February 15. Tuition remission given: full. Research assistantships available for first-year. Average amount paid per academic year: $2,700. Average number of hours worked per week: 8. Apply by February 15. Tuition remission given: full. Traineeships available for first-year. Average amount paid per academic year: $5,412. Average number of hours worked per week: 16. Apply by February 15. Tuition remission given: full. Fellowships and scholarships available for first-year. Average amount paid per academic year: $3,500. Average number of hours worked per week: 0. Apply by March 15. Tuition remission given: full.

Advanced Students: Teaching assistantships available for advanced students. Average amount paid per academic year: $4,390. Average number of hours worked per week: 10. Apply by March 15. Tuition remission given: full. Research assistantships available for advanced students. Average amount paid per academic year: $0. Average number of hours worked per week: 0. Apply by March 15. Tuition remission given: full. Traineeships available for advanced students. Average amount paid per academic year: $5,365. Average number of hours worked per week: 14. Apply by March 15. Tuition remission given: full. Fellowships and scholarships available for advanced students. Average amount paid per academic year: $1,950. Average number of hours worked per week: 0. Apply by March 15.

Contact Information: Of all students currently enrolled full-time, 75% benefitted from one or more of the listed financial assistance programs. Application and information available online at: http://www.fao.ilstu.edu.

Internships/Practica: Students in the clinical-counseling master's program are provided with extensive supervised experience in practica in external mental health agencies. Students in the School Psychology specialist (SSP) and doctoral (PhD) programs participate from their first semester in supervised practica in public and private schools, Head Start centers, and the on-campus Psychological Services Center. Full-time internships are required for all school psychology students. For those doctoral students for whom a professional internship is required prior to graduation, 6 applied in 2003–2004. Of those who applied, 5 were placed in internships listed by the Association of Psychology Postdoctoral and Internship Programs (APPIC); 1 were placed in APA accredited internships.

Housing and Day Care: On-campus housing is available. See the following Web site for more information: Housing: www.uhs. ilstu.edu/;. On-campus day care facilities are available. See the following Web site for more information: child care: www.child carecenter.ilstu.edu/.

Employment of Department Graduates:

Master's Degree Graduates: Of those who graduated in the academic year 2003–2004, the following categories and numbers represent the post-graduate activities and employment of master's degree graduates: Enrolled in a psychology doctoral program (1), enrolled in another graduate/professional program (0), enrolled in a post-doctoral residency/fellowship (n/a), employed in independent practice (n/a), employed in an academic position at a university (1), employed in an academic position at a 2-year/4-year college (0), employed in other positions at a higher education institution (0), employed in a professional position in a school system (7), employed in business or industry (research/consulting) (5), employed in business or industry (management) (1), employed in a government agency (research) (0), employed in a government agency (professional services) (0), employed in a community mental health/counseling center (11), employed in a hospital/medical center (0), still seeking employment (2), other employment position (2), do not know (3), total from the above (master's) (33).

Doctoral Degree Graduates: Of those who graduated in the academic year 2003–2004, the following categories and numbers represent the post-graduate activities and employment of doctoral degree graduates: Enrolled in a psychology doctoral program (n/a), enrolled in another graduate/professional program (0), enrolled in a post-doctoral residency/fellowship (0), employed in independent practice (0), employed in an academic position at a university (0), employed in an academic position at a 2-year/4-year college (0), employed in other positions at a higher education institution (0), employed in a professional position in a school system (1), employed in business or industry (research/consulting) (0), employed in business or industry (management) (0), employed in a government agency (research) (0), employed in a government agency (professional services) (0), employed in a community mental health/counseling center (0), employed in a hospital/medical center (0), still seeking employment (0), other employment position (0), do not know (0), total from the above (doctoral) (1).

Additional Information:

Orientation, Objectives, and Emphasis of Department: The department provides training in professional areas supplemented by options in developmental, cognitive and behavioral sciences, and quantitative. Training in the professional areas takes advantage of the professional experience of the faculty in human service settings and industry so that instruction is both practical and theoretical. While comprehensive examinations provide an alternative, most programs require a master's thesis or doctoral dissertation.

Special Facilities or Resources: The department has computer facilities and human and animal laboratories. The department also has a Psychological Services Center for assessment and treatment of children and families. For the clinical-counseling and school psychology programs, a large number of community agencies participate in the one-year practicum (schools, hospitals, mental health centers, and alcohol and drug rehabilitation centers).

Information for Students With Physical Disabilities: See the following Web site for more information: www.ilstu.edu/depts/ disabilityconcerns; e-mail: ableisu@ilstu.edu.

Application Information:

Send to: Illinois State University, Department of Psychology, Graduate Psychology Programs, Campus Box 4620, Normal, IL 61790-4620. Students are admitted in the Fall, application deadline January 15. Fall and Summer application deadline for the PhD program in School Psychology only is January 15. Fall and Summer application deadline for SSP program in School Psychology only is February 1. Fall application deadline for all master's programs is February 10. *Fee:* $30. Fee waiver based on documented financial need, veteran service (active duty for one year or more), McNair, Project 1000 and Fulbright Scholar applicants.

Illinois, University of, Chicago
Department of Psychology (M/C 285)
Liberal Arts and Sciences
1007 West Harrison Street
Chicago, IL 60607-7137
Telephone: (312) 996-2434
Fax: (312) 413-4122
E-mail: *pschinfo@uic.edu*
Web: *http://www3.psch.uic.edu/*

Department Information:

1965. Chairperson: Gary E. Raney. Number of Faculty: total–full-time 24, part-time 8; women–full-time 8, part-time 3; minority–full-time 2, part-time 2.

Programs and Degrees Offered:

Listed in the following order: Program area, degree type (T if terminal Master's), number awarded 7/03–6/04. Behavioral Neuroscience PhD (Doctor of Philosophy) 0, Clinical PhD (Doctor of Philosophy) 3, Cognitive PhD (Doctor of Philosophy) 2, Community and Prevention Research PhD (Doctor of Philosophy) 1, Social and Personality PhD (Doctor of Philosophy) 3.

APA Accreditation: Clinical PhD (Doctor of Philosophy).

Student Applications/Admissions:

Student Applications

Behavioral Neuroscience PhD (Doctor of Philosophy)—Applications 2004–2005, 11. Total applicants accepted 2004–2005,

4. Number enrolled (new admits only) 2004–2005 full-time, 2. Total enrolled 2004–2005 full-time, 7. Openings 2005–2006, 4. The number of students enrolled full and part-time who were dismissed or voluntarily withdrew from this program area were 1. *Clinical PhD (Doctor of Philosophy)*—Applications 2004–2005, 222. Total applicants accepted 2004–2005, 9. Number enrolled (new admits only) 2004–2005 full-time, 5. Total enrolled 2004–2005 full-time, 42. Openings 2005–2006, 5. The Median number of years required for completion of a degree are 7. The number of students enrolled full and part-time who were dismissed or voluntarily withdrew from this program area were 2. *Cognitive PhD (Doctor of Philosophy)*—Applications 2004–2005, 15. Total applicants accepted 2004–2005, 6. Number enrolled (new admits only) 2004–2005 full-time, 4. Total enrolled 2004–2005 full-time, 19. Openings 2005–2006, 4. The Median number of years required for completion of a degree are 6. The number of students enrolled full and part-time who were dismissed or voluntarily withdrew from this program area were 2. *Community and Prevention Research PhD (Doctor of Philosophy)*—Applications 2004–2005, 50. Total applicants accepted 2004–2005, 5. Number enrolled (new admits only) 2004–2005 full-time, 3. Total enrolled 2004–2005 full-time, 30. Openings 2005–2006, 5. The Median number of years required for completion of a degree are 7. The number of students enrolled full and part-time who were dismissed or voluntarily withdrew from this program area were 2. *Social and Personality PhD (Doctor of Philosophy)*—Applications 2004–2005, 57. Total applicants accepted 2004–2005, 10. Number enrolled (new admits only) 2004–2005 full-time, 5. Total enrolled 2004–2005 full-time, 21. Openings 2005–2006, 5. The Median number of years required for completion of a degree are 6. The number of students enrolled full and part-time who were dismissed or voluntarily withdrew from this program area were 1.

Admissions Requirements:

Scores: Entries appear in this order: required test or GPA, minimum score (if required), median score of students entering in 2003–2004. Doctoral Programs: GRE-V no minimum stated, 570; GRE-Q no minimum stated, 670; GRE-Analytical no minimum stated, 730; GRE-Subject(Psych) no minimum stated, 630; last 2 years GPA 3.2, 3.8.

Other Criteria: (importance of criteria rated low, medium, or high): GRE/MAT scores medium, research experience high, work experience low, extracurricular activity medium, clinically related public service low, GPA high, letters of recommendation high, interview high, statement of goals and objectives high, fit with faculty research high. For additional information on admission requirements, go to: www.uic.edu/depts/psch.

Student Characteristics: The following represents characteristics of students in 2004–2005 in all graduate psychology programs in the department: Female–full-time 87, part-time 0; Male–full-time 32, part-time 0; African American/Black–full-time 10, part-time 0; Hispanic/Latino(a)–full-time 2, part-time 0; Asian/Pacific Islander–full-time 12, part-time 0; American Indian/Alaska Native–full-time 2, part-time 0; Caucasian–full-time 93, part-time 0; Multi-ethnic–full-time 0, part-time 0; students subject to the Americans With Disabilities Act–full-time 3, part-time 0.

Financial Information/Assistance:

Tuition for Full-Time Study: *Doctoral:* State residents: per academic year $6,100; Nonstate residents: per academic year $17,314. Tuition is subject to change. See the following Web site for updates and changes in tuition costs: www.uic.edu/depts/oar/rr/tuition.shtml.

Financial Assistance:

First Year Students: Teaching assistantships available for first-year. Average amount paid per academic year: $12,000. Average number of hours worked per week: 18. Apply by January 1. Tuition remission given: full. Research assistantships available for first-year. Average amount paid per academic year: $12,000. Average number of hours worked per week: 18. Apply by January 1. Tuition remission given: full. Traineeships available for first-year. Average amount paid per academic year: $12,000. Average number of hours worked per week: 0. Apply by January 1. Tuition remission given: full. Fellowships and scholarships available for first-year. Average amount paid per academic year: $18,000. Average number of hours worked per week: 0. Apply by January 1. Tuition remission given: full.

Advanced Students: Teaching assistantships available for advanced students. Average amount paid per academic year: $13,500. Average number of hours worked per week: 18. Tuition remission given: full. Research assistantships available for advanced students. Average amount paid per academic year: $13,500. Average number of hours worked per week: 18. Tuition remission given: full. Traineeships available for advanced students. Average amount paid per academic year: $13,500. Average number of hours worked per week: 0. Tuition remission given: full. Fellowships and scholarships available for advanced students. Average amount paid per academic year: $18,000. Average number of hours worked per week: 0. Tuition remission given: full.

Contact Information: Of all students currently enrolled full-time, 100% benefitted from one or more of the listed financial assistance programs. Application and information available online at: http://www3.psch.uic.edu/.

Internships/Practica: Access to a wide variety of practicum and research sites is available to advanced students. These include the UIC Counseling Service, Cook County Hospital, Rush-Presbyterian-Street Lukes Medical Center, the Institute for Juvenile Research, the Institute on Disabilities and Human Development, several Veterans Administration hospitals and mental health clinics, schools, and diverse community agencies throughout the Chicago area, in addition to our own Office of Applied Psychology. For those doctoral students for whom a professional internship is required prior to graduation, 2 applied in 2003–2004. Of those who applied, 2 were placed in internships listed by the Association of Psychology Postdoctoral and Internship Programs (APPIC); 2 were placed in APA accredited internships.

Housing and Day Care: On-campus housing is available. See the following Web site for more information: www.housing.uic.edu. On-campus day care facilities are available. See the following Web site for more information: www.uic.edu/depts/children.

Employment of Department Graduates:

Master's Degree Graduates: Of those who graduated in the academic year 2003–2004, the following categories and numbers represent the post-graduate activities and employment of master's degree graduates: Enrolled in a post-doctoral residency/fellowship

(n/a), employed in independent practice (n/a), total from the above (master's) (0).

Doctoral Degree Graduates: Of those who graduated in the academic year 2003–2004, the following categories and numbers represent the post-graduate activities and employment of doctoral degree graduates: Enrolled in a psychology doctoral program (n/a), enrolled in a post-doctoral residency/fellowship (3), employed in an academic position at a university (1), employed in business or industry (research/consulting) (2), employed in a government agency (research) (1), employed in a hospital/medical center (1), do not know (1), total from the above (doctoral) (9).

Additional Information:

Orientation, Objectives, and Emphasis of Department: The goal of the psychology department's doctoral program is to educate scholars and researchers who will contribute to the growth of psychological knowledge whether they work in academic, applied, or policy settings. Within the framework of satisfying the requirements of a major division and a minor, the department encourages students in consultation with their advisors to construct programs individually tailored to their research interests. The psychology department has more than 30 faculty and over 100 graduate students. It has 5 major divisions: biopsychology, clinical, cognitive, community and prevention research, and social and personality. It has a psychology and law minor; a statistics, methods, and measurement minor; and an interdepartmental specialization in neuroscience. We have close collaborations with the Institute for Juvenile Research, the Institute for Disabilities and Human Development, the School of Public Health, the Center for Urban Educational Research and Development, the Center for the Study of Learning, Instruction and Teacher Development, the Center for Literacy, and the Institute of Government and Public Affairs. These partnerships provide students and faculties having interest in interdisciplinary research an opportunity to work with scholars from diverse fields.

Special Facilities or Resources: The department is located in the 4-floor Behavioral Sciences Building, a fully equipped facility designed to serve the needs of the behavioral and social sciences. Physical facilities include seminar rooms, animal laboratories, human research labs, clinical observation rooms with one-way observational windows and video-recording and biofeedback equipment, a well-equipped electronics and mechanics shop with an on-staff engineer, a department library, the Office of Applied Psychological Services, which coordinates clinical and community interventions, the Office of Social Science Research, which provides research support, and a faculty-student lounge. The Department maintains its own computer lab, in which personal computer workstations connected to a mainframe and stand alone PCs (MS-DOS based and Macintosh) are offered for student use. The department also offers wireless internet access.

Information for Students With Physical Disabilities: See the following Web site for more information: www.uic.edu/depts/counselctr/disability/diswebpg.htm.

Application Information:
Send to: Graduate Admissions, University of Illinois at Chicago, Department of Psychology, MC 285, 1007 W. Harrison Street, Chicago, IL 60607-7137. Application available online. Students are admitted in the Fall, application deadline January 1. *Fee:* $40. There are no application fee waivers.

Illinois, University of, Urbana–Champaign

Department of Educational Psychology
College of Education
226 Education Building, 1310 South Sixth Street
Champaign, IL 61820
Telephone: (217) 333-2245
Fax: (217) 244-7620
E-mail: *edpsy@uiuc.edu*
Web: *http://www.ed.uiuc.edu/edpsy*

Department Information:
1962. Chairperson: Michelle Perry. Number of Faculty: total–full-time 25, part-time 6; women–full-time 15, part-time 3; minority–full-time 10, part-time 3; faculty subject to the Americans With Disabilities Act 1.

Programs and Degrees Offered:
Listed in the following order: Program area, degree type (T if terminal Master's), number awarded 7/03–6/04. Counseling Psychology PhD (Doctor of Philosophy) 2, Child and Adolescent Development PhD (Doctor of Philosophy) 0, Quantitative and Evaluation (QUERIES) PhD (Doctor of Philosophy) 2, Cognition, Language, Culture (CLLIC) PhD (Doctor of Philosophy) 4, Curriculum, Technology and Education Reform (CTER) Other 20.

Student Applications/Admissions:

Student Applications

Counseling Psychology PhD (Doctor of Philosophy)—Applications 2004–2005, 76. Total applicants accepted 2004–2005, 6. Number enrolled (new admits only) 2004–2005 full-time, 5. Number enrolled (new admits only) 2004–2005 part-time, 0. The Median number of years required for completion of a degree are 6. The number of students enrolled full and part-time who were dismissed or voluntarily withdrew from this program area were 0. *Child and Adolescent Development PhD (Doctor of Philosophy)*—Applications 2004–2005, 9. Total applicants accepted 2004–2005, 3. Number enrolled (new admits only) 2004–2005 full-time, 2. The number of students enrolled full and part-time who were dismissed or voluntarily withdrew from this program area were 0. *Quantitative and Evaluation (QUERIES) PhD (Doctor of Philosophy)*—Applications 2004–2005, 35. Total applicants accepted 2004–2005, 6. Number enrolled (new admits only) 2004–2005 full-time, 11. The Median number of years required for completion of a degree are 5. The number of students enrolled full and part-time who were dismissed or voluntarily withdrew from this program area were 2. *Cognition, Language, Culture (CLLIC) PhD (Doctor of Philosophy)*—Applications 2004–2005, 47. Total applicants accepted 2004–2005, 14. Number enrolled (new admits only) 2004–2005 full-time, 9. Number enrolled (new admits only) 2004–2005 part-time, 0. The Median number of years required for completion of a degree are 5. The number of students enrolled full and part-time who were dismissed or voluntarily withdrew from this program area were 3. *Curriculum, Technology and Education Reform (CTER) Other*—Applications 2004–2005, 27. Total applicants accepted 2004–2005, 24. Number enrolled (new admits only) 2004–2005 full-time, 0. Number enrolled (new admits only) 2004–2005 part-time, 21. The Median number of years required for completion of a degree

are 2. The number of students enrolled full and part-time who were dismissed or voluntarily withdrew from this program area were 0.

Admissions Requirements:

Scores: Entries appear in this order: required test or GPA, minimum score (if required), median score of students entering in 2003–2004. Master's Programs: last 2 years GPA 3.0, 3.5. Doctoral Programs: GRE-V no minimum stated, 600; GRE-Q no minimum stated, 600; GRE-V+Q no minimum stated, 1200; last 2 years GPA 3.0, 3.5.

Other Criteria: (importance of criteria rated low, medium, or high): GRE/MAT scores medium, research experience high, work experience medium, extracurricular activity medium, clinically related public service medium, GPA medium, letters of recommendation high, interview low, statement of goals and objectives high. GRE scores not required for CTER applicants.

Student Characteristics: The following represents characteristics of students in 2004–2005 in all graduate psychology programs in the department: Female–full-time 91, part-time 28; Male–full-time 33, part-time 9; African American/Black–full-time 9, part-time 0; Hispanic/Latino(a)–full-time 6, part-time 0; Asian/Pacific Islander–full-time 57, part-time 0; American Indian/Alaska Native–full-time 1, part-time 1; Caucasian–full-time 51, part-time 36; students subject to the Americans With Disabilities Act–full-time 0, part-time 0.

Financial Information/Assistance:

Tuition for Full-Time Study: *Master's:* State residents: $367 per credit hour; Nonstate residents: $367 per credit hour. *Doctoral:* State residents: per academic year $6,692; Nonstate residents: per academic year $18,000. Tuition is subject to change. See the following Web site for updates and changes in tuition costs: http://www.oar.uiuc.edu.

Financial Assistance:

First Year Students: Teaching assistantships available for first-year. Average amount paid per academic year: $12,222. Average number of hours worked per week: 20. Apply by Varies. Tuition remission given: full. Research assistantships available for first-year. Average amount paid per academic year: $12,222. Average number of hours worked per week: 20. Apply by Varies. Tuition remission given: full. Fellowships and scholarships available for first-year. Apply by Varies. Tuition remission given: full.

Advanced Students: Teaching assistantships available for advanced students. Average amount paid per academic year: $13,558. Average number of hours worked per week: 20. Apply by Varies. Tuition remission given: full. Research assistantships available for advanced students. Average amount paid per academic year: $13,558. Average number of hours worked per week: 20. Apply by Varies. Tuition remission given: full. Fellowships and scholarships available for advanced students. Apply by Varies. Tuition remission given: full.

Contact Information: Of all students currently enrolled full-time, 90% benefitted from one or more of the listed financial assistance programs.

Internships/Practica: The Counseling Division offers a variety of practica and students are placed for practicum work within University-affiliated agencies, such as the Counseling Center, the Career Development and Placement Center, McKinley Health Center, and the Psychological Services Center or in a variety of community agencies such as the Champaign County Mental Health Center, Carle Clinic, Veterans Administration Medical Center, Cunningham Children's Home, and the Illinois State University Counseling Center. Supervision is provided by on-site supervisors and by faculty members. Each doctoral student is required to complete a year long, formal, full-time predoctoral internship at an outside service agency that is approved by the Association of Psychology Internship Centers, or the equivalent. Sites to which students apply for internships include university counseling centers, hospitals, and community mental health agencies across the nation. For those doctoral students for whom a professional internship is required prior to graduation, 3 applied in 2003–2004. Of those who applied, 3 were placed in APA accredited internships.

Housing and Day Care: On-campus housing is available. See the following Web site for more information: http://www.housing.uiuc.edu. On-campus day care facilities are available. See the following Web site for more information: http://cdl.uiuc.edu.

Employment of Department Graduates:

Master's Degree Graduates: Of those who graduated in the academic year 2003–2004, the following categories and numbers represent the post-graduate activities and employment of master's degree graduates: Enrolled in a post-doctoral residency/fellowship (n/a), employed in independent practice (n/a), employed in a professional position in a school system (20), total from the above (master's) (20).

Doctoral Degree Graduates: Of those who graduated in the academic year 2003–2004, the following categories and numbers represent the post-graduate activities and employment of doctoral degree graduates: Enrolled in a psychology doctoral program (n/a), employed in an academic position at a university (3), employed in other positions at a higher education institution (1), employed in a government agency (professional services) (1), do not know (4), total from the above (doctoral) (9).

Additional Information:

Orientation, Objectives, and Emphasis of Department: The Department of Educational Psychology is located within the College of Education. Programs in the department are all at the graduate level and come under the purview of the Graduate College. The Department is divided into four on-campus full-time instructional doctoral divisions: Counseling Psychology; Development and Socialization Processes (Developmental); Quantitative and Evaluative; Research Methodologies (QUERIES); Cognition, Learning, Language, Instruction and Culture (CLLIC). Also, we have one online Master's program, Curriculum, Technology and Education Reform (CTER), for teachers. Placement of doctoral graduates from this department includes positions as university/college professors, administrators, research assistants, counselors, psychologists/therapists, and in private and government agencies, and post doctoral fellowships.

Special Facilities or Resources: The Department of Educational Psychology is under the purview of the College of Education which is rated one of the top 5 education colleges in the nation. The University of Illinois offers a rich academic environment which includes top-ranked departments: Departments of Psychology, Computer Science, Anthropology, and Speech Communication. There are also strong programs in Cognitive Neuroscience,

Artificial Intelligence, Human Development and Family Studies, Women's Studies, Afro-American Studies, Childrens Research Center, and Latin American and Caribbean Studies. Other academic and research facilities available for students and faculty are the second largest university library system in the nation. Computer facilities available include the Educational Psychology Statistical Laboratory, the college of Education Computer Laboratory, and numerous computer sites across campus. Research facilities available for use: Computer-based Education Research Laboratory, Computer-based Eye Movement Laboratory, Institute for Research on Human Development, Model-based Measurement Laboratory, Survey Research Laboratory, Statistical Consulting Services, Teaching Techniques Laboratory, Interview and experimental rooms equipped with video-and audio-taping, classrooms for video demonstration, telecommunications, and computer-based education. Research centers on campus include Beckman Institute for Advanced Science and Technology, Bureau of Educational Research, Office of Multicultural and Bilingual Education, Office of International Mathematics Study, Center for the Study of Reading. Among academic libraries in the U.S., this university has the 3rd largest system, ranking only behind Harvard and Yale.

Information for Students With Physical Disabilities: See the following Web site for more information: http://www.disability. uiuc.edu/.

Application Information:
Send to: Admissions Secretary, Department of Educational Psychology, 226 Education, 1310 S. Sixth Street, Champaign, IL 61820. Application available online. URL of online application: www.ed.uiuc.edu/edpsy. Students are admitted in the Fall, application deadline December 15; Summer, application deadline (see below). Only the CTER program accepts for Summer, and it does not accept applicants for any other term. The Summer deadline is February 15. *Fee:* $40. Domestic fee $40. International fee $50.

Illinois, University of, Urbana–Champaign
Department of Psychology
Psychology Building, 603 East Daniel Street
Champaign, IL 61820
Telephone: (217) 333-2169
Fax: (217) 244-5876
E-mail: *gradstdy@s.psych.uiuc.edu*
Web: *http://www.psych.uiuc.edu*

Department Information:
1893. Head: Lawrence Hubert. Number of Faculty: total–full-time 47, part-time 12; women–full-time 17, part-time 5; minority–full-time 8.

Programs and Degrees Offered:
Listed in the following order: Program area, degree type (T if terminal Master's), number awarded 7/03–6/04. Applied Measurement MA/MS (Master of Arts/Science) (T) 0, Applied Personnel MA/MS (Master of Arts/Science) (T) 2, Biological PhD (Doctor

of Philosophy) 2, Clinical PhD (Doctor of Philosophy) 16, Cognitive PhD (Doctor of Philosophy) 3, Developmental PhD (Doctor of Philosophy) 5, Visual Cognitive & Human Performance PhD (Doctor of Philosophy) 5, Social-Personality-Organizational PhD (Doctor of Philosophy) 10, Quantitative PhD (Doctor of Philosophy) 3, Brain and Cognition PhD (Doctor of Philosophy) 1, Applied Engineering MA/MS (Master of Arts/Science) (T) 1.

APA Accreditation: Clinical PhD (Doctor of Philosophy).

Student Applications/Admissions:
Student Applications
Applied Measurement MA/MS (Master of Arts/Science)—Applications 2004–2005, 1. Total applicants accepted 2004–2005, 0. The Median number of years required for completion of a degree are 2. The number of students enrolled full and part-time who were dismissed or voluntarily withdrew from this program area were 0. *Applied Personnel MA/MS (Master of Arts/Science)*—Applications 2004–2005, 1. Total applicants accepted 2004–2005, 0. The Median number of years required for completion of a degree are 2. The number of students enrolled full and part-time who were dismissed or voluntarily withdrew from this program area were 0. *Biological PhD (Doctor of Philosophy)*—Applications 2004–2005, 15. Total applicants accepted 2004–2005, 0. Number enrolled (new admits only) 2004–2005 full-time, 0. The Median number of years required for completion of a degree are 6. The number of students enrolled full and part-time who were dismissed or voluntarily withdrew from this program area were 0. *Clinical PhD (Doctor of Philosophy)*—Applications 2004–2005, 128. Total applicants accepted 2004–2005, 8. Number enrolled (new admits only) 2004–2005 full-time, 2. The Median number of years required for completion of a degree are 6. *Cognitive PhD (Doctor of Philosophy)*—Applications 2004–2005, 31. Total applicants accepted 2004–2005, 9. Number enrolled (new admits only) 2004–2005 full-time, 3. The Median number of years required for completion of a degree are 6. *Developmental PhD (Doctor of Philosophy)*—Applications 2004–2005, 32. Total applicants accepted 2004–2005, 7. Number enrolled (new admits only) 2004–2005 full-time, 6. The Median number of years required for completion of a degree are 6. *Visual Cognitive & Human Performance PhD (Doctor of Philosophy)*—Applications 2004–2005, 20. Total applicants accepted 2004–2005, 5. Number enrolled (new admits only) 2004–2005 full-time, 1. The Median number of years required for completion of a degree are 6. *Social-Personality-Organizational PhD (Doctor of Philosophy)*—Applications 2004–2005, 102. Total applicants accepted 2004–2005, 15. Number enrolled (new admits only) 2004–2005 full-time, 8. The Median number of years required for completion of a degree are 6. *Quantitative PhD (Doctor of Philosophy)*—Applications 2004–2005, 10. Total applicants accepted 2004–2005, 4. Number enrolled (new admits only) 2004–2005 full-time, 3. The Median number of years required for completion of a degree are 6. *Brain and Cognition PhD (Doctor of Philosophy)*—Applications 2004–2005, 12. Total applicants accepted 2004–2005, 4. Number enrolled (new admits only) 2004–2005 full-time, 4. Total enrolled 2004–2005 full-time, 15. The Median number of years required for completion of a degree are 6. *Applied Engineering MA/MS (Master of Arts/Science)*—Total enrolled 2004–2005 full-time, 3. The Median number of years required for completion of a degree are 2.

Admissions Requirements:

Scores: Entries appear in this order: required test or GPA, minimum score (if required), median score of students entering in 2003–2004. Master's Programs: GRE-V no minimum stated, 540; GRE-Q no minimum stated, 704; GRE-Subject(Psych) no minimum stated; last 2 years GPA 3.0, 3.77. Subject test is recommended but not required. GPA above a B average. Doctoral Programs: GRE-V no minimum stated, 640; GRE-Q no minimum stated, 718; GRE-Subject(Psych) no minimum stated, 578; last 2 years GPA 3.0, 3.73. Subject test is recommended but not required.

Other Criteria: (importance of criteria rated low, medium, or high): GRE/MAT scores high, research experience high, work experience medium, clinically related public service high, GPA high, letters of recommendation high, interview high, statement of goals and objectives high. For additional information on admission requirements, go to: www.psych.uiuc.edu.

Student Characteristics: The following represents characteristics of students in 2004–2005 in all graduate psychology programs in the department: Female–full-time 127, part-time 0; Male–full-time 62, part-time 0; African American/Black–full-time 6, part-time 0; Hispanic/Latino(a)–full-time 11, part-time 0; Asian/Pacific Islander–full-time 21, part-time 0; American Indian/Alaska Native–full-time 0, part-time 0; Caucasian–full-time 99, part-time 0; Multi-ethnic–full-time 1, part-time 0; students subject to the Americans With Disabilities Act–part-time 0.

Financial Information/Assistance:

Tuition for Full-Time Study: *Master's:* State residents: per academic year $7,160; Nonstate residents: per academic year $20,000. *Doctoral:* State residents: per academic year $7,160; Nonstate residents: per academic year $20,000. Tuition is subject to change. See the following Web site for updates and changes in tuition costs: www.oar.uiuc.edu.

Financial Assistance:

First Year Students: Teaching assistantships available for first-year. Average amount paid per academic year: $14,412. Average number of hours worked per week: 20. Apply by December 1. Tuition remission given: full. Research assistantships available for first-year. Average amount paid per academic year: $14,412. Average number of hours worked per week: 20. Apply by December 1. Tuition remission given: full. Traineeships available for first-year. Average amount paid per academic year: $20,772. Apply by December 1. Tuition remission given: full. Fellowships and scholarships available for first-year. Average amount paid per academic year: $15,000. Apply by December 1. Tuition remission given: full.

Advanced Students: Teaching assistantships available for advanced students. Average amount paid per academic year: $14,412. Average number of hours worked per week: 20. Apply by December 1. Tuition remission given: full. Research assistantships available for advanced students. Average amount paid per academic year: $14,412. Average number of hours worked per week: 20. Apply by December 1. Tuition remission given: full. Traineeships available for advanced students. Average amount paid per academic year: $20,772. Apply by December 1. Tuition remission

given: full. Fellowships and scholarships available for advanced students. Average amount paid per academic year: $15,000. Apply by December 1. Tuition remission given: full.

Contact Information: Of all students currently enrolled full-time, 100% benefitted from one or more of the listed financial assistance programs. Application and information available online at: http://www.psych.uiuc.edu.

Internships/Practica: Laboratories in Clinical Psychology—Intensive practice in techniques of clinical assessment and behavior modification with emphasis on recent innovations; small sections of the course formed according to the specialized interests of students and staff. For those doctoral students for whom a professional internship is required prior to graduation, 3 applied in 2003–2004. Of those who applied, 2 were placed in internships listed by the Association of Psychology Postdoctoral and Internship Programs (APPIC); 2 were placed in APA accredited internships.

Housing and Day Care: On-campus housing is available. See the following Web site for more information: www.housing.uiuc.edu/ or Family & Graduate Housing: famhous@uiuc.edu. On-campus day care facilities are available. See the following Web site for more information: Child Care Resource Service, 314 Bevier, 905 S. Goodwin, Urbana, IL 61801, (217) 333-3252 Early Child Development Laboratory, 100 Early Child Dev Lab, 1005 W. Nevada, Urbana, IL 61801, (217) 244-6883, http://www.cdl.uiuc.edu.

Employment of Department Graduates:

Master's Degree Graduates: Of those who graduated in the academic year 2003–2004, the following categories and numbers represent the post-graduate activities and employment of master's degree graduates: Enrolled in a post-doctoral residency/fellowship (n/a), employed in independent practice (n/a), total from the above (master's) (0).

Doctoral Degree Graduates: Of those who graduated in the academic year 2003–2004, the following categories and numbers represent the post-graduate activities and employment of doctoral degree graduates: Enrolled in a psychology doctoral program (n/a), total from the above (doctoral) (0).

Additional Information:

Orientation, Objectives, and Emphasis of Department: The department trains students at the doctoral level for basic research in all areas. Students are admitted in one of the eight divisions: biological, brain and cognition, cognitive, clinical/community, developmental, quantitative, social-personality-organizational, and visual cognition and human performance. Interactions with faculty in other divisions are quite common; interdisciplinary training is encouraged. Applied research training is offered in measurement and personnel psychology. There is a strong emphasis on individualized training programs in an apprenticeship model. Each student's program is tailored to his or her research interests. Wide opportunities exist for students to participate in ongoing research programs. Students are encouraged to develop their own programs. The department offered a master's degree in applied engineering, but it was transferred to the Institute of Aviation effective Fall 2003. Applicants interested in this program should contact the Institute of Aviation for admissions information: http://www.aviation.uiuc.edu/.

Special Facilities or Resources: The department has extensive laboratory facilities in all areas, including biological psychology. Excellent departmental and university computer facilities are readily available to graduate students. Most faculty laboratories are computerized. The department maintains a computer system that supports text processing, data management, and communication between laboratories and campus computers. There are very advanced facilities for research in all areas, including psychophysiology, cognitive psychology, neurochemistry, and neuroanatomy. A first-rate animal colony is maintained by the department. There is an excellent machine shop and a fine electronics shop. The department's library carries most important journals in psychology. Programs are coordinated with other campus departments and institutes, including life sciences, communications, labor, education, and child study.

Information for Students With Physical Disabilities: See the following Web site for more information: http://www.rehab. uiuc.edu/.

Application Information:

Send to: Graduate Student Affairs Office, 314 Psychology Building, 603 E. Daniel Street, Champaign, IL 61820. Application available online. URL of online application: www.psych.uiuc.edu. Students are admitted in the Fall, application deadline January 2. *Fee:* $40. The fee for an international application is $50.

Illinois, University of, Urbana–Champaign

Human and Community Development/Human Development
 and Family Studies
Agricultural, Consumer and Environmental Sciences
274 Bevier Hall, MC-180
Urbana, IL 61801
Telephone: (217) 333-3790
Fax: (217) 244-7877
E-mail: *roswald@uiuc.edu*
Web: *http://www.hcd.uiuc.edu/*

Department Information:

1996. Department Head: Robert Hughes, PhD Number of Faculty: total–full-time 17, part-time 2; women–full-time 15, part-time 2; minority–full-time 2; faculty subject to the Americans With Disabilities Act 1.

Programs and Degrees Offered:

Listed in the following order: Program area, degree type (T if terminal Master's), number awarded 7/03–6/04. Human Development and Family Studies PhD (Doctor of Philosophy) 3, Marriage and Family Services (MS/MSW) MA/MS (Master of Arts/Science) (T) 5.

Student Applications/Admissions:

Student Applications

Human Development and Family Studies PhD (Doctor of Philosophy)—Applications 2004–2005, 20. Number enrolled (new admits only) 2004–2005 full-time, 1. Number enrolled (new admits only) 2004–2005 part-time, 0. Openings 2005–2006, 5. The Median number of years required for completion of a degree are 5. The number of students enrolled full and part-time who were dismissed or voluntarily withdrew from this program area were 1. *Marriage and Family Services (MS/MSW) MA/MS (Master of Arts/Science)*—Applications 2004–2005, 15. Total applicants accepted 2004–2005, 5. Number enrolled (new admits only) 2004–2005 full-time, 5. Number enrolled (new admits only) 2004–2005 part-time, 0. Openings 2005–2006, 5. The Median number of years required for completion of a degree are 2. The number of students enrolled full and part-time who were dismissed or voluntarily withdrew from this program area were 0.

Admissions Requirements:

Scores: Entries appear in this order: required test or GPA, minimum score (if required), median score of students entering in 2003–2004. Master's Programs: GRE-V 500; GRE-Q 500; GRE-Analytical 4.5; last 2 years GPA 3.0. Doctoral Programs: GRE-V 550, 560; GRE-Q 550, 615; GRE-Analytical 550, 655. *Other Criteria:* (importance of criteria rated low, medium, or high): GRE/MAT scores medium, research experience high, GPA medium, letters of recommendation high, statement of goals and objectives high, fit with program high. For additional information on admission requirements, go to: http://www. hcd.uiuc.edu/grad/.

Student Characteristics: The following represents characteristics of students in 2004–2005 in all graduate psychology programs in the department: Female–full-time 20, part-time 0; Male–full-time 4, part-time 0; African American/Black–full-time 3, part-time 0; Hispanic/Latino(a)–full-time 0, part-time 0; Asian/Pacific Islander–full-time 7, part-time 0; American Indian/Alaska Native–full-time 0, part-time 0; Caucasian–full-time 7, part-time 0; Multi-ethnic–full-time 2, part-time 0; students subject to the Americans With Disabilities Act–full-time 0, part-time 0.

Financial Information/Assistance:

Tuition for Full-Time Study: *Master's:* State residents: per academic year $4,099; Nonstate residents: per academic year $10,099. *Doctoral:* State residents: per academic year $4,099; Nonstate residents: per academic year $10,099. Tuition is subject to change. See the following Web site for updates and changes in tuition costs: http://www.oar.uiuc.edu/current/tuitassess.html.

Financial Assistance:

First Year Students: Teaching assistantships available for first-year. Average amount paid per academic year: $5,932. Average number of hours worked per week: 10. Tuition remission given: full. Research assistantships available for first-year. Average amount paid per academic year: $5,932. Average number of hours worked per week: 10. Tuition remission given: full. Fellowships and scholarships available for first-year. Average amount paid per academic year: $15,000. Average number of hours worked per week: 0. Tuition remission given: full.

Advanced Students: Teaching assistantships available for advanced students. Average amount paid per academic year: $6,217. Average number of hours worked per week: 10. Tuition remission given: full. Research assistantships available for advanced students. Average amount paid per academic year: $6,217. Average number of hours worked per week: 10. Tuition remission given: full. Fellowships and scholarships available for advanced students. Average amount paid per academic year: $17,500. Average number of hours worked per week: 0. Tuition remission given: full.

Contact Information: Of all students currently enrolled full-time, 100% benefitted from one or more of the listed financial assistance programs. Application and information available online at: http://www.hcd.uiuc.edu/grad/fellow.html.

Internships/Practica: Master's students and doctoral students with the applied option complete at least one semester-long internship, usually within a human services setting.

Housing and Day Care: On-campus housing is available. See the following Web site for more information: http://www.housing.uiuc.edu/. On-campus day care facilities are available. See the following Web site for more information: http://cdl.uiuc.edu/ http://www.aces.uiuc.edu/%7ECCRSCare/.

Employment of Department Graduates:

Master's Degree Graduates: Of those who graduated in the academic year 2003–2004, the following categories and numbers represent the post-graduate activities and employment of master's degree graduates: Enrolled in a post-doctoral residency/fellowship (n/a), employed in independent practice (n/a), employed in business or industry (management) (1), employed in a community mental health/counseling center (4), total from the above (master's) (5).

Doctoral Degree Graduates: Of those who graduated in the academic year 2003–2004, the following categories and numbers represent the post-graduate activities and employment of doctoral degree graduates: Enrolled in a psychology doctoral program (n/a), employed in an academic position at a university (3), total from the above (doctoral) (3).

Additional Information:

Orientation, Objectives, and Emphasis of Department: Our doctoral program focuses on the positive development and resilience of children, youth, and families within everyday life contexts. Emphases include the social and emotional development of children and youth; parent–child and sibling relationships; racial, ethnic, and sexual orientation diversity. All topics are studied within specific settings. Faculty have expertise in both qualitative and quantiative research. Students may choose an applied supporting option in program development, evaluation, and outreach.

Special Facilities or Resources: Our department includes a Laboratory Preschool, Child Care Resource and Referral Service, Lab for Community and Economic Development, and Program for Family Resiliency.

Information for Students With Physical Disabilities: See the following Web site for more information: http://www.disability.uiuc.edu/.

Application Information:
Send to: Graduate Secretary, 274 Bevier Hall, 905 South Goodwin, Urbana, IL, 61801. Application available online. URL of online application: http://www.oar.uiuc.edu/prospective. Students are admitted in the Winter, application deadline January 15. *Fee:* $40.00 for Domestic applicants; $50.00 for International applicants.

Lewis University
Department of Psychology
One University Parkway
Romeoville, IL 60446
Telephone: (815) 836-5594
Fax: (815) 836-5032
E-mail: *Helmka@lewisu.ed*
Web: *http://www.lewisu.edu*

Department Information:
1993. Graduate Program Director: Katherine Helm. Number of Faculty: total–full-time 9, part-time 10; women–full-time 4, part-time 6; minority–full-time 2, part-time 1.

Programs and Degrees Offered:
Listed in the following order: Program area, degree type (T if terminal Master's), number awarded 7/03–6/04. Guidance counseling MA/MS (Master of Arts/Science) (T) 40, Counseling Psychology MA/MS (Master of Arts/Science) 15.

Student Applications/Admissions:

Student Applications
Guidance counseling MA/MS (Master of Arts/Science)—Applications 2004–2005, 60. Total applicants accepted 2004–2005, 33. Total enrolled 2004–2005 full-time, 20, part-time, 130. Openings 2005–2006, 38. The Median number of years required for completion of a degree are 3. *Counseling Psychology MA/MS (Master of Arts/Science)*—Applications 2004–2005, 35. Total applicants accepted 2004–2005, 30. Total enrolled 2004–2005 full-time, 15, part-time, 65. Openings 2005–2006, 28. The Median number of years required for completion of a degree are 3.

Admissions Requirements:
Scores: Entries appear in this order: required test or GPA, minimum score (if required), median score of students entering in 2003–2004. Master's Programs: overall undergraduate GPA no minimum stated, 3.0; last 2 years GPA no minimum stated, 3.0; psychology GPA no minimum stated, 3.0.
Other Criteria: (importance of criteria rated low, medium, or high): research experience low, work experience high, extracurricular activity medium, clinically related public service high, GPA high, letters of recommendation medium, interview low, statement of goals and objectives high.

Student Characteristics: The following represents characteristics of students in 2004–2005 in all graduate psychology programs in the department: Female–full-time 12, part-time 118; Male–full-time 5, part-time 22; African American/Black–full-time 0, part-time 18; Hispanic/Latino(a)–full-time 0, part-time 4; Asian/Pacific Islander–full-time 0, part-time 0; American Indian/Alaska

Native–full-time 0, part-time 0; Caucasian–full-time 0, part-time 0; Multi-ethnic–part-time 4.

Financial Information/Assistance:

Tuition for Full-Time Study: *Master's:* State residents: $572 per credit hour; Nonstate residents: $572 per credit hour. Tuition is subject to change.

Financial Assistance:

First Year Students: Research assistantships available for first-year. Average number of hours worked per week: 10. Tuition remission given: partial.

Advanced Students: Research assistantships available for advanced students. Average amount paid per academic year: $0. Average number of hours worked per week: 10. Tuition remission given: partial.

Contact Information: Of all students currently enrolled full-time, 5% benefitted from one or more of the listed financial assistance programs.

Internships/Practica: Numerous practica and internship sites available in the community.

Housing and Day Care: No on-campus housing is available. No on-campus day care facilities are available.

Employment of Department Graduates:

Master's Degree Graduates: Of those who graduated in the academic year 2003–2004, the following categories and numbers represent the post-graduate activities and employment of master's degree graduates: Enrolled in a post-doctoral residency/fellowship (n/a), employed in independent practice (n/a), total from the above (master's) (0).

Doctoral Degree Graduates: Of those who graduated in the academic year 2003–2004, the following categories and numbers represent the post-graduate activities and employment of doctoral degree graduates: Enrolled in a psychology doctoral program (n/a), total from the above (doctoral) (0).

Additional Information:

Orientation, Objectives, and Emphasis of Department: The program in counseling psychology is oriented toward individuals who have some experience or great interest in mental health, behavioral, social service or educational interventions or assessment. It is designed primarily as part-time with courses offered primarily in the evenings and on occasional weekends. The Program has two subspecialty areas: 1. Mental Health counseling; 2. Child and Adolescent Counseling. There is a second program in School Counseling and Guidance designed for those individuals who want to work in the public or private school systems.

Application Information:
Send to: Graduate Program Director, Department of Psychology, Lewis University, One University Parkway, Romeoville, IL 60446. Application available online. Students are admitted in the Fall, application deadline; Spring, application deadline; Summer, application deadline; Programs have rolling admissions. *Fee:* $35. Need based waiver.

Loyola University of Chicago
Counseling Psychology Program
School of Education
820 N. Michigan Avenue
Chicago, IL 60611
Telephone: (312) 915-6311
Fax: (312) 915-6660
E-mail: *sbrown@luc.edu*
Web: *http://www.luc.edu*

Department Information:
1969. Graduate Program Director: Steven D. Brown. Number of Faculty: total–full-time 4; women–full-time 3, part-time 1; minority–full-time 3.

Programs and Degrees Offered:
Listed in the following order: Program area, degree type (T if terminal Master's), number awarded 7/03–6/04. Counseling Psychology PhD (Doctor of Philosophy) 7, Community Counseling MA/MS (Master of Arts/Science) (T) 20, School Counseling Other 10.

APA Accreditation: Counseling PhD (Doctor of Philosophy).

Student Applications/Admissions:
Student Applications

Counseling Psychology PhD (Doctor of Philosophy)—Applications 2004–2005, 67. Total applicants accepted 2004–2005, 12. Number enrolled (new admits only) 2004–2005 full-time, 10. Openings 2005–2006, 8. The Median number of years required for completion of a degree are 6. The number of students enrolled full and part-time who were dismissed or voluntarily withdrew from this program area were 1. *Community Counseling MA/MS (Master of Arts/Science)*—Applications 2004–2005, 80. Total applicants accepted 2004–2005, 40. Number enrolled (new admits only) 2004–2005 full-time, 30. Total enrolled 2004–2005 full-time, 50, part-time, 5. Openings 2005–2006, 30. The Median number of years required for completion of a degree are 2. The number of students enrolled full and part-time who were dismissed or voluntarily withdrew from this program area were 0. *School Counseling Other*—Applications 2004–2005, 30. Total applicants accepted 2004–2005, 15. Number enrolled (new admits only) 2004–2005 full-time, 8. Number enrolled (new admits only) 2004–2005 part-time, 2. Total enrolled 2004–2005 full-time, 10, part-time, 8. Openings 2005–2006, 20. The Median number of years required for completion of a degree are 2. The number of students enrolled full and part-time who were dismissed or voluntarily withdrew from this program area were 0.

Admissions Requirements:

Scores: Entries appear in this order: required test or GPA, minimum score (if required), median score of students entering in 2003–2004. Master's Programs: GRE-V no minimum stated; GRE-Q no minimum stated; GRE-V+Q no minimum stated; GRE-Analytical no minimum stated; overall undergraduate GPA 3.00. Doctoral Programs: GRE-V no minimum stated, 530; GRE-Q no minimum stated, 590; GRE-V+Q no minimum stated; GRE-Analytical no minimum stated, 570; GRE-Subject(Psych) no minimum stated, 550; overall undergraduate GPA 3.00, 3.25. These scores refer to the PhD program in Counseling Psychology.

Other Criteria: (importance of criteria rated low, medium, or high): GRE/MAT scores medium, research experience high, work experience medium, clinically related public service high, GPA high, letters of recommendation high, interview high, statement of goals and objectives high. These are for the PhD program in Counseling Psychology. For additional information on admission requirements, go to: http:///www.luc.edu/.

Student Characteristics: The following represents characteristics of students in 2004–2005 in all graduate psychology programs in the department: Female–full-time 78, part-time 9; Male–full-time 20, part-time 4; African American/Black–full-time 10, part-time 3; Hispanic/Latino(a)–full-time 8, part-time 4; Asian/Pacific Islander–full-time 6, part-time 0; American Indian/Alaska Native–full-time 0, part-time 0; Caucasian–full-time 74, part-time 6; Multi-ethnic–full-time 0, part-time 0; students subject to the Americans With Disabilities Act–full-time 0, part-time 0.

Financial Information/Assistance:

Tuition for Full-Time Study: *Master's:* State residents: $610 per credit hour; Nonstate residents: $610 per credit hour. *Doctoral:* State residents: $610 per credit hour; Nonstate residents: $610 per credit hour. Tuition is subject to change. See the following Web site for updates and changes in tuition costs: http:///www. luc.edu/.

Financial Assistance:

First Year Students: Teaching assistantships available for first-year. Average amount paid per academic year: $11,000. Average number of hours worked per week: 20. Apply by January 3. Tuition remission given: full. Research assistantships available for first-year. Average amount paid per academic year: $11,000. Average number of hours worked per week: 20. Apply by January 3. Tuition remission given: full. Traineeships available for first-year. Average amount paid per academic year: $11,000. Average number of hours worked per week: 20. Apply by January 3. Tuition remission given: full. Fellowships and scholarships available for first-year. Average amount paid per academic year: $11,000. Average number of hours worked per week: 20. Apply by Varies. Tuition remission given: full.

Advanced Students: Teaching assistantships available for advanced students. Average amount paid per academic year: $11,000. Average number of hours worked per week: 20. Apply by January 3. Tuition remission given: full. Research assistantships available for advanced students. Average amount paid per academic year: $11,000. Average number of hours worked per week: 20. Apply by January 3. Tuition remission given: full. Traineeships available for advanced students. Average amount paid per academic year: $11,000. Average number of hours worked per week: 20. Apply by January 3. Tuition remission given: full. Fellowships and scholarships available for advanced students. Average amount paid per academic year: $11,000. Average number of hours worked per week: 20. Apply by Varies. Tuition remission given: full.

Contact Information: Of all students currently enrolled full-time, 50% benefitted from one or more of the listed financial assistance programs. Application and information available online at: http://www.luc.edu/.

Internships/Practica: Internships and practica are available at many excellent training facilities in the greater Chicago-land area, including university counseling centers, hospitals, VA Centers, and mental health clinics. There are both therapy-oriented and diagnostic/assessment-oriented practica. Most practicum sites serve a diverse clientele. For those doctoral students for whom a professional internship is required prior to graduation, 5 applied in 2003–2004. Of those who applied, 5 were placed in internships listed by the Association of Psychology Postdoctoral and Internship Programs (APPIC); 5 were placed in APA accredited internships.

Housing and Day Care: On-campus housing is available. See the following Web site for more information: Apartment style housing is available for graduate students. Information is available at: www. luc.edu/students. No on-campus day care facilities are available.

Employment of Department Graduates:

Master's Degree Graduates: Of those who graduated in the academic year 2003–2004, the following categories and numbers represent the post-graduate activities and employment of master's degree graduates: Enrolled in a post-doctoral residency/fellowship (n/a), employed in independent practice (n/a), total from the above (master's) (0).

Doctoral Degree Graduates: Of those who graduated in the academic year 2003–2004, the following categories and numbers represent the post-graduate activities and employment of doctoral degree graduates: Enrolled in a psychology doctoral program (n/a), enrolled in a post-doctoral residency/fellowship (2), employed in an academic position at a university (2), employed in other positions at a higher education institution (1), employed in business or industry (research/consulting) (1), employed in a government agency (research) (1), employed in a community mental health/counseling center (3), total from the above (doctoral) (10).

Additional Information:

Orientation, Objectives, and Emphasis of Department: The PhD program, accredited by APA, is based on the scientist-practitioner model of graduate education and emphasizes the interdependence of science and practice. Doctoral students are provided with opportunities to collaborate with faculty in terms of research, prevention/intervention, and teaching activites from the first year of enrollment. Additionally, the doctoral program in counseling psychology offers minors for specialized training, including applied psychological measurement, career development, marital and family counseling, and multicultural counseling and consultation. Students are required to choose one of these areas for special concentration. Regardless of the field of interest, each student is exposed to the scientist-practitioner model. Graduates are prepared for teaching, research, and professional practice.

Special Facilities or Resources: The school has excellent library and research facilities and computer resources available to students.

Information for Students With Physical Disabilities: See the following Web site for more information: http://www.luc.edu.

Application Information:

Send to: Graduate Enrollment Management, Loyola University of Chicago, 820 N. Michigan Avenue, Chicago, IL 60611. Application available online. URL of online application: http://luc.edu/schools/grad/homedata/9applica/applica.htm/. Students are admitted in the Fall, application deadline January 2. Master's programs have an application deadline of February 15. *Fee:* $40. Contact the Dean of the Graduate School.

Loyola University of Chicago

Department of Psychology
Arts and Sciences
6525 North Sheridan Road
Chicago, IL 60626
Telephone: (773) 508-3001
Fax: (773) 508-8713
E-mail: *grad-psyc@luc.edu*
Web: *http://www.luc.edu*

Department Information:

1930. Chairperson: R. Scott Tindale. Number of Faculty: total–full-time 27; women–full-time 10; minority–full-time 2.

Programs and Degrees Offered:

Listed in the following order: Program area, degree type (T if terminal Master's), number awarded 7/03–6/04. Developmental PhD (Doctor of Philosophy) 3, Social PhD (Doctor of Philosophy) 3, Clinical PhD (Doctor of Philosophy) 7, Applied Social MA/MS (Master of Arts/Science) 4.

APA Accreditation: Clinical PhD (Doctor of Philosophy).

Student Applications/Admissions:

Student Applications

Developmental PhD (Doctor of Philosophy)—Applications 2004–2005, 12. Total applicants accepted 2004–2005, 4. Number enrolled (new admits only) 2004–2005 full-time, 4. Openings 2005–2006, 2. The Median number of years required for completion of a degree are 6. The number of students enrolled full and part-time who were dismissed or voluntarily withdrew from this program area were 0. *Social PhD (Doctor of Philosophy)*—Applications 2004–2005, 46. Total applicants accepted 2004–2005, 10. Number enrolled (new admits only) 2004–2005 full-time, 3. Openings 2005–2006, 4. The Median number of years required for completion of a degree are 6. The number of students enrolled full and part-time who were dismissed or voluntarily withdrew from this program area were 0. *Clinical PhD (Doctor of Philosophy)*—Applications 2004–2005, 295. Total applicants accepted 2004–2005, 15. Number enrolled (new admits only) 2004–2005 full-time, 6. Openings 2005–2006, 6. The Median number of years required for completion of a degree are 6. The number of students enrolled full and part-time who were dismissed or voluntarily withdrew from this program area were 0. *Applied Social MA/MS (Master of Arts/Science)*—Applications 2004–2005, 15. Total applicants accepted 2004–2005, 4. Number enrolled (new admits only) 2004–2005 full-time, 3. Openings 2005–2006, 4. The Median number of years required for completion of a degree are 2. The number of students enrolled full and part-time who were dismissed or voluntarily withdrew from this program area were 0.

Admissions Requirements:

Scores: Entries appear in this order: required test or GPA, minimum score (if required), median score of students entering in 2003–2004. Master's Programs: GRE-V no minimum stated, 525; GRE-Q no minimum stated, 600; GRE-V+Q no minimum stated, 1125; GRE-Analytical no minimum stated; GRE-Subject(Psych) no minimum stated, 550; overall undergraduate GPA 3.00, 3.4. These are the scores for the Terminal Master's Program in applied social psychology. Doctoral Programs: GRE-V 520, 600; GRE-Q 520, 670; GRE-V+Q 1040, 1255; GRE-Subject(Psych) 550, 670; overall undergraduate GPA 3.00, 3.70.

Other Criteria: (importance of criteria rated low, medium, or high): GRE/MAT scores high, research experience high, work experience low, extracurricular activity low, clinically related public service medium, GPA high, letters of recommendation high, interview high, statement of goals and objectives high. Only the Clinical Program requires an interview and clinically related public service. For additional information on admission requirements, go to: http://www.luc.edu/psychology/.

Student Characteristics: The following represents characteristics of students in 2004–2005 in all graduate psychology programs in the department: Female–full-time 78, part-time 0; Male–full-time 29, part-time 0; African American/Black–full-time 8, part-time 0; Hispanic/Latino(a)–full-time 8, part-time 0; Asian/Pacific Islander–full-time 10, part-time 0; American Indian/Alaska Native–full-time 0, part-time 0; Caucasian–full-time 0, part-time 0; Multi-ethnic–full-time 0, part-time 0; students subject to the Americans With Disabilities Act–full-time 0, part-time 0.

Financial Information/Assistance:

Tuition for Full-Time Study: *Master's:* State residents: per academic year $10,908, $606 per credit hour. *Doctoral:* State residents: per academic year $10,908, $606 per credit hour.

Financial Assistance:

First Year Students: Research assistantships available for first-year. Average amount paid per academic year: $10,000. Average number of hours worked per week: 20. Apply by December 15. Tuition remission given: full.

Advanced Students: Teaching assistantships available for advanced students. Average amount paid per academic year: $10,000. Average number of hours worked per week: 20. Apply by March 1. Tuition remission given: full. Research assistantships available for advanced students. Average amount paid per academic year: $10,000. Average number of hours worked per week: 20. Apply by March 1. Tuition remission given: full.

Contact Information: Of all students currently enrolled full-time, 80% benefitted from one or more of the listed financial assistance programs. Application and information available online at: http://www.luc.edu/psychology/.

Internships/Practica: Externship experiences are available for clinical psychology students through our in-house Training Clinic and Student Counseling Center. In addition, numerous training opportunities are available throughout the Chicago metropolitan area. Students in the doctoral applied social psychology program serve a 1000-hour planning, research and evaluation internship during their third year, while students in the developmental program complete a 250-hour internship. These positions are usually found in health-related, governmental, and research organizations in the Chicago area. For those doctoral students for whom a professional internship is required prior to graduation, 6 applied in 2003–2004. Of those who applied, 6 were placed in internships listed by the Association of Psychology Postdoctoral and Internship Programs (APPIC); 6 were placed in APA accredited internships.

Housing and Day Care: On-campus housing is available. See the following Web site for more information: www.luc.edu. On-campus day care facilities are available.

Employment of Department Graduates:

Master's Degree Graduates: Of those who graduated in the academic year 2003–2004, the following categories and numbers represent the post-graduate activities and employment of master's degree graduates: Enrolled in a psychology doctoral program (6), enrolled in another graduate/professional program (0), enrolled in a post-doctoral residency/fellowship (n/a), employed in independent practice (n/a), employed in an academic position at a university (0), employed in an academic position at a 2-year/4-year college (0), employed in other positions at a higher education institution (0), employed in a professional position in a school system (0), employed in business or industry (research/consulting) (2), employed in business or industry (management) (0), employed in a government agency (research) (0), employed in a government agency (professional services) (0), employed in a community mental health/counseling center (0), employed in a hospital/medical center (0), still seeking employment (0), total from the above (master's) (8).

Doctoral Degree Graduates: Of those who graduated in the academic year 2003–2004, the following categories and numbers represent the post-graduate activities and employment of doctoral degree graduates: Enrolled in a psychology doctoral program (n/a), enrolled in a post-doctoral residency/fellowship (5), employed in independent practice (0), employed in an academic position at a university (4), employed in an academic position at a 2-year/4-year college (0), employed in other positions at a higher education institution (0), employed in a professional position in a school system (1), employed in business or industry (research/consulting) (5), employed in business or industry (management) (1), employed in a government agency (research) (0), employed in a government agency (professional services) (0), employed in a community mental health/counseling center (3), employed in a hospital/medical center (3), still seeking employment (0), total from the above (doctoral) (22).

Additional Information:

Orientation, Objectives, and Emphasis of Department: Graduate study is organized into three areas: clinical, developmental, and social. All programs offer the PhD; only the social program offers a terminal MA in applied social psychology. The clinical program emphasizes the scientist-practitioner model, with students receiving extensive training in both areas. Students may specialize in work with children or adults. The developmental program provides training for students wishing to pursue the study of human development, particularly among infants, children, and

adolescents. Cognition, social, gender role, and personality development are covered. The social psychology program includes training in both basic and applied social psychology. The emphasis in the applied program is on developing social psychologists who are capable of conducting applied research on the planning, evaluating, and modification of social programs in the areas of law and criminal justice, educational systems, health and/or community services, and organizational behavior.

Special Facilities or Resources: Excellent libraries and computer support are available. Departmental facilities include specialized laboratories for audition, vision, and neurophysiology research; a general purpose laboratory for sensory processes; suites of research and observation rooms for clinical research; observation and videotaping rooms and equipment; an extensive psychological test library; a psychophysiology and biofeedback laboratory; and computer facilities.

Information for Students With Physical Disabilities: See the following Web site for more information: www.luc.edu.

Application Information:
Send to: Department of Psychology, [Name of Program,] Loyola University of Chicago, 6525 N. Sheridan Road, Chicago, IL 60626. Students are admitted in the Fall, application deadline December 15. For the Fall semester, the deadlines for each program are as follows: Developmental, February 1; Social, February 1; Clinical, December 15. Fee: $40.

Midwestern University
Department of Behavioral Medicine/Clinical Psychology
  Program
College of Health Sciences
555 31st Street
Downers Grove, IL 60515
Telephone: (630) 515-7650
Fax: (630) 515-7655
E-mail: fprero@midwestern.edu
Web: http://www.midwestern.edu

Department Information:
2001. Chairperson: Frank J. Prerost, PhD Number of Faculty: total–full-time 8, part-time 9; women–full-time 5, part-time 5; minority–full-time 2, part-time 3.

Programs and Degrees Offered:
Listed in the following order: Program area, degree type (T if terminal Master's), number awarded 7/03–6/04. Clinical Psychology PsyD (Doctor of Psychology) 0, Master of Arts in Clinical Psychology MA/MS (Master of Arts/Science) 0.

Student Applications/Admissions:
Student Applications
Clinical Psychology PsyD (Doctor of Psychology)—Applications 2004–2005, 40. Total applicants accepted 2004–2005, 20. Number enrolled (new admits only) 2004–2005 full-time, 16. Openings 2005–2006, 15. The number of students enrolled full and part-time who were dismissed or voluntarily withdrew

from this program area were 0. *Master of Arts in Clinical Psychology MA/MS (Master of Arts/Science)*—Applications 2004–2005, 0. Total applicants accepted 2004–2005, 0. Number enrolled (new admits only) 2004–2005 full-time, 0. The number of students enrolled full and part-time, who were dismissed or voluntarily withdrew from this program area were 0.

Admissions Requirements:

Scores: Entries appear in this order: required test or GPA, minimum score (if required), median score of students entering in 2003–2004. Master's Programs: GRE-V no minimum stated; GRE-Q no minimum stated; GRE-V+Q no minimum stated; GRE-Analytical no minimum stated; overall undergraduate GPA 2.75. Applicants can submit scores from the MCAT, LSAT, MAT, or GMAT in lieu of GRE. Doctoral Programs: GRE-V no minimum stated; GRE-Q no minimum stated; GRE-V+Q no minimum stated; GRE-Analytical no minimum stated; overall undergraduate GPA 2.75. Clinical Psychology program will accept submission of applicant's scores from the MCAT, LSAT, Millers Analogy, or GMAT as a substitute for the GRE requirement. Scores on GRE (or substitute) are considered together with work experience, interview, letters of recommendation, and GPA in decision process.

Other Criteria: (importance of criteria rated low, medium, or high): GRE/MAT scores medium, research experience medium, work experience high, extracurricular activity medium, clinically related public service high, GPA medium, letters of recommendation high, interview high, statement of goals and objectives low. Applicants are selected for interview before admission decisions are completed. For additional information on admission requirements, go to: http://www.midwestern.edu.

Student Characteristics: The following represents characteristics of students in 2004–2005 in all graduate psychology programs in the department: Female–full-time 20, part-time 0; Male–full-time 4, part-time 0; African American/Black–full-time 4, part-time 0; Hispanic/Latino(a)–full-time 1, part-time 0; Asian/Pacific Islander–full-time 3, part-time 0; American Indian/Alaska Native–full-time 0, part-time 0; Caucasian–full-time 16, part-time 0; Multi-ethnic–full-time 0, part-time 0; students subject to the Americans With Disabilities Act–full-time 0, part-time 0.

Financial Information/Assistance:

Tuition for Full-Time Study: *Doctoral:* State residents: per academic year $18,020; Nonstate residents: per academic year $18,020. Tuition is subject to change. See the following Web site for updates and changes in tuition costs: http:www.midwestern.edu.

Financial Assistance:

First Year Students: Fellowships and scholarships available for first-year. Average amount paid per academic year: $2,000. Apply by June 1.

Advanced Students: Fellowships and scholarships available for advanced students. Average amount paid per academic year: $2,000. Apply by June 1.

Contact Information: Of all students currently enrolled full-time, 10% benefitted from one or more of the listed financial assistance programs. Application and information available online at: http://www.midwestern.edu (Work study is available for most students).

Internships/Practica: Currently, all first year students participate in supervised clerkship experiences. For example, one clerkship enables students to provide behavioral health services to primary care patients at a large teaching hospital. Another clerkship permits students to serve as facilitators for support groups. In addition to the clerkships, the program has established a number of practicum experiences including an affiliation with a nationally known center serving children with autism spectrum disorders. In general, Midwestern University's location in the western suburbs of Chicago presents the opportunity for a wide variety of potential training sites in various specializations. Because of small class size, the Director of Training for the program provides individualized attention in matching practica with student interests and training needs. Since this is a new program, students have not yet applied for internships.

Housing and Day Care: On-campus housing is available. In addition to on-campus housing, a number of off-campus housing sites are in close proximity to the campus. Additional information is available at: http://www.midwestern.edu. No on-campus day care facilities are available.

Employment of Department Graduates:

Master's Degree Graduates: Of those who graduated in the academic year 2003–2004, the following categories and numbers represent the post-graduate activities and employment of master's degree graduates: Enrolled in a post-doctoral residency/fellowship (n/a), employed in independent practice (n/a), total from the above (master's) (0).

Doctoral Degree Graduates: Of those who graduated in the academic year 2003–2004, the following categories and numbers represent the post-graduate activities and employment of doctoral degree graduates: Enrolled in a psychology doctoral program (n/a), total from the above (doctoral) (0).

Additional Information:

Orientation, Objectives, and Emphasis of Department: This is a new PsyD program in clinical psychology that admitted its first class in the fall of 2003. The program is grounded in the biopsychosocial aspects of clinical psychology. It is designed to provide an extensive generalist approach in the education and training of future practitioners. The Clinical Psychology program offers small class sizes presented on a spacious suburban campus in the Chicago metropolitan area dedicated to the health care professions. The Program emphasizes a professional milieu and assigns each student a mentor at the time of matriculation. Students will receive individualized attention and mentoring throughout the didactic and clinical years. The founding college of Midwestern University opened in 1900 as the Chicago College of Osteopathic Medicine and has an outstanding reputation in the professional community.

Special Facilities or Resources: This new program utilizes the existing resources currently supporting Midwestern University's osteopathic school of medicine, the Chicago School of pharmacy, and graduate programs in physician assistant studies, physical therapy, occupational therapy, and biomedical sciences. An extensive array of biomedical research laboratories are available for students in this new program. Midwestern University has recently completed a $40 million building project involving construction of a number of new buildings providing state of the art technical support for classroom instruction.

Information for Students With Physical Disabilities: See the following Web site for more information: http://www.midwestern.edu.

Application Information:
Send to: Office of Admissions, Midwestern University, 555 31st Street, Downers Grove, IL 60515. Application available online. URL of online application: http://www.midwestern.edu. Students are admitted in the Fall, application deadline; Winter, application deadline; Spring, application deadline; Summer, application deadline. Programs have rolling admissions. *Fee:* $50. Non-refundable, non-waivable fee.

Northern Illinois University
Department of Psychology
College of Liberal Arts and Sciences
DeKalb, IL 60115-2892
Telephone: (815) 753-0372
Fax: (815) 753-8088
E-mail: *mholliday@niu.edu*
Web: *http://www.niu.edu/acad/psych*

Department Information:
1959. Chairperson: Charles E. Miller. Number of Faculty: total–full-time 33; women–full-time 14; minority–full-time 3.

Programs and Degrees Offered:
Listed in the following order: Program area, degree type (T if terminal Master's), number awarded 7/03–6/04. Clinical PhD (Doctor of Philosophy) 9, Cognitive-Development-School PhD (Doctor of Philosophy) 1, Neuroscience and Behavior PhD (Doctor of Philosophy) 1, Social/I-O PhD (Doctor of Philosophy) 2.

APA Accreditation: Clinical PhD (Doctor of Philosophy).

Student Applications/Admissions:
Student Applications
Clinical PhD (Doctor of Philosophy)—Applications 2004–2005, 145. Total applicants accepted 2004–2005, 11. Total enrolled 2004–2005 full-time, 54. Openings 2005–2006, 10. *Cognitive-Development-School PhD (Doctor of Philosophy)*—Applications 2004–2005, 82. Total applicants accepted 2004–2005, 14. Number enrolled (new admits only) 2004–2005 full-time, 8. Total enrolled 2004–2005 full-time, 39, part-time, 2. Openings 2005–2006, 8. *Neuroscience and Behavior PhD (Doctor of Philosophy)*—Applications 2004–2005, 14. Total applicants accepted 2004–2005, 3. Number enrolled (new admits only) 2004–2005 full-time, 2. Total enrolled 2004–2005 full-time, 7, part-time, 1. Openings 2005–2006, 4. The Median number of years required for completion of a degree are 7. *Social/I-O PhD (Doctor of Philosophy)*—Applications 2004–2005, 36. Total applicants accepted 2004–2005, 8. Number enrolled (new admits only) 2004–2005 full-time, 4. Total enrolled 2004–2005 full-time, 45, part-time, 2. Openings 2005–2006, 6. The Median number of years required for completion of a degree are 7.

Admissions Requirements:
Scores: Entries appear in this order: required test or GPA, minimum score (if required), median score of students entering in 2003–2004. Doctoral Programs: overall undergraduate GPA no minimum stated, 3.59.

Other Criteria: (importance of criteria rated low, medium, or high): GRE/MAT scores medium, research experience medium, work experience low, extracurricular activity low, clinically related public service low, GPA high, letters of recommendation high, interview medium, statement of goals and objectives high. Clinical and School programs interview students; other programs generally do not.

Student Characteristics: The following represents characteristics of students in 2004–2005 in all graduate psychology programs in the department: Female–full-time 113, part-time 3; Male–full-time 37, part-time 4; African American/Black–full-time 4, part-time 0; Hispanic/Latino(a)–full-time 5, part-time 0; Asian/Pacific Islander–full-time 10, part-time 1; American Indian/Alaska Native–full-time 1, part-time 0; Caucasian–full-time 130, part-time 6.

Financial Information/Assistance:
Tuition for Full-Time Study: *Master's:* State residents: per academic year $3,543; Nonstate residents: per academic year $7,086. *Doctoral:* State residents: per academic year $3,543; Nonstate residents: per academic year $7,086.

Financial Assistance:
First Year Students: Teaching assistantships available for first-year. Average amount paid per academic year: $10,139. Average number of hours worked per week: 20. Tuition remission given: full. Research assistantships available for first-year. Average amount paid per academic year: $10,139. Average number of hours worked per week: 20. Tuition remission given: full. Traineeships available for first-year. Tuition remission given: full. Fellowships and scholarships available for first-year. Tuition remission given: full.

Advanced Students: Teaching assistantships available for advanced students. Average amount paid per academic year: $10,139. Average number of hours worked per week: 20. Tuition remission given: full. Research assistantships available for advanced students. Average amount paid per academic year: $10,139. Average number of hours worked per week: 20. Tuition remission given: full. Traineeships available for advanced students. Tuition remission given: full. Fellowships and scholarships available for advanced students. Tuition remission given: full.

Contact Information: Of all students currently enrolled full-time, 93% benefitted from one or more of the listed financial assistance programs.

Internships/Practica: Clinical and school psychology internships are required for students in those areas. Clinical externships (equivalent to in-residence assistantships) are available and recommended. For those doctoral students for whom a professional internship is required prior to graduation, 12 applied in 2003–2004. Of those who applied, 11 were placed in internships listed by the Association of Psychology Postdoctoral and Internship Programs (APPIC); 10 were placed in APA accredited internships.

Housing and Day Care: On-campus housing is available. See the following Web site for more information: www.niu.edu; then "A - Z Index," and "Campus Child Care Services" or "Student Housing and Dining Services." On-campus day care facilities are available.

Employment of Department Graduates:

    Master's Degree Graduates: Of those who graduated in the academic year 2003–2004, the following categories and numbers represent the post-graduate activities and employment of master's degree graduates: Enrolled in a post-doctoral residency/fellowship (n/a), employed in independent practice (n/a), total from the above (master's) (0).

    Doctoral Degree Graduates: Of those who graduated in the academic year 2003–2004, the following categories and numbers represent the post-graduate activities and employment of doctoral degree graduates: Enrolled in a psychology doctoral program (n/a), total from the above (doctoral) (0).

Additional Information:

    Orientation, Objectives, and Emphasis of Department: The PhD program in psychology is designed to prepare graduate students to function in a variety of settings such as academic institutions, which emphasize research and/or teaching; non-academic institutions, which emphasize research on mental health; human factors, or skill acquisition; and various consultative modalities, which emphasize practitioner applications and the delivery of human services. Doctorates in psychology are awarded in four specialty areas: a fully accredited APA program in clinical psychology; cognitive/instructional, developmental, and school psychology (NASP approved); neuroscience and behavior; and social and organizational psychology. Faculty in all areas endorse the value of well-trained researchers and practitioners. Students are equipped to conduct sophisticated theoretically based empirical research and to teach at the graduate or undergraduate level. In addition to academic placements, students can also find suitable employment as applied researchers or service practitioners in a variety of mental health (clinical), educational (instructional, developmental, school), physical health (neuroscience), or business (social and organizational) settings. The overall goal of the graduate program is to produce doctoral graduates who appreciate and are deeply committed to the study of psychological processes and behavior, who are familiar with fundamental knowledge in the field, and who are well-trained in methodology and modern techniques of data analysis.

    Special Facilities or Resources: The department has a modern psychology building with offices for faculty, staff, and graduate students; classrooms; shops; a six-story research wing with research equipment, including minicomputers and direct access to the university computer and Internet applications; and a Psychological Services Center for practicum training in clinical, school, organizational, and other applied psychological areas.

Application Information:

Send to: The Graduate School, Northern Illinois University, DeKalb, IL 60115-2864. Application available online. URL of online application: www.grad.niu.edu. Students are admitted in the Fall, application deadline January 1; Spring, application deadline October 1. Spring admissions are rare. January 1 deadline for clinical applicants. January 15 deadline for Social/Industrial Organizational. February 1 deadline for Cognitive/Instructional, Developmental, or School. March 1 deadline for Neuroscience and Behavior. *Fee:* $30. Fees waived/deferred if applicant was exempt from GRE fees, is NIU employee, or is currently enrolled in graduate program at NIU.

Northwestern University

Department of Psychology
102 Swift Hall, 2029 Sheridan Road
Evanston, IL 60208-2710
Telephone: (847) 491-5190
Fax: (847) 491-7859
E-mail: *psych-chair@northwestern.edu*
Web: *http://www.psych.nwu.edu*

Department Information:

    1909. Chairperson: Alice H. Eagly. Number of Faculty: total–full-time 26, part-time 1; women–full-time 9, part-time 1; minority–full-time 3.

Programs and Degrees Offered:

    Listed in the following order: Program area, degree type (T if terminal Master's), number awarded 7/03–6/04. Clinical Psychology PhD (Doctor of Philosophy) 1, Cognitive Psychology PhD (Doctor of Philosophy) 1, Personality Psychology PhD (Doctor of Philosophy) 0, Brain, Behavior, and Cognition PhD (Doctor of Philosophy) 1, Social Psychology PhD (Doctor of Philosophy) 2.

APA Accreditation: Clinical PhD (Doctor of Philosophy).

Student Applications/Admissions:

    Student Applications

    Clinical Psychology PhD (Doctor of Philosophy)—Applications 2004–2005, 148. Total applicants accepted 2004–2005, 9. Number enrolled (new admits only) 2004–2005 full-time, 4. Number enrolled (new admits only) 2004–2005 part-time, 0. Openings 2005–2006, 2. The Median number of years required for completion of a degree are 6. The number of students enrolled full and part-time who were dismissed or voluntarily withdrew from this program area were 0. *Cognitive Psychology PhD (Doctor of Philosophy)*—Applications 2004–2005, 60. Total applicants accepted 2004–2005, 11. Number enrolled (new admits only) 2004–2005 full-time, 5. Number enrolled (new admits only) 2004–2005 part-time, 0. Openings 2005–2006, 3. The Median number of years required for completion of a degree are 5. The number of students enrolled full and part-time who were dismissed or voluntarily withdrew from this program area were 0. *Personality Psychology PhD (Doctor of Philosophy)*—Applications 2004–2005, 11. Total applicants accepted 2004–2005, 0. Number enrolled (new admits only) 2004–2005 full-time, 0. Number enrolled (new admits only) 2004–2005 part-time, 0. The Median number of years required for completion of a degree are 5. The number of students enrolled full and part-time who were dismissed or voluntarily withdrew from this program area were 0. *Brain, Behavior, and Cognition PhD (Doctor of Philosophy)*—Applications 2004–2005, 27. Total applicants accepted 2004–2005, 2. Number enrolled (new admits only) 2004–2005 full-time, 0. Number enrolled (new admits only) 2004–2005 part-time, 0. Openings 2005–2006, 3. The Median number of years required for completion of a degree are 5. The number of students enrolled full and part-time who were dismissed or voluntarily withdrew from this program area were 0. *Social Psychology PhD (Doctor of Philosophy)*—Applications 2004–2005, 99. Total applicants accepted 2004–2005, 7. Number enrolled (new admits only) 2004–2005 full-time, 4. Number enrolled (new admits only)

2004–2005 part-time, 0. Openings 2005–2006, 3. The Median number of years required for completion of a degree are 5. The number of students enrolled full and part-time who were dismissed or voluntarily withdrew from this program area were 0.

Admissions Requirements:

Scores: Entries appear in this order: required test or GPA, minimum score (if required), median score of students entering in 2003–2004. Doctoral Programs: GRE-V no minimum stated, 678; GRE-Q no minimum stated, 817; GRE-V+Q no minimum stated, 1495; GRE-Analytical no minimum stated, 375; overall undergraduate GPA no minimum stated. GRE-Analytical is substantially lower because applicants are not reporting Analytical scores or are now reporting Analytical Writing scores. The Graduate School no longer calculates GPAs.

Other Criteria: (importance of criteria rated low, medium, or high): GRE/MAT scores high, research experience high, GPA high, letters of recommendation medium, statement of goals and objectives medium.

Student Characteristics: The following represents characteristics of students in 2004–2005 in all graduate psychology programs in the department: Female–full-time 31, part-time 0; Male–full-time 22, part-time 0; African American/Black–full-time 0, part-time 0; Hispanic/Latino(a)–full-time 0, part-time 0; Asian/Pacific Islander–full-time 4, part-time 0; American Indian/Alaska Native–full-time 0, part-time 0; Caucasian–full-time 49, part-time 0; Multi-ethnic–full-time 0, part-time 0; students subject to the Americans With Disabilities Act–full-time 0, part-time 0.

Financial Information/Assistance:

Tuition for Full-Time Study: *Doctoral:* State residents: per academic year $29,940; Nonstate residents: per academic year $29,940. Tuition is subject to change.

Financial Assistance:

First Year Students: Fellowships and scholarships available for first-year. Average amount paid per academic year: $18,000. Apply by December 31. Tuition remission given: full.

Advanced Students: Teaching assistantships available for advanced students. Average amount paid per academic year: $14,157. Average number of hours worked per week: 10. Tuition remission given: full. Research assistantships available for advanced students. Average amount paid per academic year: $14,157. Tuition remission given: partial. Fellowships and scholarships available for advanced students. Average amount paid per academic year: $14,157. Tuition remission given: full.

Contact Information: Of all students currently enrolled full-time, 100% benefitted from one or more of the listed financial assistance programs.

Internships/Practica: A variety of internships in community settings is available. For those doctoral students for whom a professional internship is required prior to graduation, 1 applied in 2003–2004. Of those who applied, 1 was placed in internships listed by the Association of Psychology Postdoctoral and Internship Programs (APPIC); 1 was placed in APA accredited internships.

Housing and Day Care: On-campus housing is available. There is a University-operated residence hall for graduate students, but no child care. Additional information is available at http://www.stuaff.nwu.edu/grad_and_off/GOCH/Evanston_Incoming.html. No on-campus day care facilities are available.

Employment of Department Graduates:

Master's Degree Graduates: Of those who graduated in the academic year 2003–2004, the following categories and numbers represent the post-graduate activities and employment of master's degree graduates: Enrolled in a post-doctoral residency/fellowship (n/a), employed in independent practice (n/a), total from the above (master's) (0).

Doctoral Degree Graduates: Of those who graduated in the academic year 2003–2004, the following categories and numbers represent the post-graduate activities and employment of doctoral degree graduates: Enrolled in a psychology doctoral program (n/a), employed in an academic position at a 2-year/4-year college (1), employed in other positions at a higher education institution (4), total from the above (doctoral) (5).

Additional Information:

Orientation, Objectives, and Emphasis of Department: The faculty in each graduate area has designed programs tailored to the needs of students in that area. Whatever a student's field of interest, the department tries to produce doctoral students with a strong research orientation. Administrative barriers between areas are permeable; most faculty members take an active part in the instruction and research programs of more than one interest area. A significant population of postdoctoral fellows enhances the informal professional education of graduate students. In addition, all graduate students are given opportunities for teaching. Teaching is independent of type of financial aid.

Special Facilities or Resources: http://www.northwestern.edu/hr/eeo/?quicklinks.

Application Information:

Send to: Florence Sales, Graduate Admissions Coordinator, 102 Swift Hall, Department of Psychology, Northwestern University, 2029 Sheridan Road, Evanston, IL 60208-2710; email: f-sales@northwestern.edu. Application available online. URL of online application: https://app.applyyourself.com/?id=nwu-grad. Students are admitted in the Fall, application deadline December 31. *Fee:* $60 for resident aliens and U.S. citizens; $75 for non-residents alien.

Northwestern University, Feinberg School of Medicine

Department of Psychiatry and Behavioral Sciences, Division of Psychology
Abbott Hall, Suite 1205, 710 North Lake Shore Drive
Chicago, IL 60611
Telephone: (312) 908-8262
Fax: (312) 908-5070
E-mail: *m-reinecke@northwestern.edu*
Web: *http://www.clinpsych.northwestern.edu*

Department Information:

1970. Chief: Mark A. Reinecke, PhD Number of Faculty: total–full-time 14, part-time 15; women–full-time 7, part-time 9; faculty subject to the Americans With Disabilities Act 1.

Programs and Degrees Offered:
Listed in the following order: Program area, degree type (T if terminal Master's), number awarded 7/03–6/04. Clinical PhD (Doctor of Philosophy) 2.

APA Accreditation: Clinical PhD (Doctor of Philosophy).

Student Applications/Admissions:

Student Applications

Clinical PhD (Doctor of Philosophy)—Applications 2004–2005, 195. Total applicants accepted 2004–2005, 6. Number enrolled (new admits only) 2004–2005 full-time, 5. Total enrolled 2004–2005 full-time, 29. Openings 2005–2006, 6. The Median number of years required for completion of a degree are 6. The number of students enrolled full and part-time who were dismissed or voluntarily withdrew from this program area were 0.

Admissions Requirements:

Scores: Entries appear in this order: required test or GPA, minimum score (if required), median score of students entering in 2003–2004. Doctoral Programs: GRE-V no minimum stated, 625; GRE-Q no minimum stated, 695; GRE-Subject(Psych) no minimum stated, 710; overall undergraduate GPA no minimum stated, 3.6.

Other Criteria: (importance of criteria rated low, medium, or high): GRE/MAT scores high, research experience high, work experience low, extracurricular activity medium, clinically related public service medium, GPA medium, letters of recommendation high, interview medium, statement of goals and objectives medium.

Student Characteristics: The following represents characteristics of students in 2004–2005 in all graduate psychology programs in the department: Female–full-time 25, part-time 0; Male–full-time 4, part-time 0; African American/Black–full-time 4, part-time 0; Hispanic/Latino(a)–full-time 0, part-time 0; Asian/Pacific Islander–full-time 0, part-time 0; American Indian/Alaska Native–full-time 1, part-time 0; Caucasian–full-time 24, part-time 0; Multi-ethnic–full-time 0, part-time 0; students subject to the Americans With Disabilities Act–full-time 0, part-time 0.

Financial Information/Assistance:

Tuition for Full-Time Study: *Doctoral:* State residents: per academic year $30,800; Nonstate residents: per academic year $30,800.

Financial Assistance:

First Year Students: Research assistantships available for first-year. Tuition remission given: full and partial. Fellowships and scholarships available for first-year. Tuition remission given: full and partial.

Advanced Students: Research assistantships available for advanced students. Tuition remission given: full and partial. Fellowships and scholarships available for advanced students. Tuition remission given: full and partial.

Contact Information: Of all students currently enrolled full-time, 75% benefitted from one or more of the listed financial assistance programs. Application and information available online at: www.clinpsych.northwestern.edu.

Internships/Practica: All practica are located at clinical sites affiliated with Northwestern University Medical School or Northwestern Memorial Hospital. They include a university counseling center, an adult outpatient psychiatry clinic, several partial hospital programs, several neuropsychological sites, and programs at several child/adolescent sites. For those doctoral students for whom a professional internship is required prior to graduation, 5 applied in 2003–2004. Of those who applied, 5 were placed in internships listed by the Association of Psychology Postdoctoral and Internship Programs (APPIC); 5 were placed in APA accredited internships.

Housing and Day Care: On-campus housing is available. Graduate and Off-campus Housing Office (312) 503-8514. On-campus day care facilities are available. Office of Child and Family Resources (847) 491-3612.

Employment of Department Graduates:

Master's Degree Graduates: Of those who graduated in the academic year 2003–2004, the following categories and numbers represent the post-graduate activities and employment of master's degree graduates: Enrolled in a post-doctoral residency/fellowship (n/a), employed in independent practice (n/a), total from the above (master's) (0).

Doctoral Degree Graduates: Of those who graduated in the academic year 2003–2004, the following categories and numbers represent the post-graduate activities and employment of doctoral degree graduates: Enrolled in a psychology doctoral program (n/a), enrolled in a post-doctoral residency/fellowship (4), total from the above (doctoral) (4).

Additional Information:

Orientation, Objectives, and Emphasis of Department: The goal of our doctoral program is to develop clinical psychologists well-trained in the scientist-practitioner model. The complete graduate is skilled both in clinical practice and research. During tenure in this five-year program, a student completes a curriculum of required courses, participates in at least two years of clinical practica, apprentices as a research assistant for one year, conducts an originally conceived small research project, acts as a teaching assistant for one year, writes and defends a major paper, completes a clinical internship, and writes a doctoral dissertation. The student's contacts with clinical populations begin during the first year in the program in a variety of treatment contexts staffed by departmental faculty. The division is committed to a training model in which intensive supervision in basic diagnostic, interviewing, and treatment skills acts as a basis for competent functioning in most clinical settings and with most patient populations. The division offers subspecialties in neuropsychology, psycho-legal studies, social policy, prevention, cognitive therapy, clinical child psychology, and health psychology.

Application Information:
Send to: Division of Psychology, Northwestern University Medical School, Abbott Hall Suite 1205, 710 North Lake Shore Drive, Chicago, IL 60611-3078. Application available online. Students are admitted in the Fall, application deadline January 15. *Fee:* $50.

Roosevelt University
School of Psychology
Arts and Sciences
430 South Michigan Avenue
Chicago, IL 60605-1394
Telephone: (312) 341-3750
Fax: (312) 341-6362
E-mail: *jchoca@roosevelt.edu*
Web: *http://www.roosevelt.edu*

Department Information:
1945. Director: Dr. James P. Choca. Number of Faculty: total–full-time 14, part-time 25; women–full-time 4, part-time 19; minority–full-time 3, part-time 7.

Programs and Degrees Offered:
Listed in the following order: Program area, degree type (T if terminal Master's), number awarded 7/03–6/04. Clinical psychology MA/MS (Master of Arts/Science) (T) 7, industrial/organizational MA/MS (Master of Arts/Science) (T) 12, clinical professional counseling MA/MS (Master of Arts/Science) 28, clinical psychology PsyD (Doctor of Psychology) 6.

APA Accreditation: Clinical PsyD (Doctor of Psychology).

Student Applications/Admissions:
Student Applications
Clinical psychology MA/MS (Master of Arts/Science)—Applications 2004–2005, 43. Total applicants accepted 2004–2005, 20. Number enrolled (new admits only) 2004–2005 full-time, 8. Number enrolled (new admits only) 2004–2005 part-time, 8. Total enrolled 2004–2005 full-time, 10, part-time, 41. Openings 2005–2006, 20. The Median number of years required for completion of a degree are 5. *Industrial/organizational MA/MS (Master of Arts/Science)*—Applications 2004–2005, 73. Total applicants accepted 2004–2005, 49. Number enrolled (new admits only) 2004–2005 full-time, 7. Number enrolled (new admits only) 2004–2005 part-time, 25. Total enrolled 2004–2005 full-time, 12, part-time, 116. Openings 2005–2006, 40. The Median number of years required for completion of a degree are 3.2. *Clinical professional counseling MA/MS (Master of Arts/Science)*—Applications 2004–2005, 113. Total applicants accepted 2004–2005, 60. Number enrolled (new admits only) 2004–2005 full-time, 18. Number enrolled (new admits only) 2004–2005 part-time, 35. Total enrolled 2004–2005 part-time, 112. Openings 2005–2006, 60. The Median number of years required for completion of a degree are 3. *Clinical psychology PsyD (Doctor of Psychology)*—Applications 2004–2005, 35. Total applicants accepted 2004–2005, 13. Number enrolled (new admits only) 2004–2005 full-time, 5. Number enrolled (new admits only) 2004–2005 part-time, 4. Total enrolled 2004–2005 full-time, 15, part-time, 40. Openings 2005–2006, 20. The Median number of years required for completion of a degree are 5.1. The number of students enrolled full and part-time who were dismissed or voluntarily withdrew from this program area were 0.

Admissions Requirements:
Scores: Entries appear in this order: required test or GPA, minimum score (if required), median score of students entering

in 2003–2004. Master's Programs: overall undergraduate GPA 2.70, 3.10; last 2 years GPA 2.70, 3.20; psychology GPA 3.00, 3.25. Doctoral Programs: GRE-V no minimum stated; GRE-Q no minimum stated; GRE-V+Q no minimum stated; GRE-Analytical no minimum stated; overall undergraduate GPA 3.25.
Other Criteria: (importance of criteria rated low, medium, or high): GRE/MAT scores high, research experience low, work experience medium, extracurricular activity low, clinically related public service medium, GPA high, letters of recommendation high, interview medium, statement of goals and objectives medium. Ratings are shown are for the PsyD program. For additional information on admission requirements, go to: http://www.roosevelt.edu/cas/sp/psyd.htm.

Student Characteristics: The following represents characteristics of students in 2004–2005 in all graduate psychology programs in the department: Female–full-time 149, part-time 201; Male–full-time 49, part-time 100; African American/Black–full-time 24, part-time 33; Hispanic/Latino(a)–full-time 4, part-time 7; Asian/Pacific Islander–full-time 2, part-time 9; American Indian/Alaska Native–full-time 1, part-time 0; Caucasian–full-time 60, part-time 84; students subject to the Americans With Disabilities Act–full-time 0, part-time 0.

Financial Information/Assistance:
Tuition for Full-Time Study: *Master's:* State residents: $688 per credit hour; Nonstate residents: $688 per credit hour. *Doctoral:* State residents: $688 per credit hour; Nonstate residents: $688 per credit hour. See the following Web site for updates and changes in tuition costs: http://www.roosevelt.edu/financialaid/tuition0506.htm.

Financial Assistance:
First Year Students: Research assistantships available for first-year. Average amount paid per academic year: $5,000. Average number of hours worked per week: 20. Apply by February 5. Tuition remission given: full. Fellowships and scholarships available for first-year. Apply by open. Tuition remission given: full.
Advanced Students: Research assistantships available for advanced students. Average amount paid per academic year: $5,000. Average number of hours worked per week: 20. Apply by February 5. Tuition remission given: full. Fellowships and scholarships available for advanced students. Apply by open. Tuition remission given: full.
Contact Information: Of all students currently enrolled full-time, 7% benefitted from one or more of the listed financial assistance programs. Application and information available online at: http://www.roosevelt.edu/financialaid/default.htm.

Internships/Practica: Students in our programs have available over 130 sites in the Chicago area for practicum experience. We have a full-time Practicum Coordinator. We have a 100% placement rate for predoctoral (full-time) internships in the PsyD program. Both I/O and Clinical MA students have ample opportunities for training; I/O students nearly always get paid practicum experience. For those doctoral students for whom a professional internship is required prior to graduation, 4 applied in 2003–2004. Of those who applied, 5 were placed in internships listed by the Association of Psychology Postdoctoral and Internship Programs (APPIC); 3 were placed in APA accredited internships.

Housing and Day Care: On-campus housing is available. See the following Web site for more information: www.roosevelt.edu. The recently opened University Center is a model program that has received national attention. The 400-unit dormitory, one block from Lake Michigan, is shared by Roosevelt University, DePaul University, and Columbia College. More traditional dormitory space is available in the Herman Crown Center, immediately adjacent to the downtown campus. On-campus day care facilities are available. Licensed child care is available at the suburban campus in Schaumburg, IL.

Employment of Department Graduates:

Master's Degree Graduates: Of those who graduated in the academic year 2003–2004, the following categories and numbers represent the post-graduate activities and employment of master's degree graduates: Enrolled in a post-doctoral residency/fellowship (n/a), employed in independent practice (n/a), total from the above (master's) (0).

Doctoral Degree Graduates: Of those who graduated in the academic year 2003–2004, the following categories and numbers represent the post-graduate activities and employment of doctoral degree graduates: Enrolled in a psychology doctoral program (n/a), enrolled in a post-doctoral residency/fellowship (5), employed in independent practice (3), employed in an academic position at a university (0), employed in an academic position at a 2-year/4-year college (1), employed in other positions at a higher education institution (0), employed in a professional position in a school system (0), employed in business or industry (research/consulting) (0), employed in business or industry (management) (0), employed in a government agency (research) (0), employed in a government agency (professional services) (1), employed in a community mental health/counseling center (5), still seeking employment (0), not seeking employment (0), other employment position (0), do not know (1), total from the above (doctoral) (16).

Additional Information:

Orientation, Objectives, and Emphasis of Department: Roosevelt University was founded sixty years ago, in 1945 ago on the principles of social justice and equal educational access for all qualified students. We have a long history of inclusion and multicultural diversity. Our programmatic orientation reflects the diversity of contemporary psychology practice. A primary goal of the School of Psychology is to prepare students to work effectively with diverse cultures in urban/metropolitan settings. Master's degree programs in Psychology have been offered since 1952, and the PsyD program, the first university based clinical PsyD program in Illinois, was added in 1996. The PsyD program is designed to provide a broad-based general background in all facets of clinical practice, in preparation for post-doctoral specialization of the student's choice. There are several programmatic emphases, described below. Three master's degree programs are offered, serving several groups of students. We offer streamlined and personally tailored predoctoral training designed to help qualified students enter PhD and PsyD programs, including our own. Approximately 85 percent of our graduates who have applied to doctoral programs have been accepted. We prepare students for professional master's level employment in mental health and I/O careers. Many of our

students are several years beyond college graduation and continue to work full- or part-time while arranging their schedules around evening, daytime, and weekend courses offered at our downtown or suburban campuses. Special attention is given to helping students develop educational and professional programs that fit their career goals.

Special Facilities or Resources: The school of psychology has an exceptional faculty who are actively involved in applied research and clinical practice, supplemented by a large and highly trained adjunct faculty who also are involved in clinical, forensic, and experimental work. In addition to the extensive Roosevelt library and other facilities, there is access to clinical, research, computer, and library facilities of major Chicago universities, hospitals, and clinics. Volunteer research assistantships are available to qualified students interested in doing publishable research, with in-house computer and audiovisual equipment available. A major resource is the urban location with varied employment, educational and cultural opportunities. The Stress Institute offers basic and advanced certificates in Stress Management, which incorporate a wide range of cognitive-behavioral courses for students and health professionals interested in enhancing their clinical stress management skills. The Children and Family Studies Initiative allows students to train in the clinical treatment of children and families.

Application Information:
Send to: Graduate Admissions, Roosevelt Univesity, 430 South Michigan Avenue, Chicago, IL 60605, http://www.roosevelt.edu/contact/default.htm. Students are admitted in the Fall, application deadline January 15 (PsyD); Spring, application deadline December 30 (MA); Summer, application deadline May 1 (MA). *Fee:* $25.

Rosalind Franklin University of Medicine and Science

Department of Psychology
(formerly Finch University of Health Sciences/The Chicago Medical School)
3333 Green Bay Road
North Chicago, IL 60064
Telephone: (847) 578-3305
Fax: (847) 578-8758
E-mail: *michael.seidenberg@rosalindfranklin.edu*
Web: *http://www.rosalindfranklin.edu/sgpds/psychology*

Department Information:
1977. Professor and Chairman: Michael Seidenberg, PhD Number of Faculty: total–full-time 11; women–full-time 4; minority–full-time 1.

Programs and Degrees Offered:
Listed in the following order: Program area, degree type (T if terminal Master's), number awarded 7/03–6/04. Clinical PhD (Doctor of Philosophy) 8.

APA Accreditation: Clinical PhD (Doctor of Philosophy).

Student Applications/Admissions:

Student Applications

Clinical PhD (Doctor of Philosophy)—Applications 2004–2005, 139. Total applicants accepted 2004–2005, 17. Number enrolled (new admits only) 2004–2005 full-time, 9. Total enrolled 2004–2005 full-time, 72. Openings 2005–2006, 9. The Median number of years required for completion of a degree are 7. The number of students enrolled full and part-time who were dismissed or voluntarily withdrew from this program area were 0.

Admissions Requirements:

Scores: Entries appear in this order: required test or GPA, minimum score (if required), median score of students entering in 2003–2004. Doctoral Programs: GRE-V 600, 700; GRE-Q 600, 620; GRE-Analytical 600, 650; GRE-Subject(Psych) 600*, 600. The Advanced Psychology GRE is required for those students who are not undergraduate Psychology majors or have a Master's degree in a non-Psychology discipline.

Other Criteria: (importance of criteria rated low, medium, or high): GRE/MAT scores medium, research experience high, work experience low, extracurricular activity medium, clinically related public service medium, GPA high, letters of recommendation high, interview high, statement of goals and objectives high, These criteria are identical for all programs. Students are welcome to visit the Department throughout the year. For additional information on admission requirements, go to: http://www.rosalindfranklin.edu/sgpds/psychology/admissions.cfm.

Student Characteristics: The following represents characteristics of students in 2004–2005 in all graduate psychology programs in the department: Female full-time 57, part-time 0; Male–full-time 15, part-time 0; African American/Black–full-time 3, part-time 0; Hispanic/Latino(a)–full-time 3, part-time 0; Asian/Pacific Islander–full-time 7, part-time 0; American Indian/Alaska Native–full-time 0, part-time 0; Caucasian–full-time 59, part-time 0.

Financial Information/Assistance:

Tuition for Full-Time Study: Doctoral: State residents: per academic year $16,881; Nonstate residents: per academic year $16,881. Tuition is subject to change.

Financial Assistance:

First Year Students: Research assistantships available for first-year. Average number of hours worked per week: 10. Tuition remission given: partial. Fellowships and scholarships available for first-year. Tuition remission given: partial.

Advanced Students: Teaching assistantships available for advanced students. Average number of hours worked per week: 10. Tuition remission given: full and partial. Research assistantships available for advanced students. Average number of hours worked per week: 10. Tuition remission given: full and partial. Traineeships available for advanced students. Average number of hours worked per week: 10. Tuition remission given: full and partial. Fellowships and scholarships available for advanced students. Average number of hours worked per week: 10. Tuition remission given: full and partial.

Contact Information: Of all students currently enrolled full-time, 50% benefitted from one or more of the listed financial assistance programs.

Internships/Practica: The Department enjoys formal relationships with many of the major clinical, health and neuropsychology facilities in the catchment area from Chicago to the south and Milwaukee to the north. These include both inpatient and outpatient facilities. Thus, students have the opportunity to obtain experience and clinical training with a diverse range of clinical populations and socio-economic strata. In addition, the University operates primary care clinics that function side by side with Department operated Psychology Clinics. The University Counseling Center is also run by the Department of Psychology and it provides a variety of assessment and intervention services to members of the University. For those doctoral students for whom a professional internship is required prior to graduation, 8 applied in 2003–2004. Of those who applied, 8 were placed in internships listed by the Association of Psychology Postdoctoral and Internship Programs (APPIC); 8 were placed in APA accredited internships.

Housing and Day Care: On-campus housing is available. The University currently has on-campus housing for students. For more infomation on housing, you may call (847) 578-8350 or e-mail campus.housing@rosalindfranklin.edu. No on-campus day care facilities are available.

Employment of Department Graduates:

Master's Degree Graduates: Of those who graduated in the academic year 2003–2004, the following categories and numbers represent the post-graduate activities and employment of master's degree graduates: Enrolled in a post-doctoral residency/fellowship (n/a), employed in independent practice (n/a), total from the above (master's) (0).

Doctoral Degree Graduates: Of those who graduated in the academic year 2003–2004, the following categories and numbers represent the post-graduate activities and employment of doctoral degree graduates: Enrolled in a psychology doctoral program (n/a), enrolled in a post-doctoral residency/fellowship (6), employed in an academic position at a university (1), employed in business or industry (research/consulting) (1), total from the above (doctoral) (8).

Additional Information:

Orientation, Objectives, and Emphasis of Department: The Department of Psychology offers an APA approved program leading to the PhD degree in clinical psychology, with specialties in Health Psychology, Psychopathology and Clinical Neuropsychology. Within the context of the general clinical training program, students select a specialty emphasis in either clinical neuropsychology, psychopathology or health/behavioral medicine. The program provides students with intensive training in the methods and theories of clinical practice with emphasis in these specialty areas. Research is a vital part of the program and students work closely with professors throughout their training. Research topics include biopsychosocial issues associated with various medical illnesses (e.g., cancer, diabetes, heart disease, chronic pain), aging, psychopathology (e.g., schizophrenia, OCD, psychopathy), and neuropsychological features of various clinical populations (e.g., epilepsy, head injury, multiple sclerosis, AIDS, Alzheimer's disease, dementia, stroke). Subject populations range in age from childhood through adulthood and include those with physical and psychiatric disorders. The Department subscribes to the philosophy that a clinical psychologist is knowledgeable in formulating and solving scientific problems, and skilled in formulating clinical problems and applying empirically supported interventions. To this end, core courses are organized as integrated theory-research-practice units with a problem solving orientation. Our goal is to graduate clinical psychologists who are highly trained, clinically effective, and able to contribute to the continuing development of the profession as practitioners, teachers, and researchers.

Special Facilities or Resources: The Department operates several specialty clinics at the Chicago Medical School including an Anxiety Disorders Clinic and Neuropsychological Assessment Clinic, which provide both clinical training and research opportunities. Research facilities within the Department include an Experimental Neuropsychology Lab, Clinical Health Psychophysiology Lab, Neuroimaging Laboratory, and a Behavioral Therapy Lab. There are ongoing research programs in arthritis, oncology, diabetes, blood pressure regulation, pain and stress, epilepsy, anxiety disorders, schizophrenia, psychopathy, aging and dementia. Collaborative research opportunities are also ongoing with a number of community and academic institutions in the area and include projects using MRI and fMRI to study higher order cognitive processes.

Application Information:
Send to: Rosalind Franklin University of Medicine and Science, Graduate Admissions Office, 3333 Green Bay Road, North Chicago, IL 60064. Application available online. URL of online application: http://www.rosalindfranklin.edu/sgpds/psychology/admissions.cfm. Students are admitted in the Fall, application deadline December 31. *Fee:* $25.

Southern Illinois University Edwardsville
Department of Psychology
Box 1121
Edwardsville, IL 62026-1121
Telephone: (618) 650-2202
Fax: (618) 650-5087
E-mail: *bsulliv@siue.edu*
Web: *http://www.siue.edu/PSYCHOLOGY/grad.htm*

Department Information:
1964. Chairperson: Bryce F. Sullivan. Number of Faculty: total—full-time 18, part-time 5; women—full-time 10; minority—full-time 1, part-time 1.

Programs and Degrees Offered:
Listed in the following order: Program area, degree type (T if terminal Master's), number awarded 7/03–6/04. School Psychology EdS (Education Specialist) 11, Clinical-Adult Psychology MA/MS (Master of Arts/Science) (T) 7, Industrial Organizational Psychology MA/MS (Master of Arts/Science) (T) 8, Clinical

Child and School Psychology MA/MS (Master of Arts/Science) (T) 11.

Student Applications/Admissions:
Student Applications
School Psychology EdS *(Education Specialist)*—Applications 2004–2005, 6. Total applicants accepted 2004–2005, 6. Number enrolled (new admits only) 2004–2005 full-time, 6. Openings 2005–2006, 10. The Median number of years required for completion of a degree are 2. The number of students enrolled full and part-time who were dismissed or voluntarily withdrew from this program area were 0. *Clinical-Adult Psychology MA/MS (Master of Arts/Science)*—Applications 2004–2005, 47. Total applicants accepted 2004–2005, 11. Number enrolled (new admits only) 2004–2005 full-time, 10. Openings 2005–2006, 10. The Median number of years required for completion of a degree are 2. The number of students enrolled full and part-time who were dismissed or voluntarily withdrew from this program area were 1. *Industrial Organizational Psychology MA/MS (Master of Arts/Science)*—Applications 2004–2005, 53. Total applicants accepted 2004–2005, 10. Number enrolled (new admits only) 2004–2005 full-time, 10. Openings 2005–2006, 10. The Median number of years required for completion of a degree are 3. The number of students enrolled full and part-time who were dismissed or voluntarily withdrew from this program area were 0. *Clinical Child and School Psychology MA/MS (Master of Arts/Science)*—Applications 2004–2005, 58. Total applicants accepted 2004–2005, 12. Number enrolled (new admits only) 2004–2005 full-time, 12. Openings 2005–2006, 10. The Median number of years required for completion of a degree are 2. The number of students enrolled full and part-time who were dismissed or voluntarily withdrew from this program area were 0.

Admissions Requirements:
Scores: Entries appear in this order: required test or GPA, minimum score (if required), median score of students entering in 2003–2004. Master's Programs: GRE-V 400, 480; GRE-Q 400, 580; GRE-V+Q 800, 1060; overall undergraduate GPA 3.0, 3.57; psychology GPA 3.0, 3.6.
Other Criteria: (importance of criteria rated low, medium, or high): GRE/MAT scores medium, research experience high, work experience medium, extracurricular activity medium, clinically related public service medium, GPA high, letters of recommendation high, interview high, statement of goals and objectives high.

Student Characteristics: The following represents characteristics of students in 2004–2005 in all graduate psychology programs in the department: Female–full-time 59, part-time 0; Male–full-time 12, part-time 0; African American/Black–full-time 5, part-time 0; Hispanic/Latino(a)–full-time 2, part-time 0; Asian/Pacific Islander–full-time 0, part-time 0; American Indian/Alaska Native–full-time 1, part-time 0; Caucasian–full-time 63, part-time 0; Multi-ethnic–full-time 0, part-time 0; students subject to the Americans With Disabilities Act–full-time 0, part-time 0.

Financial Information/Assistance:
Tuition for Full-Time Study: *Master's:* State residents: per academic year $3,216; Nonstate residents: per academic year $8,040. See the following Web site for updates and changes in tuition costs: http://www.registrar.siue.edu.

Financial Assistance:

First Year Students: Research assistantships available for first-year. Average amount paid per academic year: $3,442. Average number of hours worked per week: 10. Apply by March 1. Tuition remission given: full. Fellowships and scholarships available for first-year. Average amount paid per academic year: $6,884. Average number of hours worked per week: 0. Apply by February 3. Tuition remission given: full.

Advanced Students: Research assistantships available for advanced students. Average amount paid per academic year: $3,690. Average number of hours worked per week: 10. Apply by March 1. Tuition remission given: full.

Contact Information: Of all students currently enrolled full-time, 75% benefitted from one or more of the listed financial assistance programs.

Internships/Practica: All graduate programs require at least four credit hours of supervised practicum experience in appropriate professional settings. The Specialist Degree Program also requires a 10-hour paid internship.

Housing and Day Care: On-campus housing is available. See the following Web site for more information: http://www.siue.edu/HOUSING/. On-campus day care facilities are available.

Employment of Department Graduates:

Master's Degree Graduates: Of those who graduated in the academic year 2003–2004, the following categories and numbers represent the post-graduate activities and employment of master's degree graduates: Enrolled in a post-doctoral residency/fellowship (n/a), employed in independent practice (n/a), total from the above (master's) (0).

Doctoral Degree Graduates: Of those who graduated in the academic year 2003–2004, the following categories and numbers represent the post-graduate activities and employment of doctoral degree graduates: Enrolled in a psychology doctoral program (n/a), total from the above (doctoral) (0).

Additional Information:

Orientation, Objectives, and Emphasis of Department: The faculty comprises members whose skills span the entire field of psychology — clinical, experimental, social, industrial/organizational, school, community, and developmental. On the whole, the department is eclectic in orientation. Students in each specialization are provided with training that is balanced between scientific and applied orientations.

Special Facilities or Resources: The psychology department facilities house faculty offices, classrooms, and approximately 10,000 square feet of laboratory space. Sophisticated research and instructional equipment is available, including mini- and microcomputers, videotaping equipment, and computer terminals. Special laboratories are available for learning, motivation, information processing, developmental, clinical, and psychometric activities.

Information for Students With Physical Disabilities: See the following Web site for more information: http://www.siue.edu/DSS/.

Application Information:

Send to: Attention: Graduate Records Secretary, Psychology Department, Box 1121, Edwardsville, IL 62026. Application available online.

URL of online application: http://www.siue.edu/PSYCHOLOGY/graduate/apintro.htm. Students are admitted in the Fall, application deadline March 1. *Fee:* $30.

Southern Illinois University, at Carbondale

Department of Psychology
Life Science Building II, Room 281
Carbondale, IL 62901
Telephone: (618) 536-2301
Fax: (618) 453-3563
E-mail: *swanson@siu.edu*
Web: *http://www.siu.edu/~psyc*

Department Information:

1948. Chairperson: Jane Swanson. Number of Faculty: total–full-time 29, part-time 2; women–full-time 16, part-time 2; minority–full-time 3.

Programs and Degrees Offered:

Listed in the following order: Program area, degree type (T if terminal Master's), number awarded 7/03–6/04. Clinical PhD (Doctor of Philosophy) 7, Counseling PhD (Doctor of Philosophy) 6, Applied Psychology PhD (Doctor of Philosophy) 3, Brain and Cognitive Sciences PhD (Doctor of Philosophy).

APA Accreditation: Clinical PhD (Doctor of Philosophy). Counseling PhD (Doctor of Philosophy).

Student Applications/Admissions:

Student Applications

Clinical PhD (Doctor of Philosophy)—Applications 2004–2005, 75. Total applicants accepted 2004–2005, 10. Number enrolled (new admits only) 2004–2005 full-time, 10. Openings 2005–2006, 8. The Median number of years required for completion of a degree are 6. The number of students enrolled full and part-time who were dismissed or voluntarily withdrew from this program area were 0. *Counseling PhD (Doctor of Philosophy)*—Applications 2004–2005, 85. Total applicants accepted 2004–2005, 10. Number enrolled (new admits only) 2004–2005 full-time, 9. Total enrolled 2004–2005 full-time, 34, part-time, 2. Openings 2005–2006, 7. The Median number of years required for completion of a degree are 5. The number of students enrolled full and part-time who were dismissed or voluntarily withdrew from this program area were 0. *Applied Psychology PhD (Doctor of Philosophy)*—Applications 2004–2005, 18. Total applicants accepted 2004–2005, 11. Number enrolled (new admits only) 2004–2005 full-time, 4. Openings 2005–2006, 5. The Median number of years required for completion of a degree are 5. The number of students enrolled full and part-time who were dismissed or voluntarily withdrew from this program area were 0. *Brain and Cognitive Sciences PhD (Doctor of Philosophy)*—Number enrolled (new admits only) 2004–2005 full-time, 5. Total enrolled 2004–2005 full-time, 17. Openings 2005–2006, 5. The number of students enrolled full and part-time who were dismissed or voluntarily withdrew from this program area were 1.

Admissions Requirements:

Scores: Entries appear in this order: required test or GPA, minimum score (if required), median score of students entering

in 2003–2004. Doctoral Programs: GRE-V no minimum stated, 620; GRE-Q no minimum stated, 700; overall undergraduate GPA no minimum stated, 3.76.

Other Criteria: (importance of criteria rated low, medium, or high): GRE/MAT scores medium, research experience high, work experience medium, extracurricular activity medium, clinically related public service medium, GPA medium, letters of recommendation high, interview high, statement of goals and objectives high, Some variation across programs. Clinical/work experiences relevant to programs are important. For additional information on admission requirements, go to: http://www.siu.edu/~psyc/.

Student Characteristics: The following represents characteristics of students in 2004–2005 in all graduate psychology programs in the department: Female–full-time 89, part-time 0; Male–full-time 27, part-time 0; African American/Black–full-time 11, part-time 0; Hispanic/Latino(a)–full-time 11, part-time 0; Asian/Pacific Islander–full-time 7, part-time 0; American Indian/Alaska Native–full-time 0, part-time 0; Caucasian–full-time 87, part-time 0; Multi-ethnic–full-time 0, part-time 0; students subject to the Americans With Disabilities Act–full-time 0, part-time 0.

Financial Information/Assistance:
Tuition for Full-Time Study: *Master's:* State residents: per academic year $5,447, $121 per credit hour; Nonstate residents: per academic year $10,894, $242 per credit hour. *Doctoral:* State residents: per academic year $5,447, $121 per credit hour; Nonstate residents: per academic year $10,894, $242 per credit hour. Tuition is subject to change.

Financial Assistance:
First Year Students: Teaching assistantships available for first-year. Average amount paid per academic year: $11,500. Average number of hours worked per week: 20. Tuition remission given: full. Research assistantships available for first-year. Average amount paid per academic year: $11,500. Average number of hours worked per week: 20. Tuition remission given: full. Fellowships and scholarships available for first-year. Average amount paid per academic year: $11,500. Average number of hours worked per week: 20. Tuition remission given: full.

Advanced Students: Teaching assistantships available for advanced students. Average amount paid per academic year: $12,500. Average number of hours worked per week: 20. Tuition remission given: full. Research assistantships available for advanced students. Average amount paid per academic year: $12,500. Average number of hours worked per week: 20. Tuition remission given: full. Traineeships available for advanced students. Average amount paid per academic year: $12,500. Average number of hours worked per week: 20. Tuition remission given: full. Fellowships and scholarships available for advanced students. Average amount paid per academic year: $12,000. Average number of hours worked per week: 20. Tuition remission given: full.

Contact Information: Of all students currently enrolled full-time, 100% benefitted from one or more of the listed financial assistance programs. Application and information available online at: http://www.gradapp.siu.edu/.

Internships/Practica: A variety of practica and field experiences are available at a university Clinical Center, campus Counseling Center, campus Health Service, Applied Research Consultants, and various local mental health centers, hospitals, and human service agencies. For those doctoral students for whom a professional internship is required prior to graduation, 10 applied in 2003–2004. Of those who applied, 9 were placed in internships listed by the Association of Psychology Postdoctoral and Internship Programs (APPIC); 9 were placed in APA accredited internships.

Housing and Day Care: On-campus housing is available. See the following Web site for more information: http://www.housing.siu.edu/. On-campus day care facilities are available. See the following Web site for more information: Rainbow's End Child Development Center: http://www.siu.edu/%7Estuddev/rainbow.html. Child Development Lab - (618) 536-4221.

Employment of Department Graduates:
Master's Degree Graduates: Of those who graduated in the academic year 2003–2004, the following categories and numbers represent the post-graduate activities and employment of master's degree graduates: Enrolled in a post-doctoral residency/fellowship (n/a), employed in independent practice (n/a), total from the above (master's) (0).

Doctoral Degree Graduates: Of those who graduated in the academic year 2003–2004, the following categories and numbers represent the post-graduate activities and employment of doctoral degree graduates: Enrolled in a psychology doctoral program (n/a), employed in independent practice (0), employed in an academic position at a university (0), employed in an academic position at a 2-year/4-year college (2), employed in other positions at a higher education institution (4), employed in a professional position in a school system (0), employed in business or industry (research/consulting) (1), employed in business or industry (management) (0), employed in a government agency (research) (2), employed in a government agency (professional services) (0), employed in a community mental health/counseling center (3), employed in a hospital/medical center (3), still seeking employment (0), other employment position (1), do not know (0), total from the above (doctoral) (16).

Additional Information:
Orientation, Objectives, and Emphasis of Department: The department maintains a collaborative learning environment that is responsive to student needs, that promotes professional development, and that sustains high academic standards. In all programs the student selects courses from a rich curriculum that promotes mastery of core material while allowing the pursuit of particular interests. A favorable student-faculty ratio permits close supervision of students, whether in student research, clinical/applied practica, or training assignments that provide graduated experience in research, teaching, and service as a complement to formal coursework. Such training serves to expose students to many of the activities in which they will be engaged after receiving their degrees. Potential applicants should explore our website to learn more about the unique features of specific programs.

Special Facilities or Resources: The department is located in a building having extensive laboratory facilities for human and animal research available to all students. Additional facilities include a clinic and a counseling center for practicum and research experiences.

Information for Students With Physical Disabilities: See the following Web site for more information: http://www.siu.edu/~dss/.

Application Information:
Send to: Psychology Graduate Admissions, SIU-C, Mailcode 6502, Carbondale, IL 62901-6502. Application available online. URL of online application: http://www.gradapp.siu.edu/. Students are admitted in the Fall, application deadline varies. Application Deadline varies by program: Clinical: December 1, Counseling: December 1, Applied Psychology: February 1, Brain and Cognitive Sciences: February 1. *Fee:* $20. Students experiencing significant financial need may apply for waiver.

Western Illinois University
Department of Psychology
Arts and Sciences
Waggoner Hall
Macomb, IL 61455
Telephone: (309) 298-1593
Fax: (309) 298-2179
E-mail: *psychology@wiu.edu*
Web: *http://www.wiu.edu/users/psychology*

Department Information:
1960. Chairperson: Virginia A. Diehl. Number of Faculty: total–full-time 20, part-time 5; women–full-time 9, part-time 2; minority–part-time 1.

Programs and Degrees Offered:
Listed in the following order: Program area, degree type (T if terminal Master's), number awarded 7/03–6/04. Clinical/Community Mental Health MA/MS (Master of Arts/Science) (T) 2, General Experimental MA/MS (Master of Arts/Science) (T) 3, School Other 8.

Student Applications/Admissions:
Student Applications
Clinical/Community Mental Health MA/MS (Master of Arts/Science)—Applications 2004–2005, 23. Total applicants accepted 2004–2005, 11. Number enrolled (new admits only) 2004–2005 full-time, 6. Total enrolled 2004–2005 full-time, 9, part-time, 1. Openings 2005–2006, 8. The Median number of years required for completion of a degree are 3. The number of students enrolled full and part-time who were dismissed or voluntarily withdrew from this program area were 1. *General Experimental MA/MS (Master of Arts/Science)*—Applications 2004–2005, 19. Total applicants accepted 2004–2005, 9. Number enrolled (new admits only) 2004–2005 full-time, 7. Number enrolled (new admits only) 2004–2005 part-time, 0. Total enrolled 2004–2005 full-time, 16, part-time, 1. Openings 2005–2006, 10. The Median number of years required for completion of a degree are 2. The number of students enrolled full and part-time who were dismissed or voluntarily withdrew from this program area were 2. *School Other*—Applications 2004–2005, 40. Total applicants accepted 2004–2005, 18. Number enrolled (new admits only) 2004–2005 full-time, 9. Openings 2005–2006, 10. The Median number of years required for completion of a degree are 3. The number of students enrolled full and part-time who were dismissed or voluntarily withdrew from this program area were 0.

Admissions Requirements:
Scores: Entries appear in this order: required test or GPA, minimum score (if required), median score of students entering in 2003–2004. Master's Programs: GRE-V 500, 540; GRE-Q 500, 532; GRE-V+Q no minimum stated, 1072; overall undergraduate GPA 2.75, 3.27; last 2 years GPA 2.75, 3.32; psychology GPA no minimum stated, 3.30.
Other Criteria: (importance of criteria rated low, medium, or high): GRE/MAT scores medium, research experience medium, work experience medium, extracurricular activity low, clinically related public service medium, GPA high, letters of recommendation high, interview low, statement of goals and objectives medium.

Student Characteristics: The following represents characteristics of students in 2004–2005 in all graduate psychology programs in the department: Female–full-time 32, part-time 1; Male–full-time 11, part-time 1; African American/Black–full-time 1, part-time 0; Hispanic/Latino(a)–full-time 0, part-time 0; Asian/Pacific Islander–full-time 2, part-time 0; American Indian/Alaska Native–full-time 0, part-time 0; Caucasian–full-time 40, part-time 2; students subject to the Americans With Disabilities Act–full-time 0, part-time 0.

Financial Information/Assistance:
Tuition for Full-Time Study: *Master's:* State residents: per academic year $4,002, $166 per credit hour; Nonstate residents: per academic year $8,004, $333 per credit hour. Tuition is subject to change. See the following Web site for updates and changes in tuition costs: www.wiu.edu/grad/resources/fees.shtml.

Financial Assistance:
First Year Students: Research assistantships available for first-year. Average amount paid per academic year: $6,072. Average number of hours worked per week: 10. Tuition remission given: full.
Advanced Students: Research assistantships available for advanced students. Average amount paid per academic year: $6,072. Average number of hours worked per week: 10. Tuition remission given: full.
Contact Information: Of all students currently enrolled full-time, 80% benefitted from one or more of the listed financial assistance programs. Application and information available online at: http://www.wiu.edu/grad/resources/fees.shtml.

Internships/Practica: The Clinical/Community Mental Health program includes a four semester practicum sequence of intensive, supervised work in the department's Psychology Clinic. A paid internship for which post-graduate credit is given prepares students for jobs in clinical psychology. Practicum work in community schools and the department's psychoeducational clinic under faculty supervision is required throughout both years of the School Psychology Program, and a paid internship for which post-graduate credit is given prepares students for certification in Illinois.

Housing and Day Care: On-campus housing is available. Office of Graduate and Family Housing in the Office of University Housing and Dining Services in Seal Hall, telephone 309/298-3331. On-campus day care facilities are available. WIU Preschool and Infant Center at Horrabin Hall.

Employment of Department Graduates:

Master's Degree Graduates: Of those who graduated in the academic year 2003–2004, the following categories and numbers represent the post-graduate activities and employment of master's degree graduates: Enrolled in a psychology doctoral program (2), enrolled in a post-doctoral residency/fellowship (n/a), employed in independent practice (n/a), employed in a professional position in a school system (8), employed in a community mental health/ counseling center (1), do not know (2), total from the above (master's) (13).

Doctoral Degree Graduates: Of those who graduated in the academic year 2003–2004, the following categories and numbers represent the post-graduate activities and employment of doctoral degree graduates: Enrolled in a psychology doctoral program (n/a), total from the above (doctoral) (0).

Additional Information:

Orientation, Objectives, and Emphasis of Department: The psychology department offers master's degrees in clinical/community mental health (Clin/CMH), and general experimental psychology, and a Specialist degree in school psychology. Clin/CMH-MS and School-Specialist degrees are three year programs with the third year consisting of a paid internship. The emphasis in the Clin/CMH program is to prepare students to assume professional responsibilities in outpatient mental health settings. Central to the program is the practicum experience offered through the University Psychology Clinic. Graduates of the Clin/CMH program have found employment in a variety of mental health agencies, with over 90 percent of all graduates currently employed in mental health positions. Students in the general psychology program engage in one to two years of coursework in psychology. The opportunity to specialize in industrial/organizational, social, developmental, or experimental psychology is available within the general psychology program. Many students completing the general program have been admitted to PhD programs in psychology. Students in the school psychology program acquire an academic background in psychology and a practical awareness of public school systems. During the first year of the program, students are placed in elementary schools for practical experience, and during their second year, students work in the university psychoeducational clinic. Graduates of the program have had no difficulty finding employment as school psychologists following their internships. Many have also pursued doctoral training.

Special Facilities or Resources: The Department of Psychology is housed in a large modern structure providing facilities for teaching, clinical training, and human and animal research. The department has 55 rooms, including regular classrooms, seminar rooms, observation rooms, small experimental cubicles, and neuroscience labs. Computers are available throughout the department and campus. The department operates a psychology clinic for community referrals, which aids in clinical training, and a psychoeducational clinic for training in school psychology.

Information for Students With Physical Disabilities: See the following Web site for more information: http://www.student. services.wiu.edu/dss/DSS.asp.

Application Information:
Send to: School of Graduate Studies, Western Illinois University, #1 University Circle, Macomb, IL 61455. Application available online. URL of online application: www.wiu.edu/grad/prospective/classifica tion.shtml. Students are admitted in the Fall, application deadline March 1st; Spring, application deadline. Spring and Fall admission only pertains to the MS in General Experimental Program. The School Psychology and Clinical/Community Mental Health Programs only take Fall semester applicants and the application deadline is March 1st. *Fee:* $30.

Wheaton College
Department of Psychology
501 College Avenue
Wheaton, IL 60187-5593
Telephone: (630) 752-5762
Fax: (630) 752-7033
E-mail: *robert.j.gregory@wheaton.edu*
Web: *http://www.wheaton.edu*

Department Information:
1979. Chairperson: Robert.J.Gregory, PhD. Number of Faculty: total–full-time 19, part-time 16; women–full-time 6, part-time 7; minority–full-time 2, part-time 5; faculty subject to the Americans With Disabilities Act 1.

Programs and Degrees Offered:
Listed in the following order: Program area, degree type (T if terminal Master's), number awarded 7/03–6/04. Clinical Psychology MA/MS (Master of Arts/Science) (T) 30, Clinical Psychology PsyD (Doctor of Psychology) 18.

Student Applications/Admissions:
Student Applications
Clinical Psychology MA/MS (Master of Arts/Science)—Applications 2004–2005, 70. Total applicants accepted 2004–2005, 31. Total enrolled 2004–2005 full-time, 62, part-time, 3. Openings 2005–2006, 30. The Median number of years required for completion of a degree are 2. The number of students enrolled full and part-time who were dismissed or voluntarily withdrew from this program area were 0. *Clinical Psychology PsyD (Doctor of Psychology)*—Applications 2004–2005, 81. Total applicants accepted 2004–2005, 31. Total enrolled 2004–2005 full-time, 91, part-time, 8. Openings 2005–2006, 22. The Median number of years required for completion of a degree are 5. The number of students enrolled full and part-time who were dismissed or voluntarily withdrew from this program area were 1.

Admissions Requirements:
Scores: Entries appear in this order: required test or GPA, minimum score (if required), median score of students entering in 2003–2004. Master's Programs: overall undergraduate GPA 2.8, 3.5. Doctoral Programs: overall undergraduate GPA 3.0, 3.6.
Other Criteria: (importance of criteria rated low, medium, or high): GRE/MAT scores medium, research experience medium, work experience medium, extracurricular activity low, clinically related public service medium, GPA medium, letters of recommendation high, interview high, statement of goals and objectives high.

Student Characteristics: The following represents characteristics of students in 2004–2005 in all graduate psychology programs in the department: Female–full-time 98, part-time 7; Male–full-time 55, part-time 4; African American/Black–full-time 5, part-time 0; Hispanic/Latino(a)–full-time 12, part-time 1; Asian/Pacific Islander–full-time 9, part-time 2; American Indian/Alaska Native–full-time 0, part-time 0; Caucasian–full-time 121, part-time 7; Multi-ethnic–full-time 6, part-time 1; students subject to the Americans With Disabilities Act–full-time 1, part-time 1.

Financial Information/Assistance:

Tuition for Full-Time Study: *Master's:* State residents: per academic year $9,840, $502 per credit hour; Nonstate residents: per academic year $9,840, $502 per credit hour. *Doctoral:* State residents: per academic year $16,598, $650 per credit hour; Nonstate residents: per academic year $16,598, $650 per credit hour. Tuition is subject to change. See the following Web site for updates and changes in tuition costs: www.wheaton.edu.

Financial Assistance:

First Year Students: Teaching assistantships available for first-year. Average amount paid per academic year: $5,000. Average number of hours worked per week: 10. Research assistantships available for first-year. Average amount paid per academic year: $5,000. Average number of hours worked per week: 10. Traineeships available for first-year. Average amount paid per academic year: $5,000. Average number of hours worked per week: 16. Fellowships and scholarships available for first-year. Average amount paid per academic year: $3,000.

Advanced Students: Teaching assistantships available for advanced students. Average amount paid per academic year: $5,000. Average number of hours worked per week: 10. Research assistantships available for advanced students. Average amount paid per academic year: $5,000. Average number of hours worked per week: 10. Traineeships available for advanced students. Average amount paid per academic year: $5,000. Average number of hours worked per week: 15. Fellowships and scholarships available for advanced students. Average amount paid per academic year: $3,500.

Contact Information: Of all students currently enrolled full-time, 100% benefitted from one or more of the listed financial assistance programs.

Internships/Practica: The Graduate Psychology Programs have liaisons with over 90 agencies in the Chicago and Suburban Area with facility types ranging from hospitals, clinics, community agencies, residential, and correctional facilities. The MA Program requires 500 on-site hours and the PsyD requires a minimum of 1200 hours. Faculty are involved through professional development groups while students are placed in field assignments. For those doctoral students for whom a professional internship is required prior to graduation, 14 applied in 2003–2004. Of those who applied, 14 were placed in internships listed by the Association of Psychology Postdoctoral and Internship Programs (APPIC); 8 were placed in APA accredited internships.

Housing and Day Care: On-campus housing is available. See the following Web site for more information: www.wheaton.edu. No on-campus day care facilities are available.

Employment of Department Graduates:

Master's Degree Graduates: Of those who graduated in the academic year 2003–2004, the following categories and numbers represent the post-graduate activities and employment of master's degree graduates: Enrolled in a post-doctoral residency/fellowship (n/a), employed in independent practice (n/a), total from the above (master's) (0).

Doctoral Degree Graduates: Of those who graduated in the academic year 2003–2004, the following categories and numbers represent the post-graduate activities and employment of doctoral degree graduates: Enrolled in a psychology doctoral program (n/a), enrolled in a post-doctoral residency/fellowship (2), employed in independent practice (4), employed in an academic position at a university (1), employed in an academic position at a 2-year/4-year college (1), employed in other positions at a higher education institution (1), employed in a professional position in a school system (1), employed in a community mental health/counseling center (5), employed in a hospital/medical center (1), do not know (1), total from the above (doctoral) (17).

Additional Information:

Orientation, Objectives, and Emphasis of Department: The doctoral program aims to produce competent scholar-practitioners in clinical psychology who will understand professional practice as service. The primary emphasis of the MA program is the professional preparation of the master's level therapist for employment in clinical settings; a secondary objective is the preparation of selected students for doctoral studies. The departmental orientation is eclectic, with students exposed to the theory, research, and practical clinical skills of the major clinical models in use today. A preeminent concern of all faculty is the interface of psychological theory and practice with Christian faith. Thus, students also take coursework in the theory and practice of integrating psychology and Christian faith, and coursework in theology/biblical studies. All students participate in a growth-oriented group therapy experience or an individual therapy experience. The objectives of the department are to produce mature, capable master's and doctoral level clinicians who are well grounded in clinical theory and the essentials of professional practice, and who responsibly and capably relate their Christian faith and professional interests.

Special Facilities or Resources: The PsyD Program has its own computer lab/reading room for research and study. Many students work with faculty research projects. Opportunities exist for professional conference presentations and involvement in international projects.

Information for Students With Physical Disabilities: See the following Web site for more information: www.wheaton.edu.

Application Information:
Send to: Graduate Admissions Office, Wheaton College, 501 College Avenue, Wheaton, IL, 60187. Students are admitted in the Fall, application deadline January 15. January deadline PsyD, March 1 deadline MA. *Fee:* $50.

Ball State University (2004 data)

Department of Counseling Psychology and Guidance Services
Teachers College, Room 622
Muncie, IN 47306-0585
Telephone: (765) 285-8040
Fax: (765) 285-2067
E-mail: *sbowman@bsu.edu*
Web: *http://www.bsu.edu/counselingpsych*

Department Information:

1967. Chairperson: Sharon L. Bowman. Number of Faculty: total–full-time 12; women–full-time 7; minority–full-time 2; faculty subject to the Americans With Disabilities Act 1.

Programs and Degrees Offered:

Listed in the following order: Program area, degree type (T if terminal Master's), number awarded 7/03–6/04. Social MA/MS (Master of Arts/Science) (T) 38, Psychology MA/MS (Master of Arts/Science) (T) 3, Counseling PhD (Doctor of Philosophy) 7.

APA Accreditation: Counseling PhD (Doctor of Philosophy).

Student Applications/Admissions:

Student Applications

Social MA/MS (Master of Arts/Science)—Applications 2004–2005, 106. Total applicants accepted 2004–2005, 81. Total enrolled 2004–2005 full-time, 111, part-time, 27. Openings 2005–2006, 35. The Median number of years required for completion of a degree are 2. The number of students enrolled full and part-time who were dismissed or voluntarily withdrew from this program area were 1. *Psychology MA/MS (Master of Arts/Science)*—Applications 2004–2005, 20. Total applicants accepted 2004–2005, 11. Total enrolled 2004–2005 full-time, 15, part-time, 5. Openings 2005–2006, 15. The Median number of years required for completion of a degree are 2. The number of students enrolled full and part-time who were dismissed or voluntarily withdrew from this program area were 0. *Counseling PhD (Doctor of Philosophy)*—Applications 2004–2005, 44. Total applicants accepted 2004–2005, 15. Total enrolled 2004–2005 full-time, 40, part-time, 11. Openings 2005–2006, 10. The Median number of years required for completion of a degree are 5. The number of students enrolled full and part-time who were dismissed or voluntarily withdrew from this program area were 1.

Admissions Requirements:

Scores: Entries appear in this order: required test or GPA, minimum score (if required), median score of students entering in 2003–2004. Master's Programs: GRE-V+Q no minimum stated, 983; overall undergraduate GPA 2.75, 3.33; psychology GPA 3.00. Doctoral Programs: GRE-V+Q 1000, 980; overall undergraduate GPA 3.20, 3.89.

Other Criteria: (importance of criteria rated low, medium, or high): GRE/MAT scores medium, research experience high, work experience high, extracurricular activity medium, clinically related public service medium, GPA high, letters of rec-

ommendation high, interview medium, statement of goals and objectives high, multicultural experience high. Interview is a requirement of the Doctoral Program, not the Master's programs. For additional information on admission requirements, go to: www.bsu.edu/counselingpsych.

Student Characteristics: The following represents characteristics of students in 2004–2005 in all graduate psychology programs in the department: Female–full-time 118, part-time 33; Male–full-time 48, part-time 10; African American/Black–full-time 7, part-time 0; Hispanic/Latino(a)–full-time 3, part-time 0; Asian/Pacific Islander–full-time 8, part-time 0; American Indian/Alaska Native–full-time 0, part-time 0; Caucasian–full-time 0, part-time 0; students subject to the Americans With Disabilities Act–full-time 3, part-time 0.

Financial Information/Assistance:

Tuition for Full-Time Study: *Master's:* State residents: per academic year $1,590; Nonstate residents: per academic year $4,085. *Doctoral:* State residents: per academic year $1,590; Nonstate residents: per academic year $4,085. Tuition is subject to change. See the following Web site for updates and changes in tuition costs: www.bsu.edu.

Financial Assistance:

First Year Students: Teaching assistantships available for first-year. Average amount paid per academic year: $8,700. Average number of hours worked per week: 20. Apply by February 1. Tuition remission given: full. Research assistantships available for first-year. Average amount paid per academic year: $8,700. Average number of hours worked per week: 20. Apply by February 1. Tuition remission given: full. Fellowships and scholarships available for first-year. Average amount paid per academic year: $12,000. Average number of hours worked per week: 0. Apply by February 1. Tuition remission given: full.

Advanced Students: Teaching assistantships available for advanced students. Average amount paid per academic year: $8,700. Average number of hours worked per week: 20. Apply by March 1. Tuition remission given: full. Traineeships available for advanced students. Average amount paid per academic year: $8,700. Apply by March 1. Fellowships and scholarships available for advanced students. Average amount paid per academic year: $12,000. Average number of hours worked per week: 0. Apply by March 1. Tuition remission given: full.

Contact Information: Of all students currently enrolled full-time, 85% benefitted from one or more of the listed financial assistance programs.

Internships/Practica: The department operates a practicum clinic that serves the surrounding community on a low-cost basis. All counseling master's students and doctoral students are required to complete at least one practicum in this clinic. Other practicum opportunities are available at the university counseling center, a local elementary school, and the nearby medical hospital. Master's students also are required to complete an internship prior to graduation. The Internship Director maintains a listing of available sites and assists students in identifying and securing such a site. Most of these sites are unpaid, although a few are paying sites. Doctoral students typically seek APA-approved pre-doctoral internship sites. There is one such site on campus, in the university's counseling center. Although that site does not guarantee a slot to students from this program, usually one student a year is placed there. For those doctoral students for whom a professional internship is required prior to graduation, 4 applied in 2003–2004. Of those who applied, 4 were placed in internships listed by the Association of Psychology Postdoctoral and Internship Programs (APPIC); 4 were placed in APA accredited internships.

Housing and Day Care: On-campus housing is available. See the following Web site for more information: www.bsu.edu/housing. On-campus day care facilities are available.

Employment of Department Graduates:

Master's Degree Graduates: Of those who graduated in the academic year 2003–2004, the following categories and numbers represent the post-graduate activities and employment of master's degree graduates: Enrolled in a psychology doctoral program (10), enrolled in another graduate/professional program (5), enrolled in a post-doctoral residency/fellowship (n/a), employed in independent practice (n/a), employed in an academic position at a university (0), employed in an academic position at a 2-year/4-year college (0), employed in other positions at a higher education institution (0), employed in a professional position in a school system (10), employed in business or industry (research/consulting) (0), employed in business or industry (management) (0), employed in a government agency (research) (0), employed in a government agency (professional services) (2), employed in a community mental health/counseling center (3), employed in a hospital/medical center (0), other employment position (3), do not know (3), total from the above (master's) (36).

Doctoral Degree Graduates: Of those who graduated in the academic year 2003–2004, the following categories and numbers represent the post-graduate activities and employment of doctoral degree graduates: Enrolled in a psychology doctoral program (n/a), enrolled in a post-doctoral residency/fellowship (2), employed in independent practice (0), employed in an academic position at a university (1), employed in an academic position at a 2-year/4-year college (0), employed in other positions at a higher education institution (3), employed in a professional position in a school system (0), employed in business or industry (research/consulting) (0), employed in business or industry (management) (0), employed in a government agency (research) (0), employed in a government agency (professional services) (0), employed in a community mental health/counseling center (1), employed in a hospital/medical center (1), still seeking employment (0), other employment position (0), do not know (1), total from the above (doctoral) (9).

Additional Information:

Orientation, Objectives, and Emphasis of Department: The objective of the master's counseling programs is to prepare persons to be effective counselors by providing students with a common professional core of courses and experiences. The faculty is committed to keeping abreast of trends, skills, and knowledge and to modifying the program to prepare students for their profession. Students will be able to practice in a variety of settings using therapeutic, preventive, or developmental counseling approaches. The counseling programs also prepare students for doctoral study in counseling psychology. The program goals are to develop an atmosphere conducive to inquiry, creativity, and learning and to

the discovery of new knowledge through research, counseling, and interactive involvement between students and faculty. The master's program in social psychology provides a conceptual background for those pursuing careers in education, counseling, criminology, personnel work, etc. and prepares students for entry into doctoral programs in social psychology. The doctoral program is designed to broaden students' knowledge beyond the master's degree. The rigorous program includes a sound theoretical basis, a substantial experiential component, a research component, and a variety of assistantship assignments. A basic core of courses stresses competence in the social, psychological, biological, cognitive, and affective bases of behavior. The counseling psychology PhD program is structured within a scientist-professional model of training.

Special Facilities or Resources: Departmental instructional and research facilities are exceptional. The facilities of the department occupy the sixth floor of the Teachers College building and include ten practicum rooms, an observation corridor, several group observation rooms, and computer access. Most of these facilities are linked to a control room for use of audio and video media. The computer terminals are connected to the university VAX computer cluster. The department operates an outpatient counseling clinic that serves as the training facility for all counseling graduate students. The clinic serves clients from Muncie and surrounding communities as well as Ball State faculty/staff. The university operates a separate state-of-the-art counseling center that serves as a training site for a select number of graduate students from the department.

Information for Students With Physical Disabilities: See the following Web site for more information: www.bsu.edu/dsd.

Application Information:
Send to: Department of Counseling Psychology and Guidance Services, Teachers College, Ball State University, Muncie, IN 47306. Application available online. Students are admitted in the Winter, application deadline February 1; Summer, application deadline June 15. Doctoral program—January 15. Counseling (Rehabilitation track) has rolling admissions. The summer deadline applies only to the master's programs. *Fee:* $25 for BSU alumni; $35 for those who have not received a degree from Ball State University.

Ball State University
Department of Psychological Science
Sciences and Humanities
Muncie, IN 47306-0520
Telephone: (765) 285-1690
Fax: (765) 285-8980
E-mail: *kpickel@bsu.edu*
Web: *http://www.bsu.edu/provost/graduate/psysc*

Department Information:
1968. Chairperson: Michael Stevenson. Number of Faculty: total–full-time 21, part-time 4; women–full-time 9, part-time 2; minority–full-time 1.

Programs and Degrees Offered:
Listed in the following order: Program area, degree type (T if terminal Master's), number awarded 7/03–6/04. Clinical MA/MS

(Master of Arts/Science) (T) 12, Cognitive and Social Processes MA/MS (Master of Arts/Science) (T) 7.

Student Applications/Admissions:

Student Applications

Clinical MA/MS (Master of Arts/Science)—Applications 2004–2005, 60. Total applicants accepted 2004–2005, 11. Number enrolled (new admits only) 2004–2005 full-time, 11. Number enrolled (new admits only) 2004–2005 part-time, 0. Openings 2005–2006, 12. The Median number of years required for completion of a degree are 2. The number of students enrolled full and part-time who were dismissed or voluntarily withdrew from this program area were 0. Cognitive and Social Processes MA/MS (Master of Arts/Science)—Applications 2004–2005, 25. Total applicants accepted 2004–2005, 8. Number enrolled (new admits only) 2004–2005 full-time, 8. Number enrolled (new admits only) 2004–2005 part-time, 0. Total enrolled 2004–2005 full-time, 15, part-time, 1. Openings 2005–2006, 8. The Median number of years required for completion of a degree are 2.

Admissions Requirements:

Scores: Entries appear in this order: required test or GPA, minimum score (if required), median score of students entering in 2003–2004. Master's Programs: GRE-V no minimum stated, 490; GRE-Q no minimum stated, 530; GRE-Analytical no minimum stated, 610; overall undergraduate GPA no minimum stated, 3.53; last 2 years GPA no minimum stated, 3.71; psychology GPA no minimum stated, 3.85.

Other Criteria: (importance of criteria rated low, medium, or high): GRE/MAT scores high, research experience high, work experience medium, extracurricular activity medium, clinically related public service medium, GPA high, letters of recommendation high, statement of goals and objectives high. Clinical service not important for Cognitive and Social Processes program. For additional information on admission requirements, go to: www.bsu.edu/provost/graduate/psysc.

Student Characteristics: The following represents characteristics of students in 2004–2005 in all graduate psychology programs in the department: Female–full-time 24, part-time 1; Male–full-time 14, part-time 0; African American/Black–full-time 1, part-time 0; Hispanic/Latino(a)–full-time 0, part-time 0; Asian/Pacific Islander–full-time 3, part-time 0; American Indian/Alaska Native–full-time 0, part-time 0; Caucasian–full-time 32, part-time 2; Multi-ethnic–full-time 1, part-time 0; students subject to the Americans With Disabilities Act–full-time 0, part-time 0.

Financial Information/Assistance:

Tuition for Full-Time Study: Master's: State residents: per academic year $5,532; Nonstate residents: per academic year $13,950. Tuition is subject to change. See the following Web site for updates and changes in tuition costs: http://www.bsu.edu/web/bursar/tuition_fees_payments/11_schedule_of_fees/index.htm.

Financial Assistance:

First Year Students: Teaching assistantships available for first-year. Average amount paid per academic year: $7,500. Average number of hours worked per week: 20. Apply by March 1. Tuition remission given: partial. Research assistantships available for first-year. Average amount paid per academic year: $7,500.

Average number of hours worked per week: 20. Apply by March 1. Tuition remission given: partial.

Advanced Students: Teaching assistantships available for advanced students. Average amount paid per academic year: $7,500. Average number of hours worked per week: 20. Apply by March 1. Tuition remission given: partial. Research assistantships available for advanced students. Average amount paid per academic year: $7,500. Average number of hours worked per week: 20. Apply by March 1. Tuition remission given: partial.

Contact Information: Of all students currently enrolled full-time, 44% benefitted from one or more of the listed financial assistance programs. Application and information available online at: www.bsu.edu/provost/graduate/psysc.

Internships/Practica: Practica for clinical students are available at the University Counseling Center, Community Mental Health Centers, Youth Opportunity Center, a V.A. hospital, and elsewhere.

Housing and Day Care: On-campus housing is available. See the following Web site for more information: http://www.bsu.edu/provost/graduate/housing.htm. On-campus day care facilities are available. See the following Web site for more information: http://www.bsu.edu/hrs/workfam/childcar.htm.

Employment of Department Graduates:

Master's Degree Graduates: Of those who graduated in the academic year 2003–2004, the following categories and numbers represent the post-graduate activities and employment of master's degree graduates: Enrolled in a post-doctoral residency/fellowship (n/a), employed in independent practice (n/a), total from the above (master's) (0).

Doctoral Degree Graduates: Of those who graduated in the academic year 2003–2004, the following categories and numbers represent the post-graduate activities and employment of doctoral degree graduates: Enrolled in a psychology doctoral program (n/a), total from the above (doctoral) (0).

Additional Information:

Orientation, Objectives, and Emphasis of Department: The department functions as an arts and sciences psychology department and offers courses in the core content areas of the discipline along with more specialized clinical courses. The faculty are diverse in their backgrounds: approximately seven have experimental backgrounds, and the remainder for the most part have more specialized backgrounds in applied fields such as clinical, counseling, industrial, and neuropsychology. Among the clinical faculty, cognitive behavioral and traditional approaches are present. The department's primary goal is to prepare students for doctoral study, although we also serve those seeking employment upon completion of the master's degree. The faculty welcome and encourage research collaborations with students.

Special Facilities or Resources: Students have access to university and departmental computers. The department maintains space for faculty and student research. For clinical majors, various cooperative agencies are available for practicum placement.

Information for Students With Physical Disabilities: See the following Web site for more information: http://www.bsu.edu/dsd/.

Application Information:

Send to: Kerri Pickel, PhD, Director of Graduate Studies, Department of Psychological Science, Ball State University, Muncie, IN 47306-0520. Application available online. URL of online application: www.bsu.edu/provost/graduate/psysc. Students are admitted in the Fall, application deadline March 1. For cognitive and social processes program, 6 weeks prior to either fall or spring semester if space permits. *Fee:* $35. Waiver for McNair Scholars; fee is $25 for applicants who have ever received any degree from Ball State University.

Ball State University

PhD Program in School Psychology
Teachers College
Muncie, IN 47306
Telephone: (765) 285-8500
Fax: (765) 285-3653
E-mail: *rdean@bsu.edu*
Web: *http://www.bsu.edu/teachers/departments/edpsy*

Department Information:

1967. Chairperson: Dan Lapsley. Number of Faculty: total–full-time 18, part-time 15; women–full-time 11, part-time 6; minority–full-time 2.

Programs and Degrees Offered:

Listed in the following order: Program area, degree type (T if terminal Master's), number awarded 7/03–6/04. School Psychology PhD (Doctor of Philosophy) 10, Educational Psychology MA/MS (Master of Arts/Science) (T) 9, School Psychology MA/MS (Master of Arts/Science) 10, School Psychology EdS (Education Specialist) 3, Educational Psychology PhD (Doctor of Philosophy) 0.

APA Accreditation: School PhD (Doctor of Philosophy).

Student Applications/Admissions:

Student Applications

School Psychology PhD (Doctor of Philosophy)—Applications 2004–2005, 37. Total applicants accepted 2004–2005, 8. Number enrolled (new admits only) 2004–2005 full-time, 8. Openings 2005–2006, 10. The Median number of years required for completion of a degree are 5. The number of students enrolled full and part-time who were dismissed or voluntarily withdrew from this program area were 0. *Educational Psychology MA MA/MS (Master of Arts/Science)*—Applications 2004–2005, 10. Total applicants accepted 2004–2005, 5. Number enrolled (new admits only) 2004–2005 full-time, 7. Openings 2005–2006, 10. The Median number of years required for completion of a degree are 2. The number of students enrolled full and part-time who were dismissed or voluntarily withdrew from this program area were 0. *School Psychology MA/MS (Master of Arts/Science)*—Applications 2004–2005, 81. Total applicants accepted 2004–2005, 10. Number enrolled (new admits only) 2004–2005 full-time, 4. Total enrolled 2004–2005 full-time, 25. Openings 2005–2006, 10. The Median number of years required for completion of a degree is 1. The number of students enrolled full and part-time who were dismissed or voluntarily withdrew from this program area were 0. *School Psychology EdS (Education Specialist)*—Applications 2004–2005, 10. Total

applicants accepted 2004–2005, 5. Number enrolled (new admits only) 2004–2005 full-time, 5. Total enrolled 2004–2005 full-time, 15. Openings 2005–2006, 5. The Median number of years required for completion of a degree are 3. The number of students enrolled full and part-time who were dismissed or voluntarily withdrew from this program area were 0. *Educational Psychology PhD (Doctor of Philosophy)*—Applications 2004–2005, 0. Total applicants accepted 2004–2005, 0. Number enrolled (new admits only) 2004–2005 full-time, 0. Number enrolled (new admits only) 2004–2005 part-time, 0. Openings 2005–2006, 5. The number of students enrolled full and part-time who were dismissed or voluntarily withdrew from this program area were 0.

Admissions Requirements:

Scores: Entries appear in this order: required test or GPA, minimum score (if required), median score of students entering in 2003–2004. Master's Programs: GRE-V no minimum stated, 480; GRE-Q no minimum stated, 560; GRE-V+Q 1000; GRE-Analytical none; overall undergraduate GPA 2.8, 3.4. Doctoral Programs: GRE-V no minimum stated, 555; GRE-Q no minimum stated, 600; GRE-V+Q 1000, 1150; GRE-Analytical no minimum stated, 575.

Other Criteria: (importance of criteria rated low, medium, or high): GRE/MAT scores high, research experience medium, work experience medium, extracurricular activity medium, clinically related public service high, GPA medium, letters of recommendation high, statement of goals and objectives medium, diversity high. These do not apply to the MA in Educational Psychology. For additional information on admission requirements, go to: http://www.bsu.edu/edpsych/.

Student Characteristics: The following represents characteristics of students in 2004–2005 in all graduate psychology programs in the department: Female–full-time 82, part-time 0; Male–full-time 23, part-time 0; African American/Black–full-time 1, part-time 0; Hispanic/Latino(a)–full-time 1, part-time 0; Asian/Pacific Islander–full-time 0, part-time 0; American Indian/Alaska Native–full-time 0, part-time 0; Caucasian–full-time 0, part-time 0; Multi-ethnic–full-time 0, part-time 0; students subject to the Americans With Disabilities Act–full-time 0, part-time 0.

Financial Information/Assistance:

Tuition for Full-Time Study: *Master's:* State residents: per academic year $4,320; Nonstate residents: per academic year $12,100. *Doctoral:* State residents: per academic year $4,320; Nonstate residents: per academic year $12,100. Tuition is subject to change. See the following Web site for updates and changes in tuition costs: Tuition is waved with a graduate fellowship—majority of students receive funding.

Financial Assistance:

First Year Students: Teaching assistantships available for first-year. Average amount paid per academic year: $9,000. Average number of hours worked per week: 20. Apply by February 15. Tuition remission given: full. Research assistantships available for first-year. Average amount paid per academic year: $9,000. Average number of hours worked per week: 20. Apply by February 15. Tuition remission given: full. Fellowships and scholarships available for first-year. Average amount paid per academic year: $9,200. Average number of hours worked per week: 0. Apply by February 15. Tuition remission given: full.

Advanced Students: Teaching assistantships available for advanced students. Average amount paid per academic year: $9,000. Average number of hours worked per week: 20. Apply by February 15. Tuition remission given: full. Research assistantships available for advanced students. Average amount paid per academic year: $9,000. Average number of hours worked per week: 20. Apply by February 15. Tuition remission given: full. Fellowships and scholarships available for advanced students. Average amount paid per academic year: $9,200. Average number of hours worked per week: 0. Apply by February 15. Tuition remission given: full.

Contact Information: Of all students currently enrolled full-time, 100% benefitted from one or more of the listed financial assistance programs. Application and information available online at: www.bsu.edu/edpsych.

Internships/Practica: School psychology students are expected to be involved in practicum experiences from very early in their programs and to continue such experiences until they enroll in internships. (500 clock hours in practicum are expected.) A school-based internship of one academic year is required of School Psychology MA/EdS students. No practicum or internship is required of the MA or PhD program in Educational Psychology. For those doctoral students for whom a professional internship is required prior to graduation, 5 applied in 2003–2004. Of those who applied, 5 were placed in APA accredited internships.

Housing and Day Care: On-campus housing is available. See the following Web site for more information: http://www.bsu.edu/web/housing/. No on-campus day care facilities are available.

Employment of Department Graduates:

Master's Degree Graduates: Of those who graduated in the academic year 2003–2004, the following categories and numbers represent the post-graduate activities and employment of master's degree graduates: Enrolled in a post-doctoral residency/fellowship (n/a), employed in independent practice (n/a), total from the above (master's) (0).

Doctoral Degree Graduates: Of those who graduated in the academic year 2003–2004, the following categories and numbers represent the post-graduate activities and employment of doctoral degree graduates: Enrolled in a psychology doctoral program (n/a), enrolled in a post-doctoral residency/fellowship (4), employed in independent practice (2), employed in an academic position at a university (3), employed in an academic position at a 2-year/4-year college (1), employed in other positions at a higher education institution (0), employed in a professional position in a school system (5), employed in business or industry (research/consulting) (0), employed in business or industry (management) (0), employed in a government agency (research) (0), employed in a government agency (professional services) (0), employed in a community mental health/counseling center (1), employed in a hospital/medical center (2), still seeking employment (0), other employment position (0), total from the above (doctoral) (18).

Additional Information:

Orientation, Objectives, and Emphasis of Department: The mission of the graduate programs is to train research scientists to make significant contributions in specialty areas and to address applied problems in educational settings. Our school psychology track further trains students to render diagnostic and remedial services and educational consultation. Specialty areas include neuropsychology, human development, learning, research methods/statistics, and gifted studies. Doctoral students are encouraged to become involved in on-going research with faculty members. The MA/EdS program is designed to train students for the professional practice of School Psychology, and to meet licensure requirements of Indiana and most states. The MA in Educational Psychology provides specialization options in human development, gifted and talented studies, and educational technology. Other specialization options can be tailored to meet the needs and interests of individual students.

Special Facilities or Resources: The department has an on-campus school psychology clinic, a neuropsychology laboratory, a computer laboratory, videotaping facilities, and adequate research facilities. The department is allied with the Office of Charter School Research and the Center for Gifted Studies and Talent Development.

Information for Students With Physical Disabilities: See the following Web site for more information: www.bsu.edu/dsd.

Application Information:
Send to: Educational Psychology, TC 524, Ball State University, Muncie, IN 47306. Application available online. URL of online application: http://www.bsu.edu/edpsych/. Students are admitted in the Spring, application deadline February 15. Application for the new PhD in Educational Psychology: March 18 Application for MA/Ed.S and PhD in School Psychology: February 15 Currently there is rolling admissions for the MA in Educational Pscyology. *Fee:* $35.

Indiana State University
Department of Counseling, Counseling Psychology Program
School of Education 1518
Terre Haute, IN 47809
Telephone: (812) 237-2832
Fax: (812) 237-2729
E-mail: *k-meeks@indstate.edu*
Web: *http://counseling.indstate.edu/dcp*

Department Information:
1968. Chairperson: Michele C. Boyer. Number of Faculty: total– full-time 7, part-time 1; women–full-time 3, part-time 1; minority– full-time 1.

Programs and Degrees Offered:
Listed in the following order: Program area, degree type (T if terminal Master's), number awarded 7/03–6/04. Counseling PhD (Doctor of Philosophy) 6.

APA Accreditation: Counseling PhD (Doctor of Philosophy).

Student Applications/Admissions:
Student Applications
Counseling PhD (Doctor of Philosophy)—Applications 2004– 2005, 36. Total applicants accepted 2004–2005, 15. Number enrolled (new admits only) 2004–2005 full-time, 8. Number enrolled (new admits only) 2004–2005 part-time, 0. Total enrolled 2004–2005 full-time, 33, part-time, 7. Openings

2005–2006, 8. The Median number of years required for completion of a degree are 4. The number of students enrolled full and part-time who were dismissed or voluntarily withdrew from this program area were 0.

Admissions Requirements:
Scores: Entries appear in this order: required test or GPA, minimum score (if required), median score of students entering in 2003–2004. Master's Programs: GRE-V 450; GRE-Q 450; overall undergraduate GPA 2.75. Doctoral Programs: GRE-V 500, 504; GRE-Q 500, 541; overall undergraduate GPA 2.5, 3.75.
Other Criteria: (importance of criteria rated low, medium, or high): GRE/MAT scores medium, research experience medium, work experience high, extracurricular activity medium, clinically related public service medium, GPA high, letters of recommendation high, interview high, statement of goals and objectives high.

Student Characteristics: The following represents characteristics of students in 2004–2005 in all graduate psychology programs in the department: Female–full-time 25, part-time 3; Male–full-time 8, part-time 4; African American/Black–full-time 4, part-time 1; Hispanic/Latino(a)–full-time 0, part-time 0; Asian/Pacific Islander–full-time 3, part-time 0; American Indian/Alaska Native–full-time 0, part-time 0; Caucasian–full-time 26, part-time 6; Multi-ethnic–full-time 0, part-time 0; students subject to the Americans With Disabilities Act–full-time 0, part-time 0.

Financial Information/Assistance:
Tuition for Full-Time Study: *Master's:* State residents: per academic year $5,292, $252 per credit hour; Nonstate residents: per academic year $10,521, $501 per credit hour. *Doctoral:* State residents: per academic year $6,048, $252 per credit hour; Nonstate residents: per academic year $12,024, $501 per credit hour. Tuition is subject to change. See the following Web site for updates and changes in tuition costs: http://www.indstate.edu/sogs/GradNewtemp/fee.html.

Financial Assistance:
First Year Students: Teaching assistantships available for first-year. Average amount paid per academic year: $5,457. Average number of hours worked per week: 15. Apply by March 1. Tuition remission given: partial. Research assistantships available for first-year. Average amount paid per academic year: $5,457. Average number of hours worked per week: 15. Apply by March 1. Tuition remission given: partial. Fellowships and scholarships available for first-year. Average amount paid per academic year: $5,457. Average number of hours worked per week: 15. Apply by March 1. Tuition remission given: partial.
Advanced Students: Teaching assistantships available for advanced students. Average amount paid per academic year: $5,457. Average number of hours worked per week: 15. Apply by March 1. Tuition remission given: partial. Research assistantships available for advanced students. Average amount paid per academic year: $5,457. Average number of hours worked per week: 15. Apply by March 1. Tuition remission given: partial. Fellowships and scholarships available for advanced students. Average amount paid per academic year: $5,457. Average number of hours worked per week: 15. Apply by March 1. Tuition remission given: partial.

Contact Information: Of all students currently enrolled full-time, 80% benefitted from one or more of the listed financial assistance programs. Application and information available online at: http://web.indstate.edu/sogs/deptforms.html.

Internships/Practica: Doctoral practica are available on campus (Student Counseling Center) and in a variety of community settings (CMHC, Schools, Hospitals, Prisons, VAMC, Primary Care Medical Settings), residential treatment facilities, and community college counseling centers. For those doctoral students for whom a professional internship is required prior to graduation, 9 applied in 2003–2004. Of those who applied, 6 were placed in internships listed by the Association of Psychology Postdoctoral and Internship Programs (APPIC); 6 were placed in APA accredited internships.

Housing and Day Care: On-campus housing is available. On-campus day care facilities are available.

Employment of Department Graduates:
Master's Degree Graduates: Of those who graduated in the academic year 2003–2004, the following categories and numbers represent the post-graduate activities and employment of master's degree graduates: Enrolled in a post-doctoral residency/fellowship (n/a), employed in independent practice (n/a), total from the above (master's) (0).
Doctoral Degree Graduates: Of those who graduated in the academic year 2003–2004, the following categories and numbers represent the post-graduate activities and employment of doctoral degree graduates: Enrolled in a psychology doctoral program (n/a), enrolled in a post-doctoral residency/fellowship (2), employed in other positions at a higher education institution (2), employed in a community mental health/counseling center (3), total from the above (doctoral) (7).

Additional Information:
Orientation, Objectives, and Emphasis of Department: The Department of Counseling is concerned with the application of principles, methods, and procedures for facilitating effective psychological functioning during the entire life-span. The focus is a developmental orientation on positive aspects of growth and preventable and remediable conditions and situations. Activities include the preparation of entry and advanced level practitioners, the conduct of research and scholarly activities, and consultation and leadership services to schools, agencies, and settings where counselors provide professional services. Such services include assessment, evaluation, and diagnosis; counseling interventions with individuals, couples, families, and groups; consultation; program development; and evaluation. These services are intended to help persons acquire or alter personal-social skills, improve adaptability to changing life demands, enhance environmental coping skills, and develop a variety of problem solving and decision making capabilities. Such services are intended to help individuals, groups, organizations, couples, or families at all age levels to cope more successfully with problems connected with education, career choice and development, work, sex, marriage, family, health, social relations, aging, and handicaps of a social or physical nature. Educative in nature, the orientation is upon avoiding or remediating problems and situations. Departmental activities and services can occur in University classrooms and laboratories, social services, mental and physical health institutions, rehabilitation and correctional institutions, and in a variety of other public and

private agencies committed to service in one or more of the problem areas cited above.

Special Facilities or Resources: The counseling psychology training area is housed in the College of Education, a 15-story modern structure. This area provides faculty and student offices, and a departmental clinic (individual and group therapy rooms, videotaping equipment with observation rooms, a biofeedback center, and a career and testing laboratory). Also available in the building are research stations, computer terminal and microcomputer labs, a statistics laboratory, a psychological evaluation library, testing rooms, and an instructional resource center.

Application Information:

Send to: For the PhD program please send applications to: Director of Training, ATTN: K. Meeks, SE 1518, Counseling Psychology, Indiana State University, Terre Haute, IN 47809. For the MS in Counseling Psychology program, please send applications to: ATTN: S. Edwards, SE 1517, Department of Counseling, Indiana State University, Terre Haute, IN 47809. Application available online. URL of online application: http://web.indstate.edu/sogs/GradNewtemp/usform.html. Students are admitted in the Fall, application deadline January 1. MS in Counseling Psychology deadline March 1. *Fee:* $35.

Indiana State University
Department of Educational and School Psychology
School of Education
Terre Haute, IN 47809
Telephone: (812) 237-3588
Fax: (812) 237-7613
E-mail: *epbisch@isugw.indstate.edu*
Web: *http://soe.indstate.edu/espy/*

Department Information:

1981. Chairperson: Michael W. Bahr. Number of Faculty: total–full-time 9; women–full-time 6.

Programs and Degrees Offered:

Listed in the following order: Program area, degree type (T if terminal Master's), number awarded 7/03–6/04. Guidance and Psychological Services PhD (Doctor of Philosophy) 4, Master's of Education in School Psychology Other, Educational Specialist in School Psychology EdS (Education Specialist) 4.

APA Accreditation: School PhD (Doctor of Philosophy).

Student Applications/Admissions:

Student Applications

Guidance and Psychological Services PhD (Doctor of Philosophy)—Applications 2004–2005, 26. Total applicants accepted 2004–2005, 12. Number enrolled (new admits only) 2004–2005 full-time, 6. Number enrolled (new admits only) 2004–2005 part-time, 0. Total enrolled 2004–2005 full-time, 17, part-time, 13. Openings 2005–2006, 6. The Median number of years required for completion of a degree are 5.5. The number of students enrolled full and part-time who were dismissed or voluntarily withdrew from this program area were 1. *Master's of Education in School Psychology Other—Educational Specialist in School Psy-*

chology EdS (Education Specialist)—Applications 2004–2005, 45. Total applicants accepted 2004–2005, 20. Number enrolled (new admits only) 2004–2005 full-time, 13. Number enrolled (new admits only) 2004–2005 part-time, 0. Openings 2005–2006, 6. The Median number of years required for completion of a degree are 3. The number of students enrolled full and part-time who were dismissed or voluntarily withdrew from this program area were 0.

Admissions Requirements:

Scores: Entries appear in this order: required test or GPA, minimum score (if required), median score of students entering in 2003–2004. Master's Programs: GRE-V 450, 480; GRE-Q 450, 590; GRE-Analytical 4.5, 5.5; overall undergraduate GPA 3.0, 3.21. The masters program is the first year of the EdS program; therefore the admission requirements for this program are the same as those for the EdS program. Doctoral Programs: GRE-V 500, 520; GRE-Q 500, 540; GRE-Analytical 5.0, 5.5; overall undergraduate GPA 3.0, 3.37.

Other Criteria: (importance of criteria rated low, medium, or high): GRE/MAT scores medium, research experience medium, work experience medium, extracurricular activity high, clinically related public service high, GPA high, letters of recommendation high, interview high, statement of goals and objectives high, vita high. For additional information on admission requirements, go to: www.indstate.edu/sogs.

Student Characteristics: The following represents characteristics of students in 2004–2005 in all graduate psychology programs in the department: Female–full-time 49, part-time 11; Male–full-time 8, part-time 2; African American/Black–full-time 2, part-time 0; Hispanic/Latino(a)–full-time 2, part-time 1; Asian/Pacific Islander–full-time 0, part-time 1; American Indian/Alaska Native–full-time 1, part-time 0; Caucasian–full-time 50, part-time 11; Multi-ethnic–full-time 2, part-time 0; students subject to the Americans With Disabilities Act–full-time 1, part-time 0.

Financial Information/Assistance:

Tuition for Full-Time Study: *Master's:* State residents: per academic year $5,048, $252 per credit hour; Nonstate residents: per academic year $12,024, $501 per credit hour. *Doctoral:* State residents: per academic year $5,048, $252 per credit hour; Nonstate residents: per academic year $12,024, $501 per credit hour. Tuition is subject to change. See the following Web site for updates and changes in tuition costs: http://web.indstate.edu/sogs.

Financial Assistance:

First Year Students: Teaching assistantships available for first-year. Average amount paid per academic year: $5,000. Average number of hours worked per week: 20. Tuition remission given: partial. Research assistantships available for first-year. Average amount paid per academic year: $5,000. Average number of hours worked per week: 20. Tuition remission given: partial. Fellowships and scholarships available for first-year. Average amount paid per academic year: $5,000. Average number of hours worked per week: 15. Tuition remission given: partial.

Advanced Students: Teaching assistantships available for advanced students. Average amount paid per academic year: $5,000. Average number of hours worked per week: 20. Tuition remission given: partial. Research assistantships available for advanced students. Average amount paid per academic year: $5,000. Average number of hours worked per week: 20. Tuition remission given: partial. Fellowships and scholarships available for advanced students. Average amount paid per academic year: $5,000. Average number of hours worked per week: 15. Tuition remission given: partial.

Contact Information: Of all students currently enrolled full-time, 100% benefitted from one or more of the listed financial assistance programs. Application and information available online at: http://www.indstate.edu/finaid/.

Internships/Practica: Students in all programs are required to complete a minimum of 160 direct contact hours each semester in which they are enrolled in the program. Practicum experiences include observation, consultation, assessment, counseling and intervention with diverse populations ranging from preschool-aged to school-aged students, as well as with college students, parents, teachers, and other professionals. Practicum sites include the local Head Start, public school settings, the Porter School Psychology Clinic, ISU ADHD Clinic, the READ Clinic and the School Psychology Autism Clinic as well as agencies such as Gibault, Inc. and Riley Children's Hospital. PhD students have the opportunity to complete advanced practicum requirements in school or clinical settings in order to gain additional experiences and to foster increasing autonomy. Final experiences include a 1200+ hour school-based internship for EdS students and a 1500+ hour predoctoral internship in clinic and/or school settings for PhD students. Predoctoral internship sites include public school settings, hospitals and mental health agencies. For those doctoral students for whom a professional internship is required prior to graduation, 4 applied in 2003–2004. Of those who applied, 3 were placed in internships listed by the Association of Psychology Postdoctoral and Internship Programs (APPIC); 3 were placed in APA accredited internships.

Housing and Day Care: On-campus housing is available. See the following Web site for more information: http://www.indstate.edu/reslife/. On-campus day care facilities are available. See the following Web site for more information: http://web.indstate.edu/childcare/.

Employment of Department Graduates:

Master's Degree Graduates: Of those who graduated in the academic year 2003–2004, the following categories and numbers represent the post-graduate activities and employment of master's degree graduates: Enrolled in a psychology doctoral program (4), enrolled in another graduate/professional program (4), enrolled in a post-doctoral residency/fellowship (n/a), employed in independent practice (n/a), employed in an academic position at a university (0), employed in an academic position at a 2-year/4-year college (0), employed in other positions at a higher education institution (0), employed in a professional position in a school system (0), employed in business or industry (research/consulting) (0), employed in business or industry (management) (0), employed in a government agency (research) (0), employed in a government agency (professional services) (0), employed in a community mental health/counseling center (0), employed in a hospital/medical center (0), still seeking employment (0), other employment position (0), total from the above (master's) (8).

Doctoral Degree Graduates: Of those who graduated in the academic year 2003–2004, the following categories and numbers represent the post-graduate activities and employment of doctoral degree graduates: Enrolled in a psychology doctoral program (n/a), enrolled in another graduate/professional program (0), enrolled in a post-doctoral residency/fellowship (0), employed in independent practice (0), employed in an academic position at a university (0), employed in an academic position at a 2-year/4-year college (0), employed in other positions at a higher education institution (0), employed in a professional position in a school system (3), employed in business or industry (research/consulting) (0), employed in business or industry (management) (0), employed in a government agency (research) (0), employed in a government agency (professional services) (0), employed in a community mental health/counseling center (0), employed in a hospital/medical center (1), still seeking employment (0), other employment position (0), total from the above (doctoral) (4).

Additional Information:

Orientation, Objectives, and Emphasis of Department: The PhD program in guidance and psychological services specialization in school psychology follows a scientist-practitioner model which serves as a foundation upon which program goals and objectives are based. The mission of the program is to prepare School Psychologists as scientist–practitioners with a primarily behavioral orientation through a program that is research-based and theory-driven, school-focused, and experiential in nature.

Special Facilities or Resources: The Department of Educational and School Psychology has a university-based clinic that provides psychological and educational services to children, youth, and families. The clinic includes programs specifically designed to serve children with autism spectrum disorders, children with reading disorders, and children with behavioral difficulties. The department partners with the Psychology Department to provide services through a university-based ADHD clinic. These clinics provide both clinical and research experiences. Community resources with which the department has established partnerships include a HeadStart facility, public and private schools, a residential facility for children and youth with behavioral disorders, and a local community center.

Information for Students With Physical Disabilities: See the following Web site for more information: http://www.indstate.edu/sasc.

Application Information:
Send to: Lisa G. Bischoff, Director of School Psychology Training Program, College of Education, Room 606, Indiana State University, Terrre Haute, IN 47809. Application available online. URL of online application: www.indstate.edu/sogs. Students are admitted in the Fall, application deadline February 15. *Fee:* $35. McNair Scholar.

Indiana State University (2004 data)
Department of Psychology
Root Hall
Terre Haute, IN 47809
Telephone: (812) 237-4314
Fax: (812) 237-4378
E-mail: *pyriggs@isugw.indstate.edu*
Web: *http://web.indstate.edu/psych*

Department Information:
1968. Chairperson: Douglas J. Herrmann. Number of Faculty: total–full-time 11; women–full-time 5.

Programs and Degrees Offered:
Listed in the following order: Program area, degree type (T if terminal Master's), number awarded 7/03–6/04. General MA/MS (Master of Arts/Science) (T) 1, Clinical PsyD (Doctor of Psychology) 8.

APA Accreditation: Clinical PsyD (Doctor of Psychology).

Student Applications/Admissions:

Student Applications

General MA/MS (Master of Arts/Science)—Applications 2004–2005, 27. Total applicants accepted 2004–2005, 5. Openings 2005–2006, 5. The Median number of years required for completion of a degree are 2. The number of students enrolled full and part-time who were dismissed or voluntarily withdrew from this program area were 0. *Clinical PsyD (Doctor of Psychology)*—Applications 2004–2005, 112. Total applicants accepted 2004–2005, 10. Openings 2005–2006, 10. The Median number of years required for completion of a degree are 5. The number of students enrolled full and part-time who were dismissed or voluntarily withdrew from this program area were 0.

Admissions Requirements:

Scores: Entries appear in this order: required test or GPA, minimum score (if required), median score of students entering in 2003–2004. Master's Programs: GRE-V 450, 555; GRE-Q 450, 520; GRE-Analytical 450, 530; overall undergraduate GPA 2.75, 3.64. GRE test criteria are not rigidly applied in all cases. Doctoral Programs: GRE-V 500, 565; GRE-Q 500, 591; GRE-Analytical 575, 646; overall undergraduate GPA 3.00, 3.38. Either the GRE or GPA criteria may be waived if other qualifications are strong. A master's degree is not required for admission, but a 3.50 GPA or above is needed if graduate work has been done.

Other Criteria: (importance of criteria rated low, medium, or high): GRE/MAT scores high, research experience high, work experience medium, extracurricular activity low, clinically related public service high, GPA medium, letters of recommendation high, interview high, statement of goals and objectives high. An interview is not required for the Master's Program. Clinically related public service is low for the Master's Program.

Student Characteristics: The following represents characteristics of students in 2004–2005 in all graduate psychology programs in the department: Female–full-time 30, part-time 0; Male–full-time 12, part-time 0; African American/Black–full-time 1, part-time 0; Hispanic/Latino(a)–full-time 3, part-time 0; Asian/Pacific Islander–full-time 0, part-time 0; American Indian/Alaska Native–full-time 0, part-time 0; Caucasian–full-time 0, part-time 0; Multi-ethnic–full-time 0, part-time 0; students subject to the Americans With Disabilities Act–full-time 0, part-time 0.

Financial Information/Assistance:
Tuition for Full-Time Study: *Master's:* State residents: per academic year $5,808, $242 per credit hour; Nonstate residents: per academic year $10,224, $426 per credit hour. *Doctoral:* State residents: per academic year $5,808, $242 per credit hour; Nonstate residents: per academic year $10,224, $426 per credit hour. Tuition is subject to change. See the following Web site for updates and changes in tuition costs: web.indstate.edu/sogs.

Financial Assistance:
First Year Students: Teaching assistantships available for first-year. Average amount paid per academic year: $5,000. Average number of hours worked per week: 20. Apply by March 15. Tuition remission given: full. Research assistantships available for first-year. Average amount paid per academic year: $5,000. Average number of hours worked per week: 20. Apply by March 15. Tuition remission given: full. Fellowships and scholarships available for first-year. Average amount paid per academic year: $5,000. Average number of hours worked per week: 15. Apply by March 15. Tuition remission given: full.

Advanced Students: Teaching assistantships available for advanced students. Average amount paid per academic year: $5,000. Average number of hours worked per week: 20. Apply by March 15. Tuition remission given: full. Research assistantships available for advanced students. Average amount paid per academic year: $5,000. Average number of hours worked per week: 20. Apply by March 15. Tuition remission given: full. Fellowships and scholarships available for advanced students. Average amount paid per academic year: $5,000. Average number of hours worked per week: 15. Apply by March 15. Tuition remission given: full.

Contact Information: Of all students currently enrolled full-time, 100% benefitted from one or more of the listed financial assistance programs.

Internships/Practica: PsyD students are expected to participate in practicum experiences from the beginning of the program, with clinical responsibilities gradually increasing throughout enrollment. Second year and third year PsyD students see clients in the Psychology Clinic and are supervised by clinical faculty. Fourth year students are placed in community mental health facilities under the supervision of a licensed psychologist. For those doctoral students for whom a professional internship is required prior to graduation, 5 applied in 2003–2004. Of those who applied, 5 were placed in internships listed by the Association of Psychology Postdoctoral and Internship Programs (APPIC); 5 were placed in APA accredited internships.

Housing and Day Care: On-campus housing is available. Residential Life: (812) 237-3993. Early Childhood Education Center: (812) 237-2547. On-campus day care facilities are available.

Employment of Department Graduates:
Master's Degree Graduates: Of those who graduated in the academic year 2003–2004, the following categories and numbers represent the post-graduate activities and employment of master's degree graduates: Enrolled in a post-doctoral residency/fellowship (n/a), employed in independent practice (n/a), still seeking employment (1), total from the above (master's) (1).

Doctoral Degree Graduates: Of those who graduated in the academic year 2003–2004, the following categories and numbers represent the post-graduate activities and employment of doctoral degree graduates: Enrolled in a psychology doctoral program (n/a), enrolled in a post-doctoral residency/fellowship (3), employed in independent practice (3), employed in an academic position at a university (1), employed in a community mental health/counseling center (1), total from the above (doctoral) (8).

Additional Information:
Orientation, Objectives, and Emphasis of Department: The Doctor of Psychology program at Indiana State University follows a practitioner-scientist model of training in clinical psychology

to guide the preparation and evaluation of its students. The primary goal is the training of skilled clinical psychologists in the assessment and treatment of psychological problems. The program seeks to develop a professional identity which values and pursues: excellence in clinical practice; a spirit of active inquiry and critical thought; a commitment to the development and application of new knowledge in the field; an active sense of social responsibility combined with an appreciation and respect for cultural and individual differences; and an enduring commitment to personal and professional development. The program philosophy is to prepare all students as broad-based general clinicians, with encouragement to specialize through electives, research area, internship selection, and postdoctoral training. The Master's program, with an emphasis on basic psychology and research, is intended to serve as preparatory to entrance into doctoral level study. Students are encouraged to become involved in research beginning with their first term in the program. Although the degree is in general psychology, some concentration is often possible. A main goal of the program is to have students leave with a sense of what it means to be a research psychologist.

Special Facilities or Resources: The department has a psychology clinic, mini- and micro-computers, and good laboratory facilities.

Information for Students With Physical Disabilities: See the following Web site for more information: http://web.indstate.edu/sasc/dss/index.htm.

Application Information:

Send to: Department of Psychology, c/o Graduate Admissions, Root Hall, Indiana State University, Terre Haute, IN 47809. Students are admitted in the Fall, application deadline January 1. Application deadline January 1 (PsyD); March 15 (Master's). *Fee:* $35.

Indiana University
Department of Counseling and Educational Psychology
School of Education
201 North Rose Avenue
Bloomington, IN 47405-1006
Telephone: (812) 856-8300
Fax: (812) 856-8333
E-mail: *mueller@indiana.edu*
Web: *http://education.indiana.edu/cep*

Department Information:

Chairperson: Daniel J. Mueller. Number of Faculty: total–full-time 29, part-time 9; women–full-time 10, part-time 4; minority–full-time 6, part-time 1.

Programs and Degrees Offered:

Listed in the following order: Program area, degree type (T if terminal Master's), number awarded 7/03–6/04. Counseling Psychology PhD (Doctor of Philosophy) 4, Educational Psychology PhD (Doctor of Philosophy) 8, School Psychology, PhD (Doctor of Philosophy) 5, School Psychology, EdS (Education Specialist) 4, Educational Psychology, MA/MS (Master of Arts/Science) 0.

APA Accreditation: Counseling PhD (Doctor of Philosophy). School PhD (Doctor of Philosophy).

Student Applications/Admissions:
Student Applications

Counseling Psychology PhD (Doctor of Philosophy)—Applications 2004–2005, 92. Total applicants accepted 2004–2005, 12. Number enrolled (new admits only) 2004–2005 full-time, 7. Openings 2005–2006, 12. The Median number of years required for completion of a degree are 9. The number of students enrolled full and part-time who were dismissed or voluntarily withdrew from this program area were 1. *Educational Psychology PhD (Doctor of Philosophy)*—Applications 2004–2005, 35. Total applicants accepted 2004–2005, 24. Number enrolled (new admits only) 2004–2005 full-time, 10. Openings 2005–2006, 12. The Median number of years required for completion of a degree are 7. The number of students enrolled full and part-time who were dismissed or voluntarily withdrew from this program area were 2. *School Psychology, PhD (Doctor of Philosophy)*—Applications 2004–2005, 42. Total applicants accepted 2004–2005, 9. Number enrolled (new admits only) 2004–2005 full-time, 4. Openings 2005–2006, 6. The Median number of years required for completion of a degree are 10. The number of students enrolled full and part-time who were dismissed or voluntarily withdrew from this program area were 1. *School Psychology, EdS (Education Specialist)*—Applications 2004–2005, 47. Total applicants accepted 2004–2005, 16. Number enrolled (new admits only) 2004–2005 full-time, 9. Total enrolled 2004–2005 full-time, 20. Openings 2005–2006, 10. The Median number of years required for completion of a degree are 4. The number of students enrolled full and part-time who were dismissed or voluntarily withdrew from this program area were 0. *Educational Psychology, MA/MS (Master of Arts/Science)*—Applications 2004–2005, 15. Total applicants accepted 2004–2005, 13. Number enrolled (new admits only) 2004–2005 full-time, 3. Total enrolled 2004–2005 full-time, 6. Openings 2005–2006, 10. The number of students enrolled full and part-time who were dismissed or voluntarily withdrew from this program area were 1.

Admissions Requirements:

Scores: Entries appear in this order: required test or GPA, minimum score (if required), median score of students entering in 2003–2004. Master's Programs: GRE-V no minimum stated, 480; GRE-Q no minimum stated, 580; GRE-V+Q 900, 1110; overall undergraduate GPA 3.0, 3.37; last 2 years GPA 3.0. Doctoral Programs: GRE-V no minimum stated, 530; GRE-Q no minimum stated, 630; GRE-V+Q 1100, 1160; overall undergraduate GPA 3.0, 3.5.

Other Criteria: (importance of criteria rated low, medium, or high): GRE/MAT scores high, research experience medium, work experience medium, extracurricular activity medium, clinically related public service medium, GPA high, letters of recommendation medium, interview high, statement of goals and objectives medium. In both the PhD in Counseling Psychology and PhD in School Psychology programs, personal interviews are required. GRE scores are interpreted differently for domestic and international applicants.

Student Characteristics: The following represents characteristics of students in 2004–2005 in all graduate psychology programs in the department: Female–full-time 126, part-time 0; Male–full-time 31, part-time 0; African American/Black–full-time 17, part-time 0; Hispanic/Latino(a)–full-time 9, part-time 0; Asian/Pacific Islander–full-time 20, part-time 0; American Indian/Alaska Native–full-time 0, part-time 0; Caucasian–full-time 111, part-time 0; students subject to the Americans With Disabilities Act–full-time 0, part-time 0.

Financial Information/Assistance:

Tuition for Full-Time Study: *Master's:* State residents: $212 per credit hour; Nonstate residents: $619 per credit hour. *Doctoral:* State residents: $212 per credit hour; Nonstate residents: $619 per credit hour. Tuition is subject to change.

Financial Assistance:

First Year Students: Teaching assistantships available for first-year. Average amount paid per academic year: $12,974. Average number of hours worked per week: 18. Tuition remission given: partial. Research assistantships available for first-year. Average amount paid per academic year: $10,863. Average number of hours worked per week: 18. Tuition remission given: partial. Fellowships and scholarships available for first-year. Average amount paid per academic year: $17,000. Tuition remission given: full.

Advanced Students: Teaching assistantships available for advanced students. Average amount paid per academic year: $12,974. Average number of hours worked per week: 18. Tuition remission given: partial. Research assistantships available for advanced students. Average amount paid per academic year: $10,863. Average number of hours worked per week: 18. Tuition remission given: partial. Fellowships and scholarships available for advanced students. Average amount paid per academic year: $17,000. Tuition remission given: full.

Contact Information: Of all students currently enrolled full-time, 80% benefitted from one or more of the listed financial assistance programs. Application and information available online at: http://www.indiana.edu/%7Ecepwp/finance.html.

Internships/Practica: Internships for doctoral level students are available by contacting the department chair. All counseling and school psychology students must take both practica and internships. For those doctoral students for whom a professional internship is required prior to graduation, 10 applied in 2003–2004. Of those who applied, 9 were placed in internships listed by the Association of Psychology Postdoctoral and Internship Programs (APPIC); 8 were placed in APA accredited internships.

Housing and Day Care: On-campus housing is available. See the following Web site for more information: http://www.rps.indiana.edu/housingrates.html. On-campus day care facilities are available. Campus Child Care Support, Poplars 734, Indiana University, Bloomington, IN 47405, (812) 855-5053.

Employment of Department Graduates:

Master's Degree Graduates: Of those who graduated in the academic year 2003–2004, the following categories and numbers represent the post-graduate activities and employment of master's degree graduates: Enrolled in a post-doctoral residency/fellowship (n/a), employed in independent practice (n/a), total from the above (master's) (0).

Doctoral Degree Graduates: Of those who graduated in the academic year 2003–2004, the following categories and numbers represent the post-graduate activities and employment of doctoral degree graduates: Enrolled in a psychology doctoral program (n/a), employed in an academic position at a university (6), employed in other positions at a higher education institution (7), employed in a professional position in a school system (1), employed in a

government agency (research) (1), employed in a government agency (professional services) (1), employed in a community mental health/counseling center (1), total from the above (doctoral) (17).

Additional Information:

Orientation, Objectives, and Emphasis of Department: The Department has multiple missions, but at the heart of our enterprise is a community of scholars working to contribute solutions to the problems faced by children, adolescents, and adults in the context of contemporary education. Additionally, the counseling psychology program promotes a broad range of interventions designed to facilitate the maximal adjustment of individuals. Faculty, staff and students share a commitment to open-mindedness and to social justice. We recognize the complex and dynamic nature of the social fabric and welcome qualified students of all ethnic, racial, national, religious, gender, social class, sexual, political, and philosophic orientations. Faculty and students collaboratively investigate numerous facets of child and adolescent development, creativity, learning, metacognition, aging, semiotics, and inquiry methodologies. Our programs require an understanding of both quantitative and qualitative research paradigms. We ascribe to the scientist-practitioner model for preparing professional psychologists. Our graduates work in various research and practice settings; universities, public schools, state departments of education, mental health centers, hospitals, and corporations.

Special Facilities or Resources: Special facilities include the Institute for Child Study, Center for Human Growth, and the Indiana Institute on Disability and Community.

Information for Students With Physical Disabilities: (812) 855-7578.

Application Information:

Send to: Applications are accepted via the Web at: www.indiana.edu/~educate/admiss.html. School Psych EdS and PhD, Counseling Psych PhD, and application deadline is January 15. Edus Psych MS has rolling admissions. Counseling/Counselor Educ has deadlines of March 1 and November 1. Application available online. Students are admitted in the Fall, application deadline January 15. School Psych EdS and PhD, Counseling Psych PhD, application deadline is January 15. Edus Psych MS has rolling admissions. Counseling/Counselor Educ has deadlines of March 1 and November 1. *Fee:* $50. application fee of $60 for international students, or $50 for domestic students.

Indiana University
Department of Psychology
Arts and Sciences
Psychology Building, 1101 E. 10th Street
Bloomington, IN 47405
Telephone: (812) 855-2012
Fax: (812) 855-4691
E-mail: *psychgrd@indiana.edu*
Web: *http://www.indiana.edu/~psych*

Department Information:
1919. Chairperson: Joseph E. Steinmetz. Number of Faculty: total–full-time 48; women–full-time 12; minority–full-time 2.

Programs and Degrees Offered:

Listed in the following order: Program area, degree type (T if terminal Master's), number awarded 7/03–6/04. Biology, Behavior, and Neuroscience PhD (Doctor of Philosophy) 2, Clinical Science PhD (Doctor of Philosophy) 4, Cognitive PhD (Doctor of Philosophy) 1, Developmental PhD (Doctor of Philosophy) 1, Social PhD (Doctor of Philosophy) 2.

APA Accreditation: Clinical PhD (Doctor of Philosophy).

Student Applications/Admissions:

Student Applications

Biology, Behavior, and Neuroscience PhD (Doctor of Philosophy)—Applications 2004–2005, 21. Total applicants accepted 2004–2005, 4. Number enrolled (new admits only) 2004–2005 full-time, 3. Number enrolled (new admits only) 2004–2005 part-time, 0. Openings 2005–2006, 8. The Median number of years required for completion of a degree are 5. The number of students enrolled full and part-time who were dismissed or voluntarily withdrew from this program area were 0. *Clinical Science PhD (Doctor of Philosophy)*—Applications 2004–2005, 89. Total applicants accepted 2004–2005, 6. Number enrolled (new admits only) 2004–2005 full-time, 3. Number enrolled (new admits only) 2004–2005 part-time, 0. Openings 2005–2006, 8. The Median number of years required for completion of a degree are 9.5. The number of students enrolled full and part-time who were dismissed or voluntarily withdrew from this program area were 1. *Cognitive PhD (Doctor of Philosophy)*—Applications 2004–2005, 40. Total applicants accepted 2004–2005, 14. Number enrolled (new admits only) 2004–2005 full-time, 7. Number enrolled (new admits only) 2004–2005 part-time, 0. Openings 2005–2006, 8. The Median number of years required for completion of a degree are 4. The number of students enrolled full and part-time who were dismissed or voluntarily withdrew from this program area were 0. *Developmental PhD (Doctor of Philosophy)*—Applications 2004–2005, 18. Total applicants accepted 2004–2005, 4. Number enrolled (new admits only) 2004–2005 full-time, 1. Number enrolled (new admits only) 2004–2005 part-time, 0. Openings 2005–2006, 8. The Median number of years required for completion of a degree are 4. The number of students enrolled full and part-time who were dismissed or voluntarily withdrew from this program area were 0. *Social PhD (Doctor of Philosophy)*—Applications 2004–2005, 46. Total applicants accepted 2004–2005, 4. Number enrolled (new admits only) 2004–2005 full-time, 2. Number enrolled (new admits only) 2004–2005 part-time, 0. Openings 2005–2006, 8. The Median number of years required for completion of a degree are 6. The number of students enrolled full and part-time who were dismissed or voluntarily withdrew from this program area were 0.

Admissions Requirements:

Scores: Entries appear in this order: required test or GPA, minimum score (if required), median score of students entering in 2003–2004. Doctoral Programs: GRE-V no minimum stated, 645; GRE-Q no minimum stated, 750; GRE-Analytical no minimum stated, 750; GRE-Subject(Psych) no minimum stated; overall undergraduate GPA 3.38, 3.81. Score for new Analytical Writing section: 5.0.

Other Criteria: (importance of criteria rated low, medium, or high): GRE/MAT scores high, research experience high, work experience low, extracurricular activity low, clinically related public service low, GPA high, letters of recommendation medium, interview high, statement of goals and objectives medium.

Student Characteristics: The following represents characteristics of students in 2004–2005 in all graduate psychology programs in the department: Female–full-time 44, part-time 0; Male–full-time 41, part-time 0; African American/Black–full-time 2, part-time 0; Hispanic/Latino(a)–full-time 3, part-time 0; Asian/Pacific Islander–full-time 6, part-time 0; American Indian/Alaska Native–full-time 1, part-time 0; Caucasian–full-time 73, part-time 0; Multi-ethnic–full-time 0, part-time 0; students subject to the Americans With Disabilities Act–full-time 0, part-time 0.

Financial Information/Assistance:

Tuition for Full-Time Study: *Doctoral:* State residents: per academic year $5,104, $213 per credit hour; Nonstate residents: per academic year $14,870, $620 per credit hour. Tuition is subject to change.

Financial Assistance:

First Year Students: Teaching assistantships available for first-year. Average amount paid per academic year: $18,500. Average number of hours worked per week: 20. Apply by same. Tuition remission given: full. Research assistantships available for first-year. Average amount paid per academic year: $18,500. Average number of hours worked per week: 20. Apply by same. Tuition remission given: full. Fellowships and scholarships available for first-year. Average amount paid per academic year: $21,000. Average number of hours worked per week: 0. Apply by same. Tuition remission given: full.

Advanced Students: Teaching assistantships available for advanced students. Average amount paid per academic year: $18,500. Average number of hours worked per week: 20. Apply by none. Tuition remission given: full. Research assistantships available for advanced students. Average amount paid per academic year: $18,500. Average number of hours worked per week: 20. Apply by none. Tuition remission given: full. Fellowships and scholarships available for advanced students. Average amount paid per academic year: $21,000. Average number of hours worked per week: 20. Apply by none. Tuition remission given: full.

Contact Information: Of all students currently enrolled full-time, 100% benefitted from one or more of the listed financial assistance programs. Application and information available online at: http://www.gradapp.indiana.edu.

Internships/Practica: Internships are required for a clinical psychology major.

Housing and Day Care: On-campus housing is available. See the following Web site for more information: http://www.rps.indiana.edu/. On-campus day care facilities are available. See the following Web site for more information: http://www.indiana.edu/~hm/child_care/.

Employment of Department Graduates:

Master's Degree Graduates: Of those who graduated in the academic year 2003–2004, the following categories and numbers represent the post-graduate activities and employment of master's degree graduates: Enrolled in a post-doctoral residency/fellowship (n/a), employed in independent practice (n/a), total from the above (master's) (0).

Doctoral Degree Graduates: Of those who graduated in the academic year 2003–2004, the following categories and numbers represent the post-graduate activities and employment of doctoral degree graduates: Enrolled in a psychology doctoral program (n/a), enrolled in another graduate/professional program (1), enrolled in a post-doctoral residency/fellowship (9), employed in an academic position at a 2-year/4-year college (1), employed in other positions at a higher education institution (1), employed in a government agency (professional services) (1), total from the above (doctoral) (13).

Additional Information:

Orientation, Objectives, and Emphasis of Department: Students acquire fundamental knowledge and are offered specialized training so that they may develop competence in research, teaching (college and university levels), and service. Close contact between faculty and students is made possible by a low ratio of graduate students to faculty. Extensive laboratory facilities are available for research in the major areas. A psychological clinic is maintained as a specialized unit of the department. The primary emphasis of the clinical training program is on the theoretical and scientific aspects of clinical psychology. However, in view of the diverse and changing nature of the field, the program's goal is to produce clinical psychologists who are well trained scientifically and clinically and who are capable of achieving excellence in their careers in either a clinical or an academic and research setting.

Information for Students With Physical Disabilities: See the following Web site for more information: http://www.indiana.edu/~iubdss/.

Application Information:

Send to: Indiana University, Department of Psychology, Graduate Admissions, 1101 East 10th Street, Bloomington, IN 47405. Application available online. URL of online application: https://www.gradapp.indiana.edu/. Students are admitted in the Fall, application deadline December 15. December 1 is the application deadline for international graduate student candidates. *Fee:* $50. The department does not give application fee waivers or deferrals. However, certain fellowship programs for which our applicants can apply might offer such waivers of the application fee.

Indiana University–Purdue University Indianapolis
Department of Psychology
Science
402 North Blackford Street, Room LD 124
Indianapolis, IN 46202-3275
Telephone: (317) 274-6945
Fax: (317) 274-6756
E-mail: *gradpsy@iupui.edu*
Web: *http://www.psych.iupui.edu*

Department Information:

1969. Chairperson: J. Gregor Fetterman, PhD Number of Faculty: total–full-time 24, part-time 16; women–full-time 5, part-time 10; minority–full-time 5.

Programs and Degrees Offered:

Listed in the following order: Program area, degree type (T if terminal Master's), number awarded 7/03–6/04. Industrial/ Organization MA/MS (Master of Arts/Science) (T) 5, Clinical Rehabilitation PhD (Doctor of Philosophy) 2, Psychobiology PhD (Doctor of Philosophy) 0.

APA Accreditation: Clinical PhD (Doctor of Philosophy).

Student Applications/Admissions:
Student Applications

Industrial/ Organization MA/MS (Master of Arts/Science)—Applications 2004–2005, 50. Total applicants accepted 2004–2005, 5. Number enrolled (new admits only) 2004–2005 full-time, 5. Openings 2005–2006, 7. The Median number of years required for completion of a degree are 4. The number of students enrolled full and part-time who were dismissed or voluntarily withdrew from this program area were 0. *Clinical Rehabilitation PhD (Doctor of Philosophy)*—Applications 2004–2005, 35. Total applicants accepted 2004–2005, 4. Number enrolled (new admits only) 2004–2005 full-time, 4. Openings 2005–2006, 5. The Median number of years required for completion of a degree are 5. The number of students enrolled full and part-time who were dismissed or voluntarily withdrew from this program area were 1. *Psychobiology PhD (Doctor of Philosophy)*—Applications 2004–2005, 10. Total applicants accepted 2004–2005, 4. Number enrolled (new admits only) 2004–2005 full-time, 4. Openings 2005–2006, 2. The number of students enrolled full and part-time who were dismissed or voluntarily withdrew from this program area were 0.

Admissions Requirements:

Scores: Entries appear in this order: required test or GPA, minimum score (if required), median score of students entering in 2003–2004. Master's Programs: GRE-V 550, 510; GRE-Q 550, 640; GRE-V+Q 1100, 1115; GRE-Analytical no minimum stated; overall undergraduate GPA 3.0, 3.59. Note: Minimum GRE scores are neither necessary nor sufficient for admission. Doctoral Programs: GRE-V 600, 550; GRE-Q 600, 675; GRE-V+Q 1200, 1200; GRE-Analytical no minimum stated; GRE-Subject(Psych) 600, 690; overall undergraduate GPA 3.2, 3.63. Note: Minimum GRE scores are neither necessary nor sufficient for admission.

Other Criteria: (importance of criteria rated low, medium, or high): GRE/MAT scores high, research experience high, work experience low, GPA high, letters of recommendation high, interview medium, statement of goals and objectives high. For additional information on admission requirements, go to: http://psych.iupui.edu.

Student Characteristics: The following represents characteristics of students in 2004–2005 in all graduate psychology programs in the department: Female–full-time 35, part-time 0; Male–full-time 14, part-time 0; African American/Black–full-time 2, part-time 0; Hispanic/Latino(a)–full-time 2, part-time 0; Asian/Pacific Islander–full-time 5, part-time 0; American Indian/Alaska Native–full-time 0, part-time 0; Caucasian–full-time 40, part-time 0; Multi-ethnic–part-time 0; students subject to the Americans With Disabilities Act–full-time 0, part-time 0.

Financial Information/Assistance:

Tuition for Full-Time Study: *Master's:* State residents: per academic year $4,844, $201 per credit hour; Nonstate residents: per academic year $13,981, $582 per credit hour. *Doctoral:* State residents: per academic year $4,844, $201 per credit hour; Nonstate residents: per academic year $13,981, $582 per credit hour. Tuition is subject to change. See the following Web site for updates and changes in tuition costs: http://www.bursar.iupui.edu.

Financial Assistance:

First Year Students: Research assistantships available for first-year. Average amount paid per academic year: $11,000. Average number of hours worked per week: 20. Apply by January 1. Tuition remission given: partial. Fellowships and scholarships available for first-year. Average amount paid per academic year: $22,000. Average number of hours worked per week: 0. Apply by January 1. Tuition remission given: partial.

Advanced Students: Teaching assistantships available for advanced students. Average amount paid per academic year: $11,000. Average number of hours worked per week: 20. Apply by January 1. Tuition remission given: partial. Research assistantships available for advanced students. Average amount paid per academic year: $11,000. Average number of hours worked per week: 20. Apply by January 1. Tuition remission given: partial. Fellowships and scholarships available for advanced students. Average amount paid per academic year: $22,000. Average number of hours worked per week: 0. Apply by January 1. Tuition remission given: partial.

Contact Information: Of all students currently enrolled full-time, 100% benefitted from one or more of the listed financial assistance programs. Application and information available online at: http://psych.iupui.edu.

Internships/Practica: Clinical practica sites are located at IUPUI and within the Indianapolis area, and involve supervised clinical training individually tailored for each student. A practicum coordinator, the site supervisor, and the student develop specific contracts that emphasize education and the acquisition of clinical skills and knowledge, rather than experience per se. These contractual activities and goals are monitored and evaluated at the end of each placement. Practicum opportunities are varied and numerous and include many different types of clinical settings with different clinical populations. On-site supervisors are usually psychologists but also include psychiatrists, physiatrists, and other health professionals. Many sites in different settings are available. General practicum sites include a university counseling center and several psychiatric clinics. More advanced settings can be categorized as 1) Neuropsychology; 2) Behavioral Medicine or Health Psychology; 3) Severe Mental Illness/Psychiatric Rehabilitation. The I/O Master's Program offers opportunities to achieve applied experience in business settings. Students have the opportunity to sign up for practicum in the spring of their second year. Students are typically placed in an organization for one 8-hour day each week of the semester. Paid summer internships (15-20 hours per week) in the community are also available. For those doctoral students for whom a professional internship is required prior to graduation, 1 applied in 2003–2004. Of those who applied, 1 was placed in internships listed by the Association of Psychology Postdoctoral and Internship Programs (APPIC); 1 was placed in APA accredited internships.

Housing and Day Care: On-campus housing is available. See the following Web site for more information: http://www.housing.iupui.edu/. On-campus day care facilities are available. See the following Web site for more information: http://www.childcare.iupui.edu/.

Employment of Department Graduates:

Master's Degree Graduates: Of those who graduated in the academic year 2003–2004, the following categories and numbers represent the post-graduate activities and employment of master's degree graduates: Enrolled in a psychology doctoral program (6), enrolled in a post-doctoral residency/fellowship (n/a), employed in independent practice (n/a), employed in a professional position in a school system (1), employed in business or industry (research/consulting) (3), total from the above (master's) (10).

Doctoral Degree Graduates: Of those who graduated in the academic year 2003–2004, the following categories and numbers represent the post-graduate activities and employment of doctoral degree graduates: Enrolled in a psychology doctoral program (n/a), enrolled in a post-doctoral residency/fellowship (2), total from the above (doctoral) (2).

Additional Information:

Orientation, Objectives, and Emphasis of Department: Graduate education is offered at the PhD level in Clinical Rehabilitation Psychology and the Psychobiology of Addictions. The APA-Accredited Clinical program follows the scientist-practitioner model. A rigorous academic and research education is combined with supervised practical training. The clinical program provides specialization in behavioral medicine/health psychology, neuropsychology, and severe mental illness/psychiatric rehabilitation. The PhD program in the psychobiological bases of addictions emphasizes the core content areas of psychology along with specialization in psychobiology and animal models of addiction. Research, scholarship, and close faculty-student mentor relationships are viewed as integral training elements within both programs. Graduate training at the MS level is designed to provide students with theory and practice that will enable them to apply psychological techniques and findings to subsequent jobs. All students are required to take departmental methods courses and then specific area core courses and electives. The MS degree areas are applied in focus and science-based, and this reflects the interests and orientation of the faculty.

Special Facilities or Resources: IUPUI is a unique urban university campus with 27,000 students enrolled in 235 degree programs at the undergraduate and graduate level. The campus includes schools of law, dentistry, and medicine, among others, along with undergraduate programs in the arts, humanities, and science. In addition, there are over 75 research institutes, centers, laboratories and specialized programs. The Department of Psychology at IUPUI occupies teaching and research facilities in a modern science building in the heart of campus. Facilities include a 4000-square foot space and self-contained area devoted to faculty and graduate student basic animal research in experimental psychology and psychobiology. Many of the research rooms are equipped for online computer recording to one of the faculty offices. Laboratories for human research, research rooms, and teaching laboratories are separately located on the first floor of the building. The Psychology Department maintains ties with the faculty and programs in other schools within IUPUI, including the School of Nursing, and the Departments of Psychiatry, Adolescent Medicine, and Neurology. The clinical program provides an unusually rich array of practicum opportunities in behavioral medicine, neuropsychology, and psychiatric rehabilitation.

Application Information:
Send to: Susie Wiesinger, IUPUI, Department of Psychology, LD124, 422 N. Blackford Street, Indianapolis, IN 46202-3275. Application

available online. URL of online application: http://psych.iupui.edu. Students are admitted in the Fall, application deadline January 1. Each program has a different application deadline. Clinical Rehabilitation application deadline is January 1. Industrial/Organizational application deadline is February 1. Psychobiology application deadline is January 1. *Fee:* $50. International - $60.

Indianapolis, University of
Graduate Psychology Program
School of Psychological Sciences
1400 East Hanna Avenue
Indianapolis, IN 46227
Telephone: (317) 788-3920
Fax: (317) 788-2120
E-mail: *psychology@uindy.edu*
Web: *http://psych.uindy.edu/*

Department Information:
1994. Dean: John McIlvried, PhD. Number of Faculty: total–full-time 12, part-time 8; women–full-time 6, part-time 3; minority–full-time 1, part-time 1.

Programs and Degrees Offered:
Listed in the following order: Program area, degree type (T if terminal Master's), number awarded 7/03–6/04. Clinical MA/MS (Master of Arts/Science) 11, Clinical PsyD (Doctor of Psychology) 8.

APA Accreditation: Clinical PsyD (Doctor of Psychology).

Student Applications/Admissions:
Student Applications
Clinical MA/MS (Master of Arts/Science)—Applications 2004–2005, 73. Total applicants accepted 2004–2005, 28. Number enrolled (new admits only) 2004–2005 full-time, 16. Number enrolled (new admits only) 2004–2005 part-time, 0. Total enrolled 2004–2005 full-time, 29, part-time, 2. Openings 2005–2006, 16. The Median number of years required for completion of a degree are 2. The number of students enrolled full and part-time who were dismissed or voluntarily withdrew from this program area were 0. *Clinical PsyD (Doctor of Psychology)*—Applications 2004–2005, 135. Total applicants accepted 2004–2005, 44. Number enrolled (new admits only) 2004–2005 full-time, 18. Number enrolled (new admits only) 2004–2005 part-time, 0. Total enrolled 2004–2005 full-time, 75, part-time, 18. Openings 2005–2006, 20. The Median number of years required for completion of a degree are 5. The number of students enrolled full and part-time who were dismissed or voluntarily withdrew from this program area were 0.

Admissions Requirements:
Scores: Entries appear in this order: required test or GPA, minimum score (if required), median score of students entering in 2003–2004. Master's Programs: GRE-V no minimum stated, 500; GRE-Q no minimum stated, 515; GRE-V+Q no minimum stated, 1015; GRE-Analytical no minimum stated, 5; GRE-Subject(Psych) no minimum stated, 535; overall undergraduate GPA no minimum stated, 3.53; last 2 years GPA no minimum stated; psychology GPA no minimum stated, 3.55.

GRE and GRE subject (Psych). Doctoral Programs: GRE-V no minimum stated, 515; GRE-Q no minimum stated, 519; GRE-V+Q no minimum stated, 1034; GRE-Analytical no minimum stated, 5; GRE-Subject(Psych) no minimum stated, 630; overall undergraduate GPA 3.0, 3.6.
Other Criteria: (importance of criteria rated low, medium, or high): GRE/MAT scores high, research experience medium, work experience medium, extracurricular activity low, clinically related public service medium, GPA high, letters of recommendation high, interview high, statement of goals and objectives high. For additional information on admission requirements, go to: http://psych.uindy.edu.

Student Characteristics: The following represents characteristics of students in 2004–2005 in all graduate psychology programs in the department: Female–full-time 87, part-time 17; Male–full-time 17, part-time 3; African American/Black–full-time 2, part-time 0; Hispanic/Latino(a)–full-time 2, part-time 0; Asian/Pacific Islander–full-time 1, part-time 0; American Indian/Alaska Native–full-time 1, part-time 0; Caucasian–full-time 95, part-time 20; Multi-ethnic–full-time 3, part-time 0; students subject to the Americans With Disabilities Act–full-time 0, part-time 0.

Financial Information/Assistance:
Tuition for Full-Time Study: *Master's:* State residents: $581 per credit hour; Nonstate residents: $581 per credit hour. *Doctoral:* State residents: $581 per credit hour; Nonstate residents: $581 per credit hour.

Financial Assistance:
First Year Students: Teaching assistantships available for first-year. Average amount paid per academic year: $0. Average number of hours worked per week: 12. Apply by January 10. Tuition remission given: partial. Research assistantships available for first-year. Average amount paid per academic year: $0. Average number of hours worked per week: 12. Apply by January 10. Tuition remission given: partial. Fellowships and scholarships available for first-year. Average amount paid per academic year: $0. Average number of hours worked per week: 0. Apply by January 10. Tuition remission given: full.
Advanced Students: Teaching assistantships available for advanced students. Average amount paid per academic year: $0. Average number of hours worked per week: 12. Apply by renewable. Tuition remission given: partial. Research assistantships available for advanced students. Average amount paid per academic year: $0. Average number of hours worked per week: 12. Apply by renewable. Tuition remission given: partial. Fellowships and scholarships available for advanced students. Average amount paid per academic year: $0. Average number of hours worked per week: 0. Apply by renewable. Tuition remission given: full.
Contact Information: Of all students currently enrolled full-time, 25% benefitted from one or more of the listed financial assistance programs. Application and information available online at: http://finaid.uindy.edu.

Internships/Practica: There are numerous clinical practica experiences available for both master's and doctoral students. Master's students obtain a minimum of 225 hours of supervised clinical practica experience (Mental Health Counseling requires 1000 hours), and doctoral students receive a minimum of 1200 hours of supervised clinical practica experience. Practica are available at numerous settings, including a major training medical center, local community hospitals, forensic settings, private practice placements, elementary schools, social service agencies, and mental health centers. At these placements, students gain supervised experience in clinical assessment and testing, psychotherapy, collaboration and consultation with interdisciplinary teams, program development and evaluation, treatment planning and case management, and participation in development and delivery of inservices to professional staff. In addition to mainstream psychological services, practicum students have opportunities to obtain specific training in forensics, psycho-diagnostic assessment, neuropsychology, health psychology, pain, substance abuse/dependence, developmental disabilities, and HIV/AIDS. All practica are supervised by licensed mental health professionals on-site. In conjunction with practica, students enroll in a professional practice seminar that addresses a wide variety of issues that confront mental health professionals and students. This professional practice seminar is taught by full time University faculty. Doctoral students also must complete a 2000 hour internship. The Director of Clinical Training provides assistance in locating training placements. For those doctoral students for whom a professional internship is required prior to graduation, 10 applied in 2003–2004. Of those who applied, 1 were placed in internships listed by the Association of Psychology Postdoctoral and Internship Programs (APPIC); 9 were placed in APA accredited internships.

Housing and Day Care: On-campus housing is available. See the following Web site for more information: http://www.uindy.edu/reslife/index.php. On-campus day care facilities are available. University Heights United Methodist Church, 4002 Otterbein Avenue, Indianapolis, IN 46227; Church office: (317) 787-5347.

Employment of Department Graduates:

Master's Degree Graduates: Of those who graduated in the academic year 2003–2004, the following categories and numbers represent the post-graduate activities and employment of master's degree graduates: Enrolled in a psychology doctoral program (8), enrolled in a post-doctoral residency/fellowship (n/a), employed in independent practice (n/a), total from the above (master's) (8).

Doctoral Degree Graduates: Of those who graduated in the academic year 2003–2004, the following categories and numbers represent the post-graduate activities and employment of doctoral degree graduates: Enrolled in a psychology doctoral program (n/a), enrolled in another graduate/professional program (0), enrolled in a post-doctoral residency/fellowship (3), employed in other positions at a higher education institution (1), employed in a government agency (professional services) (1), employed in a community mental health/counseling center (1), employed in a hospital/medical center (1), not seeking employment (1), total from the above (doctoral) (8).

Additional Information:

Orientation, Objectives, and Emphasis of Department: The graduate program in clinical psychology at the University of Indianapolis is based on a practitioner-scholar model of training. As such, the program is committed to developing highly competent and qualified professionals. The focus of the program is on preparing individuals to aid in the prevention and treatment of human problems, as well as the enhancement of human functioning and potential. The program trains students in the general, integrative practice of professional psychology through a broad-based exposure to a variety of psychological approaches and modalities. In addition, the program offers specialized training in four clinical emphasis areas: health psychology/behavioral medicine, childhood and adolescent psychology, adult development and geropsychology, and a generalist track. The faculty believe that education is most effective when the relationship between students and faculty is characterized by mutual respect, responsibility, and dedication to excellence. The program is founded on a deep and abiding respect for diversity in individuals, the ethical practice of psychology, and a commitment to service to others. These core values are reflected in the selection of students, the coursework and training experiences offered, and the faculty who serve as role models and mentors.

Special Facilities or Resources: Specialized training facilities include several clinical therapy labs designed for supervised assessment, testing, and therapy, and for videotaping of clinical sessions utilized in feedback and instruction. The Large Groups Lab includes interconnected classrooms used for videotaping and monitoring of experiential group or class exercises, psychoeducational programs, and other large group activities. Individualized Study and Research Labs equipped with computers are available for research projects, classroom assignments, and personal study. Computer facilities in the School of Psychology and throughout the university allow access to word processing, spreadsheets, database operations, statistical packages, e-mail, Internet connection, and online searching of library holdings. In addition, they offer the capability of conducting direct, online literature searches using a variety of different databases (e.g., PsycINFO, MedLine). The library subscribes to the major psychology journals and contains the latest publications in the field of clinical psychology. The department has a graduate student lounge in which students meet to confer about class assignments, have group study sessions, practice presentations, or just relax between classes. The School also has an on-site Psychological Services Center, which offers treatment services to community residents on a sliding fee scale. Students receive applied training experience at the Center while conducting intake assessments or providing therapeutic services.

Application Information:
Send to: Donna Hood, Coordinator of Graduate Admissions. Application available online. URL of online application: http://psych.uindy.edu/psyd/admissionapp.php. Students are admitted in the Fall, application deadline January 10. Febraury 25 MA deadline. *Fee:* $50.

Notre Dame, University of
Department of Psychology
Arts & Letters
118 Haggar Hall
Notre Dame, IN 46556
Telephone: (574) 631-6650
Fax: (574) 631-8883
E-mail: *LCarlson@nd.edu*
Web: *http://www.nd.edu*

Department Information:
1965. Chairperson: Cindy Bergeman. Number of Faculty: total–full-time 29, part-time 10; women–full-time 13, part-time 7; minority–full-time 6.

Programs and Degrees Offered:

Listed in the following order: Program area, degree type (T if terminal Master's), number awarded 7/03–6/04. Cognitive Psychology PhD (Doctor of Philosophy) 1, Counseling Psychology PhD (Doctor of Philosophy) 3, Developmental Psychology PhD (Doctor of Philosophy) 6, Quantitative Psychology PhD (Doctor of Philosophy) 0.

APA Accreditation: Counseling PhD (Doctor of Philosophy).

Student Applications/Admissions:

Student Applications

Cognitive Psychology PhD (Doctor of Philosophy)—Applications 2004–2005, 19. Total applicants accepted 2004–2005, 2. Number enrolled (new admits only) 2004–2005 full-time, 2. Total enrolled 2004–2005 full-time, 4. Openings 2005–2006, 3. The Median number of years required for completion of a degree are 6. The number of students enrolled full and part-time who were dismissed or voluntarily withdrew from this program area were 1. *Counseling Psychology PhD (Doctor of Philosophy)*—Applications 2004–2005, 105. Total applicants accepted 2004–2005, 5. Number enrolled (new admits only) 2004–2005 full-time, 5. Total enrolled 2004–2005 full-time, 22. Openings 2005–2006, 3. The Median number of years required for completion of a degree are 6.3. The number of students enrolled full and part-time who were dismissed or voluntarily withdrew from this program area were 0. *Developmental Psychology PhD (Doctor of Philosophy)*—Applications 2004–2005, 28. Total applicants accepted 2004–2005, 3. Number enrolled (new admits only) 2004–2005 full-time, 3. Total enrolled 2004–2005 full-time, 26. Openings 2005–2006, 3. The Median number of years required for completion of a degree are 5.1. The number of students enrolled full and part-time, who were dismissed or voluntarily withdrew from this program area were 0. *Quantitative Psychology PhD (Doctor of Philosophy)*—Applications 2004–2005, 14. Total applicants accepted 2004–2005, 3. Number enrolled (new admits only) 2004–2005 full-time, 3. Openings 2005–2006, 3. The number of students enrolled full and part-time who were dismissed or voluntarily withdrew from this program area were 0.

Admissions Requirements:

Scores: Entries appear in this order: required test or GPA, minimum score (if required), median score of students entering in 2003–2004. Doctoral Programs: GRE-V no minimum stated, 562; GRE-Q no minimum stated, 674; GRE-Analytical no minimum stated, 5.0; overall undergraduate GPA no minimum stated, 3.78.

Other Criteria: (importance of criteria rated low, medium, or high): GRE/MAT scores high, research experience high, extracurricular activity low, clinically related public service low, GPA high, letters of recommendation high, interview medium, statement of goals and objectives high.

Student Characteristics: The following represents characteristics of students in 2004–2005 in all graduate psychology programs in the department: Female–full-time 45, part-time 0; Male–full-time 16, part-time 0; African American/Black–full-time 4, part-time 0; Hispanic/Latino(a)–full-time 5, part-time 0; Asian/Pacific Islander–full-time 6, part-time 0; American Indian/Alaska Native–full-time 0, part-time 0; Caucasian–full-time 43, part-time 0;

Multi-ethnic–full-time 3, part-time 0; students subject to the Americans With Disabilities Act–full-time 0, part-time 0.

Financial Information/Assistance:

Tuition for Full-Time Study: *Doctoral:* State residents: per academic year $31,000; Nonstate residents: per academic year $31,000.

Financial Assistance:

First Year Students: Teaching assistantships available for first-year. Average amount paid per academic year: $15,000. Tuition remission given: full. Research assistantships available for first-year. Average amount paid per academic year: $15,000. Tuition remission given: full. Fellowships and scholarships available for first-year. Average amount paid per academic year: $15,000. Tuition remission given: full.

Advanced Students: Teaching assistantships available for advanced students. Average amount paid per academic year: $15,000. Tuition remission given: full. Research assistantships available for advanced students. Average amount paid per academic year: $15,000. Tuition remission given: full. Fellowships and scholarships available for advanced students. Average amount paid per academic year: $15,000.

Contact Information: Of all students currently enrolled full-time, 100% benefitted from one or more of the listed financial assistance programs. Application and information available online at: http://www.nd.edu/~gradsch/.

Internships/Practica: All students in the APA-accredited counseling program have an initial practicum 13-17 hours per week at the University Counseling Center. These same students have opportunities for additional practicum placements in agencies in the community. The University Counseling Center also houses an APA-accredited internship. Advanced students in the accredited program are eligible to apply. For those doctoral students for whom a professional internship is required prior to graduation, 4 applied in 2003–2004. Of those who applied, 4 were placed in internships listed by the Association of Psychology Postdoctoral and Internship Programs (APPIC); 4 were placed in APA accredited internships.

Housing and Day Care: On-campus housing is available. See the following Web site for more information: www.nd.edu/~orlh. On-campus day care facilities are available.

Employment of Department Graduates:

Master's Degree Graduates: Of those who graduated in the academic year 2003–2004, the following categories and numbers represent the post-graduate activities and employment of master's degree graduates: Enrolled in a post-doctoral residency/fellowship (n/a), employed in independent practice (n/a), total from the above (master's) (0).

Doctoral Degree Graduates: Of those who graduated in the academic year 2003–2004, the following categories and numbers represent the post-graduate activities and employment of doctoral degree graduates: Enrolled in a psychology doctoral program (n/a), enrolled in a post-doctoral residency/fellowship (3), employed in an academic position at a university (6), employed in a government agency (professional services) (2), employed in a community mental health/counseling center (1), total from the above (doctoral) (12).

Additional Information:

Orientation, Objectives, and Emphasis of Department: The Department of Psychology at the University of Notre Dame is committed to excellence in psychological science and its applications. To realize this commitment a major focus is upon developing knowledge and expertise in the increasingly sophisticated methodology of the discipline. With this methodological core as its major emphasis and integrating link, the department has emphasized four content areas: cognitive, counseling, developmental and quantitative psychology. In the context of the mores of the academy, the faculty of each content area organize and coordinate work in the three domains of research, graduate education and undergraduate education. Using our methodological understandings as a base, we strive to find intellectual common ground among the content areas within our department and other disciplines throughout the social sciences and the academy.

Special Facilities or Resources: We are involved in the development of innovative science and practice experiences for undergraduate and graduate students in the local community. Currently, many faculty have excellent relationships with community groups (e.g., the local schools, hospitals, Madison Center, Logan center, Center for the Homeless, Head Start). Many faculty conduct research with undergraduate and graduate students in these settings. Over and above these research activities, many students volunteer in these agencies. Finally, counseling psychology graduate students receive supervision to work in Madison Center, Family and Children's Ctr., Michiana EAP, Oaklawn, Street Joseph Medical Ctr., and the Center for the Homeless and, in a new initiative, postdoctoral positions exist in the Multicultural Research Institute.

Information for Students With Physical Disabilities: See the following Web site for more information: www.nd.edu/~osd.

Application Information:

Send to: Graduate Admissions, The Graduate School, University of Notre Dame, Notre Dame, IN 46556. Application available online. URL of online application: http://graduateschool.nd.edu/html/admissions/application-gateway.html. Students are admitted in the Fall, application deadline January 2. *Fee:* $50. In certain circumstances the Graduate School (at the address above) can approve the waiver of fees. Fee is $35 for applications received before December 1st.

Purdue University
Department of Psychological Sciences
College of Liberal Arts
703 Third Street
West Lafayette, IN 47907
Telephone: (765) 494-6067
Fax: (765) 496-1264
E-mail: nobrien@psych.purdue.edu
Web: http://www.psych.purdue.edu

Department Information:
1954. Professor and Head: Howard M. Weiss. Number of Faculty: total–full-time 48, part-time 2; women–full-time 13, part-time 1; minority–full-time 3.

Programs and Degrees Offered:
Listed in the following order: Program area, degree type (T if terminal Master's), number awarded 7/03–6/04. Clinical PhD (Doctor of Philosophy) 4, cognitive PhD (Doctor of Philosophy) 1, developmental PhD (Doctor of Philosophy) 1, industrial/organizational PhD (Doctor of Philosophy) 0, learning and memory PhD (Doctor of Philosophy) 1, psychobiology PhD (Doctor of Philosophy) 0, quantitative PhD (Doctor of Philosophy) 0, social PhD (Doctor of Philosophy) 3.

APA Accreditation: Clinical PhD (Doctor of Philosophy).

Student Applications/Admissions:
Student Applications

Clinical PhD (Doctor of Philosophy)—Applications 2004–2005, 201. Total applicants accepted 2004–2005, 6. Number enrolled (new admits only) 2004–2005 full-time, 3. Number enrolled (new admits only) 2004–2005 part-time, 0. Openings 2005–2006, 6. The number of students enrolled full and part-time who were dismissed or voluntarily withdrew from this program area were 2. *Cognitive PhD (Doctor of Philosophy)*—Applications 2004–2005, 31. Total applicants accepted 2004–2005, 4. Number enrolled (new admits only) 2004–2005 full-time, 3. Number enrolled (new admits only) 2004–2005 part-time, 0. Openings 2005–2006, 1. The Median number of years required for completion of a degree are 5. The number of students enrolled full and part-time who were dismissed or voluntarily withdrew from this program area were 0. *Developmental PhD (Doctor of Philosophy)*—Applications 2004–2005, 30. Total applicants accepted 2004–2005, 6. Number enrolled (new admits only) 2004–2005 full-time, 2. Number enrolled (new admits only) 2004–2005 part-time, 0. Openings 2005–2006, 4. The Median number of years required for completion of a degree are 5. The number of students enrolled full and part-time who were dismissed or voluntarily withdrew from this program area were 0. *Industrial/organizational PhD (Doctor of Philosophy)*—Applications 2004–2005, 77. Total applicants accepted 2004–2005, 8. Number enrolled (new admits only) 2004–2005 full-time, 3. Number enrolled (new admits only) 2004–2005 part-time, 0. Openings 2005–2006, 3. The number of students enrolled full and part-time who were dismissed or voluntarily withdrew from this program area were 0. *Learning and Memory PhD (Doctor of Philosophy)*—Applications 2004–2005, 77. Total applicants accepted 2004–2005, 8. Number enrolled (new admits only) 2004–2005 full-time, 3. Number enrolled (new admits only) 2004–2005 part-time, 0. The Median number of years required for completion of a degree are 5. The number of students enrolled full and part-time who were dismissed or voluntarily withdrew from this program area were 0. *Psychobiology PhD (Doctor of Philosophy)*—Applications 2004–2005, 4. Total applicants accepted 2004–2005, 3. Number enrolled (new admits only) 2004–2005 full-time, 2. Number enrolled (new admits only) 2004–2005 part-time, 0. Openings 2005–2006, 3. The number of students enrolled full and part-time who were dismissed or voluntarily withdrew from this program area were 0. *Quantitative PhD (Doctor of Philosophy)*—Applications 2004–2005, 7. Total applicants accepted 2004–2005, 4. Number enrolled (new admits only) 2004–2005 full-time, 0. Number enrolled (new admits only) 2004–2005 part-time, 0. Openings 2005–2006, 3. The number of students enrolled full and part-time, who were dismissed or voluntarily withdrew from this program area were 0. *Social PhD (Doctor of Philosophy)*—Applications 2004–2005, 73. Total applicants accepted 2004–2005, 5. Number enrolled (new admits only) 2004–2005 full-time, 3. Number enrolled (new admits only) 2004–2005 part-time, 0. Openings 2005–2006, 3. The Median number of years required for completion of a degree are 5. The number of students enrolled full and part-time who were dismissed or voluntarily withdrew from this program area were 0.

Admissions Requirements:

Scores: Entries appear in this order: required test or GPA, minimum score (if required), median score of students entering in 2003–2004. Doctoral Programs: GRE-V no minimum stated, 580; GRE-Q no minimum stated, 675; GRE-Analytical no minimum stated, 4.5; overall undergraduate GPA 3.0, 3.60.

Other Criteria: (importance of criteria rated low, medium, or high): GRE/MAT scores medium, research experience medium, work experience medium, extracurricular activity low, clinically related public service high, GPA high, letters of recommendation medium, interview high, statement of goals and objectives medium. Not all areas hold formal interviews. Clinically related public service is important if you are applying to the clinical program.

Student Characteristics: The following represents characteristics of students in 2004–2005 in all graduate psychology programs in the department: Female–full-time 73, part-time 0; Male–full-time 34, part-time 0; African American/Black–full-time 7, part-time 0; Hispanic/Latino(a)–full-time 3, part-time 0; Asian/Pacific Islander–full-time 26, part-time 0; American Indian/Alaska Native–full-time 0, part-time 0; Caucasian–full-time 60, part-time 0; Multi-ethnic–full-time 11, part-time 0; students subject to the Americans With Disabilities Act–full-time 1, part-time 0.

Financial Information/Assistance:

Tuition for Full-Time Study: *Master's:* State residents: per academic year $6,092, $218 per credit hour; Nonstate residents: per academic year $18,700, $621 per credit hour. *Doctoral:* State residents: per academic year $6,092, $218 per credit hour; Nonstate residents: per academic year $18,700, $621 per credit hour. Tuition is subject to change.

Financial Assistance:

First Year Students: Teaching assistantships available for first-year. Average amount paid per academic year: $11,650. Average number of hours worked per week: 20. Apply by January 1. Tuition remission given: partial. Research assistantships available for first-year. Average amount paid per academic year: $11,650. Average number of hours worked per week: 20. Apply by January 1. Tuition remission given: partial. Fellowships and scholarships available for first-year. Average amount paid per academic year: $17,000. Apply by January 1. Tuition remission given: partial.

Advanced Students: Teaching assistantships available for advanced students. Average amount paid per academic year: $12,150. Average number of hours worked per week: 20. Apply by January 1. Tuition remission given: partial. Research assistantships available for advanced students. Average amount paid per academic year: $12,150. Average number of hours worked per week:

20. Apply by January 1. Tuition remission given: partial. Fellowships and scholarships available for advanced students. Average amount paid per academic year: $17,000. Average number of hours worked per week: 20. Apply by January 1. Tuition remission given: partial.

Contact Information: Of all students currently enrolled full-time, 100% benefitted from one or more of the listed financial assistance programs.

Internships/Practica: After the first year requirements, clinical psychology students enroll in clinical practica carried out in the Purdue Psychology Traetment and Research Clinics. Practica include providing services for anxiety disorders, depression, personality disorders, Attention Deficit Hyperactivity Disorder, and oppositional disorders. Practicum training emphasizes use of empirically corroborated interventions for particular problems. A year-long clinical internship is required in order to complete training. For those doctoral students for whom a professional internship is required prior to graduation, 4 applied in 2003–2004. Of those who applied, 4 were placed in internships listed by the Association of Psychology Postdoctoral and Internship Programs (APPIC); 4 were placed in APA accredited internships.

Housing and Day Care: On-campus housing is available. See the following Web site for more information: http://www.housing.purdue.edu. No on-campus day care facilities are available.

Employment of Department Graduates:

Master's Degree Graduates: Of those who graduated in the academic year 2003–2004, the following categories and numbers represent the post-graduate activities and employment of master's degree graduates: Enrolled in a post-doctoral residency/fellowship (n/a), employed in independent practice (n/a), total from the above (master's) (0).

Doctoral Degree Graduates: Of those who graduated in the academic year 2003–2004, the following categories and numbers represent the post-graduate activities and employment of doctoral degree graduates: Enrolled in a psychology doctoral program (n/a), total from the above (doctoral) (0).

Additional Information:

Orientation, Objectives, and Emphasis of Department: The dominant emphasis of the department is a commitment to research and scholarship as the major core of graduate education. All programs are structured so that students become involved in research activities almost immediately upon beginning their graduate education, and this involvement is expected to continue throughout an individual's entire graduate career.

Special Facilities or Resources: The department moved into the new psychological sciences building in 1980. Excellent research facilities are available in many areas, including more than 35 computer-controlled laboratories.

Information for Students With Physical Disabilities: See the following Web site for more information: www.psych.purdue.edu.

Application Information:

Send to: Nancy O'Brien, Administrative Assistant, Psychological Sciences, 703 Third Street, Purdue University, West Lafayette, IN 47907-2004. Application available online. URL of online application: http://www.gradschool.purdue.edu/admissions. Students are admitted in the Fall, application deadline January 1. *Fee:* $55.

Saint Francis, University of (2004 data)

Psychology and Counseling
2701 Spring Street
Fort Wayne, IN 46808
Telephone: (260) 434-7443
Fax: (260) 434-7562
E-mail: *rdaniel@sf.edu*
Web: *http://www.sf.edu*

Department Information:

1971. Chairperson: Rolf Daniel, PhD Number of Faculty: total–full-time 5, part-time 4; women–full-time 2, part-time 2; minority–full-time 1.

Programs and Degrees Offered:

Listed in the following order: Program area, degree type (T if terminal Master's), number awarded 7/03–6/04. General Psychology MA/MS (Master of Arts/Science) (T) 2, Mental Health Counseling MA/MS (Master of Arts/Science) (T) 8.

Student Applications/Admissions:

Student Applications

General Psychology MA/MS (Master of Arts/Science)—Applications 2004–2005, 10. Total applicants accepted 2004–2005, 8. Openings 2005–2006, 8. The Median number of years required for completion of a degree are 2. The number of students enrolled full and part-time who were dismissed or voluntarily withdrew from this program area were 0. *Mental Health Counseling MA/MS (Master of Arts/Science)*—Applications 2004–2005, 15. Total applicants accepted 2004–2005, 9. Total enrolled 2004–2005 full-time, 18, part-time, 4. Openings 2005–2006, 10. The Median number of years required for completion of a degree are 3. The number of students enrolled full and part-time who were dismissed or voluntarily withdrew from this program area were 0.

Admissions Requirements:

Scores: Entries appear in this order: required test or GPA, minimum score (if required), median score of students entering in 2003–2004. Master's Programs: overall undergraduate GPA 3.0, 3.3.

Other Criteria: (importance of criteria rated low, medium, or high): GRE/MAT scores medium, research experience medium, work experience high, extracurricular activity low, clinically related public service high, GPA high, letters of recommendation high, interview high, statement of goals and objectives high.

Student Characteristics: The following represents characteristics of students in 2004–2005 in all graduate psychology programs in the department: Female–full-time 29, part-time 4; Male–full-time 4, part-time 0; African American/Black–full-time 2, part-time 0; Hispanic/Latino(a)–full-time 2, part-time 0; Asian/Pacific Islander–full-time 0, part-time 0; American Indian/Alaska Native–full-time 1, part-time 0; Caucasian–full-time 28, part-time 4; Multi-ethnic–full-time 0, part-time 0; students subject to the Americans With Disabilities Act–full-time 1, part-time 0.

Financial Information/Assistance:

Tuition for Full-Time Study: *Master's:* State residents: $530 per credit hour; Nonstate residents: $530 per credit hour.

Financial Assistance:

First Year Students: Teaching assistantships available for first-year. Average amount paid per academic year: $4,770. Average number of hours worked per week: 10. Apply by June 30.

Advanced Students: Teaching assistantships available for advanced students. Average amount paid per academic year: $4,770. Average number of hours worked per week: 10. Apply by June 30.

Contact Information: Of all students currently enrolled full-time, 16% benefitted from one or more of the listed financial assistance programs.

Internships/Practica: General Psychology Students can elect to do a practicum experience. This experience would be 150 clock hours (10 hours/week) of supervised practical field experience tailored to the individual needs/interests of the students. Students choosing to have a practicum experience have an "on-site" supervisor who helps define, mentor, and direct the student's activities. Students also have 15 hours of supervision on campus. This experience is designed to give students an opportunity to integrate formal education with work experience. Mental Health Counseling (MS) has required practicum and internship: Practicum: 1 semester-100 hours/60 face-to-face client contact hours. Internship: 1 or 2 semesters—600 hours/240 face-to-face client contact hours. Advanced Internship: 1 semester—300 hours/120 face-to-face client contact hours.

Housing and Day Care: On-campus housing is available. No on-campus day care facilities are available.

Employment of Department Graduates:

Master's Degree Graduates: Of those who graduated in the academic year 2003–2004, the following categories and numbers represent the post-graduate activities and employment of master's degree graduates: Enrolled in a psychology doctoral program (1), enrolled in another graduate/professional program (0), enrolled in a post-doctoral residency/fellowship (n/a), employed in independent practice (n/a), employed in an academic position at a university (0), employed in an academic position at a 2-year/4-year college (0), employed in other positions at a higher education institution (0), employed in a professional position in a school system (0), employed in business or industry (research/consulting) (0), employed in business or industry (management) (0), employed in a government agency (research) (0), employed in a government agency (professional services) (0), employed in a community mental health/counseling center (7), employed in a hospital/medical center (2), still seeking employment (0), other employment position (0), total from the above (master's) (10).

Doctoral Degree Graduates: Of those who graduated in the academic year 2003–2004, the following categories and numbers represent the post-graduate activities and employment of doctoral

degree graduates: Enrolled in a psychology doctoral program (n/a), total from the above (doctoral) (0).

Additional Information:

Orientation, Objectives, and Emphasis of Department: The MS in Psychology Program is designed for people who are either interested in preparation for doctoral work, or furthering their professional careers through a greater understanding of basic psychological principles. The primary goal of the program is to give students a solid, graduate-level grounding in psychology. This program emphasizes a mastery of psychological fundamentals, i.e., theories and research methods, areas of specialization (development, social, abnormal behavior, physiological data, personality development and behavior management techniques). Mental Health Counseling (MS) —The program of study leading to the MS Degree in Mental Health Counseling is designed to prepare persons to function as Licensed Mental Health Counselors (LMHC) in health care residential, private practice, community agency, governmental, business, and industrial settings. The scope of practice for mental health counseling is defined in Section 24. IC 25-23.6-1-7.5 of the Indiana Code, which is available from the Psychology & Counseling Department. To successfully complete the MS in Mental Health Counseling, students will: 1. Demonstrate an ability to analyze, synthesize, and critique in a scholarly manner academic subject matter, professional journal articles, and other professional resources. Students will also demonstrate an ability to write coherently and professionally according to the *Publication Manual of the American Psychological Association* (4th edition) standards. 2. Promote and adhere to the standards/ guidelines for ethical and professional conduct in all classroom and field experiences (i.e., American Counseling Association's Ethical Standards for Mental Health Professionals and the American Psychological Association's Ethical Principles) as well as legal mandates regarding the practice of their profession. 3. Demonstrate an ability to synthesize, evaluate, and articulate broad knowledge of counseling theories and approaches. This will include ability to apply scientific and measurement principles to the study of psychology. 4. Develop a capacity to communicate respect, empathy, and unconditional positive regard toward others, including demonstration of a tolerant, non-judgmental attitude toward different ethnic/cultural heritage, value orientations, and lifestyles. 5. Recognize and effectively conceptualize the special needs of persons with varying mental, adjustment, developmental and/or chemical dependence disorders. Students will recognize the need for, request, and benefit from consultation and supervision when practicing in areas of insufficient competence. 6. Demonstrate competence to counsel/interview using basic listening and influencing skills in one-to-one, marital, family, and group counseling modalities. 7. Be prepared to seek employment as a Licensed Mental Health Counselor, enter a program of additional education/training, and/or seek other appropriate certifications.

Application Information:

Send to: Office of Admissions, Trinity Hall, Room 110A, University of Saint Francis, Fort Wayne, IN 46808. Application available online. Students are admitted in the Fall, application deadline May 30; Spring, application deadline October 15; Summer, application deadline May 1; Programs have rolling admissions. *Fee:* $20.

Valparaiso University
Department of Psychology
Arts & Sciences, Graduate Division
Dickmeyer Hall
Valparaiso, IN 46383
Telephone: (219) 464-5440
Fax: (219) 464-6878
E-mail: *daniel.arkkelin@valpo.edu*
Web: *http://www.valpo.edu/psych/graduate*

Department Information:

1958. Chairperson: Daniel Arkkelin. Number of Faculty: total– full-time 9, part-time 6; women–full-time 2, part-time 4; minority– full-time 1.

Programs and Degrees Offered:

Listed in the following order: Program area, degree type (T if terminal Master's), number awarded 7/03–6/04. Counseling and Clinical Mental Health Counseling MA/MS (Master of Arts/ Science) (T) 7, Psychology/ Law Other 2, School Psychology EdS (Education Specialist) 9.

Student Applications/Admissions:

Student Applications

Counseling and Clinical Mental Health Counseling MA/MS (Master of Arts/Science)—Applications 2004–2005, 58. Total applicants accepted 2004–2005, 37. Number enrolled (new admits only) 2004–2005 full-time, 12. Number enrolled (new admits only) 2004–2005 part-time, 4. Total enrolled 2004–2005 full-time, 23, part-time, 19. Openings 2005–2006, 17. The Median number of years required for completion of a degree are 3. The number of students enrolled full and part-time who were dismissed or voluntarily withdrew from this program area were 3. *Psychology/ Law Other*—Applications 2004–2005, 23. Total applicants accepted 2004–2005, 7. Number enrolled (new admits only) 2004–2005 full-time, 5. Number enrolled (new admits only) 2004–2005 part-time, 0. Openings 2005–2006, 5. The Median number of years required for completion of a degree are 4. The number of students enrolled full and part-time who were dismissed or voluntarily withdrew from this program area were 0. *School Psychology EdS (Education Specialist)*—Applications 2004–2005, 22. Total applicants accepted 2004–2005, 17. Openings 2005–2006, 8.

Admissions Requirements:

Scores: Entries appear in this order: required test or GPA, minimum score (if required), median score of students entering in 2003–2004. Master's Programs: overall undergraduate GPA 3.0, 3.40.

Other Criteria: (importance of criteria rated low, medium, or high): research experience medium, work experience medium, extracurricular activity low, clinically related public service medium, GPA high, letters of recommendation high, interview medium, statement of goals and objectives high. For additional information on admission requirements, go to: http://www. valpo.edu/gce/graduate/admissions.php.

Student Characteristics: The following represents characteristics of students in 2004–2005 in all graduate psychology programs in the department: Female–full-time 27, part-time 15; Male–full-

time 5, part-time 4; African American/Black–full-time 3, part-time 1; Hispanic/Latino(a)–full-time 2, part-time 1; Asian/Pacific Islander–full-time 0, part-time 0; American Indian/Alaska Native–full-time 0, part-time 0; Caucasian–full-time 27, part-time 17; Multi-ethnic–full-time 0, part-time 0; students subject to the Americans With Disabilities Act–full-time 0, part-time 0.

Financial Information/Assistance:

Tuition for Full-Time Study: *Master's:* State residents: $355 per credit hour; Nonstate residents: $355 per credit hour. See the following Web site for updates and changes in tuition costs: http://www.valpo.edu/gce/graduate/costs.php.

Financial Assistance:

First Year Students: Teaching assistantships available for first-year. Average amount paid per academic year: $1,000. Apply by March 1. Research assistantships available for first-year. Average amount paid per academic year: $2,000. Average number of hours worked per week: 5. Apply by March 1. Traineeships available for first-year. Average amount paid per academic year: $8,000. Average number of hours worked per week: 20. Apply by March 1. Tuition remission given: partial.

Advanced Students: Teaching assistantships available for advanced students. Average amount paid per academic year: $1,000. Apply by March 1. Research assistantships available for advanced students. Average amount paid per academic year: $2,000. Average number of hours worked per week: 5. Apply by March 1. Traineeships available for advanced students. Average amount paid per academic year: $8,000. Average number of hours worked per week: 20. Apply by March 1. Tuition remission given: partial.

Contact Information: Of all students currently enrolled full-time, 31% benefitted from one or more of the listed financial assistance programs.

Internships/Practica: Counseling and clinical mental health counseling students obtain practical training (practica and internships) in a variety of mental health settings in Northwest Indiana. School psychology students obtain practica training (practica and internships) in school systems and special education cooperatives in Northwest Indiana.

Housing and Day Care: No on-campus housing is available. No on-campus day care facilities are available.

Employment of Department Graduates:

Master's Degree Graduates: Of those who graduated in the academic year 2003–2004, the following categories and numbers represent the post-graduate activities and employment of master's degree graduates: Enrolled in a post-doctoral residency/fellowship (n/a), employed in independent practice (n/a), total from the above (master's) (0).

Doctoral Degree Graduates: Of those who graduated in the academic year 2003–2004, the following categories and numbers represent the post-graduate activities and employment of doctoral degree graduates: Enrolled in a psychology doctoral program (n/a), total from the above (doctoral) (0).

Additional Information:

Orientation, Objectives, and Emphasis of Department: The counseling program is designed to provide advanced training to persons planning or continuing in a counseling career. The program combines a strong theoretical background in counseling with applied work through both coursework and supervised practica. A thesis option is available. The clinical mental health counseling program is designed to lead toward licensure or certification in most of the 50 states. It involves additional coursework and experiential requirements. The school psychology program is designed to provide advanced training to persons seeking certification in Indiana as school psychologists. The program is offered jointly by the psychology and education departments. The JD/MA program provides traditional legal training, exposure to psychological theory and methods, and integrated training in the application of psychological foundations to the practice of law. The program is offered jointly by the law school and psychology department. The JD/MA in clinical mental health counseling combines legal training and training in clinical mental health counseling and is designed to lead to licensure or certification as a counselor in most of the 50 states.

Special Facilities or Resources: The Department maintains strong contacts with community and regional agencies involved in mental health and counseling as well as with the campus counseling center. In addition, an in-house clinical training lab utilizing audio-video taping may be used in student training of clinical skills. Extensive computer facilities and networks are available in the department and throughout campus.

Information for Students With Physical Disabilities: See the following Web site for more information: http://www.valpo.edu/cas/dss.

Application Information:
Send to: Office of Graduate Studies, Kretzmann Hall, Valparaiso University, Valparaiso, IN 46383. Application available online. URL of online application: http://www.valpo.edu/gce/forms/main.htm. Students are admitted in the Fall, application deadline March 1. *Fee:* $30.

Iowa State University
Department of Psychology
Liberal Arts & Sciences
Lagomarcino Hall
Ames, IA 50011-3180
Telephone: (515) 294-1742
Fax: (515) 294-6424
E-mail: *psychadm@iastate.edu*
Web: *http://www.psychology.iastate.edu/*

Department Information:
1924. Chair: Craig A. Anderson. Number of Faculty: total–full-time 24, part-time 7; women–full-time 10, part-time 2; minority–full-time 1.

Programs and Degrees Offered:
Listed in the following order: Program area, degree type (T if terminal Master's), number awarded 7/03–6/04. Counseling PhD (Doctor of Philosophy) 0, General MA/MS (Master of Arts/Science) (T) 4, Social PhD (Doctor of Philosophy) 0, Cognitive PhD (Doctor of Philosophy) 1.

APA Accreditation: Counseling PhD (Doctor of Philosophy).

Student Applications/Admissions:
Student Applications
Counseling PhD (Doctor of Philosophy)—Applications 2004–2005, 46. Total applicants accepted 2004–2005, 9. Number enrolled (new admits only) 2004–2005 full-time, 6. Number enrolled (new admits only) 2004–2005 part-time, 0. Openings 2005–2006, 5. The number of students enrolled full and part-time who were dismissed or voluntarily withdrew from this program area were 0. *General MA/MS (Master of Arts/Science)*—Applications 2004–2005, 28. Total applicants accepted 2004–2005, 3. Number enrolled (new admits only) 2004–2005 full-time, 3. Number enrolled (new admits only) 2004–2005 part-time, 0. Openings 2005–2006, 5. The Median number of years required for completion of a degree are 2. The number of students enrolled full and part-time who were dismissed or voluntarily withdrew from this program area were 0. *Social PhD (Doctor of Philosophy)*—Applications 2004–2005, 35. Total applicants accepted 2004–2005, 8. Number enrolled (new admits only) 2004–2005 full-time, 5. Number enrolled (new admits only) 2004–2005 part-time, 0. Openings 2005–2006, 4. The number of students enrolled full and part-time who were dismissed or voluntarily withdrew from this program area were 0. *Cognitive PhD (Doctor of Philosophy)*—Applications 2004–2005, 10. Total applicants accepted 2004–2005, 3. Number enrolled (new admits only) 2004–2005 full-time, 2. Number enrolled (new admits only) 2004–2005 part-time, 0. Openings 2005–2006, 3. The Median number of years required for completion of a degree are 7. The number of students enrolled full and part-time who were dismissed or voluntarily withdrew from this program area were 0.

Admissions Requirements:
Scores: Entries appear in this order: required test or GPA, minimum score (if required), median score of students entering in 2003–2004. Master's Programs: GRE-V no minimum stated, 540; GRE-Q no minimum stated, 690; GRE-Analytical no minimum stated, 770; GRE-Subject(Psych) no minimum stated, 630; overall undergraduate GPA no minimum stated, 3.5; last 2 years GPA no minimum stated, 3.5; psychology GPA no minimum stated, 3.62. TOEFL required for international applicants. Doctoral Programs: GRE-V no minimum stated, 555; GRE-Q no minimum stated, 681; GRE-Analytical no minimum stated, 699; GRE-Subject(Psych) no minimum stated, 600; overall undergraduate GPA no minimum stated, 3.59; psychology GPA no minimum stated, 3.73. TOEFL required for international applicants.

Other Criteria: (importance of criteria rated low, medium, or high): GRE/MAT scores high, research experience high, work experience low, extracurricular activity low, clinically related public service low, GPA high, letters of recommendation high, interview medium, statement of goals and objectives high. Our applied/professional program places greater weight on the interview and relevant work/service experience. For additional information on admission requirements, go to: www.psychology.iastate.edu.

Student Characteristics: The following represents characteristics of students in 2004–2005 in all graduate psychology programs in the department: Female–full-time 34, part-time 0; Male–full-time 19, part-time 0; African American/Black–full-time 1, part-time 0; Hispanic/Latino(a)–full-time 2, part-time 1; Asian/Pacific Islander–full-time 2, part-time 0; American Indian/Alaska Native–full-time 1, part-time 0; Caucasian–full-time 48, part-time 0; Multi-ethnic–full-time 1, part-time 0; students subject to the Americans With Disabilities Act–full-time 0, part-time 0.

Financial Information/Assistance:
Tuition for Full-Time Study: *Master's:* State residents: per academic year $5,708, $280 per credit hour; Nonstate residents: per academic year $15,720, $790 per credit hour. *Doctoral:* State residents: per academic year $5,708, $280 per credit hour; Nonstate residents: per academic year $15,720, $790 per credit hour. Tuition is subject to change. See the following Web site for updates and changes in tuition costs: http://www.iastate.edu/~registrar/fees/.

Financial Assistance:
First Year Students: Teaching assistantships available for first-year. Average amount paid per academic year: $12,000. Average number of hours worked per week: 20. Apply by January 2. Tuition remission given: full. Research assistantships available for first-year. Average amount paid per academic year: $12,000. Average number of hours worked per week: 20. Apply by January 2. Tuition remission given: full. Fellowships and scholarships available for first-year. Average amount paid per academic year: $12,000. Average number of hours worked per week: 20. Apply by January 2. Tuition remission given: full.

Advanced Students: Teaching assistantships available for advanced students. Average amount paid per academic year:

$12,000. Average number of hours worked per week: 20. Tuition remission given: full. Research assistantships available for advanced students. Average amount paid per academic year: $12,000. Average number of hours worked per week: 20. Tuition remission given: full.

Contact Information: Of all students currently enrolled full-time, 100% benefitted from one or more of the listed financial assistance programs. Application and information available online at: http://www.psychology.iastate.edu.

Internships/Practica: Sequential, progressive practica provide students in our professional programs with individually supervised applied training in their specialty area. All supervision is provided by appropriately certified/licensed faculty and adjuncts in a range of settings, including university counseling centers, major hospitals, outpatient clinics, child and adolescent treatment centers, correctional facilities, and the public school system. Based on such practica experience and their academic training, ISU students compete successfully for select predoctoral internships across the country. For those doctoral students for whom a professional internship is required prior to graduation, 6 applied in 2003–2004. Of those who applied, 6 were placed in internships listed by the Association of Psychology Postdoctoral and Internship Programs (APPIC); 6 were placed in APA accredited internships.

Housing and Day Care: On-campus housing is available. See the following Web site for more information: http://www.iastate.edu/~dor/living.html. On-campus day care facilities are available. See the following Web site for more information: http://www.hrs.iastate.edu/childcare/homepage.shtml.

Employment of Department Graduates:

Master's Degree Graduates: Of those who graduated in the academic year 2003–2004, the following categories and numbers represent the post-graduate activities and employment of master's degree graduates: Enrolled in a psychology doctoral program (9), enrolled in another graduate/professional program (2), enrolled in a post-doctoral residency/fellowship (n/a), employed in independent practice (n/a), employed in an academic position at a university (0), employed in an academic position at a 2-year/4-year college (0), employed in other positions at a higher education institution (0), employed in a professional position in a school system (0), employed in business or industry (research/consulting) (0), employed in business or industry (management) (0), employed in a government agency (research) (1), employed in a government agency (professional services) (0), employed in a community mental health/counseling center (1), employed in a hospital/medical center (0), still seeking employment (1), other employment position (0), do not know (0), total from the above (master's) (14).

Doctoral Degree Graduates: Of those who graduated in the academic year 2003–2004, the following categories and numbers represent the post-graduate activities and employment of doctoral degree graduates: Enrolled in a psychology doctoral program (n/a), enrolled in a post-doctoral residency/fellowship (0), employed in independent practice (0), employed in an academic position at a university (1), employed in an academic position at a 2-year/4-year college (0), employed in other positions at a higher education institution (0), employed in a professional position in a school system (0), employed in business or industry (research/consulting) (0), employed in business or industry (management) (0), employed in a government agency (research) (0), employed in a government agency (professional services) (0), employed in a community mental health/counseling center (0), employed in a hospital/medical center (0), still seeking employment (0), other employment position (0), do not know (0), total from the above (doctoral) (1).

Additional Information:

Orientation, Objectives, and Emphasis of Department: Graduate programs emphasize the acquisition of a broad base of knowledge in psychology as well as concentration on the content and methodological skills requisite to performance in teaching, research, and applied activities. A strong research orientation is evident in all areas of the department, with involvement in research being required of all doctoral students throughout their graduate studies. Curriculum requirements for the degrees are based on a core course system, which is designed to enable students to tailor a program best suited to their particular objectives. Subsequent courses, seminars, research, and applied experiences are determined by the student and his or her graduate advisory committee. Additionally, teaching experience is available to all doctoral students, and extensive supervised practica experience is required of students in the applied programs.

Special Facilities or Resources: The department maintains the full array of physical facilities and equipment required for behavioral research. Observational and videotaping facilities are available for research and applied training. The department maintains a microcomputer lab, and the university maintains a superior computation center.

Application Information:

Send to: Iowa State University Graduate Admissions, Department of Psychology, W112 Lagomarcino, Ames, IA 50011. Application available online. URL of online application: www.psychology.iastate.edu. Students are admitted in the Fall, application deadline January 2. MS deadline is March 10 for Fall admission. *Fee:* $30. $70 fee for international application (paper application).

Iowa, University of
Department of Psychology
Liberal Arts and Sciences
11 Seashore Hall East
Iowa City, IA 52242-1407
Telephone: (319) 335-2406
Fax: (319) 335-0191
E-mail: *psychology@uiowa.edu*
Web: *http://www.psychology.uiowa.edu.*

Department Information:

1887. Chairperson: Gregg C. Oden. Number of Faculty: total–full-time 34, part-time 3; women–full-time 10.

Programs and Degrees Offered:

Listed in the following order: Program area, degree type (T if terminal Master's), number awarded 7/03–6/04. Behavioral and Cognitive Neuroscience PhD (Doctor of Philosophy) 1, Clinical PhD (Doctor of Philosophy) 4, Cognition and Perception PhD (Doctor of Philosophy) 1, Developmental Science PhD (Doctor of Philosophy) 2, Personality and Social PhD (Doctor of Philosophy) 2, Health PhD (Doctor of Philosophy) 0.

APA Accreditation: Clinical PhD (Doctor of Philosophy).

Student Applications/Admissions:

Student Applications

Behavioral and Cognitive Neuroscience PhD (Doctor of Philosophy)—Applications 2004–2005, 21. Total applicants accepted 2004–2005, 9. Number enrolled (new admits only) 2004–2005 full-time, 5. Number enrolled (new admits only) 2004–2005 part-time, 0. Openings 2005–2006, 4. The Median number of years required for completion of a degree are 7. The number of students enrolled full and part-time who were dismissed or voluntarily withdrew from this program area were 0. *Clinical PhD (Doctor of Philosophy)*—Applications 2004–2005, 133. Total applicants accepted 2004–2005, 11. Number enrolled (new admits only) 2004–2005 full-time, 6. Number enrolled (new admits only) 2004–2005 part-time, 0. Openings 2005–2006, 5. The Median number of years required for completion of a degree are 6.5. The number of students enrolled full and part-time who were dismissed or voluntarily withdrew from this program area were 1. *Cognition and Perception PhD (Doctor of Philosophy)*—Applications 2004–2005, 20. Total applicants accepted 2004–2005, 4. Number enrolled (new admits only) 2004–2005 full-time, 3. Number enrolled (new admits only) 2004–2005 part-time, 0. Openings 2005–2006, 3. The Median number of years required for completion of a degree are 7.3. The number of students enrolled full and part-time who were dismissed or voluntarily withdrew from this program area were 0. *Developmental Science PhD (Doctor of Philosophy)*—Applications 2004–2005, 13. Total applicants accepted 2004–2005, 4. Number enrolled (new admits only) 2004–2005 full-time, 1. Number enrolled (new admits only) 2004–2005 part-time, 0. Openings 2005–2006, 3. The Median number of years required for completion of a degree are 7.5. The number of students enrolled full and part-time who were dismissed or voluntarily withdrew from this program area were 0. *Personality and Social PhD (Doctor of Philosophy)*—Applications 2004–2005, 56. Total applicants accepted 2004–2005, 5. Number enrolled (new admits only) 2004–2005 full-time, 2. Number enrolled (new admits only) 2004–2005 part-time, 0. Openings 2005–2006, 3. The Median number of years required for completion of a degree are 6. The number of students enrolled full and part-time who were dismissed or voluntarily withdrew from this program area were 0. *Health PhD (Doctor of Philosophy)*—Applications 2004–2005, 11. Total applicants accepted 2004–2005, 2. Number enrolled (new admits only) 2004–2005 full-time, 1. Number enrolled (new admits only) 2004–2005 part-time, 0. Openings 2005–2006, 3. The number of students enrolled full and part-time who were dismissed or voluntarily withdrew from this program area were 0.

Admissions Requirements:

Scores: Entries appear in this order: required test or GPA, minimum score (if required), median score of students entering in 2003–2004. Doctoral Programs: GRE-V no minimum stated; GRE-Q no minimum stated; GRE-V+Q no minimum stated, 1210; GRE-Analytical no minimum stated; overall undergraduate GPA no minimum stated; last 2 years GPA no minimum stated; psychology GPA no minimum stated.

Other Criteria: (importance of criteria rated low, medium, or high): GRE/MAT scores high, research experience high, work experience low, extracurricular activity low, clinically related public service medium, GPA high, letters of recommendation high, interview high, statement of goals and objectives high. Formal interviews are required for most but not all areas (contact the department for more information). For additional information on admission requirements, go to: www.psychology.uiowa.edu.

Student Characteristics: The following represents characteristics of students in 2004–2005 in all graduate psychology programs in the department: Female–full-time 47, part-time 0; Male–full-time 33, part-time 0; African American/Black–full-time 2, part-time 0; Hispanic/Latino(a)–full-time 5, part-time 0; Asian/Pacific Islander–full-time 12, part-time 0; American Indian/Alaska Native–full-time 0, part-time 0; Caucasian–full-time 61, part-time 0; Multi-ethnic–full-time 0, part-time 0; students subject to the Americans With Disabilities Act–full-time 0, part-time 0.

Financial Information/Assistance:

Tuition for Full-Time Study: *Doctoral:* State residents: per academic year $5,976; Nonstate residents: per academic year $16,666. Tuition is subject to change. See the following Web site for updates and changes in tuition costs: http://www.registrar.uiowa.edu/tuition/.

Financial Assistance:

First Year Students: Teaching assistantships available for first-year. Average amount paid per academic year: $18,932. Average number of hours worked per week: 20. Tuition remission given: partial. Research assistantships available for first-year. Average amount paid per academic year: $18,932. Average number of hours worked per week: 20. Tuition remission given: partial. Fellowships and scholarships available for first-year. Average amount paid per academic year: $21,000. Average number of hours worked per week: 0. Tuition remission given: full.

Advanced Students: Teaching assistantships available for advanced students. Average amount paid per academic year: $19,111. Average number of hours worked per week: 20. Tuition remission given: partial. Research assistantships available for advanced students. Average amount paid per academic year: $19,111. Average number of hours worked per week: 20. Tuition remission given: partial. Fellowships and scholarships available for advanced students. Average amount paid per academic year: $25,000. Average number of hours worked per week: 0. Tuition remission given: full.

Contact Information: Of all students currently enrolled full-time, 100% benefitted from one or more of the listed financial assistance programs. Application and information available online at: http://www.uiowa.edu/financial-aid/graduate/.

Internships/Practica: Students in our Clinical Psychology program participate in clinical assessment and treatment practica at our department-run clinic (the Carl E. Seashore Psychology Training Clinic) and in clinics run by departments such as Psychiatry and Neurology at the University of Iowa Hospitals and Clinics. For those doctoral students for whom a professional internship is required prior to graduation, 4 applied in 2003–2004. Of those who applied, 4 were placed in internships listed by the Association of Psychology Postdoctoral and Internship Programs (APPIC); 4 were placed in APA accredited internships.

Housing and Day Care: On-campus housing is available. See the following Web sites for more information: http://www.uiowa.edu/admissions/graduate/housing.html; http://www.uiowa.edu/hr/famserv/housing/. On-campus day care facilities are available. See the following Web site for more information: http://www.uiowa.edu/hr/famserv/ccs.

Employment of Department Graduates:

Master's Degree Graduates: Of those who graduated in the academic year 2003–2004, the following categories and numbers represent the post-graduate activities and employment of master's degree graduates: Enrolled in a post-doctoral residency/fellowship (n/a), employed in independent practice (n/a), total from the above (master's) (0).

Doctoral Degree Graduates: Of those who graduated in the academic year 2003–2004, the following categories and numbers represent the post-graduate activities and employment of doctoral degree graduates: Enrolled in a psychology doctoral program (n/a), enrolled in a post-doctoral residency/fellowship (3), employed in an academic position at a university (2), employed in an academic position at a 2-year/4-year college (1), employed in other positions at a higher education institution (1), total from the above (doctoral) (7).

Additional Information:

Orientation, Objectives, and Emphasis of Department: The mission of the PhD program is to produce professional scholars who contribute significantly to the advancement of scientific psychological knowledge and who can effectively teach students about the science of psychology. Some of these scholars are also prepared to deliver psychological services. Our goal is to produce PhDs who have developed world-class programs of research, who have published extensively, and who have both broad and deep knowledge. Graduate training is organized into six broad training areas: Behavioral and Cognitive Neuroscience, Clinical Psychology, Cognition and Perception, Developmental Science, Health Psychology, and Personality and Social Psychology. The training programs are flexible, and there is considerable overlap and interaction among students and faculty in all areas, leading to an exciting intellectual environment. Students in good standing receive full support for at least five years. The student-faculty ratio remains quite low, usually less than 2 to 1. The department has been successful in establishing strong ties with other campus units such as Psychiatry, Neurology, the law school, and the business school. Through these associations, one may study such topics as the law and psychology, aging, consumer behavior, and neuroscience.

Special Facilities or Resources: The Kenneth W. Spence Laboratories of Psychology and adjoining space in Seashore Hall include automated data acquisition and analysis systems, extensive computing facilities, observation suites with remote audiovisual control and recording equipment, multiple animal facilities, several surgeries, a histology laboratory, soundproof chambers, closed-circuit TV systems, electrophysiological recording rooms, conditioning laboratories, the Carl E. Seashore Psychology Training Clinic, and well-equipped electronic, mechanical, woodworking, and computer shops. Well over half of the departmental laboratories have been extensively renovated or created anew within the past 5 years. In addition, many resources are available through collaboration with colleagues at the university hospital, the Iowa Veterans Administration Hospital, community service centers, and the Colleges of Medicine, Nursing, Dentistry, Engineering, Business, Education, and Law.

Information for Students With Physical Disabilities: See the following Web site for more information: http://www.uiowa.edu/~sds/.

Application Information:
Send to: Graduate Admissions Office, University of Iowa, 11 Seashore Hall E., Iowa City, IA 52242-1407. Application available online. URL of online application: www.uiowa.edu/admissions/applications/graduate. Students are admitted in the Fall, application deadline January 1. *Fee:* $60. $85 for international applicants.

Iowa, University of
Division of Psychological and Quantitative Foundations
College of Education
361 Lindquist Center
Iowa City, IA 52242
Telephone: (319) 335-5577
Fax: (319) 335-6145
E-mail: *janet-ervin@uiowa.edu*
Web: *www.uiowa.edu*

Department Information:
Chairperson: Elizabeth Altmaier. Number of Faculty: total–full-time 15, part-time 11; women–full-time 6, part-time 3; minority–full-time 2, part-time 1.

Programs and Degrees Offered:
Listed in the following order: Program area, degree type (T if terminal Master's), number awarded 7/03–6/04. Educational PhD (Doctor of Philosophy) 1, Educational Measurement & Statistics MA/MS (Master of Arts/Science) 7, Educational Measurement and Statistics PhD (Doctor of Philosophy) 3, School PhD (Doctor of Philosophy) 4, Counseling PhD (Doctor of Philosophy) 7.

APA Accreditation: School PhD (Doctor of Philosophy). Counseling PhD (Doctor of Philosophy).

Student Applications/Admissions:
Student Applications

Educational PhD (Doctor of Philosophy)—Applications 2004–2005, 20. Total applicants accepted 2004–2005, 7. Total enrolled 2004–2005 full-time, 28. *Educational Measurement & Statistics MA/MS (Master of Arts/Science)*—Applications 2004–2005, 5. Total applicants accepted 2004–2005, 3. Total enrolled 2004–2005 full-time, 26. *Educational Measurement and Statistics PhD (Doctor of Philosophy)*—Applications 2004–2005, 15. Total applicants accepted 2004–2005, 13. Total enrolled 2004–2005 full-time, 52. *School PhD (Doctor of Philosophy)*—Applications 2004–2005, 40. Total applicants accepted 2004–2005, 8. Openings 2005–2006, 6. *Counseling PhD (Doctor of Philosophy)*—Applications 2004–2005, 82. Total applicants accepted 2004–2005, 13. Openings 2005–2006, 8. The number of students enrolled full and part-time who were dismissed or voluntarily withdrew from this program area were 0.

Admissions Requirements:

Scores: Entries appear in this order: required test or GPA, minimum score (if required), median score of students entering in 2003–2004. Master's Programs: GRE-V+Q 1100. Doctoral Programs: GRE-V+Q 1200; overall undergraduate GPA 3.00. *Other Criteria:* (importance of criteria rated low, medium, or high): GRE/MAT scores high, research experience high, work experience medium, extracurricular activity low, clinically related public service high, GPA high, letters of recommendation high, interview medium, statement of goals and objectives high. School psychology PhD/education specialist in school psychology: GRE/MAT scores high, work experience high, clinically related public service high, GPA high, letters of recommendation high, interview high, statement of goals and objectives high, research experience medium, extracurricular activity low. For the counseling psychology program: GPA high, letters of recommendation high, statement of goals and objectives high, GRE/MAT scores medium, research experience medium, work experience medium, clinically related public service medium, interview none.

Student Characteristics: The following represents characteristics of students in 2004–2005 in all graduate psychology programs in the department: Female–full-time 138, part-time 0; Male–full-time 58, part-time 0; African American/Black–full-time 15, part-time 0; Hispanic/Latino(a)–full-time 10, part-time 0; Asian/Pacific Islander–full-time 5, part-time 0; American Indian/Alaska Native–full-time 2, part-time 0; Caucasian–full-time 108, part-time 0.

Financial Information/Assistance:

Tuition for Full-Time Study: *Master's:* State residents: $206 per credit hour; Nonstate residents: $206 per credit hour. *Doctoral:* State residents: $206 per credit hour; Nonstate residents: $206 per credit hour.

Financial Assistance:

First Year Students: Research assistantships available for first-year. Average amount paid per academic year: $15,490. Average number of hours worked per week: 20. Apply by April 1. Tuition remission given: partial.

Advanced Students: Research assistantships available for advanced students. Average amount paid per academic year: $15,490. Average number of hours worked per week: 20. Apply by April 1. Tuition remission given: partial. Fellowships and scholarships available for advanced students. Average amount paid per academic year: $15,490. Average number of hours worked per week: 20. Tuition remission given: partial.

Contact Information: Of all students currently enrolled full-time, 5% benefitted from one or more of the listed financial assistance programs.

Internships/Practica: There are multiple practicum sites at a variety of agencies, (e.g., university counseling centers, VA medical centers, community mental health centers). Educational Psychology Program: Formal internship and practica experiences are not available for MA students, although some students do find paid positions as teaching or research assistants in fields in which they have prior experience. At the PhD level, most students are supported by half-time fellowships or assistantships. In a research-oriented program, these paid positions serve the purpose of an internship or fellowship. School Psychology Program—Practica:

Available in the public schools, The University of Iowa Hospitals and Clinics (Department of Pediatrics, Psychiatry and Neurology), the Berlin-Blank National Center for Gifted, located in the College of Education, The Wendell Johnson Speech and Hearing Clinic at the University of Iowa, and in local mental health agencies.

Housing and Day Care: On-campus housing is available. See the following Web site for more information: www.uiowa.edu. On-campus day care facilities are available.

Employment of Department Graduates:

Master's Degree Graduates: Of those who graduated in the academic year 2003–2004, the following categories and numbers represent the post-graduate activities and employment of master's degree graduates: Enrolled in a psychology doctoral program (4), enrolled in a post-doctoral residency/fellowship (n/a), employed in independent practice (n/a), total from the above (master's) (4).

Doctoral Degree Graduates: Of those who graduated in the academic year 2003–2004, the following categories and numbers represent the post-graduate activities and employment of doctoral degree graduates: Enrolled in a psychology doctoral program (n/a), enrolled in a post-doctoral residency/fellowship (1), employed in an academic position at a university (2), employed in other positions at a higher education institution (4), employed in a hospital/medical center (2), do not know (9), total from the above (doctoral) (18).

Additional Information:

Orientation, Objectives, and Emphasis of Department: The counseling psychology program endorses a scientist-practitioner model and expects students to be competent researchers and practitioners at the completion of their program. At the PhD level, the educational psychology program at the University of Iowa is designed to provide students with a strong grounding in the psychology of learning and instruction. Students are encouraged to become proficient in both quantitative and qualitative research methods with an emphasis on the former. The study of individual differences is one program emphasis. At the MA level, the program provides a broad introduction to educational psychology and flexible accommodation of individual students' interest in diverse areas such as instructional technology, reading acquisition and program evaluation. The doctoral program in school psychology is committed to training professional psychologists who are knowledgeable about providing services to children in school, medical and mental health settings. The students will possess expertise in addressing children's social/emotional needs and learning processes. The program's curriculum has been developed to reflect consideration of multicultural issues within psychological theory, research and professional development. The program strives to produce psychologists who are competent in working in a variety of settings with children/adolescents with a wide array of problems and be able to provide a wide range of psychological services to children and the adults in their lives.

Special Facilities or Resources: The University of Iowa Hospitals and Clinics provide multiple research opportunities. Outstanding computer facilities exist on the campus. Educational Psychology Program—Students in the educational psychology program frequently make use of two important resources of the University of Iowa College of Education. The Iowa Testing Programs, creator of the Iowa Tests of Basic Skills and the Iowa Tests of Educational

Development, are housed here. Students have access to test databases for research and may work with faculty or research assistantships supported by the Iowa Measurement Research Foundation. The Berlin/Blank International Center for Gifted Education also provides opportunities for research, teaching, and counseling experiences as well as assistantship support. School Psychology Program—All of the above settings are open to applied research and have existing data available to students as do American College Testing and National Computer Systems, located in Iowa City, IA.

Application Information:
Send to: Susan Cline, Student Services Admissions, College of Education, N310 Lindquist Center, Iowa City, IA 52242. For students admitted in the Fall, application deadlines are: MA: May 1-MS, January 1-EP; PhD: January 1-EP, March 1-MS, January 1-CP, January 1-SP. For students admitted in the Spring, deadlines are: MA November 1-MS; PhD September 1-MS. *Fee:* $50.

Northern Iowa, University of
Department of Psychology
Social and Behavioral Sciences
334 Baker Hall
Cedar Falls, IA 50614-0505
Telephone: (319) 273-2303
Fax: (319) 273-6188
E-mail: *harton@uni.edu*
Web: *http://www.uni.edu/psych*

Department Information:
1968. Head: Frank Barrios. Number of Faculty: total–full-time 16, part-time 7; women–full-time 4, part-time 6; minority–full-time 2, part-time 1.

Programs and Degrees Offered:
Listed in the following order: Program area, degree type (T if terminal Master's), number awarded 7/03–6/04. Social MA/MS (Master of Arts/Science) (T) 1, Industrial/Organizational MA/MS (Master of Arts/Science) (T) 2, Clinical Science MA/MS (Master of Arts/Science) (T) 6, Individualized Study MA/MS (Master of Arts/Science) 0.

Student Applications/Admissions:
Student Applications
Social MA/MS (Master of Arts/Science)—Applications 2004–2005, 13. Total applicants accepted 2004–2005, 6. Number enrolled (new admits only) 2004–2005 full-time, 5. Number enrolled (new admits only) 2004–2005 part-time, 0. Openings 2005–2006, 4. The Median number of years required for completion of a degree are 2. The number of students enrolled full and part-time who were dismissed or voluntarily withdrew from this program area were 0. *Industrial/Organizational MA/MS (Master of Arts/Science)*—Applications 2004–2005, 28. Total applicants accepted 2004–2005, 17. Number enrolled (new admits only) 2004–2005 full-time, 7. Number enrolled (new admits only) 2004–2005 part-time, 0. Openings 2005–2006, 7. The Median number of years required for completion of a degree are 2. The number of students enrolled full and part-time who were dismissed or voluntarily withdrew from

this program area were 1. *Clinical Science MA/MS (Master of Arts/Science)*—Applications 2004–2005, 35. Total applicants accepted 2004–2005, 17. Number enrolled (new admits only) 2004–2005 full-time, 10. Number enrolled (new admits only) 2004–2005 part-time, 0. Openings 2005–2006, 7. The Median number of years required for completion of a degree are 2. The number of students enrolled full and part-time who were dismissed or voluntarily withdrew from this program area were 0. *Individualized Study MA/MS (Master of Arts/Science)*—Applications 2004–2005, 0. Total applicants accepted 2004–2005, 0. Number enrolled (new admits only) 2004–2005 full-time, 0. Openings 2005–2006, 1. The Median number of years required for completion of a degree are 2. The number of students enrolled full and part-time who were dismissed or voluntarily withdrew from this program area were 0.

Admissions Requirements:
Scores: Entries appear in this order: required test or GPA, minimum score (if required), median score of students entering in 2003–2004. Master's Programs: GRE-V 450, 490; GRE-Q 450, 562; GRE-V+Q 900, 1052; GRE-Analytical 3.5, 4.7; overall undergraduate GPA 3.00, 3.59.

Other Criteria: (importance of criteria rated low, medium, or high): GRE/MAT scores high, research experience high, work experience medium, extracurricular activity low, clinically related public service medium, GPA high, letters of recommendation high, interview medium, statement of goals and objectives high. Clinically related public service is less important for the social and industrial/organizational emphases; work experience is less important for the social emphasis. For additional information on admission requirements, go to: www. uni.edu/psych/grad.

Student Characteristics: The following represents characteristics of students in 2004–2005 in all graduate psychology programs in the department: Female–full-time 25, part-time 0; Male–full-time 13, part-time 0; African American/Black–full-time 3, part-time 0; Hispanic/Latino(a)–full-time 2, part-time 0; Asian/Pacific Islander–full-time 1, part-time 0; American Indian/Alaska Native–full-time 0, part-time 0; Caucasian–full-time 32, part-time 0; students subject to the Americans With Disabilities Act–full-time 0, part-time 0.

Financial Information/Assistance:
Tuition for Full-Time Study: *Master's:* State residents: per academic year $5,708; Nonstate residents: per academic year $13,532.

Financial Assistance:
First Year Students: Teaching assistantships available for first-year. Average amount paid per academic year: $3,736. Average number of hours worked per week: 10. Apply by February 1. Research assistantships available for first-year. Average amount paid per academic year: $3,736. Average number of hours worked per week: 10. Apply by February 1. Traineeships available for first-year. Average amount paid per academic year: $3,736. Average number of hours worked per week: 10. Apply by February 1. Fellowships and scholarships available for first-year. Average amount paid per academic year: $2,744. Average number of hours worked per week: 0. Apply by February 1.

Advanced Students: Teaching assistantships available for advanced students. Average amount paid per academic year:

$3,736. Average number of hours worked per week: 10. Apply by February 1. Research assistantships available for advanced students. Average amount paid per academic year: $3,736. Average number of hours worked per week: 10. Apply by February 1. Traineeships available for advanced students. Average amount paid per academic year: $3,736. Average number of hours worked per week: 10. Apply by February 1. Fellowships and scholarships available for advanced students. Average amount paid per academic year: $2,744. Average number of hours worked per week: 0. Apply by February 1.

Contact Information: Of all students currently enrolled full-time, 100% benefitted from one or more of the listed financial assistance programs. Application and information available online at: www.uni.edu/psych/grad.

Internships/Practica: A variety of practicum sites are available for second year students in the clinical science and industrial/organizational emphases. Clinical practicum sites have included the University Counseling Center, the State Psychiatric Hospital, correctional facilities, private hospitals, educational settings, and community-based agencies. I/O practicum sites have included the University's Human Resources Office, local businesses, and some nationally known out-of-state businesses (during the summer terms). Students in the social emphasis conduct independent first-year research projects under faculty supervision and present these research projects at regional and national professional conferences.

Housing and Day Care: On-campus housing is available. See the following Web site for more information: Department of Residence, University of Northern Iowa, Cedar Falls, IA 50614-0252; http://www.uni.edu/dor/. On-campus day care facilities are available. See the following Web site for more information: Child Development Center, Price Laboratory School, Cedar Falls, IA 50614-0611; http://fp.uni.edu/pls/CDC.htm.

Employment of Department Graduates:
Master's Degree Graduates: Of those who graduated in the academic year 2003–2004, the following categories and numbers represent the post-graduate activities and employment of master's degree graduates: Enrolled in a psychology doctoral program (6), enrolled in a post-doctoral residency/fellowship (n/a), employed in independent practice (n/a), employed in a community mental health/counseling center (2), employed in a hospital/medical center (1), total from the above (master's) (9).
Doctoral Degree Graduates: Of those who graduated in the academic year 2003–2004, the following categories and numbers represent the post-graduate activities and employment of doctoral degree graduates: Enrolled in a psychology doctoral program (n/a), total from the above (doctoral) (0).

Additional Information:
Orientation, Objectives, and Emphasis of Department: The MA program in General Psychology provides a strong empirical, research-based approach to the study of human behavior. Students may select one of three emphases: a) clinical science; b) social psychology; or c) industrial-organizational psychology. They may also choose to complete an individualized study program in conjunction with a faculty mentor. The objectives of the program are: a) to develop skills in research methodology; b) to gain knowledge of basic areas of scientific psychology; and c) to obtain competence in research, consulting, and/or clinical skills. The clinical science emphasis is designed for those who wish to either obtain doctoral degrees in clinical or counseling psychology or become master's-level providers of services operating in clinical settings under appropriate supervision. The social emphasis is designed for students who wish to pursue doctoral degrees in social psychology or master's-level research or teaching positions. The industrial/organizational emphasis is designed for those planning doctoral study in I/O psychology or a position in human resources or consulting.

Special Facilities or Resources: The department provides laboratory space for research with human participants; access to community facilities and populations for applied research; good access to computers for graduate students; and office space for graduate students. We are affiliated with two laboratory schools and a center for social research, and students have access to psychiatric, work, and community populations for research projects.

Information for Students With Physical Disabilities: See the following Web site for more information: http://www.uni.edu/disability/.

Application Information:
Send to: Graduate Coordinator, Department of Psychology, University of Northern Iowa, Cedar Falls, IA 50614-0505. Application available online. URL of online application: www.uni.edu/psych/grad. Students are admitted in the Fall, application deadline April 30. Programs have rolling admissions. For full consideration, applications should be received by February 1, although applications will be considered if received by April 30 as space permits. *Fee:* $30. Application fee for international students is $50.

Emporia State University

Department of Psychology and Special Education
The Teachers College
1200 Commercial Street
Emporia, KS 66801-5087
Telephone: (620) 341-5317
Fax: (620) 341-5801
E-mail: *weaverke@emporia.edu*
Web: *http://psychspe.emporia.edu*

Department Information:

1932. Chairperson: Kenneth A. Weaver. Number of Faculty: total–full-time 18, part-time 3; women–full-time 6, part-time 3; faculty subject to the Americans With Disabilities Act 1.

Programs and Degrees Offered:

Listed in the following order: Program area, degree type (T if terminal Master's), number awarded 7/03–6/04. General MA/MS (Master of Arts/Science) (T) 16, School EdS (Education Specialist) 13, Special Education MA/MS (Master of Arts/Science) (T) 57, Art Therapy MA/MS (Master of Arts/Science) (T) 4, Mental Health Counseling MA/MS (Master of Arts/Science) 4, Clinical Psychology MA/MS (Master of Arts/Science) 13.

Student Applications/Admissions:

Student Applications

General MA/MS (Master of Arts/Science)—Applications 2004–2005, 36. Total applicants accepted 2004–2005, 35. Number enrolled (new admits only) 2004–2005 full-time, 30. Total enrolled 2004–2005 full-time, 41, part-time, 18. Openings 2005–2006, 45. The Median number of years required for completion of a degree are 3. The number of students enrolled full and part-time who were dismissed or voluntarily withdrew from this program area were 0. *School EdS (Education Specialist)*—Applications 2004–2005, 23. Total applicants accepted 2004–2005, 22. Number enrolled (new admits only) 2004–2005 full-time, 15. Number enrolled (new admits only) 2004–2005 part-time, 7. Total enrolled 2004–2005 full-time, 35, part-time, 10. Openings 2005–2006, 20. The Median number of years required for completion of a degree are 3. The number of students enrolled full and part-time who were dismissed or voluntarily withdrew from this program area were 0. *Special Education MA/MS (Master of Arts/Science)*—Applications 2004–2005, 82. Total applicants accepted 2004–2005, 80. Number enrolled (new admits only) 2004–2005 part-time, 82. Total enrolled 2004–2005 part-time, 155. Openings 2005–2006, 70. The Median number of years required for completion of a degree are 4. The number of students enrolled full and part-time who were dismissed or voluntarily withdrew from this program area were 0. *Art Therapy MA/MS (Master of Arts/Science)*—Applications 2004–2005, 8. Total applicants accepted 2004–2005, 8. Number enrolled (new admits only) 2004–2005 full-time, 8. Number enrolled (new admits only) 2004–2005 part-time, 0. Total enrolled 2004–2005 full-time, 18, part-time, 1. Openings 2005–2006, 15. The Median number of years required for completion of a degree are 2. The

number of students enrolled full and part-time who were dismissed or voluntarily withdrew from this program area were 1. *Mental Health Counseling MA/MS (Master of Arts/Science)*—Applications 2004–2005, 8. Total applicants accepted 2004–2005, 8. Number enrolled (new admits only) 2004–2005 full-time, 8. Total enrolled 2004–2005 full-time, 25. Openings 2005–2006, 18. The Median number of years required for completion of a degree are 2. *Clinical Psychology MA/MS (Master of Arts/Science)*—Applications 2004–2005, 15. Total applicants accepted 2004–2005, 14. Number enrolled (new admits only) 2004–2005 full-time, 11. Total enrolled 2004–2005 full-time, 31, part-time, 2. Openings 2005–2006, 15. The Median number of years required for completion of a degree are 2.

Admissions Requirements:

Scores: Entries appear in this order: required test or GPA, minimum score (if required), median score of students entering in 2003–2004. Master's Programs: GRE-V no minimum stated; GRE-Q no minimum stated; GRE-V+Q no minimum stated; MAT no minimum stated; overall undergraduate GPA 3.00; last 2 years GPA 3.25. 2.75 for Special Education. No MAT or GRE required for Special Education

Other Criteria: (importance of criteria rated low, medium, or high): GRE/MAT scores low, research experience medium, work experience medium, extracurricular activity low, GPA high, letters of recommendation medium, statement of goals and objectives medium. Special Education does not require GRE/MAT scores. For additional information on admission requirements, go to: http://psychspe.emporia.edu.

Student Characteristics: The following represents characteristics of students in 2004–2005 in all graduate psychology programs in the department: Female–full-time 40, part-time 20; Male–full-time 30, part-time 17; African American/Black–full-time 4, part-time 3; Hispanic/Latino(a)–full-time 2, part-time 0; Asian/Pacific Islander–full-time 4, part-time 0; American Indian/Alaska Native–full-time 0, part-time 0; Caucasian–full-time 54, part-time 34; Multi-ethnic–full-time 6, part-time 0; students subject to the Americans With Disabilities Act–full-time 1, part-time 0.

Financial Information/Assistance:

Tuition for Full-Time Study: *Master's:* State residents: per academic year $3,516, $158 per credit hour; Nonstate residents: per academic year $9,884, $424 per credit hour.

Financial Assistance:

First Year Students: Teaching assistantships available for first-year. Average amount paid per academic year: $6,412. Average number of hours worked per week: 20. Apply by March 15. Tuition remission given: full. Research assistantships available for first-year. Average amount paid per academic year: $6,412. Average number of hours worked per week: 20. Apply by March 15. Tuition remission given: full. Fellowships and scholarships available for first-year. Average amount paid per academic year: $300. Apply by ongoing. Tuition remission given: partial.

Advanced Students: Teaching assistantships available for advanced students. Average amount paid per academic year: $6,412. Average number of hours worked per week: 20. Apply by March 15. Tuition remission given: full. Research assistantships available for advanced students. Average amount paid per academic year: $6,412. Average number of hours worked per week: 20. Apply by March 15. Tuition remission given: full. Fellowships and scholarships available for advanced students. Average amount paid per academic year: $300. Apply by ongoing. Tuition remission given: partial.

    Contact Information: Of all students currently enrolled full-time, 90% benefitted from one or more of the listed financial assistance programs. Application and information available online at: http://www.emporia.edu/grad/load.htm.

Internships/Practica: MS Psychology students must do internships. For Clinical students, it is 750 clock hours in a mental health setting supervised by a PhD psychologist. For I/O students it is 350 clock hours in a business setting. For Experimental students, the internship is defined as experiences working in a laboratory setting. Art Therapy students do a 750 clock hour internship. School Psychology and Special Education students do semester internships in the schools. In addition, there is a one-year, paid, post-EdS internship for School Psychology.

Housing and Day Care: On-campus housing is available. See the following Web site for more information: http://www.emporia.edu/reslife/index.htm. On-campus day care facilities are available.

Employment of Department Graduates:

    Master's Degree Graduates: Of those who graduated in the academic year 2003–2004, the following categories and numbers represent the post-graduate activities and employment of master's degree graduates: Enrolled in a psychology doctoral program (8), enrolled in another graduate/professional program (0), enrolled in a post-doctoral residency/fellowship (n/a), employed in independent practice (n/a), employed in an academic position at a university (1), employed in an academic position at a 2-year/4-year college (2), employed in other positions at a higher education institution (2), employed in a professional position in a school system (4), employed in business or industry (research/consulting) (3), employed in business or industry (management) (0), employed in a community mental health/counseling center (4), still seeking employment (0), total from the above (master's) (24).

    Doctoral Degree Graduates: Of those who graduated in the academic year 2003–2004, the following categories and numbers represent the post-graduate activities and employment of doctoral degree graduates: Enrolled in a psychology doctoral program (n/a), total from the above (doctoral) (0).

Additional Information:

    Orientation, Objectives, and Emphasis of Department: Emporia State offers the Master of Science degree in psychology, school psychology, art therapy, and special education. Emporia State also offers a Specialist in Education degree in school psychology. The MS degree in psychology is offered with specialization in the following areas: clinical, industrial/organizational, and general experimental. The MS degree in special education is offered with specialization in adaptive special education and gifted education. Additionally, students may opt to pursue the MS and EdS degrees in school psychology, or the MS degree in art therapy.

    Special Facilities or Resources: In 1999, all classrooms in the Department of Psychology and Special Education were upgraded with multimedia technology. Facilities include cognitive and animal behavior, and physiological psychology laboratories; a complete animal vivarium; suites of rooms for administration of psychological tests and observation of testing or clinical and counseling sessions; and microprocessors and mainframe computer facilities.

    Information for Students With Physical Disabilities: See the following Web site for more information: http://www.emporia.edu/disability/.

Application Information:
Send to: Dean of Graduate Studies and Research. Application available online. URL of online application: http://psychspe.emporia.edu. Students are admitted in the Fall, application deadline October 1; Spring, application deadline March 1; Summer, application deadline June 1. School Psychology Program and Special Education Program have no deadlines. *Fee:* $30.

Fort Hays State University
Department of Psychology
600 Park Street
Hays, KS 67601-4099
Telephone: (785) 628-4405
Fax: (785) 628-5861
E-mail: *cpatrick@fhsu.edu*
Web: *http://www.fhsu.edu/psych/*

Department Information:
    1929. Chair: Carol Patrick Land. Number of Faculty: total–full-time 8, part-time 6; women–full-time 3, part-time 2.

Programs and Degrees Offered:
    Listed in the following order: Program area, degree type (T if terminal Master's), number awarded 7/03–6/04. Applied Clinical MA/MS (Master of Arts/Science) (T) 3, General MA/MS (Master of Arts/Science) (T) 0, School EdS (Education Specialist) 6.

Student Applications/Admissions:
    Student Applications
    Applied Clinical MA/MS (Master of Arts/Science)—Applications 2004–2005, 18. Total applicants accepted 2004–2005, 16. Number enrolled (new admits only) 2004–2005 full-time, 7. Number enrolled (new admits only) 2004–2005 part-time, 0. Total enrolled 2004–2005 full-time, 13, part-time, 6. Openings 2005–2006, 7. The Median number of years required for completion of a degree are 2. The number of students enrolled full and part-time who were dismissed or voluntarily withdrew from this program area were 0. *General MA/MS (Master of Arts/Science)*—Applications 2004–2005, 4. Total applicants accepted 2004–2005, 4. Number enrolled (new admits only) 2004–2005 full-time, 1. Total enrolled 2004–2005 full-time, 3, part-time, 1. Openings 2005–2006, 5. The Median number of years required for completion of a degree are 2. The number of students enrolled full and part-time who were dismissed or voluntarily withdrew from this program area were 0. *School EdS (Education Specialist)*—Applications 2004–2005, 7. Total applicants accepted 2004–2005, 7. Number enrolled (new admits only) 2004–2005 full-time, 8. Number enrolled (new admits only) 2004–2005 part-time, 0. Total enrolled 2004–

2005 full-time, 14, part-time, 2. Openings 2005–2006, 7. The Median number of years required for completion of a degree are 2.

Admissions Requirements:

Scores: Entries appear in this order: required test or GPA, minimum score (if required), median score of students entering in 2003–2004. Master's Programs: GRE-V no minimum stated, 460; GRE-Q no minimum stated, 540; overall undergraduate GPA 2.85, 3.54; psychology GPA 2.54, 3.37.

Other Criteria: (importance of criteria rated low, medium, or high): GRE/MAT scores medium, research experience high, work experience low, extracurricular activity low, clinically related public service medium, GPA high, letters of recommendation medium, interview medium, statement of goals and objectives medium.

Student Characteristics: The following represents characteristics of students in 2004–2005 in all graduate psychology programs in the department: Female–full-time 21, part-time 4; Male–full-time 11, part-time 3; African American/Black–full-time 0, part-time 0; Hispanic/Latino(a)–full-time 2, part-time 0; Asian/Pacific Islander–full-time 0, part-time 0; American Indian/Alaska Native–full-time 0, part-time 0; Caucasian–full-time 0, part-time 0; Multiethnic–part-time 1; students subject to the Americans With Disabilities Act–full-time 0, part-time 0.

Financial Information/Assistance:

Tuition for Full-Time Study: *Master's:* State residents: $133 per credit hour; Nonstate residents: $349 per credit hour. Tuition is subject to change. See the following Web site for updates and changes in tuition costs: www.fhsu.edu/gradschl/.

Financial Assistance:

First Year Students: Teaching assistantships available for first-year. Average amount paid per academic year: $3,334. Average number of hours worked per week: 16. Apply by March 1. Tuition remission given: partial.

Advanced Students: Teaching assistantships available for advanced students. Average amount paid per academic year: $3,334. Average number of hours worked per week: 8. Apply by March 1. Traineeships available for advanced students. Average amount paid per academic year: $5,000. Average number of hours worked per week: 20. Apply by March 1. Tuition remission given: partial. Fellowships and scholarships available for advanced students. Average amount paid per academic year: $600. Apply by March 15.

Contact Information: Of all students currently enrolled full-time, 70% benefitted from one or more of the listed financial assistance programs. Application and information available online at: www.fhsu.edu/gradschl/.

Internships/Practica: All students in the applied psychology programs (clinical, school) are required to take a practicum in their specialty area. Students in the clinical psychology program receive initial practicum experience in the Kelly Center (an on-campus psychological services center), and then are required to complete an internship off-campus at a regional mental health agency or other approved agency. Students in the school psychology program receive initial practicum experience in the local school district, and then are required to complete additional practicum training at the same or another school district. School psychology graduates are also required to complete one year of paid, supervised post-EdS internship before being recommended for full Licensure (certification). Students in the general psychology program have the opportunity to take apprenticeships concentrating on the teaching of psychology.

Housing and Day Care: On-campus housing is available. See the following Web site for more information: www.fhsu.edu/reslife/. On-campus day care facilities are available. See the following Web site for more information: Tiger Tots Nurturery Center: www.fhsu.edu/te/tig/index.html.

Employment of Department Graduates:

Master's Degree Graduates: Of those who graduated in the academic year 2003–2004, the following categories and numbers represent the post-graduate activities and employment of master's degree graduates: Enrolled in another graduate/professional program (1), enrolled in a post-doctoral residency/fellowship (n/a), employed in independent practice (n/a), employed in a professional position in a school system (8), employed in a community mental health/counseling center (3), still seeking employment (1), total from the above (master's) (13).

Doctoral Degree Graduates: Of those who graduated in the academic year 2003–2004, the following categories and numbers represent the post-graduate activities and employment of doctoral degree graduates: Enrolled in a psychology doctoral program (n/a), total from the above (doctoral) (0).

Additional Information:

Orientation, Objectives, and Emphasis of Department: The department emphasizes a research approach to the understanding of behavior. We strive to provide basic empirical and theoretical foundations of psychology to prepare the student for doctoral study, for teaching, or for employment in a service or professional agency. The school program offers broad preparation for students in both psychology and education and includes training as a consultant to work with educators and parents as well as with children. The clinical program emphasizes the preparation of rural mental health workers, although many graduates go on to doctoral programs. The general program is intended to prepare the student for doctoral study.

Special Facilities or Resources: The department of psychology now occupies a newly remodeled building in the center of campus. Some of the new facilities in this building include: a 25-machine computer facility with separate spaces for individualized research and full Internet connections; testing and observation rooms for children, adults, and small groups; separate research and teaching labs for the major areas of psychology; an isolated small animal facility; and several seminar rooms. We are located adjacent to the student psychological services center. There is an active social organization for psychology graduate students. All students at the university have free remote Internet access.

Application Information:

Send to: Dean of the Graduate School, Fort Hays State University, 600 Park Street, Hays, KS 67601-4099. Application available online. Students are admitted in the Fall, application deadline; Summer, application deadline. Programs have rolling admissions. Deadline for financial aid is March 1st. *Fee:* $30.

Kansas State University

Department of Psychology
College of Arts and Sciences
492 Bluemont Hall - 1100 Mid-Campus Drive
Manhattan, KS 66506-5302
Telephone: (785) 532-6850
Fax: (785) 532-5401
E-mail: *psych@ksu.edu*
Web: *http://www.ksu.edu/psych*

Department Information:
1951. Head; Director of Graduate Studies: Stephen W. Kiefer; John Uhlarik. Number of Faculty: total–full-time 15, part-time 1; women–full-time 3, part-time 1.

Programs and Degrees Offered:
Listed in the following order: Program area, degree type (T if terminal Master's), number awarded 7/03–6/04. General Experimental MA/MS (Master of Arts/Science) 25, Industrial/Organizational PhD (Doctor of Philosophy) 1, Animal Learning PhD (Doctor of Philosophy) 1, Behavioral Neuroscience PhD (Doctor of Philosophy) 1, Social-Personality PhD (Doctor of Philosophy) 2, Perception-Sensation PhD (Doctor of Philosophy) 0, Human Judgment PhD (Doctor of Philosophy) 1, Psycholinguistics PhD (Doctor of Philosophy) 1, Applied Experimental PhD (Doctor of Philosophy) 0, Human Factors PhD (Doctor of Philosophy) 1.

Student Applications/Admissions:
Student Applications
General Experimental MA/MS (Master of Arts/Science)—Applications 2004–2005, 0. Total applicants accepted 2004–2005, 0. Number enrolled (new admits only) 2004–2005 part-time, 10. The Median number of years required for completion of a degree are 4. *Industrial/Organizational PhD (Doctor of Philosophy)*—Applications 2004–2005, 27. Total applicants accepted 2004–2005, 2. Number enrolled (new admits only) 2004–2005 full-time, 2. Total enrolled 2004–2005 full-time, 15, part-time, 5. Openings 2005–2006, 3. The Median number of years required for completion of a degree are 6. *Animal Learning PhD (Doctor of Philosophy)*—Applications 2004–2005, 5. Total applicants accepted 2004–2005, 1. Number enrolled (new admits only) 2004–2005 full-time, 1. Total enrolled 2004–2005 full-time, 3, part-time, 2. Openings 2005–2006, 1. The Median number of years required for completion of a degree are 5. The number of students enrolled full and part-time who were dismissed or voluntarily withdrew from this program area were 0. *Behavioral Neuroscience PhD (Doctor of Philosophy)*—Applications 2004–2005, 10. Total applicants accepted 2004–2005, 2. Openings 2005–2006, 2. The Median number of years required for completion of a degree are 5. The number of students enrolled full and part-time who were dismissed or voluntarily withdrew from this program area were 0. *Social-Personality PhD (Doctor of Philosophy)*—Applications 2004–2005, 26. Total applicants accepted 2004–2005, 5. Number enrolled (new admits only) 2004–2005 full-time, 1. Total enrolled 2004–2005 full-time, 7, part-time, 3. Openings 2005–2006, 3. The Median number of years required for completion of a degree are 5. *Perception-Sensation PhD (Doctor of Philosophy)*—Applications 2004–2005, 5. Total applicants accepted 2004–2005, 0. Number enrolled (new admits only) 2004–2005 full-time,

1. Openings 2005–2006, 1. *Human Judgment PhD (Doctor of Philosophy)*—Applications 2004–2005, 5. Total applicants accepted 2004–2005, 0. Total enrolled 2004–2005 full-time, 4, part-time, 1. Openings 2005–2006, 2. The Median number of years required for completion of a degree are 5. *Psycholinguistics PhD (Doctor of Philosophy)*—Applications 2004–2005, 4. Total applicants accepted 2004–2005, 2. Number enrolled (new admits only) 2004–2005 full-time, 1. Openings 2005–2006, 2. The Median number of years required for completion of a degree are 4. *Applied Experimental PhD (Doctor of Philosophy)*—Applications 2004–2005, 11. Total applicants accepted 2004–2005, 0. Openings 2005–2006, 2. *Human Factors PhD (Doctor of Philosophy)*—Applications 2004–2005, 23. Total applicants accepted 2004–2005, 5. Number enrolled (new admits only) 2004–2005 full-time, 1. Openings 2005–2006, 1.

Admissions Requirements:
Scores: Entries appear in this order: required test or GPA, minimum score (if required), median score of students entering in 2003–2004. Master's Programs: GRE-V no minimum stated; GRE-Q no minimum stated; GRE-Analytical no minimum stated; overall undergraduate GPA no minimum stated. Doctoral Programs: GRE-V no minimum stated, 499; GRE-Q no minimum stated, 591; GRE-V+Q no minimum stated, 460; GRE-Analytical no minimum stated, 608; overall undergraduate GPA no minimum stated, 3.81.
Other Criteria: (importance of criteria rated low, medium, or high): GRE/MAT scores high, research experience high, work experience low, extracurricular activity low, clinically related public service low, GPA high, letters of recommendation high, statement of goals and objectives high.

Student Characteristics: The following represents characteristics of students in 2004–2005 in all graduate psychology programs in the department: Female–full-time 23, part-time 20; Male–full-time 16, part-time 21; African American/Black–full-time 0, part-time 3; Hispanic/Latino(a)–full-time 0, part-time 2; Asian/Pacific Islander–full-time 4, part-time 0; American Indian/Alaska Native–full-time 0, part-time 0; Caucasian–full-time 35, part-time 36.

Financial Information/Assistance:
Tuition for Full-Time Study: *Master's:* State residents: $154 per credit hour; Nonstate residents: $427 per credit hour. *Doctoral:* State residents: $154 per credit hour; Nonstate residents: $427 per credit hour. Tuition is subject to change. See the following Web site for updates and changes in tuition costs: http://www.ksu.edu/controller/cashiers/ManhattanSummarized05.pdf.

Financial Assistance:
First Year Students: Teaching assistantships available for first-year. Average amount paid per academic year: $9,468. Average number of hours worked per week: 20. Tuition remission given: full. Research assistantships available for first-year. Average amount paid per academic year: $11,000. Average number of hours worked per week: 20. Tuition remission given: partial.
Advanced Students: Teaching assistantships available for advanced students. Average amount paid per academic year: $10,366. Average number of hours worked per week: 20. Tuition remission given: full. Research assistantships available for advanced students. Average amount paid per academic year:

$12,000. Average number of hours worked per week: 20. Tuition remission given: partial.

Contact Information: Of all students currently enrolled full-time, 90% benefitted from one or more of the listed financial assistance programs.

Internships/Practica: Arrangements for internships in human factors/applied experimental and industrial/organizational psychology vary widely and are made on an individual basis.

Housing and Day Care: On-campus housing is available. See the following Web site for more information: http://www.ksu.edu/housing/family.html http://www.ksu.edu/ksucdc/. On-campus day care facilities are available.

Employment of Department Graduates:

Master's Degree Graduates: Of those who graduated in the academic year 2003–2004, the following categories and numbers represent the post-graduate activities and employment of master's degree graduates: Enrolled in a psychology doctoral program (4), enrolled in a post-doctoral residency/fellowship (n/a), employed in independent practice (n/a), employed in a professional position in a school system (1), employed in business or industry (management) (20), total from the above (master's) (25).

Doctoral Degree Graduates: Of those who graduated in the academic year 2003–2004, the following categories and numbers represent the post-graduate activities and employment of doctoral degree graduates: Enrolled in a psychology doctoral program (n/a), employed in an academic position at a university (1), employed in an academic position at a 2-year/4-year college (3), employed in other positions at a higher education institution (2), employed in business or industry (research/consulting) (1), total from the above (doctoral) (7).

Additional Information:

Orientation, Objectives, and Emphasis of Department: Both teaching and research are heavily emphasized. Training prepares students for a variety of positions, including teaching and research positions in colleges and universities. Students have also assumed research and evaluative positions in hospitals, clinics, governmental agencies, and industry.

Special Facilities or Resources: The department has rooms for individual and group research; several computer laboratories and remote terminal access to mainframe computers; a photographic darkroom; one-way observation facilities; an electrically shielded, light-tight, sound-deadened room for auditory and visual research; laboratories for behavioral research with animals; surgical and histological facilities; and colony rooms.

Information for Students With Physical Disabilities: See the following Web site for more information: http://www.ksu.edu/dss/.

Application Information:

Send to: Graduate Admissions, Department of Psychology, 492 Bluemont Hall, 1100 Mid-campus Drive, Kansas State University, Manhattan, KS 66506-5302. Application available online. Students are admitted in the Fall, application deadline February 15. *Fee:* $30. International applicants must pay a $55 application fee in the form of an international cashier's check or money order.

Kansas, University of
Department of Applied Behavioral Science (formerly Human Development)
College of Arts and Sciences
1000 Sunnyside Avenue
Lawrence, KS 66045-7555
Telephone: (785) 864-4840
Fax: (785) 864-5202
E-mail: *absc@ku.edu*
Web: *http://www.ku.edu/~absc*

Department Information:
1968. Chairperson: Edward K. Morris. Number of Faculty: total–full-time 18; women–full-time 4; minority–full-time 2; faculty subject to the Americans With Disabilities Act 1.

Programs and Degrees Offered:
Listed in the following order: Program area, degree type (T if terminal Master's), number awarded 7/03–6/04. Behavioral Psychology PhD (Doctor of Philosophy) 9.

Student Applications/Admissions:
Student Applications
Behavioral Psychology PhD (Doctor of Philosophy)—Applications 2004–2005, 39. Total applicants accepted 2004–2005, 17. Number enrolled (new admits only) 2004–2005 full-time, 15. Total enrolled 2004–2005 full-time, 77. Openings 2005–2006, 12. The Median number of years required for completion of a degree are 6.5. The number of students enrolled full and part-time who were dismissed or voluntarily withdrew from this program area were 3.

Admissions Requirements:
Scores: Entries appear in this order: required test or GPA, minimum score (if required), median score of students entering in 2003–2004. Doctoral Programs: GRE scores are not required for admission; however, several competitive fellowship programs are available through the University which do require the GRE.

Other Criteria: (importance of criteria rated low, medium, or high): GRE/MAT scores medium, research experience high, work experience high, extracurricular activity low, clinically related public service medium, GPA high, letters of recommendation high, interview high, statement of goals and objectives high. All admission decisions are made by individual faculty members, thus the admissions criteria vary by faculty members.

Student Characteristics: The following represents characteristics of students in 2004–2005 in all graduate psychology programs in the department: Female–full-time 59, part-time 0; Male–full-time 18, part-time 0; African American/Black–full-time 6, part-time 0; Hispanic/Latino(a)–full-time 4, part-time 0; Asian/Pacific Islander–full-time 3, part-time 0; American Indian/Alaska Native–full-time 1, part-time 0; Caucasian–full-time 61, part-time 0; Multi-ethnic–full-time 2, part-time 0; students subject to the Americans With Disabilities Act–full-time 5, part-time 0.

Financial Information/Assistance:
Tuition for Full-Time Study: *Master's:* State residents: per academic year $2,034, $113 per credit hour; Nonstate residents:

per academic year $6,444, $358 per credit hour. *Doctoral:* State residents: per academic year $2,034, $113 per credit hour; Non-state residents: per academic year $6,444, $358 per credit hour. Tuition is subject to change. See the following Web site for updates and changes in tuition costs: www.ku.edu.

Financial Assistance:

First Year Students: Teaching assistantships available for first-year. Apply by January 15. Tuition remission given: full. Research assistantships available for first-year. Apply by January 15. Tuition remission given: full. Traineeships available for first-year. Apply by January 15. Tuition remission given: full. Fellowships and scholarships available for first-year. Apply by January 15. Tuition remission given: full.

Advanced Students: Teaching assistantships available for advanced students. Apply by vary. Tuition remission given: full. Research assistantships available for advanced students. Apply by vary. Tuition remission given: full. Traineeships available for advanced students. Apply by vary. Tuition remission given: full. Fellowships and scholarships available for advanced students. Apply by vary. Tuition remission given: full.

Contact Information: Of all students currently enrolled full-time, 80% benefitted from one or more of the listed financial assistance programs. Application and information available online at: www.ku.edu~absc.

Internships/Practica: A wide variety of research settings and practica sites are available to graduate students. They include: Behavioral Pediatrics; Center for Independent Living; Center for the Study of Mental Retardation and Related Problems; Child and Family Research Center; Community Programs for Adults with Mental Retardation; Edna A. Hill Child Development Center; Experimental Analysis of Behavior Laboratories; Family Enhancement Project; Gerontology Center; Juniper Gardens Project; Research on Children with Retardation; Schiefelbusch Institute for Life Span Studies; Work Group on Health Promotion and Community Development.

Housing and Day Care: On-campus housing is available. See the following Web site for more information: www.ku.edu/~absc. On-campus day care facilities are available.

Employment of Department Graduates:

Master's Degree Graduates: Of those who graduated in the academic year 2003–2004, the following categories and numbers represent the post-graduate activities and employment of master's degree graduates: Enrolled in a psychology doctoral program (5), enrolled in a post-doctoral residency/fellowship (n/a), employed in independent practice (n/a), employed in a professional position in a school system (1), employed in a government agency (professional services) (1), total from the above (master's) (7).

Doctoral Degree Graduates: Of those who graduated in the academic year 2003–2004, the following categories and numbers represent the post-graduate activities and employment of doctoral degree graduates: Enrolled in a psychology doctoral program (n/a), enrolled in a post-doctoral residency/fellowship (3), employed in

an academic position at a university (2), employed in other positions at a higher education institution (1), employed in a professional position in a school system (1), employed in a government agency (research) (2), employed in a community mental health/counseling center (1), total from the above (doctoral) (10).

Additional Information:

Orientation, Objectives, and Emphasis of Department: The primary purpose of the program is to train students in basic and applied research on typical and atypical development. It features emphases in applied behavior analysis, early childhood, developmental disabilities, community health and development, the experimental and conceptual analysis of behavior, applied gerontology, independent living, and rehabilitation. Junior Colleague Model: Throughout the PhD training sequence, students work closely as junior colleagues with a faculty adviser and a research group. Although students typically work with one faculty adviser, they are free to select a different adviser if their interests change during the course of their training. Continuous Research Involvement: Students participate in research throughout their graduate careers in an individualized, intensive program. As a result, most students complete more research projects than those required for the degree.

Special Facilities or Resources: A wide range of research settings are available to graduate students. Populations and settings include both typically developing and disabled infants, toddlers, preschool children, elementary school settings, adolescents, adults, and elders.

Information for Students With Physical Disabilities: See the following Web site for more information: www.ku.edu/~ssdis/.

Application Information:

Send to: Graduate School, 300 Strong Hall, (785) 864-6161, http://www.ku.edu/~graduate/, for admissions information, to apply online, Graduate School catalog, Graduate Student Organizations, graduation and commencement information, graduate faculty appointments, and the Graduate School Handbook. Application available online. URL of online application: http://www.ku.edu/~graduate/. Students are admitted in the Fall, application deadline January 15. All admissions are based on selections by individual faculty members willing to serve as a mentor to the student; there is no centralized admission. There is no set number of students admitted in any year. Some admissions occur throughout the year. *Fee:* $35.

Kansas, University of
Department of Psychology
426 Fraser Hall, 1415 Jayhawk Boulevard
Lawrence, KS 66045-7556
Telephone: (785) 864-4131
Fax: (785) 864-5696
E-mail: *psycgrad@ku.edu*
Web: *http://www.psych.ku.edu*

Department Information:

1916. Chairperson: Greg B. Simpson. Number of Faculty: total–full-time 35, part-time 1; women–full-time 11; minority–full-time 2.

Programs and Degrees Offered:
Listed in the following order: Program area, degree type (T if terminal Master's), number awarded 7/03–6/04. Clinical Child PhD (Doctor of Philosophy) 6, Clinical PhD (Doctor of Philosophy) 6, Cognitive PhD (Doctor of Philosophy) 4, Quantitative PhD (Doctor of Philosophy) 2, Social PhD (Doctor of Philosophy) 2, Developmental PhD (Doctor of Philosophy) 0.

APA Accreditation: Clinical PhD (Doctor of Philosophy). Clinical PhD (Doctor of Philosophy).

Student Applications/Admissions:
Student Applications
Clinical Child PhD (Doctor of Philosophy)—Applications 2004–2005, 126. Total applicants accepted 2004–2005, 5. Number enrolled (new admits only) 2004–2005 full-time, 4. Openings 2005–2006, 5. The Median number of years required for completion of a degree are 6.5. The number of students enrolled full and part-time who were dismissed or voluntarily withdrew from this program area were 0. *Clinical PhD (Doctor of Philosophy)*—Applications 2004–2005, 140. Total applicants accepted 2004–2005, 15. Number enrolled (new admits only) 2004–2005 full-time, 10. Openings 2005–2006, 5. The Median number of years required for completion of a degree are 6. The number of students enrolled full and part-time who were dismissed or voluntarily withdrew from this program area were 1. *Cognitive PhD (Doctor of Philosophy)*—Applications 2004–2005, 22. Total applicants accepted 2004–2005, 8. Number enrolled (new admits only) 2004–2005 full-time, 5. Openings 2005–2006, 5. The Median number of years required for completion of a degree are 6. The number of students enrolled full and part-time who were dismissed or voluntarily withdrew from this program area were 1. *Quantitative PhD (Doctor of Philosophy)*—Applications 2004–2005, 6. Total applicants accepted 2004–2005, 2. Number enrolled (new admits only) 2004–2005 full-time, 10. Openings 2005–2006, 1. The Median number of years required for completion of a degree are 5. The number of students enrolled full and part-time who were dismissed or voluntarily withdrew from this program area were 0. *Social PhD (Doctor of Philosophy)*—Applications 2004–2005, 58. Total applicants accepted 2004–2005, 12. Number enrolled (new admits only) 2004–2005 full-time, 3. Openings 2005–2006, 4. The Median number of years required for completion of a degree are 6. The number of students enrolled full and part-time who were dismissed or voluntarily withdrew from this program area were 1. *Developmental PhD (Doctor of Philosophy)*—Applications 2004–2005, 0. Total applicants accepted 2004–2005, 0. Number enrolled (new admits only) 2004–2005 full-time, 0. The number of students enrolled full and part-time who were dismissed or voluntarily withdrew from this program area were 0.

Admissions Requirements:
Scores: Entries appear in this order: required test or GPA, minimum score (if required), median score of students entering in 2003–2004. Doctoral Programs: GRE-V no minimum stated, 580; GRE-Q no minimum stated, 664; GRE-Analytical no minimum stated, 5.0; overall undergraduate GPA 3.0, 3.71.

Other Criteria: (importance of criteria rated low, medium, or high): GRE/MAT scores high, research experience high, work experience low, extracurricular activity low, clinically related public service medium, GPA high, letters of recommendation high, statement of goals and objectives high. Writing sample for Clinical programs only. Interview in Clinical and Clinical Child only. For additional information on admission requirements, go to: www.psycgrad.ku.edu.

Student Characteristics: The following represents characteristics of students in 2004–2005 in all graduate psychology programs in the department: Female–full-time 115, part-time 0; Male–full-time 42, part-time 0; African American/Black–full-time 4, part-time 0; Hispanic/Latino(a)–full-time 6, part-time 0; Asian/Pacific Islander–full-time 13, part-time 0; American Indian/Alaska Native–full-time 5, part-time 0; Caucasian–full-time 127, part-time 0; Multi-ethnic–full-time 2, part-time 0; students subject to the Americans With Disabilities Act–full-time 0, part-time 0.

Financial Information/Assistance:
Tuition for Full-Time Study: *Master's:* State residents: $178 per credit hour; Nonstate residents: $459 per credit hour. *Doctoral:* State residents: $178 per credit hour; Nonstate residents: $459 per credit hour. Tuition is subject to change. See the following Web site for updates and changes in tuition costs: www.timetable.ku.edu.

Financial Assistance:
First Year Students: Teaching assistantships available for first-year. Average amount paid per academic year: $10,000. Average number of hours worked per week: 20. Apply by January 15. Tuition remission given: full. Research assistantships available for first-year. Average amount paid per academic year: $10,000. Average number of hours worked per week: 20. Apply by January 15. Fellowships and scholarships available for first-year. Average amount paid per academic year: $12,000. Average number of hours worked per week: 0. Apply by January 15. Tuition remission given: full.

Advanced Students: Teaching assistantships available for advanced students. Average amount paid per academic year: $12,000. Average number of hours worked per week: 20. Apply by January 15. Tuition remission given: full. Research assistantships available for advanced students. Average amount paid per academic year: $12,000. Average number of hours worked per week: 20. Apply by January 15. Fellowships and scholarships available for advanced students. Average amount paid per academic year: $12,000. Average number of hours worked per week: 0. Apply by January 15. Tuition remission given: full.

Contact Information: Of all students currently enrolled full-time, 48% benefitted from one or more of the listed financial assistance programs. Application and information available online at: http://www.psych.ku.edu.

Internships/Practica: For those doctoral students for whom a professional internship is required prior to graduation, 11 applied in 2003–2004. Of those who applied, 11 were placed in internships listed by the Association of Psychology Postdoctoral and Internship Programs (APPIC); 11 were placed in APA accredited internships.

Housing and Day Care: On-campus housing is available. See the following Web site for more information: Housing: www.ku.edu/

~dshweb/. Child Care: www.ku.edu/~hilltop/. On-campus day care facilities are available.

Employment of Department Graduates:

Master's Degree Graduates: Of those who graduated in the academic year 2003–2004, the following categories and numbers represent the post-graduate activities and employment of master's degree graduates: Enrolled in a post-doctoral residency/fellowship (n/a), employed in independent practice (n/a), total from the above (master's) (0).

Doctoral Degree Graduates: Of those who graduated in the academic year 2003–2004, the following categories and numbers represent the post-graduate activities and employment of doctoral degree graduates: Enrolled in a psychology doctoral program (n/a), enrolled in a post-doctoral residency/fellowship (7), employed in independent practice (2), employed in an academic position at a university (6), employed in an academic position at a 2-year/4-year college (2), employed in a professional position in a school system (1), employed in a community mental health/counseling center (1), other employment position (1), do not know (1), total from the above (doctoral) (21).

Additional Information:

Orientation, Objectives, and Emphasis of Department: With 34 full-time faculty, the department offers a wide range of opportunities for the study and treatment of human psychological and behavioral functioning. Students develop skills in statistics, research methods, and specific content areas with basic and applied emphases, with the flexibility to tailor programs to individual students' needs. Students in all programs (Clinical, Clinical Child, Developmental, Quantitative, Cognitive or Social) may also complete coursework toward a minor in quantitative psychology. The Developmental Program is new in 2005, and will begin admitting students in 2006.

Special Facilities or Resources: The department has well-equipped computer labs, and access to university mainframe computers. The department maintains a computer and electronics shop, for the construction of specialized equipment. Clinical and research support facilities include an on-site clinic with a test resource library, individual and group therapy rooms, and play and psychodrama rooms. Specialized research facilities include interview rooms with audio and video capacities, psychophysiological and stress laboratories, ERP facilities, eye-movement monitoring laboratories, and an anechoic chamber. The Kansas University Medical Center houses the Hoglund Brain Imaging Center, a state-of-the-art facility with fMRI and MEG laboratories.

Information for Students With Physical Disabilities: See the following Web site for more information: www.ku.edu/~ssdis/.

Application Information:
Send to: The University of Kansas Graduate School, 1450 Jayhawk Boulevard, Room 300, Lawrence, KS 66045-7535. Application available online. URL of online application: http://www.applyweb.com/apply/ukgpsy/menu.html. Students are admitted in the Fall, application deadline January 15. *Fee:* $55.

Kansas, University of
Psychology and Research in Education
School of Education
Joseph R. Pearson Hall, 1122 West Campus Road, Room 621
Lawrence, KS 66045-3101
Telephone: (785) 864-3931
Fax: (785) 864-3820
E-mail: *preadmit@ku.edu*
Web: *http://www.soe.ku.edu/pre/*

Department Information:
1955. Chairperson: Karen D. Multon, PhD Number of Faculty: total–full-time 14, part-time 2; women–full-time 5, part-time 1; minority–full-time 1, part-time 1.

Programs and Degrees Offered:
Listed in the following order: Program area, degree type (T if terminal Master's), number awarded 7/03–6/04. School Psychology PhD (Doctor of Philosophy) 2, Counseling Psychology MA/MS (Master of Arts/Science) (T) 19, Educational Psych and Research PhD (Doctor of Philosophy) 0, Educational Psych and Research Other 3, Counseling Psychology PhD (Doctor of Philosophy) 7, School Psychology EdS (Education Specialist) 7.

APA Accreditation: School PhD (Doctor of Philosophy). Counseling PhD (Doctor of Philosophy).

Student Applications/Admissions:
Student Applications

School Psychology PhD (Doctor of Philosophy)—Applications 2004–2005, 20. Total applicants accepted 2004–2005, 5. Number enrolled (new admits only) 2004–2005 full-time, 1. Number enrolled (new admits only) 2004–2005 part-time, 0. Total enrolled 2004–2005 full-time, 10, part-time, 4. Openings 2005–2006, 4. The Median number of years required for completion of a degree are 8.5. The number of students enrolled full and part-time who were dismissed or voluntarily withdrew from this program area were 1. *Counseling Psychology MA/MS (Master of Arts/Science)*—Applications 2004–2005, 47. Total applicants accepted 2004–2005, 22. Number enrolled (new admits only) 2004–2005 full-time, 11. Number enrolled (new admits only) 2004–2005 part-time, 1. Total enrolled 2004–2005 full-time, 36, part-time, 15. Openings 2005–2006, 25. The Median number of years required for completion of a degree are 2. The number of students enrolled full and part-time who were dismissed or voluntarily withdrew from this program area were 0. *Educational Psych and Research PhD (Doctor of Philosophy)*—Applications 2004–2005, 10. Total applicants accepted 2004–2005, 5. Number enrolled (new admits only) 2004–2005 full-time, 2. Number enrolled (new admits only) 2004–2005 part-time, 1. Total enrolled 2004–2005 full-time, 14, part-time, 7. Openings 2005–2006, 5. The number of students enrolled full and part-time who were dismissed or voluntarily withdrew from this program area were 0. *Educational Psych and Research Other*—Applications 2004–2005, 6. Total applicants accepted 2004–2005, 3. Number enrolled (new admits only) 2004–2005 full-time, 1. Total enrolled 2004–2005 full-time, 2, part-time, 1. Openings 2005–2006, 5. The Median number of years required for completion of a degree are 2.5. The number of students enrolled full and part-time who were dismissed or voluntarily withdrew from this program area were 0. *Counseling Psychology PhD (Doctor of Philosophy)*—Applications 2004–2005, 58. Total applicants accepted 2004–2005, 12. Number enrolled (new admits only) 2004–2005 full-time, 7. Number enrolled (new admits only) 2004–2005 part-time, 0. Total enrolled 2004–2005 full-time, 28, part-time, 8. Openings 2005–2006, 7. The Median number of years required for completion of a degree are 6. The number of students enrolled full and part-time who were dismissed or voluntarily withdrew from this program area were 1. *School Psychology EdS (Education Specialist)*—Applications 2004–2005, 40. Total applicants accepted 2004–2005, 14. Number enrolled (new admits only) 2004–2005 full-time, 10. Number enrolled (new admits only) 2004–2005 part-time, 0. Openings 2005–2006, 10. The Median number of years required for completion of a degree are 3. The number of students enrolled full and part-time who were dismissed or voluntarily withdrew from this program area were 0.

Admissions Requirements:

Scores: Entries appear in this order: required test or GPA, minimum score (if required), median score of students entering in 2003–2004. Master's Programs: GRE-V 500, 510; GRE-Q 500, 615; GRE-Analytical no minimum stated, 5.0; overall undergraduate GPA 3.0, 3.5. The minimum requirements listed are for regular degree-seeking admission to the University of Kansas. However, there are instances when students are admitted under provisional or probationary status. The mean scores for students who entered the MS program in Counseling Psychology are: V- 471, Q-524, A-4.68, UGPA-3.41. The mean scores for students who entered the EdS program in School Psychology are: V-523, Q-661, A-4.93, UGPA-3.63. The mean scores for students who entered the MSEd program in Educational Psychology and Research are: V-552, Q-630, A-4.5, UGPA-3.75. Doctoral Programs: GRE-V 500, 540; GRE-Q 500, 700; GRE-Analytical no minimum stated, 4.77; overall undergraduate GPA no minimum stated, 3.6. The minimum requirements listed are for regular degree-seeking admission for the University of Kansas. However, there are instances when students are admitted under provisional or probationary status. The mean scores for students who entered the PhD program in Counseling Psychology are: V- 552, Q-637, A-4.61, UGPA-3.46. The mean scores for students who entered the PhD program in School Psychology are: V-650, Q-710, A-6.0, UGPA-3.99. The mean scores for students who entered the PhD program in Educational Psychology and Research are: V-453, Q-660, A-623 (old scoring system), UGPA-3.62.

Other Criteria: (importance of criteria rated low, medium, or high): GRE/MAT scores high, research experience medium, work experience medium, extracurricular activity low, clinically related public service low, GPA high, letters of recommendation high, interview high, statement of goals and objectives high, The admission criteria above are for applicants to the Counseling Psychology PhD program. The admission criteria for applicants to the School Psychology PhD program are: GRE/MAT scores-high; research experience-high; work experience-medium; extracurricular activity-low; clinically related public service-high; GPA-high; letters of recommendation-high; statement of goals and objectives-high. For additional information on admission requirements, go to: http://www.soe.ku.edu (KU School of Education).

Student Characteristics: The following represents characteristics of students in 2004–2005 in all graduate psychology programs in the department: Female–full-time 88, part-time 25; Male–full-time 24, part-time 10; African American/Black–full-time 3, part-time 1; Hispanic/Latino(a)–full-time 4, part-time 3; Asian/Pacific Islander–full-time 5, part-time 0; American Indian/Alaska Native–full-time 2, part-time 0; Caucasian–full-time 0, part-time 0; Multi-ethnic–full-time 1, part-time 0; students subject to the Americans With Disabilities Act–part-time 1.

Financial Information/Assistance:

Tuition for Full-Time Study: *Master's:* State residents: $179 per credit hour; Nonstate residents: $459 per credit hour. *Doctoral:* State residents: $179 per credit hour; Nonstate residents: $459 per credit hour. Tuition is subject to change. See the following Web site for updates and changes in tuition costs: http://www.ku.edu/~registr/CFS/index.shtml.

Financial Assistance:

First Year Students: Teaching assistantships available for first-year. Average amount paid per academic year: $6,000. Average number of hours worked per week: 12. Apply by February 15. Tuition remission given: full and partial. Research assistantships available for first-year. Average amount paid per academic year: $6,000. Average number of hours worked per week: 12. Apply by Varies. Tuition remission given: full and partial. Fellowships and scholarships available for first-year. Apply by Varies. Tuition remission given: full and partial.

Advanced Students: Teaching assistantships available for advanced students. Average amount paid per academic year: $6,000. Average number of hours worked per week: 12. Apply by February 15. Tuition remission given: full and partial. Research assistantships available for advanced students. Average amount paid per academic year: $6,000. Average number of hours worked per week: 12. Apply by Varies. Tuition remission given: full and partial. Traineeships available for advanced students. Apply by Varies. Fellowships and scholarships available for advanced students. Apply by Varies. Tuition remission given: full and partial.

Contact Information: Of all students currently enrolled full-time, 75% benefitted from one or more of the listed financial assistance programs. Application and information available online at: http://www.ku.edu/~osfa/; http://www.graduate.ku.edu/Awards/; http://www.soe.ku.edu/students/scholar.

Internships/Practica: Both master's and doctoral students in the School Psychology and Counseling Psychology programs complete their practica in a variety of local applied settings. Our doctoral students in Counseling Psychology have been successful in obtaining APA accredited internships in university counseling centers, veterans administration medical centers, community mental health centers, and other human service agencies. Students in the School Psychology program have received practica and internships in a variety of elementary, secondary, and special needs school settings throughout the country. The Center for Psychoeducational Services (CPS) offers excellent training and research opportunities for School Psychology and Counseling Psychology students. The CPS is an interdisciplinary School of Education facility serving the needs of local schools and community members. Graduate students may work with preschool, school-age children and their families, and college students from the local area. Students have training and research opportunities with adult populations at the Counseling and Psychological Services facility, the Gerontology Center, and the University Career Center. For those doctoral students for whom a professional internship is required prior to graduation, 3 applied in 2003–2004. Of those who applied, 3 were placed in internships listed by the Association of Psychology Postdoctoral and Internship Programs (APPIC); 3 were placed in APA accredited internships.

Housing and Day Care: On-campus housing is available. See the following Web site for more information: Department of Student Housing: http://www.housing.ku.edu/. On-campus day care facilities are available. See the following Web site for more information: Child Care, Hill Top: http://www.ku.edu/~hilltop/.

Employment of Department Graduates:
Master's Degree Graduates: Of those who graduated in the academic year 2003–2004, the following categories and numbers represent the post-graduate activities and employment of master's degree graduates: Enrolled in a post-doctoral residency/fellowship (n/a), employed in independent practice (n/a), total from the above (master's) (0).
Doctoral Degree Graduates: Of those who graduated in the academic year 2003–2004, the following categories and numbers represent the post-graduate activities and employment of doctoral degree graduates: Enrolled in a psychology doctoral program (n/a), total from the above (doctoral) (0).

Additional Information:
Orientation, Objectives, and Emphasis of Department: Psychology and Research in Education offers graduate training in Counseling Psychology, Educational Psychology and Research, and School Psychology. The PhD programs in Counseling Psychology and School Psychology are APA accredited. Both School Psychology degree programs (EdS and PhD) are NASP accredited. Counseling Psychology trains professionals to possess the generalist skills to function in a wide array of work settings. This program is strongly committed to the training of scientist–practitioners focused on facilitating the personal, social, educational, and vocational development of individuals. School Psychology endorses the training model of the psychoeducational consultant with multifaceted skills drawn from psychology and education to assist children toward greater realization of their potential. The psychoeducational consultant is vitally concerned with enhancing teacher effectiveness, creating a positive classroom environment for children, and influencing educational thought within the school system. The Educational Psychology and Research Program offers instruction in cognition and learning; applied human development; instructional psychology as related to educational practice; applied statistics, measurement, program evaluation, and research methods. Graduate study includes experiences in designing, conducting, and evaluating research and field experiences in a variety of settings. The objectives of the program are to prepare students to become faculty members, researchers, and measurement specialists.

Special Facilities or Resources: The KU School of Education provides extensive media and internet technology in its state-of-the-art facility. Students have access to mediated classrooms and laboratories, instructional and assessment materials libraries, audio visual resources, computer labs, and KU's Law and Medical School libraries. KU students have opportunities to conduct research in a variety of settings including public and private schools, the Center for Educational Testing and Evaluation, the Center for

Psychoeducational Services, the Life Span Institute, and the Multicultural Resource Center. Students working in the Center for Educational Testing and Evaluation help design assessment instruments, analyze test results, and evaluate tests and programs. The Center for Psychoeducational Services offers excellent training opportunities for School Psychology and Counseling Psychology students to work with school-age children and their families from local communities. School Psychology students have additional access to special preschool programs. The Life Span Institute supports a wide variety of social science research (e.g., mental retardation, human development, aging, and speech development.). The Research and Training Center on Independent Living (Life Span Institute) develops systematic approaches to enable individuals with disabilities to live independently. The Multicultural Resource Center seeks to reshape notions of education, research and public service to include a multicultural focus.

Information for Students With Physical Disabilities: See the following Web site for more information: http://www.disability.ku.edu/; http://www.lsi.ku.edu/lsi/centers/.

Application Information:
Send to: KU Psychology and Research in Education, Attn: Admissions Committee, 1122 West Campus Road, Rm 621, JRP, Lawrence, KS 66045-3101 (785) 864-3931 phone; (785) 864-3820 fax; pre-admit@ku.edu. Application available online. URL of online application: http://www.graduate.ku.edu/. Students are admitted in the Fall; Spring; Summer. January 15: Counseling Psychology, PhD program, Summer/Fall Admission February 15: Counseling Psychology, MS program, Summer/Fall Admission February 15: Educational Psychology & Research, PhD or MSEd programs, Summer/Fall Admission November 15: Educational Psychology & Research, PhD or MSEd programs, Spring Admission February 15: School Psychology, PhD and EdS programs, Summer/Fall Admission. Fee: $45. 1. The application fee of $45 is for the online domestic application fee process. Further application fee information may be viewed at http://www.graduate.ku.edu/GAPC/fees.shtml 2. Application for fee waiver must be made directly to the Department of Psychology and Research in Education.

Pittsburg State University
Department of Psychology and Counseling
College of Education
112 Hughes Hall, 1701 S. Broadway
Pittsburg, KS 66762-7551
Telephone: (620) 235-4523
Fax: (620) 235-4520
E-mail: *psych@pittstate.edu*
Web: *http://www.pittstate.edu/psych/*

Department Information:
1929. Chairperson: David P. Hurford. Number of Faculty: total–full-time 14, part-time 6; women–full-time 6, part-time 4; minority–full-time 1, part-time 1.

Programs and Degrees Offered:
Listed in the following order: Program area, degree type (T if terminal Master's), number awarded 7/03–6/04. Clinical Psychology MA/MS (Master of Arts/Science) (T) 9, Community Counseling MA/MS (Master of Arts/Science) (T) 21, General Psychol-

ogy MA/MS (Master of Arts/Science) (T) 12, School Psychology EdS (Education Specialist) 9, School Counseling MA/MS (Master of Arts/Science) (T) 12.

Student Applications/Admissions:

Student Applications

Clinical Psychology MA/MS (Master of Arts/Science)—Applications 2004–2005, 31. Total applicants accepted 2004–2005, 12. Total enrolled 2004–2005 full-time, 9, part-time, 1. Openings 2005–2006, 10. *Community Counseling MA/MS (Master of Arts/Science)*—Applications 2004–2005, 38. Total applicants accepted 2004–2005, 20. Total enrolled 2004–2005 full-time, 12, part-time, 7. Openings 2005–2006, 15. *General Psychology MA/MS (Master of Arts/Science)*—Applications 2004–2005, 16. Total applicants accepted 2004–2005, 12. Total enrolled 2004–2005 full-time, 7, part-time, 5. Openings 2005–2006, 12. *School Psychology EdS (Education Specialist)*—Applications 2004–2005, 15. Total applicants accepted 2004–2005, 10. Total enrolled 2004–2005 full-time, 8, part-time, 2. Openings 2005–2006, 10. *School Counseling MA/MS (Master of Arts/Science)*—Applications 2004–2005, 23. Total applicants accepted 2004–2005, 16. Total enrolled 2004–2005 full-time, 1, part-time, 14. Openings 2005–2006, 10.

Admissions Requirements:

Scores: Entries appear in this order: required test or GPA, minimum score (if required), median score of students entering in 2003–2004. Master's Programs: GRE-V 400, 470; GRE-Q 400, 530; GRE-Analytical 400, 540; overall undergraduate GPA 3.00, 3.43; last 2 years GPA 3.00, 3.56; psychology GPA 3.00, 3.65. Same for all programs, but medians differ by program area.

Other Criteria: (importance of criteria rated low, medium, or high): GRE/MAT scores high, research experience medium, work experience high, extracurricular activity low, clinically related public service medium, GPA high, letters of recommendation high, interview medium, statement of goals and objectives high.

Student Characteristics: The following represents characteristics of students in 2004–2005 in all graduate psychology programs in the department: Female–full-time 26, part-time 1; Male–full-time 11, part-time 4; African American/Black–full-time 0, part-time 1; Hispanic/Latino(a)–full-time 0, part-time 0; Asian/Pacific Islander–full-time 1, part-time 0; American Indian/Alaska Native–full-time 0, part-time 1; Caucasian–full-time 0, part-time 0.

Financial Information/Assistance:

Tuition for Full-Time Study: *Master's:* State residents: per academic year $1,864, $158 per credit hour; Nonstate residents: per academic year $4,578, $384 per credit hour. Tuition is subject to change.

Financial Assistance:

First Year Students: Teaching assistantships available for first-year. Average amount paid per academic year: $4,660. Average number of hours worked per week: 20. Apply by March 1. Tuition remission given: full.

Advanced Students: Teaching assistantships available for advanced students. Average amount paid per academic year: $4,660. Average number of hours worked per week: 20. Apply by March 1. Tuition remission given: full.

Contact Information: Of all students currently enrolled full-time, 5% benefitted from one or more of the listed financial assistance programs.

Internships/Practica: All MS and EdS practitioner programs include a 3–8 semester hour (150–400 clock hour) practicum sequence and a 4–32 semester hour (600–1200 clock hour) internship at a site appropriate to the specialty, and under the supervision of faculty and site supervisors. The internship in school psychology is post-degree, and is typically a paid internship. Some internships in other programs are also paid. All internships meet guidelines of the professional association or accrediting body of the specialty (i.e., CACREP, MPAC, NASP).

Housing and Day Care: On-campus housing is available. See the following Web site for more information: Web site for University Housing: www.pittstate.edu/house/. No on-campus day care facilities are available.

Employment of Department Graduates:

Master's Degree Graduates: Of those who graduated in the academic year 2003–2004, the following categories and numbers represent the post-graduate activities and employment of master's degree graduates: Enrolled in a psychology doctoral program (2), enrolled in another graduate/professional program (3), enrolled in a post-doctoral residency/fellowship (n/a), employed in independent practice (n/a), employed in an academic position at a university (1), employed in an academic position at a 2-year/4-year college (2), employed in other positions at a higher education institution (0), employed in a professional position in a school system (20), employed in business or industry (research/consulting) (0), employed in business or industry (management) (5), employed in a government agency (research) (0), employed in a government agency (professional services) (3), employed in a community mental health/counseling center (16), employed in a hospital/medical center (2), still seeking employment (2), other employment position (3), total from the above (master's) (59).

Doctoral Degree Graduates: Of those who graduated in the academic year 2003–2004, the following categories and numbers represent the post-graduate activities and employment of doctoral degree graduates: Enrolled in a psychology doctoral program (n/a), total from the above (doctoral) (0).

Additional Information:

Orientation, Objectives, and Emphasis of Department: The Department of Psychology and Counseling uses an interdisciplinary model to provide broad-based training, understanding and appreciation of the specialties that we represent. The major objective of the department is to prepare graduates with knowledge in scientific foundations and practical applied skills to function as mental health service providers or to pursue study at the doctoral level. Faculty in the department represent a diverse collection of theoretical backgrounds in scientific and applied psychology. All faculty teach coursework in each program area, providing students with the opportunity to learn multidisciplinary approaches and models. The emphasis in the department is on integrated, cross-disciplinary studies within a close faculty-student colleague model that promotes frequent contact and close supervision, aimed at developing practitioner skills. The department is pleased to have the first accredited master's degree program in clinical psychology in the nation (MPAC accreditation received in May 1997), and enjoys CACREP accreditation of the master's degree program in community counseling. The department also enjoys NCATE accreditation of the MS Degree program in school counseling and the EdS Degree program in school psychology.

Special Facilities or Resources: The department has counseling and psychotherapy training facilities equipped with one-way mirrors and audio and video taping equipment. Microcomputer laboratories with network capacity, word processing, and SAS and SPSS software are available in the department. The university library, in addition to a large book collection, currently maintains over 150 periodical subscriptions in psychology. The department operates the Center for Human Services, an on-campus training, research, and service facility, which includes University Testing Services, a family counseling center, an adult assessment center, the Center for Assessment and Remediation of Reading Difficulties, the Attention Deficit/Hyperactivity Disorder Neurofeedback Diagnostic and Treatment Center, and the Welfare to Work Assessment Center. The department has a close working relationship with local hospitals and mental health facilities, and is a constituent member of the regional community service coalition.

Information for Students With Physical Disabilities: See the following Web site for more information: www.pittstate.edu/eoaa/.

Application Information:

Send to: Chairperson, Department of Psychology and Counseling, Pittsburg State University, 1701 S. Broadway, Pittsburg, KS 66762-7551. Students are admitted in the Fall, application deadline March 1; Spring, application deadline October 1; Summer, application deadline March 1. Clinical Psychology admitted only for Fall Semester. *Fee:* $30.

Washburn University (2004 data)
Department of Psychology
1700 College
Topeka, KS 66621
Telephone: (785) 231-1010
Fax: (785) 231-1004
E-mail: *zzdppy@washburn.edu*
Web: *http://www.washburn.edu/cas/psychology/*

Department Information:
1940. Chairperson: Dave Provorse. Number of Faculty: total–full-time 8; women–full-time 4.

Programs and Degrees Offered:
Listed in the following order: Program area, degree type (T if terminal Master's), number awarded 7/03–6/04. Clinical MA/MS (Master of Arts/Science) (T) 3.

Student Applications/Admissions:
Student Applications

Clinical MA/MS (Master of Arts/Science)—Applications 2004–2005, 25. Total applicants accepted 2004–2005, 19. Total enrolled 2004–2005 full-time, 20, part-time, 6. Openings 2005–2006, 15. The Median number of years required for completion of a degree are 3. The number of students enrolled full and part-time who were dismissed or voluntarily withdrew from this program area were 1.

Admissions Requirements:
Scores: Entries appear in this order: required test or GPA, minimum score (if required), median score of students entering in 2003–2004. Master's Programs: GRE-V no minimum stated, 430; GRE-Q no minimum stated, 510; GRE-Analytical no minimum stated, 4.5; overall undergraduate GPA no minimum stated, 3.37; last 2 years GPA no minimum stated, 3.51; psychology GPA no minimum stated, 3.57.

Other Criteria: (importance of criteria rated low, medium, or high): GRE/MAT scores medium, research experience medium, work experience medium, extracurricular activity low, clinically related public service medium, GPA medium, letters of recommendation high, statement of goals and objectives high.

Student Characteristics: The following represents characteristics of students in 2004–2005 in all graduate psychology programs in the department: Female–full-time 16, part-time 3; Male–full-time 4, part-time 3; African American/Black–full-time 1, part-time 0; Hispanic/Latino(a)–full-time 1, part-time 0; Asian/Pacific Islander–full-time 0, part-time 1; American Indian/Alaska Native–full-time 0, part-time 0; Caucasian–full-time 0, part-time 0; Multi-ethnic–full-time 1, part-time 0.

Financial Information/Assistance:
Tuition for Full-Time Study: Master's: State residents: per academic year $5,550, $185 per credit hour; Nonstate residents: per academic year $5,550, $185 per credit hour. Tuition is subject to change.

Financial Assistance:
First Year Students: Teaching assistantships available for first-year. Average amount paid per academic year: $4,000. Average number of hours worked per week: 10. Apply by March 15.

Advanced Students: Teaching assistantships available for advanced students. Average amount paid per academic year: $4,000. Average number of hours worked per week: 10. Apply by May 15.

Contact Information: Of all students currently enrolled full-time, 55% benefitted from one or more of the listed financial assistance programs.

Internships/Practica: Psychological Services are offered to the community through a clinic staffed by graduate students enrolled in practica. Services offered focus on remediation of anxiety and depression. Student therapists practice skills of diagnostic interviewing, and integrating interview information with personality and intelligence testing into the formulation of a *DSM–IV–TR* diagnosis. Under the close supervision of a faculty clinical psychologist, they use this information to conceptualize etiologies and develop and deliver therapeutic treatment options. The therapy processes implemented reflect several theoretical orientations, including Interpersonal Process, Cognitive, Behavioral and Brief approaches. Issues of suicide, cross-cultural sensitivity and individual therapist development are also addressed. An internship consisting of 750 supervised hours over an academic year is required of each student prior to graduation. This requirement is met by working twenty hours per week at an assigned site and meeting three hours weekly in a classroom setting. Both on-site and academic supervisors are available to the student throughout the internship. The types of experiences provided student interns include: provision of individual adult and child therapy; cofacilitation of group therapy; psychological testing/assessment; and involvement in multidisciplinary treatment teams.

Housing and Day Care: No on-campus housing is available. No on-campus day care facilities are available.

Employment of Department Graduates:

Master's Degree Graduates: Of those who graduated in the academic year 2003–2004, the following categories and numbers represent the post-graduate activities and employment of master's degree graduates: Enrolled in a post-doctoral residency/fellowship (n/a), employed in independent practice (n/a), employed in an academic position at a 2-year/4-year college (1), employed in a community mental health/counseling center (5), other employment position (1), total from the above (master's) (7).

Doctoral Degree Graduates: Of those who graduated in the academic year 2003–2004, the following categories and numbers represent the post-graduate activities and employment of doctoral degree graduates: Enrolled in a psychology doctoral program (n/a), total from the above (doctoral) (0).

Additional Information:

Orientation, Objectives, and Emphasis of Department: Training is designed to establish a strong foundation in the content and methods of psychology. Students obtain experience and skills in research, psychological assessment and individual and group therapy. Clinical training reflects an integrative blend of humanistic, behavioral, cognitive, interpersonal process and brief therapies. The MA program is designed to prepare students for the pursuit of a doctoral degree in psychology, or for future employment as providers of psychological services in community mental health centers, hospitals and other social service agencies and clinics that require master's level training. Students with special interests in children, rural psychology or correctional settings have the opportunity to pursue these in their thesis research and internship placement.

Special Facilities or Resources: The psychology department, housed with other departments in a modern building, has well-equipped laboratories available for human experimentation. These facilities also include observation areas designed for the direct supervision of psychotherapy and psychological testing. The psychology department provides access to the University Academic Computer Center for computer hardware and software resources. Thesis research can be conducted by accessing participants from the undergraduate subject pool, or a wide array of community-based agencies.

Information for Students With Physical Disabilities: See the following Web site for more information: www.washburn.edu/services/studentaffairs/stuservices/disabilitiesguide.html.

Application Information:
Send to: Department of Psychology, Washburn University, Topeka, KS 66621. Application available online. Students are admitted in the Fall, application deadline March 15; Spring, application deadline December 1. *Fee:* $0.

Wichita State University
Department of Psychology
Fairmount College of Liberal Arts and Sciences
1845 Fairmount
Wichita, KS 67260-0034
Telephone: (316) 978-3170
Fax: (316) 978-3086
E-mail: *charles.burdsal@wichita.edu*
Web: *http://psychology.wichita.edu*

Department Information:
1948. Chairperson: Charles A. Burdsal. Number of Faculty: total–full-time 16; women–full-time 5; minority–full-time 2.

Programs and Degrees Offered:
Listed in the following order: Program area, degree type (T if terminal Master's), number awarded 7/03–6/04. Clinical Psychology PhD (Doctor of Philosophy) 8, Human Factors PhD (Doctor of Philosophy) 8, Community PhD (Doctor of Philosophy) 3.

Student Applications/Admissions:

Student Applications

Clinical Psychology PhD (Doctor of Philosophy)—Applications 2004–2005, 30. Total applicants accepted 2004–2005, 5. Number enrolled (new admits only) 2004–2005 full-time, 5. Openings 2005–2006, 3. The Median number of years required for completion of a degree are 7. The number of students enrolled full and part-time who were dismissed or voluntarily withdrew from this program area were 1. *Human Factors PhD (Doctor of Philosophy)*—Applications 2004–2005, 15. Total applicants accepted 2004–2005, 8. Number enrolled (new admits only) 2004–2005 full-time, 5. Openings 2005–2006, 6. The Median number of years required for completion of a degree are 5. The number of students enrolled full and part-time who were dismissed or voluntarily withdrew from this program area were 0. *Community PhD (Doctor of Philosophy)*—Applications 2004–2005, 14. Total applicants accepted 2004–2005, 6. Number enrolled (new admits only) 2004–2005 full-time, 6. Openings 2005–2006, 4. The Median number of years required for completion of a degree are 5. The number of students enrolled full and part-time who were dismissed or voluntarily withdrew from this program area were 0.

Admissions Requirements:

Scores: Entries appear in this order: required test or GPA, minimum score (if required), median score of students entering in 2003–2004. Doctoral Programs: GRE-V no minimum stated, 525; GRE-Q no minimum stated, 515; GRE-V+Q no minimum stated, 1020; overall undergraduate GPA 3.00, 3.3; last 2 years GPA no minimum stated, 3.4; psychology GPA no minimum stated, 3.6.

Other Criteria: (importance of criteria rated low, medium, or high): GRE/MAT scores medium, research experience high, work experience medium, clinically related public service medium, GPA high, letters of recommendation medium, interview low, statement of goals and objectives high. For additional information on admission requirements, go to: psychology.wichita.edu.

Student Characteristics: The following represents characteristics of students in 2004–2005 in all graduate psychology programs in the department: Female–full-time 42, part-time 0; Male–full-time 30, part-time 0; African American/Black–full-time 5, part-time 0; Hispanic/Latino(a)–full-time 2, part-time 0; Asian/Pacific Islander–full-time 3, part-time 0; American Indian/Alaska Native–part-time 0; Caucasian–full-time 61, part-time 0; Multi-ethnic–full-time 1, part-time 0; students subject to the Americans With Disabilities Act–full-time 1, part-time 0.

Financial Information/Assistance:

Tuition for Full-Time Study: *Doctoral:* State residents: per academic year $4,093, $170 per credit hour; Nonstate residents: per academic year $11,293, $470 per credit hour. Tuition is subject to change. See the following Web site for updates and changes in tuition costs: http://webs.wichita.edu/gradsch/.

Financial Assistance:

First Year Students: Teaching assistantships available for first-year. Average amount paid per academic year: $6,000. Average number of hours worked per week: 20. Tuition remission given: full and partial.

Advanced Students: Teaching assistantships available for advanced students. Average amount paid per academic year: $7,000. Average number of hours worked per week: 20. Tuition remission given: full and partial. Research assistantships available for advanced students. Average amount paid per academic year: $8,800. Average number of hours worked per week: 20.

Contact Information: Of all students currently enrolled full-time, 77% benefitted from one or more of the listed financial assistance programs.

Internships/Practica: An important aspect of the Human Factors Program is its requirement that all students complete a minimum six-month internship. The internship is designed to provide students with practical experience integrating their education in real-world situations. The internships have included positions with the FAA, National Cash Register, Pizza Hut, Bell Laboratories, IBM, Microsoft, and other similar settings. These placements have often led to post-PhD employment opportunities. In the Clinical and Community Programs, practicum opportunities, most of them funded, are available in on-campus training facilities and community agencies. Settings include the Psychology Clinic and the Counseling and Testing Center, both at Wichita State University; the Sedgwick County Department of Mental Health; Head Start, and various community-based projects. Students in the Clinical Program are required to complete one year of internship experience towards the end of their graduate studies. For those doctoral students for whom a professional internship is required prior to graduation, 4 applied in 2003–2004. Of those who applied, 4 were placed in internships listed by the Association of Psychology Postdoctoral and Internship Programs (APPIC); 4 were placed in APA accredited internships.

Housing and Day Care: On-campus housing is available. See the following Web site for more information: www.wichita.edu. On-campus day care facilities are available.

Employment of Department Graduates:

Master's Degree Graduates: Of those who graduated in the academic year 2003–2004, the following categories and numbers represent the post-graduate activities and employment of master's degree graduates: Enrolled in a post-doctoral residency/fellowship (n/a), employed in independent practice (n/a), total from the above (master's) (0).

Doctoral Degree Graduates: Of those who graduated in the academic year 2003–2004, the following categories and numbers represent the post-graduate activities and employment of doctoral degree graduates: Enrolled in a psychology doctoral program (n/a), enrolled in a post-doctoral residency/fellowship (1), employed in an academic position at a university (0), employed in other positions at a higher education institution (1), employed in a government agency (professional services) (1), employed in a community mental health/counseling center (1), total from the above (doctoral) (4).

Additional Information:

Orientation, Objectives, and Emphasis of Department: The Psychology Department, open to various theoretical orientations, emphasizes research in all three of its programs. The Human Factors Program is accredited by the Education Committee of the Human Factors and Ergonomics Society. This program seeks to provide students wide exposure to research training, practice, and literature, as well as to theory in the wider context of issues in basic and applied experimental psychology. Current human factors research involves cognitive functioning, aging, development, human-computer interactions, aerospace issues, music cognition, perception, vision, and driving related issues, especially with the elderly. The Clinical Program seeks to integrate community and clinical psychology. The goal of the program is to train students to be licensed clinical psychologists competent to conceptualize, research, intervene, and treat problems at the individual, group, organizational and societal levels. Special areas of interest and research include parent-child interaction, treatment and prevention of depression, treatment and prevention of delinquency, adolescent health and development, and assessment of personality and psychopathology. The Community Program seeks to educate students in Community Psychology with an emphasis on assessing and solving problems at the group, organizational and societal levels. Special areas of research and practice include: adolescent health and development, self-help groups, voluntary and paid helping relationships especially with the elderly, animal welfare, and treatment and prevention of delinquency. All three programs have an applied research focus.

Special Facilities or Resources: The department is located in Jabara Hall and maintains fully equipped laboratories. The facilities include the Human Computer Interaction Lab, Perception/Action Lab, Micro-Experimental Lab, Cognitive Research Lab, Software Usability Lab, Visual Psychophysics Lab, and Music Cognition and Audio-Visual Perception Lab. Our computer facilities are state-of-the-art and are available to students for coursework and research. The department also has access to the National Institute of Aviation Research, the Social Science Research Laboratory, and the University Computing Center. The Psychology Clinic, which is part of the psychology department, provides outpatient services via individual, group, and family modalities. The clinic has facilities for individual and group research. A state-wide Self-Help Network, with a computerized database and an 800 number, also operates out of the psychology department. Faculty maintain working relationships with a number of governmental and community agencies which facilitate student involvement in community practice and research. The agencies include the public school system, the Sedgwick County Department of Mental Health, and COMCARE.

Information for Students With Physical Disabilities: webs.wichita.edu/disserv/.

Application Information:
Send to: Graduate Coordinator, Psychology Department. Students are admitted in the Fall, application deadline see below. Community-Clinical Program, February 1; Community Program, March 1; Human Factors Program, March 15. *Fee:* $35. International Students $50.

Eastern Kentucky University

Department of Psychology
Arts and Sciences
Cammack 127
Richmond, KY 40475
Telephone: (859) 622-1105
Fax: (859) 622-5871
E-mail: *robert.brubaker@eku.edu*
Web: *http://www.psychology.eku.edu*

Department Information:

1967. Chairperson: Robert G. Brubaker. Number of Faculty: total–full-time 21, part-time 12; women–full-time 10, part-time 8; minority–full-time 1; faculty subject to the Americans With Disabilities Act 2.

Programs and Degrees Offered:

Listed in the following order: Program area, degree type (T if terminal Master's), number awarded 7/03–6/04. Clinical Psychology MA/MS (Master of Arts/Science) (T) 13, Industrial/ Organizational MA/MS (Master of Arts/Science) (T) 4, School Psychology EdS (Education Specialist) 11, General Psychology MA/MS (Master of Arts/Science) (T).

Student Applications/Admissions:

Student Applications

Clinical Psychology MA/MS (Master of Arts/Science)—Applications 2004–2005, 65. Total applicants accepted 2004–2005, 13. Number enrolled (new admits only) 2004–2005 full-time, 13. Total enrolled 2004–2005 full-time, 21. Openings 2005–2006, 13. The Median number of years required for completion of a degree are 2. The number of students enrolled full and part-time who were dismissed or voluntarily withdrew from this program area were 0. *Industrial/ Organizational MA/MS (Master of Arts/Science)*—Applications 2004–2005, 30. Total applicants accepted 2004–2005, 8. Number enrolled (new admits only) 2004–2005 full-time, 8. Number enrolled (new admits only) 2004–2005 part-time, 0. Openings 2005–2006, 10. The Median number of years required for completion of a degree are 2. The number of students enrolled full and part-time who were dismissed or voluntarily withdrew from this program area were 0. *School Psychology EdS (Education Specialist)*—Applications 2004–2005, 32. Total applicants accepted 2004–2005, 10. Number enrolled (new admits only) 2004–2005 full-time, 10. Number enrolled (new admits only) 2004–2005 part-time, 0. Openings 2005–2006, 10. The Median number of years required for completion of a degree are 3. The number of students enrolled full and part-time who were dismissed or voluntarily withdrew from this program area were 0. *General Psychology MA/MS (Master of Arts/Science)*—Applications 2004–2005, 2. Total applicants accepted 2004–2005, 2. Number enrolled (new admits only) 2004–2005 full-time, 2. Total enrolled 2004–2005 full-time, 2. Openings 2005–2006, 2. The number of students enrolled full and part-time who were dismissed or voluntarily withdrew from this program area were 0.

Admissions Requirements:

Scores: Entries appear in this order: required test or GPA, minimum score (if required), median score of students entering in 2003–2004. Master's Programs: GRE-V+Q 750, 1000; overall undergraduate GPA 2.5, 3.4.

Other Criteria: (importance of criteria rated low, medium, or high): GRE/MAT scores medium, research experience medium, work experience medium, extracurricular activity low, clinically related public service medium, GPA medium, letters of recommendation high, statement of goals and objectives high.

Student Characteristics: The following represents characteristics of students in 2004–2005 in all graduate psychology programs in the department: Female–full-time 58, part-time 0; Male–full-time 8, part-time 0; African American/Black–full-time 7, part-time 0; Hispanic/Latino(a)–full-time 0, part-time 0; Asian/Pacific Islander–full-time 1, part-time 0; American Indian/Alaska Native–full-time 0, part-time 0; Caucasian–full-time 58, part-time 0.

Financial Information/Assistance:

Tuition for Full-Time Study: *Master's:* State residents: per academic year $1,825; Nonstate residents: per academic year $4,976. See the following Web site for updates and changes in tuition costs: http://www.billings.eku.edu/fees/regfee.php.

Financial Assistance:

First Year Students: Research assistantships available for first-year. Average amount paid per academic year: $3,200. Average number of hours worked per week: 20. Apply by March 15. Tuition remission given: full and partial.

Advanced Students: Research assistantships available for advanced students. Average amount paid per academic year: $3,200. Average number of hours worked per week: 20. Apply by May 1. Tuition remission given: full and partial.

Contact Information: Of all students currently enrolled full-time, 80% benefitted from one or more of the listed financial assistance programs. Application and information available online at: http://www.finaid.eku.edu/.

Internships/Practica: A variety of field placements are available within easy commuting distance from Richmond. Practicum sites have included private psychiatric and V.A. hospitals, the University counseling center, a residential treatment facility for children, alcohol and drug abuse treatment programs, and several adult and child outpatient mental health centers. School psychology students can choose from a variety of public and private elementary and secondary schools. Students have completed internships in Kentucky as well as many other states. Students in the I-O program work on practicum projects with various for-profit and non-profit organizations in the region.

Housing and Day Care: On-campus housing is available. See the following Web site for more information: http://www.housing.eku.edu/. On-campus day care facilities are available.

Employment of Department Graduates:

Master's Degree Graduates: Of those who graduated in the academic year 2003–2004, the following categories and numbers

represent the post-graduate activities and employment of master's degree graduates: Enrolled in a psychology doctoral program (6), enrolled in a post-doctoral residency/fellowship (n/a), employed in independent practice (n/a), employed in other positions at a higher education institution (2), employed in a professional position in a school system (7), employed in business or industry (research/consulting) (5), employed in a community mental health/counseling center (10), total from the above (master's) (30).

Doctoral Degree Graduates: Of those who graduated in the academic year 2003–2004, the following categories and numbers represent the post-graduate activities and employment of doctoral degree graduates: Enrolled in a psychology doctoral program (n/a), total from the above (doctoral) (0).

Additional Information:

Orientation, Objectives, and Emphasis of Department: The MS program in clinical psychology is designed to train professional psychologists to work in clinics, hospitals, or other agencies. In the clinical program, approximately one-third of the course hours are devoted to theory and research, one-third to clinical skills training, and one-third to practicum and internship placements in the community. The clinical program also offers a certification in mental health services to deaf and hard of hearing individuals. The PsyS program in school psychology is designed to train professional psychologists to work in schools and school-related agencies. The program involves 71 graduate hours including internship, is NASP approved and meets Kentucky certification requirements. The certification program in school psychology is designed individually for the student with a degree in a related area who wishes to meet school psychology certification standards. Both programs meet the curriculum standards required for membership in the Council of Applied Master's Programs in Psychology and the North American Association for Master's Psychology, in which the department is an active participant. The clinical program is one of seven approved nationally by the Master's Program Accreditation Council. The I-O program is designed to meet the education and training guidelines established by the Society for Industrial and Organizational Psychology. The scientist-practitioner I-O program prepares students to work in organizations and/or pursue a doctoral degree. Degree requirements include intensive required courses and electives, and practicum. Research opportunities are available in all programs, and all programs prepare students for doctoral study. The M.S General Psychology program is a new offering this year. The flexible curriculum is designed to prepare students for further graduate study in psychology or for a variety of nonapplied career options.

Special Facilities or Resources: Laboratories include several multipurpose rooms. The clinical training facility includes a group therapy room, individual therapy rooms, a testing room, and a play therapy room. All rooms have two-way mirror viewing and videotape facilities. The department operates a child and family clinic providing services to the community, with its primary mission the training of students.

Information for Students With Physical Disabilities: See the following Web site for more information: http://www.disabled.eku.edu/.

Application Information:
Send to: Graduate School, Eastern Kentucky University, 521 Lancaster Avenue, Richmond, KY 40475; (Letters of recommendation should be sent to the Department Chair). Application available online. URL of online application: http://www.gradschool.eku.edu/. Students are admitted in the Fall, application deadline March 15. March 15 is the deadline for all programs. Applications after this date are considered on a space-available basis. *Fee:* $35.

Kentucky, University of (2004 data)
Department of Educational and Counseling Psychology
Counseling, School, and Educational Psychology
Dickey Hall, Room 245
Lexington, KY 40506-0017
Telephone: (859) 257-7881
Fax: (859) 257-5662
E-mail: *eande1@uky.edu*
Web: *http://www.uky.edu/education/edphead.html*

Department Information:
1968. Chairperson: Thomas Prout. Number of Faculty: total–full-time 16, part-time 3; women–full-time 7; minority–full-time 1.

Programs and Degrees Offered:
Listed in the following order: Program area, degree type (T if terminal Master's), number awarded 7/03–6/04. Counseling MA/MS (Master of Arts/Science), Educational MA/MS (Master of Arts/Science) 0, School MA/MS (Master of Arts/Science), Counseling PhD (Doctor of Philosophy), Educational PhD (Doctor of Philosophy), School PhD (Doctor of Philosophy).

APA Accreditation: Counseling PhD (Doctor of Philosophy). School PhD (Doctor of Philosophy).

Student Applications/Admissions:
Student Applications
Counseling MA/MS *(Master of Arts/Science)*—The Median number of years required for completion of a degree are 2. The number of students enrolled full and part-time who were dismissed or voluntarily withdrew from this program area were 0. *Educational MA/MS (Master of Arts/Science)*—The Median number of years required for completion of a degree are 2. The number of students enrolled full and part-time who were dismissed or voluntarily withdrew from this program area were 0. *School MA/MS (Master of Arts/Science)*—The Median number of years required for completion of a degree is 1. The number of students enrolled full and part-time who were dismissed or voluntarily withdrew from this program area were 0. *Counseling PhD (Doctor of Philosophy)*—Applications 2004–2005, 45. Total applicants accepted 2004–2005, 10. Openings 2005–2006, 10. The Median number of years required for completion of a degree are 5. *Educational PhD (Doctor of Philosophy)*—Total applicants accepted 2004–2005, 4. Openings 2005–2006, 4. *School PhD (Doctor of Philosophy)*—Applications 2004–2005, 26. Total applicants accepted 2004–2005, 4. Openings 2005–2006, 4.

Admissions Requirements:
Scores: Entries appear in this order: required test or GPA, minimum score (if required), median score of students entering in 2003–2004. Master's Programs: GRE-V no minimum stated; GRE-Q no minimum stated; GRE-V+Q no minimum stated.

Doctoral Programs: GRE-V no minimum stated; GRE-Q no minimum stated; GRE-V+Q no minimum stated; overall undergraduate GPA 3.00, 3.37.

Other Criteria: (importance of criteria rated low, medium, or high): GRE/MAT scores medium, research experience high, work experience high, extracurricular activity medium, clinically related public service high, GPA medium, letters of recommendation high, interview high, statement of goals and objectives high.

Student Characteristics: The following represents characteristics of students in 2004–2005 in all graduate psychology programs in the department: Female–full-time 252, part-time 0; Male–full-time 51, part-time 0; African American/Black–full-time 23, part-time 0; Hispanic/Latino(a)–full-time 0, part-time 0; Asian/Pacific Islander–full-time 9, part-time 0; American Indian/Alaska Native–full-time 0, part-time 0; Caucasian–full-time 0, part-time 0; Multi-ethnic–full-time 0, part-time 0; students subject to the Americans With Disabilities Act–full-time 1, part-time 0.

Financial Information/Assistance:

Tuition for Full-Time Study: *Master's:* State residents: per academic year $2,487, $261 per credit hour; Nonstate residents: per academic year $6,157, $668 per credit hour. *Doctoral:* State residents: per academic year $2,487, $261 per credit hour; Nonstate residents: per academic year $6,157, $668 per credit hour. Tuition is subject to change.

Financial Assistance:

   First Year Students: No information provided.
   Advanced Students: No information provided.
   Contact Information: No information provided.

Internships/Practica: For those doctoral students for whom a professional internship is required prior to graduation, 6 applied in 2003–2004. Of those who applied, 6 were placed in APA accredited internships.

Housing and Day Care: On-campus housing is available. See the following Web site for more information: http://www.uky.edu/AuxServ/apartment.html. On-campus day care facilities are available.

Employment of Department Graduates:

   Master's Degree Graduates: Of those who graduated in the academic year 2003–2004, the following categories and numbers represent the post-graduate activities and employment of master's degree graduates: Enrolled in a post-doctoral residency/fellowship (n/a), employed in independent practice (n/a), total from the above (master's) (0).

   Doctoral Degree Graduates: Of those who graduated in the academic year 2003–2004, the following categories and numbers represent the post-graduate activities and employment of doctoral degree graduates: Enrolled in a psychology doctoral program (n/a), employed in an academic position at a university (3), employed in other positions at a higher education institution (3), employed in a government agency (professional services) (1), employed in a hospital/medical center (1), total from the above (doctoral) (8).

Additional Information:

   Orientation, Objectives, and Emphasis of Department: Three programs are housed within the department: counseling psychology, educational psychology, and school psychology. The program faculties in counseling psychology and in school psychology are committed to the scientist-practitioner model for professional training, while educational psychology faculty emphasize the researcher-teacher model. A strong emphasis has been placed upon the psychology core for all professional training. Counseling faculty research interests focus upon cognitive social learning theory, consultation models, experiential therapies, and humanistic psychology. The school psychology faculty research interests focus upon consultation strategies, evaluation and assessment, training, and direct interventions. The educational psychology faculty research interests include motivation, cardiovascular stress in minority children, engagement in risky behaviors, forgiveness, and sleep deprivation. Students in each program are encouraged to establish mentoring relationships with their major professor by the beginning of their second semester. The counseling faculty intends to prepare professionals for diverse settings, e.g., colleges and universities, research facilities, hospitals, regional mental health centers, and private practice. The school psychology faculty aims to prepare scientist–practitioners who will function in school and university settings, in mental health consortia, and in private practice. The educational psychology faculty prepares graduates for research and teaching careers within higher education and applied research settings.

Special Facilities or Resources: The University of Kentucky is located on the western edge of Appalachia, which provides students with the opportunity to interact with a rich and varied American culture. The uniqueness of this potential client and research pool allows our students to examine attributes of the bridge between old, rural America and the future, more technological America. Microcomputer facilities are available within the department and within the college for student use in word processing, model development, simulation and evaluation, and data analysis. The university provides all the facilities and resources expected of a major research institution (e.g., extensive libraries, computer facilities, research environment, and medical center).

Application Information:
Send to: Dr. Eric Anderman, Director of Graduate Study, Department of Educational and Counseling Psychology, College of Education, University of Kentucky, 245 Dickey Hall, Lexington, KY 40506-0017. Students are admitted in the Fall. January 15 deadline for PhD; March 1 deadline for Master's program. *Fee:* $35. $45 International.

Kentucky, University of
Department of Psychology
Arts and Sciences
Kastle Hall
Lexington, KY 40506-0044
Telephone: (859) 257-9640
Fax: (859) 323-1979
E-mail: *tdherr2@uky.edu*
Web: *http://www.uky.edu/ArtsSciences/Psychology*

Department Information:

   1917. Chairperson: Charles R. Carlson, PhD, ABPP. Number of Faculty: total–full-time 31; women–full-time 13; minority–full-time 3; faculty subject to the Americans With Disabilities Act 1.

Programs and Degrees Offered:

Listed in the following order: Program area, degree type (T if terminal Master's), number awarded 7/03–6/04. Clinical PhD (Doctor of Philosophy) 4, Experimental PhD (Doctor of Philosophy) 5.

APA Accreditation: Clinical PhD (Doctor of Philosophy).

Student Applications/Admissions:

Student Applications

Clinical PhD (Doctor of Philosophy)—Applications 2004–2005, 185. Total applicants accepted 2004–2005, 8. Number enrolled (new admits only) 2004–2005 full-time, 8. Openings 2005–2006, 8. The Median number of years required for completion of a degree are 6. The number of students enrolled full and part-time who were dismissed or voluntarily withdrew from this program area were 0. *Experimental PhD (Doctor of Philosophy)*—Applications 2004–2005, 78. Total applicants accepted 2004–2005, 18. Number enrolled (new admits only) 2004–2005 full-time, 8. Openings 2005–2006, 6. The Median number of years required for completion of a degree are 5. The number of students enrolled full and part-time who were dismissed or voluntarily withdrew from this program area were 2.

Admissions Requirements:

Scores: Entries appear in this order: required test or GPA, minimum score (if required), median score of students entering in 2003–2004. Doctoral Programs: overall undergraduate GPA 2.75.

Other Criteria: (importance of criteria rated low, medium, or high): GRE/MAT scores high, research experience high, work experience low, clinically related public service medium, GPA high, letters of recommendation high, interview high, statement of goals and objectives high.

Student Characteristics: The following represents characteristics of students in 2004–2005 in all graduate psychology programs in the department: Female–full-time 55, part-time 0; Male–full-time 25, part-time 0; African American/Black–full-time 2, part-time 0; Hispanic/Latino(a)–full-time 2, part-time 0; Asian/Pacific Islander–full-time 1, part-time 0; American Indian/Alaska Native–full-time 1, part-time 0; Caucasian–full-time 74, part-time 0; Multi-ethnic–full-time 0, part-time 0; students subject to the Americans With Disabilities Act–full-time 0, part-time 0.

Financial Information/Assistance:

Tuition for Full-Time Study: *Master's:* State residents: per academic year $2,826, $299 per credit hour; Nonstate residents: per academic year $6,546, $712 per credit hour. *Doctoral:* State residents: per academic year $2,826, $299 per credit hour; Nonstate residents: per academic year $6,546, $712 per credit hour. Tuition is subject to change.

Financial Assistance:

First Year Students: Teaching assistantships available for first-year. Average amount paid per academic year: $11,076. Average number of hours worked per week: 20. Apply by January 16. Tuition remission given: full. Research assistantships available for first-year. Average amount paid per academic year: $11,076.

Average number of hours worked per week: 20. Apply by January 16. Tuition remission given: full. Fellowships and scholarships available for first-year. Average amount paid per academic year: $15,000. Average number of hours worked per week: 20. Apply by January 16. Tuition remission given: full.

Advanced Students: Teaching assistantships available for advanced students. Average amount paid per academic year: $11,076. Average number of hours worked per week: 20. Apply by January 16. Tuition remission given: full. Research assistantships available for advanced students. Average amount paid per academic year: $11,076. Average number of hours worked per week: 20. Apply by January 16. Tuition remission given: full. Fellowships and scholarships available for advanced students. Average amount paid per academic year: $15,000. Average number of hours worked per week: 20. Apply by January 16. Tuition remission given: full.

Contact Information: Of all students currently enrolled full-time, 99% benefitted from one or more of the listed financial assistance programs.

Internships/Practica: For those doctoral students for whom a professional internship is required prior to graduation, 3 applied in 2003–2004. Of those who applied, 3 were placed in internships listed by the Association of Psychology Postdoctoral and Internship Programs (APPIC); 3 were placed in APA accredited internships.

Housing and Day Care: On-campus housing is available. No on-campus day care facilities are available.

Employment of Department Graduates:

Master's Degree Graduates: Of those who graduated in the academic year 2003–2004, the following categories and numbers represent the post-graduate activities and employment of master's degree graduates: Enrolled in a psychology doctoral program (0), enrolled in another graduate/professional program (0), enrolled in a post-doctoral residency/fellowship (n/a), employed in independent practice (n/a), employed in an academic position at a university (0), employed in an academic position at a 2-year/4-year college (0), employed in other positions at a higher education institution (0), employed in a professional position in a school system (0), employed in business or industry (research/consulting) (0), employed in business or industry (management) (0), employed in a government agency (research) (0), employed in a government agency (professional services) (0), employed in a community mental health/counseling center (0), employed in a hospital/medical center (0), still seeking employment (0), other employment position (0), do not know (0), total from the above (master's) (0).

Doctoral Degree Graduates: Of those who graduated in the academic year 2003–2004, the following categories and numbers represent the post-graduate activities and employment of doctoral degree graduates: Enrolled in a psychology doctoral program (n/a), enrolled in a post-doctoral residency/fellowship (5), employed in independent practice (0), employed in an academic position at a university (2), employed in an academic position at a 2-year/4-year college (1), employed in other positions at a higher education institution (0), employed in a professional position in a school system (0), employed in business or industry (research/consulting) (1), employed in business or industry (management) (0), employed in a government agency (research) (0), employed in a government agency (professional services) (0), employed in a community mental health/counseling center (0), employed in a hospital/medical center (0), still seeking employment (0), other employment position (0), do not know (0), total from the above (doctoral) (9).

Additional Information:

Orientation, Objectives, and Emphasis of Department: The goals of the doctoral program depend partly upon the specific program area in which a student enrolls. The program in Clinical Psychology follows the Boulder scientist-practitioner model. Students in the program receive broad exposure to the major theoretical perspectives influencing clinical psychology. All students are actively engaged in research throughout their graduate training. Beginning in the second year of study, each student also receives extensive clinical experience via placements in mental or behavioral health settings. Graduates of the program are prepared to pursue an academic career or to be a practitioner. Students in the program in Experimental Psychology, Cognitive, Developmental, Social, Animal Learning and Behavioral Neuroscience are trained as research scientists. They are exposed to the important theoretical perspectives and research paradigms of their respective areas. There is considerable latitude for individuals to define their specific programs of study. Graduates are prepared to pursue an academic career or a research position in an applied setting. Graduate study is based on a core curriculum model with no set number of hours required for the PhD degree. All students complete a Master's thesis, written and oral doctoral qualifying examinations, and a dissertation demonstrating accomplishment in independent research.

Special Facilities or Resources: The psychology department occupies its own three-story building located by the computer center and main campus library. Kastle Hall houses faculty and student offices, classrooms, and research space. Research facilities in the building include: animal laboratories for behavioral and physiological research; observation rooms with one-way mirrors; extensive video equipment; and microcomputer equipped rooms for cognitive research. Two additional buildings on campus are available for behavioral research. Current faculty have collaborative arrangements with several facilities on campus, including: the neuropsychology laboratories in the Department of Neurology; the OroFacial Pain Clinic in the College of Dentistry; the Central Animal Research Facility; and the Sanders-Brown Center on Aging. The department maintains a large undergraduate subject pool. Clinical training facilities are excellent and include a departmental clinic housed in a separate building and clinical placement arrangements with a variety of mental and behavioral health facilities in Lexington.

Application Information:

Send to: 116 Kastle Hall, Department of Psychology, University of Kentucky, Lexington, KY 40506-0044. Application available online. URL of online application: http://www.uky.edu/AS/Psychology/gradu ate/. Students are admitted in the Fall, application deadline January 13. *Fee:* $35.

Louisville, University of
Psychological and Brain Sciences
Arts and Sciences
317 Life Sciences Building
Louisville, KY 40292
Telephone: (502) 852-6775
Fax: (502) 852-8904
E-mail: *dmolfese@louisville.edu*
Web: *http://www.louisville.edu/a-s/psychology/*

Department Information:

1963. Chairperson: Dennis L. Molfese. Number of Faculty: total–full-time 22; women–full-time 8; minority–full-time 2.

Programs and Degrees Offered:

Listed in the following order: Program area, degree type (T if terminal Master's), number awarded 7/03–6/04. Clinical PhD (Doctor of Philosophy) 8, Experimental PhD (Doctor of Philosophy) 2, Master of Arts in Psychology MA/MS (Master of Arts/Science) 9.

APA Accreditation: Clinical PhD (Doctor of Philosophy).

Student Applications/Admissions:

Student Applications

Clinical PhD (Doctor of Philosophy)—Applications 2004–2005, 92. Total applicants accepted 2004–2005, 8. Number enrolled (new admits only) 2004–2005 full-time, 8. Number enrolled (new admits only) 2004–2005 part-time, 0. Openings 2005–2006, 8. The Median number of years required for completion of a degree are 7. The number of students enrolled full and part-time who were dismissed or voluntarily withdrew from this program area were 1. *Experimental PhD (Doctor of Philosophy)*—Applications 2004–2005, 18. Total applicants accepted 2004–2005, 8. Number enrolled (new admits only) 2004–2005 full-time, 7. Number enrolled (new admits only) 2004–2005 part-time, 0. Openings 2005–2006, 8. The Median number of years required for completion of a degree are 6. The number of students enrolled full and part-time who were dismissed or voluntarily withdrew from this program area were 0. *Master of Arts in Psychology MA/MS (Master of Arts/Science)*—Applications 2004–2005, 44. Total applicants accepted 2004–2005, 21. Number enrolled (new admits only) 2004–2005 full-time, 19. Total enrolled 2004–2005 full-time, 41. Openings 2005–2006, 15. The Median number of years required for completion of a degree is 1. The number of students enrolled full and part-time who were dismissed or voluntarily withdrew from this program area were 0.

Admissions Requirements:

Scores: Entries appear in this order: required test or GPA, minimum score (if required), median score of students entering in 2003–2004. Master's Programs: GRE-V 550, 500; GRE-Q 550, 500; GRE-V+Q 1100; overall undergraduate GPA 3.0. Doctoral Programs: GRE-V 550, 505; GRE-Q 550, 610; GRE-V+Q 1100; overall undergraduate GPA 3.0.

Other Criteria: (importance of criteria rated low, medium, or high): GRE/MAT scores high, research experience high, work experience medium, extracurricular activity medium, clinically related public service medium, GPA high, letters of recommendation high, interview high, statement of goals and objectives medium. Experimental PhD does not require clinically related public service or interview.

Student Characteristics: The following represents characteristics of students in 2004–2005 in all graduate psychology programs in the department: Female–full-time 81, part-time 0; Male–full-time 35, part-time 0; African American/Black–full-time 12, part-time 0; Hispanic/Latino(a)–full-time 3, part-time 0; Asian/Pacific Islander–full-time 9, part-time 0; American Indian/Alaska Native–full-time 0, part-time 0; Caucasian–full-time 91, part-time 0; Multi-ethnic–full-time 1, part-time 0; students subject to the Americans With Disabilities Act–full-time 1, part-time 0.

Financial Information/Assistance:
Tuition for Full-Time Study: *Master's:* State residents: per academic year $5,472, $304 per credit hour; Nonstate residents: per academic year $15,084, $838 per credit hour. *Doctoral:* State residents: per academic year $5,472, $304 per credit hour; Nonstate residents: per academic year $15,084, $838 per credit hour. Tuition is subject to change. See the following Web site for updates and changes in tuition costs: www.louisville.edu/vpf/bursar/student/tuition.htm.

Financial Assistance:
First Year Students: Teaching assistantships available for first-year. Average amount paid per academic year: $13,500. Average number of hours worked per week: 20. Apply by July 1. Tuition remission given: full. Research assistantships available for first-year. Average amount paid per academic year: $13,500. Average number of hours worked per week: 20. Apply by July 1. Tuition remission given: full. Fellowships and scholarships available for first-year. Average amount paid per academic year: $18,000. Average number of hours worked per week: 0. Apply by February 1. Tuition remission given: full.

Advanced Students: Teaching assistantships available for advanced students. Average amount paid per academic year: $13,500. Average number of hours worked per week: 20. Apply by July 1. Tuition remission given: full. Research assistantships available for advanced students. Average amount paid per academic year: $13,500. Average number of hours worked per week: 20. Apply by July 1. Tuition remission given: full. Traineeships available for advanced students. Average amount paid per academic year: $0. Average number of hours worked per week: 0. Apply by varies. Fellowships and scholarships available for advanced students. Average amount paid per academic year: $18,000. Average number of hours worked per week: 0. Apply by February 1. Tuition remission given: full.

Contact Information: Of all students currently enrolled full-time, 53% benefitted from one or more of the listed financial assistance programs.

Internships/Practica: Internship and practica are available in a number of community and government agencies. These include the Department of Psychiatry and Behavioral Sciences, The Child Evaluation Center, Central State Hospital, Veterans Administration Medical Center, Seven Counties Services, and numerous other agencies. For those doctoral students for whom a professional internship is required prior to graduation, 10 applied in 2003–2004. Of those who applied, 10 were placed in internships listed by the Association of Psychology Postdoctoral and Internship Programs (APPIC); 10 were placed in APA accredited internships.

Housing and Day Care: On-campus housing is available. See the following Web site for more information: www.louisville.edu/student/life/housing/. No on-campus day care facilities are available.

Employment of Department Graduates:
Master's Degree Graduates: Of those who graduated in the academic year 2003–2004, the following categories and numbers represent the post-graduate activities and employment of master's degree graduates: Enrolled in a psychology doctoral program (1), enrolled in a post-doctoral residency/fellowship (n/a), employed in independent practice (n/a), employed in a government agency (professional services) (1), other employment position (7), total from the above (master's) (9).
Doctoral Degree Graduates: Of those who graduated in the academic year 2003–2004, the following categories and numbers represent the post-graduate activities and employment of doctoral degree graduates: Enrolled in a psychology doctoral program (n/a), enrolled in a post-doctoral residency/fellowship (5), employed in an academic position at a university (4), employed in business or industry (research/consulting) (1), total from the above (doctoral) (10).

Additional Information:
Orientation, Objectives, and Emphasis of Department: The experimental program offers two areas of specialization: 1) Cognitive: which focuses on memory, conceptual behavior, problem solving, language, judgment, decision making, attention, cognitive development, and mathematical models; and 2) Vision Science: which focuses on visual perception, visual neurosciences, and the physiology of the visual system. The Clinical Program adheres to a scientist-practitioner model and is designed to provide training in research, psychological assessment, psychological intervention, and legal and professional issues. The program covers basic theories, current state of knowledge, and skill training in clinical psychology. Faculty expertise is strongest in the areas of anxiety disorders in children and adults, mental health and adjustments of older adults, stress management and behavioral medicine, ethnic mental health, interpersonal relations, social influence, social cognition, aggression, group behavior, and health psychology. Clinical emphasis includes interpersonal and cognitive-behavioral approaches.

Special Facilities or Resources: Departmental facilities include several computerized laboratories, an electronic shop, physiological laboratories, and a Psychological Services Center. The University also has a Computer Center that is available from departmental stations via a campus-wide network. Additional training opportunities are available through such facilities as the Department of Psychiatry and Behavioral Sciences, the Child Evaluation Center, Central State Hospital, and numerous other community agencies.

Application Information:
Send to: Graduate Admissions Office, University of Louisville, Houchens Room 6, Louisville, KY 40292-0001. Application available online. URL of online application: http://graduate.louisville.edu/app/. Students are admitted in the Fall, application deadline December 1. MA

Program: Application Deadline is April 1 for Fall semester; November 1 for Spring semester. *Fee:* $50.

Morehead State University (Kentucky)

Department of Psychology
Science & Technology
601 Ginger Hall
Morehead, KY 40351
Telephone: (606) 783-2981
Fax: (606) 783-5077
E-mail: *b.mattin@morehead-st.edu*
Web: *http://www.morehead-st.edu/colleges/science/psych*

Department Information:

1968. Chairperson: Bruce A. Mattingly. Number of Faculty: total–full-time 11, part-time 7; women–full-time 4, part-time 4; minority–full-time 2.

Programs and Degrees Offered:

Listed in the following order: Program area, degree type (T if terminal Master's), number awarded 7/03–6/04. Clinical Psychology MA/MS (Master of Arts/Science) (T) 12, Counseling Psychology MA/MS (Master of Arts/Science) (T) 5, Experimental-General MA/MS (Master of Arts/Science) (T) 6.

Student Applications/Admissions:

Student Applications

Clinical Psychology MA/MS (Master of Arts/Science)—Applications 2004–2005, 35. Total applicants accepted 2004–2005, 20. Number enrolled (new admits only) 2004–2005 full-time, 14. Number enrolled (new admits only) 2004–2005 part-time, 0. Openings 2005–2006, 15. The Median number of years required for completion of a degree are 2. The number of students enrolled full and part-time who were dismissed or voluntarily withdrew from this program area were 2. *Counseling Psychology MA/MS (Master of Arts/Science)*—Applications 2004–2005, 10. Total applicants accepted 2004–2005, 5. Number enrolled (new admits only) 2004–2005 full-time, 2. Total enrolled 2004–2005 full-time, 5. Openings 2005–2006, 6. The Median number of years required for completion of a degree are 2. The number of students enrolled full and part-time who were dismissed or voluntarily withdrew from this program area were 0. *Experimental-General MA/MS (Master of Arts/Science)*—Applications 2004–2005, 8. Total applicants accepted 2004–2005, 5. Number enrolled (new admits only) 2004–2005 full-time, 4. Total enrolled 2004–2005 full-time, 6, part-time, 7. Openings 2005–2006, 7. The Median number of years required for completion of a degree are 2. The number of students enrolled full and part-time who were dismissed or voluntarily withdrew from this program area were 1.

Admissions Requirements:

Scores: Entries appear in this order: required test or GPA, minimum score (if required), median score of students entering in 2003–2004. Master's Programs: GRE-V+Q 800, 1000; overall undergraduate GPA 3.0.

Other Criteria: (importance of criteria rated low, medium, or high): GRE/MAT scores medium, research experience medium, work experience low, extracurricular activity low, clini-cally related public service low, GPA high, letters of recommendation high, interview low, statement of goals and objectives medium. Research experience highly valued for admission to experimental program.

Student Characteristics: The following represents characteristics of students in 2004–2005 in all graduate psychology programs in the department: Female–full-time 27, part-time 3; Male–full-time 8, part-time 4; African American/Black–full-time 1, part-time 0; Hispanic/Latino(a)–full-time 0, part-time 0; Asian/Pacific Islander–full-time 1, part-time 0; American Indian/Alaska Native–full-time 0, part-time 0; Caucasian–full-time 33, part-time 7; students subject to the Americans With Disabilities Act–full-time 0, part-time 0.

Financial Information/Assistance:

Tuition for Full-Time Study: *Master's:* State residents: per academic year $1,584, $176 per credit hour; Nonstate residents: per academic year $4,247, $472 per credit hour. Tuition is subject to change. See the following Web site for updates and changes in tuition costs: www.moreheadstate.edu.

Financial Assistance:

First Year Students: Teaching assistantships available for first-year. Average amount paid per academic year: $5,000. Average number of hours worked per week: 20. Tuition remission given: partial. Research assistantships available for first-year. Average amount paid per academic year: $5,000. Average number of hours worked per week: 20. Tuition remission given: partial.

Advanced Students: Teaching assistantships available for advanced students. Average amount paid per academic year: $5,000. Average number of hours worked per week: 20. Tuition remission given: partial. Research assistantships available for advanced students. Average amount paid per academic year: $5,000. Average number of hours worked per week: 20. Tuition remission given: partial.

Contact Information: Of all students currently enrolled full-time, 100% benefitted from one or more of the listed financial assistance programs.

Internships/Practica: Internships and practica placement sites are available in several different states.

Housing and Day Care: On-campus housing is available. See the following Web site for more information: http://www.morehead-st.edu/units/housing/. On-campus day care facilities are available. See the following Web site for more information: http://www.morehead-st.edu/units/hr/child_development_center.html.

Employment of Department Graduates:

Master's Degree Graduates: Of those who graduated in the academic year 2003–2004, the following categories and numbers represent the post-graduate activities and employment of master's degree graduates: Enrolled in a post-doctoral residency/fellowship (n/a), employed in independent practice (n/a), total from the above (master's) (0).

Doctoral Degree Graduates: Of those who graduated in the academic year 2003–2004, the following categories and numbers represent the post-graduate activities and employment of doctoral degree graduates: Enrolled in a psychology doctoral program (n/a), total from the above (doctoral) (0).

Additional Information:

Orientation, Objectives, and Emphasis of Department: The clinical and counseling programs are designed primarily to train MA level psychologists to practice in a variety of settings, and lead to certification in states that provide for certification of master's level psychologists. However, approximately 25% of our students enter doctoral level programs upon graduation. The practitioner model is emphasized in the program, with primary emphases on acquisition of applied clinical skills and knowledge of the general field of psychology. Consequently, competencies in critical analysis of theories, experimental design, and quantitative data analysis are expected. Clinical and counseling students are encouraged to participate in or conduct research ongoing in the department. Students interested in pursuing doctoral level training are encouraged to complete a thesis. The purpose of the experimental program is primarily to prepare students for entry into doctoral programs. Students and faculty are involved in research in several areas including cognitive, perception, animal learning and motivation, psychopharmacology, neurophysiology, developmental, social, and personality.

Special Facilities or Resources: The psychology program provides excellent laboratory facilities for the study of animal and human behavior. Faculty/student research programs are funded through both intra- and extramural grants. The department maintains two microcomputer laboratories, and offers training in statistical packages such as SAS and SPSS. All accepted students are supported by graduate assistantships. Financial assistance for paper presentations at professional conferences is normally available.

Application Information:

Send to: Graduate Office, Morehead State University, Ginger Hall room 701, Morehead, KY 40351. Application available online. URL of online application: http://www.morehead-st.edu/units/Graduate/forms.html. Students are admitted in the Fall, application deadline June 15; Spring, application deadline November 15; Programs have rolling admissions. Rolling admission procedure for fall semester beginning March 1. Spring admission usually for Experimental program only. Contact chair for information for clinical/counseling Spring admissions. *Fee:* $0.

Murray State University
Department of Psychology
Humanities and Fine Arts
212 Wells Hall
Murray, KY 42071-3318
Telephone: (270) 762-2851
Fax: (270) 762-2991
E-mail: *sherry.fortner@murraystate.edu*
Web: *http://www.mursuky.edu/qacd/chs/psychology/psyhom.*

Department Information:

1966. Chairperson: Dr. Renae D. Duncan. Number of Faculty: total–full-time 8, part-time 6; women–full-time 6, part-time 2.

Programs and Degrees Offered:

Listed in the following order: Program area, degree type (T if terminal Master's), number awarded 7/03–6/04. Clinical MA/MS (Master of Arts/Science) (T) 9, General MA/MS (Master of Arts/Science) (T) 0.

Student Applications/Admissions:

Student Applications

Clinical MA/MS (Master of Arts/Science)—Applications 2004–2005, 29. Total applicants accepted 2004–2005, 17. Number enrolled (new admits only) 2004–2005 full-time, 11. Total enrolled 2004–2005 full-time, 26, part-time, 1. Openings 2005–2006, 7. The Median number of years required for completion of a degree are 2. The number of students enrolled full and part-time who were dismissed or voluntarily withdrew from this program area were 1. *General MA/MS (Master of Arts/Science)*—Applications 2004–2005, 10. Total applicants accepted 2004–2005, 6. Number enrolled (new admits only) 2004–2005 full-time, 5. Openings 2005–2006, 3. The Median number of years required for completion of a degree are 2. The number of students enrolled full and part-time who were dismissed or voluntarily withdrew from this program area were 0.

Admissions Requirements:

Scores: Entries appear in this order: required test or GPA, minimum score (if required), median score of students entering in 2003–2004. Master's Programs: GRE-V no minimum stated; GRE-Q no minimum stated; GRE-V+Q 800, 1020; overall undergraduate GPA 3.00, 3.33; psychology GPA 3.00, 3.41. *Other Criteria:* (importance of criteria rated low, medium, or high): GRE/MAT scores medium, research experience medium, work experience low, clinically related public service low, GPA high, letters of recommendation high, statement of goals and objectives high.

Student Characteristics: The following represents characteristics of students in 2004–2005 in all graduate psychology programs in the department: Female–full-time 24, part-time 1; Male–full-time 8, part-time 0; African American/Black–full-time 4, part-time 0; Hispanic/Latino(a)–full-time 2, part-time 0; Asian/Pacific Islander–full-time 1, part-time 0; American Indian/Alaska Native–full-time 0, part-time 0; Caucasian–full-time 25, part-time 1; Multi-ethnic–full-time 0, part-time 0; students subject to the Americans With Disabilities Act–full-time 0, part-time 0.

Financial Information/Assistance:

Tuition for Full-Time Study: *Master's:* State residents: per academic year $2,092, $232 per credit hour; Nonstate residents: per academic year $5,850, $650 per credit hour. Tuition is subject to change. See the following Web site for updates and changes in tuition costs: www.murraystate.edu.

Financial Assistance:

First Year Students: Research assistantships available for first-year. Average amount paid per academic year: $4,200. Average number of hours worked per week: 10. Apply by March 15. Tuition remission given: partial.

Advanced Students: Research assistantships available for advanced students. Average amount paid per academic year: $4,200. Average number of hours worked per week: 10. Apply by March 15. Tuition remission given: partial.

Contact Information: Of all students currently enrolled full-time, 40% benefitted from one or more of the listed financial assistance programs.

Internships/Practica: To gain experience conducting therapy and psychological evaluations, a supervised two-semester, 20 hour per week clinical practicum is required. Clinical psychology students serve their practica at the MSU Psychological Center, an on-campus treatment center, which provides therapy and assessments for children, adults and families from the community as well as for university students and staff. In addition to gaining experience conducting therapy and assessments, our clinical graduate students receive 2½ hours per week of supervision with our PhD level licensed clinical psychologists. This allows for a fine-tuning of clinical skills as well as an added assurance that the clinician is providing the best and most ethical services to the Center's clients.

Housing and Day Care: On-campus housing is available. See the following Web site for more information: http://www.mursuky. edu/secsv/hous/colcts.htm. On-campus day care facilities are available.

Employment of Department Graduates:

Master's Degree Graduates: Of those who graduated in the academic year 2003–2004, the following categories and numbers represent the post-graduate activities and employment of master's degree graduates: Enrolled in a psychology doctoral program (0), enrolled in another graduate/professional program (0), enrolled in a post-doctoral residency/fellowship (n/a), employed in independent practice (n/a), employed in an academic position at a university (0), employed in an academic position at a 2-year/4-year college (0), employed in other positions at a higher education institution (0), employed in business or industry (research/consulting) (0), employed in business or industry (management) (0), employed in a government agency (research) (0), employed in a government agency (professional services) (0), employed in a community mental health/counseling center (5), employed in a hospital/medical center (0), still seeking employment (0), other employment position (1), total from the above (master's) (6).

Doctoral Degree Graduates: Of those who graduated in the academic year 2003–2004, the following categories and numbers represent the post-graduate activities and employment of doctoral degree graduates: Enrolled in a psychology doctoral program (n/a), total from the above (doctoral) (0).

Additional Information:

Orientation, Objectives, and Emphasis of Department: The clinical program is based on the philosophy that the master's degree is first and foremost a degree in psychology and that students should achieve a broad base of knowledge in the field. Thus, students are required to take 5 psychological foundations courses which prepare the graduate to enter the field of psychology and also provide the general psychology courses required by state licensing boards. Clinical students also receive intensive instruction in psychodiagnostics, which emphasizes the administration, scoring, and interpretation of a variety of intelligence and personality tests. The psychotherapy curriculum is primarily cognitive-behavioral in nature, though a variety of techniques and orientations are presented which teach the student how best to conduct psychotherapy with adults, children, families, and couples. Students are expected to participate in research and a master's thesis is required. The general program emphasizes psychological foundations and research methodology as preparation for doctoral studies, community college teaching, or applied research.

Special Facilities or Resources: The department has research laboratories, an on-site psychological clinic with testing and obser-

vation rooms, and complete facilities for practica in diagnostics and therapy. Students also share offices in the department. Each student is assigned a locking desk with personal computer.

Application Information:

Send to: Department Chair. Application available online. URL of online application: http://www.murraystate.edu/main_entry/g_admissions.htm. Students are admitted in the Fall, application deadline March 15; Spring, application deadline rolling. Applications will be accepted after the deadline. However, late applications will be considered only if openings remain after review of applications received before the due date. *Fee: $25.*

Spalding University
School of Professional Psychology
College of Social Sciences & Humanities
851 South Fourth Street
Louisville, KY 40203
Telephone: (502) 585-7127
Fax: (502) 585-7159
E-mail: *esimpson@spalding.edu*
Web: *http://www.spalding.edu*

Department Information:

1952. Chairperson: Andrew Meyer, PhD. Number of Faculty: total–full-time 9, part-time 23; women–full-time 3, part-time 13.

Programs and Degrees Offered:

Listed in the following order: Program area, degree type (T if terminal Master's), number awarded 7/03–6/04. Master of Arts in Clinical Psychology MA/MS (Master of Arts/Science) (T) 21, Doctor of Psychology in Clinical Psychology PsyD (Doctor of Psychology) 13.

APA Accreditation: Clinical PsyD (Doctor of Psychology).

Student Applications/Admissions:

Student Applications

Master of Arts in Clinical Psychology MA/MS (Master of Arts/ Science)—Applications 2004–2005, 19. Total applicants accepted 2004–2005, 10. Number enrolled (new admits only) 2004–2005 full-time, 8. Number enrolled (new admits only) 2004–2005 part-time, 1. Total enrolled 2004–2005 full-time, 18, part-time, 4. Openings 2005–2006, 10. The Median number of years required for completion of a degree are 3. The number of students enrolled full and part-time who were dismissed or voluntarily withdrew from this program area were 3. *Doctor of Psychology in Clinical Psychology PsyD (Doctor of Psychology)*—Applications 2004–2005, 101. Total applicants accepted 2004–2005, 63. Number enrolled (new admits only) 2004–2005 full-time, 29. Number enrolled (new admits only) 2004–2005 part-time, 1. Total enrolled 2004–2005 full-time, 86, part-time, 44. Openings 2005–2006, 48. The Median number of years required for completion of a degree are 7. The number of students enrolled full and part-time who were dismissed or voluntarily withdrew from this program area were 3.

Admissions Requirements:

Scores: Entries appear in this order: required test or GPA, minimum score (if required), median score of students entering

in 2003–2004. Master's Programs: GRE-V no minimum stated, 430; GRE-Q no minimum stated, 510; GRE-V+Q 1000, 940; overall undergraduate GPA 3.0, 3.5. Doctoral Programs: GRE-V no minimum stated, 480; GRE-Q no minimum stated, 560; GRE-V+Q 1000, 1040; overall undergraduate GPA 3.0, 3.6. *Other Criteria:* (importance of criteria rated low, medium, or high): GRE/MAT scores medium, research experience low, work experience medium, extracurricular activity medium, clinically related public service high, GPA medium, letters of recommendation high, interview high, statement of goals and objectives high.

Student Characteristics: The following represents characteristics of students in 2004–2005 in all graduate psychology programs in the department: Female–full-time 80, part-time 32; Male–full-time 24, part-time 16; African American/Black–full-time 3, part-time 3; Hispanic/Latino(a)–full-time 0, part-time 1; Asian/Pacific Islander–full-time 9, part-time 0; American Indian/Alaska Native–full-time 0, part-time 1; Caucasian–full-time 90, part-time 43; Multi-ethnic–full-time 2, part-time 0; students subject to the Americans With Disabilities Act–full-time 0, part-time 0.

Financial Information/Assistance:

Tuition for Full-Time Study: *Master's:* State residents: $495 per credit hour; Nonstate residents: $495 per credit hour. *Doctoral:* State residents: $560 per credit hour; Nonstate residents: $560 per credit hour.

Financial Assistance:

First Year Students: Research assistantships available for first-year. Average amount paid per academic year: $5,000. Apply by March 15. Tuition remission given: partial. Fellowships and scholarships available for first-year. Average amount paid per academic year: $6,000. Apply by March 15. Tuition remission given: partial.

Advanced Students: No information provided.

Contact Information: Of all students currently enrolled full-time, 25% benefitted from one or more of the listed financial assistance programs.

Internships/Practica: In the School of Professional Psychology at Spalding University, we pride ourselves on our extensive network of practica experiences. While we have a University Counseling Center with practica available, we are more broadly known for the extensive practica available through community contacts. These include regional community mental health centers, medical and psychiatric hospitals, residential treatment centers, primary care clinics, state prisons, a military hospital, private practices, public and private schools, university counseling centers, and children and family service centers. Students experience this diversity of settings beginning in their second year with assessment and intervention practica, and continuing through their Practica IV, during which they supervise a beginning level psychotherapy student under the university supervision of a skilled practitioner. A select list of specific clinical sites available include the following: Archdiocese of Louisville (Family Counseling), Ireland Army Community Hospital, Bellarmine University Counseling Center, Brooklawn Psychiatric Residential Treatment Facilities, Central State Hospital, Jefferson County Division of Family Services, Department of Juvenile Justice Center, Department of Corrections (Division of Mental Health), Lifespring Mental Health Services, Solutions Center for Brief Therapy, Spalding University

Counseling Center, and the VA Medical Center. These diverse practica placements prepare our students well for an equally diverse number of internship placements. For those doctoral students for whom a professional internship is required prior to graduation, 31 applied in 2003–2004. Of those who applied, 28 were placed in APA accredited internships.

Housing and Day Care: On-campus housing is available. No on-campus day care facilities are available.

Employment of Department Graduates:

Master's Degree Graduates: Of those who graduated in the academic year 2003–2004, the following categories and numbers represent the post-graduate activities and employment of master's degree graduates: Enrolled in a psychology doctoral program (15), enrolled in a post-doctoral residency/fellowship (n/a), employed in independent practice (n/a), total from the above (master's) (15).

Doctoral Degree Graduates: Of those who graduated in the academic year 2003–2004, the following categories and numbers represent the post-graduate activities and employment of doctoral degree graduates: Enrolled in a psychology doctoral program (n/a), total from the above (doctoral) (0).

Additional Information:

Orientation, Objectives, and Emphasis of Department: The training model of the Spalding School of Professional Psychology is a competency-based disciplined inquiry model. This model integrates professional activity as disciplined inquiry with the goal of professional activities as achieving professional competencies as identified by NCSPP. These competencies are relationship, assessment, intervention, research, supervision, and consultation. In the Spalding Model, professional activities start with issues the client brings to the situation. The professional brings all the relevant knowledge available to address the presenting situation. Relevant knowledge includes scientific knowledge, training in the various competencies identified by NCSPP, and personal knowledge from professional experience. Thus, we educate and train students simultaneously in scientifically based knowledge relevant to the local situations encountered and in the professional competencies needed to address the specific issues raised by clients. The academic scientific core content specified by APA includes: biological basis of behavior, cognitive-affective bases (learning), social bases of behavior, individual differences, history and systems of psychology, and research methods and statistics. These areas cover the theoretical and research basis for guiding conceptions relevant to situations that the professional encounters. The degree is a PsyD in clinical psychology, with an emphasis. The Spalding Program offers four emphasis areas: Adult Psychology Emphasis Area, Health Psychology Emphasis Area, Child/Adolescent/Family Emphasis Area, and Forensic/Correctional Psychology.

Special Facilities or Resources: The faculty have various areas of expertise and interest and form research groups around these areas of interest. For example, Dr. Ken Linfield has an interest group around issues of religion/spirituality and how this integrates with the practice of professional psychology. Dr. Tom Bergandi has an interest in longer-term psychotherapy, forensic psychology and organizational development. Dr. Catherine Aponte has a group research project underway teaching undergraduates relationship skills. Those interested in child and family research usually contact Dr. DeDe Wohlfarth, who works with them to design and implement professionally relevant research. Because we are a professional training model, research is conducted in action settings. Students who are active in the Health Psychology Research Interest Group, led by Dr. Abbie Beacham, are involved in all phases of research projects. Students and faculty collaborate with other universities, medical centers and specialty medical clinics in conducting clinical research. Students also actively participate in State, Regional and National Conferences in the presentation of these projects. Students are encouraged to select dissertation and other research projects based on their own desires as well as the interests of the faculty.

Application Information:
Send to: Administrative Assistant, School of Professional Psychology. Application available online. URL of online application: www.spalding.edu/psychology/welcome. Students are admitted in the Fall, application deadline January 15. *Fee:* $30.

Western Kentucky University

Department of Psychology
College of Education and Behavioral Sciences
1 Big Red Way
Bowling Green, KY 42104
Telephone: (270) 745-2695
Fax: (279) 745-6934
E-mail: *psych@edtech.wku.edu*
Web: *http://edtech.wku.edu/~psych/*

Department Information:
1931. Head: Steven J. Haggbloom. Number of Faculty: total–full-time 33, part-time 19; women–full-time 15, part-time 8; minority–full-time 2, part-time 1; faculty subject to the Americans With Disabilities Act 2.

Programs and Degrees Offered:
Listed in the following order: Program area, degree type (T if terminal Master's), number awarded 7/03–6/04. School Psychology EdS (Education Specialist) 12, Clinical Psychology MA/MS (Master of Arts/Science) (T) 9, Experimental Psychology MA/MS (Master of Arts/Science) (T) 5, Industrial and Organizational Psychology MA/MS (Master of Arts/Science) (T) 9.

Student Applications/Admissions:
Student Applications
School Psychology EdS (Education Specialist)—Applications 2004–2005, 32. Total applicants accepted 2004–2005, 12. Number enrolled (new admits only) 2004–2005 full-time, 12. Number enrolled (new admits only) 2004–2005 part-time, 0. Openings 2005–2006, 10. The Median number of years required for completion of a degree are 3. The number of students enrolled full and part-time who were dismissed or voluntarily withdrew from this program area were 0. *Clinical Psychology MA/MS (Master of Arts/Science)*—Applications 2004–2005, 30. Total applicants accepted 2004–2005, 9. Number enrolled (new admits only) 2004–2005 full-time, 9. Number enrolled (new admits only) 2004–2005 part-time, 0. Openings 2005–2006, 10. The Median number of years required for completion of a degree are 2. The number of students enrolled full and part-time who were dismissed or voluntarily withdrew from

this program area were 4. *Experimental Psychology MA/MS (Master of Arts/Science)*—Applications 2004–2005, 12. Total applicants accepted 2004–2005, 8. Number enrolled (new admits only) 2004–2005 full-time, 8. Number enrolled (new admits only) 2004–2005 part-time, 0. Openings 2005–2006, 8. The Median number of years required for completion of a degree are 2. The number of students enrolled full and part-time who were dismissed or voluntarily withdrew from this program area were 1. *Industrial and Organizational Psychology MA/MS (Master of Arts/Science)*—Applications 2004–2005, 27. Total applicants accepted 2004–2005, 10. Number enrolled (new admits only) 2004–2005 full-time, 10. Number enrolled (new admits only) 2004–2005 part-time, 0. Openings 2005–2006, 10. The Median number of years required for completion of a degree are 2. The number of students enrolled full and part-time who were dismissed or voluntarily withdrew from this program area were 0.

Admissions Requirements:
Scores: Entries appear in this order: required test or GPA, minimum score (if required), median score of students entering in 2003–2004. Master's Programs: GRE-V+Q 850, 1025; overall undergraduate GPA 2.75, 3.52. Minimum Overall GPA of 3.00 for School Psychology program. Minimum quantitative GRE of 500 for I/O program.
Other Criteria: (importance of criteria rated low, medium, or high): GRE/MAT scores high, research experience low, work experience low, extracurricular activity low, clinically related public service medium, GPA high, letters of recommendation high, statement of goals and objectives medium. Research experience is more important for the experimental program and clinically related public service is less important.

Student Characteristics: The following represents characteristics of students in 2004–2005 in all graduate psychology programs in the department: Female–full-time 43, part-time 0; Male–full-time 23, part-time 0; African American/Black–full-time 4, part-time 0; Hispanic/Latino(a)–full-time 0, part-time 0; Asian/Pacific Islander–full-time 0, part-time 0; American Indian/Alaska Native–full-time 0, part-time 0; Caucasian–full-time 62, part-time 0; Multi-ethnic–full-time 0, part-time 0; students subject to the Americans With Disabilities Act–full-time 0, part-time 0.

Financial Information/Assistance:
Tuition for Full-Time Study: *Master's:* State residents: per academic year $2,860, $286 per credit hour; Nonstate residents: per academic year $3,130, $313 per credit hour. Tuition is subject to change. See the following Web site for updates and changes in tuition costs: http://www.wku.edu/bursar/.

Financial Assistance:
First Year Students: Teaching assistantships available for first-year. Average amount paid per academic year: $8,000. Average number of hours worked per week: 20. Apply by August 1. Tuition remission given: partial. Research assistantships available for first-year. Average amount paid per academic year: $8,000. Average number of hours worked per week: 20. Apply by August 1. Tuition remission given: partial.
Advanced Students: Teaching assistantships available for advanced students. Average amount paid per academic year: $8,000. Average number of hours worked per week: 20. Apply by August 1. Tuition remission given: partial. Research assistantships

available for advanced students. Average amount paid per academic year: $8,000. Average number of hours worked per week: 20. Apply by August 1. Tuition remission given: partial.

Contact Information: Of all students currently enrolled full-time, 95% benefitted from one or more of the listed financial assistance programs. Application and information available online at: http://edtech.tph.wku.edu/~psych/grad_program.htm.

Internships/Practica: No information provided.

Housing and Day Care: On-campus housing is available. See the following Web site for more information: http://www.wku.edu/Dept/Support/Housing/HRL/HOME/. No on-campus day care facilities are available.

Employment of Department Graduates:

Master's Degree Graduates: Of those who graduated in the academic year 2003–2004, the following categories and numbers represent the post-graduate activities and employment of master's degree graduates: Enrolled in a post-doctoral residency/fellowship (n/a), employed in independent practice (n/a), total from the above (master's) (0).

Doctoral Degree Graduates: Of those who graduated in the academic year 2003–2004, the following categories and numbers represent the post-graduate activities and employment of doctoral degree graduates: Enrolled in a psychology doctoral program (n/a), total from the above (doctoral) (0).

Additional Information:

Special Facilities or Resources: The department has a training clinic for use by clinical and school psychology students, and laboratory space for experimental research in perception, cognition, motivation, and developmental psychology. Office space is available for most graduate students.

Information for Students With Physical Disabilities: See the following Web site for more information: http://www.wku.edu/Info/Student/disabil.htm.

Application Information:
Send to: Graduate Admissions Department of Psychology, Western Kentucky University, 1 Big Red Way, Bowling Green, KY 42101. Application available online. URL of online application: http://www.wku.edu/graduate/app.htm. Students are admitted in the Fall, application deadline March 1. *Fee:* $35.

Louisiana State University

Department of Psychology
Audubon Hall
Baton Rouge, LA 70803
Telephone: (225) 578-8745
Fax: (225) 578-4125
E-mail: *abaumei@lsu.edu*
Web: *http://www.psych.lsu.edu/graduate/index.html*

Department Information:
1916. Chairperson: Alan Baumeister. Number of Faculty: total–full-time 19; women–full-time 8.

Programs and Degrees Offered:
Listed in the following order: Program area, degree type (T if terminal Master's), number awarded 7/03–6/04. Biological PhD (Doctor of Philosophy) 0, Clinical PhD (Doctor of Philosophy) 13, Cognitive and Developmental PhD (Doctor of Philosophy) 1, Industrial/ Organizational PhD (Doctor of Philosophy) 0, School PhD (Doctor of Philosophy) 2.

APA Accreditation: Clinical PhD (Doctor of Philosophy). School PhD (Doctor of Philosophy).

Student Applications/Admissions:
Student Applications
Biological PhD (Doctor of Philosophy)—Applications 2004–2005, 8. Total applicants accepted 2004–2005, 1. Number enrolled (new admits only) 2004–2005 full-time, 1. Openings 2005–2006, 1. The number of students enrolled full and part-time who were dismissed or voluntarily withdrew from this program area were 0. *Clinical PhD (Doctor of Philosophy)*—Applications 2004–2005, 154. Total applicants accepted 2004–2005, 8. Number enrolled (new admits only) 2004–2005 full-time, 7. Openings 2005–2006, 10. The Median number of years required for completion of a degree are 6. The number of students enrolled full and part-time who were dismissed or voluntarily withdrew from this program area were 0. *Cognitive and Developmental PhD (Doctor of Philosophy)*—Applications 2004–2005, 17. Total applicants accepted 2004–2005, 10. Number enrolled (new admits only) 2004–2005 full-time, 5. Openings 2005–2006, 3. The Median number of years required for completion of a degree are 7.5. The number of students enrolled full and part-time who were dismissed or voluntarily withdrew from this program area were 1. *Industrial/ Organizational PhD (Doctor of Philosophy)*—Applications 2004–2005, 25. Total applicants accepted 2004–2005, 0. Number enrolled (new admits only) 2004–2005 full-time, 0. Openings 2005–2006, 2. The number of students enrolled full and part-time who were dismissed or voluntarily withdrew from this program area were 0. *School PhD (Doctor of Philosophy)*—Applications 2004–2005, 17. Total applicants accepted 2004–2005, 1. Number enrolled (new admits only) 2004–2005 full-time, 1. Openings 2005–2006, 4. The Median number of years required for completion of a degree are 6.5. The number of students en-rolled full and part-time, who were dismissed or voluntarily withdrew from this program area were 0.

Admissions Requirements:
Scores: Entries appear in this order: required test or GPA, minimum score (if required), median score of students entering in 2003–2004. Doctoral Programs: GRE-V 500, 538; GRE-Q 500, 646; GRE-V+Q 1000, 1184; overall undergraduate GPA 3.0, 3.54.
Other Criteria: (importance of criteria rated low, medium, or high): GRE/MAT scores high, research experience high, work experience medium, extracurricular activity medium, clinically related public service medium, GPA high, letters of recommen-dation high, interview medium, statement of goals and objec-tives high, Interview-clinical and school only. For additional information on admission requirements, go to: http://www.psych.lsu.edu/graduate/prospectivestudents.html.

Student Characteristics: The following represents characteristics of students in 2004–2005 in all graduate psychology programs in the department: Female–full-time 63, part-time 0; Male–full-time 28, part-time 0; African American/Black–full-time 4, part-time 0; Hispanic/Latino(a)–full-time 1, part-time 0; Asian/Pacific Is-lander–full-time 3, part-time 0; American Indian/Alaska Native–full-time 1, part-time 0; Caucasian–full-time 79, part-time 0; Multi-ethnic–full-time 3, part-time 0; students subject to the Americans With Disabilities Act–full-time 2, part-time 0.

Financial Information/Assistance:
Tuition for Full-Time Study: *Doctoral:* State residents: per aca-demic year $4,197; Nonstate residents: per academic year $10,997. Tuition is subject to change. See the following Web site for updates and changes in tuition costs: http://www.bgtplan.lsu.edu/fees/05-06/Grad.htm.

Financial Assistance:
First Year Students: Teaching assistantships available for first-year. Average amount paid per academic year: $9,500. Aver-age number of hours worked per week: 20. Apply by January 15. Tuition remission given: full. Traineeships available for first-year. Average amount paid per academic year: $12,000. Average num-ber of hours worked per week: 20. Apply by January 15. Tuition remission given: full. Fellowships and scholarships available for first-year. Average amount paid per academic year: $15,000. Apply by January 15. Tuition remission given: full.
Advanced Students: Teaching assistantships available for advanced students. Average amount paid per academic year: $9,500. Average number of hours worked per week: 20. Tuition remission given: full. Traineeships available for advanced stu-dents. Average amount paid per academic year: $12,000. Average number of hours worked per week: 20. Tuition remission given: full. Fellowships and scholarships available for advanced students. Average amount paid per academic year: $15,000. Tuition remis-sion given: full.
Contact Information: Of all students currently enrolled full-time, 80% benefitted from one or more of the listed financial assistance programs. Application and information available online at: Admission application used for assistantship application.

Internships/Practica: For those doctoral students for whom a professional internship is required prior to graduation, 4 applied in 2003–2004. Of those who applied, 4 were placed in internships listed by the Association of Psychology Postdoctoral and Internship Programs (APPIC); 4 were placed in APA accredited internships.

Housing and Day Care: On-campus housing is available. See the following Web site for more information: On campus housing is available. For information go to http://appl003.lsu.edu/slas/reslife.nsf/index. On-campus day care facilities are available. See the following Web site for more information: http://appl003.lsu.edu/slas/lsuchildcare.nsf/$Content/The+Sound+of+Quality+Child+Care?OpenDocument.

Employment of Department Graduates:

Master's Degree Graduates: Of those who graduated in the academic year 2003–2004, the following categories and numbers represent the post-graduate activities and employment of master's degree graduates: Enrolled in a post-doctoral residency/fellowship (n/a), employed in independent practice (n/a), total from the above (master's) (0).

Doctoral Degree Graduates: Of those who graduated in the academic year 2003–2004, the following categories and numbers represent the post-graduate activities and employment of doctoral degree graduates: Enrolled in a psychology doctoral program (n/a), enrolled in a post-doctoral residency/fellowship (5), employed in an academic position at a university (4), employed in business or industry (research/consulting) (1), employed in a community mental health/counseling center (3), employed in a hospital/medical center (1), do not know (2), total from the above (doctoral) (16).

Additional Information:

Orientation, Objectives, and Emphasis of Department: The Department of Psychology at Louisiana State University is committed to the view that psychology is both a science and a profession, and it regards all areas of specialization as interdependent. All graduate students, regardless of intended areas of specialization, receive broad training to develop the research skills needed to make scholarly contributions to the discipline of psychology throughout their subsequent careers. A student interested only in professional application of psychology without regard for research will not be comfortable in the graduate training program in this department. Both faculty and students in psychology recognize, however, that the model of the psychologist as a practitioner is a legitimate one. Those students whose main interest is in research are encouraged to develop familiarity with clinical, industrial, or developmental and educational settings as potential research environments. The sequence of graduate education reflects these emphases on research and on professional aspects of psychology.

Special Facilities or Resources: The department occupies a centrally located building, designed specifically to accommodate our program. Audubon Hall houses faculty offices, instructional space, desk space for graduate assistants, and research facilities for a wide array of human studies. Animal laboratories are separately housed. A training clinic is located in the Johnston Hall. Additional research and clinical training facilities are located at the Earl K. Long Memorial Hospital, and Pennington Biomedical Research Center.

Information for Students With Physical Disabilities: See the following Web site for more information: http://appl003.lsu.edu/slas/ods.nsf/index.

Application Information:

Send to: Admissions Committee, Graduate Secretary, 236 Audubon Hall, Department of Psychology, Louisiana State University, Baton Rouge, LA 70803-5501. Application available online. URL of online application: http://www.psych.lsu.edu/graduate/prospectivestudents.html. Students are admitted in the Fall, application deadline January 15. *Fee:* $0. There is no fee for the Department of Psychology application. There is a $25 fee for the Graduate School application.

Louisiana State University in Shreveport (2004 data)
Department of Psychology
College of Education and Human Development (CEHD)
One University Place
Shreveport, LA 71115
Telephone: (318) 797-5044
Fax: (318) 798-4171
E-mail: *gjones@pilot.lsus.edu*
Web: *http://www.lsus.edu/ehd/psyc/*

Department Information:

1967. Chairperson: Gary E. Jones, PhD Number of Faculty: total–full-time 11, part-time 13; women–full-time 7, part-time 8; minority–part-time 2.

Programs and Degrees Offered:

Listed in the following order: Program area, degree type (T if terminal Master's), number awarded 7/03–6/04. School Psychology Other 4, Counseling Psychology MA/MS (Master of Arts/Science) (T) 0.

Student Applications/Admissions:

Student Applications

School Psychology Other—Applications 2004–2005, 14. Total applicants accepted 2004–2005, 14. Openings 2005–2006, 10. The Median number of years required for completion of a degree are 3. The number of students enrolled full and part-time who were dismissed or voluntarily withdrew from this program area were 0. *Counseling Psychology MA/MS (Master of Arts/Science)*—Applications 2004–2005, 20. Total applicants accepted 2004–2005, 17. Total enrolled 2004–2005 full-time, 40, part-time, 20. Openings 2005–2006, 20. The Median number of years required for completion of a degree are 3. The number of students enrolled full and part-time who were dismissed or voluntarily withdrew from this program area were 7.

Admissions Requirements:

Scores: Entries appear in this order: required test or GPA, minimum score (if required), median score of students entering in 2003–2004. Master's Programs: GRE-V 400; GRE-Q 400; overall undergraduate GPA 2.75. These requirements are for the psychology specialist degree. Those not meeting these requirements may be admitted on a provisional basis.

Other Criteria: (importance of criteria rated low, medium, or high): GRE/MAT scores medium, clinically related public service low, GPA medium, letters of recommendation high, interview medium, statement of goals and objectives high.

Student Characteristics: The following represents characteristics of students in 2004–2005 in all graduate psychology programs in the department: Female–full-time 61, part-time 18; Male–full-time 20, part-time 2; African American/Black–full-time 4, part-time 3; Hispanic/Latino(a)–full-time 1, part-time 2; Asian/Pacific Islander–full-time 0, part-time 1; American Indian/Alaska Native–full-time 0, part-time 0; Caucasian–full-time 73, part-time 13; Multi-ethnic–full-time 3, part-time 0; students subject to the Americans With Disabilities Act–full-time 2, part-time 0.

Financial Information/Assistance:

Tuition for Full-Time Study: *Master's:* State residents: per academic year $1,511, $185 per credit hour; Nonstate residents: per academic year $3,991, $410 per credit hour. See the following Web site for updates and changes in tuition costs: www.lsus.edu.

Financial Assistance:

First Year Students: Research assistantships available for first-year. Average amount paid per academic year: $750. Average number of hours worked per week: 10. Apply by August 1. Tuition remission given: partial.

Advanced Students: Teaching assistantships available for advanced students. Average amount paid per academic year: $1,500. Average number of hours worked per week: 20. Apply by August 1.

Contact Information: Of all students currently enrolled full-time, 15% benefitted from one or more of the listed financial assistance programs.

Internships/Practica: Practica for our Specialist degree students are carried out in surrounding parishes which have cooperative agreements with the university for training purposes. There are two distinct practica experiences for our students. The first involves an observational practica required during the Introduction to School Psychology course. The second occurs during Psych 754- a formal 200 plus hour practica that is carried out in cooperating training parishes with supervisory field school psychologists. Internships are available within the state or students may pursue internships in other states.

Housing and Day Care: On-campus housing is available. LSUS provides housing through University Court apartments. No on-campus day care facilities are available.

Employment of Department Graduates:

Master's Degree Graduates: Of those who graduated in the academic year 2003–2004, the following categories and numbers represent the post-graduate activities and employment of master's degree graduates: Enrolled in a psychology doctoral program (1), enrolled in another graduate/professional program (0), enrolled in a post-doctoral residency/fellowship (n/a), employed in independent practice (n/a), employed in an academic position at a university (0), employed in an academic position at a 2-year/4-year college (0), employed in other positions at a higher education institution (0), employed in a professional position in a school system (0), employed in business or industry (research/consulting) (0), employed in business or industry (management) (0), employed in a government agency (research) (0), employed in a government agency (professional services) (0), employed in a

community mental health/counseling center (0), employed in a hospital/medical center (0), still seeking employment (0), other employment position (0), total from the above (master's) (1).

Doctoral Degree Graduates: Of those who graduated in the academic year 2003–2004, the following categories and numbers represent the post-graduate activities and employment of doctoral degree graduates: Enrolled in a psychology doctoral program (n/a), total from the above (doctoral) (0).

Additional Information:

Orientation, Objectives, and Emphasis of Department: The curriculum model upon which the program rests is based on the National Association of School Psychologists Training Standards outlined in School Psychology: A Blueprint for Training and Practice II. The model to which the program adheres is the data-based decision maker. It is important for school psychologists to establish accountability within the system by providing data that demonstrate their effectiveness. The School Psychology Training committee advocates a practitioner approach to fulfilling this goal. As a result, students are required to participate in two practica in the school system as well as a minimum 1200 hour internship.

Special Facilities or Resources: The master's in Counseling Psychology in conjunction with the Specialist in School Psychology have state of the art audio/video equipment for counseling techniques and skills/play therapy, all housed in a psychology clinic on campus.

Information for Students With Physical Disabilities: See the following Web site for more information: www.lsus.edu.

Application Information:
Send to: Merikay M. Ringer, Psychology Department, Lousiana State University Shreveport, One University Place, Shreveport, LA 71115. Students are admitted in the Fall, application deadline June 1; Spring, application deadline November 1; Summer, application deadline April 1. *Fee:* $15.

Louisiana Tech University
Department of Psychology and Behavioral Sciences
Box 10048, T.S.
Ruston, LA 71272
Telephone: (318) 257-4315
Fax: (318) 257-3442
E-mail: *psychology@latech.edu*
Web: *http://www.latech.edu*

Department Information:
1972. Department Head: Tony R. Young, PhD. Number of Faculty: total–full-time 17, part-time 1; women–full-time 4; minority–part-time 1.

Programs and Degrees Offered:
Listed in the following order: Program area, degree type (T if terminal Master's), number awarded 7/03–6/04. Counseling and Guidance MA/MS (Master of Arts/Science) (T), Counseling Psychology PhD (Doctor of Philosophy) 5, Educational Psychology

MA/MS (Master of Arts/Science) (T), Industrial/ Organizational MA/MS (Master of Arts/Science) (T) 60.

APA Accreditation: Counseling PhD (Doctor of Philosophy).

Student Applications/Admissions:

Student Applications

Counseling and Guidance MA/MS (Master of Arts/Science)—The Median number of years required for completion of a degree are 2. *Counseling Psychology PhD (Doctor of Philosophy)*—Applications 2004–2005, 27. Total applicants accepted 2004–2005, 7. Openings 2005–2006, 7. The Median number of years required for completion of a degree are 6. The number of students enrolled full and part-time who were dismissed or voluntarily withdrew from this program area were 0. *Educational Psychology MA/MS (Master of Arts/Science)*—The Median number of years required for completion of a degree are 2. *Industrial/ Organizational MA/MS (Master of Arts/Science)*—Applications 2004–2005, 65. Total applicants accepted 2004–2005, 62. Total enrolled 2004–2005 full-time, 120. Openings 2005–2006, 60. The Median number of years required for completion of a degree is 1.2. The number of students enrolled full and part-time who were dismissed or voluntarily withdrew from this program area were 5.

Admissions Requirements:

Scores: Entries appear in this order: required test or GPA, minimum score (if required), median score of students entering in 2003–2004. Master's Programs: GRE-V no minimum stated; GRE-Q no minimum stated; GRE-V+Q no minimum stated; overall undergraduate GPA no minimum stated; last 2 years GPA no minimum stated; psychology GPA no minimum stated. Admission requires a total score of at least 1200 for probationary admission or 1300 for full admission from the following equation: 200 x UGPA + VGRE + QGRE =1300. Doctoral Programs: GRE-V no minimum stated, 550; GRE-Q no minimum stated, 610; GRE-V+Q 1000, 1160; overall undergraduate GPA no minimum stated, 3.50. Comment: Minimal composite GRE (V + Q) score for admission consideration is normally 1000.

Other Criteria: (importance of criteria rated low, medium, or high): GRE/MAT scores high, research experience high, work experience medium, extracurricular activity low, clinically related public service medium, GPA high, letters of recommendation high, interview high, statement of goals and objectives medium. These criteria apply to the PhD program.

Student Characteristics: The following represents characteristics of students in 2004–2005 in all graduate psychology programs in the department: Female–full-time 90, part-time 1; Male–full-time 56, part-time 0; African American/Black–full-time 40, part-time 0; Hispanic/Latino(a)–full-time 3, part-time 0; Asian/Pacific Islander–full-time 0, part-time 0; American Indian/Alaska Native–full-time 0, part-time 0; Caucasian–full-time 103, part-time 0.

Financial Information/Assistance:

Financial Assistance:

First Year Students: Research assistantships available for first-year. Average amount paid per academic year: $10,000. Average number of hours worked per week: 20.

Advanced Students: Teaching assistantships available for advanced students. Average amount paid per academic year: $10,000. Average number of hours worked per week: 20. Research assistantships available for advanced students. Average amount paid per academic year: $10,000. Average number of hours worked per week: 20.

Contact Information: Of all students currently enrolled full-time, 20% benefitted from one or more of the listed financial assistance programs.

Internships/Practica: PhD counseling psychology students must complete a year-long internship. Practica are available throughout the region for PhD and MA students in their respective areas. For those doctoral students for whom a professional internship is required prior to graduation, 3 applied in 2003–2004. Of those who applied, 3 were placed in internships listed by the Association of Psychology Postdoctoral and Internship Programs (APPIC); 3 were placed in APA accredited internships.

Housing and Day Care: On-campus housing is available. Housing Office (318) 257-4917. On-campus day care facilities are available.

Employment of Department Graduates:

Master's Degree Graduates: Of those who graduated in the academic year 2003–2004, the following categories and numbers represent the post-graduate activities and employment of master's degree graduates: Enrolled in a post-doctoral residency/fellowship (n/a), employed in independent practice (n/a), total from the above (master's) (0).

Doctoral Degree Graduates: Of those who graduated in the academic year 2003–2004, the following categories and numbers represent the post-graduate activities and employment of doctoral degree graduates: Enrolled in a psychology doctoral program (n/a), enrolled in another graduate/professional program (0), employed in an academic position at a university (2), employed in a government agency (professional services) (1), employed in a hospital/ medical center (1), other employment position (1), total from the above (doctoral) (5).

Additional Information:

Orientation, Objectives, and Emphasis of Department: The Department of Psychology and Behavioral Sciences offers master's degree programs in counseling and guidance, educational psychology, and industrial/organizational psychology, in addition to the PhD in counseling psychology. The department features excellent faculty who strive to provide an eclectic and integrated approach to theory, research, and practice. The scientist-practitioner model provides the framework for most graduate programs. Successful degree candidates are provided knowledge and skills necessary for appropriate level positions in their respective fields in settings such as education, business, mental health, and government. The counseling psychology PhD explores assessment, career/vocational, and psychotherapy and is accredited by the American Psychological Association.

Application Information:

Send to: Department Chair, Department of Psychology and Behavioral Sciences. Applications to the Doctoral Program should be sent to the Director of Training. Students are admitted in the Fall, application deadline September 1; Winter, application deadline November 30; Spring, application deadline March 2; Summer, application deadline May 31. PhD: full admissions in the Fall only, deadline December 15. *Fee:* $20.

Louisiana, University of, Lafayette

Department of Psychology
P.O. Box 43131 UL-Lafayette Station
Lafayette, LA 70504-3131
Telephone: (337) 482-6597
Fax: (337) 482-6587
E-mail: *psychology@louisiana.edu*
Web: *http://www.louisiana.edu/Academic/LiberalArts/PSYC*

Department Information:
1970. Department Head: Theresa A. Wozencraft. Number of Faculty: total–full-time 13, part-time 5; women–full-time 4, part-time 6; minority–full-time 1, part-time 1.

Programs and Degrees Offered:
Listed in the following order: Program area, degree type (T if terminal Master's), number awarded 7/03–6/04. Experimental, applied MA/MS (Master of Arts/Science) (T) 7, counselor education MA/MS (Master of Arts/Science) (T) 12.

Student Applications/Admissions:

Student Applications
Experimental, applied MA/MS (Master of Arts/Science)—Applications 2004–2005, 23. Total applicants accepted 2004–2005, 10. Number enrolled (new admits only) 2004–2005 full-time, 9. Number enrolled (new admits only) 2004–2005 part-time, 1. Total enrolled 2004–2005 full-time, 16, part-time, 12. Openings 2005–2006, 12. The Median number of years required for completion of a degree are 2. The number of students enrolled full and part-time who were dismissed or voluntarily withdrew from this program area were 1. *Counselor education MA/MS (Master of Arts/Science)*—Applications 2004–2005, 45. Total applicants accepted 2004–2005, 36. Number enrolled (new admits only) 2004–2005 full-time, 10. Number enrolled (new admits only) 2004–2005 part-time, 26. Total enrolled 2004–2005 full-time, 18, part-time, 35. Openings 2005–2006, 30. The Median number of years required for completion of a degree are 2. The number of students enrolled full and part-time who were dismissed or voluntarily withdrew from this program area were 0.

Admissions Requirements:
Scores: Entries appear in this order: required test or GPA, minimum score (if required), median score of students entering in 2003–2004. Master's Programs: GRE-V+Q 1000, 1073; last 2 years GPA 3.0. Exceptions to the minimum scores will be considered on a case-by-case basis if there is high strength/promise through another indicator. Also, scores in the right-hand column are for the Fall 2004 entering class.
Other Criteria: (importance of criteria rated low, medium, or high): GRE/MAT scores medium, research experience medium, work experience medium, extracurricular activity low, clinically related public service medium, GPA medium, letters of recommendation high, statement of goals and objectives medium.

Student Characteristics: The following represents characteristics of students in 2004–2005 in all graduate psychology programs in the department: Female–full-time 11, part-time 6; Male–full-time 5, part-time 6; African American/Black–full-time 1, part-time 0; Hispanic/Latino(a)–full-time 0, part-time 0; Asian/Pacific Islander–full-time 0, part-time 1; American Indian/Alaska Native–full-time 0, part-time 0; Caucasian–full-time 13, part-time 11; Multi-ethnic–full-time 2, part-time 0; students subject to the Americans With Disabilities Act–full-time 0, part-time 0.

Financial Information/Assistance:
Tuition for Full-Time Study: *Master's:* State residents: per academic year $1,602; Nonstate residents: per academic year $4,692. Tuition is subject to change. See the following Web site for updates and changes in tuition costs: http://bursar.louisiana.edu/schedule-spring.shtml#graduate.

Financial Assistance:
First Year Students: Teaching assistantships available for first-year. Average amount paid per academic year: $5,500. Average number of hours worked per week: 15. Apply by April 12. Tuition remission given: full.
Advanced Students: Teaching assistantships available for advanced students. Average amount paid per academic year: $5,500. Average number of hours worked per week: 15. Apply by April 12. Tuition remission given: full.
Contact Information: Of all students currently enrolled full-time, 30% benefitted from one or more of the listed financial assistance programs. Application and information available online at: http://gradschool.louisiana.edu/.

Internships/Practica: Internships for master's students in the applied option are available at the Community Mental Health Center, local psychiatric and rehabilitation hospitals and facilities, private agencies and practices, and at the University Counseling and Testing Center.

Housing and Day Care: On-campus housing is available. See the following Web site for more information: http://www.louisiana.edu/Student/Housing/. On-campus day care facilities are available. See the following Web site for more information: http://www.louisiana.edu/Student/ChildDev/.

Employment of Department Graduates:
Master's Degree Graduates: Of those who graduated in the academic year 2003–2004, the following categories and numbers represent the post-graduate activities and employment of master's degree graduates: Enrolled in a psychology doctoral program (3), enrolled in a post-doctoral residency/fellowship (n/a), employed in independent practice (n/a), employed in an academic position at a university (2), employed in business or industry (management) (1), do not know (1), total from the above (master's) (7).
Doctoral Degree Graduates: Of those who graduated in the academic year 2003–2004, the following categories and numbers represent the post-graduate activities and employment of doctoral degree graduates: Enrolled in a psychology doctoral program (n/a), total from the above (doctoral) (0).

Additional Information:
Orientation, Objectives, and Emphasis of Department: The Department of Psychology at the University of Louisiana at Lafayette strives to promote the study of psychology as a science, as a profession, and as a means of promoting human welfare. A master's program is offered with options in general experimental or applied psychology. After obtaining their degree, general experimental students pursue the doctorate at other universities. Qualified stu-

dents also have the option of applying to the university's doctoral program in Cognitive Science. Applied program students have found employment in the locality working for private and public agencies.

Special Facilities or Resources: The Psychology Department houses a computer laboratory for cognitive and social research. Computer assisted instruction is available for several courses. Major physiological research is conducted at the nearby primate center, The New Iberia Research Center. An additional smaller physiological laboratory is housed in the Psychology Department. The University of Louisiana at Lafayette has excellent computer facilities. Many members of the department are also affiliated with the university's Institute for Cognitive Science, providing additional opportunities for research. There is also the possibility that students may be simultaneously enrolled in the Psychology MS program and the Cognitive Science PhD program.

Information for Students With Physical Disabilities: See the following Web site for more information: http://disability.louisiana.edu/.

Application Information:
Send to: Graduate School Director, Martin Hall, University of Louisiana, Lafayette, LA 70504. Application available online. URL of online application: http://gradschool.louisiana.edu/. Students are admitted in the Fall, application deadline 30 days; Spring, application deadline 30 days; Summer, application deadline 30 days. Fellowships have a deadline of February 15; applicants seeking an assistantship ought to have all materials in by the start of April (for the Fall semester). *Fee:* $20. U.S. students' applications are due 30 days prior to start of semester. For international students, the fee is $30, and the deadline is 90 days prior to the semester.

Louisiana, University of, Monroe
Department of Psychology
700 University Avenue
Monroe, LA 71209
Telephone: (318) 342-1330
Fax: (318) 342-1352
E-mail: williamson@ulm.edu

Department Information:
1965. Head: David Williamson. Number of Faculty: total–full-time 12, part-time 7; women–full-time 4, part-time 6; minority–full-time 1, part-time 1.

Programs and Degrees Offered:
Listed in the following order: Program area, degree type (T if terminal Master's), number awarded 7/03–6/04. Specialist in School Psychology EdS (Education Specialist) 3, General MA/MS (Master of Arts/Science) (T) 12.

Student Applications/Admissions:
Student Applications
Specialist in School Psychology EdS (Education Specialist)—Applications 2004–2005, 9. Total applicants accepted 2004–2005, 7. Number enrolled (new admits only) 2004–2005 full-time,

5. Total enrolled 2004–2005 full-time, 16. Openings 2005–2006, 15. The Median number of years required for completion of a degree are 2. The number of students enrolled full and part-time who were dismissed or voluntarily withdrew from this program area were 0. *General MA/MS (Master of Arts/Science)*—Applications 2004–2005, 16. Total applicants accepted 2004–2005, 12. Number enrolled (new admits only) 2004–2005 full-time, 12. Total enrolled 2004–2005 full-time, 23. Openings 2005–2006, 20.

Admissions Requirements:
Scores: Entries appear in this order: required test or GPA, minimum score (if required), median score of students entering in 2003–2004. Master's Programs: GRE-V+Q 900; overall undergraduate GPA 2.75. For MS Program two of the three following are required: 900 Verbal/Quant GRE, 2.75 GPA, and 1900 when GPA *400 + GRE. For SSP Program two of the three following are required: 1000 Verbal/Quant GRE, 3.00 GPA, and 2000 on combined.
Other Criteria: (importance of criteria rated low, medium, or high): GRE/MAT scores high, research experience medium, work experience medium, extracurricular activity low, clinically related public service medium, GPA high, letters of recommendation high.

Student Characteristics: The following represents characteristics of students in 2004–2005 in all graduate psychology programs in the department: Female–full-time 30, part-time 0; Male–full-time 9, part-time 0; African American/Black–full-time 8, part-time 0; Hispanic/Latino(a)–full-time 0, part-time 0; Asian/Pacific Islander–full-time 1, part-time 0; American Indian/Alaska Native–full-time 0, part-time 0; Caucasian–full-time 0, part-time 0.

Financial Information/Assistance:
Tuition for Full-Time Study: *Master's:* State residents: per academic year $3,206; Nonstate residents: per academic year $9,165.

Financial Assistance:
First Year Students: Research assistantships available for first-year. Average amount paid per academic year: $5,000. Average number of hours worked per week: 20. Tuition remission given: full.
Advanced Students: Research assistantships available for advanced students. Average amount paid per academic year: $5,000. Tuition remission given: full.
Contact Information: Of all students currently enrolled full-time, 25% benefitted from one or more of the listed financial assistance programs.

Internships/Practica: Practica and internships are required for the psychometric concentration of the MS program. Field, practica, and internships are included as an integral part of the specialist in school psychology program.

Housing and Day Care: On-campus housing is available. See the following Web site for more information: www.ulm.edu, search - residential life. On-campus day care facilities are available. See the following Web site for more information: www.ulm.edu, search - residential life.

Employment of Department Graduates:
Master's Degree Graduates: Of those who graduated in the academic year 2003–2004, the following categories and numbers

represent the post-graduate activities and employment of master's degree graduates: Enrolled in a psychology doctoral program (1), enrolled in another graduate/professional program (3), enrolled in a post-doctoral residency/fellowship (n/a), employed in independent practice (n/a), employed in an academic position at a 2-year/4-year college (3), employed in a professional position in a school system (3), employed in a community mental health/counseling center (5), total from the above (master's) (15).

Doctoral Degree Graduates: Of those who graduated in the academic year 2003–2004, the following categories and numbers represent the post-graduate activities and employment of doctoral degree graduates: Enrolled in a psychology doctoral program (n/a), total from the above (doctoral) (0).

Additional Information:

Orientation, Objectives, and Emphasis of Department: Two areas of concentration are available in the MS program. The general-experimental option focuses upon the basic science areas of psychology. The psychometric (preclinical) option is structured for those whose primary interest is employment in mental health or related settings. The specialist in school psychology program is designed so that a MS degree is awarded upon completion of the first phase of the program. All programs require a comprehensive examination and a thesis.

Special Facilities or Resources: The department facilities include laboratories in sensation-perception and learning and motivation, as well as a small animal colony. A psychological services center includes a test library and special rooms. The department also has a computer room with 13 personal computers with printers for general student use.

Information for Students With Physical Disabilities: See the following Web site for more information: www.ulm.edu.

Application Information:

Send to: Graduate School. Students are admitted in the Fall, application deadline rolling; Winter, application deadline rolling; Spring, application deadline rolling; Summer, application deadline rolling. *Fee:* $20.

New Orleans, University of
Department of Psychology
College of Science
2001 Geology and Psychology Bldg.
New Orleans, LA 70148
Telephone: (504) 280-6291
Fax: (504) 280-6049
E-mail: *pfrick@uno.edu*
Web: *http://www.uno.edu/~psyc/*

Department Information:

1982. Chairperson: Leighton Stamps. Number of Faculty: total–full-time 16, part-time 9; women–full-time 8, part-time 3; minority–full-time 2; faculty subject to the Americans With Disabilities Act 1.

Programs and Degrees Offered:

Listed in the following order: Program area, degree type (T if terminal Master's), number awarded 7/03–6/04. Applied Biopsy-chology PhD (Doctor of Philosophy) 1, Applied Developmental Psychology PhD (Doctor of Philosophy) 3.

Student Applications/Admissions:
Student Applications

Applied Biopsychology PhD (Doctor of Philosophy)—Applications 2004–2005, 18. Total applicants accepted 2004–2005, 5. Number enrolled (new admits only) 2004–2005 full-time, 4. Openings 2005–2006, 4. The Median number of years required for completion of a degree are 5. The number of students enrolled full and part-time who were dismissed or voluntarily withdrew from this program area were 2. *Applied Developmental Psychology PhD (Doctor of Philosophy)*—Applications 2004–2005, 30. Total applicants accepted 2004–2005, 6. Number enrolled (new admits only) 2004–2005 full-time, 6. Openings 2005–2006, 5. The Median number of years required for completion of a degree are 6. The number of students enrolled full and part-time who were dismissed or voluntarily withdrew from this program area were 0.

Admissions Requirements:

Scores: Entries appear in this order: required test or GPA, minimum score (if required), median score of students entering in 2003–2004. Doctoral Programs: GRE-V no minimum stated, 535; GRE-Q no minimum stated, 630; GRE-V+Q no minimum stated, 1150; overall undergraduate GPA no minimum stated, 3.5.

Other Criteria: (importance of criteria rated low, medium, or high): GRE/MAT scores high, research experience high, work experience low, extracurricular activity low, clinically related public service medium, GPA high, letters of recommendation high, statement of goals and objectives high. For additional information on admission requirements, go to: www.uno. edu/~psyc.

Student Characteristics: The following represents characteristics of students in 2004–2005 in all graduate psychology programs in the department: Female–full-time 28, part-time 0; Male–full-time 6, part-time 0; African American/Black–full-time 4, part-time 0; Hispanic/Latino(a)–full-time 1, part-time 0; Asian/Pacific Islander–full-time 0, part-time 0; American Indian/Alaska Native–full-time 1, part-time 0; Caucasian–full-time 27, part-time 0; Multi-ethnic–full-time 1, part-time 0; students subject to the Americans With Disabilities Act–full-time 0, part-time 0.

Financial Information/Assistance:

Tuition for Full-Time Study: *Doctoral:* State residents: per academic year $3,184; Nonstate residents: per academic year $10,228. Tuition is subject to change. See the following Web site for updates and changes in tuition costs: www.uno.edu.

Financial Assistance:

First Year Students: Teaching assistantships available for first-year. Average amount paid per academic year: $11,684. Average number of hours worked per week: 20. Tuition remission given: partial. Research assistantships available for first-year. Average amount paid per academic year: $15,421. Average number of hours worked per week: 20. Tuition remission given: full. Fellowships and scholarships available for first-year. Average amount paid per academic year: $16,000. Tuition remission given: full.

Advanced Students: Teaching assistantships available for advanced students. Average amount paid per academic year:

$11,684. Average number of hours worked per week: 20. Tuition remission given: partial. Research assistantships available for advanced students. Average amount paid per academic year: $15,421. Average number of hours worked per week: 20. Tuition remission given: full. Fellowships and scholarships available for advanced students. Average amount paid per academic year: $16,000. Tuition remission given: full.

Contact Information: Of all students currently enrolled full-time, 100% benefitted from one or more of the listed financial assistance programs.

Internships/Practica: Students in both applied specialties are required to complete 12 semester hours of practicum for the doctoral degree. There are a wide array of practicum experiences available and student's choice of practicum is based on his or her specific career objectives.

Housing and Day Care: On-campus housing is available. See the following Web site for more information: www.uno.edu. On-campus day care facilities are available.

Employment of Department Graduates:

Master's Degree Graduates: Of those who graduated in the academic year 2003–2004, the following categories and numbers represent the post-graduate activities and employment of master's degree graduates: Enrolled in a post-doctoral residency/fellowship (n/a), employed in independent practice (n/a), total from the above (master's) (0).

Doctoral Degree Graduates: Of those who graduated in the academic year 2003–2004, the following categories and numbers represent the post-graduate activities and employment of doctoral degree graduates: Enrolled in a psychology doctoral program (n/a), enrolled in a post-doctoral residency/fellowship (1), employed in independent practice (2), employed in a government agency (research) (1), total from the above (doctoral) (4).

Additional Information:

Orientation, Objectives, and Emphasis of Department: The University of New Orleans, Department of Psychology offers a PhD program with specializations in applied biopsychology and applied developmental psychology. The program was established in 1980 in response to a growing need for persons who are thoroughly trained in the basic content areas of human development or biopsychology, and who are able to translate that knowledge into practical applications. Both specialties emphasize research and service delivery in applied contexts. Graduates will be able to conduct original research as well as provide consulting and services to agencies concerned with problems of human health and development. Applied biopsychologists, for example, might be involved in research and service concerning the neuropsychological evaluation and rehabilitation of stroke patients, or in the behavioral or electrophysiological testing of sensory disturbances caused by diseases like multiple sclerosis. Others might research the psychological aspects of drug addiction or hormone disturbances with anatomists, physiologists, or pharmacologists. The applied developmental program has chosen to focus its training in the area of developmental psychopathology. Graduates are trained to work in a variety of settings where they can advance programmatic research focused on understanding psychopathological conditions from a developmental perspective and where they can make practical applications from this research (e.g., design and implement innovative prevention programs, or develop assessments for at risk children).

Special Facilities or Resources: Special resources of the department include laboratory computers, computer terminal room, specialized surgical equipment, videotape equipment, psychophysiological recording equipment, and a psychology department clinic.

Application Information:
Send to: Graduate Coordinator, Department of Psychology, 2001 Geology & Psychology Bldg., New Orleans, LA 70148. Application available online. URL of online application: www.uno.edu/~psyc. Students are admitted in the Fall, application deadline February 15. *Fee:* $40.

Southeastern Louisiana University
Department of Psychology
Arts and Sciences
SLU 10831
Hammond, LA 70402
Telephone: (985) 549-2154
Fax: (985) 549-3892
E-mail: *jworthen@selu.edu*
Web: *http://www.selu.edu/Academic/Dept/Psyc*

Department Information:
Chairperson: Alvin G. Burstein. Number of Faculty: total–full-time 10, part-time 3; women–full-time 4, part-time 1; minority–full-time 1.

Programs and Degrees Offered:
Listed in the following order: Program area, degree type (T if terminal Master's), number awarded 7/03–6/04. General psychology MA/MS (Master of Arts/Science) (T) 4.

Student Applications/Admissions:
Student Applications
General psychology MA/MS (Master of Arts/Science)—Applications 2004–2005, 30. Total applicants accepted 2004–2005, 10. Number enrolled (new admits only) 2004–2005 full-time, 8. Number enrolled (new admits only) 2004–2005 part-time, 0. Total enrolled 2004–2005 full-time, 25, part-time, 5. Openings 2005–2006, 10. The Median number of years required for completion of a degree are 2. The number of students enrolled full and part-time who were dismissed or voluntarily withdrew from this program area were 1.

Admissions Requirements:
Scores: Entries appear in this order: required test or GPA, minimum score (if required), median score of students entering in 2003–2004. Master's Programs: GRE-V no minimum stated; GRE-Q no minimum stated; GRE-V+Q 950, 1050; overall undergraduate GPA 3.0, 3.5; psychology GPA 3.0, 3.5. Minimum GPA of 2.5 and Minimum GRE (V+Q) of 850 required for conditional admittance.
Other Criteria: (importance of criteria rated low, medium, or high): GRE/MAT scores high, research experience high, work experience low, extracurricular activity low, clinically related public service low, GPA high, letters of recommendation high, statement of goals and objectives medium.

343

Student Characteristics: The following represents characteristics of students in 2004–2005 in all graduate psychology programs in the department: Female–full-time 22, part-time 3; Male–full-time 3, part-time 2; African American/Black–full-time 1, part-time 1; Hispanic/Latino(a)–full-time 1, part-time 1; Asian/Pacific Islander–full-time 1, part-time 0; American Indian/Alaska Native–full-time 0, part-time 0; Caucasian–full-time 22, part-time 3; Multi-ethnic–full-time 0, part-time 0; students subject to the Americans With Disabilities Act–full-time 0, part-time 0.

Financial Information/Assistance:

Tuition for Full-Time Study: *Master's:* State residents: per academic year $2,318; Nonstate residents: per academic year $6,314. Tuition is subject to change.

Financial Assistance:

First Year Students: Research assistantships available for first-year. Average amount paid per academic year: $5,500. Average number of hours worked per week: 20. Apply by March 15. Tuition remission given: full. Fellowships and scholarships available for first-year. Average amount paid per academic year: $3,500. Average number of hours worked per week: 0. Apply by March 15. Tuition remission given: full.

Advanced Students: Research assistantships available for advanced students. Average amount paid per academic year: $5,500. Average number of hours worked per week: 20. Apply by March 15. Tuition remission given: full.

Contact Information: Of all students currently enrolled full-time, 40% benefitted from one or more of the listed financial assistance programs.

Internships/Practica: Practica are available in clinical and counseling settings.

Housing and Day Care: On-campus housing is available. See the following Web site for more information: http://www.selu.edu/ACVS/housing.html. On-campus day care facilities are available. See the following Web site for more information: http://www.selu.edu/ACVS/childcare.html.

Employment of Department Graduates:

Master's Degree Graduates: Of those who graduated in the academic year 2003–2004, the following categories and numbers represent the post-graduate activities and employment of master's degree graduates: Enrolled in a psychology doctoral program (4), enrolled in another graduate/professional program (0), enrolled in a post-doctoral residency/fellowship (n/a), employed in independent practice (n/a), employed in an academic position at a university (0), employed in an academic position at a 2-year/4-year college (0), employed in other positions at a higher education institution (0), employed in a professional position in a school system (0), employed in business or industry (research/consulting) (0), employed in business or industry (management) (0), employed in a government agency (research) (0), employed in a government agency (professional services) (0), employed in a community mental health/counseling center (0), employed in a hospital/medical center (0), still seeking employment (0), not seeking employment (0), other employment position (0), do not know (0), total from the above (master's) (4).

Doctoral Degree Graduates: Of those who graduated in the academic year 2003–2004, the following categories and numbers represent the post-graduate activities and employment of doctoral degree graduates: Enrolled in a psychology doctoral program (n/a), total from the above (doctoral) (0).

Additional Information:

Orientation, Objectives, and Emphasis of Department: The primary purpose of the MA in general psychology is to prepare the student for doctoral study. This goal is achieved by providing extensive research experience and advanced knowledge in several basic areas within psychology. In recent years, 90% of students who have successfully completed our Master's program in psychology have been placed into doctoral programs.

Special Facilities or Resources: The department has three 5-room laboratory suites for conducting research with humans. There are about 40 microcomputers and 7 printers in the department, about half of which are in a microcomputer laboratory. Statistical packages, such as SPSS, are available on the microcomputers and (via departmental terminal) on the university's mainframe computers.

Application Information:

Official transcripts, GRE scores, Application for Admission form, immunization form, and application fee should be sent to the following address: Enrollment Services, Graduate Admissions, SLU, 10752 Hammond, LA 70402-0752. Your letter of application and the letters from your three references should be sent directly to the Graduate Coordinator. In addition, send copies of everything sent to Enrollment Services (unofficial copies are acceptable). Send these to the following address: James B. Worthen, PhD, SLU, Box 10831, Hammond, LA 70402. Students are admitted in the Fall, application deadline March 15; Spring, application deadline November 15. *Fee:* $20.

Tulane University
Department of Psychology
2007 Stern Hall
New Orleans, LA 70118
Telephone: (504) 865-5331
Fax: (504) 862-8744
E-mail: *psych@tulane.edu*
Web: *http://www.tulane.edu/~psych/psychome.html*

Department Information:
1911. Chairperson: Janet B. Ruscher. Number of Faculty: total–full-time 16; women–full-time 4; minority–full-time 3.

Programs and Degrees Offered:
Listed in the following order: Program area, degree type (T if terminal Master's), number awarded 7/03–6/04. Industrial/ Organizational PhD (Doctor of Philosophy) 4, Social PhD (Doctor of Philosophy) 1, School PhD (Doctor of Philosophy) 4, Developmental PhD (Doctor of Philosophy) 0, Psychobiology PhD (Doctor of Philosophy) 1, Quantitative PhD (Doctor of Philosophy) 0, Animal Behavior PhD (Doctor of Philosophy) 0.

APA Accreditation: School PhD (Doctor of Philosophy).

Student Applications/Admissions:
Student Applications
Industrial/ Organizational PhD (Doctor of Philosophy)—Applications 2004–2005, 40. Total applicants accepted 2004–2005,

7. Openings 2005–2006, 5. The Median number of years required for completion of a degree are 5. *Social PhD (Doctor of Philosophy)*—Applications 2004–2005, 15. Total applicants accepted 2004–2005, 3. Openings 2005–2006, 2. The Median number of years required for completion of a degree are 5. The number of students enrolled full and part-time who were dismissed or voluntarily withdrew from this program area were 1. *School PhD (Doctor of Philosophy)*—Applications 2004–2005, 30. Total applicants accepted 2004–2005, 8. Openings 2005–2006, 4. The Median number of years required for completion of a degree are 5. The number of students enrolled full and part-time who were dismissed or voluntarily withdrew from this program area were 0. *Developmental PhD (Doctor of Philosophy)*—Applications 2004–2005, 7. Total applicants accepted 2004–2005, 0. Openings 2005–2006, 2. *Psychobiology PhD (Doctor of Philosophy)*—Applications 2004–2005, 12. Total applicants accepted 2004–2005, 3. Total enrolled 2004–2005 full-time, 2, part-time, 1. Openings 2005–2006, 3. The Median number of years required for completion of a degree are 4. *Quantitative PhD (Doctor of Philosophy)*—Applications 2004–2005, 2. Total applicants accepted 2004–2005, 0. Openings 2005–2006, 1. The Median number of years required for completion of a degree are 4. *Animal Behavior PhD (Doctor of Philosophy)*—Applications 2004–2005, 3. Total applicants accepted 2004–2005, 0. Openings 2005–2006, 1.

Admissions Requirements:

Scores: Entries appear in this order: required test or GPA, minimum score (if required), median score of students entering in 2003–2004. Master's Programs: GRE-V+Q 1100; GRE-Subject(Psych) no minimum stated; overall undergraduate GPA 3.2; psychology GPA 3.4. Doctoral Programs: GRE-V no minimum stated; GRE-Q no minimum stated; GRE-V+Q 1220; overall undergraduate GPA 3.5. Subject test is required for I/O and recommended for other programs.

Other Criteria: (importance of criteria rated low, medium, or high): GRE/MAT scores high, research experience high, work experience medium, extracurricular activity low, clinically related public service medium, GPA high, letters of recommendation high, interview medium, statement of goals and objectives medium, Clinical experience and interview important for school psychology. Relevant work experience can be looked upon favorably in other programs (e.g., statistical consulting; market research).

Student Characteristics: The following represents characteristics of students in 2004–2005 in all graduate psychology programs in the department: Female–full-time 30, part-time 1; Male–full-time 10, part-time 0; African American/Black–full-time 7, part-time 0; Hispanic/Latino(a)–full-time 1, part-time 0; Asian/Pacific Islander–full-time 2, part-time 0; American Indian/Alaska Native–full-time 0, part-time 0; Caucasian–full-time 30, part-time 0; students subject to the Americans With Disabilities Act–full-time 0, part-time 0.

Financial Information/Assistance:

Tuition for Full-Time Study: *Doctoral:* State residents: per academic year $29,900; Nonstate residents: per academic year $29,900. Tuition is subject to change. See the following Web site for updates and changes in tuition costs: http://www2.tulane.edu/main.cfm.

Financial Assistance:

First Year Students: Teaching assistantships available for first-year. Average amount paid per academic year: $14,250. Average number of hours worked per week: 12. Apply by February 1. Tuition remission given: full. Research assistantships available for first-year. Average amount paid per academic year: $14,250. Average number of hours worked per week: 12. Apply by February 1. Tuition remission given: full. Fellowships and scholarships available for first-year. Average amount paid per academic year: $14,250. Average number of hours worked per week: 12. Apply by February 1. Tuition remission given: full.

Advanced Students: Teaching assistantships available for advanced students. Average amount paid per academic year: $14,250. Average number of hours worked per week: 12. Tuition remission given: full. Research assistantships available for advanced students. Average amount paid per academic year: $14,250. Average number of hours worked per week: 12. Tuition remission given: full. Fellowships and scholarships available for advanced students. Average amount paid per academic year: $15,000. Tuition remission given: full.

Contact Information: Of all students currently enrolled full-time, 100% benefitted from one or more of the listed financial assistance programs. Application and information available online at: http://www.tulane.edu/~gradprog/.

Internships/Practica: Practice in Psychoeducational Assessment, School Consultation, Family-School Intervention, Cognitive-Behavioral Assessment/Intervention, Industrial/Organizational Psychology. For those doctoral students for whom a professional internship is required prior to graduation, 4 applied in 2003–2004. Of those who applied, 4 were placed in APA accredited internships.

Housing and Day Care: On-campus housing is available. See the following Web site for more information: http://www2.tulane.edu/main.cfm. On-campus day care facilities are available.

Employment of Department Graduates:

Master's Degree Graduates: Of those who graduated in the academic year 2003–2004, the following categories and numbers represent the post-graduate activities and employment of master's degree graduates: Enrolled in a psychology doctoral program (3), enrolled in a post-doctoral residency/fellowship (n/a), employed in independent practice (n/a), total from the above (master's) (3).

Doctoral Degree Graduates: Of those who graduated in the academic year 2003–2004, the following categories and numbers represent the post-graduate activities and employment of doctoral degree graduates: Enrolled in a psychology doctoral program (n/a), enrolled in a post-doctoral residency/fellowship (3), employed in an academic position at a university (2), employed in business or industry (research/consulting) (1), total from the above (doctoral) (6).

Additional Information:

Orientation, Objectives, and Emphasis of Department: Tulane's department of psychology offers the PhD in the research areas listed above, as well as in applied areas of school and industrial/organizational psychology. The department does not offer programs in clinical or counseling psychology. All students are expected to articulate an individualized plan of study by the end of the first year of training, a plan developed in consultation with an advisor and a committee of faculty members. This plan will guide students' coursework and form the basis for the preliminary examinations for the PhD. Students are required to complete empirical studies for the master's thesis and the dissertation, and are expected to carry out additional research while in training. The program in school psychology, which emphasizes normal developmental processes, will take a minimum of four years to complete, including a year's internship. The industrial/organizational program provides the student with a strong theoretical background in industrial/organizational psychology, with an emphasis on personnel psychology. Applied skills in industrial/organizational psychology are developed through a series of practicum experiences. Applicants for admission should be adequately prepared in basic principles and theories of psychology and in the commonly used quantitative and experimental techniques.

Special Facilities or Resources: The department has research laboratories and computer resources to facilitate research efforts requiring special equipment or space, including physiological, social, sensory, comparative, cognitive, and developmental psychology and human and animal learning. The Newcomb Children's Center, the Hebert facilities at Riverside for natural observation of animals, the laboratories of the Delta Primate Center, and the Audubon Zoological Gardens are available as research sites. There are also opportunities for research in the New Orleans area in organizations and industries, in public and private schools, and in hospitals and other settings serving children.

Information for Students With Physical Disabilities: See the following Web site for more information: http://www.tulane.edu/~erc/disability/index.html.

Application Information:
Send to: Dean of the Graduate School, Tulane University, New Orleans, LA 70118. Students are admitted in the Fall, application deadline January 15. *Fee:* $45.

Maine, University of
Department of Psychology
Liberal Arts and Sciences
5742 Little Hall
Orono, ME 04469-5742
Telephone: (207) 581-2030
Fax: (207) 581-6128
E-mail: *Jeff_Hecker@umit.maine.edu*
Web: *http://www.hutchinsoncenter.umaine.edu/psych*

Department Information:
1926. Chairperson: Jeffrey E. Hecker. Number of Faculty: total–full-time 17, part-time 2; women–full-time 4, part-time 1.

Programs and Degrees Offered:
Listed in the following order: Program area, degree type (T if terminal Master's), number awarded 7/03–6/04. Clinical PhD (Doctor of Philosophy) 4, Development PhD (Doctor of Philosophy) 0, General MA/MS (Master of Arts/Science) 1, Social PhD (Doctor of Philosophy) 0, Biological-Cognitive PhD (Doctor of Philosophy) 0.

APA Accreditation: Clinical PhD (Doctor of Philosophy).

Student Applications/Admissions:
Student Applications
Clinical PhD (Doctor of Philosophy)—Applications 2004–2005, 109. Total applicants accepted 2004–2005, 6. Number enrolled (new admits only) 2004–2005 full-time, 6. Openings 2005–2006, 5. The Median number of years required for completion of a degree are 6. The number of students enrolled full and part-time who were dismissed or voluntarily withdrew from this program area were 0. *Development PhD (Doctor of Philosophy)*—Applications 2004–2005, 6. Total applicants accepted 2004–2005, 0. Openings 2005–2006, 2. The number of students enrolled full and part-time, who were dismissed or voluntarily withdrew from this program area were 0. *General MA/MS (Master of Arts/Science)*—Applications 2004–2005, 5. Total applicants accepted 2004–2005, 0. Openings 2005–2006, 2. The Median number of years required for completion of a degree are 4. The number of students enrolled full and part-time who were dismissed or voluntarily withdrew from this program area were 0. *Social PhD (Doctor of Philosophy)*—Applications 2004–2005, 9. Total applicants accepted 2004–2005, 0. Openings 2005–2006, 1. The number of students enrolled full and part-time who were dismissed or voluntarily withdrew from this program area were 0. *Biological-Cognitive PhD (Doctor of Philosophy)*—Applications 2004–2005, 4. Total applicants accepted 2004–2005, 2. Total enrolled 2004–2005 full-time, 2. Openings 2005–2006, 4. The number of students enrolled full and part-time who were dismissed or voluntarily withdrew from this program area were 0.

Admissions Requirements:
Scores: Entries appear in this order: required test or GPA, minimum score (if required), median score of students entering in 2003–2004. Master's Programs: GRE-V no minimum stated, 575; GRE-Q no minimum stated, 690; GRE-Analytical no minimum stated, 625; GRE-Subject(Psych) no minimum stated, 620; overall undergraduate GPA no minimum stated, 3.48. Doctoral Programs: GRE-V no minimum stated, 565; GRE-Q no minimum stated, 627; GRE-Analytical no minimum stated, 625; GRE-Subject(Psych) no minimum stated, 638; overall undergraduate GPA no minimum stated, 3.49.
Other Criteria: (importance of criteria rated low, medium, or high): GRE/MAT scores high, research experience high, work experience low, extracurricular activity low, clinically related public service medium, GPA high, letters of recommendation high, interview high, statement of goals and objectives high.

Student Characteristics: The following represents characteristics of students in 2004–2005 in all graduate psychology programs in the department: Female–full-time 24, part-time 0; Male–full-time 8, part-time 0; African American/Black–full-time 0, part-time 0; Hispanic/Latino(a)–full-time 0, part-time 0; Asian/Pacific Islander–full-time 1, part-time 0; American Indian/Alaska Native–full-time 1, part-time 0; Caucasian–full-time 29, part-time 0; Multi-ethnic–full-time 1, part-time 0; students subject to the Americans With Disabilities Act–full-time 2, part-time 0.

Financial Information/Assistance:
Tuition for Full-Time Study: *Master's:* State residents: $218 per credit hour; Nonstate residents: $623 per credit hour. *Doctoral:* State residents: $218 per credit hour; Nonstate residents: $623 per credit hour. Tuition is subject to change.

Financial Assistance:
First Year Students: Teaching assistantships available for first-year. Average number of hours worked per week: 12. Apply by No deadline. Tuition remission given: full. Research assistantships available for first-year. Average number of hours worked per week: 20. Apply by No deadline. Tuition remission given: full.
Advanced Students: Teaching assistantships available for advanced students. Average number of hours worked per week: 12. Apply by No deadline. Tuition remission given: full. Research assistantships available for advanced students. Average number of hours worked per week: 12. Apply by No deadline. Tuition remission given: full. Traineeships available for advanced students. Average number of hours worked per week: 12. Apply by No deadline. Tuition remission given: full. Fellowships and scholarships available for advanced students. Average number of hours worked per week: 0. Apply by No deadline. Tuition remission given: full.
Contact Information: Of all students currently enrolled full-time, 100% benefitted from one or more of the listed financial assistance programs.

Internships/Practica: Several settings are used for practicum training: The Psychological Services Center housed within the department, Penobscot Job Corps, Kennebec Valley Mental Health Center, Penqis CAPS Head Start, School Administrative District #4, #68, KidsPeace New England. For those doctoral students for whom a professional internship is required prior to graduation, 5 applied in 2003–2004. Of those who applied, 5 were placed in internships listed by the Association of Psychology Postdoctoral and Internship Programs (APPIC); 5 were placed in APA accredited internships.

Housing and Day Care: On-campus housing is available. On-campus day care facilities are available.

Employment of Department Graduates:

Master's Degree Graduates: Of those who graduated in the academic year 2003–2004, the following categories and numbers represent the post-graduate activities and employment of master's degree graduates: Enrolled in a post-doctoral residency/fellowship (n/a), employed in independent practice (n/a), total from the above (master's) (0).

Doctoral Degree Graduates: Of those who graduated in the academic year 2003–2004, the following categories and numbers represent the post-graduate activities and employment of doctoral degree graduates: Enrolled in a psychology doctoral program (n/a), enrolled in a post-doctoral residency/fellowship (4), do not know (1), total from the above (doctoral) (5).

Additional Information:

Orientation, Objectives, and Emphasis of Department: The department believes that the best graduate education involves close working relationships between the faculty and the student. Thus, a high faculty-to-student ratio and small class sizes characterize the department. In addition, incoming students are selected to work with a faculty research mentor. There are also opportunities for individualized study and experience in directed readings, research, and teaching. A faculty committee, selected to represent the student's interests, will assist the student in planning an appropriate graduate program.

Special Facilities or Resources: Psychophysiological, perception, EEG laboratories; animal research laboratory; on-site practicum training center; department-run preschool.

Information for Students With Physical Disabilities: See the following Web site for more information: www.ume.maine.edu/onward/disable.htm.

Application Information:
Send to: Graduate School, 5782 Winslow Hall, University of Maine, Orono, ME 04469-5782. Application available online. Students are admitted in the Spring, application deadline December 31. *Fee:* $50.

Baltimore, University of
Division of Applied Behavioral Sciences
Yale Gordon College of Liberal Arts
1420 North Charles Street
Baltimore, MD 21201-5779
Telephone: (410) 837-5310
Fax: (410) 837-4059
E-mail: *tmitchell@ubalt.edu*
Web: *http://www.ubalt.edu/dapqm*

Department Information:
1970. Graduate Program Director: Tom Mitchell, PhD Number of Faculty: total–full-time 7, part-time 2; women–full-time 3; minority–part-time 1.

Programs and Degrees Offered:
Listed in the following order: Program area, degree type (T if terminal Master's), number awarded 7/03–6/04. Psychological Applications MA/MS (Master of Arts/Science) (T) 2, Counseling MA/MS (Master of Arts/Science) (T) 14, Industrial/Organizational MA/MS (Master of Arts/Science) (T) 22.

Student Applications/Admissions:
Student Applications

Psychological Applications MA/MS (Master of Arts/Science)—Applications 2004–2005, 20. Total applicants accepted 2004–2005, 15. Number enrolled (new admits only) 2004–2005 full-time, 3. Number enrolled (new admits only) 2004–2005 part-time, 8. Total enrolled 2004–2005 full-time, 8, part-time, 10. Openings 2005–2006, 10. The Median number of years required for completion of a degree are 3.5. The number of students enrolled full and part-time who were dismissed or voluntarily withdrew from this program area were 0. *Counseling MA/MS (Master of Arts/Science)*—Applications 2004–2005, 43. Total applicants accepted 2004–2005, 30. Number enrolled (new admits only) 2004–2005 full-time, 10. Number enrolled (new admits only) 2004–2005 part-time, 35. Total enrolled 2004–2005 full-time, 12, part-time, 35. Openings 2005–2006, 25. The Median number of years required for completion of a degree are 4. The number of students enrolled full and part-time who were dismissed or voluntarily withdrew from this program area were 0. *Industrial/Organizational MA/MS (Master of Arts/Science)*—Applications 2004–2005, 68. Total applicants accepted 2004–2005, 54. Number enrolled (new admits only) 2004–2005 full-time, 13. Number enrolled (new admits only) 2004–2005 part-time, 22. Total enrolled 2004–2005 full-time, 20, part-time, 31. Openings 2005–2006, 24. The Median number of years required for completion of a degree are 3.5. The number of students enrolled full and part-time who were dismissed or voluntarily withdrew from this program area were 1.

Admissions Requirements:
Scores: Entries appear in this order: required test or GPA, minimum score (if required), median score of students entering in 2003–2004. Master's Programs: GRE-V no minimum stated, 460; GRE-Q no minimum stated, 550; GRE-Analytical no minimum stated; overall undergraduate GPA 3.0, 3.43.
Other Criteria: (importance of criteria rated low, medium, or high): GRE/MAT scores medium, GPA high, letters of recommendation low, statement of goals and objectives low.

Student Characteristics: The following represents characteristics of students in 2004–2005 in all graduate psychology programs in the department: Female–full-time 22, part-time 50; Male–full-time 9, part-time 20; African American/Black–full-time 6, part-time 25; Hispanic/Latino(a)–full-time 2, part-time 2; Asian/Pacific Islander–full-time 2, part-time 1; American Indian/Alaska Native–full-time 0, part-time 0; Caucasian–full-time 20, part-time 53; Multi-ethnic–full-time 0, part-time 0; students subject to the Americans With Disabilities Act–full-time 3, part-time 6.

Financial Information/Assistance:
Tuition for Full-Time Study: *Master's:* State residents: per academic year $9,181, $510 per credit hour; Nonstate residents: per academic year $13,537, $752 per credit hour. Tuition is subject to change.

Financial Assistance:
First Year Students: Research assistantships available for first-year. Average amount paid per academic year: $1,250. Average number of hours worked per week: 20. Apply by March 1. Tuition remission given: full.
Advanced Students: Research assistantships available for advanced students. Average amount paid per academic year: $1,250. Average number of hours worked per week: 10. Apply by March 1. Tuition remission given: full.
Contact Information: Of all students currently enrolled full-time, 12% benefitted from one or more of the listed financial assistance programs.

Internships/Practica: The Baltimore/Washington Metropolitan area provides a wide range of settings for paid practicum and internships. The academic and site supervisors work closely with the intern to insure a quality experience.

Housing and Day Care: No on-campus housing is available. No on-campus day care facilities are available.

Employment of Department Graduates:
Master's Degree Graduates: Of those who graduated in the academic year 2003–2004, the following categories and numbers represent the post-graduate activities and employment of master's degree graduates: Enrolled in a post-doctoral residency/fellowship (n/a), employed in independent practice (n/a), total from the above (master's) (0).
Doctoral Degree Graduates: Of those who graduated in the academic year 2003–2004, the following categories and numbers represent the post-graduate activities and employment of doctoral degree graduates: Enrolled in a psychology doctoral program (n/a), total from the above (doctoral) (0).

Additional Information:
Orientation, Objectives, and Emphasis of Department: The Division of Applied Behavioral Sciences has a practitioner oriented

faculty of applied psychologists and researchers. For more information visit www.ubalt.edu/dapqm on the Web.

Special Facilities or Resources: We are developing an Organizational Assessment and Development Laboratory to house current and future grants/contracts. Four different university labs and over 90% of our classrooms provide Internet access, MS Office, and SPSS for students and faculty members.

Application Information:

Send to: Office of Graduate Admissions, University of Baltimore, 1420 N. Charles Street, Baltimore, MD 21201-5779. Students are admitted in the Fall, application deadline July 1; Spring, application deadline December 1. *Fee:* $45 paper application; $30 online.

Frostburg State University
MS in Counseling Psychology Program
College of Liberal Arts and Sciences
Department of Psychology, 101 Braddock Road
Frostburg, MD 21532
Telephone: (301) 687-4446
Fax: (301) 687-7418
E-mail: *abristow@frostburg.edu*
Web: *http://www.frostburg.edu/dept/psyc/graduate/coupsy.htm*

Department Information:

1977. Ann R. Bristow, Graduate Program Coordinator: Kevin Peterson, Chair. Number of Faculty: total–full-time 10, part-time 1; women–full-time 6, part-time 1; minority–full-time 1.

Programs and Degrees Offered:

Listed in the following order: Program area, degree type (T if terminal Master's), number awarded 7/03–6/04. Counseling MA/MS (Master of Arts/Science) (T) 10.

Student Applications/Admissions:

Student Applications

Counseling MA/MS (Master of Arts/Science)—Applications 2004–2005, 45. Total applicants accepted 2004–2005, 20. Number enrolled (new admits only) 2004–2005 full-time, 7. Number enrolled (new admits only) 2004–2005 part-time, 4. Total enrolled 2004–2005 full-time, 34, part-time, 11. Openings 2005–2006, 14. The Median number of years required for completion of a degree are 3. The number of students enrolled full and part-time who were dismissed or voluntarily withdrew from this program area were 2.

Admissions Requirements:

Scores: Entries appear in this order: required test or GPA, minimum score (if required), median score of students entering in 2003–2004. Master's Programs: overall undergraduate GPA 3.0. Minimum score on GRE (V + Q = 1000) or MAT (50) required only if the GPA is less than 3.0. Otherwise, scores do not need to be submitted.

Other Criteria: (importance of criteria rated low, medium, or high): GRE/MAT scores low, research experience low, work experience high, extracurricular activity low, clinically related public service high, GPA high, letters of recommendation high, interview high, statement of goals and objectives high, undergraduate internship high.

Student Characteristics: The following represents characteristics of students in 2004–2005 in all graduate psychology programs in the department: Female–full-time 28, part-time 9; Male–full-time 6, part-time 2; African American/Black–full-time 2, part-time 1; Hispanic/Latino(a)–full-time 0, part-time 1; Asian/Pacific Islander–full-time 0, part-time 0; American Indian/Alaska Native–full-time 0, part-time 0; Caucasian–full-time 32, part-time 9; Multi-ethnic–full-time 0, part-time 0; students subject to the Americans With Disabilities Act–full-time 1, part-time 0.

Financial Information/Assistance:

Tuition for Full-Time Study: *Master's:* State residents: $280 per credit hour; Nonstate residents: $321 per credit hour. Tuition is subject to change. See the following Web site for updates and changes in tuition costs: http://www.frostburg.edu/admin/billing/.

Financial Assistance:

First Year Students: Teaching assistantships available for first-year. Average amount paid per academic year: $5,000. Average number of hours worked per week: 20. Apply by March 15. Tuition remission given: full. Research assistantships available for first-year. Average amount paid per academic year: $5,000. Average number of hours worked per week: 20. Apply by March 15. Tuition remission given: full.

Advanced Students: No information provided.

Contact Information: Of all students currently enrolled full-time, 39% benefitted from one or more of the listed financial assistance programs. Application and information available online at: http://www.frostburg.edu/grad/pdf/ga_booklet.pdf.

Internships/Practica: An extensive, two semester internship experience is required which facilitates students' receptivity to supervisory feedback, enhances self-awareness, and provides a setting in which the transition from student to professional is accomplished. In addition to on-site supervision, students participate in individual and group supervision with FSU faculty. Past graduate internship sites for the MS Counseling Psychology program have included: outpatient community mental health (the most frequent internship setting); college counseling; inpatient psychiatric; inpatient and outpatient addictions; family services; K–12 psychological assessment and alternative classroom and after school care programs; community health advocacy and counseling; criminal justice system; nursing homes; hospital-based crisis services; hospice; domestic violence programs. Students construct their internship experiences in order to meet training goals they formulate. Students electing to complete graduate certificate programs in Addictions Counseling Psychology and Child and Family Counseling Psychology must complete at least one of their two semesters of internship providing services in settings consistent with the certificate program's focus. Internship experiences, in addition to at least four academic semesters of study, prepare graduates for positions as mental health counselors, marriage and family counselors, crisis counselors, drug and alcohol counselors, community health specialists, and in supervisory positions in a variety of settings.

Housing and Day Care: On-campus housing is available. See the following Web site for more information: http://www.frostburg.edu/clife/reslife.htm. On-campus day care facilities are available.

See the following Web site for more information: http://www.frostburg.edu/about/vt/children.htm.

Employment of Department Graduates:

Master's Degree Graduates: Of those who graduated in the academic year 2003–2004, the following categories and numbers represent the post-graduate activities and employment of master's degree graduates: Enrolled in a psychology doctoral program (0), enrolled in another graduate/professional program (0), enrolled in a post-doctoral residency/fellowship (n/a), employed in independent practice (n/a), employed in an academic position at a university (0), employed in an academic position at a 2-year/4-year college (0), employed in other positions at a higher education institution (1), employed in a professional position in a school system (0), employed in business or industry (research/consulting) (0), employed in business or industry (management) (0), employed in a government agency (research) (0), employed in a government agency (professional services) (0), employed in a community mental health/counseling center (8), employed in a hospital/medical center (1), still seeking employment (0), total from the above (master's) (10).

Doctoral Degree Graduates: Of those who graduated in the academic year 2003–2004, the following categories and numbers represent the post-graduate activities and employment of doctoral degree graduates: Enrolled in a psychology doctoral program (n/a), total from the above (doctoral) (0).

Additional Information:

Orientation, Objectives, and Emphasis of Department: Providing training in professional psychology at the Master's level, FSU's program is designed for those pursuing further study in science-based counseling psychology. Our theoretical perspective is integrative, including cognitive-behavioral, family systems, developmental, feminist, multicultural, humanistic, and brief therapies. We emphasize training in empirically-supported treatments for children, adolescents, families and adults. Students develop counseling skills through learning about self, client, counselor-client relationships, and the importance of cultural contexts. Considerable attention is given not only to development of professional skills but also to personal development and multicultural awareness. These emphases reflect our belief that an effective counselor is one who is self-aware and receptive to consultation. For continuing study at the doctoral level, experience and knowledge gained in this program provide a firm foundation. Optional research opportunities prepare students for advanced graduate study in psychology. The Center for Children and Families offers unique research, educational and service experiences. Two certificate programs provide specialized training in Addictions Counseling Psychology and Child and Family Counseling Psychology. These can be completed within the three-year program of study, as well as courses required for licensure. All National Counselor Exam course areas are offered, and FSU offers this exam. The Master's in Psychology Accreditation Council accredits this program.

Special Facilities or Resources: Resources include specially designed counseling practice rooms for individual and group counseling. Two-way mirrors with adjacent observation rooms are available for supervision. Audiotaping and videotaping resources are available for faculty and student use. There is a separate library and reading room available, as well as a number of audio, video, and film media demonstrating various counseling techniques or explaining theory. The program's library includes a variety of journals and books for reference, including microfiche of various articles. The faculty have made several of their personal library book holdings available on loan to the graduate students in our program library. In addition, students' audiotapes, videotapes, and case conceptualization write-ups; all previous internship papers; and several thousand journal abstracts are available for restricted use by students.

Information for Students With Physical Disabilities: See the following Web site for more information: http://www.frostburg.edu/clife/studev.htm.

Application Information:
Send to: Ms. Patty Spiker, Director, Office of Graduate Services, Frostburg State University, Frostburg, MD 21532. Application available online. URL of online application: http://www.acaff.usmh.usmd.edu/gradapp/index.html. Students are admitted in the Fall, application deadline February 1; Programs have rolling admissions. March 15 for Graduate Assistantship applications. *Fee:* $30.

Johns Hopkins University
Department of Psychological and Brain Sciences
3400 North Charles Street
Baltimore, MD 21218
Telephone: (410) 516-6175
Fax: (410) 516-4478
E-mail: *rseitz@jhu.edu*
Web: *http://psy.jhu.edu*

Department Information:

1881. Chairperson: Dr. Michela Gallagher. Number of Faculty: total full-time 13, part-time 11; women–full-time 4, part-time 2; faculty subject to the Americans With Disabilities Act 1.

Programs and Degrees Offered:

Listed in the following order: Program area, degree type (T if terminal Master's), number awarded 7/03–6/04. Biopsychology PhD (Doctor of Philosophy) 2, Cognitive PhD (Doctor of Philosophy) 1, Cognitive Neuroscience PhD (Doctor of Philosophy) 3, Developmental PhD (Doctor of Philosophy) 0.

Student Applications/Admissions:

Student Applications

Biopsychology PhD (Doctor of Philosophy)—Applications 2004–2005, 41. Total applicants accepted 2004–2005, 5. Number enrolled (new admits only) 2004–2005 full-time, 4. Openings 2005–2006, 3. The Median number of years required for completion of a degree are 5. The number of students enrolled full and part-time who were dismissed or voluntarily withdrew from this program area were 0. *Cognitive PhD (Doctor of Philosophy)*—Applications 2004–2005, 17. Total applicants accepted 2004–2005, 1. Number enrolled (new admits only) 2004–2005 full-time, 0. Total enrolled 2004–2005 full-time, 3. Openings 2005–2006, 2. The Median number of years required for completion of a degree are 5. The number of students enrolled full and part-time who were dismissed or voluntarily withdrew from this program area were 0. *Cognitive Neuroscience PhD (Doctor of Philosophy)*—Applications 2004–2005, 40. Total applicants accepted 2004–2005, 3. Number enrolled (new admits only) 2004–2005 full-time, 1. Openings 2005–2006, 4. The Median number of years required for completion of a degree are 5. The number of students enrolled full and part-time who were dismissed or voluntarily withdrew from this program area were 1. *Developmental PhD (Doctor of Philosophy)*—Applications 2004–2005, 23. Total applicants accepted 2004–2005, 3. Number enrolled (new admits only) 2004–2005 full-time, 2. Openings 2005–2006, 2. The number of students enrolled full and part-time who were dismissed or voluntarily withdrew from this program area were 0.

Admissions Requirements:

Scores: Entries appear in this order: required test or GPA, minimum score (if required), median score of students entering in 2003–2004. Master's Programs: GRE-V no minimum stated, 602; GRE-Q no minimum stated, 690; GRE-V+Q no minimum stated; GRE-Analytical no minimum stated, 680. Doctoral Programs: GRE-V no minimum stated, 650; GRE-Q no minimum stated, 693; GRE-V+Q no minimum stated, 670; GRE-Analytical no minimum stated, 620; overall undergraduate GPA no minimum stated.

Other Criteria: (importance of criteria rated low, medium, or high): GRE/MAT scores high, research experience high, work experience medium, extracurricular activity low, clinically related public service low, GPA high, letters of recommendation high, interview high, statement of goals and objectives high, sample of work medium.

Student Characteristics: The following represents characteristics of students in 2004–2005 in all graduate psychology programs in the department: Female–full-time 11, part-time 0; Male–full-time 15, part-time 0; African American/Black–full-time 0, part-time 0; Hispanic/Latino(a)–full-time 1, part-time 0; Asian/Pacific Islander–full-time 9, part-time 0; American Indian/Alaska Native–full-time 0, part-time 0; Caucasian–full-time 16, part-time 0; Multi-ethnic–full-time 0, part-time 0; students subject to the Americans With Disabilities Act–full-time 0, part-time 0.

Financial Information/Assistance:

Financial Assistance:

First Year Students: Teaching assistantships available for first-year. Tuition remission given: full. Research assistantships available for first-year.

Advanced Students: Teaching assistantships available for advanced students. Tuition remission given: full. Research assistantships available for advanced students.

Contact Information: Of all students currently enrolled full-time, 100% benefitted from one or more of the listed financial assistance programs. Application and information available online at: http://www.psy.jhu.edu.

Internships/Practica: No information provided.

Housing and Day Care: No on-campus housing is available. No on-campus day care facilities are available.

Employment of Department Graduates:

Master's Degree Graduates: Of those who graduated in the academic year 2003–2004, the following categories and numbers represent the post-graduate activities and employment of master's degree graduates: Enrolled in a post-doctoral residency/fellowship (n/a), employed in independent practice (n/a), total from the above (master's) (0).

Doctoral Degree Graduates: Of those who graduated in the academic year 2003–2004, the following categories and numbers represent the post-graduate activities and employment of doctoral degree graduates: Enrolled in a psychology doctoral program (n/a), enrolled in another graduate/professional program (2), enrolled in a post-doctoral residency/fellowship (4), total from the above (doctoral) (6).

Additional Information:

Orientation, Objectives, and Emphasis of Department: The graduate program in psychology at The Johns Hopkins University emphasizes research training, stressing the application of basic research methodology to theoretical problems in psychology. Students are actively engaged in research projects within the first semester. There is a low student/faculty ratio; students work closely with their advisors. Courses, seminars, and research activities provide training so that students will emerge as independent investigators who can embark on successful research careers in psychology. Courses cover fundamental issues in experimental design and analysis, and provide a broad background in all the major areas of psychology. Advanced seminars deal with topics of current interest in various specific areas. The department has programs in cognitive psychology (including perceptual and cognitive development), cognitive neuroscience, quantitative psychology, and biopsychology. The evaluation of applications to our graduate program is based on many factors. They include both objective indicators, such as required GRE scores and undergraduate GPA, and more subjective information, such as a statement of purpose, a description of applicant's background and experience, and letters of recommendation. To select among the top candidates, we rely on letters of recommendation to provide a personal assessment of applicant's potential for graduate work by faculty mentors and advisors who know the applicant well. Students in good standing can expect to receive both tuition remission and salary.

Special Facilities or Resources: Each faculty member in the Department of Psychology maintains a laboratory for conducting research. The psychology building was recently renovated, and the research space is both excellent and plentiful. Every lab contains multiple microcomputer systems for experimentation, analysis, and word processing; most machines are connected via a local-area network to one another and to the Internet. In addition, individual laboratories contain special-purpose equipment designed for the research carried out there. Laboratories in cognition, for example, include high-resolution display devices for experiments in visual. Quantitative psychology laboratories include UNIX work stations for computational analysis and simulation studies. Biopsychology laboratories have facilities for animal surgery, histology, electrophysiological recording of single units and evoked potentials, analysis of neurotransmitters through assays and high-pressure liquid chromatography, bioacoustics, and for general behavioral testing.

Application Information:

Send to: Renee Seitz, Academic Program Coordinator, JHU, Department of Psychological and Brain Sciences, 204 Ames Hall, Charles & 34th Streets, Baltimore, MD 21218 Applications on line at http://www.psy.jhu.edu. Students are admitted in the Fall, application deadline December 15. *Fee:* $65.

Loyola College
Department of Psychology
4501 North Charles Street
Baltimore, MD 21210
Telephone: (410) 617-2696
Fax: (410) 617-5341
E-mail: *Psychology@loyola.edu*
Web: *http://www.Loyola.edu/Psychology*

Department Information:
1968. Chairperson: Dr. David V. Powers. Number of Faculty: total–full-time 17, part-time 18; women–full-time 9, part-time 8; minority–full-time 2, part-time 1.

Programs and Degrees Offered:
Listed in the following order: Program area, degree type (T if terminal Master's), number awarded 7/03–6/04. Clinical MA/MS (Master of Arts/Science) (T) 31, Counseling MA/MS (Master of Arts/Science) (T) 18, Clinical PsyD (Doctor of Psychology) 8.

APA Accreditation: Clinical PsyD (Doctor of Psychology).

Student Applications/Admissions:
Student Applications

Clinical MA/MS (Master of Arts/Science)—Applications 2004–2005, 140. Total applicants accepted 2004–2005, 104. Openings 2005–2006, 45. The Median number of years required for completion of a degree are 2. The number of students enrolled full and part-time who were dismissed or voluntarily withdrew from this program area were 4. *Counseling MA/MS (Master of Arts/Science)*—Applications 2004–2005, 111. Total applicants accepted 2004–2005, 68. Openings 2005–2006, 45. The Median number of years required for completion of a degree are 2. The number of students enrolled full and part-time who were dismissed or voluntarily withdrew from this program area were 2. *Clinical PsyD (Doctor of Psychology)*—Applications 2004–2005, 266. Total applicants accepted 2004–2005, 34. Number enrolled (new admits only) 2004–2005 full-time, 11. Total enrolled 2004–2005 full-time, 69. Openings 2005–2006, 15. The Median number of years required for completion of a degree are 4. The number of students enrolled full and part-time who were dismissed or voluntarily withdrew from this program area were 0.

Admissions Requirements:
Scores: Entries appear in this order: required test or GPA, minimum score (if required), median score of students entering in 2003–2004. Master's Programs: GRE-V no minimum stated, 500; GRE-Q no minimum stated, 560; GRE-V+Q no minimum stated, 1060; overall undergraduate GPA 3.0, 3.4; psychology GPA 3.0. Doctoral Programs: GRE-V no minimum stated, 510; GRE-Q no minimum stated, 555; GRE-V+Q no minimum stated, 1065; overall undergraduate GPA 3.0, 3.6.
Other Criteria: (importance of criteria rated low, medium, or high): GRE/MAT scores high, research experience high, work experience high, extracurricular activity medium, clinically related public service high, GPA high, letters of recommendation high, interview high, statement of goals and objectives medium. Interviews by invitation only for PsyD program. Interviews for Master's Program not applicable. For additional infor-

mation on admission requirements, go to: http://Graduate.loyola.edu.

Student Characteristics: The following represents characteristics of students in 2004–2005 in all graduate psychology programs in the department: Female–full-time 124, part-time 83; Male–full-time 38, part-time 31; African American/Black–full-time 15, part-time 11; Hispanic/Latino(a)–full-time 4, part-time 1; Asian/Pacific Islander–full-time 8, part-time 3; American Indian/Alaska Native–full-time 0, part-time 1; Caucasian–full-time 124, part-time 87; Multi-ethnic–full-time 0, part-time 0.

Financial Information/Assistance:
Tuition for Full-Time Study: Master's: State residents: $430 per credit hour; Nonstate residents: $430 per credit hour. *Doctoral:* State residents: per academic year $21,678; Nonstate residents: per academic year $21,678. Tuition is subject to change.

Financial Assistance:
First Year Students: No information provided.
Advanced Students: Teaching assistantships available for advanced students. Average amount paid per academic year: $1,200. Average number of hours worked per week: 10. Apply by May/November. Research assistantships available for advanced students. Average amount paid per academic year: $1,200. Average number of hours worked per week: 10. Apply by May/November. Fellowships and scholarships available for advanced students. Apply by varies. Tuition remission given: partial.
Contact Information: Of all students currently enrolled full-time, 30% benefitted from one or more of the listed financial assistance programs.

Internships/Practica: The MS program, Practitioner Track requires 300 hours of externship experience. The MS program, Thesis Track requires 300 hours of externship experience. Students are able to choose from a wide variety of sites approved by the Department. The PsyD program incorporates field placement training throughout the curriculum; a minimum total of 1,260 hours of field training is required. The Final (fifth) year of the PsyD program is a full-time internship. For those doctoral students for whom a professional internship is required prior to graduation, 14 applied in 2003–2004. Of those who applied, 13 were placed in internships listed by the Association of Psychology Postdoctoral and Internship Programs (APPIC); 13 were placed in APA accredited internships.

Housing and Day Care: No on-campus housing is available. No on-campus day care facilities are available.

Employment of Department Graduates:
Master's Degree Graduates: Of those who graduated in the academic year 2003–2004, the following categories and numbers represent the post-graduate activities and employment of master's degree graduates: Enrolled in a psychology doctoral program (5), enrolled in another graduate/professional program (6), enrolled in a post-doctoral residency/fellowship (n/a), employed in independent practice (n/a), employed in a community mental health/counseling center (2), employed in a hospital/medical center (5), do not know (31), total from the above (master's) (49).
Doctoral Degree Graduates: Of those who graduated in the academic year 2003–2004, the following categories and numbers represent the post-graduate activities and employment of doctoral

degree graduates: Enrolled in a psychology doctoral program (n/a), enrolled in a post-doctoral residency/fellowship (8), employed in independent practice (0), total from the above (doctoral) (8).

Additional Information:

Orientation, Objectives, and Emphasis of Department: The Master's programs in Clinical and Counseling Psychology at Loyola College provide training to individuals who wish to promote mental health in individuals, families, organizations, and communities though careers in direct service, leadership, research, and education. We strive to provide a learning environment that facilitates the development of skills in critical thinking, scholarship, assessment and intervention, and that is grounded in an appreciation for both psychological science and human diversity. The goals of the PsyD program in Clinical Psychology are based on the "scholar-professional" model of training, designed to train autonomous practitioners of professional psychology who will deliver mental health services and lead others in service to the general public in diverse settings.

Special Facilities or Resources: Departmental facilities include the Loyola Clinic, a health psychology/behavioral medicine laboratory, audiovisual recording facilities, assessment and therapy training rooms, and a student lounge. Students have access to a campus-wide computer system, including SPSS and SASS software. All graduate students have telephone voicemail and e-mail addresses. Advanced doctoral students are provided with individual workstations with computers.

Information for Students With Physical Disabilities: See the following Web site for more information: http://www.loyola.edu/dss.

Application Information:

Send to: Office of Graduate Admissions, Loyola College in Maryland, 4501 N. Charles Street, Baltimore, MD 21210. Students are admitted in the Fall, application deadline January 1; Spring, application deadline November 15; Summer, application deadline April 15. For Fall, deadlines are as follows: PsyD January 1; MS Thesis Track March 15; MS Practitioner Track April 15. For both Spring (November 15) and Summer (April 15), applications are accepted for MS, Practitioner Track only. *Fee:* $50.

Maryland, University of
Department of Psychology
College of Behavioral and Social Sciences
Biology-Psychology Building
College Park, MD 20742-4411
Telephone: (301) 405-5865
Fax: (301) 314-9566
E-mail: *psycgrad@deans.umd.edu*
Web: *http://www.bsos.umd.edu/psyc/*

Department Information:

1937. Chairperson: Professor William S. Hall. Number of Faculty: total–full-time 35; women–full-time 8; minority–full-time 2.

Programs and Degrees Offered:

Listed in the following order: Program area, degree type (T if terminal Master's), number awarded 7/03–6/04. Clinical PhD

(Doctor of Philosophy) 1, Cognitive PhD (Doctor of Philosophy) 0, Counseling PhD (Doctor of Philosophy) 4, Developmental PhD (Doctor of Philosophy) 0, Industrial and Organizational PhD (Doctor of Philosophy) 3, Integrative Neuroscience PhD (Doctor of Philosophy) 0, Sensorineural and Perceptual PhD (Doctor of Philosophy) 1, Social PhD (Doctor of Philosophy) 0.

APA Accreditation: Clinical PhD (Doctor of Philosophy). Counseling PhD (Doctor of Philosophy).

Student Applications/Admissions:

Student Applications

Clinical PhD (Doctor of Philosophy)—Applications 2004–2005, 269. Total applicants accepted 2004–2005, 5. Number enrolled (new admits only) 2004–2005 full-time, 5. Openings 2005–2006, 5. The Median number of years required for completion of a degree are 9. The number of students enrolled full and part-time who were dismissed or voluntarily withdrew from this program area were 0. *Cognitive PhD (Doctor of Philosophy)*—Applications 2004–2005, 18. Total applicants accepted 2004–2005, 2. Number enrolled (new admits only) 2004–2005 full-time, 2. The number of students enrolled full and part-time who were dismissed or voluntarily withdrew from this program area were 0. *Counseling PhD (Doctor of Philosophy)*—Applications 2004–2005, 85. Total applicants accepted 2004–2005, 2. Number enrolled (new admits only) 2004–2005 full-time, 2. Openings 2005–2006, 4. The Median number of years required for completion of a degree are 6. The number of students enrolled full and part-time who were dismissed or voluntarily withdrew from this program area were 0. *Developmental PhD (Doctor of Philosophy)*—Applications 2004–2005, 21. Total applicants accepted 2004–2005, 1. Number enrolled (new admits only) 2004–2005 full-time, 1. Openings 2005–2006, 2. The number of students enrolled full and part-time who were dismissed or voluntarily withdrew from this program area were 0. *Industrial and Organizational PhD (Doctor of Philosophy)*—Applications 2004–2005, 121. Total applicants accepted 2004–2005, 0. Number enrolled (new admits only) 2004–2005 full-time, 0. Openings 2005–2006, 3. The Median number of years required for completion of a degree are 7. The number of students enrolled full and part-time who were dismissed or voluntarily withdrew from this program area were 1. *Integrative Neuroscience PhD (Doctor of Philosophy)*—Applications 2004–2005, 5. Total applicants accepted 2004–2005, 1. Number enrolled (new admits only) 2004–2005 full-time, 1. The number of students enrolled full and part-time who were dismissed or voluntarily withdrew from this program area were 0. *Sensorineural and Perceptual PhD (Doctor of Philosophy)*—Applications 2004–2005, 1. Total applicants accepted 2004–2005, 0. Number enrolled (new admits only) 2004–2005 full-time, 0. The Median number of years required for completion of a degree are 5. The number of students enrolled full and part-time who were dismissed or voluntarily withdrew from this program area were 0. *Social PhD (Doctor of Philosophy)*—Applications 2004–2005, 54. Total applicants accepted 2004–2005, 3. Number enrolled (new admits only) 2004–2005 full-time, 4. Openings 2005–2006, 2. The number of students enrolled full and part-time who were dismissed or voluntarily withdrew from this program area were 0.

Admissions Requirements:

Scores: Entries appear in this order: required test or GPA, minimum score (if required), median score of students entering

in 2003–2004. Doctoral Programs: GRE-V no minimum stated, 660; GRE-Q no minimum stated, 730; GRE-V+Q no minimum stated, 1390; GRE-Analytical no minimum stated, 760; overall undergraduate GPA no minimum stated, 3.8. Each area sets its own specific requirements.

Other Criteria: (importance of criteria rated low, medium, or high): GRE/MAT scores high, research experience high, work experience low, extracurricular activity low, clinically related public service low, GPA high, letters of recommendation high, interview high, statement of goals and objectives high. The specific criteria vary across our 8 programs. Some require extracurricular activity, service, and interview—whereas others do not. Currently clinical holds a formal interview for applicants who rank in their top group.

Student Characteristics: The following represents characteristics of students in 2004–2005 in all graduate psychology programs in the department: Female–full-time 70, part-time 0; Male–full-time 35, part-time 0; African American/Black–full-time 8, part-time 0; Hispanic/Latino(a)–full-time 3, part-time 0; Asian/Pacific Islander–full-time 7, part-time 0; American Indian/Alaska Native–full-time 2, part-time 0; Caucasian–full-time 64, part-time 0; Multi-ethnic–full-time 0, part-time 0; students subject to the Americans With Disabilities Act–full-time 0, part-time 0.

Financial Information/Assistance:
Tuition for Full-Time Study: *Doctoral:* State residents: $371 per credit hour; Nonstate residents: $701 per credit hour. Tuition is subject to change.

Financial Assistance:
First Year Students: Teaching assistantships available for first-year. Average amount paid per academic year: $12,044. Average number of hours worked per week: 20. Tuition remission given: full. Research assistantships available for first-year. Average amount paid per academic year: $12,044. Average number of hours worked per week: 20. Tuition remission given: full. Fellowships and scholarships available for first-year. Average amount paid per academic year: $12,131. Tuition remission given: full.
Advanced Students: Teaching assistantships available for advanced students. Average amount paid per academic year: $12,621. Average number of hours worked per week: 20. Tuition remission given: full. Research assistantships available for advanced students. Average amount paid per academic year: $12,621. Average number of hours worked per week: 20. Tuition remission given: full. Fellowships and scholarships available for advanced students. Average amount paid per academic year: $12,505. Average number of hours worked per week: 20. Tuition remission given: full.
Contact Information: Of all students currently enrolled full-time, 100% benefitted from one or more of the listed financial assistance programs.

Internships/Practica: The metropolitan area also has many psychologists who can provide students with excellent opportunities for collaboration and/or consultation. The specialty areas have established collaborative relationships with several federal and community agencies and hospitals as well as with businesses and consulting firms, where it is possible for students to arrange for research, practicum and internship placement. These opportunities are available for Clinical, and Counseling students at the National Institutes of Health, Veteran's Administration clinics

and hospitals in Washington, DC, Baltimore Perry Point, Coatesville, Martinsburg, Kecoughton, and a number of others within a hundred mile radius of the University. Experiences include a wide range of research activities, as well as psychodiagnostic work, psychotherapy, and work within drug and alcohol abuse clinics. Various other hospitals, clinics and research facilities in the Washington, DC and Baltimore metropolitan area are also available. Industrial/Organizational students also have opportunities for practitioner experiences in organizations such as The U.S. Office of Personnel Management, GEICO, Bell Atlantic, and various consulting firms. For those doctoral students for whom a professional internship is required prior to graduation, 7 applied in 2003–2004. Of those who applied, 6 were placed in internships listed by the Association of Psychology Postdoctoral and Internship Programs (APPIC); 6 were placed in APA accredited internships.

Housing and Day Care: On-campus housing is available. Graduate Housing: (301) 422-0147. On-campus day care facilities are available. Center for Young Children: (301) 405-3168.

Employment of Department Graduates:
Master's Degree Graduates: Of those who graduated in the academic year 2003–2004, the following categories and numbers represent the post-graduate activities and employment of master's degree graduates: Enrolled in a post-doctoral residency/fellowship (n/a), employed in independent practice (n/a), total from the above (master's) (0).
Doctoral Degree Graduates: Of those who graduated in the academic year 2003–2004, the following categories and numbers represent the post-graduate activities and employment of doctoral degree graduates: Enrolled in a psychology doctoral program (n/a), total from the above (doctoral) (0).

Additional Information:
Orientation, Objectives, and Emphasis of Department: The department offers a full-time graduate program with an emphasis on intensive individual training made possible by a 4-to-1 student/faculty ratio. All students are expected to participate in a variety of relevant experiences that, in addition to coursework and research training, can include practicum experiences, field training, and teaching. The department offers a variety of programs described in the admissions brochure as well as other emphases that cut across the various specialties. All programs have a strong research emphasis with programs in clinical, counseling, and industrial advocating the scientist-practitioner model. Please note that the Department of Psychology receives a large number of applications. As required by the Graduate School, we will consider any applicant who has all materials in by December 15. Website: www.bsos.umd.edu/psyc.

Special Facilities or Resources: The Department of Psychology has all of the advantages of a large state university, and also has advantages offered by the many resources available in the metropolitan Washington-Baltimore area. The University is approximately 15 miles from the center of Washington, DC and is in close proximity to a number of libraries, and state and federal agencies. Students are able to benefit from the excellent additional library resources of the community, such as the Library of Congress, National Library of Medicine, and the National Archives (which is located on the UMCP campus). The building in which the Department is housed was designed by the faculty to incorporate research and educational facilities for all specialty areas. The building contains special centers for research, with acoustical centers, observational units, video equipment, computer facilities, surgical facilities, and radio frequency shielding. Departmental laboratories are well equipped for research in animal behavior, audition, biopsychology, cognition, coordinated motor control, counseling, industrial/organizational psychology, learning, life-span development, psycholinguistics, psychotherapy, social psychology, and vision.

Application Information:

Send to: Ms. Carol Gorham, Graduate Program Coordinator, Department of Psychology, University of Maryland, College Park, MD, 20742-4411. Application available online. URL of online application: www.vprgs.umd.edu. Students are admitted in the Fall, application deadline December 15. *Fee:* $50.

Maryland, University of
Institute for Child Study/Department of Human Development
College of Education
College Park, MD 20742
Telephone: (301) 405-2827
Fax: (301) 405-2891
E-mail: *cflatter@umd.edu*
Web: *http://www.inform.umd.edu/educ/depts/edhd*

Department Information:

1947. Chair: Charles H. Flatter. Number of Faculty: total–full-time 17, part-time 4; women–full-time 10, part-time 4; minority–full-time 1.

Programs and Degrees Offered:

Listed in the following order: Program area, degree type (T if terminal Master's), number awarded 7/03–6/04. Developmental MA/MS (Master of Arts/Science) 8, educational psychology PhD (Doctor of Philosophy) 2.

Student Applications/Admissions:
Student Applications

Developmental MA/MS *(Master of Arts/Science)*—Applications 2004–2005, 26. Total applicants accepted 2004–2005, 11. Total enrolled 2004–2005 full-time, 6, part-time, 4. Openings 2005–2006, 20. *Educational psychology PhD (Doctor of Philosophy)*—Applications 2004–2005, 14. Total applicants accepted 2004–2005, 9. Total enrolled 2004–2005 full-time, 15, part-time, 5. Openings 2005–2006, 10.

Admissions Requirements:

Scores: Entries appear in this order: required test or GPA, minimum score (if required), median score of students entering in 2003–2004. Master's Programs: GRE-V 450, 560; GRE-Q 485, 600; overall undergraduate GPA 3.0, 3.25. Doctoral Programs: GRE-V 450, 580; GRE-Q 485, 620; overall undergraduate GPA 3.0, 3.32.

Other Criteria: (importance of criteria rated low, medium, or high): GRE/MAT scores high, research experience high, work experience medium, clinically related public service medium, GPA medium, letters of recommendation high, interview medium, statement of goals and objectives high.

Student Characteristics: The following represents characteristics of students in 2004–2005 in all graduate psychology programs in the department: Female–full-time 9, part-time 2; Male–full-time 4, part-time 0; African American/Black–full-time 0, part-time 0; Hispanic/Latino(a)–full-time 0, part-time 0; Asian/Pacific Islander–full-time 5, part-time 1; American Indian/Alaska Native–full-time 5, part-time 0; Caucasian–full-time 0, part-time 0; Multi-ethnic–full-time 0, part-time 0; students subject to the Americans With Disabilities Act–full-time 0, part-time 0.

Financial Information/Assistance:
Financial Assistance:

First Year Students: No information provided.

Advanced Students: Teaching assistantships available for advanced students. Tuition remission given: partial. Traineeships available for advanced students. Tuition remission given: partial. Fellowships and scholarships available for advanced students. Tuition remission given: full.

Contact Information: Of all students currently enrolled full-time, 90% benefitted from one or more of the listed financial assistance programs.

Internships/Practica: No information provided.

Housing and Day Care: On-campus housing is available. No on-campus day care facilities are available.

Employment of Department Graduates:

Master's Degree Graduates: Of those who graduated in the academic year 2003–2004, the following categories and numbers represent the post-graduate activities and employment of master's degree graduates: Enrolled in another graduate/professional program (8), enrolled in a post-doctoral residency/fellowship (n/a), employed in independent practice (n/a), employed in an academic position at a university (0), employed in an academic position at a 2-year/4-year college (0), employed in other positions at a higher education institution (8), employed in a professional position in a school system (8), employed in business or industry (research/consulting) (0), employed in business or industry (management) (0), employed in a government agency (research) (0), employed in a government agency (professional services) (2), employed in a community mental health/counseling center (0), employed in a hospital/medical center (0), total from the above (master's) (26).

Doctoral Degree Graduates: Of those who graduated in the academic year 2003–2004, the following categories and numbers represent the post-graduate activities and employment of doctoral degree graduates: Enrolled in a psychology doctoral program (n/a), employed in an academic position at a university (7), employed in an academic position at a 2-year/4-year college (4), employed in other positions at a higher education institution (3), employed in a professional position in a school system (0), employed in business or industry (research/consulting) (0), employed in business or industry (management) (0), employed in a government agency (research) (6), employed in a government agency (professional services) (0), employed in a community mental health/counseling center (0), employed in a hospital/medical center (0), total from the above (doctoral) (20).

Additional Information:

Orientation, Objectives, and Emphasis of Department: Human development courses are psychological in nature and are intended to increase the student's understanding of human behavior, including development, learning, and adjustment. Areas of concentration that relate to the institute's goals and interests include, but are not limited to, infancy and early childhood, adolescence, adult development and aging, development over the life span, cultural processes, neuropsychology, cognitive processes, personality, and learning. Information is drawn primarily from the major fields of psychology, sociology, and physiology. The graduate specialization in educational psychology program is intended to prepare educational psychologists for service in schools and other community agencies dealing with individuals of all ages, to prepare teachers of human development and educational psychology in higher education, and to prepare research-oriented individuals for service in public (state or federal) or private organizations. A graduate joint specialization in development science with the psychology department is also available. The research thrust of this specialization is primarily concerned with social and cognitive aspects of development. The developmental science specialization is designed to prepare researchers and teachers in higher education.

Special Facilities or Resources: Special facilities or resources include extensive research and computer facilities. Videotaping studios and observation rooms are located in the building. The Child Development Assessment Laboratory is associated with the department and is heavily used for neuropsychological assessments on children. Testing and observation rooms are available in the Center for Family Relationships and Culture. In addition, the Center for Young Children, a child care center for preschool children, is under the auspices of the unit and is a resource for students studying and researching this age group.

Application Information:
Send to: Department Chair. Students are admitted in the Fall, application deadline June 1; Spring, application deadline October 1; Summer, application deadline February 1. Deadline for financial aid consideration is January 2. *Fee:* $50.

Maryland, University of
School and Counseling Psychology Programs, Department of Counseling and Personnel Services
College of Education
3214 Benjamin Building
College Park, MD 20742
Telephone: (301) 405-2858
Fax: (301) 405-9995
E-mail: *cw68@umail.umd.edu*
Web: *http://www.education.umd.edu/EDCP/*

Department Information:
1967. Chairperson: Dennis M. Kivlighan Jr. Number of Faculty: total–full-time 17, part-time 5; women–full-time 11, part-time 4; minority–full-time 5, part-time 1.

Programs and Degrees Offered:
Listed in the following order: Program area, degree type (T if terminal Master's), number awarded 7/03–6/04. Counseling psychology PhD (Doctor of Philosophy) 5, school PhD (Doctor of Philosophy) 5.

APA Accreditation: Counseling PhD (Doctor of Philosophy). School PhD (Doctor of Philosophy).

Student Applications/Admissions:
Student Applications
Counseling psychology PhD (Doctor of Philosophy)—Applications 2004–2005, 201. Total applicants accepted 2004–2005, 6. Number enrolled (new admits only) 2004–2005 full-time, 5. Number enrolled (new admits only) 2004–2005 part-time, 0. Openings 2005–2006, 5. The Median number of years required for completion of a degree are 6. The number of students enrolled full and part-time who were dismissed or voluntarily withdrew from this program area were 0. *School PhD (Doctor of Philosophy)*—Applications 2004–2005, 63. Total applicants accepted 2004–2005, 21. Number enrolled (new admits only) 2004–2005 full-time, 6. Number enrolled (new admits only) 2004–2005 part-time, 0. Total enrolled 2004–2005 full-time, 19, part-time, 12. Openings 2005–2006, 8. The Median number of years required for completion of a degree are 8. The number of students enrolled full and part-time who were dismissed or voluntarily withdrew from this program area were 0.

Admissions Requirements:
Scores: Entries appear in this order: required test or GPA, minimum score (if required), median score of students entering in 2003–2004. Master's Programs: GRE-V no minimum stated; GRE-Q no minimum stated; GRE-V+Q no minimum stated; GRE-Analytical no minimum stated; GRE-Subject(Psych) no minimum stated; MAT no minimum stated; overall undergraduate GPA no minimum stated; last 2 years GPA no minimum stated; psychology GPA no minimum stated. Doctoral Programs: GRE-V no minimum stated, 630; GRE-Q no minimum stated, 640; GRE-V+Q no minimum stated, 1280; overall undergraduate GPA no minimum stated, 3.65; last 2 years GPA no minimum stated, 3.75; psychology GPA no minimum stated.
Other Criteria: (importance of criteria rated low, medium, or high): GRE/MAT scores medium, research experience high, work experience medium, extracurricular activity medium, clinically related public service low, GPA high, letters of recommendation high, interview medium, statement of goals and objectives high, Criteria vary by program. Applicants should contact specific programs for detailed information.

Student Characteristics: The following represents characteristics of students in 2004–2005 in all graduate psychology programs in the department: Female–full-time 40, part-time 12; Male–full-time 12, part-time 0; African American/Black–full-time 5, part-time 2; Hispanic/Latino(a)–full-time 2, part-time 0; Asian/Pacific Islander–full-time 7, part-time 0; American Indian/Alaska Native–full-time 0, part-time 0; Caucasian–full-time 36, part-time 10; Multi-ethnic–full-time 2, part-time 0; students subject to the Americans With Disabilities Act–full-time 0, part-time 0.

Financial Information/Assistance:
Financial Assistance:
First Year Students: Teaching assistantships available for first-year. Average amount paid per academic year: $15,000. Average number of hours worked per week: 20. Apply by December 15. Tuition remission given: full. Research assistantships available for first-year. Average amount paid per academic year: $15,000. Average number of hours worked per week: 20. Apply by Decem-

ber 15. Tuition remission given: full. Fellowships and scholarships available for first-year. Average amount paid per academic year: $15,000. Apply by December 15. Tuition remission given: full.

Advanced Students: Teaching assistantships available for advanced students. Average amount paid per academic year: $15,000. Average number of hours worked per week: 20. Apply by April 15. Tuition remission given: full. Research assistantships available for advanced students. Average amount paid per academic year: $15,000. Average number of hours worked per week: 20. Apply by April 15. Tuition remission given: full.

Contact Information: Of all students currently enrolled full-time, 90% benefitted from one or more of the listed financial assistance programs. Application and information available online at: http://www.education.umd.edu/studentinfo/graduate_info/admissionsreq.html.

Internships/Practica: The Washington DC area offers an abundance of training settings which supplement our on-campus training facilities. A number of practica are offered at the University of Maryland Counseling Center. In addition, other practica and externships are offered at schools, community agencies, hospitals, and other counseling centers. For those doctoral students for whom a professional internship is required prior to graduation, 14 applied in 2003–2004. Of those who applied, 8 were placed in internships listed by the Association of Psychology Postdoctoral and Internship Programs (APPIC); 8 were placed in APA accredited internships.

Housing and Day Care: No on-campus housing is available. No on-campus day care facilities are available.

Employment of Department Graduates:
Master's Degree Graduates: Of those who graduated in the academic year 2003–2004, the following categories and numbers represent the post-graduate activities and employment of master's degree graduates: Enrolled in a post-doctoral residency/fellowship (n/a), employed in independent practice (n/a), total from the above (master's) (0).

Doctoral Degree Graduates: Of those who graduated in the academic year 2003–2004, the following categories and numbers represent the post-graduate activities and employment of doctoral degree graduates: Enrolled in a psychology doctoral program (n/a), total from the above (doctoral) (0).

Additional Information:
Orientation, Objectives, and Emphasis of Department: Both the Counseling Psychology and School Psychology programs espouse the scientist practitioner model of training. These programs enable students to become psychologists who are trained in general psychology, competent in providing effective assessment and intervention from a variety of theoretical perspectives, and in conducting research on a wide range of psychological topics. Note: The Counseling Psychology program is administered collaboratively by the departments of Counseling and Personnel Services and Psychology.

Special Facilities or Resources: Observation/training facilities and access to extensive library facilities both on and off campus (e.g., NIH Library of Medicine, Library of Congress).

Application Information:
Send to: Graduate Admission, College of Education, 1210 Benjamin Building, University of Maryland, College Park, MD 20742. Application available online. URL of online application: https://was-1.umd.edu/admissions/Entry.jsp. Students are admitted in the Fall, application deadline December 15. *Fee:* $50.

Maryland, University of, Baltimore County

Department of Psychology
Arts and Sciences
1000 Hilltop Circle
Baltimore, MD 21250
Telephone: (410) 455-2567
Fax: (410) 455-1055
E-mail: *psycdept@umbc.edu*
Web: *http://www.umbc.edu/psyc/index.html*

Department Information:
1966. Chairperson: Carlo C. DiClemente, PhD. Number of Faculty: total–full-time 30, part-time 11; women–full-time 15, part-time 6; minority–full-time 2, part-time 1; faculty subject to the Americans With Disabilities Act 1.

Programs and Degrees Offered:
Listed in the following order: Program area, degree type (T if terminal Master's), number awarded 7/03–6/04. Applied Behavior Analysis MA/MS (Master of Arts/Science) (T) 3, Applied Developmental PhD (Doctor of Philosophy) 3, Human Services (Clinical, Beh. Med, Comunity) PhD (Doctor of Philosophy) 8.

APA Accreditation: Clinical PhD (Doctor of Philosophy).

Student Applications/Admissions:
Student Applications
Applied Behavior Analysis MA/MS (Master of Arts/Science)— Applications 2004–2005, 38. Total applicants accepted 2004–2005, 12. Number enrolled (new admits only) 2004–2005 full-time, 11. Number enrolled (new admits only) 2004–2005 part-time, 0. Openings 2005–2006, 12. The Median number of years required for completion of a degree are 2. The number of students enrolled full and part-time who were dismissed or voluntarily withdrew from this program area were 1. *Applied Developmental PhD (Doctor of Philosophy)*—Applications 2004–2005, 37. Total applicants accepted 2004–2005, 7. Number enrolled (new admits only) 2004–2005 full-time, 7. Number enrolled (new admits only) 2004–2005 part-time, 0. Total enrolled 2004–2005 full-time, 25, part-time, 11. Openings 2005–2006, 10. The Median number of years required for completion of a degree are 5. The number of students enrolled full and part-time who were dismissed or voluntarily withdrew from this program area were 1. *Human Services (Clinical, Beh. Med, Comunity) PhD (Doctor of Philosophy)*—Applications 2004–2005, 119. Total applicants accepted 2004–2005, 11. Number enrolled (new admits only) 2004–2005 full-time, 11. Number enrolled (new admits only) 2004–2005 part-time, 0. Total enrolled 2004–2005 full-time, 55, part-time, 23. Openings 2005–2006, 12. The Median number of years required for completion of a degree are 6. The number of students enrolled full and part-time who were dismissed or voluntarily withdrew from this program area were 1.

Admissions Requirements:

Scores: Entries appear in this order: required test or GPA, minimum score (if required), median score of students entering in 2003–2004. Master's Programs: GRE-V no minimum stated; GRE-Q no minimum stated; GRE-Analytical no minimum stated; GRE-Subject(Psych) no minimum stated; overall undergraduate GPA 3.0. Doctoral Programs: GRE-V no minimum stated; GRE-Q no minimum stated; GRE-Analytical no minimum stated; GRE-Subject(Psych) 550; overall undergraduate GPA 3.0; last 2 years GPA no minimum stated; psychology GPA no minimum stated.

Other Criteria: (importance of criteria rated low, medium, or high): GRE/MAT scores high, research experience high, work experience medium, extracurricular activity medium, clinically related public service medium, GPA high, letters of recommendation high, interview high, statement of goals and objectives high, the Applied Developmental (ADP) program puts less weight on clinical service than does the Human Services (HSP) program (low).

Student Characteristics: The following represents characteristics of students in 2004–2005 in all graduate psychology programs in the department: Female–full-time 87, part-time 28; Male–full-time 11, part-time 6; African American/Black–full-time 12, part-time 5; Hispanic/Latino(a)–full-time 4, part-time 1; Asian/Pacific Islander–full-time 3, part-time 2; American Indian/Alaska Native–full-time 0, part-time 0; Caucasian–full-time 66, part-time 24; Multi-ethnic–full-time 13, part-time 2; students subject to the Americans With Disabilities Act–full-time 0, part-time 0.

Financial Information/Assistance:

Tuition for Full-Time Study: *Master's:* State residents: $373 per credit hour; Nonstate residents: $606 per credit hour. *Doctoral:* State residents: $373 per credit hour; Nonstate residents: $606 per credit hour. Tuition is subject to change.

Financial Assistance:

First Year Students: Teaching assistantships available for first-year. Average amount paid per academic year: $13,462. Average number of hours worked per week: 20. Tuition remission given: full. Research assistantships available for first-year. Average amount paid per academic year: $13,462. Average number of hours worked per week: 20. Tuition remission given: full. Fellowships and scholarships available for first-year. Average amount paid per academic year: $13,462. Tuition remission given: full.

Advanced Students: Teaching assistantships available for advanced students. Average amount paid per academic year: $13,462. Average number of hours worked per week: 20. Tuition remission given: full. Research assistantships available for advanced students. Average number of hours worked per week: 20. Tuition remission given: full. Fellowships and scholarships available for advanced students. Tuition remission given: full.

Contact Information: Of all students currently enrolled full-time, 86% benefitted from one or more of the listed financial assistance programs.

Internships/Practica: Course-linked practica provide students with a focused experience in the application of the skills and knowledge presented in the associated course. The course instructor is responsible for arranging these practica. Beyond the course-linked practica, students in the HSP and ADP programs are required to take a minimum of six additional credits of practicum,

usually in their second and third years. These practica, in various clinical, research, and human services settings, are intended to give students a broader and more integrative experience in the application of the skills and knowledge that they have acquired in the various courses they have taken. For those doctoral students for whom a professional internship is required prior to graduation, 5 applied in 2003–2004. Of those who applied, 5 were placed in internships listed by the Association of Psychology Postdoctoral and Internship Programs (APPIC); 5 were placed in APA accredited internships.

Housing and Day Care: On-campus housing is available. See the following Web site for more information: www.walkeravenueapts.com. On-campus day care facilities are available. Child Care Center: (410) 455-6830.

Employment of Department Graduates:

Master's Degree Graduates: Of those who graduated in the academic year 2003–2004, the following categories and numbers represent the post-graduate activities and employment of master's degree graduates: Enrolled in a psychology doctoral program (1), enrolled in a post-doctoral residency/fellowship (n/a), employed in independent practice (n/a), employed in business or industry (research/consulting) (1), employed in a hospital/medical center (1), total from the above (master's) (3).

Doctoral Degree Graduates: Of those who graduated in the academic year 2003–2004, the following categories and numbers represent the post-graduate activities and employment of doctoral degree graduates: Enrolled in a psychology doctoral program (n/a), enrolled in a post-doctoral residency/fellowship (2), employed in an academic position at a university (2), employed in other positions at a higher education institution (3), employed in a hospital/medical center (2), still seeking employment (1), other employment position (1), total from the above (doctoral) (11).

Additional Information:

Orientation, Objectives, and Emphasis of Department: UMBC Psychology is committed to a scientist-practitioner model and emphasizes science with an applied psychological research focus. The department uses a biopsychosocial interactive framework as the foundation for exploring various problems and issues in psychology. Two graduate programs are housed in the department: Applied Developmental Psychology (ADP) and Human Services Psychology (HSP). The ADP program has two concentrations: Early Development/Early Intervention, and Educational Contexts of Development, and students can affiliate flexibly with either or both. The ADP program is accredited by the ASPPB/National Register of Health Service Providers in Psychology. The HSP program consists of three subprograms - community/social, behavioral medicine, and an APA approved clinical subprogram. Many HSP students take cross-area training in clinical/behavioral medicine or clinical/community areas. Faculty represent a broad range of theoretical perspectives and maintain active research programs. The psychology department has many collaborative relationships for research and clinical and practical training opportunities with institutions in the Baltimore-Washington Corridor.

Special Facilities or Resources: The Psychology Department at UMBC has numerous faculty research laboratories on campus in close proximity to faculty offices. Laboratories include equipment for psychological assessments, videotaping and coding, observation as well as an animal laboratory. The department has access to several large computer laboratories on campus and has a small computer laboratory for graduate students. Through collaborative arrangements with the medical school and other University of Maryland System facilities, graduate students have access to different patient populations and opportunities for community based projects.

Application Information:
Send to: Dean of Graduate School, 1000 Hilltop Circle, Baltimore, MD 21250. Application available online. Students are admitted in the Fall, application deadline December 1. Applied Behavior Analysis Masters program deadline is May 1. Doctoral Program in Applied Developmental Psychology is January 9. *Fee:* $50.

Towson University
Department of Psychology
8000 York Road
Towson, MD 21252
Telephone: (410) 704-3080
Fax: (410) 704-3800
E-mail: cjohnson@towson.edu
Web: http://www.towson.edu/psychology/

Department Information:
1965. Chairperson: Craig T. Johnson, PhD Number of Faculty: total–full-time 31, part-time 54; women–full-time 13, part-time 26; minority–full-time 3, part-time 4.

Programs and Degrees Offered:
Listed in the following order: Program area, degree type (T if terminal Master's), number awarded 7/03–6/04. Clinical MA/MS (Master of Arts/Science) (T) 12, Counseling MA/MS (Master of Arts/Science) (T) 15, Experimental MA/MS (Master of Arts/Science) (T) 10, School MA/MS (Master of Arts/Science) 14.

Student Applications/Admissions:
Student Applications
Clinical MA/MS (Master of Arts/Science)—Applications 2004–2005, 70. Total applicants accepted 2004–2005, 14. Number enrolled (new admits only) 2004–2005 full-time, 10. Number enrolled (new admits only) 2004–2005 part-time, 0. Openings 2005–2006, 16. The Median number of years required for completion of a degree are 2. Counseling MA/MS (Master of Arts/Science)—Applications 2004–2005, 80. Total applicants accepted 2004–2005, 16. Number enrolled (new admits only) 2004–2005 full-time, 15. Number enrolled (new admits only) 2004–2005 part-time, 1. Total enrolled 2004–2005 full-time, 57, part-time, 12. Openings 2005–2006, 18. The Median number of years required for completion of a degree are 3. The number of students enrolled full and part-time who were dismissed or voluntarily withdrew from this program area were 2. Experimental MA/MS (Master of Arts/Science)—Applications 2004–2005, 41. Total applicants accepted 2004–2005, 29. Number enrolled (new admits only) 2004–2005 full-time, 11.

Number enrolled (new admits only) 2004–2005 part-time, 3. Total enrolled 2004–2005 full-time, 35, part-time, 17. Openings 2005–2006, 15. The Median number of years required for completion of a degree are 2. The number of students enrolled full and part-time who were dismissed or voluntarily withdrew from this program area were 0. School MA/MS (Master of Arts/Science)—Applications 2004–2005, 88. Total applicants accepted 2004–2005, 16. Number enrolled (new admits only) 2004–2005 full-time, 15. Number enrolled (new admits only) 2004–2005 part-time, 1. Total enrolled 2004–2005 full-time, 46, part-time, 3. Openings 2005–2006, 15. The Median number of years required for completion of a degree are 3. The number of students enrolled full and part-time who were dismissed or voluntarily withdrew from this program area was 1.

Admissions Requirements:
Scores: Entries appear in this order: required test or GPA, minimum score (if required), median score of students entering in 2003–2004. Master's Programs: GRE-V no minimum stated, 510; GRE-Q no minimum stated, 520; GRE-V+Q no minimum stated, 1000; GRE-Analytical no minimum stated, 550; last 2 years GPA 3.0, 3.25. The reported GRE statistics are an average across three of the four tracks of the Masters degree program; GRE is required for Clinical, Counseling, and School only. School Psychology has a minimum score of 400 in each section and a minimum score of 4.0 for the writing section. GPA statistics represent an average across all four tracks.
Other Criteria: (importance of criteria rated low, medium, or high): GRE/MAT scores medium, research experience medium, work experience medium, clinically related public service medium, GPA high, letters of recommendation high, interview high, statement of goals and objectives medium. Clinically related public service, letters of recommendation and interview are all used by the clinical, counseling, and school psychology programs only. Research experience is very important for the experimental program. Counseling, experimental, and school psychology also use a letter of intent and consider it very important. For additional information on admission requirements, go to: http://wwwnew.towson.edu/psychology/Graduate.htm.

Student Characteristics: The following represents characteristics of students in 2004–2005 in all graduate psychology programs in the department: Female–full-time 129, part-time 22; Male–full-time 31, part-time 10; Caucasian–full-time 0, part-time 0.

Financial Information/Assistance:
Tuition for Full-Time Study: *Master's:* State residents: $257 per credit hour; Nonstate residents: $538 per credit hour. Tuition is subject to change. See the following Web site for updates and changes in tuition costs: www.towson.edu.

Financial Assistance:
First Year Students: Teaching assistantships available for first-year. Average amount paid per academic year: $8,000. Average number of hours worked per week: 20. Apply by February 1. Tuition remission given: full and partial. Research assistantships

available for first-year. Average amount paid per academic year: $5,000. Average number of hours worked per week: 20. Apply by February 1. Tuition remission given: full and partial.

Advanced Students: Teaching assistantships available for advanced students. Average amount paid per academic year: $8,000. Average number of hours worked per week: 20. Apply by February 1. Tuition remission given: full and partial. Research assistantships available for advanced students. Average amount paid per academic year: $5,000. Average number of hours worked per week: 20. Apply by February 1. Tuition remission given: full and partial.

Contact Information: Of all students currently enrolled full-time, 10% benefitted from one or more of the listed financial assistance programs.

Internships/Practica: School Psychology students are required to complete two 100-hour practica over two consecutive semesters in a local school system. The program culminates in a 1200-hour internship that is to be completed full-time over one year or part-time over two consecutive years. At least 50% of the 1200 hours must be completed in a public school system; however most students complete all hours in public schools. Students in clinical psychology can specialize by working in either an inpatient or outpatient facility. Among the internship placement sites for students in the clinical psychology program are community mental health centers and clinics, state psychiatric hospitals, and government agencies including the Department of Veteran Affairs and other specialized psychological service centers. Counseling students complete a semester of practicum and a full-time internship experience in community mental health centers, college counseling centers, drug and alcohol rehabilitation agencies, domestic violence centers, and other psychological service agencies. A limited number of nonteaching graduate assistantships are available for students in the experimental psychology program.

Housing and Day Care: No on-campus housing is available. On-campus day care facilities are available.

Employment of Department Graduates:

Master's Degree Graduates: Of those who graduated in the academic year 2003–2004, the following categories and numbers represent the post-graduate activities and employment of master's degree graduates: Enrolled in a psychology doctoral program (0), enrolled in a post-doctoral residency/fellowship (n/a), employed in independent practice (n/a), employed in a professional position in a school system (13), employed in a community mental health/counseling center (1), total from the above (master's) (14).

Doctoral Degree Graduates: Of those who graduated in the academic year 2003–2004, the following categories and numbers represent the post-graduate activities and employment of doctoral degree graduates: Enrolled in a psychology doctoral program (n/a), total from the above (doctoral) (0).

Additional Information:

Orientation, Objectives, and Emphasis of Department: The Experimental Psychology MA Program is designed to prepare students for enrollment in PhD programs or for conducting research in industrial, government, private consulting, or hospital settings.

Students receive comprehensive instruction in research design, statistical methods (both univariate and multivariate), computer applications (both for data collection and analysis), professional writing, and specialized areas of psychology. Areas of specialization include cognitive, ethnology/comparative, industrial, social/personality, sensation/perception and physiological psychology and human neuropsychology. A meaningful individualized program of electives may be pursued by taking courses in a number of different areas. The Master of Arts in Clinical Psychology is designed for students seeking training and experience in the applied professional aspects of clinical psychology. Although approximately 50% of graduates go on to further graduate study in psychology, the primary focus of the program is the preparation of master's-level psychologists for employment in state and other non-profit organizations. Because of the applied professional emphasis, the majority of required clinical courses address the theoretical and practical issues involved in providing direct clinical services. Students take courses in psychotherapy and behavior change, preparing them to practice individual, family, and group intervention techniques. Other courses in assessment prepare students to administer and interpret psychometric instruments used to conduct intellectual, neurological, and personality assessments. Advanced seminars in cognitive-behavior therapy are offered regularly. Practical supervised clinical experiences constitute a major portion of the program. Students complete a nine-month half-time internship during which they provide supervised psychological services to clients in an off-campus mental health setting. The Counseling Psychology Program trains individuals who will be capable of facilitating a counselee's personal growth and development. Students are trained to help clients explore vocational and personal goals through individual and group counseling. Graduates of the program may go on to meet the requirements of the Licensed Clinical Professional Counselor and find employment in a wide variety of counseling agencies. The Towson University School Psychology Program is fully approved by the National Association of School Psychologists (NASP) and trains graduate students to become school psychologists. The program emphasizes consultation and early intervention. It is unique in its close relationship with its surrounding urban and suburban communities, which welcomes Towson's school psychology students in both practicum and internship settings. The Program offers a single 63-credit degree: the Master of Arts in Psychology with a concentration in School Psychology and the Certificate of Advanced Study (CAS) in School Psychology.

Special Facilities or Resources: The Psychology Building houses laboratories for histology, and computer analysis as well as for the conduct of research in learning/motivation, physiological, comparative, and general experimental psychology. Additionally, because of the popularity of the undergraduate Psychology major, there are many students willing to participate in research studies.

Application Information:
Send to: Graduate School, Towson University, Towson, MD 21252. Application available online. Students are admitted in the Fall, application deadline February 1; Spring, application deadline October 1. Counseling and School admit for the Fall with an application deadline of January 15. Clinical admits for Fall with an application deadline of February 1. The Experimental program has deadlines of February 1 and March 1. *Fee:* $40.

Uniformed Services University of the Health Sciences

Medical and Clinical Psychology
F Edward Hebert School of Medicine
4301 Jones Bridge Road
Bethesda, MD 20814
Telephone: (301) 295-9669
Fax: (301) 295-3034
E-mail: *csimmons@usuhs.mil*
Web: *www.usuhs.mil/mps*

Department Information:

1977. Chairperson: David S. Krantz, PhD Number of Faculty: total–full-time 8, part-time 2; women–full-time 4, part-time 1; faculty subject to the Americans With Disabilities Act 1.

Programs and Degrees Offered:

Listed in the following order: Program area, degree type (T if terminal Master's), number awarded 7/03–6/04. Medical Psychology PhD (Doctor of Philosophy) 2, Clinical Psychology PhD (Doctor of Philosophy) 1, Medical Psychology—Clinical Track PhD (Doctor of Philosophy) 0.

APA Accreditation: Clinical PhD (Doctor of Philosophy).

Student Applications/Admissions:

Student Applications

Medical Psychology PhD (Doctor of Philosophy)—Applications 2004–2005, 10. Total applicants accepted 2004–2005, 2. Number enrolled (new admits only) 2004–2005 full-time, 2. Number enrolled (new admits only) 2004–2005 part-time, 0. Openings 2005–2006, 4. The Median number of years required for completion of a degree are 5. The number of students enrolled full and part-time who were dismissed or voluntarily withdrew from this program area were 0. *Clinical Psychology PhD (Doctor of Philosophy)*—Applications 2004–2005, 31. Total applicants accepted 2004–2005, 3. Number enrolled (new admits only) 2004–2005 full-time, 3. Number enrolled (new admits only) 2004–2005 part-time, 0. Openings 2005–2006, 3. The Median number of years required for completion of a degree are 5. The number of students enrolled full and part-time who were dismissed or voluntarily withdrew from this program area were 0. *Medical Psychology—Clinical Track PhD (Doctor of Philosophy)*—Applications 2004–2005, 4. Total applicants accepted 2004–2005, 1. Number enrolled (new admits only) 2004–2005 full-time, 1. Number enrolled (new admits only) 2004–2005 part-time, 0. Openings 2005–2006, 1. The Median number of years required for completion of a degree are 5. The number of students enrolled full and part-time who were dismissed or voluntarily withdrew from this program area were 0.

Admissions Requirements:

Scores: Entries appear in this order: required test or GPA, minimum score (if required), median score of students entering in 2003–2004. Doctoral Programs: GRE-V+Q 1100; overall undergraduate GPA 3.0.

Other Criteria: (importance of criteria rated low, medium, or high): GRE/MAT scores high, research experience high, work experience low, extracurricular activity low, clinically related public service medium, GPA high, letters of recommendation high, interview high, statement of goals and objectives high. For additional information on admission requirements, go to: www.usuhs.mil/mps.

Student Characteristics: The following represents characteristics of students in 2004–2005 in all graduate psychology programs in the department: Female–full-time 22, part-time 0; Male–full-time 6, part-time 0; African American/Black–full-time 4, part-time 0; Hispanic/Latino(a)–full-time 2, part-time 0; Asian/Pacific Islander–full-time 1, part-time 0; American Indian/Alaska Native–full-time 1, part-time 0; Caucasian–full-time 20, part-time 0; Multi-ethnic–full-time 0, part-time 0; students subject to the Americans With Disabilities Act–full-time 0, part-time 0.

Financial Information/Assistance:

Tuition for Full-Time Study: *Master's:* State residents: per academic year $0; Nonstate residents: per academic year $0. *Doctoral:* State residents: per academic year $0; Nonstate residents: per academic year $0.

Financial Assistance:

First Year Students: Traineeships available for first-year. Average amount paid per academic year: $22,000. Average number of hours worked per week: 20. Fellowships and scholarships available for first-year. Average amount paid per academic year: $22,000. Average number of hours worked per week: 20.

Advanced Students: Teaching assistantships available for advanced students. Average amount paid per academic year: $22,000. Average number of hours worked per week: 20. Research assistantships available for advanced students. Average amount paid per academic year: $22. Average number of hours worked per week: 20. Traineeships available for advanced students. Average amount paid per academic year: $22,000. Average number of hours worked per week: 20. Fellowships and scholarships available for advanced students. Average amount paid per academic year: $22,000. Average number of hours worked per week: 20.

Contact Information: Of all students currently enrolled full-time, 90% benefitted from one or more of the listed financial assistance programs. Application and information available online at: www.usuhs.mil/mps.

Internships/Practica: Military Clinical Psychology and Clinical/Medical Psychology students complete the 12-month internship during the fifth and final year of the program within an APA-approved military or civilian clinical psychology training program. Practicum training occurs during the Fall, Winter, and Spring quarters of the second, third and fourth years. Students work at practica sites at local facilities for 6 to 10 hours per week. For those doctoral students for whom a professional internship is required prior to graduation, 3 applied in 2003–2004. Of those who applied, 3 were placed in internships listed by the Association of Psychology Postdoctoral and Internship Programs (APPIC); 3 were placed in APA accredited internships.

Housing and Day Care: No on-campus housing is available. No on-campus day care facilities are available.

Employment of Department Graduates:

Master's Degree Graduates: Of those who graduated in the academic year 2003–2004, the following categories and numbers represent the post-graduate activities and employment of master's degree graduates: Enrolled in a post-doctoral residency/fellowship (n/a), employed in independent practice (n/a), total from the above (master's) (0).

Doctoral Degree Graduates: Of those who graduated in the academic year 2003–2004, the following categories and numbers represent the post-graduate activities and employment of doctoral degree graduates: Enrolled in a psychology doctoral program (n/a), employed in an academic position at a university (1), employed in an academic position at a 2-year/4-year college (1), employed in a hospital/medical center (1), total from the above (doctoral) (3).

Additional Information:

Orientation, Objectives, and Emphasis of Department: The Department's educational programs provide a background in general psychological principles. However, two content areas are emphasized: Health Psychology and Clinical Psychology. Educational and research activities focus on the application of principles and methods of scientific psychology relevant to physical and mental health. The Department is set in a school of medicine and has an interdisciplinary focus. A Clinical Psychology program for uniformed military personnel and a Medical Psychology specialty track for civilians are APA accredited and follow the scientist-practitioner model. A research/academic program in Medical Psychology encompasses the fields of Health Psychology and Behavioral Medicine. The Department provides many research opportunities for students in the graduate programs and opportunities for mentorship because of the active and varied research programs conducted by the full-time faculty. Research opportunities available for students all involve the study of behavioral, psychological and biobehavioral factors in physical and mental health. In addition, several faculty in the Department participate in an NIH-funded predoctoral and postdoctoral training programs in cardiovascular behavioral medicine.

Special Facilities or Resources: The Department has office space, laboratory space for human and animal experimentation, multiple psychophysiology laboratories, and a biochemistry laboratory. There is access to classrooms, conference rooms, an excellent library, a computer center, audiovisual support, teaching hospitals, and a laboratory animal facility that is accredited by the Association for the Assessment and Accreditation of Laboratory Animal Care (AAALAC). The Bethesda campus of the National Institutes of Health, including the National Library of Medicine, is within walking distance from USUHS. The NIH is a resource for lecture series, specialized courses, funding information, and research collaborations. The major military training hospitals also are nearby, as are all the social and cultural offerings of Washington, D.C.

Information for Students With Physical Disabilities: See the following Web site for more information: www.usuhs.mil/mps.

Application Information:

Application available online. URL of online application: http://cim.usuhs.mil/geo. Students are admitted in the Winter, application deadline January 15th. *Fee:* $0.

Washington College
Department of Psychology
Washington Avenue
Chestertown, MD 21620-1197
Telephone: (410) 778-2800
Fax: (410) 778-7275
E-mail: *mkerchner2@washcoll.edu*
Web: *http://psychology.washcoll.edu*

Department Information:

1953. Chairperson: Michael Kerchner. Number of Faculty: total–full-time 6, part-time 4; women–full-time 2; minority–full-time 1, part-time 1.

Programs and Degrees Offered:

Listed in the following order: Program area, degree type (T if terminal Master's), number awarded 7/03–6/04. General Experimental MA/MS (Master of Arts/Science) (T) 7.

Student Applications/Admissions:

Student Applications

General Experimental MA/MS (Master of Arts/Science)—Applications 2004–2005, 13. Total applicants accepted 2004–2005, 12. Number enrolled (new admits only) 2004–2005 full-time, 1. Number enrolled (new admits only) 2004–2005 part-time, 3. Total enrolled 2004–2005 full-time, 5, part-time, 15. Openings 2005–2006, 20. The number of students enrolled full and part-time who were dismissed or voluntarily withdrew from this program area were 0.

Admissions Requirements:

Scores: Entries appear in this order: required test or GPA, minimum score (if required), median score of students entering in 2003–2004. Master's Programs: GRE-V+Q 1000; psychology GPA 3.0.

Other Criteria: (importance of criteria rated low, medium, or high). GRE/MAT scores medium, research experience medium, work experience medium, clinically related public service medium, GPA high, letters of recommendation high, statement of goals and objectives medium. Applicants who do not have an undergraduate degree in Psychology may have this requirement waived either by completing the Proseminar (PSY 499) with a grade of B or better, or by earning a score at or above the 50th percentile on the Psychology GRE achievement test. PSY499 is offered each Fall Semester. In unusual circumstances, individuals with degrees in areas other than Psychology but with a minimum of five courses in Psychology will be considered for a waiver of Psychology 499. For additional information on admission requirements, go to: http://grad.washcoll.edu/.

Student Characteristics: The following represents characteristics of students in 2004–2005 in all graduate psychology programs in the department: Female–full-time 2, part-time 14; Male–full-time 3, part-time 1; African American/Black–full-time 0, part-time 1; Hispanic/Latino(a)–full-time 0, part-time 0; Asian/Pacific Islander–full-time 0, part-time 0; American Indian/Alaska Native–full-time 0, part-time 1; Caucasian–full-time 3, part-time 10; Multi-ethnic–full-time 2, part-time 3.

Financial Information/Assistance:

Tuition for Full-Time Study: *Master's:* State residents: $275 per credit hour; Nonstate residents: $275 per credit hour. Tuition is subject to change.

Financial Assistance:

First Year Students: No information provided.
Advanced Students: No information provided.
Contact Information: No information provided.

Internships/Practica: The department enjoys excellent ties to local agencies such as the Upper Shore Community Mental Health Center (the regional residential facility located in Chestertown), Upper Shore Aging, both Kent and Queen Anne's counties school systems, residential facilities for developmentally disadvantaged individuals, troubled adolescents, etc. A variety of internships are available through the cooperation of these agencies.

Housing and Day Care: No on-campus housing is available. No on-campus day care facilities are available.

Employment of Department Graduates:

Master's Degree Graduates: Of those who graduated in the academic year 2003–2004, the following categories and numbers represent the post-graduate activities and employment of master's degree graduates: Enrolled in a post-doctoral residency/fellowship (n/a), employed in independent practice (n/a), total from the above (master's) (0).

Doctoral Degree Graduates: Of those who graduated in the academic year 2003–2004, the following categories and numbers represent the post-graduate activities and employment of doctoral degree graduates: Enrolled in a psychology doctoral program (n/a), total from the above (doctoral) (0).

Additional Information:

Orientation, Objectives, and Emphasis of Department: The goal of this program is to prepare graduate students for entry into a doctoral program of their choice and to generate master's level professionals. The emphasis of the curriculum is on psychology as a scientific endeavor and the applications of that scientific discipline to real-world problems.

Special Facilities or Resources: The department enjoys a computerize learning lab, video and audio taping facilities, biofeedback, equipment, both 16 and 64 channel EEG/ERP labs, an eye movement lab, acoustic startle lab, small mammal surgery suite, a computerized psychological testing laboratory, and a social psychology lab.

Application Information:

Send to: Director of the Graduate Programs, 300 Washington Avenue, Chestertown, MD 21620-1197. Application available online. URL of online application: http://grad.washcoll.edu/. Students are admitted on a rolling admissions basis. *Fee:* $40.

American International College
Department of Graduate Psychology
1000 State Street
Springfield, MA 01109
Telephone: (413) 737-7000
Fax: (413) 737-2803
E-mail: *inquiry@www.aic.edu*
Web: *http://www.aic.edu/web*

Department Information:
1979. Chairperson: Richard C. Sprinthall. Number of Faculty: total–full-time 15, part-time 8; women–full-time 8, part-time 4; minority–part-time 2.

Programs and Degrees Offered:
Listed in the following order: Program area, degree type (T if terminal Master's), number awarded 7/03–6/04. Clinical MA/MS (Master of Arts/Science) (T) 7, educational MA/MS (Master of Arts/Science) 9, Forensic Psychology MA/MS (Master of Arts/Science) 8, Educational Psychology EdD (Doctor of Education) 3.

Student Applications/Admissions:
Student Applications
Clinical MA/MS (Master of Arts/Science)—Applications 2004–2005, 26. Total applicants accepted 2004–2005, 15. Number enrolled (new admits only) 2004–2005 full-time, 6. Number enrolled (new admits only) 2004–2005 part-time, 9. Total enrolled 2004–2005 full-time, 16, part-time, 15. Openings 2005–2006, 15. The Median number of years required for completion of a degree are 3. The number of students enrolled full and part-time who were dismissed or voluntarily withdrew from this program area were 3. *Educational MA/MS (Master of Arts/Science)*—Applications 2004–2005, 18. Total applicants accepted 2004–2005, 10. Number enrolled (new admits only) 2004–2005 full-time, 4. Number enrolled (new admits only) 2004–2005 part-time, 6. Total enrolled 2004–2005 full-time, 7, part-time, 14. Openings 2005–2006, 15. The Median number of years required for completion of a degree are 3. The number of students enrolled full and part-time who were dismissed or voluntarily withdrew from this program area were 2. *Forensic Psychology MA/MS (Master of Arts/Science)*—Applications 2004–2005, 34. Total applicants accepted 2004–2005, 15. Number enrolled (new admits only) 2004–2005 full-time, 7. Number enrolled (new admits only) 2004–2005 part-time, 6. Total enrolled 2004–2005 full-time, 10, part-time, 8. Openings 2005–2006, 15. The Median number of years required for completion of a degree are 3. The number of students enrolled full and part-time who were dismissed or voluntarily withdrew from this program area were 1. *Educational Psychology EdD (Doctor of Education)*—Applications 2004–2005, 27. Total applicants accepted 2004–2005, 10. Number enrolled (new admits only) 2004–2005 full-time, 4. Number enrolled (new admits only) 2004–2005 part-time, 6. Total enrolled 2004–2005 full-time, 18, part-time, 22. Openings 2005–2006, 10. The Median number of years required for completion of a degree are 5. The number of students enrolled full and part-time who were dismissed or voluntarily withdrew from this program area were 2.

Admissions Requirements:
Scores: Entries appear in this order: required test or GPA, minimum score (if required), median score of students entering in 2003–2004. Master's Programs: overall undergraduate GPA no minimum stated, 3.00; last 2 years GPA no minimum stated, 3.15; psychology GPA no minimum stated, 3.35. Doctoral Programs: GRE-V no minimum stated, 580; GRE-Q no minimum stated, 500; GRE-V+Q no minimum stated, 1080; overall undergraduate GPA no minimum stated, 3.00.

Other Criteria: (importance of criteria rated low, medium, or high): GRE/MAT scores medium, research experience high, work experience high, extracurricular activity medium, clinically related public service medium, GPA high, letters of recommendation high, interview high, statement of goals and objectives high, GRE only for EdD.

Student Characteristics: The following represents characteristics of students in 2004–2005 in all graduate psychology programs in the department: Female–full-time 31, part-time 35; Male–full-time 20, part-time 24; African American/Black–full-time 5, part-time 3; Hispanic/Latino(a)–full-time 6, part-time 5; Asian/Pacific Islander–full-time 0, part-time 0; American Indian/Alaska Native–full-time 0, part-time 0; Caucasian–full-time 40, part-time 52; Multi-ethnic–full-time 0, part-time 0; students subject to the Americans With Disabilities Act–full-time 0, part-time 0.

Financial Information/Assistance:
Tuition for Full-Time Study: *Master's:* State residents: per academic year $9,810, $545 per credit hour; Nonstate residents: per academic year $9,810, $545 per credit hour. *Doctoral:* State residents: per academic year $9,810, $545 per credit hour; Nonstate residents: per academic year $9,810, $545 per credit hour.

Financial Assistance:
First Year Students: Teaching assistantships available for first-year. Average number of hours worked per week: 10. Apply by April 15. Tuition remission given: full. Research assistantships available for first-year. Average number of hours worked per week: 10. Apply by April 15. Tuition remission given: full. Fellowships and scholarships available for first-year. Average number of hours worked per week: 10. Apply by April 15. Tuition remission given: full.

Advanced Students: Teaching assistantships available for advanced students. Apply by April 15. Tuition remission given: full. Research assistantships available for advanced students. Apply by April 15. Tuition remission given: full. Fellowships and scholarships available for advanced students. Apply by April 15. Tuition remission given: full.

Contact Information: Of all students currently enrolled full-time, 20% benefitted from one or more of the listed financial assistance programs.

Internships/Practica: Internships for doctoral candidates are available at the Curtis Blake Center for Learning Disabilities and at the college-operated Curtis Blake Day School for learning-disabled children.

Housing and Day Care: On-campus housing is available. Dean Blaine Stevens, American International College, 1000 State Street, Springfield, MA 01109. No on-campus day care facilities are available.

Employment of Department Graduates:

Master's Degree Graduates: Of those who graduated in the academic year 2003–2004, the following categories and numbers represent the post-graduate activities and employment of master's degree graduates: Enrolled in a post-doctoral residency/fellowship (n/a), employed in independent practice (n/a), total from the above (master's) (0).

Doctoral Degree Graduates: Of those who graduated in the academic year 2003–2004, the following categories and numbers represent the post-graduate activities and employment of doctoral degree graduates: Enrolled in a psychology doctoral program (n/a), total from the above (doctoral) (0).

Additional Information:

Orientation, Objectives, and Emphasis of Department: All graduate programs are based on an integrated curriculum designed to produce psychologists trained in both theory and clinical skills. Solid courses in history, systems, learning theory, and research are included. Heavy emphasis is placed on experience in the context of a broad academic and research-oriented curriculum. The program includes an extensive practicum experience, affording opportunity for the student to gain familiarity with the field and to apply and sharpen skills developed previously. The school psychology program (60 hours) leads to certification by the Commonwealth of Massachusetts. The EdD program in educational psychology is focused primarily on the area of learning disabilities. Supervision is provided both on campus and at the practicum site.

Special Facilities or Resources: A wide range of supervised internship sites is available to MA and EdD candidates in mental health centers, the college counseling center, and professional agencies.

Application Information:

Send to: Department Chair. Students are admitted in the Fall, application deadline March 15. *Fee:* $25.

Assumption College
Division of Counseling Psychology
500 Salisbury Street
Worcester, MA 01609-1296
Telephone: (508) 767-7390
Fax: (508) 767-7263
E-mail: *doerfler@.assumption.edu*
Web: *http://www.assumption.edu*

Department Information:

1962. Program Director: Leonard A. Doerfler. Number of Faculty: total–full-time 9, part-time 14; women–full-time 5, part-time 5; minority–full-time 1, part-time 2.

Programs and Degrees Offered:

Listed in the following order: Program area, degree type (T if terminal Master's), number awarded 7/03–6/04. Counseling MA/MS (Master of Arts/Science) (T) 14.

Student Applications/Admissions:
Student Applications

Counseling MA/MS (*Master of Arts/Science*)—Applications 2004–2005, 50. Total applicants accepted 2004–2005, 37. Total enrolled 2004–2005 full-time, 50, part-time, 50. Openings 2005–2006, 35. The Median number of years required for completion of a degree are 3.

Admissions Requirements:

Scores: Entries appear in this order: required test or GPA, minimum score (if required), median score of students entering in 2003–2004. Master's Programs: overall undergraduate GPA 3.0, 3.4; psychology GPA 3.0, 3.4.

Other Criteria: (importance of criteria rated low, medium, or high): research experience low, work experience medium, extracurricular activity low, clinically related public service low, GPA high, letters of recommendation high, statement of goals and objectives medium.

Student Characteristics: The following represents characteristics of students in 2004–2005 in all graduate psychology programs in the department: Female–full-time 50, part-time 20; Male–full-time 10, part-time 10; African American/Black–full-time 1, part-time 4; Hispanic/Latino(a)–full-time 2, part-time 2; Asian/Pacific Islander–full-time 0, part-time 0; American Indian/Alaska Native–full-time 0, part-time 0; Caucasian–full-time 57, part-time 26; students subject to the Americans With Disabilities Act–part-time 2.

Financial Information/Assistance:

Tuition for Full-Time Study: *Master's:* State residents: $407 per credit hour; Nonstate residents: $407 per credit hour.

Financial Assistance:

First Year Students: Fellowships and scholarships available for first-year. Apply by March 1. Tuition remission given: partial.

Advanced Students: Fellowships and scholarships available for advanced students. Apply by March 1. Tuition remission given: partial.

Contact Information: Of all students currently enrolled full-time, 15% benefitted from one or more of the listed financial assistance programs. Application and information available online at: http://www.assumption.edu.

Internships/Practica: Practicum and internship placements are available in a wide range of community settings. Students can elect to work in outpatient/community, college counseling centers, substance abuse, inpatient, residential, and correctional settings. Opportunities to work with children, adolescents, adults, and families are available. The department maintains a close working relationship with the University of Massachusetts Medical Center, McLean Hospital/Harvard Medical School, and other mental health training agencies; students attend clinical case conferences, workshops, and lectures at these agencies. Students often receive training in innovative treatment models like home-based, brief problem-focused, or cognitive-behavioral treatments.

Housing and Day Care: On-campus housing is available. Information can be obtained from the Graduate School office regarding the possibility of living on campus: (508) 767-7387. No on-campus day care facilities are available.

Employment of Department Graduates:

Master's Degree Graduates: Of those who graduated in the academic year 2003–2004, the following categories and numbers represent the post-graduate activities and employment of master's degree graduates: Enrolled in a psychology doctoral program (1), enrolled in a post-doctoral residency/fellowship (n/a), employed in independent practice (n/a), employed in a professional position in a school system (2), employed in a government agency (research) (1), employed in a community mental health/counseling center (10), total from the above (master's) (14).

Doctoral Degree Graduates: Of those who graduated in the academic year 2003–2004, the following categories and numbers represent the post-graduate activities and employment of doctoral degree graduates: Enrolled in a psychology doctoral program (n/a), total from the above (doctoral) (0).

Additional Information:

Orientation, Objectives, and Emphasis of Department: The program is organized to prepare students for entrance into doctoral programs in clinical and counseling psychology and for master's degree entry-level positions in a variety of mental health and related social service settings. Students are given conceptual preparation in a variety of theoretical positions in clinical and counseling psychology. A number of skill courses in counseling, testing, and research are an integral part of the program at both the entry and advanced levels. The goal of the program is to produce master's level psychologists who show conceptual versatility in theory and practice and depth of preparation in one of several special areas of counseling work. The student takes classwork in areas such as personality theory, abnormal psychology, child development, counseling, advanced therapeutic procedure, measurement and research. Outside of class the student gains applied experience in clinical practice in the one-semester practicum and two-semester internship.

Special Facilities or Resources: Special facilities on campus include a well-equipped media center and an observation laboratory. Students also have access to in-service training at a local medical school, agencies, and hospitals. The college is located within commuting distance of Boston training facilities. College libraries in Worcester operate on a consortium basis. Programs of study are available on campus in the summer.

Application Information:

Send to: Dean of Graduate Studies, Graduate Office, Assumption College, 500 Salisbury Street, Worcester, MA 01609-1296. Students are admitted in the Fall, application deadline rolling; Spring, application deadline rolling; Summer, application deadline rolling. *Fee:* $30. Application fee waived for Assumption College alumni.

Boston College (2004 data)
Department of Counseling, Developmental, and Educational Psychology
309 Campion Hall, School of Education
Chestnut Hill, MA 02467
Telephone: (617) 552-4710
Fax: (617) 552-1981
E-mail: *sparks@bc.edu*
Web: *http://www.bc.edu/bc_org/avp/soe/counselpsy/*

Department Information:

1950. Chairperson: Elizabeth Sparks, PhD Number of Faculty: total–full-time 19; women–full-time 14; minority–full-time 4.

Programs and Degrees Offered:

Listed in the following order: Program area, degree type (T if terminal Master's), number awarded 7/03–6/04. Counseling-School MA/MS (Master of Arts/Science) (T) 8, Counseling Psychology PhD (Doctor of Philosophy) 13, Counseling-Mental Health MA/MS (Master of Arts/Science) (T) 63, Developmental Educational Psychology MA/MS (Master of Arts/Science) (T) 10, Developmental/ Educational Psychology PhD (Doctor of Philosophy) 6.

Student Applications/Admissions:

Student Applications

Counseling- School MA/MS (Master of Arts/Science)—Applications 2004–2005, 81. Total applicants accepted 2004–2005, 61. Total enrolled 2004–2005 full-time, 44. Openings 2005–2006, 25. The Median number of years required for completion of a degree are 2. The number of students enrolled full and part-time who were dismissed or voluntarily withdrew from this program area were 0. *Counseling Psychology PhD (Doctor of Philosophy)*—Applications 2004–2005, 99. Total applicants accepted 2004–2005, 9. Openings 2005–2006, 8. The Median number of years required for completion of a degree are 7. The number of students enrolled full and part-time who were dismissed or voluntarily withdrew from this program area were 0. *Counseling- Mental Health MA/MS (Master of Arts/Science)*—Applications 2004–2005, 209. Total applicants accepted 2004–2005, 164. Total enrolled 2004–2005 full-time, 121. Openings 2005–2006, 65. The Median number of years required for completion of a degree are 2. The number of students enrolled full and part-time who were dismissed or voluntarily withdrew from this program area were 3. *Developmental Educational Psychology MA/MS (Master of Arts/Science)*—Applications 2004–2005, 92. Total applicants accepted 2004–2005, 56. Total enrolled 2004–2005 full-time, 33. Openings 2005–2006, 25. The Median number of years required for completion of a degree is 1. The number of students enrolled full and part-time who were dismissed or voluntarily withdrew from this program area were 0. *Developmental/ Educational Psychology PhD (Doctor of Philosophy)*—Applications 2004–2005, 37. Total applicants accepted 2004–2005, 10. Total enrolled 2004–2005 full-time, 22. Openings 2005–2006, 5. The Median number of years required for completion of a degree are 6. The number of students enrolled full and part-time who were dismissed or voluntarily withdrew from this program area were 0.

Admissions Requirements:

Scores: Entries appear in this order: required test or GPA, minimum score (if required), median score of students entering in 2003–2004. Master's Programs: GRE-V no minimum stated, 510; GRE-Q no minimum stated, 570; GRE-V+Q no minimum stated, 1080; GRE-Analytical no minimum stated, 600; overall undergraduate GPA no minimum stated, 3.4. Doctoral Programs: GRE-V no minimum stated, 550; GRE-Q no minimum stated, 600; GRE-V+Q no minimum stated, 1150; GRE-Analytical no minimum stated, 670; overall undergraduate GPA no minimum stated, 3.51.

Other Criteria: (importance of criteria rated low, medium, or high): GRE/MAT scores medium, research experience high, work experience medium, extracurricular activity low, clinically related public service high, GPA high, letters of recommendation high, interview medium, statement of goals and objectives high. For developmental programs, clinically related public service is low.

Student Characteristics: The following represents characteristics of students in 2004–2005 in all graduate psychology programs in the department: Female–full-time 209, part-time 0; Male–full-time 52, part-time 0; African American/Black–full-time 12, part-time 0; Hispanic/Latino(a)–full-time 14, part-time 0; Asian/Pacific Islander–full-time 14, part-time 0; American Indian/Alaska Native–full-time 1, part-time 0; Caucasian–full-time 0, part-time 0; students subject to the Americans With Disabilities Act–full-time 0, part-time 0.

Financial Information/Assistance:

Tuition for Full-Time Study: *Master's:* State residents: $722 per credit hour; Nonstate residents: $722 per credit hour. *Doctoral:* State residents: $722 per credit hour; Nonstate residents: $722 per credit hour. Tuition is subject to change.

Financial Assistance:

First Year Students: Research assistantships available for first-year. Average amount paid per academic year: $12,000. Average number of hours worked per week: 20. Apply by variable. Tuition remission given: partial.

Advanced Students: Teaching assistantships available for advanced students. Average amount paid per academic year: $12,000. Average number of hours worked per week: 20. Apply by variable. Tuition remission given: partial. Research assistantships available for advanced students. Average amount paid per academic year: $13,000. Apply by variable. Tuition remission given: partial.

Contact Information: Of all students currently enrolled full-time, 50% benefitted from one or more of the listed financial assistance programs.

Internships/Practica: Doctoral students in Counseling Psychology complete an Advanced Practicum in community mental health agencies, schools, clinics, hospitals, and college counseling centers. They also complete a one year pre-doctoral internship. Master's students in mental health and school counseling work with the Masters Program Coordinator to identify internships that meet requirements for mental health licensure or school counselor certification. For those doctoral students for whom a professional internship is required prior to graduation, 11 applied in 2003–2004. Of those who applied, 9 were placed in internships listed by the Association of Psychology Postdoctoral and Internship Programs (APPIC); 9 were placed in APA accredited internships.

Housing and Day Care: On-campus housing is available. On-campus day care facilities are available.

Employment of Department Graduates:

Master's Degree Graduates: Of those who graduated in the academic year 2003–2004, the following categories and numbers represent the post-graduate activities and employment of master's degree graduates: Enrolled in a post-doctoral residency/fellowship (n/a), employed in independent practice (n/a), total from the above (master's) (0).

Doctoral Degree Graduates: Of those who graduated in the academic year 2003–2004, the following categories and numbers represent the post-graduate activities and employment of doctoral degree graduates: Enrolled in a psychology doctoral program (n/a), total from the above (doctoral) (0).

Additional Information:

Orientation, Objectives, and Emphasis of Department: The Programs in Counseling, Developmental and Educational Psychology emphasize a foundation in developmental theory, research skills, and a commitment to preparing professionals to work in public practice, public service, academic or research institutions. The counseling psychology doctoral program espouses a scientist-practitioner model and provides broad-based training with special attention to group and individual counseling processes, theory and skill in research and assessment, and understanding individual development within a social context. Master's counseling students specialize in mental health counseling or school counseling. The program in Applied Developmental and Educational Psychology focuses on application and draws on psychology, educational and community programs, and engages public policies to enhance the development of individuals and their key institutional contexts-schools, families, and work settings across the life span. Faculty research interests include psychotherapy, process and outcome, career and moral development, individual differences in cognitive and affective development including developmental disabilities, influence of gender role strain on the well-being of men, Asian-American and Latino mental health, racial identity, marital and community violence, marital satisfaction, and prevention and intervention for promoting positive development among youth.

Special Facilities or Resources: Boston College offers ample student access to computing facilities (Alpha mainframe, Macintosh and PCs) at no charge to students. The Educational Resource Center houses current psychological assessment kits and computerized instructional software. The Thomas P. O'Neill Library is fully automated with all major computerized databases. Through the consortium, students may cross-register in courses in other greater Boston universities (Boston University, Brandeis, and Tufts). The career center provides comprehensive resources and information regarding career planning and placement.

Application Information:
Send to: Graduate Admissions, Boston College, School of Education, Champion Hall 103, Chestnut Hill, MA 02467. Students are admitted in the Fall, application deadline January 1; Summer, application deadline June 15. Counseling MA programs January 1; Counseling PhD December 15. Developmental PhD January 1. Developmental MA

June 15 and January 1. *Fee:* $40. All MA programs February 1; all PhD January 1.

Boston College
Department of Psychology
College of Arts and Sciences
140 Commonwealth Avenue, McGuinn 301
Chestnut Hill, MA 02467
Telephone: (617) 552-4100
Fax: (617) 552-0523
E-mail: *winner@bc.edu*
Web: *http://www.bc.edu/schools/cas/psych/*

Department Information:
1950. Chairperson: James Russell. Number of Faculty: total–full-time 19, part-time 6; women–full-time 8, part-time 5; minority–full-time 1.

Programs and Degrees Offered:
Listed in the following order: Program area, degree type (T if terminal Master's), number awarded 7/03–6/04. Cognition and Perception PhD (Doctor of Philosophy) 2, Cultural PhD (Doctor of Philosophy) 0, Developmental PhD (Doctor of Philosophy) 1, Social PhD (Doctor of Philosophy), Behavioral Neuroscience PhD (Doctor of Philosophy) 0.

Student Applications/Admissions:
Student Applications
Cognition and Perception PhD (Doctor of Philosophy)—Applications 2004–2005, 18. Total applicants accepted 2004–2005, 0. Openings 2005–2006, 1. The Median number of years required for completion of a degree are 4. *Cultural PhD (Doctor of Philosophy)*—Applications 2004–2005, 32. Total applicants accepted 2004–2005, 1. Number enrolled (new admits only) 2004–2005 full-time, 1. The Median number of years required for completion of a degree are 4. *Developmental PhD (Doctor of Philosophy)*—Applications 2004–2005, 33. Total applicants accepted 2004–2005, 2. Number enrolled (new admits only) 2004–2005 full-time, 2. Openings 2005–2006, 2. The Median number of years required for completion of a degree are 4. *Social PhD (Doctor of Philosophy)*—Applications 2004–2005, 70. Total applicants accepted 2004–2005, 2. Number enrolled (new admits only) 2004–2005 full-time, 2. Openings 2005–2006, 1. The Median number of years required for completion of a degree are 4. The number of students enrolled full and part-time who were dismissed or voluntarily withdrew from this program area were 1. *Behavioral Neuroscience PhD (Doctor of Philosophy)*—Applications 2004–2005, 16. Total enrolled 2004–2005 full-time, 5. The Median number of years required for completion of a degree are 4.

Admissions Requirements:
Scores: Entries appear in this order: required test or GPA, minimum score (if required), median score of students entering in 2003–2004. Master's Programs: GRE-V no minimum stated; GRE-Q no minimum stated; GRE-V+Q no minimum stated; GRE-Analytical no minimum stated; overall undergraduate GPA no minimum stated; psychology GPA no minimum stated. Doctoral Programs: GRE-Subject(Psych) no minimum stated; overall undergraduate GPA no minimum stated; psychology GPA no minimum stated.
Other Criteria: (importance of criteria rated low, medium, or high): GRE/MAT scores high, research experience high, work experience low, extracurricular activity low, clinically related public service low, GPA high, letters of recommendation high, interview high, statement of goals and objectives high.

Student Characteristics: The following represents characteristics of students in 2004–2005 in all graduate psychology programs in the department: Female–full-time 18, part-time 0; Male–full-time 5, part-time 0; African American/Black–full-time 0, part-time 0; Hispanic/Latino(a)–full-time 1, part-time 0; Asian/Pacific Islander–full-time 2, part-time 0; American Indian/Alaska Native–full-time 0, part-time 0; Caucasian–full-time 15, part-time 0; Multi-ethnic–full-time 0, part-time 0; students subject to the Americans With Disabilities Act–full-time 0, part-time 0.

Financial Information/Assistance:
Tuition for Full-Time Study: *Master's:* State residents: $990 per credit hour; Nonstate residents: $990 per credit hour. *Doctoral:* State residents: $990 per credit hour; Nonstate residents: $990 per credit hour.

Financial Assistance:
First Year Students: Research assistantships available for first-year. Average amount paid per academic year: $14,400. Average number of hours worked per week: 20. Apply by January 2. Tuition remission given: full.
Advanced Students: Teaching assistantships available for advanced students. Average amount paid per academic year: $14,400. Average number of hours worked per week: 20. Apply by January 2. Tuition remission given: full. Fellowships and scholarships available for advanced students. Tuition remission given: partial.
Contact Information: Of all students currently enrolled full-time, 100% benefitted from one or more of the listed financial assistance programs.

Internships/Practica: No information provided.

Housing and Day Care: No on-campus housing is available. On-campus day care facilities are available.

Employment of Department Graduates:
Master's Degree Graduates: Of those who graduated in the academic year 2003–2004, the following categories and numbers represent the post-graduate activities and employment of master's degree graduates: Enrolled in a post-doctoral residency/fellowship (n/a), employed in independent practice (n/a), total from the above (master's) (0).
Doctoral Degree Graduates: Of those who graduated in the academic year 2003–2004, the following categories and numbers represent the post-graduate activities and employment of doctoral degree graduates: Enrolled in a psychology doctoral program (n/a), enrolled in a post-doctoral residency/fellowship (1), employed in an academic position at a university (1), total from the above (doctoral) (2).

Additional Information:
Orientation, Objectives, and Emphasis of Department: We emphasize rigorous research and a close working relationship between student and professor.

Special Facilities or Resources: The Psychology Department has a computer lab with 13 workstations. Individual faculty maintain research laboratories. The Biopsychology concentration has fully equipped new research laboratories. The new lab facility contains two components: An animal facility and research laboratory space. The animal facility includes state of the art small animal housing and behavioral testing rooms, a surgery suite, and special procedure rooms that are equipped with hoods. The research laboratories consist of (1) Microscopy suite, (2) Dark room, (3) Data analysis room, (4) 3 Research labs/wet labs equipped with hoods, sinks, and workspace.

Application Information:
Send to: Boston College, Graduate School of Arts and Sciences, 140 Commonwealth Avenue, McGuinn 221, Chestnut Hill, MA 02467. Application available online. Students are admitted in the Fall, application deadline January 2nd. *Fee:* $70. $30 for online subscription.

Boston University
Department of Psychology
64 Cummington Street
Boston, MA 02215
Telephone: (617) 353-2580
Fax: (617) 353-6933
E-mail: *hbe@bu.edu*
Web: *http://www.bu.edu/psych*

Department Information:
1935. Chairperson: Howard Eichenbaum. Number of Faculty: total–full-time 28, part-time 15; women–full-time 14, part-time 4; minority–part-time 1.

Programs and Degrees Offered:
Listed in the following order: Program area, degree type (T if terminal Master's), number awarded 7/03–6/04. Brain, Behavior, and Cognition PhD (Doctor of Philosophy) 2, Clinical PhD (Doctor of Philosophy) 8, General MA/MS (Master of Arts/Science) (T) 35, Human Development PhD (Doctor of Philosophy) 3.

APA Accreditation: Clinical PhD (Doctor of Philosophy).

Student Applications/Admissions:
Student Applications
Brain, Behavior, and Cognition PhD (Doctor of Philosophy)— Applications 2004–2005, 86. Total applicants accepted 2004–2005, 6. Number enrolled (new admits only) 2004–2005 full-time, 3. Openings 2005–2006, 4. The number of students enrolled full and part-time, who were dismissed or voluntarily withdrew from this program area were 3. *Clinical PhD (Doctor of Philosophy)*—Applications 2004–2005, 586. Total applicants accepted 2004–2005, 11. Number enrolled (new admits only) 2004–2005 full-time, 11. Number enrolled (new admits only) 2004–2005 part-time, 0. Openings 2005–2006, 10. The Median number of years required for completion of a degree are 7. The number of students enrolled full and part-time who were dismissed or voluntarily withdrew from this program area were 0. *General MA/MS (Master of Arts/Science)*—Applications 2004–2005, 171. Total applicants accepted 2004–2005, 130. Number enrolled (new admits only) 2004–2005 full-time,

26. Number enrolled (new admits only) 2004–2005 part-time, 14. Total enrolled 2004–2005 full-time, 26, part-time, 34. Openings 2005–2006, 40. The number of students enrolled full and part-time who were dismissed or voluntarily withdrew from this program area were 2. *Human Development PhD (Doctor of Philosophy)*—Applications 2004–2005, 72. Total applicants accepted 2004–2005, 1. Number enrolled (new admits only) 2004–2005 full-time, 0. Total enrolled 2004–2005 full-time, 18. Openings 2005–2006, 1. The number of students enrolled full and part-time who were dismissed or voluntarily withdrew from this program area were 1.

Admissions Requirements:
Scores: Entries appear in this order: required test or GPA, minimum score (if required), median score of students entering in 2003–2004. Master's Programs: overall undergraduate GPA no minimum stated; last 2 years GPA no minimum stated; psychology GPA no minimum stated. Doctoral Programs: overall undergraduate GPA no minimum stated; last 2 years GPA no minimum stated; psychology GPA no minimum stated.
Other Criteria: (importance of criteria rated low, medium, or high): GRE/MAT scores high, research experience high, work experience low, extracurricular activity low, clinically related public service high, GPA high, letters of recommendation high, interview high, statement of goals and objectives high.

Student Characteristics: The following represents characteristics of students in 2004–2005 in all graduate psychology programs in the department: Female–full-time 115, part-time 27; Male–full-time 26, part-time 7; Caucasian–full-time 0, part-time 0.

Financial Information/Assistance:
Tuition for Full-Time Study: *Master's:* State residents: per academic year $29,988, $937 per credit hour. *Doctoral:* State residents: per academic year $29,988, $937 per credit hour.

Financial Assistance:
First Year Students: Teaching assistantships available for first-year. Average amount paid per academic year: $15,500. Average number of hours worked per week: 20. Tuition remission given: full. Research assistantships available for first-year. Average amount paid per academic year: $23,250. Average number of hours worked per week: 20. Apply by for 12 mos. Tuition remission given: full. Fellowships and scholarships available for first-year. Tuition remission given: full.
Advanced Students: Teaching assistantships available for advanced students. Average amount paid per academic year: $15,500. Average number of hours worked per week: 20. Tuition remission given: full. Research assistantships available for advanced students. Average amount paid per academic year: $23,250. Average number of hours worked per week: 20. Apply by for 12 mos. Tuition remission given: full.
Contact Information: No information provided.

Internships/Practica: Students in the clinical doctoral program are involved in internships and practica as part of their degree requirements. For those doctoral students for whom a professional internship is required prior to graduation, 11 applied in 2003–2004. Of those who applied, 11 were placed in APA accredited internships.

Housing and Day Care: No on-campus housing is available. No on-campus day care facilities are available.

Employment of Department Graduates:

Master's Degree Graduates: Of those who graduated in the academic year 2003–2004, the following categories and numbers represent the post-graduate activities and employment of master's degree graduates: Enrolled in a post-doctoral residency/fellowship (n/a), employed in independent practice (n/a), total from the above (master's) (0).

Doctoral Degree Graduates: Of those who graduated in the academic year 2003–2004, the following categories and numbers represent the post-graduate activities and employment of doctoral degree graduates: Enrolled in a psychology doctoral program (n/a), total from the above (doctoral) (0).

Additional Information:

Orientation, Objectives, and Emphasis of Department: The department offers specialized training leading to the PhD degree in three areas of concentration: clinical; brain, behavior, and cognition; and human development with specializations in developmental, personality, social, and family. The PhD degree in psychology is awarded to students of scholarly competence as reflected by course achievement and by performance on written and oral examinations and of research competence as reflected by student's skillful application and communication of knowledge in the area of specialization. Breadth is encouraged within psychology and in related social, behavioral, and biological sciences, but it is also expected that the student will engage in intensive and penetrating study of a specialized area of the field.

Special Facilities or Resources: Laboratories for research pursuits in animal behavior, behavior disorders, child development, cognition, neurophysiology, molecular biology and psychopharmacology add to the department's facilities. The Center for Anxiety and Related Disorders (CARD), a nationally recognized clinical research and treatment center, is a recent addition to the department and allows students to engage in a variety of ongoing research projects and receive training in focused clinical interventions. In addition, the Boston area is fortunate to have a number of nationally known hospitals, counseling centers, and community mental health centers directly affiliated with our clinical program, where students have opportunities to gain experience in a variety of clinical settings with different client populations. The New England Regional Primate Center, which is supported by the National Institutes of Health, is also available to Boston University faculty and students.

Application Information:

Send to: Graduate School of Arts and Sciences, 705 Commonwealth Avenue, Boston, MA 02215. Application available online. URL of online application: www.bu.edu/cas/graduate. Students are admitted in the Fall. The deadline for applications to the Clinical PhD program is December 1. Please note, applications, as well as all credentials and supplementary materials, must be submitted in one packet by the deadline. Incomplete applications will not be reviewed. The deadline for applications to the Brain, Behavior & Cognition PhD Program and the Human Development PhD Program is January 15. Applicants for the MA-only program are reviewed in two rounds. The first deadline for completed applications is March 1. The second deadline for completed applications is June 1. *Fee:* $65.

Boston University

Divison of Graduate Medical Sciences, Program in Mental Health and Behavioral Medicine
School of Medicine
715 Albany Street, Robinson Bldg, Suite B-2903
Boston, MA 02118
Telephone: (617) 414-2320
Fax: (617) 414-2323
E-mail: *nicey@bu.edu*
Web: *www.bumc.bu.edu/mhbm*

Department Information:

2001. Chairperson: Stephen Brady, PhD Number of Faculty: total–full-time 3, part-time 10; women–full-time 4, part-time 2; minority–full-time 1, part-time 1.

Programs and Degrees Offered:

Listed in the following order: Program area, degree type (T if terminal Master's), number awarded 7/03–6/04. Mental Health and Behavioral Medicine MA/MS (Master of Arts/Science) (T) 10.

Student Applications/Admissions:

Student Applications

Mental Health and Behavioral Medicine MA/MS (Master of Arts/Science)—Applications 2004–2005, 65. Total applicants accepted 2004–2005, 38. Number enrolled (new admits only) 2004–2005 full-time, 20. Number enrolled (new admits only) 2004–2005 part-time, 5. Total enrolled 2004–2005 full-time, 36, part-time, 9. Openings 2005–2006, 25. The Median number of years required for completion of a degree are 2. The number of students enrolled full and part-time who were dismissed or voluntarily withdrew from this program area was 1.

Admissions Requirements:

Scores: Entries appear in this order: required test or GPA, minimum score (if required), median score of students entering in 2003–2004. Master's Programs: GRE-V no minimum stated, 490; GRE-Q no minimum stated, 605; GRE-V+Q no minimum stated, 1080; GRE-Analytical no minimum stated; overall undergraduate GPA no minimum stated, 3.24.

Other Criteria: (importance of criteria rated low, medium, or high): GRE/MAT scores medium, research experience low, work experience medium, extracurricular activity medium, clinically related public service medium, GPA medium, letters of recommendation high, interview high, statement of goals and objectives high. For additional information on admission requirements, go to: www.bumc.bu.edu/mhbm.

Student Characteristics: The following represents characteristics of students in 2004–2005 in all graduate psychology programs in the department: Female–full-time 27, part-time 9; Male–full-time 9, part-time 0; African American/Black–full-time 5, part-time 2; Hispanic/Latino(a)–full-time 1, part-time 0; Asian/Pacific Islander–full-time 2, part-time 0; American Indian/Alaska Native–full-time 0, part-time 0; Caucasian–full-time 28, part-time 7; Multi-ethnic–full-time 0, part-time 0; students subject to the Americans With Disabilities Act–full-time 1, part-time 0.

Financial Information/Assistance:

Tuition for Full-Time Study: *Master's:* State residents: per academic year $31,530, $985 per credit hour; Nonstate residents: per academic year $31,530, $985 per credit hour. Tuition is subject to change.

Financial Assistance:

First Year Students: No information provided.
Advanced Students: No information provided.
Contact Information: No information provided.

Internships/Practica: Completion of the Masters in Mental Health and Behavioral Medicine program prepares students for independent licensure as a Mental Health Counselor (LMHC). Our students are primarily trained to conduct clinical practice with urban multicultural underserved populations. Our clinical training program includes curricula in mental health, behavioral medicine, and neuroscience offered in an urban hospital and medical school environment. The coursework is intended to prepare students to provide clinical services to a range of individuals in diversified settings. More specifically, students are trained to perform brief forms of assessment and psychotherapeutic interventions in medical and behavioral health care settings. We offer clinical training opportunities in diverse settings such as psychiatric emergency department services, child, adolescent, and adult outpatient psychiatric clinics, medical and psychiatric inpatient services, adolescent substance abuse treatment centers, college counseling centers, and community mental health clinics. Our practicum program is a 16 hour a week commitment over the course of one semester and our internship training is a 24 hour a week commitment over the course of an academic year. At the completion of the Program students will have accumulated approximately 1,000 hours of clinical training.

Housing and Day Care: On-campus housing is available. No on-campus day care facilities are available.

Employment of Department Graduates:

Master's Degree Graduates: Of those who graduated in the academic year 2003–2004, the following categories and numbers represent the post-graduate activities and employment of master's degree graduates: Enrolled in a psychology doctoral program (1), enrolled in another graduate/professional program (1), enrolled in a post-doctoral residency/fellowship (n/a), employed in independent practice (n/a), employed in a professional position in a school system (1), employed in a community mental health/counseling center (3), other employment position (1), do not know (3), total from the above (master's) (10).

Doctoral Degree Graduates: Of those who graduated in the academic year 2003–2004, the following categories and numbers represent the post-graduate activities and employment of doctoral degree graduates: Enrolled in a psychology doctoral program (n/a), total from the above (doctoral) (0).

Additional Information:

Orientation, Objectives, and Emphasis of Department: The Mental Health and Behavioral Medicine Program is the first of its kind in the United States, as it is located within a School of Medicine. Our program curriculum blends scholarship, practical experience and an appreciation of the scientific bases of assessment and treatments for behavioral and neurological disorders. Our objective is to provide Master's level counselors with a strong foundation in psychopathology and psychotherapeutic intervention, as well as a background in behavioral medicine and neuroscience. Our primary focus is the development of professional counselors with the skills to develop as scholars, teachers, researchers and clinicians. Our program fills a major gap in the delivery of mental health services in health care settings and to patients with health care concerns. Students have a unique opportunity to work with outstanding mentors in psychology, psychiatry, neuroscience and medicine. Graduates of the Program assume positions in a variety of settings, including community mental health centers, college/university settings, clinical research settings, and government facilities. Approximately one-half of our students pursue doctoral level training either immediately upon graduation or soon thereafter. More specific information about course requirements, etc., can be found on our website: www.bumc.bu.edu/mhbm.

Special Facilities or Resources: Because the program is housed within the Boston University School of Medicine and is part of Boston University, our students and faculty have access to a wide variety of academic and medical resources. Although not a required part of students' experiences in the program, many of our students collaborate in clinical research activities, which are always a part of our campus. Students also engage in a wide variety of clinical experiences, as described above in "Internships/Practica." Books, journals, and access to computerized literature searches currently are available in the Alumni Medical Library at BUSM. This full service medical library contains most relevant publications for students in a mental health related program. On the Charles River Campus, the Charles Mugar Library is available for any students who wish further supplementary readings in the behavioral and social sciences. As a member of the Boston Library Consortium, Boston University students have access to additional library collections through inter-library loans. Overall, the library resources available to these students are excellent and do not require additional acquisitions. The current Mental Health and Behavioral Medicine Program occupies a newly renovated space with approximately 1,200 square feet for its administrative and core faculty office space.

Application Information:
Application available online. URL of online application: www.bumc.bu.edu/mhbm. Students are admitted in the Fall, application deadline rolling; Winter, application deadline rolling; Spring, application deadline rolling. Programs have rolling admissions. *Fee:* $60.

Brandeis University
Department of Psychology
415 South Street, Mail Stop 62
Waltham, MA 02454-9110
Telephone: (781) 736-3300
Fax: (781) 736-3291
E-mail: *mcdonough@brandeis.edu*
Web: *http://www.brandeis.edu/departments/psych*

Department Information:
1948. Chairperson: Margie Lachman. Number of Faculty: total–full-time 18, part-time 8; women–full-time 5, part-time 5; minority–part-time 1.

Programs and Degrees Offered:

Listed in the following order: Program area, degree type (T if terminal Master's), number awarded 7/03–6/04. Cognitive Neuroscience PhD (Doctor of Philosophy) 0, General MA/MS (Master of Arts/Science) (T) 5, Social/ Developmental PhD (Doctor of Philosophy) 4.

Student Applications/Admissions:

Student Applications

Cognitive Neuroscience PhD (Doctor of Philosophy)—Applications 2004–2005, 15. Total applicants accepted 2004–2005, 3. Number enrolled (new admits only) 2004–2005 full-time, 2. Number enrolled (new admits only) 2004–2005 part-time, 0. Openings 2005–2006, 2. The Median number of years required for completion of a degree are 5. The number of students enrolled full and part-time who were dismissed or voluntarily withdrew from this program area were 0. *General MA/MS (Master of Arts/Science)*—Applications 2004–2005, 34. Total applicants accepted 2004–2005, 7. Number enrolled (new admits only) 2004–2005 full-time, 5. Number enrolled (new admits only) 2004–2005 part-time, 0. Total enrolled 2004–2005 full-time, 3, part-time, 2. Openings 2005–2006, 6. The Median number of years required for completion of a degree is 1. The number of students enrolled full and part-time who were dismissed or voluntarily withdrew from this program area were 3. *Social/ Developmental PhD (Doctor of Philosophy)*—Applications 2004–2005, 41. Total applicants accepted 2004–2005, 6. Number enrolled (new admits only) 2004–2005 full-time, 4. Number enrolled (new admits only) 2004–2005 part-time, 0. Openings 2005–2006, 3. The Median number of years required for completion of a degree are 7. The number of students enrolled full and part-time who were dismissed or voluntarily withdrew from this program area were 0.

Admissions Requirements:

Scores: Entries appear in this order: required test or GPA, minimum score (if required), median score of students entering in 2003–2004. Master's Programs: GRE-V no minimum stated; GRE-Q no minimum stated; GRE-Analytical no minimum stated; overall undergraduate GPA no minimum stated. Doctoral Programs: GRE-V no minimum stated; GRE-Q no minimum stated; GRE-Analytical no minimum stated; overall undergraduate GPA no minimum stated. GRE Subject strongly recommended.

Other Criteria: (importance of criteria rated low, medium, or high): GRE/MAT scores high, research experience high, work experience medium, extracurricular activity low, clinically related public service low, GPA high, letters of recommendation high, interview high, statement of goals and objectives high. For additional information on admission requirements, go to: http://www.brandeis.edu/departments/psych/grad.html.

Student Characteristics: The following represents characteristics of students in 2004–2005 in all graduate psychology programs in the department: Female–full-time 24, part-time 2; Male–full-time 4, part-time 0; African American/Black–full-time 0, part-time 0; Hispanic/Latino(a)–full-time 2, part-time 0; Asian/Pacific Islander–full-time 8, part-time 0; American Indian/Alaska Native–full-time 0, part-time 0; Caucasian–full-time 16, part-time 2; Multi-ethnic–full-time 0, part-time 0; students subject to the Americans With Disabilities Act–full-time 0, part-time 1.

Financial Information/Assistance:

Tuition for Full-Time Study: *Master's:* State residents: per academic year $30,160; Nonstate residents: per academic year $30,160. See the following Web site for updates and changes in tuition costs: http://www.brandeis.edu/gsas/students/aid-handbook/costofattendance.html.

Financial Assistance:

First Year Students: Research assistantships available for first-year. Fellowships and scholarships available for first-year. Average amount paid per academic year: $16,500. Apply by January 15. Tuition remission given: full.

Advanced Students: Teaching assistantships available for advanced students. Fellowships and scholarships available for advanced students. Average amount paid per academic year: $16,500. Tuition remission given: full.

Contact Information: Of all students currently enrolled full-time, 80% benefitted from one or more of the listed financial assistance programs. Application and information available online at: http://www.brandeis.edu/gsas/prospectives/financial-assistance.html; http://www.brandeis.edu/gsas/ap.

Internships/Practica: No information provided.

Housing and Day Care: On-campus housing is available. On-campus day care facilities are available. See the following Web site for more information: On-site day care available with cost based on sliding-fee scale. Web address: http://www.brandeis.edu/lemberg/.

Employment of Department Graduates:

Master's Degree Graduates: Of those who graduated in the academic year 2003–2004, the following categories and numbers represent the post-graduate activities and employment of master's degree graduates: Enrolled in a psychology doctoral program (1), enrolled in another graduate/professional program (0), enrolled in a post-doctoral residency/fellowship (n/a), employed in independent practice (n/a), employed in an academic position at a university (0), employed in an academic position at a 2-year/4-year college (0), employed in other positions at a higher education institution (1), employed in a professional position in a school system (0), employed in business or industry (research/consulting) (0), employed in business or industry (management) (0), employed in a government agency (research) (0), employed in a government agency (professional services) (0), employed in a community mental health/counseling center (0), employed in a hospital/medical center (2), still seeking employment (0), other employment position (1), total from the above (master's) (5).

Doctoral Degree Graduates: Of those who graduated in the academic year 2003–2004, the following categories and numbers represent the post-graduate activities and employment of doctoral degree graduates: Enrolled in a psychology doctoral program (n/a), enrolled in another graduate/professional program (0), enrolled in a post-doctoral residency/fellowship (1), employed in independent practice (0), employed in an academic position at a university (1), employed in an academic position at a 2-year/4-year college (0), employed in other positions at a higher education institution (1), employed in a professional position in a school system (0), employed in business or industry (research/consulting) (0), employed in business or industry (management) (0), employed in a government agency (research) (0), employed in a government agency (professional services) (0), employed in a community mental health/counseling center (0), employed in a hospital/medical center (0), still seeking employment (0), other employment position (1), total from the above (doctoral) (4).

Additional Information:

Orientation, Objectives, and Emphasis of Department: The goal of the PhD Program is to develop excellent researchers and teachers who will become leaders in psychological science. From the start of graduate study, research activity is emphasized. The program helps students develop an area of research specialization, and gives them opportunities to work in one of two general areas: social/developmental psychology or cognitive neuroscience. In both areas, dissertation supervisors are leaders in the following areas: motor control, visual perception, taste physiology and psychophysics, memory, learning, aggression, emotion, personality and cognition in adulthood and old age, social relations and health, stereotypes, and nonverbal communication.

Special Facilities or Resources: Laboratories in the Psychology Department are well-equipped for research on memory, speech recognition, psycholinguistics, visual psychophysics, visual perception, motor control, and spatial orientation, including a NASA-sponsored laboratory for research on human spatial orientation in unusual gravatational environments. Social and developmental psychology laboratories include one-way observation rooms, videorecording and eye-tracking apparatus. There are also opportunities for social neuroscience research through a collaborative grant with the MGH-NMR center. Child development research is facilitated by cooperative relations with the Lemberg Children's Center on the Brandeis campus; applied social research is facilitated by cooperative relations with the Brandeis University Florence Heller Graduate School for Advanced Studies in Social Welfare and the Graduate School of International Economics and Finance. Research on cognitive aging is supported by a training grant from the National Institute on Aging. A special feature of the aging program is an interest in the interaction of cognitive, social and personality factors in healthy aging. The psychology department also participates in an interdisciplinary neuroscience program at the Volen National Center for Complex Systems located on the Brandeis Campus.

Application Information:

Send to: Graduate School of Arts & Sciences, MS 31, Brandeis University, Waltham, MA 02454-9110. Application available online. URL of online application: http://www.brandeis.edu/gsas/apply/index.html. Students are admitted in the Fall. PhD Fall Deadline is January 15. Master's Fall Deadline is May 1. Brandeis offers 3 ways to obtain an application: 1. Fill out our online application and submit electronically. 2. Download and print out an application from our Web site. 3. Request a hard copy application be sent to you by mail. Web site address: http://www.brandeis.edu/gsas/apply/index.html. *Fee:* $55.

Clark University (2004 data)
Frances L. Hiatt School of Psychology
950 Main Street
Worcester, MA 01610
Telephone: (508) 793-7274
Fax: (508) 793-7265
E-mail: *jvalsiner@clarku.edu*
Web: *http://www.clarku.edu/~psydept/*

Department Information:
1889. Chairperson: Jaan Valsiner, PhD Number of Faculty: total–full-time 16, part-time 10; women–full-time 6, part-time 3; minority–full-time 2.

Programs and Degrees Offered:
Listed in the following order: Program area, degree type (T if terminal Master's), number awarded 7/03–6/04. Clinical PhD (Doctor of Philosophy) 7, Developmental PhD (Doctor of Philosophy) 3, Social, Cultural and Evolutionary PhD (Doctor of Philosophy) 2.

APA Accreditation: Clinical PhD (Doctor of Philosophy).

Student Applications/Admissions:
Student Applications
Clinical PhD (Doctor of Philosophy)—Applications 2004–2005, 127. Total applicants accepted 2004–2005, 19. Total enrolled 2004–2005 full-time, 33. Openings 2005–2006, 6. The Median number of years required for completion of a degree are 7. The number of students enrolled full and part-time who were dismissed or voluntarily withdrew from this program area were 0. *Developmental PhD (Doctor of Philosophy)*—Applications 2004–2005, 22. Total applicants accepted 2004–2005, 2. Total enrolled 2004–2005 full-time, 12. Openings 2005–2006, 6. The Median number of years required for completion of a degree are 6. The number of students enrolled full and part-time who were dismissed or voluntarily withdrew from this program area were 0. *Social, Cultural and Evolutionary PhD (Doctor of Philosophy)*—Applications 2004–2005, 26. Total applicants accepted 2004–2005, 2. Total enrolled 2004–2005 full-time, 7. Openings 2005–2006, 2. The Median number of years required for completion of a degree are 6.

Admissions Requirements:
Scores: Entries appear in this order: required test or GPA, minimum score (if required), median score of students entering in 2003–2004. Doctoral Programs: GRE-V no minimum stated, 675; GRE-Q no minimum stated, 660; GRE-V+Q no minimum stated, 1335; overall undergraduate GPA no minimum stated, 3.80.
Other Criteria: (importance of criteria rated low, medium, or high): GRE/MAT scores medium, research experience high, work experience medium, extracurricular activity medium, clinically related public service medium, GPA medium, letters of recommendation high, statement of goals and objectives high.

Student Characteristics: The following represents characteristics of students in 2004–2005 in all graduate psychology programs in the department: Female–full-time 52, part-time 0; Male–full-time 9, part-time 0; African American/Black–full-time 0, part-time 0; Hispanic/Latino(a)–full-time 5, part-time 0; Asian/Pacific Islander–full-time 5, part-time 0; American Indian/Alaska Native–full-time 0, part-time 0; Caucasian–full-time 50, part-time 0; Multi-ethnic–full-time 1, part-time 0; students subject to the Americans With Disabilities Act–full-time 0, part-time 0.

Financial Information/Assistance:

Tuition for Full-Time Study: *Doctoral:* State residents: per academic year $28,000; Nonstate residents: per academic year $28,000.

Financial Assistance:

First Year Students: Teaching assistantships available for first-year. Average amount paid per academic year: $13,000. Average number of hours worked per week: 17. Tuition remission given: full. Research assistantships available for first-year. Average amount paid per academic year: $13,000. Average number of hours worked per week: 17. Tuition remission given: full. Fellowships and scholarships available for first-year. Average amount paid per academic year: $13,000. Average number of hours worked per week: 0. Tuition remission given: full.

Advanced Students: Teaching assistantships available for advanced students. Average amount paid per academic year: $13,000. Average number of hours worked per week: 17. Tuition remission given: full. Research assistantships available for advanced students. Average amount paid per academic year: $13,000. Average number of hours worked per week: 17. Tuition remission given: full. Fellowships and scholarships available for advanced students. Average amount paid per academic year: $13,000. Average number of hours worked per week: 0. Tuition remission given: full.

Contact Information: Of all students currently enrolled full-time, 100% benefitted from one or more of the listed financial assistance programs.

Internships/Practica: Doctoral students in clinical psychology enroll in a supervised practicum each year. These practica involve college students, children, couples and families. In the 3rd year, practicum sites are individually arranged to provide experience in the student's special area of interest. These sites have included state mental institutions, VA neuropsychological units, residential child treatment facilities, etc. Doctoral clinical students also take one full-time year of internship training in APA accredited agencies around the country. For those doctoral students for whom a professional internship is required prior to graduation, 3 applied in 2003–2004. Of those who applied, 4 were placed in internships listed by the Association of Psychology Postdoctoral and Internship Programs (APPIC); 4 were placed in APA accredited internships.

Housing and Day Care: On-campus housing is available. See the following Web site for more information: http://www.clarku.edu/ offices/housing/index.cfm. On-campus day care facilities are available.

Employment of Department Graduates:

Master's Degree Graduates: Of those who graduated in the academic year 2003–2004, the following categories and numbers represent the post-graduate activities and employment of master's degree graduates: Enrolled in a psychology doctoral program (6), enrolled in a post-doctoral residency/fellowship (n/a), employed in independent practice (n/a), total from the above (master's) (6).

Doctoral Degree Graduates: Of those who graduated in the academic year 2003–2004, the following categories and numbers represent the post-graduate activities and employment of doctoral degree graduates: Enrolled in a psychology doctoral program (n/a), employed in business or industry (research/consulting) (1), employed in a community mental health/counseling center (1), total from the above (doctoral) (2).

Additional Information:

Orientation, Objectives, and Emphasis of Department: The Department's philosophy affirms the unity of psychology as a subject matter and discourages rigid distinctions among kinds of psychologists and kinds of department programs. Nonetheless, the Department provides in-depth training in the student's area of specialization with a primary concern for theory development, conceptual analysis and empirical investigation. A diversity of theoretical viewpoints is represented, including various developmental viewpoints. Students become acquainted with a variety of methods of investigation, not only with traditional experimental and naturalistic methods, but also with phenomenological, structural, hermeneutic, and other qualitative methodologies. Each student's program is individualized to some degree, and education takes place through small seminars, one-to-one research and practicum training, individualized papers, and MA thesis and PhD dissertation work. Research and other scholarly work are strongly encouraged throughout the graduate experience.

Special Facilities or Resources: The Psychology Department possesses ample space, two entire floors and substantial parts of two others, most of it recently renovated, for offices, classes, laboratories, and clinical training. These include a child study area, facilities for studying family interactions, a human physiology laboratory, a personality-social research area, and dyadic and group clinical training facilities, all with one-way vision and recording facilities, as well as a chemosensory laboratory. The Heinz Werner Institute for Developmental Analysis functions in close connection with the Department. Additional opportunities for research exist in connection with the University of Massachusetts Medical School, the Worcester Foundation for Experimental Biology, schools, and other community settings. Clinical practicum settings include various area agencies.

Application Information:

Send to: Graduate Admissions Secretary, Frances L. Hiatt School of Psychology, Clark University, 950 Main Street, Worcester, MA 01610. Students are admitted in the Fall, application deadline January 15. *Fee:* $40. Fees waived in cases of financial need.

Harvard University

Department of Psychology
33 Kirkland Street
Cambridge, MA 02138
Telephone: (617) 495-3800
E-mail: *psyinfo@wjh.harvard.edu*
Web: *http://www.wjh.harvard.edu/psych/grad_main.html*

Department Information:

1936. Chairperson: Daniel Schacter. Number of Faculty: total–full-time 22, part-time 10; women–full-time 8, part-time 3; minority–full-time 1.

Programs and Degrees Offered:

Listed in the following order: Program area, degree type (T if terminal Master's), number awarded 7/03–6/04. Clinical Psychology PhD (Doctor of Philosophy) 0, Cognition, Brain, and Behavior PhD (Doctor of Philosophy) 6, Developmental PhD (Doctor of Philosophy) 1, Experimental Psychopathology PhD (Doctor of Philosophy) 3, Organizational Behavior PhD (Doctor of Philosophy) 2, Social PhD (Doctor of Philosophy) 3.

Student Applications/Admissions:

Student Applications

Clinical Psychology PhD (Doctor of Philosophy)—Applications 2004–2005, 145. Total applicants accepted 2004–2005, 4. Number enrolled (new admits only) 2004–2005 full-time, 3. Openings 2005–2006, 6. The Median number of years required for completion of a degree are 5. The number of students enrolled full and part-time who were dismissed or voluntarily withdrew from this program area were 1. *Cognition, Brain, and Behavior PhD (Doctor of Philosophy)*—Applications 2004–2005, 99. Total applicants accepted 2004–2005, 6. Number enrolled (new admits only) 2004–2005 full-time, 5. Openings 2005–2006, 4. The Median number of years required for completion of a degree are 5. The number of students enrolled full and part-time who were dismissed or voluntarily withdrew from this program area were 0. *Developmental PhD (Doctor of Philosophy)*—Applications 2004–2005, 33. Total applicants accepted 2004–2005, 3. Number enrolled (new admits only) 2004–2005 full-time, 2. Openings 2005–2006, 5. The Median number of years required for completion of a degree are 7. The number of students enrolled full and part-time who were dismissed or voluntarily withdrew from this program area were 0. *Experimental Psychopathology PhD (Doctor of Philosophy)*—Applications 2004–2005, 145. Total applicants accepted 2004–2005, 0. The Median number of years required for completion of a degree are 6. *Organizational Behavior PhD (Doctor of Philosophy)*—Number enrolled (new admits only) 2004–2005 full-time, 2. Openings 2005–2006, 2. The Median number of years required for completion of a degree are 7. The number of students enrolled full and part-time who were dismissed or voluntarily withdrew from this program area were 0. *Social PhD (Doctor of Philosophy)*—Applications 2004–2005, 101. Total applicants accepted 2004–2005, 3. Number enrolled (new admits only) 2004–2005 full-time, 3. Openings 2005–2006, 2. The Median number of years required for completion of a degree are 6. The number of students enrolled full and part-time who were dismissed or voluntarily withdrew from this program area were 0.

Admissions Requirements:

Scores: Entries appear in this order: required test or GPA, minimum score (if required), median score of students entering in 2003–2004. Doctoral Programs: GRE-V no minimum stated; GRE-Q no minimum stated; GRE-V+Q no minimum stated, 1390; GRE-Analytical no minimum stated. TOEFL exam with minimum score of 550 required for foreign applicants. We don't track average GPA.

Other Criteria: (importance of criteria rated low, medium, or high): GRE/MAT scores high, research experience high, work experience medium, extracurricular activity low, clinically related public service medium, GPA high, letters of recommendation high, interview medium, statement of goals and objectives high.

Student Characteristics: The following represents characteristics of students in 2004–2005 in all graduate psychology programs in the department: Female–full-time 56, part-time 0; Male–full-time 34, part-time 0; African American/Black–full-time 3, part-time 0; Hispanic/Latino(a)–full-time 2, part-time 0; Asian/Pacific Islander–full-time 15, part-time 0; American Indian/Alaska Native–full-time 1, part-time 0; Caucasian–full-time 69, part-time 0; Multi-ethnic–full-time 0, part-time 0.

Financial Information/Assistance:

Tuition for Full-Time Study: *Doctoral:* State residents: per academic year $31,364; Nonstate residents: per academic year $31,364. Tuition is subject to change. See the following Web site for updates and changes in tuition costs: http://www.gsas.harvard.edu/publications/handbook/financial_req.html.

Financial Assistance:

First Year Students: Fellowships and scholarships available for first-year. Average amount paid per academic year: $18,500. Apply by December 15. Tuition remission given: full.

Advanced Students: Teaching assistantships available for advanced students. Average amount paid per academic year: $18,500. Average number of hours worked per week: 20. Apply by May 1. Research assistantships available for advanced students. Apply by varies. Fellowships and scholarships available for advanced students. Apply by varies.

Contact Information: Of all students currently enrolled full-time, 90% benefitted from one or more of the listed financial assistance programs. Application and information available online at: http://apply.embark.com/grad/harvard/gsas/ for incoming students; dept. for continuing students.

Internships/Practica: Students in the clinical program will have pre-doctoral practicum placements in a local Harvard-affiliated hospital. Students are required to have defended their thesis prospectus, and are strongly encouraged to collect most of the data prior to departing for internship, but the thesis project need not be completed before beginning the internship. Clinical internship applicants use the APPIC system. For those doctoral students for whom a professional internship is required prior to graduation, 2 applied in 2003–2004. Of those who applied, 2 were placed in internships listed by the Association of Psychology Postdoctoral and Internship Programs (APPIC); 2 were placed in APA accredited internships.

Housing and Day Care: On-campus housing is available. See the following Web site for more information: http://www.gsas.harvard.

edu/publications/handbook/housing.html. On-campus day care facilities are available. See the following Web site for more information: http://www.gsas.harvard.edu/publications/handbook/service.html#child.

Employment of Department Graduates:

Master's Degree Graduates: Of those who graduated in the academic year 2003–2004, the following categories and numbers represent the post-graduate activities and employment of master's degree graduates: Enrolled in a post-doctoral residency/fellowship (n/a), employed in independent practice (n/a), total from the above (master's) (0).

Doctoral Degree Graduates: Of those who graduated in the academic year 2003–2004, the following categories and numbers represent the post-graduate activities and employment of doctoral degree graduates: Enrolled in a psychology doctoral program (n/a), enrolled in another graduate/professional program (1), enrolled in a post-doctoral residency/fellowship (7), employed in business or industry (research/consulting) (3), still seeking employment (1), do not know (1), total from the above (doctoral) (13).

Additional Information:

Orientation, Objectives, and Emphasis of Department: The psychology department offers PhDs in psychology and social psychology. In conjunction with the Harvard Business School, there is also a PhD program in organizational behavior. The psychology department is divided into a social psychology program; a cognition, brain, and behavior program; and research and training groups in developmental psychology, experimental psychopathology, including a clinical track. The aim of the program is to train students for careers in psychological research and teaching. These careers are mainly in academia. The emphasis of the program is heavily on research training; in addition to a small number of required courses, students do a first-year research project, a second-year research project, and the doctoral dissertation. Students take a major examination or intense seminar(s) in their major specialty fields. Since most students prepare for academic careers, there is ample opportunity to serve as teaching fellows.

Special Facilities or Resources: The department is well equipped with facilities for conducting research. Faculty are the recipients of many grants in various areas of psychology, and graduate students play an essential role in the conduct of most of this research. William James Hall houses a well-staffed computer lab to serve faculty and students. The building also houses a psychology research library. Students are given offices, the use of laboratory space, and a sum of money for research support. The department encourages interdisciplinary study, and students have the benefit of taking courses and working with the faculty at other Harvard graduate schools (Education, Medical School, Public Health, etc.), and at MIT. The Cambridge and Boston areas are well endowed with research facilities and hospitals that offer resources, such as MRI equipment, to students.

Information for Students With Physical Disabilities: See the following Web site for more information: http://www.gsas.harvard.edu/publications/handbook/service.html#disability.

Application Information:
Send to: Harvard University, Office of Admissions, The Graduate School of Arts and Sciences, P.O. Box 9129, Cambridge, MA 02238-9129. Application available online. URL of online application: http://

apply.embark.com/grad/harvard/gsas/. Students are admitted in the Fall, application deadline December 15. *Fee:* $70.

Lesley University
Division of Counseling and Psychology
29 Everett Street
Cambridge, MA 02138-2790
Telephone: (617) 349-8370
Fax: (617) 349-8333
E-mail: *sgere@mail.lesley.edu*
Web: *http://www.lesley.edu/gsass/30cpp.html*

Department Information:
1975. Division Director: Susan H. Gere, PhD. Number of Faculty: total–full-time 8, part-time 71; women–full-time 5, part-time 39; minority–full-time 3, part-time 6.

Programs and Degrees Offered:
Listed in the following order: Program area, degree type (T if terminal Master's), number awarded 7/03–6/04. Clinical Mental Health Counseling MA/MS (Master of Arts/Science) (T) 45, counseling and psychology MA/MS (Master of Arts/Science) 20, Counseling Psychology- School MA/MS (Master of Arts/Science) (T) 8, Counseling Psychology- Professional Counseling MA/MS (Master of Arts/Science) (T) 20, CAGS in Counseling and Psychology Other 3, Advanced Professional Certificate Other, Advanced Professional Certificate - Trauma Studies Respecialization Diploma.

Student Applications/Admissions:
Student Applications
Clinical Mental Health Counseling MA/MS (Master of Arts/Science)—Applications 2004–2005, 72. Total applicants accepted 2004–2005, 63. Number enrolled (new admits only) 2004–2005 full-time, 32. Number enrolled (new admits only) 2004–2005 part-time, 31. Total enrolled 2004–2005 full-time, 89, part-time, 53. Openings 2005–2006, 50. The Median number of years required for completion of a degree are 4. The number of students enrolled full and part-time who were dismissed or voluntarily withdrew from this program area were 0. *Counseling and psychology MA/MS (Master of Arts/Science)*—Applications 2004–2005, 5. Total applicants accepted 2004–2005, 5. Number enrolled (new admits only) 2004–2005 full-time, 3. Number enrolled (new admits only) 2004–2005 part-time, 2. Total enrolled 2004–2005 full-time, 5, part-time, 10. Openings 2005–2006, 30. The Median number of years required for completion of a degree are 3. The number of students enrolled full and part-time who were dismissed or voluntarily withdrew from this program area were 0. *Counseling Psychology- School MA/MS (Master of Arts/Science)*—Applications 2004–2005, 12. Total applicants accepted 2004–2005, 8. Number enrolled (new admits only) 2004–2005 full-time, 4. Number enrolled (new admits only) 2004–2005 part-time, 4. Total enrolled 2004–2005 full-time, 13, part-time, 20. Openings 2005–2006, 15. The Median number of years required for completion of a degree are 3. The number of students enrolled full and part-time who were dismissed or voluntarily withdrew from this program area were 0. *Counseling Psychology- Professional Counseling MA/MS (Master of Arts/Science)*—Applications 2004–

2005, 40. Total applicants accepted 2004–2005, 31. Number enrolled (new admits only) 2004–2005 full-time, 8. Number enrolled (new admits only) 2004–2005 part-time, 23. Total enrolled 2004–2005 full-time, 15, part-time, 72. Openings 2005–2006, 30. The Median number of years required for completion of a degree are 4. The number of students enrolled full and part-time who were dismissed or voluntarily withdrew from this program area were 0. *CAGS in Counseling and Psychology Other*—Applications 2004–2005, 6. Total applicants accepted 2004–2005, 5. Number enrolled (new admits only) 2004–2005 full-time, 2. Number enrolled (new admits only) 2004–2005 part-time, 1. Total enrolled 2004–2005 full-time, 2, part-time, 5. Openings 2005–2006, 5. The Median number of years required for completion of a degree are 2. The number of students enrolled full and part-time who were dismissed or voluntarily withdrew from this program area were 2. *Advanced Professional Certificate Other*—Applications 2004–2005, 2. Total applicants accepted 2004–2005, 2. Number enrolled (new admits only) 2004–2005 part-time, 2. Total enrolled 2004–2005 part-time, 6. Openings 2005–2006, 4. The Median number of years required for completion of a degree are 1.5. The number of students enrolled full and part-time who were dismissed or voluntarily withdrew from this program area were 0. *Advanced Professional Certificate - Trauma Studies Respecialization Diploma*—Applications 2004–2005, 2. Total applicants accepted 2004–2005, 2. Number enrolled (new admits only) 2004–2005 part-time, 2. Total enrolled 2004–2005 part-time, 2. Openings 2005–2006, 10. The Median number of years required for completion of a degree are 1.5. The number of students enrolled full and part-time who were dismissed or voluntarily withdrew from this program area were 0.

Admissions Requirements:

Scores: Entries appear in this order: required test or GPA, minimum score (if required), median score of students entering in 2003–2004. Master's Programs: MAT 40, 47; overall undergraduate GPA 3.0, 3.2.

Other Criteria: (importance of criteria rated low, medium, or high): GRE/MAT scores medium, research experience low, work experience medium, extracurricular activity medium, clinically related public service high, GPA high, letters of recommendation high, interview high, statement of goals and objectives high. Admissions review is holistically based. All elements are given full consideration. For additional information on admission requirements, go to: http://www.lesley.edu/grad_admiss.html.

Student Characteristics: The following represents characteristics of students in 2004–2005 in all graduate psychology programs in the department: Female–full-time 89, part-time 172; Male–full-time 13, part-time 26; African American/Black–full-time 1, part-time 12; Hispanic/Latino(a)–full-time 0, part-time 3; Asian/Pacific Islander–full-time 0, part-time 2; American Indian/Alaska Native–full-time 0, part-time 2; Caucasian–full-time 10, part-time 95.

Financial Information/Assistance:

Tuition for Full-Time Study: *Master's:* State residents: $625 per credit hour; Nonstate residents: $625 per credit hour. Tuition is subject to change. Tuition costs vary by program.

Financial Assistance:

First Year Students: Research assistantships available for first-year. Average amount paid per academic year: $3,400. Average number of hours worked per week: 10. Apply by June 27.

Advanced Students: Research assistantships available for advanced students. Average amount paid per academic year: $3,400. Average number of hours worked per week: 10. Apply by June 27.

Contact Information: No information provided.

Internships/Practica: Field-based training is a vital component of the Counseling and Psychology programs. These experiences offer a way for students to verify, clarify, and challenge the theory acquired in the classroom as well as examine their own role as a clinician. The Field Training Office works closely with several hundred placement sites nationwide to ensure students diverse and personalized learning experiences that provide closely supervised opportunities to do counseling and consultative work with individuals, groups, and families. Students choose sites that fit their professional interests, and their own schedules and locations. Students are required to complete 100 hours of practicum and 600 hours of internship. Some programs require additional 600 hours of internship. Students receive group supervision in the year-long seminar Clinical Practice and Supervision. Most placements are contracted with schools and agencies on a volunteer basis.

Housing and Day Care: No on-campus housing is available. No on-campus day care facilities are available.

Employment of Department Graduates:

Master's Degree Graduates: Of those who graduated in the academic year 2003–2004, the following categories and numbers represent the post-graduate activities and employment of master's degree graduates: Enrolled in a post-doctoral residency/fellowship (n/a), employed in independent practice (n/a), total from the above (master's) (0).

Doctoral Degree Graduates: Of those who graduated in the academic year 2003–2004, the following categories and numbers represent the post-graduate activities and employment of doctoral degree graduates: Enrolled in a psychology doctoral program (n/a), total from the above (doctoral) (0).

Additional Information:

Orientation, Objectives, and Emphasis of Department: The counseling and psychology degree programs prepare professionals in the fields of counseling and psychology at the master's and CAGS levels. The Master of Arts in Clinical Mental Health Counseling program is a 60-credit option for those wishing the most comprehensive clinical training available at the master's level to support clinical mental health counseling practice and to pursue professional licensure in most states. Within the clinical mental health counseling program, a student has the option of specializing in holistic studies, nonspecialization, and school and community counseling (licensure options in either school guidance or school adjustment counseling). The Master of Arts in Counseling Psychology degree program is a 48-credit option. Within this program a school counseling specialization leads to guidance counselor licensure. The Master of Arts in Counseling

Psychology, Professional Counseling Specialization program is a 60-credit option for those who have some clinical experience and wish to gain comprehensive clinical training at the master's level to support clinical mental health counseling practice and to pursue professional licensure in most states. All programs integrate theory and practice through course-based learning and field training. The self of the clinician as an instrument of change is a primary focus as is the understanding of the impact of power, privilege and oppression in all our lives. Graduates are prepared for clinical positions in mental health and school settings. Graduates are prepared for clinical positions, or may elect to use the program to support further graduate work at the doctoral level.

Special Facilities or Resources: Counseling Psychology students have available to them all of the general resource facilities of Lesley University, such as the university library (including a testing center), computer facilities, the Kresge Student Center, and the Career Resource Center. In addition, the department has its own resource center, where bulletins announce area resources and opportunities for further professional study both locally and nationally. Additionally, audio- and videotape equipment is available to degree students for special projects.

Information for Students With Physical Disabilities: See the following Web site for more information: http://www.lesley.edu/services/student_affairs/disabilities.html.

Application Information:

Send to: Office of Graduate Admissions, Lesley University, 29 Everett Street, Cambridge, MA 02138-2790. Application available online. URL of online application: http://www.lesley.edu/grad_admiss/printapp.html. Students are admitted in the Fall, application deadline rolling; Spring, application deadline rolling. Programs have rolling admissions. *Fee:* $50.

Massachusetts School of Professional Psychology
Professional School
221 Rivermoor Street
Boston, MA 02132
Telephone: (617) 327-6777
Fax: (617) 327-4447
E-mail: *admissions@mspp.edu*
Web: *http://www.mspp.edu*

Department Information:
1974. President: Nicholas A. Covino, PsyD Number of Faculty: total– part-time 35; women–part-time 17; minority–part-time 4.

Programs and Degrees Offered:
Listed in the following order: Program area, degree type (T if terminal Master's), number awarded 7/03–6/04. Clinical PsyD (Doctor of Psychology) 23, respecialization diploma PsyD (Doctor of Psychology) 1.

APA Accreditation: Clinical PsyD (Doctor of Psychology).

Student Applications/Admissions:
Student Applications
Clinical PsyD (Doctor of Psychology)—Applications 2004–2005, 298. Total applicants accepted 2004–2005, 91. Number enrolled (new admits only) 2004–2005 full-time, 51. Number enrolled (new admits only) 2004–2005 part-time, 0. Total enrolled 2004–2005 full-time, 165, part-time, 43. Openings 2005–2006, 48. The Median number of years required for completion of a degree are 4.8. The number of students enrolled full and part-time who were dismissed or voluntarily withdrew from this program area were 8. *Respecialization diploma PsyD (Doctor of Psychology)*—Applications 2004–2005, 3. Total applicants accepted 2004–2005, 3. Number enrolled (new admits only) 2004–2005 part-time, 3. Total enrolled 2004–2005 part-time, 3. Openings 2005–2006, 3. The Median number of years required for completion of a degree are 3. The number of students enrolled full and part-time who were dismissed or voluntarily withdrew from this program area were 1.

Admissions Requirements:
Scores: Entries appear in this order: required test or GPA, minimum score (if required), median score of students entering in 2003–2004. Doctoral Programs: GRE-V no minimum stated, 550; GRE-Q no minimum stated, 600; GRE-V+Q 1150; overall undergraduate GPA 3.00.

Other Criteria: (importance of criteria rated low, medium, or high): GRE/MAT scores medium, research experience low, work experience medium, extracurricular activity high, clinically related public service high, GPA high, letters of recommendation high, interview high, statement of goals and objectives high.

Student Characteristics: The following represents characteristics of students in 2004–2005 in all graduate psychology programs in the department: Female–full-time 137, part-time 37; Male–full-time 28, part-time 6; African American/Black–full-time 3, part-time 1; Hispanic/Latino(a)–full-time 6, part-time 0; Asian/Pacific Islander–full-time 6, part-time 1; American Indian/Alaska Native–full-time 1, part-time 0; Caucasian–full-time 149, part-time 41; Multi-ethnic–full-time 0, part-time 0; students subject to the Americans With Disabilities Act–full-time 0, part-time 0.

Financial Information/Assistance:
Tuition for Full-Time Study: *Doctoral:* State residents: per academic year $21,920, $685 per credit hour; Nonstate residents: per academic year $21,920, $685 per credit hour.

Financial Assistance:
First Year Students: Fellowships and scholarships available for first-year. Average amount paid per academic year: $1,739. Apply by February 14.

Advanced Students: Teaching assistantships available for advanced students. Average amount paid per academic year: $3,000. Average number of hours worked per week: 10. Apply by July 1. Fellowships and scholarships available for advanced students. Average amount paid per academic year: $3,526. Apply by April 15.

Contact Information: Of all students currently enrolled full-time, 59% benefitted from one or more of the listed financial assistance programs.

Internships/Practica: Field placements are an integral part of the program throughout the four years. The practica and internship experiences are integrated with the curriculum and individual's educational needs at each level of the program. Over 150 training sites are available in the greater Boston area including hospitals, mental health centers, court clinics, and other agencies offering mental health services. They provide students the opportunity to work with varied populations, life span issues, theoretical orientations, and treatment modalities in the context of supervised training. The large number of qualified agencies included in our training network enable students the option of applying for full or half-time APA-approved internships or securing suitable, high quality, local internships.

Housing and Day Care: No on-campus housing is available. No on-campus day care facilities are available.

Employment of Department Graduates:

Master's Degree Graduates: Of those who graduated in the academic year 2003–2004, the following categories and numbers represent the post-graduate activities and employment of master's degree graduates: Enrolled in a post-doctoral residency/fellowship (n/a), employed in independent practice (n/a), total from the above (master's) (0).

Doctoral Degree Graduates: Of those who graduated in the academic year 2003–2004, the following categories and numbers represent the post-graduate activities and employment of doctoral degree graduates: Enrolled in a psychology doctoral program (n/a), total from the above (doctoral) (0).

Additional Information:

Orientation, Objectives, and Emphasis of Department: The mission is to improve the quality of life by educating psychology practitioners to be capable of providing high quality human services. Graduates should be able to help evaluate, ameliorate, and prevent psychosocial problems; help individuals, families, groups, organizations, and communities function effectively; exhibit competence in the practical application of existing psychosocial knowledge and an awareness of the possibility of extending this knowledge; and develop new professional roles, service models, and delivery systems capable of meeting the changing needs of society. The educational philosophy is evident in several characteristics that distinguish it from the traditional PhD program. Course content is presented as a foundation for professional practice rather than as scientific inquiry. This entails more of a difference in course objectives and emphasis than in content. Curriculum stresses seminars integrated with field placements, focusing on helping students to coordinate theory with skills and the development of insights useful in the practice of psychology. Courses are taught by psychologists experienced in the application of knowledge in their teaching areas. The first two years of the program provide students with a solid generic foundation for psychological practice; third and fourth years allow for concentration in areas of individual interest.

Application Information:

Send to: Admissions Office. Students are admitted in the Fall, application deadline January 7. Respecialization Diploma-Rolling Admissions. *Fee:* $50.

Massachusetts, University of

Department of Psychology
Tobin Hall
Amherst, MA 01003
Telephone: (413) 545-2383
Fax: (413) 545-0996
E-mail: *berthier@psych.umass.edu*
Web: *http://www.umass.edu/psychology*

Department Information:
1947. Chairperson: Melinda Novak. Number of Faculty: total–full-time 43, part-time 5; women–full-time 18, part-time 4; minority–full-time 3.

Programs and Degrees Offered:
Listed in the following order: Program area, degree type (T if terminal Master's), number awarded 7/03–6/04. Clinical PhD (Doctor of Philosophy) 8, Cognitive PhD (Doctor of Philosophy) 3, Developmental PhD (Doctor of Philosophy) 3, Learning- Animal PhD (Doctor of Philosophy) 0, Neuroscience and Behavior MA/MS (Master of Arts/Science) (T) 0, Personality Social PhD (Doctor of Philosophy) 2, Psychology of Peace and the Prevention of Violence PhD (Doctor of Philosophy) 0.

APA Accreditation: Clinical PhD (Doctor of Philosophy).

Student Applications/Admissions:
Student Applications

Clinical PhD (Doctor of Philosophy)—Applications 2004–2005, 264. Total applicants accepted 2004–2005, 9. Openings 2005–2006, 8. The Median number of years required for completion of a degree are 5. *Cognitive PhD (Doctor of Philosophy)*—Applications 2004–2005, 35. Total applicants accepted 2004–2005, 5. Openings 2005–2006, 3. The Median number of years required for completion of a degree are 5. *Developmental PhD (Doctor of Philosophy)*—Applications 2004–2005, 21. Total applicants accepted 2004–2005, 3. Openings 2005–2006, 3. The Median number of years required for completion of a degree are 5. *Learning-Animal PhD (Doctor of Philosophy)*—Applications 2004–2005, 0. Total applicants accepted 2004–2005, 0. *Neuroscience and Behavior MA/MS (Master of Arts/Science)*—Applications 2004–2005, 0. Total applicants accepted 2004–2005, 0. *Personality Social PhD (Doctor of Philosophy)*—Applications 2004–2005, 72. Total applicants accepted 2004–2005, 9. Openings 2005–2006, 3. The Median number of years required for completion of a degree are 5. *Psychology of Peace and the Prevention of Violence PhD (Doctor of Philosophy)*—Applications 2004–2005, 20. Total applicants accepted 2004–2005, 3. Number enrolled (new admits only) 2004–2005 full-time, 3. Total enrolled 2004–2005 full-time, 3. Openings 2005–2006, 3.

Admissions Requirements:
Scores: Entries appear in this order: required test or GPA, minimum score (if required), median score of students entering in 2003–2004. Doctoral Programs: GRE-V no minimum stated, 596; GRE-Q no minimum stated, 662; GRE-V+Q no minimum stated, 1258; GRE-Analytical no minimum stated, 640; overall undergraduate GPA no minimum stated, 3.79.

Other Criteria: (importance of criteria rated low, medium, or high): GRE/MAT scores high, research experience high, work experience low, GPA high, letters of recommendation high, interview medium, statement of goals and objectives medium. Only clinical requires an interview. Clinically related public service also is a criteria (low) in admission to clinical.

Student Characteristics: The following represents characteristics of students in 2004–2005 in all graduate psychology programs in the department: Female–full-time 52, part-time 0; Male–full-time 27, part-time 0; African American/Black–full-time 2, part-time 0; Hispanic/Latino(a)–full-time 4, part-time 0; Asian/Pacific Islander–full-time 2, part-time 0; American Indian/Alaska Native–full-time 0, part-time 0; Caucasian–full-time 71, part-time 0; Multi-ethnic–full-time 0, part-time 0; students subject to the Americans With Disabilities Act–full-time 0, part-time 0.

Financial Information/Assistance:

Tuition for Full-Time Study: *Doctoral:* State residents: $110 per credit hour; Nonstate residents: $415 per credit hour. Tuition is subject to change. See the following Web site for updates and changes in tuition costs: http://www.umass.edu/gradschool/tuitfee/index.html.

Financial Assistance:

First Year Students: Teaching assistantships available for first-year. Average amount paid per academic year: $12,000. Average number of hours worked per week: 20. Tuition remission given: full. Research assistantships available for first-year. Average amount paid per academic year: $12,000. Average number of hours worked per week: 20. Tuition remission given: full. Traineeships available for first-year. Average amount paid per academic year: $12,000. Average number of hours worked per week: 20. Tuition remission given: full. Fellowships and scholarships available for first-year. Average amount paid per academic year: $10,500. Average number of hours worked per week: 0. Tuition remission given: full.

Advanced Students: Teaching assistantships available for advanced students. Average amount paid per academic year: $12,500. Average number of hours worked per week: 20. Tuition remission given: full. Research assistantships available for advanced students. Average amount paid per academic year: $12,000. Average number of hours worked per week: 20. Tuition remission given: full. Traineeships available for advanced students. Average amount paid per academic year: $12,000. Average number of hours worked per week: 20. Tuition remission given: full. Fellowships and scholarships available for advanced students. Average amount paid per academic year: $10,500. Average number of hours worked per week: 0. Tuition remission given: full.

Contact Information: Of all students currently enrolled full-time, 100% benefitted from one or more of the listed financial assistance programs. Application and information available online at: http://www.umass.edu/umfa.

Internships/Practica: Clinical students must complete an APA-approved clinical internship. None of these required internships are offered by our program. For those doctoral students for whom a professional internship is required prior to graduation, 6 applied in 2003–2004. Of those who applied, 6 were placed in APA accredited internships.

Housing and Day Care: On-campus housing is available. See the following Web site for more information: http://www.umass.edu/grad_catalog/housing.html. On-campus day care facilities are available. See the following Web site for more information: http://home.oit.umass.edu/~cshrc/childcare/main.html.

Employment of Department Graduates:

Master's Degree Graduates: Of those who graduated in the academic year 2003–2004, the following categories and numbers represent the post-graduate activities and employment of master's degree graduates: Enrolled in a post-doctoral residency/fellowship (n/a), employed in independent practice (n/a), total from the above (master's) (0).

Doctoral Degree Graduates: Of those who graduated in the academic year 2003–2004, the following categories and numbers represent the post-graduate activities and employment of doctoral degree graduates: Enrolled in a psychology doctoral program (n/a), total from the above (doctoral) (0).

Additional Information:

Orientation, Objectives, and Emphasis of Department: The psychology program is designed to develop research scholars, college teachers, and scientific/professional psychologists in the six areas listed. Individual student programs combine basic courses and seminars in a variety of specialized areas, research experience, and practica in both on- and off-campus settings. Students may elect to minor in certain areas as well, including personality-social, quantitative methods, and applied social research. In addition, the social-personality area has begun a new specialization in the Psychology of Peace and Prevention of Violence. Students with applied interests, such as clinical and developmental, have ample opportunity for in-depth practical experience.

Special Facilities or Resources: The Department has specialized laboratory facilities, including biochemistry, eyetracking, video data analysis, and other laboratories. It maintains its own clinic for research, clinical training, and service to the community. It provides students with access to microcomputers and to the VAX mainframes at University Computing Services. Departmental facilities and faculty are supplemented by the University's participation in Five-College programs (with Amherst, Hampshire, Mount Holyoke, and Smith Colleges) and by cooperation with other University departments including Computer and Information Science, Industrial Engineering, Education, Linguistics, Sociology, and Biology. The University of Massachusetts also offers a separate PhD degree-granting program in neuroscience and behavior. Many of the students in this program receive the bulk of their training in the Psychology Department and work primarily with Psychology faculty. Students interested in training in neuroscience and behavior should apply for admission directly to that program.

Information for Students With Physical Disabilities: See the following Web site for more information: http://www.umass.edu/disability/.

Application Information:
Send to: Graduate Admissions Office, Goodell Building; University of Massachusetts, Amherst, MA 01003. Application available online. Students are admitted in the Fall, application deadline see below. January 2 for Clinical; January 15 for Neuroscience & Behavior; February 1 for all other programs. *Fee:* $45. Application fee can be waived if GRE fees were waived.

Massachusetts, University of, at Dartmouth
Psychology Department
North Dartmouth, MA 02747
Telephone: (508) 999-8334
Fax: (508) 999-9169
E-mail: *PDONNELLY@umassd.edu*
Web: *http://www.umassd.edu*

Department Information:
1962. Director, Graduate Program/ Clinical: Paul Donnelly. Number of Faculty: total–full-time 11, part-time 8; women–full-time 5, part-time 4; minority–full-time 1, part-time 1; faculty subject to the Americans With Disabilities Act 1.

Programs and Degrees Offered:
Listed in the following order: Program area, degree type (T if terminal Master's), number awarded 7/03–6/04. Clinical MA/MS (Master of Arts/Science) (T) 7, General/ Research MA/MS (Master of Arts/Science) (T) 3.

Student Applications/Admissions:
Student Applications
Clinical MA/MS (Master of Arts/Science)—Applications 2004–2005, 50. Total applicants accepted 2004–2005, 14. Total enrolled 2004–2005 full-time, 30. Openings 2005–2006, 12. The Median number of years required for completion of a degree are 3. *General/ Research MA/MS (Master of Arts/Science)*—Applications 2004–2005, 10. Total applicants accepted 2004–2005, 5. Openings 2005–2006, 5. The Median number of years required for completion of a degree are 2.

Admissions Requirements:
Scores: Entries appear in this order: required test or GPA, minimum score (if required), median score of students entering in 2003–2004. Master's Programs: overall undergraduate GPA no minimum stated; last 2 years GPA no minimum stated; psychology GPA no minimum stated. Minimums are applied differently across programs. General program requires GRE V&Q.
Other Criteria: (importance of criteria rated low, medium, or high): GRE/MAT scores medium, work experience high, clinically related public service high, GPA medium, letters of recommendation high, interview high. These criteria vary across programs and apply on an individual basis.

Student Characteristics: The following represents characteristics of students in 2004–2005 in all graduate psychology programs in the department: Female–full-time 35, part-time 0; Male–full-time 3, part-time 0; African American/Black–full-time 0, part-time 0; Hispanic/Latino(a)–full-time 3, part-time 0; Asian/Pacific Islander–full-time 0, part-time 0; American Indian/Alaska Native–full-time 0, part-time 0; Caucasian–full-time 33, part-time 0; Multi-ethnic–full-time 2, part-time 0; students subject to the Americans With Disabilities Act–full-time 0, part-time 0.

Financial Information/Assistance:
Tuition for Full-Time Study: *Master's:* State residents: per academic year $4,703; Nonstate residents: per academic year $9,500.

Financial Assistance:
First Year Students: Teaching assistantships available for first-year. Average amount paid per academic year: $3,500. Average number of hours worked per week: 10. Tuition remission given: full. Research assistantships available for first-year. Average amount paid per academic year: $7,000. Average number of hours worked per week: 20.
Advanced Students: Research assistantships available for advanced students. Average amount paid per academic year: $7,000. Average number of hours worked per week: 20.
Contact Information: Of all students currently enrolled full-time, 50% benefitted from one or more of the listed financial assistance programs.

Internships/Practica: We have a wide variety of internship and practica experiences available. Field experiences are tailored to specific student needs.u.

Housing and Day Care: No on-campus housing is available. No on-campus day care facilities are available.

Employment of Department Graduates:
Master's Degree Graduates: Of those who graduated in the academic year 2003–2004, the following categories and numbers represent the post-graduate activities and employment of master's degree graduates: Enrolled in a post-doctoral residency/fellowship (n/a), employed in independent practice (n/a), total from the above (master's) (0).
Doctoral Degree Graduates: Of those who graduated in the academic year 2003–2004, the following categories and numbers represent the post-graduate activities and employment of doctoral degree graduates: Enrolled in a psychology doctoral program (n/a), total from the above (doctoral) (0).

Additional Information:
Orientation, Objectives, and Emphasis of Department: The general psychology option of the MA program in psychology is designed to prepare students for doctoral work in psychology and related fields, including cognitive science. The program combines coursework in basic areas of psychology with the opportunity to do collaborative research with faculty members. Students have considerable flexibility to tailor their programs to their individual needs. The outstanding feature of this program is the opportunity for close interaction between faculty and students, both in the classroom and in the laboratory, because of the low student/faculty ratio. The objectives of the Clinical/Behavioral Analysis option are to provide students with specific and applied research and problem-solving skills; to provide all clinical students with a broad exposure to a variety of therapy modalities; to provide students with extensive experiential learning opportunities, practica, internships and intensive supervision; and to prepare students for licensure as Certified Mental Health Counselors.

Application Information:
Please send applications to Office of Graduate Studies. Application available online. Students are admitted in the Fall, application deadline March 31. Office of Graduate Studies (508) 999-8026 No set deadline for general option. *Fee:* $40. $20 in state.

Massachusetts, University of, Boston

Counseling and School Psychology
Graduate College of Education
100 Morrissey Blvd.
Boston, MA 02125-3393
Telephone: (617) 287-7602
Fax: (617) 287-7664
E-mail: *virginia.harvey@umb.edu*

Department Information:

1982. Chairperson: Virginia Smith Harvey. Number of Faculty: total–full-time 12, part-time 13; women–full-time 8, part-time 5; minority–full-time 4, part-time 1; faculty subject to the Americans With Disabilities Act 16.

Programs and Degrees Offered:

Listed in the following order: Program area, degree type (T if terminal Master's), number awarded 7/03–6/04. School Psychology Other 21, Mental Health Counseling Other 45, Rehabilitation Counseling Other 7, School Counseling Other 16, Family Therapy Other 6.

Student Applications/Admissions:

Student Applications

School Psychology Other—Applications 2004–2005, 94. Total applicants accepted 2004–2005, 40. Number enrolled (new admits only) 2004–2005 part-time, 21. Total enrolled 2004–2005 full-time, 40, part-time, 50. Openings 2005–2006, 30. The Median number of years required for completion of a degree are 3. *Mental Health Counseling Other*—Applications 2004–2005, 104. Total applicants accepted 2004–2005, 51. Number enrolled (new admits only) 2004–2005 part-time, 23. Total enrolled 2004–2005 part-time, 77. Openings 2005–2006, 30. *Rehabilitation Counseling Other*—Applications 2004–2005, 15. Total applicants accepted 2004–2005, 11. Number enrolled (new admits only) 2004–2005 part-time, 6. Total enrolled 2004–2005 part-time, 18. Openings 2005–2006, 15. *School Counseling Other*—Applications 2004–2005, 85. Total applicants accepted 2004–2005, 39. Number enrolled (new admits only) 2004–2005 part-time, 20. Total enrolled 2004–2005 part-time, 62. Openings 2005–2006, 20. *Family Therapy Other*—Applications 2004–2005, 57. Total applicants accepted 2004–2005, 17. Number enrolled (new admits only) 2004–2005 part-time, 6. Total enrolled 2004–2005 part-time, 25. Openings 2005–2006, 15.

Admissions Requirements:

Scores: Entries appear in this order: required test or GPA, minimum score (if required), median score of students entering in 2003–2004. Master's Programs: MAT no minimum stated; overall undergraduate GPA no minimum stated; last 2 years GPA no minimum stated. Either the GRE or the MAT is required for School Psychology, Family Therapy, Mental Health, and Rehabilitation Counseling. The Massachusetts Educator's Test of Literacy may be substituted for the GRE or MAT in School Counseling. The Massachusetts Educator's Test of Literacy is required for full admission to the School Psychology program. Recommended scores on all tests: 50th percentile. Recommended GPAs for all programs: 3.0

Other Criteria: (importance of criteria rated low, medium, or high): GRE/MAT scores medium, research experience low, work experience high, extracurricular activity high, clinically related public service high, GPA high, letters of recommendation high, interview high, statement of goals and objectives high.

Student Characteristics: The following represents characteristics of students in 2004–2005 in all graduate psychology programs in the department: Female–full-time 35, part-time 203; Male–full-time 5, part-time 50; African American/Black–part-time 21; Hispanic/Latino(a)–part-time 12; Asian/Pacific Islander–part-time 10; American Indian/Alaska Native–part-time 1; Caucasian–full-time 0, part-time 253; Multi-ethnic–part-time 18.

Financial Information/Assistance:

Tuition for Full-Time Study: *Master's:* State residents: per academic year $8,920; Nonstate residents: per academic year $18,790. Tuition is subject to change. See the following Web site for updates and changes in tuition costs: http://www.umb.edu/admissions/financing.html.

Financial Assistance:

First Year Students: Research assistantships available for first-year. Average amount paid per academic year: $3,200. Average number of hours worked per week: 5. Apply by July 1. Tuition remission given: partial.

Advanced Students: Research assistantships available for advanced students. Average amount paid per academic year: $3,200. Average number of hours worked per week: 5. Apply by July 1. Tuition remission given: partial.

Contact Information: Of all students currently enrolled full-time, 10% benefitted from one or more of the listed financial assistance programs. Application and information available online at: http://www.umb.edu/students/financial_aid/gradstudents.html.

Internships/Practica: The department maintains collaborative partnerships with a number of Boston area schools, mental health clinics, rehabilitation centers, and other facilities which provide practicum and internship sites for students.

Housing and Day Care: No on-campus housing is available. No on-campus day care facilities are available.

Employment of Department Graduates:

Master's Degree Graduates: Of those who graduated in the academic year 2003–2004, the following categories and numbers represent the post-graduate activities and employment of master's degree graduates: Enrolled in a post-doctoral residency/fellowship (n/a), employed in independent practice (n/a), total from the above (master's) (0).

Doctoral Degree Graduates: Of those who graduated in the academic year 2003–2004, the following categories and numbers represent the post-graduate activities and employment of doctoral degree graduates: Enrolled in a psychology doctoral program (n/a), total from the above (doctoral) (0).

Additional Information:

Orientation, Objectives, and Emphasis of Department: The University of Massachusetts Boston's Department of Counseling and School Psychology mission is to prepare thoughtful and responsive school counselors, mental health counselors, rehabilitation counselors, family therapists, and school psychologists. We are committed to fostering and enhancing the abilities of professionals to address the needs of children, adolescents, adults, and families with a diversity of cultural, linguistic, and ethnic backgrounds, race, socio-economic status, sexual orientation, and abilities. We offer courses integrated with experiences that address multicultural differences, individual diversity, and the demands of living in an urban environment. Our commitment to multicultural differences and individual diversity is reflected in our admission and hiring policies: 50% of our faculty are bilingual. Our curriculum is organized to meet state licensing requirements as well as national training standards at the master's and specialist level for the National Association of School Psychologists (NASP), the Council for the Accreditation of Marriage and Family Training Programs (COAMFTE), the Council for Rehabilitation Education (CORE), the National Council for Accreditation of Teacher Education (NCATE), and the Council for the Accreditation of Counseling Education Programs (CACREP). We currently are accredited or approved by the first four of these organizations, and graduates satisfy requirements for licensure in their respective fields.

Information for Students With Physical Disabilities: See the following Web site for more information: www.umb.edu.

Application Information:
Send to: Graduate Admissions, Quinn Adminstration Building, University of Massachusetts Boston, 100 Morrissey Blvd., Boston, MA 02125. Application available online. URL of online application: http://www.umb.edu/admissions/graduate/apply/index.html. Students are admitted in the Fall, application deadline February 1. $40 application fee for Massachusetts residents, $60 for non-residents.

Massachusetts, University of, Boston
Department of Psychology
College of Arts and Sciences
Harbor Campus
Boston, MA 02125-3393
Telephone: (617) 287-6000
Fax: (617) 287-6336
E-mail: *clinical.psych@umb.edu*
Web: *http://www.umb.edu/academics/graduate/ clinical_psychology/*

Department Information:
1967. Department Chair: Celia Moore. Number of Faculty: total–full-time 21, part-time 32; women–full-time 16, part-time 14; minority–full-time 5, part-time 3.

Programs and Degrees Offered:
Listed in the following order: Program area, degree type (T if terminal Master's), number awarded 7/03–6/04. Clinical PhD (Doctor of Philosophy) 7.

APA Accreditation: Clinical PhD (Doctor of Philosophy).

Student Applications/Admissions:
Student Applications
Clinical PhD (Doctor of Philosophy)—Applications 2004–2005, 287. Total applicants accepted 2004–2005, 12. Number en-

rolled (new admits only) 2004–2005 full-time, 9. Openings 2005–2006, 8. The Median number of years required for completion of a degree are 6.5. The number of students enrolled full and part-time who were dismissed or voluntarily withdrew from this program area were 0.

Admissions Requirements:
Scores: Entries appear in this order: required test or GPA, minimum score (if required), median score of students entering in 2003–2004. Doctoral Programs: GRE-V no minimum stated, 640; GRE-Q no minimum stated, 680; GRE-V+Q no minimum stated, 1320; GRE-Analytical no minimum stated, 700; GRE-Subject(Psych) no minimum stated, 670; overall undergraduate GPA no minimum stated, 3.82; last 2 years GPA no minimum stated, 3.70; psychology GPA no minimum stated, 3.89.

Other Criteria: (importance of criteria rated low, medium, or high): GRE/MAT scores medium, research experience high, work experience high, extracurricular activity medium, clinically related public service high, GPA high, letters of recommendation high, interview high, statement of goals and objectives high. For additional information on admission requirements, go to: www.umb.edu/academics/graduate/clinical_psychology.

Student Characteristics: The following represents characteristics of students in 2004–2005 in all graduate psychology programs in the department: Female–full-time 46, part-time 0; Male–full-time 13, part-time 0; African American/Black–full-time 6, part-time 0; Hispanic/Latino(a)–full-time 6, part-time 0; Asian/Pacific Islander–full-time 9, part-time 0; American Indian/Alaska Native–full-time 0, part-time 0; Caucasian–full-time 37, part-time 0; Multi-ethnic–full-time 1, part-time 0; students subject to the Americans With Disabilities Act–full-time 0, part-time 0.

Financial Information/Assistance:
Financial Assistance:
First Year Students: Teaching assistantships available for first-year. Average amount paid per academic year: $12,600. Average number of hours worked per week: 20. Tuition remission given: full. Research assistantships available for first-year. Average amount paid per academic year: $12,600. Average number of hours worked per week: 20. Tuition remission given: full.

Advanced Students: Teaching assistantships available for advanced students. Average amount paid per academic year: $13,600. Average number of hours worked per week: 20. Tuition remission given: full. Research assistantships available for advanced students. Average amount paid per academic year: $12,600. Average number of hours worked per week: 20. Tuition remission given: full.

Contact Information: Of all students currently enrolled full-time, 80% benefitted from one or more of the listed financial assistance programs. Application and information available online at: http://www.umb.edu/academics/graduate/clinical_psychology/admission.html.

Internships/Practica: Students do a 15 hour per week clinical practicum in the University Counseling Center in their second year. They obtain supervised clinical experience doing intake evaluations, short-term dynamic and cognitive behavioral therapy, and some group and couples treatment. Students also do 20 hour per week clinical practica in a training hospital or community health center in their third year. Examples of external practica include: Cambridge Hospital, Children's Hospital, McLean Hospital, The Brookline Center, South Cove Health Center, and Chelsea Memorial Health Center. These agencies all serve a significant number of low income and ethnic minority clients. Students get supervised clinical training in testing and assessment and a range of psychotherapeutic interventions with children, adolescents, and adults at their external practica. Students do a full-time APA approved clinical internship in their fifth year. For those doctoral students for whom a professional internship is required prior to graduation, 6 applied in 2003–2004. Of those who applied, 6 were placed in internships listed by the Association of Psychology Postdoctoral and Internship Programs (APPIC); 6 were placed in APA accredited internships.

Housing and Day Care: No on-campus housing is available. No on-campus day care facilities are available.

Employment of Department Graduates:

Master's Degree Graduates: Of those who graduated in the academic year 2003–2004, the following categories and numbers represent the post-graduate activities and employment of master's degree graduates: Enrolled in a post-doctoral residency/fellowship (n/a), employed in independent practice (n/a), total from the above (master's) (0).

Doctoral Degree Graduates: Of those who graduated in the academic year 2003–2004, the following categories and numbers represent the post-graduate activities and employment of doctoral degree graduates: Enrolled in a psychology doctoral program (n/a), enrolled in a post-doctoral residency/fellowship (5), employed in an academic position at a university (1), employed in other positions at a higher education institution (1), total from the above (doctoral) (7).

Additional Information:

Orientation, Objectives, and Emphasis of Department: The Clinical Psychology PhD Program follows the scientist-practitioner model of clinical training. It provides a strong theoretical background in psychology and related social science disciplines as well as training in essential clinical skills and in conducting research. Its graduates function as professional psychologists who can translate their basic knowledge into practical applications and who can advance understanding of key problems through research or other scholarly activities. The program's primary goals and objectives are to provide students with (a) a strong theoretical and empirical foundation in normal and abnormal development from early childhood through adolescence and adulthood; (b) a strong theoretical and empirical foundation in social and cultural perspectives on development, especially as they affect students; understanding of ethnic minority and low income groups; (c) to provide students with solid grounding in the bio-psycho-social approach to explaining and treating problems in living, symptomatic behavior, and mental illness, and with learning opportunities that foster interdisciplinary thinking; (d) a broad range of assessment and intervention skills that will help them treat problem behavior, promote healthy adaptation, and prevent individual and social problems from developing; (e) opportunities to develop competence in the basic research methodologies and data analytic techniques of psychology and their application to clinical issues. The program was one of three recipients of the 2001 APA Suinn Minority Achievement Award in recognition or our program's

success in recruiting, educating, supporting, retaining, and graduating significant numbers of ethnic minority doctoral students.

Special Facilities or Resources: The Psychology Department's research laboratories support a wide range of research and teaching functions. There are several interaction rooms with one-way mirrors that can be used for clinical, social, and developmental research. These rooms are equipped with state-of-the-art audio and video recording equipment. The animal laboratories are fully equipped to conduct research in animal behavior, learning, and physiology. Other laboratories in the department support ongoing research in cognition, perception, and human electrophysiology. The department maintains a network of microcomputers that can be used for research, data analysis, and other related functions. For larger projects, the University Computing Center operates a VAX cluster and a CDC Cyber 175 computer (housed at the University of Massachusetts at Amherst). The department's laboratory facilities also include woodworking and electronic shops, which are staffed by full-time experienced technicians. The technical staff provides programming, electronic, and other related support to the faculty and students in the department. Students in the clinical psychology program may also gain experience and have access to the facilities of other research centers and the university, including the Center for Survey Research, the Center for the Study of Social Acceptance, the William Monroe Trotter Institute for the Study of Black Culture, and the William Joiner Center for the Study of War and Social Consequences.

Application Information:

Send to: Graduate Admissions, University of Massachusetts at Boston, 100 Morrissey Blvd., Boston, MA 02125. Application available online. URL of online application: http://www.umb.edu/academics/graduate/ clinical_psychology/admission.html. Students are admitted in the Fall, application deadline December 1. *Fee:* $50. Need basis waivers.

Massachusetts, University of, Lowell
Community Social Psychology Master's Program
Arts and Sciences
870 Broadway Street, Suite 1
Lowell, MA 01854-3043
Telephone: (978) 934-3950
Fax: (978) 934-3074
E-mail: *Richard_Siegel@uml.edu*
Web: *http://www.uml.edu/Dept/Psychology/csp*

Department Information:

1980. Graduate Program Co-Coordinator: Richard Siegel. Number of Faculty: total–full-time 9, part-time 1; women–full-time 7; minority–full-time 2.

Programs and Degrees Offered:

Listed in the following order: Program area, degree type (T if terminal Master's), number awarded 7/03–6/04. Community Social MA/MS (Master of Arts/Science) (T) 13.

Student Applications/Admissions:

Student Applications

Community Social MA/MS (Master of Arts/Science)—Applications 2004–2005, 18. Total applicants accepted 2004–2005,

15. Number enrolled (new admits only) 2004–2005 full-time, 6. Number enrolled (new admits only) 2004–2005 part-time, 3. Total enrolled 2004–2005 full-time, 11, part-time, 30. Openings 2005–2006, 25. The Median number of years required for completion of a degree are 3. The number of students enrolled full and part-time who were dismissed or voluntarily withdrew from this program area were 2.

Admissions Requirements:

Scores: Entries appear in this order: required test or GPA, minimum score (if required), median score of students entering in 2003–2004. Master's Programs: GRE-V no minimum stated, 470; GRE-Q no minimum stated, 530; MAT no minimum stated, 35; overall undergraduate GPA 3.0, 3.22. Either the GRE V+Q or the MAT is required.

Other Criteria: (importance of criteria rated low, medium, or high): GRE/MAT scores medium, research experience medium, work experience high, extracurricular activity low, clinically related public service medium, GPA high, letters of recommendation high, interview low, statement of goals and objectives high.

Student Characteristics: The following represents characteristics of students in 2004–2005 in all graduate psychology programs in the department: Female–full-time 8, part-time 27; Male–full-time 3, part-time 3; African American/Black–full-time 1, part-time 1; Hispanic/Latino(a)–full-time 0, part-time 1; Asian/Pacific Islander–full-time 1, part-time 0; American Indian/Alaska Native–full-time 0, part-time 0; Caucasian–full-time 9, part-time 28; Multi-ethnic–full-time 0, part-time 0; students subject to the Americans With Disabilities Act–full-time 0, part-time 0.

Financial Information/Assistance:

Tuition for Full-Time Study: *Master's:* State residents: per academic year $7,448, $427 per credit hour; Nonstate residents: per academic year $14,722, $831 per credit hour. See the following Web site for updates and changes in tuition costs: http://www.uml.edu/grad/TuitionFees03_04.htm.

Financial Assistance:

First Year Students: Teaching assistantships available for first-year. Average amount paid per academic year: $6,033. Average number of hours worked per week: 9. Apply by May 1. Tuition remission given: full. Research assistantships available for first-year. Average amount paid per academic year: $6,033. Average number of hours worked per week: 9. Apply by May 1. Tuition remission given: full.

Advanced Students: Teaching assistantships available for advanced students. Average amount paid per academic year: $6,033. Average number of hours worked per week: 9. Apply by May 1. Tuition remission given: full. Research assistantships available for advanced students. Average amount paid per academic year: $6,033. Average number of hours worked per week: 9. Apply by May 1. Tuition remission given: full.

Contact Information: Of all students currently enrolled full-time, 63% benefitted from one or more of the listed financial assistance programs.

Internships/Practica: There is a one-year practicum requirement of 10 to 12 hours a week. Settings vary but have a community emphasis.

Housing and Day Care: On-campus housing is available. See the following Web site for more information: http://www.uml.edu/grad; select "More Information," then "Student Services." On-campus day care facilities are available.

Employment of Department Graduates:

Master's Degree Graduates: Of those who graduated in the academic year 2003–2004, the following categories and numbers represent the post-graduate activities and employment of master's degree graduates: Enrolled in a psychology doctoral program (0), enrolled in another graduate/professional program (2), enrolled in a post-doctoral residency/fellowship (n/a), employed in independent practice (n/a), employed in an academic position at a university (0), employed in an academic position at a 2-year/4-year college (0), employed in other positions at a higher education institution (0), employed in a professional position in a school system (1), employed in business or industry (research/consulting) (0), employed in business or industry (management) (0), employed in a government agency (research) (0), employed in a government agency (professional services) (4), employed in a community mental health/counseling center (0), still seeking employment (0), other employment position (3), do not know (3), total from the above (master's) (13).

Doctoral Degree Graduates: Of those who graduated in the academic year 2003–2004, the following categories and numbers represent the post-graduate activities and employment of doctoral degree graduates: Enrolled in a psychology doctoral program (n/a), total from the above (doctoral) (0).

Additional Information:

Orientation, Objectives, and Emphasis of Department: The program is designed to benefit recent college graduates interested in community service careers as well as older and nontraditional students with experience in community settings. The goal of the program is to provide both kinds of students with an understanding of how urban environments affect people; the research skills necessary for program development and evaluation; the opportunity to apply their learning in community settings in the greater Merrimack Valley and to gain skills through direct experience and supervision in those settings; and the ability to apply psychological principles to community problem-solving in such areas as discrimination, inadequate housing, and organizational change.

Special Facilities or Resources: Special facilities and resources consist of computer facilities, a campus-based elementary magnet school, grant-related technical services from the University Research Foundation, numerous research centers such as the Center for Family, Work and Community and the Center for Women and Work, and a unique multi-ethnic urban setting in a middle-sized city accessible to Boston.

Information for Students With Physical Disabilities: See the following Web site for more information: http://www.uml.edu/student-services/disab/index.html.

Application Information:

Send to: Graduate School Admissions, 1 University Avenue, Lowell, MA 01854. Students are admitted in the Fall, application deadline November 1; Winter, application deadline January 15; Spring, application deadline April 1; Summer, application deadline July 1. Rolling admission. Fee: $20 for Massachusetts residents, $35 all others.

Northeastern University
Department of Counseling & Applied Educational Psychology
Bouve College of Health Sciences
203 Lake Hall
Boston, MA 02115
Telephone: (617) 373-2485
Fax: (617) 373-8892
E-mail: *j.nascarella@neu.edu*
Web: *http://www.bouve.neu.edu/department/crs/caep.html*

Department Information:
1983. Interim Chair: William Sanchez, PhD Number of Faculty: total–full-time 18, part-time 23; women–full-time 13, part-time 14; minority–full-time 6, part-time 2.

Programs and Degrees Offered:
Listed in the following order: Program area, degree type (T if terminal Master's), number awarded 7/03–6/04. Combined PhD (Doctor of Philosophy) 6, College Student Development MA/MS (Master of Arts/Science) (T) 9, counseling psychology MA/MS (Master of Arts/Science) (T) 18, applied behavioral analysis MA/MS (Master of Arts/Science) (T) 11, School Psychology MS/CAGS MA/MS (Master of Arts/Science) 24, school counseling MA/MS (Master of Arts/Science) (T) 11.

APA Accreditation: Combination PhD (Doctor of Philosophy).

Student Applications/Admissions:
Student Applications
Combined PhD (Doctor of Philosophy)—Applications 2004–2005, 50. Total applicants accepted 2004–2005, 12. Number enrolled (new admits only) 2004–2005 full-time, 13. Number enrolled (new admits only) 2004–2005 part-time, 0. Total enrolled 2004–2005 full-time, 30, part-time, 2. Openings 2005–2006, 8. The Median number of years required for completion of a degree are 6. The number of students enrolled full and part-time who were dismissed or voluntarily withdrew from this program area were 0. *College Student Development MA/MS (Master of Arts/Science)*—Applications 2004–2005, 29. Total applicants accepted 2004–2005, 27. Number enrolled (new admits only) 2004–2005 full-time, 5. Number enrolled (new admits only) 2004–2005 part-time, 3. Total enrolled 2004–2005 full-time, 18, part-time, 10. Openings 2005–2006, 14. The Median number of years required for completion of a degree are 2. The number of students enrolled full and part-time who were dismissed or voluntarily withdrew from this program area were 1. *Counseling psychology MA/MS (Master of Arts/Science)*—Applications 2004–2005, 110. Total applicants accepted 2004–2005, 35. Number enrolled (new admits only) 2004–2005 full-time, 23. Number enrolled (new admits only) 2004–2005 part-time, 1. Total enrolled 2004–2005 full-time, 45, part-time, 7. Openings 2005–2006, 25. The Median number of years required for completion of a degree are 2. The number of students enrolled full and part-time who were dismissed or voluntarily withdrew from this program area were 2. *Applied behavioral analysis MA/MS (Master of Arts/Science)*—Applications 2004–2005, 62. Total applicants accepted 2004–2005, 18. Number enrolled (new admits only) 2004–2005 full-time, 4. Number enrolled (new admits only) 2004–2005 part-time, 25. Total enrolled 2004–2005 full-time, 22, part-time,

52. Openings 2005–2006, 10. The Median number of years required for completion of a degree are 2. The number of students enrolled full and part-time who were dismissed or voluntarily withdrew from this program area were 2. *School Psychology MS/CAGS MA/MS (Master of Arts/Science)*—Applications 2004–2005, 80. Total applicants accepted 2004–2005, 53. Number enrolled (new admits only) 2004–2005 full-time, 29. Number enrolled (new admits only) 2004–2005 part-time, 1. Total enrolled 2004–2005 full-time, 49, part-time, 1. Openings 2005–2006, 20. The Median number of years required for completion of a degree are 3. The number of students enrolled full and part-time who were dismissed or voluntarily withdrew from this program area were 1. *School counseling MA/MS (Master of Arts/Science)*—Applications 2004–2005, 20. Total applicants accepted 2004–2005, 12. Number enrolled (new admits only) 2004–2005 full-time, 4. Number enrolled (new admits only) 2004–2005 part-time, 2. Total enrolled 2004–2005 full-time, 18, part-time, 7. Openings 2005–2006, 16. The Median number of years required for completion of a degree are 2. The number of students enrolled full and part-time who were dismissed or voluntarily withdrew from this program area were 0.

Admissions Requirements:
Scores: Entries appear in this order: required test or GPA, minimum score (if required), median score of students entering in 2003–2004. Master's Programs: GRE-V 400, 470; GRE-Q 400, 540; GRE-V+Q no minimum stated; overall undergraduate GPA 3.0, 3.28; psychology GPA no minimum stated. Programs scores are competitive. Department prefers 500 minimum in GRE Q and V. TOEFL scores for international applicants who do not hold undergraduate or graduate degrees from U.S. institutions, and whose native language is not English. Doctoral Programs: GRE-V 500, 560; GRE-Q 500, 560; GRE-V+Q no minimum stated; overall undergraduate GPA 3.00, 3.47.
Other Criteria: (importance of criteria rated low, medium, or high): GRE/MAT scores medium, research experience medium, work experience high, extracurricular activity medium, clinically related public service high, GPA medium, letters of recommendation high, interview high, statement of goals and objectives high.

Student Characteristics: The following represents characteristics of students in 2004–2005 in all graduate psychology programs in the department: Female–full-time 113, part-time 59; Male–full-time 250, part-time 64; African American/Black–full-time 11, part-time 3; Hispanic/Latino(a)–full-time 9, part-time 5; Asian/Pacific Islander–full-time 6, part-time 2; American Indian/Alaska Native–full-time 0, part-time 0; Caucasian–full-time 0, part-time 0; Multi-ethnic–part-time 2; students subject to the Americans With Disabilities Act–part-time 1.

Financial Information/Assistance:
Tuition for Full-Time Study: *Master's:* State residents: $875 per credit hour; Nonstate residents: $875 per credit hour. *Doctoral:* State residents: $875 per credit hour; Nonstate residents: $875 per credit hour. Tuition is subject to change.

Financial Assistance:
First Year Students: Teaching assistantships available for first-year. Average number of hours worked per week: 10. Tuition

remission given: partial. Research assistantships available for first-year. Average number of hours worked per week: 0. Traineeships available for first-year. Average number of hours worked per week: 0. Tuition remission given: partial. Fellowships and scholarships available for first-year. Average number of hours worked per week: 0. Tuition remission given: partial.

Advanced Students: Teaching assistantships available for advanced students. Average number of hours worked per week: 10. Tuition remission given: full and partial. Research assistantships available for advanced students. Average amount paid per academic year: $12,500. Average number of hours worked per week: 20. Tuition remission given: full and partial. Fellowships and scholarships available for advanced students. Average number of hours worked per week: 0. Tuition remission given: full and partial.

Contact Information: Of all students currently enrolled full-time, 10% benefitted from one or more of the listed financial assistance programs.

Internships/Practica: Internship and field placement sites are varied depending on the program and specialization. Sites are in the Boston metropolitan area and include some of the most desirable and prestigious settings in the field. For those doctoral students for whom a professional internship is required prior to graduation, 11 applied in 2003–2004. Of those who applied, 1 were placed in internships listed by the Association of Psychology Postdoctoral and Internship Programs (APPIC); 9 were placed in APA accredited internships.

Housing and Day Care: No on-campus housing is available. On-campus day care facilities are available. Child care services are available to campus personnel.

Employment of Department Graduates:

Master's Degree Graduates: Of those who graduated in the academic year 2003–2004, the following categories and numbers represent the post-graduate activities and employment of master's degree graduates: Enrolled in a post-doctoral residency/fellowship (n/a), employed in independent practice (n/a), total from the above (master's) (0).

Doctoral Degree Graduates: Of those who graduated in the academic year 2003–2004, the following categories and numbers represent the post-graduate activities and employment of doctoral degree graduates: Enrolled in a psychology doctoral program (n/a), total from the above (doctoral) (0).

Additional Information:

Orientation, Objectives, and Emphasis of Department: Philosophically, the combined school and counseling doctoral program is based on an ecological model. This model focuses on the contexts in which people and their environments intersect, including individuals' families, groups, cultures, and social, political, and economic institutions. Thus, the ecological model includes individual and interpersonal relationships along with their interactive physical and sociocultural environments. It employs a general systems perspective to understand the mutually reciprocal interactions of all of these elements. Central to this theoretical stance are assumptions of interdependence, circular and multilevel influence and causality, and interactive identities. Issues of gender, status, and culture are given special emphasis as well as the developmental stages of the individual, family, or group. The ecological model is large enough and sufficiently comprehensive to allow for teaching and using other models such as psychodynamic, be-haviorist, and humanistic, as they help to explain behavior and phenomena in individuals, families, and groups. This allows faculty and students to teach, understand, and use many explanations of human activities. This ecological orientation provides the lenses through which students study psychological and counseling theory and research. In their varied fieldwork settings, students have the opportunity to translate this orientation into practice.

Special Facilities or Resources: Northeastern University, one of the largest private universities in the country, is located in Boston, a center of academic excellence and psychological research. There are numerous opportunities for diverse experiences, such as placements specializing in neuropsychology, early intervention, and sexual abuse. The campus is in the Back Bay, an area with a large student population and rich cultural opportunities. The Snell Library, one of the most advanced college libraries in the Boston area, provides access for students not only to its large psychology and education collections, but also to media and microcomputer centers and an extensive global academic computer networking system. Northeastern students also have privileges at the other Boston area research libraries.

Information for Students With Physical Disabilities: See the following Web site for more information: http://www.access-disability-deaf.neu.edu/.

Application Information:
Send to: Graduate Dean, Bouve College of Health Sciences, 103 Mugar, Northeastern University, Boston, MA 02169. URL of online application: http://www.applyweb.com/aw?neugh. Students are admitted in the Fall, application deadline. Deadlines: combined School and Counseling Psychology PhD—January 15 for admission following fall; MS Counseling Psychology—December 1 for admission following fall; MS/CAGS School Psychology—Suggested January 15 for admission following fall. All other program have a suggested May 1 deadline. *Fee:* $50.

Northeastern University
Department of Psychology
Arts and Sciences
125 Nightingale Hall
Boston, MA 02115
Telephone: (617) 373-3076
Fax: (617) 373-8714
E-mail: *psychology@neu.edu*
Web: *http://www.psych.neu.edu*

Department Information:
1966. Chairperson: Stephen G. Harkins. Number of Faculty: total–full-time 18, part-time 4; women–full-time 4, part-time 2; minority–full-time 3, part-time 1.

Programs and Degrees Offered:
Listed in the following order: Program area, degree type (T if terminal Master's), number awarded 7/03–6/04. Cognitive PhD (Doctor of Philosophy) 1, Psychobiology PhD (Doctor of Philosophy) 0, Social/ Personality PhD (Doctor of Philosophy) 1, Sensation PhD (Doctor of Philosophy) 0.

Student Applications/Admissions:

Student Applications

Cognitive PhD (Doctor of Philosophy)—Applications 2004–2005, 9. Total applicants accepted 2004–2005, 3. Number enrolled (new admits only) 2004–2005 full-time, 2. Openings 2005–2006, 4. The Median number of years required for completion of a degree are 6. The number of students enrolled full and part-time who were dismissed or voluntarily withdrew from this program area were 0. *Psychobiology PhD (Doctor of Philosophy)*—Applications 2004–2005, 22. Total applicants accepted 2004–2005, 0. Openings 2005–2006, 4. The number of students enrolled full and part-time who were dismissed or voluntarily withdrew from this program area were 0. *Social/Personality PhD (Doctor of Philosophy)*—Applications 2004–2005, 48. Total applicants accepted 2004–2005, 10. Number enrolled (new admits only) 2004–2005 full-time, 4. Openings 2005–2006, 4. The Median number of years required for completion of a degree are 5. *Sensation PhD (Doctor of Philosophy)*—Applications 2004–2005, 6. Total applicants accepted 2004–2005, 2. Number enrolled (new admits only) 2004–2005 full-time, 2. Openings 2005–2006, 3.

Admissions Requirements:

Scores: Entries appear in this order: required test or GPA, minimum score (if required), median score of students entering in 2003–2004. Master's Programs: GRE-V+Q is recommended strongly. Doctoral Programs: GRE-V no minimum stated, 616; GRE-Q no minimum stated, 681; GRE-V+Q no minimum stated, 1297.

Other Criteria: (importance of criteria rated low, medium, or high): GRE/MAT scores high, research experience high, work experience low, extracurricular activity low, clinically related public service low, GPA high, letters of recommendation high, interview high, statement of goals and objectives high.

Student Characteristics: The following represents characteristics of students in 2004–2005 in all graduate psychology programs in the department: Female–full-time 15, part-time 0; Male–full-time 8, part-time 0; African American/Black–full-time 3, part-time 0; Hispanic/Latino(a)–full-time 0, part-time 0; Asian/Pacific Islander–full-time 2, part-time 0; American Indian/Alaska Native–part-time 0; Caucasian–full-time 18, part-time 0; students subject to the Americans With Disabilities Act–full-time 0, part-time 0.

Financial Information/Assistance:

Tuition for Full-Time Study: *Doctoral:* State residents: $825 per credit hour; Nonstate residents: $825 per credit hour.

Financial Assistance:

First Year Students: Teaching assistantships available for first-year. Average amount paid per academic year: $20,772. Average number of hours worked per week: 20. Apply by January 15. Tuition remission given: full. Research assistantships available for first-year. Average amount paid per academic year: $20,772. Average number of hours worked per week: 20. Apply by January 15. Tuition remission given: full. Traineeships available for first-year. Average amount paid per academic year: $20,772. Average number of hours worked per week: 20. Apply by January 15. Tuition remission given: full.

Advanced Students: Teaching assistantships available for advanced students. Average amount paid per academic year: $20,772. Average number of hours worked per week: 20. Apply by January 15. Tuition remission given: full. Research assistantships available for advanced students. Average amount paid per academic year: $20,772. Average number of hours worked per week: 20. Apply by January 15. Tuition remission given: full. Traineeships available for advanced students. Average amount paid per academic year: $20,772. Average number of hours worked per week: 20. Apply by January 15. Tuition remission given: full.

Contact Information: Of all students currently enrolled full-time, 100% benefitted from one or more of the listed financial assistance programs.

Internships/Practica: No information provided.

Housing and Day Care: On-campus housing is available. On-campus day care facilities are available.

Employment of Department Graduates:

Master's Degree Graduates: Of those who graduated in the academic year 2003–2004, the following categories and numbers represent the post-graduate activities and employment of master's degree graduates: Enrolled in a post-doctoral residency/fellowship (n/a), employed in independent practice (n/a), total from the above (master's) (0).

Doctoral Degree Graduates: Of those who graduated in the academic year 2003–2004, the following categories and numbers represent the post-graduate activities and employment of doctoral degree graduates: Enrolled in a psychology doctoral program (n/a), enrolled in a post-doctoral residency/fellowship (2), total from the above (doctoral) (2).

Additional Information:

Orientation, Objectives, and Emphasis of Department: The PhD program aims to train students to undertake basic research in the following areas: neuropsychology and psychobiology; sensation and perception; language and cognition; and experimental-social and personality. Students may expect to collaborate with faculty in conducting research in these areas, using technically sophisticated research laboratories. The doctoral program also provides opportunities to gain teaching experience. It does not, however, provide clinical training.

Special Facilities or Resources: The department has a wide range of research laboratories containing state-of-the-art facilities in the following areas: neuropsychology and psychobiology; sensation and perception; language and cognition; and experimental-social and personality. These facilities include an array of mini- and microcomputers used for subject testing, data acquisition and analysis, graphics, and word processing. The facilities also house numerous special-purpose systems (e.g., eye-tracker, histology facilities, and speech processing system). In addition, laboratory resources outside the department are available to students through the collaborative network the department maintains with other institutions in the Boston/Cambridge area.

Application Information:

Send to: Department of Psychology, 125 NI, Northeastern University, Boston, MA 02115. Students are admitted in the Fall, application deadline January 15. *Fee:* $50. Fee waived for financial need.

Springfield College

Department of Psychology
School of Arts and Sciences and Professional Studies
263 Alden Street
Springfield, MA 01109
Telephone: (413) 748-3328
Fax: (413) 748-3854
E-mail: *Anna_L_Moriarty@Spfldcol.edu*
Web: *http://www.spfldcol.edu*

Department Information:

1946. Chairperson: Ann Moriarty. Number of Faculty: total–full-time 14, part-time 18; women–full-time 8, part-time 11; minority–part-time 1.

Programs and Degrees Offered:

Listed in the following order: Program area, degree type (T if terminal Master's), number awarded 7/03–6/04. Athletic Counseling MA/MS (Master of Arts/Science) (T) 9, Industrial/ Organizational MA/MS (Master of Arts/Science) (T) 18, Marriage and Family Therapy MA/MS (Master of Arts/Science) (T) 8, Mental Health Counseling MA/MS (Master of Arts/Science) (T) 12, School Guidance Counseling Other 18, Students & Personnel Administration MA/MS (Master of Arts/Science) (T) 17.

Student Applications/Admissions:

Student Applications

Athletic Counseling MA/MS (Master of Arts/Science)—Applications 2004–2005, 50. Total applicants accepted 2004–2005, 20. Number enrolled (new admits only) 2004–2005 full-time, 12. Total enrolled 2004–2005 full-time, 25. Openings 2005–2006, 12. The Median number of years required for completion of a degree are 2. The number of students enrolled full and part-time who were dismissed or voluntarily withdrew from this program area were 1. *Industrial/ Organizational MA/MS (Master of Arts/Science)*—Applications 2004–2005, 60. Total applicants accepted 2004–2005, 38. Number enrolled (new admits only) 2004–2005 full-time, 16. Number enrolled (new admits only) 2004–2005 part-time, 5. Total enrolled 2004–2005 full-time, 40, part-time, 10. Openings 2005–2006, 17. The Median number of years required for completion of a degree are 2. The number of students enrolled full and part-time who were dismissed or voluntarily withdrew from this program area were 1. *Marriage and Family Therapy MA/MS (Master of Arts/Science)*—Applications 2004–2005, 23. Total applicants accepted 2004–2005, 20. Number enrolled (new admits only) 2004–2005 full-time, 18. Number enrolled (new admits only) 2004–2005 part-time, 2. Total enrolled 2004–2005 full-time, 34, part-time, 4. Openings 2005–2006, 15. The Median number of years required for completion of a degree are 2. The number of students enrolled full and part-time who were dismissed or voluntarily withdrew from this program area were 1. *Mental Health Counseling MA/MS (Master of Arts/Science)*—Applications 2004–2005, 43. Total applicants accepted 2004–2005, 34. Number enrolled (new admits only) 2004–2005 full-time, 27. Number enrolled (new admits only) 2004–2005 part-time, 3. Total enrolled 2004–2005 full-time, 53, part-time, 3. Openings 2005–2006, 15. The Median number of years required for completion of a degree are 2. The number of students enrolled full and part-time who were dis-

missed or voluntarily withdrew from this program area were 1. *School Guidance Counseling Other*—Applications 2004–2005, 40. Total applicants accepted 2004–2005, 20. Number enrolled (new admits only) 2004–2005 full-time, 10. Number enrolled (new admits only) 2004–2005 part-time, 8. Total enrolled 2004–2005 full-time, 20, part-time, 14. Openings 2005–2006, 15. The Median number of years required for completion of a degree are 2. The number of students enrolled full and part-time who were dismissed or voluntarily withdrew from this program area were 0. *Students & Personnel Administration MA/MS (Master of Arts/Science)*—Applications 2004–2005, 30. Total applicants accepted 2004–2005, 25. Number enrolled (new admits only) 2004–2005 full-time, 15. Number enrolled (new admits only) 2004–2005 part-time, 2. Total enrolled 2004–2005 full-time, 27, part-time, 6. Openings 2005–2006, 13. The Median number of years required for completion of a degree are 2.

Admissions Requirements:

Scores: Entries appear in this order: required test or GPA, minimum score (if required), median score of students entering in 2003–2004. Master's Programs: overall undergraduate GPA 2.6, 3.3; last 2 years GPA no minimum stated; psychology GPA no minimum stated. Different GPAs are required for different programs.

Other Criteria: (importance of criteria rated low, medium, or high): research experience low, work experience medium, extracurricular activity medium, clinically related public service high, GPA medium, letters of recommendation high, interview medium, statement of goals and objectives high. These criteria vary for different program areas.

Student Characteristics: The following represents characteristics of students in 2004–2005 in all graduate psychology programs in the department: Female–full-time 124, part-time 30; Male–full-time 75, part-time 7; African American/Black–full-time 13, part-time 7; Hispanic/Latino(a)–full-time 8, part-time 0; Asian/Pacific Islander–full-time 5, part-time 0; American Indian/Alaska Native–full-time 0, part-time 0; Caucasian–full-time 151, part-time 20; Multi-ethnic–full-time 22, part-time 10; students subject to the Americans With Disabilities Act–full-time 0, part-time 0.

Financial Information/Assistance:

Tuition for Full-Time Study: *Master's:* State residents: $586 per credit hour; Nonstate residents: $586 per credit hour. Tuition is not available at this time.

Financial Assistance:

First Year Students: Teaching assistantships available for first-year. Apply by As needed. Tuition remission given: full and partial. Research assistantships available for first-year. Apply by As needed. Fellowships and scholarships available for first-year. Average amount paid per academic year: $2,000. Apply by March 1. Tuition remission given: full and partial.

Advanced Students: Teaching assistantships available for advanced students. Apply by As needed. Tuition remission given: full and partial. Research assistantships available for advanced students. Apply by As needed. Fellowships and scholarships available for advanced students. Average amount paid per academic year: $2,000. Apply by March 1. Tuition remission given: full and partial.

Contact Information: Of all students currently enrolled full-time, 30% benefitted from one or more of the listed financial assistance programs.

Internships/Practica: Numerous internships, paid and unpaid, exist for students in their field of study. Established affiliation agreements are in place with regional corporate, clinical and counseling settings. A Cooperative Education Program provides students with opportunities for credited, paid internships.

Housing and Day Care: On-campus housing is available. Springfield College Student Affairs, 263 Alden Street, Sprigfield, MA 01109. On-campus day care facilities are available.

Employment of Department Graduates:

Master's Degree Graduates: Of those who graduated in the academic year 2003–2004, the following categories and numbers represent the post-graduate activities and employment of master's degree graduates: Enrolled in a post-doctoral residency/fellowship (n/a), employed in independent practice (n/a), total from the above (master's) (0).

Doctoral Degree Graduates: Of those who graduated in the academic year 2003–2004, the following categories and numbers represent the post-graduate activities and employment of doctoral degree graduates: Enrolled in a psychology doctoral program (n/a), total from the above (doctoral) (0).

Additional Information:

Orientation, Objectives, and Emphasis of Department: Understanding of personal values, attitudes, and needs is a primary characteristic of effective facilitators. The psychology and counseling programs, therefore, design many of the experiences to help students increase their awareness of self and the ways in which personal behavior affects others. While mastery of content areas is expected, continual reference to personal relevance of that content is encouraged. Frequent opportunities are afforded for students to understand themselves better through participation in group and individual experiences. As a reflection of the value placed upon individual program development, the comprehensive examination requirement is not the traditional written and oral exercise. Some of the Psychology and Counseling programs use the portfolio system, which is an ongoing, active evaluation process. A more traditional thesis or research project is also offered and supported when chosen, and individual attention is readily available for both options.

Special Facilities or Resources: The department offers fully equipped counseling and research laboratories and an audiovisual facility. Access to computers, a well-equipped behavior modification laboratory, and an excellent physiological and fitness laboratories are available. The Department also sponsors the Center for Performance Enhancement and Applied Research (CPEAR), which serves as a clearinghouse for information about grants and research opportunities.

Information for Students With Physical Disabilities: Deborah_Dickens@Spfldcol.edu.

Application Information:

Send to: Graduate Admissions, 263 Alden Street, Springfield, MA 01109. Students are admitted in the Fall, application deadline rolling; Winter, application deadline rolling; Spring, application deadline rolling; Summer, application deadline rolling. *Fee:* $50.

Suffolk University

Department of Psychology
College of Arts and Sciences
41 Temple Street
Boston, MA 02114
Telephone: (617) 573-8293
Fax: (617) 367-2924
E-mail: *phd@suffolk.edu*
Web: *http://www.cas.suffolk.edu/psychology*

Department Information:

1968. Chairperson: Robert C. Webb. Number of Faculty: total–full-time 14, part-time 24; women–full-time 9, part-time 17; minority–full-time 2, part-time 1.

Programs and Degrees Offered:

Listed in the following order: Program area, degree type (T if terminal Master's), number awarded 7/03–6/04. Clinical Psychology PhD (Doctor of Philosophy) 6, Clinical Psychology Respecialization Diploma 0.

APA Accreditation: Clinical PhD (Doctor of Philosophy).

Student Applications/Admissions:

Student Applications

Clinical Psychology PhD (Doctor of Philosophy)—Applications 2004–2005, 228. Total applicants accepted 2004–2005, 26. Number enrolled (new admits only) 2004–2005 full-time, 14. Total enrolled 2004–2005 full-time, 37, part-time, 46. Openings 2005–2006, 14. The Median number of years required for completion of a degree are 6. The number of students enrolled full and part-time who were dismissed or voluntarily withdrew from this program area were 0. *Clinical Psychology Respecialization Diploma*—Applications 2004–2005, 1. Total applicants accepted 2004–2005, 1. Number enrolled (new admits only) 2004–2005 full-time, 1. Number enrolled (new admits only) 2004–2005 part-time, 0. Openings 2005–2006, 1. The number of students enrolled full and part-time who were dismissed or voluntarily withdrew from this program area were 0.

Admissions Requirements:

Scores: Entries appear in this order: required test or GPA, minimum score (if required), median score of students entering in 2003–2004. Doctoral Programs: GRE-V no minimum stated, 585; GRE-Q no minimum stated, 616; GRE-Analytical no minimum stated, 636; overall undergraduate GPA no minimum stated, 3.57.

Other Criteria: (importance of criteria rated low, medium, or high): GRE/MAT scores medium, research experience high, work experience medium, extracurricular activity low, clinically related public service medium, GPA high, letters of recommendation medium, interview high, statement of goals and objectives high, interest/program match high. For additional information on admission requirements, go to: http://www.cas.suffolk.edu/psychology.

Student Characteristics: The following represents characteristics of students in 2004–2005 in all graduate psychology programs in the department: Female–full-time 31, part-time 39; Male–full-time 6, part-time 7; African American/Black–full-time 2, part-time 2; Hispanic/Latino(a)–full-time 4, part-time 3; Asian/Pacific Islander–full-time 6, part-time 2; American Indian/Alaska Native–full-time 0, part-time 0; Caucasian–full-time 24, part-time 39; Multi-ethnic–full-time 1, part-time 0; students subject to the Americans With Disabilities Act–full-time 0, part-time 0.

Financial Information/Assistance:

Tuition for Full-Time Study: *Doctoral:* State residents: per academic year $23,900, $918 per credit hour; Nonstate residents: per academic year $23,900, $918 per credit hour. Tuition is subject to change. See the following Web site for updates and changes in tuition costs: http://www.suffolk.edu/stdact/cas_ssom_rates.html.

Financial Assistance:

First Year Students: Teaching assistantships available for first-year. Average amount paid per academic year: $3,500. Average number of hours worked per week: 7. Apply by March 15th. Tuition remission given: partial. Research assistantships available for first-year. Average amount paid per academic year: $3,500. Average number of hours worked per week: 7. Apply by March 15. Tuition remission given: partial. Fellowships and scholarships available for first-year. Average amount paid per academic year: $12,000. Average number of hours worked per week: 7. Apply by March 15. Tuition remission given: partial.

Advanced Students: Teaching assistantships available for advanced students. Average amount paid per academic year: $3,500. Average number of hours worked per week: 7. Apply by March 15. Tuition remission given: partial. Research assistantships available for advanced students. Average amount paid per academic year: $3,500. Average number of hours worked per week: 7. Apply by March 15. Tuition remission given: partial. Fellowships and scholarships available for advanced students. Average amount paid per academic year: $10,500. Average number of hours worked per week: 7. Apply by March 15. Tuition remission given: partial.

Contact Information: Of all students currently enrolled full-time, 100% benefitted from one or more of the listed financial assistance programs. Application and information available online at: https://www.applyweb.com/apply/suffcas.

Internships/Practica: Suffolk University's clinical psychology doctoral program is committed to providing the highest-quality program experiences available. Practicum sites have been chosen that provide students with supervision by appropriate professionals as well as offer training that is holistic and integrated in nature. Each practicum is designed to be consistent with the goal of the doctoral program, which emphasizes using a clinical-developmental framework to address psychological problems in the context of direct client service, consultation, and applied research. Internship/Practica: Two years of practicum experience, beginning in the second year, are required of our doctoral students; a third year is optional. Students receive weekly supervision by professionals at their practicum sites and attend a weekly practicum seminar at Suffolk University, where they are able to integrate

their practical experiences and educational training within the program. Students receive a total of 4 hours per week, on average, of individual and group supervision during each of their 2–3 years of practicum training. Students' first practicum experience occurs at one of five locations: Juvenile Court Clinic, May Institute, The Walker Home & School, Bournewood Hospital or The Manville School. The second practicum experience occurs at the Intensive Psychiatric Community Care program at the Edith Nourse Rogers Memorial Veterans Hospital in Bedford, MA or at Lemuel Shattuck Hospital in Jamaica Plain, MA. Students may choose a third practicum experience for more advanced training and preparation for internships at one of a selected set of approved sites during their fourth year of academic training. Students can choose among inpatient, outpatient, school-based, children, adolescents, adults, and/or neuropsychology based sites. After students have completed 2-3 years of practica and have submitted a dissertation prospectus, students must complete a 1600-hour predoctoral internship in their chosen area. For those doctoral students for whom a professional internship is required prior to graduation, 9 applied in 2003–2004. Of those who applied, 5 were placed in internships listed by the Association of Psychology Postdoctoral and Internship Programs (APPIC); 5 were placed in APA accredited internships.

Housing and Day Care: No on-campus housing is available. No on-campus day care facilities are available.

Employment of Department Graduates:

Master's Degree Graduates: Of those who graduated in the academic year 2003–2004, the following categories and numbers represent the post-graduate activities and employment of master's degree graduates: Enrolled in a post-doctoral residency/fellowship (n/a), employed in independent practice (n/a), total from the above (master's) (0).

Doctoral Degree Graduates: Of those who graduated in the academic year 2003–2004, the following categories and numbers represent the post-graduate activities and employment of doctoral degree graduates: Enrolled in a psychology doctoral program (n/a), enrolled in a post-doctoral residency/fellowship (2), employed in other positions at a higher education institution (1), employed in a hospital/medical center (1), total from the above (doctoral) (4).

Additional Information:

Orientation, Objectives, and Emphasis of Department: Suffolk University's PhD program in clinical psychology is unique among clinical doctoral programs in several respects: (1) It emphasizes a clinical-developmental perspective—the view that clinical problems are best understood in the context of knowledge about normal and optimal development over the life span; (2) Conceptualizing clinical and developmental psychology in broad terms, it prepares students to work as creative problem-solvers in a wide range of research, clinical, educational, organizational, and public policy settings; and (3) In the tradition of the scientist-practitioner model, it emphasizes a rigorous understanding of the interrelations between basic and applied research and between qualitative and quantitative methodologies in contributing to theoretical and practical knowledge. The program combines a strong theoretical/research background in a wide range of subfields of psychology with preparation to deliver high-quality psychological services to children, adolescents and adults. Training emphasizes students' abilities to think critically about knowledge, to conduct original research, and to design and carry out effective interventions at individual, family, community or societal levels.

Special Facilities or Resources: The department has a variety of laboratory spaces available for general use by faculty and doctoral students. Special equipment includes one-way mirrors and video cameras. A great deal of research occurs off-site in the clinical, medical, and scholastic institutions of the Boston area. There is a computer lab for graduate student use within the department in addition to larger computer labs throughout the university. All computers provide access to SPSS, the Internet, and major academic search systems. Graduate students receive inter-library loan and online document delivery privileges and have access to most of the academic libraries in the Boston area.

Information for Students With Physical Disabilities: See the following Web site for more information: http://www.suffolk.edu/studentservices/disabilities/disabilities.html.

Application Information:
Send to: Office of Graduate Admissions, 8 Ashburton Place, Boston, MA 02108. Application available online. URL of online application: https://www.applyweb.com/apply/suffcas. Students are admitted in the Fall, application deadline January 1. Same deadline for all. *Fee:* $50.

Tufts University
Department of Education; School Psychology Program
Graduate School of Arts and Sciences
Paige Hall
Medford, MA 02155
Telephone: (617) 627-2393
Fax: (617) 627-3901
E-mail: *caroline.wandle@tufts.edu*
Web: *http://www.tufts.edu/as/ed*

Department Information:
1910. Program Director-School Psychology: Caroline Wandle. Number of Faculty: total–full-time 14, part-time 16; women–full-time 9, part-time 9; minority–full-time 4, part-time 3.

Programs and Degrees Offered:
Listed in the following order: Program area, degree type (T if terminal Master's), number awarded 7/03–6/04. School MA/MS (Master of Arts/Science) 14.

Student Applications/Admissions:
Student Applications
School MA/MS (Master of Arts/Science)—Applications 2004–2005, 90. Total applicants accepted 2004–2005, 35. Number enrolled (new admits only) 2004–2005 full-time, 16. Number enrolled (new admits only) 2004–2005 part-time, 0. Total enrolled 2004–2005 full-time, 44, part-time, 3. Openings 2005–2006, 18. The Median number of years required for completion of a degree are 3. The number of students enrolled full and part-time who were dismissed or voluntarily withdrew from this program area were 0.

Admissions Requirements:
Scores: Entries appear in this order: required test or GPA, minimum score (if required), median score of students entering in 2003–2004. Master's Programs: GRE-V no minimum stated, 550; GRE-Q no minimum stated, 550; GRE-V+Q no minimum stated, 1100; GRE-Analytical no minimum stated, 550; overall undergraduate GPA 3.0, 3.6; last 2 years GPA no minimum stated. GRE writing score may be substituted for GRE analytic. Last two years GPA may be considered with more weight in some cases.
Other Criteria: (importance of criteria rated low, medium, or high): GRE/MAT scores medium, research experience medium, work experience high, extracurricular activity medium, clinically related public service high, GPA high, letters of recommendation high, interview high, statement of goals and objectives high.

Student Characteristics: The following represents characteristics of students in 2004–2005 in all graduate psychology programs in the department: Female–full-time 41, part-time 2; Male–full-time 3, part-time 1; African American/Black–full-time 1, part-time 0; Hispanic/Latino(a)–full-time 2, part-time 0; Asian/Pacific Islander–full-time 7, part-time 0; American Indian/Alaska Native–full-time 0, part-time 0; Caucasian–full-time 33, part-time 3; Multi-ethnic–full-time 1, part-time 0; students subject to the Americans With Disabilities Act–full-time 1, part-time 0.

Financial Information/Assistance:
Tuition for Full-Time Study: *Master's:* State residents: per academic year $28,300; Nonstate residents: per academic year $28,300. Tuition is subject to change.

Financial Assistance:
First Year Students: Teaching assistantships available for first-year. Average amount paid per academic year: $1,300. Average number of hours worked per week: 4. Apply by September 1. Research assistantships available for first-year. Average amount paid per academic year: $1,300. Average number of hours worked per week: 4. Apply by September 1. Fellowships and scholarships available for first-year. Average amount paid per academic year: $8,000. Apply by February 1. Tuition remission given: partial.
Advanced Students: Teaching assistantships available for advanced students. Average amount paid per academic year: $1,300. Average number of hours worked per week: 4. Apply by September 1. Research assistantships available for advanced students. Average amount paid per academic year: $1,300. Average number of hours worked per week: 4. Apply by September 1. Fellowships and scholarships available for advanced students. Average amount paid per academic year: $8,000. Apply by February 1. Tuition remission given: partial.
Contact Information: Of all students currently enrolled full-time, 80% benefitted from one or more of the listed financial assistance programs. Application and information available online at: ase.tufts.edu.

Internships/Practica: Students complete a school-based pre-practicum experience of 150 hours during their first year and a school-based practicum of 600 hours during their second year. Students complete a 1200-hour internship during their third year. This may be completed through 600 hours in a school setting and 600 hours in a clinical setting, or all 1200 hours in a school setting.

Housing and Day Care: On-campus housing is available. See the following Web site for more information: ase.tufts.edu. On-campus day care facilities are available.

Employment of Department Graduates:

Master's Degree Graduates: Of those who graduated in the academic year 2003–2004, the following categories and numbers represent the post-graduate activities and employment of master's degree graduates: Enrolled in a psychology doctoral program (0), enrolled in another graduate/professional program (0), enrolled in a post-doctoral residency/fellowship (n/a), employed in independent practice (n/a), employed in an academic position at a university (0), employed in an academic position at a 2-year/4-year college (0), employed in other positions at a higher education institution (0), employed in a professional position in a school system (14), employed in business or industry (research/consulting) (0), employed in business or industry (management) (0), employed in a government agency (research) (0), employed in a government agency (professional services) (0), employed in a community mental health/counseling center (0), employed in a hospital/medical center (0), still seeking employment (0), other employment position (0), total from the above (master's) (14).
Doctoral Degree Graduates: Of those who graduated in the academic year 2003–2004, the following categories and numbers represent the post-graduate activities and employment of doctoral degree graduates: Enrolled in a psychology doctoral program (n/a), total from the above (doctoral) (0).

Additional Information:

Orientation, Objectives, and Emphasis of Department: Students are exposed to a broad spectrum of assessment and intervention techniques from various theoretical perspectives including psychodynamic, humanistic, cognitive-behavioral, and family systems. Assessment and intervention strategies are anchored in a developmental perspective which stresses the social, intellectual, and emotional growth of the individual from childhood through the early adult years. The school psychology program is approved by the Massachusetts Department of Education. Graduates who complete program requirements will be eligible for state licensure as a school psychologist. The program also is approved by the National Association of School Psychologists.

Special Facilities or Resources: Several courses of interest are offered through the Eliot-Pearson Department of Child Development. Tufts students may also cross-register for courses at several other Boston universities at no additional charge through a consortium arrangement.

Information for Students With Physical Disabilities: ase.tufts.edu.

Application Information:
Send to: Office of Graduate and Professional Studies, Tufts University, Ballou Hall, Medford, MA 02155. Application available online. URL of online application: ase.tufts.edu. Students are admitted in the Fall, application deadline February 1. *Fee:* $50.

Tufts University
Department of Psychology
Psychology Building
Medford, MA 02155
Telephone: (617) 627-3523
Fax: (617) 627-3181
E-mail: *holly.taylor@tufts.edu*
Web: *http://ase.tufts.edu/psychology/*

Department Information:
Chair: Joseph DeBold. Number of Faculty: total–full-time 16, part-time 17; women–full-time 6, part-time 10; minority–full-time 2, part-time 1.

Programs and Degrees Offered:
Listed in the following order: Program area, degree type (T if terminal Master's), number awarded 7/03–6/04. General Experimental PhD (Doctor of Philosophy).

Student Applications/Admissions:
Student Applications
General Experimental PhD (Doctor of Philosophy)—Applications 2004–2005, 75. Total applicants accepted 2004–2005, 10. Number enrolled (new admits only) 2004–2005 full-time, 7. Total enrolled 2004–2005 full-time, 32. Openings 2005–2006, 7. The Median number of years required for completion of a degree are 5.

Admissions Requirements:
Scores: Entries appear in this order: required test or GPA, minimum score (if required), median score of students entering in 2003–2004. Master's Programs: GRE-Subject is not required, but it is strongly recommended. Doctoral Programs: GRE-Subject is not required but is strongly recommended.
Other Criteria: (importance of criteria rated low, medium, or high): GRE/MAT scores medium, research experience high, work experience medium, extracurricular activity low, GPA low, letters of recommendation high, interview medium, statement of goals and objectives high.

Student Characteristics: The following represents characteristics of students in 2004–2005 in all graduate psychology programs in the department: Female–full-time 28, part-time 0; Male–full-time 4, part-time 0; African American/Black–full-time 1, part-time 0; Hispanic/Latino(a)–full-time 0, part-time 0; Asian/Pacific Islander–full-time 3, part-time 0; American Indian/Alaska Native–full-time 0, part-time 0; Caucasian–full-time 28, part-time 0; Multi-ethnic–full-time 0, part-time 0.

Financial Information/Assistance:
Tuition for Full-Time Study: *Doctoral:* State residents: per academic year $28,264.

Financial Assistance:
First Year Students: Teaching assistantships available for first-year. Average amount paid per academic year: $16,000. Aver-

age number of hours worked per week: 20. Tuition remission given: full. Research assistantships available for first-year. Average amount paid per academic year: $16,000. Average number of hours worked per week: 20. Tuition remission given: full.

Advanced Students: Teaching assistantships available for advanced students. Average amount paid per academic year: $18,000. Tuition remission given: full. Research assistantships available for advanced students. Average amount paid per academic year: $18,000. Tuition remission given: full.

Contact Information: Of all students currently enrolled full-time, 100% benefitted from one or more of the listed financial assistance programs.

Internships/Practica: No information provided.

Housing and Day Care: No on-campus housing is available. On-campus day care facilities are available. See the following Web site for more information: http://ase.tufts.edu/tedcc/.

Employment of Department Graduates:

Master's Degree Graduates: Of those who graduated in the academic year 2003–2004, the following categories and numbers represent the post-graduate activities and employment of master's degree graduates: Enrolled in a post-doctoral residency/fellowship (n/a), employed in independent practice (n/a), total from the above (master's) (0).

Doctoral Degree Graduates: Of those who graduated in the academic year 2003–2004, the following categories and numbers represent the post-graduate activities and employment of doctoral degree graduates: Enrolled in a psychology doctoral program (n/a), total from the above (doctoral) (0).

Additional Information:

Orientation, Objectives, and Emphasis of Department: The Department of Psychology offers a graduate program in experimental psychology, with specializations in cognition, neuroscience, psychopathology, and developmental, and social psychology. The program is designed to produce broadly trained graduates who are prepared for careers in teaching, research, or applied psychology. The department does not offer clinical training. Accepted applicants generally possess a substantial college background in psychology, including familiarity with fundamental statistical concepts and research design. The university is a PhD track program although completion of an MS is required as an integral part of the program. Students who already possess a master's degree may be admitted to the PhD program if a sufficient number of credits are acceptable for transfer and a thesis has been done. Areas of faculty research include infant perception, memory processes, animal cognition and learning, neural and hormonal control of animal sexual behavior, psychopharmacology, event-related brain potentials, neuropsychology of language processes, nutrition and behavior, human factors, decision making, development of emotion understanding, spatial cognition, psychology and law, and the social psychology of prejudicial attitudes. All graduate students participate in supervised research and/or teaching activities each semester. The department provides laboratory space and equipment for many kinds of research, and facilities are available for the behavioral and physiological study of humans and experimental animals.

Special Facilities or Resources: Department has brand new research facilities for both human and animal research in areas of cognition, biopsychology, neuroscience, developmental and social psychology.

Application Information:
Send to: Graduate School, Tufts University, Ballou Hall, Medford, MA 02155. Students are admitted in the Fall, application deadline January 15. *Fee:* $50.

Tufts University
Eliot-Pearson Department of Child Development
Graduate School of Arts and Sciences
105 College Avenue
Medford, MA 02155
Telephone: (617) 627-3355
Fax: (617) 627-3503
E-mail: *Fred.Rothbaum@tufts.edu*
Web: *http://ase.tufts.edu/epcd*

Department Information:
1964. Chairperson: Fred Rothbaum. Number of Faculty: total–full-time 22, part-time 18; women–full-time 13, part-time 15; minority–full-time 6, part-time 1.

Programs and Degrees Offered:
Listed in the following order: Program area, degree type (T if terminal Master's), number awarded 7/03–6/04. MA/MS (Master of Arts/Science) 40, PhD (Doctor of Philosophy) 5, CAGS Other 0, MAT Other 18.

Student Applications/Admissions:
Student Applications
MA/MS *(Master of Arts/Science)*—Applications 2004–2005, 128. Total applicants accepted 2004–2005, 83. Number enrolled (new admits only) 2004–2005 full-time, 30. Number enrolled (new admits only) 2004–2005 part-time, 6. Total enrolled 2004–2005 full-time, 67, part-time, 11. Openings 2005–2006, 60. The number of students enrolled full and part-time who were dismissed or voluntarily withdrew from this program area were 0. *PhD (Doctor of Philosophy)*—Applications 2004–2005, 67. Total applicants accepted 2004–2005, 7. Number enrolled (new admits only) 2004–2005 full-time, 4. Number enrolled (new admits only) 2004–2005 part-time, 0. Openings 2005–2006, 5. The number of students enrolled full and part-time who were dismissed or voluntarily withdrew from this program area were 0. *CAGS Other*—Applications 2004–2005, 0. Total applicants accepted 2004–2005, 0. Number enrolled (new admits only) 2004–2005 full-time, 0. Number enrolled (new admits only) 2004–2005 part-time, 0. Openings 2005–2006, 1. The number of students enrolled full and part-time who were dismissed or voluntarily withdrew from this program area were 0. *MAT Other*—Applications 2004–2005, 41. Total applicants accepted 2004–2005, 35. Number enrolled (new admits only) 2004–2005 full-time, 11. Number enrolled (new admits only) 2004–2005 part-time, 0. Total enrolled 2004–2005 full-time, 24, part-time, 3. Openings 2005–2006, 20. The number of students enrolled full and part-time who were dismissed or voluntarily withdrew from this program area were 0.

Admissions Requirements:

Scores: Entries appear in this order: required test or GPA, minimum score (if required), median score of students entering in 2003–2004. Master's Programs: GRE-V no minimum stated; GRE-Q no minimum stated; GRE-V+Q no minimum stated; GRE-Analytical no minimum stated; overall undergraduate GPA no minimum stated; last 2 years GPA no minimum stated. Doctoral Programs: GRE-V no minimum stated; GRE-Q no minimum stated; GRE-V+Q no minimum stated; GRE-Analytical no minimum stated; overall undergraduate GPA no minimum stated; last 2 years GPA no minimum stated.

Other Criteria: (importance of criteria rated low, medium, or high): GRE/MAT scores high, research experience medium, work experience medium, extracurricular activity low, clinically related public service medium, GPA medium, letters of recommendation high, statement of goals and objectives high. For additional information on admission requirements, go to: http://ase.tufts.edu/GradStudy.

Student Characteristics: The following represents characteristics of students in 2004–2005 in all graduate psychology programs in the department: Female–full-time 111, part-time 12; Male–full-time 14, part-time 2; African American/Black–full-time 7, part-time 0; Hispanic/Latino(a)–full-time 10, part-time 0; Asian/Pacific Islander–full-time 10, part-time 0; American Indian/Alaska Native–full-time 0, part-time 0; Caucasian–full-time 78, part-time 12; Multi-ethnic–full-time 20, part-time 2; students subject to the Americans With Disabilities Act–full-time 0, part-time 0.

Financial Information/Assistance:

Tuition for Full-Time Study: *Master's:* State residents: per academic year $32,360, $3,236 per credit hour; Nonstate residents: per academic year $32,360, $3,236 per credit hour. *Doctoral:* State residents: per academic year $32,360, $3,236 per credit hour; Nonstate residents: per academic year $32,360, $3,236 per credit hour. See the following Web site for updates and changes in tuition costs: http://ase.tufts.edu/GradStudy.

Financial Assistance:

First Year Students: Teaching assistantships available for first-year. Average amount paid per academic year: $17,000. Average number of hours worked per week: 20. Apply by January 15. Tuition remission given: full. Research assistantships available for first-year. Apply by Varies. Fellowships and scholarships available for first-year. Apply by January 15. Tuition remission given: full.

Advanced Students: Teaching assistantships available for advanced students. Average amount paid per academic year: $17,000. Average number of hours worked per week: 20. Apply by January 15. Tuition remission given: full. Research assistantships available for advanced students. Apply by Varies. Fellowships and scholarships available for advanced students. Apply by January 15. Tuition remission given: full and partial.

Contact Information: Of all students currently enrolled full-time, 80% benefitted from one or more of the listed financial assistance programs. Application and information available online at: http://ase.tufts.edu/GradStudy.

Internships/Practica: MA-students engage in a semester-long internship in applied settings such as hospitals, mental health clinics, policy centers, museums. PhD students engage in full-time 1-semester or half-time full-year applied internships in varied settings.

Housing and Day Care: On-campus housing is available. See the following Web site for more information: Please contact the Graduate and Professional Studies office at http://ase.tufts.edu/Gradstudy and the Residential Life office (ask for the off-campus housing) at (617) 627-3248 or at http://ase.tufts.edu/reslife/LEFT/Graduates/grad_students.html. Off-campus listings, along with other information, can be found online at http://ase.tufts.edu/och. On-campus day care facilities are available.

Employment of Department Graduates:

Master's Degree Graduates: Of those who graduated in the academic year 2003–2004, the following categories and numbers represent the post-graduate activities and employment of master's degree graduates: Enrolled in a post-doctoral residency/fellowship (n/a), employed in independent practice (n/a), total from the above (master's) (0).

Doctoral Degree Graduates: Of those who graduated in the academic year 2003–2004, the following categories and numbers represent the post-graduate activities and employment of doctoral degree graduates: Enrolled in a psychology doctoral program (n/a), total from the above (doctoral) (0).

Additional Information:

Orientation, Objectives, and Emphasis of Department: The department prepares students for a variety of careers that have, as their common prerequisite, a comprehensive understanding of children and their development. Students receive a foundation in psychological theory and research concerning the social, emotional, intellectual, linguistic, and physiological growth of children. Course material is complemented with progressively more involved practica encompassing observations and works with children in a wide variety of applied and research settings. The major aim of the program is to train people who can translate their knowledge about development into effective strategies for working with and on behalf of children. We believe that a background in child development is the best possible preparation for teaching and administrative careers in schools, children's advocacy and mental health agencies, hospitals, the media, government agencies concerned with the rights and welfare of children, and related fields. There is considerable room for flexibility in the program. For example, students with proficiency in one area, such as field experience, may concentrate on others, such as clinical theory and research. Also, students may choose from a rich variety of elective courses that touch upon such diverse topics as child advocacy, divorce and the family, and children's literature. The largest number of courses are in the area of developmental psychology, but there are also several courses in clinical and educational psychology and in the study of children and family policy.

Special Facilities or Resources: The department is housed in a complex of buildings on the Medford campus. The main building contains faculty, staff and TA offices, class meeting rooms, a library and a curriculum research lab. This building also includes the Eliot-Pearson Children's School, which serves normal and special-needs children aged 2 to 6. The school has observation booths for student use. Other buildings on campus house several faculty research projects, classrooms and meeting rooms - Center for Reading and Language Research; Institute for Applied Research in Youth Development. The department is also associated with the Tufts Educational Day Care Center. Students may work, as well as observe, in all of these settings. Both facilities are integrated into faculty research and research training for graduate students.

Information for Students With Physical Disabilities: See the following Web site for more information: http://www.studentservices.tufts.edu/DisabilityServices/information.htm.

Application Information:
Send to: Tufts University, Graduate and Professional Studies, Ballou Hall, Medford, MA 02155. Application available online. URL of online application: http://ase.tufts.edu/gradstudy/admisApply.htm. Students are admitted in the Fall, application deadline January 15; Programs have rolling admissions. February 1 for joint-degree programs. *Fee:* $60.

Andrews University

Department of Educational and Counseling Psychology
Bell Hall Room 160
Berrien Springs, MI 49104-0104
Telephone: (616) 471-3113
Fax: (616) 471-6374
E-mail: *ecp@andrews.edu*
Web: *http://www.educ.andrews.edu*

Department Information:

Chairperson: Jerome D. Thayer. Number of Faculty: total–full-time 9; women–full-time 2; minority–full-time 4.

Programs and Degrees Offered:

Listed in the following order: Program area, degree type (T if terminal Master's), number awarded 7/03–6/04. Community Counseling MA/MS (Master of Arts/Science) (T) 11, Counseling Psychology PhD (Doctor of Philosophy) 3, Educational Psychology MA/MS (Master of Arts/Science) 8, School Counseling MA/MS (Master of Arts/Science) (T) 5, School Psychology EdS (Education Specialist) 2.

Student Applications/Admissions:

Student Applications

Community Counseling MA/MS (Master of Arts/Science)—Applications 2004–2005, 28. Total applicants accepted 2004–2005, 20. Total enrolled 2004–2005 full-time, 18, part-time, 4. Openings 2005–2006, 25. The Median number of years required for completion of a degree are 2. The number of students enrolled full and part-time who were dismissed or voluntarily withdrew from this program area were 2. *Counseling Psychology PhD (Doctor of Philosophy)*—Applications 2004–2005, 10. Total applicants accepted 2004–2005, 6. Total enrolled 2004–2005 full-time, 10, part-time, 19. Openings 2005–2006, 25. The Median number of years required for completion of a degree are 6. The number of students enrolled full and part-time who were dismissed or voluntarily withdrew from this program area were 0. *Educational Psychology MA/MS (Master of Arts/Science)*—Applications 2004–2005, 16. Total applicants accepted 2004–2005, 10. Total enrolled 2004–2005 full-time, 7, part-time, 6. Openings 2005–2006, 12. The Median number of years required for completion of a degree are 2. The number of students enrolled full and part-time who were dismissed or voluntarily withdrew from this program area were 1. *School Counseling MA/MS (Master of Arts/Science)*—Applications 2004–2005, 7. Total applicants accepted 2004–2005, 4. Total enrolled 2004–2005 full-time, 5, part-time, 6. Openings 2005–2006, 5. The Median number of years required for completion of a degree are 2. The number of students enrolled full and part-time who were dismissed or voluntarily withdrew from this program area were 0. *School Psychology EdS (Education Specialist)*—Applications 2004–2005, 9. Total applicants accepted 2004–2005, 7. Total enrolled 2004–2005 full-time, 7, part-time, 5. Openings 2005–2006, 5. The Median number of years required for completion of a degree are 3. The number

of students enrolled full and part-time who were dismissed or voluntarily withdrew from this program area were 0.

Admissions Requirements:

Scores: Entries appear in this order: required test or GPA, minimum score (if required), median score of students entering in 2003–2004. Master's Programs: GRE-V no minimum stated; GRE-Q no minimum stated; overall undergraduate GPA 2.6. Doctoral Programs: GRE-V no minimum stated; GRE-Q no minimum stated; overall undergraduate GPA 3.0.

Other Criteria: (importance of criteria rated low, medium, or high): GRE/MAT scores medium, research experience low, work experience low, extracurricular activity low, clinically related public service low, GPA high, letters of recommendation high, interview high, statement of goals and objectives high.

Student Characteristics: The following represents characteristics of students in 2004–2005 in all graduate psychology programs in the department: Female–full-time 66, part-time 14; Male–full-time 15, part-time 7; African American/Black–full-time 20, part-time 6; Hispanic/Latino(a)–full-time 3, part-time 2; Asian/Pacific Islander–full-time 2, part-time 0; American Indian/Alaska Native–full-time 0, part-time 0; Caucasian–full-time 56, part-time 13; Multi-ethnic–full-time 0, part-time 0; students subject to the Americans With Disabilities Act–full-time 0, part-time 0.

Financial Information/Assistance:

Tuition for Full-Time Study: *Master's:* State residents: per academic year $14,880, $620 per credit hour; Nonstate residents: per academic year $14,880, $620 per credit hour. *Doctoral:* State residents: per academic year $17,400, $725 per credit hour; Nonstate residents: per academic year $17,400, $725 per credit hour. Tuition is subject to change. See the following Web site for updates and changes in tuition costs: http://www.andrews.edu/SF/.

Financial Assistance:

First Year Students: Teaching assistantships available for first-year. Average amount paid per academic year: $4,000. Average number of hours worked per week: 20. Apply by no deadline. Research assistantships available for first-year. Average amount paid per academic year: $4,000. Average number of hours worked per week: 20. Apply by no deadline.

Advanced Students: Teaching assistantships available for advanced students. Average amount paid per academic year: $4,000. Average number of hours worked per week: 20. Apply by no deadline. Research assistantships available for advanced students. Average amount paid per academic year: $4,000. Average number of hours worked per week: 20. Apply by no deadline.

Contact Information: Of all students currently enrolled full-time, 18% benefitted from one or more of the listed financial assistance programs.

Internships/Practica: The professional training programs in counseling and counseling psychology are designed to produce professionals who have well developed skills in assesssment, diagnosis, and counseling. All trainees in the counseling and counseling psychology programs work in the department's Counseling and

Psychological Services Center, where they see clients from the surrounding community who present a wide range of concerns, in order to prepare them for their internship experience. Master's students in the school counseling or community counseling programs must complete a 600-clock-hour internship in a school or community agency setting. These agencies include community mental health centers, youth/adolescent treatment centers, drug-alcohol treatment programs, private counseling centers, schools, and other human service agencies. Counseling psychology doctoral students must complete a 2,000 clock-hour internship in an approved health care setting under the direct supervision of a psychologist licensed to practice independently. Students are strongly encouraged to seek APA-approved or APPIC internships. Students in the master's and doctoral programs in educational psychology are provided with opportunities to do field work in educational psychology. Students in school psychology must complete a 1,200-clock-hour internship under the supervision of a certified or licensed school psychologist in a local school district. For those doctoral students for whom a professional internship is required prior to graduation, 4 applied in 2003–2004. Of those who applied, 3 were placed in internships listed by the Association of Psychology Postdoctoral and Internship Programs (APPIC); 3 were placed in APA accredited internships.

Housing and Day Care: On-campus housing is available. See the following Web site for more information: http://www.andrews.edu/HOUSING/. On-campus day care facilities are available. See the following Web site for more information: http://www.andrews.edu/CAS/CrayonBox/.

Employment of Department Graduates:

Master's Degree Graduates: Of those who graduated in the academic year 2003–2004, the following categories and numbers represent the post-graduate activities and employment of master's degree graduates: Enrolled in a psychology doctoral program (2), enrolled in another graduate/professional program (2), enrolled in a post-doctoral residency/fellowship (n/a), employed in independent practice (n/a), employed in an academic position at a university (0), employed in an academic position at a 2-year/4-year college (0), employed in other positions at a higher education institution (1), employed in a professional position in a school system (6), employed in business or industry (research/consulting) (0), employed in business or industry (management) (1), employed in a government agency (research) (0), employed in a government agency (professional services) (0), employed in a community mental health/counseling center (3), employed in a hospital/medical center (3), still seeking employment (0), other employment position (0), do not know (2), total from the above (master's) (20).

Doctoral Degree Graduates: Of those who graduated in the academic year 2003–2004, the following categories and numbers represent the post-graduate activities and employment of doctoral degree graduates: Enrolled in a psychology doctoral program (n/a), enrolled in another graduate/professional program (0), enrolled in a post-doctoral residency/fellowship (0), employed in independent practice (0), employed in an academic position at a university (0), employed in an academic position at a 2-year/4-year college (1), employed in other positions at a higher education institution (0), employed in a professional position in a school system (1), employed in business or industry (research/consulting) (0), employed in business or industry (management) (0), employed in a government agency (research) (0), employed in a government agency (professional services) (0), employed in a community mental health/counseling center (1), employed in a hospital/medical center (0), still seeking employment (1), other employment position (1), do not know (5), total from the above (doctoral) (10).

Additional Information:

Orientation, Objectives, and Emphasis of Department: The objective of the master's programs is to prepare students for professional employment in educational and mental health settings as counselors and learning specialists. Students obtaining an EdS in school psychology are prepared for a professional career as certified or licensed school psychologists to work in public or private schools, preschools, and child development centers. Doctoral students are prepared for teaching, research, and professional practice. Students are exposed to a variety of theoretical orientations and are expected to develop an eclectic model for delivering counseling and psychological services. The university is sponsored by the Seventh-Day Adventist Church. However, students from all religious persuasions are welcome and considered without bias. While there is an emphasis in the department on the relationship between psychological theory, research, and practice and Christian theology and religious experience, respect is maintained for individual differences. PhD students in counseling psychology are trained using the scientist-practitioner model. They are given instruction in scientific and professional ethics and standards, research design and methodology, statistics and psychometrics. In addition, coursework in the following areas is required: biological bases of behavior, cognitive-affective bases of behavior, social bases of behavior, and individual differences. Special emphases are available in marital and family therapy, substance abuse counseling, adult or child mental health services.

Personal Behavior Statement: With rights come responsibilities. Students who enroll at Andrews University are expected to maintain and contribute to the university's high standards of honor, integrity, morality, and respect for self and others. Students play an important role in creating and maintaining a healthy climate for campus learning, living, and working. As far as possible, the goal of the University is to permit and foster the exercise of sound judgment by individual students. It is from this perspective that this student responsibilities section is written. Students are expected to conduct themselves at all times in a manner that is honest and is consistent with the traditions and beliefs of the Seventh-day Adventist Church. Students may be disciplined for conduct that is hazardous to the health, safety, or well-being of members of the university community; is incompatible with Biblical standards of morality as interpreted by the Seventh-day Adventist Church; or is detrimental to the university's interest whether such conduct occurs on or off campus or at university-sponsored events.

Special Facilities or Resources: The department operates a Counseling and Psychological Services Center that provides mental health services to children, adolescents, and adults who reside in the surrounding area. The Center includes space for individual, family, group, and child therapy. Video monitors and videotape are used in the supervision of all trainees. The department also has access to a statistical research center with mainframe accessibility and a number of microcomputers. A separate microcomputer lab is also available.

Application Information:

Send to: Eileen Lesher/Graduate Admissions, Andrews University, Berrien Springs, MI 49104-0740. Application available online. URL of online application: http://www.andrews.edu/admissions/apply.php3. Students are admitted in the Fall. Programs have rolling admissions. Rolling deadline, ask for details. *Fee:* $40.

Center for Humanistic Studies Graduate School

26811 Orchard Lake Road
Farmington Hills, MI 48334-4512
Telephone: (248) 476-1122
Fax: (248) 476-1125
E-mail: *chs@humanpsych.edu*
Web: *http://www.humanpsych.edu*

Department Information:

1980. President: Kerry Moustakas, PhD Number of Faculty: total–full-time 3, part-time 14; women–full-time 2, part-time 6; minority–part-time 1.

Programs and Degrees Offered:

Listed in the following order: Program area, degree type (T if terminal Master's), number awarded 7/03–6/04. PsyD (Doctor of Psychology) 8, MA/MS (Master of Arts/Science) 24.

Student Applications/Admissions:

Student Applications

PsyD (Doctor of Psychology)—Applications 2004–2005, 21. Total applicants accepted 2004–2005, 15. Number enrolled (new admits only) 2004–2005 full-time, 14. Number enrolled (new admits only) 2004–2005 part-time, 0. Total enrolled 2004–2005 full-time, 47, part-time, 5. Openings 2005–2006, 18. The Median number of years required for completion of a degree are 4. The number of students enrolled full and part-time who were dismissed or voluntarily withdrew from this program area were 1. *Masters MA/MS (Master of Arts/Science)*—Applications 2004–2005, 53. Total applicants accepted 2004–2005, 44. Number enrolled (new admits only) 2004–2005 full-time, 33. Number enrolled (new admits only) 2004–2005 part-time, 0. Total enrolled 2004–2005 full-time, 33, part-time, 8. Openings 2005–2006, 36. The Median number of years required for completion of a degree is 1. The number of students enrolled full and part-time who were dismissed or voluntarily withdrew from this program area were 3.

Admissions Requirements:

Scores: Entries appear in this order: required test or GPA, minimum score (if required), median score of students entering in 2003–2004. Master's Programs: overall undergraduate GPA 3.0, 3.0; psychology GPA 3.0, 3.0. Doctoral Programs: overall undergraduate GPA 3.0, 3.0; psychology GPA 3.0, 3.0.

Other Criteria: (importance of criteria rated low, medium, or high): research experience medium, work experience high, extracurricular activity medium, clinically related public service high, GPA high, letters of recommendation high, interview high, statement of goals and objectives high.

Student Characteristics: The following represents characteristics of students in 2004–2005 in all graduate psychology programs in the department: Female–full-time 62, part-time 9; Male–full-time 18, part-time 4; African American/Black–full-time 9, part-time 3; Hispanic/Latino(a)–full-time 4, part-time 0; Asian/Pacific Islander–full-time 1, part-time 1; American Indian/Alaska Native–full-time 0, part-time 0; Caucasian–full-time 66, part-time 9; Multi-ethnic–full-time 0, part-time 0; students subject to the Americans With Disabilities Act–full-time 0, part-time 0.

Financial Information/Assistance:

Tuition for Full-Time Study: *Master's:* State residents: per academic year $16,530, $375 per credit hour; Nonstate residents: per academic year $16,530, $375 per credit hour. *Doctoral:* State residents: per academic year $16,530, $425 per credit hour; Nonstate residents: per academic year $16,530, $425 per credit hour. Tuition is subject to change. Above tuition for academic year 2005-06.

Financial Assistance:

First Year Students: No information provided.
Advanced Students: No information provided.
Contact Information: Of all students currently enrolled full-time, 0% benefitted from one or more of the listed financial assistance programs.

Internships/Practica: *Master's:* is required prior to graduation, 9 applied in 2003–2004.

Housing and Day Care: No on-campus housing is available. No on-campus day care facilities are available.

Employment of Department Graduates:

Master's Degree Graduates: Of those who graduated in the academic year 2003–2004, the following categories and numbers represent the post-graduate activities and employment of master's degree graduates: Enrolled in a psychology doctoral program (15), enrolled in another graduate/professional program (3), enrolled in a post-doctoral residency/fellowship (n/a), employed in independent practice (n/a), employed in a community mental health/counseling center (12), employed in a hospital/medical center (3), do not know (15), total from the above (master's) (48).

Doctoral Degree Graduates: Of those who graduated in the academic year 2003–2004, the following categories and numbers represent the post-graduate activities and employment of doctoral degree graduates: Enrolled in a psychology doctoral program (n/a), employed in an academic position at a 2-year/4-year college (4), employed in a professional position in a school system (2), do not know (4), total from the above (doctoral) (10).

Additional Information:

Orientation, Objectives, and Emphasis of Department: The mission of the Center for Humanistic Studies Graduate School is to educate and train individuals to become reflective scholar-practitioners with the competencies necessary to serve diverse populations as professional humanistic psychologists and psychotherapists.

Special Facilities or Resources: n/a.

Information for Students With Physical Disabilities: Our new facility is accessible to students with physical disabilities.

Application Information:
Send to: Admissions Department, CHS, 26811 Orchard Lake Road, Farmington Hills, MI 48334-4512. Students are admitted in the Fall. We accept on a rolling admissions policy. Our deadline is March 1 but will still accept applications if there are openings. Students may be wait-listed. *Fee:* $75.

Central Michigan University
Department of Psychology
Humanities and Social and Behavioral Sciences
Sloan Hall
Mt. Pleasant, MI 48859
Telephone: (989) 774-3001
Fax: (989) 774-2553
E-mail: *psy@cmich.edu*
Web: *http://www.chsbs.cmich.edu/psychology*

Department Information:
1965. Chairperson: Gary Dunbar. Number of Faculty: total–full-time 34, part-time 3; women–full-time 12, part-time 2; minority–full-time 5.

Programs and Degrees Offered:
Listed in the following order: Program area, degree type (T if terminal Master's), number awarded 7/03–6/04. Clinical PhD (Doctor of Philosophy) 5, Experimental PhD (Doctor of Philosophy) 0, General MA/MS (Master of Arts/Science) 2, School PhD (Doctor of Philosophy) 2, Industrial/ Organizational MA/MS (Master of Arts/Science) 0, Industrial/Organizational PhD (Doctor of Philosophy) 1, School Master/Specialists Other 5.

APA Accreditation: Clinical PhD (Doctor of Philosophy). School PhD (Doctor of Philosophy).

Student Applications/Admissions:
Student Applications
Clinical PhD (Doctor of Philosophy)—Applications 2004–2005, 96. Total applicants accepted 2004–2005, 6. Number enrolled (new admits only) 2004–2005 full-time, 6. Openings 2005–2006, 6. The Median number of years required for completion of a degree are 7. The number of students enrolled full and part-time who were dismissed or voluntarily withdrew from this program area were 0. *Experimental PhD (Doctor of Philosophy)*—Applications 2004–2005, 12. Total applicants accepted 2004–2005, 4. Number enrolled (new admits only) 2004–2005 full-time, 4. Openings 2005–2006, 2. *General MA/MS (Master of Arts/Science)*—Applications 2004–2005, 18. Total applicants accepted 2004–2005, 8. Number enrolled (new admits only) 2004–2005 full-time, 8. Openings 2005–2006, 5. The Median number of years required for completion of a degree are 2. The number of students enrolled full and part-time who were dismissed or voluntarily withdrew from this program area were 0. *School - PhD (Doctor of Philosophy)*—Applications 2004–2005, 24. Total applicants accepted 2004–2005, 4. Number enrolled (new admits only) 2004–2005 full-time, 4. Total enrolled 2004–2005 full-time, 14. Openings 2005–2006, 3. The Median number of years required for completion of a degree are 7. The number of students enrolled full and part-time who were dismissed or voluntarily withdrew from this program area

were 0. *Industrial/ Organizational - Master's MA/MS (Master of Arts/Science)*—Applications 2004–2005, 27. Total applicants accepted 2004–2005, 3. Number enrolled (new admits only) 2004–2005 full-time, 3. Total enrolled 2004–2005 full-time, 4. Openings 2005–2006, 3. The number of students enrolled full and part-time who were dismissed or voluntarily withdrew from this program area were 0. *Industrial/Organizational - PhD (Doctor of Philosophy)*—Applications 2004–2005, 57. Total applicants accepted 2004–2005, 2. Number enrolled (new admits only) 2004–2005 full-time, 2. Total enrolled 2004–2005 full-time, 30. The Median number of years required for completion of a degree are 4. *School Master/Specialists Other*—Applications 2004–2005, 34. Total applicants accepted 2004–2005, 3. Number enrolled (new admits only) 2004–2005 full-time, 3. Total enrolled 2004–2005 full-time, 32. The Median number of years required for completion of a degree are 5.

Admissions Requirements:
Scores: Entries appear in this order: required test or GPA, minimum score (if required), median score of students entering in 2003–2004. Master's Programs: GRE-V no minimum stated; GRE-Q no minimum stated; overall undergraduate GPA 3.00; psychology GPA 3.00. GRE-V and GRE-Q score requirements vary with each application pool. Doctoral Programs: GRE-V no minimum stated; GRE-Q no minimum stated; overall undergraduate GPA 3.00. GRE-V & GRE-Q requirements vary with each application pool.
Other Criteria: (importance of criteria rated low, medium, or high): GRE/MAT scores medium, research experience high, work experience medium, extracurricular activity low, clinically related public service medium, GPA high, letters of recommendation high, statement of goals and objectives high.

Student Characteristics: The following represents characteristics of students in 2004–2005 in all graduate psychology programs in the department: Female–full-time 101, part-time 0; Male–full-time 62, part-time 0; African American/Black–full-time 3, part-time 0; Hispanic/Latino(a)–full-time 3, part-time 0; Asian/Pacific Islander–full-time 13, part-time 0; American Indian/Alaska Native–full-time 1, part-time 0; Caucasian–full-time 142, part-time 0; Multi-ethnic–full-time 1, part-time 0.

Financial Information/Assistance:
Tuition for Full-Time Study: *Master's:* State residents: $205 per credit hour; Nonstate residents: $408 per credit hour. *Doctoral:* State residents: $222 per credit hour; Nonstate residents: $441 per credit hour. Tuition is subject to change.

Financial Assistance:
First Year Students: Teaching assistantships available for first-year. Average amount paid per academic year: $10,500. Average number of hours worked per week: 20. Apply by February 6. Tuition remission given: partial. Research assistantships available for first-year. Average amount paid per academic year: $9,050. Average number of hours worked per week: 20. Apply by February 6. Tuition remission given: partial. Fellowships and scholarships available for first-year. Average amount paid per academic year: $8,550. Average number of hours worked per week: 30. Apply by February 6. Tuition remission given: partial.
Advanced Students: Teaching assistantships available for advanced students. Average amount paid per academic year: $11,200. Average number of hours worked per week: 20. Apply

by February 6. Tuition remission given: partial. Research assistantships available for advanced students. Average amount paid per academic year: $10,200. Average number of hours worked per week: 20. Apply by February 6. Tuition remission given: partial. Fellowships and scholarships available for advanced students. Average amount paid per academic year: $9,900. Average number of hours worked per week: 30. Apply by February 6. Tuition remission given: partial.

Contact Information: Of all students currently enrolled full-time, 43% benefitted from one or more of the listed financial assistance programs. Application and information available online at: www.chsbs.cmich.edu/psychology.

Internships/Practica: Most practica and internships are arranged through agencies and schools outside the University. However, practica experiences are available through the Department's Psychological Training and Consultation Center. Second-year clinical students routinely have their first practicum at the Center. For those doctoral students for whom a professional internship is required prior to graduation, 10 applied in 2003–2004. Of those who applied, 10 were placed in internships listed by the Association of Psychology Postdoctoral and Internship Programs (APPIC); 10 were placed in APA accredited internships.

Housing and Day Care: On-campus housing is available. Office of Residence Life, Bovee University Center, Room 201, Central Michigan University, Mt. Pleasant, MI 48859-0001. No on-campus day care facilities are available.

Employment of Department Graduates:

Master's Degree Graduates: Of those who graduated in the academic year 2003–2004, the following categories and numbers represent the post-graduate activities and employment of master's degree graduates: Enrolled in a post-doctoral residency/fellowship (n/a), employed in independent practice (n/a), total from the above (master's) (0).

Doctoral Degree Graduates: Of those who graduated in the academic year 2003–2004, the following categories and numbers represent the post-graduate activities and employment of doctoral degree graduates: Enrolled in a psychology doctoral program (n/a), total from the above (doctoral) (0).

Additional Information:

Orientation, Objectives, and Emphasis of Department: Specialization is possible in the areas of clinical, applied experimental, industrial/organizational, and school psychology. There is also a general/experimental MS program with emphasis on foundations, statistics, methodology, and research, which is designed to prepare students for doctoral training or research positions in the public or private sectors. The clinical program follows a practitioner-scientist model, focusing on training for applied settings. The industrial/organizational program is oriented toward training students for careers in research, university, or business settings. The school program prepares school psychologists to provide consultation, intervention, and diagnostic services to schools and school children. The program meets Michigan requirements for certification.

Special Facilities or Resources: Space is reserved for student research with human subjects. Special equipment permits studies in learning, cognition, human factors, psychophysiology, neuropsychology, and perception. Computer laboratories are available,

one specifically designated for clinical and school students. All computer labs have direct email, and Internet access, as well as statistical and research software. The Psychology Training and Consultation Center provides training, research, and service functions. In a separate building, space is devoted to animal research and teaching of behavioral neuroscience and experimental behavior analysis. The behavioral neuroscience laboratory contains a fully equipped surgical/historological suite, behavioral testing area and equipment, and a data analysis room including microscopes and an image analysis system. The experimental analysis laboratory is equipped with automated operant chambers for both birds and rodents. A Life-Span Development Research Center has been established in the Department.

Information for Students With Physical Disabilities: See the following Web site for more information: http://www.cmich.edu/student-disability/.

Application Information:
Send to: Psychology Department, Sloan Hall, Central Michigan University, Mt. Pleasant, MI 48859. Application available online. URL of online application: www.chsbs.cmich.edu/psychology. Students are admitted in the Fall. Clinical and School deadlines are January 15, Experimental & Industrial/Organizational deadlines are February 1. *Fee:* $30.

Detroit–Mercy, University of
Department of Psychology
College of Liberal Arts and Education
4001 W. McNichols/ P.O. Box 19900
Detroit, MI 48219-0900
Telephone: (313) 578-0392
Fax: (313) 578-0507
E-mail: *abellsc@udmercy.edu*
Web: *http://www.udmercy.edu/catalog*

Department Information:
1946. Chairperson: Steven Abell, PhD Number of Faculty: total–full-time 16, part-time 20; women–full-time 11; minority–full-time 3; faculty subject to the Americans With Disabilities Act 1.

Programs and Degrees Offered:
Listed in the following order: Program area, degree type (T if terminal Master's), number awarded 7/03–6/04. Industrial/ Organizational MA/MS (Master of Arts/Science) (T) 7, Specialist in School Psychology Other 12, Clinical Psychology PhD (Doctor of Philosophy) 7, Clinical Psychology MA/MS (Master of Arts/Science) (T) 6.

APA Accreditation: Clinical PhD (Doctor of Philosophy).

Student Applications/Admissions:
Student Applications
Industrial/ Organizational MA/MS (Master of Arts/Science)— Applications 2004–2005, 20. Total applicants accepted 2004–2005, 16. Total enrolled 2004–2005 full-time, 12, part-time, 10. Openings 2005–2006, 14. The Median number of years required for completion of a degree are 2. *Specialist in School*

Psychology Other—Applications 2004–2005, 40. Total applicants accepted 2004–2005, 12. Number enrolled (new admits only) 2004–2005 full-time, 8. Number enrolled (new admits only) 2004–2005 part-time, 4. Total enrolled 2004–2005 full-time, 16, part-time, 12. Openings 2005–2006, 12. The Median number of years required for completion of a degree are 3. The number of students enrolled full and part-time who were dismissed or voluntarily withdrew from this program area were 0. *Clinical Psychology PhD (Doctor of Philosophy)*—Applications 2004–2005, 62. Total applicants accepted 2004–2005, 10. Number enrolled (new admits only) 2004–2005 full-time, 10. Number enrolled (new admits only) 2004–2005 part-time, 0. Openings 2005–2006, 10. The Median number of years required for completion of a degree are 6. The number of students enrolled full and part-time who were dismissed or voluntarily withdrew from this program area were 0. *Clinical Psychology MA/MS (Master of Arts/Science)*—Applications 2004–2005, 60. Total applicants accepted 2004–2005, 18. Number enrolled (new admits only) 2004–2005 full-time, 9. Number enrolled (new admits only) 2004–2005 part-time, 1. Total enrolled 2004–2005 full-time, 24, part-time, 4. Openings 2005–2006, 14. The Median number of years required for completion of a degree are 2. The number of students enrolled full and part-time who were dismissed or voluntarily withdrew from this program area were 2.

Admissions Requirements:

Scores: Entries appear in this order: required test or GPA, minimum score (if required), median score of students entering in 2003–2004. Master's Programs: GRE-V 450, 550; GRE-Q 450, 500; GRE-V+Q 900, 1050; overall undergraduate GPA 3.0, 3.3; last 2 years GPA 3.0, 3.4; psychology GPA 3.0, 3.5. Doctoral Programs: GRE-V 500, 550; GRE-Q 500, 630; GRE-V+Q 1000, 1180; GRE-Analytical 4.0, 4.5; overall undergraduate GPA 3.0, 3.7.

Other Criteria: (importance of criteria rated low, medium, or high): GRE/MAT scores high, research experience medium, work experience medium, extracurricular activity medium, clinically related public service medium, GPA high, letters of recommendation high, interview high, statement of goals and objectives high. For the Clinical MA program, GRE scores are not given as much weight as GPA, letters of recommendation, and previous relevant work experience. For additional information on admission requirements, go to: www.udmercy.edu/catalog.

Student Characteristics: The following represents characteristics of students in 2004–2005 in all graduate psychology programs in the department: Female–full-time 74, part-time 20; Male–full-time 30, part-time 10; African American/Black–full-time 5, part-time 0; Hispanic/Latino(a)–full-time 1, part-time 0; Asian/Pacific Islander–full-time 2, part-time 3; American Indian/Alaska Native–full-time 0, part-time 0; Caucasian–full-time 0, part-time 0.

Financial Information/Assistance:

Tuition for Full-Time Study: *Master's:* State residents: $760 per credit hour; Nonstate residents: $760 per credit hour. *Doctoral:* State residents: $760 per credit hour; Nonstate residents: $760 per credit hour. Tuition is subject to change. See the following Web site for updates and changes in tuition costs: www.udmercy.edu.

Financial Assistance:

First Year Students: Teaching assistantships available for first-year. Average number of hours worked per week: 15. Apply by January 1. Research assistantships available for first-year. Average number of hours worked per week: 15. Apply by January 1. Tuition remission given: partial.

Advanced Students: Teaching assistantships available for advanced students. Average number of hours worked per week: 15. Apply by January 1. Tuition remission given: partial. Research assistantships available for advanced students. Average number of hours worked per week: 15. Apply by January 1. Tuition remission given: partial.

Contact Information: Application and information available online at: www.udmercy.edu.

Internships/Practica: Students have available for practicum and internship experiences a wide range of settings ranging from hospitals, inpatient and outpatient units, schools, community agencies, and businesses. Populations served can range from children, adolescents, and adults to prisoners and those requiring rehabilitation services. Assessments and interventions of various kinds are performed under the supervision of licensed or appropriately credentialed psychologists. For those doctoral students for whom a professional internship is required prior to graduation, 8 applied in 2003–2004. Of those who applied, 8 were placed in internships listed by the Association of Psychology Postdoctoral and Internship Programs (APPIC); 8 were placed in APA accredited internships.

Housing and Day Care: On-campus housing is available. While the University does not have on-campus housing specifically for graduate students, graduate students are eligible to live in the University's residence halls on the McNichols campus, which is also home to the Psychology Department. On-campus day care facilities are available. A licensed child care facility is currently located on the University's Outer Drive Campus, which has both a daytime and evening program.

Employment of Department Graduates:

Master's Degree Graduates: Of those who graduated in the academic year 2003–2004, the following categories and numbers represent the post-graduate activities and employment of master's degree graduates: Enrolled in a post-doctoral residency/fellowship (n/a), employed in independent practice (n/a), total from the above (master's) (0).

Doctoral Degree Graduates: Of those who graduated in the academic year 2003–2004, the following categories and numbers represent the post-graduate activities and employment of doctoral degree graduates: Enrolled in a psychology doctoral program (n/a), employed in independent practice (4), employed in a community mental health/counseling center (2), employed in a hospital/medical center (1), total from the above (doctoral) (7).

Additional Information:

Orientation, Objectives, and Emphasis of Department: The overall goal of graduate education in the Psychology Department is to train psychologists who are well-grounded in theory and research and who can function in a variety of settings. The theoretical emphasis of the doctoral program in clinical psychology is psychodynamic, while the orientations of the other programs are more eclectic. Regardless of orientation, however, students are exposed to different kinds of intervention techniques, each with its own theoretical rationale. The master's program in clinical psychology allows students to specialize in working with substance abusers or children. The specialist program in school psychology prepares students to function as psychologists in school settings, dealing with children and families. The master's program in industrial psychology focuses on human resource development and personnel management.

Special Facilities or Resources: The University of Detroit-Mercy runs the University Psychology Clinic, which serves the metropolitan area as a community mental health clinic. The clinic work is directed or supervised by faculty members and psychologists from the community. Students in the doctoral and masters programs in clinical and students in the specialist program in school psychology begin their clinical work in their second year and continue with increasingly responsible supervised experiences.

Application Information:
Send to: Mr. Steven Coddington, Admissions Office, University of Detroit–Mercy, 4001 W. McNichols, Detroit, MI 48221. Online applications available at www.udmercy.edu. Students are admitted in the Fall. The application deadline for the fall semester varies by program: PhD Clinical, January 1, School Psychology—February 1, Industrial/Organizational Psychology MA—March 1, Clinical MA—March 31. Application materials available online. The amount of fee is $30 for the Clinical MA or Specialist program and $50 for the PhD program. The application fee is waived when students apply online at www.udmercy.edu.

Eastern Michigan University
Department of Psychology
College of Arts and Sciences
537 Mark Jefferson Hall
Ypsilanti, MI 48197
Telephone: (313) 487-1155
Fax: (313) 487-6553
E-mail: *jknapp@emich.edu*
Web: *http://www.emich.edu*

Department Information:
1962. Department Head: John R. Knapp. Number of Faculty: total–full-time 25, part-time 9; women–full-time 11, part-time 5; minority–full-time 1, part-time 3.

Programs and Degrees Offered:
Listed in the following order: Program area, degree type (T if terminal Master's), number awarded 7/03–6/04. General Clinical Psychology MA/MS (Master of Arts/Science) (T) 5, Clinical Behavioral Psychology MA/MS (Master of Arts/Science) (T) 7, General Experimental Psych. MA/MS (Master of Arts/Science) (T) 1, Clinical Psychology PhD (Doctor of Philosophy) 0.

Student Applications/Admissions:
Student Applications
General Clinical Psychology MA/MS (Master of Arts/Science)—Applications 2004–2005, 40. Total applicants accepted 2004–2005, 17. Number enrolled (new admits only) 2004–2005 full-time, 4. Number enrolled (new admits only) 2004–2005 part-time, 0. Openings 2005–2006, 5. The Median number of years

required for completion of a degree are 2. The number of students enrolled full and part-time who were dismissed or voluntarily withdrew from this program area were 0. *Clinical Behavioral Psychology MA/MS (Master of Arts/Science)*—Applications 2004–2005, 23. Total applicants accepted 2004–2005, 13. Number enrolled (new admits only) 2004–2005 full-time, 9. Number enrolled (new admits only) 2004–2005 part-time, 0. Total enrolled 2004–2005 full-time, 18. Openings 2005–2006, 10. The Median number of years required for completion of a degree are 2. The number of students enrolled full and part-time who were dismissed or voluntarily withdrew from this program area were 1. *General Experimental Psych. MA/MS (Master of Arts/Science)*—Applications 2004–2005, 8. Total applicants accepted 2004–2005, 4. Number enrolled (new admits only) 2004–2005 full-time, 4. Number enrolled (new admits only) 2004–2005 part-time, 0. Openings 2005–2006, 3. The Median number of years required for completion of a degree are 2. The number of students enrolled full and part-time who were dismissed or voluntarily withdrew from this program area were 0. *Clinical Psychology PhD (Doctor of Philosophy)*—Applications 2004–2005, 63. Total applicants accepted 2004–2005, 10. Number enrolled (new admits only) 2004–2005 full-time, 10. Total enrolled 2004–2005 full-time, 38. Openings 2005–2006, 10. The Median number of years required for completion of a degree are 5. The number of students enrolled full and part-time who were dismissed or voluntarily withdrew from this program area was 1.

Admissions Requirements:
Scores: Entries appear in this order: required test or GPA, minimum score (if required), median score of students entering in 2003–2004. Master's Programs: GRE-V+Q 1000; overall undergraduate GPA 3.0. The GRE scores of 500 and 500 (or 1000 combined) are our suggested scores, however this is not an absolute cut-off point. There is also a minimum GPA of 3.0 that is advised. At least three letters of recommendation are necessary and a personal statement/writing sample are required for some programs. Please request information from the department for complete requirements. Doctoral Programs: GRE-V+Q 1000; GRE-Subject(Psych) no minimum stated; overall undergraduate GPA 3.0. The Subject Test in Psychology is a requirement, but there is not a minimum score. Typically with a major or minor in Psychology, a satisfactory score can be achieved.
Other Criteria: (importance of criteria rated low, medium, or high): GRE/MAT scores medium, research experience medium, work experience medium, extracurricular activity medium, clinically related public service medium, GPA medium, letters of recommendation medium, interview medium, statement of goals and objectives medium. Weight given to criteria vary among each of three programs.

Student Characteristics: The following represents characteristics of students in 2004–2005 in all graduate psychology programs in the department: Female–full-time 45, part-time 0; Male–full-time 24, part-time 0; African American/Black–full-time 3, part-time 0; Hispanic/Latino(a)–full-time 2, part-time 0; Asian/Pacific Islander–full-time 3, part-time 0; American Indian/Alaska Native–full-time 3, part-time 0; Caucasian–full-time 53, part-time 0; Multi-ethnic–full-time 5, part-time 0; students subject to the Americans With Disabilities Act–full-time 0, part-time 0.

Financial Information/Assistance:

Tuition for Full-Time Study: *Master's:* State residents: $246 per credit hour; Nonstate residents: $500 per credit hour. *Doctoral:* State residents: $285 per credit hour; Nonstate residents: $567 per credit hour. Tuition is subject to change.

Financial Assistance:

First Year Students: Teaching assistantships available for first-year. Average amount paid per academic year: $7,800. Average number of hours worked per week: 20. Apply by February 15. Tuition remission given: partial. Traineeships available for first-year. Average amount paid per academic year: $12,000. Average number of hours worked per week: 20. Apply by January 15. Tuition remission given: full. Fellowships and scholarships available for first-year. Average amount paid per academic year: $4,000. Average number of hours worked per week: 20. Apply by February 15. Tuition remission given: full and partial.

Advanced Students: Teaching assistantships available for advanced students. Average amount paid per academic year: $8,400. Average number of hours worked per week: 20. Apply by February 15. Tuition remission given: partial. Traineeships available for advanced students. Average amount paid per academic year: $12,000. Average number of hours worked per week: 20. Apply by January 15. Tuition remission given: full. Fellowships and scholarships available for advanced students. Average amount paid per academic year: $4,000. Average number of hours worked per week: 20. Apply by February 15. Tuition remission given: full and partial.

Contact Information: Of all students currently enrolled full-time, 22% benefitted from one or more of the listed financial assistance programs.

Internships/Practica: Practicum settings (unpaid) are available in the surrounding community for clinical and clinical behavioral students. In addition, the university offers mental health services involving practicum experiences at both the campus Snow Health Center and the EMU Psychology Clinic. Both terminal MS and PhD programs require sufficient practicum hours to meet the State of Michigan requirements for the Limited License in Psychology (LLP).

Housing and Day Care: On-campus housing is available. Contact Housing and Dining services : (734) 487-1300. The University offers married student/family housing as well as residence hall environments. On-campus day care facilities are available. Contact The Children's Institute, an on-campus facility: (734) 487-2348. Other private care facilities are located within a reasonable distance of campus.

Employment of Department Graduates:

Master's Degree Graduates: Of those who graduated in the academic year 2003–2004, the following categories and numbers represent the post-graduate activities and employment of master's degree graduates: Enrolled in a psychology doctoral program (3), enrolled in a post-doctoral residency/fellowship (n/a), employed in independent practice (n/a), employed in business or industry (research/consulting) (3), employed in a community mental health/counseling center (15), employed in a hospital/medical center (2), total from the above (master's) (23).

Doctoral Degree Graduates: Of those who graduated in the academic year 2003–2004, the following categories and numbers represent the post-graduate activities and employment of doctoral degree graduates: Enrolled in a psychology doctoral program (n/a), total from the above (doctoral) (0).

Additional Information:

Orientation, Objectives, and Emphasis of Department: The Psychology Department offers three terminal Master's Degree programs and courses in several orientations, including behavioral, social, insight, developmental, and physiological. Within the two Master's clinical programs, the major emphases are on psychological assessment (Clinical Program) and behavioral treatment (Clinical Behavioral Program). Within each program there are a wide variety of theoretical, applied, and research interests. The goal of the Clinical and Clinical Behavioral programs is on giving students the background to immediately begin work in clinical treatment settings or to prepare them for entry into doctoral programs, as matches the student's educational objectives. The emphasis of the Master's in General Experimental Psychology is to prepare students for entry into higher level study in psychology or as researchers in applied/research settings. Because Psychology is considered a natural science at Eastern Michigan University, there is also an emphasis on basing clinical practice on research findings. Theses, although optional in the clinical programs, are expected to be research based. A new five-year PhD program in Clinical Psychology, designed to give advanced training in the supervision of mental health professionals in mental health care settings, accepted the first class in the Fall 2001. The entry requirements for this program are somewhat more stringent than those of our Master's Program, with a more competitive applicant pool. The PhD offers specializations in either general clinical or behavioral psychology, a terminal Master's Degree en route, a full four-year doctoral fellowship which covers tuition plus a stipend. For more information on this program, please contact: Graduate Secretary, 537 Mark Jefferson, Psychology Department, Eastern Michigan University, Ypsilanti, MI; (734) 487-1155. Information is also available at on the EMU-Psychology Department Web site: http://164.76.13.213/EMUPsych/index.html.

Special Facilities or Resources: The faculty, which consists of approximately 25 full-time members with PhDs and varying numbers of part-time lecturers, is eclectic in orientation with a wide variety of interests and professional backgrounds. Research interests and publication records of the faculty includes psychological test construction and validation, basic behavioral research with humans and non-humans, the history of psychology, consumer fraud, applied behavior analysis, physiological psychology, forensic psychology, personality, social psychology, and many more. Student enrollment is intentionally kept low in order to provide the students with ample opportunities to develop close working relationships with the faculty. Students regularly present at regional, national, and international conventions, as well as co-author published papers with faculty. The facilities of the Psychology Department are located in the Mark Jefferson Science building and in the newly renovated Psychology Clinic at 611 West Cross. The department features a state-of-the-art computer laboratory, IEEE 802.11 (AirPort) wireless networking capabilities, human and animal research facilities, seminar rooms, a clinic with one-way observation capabilities, a new university library less than three minutes away on foot, and other equipment and supplies needed for advanced study.

Application Information:

Send to: Graduate Admissions, 401 Pierce Hall, Eastern Michigan University, Ypsilanti, MI 48197. Students are admitted in the Fall, application deadline January 15. February 15 is a "priority deadline." Applications received after that date may be considered if places remain open. A January 15 deadline applies to our PhD Psychology Program. February 15 refers to our MS programs. Submit duplicate application directly to: Graduate Secretary, 537 Mark Jefferson, Department of Psychology, Eastern Michigan University, Ypsilanti, MI 48197. *Fee:* $35.

Michigan State University
Department of Psychology
Social Science
202 Psychology Building
East Lansing, MI 48824-1116
Telephone: (517) 353-5258
Fax: (517) 432-2476
E-mail: *detwiler@msu.edu*
Web: *http://psychology.msu.edu*

Department Information:
1946. Chairperson: Neal Schmitt. Number of Faculty: total–full-time 57, part-time 4; women–full-time 27, part-time 1; minority–full-time 6.

Programs and Degrees Offered:
Listed in the following order: Program area, degree type (T if terminal Master's), number awarded 7/03–6/04. Behavioral Neuroscience PhD (Doctor of Philosophy) 1, Clinical PhD (Doctor of Philosophy) 7, Ecological/Community PhD (Doctor of Philosophy), Industrial/Organizational PhD (Doctor of Philosophy) 6, Cognitive PhD (Doctor of Philosophy), Social/Personality PhD (Doctor of Philosophy).

APA Accreditation: Clinical PhD (Doctor of Philosophy).

Student Applications/Admissions:
Student Applications
Behavioral Neuroscience PhD (Doctor of Philosophy)—Applications 2004–2005, 7. Total applicants accepted 2004–2005, 5. Openings 2005–2006, 4. The Median number of years required for completion of a degree are 6. The number of students enrolled full and part-time who were dismissed or voluntarily withdrew from this program area were 0. *Clinical PhD (Doctor of Philosophy)*—Applications 2004–2005, 218. Total applicants accepted 2004–2005, 5. Openings 2005–2006, 5. The Median number of years required for completion of a degree are 6. The number of students enrolled full and part-time who were dismissed or voluntarily withdrew from this program area were 4. *Ecological/Community PhD (Doctor of Philosophy)*—Applications 2004–2005, 21. Total applicants accepted 2004–2005, 5. Openings 2005–2006, 5. The Median number of years required for completion of a degree are 6. *Industrial/Organizational PhD (Doctor of Philosophy)*—Applications 2004–2005, 70. Total applicants accepted 2004–2005, 5. Openings 2005–2006, 5. The Median number of years required for completion of a

degree are 5. The number of students enrolled full and part-time who were dismissed or voluntarily withdrew from this program area were 0. *Cognitive PhD (Doctor of Philosophy)*—Applications 2004–2005, 29. Total applicants accepted 2004–2005, 5. Openings 2005–2006, 5. The Median number of years required for completion of a degree are 6. The number of students enrolled full and part-time who were dismissed or voluntarily withdrew from this program area were 0. *Social/Personality PhD (Doctor of Philosophy)*—Applications 2004–2005, 42. Total applicants accepted 2004–2005, 5. Openings 2005–2006, 5. The Median number of years required for completion of a degree are 6. The number of students enrolled full and part-time who were dismissed or voluntarily withdrew from this program area were 0.

Admissions Requirements:
Scores: Entries appear in this order: required test or GPA, minimum score (if required), median score of students entering in 2003–2004. Master's Programs: GRE-V no minimum stated; GRE-Q no minimum stated; GRE-Analytical no minimum stated; GRE-Subject(Psych) no minimum stated; overall undergraduate GPA no minimum stated; last 2 years GPA no minimum stated. Doctoral Programs: GRE-V no minimum stated; GRE-Q no minimum stated; GRE-Analytical no minimum stated; GRE-Subject(Psych) no minimum stated; overall undergraduate GPA no minimum stated; last 2 years GPA no minimum stated.

Other Criteria: (importance of criteria rated low, medium, or high): GRE/MAT scores medium, research experience high, work experience medium, extracurricular activity low, clinically related public service low, GPA medium, letters of recommendation high, statement of goals and objectives high. Extra curricular, public service and clinical activities are important for applicants to the clinical and ecological/community programs. For additional information on admission requirements, go to: http://psychology.msu.edu.

Student Characteristics: The following represents characteristics of students in 2004–2005 in all graduate psychology programs in the department: Female–full-time 73, part-time 23; Male–full-time 30, part-time 12; African American/Black–full-time 5, part-time 0; Hispanic/Latino(a)–full-time 2, part-time 0; Asian/Pacific Islander–full-time 3, part-time 0; American Indian/Alaska Native–full-time 0, part-time 0; Caucasian–full-time 0, part-time 0.

Financial Information/Assistance:
Financial Assistance:
First Year Students: Teaching assistantships available for first-year. Average amount paid per academic year: $11,493. Average number of hours worked per week: 20. Apply by December 15. Tuition remission given: partial. Research assistantships available for first-year. Average amount paid per academic year: $11,493. Average number of hours worked per week: 20. Apply by December 15. Tuition remission given: partial. Fellowships and scholarships available for first-year. Average amount paid per academic year: $23,000. Average number of hours worked per week: 0. Apply by December 15. Tuition remission given: partial.

Advanced Students: Teaching assistantships available for advanced students. Average amount paid per academic year: $12,276. Average number of hours worked per week: 20. Apply by none. Tuition remission given: partial. Research assistantships available for advanced students. Average amount paid per academic year: $12,276. Average number of hours worked per week: 20. Apply by none. Tuition remission given: partial. Fellowships and scholarships available for advanced students. Average amount paid per academic year: $22,000. Apply by none. Tuition remission given: partial.

Contact Information: Of all students currently enrolled full-time, 85% benefitted from one or more of the listed financial assistance programs. Application and information available online at: http://psychology.msu.edu.

Internships/Practica: Clinical practica provided by the clinical program at the department's Psychological Clinic. For those doctoral students for whom a professional internship is required prior to graduation, 12 applied in 2003–2004. Of those who applied, 12 were placed in internships listed by the Association of Psychology Postdoctoral and Internship Programs (APPIC); 12 were placed in APA accredited internships.

Housing and Day Care: On-campus housing is available. See the following Web site for more information: http://www.hfs.msu.edu/uh/. On-campus day care facilities are available. See the following Web site for more information: http://www.vps.msu.edu/scdc/.

Employment of Department Graduates:

Master's Degree Graduates: Of those who graduated in the academic year 2003–2004, the following categories and numbers represent the post-graduate activities and employment of master's degree graduates: Enrolled in a post-doctoral residency/fellowship (n/a), employed in independent practice (n/a), total from the above (master's) (0).

Doctoral Degree Graduates: Of those who graduated in the academic year 2003–2004, the following categories and numbers represent the post-graduate activities and employment of doctoral degree graduates: Enrolled in a psychology doctoral program (n/a), total from the above (doctoral) (0).

Additional Information:

Orientation, Objectives, and Emphasis of Department: The main objective of our programs is to train researchers who will engage in the generation and application of knowledge in a wide range of areas in psychology.

Special Facilities or Resources: Facilities include the Psychological Clinic for the clinical program, which includes playrooms equipped for audio and video recording, testing equipment, computer-based record keeping system, and neuropsychological assessment lab. The Neuroscience-Biological Psychology Laboratories include research animal facilities, computers, light and electronmicroscopy, histology and endocrinology labs. The Vision Research Laboratory, Cognitive Processes Laboratories, Eye-Movement Lab, and Speech Processing Lab provide automated facilities for conducting research in cognitive science. Additional observational labs equipped with video remote control equipment, one-way windows, and automated data recording equipment are available. Computer labs are available within the department and across campus.

Information for Students With Physical Disabilities: See the following Web site for more information: http://www2.rcpd.msu.edu/Home/.

Application Information:
Send to: Graduate Secretary, Department of Psychology, 202 Psychology Building, Michigan State University, East Lansing, MI 48824. Application available online. URL of online application: http://www.psychology.msu.edu/. Students are admitted in the Fall, application deadline December 15. Department application, as well as university application, is required by December 15. *Fee:* $50.

Michigan, University of (2004 data)
Combined Program in Education and Psychology
1406 School of Education, 610 E. University Avenue
Ann Arbor, MI 48109-1259
Telephone: (734) 647-0626
Fax: (734) 615-2164
E-mail: *CPEP@umich.edu*
Web: *http://www.soe.umich.edu/programs/comb.html*

Department Information:
1956. Chairperson: Jacquelynne Eccles and Phyllis Blumenfeld. Number of Faculty: total–full-time 3, part-time 17; women–full-time 2, part-time 6; minority–part-time 4.

Programs and Degrees Offered:
Listed in the following order: Program area, degree type (T if terminal Master's), number awarded 7/03–6/04. Education and Psychology PhD (Doctor of Philosophy) 4.

Student Applications/Admissions:

Student Applications
Education and Psychology PhD (Doctor of Philosophy)—Applications 2004–2005, 76. Total applicants accepted 2004–2005, 10. Total enrolled 2004–2005 full-time, 28. Openings 2005–2006, 5. The Median number of years required for completion of a degree are 5. The number of students enrolled full and part-time who were dismissed or voluntarily withdrew from this program area were 2.

Admissions Requirements:

Scores: Entries appear in this order: required test or GPA, minimum score (if required), median score of students entering in 2003–2004. Doctoral Programs: GRE-V no minimum stated, 635; GRE-Q no minimum stated, 727; GRE-V+Q no minimum stated, 1362; GRE-Analytical no minimum stated, 693; overall undergraduate GPA no minimum stated, 3.69.

Other Criteria: (importance of criteria rated low, medium, or high): GRE/MAT scores medium, research experience high, work experience medium, extracurricular activity medium, clinically related public service low, GPA medium, letters of recommendation high, interview high, statement of goals and objectives high.

Student Characteristics: The following represents characteristics of students in 2004–2005 in all graduate psychology programs in the department: Female–full-time 19, part-time 0; Male–full-time

9, part-time 0; African American/Black–full-time 4, part-time 0; Hispanic/Latino(a)–full-time 1, part-time 0; Asian/Pacific Islander–full-time 1, part-time 0; American Indian/Alaska Native–full-time 0, part-time 0; Caucasian–full-time 22, part-time 0.

Financial Information/Assistance:

Tuition for Full-Time Study: *Doctoral:* State residents: per academic year $12,746, $989 per credit hour; Nonstate residents: per academic year $25,812, $1,714 per credit hour. See the following Web site for updates and changes in tuition costs: http://www.umich.edu/~regoff/.

Financial Assistance:

First Year Students: Research assistantships available for first-year. Average amount paid per academic year: $20,271. Average number of hours worked per week: 20. Apply by January 1. Tuition remission given: full. Fellowships and scholarships available for first-year. Average amount paid per academic year: $18,000. Average number of hours worked per week: 20. Apply by January 1. Tuition remission given: full.

Advanced Students: Teaching assistantships available for advanced students. Average amount paid per academic year: $20,355. Average number of hours worked per week: 20. Apply by varies. Tuition remission given: full. Research assistantships available for advanced students. Average amount paid per academic year: $20,271. Average number of hours worked per week: 20. Apply by varies. Tuition remission given: full. Fellowships and scholarships available for advanced students. Average amount paid per academic year: $18,000. Average number of hours worked per week: 20. Apply by varies. Tuition remission given: full.

Contact Information: Of all students currently enrolled full-time, 89% benefitted from one or more of the listed financial assistance programs.

Internships/Practica: No information provided.

Housing and Day Care: On-campus housing is available. See the following Web site for more information: http://www.housing.umich.edu or call the following phone number for more information: (734) 763-3164. On-campus day care facilities are available. See the following Web site for more information: http://www.umich.edu/~hraa/worklife/. For more childcare information call: (734) 936-8677.

Employment of Department Graduates:

Master's Degree Graduates: Of those who graduated in the academic year 2003–2004, the following categories and numbers represent the post-graduate activities and employment of master's degree graduates: Enrolled in a post-doctoral residency/fellowship (n/a), employed in independent practice (n/a), total from the above (master's) (0).

Doctoral Degree Graduates: Of those who graduated in the academic year 2003–2004, the following categories and numbers represent the post-graduate activities and employment of doctoral degree graduates: Enrolled in a psychology doctoral program (n/a), employed in an academic position at a university (2), employed in an academic position at a 2-year/4-year college (1), employed in other positions at a higher education institution (1), total from the above (doctoral) (4).

Additional Information:

Orientation, Objectives, and Emphasis of Department: The Combined Program in Education and Psychology focuses on re-search training in instructional psychology, broadly defined. Students are trained to study educational issues and do research in educational settings, on significant educational problems related to learning. There are currently four main research foci: 1) human development in the context of schools, families, and communities; 2) cognitive and learning sciences; 3) motivation and self-regulated learning; 4) resilience and development. Faculty affiliated with the program have ongoing research programs on various important issues. These include projects on children's cognitive development and reading skills, children's achievement motivation, socialization in the schools, how computers are changing the ways in which children learn, and learning and achievement of ethnically diverse students. Students in the program work with faculty on these projects, and learn to design projects in their own areas of interest. They take courses taught by faculty members in the program, and also courses taught by faculty in the Psychology Department and the School of Education. Because the department is an independent interdepartmental unit, students have the unique opportunity to work with faculty in both the Psychology Department and the School of Education, in addition to the faculty directly affiliated with the program. Graduates are well prepared for teaching and research careers in academic and non-academic settings. We are not a School Psychology or a Counseling Psychology program.

Special Facilities or Resources: The University of Michigan is blessed with an extensive scientific-scholarly community of psychologists that is virtually unique in breadth, diversity, and quality. Because of the close collaborative relationships that have evolved over the years, graduate and postgraduate students have the opportunity to learn and work in a wide variety of well-developed specialty centers. These include: the Center for Human Growth and Development, the Center for Research on Learning and Teaching, the Center for Research on Women and Gender, the Human Performance Center, the Institute of Gerontology, the Institute for Social Research (i.e., Survey Research Center, Research Center for Group Dynamics, Center for Political Studies), the NASA Center of Excellence in Man-Systems Research, the Cognitive Science and Machine Intelligence Laboratory, the Human Factors Division of the University of Michigan Transportation Research Institute, the Kresge Hearing Research Institute, the Neuroscience Laboratory, the Evolution and Human Behavior Program, the Children's Center, the Vision Research Laboratory, and the Women's Studies Program. In addition to these resources, the Michigan campus also offers an unusually diverse series of stimulating colloquium and seminar presentations, involving both local and visiting speakers, that contributes significantly to the available opportunities for professional growth and development.

Information for Students With Physical Disabilities: See the following Web site for more information: http://www.umich.edu/~sswd/.

Application Information:

Send to: Department Chair. Students are admitted in the Fall, application deadline January 1. Application fees: $60 for U.S. citizens and permanent resident aliens; $75 for non-U.S. citizens.

Michigan, University of
Department of Psychology
Letters, Science & Arts
525 East University, 1223 East Hall
Ann Arbor, MI 48109-1109
Telephone: (734) 764-6316
Fax: (734) 615-7584
E-mail: *psych.grad.office@umich.edu*
Web: *http://www.lsa.umich.edu/psych/grad/*

Department Information:

1929. Chairperson: Scott G. Paris. Number of Faculty: total–full-time 84, part-time 68; women–full-time 38, part-time 39; minority–full-time 25, part-time 20.

Programs and Degrees Offered:

Listed in the following order: Program area, degree type (T if terminal Master's), number awarded 7/03–6/04. Biopsychology PhD (Doctor of Philosophy) 5, Cognition and Perception PhD (Doctor of Philosophy) 4, Developmental PhD (Doctor of Philosophy) 6, Social PhD (Doctor of Philosophy) 5, Organizational PhD (Doctor of Philosophy) 2, Personality PhD (Doctor of Philosophy) 4, Clinical PhD (Doctor of Philosophy) 4.

APA Accreditation: Clinical PhD (Doctor of Philosophy).

Student Applications/Admissions:

Student Applications

Biopsychology PhD (Doctor of Philosophy)—Applications 2004–2005, 44. Total applicants accepted 2004–2005, 10. Number enrolled (new admits only) 2004–2005 full-time, 6. Total enrolled 2004–2005 full-time, 25. Openings 2005–2006, 5. The Median number of years required for completion of a degree are 5. The number of students enrolled full and part-time who were dismissed or voluntarily withdrew from this program area were 0. *Cognition and Perception PhD (Doctor of Philosophy)*—Applications 2004–2005, 44. Total applicants accepted 2004–2005, 6. Number enrolled (new admits only) 2004–2005 full-time, 0. Total enrolled 2004–2005 full-time, 18. Openings 2005–2006, 5. The Median number of years required for completion of a degree are 5. The number of students enrolled full and part-time who were dismissed or voluntarily withdrew from this program area were 0. *Developmental PhD (Doctor of Philosophy)*—Applications 2004–2005, 66. Total applicants accepted 2004–2005, 12. Number enrolled (new admits only) 2004–2005 full-time, 5. Total enrolled 2004–2005 full-time, 27. Openings 2005–2006, 6. The Median number of years required for completion of a degree are 5. The number of students enrolled full and part-time who were dismissed or voluntarily withdrew from this program area were 0. *Social PhD (Doctor of Philosophy)*—Applications 2004–2005, 127. Total applicants accepted 2004–2005, 14. Number enrolled (new admits only) 2004–2005 full-time, 7. Total enrolled 2004–2005 full-time, 24. Openings 2005–2006, 6. The Median number of years required for completion of a degree are 5. The number of students enrolled full and part-time who were dismissed or voluntarily withdrew from this program area were 0. *Organizational PhD (Doctor of Philosophy)*—Applications 2004–2005, 32. Total applicants accepted 2004–2005, 2. Number enrolled (new admits only) 2004–2005 full-time, 2. Total

enrolled 2004–2005 full-time, 11. Openings 2005–2006, 2. The Median number of years required for completion of a degree are 5. The number of students enrolled full and part-time who were dismissed or voluntarily withdrew from this program area were 0. *Personality PhD (Doctor of Philosophy)*—Applications 2004–2005, 16. Total applicants accepted 2004–2005, 4. Number enrolled (new admits only) 2004–2005 full-time, 2. Total enrolled 2004–2005 full-time, 14. Openings 2005–2006, 3. The Median number of years required for completion of a degree are 5. The number of students enrolled full and part-time who were dismissed or voluntarily withdrew from this program area were 0. *Clinical PhD (Doctor of Philosophy)*—Applications 2004–2005, 288. Total applicants accepted 2004–2005, 4. Number enrolled (new admits only) 2004–2005 full-time, 4. Total enrolled 2004–2005 full-time, 26. Openings 2005–2006, 6. The Median number of years required for completion of a degree are 5. The number of students enrolled full and part-time who were dismissed or voluntarily withdrew from this program area were 0.

Admissions Requirements:

Scores: Entries appear in this order: required test or GPA, minimum score (if required), median score of students entering in 2003–2004. Master's Programs: GRE-V no minimum stated, 670; GRE-Q no minimum stated, 700; GRE-V+Q no minimum stated, 1264; GRE-Analytical no minimum stated, 700; overall undergraduate GPA 3.7, 3.71; last 2 years GPA 3.5, 3.5; psychology GPA 3.5, 3.5. Doctoral Programs: GRE-V no minimum stated, 602; GRE-Q no minimum stated, 662; GRE-V+Q no minimum stated, 1264; GRE-Analytical no minimum stated, 682; overall undergraduate GPA 3.0, 3.66.

Other Criteria: (importance of criteria rated low, medium, or high): GRE/MAT scores medium, research experience high, work experience high, extracurricular activity low, clinically related public service low, GPA medium, letters of recommendation high, interview high, statement of goals and objectives high. For additional information on admission requirements, go to: http://www.lsa.umich.edu/psych/grad/prospective/.

Student Characteristics: The following represents characteristics of students in 2004–2005 in all graduate psychology programs in the department: Female–full-time 141, part-time 0; Male–full-time 44, part-time 0; African American/Black–full-time 25, part-time 0; Hispanic/Latino(a)–full-time 13, part-time 0; Asian/Pacific Islander–full-time 20, part-time 0; American Indian/Alaska Native–full-time 2, part-time 0; Caucasian–full-time 90, part-time 0; Multi-ethnic–full-time 1, part-time 0; students subject to the Americans With Disabilities Act–full-time 0, part-time 0.

Financial Information/Assistance:

Tuition for Full-Time Study: *Doctoral:* State residents: per academic year $13,545, $804 per credit hour; Nonstate residents: per academic year $27,311, $1,529 per credit hour. Tuition is subject to change. See the following Web site for updates and changes in tuition costs: http://www.umich.edu/~regoff.

Financial Assistance:

First Year Students: Fellowships and scholarships available for first-year. Average amount paid per academic year: $16,500. Average number of hours worked per week: 22. Apply by December 15. Tuition remission given: full.

Advanced Students: Teaching assistantships available for advanced students. Average amount paid per academic year: $27,141. Average number of hours worked per week: 22. Apply by December 15. Tuition remission given: full. Research assistantships available for advanced students. Average amount paid per academic year: $27,141. Average number of hours worked per week: 22. Apply by December 15. Tuition remission given: full. Fellowships and scholarships available for advanced students. Average amount paid per academic year: $12,000. Average number of hours worked per week: 22. Apply by December 15.

Contact Information: Of all students currently enrolled full-time, 100% benefitted from one or more of the listed financial assistance programs.

Internships/Practica: No information provided.

Housing and Day Care: On-campus housing is available. See the following Web site for more information: http://www.housing.umich.edu. On-campus day care facilities are available. For childcare info call: (734) 936-8677.

Employment of Department Graduates:
Master's Degree Graduates: Of those who graduated in the academic year 2003–2004, the following categories and numbers represent the post-graduate activities and employment of master's degree graduates: Enrolled in a post-doctoral residency/fellowship (n/a), employed in independent practice (n/a), total from the above (master's) (0).
Doctoral Degree Graduates: Of those who graduated in the academic year 2003–2004, the following categories and numbers represent the post-graduate activities and employment of doctoral degree graduates: Enrolled in a psychology doctoral program (n/a), enrolled in a post-doctoral residency/fellowship (4), employed in an academic position at a university (3), employed in business or industry (research/consulting) (6), employed in a community mental health/counseling center (4), still seeking employment (3), do not know (3), total from the above (doctoral) (23).

Additional Information:
Orientation, Objectives, and Emphasis of Department: The general objectives of the PhD program are to permit the student to achieve: 1) a general knowledge of the broad subject matter of psychology; 2) mastery of a specialized field; 3) competence in organizing, interpreting, and communicating effectively; 4) competence in research skills and creative work; and 5) professional skills relevant to their field of specialization. At its best, graduate education requires an intensive and intimate form of instruction. Psychology department faculty members are very accessible to students and research opportunities are available in a wide variety of labs and projects. Although the department is one of the largest in the country, we have developed procedures that not only allow each student freedom in planning an individualized program of study but also permit collaborative work with a small group of staff members.

Special Facilities or Resources: The University of Michigan provides a rich environment for graduate studies. The faculty in both education and psychology are internationally known for their scholarly productivity, and so students receive excellent training in how to conduct educational research. Faculty in the Psychology Department have ties to school officials in Ann Arbor and the greater Detroit area, which means students receive ample opportu-nities for working on many different kinds of educational projects. Students can take advantage of the university's excellent library and computer facilities, both of which are among the best in the country. A distinct advantage of the program is that it is interdepartmental in the graduate school with full resources and faculty available from both the Psychology Department and the School of Education. The department has close collaborative relationships with the Center for Human Growth and Development, the Center for Research on Learning and Teaching, the Center for Research on Women and Gender, the Human Performance Center, the Institute of Gerontology, the Institute for Social Research, the Cognitive Science and Machine Intelligence Laboratory, the Evolution and Human Behavior Program, and the Children's Center.

Application Information:
Send to: Psychology Graduate Office, 1223 East Hall, 525 East University, University of Michigan, Ann Arbor, MI 48109-1109. Application available online. URL of online application: www.lsa.umich.edu/psych. Students are admitted in the Fall, application deadline December 15. May apply to up to 3 separate sub-plans within Psychology in the Rackham School of Graduate Studies with one fee payment. Read all application materials. *Fee:* $60. $75 for International Applications.

Northern Michigan University
Department of Psychology
Arts and Sciences
1401 Presque Isle Avenue
Marquette, MI 49855
Telephone: (906) 227 2935
Fax: (906) 227-2954
E-mail: *jsuksi@nmu.edu; hwhitake@nmu.edu*
Web: *http://www.nmu.edu/departments/psych.htm*

Department Information:
1950. Head and Professor: Harry Whitaker. Number of Faculty: total–full-time 12; women–full-time 5.

Programs and Degrees Offered:
Listed in the following order: Program area, degree type (T if terminal Master's), number awarded 7/03–6/04. Psychology MA/MS (Master of Arts/Science) 4.

Student Applications/Admissions:
Student Applications
Psychology MA/MS (Master of Arts/Science)—Applications 2004–2005, 20. Total applicants accepted 2004–2005, 12. Number enrolled (new admits only) 2004–2005 full-time, 5. Number enrolled (new admits only) 2004–2005 part-time, 7. Total enrolled 2004–2005 full-time, 25, part-time, 30. Openings 2005–2006, 25. The Median number of years required for completion of a degree are 2. The number of students enrolled full and part-time who were dismissed or voluntarily withdrew from this program area were 0.

Admissions Requirements:
Scores: Entries appear in this order: required test or GPA, minimum score (if required), median score of students entering in 2003–2004. Master's Programs: GRE-V no minimum stated;

GRE-Q no minimum stated; GRE-V+Q no minimum stated; GRE-Subject(Psych) no minimum stated; overall undergraduate GPA 3.00; psychology GPA 3.00. If other components of the application dossier warrant, an exception to the combined GRE V+Q of 1000 may be considered.

Other Criteria: (importance of criteria rated low, medium, or high): GRE/MAT scores medium, research experience medium, work experience medium, extracurricular activity medium, clinically related public service low, GPA high, letters of recommendation high, statement of goals and objectives high.

Student Characteristics: The following represents characteristics of students in 2004–2005 in all graduate psychology programs in the department: African American/Black–full-time 0, part-time 0; Hispanic/Latino(a)–full-time 0, part-time 0; Asian/Pacific Islander–full-time 1, part-time 0; American Indian/Alaska Native–full-time 0, part-time 0; Caucasian–full-time 0, part-time 0; Multi-ethnic–full-time 0, part-time 0; students subject to the Americans With Disabilities Act–full-time 1, part-time 0.

Financial Information/Assistance:

Financial Assistance:

First Year Students: Teaching assistantships available for first-year. Average amount paid per academic year: $4,000. Average number of hours worked per week: 8. Apply by May. Tuition remission given: full.

Advanced Students: Fellowships and scholarships available for advanced students. Average amount paid per academic year: $5,000. Average number of hours worked per week: 0.

Contact Information: Of all students currently enrolled full-time, 10% benefitted from one or more of the listed financial assistance programs.

Internships/Practica: No information provided.

Housing and Day Care: On-campus housing is available. See the following Web site for more information: http://www.nmu.edu/. No on-campus day care facilities are available.

Employment of Department Graduates:

Master's Degree Graduates: Of those who graduated in the academic year 2003–2004, the following categories and numbers represent the post-graduate activities and employment of master's degree graduates: Enrolled in a psychology doctoral program (4), enrolled in another graduate/professional program (0), enrolled in a post-doctoral residency/fellowship (n/a), employed in independent practice (n/a), employed in an academic position at a university (0), employed in an academic position at a 2-year/4-year college (0), employed in other positions at a higher education institution (0), employed in a professional position in a school system (0), employed in business or industry (research/consulting) (0), employed in business or industry (management) (0), employed in a government agency (research) (0), employed in a government agency (professional services) (0), employed in a community mental health/counseling center (0), employed in a hospital/medical center (0), still seeking employment (0), other employment position (0), total from the above (master's) (4).

Doctoral Degree Graduates: Of those who graduated in the academic year 2003–2004, the following categories and numbers represent the post-graduate activities and employment of doctoral degree graduates: Enrolled in a psychology doctoral program (n/a), enrolled in a post-doctoral residency/fellowship (0), employed in independent practice (0), employed in an academic position at a university (0), employed in an academic position at a 2-year/4-year college (0), employed in other positions at a higher education institution (0), employed in a professional position in a school system (0), employed in business or industry (research/consulting) (0), employed in business or industry (management) (0), employed in a government agency (research) (0), employed in a government agency (professional services) (0), employed in a community mental health/counseling center (0), employed in a hospital/medical center (0), still seeking employment (0), other employment position (0), total from the above (doctoral) (0).

Additional Information:

Orientation, Objectives, and Emphasis of Department: Our MS program is a training, development and human performance program; students may to some degree develop their own program of study.

Special Facilities or Resources: Active research labs in the department: learning, perception, developmental, social, physiological (2), behavioral and historical. There is an up-to-date statistics lab. Grad students are provided office and research space.

Information for Students With Physical Disabilities: See the following Web site for more information: http://www.nmu.edu/.

Application Information:

Send to: James Suksi, PhD, Director of Graduate Studies, Department of Psychology, Northern Michigan University, Marquette, MI 49855. Application available online. URL of online application: www.nmu.edu. Students are admitted in the Fall, application deadline. *Fee:* $35.

Wayne State University
Department of Psychology
Science
71 West Warren
Detroit, MI 48202
Telephone: (313) 577-2800
Fax: (313) 577-7636
E-mail: *aallen@wayne.edu*
Web: *http://www.psych.wayne.edu*

Department Information:

1923. Interim Chair: R. Douglas Whitman. Number of Faculty: total–full-time 35, part-time 10; women–full-time 15; minority–full-time 2; faculty subject to the Americans With Disabilities Act 1.

Programs and Degrees Offered:

Listed in the following order: Program area, degree type (T if terminal Master's), number awarded 7/03–6/04. Clinical Psychology PhD (Doctor of Philosophy) 15, Behavioral and Cognitive Neuroscience PhD (Doctor of Philosophy) 2, Industrial/Organizational Psychology PhD (Doctor of Philosophy) 6, Human Development (Terminal MA) MA/MS (Master of Arts/Science) (T) 1, Cognitive & Social Psychology Across the Lifespan PhD (Doctor of Philosophy) 2, Industrial/Organizational Psychology (Terminal MA) MA/MS (Master of Arts/Science) 0.

APA Accreditation: Clinical PhD (Doctor of Philosophy).

Student Applications/Admissions:

Student Applications

Clinical Psychology PhD (Doctor of Philosophy)—Applications 2004–2005, 158. Total applicants accepted 2004–2005, 25. Number enrolled (new admits only) 2004–2005 full-time, 13. Total enrolled 2004–2005 full-time, 65. Openings 2005–2006, 10. The Median number of years required for completion of a degree are 7. The number of students enrolled full and part-time who were dismissed or voluntarily withdrew from this program area were 0. *Behavioral and Cognitive Neuroscience PhD (Doctor of Philosophy)*—Applications 2004–2005, 14. Total applicants accepted 2004–2005, 7. Number enrolled (new admits only) 2004–2005 full-time, 2. Total enrolled 2004–2005 full-time, 10. Openings 2005–2006, 5. *Industrial/Organizational Psychology PhD (Doctor of Philosophy)*—Applications 2004–2005, 32. Total applicants accepted 2004–2005, 6. Number enrolled (new admits only) 2004–2005 full-time, 4. Total enrolled 2004–2005 full-time, 32. Openings 2005–2006, 6. The Median number of years required for completion of a degree are 5. The number of students enrolled full and part-time who were dismissed or voluntarily withdrew from this program area were 0. *Human Development (Terminal MA) MA/MS (Master of Arts/Science)*—Applications 2004–2005, 10. Total applicants accepted 2004–2005, 4. Number enrolled (new admits only) 2004–2005 part-time, 3. Openings 2005–2006, 6. The Median number of years required for completion of a degree are 3. The number of students enrolled full and part-time who were dismissed or voluntarily withdrew from this program area were 0. *Cognitive & Social Psychology Across the Lifespan PhD (Doctor of Philosophy)*—Applications 2004–2005, 35. Total applicants accepted 2004–2005, 10. Number enrolled (new admits only) 2004–2005 full-time, 4. Total enrolled 2004–2005 full-time, 27. Openings 2005–2006, 5. The Median number of years required for completion of a degree are 5. The number of students enrolled full and part-time who were dismissed or voluntarily withdrew from this program area were 0. *Industrial/Organizational Psychology (Terminal MA) MA/MS (Master of Arts/Science)*—Applications 2004–2005, 0. Total applicants accepted 2004–2005, 0. Number enrolled (new admits only) 2004–2005 full-time, 0. Number enrolled (new admits only) 2004–2005 part-time, 0. Openings 2005–2006, 10. The number of students enrolled full and part-time who were dismissed or voluntarily withdrew from this program area were 0.

Admissions Requirements:

Scores: Entries appear in this order: required test or GPA, minimum score (if required), median score of students entering in 2003–2004. Master's Programs: GRE-V no minimum stated, 500; GRE-Q no minimum stated, 480; GRE-Analytical no minimum stated, 500; overall undergraduate GPA 2.80; last 2 years GPA 3.00. Doctoral Programs: GRE-V no minimum stated, 610; GRE-Q no minimum stated, 620; GRE-Analytical no minimum stated, 600; overall undergraduate GPA 3.00, 3.50; last 2 years GPA 3.00.

Other Criteria: (importance of criteria rated low, medium, or high): GRE/MAT scores high, research experience high, work experience low, extracurricular activity low, clinically related public service low, GPA high, letters of recommendation high, interview high, statement of goals and objectives high. For additional information on admission requirements, go to: http://www.psych.wayne.edu/graduate/gradprostu.htm.

Student Characteristics: The following represents characteristics of students in 2004–2005 in all graduate psychology programs in the department: Female–full-time 97, part-time 12; Male–full-time 37, part-time 1; African American/Black–full-time 13, part-time 0; Hispanic/Latino(a)–full-time 4, part-time 0; Asian/Pacific Islander–full-time 14, part-time 0; American Indian/Alaska Native–full-time 0, part-time 0; Caucasian–full-time 106, part-time 0; Multi-ethnic–full-time 3, part-time 0; students subject to the Americans With Disabilities Act–full-time 0, part-time 0.

Financial Information/Assistance:

Tuition for Full-Time Study: *Master's:* State residents: $405 per credit hour; Nonstate residents: $750 per credit hour. *Doctoral:* State residents: $405 per credit hour; Nonstate residents: $750 per credit hour. Tuition is subject to change. See the following Web site for updates and changes in tuition costs: http://sdcl.wayne.edu/registrar/registrarhome.

Financial Assistance:

First Year Students: Teaching assistantships available for first-year. Average amount paid per academic year: $12,500. Average number of hours worked per week: 20. Tuition remission given: full. Research assistantships available for first-year. Average amount paid per academic year: $12,500. Average number of hours worked per week: 20. Tuition remission given: full. Fellowships and scholarships available for first-year. Average amount paid per academic year: $12,500. Average number of hours worked per week: 20. Tuition remission given: full.

Advanced Students: Teaching assistantships available for advanced students. Average amount paid per academic year: $12,500. Average number of hours worked per week: 20. Tuition remission given: full. Research assistantships available for advanced students. Average amount paid per academic year: $12,500. Average number of hours worked per week: 20. Tuition remission given: full. Fellowships and scholarships available for advanced students. Average amount paid per academic year: $12,500. Average number of hours worked per week: 20. Tuition remission given: full.

Contact Information: Application and information available online at: http://www.gradschool.wayne.edu/Funding.html.

Internships/Practica: No information provided.

Housing and Day Care: On-campus housing is available. See the following Web site for more information: www.housing.wayne.edu/; www.detroitmidtown.com. On-campus day care facilities are available.

Employment of Department Graduates:

Master's Degree Graduates: Of those who graduated in the academic year 2003–2004, the following categories and numbers represent the post-graduate activities and employment of master's degree graduates: Enrolled in a post-doctoral residency/fellowship (n/a), employed in independent practice (n/a), total from the above (master's) (0).

Doctoral Degree Graduates: Of those who graduated in the academic year 2003–2004, the following categories and numbers represent the post-graduate activities and employment of doctoral degree graduates: Enrolled in a psychology doctoral program (n/a), total from the above (doctoral) (0).

Additional Information:

Orientation, Objectives, and Emphasis of Department: This department strives to select graduate students with a strong educational background and outstanding potential and to train them to be knowledgeable, ethical practitioners and research scholars in their chosen areas. Program admission is limited to persons planning to obtain the doctoral degree. Initial broad training is followed by specialized training.

Special Facilities or Resources: The biopsychology area participates in the university neuroscience program. Excellent laboratory facilities are available in neurobiology, neuropharmacology, psychopharmacology, neuropsychology, and ethology. Several faculty in biopsychology and other areas in the department work in the area of substance abuse. The clinical program emphasizes psychotherapy, community mental health, diagnostics, alcohol abuse issues, neuropsychology, and child and geropsychology. Clinical practice and research experience are obtained in a variety of clinical placements and in our own clinic. The cognitive program emphasizes cognition theory and its application to applied problems. The developmental area emphasizes life-span studies and is affiliated with the Institute of Gerontology. The social psychology program has both basic and applied research emphases. Well-equipped laboratories in the department and at the Merrill-Palmer Institute, which is affiliated with the department, are available for cognitive, social, and developmental research. In addition, social psychology uses its urban setting to carry out field studies. The industrial/organizational area emphasizes organizational psychology, personnel research, and field placements. Excellent computer facilities and libraries support research in all areas.

Application Information:
Send to: Graduate Office, Psychology Department, WSU, 71 W. Warren, Detroit, MI 48202. Application available online. URL of online application: http://www.psych.wayne.edu/graduate/gradprostu2.htm. Students are admitted in the Fall, application deadline January 1. MA Human Development Fall application deadline July 1; Winter application deadline October 1. *Fee:* $50.

Wayne State University
Division of Theoretical and Behavioral Foundations-
   Educational Psychology
College of Education
Detroit, MI 48202
Telephone: (313) 557-1614
Fax: (313) 577-5235
E-mail: *s.b.hillman@wayne.edu*

Department Information:
1957. Chairperson: Stephen B. Hillman. Number of Faculty: total–full-time 5, part-time 12; women–full-time 2, part-time 5; minority–part-time 2.

Programs and Degrees Offered:
Listed in the following order: Program area, degree type (T if terminal Master's), number awarded 7/03–6/04. Educational PhD (Doctor of Philosophy) 8, School MA/MS (Master of Arts/Science) 30.

Student Applications/Admissions:
Student Applications
Educational PhD (Doctor of Philosophy)—Applications 2004–2005, 18. Total applicants accepted 2004–2005, 7. Number enrolled (new admits only) 2004–2005 part-time, 7. Openings 2005–2006, 15. The Median number of years required for completion of a degree are 6.5. The number of students enrolled full and part-time, who were dismissed or voluntarily withdrew from this program area were 0. School MA/MS (Master of Arts/Science)—Applications 2004–2005, 72. Total applicants accepted 2004–2005, 28. Number enrolled (new admits only) 2004–2005 part-time, 28. Total enrolled 2004–2005 part-time, 28. Openings 2005–2006, 32. The Median number of years required for completion of a degree are 2.5. The number of students enrolled full and part-time who were dismissed or voluntarily withdrew from this program area were 2.

Admissions Requirements:
Scores: Entries appear in this order: required test or GPA, minimum score (if required), median score of students entering in 2003–2004. Master's Programs: GRE-V no minimum stated; GRE-Q no minimum stated; GRE-V+Q no minimum stated; overall undergraduate GPA no minimum stated. GRE for MA Program (School Psychology) only. Doctoral Programs: overall undergraduate GPA no minimum stated.
Other Criteria: (importance of criteria rated low, medium, or high): research experience medium, work experience medium, extracurricular activity medium, clinically related public service medium, GPA high, letters of recommendation high, interview high, statement of goals and objectives high.

Student Characteristics: The following represents characteristics of students in 2004–2005 in all graduate psychology programs in the department: Female–full-time 7, part-time 42; Male–full-time 0, part-time 3; African American/Black–full-time 0, part-time 6; Hispanic/Latino(a)–full-time 0, part-time 0; Asian/Pacific Islander–full-time 0, part-time 1; American Indian/Alaska Native–full-time 0, part-time 1; Caucasian–full-time 0, part-time 54; students subject to the Americans With Disabilities Act–full-time 0, part-time 0.

Financial Information/Assistance:
Tuition for Full-Time Study: Master's: State residents: per academic year $3,800, $186 per credit hour; Nonstate residents: per academic year $7,600, $186 per credit hour. *Doctoral:* State residents: per academic year $3,800, $186 per credit hour; Nonstate residents: per academic year $7,600, $186 per credit hour. Tuition is subject to change.

Financial Assistance:
First Year Students: Fellowships and scholarships available for first-year. Apply by March 1. Tuition remission given: full.
Advanced Students: Fellowships and scholarships available for advanced students. Apply by March 1. Tuition remission given: full.
Contact Information: Of all students currently enrolled full-time, 15% benefitted from one or more of the listed financial assistance programs.

Internships/Practica: No information provided.

Housing and Day Care: On-campus housing is available. On-campus day care facilities are available.

Employment of Department Graduates:

Master's Degree Graduates: Of those who graduated in the academic year 2003–2004, the following categories and numbers represent the post-graduate activities and employment of master's degree graduates: Enrolled in another graduate/professional program (6), enrolled in a post-doctoral residency/fellowship (n/a), employed in independent practice (n/a), employed in a professional position in a school system (15), employed in a hospital/medical center (2), total from the above (master's) (23).

Doctoral Degree Graduates: Of those who graduated in the academic year 2003–2004, the following categories and numbers represent the post-graduate activities and employment of doctoral degree graduates: Enrolled in a psychology doctoral program (n/a), employed in independent practice (2), employed in a professional position in a school system (6), employed in a hospital/medical center (1), total from the above (doctoral) (9).

Additional Information:

Orientation, Objectives, and Emphasis of Department: The department offers MA programs in school and community psychology , marriage and family psychology, and MEd and PhD programs in educational psychology. The program orientations are eclectic, using the scientific-practitioner model, with emphasis on application of theory at the master's degree level and on theoretical issues at the PhD level.

Application Information:

Send to: Department Chair. Students are admitted in the Spring, application deadline February 15. MEd Program rolling admissions throughout the year. *Fee:* $20.

Western Michigan University

Counselor Education & Counseling Psychology
College of Education
3102 Sangren Hall, WMU, 1201 Oliver Street
Kalamazoo, MI 49008-5226
Telephone: (269) 387-5100
Fax: (269) 387-5090
E-mail: *joseph.morris@wmich.edu*
Web: *http://www.wmich.edu/cecp*

Department Information:

1970. Professor & Chair: Joseph R. Morris. Number of Faculty: total–full-time 19, part-time 8; women–full-time 4, part-time 5; minority–full-time 4, part-time 4; faculty subject to the Americans With Disabilities Act 1.

Programs and Degrees Offered:

Listed in the following order: Program area, degree type (T if terminal Master's), number awarded 7/03–6/04. Counseling Psychology MA/MS (Master of Arts/Science) 45, Counseling Psycholgy PhD (Doctor of Philosophy) 1.

APA Accreditation: Counseling PhD (Doctor of Philosophy).

Student Applications/Admissions:

Student Applications

Counseling Psychology MA/MS (Master of Arts/Science)—Applications 2004–2005, 96. Total applicants accepted 2004–2005,

88. Number enrolled (new admits only) 2004–2005 full-time, 65. Number enrolled (new admits only) 2004–2005 part-time, 23. Total enrolled 2004–2005 full-time, 195, part-time, 68. Openings 2005–2006, 50. The Median number of years required for completion of a degree are 3. The number of students enrolled full and part-time who were dismissed or voluntarily withdrew from this program area were 0. *Counseling Psychology PhD (Doctor of Philosophy)*—Applications 2004–2005, 40. Total applicants accepted 2004–2005, 9. Number enrolled (new admits only) 2004–2005 full-time, 8. Number enrolled (new admits only) 2004–2005 part-time, 0. Openings 2005–2006, 8. The Median number of years required for completion of a degree are 6. The number of students enrolled full and part-time who were dismissed or voluntarily withdrew from this program area were 1.

Admissions Requirements:

Scores: Entries appear in this order: required test or GPA, minimum score (if required), median score of students entering in 2003–2004. Master's Programs: overall undergraduate GPA 3.0; last 2 years GPA 3.0. Doctoral Programs: GRE-V 500; GRE-Q 500; GRE-V+Q 1000; overall undergraduate GPA 3.20.

Other Criteria: (importance of criteria rated low, medium, or high): GRE/MAT scores high, research experience high, work experience medium, extracurricular activity low, clinically related public service low, GPA high, letters of recommendation high, interview high, statement of goals and objectives high. For additional information on admission requirements, go to: http://www.wmich.edu/cecp/admission/.

Student Characteristics: The following represents characteristics of students in 2004–2005 in all graduate psychology programs in the department: Female–full-time 185, part-time 53; Male–full-time 61, part-time 15; African American/Black–full-time 25, part-time 4; Hispanic/Latino(a)–full-time 4, part-time 1; Asian/Pacific Islander–full-time 14, part-time 4; American Indian/Alaska Native–full-time 1, part-time 0; Caucasian–full-time 201, part-time 59; Multi-ethnic–full-time 1, part-time 0; students subject to the Americans With Disabilities Act–full-time 0, part-time 0.

Financial Information/Assistance:

Tuition for Full-Time Study: *Master's:* State residents: $265 per credit hour; Nonstate residents: $599 per credit hour. *Doctoral:* State residents: $265 per credit hour; Nonstate residents: $599 per credit hour. See the following Web site for updates and changes in tuition costs: http://www.wmich.edu/registrar/tuition.html.

Financial Assistance:

First Year Students: Teaching assistantships available for first-year. Average amount paid per academic year: $14,884. Average number of hours worked per week: 20. Apply by February 15. Tuition remission given: full. Research assistantships available for first-year. Average amount paid per academic year: $14,884. Average number of hours worked per week: 20. Apply by February 15. Tuition remission given: full. Fellowships and scholarships available for first-year. Average amount paid per academic year: $9,639. Average number of hours worked per week: 20. Apply by February 15. Tuition remission given: full.

Advanced Students: Teaching assistantships available for advanced students. Average amount paid per academic year: $15,403. Average number of hours worked per week: 20. Apply by

February 15. Tuition remission given: full. Research assistantships available for advanced students. Average amount paid per academic year: $15,403. Average number of hours worked per week: 20. Apply by February 15. Tuition remission given: full.

Contact Information: Application and information available online at: http://www.wmich.edu/grad/funding/.

Internships/Practica: Master's level practica are available in a wide range of settings. Doctoral practica are also available in hospitals, clinics, university counseling centers, etc. For those doctoral students for whom a professional internship is required prior to graduation, 7 applied in 2003–2004. Of those who applied, 7 were placed in internships listed by the Association of Psychology Postdoctoral and Internship Programs (APPIC); 7 were placed in APA accredited internships.

Housing and Day Care: On-campus housing is available. See the following Web sites for more information: http://www.reslife. wmich.edu/; http://www.wmich.edu/apartmnt/. On-campus day care facilities are available. See the following Web site for more information: http://www.wmich.edu/childrensplace/index.html.

Employment of Department Graduates:

Master's Degree Graduates: Of those who graduated in the academic year 2003–2004, the following categories and numbers represent the post-graduate activities and employment of master's degree graduates: Enrolled in a post-doctoral residency/fellowship (n/a), employed in independent practice (n/a), total from the above (master's) (0).

Doctoral Degree Graduates: Of those who graduated in the academic year 2003–2004, the following categories and numbers represent the post-graduate activities and employment of doctoral degree graduates: Enrolled in a psychology doctoral program (n/a), employed in independent practice (1), employed in other positions at a higher education institution (1), employed in business or industry (research/consulting) (1), employed in a hospital/medical center (1), total from the above (doctoral) (4).

Additional Information:

Orientation, Objectives, and Emphasis of Department: The department prepares professional counseling psychologists at the master's and doctoral levels. The philosophy of the counseling psychology doctoral program is that theory, research, and practice are interdependent and complementary dimensions of a professional education within a scientist-practitioner training model. The curriculum and the practical experiences of the program are designed to ensure competency in all three dimensions and to facilitate their integration into the development of a professional identity as a counseling psychologist. Counseling psychologists are employed in a variety of professional settings including academic departments, college and university counseling and student development centers, private practices, mental health systems and agencies, and in business, government, and industry. Consistent with the philosophy of training, the development of professional identity, and the employment objectives of counseling psychology students, the program consists of courses and related experiences in (1) the science of psychology, (2) counseling psychology specialization, (3) counseling and psychotherapy, and (4) research. Persons considering admission to the Counseling Psychology Doctoral Program need to know that the program recognizes the importance of increasing the educational opportunities of minority students, as well as ensuring a diversity of role models in the counseling psychology program. Therefore, the department of counselor education and counseling psychology in which the counseling psychology program is housed, strives to create an atmosphere conducive to the concerns of diverse populations, to integrate these concerns into programs and courses, and to fulfill its commitment to recruit, admit, and graduate minority students prepared for their chosen careers. To this end, the department, the College of Education and the Graduate College provide financial support for eligible minority students. Additional information: The department uses an affirmative recruitment program.

Special Facilities or Resources: The department's primary training facility is the Center for Counseling and Psychological Services, which includes interview rooms, two group/family therapy rooms, and a seminar room; it is equipped with audio and video recording systems and provides for observation and telephone supervision. The department also maintains a comparable training clinic at the Graduate Center in Grand Rapids, Michigan. A wide variety of regional resources, including community clinics, schools, hospitals, and private clinics, are available to students.

Information for Students With Physical Disabilities: See the following Web site for more information: http://www.dsrs. wmich.edu.

Application Information:
Send to: Department of Counselor Education & Counseling Psychology, 3102 Sangren Hall, WMU, Kalamazoo, MI 49008-5226. Application available online. URL of online application: http://www.wmich. edu/cecp/admission/us.htm. Students are admitted in the Fall, application deadline January 10. Application deadline for MA admission is January 15 and August 1. *Fee:* $40.

Western Michigan University
Department of Psychology
Room 3740, Wood Hall
Kalamazoo, MI 49008
Telephone: (616) 387-4474
Fax: (616) 387-4550
E-mail: *r.wayne.fuqua@wmich.edu*
Web: *http://www.wmich.edu/psychology*

Department Information:
1952. Chairperson: R. Wayne Fuqua. Number of Faculty: total–full-time 18, part-time 5; women–full-time 6, part-time 3; minority–full-time 1.

Programs and Degrees Offered:
Listed in the following order: Program area, degree type (T if terminal Master's), number awarded 7/03–6/04. Behavior analysis MA/MS (Master of Arts/Science) 14, industrial/organizational MA/MS (Master of Arts/Science) 4, behavior analysis PhD (Doctor of Philosophy) 9, clinical PhD (Doctor of Philosophy) 4.

APA Accreditation: Clinical PhD (Doctor of Philosophy).

Student Applications/Admissions:
Student Applications
Behavior analysis MA/MS (Master of Arts/Science)—Applications 2004–2005, 75. Total applicants accepted 2004–2005,

43. Number enrolled (new admits only) 2004–2005 full-time, 18. Openings 2005–2006, 20. The Median number of years required for completion of a degree are 2. The number of students enrolled full and part-time who were dismissed or voluntarily withdrew from this program area were 0. *Industrial/ organizational MA/MS (Master of Arts/Science)*—Applications 2004–2005, 34. Total applicants accepted 2004–2005, 6. Number enrolled (new admits only) 2004–2005 full-time, 4. Openings 2005–2006, 4. The Median number of years required for completion of a degree are 3. *Behavior analysis PhD (Doctor of Philosophy)*—Applications 2004–2005, 32. Total applicants accepted 2004–2005, 10. Number enrolled (new admits only) 2004–2005 full-time, 7. Openings 2005–2006, 6. The Median number of years required for completion of a degree are 5. The number of students enrolled full and part-time who were dismissed or voluntarily withdrew from this program area were 0. *Clinical PhD (Doctor of Philosophy)*—Applications 2004–2005, 91. Total applicants accepted 2004–2005, 9. Number enrolled (new admits only) 2004–2005 full-time, 5. Openings 2005–2006, 6. The Median number of years required for completion of a degree are 5. The number of students enrolled full and part-time who were dismissed or voluntarily withdrew from this program area were 0.

Admissions Requirements:

Scores: Entries appear in this order: required test or GPA, minimum score (if required), median score of students entering in 2003–2004. Master's Programs: GRE-V 500, 556; GRE-Q 500, 569; overall undergraduate GPA 3.00, 3.69. Behavior Analysis Master's Minimum Score: No subscore below 400 and a minimum combined score of 900. Doctoral Programs: GRE-V 500, 579; GRE-Q 500, 572; overall undergraduate GPA 3.0, 3.72. Behavior Analysis GRE: no subscore below 400 and combined total minimum of 900.

Other Criteria: (importance of criteria rated low, medium, or high): GRE/MAT scores high, research experience high, work experience medium, extracurricular activity medium, clinically related public service medium, GPA medium, letters of recommendation high, interview high, statement of goals and objectives high, behavior analysis background high. High importance placed on interpersonal skills. For additional information on admission requirements, go to: www.wmich.edu/psychology.

Student Characteristics: The following represents characteristics of students in 2004–2005 in all graduate psychology programs in the department: Female–full-time 69, part-time 0; Male–full-time 35, part-time 0; African American/Black–full-time 3, part-time 0; Hispanic/Latino(a)–full-time 4, part-time 0; Asian/Pacific Islander–full-time 2, part-time 0; American Indian/Alaska Native–full-time 1, part-time 0; Caucasian–full-time 94, part-time 0; Multi-ethnic–full-time 0, part-time 0; students subject to the Americans With Disabilities Act–full-time 1, part-time 0.

Financial Information/Assistance:

Tuition for Full-Time Study: *Master's:* State residents: $265 per credit hour; Nonstate residents: $599 per credit hour. *Doctoral:* State residents: $265 per credit hour; Nonstate residents: $599 per credit hour. Tuition is subject to change.

Financial Assistance:

First Year Students: Teaching assistantships available for first-year. Average amount paid per academic year: $9,498. Aver-

age number of hours worked per week: 20. Tuition remission given: partial. Research assistantships available for first-year. Average amount paid per academic year: $9,498. Average number of hours worked per week: 20. Tuition remission given: partial. Fellowships and scholarships available for first-year. Average amount paid per academic year: $12,104. Average number of hours worked per week: 0. Tuition remission given: partial.

Advanced Students: Teaching assistantships available for advanced students. Average amount paid per academic year: $9,806. Average number of hours worked per week: 20. Tuition remission given: partial. Research assistantships available for advanced students. Average amount paid per academic year: $9,806. Average number of hours worked per week: 20. Tuition remission given: partial. Fellowships and scholarships available for advanced students. Average amount paid per academic year: $12,104. Average number of hours worked per week: 20. Tuition remission given: partial.

Contact Information: Of all students currently enrolled full-time, 80% benefitted from one or more of the listed financial assistance programs. Application and information available online at: www.wmich.edu/psychology.

Internships/Practica: No information provided.

Housing and Day Care: On-campus housing is available. See the following Web site for more information: www.wmich.edu/apartments; www.ocl.wmich.edu. On-campus day care facilities are available.

Employment of Department Graduates:

Master's Degree Graduates: Of those who graduated in the academic year 2003–2004, the following categories and numbers represent the post-graduate activities and employment of master's degree graduates: Enrolled in a post-doctoral residency/fellowship (n/a), employed in independent practice (n/a), total from the above (master's) (0).

Doctoral Degree Graduates: Of those who graduated in the academic year 2003–2004, the following categories and numbers represent the post-graduate activities and employment of doctoral degree graduates: Enrolled in a psychology doctoral program (n/a), total from the above (doctoral) (0).

Additional Information:

Orientation, Objectives, and Emphasis of Department: The Department of Psychology has a pervasive behavior analytic orientation which is reflected in all of its graduate programs. Although the student may design a program of study to meet specific career goals, all programs require courses in behavior analysis. Applicants accepted into the program receive a personal appointment to an advisor and two faculty sponsors who serve as the thesis-dissertation committee and provide both academic and professional advising throughout the student's tenure at the University. The emphasis of the program is upon cooperation between student and faculty, and students are expected to assume positions of responsibility in teaching, research, and service within the department and in community-based programs. The faculty are involved in professional organizations and publish in a variety of scholarly journals. Students are also expected to become involved in these activities and contribute to research projects as co-investigators, and to publications as co-authors.

Personal Behavior Statement: I have received a copy of the Department of Psychology Graduate Student Handbook and agree to abide by the program requirements and expectations described therein during the course of my training in the Department of Psychology. This includes agreement to adhere to the Ethical Standards of the American Psychological Association, codes of ethics that are relevant to my area of specialization, the WMU Student Code, and the Student Academic Rights and Responsibilities as stipulated in the Graduate Catalog.

Special Facilities or Resources: Western Michigan University emphasizes computer usage and maintains several microcomputer laboratories for student use as well as a state-of-the-art mainframe computer system. The department research laboratories include microcomputer control systems and other support equipment for research with birds and small mammals. The clinical research laboratories include equipment for electrophysiological recording, fitness testing, and human operant research. The department also maintains an in-house clinic for training in therapeutic techniques under faculty supervision; the clinic includes facilities for adult, child, and family therapy.

Information for Students With Physical Disabilities: See the following Web site for more information: www.wmich.edu/psy chology.

Application Information:
Send to: Psychology Graduate Training, Department of Psychology, Western Michigan University, Kalamazoo, MI 49008. URL of online application: http://www.wmich.edu/psychology/grad/index.html. Students are admitted in the Fall, application deadline January 20. *Fee:* $40.

Argosy University/Twin Cities

Clinical Psychology
Minnesota School of Professional Psychology
1515 Central Parkway
Eagan, MN 55121
Telephone: (651) 846-2882
Fax: (651) 994-0144
E-mail: tcadmissions@argosyu.edu
Web: http://www.argosyu.edu

Department Information:
1987. Program Chair: Kenneth B. Solberg. Number of Faculty: total–full-time 15, part-time 19; women–full-time 8, part-time 9; minority–full-time 2, part-time 2; faculty subject to the Americans With Disabilities Act 1.

Programs and Degrees Offered:
Listed in the following order: Program area, degree type (T if terminal Master's), number awarded 7/03–6/04. Clinical Psychology PsyD (Doctor of Psychology) 69, Clinical Psychology MA/MS (Master of Arts/Science) (T) 15, Marriage & Family Therapy MA/MS (Master of Arts/Science) (T) 53.

APA Accreditation: Clinical PsyD (Doctor of Psychology).

Student Applications/Admissions:
Student Applications

Clinical Psychology PsyD (Doctor of Psychology)—Applications 2004–2005, 175. Total applicants accepted 2004–2005, 105. Total enrolled 2004–2005 full-time, 144, part-time, 98. Openings 2005–2006, 50. The Median number of years required for completion of a degree are 5. The number of students enrolled full and part-time who were dismissed or voluntarily withdrew from this program area were 7. *Clinical Psychology MA/MS (Master of Arts/Science)*—Applications 2004–2005, 35. Total applicants accepted 2004–2005, 19. Total enrolled 2004–2005 full-time, 34, part-time, 6. Openings 2005–2006, 20. The Median number of years required for completion of a degree are 2. The number of students enrolled full and part-time who were dismissed or voluntarily withdrew from this program area were 2. *Marriage & Family Therapy MA/MS (Master of Arts/Science)*—Applications 2004–2005, 77. Total applicants accepted 2004–2005, 50. Total enrolled 2004–2005 full-time, 117, part-time, 21. Openings 2005–2006, 50. The Median number of years required for completion of a degree are 2. The number of students enrolled full and part-time who were dismissed or voluntarily withdrew from this program area were 1.

Admissions Requirements:
Scores: Entries appear in this order: required test or GPA, minimum score (if required), median score of students entering in 2003–2004. Master's Programs: The GRE/MAT are not required for the Marriage & Family Therapy MA program. They are required for the MA Clinical program. Doctoral Programs: GRE-V no minimum stated, 536; GRE-Q no minimum stated, 565; GRE-V+Q no minimum stated, 1101; GRE-Analytical no minimum stated, 577; MAT no minimum stated, 57; overall undergraduate GPA no minimum stated, 3.6; last 2 years GPA no minimum stated, 3.7; psychology GPA no minimum stated, 3.7. The applicant may submit either the MAT or the GRE.

Other Criteria: (importance of criteria rated low, medium, or high): GRE/MAT scores medium, research experience low, work experience medium, extracurricular activity low, clinically related public service medium, GPA high, letters of recommendation medium, interview high, statement of goals and objectives medium.

Student Characteristics: The following represents characteristics of students in 2004–2005 in all graduate psychology programs in the department: Female–full-time 290, part-time 68; Male–full-time 70, part-time 20; African American/Black–full-time 8, part-time 4; Hispanic/Latino(a)–full-time 4, part-time 2; Asian/Pacific Islander–full-time 9, part-time 4; American Indian/Alaska Native–full-time 3, part-time 1; Caucasian–full-time 268, part-time 113; Multi-ethnic–full-time 3, part-time 1; students subject to the Americans With Disabilities Act–full-time 1, part-time 1.

Financial Information/Assistance:
Tuition for Full-Time Study: *Master's:* State residents: $475 per credit hour; Nonstate residents: $475 per credit hour. *Doctoral:* State residents: $750 per credit hour; Nonstate residents: $750 per credit hour. Tuition is subject to change. Tuition costs vary by program. See the following Web site for updates and changes in tuition costs: www.argosyu.edu.

Financial Assistance:
First Year Students: Fellowships and scholarships available for first-year. Average amount paid per academic year: $3,000. Average number of hours worked per week: 3. Apply by March. Tuition remission given: full and partial.

Advanced Students: Teaching assistantships available for advanced students. Average amount paid per academic year: $1,920. Average number of hours worked per week: 6. Apply by per term. Tuition remission given: full and partial. Fellowships and scholarships available for advanced students. Average amount paid per academic year: $3,000. Average number of hours worked per week: 3. Apply by March. Tuition remission given: full and partial.

Contact Information: No information provided.

Internships/Practica: AU/TC places students in over 50 practicum sites. These training sites cover a wide range of training interests, including medical centers, clinics, counseling centers, prisons, state hospitals, schools, private practice, chemical dependency treatment centers, neuropsychological/rehabilitation centers, pain treatment centers, and managed care facilities. Students are placed in these sites based on their interests and training needs. Each practicum lasts nine months and 600 hours. Students in the PsyD program focus on assessment skills during their first practicum and intervention skills during their second practicum, and are supervised by a licensed, doctoral-level psychologist. For those doctoral students for whom a professional internship is required prior to graduation, 37 applied in 2003–2004. Of those who applied, 18 were placed in internships listed by the Association of Psychology Postdoctoral and Internship Programs (AP-PIC); 10 were placed in APA accredited internships.

Housing and Day Care: No on-campus housing is available. No on-campus day care facilities are available.

Employment of Department Graduates:
Master's Degree Graduates: Of those who graduated in the academic year 2003–2004, the following categories and numbers represent the post-graduate activities and employment of master's degree graduates: Enrolled in a psychology doctoral program (14), enrolled in a post-doctoral residency/fellowship (n/a), employed in independent practice (n/a), do not know (1), total from the above (master's) (15).
Doctoral Degree Graduates: Of those who graduated in the academic year 2003–2004, the following categories and numbers represent the post-graduate activities and employment of doctoral degree graduates: Enrolled in a psychology doctoral program (n/a), enrolled in a post-doctoral residency/fellowship (12), employed in independent practice (6), employed in an academic position at a 2-year/4-year college (2), employed in business or industry (research/consulting) (3), employed in business or industry (management) (3), employed in a government agency (professional services) (4), employed in a community mental health/counseling center (17), employed in a hospital/medical center (8), still seeking employment (1), other employment position (2), do not know (11), total from the above (doctoral) (69).

Additional Information:
Orientation, Objectives, and Emphasis of Department: The APA Accredited PsyD Program at AU/TC's Minnesota School of Professional Psychology requires 98 semester hours and is eclectic, experiential, and competency-based. Faculty represent a range of orientations including psychodynamic, cognitive behavioral, systemic, interpersonal, narrative, and experiential. The program is committed to fostering the growth and development of each student's identity as a professional psychologist. The MA in Professional Counseling/Marriage & Family Therapy emphasizes development of a working theory and practice in interactional, systemic, and contextual therapy across interpersonal, intrapersonal, and social-cultural relationships. This MA program requires 45 semester credits, and includes a required portfolio process.

Special Facilities or Resources: Predoctoral concentrations in the PsyD program are available in Marriage & Family Therapy, Clinical Health Psychology, Forensic Psychology, and Clinical Child Psychology, and Neuropsychology. We maintain both a university counseling clinic and a community based clinic staffed by practicum students.

Application Information:
Send to: Admissions Department, Argosy University/Twin Cities, 1515 Central Parkway, Eagan, MN 55121. Application available online. URL of online application: www.argosyu.edu. Students are admitted in the Fall, application deadline May 15; Winter, application deadline October 15; Programs have rolling admissions. Early application deadline is January 15. *Fee:* $50.

Metropolitan State University
Psychology/ MA in Psychology Program
College of Professional Studies
700 E. 7th Street
Street Paul, MN 55106
Telephone: (651) 793-1370
Fax: (651) 793-1368
E-mail: *kelly.hazel@metrostate.edu*
Web: *www.metrostate.edu/cps/psych/grad*

Department Information:
1990. Chairperson: Deborah Bushway. Number of Faculty: total–full-time 7, part-time 55; women–full-time 5, part-time 33; minority–full-time 1, part-time 5.

Programs and Degrees Offered:
Listed in the following order: Program area, degree type (T if terminal Master's), number awarded 7/03–6/04. Psychology MA/MS (Master of Arts/Science) (T) 3.

Student Applications/Admissions:
Student Applications
MA Psychology MA/MS *(Master of Arts/Science)*—Applications 2004–2005, 26. Total applicants accepted 2004–2005, 12. Number enrolled (new admits only) 2004–2005 full-time, 3. Number enrolled (new admits only) 2004–2005 part-time, 3. Total enrolled 2004–2005 full-time, 5, part-time, 22. Openings 2005–2006, 15. The Median number of years required for completion of a degree are 2. The number of students enrolled full and part-time who were dismissed or voluntarily withdrew from this program area were 4.

Admissions Requirements:
Scores: Entries appear in this order: required test or GPA, minimum score (if required), median score of students entering in 2003–2004. Master's Programs: overall undergraduate GPA 3.0.
Other Criteria: (importance of criteria rated low, medium, or high): research experience medium, work experience high, extracurricular activity medium, clinically related public service low, GPA high, letters of recommendation medium, interview high, statement of goals and objectives high, community-based work high. For additional information on admission requirements, go to: www.metrostate.edu/cps/psych/grad.

Student Characteristics: The following represents characteristics of students in 2004–2005 in all graduate psychology programs in the department: Female–full-time 4, part-time 14; Male–full-time 1, part-time 4; African American/Black–full-time 0, part-time 4; Hispanic/Latino(a)–full-time 0, part-time 0; Asian/Pacific Islander–full-time 1, part-time 1; American Indian/Alaska Native–full-time 0, part-time 1; Caucasian–full-time 4, part-time 13; Multi-ethnic–full-time 0, part-time 0; students subject to the Americans With Disabilities Act–full-time 1, part-time 1.

Financial Information/Assistance:
  Tuition for Full-Time Study: *Master's:* State residents: $217 per credit hour; Nonstate residents: $369 per credit hour. Tuition is subject to change. See the following Web site for updates and changes in tuition costs: http://www.metrostate.edu/tuition/.

  Financial Assistance:
    First Year Students: No information provided.
    Advanced Students: No information provided.
    Contact Information: Of all students currently enrolled full-time, 0% benefitted from one or more of the listed financial assistance programs. Application and information available online at: http://www.metrostate.edu/aid/index.html.

  Internships/Practica: Community-based practica are arranged in consultation between the student and their faculty advisor. Practica are developed and implemented in cooperation with Metropolitan State University's Center for Community Based Learning (www.metrostate.edu/ccbl).

  Housing and Day Care: No on-campus housing is available. No on-campus day care facilities are available.

Employment of Department Graduates:
  Master's Degree Graduates: Of those who graduated in the academic year 2003–2004, the following categories and numbers represent the post-graduate activities and employment of master's degree graduates: Enrolled in a post-doctoral residency/fellowship (n/a), employed in independent practice (n/a), employed in other positions at a higher education institution (1), other employment position (2), total from the above (master's) (3).
  Doctoral Degree Graduates: Of those who graduated in the academic year 2003–2004, the following categories and numbers represent the post-graduate activities and employment of doctoral degree graduates: Enrolled in a psychology doctoral program (n/a), total from the above (doctoral) (0).

Additional Information:
  Orientation, Objectives, and Emphasis of Department: The Master of Arts in Psychology Program emphasizes the application of psychology in the form of community-based interventions that are rooted in the wisdom and work of members of each community. It is an innovative program, rooted in a community psychology model, in which students learn to combine theory, research, and practice to achieve positive social and community change. Prevention (rather than treatment) is a primary focus along with empowerment, health promotion, community organizing and community development.

  Information for Students With Physical Disabilities: See the following Web site for more information: www.metrostate.edu/studentaff/disability.html.

Application Information:
Send to: Kelly Hazel, MA, Psychology Program Coordinator, 700 E. 7th Street, Street Paul, MN 55106-5000. Application available online. URL of online application: www.metrostate.edu/cps/psych/grad. Students are admitted in the Fall, application deadline March 1. *Fee:* $20. Metropolitan State University graduates are exempt from this fee.

Minnesota State University—Mankato
Department of Psychology
AH 23
Mankato, MN 56001
Telephone: (507) 389-2724
Fax: (507) 389-5831
E-mail: *carol.seifert@mnsu.edu*
Web: *http://www.mnsu.edu/psych/psych.html*

Department Information:
  1964. Chairperson: Rosemary Krawczyk. Number of Faculty: total–full-time 17; women–full-time 5; minority–full-time 2.

Programs and Degrees Offered:
  Listed in the following order: Program area, degree type (T if terminal Master's), number awarded 7/03–6/04. Clinical MA/MS (Master of Arts/Science) 10, Industrial/Organizational MA/MS (Master of Arts/Science) (T) 12.

Student Applications/Admissions:
  Student Applications
    Clinical MA/MS (Master of Arts/Science)—Applications 2004–2005, 44. Total applicants accepted 2004–2005, 17. Number enrolled (new admits only) 2004–2005 full-time, 9. Total enrolled 2004–2005 full-time, 17. Openings 2005–2006, 10. The Median number of years required for completion of a degree are 2. The number of students enrolled full and part-time who were dismissed or voluntarily withdrew from this program area were 1. *Industrial/Organizational MA/MS (Master of Arts/Science)*—Applications 2004–2005, 38. Total applicants accepted 2004–2005, 14. Number enrolled (new admits only) 2004–2005 full-time, 9. Total enrolled 2004–2005 full-time, 19. Openings 2005–2006, 10. The Median number of years required for completion of a degree are 2. The number of students enrolled full and part-time who were dismissed or voluntarily withdrew from this program area were 1.

  Admissions Requirements:
    Scores: Entries appear in this order: required test or GPA, minimum score (if required), median score of students entering in 2003–2004. Master's Programs: GRE-V 500, 500; GRE-Q 500, 520; GRE-V+Q 1000, 1020; overall undergraduate GPA 3.0, 3.4.
    Other Criteria: (importance of criteria rated low, medium, or high): GRE/MAT scores high, research experience high, work experience low, extracurricular activity low, clinically related public service low, GPA medium, letters of recommendation high, statement of goals and objectives medium.

  Student Characteristics: The following represents characteristics of students in 2004–2005 in all graduate psychology programs in the department: Female–full-time 22, part-time 0; Male–full-time 14, part-time 0; Hispanic/Latino(a)–full-time 1, part-time 0; Caucasian–full-time 35, part-time 0; students subject to the Americans With Disabilities Act–full-time 0, part-time 0.

Financial Information/Assistance:
  Tuition for Full-Time Study: *Master's:* State residents: $226 per credit hour; Nonstate residents: $356 per credit hour. Tuition is subject to change. See the following Web site for updates and

changes in tuition costs: http://www.mnsu.edu/busoff/acctsrec/tuition_fees/.

Financial Assistance:

First Year Students: Teaching assistantships available for first-year. Average amount paid per academic year: $4,000. Average number of hours worked per week: 10. Apply by March 15. Tuition remission given: partial.

Advanced Students: Teaching assistantships available for advanced students. Average amount paid per academic year: $4,000. Average number of hours worked per week: 10. Tuition remission given: partial.

Contact Information: Of all students currently enrolled full-time, 50% benefitted from one or more of the listed financial assistance programs.

Internships/Practica: A variety of clinical practica are available to our clinical students. Sites have included the Mayo Clinic, The Munroe-Meyer Institute, Minneapolis VA Hospital and local Riverview Clinic. I/O internship sites include Chiquita, ePredix, Minnesota Twins, Thrivent, Midwest Wireless, 3M and Army research labs.

Housing and Day Care: On-campus housing is available. See the following Web site for more information: http://www2.mnsu.edu/reslife/. On-campus day care facilities are available. See the following Web site for more information: http://www.coled.mnsu.edu/NewWeb/ChildrensHouse/tourtotheinsidehouse.html.

Employment of Department Graduates:

Master's Degree Graduates: Of those who graduated in the academic year 2003–2004, the following categories and numbers represent the post-graduate activities and employment of master's degree graduates: Enrolled in a psychology doctoral program (5), enrolled in another graduate/professional program (2), enrolled in a post-doctoral residency/fellowship (n/a), employed in independent practice (n/a), employed in business or industry (management) (11), employed in a community mental health/counseling center (2), other employment position (2), total from the above (master's) (22).

Doctoral Degree Graduates: Of those who graduated in the academic year 2003–2004, the following categories and numbers represent the post-graduate activities and employment of doctoral degree graduates: Enrolled in a psychology doctoral program (n/a), total from the above (doctoral) (0).

Additional Information:

Orientation, Objectives, and Emphasis of Department: The clinical program is a research-based, predoctoral program with a strong behavioral emphasis. The goal of the I/O program is to provide broad theoretical and technical training for individuals who will function as human resource professionals or who will go on to doctoral programs in I/O psychology.

Special Facilities or Resources: I/O faculty have ongoing research partnerships with major organizations such as Midwest Wireless, Nokia, ePredix, United States Air Force. Clinical faculty maintain professional relationships with Immanuel-Street Joseph Hospital, Mayo Health System and with area schools.

Information for Students With Physical Disabilities: See the following Web site for more information: http://www.mnsu.edu/dso/.

Application Information:
Send to: Department of Psychology, AH 23, Minnesota State University, Mankato, Mankato, MN 56001. Students are admitted in the Fall, application deadline March 1. *Fee:* $40.

Minnesota State University Moorhead
School Psychology Program
Social and Natural Sciences
1104 7th Avenue S.
Moorhead, MN 56563
Telephone: (218) 477-2802
Fax: (218) 477-2602
E-mail: *potter@mnstate.edu*
Web: *http://www.mnstate.edu/gradpsyc*

Department Information:
1970. Program Director: Margaret L. Potter. Number of Faculty: total–full-time 11; women–full-time 6; minority–full-time 1.

Programs and Degrees Offered:
Listed in the following order: Program area, degree type (T if terminal Master's), number awarded 7/03–6/04. School Psychology EdS (Education Specialist) 6.

Student Applications/Admissions:
Student Applications

School Psychology EdS (Education Specialist)—Applications 2004–2005, 28. Total applicants accepted 2004–2005, 14. Number enrolled (new admits only) 2004–2005 full-time, 8. Total enrolled 2004–2005 full-time, 19, part-time, 3. Openings 2005–2006, 9. The Median number of years required for completion of a degree are 3. The number of students enrolled full and part-time who were dismissed or voluntarily withdrew from this program area were 2.

Admissions Requirements:

Scores: Entries appear in this order: required test or GPA, minimum score (if required), median score of students entering in 2003–2004. Master's Programs: GRE-V+Q 1000, 1050; overall undergraduate GPA 3.00, 3.6; last 2 years GPA 3.25.
Other Criteria: (importance of criteria rated low, medium, or high): GRE/MAT scores high, research experience medium, work experience medium, extracurricular activity medium, clinically related public service low, GPA high, letters of recommendation high, interview medium, statement of goals and objectives high.

Student Characteristics: The following represents characteristics of students in 2004–2005 in all graduate psychology programs in the department: Female–full-time 17, part-time 3; Male–full-time 2, part-time 0; African American/Black–full-time 0, part-time 0; Hispanic/Latino(a)–full-time 0, part-time 0; Asian/Pacific Islander–full-time 0, part-time 0; American Indian/Alaska Native–full-time 0, part-time 0; Caucasian–full-time 20, part-time 0; Multi-ethnic–full-time 1, part-time 0; students subject to the Americans With Disabilities Act–full-time 0, part-time 0.

Financial Information/Assistance:
Tuition for Full-Time Study: *Master's:* State residents: per academic year $4,240, $212 per credit hour; Nonstate residents: per

421

academic year $4,240, $212 per credit hour. Tuition is subject to change. See the following Web site for updates and changes in tuition costs: http://www.mnstate.edu/busoff/tuitionfees.htm.

Financial Assistance:

First Year Students: Research assistantships available for first-year. Average amount paid per academic year: $1,700. Average number of hours worked per week: 5. Apply by May 15.

Advanced Students: Research assistantships available for advanced students. Average amount paid per academic year: $2,000. Average number of hours worked per week: 6. Apply by May 15.

Contact Information: Of all students currently enrolled full-time, 90% benefitted from one or more of the listed financial assistance programs.

Internships/Practica: Field-based practica in both first and second years of study provide actual experience to students. Practica are supervised by local educators and school psychologists and are coordinated with on-campus course work so students can apply concepts and techniques learned in class. A 1200-hour internship during the third year of study serves as the capstone experience for student's training. Internships are usually positions within school districts or special education cooperatives in the tri-state area.

Housing and Day Care: On-campus housing is available. See the following Web site for more information: www.mnstate.edu/housing. On-campus day care facilities are available. See the following Web site for more information: www.mnstate.edu/childcare.

Employment of Department Graduates:

Master's Degree Graduates: Of those who graduated in the academic year 2003–2004, the following categories and numbers represent the post-graduate activities and employment of master's degree graduates: Enrolled in a psychology doctoral program (0), enrolled in another graduate/professional program (0), enrolled in a post-doctoral residency/fellowship (n/a), employed in independent practice (n/a), employed in an academic position at a university (0), employed in an academic position at a 2-year/4-year college (0), employed in other positions at a higher education institution (0), employed in a professional position in a school system (6), total from the above (master's) (6).

Doctoral Degree Graduates: Of those who graduated in the academic year 2003–2004, the following categories and numbers represent the post-graduate activities and employment of doctoral degree graduates: Enrolled in a psychology doctoral program (n/a), total from the above (doctoral) (0).

Additional Information:

Orientation, Objectives, and Emphasis of Department: Our goal is to provide the training necessary for our graduates to be skilled problem solvers in dealing with the needs of children, families, and others involved in the learning enterprise. Within a scientist-practitioner model and integrative perspective, the program's primary focus is on educating specialist-level professionals capable of working effectively in educational agencies and in collaboration with other human services providers. Our graduates are highly regarded by the schools and agencies within which they work because of their knowledge of current best practices in the field and because of their skills as team members.

Information for Students With Physical Disabilities: See the following Web site for more information: www.mnstate.edu/disability.

Application Information:
Send to: Graduate Studies Office, Minnesota State University Moorhead, 1104 7th Avenue S., Moorhead, MN 56563. Application available online. URL of online application: www.mnstate.edu/graduate. Students are admitted in the Fall, application deadline February 15. Applications will be accepted after February 15 if space is available. *Fee:* $20.

Minnesota, University of
Department of Educational Psychology: Counseling and Student Personnel; School Psychology
Education and Human Development
178 Pillsbury Drive SE, 206 Burton Hall
Minneapolis, MN 55455
Telephone: (612) 624-1698
Fax: (612) 624-8241
E-mail: *roman001@umn.edu*
Web: *http://www.education.umn.edu/EdPsych*

Department Information:
1947. Chair: John L. Romano. Number of Faculty: total–full-time 35; women–full-time 13; minority–full-time 5.

Programs and Degrees Offered:
Listed in the following order: Program area, degree type (T if terminal Master's), number awarded 7/03–6/04. Counseling & Student Personnel MA/MS (Master of Arts/Science) (T) 23, School Psychology PhD (Doctor of Philosophy) 6, Counseling and Student Personnel PhD (Doctor of Philosophy) 8, School Psychology MA/MS (Master of Arts/Science) 13.

APA Accreditation: School PhD (Doctor of Philosophy). Counseling PhD (Doctor of Philosophy).

Student Applications/Admissions:
Student Applications
Counseling & Student Personnel MA/MS (Master of Arts/Science)—Applications 2004–2005, 78. Total applicants accepted 2004–2005, 53. Number enrolled (new admits only) 2004–2005 full-time, 37. Total enrolled 2004–2005 full-time, 69. The Median number of years required for completion of a degree are 2. *School Psychology PhD (Doctor of Philosophy)*—Applications 2004–2005, 28. Total applicants accepted 2004–2005, 13. Number enrolled (new admits only) 2004–2005 full-time, 6. Total enrolled 2004–2005 full-time, 39. The Median number of years required for completion of a degree are 6. *Counseling and Student Personnel PhD (Doctor of Philosophy)*—Applications 2004–2005, 47. Total applicants accepted 2004–2005, 12. Number enrolled (new admits only) 2004–2005 full-time, 7. Total enrolled 2004–2005 full-time, 42. The Median number of years required for completion of a degree are 8. *School Psychology MA/MS (Master of Arts/Science)*—Applications 2004–2005, 10. Total applicants accepted 2004–2005, 0. Total enrolled 2004–2005 full-time, 19. The Median number of years required for completion of a degree are 3.

Admissions Requirements:

Scores: Entries appear in this order: required test or GPA, minimum score (if required), median score of students entering in 2003–2004. Master's Programs: overall undergraduate GPA no minimum stated; last 2 years GPA no minimum stated; psychology GPA no minimum stated. Complete application is reviewed. Decision not based solely on GRE or GPA. Doctoral Programs: overall undergraduate GPA no minimum stated; last 2 years GPA no minimum stated; psychology GPA no minimum stated. Decision is not solely based on GRE or GPA.

Other Criteria: (importance of criteria rated low, medium, or high): GRE/MAT scores high, research experience medium, work experience medium, extracurricular activity medium, clinically related public service low, GPA medium, letters of recommendation high, interview high, statement of goals and objectives high. CSPP/PhD: Research: high; Work: high; Extracurricular: high; Public Service: high; Letters of Rec: high; Statement of Goals: high; interview: none. For additional information on admission requirements, go to: http://www.education.umn.edu/EdPsych.

Student Characteristics: The following represents characteristics of students in 2004–2005 in all graduate psychology programs in the department: Female–full-time 189, part-time 54; Male–full-time 56, part-time 15; African American/Black–full-time 11, part-time 3; Hispanic/Latino(a)–full-time 6, part-time 0; Asian/Pacific Islander–full-time 12, part-time 5; American Indian/Alaska Native–full-time 3, part-time 1; Caucasian–full-time 157, part-time 52; Multi-ethnic–full-time 56, part-time 8.

Financial Information/Assistance:

Tuition for Full-Time Study: *Master's:* State residents: per academic year $8,174, $681 per credit hour; Nonstate residents: per academic year $15,274, $1,273 per credit hour. *Doctoral:* State residents: per academic year $8,174, $681 per credit hour; Nonstate residents: per academic year $15,274, $1,273 per credit hour. Tuition is subject to change. See the following Web site for updates and changes in tuition costs: www.onestop.umn.edu.

Financial Assistance:

First Year Students: Teaching assistantships available for first-year. Average amount paid per academic year: $9,179. Average number of hours worked per week: 17. Apply by December 1. Tuition remission given: partial. Research assistantships available for first-year. Average amount paid per academic year: $9,179. Average number of hours worked per week: 17. Apply by December 1. Tuition remission given: partial. Fellowships and scholarships available for first-year. Average amount paid per academic year: $16,000. Average number of hours worked per week: 0. Apply by December 1. Tuition remission given: full.

Advanced Students: Teaching assistantships available for advanced students. Average amount paid per academic year: $9,179. Average number of hours worked per week: 17. Apply by December 1. Tuition remission given: partial. Research assistantships available for advanced students. Average amount paid per academic year: $9,179. Average number of hours worked per week: 17. Apply by December 1. Tuition remission given: partial. Fellowships and scholarships available for advanced students.

Contact Information: Of all students currently enrolled full-time, 75% benefitted from one or more of the listed financial assistance programs. Application and information available online at: we use departmental application files for new students; knowledge of current students.

Internships/Practica: Counseling and Student Personnel Psychology - MA students complete an academic year practicum in the second year with a focus on community counseling, school counseling or college student development. The practicum consists of direct work with clients/students, individual supervision on-site and an academic seminar at the university. PhD students complete one or more practica and then a year-long internship. Some students stay in the Twin Cities for the internship; others go nationally. School Psychology - Doctoral students have three tiers of applied training. Tier 1 - Year-long practica tied to assessment coursework followed by a second year of practica tied to intervention coursework. Most of these experiences occur in metro area schools. Tier 2 - Formal school practicum under the supervision of a school psychologist in Twin Cities area schools. In addition, doctoral students complete a community/clinical practica. These practica occur in a wide variety of settings including mental health and community agencies such as Indian Health Board, Washburn Child Guidance Center, Community University Health Care Center, Fraser Family and Children services. Tier 3 - Internship. The majority completes their year-long internships in public schools settings, although some have found internships in settings that are a collaboration of community and educational settings. In one setting, interns work as part of a mental health and educational team providing school based services to identified students with emotional and behavioral disorders. For those doctoral students for whom a professional internship is required prior to graduation, 9 applied in 2003–2004. Of those who applied, 5 were placed in internships listed by the Association of Psychology Postdoctoral and Internship Programs (APPIC); 5 were placed in APA accredited internships.

Housing and Day Care: On-campus housing is available. See the following Web site for more information: www.umn.edu/housing housing@umn.edu. On-campus day care facilities are available. University Child Care Center, 1600 Rollins Avenue SE, Minneapolis (few blocks from campus); (612) 627-4014.

Employment of Department Graduates:

Master's Degree Graduates: Of those who graduated in the academic year 2003–2004, the following categories and numbers represent the post-graduate activities and employment of master's degree graduates: Enrolled in a psychology doctoral program (11), enrolled in another graduate/professional program (1), enrolled in a post-doctoral residency/fellowship (n/a), employed in independent practice (n/a), employed in a professional position in a school system (6), other employment position (1), do not know (21), total from the above (master's) (40).

Doctoral Degree Graduates: Of those who graduated in the academic year 2003–2004, the following categories and numbers represent the post-graduate activities and employment of doctoral degree graduates: Enrolled in a psychology doctoral program (n/a), enrolled in a post-doctoral residency/fellowship (0), employed in independent practice (1), employed in an academic position at a university (4), employed in a professional position in a school system (4), employed in business or industry (research/consulting) (1), employed in a hospital/medical center (1), do not know (7), total from the above (doctoral) (18).

Additional Information:

Orientation, Objectives, and Emphasis of Department: Counseling and Student Personnel Psychology is intended to provide a fundamental body of knowledge and skills to prepare counselors and counseling psychologists for work in a variety of settings—counseling and human development, career development, staff development, and student personnel work. While the focus is primarily on facilitating human development in educational settings, it is possible for individuals to prepare for community and agency settings as well. The faculty is committed to addressing current social issues such as diversity concerns and adolescent well-being. The CSPP program is designed for a select group of individuals with a demonstrated capacity for leadership and a commitment in the human services. School Psychology: The range of the school psychologist's impact includes, but is not limited to, the application of theory and research in the psychosocial development and learning of children and youth, social interaction processes, prevention and competence enhancement strategies, instructional intervention and program development, and delivery of mental health services. Our major training goal is to prepare school psychologists for roles within the educational enterprise. Competencies needed include knowledge in developmental psychology, personality and learning theory, and social psychology; assessing individual and systems needs; generating and implementing prevention programs and intervention strategies; collaborative consultation; diversity; and evaluating and redesigning programs. Training modalities include a variety of seminars and independent study projects. A wide range of community resources is available to facilitate goals of the program.

Special Facilities or Resources: Our graduate program is located within a major research university where many research projects are ongoing. The program is also located within a state—Minnesota—and major metropolitan area—the Twin Cities—that are known for innovations in human services. The result is that both the research climate and the practice climate are good ones for students. CSPP: The department has some flexibility in the design of student programs. Excellent facilities for research opportunities exist throughout the university. There is a time-shared instructional computing laboratory with batch and online computer facilities available for student use; and free access to the central university computer. Students may borrow laptops, video cameras, LCD projectors, audiorecorders, overheads, and VCRs. School Psychology: Two job files (academic and professional service positions) exist. School Psychology Resources houses journals, books, and intervention and assessment materials. This collection supplements the Psychology Department Journal Seminar Room (for psychology majors) and the Florence Goodenough Reading Room (for child psychology majors), the University Psychology and Educational Library with its specialized computer search facilities, and the extensive University libraries system with holdings numbering approximately 3.5 million volumes. School psychology also maintains a collection of standardized, individual, and group psychometric tests, measures, and protocols which can be borrowed for coursework use.

Information for Students With Physical Disabilities: See the following Web site for more information: http://ds.umn.edu.

Application Information:
Send to: School Psych Program, 344 Elliott Hall, University of Minnesota, Minneapolis, MN 55455. Counseling and Student Personnel Psychology, 206 Burton Hall, University of Minnesota, Minneapolis, MN 55455. Students are admitted in the Fall, application deadline December 1. *Fee:* $55.

Minnesota, University of
Department of Psychology
N218 Elliott Hall, 75 East River Road
Minneapolis, MN 55455
Telephone: (612) 625-4042
Fax: (612) 626-2079
E-mail: *psyapply@tc.umn.edu*
Web: *http://www.psych.umn.edu*

Department Information:
1919. Chairperson: John Campbell, until 6/30/05. Number of Faculty: total–full-time 38, part-time 36; women–full-time 9, part-time 14; minority–full-time 3, part-time 2; faculty subject to the Americans With Disabilities Act 1.

Programs and Degrees Offered:
Listed in the following order: Program area, degree type (T if terminal Master's), number awarded 7/03–6/04. Biological Psychopathology PhD (Doctor of Philosophy) 0, Clinical PhD (Doctor of Philosophy) 6, Cognitive and Biological PhD (Doctor of Philosophy) 3, Counseling PhD (Doctor of Philosophy) 3, Differential/ Behavioral Genetics PhD (Doctor of Philosophy) 2, Industrial/ Organizational PhD (Doctor of Philosophy) 4, Personality Research PhD (Doctor of Philosophy) 1, Quantitative Methods PhD (Doctor of Philosophy) 0, School PhD (Doctor of Philosophy) 0, Social PhD (Doctor of Philosophy) 3.

APA Accreditation: Clinical PhD (Doctor of Philosophy). Counseling PhD (Doctor of Philosophy).

Student Applications/Admissions:
Student Applications

Biological Psychopathology PhD (Doctor of Philosophy)—Applications 2004–2005, 9. Total applicants accepted 2004–2005, 1. Number enrolled (new admits only) 2004–2005 full-time, 1. Openings 2005–2006, 1. The number of students enrolled full and part-time who were dismissed or voluntarily withdrew from this program area were 0. *Clinical PhD (Doctor of Philosophy)*—Applications 2004–2005, 131. Total applicants accepted 2004–2005, 8. Number enrolled (new admits only) 2004–2005 full-time, 4. Openings 2005–2006, 4. The number of students enrolled full and part-time who were dismissed or voluntarily withdrew from this program area were 0. *Cognitive and Biological PhD (Doctor of Philosophy)*—Applications 2004–2005, 52. Total applicants accepted 2004–2005, 20. Number enrolled (new admits only) 2004–2005 full-time, 12. Openings 2005–2006, 5. The number of students enrolled full and part-time who were dismissed or voluntarily withdrew from this program area were 0. *Counseling PhD (Doctor of Philosophy)*—Applications 2004–2005, 69. Total applicants accepted 2004–2005, 6. Number enrolled (new admits only) 2004–2005 full-time, 3. Openings 2005–2006, 4. The number of students enrolled full and part-time, who were dismissed or voluntarily withdrew from this program area were 0. *Differential/ Behavioral Genetics PhD (Doctor of Philosophy)*—Applications 2004–2005, 12. Total applicants accepted 2004–2005, 3. Number enrolled (new admits only) 2004–2005 full-time, 2. Openings 2005–2006, 1. The number of students enrolled full and part-time who were dismissed or voluntarily withdrew from this program area were 0. *Industrial/ Organizational PhD (Doctor of Philosophy)*—Applications 2004–2005, 87. Total applicants accepted 2004–2005, 8. Number enrolled (new admits only) 2004–2005 full-time, 7. Openings 2005–2006, 4. The number of students enrolled full and part-time who were dismissed or voluntarily withdrew from this program area were 1. *Personality Research PhD (Doctor of Philosophy)*—Applications 2004–2005, 6. Total applicants accepted 2004–2005, 0. Number enrolled (new admits only) 2004–2005 full-time, 0. Openings 2005–2006, 1. The number of students enrolled full and part-time who were dismissed or voluntarily withdrew from this program area were 0. *Quantitative Methods PhD (Doctor of Philosophy)*—Applications 2004–2005, 9. Total applicants accepted 2004–2005, 3. Number enrolled (new admits only) 2004–2005 full-time, 2. Openings 2005–2006, 2. The number of students enrolled full and part-time who were dismissed or voluntarily withdrew from this program area were 1. *School PhD (Doctor of Philosophy)*—Applications 2004–2005, 0. Total applicants accepted 2004–2005, 0. Number enrolled (new admits only) 2004–2005 full-time, 0. Openings 2005–2006, 1. The number of students enrolled full and part-time who were dismissed or voluntarily withdrew from this program area were 0. *Social PhD (Doctor of Philosophy)*—Applications 2004–2005, 71. Total applicants accepted 2004–2005, 10. Number enrolled (new admits only) 2004–2005 full-time, 7. Openings 2005–2006, 6. The number of students enrolled full and part-time who were dismissed or voluntarily withdrew from this program area were 0.

Admissions Requirements:

Scores: Entries appear in this order: required test or GPA, minimum score (if required), median score of students entering in 2003–2004. Master's Programs: GRE-V no minimum stated; GRE-Q no minimum stated; overall undergraduate GPA no minimum stated. Doctoral Programs: GRE-V no minimum stated, 625; GRE-Q no minimum stated, 730; overall undergraduate GPA no minimum stated, 3.67. While we have no fixed requirements and admission decisions are based on an individual's complete record, it is desirable that applicants have either a GPA of 3.0 and GRE scores of at least 600 on both the verbal and quantitative sections or a GPA of 3.3 and scores of 500 or greater on the GRE verbal and quantitative sections. For the clinical program and the personality research program, it is desirable that applicants have at least a 3.5 GPA and scores of at least 600 on the verbal and quantitative sections of the GRE. The GRE Subject Test in Psychology is recommended.

Other Criteria: (importance of criteria rated low, medium, or high): GRE/MAT scores high, research experience high, work experience medium, extracurricular activity medium, clinically related public service medium, GPA high, letters of recommendation high, statement of goals and objectives high. For additional information on admission requirements, go to: http://www.psych.umn.edu.

Student Characteristics:

The following represents characteristics of students in 2004–2005 in all graduate psychology programs in the department: Female–full-time 90, part-time 0; Male–full-time 77, part-time 0; African American/Black–full-time 5, part-time 0; Hispanic/Latino(a)–full-time 2, part-time 0; Asian/Pacific Islander–full-time 14, part-time 0; American Indian/Alaska Native–full-time 0, part-time 0; Caucasian–full-time 146, part-time 0; Multi-ethnic–full-time 0, part-time 0; students subject to the Americans With Disabilities Act–full-time 3, part-time 0.

Financial Information/Assistance:

Tuition for Full-Time Study: *Master's:* State residents: per academic year $8,174, $681 per credit hour; Nonstate residents: per academic year $15,274, $1,273 per credit hour. *Doctoral:* State residents: per academic year $8,174, $681 per credit hour; Nonstate residents: per academic year $15,274, $1,273 per credit hour. Tuition is subject to change. See the following Web site for updates and changes in tuition costs: http://www.grad.umn.edu/admissions.

Financial Assistance:

First Year Students: Teaching assistantships available for first-year. Average amount paid per academic year: $10,538. Average number of hours worked per week: 20. Apply by December 30. Tuition remission given: full. Research assistantships available for first-year. Average amount paid per academic year: $10,538. Average number of hours worked per week: 20. Apply by December 30. Tuition remission given: full. Traineeships available for first-year. Average amount paid per academic year: $19,968. Average number of hours worked per week: 0. Apply by December 30. Tuition remission given: full. Fellowships and scholarships available for first-year. Average amount paid per academic year: $16,000. Average number of hours worked per week: 0. Apply by December 30. Tuition remission given: full.

Advanced Students: Teaching assistantships available for advanced students. Average amount paid per academic year: $10,538. Average number of hours worked per week: 20. Tuition remission given: full. Research assistantships available for advanced students. Average amount paid per academic year: $10,538. Average number of hours worked per week: 20. Tuition remission given: full. Traineeships available for advanced students. Average amount paid per academic year: $19,968. Average number of hours worked per week: 0. Tuition remission given: full. Fellowships and scholarships available for advanced students. Average amount paid per academic year: $16,000. Average number of hours worked per week: 0. Tuition remission given: full.

Contact Information: Of all students currently enrolled full-time, 84% benefitted from one or more of the listed financial assistance programs. Application and information available online at: http://www.psych.umn.edu.

Internships/Practica: Internships are available at the university hospitals, the department's Vocational Assessment Clinic, the University Counseling and Consulting Services, the Veterans Administration, and several other governmental and private agencies throughout the area. For those doctoral students for whom a professional internship is required prior to graduation, 8 applied in 2003–2004. Of those who applied, 7 were placed in internships listed by the Association of Psychology Postdoctoral and Internship Programs (APPIC); 7 were placed in APA accredited internships.

Housing and Day Care: On-campus housing is available. See the following Web site for more information: www.umn.edu/housing. On-campus day care facilities are available.

Employment of Department Graduates:

Master's Degree Graduates: Of those who graduated in the academic year 2003–2004, the following categories and numbers represent the post-graduate activities and employment of master's degree graduates: Enrolled in a psychology doctoral program (3), enrolled in a post-doctoral residency/fellowship (n/a), employed in independent practice (n/a), employed in a government agency (professional services) (1), total from the above (master's) (4).

Doctoral Degree Graduates: Of those who graduated in the academic year 2003–2004, the following categories and numbers represent the post-graduate activities and employment of doctoral degree graduates: Enrolled in a psychology doctoral program (n/a), enrolled in another graduate/professional program (1), enrolled in a post-doctoral residency/fellowship (5), employed in independent practice (1), employed in an academic position at a university (4), employed in an academic position at a 2-year/4-year college (2), employed in other positions at a higher education institution (1), employed in business or industry (research/consulting) (1), employed in a community mental health/counseling center (1), employed in a hospital/medical center (1), do not know (1), total from the above (doctoral) (18).

Additional Information:

Orientation, Objectives, and Emphasis of Department: Minnesota has a broad range of areas of specialization in the department, which cannot be described in detail here. The departmental application materials and program information available on the Web contain detailed relevant information on each program area. In general, the overall goal is to train the people who will become leaders in their chosen area of specialization. Consequently, the graduate training programs in the department are oriented first to the training of skilled researchers and teachers in psychology, and then to the training of specialists and practitioners. The PhD programs in Clinical, Counseling, and School Psychology are accredited by APA. Department faculty also participate in independent degree programs in neuroscience and cognitive science. The Department of Psychology and the Institute of Child Development offer a training program in child clinical psychology focused on the study of psychopathology in the context of development. The Developmental Psychopathology and Clinical Science (DPCS) Training Program is APA-accredited as part of the Clinical Psychology Program. Admission to the DPCS program is coordinated by the Institute of Child Development, 51 East River Road, University of Minnesota, Minneapolis, MN 55455. The school psychology PhD is offered jointly with the School Psychology Program. For information about this program, please write directly to the School Psychology Program, 344 Elliott Hall, 75 East River Road, University of Minnesota, Minneapolis, MN 55455.

Special Facilities or Resources: The department offers extensive laboratory and computer facilities, a wide variety of resources and collaborative relationships both on and off campus, and several federally funded research projects. For example, three research centers are headquartered in the Department: Center for Cognitive Sciences, Center for the Study of Political Psychology, and the Center for the Study of the Individual and Society. Other research centers with which the faculty are involved are located in Neuroscience, Radiology, Epidemiology, and Public Health. We have adjunct faculty at the University of Minnesota Counseling and Consulting Services, Carlson School of Management, Institute of Child Development, and Department of Educational

Psychology; and in the VA Medical Center, Hennepin County Medical Center (Minneapolis), Ramsey County Medical Center (Street Paul), and Personnel Decisions International (Minneapolis).

Information for Students With Physical Disabilities: See the following Web site for more information: http://ds.umn.edu.

Application Information:

Send to: Coordinator of Graduate Admissions, University of Minnesota, Department of Psychology, 249 Elliott Hall, 75 East River Road, Minneapolis, MN 55455. Students are admitted in the Fall, application deadline December 30. Two applications are required to apply for graduate studies: the Graduate School On-line Application for Admission and the Department of Psychology Application for Graduate Work. Processing of the Graduate School Application can take up to 30 days, so please allow enough time to meet the December 30 application deadline. The departmental application and supporting materials should be sent to the Department of Psychology by December 30. *Fee:* $55. $75 for international applicants. The application fee cannot be waived or deferred and is not refundable.

Minnesota, University of
Institute of Child Development
College of Education and Human Development
51 East River Road
Minneapolis, MN 55455
Telephone: (612) 624-0526
Fax: (612) 624-6373
E-mail: *icd@umn.edu*
Web: *http://www.education.umn.edu/icd/*

Department Information:

1925. Director: Nicki Crick. Number of Faculty: total–full-time 15, part-time 2; women–full-time 7; minority–full-time 1.

Programs and Degrees Offered:

Listed in the following order: Program area, degree type (T if terminal Master's), number awarded 7/03–6/04. Child Psychology PhD (Doctor of Philosophy) 6, Child/Clinical Psychology PhD (Doctor of Philosophy) 2, Child/School Psychology PhD (Doctor of Philosophy) 0.

Student Applications/Admissions:

Student Applications

Child Psychology PhD (Doctor of Philosophy)—Applications 2004–2005, 32. Total applicants accepted 2004–2005, 11. Number enrolled (new admits only) 2004–2005 full-time, 7. Total enrolled 2004–2005 full-time, 41. Openings 2005–2006, 8. The Median number of years required for completion of a degree are 5.5. The number of students enrolled full and part-time who were dismissed or voluntarily withdrew from this program area were 0. *Child/Clinical Psychology PhD (Doctor of Philosophy)*—Applications 2004–2005, 33. Total applicants accepted 2004–2005, 4. Number enrolled (new admits only) 2004–2005 full-time, 4. Total enrolled 2004–2005 full-time, 18. Openings 2005–2006, 4. The Median number of years required for completion of a degree are 6. The number of students enrolled full and part-time who were dismissed or voluntarily withdrew from this program area were 0. *Child/ School Psychology PhD (Doctor of Philosophy)*—Applications 2004–2005, 2. Total applicants accepted 2004–2005, 1. Number enrolled (new admits only) 2004–2005 full-time, 1. Total enrolled 2004–2005 full-time, 4. Openings 2005–2006, 1. The number of students enrolled full and part-time who were dismissed or voluntarily withdrew from this program area were 0.

Admissions Requirements:

Scores: Entries appear in this order: required test or GPA, minimum score (if required), median score of students entering in 2003–2004. Doctoral Programs: GRE-V no minimum stated; GRE-Q no minimum stated; GRE-V+Q no minimum stated; GRE-Analytical no minimum stated; overall undergraduate GPA no minimum stated.

Other Criteria: (importance of criteria rated low, medium, or high): GRE/MAT scores medium, research experience high, work experience low, extracurricular activity low, clinically related public service low, GPA high, letters of recommendation high, statement of goals and objectives high. Clinically related public service rated low for joint child/clinical program. K-12 work/volunteer experience applies only to joint school psychology program. For additional information on admission requirements, go to: http://education.umn.edu/ICD/GradInfo/.

Student Characteristics: The following represents characteristics of students in 2004–2005 in all graduate psychology programs in the department: Female–full-time 56, part-time 0; Male–full-time 7, part-time 0; African American/Black–full-time 1, part-time 0; Hispanic/Latino(a)–full-time 2, part-time 0; Asian/Pacific Islander–full-time 4, part-time 0; American Indian/Alaska Native– full-time 0, part-time 0; Caucasian–full-time 55, part-time 0; Multi-ethnic–full-time 1, part-time 0; students subject to the Americans With Disabilities Act–full-time 2, part-time 0.

Financial Information/Assistance:

Tuition for Full-Time Study: *Doctoral:* State residents: per academic year $8,174, $681 per credit hour; Nonstate residents: per academic year $15,274, $1,273 per credit hour. Tuition is subject to change. See the following Web site for updates and changes in tuition costs: http://www.grad.umn.edu/Prospective_Students/Financing/index.html.

Financial Assistance:

First Year Students: Teaching assistantships available for first-year. Average amount paid per academic year: $10,663. Average number of hours worked per week: 20. Tuition remission given: full. Research assistantships available for first-year. Average amount paid per academic year: $10,663. Average number of hours worked per week: 20. Tuition remission given: full. Fellowships and scholarships available for first-year. Average amount paid per academic year: $16,000. Tuition remission given: full.

Advanced Students: Teaching assistantships available for advanced students. Average amount paid per academic year: $10,663. Average number of hours worked per week: 20. Tuition remission given: full. Research assistantships available for advanced students. Average amount paid per academic year: $10,663. Average number of hours worked per week: 20. Tuition remission given: full. Traineeships available for advanced students. Average amount paid per academic year: $20,772. Tuition remission given: full. Fellowships and scholarships available for advanced students. Average amount paid per academic year: $30,000. Tuition remission given: full.

Contact Information: Of all students currently enrolled full-time, 100% benefitted from one or more of the listed financial assistance programs.

Internships/Practica: Clinical and school psychology practica and internships are available within the local community to joint program students and are offered through our departmental affiliates. Field experiences are also offered to students in our Applied Developmental Psychology Certificate program. For those doctoral students for whom a professional internship is required prior to graduation, 6 applied in 2003–2004. Of those who applied, 6 were placed in internships listed by the Association of Psychology Postdoctoral and Internship Programs (APPIC); 6 were placed in APA accredited internships.

Housing and Day Care: On-campus housing is available. On-campus housing for graduate students is limited to those with families. Off-campus student housing is available in the surrounding area. See: http://www.grad.umn.edu/current_students/handbook/housing.html and http://www.housing.umn.edu/. On-campus day care facilities are available. Child-care is available at the University Child Care Center. See: http://education.umn.edu/ChildCareCenter/.

Employment of Department Graduates:

Master's Degree Graduates: Of those who graduated in the academic year 2003–2004, the following categories and numbers represent the post-graduate activities and employment of master's degree graduates: Enrolled in a post-doctoral residency/fellowship (n/a), employed in independent practice (n/a), total from the above (master's) (0).

Doctoral Degree Graduates: Of those who graduated in the academic year 2003–2004, the following categories and numbers represent the post-graduate activities and employment of doctoral degree graduates: Enrolled in a psychology doctoral program (n/a), enrolled in a post-doctoral residency/fellowship (1), employed in an academic position at a university (2), employed in an academic position at a 2-year/4-year college (1), employed in other positions at a higher education institution (1), employed in a professional position in a school system (0), employed in a community mental health/counseling center (1), other employment position (2), total from the above (doctoral) (8).

Additional Information:

Orientation, Objectives, and Emphasis of Department: The Institute program emphasizes training for research and academic careers and provides supplementary opportunities in areas of applied developmental psychology. The program offers a diversity of substantive and methodological approaches. In the core program, special strengths are in infancy, personality and social development, perception, cognitive processes, language development, biological bases of development, and developmental neuroscience. Formal applied training is available through the Developmental Psychopathology and Clinical Science (DPCS) and School Psychology joint programs. Formal minor programs are offered in Neuroscience, Cognitive Science, and Interpersonal Relationships Research. Students can complete an Applied Developmental Psychology Certificate program, focusing on such areas as educational programs and research, public policy, and policy-relevant research. Special training is also available through affiliations with the Center for Cognitive Sciences, the Harris Center, the Center for Neurobehavioral Development, the Center for Early Education and Development and the Consortium on Children, Youth, and Families.

Special Facilities or Resources: Physical and research facilities include an office for every student, each equipped with an Ethernet connected computer and printer, a reference room with more than 4,500 volumes, twenty-five experiment rooms, a computer laboratory, a shop for construction of apparatus, and a laboratory nursery school. In addition, state-of-the-art research facilities and interdisciplinary collaborations facilitate cutting-edge neuroscience research in the areas of cognitive, behavioral, and social/emotional development. Onsite facilities include both high density (128 channels) and low density (32 channels) electrophysiological recording equipment and eyetracking equipment. Facilities at the Center for Neurobehavioral Development (opened in 2001) include autonomic and electrophysiological laboratories equipped with functional magnetic resonance imaging (fMRI) and event-related potential (ERP) equipment; audio/visual systems for online data collection, videotaping, presentations, and training; research suites, computer workroom, library/conference room; and subject exam rooms and family waiting/play rooms. At the Center for Magnetic Resonance Research, structural and functional MRI equipment is available.

Information for Students With Physical Disabilities: See the following Web site for more information: http://ds.umn.edu/.

Application Information:

Send to: Chair of Admissions, Institute of Child Development, University of Minnesota, 51 East River Road, Minneapolis, MN 55455-0345. Application available online. URL of online application: http://www.education.umn.edu/icd/GradInfo/. Students are admitted in the Fall, application deadline December. *Fee:* $55. $75 for international applicants. Visa, Mastercard, Discover accepted. Waivers for extreme financial hardship upon written request to the director of graduate studies.

Saint Mary's University of Minnesota
Counseling and Psychological Services
School of Graduate Studies
2500 Park Avenue
Minneapolis, MN 55404
Telephone: (612) 728-5113
Fax: (612) 728-5121
E-mail: *chuck@smumn.edu*
Web: *http://www.smumn.edu*

Department Information:

1983. Program Director: Christina Huck, PhD, L.P. Number of Faculty: total–full-time 2, part-time 71; women–full-time 2, part-time 36; minority–part-time 3.

Programs and Degrees Offered:

Listed in the following order: Program area, degree type (T if terminal Master's), number awarded 7/03–6/04. Counseling and Psychological MA/MS (Master of Arts/Science) (T) 62, Master of Arts in Marriage and Family Therapy MA/MS (Master of Arts/

Science) 0, Graduate Certificate - Marriage and Family Therapy Other 22.

Student Applications/Admissions:
Student Applications

Counseling and Psychological MA/MS (Master of Arts/Science)— Applications 2004–2005, 165. Total applicants accepted 2004–2005, 137. Number enrolled (new admits only) 2004–2005 full-time, 31. Number enrolled (new admits only) 2004–2005 part-time, 92. Total enrolled 2004–2005 full-time, 71, part-time, 248. *Master of Arts in Marriage and Family Therapy MA/MS (Master of Arts/Science)*—Applications 2004–2005, 15. Total applicants accepted 2004–2005, 9. Number enrolled (new admits only) 2004–2005 full-time, 3. Number enrolled (new admits only) 2004–2005 part-time, 4. Total enrolled 2004–2005 full-time, 11, part-time, 13. *Graduate Certificate - Marriage and Family Therapy Other*—Applications 2004–2005, 41. Total applicants accepted 2004–2005, 39. Number enrolled (new admits only) 2004–2005 full-time, 8. Number enrolled (new admits only) 2004–2005 part-time, 25. Total enrolled 2004–2005 full-time, 11, part-time, 74.

Admissions Requirements:

Scores: Entries appear in this order: required test or GPA, minimum score (if required), median score of students entering in 2003–2004. Master's Programs: overall undergraduate GPA 2.75.

Other Criteria: (importance of criteria rated low, medium, or high): research experience medium, work experience high, extracurricular activity medium, clinically related public service high, GPA high, letters of recommendation high, interview high, statement of goals and objectives high.

Student Characteristics: The following represents characteristics of students in 2004–2005 in all graduate psychology programs in the department: Female–full-time 78, part-time 276; Male–full-time 15, part-time 59; African American/Black–full-time 15, part-time 18; Hispanic/Latino(a)–full-time 2, part-time 7; Asian/Pacific Islander–full-time 1, part-time 5; American Indian/Alaska Native–full-time 1, part-time 3; Caucasian–full-time 84, part-time 302.

Financial Information/Assistance:

Tuition for Full-Time Study: *Master's:* State residents: $275 per credit hour; Nonstate residents: $275 per credit hour.

Financial Assistance:

First Year Students: No information provided.

Advanced Students: No information provided.

Contact Information: Of all students currently enrolled full-time, 0% benefitted from one or more of the listed financial assistance programs.

Internships/Practica: A wide variety of practicum sites are available for students.

Housing and Day Care: No on-campus housing is available. No on-campus day care facilities are available.

Employment of Department Graduates:

Master's Degree Graduates: Of those who graduated in the academic year 2003–2004, the following categories and numbers

represent the post-graduate activities and employment of master's degree graduates: Enrolled in a post-doctoral residency/fellowship (n/a), employed in independent practice (n/a), total from the above (master's) (0).

Doctoral Degree Graduates: Of those who graduated in the academic year 2003–2004, the following categories and numbers represent the post-graduate activities and employment of doctoral degree graduates: Enrolled in a psychology doctoral program (n/a), total from the above (doctoral) (0).

Additional Information:
Orientation, Objectives, and Emphasis of Department: The Master of Arts Program in Counseling and Psychological Services prepares graduates for professional work in counseling, psychotherapy, and other psychological services. It is designed to enhance the student's understanding of the complex nature of human behavior and social interaction, and to develop tools for assessing human problems and assisting individuals in developing greater understanding and acceptance of themselves and their relationships with others. The program is designed to meet the educational requirements for Minnesota licensure for Licensed Professional Counselors. Students planning to seek licensure with the Minnesota Board of Psychology after earning a doctorate can work toward some of their educational requirements in the Master's program. This program is offered in Rochester, MN, as well as in Minneapolis.

Special Facilities or Resources: The majority of our faculty are adjunct (part-time) instructors who are practicing in the field. They bring a wealth of real-world experience to their teaching and possess strong academic credentials. Since our emphasis is on applied psychological competence, we consider the backgrounds of these practitioner-scholars to be a major strength of the program.

Application Information:
Send to: Admissions, Saint Mary's University of Minnesota, 2500 Park Avenue, Minneapolis, MN 55404. Application available online. URL of online application: www.smumn.edu. Students are admitted in the Fall. No deadline dates; recommended applying 3 months before the start of the semester. *Fee:* $25.

Street Cloud State University
Counseling and Educational Psychology
College of Education
Education Building, 720 4th Avenue S.
Street Cloud, MN 56301
Telephone: (320) 308-3131
Fax: (320) 308-4082
E-mail: *jpreble@stcloudstate.edu*
Web: *http://www.saintcloudstate.edu*

Department Information:
2001. Chairperson: Jana Preble. Number of Faculty: total–full-time 12, part-time 5; women–full-time 4, part-time 3; minority–full-time 2, part-time 1.

Programs and Degrees Offered:
Listed in the following order: Program area, degree type (T if terminal Master's), number awarded 7/03–6/04. College Student Development MA/MS (Master of Arts/Science) (T) 10, Rehabilitation Counseling Psyc MA/MS (Master of Arts/Science) (T) 11, School Counseling Psychology MA/MS (Master of Arts/Science) (T) 25.

Student Applications/Admissions:
Student Applications
*College Student Development MA/MS (Master of Arts/Science)—*Applications 2004–2005, 11. Total applicants accepted 2004–2005, 10. Number enrolled (new admits only) 2004–2005 full-time, 8. Number enrolled (new admits only) 2004–2005 part-time, 2. Total enrolled 2004–2005 full-time, 15, part-time, 3. Openings 2005–2006, 12. *Rehabilitation Counseling Psyc MA/MS (Master of Arts/Science)—*Applications 2004–2005, 8. Total applicants accepted 2004–2005, 7. Number enrolled (new admits only) 2004–2005 full-time, 6. Number enrolled (new admits only) 2004–2005 part-time, 1. Total enrolled 2004–2005 full-time, 12, part-time, 9. Openings 2005–2006, 12. The Median number of years required for completion of a degree are 2. The number of students enrolled full and part-time who were dismissed or voluntarily withdrew from this program area were 0. *School Counseling Psychology MA/MS (Master of Arts/Science)—*Applications 2004–2005, 38. Total applicants accepted 2004–2005, 25. Number enrolled (new admits only) 2004–2005 full-time, 16. Number enrolled (new admits only) 2004–2005 part-time, 6. Total enrolled 2004–2005 full-time, 36, part-time, 57. Openings 2005–2006, 20. The Median number of years required for completion of a degree are 2. The number of students enrolled full and part-time who were dismissed or voluntarily withdrew from this program area were 0.

Admissions Requirements:
Scores: Entries appear in this order: required test or GPA, minimum score (if required), median score of students entering in 2003–2004. Master's Programs: GRE-V no minimum stated; GRE-Q no minimum stated; GRE-V+Q no minimum stated; GRE-Analytical no minimum stated; overall undergraduate GPA no minimum stated; last 2 years GPA no minimum stated.
Other Criteria: (importance of criteria rated low, medium, or high): GRE/MAT scores medium, research experience medium, work experience high, extracurricular activity medium, clinically related public service high, GPA high, letters of recommendation high, interview high, statement of goals and objectives high.

Student Characteristics: The following represents characteristics of students in 2004–2005 in all graduate psychology programs in the department: Female–full-time 42, part-time 61; Male–full-time 7, part-time 8; African American/Black–full-time 1, part-time 0; Hispanic/Latino(a)–full-time 2, part-time 0; Asian/Pacific Islander–full-time 2, part-time 0; American Indian/Alaska Native–full-time 2, part-time 0; Caucasian–full-time 42, part-time 69; students subject to the Americans With Disabilities Act–full-time 6, part-time 3.

Financial Information/Assistance:
Tuition for Full-Time Study: *Master's:* State residents: $176 per credit hour; Nonstate residents: $275 per credit hour. Tuition is subject to change. See the following Web site for updates and changes in tuition costs: www.stcloudstate.edu.

Financial Assistance:

First Year Students: Teaching assistantships available for first-year. Average amount paid per academic year: $5,000. Average number of hours worked per week: 10. Tuition remission given: partial. Research assistantships available for first-year. Average amount paid per academic year: $5,000. Average number of hours worked per week: 10. Tuition remission given: partial. Fellowships and scholarships available for first-year. Average amount paid per academic year: $500.

Advanced Students: No information provided.

Contact Information: Of all students currently enrolled full-time, 50% benefitted from one or more of the listed financial assistance programs. Application and information available online at: www.stcloudstate.edu.

Internships/Practica: Internship opportunities exist in mental health centers, university counseling centers, Veterans Administration hospitals, general hospitals, social service and welfare agencies, state rehabilitation offices, private rehabilitation companies, rehabilitation workshops and facilities, medical rehabilitation centers, and a number of human services agencies and school and college settings.

Housing and Day Care: On-campus housing is available. See the following Web site for more information: www.stcloudstate.edu. On-campus day care facilities are available.

Employment of Department Graduates:

Master's Degree Graduates: Of those who graduated in the academic year 2003–2004, the following categories and numbers represent the post-graduate activities and employment of master's degree graduates: Enrolled in a psychology doctoral program (4), enrolled in another graduate/professional program (3), enrolled in a post-doctoral residency/fellowship (n/a), employed in independent practice (n/a), employed in other positions at a higher education institution (10), employed in a professional position in a school system (17), employed in business or industry (research/consulting) (13), employed in a government agency (professional services) (6), employed in a community mental health/counseling center (2), total from the above (master's) (55).

Doctoral Degree Graduates: Of those who graduated in the academic year 2003–2004, the following categories and numbers represent the post-graduate activities and employment of doctoral degree graduates: Enrolled in a psychology doctoral program (n/a), total from the above (doctoral) (0).

Additional Information:

Orientation, Objectives, and Emphasis of Department: The college student development program prepares students to work in college counseling centers, career centers, and other student affairs positions in higher education. The Rehabilitation Counseling Program is accredited by the Council on Rehabilitation Education and prepares students to work in a variety of public and private rehabilitation settings. The School Counseling Program prepares students for licensure as elementary or secondary school counselors and is accredited by the Council for the Accreditation of Counseling and Related Educational Programs (CACREP).

Special Facilities or Resources: A counseling classroom surrounded by 10 counseling and observation suites allows for both individual and group counseling experiences. Audio and video equipment is available for taping and reviewing counseling sessions. A separate group room is also available for training and observation experiences. There is an animal laboratory containing pigeon and rat boxes with events controlled via a PDP-8.

Information for Students With Physical Disabilities: jkoshiol@stcloudstate.edu.

Application Information:

Send to: Department of Counselor and Educational Psychology. Application available online. Students are admitted in the Spring, application deadline March 1; Summer, application deadline June 15. Summer admissions occur only if there are vacancies remaining in the programs after the spring deadline and interviews. *Fee:* $20. (subject to change with revision of university graduate bulletin).

Street Cloud State University
Department of Psychology
Social Sciences
720 4th Avenue S.
Saint Cloud, MN 56301
Telephone: (320) 308-4157
Fax: (320) 308-3098
E-mail: *jjillies@stcloudstate.edu*
Web: *http://www.stcloudstate.edu/~psy/io/*

Department Information:

1963. Chairperson: Dr. Leslie Valdes. Number of Faculty: total–full-time 11; women–full-time 5; minority–full-time 1.

Programs and Degrees Offered:

Listed in the following order: Program area, degree type (T if terminal Master's), number awarded 7/03–6/04. Industrial/Organizational Psychology MA/MS (Master of Arts/Science) (T).

Student Applications/Admissions:

Student Applications

Industrial/Organizational Psychology MA/MS (Master of Arts/Science)—Applications 2004–2005, 30. Total applicants accepted 2004–2005, 10. Number enrolled (new admits only) 2004–2005 full-time, 5. Openings 2005–2006, 10. The number of students enrolled full and part-time who were dismissed or voluntarily withdrew from this program area were 0.

Admissions Requirements:

Scores: Entries appear in this order: required test or GPA, minimum score (if required), median score of students entering in 2003–2004. Master's Programs: GRE-V no minimum stated; GRE-Q no minimum stated; GRE-V+Q 1000; overall undergraduate GPA 2.75; last 2 years GPA 2.75.

Other Criteria: (importance of criteria rated low, medium, or high): GRE/MAT scores high, research experience medium, work experience medium, extracurricular activity low, GPA high, letters of recommendation medium, statement of goals and objectives medium.

Student Characteristics: The following represents characteristics of students in 2004–2005 in all graduate psychology programs in the department: Female–full-time 8, part-time 0; Male–full-time

4, part-time 0; Asian/Pacific Islander–full-time 3, part-time 0; Caucasian–full-time 9, part-time 0.

Financial Information/Assistance:

Tuition for Full-Time Study: *Master's:* State residents: $233 per credit hour; Nonstate residents: $364 per credit hour. Tuition is subject to change. See the following Web site for updates and changes in tuition costs: http://www.stcloudstate.edu/graduatestudies.

Financial Assistance:

First Year Students: Teaching assistantships available for first-year. Average amount paid per academic year: $4,100. Average number of hours worked per week: 10. Tuition remission given: partial. Research assistantships available for first-year. Average amount paid per academic year: $4,100. Average number of hours worked per week: 10. Tuition remission given: partial. Fellowships and scholarships available for first-year.

Advanced Students: Teaching assistantships available for advanced students. Average amount paid per academic year: $4,100. Average number of hours worked per week: 10. Tuition remission given: partial. Research assistantships available for advanced students. Average amount paid per academic year: $4,100. Average number of hours worked per week: 10. Tuition remission given: partial. Fellowships and scholarships available for advanced students.

Contact Information: Of all students currently enrolled full-time, 75% benefitted from one or more of the listed financial assistance programs. Application and information available online at: http://www.stcloudstate.edu/graduatestudies.

Internships/Practica: Students pursuing the Master's Degree in Industrial-Organizational Psychology have the option of completing either a practicum/internship or a thesis. The practicum/internship option is designed for students planning to seek employment upon completion of their degree. The thesis option is designed for students planning to seek a doctoral degree in Industrial-Organizational Psychology.

Housing and Day Care: On-campus housing is available. See the following Web site for more information: http://www.stcloudstate.edu/~reslife. On-campus day care facilities are available. See the following Web site for more information: Lindgren Child Care Center; 320-308-3296; http://www.stcloudstate.edu/childcare/.

Employment of Department Graduates:

Master's Degree Graduates: Of those who graduated in the academic year 2003–2004, the following categories and numbers represent the post-graduate activities and employment of master's degree graduates: Enrolled in a post-doctoral residency/fellowship (n/a), employed in independent practice (n/a), total from the above (master's) (0).

Doctoral Degree Graduates: Of those who graduated in the academic year 2003–2004, the following categories and numbers represent the post-graduate activities and employment of doctoral degree graduates: Enrolled in a psychology doctoral program (n/a), total from the above (doctoral) (0).

Additional Information:

Orientation, Objectives, and Emphasis of Department: The Street Cloud State University Department of Psychology is dedicated to providing students with a quality graduate education. The Industrial-Organizational Psychology Master's Degree Program is designed to provide graduate students with the knowledge and skills that will prepare them for jobs in consulting, business, and government, or to continue their education. The curriculum reflects a commitment to the scientist-practitioner model of graduate education in psychology by including training in the theoretical and empirical bases of industrial-organizational psychology and in the application of these perspectives to work settings. Following the recommendations of the Society for Industrial-Organizational Psychology for master's level education, students' graduate experience will include: (a) training in the core areas of industrial-organizational psychology, including personnel selection, training and organizational development, criterion development, and organizational theory, (b) a firm foundation in psychological theory, research methods, statistics, and psychometrics, and (c) the opportunity to obtain both research experience and applied experience while completing their education.

Special Facilities or Resources: The Street Cloud State University Psychology Department has a dedicated psychology laboratory facility (new space established in 1999). It has 10 rooms for individual and group testing. The lab has networked computers and a laser printer. Activities that take place in this lab include: faculty and student research, meetings of student organizations, research seminars, and classroom demonstrations.

Information for Students With Physical Disabilities: See the following Web site for more information: http://www.stcloudstate.edu/~sds/.

Application Information:
Send to: School of Graduate Studies, 121 Administrative Services, Street Cloud State University, 720 4th Avenue S., Street Cloud, MN 56301. Application available online. URL of online application: www.stcloudstate.edu/graduatestudies/. Students are admitted in the Fall, application deadline March 1. *Fee:* $35.

Street Thomas, University of
Graduate School of Professional Psychology
TMH451, 1000 La Salle Avenue
Minneapolis, MN 55403
Telephone: (651) 962-4650
Fax: (651) 962-4651
E-mail: *gradpsych@stthomas.edu*
Web: *http://www.stthomas.edu/gradpsych*

Department Information:
1960. Dean: David Welch. Number of Faculty: total–full-time 8, part-time 10; women–full-time 4, part-time 4; minority–full-time 1, part-time 1.

Programs and Degrees Offered:
Listed in the following order: Program area, degree type (T if terminal Master's), number awarded 7/03–6/04. Counseling MA/MS (Master of Arts/Science) (T) 53, Counseling Psychology PsyD (Doctor of Psychology) 10.

APA Accreditation: Counseling PsyD (Doctor of Psychology).

Student Applications/Admissions:

Student Applications

Counseling MA/MS (Master of Arts/Science)—Applications 2004–2005, 83. Total applicants accepted 2004–2005, 40. Total enrolled 2004–2005 full-time, 35, part-time, 154. Openings 2005–2006, 45. The Median number of years required for completion of a degree are 4. The number of students enrolled full and part-time who were dismissed or voluntarily withdrew from this program area were 0. Counseling Psychology PsyD (Doctor of Psychology)—Applications 2004–2005, 45. Total applicants accepted 2004–2005, 15. Number enrolled (new admits only) 2004–2005 full-time, 15. Number enrolled (new admits only) 2004–2005 part-time, 0. Total enrolled 2004–2005 full-time, 55, part-time, 15. Openings 2005–2006, 15. The Median number of years required for completion of a degree are 5. The number of students enrolled full and part-time who were dismissed or voluntarily withdrew from this program area were 0.

Admissions Requirements:

Scores: Entries appear in this order: required test or GPA, minimum score (if required), median score of students entering in 2003–2004. Master's Programs: GRE-V no minimum stated; GRE-Q no minimum stated; GRE-V+Q no minimum stated; GRE-Analytical no minimum stated; MAT no minimum stated, 50; overall undergraduate GPA 2.75. Accept either the GRE or MAT. Doctoral Programs: MAT no minimum stated, 50. Accept either the GRE or MAT.

Other Criteria: (importance of criteria rated low, medium, or high): GRE/MAT scores medium, research experience low, work experience medium, extracurricular activity low, clinically related public service high, GPA high, letters of recommendation high, interview high, statement of goals and objectives high. For additional information on admission requirements, go to: www.stthomas.edu/gradpsych.

Student Characteristics: The following represents characteristics of students in 2004–2005 in all graduate psychology programs in the department: Female–full-time 72, part-time 135; Male–full-time 18, part-time 34; African American/Black–full-time 1, part-time 3; Hispanic/Latino(a)–full-time 0, part-time 3; Asian/Pacific Islander–full-time 1, part-time 3; American Indian/Alaska Native–full-time 0, part-time 0; Caucasian–full-time 88, part-time 160; students subject to the Americans With Disabilities Act–full-time 1, part-time 1.

Financial Information/Assistance:

Tuition for Full-Time Study: Master's: State residents: $486 per credit hour; Nonstate residents: $486 per credit hour. Doctoral: State residents: $643 per credit hour; Nonstate residents: $643 per credit hour. See the following Web site for updates and changes in tuition costs: www.stthomas.edu/gradpsych.

Financial Assistance:

First Year Students: Fellowships and scholarships available for first-year. Average amount paid per academic year: $2,500. Average number of hours worked per week: 0. Apply by April 1.

Advanced Students: Research assistantships available for advanced students. Average amount paid per academic year: $2,500. Average number of hours worked per week: 5. Apply by April 1.

Contact Information: Of all students currently enrolled full-time, 0% benefitted from one or more of the listed financial assistance programs. Application and information available online at: http://www.stthomas.edu/financialservices.

Internships/Practica: Master's and doctoral students have available a wide variety of practica and internships in the surrounding community in the Twin Cities area. Application is competitive and supported by the training coordinator at UST. Students also participate in APPIC internships locally and across the country. Recent sites have included community mental health centers, regional hospitals, VA medical centers, residential chemical dependency centers, career and vocational services, college/university counseling and career centers, vocational rehabilitation programs, employee assistance counseling programs, health maintenance organizations, MN state hospitals, and the MN state prison system. For those doctoral students for whom a professional internship is required prior to graduation, 16 applied in 2003–2004. Of those who applied, 15 were placed in internships listed by the Association of Psychology Postdoctoral and Internship Programs (APPIC); 13 were placed in APA accredited internships.

Housing and Day Care: No on-campus housing is available. On-campus day care facilities are available. See the following Web site for more information: www.ssthomas.edu/childdevelopment.

Employment of Department Graduates:

Master's Degree Graduates: Of those who graduated in the academic year 2003–2004, the following categories and numbers represent the post-graduate activities and employment of master's degree graduates: Enrolled in a post-doctoral residency/fellowship (n/a), employed in independent practice (n/a), total from the above (master's) (0).

Doctoral Degree Graduates: Of those who graduated in the academic year 2003–2004, the following categories and numbers represent the post-graduate activities and employment of doctoral degree graduates: Enrolled in a psychology doctoral program (n/a), total from the above (doctoral) (0).

Additional Information:

Orientation, Objectives, and Emphasis of Department: The Graduate School of Professional Psychology is dedicated to the development of general practitioners who will make ethical, professional, and creative contributions to their communities and their profession. The programs strive toward leadership in emphasizing a practitioner focus with adult learners. Teaching, scholarship, and service are responsive to diverse perspectives, a blend of practical and reflective inquiry, and social needs. The recently developed PsyD program meets designation criteria of the ASPPB/National Register Joint Designation Project.

Personal Behavior Statement: They may email the school at gradpsych@stthomas.edu and request a copy of the Personal Characteristics that enrolled students sign when they enter the program.

Information for Students With Physical Disabilities: See the following Web site for more information: www.stthomas.edu/enhancementprog.

Application Information:
Send to: Admissions Chair, Graduate School of Professional Psychology, University of Street Thomas, 1000 La Salle Avenue, TMH451, Minneapolis, MN 55403. Application available online. URL of online application: www.stthomas.edu/gradpsych. Students are admitted in the Fall: application deadlines—April 1 for MA; February 1 for PsyD. *Fee:* $50.

Walden University
Psychology Program
School of Psychology
155 Fifth Avenue S.
Minneapolis, MN 55401
Telephone: (800) WALDENU
Fax: (612) 338-5092
E-mail: *ddezolt@waldenu.edu*
Web: *http://www.waldnu.edu*

Department Information:
1996. Dean: Denise DeZolt. Number of Faculty: total–full-time 4, part-time 110; women–full-time 2, part-time 54; minority–full-time 2, part-time 13; faculty subject to the Americans With Disabilities Act 2.

Programs and Degrees Offered:
Listed in the following order: Program area, degree type (T if terminal Master's), number awarded 7/03–6/04. General Psychology MA/MS (Master of Arts/Science), Clinical Psychology PhD (Doctor of Philosophy), Counseling Psychology PhD (Doctor of Philosophy), Organizational Psychology PhD (Doctor of Philosophy), Health Psychology PhD (Doctor of Philosophy), Academic Psychology PhD (Doctor of Philosophy), School Psychology PhD (Doctor of Philosophy), Industrial/Organizational MA/MS (Master of Arts/Science).

Student Applications/Admissions:
Student Applications
General Psychology MA/MS (Master of Arts/Science)—Total enrolled 2004–2005 full-time, 505. *Clinical Psychology PhD (Doctor of Philosophy)*—Total enrolled 2004–2005 full-time, 261. The Median number of years required for completion of a degree are 5. *Counseling Psychology PhD (Doctor of Philosophy)*—Total enrolled 2004–2005 full-time, 150. The Median number of years required for completion of a degree are 5. *Organizational Psychology PhD (Doctor of Philosophy)*—Total enrolled 2004–2005 full-time, 84. The Median number of years required for completion of a degree are 3. *Health Psychology PhD (Doctor of Philosophy)*—Total enrolled 2004–2005 full-time, 73. *Academic Psychology PhD (Doctor of Philosophy)*—Total enrolled 2004–2005 full-time, 123. *School Psychology PhD (Doctor of Philosophy)*—Total enrolled 2004–2005 full-time, 22. *Industrial/Organizational MA/MS (Master of Arts/Science)*—Total enrolled 2004–2005 full-time, 75.

Admissions Requirements:
Scores: Entries appear in this order: required test or GPA, minimum score (if required), median score of students entering in 2003–2004. Master's Programs: overall undergraduate GPA 3.0, 3.5; last 2 years GPA 3.0, 3.5; psychology GPA 3.0, 3.5. Doctoral Programs: last 2 years GPA 3.0; psychology GPA 3.0.
Other Criteria: (importance of criteria rated low, medium, or high): research experience low, work experience high, extracurricular activity high, clinically related public service high, GPA high, letters of recommendation low, interview low, statement of goals and objectives high.

Student Characteristics: The following represents characteristics of students in 2004–2005 in all graduate psychology programs in the department: African American/Black–full-time 122, part-time 0; Hispanic/Latino(a)–full-time 26, part-time 0; Asian/Pacific Islander–full-time 10, part-time 0; American Indian/Alaska Native–full-time 9, part-time 0; Caucasian–full-time 0, part-time 0; Multi-ethnic–full-time 13, part-time 0; students subject to the Americans With Disabilities Act–full-time 9, part-time 0.

Financial Information/Assistance:
Tuition for Full-Time Study: *Master's:* State residents: $300 per credit hour; Nonstate residents: $300 per credit hour. *Doctoral:* State residents: $370 per credit hour; Nonstate residents: $370 per credit hour. Tuition is subject to change. See the following Web site for updates and changes in tuition costs: http://www.waldenu.edu/catalog/2004/introduction/financial_01tuition.html.

Financial Assistance:
First Year Students: No information provided.
Advanced Students: Teaching assistantships available for advanced students. Average amount paid per academic year: $6,000. Average number of hours worked per week: 10. Apply by varies. Research assistantships available for advanced students. Average amount paid per academic year: $6,000. Average number of hours worked per week: 10. Apply by varies.
Contact Information: Of all students currently enrolled full-time, 1% benefitted from one or more of the listed financial assistance programs. Application and information available online at: http://www.ealdenu.edu/financial for financial aid info; psychologyresumes@waldenu.edu for assistant.

Internships/Practica: For those doctoral students for whom a professional internship is required prior to graduation, 65 applied in 2003–2004. Of those who applied, 3 were placed in internships listed by the Association of Psychology Postdoctoral and Internship Programs (APPIC).

Housing and Day Care: No on-campus housing is available. No on-campus day care facilities are available.

Employment of Department Graduates:
Master's Degree Graduates: Of those who graduated in the academic year 2003–2004, the following categories and numbers represent the post-graduate activities and employment of master's degree graduates: Enrolled in a post-doctoral residency/fellowship (n/a), employed in independent practice (n/a), total from the above (master's) (0).
Doctoral Degree Graduates: Of those who graduated in the academic year 2003–2004, the following categories and numbers represent the post-graduate activities and employment of doctoral degree graduates: Enrolled in a psychology doctoral program (n/a), total from the above (doctoral) (0).

Additional Information:

Orientation, Objectives, and Emphasis of Department: Students have the opportunity to work with faculty with a diverse array of theoretical orientations.

Information for Students With Physical Disabilities: See the following Web site for more information: www.waldenu.edu.

Application Information:

Send to: Office of Student Enrollment, Walden University, 1001 Fleet Street, Baltimore, MD 21202 USA. Application available online. URL of online application: http://www.waldenu.edu/prospect/apply/index.html. Students are admitted in the Fall, application deadline August 15; Winter, application deadline November 15; Spring, application deadline February 15; Summer, application deadline May 15. Programs have rolling admissions. *Fee:* $50.

Jackson State University

Department of Psychology
Liberal Arts
P.O. Box 17550
Jackson, MS 39217-0350
Telephone: (601) 979-3385
Fax: (601) 979-3947
E-mail: *jeffrey.e.cassisi@jsums.edu*
Web: *http://ccaix.jsums.edu/~psycdept/*

Department Information:
1971. Professor and Chair: Shih-Sung Wen. Number of Faculty: total–full-time 13, part-time 1; women–full-time 5; minority–full-time 6.

Programs and Degrees Offered:
Listed in the following order: Program area, degree type (T if terminal Master's), number awarded 7/03–6/04. Clinical psychology PhD (Doctor of Philosophy) 1.

APA Accreditation: Clinical PhD (Doctor of Philosophy).

Student Applications/Admissions:
Student Applications
Clinical psychology PhD (Doctor of Philosophy)—Applications 2004–2005, 35. Total applicants accepted 2004–2005, 10. Total enrolled 2004–2005 full-time, 30, part-time, 1. Openings 2005–2006, 8. The Median number of years required for completion of a degree are 5. The number of students enrolled full and part-time who were dismissed or voluntarily withdrew from this program area were 4.

Admissions Requirements:
Scores: Entries appear in this order: required test or GPA, minimum score (if required), median score of students entering in 2003–2004. Doctoral Programs: GRE-V no minimum stated, 460; GRE-Q no minimum stated, 470; GRE-V+Q no minimum stated, 930; overall undergraduate GPA no minimum stated, 3.7.
Other Criteria: (importance of criteria rated low, medium, or high): GRE/MAT scores low, research experience high, work experience high, extracurricular activity low, clinically related public service medium, GPA high, letters of recommendation high, interview high, statement of goals and objectives medium.

Student Characteristics: The following represents characteristics of students in 2004–2005 in all graduate psychology programs in the department: Female–full-time 22, part-time 1; Male–full-time 8, part-time 0; African American/Black–full-time 11, part-time 0; Hispanic/Latino(a)–full-time 0, part-time 0; Asian/Pacific Islander–full-time 1, part-time 0; American Indian/Alaska Native–full-time 0, part-time 0; Caucasian–full-time 0, part-time 0; students subject to the Americans With Disabilities Act–full-time 0, part-time 0.

Financial Information/Assistance:
Tuition for Full-Time Study: *Doctoral:* State residents: per academic year $3,612, $201 per credit hour; Nonstate residents: per academic year $8,116. Tuition is subject to change.

Financial Assistance:
First Year Students: Teaching assistantships available for first-year. Average amount paid per academic year: $11,000. Average number of hours worked per week: 14. Research assistantships available for first-year. Average amount paid per academic year: $11,000. Average number of hours worked per week: 14. Fellowships and scholarships available for first-year. Average number of hours worked per week: 0. Tuition remission given: partial.
Advanced Students: Teaching assistantships available for advanced students. Average amount paid per academic year: $11,000. Average number of hours worked per week: 14. Research assistantships available for advanced students. Average amount paid per academic year: $11,000. Average number of hours worked per week: 14. Fellowships and scholarships available for advanced students. Average number of hours worked per week: 0. Tuition remission given: partial.
Contact Information: Of all students currently enrolled full-time, 90% benefitted from one or more of the listed financial assistance programs.

Internships/Practica: Extensive Practicum and Externship experiences are required. Students have recently been placed at the Mississippi State Hospital at Whitfield, Street Dominic's Medical Center, and the University of Mississippi Medical Center, and the Jackson Veteran's Administration Medical Center. For those doctoral students for whom a professional internship is required prior to graduation, 4 applied in 2003–2004. Of those who applied, 4 were placed in internships listed by the Association of Psychology Postdoctoral and Internship Programs (APPIC); 4 were placed in APA accredited internships.

Housing and Day Care: No on-campus housing is available. On-campus day care facilities are available.

Employment of Department Graduates:
Master's Degree Graduates: Of those who graduated in the academic year 2003–2004, the following categories and numbers represent the post-graduate activities and employment of master's degree graduates: Enrolled in a post-doctoral residency/fellowship (n/a), employed in independent practice (n/a), total from the above (master's) (0).
Doctoral Degree Graduates: Of those who graduated in the academic year 2003–2004, the following categories and numbers represent the post-graduate activities and employment of doctoral degree graduates: Enrolled in a psychology doctoral program (n/a), employed in an academic position at a university (1), total from the above (doctoral) (1).

Additional Information:
Orientation, Objectives, and Emphasis of Department: The mission of the Clinical Psychology Doctoral Program at Jackson State University (JSU) is fourfold: a) To produce highly skilled, license eligible graduates who can function as both scientists and clini-

cians; b) To increase the awareness, knowledge, and skills of students, faculty, and professionals in the area of multicultural psychology; c) To support the progress of ethnic minority psychologists; and d) To provide field experiences designed to meet the diverse psychological, health, and service needs of ethnic minority populations. Participants in this program are guided by a curriculum anchored in the cumulative body of psychological knowledge with a firm basis in statistics, research design, and experimental methodology. The program develops in the student the knowledge and skills required for effective functioning as an empirically-oriented clinical psychologist in diverse settings. This is accomplished through a sequence of formal clinical courses, distinguished by in-depth exploration of multicultural issues and exposure to ethnic minority communities, including interdisciplinary and interorganizational collaboration and consultation. Jackson State University is located in Jackson, Mississippi, the capital and largest city of the state. The metropolitan area consists of a growing population estimated to be 400,000. The campus is located on a scenic 106-acre tract situated one mile west of the main business district of the city. Jackson is also the hub for healthcare in the state. A Veteran's Administration medical center, the University of Mississippi Medical School, Whitfield State Hospital, and Street Dominic's Medical Center are all within a 20-minute radius of the campus. These sites and others offer many potential research and practicum opportunities.

Special Facilities or Resources: The Department of Psychology is located in a new $16-million Liberal Arts Building; it contains faculty offices, computing facilities, and a Psychology Clinic. A $12-million expansion of the H.T. Sampson Library has just been completed. The Community Health Program is administered by the Department of Psychology and is an important resource for graduate student research. This program has been awarded several multiyear grants from the National Institutes of Health and the Centers for Disease Control. Several students have chosen to conduct their dissertations at this facility. The Community Health Program is located at the Jackson Medical Mall.

Application Information:
Send to: Clinical Program Admissions, Department of Psychology, Jackson State University, P.O. Box 17550, Jackson, MS 39217-0350. Students are admitted in the Fall, application deadline March 1. *Fee:* $20. Application fee applies to out-of-state applicants only.

Mississippi State University
Department of Counseling, Educational Psychology, & Special
  Education
College of Education
P.O. Box 9727
Mississippi State, MS 39762-5670
Telephone: (662) 325-3426
Fax: (662) 325-3263
E-mail: *hosie@colled.msstate.edu*
Web: *http://www.educ.msstate.edu/CEdEPy/cedepy.html*

Department Information:
  1954. Department Head: Thomas W. Hosie. Number of Faculty: total–full-time 25, part-time 2; women–full-time 12, part-time 1; minority–full-time 2.

Programs and Degrees Offered:
  Listed in the following order: Program area, degree type (T if terminal Master's), number awarded 7/03–6/04. School PhD (Doctor of Philosophy) 5, educational PhD (Doctor of Philosophy) 2.

APA Accreditation: School PhD (Doctor of Philosophy).

Student Applications/Admissions:
  Student Applications
    School PhD (Doctor of Philosophy)—Applications 2004–2005, 16. Total applicants accepted 2004–2005, 6. Number enrolled (new admits only) 2004–2005 full-time, 5. Number enrolled (new admits only) 2004–2005 part-time, 0. Openings 2005–2006, 6. The Median number of years required for completion of a degree are 5. The number of students enrolled full and part-time who were dismissed or voluntarily withdrew from this program area were 1. *Educational PhD (Doctor of Philosophy)*— Applications 2004–2005, 4. Total applicants accepted 2004–2005, 2. Total enrolled 2004–2005 full-time, 9, part-time, 3. Openings 2005–2006, 6. The Median number of years required for completion of a degree are 4. The number of students enrolled full and part-time who were dismissed or voluntarily withdrew from this program area were 1.

  Admissions Requirements:
    Scores: Entries appear in this order: required test or GPA, minimum score (if required), median score of students entering in 2003–2004. Master's Programs: overall undergraduate GPA 3.0, 3.00; last 2 years GPA 3.0, 3.4. Doctoral Programs: overall undergraduate GPA no minimum stated, 3.00.
    Other Criteria: (importance of criteria rated low, medium, or high): GRE/MAT scores medium, research experience medium, work experience medium, extracurricular activity low, clinically related public service low, GPA high, letters of recommendation high, interview high, statement of goals and objectives high.

  Student Characteristics: The following represents characteristics of students in 2004–2005 in all graduate psychology programs in the department: Female–full-time 30, part-time 14; Male–full-time 6, part-time 3; African American/Black–full-time 5, part-time 2; Hispanic/Latino(a)–full-time 0, part-time 1; Asian/Pacific Islander–full-time 0, part-time 0; American Indian/Alaska Native–full-time 0, part-time 0; Caucasian–full-time 24, part-time 11; Multi-ethnic–full-time 1, part-time 0; students subject to the Americans With Disabilities Act–full-time 0, part-time 0.

Financial Information/Assistance:
  Tuition for Full-Time Study: *Master's:* State residents: $228 per credit hour; Nonstate residents: $517 per credit hour. *Doctoral:* State residents: $228 per credit hour; Nonstate residents: $517 per credit hour.

  Financial Assistance:
    First Year Students: Teaching assistantships available for first-year. Average amount paid per academic year: $6,363. Average number of hours worked per week: 20. Tuition remission given: full. Research assistantships available for first-year. Average amount paid per academic year: $9,000. Average number of hours worked per week: 20. Tuition remission given: full.

Advanced Students: Teaching assistantships available for advanced students. Average amount paid per academic year: $8,900. Average number of hours worked per week: 20. Tuition remission given: full. Research assistantships available for advanced students. Average amount paid per academic year: $9,000. Average number of hours worked per week: 20. Tuition remission given: full.

Contact Information: Of all students currently enrolled full-time, 95% benefitted from one or more of the listed financial assistance programs.

Internships/Practica: The school psychology program offers students numerous practica and internship opportunities. Most practica are coordinated with school districts, medical centers/hospitals, community counseling centers, and the like. Internship and practica opportunities are tailored to meet the individual needs of students and a variety of options can be arranged. In general, students are encouraged to seek APA-approved internships.

Housing and Day Care: On-campus housing is available. See the following Web site for more information: http://www.msstate.edu/dept/housing/index.php. On-campus day care facilities are available.

Employment of Department Graduates:

Master's Degree Graduates: Of those who graduated in the academic year 2003–2004, the following categories and numbers represent the post-graduate activities and employment of master's degree graduates: Enrolled in a psychology doctoral program (6), enrolled in another graduate/professional program (0), enrolled in a post-doctoral residency/fellowship (n/a), employed in independent practice (n/a), employed in an academic position at a university (0), employed in an academic position at a 2-year/4-year college (0), employed in other positions at a higher education institution (0), employed in a professional position in a school system (2), employed in business or industry (research/consulting) (1), employed in business or industry (management) (0), employed in a government agency (research) (0), employed in a government agency (professional services) (0), employed in a community mental health/counseling center (0), employed in a hospital/medical center (0), still seeking employment (0), other employment position (0), do not know (1), total from the above (master's) (10).

Doctoral Degree Graduates: Of those who graduated in the academic year 2003–2004, the following categories and numbers represent the post-graduate activities and employment of doctoral degree graduates: Enrolled in a psychology doctoral program (n/a), enrolled in another graduate/professional program (0), enrolled in a post-doctoral residency/fellowship (0), employed in independent practice (0), employed in an academic position at a university (2), employed in an academic position at a 2-year/4-year college (0), employed in other positions at a higher education institution (0), employed in a professional position in a school system (2), employed in business or industry (research/consulting) (0), employed in business or industry (management) (0), employed in a government agency (research) (0), employed in a government agency (professional services) (0), employed in a community mental health/counseling center (0), employed in a hospital/medical center (1), still seeking employment (0), other employment position (0), do not know (0), total from the above (doctoral) (5).

Additional Information:

Orientation, Objectives, and Emphasis of Department: Our graduate programs are designed primarily to help develop and train competent and ethical psychologists in several areas: school psychology and educational psychology. The programs are based on a scientist-practitioner model. The flexibility of these offerings gives the student the option of functioning as an educational psychologist in a variety of settings, thereby enhancing employment opportunities.

Special Facilities or Resources: The Educational Psychology faculty maintain close working relationships with the Department of Psychology, the Department of Counseling and Special Education, and others. Such relationships afford students the opportunity to work closely with diverse faculty members with various human services backgrounds. Moreover, students are encouraged to work closely with faculty on various creative projects and research. Additional opportunities exist at the Rehabilitation Research and Training Center on Blindness and Low Vision, the Bureau of Educational Research and Evaluation, and the Research and Curriculum Unit for Vocational-Technical Education, Social Science Research Center, all of which are connected with Mississippi State University.

Information for Students With Physical Disabilities: See the following Web site for more information: http://www.msstate.edu/dept/students/sss.htm.

Application Information:
Send to: Department Chair. Students are admitted in the Fall, application deadline Feburary 1. MS for Fall due March 1; Educational psychology programs offer spring and summer admission as well. *Fee:* $0. $25 admission fee for out of state applicants.

Mississippi State University
Department of Psychology
Arts and Sciences
P.O. Drawer 6161
Mississippi State, MS 39762
Telephone: (662) 325-3202
Fax: (662) 325-7212
E-mail: *kja3@ra.msstate.edu*
Web: *http://www.msstate.edu/Dept/Psychology/psych.html*

Department Information:
1966. Department Head: Stephen B. Klein. Number of Faculty: total–full-time 14, part-time 9; women–full-time 5, part-time 5; minority–part-time 1.

Programs and Degrees Offered:
Listed in the following order: Program area, degree type (T if terminal Master's), number awarded 7/03–6/04. Clinical Psychology MA/MS (Master of Arts/Science) (T) 7, Experimental Psychology MA/MS (Master of Arts/Science) (T) 0, Cognitive Science PhD (Doctor of Philosophy) 0.

Student Applications/Admissions:
Student Applications
Clinical Psychology MA/MS (Master of Arts/Science)—Applications 2004–2005, 35. Total applicants accepted 2004–2005,

19. Number enrolled (new admits only) 2004–2005 full-time, 9. Number enrolled (new admits only) 2004–2005 part-time, 0. Openings 2005–2006, 10. The Median number of years required for completion of a degree are 3. The number of students enrolled full and part-time who were dismissed or voluntarily withdrew from this program area were 2. *Experimental Psychology MA/MS (Master of Arts/Science)*—Applications 2004–2005, 8. Total applicants accepted 2004–2005, 4. Number enrolled (new admits only) 2004–2005 full-time, 2. Openings 2005–2006, 3. The number of students enrolled full and part-time who were dismissed or voluntarily withdrew from this program area were 0. *Cognitive Science PhD (Doctor of Philosophy)*—Applications 2004–2005, 1. Total applicants accepted 2004–2005, 0. Number enrolled (new admits only) 2004–2005 full-time, 0. Number enrolled (new admits only) 2004–2005 part-time, 0. Total enrolled 2004–2005 full-time, 7, part-time, 1. Openings 2005–2006, 3. The number of students enrolled full and part-time who were dismissed or voluntarily withdrew from this program area was 1.

Admissions Requirements:

Scores: Entries appear in this order: required test or GPA, minimum score (if required), median score of students entering in 2003–2004. Master's Programs: GRE-V 500, 520; GRE-Q 500, 595; GRE-V+Q 1000, 1125; last 2 years GPA 2.75, 3.77. The GPA of 2.75 is the minimum our Office of Graduate Admissions will accept for entry into the Graduate School. We look for a minimum GRE of 1000 (quantitative and verbal), but it's not an absolute requirement. The numbers under median are the figures for the latest group of applicants we accepted and who are actually enrolled in the clinical program. Doctoral Programs: GRE-V 500, 550; GRE-Q 500, 650; GRE-V+Q 1000, 1180. The numbers under median scores are the actual figures for the last 2 groups of applicants we accepted into the program.

Other Criteria: (importance of criteria rated low, medium, or high): GRE/MAT scores medium, research experience medium, work experience medium, extracurricular activity low, clinically related public service medium, GPA medium, letters of recommendation medium, interview low, statement of goals and objectives medium. The clinically related public service would be relevant for applicants to the master's program, clinical concentration. Computer-related experience is relevant to the Cognitive PhD program.

Student Characteristics: The following represents characteristics of students in 2004–2005 in all graduate psychology programs in the department: Female–full-time 27, part-time 0; Male–full-time 15, part-time 1; African American/Black–full-time 3, part-time 0; Hispanic/Latino(a)–full-time 0, part-time 0; Asian/Pacific Islander–full-time 1, part-time 0; American Indian/Alaska Native–full-time 0, part-time 0; Caucasian–full-time 37, part-time 1; Multi-ethnic–full-time 1, part-time 0; students subject to the Americans With Disabilities Act–full-time 0, part-time 0.

Financial Information/Assistance:

Tuition for Full-Time Study: *Master's:* State residents: per academic year $1,937, $215 per credit hour; Nonstate residents: per academic year $4,390, $488 per credit hour. *Doctoral:* State residents: per academic year $1,937, $215 per credit hour; Nonstate residents: per academic year $4,390, $488 per credit hour. Tuition is subject to change. See the following Web site for updates and changes in tuition costs: http://www.sfa.msstate.edu/policies/cost.php.

Financial Assistance:

First Year Students: Teaching assistantships available for first-year. Average amount paid per academic year: $5,940. Average number of hours worked per week: 20. Apply by May 1. Tuition remission given: full.

Advanced Students: Teaching assistantships available for advanced students. Average amount paid per academic year: $10,000. Average number of hours worked per week: 20. Apply by May 1. Tuition remission given: full. Research assistantships available for advanced students. Average amount paid per academic year: $10,000. Average number of hours worked per week: 20. Apply by May 1. Tuition remission given: full.

Contact Information: Of all students currently enrolled full-time, 90% benefitted from one or more of the listed financial assistance programs.

Internships/Practica: Students in the clinical-emphasis program complete two 300 clock-hour practicum courses. These practica occur in a variety of settings, including public and private psychiatric hospitals and mental retardation facilities, community mental health centers, etc. Students are exposed to diverse client populations (e.g., in- and outpatient, children and adults with varied diagnoses and ethnic backgrounds).

Housing and Day Care: On-campus housing is available. See the following Web site for more information: http://www.housing.msstate.edu/grad/. No on-campus day care facilities are available.

Employment of Department Graduates:

Master's Degree Graduates: Of those who graduated in the academic year 2003–2004, the following categories and numbers represent the post-graduate activities and employment of master's degree graduates: Enrolled in a psychology doctoral program (3), enrolled in a post-doctoral residency/fellowship (n/a), employed in independent practice (n/a), employed in an academic position at a 2-year/4-year college (1), employed in a hospital/medical center (1), do not know (2), total from the above (master's) (7).

Doctoral Degree Graduates: Of those who graduated in the academic year 2003–2004, the following categories and numbers represent the post-graduate activities and employment of doctoral degree graduates: Enrolled in a psychology doctoral program (n/a), total from the above (doctoral) (0).

Additional Information:

Orientation, Objectives, and Emphasis of Department: Currently we offer both a MS and a PhD degree through different programs. Our master's degree programs offer concentrations in either experimental or clinical psychology. The clinical masters program is accredited by the Master's in Psychology Accreditation Council (MPAC). Our PhD program awards a degree in Applied Cognitive Science through an interdisciplinary program housed in the Psychology Department but operated in cooperation with the Computer Science Department, the Industrial Engineering Department, and other units on campus. You can learn more about any of our programs by visiting the department's website at http://www.psychology.msstate.edu.

Special Facilities or Resources: The department houses a state-of-the-art computer lab for human subject data collection. Faculty laboratories include extensive computer labs for data collection, eye trackers, high-speed servers, and fast network access. Other research facilities, including a 3-D "CAVE" environment, are available through connections to other research facilities, both on-campus and off. Clinical students have research/training opportunities in the on-site Psychology Training Clinic and in several off-campus practicum placements.

Application Information:

Send to: Graduate Admissions, Drawer 6305, Mississippi State, MS 39762. Online applications can be completed at http://www.msstate.edu/dept/grad/application.htm. Students are admitted in the Fall, application deadline January 15; Spring, application deadline November 1. The application deadline for the Cognitive Science PhD program is January 15. Although the deadline for full financial consideration is January 15, we will continue to review applications until May 1. The application deadline for the Master's Degree concentrations in Clinical and Experimental Psychology is May 1, although applications are reviewed beginning in mid-March. Earlier applicants receive earlier decisions and outstanding early applicants have a better chance of obtaining financial support. There is no application fee for in-state applicants; $25 fee for out-of-state and foreign applicants.

Mississippi, University of
Department of Psychology
Liberal Arts
205 Peabody
University, MS 38677
Telephone: (662) 915-7383
Fax: (662) 915-5398
E-mail: psych@olemiss.edu
Web: http://www.olemiss.edu/depts/psychology

Department Information:

1932. Chairperson: Michael T. Allen. Number of Faculty: total–full-time 14, part-time 3; women–full-time 6.

Programs and Degrees Offered:

Listed in the following order: Program area, degree type (T if terminal Master's), number awarded 7/03–6/04. Clinical PhD (Doctor of Philosophy) 4, Experimental PhD (Doctor of Philosophy) 3.

APA Accreditation: Clinical PhD (Doctor of Philosophy).

Student Applications/Admissions:

Student Applications

Clinical PhD (Doctor of Philosophy)—Applications 2004–2005, 95. Total applicants accepted 2004–2005, 8. Number enrolled (new admits only) 2004–2005 full-time, 7. Openings 2005–2006, 6. The Median number of years required for completion of a degree are 6. The number of students enrolled full and part-time who were dismissed or voluntarily withdrew from this program area were 2. *Experimental PhD (Doctor of Philosophy)*—Applications 2004–2005, 5. Total applicants accepted 2004–2005, 3. Number enrolled (new admits only) 2004–2005 full-time, 1. Number enrolled (new admits only) 2004–2005 part-time, 0. Openings 2005–2006, 4. The Median number of years required for completion of a degree are 5. The number of students enrolled full and part-time who were dismissed or voluntarily withdrew from this program area were 1.

Admissions Requirements:

Scores: Entries appear in this order: required test or GPA, minimum score (if required), median score of students entering in 2003–2004. Master's Programs: No terminal Master's degree programs are offered. Doctoral Programs: GRE-V no minimum stated, 560; GRE-Q no minimum stated, 635; GRE-V+Q no minimum stated, 1195; GRE-Analytical no minimum stated, 630; GRE-Subject(Psych) no minimum stated, 640; overall undergraduate GPA no minimum stated, 3.5; last 2 years GPA 3.0. Master's GPA only applies to students entering with Master's degrees. The Graduate School requires a GPA of 3.0 or equivalent average on the last 60 hours of undergraduate course work in order to be admitted with full standing.

Other Criteria: (importance of criteria rated low, medium, or high): GRE/MAT scores medium, research experience high, work experience medium, extracurricular activity medium, clinically related public service medium, GPA medium, letters of recommendation high, interview high, statement of goals and objectives high.

Student Characteristics: The following represents characteristics of students in 2004–2005 in all graduate psychology programs in the department: Female–full-time 41, part-time 0; Male–full-time 21, part-time 0; African American/Black–full-time 6, part-time 0; Hispanic/Latino(a)–full-time 3, part-time 0; Asian/Pacific Islander–full-time 2, part-time 0; American Indian/Alaska Native–full-time 0, part-time 0; Caucasian–full-time 51, part-time 0; Multi-ethnic–full-time 0, part-time 0; students subject to the Americans With Disabilities Act–full-time 0, part-time 0.

Financial Information/Assistance:

Tuition for Full-Time Study: *Master's:* State residents: per academic year $4,108, $228 per credit hour; Nonstate residents: per academic year $9,261, $515 per credit hour. *Doctoral:* State residents: per academic year $4,108, $228 per credit hour; Nonstate residents: per academic year $9,261, $515 per credit hour. Tuition is subject to change. See the following Web site for updates and changes in tuition costs: www.olemiss.edu.

Financial Assistance:

First Year Students: Teaching assistantships available for first-year. Average amount paid per academic year: $4,000. Average number of hours worked per week: 10. Apply by January 15. Tuition remission given: partial. Research assistantships available for first-year. Average amount paid per academic year: $4,000. Average number of hours worked per week: 10. Apply by January 15. Tuition remission given: partial.

Advanced Students: Teaching assistantships available for advanced students. Average amount paid per academic year: $4,000. Average number of hours worked per week: 10. Apply by January 15. Tuition remission given: partial. Research assistantships available for advanced students. Average amount paid per academic year: $4,000. Average number of hours worked per week: 10. Apply by January 15. Tuition remission given: partial. Traineeships available for advanced students. Average amount paid per academic year: $8,000. Average number of hours worked per week: 20. Apply by January 15. Tuition remission given: partial. Fellowships and scholarships available for advanced students. Average amount paid per academic year: $2,000. Apply by January 15.

Contact Information: Of all students currently enrolled full-time, 95% benefitted from one or more of the listed financial assistance programs. Application and information available online at: www.olemiss.edu/depts/graduate_school/apply.html.

Internships/Practica: Practica or Field Placements are available for clinical students beginning in the second year of the program. Students serve as therapists on practicum teams in our in house clinic for a minimum of three years under the direct supervision of the members of our clinical faculty, all of whom are licensed psychologists. After students have demonstrated a minimum level of competence in the clinic, they are allowed to apply for practicum positions at field placement agencies in the community where they are supervised by licensed practitioners who are employed by the field placement agency. In recent years, students have completed field placements at Community Mental Health Centers in Oxford and Tupelo; North Mississippi Regional Center in Oxford; North Mississippi Medical Center in Tupelo; Street Jude Children's Research Hospital in Memphis, and the DeSoto County (MS) School District. Students are assisted and advised by faculty in choosing field placements most appropriate to their individual career goals. For those doctoral students for whom a professional internship is required prior to graduation, 12 applied in 2003–2004. Of those who applied, 12 were placed in internships listed by the Association of Psychology Postdoctoral and Internship Programs (APPIC); 12 were placed in APA accredited internships.

Housing and Day Care: On-campus housing is available. See the following Web site for more information: housing@olemiss.edu. On-campus day care facilities are available. The Willie Price University Nursery School is housed on campus and serves children aged 3–5 years. More information may be found at www.outreach.olemiss.edu/willieprice/.

Employment of Department Graduates:
Master's Degree Graduates: Of those who graduated in the academic year 2003–2004, the following categories and numbers represent the post-graduate activities and employment of master's degree graduates: Enrolled in a post-doctoral residency/fellowship (n/a), employed in independent practice (n/a), total from the above (master's) (0).
Doctoral Degree Graduates: Of those who graduated in the academic year 2003–2004, the following categories and numbers represent the post-graduate activities and employment of doctoral degree graduates: Enrolled in a psychology doctoral program (n/a), enrolled in a post-doctoral residency/fellowship (6), employed in independent practice (1), employed in an academic position at a 2-year/4-year college (1), employed in other positions at a higher education institution (1), employed in a community mental health/counseling center (1), total from the above (doctoral) (10).

Additional Information:
Orientation, Objectives, and Emphasis of Department: The Department of Psychology offers programs of study in clinical and experimental psychology leading to the Doctor of Philosophy degree. The clinical program, which is fully accredited by the American Psychological Association, ordinarily requires five years beyond the bachelor's level to complete. Four of the five years are devoted to coursework and research, and the remaining year

entails a clinical internship at an APA-approved training site. Requirements for the master's degree are also fulfilled during this period; however, the MA is considered to be a step in the doctoral training. The clinical program adheres to the scientist-practitioner model and emphasizes an empirical approach to clinical practice. A social learning or behavioral approach characterizes the clinical training offered. The experimental program is designed to prepare psychologists for careers in teaching and research. Specific programs include Behavioral Neuroscience, Cognitive Psychology, and Social Psychology. Students entering the experimental program are assigned a faculty mentor (major professor) whose research interests match their training goals. All students are required to engage in significant research projects.

Special Facilities or Resources: Most of the department's offices and laboratories are housed in the George Peabody Building. State-of-the-art facilities for animal research are available in a new centralized animal facility on campus. The psychology clinic has recently moved to a new location on campus which provides for a more professional office environment and better client accessibility. The psychology clinic includes multipurpose rooms for evaluation, consultation, and therapy and observation rooms equipped with one-way mirrors and videotape equipment. The department offers computer-based laboratories for psychopharmacology, psychophysiology, operant conditioning, and behavioral toxicology. The department has close ties with the pharmacy and law schools (located on the Oxford campus) and with the medical school in Jackson.

Information for Students With Physical Disabilities: sds@olemiss.edu.

Application Information:
Send to: Admissions Chairperson for desired program. Application available online. URL of online application: https://secure.olemiss.edu/services/appl_index.html. Students are admitted in the Fall, application deadline January 15. *Fee:* $25. If an application is transmitted via an online application service, an additional charge may be required by the service.

Southern Mississippi, The University of
Department of Psychology
College of Education and Psychology
118 College Drive # 5025
Hattiesburg, MS 39401
Telephone: (601) 266-4177
Fax: (601) 266-5580
E-mail: *s.kuczaj@usm.edu*
Web: *http://www.usm.edu/psy/*

Department Information:
1960. Chairperson: Stan Kuczaj. Number of Faculty: total–full-time 31, part-time 4; women–full-time 11; minority–full-time 2, part-time 1.

Programs and Degrees Offered:
Listed in the following order: Program area, degree type (T if terminal Master's), number awarded 7/03–6/04. Counseling PhD (Doctor of Philosophy) 1, Clinical Psychology PhD (Doctor of

Philosophy) 5, Counseling MA/MS (Master of Arts/Science) (T) 13, Experimental PhD (Doctor of Philosophy) 1, School Psychology PhD (Doctor of Philosophy) 1.

APA Accreditation: Counseling PhD (Doctor of Philosophy). Clinical PhD (Doctor of Philosophy). School PhD (Doctor of Philosophy).

Student Applications/Admissions:

Student Applications

Counseling PhD (Doctor of Philosophy)—Applications 2004–2005, 44. Total applicants accepted 2004–2005, 7. Number enrolled (new admits only) 2004–2005 full-time, 7. Number enrolled (new admits only) 2004–2005 part-time, 0. Openings 2005–2006, 6. The Median number of years required for completion of a degree are 5. The number of students enrolled full and part-time who were dismissed or voluntarily withdrew from this program area were 3. *Clinical Psychology PhD (Doctor of Philosophy)*—Applications 2004–2005, 78. Total applicants accepted 2004–2005, 9. Number enrolled (new admits only) 2004–2005 full-time, 9. Number enrolled (new admits only) 2004–2005 part-time, 0. Openings 2005–2006, 8. The Median number of years required for completion of a degree are 5. The number of students enrolled full and part-time who were dismissed or voluntarily withdrew from this program area were 0. *Counseling MA/MS (Master of Arts/Science)*—Applications 2004–2005, 70. Total applicants accepted 2004–2005, 18. Number enrolled (new admits only) 2004–2005 full-time, 17. Number enrolled (new admits only) 2004–2005 part-time, 0. Openings 2005–2006, 15. The Median number of years required for completion of a degree are 2. The number of students enrolled full and part-time who were dismissed or voluntarily withdrew from this program area were 2. *Experimental PhD (Doctor of Philosophy)*—Applications 2004–2005, 15. Total applicants accepted 2004–2005, 7. Number enrolled (new admits only) 2004–2005 full-time, 4. Number enrolled (new admits only) 2004–2005 part-time, 0. Openings 2005–2006, 5. The Median number of years required for completion of a degree are 5. The number of students enrolled full and part-time who were dismissed or voluntarily withdrew from this program area were 2. *School Psychology PhD (Doctor of Philosophy)*—Applications 2004–2005, 22. Total applicants accepted 2004–2005, 14. Number enrolled (new admits only) 2004–2005 full-time, 7. Number enrolled (new admits only) 2004–2005 part-time, 0. Openings 2005–2006, 8. The Median number of years required for completion of a degree are 10. The number of students enrolled full and part-time who were dismissed or voluntarily withdrew from this program area were 2.

Admissions Requirements:

Scores: Entries appear in this order: required test or GPA, minimum score (if required), median score of students entering in 2003–2004. Master's Programs: GRE-V no minimum stated, 510; GRE-Q no minimum stated, 570; GRE-V+Q no minimum stated, 1070. Doctoral Programs: GRE-V no minimum stated, 510; GRE-Q no minimum stated, 600; GRE-V+Q no minimum stated, 1120; overall undergraduate GPA no minimum stated, 3.55. Check with program directors.

Other Criteria: (importance of criteria rated low, medium, or high): GRE/MAT scores high, research experience high, work experience medium, extracurricular activity low, clinically related public service low, GPA high, letters of recommendation high, interview high, statement of goals and objectives high. Criteria vary by program. Check with program directors.

Student Characteristics: The following represents characteristics of students in 2004–2005 in all graduate psychology programs in the department: Female–full-time 102, part-time 0; Male–full-time 35, part-time 0; African American/Black–full-time 4, part-time 0; Hispanic/Latino(a)–full-time 0, part-time 0; Asian/Pacific Islander–full-time 1, part-time 0; American Indian/Alaska Native–full-time 0, part-time 0; Caucasian–full-time 130, part-time 0; Multi-ethnic–full-time 2, part-time 0; students subject to the Americans With Disabilities Act–full-time 1, part-time 0.

Financial Information/Assistance:

Tuition for Full-Time Study: *Master's:* State residents: per academic year $3,874; Nonstate residents: per academic year $8,752. *Doctoral:* State residents: per academic year $3,874; Nonstate residents: per academic year $8,752. Tuition is subject to change. See the following Web site for updates and changes in tuition costs: http://www.usm.edu/admissions/cost/.

Financial Assistance:

First Year Students: Research assistantships available for first-year. Average amount paid per academic year: $4,590. Average number of hours worked per week: 20. Apply by January 15. Tuition remission given: full.

Advanced Students: Teaching assistantships available for advanced students. Average amount paid per academic year: $5,270. Average number of hours worked per week: 20. Apply by January 15. Tuition remission given: full. Research assistantships available for advanced students. Average amount paid per academic year: $5,270. Average number of hours worked per week: 20. Apply by January 15. Tuition remission given: full.

Contact Information: Of all students currently enrolled full-time, 99% benefitted from one or more of the listed financial assistance programs. Application and information available online at: http://www.usm.edu/financialaid/.

Internships/Practica: Doctoral students from our three APA-approved programs (Clinical, Counseling, and School) begin practicum experiences in the on-campus clinics and progress to community externship placements, as they gain experience and training. A student's final year is a full-time internship in an APA-accredited internship. Students have been placed throughout the United States, with the majority in health service settings, such as Veterans Administration Medical Centers, medical schools, and comprehensive community mental health centers. For those doctoral students for whom a professional internship is required prior to graduation, 13 applied in 2003–2004. Of those who applied, 13 were placed in internships listed by the Association of Psychology Postdoctoral and Internship Programs (APPIC); 13 were placed in APA accredited internships.

Housing and Day Care: On-campus housing is available. See the following Web site for more information: www.usm.edu/pinehaven. On-campus day care facilities are available. See the following Web site for more information: http://www.usm.edu/childandfamilystudies/main_ccdev.htm.

Employment of Department Graduates:

Master's Degree Graduates: Of those who graduated in the academic year 2003–2004, the following categories and numbers

represent the post-graduate activities and employment of master's degree graduates: Enrolled in a psychology doctoral program (0), enrolled in another graduate/professional program (0), enrolled in a post-doctoral residency/fellowship (n/a), employed in independent practice (n/a), employed in a government agency (professional services) (0), employed in a community mental health/counseling center (13), total from the above (master's) (13).

Doctoral Degree Graduates: Of those who graduated in the academic year 2003–2004, the following categories and numbers represent the post-graduate activities and employment of doctoral degree graduates: Enrolled in a psychology doctoral program (n/a), enrolled in another graduate/professional program (0), enrolled in a post-doctoral residency/fellowship (1), employed in independent practice (0), employed in an academic position at a university (2), employed in an academic position at a 2-year/4-year college (0), employed in other positions at a higher education institution (0), employed in a professional position in a school system (0), employed in business or industry (research/consulting) (0), employed in business or industry (management) (0), employed in a government agency (research) (0), employed in a government agency (professional services) (1), employed in a community mental health/counseling center (0), employed in a hospital/medical center (1), still seeking employment (0), not seeking employment (0), other employment position (0), do not know (2), total from the above (doctoral) (7).

Additional Information:

Orientation, Objectives, and Emphasis of Department: The department has four psychology doctoral programs (Clinical, Counseling, Experimental, and School), each with different emphases and orientations. Specific information about each program can be obtained from our Web site (http://www.usm.edu/psy). The departmental philosophy is built on the assumption that psychology is first and foremost a scientific discipline. Therefore, a common element of all the programs is a commitment to science and research, with exposure to the breadth and depth of the field of psychology. Students are challenged to develop critical thinking skills, and are taught to respect discovery and inquiry. The applied programs espouse the scientist-practitioner model of training and emphasize training in research as well as delivery of psychological services. The department offers opportunities for research and clinical training in several subareas, such as child clinical, multicultural issues, and child/family interventions.

Special Facilities or Resources: The department houses three psychology service training clinics. Research laboratories provide training in various areas such as sleep, behavioral neuroscience, and personality and experimental psychopathology. Off-campus facilities provide opportunities for research with marine mammals. Opportunities for research are also available at community facilities such as local hospitals and schools.

Information for Students With Physical Disabilities: See the following Web site for more information: http://www.usm.edu/ids/.

Application Information:

Send to: Admissions Coordinator; specify program. Students are admitted in the Fall, application deadline February 15. Counseling MS application deadline—March 1. *Fee:* $25. Legal residents of Mississippi are exempt from the application fee.

Avila University
School of Psychology
11901 Wornall Road
Kansas City, MO 64145-1698
Telephone: (816) 501-3665
Fax: (816) 501-2455
E-mail: *gradpsych@mail.avila.edu*
Web: *www.avila.edu/gradpsych*

Department Information:
1977. Dean of the School of Psychology: Maria Hunt, PhD Number of Faculty: total–full-time 4, part-time 22; women–full-time 3, part-time 17; minority–part-time 3.

Programs and Degrees Offered:
Listed in the following order: Program area, degree type (T if terminal Master's), number awarded 7/03–6/04. Counseling Psychology MA/MS (Master of Arts/Science) (T) 14, General Psychology MA/MS (Master of Arts/Science) (T), Organizational Development Psychology MA/MS (Master of Arts/Science) (T).

Student Applications/Admissions:
Student Applications
Counseling Psychology MA/MS (Master of Arts/Science)—Applications 2004–2005, 104. Total applicants accepted 2004–2005, 85. Total enrolled 2004–2005 full-time, 85, part-time, 20. Openings 2005–2006, 30. The Median number of years required for completion of a degree are 3. The number of students enrolled full and part-time who were dismissed or voluntarily withdrew from this program area were 5. *General Psychology MA/MS (Master of Arts/Science)*—Openings 2005–2006, 10. *Organizational Development Psychology MA/MS (Master of Arts/Science)*—Applications 2004–2005, 14. Total applicants accepted 2004–2005, 14. Number enrolled (new admits only) 2004–2005 full-time, 14. Total enrolled 2004–2005 full-time, 14. Openings 2005–2006, 15.

Admissions Requirements:
Scores: Entries appear in this order: required test or GPA, minimum score (if required), median score of students entering in 2003–2004. Master's Programs: GRE-V 450, 500; GRE-Q 425, 465; GRE-Analytical 3.5, 4.0; last 2 years GPA 3.0, 3.25. General Psychology requires a GPA of 3.25. Organizational Development Psychology also requires a 3.25 GPA but does not require the Graduate Record Examination (GRE)
Other Criteria: (importance of criteria rated low, medium, or high): GRE/MAT scores high, research experience low, work experience medium, extracurricular activity medium, clinically related public service medium, GPA high, letters of recommendation high, statement of goals and objectives high.

Student Characteristics: The following represents characteristics of students in 2004–2005 in all graduate psychology programs in the department: Female–full-time 79, part-time 15; Male–full-time 6, part-time 5; African American/Black–full-time 11, part-time 0; Hispanic/Latino(a)–full-time 2, part-time 0; Asian/Pacific Islander–full-time 3, part-time 0; American Indian/Alaska Native–full-time 0, part-time 0; Caucasian–full-time 69, part-time 17; students subject to the Americans With Disabilities Act–full-time 1, part-time 1.

Financial Information/Assistance:
Tuition for Full-Time Study: *Master's:* State residents: $395 per credit hour; Nonstate residents: $395 per credit hour. Tuition is subject to change. See the following Web site for updates and changes in tuition costs: http://www.avila.edu/gradpsych.

Financial Assistance:
First Year Students: Fellowships and scholarships available for first-year. Average amount paid per academic year: $500. Apply by July 2.

Advanced Students: Teaching assistantships available for advanced students. Average number of hours worked per week: 20. Apply by April 1. Tuition remission given: partial.

Contact Information: Of all students currently enrolled full-time, 5% benefitted from one or more of the listed financial assistance programs. Application and information available online at: http://www.avila.edu/gradpsych.

Internships/Practica: There is a 750 contact hour internship (6 credit hours) at a site chosen by the student. There are a wide variety of internship sites—mental health agencies, psychiatric hospitals, and residential treatment programs, for example. Some students choose to work with specific populations, such as children and adolescents, the chronically mentally ill, and those in substance abuse treatment, to name a few. All interns have an approved on-site supervisor and also meet once a week with the faculty internship advisor.

Housing and Day Care: On-campus housing is available. See the following Web site for more information: http://www.avila.edu. On-campus day care facilities are available. Carol Frevert (816) 501-3668.

Employment of Department Graduates:
Master's Degree Graduates: Of those who graduated in the academic year 2003–2004, the following categories and numbers represent the post-graduate activities and employment of master's degree graduates: Enrolled in a psychology doctoral program (1), enrolled in another graduate/professional program (1), enrolled in a post-doctoral residency/fellowship (n/a), employed in independent practice (n/a), employed in an academic position at a university (1), employed in an academic position at a 2-year/4-year college (1), employed in other positions at a higher education institution (1), employed in a professional position in a school system (2), employed in business or industry (research/consulting) (0), employed in business or industry (management) (0), employed in a government agency (research) (0), employed in a government agency (professional services) (0), employed in a community mental health/counseling center (3), employed in a hospital/medical center (0), still seeking employment (0), other employment position (0), do not know (1), total from the above (master's) (11).

Doctoral Degree Graduates: Of those who graduated in the academic year 2003–2004, the following categories and numbers represent the post-graduate activities and employment of doctoral degree graduates: Enrolled in a psychology doctoral program (n/a), total from the above (doctoral) (0).

Additional Information:

Orientation, Objectives, and Emphasis of Department: The Master of Science in Psychology degree programs at Avila University are part of a values-based community of learning which respects the worth and dignity of all persons. Within this context, we are committed to the scientist-practitioner model. Each program's curriculum is designed around a set of educational outcomes that specifies the knowledge and skills students are expected to demonstrate upon graduation. The Master of Science in Counseling Psychology (MSCP) is a 60-credit degree program intended to train master's-level counseling psychologists for the delivery of mental health services in a variety of settings, such as mental health clinics, counseling centers, and human service agencies. The MSCP program meets the Missouri state educational requirements for licensure as a Licensed Professional Counselor (LPC) and the Kansas state educational requirements for licensure as a Licensed Master's-level Psychologist (LMLP). The 36-credit Master of Science in General Psychology (MSGP) degree offers students an in-depth survey of the diverse research, theory and practices of psychology's many sub-disciplines. It is designed for students interested in discovering and studying non-clinical applications in the field and/or who want greater preparation for doctoral programs. The Master of Science in Organizational Development Psychology (MSOD) degree is a 37-credit degree designed to provide students with practical, empirically tested principles, tools, and methodologies associated with effective change management. The school is a member of the Council of Applied Master's Programs in Psychology (CAMPP), the Council of Graduate Departments of Psychology (COGDOP), the Organizational Development Network, and is accredited by the Masters in Psychology Accreditation Council (MPAC).

Application Information:

Send to: Cyndi Lestyk, Administrative Director of Graduate Psychology, Avila University, 11901 Wornall Road, Kansas City, MO 64145. Application available online. URL of online application: www.avila.edu/gradpsych. Students are admitted in the Fall, application deadline August 1; Spring, application deadline December 31; Summer, application deadline May 1; Programs have rolling admissions. *Fee:* $0. no application fee.

Forest Institute of Professional Psychology (2004 data)

Programs in Clinical Psychology
2885 W. Battlefield Road
Springfield, MO 65807
Telephone: (417) 823-3477
Fax: (417) 823-3442
E-mail: *praleigh@forest.edu*
Web: *http://www.forest.edu*

Department Information:

1979. President: Mark E. Skrade, PsyD Number of Faculty: total–full-time 16, part-time 11; women–full-time 9, part-time 6; minor-

ity–full-time 3; faculty subject to the Americans With Disabilities Act 2.

Programs and Degrees Offered:

Listed in the following order: Program area, degree type (T if terminal Master's), number awarded 7/03–6/04. Clinical Psychology MA/MS (Master of Arts/Science) (T) 38, Clinical Psychology PsyD (Doctor of Psychology) 70.

APA Accreditation: Clinical PsyD (Doctor of Psychology).

Student Applications/Admissions:

Student Applications

Clinical Psychology MA/MS (Master of Arts/Science)—Applications 2004–2005, 8. Total applicants accepted 2004–2005, 5. Total enrolled 2004–2005 full-time, 1, part-time, 1. Openings 2005–2006, 10. The Median number of years required for completion of a degree are 2. The number of students enrolled full and part-time who were dismissed or voluntarily withdrew from this program area were 0. *Clinical Psychology PsyD (Doctor of Psychology)*—Applications 2004–2005, 130. Total applicants accepted 2004–2005, 50. Total enrolled 2004–2005 full-time, 210, part-time, 13. Openings 2005–2006, 75. The Median number of years required for completion of a degree are 4. The number of students enrolled full and part-time who were dismissed or voluntarily withdrew from this program area were 2.

Admissions Requirements:

Scores: Entries appear in this order: required test or GPA, minimum score (if required), median score of students entering in 2003–2004. Master's Programs: overall undergraduate GPA 3.0; last 2 years GPA 3.0; psychology GPA 3.0. Doctoral Programs: overall undergraduate GPA 3.00; last 2 years GPA 3.00; psychology GPA 3.00.

Other Criteria: (importance of criteria rated low, medium, or high): GRE/MAT scores medium, research experience medium, work experience medium, clinically related public service medium, GPA high, letters of recommendation high, interview high, statement of goals and objectives high.

Student Characteristics: The following represents characteristics of students in 2004–2005 in all graduate psychology programs in the department: Female–full-time 136, part-time 9; Male–full-time 75, part-time 7; African American/Black–full-time 16, part-time 0; Hispanic/Latino(a)–full-time 3, part-time 0; Asian/Pacific Islander–full-time 8, part-time 0; American Indian/Alaska Native–full-time 3, part-time 0; Caucasian–full-time 0, part-time 0; Multi-ethnic–full-time 4, part-time 0; students subject to the Americans With Disabilities Act–full-time 12, part-time 0.

Financial Information/Assistance:

Tuition for Full-Time Study: *Master's:* State residents: $436 per credit hour; Nonstate residents: $436 per credit hour. *Doctoral:* State residents: $436 per credit hour; Nonstate residents: $436 per credit hour. Tuition is subject to change. See the following Web site for updates and changes in tuition costs: http://www.forest.edu.

Financial Assistance:

First Year Students: Fellowships and scholarships available for first-year. Apply by May 9. Tuition remission given: full and partial.

Advanced Students: Teaching assistantships available for advanced students. Tuition remission given: partial.

Contact Information: No information provided.

Internships/Practica: Forest Institute of Professional Psychology enjoys a close relationship with the major state and city mental health facilities in the metropolitan and rural areas. Currently, there are 55 practica experiences available to students. These opportunities provide a vast array of clinical experiences for a total of 1,200 practicum hours accumulated by the end of your required coursework. During the fourth year of study, all students are required to complete a 2000 hour internship. Forest Institute has several on-site internship opportunities ranging in a number of clinical experiences. For those doctoral students for whom a professional internship is required prior to graduation, 71 applied in 2003–2004. Of those who applied, 44 were placed in internships listed by the Association of Psychology Postdoctoral and Internship Programs (APPIC); 22 were placed in APA accredited internships.

Housing and Day Care: On-campus housing is available. One and two-bedroom apartments are available. No on-campus day care facilities are available.

Employment of Department Graduates:

Master's Degree Graduates: Of those who graduated in the academic year 2003–2004, the following categories and numbers represent the post-graduate activities and employment of master's degree graduates: Enrolled in a post-doctoral residency/fellowship (n/a), employed in independent practice (n/a), total from the above (master's) (0).

Doctoral Degree Graduates: Of those who graduated in the academic year 2003–2004, the following categories and numbers represent the post-graduate activities and employment of doctoral degree graduates: Enrolled in a psychology doctoral program (n/a), enrolled in a post-doctoral residency/fellowship (70), total from the above (doctoral) (70).

Additional Information:

Orientation, Objectives, and Emphasis of Department: The design of the clinical psychology PsyD program is based on the belief that a thorough understanding of the comprehensive body of psychological knowledge, skills, and attitudes is essential for professional practitioners. The acquisition of this broad-based understanding and these abilities requires that the curriculum cover a combination of didactic knowledge, skill training, and supervised clinical experience with faculty and supervisors who provide appropriate role models. The PsyD degree is designed for individuals seeking an educational and training program geared toward professional application. Students are prepared to offer professional services in diagnostic, therapeutic, consultative, and administrative settings. Research and investigation skills are complemented by an increased focus on the use of research findings and theoretical formulations. The field practicum and internship are supervised clinical experiences that are integrated with the academic coursework. The faculty represents a variety of theoretical orientations and is committed to the rigorous preparation of students to become competent providers of service as well as ethical contributing members of the professional community. The MA in psychology program is intended to provide a comprehensive exposure to the scientific foundations of psychology, including theories, concepts, and empirical knowledge of human development and

behavior. The master's program is valuable to those who wish to increase their understanding of human behavior. These would include teachers, clergy, and training and personnel officers. The program also provides a solid foundation for eventual pursuit of a doctoral program. The MA program provides the necessary coursework to obtain a counseling licensure at the master's level in most, if not all states.

Special Facilities or Resources: Forest Institute is located in the heart of the Ozarks. The academic/administrative center sits on 58 acres of land and provides students with a modern facility and state of the art equipment. Forest has both an on-site outpatient community mental health clinic and a rehabilitation-health psychology-neuropsychology clinic. Practicum involves a high degree of community services and resources. Students provide services in the rural Ozarks, are actively involved with the homeless organizations of the Ozarks, correctional facilities, and many other community based opportunities.

Information for Students With Physical Disabilities: equalopportuniticsofficcr@forest.edu.

Application Information:
Send to: Forest Institute of Professional Psychology, Office of Admissions, 2885 W. Battlefield Road, Springfield, MO 65807. Students are admitted in the Fall. Applications for admission are accepted on a rolling basis. *Fee:* $50.

Missouri, University of, Columbia
Department of Educational, School, and Counseling
   Psychology
College of Education
16 Hill Hall
Columbia, MO 65211
Telephone: (573) 882-7731
Fax: (573) 884-5989
E-mail: ecpgrad@coe.missouri.edu
Web: http://escp.coe.missouri.edu

Department Information:
1953. Chairperson: Richard H. Cox. Number of Faculty: total–full-time 22; women–full-time 6; minority–full-time 5; faculty subject to the Americans With Disabilities Act 2.

Programs and Degrees Offered:
Listed in the following order: Program area, degree type (T if terminal Master's), number awarded 7/03–6/04. Counseling Psychology MA/MS (Master of Arts/Science) (T) 30, Educational Psychology MA/MS (Master of Arts/Science) (T) 1, School Psychology MA/MS (Master of Arts/Science) 3, Counseling Psychology EdS (Education Specialist) 1, Counseling Psychology PhD (Doctor of Philosophy) 14, Educational Specialist EdS (Education Specialist) 0, Educational Psychology PhD (Doctor of Philosophy) 1, School Psychology EdS (Education Specialist) 0, School Psychology PhD (Doctor of Philosophy) 2.

APA Accreditation: Counseling PhD (Doctor of Philosophy). School PhD (Doctor of Philosophy).

Student Applications/Admissions:

Student Applications

Counseling Psychology MA/MS (Master of Arts/Science)—Applications 2004–2005, 98. Total applicants accepted 2004–2005, 26. Number enrolled (new admits only) 2004–2005 full-time, 24. Number enrolled (new admits only) 2004–2005 part-time, 0. Openings 2005–2006, 28. The Median number of years required for completion of a degree are 2. The number of students enrolled full and part-time who were dismissed or voluntarily withdrew from this program area were 2. *Educational Psychology MA/MS (Master of Arts/Science)*—Applications 2004–2005, 1. Total applicants accepted 2004–2005, 1. Number enrolled (new admits only) 2004–2005 full-time, 1. Number enrolled (new admits only) 2004–2005 part-time, 0. Openings 2005–2006, 3. The Median number of years required for completion of a degree are 2. The number of students enrolled full and part-time who were dismissed or voluntarily withdrew from this program area were 1. *School Psychology MA/MS (Master of Arts/Science)*—Applications 2004–2005, 0. Total applicants accepted 2004–2005, 0. Number enrolled (new admits only) 2004–2005 full-time, 0. Number enrolled (new admits only) 2004–2005 part-time, 0. The Median number of years required for completion of a degree are 3. The number of students enrolled full and part-time who were dismissed or voluntarily withdrew from this program area were 0. *Counseling Psychology EdS (Education Specialist)*—Applications 2004–2005, 1. Total applicants accepted 2004–2005, 1. Number enrolled (new admits only) 2004–2005 full-time, 1. Number enrolled (new admits only) 2004–2005 part-time, 0. Total enrolled 2004–2005 full-time, 1, part-time, 1. Openings 2005–2006, 1. The Median number of years required for completion of a degree are 2. The number of students enrolled full and part-time who were dismissed or voluntarily withdrew from this program area were 0. *Counseling Psychology PhD (Doctor of Philosophy)*—Applications 2004–2005, 113. Total applicants accepted 2004–2005, 8. Number enrolled (new admits only) 2004–2005 full-time, 8. Number enrolled (new admits only) 2004–2005 part-time, 0. Openings 2005–2006, 8. The Median number of years required for completion of a degree are 7. The number of students enrolled full and part-time who were dismissed or voluntarily withdrew from this program area were 0. *Educational Psychology EdS (Education Specialist)*—Applications 2004–2005, 1. Total applicants accepted 2004–2005, 1. Number enrolled (new admits only) 2004–2005 full-time, 1. Number enrolled (new admits only) 2004–2005 part-time, 0. The number of students enrolled full and part-time who were dismissed or voluntarily withdrew from this program area were 0. *Educational Psychology PhD (Doctor of Philosophy)*—Applications 2004–2005, 12. Total applicants accepted 2004–2005, 4. Number enrolled (new admits only) 2004–2005 full-time, 2. Number enrolled (new admits only) 2004–2005 part-time, 0. Openings 2005–2006, 3. The Median number of years required for completion of a degree are 3. The number of students enrolled full and part-time who were dismissed or voluntarily withdrew from this program area were 0. *School Psychology EdS (Education Specialist)*—Applications 2004–2005, 11. Total applicants accepted 2004–2005, 7. Number enrolled (new admits only) 2004–2005 full-time, 5. Number enrolled (new admits only) 2004–2005 part-time, 0. Openings 2005–2006, 5. The number of students enrolled full and part-time who were dismissed or voluntarily withdrew from this program area were 1. *School Psychology PhD (Doctor of Philosophy)*—Applica-

tions 2004–2005, 7. Total applicants accepted 2004–2005, 4. Number enrolled (new admits only) 2004–2005 full-time, 3. Number enrolled (new admits only) 2004–2005 part-time, 0. Openings 2005–2006, 6. The Median number of years required for completion of a degree are 6. The number of students enrolled full and part-time who were dismissed or voluntarily withdrew from this program area were 0.

Admissions Requirements:

Scores: Entries appear in this order: required test or GPA, minimum score (if required), median score of students entering in 2003–2004. Master's Programs: GRE-V no minimum stated, 508; GRE-Q no minimum stated, 556; GRE-V+Q no minimum stated; GRE-Analytical no minimum stated, 595; overall undergraduate GPA 3.00; last 2 years GPA 3.00. MAT not accepted for admission. Doctoral Programs: GRE-V no minimum stated, 549; GRE-Q no minimum stated, 616; GRE-V+Q no minimum stated; GRE-Analytical no minimum stated, 632; overall undergraduate GPA 3.00; last 2 years GPA 3.00. MAT not accepted for admission.

Other Criteria: (importance of criteria rated low, medium, or high): GRE/MAT scores high, research experience high, work experience medium, extracurricular activity medium, clinically related public service medium, GPA high, letters of recommendation high, interview low, statement of goals and objectives high.

Student Characteristics: The following represents characteristics of students in 2004–2005 in all graduate psychology programs in the department: Female–full-time 123, part-time 1; Male–full-time 47, part-time 0; African American/Black–full-time 20, part-time 0; Hispanic/Latino(a)–full-time 10, part-time 0; Asian/Pacific Islander–full-time 5, part-time 0; American Indian/Alaska Native–full-time 1, part-time 0; Caucasian–full-time 115, part-time 1; students subject to the Americans With Disabilities Act–full-time 10, part-time 0.

Financial Information/Assistance:

Tuition for Full-Time Study: *Master's:* State residents: $254 per credit hour; Nonstate residents: $656 per credit hour. *Doctoral:* State residents: $254 per credit hour; Nonstate residents: $656 per credit hour. Tuition is subject to change. See the following Web site for updates and changes in tuition costs: http://web.missouri.edu/~gradschl/.

Financial Assistance:

First Year Students: Teaching assistantships available for first-year. Average amount paid per academic year: $4,500. Average number of hours worked per week: 10. Apply by December 1. Tuition remission given: full. Research assistantships available for first-year. Average amount paid per academic year: $4,500. Average number of hours worked per week: 10. Apply by December 1. Tuition remission given: partial. Fellowships and scholarships available for first-year. Average amount paid per academic year: $8,000. Apply by February 11. Tuition remission given: full.

Advanced Students: Teaching assistantships available for advanced students. Average amount paid per academic year: $4,500. Average number of hours worked per week: 10. Apply by April 1. Tuition remission given: full. Research assistantships available for advanced students. Tuition remission given: partial. Fellowships and scholarships available for advanced students. Tuition remission given: partial.

Contact Information: Of all students currently enrolled full-time, 70% benefitted from one or more of the listed financial assistance programs. Application and information available online at: https://sfa.missouri.edu/.

Internships/Practica: Internships are available in counseling psychology: VA hospitals, rehabilitation centers, mental health centers, university student counseling services; in school psychology: public schools, schools of medicine; in school counseling: public schools; in rehabilitation counseling: rehabilitation centers, mental health centers, and drug and alcohol centers. For those doctoral students for whom a professional internship is required prior to graduation, 10 applied in 2003–2004. Of those who applied, 8 were placed in internships listed by the Association of Psychology Postdoctoral and Internship Programs (APPIC); 8 were placed in APA accredited internships.

Housing and Day Care: On-campus housing is available. See the following Web site for more information: http://web.missouri.edu/~gradschl/studentlife/life.htm. No on-campus day care facilities are available.

Employment of Department Graduates:

Master's Degree Graduates: Of those who graduated in the academic year 2003–2004, the following categories and numbers represent the post-graduate activities and employment of master's degree graduates: Enrolled in a psychology doctoral program (11), enrolled in another graduate/professional program (1), enrolled in a post-doctoral residency/fellowship (n/a), employed in independent practice (n/a), employed in other positions at a higher education institution (1), employed in a community mental health/counseling center (1), employed in a hospital/medical center (1), other employment position (2), do not know (17), total from the above (master's) (34).

Doctoral Degree Graduates: Of those who graduated in the academic year 2003–2004, the following categories and numbers represent the post-graduate activities and employment of doctoral degree graduates: Enrolled in a psychology doctoral program (n/a), enrolled in a post-doctoral residency/fellowship (1), employed in an academic position at a university (1), employed in other positions at a higher education institution (4), employed in business or industry (management) (1), employed in a government agency (professional services) (1), employed in a hospital/medical center (1), do not know (8), total from the above (doctoral) (17).

Additional Information:

Orientation, Objectives, and Emphasis of Department: The goals of the department include the preparation of students in the professional specialties of counseling, school and educational psychology, rehabilitation counseling, school counseling and student personnel work, and the conduct of research on the applications of psychological knowledge to counseling and educational settings. The department emphasizes general psychological foundations, assessment, career development, counselor training and supervision, group processes, and research on counseling processes and psychological measurement and assessment. The theoretical orientation of the faculty is eclectic.

Special Facilities or Resources: Individual and group counseling and psychological assessment training facilities are available in the department, the College of Education and the department's assessment and consultation clinic, and on campus in the Student Counseling Services. Supervised training opportunities also occur in the Career Planning and Placement Center and with the Vocational Assessment Program. A well-stocked library of references in the specialty areas is located in the department. Access to computer services is available across the campus.

Information for Students With Physical Disabilities: See the following Web site for more information: www.missouri.edu/services.htm#disability.

Application Information:
Send to: Graduate Secretary, 16 Hill Hall, University of Missouri—Columbia, Educational, School, and Counseling Psychology, Columbia, MO 65211. Application available online. URL of online application: http://escp.coe.missouri.edu. Students are admitted in the Fall, application deadline December 1. *Fee:* $45. International applicants pay a $60 admissions fee. Fee is sent directly to the International Admissions Office, 210 Jesse Hall.

Missouri, University of, Columbia
Department of Psychological Sciences
210 McAlester Hall
Columbia, MO 65211
Telephone: (573) 882-0838
Fax: (573) 882-7710
E-mail: *garibaymendozabj@missouri.edu*
Web: *http://www.missouri.edu/~psywww*

Department Information:
1900. Chairperson: Ann Bettencourt. Number of Faculty: total–full-time 42, part-time 6; women–full-time 14, part-time 5; minority–full-time 2, part-time 1.

Programs and Degrees Offered:
Listed in the following order: Program area, degree type (T if terminal Master's), number awarded 7/03–6/04. Clinical PhD (Doctor of Philosophy) 10, Cognition and Neuroscience PhD (Doctor of Philosophy) 3, Social PhD (Doctor of Philosophy) 3, Quantitative PhD (Doctor of Philosophy) 0, Developmental PhD (Doctor of Philosophy) 1, Joint Developmental/ Child Clinical PhD (Doctor of Philosophy) 0.

APA Accreditation: Clinical PhD (Doctor of Philosophy).

Student Applications/Admissions:
Student Applications
Clinical PhD (Doctor of Philosophy)—Applications 2004–2005, 96. Total applicants accepted 2004–2005, 7. Number enrolled (new admits only) 2004–2005 full-time, 7. Number enrolled (new admits only) 2004–2005 part-time, 0. Openings 2005–2006, 8. The Median number of years required for completion of a degree are 5. The number of students enrolled full and part-time who were dismissed or voluntarily withdrew from this program area were 0. *Cognition and Neuroscience PhD (Doctor of Philosophy)*—Applications 2004–2005, 229. Total applicants accepted 2004–2005, 5. Number enrolled (new admits only) 2004–2005 full-time, 4. Openings 2005–2006, 5. The Median number of years required for completion of a

degree are 5. The number of students enrolled full and part-time who were dismissed or voluntarily withdrew from this program area were 1. *Social PhD (Doctor of Philosophy)*—Applications 2004–2005, 40. Total applicants accepted 2004–2005, 5. Number enrolled (new admits only) 2004–2005 full-time, 4. Number enrolled (new admits only) 2004–2005 part-time, 0. Openings 2005–2006, 4. The Median number of years required for completion of a degree are 5. The number of students enrolled full and part-time who were dismissed or voluntarily withdrew from this program area were 0. *Quantitative PhD (Doctor of Philosophy)*—Applications 2004–2005, 10. Total applicants accepted 2004–2005, 4. Number enrolled (new admits only) 2004–2005 full-time, 1. Number enrolled (new admits only) 2004–2005 part-time, 0. Openings 2005–2006, 3. The number of students enrolled full and part-time who were dismissed or voluntarily withdrew from this program area were 0. *Developmental PhD (Doctor of Philosophy)*—Applications 2004–2005, 14. Total applicants accepted 2004–2005, 2. Number enrolled (new admits only) 2004–2005 full-time, 1. Total enrolled 2004–2005 full-time, 7. Openings 2005–2006, 2. The Median number of years required for completion of a degree are 5. The number of students enrolled full and part-time who were dismissed or voluntarily withdrew from this program area were 0. *Joint Developmental/ Child Clinical PhD (Doctor of Philosophy)*—Applications 2004–2005, 24. Total applicants accepted 2004–2005, 2. Number enrolled (new admits only) 2004–2005 full-time, 1. Total enrolled 2004–2005 full-time, 3. Openings 2005–2006, 2. The number of students enrolled full and part-time who were dismissed or voluntarily withdrew from this program area were 0.

Admissions Requirements:

Scores: Entries appear in this order: required test or GPA, minimum score (if required), median score of students entering in 2003–2004. Doctoral Programs: GRE-V no minimum stated, 630; GRE-Q no minimum stated, 700; GRE-V+Q 1000, 1330; GRE-Analytical no minimum stated, 720; overall undergraduate GPA 3.0, 3.65; last 2 years GPA no minimum stated, 3.78; psychology GPA no minimum stated, 3.91.

Other Criteria: (importance of criteria rated low, medium, or high): GRE/MAT scores high, research experience high, work experience low, extracurricular activity low, clinically related public service low, GPA high, letters of recommendation high, statement of goals and objectives medium. The clinical program requires an interview.

Student Characteristics: The following represents characteristics of students in 2004–2005 in all graduate psychology programs in the department: Female–full-time 54, part-time 0; Male–full-time 22, part-time 0; African American/Black–full-time 2, part-time 0; Hispanic/Latino(a)–full-time 5, part-time 0; Asian/Pacific Islander–full-time 5, part-time 0; American Indian/Alaska Native–full-time 1, part-time 0; Caucasian–full-time 63, part-time 0; Multi-ethnic–full-time 0, part-time 0; students subject to the Americans With Disabilities Act–full-time 0, part-time 0.

Financial Information/Assistance:

Tuition for Full-Time Study: *Doctoral:* State residents: $282 per credit hour; Nonstate residents: $698 per credit hour. Tuition is subject to change.

Financial Assistance:

First Year Students: Teaching assistantships available for first-year. Average amount paid per academic year: $11,236. Average number of hours worked per week: 20. Tuition remission given: full. Research assistantships available for first-year. Average amount paid per academic year: $11,236. Average number of hours worked per week: 20. Tuition remission given: full. Fellowships and scholarships available for first-year. Average amount paid per academic year: $13,500. Average number of hours worked per week: 20. Tuition remission given: full.

Advanced Students: Teaching assistantships available for advanced students. Average amount paid per academic year: $11,965. Average number of hours worked per week: 20. Tuition remission given: full. Research assistantships available for advanced students. Average amount paid per academic year: $11,965. Average number of hours worked per week: 20. Tuition remission given: full. Traineeships available for advanced students. Average amount paid per academic year: $11,965. Average number of hours worked per week: 20. Tuition remission given: partial. Fellowships and scholarships available for advanced students. Average amount paid per academic year: $13,500. Average number of hours worked per week: 20. Tuition remission given: full.

Contact Information: Of all students currently enrolled full-time, 100% benefitted from one or more of the listed financial assistance programs.

Internships/Practica: In clinical psychology, an APA-approved internship is required for the PhD degree. For those doctoral students for whom a professional internship is required prior to graduation, 5 applied in 2003–2004. Of those who applied, 5 were placed in APA accredited internships.

Housing and Day Care: On-campus housing is available. See the following Web site for more information: http://admissions. missouri.edu/campus_life/residential_life/. On-campus day care facilities are available. See the following Web site for more information: http://cdl.missouri.edu.

Employment of Department Graduates:

Master's Degree Graduates: Of those who graduated in the academic year 2003–2004, the following categories and numbers represent the post-graduate activities and employment of master's degree graduates: Enrolled in a post-doctoral residency/fellowship (n/a), employed in independent practice (n/a), total from the above (master's) (0).

Doctoral Degree Graduates: Of those who graduated in the academic year 2003–2004, the following categories and numbers represent the post-graduate activities and employment of doctoral degree graduates: Enrolled in a psychology doctoral program (n/a), total from the above (doctoral) (0).

Additional Information:

Orientation, Objectives, and Emphasis of Department: The clinical program is fully accredited by the American Psychological Association and is a charter member of the Academy of Psychological Clinical Science. All programs offer broad empirical and theoretical training with a research emphasis.

Special Facilities or Resources: The department has the following special facilities or resources: a psychology research facility, a psychological clinic, a medical school, a VA hospital, Mid-Missouri Mental Health Center, a counseling center, human experimental laboratories, a central computer system with extensive program library and remote terminal support, and departmental computers.

Application Information:

Send to: Director of Graduate Admissions Department of Psychological Sciences, University of Missouri, 210 McAlester Hall, Columbia, MO 65211. Application available online. URL of online application: http://psychology.missouri.edu/programs/application.htm. Students are admitted in the Fall, application deadline December 31. *Fee:* $45. There is a $60 application fee for international students.

Missouri, University of, Kansas City
Department of Psychology
4825 Troost Suite 215
Kansas City, MO 64110
Telephone: (816) 235-1318
Fax: (816) 235-1062
E-mail: *psychology@umkc.edu*
Web: *www.umkc.edu/psychology*

Department Information:

1940. Chairperson: Diane L. Filion, PhD Number of Faculty: total–full-time 14; women–full-time 8; minority–full-time 1.

Programs and Degrees Offered:

Listed in the following order: Program area, degree type (T if terminal Master's), number awarded 7/03–6/04. Psychology MA/MS (Master of Arts/Science) (T) 3, Interdisciplinary Pyschology PhD (Doctor of Philosophy) 3, Clinical Psychology PhD (Doctor of Philosophy) 0.

APA Accreditation: Clinical PhD (Doctor of Philosophy).

Student Applications/Admissions:

Student Applications

Psychology MA/MS (Master of Arts/Science)—Applications 2004–2005, 10. Total applicants accepted 2004–2005, 1. Number enrolled (new admits only) 2004–2005 full-time, 1. Number enrolled (new admits only) 2004–2005 part-time, 0. Openings 2005–2006, 4. The Median number of years required for completion of a degree are 2. The number of students enrolled full and part-time who were dismissed or voluntarily withdrew from this program area were 0. *Interdisciplinary Pyschology PhD (Doctor of Philosophy)*—Applications 2004–2005, 10. Total applicants accepted 2004–2005, 3. Number enrolled (new admits only) 2004–2005 full-time, 3. Number enrolled (new admits only) 2004–2005 part-time, 0. Openings 2005–2006, 2. The Median number of years required for completion of a degree are 4. The number of students enrolled full and part-time who were dismissed or voluntarily withdrew from this program area were 0. *Clinical Psychology PhD (Doctor of Philosophy)*—Applications 2004–2005, 24. Total applicants accepted 2004–2005, 4. Number enrolled (new admits only) 2004–2005 full-time, 4. Number enrolled (new admits only) 2004–2005 part-time, 0. Openings 2005–2006, 4. The Median number of years required for completion of a degree are 5. The number

of students enrolled full and part-time who were dismissed or voluntarily withdrew from this program area were 0.

Admissions Requirements:

Scores: Entries appear in this order: required test or GPA, minimum score (if required), median score of students entering in 2003–2004. Doctoral Programs: Please check the department website at www.umkc.edu/psychology for program-specific admissions requirements.

Other Criteria: (importance of criteria rated low, medium, or high): GRE/MAT scores high, research experience high, work experience medium, extracurricular activity low, clinically related public service medium, GPA high, letters of recommendation high, interview high, statement of goals and objectives high. Please refer to the department website at www.umkc.edu/psychology for more program-specific requirements/criteria/information. For additional information on admission requirements, go to: www.umkc.edu/psychology.

Student Characteristics: The following represents characteristics of students in 2004–2005 in all graduate psychology programs in the department: Female–full-time 23, part-time 0; Male–full-time 12, part-time 0; African American/Black–full-time 2, part-time 0; Hispanic/Latino(a)–full-time 2, part-time 0; Asian/Pacific Islander–full-time 1, part-time 0; American Indian/Alaska Native–full-time 0, part-time 0; Caucasian–full-time 30, part-time 0; students subject to the Americans With Disabilities Act–full-time 0, part-time 0.

Financial Information/Assistance:

Tuition for Full-Time Study: *Master's:* State residents: $254 per credit hour; Nonstate residents: $656 per credit hour. *Doctoral:* State residents: $254 per credit hour; Nonstate residents: $656 per credit hour. Tuition is subject to change. See the following Web site for updates and changes in tuition costs: www.umkc.edu.

Financial Assistance:

First Year Students: Teaching assistantships available for first-year. Average amount paid per academic year: $9,000. Average number of hours worked per week: 20. Apply by 0. Tuition remission given: partial. Research assistantships available for first-year. Average amount paid per academic year: $9,000. Average number of hours worked per week: 20. Apply by 0. Tuition remission given: partial. Fellowships and scholarships available for first-year. Apply by varies. Tuition remission given: partial.

Advanced Students: Teaching assistantships available for advanced students. Average amount paid per academic year: $9,000. Average number of hours worked per week: 20. Apply by 0. Tuition remission given: partial. Research assistantships available for advanced students. Average amount paid per academic year: $9,000. Average number of hours worked per week: 20. Apply by 0. Tuition remission given: partial. Fellowships and scholarships available for advanced students. Apply by varies. Tuition remission given: partial.

Contact Information: Of all students currently enrolled full-time, 75% benefitted from one or more of the listed financial assistance programs. Application and information available online at: umkc.edu/psychology.

Internships/Practica: With a population of over 1.5 million, Kansas City offers numerous opportunities for practicum and research opportunities. Formal community practicum opportunities are offered to both Master's and Clinical Psychology PhD students. Kansas City offers numerous practicum opportunities for clinical psychology doctoral students. A variety of community agencies, medical centers, and other applied settings are available for clinical practica. Clinical psychology students are required to enroll in six semesters of practicum during which they are involved in many different types of clinical experiences, ranging from supervised work in specialized health care programs to more general outpatient settings for psychotherapy and psychological assessment. Basic clinical practica include training in general mental health assessment and treatment areas such as crisis intervention, depression screening, personnel and disability evaluations, and treatment of adjustment problems, depression, and anxiety disorders. Advanced training opportunities in the assessment and treatment of obesity and eating disorders, smoking and other substance abuse, and managed care. In the fifth year of study, students are required to complete a one year clinical internship. For those doctoral students for whom a professional internship is required prior to graduation, 2 applied in 2003–2004. Of those who applied, 2 were placed in internships listed by the Association of Psychology Postdoctoral and Internship Programs (APPIC).

Housing and Day Care: On-campus housing is available. See the following Web site for more information: http://www.umkc.edu/housing/housingoptions.asp. On-campus day care facilities are available.

Employment of Department Graduates:
   Master's Degree Graduates: Of those who graduated in the academic year 2003–2004, the following categories and numbers represent the post-graduate activities and employment of master's degree graduates: Enrolled in a post-doctoral residency/fellowship (n/a), employed in independent practice (n/a), total from the above (master's) (0).
   Doctoral Degree Graduates: Of those who graduated in the academic year 2003–2004, the following categories and numbers represent the post-graduate activities and employment of doctoral degree graduates: Enrolled in a psychology doctoral program (n/a), total from the above (doctoral) (0).

Additional Information:
   Orientation, Objectives, and Emphasis of Department: The orientation of the Department of Psychology is broadly eclectic with an empirical emphasis. A broad range of points of view are represented by faculty and by research in the department. The major educational goal within the department is to convey methodological and problem-solving techniques to the students. Also, we attempt to provide students with tools to evaluate the research of others and to produce research.

   Special Facilities or Resources: The Department of Psychology is committed to making cutting-edge behavioral science research contributions to health and health care. Our faculty of nationally and internationally recognized leaders in Health Outcomes Research in areas such as HIV/AIDS, tobacco use, obesity and eating disorders, cancer, neuropsychological functioning, safety and violence, and community factors in health have an exceptional track record of extramural funding and collaborative partnership building. We have strong and active partnerships with important community health care institutions such as Saint Luke's Hospital, The Cancer Institute, Mid America Heart Institute, the Kansas City Free Clinic, University of Kansas Medical Center, and Truman Medical Center. In addition, we have established strong interdisciplinary collaborations with other UMKC divisions and schools such as the Schools of Medicine, Dentistry, Nursing, Education and Law. Our extramural research funding (> $6.5 million) has come from prestigious sources such as the National Institutes of Health, Fogerty International, Department of Defense, Substance Abuse and Mental Health Services Administration, as well as several prominent foundations.

Application Information:
Send to: For MA and PhD Degrees: University of Missouri-Kansas City, Office of Admissions, Administrative Center, 5115 Oak, Kansas City, MO 64110. For any Interdisciplinary PhD: Ms. Quincy Bennett, School of Graduate Studies, University of Missouri—Kansas City, 5115 Oak, Kansas City, MO 64110. Application available online. Students are admitted in the Fall, application deadline December 15. Refer to department Web site at www.umkc.edu/psychology for MA and PhD deadlines, which are different. *Fee:* $35.

Missouri, University of, Kansas City
Division of Counseling, Educational Psychology, and Exercise
   Science
School of Education
5100 Rockhill Road, 215
Kansas City, MO 64110
Telephone: (816) 235-2722
Fax: (816) 235-5270
E-mail: *Duanc@umkc.edu*
Web: *http://umkc.edu/education/divs/cpce/*

Department Information:
   Chairperson: Changming Duan, PhD Number of Faculty: total–full-time 16; women–full-time 8; minority–full-time 5.

Programs and Degrees Offered:
   Listed in the following order: Program area, degree type (T if terminal Master's), number awarded 7/03–6/04. Counseling Psychology PhD (Doctor of Philosophy) 7, Counseling and Guidance MA/MS (Master of Arts/Science) (T) 15, Counseling and Guidance EdS (Education Specialist) 0.

APA Accreditation: Counseling PhD (Doctor of Philosophy).

Student Applications/Admissions:
   Student Applications
   Counseling Psychology PhD (Doctor of Philosophy)—Applications 2004–2005, 97. Total applicants accepted 2004–2005, 7. Openings 2005–2006, 8. The Median number of years required for completion of a degree are 6. The number of students enrolled full and part-time who were dismissed or voluntarily

withdrew from this program area were 1. *Counseling and Guidance MA/MS (Master of Arts/Science)*—Applications 2004–2005, 147. Total applicants accepted 2004–2005, 85. Openings 2005–2006, 50. The number of students enrolled full and part-time who were dismissed or voluntarily withdrew from this program area were 0. *Counseling and Guidance EdS (Education Specialist)*—Applications 2004–2005, 8. Total applicants accepted 2004–2005, 8. Openings 2005–2006, 6. The number of students enrolled full and part-time who were dismissed or voluntarily withdrew from this program area were 0.

Admissions Requirements:

Scores: Entries appear in this order: required test or GPA, minimum score (if required), median score of students entering in 2003–2004. Master's Programs: overall undergraduate GPA 2.75, *. Applicants may choose between the GRE or MAT. *Indicates information not available. Doctoral Programs: GRE-V+Q 1000, 1160; overall undergraduate GPA 3.0, 3.7. *Other Criteria:* (importance of criteria rated low, medium, or high): GRE/MAT scores medium, research experience high, work experience medium, extracurricular activity medium, clinically related public service medium, GPA medium, letters of recommendation high, interview high, statement of goals and objectives high.

Student Characteristics: The following represents characteristics of students in 2004–2005 in all graduate psychology programs in the department: Female–full-time 36, part-time 0; Male–full-time 6, part-time 0; African American/Black–full-time 3, part-time 0; Hispanic/Latino(a)–full-time 2, part-time 0; Asian/Pacific Islander–full-time 4, part-time 0; American Indian/Alaska Native–full-time 2, part-time 0; Caucasian–full-time 30, part-time 0; Multi-ethnic–full-time 1, part-time 0; students subject to the Americans With Disabilities Act–full-time 1, part-time 0.

Financial Information/Assistance:

Tuition for Full-Time Study: *Master's:* State residents: $236 per credit hour; Nonstate residents: $639 per credit hour. *Doctoral:* State residents: $236 per credit hour; Nonstate residents: $236 per credit hour. Tuition is subject to change.

Financial Assistance:

First Year Students: Teaching assistantships available for first-year. Average amount paid per academic year: $10,560. Average number of hours worked per week: 20. Apply by varies. Tuition remission given: partial. Research assistantships available for first-year. Average amount paid per academic year: $10,560. Average number of hours worked per week: 20. Apply by varies. Tuition remission given: partial. Fellowships and scholarships available for first-year. Apply by February 15. Tuition remission given: partial.

Advanced Students: No information provided.

Contact Information: Of all students currently enrolled full-time, 60% benefitted from one or more of the listed financial assistance programs. Application and information available online at: http://www.umkc.edu/sgs/financial.

Internships/Practica: All programs offer a wide range of practicum and internship placements. The Division of Counseling Psychology and Counselor Education operates the Community Counseling Services, an in-house training facility serving individuals, couples, and families in the surrounding community. Advanced practica are also available in a variety of agencies including local community mental health centers, Veterans Affairs Hospitals, and other local service provision agencies. For those doctoral students for whom a professional internship is required prior to graduation, 3 applied in 2003–2004. Of those who applied, 2 were placed in internships listed by the Association of Psychology Postdoctoral and Internship Programs (APPIC); 2 were placed in APA accredited internships.

Housing and Day Care: On-campus housing is available. See the following Web site for more information: www.umkc.edu/housing. No on-campus day care facilities are available.

Employment of Department Graduates:

Master's Degree Graduates: Of those who graduated in the academic year 2003–2004, the following categories and numbers represent the post-graduate activities and employment of master's degree graduates: Enrolled in a post-doctoral residency/fellowship (n/a), employed in independent practice (n/a), total from the above (master's) (0).

Doctoral Degree Graduates: Of those who graduated in the academic year 2003–2004, the following categories and numbers represent the post-graduate activities and employment of doctoral degree graduates: Enrolled in a psychology doctoral program (n/a), employed in independent practice (1), employed in other positions at a higher education institution (4), employed in a hospital/medical center (2), total from the above (doctoral) (7).

Additional Information:

Orientation, Objectives, and Emphasis of Department: Our Counseling Psychology program emphasizes the study of multicultural and individual diversity within a scientist-practitioner model. Consistent with the University of Missouri-Kansas City urban/metropolitan mission, the faculty is committed to educating future Counseling Psychologists to improve the welfare of individuals and communities through scholarship and applied interventions. 1. The program faculty encourages students to develop primary identification with the core values of counseling psychology. These values emphasize: a) assets, strengths, and positive mental health; b) respect for cultural and individual diversity; c) scientific foundation for all activities; d) developmental models of human growth; e) relatively brief counseling interventions; f) person-environment interaction; g) education and prevention; h) career/vocational development. 2. Our commitment to cultural and individual diversity is reflected in: a) faculty composition; b) student recruitment; c) scholarship; d) course content and offerings; e) practicum opportunities; f) community service and consultation. 3. Education in counseling psychology follows a developmental model in which science-practice integration is emphasized throughout the program. Early and progressive training is provided in research, culminating in professionals who can design, conduct, and evaluate research relevant for counseling psychologists. Similarly, early and progressive training in practice activity is emphasized. 4. Program graduates will apply the values of counseling psychology to their work in a variety of employment settings, and as scientist–practitioners, their practice is informed by research and approached with a scientific attitude. 5. Counseling psychologists abide by the American Psychological Association code of conduct. Students will understand the ethical, legal, and professional issues related to the science and practice of counseling psychology.

Information for Students With Physical Disabilities: See the following Web site for more information: www.umkc.edu/dis ability.

Application Information:
Send to: PhD in Counseling Psychology Program: Applications go to two places: Office of Admissions, University of Missouri—Kansas City, 5115 Oak, 5100 Rockhill Road, Kansas City, MO 64110; and Counseling Psychology Program, University of Missouri—Kansas City, ED 215, 5100 Rockhill Road, Kansas City, MO 64110. Students are admitted in the Fall, application deadline January 15. Please see program Web site for more details on application requirements and process (www.umkc.edu/education/divs/cpce). *Fee:* $25.

Northwest Missouri State University (2004 data)
Department of Psychology/Sociology/Counseling
Colden Hall 2440
Maryville, MO 64468
Telephone: (660) 562-1260
Fax: (660) 562-1731
E-mail: *teaneyc@mail.nwmissouri.edu*
Web: *www.nwmissouri.edu/~0500605/psychomepage.htm*

Department Information:
1968. Chairperson: Jerrold E. Barnett. Number of Faculty: total–full-time 13, part-time 3; women–full-time 6, part-time 3; minority–full-time 1, part-time 1.

Programs and Degrees Offered:
Listed in the following order: Program area, degree type (T if terminal Master's), number awarded 7/03–6/04. Counseling Psychology MA/MS (Master of Arts/Science) (T) 5, School Counseling MA/MS (Master of Arts/Science) 7.

Student Applications/Admissions:
Student Applications
Counseling Psychology MA/MS (Master of Arts/Science)—Applications 2004–2005, 0. Total applicants accepted 2004–2005, 0. Total enrolled 2004–2005 full-time, 15, part-time, 1. The Median number of years required for completion of a degree are 5. The number of students enrolled full and part-time who were dismissed or voluntarily withdrew from this program area were 1. *School Counseling MA/MS (Master of Arts/Science)*—Applications 2004–2005, 19. Total applicants accepted 2004–2005, 14. Total enrolled 2004–2005 full-time, 33, part-time, 1. Openings 2005–2006, 15. The Median number of years required for completion of a degree are 4.

Admissions Requirements:
Scores: Entries appear in this order: required test or GPA, minimum score (if required), median score of students entering in 2003–2004. Master's Programs: GRE-Subject(Psych) 500, 504; overall undergraduate GPA 2.75, 3.5; psychology GPA 3.0, 3.6. MSEd: minimum GPA of 2.5 in declared major; submission of GRE scores.
Other Criteria: (importance of criteria rated low, medium, or high): GRE/MAT scores medium, research experience medium, work experience medium, extracurricular activity low,

clinically related public service medium, GPA high, letters of recommendation high, statement of goals and objectives high.

Student Characteristics: The following represents characteristics of students in 2004–2005 in all graduate psychology programs in the department: Female–full-time 20, part-time 0; Male–full-time 2, part-time 0; African American/Black–full-time 0, part-time 0; Hispanic/Latino(a)–full-time 0, part-time 0; Asian/Pacific Islander–full-time 0, part-time 0; American Indian/Alaska Native–full-time 0, part-time 0; Caucasian–full-time 0, part-time 0.

Financial Information/Assistance:
Financial Assistance:
First Year Students: Teaching assistantships available for first-year. Average amount paid per academic year: $5,250. Average number of hours worked per week: 20. Apply by open. Tuition remission given: full.
Advanced Students: Teaching assistantships available for advanced students. Average amount paid per academic year: $5,250. Average number of hours worked per week: 20. Apply by open. Tuition remission given: full.
Contact Information: Of all students currently enrolled full-time, 20% benefitted from one or more of the listed financial assistance programs.

Internships/Practica: No information provided.

Housing and Day Care: No on-campus housing is available. No on-campus day care facilities are available.

Employment of Department Graduates:
Master's Degree Graduates: Of those who graduated in the academic year 2003–2004, the following categories and numbers represent the post-graduate activities and employment of master's degree graduates: Enrolled in a post-doctoral residency/fellowship (n/a), employed in independent practice (n/a), employed in a community mental health/counseling center (3), total from the above (master's) (3).
Doctoral Degree Graduates: Of those who graduated in the academic year 2003–2004, the following categories and numbers represent the post-graduate activities and employment of doctoral degree graduates: Enrolled in a psychology doctoral program (n/a), total from the above (doctoral) (0).

Additional Information:
Orientation, Objectives, and Emphasis of Department: Professional counselors provide services to assist people in coping with the stresses and strains engendered by the changing and complex world in which they live. This program is designed to prepare students to provide counseling services in a variety of settings ranging from mental health clinics and psychiatric hospitals to private practice clinics and social service agencies. Particular emphasis is given to assessment, both in terms of theory and practice. The MSEd program prepares professional counselors for careers in elementary and secondary schools.

Special Facilities or Resources: Training rooms for individual and group therapy; association with the university counseling center; association with laboratory school.

Application Information:
Send to: Dean, Graduate School. Students are admitted in the Fall, application deadline March 1. *Fee:* $50.

Saint Louis University

Department of Psychology
Arts and Sciences
3511 Laclede, 104 Shannon Hall
Street Louis, MO 63103-2010
Telephone: (314) 977-2300
Fax: (314) 977-1014
E-mail: *kelloggr@slu.edu*
Web: *http://www.slu.edu/colleges/AS/PSY/*

Department Information:

1926. Chairperson: Ronald T. Kellogg. Number of Faculty: total–full-time 24, part-time 1; women–full-time 8; minority–full-time 3.

Programs and Degrees Offered:

Listed in the following order: Program area, degree type (T if terminal Master's), number awarded 7/03–6/04. Cognition & Neuroscience PhD (Doctor of Philosophy) 3, Clinical PhD (Doctor of Philosophy) 10, Developmental PhD (Doctor of Philosophy) 1, Social PhD (Doctor of Philosophy) 2, Industrial Organizational PhD (Doctor of Philosophy) 4.

APA Accreditation: Clinical PhD (Doctor of Philosophy).

Student Applications/Admissions:

Student Applications

Cognition & Neuroscience PhD (Doctor of Philosophy)—Applications 2004–2005, 16. Total applicants accepted 2004–2005, 2. Number enrolled (new admits only) 2004–2005 full-time, 3. Number enrolled (new admits only) 2004–2005 part-time, 0. Openings 2005–2006, 2. The Median number of years required for completion of a degree are 5. The number of students enrolled full and part-time who were dismissed or voluntarily withdrew from this program area were 0. *Clinical PhD (Doctor of Philosophy)*—Applications 2004–2005, 125. Total applicants accepted 2004–2005, 12. Number enrolled (new admits only) 2004–2005 full-time, 8. Number enrolled (new admits only) 2004–2005 part-time, 0. Openings 2005–2006, 8. The Median number of years required for completion of a degree are 5. The number of students enrolled full and part-time who were dismissed or voluntarily withdrew from this program area were 0. *Developmental PhD (Doctor of Philosophy)*—Applications 2004–2005, 4. Total applicants accepted 2004–2005, 2. Number enrolled (new admits only) 2004–2005 full-time, 1. Number enrolled (new admits only) 2004–2005 part-time, 0. Openings 2005–2006, 2. The Median number of years required for completion of a degree are 5. The number of students enrolled full and part-time who were dismissed or voluntarily withdrew from this program area were 1. *Social PhD (Doctor of Philosophy)*—Applications 2004–2005, 20. Total applicants accepted 2004–2005, 2. Number enrolled (new admits only) 2004–2005 full-time, 2. Number enrolled (new admits only) 2004–2005 part-time, 0. Openings 2005–2006, 2. The Median number of years required for completion of a degree are 5. The number of students enrolled full and part-time who were dismissed or voluntarily withdrew from this program area were 1. *Industrial Organizational PhD (Doctor of Philosophy)*—Applications 2004–2005, 30. Total applicants accepted 2004–2005, 9. Number enrolled (new admits only) 2004–2005 full-time, 2. Number enrolled (new admits only) 2004–2005 part-time, 0. Openings 2005–2006, 4. The Median number of years required for completion of a degree are 5. The number of students enrolled full and part-time who were dismissed or voluntarily withdrew from this program area were 1.

Admissions Requirements:

Scores: Entries appear in this order: required test or GPA, minimum score (if required), median score of students entering in 2003–2004. Doctoral Programs: GRE-V no minimum stated, 535; GRE-Q no minimum stated, 615; GRE-Analytical no minimum stated, 4.5; overall undergraduate GPA 3.65. Clinical prefers verbal (550), quantitative (550). Others prefer verbal + quantitative = 1000.

Other Criteria: (importance of criteria rated low, medium, or high): GRE/MAT scores high, research experience high, work experience medium, extracurricular activity medium, clinically related public service high, GPA high, letters of recommendation high, interview high, statement of goals and objectives high. For nonclinical specialties, clinically related public service is low and interview is medium.

Student Characteristics: The following represents characteristics of students in 2004–2005 in all graduate psychology programs in the department: Female–full-time 64, part-time 0; Male–full-time 36, part-time 0; African American/Black–full-time 12, part-time 0; Hispanic/Latino(a)–full-time 2, part-time 0; Asian/Pacific Islander–full-time 1, part-time 0; American Indian/Alaska Native–full-time 0, part-time 0; Caucasian–full-time 83, part-time 0; Multi-ethnic–full-time 2, part-time 0; students subject to the Americans With Disabilities Act–full-time 0, part-time 0.

Financial Information/Assistance:

Tuition for Full-Time Study: *Master's:* State residents: $725 per credit hour; Nonstate residents: $725 per credit hour. *Doctoral:* State residents: $725 per credit hour; Nonstate residents: $725 per credit hour. Tuition is subject to change.

Financial Assistance:

First Year Students: Teaching assistantships available for first-year. Average amount paid per academic year: $11,000. Average number of hours worked per week: 20. Tuition remission given: full. Research assistantships available for first-year. Average amount paid per academic year: $13,000. Average number of hours worked per week: 20. Tuition remission given: full. Fellowships and scholarships available for first-year. Average amount paid per academic year: $13,000. Average number of hours worked per week: 20. Tuition remission given: full.

Advanced Students: Teaching assistantships available for advanced students. Average amount paid per academic year: $11,000. Average number of hours worked per week: 20. Tuition remission given: full. Research assistantships available for advanced students. Average amount paid per academic year: $13,000. Average number of hours worked per week: 20. Tuition remission given: full. Traineeships available for advanced students. Average amount paid per academic year: $13,000. Average number of hours worked per week: 20. Tuition remission given: full. Fellowships and scholarships available for advanced students. Average amount paid per academic year: $13,000. Average number of hours worked per week: 20. Tuition remission given: full.

Contact Information: Of all students currently enrolled full-time, 65% benefitted from one or more of the listed financial

assistance programs. Application and information available online at: http://www.slu.edu/colleges/AS/PSY/.

Internships/Practica: Opportunities for additional training and experience in clinical practice, research and teaching are available through graduate assistantships and clerkships either within the university or at external placements in the community. These assistantships and clerkships provide financial support for students, as well as opportunities for supervised teaching, research and clinical experience.

Housing and Day Care: No on-campus housing is available. No on-campus day care facilities are available.

Employment of Department Graduates:

Master's Degree Graduates: Of those who graduated in the academic year 2003–2004, the following categories and numbers represent the post-graduate activities and employment of master's degree graduates: Enrolled in a post-doctoral residency/fellowship (n/a), employed in independent practice (n/a), total from the above (master's) (0).

Doctoral Degree Graduates: Of those who graduated in the academic year 2003–2004, the following categories and numbers represent the post-graduate activities and employment of doctoral degree graduates: Enrolled in a psychology doctoral program (n/a), enrolled in a post-doctoral residency/fellowship (8), employed in a hospital/medical center (8), total from the above (doctoral) (16).

Additional Information:

Orientation, Objectives, and Emphasis of Department: Our mission is to educate students in the discipline of psychology and its applications. We encourage intellectual curiosity, critical thinking, and ethical responsibility in our teaching, research, and practice. Our commitment to value-based, holistic education and our enthusiasm for psychology is realized in the products of our research, in our graduates, and in service to others. The Clinical Psychology Program offers broad-based education and training in both the science and practice of psychology to prepare its graduates to function as competent, ethical scientist–practitioners across a wide range of settings with diverse populations, problems and approaches. The Applied–Experimental program includes three specializations (Developmental, Cognition & Neuroscience, and Social) and one formal program (Organizational Psychology) of training. The Developmental specialty emphasizes the development of children and adolescents with a focus on diversity, including gender, race, ethnicity, and culture. The Cognition & Neuroscience specialty reflects the interests of the faculty in the areas of memory, cognitive aging, physiology, sleep, and neuroscience. Social psychology includes the study of attitudes and social influence, close relationships, eyewitness testimony, prejudice, stigma and racial identity, self and self-concept change, and the social psychology of health. Organizational psychology is concerned with the individual, groups, and organizational interventions in the workplace.

Special Facilities or Resources: The clinical program operates an on-campus Psychological Services Center which serves as a primary site for supervised clinical experiences with children, adolescents, adults, couples and families. The Clinical program also has established collaborative relationships with various hospitals, agencies, institutions, and private practitioners throughout the community to provide advanced training and experience in the science and practice of psychology. Resources available to the experimental students include animal housing; research suites for neuroscience and sleep research; an undergraduate laboratory room; and several laboratory suites for social, cognitive, and developmental research. In addition to space for laboratory research, the students in the Industrial/Organizational program are involved with the Center for the Application of the Behavioral Science. Housed within the department, this Center provides opportunities for training in organizational consulting and program evaluation in field settings.

Application Information:

Send to: The Graduate School, Saint Louis University, 3663 Lindell Boulevard, Street Louis, MO 63108, (314) 977-2240. Students are admitted in the Fall, application deadline January 1. *Fee:* $40.

Southwest Missouri State University
Psychology Department
Health and Human Services
901 South National Avenue
Springfield, MO 65804-0095
Telephone: (417) 836-5797
Fax: (417) 836-8330
E-mail: *fredmaxwell@smsu.edu*
Web: *http://www.smsu.edu/chhs/chhs.html*

Department Information:

1967. Head: Fred Maxwell. Number of Faculty: total–full-time 34, part-time 5; women–full-time 14; minority–full-time 1.

Programs and Degrees Offered:

Listed in the following order: Program area, degree type (T if terminal Master's), number awarded 7/03–6/04. Clinical MA/MS (Master of Arts/Science) (T) 15, Experimental MA/MS (Master of Arts/Science) (T) 1, Industrial/ Organizational MA/MS (Master of Arts/Science) (T) 8.

Student Applications/Admissions:

Student Applications

Clinical MA/MS (Master of Arts/Science)—Applications 2004–2005, 24. Total applicants accepted 2004–2005, 8. Number enrolled (new admits only) 2004–2005 full-time, 8. Number enrolled (new admits only) 2004–2005 part-time, 0. Openings 2005–2006, 8. The Median number of years required for completion of a degree are 2. The number of students enrolled full and part-time who were dismissed or voluntarily withdrew from this program area were 0. *Experimental MA/MS (Master of Arts/Science)*—Applications 2004–2005, 5. Total applicants accepted 2004–2005, 3. Number enrolled (new admits only) 2004–2005 full-time, 3. Number enrolled (new admits only) 2004–2005 part-time, 0. Openings 2005–2006, 3. The Median number of years required for completion of a degree are 2. The number of students enrolled full and part-time who were dismissed or voluntarily withdrew from this program area were 0. *Industrial/ Organizational MA/MS (Master of Arts/Science)*—Applications 2004–2005, 32. Total applicants accepted 2004–2005, 14. Number enrolled (new admits only) 2004–2005 full-time, 14. Number enrolled (new admits only) 2004–2005 part-time, 0. Openings 2005–2006, 10. The Median number of years required for completion of a degree are 2. The number of students enrolled full and part-time who were dismissed or voluntarily withdrew from this program area were 1.

Admissions Requirements:

Scores: Entries appear in this order: required test or GPA, minimum score (if required), median score of students entering in 2003–2004. Master's Programs: GRE-V 475, 542; GRE-Q 475, 550; GRE-V+Q 1000, 1092; GRE-Subject(Psych) 550, 615; overall undergraduate GPA 3.00, 3.72; psychology GPA 3.25, 3.88.

Other Criteria: (importance of criteria rated low, medium, or high): GRE/MAT scores medium, research experience high, work experience medium, extracurricular activity medium, clinically related public service high, GPA high, letters of recommendation high, statement of goals and objectives high.

Student Characteristics: The following represents characteristics of students in 2004–2005 in all graduate psychology programs in the department: Female–full-time 37, part-time 0; Male–full-time 11, part-time 0; African American/Black–full-time 4, part-time 0; Hispanic/Latino(a)–full-time 0, part-time 0; Asian/Pacific Islander–full-time 0, part-time 0; American Indian/Alaska Native–full-time 1, part-time 0; Caucasian–full-time 42, part-time 1; Multi-ethnic–full-time 1, part-time 0; students subject to the Americans With Disabilities Act–full-time 1, part-time 0.

Financial Information/Assistance:

Tuition for Full-Time Study: *Master's:* State residents: per academic year $4,248, $177 per credit hour; Nonstate residents: per academic year $8,496, $354 per credit hour.

Financial Assistance:

First Year Students: Research assistantships available for first-year. Average amount paid per academic year: $6,300. Average number of hours worked per week: 20. Apply by July. Tuition remission given: full.

Advanced Students: Teaching assistantships available for advanced students. Average amount paid per academic year: $8,400. Average number of hours worked per week: 20. Apply by March. Tuition remission given: full. Research assistantships available for advanced students. Average amount paid per academic year: $6,300. Average number of hours worked per week: 20. Apply by July. Tuition remission given: full.

Contact Information: Of all students currently enrolled full-time, 75% benefitted from one or more of the listed financial assistance programs.

Internships/Practica: Clinical—students must complete two 175 contact hour practica. Placements are in a variety of mental health settings. Students who choose a non-thesis option must complete an additional 175 contact hour internship. Experimental—practicum experience is acquired through basic laboratory research work tailored specifically to the graduate student's research area of interest. The goal of the practicum(s) is for the student to develop or acquire competence in various research methods and behavioral/cognitive measurement skills that will prepare the student for later doctoral work.

Housing and Day Care: On-campus housing is available. See the following Web site for more information: http://www.smsu.edu/reslife/. On-campus day care facilities are available. (417) 866-0980.

Employment of Department Graduates:

Master's Degree Graduates: Of those who graduated in the academic year 2003–2004, the following categories and numbers represent the post-graduate activities and employment of master's degree graduates: Enrolled in a psychology doctoral program (6), enrolled in another graduate/professional program (1), enrolled in a post-doctoral residency/fellowship (n/a), employed in independent practice (n/a), employed in an academic position at a university (1), employed in an academic position at a 2-year/4-year college (0), employed in other positions at a higher education institution (0), employed in a professional position in a school system (0), employed in business or industry (research/consulting) (2), employed in business or industry (management) (4), employed in a government agency (research) (0), employed in a government agency (professional services) (0), employed in a community mental health/counseling center (7), employed in a hospital/medical center (0), still seeking employment (2), other employment position (0), do not know (0), total from the above (master's) (23).

Doctoral Degree Graduates: Of those who graduated in the academic year 2003–2004, the following categories and numbers represent the post-graduate activities and employment of doctoral degree graduates: Enrolled in a psychology doctoral program (n/a), total from the above (doctoral) (0).

Additional Information:

Orientation, Objectives, and Emphasis of Department: We are an eclectic department of 34 full-time faculty serving over 500 undergraduate majors. The faculty have diverse research interests including clinical, I/O, stress management, sport psychology, human learning, perception, motivation, animal learning, human skills, and memory. The department operates the Learning Diagnostic Clinic for diagnosis and remediation of special populations as well as limited therapy for other psychological disorders.

Special Facilities or Resources: The experimental track has 5 research labs that provide the means and opportunity for graduate students to conduct basic research. A brief description of each lab is as follows: the Infant Perception Laboratory which houses basic computer hardware and software to accommodate basic research in visual scanning and psycho-physiological testing; the Music Perception and Cognition Lab; which houses computer hardware and software to generate a variety of auditory stimuli and the facilities to conduct auditory learning and cognition research; the Implicit and Explicit Motivation Research Lab, which houses computer hardware and software to conduct research in automatic processing and to conduct Structural Equation Modeling and HLM analyses; the Animal Research Lab, which houses computer software, hardware and a small animal testing chamber designed to conduct research in visual discrimination learning; and the Cognitive Strategies Research Lab, which provides the facility to test and design stimulus materials to conduct applied memory research. The department has 14 separate labs that serve the Experimental, Clinical and Industrial Organizational tracks. Research focusing on Cognition, Gender Issues, Life-Span Development, Motivation, Body Image, Music, Sports Psychology, and Animal Behavior are available to all students regardless of their track. The department also has excellent computer support facilities in all labs. The department also oversees a clinic that primarily supports the University's desire to comply with the ADA. The clinic provides an excellent training facility for our clinical graduate students.

Information for Students With Physical Disabilities: See the following Web site for more information: http://www.smsu.edu/disability.

Application Information:

Send to: Admissions Secretary. Students are admitted in the Spring, application deadline March 1. Will accept applications up to June 1 if all 8 openings in each track aren't filled. *Fee:* $0.

University of Missouri—Street Louis

Department of Psychology
One University Boulevard
Street Louis, MO 63121
Telephone: (314) 516-5391
Fax: (314) 516-5392
E-mail: *robert_calsyn@UMSL.EDU*
Web: *www.umsl.edu/divisions/artscience/psychology*

Department Information:

1967. Chairperson: Robert J. Calsyn. Number of Faculty: total–full-time 15; women–full-time 5.

Programs and Degrees Offered:

Listed in the following order: Program area, degree type (T if terminal Master's), number awarded 7/03–6/04. Clinical PhD (Doctor of Philosophy) 8, Industrial/ Organizational PhD (Doctor of Philosophy) 4, Experimental PhD (Doctor of Philosophy) 0.

APA Accreditation: Clinical PhD (Doctor of Philosophy).

Student Applications/Admissions:

Student Applications

Clinical PhD (Doctor of Philosophy)—Applications 2004–2005, 120. Total applicants accepted 2004–2005, 13. Number enrolled (new admits only) 2004–2005 full-time, 6. Number enrolled (new admits only) 2004–2005 part-time, 0. Openings 2005–2006, 6. The Median number of years required for completion of a degree are 6. The number of students enrolled full and part-time who were dismissed or voluntarily withdrew from this program area were 1. *Industrial/ Organizational PhD (Doctor of Philosophy)*—Applications 2004–2005, 75. Total applicants accepted 2004–2005, 15. Number enrolled (new admits only) 2004–2005 full-time, 5. Total enrolled 2004–2005 full-time, 31, part-time, 2. Openings 2005–2006, 4. The Median number of years required for completion of a degree are 7. The number of students enrolled full and part-time who were dismissed or voluntarily withdrew from this program area were 1. *Experimental PhD (Doctor of Philosophy)*—Applications 2004–2005, 10. Total applicants accepted 2004–2005, 1. Number enrolled (new admits only) 2004–2005 full-time, 1. Total enrolled 2004–2005 full-time, 6. Openings 2005–2006, 2. The Median number of years required for completion of a degree are 6. The number of students enrolled full and part-time who were dismissed or voluntarily withdrew from this program area were 1.

Admissions Requirements:

Scores: Entries appear in this order: required test or GPA, minimum score (if required), median score of students entering in 2003–2004. Master's Programs: GRE-V no minimum stated; GRE-Q no minimum stated; GRE-V+Q no minimum stated; GRE-Analytical no minimum stated; GRE-Subject(Psych) no minimum stated; overall undergraduate GPA no minimum stated; psychology GPA no minimum stated. There are no minimum requirements. Median values vary by program. GRE-Subject not required for Clinical Doctoral Program. Doctoral Programs: GRE-V no minimum stated, 620; GRE-Q no minimum stated, 640; GRE-Analytical no minimum stated, 660; GRE-Subject(Psych) no minimum stated, 630; overall undergraduate GPA no minimum stated, 3.55.

Other Criteria: (importance of criteria rated low, medium, or high): GRE/MAT scores high, research experience high, work experience medium, extracurricular activity medium, clinically related public service medium, GPA high, letters of recommendation high, interview high, statement of goals and objectives high. Only the clinical program has a formal interview procedure. Importance of criteria varies by program.

Student Characteristics: The following represents characteristics of students in 2004–2005 in all graduate psychology programs in the department: Female–full-time 53, part-time 19; Male–full-time 19, part-time 2; African American/Black–full-time 3, part-time 0; Hispanic/Latino(a)–full-time 1, part-time 1; Asian/Pacific Islander–full-time 4, part-time 0; American Indian/Alaska Native–full-time 1, part-time 0; Caucasian–full-time 63, part-time 2; Multi-ethnic–full-time 0, part-time 0; students subject to the Americans With Disabilities Act–full-time 0, part-time 0.

Financial Information/Assistance:

Tuition for Full-Time Study: *Master's:* State residents: $236 per credit hour; Nonstate residents: $639 per credit hour. *Doctoral:* State residents: $236 per credit hour; Nonstate residents: $639 per credit hour. Tuition is subject to change.

Financial Assistance:

First Year Students: Teaching assistantships available for first-year. Average amount paid per academic year: $9,500. Average number of hours worked per week: 20. Apply by January 15. Tuition remission given: full. Research assistantships available for first-year. Average amount paid per academic year: $9,500. Average number of hours worked per week: 20. Apply by January 15. Tuition remission given: full.

Advanced Students: Teaching assistantships available for advanced students. Average amount paid per academic year: $9,500. Average number of hours worked per week: 20. Apply by January 15. Tuition remission given: full and partial. Research assistantships available for advanced students. Average amount paid per academic year: $9,500. Average number of hours worked per week: 20. Apply by January 15. Tuition remission given: full and partial.

Contact Information: Of all students currently enrolled full-time, 50% benefitted from one or more of the listed financial assistance programs.

Internships/Practica:

Students (clinical) participate in practica in our Community Psychological Service (the psychology clinic), and a paid clinical clerkship, which may be in a community or university-based program. For those doctoral students for whom a professional internship is required prior to graduation, 6 applied in 2003–2004. Of those who applied, 6 were placed in internships listed by the Association of Psychology Postdoctoral and Internship Programs (APPIC); 6 were placed in APA accredited internships.

Housing and Day Care: On-campus housing is available. For information regarding on-campus housing, please call the Residence Hall at: (314) 516-6877. Affordable housing for students is also available off campus. For example, a two-bedroom apartment is approximately $500-600/month within a close commuting distance from campus. On-campus day care facilities are available. Child Development Center: (314) 516-5658.

Employment of Department Graduates:
Master's Degree Graduates: Of those who graduated in the academic year 2003–2004, the following categories and numbers represent the post-graduate activities and employment of master's degree graduates: Enrolled in a post-doctoral residency/fellowship (n/a), employed in independent practice (n/a), total from the above (master's) (0).
Doctoral Degree Graduates: Of those who graduated in the academic year 2003–2004, the following categories and numbers represent the post-graduate activities and employment of doctoral degree graduates: Enrolled in a psychology doctoral program (n/a), total from the above (doctoral) (0).

Additional Information:
Orientation, Objectives, and Emphasis of Department: The orientation of the department emphasizes psychology as science yet also recognizes the important social responsibilities of psychology, especially in the clinical and applied areas. Emphasis of experimental is in behavioral neuropharmacology/endocrinology with a secondary interest in neuroscience. The department offers a broad spectrum of high-quality programs at the undergraduate and graduate levels.

Special Facilities or Resources: The Department of Psychology is housed in Stadler Hall, and research laboratories and computers are conveniently located in the building. The psychological clinic (Community Psychological Service) is also contained within Stadler Hall. The Center for Trauma Recovery and Child Advocacy Center each have community clinics, which are housed on campus. Physical facilities include workshops and comparative, social, and human experimental laboratories. A wide range of research equipment is available, including videotaping facilities, computer terminals, and personal computers.

Information for Students With Physical Disabilities: See the following Web site for more information: http://www.umsl.edu/services/disabled/.

Application Information:
Send to: Graduate Admissions, University of Missouri—Street Louis, 358 Millennium Student Center, 8001 Natural Bridge, Street Louis, MO 63121. Application available online. URL of online application: http://www.umsl.edu/divisions/graduate/pdf/gs-appl.pdf. Students are admitted in the Fall; Clinical deadline is January 15, I/O deadline is February 1, Experimental is February 1. *Fee:* $25. Fee for McNair Scholars is waived.

Washington University in Street Louis
Department of Psychology
One Brookings Drive, Box 1125
Street Louis, MO 63130
Telephone: (314) 935-6520
Fax: (314) 935-7588
E-mail: *psych@artsci.wustl.edu*
Web: *http://www.artsci.wustl.edu/~psych/index.html*

Department Information:
1924. Chairperson: Randy J. Larsen. Number of Faculty: total–full-time 32, part-time 5; women–full-time 10, part-time 1; minority–full-time 2.

Programs and Degrees Offered:
Listed in the following order: Program area, degree type (T if terminal Master's), number awarded 7/03–6/04. Clinical PhD (Doctor of Philosophy) 4, Aging and Development PhD (Doctor of Philosophy) 0, Behavior/Brain/Cognition PhD (Doctor of Philosophy) 2, Social/Personality PhD (Doctor of Philosophy) 2.

APA Accreditation: Clinical PhD (Doctor of Philosophy).

Student Applications/Admissions:
Student Applications
Clinical PhD (Doctor of Philosophy)—Applications 2004–2005, 168. Total applicants accepted 2004–2005, 6. Number enrolled (new admits only) 2004–2005 full-time, 6. Number enrolled (new admits only) 2004–2005 part-time, 0. Openings 2005–2006, 8. The Median number of years required for completion of a degree are 6. The number of students enrolled full and part-time who were dismissed or voluntarily withdrew from this program area were 0. *Aging and Development PhD (Doctor of Philosophy)*—Applications 2004–2005, 7. Total applicants accepted 2004–2005, 1. Number enrolled (new admits only) 2004–2005 full-time, 1. Number enrolled (new admits only) 2004–2005 part-time, 0. Openings 2005–2006, 2. The number of students enrolled full and part-time who were dismissed or voluntarily withdrew from this program area were 0. *Behavior/Brain/Cognition PhD (Doctor of Philosophy)*—Applications 2004–2005, 86. Total applicants accepted 2004–2005, 12. Number enrolled (new admits only) 2004–2005 full-time, 12. Number enrolled (new admits only) 2004–2005 part-time, 0. Openings 2005–2006, 15. The Median number of years required for completion of a degree are 6. The number of students enrolled full and part-time who were dismissed or voluntarily withdrew from this program area were 0. *Social/Personality PhD (Doctor of Philosophy)*—Applications 2004–2005, 24. Total applicants accepted 2004–2005, 1. Number enrolled (new admits only) 2004–2005 full-time, 1. Number enrolled (new admits only) 2004–2005 part-time, 0. Openings 2005–2006, 1. The Median number of years required for completion of a degree are 6. The number of students enrolled full and part-time who were dismissed or voluntarily withdrew from this program area were 0.

Admissions Requirements:
Scores: Entries appear in this order: required test or GPA, minimum score (if required), median score of students entering in 2003–2004. Doctoral Programs: GRE-V no minimum stated,

600; GRE-Q no minimum stated, 690; GRE-Analytical no minimum stated, 690.

Other Criteria: (importance of criteria rated low, medium, or high): GRE/MAT scores high, research experience high, work experience medium, clinically related public service low, GPA medium, letters of recommendation high, interview high, statement of goals and objectives high. Interview is required for applicants prior to acceptance.

Student Characteristics: The following represents characteristics of students in 2004–2005 in all graduate psychology programs in the department: Female–full-time 48, part-time 0; Male–full-time 32, part-time 0; African American/Black–full-time 2, part-time 0; Hispanic/Latino(a)–full-time 1, part-time 0; Asian/Pacific Islander–full-time 6, part-time 0; American Indian/Alaska Native–full-time 0, part-time 0; Caucasian–full-time 54, part-time 0; Multi-ethnic–full-time 17, part-time 0; students subject to the Americans With Disabilities Act–full-time 0, part-time 0.

Financial Information/Assistance:

Tuition for Full-Time Study: *Doctoral:* State residents: per academic year $31,100; Nonstate residents: per academic year $31,100.

Financial Assistance:

First Year Students: Research assistantships available for first-year. Average amount paid per academic year: $17,000. Average number of hours worked per week: 10. Tuition remission given: full. Traineeships available for first-year. Average amount paid per academic year: $18,000. Average number of hours worked per week: 0. Tuition remission given: full. Fellowships and scholarships available for first-year. Average amount paid per academic year: $20,000. Average number of hours worked per week: 0. Apply by January 25. Tuition remission given: full.

Advanced Students: Teaching assistantships available for advanced students. Average amount paid per academic year: $16,500. Average number of hours worked per week: 10. Tuition remission given: full. Research assistantships available for advanced students. Average amount paid per academic year: $16,500. Average number of hours worked per week: 15. Tuition remission given: full. Traineeships available for advanced students. Average amount paid per academic year: $20,772. Average number of hours worked per week: 0. Tuition remission given: full. Fellowships and scholarships available for advanced students. Average amount paid per academic year: $16,500. Average number of hours worked per week: 0. Tuition remission given: full.

Contact Information: Of all students currently enrolled full-time, 100% benefitted from one or more of the listed financial assistance programs.

Internships/Practica: For those doctoral students for whom a professional internship is required prior to graduation, 3 applied in 2003–2004. Of those who applied, 3 were placed in internships listed by the Association of Psychology Postdoctoral and Internship Programs (APPIC); 3 were placed in APA accredited internships.

Housing and Day Care: On-campus housing is available. Although on-campus housing is available, this is an option that is reserved to undergraduates. On-campus day care facilities are available.

Employment of Department Graduates:

Master's Degree Graduates: Of those who graduated in the academic year 2003–2004, the following categories and numbers represent the post-graduate activities and employment of master's degree graduates: Enrolled in a post-doctoral residency/fellowship (n/a), employed in independent practice (n/a), total from the above (master's) (0).

Doctoral Degree Graduates: Of those who graduated in the academic year 2003–2004, the following categories and numbers represent the post-graduate activities and employment of doctoral degree graduates: Enrolled in a psychology doctoral program (n/a), enrolled in a post-doctoral residency/fellowship (3), employed in business or industry (research/consulting) (1), employed in a hospital/medical center (3), still seeking employment (1), total from the above (doctoral) (8).

Additional Information:

Orientation, Objectives, and Emphasis of Department: The emphasis within the clinical program is on training clinical scientists and promoting an integration of science and practice. Its goal is to train students who will lead the search for knowledge regarding the assessment, understanding, and treatment of psychological disorders. In the experimental programs, the development of generalists with one or more areas of specialization is the department's orientation.

Special Facilities or Resources: The department's extensive facilities include animal, human psychophysiological, psychoacoustic, and clinical training laboratories; computer labs; closed circuit TV; and Neuroimaging (fMRI) and Image Analysis Laboratory.

Application Information:

Send to: Meg McClelland, Graduate Program Coordinator, Washington University, Department of Psychology, Campus Box 1125, Street Louis, MO 63130-4899. Application available online. URL of online application: https://apply.embark.com/grad/washu/gsas/. Students are admitted in the Fall, application deadline January 15. January 25—Chancellor's Fellowship (for African-American candidates); February 1—Olin Women's Fellowship (for female candidates). *Fee:* $35. Candidate must have attended an undergraduate institution within the United States and have received financial assistance. Fee waiver must be completed by a representative from the financial aid office at the undergraduate institution.

Montana State University
Department of Psychology
Letters and Science
304 Traphagen Hall
Bozeman, MT 59717-3440
Telephone: (406) 994-3801
Fax: (406) 994-3804
E-mail: *jboldry@montana.edu*
Web: *htt://www.montana.edu/wwwpy*

Department Information:
1950. Chairperson: Wes Lynch, PhD. Number of Faculty: total–full-time 6; women–full-time 1.

Programs and Degrees Offered:
Listed in the following order: Program area, degree type (T if terminal Master's), number awarded 7/03–6/04. Applied Psychology MA/MS (Master of Arts/Science) (T) 2.

Student Applications/Admissions:

Student Applications
Applied Psychology MA/MS (Master of Arts/Science)—Applications 2004–2005, 16. Total applicants accepted 2004–2005, 8. Openings 2005–2006, 6. The Median number of years required for completion of a degree are 2. The number of students enrolled full and part-time who were dismissed or voluntarily withdrew from this program area were 0.

Admissions Requirements:
Scores: Entries appear in this order: required test or GPA, minimum score (if required), median score of students entering in 2003–2004. Master's Programs: GRE-V 500, 535; GRE-Q 500, 558; GRE-V+Q 1000, 1100; GRE-Analytical 5, 5.5; overall undergraduate GPA 3.00, 3.50; last 2 years GPA 3.00; psychology GPA 3.00, 3.71. GRE subject test in psychology required if not an undergrad psychology major.
Other Criteria: (importance of criteria rated low, medium, or high): GRE/MAT scores high, research experience high, work experience low, extracurricular activity low, GPA high, letters of recommendation high, interview medium, statement of goals and objectives high. For additional information on admission requirements, go to: http://www.montana.edu/wwwpy.

Student Characteristics: The following represents characteristics of students in 2004–2005 in all graduate psychology programs in the department: Female–full-time 6, part-time 0; Male–full-time 7, part-time 0; African American/Black–full-time 0, part-time 0; Hispanic/Latino(a)–full-time 0, part-time 0; Asian/Pacific Islander–full-time 0, part-time 0; American Indian/Alaska Native–full-time 0, part-time 0; Caucasian–full-time 13, part-time 0; Multi-ethnic–full-time 0, part-time 0; students subject to the Americans With Disabilities Act–full-time 0, part-time 0.

Financial Information/Assistance:
Tuition for Full-Time Study: *Master's:* State residents: $257 per credit hour; Nonstate residents: $657 per credit hour. Tuition is subject to change. See the following Web site for updates and changes in tuition costs: http://www.montana.edu/gradstudies.

Financial Assistance:
First Year Students: Teaching assistantships available for first-year. Average amount paid per academic year: $6,500. Apply by February 1. Tuition remission given: full. Fellowships and scholarships available for first-year. Average amount paid per academic year: $1,000. Apply by February 1.
Advanced Students: Teaching assistantships available for advanced students. Average amount paid per academic year: $6,500. Apply by February 1. Tuition remission given: partial.
Contact Information: Of all students currently enrolled full-time, 80% benefitted from one or more of the listed financial assistance programs. Application and information available online at: http://www.montana.edu/wwwpy.

Internships/Practica: No information provided.

Housing and Day Care: On-campus housing is available. On-campus day care facilities are available.

Employment of Department Graduates:
Master's Degree Graduates: Of those who graduated in the academic year 2003–2004, the following categories and numbers represent the post-graduate activities and employment of master's degree graduates: Enrolled in a psychology doctoral program (0), enrolled in another graduate/professional program (1), enrolled in a post-doctoral residency/fellowship (n/a), employed in independent practice (n/a), employed in an academic position at a university (0), employed in an academic position at a 2-year/4-year college (0), employed in other positions at a higher education institution (0), employed in a professional position in a school system (0), employed in business or industry (research/consulting) (1), employed in business or industry (management) (0), employed in a government agency (research) (0), employed in a government agency (professional services) (0), employed in a community mental health/counseling center (0), employed in a hospital/medical center (0), still seeking employment (0), other employment position (0), total from the above (master's) (2).
Doctoral Degree Graduates: Of those who graduated in the academic year 2003–2004, the following categories and numbers represent the post-graduate activities and employment of doctoral degree graduates: Enrolled in a psychology doctoral program (n/a), total from the above (doctoral) (0).

Additional Information:
Orientation, Objectives, and Emphasis of Department: Our two-year, research-oriented MS program in applied psychology is designed for students interested in cognitive psychology, social psychology, industrial/organizational psychology, and physiological psychology. Areas of faculty interest include cognitive psychology, social psychology, industrial/organizational psychology, physiological psychology, health psychology, research methods, and applied statistics.

Special Facilities or Resources: Laboratory space for human and animal research is available for faculty-sponsored research.

Application Information:
Send to: Dr. Jennifer Boldry, Department of Psychology, 304 Trapha-gen Hall, Montana State University, Bozeman, MT 59717-3440. Application available online. URL of online application: www.montana.edu/gradstudies. Students are admitted in the Fall, application deadline February 1. *Fee:* $50.

Montana, The University of
Department of Psychology
Arts and Sciences
143 Skaggs Building
Missoula, MT 59812-1584
Telephone: (406) 243-4521
Fax: (406) 243-6366
E-mail: *psychgrad@umontana.edu*
Web: *http://www.umt.edu/psych/*

Department Information:
1920. Chairperson: Nabil Haddad. Number of Faculty: total–full-time 22; women–full-time 11; minority–full-time 1.

Programs and Degrees Offered:
Listed in the following order: Program area, degree type (T if terminal Master's), number awarded 7/03–6/04. Clinical PhD (Doctor of Philosophy) 6, Developmental PhD (Doctor of Philosophy) 0, Learning/ Comparative PhD (Doctor of Philosophy) 0, School MA/MS (Master of Arts/Science) (T) 5.

APA Accreditation: Clinical PhD (Doctor of Philosophy).

Student Applications/Admissions:
Student Applications
Clinical PhD (Doctor of Philosophy)—Applications 2004–2005, 152. Total applicants accepted 2004–2005, 8. Number enrolled (new admits only) 2004–2005 full-time, 8. Total enrolled 2004–2005 full-time, 25, part-time, 10. Openings 2005–2006, 7. The Median number of years required for completion of a degree are 7. The number of students enrolled full and part-time who were dismissed or voluntarily withdrew from this program area were 1. *Developmental PhD (Doctor of Philosophy)*—Applications 2004–2005, 7. Total applicants accepted 2004–2005, 5. Number enrolled (new admits only) 2004–2005 full-time, 5. Total enrolled 2004–2005 full-time, 6, part-time, 2. Openings 2005–2006, 3. The number of students enrolled full and part-time who were dismissed or voluntarily withdrew from this program area were 0. *Learning/Comparative PhD (Doctor of Philosophy)*—Applications 2004–2005, 6. Total applicants accepted 2004–2005, 2. Number enrolled (new admits only) 2004–2005 full-time, 1. Openings 2005–2006, 3. The number of students enrolled full and part-time who were dismissed or voluntarily withdrew from this program area were 0. *School MA/MS (Master of Arts/Science)*—Applications 2004–2005, 24. Total applicants accepted 2004–2005, 4. Number enrolled (new admits only) 2004–2005 full-time, 4. Total enrolled 2004–2005 full-time, 8, part-time, 4. Openings 2005–2006, 10. The Median number of years required for completion of a degree are 2. The number of students enrolled full and part-time who were dismissed or voluntarily withdrew from this program area were 0.

Admissions Requirements:
Scores: Entries appear in this order: required test or GPA, minimum score (if required), median score of students entering in 2003–2004. Master's Programs: GRE-V 500, 410; GRE-Q 500, 460; last 2 years GPA 3.25, 3.30. Above (#11) information is for school psychology. Doctoral Programs: GRE-V 525, 535; GRE-Q 525, 630; GRE-V+Q no minimum stated; GRE-Subject(Psych) no minimum stated; overall undergraduate GPA 3.25, 3.5. The Clinical program requires scores at 50th percentile or above for GRE Quantitative and Verbal.
Other Criteria: (importance of criteria rated low, medium, or high): GRE/MAT scores high, research experience medium, work experience medium, extracurricular activity low, clinically related public service medium, GPA high, letters of recommendation high, interview medium, statement of goals and objectives medium, Clinical service is a criterion for clinical program only. For additional information on admission requirements, go to: www2.umt.edu/psych/gradinfo.htm.

Student Characteristics: The following represents characteristics of students in 2004–2005 in all graduate psychology programs in the department: Female–full-time 33, part-time 12; Male–full-time 11, part-time 4; African American/Black–full-time 0, part-time 0; Hispanic/Latino(a)–full-time 0, part-time 0; Asian/Pacific Islander–full-time 1, part-time 0; American Indian/Alaska Native–full-time 10, part-time 3; Caucasian–full-time 0, part-time 0; students subject to the Americans With Disabilities Act–full-time 0, part-time 1.

Financial Information/Assistance:
Tuition for Full-Time Study: *Master's:* State residents: per academic year $2,484, $251 per credit hour; Nonstate residents: per academic year $6,866, $616 per credit hour. *Doctoral:* State residents: per academic year $2,731, $271 per credit hour; Nonstate residents: per academic year $7,114, $636 per credit hour. Tuition is subject to change. See the following Web site for updates and changes in tuition costs: www.umt.edu/grad/money/.

Financial Assistance:
First Year Students: Teaching assistantships available for first-year. Average amount paid per academic year: $14,000. Average number of hours worked per week: 15. Apply by January 15. Tuition remission given: full. Research assistantships available for first-year. Average amount paid per academic year: $12,000. Average number of hours worked per week: 15. Apply by Open.
Advanced Students: Teaching assistantships available for advanced students. Average amount paid per academic year: $14,000. Average number of hours worked per week: 15. Apply by January 15. Tuition remission given: full. Research assistantships available for advanced students. Average amount paid per academic year: $12,000. Average number of hours worked per week: 15. Apply by Open.
Contact Information: Of all students currently enrolled full-time, 73% benefitted from one or more of the listed financial assistance programs. Application and information available online at: www.umt.edu/grad/.

Internships/Practica: For those doctoral students for whom a professional internship is required prior to graduation, 5 applied in 2003–2004. Of those who applied, 5 were placed in internships listed by the Association of Psychology Postdoctoral and Internship Programs (APPIC); 5 were placed in APA accredited internships.

Housing and Day Care: On-campus housing is available. Contact University Villages, phone (406) 243-6030. On-campus day care facilities are available. Contact ASUM Office of Child Care, phone (406) 243-2542.

Employment of Department Graduates:

Master's Degree Graduates: Of those who graduated in the academic year 2003–2004, the following categories and numbers represent the post-graduate activities and employment of master's degree graduates: Enrolled in another graduate/professional program (1), enrolled in a post-doctoral residency/fellowship (n/a), employed in independent practice (n/a), employed in a professional position in a school system (4), total from the above (master's) (5).

Doctoral Degree Graduates: Of those who graduated in the academic year 2003–2004, the following categories and numbers represent the post-graduate activities and employment of doctoral degree graduates: Enrolled in a psychology doctoral program (n/a), enrolled in a post-doctoral residency/fellowship (5), other employment position (1), total from the above (doctoral) (6).

Additional Information:

Orientation, Objectives, and Emphasis of Department: The clinical psychology PhD program trains students in basic psychological science and clinical skills including assessment, diagnosis, and therapeutic interventions. The program is based on the scientist-practitioner model and is eclectically oriented. The training is a balanced combination of coursework, practicum and research. Upon completion of coursework, research practicum, and internship experiences, the graduates are well prepared for professional careers as clinical psychologists in institutional, academic, and private settings. The experimental psychology PhD program offers major emphases in the fields of learning-comparative and developmental psychology. Minor areas are offered in quantitative, program evaluation, and special areas of psychology, as well as those fields in which majors are offered. Graduates have found placement in both academic and business settings. The EdS program is offered in conjunction with the School of Education. Coursework in the Psychology Department and the School of Education provides an integrated foundation upon which practicum and internship experiences build such that a graduate has the knowledge and the experience to become an effective school psychologist.

Special Facilities or Resources: The Department of Psychology is housed in a modern building. It has classrooms; offices; research laboratories for social, developmental, and learning experimentation; a shop; and colony rooms for small animals. A clinical psychology center opened in the fall of 1983 and serves as a meeting place for clinical classes, seminars, research groups, and clinical services.

Information for Students With Physical Disabilities: See the following Web site for more information: http://www.umt.edu/dss/.

Application Information:

Send to: Graduate Admissions, Department of Psychology, The University of Montana, Skaggs Building 143, Missoula, MT 59812-1584. Application available online. URL of online application: http://www.applyweb.com/apply/uomont/menu.html. Students are admitted in the Fall, application deadline January 1. For developmental and learning/comparative, October 15 is also acceptable. Fall application deadline for School Psychology is January 15. All deadlines are postmark dates. *Fee:* $45.

Nebraska, University of, Lincoln

Department of Educational Psychology
Teachers College
114 Teachers College Hall
Lincoln, NE 68588-0345
Telephone: (402) 472-2223
Fax: (402) 472-8319
E-mail: *rdeayala@unlserve.unl.edu*
Web: *http://cehsdept.unl.edu/index.php?Page=1011*

Department Information:
1920. Chairperson: R.J. De Ayala. Number of Faculty: total–full-time 21; women–full-time 8; minority–full-time 3.

Programs and Degrees Offered:
Listed in the following order: Program area, degree type (T if terminal Master's), number awarded 7/03–6/04. Cognition, Learning, Development PhD (Doctor of Philosophy) 0, Counseling PhD (Doctor of Philosophy) 3, Quantitative and Qualitative Methods PhD (Doctor of Philosophy) 1, School PhD (Doctor of Philosophy) 5.

APA Accreditation: Counseling PhD (Doctor of Philosophy). School PhD (Doctor of Philosophy).

Student Applications/Admissions:
Student Applications
Cognition, Learning, Development PhD (Doctor of Philosophy)—Applications 2004–2005, 12. Total applicants accepted 2004–2005, 8. Number enrolled (new admits only) 2004–2005 full-time, 3. Total enrolled 2004–2005 full-time, 35, part-time, 2. Openings 2005–2006, 5. *Counseling PhD (Doctor of Philosophy)*—Applications 2004–2005, 55. Total applicants accepted 2004–2005, 20. Openings 2005–2006, 10. *Quantitative and Qualitative Methods (QQME) PhD (Doctor of Philosophy)*—Applications 2004–2005, 14. Total applicants accepted 2004–2005, 7. Number enrolled (new admits only) 2004–2005 full-time, 6. Total enrolled 2004–2005 full-time, 28, part-time, 6. Openings 2005–2006, 5. *School PhD (Doctor of Philosophy)*—Applications 2004–2005, 33. Total applicants accepted 2004–2005, 18. Number enrolled (new admits only) 2004–2005 full-time, 13. Openings 2005–2006, 10.

Admissions Requirements:
Scores: Entries appear in this order: required test or GPA, minimum score (if required), median score of students entering in 2003–2004. Master's Programs: GRE-V no minimum stated, 500; GRE-Q no minimum stated, 575; GRE-V+Q no minimum stated, 1075; GRE-Analytical no minimum stated, 500; overall undergraduate GPA no minimum stated, 3.00; psychology GPA no minimum stated. Doctoral Programs: GRE-V no

minimum stated, 550; GRE-Q no minimum stated, 550; GRE-V+Q no minimum stated, 1100; GRE-Analytical no minimum stated, 500; overall undergraduate GPA no minimum stated, 3.00.
Other Criteria: (importance of criteria rated low, medium, or high): GRE/MAT scores high, research experience high, work experience high, extracurricular activity medium, clinically related public service high, GPA high, letters of recommendation high, interview high, statement of goals and objectives high. Minimum TOEFL score of 550.

Student Characteristics: The following represents characteristics of students in 2004–2005 in all graduate psychology programs in the department: Female–full-time 108, part-time 0; Male–full-time 55, part-time 0; African American/Black–full-time 4, part-time 0; Hispanic/Latino(a)–full-time 3, part-time 0; Asian/Pacific Islander–full-time 4, part-time 0; American Indian/Alaska Native–full-time 0, part-time 0; Caucasian–full-time 0, part-time 0; Multi-ethnic–full-time 1, part-time 0; students subject to the Americans With Disabilities Act–full-time 1, part-time 0.

Financial Information/Assistance:
Tuition for Full-Time Study: *Master's:* State residents: $190 per credit hour; Nonstate residents: $512 per credit hour. *Doctoral:* State residents: $190 per credit hour; Nonstate residents: $512 per credit hour. Tuition is subject to change.

Financial Assistance:
First Year Students: Teaching assistantships available for first-year. Average amount paid per academic year: $12,679. Average number of hours worked per week: 20. Tuition remission given: full. Research assistantships available for first-year. Average amount paid per academic year: $12,679. Average number of hours worked per week: 20. Tuition remission given: full. Fellowships and scholarships available for first-year. Average amount paid per academic year: $7,725. Average number of hours worked per week: 13. Tuition remission given: full.
Advanced Students: Teaching assistantships available for advanced students. Average amount paid per academic year: $12,679. Average number of hours worked per week: 20. Tuition remission given: full. Research assistantships available for advanced students. Average amount paid per academic year: $12,679. Average number of hours worked per week: 20. Tuition remission given: full. Fellowships and scholarships available for advanced students. Average amount paid per academic year: $7,725. Average number of hours worked per week: 13. Tuition remission given: full.
Contact Information: Of all students currently enrolled full-time, 42% benefitted from one or more of the listed financial assistance programs.

Internships/Practica: The Counseling Psychology and School Psychology Programs both have sets of practicum courses wherein students provide direct and consultation services to students, staff and families in urban school settings. The Nebraska Internship

Consortium in Professional Psychology is affiliated with the School Psychology Programs. Doctoral students in the QQME program are encouraged to obtain internships.

Housing and Day Care: On-campus housing is available. See the following Web site for more information: http://www.unl.edu/gradstudies/prospective/housing.shtml. On-campus day care facilities are available. See the following Web site for more information: http://hr.unl.edu/er/childcare.cfm and www.unl.edu/neunion/ChildCare/ChildFee.html.

Employment of Department Graduates:
Master's Degree Graduates: Of those who graduated in the academic year 2003–2004, the following categories and numbers represent the post-graduate activities and employment of master's degree graduates: Enrolled in a post-doctoral residency/fellowship (n/a), employed in independent practice (n/a), total from the above (master's) (0).
Doctoral Degree Graduates: Of those who graduated in the academic year 2003–2004, the following categories and numbers represent the post-graduate activities and employment of doctoral degree graduates: Enrolled in a psychology doctoral program (n/a), total from the above (doctoral) (0).

Additional Information:
Orientation, Objectives, and Emphasis of Department: The objective of the program is to develop applied behavioral scientists able to function in a variety of settings and roles ranging from educational settings to private practice. The broad base of the department offers a diversity of orientations and role models for students.

Special Facilities or Resources: The department operates the Counseling and School Psychology Clinic, which serves as a practicum site for School Psychology and Counseling Psychology programs. In addition, the department maintains excellent contact with the community, which promotes access to practical experiences and research subject pools. The department contains the Buros Center for Testing and its comprehensive reference library of assessment devices. The department also is home to the Center for Instructional Innovation, which conducts research on teaching and learning as well as the Nebraska Research Center on Children, Youth, Families and Schools.

Information for Students With Physical Disabilities: See the following Web site for more information: http://www.unl.edu/equity/.

Application Information:
Send to: University of Nebraska-Lincoln Attention: Tania Aguilar, Admissions Coordinator, Graduate Student Services, 116 Henzlik Hall Lincoln, NE 68588-0355. Application available online. URL of online application: http://cehs.unl.edu/edpsych/graduate/apply.shtml. Students are admitted in the Fall, application deadline January 15; Spring, application deadline October 1. School Psychology program considers applications for admission December 1; Counseling Psychology program considers applications for admission December 15; Cognition, Learning, & Developmental considers applications for admissions at October 1, January 15, and May 15 deadlines. Quantitative and Qualitative Methods in Education (QQME) considers applications for admissions at October 1 and January 15 deadlines. *Fee:* $45. Written request for waiver of fee indicating need/justification for waiver or deferral of application fee.

Nebraska, University of, Lincoln
Department of Psychology
Arts & Sciences
238 Burnett Hall
Lincoln, NE 68588-0308
Telephone: (402) 472-3721
Fax: (402) 472-4637
E-mail: *rbarnes1@unl.edu*
Web: *http://www.unl.edu/psypage*

Department Information:
1889. Chairperson: David J. Hansen. Number of Faculty: total–full-time 25, part-time 2; women–full-time 7; minority–full-time 2.

Programs and Degrees Offered:
Listed in the following order: Program area, degree type (T if terminal Master's), number awarded 7/03–6/04. Clinical PhD (Doctor of Philosophy) 7, Cognitive PhD (Doctor of Philosophy) 2, Law and Psychology, MLS PhD (Doctor of Philosophy) 3, Comparative/ Biopsychology PhD (Doctor of Philosophy) 1, Developmental PhD (Doctor of Philosophy) 0, Social-Personality PhD (Doctor of Philosophy) 0.

APA Accreditation: Clinical PhD (Doctor of Philosophy).

Student Applications/Admissions:
Student Applications
Clinical PhD (Doctor of Philosophy)—Applications 2004–2005, 163. Total applicants accepted 2004–2005, 11. Total enrolled 2004–2005 full-time, 58. Openings 2005–2006, 10. The Median number of years required for completion of a degree are 6. *Cognitive PhD (Doctor of Philosophy)*—Applications 2004–2005, 9. Total applicants accepted 2004–2005, 0. Openings 2005–2006, 2. The Median number of years required for completion of a degree are 5. *Law and Psychology, MLS PhD (Doctor of Philosophy)*—Applications 2004–2005, 25. Total applicants accepted 2004–2005, 6. Total enrolled 2004–2005 full-time, 16. Openings 2005–2006, 4. The Median number of years required for completion of a degree are 6. The number of students enrolled full and part-time who were dismissed or voluntarily withdrew from this program area were 1. *Comparative/ Biopsychology PhD (Doctor of Philosophy)*—Applications 2004–2005, 10. Total applicants accepted 2004–2005, 3. Openings 2005–2006, 3. The Median number of years required for completion of a degree are 5. *Developmental PhD (Doctor of Philosophy)*—Applications 2004–2005, 10. Total applicants accepted 2004–2005, 2. Openings 2005–2006, 3. The Median number of years required for completion of a degree are 5. *Social-Personality PhD (Doctor of Philosophy)*—Applications 2004–2005, 35. Total applicants accepted 2004–2005, 1. Openings 2005–2006, 2. The Median number of years required for completion of a degree are 5.

Admissions Requirements:
Scores: Entries appear in this order: required test or GPA, minimum score (if required), median score of students entering

in 2003–2004. Master's Programs: GRE-V no minimum stated, 610; GRE-Q no minimum stated, 630; GRE-Analytical no minimum stated, 640; GRE-Subject(Psych) no minimum stated, 630; overall undergraduate GPA 3.0, 3.50. Doctoral Programs: GRE-V no minimum stated, 610; GRE-Q no minimum stated, 630; GRE-Analytical no minimum stated, 640; GRE-Subject(Psych) no minimum stated, 630; overall undergraduate GPA 3.0, 3.5.

Other Criteria: (importance of criteria rated low, medium, or high): GRE/MAT scores medium, research experience medium, work experience medium, extracurricular activity low, clinically related public service medium, GPA medium, letters of recommendation high, interview medium, statement of goals and objectives medium.

Student Characteristics: The following represents characteristics of students in 2004–2005 in all graduate psychology programs in the department: Female–full-time 76, part-time 0; Male–full-time 31, part-time 0; African American/Black–full-time 2, part-time 0; Hispanic/Latino(a)–full-time 7, part-time 0; Asian/Pacific Islander–full-time 6, part-time 0; American Indian/Alaska Native–full-time 3, part-time 0; Caucasian–full-time 0, part-time 0; Multi-ethnic–full-time 3, part-time 0.

Financial Information/Assistance:

Tuition for Full-Time Study: *Master's:* State residents: $190 per credit hour; Nonstate residents: $512 per credit hour. *Doctoral:* State residents: $190 per credit hour; Nonstate residents: $512 per credit hour. Tuition is subject to change. See the following Web site for updates and changes in tuition costs: www.unl.edu/gradstudies.

Financial Assistance:

First Year Students: Teaching assistantships available for first-year. Average number of hours worked per week: 19. Tuition remission given: full. Research assistantships available for first-year. Average number of hours worked per week: 19. Tuition remission given: full. Fellowships and scholarships available for first-year. Average number of hours worked per week: 19.

Advanced Students: Teaching assistantships available for advanced students. Average number of hours worked per week: 19. Tuition remission given: full. Research assistantships available for advanced students. Average number of hours worked per week: 19. Tuition remission given: full. Traineeships available for advanced students. Average number of hours worked per week: 19. Tuition remission given: full. Fellowships and scholarships available for advanced students.

Contact Information: Of all students currently enrolled full-time, 100% benefitted from one or more of the listed financial assistance programs. Application and information available online at: http://www.unl.edu/psypage.

Internships/Practica: The clinical program offers numerous internship opportunities for students. We have an excellent record of placements for our students at high-quality internship sites throughout North America and participate in the APPIC internship process. For those doctoral students for whom a professional internship is required prior to graduation, 9 applied in 2003–2004. Of those who applied, 8 were placed in internships listed by the Association of Psychology Postdoctoral and Internship Programs (APPIC); 8 were placed in APA accredited internships.

Housing and Day Care: On-campus housing is available. No on-campus day care facilities are available.

Employment of Department Graduates:

Master's Degree Graduates: Of those who graduated in the academic year 2003–2004, the following categories and numbers represent the post-graduate activities and employment of master's degree graduates: Enrolled in a post-doctoral residency/fellowship (n/a), employed in independent practice (n/a), total from the above (master's) (0).

Doctoral Degree Graduates: Of those who graduated in the academic year 2003–2004, the following categories and numbers represent the post-graduate activities and employment of doctoral degree graduates: Enrolled in a psychology doctoral program (n/a), enrolled in a post-doctoral residency/fellowship (3), employed in an academic position at a university (1), employed in an academic position at a 2-year/4-year college (6), employed in business or industry (research/consulting) (3), employed in a government agency (research) (1), employed in a community mental health/counseling center (1), other employment position (0), total from the above (doctoral) (15).

Additional Information:

Orientation, Objectives, and Emphasis of Department: The Department of Psychology at the University of Nebraska-Lincoln offers PhD programs that emphasize the development of research and teaching excellence, collegial partnerships between students and faculty, and the cross-fertilization of ideas between specializations in the context of a rigorous, but flexible, training program. The goal of the clinical program is to produce broadly trained, scientifically oriented psychologists who have skills in both research and professional activities. The cognitive, comparative, developmental, and social-personality programs all emphasize research training but also place equal importance upon training for college or university teaching and policy/applied careers. Students in the PhD/JD program take their first year in the Law College, and then concentrate on psychology plus law to graduate with a double doctorate.

Special Facilities or Resources: The department has a number of resources including the Ruth Staples Child Development Laboratory, the Center for Children, Families and the Law, the BUROS Mental Measurement Institute, the NEAR Center, the UNL Public Policy Center, and the Lincoln Regional Mental Health Center.

Information for Students With Physical Disabilities: See the following Web site for more information: http://www.unl.edu.

Application Information:
Send to: Admissions Coordinator, Dept. of Psychology, UNL, 238 Burnett, Lincoln, NE 68588-0308. Students are admitted in the Fall; deadlines are January 3 for clinical, January 15 for all others. *Fee:* $45.

Nebraska, University of, Omaha

Department of Psychology
Arts and Sciences
60th & Dodge Streets
Omaha, NE 68182-0274
Telephone: (402) 554-2592; 2313 Joseph Brown
Fax: (402) 554-2556
E-mail: *kdeffenbacher@mail.unomaha.edu*
Web: *http://www.unomaha.edu/~psychweb/*

Department Information:

Chairperson: Kenneth A. Deffenbacher. Number of Faculty: total–full-time 18, part-time 4; women–full-time 8; minority–full-time 2.

Programs and Degrees Offered:

Listed in the following order: Program area, degree type (T if terminal Master's), number awarded 7/03–6/04. Industrial/Organizational MA/MS (Master of Arts/Science) 7, School-MS MS (Master of Science) 6, Psychobiology PhD (Doctor of Philosophy) 1, Developmental MA/MS (Master of Arts/Science) 4, Experimental MA/MS (Master of Arts/Science) 0, Developmental PhD (Doctor of Philosophy) 3, School EdS (Education Specialist) 5, Industrial/Organizational MS (Master of Science) (T) 6, Industrial/Organizational PhD (Doctor of Philosophy) 3.

Student Applications/Admissions:

Student Applications

Industrial/Organizational MA/MS (Master of Arts/Science)—Applications 2004–2005, 15. Total applicants accepted 2004–2005, 7. Number enrolled (new admits only) 2004–2005 full-time, 5. Number enrolled (new admits only) 2004–2005 part-time, 0. Openings 2005–2006, 5. The Median number of years required for completion of a degree are 3. The number of students enrolled full and part-time who were dismissed or voluntarily withdrew from this program area were 0. *School MS (Master Science)*—Applications 2004–2005, 23. Total applicants accepted 2004–2005, 12. Number enrolled (new admits only) 2004–2005 full-time, 6. Openings 2005–2006, 6. The Median number of years required for completion of a degree are 2. The number of students enrolled full and part-time who were dismissed or voluntarily withdrew from this program area were 0. *Psychobiology PhD (Doctor of Philosophy)*—Applications 2004–2005, 4. Total applicants accepted 2004–2005, 3. Number enrolled (new admits only) 2004–2005 full-time, 0. Number enrolled (new admits only) 2004–2005 part-time, 0. Openings 2005–2006, 3. The number of students enrolled full and part-time who were dismissed or voluntarily withdrew from this program area were 0. *Developmental MA/MS (Master of Arts/Science)*—Applications 2004–2005, 6. Total applicants accepted 2004–2005, 4. Number enrolled (new admits only) 2004–2005 full-time, 0. Openings 2005–2006, 3. The Median number of years required for completion of a degree are 3. The number of students enrolled full and part-time who were dismissed or voluntarily withdrew from this program area were 0. *Experimental MA/MS (Master of Arts/Science)*—Applications 2004–2005, 3. Total applicants accepted 2004–2005, 1. Number enrolled (new admits only) 2004–2005 full-time, 1. Number enrolled (new admits only) 2004–2005 part-time, 0. Openings 2005–2006, 3. The number of students enrolled full and part-time who were dismissed or voluntarily withdrew from this program area were 0. *Developmental PhD (Doctor of Philosophy)*—Applications 2004–2005, 2. Total applicants accepted 2004–2005, 2. Number enrolled (new admits only) 2004–2005 full-time, 0. Number enrolled (new admits only) 2004–2005 part-time, 0. Openings 2005–2006, 2. The Median number of years required for completion of a degree are 6. The number of students enrolled full and part-time who were dismissed or voluntarily withdrew from this program area were 1. *School EdS (Education Specialist)*—Applications 2004–2005, 4. Total applicants accepted 2004–2005, 4. Number enrolled (new admits only) 2004–2005 full-time, 4. Number enrolled (new admits only) 2004–2005 part-time, 0. Openings 2005–2006, 5. The Median number of years required for completion of a degree are 4. The number of students enrolled full and part-time who were dismissed or voluntarily withdrew from this program area were 0. *Industrial/Organizational-MS MA/MS (Master of Arts/Science)*—Applications 2004–2005, 19. Total applicants accepted 2004–2005, 9. Number enrolled (new admits only) 2004–2005 full-time, 6. Number enrolled (new admits only) 2004–2005 part-time, 0. Openings 2005–2006, 6. The Median number of years required for completion of a degree are 2. The number of students enrolled full and part-time who were dismissed or voluntarily withdrew from this program area were 1. *Industrial/Organizational PhD (Doctor of Philosophy)*—Applications 2004–2005, 4. Total applicants accepted 2004–2005, 4. Number enrolled (new admits only) 2004–2005 full-time, 4. Total enrolled 2004–2005 full-time, 12. Openings 2005–2006, 3. The Median number of years required for completion of a degree are 6. The number of students enrolled full and part-time who were dismissed or voluntarily withdrew from this program area were 0.

Admissions Requirements:

Scores: Entries appear in this order: required test or GPA, minimum score (if required), median score of students entering in 2003–2004. Master's Programs: GRE-V no minimum stated, 500; GRE-Q no minimum stated, 605; GRE-V+Q no minimum stated, 1105; GRE-Analytical no minimum stated, 660; overall undergraduate GPA no minimum stated, 3.69. Doctoral Programs: GRE-V no minimum stated, 580; GRE-Q no minimum stated, 630; GRE-V+Q no minimum stated, 1200; GRE-Analytical no minimum stated, 660; GRE-Subject(Psych) no minimum stated, 645; overall undergraduate GPA no minimum stated, 3.79.

Other Criteria: (importance of criteria rated low, medium, or high): GRE/MAT scores high, research experience high, work experience medium, extracurricular activity medium, clinically related public service low, GPA high, letters of recommendation high, interview medium, statement of goals and objectives high.

Student Characteristics: The following represents characteristics of students in 2004–2005 in all graduate psychology programs in the department: Female–full-time 53, part-time 0; Male–full-time 21, part-time 0; African American/Black–full-time 1, part-time 0; Hispanic/Latino(a)–full-time 1, part-time 0; Asian/Pacific Islander–full-time 4, part-time 0; American Indian/Alaska Native–full-time 0, part-time 0; Caucasian–full-time 68, part-time 0.

Financial Information/Assistance:

Tuition for Full-Time Study: *Master's:* State residents: $146 per credit hour; Nonstate residents: $334 per credit hour. *Doctoral:* State residents: $199 per credit hour; Nonstate residents: $512 per credit hour. Tuition is subject to change.

Financial Assistance:

First Year Students: Teaching assistantships available for first-year. Average amount paid per academic year: $10,142. Average number of hours worked per week: 20. Apply by February 1. Tuition remission given: full. Research assistantships available for first-year. Average amount paid per academic year: $10,142. Average number of hours worked per week: 20. Apply by February 1. Tuition remission given: full. Fellowships and scholarships available for first-year. Average amount paid per academic year: $10,142. Average number of hours worked per week: 20. Apply by February 1. Tuition remission given: full.

Advanced Students: Teaching assistantships available for advanced students. Average amount paid per academic year: $10,142. Average number of hours worked per week: 20. Apply by February 1. Tuition remission given: full. Research assistantships available for advanced students. Average amount paid per academic year: $10,142. Average number of hours worked per week: 20. Apply by February 1. Tuition remission given: full. Traineeships available for advanced students. Average number of hours worked per week: 20. Tuition remission given: full and partial. Fellowships and scholarships available for advanced students. Average amount paid per academic year: $10,142. Average number of hours worked per week: 20. Apply by February 1. Tuition remission given: full and partial.

Contact Information: Of all students currently enrolled full-time, 50% benefitted from one or more of the listed financial assistance programs.

Internships/Practica: An internship in school psychology is available and required within the EdS program leading to certification in the field of school psychology. Practica are also available (and for some degrees required) in industrial/organizational psychology and developmental psychology.

Housing and Day Care: On-campus housing is available. See the following Web site for more information: www.campushousing.com/uneb. On-campus day care facilities are available. See the following Web site for more information: http://mbsc.unomaha.edu/child.htm.

Employment of Department Graduates:

Master's Degree Graduates: Of those who graduated in the academic year 2003–2004, the following categories and numbers represent the post-graduate activities and employment of master's degree graduates: Enrolled in a post-doctoral residency/fellowship (n/a), employed in independent practice (n/a), total from the above (master's) (0).

Doctoral Degree Graduates: Of those who graduated in the academic year 2003–2004, the following categories and numbers represent the post-graduate activities and employment of doctoral degree graduates: Enrolled in a psychology doctoral program (n/a), total from the above (doctoral) (0).

Additional Information:

Orientation, Objectives, and Emphasis of Department: The department is broadly eclectic, placing emphasis on theory, research, and application. The MA program is primarily for students who anticipate continuing their education at the PhD level. The MA degree may be completed in eight areas of psychology. The MS program is primarily for students who view the master's degree as terminal and who wish to emphasize application in the fields of educational-school or industrial/organizational psychology. These two areas may be emphasized within the MA program as well.

Special Facilities or Resources: The department maintains extensive laboratory facilities in a variety of experimental areas, both human and animal. The animal colony consists of rats, gerbils, mice, and golden-lion tamarins. Up-to-date interactive computer facilities are readily available. The Center for Applied Psychological Services is a departmentally controlled, faculty-student consulting service that provides an opportunity to gain practical experience in industrial psychology and school psychology. The department maintains working relations with the Children's Rehabilitation Institute, the Department of Pediatrics, the Department of Physiology, and the University of Nebraska Medical Center. In addition, contact exists with the Boys Town Institute, Boys Town Home, Henry Doorly Zoo, Union Pacific Railroad, and Mutual of Omaha.

Application Information:

Send to: Department Chair. Students are admitted in the Fall, application deadline February 1. *Fee:* $45.

Nevada, University of, Las Vegas
Department of Psychology
Liberal Arts
4505 Maryland Parkway
Las Vegas, NV 89154-5030
Telephone: (702) 895-3305
Fax: (702) 895-0195
E-mail: *psyunlv@unlv.nevada.edu*
Web: *http://psychology.unlv.edu*

Department Information:
1960. Chairperson: Mark H. Ashcraft. Number of Faculty: total–full-time 18, part-time 10; women–full-time 5, part-time 3; minority–full-time 1.

Programs and Degrees Offered:
Listed in the following order: Program area, degree type (T if terminal Master's), number awarded 7/03–6/04. Clinical PhD (Doctor of Philosophy) 0, Experimental PhD (Doctor of Philosophy) 0.

Student Applications/Admissions:
Student Applications
Clinical PhD (Doctor of Philosophy)—Applications 2004–2005, 82. Total applicants accepted 2004–2005, 11. Number enrolled (new admits only) 2004–2005 full-time, 10. Openings 2005–2006, 7. The number of students enrolled full and part-time who were dismissed or voluntarily withdrew from this program area were 1. *Experimental PhD (Doctor of Philosophy)*—Applications 2004–2005, 14. Total applicants accepted 2004–2005, 4. Number enrolled (new admits only) 2004–2005 full-time, 4. Number enrolled (new admits only) 2004–2005 part-time, 0. Openings 2005–2006, 5. The number of students enrolled full and part-time who were dismissed or voluntarily withdrew from this program area were 1.

Admissions Requirements:
Scores: Entries appear in this order: required test or GPA, minimum score (if required), median score of students entering in 2003–2004. Doctoral Programs: GRE-V 500, 545; GRE-Q 500, 625; GRE-Subject(Psych) 500, 590; overall undergraduate GPA 3.2, 3.63; psychology GPA 3.2, 3.77.
Other Criteria: (importance of criteria rated low, medium, or high): GRE/MAT scores high, research experience high, work experience low, clinically related public service medium, GPA high, letters of recommendation high, interview high, statement of goals and objectives high. Experimental program ranks clinical related public services as low.

Student Characteristics: The following represents characteristics of students in 2004–2005 in all graduate psychology programs in the department: Female–full-time 60, part-time 0; Male–full-time 16, part-time 0; African American/Black–full-time 2, part-time 0; Hispanic/Latino(a)–full-time 9, part-time 0; Asian/Pacific Islander–full-time 3, part-time 0; American Indian/Alaska Native–full-time 1, part-time 0; Caucasian–full-time 60, part-time 0;

Multi-ethnic–full-time 1, part-time 0; students subject to the Americans With Disabilities Act–full-time 0, part-time 0.

Financial Information/Assistance:
Tuition for Full-Time Study: *Doctoral:* State residents: $126 per credit hour; Nonstate residents: $126 per credit hour. See the following Web site for updates and changes in tuition costs: http://www.unlv.edu/Colleges/Graduate/financing/cost_fees.htm.

Financial Assistance:
First Year Students: Teaching assistantships available for first-year. Average amount paid per academic year: $12,000. Average number of hours worked per week: 20. Apply by January 15. Tuition remission given: partial. Research assistantships available for first-year. Average amount paid per academic year: $12,000. Average number of hours worked per week: 20. Apply by January 15. Tuition remission given: partial.
Advanced Students: Teaching assistantships available for advanced students. Average amount paid per academic year: $12,000. Average number of hours worked per week: 20. Apply by March 1. Tuition remission given: partial. Research assistantships available for advanced students. Average amount paid per academic year: $12,000. Average number of hours worked per week: 20. Apply by March 1. Tuition remission given: partial. Fellowships and scholarships available for advanced students. Average amount paid per academic year: $15,000. Average number of hours worked per week: 0. Apply by March 1. Tuition remission given: full.
Contact Information: Of all students currently enrolled full-time, 96% benefitted from one or more of the listed financial assistance programs. Application and information available online at: http://www.unlv.edu/Colleges/Graduate/financing/financing.htm.

Internships/Practica: Students work in various community settings as part of their training experience. Additional information is available on the program website: psychology.unlv.edu. For those doctoral students for whom a professional internship is required prior to graduation, 6 applied in 2003–2004. Of those who applied, 5 were placed in internships listed by the Association of Psychology Postdoctoral and Internship Programs (APPIC); 5 were placed in APA accredited internships.

Housing and Day Care: No on-campus housing is available. On-campus day care facilities are available.

Employment of Department Graduates:
Master's Degree Graduates: Of those who graduated in the academic year 2003–2004, the following categories and numbers represent the post-graduate activities and employment of master's degree graduates: Enrolled in a post-doctoral residency/fellowship (n/a), employed in independent practice (n/a), total from the above (master's) (0).
Doctoral Degree Graduates: Of those who graduated in the academic year 2003–2004, the following categories and numbers represent the post-graduate activities and employment of doctoral degree graduates: Enrolled in a psychology doctoral program (n/a), total from the above (doctoral) (0).

Additional Information:

Orientation, Objectives, and Emphasis of Department: The UNLV Clinical Psychology Doctoral Program trains students to address human concerns through both scholarly research and the application of psychological knowledge and skills. We train students as generalist scientist–practitioners prepared to conduct scientific research and clinical interventions with children and adults. Our program began in 1999. We will seek accreditation from the American Psychological Association during the 2005/2006 academic year. The UNLV Experimental Psychology Doctoral Program is designed to prepare experimental psychologists for the rich opportunities that are presented by a changing employment picture. This program addresses the training needs of new psychologists in ways that traditional programs do not. Specifically, the program combines a strong focus on the major content areas of experimental psychology and methodology/statistics, while also providing opportunities to learn skills and conduct research that can be applied to real-world problems. In short, graduate training will produce experimental psychologists who can be employed in both academic and non-academic settings.

Special Facilities or Resources: The strongest resource of the psychology department is the many talents of its diverse faculty. Our graduate program is small enough to provide close personal interaction experiences for training, and yet we encourage students to demonstrate initiative and to undertake the major responsibility for their graduate learning experiences. Student research is encouraged within the department and throughout the university.

Information for Students With Physical Disabilities: See the following Web site for more information: http://www.unlv.edu/studentlife/disability/index.html.

Application Information:

Send to: See Web site for application information: http://psychology.unlv.edu/index.html. Application available online. URL of online application: http://psychology.unlv.edu/html/unlvpsy_graduate_programs.html. Students are admitted in the Fall, application deadline January 15. *Fee:* $60. Waivers are obtained through the Graduate College office.

Nevada, University of, Reno

Department of Psychology/296
Liberal Arts
1664 N. Virginia
Reno, NV 89557
Telephone: (775) 784-6828
Fax: (775) 784-1126
E-mail: *vmf@unr.edu*
Web: *http://www.unr.edu/psych/*

Department Information:

1920. Chair: Victoria M. Follette. Number of Faculty: total–full-time 17, part-time 5; women–full-time 7, part-time 2; minority–full-time 1, part-time 1.

Programs and Degrees Offered:

Listed in the following order: Program area, degree type (T if terminal Master's), number awarded 7/03–6/04. Behavior Analysis PhD (Doctor of Philosophy) 6, Experimental PhD (Doctor of Philosophy) 4, Clinical PhD (Doctor of Philosophy) 8.

APA Accreditation: Clinical PhD (Doctor of Philosophy).

Student Applications/Admissions:

Student Applications

Behavior Analysis PhD (Doctor of Philosophy)—Applications 2004–2005, 27. Total applicants accepted 2004–2005, 6. Number enrolled (new admits only) 2004–2005 full-time, 6. Number enrolled (new admits only) 2004–2005 part-time, 0. Openings 2005–2006, 4. The Median number of years required for completion of a degree are 6. The number of students enrolled full and part-time who were dismissed or voluntarily withdrew from this program area were 1. *Experimental PhD (Doctor of Philosophy)*—Applications 2004–2005, 8. Total applicants accepted 2004–2005, 6. Number enrolled (new admits only) 2004–2005 full-time, 3. Number enrolled (new admits only) 2004–2005 part-time, 0. Openings 2005–2006, 5. The Median number of years required for completion of a degree are 5. The number of students enrolled full and part-time who were dismissed or voluntarily withdrew from this program area were 2. *Clinical PhD (Doctor of Philosophy)*—Applications 2004–2005, 100. Total applicants accepted 2004–2005, 8. Number enrolled (new admits only) 2004–2005 full-time, 8. Number enrolled (new admits only) 2004–2005 part-time, 0. Openings 2005–2006, 8. The Median number of years required for completion of a degree are 7. The number of students enrolled full and part-time who were dismissed or voluntarily withdrew from this program area were 2.

Admissions Requirements:

Scores: Entries appear in this order: required test or GPA, minimum score (if required), median score of students entering in 2003–2004. Master's Programs: GRE-V no minimum stated, 470; GRE-Q no minimum stated, 510; GRE-Analytical no minimum stated, 600; GRE-Subject(Psych) 550; overall undergraduate GPA 3.0. For the GRE-V+Q, the minimum score is 1200 for clinical. For the Undergraduate GPA, 3.5 is suggested for Clinical. Doctoral Programs: GRE-V no minimum stated, 550; GRE-Q no minimum stated, 545; GRE-Analytical no minimum stated, 505; GRE-Subject(Psych) 550, 550; overall undergraduate GPA 3.0; 1200 for clinical for the GRE-V+Q. For the Undergraduate GPA, 3.5 suggested for clinical. *Other Criteria:* (importance of criteria rated low, medium, or high): GRE/MAT scores high, research experience high, work experience high, extracurricular activity medium, clinically related public service medium, GPA high, letters of recommendation high, interview high, statement of goals and objectives high. Interviews for admission into behavior analysis and clinical is required.

Student Characteristics: The following represents characteristics of students in 2004–2005 in all graduate psychology programs in the department: Female–full-time 71, part-time 0; Male–full-time 40, part-time 0; African American/Black–full-time 1, part-time 0; Hispanic/Latino(a)–full-time 12, part-time 0; Asian/Pacific Islander–full-time 4, part-time 0; American Indian/Alaska Native–full-time 2, part-time 0; Caucasian–full-time 89, part-time 0;

Multi-ethnic–full-time 3, part-time 0; students subject to the Americans With Disabilities Act–full-time 0, part-time 0.

Financial Information/Assistance:

Tuition for Full-Time Study: *Master's:* State residents: $127 per credit hour; Nonstate residents: per academic year $4,337, $127 per credit hour. *Doctoral:* State residents: $127 per credit hour; Nonstate residents: per academic year $4,337, $127 per credit hour. Tuition is subject to change.

Financial Assistance:

First Year Students: Teaching assistantships available for first-year. Average amount paid per academic year: $14,000. Average number of hours worked per week: 20. Tuition remission given: full. Research assistantships available for first-year. Average amount paid per academic year: $14,000. Average number of hours worked per week: 20. Tuition remission given: full.

Advanced Students: Teaching assistantships available for advanced students. Average amount paid per academic year: $14,000. Average number of hours worked per week: 20. Tuition remission given: full. Research assistantships available for advanced students. Average amount paid per academic year: $14,000. Average number of hours worked per week: 20. Tuition remission given: full.

Contact Information: Of all students currently enrolled full-time, 80% benefitted from one or more of the listed financial assistance programs.

Internships/Practica: The department offers several teaching/research assistantships. Experimental—Some students receive support as research assistants through individual faculty grants. Behavior Analysis—All doctoral students and most master's students receive full support from assistantships or consultation services. Clinical—Participation in clinical practica is required for students. From the last half of the first year through the third year, students see clients at the Psychological Service Center, an in-house clinic. During the fourth year, students are required to complete a 1000 hour practicum (externship) on campus or at agencies in the area. Finally, students are required to complete a 2000 hour, APA-approved internship during their final year. For those doctoral students for whom a professional internship is required prior to graduation, 6 applied in 2003–2004. Of those who applied, 6 were placed in internships listed by the Association of Psychology Postdoctoral and Internship Programs (APPIC); 5 were placed in APA accredited internships.

Housing and Day Care: On-campus housing is available. See the following Web site for more information: www.unr.edu/reslife/html/oncampus.html. On-campus day care facilities are available.

Employment of Department Graduates:

Master's Degree Graduates: Of those who graduated in the academic year 2003–2004, the following categories and numbers represent the post-graduate activities and employment of master's degree graduates: Enrolled in a psychology doctoral program (0), enrolled in another graduate/professional program (0), enrolled in a post-doctoral residency/fellowship (n/a), employed in independent practice (n/a), employed in an academic position at a university (0), employed in an academic position at a 2-year/4-year college (0), employed in business or industry (research/consulting) (0), employed in business or industry (management) (0), employed in a government agency (research) (0), employed in a government agency (professional services) (0), employed in a community mental health/counseling center (2), employed in a hospital/medical center (2), still seeking employment (0), not seeking employment (0), other employment position (0), total from the above (master's) (4).

Doctoral Degree Graduates: Of those who graduated in the academic year 2003–2004, the following categories and numbers represent the post-graduate activities and employment of doctoral degree graduates: Enrolled in a psychology doctoral program (n/a), enrolled in another graduate/professional program (0), enrolled in a post-doctoral residency/fellowship (3), employed in independent practice (2), employed in an academic position at a university (2), employed in an academic position at a 2-year/4-year college (0), employed in business or industry (research/consulting) (1), employed in business or industry (management) (0), employed in a government agency (research) (0), employed in a government agency (professional services) (4), employed in a community mental health/counseling center (0), employed in a hospital/medical center (2), still seeking employment (0), not seeking employment (0), other employment position (0), total from the above (doctoral) (14).

Additional Information:

Orientation, Objectives, and Emphasis of Department: The experimental program in psychology is research-oriented. The experimental division offers specialized work in human cognition and cognitive neuroscience; learning, perception and psychophysics; and animal communication. The clinical program has a scientist-practitioner emphasis and offers skills in psychotherapy, assessment, evaluation, and community psychology. The behavior analysis program emphasizes applied behavior analysis, especially in institutional settings, and examines both the theoretical and applied ramifications of the behavioral programs.

Special Facilities or Resources: Experimental— the program has active labs with facilities for research in visual perception, memory, cognition, and animal behavior and communication (including opportunities for research at the primate center at Central Washington University). Behavior Analysis—the program has a lab where they work with autistic children and developmentally disabled clients. Clinical—the primary academic/research facility of the program is the Psychological Service Center, an in-house training clinic that serves the community by offering services on a sliding fee basis.

Application Information:
Specify Clinical, Behavioral Analysis or Experimental Admissions, Psychology Department/296, University of Nevada, Reno, NV 89557. URL of online application: http://www.unr.edu/psych/gradappl.html. For the Fall semester, the deadline for Clinical is January 1; February 1 for Behavior Analysis, and March 1 for Experimental. For the Spring semester, the deadline is November 1 for Experimental only. *Fee:* $40. $20 if previously enrolled in UNR.

Antioch New England Graduate School

Clinical Psychology
40 Avon Street
Keene, NH 03431-3552
Telephone: (603) 357-3122
Fax: (603) 357-1679
E-mail: *admissions@antiochne.edu*
Web: *http://www.antiochne.edu*

Department Information:

1982. Chairperson: Roger L. Peterson, PhD, ABPP. Number of Faculty: total–full-time 10, part-time 17; women–full-time 5, part-time 6; minority–full-time 1.

Programs and Degrees Offered:

Listed in the following order: Program area, degree type (T if terminal Master's), number awarded 7/03–6/04. Clinical PsyD (Doctor of Psychology) 22.

APA Accreditation: Clinical PsyD (Doctor of Psychology).

Student Applications/Admissions:

Student Applications

Clinical PsyD (Doctor of Psychology)—Applications 2004–2005, 110. Total applicants accepted 2004–2005, 60. Number enrolled (new admits only) 2004–2005 full-time, 30. Number enrolled (new admits only) 2004–2005 part-time, 0. Total enrolled 2004–2005 full-time, 125, part-time, 40. Openings 2005–2006, 26. The Median number of years required for completion of a degree are 6. The number of students enrolled full and part-time who were dismissed or voluntarily withdrew from this program area were 6.

Admissions Requirements:

Scores: Entries appear in this order: required test or GPA, minimum score (if required), median score of students entering in 2003–2004. Master's Programs: The Department of Clinical Psychology does not have separate master's program. Doctoral Programs: GRE-V n/a, 530; GRE-Q n/a, 540; GRE-V+Q n/a, 1070; GRE-Analytical n/a, 555; GRE-Subject(Psych) n/a, 580; overall undergraduate GPA n/a, 3.28.

Other Criteria: (importance of criteria rated low, medium, or high): GRE/MAT scores medium, research experience medium, work experience medium, extracurricular activity low, clinically related public service medium, GPA high, letters of recommendation high, interview high, statement of goals and objectives high. Requires evidence of academic promise, personal and interpersonal competence, and clinical and professional promise. For additional information on admission requirements, go to: www.antiochne.edu.

Student Characteristics: The following represents characteristics of students in 2004–2005 in all graduate psychology programs in the department: Female–full-time 130, part-time 0; Male–full-time 35, part-time 0; African American/Black–full-time 2, part-time 0; Hispanic/Latino(a)–full-time 4, part-time 0; Asian/Pacific Islander–full-time 1, part-time 0; American Indian/Alaska Native–full-time 0, part-time 0; Caucasian–full-time 150, part-time 0; Multi-ethnic–full-time 8, part-time 0; students subject to the Americans With Disabilities Act–full-time 5, part-time 0.

Financial Information/Assistance:

Tuition for Full-Time Study: *Doctoral:* State residents: per academic year $21,500; Nonstate residents: per academic year $21,500. Tuition is subject to change.

Financial Assistance:

First Year Students: Teaching assistantships available for first-year. Average amount paid per academic year: $1,200. Average number of hours worked per week: 6. Research assistantships available for first-year. Average amount paid per academic year: $1,730. Average number of hours worked per week: 6.

Advanced Students: Teaching assistantships available for advanced students. Average amount paid per academic year: $1,667. Average number of hours worked per week: 6. Research assistantships available for advanced students. Average amount paid per academic year: $2,425. Average number of hours worked per week: 6.

Contact Information: Of all students currently enrolled full-time, 17% benefitted from one or more of the listed financial assistance programs. Application and information available online at: www.antiochne.edu.

Internships/Practica: Students complete practica at agencies within driving distance around New England. About 12 students per year do a practicum at the Antioch Psychological Services Center (PSC), within the Department of Clinical Psychology. It functions as a mental health clinic providing a range of psychological services to residents from Keene and surrounding communities, and to Antioch New England students in departments other than Clinical Psychology. These services include individual psychotherapy, couple and family therapy, individual and family assessment, and various problem-specific psychoeducational groups and seminars. In addition, the PSC is actively involved in community outreach services; clinicians are encouraged to develop public psychoeducation and consultation activities, and to work in collaboration with other social service agencies for the purpose of ongoing community needs assessment and program development. A practicum at the PSC offers the student a unique opportunity for more concentrated interaction with core faculty—through supervision, training, and involvement in applied clinical and research projects of mutual interest. Specialized training opportunities exist for students interested in health psychology, family therapy, and assessment. For those doctoral students for whom a professional internship is required prior to graduation, 19 applied in 2003–2004. Of those who applied, 17 were placed in internships listed by the Association of Psychology Postdoctoral and Internship Programs (APPIC); 14 were placed in APA accredited internships.

Housing and Day Care: No on-campus housing is available. No on-campus day care facilities are available.

Employment of Department Graduates:

Master's Degree Graduates: Of those who graduated in the academic year 2003–2004, the following categories and numbers represent the post-graduate activities and employment of master's degree graduates: Enrolled in a post-doctoral residency/fellowship (n/a), employed in independent practice (n/a), total from the above (master's) (0).

Doctoral Degree Graduates: Of those who graduated in the academic year 2003–2004, the following categories and numbers represent the post-graduate activities and employment of doctoral degree graduates: Enrolled in a psychology doctoral program (n/a), enrolled in another graduate/professional program (0), enrolled in a post-doctoral residency/fellowship (0), employed in independent practice (3), employed in an academic position at a university (0), employed in an academic position at a 2-year/4-year college (0), employed in other positions at a higher education institution (4), employed in a professional position in a school system (2), employed in business or industry (research/consulting) (0), employed in business or industry (management) (0), employed in a government agency (research) (0), employed in a government agency (professional services) (0), employed in a community mental health/counseling center (6), employed in a hospital/medical center (2), still seeking employment (0), not seeking employment (1), other employment position (0), do not know (4), total from the above (doctoral) (22).

Additional Information:

Orientation, Objectives, and Emphasis of Department: Our practitioner-scholar program prepares professional psychologists for multiple roles for the expanded world of 21st century clinical psychology, including not only intervention, assessment, and research but also supervision, management, administration, consultation, and public policy. With a commitment to social responsibility, social justice, and diversity, we emphasize a social vision of clinical psychology, responsive to the needs of the larger society. The program includes broad training with a range of theoretical perspectives, a sound psychological knowledge base, and supervised practice. It follows the educational model developed by the National Council of Schools and Programs of Professional Psychology (NCSPP). This model specifies seven core professional competency areas: relationship, assessment, intervention, research and evaluation, consultation and education, management and supervision, and diversity (we have required courses in each) and, of course, includes basic psychological science. Research for clinical psychology is rooted in solving professional and social problems, where science and practice are integrated and complementary in the required dissertation. Preparation as "local clinical scientists" includes opportunities for training in program evaluation, as well as a range of other psychological topics and methodologies. Our pedagogy brings together theory, practice, and research through integrative, reflective learning experiences which help students develop their professional "voice."

Special Facilities or Resources: The Center for Research on Psychological Practice (CROPP) in the Department of Clinical Psychology serves both the department and the community. This center is designed to address particular emerging educational aspects of doctoral training in clinical psychology that are not regularly included within the usual professional psychology curriculum—those relevant to applied clinical research skills and the associated administrative, consultative, and policy-creation roles of doctoral level psychologists. Several specific areas of research

are priorities for CROPP. These include program evaluation and quality assurance issues, such as needs assessment, outcome and satisfaction research, cost-benefit analysis, policy analysis, and other topics relevant to mental health service management: public welfare issues such as treatment access, utilization, and outcome for underserved, rural, low socioeconomic, and minority populations; development of novel treatment and delivery systems; and methodological issues including the assessment and development of methods and measures appropriate for practice research. The research is done primarily in community service settings and entails collaboration with agencies and caregivers throughout the region. The development of this kind of research center, particularly within the context of a doctoral program in clinical psychology, has not, to our knowledge, been done elsewhere in the country. The Antioch New England Multicultural Center for Research and Practice addresses the diverse array of emerging multicultural information, which represents an enormous and unique opportunity to revolutionize and improve education, training, research, and human services while addressing concerns of social justice. The Center has a particular focus on racial and ethnic minority and immigrant youth, adults, and families. It provides an excellent model of how the combination of research and practice can have a positive impact on communities across New England and beyond. The services of the Multicultural Center include social support for racial and ethnic minority people; individual and group multicultural interactions; workshops on multicultural awareness and acceptance; workshops on racism and stereotypes; consultation with professionals, educators, and businesses on multicultural applications and services; and coalition-building among disenfranchised groups. Its Web-based services include access to multicultural tests housed in the Center, resources of multicultural test titles and reviews, multicultural lecture notes, awareness exercises, documentation of process and outcome of multicultural service delivery, and a national multicultural course syllabus archive.

Application Information:

Send to: Office of Doctoral Admissions, Antioch New England Graduate School, 40 Avon Street, Keene, NH, 03431-3552. Application available online. Students are admitted in the Fall, application deadline January 14. *Fee:* $75.

Dartmouth College
Psychological and Brain Sciences
6207 Moore Hall
Hanover, NH 03755-3578
Telephone: (603) 646-3181
Fax: (603) 646-1419
E-mail: *psychological.and.brain.sciences@dartmouth.edu*
Web: *http://www.dartmouth.edu/artsci/psych/grad.html*

Department Information:

1894. Chairperson: Todd Heatherton. Number of Faculty: total—full-time 20, part-time 10; women—full-time 5, part-time 4; minority—full-time 2.

Programs and Degrees Offered:

Listed in the following order: Program area, degree type (T if terminal Master's), number awarded 7/03–6/04. General Experimental PhD (Doctor of Philosophy) 4.

Student Applications/Admissions:

Student Applications

General Experimental PhD (Doctor of Philosophy)—Applications 2004–2005, 96. Total applicants accepted 2004–2005, 12. Number enrolled (new admits only) 2004–2005 full-time, 4. Openings 2005–2006, 4. The Median number of years required for completion of a degree are 4. The number of students enrolled full and part-time who were dismissed or voluntarily withdrew from this program area were 0.

Admissions Requirements:

Scores: Entries appear in this order: required test or GPA, minimum score (if required), median score of students entering in 2003–2004. Doctoral Programs: GRE-V no minimum stated; GRE-Q no minimum stated; GRE-Analytical no minimum stated; overall undergraduate GPA no minimum stated.

Other Criteria: (importance of criteria rated low, medium, or high): GRE/MAT scores high, research experience high, work experience medium, extracurricular activity low, GPA high, letters of recommendation high, interview medium, statement of goals and objectives high.

Student Characteristics: The following represents characteristics of students in 2004–2005 in all graduate psychology programs in the department: Female–full-time 15, part-time 0; Male–full-time 12, part-time 0; African American/Black–full-time 0, part-time 0; Hispanic/Latino(a)–full-time 1, part-time 0; Asian/Pacific Islander–full-time 0, part-time 0; American Indian/Alaska Native–full-time 1, part-time 0; Caucasian–full-time 25, part-time 0.

Financial Information/Assistance:

Financial Assistance:

First Year Students: Fellowships and scholarships available for first-year. Average amount paid per academic year: $17,386. Apply by none. Tuition remission given: full.

Advanced Students: Fellowships and scholarships available for advanced students. Average amount paid per academic year: $19,020. Tuition remission given: full.

Contact Information: Of all students currently enrolled full-time, 100% benefitted from one or more of the listed financial assistance programs.

Internships/Practica: No information provided.

Housing and Day Care: On-campus housing is available. No on-campus day care facilities are available.

Employment of Department Graduates:

Master's Degree Graduates: Of those who graduated in the academic year 2003–2004, the following categories and numbers represent the post-graduate activities and employment of master's degree graduates: Enrolled in a post-doctoral residency/fellowship (n/a), employed in independent practice (n/a), total from the above (master's) (0).

Doctoral Degree Graduates: Of those who graduated in the academic year 2003–2004, the following categories and numbers represent the post-graduate activities and employment of doctoral degree graduates: Enrolled in a psychology doctoral program (n/a), total from the above (doctoral) (0).

Additional Information:

Orientation, Objectives, and Emphasis of Department: The graduate program offers training in social psychology, cognition/

perception, cognitive neuroscience, and behavioral neuroscience. Many of our students pursue research that bridges these areas. Because of its moderate size, the program emphasizes a close working relationship between faculty and students. The program has a strong experimental orientation in which students serve research and teaching apprenticeships with faculty. The emphasis is on professional development for academic careers.

Special Facilities or Resources: The department has excellent laboratories with ample equipment and superior computer facilities.

Application Information:
Send to: Chair, Graduate Committee, 6207 Moore Hall, Hanover, NH 03755-3578. Students are admitted in the Fall, application deadline January 15. *Fee:* $40.

New Hampshire, University of
Department of Psychology
Conant Hall
Durham, NH 03824
Telephone: (603) 862-2360
Fax: (603) 862-4986
E-mail: *janicec@cisunix.unh.edu*
Web: *http://www.unh.edu/psychology/*

Department Information:
1923. Chairperson: Kenneth Fuld. Number of Faculty: total–full-time 27, part-time 1; women–full-time 12; minority–full-time 1.

Programs and Degrees Offered:
Listed in the following order: Program area, degree type (T if terminal Master's), number awarded 7/03–6/04. Developmental PhD (Doctor of Philosophy), History PhD (Doctor of Philosophy), Sensation/Perception PhD (Doctor of Philosophy), Social/Personality PhD (Doctor of Philosophy), Cognitive Neuroscience PhD (Doctor of Philosophy), Behavioral Neuroscience PhD (Doctor of Philosophy).

Student Applications/Admissions:

Student Applications

Developmental PhD (Doctor of Philosophy)—History PhD (Doctor of Philosophy)—Sensation/Perception PhD (Doctor of Philosophy)—Social/Personality PhD (Doctor of Philosophy)—Cognitive Neuroscience PhD (Doctor of Philosophy)—Behavioral Neuroscience PhD (Doctor of Philosophy).

Admissions Requirements:

Scores: Entries appear in this order: required test or GPA, minimum score (if required), median score of students entering in 2003–2004. Doctoral Programs: GRE-V no minimum stated; GRE-Q no minimum stated; GRE-Analytical no minimum stated; GRE-Subject(Psych) no minimum stated; overall undergraduate GPA no minimum stated; psychology GPA no minimum stated.

Other Criteria: (importance of criteria rated low, medium, or high): GRE/MAT scores high, research experience high, work experience low, extracurricular activity low, GPA high, letters of recommendation high, interview low, statement of goals and objectives high.

Student Characteristics: The following represents characteristics of students in 2004–2005 in all graduate psychology programs in the department: Female–full-time 18, part-time 0; Male–full-time 13, part-time 0; African American/Black–full-time 1, part-time 0; Hispanic/Latino(a)–full-time 0, part-time 0; Asian/Pacific Islander–full-time 1, part-time 0; American Indian/Alaska Native–full-time 0, part-time 0; Caucasian–full-time 29, part-time 0.

Financial Information/Assistance:
Financial Assistance:
First Year Students: Teaching assistantships available for first-year. Average amount paid per academic year: $12,875. Average number of hours worked per week: 20. Apply by February 15. Tuition remission given: full.

Advanced Students: Teaching assistantships available for advanced students. Average amount paid per academic year: $13,175. Average number of hours worked per week: 20. Tuition remission given: full. Fellowships and scholarships available for advanced students. Average amount paid per academic year: $13,750. Average number of hours worked per week: 0. Tuition remission given: full.

Contact Information: Of all students currently enrolled full-time, 100% benefitted from one or more of the listed financial assistance programs.

Internships/Practica: No information provided.

Housing and Day Care: On-campus housing is available. See the following Web sites for more information: http://unhinfo.unh.edu/housing/gradhousing/gradhousing.html; http://unhinfo.unh.edu/housing/famhousing/famhousing.html. On-campus day care facilities are available. See the following Web site for more information: http://www.unh.edu/csdc/.

Employment of Department Graduates:
Master's Degree Graduates: Of those who graduated in the academic year 2003–2004, the following categories and numbers represent the post-graduate activities and employment of master's degree graduates: Enrolled in a post-doctoral residency/fellowship (n/a), employed in independent practice (n/a), total from the above (master's) (0).

Doctoral Degree Graduates: Of those who graduated in the academic year 2003–2004, the following categories and numbers represent the post-graduate activities and employment of doctoral degree graduates: Enrolled in a psychology doctoral program (n/a), enrolled in a post-doctoral residency/fellowship (1), employed in an academic position at a university (3), employed in business or industry (research/consulting) (1), total from the above (doctoral) (5).

Additional Information:
Orientation, Objectives, and Emphasis of Department: The program's basic goal is the development of psychologists who have a broad knowledge of psychology, who can teach and communicate effectively, and who can carry out sound research in one of the following areas of specialization: Brain, Behavior, and Cognition; Developmental Psychology; History of Psychology; or Social Psychology/Personality. Besides the usual academic courses, our program places a distinctive emphasis on preparing graduate students for future roles as faculty members in college or university settings. Students complete a year-long seminar and practicum in the teaching of psychology, which introduces them to the theory and practice of teaching, while they concurrently teach under the supervision of master-teachers. Students also gain experience in other faculty roles such as sponsoring undergraduate students' research and serving on committees. After graduation, most students secure academic positions. All students receive tuition waivers and stipends for at least 4 years, in exchange for serving as teaching or research assistants in their early years and as teachers in their later years. Students can apply for research funds.

Special Facilities or Resources: The department occupies several buildings and offers research facilities, equipment, and resources in all of its areas of specialization. In addition, the department has many microcomputers and terminals that may be used to access the university's mainframe computer.

Application Information:
Send to: Dean of the Graduate School, University of New Hampshire, Thompson Hall, Durham, NH 03824. Application available online. Students are admitted in the Fall, application deadline February 15. *Fee:* $60. Financial aid applications are available.

Fairleigh Dickinson University, Madison
Department of Psychology M-AB2-01
College at Florham
285 Madison Avenue
Madison, NJ 07940
Telephone: (973) 443-8547
Fax: (973) 443-8562
E-mail: *chell@fdu.edu*
Web: *http://alpha.fdu.edu/psychweb*

Department Information:
1962. Chairperson: Dr. Robert M. Chell. Number of Faculty: total–full-time 11, part-time 16; women–full-time 6, part-time 7; minority–full-time 1, part-time 1.

Programs and Degrees Offered:
Listed in the following order: Program area, degree type (T if terminal Master's), number awarded 7/03–6/04. Clinical/counseling MA/MS (Master of Arts/Science) (T) 43, Industrial/Organizational MA/MS (Master of Arts/Science) (T) 15, Organizational Behavior MA/MS (Master of Arts/Science) (T) 10.

Student Applications/Admissions:
Student Applications
Clinical/counseling MA/MS (Master of Arts/Science)—Applications 2004–2005, 132. Total applicants accepted 2004–2005, 112. Total enrolled 2004–2005 full-time, 66, part-time, 46. Openings 2005–2006, 50. The Median number of years required for completion of a degree are 3. The number of students enrolled full and part-time who were dismissed or voluntarily withdrew from this program area were 4. *Industrial/Organizational MA/MS (Master of Arts/Science)*—Applications 2004–2005, 30. Total applicants accepted 2004–2005, 22. Total enrolled 2004–2005 full-time, 10, part-time, 19. Openings 2005–2006, 20. The Median number of years required for completion of a degree are 3. The number of students enrolled full and part-time who were dismissed or voluntarily withdrew from this program area were 2. *Organizational Behavior MA/MS (Master of Arts/Science)*—Applications 2004–2005, 11. Total applicants accepted 2004–2005, 10. Openings 2005–2006, 15. The Median number of years required for completion of a degree are 2. The number of students enrolled full and part-time who were dismissed or voluntarily withdrew from this program area were 0.

Admissions Requirements:
Scores: Entries appear in this order: required test or GPA, minimum score (if required), median score of students entering in 2003–2004. Master's Programs: GRE-V 500, 550; GRE-Q 500, 550; GRE-V+Q 1000, 1100; GRE-Subject(Psych) 500, 550; overall undergraduate GPA 3.0, 3.4; psychology GPA 3.0, 3.4.
Other Criteria: (importance of criteria rated low, medium, or high): GRE/MAT scores medium, research experience medium, work experience medium, extracurricular activity medium, clinically related public service low, GPA high, letters

of recommendation high, interview medium, statement of goals and objectives high. Organizational program has a minimum work experience requirement. For additional information on admission requirements, go to: www.fdu.edu.

Student Characteristics: The following represents characteristics of students in 2004–2005 in all graduate psychology programs in the department: Female–full-time 64, part-time 51; Male–full-time 20, part-time 14; African American/Black–full-time 4, part-time 3; Hispanic/Latino(a)–full-time 4, part-time 6; Asian/Pacific Islander–full-time 2, part-time 3; American Indian/Alaska Native–full-time 1, part-time 0; Caucasian–full-time 71, part-time 53; Multi-ethnic–full-time 2, part-time 0; students subject to the Americans With Disabilities Act–full-time 1, part-time 0.

Financial Information/Assistance:
Tuition for Full-Time Study: *Master's:* State residents: $735 per credit hour; Nonstate residents: $735 per credit hour. Tuition is subject to change. See the following Web site for updates and changes in tuition costs: www.fdu.edu.

Financial Assistance:
First Year Students: Teaching assistantships available for first-year. Average amount paid per academic year: $2,000. Average number of hours worked per week: 20. Apply by March 31. Tuition remission given: partial.
Advanced Students: Teaching assistantships available for advanced students. Average amount paid per academic year: $0. Average number of hours worked per week: 20. Apply by March 31. Tuition remission given: full.
Contact Information: Of all students currently enrolled full-time, 8% benefitted from one or more of the listed financial assistance programs. Application and information available online at: http://www.fdu.edu.

Internships/Practica: Both the Masters in Clinical/Counseling Psychology and Industrial/Organizational Psychology have practica and/or internships in a variety of program related settings. Clinical/Counseling students complete their practica and become eligible to sit for the New Jersey Licensed Professional Counselor designation if so desired.

Housing and Day Care: On-campus housing is available. See the following Web site for more information: www.fdu.edu. On-campus day care facilities are available.

Employment of Department Graduates:
Master's Degree Graduates: Of those who graduated in the academic year 2003–2004, the following categories and numbers represent the post-graduate activities and employment of master's degree graduates: Enrolled in a psychology doctoral program (5), enrolled in another graduate/professional program (3), enrolled in a post-doctoral residency/fellowship (n/a), employed in independent practice (n/a), total from the above (master's) (8).
Doctoral Degree Graduates: Of those who graduated in the academic year 2003–2004, the following categories and numbers represent the post-graduate activities and employment of doctoral

degree graduates: Enrolled in a psychology doctoral program (n/a), total from the above (doctoral) (0).

Additional Information:

Orientation, Objectives, and Emphasis of Department: The programs and courses offered by the psychology department are designed to meet the needs of students who wish to prepare for employment in various scientific and professional areas of psychology such as research, teaching, and practice in a variety of organizational settings (e.g. treatment centers, school settings, counseling centers, human resource departments, consulting organizations). In addition, programs and courses also may be taken by those students who wish to develop a background for subsequent work leading to a doctoral degree.

Personal Behavior Statement: www.fdu.edu.

Special Facilities or Resources: The department is able to provide facilities for research in counseling and industrial/organizational behavior. Most faculty members are practicing psychologists and provide intern-type experiences for students.

Information for Students With Physical Disabilities: See the following Web site for more information: www.fdu.edu.

Application Information:

Send to: Office of Admissions, Fairleigh Dickinson University, 285 Madison Avenue, Madison, NJ 07940. See the FDU Web site to apply, www.fdu.edu. Application available online. Students are admitted in the Fall. Programs have rolling admissions. *Fee:* $40.

Fairleigh Dickinson University, Metropolitan Campus (2004 data)

School of Psychology
University College: Arts-Sciences-Professional Studies
1000 River Road
Teaneck, NJ 07666
Telephone: (201) 692-2300
Fax: (201) 692-2304
E-mail: *capuano@fdu.edu*
Web: *http://www.fdu.edu*

Department Information:

1960. Director: Christopher A. Capuano, PhD Number of Faculty: total–full-time 19, part-time 19; women–full-time 9, part-time 8; minority–full-time 1, part-time 1.

Programs and Degrees Offered:

Listed in the following order: Program area, degree type (T if terminal Master's), number awarded 7/03–6/04. General/ Theoretical MA/MS (Master of Arts/Science) (T) 17, Clinical PhD (Doctor of Philosophy) 15, School PsyD (Doctor of Psychology) 12, Psychopharmacology MA/MS (Master of Arts/Science) (T) 0, School MA/MS (Master of Arts/Science) (T) 7.

Student Applications/Admissions:

Student Applications

General/ Theoretical MA/MS (Master of Arts/Science)—Applications 2004–2005, 48. Total applicants accepted 2004–2005,

22. Total enrolled 2004–2005 full-time, 13, part-time, 24. Openings 2005–2006, 15. The Median number of years required for completion of a degree are 3. The number of students enrolled full and part-time who were dismissed or voluntarily withdrew from this program area were 2. *Clinical PhD (Doctor of Philosophy)*—Applications 2004–2005, 127. Total applicants accepted 2004–2005, 35. Openings 2005–2006, 12. The Median number of years required for completion of a degree are 5. The number of students enrolled full and part-time who were dismissed or voluntarily withdrew from this program area were 1. *School PsyD (Doctor of Psychology)*—Applications 2004–2005, 34. Total applicants accepted 2004–2005, 14. Openings 2005–2006, 15. The Median number of years required for completion of a degree are 3. The number of students enrolled full and part-time who were dismissed or voluntarily withdrew from this program area were 1. *Psychopharmacology MA/MS (Master of Arts/Science)*—Applications 2004–2005, 35. Total applicants accepted 2004–2005, 35. Total enrolled 2004–2005 part-time, 39. Openings 2005–2006, 15. The Median number of years required for completion of a degree are 2. The number of students enrolled full and part-time who were dismissed or voluntarily withdrew from this program area were 7. *School MA/MS (Master of Arts/Science)*—Applications 2004–2005, 27. Total applicants accepted 2004–2005, 15. Total enrolled 2004–2005 part-time, 47. Openings 2005–2006, 13. The Median number of years required for completion of a degree are 3. The number of students enrolled full and part-time who were dismissed or voluntarily withdrew from this program area were 0.

Admissions Requirements:

Scores: Entries appear in this order: required test or GPA, minimum score (if required), median score of students entering in 2003–2004. Master's Programs: GRE-V 500, 560; GRE-Q 500, 580; GRE-V+Q 1000, 1140; GRE-Subject(Psych) 500, 570; overall undergraduate GPA 3.00, 3.20; psychology GPA 3.25, 3.40. Minimum scores/GPAs indicated are preferred, not required. Doctoral Programs: GRE-V 550, 590; GRE-Q 550, 610; GRE-V+Q 1100, 1200; GRE-Subject(Psych) 600, 640; overall undergraduate GPA 3.25, 3.50. Minimum scores/GPAs indicated are preferred, not required.

Other Criteria: (importance of criteria rated low, medium, or high): research experience high, work experience medium, extracurricular activity medium, clinically related public service high, letters of recommendation high, interview high, statement of goals and objectives high. These criteria are used for admission to PhD and PsyD programs. For PsyD program, research experience would be low and work experience would be medium-high.

Student Characteristics: The following represents characteristics of students in 2004–2005 in all graduate psychology programs in the department: Female–full-time 91, part-time 73; Male–full-time 26, part-time 37; Caucasian–full-time 0, part-time 0.

Financial Information/Assistance:

Tuition for Full-Time Study: *Master's:* State residents: $700 per credit hour; Nonstate residents: $700 per credit hour. *Doctoral:* State residents: per academic year $21,396; Nonstate residents: per academic year $21,396.

Financial Assistance:

First Year Students: Research assistantships available for first-year. Average amount paid per academic year: $10,698. Average number of hours worked per week: 20. Apply by PhD students.

Advanced Students: Research assistantships available for advanced students. Average amount paid per academic year: $8,698. Average number of hours worked per week: 20. Apply by PhD students.

Contact Information: Of all students currently enrolled full-time, 33% benefitted from one or more of the listed financial assistance programs.

Internships/Practica: All PhD students are required to complete research and clinical practica during their first three years. Clinical practica may be completed on-campus at the University's Center for Psychological Services. For those doctoral students for whom a professional internship is required prior to graduation, 20 applied in 2003–2004. Of those who applied, 20 were placed in internships listed by the Association of Psychology Postdoctoral and Internship Programs (APPIC); 18 were placed in APA accredited internships.

Housing and Day Care: No on-campus housing is available. No on-campus day care facilities are available.

Employment of Department Graduates:

Master's Degree Graduates: Of those who graduated in the academic year 2003–2004, the following categories and numbers represent the post-graduate activities and employment of master's degree graduates: Enrolled in a post-doctoral residency/fellowship (n/a), employed in independent practice (n/a), total from the above (master's) (0).

Doctoral Degree Graduates: Of those who graduated in the academic year 2003–2004, the following categories and numbers represent the post-graduate activities and employment of doctoral degree graduates: Enrolled in a psychology doctoral program (n/a), total from the above (doctoral) (0).

Additional Information:

Orientation, Objectives, and Emphasis of Department: The orientation of the department is essentially based on the scientist-practitioner model. In terms of theoretical orientations, some faculty are dynamicists, some behaviorists, and some humanists, though there is a sense of eclecticism that pervades those who are practitioners. There is a considerable emphasis on empirical research as the preferred basis for developing a theoretical orientation.

Special Facilities or Resources: The department operates the Center for Psychological Services, which provides students in the PhD and PsyD programs opportunities in therapy and assessment with adults, children, families, and couples. The department has research laboratories equipped for experiments with humans as well as with small animals. Equipment includes computer facilities, both micro- and mainframe, a four-channel physiograph, electro-physiological stimulating and recording equipment, operant equipment for programming and recording behavior, two- and four-channel tachistoscopes, various other sensory apparatus, standard and computer-based EEG recorders, and equipment and supplies for psychopharmacological studies.

Application Information:
Send to: School of Psychology (T-WH1-01), Fairleigh Dickinson University, 1000 River Road, Teaneck, NJ 07666. Students are admitted in the Fall: February 1, PhD; March 1, PsyD; March 15, MA-School. Spring admission is only for applicants to the BA/MA and MA programs in general/theoretical psychology. *Fee:* $40. The application fee is waived or deferred for Fairleigh Dickinson graduates. $40 for doctoral programs and $35 for MA programs.

Georgian Court University

Psychology Department/Counseling Psychology
900 Lakewood Avenue
Lakewood, NJ 08701-2697
Telephone: (732) 987-2617
Fax: (732) 376-7301
E-mail: *james@georgian.edu*
Web: *http://www.georgian.edu/psychgy/ps-wwd.htm*

Department Information:
1972. Chairperson: Elaine Thompson. Number of Faculty: total–full-time 11, part-time 8; women–full-time 4, part-time 3.

Programs and Degrees Offered:
Listed in the following order: Program area, degree type (T if terminal Master's), number awarded 7/03–6/04. Counseling MA/MS (Master of Arts/Science) (T) 11, School MA/MS (Master of Arts/Science) 2.

Student Applications/Admissions:

Student Applications

Counseling MA/MS (Master of Arts/Science)—Applications 2004–2005, 28. Total applicants accepted 2004–2005, 19. Number enrolled (new admits only) 2004–2005 full-time, 5. Number enrolled (new admits only) 2004–2005 part-time, 10. Total enrolled 2004–2005 full-time, 21, part-time, 67. Openings 2005–2006, 20. The Median number of years required for completion of a degree are 3. The number of students enrolled full and part-time who were dismissed or voluntarily withdrew from this program area were 1. *School MA/MS (Master of Arts/Science)*—Applications 2004–2005, 5. Total applicants accepted 2004–2005, 5. Number enrolled (new admits only) 2004–2005 part-time, 5. Total enrolled 2004–2005 part-time, 8. Openings 2005–2006, 8. The Median number of years required for completion of a degree are 3. The number of students enrolled full and part-time who were dismissed or voluntarily withdrew from this program area were 0.

Admissions Requirements:

Scores: Entries appear in this order: required test or GPA, minimum score (if required), median score of students entering in 2003–2004. Master's Programs: GRE-V no minimum stated, 450; GRE-Q no minimum stated, 510; GRE-Analytical no minimum stated, 490; GRE-Subject(Psych) no minimum stated, 500; overall undergraduate GPA 3.00.

Other Criteria: (importance of criteria rated low, medium, or high): GRE/MAT scores medium, research experience low, work experience medium, extracurricular activity medium, clinically related public service medium, GPA high, letters of recommendation high, interview medium, statement of goals and objectives high.

Student Characteristics: The following represents characteristics of students in 2004–2005 in all graduate psychology programs in the department: Female–full-time 20, part-time 71; Male–full-time 1, part-time 4; African American/Black–full-time 0, part-time 2; Hispanic/Latino(a)–full-time 0, part-time 4; Asian/Pacific Islander–full-time 0, part-time 1; American Indian/Alaska Native–full-time 0, part-time 0; Caucasian–full-time 21, part-time 68; students subject to the Americans With Disabilities Act–full-time 1, part-time 3.

Financial Information/Assistance:

Tuition for Full-Time Study: *Master's:* State residents: $530 per credit hour; Nonstate residents: $530 per credit hour.

Financial Assistance:

First Year Students: No information provided.

Advanced Students: Research assistantships available for advanced students. Average number of hours worked per week: 9. Apply by April 30. Tuition remission given: partial.

Contact Information: Of all students currently enrolled full-time, 8% benefitted from one or more of the listed financial assistance programs.

Internships/Practica: Practicum experiences take place in college counseling centers, mental health outpatient facilities, inpatient state and private hospitals and schools.

Housing and Day Care: No on-campus housing is available. No on-campus day care facilities are available.

Employment of Department Graduates:

Master's Degree Graduates: Of those who graduated in the academic year 2003–2004, the following categories and numbers represent the post-graduate activities and employment of master's degree graduates: Enrolled in a post-doctoral residency/fellowship (n/a), employed in independent practice (n/a), employed in a professional position in a school system (1), employed in a community mental health/counseling center (1), total from the above (master's) (2).

Doctoral Degree Graduates: Of those who graduated in the academic year 2003–2004, the following categories and numbers represent the post-graduate activities and employment of doctoral degree graduates: Enrolled in a psychology doctoral program (n/a), total from the above (doctoral) (0).

Additional Information:

Orientation, Objectives, and Emphasis of Department: Course work for both the Master's and School Psychology Certificate program is designed to provide sound clinical training based in theory. The Professional Counselor Certificate Program is for students who have an MA degree who wish to pursue additional coursework necessary to academically qualify for the Licensed Professional Counselor designation through the State of New Jersey. The majority of the faculty is full-time with experience in clinical and school settings. Four full-time faculty and three adjuncts are licensed to practice psychology in New Jersey and bring a wealth of diverse clinical experience. Four of the full-time faculty and one adjunct are certified school psychologists with many years of experience in the public and parochial schools.

Coursework will prepare the students to work in diverse settings, to make assessments of children and adults, to develop clinical skills with strong theoretical underpinnings, to become competent professionals. Practica experiences are provided in a variety of settings in the surrounding community, with supervision provided on-site and within the classroom. School psychology externships meet New Jersey state requirements. Courses meet in the late afternoon and evening. Students may attend either part-time or full-time. Georgian Court College is a private Catholic college.

Special Facilities or Resources: There are 4 computer labs available on campus and an interactive television lab.

Application Information:
Send to: Department Chair. Students are admitted in the Fall, application deadline November 15; Spring, application deadline June 1. *Fee:* $40.

Kean University
Department of Psychology
Morris Avenue
Union, NJ 07083
Telephone: (908) 737-4000
Fax: (908) 737-4004
E-mail: *grad-adm@cougar.kean.edu*
Web: *http://www.kean.edu*

Department Information:
1969. Chairperson: Dr. Suzanne Bousquet. Number of Faculty: total–full-time 21; women–full-time 12; minority–full-time 3; faculty subject to the Americans With Disabilities Act 1.

Programs and Degrees Offered:
Listed in the following order: Program area, degree type (T if terminal Master's), number awarded 7/03–6/04. Marriage and Family Therapy Other 4, Human Behavior and Organizational Psychology MA/MS (Master of Arts/Science) (T) 14, Psychological Services MA/MS (Master of Arts/Science) (T) 11, School Psychology MA/MS (Master of Arts/Science) (T) 8, Educational Psychology MA/MS (Master of Arts/Science) 5.

Student Applications/Admissions:
Student Applications

Marriage and Family Therapy Other—Applications 2004–2005, 8. Total applicants accepted 2004–2005, 4. Total enrolled 2004–2005 full-time, 9, part-time, 10. Openings 2005–2006, 12. The Median number of years required for completion of a degree are 3. The number of students enrolled full and part-time who were dismissed or voluntarily withdrew from this program area were 0. *Human Behavior and Organizational Psychology MA/MS (Master of Arts/Science)*—Applications 2004–2005, 18. Total applicants accepted 2004–2005, 4. Total enrolled 2004–2005 full-time, 11, part-time, 28. Openings 2005–2006, 20. The number of students enrolled full and part-time who were dismissed or voluntarily withdrew from this program area were 0. *Psychological Services MA/MS (Master of Arts/Science)*—Applications 2004–2005, 19. Total applicants accepted 2004–2005, 13. Total enrolled 2004–2005 full-time, 7, part-time, 30. Openings 2005–2006, 15. The Median number of years required for completion of a degree are 3. The number of students enrolled full and part-time who were dismissed or voluntarily withdrew from this program area were 0. *School Psychology MA/MS (Master of Arts/Science)*—Applications 2004–2005, 51. Total applicants accepted 2004–2005, 13. Total enrolled 2004–2005 full-time, 10, part-time, 23. Openings 2005–2006, 12. The number of students enrolled full and part-time who were dismissed or voluntarily withdrew from this program area were 0. *Educational Psychology MA/MS (Master of Arts/Science)*—Applications 2004–2005, 15. Total applicants accepted 2004–2005, 7. Total enrolled 2004–2005 full-time, 11, part-time, 6. Openings 2005–2006, 12. The Median number of years required for completion of a degree are 3.

Admissions Requirements:
Scores: Entries appear in this order: required test or GPA, minimum score (if required), median score of students entering in 2003–2004. Master's Programs: GRE-V no minimum stated, 520; GRE-Q no minimum stated, 540; GRE-V+Q no minimum stated, 1060; GRE-Analytical no minimum stated; overall undergraduate GPA 3.0; last 2 years GPA 3.0; psychology GPA 3.0.
Other Criteria: (importance of criteria rated low, medium, or high): GRE/MAT scores high, research experience medium, work experience medium, extracurricular activity low, clinically related public service high, GPA high, letters of recommendation high, interview medium, statement of goals and objectives medium.

Student Characteristics: The following represents characteristics of students in 2004–2005 in all graduate psychology programs in the department: Female–full-time 39, part-time 58; Male–full-time 22, part-time 33; African American/Black–full-time 0, part-time 0; Hispanic/Latino(a)–full-time 0, part-time 0; Asian/Pacific Islander–full-time 0, part-time 0; American Indian/Alaska Native–full-time 0, part-time 0; Caucasian–full-time 0, part-time 0.

Financial Information/Assistance:
Tuition for Full-Time Study: *Master's:* State residents: per academic year $3,936, $437 per credit hour; Nonstate residents: per academic year $5,004, $556 per credit hour. Tuition is subject to change. See the following Web site for updates and changes in tuition costs: www.kean.edu.

Financial Assistance:
First Year Students: Teaching assistantships available for first-year. Average amount paid per academic year: $3,600. Average number of hours worked per week: 15. Apply by June 1. Tuition remission given: full.
Advanced Students: Teaching assistantships available for advanced students. Average amount paid per academic year: $3,600. Average number of hours worked per week: 15. Apply by June 1. Tuition remission given: full.
Contact Information: Of all students currently enrolled full-time, 25% benefitted from one or more of the listed financial assistance programs. Application and information available online at: www.kean.edu.

Internships/Practica: Internships are available for school psychology, marriage and family therapy and behavioral science students in a variety of settings.

Housing and Day Care: No on-campus housing is available. On-campus day care facilities are available. See the following Web site for more information: www.kean.edu.

Employment of Department Graduates:
Master's Degree Graduates: Of those who graduated in the academic year 2003–2004, the following categories and numbers represent the post-graduate activities and employment of master's degree graduates: Enrolled in a post-doctoral residency/fellowship (n/a), employed in independent practice (n/a).
Doctoral Degree Graduates: Of those who graduated in the academic year 2003–2004, the following categories and numbers represent the post-graduate activities and employment of doctoral degree graduates: Enrolled in a psychology doctoral program (n/a).

Additional Information:
Orientation, Objectives, and Emphasis of Department: Our academic emphasis is eclectic. All classes are small, which facilitates the opportunity for personal growth.

Special Facilities or Resources: Special resources include two complete computer facilities. One is integrated with statistics, tests and measurement, and experimental psychology courses; the other is used in conjunction with professional psychology testing courses and general instruction.

Application Information:
Send to: Office of Graduate Admissions, Joanne Morris, Director, Kean University, Union, NJ 07083. Application available online at www.kean.edu. Students are admitted in the Fall, application deadline June 1; Spring, application deadline November 1. For School Psychology, deadline is March 15. Spring admits for all programs except School Psychology and Educational Psychology. *Fee:* $60.

Monmouth University
Department of Psychology
Monmouth University
West Long Branch, NJ 07764-1898
Telephone: (732) 571-3400/3570
Fax: (732) 263-5159
E-mail: *acavaiol@monmouth.edu*
Web: *http://www.monmouth.edu*

Department Information:
1993. Chairperson: Fran Trotman, PhD. Number of Faculty: total–full-time 7, part-time 2; women–full-time 3, part-time 2; minority–full-time 1, part-time 1.

Programs and Degrees Offered:
Listed in the following order: Program area, degree type (T if terminal Master's), number awarded 7/03–6/04. Psychological Counseling MA/MS (Master of Arts/Science), Professional Counseling (Certificate) Other.

Student Applications/Admissions:
Student Applications
Psychological Counseling MA/MS (Master of Arts/Science)—Professional Counseling (Certificate) Other—No information provided.

Admissions Requirements:

Scores: Entries appear in this order: required test or GPA, minimum score (if required), median score of students entering in 2003–2004. Master's Programs: Graduates of colleges of recognized standing, whose records show evidence of ability to do graduate work, may apply for admission. Selection for all programs is based in the student's ability to do graduate work of high quality as shown by the distinction of the undergraduate record, particularly in the major, scores on appropriate admission tests, and/or other supporting documentation where required. All admission decisions are approved by the program director of the department in which the student plans to earn a graduate degree.

Other Criteria: (importance of criteria rated low, medium, or high): The two main criteria used in evaluating an application are cumulative high school grade point average and SAT or ACT scores. Students accepted to Monmouth for the fall 2001 semester typically scored between 990-1120 on the SAT and had about a B average. There are students who scored higher and lower than these figures.

Student Characteristics: The following represents characteristics of students in 2004–2005 in all graduate psychology programs in the department: Female–full-time 29, part-time 69; Male–full-time 12, part-time 18; African American/Black–full-time 8, part-time 9; Hispanic/Latino(a)–full-time 3, part-time 6; Asian/Pacific Islander–full-time 4, part-time 7; American Indian/Alaska Native–full-time 0, part-time 1; Caucasian–full-time 0, part-time 0; Multi-ethnic–full-time 2, part-time 4.

Financial Information/Assistance:

Tuition for Full-Time Study: *Master's:* State residents: $549 per credit hour. Tuition is subject to change.

Financial Assistance:

First Year Students: Research assistantships available for first-year. Tuition remission given: full and partial. Fellowships and scholarships available for first-year. Tuition remission given: full and partial.

Advanced Students: Research assistantships available for advanced students. Tuition remission given: full and partial. Fellowships and scholarships available for advanced students. Tuition remission given: full and partial.

Contact Information: Of all students currently enrolled full-time, 60% benefitted from one or more of the listed financial assistance programs. Application and information available online at: http://www.Monmouth.edu/admission/adm_finaid.asp.

Internships/Practica: No information provided.

Housing and Day Care: No on-campus housing is available. No on-campus day care facilities are available.

Employment of Department Graduates:

Master's Degree Graduates: Of those who graduated in the academic year 2003–2004, the following categories and numbers represent the post-graduate activities and employment of master's degree graduates: Enrolled in a post-doctoral residency/fellowship (n/a), employed in independent practice (n/a), total from the above (master's) (0).

Doctoral Degree Graduates: Of those who graduated in the academic year 2003–2004, the following categories and numbers represent the post-graduate activities and employment of doctoral degree graduates: Enrolled in a psychology doctoral program (n/a), total from the above (doctoral) (0).

Additional Information:

Orientation, Objectives, and Emphasis of Department: The psychology curriculum is designed to focus on the scientific study of human and animal behavior and related mental and physiological processes. Training in psychology can lead to employment in business and industry, government, social agencies, hospitals, clinics, and in fields such as personnel, sales, management, psychological testing, vocational guidance, clinical work, school psychology, college teaching, social service, or research. Monmouth offers two graduate programs in psychological counseling: a Master of Arts in Psychological Counseling and a post-master's certificate in Professional Counseling that builds on the Master's program. The MA program provides a broad-based exploration of the field that equips students with the theoretical and practical applications vital to positions in human service agencies. Graduates will be prepared for employment in drug and alcohol counseling centers, rehabilitation clinics, human resources agencies, and various mental health and other health care settings where psychological counseling is needed. The MA program offers a core curriculum that gives students a solid foundation in counseling procedure, intervention skills, quantitative methods, assessment methods, and interpretation of psychological assessments. By combining academic course work with experiential study, the MA program prepares students to excel in the traditional counseling field, as well as in emerging areas.

Information for Students With Physical Disabilities: See the following Web site for more information: www.monmouth.edu/acedemics/lcac/disabilities/specialist.asp.

Application Information:

Send to: Office of Graduate Admissions, (732) 571-3452, (732) 571-5247. Application available online. URL of online application: www.monmouth.edu. Students are admitted in the Fall, application deadline August 15; Spring, application deadline December 15; Summer, application deadline April 15. Programs have rolling admissions.

Princeton University
Psychology Department
Green Hall
Princeton, NJ 08544-1010
Telephone: (609) 258-5289
Fax: (609) 258-1113
E-mail: *arlener@princeton.edu*
Web: *http://www.princeton.edu/~psych/*

Department Information:

1901. Chairperson: Deborah Prentice. Number of Faculty: total–full-time 21, part-time 5; women–full-time 9, part-time 1; minority–full-time 1.

Programs and Degrees Offered:

Listed in the following order: Program area, degree type (T if terminal Master's), number awarded 7/03–6/04. Cognitive PhD

(Doctor of Philosophy) 2, Neuroscience PhD (Doctor of Philosophy) 2, Social/ Personality PhD (Doctor of Philosophy) 3.

Student Applications/Admissions:

Student Applications

Cognitive PhD (Doctor of Philosophy)—Applications 2004–2005, 21. Total applicants accepted 2004–2005, 3. Number enrolled (new admits only) 2004–2005 full-time, 3. Openings 2005–2006, 4. The Median number of years required for completion of a degree are 5. The number of students enrolled full and part-time who were dismissed or voluntarily withdrew from this program area were 0. *Neuroscience PhD (Doctor of Philosophy)*—Applications 2004–2005, 77. Total applicants accepted 2004–2005, 4. Number enrolled (new admits only) 2004–2005 full-time, 3. Openings 2005–2006, 7. The Median number of years required for completion of a degree are 5. The number of students enrolled full and part-time who were dismissed or voluntarily withdrew from this program area were 0. *Social/ Personality PhD (Doctor of Philosophy)*—Applications 2004–2005, 95. Total applicants accepted 2004–2005, 12. Number enrolled (new admits only) 2004–2005 full-time, 7. Openings 2005–2006, 5. The Median number of years required for completion of a degree are 5. The number of students enrolled full and part-time who were dismissed or voluntarily withdrew from this program area were 0.

Admissions Requirements:

Scores: Entries appear in this order: required test or GPA, minimum score (if required), median score of students entering in 2003–2004. Doctoral Programs: GRE-V no minimum stated, 620; GRE-Q no minimum stated, 675; overall undergraduate GPA no minimum stated, 3.77; psychology GPA no minimum stated, 3.88.

Other Criteria: (importance of criteria rated low, medium, or high): GRE/MAT scores high, research experience high, work experience high, extracurricular activity low, GPA high, letters of recommendation high, interview medium, statement of goals and objectives high. The regular application provides a place to indicate whether you are seeking aid from the University. All graduate students in psychology receive a full fellowship during their first year at Princeton. In subsequent years, full support is available through fellowships, teaching assistantships and research assistantships. For additional information on admission requirements, go to: http://www.princeton.edu/~psych/ OR gso.princeton.edu.

Student Characteristics: The following represents characteristics of students in 2004–2005 in all graduate psychology programs in the department: Female–full-time 23, part-time 0; Male–full-time 19, part-time 0; African American/Black–full-time 3, part-time 0; Hispanic/Latino(a)–full-time 0, part-time 0; Asian/Pacific Islander–full-time 1, part-time 0; American Indian/Alaska Native–full-time 0, part-time 0; Caucasian–full-time 38, part-time 0; Multi-ethnic–full-time 0, part-time 0; students subject to the Americans With Disabilities Act–full-time 0, part-time 0.

Financial Information/Assistance:

Tuition for Full-Time Study: *Doctoral:* State residents: per academic year $30,720; Nonstate residents: per academic year $30,720. See the following Web site for updates and changes in tuition costs: gso.princeton.edu.

Financial Assistance:

First Year Students: Fellowships and scholarships available for first-year. Average amount paid per academic year: $16,000. Tuition remission given: full.

Advanced Students: Teaching assistantships available for advanced students. Average amount paid per academic year: $19,300. Average number of hours worked per week: 18. Tuition remission given: full. Research assistantships available for advanced students. Average amount paid per academic year: $18,200. Average number of hours worked per week: 20. Tuition remission given: full. Fellowships and scholarships available for advanced students. Average amount paid per academic year: $16,000. Tuition remission given: full.

Contact Information: Of all students currently enrolled full-time, 100% benefitted from one or more of the listed financial assistance programs. Application and information available online at: apply.embark.com/grad/princeton/edu OR gso.princeton.edu.

Internships/Practica: No information provided.

Housing and Day Care: On-campus housing is available. Graduate Housing Office, MacMillan Building, Princeton University, Princeton, NJ 08544-5264. Fax number: (609) 258-5898. On-campus day care facilities are available.

Employment of Department Graduates:

Master's Degree Graduates: Of those who graduated in the academic year 2003–2004, the following categories and numbers represent the post-graduate activities and employment of master's degree graduates: Enrolled in a post-doctoral residency/fellowship (n/a), employed in independent practice (n/a), total from the above (master's) (0).

Doctoral Degree Graduates: Of those who graduated in the academic year 2003–2004, the following categories and numbers represent the post-graduate activities and employment of doctoral degree graduates: Enrolled in a psychology doctoral program (n/a), enrolled in a post-doctoral residency/fellowship (6), employed in business or industry (research/consulting) (1), total from the above (doctoral) (7).

Additional Information:

Orientation, Objectives, and Emphasis of Department: Graduate students in our department follow a research apprenticeship program, and become affiliated with a faculty research adviser during their first year of study. Although one faculty person will usually serve as the student's major advisor during her or his graduate career, the student is also encouraged to work with other faculty. The program of graduate work in psychology emphasizes preparation for teaching and research in psychology, with specialization in the following broad areas: neuroscience, cognition, social and personality, and public policy. All students are required to assist in teaching as a significant part of their graduate education as determined by the department (at least three class hours, during their graduate career). The program is designed to prepare students for attaining the degree of doctor of philosophy and a career of productive scholarship in psychology. The department requires that candidates for admission take the Graduate Record Examination (GRE). Instruction is based on the assumption that first-year students have had the equivalent of an undergraduate major in psychology or related fields. Basic undergraduate training in science and mathematics is also considered desirable. A program leading to the degree of doctor of philosophy in psychology and neuroscience is also offered. The program is oriented toward the study of the role of the central nervous system in behavior.

Special Facilities or Resources: Facilities and specialized equipment needed for thorough training in modern psychology are available in the departmental laboratories in John C. Green Hall. Laboratory units are organized around the research programs of the faculty. In addition to these traditional areas of psychology, the department is actively engaged in two ambitious new initiatives. One is the Program in Social Policy and Decision Making, in collaboration with the Woodrow Wilson School of Public Policy. The other is in cognitive neuroscience, together with the Center for the Study of Brain, Mind and Behavior (CSBMB). The CSBMB houses an onsite, fully research-dedicated brain imaging facility, including a state-of-the-art fMRI scanner and high density scalp electrical recording apparatus. The Psychology Library is also located in Green Hall. It comprises an extensive collection of more than 21,000 volumes, including about 450 of the principal journals in the various areas of psychology, as well as standard reference works, texts, and monographs. A computer terminal in the Psychology Library provides online access to psychological and related bibliographic databases.

Application Information:

Send to: Princeton University, Office of Graduate Admissions, P.O. Box 270, Princeton, NJ 08544-0270. Application available online. URL of online application: apply.embark.com/grad/princeton.edu. Students are admitted in the Fall, application deadline December 31. Contact the Office of Graduate Admissions for the exact deadline date. Fee: $55 before December 1 and $80 after December 1 until the deadline date.

Rowan University
Department of Psychology
College of Liberal Arts and Sciences
201 Mullica Hill Road
Glassboro, NJ 08028-1701
Telephone: (856) 256-4500 ext 3781
Fax: (856) 256-4892
E-mail: *haugh@rowan.edu*
Web: *http://www.rowan.edu/mars/depts/psychology/*

Department Information:

1969. Program Coordinator: Jim A. Haugh. Number of Faculty: total–full-time 23; women–full-time 15; minority–full-time 4.

Programs and Degrees Offered:

Listed in the following order: Program area, degree type (T if terminal Master's), number awarded 7/03–6/04. Mental Health Counseling MA/MS (Master of Arts/Science) (T) 15.

Student Applications/Admissions:

Student Applications

Mental Health Counseling MA/MS (Master of Arts/Science)— Applications 2004–2005, 50. Total applicants accepted 2004–2005, 15. Number enrolled (new admits only) 2004–2005 full-time, 8. Number enrolled (new admits only) 2004–2005 part-time, 7. Total enrolled 2004–2005 full-time, 14, part-time, 22. Openings 2005–2006, 20. The Median number of years

required for completion of a degree are 3. The number of students enrolled full and part-time who were dismissed or voluntarily withdrew from this program area were 2.

Admissions Requirements:

Scores: Entries appear in this order: required test or GPA, minimum score (if required), median score of students entering in 2003–2004. Master's Programs: GRE-V no minimum stated; GRE-Q no minimum stated; GRE-V+Q no minimum stated; overall undergraduate GPA 3.0; psychology GPA no minimum stated.

Other Criteria: (importance of criteria rated low, medium, or high): GRE/MAT scores medium, research experience medium, work experience medium, extracurricular activity low, clinically related public service high, GPA high, letters of recommendation high, interview high, statement of goals and objectives high.

Student Characteristics: The following represents characteristics of students in 2004–2005 in all graduate psychology programs in the department: Caucasian–full-time 0, part-time 0.

Financial Information/Assistance:

Tuition for Full-Time Study: *Master's:* State residents: per academic year $9,914, $450 per credit hour; Nonstate residents: per academic year $15,014, $682 per credit hour. Tuition is subject to change. See the following Web site for updates and changes in tuition costs: http://www2.rowan.edu/open/depts/bursar.

Financial Assistance:

First Year Students: Research assistantships available for first-year. Fellowships and scholarships available for first-year. Tuition remission given: full and partial.

Advanced Students: Research assistantships available for advanced students. Tuition remission given: full and partial. Fellowships and scholarships available for advanced students. Tuition remission given: full and partial.

Contact Information: Of all students currently enrolled full-time, 13% benefitted from one or more of the listed financial assistance programs. Application and information available online at: http://www.rowan.edu/elan/graduate/financial_aid/index.htm.

Internships/Practica: Practica are available in a wide range of mental health settings.

Housing and Day Care: On-campus housing is available. See the following Web site for more information: http://www.rowan.edu/studentaffairs/reslife/. On-campus day care facilities are available. See the following Web site for more information: http://users.rowan.edu/~coughlin/.

Employment of Department Graduates:

Master's Degree Graduates: Of those who graduated in the academic year 2003–2004, the following categories and numbers represent the post-graduate activities and employment of master's degree graduates: Enrolled in a post-doctoral residency/fellowship (n/a), employed in independent practice (n/a), total from the above (master's) (0).

Doctoral Degree Graduates: Of those who graduated in the academic year 2003–2004, the following categories and numbers represent the post-graduate activities and employment of doctoral

degree graduates: Enrolled in a psychology doctoral program (n/a), total from the above (doctoral) (0).

Additional Information:

Orientation, Objectives, and Emphasis of Department: This 48 credit Master's program prepares students to become mental health counselors and is designed to meet the coursework and practicum requirements of the National Board of Certified Counselors. Students completing a 12 credit hour post-master's course sequence and additional supervised hours will be eligible to apply for the New Jersey Licensed Professional Counseling Certification. The program uses a competency based approach. Emphasis is placed upon differential diagnosis, the use of empirically validated treatment approaches, and outcome measurement.

Special Facilities or Resources: Rowan's Child and Family Assessment Clinic provides opportunities for both clinical assessments and research. The clinic uses a broad range of assessment tools and techniques to evaluate the functioning and needs of children and families involved in the child welfare system.

Application Information:

Send to: The Graduate School, Rowan University, 201 Mullica Hill Road, Glassboro, NJ 08028-1701. Application available online. URL of online application: http://www.rowan.edu/elan/graduate/. Students are admitted in the Fall, application deadline April 1. Early admissions deadline, November 15. *Fee:* $50.

Rutgers University—New Brunswick
Graduate Program in Psychology
Faculty of Arts and Sciences
152 Frelinghuysen Road
Piscataway, NJ 08854-8020
Telephone: (732) 445-2556
Fax: (732) 445-2987
E-mail: *matzel@rci.rutgers.edu*
Web: *http://psych.rutgers.edu/graduate/*

Department Information:

1942. Chair and Graduate Director: Louis D. Matzel. Number of Faculty: total–full-time 49; women–full-time 15; minority–full-time 1; faculty subject to the Americans With Disabilities Act 1.

Programs and Degrees Offered:

Listed in the following order: Program area, degree type (T if terminal Master's), number awarded 7/03–6/04. Clinical PhD (Doctor of Philosophy) 5, Behavioral neuroscience PhD (Doctor of Philosophy) 3, Cognitive PhD (Doctor of Philosophy) 4, Social PhD (Doctor of Philosophy) 2.

APA Accreditation: Clinical PhD (Doctor of Philosophy).

Student Applications/Admissions:

Student Applications

Clinical PhD (Doctor of Philosophy)—Applications 2004–2005, 340. Total applicants accepted 2004–2005, 9. Number enrolled (new admits only) 2004–2005 full-time, 7. Total enrolled 2004–2005 full-time, 39. Openings 2005–2006, 5. The Median number of years required for completion of a degree are 6.5. The number of students enrolled full and part-time who were dismissed or voluntarily withdrew from this program area were 1. *Behavioral neuroscience PhD (Doctor of Philosophy)*—Applications 2004–2005, 47. Total applicants accepted 2004–2005, 4. Number enrolled (new admits only) 2004–2005 full-time, 1. Total enrolled 2004–2005 full-time, 24. Openings 2005–2006, 5. The Median number of years required for completion of a degree are 6. The number of students enrolled full and part-time who were dismissed or voluntarily withdrew from this program area were 0. *Cognitive PhD (Doctor of Philosophy)*—Applications 2004–2005, 38. Total applicants accepted 2004–2005, 9. Number enrolled (new admits only) 2004–2005 full-time, 3. Total enrolled 2004–2005 full-time, 24. Openings 2005–2006, 5. The Median number of years required for completion of a degree are 6. The number of students enrolled full and part-time who were dismissed or voluntarily withdrew from this program area were 0. *Social PhD (Doctor of Philosophy)*—Applications 2004–2005, 76. Total applicants accepted 2004–2005, 6. Number enrolled (new admits only) 2004–2005 full-time, 3. Total enrolled 2004–2005 full-time, 19. Openings 2005–2006, 5. The Median number of years required for completion of a degree are 5. The number of students enrolled full and part-time who were dismissed or voluntarily withdrew from this program area were 0.

Admissions Requirements:

Scores: Entries appear in this order: required test or GPA, minimum score (if required), median score of students entering in 2003–2004. Doctoral Programs: GRE-V no minimum stated, 630; GRE-Q no minimum stated, 750; GRE-V+Q no minimum stated, 1380; GRE-Analytical no minimum stated, 640; overall undergraduate GPA no minimum stated, 3.45. GRE Subject test in Psychology is highly recommended.

Other Criteria: (importance of criteria rated low, medium, or high): GRE/MAT scores high, research experience high, clinically related public service low, GPA high, letters of recommendation high, interview medium, statement of goals and objectives high. For additional information on admission requirements, go to: http://www.psychology.rutgers.edu/graduate/.

Student Characteristics: The following represents characteristics of students in 2004–2005 in all graduate psychology programs in the department: Female–full-time 75, part-time 0; Male–full-time 31, part-time 0; African American/Black–full-time 3, part-time 0; Hispanic/Latino(a)–full-time 5, part-time 0; Asian/Pacific Islander–full-time 13, part-time 0; American Indian/Alaska Native–full-time 0, part-time 0; Caucasian–full-time 85, part-time 0; Multi-ethnic–full-time 0, part-time 0; students subject to the Americans With Disabilities Act–full-time 1, part-time 0.

Financial Information/Assistance:

Tuition for Full-Time Study: *Doctoral:* State residents: per academic year $9,668, $402 per credit hour; Nonstate residents: per academic year $14,371, $598 per credit hour. Tuition is subject to change. See the following Web site for updates and changes in tuition costs: http://gradstudy.rutgers.edu/costs.html.

Financial Assistance:

First Year Students: Teaching assistantships available for first-year. Average amount paid per academic year: $16,988. Aver-

age number of hours worked per week: 15. Apply by December 15. Tuition remission given: full. Research assistantships available for first-year. Average amount paid per academic year: $16,988. Average number of hours worked per week: 15. Apply by December 15. Tuition remission given: full. Traineeships available for first-year. Average amount paid per academic year: $20,000. Apply by December 15. Tuition remission given: full. Fellowships and scholarships available for first-year. Average amount paid per academic year: $18,000. Apply by December 15. Tuition remission given: full.

Advanced Students: Teaching assistantships available for advanced students. Average amount paid per academic year: $16,988. Average number of hours worked per week: 15. Apply by December 15. Tuition remission given: full. Research assistantships available for advanced students. Average amount paid per academic year: $16,988. Average number of hours worked per week: 15. Apply by December 15. Tuition remission given: full. Traineeships available for advanced students. Average amount paid per academic year: $20,000. Apply by December 15. Tuition remission given: full. Fellowships and scholarships available for advanced students. Average amount paid per academic year: $18,000. Apply by December 15. Tuition remission given: full.

Contact Information: Of all students currently enrolled full-time, 98% benefitted from one or more of the listed financial assistance programs. Application and information available online at: http://studentaid.rutgers.edu/.

Internships/Practica: Clinical students must complete an APA-approved clinical internship. None of these required internships are offered by our program. There are several university-based practica, including both general and specialty outpatient clinics, however, where clinical students do training before their internships. For those doctoral students for whom a professional internship is required prior to graduation, 6 applied in 2003–2004. Of those who applied, 6 were placed in internships listed by the Association of Psychology Postdoctoral and Internship Programs (APPIC); 6 were placed in APA accredited internships.

Housing and Day Care: On-campus housing is available. See the following Web site for more information: http://housing.rutgers.edu/ns/. On-campus day care facilities are available.

Employment of Department Graduates:

Master's Degree Graduates: Of those who graduated in the academic year 2003–2004, the following categories and numbers represent the post-graduate activities and employment of master's degree graduates: Enrolled in a psychology doctoral program (0), enrolled in another graduate/professional program (0), enrolled in a post-doctoral residency/fellowship (n/a), employed in independent practice (n/a), employed in an academic position at a university (0), employed in an academic position at a 2-year/4-year college (0), employed in other positions at a higher education institution (0), employed in a professional position in a school system (0), employed in business or industry (research/consulting) (0), employed in business or industry (management) (0), employed in a government agency (research) (0), employed in a government agency (professional services) (0), employed in a community mental health/counseling center (0), employed in a hospital/medical center (0), still seeking employment (0), other employment position (0), total from the above (master's) (0).

Doctoral Degree Graduates: Of those who graduated in the academic year 2003–2004, the following categories and numbers represent the post-graduate activities and employment of doctoral degree graduates: Enrolled in a psychology doctoral program (n/a), enrolled in a post-doctoral residency/fellowship (4), employed in independent practice (0), employed in an academic position at a university (1), employed in an academic position at a 2-year/4-year college (1), employed in other positions at a higher education institution (2), employed in a professional position in a school system (0), employed in business or industry (research/consulting) (1), employed in business or industry (management) (0), employed in a government agency (research) (1), employed in a government agency (professional services) (0), employed in a community mental health/counseling center (2), employed in a hospital/medical center (1), still seeking employment (0), other employment position (1), total from the above (doctoral) (14).

Additional Information:

Orientation, Objectives, and Emphasis of Department: The Rutgers University Graduate Program in Psychology has one of the country's largest faculties, including fifty full-time professors of psychology. The graduate program trains students for careers as professors; researchers in government, corporate, and non-profit settings; and clinical researchers. There are four main areas (Biopsychology and Behavioral Neuroscience, Cognitive Psychology, Clinical Psychology and Social Psychology) and two intradisciplinary programs: Health Psychology and Developmental Psychology (students with intradisciplinary interest must apply to one of the four main areas). Faculty advisors closely mentor students through a series of progressively more sophisticated research experiences. Basic courses and more advanced specialty seminars are available within each area of psychology. The clinical program is designed to develop clinical scientists.

Information for Students With Physical Disabilities: See the following Web site for more information: http://www.rci.rutgers.edu/~polcomp/disab.shtml.

Application Information:
Send to: Office of Graduate and Professional Admissions, Rutgers, The State University of New Jersey, 18 Bishop Place, New Brunswick, NJ 08901-8530. Students are admitted in the Fall. Social, Clinical and Cognitive deadline is December 15. Biopsychology and Behavioral Neuroscience deadline is January 15. *Fee:* $50.

Rutgers University—Newark Campus
Department of Psychology
101 Warren Street
Newark, NJ 07102
Telephone: (973) 353-5440 x221
Fax: (973) 353-1171
E-mail: *gradprog@psychology.rutgers.edu*
Web: *http://www.psych.rutgers.edu*

Department Information:
1946. Chairperson: Maggie Shiffrar. Number of Faculty: total–full-time 16, part-time 5; women–full-time 5, part-time 3.

Programs and Degrees Offered:
Listed in the following order: Program area, degree type (T if terminal Master's), number awarded 7/03–6/04. Experimental Psychology PhD (Doctor of Philosophy) 4.

Student Applications/Admissions:

Student Applications
Experimental Psychology PhD (Doctor of Philosophy)—Applications 2004–2005, 35. Total applicants accepted 2004–2005, 7. Openings 2005–2006, 4. The Median number of years required for completion of a degree are 5. The number of students enrolled full and part-time who were dismissed or voluntarily withdrew from this program area were 1.

Admissions Requirements:
Scores: Entries appear in this order: required test or GPA, minimum score (if required), median score of students entering in 2003–2004. Doctoral Programs: GRE-V 500, 570; GRE-Q 500, 638; GRE-Analytical 500, 684; overall undergraduate GPA 3.0, 3.5.
Other Criteria: (importance of criteria rated low, medium, or high): GRE/MAT scores medium, research experience high, work experience medium, extracurricular activity low, clinically related public service low, GPA medium, letters of recommendation high, interview high, statement of goals and objectives high.

Student Characteristics: The following represents characteristics of students in 2004–2005 in all graduate psychology programs in the department: Female–full-time 16, part-time 0; Male–full-time 8, part-time 0; African American/Black–full-time 1, part-time 0; Hispanic/Latino(a)–full-time 2, part-time 0; Asian/Pacific Islander–full-time 3, part-time 0; American Indian/Alaska Native–full-time 0, part-time 0; Caucasian–full-time 0, part-time 0; Multiethnic–full-time 1, part-time 0; students subject to the Americans With Disabilities Act–full-time 1, part-time 0.

Financial Information/Assistance:
Tuition for Full-Time Study: *Doctoral:* State residents: per academic year $9,668; Nonstate residents: per academic year $14,370. Tuition is subject to change. See the following Web site for updates and changes in tuition costs: gradstudy.rutgers.edu/costs.html.

Financial Assistance:
First Year Students: Teaching assistantships available for first-year. Average amount paid per academic year: $18,000. Average number of hours worked per week: 15. Tuition remission given: full. Research assistantships available for first-year. Average amount paid per academic year: $18,000. Average number of hours worked per week: 15. Tuition remission given: full. Fellowships and scholarships available for first-year. Average amount paid per academic year: $18,000. Average number of hours worked per week: 15. Tuition remission given: full.
Advanced Students: Teaching assistantships available for advanced students. Average amount paid per academic year: $18,000. Average number of hours worked per week: 15. Tuition remission given: full. Research assistantships available for advanced students. Average amount paid per academic year: $18,000. Average number of hours worked per week: 15. Tuition remission given: full. Fellowships and scholarships available for advanced students. Average amount paid per academic year:

$16,000. Average number of hours worked per week: 15. Tuition remission given: full.
Contact Information: Of all students currently enrolled full-time, 90% benefitted from one or more of the listed financial assistance programs.

Internships/Practica: None.

Housing and Day Care: On-campus housing is available. See the following Web site for more information: http://newark.rutgers.edu/~reslife/. No on-campus day care facilities are available.

Employment of Department Graduates:
Master's Degree Graduates: Of those who graduated in the academic year 2003–2004, the following categories and numbers represent the post-graduate activities and employment of master's degree graduates: Enrolled in a post-doctoral residency/fellowship (n/a), employed in independent practice (n/a), total from the above (master's) (0).
Doctoral Degree Graduates: Of those who graduated in the academic year 2003–2004, the following categories and numbers represent the post-graduate activities and employment of doctoral degree graduates: Enrolled in a psychology doctoral program (n/a), enrolled in a post-doctoral residency/fellowship (3), employed in business or industry (research/consulting) (1), total from the above (doctoral) (4).

Additional Information:
Orientation, Objectives, and Emphasis of Department: Our doctoral program emphasizes research in five areas: Cognitive Science and Perception, Cognitive Neuroscience, Social Psychology and the Biopsychology of Emotion and Adaptive Behavior. Specific research areas include: visual perception, categorization, perceptual development and learning, computational modeling, conflict mediation, social cognition, attachment, parental behavior, attention, language, analgesia, brain imaging (fMRI and EEG), and the neuroendocrine system. With a faculty to graduate student ratio of 1:2, we emphasize hands-on, integrative research training in state of the art research facilities. Generally, graduate students take classes and conduct research during their first two years. A comprehensive exam is given at the beginning of the third year. After this, students focus on their dissertation research. After graduating, our doctoral students successfully obtain post-doctoral research positions, faculty positions, and/or research and development positions in industrial and government settings. You can learn more about our program at http://psychology.rutgers.edu/.

Special Facilities or Resources: The Psychology Department occupies about 42,000 square feet on the first, third, and fourth floors of Smith Hall and has its own servers (psychology.rutgers.edu), computing laboratory and individual laboratories for behavioral, neurophysiological, neuroanatomical, and neuropharmacological research. There are 16,400 square feet available for animal holding, animal testing, and animal support areas. In the Cognitive Science and Perception areas, research is conducted using one-way observation rooms, video equipment, high-speed graphics computers (SGI, SUN, P6s, Macs, etc.), cutting-edge driving simulators and an active optical motion tracking system as well as access to a newly acquired high performance parallel supercomputer (IBM-SP). The Psychology Department with UMDNJ also supports an ERP and a fMRI brain imaging facility for general usage throughout the various programs of study. Students have the use of the John Cotton Dana Library, with a collection of over 550,000 volumes as well as rapid and easy access to the Rutgers University libraries in New Brunswick and to the University of Medicine and Dentistry of New Jersey library in Newark.

Information for Students With Physical Disabilities: See the following Web site for more information: http://lrc.rutgers.edu/disabilities.html.

Application Information:
Send to: Office of Graduate Admissions, Rutgers, The State University of New Jersey, 249 University Avenue, Newark, NJ 07102-1896; telephone (973) 353-5205 or online at gradstudy.rutgers.edu. Application available online. URL of online application: gradstudy.rutgers.edu. Students are admitted in the Fall, application deadline February 1; Spring, application deadline November 1. Applications can be obtained and submitted online at gradstudy.rutgers.edu For additional information about this doctoral Psychology program, consult www.psych.rutgers.edu. *Fee:* $50.

Rutgers—The State University of New Jersey
Department of Applied Professional Psychology
Graduate School of Applied and Professional Psychology
152 Frelinghuysen Road, Busch Campus, Psychology
  Building, New Addition
Piscataway, NJ 08854-8085
Telephone: (732) 445-2000 Ext. 106
Fax: (732) 445-4888
E-mail: *schpsyd@rci.rutgers.edu*
Web: *http://gsappweb.rutgers.edu*

Department Information:
1974. Chairperson: Kenneth Schneider, PhD Number of Faculty: total–full-time 7, part-time 7; women–full-time 2, part-time 7.

Programs and Degrees Offered:
Listed in the following order: Program area, degree type (T if terminal Master's), number awarded 7/03–6/04. Organizational PsyD (Doctor of Psychology) 8, School PsyD (Doctor of Psychology) 6.

APA Accreditation: School PsyD (Doctor of Psychology).

Student Applications/Admissions:
Student Applications
Organizational PsyD (Doctor of Psychology)—Applications 2004–2005, 29. Total applicants accepted 2004–2005, 8. Number enrolled (new admits only) 2004–2005 full-time, 5. Openings 2005–2006, 6. The Median number of years required for completion of a degree are 5.7. The number of students enrolled full and part-time who were dismissed or voluntarily withdrew from this program area were 0. *School PsyD (Doctor of Psychology)*—Applications 2004–2005, 71. Total applicants accepted 2004–2005, 16. Number enrolled (new admits only) 2004–2005 full-time, 7. Number enrolled (new admits only) 2004–2005 part-time, 1. Total enrolled 2004–2005 full-time, 47, part-time, 9. Openings 2005–2006, 10. The Median number of years required for completion of a degree are 5.5. The number of students enrolled full and part-time who were dismissed or voluntarily withdrew from this program area were 0.

Admissions Requirements:
Scores: Entries appear in this order: required test or GPA, minimum score (if required), median score of students entering in 2003–2004. Doctoral Programs: GRE-Subject(Psych) no minimum stated; overall undergraduate GPA no minimum stated; last 2 years GPA no minimum stated; psychology GPA no minimum stated.
Other Criteria: (importance of criteria rated low, medium, or high): GRE/MAT scores high, research experience medium, work experience high, extracurricular activity medium, clinically related public service high, GPA high, letters of recommendation high, interview high, statement of goals and objectives high, MAT not required for admission into the PsyD programs. For additional information on admission requirements, go to: http://gsappweb.rutgers.edu.

Student Characteristics: The following represents characteristics of students in 2004–2005 in all graduate psychology programs in the department: Female–full-time 62, part-time 8; Male–full-time 16, part-time 1; African American/Black–full-time 8, part-time 0; Hispanic/Latino(a)–full-time 3, part-time 0; Asian/Pacific Islander–full-time 5, part-time 0; American Indian/Alaska Native–full-time 0, part-time 0; Caucasian–full-time 61, part-time 9; Multi-ethnic–full-time 1, part-time 0; students subject to the Americans With Disabilities Act–full-time 0, part-time 0.

Financial Information/Assistance:
Tuition for Full-Time Study: *Doctoral:* State residents: per academic year $10,687, $445 per credit hour; Nonstate residents: per academic year $15,878, $661 per credit hour. Tuition is subject to change.

Financial Assistance:
First Year Students: Teaching assistantships available for first-year. Average amount paid per academic year: $15,730. Tuition remission given: full. Research assistantships available for first-year. Average amount paid per academic year: $15,730. Tuition remission given: full. Traineeships available for first-year. Fellowships and scholarships available for first-year. Average amount paid per academic year: $2,000.
Advanced Students: Teaching assistantships available for advanced students. Average amount paid per academic year: $15,730. Tuition remission given: full. Research assistantships available for advanced students. Average amount paid per academic year: $15,730. Tuition remission given: full. Traineeships available for advanced students. Fellowships and scholarships available for advanced students. Average amount paid per academic year: $2,000.
Contact Information: Of all students currently enrolled full-time, 36% benefitted from one or more of the listed financial assistance programs. Application and information available online at: http://studentaid.rutgers.edu.

Internships/Practica: Required prior to graduation, 11 applied in 2003–2004.

Housing and Day Care: On-campus housing is available. See the following Web site for more information: http://housing.rutgers.edu or http://www.rutgers.edu, click on INFOdex and type in "on-campus housing." On-campus day care facilities are available. See the following Web site for more information: Child Care: (732) 932-7823, or at http://www.rutgers.edu, click on INFOdex and type in "child care."

Employment of Department Graduates:

Master's Degree Graduates: Of those who graduated in the academic year 2003–2004, the following categories and numbers represent the post-graduate activities and employment of master's degree graduates: Enrolled in a post-doctoral residency/fellowship (n/a), employed in independent practice (n/a), total from the above (master's) (0).

Doctoral Degree Graduates: Of those who graduated in the academic year 2003–2004, the following categories and numbers represent the post-graduate activities and employment of doctoral degree graduates: Enrolled in a psychology doctoral program (n/a), enrolled in another graduate/professional program (0), enrolled in a post-doctoral residency/fellowship (0), employed in independent practice (0), employed in an academic position at a university (1), employed in an academic position at a 2-year/4-year college (0), employed in other positions at a higher education institution (0), employed in a professional position in a school system (5), employed in business or industry (research/consulting) (5), employed in business or industry (management) (0), employed in a government agency (research) (0), employed in a government agency (professional services) (0), employed in a community mental health/counseling center (0), employed in a hospital/medical center (0), still seeking employment (0), other employment position (2), total from the above (doctoral) (13).

Additional Information:

Orientation, Objectives, and Emphasis of Department: The department of applied psychology is a multi-dimensional organizational unit dedicated (1) to enhancement of instruction and learning of children, adolescents, and adults in school and related educational settings, and (2) to development of organizations that allow schooling to occur in effective and efficient ways. Three interrelated dimensions serve to structure the department. An applied research dimension signifies the important weight placed on generating new knowledge; an education and training dimension reflects concern for development of high-level practitioners and leaders of school psychology; an organizational and community services dimension is targeted at providing schools and related educational settings with consultation and technical assistance in areas of instruction and learning. A specialization in organizational psychology is available in the department of applied psychology. A continuum of instruction ranges from observation and assessment through intervention models that include supervised experience as an essential component of didactic instruction. Core faculty are augmented by senior psychologists whose major professional involvement is in the schools or organizational and community settings.

Special Facilities or Resources: There are two special facilities that are an integrated part of the training program. One is an on-site psychological clinic which serves the university and state communities. Assessment and intervention programs are offered. The other is the Center for Applied Psychology, a division of GSAPP, which develops, implements, and evaluates projects involving faculty, students and others from the community. Included in these projects are the Eating Disorders Clinic, Foster Care Counseling, a home-based intervention program for developmen-

tally disabled individuals, and a family business consultation program.

Information for Students With Physical Disabilities: See the following Web site for more information: http://gsappweb.rutgers.edu.

Application Information:
Send to: Rutgers University, Graduate Admissions, 18 Bishop Place, New Brunswick, NJ 08901, or request application and catalog online at http://gradstudy.rutgers.edu. Application available online. URL of online application: http://gradstudy.rutgers.edu. Students are admitted in the Fall, application deadline January 5. *Fee:* $50. Project 1000 application fee is waived. Contact Graduate Admissions at (732) 932-7711 to find about other application fee waivers.

Rutgers—The State University of New Jersey
Department of Clinical Psychology
Graduate School of Applied and Professional Psychology, 152
   Frelinghuysen Road
Piscataway, NJ 08854-8085
Telephone: (732) 445-2000 x117
Fax: (732) 445-4888
E-mail: *clinpsyd@rci.rutgers.edu*
Web: *http://gsappweb.rutgers.edu*

Department Information:
1974. Chair: Brenna H. Bry. Number of Faculty: total–full-time 12, part-time 14; women–full-time 5, part-time 7; minority–full-time 3.

Programs and Degrees Offered:
Listed in the following order: Program area, degree type (T if terminal Master's), number awarded 7/03–6/04. Clinical PsyD (Doctor of Psychology) 19.

APA Accreditation: Clinical PsyD (Doctor of Psychology).

Student Applications/Admissions:
Student Applications
Clinical PsyD (Doctor of Psychology)—Applications 2004–2005, 426. Total applicants accepted 2004–2005, 25. Number enrolled (new admits only) 2004–2005 full-time, 16. Number enrolled (new admits only) 2004–2005 part-time, 0. Total enrolled 2004–2005 full-time, 113. Openings 2005–2006, 16. The Median number of years required for completion of a degree are 6.0. The number of students enrolled full and part-time, who were dismissed or voluntarily withdrew from this program area were 0.

Admissions Requirements:
Scores: Entries appear in this order: required test or GPA, minimum score (if required), median score of students entering in 2003–2004. Doctoral Programs: GRE-V+Q no minimum stated; GRE-Subject(Psych) n/a; overall undergraduate GPA n/a; last 2 years GPA n/a; psychology GPA n/a.
Other Criteria: (importance of criteria rated low, medium, or high): GRE/MAT scores medium, research experience me-

dium, work experience high, extracurricular activity low, clinically related public service high, GPA high, letters of recommendation high, interview high, statement of goals and objectives high. MAT not required for admission to PsyD program. For additional information on admission requirements, go to: http://gsappweb.rutgers.edu.

Student Characteristics: The following represents characteristics of students in 2004–2005 in all graduate psychology programs in the department: Female–full-time 80, part-time 0; Male–full-time 30, part-time 0; African American/Black–full-time 17, part-time 0; Hispanic/Latino(a)–full-time 16, part-time 0; Asian/Pacific Islander–full-time 7, part-time 0; American Indian/Alaska Native–full-time 1, part-time 0; Caucasian–full-time 69, part-time 0; Multi-ethnic–full-time 0, part-time 0; students subject to the Americans With Disabilities Act–full-time 0, part-time 0.

Financial Information/Assistance:

Tuition for Full-Time Study: *Doctoral:* State residents: per academic year $10,687, $445 per credit hour; Nonstate residents: per academic year $15,879, $661 per credit hour. Tuition is subject to change. See the following Web site for updates and changes in tuition costs: www.rci.rutgers.edu/~sfs/index.html.

Financial Assistance:

First Year Students: Teaching assistantships available for first-year. Average amount paid per academic year: $15,730. Tuition remission given: full. Research assistantships available for first-year. Average amount paid per academic year: $15,730. Tuition remission given: full. Traineeships available for first-year. Fellowships and scholarships available for first-year. Tuition remission given: partial.

Advanced Students: Teaching assistantships available for advanced students. Average amount paid per academic year: $15,730. Tuition remission given: full. Research assistantships available for advanced students. Average amount paid per academic year: $15,730. Tuition remission given: full. Traineeships available for advanced students. Fellowships and scholarships available for advanced students. Tuition remission given: partial.

Contact Information: Of all students currently enrolled full-time, 25% benefitted from one or more of the listed financial assistance programs. Application and information available online at: http://gsappweb.rutgers.edu.

Internships/Practica: The PsyD program provides a broadly based practicum program which is structured around the needs and interests of our students. Students can choose placements in hospitals which include a hospice program, neuropsych testing, long and short term inpatient treatment programs for both adolescents and adults. They can choose to be placed in traditional community mental health centers, college counseling centers, specialized schools for children (autism, learning disabled, emotionally disturbed). Students can be placed in public school based mental health clinics, in programs which provide service to homeless people and in programs for battered women and programs for addictive disorders. Our programs are selected for their attention to supervision but also for their balance regarding gender, race and socio-economic levels. For those doctoral students for whom a professional internship is required prior to graduation, 16 applied in 2003–2004. Of those who applied, 15 were placed in internships listed by the Association of Psychology Postdoctoral and Internship Programs (APPIC); 13 were placed in APA accredited internships.

Housing and Day Care: On-campus housing is available. See the following Web site for more information: http://housing.rutgers.edu. On-campus day care facilities are available. See the following Web site for more information: http://ruinfo.rutgers.edu/.

Employment of Department Graduates:

Master's Degree Graduates: Of those who graduated in the academic year 2003–2004, the following categories and numbers represent the post-graduate activities and employment of master's degree graduates: Enrolled in a post-doctoral residency/fellowship (n/a), employed in independent practice (n/a), total from the above (master's) (0).

Doctoral Degree Graduates: Of those who graduated in the academic year 2003–2004, the following categories and numbers represent the post-graduate activities and employment of doctoral degree graduates: Enrolled in a psychology doctoral program (n/a), enrolled in another graduate/professional program (0), enrolled in a post-doctoral residency/fellowship (4), employed in independent practice (0), employed in an academic position at a university (0), employed in an academic position at a 2-year/4-year college (0), employed in other positions at a higher education institution (0), employed in a professional position in a school system (0), employed in business or industry (research/consulting) (0), employed in business or industry (management) (0), employed in a government agency (research) (0), employed in a government agency (professional services) (0), employed in a community mental health/counseling center (2), employed in a hospital/medical center (4), still seeking employment (0), other employment position (2), do not know (7), total from the above (doctoral) (19).

Additional Information:

Orientation, Objectives, and Emphasis of Department: The PsyD program emphasizes pragmatic training in problem solving and planned change techniques. Didactic training in basic psychological principles is coupled with practical, graduate instruction in a range of assessment and intervention modes. The level of involvement becomes progressively more intense during the student's course of training. Most courses include (1) a seminar component oriented around case discussions and substantive theoretical issues of clinical import, (2) a practicum component during which students see clients in the intervention mode or problem area under study, and (3) a supervision component by which the student receives guidance from an experienced clinical instructor in a wide range of applied clinical settings. All three components are coordinated around a central conceptual issue, such as a mode of intervention or a clinical problem area. Instruction and supervision are offered by full-time faculty and senior psychologists whose primary professional involvement is in applied clinical settings throughout the state. In addition to required general core courses, students may emphasize training within any of three perspectives: psychodynamic, behavioral, or systems approaches. This last perspective focuses on family, organizational and community services.

Special Facilities or Resources: The Center for Applied Psychology at GSAPP is the focal point for the field experiences that are critical in the development of professional psychologists. The projects overseen by the Center are cornerstones of training for our students; the GSAPP Psychological Clinic, the Foster Care Counseling project, the Natural Setting Therapeutic Management program, the Family Business Forum and our extensive network of practicum placements are all available to our students. Students are placed in community-based organizations where the recipients of the services we provide are often underserved. These placements include community mental health centers, hospitals, special schools, shelters, and other programs. All students are placed in a practicum setting for at least one full day per week during their years at GSAPP. All students see clients through our Clinic and receive one-hour of individual supervision for each hour of therapy. The Clinic is developing specialty sub-clinics which will allow students to gain experience and supervision in specific treatment approaches working with Faculty experts.

Information for Students With Physical Disabilities: See the following Web site for more information: http://www.rcstudentservice.rutgers.edu/disability.html.

Application Information:

Send to: Graduate and Professional Admissions, Rutgers—The State University of New Jersey, 18 Bishop Place, New Brunswick, NJ 08901-8530. Application available online. URL of online application: www.rutgers.edu. Students are admitted in the Fall, application deadline January 5. *Fee:* $50. Project 1000—Fee waived.

Rutgers—The State University of New Jersey, New Brunswick

Department of Educational Psychology
Graduate School of Education
10 Seminary Place
New Brunswick, NJ 08901-1183
Telephone: (732) 932-7496 x8327
Fax: (732) 932-6829
E-mail: *carmbre@rci.rutgers.edu*
Web: *http://www.gse.rutgers.edu*

Department Information:

1923. Chairperson: Jeffrey K. Smith. Number of Faculty: total–full-time 19; women–full-time 8; minority–full-time 4.

Programs and Degrees Offered:

Listed in the following order: Program area, degree type (T if terminal Master's), number awarded 7/03–6/04. Learning, Cognition, & Development Other 5, Special Education Other 33, Counseling Psychology EdD (Doctor of Education) 2, Educational Psychology PhD (Doctor of Philosophy) 3, Educational Statistics & Measurement Other 2, Educational Statistics & Measurement EdD (Doctor of Education) 0, Learning, Cognition, & Development EdD (Doctor of Education) 2, Special Education EdD (Doctor of Education) 4, Counseling Psychology Other 25.

Student Applications/Admissions:

Student Applications

Learning, Cognition, & Development Other—Applications 2004–2005, 21. Total applicants accepted 2004–2005, 10. Number enrolled (new admits only) 2004–2005 full-time, 2. Number enrolled (new admits only) 2004–2005 part-time, 4. Total enrolled 2004–2005 full-time, 2, part-time, 19. Openings 2005–2006, 10. The Median number of years required for completion of a degree are 7.25. The number of students enrolled full and part-time who were dismissed or voluntarily withdrew from this program area were 3. *Special Education Other*—Applications 2004–2005, 84. Total applicants accepted 2004–2005, 49. Number enrolled (new admits only) 2004–2005 full-time, 30. Number enrolled (new admits only) 2004–2005 part-time, 15. Total enrolled 2004–2005 full-time, 26, part-time, 40. Openings 2005–2006, 35. The Median number of years required for completion of a degree is 1. The number of students enrolled full and part-time who were dismissed or voluntarily withdrew from this program area were 8. *Counseling Psychology EdD (Doctor of Education)*—Applications 2004–2005, 0. Total applicants accepted 2004–2005, 0. Number enrolled (new admits only) 2004–2005 full-time, 0. Number enrolled (new admits only) 2004–2005 part-time, 0. The Median number of years required for completion of a degree are 10. The number of students enrolled full and part-time who were dismissed or voluntarily withdrew from this program area were 3. *Educational Psychology PhD (Doctor of Philosophy)*—Applications 2004–2005, 29. Total applicants accepted 2004–2005, 10. Number enrolled (new admits only) 2004–2005 full-time, 5. Number enrolled (new admits only) 2004–2005 part-time, 0. Total enrolled 2004–2005 full-time, 26, part-time, 15. Openings 2005–2006, 15. The Median number of years required for completion of a degree are 7.3. The number of students enrolled full and part-time who were dismissed or voluntarily withdrew from this program area were 5. *Educational Statistics & Measurement Other*—Applications 2004–2005, 13. Total applicants accepted 2004–2005, 6. Number enrolled (new admits only) 2004–2005 full-time, 0. Number enrolled (new admits only) 2004–2005 part-time, 4. Total enrolled 2004–2005 full-time, 1, part-time, 4. Openings 2005–2006, 10. The Median number of years required for completion of a degree are 5.75. The number of students enrolled full and part-time who were dismissed or voluntarily withdrew from this program area were 2. *Educational Statistics & Measurement EdD (Doctor of Education)*—Applications 2004–2005, 0. Total applicants accepted 2004–2005, 0. Number enrolled (new admits only) 2004–2005 full-time, 0. Number enrolled (new admits only) 2004–2005 part-time, 0. The number of students enrolled full and part-time who were dismissed or voluntarily withdrew from this program area were 3. *Learning, Cognition, & Development EdD (Doctor of Education)*—Applications 2004–2005, 0. Total applicants accepted 2004–2005, 0. Number enrolled (new admits only) 2004–2005 full-time, 0. Number enrolled (new admits only) 2004–2005 part-time, 0. Total enrolled 2004–2005 full-time, 1, part-time, 4. The Median number of years required for completion of a degree are 9. The number of students enrolled full and part-time who were dismissed or voluntarily withdrew from this program area were 1. *Special Education EdD (Doctor of Education)*—Applications 2004–2005, 15. Total applicants accepted 2004–2005, 3. Number enrolled (new admits only) 2004–2005 full-time, 0. Number enrolled (new admits only) 2004–2005 part-time, 2. Openings 2005–2006, 5. The Median number of years required for completion of a degree are 8. The number of students enrolled full and part-time who were dismissed or voluntarily withdrew from this program area were 0. *Counseling Psychology Other*—Applications 2004–2005, 96. Total applicants accepted 2004–2005, 46. Number enrolled (new admits only) 2004–2005 full-time, 15. Number enrolled (new admits only) 2004–2005 part-time, 15. Total enrolled 2004–2005 full-time, 21, part-time, 35. Openings 2005–2006, 50. The Median number of years required for completion of a degree are 1.5. The number of students enrolled full and part-time, who were dismissed or voluntarily withdrew from this program area were 7.

Admissions Requirements:

Scores: Entries appear in this order: required test or GPA, minimum score (if required), median score of students entering in 2003–2004. Master's Programs: GRE-V+Q 1000, 1021; overall undergraduate GPA 3.00, 3.31. For international students TOEFL is required with a minimum score of 213 (computerized) / 550 (paper). Doctoral Programs: GRE-V+Q 1100, 1135; overall undergraduate GPA 3.00, 3.35. For PhD candidates the GRE V+Q average is 1250. For international students TOEFL is required with a minimum score of 213 (computerized) / 550 (paper).

Other Criteria: (importance of criteria rated low, medium, or high): GRE/MAT scores high, research experience high, work experience medium, GPA high, letters of recommendation high, statement of goals and objectives high. For additional information on admission requirements, go to: http://grads tudy.rutgers.edu.

Student Characteristics: The following represents characteristics of students in 2004–2005 in all graduate psychology programs in the department: Female–full-time 60, part-time 121; Male–full-time 17, part-time 18; African American/Black–full-time 5, part-time 4; Hispanic/Latino(a)–full-time 6, part-time 5; Asian/Pacific Islander–full-time 14, part-time 8; American Indian/Alaska Native–full-time 0, part-time 1; Caucasian–full-time 37, part-time 96; Multi-ethnic–full-time 3, part-time 2.

Financial Information/Assistance:

Tuition for Full-Time Study: *Master's:* State residents: per academic year $9,668, $403 per credit hour; Nonstate residents: per academic year $14,371, $599 per credit hour. *Doctoral:* State residents: per academic year $9,668, $403 per credit hour; Nonstate residents: per academic year $14,371, $589 per credit hour. Tuition is subject to change. See the following Web site for updates and changes in tuition costs: http://www.studentabc.rutg ers.edu.

Financial Assistance:

First Year Students: Teaching assistantships available for first-year. Average amount paid per academic year: $15,730. Average number of hours worked per week: 15. Apply by March 1. Tuition remission given: full. Research assistantships available for first-year. Average amount paid per academic year: $15,730. Average number of hours worked per week: 15. Apply by March 1. Tuition remission given: full. Fellowships and scholarships available for first-year. Average number of hours worked per week: 0.

Advanced Students: Teaching assistantships available for advanced students. Average amount paid per academic year: $15,730. Average number of hours worked per week: 15. Apply by March 1. Tuition remission given: full. Research assistantships available for advanced students. Average amount paid per academic year: $15,730. Average number of hours worked per week: 15. Apply by March 1. Tuition remission given: full. Fellowships and scholarships available for advanced students.

Contact Information: Of all students currently enrolled full-time, 70% benefitted from one or more of the listed financial assistance programs. Application and information available online at: http://studentaid.rutgers.edu/.

Internships/Practica: No information provided. For those doctoral students for whom a professional internship is required prior to graduation, 2 applied in 2003–2004. Of those who applied, 2 were placed in internships listed by the Association of Psychology Postdoctoral and Internship Programs (APPIC); 1 was placed in APA accredited internships.

Housing and Day Care: On-campus housing is available. See the following Web site for more information: For on-campus housing go to http:/housing.rutgers.edu/ie. For off-campus housing go to http:/ruoffcampus.rutgers.edu. On-campus day care facilities are available. See the following Web site for more information: http://nbpweb.rutgers.edu/menus/childcare.shtml.

Employment of Department Graduates:

Master's Degree Graduates: Of those who graduated in the academic year 2003–2004, the following categories and numbers represent the post-graduate activities and employment of master's degree graduates: Enrolled in a post-doctoral residency/fellowship (n/a), employed in independent practice (n/a), total from the above (master's) (0).

Doctoral Degree Graduates: Of those who graduated in the academic year 2003–2004, the following categories and numbers represent the post-graduate activities and employment of doctoral degree graduates: Enrolled in a psychology doctoral program (n/a), total from the above (doctoral) (0).

Additional Information:

Orientation, Objectives, and Emphasis of Department: The Department of Educational Psychology offers a PhD in Educational Psychology that seeks to prepare scholarly researchers in areas that include theory and methods of statistical analysis, evaluation, and measurement as applied to educational issues; and the psychology of human learning, cognition and development in schools, families, and communities. An EdD in Special Education, which prepares individuals seeking professional positions in the field, is also offered. At the master's level, the Department offers graduate Master's in Education (Ed.M.) degree programs of study in (a) counseling psychology, (b) educational statistics and measurement, (c) learning, cognition, & development, and (d) special education. Completion of these master's degree programs can also result in various professional credentials including certification as Teacher of the Handicapped, Learning Disabilities Teacher Consultant, and School Counselor. The Department also offers a certificate program in Interdisciplinary Infant Studies. All programs in the Department include research training and pertain to the description, explanation and optimization of human development in various contexts.

Special Facilities or Resources: We have all the resources normally associated with a major research university. www.rutgers.edu.

Information for Students With Physical Disabilities: See the following Web site for more information: http://www.rci.rutgers.edu/~divcoaff/.

Application Information:

Send to: Office of Graduate and Professional Admissions, Rutgers, The State University of New Jersey, 18 Bishop Place, New Brunswick,

NJ 08901-8530; phone: (732) 932-7711; fax: (732) 932-8231; http://gradstudy.rutgers.edu/index.html. Application available online. URL of online application: http://gradstudy.rutgers.edu. Students are admitted in the Fall, application deadline November 1; Spring, application deadline March 1. PhD program has Fall admission only: February 1 deadline. EdD admissions is temporarily suspended in Counseling Psychology. Students interested in EdD in Learning Cognition & Development, or Educational Statistics & Measurement should refer to PhD in Educational Psychology. Admissions to EdD in Learning Cognition & Development, and Educational Statistics & Measurement suspended. *Fee:* $50.

Seton Hall University
Professional Psychology and Family Therapy
Education and Human Services
400 South Orange Avenue
South Orange, NJ 07079
Telephone: (973) 761-9451
Fax: (973) 275-2188
E-mail: *palmerla@shu.edu*
Web: *www.shu.edu*

Department Information:
1965. Chairperson: Laura Palmer. Number of Faculty: total–full-time 10, part-time 1; women–full-time 5; minority–full-time 1.

Programs and Degrees Offered:
Listed in the following order: Program area, degree type (T if terminal Master's), number awarded 7/03–6/04. Counseling Psychology PhD (Doctor of Philosophy) 6, MA Psych Studies/EdS Marriage and Family Therapy EdS (Education Specialist) 3, MA Psych Studies/EdS School and Community EdS (Education Specialist) 6, Psychological Studies MA/MS (Master of Arts/Science) (T) 4, MA Psych Studies/EdS Mental Health Counseling EdS (Education Specialist) 0.

APA Accreditation: Counseling PhD (Doctor of Philosophy).

Student Applications/Admissions:
Student Applications
Counseling Psychology PhD (Doctor of Philosophy)—Applications 2004–2005, 86. Total applicants accepted 2004–2005, 5. Total enrolled 2004–2005 full-time, 20. Openings 2005–2006, 5. The Median number of years required for completion of a degree are 5. The number of students enrolled full and part-time who were dismissed or voluntarily withdrew from this program area were 0. *MA Psych Studies/EdS Marriage and Family Therapy EdS (Education Specialist)*—Applications 2004–2005, 6. Total applicants accepted 2004–2005, 5. Total enrolled 2004–2005 full-time, 15, part-time, 4. Openings 2005–2006, 6. The Median number of years required for completion of a degree are 3. The number of students enrolled full and part-time who were dismissed or voluntarily withdrew from this program area were 0. *MA Psych Studies/EdS School and Community EdS (Education Specialist)*—Applications 2004–2005, 25. Total applicants accepted 2004–2005, 15. Total enrolled 2004–2005 full-time, 25, part-time, 6. Openings 2005–2006, 15. The Median number of years required for completion of a degree are 4. The number of students enrolled

full and part-time who were dismissed or voluntarily withdrew from this program area were 3. *Psychological Studies MA/MS (Master of Arts/Science)*—Applications 2004–2005, 12. Total applicants accepted 2004–2005, 12. Openings 2005–2006, 8. The Median number of years required for completion of a degree are 3. The number of students enrolled full and part-time who were dismissed or voluntarily withdrew from this program area were 0. *MA Psych Studies/EdS Mental Health Counseling EdS (Education Specialist)*—Applications 2004–2005, 13. Total applicants accepted 2004–2005, 13. Total enrolled 2004–2005 full-time, 10, part-time, 3. Openings 2005–2006, 5. The Median number of years required for completion of a degree are 3. The number of students enrolled full and part-time who were dismissed or voluntarily withdrew from this program area were 0.

Admissions Requirements:
Scores: Entries appear in this order: required test or GPA, minimum score (if required), median score of students entering in 2003–2004. Master's Programs: GRE-V no minimum stated; GRE-Q no minimum stated; MAT no minimum stated. Doctoral Programs: overall undergraduate GPA no minimum stated.
Other Criteria: (importance of criteria rated low, medium, or high): GRE/MAT scores medium, research experience high, work experience medium, extracurricular activity medium, clinically related public service medium, GPA medium, letters of recommendation high, interview high, statement of goals and objectives high, PhD program scientist/practitioner model of training; Master's and EdS programs clinically focused. For additional information on admission requirements, go to: www.shu.edu.

Student Characteristics: The following represents characteristics of students in 2004–2005 in all graduate psychology programs in the department: Caucasian–full-time 0, part-time 0; Multi-ethnic–full-time 0, part-time 0; students subject to the Americans With Disabilities Act–full-time 0, part-time 0.

Financial Information/Assistance:
Tuition for Full-Time Study: *Master's:* State residents: $645 per credit hour; Nonstate residents: $645 per credit hour. *Doctoral:* State residents: $645 per credit hour; Nonstate residents: $645 per credit hour. Tuition is subject to change. See the following Web site for updates and changes in tuition costs: www.shu.edu.

Financial Assistance:
First Year Students: Research assistantships available for first-year. Average amount paid per academic year: $4,500. Average number of hours worked per week: 20. Apply by early spring. Tuition remission given: full.
Advanced Students: Research assistantships available for advanced students. Average amount paid per academic year: $4,500. Average number of hours worked per week: 20. Apply by spring. Tuition remission given: full.
Contact Information: Of all students currently enrolled full-time, 90% benefitted from one or more of the listed financial assistance programs. Application and information available online at: www.shu.edu.

Internships/Practica: The Marriage and Family students follow the standards of the Commission on Accreditation for Marriage and Family Therapy Education. The doctoral students adhere to Psychology guidelines. For those doctoral students for whom a professional internship is required prior to graduation, 5 applied in 2003–2004. Of those who applied, 5 were placed in internships listed by the Association of Psychology Postdoctoral and Internship Programs (APPIC).

Housing and Day Care: No on-campus housing is available. No on-campus day care facilities are available.

Employment of Department Graduates:

Master's Degree Graduates: Of those who graduated in the academic year 2003–2004, the following categories and numbers represent the post-graduate activities and employment of master's degree graduates: Enrolled in a psychology doctoral program (0), enrolled in another graduate/professional program (0), enrolled in a post-doctoral residency/fellowship (n/a), employed in independent practice (n/a), employed in an academic position at a university (0), employed in an academic position at a 2-year/4-year college (0), employed in other positions at a higher education institution (0), employed in a professional position in a school system (0), employed in business or industry (research/consulting) (0), employed in business or industry (management) (0), employed in a government agency (research) (0), employed in a government agency (professional services) (0), employed in a community mental health/counseling center (0), employed in a hospital/medical center (0), still seeking employment (0), other employment position (0), total from the above (master's) (0).

Doctoral Degree Graduates: Of those who graduated in the academic year 2003–2004, the following categories and numbers represent the post-graduate activities and employment of doctoral degree graduates: Enrolled in a psychology doctoral program (n/a), enrolled in a post-doctoral residency/fellowship (0), employed in independent practice (0), employed in an academic position at a university (0), employed in an academic position at a 2-year/4-year college (0), employed in other positions at a higher education institution (0), employed in a professional position in a school system (0), employed in business or industry (research/consulting) (0), employed in business or industry (management) (0), employed in a government agency (research) (0), employed in a government agency (professional services) (0), employed in a community mental health/counseling center (0), employed in a hospital/medical center (0), still seeking employment (0), other employment position (0), total from the above (doctoral) (0).

Additional Information:

Orientation, Objectives, and Emphasis of Department: The Marriage and Family programs are based on a systemic orientation to family psychology and family therapy. The goals of Counseling Psychology encompass knowledge of the science of psychology and counseling psychology as a specialty, integration of research and practice, and commitment to ongoing professional development. Professional counselors are mental health practitioners trained to help individual clients and groups address common developmental challenges and transitions as well as more severe emotional difficulties. School psychology students learn to specialize in assessment and evaluations in schools. Programs listed as MA/EdS are combined programs in which students are afforded the opportunity to continue their studies without applying for the advanced degree.

Special Facilities or Resources: The department has individual counseling/assessment rooms, family and couple laboratories, and group therapy rooms, all of which are wired with state-of-the-art audiovisual equipment with centralized viewing in a control room. There are rooms for data analyses as well.

Information for Students With Physical Disabilities: See the following Web site for more information: www.shu.edu.

Application Information:
Send to: Graduate Admissions, College of Education and Human Services, Seton Hall University, South Orange, NJ 07079. Application available online. Students are admitted in the Fall. Counseling Psychology PhD (January 15), all other programs rolling admissions. *Fee:* $50.

Seton Hall University
Psychology/ Experimental Psychology
Arts and Sciences
400 South Orange Avenue
South Orange, NJ 07079
Telephone: (973) 761-9484
Fax: (973) 275-5829
E-mail: *psych@shu.edu*
Web: *http://artsci.shu.edu/psychology/*

Department Information:
1952. Chairperson: Jeffrey C. Levy, PhD Number of Faculty: total–full-time 12; women–full-time 7.

Programs and Degrees Offered:
Listed in the following order: Program area, degree type (T if terminal Master's), number awarded 7/03–6/04. Experimental Psychology MA/MS (Master of Arts/Science).

Student Applications/Admissions:
Student Applications
Experimental Psychology MA/MS (Master of Arts/Science)— Number enrolled (new admits only) 2004–2005 full-time, 5. Number enrolled (new admits only) 2004–2005 part-time, 1. Total enrolled 2004–2005 full-time, 5, part-time, 1. Openings 2005–2006, 10. The number of students enrolled full and part-time who were dismissed or voluntarily withdrew from this program area were 1.

Admissions Requirements:
Scores: Entries appear in this order: required test or GPA, minimum score (if required), median score of students entering in 2003–2004. Master's Programs: GRE-V 500, 510; GRE-Q 500, 630; GRE-V+Q 1000, 1110; overall undergraduate GPA 3.00, 3.43; psychology GPA no minimum stated.
Other Criteria: (importance of criteria rated low, medium, or high): GRE/MAT scores high, research experience high, GPA high, letters of recommendation high, statement of goals and objectives high.

Student Characteristics: The following represents characteristics of students in 2004–2005 in all graduate psychology programs in the department: Female–full-time 3, part-time 0; Male–full-time 2, part-time 1; Caucasian–full-time 5, part-time 1.

Financial Information/Assistance:

Tuition for Full-Time Study: *Master's:* State residents: per academic year $13,420, $675 per credit hour. Tuition is subject to change. See the following Web site for updates and changes in tuition costs: http://www.shu.edu/finplan.html#costs.

Financial Assistance:

First Year Students: Teaching assistantships available for first-year. Average amount paid per academic year: $5,200. Average number of hours worked per week: 20. Tuition remission given: full. Research assistantships available for first-year. Average amount paid per academic year: $5,200. Average number of hours worked per week: 20. Tuition remission given: full.

Advanced Students: Teaching assistantships available for advanced students. Average amount paid per academic year: $5,200. Average number of hours worked per week: 20. Tuition remission given: full. Research assistantships available for advanced students. Average amount paid per academic year: $5,200. Average number of hours worked per week: 20. Tuition remission given: full.

Contact Information: Application and information available online at: http://artsci.shu.edu/onlineapp.html.

Internships/Practica: No information provided.

Housing and Day Care: No on-campus housing is available. No on-campus day care facilities are available.

Employment of Department Graduates:

Master's Degree Graduates: Of those who graduated in the academic year 2003–2004, the following categories and numbers represent the post-graduate activities and employment of master's degree graduates: Enrolled in a post-doctoral residency/fellowship (n/a), employed in independent practice (n/a), total from the above (master's) (0).

Doctoral Degree Graduates: Of those who graduated in the academic year 2003–2004, the following categories and numbers represent the post-graduate activities and employment of doctoral degree graduates: Enrolled in a psychology doctoral program (n/a), total from the above (doctoral) (0).

Additional Information:

Orientation, Objectives, and Emphasis of Department: The MS degree in experimental psychology is designed specifically for students seeking to gain a solid foundation in empirical research for eventual entry into PhD programs in scientific psychology or for students desiring to explore the field. The Experimental Psychology program consists of 36 credits to be completed in 2 years. All incoming students are required to participate in experimental research each semester. The courses offered (including a research thesis) comprise traditional areas in experimental psychology with optional concentrations in General Psychology and Behavioral Neuroscience. The Behavioral Neuroscience concentration represents courses that are most directly relevant to behavioral studies of brain functioning.

Special Facilities or Resources: Faculty have private offices of approximately 150 square feet each. A suite of nine 8' X 8' cubicles are available for graduate student use. A Conditioning Laboratory consists of eight test cubicles, each equipped with an operant chamber interfaced to an IBM Desktop Pentium 233MHz laboratory control computer. A five room Physiological Psychology Suite of approximately 400 square feet is used for surgical preparations, histology, and behavioral observation of rodents. Several mazes are also available for the study of learning and memory. The laboratories share access to two animal colony rooms for housing rodents. Research space for human experimental psychology investigations includes a corridor lined by eleven research cubicles, each one approximately 90 square feet and a research participant reception area of approximately 200 square feet. Equipment for these cubicles includes seven desktop computers powered by 433MHz Intel Celeron processors with 15§ monitors and associated equipment that allows them to function as laboratory control devices. Three of these machines have video capture cards permitting still frame capture and video-conferencing with Sony video camcorders. In addition, the department's Perceptual Laboratory consists of a three-room suite totaling 650 square feet. A one-way vision room is also available.

Application Information:

Send to: Office of the Dean College of Arts and Sciences, Fahy Hall, Room 128, Seton Hall University, South Orange, NJ 07079. Application available online. Students are admitted in the Fall, application deadline July 1. Strong applications submitted before April 1 have a greater chance of admittance and receiving financial aid. *Fee:* $50.

William Paterson University

Psychology/MA in Applied Clinical Psychology
Humanities & Social Sciences
300 Pompton Road
Wayne, NJ 07470
Telephone: (973) 720-2643
Fax: (973) 720-3392
E-mail: *PAKIZEGIB@WPUNJ.EDU*
Web: *http://www.wpunj.edu/cohss/psychology/Masters.htm*

Department Information:

1999. Graduate Director: Behnaz Pakizegi, PhD. Number of Faculty: total–full-time 7, part-time 3; women–full-time 5, part-time 1.

Programs and Degrees Offered:

Listed in the following order: Program area, degree type (T if terminal Master's), number awarded 7/03–6/04. Applied Clinical Psychology MA/MS (Master of Arts/Science) (T) 7.

Student Applications/Admissions:

Student Applications

Applied Clinical Psychology MA/MS (Master of Arts/Science)— Applications 2004–2005, 64. Total applicants accepted 2004–2005, 42. Number enrolled (new admits only) 2004–2005 full-time, 6. Number enrolled (new admits only) 2004–2005 part-time, 14. Total enrolled 2004–2005 full-time, 11, part-time, 33. Openings 2005–2006, 20. The Median number of years required for completion of a degree are 3. The number of students enrolled full and part-time who were dismissed or voluntarily withdrew from this program area were 3.

Admissions Requirements:

Scores: Entries appear in this order: required test or GPA, minimum score (if required), median score of students entering in 2003–2004. Master's Programs: GRE-V 450; GRE-Analytical 5.0; overall undergraduate GPA 3.0. We require a minimum score of 5.0 out of 6.0 on the Analytical Section (essay).

Other Criteria: (importance of criteria rated low, medium, or high): GRE/MAT scores high, research experience medium, work experience medium, extracurricular activity medium, clinically related public service medium, GPA high, letters of recommendation high, interview medium, statement of goals and objectives high, Also required: Undergraduate background including the following courses (1) General Psychology, (2) Abnormal or Personality Psychology, (3) Statistics or Experimental Design, and (4) Developmental or Child Psychology. For additional information on admission requirements, go to: http://www.wpunj.edu/cohss/psychology/masters.htm.

Student Characteristics: The following represents characteristics of students in 2004–2005 in all graduate psychology programs in the department: Female–full-time 12, part-time 24; Male–full-time 2, part-time 9; African American/Black–full-time 0, part-time 3; Hispanic/Latino(a)–full-time 0, part-time 4; Asian/Pacific Islander–full-time 0, part-time 1; American Indian/Alaska Native–full-time 0, part-time 0; Caucasian–full-time 14, part-time 25; Multi-ethnic–full-time 0, part-time 0; students subject to the Americans With Disabilities Act–full-time 0, part-time 0.

Financial Information/Assistance:

Tuition for Full-Time Study: *Master's:* State residents: per academic year $10,740, $358 per credit hour; Nonstate residents: per academic year $16,050, $535 per credit hour.

Financial Assistance:

First Year Students: Traineeships available for first-year. Average amount paid per academic year: $6,000. Average number of hours worked per week: 20. Apply by March 1. Tuition remission given: full.

Advanced Students: Traineeships available for advanced students. Average amount paid per academic year: $6,000. Average number of hours worked per week: 20. Apply by March 1. Tuition remission given: full.

Contact Information: Of all students currently enrolled full-time, 27% benefitted from one or more of the listed financial assistance programs.

Internships/Practica: Our program trains master's level practitioners for work in a wide variety of inpatient and outpatient clinical settings including hospitals, community mental health clinics, group homes, drug treatment facilities, physical rehabilitation centers, correctional facilities, gerontology programs, and, after licensure, private practice. Under supervision, graduates of our program are able to conduct diagnostic and psychological assessments; counsel individuals, groups and families using appropriate interview and intervention techniques; participate in institutional and organizational research projects involving study design, data collection and analysis; and work on an elective basis

with such populations as children, adolescents, the aged, the severely mentally ill, the neurologically impaired, substance abusers, and others.

Housing and Day Care: On-campus housing is available. See the following Web site for more information: www.wpunj.edu. On-campus day care facilities are available.

Employment of Department Graduates:

Master's Degree Graduates: Of those who graduated in the academic year 2003–2004, the following categories and numbers represent the post-graduate activities and employment of master's degree graduates: Enrolled in a psychology doctoral program (1), enrolled in another graduate/professional program (0), enrolled in a post-doctoral residency/fellowship (n/a), employed in independent practice (n/a), employed in an academic position at a university (2), employed in an academic position at a 2-year/4-year college (0), employed in other positions at a higher education institution (0), employed in a professional position in a school system (0), employed in business or industry (research/consulting) (0), employed in business or industry (management) (0), employed in a government agency (research) (0), employed in a government agency (professional services) (0), employed in a community mental health/counseling center (9), employed in a hospital/medical center (1), still seeking employment (0), not seeking employment (0), other employment position (0), do not know (0), total from the above (master's) (13).

Doctoral Degree Graduates: Of those who graduated in the academic year 2003–2004, the following categories and numbers represent the post-graduate activities and employment of doctoral degree graduates: Enrolled in a psychology doctoral program (n/a), total from the above (doctoral) (0).

Additional Information:

Orientation, Objectives, and Emphasis of Department: The Master's Program in Applied Clinical Psychology prepares students for psychological counseling, assessment and mental health research in non-school settings. Graduates meet the academic requirements for eligibility to take the National Counselor Examination, currently required for licensure as a Licensed Professional Counselor in New Jersey and in the majority of the states in the country. Graduates must successfully complete 60 credit hours of coursework and supervised fieldwork. The curriculum emphasizes intervention and consists of required and elective courses in the theoretical, empirical, and ethical foundations of clinical psychology. Supervised fieldwork in clinical settings enables students to apply the theories and empirical findings discussed in the classroom to develop the competency needed for practice with clients. Students may opt to complete this program on either a full-time (two years including summers) or part-time basis (three to six years including summers). Full-time students may not be employed for more than 20 hours per week. As much as possible, courses will be offered in consecutive time slots 2 to 3 days per week, in the late afternoon and evening slots, as well as during the summer.

Special Facilities or Resources: William Paterson University is equipped with several computer and research labs, a large library, and access to several online databases. The Psych Dept. and graduate program own a wide array of assessment kits and dozens of relevant videos which are available to faculty and students.

The graduate program faculty currently have ongoing research in the areas of mind-body approaches to well-being, life span issues, trauma, substance abuse and addiction, gerontology, serious and persistent psychiatric disorders, and neuropsychology. The university is close to urban settings and 30 minutes from NYC.

Information for Students With Physical Disabilities: See the following Web site for more information: www.wpunj.edu.

Application Information:
Send to: Office of Graduate Studies, Raubinger Hall, Room 139, William Paterson University, 300 Pompton Road, Wayne, NJ 07470. Application available online. Students are admitted in the Fall, application deadline March 1; Spring, application deadline October 15. *Fee:* $35.

New Mexico Highlands University
Division of Psychology
Department of Behavioral Sciences
Hewett Hall
Las Vegas, NM 87701-4073
Telephone: (505) 454-3343
Fax: (505) 454-3331
E-mail: *jlhill@nmhu.edu*
Web: *http://www.nmhu.edu/psychology/*

Department Information:
1946. Psychology Program Coordinator: Jean L. Hill. Number of Faculty: total–full-time 4, part-time 2; women–full-time 2, part-time 1; minority–part-time 1.

Programs and Degrees Offered:
Listed in the following order: Program area, degree type (T if terminal Master's), number awarded 7/03–6/04. General/ Clinical/ Counseling MA/MS (Master of Arts/Science) (T) 4.

Student Applications/Admissions:
Student Applications
General/ Clinical/ Counseling MA/MS (Master of Arts/Science)— Applications 2004–2005, 13. Total applicants accepted 2004–2005, 13. Number enrolled (new admits only) 2004–2005 full-time, 8. Number enrolled (new admits only) 2004–2005 part-time, 0. Total enrolled 2004–2005 full-time, 17, part-time, 9. Openings 2005–2006, 15. The Median number of years required for completion of a degree are 3. The number of students enrolled full and part-time who were dismissed or voluntarily withdrew from this program area were 1.

Admissions Requirements:
Scores: Entries appear in this order: required test or GPA, minimum score (if required), median score of students entering in 2003–2004. Master's Programs: psychology GPA 3.00, 3.45.
Other Criteria: (importance of criteria rated low, medium, or high): research experience medium, work experience medium, extracurricular activity low, clinically related public service medium, letters of recommendation medium, statement of goals and objectives high.

Student Characteristics: The following represents characteristics of students in 2004–2005 in all graduate psychology programs in the department: Female–full-time 9, part-time 5; Male–full-time 8, part-time 4; African American/Black–full-time 1, part-time 0; Hispanic/Latino(a)–full-time 7, part-time 1; Asian/Pacific Islander–full-time 0, part-time 1; American Indian/Alaska Native–full-time 1, part-time 0; Caucasian–full-time 8, part-time 7; Multi-ethnic–full-time 0, part-time 0; students subject to the Americans With Disabilities Act–full-time 0, part-time 0.

Financial Information/Assistance:
Tuition for Full-Time Study: *Master's:* State residents: per academic year $2,238; Nonstate residents: per academic year $8,776. Tuition is subject to change.

Financial Assistance:
First Year Students: Teaching assistantships available for first-year. Average amount paid per academic year: $6,500. Average number of hours worked per week: 20. Tuition remission given: full and partial. Research assistantships available for first-year. Average amount paid per academic year: $6,500. Average number of hours worked per week: 20. Tuition remission given: full and partial. Fellowships and scholarships available for first-year. Average amount paid per academic year: $6,500. Average number of hours worked per week: 20. Tuition remission given: full and partial.

Advanced Students: Teaching assistantships available for advanced students. Average amount paid per academic year: $6,500. Average number of hours worked per week: 20. Tuition remission given: full and partial. Research assistantships available for advanced students. Average amount paid per academic year: $6,500. Average number of hours worked per week: 20. Tuition remission given: full and partial. Fellowships and scholarships available for advanced students. Average amount paid per academic year: $6,500. Average number of hours worked per week: 20. Tuition remission given: full and partial.

Contact Information: Of all students currently enrolled full-time, 100% benefitted from one or more of the listed financial assistance programs.

Internships/Practica: Students in the Clinical Psychology/Counseling track must complete 12 credit hours of Field Experience. Completion of the 12 credit hours ensures that each student in this track gains 720 hours of direct clinical experience while completing the program. Field Experience placements are arranged through cooperative planning by the student, the program, and the agency. Students from our program have been placed with the following agencies: the forensic, adolescent, and adult units of the state psychiatric hospital; the local community mental health center; the state juvenile correctional facility; local schools; an equine therapy program; and many others.

Housing and Day Care: On-campus housing is available. On-campus day care facilities are available.

Employment of Department Graduates:
Master's Degree Graduates: Of those who graduated in the academic year 2003–2004, the following categories and numbers represent the post-graduate activities and employment of master's degree graduates: Enrolled in a post-doctoral residency/fellowship (n/a), employed in independent practice (n/a), total from the above (master's) (0).
Doctoral Degree Graduates: Of those who graduated in the academic year 2003–2004, the following categories and numbers represent the post-graduate activities and employment of doctoral degree graduates: Enrolled in a psychology doctoral program (n/a), total from the above (doctoral) (0).

Additional Information:
Orientation, Objectives, and Emphasis of Department: The department offers two tracks that lead to a Master of Science degree in psychology. The General Psychology track requires 36 credit hours and is intended to provide a background similar to that

given in many PhD programs. This track is organized around a general core of courses designed to educate the student in all areas of psychology with the opportunity to further pursue an area of interest such as physiological experimental, neuropsychological, or social psychology. This track is especially useful for those students whose goals include either entering a doctoral program or working in a non-clinical position (research, etc.) upon completing the master's degree. The Clinical Psychology/Counseling track is a 63-credit hour emphasis area that is unique because it is one of the only programs in the U.S. that provides comprehensive training in psychological training and assessment in four areas: neuropsychological, behavioral, intelligence, and personality. This track is designed to prepare students to continue their education at the doctoral level or to work as a master's level clinician. The student successfully completing this track will qualify for licensure as a master's level clinican in approximately 40 states.

Special Facilities or Resources: The department offers excellent animal laboratory facilities for experimental-physiological research, as well as laboratories for human subjects research. In addition, the department has an extensive computer laboratory. We also have a close relationship with the state psychiatric hospital, which is located in the community.

Application Information:

Send to: Psychology Program Coordinator. Students are admitted in the Fall, application deadline June 1. Earlier applications receive preferential treatment for financial aid. *Fee:* $15.

New Mexico State University

Counseling and Educational Psychology
College of Education
Box 30001 MSC 3CEP
Las Cruces, NM 88003-8001
Telephone: (505) 646-2121
Fax: (505) 646-8035
E-mail: *eadams@nmsu.edu*
Web: *http://education.nmsu.edu/cep/*

Department Information:

1905. Dept Head: Luiz A. Vazquez. Number of Faculty: total–full-time 10; women–full-time 3; minority–full-time 1.

Programs and Degrees Offered:

Listed in the following order: Program area, degree type (T if terminal Master's), number awarded 7/03–6/04. Counseling and Guidance MA/MS (Master of Arts/Science) (T) 20, School Psychology EdS (Education Specialist) 1, Counseling Psychology PhD (Doctor of Philosophy) 6.

APA Accreditation: Counseling PhD (Doctor of Philosophy).

Student Applications/Admissions:

Student Applications

*Counseling and Guidance MA/MS (Master of Arts/Science)—*Applications 2004–2005, 26. Total applicants accepted 2004–2005, 14. Number enrolled (new admits only) 2004–2005 full-time, 9. Number enrolled (new admits only) 2004–2005 part-time, 3. Total enrolled 2004–2005 full-time, 18, part-time, 6. Openings 2005–2006, 14. The Median number of years required for completion of a degree are 2. The number of students enrolled full and part-time who were dismissed or voluntarily withdrew from this program area were 2. *School Psychology EdS (Education Specialist)—*Applications 2004–2005, 17. Total applicants accepted 2004–2005, 12. Number enrolled (new admits only) 2004–2005 full-time, 6. Number enrolled (new admits only) 2004–2005 part-time, 6. Total enrolled 2004–2005 full-time, 22, part-time, 10. Openings 2005–2006, 12. The Median number of years required for completion of a degree are 3. The number of students enrolled full and part-time who were dismissed or voluntarily withdrew from this program area were 0. *Counseling Psychology PhD (Doctor of Philosophy)—*Applications 2004–2005, 34. Total applicants accepted 2004–2005, 12. Number enrolled (new admits only) 2004–2005 full-time, 6. Number enrolled (new admits only) 2004–2005 part-time, 0. Openings 2005–2006, 6. The Median number of years required for completion of a degree are 5. The number of students enrolled full and part-time who were dismissed or voluntarily withdrew from this program area were 0.

Admissions Requirements:

Scores: Entries appear in this order: required test or GPA, minimum score (if required), median score of students entering in 2003–2004. Master's Programs: GRE-V no minimum stated, 370; GRE-Q no minimum stated, 490; GRE-V+Q no minimum stated; GRE-Analytical no minimum stated; overall undergraduate GPA no minimum stated, 3.43; last 2 years GPA no minimum stated. Doctoral Programs: GRE-V no minimum stated; GRE-Q no minimum stated; GRE-V+Q no minimum stated, 984; GRE-Analytical no minimum stated; overall undergraduate GPA no minimum stated, 3.3. Median scores for EdS Program are: GRE Verbal - 430, Quantitative - 430, and MA GPA - 3.35.

Other Criteria: (importance of criteria rated low, medium, or high): GRE/MAT scores medium, research experience high, work experience medium, extracurricular activity medium, clinically related public service medium, GPA high, letters of recommendation high, interview high, statement of goals and objectives high, writing sample medium. Criteria do vary for different programs. For additional information on admission requirements, go to: http://education.nmsu.edu/cep/.

Student Characteristics: The following represents characteristics of students in 2004–2005 in all graduate psychology programs in the department: Female–full-time 43, part-time 14; Male–full-time 25, part-time 2; African American/Black–full-time 7, part-time 0; Hispanic/Latino(a)–full-time 28, part-time 7; Asian/Pacific Islander–full-time 0, part-time 0; American Indian/Alaska Native–full-time 2, part-time 1; Caucasian–full-time 29, part-time 8; Multi-ethnic–full-time 2, part-time 0; students subject to the Americans With Disabilities Act–full-time 2, part-time 0.

Financial Information/Assistance:

Tuition for Full-Time Study: *Master's:* State residents: per academic year $4,000; Nonstate residents: per academic year $13,000. *Doctoral:* State residents: per academic year $4,000; Nonstate residents: per academic year $13,000. Tuition is subject to change. See the following Web site for updates and changes in tuition costs: http://gradschool.nmsu.edu.

Financial Assistance:

First Year Students: Teaching assistantships available for first-year. Average amount paid per academic year: $7,000. Average number of hours worked per week: 10. Apply by varies. Research assistantships available for first-year. Average amount paid per academic year: $7,000. Average number of hours worked per week: 10. Apply by varies. Fellowships and scholarships available for first-year. Apply by varies. Tuition remission given: full.

Advanced Students: Teaching assistantships available for advanced students. Average amount paid per academic year: $7,000. Average number of hours worked per week: 10. Apply by varies. Research assistantships available for advanced students. Average amount paid per academic year: $7,000. Average number of hours worked per week: 10. Apply by varies. Fellowships and scholarships available for advanced students. Apply by varies. Tuition remission given: full.

Contact Information: Of all students currently enrolled full-time, 75% benefitted from one or more of the listed financial assistance programs. Application and information available online at: Doctoral students are guarenteed funding. Other grad applicants are not.

Internships/Practica: Practicum placements include the NMSU Counseling Center, the Las Cruces Public Schools, a primary care setting, community mental health centers, hospitals, adolescent residential centers, the Department of Vocational Rehabilitation, military bases, and nursing homes. For those doctoral students for whom a professional internship is required prior to graduation, 6 applied in 2003–2004. Of those who applied, 6 were placed in internships listed by the Association of Psychology Postdoctoral and Internship Programs (APPIC); 5 were placed in APA accredited internships.

Housing and Day Care: On-campus housing is available. See the following Web site for more information: http://www.nmsu.edu/~housing/. On-campus day care facilities are available. Call (505) 646-3206 for university child care. Call (505) 527-1149 for community resources.

Employment of Department Graduates:

Master's Degree Graduates: Of those who graduated in the academic year 2003–2004, the following categories and numbers represent the post-graduate activities and employment of master's degree graduates: Enrolled in a psychology doctoral program (2), enrolled in another graduate/professional program (0), enrolled in a post-doctoral residency/fellowship (n/a), employed in independent practice (n/a), employed in an academic position at a university (0), employed in an academic position at a 2-year/4-year college (0), employed in other positions at a higher education institution (0), employed in a professional position in a school system (5), employed in business or industry (research/consulting) (0), employed in business or industry (management) (0), employed in a government agency (research) (0), employed in a government agency (professional services) (0), employed in a community mental health/counseling center (5), employed in a hospital/medical center (0), still seeking employment (0), not seeking employment (0), other employment position (0), do not know (0), total from the above (master's) (12).

Doctoral Degree Graduates: Of those who graduated in the academic year 2003–2004, the following categories and numbers represent the post-graduate activities and employment of doctoral degree graduates: Enrolled in a psychology doctoral program (n/a), enrolled in another graduate/professional program (0), enrolled in a post-doctoral residency/fellowship (1), employed in independent practice (1), employed in an academic position at a university (0), employed in an academic position at a 2-year/4-year college (0), employed in other positions at a higher education institution (2), employed in a professional position in a school system (0), employed in business or industry (research/consulting) (0), employed in business or industry (management) (0), employed in a government agency (research) (0), employed in a government agency (professional services) (0), employed in a community mental health/counseling center (2), employed in a hospital/medical center (0), still seeking employment (0), not seeking employment (0), other employment position (0), do not know (0), total from the above (doctoral) (6).

Additional Information:

Orientation, Objectives, and Emphasis of Department: The major thrust of the department is the preparation of professionals for licensure and positions in counseling psychology, mental health and school counseling, school psychology, and related areas. Three graduate degrees are available: (1) Doctor of Philosophy, (2) Masters of Arts, and (3) Specialist in Education. The PhD in Counseling Psychology, which is accredited by the American Psychological Association, is based on the scientist-practitioner model through which both research and service delivery skills are acquired. Graduates of the program are prepared to conduct research, provide service, teach, and supervise. Emphases in the Counseling Psychology program include cultural diversity, group and family counseling, and counselor training, supervision and consultation. The Master of Arts in Counseling and Guidance prepares professional counselors to offer individual, family, and group counseling in schools, agencies, hospitals, and private practice. The curriculum covers human development; appraisal; diagnosis; treatment planning; individual, professional issues. The School Psychology Program (EdS) prepares professionals for positions in public schools and other organizations which require advanced assessment, counseling, consultation and supervision skills. A major research project (thesis) is a degree requirement.

Special Facilities or Resources: The Counseling and School Psychology Training and Research Center is a training/service facility sponsored by the Department of Counseling and Educational Psychology, which provides excellent opportunities for supervised counseling and supervision-of-supervision. Four rooms are available for videotaping, and have one-way mirrors, telephones, and microphone-speakers for live supervision of counseling and live supervision of supervision. A portable video camera is available for use in other rooms. The facility has a "state-of-the-art" bug in the ear system which helps facilitate live supervision for immediate feedback to the counselor in training.

Information for Students With Physical Disabilities: See the following Web site for more information: http://www.nmsu.edu/~ssd/.

Application Information:

Application to the department should be mailed to: Training Director, Department of Counseling and Educational Psychology, MSC 3CEP/Box 30001, Las Cruces, NM 88003-8001 Applications to the Graduate School should be mailed to: The Graduate School, MSC 3G/Box 30001, Las Cruces, NM 88003-8001. Application available online. URL of online application: http://www.nmsu.edu/~gradcolg/app.html.

Students are admitted in the Fall, application deadline March 15; Summer, application deadline December 15. The PhD Program deadline is December 15. The EdS Program deadline is January 15. The MA Program deadline is March 15. The Graduate School does not have any deadlines. Students must check with the department for their deadlines, if any. We accept applications all year round. *Fee:* $30. McNair scholars can have their fees waived.

New Mexico State University

Department of Psychology
Department 3452, PO Box 30001
Las Cruces, NM 88003
Telephone: (505) 646-2502
Fax: (505) 646-6212
E-mail: *gillan@crl.nmsu.edu*
Web: *http://www-psych.nmsu.edu*

Department Information:
1950. Head: Douglas J. Gillan. Number of Faculty: total–full-time 14, part-time 3; women–full-time 5, part-time 1; minority–full-time 1.

Programs and Degrees Offered:
Listed in the following order: Program area, degree type (T if terminal Master's), number awarded 7/03–6/04. Cognitive MA/MS (Master of Arts/Science) (T) 2, Engineering MA/MS (Master of Arts/Science) (T) 3, Experimental- General MA/MS (Master of Arts/Science) (T) 1, Social MA/MS (Master of Arts/Science) (T) 3, Cognitive PhD (Doctor of Philosophy) 1, Engineering PhD (Doctor of Philosophy) 0, Social PhD (Doctor of Philosophy) 1.

Student Applications/Admissions:
Student Applications
Cognitive MA/MS (Master of Arts/Science)—Applications 2004–2005, 5. Total applicants accepted 2004–2005, 2. Total enrolled 2004–2005 full-time, 6, part-time, 2. Openings 2005–2006, 5. The Median number of years required for completion of a degree are 3. The number of students enrolled full and part-time who were dismissed or voluntarily withdrew from this program area were 0. *Engineering MA/MS (Master of Arts/Science)*—Applications 2004–2005, 10. Total applicants accepted 2004–2005, 5. Number enrolled (new admits only) 2004–2005 full-time, 2. Number enrolled (new admits only) 2004–2005 part-time, 0. Total enrolled 2004–2005 full-time, 8, part-time, 7. Openings 2005–2006, 6. The Median number of years required for completion of a degree are 3. The number of students enrolled full and part-time who were dismissed or voluntarily withdrew from this program area were 0. *Experimental-General MA/MS (Master of Arts/Science)*—Applications 2004–2005, 3. Total applicants accepted 2004–2005, 0. Number enrolled (new admits only) 2004–2005 full-time, 0. Number enrolled (new admits only) 2004–2005 part-time, 0. Openings 2005–2006, 5. The number of students enrolled full and part-time who were dismissed or voluntarily withdrew from this program area were 0. *Social MA/MS (Master of Arts/Science)*—Applications 2004–2005, 10. Total applicants accepted 2004–2005, 6. Number enrolled (new admits only) 2004–2005 full-time, 3. Number enrolled (new admits only) 2004–2005 part-time, 0. Openings 2005–2006, 6. The Median number of years

required for completion of a degree are 3. The number of students enrolled full and part-time who were dismissed or voluntarily withdrew from this program area were 0. *Cognitive PhD (Doctor of Philosophy)*—Applications 2004–2005, 3. Total applicants accepted 2004–2005, 0. Number enrolled (new admits only) 2004–2005 full-time, 0. Number enrolled (new admits only) 2004–2005 part-time, 0. Total enrolled 2004–2005 full-time, 3, part-time, 2. Openings 2005–2006, 2. The Median number of years required for completion of a degree are 3. The number of students enrolled full and part-time who were dismissed or voluntarily withdrew from this program area were 0. *Engineering PhD (Doctor of Philosophy)*—Applications 2004–2005, 3. Total applicants accepted 2004–2005, 1. Number enrolled (new admits only) 2004–2005 full-time, 0. Number enrolled (new admits only) 2004–2005 part-time, 0. Total enrolled 2004–2005 full-time, 3, part-time, 1. Openings 2005–2006, 2. The number of students enrolled full and part-time who were dismissed or voluntarily withdrew from this program area were 0. *Social PhD (Doctor of Philosophy)*—Applications 2004–2005, 4. Total applicants accepted 2004–2005, 1. Number enrolled (new admits only) 2004–2005 full-time, 0. Number enrolled (new admits only) 2004–2005 part-time, 0. Total enrolled 2004–2005 full-time, 6, part-time, 1. Openings 2005–2006, 2. The Median number of years required for completion of a degree are 3. The number of students enrolled full and part-time who were dismissed or voluntarily withdrew from this program area were 0.

Admissions Requirements:
Scores: Entries appear in this order: required test or GPA, minimum score (if required), median score of students entering in 2003–2004. Master's Programs: GRE-V no minimum stated, 550; GRE-Q no minimum stated; overall undergraduate GPA no minimum stated. Doctoral Programs: GRE-V no minimum stated; GRE-Q no minimum stated; overall undergraduate GPA no minimum stated.
Other Criteria: (importance of criteria rated low, medium, or high): GRE/MAT scores high, research experience medium, work experience low, GPA high, letters of recommendation high, statement of goals and objectives medium.

Student Characteristics: The following represents characteristics of students in 2004–2005 in all graduate psychology programs in the department: Female–full-time 25, part-time 7; Male–full-time 12, part-time 6; African American/Black–full-time 1, part-time 0; Hispanic/Latino(a)–full-time 7, part-time 0; Asian/Pacific Islander–full-time 0, part-time 0; American Indian/Alaska Native–full-time 0, part-time 0; Caucasian–full-time 29, part-time 13; Multi-ethnic–full-time 0, part-time 0; students subject to the Americans With Disabilities Act–full-time 0, part-time 0.

Financial Information/Assistance:
Tuition for Full-Time Study: *Master's:* State residents: per academic year $3,624, $151 per credit hour; Nonstate residents: per academic year $11,550, $481 per credit hour. *Doctoral:* State residents: per academic year $3,624, $151 per credit hour; Nonstate residents: per academic year $11,550, $481 per credit hour. Tuition is subject to change. See the following Web site for updates and changes in tuition costs: http://www.nmsu.edu/%7Egradcolg/Catalog/tuition_fees.html.

Financial Assistance:

First Year Students: Teaching assistantships available for first-year. Average amount paid per academic year: $12,200. Average number of hours worked per week: 20. Apply by February 15. Tuition remission given: partial. Research assistantships available for first-year. Average amount paid per academic year: $12,200. Average number of hours worked per week: 20. Apply by February 15. Tuition remission given: partial. Fellowships and scholarships available for first-year. Apply by February 15.

Advanced Students: Teaching assistantships available for advanced students. Average amount paid per academic year: $12,600. Average number of hours worked per week: 20. Apply by February 15. Tuition remission given: partial. Research assistantships available for advanced students. Average amount paid per academic year: $12,600. Average number of hours worked per week: 20. Apply by February 15. Tuition remission given: partial.

Contact Information: Of all students currently enrolled full-time, 100% benefitted from one or more of the listed financial assistance programs.

Internships/Practica: For the PhD degree in Engineering Psychology, students must complete an internship in an industrial, government, or other laboratory setting of at least three months in duration. Many master's students in Engineering Psychology and Cognitive Psychology spend a summer or half-year as an intern in industry, but it is not required for the MA degree.

Housing and Day Care: On-campus housing is available. Housing Information: Department of Housing and Dining Services, MSC 3BB, New Mexico State University, P.O. Box 30001, Las Cruces, NM 88003-8001. On-campus day care facilities are available.

Employment of Department Graduates:

Master's Degree Graduates: Of those who graduated in the academic year 2003–2004, the following categories and numbers represent the post-graduate activities and employment of master's degree graduates: Enrolled in a psychology doctoral program (6), enrolled in a post-doctoral residency/fellowship (n/a), employed in independent practice (n/a), employed in business or industry (research/consulting) (3), total from the above (master's) (9).

Doctoral Degree Graduates: Of those who graduated in the academic year 2003–2004, the following categories and numbers represent the post-graduate activities and employment of doctoral degree graduates: Enrolled in a psychology doctoral program (n/a), employed in an academic position at a 2-year/4-year college (2), total from the above (doctoral) (2).

Additional Information:

Orientation, Objectives, and Emphasis of Department: The department offers an MA degree in general experimental psychology that allows an emphasis in cognitive, engineering, or social psychology. The PhD is offered in the major areas of cognitive, engineering, and social psychology. Within these areas there is special emphasis on language processing, human-computer interaction, and cross-cultural psychology, respectively. Students must earn an MA degree before being admitted to the doctoral program. All programs are experimentally oriented and have the distinctive characteristic of pursuing and extending basic research questions in applied settings.

Special Facilities or Resources: All faculty members have specialized laboratories with a wide variety of computer hardware and software. These include a Teamwork lab that is used to conduct research on team cognition in complex task environments, an Eye Tracking lab used to study perceptual and cognitive issues, a biopsychology lab equipped to measure ERPs, and a developmental laboratory equipped with sophisticated equipment for recording, analyzing, and editing mother-infant interactions, etc. Many members of the department have joint appointments in the Computing Research Laboratory, a nonacademic research center that specializes in computational linguistics, machine translation, and intelligent tutoring.

Application Information:
Send to: Chair of Graduate Committee, Department of Psychology, MSC 3452, New Mexico State University, Las Cruces, NM 88003-8001. Application available online. URL of online application: http://gradschool.nmsu.edu/admit-form.html. Students are admitted in the Fall, application deadline February 15; Spring, application deadline November 1. *Fee:* $30. On-line application is for NMSU graduate school only. Separate application materials (including forms for letters of reference) must be requested from the Psychology Department.

New Mexico, The University of
Department of Psychology
Arts and Science
Logan Hall
Albuquerque, NM 87131-1161
Telephone: (505) 277-5009
Fax: (505) 277-1394
E-mail: *psych@unm.edu*
Web: *http://psych.unm.edu*

Department Information:
1960. Chairperson: Ron Yeo. Number of Faculty: total–full-time 21, part-time 1; women–full-time 7, part-time 1; minority–full-time 1.

Programs and Degrees Offered:
Listed in the following order: Program area, degree type (T if terminal Master's), number awarded 7/03–6/04. Behavioral Neuroscience PhD (Doctor of Philosophy) 6, Clinical PhD (Doctor of Philosophy) 13, Cognitive/ Learning PhD (Doctor of Philosophy) 7, Developmental PhD (Doctor of Philosophy) 0, Quantitative PhD (Doctor of Philosophy) 1, Evolutionary PhD (Doctor of Philosophy) 1.

APA Accreditation: Clinical PhD (Doctor of Philosophy).

Student Applications/Admissions:
Student Applications
Behavioral Neuroscience PhD (Doctor of Philosophy)—Applications 2004–2005, 6. Total applicants accepted 2004–2005, 0. Number enrolled (new admits only) 2004–2005 full-time, 0. Number enrolled (new admits only) 2004–2005 part-time, 0. Openings 2005–2006, 1. The Median number of years required for completion of a degree are 5. The number of students enrolled full and part-time who were dismissed or voluntarily withdrew from this program area were 0. *Clinical PhD (Doctor of Philosophy)*—Applications 2004–2005, 104. Total applicants accepted 2004–2005, 11. Number enrolled (new admits only)

2004–2005 full-time, 8. Number enrolled (new admits only) 2004–2005 part-time, 0. Openings 2005–2006, 4. The Median number of years required for completion of a degree are 6. The number of students enrolled full and part-time who were dismissed or voluntarily withdrew from this program area were 3. *Cognitive/ Learning PhD (Doctor of Philosophy)*—Applications 2004–2005, 12. Total applicants accepted 2004–2005, 4. Number enrolled (new admits only) 2004–2005 full-time, 3. Number enrolled (new admits only) 2004–2005 part-time, 0. The Median number of years required for completion of a degree are 5. The number of students enrolled full and part-time who were dismissed or voluntarily withdrew from this program area were 2. *Developmental PhD (Doctor of Philosophy)*—Applications 2004–2005, 2. Total applicants accepted 2004–2005, 1. Number enrolled (new admits only) 2004–2005 full-time, 1. Number enrolled (new admits only) 2004–2005 part-time, 0. Openings 2005–2006, 1. The Median number of years required for completion of a degree are 5. The number of students enrolled full and part-time who were dismissed or voluntarily withdrew from this program area were 0. *Quantitative PhD (Doctor of Philosophy)*—Applications 2004–2005, 2. Total applicants accepted 2004–2005, 0. Number enrolled (new admits only) 2004–2005 full-time, 0. Number enrolled (new admits only) 2004–2005 part-time, 0. Openings 2005–2006, 1. The Median number of years required for completion of a degree are 5. The number of students enrolled full and part-time who were dismissed or voluntarily withdrew from this program area were 0. *Evolutionary PhD (Doctor of Philosophy)*—Applications 2004–2005, 15. Total applicants accepted 2004–2005, 4. Number enrolled (new admits only) 2004–2005 full-time, 4. Number enrolled (new admits only) 2004–2005 part-time, 0. Openings 2005–2006, 1. The Median number of years required for completion of a degree are 5. The number of students enrolled full and part-time who were dismissed or voluntarily withdrew from this program area were 0.

Admissions Requirements:

Scores: Entries appear in this order: required test or GPA, minimum score (if required), median score of students entering in 2003–2004. Doctoral Programs: GRE-V no minimum stated, 557; GRE-Q no minimum stated, 621; GRE-Analytical no minimum stated, 654; GRE-Subject(Psych) no minimum stated, 628; overall undergraduate GPA 3.0, 3.58.

Other Criteria: (importance of criteria rated low, medium, or high): GRE/MAT scores high, research experience high, work experience medium, extracurricular activity medium, clinically related public service medium, GPA high, letters of recommendation high, interview medium, statement of goals and objectives high. The importance for the interview and special skills varies. For additional information on admission requirements, go to: http://psych.unm.edu/grad_home.htm.

Student Characteristics: The following represents characteristics of students in 2004–2005 in all graduate psychology programs in the department: Female–full-time 55, part-time 0; Male–full-time 22, part-time 0; African American/Black–full-time 1, part-time 0; Hispanic/Latino(a)–full-time 7, part-time 0; Asian/Pacific Islander–full-time 1, part-time 0; American Indian/Alaska Native–full-time 0, part-time 0; Caucasian–full-time 63, part-time 0; Multi-ethnic–full-time 5, part-time 0.

Financial Information/Assistance:

Tuition for Full-Time Study: *Master's:* State residents: per academic year $4,070, $171 per credit hour; Nonstate residents: per academic year $12,810. *Doctoral:* State residents: per academic year $4,070, $171 per credit hour; Nonstate residents: per academic year $12,810. Tuition is subject to change. See the following Web site for updates and changes in tuition costs: http://www.unm.edu/~bursar/tuitionrates.html.

Financial Assistance:

First Year Students: Teaching assistantships available for first-year. Average amount paid per academic year: $10,815. Average number of hours worked per week: 20. Apply by January 15. Tuition remission given: full. Research assistantships available for first-year. Average amount paid per academic year: $14,000. Average number of hours worked per week: 20. Apply by January 15. Tuition remission given: full. Fellowships and scholarships available for first-year. Average amount paid per academic year: $3,000. Apply by March 1.

Advanced Students: Teaching assistantships available for advanced students. Average amount paid per academic year: $11,896. Average number of hours worked per week: 20. Apply by January 15. Tuition remission given: full. Research assistantships available for advanced students. Average amount paid per academic year: $14,500. Average number of hours worked per week: 20. Apply by January 15. Tuition remission given: full. Fellowships and scholarships available for advanced students. Average amount paid per academic year: $8,000. Apply by March 1.

Contact Information: Of all students currently enrolled full-time, 75% benefitted from one or more of the listed financial assistance programs. Application and information available online at: http://www.unm.edu/~grad/funding/funding.html.

Internships/Practica: For those doctoral students for whom a professional internship is required prior to graduation, 8 applied in 2003–2004. Of those who applied, 7 were placed in internships listed by the Association of Psychology Postdoctoral and Internship Programs (APPIC); 7 were placed in APA accredited internships.

Housing and Day Care: On-campus housing is available. See the following Web site for more information: Residence housing: http://www.unm.edu/~reshalls/ Off campus housing: http://och.unm.edu. On-campus day care facilities are available. See the following Web site for more information: http://www.unm.edu/~weecare.

Employment of Department Graduates:

Master's Degree Graduates: Of those who graduated in the academic year 2003–2004, the following categories and numbers represent the post-graduate activities and employment of master's degree graduates: Enrolled in a post-doctoral residency/fellowship (n/a), employed in independent practice (n/a), total from the above (master's) (0).

Doctoral Degree Graduates: Of those who graduated in the academic year 2003–2004, the following categories and numbers represent the post-graduate activities and employment of doctoral degree graduates: Enrolled in a psychology doctoral program (n/a), total from the above (doctoral) (0).

Additional Information:

Orientation, Objectives, and Emphasis of Department: Founded in 1960, the doctoral training program in psychology is based on the premise that psychology, in all of its areas, is fundamentally an experimental discipline. For all students, the PhD degree is awarded in general experimental psychology, and students acquire a solid foundation in both scientific methodology and general psychology. Within this framework, students specialize in any of several competency areas. The well-trained psychologist, within this perspective, is one who combines competence in the general discipline of psychology with excellence in his or her chosen specialization.

Special Facilities or Resources: The department is housed in a building on the central campus. In addition to faculty and administrative offices and seminar rooms, the building is equipped for sophisticated research. There are soundproof chambers for conducting experiments, a variety of timing devices, computer terminals, and electromechanical measuring equipment. Laboratory facilities exist for research in human memory, learning, cognitive psychology, perception, information processing, attention, decision making, developmental, social, personality, neuropsychology, psychophysiology, and clinical psychology. The building also has a large animal research facility with primates and rodents. The campus animal research facility is equipped for surgery and for delicate measurements of brain activities as well as for tests of physical, cognitive, and emotional responses. Microcomputers are widely used in individual faculty laboratories and in a graduate student computer room. The Department of Psychology Clinic opened in 1982 and offers diagnostic and therapeutic services to the Albuquerque community while providing an excellent training facility for clinical students.

Application Information:
Send to: The University of New Mexico, Office of Graduate Studies, 107 Humanities Building, Albuquerque, NM 87131. Application available online. URL of online application: http://www.unm.edu/~grad/admissions/admissions.html. Students are admitted in the Fall, application deadline January 15. The deadline for full financial consideration is January 15, however we accept applications through May 1. *Fee:* $40.

Adelphi University

The Derner Institute of Advanced Psychological Studies,
  School of Professional Psychology
Adelphi University
Garden City, NY 11530
Telephone: (516) 877-4800
Fax: (516) 877-4805
E-mail: *primaver@adelphi.edu*
Web: *http://www.adelphi.edu*

Department Information:

1952. Dean: Louis Primavera. Number of Faculty: total–full-time 23, part-time 23; women–full-time 10, part-time 16; minority–full-time 2, part-time 2.

Programs and Degrees Offered:

Listed in the following order: Program area, degree type (T if terminal Master's), number awarded 7/03–6/04. Clinical PhD (Doctor of Philosophy) 25, Psychoanalysis Other 15, Respecialization Diploma PhD (Doctor of Philosophy) 1, General Psychology MA/MS (Master of Arts/Science) (T) 50, School Psychology MA/MS (Master of Arts/Science) 0.

APA Accreditation: Clinical PhD (Doctor of Philosophy).

Student Applications/Admissions:

Student Applications

Clinical PhD (Doctor of Philosophy)—Applications 2004–2005, 240. Total applicants accepted 2004–2005, 40. Openings 2005–2006, 20. The Median number of years required for completion of a degree are 6. The number of students enrolled full and part-time who were dismissed or voluntarily withdrew from this program area were 2. *Psychoanalysis Other*—Applications 2004–2005, 45. Total applicants accepted 2004–2005, 36. Openings 2005–2006, 36. The Median number of years required for completion of a degree are 4. The number of students enrolled full and part-time who were dismissed or voluntarily withdrew from this program area were 5. *Respecialization Diploma PhD (Doctor of Philosophy)*—Applications 2004–2005, 1. Total applicants accepted 2004–2005, 1. Openings 2005–2006, 1. The Median number of years required for completion of a degree are 3. The number of students enrolled full and part-time who were dismissed or voluntarily withdrew from this program area were 0. *General Psychology MA/MS (Master of Arts/Science)*—Applications 2004–2005, 139. Total applicants accepted 2004–2005, 89. Total enrolled 2004–2005 full-time, 100, part-time, 40. Openings 2005–2006, 90. The Median number of years required for completion of a degree is 1. The number of students enrolled full and part-time who were dismissed or voluntarily withdrew from this program area were 4. *School Psychology MA/MS (Master of Arts/Science)*—Applications 2004–2005, 60. Total applicants accepted 2004–2005, 48. Total enrolled 2004–2005 part-time, 45. Openings 2005–2006, 30. The number of students enrolled full and part-time who were dismissed or voluntarily withdrew from this program area were 7.

Admissions Requirements:

Scores: Entries appear in this order: required test or GPA, minimum score (if required), median score of students entering in 2003–2004. Master's Programs: overall undergraduate GPA 3.00, 3.20; last 2 years GPA no minimum stated, 3.00. Doctoral Programs: GRE-V 550, 620; GRE-Q 550, 630; GRE-V+Q no minimum stated; GRE-Subject(Psych) 550, 640; overall undergraduate GPA 3.00, 3.40. We consider all applications, and will admit students below 550 GRE's if there are compensatory situations, but applicants with scores below the listed minima are infrequently accepted.

Other Criteria: (importance of criteria rated low, medium, or high): GRE/MAT scores high, research experience high, work experience high, extracurricular activity low, clinically related public service high, GPA high, letters of recommendation high, interview high, statement of goals and objectives high.

Student Characteristics: The following represents characteristics of students in 2004–2005 in all graduate psychology programs in the department: Female–full-time 171, part-time 91; Male–full-time 90, part-time 49; African American/Black–full-time 6, part-time 35; Hispanic/Latino(a)–full-time 6, part-time 8; Asian/Pacific Islander–full-time 10, part-time 5; American Indian/Alaska Native–full-time 0, part-time 0; Caucasian–full-time 0, part-time 0; Multi-ethnic–full-time 0, part-time 0; students subject to the Americans With Disabilities Act–full-time 0, part-time 0.

Financial Information/Assistance:

Tuition for Full-Time Study: *Master's:* State residents: $700 per credit hour; Nonstate residents: $700 per credit hour. *Doctoral:* State residents: per academic year $25,000; Nonstate residents: per academic year $25,000. See the following Web site for updates and changes in tuition costs: www.adelphi.edu.

Financial Assistance:

First Year Students: Teaching assistantships available for first-year. Average amount paid per academic year: $5,000. Average number of hours worked per week: 5. Apply by April 15. Tuition remission given: partial. Research assistantships available for first-year. Average amount paid per academic year: $5,000. Average number of hours worked per week: 5. Apply by April 15. Tuition remission given: partial.

Advanced Students: Teaching assistantships available for advanced students. Average amount paid per academic year: $5,000. Average number of hours worked per week: 5. Apply by April 15. Tuition remission given: partial. Research assistantships available for advanced students. Average amount paid per academic year: $5,000. Average number of hours worked per week: 5. Apply by April 15. Tuition remission given: partial.

Contact Information: Of all students currently enrolled full-time, 60% benefitted from one or more of the listed financial assistance programs.

Internships/Practica: For the doctoral program, students are assigned to the Psychological Services Clinic, the training facility of the PhD Program. Beginning in the first year of the doctoral program, students are trained to perform intake evaluations. In the following years, students are to perform psychodiagnostic evaluations and psychotherapy. Students are also assigned to externships at full service mental health centers during their second year of training. During their fifth year, students complete a one-year internship in clinical psychology. For the Postdoctoral Program, students are assigned to the Postdoctoral Psychotherapy Center, the training facility of the Postdoctoral Program. For those doctoral students for whom a professional internship is required prior to graduation, 30 applied in 2003–2004. Of those who applied, 29 were placed in internships listed by the Association of Psychology Postdoctoral and Internship Programs (APPIC); 29 were placed in APA accredited internships.

Housing and Day Care: On-campus housing is available. There is little on-campus housing for graduate students, but 1–2 students in the PhD program each year elect to live in the undergraduate student dormitories. On-campus day care facilities are available. There is a Child Activity Center available to faculty and students.

Employment of Department Graduates:

Master's Degree Graduates: Of those who graduated in the academic year 2003–2004, the following categories and numbers represent the post-graduate activities and employment of master's degree graduates: Enrolled in a psychology doctoral program (24), enrolled in another graduate/professional program (14), enrolled in a post-doctoral residency/fellowship (n/a), employed in independent practice (n/a), employed in business or industry (research/consulting) (3), employed in business or industry (management) (3), employed in a government agency (professional services) (6), employed in a community mental health/counseling center (6), employed in a hospital/medical center (5), do not know (5), total from the above (master's) (66).

Doctoral Degree Graduates: Of those who graduated in the academic year 2003–2004, the following categories and numbers represent the post-graduate activities and employment of doctoral degree graduates: Enrolled in a psychology doctoral program (n/a), enrolled in a post-doctoral residency/fellowship (3), employed in independent practice (2), employed in an academic position at a university (2), employed in other positions at a higher education institution (1), employed in a community mental health/counseling center (5), employed in a hospital/medical center (9), total from the above (doctoral) (22).

Additional Information:

Orientation, Objectives, and Emphasis of Department: The Derner Institute of Advanced Psychological Studies is the first university-based professional school of psychology. The orientation is psychodynamic and scholar-professional. The doctoral program in clinical and the respecialization program are oriented toward community service and prepare the students for careers in clinical service; the postdoctoral programs prepare graduates for the practice of psychoanalysis and psychotherapy. All doctoral programs offer supervised experience in research and theory. The clinical program consists of four years of coursework, which includes at least one day a week of supervised practice each year and a fifth-year full-time internship; the respecialization program consists of two years of coursework, including at least one day a week of supervised practice each year and a third-year full-time internship; the postdoctoral programs consist of four years of seminars, case conferences, personal therapy, and supervised practice, the master's program consists of two years of course work, which includes a thesis or project. A new MA program in School Psychology was begun in Spring 2003; it is a three-year program, with a joint emphasis on didactic instruction and supervised practice.

Special Facilities or Resources: Facilities include a videotape recording studio and perception, learning, developmental, cognition, and applied research laboratories. The Institute has close interaction with two health-related professional schools, the Adelphi School of Nursing and the Adelphi School of Social Work, and with affiliated community school and clinical facilities. The Institute maintains two major clinical facilities, the Adelphi University Psychological Services Center and the Postdoctoral Psychotherapy Center. An APA-accredited continuing education program brings a series of distinguished workshops to the campus.

Application Information:
Send to: Graduate Admissions. Students are admitted in the Winter, application deadline January 15. Applicants for the PhD program have a January 15 deadline. MA applicants may begin in either Fall or Spring semester. There is no application deadline for the MA in General Psychology. For School Psychology the application deadline March 1 for the Fall semester and November 30 for Spring semester. Postdoctoral applicants begin in Fall only, but no application deadline. *Fee:* $50. Graduate admissions will waive application fee if a request for waiver is completed.

Alfred University
Division of School Psychology
Graduate School
Saxon Drive
Alfred, NY 14802-1205
Telephone: (607) 871-2212
Fax: (607) 871-3422
E-mail: *fcerio@alfred.edu*
Web: *http://www.alfred.edu*

Department Information:
1953. Chairperson: John D. Cerio. Number of Faculty: total–full-time 7, part-time 2; women–full-time 4, part-time 2; minority–full-time 1.

Programs and Degrees Offered:
Listed in the following order: Program area, degree type (T if terminal Master's), number awarded 7/03–6/04. School EdS (Education Specialist) 18, School PsyD (Doctor of Psychology) 4.

APA Accreditation: School PsyD (Doctor of Psychology).

Student Applications/Admissions:
Student Applications

School EdS (Education Specialist)—Applications 2004–2005, 77. Total applicants accepted 2004–2005, 34. Number enrolled (new admits only) 2004–2005 full-time, 26. Number enrolled (new admits only) 2004–2005 part-time, 0. Total enrolled 2004–2005 full-time, 43, part-time, 9. Openings 2005–2006, 18. The Median number of years required for completion of a degree are 2. The number of students enrolled full and part-time who were dismissed or voluntarily withdrew from this program area were 1. *School PsyD (Doctor of Psychology)*—

Applications 2004–2005, 33. Total applicants accepted 2004–2005, 12. Number enrolled (new admits only) 2004–2005 full-time, 8. Number enrolled (new admits only) 2004–2005 part-time, 0. Total enrolled 2004–2005 full-time, 15, part-time, 28. Openings 2005–2006, 7. The Median number of years required for completion of a degree are 4.25. The number of students enrolled full and part-time who were dismissed or voluntarily withdrew from this program area were 1.

Admissions Requirements:

Scores: Entries appear in this order: required test or GPA, minimum score (if required), median score of students entering in 2003–2004. Master's Programs: GRE-V no minimum stated, 444; GRE-Q no minimum stated, 539; GRE-V+Q no minimum stated, 983; overall undergraduate GPA no minimum stated, 3.5. Doctoral Programs: GRE-V no minimum stated, 470; GRE-Q no minimum stated, 525; GRE-V+Q no minimum stated, 995; overall undergraduate GPA no minimum stated, 3.4.

Other Criteria: (importance of criteria rated low, medium, or high): GRE/MAT scores medium, research experience low, work experience medium, extracurricular activity medium, clinically related public service low, GPA high, letters of recommendation medium, interview high, statement of goals and objectives high. The PsyD program places a higher emphasis on research experience.

Student Characteristics: The following represents characteristics of students in 2004–2005 in all graduate psychology programs in the department: Female–full-time 47, part-time 28; Male–full-time 11, part-time 9; African American/Black–full-time 0, part-time 2; Hispanic/Latino(a)–full-time 1, part-time 1; Asian/Pacific Islander–full-time 0, part-time 1; American Indian/Alaska Native–full-time 0, part-time 0; Caucasian–full-time 68, part-time 12; Multi-ethnic–full-time 1, part-time 0; students subject to the Americans With Disabilities Act–full-time 0, part-time 0.

Financial Information/Assistance:

Tuition for Full-Time Study: *Master's:* State residents: per academic year $28,450; Nonstate residents: per academic year $28,450. *Doctoral:* State residents: per academic year $28,450; Nonstate residents: per academic year $28,450. Tuition is subject to change. See the following Web site for updates and changes in tuition costs: www.alfred.edu.

Financial Assistance:

First Year Students: Research assistantships available for first-year. Average amount paid per academic year: $14,225. Average number of hours worked per week: 7. Apply by None. Tuition remission given: partial.

Advanced Students: Teaching assistantships available for advanced students. Average amount paid per academic year: $14,225. Average number of hours worked per week: 7. Apply by None. Tuition remission given: partial. Research assistantships available for advanced students. Average amount paid per academic year: $14,225. Average number of hours worked per week: 7. Apply by None. Tuition remission given: partial. Fellowships and scholarships available for advanced students. Average amount paid per academic year: $14,225. Average number of hours worked per week: 7. Apply by Variable. Tuition remission given: partial.

Contact Information: Of all students currently enrolled full-time, 100% benefitted from one or more of the listed financial assistance programs.

Internships/Practica: *Master's:* State residents: per academic year $28,450; Nonstate residents: per academic year $28,450. is required prior to graduation, 7 applied in 2003–2004.

Housing and Day Care: Limited housing is available for graduate students. Most graduate students live off campus. For information contact: Residence Life Office, Alfred University, Saxon Drive, Alfred, NY 14802; or go to the university Web site: www.alfred.edu. On-campus day care facilities are available. A private Montessori School is located on campus. For information, contact: Alfred Montessori School, 8 1/2 South Main Street, Alfred, NY 14802.

Employment of Department Graduates:

Master's Degree Graduates: Of those who graduated in the academic year 2003–2004, the following categories and numbers represent the post-graduate activities and employment of master's degree graduates: Enrolled in a psychology doctoral program (4), enrolled in another graduate/professional program (0), enrolled in a post-doctoral residency/fellowship (n/a), employed in independent practice (n/a), employed in an academic position at a university (0), employed in an academic position at a 2-year/4-year college (0), employed in other positions at a higher education institution (0), employed in a professional position in a school system (12), employed in business or industry (research/consulting) (0), employed in business or industry (management) (0), employed in a government agency (research) (0), employed in a government agency (professional services) (0), employed in a community mental health/counseling center (0), employed in a hospital/medical center (0), still seeking employment (0), other employment position (0), total from the above (master's) (16).

Doctoral Degree Graduates: Of those who graduated in the academic year 2003–2004, the following categories and numbers represent the post-graduate activities and employment of doctoral degree graduates: Enrolled in a psychology doctoral program (n/a), enrolled in another graduate/professional program (0), enrolled in a post-doctoral residency/fellowship (0), employed in independent practice (0), employed in an academic position at a university (0), employed in an academic position at a 2-year/4-year college (0), employed in other positions at a higher education institution (1), employed in a professional position in a school system (3), employed in business or industry (research/consulting) (0), employed in business or industry (management) (0), employed in a government agency (research) (0), employed in a government agency (professional services) (0), employed in a community mental health/counseling center (0), employed in a hospital/medical center (0), other employment position (0), total from the above (doctoral) (4).

Additional Information:

Orientation, Objectives, and Emphasis of Department: The Alfred School Psychology program emphasizes a field-centered, systems-oriented, Practitioner–Scientist approach. The primary goal of the program is the preparation of problem-solving psychologists with special concern for the application of psychological knowledge in a variety of child and family related settings. Students acquire knowledge in a wide variety of psychological theories and practices; skills are learned and then demonstrated in a number of different applied settings. They develop the personal characteristics and academic competencies necessary to work effectively with others in the identification, prevention and remediation of psychological and educational problems with children and adults.

Training in school psychology at Alfred University offers extensive one-to-one contact between students and faculty members to encourage the personalized learning process. Students are involved in field experience and research orientation (PsyD) from the first semester on. Training in the following areas is provided: knowledge base in psychology and education, assessment, intervention and remediation including counseling, play therapy and family work, consulting/training with teachers, administrators and parents, research methodology, program evaluation, and professional identification and functioning. Training at the doctoral level emphasizes applied research and the development of an area of specialization.

Special Facilities or Resources: Departmental resources include 6 one-way mirror observation rooms, counseling cubicles, an audio-video tape library, and an extensive library of psychological and educational assessment materials. In addition, all students gain practicum experience in the on-campus Child and Family Services Center, operated by the Division of School Psychology. The Center provides consultation, assessment, and counseling services to children and families of the region. The Center is a state of the art facility with all consultation rooms equipped with observation mirrors and remote audio-video recording equipment. The Center serves training, service and research functions for faculty and students. Graduate students have a work/computer room and a spacious lounge. Additionally, all graduate students have access to the mainframe computer and numerous PCs at no cost.

Information for Students With Physical Disabilities: taggarmt@alfred.edu.

Application Information:

Send to: Graduate Admissions, Alfred University, Saxon Drive, Alfred, NY 14802. Application available online. Students are admitted in the Fall, application deadline January 15. Deadline for fall admission to the MA/CAS program is February 15; for the PsyD program, January 15. Late applications may be considered if places in the class still exist for qualified applicants. *Fee:* $50. Waiver of fee available for online application submission only.

Binghamton University
Psychology
P.O. Box 6000
Binghamton, NY 13902-6000
Telephone: (607) 777-2449
Fax: (607) 777-4890
E-mail: *inhoff@binghamton.edu*
Web: *http://psychology.binghamton.edu*

Department Information:

65. Chairperson: Albrecht Inhoff. Number of Faculty: total–full-time 27; women–full-time 11, part-time 2; minority–full-time 2.

Programs and Degrees Offered:

Listed in the following order: Program area, degree type (T if terminal Master's), number awarded 7/03–6/04. Behavioral Neuroscience PhD (Doctor of Philosophy) 6, Clinical PhD (Doctor of Philosophy) 5, Cognitive PhD (Doctor of Philosophy) 4.

APA Accreditation: Clinical PhD (Doctor of Philosophy).

Student Applications/Admissions:
Student Applications

Behavioral Neuroscience PhD (Doctor of Philosophy)—Applications 2004–2005, 25. Total applicants accepted 2004–2005, 6. Openings 2005–2006, 3. The Median number of years required for completion of a degree are 5. The number of students enrolled full and part-time who were dismissed or voluntarily withdrew from this program area were 1. *Clinical PhD (Doctor of Philosophy)*—Applications 2004–2005, 197. Total applicants accepted 2004–2005, 12. Openings 2005–2006, 10. The Median number of years required for completion of a degree are 6. The number of students enrolled full and part-time who were dismissed or voluntarily withdrew from this program area were 1. *Cognitive PhD (Doctor of Philosophy)*—Applications 2004–2005, 26. Total applicants accepted 2004–2005, 6. Openings 2005–2006, 4. The Median number of years required for completion of a degree are 5. The number of students enrolled full and part-time who were dismissed or voluntarily withdrew from this program area were 1.

Admissions Requirements:

Scores: Entries appear in this order: required test or GPA, minimum score (if required), median score of students entering in 2003–2004. Master's Programs: GRE-V no minimum stated, 570; GRE-Q no minimum stated, 640; GRE-V+Q no minimum stated, 1210; GRE-Analytical no minimum stated, 665; GRE-Subject(Psych) no minimum stated, 675; overall undergraduate GPA no minimum stated, 3.57; psychology GPA no minimum stated. Doctoral Programs: GRE-V no minimum stated, 570; GRE-Q no minimum stated, 640; GRE-V+Q no minimum stated, 1210; GRE-Analytical no minimum stated, 665; GRE-Subject(Psych) no minimum stated; overall undergraduate GPA no minimum stated. Although we don't require a minimum GRE in all areas, we look at each applicant on an individual basis.

Other Criteria: (importance of criteria rated low, medium, or high): GRE/MAT scores high, research experience high, work experience medium, extracurricular activity low, clinically related public service low, GPA medium, letters of recommendation high, interview high, statement of goals and objectives high.

Student Characteristics: The following represents characteristics of students in 2004–2005 in all graduate psychology programs in the department: Female–full-time 51, part-time 0; Male–full-time 31, part-time 0; African American/Black–full-time 3, part-time 0; Hispanic/Latino(a)–full-time 4, part-time 0; Asian/Pacific Islander–full-time 3, part-time 0; American Indian/Alaska Native–full-time 0, part-time 0; Caucasian–full-time 0, part-time 0.

Financial Information/Assistance:

Tuition for Full-Time Study: *Doctoral:* State residents: per academic year $5,200; Nonstate residents: per academic year $8,500. Tuition is subject to change.

Financial Assistance:

First Year Students: Teaching assistantships available for first-year. Average amount paid per academic year: $12,000. Average number of hours worked per week: 15. Tuition remission given: full. Research assistantships available for first-year. Average amount paid per academic year: $12,000. Tuition remission given: full. Fellowships and scholarships available for first-year. Average amount paid per academic year: $12,000. Tuition remission given: full.

Advanced Students: Teaching assistantships available for advanced students. Average amount paid per academic year: $12,000. Average number of hours worked per week: 15. Tuition remission given: full. Research assistantships available for advanced students. Average amount paid per academic year: $12,000. Tuition remission given: full. Fellowships and scholarships available for advanced students. Average amount paid per academic year: $12,000. Tuition remission given: full.

Contact Information: Of all students currently enrolled full-time, 98% benefitted from one or more of the listed financial assistance programs.

Internships/Practica: Students in the clinical area are required to complete two practica, a psychotherapy practicum and a community practicum. The psychotherapy practicum is conducted in the department clinic under the supervision of a faculty member and generally involves the joint treatment of a variety of problems across a broad range of ages and diagnoses. The community practicum consists of supervised clinical activity and/or research at one of a wide range of local agencies, hospitals, or clinics. Students in cognitive psychology are invited—but not required—to complete a research-related practicum in industry. Past internships included training at GE, IBM, Microsoft, Lockheed Martin, and others.

Housing and Day Care: No on-campus housing is available. On-campus day care facilities are available.

Employment of Department Graduates:

Master's Degree Graduates: Of those who graduated in the academic year 2003–2004, the following categories and numbers represent the post-graduate activities and employment of master's degree graduates: Enrolled in a post-doctoral residency/fellowship (n/a), employed in independent practice (n/a), total from the above (master's) (0).

Doctoral Degree Graduates: Of those who graduated in the academic year 2003–2004, the following categories and numbers represent the post-graduate activities and employment of doctoral degree graduates: Enrolled in a psychology doctoral program (n/a), enrolled in a post-doctoral residency/fellowship (4), employed in independent practice (3), employed in an academic position at a university (2), employed in an academic position at a 2-year/4-year college (1), employed in other positions at a higher education institution (0), employed in a professional position in a school system (0), employed in business or industry (research/consulting) (3), employed in business or industry (management) (0), employed in a government agency (research) (0), employed in a government agency (professional services) (0), employed in a community mental health/counseling center (0), employed in a hospital/medical center (0), still seeking employment (0), other employment position (0), total from the above (doctoral) (13).

Additional Information:

Orientation, Objectives, and Emphasis of Department: The psychology department emphasizes basic and applied research in its three areas of specialization, clinical psychology, cognitive psychology, and behavioral neuroscience. The goal of our APA-accredited Clinical Program is to develop scientists and practitioners. By virtue of ongoing research involvement, students are expected to contribute to knowledge about psychopathology, assessment, and treatment. Our cognitive program has two major research emphases, one on perception and language (both in the visual and auditory domains) and one on learning and memory. Researchers in this area also work in industrial settings and collaborate with local industry. Our behavioral neuroscience program emphasizes the study of neural and hormonal bases of normal and abnormal behavior and their developmental antecedents in preclinical animal models.

Special Facilities or Resources: All faculty have state-of-the-art, spacious laboratories. The clinical program supports an active in-house mental-health clinic. Members of the cognitive area have access to sophisticated systems for the manipulation of auditory and visual stimuli and the online measurement of cognitive processes, and members of the behavioral neurosciences area share multi-user histology, microneuroimaging, and neurochemistry laboratories.

Application Information:
Send to: Graduate Admissions Office. Application available online. Students are admitted in the Spring; Clinical application deadline is January 1; Behavioral Neuroscience deadline and Cognitive deadline is January 15. *Fee:* $50.

City University of New York
Department of Psychology
Hunter College
695 Park Avenue
New York, NY 10021
Telephone: (212) 772-5550
E-mail: *gradpsych@hunter.cuny.edu*
Web: *http://maxweber.hunter.cuny.edu/psych*

Department Information:
Chairperson: Vita Rabinowitz. Number of Faculty: total–full-time 27, part-time 44; women–full-time 14, part-time 20; minority–full-time 5, part-time 5.

Programs and Degrees Offered:
Listed in the following order: Program area, degree type (T if terminal Master's), number awarded 7/03–6/04. Psychology MA/MS (Master of Arts/Science) (T) 3.

Student Applications/Admissions:
Student Applications
Psychology MA/MS (Master of Arts/Science)—Applications 2004–2005, 126. Total applicants accepted 2004–2005, 48. Number enrolled (new admits only) 2004–2005 full-time, 12. Number enrolled (new admits only) 2004–2005 part-time, 14. Total enrolled 2004–2005 full-time, 17, part-time, 49. The Median number of years required for completion of a degree are 3.

Admissions Requirements:
Scores: Entries appear in this order: required test or GPA, minimum score (if required), median score of students entering

in 2003–2004. Master's Programs: overall undergraduate GPA no minimum stated.

Other Criteria: (importance of criteria rated low, medium, or high): GRE/MAT scores high, research experience medium, GPA high, letters of recommendation high, statement of goals and objectives high. For additional information on admission requirements, go to: http://maxweber.hunter.cuny.edu/psych/maprog/.

Student Characteristics: The following represents characteristics of students in 2004–2005 in all graduate psychology programs in the department: Female–full-time 15, part-time 37; Male–full-time 2, part-time 12; African American/Black–full-time 0, part-time 5; Hispanic/Latino(a)–full-time 2, part-time 5; Asian/Pacific Islander–full-time 3, part-time 2; American Indian/Alaska Native–full-time 0, part-time 0; Caucasian–full-time 8, part-time 32; Multi-ethnic–full-time 4, part-time 5.

Financial Information/Assistance:

Tuition for Full-Time Study: *Master's:* State residents: per academic year $5,440, $230 per credit hour; Nonstate residents: per academic year $10,200, $425 per credit hour. Tuition costs vary by program. See the following Web site for updates and changes in tuition costs: http://registrar.hunter.cuny.edu/subpages/oasispages/tuition_fees.shtml.

Financial Assistance:

First Year Students: Fellowships and scholarships available for first-year. Average amount paid per academic year: $1,250.

Advanced Students: No information provided.

Contact Information: Of all students currently enrolled full-time, 6% benefitted from one or more of the listed financial assistance programs.

Internships/Practica: No information provided.

Housing and Day Care: On-campus housing is available. See the following Web site for more information: http://admissions.hunter.cuny.edu/~graduate/house.html. No on-campus day care facilities are available.

Employment of Department Graduates:

Master's Degree Graduates: Of those who graduated in the academic year 2003–2004, the following categories and numbers represent the post-graduate activities and employment of master's degree graduates: Enrolled in a post-doctoral residency/fellowship (n/a), employed in independent practice (n/a), total from the above (master's) (0).

Doctoral Degree Graduates: Of those who graduated in the academic year 2003–2004, the following categories and numbers represent the post-graduate activities and employment of doctoral degree graduates: Enrolled in a psychology doctoral program (n/a), total from the above (doctoral) (0).

Additional Information:

Orientation, Objectives, and Emphasis of Department: Hunter College offers a Master of Arts program in general psychology. Students may focus their courses, independent study, and thesis research in one of three content areas: (1) applied and evaluative psychology; (2) social, cognitive, and developmental psychology; (3) biopsychology and comparative psychology, with a focus on animal behavior and conservation. The Department offers theoretical courses on clinical topics, but it does not offer supervision in counseling or therapy.

Information for Students With Physical Disabilities: See the following Web site for more information: http://studentservices.hunter.cuny.edu/DisabilitiesOffice.html.

Application Information:

Send to: Graduate Admissions, Hunter College of the City University of New York, 695 Park Avenue, New York, NY 10021. Application available online. URL of online application: http://admissions.hunter.cuny.edu/~graduate/GradWebFilingPackage.pdf. Students are admitted in the Fall, application deadline April 1; Spring, application deadline November 1. We strongly advise international applicants [those who either have undergraduate credits from a non-U.S. institution and/or who require student (F-1) or Exchange (IAP-66) visas] to submit their applications as early as possible, but at least two months prior to established deadlines. *Fee:* $125.

City University of New York
Department of Psychology/Biopsychology PhD Subprogram
Hunter College (all data for PhD Subprogram)
695 Park Avenue - Rm. 611 North Building
New York, NY 10021
Telephone: (212) 772-5550 Psych; (212) 772-5621 Bio
Fax: (212) 772-5620
E-mail: *biopsych@hunter.cuny.edu*
Web: *http://maxweber.hunter.cuny.edu/psych/biopsych.htm*

Department Information:

1962. Program Head for Biopsychology: Peter Moller. Number of Faculty: total–full-time 12; women–full-time 5; minority–full-time 1.

Programs and Degrees Offered:

Listed in the following order: Program area, degree type (T if terminal Master's), number awarded 7/03–6/04. Biopsychology PhD (Doctor of Philosophy) 6.

Student Applications/Admissions:

Student Applications

Biopsychology PhD (Doctor of Philosophy)—Applications 2004–2005, 15. Total applicants accepted 2004–2005, 5. Number enrolled (new admits only) 2004–2005 full-time, 4. Openings 2005–2006, 3. The Median number of years required for completion of a degree are 7. The number of students enrolled full and part-time who were dismissed or voluntarily withdrew from this program area were 1.

Admissions Requirements:

Scores: Entries appear in this order: required test or GPA, minimum score (if required), median score of students entering in 2003–2004. Master's Programs: GRE-V no minimum stated; GRE-Q no minimum stated; GRE-Analytical no minimum stated; GRE-Subject(Psych) no minimum stated; overall undergraduate GPA no minimum stated; psychology GPA no minimum stated. Doctoral Programs: GRE-V 600; GRE-Q 600; GRE-V+Q 1200; GRE-Analytical 600; GRE-Subject(Psych)

600; overall undergraduate GPA 3.00. GRE in Subject area by end of first year of program.

Other Criteria: (importance of criteria rated low, medium, or high): GRE/MAT scores medium, research experience high, extracurricular activity low, GPA medium, letters of recommendation high, interview medium, statement of goals and objectives high.

Student Characteristics: The following represents characteristics of students in 2004–2005 in all graduate psychology programs in the department: Female–full-time 28, part-time 0; Male–full-time 7, part-time 0; African American/Black–full-time 2, part-time 0; Hispanic/Latino(a)–full-time 4, part-time 0; Asian/Pacific Islander–full-time 3, part-time 0; American Indian/Alaska Native–full-time 0, part-time 0; Caucasian–full-time 26, part-time 0.

Financial Information/Assistance:

Tuition for Full-Time Study: *Doctoral:* State residents: per academic year $4,870; Nonstate residents: $475 per credit hour. Tuition is subject to change.

Financial Assistance:

First Year Students: Teaching assistantships available for first-year. Average amount paid per academic year: $16,000. Tuition remission given: partial. Fellowships and scholarships available for first-year. Average amount paid per academic year: $24,000. Tuition remission given: full.

Advanced Students: Teaching assistantships available for advanced students. Average amount paid per academic year: $17,000. Tuition remission given: partial. Fellowships and scholarships available for advanced students. Average amount paid per academic year: $24,000. Tuition remission given: full.

Contact Information: Of all students currently enrolled full-time, 50% benefitted from one or more of the listed financial assistance programs.

Internships/Practica: No information provided.

Housing and Day Care: On-campus housing is available. We have a limited number of dorm rooms available. No on-campus day care facilities are available.

Employment of Department Graduates:

Master's Degree Graduates: Of those who graduated in the academic year 2003–2004, the following categories and numbers represent the post-graduate activities and employment of master's degree graduates: Enrolled in a post-doctoral residency/fellowship (n/a), employed in independent practice (n/a), total from the above (master's) (0).

Doctoral Degree Graduates: Of those who graduated in the academic year 2003–2004, the following categories and numbers represent the post-graduate activities and employment of doctoral degree graduates: Enrolled in a psychology doctoral program (n/a), enrolled in a post-doctoral residency/fellowship (6), employed in other positions at a higher education institution (4), employed in a government agency (research) (1), employed in a hospital/medical center (1), total from the above (doctoral) (12).

Additional Information:

Orientation, Objectives, and Emphasis of Department: The doctoral program in biopsychology interrelates the concepts and methods of neuroscience, cognitive science, the biological disciplines, and behavior analysis to offer a comparative and ontogenetic perspective on species-typical behavior and behavior acquired and modified during the individual's life-cycle. Basic psychological processes are studied in conjunction with contributions from neurobiology, ethology, ecology, evolutionary biology, genetics, endocrinology, pharmacology, and other sciences to illuminate the many ways in which all species adapt, survive, reproduce, and evolve. Through diversified laboratory experiences plus core courses, electives, seminars, colloquia, and field studies, students develop an interdisciplinary perspective. Neuroscience and animal behavior are taught jointly with the biology faculty. Electives address a wide range of topics in basic and applied areas of traditional psychology, neuroscience, and cognitive science. The biopsychology program provides unique training for basic research and teaching in the field of animal and human behavior, and in the application of biobehavioral knowledge to problems in industrial, business, institutional, health, and environmental settings. Students in the MA program may take courses in social, developmental, cognitive, and other areas of psychology as well as in biopsychology. We try to arrange individualized programs for two populations of students: those oriented toward the PhD, for whom research training is a prime concern, and those with diverse career aspirations who are oriented toward a general graduate background in psychology.

Special Facilities or Resources: Laboratories for research with human subjects and with a variety of animal species are located at Hunter College. The College has a modern animal-care facility. Facilities for field research in animal behavior are available at the Southwest Field Station of the American Museum of Natural History in the Chiricahua Mountains of Arizona. Additional research opportunities are available through minority programs such as RCMI, MBRS, MIDARP and also through the Center for the Study of Gene Structure and Function. There is also collaboration with programs such as Biology, Chemistry and Physiology and faculty affiliations with many other academic and research institutes in New York City. Hunter College lab facilities include equipment for electrophysiology, phase-fluorescence, and transmission microscopy, electron- and scanning-electron microscopy, radio immunoassay, high-performance liquid chromatography, autoradiography and other radioreceptor techniques, human and animal psychophysiology, histology, operant and classical conditioning, and video/cinematographic analysis. Computer facilities include a variety of micro- and minicomputers as well as access to the University computer center. Doctoral students may register for specialized courses at any CUNY campus and have privileges at all CUNY libraries.

Application Information:

Send to: Graduate Admissions, 695 Park Avenue, Hunter College, CUNY, New York, NY 10021 for the Master's Program. Office of Admissions, Graduate School-CUNY, 365 Fifth Avenue, New York, NY 10016-4309 for the Psychology PhD Program; a copy should be sent to the Biopsychology Program here at Hunter College-Rm. 611 North Building as well. Students are admitted in the Fall, application deadline February 1. Fall deadline; November 7—MA, February 1—PhD. Applications for Biospsychology PhD are sent to: Admissions Office, City University Graduate Center, 365 Fifth Avenue, New York, NY 10016-4309, (212) 817-7000. *Fee:* $125.

City University of New York: Brooklyn College

School Psychologist Graduate Program, School of Education
2900 Bedford Avenue, Room 1205 James
Brooklyn, NY 11210
Telephone: (718) 951-5876
Fax: (718) 951-4232
E-mail: *rubinson@brooklyn.cuny.edu*
Web: *http://depthome.brooklyn.cuny.edu/schooled*

Department Information:

1968. Program Head: Florence Rubinson. Number of Faculty: total–full-time 5, part-time 4; women–full-time 3, part-time 2; minority–full-time 2, part-time 1.

Programs and Degrees Offered:

Listed in the following order: Program area, degree type (T if terminal Master's), number awarded 7/03–6/04. School MA/MS (Master of Arts/Science) 24.

Student Applications/Admissions:

Student Applications

School MA/MS (Master of Arts/Science)—Applications 2004–2005, 160. Total applicants accepted 2004–2005, 40. Number enrolled (new admits only) 2004–2005 full-time, 16. Number enrolled (new admits only) 2004–2005 part-time, 13. Total enrolled 2004–2005 full-time, 44, part-time, 59. Openings 2005–2006, 32. The Median number of years required for completion of a degree are 3. The number of students enrolled full and part-time who were dismissed or voluntarily withdrew from this program area were 1.

Admissions Requirements:

Scores: Entries appear in this order: required test or GPA, minimum score (if required), median score of students entering in 2003–2004. Master's Programs: overall undergraduate GPA 3.0, 3.5.

Other Criteria: (importance of criteria rated low, medium, or high): GRE/MAT scores low, research experience medium, work experience high, extracurricular activity medium, clinically related public service high, GPA high, letters of recommendation high, interview high, statement of goals and objectives high, writing sample high.

Student Characteristics: The following represents characteristics of students in 2004–2005 in all graduate psychology programs in the department: Female–full-time 38, part-time 53; Male–full-time 6, part-time 6; African American/Black–full-time 3, part-time 10; Hispanic/Latino(a)–full-time 6, part-time 15; Asian/Pacific Islander–full-time 0, part-time 2; American Indian/Alaska Native–full-time 0, part-time 0; Caucasian–full-time 35, part-time 32; students subject to the Americans With Disabilities Act–full-time 0, part-time 0.

Financial Information/Assistance:

Tuition for Full-Time Study: *Master's:* State residents: $230 per credit hour; Nonstate residents: $320 per credit hour.

Financial Assistance:

First Year Students: Fellowships and scholarships available for first-year. Apply by March 15.

Advanced Students: Fellowships and scholarships available for advanced students. Apply by March 15.

Contact Information: Of all students currently enrolled full-time, 10% benefitted from one or more of the listed financial assistance programs.

Internships/Practica: Internships are available and coordinated through our program with various schools, both public and private, working with both the mainstream population, as well as special populations. In addition, internships are available in mental health clinics, agencies, and hospitals. Practica are designed to be part of the students' coursework. Practicum is an intensive five-hour, four-credit course the students take during their internship year that represents an opportunity to incorporate and share with their classmates experiences from their internship sites into the academic setting.

Housing and Day Care: No on-campus housing is available. On-campus day care facilities are available.

Employment of Department Graduates:

Master's Degree Graduates: Of those who graduated in the academic year 2003–2004, the following categories and numbers represent the post-graduate activities and employment of master's degree graduates: Enrolled in a psychology doctoral program (4), enrolled in another graduate/professional program (0), enrolled in a post-doctoral residency/fellowship (n/a), employed in independent practice (n/a), employed in an academic position at a 2-year/4-year college (1), employed in other positions at a higher education institution (1), employed in a professional position in a school system (17), still seeking employment (1), total from the above (master's) (24).

Doctoral Degree Graduates: Of those who graduated in the academic year 2003–2004, the following categories and numbers represent the post-graduate activities and employment of doctoral degree graduates: Enrolled in a psychology doctoral program (n/a), total from the above (doctoral) (0).

Additional Information:

Orientation, Objectives, and Emphasis of Department: The aim of the school psychologists' training program is to meet the community needs for professionally competent personnel to function in the schools as consultants on psychological aspects of learning and mental health. They will be prepared to make assessments of situations involving children, parents, and school personnel to achieve the more optimal functioning of children in the school setting. Coursework will prepare students in the areas of measurement and evaluation, personality understanding, educational objectives and procedures, curriculum development, and research. They will also be trained to achieve greater integration between school and community. Elements of the program will provide students with opportunities for self-exploration and understanding. Completion of this program will train students to work in public or private schools, as well as mental health centers, clinics, hospitals, and other community agencies.

Special Facilities or Resources: In addition to the use of the Brooklyn College library, students are welcome to use all the libraries at other colleges within the CUNY system. The School Psychology Program also has a small library of texts and journals for the students' use.

Application Information:
Send to: Department Chair. Application available online. Students are admitted in the Fall, application deadline March 1. There are two admissions applications, one for the program and one for graduate admissions. *Fee:* $40.

City University of New York: Brooklyn College
Department of Psychology
2900 Bedford Ave
Brooklyn, NY 11210
Telephone: (718) 951-5601
Fax: (718) 951-4814
E-mail: *psych-phd@brooklyn.cuny.edu or psych-ma@brooklyn.cuny.edu*
Web: *http://depthome.brooklyn.cuny.edu/psych*

Department Information:
1935. PhD Program Head or MA Program Head: Elisabeth Brauner or Benzion Chanowitz. Number of Faculty: total–full-time 28, part-time 12; women–full-time 11, part-time 9; minority–full-time 2, part-time 2.

Programs and Degrees Offered:
Listed in the following order: Program area, degree type (T if terminal Master's), number awarded 7/03–6/04. Experimental Psychology: Cognition, Learning, and Perception PhD (Doctor of Philosophy) 5, General Experimental Psychology MA/MS (Master of Arts/Science) (T) 7, Industrial and Organizational Psychology MA/MS (Master of Arts/Science) (T) 46.

Student Applications/Admissions:
Student Applications
Experimental Psychology: Cognition, Learning, and Perception PhD (Doctor of Philosophy)—Applications 2004–2005, 19. Total applicants accepted 2004–2005, 13. Number enrolled (new admits only) 2004–2005 full-time, 7. Number enrolled (new admits only) 2004–2005 part-time, 0. Openings 2005–2006, 6. The Median number of years required for completion of a degree are 7. The number of students enrolled full and part-time who were dismissed or voluntarily withdrew from this program area were 0. *General Experimental Psychology MA/MS (Master of Arts/Science)*—Applications 2004–2005, 53. Total applicants accepted 2004–2005, 15. Number enrolled (new admits only) 2004–2005 full-time, 8. Number enrolled (new admits only) 2004–2005 part-time, 0. Openings 2005–2006, 15. The Median number of years required for completion of a degree are 3. The number of students enrolled full and part-time who were dismissed or voluntarily withdrew from this program area were 0. *Industrial and Organizational Psychology MA/MS (Master of Arts/Science)*—Applications 2004–2005, 155. Total applicants accepted 2004–2005, 46. Number enrolled (new admits only) 2004–2005 full-time, 28. Number enrolled (new admits only) 2004–2005 part-time, 0. Openings 2005–2006, 35. The Median number of years required for

completion of a degree are 3. The number of students enrolled full and part-time who were dismissed or voluntarily withdrew from this program area were 2.

Admissions Requirements:
Scores: Entries appear in this order: required test or GPA, minimum score (if required), median score of students entering in 2003–2004. Master's Programs: overall undergraduate GPA 3.0.
Other Criteria: (importance of criteria rated low, medium, or high): GRE/MAT scores medium, research experience high, work experience medium, extracurricular activity low, clinically related public service low, GPA medium, letters of recommendation high, statement of goals and objectives high. The MA program in Industrial and Organizational has a greater emphasis on applications of psychology. The MA in General Experimental and the PhD program looks for a strong background in research.

Student Characteristics: The following represents characteristics of students in 2004–2005 in all graduate psychology programs in the department: Female–full-time 61, part-time 0; Male–full-time 65, part-time 0; African American/Black–full-time 24, part-time 0; Hispanic/Latino(a)–full-time 14, part-time 0; Asian/Pacific Islander–full-time 7, part-time 0; American Indian/Alaska Native–full-time 0, part-time 0; Caucasian–full-time 71, part-time 0; Multi-ethnic–full-time 0, part-time 0; students subject to the Americans With Disabilities Act–full-time 1, part-time 0.

Financial Information/Assistance:
Tuition for Full-Time Study: *Master's:* State residents: per academic year $2,175, $185 per credit hour; Nonstate residents: per academic year $3,800, $320 per credit hour. *Doctoral:* State residents: per academic year $2,435, $475 per credit hour; Nonstate residents: per academic year $4,750, $475 per credit hour. Tuition is subject to change. See the following Web site for updates and changes in tuition costs: http://www.cuny.edu.

Financial Assistance:
First Year Students: Teaching assistantships available for first-year. Average amount paid per academic year: $12,000. Average number of hours worked per week: 20. Apply by March 1. Tuition remission given: partial. Research assistantships available for first-year. Average amount paid per academic year: $14,000. Average number of hours worked per week: 20. Apply by March 1. Tuition remission given: partial. Fellowships and scholarships available for first-year. Average amount paid per academic year: $2,000. Apply by March 1. Tuition remission given: partial.
Advanced Students: Teaching assistantships available for advanced students. Average amount paid per academic year: $12,000. Average number of hours worked per week: 20. Apply by March 1. Tuition remission given: partial. Research assistantships available for advanced students. Average amount paid per academic year: $14,000. Average number of hours worked per week: 20. Apply by March 1. Tuition remission given: partial. Fellowships and scholarships available for advanced students. Average amount paid per academic year: $2,000. Apply by March 1. Tuition remission given: partial.

Contact Information: Of all students currently enrolled full-time, 80% benefitted from one or more of the listed financial assistance programs. Application and information available online at: http://depthome.brooklyn.cuny.edu/psych.

Internships/Practica: The MA program in Industrial and Organizational psychology has an internship component that most students avail themselves of. It functions as both training and as an opportunity to experience the hands-on application of principles in a work setting.

Housing and Day Care: No on-campus housing is available. On-campus day care facilities are available. See the following Web site for more information: http://depthome.brooklyn.cuny.edu/ecc.

Employment of Department Graduates:

Master's Degree Graduates: Of those who graduated in the academic year 2003–2004, the following categories and numbers represent the post-graduate activities and employment of master's degree graduates: Enrolled in a psychology doctoral program (5), enrolled in another graduate/professional program (2), enrolled in a post-doctoral residency/fellowship (n/a), employed in independent practice (n/a), employed in an academic position at a 2-year/4-year college (1), employed in other positions at a higher education institution (2), employed in a professional position in a school system (3), employed in business or industry (research/consulting) (3), employed in business or industry (management) (23), employed in a government agency (professional services) (1), employed in a community mental health/counseling center (2), do not know (4), total from the above (master's) (46).

Doctoral Degree Graduates: Of those who graduated in the academic year 2003–2004, the following categories and numbers represent the post-graduate activities and employment of doctoral degree graduates: Enrolled in a psychology doctoral program (n/a), employed in an academic position at a 2-year/4-year college (2), employed in a government agency (research) (1), employed in a hospital/medical center (2), total from the above (doctoral) (5).

Additional Information:

Orientation, Objectives, and Emphasis of Department: The PhD program is broadly based, with concentrations in cognitive and cognitive neuropsychology, learning, perception, social and developmental. These diverse areas are bound by a commitment to empirical methods and theory development. The focus is on training scientists in both pure and applied approaches. By virtue of our participation in the CUNY consortium, our students also have the opportunity to work with faculty at other CUNY campuses and several other research universities in New York. The training is primarily in the apprenticeship mode. Students work with faculty in chosen areas of specialization. Collaboration with several faculty and other students is common and encouraged. The emphasis of the program is on research. Historically, the majority of our graduates have gone on to careers in teaching and research, although many have used their training for work in applied fields. The MA program in General Experimental mirrors the first two years of the PhD program. The programs in Industrial and Organizational psychology are more oriented toward training individuals in applied fields. One concentration focuses on Human Relations Training and a second, parallel concentration is oriented more toward Organizational Behavior.

Special Facilities or Resources: There are over a dozen active laboratories in the department focusing on topics as diverse as the physiology of taste and preference formation, children's acquisition of spatial knowledge, transactive knowledge in organizations, implicit learning in cognitive disorders, visual functions in Down syndrome, creativity and cognition in the arts, cognition without a spine (i.e., in octopus), hippocampal atrophy in early Alzheimer's disease, implicit impression formation, Darwinian models of mate selection, biomemetic robotics, neurodegeneration in the aged and parent-child communication. All labs are well equipped and many supported by grants from NSF, NIH, NASA, DARPA, and other organizations. Several faculty have appointments and working collaborations with research labs in city hospitals and medical schools with access to frontier technologies such as MRI.

Application Information:

Send to: PhD Program, Office of Admissions Graduate Center of CUNY, 365 Fifth Avenue, New York, NY 10016-4309. MA Program, apply to: Office of Graduate Admissions, Brooklyn College, 2900 Bedford Avenue, Brooklyn, NY 11210. Application available online. URL of online application: http://www.gc.cuny.edu or http://www.brooklyn.cuny.edu. Students are admitted in the Fall, application deadline March 1; Spring, application deadline November 1 (MA). *Fee:* $125. Requests can be made of Office of Admissions.

City University of New York: Graduate Center
Learning Processes Doctoral Subprogram
Queens College
65-30 Kissena Boulevard
Flushing, NY 11367
Telephone: (718) 997-3630
Fax: (718) 997-3257
E-mail: *bruce_brown@qc.edu*
Web: *http://www.qc.edu/Psychology/lph.htm*

Department Information:
1967. Program Head: Bruce L. Brown. Number of Faculty: total–full-time 9; women–full-time 3; minority–full-time 1.

Programs and Degrees Offered:
Listed in the following order: Program area, degree type (T if terminal Master's), number awarded 7/03–6/04. Learning Processes PhD (Doctor of Philosophy) 4.

Student Applications/Admissions:
Student Applications

Learning Processes PhD (Doctor of Philosophy)—Applications 2004–2005, 20. Total applicants accepted 2004–2005, 11. Openings 2005–2006, 8. The Median number of years required for completion of a degree are 9. The number of students enrolled full and part-time who were dismissed or voluntarily withdrew from this program area were 0.

Admissions Requirements:
Scores: Entries appear in this order: required test or GPA, minimum score (if required), median score of students entering in 2003–2004. Doctoral Programs: Complete transcripts are required for applications to the Learning Processes program.

Other Criteria: (importance of criteria rated low, medium, or high): GRE/MAT scores medium, research experience medium, work experience low, extracurricular activity low, clinically related public service low, GPA high, letters of recommendation high, interview low, statement of goals and objectives medium.

Student Characteristics: The following represents characteristics of students in 2004–2005 in all graduate psychology programs in the department: Female–full-time 35, part-time 0; Male–full-time 7, part-time 0; African American/Black–full-time 0, part-time 0; Hispanic/Latino(a)–full-time 1, part-time 0; Asian/Pacific Islander–full-time 3, part-time 0; American Indian/Alaska Native–full-time 0, part-time 0; Caucasian–full-time 38, part-time 0; Multi-ethnic–full-time 0, part-time 0; students subject to the Americans With Disabilities Act–full-time 0, part-time 0.

Financial Information/Assistance:

Tuition for Full-Time Study: *Doctoral:* State residents: per academic year $4,870, $275 per credit hour; Nonstate residents: $475 per credit hour. Tuition is subject to change.

Financial Assistance:

First Year Students: Fellowships and scholarships available for first-year. Average amount paid per academic year: $24,000. Average number of hours worked per week: 20. Apply by January 1. Tuition remission given: full.

Advanced Students: Teaching assistantships available for advanced students. Average amount paid per academic year: $10,000. Average number of hours worked per week: 4. Tuition remission given: partial. Research assistantships available for advanced students. Average amount paid per academic year: $8,307. Average number of hours worked per week: 20. Tuition remission given: partial.

Contact Information: Of all students currently enrolled full-time, 17% benefitted from one or more of the listed financial assistance programs. Application and information available online at: http://www.gc.cuny.edu/prospective_students/prospective_index.htm.

Internships/Practica: Information concerning practica and internships is available on request. Internships are available, but not required.

Housing and Day Care: No on-campus housing is available. No on-campus day care facilities are available.

Employment of Department Graduates:

Master's Degree Graduates: Of those who graduated in the academic year 2003–2004, the following categories and numbers represent the post-graduate activities and employment of master's degree graduates: Enrolled in a psychology doctoral program (0), enrolled in another graduate/professional program (0), enrolled in a post-doctoral residency/fellowship (n/a), employed in independent practice (n/a), employed in an academic position at a university (0), employed in an academic position at a 2-year/4-year college (0), employed in other positions at a higher education institution (0), employed in a professional position in a school system (0), employed in business or industry (research/consulting) (0), employed in business or industry (management) (0), employed in a government agency (research) (0), employed in a government agency (professional services) (0), employed in a community mental health/counseling center (0), employed in a hospital/medical center (0), still seeking employment (0), other employment position (0), total from the above (master's) (0).

Doctoral Degree Graduates: Of those who graduated in the academic year 2003–2004, the following categories and numbers represent the post-graduate activities and employment of doctoral degree graduates: Enrolled in a psychology doctoral program (n/a), enrolled in a post-doctoral residency/fellowship (0), employed in independent practice (0), employed in an academic position at a university (0), employed in an academic position at a 2-year/4-year college (1), employed in other positions at a higher education institution (0), employed in a professional position in a school system (3), employed in business or industry (research/consulting) (0), employed in business or industry (management) (0), employed in a government agency (research) (0), employed in a government agency (professional services) (0), employed in a community mental health/counseling center (3), employed in a hospital/medical center (0), still seeking employment (0), other employment position (0), total from the above (doctoral) (7).

Additional Information:

Orientation, Objectives, and Emphasis of Department: The Learning Processes program offers doctoral students in Psychology training in the experimental analysis of human and animal behavior and in applied behavior analysis. Students and faculty investigate a wide spectrum of behavioral processes through lectures and experimental laboratory coursework, advanced seminars, informal student-faculty discussions, practica, internships, and individual research projects. Faculty and students publish regularly in peer-reviewed journals and are strongly represented at major national and international conferences. Their current research interests include such topics as categorization and concept formation, language acquisition, affective behavior, behavioral assessment, human and animal timing, pattern recognition, stimulus control, behavioral community psychology, education and training of children with autism, and staff training in organizational settings. The Learning Processes program is accredited in behavior analysis by the Association for Behavior Analysis, and its curriculum is licensure-qualifing in New York State. In addition, the Behavior Analyst Certification Board, Inc., has approved a subset of the curriculum as a course sequence that meets the coursework requirements for eligibility to take the Board Certified Behavior Analyst Examination. Applicants will have to meet additional requirements to qualify.

Special Facilities or Resources: A full description of the program can be found on our website: http://www.qc.edu/Psychology/lph.htm.

Application Information:

Send to: Office of Admissions, The Graduate School & University Center of the City University of New York, 365 Fifth Avenue, New York, NY 10016-4309. Application available online. URL of online application: http://www.gc.cuny.edu/prospective_students/admissions_index.htm. Students are admitted in the Fall, application deadline March 1. January 1 deadline for financial aid applications. *Fee:* $50.

City University of New York: Graduate Center

Neuropsychology Doctoral Program
Queens College
65-30 Kissena Boulevard
Flushing, NY 11367
Telephone: (718) 997-3630
Fax: (718) 997-3257
E-mail: *mschimat@qc1.qc.edu*
Web: *http://www.qc.edu/Psychology/neuro/homepage.htm*

Department Information:

1968. Program head: Howard Ehrlichman, PhD Number of Faculty: total–full-time 18; women–full-time 8; minority–full-time 1.

Programs and Degrees Offered:

Listed in the following order: Program area, degree type (T if terminal Master's), number awarded 7/03–6/04. Neuropsychology PhD (Doctor of Philosophy) 9.

Student Applications/Admissions:

Student Applications

Neuropsychology PhD (Doctor of Philosophy)—Applications 2004–2005, 43. Total applicants accepted 2004–2005, 19. Number enrolled (new admits only) 2004–2005 full-time, 15. Openings 2005–2006, 10. The Median number of years required for completion of a degree are 7. The number of students enrolled full and part-time who were dismissed or voluntarily withdrew from this program area were 2.

Admissions Requirements:

Scores: Entries appear in this order: required test or GPA, minimum score (if required), median score of students entering in 2003–2004. Doctoral Programs: GRE-V no minimum stated; GRE-Q no minimum stated; GRE-V+Q no minimum stated; GRE-Analytical no minimum stated; GRE-Subject(Psych) no minimum stated; overall undergraduate GPA no minimum stated.

Other Criteria: (importance of criteria rated low, medium, or high): GRE/MAT scores medium, research experience high, work experience low, extracurricular activity low, clinically related public service low, GPA high, letters of recommendation high, interview high, statement of goals and objectives high. Interviews will be carried out for the clinical track only.

Student Characteristics: The following represents characteristics of students in 2004–2005 in all graduate psychology programs in the department: Female–full-time 45, part-time 0; Male–full-time 17, part-time 0; African American/Black–full-time 2, part-time 0; Hispanic/Latino(a)–full-time 2, part-time 0; Asian/Pacific Islander–full-time 4, part-time 0; American Indian/Alaska Native–full-time 0, part-time 0; Caucasian–full-time 54, part-time 0; Multi-ethnic–full-time 0, part-time 0; students subject to the Americans With Disabilities Act–full-time 0, part-time 0.

Financial Information/Assistance:

Tuition for Full-Time Study: *Doctoral:* State residents: per academic year $4,870; Nonstate residents: $475 per credit hour. Tuition is subject to change. See the following Web site for updates and changes in tuition costs: http://www.gc.cuny.edu/academic_matters/tuition_and_fees.htm.

Financial Assistance:

First Year Students: Fellowships and scholarships available for first-year. Average amount paid per academic year: $0. Average number of hours worked per week: 0.

Advanced Students: Teaching assistantships available for advanced students. Average number of hours worked per week: 0. Research assistantships available for advanced students. Average number of hours worked per week: 0. Fellowships and scholarships available for advanced students. Average number of hours worked per week: 0.

Contact Information: Of all students currently enrolled full-time, 40% benefitted from one or more of the listed financial assistance programs.

Internships/Practica: For those doctoral students for whom a professional internship is required prior to graduation, 4 applied in 2003–2004. Of those who applied, 3 were placed in internships listed by the Association of Psychology Postdoctoral and Internship Programs (APPIC); 3 were placed in APA accredited internships.

Housing and Day Care: No on-campus housing is available. On-campus day care facilities are available.

Employment of Department Graduates:

Master's Degree Graduates: Of those who graduated in the academic year 2003–2004, the following categories and numbers represent the post-graduate activities and employment of master's degree graduates: Enrolled in a psychology doctoral program (0), enrolled in another graduate/professional program (0), enrolled in a post-doctoral residency/fellowship (n/a), employed in independent practice (n/a), employed in an academic position at a university (0), employed in an academic position at a 2-year/4-year college (0), employed in other positions at a higher education institution (0), employed in a professional position in a school system (0), employed in business or industry (research/consulting) (0), employed in business or industry (management) (0), employed in a government agency (research) (0), employed in a government agency (professional services) (0), employed in a community mental health/counseling center (0), employed in a hospital/medical center (0), still seeking employment (0), other employment position (0), total from the above (master's) (0).

Doctoral Degree Graduates: Of those who graduated in the academic year 2003–2004, the following categories and numbers represent the post-graduate activities and employment of doctoral degree graduates: Enrolled in a psychology doctoral program (n/a), enrolled in a post-doctoral residency/fellowship (6), employed in independent practice (0), employed in an academic position at a university (0), employed in an academic position at a 2-year/4-year college (0), employed in other positions at a higher education institution (0), employed in a professional position in a school system (0), employed in business or industry (research/consulting) (0), employed in business or industry (management) (0), employed in a government agency (research) (1), employed in a government agency (professional services) (0), employed in a community mental health/counseling center (0), employed in a hospital/medical center (2), still seeking employment (0), other employment position (0), total from the above (doctoral) (9).

Additional Information:

Orientation, Objectives, and Emphasis of Department: The Neuropsychology Subprogram is an academically-oriented PhD program with a core philosophy based on two premises. The first of these is that productive research, effective teaching, and responsible clinical practice are integrally interdependent. That is, effective teaching must include critical analysis of current research data, and clinical assessment and treatment procedures must be empirically validated. The second premise is that the understanding of impaired or disordered brain function in humans requires rigorous training in the neurosciences as well as in the traditional clinical topics. The Subprogram was designed to train professionals with competence in research and/or teaching in the area of brain-behavior relationships, and in the application of these competencies in clinical settings. There are two tracks within the program: the basic track requires 60 course credits; the clinical track requires 83 credits including at least two years of practicum training. Both tracks focus heavily on neuroscience topics, and provides intensive experience in human and animal experimentation. The clinical track also provides students the opportunity to acquire and apply the skills appropriate to the practice of clinical neuropsychology. Students in the clinical track thus receive training in the evaluation of psychological and neuropsychological function in various clinical populations, which may include children or adults, neurological, neurosurgical, rehabilitation medicine and psychiatric patients, as well as in the use of rehabilitative, psychotherapeutic, and remediative techniques. A full-year internship is required for graduation from the clinical track.

Special Facilities or Resources: http://www.qc.edu/Psychology/neuro/homepage.htm.

Application Information:
Send to: Office of Admissions, The Graduate School & University Center of the City University of New York, 365 Fifth Avenue, New York, NY 10016-4309. Application available online. URL of online application: http://www.gc.cuny.edu/prospective_students/admissions_index.htm. Students are admitted in the Fall, application deadline January 1. *Fee:* $125.

City University of New York: Graduate School and University Center
PhD Program in Educational Psychology
365 Fifth Avenue
New York, NY 10016-4309
Telephone: (212) 817-8285
Fax: (212) 817-1516
E-mail: *agross@gc.cuny.edu*
Web: *http://www.gc.cuny.edu*

Department Information:
1969. Executive Officer: Alan L. Gross. Number of Faculty: total–full-time 33, part-time 1; women–full-time 15; minority–full-time 6.

Programs and Degrees Offered:
Listed in the following order: Program area, degree type (T if terminal Master's), number awarded 7/03–6/04. Educational Psychology PhD (Doctor of Philosophy) 6.

APA Accreditation: School PhD (Doctor of Philosophy).

Student Applications/Admissions:
Student Applications
Educational Psychology PhD (Doctor of Philosophy)—Applications 2004–2005, 102. Total applicants accepted 2004–2005, 35. Number enrolled (new admits only) 2004–2005 full-time, 14. Number enrolled (new admits only) 2004–2005 part-time, 4. Total enrolled 2004–2005 full-time, 86, part-time, 13. Openings 2005–2006, 25. The Median number of years required for completion of a degree are 7. The number of students enrolled full and part-time who were dismissed or voluntarily withdrew from this program area were 2.

Admissions Requirements:
Scores: Entries appear in this order: required test or GPA, minimum score (if required), median score of students entering in 2003–2004. Doctoral Programs: GRE-V no minimum stated; GRE-Q no minimum stated; GRE-Analytical no minimum stated; overall undergraduate GPA no minimum stated.
Other Criteria: (importance of criteria rated low, medium, or high): GRE/MAT scores high, research experience medium, work experience medium, extracurricular activity low, clinically related public service low, GPA medium, letters of recommendation high, interview high, statement of goals and objectives high.

Student Characteristics: The following represents characteristics of students in 2004–2005 in all graduate psychology programs in the department: Female–full-time 63, part-time 11; Male–full-time 23, part-time 2; African American/Black–full-time 9, part-time 1; Hispanic/Latino(a)–full-time 7, part-time 2; Asian/Pacific Islander–full-time 5, part-time 1; American Indian/Alaska Native–full-time 0, part-time 0; Caucasian–full-time 0, part-time 0; Multi-ethnic–full-time 1, part-time 0; students subject to the Americans With Disabilities Act–full-time 2, part-time 0.

Financial Information/Assistance:
Tuition for Full-Time Study: Nonstate residents: $475 per credit hour. *Doctoral:* State residents: per academic year $4,870; Nonstate residents: per academic year $8,550.

Financial Assistance:
First Year Students: Teaching assistantships available for first-year. Average amount paid per academic year: $13,000. Average number of hours worked per week: 10. Apply by April 15. Research assistantships available for first-year. Average amount paid per academic year: $5,000. Average number of hours worked per week: 5. Apply by April 15. Fellowships and scholarships available for first-year. Average amount paid per academic year: $14,000. Average number of hours worked per week: 5. Apply by February 1.

Advanced Students: Teaching assistantships available for advanced students. Average amount paid per academic year: $12,000. Average number of hours worked per week: 10. Apply by April 15. Research assistantships available for advanced students. Average amount paid per academic year: $5,000. Average number of hours worked per week: 5. Apply by April 15. Fellowships and scholarships available for advanced students. Average amount paid per academic year: $14,000. Average number of hours worked per week: 5. Apply by February 1.

Contact Information: Of all students currently enrolled full-time, 50% benefitted from one or more of the listed financial assistance programs.

Internships/Practica: Required prior to graduation, 3 applied in 2003–2004.

Housing and Day Care: On-campus housing is available. Contact Office of Residence Life: reslife@gc.cuny.edu. On-campus day care facilities are available. There is a Child Development & Learning Center (Rm. 3201) under the direction of Linda Perrotta.

Employment of Department Graduates:

Master's Degree Graduates: Of those who graduated in the academic year 2003–2004, the following categories and numbers represent the post-graduate activities and employment of master's degree graduates: Enrolled in a post-doctoral residency/fellowship (n/a), employed in independent practice (n/a), total from the above (master's) (0).

Doctoral Degree Graduates: Of those who graduated in the academic year 2003–2004, the following categories and numbers represent the post-graduate activities and employment of doctoral degree graduates: Enrolled in a psychology doctoral program (n/a), enrolled in a post-doctoral residency/fellowship (0), employed in independent practice (0), employed in an academic position at a 2-year/4-year college (4), employed in a professional position in a school system (4), employed in a hospital/medical center (1), total from the above (doctoral) (9).

Additional Information:

Orientation, Objectives, and Emphasis of Department: The PhD Program in Educational Psychology is research oriented, preparing students for teaching, research, and program development in various educational settings such as universities, school systems, research institutions, community agencies, as well as in educational publishing, television, and other agencies with training programs. Four areas of concentration are offered: quantitative methods in educational and psychological research, learning development and instruction, school psychology and educational policy analysis.

Special Facilities or Resources: The Educational Psychology Program is affiliated with a university based research institute, CASE (Center for Advanced Study in Education). CASE is heavily involved in the evaluation and implementation of various applied educational programs. Our faculty and students have worked as principal investigators and research assistants on CASE projects.

Information for Students With Physical Disabilities: slerner@gc.cuny.edu.

Application Information:

Send to: Admissions Office, CUNY Graduate Center, 365 Fifth Avenue, New York, NY 10016-4309. Application available online. URL of online application: www.gc.cuny.edu. Students are admitted in the Fall, application deadline. February 15 for School Psychology; April 15 for all others. *Fee:* $125.

City University of New York: Graduate School and University Center

PhD Program in Psychology
365 Fifth Avenue
New York, NY 10016-4309
Telephone: (212) 817-8705/8753/8706
Fax: (212) 817-1533
E-mail: *psychology@gc.cuny.edu*
Web: *http://www.gc.cuny.edu*

Department Information:

1961. Executive Officer: Joseph Glick. Number of Faculty: total–full-time 121, part-time 47; women–full-time 46, part-time 18; minority–full-time 8, part-time 1.

Programs and Degrees Offered:

Listed in the following order: Program area, degree type (T if terminal Master's), number awarded 7/03–6/04. Biopsychology PhD (Doctor of Philosophy) 4, Clinical PhD (Doctor of Philosophy) 17, Developmental PhD (Doctor of Philosophy) 2, Experimental PhD (Doctor of Philosophy) 1, Experimental Cognition PhD (Doctor of Philosophy) 1, Environmental PhD (Doctor of Philosophy) 4, Industrial/Organizational PhD (Doctor of Philosophy) 5, Learning Processes PhD (Doctor of Philosophy) 2, Neuropsychology PhD (Doctor of Philosophy) 4, Social/Personality PhD (Doctor of Philosophy) 4, Forensic Psychology PhD (Doctor of Philosophy).

Student Applications/Admissions:

Student Applications

Biopsychology PhD (Doctor of Philosophy)—Applications 2004–2005, 17. Total applicants accepted 2004–2005, 6. Openings 2005–2006, 12. The Median number of years required for completion of a degree are 6. *Clinical PhD (Doctor of Philosophy)*—Applications 2004–2005, 345. Total applicants accepted 2004–2005, 12. Openings 2005–2006, 12. The Median number of years required for completion of a degree are 6. *Developmental PhD (Doctor of Philosophy)*—Applications 2004–2005, 32. Total applicants accepted 2004–2005, 12. Openings 2005–2006, 10. *Experimental PhD (Doctor of Philosophy)*—Applications 2004–2005, 13. Total applicants accepted 2004–2005, 8. Openings 2005–2006, 8. The Median number of years required for completion of a degree are 7. *Experimental Cognition PhD (Doctor of Philosophy)*—Applications 2004–2005, 10. Total applicants accepted 2004–2005, 7. Openings 2005–2006, 5. The Median number of years required for completion of a degree are 8. *Environmental PhD (Doctor of Philosophy)*—Applications 2004–2005, 21. Total applicants accepted 2004–2005, 10. Openings 2005–2006, 10. The Median number of years required for completion of a degree are 7. *Industrial/Organizational PhD (Doctor of Philosophy)*—Applications 2004–2005, 61. Total applicants accepted 2004–2005, 5. Openings 2005–2006, 7. The Median number of years required for completion of a degree are 7. *Learning Processes PhD (Doctor of Philosophy)*—Applications 2004–2005, 18. Total applicants accepted 2004–2005, 7. Openings 2005–2006, 10. The Median number of years required for completion of a degree are 6. *Neuropsychology PhD (Doctor of Philosophy)*—Applications 2004–2005, 55. Total applicants accepted 2004–2005, 9. Openings 2005–2006, 8. *Social/Personality PhD (Doctor of*

Philosophy)—Applications 2004–2005, 66. Total applicants accepted 2004–2005, 10. Openings 2005–2006, 7. *Forensic Psychology PhD (Doctor of Philosophy)*—Applications 2004–2005, 145. Total applicants accepted 2004–2005, 10. Number enrolled (new admits only) 2004–2005 full-time, 10. Openings 2005–2006, 10.

Admissions Requirements:

Scores: Entries appear in this order: required test or GPA, minimum score (if required), median score of students entering in 2003–2004. Master's Programs: GRE-V no minimum stated; GRE-Q no minimum stated; GRE-V+Q no minimum stated; GRE-Analytical no minimum stated. Clinical requires the Psychology subject test. Doctoral Programs: GRE-V 550; GRE-Q 550; GRE-Analytical 550; GRE-Subject(Psych) 550; overall undergraduate GPA 3.0. "Minimum scores" are flexible depending on the complete application package and any special circumstances that may apply.

Other Criteria: (importance of criteria rated low, medium, or high): GRE/MAT scores medium, research experience medium, work experience low, extracurricular activity low, clinically related public service medium, GPA medium, letters of recommendation high, interview high, statement of goals and objectives high.

Student Characteristics: The following represents characteristics of students in 2004–2005 in all graduate psychology programs in the department: Female–full-time 340, part-time 2; Male–full-time 128, part-time 2; African American/Black–full-time 39, part-time 0; Hispanic/Latino(a)–full-time 72, part-time 0; Asian/Pacific Islander–full-time 20, part-time 0; American Indian/Alaska Native–full-time 1, part-time 0; Caucasian–full-time 0, part-time 0.

Financial Information/Assistance:

Tuition for Full-Time Study: *Doctoral:* State residents: per academic year $2,435, $275 per credit hour; Nonstate residents: per academic year $3,390, $475 per credit hour. Tuition is subject to change.

Financial Assistance:

First Year Students: Teaching assistantships available for first-year. Average amount paid per academic year: $11,000. Average number of hours worked per week: 20. Research assistantships available for first-year. Average amount paid per academic year: $7,552. Fellowships and scholarships available for first-year. Average amount paid per academic year: $13,500. Average number of hours worked per week: 20. Tuition remission given: full.

Advanced Students: Teaching assistantships available for advanced students. Average amount paid per academic year: $6,000. Average number of hours worked per week: 12. Research assistantships available for advanced students. Fellowships and scholarships available for advanced students. Average amount paid per academic year: $20,000.

Contact Information: Of all students currently enrolled full-time, 90% benefitted from one or more of the listed financial assistance programs.

Internships/Practica: Clinical students are placed at agencies or hospitals. Neuropsychology students are placed at hospitals or clinics. Learning Processes students are placed in service agencies and treatment facilities. Forensic students find placement in various justice system related positions.

Housing and Day Care: No on-campus housing is available. On-campus day care facilities are available.

Employment of Department Graduates:

Master's Degree Graduates: Of those who graduated in the academic year 2003–2004, the following categories and numbers represent the post-graduate activities and employment of master's degree graduates: Enrolled in a post-doctoral residency/fellowship (n/a), employed in independent practice (n/a), total from the above (master's) (0).

Doctoral Degree Graduates: Of those who graduated in the academic year 2003–2004, the following categories and numbers represent the post-graduate activities and employment of doctoral degree graduates: Enrolled in a psychology doctoral program (n/a), enrolled in a post-doctoral residency/fellowship (4), employed in an academic position at a university (16), employed in an academic position at a 2-year/4-year college (9), employed in a professional position in a school system (13), employed in business or industry (research/consulting) (2), total from the above (doctoral) (44).

Additional Information:

Orientation, Objectives, and Emphasis of Department: The developmental subprogram offers training in all areas of developmental research, with emphasis on social, cognitive, and language development. The Environmental subprogram provides interdisciplinary training with relationships between the physical environment and behavior. Concepts and approaches of fields such as urban planning, psychology, architecture, geography, anthropology, landscape architecture, and sociology are learned in a context that emphasizes the integration of systematic research and applied work with the development of theory. The social-personality subprogram trains students in the theory and research methods of both social and personality psychology. A health psychology concentration is available to students in all subprograms. Through courses, research projects, and practica, the concentration seeks to train psychologists to be able to work in a variety of health-related settings. Industrial/Organizational psychology trains people to do research in organizations and in personnel issues. Neuropsychology trains students in both basic and clinical neuroscience. Learning Processes offers training in Applied Behavior Analysis. Clinical offers training in psychodynamic approaches to mental health with particular attention paid to minority populations. Experimental Psychology and Experimental Cognition focus on the experimental approach to a wide variety of phenomena. Forensic psychology has two tracks, clinical (90 credits) and experimental (60 credits). The clinical track prepares people to work within the criminal justice system in a variety of clinical roles. The experimental track prepares people in basic research dealing with the interface of psychology and the law.

Special Facilities or Resources: Computers for student use are available in the library; computer hubs, on most academic floors; and student carrel spaces, in the academic program offices. An assortment of programming languages and statistical, graphical, word processing, and specialty software applications are provided. Also available are laser printers, file format translation, image scanning, and optical character recognition facilities. Adaptive technology for students with disabilities is available and includes screen-access software and such peripheral devices as reading machines, a computer-linked closed-circuit TV, and a Braille printer. Most computers designated for students are 400Mhz Celeron processor systems with 6GB hard drives, 64 MB Ram, and 15-inch flat-screen monitors. Five special-purpose classrooms, with a total of more than 100 computers, are furnished with 450 Mhz Pentium III computers and 15-inch flat-screen monitors. Students may access UNIX-based academic software from home or via a telnet session upon request. The UNIX accounts provide access to statistical or other academic software but not e-mail support. Information Resources maintains an ongoing program of equipment, computer hardware, and software modernization and provides such client services as documentation, training, and lab consulting. Workshops are held throughout the year on a wide range of topics and include many hands-on training programs.

Information for Students With Physical Disabilities: slerner@gc.cuny.edu.

Application Information:
Send to: Admissions Office, City University Graduate Center, 365 Fifth Avenue, New York, NY 10016-4309; Phone: (212) 817-7470; E-mail: admissions@gc.cuny.edu. Students are admitted in the Fall. Deadline is January 1 for Clinical and Neuropsychology; January 15 for Developmental, Environmental and Social-Personality. Forensic; February 1 for Experimental Cognition, Industrial/ Organizational; March 1 for Biopsychology; March 15 for Learning Processes, Experimental. *Fee:* $125.

City University of New York: John Jay College of Criminal Justice
Department of Psychology
445 West 59th Street
New York, NY 10019
Telephone: (212) 237-8782
Fax: (212) 237-8742
E-mail: *Jwulach@jjay.cuny.edu*
Web: *www.jjay.cuny.edu*

Department Information:
1976. Director: James S. Wulach, PhD, J.D. Number of Faculty: total–full-time 27, part-time 3; women–full-time 15; minority–full-time 4.

Programs and Degrees Offered:
Listed in the following order: Program area, degree type (T if terminal Master's), number awarded 7/03–6/04. Forensic Psychology MA/MS (Master of Arts/Science) (T) 148, Forensic Psychology PhD (Doctor of Philosophy).

Student Applications/Admissions:
Student Applications
Forensic Psychology MA/MS (Master of Arts/Science)—Applications 2004–2005, 249. Total applicants accepted 2004–2005, 166. Total enrolled 2004–2005 full-time, 216, part-time, 208. Openings 2005–2006, 175. The Median number of years required for completion of a degree are 2. The number of students enrolled full and part-time who were dismissed or voluntarily withdrew from this program area were 26. *Forensic Psychology*

PhD (Doctor of Philosophy)—Applications 2004–2005, 160. Total applicants accepted 2004–2005, 10. Number enrolled (new admits only) 2004–2005 full-time, 9. Number enrolled (new admits only) 2004–2005 part-time, 0. Openings 2005–2006, 15. The number of students enrolled full and part-time who were dismissed or voluntarily withdrew from this program area were 0.

Admissions Requirements:
Scores: Entries appear in this order: required test or GPA, minimum score (if required), median score of students entering in 2003–2004. Master's Programs: GRE-V+Q 1000, 1050; overall undergraduate GPA 3.0, 3.2. Doctoral Programs: No required minimum scores. Each candidate is evaluated individually.
Other Criteria: (importance of criteria rated low, medium, or high): GRE/MAT scores high, research experience low, work experience low, GPA high, letters of recommendation low, statement of goals and objectives low. Doctoral Program: GRE Scores (High); Research Experience (Medium); Work Experience (Low); Extracurricular activity (Low); Clinically related public service (Medium); GPA (High); Letters of recommendation (High); Interview (Medium); Statement of Goals and Objectives (High). MA Program: GPA & GRE Scores weighted most heavily. For additional information on admission requirements, go to: web.gc.cuny.edu/psychology (for Doctoral Program); www.jjay.cuny.edu for MA Program.

Student Characteristics: The following represents characteristics of students in 2004–2005 in all graduate psychology programs in the department: Female–full-time 150, part-time 146; Male–full-time 66, part-time 62; African American/Black–full-time 14, part-time 35; Hispanic/Latino(a)–full-time 17, part-time 26; Asian/Pacific Islander–full-time 2, part-time 9; American Indian/Alaska Native–full-time 1, part-time 0; Caucasian–full-time 0, part-time 0.

Financial Information/Assistance:
Tuition for Full-Time Study: *Master's:* State residents: per academic year $5,440, $230 per credit hour; Nonstate residents: $425 per credit hour. *Doctoral:* State residents: per academic year $4,870; Nonstate residents: $475 per credit hour. See the following Web site for updates and changes in tuition costs: www.jjay.cuny.edu (MA) or http://www.gc.cuny.edu/academic_matters/tuition_and_fees.htm (PhD).

Financial Assistance:
First Year Students: No information provided.
Advanced Students: No information provided.
Contact Information: Of all students currently enrolled full-time, 0% benefitted from one or more of the listed financial assistance programs. Application and information available online at: http://www.gc.cuny.edu/administrative_offices/financial_aid.htm (PhD Program only).

Internships/Practica: (MA Program): Most students complete a 400-hour externship in local forensic psychology settings, such as hospitals or prisons. (Doctoral Program): Doctoral students are required to complete a one-year internship and will be eligible to apply via APPIC application procedures.

Housing and Day Care: No on-campus housing is available. On-campus day care facilities are available. See the following Web site for more information: www.jjay.cuny.edu.

Employment of Department Graduates:

Master's Degree Graduates: Of those who graduated in the academic year 2003–2004, the following categories and numbers represent the post-graduate activities and employment of master's degree graduates: Enrolled in a post-doctoral residency/fellowship (n/a), employed in independent practice (n/a), total from the above (master's) (0).

Doctoral Degree Graduates: Of those who graduated in the academic year 2003–2004, the following categories and numbers represent the post-graduate activities and employment of doctoral degree graduates: Enrolled in a psychology doctoral program (n/a), total from the above (doctoral) (0).

Additional Information:

Orientation, Objectives, and Emphasis of Department: (MA Program) Our program is designed to train students to provide professional psychological services to, and within, the legal system—especially the criminal justice system. Thus, in addition to offering (and requiring) traditional master's level clinical psychology courses, we offer specialized courses in psychology and the law; the psychology and treatment of juvenile and adult offenders and the victims of crime; forensic evaluation and testimony; jury research; eyewitness research; psychological profiles of homicidal offenders; psychology of terrorism; and forensic psychological research. Courses are primarily offered in the afternoon and evening. Many of our 27 full-time faculty members have postdoctoral psychological certifications; 4 are lawyers as well as psychologists; and many have extensive forensic experience as practitioners and/or researchers. In addition, the full educational resources of the John Jay College of Criminal Justice are available to our students. Some of our graduates become psychological counselors and psychologists within the criminal justice system, working with offenders, delinquents, and victims. Other graduates enhance their present careers in law enforcement, probation, or parole by completing the program. Many of our graduates continue their education in psychology doctoral programs, in John Jay's doctoral program in criminal justice, or in law.

Special Facilities or Resources: The department maintains affiliations with the major forensic psychology institutions in the New York metropolitan area. The Program is endowed for student-psychology research, in the Forensic Psychology Research Institute. In addition, the full academic resources and educational milieu of John Jay College of Criminal Justice, CUNY, are available to our students.

Application Information:

Send to: MA Program: Graduate Admissions, John Jay College of Criminal Justice, CUNY, Room 4205N, 445 West 59th Street, New York, NY 10019, Phone number: (212) 237-8863. Doctoral Program: Office of Admissions, The Graduate Center, The City University of New York, 365 Fifth Avenue, New York, NY 10016, Phone number: (212) 817-7470. Application available online. Students are admitted in the Fall, application deadline June 30; Spring, application deadline December 1; Summer, application deadline December 1. Doctoral Program deadline is January 1. *Fee:* $40.

Columbia University

Health and Behavior Studies/School Psychology
Teachers College
525 West 120th Street, Box 120
New York, NY 10027
Telephone: (212) 678-3942
Fax: (212) 678-4034
E-mail: *peverly@exchange.tc.columbia.edu*
Web: *http://www.tc.columbia.edu/hbs/schoolpsych/*

Department Information:

1986. Chairperson: Charles Basch. Number of Faculty: total–full-time 3, part-time 10; women–full-time 1, part-time 8.

Programs and Degrees Offered:

Listed in the following order: Program area, degree type (T if terminal Master's), number awarded 7/03–6/04. School Psychology PhD (Doctor of Philosophy) 3, School Psychology Other 13.

APA Accreditation: School PhD (Doctor of Philosophy).

Student Applications/Admissions:

Student Applications

School Psychology PhD (Doctor of Philosophy)—Applications 2004–2005, 40. Total applicants accepted 2004–2005, 6. Number enrolled (new admits only) 2004–2005 full-time, 5. Total enrolled 2004–2005 full-time, 14, part-time, 23. Openings 2005–2006, 4. The Median number of years required for completion of a degree are 7. The number of students enrolled full and part-time who were dismissed or voluntarily withdrew from this program area were 0. *School Psychology Other*—Applications 2004–2005, 90. Total applicants accepted 2004–2005, 40. Number enrolled (new admits only) 2004–2005 full-time, 25. Total enrolled 2004–2005 full-time, 62. Openings 2005–2006, 20. The Median number of years required for completion of a degree are 3. The number of students enrolled full and part-time who were dismissed or voluntarily withdrew from this program area were 4.

Admissions Requirements:

Scores: Entries appear in this order: required test or GPA, minimum score (if required), median score of students entering in 2003–2004. Master's Programs: GRE-V no minimum stated, 500; GRE-Q no minimum stated, 570; GRE-V+Q no minimum stated, 1070; GRE-Analytical no minimum stated, 640; overall undergraduate GPA no minimum stated, 3.52. Doctoral Programs: GRE-V no minimum stated, 650; GRE-Q no minimum stated, 660; GRE-V+Q no minimum stated, 1300; GRE-Analytical no minimum stated, 690; overall undergraduate GPA no minimum stated, 3.51.

Other Criteria: (importance of criteria rated low, medium, or high): GRE/MAT scores medium, research experience high, work experience medium, extracurricular activity medium, clinically related public service medium, GPA high, letters of recommendation high, interview high, statement of goals and objectives high.

Student Characteristics: The following represents characteristics of students in 2004–2005 in all graduate psychology programs in the department: Female–full-time 68, part-time 19; Male–full-

time 8, part-time 4; African American/Black–full-time 7, part-time 3; Hispanic/Latino(a)–full-time 2, part-time 1; Asian/Pacific Islander–full-time 11, part-time 4; American Indian/Alaska Native–full-time 0, part-time 0; Caucasian–full-time 57, part-time 15; Multi-ethnic–full-time 0, part-time 0; students subject to the Americans With Disabilities Act–full-time 2, part-time 0.

Financial Information/Assistance:

Tuition for Full-Time Study: *Master's:* State residents: $875 per credit hour; Nonstate residents: $875 per credit hour. *Doctoral:* State residents: $875 per credit hour; Nonstate residents: $875 per credit hour. Tuition is subject to change. See the following Web site for updates and changes in tuition costs: www.tc.columbia.edu.

Financial Assistance:

First Year Students: No information provided.
Advanced Students: No information provided.
Contact Information: Of all students currently enrolled full-time, 25% benefitted from one or more of the listed financial assistance programs.

Internships/Practica: First year—Two practica in our Center for Educational and Psychological Services: (1) Practicum in Assessment of Reading and School Subject Difficulties (Fall); (2) Practicum in Psychoeducational Assessment with Culturally Diverse Students (Spring); Second year—Students engage in (1) Fieldwork (2 days/week over the academic year in one of our cooperating inner-city schools), (2) a practicum in psychoeducational groups (the groups are run within students' fieldwork sites); Third year—Externship (2 days/week over an academic year; most students are required to do 2 externships: one in a school and one in a hospital or clinic); Fourth or Fifth year—Internship (full calendar year; students must have an approved dissertation proposal before they begin to do the internship after completing most or all of their dissertation). For those doctoral students for whom a professional internship is required prior to graduation, 1 applied in 2003–2004. Of those who applied, 1 was placed in an internship listed by the Association of Psychology Postdoctoral and Internship Programs (APPIC); 1 was placed in an APA accredited internship.

Housing and Day Care: On-campus housing is available. See the following Web site for more information: http://www.tc.columbia.edu. On-campus day care facilities are available.

Employment of Department Graduates:

Master's Degree Graduates: Of those who graduated in the academic year 2003–2004, the following categories and numbers represent the post-graduate activities and employment of master's degree graduates: Enrolled in a psychology doctoral program (1), enrolled in another graduate/professional program (0), enrolled in a post-doctoral residency/fellowship (n/a), employed in independent practice (n/a), employed in a professional position in a school system (14), total from the above (master's) (15).
Doctoral Degree Graduates: Of those who graduated in the academic year 2003–2004, the following categories and numbers represent the post-graduate activities and employment of doctoral degree graduates: Enrolled in a psychology doctoral program (n/a), enrolled in a post-doctoral residency/fellowship (1), employed in an academic position at a university (1), employed in a profes-

sional position in a school system (1), total from the above (doctoral) (3).

Additional Information:

Orientation, Objectives, and Emphasis of Department: The primary theoretical orientation of our program is cognitive with strong applications to instruction and mental health. We place a particularly strong emphasis on prevention and intervention in these areas. Throughout the curriculum, there is a balance between science and practice, and we ensure that all students are well grounded in the theory and methods of psychological science. Most students opt to go through the general curriculum. However, some have adopted a specialization in the deaf and hearing impaired.

Special Facilities or Resources: The School Psychology program has strong collaborative relationships with 3 inner-city schools that serve as fieldwork and sites for our master's and doctoral students.

Information for Students With Physical Disabilities: See the following Web site for more information: www.tc.columbia.edu.

Application Information:

Send to: Office of Admissions, Box 302, Teachers College, Columbia University, 525 West 120th Street, New York, NY 10027; (212) 678-3710. Application available online. URL of online application: www.tc.columbia.edu/admissions. Students are admitted in the Fall, application deadline December 15. *Fee:* $60. Re-applicants—$35.

Columbia University
Psychology
Graduate School of Arts and Sciences
1190 Amsterdam Aveunue, 406 Schermerhorn Hall
New York, NY 10027
Telephone: (212) 854-3608
Fax: (212) 854-3609
E-mail: *veronica@psych.columbia.edu*
Web: *http://www.columbia.edu/cu/psychology*

Department Information:

1867. Chairperson: Dr. Geraldine Downey. Number of Faculty: total–full-time 21, part-time 8; women–full-time 8, part-time 3; minority–part-time 1; faculty subject to the Americans With Disabilities Act 1.

Student Applications/Admissions:

Admissions Requirements:

Scores: Entries appear in this order: required test or GPA, minimum score (if required), median score of students entering in 2003–2004. Doctoral Programs: GRE-V+Q 1200.
Other Criteria: (importance of criteria rated low, medium, or high): GRE/MAT scores high, research experience high, work experience medium, extracurricular activity medium, clinically related public service medium, GPA high, letters of recommendation high, interview high, statement of goals and objectives high. For additional information on admission requirements, go to: http://www.columbia.edu/cu/gsas.

Student Characteristics: The following represents characteristics of students in 2004–2005 in all graduate psychology programs in the department: Female–full-time 22, part-time 0; Male–full-time 13, part-time 0; African American/Black–full-time 2, part-time 0; Hispanic/Latino(a)–full-time 1, part-time 0; Asian/Pacific Islander–full-time 3, part-time 0; American Indian/Alaska Native–full-time 0, part-time 0; Caucasian–full-time 28, part-time 0; Multi-ethnic–full-time 1, part-time 0; students subject to the Americans With Disabilities Act–full-time 0, part-time 0.

Financial Information/Assistance:
Financial Assistance:
First Year Students: Fellowships and scholarships available for first-year. Tuition remission given: full.

Advanced Students: No information provided.

Contact Information: Application and information available online at: http://www.columbia.edu/cu/psychology/dept/grad/admitcop.html.

Internships/Practica: All are required to serve as teaching assistants for one semester per year.

Housing and Day Care: On-campus housing is available. See the following Web site for more information: http://www.columbia.edu/cu/ire. On-campus day care facilities are available. See the following Web site for more information: http://www.columbia.edu/cu/provost/childcare/.

Employment of Department Graduates:
Master's Degree Graduates: Of those who graduated in the academic year 2003–2004, the following categories and numbers represent the post-graduate activities and employment of master's degree graduates: Enrolled in a psychology doctoral program (31), enrolled in a post-doctoral residency/fellowship (n/a), employed in independent practice (n/a), total from the above (master's) (31).
Doctoral Degree Graduates: Of those who graduated in the academic year 2003–2004, the following categories and numbers represent the post-graduate activities and employment of doctoral degree graduates: Enrolled in a psychology doctoral program (n/a), enrolled in a post-doctoral residency/fellowship (2), employed in an academic position at a university (3), total from the above (doctoral) (5).

Additional Information:
Orientation, Objectives, and Emphasis of Department: The program has a research-apprenticeship orientation and trains students for careers in basic and applied research and teaching. Teaching and research experience are considered an important aspect of the training of graduate students.

Special Facilities or Resources: All students accepted to the five-year program receive a Faculty Fellowship, which supports tuition, health and insurance fees, and an annual stipend. All fellows receive equal awards, and the stipend level is adjusted each year to keep pace with inflation.

Information for Students With Physical Disabilities: See the following Web site for more information: http://www.health.columbia.edu/ods/.

Application Information:
Send to: Graduate School of Arts and Sciences, Columbia University, 107 Low Library, MC 4304 535, West 116th Street, New York, NY 10027-7004. Application available online. URL of online application: http://www.columbia.edu/cu/gsas/. Students are admitted in the Fall, application deadline December 1. *Fee:* $75. Financial hardship waiver conditions: Must be enrolled at another University and be on financial aid at the University. The Graduate School of Arts and Sciences is no longer printing applications to be mailed. Also, please note that the application fee is $75 for the online application, but $90 for students who mail in the paper version.

Cornell University
Department of Human Development
The New York State College of Human Ecology
G77 Martha Van Rensselaer Hall
Ithaca, NY 14853-4401
Telephone: (607) 255-7620
Fax: (607) 255-9856
E-mail: *hdfs@cornell.edu*
Web: *http://human.cornell.edu/units/hd/grad_progs.cfm*

Department Information:
1925. Chairperson: Ritch Savin-Williams. Number of Faculty: total–full-time 21; women–full-time 10; minority–full-time 2.

Programs and Degrees Offered:
Listed in the following order: Program area, degree type (T if terminal Master's), number awarded 7/03–6/04. Developmental PhD (Doctor of Philosophy) 3, Human Development Family Studies PhD (Doctor of Philosophy) 1.

Student Applications/Admissions:
Student Applications
Developmental PhD (Doctor of Philosophy)—Applications 2004–2005, 51. Total applicants accepted 2004–2005, 15. Number enrolled (new admits only) 2004–2005 full-time, 7. Number enrolled (new admits only) 2004–2005 part-time, 0. Openings 2005–2006, 7. The Median number of years required for completion of a degree are 5. The number of students enrolled full and part-time who were dismissed or voluntarily withdrew from this program area were 0. *Human Development Family Studies PhD (Doctor of Philosophy)*—Applications 2004–2005, 18. Total applicants accepted 2004–2005, 3. Number enrolled (new admits only) 2004–2005 full-time, 2. Number enrolled (new admits only) 2004–2005 part-time, 0. Openings 2005–2006, 2. The Median number of years required for completion of a degree are 5. The number of students enrolled full and part-time who were dismissed or voluntarily withdrew from this program area were 0.

Admissions Requirements:
Scores: Entries appear in this order: required test or GPA, minimum score (if required), median score of students entering in 2003–2004. Doctoral Programs: GRE-V 600, 560; GRE-Q 600, 700; GRE-V+Q 1200, 1240; GRE-Analytical 600; overall undergraduate GPA 3.3.
Other Criteria: (importance of criteria rated low, medium, or high): GRE/MAT scores high, research experience high, work experience medium, extracurricular activity low, clinically related public service low, GPA high, letters of recommendation high, statement of goals and objectives high.

Student Characteristics: The following represents characteristics of students in 2004–2005 in all graduate psychology programs in the department: Female–full-time 23, part-time 0; Male–full-time 8, part-time 0; African American/Black–full-time 2, part-time 0; Hispanic/Latino(a)–full-time 1, part-time 0; Asian/Pacific Islander–full-time 7, part-time 0; American Indian/Alaska Native–full-time 0, part-time 0; Caucasian–full-time 21, part-time 0; Multi-ethnic–full-time 0, part-time 0; students subject to the Americans With Disabilities Act–full-time 0, part-time 0.

Financial Information/Assistance:

Tuition for Full-Time Study: *Doctoral:* State residents: per academic year $19,300; Nonstate residents: per academic year $19,300. Tuition is subject to change.

Financial Assistance:

First Year Students: Teaching assistantships available for first-year. Average amount paid per academic year: $17,600. Average number of hours worked per week: 15. Apply by January 15. Tuition remission given: full. Research assistantships available for first-year. Average amount paid per academic year: $17,600. Average number of hours worked per week: 15. Apply by January 15. Tuition remission given: full. Traineeships available for first-year. Average amount paid per academic year: $17,600. Average number of hours worked per week: 15. Apply by January 15. Tuition remission given: full. Fellowships and scholarships available for first-year. Average amount paid per academic year: $17,600. Average number of hours worked per week: 0. Apply by January 15. Tuition remission given: full.

Advanced Students: Teaching assistantships available for advanced students. Average amount paid per academic year: $17,600. Average number of hours worked per week: 15. Apply by January 15. Tuition remission given: full. Research assistantships available for advanced students. Average amount paid per academic year: $17,600. Average number of hours worked per week: 15. Apply by January 15. Tuition remission given: full. Traineeships available for advanced students. Average amount paid per academic year: $17,600. Average number of hours worked per week: 15. Apply by January 15. Tuition remission given: full. Fellowships and scholarships available for advanced students. Average amount paid per academic year: $17,600. Average number of hours worked per week: 0. Apply by January 15. Tuition remission given: full.

Contact Information: Of all students currently enrolled full-time, 100% benefitted from one or more of the listed financial assistance programs.

Internships/Practica: No information provided.

Housing and Day Care: On-campus housing is available. See the following Web site for more information: www.campuslife.cornell.edu/graduate_housing/. On-campus day care facilities are available. See the following Web site for more information: www.ohr.cornell.edu/benefits/lifeEvents/childcare.html.

Employment of Department Graduates:

Master's Degree Graduates: Of those who graduated in the academic year 2003–2004, the following categories and numbers represent the post-graduate activities and employment of master's degree graduates: Enrolled in a post-doctoral residency/fellowship (n/a), employed in independent practice (n/a), total from the above (master's) (0).

Doctoral Degree Graduates: Of those who graduated in the academic year 2003–2004, the following categories and numbers represent the post-graduate activities and employment of doctoral degree graduates: Enrolled in a psychology doctoral program (n/a), enrolled in a post-doctoral residency/fellowship (1), employed in an academic position at a university (3), total from the above (doctoral) (4).

Additional Information:

Orientation, Objectives, and Emphasis of Department: The field offers two general majors. The major in Developmental Psychology focuses on individual development and the effects on it of various intrinsic and extrinsic factors. The major in Human Development and Family Studies focuses on the interrelationships among the individual, the family, and the larger society. The PhD in Developmental Psychology is intended to provide students with strong training in the general discipline of developmental psychology as well as more focused training within one or more of its sub-areas (cognitive, social-personality, biological, infancy, childhood, adolescence, and adulthood). The Human and Family Studies Development major is designed to meet the needs of students seeking advanced training that bridges basic and applied research in human development from a life course perspective. The program places heavy emphasis on research training. Students are prepared for careers in academic life in departments of psychology, sociology, or human development, in government agencies concerned with research or social policy, and in a range of programs involving community agencies or private enterprise. Training is not offered in clinical or counseling psychology, marriage counseling, or family therapy, nor is teacher certification offered.

Special Facilities or Resources: The department houses a number of laboratories directed by individual faculty conducting observational and experimental studies of basic processes in development. In addition, the Cornell Early Childhood Program operates a day care program that provides numerous opportunities for research. Students may become involved in research or demonstration projects in the College's Family Life Development Center (child maltreatment and families under stress) and Bronfenbrenner Life Course Institute (adulthood and aging). The department also maintains close relationships with many public schools, nursery schools, day care centers, and youth service agencies, and much research is conducted in those settings. Additionally, there are several experimental labs as well as graduate student computer facilities and data decoding rooms.

Information for Students With Physical Disabilities: See the following Web site for more information: www.sas.cornell.edu/CLT/campus/sds/index.html.

Application Information:

Send to: The Graduate School, Caldwell Hall, Cornell University, Ithaca, NY 14853. Application available online. URL of online application: http://www.gradschool.edu/?p=2. Students are admitted in the Fall, application deadline January 15. *Fee:* $70. In cases of extreme financial need, a fee waiver will be considered. A letter of request for a waiver and documentation of need such as a letter from the college financial aid office needs to be submitted.

Cornell University

Graduate Field of Psychology
Arts
211D Uris Hall
Ithaca, NY 14853-7601
Telephone: (607) 255-6364
Fax: (607) 255-8433
E-mail: *lap5@cornell.edu*
Web: *www.psych.cornell.edu*

Department Information:
   1885. Director of Graduate Studies: Barb Finlay. Number of Faculty: total–full-time 22, part-time 1; women–full-time 5.

Programs and Degrees Offered:
   Listed in the following order: Program area, degree type (T if terminal Master's), number awarded 7/03–6/04. Bio-Psychology and Neuroscience PhD (Doctor of Philosophy) 4, Cognition and Perception PhD (Doctor of Philosophy) 2, Personality and Social PhD (Doctor of Philosophy) 3.

Student Applications/Admissions:
   Student Applications
   Bio-Psychology and Neuroscience PhD (Doctor of Philosophy)— Applications 2004–2005, 20. Total applicants accepted 2004–2005, 4. Number enrolled (new admits only) 2004–2005 full-time, 4. Openings 2005–2006, 2. The number of students enrolled full and part-time, who were dismissed or voluntarily withdrew from this program area were 0. *Cognition and Perception PhD (Doctor of Philosophy)*—Applications 2004–2005, 52. Total applicants accepted 2004–2005, 3. Number enrolled (new admits only) 2004–2005 full-time, 3. Openings 2005–2006, 2. The number of students enrolled full and part-time who were dismissed or voluntarily withdrew from this program area were 0. *Personality and Social PhD (Doctor of Philosophy)*— Applications 2004–2005, 100. Total applicants accepted 2004–2005, 2. Number enrolled (new admits only) 2004–2005 full-time, 2. Openings 2005–2006, 2.

   Admissions Requirements:
   Scores: Entries appear in this order: required test or GPA, minimum score (if required), median score of students entering in 2003–2004. Doctoral Programs: GRE-V no minimum stated, 562; GRE-Q no minimum stated, 685; GRE-V+Q no minimum stated, 1247; GRE-Analytical no minimum stated, 707; GRE-Subject(Psych) no minimum stated, 720; overall undergraduate GPA no minimum stated.
   Other Criteria: (importance of criteria rated low, medium, or high): GRE/MAT scores high, research experience high, work experience low, extracurricular activity low, GPA high, letters of recommendation high, statement of goals and objectives high.

   Student Characteristics: The following represents characteristics of students in 2004–2005 in all graduate psychology programs in the department: Female–full-time 15, part-time 0; Male–full-time 16, part-time 0; African American/Black–full-time 0, part-time 0; Hispanic/Latino(a)–full-time 2, part-time 0; Asian/Pacific Islander–full-time 6, part-time 0; American Indian/Alaska Native– full-time 0, part-time 0; Caucasian–full-time 23, part-time 0.

Financial Information/Assistance:
   Financial Assistance:
      First Year Students: Teaching assistantships available for first-year. Average amount paid per academic year: $17,600. Average number of hours worked per week: 20. Fellowships and scholarships available for first-year. Average amount paid per academic year: $17,600.
      Advanced Students: No information provided.
      Contact Information: Of all students currently enrolled full-time, 100% benefitted from one or more of the listed financial assistance programs.

   Internships/Practica: No information provided.

   Housing and Day Care: On-campus housing is available. On-campus day care facilities are available.

Employment of Department Graduates:
   Master's Degree Graduates: Of those who graduated in the academic year 2003–2004, the following categories and numbers represent the post-graduate activities and employment of master's degree graduates: Enrolled in a post-doctoral residency/fellowship (n/a), employed in independent practice (n/a), total from the above (master's) (0).
   Doctoral Degree Graduates: Of those who graduated in the academic year 2003–2004, the following categories and numbers represent the post-graduate activities and employment of doctoral degree graduates: Enrolled in a psychology doctoral program (n/a), enrolled in a post-doctoral residency/fellowship (5), employed in an academic position at a university (6), total from the above (doctoral) (11).

Additional Information:
   Orientation, Objectives, and Emphasis of Department: The Psychology Department of the College of Arts and Sciences at Cornell has a faculty of 27 psychologists and is divided into three areas—cognition & perception (encompassing cognition, language, perception, and its developmental perspectives), biopsychology & neuroscience (focusing on hormones and behavior, neural development, and sensory systems), and social/personality (social cognition, judgment, and decision making). We do not have clinical, community, or counseling programs. We have a strong research orientation, training our students to become professional academics or researchers. Our 33 students design their graduate programs under the supervision of their special committees. These committees consist of at least four members of the graduate faculty at Cornell; at least three are from within the department. The chair of the committee is a member of the Graduate Field of Psychology, which consists of the 27 members of our department plus 20 researchers in allied fields (human development, education, industrial and labor relations, and neurobiology and behavior). Two other committee members serve as minor members, one of whom can be outside the Graduate Field of Psychology, and the fourth member oversees breadth requirements.

   Special Facilities or Resources: The three areas of our program each have laboratories associated with them. Each of the members of the cognition and perception program has a separate laboratory, fully equipped with state-of-the-art computer equipment. In addition, the program has several computer-based teaching laboratories. The biopsychologists each have separate labs and computers, and animal housing facilities where relevant, but they share much equipment and lab space. There is also a teaching lab associated with the biopsychology group labs. The social-personality psychologists share a large lab space with the sociology department. The department also has a small research library and machine, wood, and electronic shops.

Application Information:
Send to: Graduate School, Caldwell Hall, Cornell University, Ithaca, NY 14853. Application available online. URL of online application: http://gradschool.cornell.edu. Students are admitted in the Fall, application deadline December 15. *Fee:* $70.

Fordham University (2004 data)
Department of Psychology
Arts and Sciences
441 East Fordham Road
Bronx, NY 10458
Telephone: (718) 817-3775
Fax: (718) 817-3785
E-mail: *wertz@fordham.edu*
Web: *http://www.fordham.edu/faculty/Undergraduate/Psych*

Department Information:
Chairperson: Frederick J. Wertz. Number of Faculty: total–full-time 31, part-time 3; women–full-time 8, part-time 2; minority–full-time 2.

Programs and Degrees Offered:
Listed in the following order: Program area, degree type (T if terminal Master's), number awarded 7/03–6/04. Clinical PhD (Doctor of Philosophy) 13, Psychometric PhD (Doctor of Philosophy) 1, Applied Developmental Psychology PhD (Doctor of Philosophy) 7.

APA Accreditation: Clinical PhD (Doctor of Philosophy).

Student Applications/Admissions:
Student Applications
Clinical PhD (Doctor of Philosophy)—Applications 2004–2005, 350. Total applicants accepted 2004–2005, 25. Openings 2005–2006, 12. The Median number of years required for completion of a degree are 6. *Psychometric PhD (Doctor of Philosophy)*—Applications 2004–2005, 11. Total applicants accepted 2004–2005, 3. Openings 2005–2006, 5. The Median number of years required for completion of a degree are 5. The number of students enrolled full and part-time who were dismissed or voluntarily withdrew from this program area were 0. *Applied Developmental Psychology PhD (Doctor of Philosophy)*—Applications 2004–2005, 30. Total applicants accepted 2004–2005, 9. Openings 2005–2006, 6. The Median number of years required for completion of a degree are 5. The number of students enrolled full and part-time who were dismissed or voluntarily withdrew from this program area were 1.

Admissions Requirements:
Scores: Entries appear in this order: required test or GPA, minimum score (if required), median score of students entering

in 2003–2004. Master's Programs: GRE-V no minimum stated; GRE-Q no minimum stated; GRE-V+Q no minimum stated; GRE-Analytical no minimum stated; GRE-Subject(Psych) no minimum stated; MAT no minimum stated; overall undergraduate GPA no minimum stated; last 2 years GPA no minimum stated; psychology GPA no minimum stated. Doctoral Programs: GRE-V no minimum stated; GRE-Q no minimum stated; GRE-V+Q no minimum stated; GRE-Analytical 650; GRE-Subject(Psych) no minimum stated; MAT no minimum stated; overall undergraduate GPA 3.5; last 2 years GPA no minimum stated; psychology GPA no minimum stated. Clinical average GRE and V+Q is 650.

Other Criteria: (importance of criteria rated low, medium, or high): GRE/MAT scores high, research experience high, work experience medium, extracurricular activity medium, clinically related public service medium, GPA high, letters of recommendation high, interview high, statement of goals and objectives high.

Student Characteristics: The following represents characteristics of students in 2004–2005 in all graduate psychology programs in the department: Female–full-time 18, part-time 0; Male–full-time 7, part-time 0; African American/Black–full-time 5, part-time 0; Hispanic/Latino(a)–full-time 4, part-time 0; Asian/Pacific Islander–full-time 3, part-time 0; American Indian/Alaska Native–full-time 0, part-time 0; Caucasian–full-time 0, part-time 0.

Financial Information/Assistance:
Tuition for Full-Time Study: *Doctoral:* State residents: $720 per credit hour; Nonstate residents: $720 per credit hour. Tuition is subject to change. See the following Web site for updates and changes in tuition costs: http://www.fordham.edu/faculty/Graduate_Schools/GSAS_Fees_for_2002206632.html.

Financial Assistance:
First Year Students: Teaching assistantships available for first-year. Average amount paid per academic year: $12,500. Average number of hours worked per week: 15. Apply by January 8. Tuition remission given: full. Research assistantships available for first-year. Average amount paid per academic year: $12,500. Average number of hours worked per week: 15. Apply by January 8. Tuition remission given: full. Fellowships and scholarships available for first-year. Average amount paid per academic year: $15,000. Average number of hours worked per week: 8. Apply by January 8. Tuition remission given: full.

Advanced Students: Teaching assistantships available for advanced students. Average amount paid per academic year: $12,500. Average number of hours worked per week: 15. Apply by February 15. Tuition remission given: full. Research assistantships available for advanced students. Average amount paid per academic year: $12,500. Average number of hours worked per week: 15. Apply by February 15. Tuition remission given: full. Fellowships and scholarships available for advanced students. Average amount paid per academic year: $15,000. Average number of hours worked per week: 15. Apply by February 15. Tuition remission given: full.

Contact Information: Of all students currently enrolled full-time, 85% benefitted from one or more of the listed financial assistance programs. Application and information available online at: http://www.fordham.edu/faculty/Graduate_Schools/Financial_Aid6667.html.

Internships/Practica: Internships in a variety of public and private facilities are available for students after they have completed their coursework in the program. For those doctoral students for whom a professional internship is required prior to graduation, 17 applied in 2003–2004. Of those who applied, 3 were placed in internships listed by the Association of Psychology Postdoctoral and Internship Programs (APPIC); 11 were placed in APA accredited internships.

Housing and Day Care: No on-campus housing is available. No on-campus day care facilities are available.

Employment of Department Graduates:

Master's Degree Graduates: Of those who graduated in the academic year 2003–2004, the following categories and numbers represent the post-graduate activities and employment of master's degree graduates: Enrolled in a post-doctoral residency/fellowship (n/a), employed in independent practice (n/a), total from the above (master's) (0).

Doctoral Degree Graduates: Of those who graduated in the academic year 2003–2004, the following categories and numbers represent the post-graduate activities and employment of doctoral degree graduates: Enrolled in a psychology doctoral program (n/a), total from the above (doctoral) (0).

Additional Information:

Orientation, Objectives, and Emphasis of Department: The clinical psychology program prepares students for practice, research, and teaching in the clinical field, emphasizing that they are both professionals and scientists. The courses in the clinical program can be grouped under four major areas: clinical theory and methodology, research topics and methods, behavioral classification and assessment, and treatment approaches, and includes a full-time, one-year internship. The developmental psychology program is designed to train professionals who can conduct both basic and applied research in developmental processes across the life span and who can share their knowledge in academic and community-based setting. A subspecialty in applied developmental psychology (ADP) focuses on the interplay between developmental processes and social contexts including design and evaluation of programs; consultation to courts, lawyers, and public policy makers; development and evaluation of programs and materials directed at children and families; and parent and family education. The psychometrics program focuses on the quantitative and research-oriented communalities relevant to most of the behavioral sciences, and their applications in industry, education, and the health services. Students in the psychometrics program become familiar with statistics, psychological testing, use of computer systems, and other research techniques, as well as with the psychology of individual differences.

Special Facilities or Resources: Clinical psychology uses three large rooms with one-way vision screens and sound recording equipment for testing, interviewing, and psychotherapy. The Human Development Laboratory, which consists of observation rooms and smaller testing rooms, is available for a wide range of psychological projects. Practicum training in both applied developmental and clinical psychology is conducted at various agencies in the metropolitan area. The department has microcomputers for student use as well as terminals connected with the university's central computer.

Application Information:

Send to: Graduate Admissions Office, Keating 216. Students are admitted in the Fall, application deadline January 8. Paper Application fee is $75; electronic application fee is $60.

Fordham University (2004 data)

Pastoral Counseling and Spiritual Care: Pastoral Psychology
Graduate School of Religion and Religious Education
441 E. Fordham Road
Bronx, NY 10458-9993
Telephone: (718) 817-4800
Fax: (718) 817-3352
E-mail: *vnovak@fordham.edu*
Web: *http://www.fordham.edu/gsre/grrb_main.html*

Department Information:

1999. Dean and Chair: Vincent M. Novak, S. J. Number of Faculty: total–full-time 8, part-time 5; women–full-time 3, part-time 3; minority–full-time 1.

Programs and Degrees Offered:

Listed in the following order: Program area, degree type (T if terminal Master's), number awarded 7/03–6/04. Pastoral Counseling and Spirit MA/MS (Master of Arts/Science) (T) 3.

Student Applications/Admissions:

Student Applications

Pastoral Counseling and Spirit MA/MS (Master of Arts/Science)— Applications 2004–2005, 6. Total applicants accepted 2004–2005, 6. Openings 2005–2006, 12. The Median number of years required for completion of a degree are 2. The number of students enrolled full and part-time who were dismissed or voluntarily withdrew from this program area were 0.

Admissions Requirements:

Scores: Entries appear in this order: required test or GPA, minimum score (if required), median score of students entering in 2003–2004. Master's Programs: MAT no minimum stated; overall undergraduate GPA no minimum stated; last 2 years GPA no minimum stated. Doctoral Programs: MAT no minimum stated.

Other Criteria: (importance of criteria rated low, medium, or high): GRE/MAT scores medium, work experience low, extracurricular activity low, GPA high, letters of recommendation high, interview high, statement of goals and objectives high.

Student Characteristics: The following represents characteristics of students in 2004–2005 in all graduate psychology programs in the department: Female–full-time 6, part-time 0; Male–full-time 18, part-time 0; African American/Black–full-time 1, part-time 0; Hispanic/Latino(a)–full-time 2, part-time 0; Asian/Pacific Islander–full-time 0, part-time 0; American Indian/Alaska Native–full-time 0, part-time 0; Caucasian–full-time 0, part-time 0.

Financial Information/Assistance:

Tuition for Full-Time Study: *Master's:* State residents: $566 per credit hour; Nonstate residents: $566 per credit hour. *Doctoral:*

State residents: $566 per credit hour; Nonstate residents: $566 per credit hour.

Financial Assistance:

First Year Students: Fellowships and scholarships available for first-year. Average number of hours worked per week: 6. Tuition remission given: partial.

Advanced Students: Fellowships and scholarships available for advanced students. Average number of hours worked per week: 6. Tuition remission given: partial.

Contact Information: Of all students currently enrolled full-time, 40% benefitted from one or more of the listed financial assistance programs.

Internships/Practica: In conjunction with the MA program, Clinical Pastoral Education (CPE) is available in neighboring hospitals in New York City. One unit of CPE can account for the equivalent of 6 graduate credits in the degree program. Field Placement will be an essential part of the core curriculum, along with Pastoral Interviewing and Diagnosis.

Housing and Day Care: No on-campus housing is available. No on-campus day care facilities are available.

Employment of Department Graduates:

Master's Degree Graduates: Of those who graduated in the academic year 2003–2004, the following categories and numbers represent the post-graduate activities and employment of master's degree graduates: Enrolled in a post-doctoral residency/fellowship (n/a), employed in independent practice (n/a), total from the above (master's) (0).

Doctoral Degree Graduates: Of those who graduated in the academic year 2003–2004, the following categories and numbers represent the post-graduate activities and employment of doctoral degree graduates: Enrolled in a psychology doctoral program (n/a), total from the above (doctoral) (0).

Additional Information:

Orientation, Objectives, and Emphasis of Department: The Master of Arts in Pastoral Counseling and Spiritual Care is a professional degree registered in 1999 with the Office of Higher Education for the State of New York. It accepted the first cohort of 8 degree candidates in this graduate school for the Fall semester 2000, commencing August 28 at Fordham University's Rose Hill campus. Its overarching goal is to integrate the human sciences and counseling skills with the spiritual insights degree candidates seek to derive from their religious faiths. It aims to train pastoral counselors for all institutional environments of church and state: Practitioners in health care and care of the elderly, nursing and medical personnel, parish personnel, clergy and lay, who minister to persons in need emotionally and spiritually. The body-mind-spirit model operates here in serving the needs of complete human beings in all facets of their personhood. With problematic HMOs, short-term hospital care, and increasing necessity for long-term home care, the program seeks to turn out knowledgeable and highly motivated leaders for the different institutions of society. Partners in Healing is the program's theme, providing a rich association with a New York ecumenical organization with that name, founded by one of our present full-time faculty.

Special Facilities or Resources: This graduate school enjoys its own professional library. The University library, it should be noted, is state-of-the-art on the Rose Hill campus. Computer facilities are available to students.

Application Information:
Send to: Dean, Graduate School of Religion and Religious Education, 441. E. Fordham Road, Bronx, NY 10458-9993. Application available online. Students are admitted in the Fall, application deadline April 15. *Fee:* $60.

Hofstra University
Department of Psychology
Hofstra College of Liberal Arts and Sciences
Hauser Hall
Hempstead, NY 11549
Telephone: (516) 463-5624
Fax: (516) 463-6052
E-mail: *psyrwm@mail1.hofstra.edu*
Web: *http://www.hofstra.edu/Academics/HCLAS/Psychology/*

Department Information:
1948. Chairperson: Robert Motta, PhD Number of Faculty: total–full-time 26, part-time 30; women–full-time 8, part-time 13; minority–full-time 1; faculty subject to the Americans With Disabilities Act 1.

Programs and Degrees Offered:
Listed in the following order: Program area, degree type (T if terminal Master's), number awarded 7/03–6/04. Combined Clinical and School PhD (Doctor of Philosophy) 20, Industrial-Organization MA/MS (Master of Arts/Science) (T) 22, School-Community PsyD (Doctor of Psychology) 1.

Student Applications/Admissions:

Student Applications

Combined Clinical and School PhD (Doctor of Philosophy)—Applications 2004–2005, 137. Total applicants accepted 2004–2005, 41. Openings 2005–2006, 16. The Median number of years required for completion of a degree are 5. The number of students enrolled full and part-time who were dismissed or voluntarily withdrew from this program area were 1. *Industrial-Organization MA/MS (Master of Arts/Science)*—Applications 2004–2005, 85. Total applicants accepted 2004–2005, 55. Total enrolled 2004–2005 full-time, 29, part-time, 10. Openings 2005–2006, 32. The Median number of years required for completion of a degree are 2. The number of students enrolled full and part-time who were dismissed or voluntarily withdrew from this program area were 1. *School-Community PsyD (Doctor of Psychology)*—Applications 2004–2005, 80. Total applicants accepted 2004–2005, 25. Total enrolled 2004–2005 full-time, 55, part-time, 25. Openings 2005–2006, 15. The Median number of years required for completion of a degree are 5.

Admissions Requirements:

Scores: Entries appear in this order: required test or GPA, minimum score (if required), median score of students entering in 2003–2004. Master's Programs: GRE-V 500, 530; GRE-Q 500, 560; overall undergraduate GPA 3.0, 3.2. Applications are accepted from students with undergraduate preparation in Psychology or Business. Doctoral Programs: GRE-V 500, 551;

GRE-Q 500, 574; GRE-V+Q 1000, 1125; GRE-Subject(Psych) no minimum stated, 610; overall undergraduate GPA 3.0, 3.3.

Other Criteria: (importance of criteria rated low, medium, or high): GRE/MAT scores high, research experience medium, work experience medium, extracurricular activity low, clinically related public service medium, GPA high, letters of recommendation medium, interview high, statement of goals and objectives medium. For Combined Clinical and School PhD program: research experience high, especially professional presentations and publications, clinically related public service high, statement of goals and objectives high. For PsyD program: research experience low, clinically related public service medium, statement of goals and objectives medium.

Student Characteristics: The following represents characteristics of students in 2004–2005 in all graduate psychology programs in the department: Caucasian–full-time 0, part-time 0.

Financial Information/Assistance:

Tuition for Full-Time Study: *Master's:* State residents: $517 per credit hour; Nonstate residents: $517 per credit hour. *Doctoral:* State residents: $517 per credit hour; Nonstate residents: $517 per credit hour. Tuition is subject to change.

Financial Assistance:

First Year Students: Teaching assistantships available for first-year. Average number of hours worked per week: 6. Apply by variable. Research assistantships available for first-year. Average number of hours worked per week: 5. Apply by variable. Tuition remission given: partial. Fellowships and scholarships available for first-year. Apply by variable. Tuition remission given: partial.

Advanced Students: Teaching assistantships available for advanced students. Average number of hours worked per week: 6. Apply by variable. Research assistantships available for advanced students. Average number of hours worked per week: 5. Apply by variable. Tuition remission given: partial. Fellowships and scholarships available for advanced students. Apply by variable. Tuition remission given: partial.

Contact Information: Of all students currently enrolled full-time, 33% benefitted from one or more of the listed financial assistance programs.

Internships/Practica: In the PhD and PsyD programs students complete a series of practica in which assessment, testing, and interviewing skills are developed. PhD students complete various courses and role playing experiences in adult psychotherapy. All doctoral students complete a diversified and extended internship over a 2-year period. PhD students are first placed in a school (2 days per week) and then in a mental health facility such as a clinic, psychiatric hospital or medical center (3 days per week). PsyD students are first placed in a school (3 days per week) and then in a community agency (2 days per week). During their second year MA students in Industrial/Organizational Psychology complete an internship in a business setting.

Housing and Day Care: On-campus housing is available. On-campus day care facilities are available. Child care is available in the Saltzman Community Services Center.

Employment of Department Graduates:

Master's Degree Graduates: Of those who graduated in the academic year 2003–2004, the following categories and numbers represent the post-graduate activities and employment of master's degree graduates: Enrolled in a post-doctoral residency/fellowship (n/a), employed in independent practice (n/a), total from the above (master's) (0).

Doctoral Degree Graduates: Of those who graduated in the academic year 2003–2004, the following categories and numbers represent the post-graduate activities and employment of doctoral degree graduates: Enrolled in a psychology doctoral program (n/a), total from the above (doctoral) (0).

Additional Information:

Orientation, Objectives, and Emphasis of Department: The PhD program in Combined Clinical and School Psychology prepares students for independent clinical practice, institutional school and mental health service, and academic careers. Established in 1967, and fully APA accredited, it immerses students into theory, research findings, and the practice of professional psychology in clinical and school settings. Students complete practica and internships in which assessment, testing, interviewing, and psychotherapy skills are developed by working with patients in hospital, school and clinic settings. In addition to classes on assessment and psychotherapy, coursework focuses upon the basic findings of psychological science. The PhD program in Combined Clinical and School Psychology develops psychologists with 1) a background in psychological theory, 2) competence in the skill sets related to assessment and psychotherapy for professional practice, and 3) the ability to evaluate and conduct research. The program is broadly based upon cognitive-behavioral theories. Students are trained in applied conditioning therapies as well as social learning and cognitive-emotive interventions. Most graduates of the PhD program are employed in schools, mental health clinics and hospitals. Some have chosen less traveled paths by becoming college and university faculty members, research scientists, or editors for psychological publishers. Many engage in full-time or part-time private practice. The PsyD program in School-Community Psychology trains practitioners who are skilled in providing psychological services to children, families, and schools. Schools are viewed as being part of the larger community. Thus, in addition to being trained in a school based, direct service model, emphasis is placed upon training students whose subject of study is the educational or community system in which children develop. PsyD students are trained as consultants who may be involved in educational and mental health program implementation and evaluation in settings such as the judicial system, the schools, personnel agencies, police departments, immigration centers, etc. Most graduates of the PsyD program are employed in schools. The MA program in Industrial/Organizational Psychology prepares students for careers in human resources, training, management, and organizational development. It provides a background in statistics, research design, social psychology, cognition and perception, and learning. The courses in I/O Psychology include selection, training, performance appraisal, worker motivation, and organization development. The curriculum is strengthened by an internship sequence which provides on-site supervised experience working on applied projects in business. The types of work that graduates perform include employee selection, management development, survey research, training, organizational development, performance appraisal, career development and program evaluation.

Special Facilities or Resources: A community services center, the Psychological Evaluation, Research, and Counseling Clinic (PERCC), provides practicum experiences for students in the areas of assessment, intervention, and research. A laboratory, instrumented for videotaping, is equipped to handle research in areas of interviewing, communication, problem solving, psychotherapy, and team building. An outstanding library and a computer center are also available, as are many department microcomputers and videotape equipment. The student workroom has six computers for exclusive doctoral student use and all major software programs are available for student use.

Application Information:
Send to: Graduate Admissions, Bernon Hall, Hofstra University, Hempstead, NY 11549. Students are admitted in the Fall, application deadline January 15. Deadline for the PhD in Combined Clinical and School Psychology is January 15. Deadline for the PsyD in School-Community Psychology is January 15. Applications for the MA in Industrial/Organizational Psychology are accepted on a rolling basis until the class is filled. *Fee:* $40.

Iona College
Department of Psychology/Masters of Arts in Psychology
715 North Avenue
New Rochelle, NY 10801
Telephone: (914) 637-7788
Fax: (914) 633-2528
E-mail: *pgreene@iona.edu*
Web: *http://www.iona.edu/academic/arts_sci/departments/*

Department Information:
1963. Chairperson: Paul Greene, PhD Number of Faculty: total–full-time 9, part-time 20; women–full-time 6, part-time 15; minority–full-time 2.

Programs and Degrees Offered:
Listed in the following order: Program area, degree type (T if terminal Master's), number awarded 7/03–6/04. School MA/MS (Master of Arts/Science) (T) 6, Industrial/Organizational MA/MS (Master of Arts/Science) (T) 0, Mental Health Counseling MA/MS (Master of Arts/Science) (T) 1, Experimental MA/MS (Master of Arts/Science) (T) 2.

Student Applications/Admissions:
Student Applications
School MA/MS (Master of Arts/Science)—Applications 2004–2005, 20. Total applicants accepted 2004–2005, 13. Number enrolled (new admits only) 2004–2005 full-time, 16. Number enrolled (new admits only) 2004–2005 part-time, 5. Total enrolled 2004–2005 full-time, 26, part-time, 10. Openings 2005–2006, 15. The Median number of years required for completion of a degree are 3. The number of students enrolled full and part-time who were dismissed or voluntarily withdrew from this program area were 3. *Industrial/Organizational MA/MS (Master of Arts/Science)*—Number enrolled (new admits only) 2004–2005 full-time, 4. Number enrolled (new admits only) 2004–2005 part-time, 2. Total enrolled 2004–2005 full-

time, 6, part-time, 4. Openings 2005–2006, 8. *Mental Health Counseling MA/MS (Master of Arts/Science)*—Applications 2004–2005, 15. Total applicants accepted 2004–2005, 8. Number enrolled (new admits only) 2004–2005 full-time, 5. Number enrolled (new admits only) 2004–2005 part-time, 2. Total enrolled 2004–2005 full-time, 13, part-time, 2. Openings 2005–2006, 15. The Median number of years required for completion of a degree are 2. The number of students enrolled full and part-time who were dismissed or voluntarily withdrew from this program area were 1. *Experimental MA/MS (Master of Arts/Science)*—Number enrolled (new admits only) 2004–2005 full-time, 2. Total enrolled 2004–2005 full-time, 4, part-time, 2. Openings 2005–2006, 6. The Median number of years required for completion of a degree are 3.

Admissions Requirements:
Scores: Entries appear in this order: required test or GPA, minimum score (if required), median score of students entering in 2003–2004. Master's Programs: overall undergraduate GPA 3.0. The Chair may grant exceptions to the minimum requrements for admission as a non-matriculated student.
Other Criteria: (importance of criteria rated low, medium, or high): research experience high, work experience medium, extracurricular activity medium, clinically related public service medium, GPA high, letters of recommendation high, interview low.

Student Characteristics: The following represents characteristics of students in 2004–2005 in all graduate psychology programs in the department: Female–full-time 39, part-time 17; Male–full-time 11, part-time 1; African American/Black–full-time 1, part-time 4; Hispanic/Latino(a)–full-time 1, part-time 4; Asian/Pacific Islander–full-time 0, part-time 0; American Indian/Alaska Native–full-time 0, part-time 0; Caucasian–full-time 0, part-time 0.

Financial Information/Assistance:
Tuition for Full-Time Study: *Master's:* State residents: $621 per credit hour; Nonstate residents: $621 per credit hour.

Financial Assistance:
First Year Students: Fellowships and scholarships available for first-year. Average amount paid per academic year: $14,500. Average number of hours worked per week: 20. Tuition remission given: partial.
Advanced Students: Fellowships and scholarships available for advanced students. Average amount paid per academic year: $14,500. Average number of hours worked per week: 20. Tuition remission given: partial.
Contact Information: Of all students currently enrolled full-time, 15% benefitted from one or more of the listed financial assistance programs.

Internships/Practica: Students specializing in areas that may meet New York State requirements for employment, certification, or licensure, are required to take appropriate internship courses. While there is no guarantee that the student will get accepted by a site, the Department fully assists its students by providing instruction and personal guidance.

Housing and Day Care: On-campus housing is available. See the following Web site for more information: www.iona.edu. No on-campus day care facilities are available.

Employment of Department Graduates:

Master's Degree Graduates: Of those who graduated in the academic year 2003–2004, the following categories and numbers represent the post-graduate activities and employment of master's degree graduates: Enrolled in a psychology doctoral program (1), enrolled in another graduate/professional program (1), enrolled in a post-doctoral residency/fellowship (n/a), employed in independent practice (n/a), employed in an academic position at a 2-year/4-year college (3), employed in a professional position in a school system (3), employed in business or industry (research/consulting) (2), employed in a hospital/medical center (1), other employment position (1), total from the above (master's) (12).

Doctoral Degree Graduates: Of those who graduated in the academic year 2003–2004, the following categories and numbers represent the post-graduate activities and employment of doctoral degree graduates: Enrolled in a psychology doctoral program (n/a), total from the above (doctoral) (0).

Additional Information:

Orientation, Objectives, and Emphasis of Department: The MA in Psychology degree, with areas of specialization in Experimental Psychology, School Psychology, Industrial/Organizational Psychology, and Applied Mental Health Counseling, has been designed for persons who are considering a career in psychology or who are en route to doctoral study in psychology, or are already employed in the field. The program provides a balance of theoretical, methodological and practical expertise, as well as extensive training in written and oral expression. It is designed to provide pertinent new experiences, to enhance knowledge in substantive areas, and to facilitate maximum development of essential professional competencies and attitudes. The masters program in Psychology has several goals. Students gain an understanding of the scientific method and training in how to frame, test, and evaluate hypotheses; an appreciation of how human problems can be resolved through the application of psychological knowledge, scientific skills, and problem solving strategies; expertise in utilizing the scientific database of psychology to advance the welfare of their fellow citizens; an opportunity to address quality of life issues and complex social problems with techniques of cooperation, social facilitation, listening, and self-improvement.

Personal Behavior Statement: Students are informed of how we expect graduate students to act and are asked to sign a document agreeing to uphold appropriate, ethical standards of behavior.

Special Facilities or Resources: The Department contains 2000 square feet of research space and supports research projects in specialties of psychology including social, perception, developmental, learning, treatment, and cognition. Extensive computer and software capabilities are available.

Application Information:

Send to: Office of Graduate Admissions, School of Arts and Sciences. Students are admitted in the Fall. Programs have rolling admissions. *Fee:* $50.

Long Island University

Department of Psychology
C.W. Post
720 Northern Boulevard
Brookville, NY 11548
Telephone: (516) 299-2377
Fax: (516) 299-3105
E-mail: *gerald.lachter@liu.edu*
Web: *www.cwpost.liunet.edu/cwis/cwp/psych/psych.htm*

Department Information:

1954. Chairperson: Gerald D. Lachter. Number of Faculty: total–full-time 17, part-time 13; women–full-time 6, part-time 7; minority–full-time 1, part-time 1.

Programs and Degrees Offered:

Listed in the following order: Program area, degree type (T if terminal Master's), number awarded 7/03–6/04. Experimental MA/MS (Master of Arts/Science) (T) 3, Clinical PsyD (Doctor of Psychology) 12, Advanced Certificate in Applied Behavior Analysis Other 3.

APA Accreditation: Clinical PsyD (Doctor of Psychology).

Student Applications/Admissions:

Student Applications

Experimental MA/MS (Master of Arts/Science)—Applications 2004–2005, 35. Total applicants accepted 2004–2005, 13. Number enrolled (new admits only) 2004–2005 full-time, 2. Total enrolled 2004–2005 full-time, 3, part-time, 1. Openings 2005–2006, 10. The Median number of years required for completion of a degree are 2. The number of students enrolled full and part-time who were dismissed or voluntarily withdrew from this program area were 1. *Clinical PsyD (Doctor of Psychology)*—Applications 2004–2005, 210. Total applicants accepted 2004–2005, 25. Number enrolled (new admits only) 2004–2005 full-time, 15. Total enrolled 2004–2005 full-time, 86. Openings 2005–2006, 16. The Median number of years required for completion of a degree are 5. *Advanced Certificate in Applied Behavior Analysis Other*—Applications 2004–2005, 20. Total applicants accepted 2004–2005, 11. Number enrolled (new admits only) 2004–2005 part-time, 11. Total enrolled 2004–2005 part-time, 11. Openings 2005–2006, 15. The Median number of years required for completion of a degree is 1. The number of students enrolled full and part-time who were dismissed or voluntarily withdrew from this program area were 0.

Admissions Requirements:

Scores: Entries appear in this order: required test or GPA, minimum score (if required), median score of students entering in 2003–2004. Master's Programs: GRE-V 500, 573; GRE-Q 500, 573; overall undergraduate GPA 3.0, 3.33. GRE's are not required for admission to the Advanced Certificate Program Doctoral Programs: GRE-V 550, 587; GRE-Q 550, 618; GRE-Subject(Psych) 610, 651; overall undergraduate GPA 3.6, 3.49. *Other Criteria:* (importance of criteria rated low, medium, or high): GRE/MAT scores medium, research experience high, work experience high, extracurricular activity low, clinically related public service high, GPA high, letters of recommendation high, interview high, statement of goals and objectives medium.

Student Characteristics: The following represents characteristics of students in 2004–2005 in all graduate psychology programs in the department: Female–full-time 56, part-time 6; Male–full-time 38, part-time 5; African American/Black–full-time 6, part-time 0; Hispanic/Latino(a)–full-time 12, part-time 2; Asian/Pacific Islander–full-time 6, part-time 0; American Indian/Alaska Native–full-time 1, part-time 0; Caucasian–full-time 62, part-time 10; Multi-ethnic–full-time 0, part-time 0; students subject to the Americans With Disabilities Act–full-time 1, part-time 0.

Financial Information/Assistance:

Tuition for Full-Time Study: *Master's:* State residents: $705 per credit hour; Nonstate residents: $705 per credit hour. *Doctoral:* State residents: per academic year $28,800; Nonstate residents: per academic year $28,800. Tuition is subject to change.

Financial Assistance:

First Year Students: Teaching assistantships available for first-year. Tuition remission given: partial. Research assistantships available for first-year. Tuition remission given: partial.

Advanced Students: Teaching assistantships available for advanced students. Tuition remission given: partial. Research assistantships available for advanced students. Tuition remission given: partial.

Contact Information: Of all students currently enrolled full-time, 75% benefitted from one or more of the listed financial assistance programs. Application and information available online at: apply@cwpost.liu.edu.

Internships/Practica: A wide range of internship and practicum placements are available. For those doctoral students for whom a professional internship is required prior to graduation, 15 applied in 2003–2004. Of those who applied, 15 were placed in internships listed by the Association of Psychology Postdoctoral and Internship Programs (APPIC); 15 were placed in APA accredited internships.

Housing and Day Care: On-campus housing is available. See the following Web site for more information: http://www.cwpost.liu.edu/cwis/cwp/stuact/housing/housing.html. On-campus day care facilities are available.

Employment of Department Graduates:

Master's Degree Graduates: Of those who graduated in the academic year 2003–2004, the following categories and numbers represent the post-graduate activities and employment of master's degree graduates: Enrolled in a psychology doctoral program (1), enrolled in another graduate/professional program (0), enrolled in a post-doctoral residency/fellowship (n/a), employed in independent practice (n/a), employed in business or industry (research/consulting) (1), employed in a community mental health/counseling center (1), total from the above (master's) (3).

Doctoral Degree Graduates: Of those who graduated in the academic year 2003–2004, the following categories and numbers represent the post-graduate activities and employment of doctoral degree graduates: Enrolled in a psychology doctoral program (n/a), enrolled in a post-doctoral residency/fellowship (1), employed in independent practice (5), employed in a community mental health/counseling center (6), total from the above (doctoral) (12).

Additional Information:

Orientation, Objectives, and Emphasis of Department: The clinical psychology doctoral program is distinctive in three ways. First, the mission of the program is to teach scholar-practitioners to provide clinical psychology services in the public sector. Second, in addition to developing clinical psychologists with the basic knowledge, skills and values necessary for competent and ethical practice, students receive advanced training in one of three areas of concentration: family violence, developmental disabilities or serious and persistent mental illness. These concentrations represent an attempt to provide underserved populations with highly trained clinical psychologists motivated and able to offer helpful services. Third, the program offers students a focus on two theoretical orientations: psychodynamic and cognitive-behavioral. Each year students receive supervised training in clinical practice at various area mental health facilities. Students also receive considerable individual attention throughout the educational experience. The Master's degree program gives students a broad background in Experimental Psychology. Faculty interests include Behavior Analysis, Cognition and Perception, and Neuroscience. The program is designed to prepare students for admission to doctoral programs, or to give them the skills necessary to obtain employment.

Special Facilities or Resources: Laboratories exist for the study of animal and human learning, cognition and perception, and neuroscience.

Application Information:

Send to: Graduate Admissions, C.W. Post, Brookville, NY 11548. Application available online. URL of online application: http://www.cwpost.liu.edu/cwis/cwp/admissions/graduate/howtoapplyg.html. Students are admitted in the Fall. Programs have rolling admissions. Fall deadlines—February 1 for PsyD; June 1 for MA; August 1 for Advanced Certificate Program. *Fee:* $30.

Long Island University
Psychology/Clinical Psychology
Richard L. Conolly College
1 University Plaza
Brooklyn, NY 11201
Telephone: (718) 488-1164
Fax: (718) 488-1179
E-mail: *nicholas.papouchis@liu.edu*

Department Information:

1967. Director, PhD Program in Clinical Psychology: Nicholas Papouchis. Number of Faculty: total–full-time 15, part-time 6; women–full-time 6, part-time 2; minority–full-time 5, part-time 2.

Programs and Degrees Offered:

Listed in the following order: Program area, degree type (T if terminal Master's), number awarded 7/03–6/04. Clinical PhD (Doctor of Philosophy) 12, general MA/MS (Master of Arts/Science) (T) 27.

APA Accreditation: Clinical PhD (Doctor of Philosophy).

Student Applications/Admissions:

Student Applications

Clinical PhD (Doctor of Philosophy)—Applications 2004–2005, 175. Total applicants accepted 2004–2005, 29. Number enrolled (new admits only) 2004–2005 full-time, 16. Number enrolled (new admits only) 2004–2005 part-time, 0. Total enrolled 2004–2005 full-time, 90, part-time, 19. Openings 2005–2006, 16. The Median number of years required for completion of a degree are 6. The number of students enrolled full and part-time who were dismissed or voluntarily withdrew from this program area were 2. General MA/MS (Master of Arts/Science)—Applications 2004–2005, 40. Total applicants accepted 2004–2005, 34. Number enrolled (new admits only) 2004–2005 full-time, 12. Number enrolled (new admits only) 2004–2005 part-time, 22. Total enrolled 2004–2005 full-time, 26, part-time, 49. Openings 2005–2006, 35. The Median number of years required for completion of a degree are 4. The number of students enrolled full and part-time who were dismissed or voluntarily withdrew from this program area were 0.

Admissions Requirements:

Scores: Entries appear in this order: required test or GPA, minimum score (if required), median score of students entering in 2003–2004. Master's Programs: overall undergraduate GPA 2.75, 3.0; psychology GPA 3.0, 3.2. Doctoral Programs: GRE-V 550, 650; GRE-Q 550, 625; GRE-V+Q 1100, 1275; GRE-Analytical 600, 625; GRE-Subject(Psych) 550, 625; overall undergraduate GPA 3.2, 3.6.

Other Criteria: (importance of criteria rated low, medium, or high): GRE/MAT scores high, research experience medium, work experience medium, extracurricular activity low, clinically related public service medium, GPA high, letters of recommendation high, interview high, statement of goals and objectives medium.

Student Characteristics: The following represents characteristics of students in 2004–2005 in all graduate psychology programs in the department: Female–full-time 90, part-time 54; Male–full-time 26, part-time 14; African American/Black–full-time 19, part-time 18; Hispanic/Latino(a)–full-time 14, part-time 17; Asian/Pacific Islander–full-time 4, part-time 1; American Indian/Alaska Native–full-time 1, part-time 0; Caucasian–full-time 76, part-time 30; Multi-ethnic–full-time 2, part-time 2; students subject to the Americans With Disabilities Act–full-time 0, part-time 0.

Financial Information/Assistance:

Tuition for Full-Time Study: Master's: State residents: $705 per credit hour; Nonstate residents: $705 per credit hour. Doctoral: State residents: per academic year $28,800, $920 per credit hour; Nonstate residents: per academic year $28,800, $920 per credit hour. Tuition is subject to change. See the following Web site for updates and changes in tuition costs: www.liu.edu click on Brooklyn Campus.

Financial Assistance:

First Year Students: Research assistantships available for first-year. Average amount paid per academic year: $1,400. Average number of hours worked per week: 10. Apply by April. Tuition remission given: partial. Fellowships and scholarships available for first-year. Average amount paid per academic year: $4,000. Average number of hours worked per week: 10. Apply by April 15. Tuition remission given: full.

Advanced Students: Teaching assistantships available for advanced students. Average amount paid per academic year: $4,800. Average number of hours worked per week: 10. Apply by April 15. Tuition remission given: partial. Research assistantships available for advanced students. Average amount paid per academic year: $1,400. Average number of hours worked per week: 10. Apply by April 15. Tuition remission given: partial. Fellowships and scholarships available for advanced students. Average amount paid per academic year: $4,000. Average number of hours worked per week: 10. Apply by April 15. Tuition remission given: full.

Contact Information: Of all students currently enrolled full-time, 100% benefitted from one or more of the listed financial assistance programs.

Internships/Practica: Students in the master's program have a variety of practica available to them. Doctoral practicum settings and internships in the New York City Metropolitan area are among the best in the country and offer training with a wide range of clinical patients and a number of specializations. Among these are child training, family training, neuropsychology and forensic training. Students in the PhD program regularly train in the best of these externship and practicum settings, and over the previous three years from 2002 to 2005 doctoral students matched 100% with their internship choices. For 2005-2006 the percentage of doctoral students matching was 90%. For those doctoral students for whom a professional internship is required prior to graduation, 10 applied in 2003–2004. Of those who applied, 10 were placed in internships listed by the Association of Psychology Postdoctoral and Internship Programs (APPIC); 10 were placed in APA accredited internships.

Housing and Day Care: On-campus housing is available. See the following Web site for more information: www.liu.edu, Brooklyn Campus. On-campus day care facilities are available. See the following Web site for more information: www.liu.edu, Brooklyn Campus.

Employment of Department Graduates:

Master's Degree Graduates: Of those who graduated in the academic year 2003–2004, the following categories and numbers represent the post-graduate activities and employment of master's degree graduates: Enrolled in a post-doctoral residency/fellowship (n/a), employed in independent practice (n/a), total from the above (master's) (0).

Doctoral Degree Graduates: Of those who graduated in the academic year 2003–2004, the following categories and numbers represent the post-graduate activities and employment of doctoral degree graduates: Enrolled in a psychology doctoral program (n/a), enrolled in a post-doctoral residency/fellowship (4), employed in a professional position in a school system (1), employed in a community mental health/counseling center (3), employed in a hospital/medical center (4), total from the above (doctoral) (12).

Additional Information:

Orientation, Objectives, and Emphasis of Department: The PhD and master's programs are housed in an urban institution with a multicultural undergraduate student body. This diversity enriches the students' appreciation of the complexity of the clinical and theoretical issues relevant to work in psychology. The theoretical orientation of the clinical training sequence reflects the spectrum of psychodynamic approaches to treatment as well as cognitive-behavioral and family systems approaches. Clinical students are exposed, in a graded series of practicum experiences, to both short-term and longer term approaches to psychotherapy with the New York area's culturally diverse clinical populations. Students are also trained in a range of psychological assessment procedures including cognitive, projective, and neuropsychological testing. The program seeks to train clinical psychologists who are competent in research and carefully grounded in the science of psychology. To this end doctoral students receive extensive training in research design and statistics early in their coursework and complete a second-year research project preparatory to beginning their dissertation. The final goal and emphasis of the department and the PhD program is to enable students to develop a broad base of knowledge in clinical psychology. To this end doctoral students are provided with opportunities for clinical training with adults, children and adolescents; training in family therapy and group therapy; and research training in a range of topics relevant to psychology.

Special Facilities or Resources: The Department of Psychology has the following facilities and resources: An on-site Psychological Services Center where clinical students' clinical work is carefully supervised by the doctoral faculty; an ongoing psychotherapy research group; research labs for the study of unconscious cognitive processes and personality and mood/anxiety disorders; training in child and adolescent clinical work at a number of New York area clinical training facilities; opportunity for specialized electives in neuropsychology; free access to computer training and computer facilities; full-tuition minority research fellowships for selected minority doctoral candidates. Finally, students in the PhD program have the spectrum of New York City's clinical and educational facilities available for them to be trained in. The PhD program has also sponsored the development of the Center for Studies in Ethnicity and Human Development under the leadership of Dr. Carol Magai. This center is devoted to research with diverse ethnic groups and minorities.

Application Information:
Send to: Admissions Office, Long Island University, Brooklyn Campus, 1 University Plaza, Brooklyn, NY 11201. URL of online application: www.liu.edu, click on the Brooklyn Campus Web site. Students are admitted in the Fall, application deadline February 1. For MA program, deadline is one month before the beginning of the semester. *Fee:* $30. For MA program, deadline is one month before.

Marist College
Department of Psychology
Poughkeepsie, NY 12601
Telephone: (845) 575-3000
Fax: (845) 575-3965
E-mail: *james.regan@marist.edu*
Web: *http://www.marist.edu/graduate*

Department Information:
1972. Graduate Program Director: James Regan PhD. Number of Faculty: total–full-time 14, part-time 21; women–full-time 5, part-time 8; minority–full-time 2, part-time 1.

Programs and Degrees Offered:
Listed in the following order: Program area, degree type (T if terminal Master's), number awarded 7/03–6/04. Counseling/Community MA/MS (Master of Arts/Science) (T) 25, Educational MA/MS (Master of Arts/Science) (T) 14, School MA/MS (Master of Arts/Science) (T) 14.

Student Applications/Admissions:
Student Applications
Counseling/ Community MA/MS (Master of Arts/Science)—Applications 2004–2005, 70. Total applicants accepted 2004–2005, 60. Total enrolled 2004–2005 full-time, 22, part-time, 35. Openings 2005–2006, 30. The Median number of years required for completion of a degree are 2. The number of students enrolled full and part-time who were dismissed or voluntarily withdrew from this program area were 3. *Educational MA/MS (Master of Arts/Science)*—Applications 2004–2005, 23. Total applicants accepted 2004–2005, 20. Total enrolled 2004–2005 full-time, 5, part-time, 20. Openings 2005–2006, 20. The Median number of years required for completion of a degree is 1. *School MA/MS (Master of Arts/Science)*—Applications 2004–2005, 96. Total applicants accepted 2004–2005, 77. Total enrolled 2004–2005 full-time, 26, part-time, 39. Openings 2005–2006, 30. The Median number of years required for completion of a degree are 3.

Admissions Requirements:
Scores: Entries appear in this order: required test or GPA, minimum score (if required), median score of students entering in 2003–2004. Master's Programs: GRE-V no minimum stated; GRE-Q no minimum stated; GRE-V+Q no minimum stated, 1000; GRE-Analytical no minimum stated; overall undergraduate GPA 3.00, 3.30; psychology GPA 3.00, 3.40.
Other Criteria: (importance of criteria rated low, medium, or high): GRE/MAT scores medium, research experience medium, work experience medium, extracurricular activity low, clinically related public service medium, GPA high, letters of recommendation medium, interview medium, statement of goals and objectives medium.

Student Characteristics: The following represents characteristics of students in 2004–2005 in all graduate psychology programs in the department: Female–full-time 45, part-time 72; Male–full-time 8, part-time 22; African American/Black–full-time 5, part-time 4; Hispanic/Latino(a)–full-time 4, part-time 9; Asian/Pacific Islander–full-time 1, part-time 3; American Indian/Alaska Native–full-time 0, part-time 3; Caucasian–full-time 0, part-time 0; Multi-ethnic–part-time 3; students subject to the Americans With Disabilities Act–full-time 1, part-time 2.

Financial Information/Assistance:
Tuition for Full-Time Study: *Master's:* State residents: per academic year $12,000, $562 per credit hour; Nonstate residents: per academic year $12,000, $562 per credit hour. Tuition is subject to change. See the following Web site for updates and changes in tuition costs: www.marist.edu.

Financial Assistance:
First Year Students: Research assistantships available for first-year. Average amount paid per academic year: $4,500. Average number of hours worked per week: 10. Apply by August 1.

Tuition remission given: partial. Fellowships and scholarships available for first-year.

Advanced Students: Research assistantships available for advanced students. Average amount paid per academic year: $4,500. Average number of hours worked per week: 10. Apply by August 1. Tuition remission given: partial.

Contact Information: Of all students currently enrolled full-time, 80% benefitted from one or more of the listed financial assistance programs. Application and information available online at: www.marist.edu.

Internships/Practica: The mid-Hudson area has many public and private agencies dealing with mental health, developmental disabilities, criminal justice, and social services. Students choose their own placement site in consultation with faculty supervisor.

Housing and Day Care: No on-campus housing is available. No on-campus day care facilities are available.

Employment of Department Graduates:

Master's Degree Graduates: Of those who graduated in the academic year 2003–2004, the following categories and numbers represent the post-graduate activities and employment of master's degree graduates: Enrolled in a psychology doctoral program (5), enrolled in another graduate/professional program (5), enrolled in a post-doctoral residency/fellowship (n/a), employed in independent practice (n/a), employed in an academic position at a 2-year/4-year college (3), employed in other positions at a higher education institution (3), employed in a professional position in a school system (22), employed in business or industry (research/consulting) (2), employed in business or industry (management) (3), employed in a government agency (research) (2), employed in a government agency (professional services) (1), employed in a community mental health/counseling center (8), employed in a hospital/medical center (2), still seeking employment (2), total from the above (master's) (58).

Doctoral Degree Graduates: Of those who graduated in the academic year 2003–2004, the following categories and numbers represent the post-graduate activities and employment of doctoral degree graduates: Enrolled in a psychology doctoral program (n/a), total from the above (doctoral) (0).

Additional Information:

Orientation, Objectives, and Emphasis of Department: The Master of Arts in Psychology focuses on counseling and community psychology. The goal of the program is to provide students with the relevant theory, skills, and practical experience that will enable them to perform competently in assessing individual differences, in counseling, and in planning and implementing effective individual, group, and system level interventions. Students interested in working in community settings will find a variety of opportunities for "hands-on" experience.

Special Facilities or Resources: Interested students can assist in research at facilities such as the Nathan Kline Research Institute, The Center for Advanced Brain Imaging, The Marist Institute for Community Research, Hudson River Psychiatric Center, Dutchess County Department of Mental Hygiene and Public Health, and the Montrose and Castlepoint Veterans Hospitals.

Information for Students With Physical Disabilities: SpecServ@Marist.edu.

Application Information:
Send to: Director of Graduate Admissions, Marist College, Poughkeepsie, NY 12601. Application available online. URL of online application: www.marist.edu/graduate. Students are admitted in the Fall, application deadline August 1; Spring, application deadline December 15; Summer, application deadline April 15. Rolling deadline until classes are full. *Fee:* $30.

New School University
Department of Psychology
Graduate Faculty
65 Fifth Avenue, F-330
New York, NY 10003
Telephone: (212) 229-5727
Fax: (212) 989-0846
E-mail: *gfwebmaster@newschool.edu*
Web: *http://www.newschool.edu/gf/psy/*

Department Information:
1936. Chairperson: Michael F. Schober, PhD Number of Faculty: total–full-time 12, part-time 2; women–full-time 5, part-time 1; minority–full-time 2.

Programs and Degrees Offered:
Listed in the following order: Program area, degree type (T if terminal Master's), number awarded 7/03–6/04. Mental Health Substance Abuse MA/MS (Master of Arts/Science) (T) 4, Clinical Psychology PhD (Doctor of Philosophy) 12, General Psychology MA/MS (Master of Arts/Science) (T) 39, General Psychology PhD (Doctor of Philosophy) 3.

APA Accreditation: Clinical PhD (Doctor of Philosophy).

Student Applications/Admissions:
Student Applications
Mental Health Substance Abuse MA/MS (Master of Arts/Science)—Applications 2004–2005, 39. Total applicants accepted 2004–2005, 26. Number enrolled (new admits only) 2004–2005 full-time, 8. Total enrolled 2004–2005 full-time, 11. Openings 2005–2006, 8. The Median number of years required for completion of a degree are 2. The number of students enrolled full and part-time who were dismissed or voluntarily withdrew from this program area were 0. *Clinical Psychology PhD (Doctor of Philosophy)*—Applications 2004–2005, 30. Total applicants accepted 2004–2005, 16. Total enrolled 2004–2005 full-time, 86. Openings 2005–2006, 16. The Median number of years required for completion of a degree are 7. The number of students enrolled full and part-time who were dismissed or voluntarily withdrew from this program area were 1. *General Psychology MA/MS (Master of Arts/Science)*—Applications 2004–2005, 284. Total applicants accepted 2004–2005, 229. Number enrolled (new admits only) 2004–2005 full-time, 70. Total enrolled 2004–2005 full-time, 65, part-time, 36. Openings 2005–2006, 53. The Median number of years required for completion of a degree are 2. The number of students enrolled full and part-time who were dismissed or voluntarily withdrew from this program area were 7. *General Psychology PhD (Doctor of Philosophy)*—Applications 2004–2005, 12. Total applicants accepted 2004–2005, 9. Number

enrolled (new admits only) 2004–2005 full-time, 9. Total enrolled 2004–2005 full-time, 27. Openings 2005–2006, 10. The Median number of years required for completion of a degree are 5. The number of students enrolled full and part-time who were dismissed or voluntarily withdrew from this program area were 0.

Admissions Requirements:

Scores: Entries appear in this order: required test or GPA, minimum score (if required), median score of students entering in 2003–2004. Master's Programs: GRE-V 400, 525; GRE-Q 400, 590; GRE-Analytical 400, 610; overall undergraduate GPA 3.30, 3.17. Doctoral Programs: overall undergraduate GPA 3.33, 3.50. GRE scores are included in applications to our Master's Programs only. Since all applicants to our PhD programs are New School Master's students, and considering that the GRE is not a consideration for admission into the PhD programs, there is no need for GRE scores to be reported a second time.

Other Criteria: (importance of criteria rated low, medium, or high): research experience high, work experience high, extracurricular activity medium, clinically related public service high, GPA high, letters of recommendation high, interview high, statement of goals and objectives high, writing sample high. Only Master's students at New School University are eligible to apply to our PhD Programs. Outside applicants with previous graduate credit must apply first to the MA program at New School University, then, once they complete 12 credits of coursework here, they may transfer credits from a previous degree. Often, students with previous graduate credit are able to enter the PhD Program after only one year of study here. Only Clinical PhD applicants are interviewed; all PhD applicants submit a detailed statement and research plan. All PhD applicants must have a 3.30 GPA in their Master's level courses and must successfully complete the MA comprehensive examinations.

Student Characteristics: The following represents characteristics of students in 2004–2005 in all graduate psychology programs in the department: Female–full-time 174, part-time 21; Male–full-time 54, part-time 6; African American/Black–full-time 10, part-time 2; Hispanic/Latino(a)–full-time 16, part-time 1; Asian/Pacific Islander–full-time 9, part-time 2; American Indian/Alaska Native–full-time 1, part-time 0; Caucasian–full-time 135, part-time 18; Multi-ethnic–full-time 5, part-time 1; students subject to the Americans With Disabilities Act–full-time 5, part-time 0.

Financial Information/Assistance:

Tuition for Full-Time Study: *Master's:* State residents: $1,200 per credit hour; Nonstate residents: $1,200 per credit hour. *Doctoral:* State residents: $1,200 per credit hour; Nonstate residents: $1,200 per credit hour. Tuition is subject to change. See the following Web site for updates and changes in tuition costs: www.newschool.edu/gf.

Financial Assistance:

First Year Students: Fellowships and scholarships available for first-year. Average amount paid per academic year: $5,877. Apply by January 15. Tuition remission given: partial.

Advanced Students: Teaching assistantships available for advanced students. Average amount paid per academic year: $6,000. Average number of hours worked per week: 10. Apply by

March 1. Research assistantships available for advanced students. Average amount paid per academic year: $6,000. Average number of hours worked per week: 16. Apply by March 1. Fellowships and scholarships available for advanced students. Average amount paid per academic year: $10,800. Apply by March 1. Tuition remission given: partial.

Contact Information: Of all students currently enrolled full-time, 78% benefitted from one or more of the listed financial assistance programs.

Internships/Practica: Depending on their research areas, students pursuing general psychology can gain internship and work experience in a range of applied settings, including industry research labs and non-profit organizations. Master's level psychology students who are interested in applying to the Clinical PhD Program are strongly encouraged to pursue volunteer clinical positions available at local hospitals or institutes. First year doctoral students in the Clinical Program participate in an assessment and diagnosis practicum in which they conduct supervised psychological intake evaluations on Beth Israel Medical Center's Psychiatry Outpatient Service for Adults. These students also spend 4 hours per week on an inpatient rotation, co-leading groups and attending relevant unit meetings. This experience provides strong preparation for the 16-20 hour per week externships in their second and third years of PhD level study at approved, affiliated sites. After completing their dissertation proposals, all Clinical PhD students are required to complete an APA-accredited internship. During the internship application process, students receive administrative and academic support services from the Assistant Director of Clinical Training and the Clinical Coordinator. For those doctoral students for whom a professional internship is required prior to graduation, 12 applied in 2003–2004. Of those who applied, 11 were placed in internships listed by the Association of Psychology Postdoctoral and Internship Programs (APPIC); 11 were placed in APA accredited internships.

Housing and Day Care: On-campus housing is available. New School University, Office of Housing, 65 5th Avenue, Rm. 269, New York, NY 10003; ricarteF@newschool.edu (Director of Housing). No on-campus day care facilities are available.

Employment of Department Graduates:

Master's Degree Graduates: Of those who graduated in the academic year 2003–2004, the following categories and numbers represent the post-graduate activities and employment of master's degree graduates: Enrolled in a post-doctoral residency/fellowship (n/a), employed in independent practice (n/a), total from the above (master's) (0).

Doctoral Degree Graduates: Of those who graduated in the academic year 2003–2004, the following categories and numbers represent the post-graduate activities and employment of doctoral degree graduates: Enrolled in a psychology doctoral program (n/a), enrolled in a post-doctoral residency/fellowship (2), employed in a community mental health/counseling center (4), employed in a hospital/medical center (3), not seeking employment (1), do not know (2), total from the above (doctoral) (12).

Additional Information:

Orientation, Objectives, and Emphasis of Department: At New School University, the Psychology Department provides a broad theoretical background emphasizing scientific study of psychology and representing the several academic approaches to human experience and behavior. One important feature of the department is the unusual degree of cooperation between clinical and non-clinical faculty, i.e., clinical students regularly choose non-clinical faculty as mentors. The master's program accommodates both full- and part-time students, with courses in cognitive, personality, developmental, social, and clinical psychology. All MA students design and carry out original individual research projects. At the PhD level, students may specialize in general psychology (cognitive, social-personality, developmental) or in clinical psychology. Admission to doctoral candidacy is based on students' academic performance in our master's program, interviews with faculty, a personal essay, and passing the psychology comprehensive examination. Students who have already completed sufficient graduate study elsewhere may apply to the PhD Program during their first year of MA level study in our program, in contrast to other students who apply during their second year. Broadly speaking, our programs prepare students as scientists with a critical eye to mainstream assumptions in the various subfields of psychology. Clinical students are prepared as scientist–practitioners equally at home in clinical, research, and teaching settings.

Special Facilities or Resources: All students may participate in collaborative research projects with faculty in labs that feature equipment and software dedicated to the particular research carried out by department members (see http://www.newschool.edu/gf/psy). Students have library access not only at New School social science libraries but also at NYU's Bobst library, the Cooper Union Library, and other libraries within a New York consortium. Various state of the art computing facilities are also available. For clinical PhD students, the New School-Beth Israel Center for Clinical Training and Research provides unusually broad training in outpatient clinics, inpatient units, and clinical research programs. First year clinical PhD students have access to the Psychology library at Beth Israel Medical Center, perform intake evaluations on Beth Israel's psychiatry outpatient clinic and provide group therapy on adult inpatient units. They also attend psychiatry grand rounds and training seminars on child abuse and assault prevention. Second and third-year clinical students may continue work at Beth Israel Medical Center conducting therapy through the Brief Psychotherapy Research Project. Psychotherapy sessions are videotaped with patients' consent, and students review these sessions in supervision with Beth Israel supervising psychologists. Cases are also discussed in externship seminars with New School University faculty.

Information for Students With Physical Disabilities: See the following Web site for more information: http://www.newschool.edu/studentaffairs/st_disability_over.html.

Application Information:
Send to: Emanual Lomax, Director of Admissions, Graduate Faculty—New School University, 65 Fifth Avenue, New York, NY 10003. Students are admitted in the Fall, application deadline January 15; Spring, application deadline December 15. Programs have rolling admissions. Applications received or completed after January 15 are considered for Admissions and Financial Aid on a rolling basis. *Fee:* $40. Deadline is January 15 for financial aid consideration. For master's level students who will be applying for admission without financial aid, admission will be made up to the begining date of fall classes.

New York University
Department of Applied Psychology
The Steinhardt School of Education
239 Greene Street, Rm. 400 and Rm. 500
New York, NY 10003
Telephone: (212) 998-5555
Fax: (212) 995-3654
E-mail: *applied.psychology@nyu.edu*
Web: *http://www.nyu.edu/education/appsych*

Department Information:
1990. Chairperson: Dr. Perry N. Halkitis. Number of Faculty: total–full-time 28, part-time 45; women–full-time 17, part-time 24; minority–full-time 8, part-time 9.

Programs and Degrees Offered:
Listed in the following order: Program area, degree type (T if terminal Master's), number awarded 7/03–6/04. Counseling and Guidance MA/MS (Master of Arts/Science) (T) 56, Counseling PhD (Doctor of Philosophy) 5, Psychological Development PhD (Doctor of Philosophy) 1, Educational Psychology MA/MS (Master of Arts/Science) (T) 22, School Psychologist PhD (Doctor of Philosophy) 2, School PsyD (Doctor of Psychology) 7.

APA Accreditation: Counseling PhD (Doctor of Philosophy). School PhD (Doctor of Philosophy). School PsyD (Doctor of Psychology).

Student Applications/Admissions:
Student Applications
Counseling and Guidance MA/MS (Master of Arts/Science)—Applications 2004–2005, 271. Total applicants accepted 2004–2005, 87. Number enrolled (new admits only) 2004–2005 full-time, 49. Number enrolled (new admits only) 2004–2005 part-time, 38. Total enrolled 2004–2005 full-time, 95, part-time, 79. Openings 2005–2006, 80. *Counseling PhD (Doctor of Philosophy)*—Applications 2004–2005, 113. Total applicants accepted 2004–2005, 2. Number enrolled (new admits only) 2004–2005 full-time, 2. Total enrolled 2004–2005 full-time, 27, part-time, 25. Openings 2005–2006, 4. *Psychological Development PhD (Doctor of Philosophy)*—Applications 2004–2005, 36. Total applicants accepted 2004–2005, 6. Number enrolled (new admits only) 2004–2005 full-time, 5. Number enrolled (new admits only) 2004–2005 part-time, 1. Total enrolled 2004–2005 full-time, 8, part-time, 13. Openings 2005–2006, 4. The number of students enrolled full and part-time who were dismissed or voluntarily withdrew from this program area were 1. *Educational Psychology MA/MS (Master of Arts/Science)*—Applications 2004–2005, 70. Total applicants accepted 2004–2005, 35. Total enrolled 2004–2005 full-time, 22, part-time, 43. Openings 2005–2006, 30. *School Psychologist PhD (Doctor of Philosophy)*—Applications 2004–2005, 48. Total applicants accepted 2004–2005, 2. Number enrolled (new admits only) 2004–2005 full-time, 2. Total enrolled 2004–2005 full-time, 11, part-time, 9. Openings 2005–2006, 4. The Median number of years required for completion of a degree are 7. *School PsyD (Doctor of Psychology)*—Applications 2004–2005, 74. Total applicants accepted 2004–2005, 0. Total enrolled 2004–2005 full-time, 20, part-time, 17. The Median number of years required for completion of a degree are 7.

Admissions Requirements:

Scores: Entries appear in this order: required test or GPA, minimum score (if required), median score of students entering in 2003–2004. Master's Programs: overall undergraduate GPA no minimum stated, 3.20. Master's programs do not require GRE scores. Doctoral Programs: GRE-V 500, 520; GRE-Q 500, 600; GRE-V+Q 1000, 1100; overall undergraduate GPA no minimum stated, 3.20.

Other Criteria: (importance of criteria rated low, medium, or high): GRE/MAT scores medium, research experience high, work experience medium, extracurricular activity low, clinically related public service medium, GPA medium, letters of recommendation high, interview high, statement of goals and objectives high. The above criteria range from "medium" to "high" for admission into the doctoral programs. Masters programs primarily consider GPA, statement of goals and objectives, and letters of recommendation; interviews sometimes required for master's applicants. For additional information on admission requirements, go to: www.nyu.edu/education/graduate.admissions.

Student Characteristics: The following represents characteristics of students in 2004–2005 in all graduate psychology programs in the department: Female–full-time 138, part-time 145; Male–full-time 45, part-time 41; African American/Black–full-time 19, part-time 14; Hispanic/Latino(a) full-time 11, part-time 3; Asian/Pacific Islander–full-time 11, part-time 6; American Indian/Alaska Native–full-time 0, part-time 0; Caucasian–full-time 142, part-time 163.

Financial Information/Assistance:

Financial Assistance:

First Year Students: Fellowships and scholarships available for first-year. Average number of hours worked per week: 20.

Advanced Students: Teaching assistantships available for advanced students. Average number of hours worked per week: 20. Tuition remission given: full. Research assistantships available for advanced students. Average number of hours worked per week: 20. Tuition remission given: full. Traineeships available for advanced students. Fellowships and scholarships available for advanced students.

Contact Information: Of all students currently enrolled full-time, 50% benefitted from one or more of the listed financial assistance programs. Application and information available online at: http://www.nyu.edu/education/appsych/.

Internships/Practica: Available in the following areas: school and university counseling; counseling in community agencies, hospitals, and business; school psychology; psychological development; measurement and evaluation.

Housing and Day Care: On-campus housing is available. See the following Web site for more information: http://www.nyu.edu/housing/. No on-campus day care facilities are available.

Employment of Department Graduates:

Master's Degree Graduates: Of those who graduated in the academic year 2003–2004, the following categories and numbers represent the post-graduate activities and employment of master's degree graduates: Enrolled in a post-doctoral residency/fellowship (n/a), employed in independent practice (n/a), total from the above (master's) (0).

Doctoral Degree Graduates: Of those who graduated in the academic year 2003–2004, the following categories and numbers represent the post-graduate activities and employment of doctoral degree graduates: Enrolled in a psychology doctoral program (n/a), total from the above (doctoral) (0).

Additional Information:

Orientation, Objectives, and Emphasis of Department: The cornerstone of our department is the marriage of theory and practice driven by the University's commitment to being a private university in the public service. To this end, the department's programs reflect both a concern for excellence in teaching and the opportunity to learn from involvement in community based data collection. Emphasis and specific core requirements differ somewhat from program to program, but include a solid foundation in the basic psychological disciplines. Departmental faculty have research projects in several areas, and students have the opportunity to participate in community based data collection. Departmental faculty have ongoing research projects in many areas, including: cognition; language; social and emotional development; health and human development; applied measurement and research methods; working people's lives; spirituality; multicultural assessment; group and organizational dynamics; psychopathology and personality; sexual and gender identity; communication and creative expression; trauma and resilience; parenting; immigration.

Special Facilities or Resources: The Infancy Studies Laboratory conducts research in infant temperament, perceptual development, learning and attention, parenting views and child rearing styles. The Measurement Laboratory contains educational and psychological tests and reference books. PC computers are available for data analysis and word processing. The Psychoeducational Center assigns school psychologists-in-training to schools, settlement houses, clinics, and day care centers and is a clearinghouse of scholarly papers resulting from collaborative activities of doctoral students and faculty. The Center for Research on Culture, Development, and Education conducts longitudinal research on the pathways to educational success in early childhood and early adolescence among New York City families of 5 ethnic groups. The Center for Health, Identity, Behavior, & Prevention Studies (CHIBPS) conducts formative and intervention research on social and psychological factors that contribute to HIV transmission and the synergy between drug use, mental health, and HIV transmission. The Child and Family Policy Center conducts research, offers technical assistance and works to disseminate state-of-the field knowledge to bring children's healthy development and school success to the forefront of policymaking, program design, and practice. The Arnold and Rosalie Weiss Resource Center in Applied Psychology provides a departmental library to assist students and researchers within the department.

Information for Students With Physical Disabilities: See the following Web site for more information: http://www.nyu.edu/osl/csd/.

Application Information:

Send to: Office of Graduate Admissions, The Steinhardt School of Education, New York University, 82 Washington Sq. East, Floor 3, New York, NY 10003. Application available online. Students are admitted in the Fall, application deadline MA—February 1; Spring, application deadline MA—December 1. Fall deadline: doctoral—January 15; Ed Psych Master's has rolling admissions. *Fee:* $40. $60 for international students.

New York University

Department of Psychology
Graduate School of Arts and Science
6 Washington Place, Room 550
New York, NY 10003
Telephone: (212) 998-7900
Fax: (212) 995-4018
E-mail: *psychq@psych.nyu.edu*
Web: *http://www.psych.nyu.edu*

Department Information:

1950. Chairperson: Marisa Carrasco. Number of Faculty: total–full-time 40; women–full-time 13; minority–full-time 5.

Programs and Degrees Offered:

Listed in the following order: Program area, degree type (T if terminal Master's), number awarded 7/03–6/04. General Psychology MA/MS (Master of Arts/Science) (T) 25, Industrial/Organizational MA/MS (Master of Arts/Science) (T) 29, Cognition and Perception PhD (Doctor of Philosophy) 3, Social PhD (Doctor of Philosophy) 7, Community PhD (Doctor of Philosophy) 4.

Student Applications/Admissions:

Student Applications

General Psychology MA/MS (Master of Arts/Science)—Applications 2004–2005, 347. Total applicants accepted 2004–2005, 127. Number enrolled (new admits only) 2004–2005 part-time, 69. Total enrolled 2004–2005 part-time, 126. Openings 2005–2006, 50. *Industrial/Organizational MA/MS (Master of Arts/Science)*—Applications 2004–2005, 238. Total applicants accepted 2004–2005, 120. Number enrolled (new admits only) 2004–2005 part-time, 42. Total enrolled 2004–2005 part-time, 114. Openings 2005–2006, 50. *Cognition and Perception PhD (Doctor of Philosophy)*—Applications 2004–2005, 133. Total applicants accepted 2004–2005, 22. Number enrolled (new admits only) 2004–2005 full-time, 9. Total enrolled 2004–2005 full-time, 29. *Social PhD (Doctor of Philosophy)*—Applications 2004–2005, 237. Total applicants accepted 2004–2005, 13. Number enrolled (new admits only) 2004–2005 full-time, 6. Total enrolled 2004–2005 full-time, 30. *Community PhD (Doctor of Philosophy)*—Applications 2004–2005, 77. Total applicants accepted 2004–2005, 4. Number enrolled (new admits only) 2004–2005 full-time, 3.

Admissions Requirements:

Scores: Entries appear in this order: required test or GPA, minimum score (if required), median score of students entering in 2003–2004. Master's Programs: GRE-V 530, 550; GRE-Q 530, 630; GRE-Analytical 530, 650; overall undergraduate GPA 3.0. The Master's program expects a minimum score of 4.5 on the GRE Analytical Writing test. The median score

of enrolled master's students is 5.0. Doctoral Programs: GRE-V no minimum stated; GRE-Q no minimum stated; GRE-Analytical no minimum stated; GRE-Subject(Psych) no minimum stated.

Other Criteria: (importance of criteria rated low, medium, or high): GRE/MAT scores medium, research experience high, work experience low, extracurricular activity low, clinically related public service low, GPA medium, letters of recommendation high, statement of goals and objectives high. These rankings are for the PhD only. For master's program, letters of recommendation and statement of goals and objectives have high importance; other criteria are low; no interviews are given. GRE/GPA varies by program.

Student Characteristics: The following represents characteristics of students in 2004–2005 in all graduate psychology programs in the department: Female–full-time 50, part-time 180; Male–full-time 24, part-time 61; African American/Black–full-time 6, part-time 7; Hispanic/Latino(a)–full-time 6, part-time 14; Asian/Pacific Islander–full-time 12, part-time 48; Caucasian–full-time 44, part-time 131; Multi-ethnic–full-time 2, part-time 7.

Financial Information/Assistance:

Financial Assistance:

First Year Students: Teaching assistantships available for first-year. Average amount paid per academic year: $18,000. Average number of hours worked per week: 20. Apply by December 15. Tuition remission given: full. Research assistantships available for first-year. Average amount paid per academic year: $18,000. Average number of hours worked per week: 20. Apply by December 15. Tuition remission given: full. Traineeships available for first-year. Tuition remission given: full. Fellowships and scholarships available for first-year. Average amount paid per academic year: $18,000. Apply by December 15. Tuition remission given: full.

Advanced Students: Teaching assistantships available for advanced students. Average amount paid per academic year: $18,000. Average number of hours worked per week: 20. Apply by December 15. Tuition remission given: full. Research assistantships available for advanced students. Average amount paid per academic year: $18,000. Average number of hours worked per week: 20. Apply by December 15. Tuition remission given: full. Traineeships available for advanced students. Tuition remission given: full. Fellowships and scholarships available for advanced students. Average amount paid per academic year: $18,000. Apply by December 15. Tuition remission given: full.

Contact Information: Of all students currently enrolled full-time, 100% benefitted from one or more of the listed financial assistance programs. Application and information available online at: http://www.nyu.edu/gsas/Admissions/ObtainApp.html.

Internships/Practica: Master's students may opt to take Fieldwork, which would enable them to obtain supervised experience in selected agencies, clinics, and industrial and non-profit organizations relevant to the career or academic objectives of the student.

Housing and Day Care: On-campus housing is available. See the following Web site for more information: www.nyu.edu/housing/. On-campus day care facilities are available.

Employment of Department Graduates:

Master's Degree Graduates: Of those who graduated in the academic year 2003–2004, the following categories and numbers represent the post-graduate activities and employment of master's degree graduates: Enrolled in a post-doctoral residency/fellowship (n/a), employed in independent practice (n/a), total from the above (master's) (0).

Doctoral Degree Graduates: Of those who graduated in the academic year 2003–2004, the following categories and numbers represent the post-graduate activities and employment of doctoral degree graduates: Enrolled in a psychology doctoral program (n/a), total from the above (doctoral) (0).

Additional Information:

Orientation, Objectives, and Emphasis of Department: The doctoral programs all emphasize research. The community psychology program addresses critical social problems in context through action, research, and theory. It trains students for direct roles in academia, action-research, and policy analysis. The cognition-perception program has faculty whose research focuses on memory, emotion, psycholinguistics, categorization, cognitive neuroscience, visual perception and attention. The social program trains researchers in theory and methods for understanding individuals and groups in social and organizational contexts. Training is provided in subareas ranging from social cognition to motivation, personality, close relationships, groups and organizations. A doctoral concentration in developmental psychology emphasizes research training cutting across the traditional areas of psychology. Students may minor in quantitative psychology or in any of the above programs. The Master's Program in General Psychology has the flexibility to suit students who wish to explore several areas of psychology to find the area that interests them most, as well as students who wish to shape their course of study to fit special interests and needs, including preparation for admission to a doctoral program. The Master's Program in Industrial/Organizational Psychology is designed to prepare graduates to apply research and principles of human behavior to a variety of organizational settings, such as human resources departments, and management consulting firms. The program can also be modified for students who are preparing for admission to doctoral programs in Industrial/Organizational and related fields. Students in the master's programs may opt for either full- or part-time status.

Special Facilities or Resources: The Department of Psychology maintains laboratories, classrooms, project rooms, and a magnetic resonance (MR) neuroimaging facility. Modern laboratories are continually improved through grants from foundations and federal agencies. The Center for Brain Imaging houses a research-dedicated 3 Tesla Seimens MR system for the use of faculty and students interested in research using functional brain imaging. The center includes faculty members from both the Department of Psychology and the Center for Neural Science, as well as individuals whose expertise is in MR physics and statistical methods for analysis. The department maintains several computer classrooms and laboratories, and the University offers technical courses on emerging computational tools. Faculty laboratories are equipped with specialized computer equipment within each of the graduate programs. The department collaborates closely with the Center for Neural Science in maintaining a technical shop.

Application Information:

Send to: New York University, Graduate School of Arts & Sciences, Graduate Enrollment Services, P.O. Box 907, New York, NY 10276-

0907. Students are admitted in the Fall. PhD students admitted only in the Fall (application deadline December 15). Master's in General Psychology: Fall deadline: July 1; Spring deadline: December 1; Summer deadline: April 15. Master's in Industrial/Organizational Psychology: Fall deadline: March 15; Spring deadline: October 15; Summer deadline: March 15. *Fee:* $75. The Graduate School of Arts & Sciences does not waive application fees.

Pace University
Department of Psychology
Dyson College of Arts and Sciences
One Pace Plaza
New York, NY 10038
Telephone: (212) 346-1506
Fax: (212) 346-1618
E-mail: *HKrauss@pace.edu*
Web: *http://www.pace.edu/dyson/psychology*

Department Information:

1961. Chairperson: Herbert H. Krauss. Number of Faculty: total–full-time 14, part-time 12; women–full-time 8, part-time 6; minority–full-time 4, part-time 2.

Programs and Degrees Offered:

Listed in the following order: Program area, degree type (T if terminal Master's), number awarded 7/03–6/04. General MA/MS (Master of Arts/Science) (T) 5, School-Clinical Child Psychology PsyD (Doctor of Psychology) 35.

APA Accreditation: Combination PsyD (Doctor of Psychology).

Student Applications/Admissions:

Student Applications

General MA/MS (*Master of Arts/Science*)—Applications 2004–2005, 20. Total applicants accepted 2004–2005, 15. Total enrolled 2004–2005 full-time, 4, part-time, 20. Openings 2005–2006, 25. *School-Clinical Child Psychology PsyD (Doctor of Psychology)*—Applications 2004–2005, 301. Total applicants accepted 2004–2005, 44. Number enrolled (new admits only) 2004–2005 full-time, 19. Number enrolled (new admits only) 2004–2005 part-time, 0. Total enrolled 2004–2005 full-time, 123, part-time, 9. Openings 2005–2006, 20. The Median number of years required for completion of a degree are 7. The number of students enrolled full and part-time who were dismissed or voluntarily withdrew from this program area was 1.

Admissions Requirements:

Scores: Entries appear in this order: required test or GPA, minimum score (if required), median score of students entering in 2003–2004. Master's Programs: GRE-V no minimum stated; GRE-Q no minimum stated; GRE-V+Q no minimum stated; GRE-Subject(Psych) no minimum stated; overall undergraduate GPA no minimum stated. Doctoral Programs: GRE-V no minimum stated, 560; GRE-Q no minimum stated, 640; GRE-V+Q no minimum stated, 1200; GRE-Analytical no minimum stated; GRE-Subject(Psych) no minimum stated, 650; overall undergraduate GPA no minimum stated, 3.60.

Other Criteria: (importance of criteria rated low, medium, or high): GRE/MAT scores high, research experience medium, work experience medium, extracurricular activity low, clinically related public service medium, GPA high, letters of recommendation high, interview high, statement of goals and objectives high. These criteria are used for the MSEd and PsyD programs only.

Student Characteristics: The following represents characteristics of students in 2004–2005 in all graduate psychology programs in the department: Female–full-time 127, part-time 23; Male–full-time 19, part-time 3; Caucasian–full-time 0, part-time 0; students subject to the Americans With Disabilities Act–full-time 0, part-time 0.

Financial Information/Assistance:

Tuition for Full-Time Study: *Master's:* State residents: $770 per credit hour; Nonstate residents: $770 per credit hour. *Doctoral:* State residents: $820 per credit hour; Nonstate residents: $820 per credit hour. Tuition is subject to change. See the following Web site for updates and changes in tuition costs: gradnyc@pace.edu.

Financial Assistance:

First Year Students: Research assistantships available for first-year. Average amount paid per academic year: $2,500. Average number of hours worked per week: 10. Apply by February 1. Tuition remission given: partial. Fellowships and scholarships available for first-year. Average amount paid per academic year: $4,000. Apply by February 1.

Advanced Students: Teaching assistantships available for advanced students. Apply by February 1. Research assistantships available for advanced students. Average amount paid per academic year: $2,500. Average number of hours worked per week: 10. Apply by February 1. Tuition remission given: partial. Fellowships and scholarships available for advanced students. Average amount paid per academic year: $4,000. Apply by February 1.

Contact Information: Of all students currently enrolled full-time, 50% benefitted from one or more of the listed financial assistance programs. Application and information available online at: gradnyc@pace.edu.

Internships/Practica: Most school psychology and bilingual school psychology internships occur in the New York metropolitan region, including Long Island, Westchester County, and school districts throughout northern New Jersey. Doctoral internships are typically secured through the APPIC system. Doctoral students typically secure internships in the New York metropolitan region.

Housing and Day Care: On-campus housing is available. There is some on-campus housing available. No on-campus day care facilities are available.

Employment of Department Graduates:

Master's Degree Graduates: Of those who graduated in the academic year 2003–2004, the following categories and numbers represent the post-graduate activities and employment of master's degree graduates: Enrolled in a post-doctoral residency/fellowship (n/a), employed in independent practice (n/a), total from the above (master's) (0).

Doctoral Degree Graduates: Of those who graduated in the academic year 2003–2004, the following categories and numbers represent the post-graduate activities and employment of doctoral degree graduates: Enrolled in a psychology doctoral program (n/a), enrolled in a post-doctoral residency/fellowship (1), employed in a professional position in a school system (12), employed in a community mental health/counseling center (3), employed in a hospital/medical center (3), total from the above (doctoral) (19).

Additional Information:

Orientation, Objectives, and Emphasis of Department: The PsyD program in School-Clinical Child Psychology at Pace University is a professional practice training program that is dedicated to the training model of school/clinical child psychologists as scholar-practitioners. The focus is on developing individuals whose theoretical and research knowledge, and professional skills enable them to deliver a broad array of direct and indirect psychological services to infants, children, adolescents, and families, and the personnel, organizations and institutions that serve them. The purpose of the program is to train school/clinical child psychology practitioners to possess broad knowledge about general psychological theoretical foundations, as well as more specific knowledge pertaining to the scientific foundations of psychological practice and professional school-clinical child psychology practice competencies. School psychologists-in-training receive instruction and supervision related to following ethical guidelines and being sensitive to diversity and multicultural issues. The program coordinates placement in university-based and field-based supervised training experiences, which are carefully integrated with theoretical coursework and a seminar, enabling practitioners in training to compare key aspects of professional functioning across a wide variety of settings. There are sixteen specific training goals of the School-Clinical Child Psychology program: 1. Psychoeducational assessment related to school difficulties and learning disorders. 2. Psychological assessment related to personality and mental disorders. 3. Delivery of psychological interventions aimed at ameliorating adjustment and personal difficulties experienced by children, adolescents, and families. 4. Delivery of psychoeducational interventions aimed at ameliorating learning difficulties experienced by children, adolescents, and families. 5. Providing psychological services with an awareness of and sensitivity to ethnic and cultural diversity. 6. Development and/or implementation of programmatic/preventive interventions. 7. Development and/or implementation of a broad range of consultation services. 8. Enlisting the aid of community agencies to secure services or prevent circumstances contributing to unsatisfactory adjustment or behavior problems. 9. Initiating and/or directing group interventions. 10. Initiating and/or directing family interventions. 11. Conducting in-service training sessions for parents and/or school personnel. 12. Coordinating inter-disciplinary assessment and intervention strategies. 13. Providing psychotherapy to children, adolescents, and families. 14. Providing diagnoses related to mental disorders. 15. Carrying out applied research. 16. Supervising the provision of direct psychological services.

Special Facilities or Resources: The Psychology Department maintains the McShane Center for Psychological Services. This on-site training facility provides practicum training for students in the MSEd, MSEd Bilingual, and PsyD programs. For example, training opportunities include biofeedback, interviewing, parent-infant observations, psychodiagnostics, and psychotherapy.

Application Information:

Send to: Graduate Admissions, Pace University, 1 Pace Plaza, New York, NY 10038. Application available online. URL of online application: gradnyc@pace.edu. Students are admitted in the Fall, application deadline February 1; Winter, application deadline August 1; Spring, application deadline December 1; Summer, application deadline May 1. February 1 deadline for MS Ed and PsyD programs. Fall deadline for MA is August 1. *Fee:* $65. Check with graduate admissions for current application fee.

Rensselaer Polytechnic Institute
Cognitive Science
110 8th Street, Carnegie Building, Room #305
Troy, NY 12180-3590
Telephone: (518) 276-6473
Fax: (518) 276-8268
E-mail: *osgane@rpi.edu*
Web: *www.cogsci.rpi.edu*

Department Information:

2000. Chairperson: Selmer Bringsjord. Number of Faculty: total–full-time 18, part-time 5; women–full-time 1, part-time 1; minority–full-time 2.

Programs and Degrees Offered:

Listed in the following order: Program area, degree type ('T' if terminal Master's), number awarded 7/03–6/04. PhD in Cognitive Science PhD (Doctor of Philosophy).

Student Applications/Admissions:

Student Applications

PhD in Cognitive Science PhD (Doctor of Philosophy)—Applications 2004–2005, 32. Total applicants accepted 2004–2005, 5. Number enrolled (new admits only) 2004–2005 full-time, 4. Total enrolled 2004–2005 full-time, 8. Openings 2005–2006, 4.

Admissions Requirements:

Scores: Entries appear in this order: required test or GPA, minimum score (if required), median score of students entering in 2003–2004. Doctoral Programs: GRE-V 600, 620; GRE-Q 600, 780; GRE-V+Q 1200, 1400; GRE-Analytical 5, 5.5.

Other Criteria: (importance of criteria rated low, medium, or high): GRE/MAT scores high, research experience high, work experience low, extracurricular activity low, GPA medium, letters of recommendation high, interview medium, statement of goals and objectives high.

Student Characteristics: The following represents characteristics of students in 2004–2005 in all graduate psychology programs in the department: Female–full-time 1, part-time 0; Male–full-time 7, part-time 0; African American/Black–full-time 0, part-time 0; Hispanic/Latino(a)–full-time 1, part-time 0; Asian/Pacific Islander–full-time 1, part-time 0; American Indian/Alaska Native–full-time 0, part-time 0; Caucasian–full-time 6, part-time 0.

Financial Information/Assistance:

Tuition for Full-Time Study: *Doctoral:* State residents: per academic year $28,950, $1,320 per credit hour; Nonstate residents: per academic year $28,950, $1,320 per credit hour.

Financial Assistance:

First Year Students: Teaching assistantships available for first-year. Average amount paid per academic year: $16,000. Average number of hours worked per week: 20. Apply by January 15. Tuition remission given: full. Research assistantships available for first-year. Average amount paid per academic year: $16,000. Average number of hours worked per week: 20. Apply by January 15. Tuition remission given: full. Fellowships and scholarships available for first-year. Average amount paid per academic year: $21,000. Apply by January 15. Tuition remission given: full.

Advanced Students: No information provided.

Contact Information: Of all students currently enrolled full-time, 100% benefitted from one or more of the listed financial assistance programs. Application and information available online at: http://gradadmissions.rpi.edu/application.

Internships/Practica: No information provided.

Housing and Day Care: On-campus housing is available. On-campus day care facilities are available.

Employment of Department Graduates:

Master's Degree Graduates: Of those who graduated in the academic year 2003–2004, the following categories and numbers represent the post-graduate activities and employment of master's degree graduates: Enrolled in a post-doctoral residency/fellowship (n/a), employed in independent practice (n/a), total from the above (master's) (0).

Doctoral Degree Graduates: Of those who graduated in the academic year 2003–2004, the following categories and numbers represent the post-graduate activities and employment of doctoral degree graduates: Enrolled in a psychology doctoral program (n/a), total from the above (doctoral) (0).

Additional Information:

Orientation, Objectives, and Emphasis of Department: The department is committed to the concept of integrated cognitive systems. Specifically, research and teaching falls into areas that together cover low- to high-level cognition, whether in minds or machines: reasoning (human and machine); computational cognitive modeling; cognitive engineering; perception and action.

Special Facilities or Resources: Modern research facilities, including the CogWorks Laboratory, Interactive and Distance Education Assessment (IDEA) Laboratory, Rensselaer Artificial Intelligence and Reasoning Laboratory (RAIR Lab), Vision and Action Lab, and dedicated space in the Institute's new Social and Behavioral Research Laboratory, provide a new expression of the Department's interests in cognitive science that intgrates the diverse research activities of the faculty in the Department.

Application Information:

Send to: Admissions, Rensselaer Polytechnic Institute, Troy, NY 12180. Application available online. Students are admitted in the Fall, application deadline January 15. *Fee:* $75.

Rochester, University of (2004 data)
Department of Clinical and Social Sciences in Psychology
Arts, Sciences and Engineering
Meliora Hall 355, RC Box 270266
Rochester, NY 14627-0266
Telephone: (585) 275-8649
Fax: (585) 273-1100
E-mail: *loretta@psych.rochester.edu*
Web: *http://www.psych.rochester.edu/scp/*

Department Information:
1935. Chairperson: Miron Zuckerman. Number of Faculty: total–full-time 16, part-time 13; women–full-time 4, part-time 6; minority–full-time 1, part-time 1.

Programs and Degrees Offered:
Listed in the following order: Program area, degree type (T if terminal Master's), number awarded 7/03–6/04. Clinical PhD (Doctor of Philosophy) 1, Developmental PhD (Doctor of Philosophy) 0, Social-Personality PhD (Doctor of Philosophy) 1.

APA Accreditation: Clinical PhD (Doctor of Philosophy).

Student Applications/Admissions:
Student Applications

Clinical PhD (Doctor of Philosophy)—Applications 2004–2005, 152. Total applicants accepted 2004–2005, 5. Openings 2005–2006, 3. The Median number of years required for completion of a degree are 7. The number of students enrolled full and part-time who were dismissed or voluntarily withdrew from this program area were 1. *Developmental PhD (Doctor of Philosophy)*—Applications 2004–2005, 31. Total applicants accepted 2004–2005, 4. Openings 2005–2006, 4. The number of students enrolled full and part-time, who were dismissed or voluntarily withdrew from this program area were 0. *Social-Personality PhD (Doctor of Philosophy)*—Applications 2004–2005, 58. Total applicants accepted 2004–2005, 7. Openings 2005–2006, 2. The Median number of years required for completion of a degree are 8. The number of students enrolled full and part-time who were dismissed or voluntarily withdrew from this program area were 0.

Admissions Requirements:

Scores: Entries appear in this order: required test or GPA, minimum score (if required), median score of students entering in 2003–2004. Doctoral Programs: GRE-V no minimum stated, 580; GRE-Q no minimum stated, 676; GRE-V+Q no minimum stated, 1256; GRE-Analytical no minimum stated, 656; overall undergraduate GPA no minimum stated, 3.4. Please note: Scores reflected above are only for clinical program.

Other Criteria: (importance of criteria rated low, medium, or high): GRE/MAT scores medium, research experience high, work experience high, extracurricular activity medium, clinically related public service medium, GPA high, letters of recommendation high, interview high, statement of goals and objectives high.

Student Characteristics: The following represents characteristics of students in 2004–2005 in all graduate psychology programs in the department: Female–full-time 36, part-time 0; Male–full-time 16, part-time 0; African American/Black–full-time 2, part-time 0; Hispanic/Latino(a)–full-time 2, part-time 0; Asian/Pacific Islander–full-time 1, part-time 0; American Indian/Alaska Native–full-time 0, part-time 0; Caucasian–full-time 46, part-time 0; Multi-ethnic–full-time 1, part-time 0; students subject to the Americans With Disabilities Act–full-time 0, part-time 0.

Financial Information/Assistance:
Financial Assistance:

First Year Students: Teaching assistantships available for first-year. Average amount paid per academic year: $12,000. Tuition remission given: full. Research assistantships available for first-year. Average amount paid per academic year: $12,000. Tuition remission given: full. Fellowships and scholarships available for first-year. Tuition remission given: full.

Advanced Students: Teaching assistantships available for advanced students. Average amount paid per academic year: $12,000. Tuition remission given: full. Research assistantships available for advanced students. Average amount paid per academic year: $12,000. Tuition remission given: full. Fellowships and scholarships available for advanced students. Tuition remission given: full.

Contact Information: Of all students currently enrolled full-time, 68% benefitted from one or more of the listed financial assistance programs. Application and information available online at: http://www.psych.rochester.edu/graduate/.

Internships/Practica: Some students are supported via teaching and research assistantships as well as part-time assignments at several local agencies including: Mt. Hope Family Center, Childrens' Institute, University of Rochester Medical Center, and the University of Rochester Counseling Center. Suitable clinical practica and a one-year clinical internship ensure continuity of clinical training throughout the student's stay in the program. For those doctoral students for whom a professional internship is required prior to graduation, 4 applied in 2003–2004. Of those who applied, 4 were placed in APA accredited internships.

Housing and Day Care: On-campus housing is available. No on-campus day care facilities are available.

Employment of Department Graduates:
Master's Degree Graduates: Of those who graduated in the academic year 2003–2004, the following categories and numbers represent the post-graduate activities and employment of master's degree graduates: Enrolled in a post-doctoral residency/fellowship (n/a), employed in independent practice (n/a), total from the above (master's) (0).

Doctoral Degree Graduates: Of those who graduated in the academic year 2003–2004, the following categories and numbers represent the post-graduate activities and employment of doctoral degree graduates: Enrolled in a psychology doctoral program (n/a), enrolled in a post-doctoral residency/fellowship (1), employed in other positions at a higher education institution (1), total from the above (doctoral) (2).

Additional Information:

Orientation, Objectives, and Emphasis of Department: The primary goal of the graduate program in the Department of Clinical and Social Sciences in Psychology is to provide highly qualified applicants a broad range of coursework, research experience, and practical training that will equip them to make independent contributions to psychology. Our department offers PhD training in three areas of Psychology: Clinical, Developmental and Social-Personality. The department also includes a research program in Human Motivation that includes faculty and students from all three areas. Two additional research units are affiliated with the department — the Mt. Hope Family Center and the Childrens' Institute. The Mt. Hope Family Center provides opportunities for training and research in developmental psychopathology. The Childrens' Institute provides similar opportunities for work on the detection and prevention of young children's adjustment problems. Graduate training emphasizes the development of research skills. To excel in any discipline, students need outstanding facilities, distinguished faculty, and an environment promoting their full integration in the research endeavor. We feel that our Department combines all of these characteristics.

Special Facilities or Resources: The Mt. Hope Family Center offers a unique combination of service, training, and research. The service component focuses on the assessment and treatment of families experiencing severe familial dysfunction and of children at risk of foster care placement and/or emotional difficulties. Treatment programs include: a) a full-time preschool program with psycho-educational treatment for families and a parent-child attachment intervention for children ages 3 to 5 and their caregivers, and b) an after school program for at-risk school-aged children. The Childrens' Institute aims to: 1) develop, implement, and evaluate programs to maximize adjustment of individuals (particularly young children) to their environments; and 2) apply psychological methods and knowledge to the solution of community problems in mental health. The Institute develops programs to address longstanding mental health problems from a preventive standpoint: a) by analyzing and modifying social environments (such as schools); b) by training young children in age-appropriate, adaptive social competencies; c) by identifying ways to reduce stress and training children to cope with it; and d) by developing programs for early identification and prevention of school adjustment problems and enhancing wellness.

Information for Students With Physical Disabilities: See the following Web site for more information: http://www.rochester.edu/ada/.

Application Information:

Send to: Maryann Gilbert, Academic Coordinator, Department of Clinical and Social Sciences in Psychology, University of Rochester, Meliora Hall 355, RC Box 270266, Rochester, NY 14627-0266. Students are admitted in the Fall, application deadline January 20. *Fee:* $25.

Sage Colleges, The
Department of Psychology
45 Ferry Street
Troy, NY 12180
Telephone: (518) 244-2221
Fax: (518) 244-4564
E-mail: *hills@sage.edu*
Web: *http://www.sage.edu*

Department Information:

Department Chair: Dr. Samuel Hill. Number of Faculty: total–full-time 11; women–full-time 9.

Programs and Degrees Offered:

Listed in the following order: Program area, degree type (T if terminal Master's), number awarded 7/03–6/04. Community MA/MS (Master of Arts/Science) (T) 15, Certificate in Forensic Psychology Other 3, Counseling and Community Psychology MA/MS (Master of Arts/Science) (T) 0.

Student Applications/Admissions:

Student Applications

Community MA/MS (Master of Arts/Science)—Applications 2004–2005, 15. Total applicants accepted 2004–2005, 10. Number enrolled (new admits only) 2004–2005 full-time, 2. Number enrolled (new admits only) 2004–2005 part-time, 8. Total enrolled 2004–2005 full-time, 5, part-time, 20. Openings 2005–2006, 20. The Median number of years required for completion of a degree are 3. The number of students enrolled full and part-time who were dismissed or voluntarily withdrew from this program area were 0. *Certificate in Forensic Psychology Other*—Openings 2005–2006, 15. The Median number of years required for completion of a degree are 2. *Counseling and Community Psychology MA/MS (Master of Arts/Science)*—Applications 2004–2005, 50. Total applicants accepted 2004–2005, 40. Number enrolled (new admits only) 2004–2005 full-time, 12. Number enrolled (new admits only) 2004–2005 part-time, 28. Total enrolled 2004–2005 full-time, 22, part-time, 60. Openings 2005–2006, 40. The Median number of years required for completion of a degree are 3.5. The number of students enrolled full and part-time who were dismissed or voluntarily withdrew from this program area were 3.

Admissions Requirements:

Scores: Entries appear in this order: required test or GPA, minimum score (if required), median score of students entering in 2003–2004. Master's Programs: overall undergraduate GPA no minimum stated. Community Psychology: 2.75 Forensic Psychology: 3.00

Other Criteria: (importance of criteria rated low, medium, or high): research experience low, work experience low, clinically related public service low, GPA high, letters of recommendation high, interview medium, statement of goals and objectives high. Forensic psychology: competitive assessment because enrollments are limited per academic year.

Student Characteristics: The following represents characteristics of students in 2004–2005 in all graduate psychology programs in the department: Female–full-time 4, part-time 63; Male–full-time 0, part-time 20; African American/Black–full-time 0, part-time

7; Hispanic/Latino(a)–full-time 0, part-time 4; Asian/Pacific Is-lander–full-time 0, part-time 3; American Indian/Alaska Native–full-time 0, part-time 1; Caucasian–full-time 4, part-time 61; Multi-ethnic–part-time 3.

Financial Information/Assistance:

Tuition for Full-Time Study: *Master's:* State residents: $415 per credit hour; Nonstate residents: $415 per credit hour.

Financial Assistance:

First Year Students: Research assistantships available for first-year. Average number of hours worked per week: 8. Apply by June 1. Tuition remission given: full.

Advanced Students: Research assistantships available for advanced students. Average number of hours worked per week: 8. Tuition remission given: full.

Contact Information: Of all students currently enrolled full-time, 10% benefitted from one or more of the listed financial assistance programs.

Internships/Practica:
As part of each degree, all students are required to complete an internship (direct services) and/or externship (not direct services) placement, depending upon the selected area of concentration. Internships comprise one year placements in a setting appropriate to the student's interests; externships are one semester projects in a setting of the student's choice.

Housing and Day Care:
On-campus housing is available. No on-campus day care facilities are available.

Employment of Department Graduates:

Master's Degree Graduates: Of those who graduated in the academic year 2003–2004, the following categories and numbers represent the post-graduate activities and employment of master's degree graduates: Enrolled in a psychology doctoral program (2), enrolled in a post-doctoral residency/fellowship (n/a), employed in independent practice (n/a), employed in business or industry (research/consulting) (2), employed in a community mental health/counseling center (3), other employment position (8), total from the above (master's) (15).

Doctoral Degree Graduates: Of those who graduated in the academic year 2003–2004, the following categories and numbers represent the post-graduate activities and employment of doctoral degree graduates: Enrolled in a psychology doctoral program (n/a), total from the above (doctoral) (0).

Additional Information:

Orientation, Objectives, and Emphasis of Department: Our two degrees (MA in Community Psychology, and MA in Forensic Psychology) provide students with the academic and skills training to become practitioners at the master's level. The programs range in credits from 39 to 48, depending on degree and, for Community Psychology, track. The emphasis is on developing and strengthening student skills for application (whether individual or systems level) in the context of strong theoretical foundations.

Special Facilities or Resources: In addition to the faculty resources one would assume at the master's level, a particular advantage for psychology programs at Sage Graduate School is our prime location in the Capital District area of New York State. The geographic size, population density, and availability of widely varied populations make possible a wide variety of experiences.

Information for Students With Physical Disabilities: See the following Web site for more information: www.sage.edu.

Application Information:
Send to: Graduate Admissions, The Sage Colleges, 45 Ferry Street, Troy, NY 12180. Students are admitted in the Fall. Community Psychology: rolling admissions; Forensic Psychology: November 1 for Spring; April 1 for Summer and Fall. *Fee:* $40. fee waived for graduates of The Sage Colleges.

Saint Bonaventure University
Department of Counselor Education
Street Bonaventure University
P.O. Box AV
Street Bonaventure, NY 14778
Telephone: (716) 375-2374
Fax: (716) 375-2360
E-mail: *czuck@sbu.edu*
Web: *http://schoolofed.sbu.edu/*

Department Information:
1950. Chairperson: Craig Zuckerman. Number of Faculty: total–full-time 6, part-time 1; women–full-time 2; minority–full-time 1.

Programs and Degrees Offered:
Listed in the following order: Program area, degree type (T if terminal Master's), number awarded 7/03–6/04. School Counseling Other 40, Agency Counseling Other 10, Advanced Certificate in School Other 15, Advanced Certificate in Agency Other 5.

Student Applications/Admissions:
Student Applications

School Counseling Other—Applications 2004–2005, 60. Total applicants accepted 2004–2005, 45. Number enrolled (new admits only) 2004–2005 full-time, 30. Number enrolled (new admits only) 2004–2005 part-time, 10. Total enrolled 2004–2005 full-time, 80, part-time, 25. Openings 2005–2006, 40. The Median number of years required for completion of a degree are 2. The number of students enrolled full and part-time who were dismissed or voluntarily withdrew from this program area were 5. *Agency Counseling Other*—Applications 2004–2005, 15. Total applicants accepted 2004–2005, 13. Number enrolled (new admits only) 2004–2005 full-time, 7. Number enrolled (new admits only) 2004–2005 part-time, 3. Total enrolled 2004–2005 full-time, 20, part-time, 5. Openings 2005–2006, 15. The Median number of years required for completion of a degree are 2. The number of students enrolled full and part-time who were dismissed or voluntarily withdrew from this program area were 2. *Advanced Certificate in School Other*—Applications 2004–2005, 10. Total applicants accepted 2004–2005, 10. Number enrolled (new admits only) 2004–2005 full-time, 0. Number enrolled (new admits only) 2004–2005 part-time, 8. Openings 2005–2006, 15. The Median number of years required for completion of a degree are 3. The number of students enrolled full and part-time who were dismissed or voluntarily withdrew from this program area were 2. *Advanced Certificate in Agency Other*—Applications 2004–2005, 7. Total applicants accepted 2004–2005, 5. Number enrolled (new admits only) 2004–2005 full-time, 0. Num-ber enrolled (new admits only) 2004–2005 full-time, 0. Number enrolled (new admits only) 2004–2005 part-time, 4. Openings 2005–2006, 10. The Median number of years required for completion of a degree are 3. The number of students enrolled full and part-time who were dismissed or voluntarily withdrew from this program area were 2.

Admissions Requirements:

Scores: Entries appear in this order: required test or GPA, minimum score (if required), median score of students entering in 2003–2004. Master's Programs: MAT no minimum stated; overall undergraduate GPA 3.0. Students may submit either the GRE or MAT

Other Criteria: (importance of criteria rated low, medium, or high): GRE/MAT scores medium, extracurricular activity low, GPA high, letters of recommendation medium, interview high, statement of goals and objectives medium.

Student Characteristics: The following represents characteristics of students in 2004–2005 in all graduate psychology programs in the department: Female–full-time 85, part-time 60; Male–full-time 15, part-time 10; African American/Black–full-time 3, part-time 2; Hispanic/Latino(a)–full-time 2, part-time 1; Asian/Pacific Islander–full-time 0, part-time 0; American Indian/Alaska Native–full-time 1, part-time 1; Caucasian–full-time 94, part-time 66; Multi-ethnic–full-time 0, part-time 0; students subject to the Americans With Disabilities Act full-time 2, part-time 1.

Financial Information/Assistance:

Tuition for Full-Time Study: Master's: State residents: $560 per credit hour; Nonstate residents: $560 per credit hour.

Financial Assistance:

First Year Students: No information provided.
Advanced Students: No information provided.
Contact Information: No information provided.

Internships/Practica: Many local opportunities exist for internships in both school counseling programs and at agency counseling sites. We have also started an on-site, outpatient mental health and academic counseling clinic on the main campus of Street Bonaventure University that offers practical experiences.

Housing and Day Care: No on-campus housing is available. No on-campus day care facilities are available.

Employment of Department Graduates:

Master's Degree Graduates: Of those who graduated in the academic year 2003–2004, the following categories and numbers represent the post-graduate activities and employment of master's degree graduates: Enrolled in a post-doctoral residency/fellowship (n/a), employed in independent practice (n/a), total from the above (master's) (0).

Doctoral Degree Graduates: Of those who graduated in the academic year 2003–2004, the following categories and numbers represent the post-graduate activities and employment of doctoral degree graduates: Enrolled in a psychology doctoral program (n/a), total from the above (doctoral) (0).

Additional Information:

Orientation, Objectives, and Emphasis of Department: The mission of the Department of Counselor Education is to prepare students for the professional practice of counseling in a multicul-

tural and diverse society. Specific program goals are: (a) support for the mission of Street Bonaventure University; and (b) adherence to the highest standards of counselor education.

Special Facilities or Resources: Street Bonaventure University's School of Education Outpatient Counseling Clinic opened in 2004 offering academic, behavioral and mental health services to children, their families, and adults in the community. The clinic serves both the college community and the surrounding underserved communities in four New York counties as well as neighboring communities in Pennsylvania. The clinic offers group and individual counseling.

Application Information:
Send to: School of Graduate Studies. Students are admitted in the Fall, application deadline August 1; Spring, application deadline December 1; Summer, application deadline April 1. Fee: $30. If applying online, the fee is waived.

Street John's University
Department of Psychology
Street John's College of Arts & Sciences
8000 Utopia Parkway
Jamaica, NY 11439
Telephone: (718) 990-6368
Fax: (718) 990-6705
E-mail: digiuser@stjohns.edu
Web: http://new.stjohns.edu

Department Information:
1958. Chairperson: Raymond DiGiuseppe. Number of Faculty: total–full-time 29, part-time 32; women–full-time 9, part-time 10; minority–full-time 4, part-time 1.

Programs and Degrees Offered:
Listed in the following order: Program area, degree type (T if terminal Master's), number awarded 7/03–6/04. Clinical Psychology PhD (Doctor of Philosophy) 12, General-Experiment Psychology MA/MS (Master of Arts/Science) (T) 5, School Psychology MA/MS (Master of Arts/Science) (T) 12, School Psychology PsyD (Doctor of Psychology) 12.

APA Accreditation: Clinical PhD (Doctor of Philosophy).

Student Applications/Admissions:

Student Applications

Clinical Psychology PhD (Doctor of Philosophy)—Applications 2004–2005, 330. Total applicants accepted 2004–2005, 25. Number enrolled (new admits only) 2004–2005 full-time, 12. Openings 2005–2006, 12. The Median number of years required for completion of a degree are 6. The number of students enrolled full and part-time who were dismissed or voluntarily withdrew from this program area were 0. General-Experiment Psychology MA/MS (Master of Arts/Science)—Applications 2004–2005, 25. Total applicants accepted 2004–2005, 10. Number enrolled (new admits only) 2004–2005 full-time, 8. Number enrolled (new admits only) 2004–2005 part-time, 3. Total enrolled 2004–2005 full-time, 16, part-time, 5. Openings

2005–2006, 10. The Median number of years required for completion of a degree are 2. The number of students enrolled full and part-time who were dismissed or voluntarily withdrew from this program area were 0. *School Psychology MA/MS (Master of Arts/Science)*—Applications 2004–2005, 62. Total applicants accepted 2004–2005, 22. Number enrolled (new admits only) 2004–2005 full-time, 6. Number enrolled (new admits only) 2004–2005 part-time, 6. Total enrolled 2004–2005 full-time, 30, part-time, 10. Openings 2005–2006, 16. The Median number of years required for completion of a degree are 3. The number of students enrolled full and part-time who were dismissed or voluntarily withdrew from this program area were 0. *School Psychology PsyD (Doctor of Psychology)*—Applications 2004–2005, 90. Total applicants accepted 2004–2005, 18. Number enrolled (new admits only) 2004–2005 full-time, 15. Number enrolled (new admits only) 2004–2005 part-time, 3. Total enrolled 2004–2005 full-time, 58, part-time, 59. Openings 2005–2006, 16. The Median number of years required for completion of a degree are 6. The number of students enrolled full and part-time who were dismissed or voluntarily withdrew from this program area were 0.

Admissions Requirements:

Scores: Entries appear in this order: required test or GPA, minimum score (if required), median score of students entering in 2003–2004. Master's Programs: GRE-V no minimum stated, 500; GRE-Q no minimum stated, 500; GRE-V+Q no minimum stated, 1000; GRE-Subject(Psych) no minimum stated, 520; overall undergraduate GPA no minimum stated, 3.3; psychology GPA no minimum stated. GRE not required for MA in General Experimental Psychology. Doctoral Programs: GRE-V no minimum stated, 630; GRE-Q no minimum stated, 650; GRE-V+Q no minimum stated, 1280; GRE-Subject(Psych) no minimum stated, 640; overall undergraduate GPA no minimum stated, 3.61.

Other Criteria: (importance of criteria rated low, medium, or high): GRE/MAT scores high, research experience high, work experience high, extracurricular activity high, clinically related public service high, GPA high, letters of recommendation high, interview high, statement of goals and objectives high. Interview for PhD and PsyD programs only. Clinically related public service is not applicable to MA program.

Student Characteristics: The following represents characteristics of students in 2004–2005 in all graduate psychology programs in the department: Female–full-time 119, part-time 64; Male–full-time 18, part-time 15; African American/Black–full-time 9, part-time 2; Hispanic/Latino(a)–full-time 9, part-time 2; Asian/Pacific Islander–full-time 3, part-time 0; American Indian/Alaska Native–full-time 0, part-time 0; Caucasian–full-time 114, part-time 70; Multi-ethnic–full-time 2, part-time 0.

Financial Information/Assistance:

Tuition for Full-Time Study: Nonstate residents: $660 per credit hour. *Doctoral:* Nonstate residents: $820 per credit hour. Tuition is subject to change.

Financial Assistance:

First Year Students: Teaching assistantships available for first-year. Average amount paid per academic year: $6,000. Average number of hours worked per week: 18. Apply by February 1. Tuition remission given: full. Research assistantships available for first-year. Average amount paid per academic year: $7,500. Average number of hours worked per week: 18. Apply by February 1. Tuition remission given: full.

Advanced Students: Teaching assistantships available for advanced students. Average amount paid per academic year: $6,000. Average number of hours worked per week: 18. Apply by February 1. Tuition remission given: full. Research assistantships available for advanced students. Average amount paid per academic year: $7,500. Average number of hours worked per week: 18. Apply by February 1. Tuition remission given: full. Fellowships and scholarships available for advanced students. Average amount paid per academic year: $8,000. Average number of hours worked per week: 0. Apply by February 1. Tuition remission given: full.

Contact Information: Of all students currently enrolled full-time, 25% benefitted from one or more of the listed financial assistance programs.

Internships/Practica: Students in the PhD program in clinical psychology see clients in our Center for Psychological Services during all four full-time years of study. They also compete a 2 day per week externship in a clinical facility during their third and fourth years. A full-time internship is required in the fifth year. Students in the MS program in school psychology complete a one year practicum at the Center for Psychological Services that includes work at the clinic and one or more area schools. They also complete a five day per week internship during their final year either in a public school setting or at an agency serving children or adolescents. Students in the PsyD program in school psychology complete two years of practice at the Center for Psychological Services and Clinical Studies in the second and fourth years of the Program. This work includes working at the clinic and in one or more area schools. Students also complete a 3-day per week internship in a public school in the third year and a 3-day per week externship in a school or facility for exceptional children in the fourth year. A full-time internship is required in the fifth year. For those doctoral students for whom a professional internship is required prior to graduation, 17 applied in 2003–2004. Of those who applied, 12 were placed in internships listed by the Association of Psychology Postdoctoral and Internship Programs (APPIC); 12 were placed in APA accredited internships.

Housing and Day Care: On-campus housing is available. E-mail reslife@stjohns.edu or call (718) 990-2417. On-campus day care facilities are available.

Employment of Department Graduates:

Master's Degree Graduates: Of those who graduated in the academic year 2003–2004, the following categories and numbers represent the post-graduate activities and employment of master's degree graduates: Enrolled in a post-doctoral residency/fellowship (n/a), employed in independent practice (n/a), total from the above (master's) (0).

Doctoral Degree Graduates: Of those who graduated in the academic year 2003–2004, the following categories and numbers represent the post-graduate activities and employment of doctoral degree graduates: Enrolled in a psychology doctoral program (n/a), total from the above (doctoral) (0).

Additional Information:

Orientation, Objectives, and Emphasis of Department: The department emphasizes advanced preparation in the science of psychology by integrating theory and practice. Training at the master's degree level is provided in school psychology (MS) and general-experimental psychology (MA). The MA program offers a thesis and non-thesis track. Training at the doctoral level is provided in clinical psychology (PhD) and school psychology (PsyD). The doctoral program in clinical psychology is anchored within the scientist-practitioner model. Students are exposed to diverse theoretical approaches in contemporary clinical practice, particularly psychoanalytic cognitive-behavioral, and family systems models. Students follow either a general track of study in clinical psychology or a track in clinical child psychology. The doctoral program in school psychology is anchored within the scholar-practitioner model. Students receive a firm foundation in the basic science of psychology upon which training in the practice of psychology is built. Students are trained to be scholars who can use their scientific background in psychology to assess and intervene with children, adolescents and their families, and to consult with parents, teachers, and organizations on the development of programs to enhance children's educational and mental health needs. A strong emphasis is placed on using empirically supported assessment instruments and interventions. The MS and PsyD programs in school psychology lead to certification as a school psychologist. Students who are bilingual may select a track of study leading to certification as a bilingual school psychologist.

Special Facilities or Resources: The Center for Psychological Services is an on-campus training site for students in clinical and school psychology. The Center provides comprehensive psychological services to the community at a modest cost. The Center also serves as a site for student and faculty research.

Application Information:

Send to: Graduate Admissions, Newman Hall Room 106, Street John's University, 8000 Utopia Pkwy, Jamaica, NY 11439. Students are admitted in the Fall, application deadline February 1; Spring, application deadline rolling; Summer, application deadline rolling. Doctoral Programs have Fall admission only, with a deadline of February 1. For the MS in School Psychology: Fall admission only, with a deadline of March 15. For the MA in General/Experimental: rolling admissions. *Fee:* $40.

State University of New York at Albany
Department of Educational and Counseling Psychology
School of Education
1400 Washington Avenue
Albany, NY 12222
Telephone: (518) 442-5050
Fax: (518) 442-4953
E-mail: *maysped@csc.albany.edu*
Web: *http://www.albany.edu/education/contact_us/acd_dep*

Department Information:

1963. Directors (counseling psych, school psych, ed psych): Myrna Friedlander, Deborah Kundert, Joan Newman. Number of Faculty: total–full-time 19, part-time 11; women–full-time 8, part-time 6; minority–full-time 3, part-time 1.

Programs and Degrees Offered:

Listed in the following order: Program area, degree type (T if terminal Master's), number awarded 7/03–6/04. Counseling Psy-

chology PhD (Doctor of Philosophy) 16, School Psychology PsyD (Doctor of Psychology) 6, Educational psychology Other 1, Educational psychology MA/MS (Master of Arts/Science) 18, Educational psychology PhD (Doctor of Philosophy) 5, School Psychology Other 0, School Counseling Other 14, Rehabilitation Counseling MA/MS (Master of Arts/Science) (T) 10, Community Counseling MA/MS (Master of Arts/Science) (T) 2.

APA Accreditation: Counseling PhD (Doctor of Philosophy). School PsyD (Doctor of Psychology).

Student Applications/Admissions:

Student Applications

Counseling Psychology PhD (Doctor of Philosophy)—Applications 2004–2005, 111. Total applicants accepted 2004–2005, 12. Number enrolled (new admits only) 2004–2005 full-time, 8. Number enrolled (new admits only) 2004–2005 part-time, 0. Total enrolled 2004–2005 full-time, 55, part-time, 5. Openings 2005–2006, 8. The Median number of years required for completion of a degree are 6.5. The number of students enrolled full and part-time who were dismissed or voluntarily withdrew from this program area were 1. *School Psychology PsyD (Doctor of Psychology)*—Applications 2004–2005, 39. Total applicants accepted 2004–2005, 7. Number enrolled (new admits only) 2004–2005 full-time, 9. Number enrolled (new admits only) 2004–2005 part-time, 0. Openings 2005–2006, 5. The Median number of years required for completion of a degree are 5.5. The number of students enrolled full and part-time who were dismissed or voluntarily withdrew from this program area were 2. *Educational psychology Other*—Applications 2004–2005, 2. Total applicants accepted 2004–2005, 2. Number enrolled (new admits only) 2004–2005 full-time, 1. Number enrolled (new admits only) 2004–2005 part-time, 2. Total enrolled 2004–2005 full-time, 3, part-time, 2. Openings 2005–2006, 3. The Median number of years required for completion of a degree are 4. The number of students enrolled full and part-time who were dismissed or voluntarily withdrew from this program area were 1. *Educational psychology MA/MS (Master of Arts/Science)*—Applications 2004–2005, 10. Total applicants accepted 2004–2005, 6. Number enrolled (new admits only) 2004–2005 full-time, 3. Number enrolled (new admits only) 2004–2005 part-time, 3. Total enrolled 2004–2005 full-time, 10, part-time, 28. Openings 2005–2006, 40. The Median number of years required for completion of a degree are 3. The number of students enrolled full and part-time who were dismissed or voluntarily withdrew from this program area were 1. *Educational psychology PhD (Doctor of Philosophy)*—Applications 2004–2005, 21. Total applicants accepted 2004–2005, 12. Number enrolled (new admits only) 2004–2005 full-time, 7. Number enrolled (new admits only) 2004–2005 part-time, 1. Total enrolled 2004–2005 full-time, 21, part-time, 15. Openings 2005–2006, 8. The Median number of years required for completion of a degree are 6. The number of students enrolled full and part-time who were dismissed or voluntarily withdrew from this program area were 0. *School Psychology Other*—Applications 2004–2005, 26. Total applicants accepted 2004–2005, 12. Number enrolled (new admits only) 2004–2005 full-time, 9. Number enrolled (new admits only) 2004–2005 part-time, 0. Openings 2005–2006, 10. The Median number of years required for completion of a degree are 3. The number of students enrolled full and part-time who were dismissed or voluntarily withdrew from this program area

545

were 0. *School Counseling Other*—Applications 2004–2005, 37. Total applicants accepted 2004–2005, 11. Number enrolled (new admits only) 2004–2005 full-time, 11. Openings 2005–2006, 10. The Median number of years required for completion of a degree are 1.5. The number of students enrolled full and part-time who were dismissed or voluntarily withdrew from this program area were 0. *Rehabilitation Counseling MA/MS (Master of Arts/Science)*—Applications 2004–2005, 24. Total applicants accepted 2004–2005, 9. Number enrolled (new admits only) 2004–2005 full-time, 9. Openings 2005–2006, 10. The Median number of years required for completion of a degree are 1.5. The number of students enrolled full and part-time, who were dismissed or voluntarily withdrew from this program area were 0. *Community Counseling MA/MS (Master of Arts/Science)*—Applications 2004–2005, 29. Total applicants accepted 2004–2005, 7. Number enrolled (new admits only) 2004–2005 full-time, 7. Openings 2005–2006, 12. The Median number of years required for completion of a degree are 1.5. The number of students enrolled full and part-time who were dismissed or voluntarily withdrew from this program area were 0.

Admissions Requirements:

Scores: Entries appear in this order: required test or GPA, minimum score (if required), median score of students entering in 2003–2004. Master's Programs: GRE-V no minimum stated; GRE-Q no minimum stated; GRE-V+Q no minimum stated; GRE-Analytical no minimum stated; overall undergraduate GPA no minimum stated; psychology GPA no minimum stated. The GRE-Analytical is required for school psychology but not counseling psychology Doctoral Programs: GRE-V no minimum stated; GRE-Q no minimum stated; GRE-V+Q no minimum stated; GRE-Analytical no minimum stated; overall undergraduate GPA no minimum stated; psychology GPA no minimum stated. Typically the scores for the master's and Certificate of Advanced Study programs are lower than those for the doctoral programs. Note that PsyD (school psychology) admissions for 2003-2004 were deferred for a year.

Other Criteria: (importance of criteria rated low, medium, or high): GRE/MAT scores high, research experience high, work experience medium, extracurricular activity medium, clinically related public service medium, GPA high, letters of recommendation high, interview high, statement of goals and objectives high. In counseling psychology, research experience is rated more highly for PhD applicants than for master's and CAS applicants. For additional information on admission requirements, go to: www.albany.edu/counseling_psych; www.albany.edu/schoolpsych; www.albany.edu/educational_psychology.

Student Characteristics: The following represents characteristics of students in 2004–2005 in all graduate psychology programs in the department: Female–full-time 155, part-time 36; Male–full-time 37, part-time 10; African American/Black–full-time 17, part-time 0; Hispanic/Latino(a)–full-time 5, part-time 1; Asian/Pacific Islander–full-time 10, part-time 6; American Indian/Alaska Native–full-time 1, part-time 0; Caucasian–full-time 157, part-time 46; Multi-ethnic–full-time 2, part-time 0; students subject to the Americans With Disabilities Act–full-time 4, part-time 1.

Financial Information/Assistance:

Tuition for Full-Time Study: *Master's:* State residents: per academic year $6,900, $288 per credit hour; Nonstate residents: per academic year $10,920, $455 per credit hour. *Doctoral:* State residents: per academic year $6,900, $288 per credit hour; Non-state residents: per academic year $10,920, $455 per credit hour. Tuition is subject to change. See the following Web site for updates and changes in tuition costs: http://www.albany.edu/grad/expenses.html#general_information.

Financial Assistance:

First Year Students: Research assistantships available for first-year. Average amount paid per academic year: $7,000. Average number of hours worked per week: 10. Apply by January 1. Tuition remission given: full. Fellowships and scholarships available for first-year. Average amount paid per academic year: $10,000. Average number of hours worked per week: 0. Apply by January 1. Tuition remission given: full.

Advanced Students: Teaching assistantships available for advanced students. Average amount paid per academic year: $7,300. Average number of hours worked per week: 20. Apply by April 1. Tuition remission given: full. Research assistantships available for advanced students. Average amount paid per academic year: $8,500. Average number of hours worked per week: 20. Apply by April 1. Tuition remission given: full. Traineeships available for advanced students. Average amount paid per academic year: $9,000. Average number of hours worked per week: 22. Apply by April 1. Tuition remission given: full. Fellowships and scholarships available for advanced students. Average amount paid per academic year: $10,000. Average number of hours worked per week: 0. Apply by April 1. Tuition remission given: full.

Contact Information: Of all students currently enrolled full-time, 60% benefitted from one or more of the listed financial assistance programs. Application and information available online at: http://www.albany.educ/financial_aid/.

Internships/Practica: In counseling psychology, PhD students take beginning and advanced practica and practica in specialized procedures. The initial year-long practicum is taken at the university-operated Psychological Services Center, a training facility for graduate students in the counseling and clinical psychology programs. Opportunities for practica in specialized procedures are typically community-based, and have included inpatient and outpatient assessment in college/university counseling centers; private, state, and general hospitals; community mental health agencies; and residential treatment settings for youth. Our doctoral students have been highly successful in obtaining their preferred APA-accredited internships. Master's students in counseling take practica and internships in public schools, hospitals, and community agencies. Both PsyD and CAS students in school psychology complete a 2-semester, school-based practicum under the supervision of the University clinical supervisor. Experiences that the students complete include assessments, individual and group counseling, classroom interventions, tutoring, and consultation. Doctoral students in school psychology complete additional field training experiences in local schools and agencies to reinforce basic skills and to develop additional skills in consultation, prevention, and systems issues. Certificate students complete a 1-year, full time internship in a public school system to develop and reinforce basic skill competencies needed for future employment. For those doctoral students for whom a professional internship is required prior to graduation, 12 applied in 2003–2004. Of those who applied, 9 were placed in internships listed by the Association of Psychology Postdoctoral and Internship Programs (APPIC); 9 were placed in APA accredited internships.

Housing and Day Care: On-campus housing is available. See the following Web sites for more information: http://www.albany.edu/housing/ or http://www.albany.edu/opsoca/off_campus_housing/. On-campus day care facilities are available. See the following Web site for more information: http://www.albany.edu/cpsp/sites/u/u1.html or contact (518) 442-2660 (U-Kids Child Care).

Employment of Department Graduates:

Master's Degree Graduates: Of those who graduated in the academic year 2003–2004, the following categories and numbers represent the post-graduate activities and employment of master's degree graduates: Enrolled in a post-doctoral residency/fellowship (n/a), employed in independent practice (n/a), do not know (26), total from the above (master's) (26).

Doctoral Degree Graduates: Of those who graduated in the academic year 2003–2004, the following categories and numbers represent the post-graduate activities and employment of doctoral degree graduates: Enrolled in a psychology doctoral program (n/a), enrolled in a post-doctoral residency/fellowship (3), employed in independent practice (1), employed in an academic position at a university (2), employed in an academic position at a 2-year/4-year college (0), employed in other positions at a higher education institution (4), employed in a professional position in a school system (0), employed in business or industry (research/consulting) (0), employed in business or industry (management) (0), employed in a government agency (research) (0), employed in a government agency (professional services) (0), employed in a community mental health/counseling center (0), employed in a hospital/medical center (7), still seeking employment (0), other employment position (0), total from the above (doctoral) (17).

Additional Information:

Orientation, Objectives, and Emphasis of Department: The master's programs in school psychology and in community, rehabilitation, and school counseling are practitioner-focused. In the school and counseling psychology doctoral programs, practice and science are viewed as complementary and interdependent, implemented through coursework in psychological foundations, research methods, intervention theory and assessment, and by research and practice opportunities via assistantships, professional development activities, practica, specialized coursework, and independent study. Our generalist training emphasizes normal development and theory and methods relating to prevention and remediation of intra- and interpersonal human concerns. We have many opportunities to explore issues of individual and cultural diversity, to learn a variety of theoretical orientations, to pursue a range of research topics and methods, to study with a multicultural array of colleagues, to work with diverse client populations in multiple work settings, and to engage in varied professional roles. The master's program in educational psychology and statistics focuses on research based knowledge of human development, learning and individual differences, and the development of skills and understanding of research methodology. The program serves two main groups of students: those students seeking professional teaching certification in NY state and students desiring introductory graduate work in psychology.

Special Facilities or Resources: fee-for-service training clinic, the Psychological Services Center, directed by a licensed psychologist. Second-year doctoral students are supervised by licensed faculty using one-way mirrors and live video monitoring. Advanced doctoral students may have assistantships at the Center, where they gain additional experience in psychodiagnostic testing and psychotherapy. Assistants also provide assessment and intervention services for outside agencies that contract with the Center for services, e.g., private schools, Family Court, etc. One unique aspect of the program in Counseling Psychology is the opportunity for PhD students who are reasonably fluent in Spanish to participate in an exchange program with a family therapy training program in northwestern Spain. The Division of School Psychology maintans ongoing training partnerships with a number of local school districts and community agencies. Faculty in the Educational Psychology and Methodology Division are associated with two centers that provide students with opportunities to gain experience to supplement their coursework. The Child Research and Study Center undertakes research into the acquisition and remediation of reading skill, and consultation with schools and parents regarding children's school related difficulties. The Evaluation Consortium contracts to evaluate a wide variety of programs provided by schools and agencies.

Information for Students With Physical Disabilities: See the following Web site for more information: www.albany.edu/studentlife/dss/dss.html.

Application Information:
Send to: Office of Graduate Studies, University of Albany, State University of New York, 1400 Washington Avenue, Albany, NY 12222. Students are admitted in the Fall; Summer, application deadline February 1. MS and CAS applicants for Community, Rehabilitation, and School Counseling are due February 1 for summer admission. MS and CAS applicants for Educational Psychology are suggested for March 1 and October 15. PhD applicants for Counseling Psychology are due January 1. PhD applicants for Educational Psychology are due January 15. *Fee:* $60.

State University of New York at Albany
Department of Psychology
College of Arts and Sciences
1400 Washington Avenue
Albany, NY 12222
Telephone: (518) 442-4820
Fax: (518) 442-4867
E-mail: *cm949@albany.edu*
Web: *http://www.albany.edu/psy/*

Department Information:
1950. Chairperson: Edelgard Wulfert. Number of Faculty: total–full-time 29; women–full-time 15; minority–full-time 5.

Programs and Degrees Offered:
Listed in the following order: Program area, degree type (T if terminal Master's), number awarded 7/03–6/04. Biopsychology PhD (Doctor of Philosophy) 2, Clinical PhD (Doctor of Philosophy) 9, Cognitive PhD (Doctor of Philosophy) 0, Industrial/Organizational PhD (Doctor of Philosophy) 0, Social/ Personality PhD (Doctor of Philosophy) 2.

APA Accreditation: Clinical PhD (Doctor of Philosophy).

Student Applications/Admissions:

Student Applications

Biopsychology PhD (Doctor of Philosophy)—Applications 2004–2005, 13. Total applicants accepted 2004–2005, 9. Number enrolled (new admits only) 2004–2005 full-time, 4. Number enrolled (new admits only) 2004–2005 part-time, 0. Total enrolled 2004–2005 full-time, 12, part-time, 4. Openings 2005–2006, 3. The Median number of years required for completion of a degree are 7. The number of students enrolled full and part-time who were dismissed or voluntarily withdrew from this program area were 0. Clinical PhD (Doctor of Philosophy)—Applications 2004–2005, 168. Total applicants accepted 2004–2005, 14. Number enrolled (new admits only) 2004–2005 full-time, 6. Number enrolled (new admits only) 2004–2005 part-time, 0. Total enrolled 2004–2005 full-time, 50, part-time, 2. Openings 2005–2006, 6. The Median number of years required for completion of a degree are 5. The number of students enrolled full and part-time who were dismissed or voluntarily withdrew from this program area were 0. Cognitive PhD (Doctor of Philosophy)—Applications 2004–2005, 9. Total applicants accepted 2004–2005, 7. Number enrolled (new admits only) 2004–2005 full-time, 1. Number enrolled (new admits only) 2004–2005 part-time, 0. Total enrolled 2004–2005 full-time, 8, part-time, 2. Openings 2005–2006, 2. The number of students enrolled full and part-time who were dismissed or voluntarily withdrew from this program area were 0. Industrial/ Organizational PhD (Doctor of Philosophy)—Applications 2004–2005, 40. Total applicants accepted 2004–2005, 15. Number enrolled (new admits only) 2004–2005 full-time, 4. Number enrolled (new admits only) 2004–2005 part-time, 0. Total enrolled 2004–2005 full-time, 13, part-time, 7. Openings 2005–2006, 3. The number of students enrolled full and part-time who were dismissed or voluntarily withdrew from this program area were 1. Social/ Personality PhD (Doctor of Philosophy)—Applications 2004–2005, 21. Total applicants accepted 2004–2005, 8. Number enrolled (new admits only) 2004–2005 full-time, 4. Number enrolled (new admits only) 2004–2005 part-time, 0. Total enrolled 2004–2005 full-time, 8, part-time, 5. Openings 2005–2006, 3. The Median number of years required for completion of a degree are 6. The number of students enrolled full and part-time who were dismissed or voluntarily withdrew from this program area were 0.

Admissions Requirements:

Scores: Entries appear in this order: required test or GPA, minimum score (if required), median score of students entering in 2003–2004. Doctoral Programs: GRE-V 500, 585; GRE-Q 600, 661; GRE-V+Q 1000, 1246; GRE-Subject(Psych) 600, 653; overall undergraduate GPA 3.0, 3.58; psychology GPA 3.25, 3.71.

Other Criteria: (importance of criteria rated low, medium, or high): GRE/MAT scores high, research experience high, work experience low, extracurricular activity low, clinically related public service medium, GPA high, letters of recommendation high, interview high, statement of goals and objectives high. The interview process and clinically related service are relevant for the clinical psychology program only.

Student Characteristics: The following represents characteristics of students in 2004–2005 in all graduate psychology programs in the department: Female–full-time 71, part-time 10; Male–full-time 20, part-time 10; African American/Black–full-time 5, part-time 0; Hispanic/Latino(a)–full-time 6, part-time 0; Asian/Pacific Islander–full-time 8, part-time 3; American Indian/Alaska Native–full-time 0, part-time 0; Caucasian–full-time 72, part-time 16; Multi-ethnic–full-time 0, part-time 1; students subject to the Americans With Disabilities Act–full-time 0, part-time 0.

Financial Information/Assistance:

Tuition for Full-Time Study: *Doctoral:* State residents: per academic year $6,900, $288 per credit hour; Nonstate residents: per academic year $10,920, $455 per credit hour. Tuition is subject to change. See the following Web site for updates and changes in tuition costs: http://www.albany.edu/studentaccounts/charges.shtml.

Financial Assistance:

First Year Students: Teaching assistantships available for first-year. Average amount paid per academic year: $10,500. Average number of hours worked per week: 20. Apply by January 15. Tuition remission given: full and partial. Research assistantships available for first-year. Average amount paid per academic year: $10,500. Average number of hours worked per week: 20. Apply by January 15. Tuition remission given: full and partial. Fellowships and scholarships available for first-year. Average amount paid per academic year: $13,500. Average number of hours worked per week: 0. Apply by January 15. Tuition remission given: full.

Advanced Students: Teaching assistantships available for advanced students. Average amount paid per academic year: $10,500. Average number of hours worked per week: 20. Apply by None. Tuition remission given: full and partial. Research assistantships available for advanced students. Average amount paid per academic year: $10,500. Average number of hours worked per week: 20. Apply by None. Tuition remission given: full and partial. Fellowships and scholarships available for advanced students. Average amount paid per academic year: $13,500. Average number of hours worked per week: 0. Apply by None. Tuition remission given: full.

Contact Information: Of all students currently enrolled full-time, 90% benefitted from one or more of the listed financial assistance programs.

Internships/Practica: During the second year of our doctoral program in Clinical Psychology, students are placed at the Psychological Services Center, a University operated center that serves the general population of the city of Albany. During this placement students are supervised by members of the Clinical faculty. In their third year, students are required to participate in a community-based practicum. These practica include community mental health centers, VA inpatient and outpatient centers, inpatient and outpatient clinics in community hospitals and rehabilitation centers, residential facilities for youth, and the University's counseling center. Students may also elect to participate in an additional community-based practicum experience during their 4th year of training. Students are encouraged to attend APA accredited internships during their 5th year of study. Our students have attended internships in a variety of settings including children's hospitals, psychiatric hospitals, VA hospitals, university affiliated medical centers, general hospitals, and rehabilitation centers. Practicum and internship placements for doctoral students in the Industrial/Organizational Psychology specialization are possible with a number of local and national corporations and government agencies. For those doctoral students for whom a professional internship is required prior to graduation, 10 applied in 2003–

2004. Of those who applied, 10 were placed in internships listed by the Association of Psychology Postdoctoral and Internship Programs (APPIC); 10 were placed in APA accredited internships.

Housing and Day Care: On-campus housing is available. See the following Web site for more information: www.albany.edu/housing. On-campus day care facilities are available. See the following Web site for more information: www.albany.edu U-Kids Child Care, (518) 442-2660.

Employment of Department Graduates:

Master's Degree Graduates: Of those who graduated in the academic year 2003–2004, the following categories and numbers represent the post-graduate activities and employment of master's degree graduates: Enrolled in a post-doctoral residency/fellowship (n/a), employed in independent practice (n/a), total from the above (master's) (0).

Doctoral Degree Graduates: Of those who graduated in the academic year 2003–2004, the following categories and numbers represent the post-graduate activities and employment of doctoral degree graduates: Enrolled in a psychology doctoral program (n/a), enrolled in another graduate/professional program (0), enrolled in a post-doctoral residency/fellowship (3), employed in independent practice (0), employed in an academic position at a university (5), employed in an academic position at a 2-year/4-year college (1), employed in other positions at a higher education institution (1), employed in a professional position in a school system (0), employed in business or industry (research/consulting) (0), employed in business or industry (management) (0), employed in a government agency (research) (1), employed in a government agency (professional services) (0), employed in a community mental health/counseling center (2), employed in a hospital/medical center (1), still seeking employment (0), not seeking employment (0), other employment position (0), do not know (1), total from the above (doctoral) (15).

Additional Information:

Orientation, Objectives, and Emphasis of Department: All facets of the graduate program reflect a commitment to the empirical tradition in psychology. Thus, involvement in research is stressed in all areas of study. Students begin an apprentice relationship with faculty members upon entry into the department and are expected to remain actively involved in research throughout their graduate careers. A major goal of the department is to train individuals who will make research contributions to the field. All areas of concentration train students for careers as teachers and research scientists. In addition, the social, clinical, and, industrial/organizational areas prepare students for careers in applied settings. The orientation of the clinical program emphasizes cognitive and behavioral approaches. Admission is offered in five areas: biopsychology, clinical, cognitive, industrial/organizational, and social-personality.

Special Facilities or Resources: Resources and facilities include university- and grant-funded student stipends, plus stipends from other campus sources; a state-of-the-art animal facility and research laboratories in the Life Sciences Building; several human research laboratories; grant-supported research and treatment clinics; the Psychological Services Center for practicum training; and a variety of research equipment.

Information for Students With Physical Disabilities: See the following Web site for more information: www.albany.edu/studentlife.

Application Information:
Send to: The Office of Graduate Admissions, University Administration Building 121, 1400 Washington Avenue, Albany, NY 12222. Application available online. URL of online application: http://www.albany.edu/graduate/applyonline.shtml. Students are admitted in the Fall, application deadline January 1 for clinical psychology, January 15 for all other areas. *Fee:* $50.

State University of New York at Buffalo
Department of Counseling, School and Educational
  Psychology
409 Baldy Hall
Buffalo, NY 14260-1000
Telephone: (716) 645-2484
Fax: (716) 645-6616
E-mail: *nmyers@buffalo.edu*
Web: *http://www.gse.buffalo.edu*

Department Information:
1949. Chairperson: Thomas T. Frantz. Number of Faculty: total–full-time 18, part-time 3; women–full-time 8, part-time 2; minority–full-time 3.

Programs and Degrees Offered:
Listed in the following order: Program area, degree type (T if terminal Master's), number awarded 7/03–6/04. Counselor Education PhD (Doctor of Philosophy) 4, Educational Psychology PhD (Doctor of Philosophy) 0, Rehabilitation Counseling MA/MS (Master of Arts/Science) (T) 7, School Counseling Other 28, Educational Psychology MA/MS (Master of Arts/Science) (T) 4, School Psychology MA/MS (Master of Arts/Science) (T) 6, Counseling/School Psychology PhD (Doctor of Philosophy) 12, Mental Health Counseling MA/MS (Master of Arts/Science) (T).

APA Accreditation: Combination PhD (Doctor of Philosophy).

Student Applications/Admissions:
Student Applications

Counselor Education PhD (Doctor of Philosophy)—Applications 2004–2005, 16. Total applicants accepted 2004–2005, 5. Number enrolled (new admits only) 2004–2005 full-time, 1. Number enrolled (new admits only) 2004–2005 part-time, 4. Total enrolled 2004–2005 full-time, 3, part-time, 27. Openings 2005–2006, 4. The Median number of years required for completion of a degree are 6. The number of students enrolled full and part-time who were dismissed or voluntarily withdrew from this program area were 2. *Educational Psychology PhD (Doctor of Philosophy)*—Applications 2004–2005, 6. Total applicants accepted 2004–2005, 4. Number enrolled (new admits only) 2004–2005 full-time, 2. Number enrolled (new admits only) 2004–2005 part-time, 2. Total enrolled 2004–2005 full-time, 3, part-time, 13. Openings 2005–2006, 5. The Median number of years required for completion of a degree are 5. The number of students enrolled full and part-time who were dismissed or voluntarily withdrew from this program area were 0. *Rehabilitation Counseling MA/MS (Master of Arts/Science)*— Applications 2004–2005, 17. Total applicants accepted 2004–2005, 10. Number enrolled (new admits only) 2004–2005 full-time, 8. Number enrolled (new admits only) 2004–2005 part-time, 2. Total enrolled 2004–2005 full-time, 15, part-time, 5. Openings 2005–2006, 10. The Median number of years required for completion of a degree are 2. The number of students enrolled full and part-time who were dismissed or voluntarily withdrew from this program area were 3. *School Counseling Other*—Applications 2004–2005, 67. Total applicants accepted 2004–2005, 31. Number enrolled (new admits only) 2004–2005 full-time, 22. Number enrolled (new admits only) 2004–2005 part-time, 7. Total enrolled 2004–2005 full-time, 22, part-time, 33. Openings 2005–2006, 30. The Median number of years required for completion of a degree is 1. The number of students enrolled full and part-time who were dismissed or voluntarily withdrew from this program area were 2. *Educational Psychology MA/MS (Master of Arts/Science)*— Applications 2004–2005, 11. Total applicants accepted 2004–2005, 3. Number enrolled (new admits only) 2004–2005 full-time, 2. Number enrolled (new admits only) 2004–2005 part-time, 1. Total enrolled 2004–2005 full-time, 6, part-time, 7. Openings 2005–2006, 5. The Median number of years required for completion of a degree are 2. The number of students enrolled full and part-time who were dismissed or voluntarily withdrew from this program area were 0. *School Psychology MA/MS (Master of Arts/Science)*—Applications 2004–2005, 93. Total applicants accepted 2004–2005, 11. Number enrolled (new admits only) 2004–2005 full-time, 11. Number enrolled (new admits only) 2004–2005 part-time, 0. Total enrolled 2004–2005 full-time, 28. Openings 2005–2006, 11. The Median number of years required for completion of a degree are 3. The number of students enrolled full and part-time who were dismissed or voluntarily withdrew from this program area were 0. *Counseling/School Psychology PhD (Doctor of Philosophy)*—Applications 2004–2005, 80. Total applicants accepted 2004–2005, 12. Number enrolled (new admits only) 2004–2005 full-time, 12. Total enrolled 2004–2005 full-time, 43. Openings 2005–2006, 12. The Median number of years required for completion of a degree are 5. The number of students enrolled full and part-time who were dismissed or voluntarily withdrew from this program area were 0. *Mental Health Counseling MA/MS (Master of Arts/Science)*—Openings 2005–2006, 10. The Median number of years required for completion of a degree are 2.

Admissions Requirements:

Scores: Entries appear in this order: required test or GPA, minimum score (if required), median score of students entering in 2003–2004. Master's Programs: GRE-V no minimum stated, 505; GRE-Q no minimum stated, 565; GRE-V+Q no minimum stated, 1070; overall undergraduate GPA no minimum stated, 3.3. Doctoral Programs: GRE-V no minimum stated, 545; GRE-Q no minimum stated, 612; GRE-V+Q no minimum stated, 1157; overall undergraduate GPA no minimum stated, 3.3.

Other Criteria: (importance of criteria rated low, medium, or high): GRE/MAT scores high, research experience medium, work experience high, extracurricular activity low, clinically related public service medium, GPA medium, letters of recommendation medium, interview high, statement of goals and objectives high. Not all programs conduct personal interviews.

Student Characteristics: The following represents characteristics of students in 2004–2005 in all graduate psychology programs in the department: Female–full-time 102, part-time 64; Male–full-time 18, part-time 21; African American/Black–full-time 5, part-time 1; Hispanic/Latino(a)–full-time 4, part-time 0; Asian/Pacific Islander–full-time 4, part-time 1; American Indian/Alaska Native–full-time 1, part-time 1; Caucasian–full-time 106, part-time 82; Multi-ethnic–full-time 0, part-time 0; students subject to the Americans With Disabilities Act–full-time 0, part-time 0.

Financial Information/Assistance:

Tuition for Full-Time Study: *Master's:* State residents: per academic year $6,900, $288 per credit hour; Nonstate residents: per academic year $10,500, $438 per credit hour. *Doctoral:* State residents: per academic year $6,900, $288 per credit hour; Nonstate residents: per academic year $10,500, $438 per credit hour. See the following Web site for updates and changes in tuition costs: www.gse.buffalo.edu.

Financial Assistance:

First Year Students: Research assistantships available for first-year. Average amount paid per academic year: $9,000. Average number of hours worked per week: 20. Apply by April 15. Tuition remission given: full and partial.

Advanced Students: Research assistantships available for advanced students. Average amount paid per academic year: $9,000. Average number of hours worked per week: 20. Apply by April 15. Tuition remission given: full and partial.

Contact Information: Application and information available online at: www.buffalo.gse.edu.

Internships/Practica: Practicum and Internships available at area schools, community agencies, and hospitals. Experience with death and end of life issues, forensics, persons with disabilities, and assessment is available. For those doctoral students for whom a professional internship is required prior to graduation, 6 applied in 2003–2004. Of those who applied, 6 were placed in internships listed by the Association of Psychology Postdoctoral and Internship Programs (APPIC); 6 were placed in APA accredited internships.

Housing and Day Care: On-campus housing is available. See the following Web site for more information: www.wings.buffalo.edu. On-campus day care facilities are available. See the following Web site for more information: www.gse.buffalo.edu.

Employment of Department Graduates:

Master's Degree Graduates: Of those who graduated in the academic year 2003–2004, the following categories and numbers represent the post-graduate activities and employment of master's degree graduates: Enrolled in a psychology doctoral program (11), enrolled in a post-doctoral residency/fellowship (n/a), employed in independent practice (n/a), employed in other positions at a higher education institution (11), employed in business or industry (research/consulting) (8), employed in a community mental health/counseling center (30), employed in a hospital/medical center (20), total from the above (master's) (80).

Doctoral Degree Graduates: Of those who graduated in the academic year 2003–2004, the following categories and numbers represent the post-graduate activities and employment of doctoral degree graduates: Enrolled in a psychology doctoral program (n/a), total from the above (doctoral) (0).

Additional Information:

Orientation, Objectives, and Emphasis of Department: Departmental emphasis is on research based counseling with adults, college students, adolescents, children, and persons with disabilities. Doctoral programs follow the scientist-practitioner model. Some focus on preparing college faculty. Increased integration of counseling, school, and educational psychology programs is developing. Field experience and research experience are continuous through the programs. A new program leading to licensure as a mental health counselor is beginning in fall 2005.

Special Facilities or Resources: Department offers training experiences in a wide variety of schools, agencies, and college in both urban and suburban settings.

Application Information:

Send to: Office of Graduate Admissions, Graduate School of Education, 372 Baldy Hall, University at Buffalo, The State University of New York, Buffalo, NY 14260-1000. Application available online. URL of online application: www.buffalo.gse.edu. Students are admitted in the Fall, application deadline February 1. Counselor Education and Mental Health Counseling fall application deadline March 1. Educational Psychology and Rehabilitation Counseling applications considered for fall and spring admission. *Fee:* $50.

State University of New York at Buffalo

Department of Psychology
College of Arts and Sciences
210 Park Hall
Buffalo, NY 14260-4110
Telephone: (716) 645-3650
Fax: (716) 645-3801
E-mail: *psych@acsu.buffalo.edu*
Web: *http://wings.buffalo.edu/psychology/*

Department Information:

1921. Chair: Paul A. Luce. Number of Faculty: total–full-time 27; women–full-time 9; minority–full-time 1.

Programs and Degrees Offered:

Listed in the following order: Program area, degree type (T if terminal Master's), number awarded 7/03–6/04. Behavioral Neuroscience PhD (Doctor of Philosophy) 2, Clinical PhD (Doctor of Philosophy) 4, Cognitive PhD (Doctor of Philosophy) 1, Social-Personality PhD (Doctor of Philosophy) 0, General MA/MS (Master of Arts/Science) (T) 4.

APA Accreditation: Clinical PhD (Doctor of Philosophy).

Student Applications/Admissions:

Student Applications

Behavioral Neuroscience PhD (Doctor of Philosophy)—Applications 2004–2005, 23. Total applicants accepted 2004–2005, 7. Number enrolled (new admits only) 2004–2005 full-time, 2. Total enrolled 2004–2005 full-time, 10. Openings 2005–2006, 3. The Median number of years required for completion of a degree are 7. The number of students enrolled full and part-time who were dismissed or voluntarily withdrew from this program area were 2. *Clinical PhD (Doctor of Philosophy)*—Applications 2004–2005, 147. Total applicants accepted 2004–2005, 14. Number enrolled (new admits only) 2004–2005 full-time, 6. Total enrolled 2004–2005 full-time, 34. Openings 2005–2006, 3. The Median number of years required for completion of a degree are 8.5. The number of students enrolled full and part-time who were dismissed or voluntarily withdrew from this program area were 1. *Cognitive PhD (Doctor of Philosophy)*—Applications 2004–2005, 23. Total applicants accepted 2004–2005, 10. Number enrolled (new admits only) 2004–2005 full-time, 4. Total enrolled 2004–2005 full-time, 15. Openings 2005–2006, 3. The Median number of years required for completion of a degree are 4. The number of students enrolled full and part-time who were dismissed or voluntarily withdrew from this program area were 0. *Social-Personality PhD (Doctor of Philosophy)*—Applications 2004–2005, 59. Total applicants accepted 2004–2005, 6. Number enrolled (new admits only) 2004–2005 full-time, 3. Total enrolled 2004–2005 full-time, 8. Openings 2005–2006, 3. The Median number of years required for completion of a degree are 5. The number of students enrolled full and part-time who were dismissed or voluntarily withdrew from this program area were 2. *General MA/MS (Master of Arts/Science)*—Applications 2004–2005, 95. Total applicants accepted 2004–2005, 8. Number enrolled (new admits only) 2004–2005 full-time, 5. Total enrolled 2004–2005 full-time, 14. Openings 2005–2006, 20. The Median number of years required for completion of a degree are 2. The number of students enrolled full and part-time who were dismissed or voluntarily withdrew from this program area were 0.

Admissions Requirements:

Scores: Entries appear in this order: required test or GPA, minimum score (if required), median score of students entering in 2003–2004. Master's Programs: GRE-V no minimum stated; GRE-Q no minimum stated; GRE-Analytical no minimum stated. Doctoral Programs: GRE-V no minimum stated; GRE-Q no minimum stated; GRE-Analytical no minimum stated.

Other Criteria: (importance of criteria rated low, medium, or high): GRE/MAT scores medium, research experience high, work experience low, extracurricular activity low, clinically related public service medium, GPA high, letters of recommendation high, interview medium, statement of goals and objectives high. Interview for clinical only. For additional information on admission requirements, go to: http://wings.buffalo.edu/psychology.

Student Characteristics: The following represents characteristics of students in 2004–2005 in all graduate psychology programs in the department: Female–full-time 46, part-time 0; Male–full-time 35, part-time 0; African American/Black–full-time 6, part-time 0; Hispanic/Latino(a)–full-time 2, part-time 0; Asian/Pacific Islander–full-time 11, part-time 0; American Indian/Alaska Native–full-time 0, part-time 0; Caucasian–full-time 62, part-time 0; Multi-ethnic–full-time 0, part-time 0; students subject to the Americans With Disabilities Act–full-time 0, part-time 0.

Financial Information/Assistance:

Tuition for Full-Time Study: *Master's:* State residents: per academic year $8,108, $288 per credit hour; Nonstate residents: per academic year $12,128, $438 per credit hour. *Doctoral:* State residents: per academic year $8,108, $288 per credit hour; Nonstate residents: per academic year $12,128, $438 per credit hour. See the following Web site for updates and changes in tuition costs: http://src.buffalo.edu.

Financial Assistance:

First Year Students: Teaching assistantships available for first-year. Average amount paid per academic year: $8,400. Average number of hours worked per week: 20. Tuition remission given: full. Research assistantships available for first-year. Average amount paid per academic year: $8,400. Average number of hours worked per week: 20. Tuition remission given: full. Fellowships and scholarships available for first-year. Average amount paid per academic year: $10,400. Tuition remission given: full.

Advanced Students: Teaching assistantships available for advanced students. Average amount paid per academic year: $9,020. Average number of hours worked per week: 20. Tuition remission given: full. Research assistantships available for advanced students. Average amount paid per academic year: $9,020. Average number of hours worked per week: 20. Tuition remission given: full. Fellowships and scholarships available for advanced students. Average amount paid per academic year: $16,400. Tuition remission given: full.

Contact Information: Of all students currently enrolled full-time, 75% benefitted from one or more of the listed financial assistance programs. Application and information available online at: http://wings.buffalo.edu/psychology.

Internships/Practica: Several clinical practica are offered each year for students in the doctoral program in Clinical Psychology and for other doctoral students with permission of the instructor. In addition, there is a summer practicum focused on treatment of children with attention deficit/hyperactivity disorder. For those doctoral students for whom a professional internship is required prior to graduation, 7 applied in 2003–2004. Of those who applied, 7 were placed in internships listed by the Association of Psychology Postdoctoral and Internship Programs (APPIC); 7 were placed in APA accredited internships.

Housing and Day Care: On-campus housing is available. See the following Web site for more information: On-campus housing: http://www.grad.buffalo.edu/admissions/housing.shtml. On-campus day care facilities are available. See the following Web site for more information: http://wings.buffalo.edu/services/ccc.

Employment of Department Graduates:

Master's Degree Graduates: Of those who graduated in the academic year 2003–2004, the following categories and numbers represent the post-graduate activities and employment of master's degree graduates: Enrolled in a post-doctoral residency/fellowship (n/a), employed in independent practice (n/a), do not know (11), total from the above (master's) (11).

Doctoral Degree Graduates: Of those who graduated in the academic year 2003–2004, the following categories and numbers represent the post-graduate activities and employment of doctoral degree graduates: Enrolled in a psychology doctoral program (n/a), total from the above (doctoral) (0).

Additional Information:

Orientation, Objectives, and Emphasis of Department: The Department of Psychology offers doctoral degrees in Behavioral Neuroscience, Clinical Psychology, Cognitive Psychology, and Social-Personality Psychology and a Master's degree in Psychology with several specializations. The department has as its defining characteristic and distinguishing mission the conduct and communication of research and scholarship that contributes to the scientific understanding of psychology and the provision of high-quality graduate education and training. The department is dedicated to offering state-of-the-art education and training to its graduate students to prepare them to become leading researchers and to assume important positions in academic institutions or professional practice. We offer students a learning environment that is exciting and challenging, one that will allow them to follow their interests and fully develop their research skills. The research emphasis in the doctoral program in Behavorial Neuroscience is on the neural, endocrine, and molecular bases of behavior. Areas of specialization in Clinical Psychology include adult mood and anxiety disorders, relationship dysfunction, behavioral medicine, attention deficit/hyperactivity disorder, and child and adolescent aggression and substance abuse. The program in Cognitive Psychology focuses on the processes underlying perception, attention, memory, spoken and written language comprehension, language acquisition, categorization, problem solving, and thinking. Faculty research interests in the Social-Personality Program include close relationships, social cognition, self-concept, and self-esteem. Complete information is available on the department's Web site, http://wings.buffalo.edu/psychology.

Special Facilities or Resources: The Department of Psychology has specialized research facilities for the study of language comprehension, auditory and speech perception, memory, categorization, animal cognition, visual perception, attention, social interaction, small group processes, animal surgery research, behavior therapy, human psychophysiology and biofeedback, and neurochemical and electrophysiological investigations into the physiological bases of behavior. Many of these laboratories are computer-based. The department also has ample facilities for individual and group therapy, marriage counseling, and therapeutic work with children. One-way vision screens and videotape equipment are available for observation and supervision. Internships are available through the department's Psychological Services Center. Excellent facilities are available for working with animals. Students have liberal access to the University's computing services on the North Campus.

Application Information:

Send to: Director of Graduate Admissions, Department of Psychology, University at Buffalo—The State University of New York, Park Hall Room 210, Buffalo, NY 14260-4110 Early deadline for PhD—December 15; Final deadline—January 5. Application available online. URL of online application: http://wings.buffalo.edu/psychology. Students are admitted in the Fall, application deadline January 5. MA Application deadline for fall enrollment is May 1. *Fee:* $35.

State University of New York at New Paltz

Department of Psychology / Graduate Program
75 South Manheim Boulevard, Suite 6
New Paltz, NY 12561-2440
Telephone: (845) 257-3467
Fax: (845) 257-3474
E-mail: *raskinj@newpaltz.edu*
Web: *http://www.newpaltz.edu/psychology/graduateprogram*

Department Information:

1969. Chairperson: Maryalice Citera. Number of Faculty: total–full-time 12, part-time 5; women–full-time 6, part-time 4; minority–full-time 3, part-time 1; faculty subject to the Americans With Disabilities Act 1.

Programs and Degrees Offered:

Listed in the following order: Program area, degree type (T if terminal Master's), number awarded 7/03–6/04. General Psychology/Concentration in Counseling MA/MS (Master of Arts/Science) (T) 12.

Student Applications/Admissions:

Student Applications

General Psychology / Concentration in Counseling MA/MS (Master of Arts/Science)—Applications 2004–2005, 38. Total applicants accepted 2004–2005, 26. Number enrolled (new admits only) 2004–2005 full-time, 14. Number enrolled (new admits only) 2004–2005 part-time, 1. Openings 2005–2006, 20. The number of students enrolled full and part-time who were dismissed or voluntarily withdrew from this program area were 0.

Admissions Requirements:

Scores: Entries appear in this order: required test or GPA, minimum score (if required), median score of students entering in 2003–2004. Master's Programs: GRE-V no minimum stated, 500; GRE-Q no minimum stated, 550; GRE-V+Q no minimum stated, 1050; GRE-Analytical no minimum stated; overall undergraduate GPA 3.0, 3.3; psychology GPA 3.0, 3.5. Students must take the General GRE (Verbal, Quantitative, and Analytical Writing sections) and have a 3.0 undergraduate GPA (overall and in psychology classes). Other admissions requirements are as follows: 1) Baccalaureate degree from a regionally accredited institution, 2) Successful completion of undergraduate General Psychology, Statistics, Experimental Methods or Research Methods in Psychology, 3) Psychology Subject GRE scores optional, 4) Completed application for admission to the Master of Arts Program in Psychology, 5) Two official transcripts of all undergraduate and graduate work, 6) Three letters of recommendation, 7) International Students must meet additional university-wide requirements for admission. For details see: http://www.newpaltz.edu/admissions/intern_academic.html

Other Criteria: (importance of criteria rated low, medium, or high): GRE/MAT scores medium, research experience high, work experience high, extracurricular activity high, clinically related public service medium, GPA high, letters of recommendation high, interview low, statement of goals and objectives high, writing ability high. For additional information on admission requirements, go to: http://www.newpaltz.edu/psychology/graduateprogram/.

Student Characteristics: The following represents characteristics of students in 2004–2005 in all graduate psychology programs in the department: Female–full-time 20, part-time 8; Male–full-time 4, part-time 2; Caucasian–full-time 0, part-time 0.

Financial Information/Assistance:

Tuition for Full-Time Study: *Master's:* State residents: per academic year $6,900, $288 per credit hour; Nonstate residents: per academic year $10,500, $438 per credit hour. Tuition is subject to change. See the following Web site for updates and changes in tuition costs: http://www.newpaltz.edu/financialaid/tuition.html.

Financial Assistance:

First Year Students: Teaching assistantships available for first-year. Average amount paid per academic year: $5,000. Average number of hours worked per week: 20. Apply by March 15. Tuition remission given: partial. Research assistantships available for first-year. Apply by varies. Fellowships and scholarships available for first-year. Average number of hours worked per week: 10. Apply by varies. Tuition remission given: partial.

Advanced Students: Teaching assistantships available for advanced students. Average amount paid per academic year: $5,000. Average number of hours worked per week: 20. Tuition remission given: partial. Research assistantships available for advanced students. Apply by varies. Fellowships and scholarships available for advanced students. Apply by varies. Tuition remission given: partial.

Contact Information: Of all students currently enrolled full-time, 30% benefitted from one or more of the listed financial assistance programs. Application and information available online at: http://www.newpaltz.edu/psychology/graduateprogram/#application.

Internships/Practica: All students in the counseling concentration complete a practicum at the college counseling center and the career advising center. Additional internship opportunities are available with regional public and private mental health agencies. In addition to practicum and internship requirements, counseling concentration students complete additional counseling related coursework. Details can be found in the Graduate Handbook online: http://www.newpaltz.edu/psychology/gradbook.htm.

Housing and Day Care: On-campus housing is available. See the following Web site for more information: http://www.newpaltz.edu/reslife/ or contact Residence Life at (845) 257-4444. On-campus day care facilities are available. See the following Web site for more information: http://www.newpaltz.edu/services/children.html or contact The Children's Center at (845) 257-2910.

Employment of Department Graduates:

Master's Degree Graduates: Of those who graduated in the academic year 2003–2004, the following categories and numbers represent the post-graduate activities and employment of master's degree graduates: Enrolled in a post-doctoral residency/fellowship (n/a), employed in independent practice (n/a), total from the above (master's) (0).

Doctoral Degree Graduates: Of those who graduated in the academic year 2003–2004, the following categories and numbers

represent the post-graduate activities and employment of doctoral degree graduates: Enrolled in a psychology doctoral program (n/a), total from the above (doctoral) (0).

Additional Information:

Orientation, Objectives, and Emphasis of Department: Founded in 1828, America's 99th oldest university is an exciting blend of tradition and vision, providing students with the skills and knowledge needed to meet the challenges of the 21st century. The State University of New York at New Paltz offers general graduate training in psychology leading to the Master of Arts degree. In addition, the 36-credit general program provides students with the opportunity to select electives in a variety of fields including social, experimental, and organizational psychology as well as counseling. The program may serve as preparation for those training for entry into a doctoral program or as additional training for those who plan to enter or are already involved in applied areas of psychology. The Department also offers students the opportunity to pursue a specialized course of study leading to a Master of Arts degree with a Concentration in Counseling. This specialization requires 48 credits of graduate work, including the core curriculum and specialization courses. Three required fieldwork courses provide unique, varied, and intense hands-on experiences. New York's recent move to license MA level counselors makes the Concentration in Counseling a very marketable degree.

Special Facilities or Resources: Laboratory facilities and equipment (computers, videotaping equipment) are available to support student and faculty research in a variety of research areas (see department Web site for research details: http://www.newpaltz.edu/psychology/). The department also maintains links to local and community organizations for research opportunities. In addition the department has a computer lab for research and instruction with Internet access. All graduate students have access to word processing, SPSS, and the world-wide Web through the campus computer network.

Information for Students With Physical Disabilities: See the following Web site for more information: http://www.newpaltz.edu/drc.

Application Information:

Send to: Applications are available online (http://www.newpaltz.edu/graduate/applications.cfm) or by contacting the program at (845) 257-3467. As soon as you have a completed application, please send it to the following address: The Graduate School HAB 804, SUNY New Paltz, 75 South Manheim Boulevard, Suite 9, New Paltz, NY 12561-2443. Application available online. URL of online application: http://www.newpaltz.edu/graduate/applications.cfm. Students are admitted in the Fall, application deadline March 15; Spring, application deadline November 15. For Fall admission, application review begins March 15 and continues until the fall class is filled. For Spring admission, applications must be received by November 15. Graduate assistantships are available to selected students each year. Current stipends are $2,500 per semester ($5,000 per academic year) plus a six-credit tuition waiver per semester. Assistantship duties involve assisting faculty in teaching and research. Contact the program at (845) 257-3467 for further information about assistantships. *Fee:* $50.

State University of New York at Stony Brook
Department of Psychology
Stony Brook, NY 11794-2500
Telephone: (631) 632-7814
Fax: (631) 632-632-7876
E-mail: *abarry@notes.cc.sunysb.edu*
Web: *http://www.psy.sunysb.edu*

Department Information:

1961. Chair: Nancy Squires. Number of Faculty: total–full-time 28; women–full-time 13; minority–full-time 3.

Programs and Degrees Offered:

Listed in the following order: Program area, degree type (T if terminal Master's), number awarded 7/03–6/04. Biopsychology PhD (Doctor of Philosophy) 3, Clinical PhD (Doctor of Philosophy) 7, Experimental PhD (Doctor of Philosophy) 5, Social/Health PhD (Doctor of Philosophy) 4.

APA Accreditation: Clinical PhD (Doctor of Philosophy).

Student Applications/Admissions:

Student Applications

Biopsychology PhD (Doctor of Philosophy)—Applications 2004–2005, 36. Total applicants accepted 2004–2005, 5. Total enrolled 2004–2005 full-time, 18. *Clinical PhD (Doctor of Philosophy)*—Applications 2004–2005, 287. Total applicants accepted 2004–2005, 13. Total enrolled 2004–2005 full-time, 47. *Experimental PhD (Doctor of Philosophy)*—Applications 2004–2005, 25. Total applicants accepted 2004–2005, 6. Total enrolled 2004–2005 full-time, 17. *Social/ Health PhD (Doctor of Philosophy)*—Applications 2004–2005, 65. Total applicants accepted 2004–2005, 7. Total enrolled 2004–2005 full-time, 20.

Admissions Requirements:

Scores: Entries appear in this order: required test or GPA, minimum score (if required), median score of students entering in 2003–2004. Master's Programs: GRE-V no minimum stated; GRE-Q no minimum stated; GRE-Analytical no minimum stated; overall undergraduate GPA 3.50. Doctoral Programs: GRE-V+Q 1250; overall undergraduate GPA 3.5.
Other Criteria: (importance of criteria rated low, medium, or high): GRE/MAT scores medium, research experience high, work experience low, extracurricular activity low, clinically related public service low, GPA medium, letters of recommendation high, statement of goals and objectives high.

Student Characteristics: The following represents characteristics of students in 2004–2005 in all graduate psychology programs in the department: Female–full-time 72, part-time 0; Male–full-time 30, part-time 0; African American/Black–full-time 3, part-time 0; Hispanic/Latino(a)–full-time 6, part-time 0; Asian/Pacific Islander–full-time 3, part-time 0; American Indian/Alaska Native–

full-time 0, part-time 0; Caucasian–full-time 0, part-time 0; students subject to the Americans With Disabilities Act–full-time 0, part-time 0.

Financial Information/Assistance:

Tuition for Full-Time Study: *Doctoral:* State residents: per academic year $6,900, $288 per credit hour; Nonstate residents: per academic year $10,500, $438 per credit hour.

Financial Assistance:

First Year Students: No information provided.

Advanced Students: No information provided.

Contact Information: Of all students currently enrolled full-time, 75% benefitted from one or more of the listed financial assistance programs. Application and information available online at: http://www.psychology.sunysb.edu/psychology/grad/gradaid.htm.

Internships/Practica: For those doctoral students for whom a professional internship is required prior to graduation, 5 applied in 2003–2004. Of those who applied, 5 were placed in APA accredited internships.

Housing and Day Care: On-campus housing is available. See the following Web site for more information: http://studentaffairs.stonybrook.edu/residence. On-campus day care facilities are available. See the following Web site for more information: http://ws.cc.stonybrook.edu/sb/childcare/.

Employment of Department Graduates:

Master's Degree Graduates: Of those who graduated in the academic year 2003–2004, the following categories and numbers represent the post-graduate activities and employment of master's degree graduates: Enrolled in a post-doctoral residency/fellowship (n/a), employed in independent practice (n/a), total from the above (master's) (0).

Doctoral Degree Graduates: Of those who graduated in the academic year 2003–2004, the following categories and numbers represent the post-graduate activities and employment of doctoral degree graduates: Enrolled in a psychology doctoral program (n/a), total from the above (doctoral) (0).

Additional Information:

Orientation, Objectives, and Emphasis of Department: In all areas, the primary emphasis is on research training through research advisement and apprenticeship. Students are encouraged to become involved in ongoing research immediately and to engage in independent research when sufficient skills and knowledge permit, with the goal of becoming active and original contributors. As the first behavioral clinical curriculum in the country, Stony Brook has served as a model for a number of other behaviorally oriented clinical programs and continues to be a leader in that field. Research in the experimental area has always included both human and animal learning and now includes spatial cognition, psycholinguistics, cognitive development, memory, attention,

judgement and choice, sensation and perception, and psychophysics. Biopsychology offers three areas of concentration: psychophysiology, neuropsychology, and behavioral neuroscience. Social psychology offers a general education and research in social and health psychology. Health psychology and psychophysiology are interarea concentrations.

Special Facilities or Resources: Besides faculty laboratories for human, animal, and physiological research, and electronics and machine shops, other campus facilities for research and graduate training include: Psychological Center, the training, research, and service unit for clinical psychology; Point of Woods Laboratory School with a special education class for elementary students; University Preschool with children from 18 months to 5 years of age; University Marital Therapy Clinic; and Suffolk Child Development Center, a private school for autistic, retarded, aphasic, and developmentally delayed children. Clinical neuropsychology uses affiliations with the University Health Sciences Center, local schools, an agency for the mentally retarded, and a Veterans Administration hospital. Departmental CRT terminals and 12 additional terminals and two printers in the division's Social Science Data Laboratory are used with campus computers.

Application Information:

Send to: Graduate Office-Department of Psychology, SUNY at Stony Brook, Stony Brook, NY 11794-2500. Application available online. URL of online application: http://www.psychology.sunysb.edu/psychology/grad/gradapply.htm. Students are admitted in the Fall, application deadline January 15. *Fee:* $60.

State University of New York, College at Brockport
Department of Psychology
350 New Campus Drive
Brockport, NY 14420
Telephone: (585) 395-2488
Fax: (585) 395-2116
E-mail: *psychdpt@brockport.edu*
Web: *http://www.brockport.edu*

Department Information:

1965. Chairperson: Robert J. Miller. Number of Faculty: total–full-time 13, part-time 5; women–full-time 6, part-time 3; minority–full-time 1.

Programs and Degrees Offered:

Listed in the following order: Program area, degree type (T if terminal Master's), number awarded 7/03–6/04. Clinical MA/MS (Master of Arts/Science) (T) 10.

Student Applications/Admissions:

Student Applications

Clinical MA/MS (Master of Arts/Science)—Applications 2004–2005, 34. Total applicants accepted 2004–2005, 11. Number enrolled (new admits only) 2004–2005 full-time, 8. Number enrolled (new admits only) 2004–2005 part-time 2. Total enrolled 2004–2005 full-time, 13, part-time, 10. Openings 2005–2006, 15. The Median number of years required for completion of a degree are 2. The number of students enrolled full and part-time who were dismissed or voluntarily withdrew from this program area were 1.

Admissions Requirements:

Scores: Entries appear in this order: required test or GPA, minimum score (if required), median score of students entering in 2003–2004. Master's Programs: GRE-V 500, 500; GRE-Q 500, 580; GRE-Analytical 500; overall undergraduate GPA 3.00, 3.50; last 2 years GPA 3.25, 3.70.

Other Criteria: (importance of criteria rated low, medium, or high): GRE/MAT scores medium, research experience high, work experience low, clinically related public service medium, GPA high, letters of recommendation high, interview high, statement of goals and objectives high. For additional information on admission requirements, go to: www.brockport.edu.

Student Characteristics: The following represents characteristics of students in 2004–2005 in all graduate psychology programs in the department: Female–full-time 13, part-time 2; Male–full-time 2, part-time 4; African American/Black–full-time 0, part-time 1; Hispanic/Latino(a)–full-time 1, part-time 0; Asian/Pacific Islander–full-time 1, part-time 0; American Indian/Alaska Native–full-time 0, part-time 0; Caucasian–full-time 4, part-time 16; Multi-ethnic–full-time 0, part-time 0; students subject to the Americans With Disabilities Act–full-time 0, part-time 0.

Financial Information/Assistance:

Tuition for Full-Time Study: *Master's:* State residents: per academic year $3,456, $288 per credit hour; Nonstate residents: per academic year $5,256, $438 per credit hour. Tuition is subject to change.

Financial Assistance:

First Year Students: Teaching assistantships available for first-year. Average amount paid per academic year: $6,000. Average number of hours worked per week: 20. Apply by April 15. Tuition remission given: partial.

Advanced Students: Teaching assistantships available for advanced students. Average amount paid per academic year: $6,000. Average number of hours worked per week: 20. Apply by April 15. Tuition remission given: partial.

Contact Information: Of all students currently enrolled full-time, 10% benefitted from one or more of the listed financial assistance programs.

Internships/Practica: Practical experience is in one of nearly 50 human service agencies in western New York, including the college counseling center, VA and academic medical centers, and state and local mental health, developmental disability/autism centers, and other community service agencies. Each practicum placement is developed individually, based on the specific student and agency involved. Each practicum is supervised by an agency staff member as well as a faculty member from the Department of Psychology. Students must successfully complete all required coursework before beginning the practicum.

Housing and Day Care: On-campus housing is available. Contact gradadmit@brockport.edu. On-campus day care facilities are available.

Employment of Department Graduates:

Master's Degree Graduates: Of those who graduated in the academic year 2003–2004, the following categories and numbers represent the post-graduate activities and employment of master's degree graduates: Enrolled in a psychology doctoral program (0), enrolled in another graduate/professional program (1), enrolled in a post-doctoral residency/fellowship (n/a), employed in independent practice (n/a), employed in an academic position at a university (0), employed in an academic position at a 2-year/4-year college (0), employed in other positions at a higher education institution (0), employed in a professional position in a school system (0), employed in business or industry (research/consulting) (0), employed in business or industry (management) (0), employed in a government agency (research) (0), employed in a government agency (professional services) (0), employed in a community mental health/counseling center (2), employed in a hospital/medical center (2), still seeking employment (1), other employment position (3), total from the above (master's) (9).

Doctoral Degree Graduates: Of those who graduated in the academic year 2003–2004, the following categories and numbers represent the post-graduate activities and employment of doctoral degree graduates: Enrolled in a psychology doctoral program (n/a), total from the above (doctoral) (0).

Additional Information:

Orientation, Objectives, and Emphasis of Department: The MA in psychology program is designed to prepare students for both doctoral work and also careers in applied psychology and the helping professions. Students are trained as scientists and practitioners, concerned with the application of psychological principles to the treatment and prevention of behavior disorders. Courses provide theoretical and practical training in contemporary methods of assessment, behavioral and cognitive-behavioral clinical intervention, and program evaluation applicable to child, adolescent and adult populations. Faculty includes board-certified applied behavior analysts and licensed psychologists.

Special Facilities or Resources: The department has facilities for research in the biobehavioral sciences, as well as sensory-perceptual, clinical, developmental, and personality psychology topics; and assessment/intervention training. Laboratory space, computer equipment, and an extensive file of psychological assessment instruments are also available.

Information for Students With Physical Disabilities: gradadmit-@brockport.edu.

Application Information:

Send to: Office of Graduate Studies, SUNY College at Brockport, 350 New Campus Drive, Brockport, NY 14420-2914. Students are admitted in the Fall, application deadline April 15. *Fee:* $50.

State University of New York, College at Plattsburgh

Psychology Department
Beaumont Hall, 101 Broad Street
Plattsburgh, NY 12901
Telephone: (518) 564-3076
Fax: (518) 564-3397
E-mail: *William.Tooke@plattsburgh.edu or Jeanne.Ryan@plattsburgh.edu*
Web: *http://www.plattsburgh.edu/psy*

Department Information:

1970. Chairperson: Dr. William Tooke and Dr. Jeanne Ryan, Co-Chairs. Number of Faculty: total–full-time 13, part-time 7; women–full-time 4, part-time 4; minority–full-time 1.

Programs and Degrees Offered:

Listed in the following order: Program area, degree type (T if terminal Master's), number awarded 7/03–6/04. School Psychology MA/MS (Master of Arts/Science) (T) 0.

Student Applications/Admissions:

Student Applications

School Psychology MA/MS (Master of Arts/Science)—Applications 2004–2005, 25. Total applicants accepted 2004–2005, 8. Openings 2005–2006, 10. The Median number of years required for completion of a degree are 4.

Admissions Requirements:

Scores: Entries appear in this order: required test or GPA, minimum score (if required), median score of students entering in 2003–2004. Master's Programs: GRE-V no minimum stated; GRE-Q no minimum stated; GRE-V+Q 1000, 1100; overall undergraduate GPA 3.00, 3.20.

Other Criteria: (importance of criteria rated low, medium, or high): GRE/MAT scores medium, research experience medium, work experience medium, clinically related public service medium, GPA medium, letters of recommendation high, interview high, statement of goals and objectives high.

Student Characteristics: The following represents characteristics of students in 2004–2005 in all graduate psychology programs in the department: Female–full-time 10, part-time 0; Male–full-time 4, part-time 0; African American/Black–full-time 0, part-time 0; Hispanic/Latino(a)–full-time 0, part-time 0; Asian/Pacific Islander–full-time 0, part-time 0; American Indian/Alaska Native–full-time 0, part-time 0; Caucasian–full-time 0, part-time 0; Multiethnic–full-time 0, part-time 0; students subject to the Americans With Disabilities Act–full-time 0, part-time 0.

Financial Information/Assistance:

Tuition for Full-Time Study: *Master's:* State residents: per academic year $2,550, $213 per credit hour; Nonstate residents: per academic year $4,208, $351 per credit hour. Tuition is subject to change.

Financial Assistance:

First Year Students: Research assistantships available for first-year. Average amount paid per academic year: $4,600. Average number of hours worked per week: 10. Apply by March 1. Tuition remission given: full and partial.

Advanced Students: Research assistantships available for advanced students. Average amount paid per academic year: $4,600. Average number of hours worked per week: 10. Apply by March 1. Tuition remission given: full and partial. Traineeships available for advanced students. Average amount paid per academic year: $5,000. Average number of hours worked per week: 15. Apply by March 1. Tuition remission given: full.

Contact Information: Of all students currently enrolled full-time, 40% benefitted from one or more of the listed financial assistance programs.

Internships/Practica: During the third and final year of graduate study, students are placed within school districts on a full-time basis. School districts sometimes offer a stipend under contractual agreement with the graduate student and the University. Stipends range from $5,000 to $9,000. Relocating to a school district in order to receive a stipend might be necessary.

Housing and Day Care: On-campus housing is available. Contact Graduate Admissions, Kehoe Building, Plattsburgh State University of New York, 101 Broad Street, Plattsburgh, NY 12901. On-campus day care facilities are available.

Employment of Department Graduates:

Master's Degree Graduates: Of those who graduated in the academic year 2003–2004, the following categories and numbers represent the post-graduate activities and employment of master's degree graduates: Enrolled in a psychology doctoral program (1), enrolled in a post-doctoral residency/fellowship (n/a), employed in independent practice (n/a), employed in a professional position in a school system (7), still seeking employment (0), total from the above (master's) (8).

Doctoral Degree Graduates: Of those who graduated in the academic year 2003–2004, the following categories and numbers represent the post-graduate activities and employment of doctoral degree graduates: Enrolled in a psychology doctoral program (n/a), total from the above (doctoral) (0).

Additional Information:

Orientation, Objectives, and Emphasis of Department: The curriculum is a three-year, 69-hour MA program in psychology. The program offers coursework in psychological theories and skill development and applied experiences in area schools and community agencies. The goal of the program is to enable students to work effectively with individuals and groups and to act as psychological resources in schools and the community. A unique feature of the program is that many courses, beginning in the first semester, combine theory and research with practicum experiences in school and clinical work. Students develop competencies in personality, research methods, psychological assessment, behavior modification, individual and group psychotherapy, and community mental health. An important aspect of graduate training is the internship served the third year of graduate study at area schools. The Psychology Department and the agencies involved provide extensive supervision of students' work.

Special Facilities or Resources: The Neuropsychology Clinic and Psychoeducational Services center provide graduate students with on-site practicum experiences. As part of course assignments, all students are required to provide supervised practicum work in the clinic to clients from the community and college.

Information for Students With Physical Disabilities: See the following Web site for more information: www.plattsburgh.edu.

Application Information:
Send to: Graduate Admissions, Kehoe Hall, SUNY-Plattsburgh, 101 Broad Street, Plattsburgh, NY 12901. Students are admitted in the Fall, application deadline March 1. *Fee:* $75.

Syracuse University
Department of Psychology
Arts & Sciences
430 Huntington Hall, 150 Marshall Street
Syracuse, NY 13244-2340
Telephone: (315) 443-2354
Fax: (315) 443-4085
E-mail: *mlcripps@syr.edu*
Web: *http://psychweb.syr.edu*

Department Information:
1952. Chairperson: Barbara H. Fiese. Number of Faculty: total–full-time 25, part-time 28; women–full-time 9, part-time 7; minority–full-time 2.

Programs and Degrees Offered:
Listed in the following order: Program area, degree type (T if terminal Master's), number awarded 7/03–6/04. Clinical PhD (Doctor of Philosophy) 1, Experimental PhD (Doctor of Philosophy) 1, School PhD (Doctor of Philosophy) 2, Social PhD (Doctor of Philosophy) 2.

APA Accreditation: Clinical PhD (Doctor of Philosophy). School PhD (Doctor of Philosophy).

Student Applications/Admissions:
Student Applications
 Clinical PhD (Doctor of Philosophy)—Applications 2004–2005, 128. Total applicants accepted 2004–2005, 8. Number enrolled (new admits only) 2004–2005 full-time, 6. Openings 2005–2006, 4. The Median number of years required for completion of a degree are 5. The number of students enrolled full and part-time who were dismissed or voluntarily withdrew from this program area were 0. *Experimental PhD (Doctor of Philosophy)*—Applications 2004–2005, 20. Total applicants accepted 2004–2005, 5. Number enrolled (new admits only) 2004–2005 full-time, 2. Openings 2005–2006, 4. The Median number of years required for completion of a degree are 5. The number of students enrolled full and part-time who were dismissed or voluntarily withdrew from this program area were 1. *School PhD (Doctor of Philosophy)*—Applications 2004–2005, 53. Total applicants accepted 2004–2005, 4. Number enrolled (new admits only) 2004–2005 full-time, 4. Openings 2005–2006, 4.

The Median number of years required for completion of a degree are 5. The number of students enrolled full and part-time who were dismissed or voluntarily withdrew from this program area were 0. *Social PhD (Doctor of Philosophy)*—Applications 2004–2005, 7. Total applicants accepted 2004–2005, 0. Openings 2005–2006, 1. The Median number of years required for completion of a degree are 5. The number of students enrolled full and part-time who were dismissed or voluntarily withdrew from this program area were 0.

Admissions Requirements:
 Scores: Entries appear in this order: required test or GPA, minimum score (if required), median score of students entering in 2003–2004. Doctoral Programs: GRE-V 500; GRE-Q 600; GRE-V+Q 1100; overall undergraduate GPA 3.0. GRE required by all programs. Subject required for Clinical Psychology Program only. Subject minimum score is 500.
 Other Criteria: (importance of criteria rated low, medium, or high): GRE/MAT scores high, research experience high, work experience medium, extracurricular activity low, clinically related public service medium, GPA high, letters of recommendation high, interview high, statement of goals and objectives high. Interview requirements vary from program to program.

Student Characteristics: The following represents characteristics of students in 2004–2005 in all graduate psychology programs in the department: Female–full-time 48, part-time 0; Male–full-time 18, part-time 0; African American/Black–full-time 0, part-time 0; Hispanic/Latino(a)–full-time 0, part-time 0; Asian/Pacific Islander–full-time 7, part-time 0; American Indian/Alaska Native–full-time 0, part-time 0; Caucasian–full-time 58, part-time 0; Multi-ethnic–full-time 1, part-time 0; students subject to the Americans With Disabilities Act–full-time 0, part-time 0.

Financial Information/Assistance:
Tuition for Full-Time Study: *Doctoral:* State residents: per academic year $19,344, $806 per credit hour; Nonstate residents: per academic year $19,344, $806 per credit hour. Tuition is subject to change. See the following Web site for updates and changes in tuition costs: http://financialaid.syr.edu.

Financial Assistance:
 First Year Students: Teaching assistantships available for first-year. Average amount paid per academic year: $10,958. Average number of hours worked per week: 20. Apply by January 10. Tuition remission given: full. Research assistantships available for first-year. Average amount paid per academic year: $10,958. Average number of hours worked per week: 20. Apply by January 10. Tuition remission given: full and partial. Fellowships and scholarships available for first-year. Average amount paid per academic year: $18,000. Average number of hours worked per week: 0. Apply by January 10. Tuition remission given: full.
 Advanced Students: Teaching assistantships available for advanced students. Average amount paid per academic year: $10,958. Average number of hours worked per week: 20. Apply by NA. Tuition remission given: full. Research assistantships available for advanced students. Average amount paid per academic year: $10,958. Average number of hours worked per week: 20. Apply by NA. Tuition remission given: full and partial. Fellowships and scholarships available for advanced students. Average amount paid per academic year: $18,000. Average number of hours worked per week: 0. Apply by NA. Tuition remission given: full.

Contact Information: Of all students currently enrolled full-time, 61% benefitted from one or more of the listed financial assistance programs.

Internships/Practica: Students in the clinical and school psychology training programs have appropriate internship and practica experiences available in hospitals, schools, and other community and University settings. Following completion of their coursework, clinical students complete APA approved internships as part of their required program of study. For those doctoral students for whom a professional internship is required prior to graduation, 4 applied in 2003–2004. Of those who applied, 4 were placed in internships listed by the Association of Psychology Postdoctoral and Internship Programs (APPIC); 3 were placed in APA accredited internships.

Housing and Day Care: On-campus housing is available. See the following Web site for more information: www.syr.edu/HousingMealplans/gradhousing.htm. On-campus day care facilities are available.

Employment of Department Graduates:

Master's Degree Graduates: Of those who graduated in the academic year 2003–2004, the following categories and numbers represent the post-graduate activities and employment of master's degree graduates: Enrolled in a post-doctoral residency/fellowship (n/a), employed in independent practice (n/a), total from the above (master's) (0).

Doctoral Degree Graduates: Of those who graduated in the academic year 2003–2004, the following categories and numbers represent the post-graduate activities and employment of doctoral degree graduates: Enrolled in a psychology doctoral program (n/a), employed in an academic position at a university (4), employed in an academic position at a 2-year/4-year college (1), employed in other positions at a higher education institution (1), employed in a professional position in a school system (1), total from the above (doctoral) (7).

Additional Information:

Orientation, Objectives, and Emphasis of Department: Our goal is to train high caliber scientists in psychology. Students work closely with a faculty advisor whose research interests are similar to the student's (one can change to a new advisor, however, if one's research interests change). Our APA-approved programs in clinical and school psychology are based on the Boulder scientist-practitioner model. There are four thematic foci in the department: Cognitive Aging; Health and Behavior; The Scholarship of the Causes, Consequences, and Remediation of Social Challenges; and the Psychology of Children in Home and School. Students can gain exposure to research in coping with chronic illness, HIV prevention, memory processes in older adults, school based intervention, substance abuse, and group process, to name a few. A second goal is training future teachers of Psychology. Students typically engage in several semesters of teaching, beginning with sections of introductory psychology and moving on to teach more specialized courses. Entering students participate in the University's "Future Professoriate Program," a teaching practicum nationally known for helping new graduate students enter the profession. Other teaching opportunities are available in the Department's Allport Project, which involves undergraduates in faculty research activities. As part of this program, graduate students may offer supervised but essentially independent seminars

for undergraduates in their specialty area. Students enrolled in the clinical and school psychology programs gain clinical experience through our university based psychological services center and placement in area schools and hospitals.

Special Facilities or Resources: The Department of Psychology is housed in Huntington Hall, an historic building that has been remodeled to provide offices and seminar rooms, as well as laboratories for the study of cognition, social psychology, behavioral medicine, family interaction, and group processes. Labs and offices are equipped with microcomputers for data collection and analysis. A separate wing houses the Department's Psychological Services Center, which offers facilities for clinical and school psychology practicum training and research. In addition, the Department has two facilities on campus and two facilities off campus that provide additional lab space. Other facilities are available through faculty collaborations with researchers at the Upstate Medical University, which is adjacent to Huntington Hall. The Department and its Center for Health and Behavior support two full-time computer technicians.

Information for Students With Physical Disabilities: See the following Web site for more information: http://sumweb.syr.edu/ss/dserv/.

Application Information:
Send to: Graduate School, Suite 303, Bowne Hall, Syracuse University, Syracuse, NY 13244-1200. Application available online. URL of online application: http://gradsch.syr.edu/application/. Students are admitted in the Fall, application deadline January 10. To be considered for a University Fellowship, completed applications must be received by January 10. Due to APA requirements, all applications (fellowship and non-fellowship) for the School and Clinical Psychology Programs are due by January 10. *Fee:* $65.

Teachers College, Columbia University
Department of Counseling and Clinical Psychology
Box 102, 525 West 120th Street
New York, NY 10027-6696
Telephone: (212) 678-3257
Fax: (212) 678-3275
E-mail: *bf39@columbia.edu*
Web: *http://www.tc.columbia.edu*

Department Information:
1996. Chairperson: Madonna G. Constantine. Number of Faculty: total–full-time 12, part-time 29; women–full-time 7, part-time 18; minority–full-time 6, part-time 4.

Programs and Degrees Offered:
Listed in the following order: Program area, degree type (T if terminal Master's), number awarded 7/03–6/04. Clinical PhD (Doctor of Philosophy) 11, Counseling PhD (Doctor of Philosophy), Pychological Counseling Other, Psychology in Education: Applied MA/MS (Master of Arts/Science) (T) 40.

APA Accreditation: Clinical PhD (Doctor of Philosophy). Counseling PhD (Doctor of Philosophy).

Student Applications/Admissions:

Student Applications

Clinical PhD (Doctor of Philosophy)—Applications 2004–2005, 250. Total applicants accepted 2004–2005, 12. Number enrolled (new admits only) 2004–2005 full-time, 7. Total enrolled 2004–2005 full-time, 30, part-time, 24. Openings 2005–2006, 8. The Median number of years required for completion of a degree are 6. The number of students enrolled full and part-time who were dismissed or voluntarily withdrew from this program area were 0. *Counseling PhD (Doctor of Philosophy)*—Applications 2004–2005, 163. Total applicants accepted 2004–2005, 10. Number enrolled (new admits only) 2004–2005 full-time, 9. Total enrolled 2004–2005 full-time, 27, part-time, 20. Openings 2005–2006, 6. The number of students enrolled full and part-time who were dismissed or voluntarily withdrew from this program area were 0. *Pychological Counseling Other*—Applications 2004–2005, 188. Total applicants accepted 2004–2005, 133. Number enrolled (new admits only) 2004–2005 full-time, 78. Total enrolled 2004–2005 full-time, 105, part-time, 71. The number of students enrolled full and part-time who were dismissed or voluntarily withdrew from this program area were 3. *Psychology in Education: Applied MA/MS (Master of Arts/Science)*—Applications 2004–2005, 80. Total applicants accepted 2004–2005, 60. Number enrolled (new admits only) 2004–2005 full-time, 35. Number enrolled (new admits only) 2004–2005 part-time, 25. Total enrolled 2004–2005 full-time, 35, part-time, 35. Openings 2005–2006, 80. The Median number of years required for completion of a degree is 1. The number of students enrolled full and part-time who were dismissed or voluntarily withdrew from this program area were 5.

Admissions Requirements:

Scores: Entries appear in this order: required test or GPA, minimum score (if required), median score of students entering in 2003–2004. Master's Programs: overall undergraduate GPA no minimum stated, 3.65; last 2 years GPA no minimum stated; psychology GPA no minimum stated. GRE scores are not required for MEd. For MA, GRE scores are strongly recommended but not required. Doctoral Programs: GRE-V no minimum stated; GRE-Q no minimum stated; GRE-V+Q 1300, 1340; GRE-Analytical no minimum stated; GRE-Subject(Psych) 650, 660.

Other Criteria: (importance of criteria rated low, medium, or high): GRE/MAT scores high, research experience high, work experience medium, extracurricular activity low, clinically related public service medium, GPA medium, letters of recommendation high, interview high, statement of goals and objectives high. For additional information on admission requirements, go to: http://www.tc.edu/ccp/Clinical/detail.asp?id=Special+Application+Requirements+and+Information.

Student Characteristics: The following represents characteristics of students in 2004–2005 in all graduate psychology programs in the department: Female–full-time 167, part-time 127; Male–full-time 30, part-time 23; African American/Black–full-time 22, part-time 11; Hispanic/Latino(a)–full-time 17, part-time 9; Asian/Pacific Islander–full-time 26, part-time 15; American Indian/Alaska Native–full-time 1, part-time 0; Caucasian–full-time 121, part-time 96; Multi-ethnic–full-time 10, part-time 19; students subject to the Americans With Disabilities Act–full-time 4, part-time 0.

Financial Information/Assistance:

Tuition for Full-Time Study: *Master's:* State residents: per academic year $21,420, $875 per credit hour; Nonstate residents: per academic year $21,420, $875 per credit hour. *Doctoral:* State residents: per academic year $21,420, $875 per credit hour; Nonstate residents: per academic year $21,420, $875 per credit hour. Tuition is subject to change.

Financial Assistance:

First Year Students: Fellowships and scholarships available for first-year. Average amount paid per academic year: $6,600. Apply by December 15. Tuition remission given: partial.

Advanced Students: Fellowships and scholarships available for advanced students. Average amount paid per academic year: $6,600. Tuition remission given: partial.

Contact Information: Of all students currently enrolled full-time, 40% benefitted from one or more of the listed financial assistance programs. Application and information available online at: http://www.tc.columbia.edu/studentaid/.

Internships/Practica: Master's students in the Department of Counseling and Clinical Psychology complete fieldwork appropriate to their track or area of interest in a variety of settings including schools, hospitals, diverse mental health clinics and rehabilitation centers. Doctoral students do externships in settings similar to the ones indicated above, in preparation for their required APA-approved internships. In addition, all PhD students as well as the MEd students engage in practicum experiences at the Center for Educational and Psychological Services at the College. The Center is a community resource that provides low-cost services for the public utilizing graduate students from several departments within the College. All students receive supervision provided by full-time and adjunct faculty. For those doctoral students for whom a professional internship is required prior to graduation, 5 applied in 2003–2004. Of those who applied, 5 were placed in internships listed by the Association of Psychology Postdoctoral and Internship Programs (APPIC); 5 were placed in APA accredited internships.

Housing and Day Care: On-campus housing is available. See the following Web site for more information: http://www.tc.columbia.edu/housing/. On-campus day care facilities are available. See the following Web site for more information: http://www.tc.edu/centers/hollingworth/; http://www.tc.edu/centers/citp/.

Employment of Department Graduates:

Master's Degree Graduates: Of those who graduated in the academic year 2003–2004, the following categories and numbers represent the post-graduate activities and employment of master's degree graduates: Enrolled in a psychology doctoral program (22), enrolled in a post-doctoral residency/fellowship (n/a), employed in independent practice (n/a), total from the above (master's) (22).

Doctoral Degree Graduates: Of those who graduated in the academic year 2003–2004, the following categories and numbers represent the post-graduate activities and employment of doctoral degree graduates: Enrolled in a psychology doctoral program (n/a), enrolled in another graduate/professional program (0), enrolled in a post-doctoral residency/fellowship (6), employed in an academic position at a university (2), employed in other positions at a higher education institution (1), employed in a government agency (professional services) (1), employed in a community mental health/counseling center (2), employed in a hospital/medical center (2), still seeking employment (1), total from the above (doctoral) (15).

Additional Information:

Orientation, Objectives, and Emphasis of Department: This department prepares students to investigate and address the psychological needs of individuals, families, groups, organizations/institutions and communities. Counseling psychology focuses on normal and optimal development across the life span, with particular attention to expanding knowledge and skills in occupational choice and transitions, and multicultural and group counseling. Clinical Psychology primarily uses a broad-based psychodynamic perspective to study and treat a variety of psychological and psychoeducational problems. In addition to sharing an interest and appreciation for the critical role of culture in development and adaptation, both programs highly value the teaching of clinical and research skills. Thus, students in this department are trained to become knowledgeable and proficient researchers, to provide psychological and educational leadership, and to be effective practitioners. Specifically, graduates from these programs seek positions in teaching, research, policy, administration, psychotherapy, and counseling.

Special Facilities or Resources: The College provides academic/research support in several ways. Students of the College have access to all the libraries of Columbia University. Of particular interest, in addition to the Milbank Memorial Library here at Teachers College, are the Psychology Library on the main Columbia campus and the library at the School of Social Work. Technology has transformed most libraries to computer-oriented environments with immediate access to information. The Library not only provides the access but instruction to students so they may avail themselves of the new technology. The ERIC system as well as Inter-Library Loan are also available. The Microcomputer Center provides students with access to PC and Mac computers, which allow for sharing disk, file and printer resources as well as email services to Columbia University and to the Internet. Other hardware includes CD-ROMs, zip drives, a color scanner, and a sound and video digitizer.

Information for Students With Physical Disabilities: See the following Web site for more information: http://www.tc.columbia.edu/administration/ossd/.

Application Information:
Send to: Admissions Office, Box 302, Teachers College, Columbia University, 525 West 120th Street, New York, NY 10027-6696. Students are admitted in the Fall. The Doctoral application deadline is December 15. For masters applications, all admissions materials must be received by January 15 for priority consideration or by April 15 for final consideration. *Fee:* $60. Waiver is available. Hardship verification is done via a letter from a Financial Aid Officer at the applicant's previous academic institution.

Yeshiva University
Ferkauf Graduate School of Psychology
1300 Morris Park Avenue
Bronx, NY 10461-1602
Telephone: (718) 430-3850
Fax: (718) 430-3960
E-mail: *gill@aecom.yu.edu*
Web: *http://www.yu.edu/ferkauf*

Department Information:
1957. Dean: Lawrence J. Siegel, PhD, ABPP. Number of Faculty: total–full-time 29, part-time 19; women–full-time 15, part-time 13; minority–full-time 4, part-time 3; faculty subject to the Americans With Disabilities Act 1.

Programs and Degrees Offered:
Listed in the following order: Program area, degree type (T if terminal Master's), number awarded 7/03–6/04. Clinical PsyD (Doctor of Psychology) 22, Clinical Health PhD (Doctor of Philosophy) 16, Developmental PhD (Doctor of Philosophy) 2, School/Clinical Child PsyD (Doctor of Psychology) 21, Applied MA/MS (Master of Arts/Science) (T) 6, School Psychology PsyD (Doctor of Psychology) 8.

APA Accreditation: Clinical PsyD (Doctor of Psychology). Combination PsyD (Doctor of Psychology). School PsyD (Doctor of Psychology).

Student Applications/Admissions:
Student Applications

Clinical PsyD (Doctor of Psychology)—Applications 2004–2005, 275. Total applicants accepted 2004–2005, 75. Number enrolled (new admits only) 2004–2005 full-time, 23. Total enrolled 2004–2005 full-time, 124, part-time, 12. Openings 2005–2006, 21. The Median number of years required for completion of a degree are 5. The number of students enrolled full and part-time who were dismissed or voluntarily withdrew from this program area were 4. *Clinical Health PhD (Doctor of Philosophy)*—Applications 2004–2005, 100. Total applicants accepted 2004–2005, 45. Number enrolled (new admits only) 2004–2005 full-time, 17. Total enrolled 2004–2005 full-time, 80, part-time, 3. Openings 2005–2006, 17. The Median number of years required for completion of a degree are 5. The number of students enrolled full and part-time who were dismissed or voluntarily withdrew from this program area were 0. *Developmental PhD (Doctor of Philosophy)*—Applications 2004–2005, 30. Total applicants accepted 2004–2005, 8. Number enrolled (new admits only) 2004–2005 full-time, 3. Total enrolled 2004–2005 full-time, 10, part-time, 2. Openings 2005–2006, 4. The Median number of years required for completion of a degree are 5. *School/Clinical Child PsyD (Doctor of Psychology)*—Applications 2004–2005, 225. Total applicants accepted 2004–2005, 60. Number enrolled (new admits only) 2004–2005 full-time, 18. Total enrolled 2004–2005 full-time, 107, part-time, 12. Openings 2005–2006, 17. The Median number of years required for completion of a degree are 5. The number of students enrolled full and part-time who were dismissed or voluntarily withdrew from this program area were 1. *Applied MA/MS (Master of Arts/Science)*—Applications 2004–2005, 45. Total applicants accepted 2004–2005, 20.

Number enrolled (new admits only) 2004–2005 full-time, 15. Number enrolled (new admits only) 2004–2005 part-time, 2. Openings 2005–2006, 15. The Median number of years required for completion of a degree are 2. The number of students enrolled full and part-time who were dismissed or voluntarily withdrew from this program area were 3. *School Psychology PsyD (Doctor of Psychology)*—Applications 2004–2005, 30. Total applicants accepted 2004–2005, 6. Number enrolled (new admits only) 2004–2005 full-time, 0. Total enrolled 2004–2005 full-time, 20, part-time, 7. The Median number of years required for completion of a degree are 3. The number of students enrolled full and part-time who were dismissed or voluntarily withdrew from this program area were 0.

Admissions Requirements:
Scores: Entries appear in this order: required test or GPA, minimum score (if required), median score of students entering in 2003–2004. Master's Programs: GRE-V no minimum stated; GRE-Q no minimum stated; GRE-V+Q 1100, 1200; overall undergraduate GPA 3.0, 3.5; psychology GPA 3.0, 3.5. Doctoral Programs: GRE-V no minimum stated; GRE-Q no minimum stated; GRE-V+Q 1100, 1200; overall undergraduate GPA 3.0, 3.5.
Other Criteria: (importance of criteria rated low, medium, or high): GRE/MAT scores high, research experience high, work experience high, extracurricular activity medium, clinically related public service high, GPA high, letters of recommendation high, interview high, statement of goals and objectives high.

Student Characteristics: The following represents characteristics of students in 2004–2005 in all graduate psychology programs in the department: Female–full-time 257, part-time 19; Male–full-time 98, part-time 17; African American/Black–full-time 9, part-time 0; Hispanic/Latino(a)–full-time 21, part-time 1; Asian/Pacific Islander–full-time 9, part-time 1; American Indian/Alaska Native–full-time 0, part-time 0; Caucasian–full-time 0, part-time 0; Multi-ethnic–full-time 4, part-time 1; students subject to the Americans With Disabilities Act–full-time 1, part-time 1.

Financial Information/Assistance:
Tuition for Full-Time Study: *Master's:* State residents: $1,075 per credit hour; Nonstate residents: $1,075 per credit hour. *Doctoral:* State residents: $1,108 per credit hour; Nonstate residents: $1,108 per credit hour. See the following Web site for updates and changes in tuition costs: http://www.yu.edu/student_aid/.

Financial Assistance:
First Year Students: Teaching assistantships available for first-year. Average amount paid per academic year: $2,000. Average number of hours worked per week: 10. Research assistantships available for first-year. Average amount paid per academic year: $7,500. Average number of hours worked per week: 20. Traineeships available for first-year. Average amount paid per academic year: $10,000. Average number of hours worked per week: 20. Fellowships and scholarships available for first-year. Average amount paid per academic year: $5,000. Average number of hours worked per week: 0.
Advanced Students: Teaching assistantships available for advanced students. Average amount paid per academic year: $2,000. Average number of hours worked per week: 10. Research assistantships available for advanced students. Average amount

paid per academic year: $7,500. Average number of hours worked per week: 20. Traineeships available for advanced students. Average amount paid per academic year: $10,000. Average number of hours worked per week: 20. Fellowships and scholarships available for advanced students. Average amount paid per academic year: $5,000. Average number of hours worked per week: 0.
Contact Information: Of all students currently enrolled full-time, 75% benefitted from one or more of the listed financial assistance programs. Application and information available online at: http://www.yu.edu/student_aid/.

Internships/Practica: Examples listed in catalog. For those doctoral students for whom a professional internship is required prior to graduation, 40 applied in 2003–2004. Of those who applied, 40 were placed in internships listed by the Association of Psychology Postdoctoral and Internship Programs (APPIC); 38 were placed in APA accredited internships.

Housing and Day Care: No on-campus housing is available. No on-campus day care facilities are available.

Employment of Department Graduates:
Master's Degree Graduates: Of those who graduated in the academic year 2003–2004, the following categories and numbers represent the post-graduate activities and employment of master's degree graduates: Enrolled in a psychology doctoral program (65), enrolled in another graduate/professional program (5), enrolled in a post-doctoral residency/fellowship (n/a), employed in independent practice (n/a), total from the above (master's) (70).
Doctoral Degree Graduates: Of those who graduated in the academic year 2003–2004, the following categories and numbers represent the post-graduate activities and employment of doctoral degree graduates: Enrolled in a psychology doctoral program (n/a), enrolled in a post-doctoral residency/fellowship (3), employed in independent practice (7), employed in an academic position at a university (2), employed in an academic position at a 2-year/4-year college (2), employed in other positions at a higher education institution (1), employed in a professional position in a school system (15), employed in business or industry (research/consulting) (3), employed in business or industry (management) (1), employed in a government agency (professional services) (2), employed in a community mental health/counseling center (11), employed in a hospital/medical center (20), still seeking employment (1), other employment position (2), do not know (1), total from the above (doctoral) (71).

Additional Information:
Orientation, Objectives, and Emphasis of Department: The objective of the Ferkauf Graduate School of Psychology is to promote a balance between the scientific-research orientation and the practitioner model. Developmental and Health psychology place greater emphasis upon applied and basic research, whereas the school and clinical psychology programs focus on the scientist-practitioner model with integrated clinical research and supervised practicum experiences. Further, Ferkauf offers PhD and PsyD degrees placing emphasis on research in the former and on application in the latter. A comprehensive theoretical orientation is offered with a psychodynamic focus and an applied behavioral emphasis. In all specialty areas, and at all levels of training, there is a strong commitment to the foundations of psychology, and a core of basic courses is required in all programs. Collaborations with the major NYC health and hospital institutions are well

established for all programs, and a joint program with Albert Einstein College of Medicine (AECOM) offers health psychology doctoral research opportunities. Ferkauf has affiliations with the AECOM Department of Pediatrics and the Rose Kennedy Center for Research in Mental Retardation and Human Development that provide interdisciplinary training for students.

Special Facilities or Resources: The clinical and school psychology programs offer practicum experience through Ferkauf's Center for Psychological and Psychoeducational Services. The Center provides a wide range of evaluation, remediation, and therapeutic services for children, adolescents, and adults in the neighboring communities, in addition to consultation services directly to the local schools. Ferkauf is located on Yeshiva University's campus of the Albert Einstein College of Medicine, which has led to the development of cooperative programs and activities with various disciplines in medicine as well as added training opportunities for students at the various service delivery agencies affiliated with the medical college. A Behavioral Medicine/Psychophysiological laboratory and Anxiety Disorders Clinic has been established to provide a research service for phobic individuals. The Leonard and Murial Marcus Family Project for the Study of the Disturbed Adolescent and the Robert M. Beren Center for Psychological Intervention support research and services for family intervention.

Application Information:
Send to: Director of Admissions, Ferkauf Graduate School of Psychology, 1300 Morris Park Avenue, Bronx, NY 10461. Application available online. URL of online application: http://www.yu.edu/ferkauf/FGS03APP.pdf. Students are admitted in the Fall, application deadline January 15. *Fee:* $50.

Appalachian State University
Department of Psychology
Arts and Science
Smith-Wright Hall
Boone, NC 28608
Telephone: (828) 262-2272
Fax: (828) 262-2974
E-mail: *psychology@appstate.edu*
Web: *http://www.als.appstate.edu/dept/psych*

Department Information:
1966. Chairperson: Paul A. Fox. Number of Faculty: total–full-time 31, part-time 4; women–full-time 10, part-time 2; minority–full-time 1.

Programs and Degrees Offered:
Listed in the following order: Program area, degree type (T if terminal Master's), number awarded 7/03–6/04. Clinical MA/MS (Master of Arts/Science) (T) 8, General MA/MS (Master of Arts/Science) (T) 4, Health MA/MS (Master of Arts/Science) (T) 7, Industrial/Organizational MA/MS (Master of Arts/Science) (T) 5, School MA/MS (Master of Arts/Science) 10.

Student Applications/Admissions:
Student Applications

Clinical MA/MS (Master of Arts/Science)—Applications 2004–2005, 90. Total applicants accepted 2004–2005, 18. Openings 2005–2006, 10. *General MA/MS (Master of Arts/Science)*—Applications 2004–2005, 14. Total applicants accepted 2004–2005, 6. Openings 2005–2006, 5. *Health MA/MS (Master of Arts/Science)*—Applications 2004–2005, 24. Total applicants accepted 2004–2005, 14. Openings 2005–2006, 10. *Industrial/Organizational MA/MS (Master of Arts/Science)*—Applications 2004–2005, 72. Total applicants accepted 2004–2005, 20. Openings 2005–2006, 10. *School MA/MS (Master of Arts/Science)*—Applications 2004–2005, 42. Total applicants accepted 2004–2005, 16. Openings 2005–2006, 10.

Admissions Requirements:
Scores: Entries appear in this order: required test or GPA, minimum score (if required), median score of students entering in 2003–2004. Master's Programs: GRE-V no minimum stated, 510; GRE-Q no minimum stated, 570; GRE-V+Q no minimum stated, 1080; overall undergraduate GPA 3.0, 3.4.
Other Criteria: (importance of criteria rated low, medium, or high): GRE/MAT scores high, research experience medium, work experience low, extracurricular activity low, clinically related public service low, GPA high, letters of recommendation medium, interview high, statement of goals and objectives high. An interview is not required for Industrial/Organizational, General-Theoretical, or Rehabilitation Psychology.

Student Characteristics: The following represents characteristics of students in 2004–2005 in all graduate psychology programs in the department: Female–full-time 21, part-time 1; Male–full-time 11, part-time 0; African American/Black–full-time 1, part-time 0; Hispanic/Latino(a)–full-time 1, part-time 0; Asian/Pacific Islander–full-time 1, part-time 0; American Indian/Alaska Native–full-time 0, part-time 0; Caucasian–full-time 74, part-time 1; students subject to the Americans With Disabilities Act–full-time 1, part-time 0.

Financial Information/Assistance:
Tuition for Full-Time Study: *Master's:* State residents: per academic year $3,012; Nonstate residents: per academic year $12,552. Tuition is subject to change.

Financial Assistance:
First Year Students: Research assistantships available for first-year. Average amount paid per academic year: $3,250. Average number of hours worked per week: 10. Fellowships and scholarships available for first-year. Average amount paid per academic year: $1,025. Average number of hours worked per week: 10. Apply by January.
Advanced Students: Teaching assistantships available for advanced students. Average amount paid per academic year: $6,500. Average number of hours worked per week: 20. Research assistantships available for advanced students. Average amount paid per academic year: $3,250. Average number of hours worked per week: 10.
Contact Information: Of all students currently enrolled full-time, 70% benefitted from one or more of the listed financial assistance programs.

Internships/Practica: Clinical—Students complete a practicum at the Unversity Counseling Center and two other practica at regional mental health institutes. Students complete a 1,000-hour internship at a mental health center. School—Students complete a practica at a regional public school and a 1200-hour internship at a regional public school. Health—Students complete a practicum and a 600-hour internship at a rehabilitation or health psychology center. Industrial/Organizational—Students have the option of completing a 600-hour internship at a local business.

Housing and Day Care: No on-campus housing is available. No on-campus day care facilities are available.

Employment of Department Graduates:
Master's Degree Graduates: Of those who graduated in the academic year 2003–2004, the following categories and numbers represent the post-graduate activities and employment of master's degree graduates: Enrolled in a post-doctoral residency/fellowship (n/a), employed in independent practice (n/a), total from the above (master's) (0).
Doctoral Degree Graduates: Of those who graduated in the academic year 2003–2004, the following categories and numbers represent the post-graduate activities and employment of doctoral degree graduates: Enrolled in a psychology doctoral program (n/a), total from the above (doctoral) (0).

Additional Information:
Orientation, Objectives, and Emphasis of Department: The department is student oriented, with a director for each graduate program. The general-experimental program is primarily predoc-

toral, but one can structure an applied orientation. The clinical, school and health programs stress professional training, and the majority of graduates obtain positions in the area of preparation after finishing their master's degree. The industrial/organizational and human resource management program is a cooperative program with the Department of Management in the College of Business.

Special Facilities or Resources: Biofeedback facilities, student computer laboratory, neuroscience laboratory, an animal operant conditioning laboratory, and a shared Psychology Clinic/Research House are available.

Application Information:
Send to: The Dean, Cratis D. Williams Graduate School, Dougherty Administration Building, Appalachian State University, Boone, NC 28608. Application available online. URL of online application: apps tate.edu. Students are admitted in the Fall, application deadline March 1. *Fee:* $35.

Duke University

Department of Psychology:Social and Health Sciences
229 Psychology / Sociology Building, P.O. Box 90085
9 Flowers Drive
Durham, NC 27708
Telephone: (919) 660-5716
Fax: (919) 660-5726
E-mail: *lkc@duke.edu*
Web: *www.psych.duke.edu*

Department Information:
1948. Chairperson: Dr. Timothy Strauman. Number of Faculty: total–full-time 16, part-time 12; women–full-time 7, part-time 4; minority–full-time 4.

Programs and Degrees Offered:
Listed in the following order: Program area, degree type (T if terminal Master's), number awarded 7/03–6/04. Clinical Psychology PhD (Doctor of Philosophy) 7, Developmental Psychology PhD (Doctor of Philosophy) 0, Social Psychology PhD (Doctor of Philosophy) 0.

APA Accreditation: Clinical PhD (Doctor of Philosophy).

Student Applications/Admissions:
Student Applications
Clinical Psychology PhD (Doctor of Philosophy)—Applications 2004–2005, 306. Total applicants accepted 2004–2005, 12. Number enrolled (new admits only) 2004–2005 full-time, 7. Openings 2005–2006, 5. The Median number of years required for completion of a degree are 5. The number of students enrolled full and part-time who were dismissed or voluntarily withdrew from this program area were 0. *Developmental Psychology PhD (Doctor of Philosophy)*—Applications 2004–2005, 30. Total applicants accepted 2004–2005, 6. Number enrolled (new admits only) 2004–2005 full-time, 3. Number enrolled (new admits only) 2004–2005 part-time, 0. Openings 2005–2006, 3. The number of students enrolled full and part-time

who were dismissed or voluntarily withdrew from this program area were 0. *Social Psychology PhD (Doctor of Philosophy)*— Applications 2004–2005, 35. Total applicants accepted 2004–2005, 10. Number enrolled (new admits only) 2004–2005 full-time, 7. Number enrolled (new admits only) 2004–2005 part-time, 0. Openings 2005–2006, 3. The number of students enrolled full and part-time, who were dismissed or voluntarily withdrew from this program area were 0.

Admissions Requirements:
Scores: Entries appear in this order: required test or GPA, minimum score (if required), median score of students entering in 2003–2004. Doctoral Programs: GRE-V no minimum stated; GRE-Q no minimum stated; GRE-V+Q no minimum stated; GRE-Analytical no minimum stated; GRE-Subject(Psych) no minimum stated; overall undergraduate GPA no minimum stated. The GRE Subject test is required for the Clinical program only. Please see our Web site for mean scores for applicants admitted.
Other Criteria: (importance of criteria rated low, medium, or high): GRE/MAT scores high, research experience high, work experience medium, extracurricular activity low, clinically related public service medium, GPA high, letters of recommendation high, interview high, statement of goals and objectives high. For additional information on admission requirements, go to: http://www.gradschool.duke.edu/.

Student Characteristics: The following represents characteristics of students in 2004–2005 in all graduate psychology programs in the department: Female–full-time 48, part-time 0; Male–full-time 11, part-time 0; African American/Black–full-time 6, part-time 0; Hispanic/Latino(a)–full-time 3, part-time 0; Asian/Pacific Islander–full-time 1, part-time 0; American Indian/Alaska Native–full-time 0, part-time 0; Caucasian–full-time 49, part-time 0; Multi-ethnic–full-time 0, part-time 0; students subject to the Americans With Disabilities Act–full-time 0, part-time 0.

Financial Information/Assistance:
Tuition for Full-Time Study: *Doctoral:* State residents: per academic year $25,650; Nonstate residents: per academic year $25,650. Tuition is subject to change. See the following Web site for updates and changes in tuition costs: http://www.gradschool.duke.edu/.

Financial Assistance:
First Year Students: Teaching assistantships available for first-year. Average amount paid per academic year: $15,500. Average number of hours worked per week: 19. Apply by December 1. Tuition remission given: full. Research assistantships available for first-year. Average amount paid per academic year: $15,500. Average number of hours worked per week: 19. Apply by December 1. Tuition remission given: full. Fellowships and scholarships available for first-year. Apply by December 1. Tuition remission given: full.
Advanced Students: No information provided.
Contact Information: Of all students currently enrolled full-time, 100% benefitted from one or more of the listed financial assistance programs. Application and information available online at: http://www.gradschool.duke.edu/.

Internships/Practica: Doctoral students in our clinical program receive experience in our own departmental clinic as well as a great number of local institutions and medical center facilities. For those doctoral students for whom a professional internship is required prior to graduation, 7 applied in 2003–2004. Of those who applied, 7 were placed in APA accredited internships.

Housing and Day Care: On-campus housing is available. More information can be found at http://communityhousing.duke.edu. No on-campus day care facilities are available.

Employment of Department Graduates:
Master's Degree Graduates: Of those who graduated in the academic year 2003–2004, the following categories and numbers represent the post-graduate activities and employment of master's degree graduates: Enrolled in a post-doctoral residency/fellowship (n/a), employed in independent practice (n/a), total from the above (master's) (0).
Doctoral Degree Graduates: Of those who graduated in the academic year 2003–2004, the following categories and numbers represent the post-graduate activities and employment of doctoral degree graduates: Enrolled in a psychology doctoral program (n/a), enrolled in a post-doctoral residency/fellowship (6), employed in a hospital/medical center (1), total from the above (doctoral) (7).

Additional Information:
Orientation, Objectives, and Emphasis of Department: The department features a strong mentor-oriented training program with areas of specialization in clinical health, adult, and child psychology. Also, programs in developmental and social psychology. Emphasis is placed on informal interaction among faculty and students; seminars and small groups of faculty and graduate students meet regularly.

Special Facilities or Resources: Collaborations are available with faculty in the Center for Cognitive Neuroscience, the Center for the Study of Aging and Human Development, and the Fuqua School of Business. Training in developmental psychology focuses on cognitive, linguistic, personality and social development. Additional collaborations are available with faculty in Medical Psychology, the Center for Aging and Human Development, the Center for Child and Family Policy, and the Carolina Consortium on Human Development and UNC-Duke Collaborative Graduate Certificate Program in Developmental Psychology. This is a joint effort between Duke's Psychology, Social and Health Sciences and the University of North Carolina at Chapel Hill Developmental Program. The Clinical Training Program is conducted jointly with the Division of Medical Psychology at Duke University Medical Center. This program has three major foci: child psychopathology and intervention, adult disorders and treatment, and health psychology. State-of-the-art facilities including specially equipped laboratories and clinics are available for student use. These include computational facilities for word processing, data analysis, and experimental programming. Collaborative ties also exist with the Center for Child and Family Policy.

Information for Students With Physical Disabilities: See the following Web site for more information: http://www.access.duke.edu/studentIssues.asp.

Application Information:
Send to: The Graduate School, 127 Allen Building, Box 90066, Durham, NC 27708. Application available online. URL of online application: http://www.gradschool.duke.edu/onlineapp.htm. Students are admitted in the Fall, application deadline December 1. Due to the high volume of Clinical applications we receive, we require that clinical applications be submitted by December 1. We encourage a December 1 deadline for the Social and Developmental programs as well but will review these applications until December 31. *Fee:* $75. There is a discount of $10 for applications received by the December 1 deadline.

East Carolina University
Department of Psychology
Arts & Sciences
104 Rawl
Greenville, NC 27858-4353
Telephone: (252) 328-6800
Fax: (252) 328-6283
E-mail: *psychology@mail.ecu.edu*
Web: *http://www.ecu.edu/psyc*

Department Information:
1959. Interim Chair: Larry Bolen. Number of Faculty: total–full-time 32, part-time 15; women–full-time 15, part-time 7; minority–full-time 3; faculty subject to the Americans With Disabilities Act 2.

Programs and Degrees Offered:
Listed in the following order: Program area, degree type (T if terminal Master's), number awarded 7/03–6/04. Clinical Psychology MA/MS (Master of Arts/Science) (T) 10, School Psychology MA/MS (Master of Arts/Science) (T) 8, General MA/MS (Master of Arts/Science) (T) 7.

Student Applications/Admissions:
Student Applications
Clinical Psychology MA/MS (Master of Arts/Science)—Applications 2004–2005, 52. Total applicants accepted 2004–2005, 8. Number enrolled (new admits only) 2004–2005 full-time, 8. Openings 2005–2006, 8. The Median number of years required for completion of a degree are 2. *School Psychology MA/MS (Master of Arts/Science)*—Applications 2004–2005, 40. Total applicants accepted 2004–2005, 12. Number enrolled (new admits only) 2004–2005 full-time, 8. Number enrolled (new admits only) 2004–2005 part-time, 0. Openings 2005–2006, 8. The Median number of years required for completion of a degree are 3. *General MA/MS (Master of Arts/Science)*—Applications 2004–2005, 47. Total applicants accepted 2004–2005, 24. Number enrolled (new admits only) 2004–2005 full-time, 9. Number enrolled (new admits only) 2004–2005 part-time, 9. Total enrolled 2004–2005 full-time, 19, part-time, 10. Openings 2005–2006, 24. The Median number of years required for completion of a degree are 2. The number of students enrolled full and part-time who were dismissed or voluntarily withdrew from this program area were 0.

Admissions Requirements:
Scores: Entries appear in this order: required test or GPA, minimum score (if required), median score of students entering in 2003–2004. Master's Programs: GRE-V 450, 500; GRE-Q 450, 600; overall undergraduate GPA 2.78, 3.47; last 2 years GPA 3.00, 3.66.

Other Criteria: (importance of criteria rated low, medium, or high): GRE/MAT scores high, research experience medium, work experience medium, extracurricular activity low, clinically related public service medium, GPA high, letters of recommendation high, interview low, statement of goals and objectives medium. Clinical requires interview.

Student Characteristics: The following represents characteristics of students in 2004–2005 in all graduate psychology programs in the department: Female–full-time 58, part-time 10; Male–full-time 6, part-time 0; African American/Black–full-time 3, part-time 0; Hispanic/Latino(a)–full-time 0, part-time 0; Asian/Pacific Islander–full-time 1, part-time 0; American Indian/Alaska Native–full-time 0, part-time 0; Caucasian–full-time 51, part-time 9; Multi-ethnic–full-time 0, part-time 0; students subject to the Americans With Disabilities Act–full-time 0, part-time 0.

Financial Information/Assistance:
Tuition for Full-Time Study: *Master's:* State residents: per academic year $3,535, $147 per credit hour; Nonstate residents: per academic year $13,851, $577 per credit hour. Tuition is subject to change.

Financial Assistance:
First Year Students: Teaching assistantships available for first-year. Average amount paid per academic year: $3,750. Average number of hours worked per week: 10. Apply by March 1. Tuition remission given: partial. Research assistantships available for first-year. Average amount paid per academic year: $3,750. Average number of hours worked per week: 10. Apply by March 1. Tuition remission given: partial. Fellowships and scholarships available for first-year. Average amount paid per academic year: $7,500. Average number of hours worked per week: 20. Apply by March 1. Tuition remission given: partial.

Advanced Students: Teaching assistantships available for advanced students. Average amount paid per academic year: $3,750. Average number of hours worked per week: 10. Apply by March 1. Research assistantships available for advanced students. Average amount paid per academic year: $3,750. Average number of hours worked per week: 10. Apply by March 1. Fellowships and scholarships available for advanced students. Average amount paid per academic year: $7,500. Average number of hours worked per week: 20. Apply by March 1. Tuition remission given: partial.

Contact Information: Of all students currently enrolled full-time, 80% benefitted from one or more of the listed financial assistance programs.

Internships/Practica: Clinical internships in mental health clinics offer stipends between $600 and $800 per month for six months; School internships in area school systems offer stipends of up to $2,450 per month for 10 months. Paid I/O internships are usually available during the summer.

Housing and Day Care: On-campus housing is available. See the following Web site for more information: http://www.ecu.edu/campusliving/. Some limited housing for graduate students is available. No on-campus day care facilities are available.

Employment of Department Graduates:
Master's Degree Graduates: Of those who graduated in the academic year 2003–2004, the following categories and numbers represent the post-graduate activities and employment of master's

degree graduates: Enrolled in a psychology doctoral program (2), enrolled in another graduate/professional program (0), enrolled in a post-doctoral residency/fellowship (n/a), employed in independent practice (n/a), employed in an academic position at a university (0), employed in an academic position at a 2-year/4-year college (0), employed in other positions at a higher education institution (0), employed in a professional position in a school system (8), employed in business or industry (research/consulting) (0), employed in business or industry (management) (6), employed in a government agency (research) (0), employed in a government agency (professional services) (2), employed in a community mental health/counseling center (2), employed in a hospital/medical center (0), still seeking employment (0), other employment position (4), do not know (1), total from the above (master's) (25).

Doctoral Degree Graduates: Of those who graduated in the academic year 2003–2004, the following categories and numbers represent the post-graduate activities and employment of doctoral degree graduates: Enrolled in a psychology doctoral program (n/a), total from the above (doctoral) (0).

Additional Information:
Orientation, Objectives, and Emphasis of Department: The primary objective of the Clinical Psychology program is to prepare students for licensure in NC as a Licensed Psychological Associate. Training is applied with a focus on psychological assessment and psychotherapy skills development. The program offers tracks in child clinical, adult, and mental retardation/developmental disabilities. The School Psychology MA/CAS program is approved by the National Association of School Psychologists and the NC Department of Public Instruction. The program provides training and experience in assessment, consultation, and intervention. Most graduates of the Clinical and School programs are employed in mental health and school settings. The General Psychology program offers students the opportunity to specialize in one of three concentrations. The Academic concentration prepares students to teach psychology at the Community/Junior College level. This concentration is offered both on campus and online beginning in Fall 2003. The Research concentration focuses on preparing the student for research and doctoral training. The Industrial/Organizational concentration prepares students for careers involving the application of psychology and human resources in organizations.

Special Facilities or Resources: The department has student computer facilities, interview and testing facilities, and animal laboratory. The Clinical and School programs work closely with community schools and mental health agencies.

Information for Students With Physical Disabilities: See the following Web site for more information: www.ecu.edu/dss.

Application Information:
Send to: East Carolina University Graduate School, Greenville, NC 27858-4353. URL of online application: http://www.ecu.edu/psyc/grad/index.htm. Students are admitted in the Fall, application deadline March 1. *Fee:* $40.

Fayetteville State University

Department of Psychology
College of Basic and Applied Sciences
1200 Murchison Road
Fayetteville, NC 28301
Telephone: (910) 672-1413
Fax: (910) 672-1043
E-mail: *jcassisi@uncfsu.edu*
Web: *http://www.uncfsu.edu/psychology/*

Department Information:

1998. Chairperson: Jeffrey E. Cassisi, PhD Number of Faculty: total–full-time 11, part-time 6; women–full-time 5, part-time 5; minority–full-time 6, part-time 2.

Programs and Degrees Offered:

Listed in the following order: Program area, degree type (T if terminal Master's), number awarded 7/03–6/04. Masters Program in Counseling Psychology MA/MS (Master of Arts/Science) (T) 5, Masters Program in Experimental Psychology MA/MS (Master of Arts/Science) (T) 0.

Student Applications/Admissions:

Student Applications

Masters Program in Counseling Psychology MA/MS (Master of Arts/Science)—Applications 2004–2005, 12. Total applicants accepted 2004–2005, 6. Number enrolled (new admits only) 2004–2005 full-time, 0. Number enrolled (new admits only) 2004–2005 part-time, 5. Openings 2005–2006, 10. The Median number of years required for completion of a degree are 4. The number of students enrolled full and part-time who were dismissed or voluntarily withdrew from this program area were 0. *Masters Program in Experimental Psychology MA/MS (Master of Arts/Science)*—Applications 2004–2005, 0. Total applicants accepted 2004–2005, 0. Number enrolled (new admits only) 2004–2005 full-time, 0. Number enrolled (new admits only) 2004–2005 part-time, 0. Openings 2005–2006, 6. The number of students enrolled full and part-time who were dismissed or voluntarily withdrew from this program area were 0.

Admissions Requirements:

Scores: Entries appear in this order: required test or GPA, minimum score (if required), median score of students entering in 2003–2004. Master's Programs: GRE-V no minimum stated, 400; GRE-Q no minimum stated, 400; GRE-V+Q no minimum stated, 850; last 2 years GPA no minimum stated, 3.5; psychology GPA no minimum stated, 3.5.

Other Criteria: (importance of criteria rated low, medium, or high): GRE/MAT scores medium, research experience medium, work experience low, extracurricular activity low, clinically related public service low, GPA high, letters of recommendation medium, interview medium, statement of goals and objectives medium, research experience is weighted more heavily for the Experimental Program. For additional information on admission requirements, go to: http://www.uncfsu.edu/psychology/gradstudents/Admissions/App_Checklist.pdf.

Student Characteristics: The following represents characteristics of students in 2004–2005 in all graduate psychology programs in the department: Female–full-time 0, part-time 18; Male–full-time 0, part-time 5; African American/Black–full-time 0, part-time 9; Hispanic/Latino(a)–full-time 0, part-time 2; Asian/Pacific Islander–full-time 0, part-time 0; American Indian/Alaska Native–full-time 0, part-time 0; Caucasian–full-time 0, part-time 12; Multi-ethnic–full-time 0, part-time 1; students subject to the Americans With Disabilities Act–full-time 0, part-time 0.

Financial Information/Assistance:

Tuition for Full-Time Study: *Master's:* State residents: $113 per credit hour; Nonstate residents: $583 per credit hour. Tuition is subject to change. See the following Web site for updates and changes in tuition costs: http://www.uncfsu.edu/bursar/fees.htm.

Financial Assistance:

First Year Students: No information provided.
Advanced Students: No information provided.
Contact Information: No information provided.

Internships/Practica: Practica and internships are provided through supervised off-site or on-site placements. Counseling graduate students may choose placement in our training facility, which provides psychotherapy services to residents of Fayetteville presenting with depression, anxiety, substance abuse, and/or relationship problems. Alternatively, counseling graduate students may choose placement at a variety of other sites in the surrounding community. These include placements that provide academic, career/vocational, mental health counseling services in surrounding area college counseling centers, community mental health centers, or correctional facilities.

Housing and Day Care: On-campus housing is available. See the following Web site for more information: http://www.uncfsu.edu/ResLife/. On-campus day care facilities are available. See the following Web site for more information: http://www.uncfsu.edu/soe/ECLC.HTM.

Employment of Department Graduates:

Master's Degree Graduates: Of those who graduated in the academic year 2003–2004, the following categories and numbers represent the post-graduate activities and employment of master's degree graduates: Enrolled in a post-doctoral residency/fellowship (n/a), employed in independent practice (n/a), total from the above (master's) (0).

Doctoral Degree Graduates: Of those who graduated in the academic year 2003–2004, the following categories and numbers represent the post-graduate activities and employment of doctoral degree graduates: Enrolled in a psychology doctoral program (n/a), total from the above (doctoral) (0).

Additional Information:

Orientation, Objectives, and Emphasis of Department: Individuals who are interested in the applied or research aspects of psychology may pursue the Master of Arts degree in either Counseling Psychology or General Experimental Psychology. The mission of the 48-unit Master of Arts in Counseling is: 1.) To produce highly skilled, license eligible graduates in counseling; 2.) to increase the knowledge of students in the area of multicultural counseling; and 3.) to provide field experiences that reflect the community counseling, health, and service needs of an increasingly pluralistic society. The program provides curricular experiences in eight core areas including Professional Identity, Cultural

Diversity, Development, Career Development, Helping Relationships, Group Work, Assessment, and Research and Program Evaluation. Field placements culminate with a supervised practicum/internship that permits the integration of theory, research, and application. The 36-unit Master of Arts in General Experimental Psychology affords the candidate an opportunity for advanced study of theory and research techniques for the following objectives: 1.) to prepare for community college or junior college teaching; 2.) to prepare for employment in business, government, and/or human factors research settings; and 3.) to prepare for additional advanced study leading to the doctorate. The program in General Experimental Psychology culminates with thesis research.

Special Facilities or Resources: The General Experimental Psychology track is new and will be accepting students for the first time in fall 2005. Many of our courses are also offered at our Ft. Bragg campus, which is approximately 8 miles north of the main campus. There are increasing opportunities for academic/research collaboration with the universities in the Raleigh/Durham/Chapel Hill area, which is approximately an hour and half drive north of the main campus. Department facilities are currently undergoing a major renovation and construction, which is projected to be finished in 2007.

Information for Students With Physical Disabilities: See the following Web site for more information: http://www.uncfsu.edu/studentaffairs/CFPD/cfpddss.htm.

Application Information:
Send originals to: Director of Admissions, Fayetteville State University, 1200 Murchison Road, Fayetteville, NC 28301-4298; Send one copy to Coordinator, Graduate Program, Department of Psychology, Fayetteville State University, 1200 Murchison Road, Fayetteville, NC 28301-4298. URL of online application: http://www.uncfsu.edu/psychology/gradstudents/Admissions/Graduate%20Application.pdf. Students are admitted in the Fall, application deadline March 15; Spring, application deadline October 15. *Fee:* $25.

North Carolina State University (2004 data)
Department of Psychology
College of Humanities and Social Sciences
640 Poe Hall, Box 7801
Raleigh, NC 27695-7801
Telephone: (919) 515-2251
Fax: (919) 515-1716
E-mail: *psych@ncsu.edu*
Web: *http://www.ncsu.edu/psychology*

Department Information:
1938. Department Head: David W. Martin. Number of Faculty: total–full-time 30, part-time 5; women–full-time 9, part-time 4; minority–full-time 3, part-time 1.

Programs and Degrees Offered:
Listed in the following order: Program area, degree type (T if terminal Master's), number awarded 7/03–6/04. Ergonomics & Experimental PhD (Doctor of Philosophy) 7, Developmental PhD (Doctor of Philosophy) 3, Industrial/Organizational PhD (Doctor

of Philosophy) 12, Public Interest PhD (Doctor of Philosophy) 4, School Psychology PhD (Doctor of Philosophy) 2.

APA Accreditation: School PhD (Doctor of Philosophy).

Student Applications/Admissions:
Student Applications
Ergonomics & Experimental PhD (Doctor of Philosophy)—Applications 2004–2005, 21. Total applicants accepted 2004–2005, 9. Total enrolled 2004–2005 full-time, 21. Openings 2005–2006, 4. The Median number of years required for completion of a degree are 7. The number of students enrolled full and part-time who were dismissed or voluntarily withdrew from this program area were 0. *Developmental PhD (Doctor of Philosophy)*—Applications 2004–2005, 24. Total applicants accepted 2004–2005, 7. Total enrolled 2004–2005 full-time, 11. Openings 2005–2006, 3. The Median number of years required for completion of a degree are 5. The number of students enrolled full and part-time who were dismissed or voluntarily withdrew from this program area were 0. *Industrial/Organizational PhD (Doctor of Philosophy)*—Applications 2004–2005, 46. Total applicants accepted 2004–2005, 5. Total enrolled 2004–2005 full-time, 19. Openings 2005–2006, 4. The Median number of years required for completion of a degree are 6. The number of students enrolled full and part-time who were dismissed or voluntarily withdrew from this program area were 0. *Public Interest PhD (Doctor of Philosophy)*—Applications 2004–2005, 19. Total applicants accepted 2004–2005, 9. Total enrolled 2004–2005 full-time, 24. Openings 2005–2006, 3. The Median number of years required for completion of a degree are 5. The number of students enrolled full and part-time who were dismissed or voluntarily withdrew from this program area were 1. *School Psychology PhD (Doctor of Philosophy)*—Applications 2004–2005, 42. Total applicants accepted 2004–2005, 4. Total enrolled 2004–2005 full-time, 21. Openings 2005–2006, 5. The Median number of years required for completion of a degree are 6. The number of students enrolled full and part-time who were dismissed or voluntarily withdrew from this program area were 1.

Admissions Requirements:
Scores: Entries appear in this order: required test or GPA, minimum score (if required), median score of students entering in 2003–2004. Master's Programs: GRE-V no minimum stated, 550; GRE-Q no minimum stated, 640; GRE-Analytical no minimum stated, 660; overall undergraduate GPA no minimum stated, 3.6. GRE Subject Test is also required for program in I/O Psychology; recommended for others. Doctoral Programs: GRE-V no minimum stated, 550; GRE-Q no minimum stated, 640; GRE-Analytical no minimum stated, 660; overall undergraduate GPA no minimum stated, 3.6. GRE Subject Test is also required for program in I/O Psychology; recommended for others.
Other Criteria: (importance of criteria rated low, medium, or high): GRE/MAT scores high, research experience high, work experience medium, extracurricular activity low, clinically related public service low, GPA high, letters of recommendation high, interview medium, statement of goals and objectives high. Psychology in the Public Interest gives greater weight to work experience and public service than do other program areas. The School Psychology program operates a by-invitation Interview Day for those applicants who pass an initial selection

process. For additional information on admission requirements, download information sheets from http://www4.ncsu.edu:8030/~mershon/FDF/Documents/.

Student Characteristics: The following represents characteristics of students in 2004–2005 in all graduate psychology programs in the department: Female–full-time 67, part-time 0; Male–full-time 29, part-time 0; African American/Black–full-time 12, part-time 0; Hispanic/Latino(a)–full-time 5, part-time 0; Asian/Pacific Islander–full-time 6, part-time 0; American Indian/Alaska Native–full-time 1, part-time 0; Caucasian–full-time 0, part-time 0; Multiethnic–full-time 0, part-time 0; students subject to the Americans With Disabilities Act–full-time 2, part-time 0.

Financial Information/Assistance:

Tuition for Full-Time Study: *Master's:* State residents: per academic year $3,262; Nonstate residents: per academic year $14,962. *Doctoral:* State residents: per academic year $3,262; Nonstate residents: per academic year $14,962. Tuition is subject to change. See the following Web site for updates and changes in tuition costs: http://www7.acs.ncsu.edu/cashier/Tuition/GradTuition2002.htm.

Financial Assistance:

First Year Students: Teaching assistantships available for first-year. Average amount paid per academic year: $12,500. Average number of hours worked per week: 20. Apply by same as appl. Tuition remission given: full. Research assistantships available for first-year. Average amount paid per academic year: $12,500. Average number of hours worked per week: 20. Apply by same as appl. Tuition remission given: full. Traineeships available for first-year. Average amount paid per academic year: $11,000. Average number of hours worked per week: 0. Apply by same as appl. Tuition remission given: full.

Advanced Students: Teaching assistantships available for advanced students. Average amount paid per academic year: $12,500. Average number of hours worked per week: 20. Tuition remission given: full. Research assistantships available for advanced students. Average amount paid per academic year: $12,500. Average number of hours worked per week: 20. Tuition remission given: full.

Contact Information: Of all students currently enrolled full-time, 40% benefitted from one or more of the listed financial assistance programs. Application and information available online at: No separate application; indicate interest on regular application and/or in personal statement.

Internships/Practica: Practica and internships are required for both master's and doctoral students in the School Psychology program. These include supervised experiences in assessment, consultation, intervention, research, and professional school psychology in a wide variety of school-related settings. Students in Ergonomics are also expected to obtain employment for at least one summer/semester in one of the many suitable companies located in the Research Triangle area. For those doctoral students for whom a professional internship is required prior to graduation, 4 applied in 2003–2004. Of those who applied, 1 was placed in APA accredited internships.

Housing and Day Care: On-campus housing is available. See the following Web site for more information: http://www.ncsu.edu/housing/. No on-campus day care facilities are available.

Employment of Department Graduates:

Master's Degree Graduates: Of those who graduated in the academic year 2003–2004, the following categories and numbers represent the post-graduate activities and employment of master's degree graduates: Enrolled in a post-doctoral residency/fellowship (n/a), employed in independent practice (n/a), total from the above (master's) (0).

Doctoral Degree Graduates: Of those who graduated in the academic year 2003–2004, the following categories and numbers represent the post-graduate activities and employment of doctoral degree graduates: Enrolled in a psychology doctoral program (n/a), total from the above (doctoral) (0).

Additional Information:

Orientation, Objectives, and Emphasis of Department: The department trains in the scientist-practitioner model. Students are expected to become knowledgeable about both research and application within their area of study. There are five specialty areas with different emphases. Developmental Psychology stresses a balance of conceptual, research-analytical, and application skills and encompasses social and cognitive development from infancy to old age. Ergonomics and Experimental Psychology includes two tracks. The ergonomics track emphasizes the cognitive/perceptual aspects of human factors, including research on visual displays, visual/auditory spatial judgments, ergonomics for older adults and the effective information transfer for complex systems. This track has a cooperative relationship with the Biomechanics Program in IE. The experimental psychology track provides extensive research training with concentrations in biopsychology, cognition and/or perception. The Psychology in the Public Interest program (formerly known as Human Resource Development/Community Psychology) is a problem-oriented program dealing with research and professional issues in communities and social systems. Industrial/Organizational (I/O) students may concentrate in areas such as performance appraisal, selection, training, job analysis, work motivation, organizational theory, and development. School Psychology develops behavioral scientists who apply psychological knowledge and techniques in school and family settings to help students, parents, and teachers.

Special Facilities or Resources: The department is housed on two floors of a modern building. Students with assistantships share offices. All programs have appropriate laboratory space and facilities. These include specialized lab facilities: Audition Laboratory, Cognitive-Development Laboratory, Ergonomics Laboratory, Neuropsychology Laboratory, Social Development Laboratory, and Visual Perception Laboratory. Ergonomics, Human Resource Development, I/O, and School students may have opportunities to work in state government, industry, schools, and community agencies to gain practical and research experience. As this area is developing rapidly, more opportunities appear each year. Students are, however, required to maintain continuous registration and carry an adequate course load each semester. Students are permitted to enroll in courses at the University of North Carolina-Chapel Hill and at Duke University as if the courses were offered on their home campus. Once basic research, statistics, and area course requirements are satisfied, students have considerable flexibility in developing tailored programs of study.

Information for Students With Physical Disabilities: See the following Web site for more information: http://www.ncsu.edu/provost/offices/affirm_action/dss/.

Application Information:

Send to: Application, Fees & Transcripts: The Graduate School, Box 7102, NCSU, Raleigh, NC 27695-7102. Or, complete an online application at http://www2.acs.ncsu.edu/grad/applygrad.htm. Letters & Questionnaires: Director of Graduate Programs, Psychology Department, Box 7801, NCSU, Raleigh, NC 27695-7801. Students are admitted in the Fall, application deadline January 15. The program in School Psychology is planning to move its deadline to an earlier date (December 1 or December 15, 2004), starting with applications for Fall 2005. Please check with department during Fall 2004 to be sure of actual application deadline. Other programs may or may not be affected. *Fee:* $55. $65 for international applications.

North Carolina, University of, at Greensboro (2004 data)

Department of Psychology
College of Arts and Sciences
296 Eberhart Building, P.O. Box 26170
Greensboro, NC 27402-6170
Telephone: (336) 334-5013
Fax: (336) 334-5066
E-mail: *decasper@uncg.edu*
Web: *http://www.uncg.edu/psy/*

Department Information:

1925. Interim, Department Head: Anthony DeCasper. Number of Faculty: total–full-time 23, part-time 2; women–full-time 6.

Programs and Degrees Offered:

Listed in the following order: Program area, degree type (T if terminal Master's), number awarded 7/03–6/04. Clinical PhD (Doctor of Philosophy) 3, Cognitive PhD (Doctor of Philosophy) 0, Developmental PhD (Doctor of Philosophy) 0, Social PhD (Doctor of Philosophy) 1.

APA Accreditation: Clinical PhD (Doctor of Philosophy).

Student Applications/Admissions:

Student Applications

Clinical PhD (Doctor of Philosophy)—Applications 2004–2005, 237. Total applicants accepted 2004–2005, 7. Openings 2005–2006, 6. The Median number of years required for completion of a degree are 6. The number of students enrolled full and part-time who were dismissed or voluntarily withdrew from this program area were 0. *Cognitive PhD (Doctor of Philosophy)*—Applications 2004–2005, 5. Total applicants accepted 2004–2005, 1. Openings 2005–2006, 1. The Median number of years required for completion of a degree are 5. The number of students enrolled full and part-time who were dismissed or voluntarily withdrew from this program area were 0. *Developmental PhD (Doctor of Philosophy)*—Applications 2004–2005, 14. Total applicants accepted 2004–2005, 1. Openings 2005–2006, 1. The Median number of years required for completion of a degree are 5. The number of students enrolled full and part-time who were dismissed or voluntarily withdrew from this program area were 0. *Social PhD (Doctor of Philosophy)*—Applications 2004–2005, 20. Total applicants accepted 2004–2005, 0. Openings 2005–2006, 1. The Median number of years required for completion of a degree are 6. The number of

students enrolled full and part-time who were dismissed or voluntarily withdrew from this program area were 0.

Admissions Requirements:

Scores: Entries appear in this order: required test or GPA, minimum score (if required), median score of students entering in 2003–2004. Master's Programs: GRE-V 590, 680; GRE-Q 640, 780; GRE-V+Q 1230, 1370; GRE-Subject(Psych) 660, 700; overall undergraduate GPA 3.4, 3.8. Doctoral Programs: GRE-V no minimum stated, 590; GRE-Q no minimum stated, 640; GRE-V+Q no minimum stated, 1290; GRE-Subject(Psych) no minimum stated; overall undergraduate GPA no minimum stated, 3.6.

Other Criteria: (importance of criteria rated low, medium, or high): GRE/MAT scores high, research experience high, work experience low, extracurricular activity low, clinically related public service medium, GPA high, letters of recommendation high, interview high, statement of goals and objectives low.

Student Characteristics: The following represents characteristics of students in 2004–2005 in all graduate psychology programs in the department: Female–full-time 46, part-time 1; Male–full-time 13, part-time 0; African American/Black–full-time 3, part-time 0; Hispanic/Latino(a)–full-time 2, part-time 0; Asian/Pacific Islander–full-time 2, part-time 0; American Indian/Alaska Native–full-time 0, part-time 0; Caucasian–full-time 52, part-time 1; Multi-ethnic–full-time 0, part-time 0; students subject to the Americans With Disabilities Act–full-time 1, part-time 0.

Financial Information/Assistance:

Tuition for Full-Time Study: *Master's:* State residents: per academic year $137, $225 per credit hour; Nonstate residents: per academic year $415, $225 per credit hour. Tuition is subject to change.

Financial Assistance:

First Year Students: Research assistantships available for first-year. Average amount paid per academic year: $8,500. Average number of hours worked per week: 12. Apply by December 15. Tuition remission given: partial.

Advanced Students: Teaching assistantships available for advanced students. Average amount paid per academic year: $3,500. Apply by December 15. Research assistantships available for advanced students. Average amount paid per academic year: $8,500. Average number of hours worked per week: 12. Apply by December 15.

Contact Information: Of all students currently enrolled full-time, 90% benefitted from one or more of the listed financial assistance programs. Application and information available online at: www.uncg.edu/grs.

Internships/Practica: For those doctoral students for whom a professional internship is required prior to graduation, 7 applied in 2003–2004. Of those who applied, 6 were placed in internships listed by the Association of Psychology Postdoctoral and Internship Programs (APPIC); 6 were placed in APA accredited internships.

Housing and Day Care: On-campus housing is available. Contact Housing and Residence Life 1st Floor, Mendenhall-Ragsdale Bldg. (336) 334-5636. On-campus day care facilities are available.

Employment of Department Graduates:

Master's Degree Graduates: Of those who graduated in the academic year 2003–2004, the following categories and numbers represent the post-graduate activities and employment of master's degree graduates: Enrolled in a post-doctoral residency/fellowship (n/a), employed in independent practice (n/a), total from the above (master's) (0).

Doctoral Degree Graduates: Of those who graduated in the academic year 2003–2004, the following categories and numbers represent the post-graduate activities and employment of doctoral degree graduates: Enrolled in a psychology doctoral program (n/a), employed in an academic position at a 2-year/4-year college (3), employed in other positions at a higher education institution (4), employed in business or industry (research/consulting) (2), employed in a community mental health/counseling center (2), employed in a hospital/medical center (2), total from the above (doctoral) (13).

Additional Information:

Orientation, Objectives, and Emphasis of Department: The objective is to provide scholarship and methodological and practical skills to enable the student to function in a variety of academic, research, and service settings. The program has an experimental orientation, with four major areas of concentration: clinical, which includes applied training and clinical research training in a variety of service settings; developmental, which includes basic research in behavioral, cognitive, language, and social development in infant, child, adolescent, and adult humans and in animals; cognitive, which includes basic research in human memory, cognition, and language; and social, designed to introduce students to theoretical issues and to applied, biological, and developmental perspectives in social psychology. Although the program is oriented toward the PhD as the terminal degree, an applicant with a bachelor's degree is admitted into the master's program. Upon successful completion of the requirements for the master's degree, the student's work is reviewed for admission into the PhD program.

Special Facilities or Resources: The Department of Psychology is located in the Life Sciences Building. Space is devoted to classrooms; research laboratories; vivaria; the Psychology Clinic; faculty, student, and secretarial offices; a computer terminal room; a library; and a lounge. Graduate students share offices with one or two other students. Active research laboratories in each of the specialty areas contain an assortment of items: animal test chambers with supporting apparatus for research in perception, learning, and the development of social behavior; automated equipment for studying concept formation and problem-solving behavior in humans, signal-averaging computers with XY plotters for analyses of electrophysical correlates of behavior; soundproof chambers; electronic psychoacoustic equipment for stimulus control in auditory research with humans and animals; videotape studio; polygraphs for psychological recording; and observation rooms with one-way mirrors. The university computer center is available to faculty members and graduate students involved in research. Facilities include interactive and batch access to the large-sized computer on campus. Virtually all computer languages and standard software packages are available. The university library has an exceptional collection of journals and books. The department also has its own library located in the Life Sciences Building.

Information for Students With Physical Disabilities: See the following Web site for more information: www.uncg.edu/psy/.

Application Information:
Send to: UNCG, Graduate School, P.O. Box 26176, UNCG, Greensboro, NC 27402-6176. Application available online. Students are admitted in the Fall, application deadline December 15. December 15 for Clinical; January 15 for all other programs. *Fee:* $35.

North Carolina, University of, Chapel Hill
Department of Psychology
Arts and Sciences
CB #3270
Chapel Hill, NC 27599-3270
Telephone: (919) 962-4155
Fax: (919) 962-2537
E-mail: *psychwww@unc.edu*
Web: *http://www.psych.unc.edu*

Department Information:
1921. Chairperson: Karen M. Gil. Number of Faculty: total–full-time 47, part-time 8; women–full-time 24, part-time 3; minority–full-time 3, part-time 1.

Programs and Degrees Offered:
Listed in the following order: Program area, degree type (T if terminal Master's), number awarded 7/03–6/04. Clinical PhD (Doctor of Philosophy) 10, Cognitive PhD (Doctor of Philosophy) 0, Developmental PhD (Doctor of Philosophy) 4, Experimental/Biological PhD (Doctor of Philosophy) 0, Quantitative PhD (Doctor of Philosophy) 2, Social PhD (Doctor of Philosophy) 2.

APA Accreditation: Clinical PhD (Doctor of Philosophy).

Student Applications/Admissions:
Student Applications
Clinical PhD (Doctor of Philosophy)—Applications 2004–2005, 299. Total applicants accepted 2004–2005, 5. Number enrolled (new admits only) 2004–2005 full-time, 4. Openings 2005–2006, 8. The Median number of years required for completion of a degree are 5. *Cognitive PhD (Doctor of Philosophy)*—Applications 2004–2005, 31. Total applicants accepted 2004–2005, 5. Number enrolled (new admits only) 2004–2005 full-time, 2. Total enrolled 2004–2005 full-time, 11. Openings 2005–2006, 3. The Median number of years required for completion of a degree are 5. *Developmental PhD (Doctor of Philosophy)*—Applications 2004–2005, 45. Total applicants accepted 2004–2005, 7. Number enrolled (new admits only) 2004–2005 full-time, 1. Openings 2005–2006, 4. The Median number of years required for completion of a degree are 5. *Experimental/Biological PhD (Doctor of Philosophy)*—Applications 2004–2005, 26. Total applicants accepted 2004–2005, 3. Number enrolled (new admits only) 2004–2005 full-time, 3. Openings 2005–2006, 3. The Median number of years required for completion of a degree are 5. *Quantitative PhD (Doctor of Philosophy)*—Applications 2004–2005, 15. Total applicants accepted 2004–2005, 4. Number enrolled (new admits only) 2004–2005 full-time, 0. Openings 2005–2006, 3. The Median number of years required for completion of a degree are 5. *Social PhD (Doctor*

of Philosophy)—Applications 2004–2005, 63. Total applicants accepted 2004–2005, 0. Number enrolled (new admits only) 2004–2005 full-time, 0. Openings 2005–2006, 3. The Median number of years required for completion of a degree are 5.

Admissions Requirements:

Scores: Entries appear in this order: required test or GPA, minimum score (if required), median score of students entering in 2003–2004. Doctoral Programs: GRE-V 50%, 627; GRE-Q 50%, 701; last 2 years GPA 3.0, 3.68.

Other Criteria: (importance of criteria rated low, medium, or high): GRE/MAT scores high, research experience high, work experience medium, clinically related public service medium, GPA high, letters of recommendation high, interview medium, statement of goals and objectives high.

Student Characteristics: The following represents characteristics of students in 2004–2005 in all graduate psychology programs in the department: Female–full-time 66, part-time 0; Male–full-time 48, part-time 0; African American/Black–full-time 11, part-time 0; Hispanic/Latino(a)–full-time 0, part-time 0; Asian/Pacific Islander–full-time 6, part-time 0; American Indian/Alaska Native–full-time 1, part-time 0; Caucasian–full-time 96, part-time 0.

Financial Information/Assistance:

Tuition for Full-Time Study: *Doctoral:* State residents: per academic year $4,651; Nonstate residents: per academic year $17,899.

Financial Assistance:

First Year Students: Research assistantships available for first-year. Average amount paid per academic year: $12,000. Average number of hours worked per week: 15. Tuition remission given: full and partial. Traineeships available for first-year. Average amount paid per academic year: $15,000. Tuition remission given: full and partial. Fellowships and scholarships available for first-year. Average amount paid per academic year: $15,000. Tuition remission given: full and partial.

Advanced Students: Teaching assistantships available for advanced students. Average amount paid per academic year: $12,280. Average number of hours worked per week: 15. Tuition remission given: full and partial. Research assistantships available for advanced students. Average amount paid per academic year: $12,000. Average number of hours worked per week: 15. Tuition remission given: full and partial. Traineeships available for advanced students. Average amount paid per academic year: $15,000. Tuition remission given: full. Fellowships and scholarships available for advanced students. Average amount paid per academic year: $15,000. Tuition remission given: full.

Contact Information: Of all students currently enrolled full-time, 75% benefitted from one or more of the listed financial assistance programs.

Internships/Practica: Students within the doctoral program in clinical psychology engage in a wide range of clinical practica activities beginning in the first year of doctoral study. A variety of sites are included in our practicum arrangements. One of these sites is the University of North Carolina Medical School, which includes opportunities in a number of areas including child, family, adolescent, and adults. There are also specialized opportunities at that site to work with children with developmental disabilities and college students in a university counseling setting. Students also receive training at John Umstead Hospital, a state psychiatric hospital; opportunities there range from child, adolescent, adult, and geriatric patients. Overall Umstead Hospital emphasizes treatment of more disturbed individuals, but opportunities are available as well for outpatient treatment. Third, students are involved in our Psychology Department Psychological Services Center, our in-house outpatient treatment facility. Students work with a wide variety of clients within that context, with specialized opportunities in the anxiety disorders and marital therapy. Among other sites, students provide consultation to the local school system, to the Orange-Person-Chatham Mental Health Center, and a variety of other sites that are arranged on an as needed basis. For those doctoral students for whom a professional internship is required prior to graduation, 2 applied in 2003–2004. Of those who applied, 1 was placed in internships listed by the Association of Psychology Postdoctoral and Internship Programs (APPIC); 1 was placed in an APA accredited internship.

Housing and Day Care: No on-campus housing is available. No on-campus day care facilities are available.

Employment of Department Graduates:

Master's Degree Graduates: Of those who graduated in the academic year 2003–2004, the following categories and numbers represent the post-graduate activities and employment of master's degree graduates: Enrolled in a post-doctoral residency/fellowship (n/a), employed in independent practice (n/a), total from the above (master's) (0).

Doctoral Degree Graduates: Of those who graduated in the academic year 2003–2004, the following categories and numbers represent the post-graduate activities and employment of doctoral degree graduates: Enrolled in a psychology doctoral program (n/a), total from the above (doctoral) (0).

Additional Information:

Orientation, Objectives, and Emphasis of Department: Each graduate training program is designed to acquaint students with the theoretical and research content of their specialty and to train them in the research and teaching skills needed to make contributions to science and society. In addition, certain programs (for example, the clinical program) include an emphasis on the development of competence in appropriate professional skills. Faculty members maintain a balance of commitments to research, teaching and service.

Special Facilities or Resources: Affiliated clinical and research facilities are the Psychological Services Center, Psychology Department; John Umstead State Hospital, Butner, NC; North Carolina Memorial Hospital, Chapel Hill; Murdoch Center for the Retarded, Butner; Division for Disorders of Development and Learning, Chapel Hill; VA Hospital, Durham; Frank Porter Graham Child Development Center, Chapel Hill; Carolina Population Center, Chapel Hill; Alcoholic Rehabilitation Center, Butner; North Carolina Highway Safety Research Center, Chapel Hill; L.L. Thurstone Psychometric Laboratory, Chapel Hill; Human Psychophysiology Laboratory, Chapel Hill; Institute for Research in Social Sciences, Chapel Hill; Laboratory for Computing and Cognition, Chapel Hill; Neurobiology Curriculum, University of North Carolina; Research Laboratories of the U.S. Environmental Protection Agency, Research Triangle Park; and TEACCH Division, North Carolina Memorial Hospital, specializing in the treatment and education of victims of autism and related disorders of communication.

Application Information:

Send to: Graduate Admissions, CB#3270, 203 Davie Hall, Department of Psychology, UNC-Chapel Hill, Chapel Hill, NC 27599-3270. Application available online. Students are admitted in the Fall, application deadline January 1. *Fee:* $65.

North Carolina, University of, Charlotte

Department of Psychology
Arts and Sciences
9201 University City Boulevard
Charlotte, NC 28223-0001
Telephone: (704) 687-4731
Fax: (704) 687-3096
E-mail: *rtedesch@email.uncc.edu or sgrogelb@email.uncc.edu*
Web: *http://www.uncc.edu/psychology/*

Department Information:

1960. Graduate Coordinator: Dr. Richard Tedeschi. Number of Faculty: total–full-time 28, part-time 10; women–full-time 10, part-time 6; minority–full-time 2.

Programs and Degrees Offered:

Listed in the following order: Program area, degree type (T if terminal Master's), number awarded 7/03–6/04. Clinical/ Community MA/MS (Master of Arts/Science) (T) 4, Industrial/ Organizational MA/MS (Master of Arts/Science) (T) 4.

Student Applications/Admissions:

Student Applications

Clinical/ Community MA/MS (Master of Arts/Science)—Applications 2004–2005, 75. Total applicants accepted 2004–2005, 10. Number enrolled (new admits only) 2004–2005 full-time, 10. Number enrolled (new admits only) 2004–2005 part-time, 0. Total enrolled 2004–2005 full-time, 17, part-time, 20. Openings 2005–2006, 12. The Median number of years required for completion of a degree are 2. The number of students enrolled full and part-time who were dismissed or voluntarily withdrew from this program area were 2. *Industrial/ Organizational MA/MS (Master of Arts/Science)*—Applications 2004–2005, 70. Total applicants accepted 2004–2005, 12. Total enrolled 2004–2005 full-time, 21, part-time, 3. Openings 2005–2006, 12. The Median number of years required for completion of a degree are 2. The number of students enrolled full and part-time who were dismissed or voluntarily withdrew from this program area was 1.

Admissions Requirements:

Scores: Entries appear in this order: required test or GPA, minimum score (if required), median score of students entering in 2003–2004. Master's Programs: GRE-V 500, 554; GRE-Q 500, 600; GRE-V+Q 1000, 1150; GRE-Subject(Psych) no minimum stated, 570; overall undergraduate GPA 3.0, 3.4. GRE Subject (Psychology) is not required for IO

Other Criteria: (importance of criteria rated low, medium, or high): GRE/MAT scores high, research experience high, work experience medium, extracurricular activity low, clinically related public service medium, GPA high, letters of recommendation high, interview low, statement of goals and objectives high. Community work for clinical/community only.

Student Characteristics: The following represents characteristics of students in 2004–2005 in all graduate psychology programs in the department: Female–full-time 29, part-time 18; Male–full-time 8, part-time 2; African American/Black–full-time 5, part-time 0; Hispanic/Latino(a)–full-time 0, part-time 0; Asian/Pacific Islander–full-time 1, part-time 0; Caucasian–full-time 0, part-time 0.

Financial Information/Assistance:

Tuition for Full-Time Study: *Master's:* State residents: per academic year $3,552, $476 per credit hour; Nonstate residents: per academic year $13,759, $1,752 per credit hour. Tuition is subject to change.

Financial Assistance:

First Year Students: Teaching assistantships available for first-year. Average amount paid per academic year: $9,000. Average number of hours worked per week: 20. Apply by March 1. Research assistantships available for first-year. Average amount paid per academic year: $8,500. Average number of hours worked per week: 20. Apply by March 1. Fellowships and scholarships available for first-year. Average amount paid per academic year: $2,150. Apply by March 1.

Advanced Students: Teaching assistantships available for advanced students. Average amount paid per academic year: $9,000. Average number of hours worked per week: 20. Research assistantships available for advanced students. Average amount paid per academic year: $8,500. Average number of hours worked per week: 20.

Contact Information: Of all students currently enrolled full-time, 60% benefitted from one or more of the listed financial assistance programs. Application and information available online at: http://www.uncc.edu/finaid.

Internships/Practica: Clinical/Community: Students are required to enroll in 2 semesters of practicum, working 22 hrs/week in community agencies such as mental health centers, prisons, hospitals, and non-profit organizations. Industrial/Organizational: An extensive practicum component utilizes the Charlotte area as a setting for applied experience. All students must complete 3 hours of Projects in I/O Pscychology and they are strongly encouraged to take 6 hours.

Housing and Day Care: On-campus housing is available. No on-campus day care facilities are available.

Employment of Department Graduates:

Master's Degree Graduates: Of those who graduated in the academic year 2003–2004, the following categories and numbers represent the post-graduate activities and employment of master's degree graduates: Enrolled in a post-doctoral residency/fellowship (n/a), employed in independent practice (n/a), total from the above (master's) (0).

Doctoral Degree Graduates: Of those who graduated in the academic year 2003–2004, the following categories and numbers represent the post-graduate activities and employment of doctoral degree graduates: Enrolled in a psychology doctoral program (n/a), total from the above (doctoral) (0).

Additional Information:

Orientation, Objectives, and Emphasis of Department: The objective of the master's degree program is to train psychologists in the knowledge and skills necessary to address problems encountered in industry, organizations, and the community. The program has an applied emphasis. Graduates of the program are eligible to apply for licensing in North Carolina as psychological associates. Although our goals emphasize application of psychological principles in organizational, clinical, and community settings, the rigorous program allows students to prepare themselves well for further education in psychology.

Special Facilities or Resources: The psychology department is housed in a modern classroom office building that provides offices, demonstration rooms, a workshop, and specialty laboratories for research. Facilities include a computerized laboratory with 37 microcomputers; many small testing, training, and interview rooms with one-way mirrors for direct observation; audio intercommunications; and closed circuit television. There is extensive audio and video equipment available as well as a research trailer, tachistoscopes, programming and timing equipment, and microcomputers. The psychometric laboratory contains an extensive inventory of current tests of intelligence, personality, and interest, as well as calculators and microcomputers for testing, test score evaluation and data analysis. A well-equipped physiological laboratory is available for work including human electrophysiology.

Application Information:
Send to: Graduate Admissions, UNC-Charlotte, 9201 University City Boulevard, Charlotte, NC 28223. Students are admitted in the Fall. February 1 is the deadline for the Industrial/Organizational program. March 1 is the deadline for Clinical/Community MA program. *Fee:* $35.

North Carolina, University of, Wilmington

Psychology
Arts and Sciences
601 South College Road
Wilmington, NC 28403-5612
Telephone: (910) 962-3370
Fax: (910) 962-7010
E-mail: *noeln@uncw.edu*
Web: *http://www.uncw.edu/psy/*

Department Information:
1972. Chairperson: Mark Galizio, PhD Number of Faculty: total–full-time 27; women–full-time 10; minority–full-time 3; faculty subject to the Americans With Disabilities Act 1.

Programs and Degrees Offered:
Listed in the following order: Program area, degree type (T if terminal Master's), number awarded 7/03–6/04. General Psychology MA/MS (Master of Arts/Science) (T) 8, Substance Abuse Treatment Psychology MA/MS (Master of Arts/Science) (T) 8, Applied Behavior Analysis MA/MS (Master of Arts/Science) (T) 0.

Student Applications/Admissions:
Student Applications
 General Psychology MA/MS (Master of Arts/Science)—Applications 2004–2005, 50. Total applicants accepted 2004–2005, 17. Number enrolled (new admits only) 2004–2005 full-time,

14. Total enrolled 2004–2005 full-time, 18, part-time, 10. Openings 2005–2006, 10. The Median number of years required for completion of a degree are 2. The number of students enrolled full and part-time who were dismissed or voluntarily withdrew from this program area were 1. *Substance Abuse Treatment Psychology MA/MS (Master of Arts/Science)*—Applications 2004–2005, 24. Total applicants accepted 2004–2005, 6. Number enrolled (new admits only) 2004–2005 full-time, 6. Total enrolled 2004–2005 full-time, 12, part-time, 1. Openings 2005–2006, 8. The Median number of years required for completion of a degree are 3. The number of students enrolled full and part-time who were dismissed or voluntarily withdrew from this program area were 0. *Applied Behavior Analysis MA/MS (Master of Arts/Science)*—Openings 2005–2006, 8.

Admissions Requirements:
Scores: Entries appear in this order: required test or GPA, minimum score (if required), median score of students entering in 2003–2004. Master's Programs: GRE-V no minimum stated, 530; GRE-Q no minimum stated, 530; GRE-V+Q no minimum stated, 1060; GRE-Analytical no minimum stated, 580; overall undergraduate GPA no minimum stated, 3.2; last 2 years GPA no minimum stated, 3.5.
Other Criteria: (importance of criteria rated low, medium, or high): GRE/MAT scores high, research experience high, work experience low, extracurricular activity low, clinically related public service medium, GPA high, letters of recommendation high, interview high, statement of goals and objectives high. In the Substance Abuse Treatment Psychology Concentration, clinically related public service may be given more weight, since this concentration emphasizes the development of clinical as well as research skills. For additional information on admission requirements, go to: http://www.uncw.edu/psy/.

Student Characteristics: The following represents characteristics of students in 2004–2005 in all graduate psychology programs in the department: Female–full-time 16, part-time 4; Male–full-time 14, part-time 7; African American/Black–full-time 2, part-time 2; Hispanic/Latino(a)–full-time 2, part-time 1; Asian/Pacific Islander–full-time 1, part-time 1; American Indian/Alaska Native–full-time 0, part-time 0; Caucasian–full-time 25, part-time 7; Multi-ethnic–full-time 0, part-time 0; students subject to the Americans With Disabilities Act–full-time 0, part-time 0.

Financial Information/Assistance:
Tuition for Full-Time Study: *Master's:* State residents: per academic year $3,701, $393 per credit hour; Nonstate residents: per academic year $13,539, $1,623 per credit hour. Tuition is subject to change. See the following Web site for updates and changes in tuition costs: http://www.uncw.edu/grad_info/grad_support.htm.

Financial Assistance:
 First Year Students: Teaching assistantships available for first-year. Average amount paid per academic year: $9,000. Average number of hours worked per week: 20. Apply by January 15. Research assistantships available for first-year. Average amount paid per academic year: $9,000. Average number of hours worked per week: 20. Apply by Varied. Tuition remission given: partial. Traineeships available for first-year. Average amount paid per academic year: $9,000. Average number of hours worked per week: 20. Apply by Varied. Fellowships and scholarships available for

first-year. Average amount paid per academic year: $7,000. Average number of hours worked per week: 0. Apply by Varied.

Advanced Students: Teaching assistantships available for advanced students. Average amount paid per academic year: $9,000. Average number of hours worked per week: 20. Apply by January 15. Research assistantships available for advanced students. Average amount paid per academic year: $9,000. Average number of hours worked per week: 20. Apply by Varied. Tuition remission given: partial. Traineeships available for advanced students. Average amount paid per academic year: $9,000. Average number of hours worked per week: 20. Apply by Varied. Fellowships and scholarships available for advanced students. Average amount paid per academic year: $7,000. Average number of hours worked per week: 0. Apply by Varied.

Contact Information: Of all students currently enrolled full-time, 83% benefitted from one or more of the listed financial assistance programs.

Internships/Practica: In the Substance Abuse Treatment Psychology Concentration and our new Applied Behavior Analysis Concentration, students are prepared for work with dual diagnosis clients or with severely developmentally disabled clients through the completion of a required practicum and internship. The required internship and practicum consist of at least 1500 hours total of supervised experience working with substance abuse, autism, mental retardation and other psychological and behavioral problems. Training sites include: Community Mental Health Centers, Correctional Institutions, University Counseling Centers, Inpatient and Outpatient Substance Abuse Treatment Centers and residential centers for autistic and mentally retarded individuals.

Housing and Day Care: On-campus housing is available. See the following Web site for more information: http://www.uncwil.edu/grad_info/housing.htm. No on-campus day care facilities are available.

Employment of Department Graduates:
Master's Degree Graduates: Of those who graduated in the academic year 2003–2004, the following categories and numbers represent the post-graduate activities and employment of master's degree graduates: Enrolled in a psychology doctoral program (5), enrolled in another graduate/professional program (1), enrolled in a post-doctoral residency/fellowship (n/a), employed in independent practice (n/a), employed in an academic position at a university (0), employed in an academic position at a 2-year/4-year college (1), employed in other positions at a higher education institution (0), employed in a professional position in a school system (0), employed in business or industry (research/consulting) (2), employed in business or industry (management) (0), employed in a government agency (research) (0), employed in a government agency (professional services) (0), employed in a community mental health/counseling center (6), employed in a hospital/medical center (0), still seeking employment (0), not seeking employment (1), total from the above (master's) (16).
Doctoral Degree Graduates: Of those who graduated in the academic year 2003–2004, the following categories and numbers represent the post-graduate activities and employment of doctoral degree graduates: Enrolled in a psychology doctoral program (n/a), total from the above (doctoral) (0).

Additional Information:
Orientation, Objectives, and Emphasis of Department: The department is committed to fostering an understanding of psychological research, and it stresses the relationship between students and professors in this process. Research methodology and application are emphasized for all students. Students in the General Psychology Concentration are prepared to continue to the PhD in a variety of content areas. Students completing the Substance Abuse Treatment Psychology Concentration are prepared for work with dual diagnosis clients in mental health clinics and other public service agencies. The Applied Behavior Analysis Concentration prepares students for work primarily with autistic and mentally retarded individuals. The SATP and ABA graduates meet all academic requirements to apply for North Carolina state licensure as a Psychological Associate and either North Carolina state certification as a Certified Clinical Addictions Specialist (SATP concentration) or national certification as an Applied Behavior Analyst (ABA concentration).

Special Facilities or Resources: Special facilities or resources include state-of-the-art microcomputers with CD-ROM, DVD and Power Point capabilities in the classrooms, research laboratories (including behavioral pharmacology laboratories and a human laboratory), an animal laboratory, videotape and digital recording equipment. All students have access to word processing, SAS, and SPSS on the university computer system.

Information for Students With Physical Disabilities: See the following Web site for more information: http://www.uncwil.edu/stuaff/SDS/disability.html.

Application Information:
Send to: Graduate School, University of North Carolina, Wilmington, 601 South College Road, Wilmington, NC 28403-5955. Application available online. URL of online application: http://www.uncw.edu/grad_info/pdf/Application%20for%202004_int.pdf. Students are admitted in the Fall, application deadline January 15. Technically, applications can be accepted until June 20, but complete applications (i.e. application forms, GREs, letters, and transcripts) received by January 15 will be given first consideration. Generally, all spaces are taken by early applicants (i.e., by people with complete applications by mid January). Admission is competitive. *Fee:* $45. Fee waived for McNair Scholars.

Wake Forest University
Department of Psychology
Arts & Sciences
P.O. Box 7778
Winston-Salem, NC 27109
Telephone: (336) 758-5424
Fax: (336) 758-4733
E-mail: *teehill@wfu.edu*
Web: *http://www.wfu.edu/academics/psychology*

Department Information:
1958. Chairperson: Mark R. Leary. Number of Faculty: total–full-time 19, part-time 5; women–full-time 10, part-time 1.

Programs and Degrees Offered:
Listed in the following order: Program area, degree type (T if terminal Master's), number awarded 7/03–6/04. General MA/MS (Master of Arts/Science) (T) 12.

Student Applications/Admissions:
Student Applications
General MA/MS (Master of Arts/Science)—Applications 2004–2005, 116. Total applicants accepted 2004–2005, 20. Number enrolled (new admits only) 2004–2005 full-time, 12. Number enrolled (new admits only) 2004–2005 part-time, 0. Openings 2005–2006, 12. The Median number of years required for completion of a degree are 2. The number of students enrolled full and part-time who were dismissed or voluntarily withdrew from this program area was 1.

Admissions Requirements:
Scores: Entries appear in this order: required test or GPA, minimum score (if required), median score of students entering in 2003–2004. Master's Programs: GRE-V no minimum stated, 600; GRE-Q no minimum stated, 695; GRE-V+Q no minimum stated, 1295; overall undergraduate GPA 3.00, 3.55; psychology GPA 3.00.
Other Criteria: (importance of criteria rated low, medium, or high): GRE/MAT scores medium, research experience high, GPA medium, letters of recommendation high, interview medium, statement of goals and objectives high.

Student Characteristics: The following represents characteristics of students in 2004–2005 in all graduate psychology programs in the department: Female–full-time 19, part-time 0; Male–full-time 5, part-time 0; African American/Black–full-time 0, part-time 0; Hispanic/Latino(a)–full-time 1, part-time 0; Asian/Pacific Islander–full-time 0, part-time 0; American Indian/Alaska Native–full-time 0, part-time 0; Caucasian–full-time 23, part-time 0; Multi-ethnic–full-time 0, part-time 0; students subject to the Americans With Disabilities Act–full-time 0, part-time 0.

Financial Information/Assistance:
Tuition for Full-Time Study: *Master's:* State residents: per academic year $24,475; Nonstate residents: per academic year $24,475. Tuition is subject to change. See the following Web site for updates and changes in tuition costs: http://www.wfubmc.edu/graduate/application.html#info.

Financial Assistance:
First Year Students: Teaching assistantships available for first-year. Average amount paid per academic year: $8,500. Average number of hours worked per week: 12. Apply by January 15. Tuition remission given: full. Research assistantships available for first-year. Average amount paid per academic year: $8,500. Average number of hours worked per week: 12. Apply by January 15. Tuition remission given: full.
Advanced Students: Teaching assistantships available for advanced students. Average amount paid per academic year: $8,500. Average number of hours worked per week: 12. Apply by January 15. Tuition remission given: full. Research assistantships available for advanced students. Average amount paid per academic year: $8,500. Average number of hours worked per week: 12. Apply by January 15. Tuition remission given: full.
Contact Information: Of all students currently enrolled full-time, 83% benefitted from one or more of the listed financial assistance programs. Application and information available online at: http://www.wfubmc.edu/graduate/application.html.

Internships/Practica: No information provided.

Housing and Day Care: No on-campus housing is available. No on-campus day care facilities are available.

Employment of Department Graduates:
Master's Degree Graduates: Of those who graduated in the academic year 2003–2004, the following categories and numbers represent the post-graduate activities and employment of master's degree graduates: Enrolled in a psychology doctoral program (9), enrolled in a post-doctoral residency/fellowship (n/a), employed in independent practice (n/a), employed in an academic position at a 2-year/4-year college (1), employed in other positions at a higher education institution (2), employed in a community mental health/counseling center (1), do not know (1), total from the above (master's) (14).
Doctoral Degree Graduates: Of those who graduated in the academic year 2003–2004, the following categories and numbers represent the post-graduate activities and employment of doctoral degree graduates: Enrolled in a psychology doctoral program (n/a), total from the above (doctoral) (0).

Additional Information:
Orientation, Objectives, and Emphasis of Department: The department aims to provide rigorous master's level training, with an emphasis on mastery of theory, research methodology, and content in the basic areas of psychology. This is a general, research-oriented MA program for capable students, most of whom will continue to the PhD.

Special Facilities or Resources: The department of psychology occupies a beautiful and spacious new building that is equipped with state-of-the art teaching and laboratory facilities. Learning resources include in-class multimedia instruction equipment, departmental mini- and microcomputers, departmental and university libraries, and information technology centers. Ample research space is available, including social, developmental, cognitive, perception, physiological, and animal behavior laboratories. Office space is available for graduate students. The department has links with the Wake Forest University School of Medicine (e.g., Neuroscience), which can provide opportunities for students. All students work closely with individual faculty on research during both years (2:1 student/faculty ratio). Wake Forest University offers the academic and technological resources, facilities, and Division I athletic programs, music, theater, and art associated with a larger university, with the individual attention that a smaller university can provide.

Application Information:
Send to: Dean of Graduate School, Wake Forest University, P.O. Box 7487, Winston-Salem, NC 27109. Application available online. URL of online application: http://www.wfubmc.edu/graduate/application.html. Students are admitted in the Spring, application deadline January 15. Fee: $25.

Western Carolina University

Department of Psychology
College of Education & Allied Professions
Killian Building
Cullowhee, NC 28723
Telephone: (828) 227-7361
Fax: (828) 227-7005
E-mail: *mccord@wcu.edu*
Web: *http://www.wcu.edu/ceap/psychology/psyhome.htm*

Department Information:

1919. Department Head: David M. McCord, PhD Number of Faculty: total–full-time 16, part-time 5; women–full-time 6, part-time 3.

Programs and Degrees Offered:

Listed in the following order: Program area, degree type (T if terminal Master's), number awarded 7/03–6/04. Clinical Psychology MA/MS (Master of Arts/Science) (T) 6, School Psychology MA/MS (Master of Arts/Science) (T) 8, General-Experimental Psychology MA/MS (Master of Arts/Science) (T) 0.

Student Applications/Admissions:

Student Applications

Clinical Psychology MA/MS (Master of Arts/Science)—Applications 2004–2005, 38. Total applicants accepted 2004–2005, 8. Number enrolled (new admits only) 2004–2005 full-time, 8. Number enrolled (new admits only) 2004–2005 part-time, 0. Openings 2005–2006, 9. The Median number of years required for completion of a degree are 2. The number of students enrolled full and part-time who were dismissed or voluntarily withdrew from this program area were 2. *School Psychology MA/MS (Master of Arts/Science)*—Applications 2004–2005, 40. Total applicants accepted 2004–2005, 9. Number enrolled (new admits only) 2004–2005 full-time, 10. Number enrolled (new admits only) 2004–2005 part-time, 0. Openings 2005–2006, 9. The Median number of years required for completion of a degree are 3. The number of students enrolled full and part-time who were dismissed or voluntarily withdrew from this program area were 2. *General-Experimental Psychology MA/MS (Master of Arts/Science)*—Applications 2004–2005, 3. Total applicants accepted 2004–2005, 2. Number enrolled (new admits only) 2004–2005 full-time, 2. Number enrolled (new admits only) 2004–2005 part-time, 0. Openings 2005–2006, 8. The Median number of years required for completion of a degree are 2. The number of students enrolled full and part-time who were dismissed or voluntarily withdrew from this program area were 0.

Admissions Requirements:

Scores: Entries appear in this order: required test or GPA, minimum score (if required), median score of students entering in 2003–2004. Master's Programs: GRE-V 500; GRE-Q 500; GRE-V+Q 1000, 1050; last 2 years GPA 3.00, 3.40; psychology GPA 3.00, 3.40. Doctoral Programs: GRE-V no minimum stated; GRE-Q no minimum stated; overall undergraduate GPA no minimum stated; last 2 years GPA no minimum stated; psychology GPA no minimum stated.

Other Criteria: (importance of criteria rated low, medium, or high): GRE/MAT scores high, research experience high, work experience medium, extracurricular activity medium, clinically related public service medium, GPA high, letters of recommendation high, interview high, statement of goals and objectives high.

Student Characteristics: The following represents characteristics of students in 2004–2005 in all graduate psychology programs in the department: Female–full-time 22, part-time 0; Male–full-time 9, part-time 0; African American/Black–full-time 1, part-time 0; Hispanic/Latino(a)–full-time 0, part-time 0; Asian/Pacific Islander–full-time 1, part-time 0; American Indian/Alaska Native–full-time 0, part-time 0; Caucasian–full-time 0, part-time 0; Multi-ethnic–full-time 0, part-time 0; students subject to the Americans With Disabilities Act–full-time 0, part-time 0.

Financial Information/Assistance:

Tuition for Full-Time Study: *Master's:* State residents: per academic year $1,127, $174 per credit hour; Nonstate residents: per academic year $4,762, $1,082 per credit hour.

Financial Assistance:

First Year Students: Teaching assistantships available for first-year. Average amount paid per academic year: $5,000. Average number of hours worked per week: 15. Apply by February 1.

Advanced Students: Teaching assistantships available for advanced students. Average amount paid per academic year: $5,000. Average number of hours worked per week: 15. Apply by Febraury 1. Research assistantships available for advanced students. Average amount paid per academic year: $5,000. Average number of hours worked per week: 15. Apply by February 1.

Contact Information: No information provided.

Internships/Practica: Public schools, mental health centers, private hospitals, psychological services center, private schools-alternative schools.

Housing and Day Care: No on-campus housing is available. No on-campus day care facilities are available.

Employment of Department Graduates:

Master's Degree Graduates: Of those who graduated in the academic year 2003–2004, the following categories and numbers represent the post-graduate activities and employment of master's degree graduates: Enrolled in a post-doctoral residency/fellowship (n/a), employed in independent practice (n/a), total from the above (master's) (0).

Doctoral Degree Graduates: Of those who graduated in the academic year 2003–2004, the following categories and numbers represent the post-graduate activities and employment of doctoral degree graduates: Enrolled in a psychology doctoral program (n/a), total from the above (doctoral) (0).

Additional Information:

Orientation, Objectives, and Emphasis of Department: The Master or Arts in Psychology program has three concentrations, Clinical, School, and General-Experimental. All three concentrations focus on empirically validated methods, with a research emphasis. Both the Clinical Psychology and School Psychology programs emphasize a scientist-practitioner model. Master of Arts in Psychology-Clinical (2 years). Purpose: 1. To provide students with professional training in the practice of clinical psychology including skills in diagnosis, assessment, therapy and research. 2.

To prepare students for doctoral training in clinical psychology. Master of Arts in Psychology - School (3 years). Purpose: The school psychology curriculum is organized to accomplish several goals: to gain an understanding of psychological theories, concepts and research regarding human behavior, and apply that knowledge to promote human welfare in the school setting. 1. They will have a basic background in both psychology and education designed to provide a general theoretical applied orientation in order to function effectively as a psychologist in an educational setting. 3. They will have sufficient academic training to interpret and apply educational and psychological research in a critical manner. 4. They will develop at least one area of expertise to make a distinct contribution as a school psychologist in a school system. 5. They will gain an understanding of the educational system. 5. They will have an understanding of professional problems and issues as well as how to follow approved ethical practices. Purpose and general description of General-Experimental track: This track is a part of a master's program in psychology that was established in 1970. The purpose of the track is to prepare students for entry into doctoral programs in areas of experimental psychology, such as cognitive, developmental, social and neuropsychology. To achieve this objective, advanced coursework is offered in research methodology and content areas of experimental psychology, and students engage in research through a thesis requirement, as well as through elective-directed study that provides opportunities for involvement in faculty research.

Special Facilities or Resources: The department includes shared offices for most graduate students, with space for research and for our psychological services clinic, which provides assessment and intervention to individuals within and outside of the university.

Application Information:
Send to: School of Research and Graduate Studies: WCU, Cullowhee, NC 28723. Application available online. Students are admitted in the Fall, application deadline February 1. *Fee:* $35.

Minot State University

Psychology
Education & Health Sciences
500 University Avenue W.
Minot, ND 58707
Telephone: (701) 858-4262
Fax: (701) 858-4260
E-mail: *ccoleman@minotstateu.edu*
Web: *http://www.misu.nodak.edu/*

Department Information:

1991. Chairperson: Donald Burke. Number of Faculty: total–full-time 12, part-time 2; women–full-time 8, part-time 2; minority–full-time 1.

Programs and Degrees Offered:

Listed in the following order: Program area, degree type (T if terminal Master's), number awarded 7/03–6/04. Education Specialist EdS (Education Specialist) 6.

Student Applications/Admissions:

Student Applications

Education Specialist EdS (Education Specialist)—Applications 2004–2005, 12. Total applicants accepted 2004–2005, 7. Number enrolled (new admits only) 2004–2005 full-time, 6. Number enrolled (new admits only) 2004–2005 part-time, 1. Total enrolled 2004–2005 full-time, 17, part-time, 1. Openings 2005–2006, 10. The Median number of years required for completion of a degree are 3. The number of students enrolled full and part-time who were dismissed or voluntarily withdrew from this program area were 0.

Admissions Requirements:

Scores: Entries appear in this order: required test or GPA, minimum score (if required), median score of students entering in 2003–2004. Master's Programs: GRE-V 450, 550; GRE-Q 450, 500; GRE-Analytical no minimum stated; overall undergraduate GPA 2.75, 3.25. Students without the overall GPA must appeal to the chairperson and receive special written permission to be considered for admission.

Other Criteria: (importance of criteria rated low, medium, or high): GRE/MAT scores high, research experience low, work experience high, extracurricular activity medium, clinically related public service medium, GPA medium, letters of recommendation low, interview medium, statement of goals and objectives medium.

Student Characteristics: The following represents characteristics of students in 2004–2005 in all graduate psychology programs in the department: Female–full-time 14, part-time 1; Male–full-time 2, part-time 0; African American/Black–full-time 0, part-time 0; Hispanic/Latino(a)–full-time 0, part-time 0; Asian/Pacific Islander–full-time 1, part-time 0; American Indian/Alaska Native–full-time 0, part-time 0; Caucasian–full-time 15, part-time 1; Multi-ethnic–full-time 0, part-time 0; students subject to the Americans With Disabilities Act–full-time 0, part-time 0.

Financial Information/Assistance:

Tuition for Full-Time Study: *Master's:* State residents: per academic year $3,273; Nonstate residents: per academic year $8,223.

Financial Assistance:

First Year Students: Research assistantships available for first-year. Average number of hours worked per week: 10. Tuition remission given: partial.

Advanced Students: Research assistantships available for advanced students. Average number of hours worked per week: 10. Tuition remission given: partial.

Contact Information: Of all students currently enrolled full-time, 10% benefitted from one or more of the listed financial assistance programs.

Internships/Practica: School Psychology Practicum I: This practicum provides students an opportunity to apply their learning from content courses to elementary and secondary students who are failing to find success in school. The assessment of processing problems that sometimes underlie learning disabilities will be examined. School Psychology Practicum II: This is a capstone course wherein the students apply information learned and skills acquired in previous courses in diagnosis and remediation planning of actual school-based cases. Theory and techniques are applied to assisting school children with challenging learning and behavior problems. Emphasis will be placed on deciding whether a diagnostic or consultative role will best meet a particular child's needs. Internship: The internship will involve spending 1200 hours in schools or a similar setting. It will also involve an integrative experience where the individual will demonstrate competencies in assessment, programming, consultation, and counseling.

Housing and Day Care: On-campus housing is available. See the following Web site for more information: http://www.minotstateu. edu/admin/housing.html. No on-campus day care facilities are available.

Employment of Department Graduates:

Master's Degree Graduates: Of those who graduated in the academic year 2003–2004, the following categories and numbers represent the post-graduate activities and employment of master's degree graduates: Enrolled in a psychology doctoral program (0), enrolled in another graduate/professional program (0), enrolled in a post-doctoral residency/fellowship (n/a), employed in independent practice (n/a), employed in an academic position at a university (0), employed in an academic position at a 2-year/4-year college (0), employed in other positions at a higher education institution (0), employed in a professional position in a school system (6), employed in business or industry (research/consulting) (0), employed in business or industry (management) (0), employed in a government agency (research) (0), employed in a government agency (professional services) (0), employed in a community mental health/counseling center (0), employed in a hospital/medical center (0), still seeking employment (0), other employment position (0), total from the above (master's) (6).

Doctoral Degree Graduates: Of those who graduated in the academic year 2003–2004, the following categories and numbers represent the post-graduate activities and employment of doctoral

degree graduates: Enrolled in a psychology doctoral program (n/a), total from the above (doctoral) (0).

Additional Information:

Orientation, Objectives, and Emphasis of Department: The Education Specialist degree in school psychology is designed to prepare students for certification by the National Association of School Psychology (NASP) and as a School Psychologist in the State of North Dakota. Graduate students participate in a rigorous three-year program. The program emphasizes hands-on experience culminating in a one-year, 1,200-hour internship. The emphasis of the program is to provide the student with the theoretical and practical skills to be an effective school psychologist. The curriculum stresses teaching assessment skills, intervention techniques, and consultative strategies through numerous practicum opportunities. The program trains practitioners who are culturally competent service providers. The school psychology program at Minot State University trains practitioners who are prepared to work as problem solvers in rurally based schools that typify a state like North Dakota. The ideal practitioner in a rural setting is a generalist who combines appropriate educational and behavioral assessments with a knowledge of educational curriculum and instruction to develop appropriate interventions for a broad range of student concerns.

Application Information:

Send to: Graduate School, Minot State University, 500 University Avenue West, Minot, ND 58707. Application available online. Students are admitted in the Fall, application deadline March 15. *Fee:* $35.

North Dakota State University
Department of Psychology
Science and Mathematics
115 Minard Hall
Fargo, ND 58105
Telephone: (701) 231-8622
Fax: (701) 231-8426
E-mail: *NDSU.psych@ndsu.edu*
Web: *http://www.ndsu.nodak.edu/ndsu/psychology*

Department Information:

1965. Chairperson: Paul D. Rokke. Number of Faculty: total–full-time 17, part-time 7; women–full-time 4, part-time 6.

Programs and Degrees Offered:

Listed in the following order: Program area, degree type (T if terminal Master's), number awarded 7/03–6/04. Clinical MA/MS (Master of Arts/Science) (T) 6, Cognitive Neuroscience PhD (Doctor of Philosophy) 0, Health/Social PhD (Doctor of Philosophy) 1.

Student Applications/Admissions:

Student Applications

Clinical MA/MS (Master of Arts/Science)—Applications 2004–2005, 30. Total applicants accepted 2004–2005, 6. Number enrolled (new admits only) 2004–2005 full-time, 6. Openings 2005–2006, 6. The Median number of years required for completion of a degree are 2. The number of students enrolled full and part-time who were dismissed or voluntarily withdrew

from this program area were 0. *Cognitive Neuroscience PhD (Doctor of Philosophy)*—Applications 2004–2005, 1. Total applicants accepted 2004–2005, 1. Number enrolled (new admits only) 2004–2005 full-time, 1. Total enrolled 2004–2005 full-time, 2. Openings 2005–2006, 4. The Median number of years required for completion of a degree are 4. The number of students enrolled full and part-time who were dismissed or voluntarily withdrew from this program area were 0. *Health/Social PhD (Doctor of Philosophy)*—Applications 2004–2005, 10. Total applicants accepted 2004–2005, 3. Number enrolled (new admits only) 2004–2005 full-time, 3. Total enrolled 2004–2005 full-time, 13. Openings 2005–2006, 4. The Median number of years required for completion of a degree are 4. The number of students enrolled full and part-time who were dismissed or voluntarily withdrew from this program area were 0.

Admissions Requirements:

Scores: Entries appear in this order: required test or GPA, minimum score (if required), median score of students entering in 2003–2004. Master's Programs: GRE-V no minimum stated, 560; GRE-Q no minimum stated, 580; GRE-V+Q no minimum stated, 1155; GRE-Analytical no minimum stated, 620; GRE-Subject(Psych) no minimum stated, 580; overall undergraduate GPA no minimum stated, 3.72. Doctoral Programs: GRE-V no minimum stated, 580; GRE-Q no minimum stated, 630; GRE-V+Q no minimum stated, 1240; GRE-Analytical no minimum stated, 620; GRE-Subject(Psych) no minimum stated, 690; overall undergraduate GPA no minimum stated, 3.72.

Other Criteria: (importance of criteria rated low, medium, or high): GRE/MAT scores high, research experience high, work experience low, extracurricular activity low, clinically related public service low, GPA high, letters of recommendation medium, statement of goals and objectives medium.

Student Characteristics: The following represents characteristics of students in 2004–2005 in all graduate psychology programs in the department: Female–full-time 17, part-time 0; Male–full-time 10, part-time 0; African American/Black–full-time 0, part-time 0; Hispanic/Latino(a)–full-time 0, part-time 0; Asian/Pacific Islander–full-time 1, part-time 0; American Indian/Alaska Native–full-time 0, part-time 0; Caucasian–full-time 27, part-time 0; students subject to the Americans With Disabilities Act–full-time 0, part-time 0.

Financial Information/Assistance:

Tuition for Full-Time Study: *Master's:* State residents: per academic year $5,010, $264 per credit hour; Nonstate residents: per academic year $12,234, $510 per credit hour. *Doctoral:* State residents: per academic year $5,010, $264 per credit hour; Nonstate residents: per academic year $12,234, $510 per credit hour.

Financial Assistance:

First Year Students: Teaching assistantships available for first-year. Average amount paid per academic year: $4,326. Average number of hours worked per week: 10. Apply by March 1. Tuition remission given: full. Research assistantships available for first-year. Average amount paid per academic year: $4,326. Average number of hours worked per week: 10. Apply by March 1. Tuition remission given: full.

Advanced Students: Teaching assistantships available for advanced students. Average amount paid per academic year: $12,000. Average number of hours worked per week: 20. Apply by March 1. Tuition remission given: full. Research assistantships available for advanced students. Average amount paid per academic year: $12,000. Average number of hours worked per week: 20. Apply by March 1. Tuition remission given: full. Fellowships and scholarships available for advanced students. Average amount paid per academic year: $16,000. Average number of hours worked per week: 20. Apply by March 1. Tuition remission given: full.

Contact Information: Of all students currently enrolled full-time, 100% benefitted from one or more of the listed financial assistance programs. Application and information available online at: http://www.ndsu.edu/finaid.

Internships/Practica: Our master's program in clinical psychology has a number of clinical practica that provide a variety of experiences. These include work with traditional one-on-one counseling, chronic pain, eating disorders, behavior analysis, developmental disabilities, child and adolescent psychotherapy, community mental health, and clinical neuropsychology. Research practica are available for doctoral students who wish to develop applied research skills and experiences. Sites include a private foundation for reseach on addictions and eating disorders, a nationally prominent organization for clinical drug trials, a chronic pain treatment program, a community mental health center, and several sites devoted to survey research.

Housing and Day Care: On-campus housing is available. See the following Web site for more information: http://www.ndsu.edu/reslife/housing/index.shtml. For information on child care, contact secretary of the NDSU Center for Child Development at Deanna.Stamnes@ndsu.nodak.edu (e-mail) or (701) 231-8283 (phone). On-campus day care facilities are available.

Employment of Department Graduates:
Master's Degree Graduates: Of those who graduated in the academic year 2003–2004, the following categories and numbers represent the post-graduate activities and employment of master's degree graduates: Enrolled in a post-doctoral residency/fellowship (n/a), employed in independent practice (n/a), total from the above (master's) (0).
Doctoral Degree Graduates: Of those who graduated in the academic year 2003–2004, the following categories and numbers represent the post-graduate activities and employment of doctoral degree graduates: Enrolled in a psychology doctoral program (n/a), total from the above (doctoral) (0).

Additional Information:
Orientation, Objectives, and Emphasis of Department: Our strong research tradition has earned us a reputation as one of the best small psychology departments in the nation. Our clinical master's program is over 30 years old, and many of our alumini have gone on to earn PhDs at top institutions. Our doctoral program emphasizes our strengths in health psychology and neuroscience. PhD training is designed to produce graduates with records in research and teaching, which will make them highly competitive for employment in both traditional academic and nontraditional government and private sector settings. Our programs are based on a mentoring model in which students work closely with specific faculty members who match their research interests. Potential applicants should visit our Web site (www.ndsu.nodak.edu/ndsu/psychology) to learn about specific faculty interests and accomplishments.

Special Facilities or Resources: The department has state-of-the-art facilities for research in electrophysiology (including ERP), vision, and cognition, as well as ample space for other research projects. A center for research on virtual reality / multisensory integration is under development. As the largest population center in the region, Fargo-Moorhead serves as a center for medical services for a large geographic area. There are three major hospitals (including a VA), a medical school Department of Neuroscience, a psychiatric hospital, a neuroscience research institute, and a private pharmaceutical research institute, which offer opportunities for collaboration. NDSU also has a Research and Technology Park, which may offer research experiences involving advanced technology.

Information for Students With Physical Disabilities: See the following Web site for more information: http://www.ndsu.nodak.edu/counseling/disability/index.shtml.

Application Information:
Send to: Office of Graduate Studies, P.O. Box 5790, NDSU, Fargo, ND 58105-5790. Application available online. URL of online application: http://www.ndsu.nodak.edu/gradschool/. Students are admitted in the Fall. Deadline for Masters Clinical program is March 1. Deadline for PhD is March 15. Applications arriving after deadlines will be considered until positions are filled. For detailed information on programs, application, forms, and fellowships, see our Web site: www.ndsu.nodak.edu/ndsu/psychology. *Fee:* $35.

North Dakota, University of
Department of Counseling/PhD in Counseling Psychology; MA in Counseling
Education and Human Development
Box 8255
Grand Forks, ND 58202
Telephone: (701) 777-2729
Fax: (701) 777-3184
E-mail: *michael.loewy@und.edu;*
david_whitcomb@und.nodak.edu
Web: *www.counseling.und.edu*

Department Information:
1963. Chairperson: Dr. Michael Loewy. Number of Faculty: total–full-time 7, part-time 1; women–full-time 4, part-time 1; minority–full-time 2; faculty subject to the Americans With Disabilities Act 2.

Programs and Degrees Offered:
Listed in the following order: Program area, degree type (T if terminal Master's), number awarded 7/03–6/04. Counseling Psychology PhD (Doctor of Philosophy) 8, Counseling MA/MS (Master of Arts/Science) (T) 16.

APA Accreditation: Counseling PhD (Doctor of Philosophy).

Student Applications/Admissions:

Student Applications

Counseling Psychology PhD (Doctor of Philosophy)—Applications 2004–2005, 29. Total applicants accepted 2004–2005, 12. Number enrolled (new admits only) 2004–2005 full-time, 5. Openings 2005–2006, 6. The Median number of years required for completion of a degree are 5. The number of students enrolled full and part-time who were dismissed or voluntarily withdrew from this program area were 0. *Counseling MA/MS (Master of Arts/Science)*—Applications 2004–2005, 41. Total applicants accepted 2004–2005, 34. Number enrolled (new admits only) 2004–2005 full-time, 17. Number enrolled (new admits only) 2004–2005 part-time, 2. Total enrolled 2004–2005 full-time, 35, part-time, 17. Openings 2005–2006, 20. The Median number of years required for completion of a degree are 2. The number of students enrolled full and part-time who were dismissed or voluntarily withdrew from this program area were 2.

Admissions Requirements:

Scores: Entries appear in this order: required test or GPA, minimum score (if required), median score of students entering in 2003–2004. Master's Programs: overall undergraduate GPA 2.75; last 2 years GPA 3.00. Doctoral Programs: GRE-Subject(Psych) no minimum stated, 635.

Other Criteria: (importance of criteria rated low, medium, or high): GRE/MAT scores medium, research experience high, work experience medium, extracurricular activity medium, clinically related public service medium, GPA medium, letters of recommendation high, interview high, statement of goals and objectives high, prerequisites medium. For additional information on admission requirements, go to: http://www.und.edu/dept/grad/pdf/PDF/04%20Supplemental%20Application%20Form.pdf.

Student Characteristics: The following represents characteristics of students in 2004–2005 in all graduate psychology programs in the department: Female–full-time 46, part-time 8; Male–full-time 14, part-time 2; African American/Black–full-time 1, part-time 0; Hispanic/Latino(a)–full-time 1, part-time 0; Asian/Pacific Islander–full-time 2, part-time 0; American Indian/Alaska Native–full-time 7, part-time 1; Caucasian–full-time 48, part-time 9; Multi-ethnic–full-time 1, part-time 0; students subject to the Americans With Disabilities Act–full-time 0, part-time 2.

Financial Information/Assistance:

Tuition for Full-Time Study: *Master's:* State residents: per academic year $5,132, $234 per credit hour. *Doctoral:* State residents: per academic year $5,132, $234 per credit hour. Tuition is subject to change. See the following Web site for updates and changes in tuition costs: http://www.und.edu/dept/busoff/tuitionrates.html.

Financial Assistance:

First Year Students: Teaching assistantships available for first-year. Average amount paid per academic year: $5,000. Average number of hours worked per week: 10. Tuition remission given: full. Research assistantships available for first-year. Average amount paid per academic year: $5,000. Average number of hours worked per week: 10. Tuition remission given: full. Fellowships and scholarships available for first-year. Average amount paid per academic year: $5,000. Average number of hours worked per week: 10. Tuition remission given: full.

Advanced Students: Teaching assistantships available for advanced students. Average amount paid per academic year: $5,000. Average number of hours worked per week: 10. Tuition remission given: full. Research assistantships available for advanced students. Average amount paid per academic year: $5,000. Average number of hours worked per week: 10. Tuition remission given: full. Fellowships and scholarships available for advanced students. Average amount paid per academic year: $5,000. Average number of hours worked per week: 10. Tuition remission given: full.

Contact Information: Of all students currently enrolled full-time, 70% benefitted from one or more of the listed financial assistance programs. Application and information available online at: http://www.und.edu/dept/finaid/ or P.O. Box 8371, Grand Forks, ND 58202-8371 Phone: (701) 777-3121.

Internships/Practica: The first Practicum for MA students is held at Northeast Human Services Center located in Grand Forks, ND. Practicum is an introduction to counseling practice with an emphasis on development, improvement, and evaluation of counseling relationships. Students use counseling skills in practice with real clients and live supervision. School counseling students' practicum experience is based in the schools of Grand Forks, ND. Doctoral and MA students undergo a two-semester, half-time, supervised counseling experience at an external site, typically completed during the second year in the program. Group, individual, couples and family counseling; individual supervision; case conferencing; administrative activities; outreach services; and professional consultations are some of the possible opportunities. Placements are in community agencies, university counseling centers, schools, and other sites to fit the career goals of the student. All MA students are supervised weekly by a supervisor at the site. The supervisor must have an MA in Counseling or equivalent preparation. In recent years predoctoral interns have been placed at university counseling centers, mental health agencies, and VA and other medical centers. The training director and program faculty assist students with this process. All doctoral students are supervised by licensed psychologists on site. For those doctoral students for whom a professional internship is required prior to graduation, 2 applied in 2003–2004. Of those who applied, 1 was placed in an internship listed by the Association of Psychology Postdoctoral and Internship Programs (APPIC); 1 was placed in an APA accredited internship.

Housing and Day Care: On-campus housing is available. See the following Web site for more information: http://www.housing.und.edu/ or P.O. Box 9029, Grand Forks, ND 58202-9029, (701) 777-4251. On-campus day care facilities are available. See the following Web site for more information: http://www.housing.und.edu/ or P.O. Box 9026, Grand Forks, ND 58202-9026, (701) 777-4251.

Employment of Department Graduates:

Master's Degree Graduates: Of those who graduated in the academic year 2003–2004, the following categories and numbers represent the post-graduate activities and employment of master's degree graduates: Enrolled in a psychology doctoral program (4), enrolled in another graduate/professional program (1), enrolled in a post-doctoral residency/fellowship (n/a), employed in independent practice (n/a), employed in an academic position at a university (0), employed in an academic position at a 2-year/4-year college (0), employed in other positions at a higher education institution (1), employed in a professional position in a school system (3), employed in business or industry (research/consulting) (0), employed in business or industry (management) (0), employed in a government agency (research) (0), employed in a government agency (professional services) (0), employed in a community mental health/counseling center (6), employed in a hospital/medical center (0), still seeking employment (0), not seeking employment (0), other employment position (0), do not know (1), total from the above (master's) (16).

Doctoral Degree Graduates: Of those who graduated in the academic year 2003–2004, the following categories and numbers represent the post-graduate activities and employment of doctoral degree graduates: Enrolled in a psychology doctoral program (n/a), enrolled in another graduate/professional program (0), enrolled in a post-doctoral residency/fellowship (1), employed in independent practice (0), employed in an academic position at a university (0), employed in an academic position at a 2-year/4-year college (1), employed in other positions at a higher education institution (2), employed in a professional position in a school system (0), employed in business or industry (research/consulting) (0), employed in business or industry (management) (0), employed in a government agency (research) (0), employed in a government agency (professional services) (0), employed in a community mental health/counseling center (2), employed in a hospital/medical center (1), still seeking employment (0), other employment position (1), total from the above (doctoral) (8).

Additional Information:

Orientation, Objectives, and Emphasis of Department: The Department of Counseling at the University of North Dakota affirms as a primary value the integration of practice and science throughout the professional life span, from training through career-long participation in the profession. Whether a counselor's or counseling psychologist's career is primarily involved with direct services to clients, or with educational services to students in academia, or with consultative services to organizations, we view science and practice as necessary and complementary aspects of our professional identity. There is no relative importance implied by the order of the words; they are mutual, reciprocal components, best depicted in a circular fashion, not a linear one. An equally important value is best captured by the word *diversity*, which is to be sought, valued, and respected. We use the word in a very broad sense. Included in diversity is the variety of cultures, backgrounds, values, religions, and experiences among our faculty and students; we seek such diversity actively. Also included, though, is the diversity of our professional ways of practice across many theoretical models, the diversity of our ways of learning and our ways of doing science, the diversity of our strengths and our needs, and the diversity of our goals and ways of achieving them.

Special Facilities or Resources: Our Practicum Clinic is in a new counseling facility that we share with Northeast Human Services in downtown Grand Forks, North Dakota. The facility has an observation area wherein we can view sessions live or through video monitors. We also are able to communicate with the counselor-in-training through a walkie-talkie system (bug in the ear).

Information for Students With Physical Disabilities: See the following Web site for more information: www.und.edu/dept/dss/.

Application Information:
Send to: Graduate School Admissions, University of North Dakota, P.O. Box 8178, Grand Forks, ND 58202-8178. Application available online. URL of online application: http://apply.embark.com/grad/northdakota. Students are admitted in the Fall, application deadline January 10. February 1 for the Masters program. *Fee:* $35. The application fee is waived if you have received a master's or doctoral degree from UND or if you are a McNair Scholar.

North Dakota, University of
Department of Psychology
Arts and Science
P.O. Box 8380
Grand Forks, ND 58202-8380
Telephone: (701) 777-3451
Fax: (701) 777-3454
E-mail: *pam_bethke@und.nodak.edu*
Web: *http://www.und.nodak.edu/dept/psychol*

Department Information:
1921. Chairperson: Jeffrey Weatherly. Number of Faculty: total– full-time 16; women–full-time 3; minority–full-time 1.

Programs and Degrees Offered:
Listed in the following order: Program area, degree type (T if terminal Master's), number awarded 7/03–6/04. Clinical PhD (Doctor of Philosophy) 4, General/ Experimental PhD (Doctor of Philosophy) 1.

APA Accreditation: Clinical PhD (Doctor of Philosophy).

Student Applications/Admissions:
Student Applications

Clinical PhD (Doctor of Philosophy)—Applications 2004–2005, 65. Total applicants accepted 2004–2005, 8. Openings 2005– 2006, 8. The number of students enrolled full and part-time who were dismissed or voluntarily withdrew from this program area were 1. *General/ Experimental PhD (Doctor of Philosophy)*— Applications 2004–2005, 4. Total applicants accepted 2004– 2005, 1. Openings 2005–2006, 4. The number of students enrolled full and part-time who were dismissed or voluntarily withdrew from this program area were 0.

Admissions Requirements:
Scores: Entries appear in this order: required test or GPA, minimum score (if required), median score of students entering in 2003–2004. Master's Programs: GRE-V no minimum stated, 553; GRE-Q no minimum stated, 577; GRE-Analytical no minimum stated, 513; GRE-Subject(Psych) no minimum stated, 472; overall undergraduate GPA no minimum stated, 3.56; last 2 years GPA no minimum stated, 3.7. Doctoral Programs: GRE-V no minimum stated; GRE-Q no minimum stated; GRE-Analytical no minimum stated; GRE-Subject(Psych) no minimum stated; last 2 years GPA no minimum stated; psychology GPA no minimum stated. Not calculated separately.
Other Criteria: (importance of criteria rated low, medium, or high): GRE/MAT scores medium, research experience high, work experience low, clinically related public service low, GPA medium, letters of recommendation medium, interview medium, statement of goals and objectives medium.

Student Characteristics: The following represents characteristics of students in 2004–2005 in all graduate psychology programs in the department: Female–full-time 28, part-time 0; Male–full-time 14, part-time 0; African American/Black–full-time 0, part-time 0; Hispanic/Latino(a)–full-time 0, part-time 0; Asian/Pacific Islander–full-time 0, part-time 0; American Indian/Alaska Native–full-time 11, part-time 0; Caucasian–full-time 0, part-time 0.

Financial Information/Assistance:

Tuition for Full-Time Study: *Master's:* State residents: per academic year $4,418; Nonstate residents: per academic year $10,604. *Doctoral:* State residents: per academic year $4,418; Nonstate residents: per academic year $10,604. Tuition is subject to change. See the following Web site for updates and changes in tuition costs: www.und.nodak.edu.

Financial Assistance:

First Year Students: Teaching assistantships available for first-year. Average amount paid per academic year: $10,413. Average number of hours worked per week: 15. Apply by January 15. Tuition remission given: full.

Advanced Students: Traineeships available for advanced students. Tuition remission given: full.

Contact Information: Of all students currently enrolled full-time, 100% benefitted from one or more of the listed financial assistance programs.

Internships/Practica: For those doctoral students for whom a professional internship is required prior to graduation, 4 applied in 2003–2004. Of those who applied, 4 were placed in internships listed by the Association of Psychology Postdoctoral and Internship Programs (APPIC); 4 were placed in APA accredited internships.

Housing and Day Care: On-campus housing is available. On-campus day care facilities are available.

Employment of Department Graduates:

Master's Degree Graduates: Of those who graduated in the academic year 2003–2004, the following categories and numbers represent the post-graduate activities and employment of master's degree graduates: Enrolled in a psychology doctoral program (8), enrolled in a post-doctoral residency/fellowship (n/a), employed in independent practice (n/a), total from the above (master's) (8).

Doctoral Degree Graduates: Of those who graduated in the academic year 2003–2004, the following categories and numbers represent the post-graduate activities and employment of doctoral degree graduates: Enrolled in a psychology doctoral program (n/a), enrolled in a post-doctoral residency/fellowship (2), employed in other positions at a higher education institution (1), employed in a community mental health/counseling center (2), total from the above (doctoral) (5).

Additional Information:

Orientation, Objectives, and Emphasis of Department: The Psychology Department at the University of North Dakota offers doctoral programs in experimental and clinical psychology. Experimental students work out individualized programs of study and research with their advisory committees and are encouraged to develop research productivity early in the program. Coursework and research opportunities are strongest in the cognitive, social, and behavioral areas. Because the clinical program leads to a PhD rather than a professional PsyD degree, the emphasis is on the understanding of general psychological theory and the application of the scientific method to research issues. Clinical students work on developing interpersonal skills, and applying both analytic thought and intuitive judgment to problems of individuals, families, and communities. A variety of ongoing research programs help train students in the scientist-practitioner model. The clinical program works closely with the Indians in Psychology Doctoral Education (INPSYDE) program to facilitate entry of Native Americans into clinical psychology and to improve services available to rural, Native American communities. Finally, all students, with specific encouragement for the experimental students, have opportunities to develop expertise in teaching.

Special Facilities or Resources: The department has practicum placements for training in rural community mental health, a low faculty-student ratio, a campus-based psychological services center, and a faculty with active research programs. The Department also has dedicated laboratories capable of computer-assisted monitoring and recording of various physiological and psychological measures in humans (e.g., eye movements, reaction time, sexual response, autonomic nervous system function) as well as in animals (e.g., operant behavior). The University's library has a wide range of holdings in psychology and is tied into an interlibrary loan network. The Department's computers are available for research and provide access to UND's main computer system. Medline, PSYCLIT, and ERIC computer literature searches are available to students. Additional research facilities have been developed in conjunction with the adjacent USDA Grand Forks Human Nutrition Research Center and include a computerized neuropsychological laboratory, sleep EEG rooms, and animal behavior laboratories.

Application Information:

Send to: Graduate School, University of North Dakota, Box 8178, Grand Forks, ND 58202. Application available online. Students are admitted in the Fall, application deadline January 15. *Fee:* $35.

Akron, University of
Department of Counseling
College of Education
127 Carroll Hall
Akron, OH 44325-5007
Telephone: (330) 972- 7779
Fax: (330) 972-5292
E-mail: jrrogers@uakron.edu
Web: http://www.uakron.edu/collges/educ/counseling

Department Information:
1968. Interim Chair: Jim Rogers. Number of Faculty: total–full-time 11, part-time 6; women–full-time 5, part-time 2; minority–full-time 2.

Programs and Degrees Offered:
Listed in the following order: Program area, degree type (T if terminal Master's), number awarded 7/03–6/04. Collaborative Program in Counseling Psychology PhD (Doctor of Philosophy) 4.

APA Accreditation: Counseling PhD (Doctor of Philosophy).

Student Applications/Admissions:
Student Applications

Collaborative Program in Counseling Psychology PhD (Doctor of Philosophy)—Applications 2004–2005, 30. Total applicants accepted 2004–2005, 5. Number enrolled (new admits only) 2004–2005 full-time, 5. Number enrolled (new admits only) 2004–2005 part-time, 0. Total enrolled 2004–2005 full-time, 12, part-time, 18. Openings 2005–2006, 5. The Median number of years required for completion of a degree are 6. The number of students enrolled full and part-time who were dismissed or voluntarily withdrew from this program area were 0.

Admissions Requirements:

Scores: Entries appear in this order: required test or GPA, minimum score (if required), median score of students entering in 2003–2004. Doctoral Programs: GRE-V 550, 566; GRE-Q 550, 626; GRE-V+Q 1100, 1192; GRE-Subject(Psych) 550, 625; overall undergraduate GPA 3.00, 3.37.

Other Criteria: (importance of criteria rated low, medium, or high): GRE/MAT scores high, research experience high, work experience medium, extracurricular activity low, clinically related public service low, GPA high, letters of recommendation high, interview high, statement of goals and objectives high. For additional information on admission requirements, go to: www.uakron.edu/psychology.

Student Characteristics: The following represents characteristics of students in 2004–2005 in all graduate psychology programs in the department: Female–full-time 10, part-time 14; Male–full-time 2, part-time 4; African American/Black–full-time 0, part-time 0; Hispanic/Latino(a)–full-time 0, part-time 0; Asian/Pacific Islander–full-time 1, part-time 1; American Indian/Alaska Native–full-time 0, part-time 0; Caucasian–full-time 11, part-time 17; Multi-ethnic–part-time 0; students subject to the Americans With Disabilities Act–full-time 0, part-time 0.

Financial Information/Assistance:
Tuition for Full-Time Study: *Doctoral:* State residents: per academic year $7,861, $327 per credit hour; Nonstate residents: per academic year $13,095, $545 per credit hour. See the following Web site for updates and changes in tuition costs: www.uakron. Edu/Buffin/Student/Grad.php.

Financial Assistance:

First Year Students: Research assistantships available for first-year. Average amount paid per academic year: $10,500. Average number of hours worked per week: 20. Apply by April 15. Tuition remission given: full.

Advanced Students: No information provided.

Contact Information: Of all students currently enrolled full-time, 100% benefitted from one or more of the listed financial assistance programs. Application and information available online at: http://www.uakron.edu/administration/studentaffairs/financialAid.

Internships/Practica: Practica are offered in the department's clinic, the counseling center on campus, and community mental health centers. For those doctoral students for whom a professional internship is required prior to graduation, 6 applied in 2003–2004. Of those who applied, 5 were placed in internships listed by the Association of Psychology Postdoctoral and Internship Programs (APPIC); 5 were placed in APA accredited internships.

Housing and Day Care: On-campus housing is available. See the following Web site for more information: http://www.uakron.edu/studentaff//reslife/housingmain.php. Child care is available on campus for a fee at the Center for Child Development. See the following Web site for more information: http://www3.uakron.edu/hefe/ccd.htm.

Employment of Department Graduates:
Master's Degree Graduates: Of those who graduated in the academic year 2003–2004, the following categories and numbers represent the post-graduate activities and employment of master's degree graduates: Enrolled in a post-doctoral residency/fellowship (n/a), employed in independent practice (n/a), total from the above (master's) (0).

Doctoral Degree Graduates: Of those who graduated in the academic year 2003–2004, the following categories and numbers represent the post-graduate activities and employment of doctoral degree graduates: Enrolled in a psychology doctoral program (n/a), enrolled in another graduate/professional program (0), employed in independent practice (0), employed in an academic position at a university (0), employed in an academic position at a 2-year/4-year college (0), employed in other positions at a higher education institution (1), employed in a professional position in a school system (0), employed in business or industry (research/consulting) (0), employed in business or industry (management) (0), employed in a government agency (research) (0), employed in a government agency (professional services) (0), employed in a community mental health/counseling center (3), employed in a hospital/medical center (0), still seeking employment (0), other employment position (0), do not know (0), total from the above (doctoral) (4).

Additional Information:

Orientation, Objectives, and Emphasis of Department: The department subscribes to a scientist-practitioner model of training. Its objective is to provide a core of courses in general psychology and courses in the specialty of counseling psychology. The emphasis is on preparation for teaching, research, and practice career paths.

Special Facilities or Resources: The department has its own computer lab and a clinic for individual, group, and family therapy.

Information for Students With Physical Disabilities: See the following Web site for more information: http://www3.uakron.edu/access/.

Application Information:

Send to: Admissions Committee, Collaborative Program in Counseling Psychology, 341 Arts and Sciences Building, The University of Akron, Akron, OH 44325-4301. Application available online. URL of online application: www.uakron.edu/gradsch/pdf/applGrad.pdf. Students are admitted in the Fall, application deadline January 15. *Fee:* $25. Minority applicants may apply for a fee waiver by contacting: The Graduate School, The University of Akron, Akron, OH 44325-2101.

Akron, University of
Department of Psychology
Buchtel College of Arts and Sciences
Arts & Sciences Bldg.
290 E. Buchtel Avenue
Akron, OH 44325-4301
Telephone: (330) 972-7280
Fax: (330) 972-5174
E-mail: *subich@uakron.edu*
Web: *http://www.uakron.edu/psychology*

Department Information:

1921. Chairperson: Linda Mezydlo Subich. Number of Faculty: total–full-time 19; women–full-time 6.

Programs and Degrees Offered:

Listed in the following order: Program area, degree type (T if terminal Master's), number awarded 7/03–6/04. Counseling PhD (Doctor of Philosophy) 7, Applied Cognitive Aging PhD (Doctor of Philosophy) 2, Applied Cognitive Aging (thesis) MA/MS (Master of Arts/Science) (T) 1, Industrial/Organizational (thesis) MA/MS (Master of Arts/Science) (T) 0, Industrial/Organizational (Personnel, non-thesis) MA/MS (Master of Arts/Science) (T) 6, Industrial/Organizational PhD (Doctor of Philosophy) 5, Industrial/Gerontological PhD (Doctor of Philosophy) 0.

APA Accreditation: Counseling PhD (Doctor of Philosophy).

Student Applications/Admissions:

Student Applications

Counseling PhD (Doctor of Philosophy)—Applications 2004–2005, 54. Total applicants accepted 2004–2005, 8. Number

enrolled (new admits only) 2004–2005 full-time, 5. Number enrolled (new admits only) 2004–2005 part-time, 0. Total enrolled 2004–2005 full-time, 20, part-time, 12. Openings 2005–2006, 5. The Median number of years required for completion of a degree are 9. The number of students enrolled full and part-time who were dismissed or voluntarily withdrew from this program area were 1. *Applied Cognitive Aging PhD (Doctor of Philosophy)*—Applications 2004–2005, 0. Total applicants accepted 2004–2005, 0. Number enrolled (new admits only) 2004–2005 full-time, 0. Number enrolled (new admits only) 2004–2005 part-time, 0. Total enrolled 2004–2005 full-time, 2, part-time, 6. The Median number of years required for completion of a degree are 5. The number of students enrolled full and part-time who were dismissed or voluntarily withdrew from this program area were 0. *Applied Cognitive Aging (thesis) MA/MS (Master of Arts/Science)*—Applications 2004–2005, 0. Total applicants accepted 2004–2005, 0. Number enrolled (new admits only) 2004–2005 full-time, 0. Number enrolled (new admits only) 2004–2005 part-time, 0. The Median number of years required for completion of a degree are 2. The number of students enrolled full and part-time who were dismissed or voluntarily withdrew from this program area were 0. *Industrial/Organizational (thesis) MA/MS (Master of Arts/Science)*—Applications 2004–2005, 1. Total applicants accepted 2004–2005, 0. Number enrolled (new admits only) 2004–2005 full-time, 0. Number enrolled (new admits only) 2004–2005 part-time, 0. The number of students enrolled full and part-time who were dismissed or voluntarily withdrew from this program area were 0. *Industrial/Organizational (Personnel, non-thesis) MA/MS (Master of Arts/Science)*—Applications 2004–2005, 17. Total applicants accepted 2004–2005, 7. Number enrolled (new admits only) 2004–2005 full-time, 3. Number enrolled (new admits only) 2004–2005 part-time, 0. Openings 2005–2006, 4. The Median number of years required for completion of a degree are 2. The number of students enrolled full and part-time who were dismissed or voluntarily withdrew from this program area were 0. *Industrial/Organizational PhD (Doctor of Philosophy)*—Applications 2004–2005, 41. Total applicants accepted 2004–2005, 8. Number enrolled (new admits only) 2004–2005 full-time, 7. Number enrolled (new admits only) 2004–2005 part-time, 0. Total enrolled 2004–2005 full-time, 26, part-time, 15. Openings 2005–2006, 6. The Median number of years required for completion of a degree are 6. The number of students enrolled full and part-time who were dismissed or voluntarily withdrew from this program area were 0. *Industrial/Gerontological PhD (Doctor of Philosophy)*—Applications 2004–2005, 3. Total applicants accepted 2004–2005, 0. Number enrolled (new admits only) 2004–2005 full-time, 0. Number enrolled (new admits only) 2004–2005 part-time, 0. Openings 2005–2006, 1. The number of students enrolled full and part-time who were dismissed or voluntarily withdrew from this program area were 0.

Admissions Requirements:

Scores: Entries appear in this order: required test or GPA, minimum score (if required), median score of students entering in 2003–2004. Master's Programs: GRE-V 500, 540; GRE-Q 500, 660; GRE-Subject(Psych) 500, 630; overall undergraduate GPA 2.75, 3.28; psychology GPA 3.00, 3.39. These minimum GRE scores and GPA values are guidelines rather than absolute thresholds. Exceptions may be made given other evidence of high potential. Doctoral Programs: GRE-V 550, 560;

GRE-Q 550, 640; GRE-Subject(Psych) 550, 590; overall undergraduate GPA 3.00, 3.90; psychology GPA 3.25, 3.75. These minimum GRE scores and GPA values are guidelines rather than absolute thresholds. Exceptions may be made given other evidence of high potential. The MA GPA is relevant only to programs admitting directly to the PhD

Other Criteria: (importance of criteria rated low, medium, or high): GRE/MAT scores high, research experience high, work experience low, extracurricular activity low, clinically related public service low, GPA high, letters of recommendation medium, interview medium, statement of goals and objectives high. Telephone interviews are used as a selection criterion only in the Counseling Psychology Program. Clinical service may be considered more heavily for admissions to the Counseling Psychology MA-PhD program. For additional information on admission requirements, go to: http://www3.uakron.edu/psychology/gradschool/minreq.html.

Student Characteristics: The following represents characteristics of students in 2004–2005 in all graduate psychology programs in the department: Female–full-time 38, part-time 24; Male–full-time 15, part-time 9; African American/Black–full-time 3, part-time 1; Hispanic/Latino(a)–full-time 0, part-time 0; Asian/Pacific Islander–full-time 7, part-time 4; American Indian/Alaska Native–full-time 0, part-time 0; Caucasian–full-time 43, part-time 28; Multi-ethnic–full-time 0, part-time 0; students subject to the Americans With Disabilities Act–full-time 0, part-time 0.

Financial Information/Assistance:

Tuition for Full-Time Study: *Master's:* State residents: per academic year $9,690, $327 per credit hour; Nonstate residents: per academic year $16,232, $545 per credit hour. *Doctoral:* State residents: per academic year $9,690, $327 per credit hour; Nonstate residents: per academic year $16,232, $545 per credit hour. Tuition is subject to change. See the following Web site for updates and changes in tuition costs: http://www.uakron.edu/busfin/studentfin/grad.php.

Financial Assistance:

First Year Students: Teaching assistantships available for first-year. Average amount paid per academic year: $12,300. Average number of hours worked per week: 20. Apply by January 15. Tuition remission given: full. Fellowships and scholarships available for first-year. Average amount paid per academic year: $0. Average number of hours worked per week: 0. Apply by January 15. Tuition remission given: full.

Advanced Students: Teaching assistantships available for advanced students. Average amount paid per academic year: $11,500. Average number of hours worked per week: 20. Apply by April 15. Tuition remission given: full. Research assistantships available for advanced students. Average amount paid per academic year: $11,500. Average number of hours worked per week: 20. Apply by April 15. Tuition remission given: full.

Contact Information: Of all students currently enrolled full-time, 90% benefitted from one or more of the listed financial assistance programs. Application and information available online at: http://www3.uakron.edu/psychology/gradschool/.

Internships/Practica: Practica are offered in the department's own Counseling Training Clinic and Center for Organizational Research. Students also have access to a wide variety of community-based practica in industrial and public settings, hospitals,

the University's Counseling Testing and Careers Center, and community mental health centers. For those doctoral students for whom a professional internship is required prior to graduation, 5 applied in 2003–2004. Of those who applied, 3 were placed in internships listed by the Association of Psychology Postdoctoral and Internship Programs (APPIC); 3 were placed in APA accredited internships.

Housing and Day Care: Limited housing is available on campus. Details may be found at: http://www.uakron.edu/studentaff/reslife/housingmain.php. Child care is available on campus for a fee at the Center for Child Development, a center run by the College of Education and College of Fine and Applied Arts; the Center's Web address is http://www3.uakron.edu/hefe/ccd/ccd.htm.

Employment of Department Graduates:

Master's Degree Graduates: Of those who graduated in the academic year 2003–2004, the following categories and numbers represent the post-graduate activities and employment of master's degree graduates: Enrolled in a psychology doctoral program (1), enrolled in another graduate/professional program (0), enrolled in a post-doctoral residency/fellowship (n/a), employed in independent practice (n/a), employed in an academic position at a university (0), employed in an academic position at a 2-year/4-year college (0), employed in other positions at a higher education institution (0), employed in a professional position in a school system (0), employed in business or industry (research/consulting) (1), employed in business or industry (management) (1), employed in a government agency (research) (0), employed in a government agency (professional services) (0), employed in a community mental health/counseling center (0), employed in a hospital/medical center (0), still seeking employment (0), not seeking employment (0), other employment position (0), do not know (4), total from the above (master's) (7).

Doctoral Degree Graduates: Of those who graduated in the academic year 2003–2004, the following categories and numbers represent the post-graduate activities and employment of doctoral degree graduates: Enrolled in a psychology doctoral program (n/a), enrolled in another graduate/professional program (0), enrolled in a post-doctoral residency/fellowship (2), employed in independent practice (1), employed in an academic position at a university (1), employed in an academic position at a 2-year/4-year college (1), employed in other positions at a higher education institution (2), employed in a professional position in a school system (0), employed in business or industry (research/consulting) (4), employed in business or industry (management) (0), employed in a government agency (research) (0), employed in a government agency (professional services) (0), employed in a community mental health/counseling center (0), employed in a hospital/medical center (2), still seeking employment (0), not seeking employment (0), other employment position (1), do not know (0), total from the above (doctoral) (14).

Additional Information:

Orientation, Objectives, and Emphasis of Department: The department's goals are to: (1) increase and diffuse psychological knowledge by advancing the discipline both as a science and as a means of promoting human welfare; (2) promote psychology in all its branches in the broadest and most liberal manner; (3) encourage research in psychology; and (4) advance high standards of education, achievement, professional ethics and conduct. The department subscribes to a scientist-practitioner model of training.

Graduate students take a common set of courses in foundational areas of psychology in addition to their specialty coursework, with study in the specialty area beginning early in graduate training. The emphasis is on preparation for teaching as well as for research, industrial, or mental health services career paths. Industrial/organizational, industrial gerontological, and counseling psychology are the specialty emphases at the MA and PhD level.

Special Facilities or Resources: To enhance research and instruction, we maintain a number of psychological research laboratories designed for individual and group studies, and equipped with computers, one-way viewing mirrors, video equipment, etc. Over 60 computers are available to faculty and students for word processing, statistical analysis, classroom instruction, e-mail correspondence, and web access. A programmer/technician provides full-time support for the hardware and software for the department and writes custom software for experimental control, stimulus display, and data collection. We maintain an in-house library of teaching resources for graduate teaching assistants, as well as a test library with over 100 tests and manuals for assessment of a broad range of constructs. We are affiliated with the university's Institute for Life-Span Development and Gerontology and the Archives of the History of American Psychology.

Information for Students With Physical Disabilities: See the following Web site for more information: http://www3.uakron.edu/access/.

Application Information:
Send to: Admissions Committee, Department of Psychology, 341 Arts and Sciences Building, 290 E. Buchtel Avenue, The University of Akron, Akron, OH 44325-4301. Application available online. URL of online application: www.uakron.edu/gradsch/admissions/applProc.php. Students are admitted in the Fall, application deadline January 15. We require the full application package be submitted at one time to the Department of Psychology per instructions on our web page at www3.uakron.edu/psychology/gradschool/checklist.html. *Fee:* $30. Fee listed above is for a domestic student; an international student's fee is $40.

Bowling Green State University
Department of Psychology
Bowling Green, OH 43403
Telephone: (419) 372-2301
Fax: (419) 372-6013
E-mail: *pwatson@bgnet.bgsu.edu*
Web: *http://www.bgsu.edu/departments/psych/*

Department Information:
1947. Chairperson: Dale S. Klopfer. Number of Faculty: total–full-time 30, part-time 6; women–full-time 11, part-time 2; minority–full-time 4, part-time 1.

Programs and Degrees Offered:
Listed in the following order: Program area, degree type (T if terminal Master's), number awarded 7/03–6/04. Clinical PhD (Doctor of Philosophy) 11, developmental PhD (Doctor of Philosophy) 1, Neural & Cognitive PhD (Doctor of Philosophy) 0, Industrial/Organizational PhD (Doctor of Philosophy) 3.

Student Applications/Admissions:
Student Applications
Clinical PhD (Doctor of Philosophy)—Applications 2004–2005, 177. Total applicants accepted 2004–2005, 15. Number enrolled (new admits only) 2004–2005 full-time, 12. Total enrolled 2004–2005 full-time, 65. Openings 2005–2006, 10. The Median number of years required for completion of a degree are 6. The number of students enrolled full and part-time who were dismissed or voluntarily withdrew from this program area were 1. Developmental PhD (Doctor of Philosophy)—Applications 2004–2005, 12. Total applicants accepted 2004–2005, 4. Number enrolled (new admits only) 2004–2005 full-time, 2. Total enrolled 2004–2005 full-time, 5. Openings 2005–2006, 3. The Median number of years required for completion of a degree are 5. The number of students enrolled full and part-time who were dismissed or voluntarily withdrew from this program area were 0. Neural & Cognitive PhD (Doctor of Philosophy)—Applications 2004–2005, 16. Total applicants accepted 2004–2005, 10. Number enrolled (new admits only) 2004–2005 full-time, 3. Total enrolled 2004–2005 full-time, 19. Openings 2005–2006, 6. The Median number of years required for completion of a degree are 6. The number of students enrolled full and part-time who were dismissed or voluntarily withdrew from this program area were 2. Industrial/Organizational PhD (Doctor of Philosophy)—Applications 2004–2005, 80. Total applicants accepted 2004–2005, 8. Number enrolled (new admits only) 2004–2005 full-time, 8. Total enrolled 2004–2005 full-time, 26. Openings 2005–2006, 6. The Median number of years required for completion of a degree are 5. The number of students enrolled full and part-time who were dismissed or voluntarily withdrew from this program area were 0.

Admissions Requirements:
Scores: Entries appear in this order: required test or GPA, minimum score (if required), median score of students entering in 2003–2004. Doctoral Programs: GRE-V no minimum stated, 568; GRE-Q no minimum stated, 674; GRE-Subject(Psych) no minimum stated, 665; overall undergraduate GPA no minimum stated, 3.77.
Other Criteria: (importance of criteria rated low, medium, or high): GRE/MAT scores high, research experience high, work experience medium, extracurricular activity medium, clinically related public service high, GPA high, letters of recommendation high, interview high, statement of goals and objectives high. Clinically related public service and interview are high for Clinical program only. For additional information on admission requirements, go to: http://www.bgsu.edu/departments/psych.

Student Characteristics: The following represents characteristics of students in 2004–2005 in all graduate psychology programs in the department: Female–full-time 76, part-time 0; Male–full-time 39, part-time 0; African American/Black–full-time 0, part-time 0; Hispanic/Latino(a)–full-time 5, part-time 0; Asian/Pacific Islander–full-time 5, part-time 0; American Indian/Alaska Native–full-time 1, part-time 0; Caucasian–full-time 104, part-time 0; Multi-ethnic–full-time 0, part-time 0; students subject to the Americans With Disabilities Act–full-time 0, part-time 0.

Financial Information/Assistance:

Tuition for Full-Time Study: *Doctoral:* State residents: per academic year $13,380; Nonstate residents: per academic year $24,342. Tuition is subject to change.

Financial Assistance:

First Year Students: Teaching assistantships available for first-year. Average amount paid per academic year: $10,115. Average number of hours worked per week: 20. Apply by January 1. Tuition remission given: full. Research assistantships available for first-year. Average amount paid per academic year: $10,115. Average number of hours worked per week: 20. Apply by January 1. Tuition remission given: full.

Advanced Students: Teaching assistantships available for advanced students. Average amount paid per academic year: $12,117. Average number of hours worked per week: 20. Apply by January 1. Tuition remission given: full. Research assistantships available for advanced students. Average amount paid per academic year: $12,117. Average number of hours worked per week: 20. Apply by January 1. Tuition remission given: full. Traineeships available for advanced students. Average amount paid per academic year: $12,117. Average number of hours worked per week: 20. Apply by January 1. Tuition remission given: full. Fellowships and scholarships available for advanced students. Average amount paid per academic year: $15,146. Average number of hours worked per week: 0. Apply by March. Tuition remission given: full.

Contact Information: Of all students currently enrolled full-time, 100% benefitted from one or more of the listed financial assistance programs. Application and information available online at: http://www.bgsu.edu/departments/psych/application.pdf.

Internships/Practica: In their beginning years, clinical students are placed on Basic Clinical Skills practicum teams through the Department's Psychological Services Center (PSC) that provide experience with a broad range of clients and clinical problems. Students focus on the application of such basic clinical skills as psychological assessment and interventions, the integration of science and practice, case conceptualization, clinical judgement and decision-making, and report writing. In their second year students begin receiving in-house training in psychotherapy through the PSC. As clinical students progress through the program they are placed on Advanced Clinical Skills teams that involve them in current projects providing "hands-on" experience with the integration of research and practice as it applies to individuals, health/behavioral medicine, the community, or special populations (e.g., children; problem drinkers). More advanced clinical students are provided practicum opportunities consistent with their interest through a number of outside placements, such as community mental health centers, a nearby medical college, the university counseling center and health service, an inpatient child and adolescent facility, hospital-based rehabilitation centers, treatment centers for children and families, and programs for individuals with severe mental disabilities and emotional disorders. Industrial/Organizational students are strongly encouraged to apply for a formal internship after completion of their Master's project. Although such experiences are encouraged and typically followed, internships are not required of I/O students for completion of the doctoral degree. Other experiences through coursework

activities and Institute for Psychological Research and Application (IPRA) projects can collectively serve the same function as an internship. For those doctoral students for whom a professional internship is required prior to graduation, 8 applied in 2003–2004. Of those who applied, 7 were placed in internships listed by the Association of Psychology Postdoctoral and Internship Programs (APPIC); 8 were placed in APA accredited internships.

Housing and Day Care: No on-campus housing is available. No on-campus day care facilities are available.

Employment of Department Graduates:

Master's Degree Graduates: Of those who graduated in the academic year 2003–2004, the following categories and numbers represent the post-graduate activities and employment of master's degree graduates: Enrolled in a post-doctoral residency/fellowship (n/a), employed in independent practice (n/a), total from the above (master's) (0).

Doctoral Degree Graduates: Of those who graduated in the academic year 2003–2004, the following categories and numbers represent the post-graduate activities and employment of doctoral degree graduates: Enrolled in a psychology doctoral program (n/a), total from the above (doctoral) (0).

Additional Information:

Orientation, Objectives, and Emphasis of Department: The primary goal of the PhD program is the development of scientists capable of advancing psychological knowledge. The program is characterized by both an emphasis on extensive academic training in general psychology and an early and continuing commitment to research. Although each graduate student will seek an area in which to develop his or her own expertise, students will be expected to be knowledgeable about many areas and will be encouraged to pursue interests that cross conventional specialty lines. The program is research oriented. Each student normally works in close association with a sponsor or chairperson whose special competence matches the student's interest, but students are free to pursue research interests with any faculty member and in any area(s) they choose. Both basic and applied research are well represented within the department. The clinical program has concentrations in clinical child, behavioral medicine, and community, as well as general clinical.

Special Facilities or Resources: The department is located in the psychology building, with excellent facilities for all forms of research. The building houses all faculty and graduate students. The department operates a community-oriented Psychological Services Center and the Institute for Psychological Research and Application. The department operates its own computer facility, with terminals to the mainframe computer available in the building, as well as a microcomputer facility.

Application Information:

Send to: Graduate Secretary. Application available online. URL of online application: http://www.bgsu.edu/departments/psych/application.pdf. Students are admitted in the Fall, application deadline January 1. Fee: $30. Application fee may be deferred for members of minority groups.

Case Western Reserve University

Department of Psychology
Arts and Sciences
Mather Memorial Building
11220 Bellflower Road, Room 103
Cleveland, OH 44106-7123
Telephone: (216) 368-2686
Fax: (216) 368-4891
E-mail: *psychdept@cwru.edu*
Web: *http://www.cwru.edu/artsci/pscl/*

Department Information:

1928. Chairperson: Douglas K. Detterman. Number of Faculty: total–full-time 13, part-time 1; women–full-time 4; minority–full-time 2.

Programs and Degrees Offered:

Listed in the following order: Program area, degree type (T if terminal Master's), number awarded 7/03–6/04. Clinical PhD (Doctor of Philosophy) 6, Experimental PhD (Doctor of Philosophy) 3, Mental Retardation PhD (Doctor of Philosophy) 0.

APA Accreditation: Clinical PhD (Doctor of Philosophy).

Student Applications/Admissions:

Student Applications

Clinical PhD (Doctor of Philosophy)—Applications 2004–2005, 140. Total applicants accepted 2004–2005, 7. Number enrolled (new admits only) 2004–2005 full-time, 5. Number enrolled (new admits only) 2004–2005 part-time, 0. Openings 2005–2006, 5. The Median number of years required for completion of a degree are 6. The number of students enrolled full and part-time who were dismissed or voluntarily withdrew from this program area were 1. *Experimental PhD (Doctor of Philosophy)*— Applications 2004–2005, 19. Total applicants accepted 2004–2005, 3. Number enrolled (new admits only) 2004–2005 full-time, 3. Number enrolled (new admits only) 2004–2005 part-time, 0. Openings 2005–2006, 2. The Median number of years required for completion of a degree are 4. The number of students enrolled full and part-time who were dismissed or voluntarily withdrew from this program area were 0. *Mental Retardation PhD (Doctor of Philosophy)*—Applications 2004–2005, 19. Total applicants accepted 2004–2005, 0. Number enrolled (new admits only) 2004–2005 full-time, 0. Number enrolled (new admits only) 2004–2005 part-time, 0. Openings 2005–2006, 2. The Median number of years required for completion of a degree are 4. The number of students enrolled full and part-time who were dismissed or voluntarily withdrew from this program area were 0.

Admissions Requirements:

Scores: Entries appear in this order: required test or GPA, minimum score (if required), median score of students entering in 2003–2004. Master's Programs: The department doesn't accept applications for a master's degree. Doctoral Programs: These scores are only preferred. Each application is evaluated on an individual basis and takes into consideration transcripts, statement of purpose and recommendation letters as well as specific test scores.

Other Criteria: (importance of criteria rated low, medium, or high): GRE/MAT scores high, research experience high, work experience low, extracurricular activity low, clinically related public service medium, GPA high, letters of recommendation medium, interview medium, statement of goals and objectives medium.

Student Characteristics: The following represents characteristics of students in 2004–2005 in all graduate psychology programs in the department: Female–full-time 32, part-time 0; Male–full-time 5, part-time 0; African American/Black–full-time 2, part-time 0; Hispanic/Latino(a)–full-time 2, part-time 0; Asian/Pacific Islander–full-time 3, part-time 0; American Indian/Alaska Native–full-time 0, part-time 0; Caucasian–full-time 30, part-time 0; Multi-ethnic–full-time 0, part-time 0; students subject to the Americans With Disabilities Act–full-time 0, part-time 0.

Financial Information/Assistance:

Tuition for Full-Time Study: *Master's:* State residents: per academic year $25,400, $1,058 per credit hour; Nonstate residents: per academic year $25,400, $1,058 per credit hour. *Doctoral:* State residents: per academic year $25,400, $1,058 per credit hour; Nonstate residents: per academic year $25,400, $1,058 per credit hour. Tuition is subject to change.

Financial Assistance:

First Year Students: Research assistantships available for first-year. Average amount paid per academic year: $19,000. Tuition remission given: full. Traineeships available for first-year. Average amount paid per academic year: $20,772. Tuition remission given: full.

Advanced Students: Teaching assistantships available for advanced students. Research assistantships available for advanced students. Average amount paid per academic year: $19,000. Tuition remission given: full. Traineeships available for advanced students. Average amount paid per academic year: $20,722. Tuition remission given: full. Fellowships and scholarships available for advanced students. Average amount paid per academic year: $19,000. Tuition remission given: full.

Contact Information: Of all students currently enrolled full-time, 85% benefitted from one or more of the listed financial assistance programs. Application and information available online at: www.case.edu/artsci/pscl.

Internships/Practica: The clinical psychology graduate program has a number of practica placements in the Cleveland area. Students spend time in different settings during their second, third, and fourth years. In addition, the department requires two in-house practica in different types of psychotherapy. For those doctoral students for whom a professional internship is required prior to graduation, 5 applied in 2003–2004. Of those who applied, 5 were placed in internships listed by the Association of Psychology Postdoctoral and Internship Programs (APPIC); 5 were placed in APA accredited internships.

Housing and Day Care: On-campus housing is available. No on-campus day care facilities are available.

Employment of Department Graduates:

Master's Degree Graduates: Of those who graduated in the academic year 2003–2004, the following categories and numbers represent the post-graduate activities and employment of master's degree graduates: Enrolled in a post-doctoral residency/fellowship (n/a), employed in independent practice (n/a), total from the above (master's) (0).

Doctoral Degree Graduates: Of those who graduated in the academic year 2003–2004, the following categories and numbers represent the post-graduate activities and employment of doctoral degree graduates: Enrolled in a psychology doctoral program (n/a), enrolled in another graduate/professional program (0), enrolled in a post-doctoral residency/fellowship (5), employed in independent practice (1), employed in an academic position at a university (0), employed in an academic position at a 2-year/4-year college (0), employed in other positions at a higher education institution (0), employed in a professional position in a school system (0), employed in business or industry (research/consulting) (0), employed in business or industry (management) (0), employed in a government agency (research) (0), employed in a government agency (professional services) (0), employed in a community mental health/counseling center (0), employed in a hospital/medical center (0), still seeking employment (0), other employment position (0), do not know (0), total from the above (doctoral) (6).

Additional Information:

Orientation, Objectives, and Emphasis of Department: The graduate program seeks to give students a thorough grounding in basic areas of fact and theory in psychology, to train them in research methods by which knowledge in the behavioral sciences is advanced, and to prepare them for careers as teachers and researchers. During the first year, students begin a research clerkship under the tutelage of a faculty member. A variety of facilities and subject populations are available for the study of developmental processes, and a number of well-equipped laboratories are used for research in perception, memory, cognition, learning, physiological psychology, and individual differences. The department offers programs in experimental and clinical psychology. Within each of these major areas of concentration, a number of subspecializations are available. For clinical psychology, these include adult, child, and pediatric psychology. For experimental psychology, the areas of specialization are determined by the faculty member with whom the student works. These include, but are not limited to, cognition, human intelligence, aging, social, and physiological psychology.

Special Facilities or Resources: A number of excellent facilities for clinical training and research are available on campus and in the surrounding community, such as the Student Counseling Center of Case Western Reserve, University Hospitals, the Cleveland Veterans Administration Hospital, and MetroHealth Medical Center. The department also maintains an extensive perceptual development laboratory to study the developmental aspects of learning, cognition, and language acquisition, and several experimental laboratories for the study of learning, perception, cognition, and physiological psychology, and social psychology.

Application Information:

Send to: Department of Psychology, Case Western Reserve University, 10900 Euclid Avenue, Cleveland, OH 44106-7123. Application available online. Students are admitted in the Fall. Deadline is December 9 for Clinical and February 15 for Experimental and Mental Retardation. *Fee:* $50.

Cincinnati, University of (2004 data)

Department of Psychology
Arts and Sciences
429 Dyer Hall
Cincinnati, OH 45221-0376
Telephone: (513) 556-5539
Fax: (513) 556-1904
E-mail: *psych@uc.edu*
Web: *http://www.ucaswww.mcm.uc.edu/psychology*

Department Information:

1901. Chairperson: Kevin J. Corcoran. Number of Faculty: total–full-time 30, part-time 5; women–full-time 8, part-time 1; minority–full-time 6, part-time 1.

Programs and Degrees Offered:

Listed in the following order: Program area, degree type (T if terminal Master's), number awarded 7/03–6/04. Clinical-Child PhD (Doctor of Philosophy), Clinical-General PhD (Doctor of Philosophy), Clinical-Health PhD (Doctor of Philosophy), Clinical-Neuropsychology PhD (Doctor of Philosophy), Experimental Neuropsychology PhD (Doctor of Philosophy), Health PhD (Doctor of Philosophy), Human Factors PhD (Doctor of Philosophy).

APA Accreditation: Clinical PhD (Doctor of Philosophy).

Student Applications/Admissions:

Student Applications

Clinical-Child PhD (Doctor of Philosophy)—Applications 2004–2005, 25. Total applicants accepted 2004–2005, 3. Openings 2005–2006, 2. The number of students enrolled full and part-time who were dismissed or voluntarily withdrew from this program area were 0. *Clinical-General PhD (Doctor of Philosophy)*—Applications 2004–2005, 55. Total applicants accepted 2004–2005, 2. Openings 2005–2006, 3. The number of students enrolled full and part-time, who were dismissed or voluntarily withdrew from this program area were 1. *Clinical-Health PhD (Doctor of Philosophy)*—Applications 2004–2005, 80. Total applicants accepted 2004–2005, 2. Openings 2005–2006, 4. *Clinical-Neuropsychology PhD (Doctor of Philosophy)*—Applications 2004–2005, 70. Total applicants accepted 2004–2005, 5. Openings 2005–2006, 4. The number of students enrolled full and part-time who were dismissed or voluntarily withdrew from this program area were 0. *Experimental Neuropsychology PhD (Doctor of Philosophy)*—Applications 2004–2005, 2. Total applicants accepted 2004–2005, 0. Openings 2005–2006, 1. The number of students enrolled full and part-time who were dismissed or voluntarily withdrew from this program area were 0. *Health PhD (Doctor of Philosophy)*—Applications 2004–2005, 3. Total applicants accepted 2004–2005, 0. Openings 2005–2006, 1. The number of students enrolled full and part-time who were dismissed or voluntarily withdrew from this program area were 0. *Human Factors PhD (Doctor of Philosophy)*—Applications 2004–2005, 20. Total applicants accepted 2004–2005, 4. Openings 2005–2006, 7. The number of students enrolled full and part-time, who were dismissed or voluntarily withdrew from this program area were 0.

Admissions Requirements:

Scores: Entries appear in this order: required test or GPA, minimum score (if required), median score of students entering in 2003–2004. Doctoral Programs: GRE-V no minimum stated, 580; GRE-Q no minimum stated, 641; GRE-Analytical no minimum stated; overall undergraduate GPA no minimum stated, 3.5.

Other Criteria: (importance of criteria rated low, medium, or high): GRE/MAT scores medium, research experience high, work experience high, extracurricular activity medium, clinically related public service high, GPA high, letters of recommendation high, interview high, statement of goals and objectives high, compatibility with faculty interests high. Clinically related public service is only relevent to students applying to clinical. For additional information on admission requirements, go to: http://asweb.artsci.uc.edu/psychology/index.html.

Student Characteristics: The following represents characteristics of students in 2004–2005 in all graduate psychology programs in the department: Female–full-time 67, part-time 0; Male–full-time 19, part-time 0; African American/Black–full-time 11, part-time 0; Hispanic/Latino(a)–full-time 1, part-time 0; Asian/Pacific Islander–full-time 3, part-time 0; American Indian/Alaska Native–full-time 0, part-time 0; Caucasian–full-time 71, part-time 0; Multi-ethnic–full-time 0, part-time 0; students subject to the Americans With Disabilities Act–full-time 0, part-time 0.

Financial Information/Assistance:

Financial Assistance:

First Year Students: Teaching assistantships available for first-year. Tuition remission given: full. Research assistantships available for first-year. Tuition remission given: full. Fellowships and scholarships available for first-year. Tuition remission given: full.

Advanced Students: Teaching assistantships available for advanced students. Tuition remission given: full. Research assistantships available for advanced students. Tuition remission given: full. Fellowships and scholarships available for advanced students. Tuition remission given: full.

Contact Information: Of all students currently enrolled full-time, 100% benefitted from one or more of the listed financial assistance programs.

Internships/Practica: All clinical students in years three and four typically perform a paid, 20 hour/week clinical (or clinical research) training placement at an external site in the Greater Cincinnati area. Often these placements are at the University of Cincinnati Medical Center, the Childrens Hospital Medical Center, or agencies affiliated with one of these centers. If students need a fifth year of support prior to going off on an APA-accredited clinical internship, we can often arrange a clinical training opportunity, although priority for placements goes to students in years 1 through 4. While most of our non-clinical students do their paid training assignments within the department, there are also paid external training slots available for some of our students in private industry or with the federal government. For those doctoral students for whom a professional internship is required prior to graduation, 18 applied in 2003–2004. Of those who applied, 16 were placed in internships listed by the Association of Psychology Postdoctoral and Internship Programs (APPIC); 16 were placed in APA accredited internships.

Housing and Day Care: No on-campus housing is available. On-campus day care facilities are available.

Employment of Department Graduates:

Master's Degree Graduates: Of those who graduated in the academic year 2003–2004, the following categories and numbers represent the post-graduate activities and employment of master's degree graduates: Enrolled in a psychology doctoral program (10), enrolled in a post-doctoral residency/fellowship (n/a), employed in independent practice (n/a), total from the above (master's) (10).

Doctoral Degree Graduates: Of those who graduated in the academic year 2003–2004, the following categories and numbers represent the post-graduate activities and employment of doctoral degree graduates: Enrolled in a psychology doctoral program (n/a), enrolled in a post-doctoral residency/fellowship (2), employed in independent practice (1), employed in an academic position at a university (2), employed in a community mental health/counseling center (1), employed in a hospital/medical center (1), do not know (1), total from the above (doctoral) (8).

Additional Information:

Orientation, Objectives, and Emphasis of Department: The University of Cincinnati offers the PhD in psychology, including an APA-accredited training program in clinical psychology. Clinical students must specify a specialty training area, which might include health, neuropsychology or general training. For students who do not want clinical training, we offer training primarily in human factors (we are part of the Southwest Ohio Human Factors/Ergonomics Consortium), ecological psychology, and experimental neuropsychology. The doctoral program is limited to full-time students who show outstanding promise. Students are admitted to the doctoral program to work with a faculty research mentor. Faculty mentors are responsible for ensuring that students are actively engaged in doing research from the very start of their graduate school career, and that this work leads successfully to a Masters thesis and a dissertation within the prescribed period.

Special Facilities or Resources: The department's clinical program has close ties to the medical centers and the UC School of Medicine (a site for fMRI research for our students) and a whole range of community agencies. The human factors faculty at UC are involved in the Southwest Ohio Human Factors/Ergonomics Consortium. Through this consortium, students have access to courses offered at nearby universities and to training sites at the Wright Patterson Air Force Base.

Application Information:

Send to: Graduate Secretary, Department of Psychology, University of Cincinnati, P.O. Box 210376, Cincinnati, OH 45221-0376. Application available online. Students are admitted in the Fall, application deadline January 5. *Fee:* $45.

Cincinnati, University of
Human Services/School Psychology
Education, Criminal Justice, and Human Services
P.O. Box 210002
Cincinnati, OH 45221-0002
Telephone: (513) 556-3334
Fax: (513) 556-3898
E-mail: *sarah.j.allen@uc.edu*
Web: *www.uc.edu/schoolpsychology/*

Department Information:
1992. Program Director: Sarah Allen. Number of Faculty: total–full-time 5, part-time 3; women–full-time 3, part-time 1.

Programs and Degrees Offered:
Listed in the following order: Program area, degree type (T if terminal Master's), number awarded 7/03–6/04. School Psychology - PhD (Doctor of Philosophy) 4, School Psychology - EdS (Education Specialist) 10.

Student Applications/Admissions:
Student Applications

School Psychology - PhD (Doctor of Philosophy)—Applications 2004–2005, 14. Total applicants accepted 2004–2005, 6. Number enrolled (new admits only) 2004–2005 full-time, 5. Number enrolled (new admits only) 2004–2005 part-time, 1. Total enrolled 2004–2005 full-time, 13, part-time, 10. Openings 2005–2006, 6. The Median number of years required for completion of a degree are 6.5. The number of students enrolled full and part-time who were dismissed or voluntarily withdrew from this program area were 2. *School Psychology - EdS (Education Specialist)*—Applications 2004–2005, 64. Total applicants accepted 2004–2005, 9. Number enrolled (new admits only) 2004–2005 full-time, 9. Number enrolled (new admits only) 2004–2005 part-time, 0. Openings 2005–2006, 10. The Median number of years required for completion of a degree are 3. The number of students enrolled full and part-time who were dismissed or voluntarily withdrew from this program area were 1.

Admissions Requirements:

Scores: Entries appear in this order: required test or GPA, minimum score (if required), median score of students entering in 2003–2004. Master's Programs: GRE-V no minimum stated, 500; GRE-Q no minimum stated, 580; GRE-V+Q no minimum stated, 1131; GRE-Analytical no minimum stated, 4.0; overall undergraduate GPA 3.0, 3.66; last 2 years GPA no minimum stated, 3.75; psychology GPA no minimum stated, 3.79. Doctoral Programs: GRE-V no minimum stated, 580; GRE-Q no minimum stated, 650; GRE-V+Q no minimum stated, 1230; GRE-Analytical no minimum stated, 635; GRE-Subject(Psych) no minimum stated, 635; overall undergraduate GPA 3.25, 3.7; last 2 years GPA no minimum stated, 3.77; psychology GPA no minimum stated, 3.81.
Other Criteria: (importance of criteria rated low, medium, or high): GRE/MAT scores high, research experience medium, work experience medium, extracurricular activity medium, clinically related public service high, GPA high, letters of recommendation medium, interview high, statement of goals and objectives high. Specific, focused goals reflected for doc-

toral study. For additional information on admission requirements, go to: www.uc.edu/schoolpsychology/.

Student Characteristics: The following represents characteristics of students in 2004–2005 in all graduate psychology programs in the department: Female–full-time 37, part-time 10; Male–full-time 2, part-time 0; African American/Black–full-time 0, part-time 0; Hispanic/Latino(a)–full-time 0, part-time 1; Asian/Pacific Islander–full-time 0, part-time 0; American Indian/Alaska Native–full-time 1, part-time 0; Caucasian–full-time 38, part-time 8; Multi-ethnic–full-time 0, part-time 1; students subject to the Americans With Disabilities Act–full-time 0, part-time 0.

Financial Information/Assistance:
Tuition for Full-Time Study: *Master's:* State residents: per academic year $9,975, $333 per credit hour; Nonstate residents: per academic year $18,405, $614 per credit hour. *Doctoral:* State residents: per academic year $9,975, $333 per credit hour; Nonstate residents: per academic year $18,405, $614 per credit hour. Tuition is subject to change. See the following Web site for updates and changes in tuition costs: www.uc.edu.

Financial Assistance:
First Year Students: Research assistantships available for first-year. Average amount paid per academic year: $10,500. Average number of hours worked per week: 20. Tuition remission given: full. Fellowships and scholarships available for first-year. Average amount paid per academic year: $15,000. Average number of hours worked per week: 20. Tuition remission given: full.
Advanced Students: Teaching assistantships available for advanced students. Average amount paid per academic year: $10,500. Average number of hours worked per week: 20. Tuition remission given: full. Research assistantships available for advanced students. Average amount paid per academic year: $10,500. Average number of hours worked per week: 20. Tuition remission given: full. Traineeships available for advanced students. Average amount paid per academic year: $25,000. Average number of hours worked per week: 40. Tuition remission given: partial. Fellowships and scholarships available for advanced students. Average amount paid per academic year: $15,000. Average number of hours worked per week: 20. Tuition remission given: full and partial.
Contact Information: Of all students currently enrolled full-time, 100% benefitted from one or more of the listed financial assistance programs. Application and information available online at: www.grad.uc.edu.

Internships/Practica: *Master's:* State residents: per academic year $9,975, $333 per credit hour; Nonstate residents: per academic year $18,405, $614 per credit hour. Internship is required prior to graduation, 2 applied in 2003–2004.

Housing and Day Care: On-campus housing is available. See the following Web site for more information: www.uc.edu/housing/. On-campus day care facilities are available. See the following Web site for more information: www.uc.edu.

Employment of Department Graduates:
Master's Degree Graduates: Of those who graduated in the academic year 2003–2004, the following categories and numbers represent the post-graduate activities and employment of master's degree graduates: Enrolled in a psychology doctoral program (1),

enrolled in a post-doctoral residency/fellowship (n/a), employed in independent practice (n/a), employed in a professional position in a school system (9), total from the above (master's) (10).

Doctoral Degree Graduates: Of those who graduated in the academic year 2003–2004, the following categories and numbers represent the post-graduate activities and employment of doctoral degree graduates: Enrolled in a psychology doctoral program (n/a), employed in a professional position in a school system (4), total from the above (doctoral) (4).

Additional Information:

Orientation, Objectives, and Emphasis of Department: The School Psychology Program at the University of Cincinnati is dedicated to preparing highly competent professional school psychologists, at the specialist (EdS) and doctoral (PhD) levels, according to the scientist-practitioner model. The program builds on foundations in psychology and education and fosters a special sensitivity to cultural diversity of all people and respect for the uniqueness and human dignity of each person. The program emphasizes the delivery of school psychological services using a collaborative consultation model from an ecological/behavioral orientation. Students learn to view problems from an ecological/systems perspective focusing on child, family, school and community and to provide comprehensive intervention-based services utilizing data-based decision making to design, implement, and evaluate strategies for preventing and resolving learning and adjustment problem situations across a tiered service delivery model. A child advocacy perspective, built on a scientist-practitioner foundation, provides a framework for guiding decisions and practices to support positive outcomes for all children. Both theoretical and empirical bases of professional practice are emphasized, and a diverse range of practical experiences are provided throughout all preparation (preschool to high school, in urban, suburban, and rural settings). The program is noted for its intervention emphasis, focusing on data-based decision making across all levels of service delivery (prevention/school-wide intervention, target and supplemental intervention, and intensive, individualized intervention). In addition to these program themes, training at the doctoral level emphasizes advanced research and evaluation training, leadership supervision and systems-level change facilitation. Doctoral students participate as research team members in schools in Years 1 through 3.

Special Facilities or Resources: The program has access to excellent field-based training and research partnerships through collaborative relationships with several local school districts and Head Start programs. The program is linked to teacher preparation through professional development schools and collaboration with teacher interns in their training. Research facilities include statistical consultation for students, a college evaluation services center, and support for student research through college-sponsored mentoring grants.

Information for Students With Physical Disabilities: uc.edu/sas/disability.

Application Information:
Send to: Admission Coordinator, School Psychology Program, University of Cincinnati, P.O. Box 210002, Cincinnati, OH 45221-0002. Application available online. Students are admitted in the Fall, application deadline January 15. *Fee:* $40.

Cleveland State University
Department of Psychology
College of Science
2121 Euclid Avenue
Cleveland, OH 44115
Telephone: (216) 687-2544
Fax: (216) 687-9294
E-mail: *m.ashcraft@popmail.csuohio.edu*
Web: *http://www.csuohio.edu/psy/*

Department Information:
1964. Chairperson: Mark H. Ashcraft. Number of Faculty: total–full-time 20, part-time 12; women–full-time 8, part-time 7; minority–full-time 4, part-time 1; faculty subject to the Americans With Disabilities Act 3.

Programs and Degrees Offered:
Listed in the following order: Program area, degree type (T if terminal Master's), number awarded 7/03–6/04. Clinical Psychology MA/MS (Master of Arts/Science) (T) 5, Consumer-Industrial MA/MS (Master of Arts/Science) (T) 7, Diversity Management MA/MS (Master of Arts/Science) (T) 13, Experimental Research MA/MS (Master of Arts/Science) (T) 2, School Psychology Other 7.

Student Applications/Admissions:
Student Applications

Clinical Psychology MA/MS (Master of Arts/Science) Applications 2004–2005, 81. Total applicants accepted 2004–2005, 10. Number enrolled (new admits only) 2004–2005 full-time, 10. Openings 2005–2006, 12. The Median number of years required for completion of a degree are 2. The number of students enrolled full and part-time who were dismissed or voluntarily withdrew from this program area were 0. *Consumer-Industrial MA/MS (Master of Arts/Science)*—Applications 2004–2005, 30. Total applicants accepted 2004–2005, 6. Number enrolled (new admits only) 2004–2005 full-time, 6. Total enrolled 2004–2005 full-time, 11, part-time, 1. Openings 2005–2006, 12. The Median number of years required for completion of a degree are 2. The number of students enrolled full and part-time who were dismissed or voluntarily withdrew from this program area were 0. *Diversity Management MA/MS (Master of Arts/Science)*—Applications 2004–2005, 20. Total applicants accepted 2004–2005, 14. Number enrolled (new admits only) 2004–2005 part-time, 14. Openings 2005–2006, 20. The Median number of years required for completion of a degree are 2. The number of students enrolled full and part-time who were dismissed or voluntarily withdrew from this program area were 0. *Experimental Research MA/MS (Master of Arts/Science)*—Applications 2004–2005, 11. Total applicants accepted 2004–2005, 4. Number enrolled (new admits only) 2004–2005 full-time, 4. Total enrolled 2004–2005 full-time, 8, part-time, 1. Openings 2005–2006, 10. The Median number of years required for completion of a degree are 3. The number of students enrolled full and part-time who were dismissed or voluntarily withdrew from this program area were 1. *School Psychology Other*—Applications 2004–2005, 32. Total applicants accepted 2004–2005, 9. Number enrolled (new admits only) 2004–2005 full-time, 9. Openings 2005–2006, 12. The Median number of years required for completion of a degree

are 3. The number of students enrolled full and part-time who were dismissed or voluntarily withdrew from this program area were 0.

Admissions Requirements:

Scores: Entries appear in this order: required test or GPA, minimum score (if required), median score of students entering in 2003–2004. Master's Programs: GRE-V no minimum stated, 493; GRE-Q no minimum stated, 608; GRE-Analytical no minimum stated, 596; GRE-Subject(Psych) no minimum stated; overall undergraduate GPA no minimum stated, 3.5. Requirements vary per program. All programs look for GREs at about the 500 level; the Diversity Management program does not require GRE.

Other Criteria: (importance of criteria rated low, medium, or high): GRE/MAT scores medium, research experience medium, work experience low, clinically related public service low, GPA medium, letters of recommendation high, interview high, statement of goals and objectives high. Only the clinical/counseling and diversity programs require an interview.

Student Characteristics: The following represents characteristics of students in 2004–2005 in all graduate psychology programs in the department: Female–full-time 46, part-time 26; Male–full-time 21, part-time 10; African American/Black–full-time 8, part-time 14; Hispanic/Latino(a)–full-time 2, part-time 1; Asian/Pacific Islander–full-time 3, part-time 1; American Indian/Alaska Native–full-time 0, part-time 0; Caucasian–full-time 54, part-time 20; Multi-ethnic–part-time 0; students subject to the Americans With Disabilities Act–full-time 0, part-time 0.

Financial Information/Assistance:

Tuition for Full-Time Study: *Master's:* State residents: per academic year $8,592, $358 per credit hour; Nonstate residents: per academic year $16,482, $697 per credit hour. Tuition is subject to change.

Financial Assistance:

First Year Students: Teaching assistantships available for first-year. Average number of hours worked per week: 10. Apply by February 15. Tuition remission given: full.

Advanced Students: Teaching assistantships available for advanced students. Average number of hours worked per week: 10. Apply by March 15. Tuition remission given: full.

Contact Information: Of all students currently enrolled full-time, 34% benefitted from one or more of the listed financial assistance programs.

Internships/Practica: Master's students and 3rd year School Psychology students complete a 20 hour/40 hour per week internship, respectively, as part of the degree requirements. Practica during the two year curriculum are integrated into coursework.

Housing and Day Care: On-campus housing is available. See the following Web site for more information: http://www.csuohio.edu. From University Web site, go to Residence Information (Viking Hall). No on-campus day care facilities are available.

Employment of Department Graduates:

Master's Degree Graduates: Of those who graduated in the academic year 2003–2004, the following categories and numbers represent the post-graduate activities and employment of master's degree graduates: Enrolled in a psychology doctoral program (2), enrolled in another graduate/professional program (0), enrolled in a post-doctoral residency/fellowship (n/a), employed in independent practice (n/a), employed in a professional position in a school system (7), employed in business or industry (research/consulting) (5), employed in business or industry (management) (8), employed in a community mental health/counseling center (3), do not know (9), total from the above (master's) (34).

Doctoral Degree Graduates: Of those who graduated in the academic year 2003–2004, the following categories and numbers represent the post-graduate activities and employment of doctoral degree graduates: Enrolled in a psychology doctoral program (n/a), total from the above (doctoral) (0).

Additional Information:

Orientation, Objectives, and Emphasis of Department: The clinical/counseling program is a CAMPP approved program. Departmental faculty provide significant breadth across the entire discipline as well as considerable depth in professional and applied areas. Substantive areas include social, developmental, cognitive-affective, clinical, industrial, and experimental psychology. The clinical-counseling program emphasizes theory, principles and application, and preparing general practitioners to provide psychological service in clinical, community, and educational settings. Orientations include psychodynamic, cognitive, and behavioral viewpoints in assessment and individual, group, family, and community intervention. A post-MA year fulfills requirements for certification as a school psychologist in Ohio. The primary goals of the experimental research program are to train students to conduct scientific research in a chosen area of psychology, and to prepare students for further graduate work in psychology or for employment in research settings and institutions. The three main components of the program are coursework in several core areas of psychology, an apprenticeship or tutorial relationship between the student and faculty adviser, and continual involvement in research activity that culminates in a master's thesis project. The program in consumer-industrial research prepares students to apply psychological concepts and research techniques in business and in institutional settings. It combines advanced quantitative research with hands-on experience involving problems and issues encountered in industrial and service organizations.

Special Facilities or Resources: Many students in the clinical-community program will apply to doctoral programs after obtaining their MA degree. To better prepare these students for doctoral study, we offer a formal thesis option, in which a student is permitted to drop two required courses and complete a research thesis instead.

Application Information:

Send to: Graduate Secretary, Dept. of Psychology, Cleveland State University, 2121 Euclid Avenue, Cleveland, OH 44115-2440. Application available online. URL of online application: http://www.csuohio.edu/admissions/gradForm.html. Students are admitted in the Fall, application deadline February 15, March 1 for Consumer-Industrial and Experimental Research. Applications received after February 15 may be considered. Rolling deadline for Diversity Management. *Fee:* $30.

Dayton, University of
Department of Psychology
300 College Park Avenue
Dayton, OH 45469-1430
Telephone: (937) 229-2713
Fax: (937) 229-3900
E-mail: *biers@udayton.edu*
Web: *http://www.udayton.edu/~psych*

Department Information:
1937. Chairperson: David W. Biers. Number of Faculty: total–full-time 17, part-time 15; women–full-time 5, part-time 8; minority–full-time 1.

Programs and Degrees Offered:
Listed in the following order: Program area, degree type (T if terminal Master's), number awarded 7/03–6/04. Clinical MA/MS (Master of Arts/Science) (T) 4, General MA/MS (Master of Arts/Science) (T) 1, Experimental Human Factors MA/MS (Master of Arts/Science) (T) 2.

Student Applications/Admissions:
Student Applications
Clinical MA/MS (Master of Arts/Science)—Applications 2004–2005, 77. Total applicants accepted 2004–2005, 33. Number enrolled (new admits only) 2004–2005 full-time, 12. Number enrolled (new admits only) 2004–2005 part-time, 0. Total enrolled 2004–2005 full-time, 20, part-time, 2. Openings 2005–2006, 12. *General MA/MS (Master of Arts/Science)*—Applications 2004–2005, 15. Total applicants accepted 2004–2005, 5. Number enrolled (new admits only) 2004–2005 full-time, 0. Number enrolled (new admits only) 2004–2005 part-time, 0. Openings 2005–2006, 5. *Experimental Human Factors MA/MS (Master of Arts/Science)*—Applications 2004–2005, 11. Total applicants accepted 2004–2005, 9. Number enrolled (new admits only) 2004–2005 full-time, 5. Number enrolled (new admits only) 2004–2005 part-time, 0. Openings 2005–2006, 6.

Admissions Requirements:
Scores: Entries appear in this order: required test or GPA, minimum score (if required), median score of students entering in 2003–2004. Master's Programs: GRE-V no minimum stated; GRE-Q no minimum stated; overall undergraduate GPA 3.0. *Other Criteria:* (importance of criteria rated low, medium, or high): GRE/MAT scores medium, research experience high, work experience medium, extracurricular activity low, clinically related public service medium, GPA high, letters of recommendation high, interview low, statement of goals and objectives high.

Student Characteristics: The following represents characteristics of students in 2004–2005 in all graduate psychology programs in the department: Female–full-time 22, part-time 2; Male–full-time 12, part-time 0; African American/Black–full-time 1, part-time 1; Hispanic/Latino(a)–full-time 0, part-time 0; Asian/Pacific Islander–full-time 3, part-time 0; American Indian/Alaska Native–full-time 0, part-time 0; Caucasian–full-time 30, part-time 1; Multi-ethnic–full-time 0, part-time 0; students subject to the Americans With Disabilities Act–full-time 0, part-time 0.

Financial Information/Assistance:
Tuition for Full-Time Study: *Master's:* State residents: $567 per credit hour; Nonstate residents: $567 per credit hour.

Financial Assistance:
First Year Students: Teaching assistantships available for first-year. Average amount paid per academic year: $9,150. Average number of hours worked per week: 20. Apply by March 1. Tuition remission given: full. Research assistantships available for first-year. Average amount paid per academic year: $9,150. Average number of hours worked per week: 20. Apply by March 1. Tuition remission given: full. Traineeships available for first-year. Average amount paid per academic year: $6,000. Average number of hours worked per week: 17. Apply by March 1. Tuition remission given: partial.

Advanced Students: Teaching assistantships available for advanced students. Average amount paid per academic year: $9,150. Average number of hours worked per week: 20. Apply by March 1. Tuition remission given: full. Research assistantships available for advanced students. Average amount paid per academic year: $9,150. Average number of hours worked per week: 20. Apply by March 1. Tuition remission given: full.

Contact Information: Of all students currently enrolled full-time, 89% benefitted from one or more of the listed financial assistance programs.

Internships/Practica: A limited number of paid traineeship placements at local mental health agencies are available for both first and second year clinical students. These traineeships satisfy the programs's practica requirements and include partial tuition remission. The human factors practicum is required of all program students and enables the student to gain practical experience working for governmental agencies or industrial firms during the summer between their first and second years.

Housing and Day Care: No on-campus housing is available. On-campus day care facilities are available.

Employment of Department Graduates:
Master's Degree Graduates: Of those who graduated in the academic year 2003–2004, the following categories and numbers represent the post-graduate activities and employment of master's degree graduates: Enrolled in a psychology doctoral program (3), enrolled in a post-doctoral residency/fellowship (n/a), employed in independent practice (n/a), employed in business or industry (research/consulting) (1), employed in a community mental health/counseling center (2), other employment position (1), total from the above (master's) (7).
Doctoral Degree Graduates: Of those who graduated in the academic year 2003–2004, the following categories and numbers represent the post-graduate activities and employment of doctoral degree graduates: Enrolled in a psychology doctoral program (n/a), total from the above (doctoral) (0).

Additional Information:
Orientation, Objectives, and Emphasis of Department: The Department of Psychology offers graduate programs leading to the MA degree in clinical, experimental-human factors, and general psychology. Emphasis is placed on integrating theory and literature with appropriate applied experience and on competence in the development of relevant research. This is the product of individual supervision and a low student-to-faculty ratio. The aim

of the department is to prepare the student for doctoral training or employment at the MA level in an applied/community setting, in research, or in teaching. A recent survey has shown that over 90% of our MA graduates who applied for doctoral programs in the last 23 years were accepted. Also, 93% of Human Factors students seeking employment at the MA level have found jobs in human factors or a closely related field.

Special Facilities or Resources: Laboratory and computer facilities are available to support student and faculty research. These include microlaboratory facilities for research in cognitive science, human factors, social psychology, and clinical psychology as well as a state-of-the-art Information Science Research Laboratory for multidisciplinary research in human-computer interaction. In additon, research opportunities are available through the university's Research Institute, the Center for Family and Community Research, and local community agencies.

Application Information:
Apply online at gradadmission.udayton.edu. Application available online. URL of online application: http://gradadmission.udayton.edu. Students are admitted in the Fall, application deadline March 1. *Fee:* $30. Fee waived if apply online.

Kent State University
Department of Psychology
Arts & Sciences
Kent, OH 44242
Telephone: (330) 672-2166
Fax: (330) 672-3786
E-mail: *ksupsych@kent.edu*
Web: *http://www.kent.edu/psychology/*

Department Information:
1936. Chairperson: Janis H. Crowther. Number of Faculty: total–full-time 28, part-time 6; women–full-time 12, part-time 3; minority–full-time 5, part-time 1; faculty subject to the Americans With Disabilities Act 2.

Programs and Degrees Offered:
Listed in the following order: Program area, degree type (T if terminal Master's), number awarded 7/03–6/04. Clinical PhD (Doctor of Philosophy) 6, Experimental PhD (Doctor of Philosophy) 10.

APA Accreditation: Clinical PhD (Doctor of Philosophy).

Student Applications/Admissions:
Student Applications

Clinical PhD (Doctor of Philosophy)—Applications 2004–2005, 240. Total applicants accepted 2004–2005, 11. Number enrolled (new admits only) 2004–2005 full-time, 11. Openings 2005–2006, 11. The Median number of years required for completion of a degree are 6. The number of students enrolled full and part-time who were dismissed or voluntarily withdrew from this program area were 1. *Experimental PhD (Doctor of Philosophy)*—Applications 2004–2005, 64. Total applicants accepted 2004–2005, 11. Number enrolled (new admits only)

2004–2005 full-time, 11. Openings 2005–2006, 10. The Median number of years required for completion of a degree are 5. The number of students enrolled full and part-time who were dismissed or voluntarily withdrew from this program area were 0.

Admissions Requirements:
Scores: Entries appear in this order: required test or GPA, minimum score (if required), median score of students entering in 2003–2004. Doctoral Programs: GRE-V no minimum stated, 596; GRE-Q no minimum stated, 655; GRE-Analytical no minimum stated; overall undergraduate GPA 3.00, 3.69. The above median scores are for applicants who were admitted to our clinical program (and accepted) in spring 2004. The median scores for students who accepted admission into our experimental program that year are: GRE-V: 559; GRE-Q: 634; Overall undergrad GPA: 3.53.

Other Criteria: (importance of criteria rated low, medium, or high): GRE/MAT scores high, research experience high, work experience low, extracurricular activity low, clinically related public service low, GPA high, letters of recommendation high, interview high, statement of goals and objectives high.

Student Characteristics: The following represents characteristics of students in 2004–2005 in all graduate psychology programs in the department: Female–full-time 85, part-time 0; Male–full-time 31, part-time 0; African American/Black–full-time 2, part-time 0; Hispanic/Latino(a)–full-time 7, part-time 0; Asian/Pacific Islander–full-time 4, part-time 0; American Indian/Alaska Native–full-time 1, part-time 0; Caucasian–full-time 102, part-time 0.

Financial Information/Assistance:
Financial Assistance:

First Year Students: Teaching assistantships available for first-year. Average amount paid per academic year: $10,500. Average number of hours worked per week: 20. Apply by January 1. Tuition remission given: full. Research assistantships available for first-year. Average amount paid per academic year: $10,500. Average number of hours worked per week: 20. Apply by January 1. Tuition remission given: full.

Advanced Students: Teaching assistantships available for advanced students. Average amount paid per academic year: $10,500. Average number of hours worked per week: 20. Apply by January 1. Tuition remission given: full. Research assistantships available for advanced students. Average amount paid per academic year: $10,500. Average number of hours worked per week: 20. Apply by January 1. Tuition remission given: full. Traineeships available for advanced students. Average amount paid per academic year: $10,000. Average number of hours worked per week: 20. Apply by January 1. Tuition remission given: full. Fellowships and scholarships available for advanced students. Average amount paid per academic year: $6,000. Average number of hours worked per week: 10. Apply by January 1. Tuition remission given: full.

Contact Information: Of all students currently enrolled full-time, 100% benefitted from one or more of the listed financial assistance programs. Application and information available online at: http://dept.kent.edu/psychology.

Internships/Practica: Seven semesters of clinical practica are required through the department's Psychological Clinic; 1,000 hours of supervised clinical experience at local field placement sites are provided with additional hours sometimes available; 2,000 hours of supervised internship experience in a program accredited by the American Psychological Association (these are competitive internships) are required. For those doctoral students for whom a professional internship is required prior to graduation, 7 applied in 2003–2004. Of those who applied, 7 were placed in internships listed by the Association of Psychology Postdoctoral and Internship Programs (APPIC); 7 were placed in APA accredited internships.

Housing and Day Care: On-campus housing is available. Residence Services Korb Hall Kent State University P.O. Box 5190 Kent, OH 44242-0001 Phone number: (330) 672-7000. On-campus day care facilities are available. Child Development Center: (330) 672-2559.

Employment of Department Graduates:

Master's Degree Graduates: Of those who graduated in the academic year 2003–2004, the following categories and numbers represent the post-graduate activities and employment of master's degree graduates: Enrolled in a psychology doctoral program (10), enrolled in a post-doctoral residency/fellowship (n/a), employed in independent practice (n/a), total from the above (master's) (10).

Doctoral Degree Graduates: Of those who graduated in the academic year 2003–2004, the following categories and numbers represent the post-graduate activities and employment of doctoral degree graduates: Enrolled in a psychology doctoral program (n/a), enrolled in a post-doctoral residency/fellowship (5), employed in independent practice (0), employed in an academic position at a university (0), employed in an academic position at a 2-year/4-year college (4), employed in other positions at a higher education institution (1), employed in a professional position in a school system (0), employed in business or industry (research/consulting) (1), employed in business or industry (management) (0), employed in a government agency (research) (0), employed in a government agency (professional services) (0), employed in a community mental health/counseling center (3), employed in a hospital/medical center (1), still seeking employment (1), do not know (0), total from the above (doctoral) (16).

Additional Information:

Orientation, Objectives, and Emphasis of Department: Doctoral training is provided in clinical and in various experimental areas. Students in clinical or experimental may major in health psychology. There is also an opportunity for subspecialization in child/developmental psychology. A common program of basic core courses is required of all students. Training facilities and laboratories are freely available to graduate students. The doctoral program requires full-time, continuous enrollment and is strongly research oriented. Students are encouraged to become involved in a variety of research projects before they begin dissertation work. The program's objective is to train those who can contribute through teaching, research, service, innovation, and administration.

Special Facilities or Resources: The department has well-equipped laboratories available for human and animal experimentation. Research opportunities are also available in various mental health settings in the area and at the SUMMA/KSU Center for the Treatment and Study of Traumatic Stress. Clinical training opportunities are available in the Psychological Clinic, which is staffed by clinical faculty and graduate students. The Applied Psychology Center supports research focused on psychological problems of social significance.

Application Information:
Send to: Chair, Graduate Admissions; Department of Psychology, Kent State University, Kent, OH 44242. Students are admitted in the Fall, application deadline January 1. *Fee:* $30.

Kent State University
Educational Foundations and Special Services/ Graduate
  Program in School Psychology
College and Graduate School of Education
405 White Hall
Kent, OH 44242
Telephone: (330) 672-2294
Fax: (330) 672-2512
E-mail: *ctelzrow@kent.edu*
Web: *http://spsy.educ.kent.edu*

Department Information:
1964. Department Chair: Paul Zionts. Number of Faculty: total–full-time 5, part-time 26; women–full-time 3, part-time 12; minority–full-time 1, part-time 1; faculty subject to the Americans With Disabilities Act 1.

Programs and Degrees Offered:
Listed in the following order: Program area, degree type (T if terminal Master's), number awarded 7/03–6/04. School Psychology PhD (Doctor of Philosophy) 2, School Psychology EdS (Education Specialist) 12.

APA Accreditation: School PhD (Doctor of Philosophy).

Student Applications/Admissions:
Student Applications

School Psychology PhD (Doctor of Philosophy)—Applications 2004–2005, 10. Total applicants accepted 2004–2005, 6. Number enrolled (new admits only) 2004–2005 full-time, 5. Number enrolled (new admits only) 2004–2005 part-time, 0. Total enrolled 2004–2005 full-time, 7, part-time, 10. Openings 2005–2006, 4. The Median number of years required for completion of a degree are 10. The number of students enrolled full and part-time who were dismissed or voluntarily withdrew from this program area were 1. *School Psychology EdS (Education Specialist)*—Applications 2004–2005, 60. Total applicants accepted 2004–2005, 18. Number enrolled (new admits only) 2004–2005 full-time, 12. Number enrolled (new admits only) 2004–2005 part-time, 3. Total enrolled 2004–2005 full-time, 43, part-time, 6. Openings 2005–2006, 15. The Median number of years required for completion of a degree are 3. The number of students enrolled full and part-time who were dismissed or voluntarily withdrew from this program area were 0.

Admissions Requirements:
Scores: Entries appear in this order: required test or GPA, minimum score (if required), median score of students entering in 2003–2004. Master's Programs: GRE-V none, 510; GRE-Q none, 570; GRE-Analytical none, 590; overall undergraduate

GPA 3.5, 3.5. Doctoral Programs: GRE-V 550, 580; GRE-Q none, 550; GRE-V+Q none, 1130; overall undergraduate GPA 3.5, 3.5.

Other Criteria: (importance of criteria rated low, medium, or high): GRE/MAT scores medium, research experience medium, work experience high, extracurricular activity medium, clinically related public service medium, GPA medium, letters of recommendation high, interview high, statement of goals and objectives high. For additional information on admission requirements, go to: http://spsy.educ.kent.edu.

Student Characteristics: The following represents characteristics of students in 2004–2005 in all graduate psychology programs in the department: Female–full-time 45, part-time 13; Male–full-time 5, part-time 3; African American/Black–full-time 2, part-time 2; Hispanic/Latino(a)–full-time 3, part-time 0; Asian/Pacific Islander–full-time 1, part-time 0; American Indian/Alaska Native–full-time 0, part-time 0; Caucasian–full-time 44, part-time 14; Multi-ethnic–full-time 0, part-time 0; students subject to the Americans With Disabilities Act–full-time 1, part-time 1.

Financial Information/Assistance:

Tuition for Full-Time Study: *Master's:* State residents: per academic year $11,265, $365 per credit hour; Nonstate residents: per academic year $21,157, $685 per credit hour. *Doctoral:* State residents: per academic year $11,265, $365 per credit hour; Nonstate residents: per academic year $21,157, $685 per credit hour. See the following Web site for updates and changes in tuition costs: www.kent.edu.

Financial Assistance:

First Year Students: Teaching assistantships available for first-year. Average amount paid per academic year: $7,000. Average number of hours worked per week: 20. Apply by May 1. Tuition remission given: full. Research assistantships available for first-year. Average amount paid per academic year: $7,000. Average number of hours worked per week: 20. Apply by May 1. Tuition remission given: full. Traineeships available for first-year. Average amount paid per academic year: $7,000. Average number of hours worked per week: 20. Apply by May 1. Tuition remission given: full. Fellowships and scholarships available for first-year. Apply by none. Tuition remission given: full.

Advanced Students: Teaching assistantships available for advanced students. Average amount paid per academic year: $9,500. Average number of hours worked per week: 20. Apply by May 1. Tuition remission given: full. Research assistantships available for advanced students. Average amount paid per academic year: $9,500. Average number of hours worked per week: 20. Apply by May 1. Tuition remission given: full. Traineeships available for advanced students. Average amount paid per academic year: $9,500. Average number of hours worked per week: 20. Apply by May 1. Tuition remission given: full.

Contact Information: Of all students currently enrolled full-time, 98% benefitted from one or more of the listed financial assistance programs.

Internships/Practica: *Master's:* State residents: per academic year $11,265, $365 per credit hour; Nonstate residents: per academic year $21,157, $685 per credit hour. Internship is required prior to graduation, 1 applied in 2003–2004.

Housing and Day Care: On-campus housing is available. See the following Web site for more information: http://www.res.kent.

edu/main.htm. On-campus day care facilities are available. See the following Web site for more information: http://cdc.educ.kent.edu.

Employment of Department Graduates:

Master's Degree Graduates: Of those who graduated in the academic year 2003–2004, the following categories and numbers represent the post-graduate activities and employment of master's degree graduates: Enrolled in a psychology doctoral program (1), enrolled in a post-doctoral residency/fellowship (n/a), employed in independent practice (n/a), employed in a professional position in a school system (11), total from the above (master's) (12).

Doctoral Degree Graduates: Of those who graduated in the academic year 2003–2004, the following categories and numbers represent the post-graduate activities and employment of doctoral degree graduates: Enrolled in a psychology doctoral program (n/a), employed in independent practice (1), employed in a professional position in a school system (1), total from the above (doctoral) (2).

Additional Information:

Orientation, Objectives, and Emphasis of Department: The KSU school psychology program embraces a preventive mental health model as a context for the study of psychological and educational principles that influence the adjustment of individuals and systems. A commitment to using the science of psychology to promote human welfare is emphasized. In addition, recognizing the pluralistic nature of our society, the program is committed to fostering in its students sensitivity to, appreciation for, and understanding of all individual differences. A scientist-practitioner model of training, which conceptualizes school psychologists as data-oriented problem-solvers and transmitters of psychological knowledge and skill, provides another organizing theme of training. The program emphasizes the provision of services to individual schools and children, in addition to attaining a functional understanding of systems-consultation and the ability to promote and implement primary and secondary prevention programs to optimize adjustment. Since the program's emphasis is on the application of psychology in applied educational and mental health settings, students are required to demonstrate competence in the substantive content areas of psychological and educational theory and practice. Other related areas outside the school psychology core include coursework in the biological, cognitive/perceptual, social, and developmental bases of behavior, as well as in the areas of curriculum and instruction, educational foundations, and research.

Special Facilities or Resources: The Center for Disability studies provides interdisciplinary research support for faculty and graduate students engaged in research on disability issues. The Child Development Center, an early childhood model laboratory school, provides opportunities for faculty and student research and practice. The Family Child Learning Center, which offers early intervention services to infants and toddlers with disabilities and their families, offers a training location for grant-funded school psychology students and for faculty research. The Counseling and Human Development Center (CHDC) provides students with a practicum experience through the supervised provision of assessment services to university students and the local community. The CHDC is equipped with one-way mirrors, split-screen videotaping facilities, and in-room telephones based around seven recently refurbished counseling cubicles. This permits observation by our students at the time of assessment and counseling and allows for videotaping for viewing at a later time. The Bureau of Educational Research provides a source of support for students who are engaged in research activities, including data entry and analysis.

Information for Students With Physical Disabilities: See the following Web site for more information: http://www.registrars.kent.edu/disability/default.htm.

Application Information:
Send to: Dr. Cathy Telzrow, Program Coordinator, 405 White Hall, Kent State University, Kent, OH 44242. Application available online. URL of online application: https://app.applyyourself.com/?id=kent-grad. Students are admitted in the Fall, application deadline October 15; Spring, application deadline February 15; Summer, application deadline June 15. Programs have rolling admissions. *Fee:* $30.

Marietta College
Department of Psychology
215 Flfth Street
Marietta, OH 45750
Telephone: (740) 376-4762
Fax: (740) 376-4459
E-mail: *sibickym@marietta.edu*
Web: *http://www.marietta.edu/*

Department Information:
1915. Chairperson: Mark E. Sibicky. Number of Faculty: total–full-time 5, part-time 3; women–full-time 2, part-time 1; minority–part-time 1.

Programs and Degrees Offered:
Listed in the following order: Program area, degree type (T if terminal Master's), number awarded 7/03–6/04. Master's Degree in General Psychology MA/MS (Master of Arts/Science) (T) 0.

Student Applications/Admissions:
Student Applications
Master's Degree in General Psychology MA/MS (Master of Arts/Science)—Applications 2004–2005, 17. Total applicants accepted 2004–2005, 10. Number enrolled (new admits only) 2004–2005 full-time, 9. Number enrolled (new admits only) 2004–2005 part-time, 0. Openings 2005–2006, 8. The number of students enrolled full and part-time who were dismissed or voluntarily withdrew from this program area were 3.

Admissions Requirements:
Scores: Entries appear in this order: required test or GPA, minimum score (if required), median score of students entering in 2003–2004. Master's Programs: GRE-V no minimum stated; GRE-Q no minimum stated; GRE-V+Q no minimum stated; GRE-Analytical no minimum stated; overall undergraduate GPA 2.8; psychology GPA 3.0.
Other Criteria: (importance of criteria rated low, medium, or high): GRE/MAT scores low, work experience low, GPA medium, letters of recommendation high, interview high, statement of goals and objectives high.

Student Characteristics: The following represents characteristics of students in 2004–2005 in all graduate psychology programs in the department: Female–full-time 7, part-time 0; Male–full-time 4, part-time 0; Asian/Pacific Islander–full-time 1, part-time 0; Caucasian–full-time 10, part-time 0; students subject to the Americans With Disabilities Act–full-time 0, part-time 0.

Financial Information/Assistance:
Tuition for Full-Time Study: *Master's:* State residents: $520 per credit hour; Nonstate residents: $520 per credit hour.

Financial Assistance:
First Year Students: Traineeships available for first-year. Average amount paid per academic year: $4,000. Average number of hours worked per week: 25. Apply by April 1.
Advanced Students: Traineeships available for advanced students. Average amount paid per academic year: $4,000. Average number of hours worked per week: 25. Apply by April 1.
Contact Information: Of all students currently enrolled full-time, 25% benefitted from one or more of the listed financial assistance programs.

Internships/Practica: Students select two three credit electives in an applied professional practica experience. The practica experience is designed to provide students with an applied experience relating to their career interests in psychology. Students choose electives from the following areas: The Teaching of Psychology - designed to train students to be effective instructors of psychology, Supervised Internship - internships in the areas of clinical, developmental, or the college's residence life program, Directed Independent Research - students pursue their own research interests under the direction of a faculty member. Students may also apply for Graduate Assistant positions in Residence Life. These paid supervised assistantships are for 10 months and provide students with room and board as well as a paid stipend.

Housing and Day Care: No on-campus housing is available. No on-campus day care facilities are available.

Employment of Department Graduates:
Master's Degree Graduates: Of those who graduated in the academic year 2003–2004, the following categories and numbers represent the post-graduate activities and employment of master's degree graduates: Enrolled in a post-doctoral residency/fellowship (n/a), employed in independent practice (n/a), total from the above (master's) (0).
Doctoral Degree Graduates: Of those who graduated in the academic year 2003–2004, the following categories and numbers represent the post-graduate activities and employment of doctoral degree graduates: Enrolled in a psychology doctoral program (n/a), total from the above (doctoral) (0).

Additional Information:
Orientation, Objectives, and Emphasis of Department: The Psychology Department at Marietta College offers a two-year Master of Arts Degree in General Psychology. The program is designed to prepare students with a strong graduate level foundation in psychology so students may pursue further education in psychology at the PhD level or so students may seek employment in a field related to psychology. The orientation of the department faculty is that psychology is a science, and that psychological research and knowledge can be applied to improving people's lives. The two year program consists of 24 core content courses in psychology, six hours of applied practicum electives in an area of professional

psychology (e.g., clinical internship, child and family center internship, the teaching of psychology), and six hours of supervised thesis research. The program offers the opportunity for students to focus their interests in the areas of clinical, social, developmental, cognitive, or applied psychology. Students are taught by outstanding teachers, with exceptional research and professional experience. Classes are small and students choose a faculty mentor/advisor who works with them throughout the program, including supervising the student's thesis research. Although the curriculum is challenging, faculty are focused on helping students achieve their personal, educational and professional goals.

Special Facilities or Resources: The Psychology Department at Marietta College has a newly remodeled human research laboratory equipped with several research cubicles, video recording equipment, one way observational windows, and computers with specialized cognitive and behavioral research software. Students interested in children and families have internship and research opportunities at the Marietta College Center for Families and Children. This on campus facility is maintained by the psychology department and provides educational and psychological services to children and families in the community. The department also maintains its own separate student computer lab equipped with word processing and statistical (SPSS) software. Students have access to graduate research and conference travel funds. There is also a designated graduate classroom and student lounge area.

Information for Students With Physical Disabilities: See the following Web site for more information: http://www.marietta.edu/~arc/.

Application Information:
Send to: Director of Graduate Programs and Continuing Education, Irvine Building, Marietta College, 215 Fifth Street, Marietta, OH, 45750-4005. Students are admitted in the Fall, application deadline April 1. *Fee:* $25.

Miami University (Ohio)
Department of Psychology
Oxford, OH 45056
Telephone: (513) 529-2400
Fax: (513) 529-2420
E-mail: *markls@muohio.edu*
Web: *http://www.muohio.edu/~psycwis/*

Department Information:
1888. Chairperson: Karen Maitland Schilling. Number of Faculty: total–full-time 32, part-time 8; women–full-time 15, part-time 2; minority–full-time 2, part-time 1.

Programs and Degrees Offered:
Listed in the following order: Program area, degree type (T if terminal Master's), number awarded 7/03–6/04. Clinical PhD (Doctor of Philosophy) 5, Brain and Cognitive Science PhD (Doctor of Philosophy) 0, Social PhD (Doctor of Philosophy) 1, Developmental Concentration PhD (Doctor of Philosophy) 0.

APA Accreditation: Clinical PhD (Doctor of Philosophy).

Student Applications/Admissions:
Student Applications
Clinical PhD (Doctor of Philosophy)—Applications 2004–2005, 144. Total applicants accepted 2004–2005, 7. Number enrolled (new admits only) 2004–2005 full-time, 7. Number enrolled (new admits only) 2004–2005 part-time, 0. Total enrolled 2004–2005 full-time, 22, part-time, 11. Openings 2005–2006, 7. The Median number of years required for completion of a degree are 7. The number of students enrolled full and part-time who were dismissed or voluntarily withdrew from this program area were 1. *Brain and Cognitive Science PhD (Doctor of Philosophy)*—Applications 2004–2005, 21. Total applicants accepted 2004–2005, 6. Number enrolled (new admits only) 2004–2005 full-time, 6. Number enrolled (new admits only) 2004–2005 part-time, 0. Total enrolled 2004–2005 full-time, 19, part-time, 2. Openings 2005–2006, 2. The number of students enrolled full and part-time, who were dismissed or voluntarily withdrew from this program area were 0. *Social PhD (Doctor of Philosophy)*—Applications 2004–2005, 41. Total applicants accepted 2004–2005, 2. Number enrolled (new admits only) 2004–2005 full-time, 3. Number enrolled (new admits only) 2004–2005 part-time, 1. Total enrolled 2004–2005 full-time, 12, part-time, 1. Openings 2005–2006, 3. The Median number of years required for completion of a degree are 5. The number of students enrolled full and part-time who were dismissed or voluntarily withdrew from this program area were 0. *Developmental Concentration PhD (Doctor of Philosophy)*—Applications 2004–2005, 5. Total applicants accepted 2004–2005, 2. Number enrolled (new admits only) 2004–2005 full-time, 2. Number enrolled (new admits only) 2004–2005 part-time, 0. Total enrolled 2004–2005 full-time, 15, part-time, 1. Openings 2005–2006, 1. The number of students enrolled full and part-time who were dismissed or voluntarily withdrew from this program area were 0.

Admissions Requirements:
Scores: Entries appear in this order: required test or GPA, minimum score (if required), median score of students entering in 2003–2004. Doctoral Programs: GRE-V no minimum stated, 610; GRE-Q no minimum stated, 690; GRE-Analytical no minimum stated, 660; GRE-Subject(Psych) no minimum stated, 690; overall undergraduate GPA no minimum stated, 3.8.
Other Criteria: (importance of criteria rated low, medium, or high): GRE/MAT scores medium, research experience high, work experience medium, extracurricular activity medium, clinically related public service medium, GPA medium, letters of recommendation high, interview medium, statement of goals and objectives high.

Student Characteristics: The following represents characteristics of students in 2004–2005 in all graduate psychology programs in the department: Female–full-time 41, part-time 10; Male–full-time 27, part-time 5; African American/Black–full-time 3, part-time 2; Hispanic/Latino(a)–full-time 1, part-time 1; Asian/Pacific Islander–full-time 1, part-time 1; American Indian/Alaska Native–full-time 0, part-time 0; Caucasian–full-time 63, part-time 11; Multi-ethnic–full-time 0, part-time 0; students subject to the Americans With Disabilities Act–full-time 0, part-time 0.

Financial Information/Assistance:
Tuition for Full-Time Study: *Doctoral:* State residents: per academic year $9,346, $390 per credit hour; Nonstate residents: per

academic year $19,926, $831 per credit hour. Tuition is subject to change.

Financial Assistance:

First Year Students: Teaching assistantships available for first-year. Average amount paid per academic year: $12,556. Average number of hours worked per week: 20. Apply by January. Tuition remission given: full. Research assistantships available for first-year. Average amount paid per academic year: $12,556. Average number of hours worked per week: 20. Apply by January. Tuition remission given: full.

Advanced Students: Teaching assistantships available for advanced students. Average amount paid per academic year: $16,834. Average number of hours worked per week: 20. Tuition remission given: full. Research assistantships available for advanced students. Average amount paid per academic year: $12,556. Average number of hours worked per week: 20. Tuition remission given: full. Fellowships and scholarships available for advanced students. Average amount paid per academic year: $16,913. Average number of hours worked per week: 20. Tuition remission given: full.

Contact Information: Of all students currently enrolled full-time, 100% benefitted from one or more of the listed financial assistance programs.

Internships/Practica: There are opportunities for students to engage in practica and internships as well as conduct applied research. Traineeships for advanced clinical students are available in a wide range of settings including community mental health centers, hospitals, and school systems. For those doctoral students for whom a professional internship is required prior to graduation, 8 applied in 2003–2004. Of those who applied, 8 were placed in internships listed by the Association of Psychology Postdoctoral and Internship Programs (APPIC); 8 were placed in APA accredited internships.

Housing and Day Care: On-campus housing is available. See the following Web site for more information: http://www.miami.muohio.edu/housing/. On-campus day care facilities are available.

Employment of Department Graduates:

Master's Degree Graduates: Of those who graduated in the academic year 2003–2004, the following categories and numbers represent the post-graduate activities and employment of master's degree graduates: Enrolled in a post-doctoral residency/fellowship (n/a), employed in independent practice (n/a), total from the above (master's) (0).

Doctoral Degree Graduates: Of those who graduated in the academic year 2003–2004, the following categories and numbers represent the post-graduate activities and employment of doctoral degree graduates: Enrolled in a psychology doctoral program (n/a), enrolled in a post-doctoral residency/fellowship (2), employed in an academic position at a university (1), employed in a community mental health/counseling center (1), other employment position (2), total from the above (doctoral) (6).

Additional Information:

Orientation, Objectives, and Emphasis of Department: The goal of the department is to provide an environment in which students thrive intellectually. We strive for a balance between enough structure to gauge student progress and provide grounding in the breadth of psychology and enough freedom for students to design programs optimal to their own professional goals. The department provides training and experience in research, teaching, and application of psychology. The department offers basic and applied research orientations in all programs. The clinical program emphasizes a theory-research-practicum combination, so that graduates will be able to function in a variety of academic and service settings. The objective of the department is to produce skilled, informed, and enthusiastic psychologists capable of contributing to their field in a variety of ways.

Special Facilities or Resources: The department has two social interaction laboratories with remote-controlled audio-visual equipment that are specially equipped for research on group processes and observing parent-child interactions. Four psychobiology laboratories offer advanced facilities for neurological recording, drug delivery, and pharmacological and histological analyses. The Center of Ergonomic Research provides a variety of ergonomic equipment used in studying human-computer interactions. The Psychology Clinic includes group and child therapy rooms, individual assessment and therapy rooms, a test library, conference room, and offices for the clinic director and a full-time secretary. Clinical services are offered in a training or research context to university students and the Oxford community. Research with children is facilitated by a good relationship with the Oxford public schools. Access to clinical populations is available through the Psychology Clinic and through cooperative arrangements with mental health centers in nearby communities.

Application Information:
Send to: The Graduate School, 102 Roudebush, Miami University, Oxford, OH 45056. Application available online. URL of online application: http://www.miami.muohio.edu/graduate/. Students are admitted in the Fall, application deadline January 1. *Fee:* $35.

Ohio State University
Department of Psychology
College of Social and Behavioral Sciences
238 Townshend Hall, 1885 Neil Avenue Mall
Columbus, OH 43210-1222
Telephone: (614) 292-4112
Fax: (614) 292-4537
E-mail: *psygrad@osu.edu*
Web: *http://www.psy.ohio-state.edu*

Department Information:
1907. Chairperson: Gifford Weary, PhD. Number of Faculty: total–full-time 47, part-time 15; women–full-time 13, part-time 8; minority–full-time 2, part-time 6.

Programs and Degrees Offered:
Listed in the following order: Program area, degree type (T if terminal Master's), number awarded 7/03–6/04. Clinical PhD (Doctor of Philosophy) 5, Cognitive/Experimental PhD (Doctor of Philosophy) 2, Counseling Psychology PhD (Doctor of Philosophy) 3, Developmental PhD (Doctor of Philosophy) 0, Industrial/Organizational PhD (Doctor of Philosophy) 1, Mental Retardation/Development PhD (Doctor of Philosophy) 2, Psychobiology and Behavioral Neuroscience PhD (Doctor of Philosophy) 0,

Quantitative PhD (Doctor of Philosophy) 0, Social PhD (Doctor of Philosophy) 3.

APA Accreditation: Clinical PhD (Doctor of Philosophy). Counseling PhD (Doctor of Philosophy).

Student Applications/Admissions:

Student Applications

Clinical PhD (Doctor of Philosophy)—Applications 2004–2005, 187. Total applicants accepted 2004–2005, 16. Number enrolled (new admits only) 2004–2005 full-time, 7. Number enrolled (new admits only) 2004–2005 part-time, 0. Total enrolled 2004–2005 full-time, 26, part-time, 3. Openings 2005–2006, 8. The Median number of years required for completion of a degree are 6. The number of students enrolled full and part-time who were dismissed or voluntarily withdrew from this program area were 1. *Cognitive/Experimental PhD (Doctor of Philosophy)*—Applications 2004–2005, 36. Total applicants accepted 2004–2005, 3. Number enrolled (new admits only) 2004–2005 full-time, 2. Number enrolled (new admits only) 2004–2005 part-time, 0. Total enrolled 2004–2005 full-time, 13, part-time, 1. Openings 2005–2006, 5. The Median number of years required for completion of a degree are 5. The number of students enrolled full and part-time who were dismissed or voluntarily withdrew from this program area were 0. *Counseling Psychology PhD (Doctor of Philosophy)*—Applications 2004–2005, 0. Total applicants accepted 2004–2005, 0. The Median number of years required for completion of a degree are 7. The number of students enrolled full and part-time who were dismissed or voluntarily withdrew from this program area were 0. *Developmental PhD (Doctor of Philosophy)*—Applications 2004–2005, 28. Total applicants accepted 2004–2005, 7. Number enrolled (new admits only) 2004–2005 full-time, 2. Number enrolled (new admits only) 2004–2005 part-time, 0. Openings 2005–2006, 3. The number of students enrolled full and part-time who were dismissed or voluntarily withdrew from this program area were 0. *Industrial/Organizational PhD (Doctor of Philosophy)*—Applications 2004–2005, 0. Total applicants accepted 2004–2005, 0. Total enrolled 2004–2005 full-time, 1, part-time, 1. The Median number of years required for completion of a degree are 5. The number of students enrolled full and part-time who were dismissed or voluntarily withdrew from this program area were 0. *Mental Retardation/Development PhD (Doctor of Philosophy)*—Applications 2004–2005, 18. Total applicants accepted 2004–2005, 4. Number enrolled (new admits only) 2004–2005 full-time, 4. Number enrolled (new admits only) 2004–2005 part-time, 0. Openings 2005–2006, 2. The Median number of years required for completion of a degree are 5. The number of students enrolled full and part-time who were dismissed or voluntarily withdrew from this program area were 0. *Psychobiology and Behavioral Neuroscience PhD (Doctor of Philosophy)*—Applications 2004–2005, 22. Total applicants accepted 2004–2005, 5. Number enrolled (new admits only) 2004–2005 full-time, 3. Number enrolled (new admits only) 2004–2005 part-time, 0. Openings 2005–2006, 5. The number of students enrolled full and part-time who were dismissed or voluntarily withdrew from this program area were 0. *Quantitative PhD (Doctor of Philosophy)*—Applications 2004–2005, 15. Total applicants accepted 2004–2005, 5. Number enrolled (new admits only) 2004–2005 full-time, 3. Number enrolled (new admits only) 2004–2005 part-time, 0. Openings 2005–2006, 3. The number

of students enrolled full and part-time who were dismissed or voluntarily withdrew from this program area were 0. *Social PhD (Doctor of Philosophy)*—Applications 2004–2005, 106. Total applicants accepted 2004–2005, 13. Number enrolled (new admits only) 2004–2005 full-time, 8. Number enrolled (new admits only) 2004–2005 part-time, 0. Openings 2005–2006, 7. The Median number of years required for completion of a degree are 6. The number of students enrolled full and part-time who were dismissed or voluntarily withdrew from this program area were 0.

Admissions Requirements:

Scores: Entries appear in this order: required test or GPA, minimum score (if required), median score of students entering in 2003–2004. Doctoral Programs: GRE-V 600, 611; GRE-Q 600, 707; GRE-V+Q 1200, 1318; GRE-Analytical 600, 714; overall undergraduate GPA 3.2, 3.79. GRE exceptions can be made when there is other evidence of high potential. Please note that to qualify for University Fellowships, the above required scores must be met.

Other Criteria: (importance of criteria rated low, medium, or high): research experience high, work experience low, extracurricular activity low, clinically related public service low, letters of recommendation high, statement of goals and objectives high. Clinical area ranks interview as high.

Student Characteristics: The following represents characteristics of students in 2004–2005 in all graduate psychology programs in the department: Female–full-time 103, part-time 4; Male–full-time 37, part-time 1; African American/Black–full-time 9, part-time 1; Hispanic/Latino(a)–full-time 7, part-time 0; Asian/Pacific Islander–full-time 4, part-time 0; American Indian/Alaska Native–full-time 1, part-time 0; Caucasian–full-time 96, part-time 4; Multi-ethnic–full-time 0, part-time 0; students subject to the Americans With Disabilities Act–full-time 0, part-time 0.

Financial Information/Assistance:

Tuition for Full-Time Study: *Doctoral:* State residents: per academic year $11,000, $350 per credit hour; Nonstate residents: per academic year $26,844, $746 per credit hour. Tuition is subject to change. See the following Web site for updates and changes in tuition costs: http://gradapply.osu.edu/BufferCosts.htm.

Financial Assistance:

First Year Students: Teaching assistantships available for first-year. Average amount paid per academic year: $10,080. Average number of hours worked per week: 20. Apply by December 30. Tuition remission given: full. Research assistantships available for first-year. Average amount paid per academic year: $10,080. Average number of hours worked per week: 20. Apply by December 30. Tuition remission given: full. Fellowships and scholarships available for first-year. Average amount paid per academic year: $12,000. Average number of hours worked per week: 0. Apply by December 30. Tuition remission given: full.

Advanced Students: Teaching assistantships available for advanced students. Average amount paid per academic year: $11,475. Average number of hours worked per week: 20. Apply by December 30. Tuition remission given: full. Research assistantships available for advanced students. Average amount paid per academic year: $11,475. Average number of hours worked per week: 20. Apply by December 30. Tuition remission given: full. Traineeships available for advanced students. Average amount paid per academic year: $11,475. Average number of hours worked per week: 20. Apply by December 30. Tuition remission given: full.

Contact Information: Of all students currently enrolled full-time, 100% benefitted from one or more of the listed financial assistance programs.

Internships/Practica: For students in the clinical training program, initial practica are conducted at the in-house Psychological Services Center (PSC), supervised by core clinical faculty. Following one year of in-house training, students progress to advanced clinical experiences at program-approved externship sites throughout the community, where students gain clinical assessment and treatment experiences in a variety of settings consistent with the program's three training tracks: Adult Psychopathology, Health Psychology, and Child-Clinical Psychology. Advanced students also have the opportunity to continue treating clients in the in-house PSC while receiving supervision from adjunct faculty in the community. Additionally, all students must complete a one-year full-time internship in clinical psychology prior to the award of the doctoral degree. Counseling psychology students complete 3 in-house practica where each counseling session is observed by a supervisor followed by 1 hour of individual supervision. External practicum sites include a variety of sites in the Central Ohio Area including university counseling centers, departments of rehabilitation psychology, VA medical centers, psychiatric hospitals, community mental health centers, forensic psychology at State correctional facilities, OPA psychology advocacy program, pain management and sport psychology clinics. For those doctoral students for whom a professional internship is required prior to graduation, 25 applied in 2003–2004. Of those who applied, 15 were placed in internships listed by the Association of Psychology Postdoctoral and Internship Programs (APPIC); 22 were placed in APA accredited internships.

Housing and Day Care: On-campus housing is available. See the following Web site for more information: http://www.osuhousing.com/gradhouse.html. For off campus information: http://www.osuoffcampus.com. On-campus day care facilities are available. See the following Web site for more information: http://hr.osu.edu/ccc/home.htm.

Employment of Department Graduates:

Master's Degree Graduates: Of those who graduated in the academic year 2003–2004, the following categories and numbers represent the post-graduate activities and employment of master's degree graduates: Enrolled in a psychology doctoral program (33), enrolled in another graduate/professional program (0), enrolled in a post-doctoral residency/fellowship (n/a), employed in independent practice (n/a), total from the above (master's) (33).

Doctoral Degree Graduates: Of those who graduated in the academic year 2003–2004, the following categories and numbers represent the post-graduate activities and employment of doctoral degree graduates: Enrolled in a psychology doctoral program (n/a), enrolled in a post-doctoral residency/fellowship (5), employed in an academic position at a university (5), employed in business or industry (research/consulting) (1), employed in a community mental health/counseling center (1), not seeking employment (1), do not know (3), total from the above (doctoral) (16).

Additional Information:

Orientation, Objectives, and Emphasis of Department: The department is comprehensive in nature, with PhD programs in nearly all the major fields of study in psychology. The programs all strive to educate psychological scientists, and there is consequently a strong emphasis on research training in the doctoral programs, even in the applied areas. Our objective is to prepare theoretically sophisticated psychologists who leave us with effective skills to build upon in their later careers and with the ability to grow as psychology develops as a science and profession.

Special Facilities or Resources: There are several research labs specializing in the various programs of the OSU psychology department. Please visit www.psy.ohio-state.edu and click on "Labs" in the header for more detailed information. In addition, since The Ohio State University is a well-known and well-established research institution, there are several non-department labs located throughout the campus that would be of possible interest to Psychology Graduate Students.

Information for Students With Physical Disabilities: See the following Web site for more information: http://www.ods.ohio-state.edu/.

Application Information:
Application must be submitted online. The online application is available at www.psy.ohio-state.edu, then click on "Graduate" for further instructions. Application available online. URL of online application: http://www.psy.ohio-state.edu/gradadv/app.htm. Students are admitted in the Fall, application deadline December 30. Our clinical program has an earlier deadline of December 15. Deadline for all international applicants—November 30. *Fee:* $40. International applications $50.

Ohio State University
School of Physical Activity and Educational Services
Education
1760 Neil Avenue
Columbus, OH 43210
Telephone: (614) 292-5909
Fax: (614) 688-4613
E-mail: *miranda.2@osu.edu*
Web: *http://www.coe.ohio-state.edu-paes*

Department Information:
1996. director: Donna Pastore. Number of Faculty: total–full-time 3; women–full-time 3; minority–full-time 1.

Programs and Degrees Offered:
Listed in the following order: Program area, degree type (T if terminal Master's), number awarded 7/03–6/04. School MA/MS (Master of Arts/Science) (T) 12, School PhD (Doctor of Philosophy) 0.

Student Applications/Admissions:
Student Applications
School MA/MS (*Master of Arts/Science*)—Applications 2004–2005, 98. Total applicants accepted 2004–2005, 15. Number enrolled (new admits only) 2004–2005 full-time, 10. Openings 2005–2006, 15. The Median number of years required for completion of a degree are 3. The number of students enrolled full and part-time who were dismissed or voluntarily withdrew

from this program area were 0. *School PhD (Doctor of Philosophy)*—Applications 2004–2005, 15. Total applicants accepted 2004–2005, 6. Number enrolled (new admits only) 2004–2005 full-time, 2. Total enrolled 2004–2005 full-time, 14. Openings 2005–2006, 5. The Median number of years required for completion of a degree are 5. The number of students enrolled full and part-time who were dismissed or voluntarily withdrew from this program area were 0.

Admissions Requirements:

Scores: Entries appear in this order: required test or GPA, minimum score (if required), median score of students entering in 2003–2004. Master's Programs: GRE-V 500, 643; GRE-Q 500, 607; GRE-V+Q 1000; overall undergraduate GPA 3.0, 3.4. Doctoral Programs: GRE-V 500, 687; GRE-Q 500, 653; GRE-V+Q 1000; overall undergraduate GPA 3.0, 3.7.

Other Criteria: (importance of criteria rated low, medium, or high): GRE/MAT scores medium, research experience medium, work experience medium, extracurricular activity low, clinically related public service medium, GPA high, letters of recommendation high, interview high, statement of goals and objectives high.

Student Characteristics: The following represents characteristics of students in 2004–2005 in all graduate psychology programs in the department: Female–full-time 31, part-time 0; Male–full-time 5, part-time 0; African American/Black–full-time 4, part-time 0; Hispanic/Latino(a)–full-time 2, part-time 0; Asian/Pacific Islander–full-time 0, part-time 0; American Indian/Alaska Native–full-time 0, part-time 0; Caucasian–full-time 0, part-time 0; students subject to the Americans With Disabilities Act–full-time 0, part-time 0.

Financial Information/Assistance:

Tuition for Full-Time Study: *Master's:* State residents: per academic year $7,479; Nonstate residents: per academic year $18,056. *Doctoral:* State residents: per academic year $7,479; Nonstate residents: per academic year $18,056. Tuition is subject to change.

Financial Assistance:

First Year Students: Fellowships and scholarships available for first-year. Average amount paid per academic year: $10,000. Apply by January 1. Tuition remission given: full.

Advanced Students: Fellowships and scholarships available for advanced students. Average amount paid per academic year: $10,000. Apply by January 1. Tuition remission given: full.

Contact Information: Of all students currently enrolled full-time, 40% benefitted from one or more of the listed financial assistance programs.

Internships/Practica: Master's students are engaged in practica during their two years of study. All students gain experience in an urban school district as well as either a rural or suburban setting. Students are involved in a 9-month school-based internship in the Central Ohio area. Internships are paid.

Housing and Day Care: On-campus housing is available. See the following Web site for more information: http://www.osuhousing.com/. On-campus day care facilities are available. See the following Web site for more information: http://hr.osu.edu/ccc/home.htm.

Employment of Department Graduates:

Master's Degree Graduates: Of those who graduated in the academic year 2003–2004, the following categories and numbers represent the post-graduate activities and employment of master's degree graduates: Enrolled in a post-doctoral residency/fellowship (n/a), employed in independent practice (n/a), employed in a professional position in a school system (10), total from the above (master's) (10).

Doctoral Degree Graduates: Of those who graduated in the academic year 2003–2004, the following categories and numbers represent the post-graduate activities and employment of doctoral degree graduates: Enrolled in a psychology doctoral program (n/a), total from the above (doctoral) (0).

Additional Information:

Orientation, Objectives, and Emphasis of Department: The Counselor Education, Rehabilitation Services, and School Psychology Section in the School of Physical Activity and Educational Services emphasizes the preparation of individuals who can function in human services settings such as public and private schools and universities, social agencies, state and federal government agencies, business and industry, hospitals and health care facilities, and rehabilitation agencies. Emphasizing primary prevention, the program will help students, learners, and clients achieve optimal levels of human functioning and advocate for organizations and systems that promote optimal levels of human functioning. Students in the program may undertake coursework to emphasize one or more of the three areas: (a) counselor education; (b) rehabilitation services; (c) school psychology.

Application Information:

Send to: School of Physical Activity and Educational Services, Student Services and Academic Programs, 215 Pomorene Hall, 1760 Neil Avenue, Columbus, OH 43210. Students are admitted in the Fall, application deadline January 15. *Fee:* $30.

Ohio University
Department of Psychology
Arts and Sciences
200 Porter Hall
Athens, OH 45701-2979
Telephone: (740) 593-1707
Fax: (740) 593-0579
E-mail: *psychology@ohiou.edu*
Web: *http://www.psych.ohiou.edu*

Department Information:

1922. Chairperson: Ben Ogles, PhD Number of Faculty: total–full-time 26, part-time 14; women–full-time 10, part-time 3; minority–full-time 2, part-time 1.

Programs and Degrees Offered:

Listed in the following order: Program area, degree type (T if terminal Master's), number awarded 7/03–6/04. Clinical PhD (Doctor of Philosophy) 8, Experimental PhD (Doctor of Philosophy) 2, Organizational PhD (Doctor of Philosophy) 2.

APA Accreditation: Clinical PhD (Doctor of Philosophy).

Student Applications/Admissions:

Student Applications

Clinical PhD (Doctor of Philosophy)—Applications 2004–2005, 173. Total applicants accepted 2004–2005, 16. Number enrolled (new admits only) 2004–2005 full-time, 10. Total enrolled 2004–2005 full-time, 37. Openings 2005–2006, 10. The Median number of years required for completion of a degree are 6. The number of students enrolled full and part-time who were dismissed or voluntarily withdrew from this program area were 1. *Experimental PhD (Doctor of Philosophy)*—Applications 2004–2005, 31. Total applicants accepted 2004–2005, 15. Number enrolled (new admits only) 2004–2005 full-time, 10. Total enrolled 2004–2005 full-time, 20. Openings 2005–2006, 7. The Median number of years required for completion of a degree are 6. The number of students enrolled full and part-time who were dismissed or voluntarily withdrew from this program area were 1. *Organizational PhD (Doctor of Philosophy)*—Applications 2004–2005, 20. Total applicants accepted 2004–2005, 6. Number enrolled (new admits only) 2004–2005 full-time, 3. Openings 2005–2006, 3. The Median number of years required for completion of a degree are 6. The number of students enrolled full and part-time who were dismissed or voluntarily withdrew from this program area were 0.

Admissions Requirements:

Scores: Entries appear in this order: required test or GPA, minimum score (if required), median score of students entering in 2003–2004. Master's Programs: overall undergraduate GPA 3.0; psychology GPA 3.3. Doctoral Programs: GRE-V no minimum stated, 550; GRE-Q no minimum stated, 660; GRE-V+Q no minimum stated; GRE-Analytical no minimum stated; GRE-Subject(Psych) no minimum stated, 650; overall undergraduate GPA no minimum stated, 3.76.

Other Criteria: (importance of criteria rated low, medium, or high): GRE/MAT scores high, research experience high, work experience low, extracurricular activity low, clinically related public service medium, GPA high, letters of recommendation high, interview medium, statement of goals and objectives medium.

Student Characteristics: The following represents characteristics of students in 2004–2005 in all graduate psychology programs in the department: Female–full-time 45, part-time 0; Male–full-time 17, part-time 0; African American/Black–full-time 0, part-time 0; Hispanic/Latino(a)–full-time 1, part-time 0; Asian/Pacific Islander–full-time 5, part-time 0; American Indian/Alaska Native–full-time 0, part-time 0; Caucasian–full-time 56, part-time 0; Multi-ethnic–full-time 0, part-time 0; students subject to the Americans With Disabilities Act–full-time 0, part-time 0.

Financial Information/Assistance:

Tuition for Full-Time Study: *Master's:* State residents: per academic year $7,167; Nonstate residents: per academic year $7,167. *Doctoral:* State residents: per academic year $7,167; Nonstate residents: per academic year $7,167. Tuition is subject to change.

Financial Assistance:

First Year Students: Teaching assistantships available for first-year. Average amount paid per academic year: $12,000. Average number of hours worked per week: 15. Tuition remission given: full. Research assistantships available for first-year. Average amount paid per academic year: $12,000. Average number of hours worked per week: 15. Tuition remission given: full. Fellowships and scholarships available for first-year. Average amount paid per academic year: $16,400. Average number of hours worked per week: 8. Tuition remission given: full.

Advanced Students: Teaching assistantships available for advanced students. Average amount paid per academic year: $12,000. Average number of hours worked per week: 15. Tuition remission given: full. Research assistantships available for advanced students. Average amount paid per academic year: $12,000. Average number of hours worked per week: 15. Tuition remission given: full. Traineeships available for advanced students. Average amount paid per academic year: $12,000. Average number of hours worked per week: 15. Tuition remission given: full. Fellowships and scholarships available for advanced students. Average amount paid per academic year: $16,400. Average number of hours worked per week: 8. Tuition remission given: full.

Contact Information: Of all students currently enrolled full-time, 100% benefitted from one or more of the listed financial assistance programs.

Internships/Practica: Clinical doctoral interns are placed in APA-approved, one-year internships throughout the country. Supervised training in clinical skills is provided for all clinical students in area mental health agencies, clinics, and the departmental psychology clinic. Such training is in addition to traineeships and internships. Supervised practicum experience is provided for organizational students in area industries and organizations. For those doctoral students for whom a professional internship is required prior to graduation, 11 applied in 2003–2004. Of those who applied, 11 were placed in internships listed by the Association of Psychology Postdoctoral and Internship Programs (APPIC); 11 were placed in APA accredited internships.

Housing and Day Care: On-campus housing is available. See the following Web site for more information: http://www.ohiou.edu/housing/. On-campus day care facilities are available.

Employment of Department Graduates:

Master's Degree Graduates: Of those who graduated in the academic year 2003–2004, the following categories and numbers represent the post-graduate activities and employment of master's degree graduates: Enrolled in a post-doctoral residency/fellowship (n/a), employed in independent practice (n/a), total from the above (master's) (0).

Doctoral Degree Graduates: Of those who graduated in the academic year 2003–2004, the following categories and numbers represent the post-graduate activities and employment of doctoral degree graduates: Enrolled in a psychology doctoral program (n/a), total from the above (doctoral) (0).

Additional Information:

Orientation, Objectives, and Emphasis of Department: The clinical doctoral program is a scientist/practitioner program, offering balanced training in research and clinical skills. Practicum training is offered in intellectual and personality assessment. Therapy sequences are offered in health psychology, individual and group psychotherapy, behavior modification, and child psychology. Traineeships are available at the university counseling center and area mental health agencies and clinics. The department has a psychology training clinic. The doctoral program in experimental psychology provides intensive training in scholarly and research activities, preparing the student for positions in academic and research settings.

Special Facilities or Resources: Anderson Laboratories, adjacent to the psychology building, are equipped for a wide variety of human research activities, including psychophysiology, cognitive, social, and health. The department has its own clinic, which is used to train clinical doctoral students. Two computer laboratories in the Psychology Department, one with 30 microcomputers and one with 8 microcomputers, are also available for student research. All computer services are free of charge. Ohio University was recently awarded the Psychology Department selective-investment funds, which represent a major increase in funding for the department.

Application Information:
Send to: Office of Graduate Studies, Ohio University, McKee House, Athens, OH 45701-2979. Students are admitted in the Fall, application deadline January 1. *Fee:* $45. The fee is waived or deferred with a statement of need from the financial aid office of the applicant's college.

Toledo, University of
Department of Psychology
Arts and Science
Mail Stop 948
Toledo, OH 43606
Telephone: (419) 530-2717
Fax: (419) 530-8479
E-mail: *joseph.hovey@utoledo.edu*
Web: *http://www.utoledo.edu/psychology/*

Department Information:
1913. Chairperson: Joseph D. Hovey. Number of Faculty: total–full-time 20, part-time 2; women–full-time 8, part-time 2; minority–full-time 4.

Programs and Degrees Offered:
Listed in the following order: Program area, degree type (T if terminal Master's), number awarded 7/03–6/04. Behavioral Science PhD (Doctor of Philosophy) 4, Clinical PhD (Doctor of Philosophy) 6.

APA Accreditation: Clinical PhD (Doctor of Philosophy).

Student Applications/Admissions:
Student Applications
Behavioral Science PhD (Doctor of Philosophy)—Applications 2004–2005, 35. Total applicants accepted 2004–2005, 5. Number enrolled (new admits only) 2004–2005 full-time, 3. Num-

ber enrolled (new admits only) 2004–2005 part-time, 0. Openings 2005–2006, 5. The Median number of years required for completion of a degree are 5. The number of students enrolled full and part-time who were dismissed or voluntarily withdrew from this program area were 1. *Clinical PhD (Doctor of Philosophy)*—Applications 2004–2005, 75. Total applicants accepted 2004–2005, 9. Number enrolled (new admits only) 2004–2005 full-time, 7. Number enrolled (new admits only) 2004–2005 part-time, 0. Openings 2005–2006, 6. The Median number of years required for completion of a degree are 6. The number of students enrolled full and part-time who were dismissed or voluntarily withdrew from this program area were 0.

Admissions Requirements:
Scores: Entries appear in this order: required test or GPA, minimum score (if required), median score of students entering in 2003–2004. Master's Programs: GRE-Subject(Psych) no minimum stated; overall undergraduate GPA no minimum stated; last 2 years GPA no minimum stated; psychology GPA no minimum stated. Doctoral Programs: overall undergraduate GPA no minimum stated; last 2 years GPA no minimum stated; psychology GPA no minimum stated.
Other Criteria: (importance of criteria rated low, medium, or high): GRE/MAT scores high, research experience high, work experience medium, extracurricular activity medium, clinically related public service low, GPA high, letters of recommendation high, interview medium, statement of goals and objectives high. For additional information on admission requirements, go to: www.utoledo.edu/psychology.

Student Characteristics: The following represents characteristics of students in 2004–2005 in all graduate psychology programs in the department: Female–full-time 34, part-time 0; Male–full-time 12, part-time 0; African American/Black–full-time 0, part-time 0; Hispanic/Latino(a)–full-time 0, part-time 0; Asian/Pacific Islander–full-time 3, part-time 0; American Indian/Alaska Native–full-time 0, part-time 0; Caucasian–full-time 43, part-time 0; Multi-ethnic–full-time 0, part-time 0; students subject to the Americans With Disabilities Act–full-time 1, part-time 0.

Financial Information/Assistance:
Financial Assistance:
First Year Students: Research assistantships available for first-year. Average amount paid per academic year: $11,000. Average number of hours worked per week: 20. Tuition remission given: full. Fellowships and scholarships available for first-year. Average amount paid per academic year: $12,000. Tuition remission given: full.
Advanced Students: Teaching assistantships available for advanced students. Average amount paid per academic year: $11,000. Average number of hours worked per week: 20. Tuition remission given: full. Research assistantships available for advanced students. Average amount paid per academic year: $11,000. Average number of hours worked per week: 20. Tuition remission given: full. Traineeships available for advanced students. Average amount paid per academic year: $11,000. Average number of hours worked per week: 20. Tuition remission given: full. Fellowships and scholarships available for advanced students. Tuition remission given: full.

Contact Information: Of all students currently enrolled full-time, 100% benefitted from one or more of the listed financial assistance programs.

Internships/Practica: For those doctoral students for whom a professional internship is required prior to graduation, 6 applied in 2003–2004. Of those who applied, 6 were placed in internships listed by the Association of Psychology Postdoctoral and Internship Programs (APPIC); 6 were placed in APA accredited internships.

Housing and Day Care: On-campus housing is available. See the following Web site for more information: www.utoledo.edu. On-campus day care facilities are available.

Employment of Department Graduates:

Master's Degree Graduates: Of those who graduated in the academic year 2003–2004, the following categories and numbers represent the post-graduate activities and employment of master's degree graduates: Enrolled in a post-doctoral residency/fellowship (n/a), employed in independent practice (n/a), total from the above (master's) (0).

Doctoral Degree Graduates: Of those who graduated in the academic year 2003–2004, the following categories and numbers represent the post-graduate activities and employment of doctoral degree graduates: Enrolled in a psychology doctoral program (n/a), total from the above (doctoral) (0).

Additional Information:

Orientation, Objectives, and Emphasis of Department: The clinical psychology program's main goal is to train scholar-practitioners. A second goal of the program is to generate research that can contribute to the fund of general knowledge. The third goal of the program is to provide public service. The program in behavioral science is founded on the assumption that we are charged with the training of students who will become researchers in one of several branches of psychology. Most of these students will also become college or university teachers. For these reasons, the program places major emphasis on the student's development as a researcher and a teacher. The department requires that students have a thorough grounding in research methods, possess a high level of knowledge in their chosen specialty, have a broad knowledge of general psychology, and show competence as a teacher. Areas of student emphasis in the behavioral science program: cognitive, developmental, psychobiology/animal learning, social psychology.

Special Facilities or Resources: http://www.utoledo.edu/psychology.

Information for Students With Physical Disabilities: See the following Web site for more information: http://www.student-services.utoledo.edu/accessibility/index.html.

Application Information:

Send to: Graduate School, University of Toledo, Toledo, OH 43606. Application available online. URL of online application: www.utoledo.edu/psychology. Students are admitted in the Fall, application deadline January 15. *Fee:* $35.

Wright State University

Department of Psychology
College of Science and Mathematics
335 Fawcett Hall, 3640 Colonel Glenn Highway
Dayton, OH 45435-0001
Telephone: (937) 775-3348
Fax: (937) 775-3347
E-mail: *psych@wright.edu*
Web: *http://www.psych.wright.edu*

Department Information:

1979. Chairperson: John M. Flach. Number of Faculty: total–full-time 21, part-time 18; women–full-time 7, part-time 8; minority–full-time 2, part-time 2.

Programs and Degrees Offered:

Listed in the following order: Program area, degree type (T if terminal Master's), number awarded 7/03 6/04. Industrial/Organizational PhD (Doctor of Philosophy) 2, Human Factors PhD (Doctor of Philosophy) 1.

Student Applications/Admissions:

Student Applications

Industrial/Organizational PhD (Doctor of Philosophy)—Applications 2004–2005, 42. Total applicants accepted 2004–2005, 3. Number enrolled (new admits only) 2004–2005 full-time, 3. Total enrolled 2004–2005 full-time, 16, part-time, 1. Openings 2005–2006, 4. The Median number of years required for completion of a degree are 7. The number of students enrolled full and part-time who were dismissed or voluntarily withdrew from this program area were 0. *Human Factors PhD (Doctor of Philosophy)*—Applications 2004–2005, 22. Total applicants accepted 2004–2005, 7. Number enrolled (new admits only) 2004–2005 full-time, 4. Number enrolled (new admits only) 2004–2005 part-time, 3. Total enrolled 2004–2005 full-time, 17, part-time, 8. Openings 2005–2006, 5. The Median number of years required for completion of a degree are 4. The number of students enrolled full and part-time who were dismissed or voluntarily withdrew from this program area were 0.

Admissions Requirements:

Scores: Entries appear in this order: required test or GPA, minimum score (if required), median score of students entering in 2003–2004. Master's Programs: GRE-V+Q 1100, 1150; overall undergraduate GPA 3.15, 3.18. Doctoral Programs: GRE-V+Q 1100, 1185; overall undergraduate GPA 3.15, 3.75. **Other Criteria:** (importance of criteria rated low, medium, or high): GRE/MAT scores high, research experience high, work experience medium, extracurricular activity low, GPA high, letters of recommendation high, interview medium, statement of goals and objectives high.

Student Characteristics: The following represents characteristics of students in 2004–2005 in all graduate psychology programs in the department: Female–full-time 20, part-time 5; Male–full-time 15, part-time 5; African American/Black–full-time 0, part-time 0; Hispanic/Latino(a)–full-time 2, part-time 1; Asian/Pacific Islander–full-time 4, part-time 1; American Indian/Alaska Native–full-time 0, part-time 0; Caucasian–full-time 29, part-time 8;

Multi-ethnic–full-time 0, part-time 0; students subject to the Americans With Disabilities Act–full-time 0, part-time 0.

Financial Information/Assistance:
Tuition for Full-Time Study: *Master's:* State residents: per academic year $2,884, $271 per credit hour; Nonstate residents: per academic year $4,889, $458 per credit hour. *Doctoral:* State residents: per academic year $2,884, $271 per credit hour; Nonstate residents: per academic year $4,889, $458 per credit hour. Tuition is subject to change.

Financial Assistance:
First Year Students: Teaching assistantships available for first-year. Average amount paid per academic year: $11,300. Average number of hours worked per week: 20. Apply by January 1. Tuition remission given: full. Research assistantships available for first-year. Average amount paid per academic year: $11,300. Average number of hours worked per week: 20. Apply by January 1. Tuition remission given: full. Fellowships and scholarships available for first-year. Average amount paid per academic year: $12,000. Average number of hours worked per week: 20. Apply by January 1. Tuition remission given: full.

Advanced Students: Teaching assistantships available for advanced students. Average amount paid per academic year: $11,300. Average number of hours worked per week: 20. Apply by January 1. Tuition remission given: full. Research assistantships available for advanced students. Average amount paid per academic year: $11,300. Average number of hours worked per week: 20. Apply by January 1. Tuition remission given: full.

Contact Information: Of all students currently enrolled full-time, 100% benefitted from one or more of the listed financial assistance programs.

Internships/Practica: No information provided.

Housing and Day Care: No on-campus housing is available. On-campus day care facilities are available: Mini University, Inc., (937) 775-4070.

Employment of Department Graduates:
Master's Degree Graduates: Of those who graduated in the academic year 2003–2004, the following categories and numbers represent the post-graduate activities and employment of master's degree graduates: Enrolled in a psychology doctoral program (0), enrolled in another graduate/professional program (0), enrolled in a post-doctoral residency/fellowship (n/a), employed in independent practice (n/a), employed in an academic position at a university (0), employed in an academic position at a 2-year/4-year college (0), employed in other positions at a higher education institution (0), employed in a professional position in a school system (0), employed in business or industry (research/consulting) (3), employed in business or industry (management) (0), employed in a government agency (research) (0), employed in a government agency (professional services) (0), employed in a community mental health/counseling center (0), employed in a hospital/medical center (0), still seeking employment (0), other employment position (0), total from the above (master's) (3).
Doctoral Degree Graduates: Of those who graduated in the academic year 2003–2004, the following categories and numbers represent the post-graduate activities and employment of doctoral degree graduates: Enrolled in a psychology doctoral program (n/a), enrolled in a post-doctoral residency/fellowship (0), employed in

independent practice (0), employed in an academic position at a university (0), employed in an academic position at a 2-year/4-year college (0), employed in other positions at a higher education institution (0), employed in a professional position in a school system (0), employed in business or industry (research/consulting) (0), employed in business or industry (management) (0), employed in a government agency (research) (0), employed in a government agency (professional services) (0), employed in a community mental health/counseling center (0), employed in a hospital/medical center (0), still seeking employment (0), other employment position (0), total from the above (doctoral) (0).

Additional Information:
Orientation, Objectives, and Emphasis of Department: The Department offers MS and PhD degrees in Human Factors and Industrial/Organizational Psychology. Students specialize in one of these areas, but the program is designed to foster an understanding of both areas and the importance of considering both aspects in the design of industrial, aerospace, or other systems. The program prepares students for careers in research, teaching, design and practice in government, consulting, business, or industry. It includes coursework, research training, and experience with system design and applications. Students work closely with faculty beginning early in the program. Human factors, also called ergonomics or engineering psychology, deals with human-machine interactions (microsystem variables), while industrial/organizational deals with individual or group behaviors in work settings (macrosystem variables). The department has a critical mass of students and faculty in these areas and is unique because its focus on applied psychology does not include students in clinical psychology or other health-related areas. Both programs are strengthened by being located in the Dayton, Ohio metropolitan region, which is a rapidly developing high technology sector, a major human factors research and development center, and a region of considerable industrial and corporate strength.

Special Facilities or Resources: The Department of Psychology has modern state-of-the-art research laboratories, well-equipped teaching laboratories, and office space for faculty and graduate assistants. Specialized equipment in dedicated research laboratories supports research on sensory processes, motor control, spatial orientation, human computer interaction and display design, flight simulation, memory, aging, expertise, teamwork, assessment, training, and stress in the workplace. Computer facilities include numerous UNIX workstations, PCs, and Macintoshes. The Department is particularly proud of its facilities for virtual environment generation, including 3-D visual displays, 3-D auditory displays, and tactile/haptic displays. The Virtual Environment Research, Interactive Technology, and Simulation (VERITAS) facility, which is owned and operated by Wright State University but housed at Wright Patterson Air Force Base, is unique in the world. The facility includes a room-size display that surrounds the user with interactive 3-D auditory and visual images. The Department of Psychology has a Memorandum of Agreement with the U.S. Air Force Research Laboratory, which facilitates utilization of its sophisticated behavioral laboratories such as flight simulators and the Auditory Localization Facility.

Information for Students With Physical Disabilities: Director of Office of Disability Services (jeff.vernooy@wright.edu).

Application Information:
Send to: School of Graduate Studies, Wright State University, E344 Student Union, 3640 Colonel Glenn Highway, Dayton, OH 45435-0001. Application available online. URL of online application: www.psych.wright.edu. Students are admitted in the Fall, application deadline January 1. Send three letters of recommendation on letterhead (no form required) to the School of Graduate Studies at the address listed above. *Fee:* $25.

Wright State University
School of Professional Psychology
3640 Colonel Glenn Highway
Dayton, OH 45435
Telephone: (937) 775-3490
Fax: (937) 775-3434
E-mail: *John.Rudisill@wright.edu*
Web: *http://www.wright.edu/sopp/*

Department Information:
1979. Dean: John R. Rudisill, PhD. Number of Faculty: total–full-time 15, part-time 9; women–full-time 9, part-time 5; minority–full-time 5, part-time 2; faculty subject to the Americans With Disabilities Act 1.

Programs and Degrees Offered:
Listed in the following order: Program area, degree type (T if terminal Master's), number awarded 7/03–6/04. Clinical PsyD (Doctor of Psychology) 24.

APA Accreditation: Clinical PsyD (Doctor of Psychology).

Student Applications/Admissions:
Student Applications
Clinical PsyD (Doctor of Psychology)—Applications 2004–2005, 148. Total applicants accepted 2004–2005, 25. Number enrolled (new admits only) 2004–2005 full-time, 25. Total enrolled 2004–2005 full-time, 123, part-time, 4. Openings 2005–2006, 27. The Median number of years required for completion of a degree are 5. The number of students enrolled full and part-time who were dismissed or voluntarily withdrew from this program area was 1.

Admissions Requirements:
Scores: Entries appear in this order: required test or GPA, minimum score (if required), median score of students entering in 2003–2004. Doctoral Programs: GRE-V no minimum stated, 500; GRE-Q no minimum stated, 520; GRE-V+Q no minimum stated, 1020; GRE-Analytical no minimum stated, 470; GRE-Subject(Psych) no minimum stated, 550; overall undergraduate GPA no minimum stated, 3.5.
Other Criteria: (importance of criteria rated low, medium, or high): GRE/MAT scores medium, research experience low, work experience medium, extracurricular activity medium, clinically related public service high, GPA high, letters of recommendation high, interview high, statement of goals and objectives high. For additional information on admission requirements, go to: www.wright.edu/sopp.

Student Characteristics: The following represents characteristics of students in 2004–2005 in all graduate psychology programs in the department: Female–full-time 86, part-time 3; Male–full-time 37, part-time 1; African American/Black–full-time 20, part-time 2; Hispanic/Latino(a)–full-time 5, part-time 0; Asian/Pacific Islander–full-time 11, part-time 0; American Indian/Alaska Native–full-time 1, part-time 0; Caucasian–full-time 86, part-time 2; Multi-ethnic–full-time 1, part-time 0; students subject to the Americans With Disabilities Act–full-time 4, part-time 0.

Financial Information/Assistance:
Tuition for Full-Time Study: *Doctoral:* State residents: per academic year $13,476, $290 per credit hour; Nonstate residents: per academic year $21,496, $460 per credit hour. Tuition is subject to change.

Financial Assistance:
First Year Students: Fellowships and scholarships available for first-year. Average amount paid per academic year: $13,456. Tuition remission given: full and partial.
Advanced Students: Traineeships available for advanced students. Average amount paid per academic year: $6,000. Average number of hours worked per week: 16. Fellowships and scholarships available for advanced students. Average amount paid per academic year: $11,484. Average number of hours worked per week: 0. Tuition remission given: partial.
Contact Information: Of all students currently enrolled full-time, 100% benefitted from one or more of the listed financial assistance programs.

Internships/Practica: During years two, three, and four of the doctoral program, students are assigned to yearlong practicum placements for 2 days (16-20 hours) per week. Most practicum placements are paid positions, at an average rate of $6,000 per year. Approximately half the practicum placements are in the two clinical/teaching facilities operated by the school. These include the Center for Psychological Services on WSU's campus, which provides psychological services for the university's student body, and the Ellis Institute, which is located in an urban, predominately African American section of the city and which provides a broad range of psychological services and special treatment programs developed in response to the needs of the Dayton community. The remaining practicum placements are located in a broad array of service settings located primarily in the Dayton and Cincinnati areas. These practicum settings include: public agencies, correctional settings, hospitals, health and mental health clinics, and a number of private practices of area psychologists. For those doctoral students for whom a professional internship is required prior to graduation, 20 applied in 2003–2004. Of those who applied, 19 were placed in internships listed by the Association of Psychology Postdoctoral and Internship Programs (APPIC); 17 were placed in APA accredited internships.

Housing and Day Care: On-campus housing is available. See the following Web site for more information: www.wright.edu/students/housing. On-campus day care facilities are available.

Employment of Department Graduates:
Master's Degree Graduates: Of those who graduated in the academic year 2003–2004, the following categories and numbers represent the post-graduate activities and employment of master's degree graduates: Enrolled in a post-doctoral residency/fellowship

(n/a), employed in independent practice (n/a), total from the above (master's) (0).

Doctoral Degree Graduates: Of those who graduated in the academic year 2003–2004, the following categories and numbers represent the post-graduate activities and employment of doctoral degree graduates: Enrolled in a psychology doctoral program (n/a), enrolled in another graduate/professional program (0), enrolled in a post-doctoral residency/fellowship (12), employed in independent practice (2), employed in an academic position at a university (0), employed in an academic position at a 2-year/4-year college (0), employed in other positions at a higher education institution (0), employed in a professional position in a school system (0), employed in business or industry (research/consulting) (0), employed in business or industry (management) (0), employed in a government agency (research) (0), employed in a government agency (professional services) (1), employed in a community mental health/counseling center (0), employed in a hospital/medical center (3), still seeking employment (1), other employment position (1), do not know (0), total from the above (doctoral) (20).

Additional Information:

Orientation, Objectives, and Emphasis of Department: The School of Professional Psychology is committed to a practitioner model of professional education that educates students at the doctoral level for the eclectic, general practice of psychology. As a part of its educational mission, the school emphasizes cultural and other aspects of diversity in the composition of its student body, faculty and curriculum. The curriculum is organized around six core competency areas that are fundamental to the practice of psychology currently and in the future, including research and evaluation, assessment, intervention, management and supervision, and consultation and education. In years 1 and 2 the curriculum is designed around foundation coursework and the development of basic competencies. Years 3 and 4 are devoted to the development of advanced competency levels.

Special Facilities or Resources: The program operates two large clinical service centers that are designed to accommodate academic teaching, clinical training, clinical program development and research. The Psychology Service Center is located in an outpatient health care facility on the university's campus. This service center provides assessment and group and individual therapy services to the university student body which numbers approximately 15,000. Opportunities are available for trainees to participate in crisis intervention, prevention programs, outreach to residence halls, and multidisciplinary training with medical and nursing students. The second service center, the Ellis Institute, is located in an urban, primarily African-American section of Dayton. The Ellis Institute provides assessment and group and individual therapy to children, adolescents and adults from the Dayton community. Several special treatment programs provide unique opportunities for trainees. These include violence prevention programs for minority adolescents, treatment programs addressing perpetrators and victims of domestic violence, anxiety and depression in children, mental health needs of deaf individuals, and the needs of clients and families of people with HIV/AIDS and herpes. Both service centers house classrooms, trainee and faculty offices and computers for student use in research and training activities, and both facilities are equipped with state of the art equipment for videotaped and live clinical supervision.

Information for Students With Physical Disabilities: See the following Web site for more information: www.wright.edu/students/dis_services/.

Application Information:
Send to: Office of Admissions/Alumni Relations, 110 Health Sciences Building, Wright State University, Dayton, OH 45435. Application available online. URL of online application: www.wright.edu/sopp. Students are admitted in the Fall, application deadline January 15. *Fee:* $50.

Xavier University
Department of Psychology
College of Social Sciences
Elet Hall
Cincinnati, OH 45207-6511
Telephone: (513) 745-3533
Fax: (513) 745-3327
E-mail: dacey@xavier.edu
Web: http://www.xu.edu

Department Information:
1964. Chairperson: Christine M. Dacey, PhD, ABPP. Number of Faculty: total–full-time 19, part-time 6; women–full-time 9, part-time 2; minority–full-time 2.

Programs and Degrees Offered:
Listed in the following order: Program area, degree type (T if terminal Master's), number awarded 7/03–6/04. Clinical PsyD (Doctor of Psychology) 20, Experimental MA/MS (Master of Arts/Science) (T) 1, Industrial/Organizational MA/MS (Master of Arts/Science) (T) 8.

APA Accreditation: Clinical PsyD (Doctor of Psychology).

Student Applications/Admissions:
Student Applications
Clinical PsyD (Doctor of Psychology)—Applications 2004–2005, 140. Total applicants accepted 2004–2005, 35. Number enrolled (new admits only) 2004–2005 full-time, 16. Total enrolled 2004–2005 full-time, 82, part-time, 10. Openings 2005–2006, 16. The Median number of years required for completion of a degree are 5. The number of students enrolled full and part-time who were dismissed or voluntarily withdrew from this program area were 1. *Experimental MA/MS (Master of Arts/Science)*—Applications 2004–2005, 6. Total applicants accepted 2004–2005, 0. Number enrolled (new admits only) 2004–2005 full-time, 0. Total enrolled 2004–2005 full-time, 1. The Median number of years required for completion of a degree are 4. The number of students enrolled full and part-time who were dismissed or voluntarily withdrew from this program area were 0. *Industrial/Organizational MA/MS (Master of Arts/Science)*—Applications 2004–2005, 37. Total applicants accepted 2004–2005, 20. Number enrolled (new admits only) 2004–2005 full-time, 9. Total enrolled 2004–2005 full-time, 17, part-time, 8. Openings 2005–2006, 11. The Median

number of years required for completion of a degree are 3. The number of students enrolled full and part-time who were dismissed or voluntarily withdrew from this program area were 0.

Admissions Requirements:

Scores: Entries appear in this order: required test or GPA, minimum score (if required), median score of students entering in 2003–2004. Master's Programs: GRE-V no minimum stated; GRE-Q no minimum stated; GRE-V+Q no minimum stated; GRE-Analytical no minimum stated; overall undergraduate GPA 3.0; psychology GPA 3.0. GRE-Subject (Psychology) is required of those without psychology as their undergraduate major or minor. Eighteen hours of psychology courses with statistics and experimental (research methods) are required for those without psychology as their major/degree. A Test and Measurement course is required for the PsyD and MA programs. An Industrial/Organizational psychology course is required for the MA in I/O program. Doctoral Programs: GRE-V no minimum stated; GRE-Q no minimum stated; GRE-V+Q no minimum stated; GRE-Analytical no minimum stated; overall undergraduate GPA 3.0. The GRE-Subject is required of those without psychology as their undergraduate major or minor. Eighteen semester hours of psychology courses with statistics and experimental (research methods) are required for those without psychology as their major/degree. A Test and Measurement course is required for the PsyD program. *Other Criteria:* (importance of criteria rated low, medium, or high): GRE/MAT scores high, research experience medium, work experience medium, extracurricular activity low, clinically related public service medium, GPA high, letters of recommendation high, interview low, statement of goals and objectives high. For additional information on admission requirements, go to: www.xu.edu/psychology.

Student Characteristics: The following represents characteristics of students in 2004–2005 in all graduate psychology programs in the department: Female–full-time 74, part-time 12; Male–full-time 26, part-time 6; African American/Black–full-time 3, part-time 0; Hispanic/Latino(a)–full-time 0, part-time 0; Asian/Pacific Islander–full-time 1, part-time 0; American Indian/Alaska Native–full-time 0, part-time 0; Caucasian–full-time 96, part-time 18; Multi-ethnic–full-time 0, part-time 0.

Financial Information/Assistance:

Tuition for Full-Time Study: *Master's:* State residents: $498 per credit hour; Nonstate residents: $498 per credit hour. *Doctoral:* State residents: $650 per credit hour; Nonstate residents: $650 per credit hour.

Financial Assistance:

First Year Students: Research assistantships available for first-year. Average number of hours worked per week: 10. Apply by January 15. Tuition remission given: partial. Fellowships and scholarships available for first-year. Apply by January 15. Tuition remission given: partial.

Advanced Students: Teaching assistantships available for advanced students. Average number of hours worked per week: 10.

Apply by March 1. Tuition remission given: partial. Traineeships available for advanced students. Apply by March 1. Tuition remission given: partial. Fellowships and scholarships available for advanced students. Apply by March 1. Tuition remission given: partial.

Contact Information: Of all students currently enrolled full-time, 43% benefitted from one or more of the listed financial assistance programs. Application and information available online at: www.xu.edu/psychology.

Internships/Practica: In an urban setting, the university has established relationships with a number of private and public agencies, hospitals, and mental health care centers. Also, in conjunction with the three areas of interest in our PsyD program (child, the elderly, and the severely mentally disabled), training sites are matched. Students are given the opportunity to work with these populations in a number of settings. For those doctoral students for whom a professional internship is required prior to graduation, 18 applied in 2003–2004. Of those who applied, 16 were placed in internships listed by the Association of Psychology Postdoctoral and Internship Programs (APPIC); 16 were placed in APA accredited internships.

Housing and Day Care: No on-campus housing is available. No on-campus day care facilities are available.

Employment of Department Graduates:

Master's Degree Graduates: Of those who graduated in the academic year 2003–2004, the following categories and numbers represent the post-graduate activities and employment of master's degree graduates: Enrolled in a post-doctoral residency/fellowship (n/a), employed in independent practice (n/a), employed in business or industry (management) (7), still seeking employment (1), total from the above (master's) (8).

Doctoral Degree Graduates: Of those who graduated in the academic year 2003–2004, the following categories and numbers represent the post-graduate activities and employment of doctoral degree graduates: Enrolled in a psychology doctoral program (n/a), enrolled in a post-doctoral residency/fellowship (1), employed in independent practice (2), employed in a community mental health/counseling center (9), employed in a hospital/medical center (3), not seeking employment (1), other employment position (4), total from the above (doctoral) (20).

Additional Information:

Orientation, Objectives, and Emphasis of Department: Both the master's and doctoral programs provide students with the knowledge and range of skills necessary to provide psychological services in today's changing professional climate. Our objective for the master's students is to prepare them for entry into a doctoral program in their field or for immediate employment. Our objective for the doctoral program is to prepare students to serve as practitioner-scientists in their communities The basic philosophy of the PsyD program is to educate skilled practitioners who have a solid appreciation of the role of science in all aspects of professional activity. It is based on a practitioner-scientist model of training.

Special Facilities or Resources: The department has affiliation with the Psychological Services Center on campus, which provides psychological services to both the university population and the Greater Cincinnati community. The center provides the opportunity for training, service, and research. There are opportunities to work in various areas (e.g., student development) in the university. The department also has established contact with care providers in the community, which provides the opportunity to learn the delivery of service and research that occurs in such organizations.

Information for Students With Physical Disabilities: See the following Web site for more information: www.xu.edu/lac.

Application Information:
Send to: Margaret Maybury, Assistant Director, Enrollment and Student Services, Psychology Department, Xavier University, 3800 Victory Parkway Cincinnati, OH 45207-6511. Application available online. URL of online application: www.xu.edu/psychology. Students are admitted in the Fall, application deadline January 15. Febraury 1 deadline for master's applicants. There is a rolling deadline for the master's program if the open slots are not filled. *Fee:* $35.

Central Oklahoma, University of
Department of Psychology
100 North University Drive
Edmond, OK 73034
Telephone: (405) 974-5455
Fax: (405) 974-3822
E-mail: *mknight@ucok.edu*

Department Information:
1968. Chairperson: Mike Knight. Number of Faculty: total–full-time 13; women–full-time 7; minority–full-time 1.

Programs and Degrees Offered:
Listed in the following order: Program area, degree type (T if terminal Master's), number awarded 7/03–6/04. Counseling Psychology MA/MS (Master of Arts/Science) (T) 34, General Psychology MA/MS (Master of Arts/Science) (T) 0, Experimental Psychology MA/MS (Master of Arts/Science) 12.

Student Applications/Admissions:
Student Applications
Counseling Psychology MA/MS (Master of Arts/Science)—Applications 2004–2005, 98. Total applicants accepted 2004–2005, 87. Total enrolled 2004–2005 full-time, 121, part-time, 41. Openings 2005–2006, 25. The Median number of years required for completion of a degree are 2.5. The number of students enrolled full and part-time who were dismissed or voluntarily withdrew from this program area were 24. *General Psychology MA/MS (Master of Arts/Science)*—Applications 2004–2005, 0. Total applicants accepted 2004–2005, 0. Openings 2005–2006, 25. The number of students enrolled full and part-time who were dismissed or voluntarily withdrew from this program area were 0. *Experimental Psychology MA/MS (Master of Arts/Science)*—Applications 2004–2005, 30. Total applicants accepted 2004–2005, 27. Openings 2005–2006, 10. The Median number of years required for completion of a degree are 2. The number of students enrolled full and part-time who were dismissed or voluntarily withdrew from this program area were 5.

Admissions Requirements:
Scores: Entries appear in this order: required test or GPA, minimum score (if required), median score of students entering in 2003–2004. Master's Programs: GRE-V no minimum stated; GRE-Q no minimum stated; GRE-Analytical no minimum stated; overall undergraduate GPA 2.5; last 2 years GPA 2.75. Attain a combined score of 900 on Verbal + Quantitative, or a 3.5 on the GRE Written Test
Other Criteria: (importance of criteria rated low, medium, or high): research experience high, work experience medium, extracurricular activity medium, clinically related public service high, letters of recommendation high.

Student Characteristics: The following represents characteristics of students in 2004–2005 in all graduate psychology programs in the department: Female–full-time 54, part-time 10; Male–full-time 24, part-time 6; African American/Black–full-time 18, part-time 4; Hispanic/Latino(a)–full-time 9, part-time 1; Asian/Pacific Islander–full-time 7, part-time 0; American Indian/Alaska Native–full-time 6, part-time 0; Caucasian–full-time 81, part-time 0; Multi-ethnic–part-time 36; students subject to the Americans With Disabilities Act–full-time 7, part-time 3.

Financial Information/Assistance:
Tuition for Full-Time Study: *Master's:* State residents: $88 per credit hour; Nonstate residents: $207 per credit hour.

Financial Assistance:
First Year Students: No information provided.
Advanced Students: No information provided.
Contact Information: Of all students currently enrolled full-time, 0% benefitted from one or more of the listed financial assistance programs.

Internships/Practica: Practicum and internships are available through our program in Counseling Psychology. Students initially work in our departmental clinic and then are placed off-campus in community mental health clinics in our area.

Housing and Day Care: No on-campus housing is available. No on-campus day care facilities are available.

Employment of Department Graduates:
Master's Degree Graduates: Of those who graduated in the academic year 2003–2004, the following categories and numbers represent the post-graduate activities and employment of master's degree graduates: Enrolled in a post-doctoral residency/fellowship (n/a), employed in independent practice (n/a), total from the above (master's) (0).
Doctoral Degree Graduates: Of those who graduated in the academic year 2003–2004, the following categories and numbers represent the post-graduate activities and employment of doctoral degree graduates: Enrolled in a psychology doctoral program (n/a), total from the above (doctoral) (0).

Additional Information:
Orientation, Objectives, and Emphasis of Department: Excellent training to pursue doctoral work/General experimental option - or Licensed Professional Counselor (LPC), or Licensed Behavioral Practitioner (LPB)—Counseling Psychology Option.

Special Facilities or Resources: The department has excellent computer facilities. It also has excellent clinic facilities with audio/visual equipment to train students in community counseling.

Application Information:
Send to: Dean of the Graduate College, 100 North University Drive, University of Central Oklahoma, Edmund, OK 73034. Students are

admitted in the Fall, application deadline open; Spring, application deadline open; Summer, application deadline open. *Fee:* $0.

East Central University
Department of Psychology
1100 E. 14th Street
Ada, OK 74820-6999
Telephone: (580) 332 8000
Fax: (580) 310 5317
E-mail: *fpatrizi@mailclerk.ecok.edu*
Web: *http://www.ecok.edu*

Department Information:
1965. Chairperson: Fred Patrizi. Number of Faculty: total–full-time 6, part-time 3; women–full-time 2, part-time 2.

Student Applications/Admissions:
Other Criteria: (importance of criteria rated low, medium, or high): GRE/MAT scores medium, research experience medium, work experience medium, extracurricular activity medium, clinically related public service medium, GPA medium, letters of recommendation medium, interview medium, statement of goals and objectives medium.

Student Characteristics: The following represents characteristics of students in 2004–2005 in all graduate psychology programs in the department: Female–full-time 7, part-time 7; Male–full-time 2, part-time 0; Asian/Pacific Islander–full-time 1, part-time 0; American Indian/Alaska Native–full-time 1, part-time 1; Caucasian–full-time 7, part-time 6.

Financial Information/Assistance:
Tuition for Full-Time Study: *Master's:* State residents: per academic year $2,010, $85 per credit hour; Nonstate residents: per academic year $3,370, $155 per credit hour. Tuition is subject to change. See the following Web site for updates and changes in tuition costs: http://www.ecok.edu.

Financial Assistance:
First Year Students: Teaching assistantships available for first-year. Average number of hours worked per week: 20. Traineeships available for first-year.

Advanced Students: Teaching assistantships available for advanced students. Average amount paid per academic year: $2,700. Average number of hours worked per week: 10. Traineeships available for advanced students. Average amount paid per academic year: $2,700. Average number of hours worked per week: 10. Fellowships and scholarships available for advanced students.

Contact Information: Of all students currently enrolled full-time, 7% benefitted from one or more of the listed financial assistance programs.

Internships/Practica:
Students are assisted in obtaining practicum sites. They also have the option of locating their own sites. Several local sites are available at community mental health centers, counseling centers, and private psychiatric hospitals.

Housing and Day Care: On-campus housing is available. See the following Web site for more information: http://www.ecok.edu. On-campus day care facilities are available.

Employment of Department Graduates:
Master's Degree Graduates: Of those who graduated in the academic year 2003–2004, the following categories and numbers represent the post-graduate activities and employment of master's degree graduates: Enrolled in a psychology doctoral program (1), enrolled in a post-doctoral residency/fellowship (n/a), employed in independent practice (n/a), employed in a professional position in a school system (1), employed in business or industry (research/consulting) (2), employed in a government agency (professional services) (1), employed in a community mental health/counseling center (2), do not know (2), total from the above (master's) (9). *Doctoral Degree Graduates:* Of those who graduated in the academic year 2003–2004, the following categories and numbers represent the post-graduate activities and employment of doctoral degree graduates: Enrolled in a psychology doctoral program (n/a), total from the above (doctoral) (0).

Additional Information:
Orientation, Objectives, and Emphasis of Department: Emphasis is on graduate training designed for individuals interested in acquiring or upgrading their skills and providing psychological services to a variety of client populations. This program has been designated as a Master of Science in psychological services. This is an innovative program covering areas of study traditionally included in master's level programs in clinical psychology, mental health specialist, and community psychology. The program of study includes a balanced combination of required academic work and supervised practical experience to prepare the student to provide the psychological services of counseling, consulting, and testing. This graduate program in psychological services is being expanded to 60 semester hours, 12 of which are for practicum experience. A student also has an option of writing a thesis in lieu of six hours of practicum. Training is provided in psychological assessment and evaluation, theory and research, techniques of counseling and behavior change, and community consultation. The 60 hour program will allow students to meet all the core course requirements for Oklahoma licensing as either a Licensed Professional Counselor or a Licensed Behavioral Practitioner.

Special Facilities or Resources: Practicum students are expected to locate their own practicum sites; however, there are several local mental health facilities which accommodate students, including a community mental health center, a psychiatric hospital, and several counseling centers. Classes are held in a central location adjacent to faculty offices and training facilities. Small classes ensure close interaction between students and faculty.

Application Information:
Send to: Dr. Alvin Turner, Dean, School of Graduate Studies, 1100 E. 14th Street, East Central University, Ada, OK 74820-6999. Students are admitted in the Fall. Programs have rolling admissions. Programs have rolling admissions. *Fee:* $0.

Oklahoma State University

Department of Psychology
Arts & Sciences
215 North Murray Hall
Stillwater, OK 74078-3064
Telephone: (405) 744-6027
Fax: (405) 744-8067
E-mail: *maureen@okstate.edu*
Web: *http://psychology.okstate.edu*

Department Information:

1920. Head: Maureen A. Sullivan. Number of Faculty: total–full-time 18, part-time 1; women–full-time 7; minority–full-time 1.

Programs and Degrees Offered:

Listed in the following order: Program area, degree type (T if terminal Master's), number awarded 7/03–6/04. Clinical PhD (Doctor of Philosophy) 6, Life-Span Developmental PhD (Doctor of Philosophy) 1.

APA Accreditation: Clinical PhD (Doctor of Philosophy).

Student Applications/Admissions:

Student Applications

Clinical PhD (Doctor of Philosophy)—Applications 2004–2005, 95. Total applicants accepted 2004–2005, 14. Number enrolled (new admits only) 2004–2005 full-time, 7. Number enrolled (new admits only) 2004–2005 part-time, 0. Openings 2005–2006, 8. The Median number of years required for completion of a degree are 5. The number of students enrolled full and part-time who were dismissed or voluntarily withdrew from this program area were 2. *Life-Span Developmental PhD (Doctor of Philosophy)*—Applications 2004–2005, 11. Total applicants accepted 2004–2005, 3. Number enrolled (new admits only) 2004–2005 full-time, 2. Number enrolled (new admits only) 2004–2005 part-time, 0. Openings 2005–2006, 3. The Median number of years required for completion of a degree are 5. The number of students enrolled full and part-time who were dismissed or voluntarily withdrew from this program area were 0.

Admissions Requirements:

Scores: Entries appear in this order: required test or GPA, minimum score (if required), median score of students entering in 2003–2004. Master's Programs: GRE-V no minimum stated; GRE-Q no minimum stated; GRE-V+Q no minimum stated; GRE-Analytical no minimum stated; overall undergraduate GPA no minimum stated; last 2 years GPA no minimum stated; psychology GPA no minimum stated. No terminal masters program. Doctoral Programs: GRE-V no minimum stated, 540; GRE-Q no minimum stated, 600; GRE-V+Q no minimum stated, 1140; GRE-Analytical no minimum stated; overall undergraduate GPA no minimum stated, 3.5; last 2 years GPA no minimum stated, 3.78; psychology GPA no minimum stated, 3.8.

Other Criteria: (importance of criteria rated low, medium, or high): GRE/MAT scores high, research experience high, work experience low, extracurricular activity low, clinically related public service low, GPA high, letters of recommendation high, interview high, statement of goals and objectives high. For additional information on admission requirements, go to: http://psychology.okstate.edu/grad/index.html#app.

Student Characteristics: The following represents characteristics of students in 2004–2005 in all graduate psychology programs in the department: Female–full-time 38, part-time 0; Male–full-time 12, part-time 0; African American/Black–full-time 0, part-time 0; Hispanic/Latino(a)–full-time 8, part-time 0; Asian/Pacific Islander–full-time 3, part-time 0; American Indian/Alaska Native–full-time 9, part-time 0; Caucasian–full-time 29, part-time 0; Multi-ethnic–full-time 1, part-time 0; students subject to the Americans With Disabilities Act–full-time 0, part-time 0.

Financial Information/Assistance:

Tuition for Full-Time Study: *Master's:* State residents: $118 per credit hour; Nonstate residents: $393 per credit hour. *Doctoral:* State residents: $118 per credit hour; Nonstate residents: $393 per credit hour. Tuition is subject to change. See the following Web site for updates and changes in tuition costs: http://bursar.okstate.edu/tuitionestimate.asp.

Financial Assistance:

First Year Students: Teaching assistantships available for first-year. Average amount paid per academic year: $9,516. Average number of hours worked per week: 20. Tuition remission given: partial. Traineeships available for first-year. Average amount paid per academic year: $12,540. Average number of hours worked per week: 20. Tuition remission given: full. Fellowships and scholarships available for first-year. Average amount paid per academic year: $1,000. Average number of hours worked per week: 0.

Advanced Students: Teaching assistantships available for advanced students. Average amount paid per academic year: $10,947. Average number of hours worked per week: 20. Tuition remission given: partial. Research assistantships available for advanced students. Tuition remission given: partial. Traineeships available for advanced students. Average amount paid per academic year: $12,540. Average number of hours worked per week: 20. Tuition remission given: full. Fellowships and scholarships available for advanced students. Average amount paid per academic year: $1,000. Average number of hours worked per week: 0.

Contact Information: Of all students currently enrolled full-time, 100% benefitted from one or more of the listed financial assistance programs. Application and information available online at: http://psychology.okstate.edu/grad/index.html#app.

Internships/Practica: For clinical students, the first 2 years of practicum experience are through our on-site clinic. Advanced students are eligible to participate in external supervised practica at affiliated agencies. For those doctoral students for whom a professional internship is required prior to graduation, 6 applied in 2003–2004. Of those who applied, 6 were placed in internships listed by the Association of Psychology Postdoctoral and Internship Programs (APPIC); 6 were placed in APA accredited internships.

Housing and Day Care: On-campus housing is available. See the following Web site for more information: http://www.reslife.okstate.edu. No on-campus day care facilities are available.

Employment of Department Graduates:

Master's Degree Graduates: Of those who graduated in the academic year 2003–2004, the following categories and numbers

represent the post-graduate activities and employment of master's degree graduates: Enrolled in a post-doctoral residency/fellowship (n/a), employed in independent practice (n/a), total from the above (master's) (0).

Doctoral Degree Graduates: Of those who graduated in the academic year 2003–2004, the following categories and numbers represent the post-graduate activities and employment of doctoral degree graduates: Enrolled in a psychology doctoral program (n/a), enrolled in a post-doctoral residency/fellowship (2), employed in an academic position at a university (2), employed in an academic position at a 2-year/4-year college (3), employed in a government agency (professional services) (2), employed in a community mental health/counseling center (1), employed in a hospital/medical center (2), do not know (1), total from the above (doctoral) (13).

Additional Information:

Orientation, Objectives, and Emphasis of Department: The doctoral program in clinical psychology is based on the scientist-practitioner model. The program emphasizes the development of knowledge and skills in basic psychology, clinical theory, assessment and treatment procedures, and research. Practica, coursework, and internships are selected to enhance the student's interests. Students are expected, through additional coursework, specialized practica, and research, to develop a subspecialty in general clinical, clinical child, or health psychology. The program in Lifespan Developmental Psychology is a true life span program that has three primary goals: instruction in content areas of developmental psychology, training in research methodology and quantitative analysis, and preparation for teaching and/or research on applied topics. Students with interests in animal behavior, personality, psycholinguistics, and quantitative methods are also encouraged to apply.

Special Facilities or Resources: The Department of Psychology is located in North Murray near the center of the OSU campus. All students are provided office space that they share with 2 or 3 others. Each graduate student office is equipped with a personal computer with server access to SPSS, MS Office, the Internet, and printers. Every student is also provided a free email account. Graduate students also share a common room with a refrigerator, microwave oven, 2 additional computers, and a printer. In addition, the Department of Psychology maintains a 24-station computer lab for student research, teaching, and other endeavors. The department operates the Psychological Services Center, an on-campus facility for clinical work and research. The center has equipment and facilities to accommodate a number of specialized services and functions, including videotaping, direct observation of clinical work using one-way mirrors, and direct supervision through telephones placed in therapy rooms. The department maintains liaisons with many off-campus organizations and agencies which provide the student with access to special populations for research as well as clinical activities. The department offers a variety of support services through the Psychology Diversified Students Program and the Psychology Graduate Students Association. Students are provided preadmission and postadmission assistance.

Information for Students With Physical Disabilities: See the following Web site for more information: www.okstate.edu/ucs/stdis.

Application Information:

Send to: Maureen A. Sullivan, Department of Psychology, OSU, 215 N. Murray Hall, Stillwater, OK 74078-3064. Application available online. URL of online application: http://psychology.okstate.edu/grad/index.html#app. Students are admitted in the Fall: January 1 deadline for Clinical; January 15 Lifespan Developmental. *Fee:* $25.

Oklahoma State University

School of Applied Health and Educational Psychology
College of Education
434 Willard Hall
Stillwater, OK 74078
Telephone: (405) 744-6040
Fax: (405) 744-6756
E-mail: *al.carlozzi@okstate.edu*
Web: *http://www.okstate.edu/education/sahepcore.html*

Department Information:

1997. School Head: Dr. Al C. Carlozzi, EdD Number of Faculty: total–full-time 33, part-time 13; women–full-time 16, part-time 10; minority–full-time 2, part-time 7.

Programs and Degrees Offered:

Listed in the following order: Program area, degree type (T if terminal Master's), number awarded 7/03–6/04. Counseling Psychology PhD (Doctor of Philosophy) 8, School Psychology PhD (Doctor of Philosophy) 4, School Psychology EdS (Education Specialist) 2, Educational Psychology PhD (Doctor of Philosophy) 7.

APA Accreditation: Counseling PhD (Doctor of Philosophy). School PhD (Doctor of Philosophy).

Student Applications/Admissions:

Student Applications

Counseling Psychology PhD (Doctor of Philosophy)—Applications 2004–2005, 34. Total applicants accepted 2004–2005, 9. Number enrolled (new admits only) 2004–2005 full-time, 9. Number enrolled (new admits only) 2004–2005 part-time, 0. Total enrolled 2004–2005 full-time, 28, part-time, 16. Openings 2005–2006, 10. The Median number of years required for completion of a degree are 5. The number of students enrolled full and part-time who were dismissed or voluntarily withdrew from this program area were 0. *School Psychology PhD (Doctor of Philosophy)*—Applications 2004–2005, 16. Total applicants accepted 2004–2005, 11. Number enrolled (new admits only) 2004–2005 full-time, 10. Total enrolled 2004–2005 full-time, 20, part-time, 9. Openings 2005–2006, 6. The Median number of years required for completion of a degree are 5. The number of students enrolled full and part-time who were dismissed or voluntarily withdrew from this program area were 3. *School Psychology EdS (Education Specialist)*—Applications 2004–2005, 8. Total applicants accepted 2004–2005, 8. Number enrolled (new admits only) 2004–2005 full-time, 7. Total enrolled 2004–2005 full-time, 10, part-time, 8. Openings 2005–2006, 8. The Median number of years required for completion of a degree are 4. The number of students enrolled full and part-time who were dismissed or voluntarily withdrew from this program area were 0. *Educational Psychology PhD*

(*Doctor of Philosophy*)—Applications 2004–2005, 15. Total applicants accepted 2004–2005, 12. Number enrolled (new admits only) 2004–2005 full-time, 3. Number enrolled (new admits only) 2004–2005 part-time, 9. Total enrolled 2004–2005 full-time, 7, part-time, 24. Openings 2005–2006, 6. The Median number of years required for completion of a degree are 5. The number of students enrolled full and part-time who were dismissed or voluntarily withdrew from this program area were 0.

Admissions Requirements:

Scores: Entries appear in this order: required test or GPA, minimum score (if required), median score of students entering in 2003–2004. Master's Programs: GRE-V+Q no minimum stated, 936; MAT no minimum stated, 48.8; overall undergraduate GPA no minimum stated, 3.21. Doctoral Programs: overall undergraduate GPA no minimum stated, 3.32.

Other Criteria: (importance of criteria rated low, medium, or high): GRE/MAT scores high, research experience medium, work experience medium, extracurricular activity medium, clinically related public service low, GPA medium, letters of recommendation high, interview high, statement of goals and objectives high. School Psychology: work experience and clinically related public service low, letters and interview are high. For additional information on admission requirements, go to: http://gradcollege.okstate.edu/default.htm.

Student Characteristics: The following represents characteristics of students in 2004–2005 in all graduate psychology programs in the department: Female–full-time 48, part-time 42; Male–full-time 17, part-time 15; African American/Black–full-time 2, part-time 1; Hispanic/Latino(a)–full-time 2, part-time 0; Asian/Pacific Islander–full-time 2, part-time 2; American Indian/Alaska Native–full-time 8, part-time 6; Caucasian–full-time 49, part-time 46; Multi-ethnic–full-time 2, part-time 2; students subject to the Americans With Disabilities Act–full-time 0, part-time 0.

Financial Information/Assistance:

Tuition for Full-Time Study: *Master's:* State residents: per academic year $2,340, $130 per credit hour; Nonstate residents: per academic year $8,010, $445 per credit hour. *Doctoral:* State residents: per academic year $2,340, $130 per credit hour; Nonstate residents: per academic year $8,010, $445 per credit hour. Tuition is subject to change. Tuition costs vary by program. See the following Web site for updates and changes in tuition costs: http://bursar.okstate.edu/tuition.html.

Financial Assistance:

First Year Students: Teaching assistantships available for first-year. Average amount paid per academic year: $3,435. Average number of hours worked per week: 10. Apply by April 15. Tuition remission given: full and partial. Research assistantships available for first-year. Average amount paid per academic year: $6,866. Average number of hours worked per week: 20. Apply by April 15. Tuition remission given: full and partial. Traineeships available for first-year. Apply by N/A. Tuition remission given: partial. Fellowships and scholarships available for first-year. Average amount paid per academic year: $250. Apply by N/A. Tuition remission given: partial.

Advanced Students: Teaching assistantships available for advanced students. Average amount paid per academic year: $3,982. Average number of hours worked per week: 10. Apply by April 15. Tuition remission given: full and partial. Research assistantships available for advanced students. Average amount paid per academic year: $3,982. Average number of hours worked per week: 10. Apply by April 15. Tuition remission given: full and partial. Traineeships available for advanced students. Average amount paid per academic year: $4,800. Average number of hours worked per week: 20. Apply by N/A. Tuition remission given: partial. Fellowships and scholarships available for advanced students. Average amount paid per academic year: $250. Apply by N/A. Tuition remission given: partial.

Contact Information: Of all students currently enrolled full-time, 83% benefitted from one or more of the listed financial assistance programs. Application and information available on-line at: http://www.okstate.edu/education/prospectivestudentsflash.html.

Internships/Practica: Internships—Multiple settings for internship experiences are available nationally on a competitive basis, faculty must approve site selection. In the past, students have obtained internships in a wide variety of settings (i.e., health centers, hospital settings). Internships must meet established standards for pre-doctoral internships in counseling psychology. Practicum—Practicums are available at on-campus agencies, including a university counseling service, a mental health clinic at the student hospital, a career information center, and a marriage and family counseling service. Several off-campus placements are within a 75 mile radius of Stillwater, particularly in and around Tulsa and Oklahoma City, and sites include a stipend and public school settings. For those doctoral students for whom a professional internship is required prior to graduation, 10 applied in 2003–2004. Of those who applied, 10 were placed in internships listed by the Association of Psychology Postdoctoral and Internship Programs (APPIC); 9 were placed in APA accredited internships.

Housing and Day Care: On-campus housing is available. See the following Web site for more information: www.reslife.okstate.edu/housing02.htm or contact OSU Residential Life, 1st Floor IBA Hall, Stillwater, OK 74078-0636, Phone: (405) 744-5592, Fax: (405) 744-6775. No on-campus day care facilities are available.

Employment of Department Graduates:

Master's Degree Graduates: Of those who graduated in the academic year 2003–2004, the following categories and numbers represent the post-graduate activities and employment of master's degree graduates: Enrolled in a psychology doctoral program (11), enrolled in a post-doctoral residency/fellowship (n/a), employed in independent practice (n/a), employed in a government agency (research) (1), total from the above (master's) (12).

Doctoral Degree Graduates: Of those who graduated in the academic year 2003–2004, the following categories and numbers represent the post-graduate activities and employment of doctoral degree graduates: Enrolled in a psychology doctoral program (n/a), employed in an academic position at a university (1), employed in other positions at a higher education institution (1), still seeking employment (1), total from the above (doctoral) (3).

Additional Information:

Orientation, Objectives, and Emphasis of Department: Counseling Psychology—The orientation of the Counseling Psychology program is consistent both with the historical development of counseling psychology and with the current roles and functions of counseling psychology. We give major emphasis to prevention/

developmental/educational interventions, and to remediation of problems that arise in the normal development of relatively well functioning people. The focus on prevention and developmental change brings us to seek knowledge and skills related to facilitation of growth, such as training in education, consultation, environmental change and self-help. It is the focus upon the assets, skills and strengths, and possibilities for further development of persons that is most reflective of the general philosophical orientation of counseling psychology and of this program. School Psychology—The School Psychology program is based on the scientist-practitioner model, which emphasizes the application of the scientific knowledge base and methodological rigor in the delivery of school psychology services and in conducting research. Training in the scientist-practitioner model at OSU is for the purpose of developing a Science-Based Learner Success (SBLS) orientation in our students. Our philosophy is that all children and youth have the right to be successful and school psychologists are important agents who assist children, families, and others to be successful. Success refers not only to accomplishment of immediate goals but also to long range goals of adulthood such as contributing to society, social integration, meaningful work, and maximizing personal potentials. The SBLS orientation focuses on prevention and intervention services related to children's psychoeducational and mental health and wellness. School Specialist and Doctoral programs are also approved by the National Association of School Psychologists. Educational Psychology is concerned with all aspects of psychology that are relevant to education, in particular, focal areas in the professions of Human Development, Education of the Gifted and Talented, and Instructional Psychology. Educational Psychology—The Educational Psychology program brings together theory and research from psychology and related disciplines in order to facilitate healthy human development and effective learning and teaching in any educational setting. The program is designed to prepare graduates to teach in college or university settings, public education, and/or to do research in university, business, and government settings.

Special Facilities or Resources: Community/School Services, Counseling Psychology Clinic and the Reading and Math Clinic Training Facility.

Information for Students With Physical Disabilities: See the following Web site for more information: http://www.okstate.edu/ucs/stdis/index.html.

Application Information:
Send to: OSU Graduate College, Oklahoma State University, 202 Whitehurst, Stillwater, OK 74078-1019, Phone: (405) 744-6368 / Fax: (405) 744-0355. Please send program admission criteria to: College of Education, Graduate Studies Records, Oklahoma State University, 325 Willard, Stillwater, OK 74078. Application available online. URL of online application: http://gradcollege.okstate.edu/apply/default.htm. Students are admitted in the Fall and Spring. Counseling Psychology application deadlines: PhD: January 15, Master's: March 15 and October 15; School Psychology application deadline: PhD: February 1; Educational Psychology application deadline: PhD: February 1, Master's: Rolling Educational Specalist application deadline: PhD: March 1. *Fee:* $25. The application fee is non-refundable. The International application fee is $50.00.

Oklahoma, University of
Department of Educational Psychology
College of Education
820 Van Vleet Oval, Rm. 321
Norman, OK 73019-2041
Telephone: (405) 325-5974
Fax: (405) 325-6655
E-mail: gpoedpsych@ou.edu
Web: http://www.ou.edu/education/edpsy/epsy.htm

Department Information:
1986. Chairperson: Professor Barbara A. Greene. Number of Faculty: total–full-time 23; women–full-time 12; minority–full-time 4.

Programs and Degrees Offered:
Listed in the following order: Program area, degree type (T if terminal Master's), number awarded 7/03–6/04. Counseling Psychology PhD (Doctor of Philosophy) 5, Community Counseling MEd Other 7, Instructional Psychology and Technology MEd Other 12, Instructional Psychology and Technology PhD (Doctor of Philosophy) 1, School Counseling MEd Other 5, Special Education MEd Other 2, Special Education PhD (Doctor of Philosophy) 0.

APA Accreditation: Counseling PhD (Doctor of Philosophy).

Student Applications/Admissions:
Student Applications
Counseling Psychology PhD (Doctor of Philosophy)—Applications 2004–2005, 53. Total applicants accepted 2004–2005, 8. Number enrolled (new admits only) 2004–2005 full-time, 7. Number enrolled (new admits only) 2004–2005 part-time, 0. Total enrolled 2004–2005 full-time, 33, part-time, 11. Openings 2005–2006, 8. The Median number of years required for completion of a degree are 4. The number of students enrolled full and part-time who were dismissed or voluntarily withdrew from this program area were 1. *Community Counseling MEd Other*—Applications 2004–2005, 47. Total applicants accepted 2004–2005, 17. Number enrolled (new admits only) 2004–2005 full-time, 17. Total enrolled 2004–2005 full-time, 26, part-time, 1. Openings 2005–2006, 16. The Median number of years required for completion of a degree are 2. The number of students enrolled full and part-time who were dismissed or voluntarily withdrew from this program area were 0. *Instructional Psychology and Technology MEd Other*—Applications 2004–2005, 31. Total applicants accepted 2004–2005, 19. Number enrolled (new admits only) 2004–2005 full-time, 7. Number enrolled (new admits only) 2004–2005 part-time, 4. Total enrolled 2004–2005 full-time, 20, part-time, 11. Openings 2005–2006, 20. The Median number of years required for completion of a degree are 2.5. The number of students enrolled full and part-time who were dismissed or voluntarily withdrew from this program area were 4. *Instructional Psychology and Technology PhD (Doctor of Philosophy)*—Applications 2004–2005, 37. Total applicants accepted 2004–2005, 11. Number enrolled (new admits only) 2004–2005 full-time, 9. Number enrolled (new admits only) 2004–2005 part-time, 2. Total enrolled 2004–2005 full-time, 18, part-time, 8. Openings 2005–2006, 10. The Median number of years re-

quired for completion of a degree are 5. The number of students enrolled full and part-time who were dismissed or voluntarily withdrew from this program area were 2. *School Counseling MEd Other*—Applications 2004–2005, 11. Total applicants accepted 2004–2005, 5. Number enrolled (new admits only) 2004–2005 full-time, 5. Number enrolled (new admits only) 2004–2005 part-time, 0. Openings 2005–2006, 8. The Median number of years required for completion of a degree are 2. The number of students enrolled full and part-time who were dismissed or voluntarily withdrew from this program area were 0. *Special Education MEd Other*—Applications 2004–2005, 33. Total applicants accepted 2004–2005, 19. Number enrolled (new admits only) 2004–2005 full-time, 5. Number enrolled (new admits only) 2004–2005 part-time, 11. Total enrolled 2004–2005 full-time, 14, part-time, 9. Openings 2005–2006, 25. The Median number of years required for completion of a degree are 2.5. The number of students enrolled full and part-time who were dismissed or voluntarily withdrew from this program area were 3. *Special Education PhD (Doctor of Philosophy)*—Applications 2004–2005, 16. Total applicants accepted 2004–2005, 11. Number enrolled (new admits only) 2004–2005 full-time, 6. Number enrolled (new admits only) 2004–2005 part-time, 5. Total enrolled 2004–2005 full-time, 10, part-time, 8. Openings 2005–2006, 10. The Median number of years required for completion of a degree are 5. The number of students enrolled full and part-time who were dismissed or voluntarily withdrew from this program area were 3.

Admissions Requirements:
Scores: Entries appear in this order: required test or GPA, minimum score (if required), median score of students entering in 2003–2004. Master's Programs: GRE-V no minimum stated, 510; GRE-Q no minimum stated, 510; GRE-Analytical no minimum stated, 500; last 2 years GPA 2.75, 3.40. Doctoral Programs: GRE-V no minimum stated, 560; GRE-Q no minimum stated, 630; GRE-Analytical no minimum stated, 630; overall undergraduate GPA 3.00, 3.80; last 2 years GPA 3.0, 3.80. GPA of 3.0 for a minimum of 18 hours coursework in psychology or a related field is required for entrance into the Counseling Psychology PhD program.
Other Criteria: (importance of criteria rated low, medium, or high): GRE/MAT scores medium, research experience medium, work experience medium, extracurricular activity low, clinically related public service medium, GPA medium, letters of recommendation medium, interview high, statement of goals and objectives high. For additional information on admission requirements, go to: http://www.ou.edu/education/edpsy/epsy.htm.

Student Characteristics: The following represents characteristics of students in 2004–2005 in all graduate psychology programs in the department: Female–full-time 138, part-time 0; Male–full-time 50, part-time 0; African American/Black–full-time 16, part-time 0; Hispanic/Latino(a)–full-time 8, part-time 0; Asian/Pacific Islander–full-time 20, part-time 0; American Indian/Alaska Native–full-time 16, part-time 0; Caucasian–full-time 120, part-time 0; Multi-ethnic–full-time 0, part-time 0; students subject to the Americans With Disabilities Act–full-time 1, part-time 0.

Financial Information/Assistance:
Tuition for Full-Time Study: *Master's:* State residents: per academic year $3,859, $160 per credit hour; Nonstate residents: per

academic year $11,268, $469 per credit hour. *Doctoral:* State residents: per academic year $3,859, $160 per credit hour; Nonstate residents: per academic year $11,268, $469 per credit hour. Tuition is subject to change. See the following Web site for updates and changes in tuition costs: http://www.ou.edu.

Financial Assistance:
First Year Students: Teaching assistantships available for first-year. Average amount paid per academic year: $10,000. Average number of hours worked per week: 20. Apply by January 10. Tuition remission given: partial. Research assistantships available for first-year. Average amount paid per academic year: $10,000. Average number of hours worked per week: 20. Apply by January 10. Tuition remission given: partial. Traineeships available for first-year. Average amount paid per academic year: $12,000. Average number of hours worked per week: 20. Apply by January 10. Tuition remission given: partial.
Advanced Students: Teaching assistantships available for advanced students. Average amount paid per academic year: $10,000. Average number of hours worked per week: 20. Apply by April 15. Tuition remission given: partial. Research assistantships available for advanced students. Average amount paid per academic year: $10,000. Average number of hours worked per week: 20. Apply by April 15. Tuition remission given: partial. Traineeships available for advanced students. Average amount paid per academic year: $12,000. Average number of hours worked per week: 20. Apply by April 15. Tuition remission given: partial.
Contact Information: Of all students currently enrolled full-time, 66% benefitted from one or more of the listed financial assistance programs.

Internships/Practica: Master's: Numerous hospitals and clinics in the local area. Doctoral: Students choose from APA-accredited sites (two in the local area, and others across the nation). For those doctoral students for whom a professional internship is required prior to graduation, 8 applied in 2003–2004. Of those who applied, 8 were placed in internships listed by the Association of Psychology Postdoctoral and Internship Programs (APPIC); 8 were placed in APA accredited internships.

Housing and Day Care: On-campus housing is available. See the following Web site for more information: www.housing.ou.edu. On-campus day care facilities are available.

Employment of Department Graduates:
Master's Degree Graduates: Of those who graduated in the academic year 2003–2004, the following categories and numbers represent the post-graduate activities and employment of master's degree graduates: Enrolled in a psychology doctoral program (1), enrolled in a post-doctoral residency/fellowship (n/a), employed in independent practice (n/a), do not know (24), total from the above (master's) (25).
Doctoral Degree Graduates: Of those who graduated in the academic year 2003–2004, the following categories and numbers represent the post-graduate activities and employment of doctoral degree graduates: Enrolled in a psychology doctoral program (n/a), employed in an academic position at a university (1), do not know (6), total from the above (doctoral) (7).

Additional Information:
Orientation, Objectives, and Emphasis of Department: The Counseling Psychology program emphasizes training in working

with couples and families with children. The program has a scientist-practitioner orientation designed to encourage the professional development of the students. Minority applications are encouraged.

Personal Behavior Statement: We require students to sign an agreement to behave in accordance with APA ethical guidelines.

Special Facilities or Resources: The Counseling Psychology Clinic is a community-based training site for our students. The clientele reflects diverse diagnostic classifications with some cultural diversity. Couples, children, and families make up a large proportion of the population served by the clinic.

Information for Students With Physical Disabilities: See the following Web site for more information: http://www.sa.ou.edu/ods/.

Application Information:

Send to: Graduate Programs Officer, Department of Educational Psychology, University of Oklahoma, 820 Van Vleet Oval, Rm. 321, Norman, OK 73019-2041. Application available online. URL of online application: http://www.ou.edu/education/edpsy/epsy.htm. Students are admitted in the Fall, Spring, and Summer. Deadline for Counseling PhD is January 10 (Begins in fall semester), deadline for Community Counseling MEd is January 31 (Begins in summer semester), deadline for School Counseling MEd is January 31 (Begins in summer semester), deadlines for Instructional Psychology & Technology MEd: Spring—October 15; Fall—March 15 and July 1, deadline for Instructional Psychology & Technology PhD: Fall only—February 1, Special Education PhD—no deadline, fall admission only, special Education MEd—no deadline, spring and fall admission only. Fee: $0.

Oklahoma, University of
Department of Psychology
Arts and Sciences
455 West Lindsey
Norman, OK 73019-2007
Telephone: (405) 325-4511, (800) 522-0772, ext 4512
Fax: (405) 325-4737
E-mail: KPaine@ou.edu
Web: http://www.ou.edu/cas/psychology/

Department Information:

1928. Chairperson: Jorge Mendoza. Number of Faculty: total–full-time 22, part-time 11; women–full-time 11, part-time 4; minority–full-time 1, part-time 1.

Programs and Degrees Offered:

Listed in the following order: Program area, degree type (T if terminal Master's), number awarded 7/03–6/04. Industrial/organizational MA/MS (Master of Arts/Science) (T) 2, social PhD (Doctor of Philosophy) 1, animal cognition PhD (Doctor of Philosophy) 1, cognitive PhD (Doctor of Philosophy) 0, development PhD (Doctor of Philosophy) 1, experimental personality PhD (Doctor of Philosophy) 0, industrial/organizational PhD (Doctor of Philosophy) 4, quantitative/measurement PhD (Doctor of Philosophy) 0.

Student Applications/Admissions:
Student Applications

Industrial/organizational MA/MS (Master of Arts/Science)—Applications 2004–2005, 13. Total applicants accepted 2004–2005, 0. Number enrolled (new admits only) 2004–2005 full-time, 0. Openings 2005–2006, 2. The Median number of years required for completion of a degree are 2. The number of students enrolled full and part-time who were dismissed or voluntarily withdrew from this program area were 1. *Social PhD (Doctor of Philosophy)*—Applications 2004–2005, 26. Total applicants accepted 2004–2005, 5. Number enrolled (new admits only) 2004–2005 full-time, 2. Total enrolled 2004–2005 full-time, 8. Openings 2005–2006, 6. The Median number of years required for completion of a degree are 5. *Animal cognition PhD (Doctor of Philosophy)*—Applications 2004–2005, 6. Total applicants accepted 2004–2005, 0. Openings 2005–2006, 1. The Median number of years required for completion of a degree are 5. *Cognitive PhD (Doctor of Philosophy)*—Applications 2004–2005, 5. Total applicants accepted 2004–2005, 3. Number enrolled (new admits only) 2004–2005 full-time, 1. Openings 2005–2006, 5. *Development PhD (Doctor of Philosophy)*—Applications 2004–2005, 3. Total applicants accepted 2004–2005, 1. Number enrolled (new admits only) 2004–2005 full-time, 0. Openings 2005–2006, 3. The Median number of years required for completion of a degree are 6. *Experimental personality PhD (Doctor of Philosophy)*—Applications 2004–2005, 1. Total applicants accepted 2004–2005, 1. Number enrolled (new admits only) 2004–2005 full-time, 1. Openings 2005–2006, 3. *Industrial/Organizational PhD (Doctor of Philosophy)*—Applications 2004–2005, 32. Total applicants accepted 2004–2005, 15. Number enrolled (new admits only) 2004–2005 full-time, 7. Openings 2005–2006, 9. The Median number of years required for completion of a degree are 5. *Quantitative/Measurement PhD (Doctor of Philosophy)*—Applications 2004–2005, 5. Total applicants accepted 2004–2005, 2. Number enrolled (new admits only) 2004–2005 full-time, 1. Total enrolled 2004–2005 full-time, 9, part-time, 1. Openings 2005–2006, 2. The number of students enrolled full and part-time who were dismissed or voluntarily withdrew from this program area were 1.

Admissions Requirements:

Scores: Entries appear in this order: required test or GPA, minimum score (if required), median score of students entering in 2003–2004. Master's Programs: GRE-V no minimum stated; GRE-Q no minimum stated; GRE-V+Q no minimum stated; GRE-Analytical no minimum stated; overall undergraduate GPA no minimum stated; last 2 years GPA no minimum stated; psychology GPA no minimum stated. Doctoral Programs: GRE-V no minimum stated, 545; GRE-Q no minimum stated, 630; GRE-V+Q no minimum stated, 1175; GRE-Analytical no minimum stated; overall undergraduate GPA no minimum stated, 3.75; last 2 years GPA no minimum stated; psychology GPA no minimum stated.

Other Criteria: (importance of criteria rated low, medium, or high): GRE/MAT scores high, research experience high, extracurricular activity low, GPA high, letters of recommendation high, interview medium, statement of goals and objectives high.

Student Characteristics: The following represents characteristics of students in 2004–2005 in all graduate psychology programs in

the department: Female–full-time 31, part-time 1; Male–full-time 20, part-time 0; African American/Black–full-time 0, part-time 0; Hispanic/Latino(a)–full-time 1, part-time 0; Asian/Pacific Islander–full-time 4, part-time 0; American Indian/Alaska Native–full-time 0, part-time 0; Caucasian–full-time 46, part-time 1; Multi-ethnic–full-time 1, part-time 0; students subject to the Americans With Disabilities Act–full-time 0, part-time 1.

Financial Information/Assistance:

Tuition for Full-Time Study: *Master's:* State residents: $122 per credit hour; Nonstate residents: $431 per credit hour. *Doctoral:* State residents: $122 per credit hour; Nonstate residents: $431 per credit hour. Tuition is subject to change. See the following Web site for updates and changes in tuition costs: http://www.ou.edu/bursar/fees.htm.

Financial Assistance:

First Year Students: Teaching assistantships available for first-year. Average amount paid per academic year: $11,157. Average number of hours worked per week: 20. Tuition remission given: partial. Research assistantships available for first-year. Average amount paid per academic year: $11,157. Average number of hours worked per week: 20. Tuition remission given: partial. Fellowships and scholarships available for first-year. Average amount paid per academic year: $18,157. Average number of hours worked per week: 20. Tuition remission given: full.

Advanced Students: Teaching assistantships available for advanced students. Average amount paid per academic year: $11,907. Average number of hours worked per week: 20. Tuition remission given: partial. Research assistantships available for advanced students. Average amount paid per academic year: $11,907. Average number of hours worked per week: 20. Tuition remission given: partial.

Contact Information: Of all students currently enrolled full-time, 90% benefitted from one or more of the listed financial assistance programs. Application and information available online at: http://www.ou.edu/cas/psychology/grad/application.htm.

Internships/Practica: No information provided.

Housing and Day Care: On-campus housing is available. See the following Web site for more information: http://www.housing.ou.edu/. On-campus day care facilities are available. See the following Web site for more information: http://gradweb.ou.edu/docs/archives/Gb2001/generalinfo.htm.

Employment of Department Graduates:

Master's Degree Graduates: Of those who graduated in the academic year 2003–2004, the following categories and numbers represent the post-graduate activities and employment of master's degree graduates: Enrolled in a post-doctoral residency/fellowship (n/a), employed in independent practice (n/a), employed in business or industry (research/consulting) (2), total from the above (master's) (2).

Doctoral Degree Graduates: Of those who graduated in the academic year 2003–2004, the following categories and numbers represent the post-graduate activities and employment of doctoral degree graduates: Enrolled in a psychology doctoral program (n/a), employed in an academic position at a university (1), employed in an academic position at a 2-year/4-year college (1), employed in business or industry (research/consulting) (2), employed in a government agency (research) (4), employed in a government

agency (professional services) (1), total from the above (doctoral) (9).

Additional Information:

Orientation, Objectives, and Emphasis of Department: All programs are highly research oriented within the broad framework of experimental psychology. The department aims to produce creative and productive psychologists to function in academic and research settings, and toward this end emphasizes early and continuing involvement in research. Achievement of orientation and objectives is demonstrated by the excellent placement record of doctoral graduates, and by the department's recent rating as ninth in the nation in percent of publishing faculty. An excellent program in Quantitative Methods in Psychology is an especially attractive feature of the quality graduate training offered.

Special Facilities or Resources: The department offers modern research facilities with microprocessor-controlled laboratories, instrumentation shops with a full-time engineer, a small animal colony, a university computing center, and graduate offices located near faculty and departmental offices.

Application Information:

Send to: Graduate Admissions Committee, Department of Psychology, University of Oklahoma, 455 W. Lindsey, Room 705, Norman, OK 73019-2007. Application available online. URL of online application: http://www.ou.edu/cas/psychology/grad/application.htm. Students are admitted in the Fall, application deadline January 1. *Fee:* $25.

Oklahoma, University of, Health Sciences Center
Biological Psychology PhD Program
Graduate
P.O. Box 26901, ORI 332
Oklahoma City, OK 73190-3000
Telephone: (405) 271-2011, ext. 47717
Fax: (405) 271-6236
E-mail: *Larry-Gonzalez@ouhsc.edu (Program Director)*
Web: *http://w3.ouhsc.edu/biopsych*

Department Information:

1966. Director, Biological Psychology Program: Larry P. Gonzalez, PhD. Number of Faculty: total–full-time 18, part-time 14; women–full-time 8, part-time 5; minority–part-time 2.

Programs and Degrees Offered:

Listed in the following order: Program area, degree type (T if terminal Master's), number awarded 7/03–6/04. Biological Psychology PhD (Doctor of Philosophy) 6.

Student Applications/Admissions:

Student Applications

Biological Psychology PhD (Doctor of Philosophy)—Applications 2004–2005, 16. Total applicants accepted 2004–2005, 4. Openings 2005–2006, 3. The Median number of years required for completion of a degree are 5. The number of students enrolled full and part-time who were dismissed or voluntarily withdrew from this program area were 0.

Admissions Requirements:

Scores: Entries appear in this order: required test or GPA, minimum score (if required), median score of students entering in 2003–2004. Doctoral Programs: GRE-V 550, 550; GRE-Q 550, 610; GRE-V+Q 1100, 1160; GRE-Analytical no minimum stated, 673; overall undergraduate GPA 3.0, 3.50.

Other Criteria: (importance of criteria rated low, medium, or high): GRE/MAT scores medium, research experience high, work experience high, extracurricular activity low, GPA high, letters of recommendation high, interview medium, statement of goals and objectives high.

Student Characteristics: The following represents characteristics of students in 2004–2005 in all graduate psychology programs in the department: Female–full-time 0, part-time 0; Male–full-time 0, part-time 0; African American/Black–full-time 0, part-time 0; Hispanic/Latino(a)–full-time 0, part-time 0; Asian/Pacific Islander–full-time 0, part-time 0; American Indian/Alaska Native–full-time 0, part-time 0; Caucasian–full-time 0, part-time 0; Multiethnic–full-time 0, part-time 0; students subject to the Americans With Disabilities Act–full-time 0, part-time 0.

Financial Information/Assistance:

Tuition for Full-Time Study: *Doctoral:* State residents: $98 per credit hour; Nonstate residents: $226 per credit hour. Tuition is subject to change. See the following Web site for updates and changes in tuition costs: http://www.ouhsc.edu.

Financial Assistance:

First Year Students: Research assistantships available for first-year. Average amount paid per academic year: $18,156. Average number of hours worked per week: 20. Apply by March 1. Tuition remission given: partial. Traineeships available for first-year. Average amount paid per academic year: $18,156. Average number of hours worked per week: 20. Apply by March 1. Tuition remission given: full. Fellowships and scholarships available for first-year. Average amount paid per academic year: $18,156. Average number of hours worked per week: 20. Tuition remission given: full.

Advanced Students: Research assistantships available for advanced students. Average amount paid per academic year: $18,156. Average number of hours worked per week: 20. Apply by March 1. Tuition remission given: partial. Traineeships available for advanced students. Average amount paid per academic year: $18,156. Average number of hours worked per week: 20. Apply by March 1. Tuition remission given: full.

Contact Information: Of all students currently enrolled full-time, 50% benefitted from one or more of the listed financial assistance programs.

Internships/Practica: No information provided.

Housing and Day Care: On-campus housing is available. See the following Web site for more information: www.ou.edu/universityvillage (405) 325-2511. On-campus day care facilities are available.

Employment of Department Graduates:

Master's Degree Graduates: Of those who graduated in the academic year 2003–2004, the following categories and numbers represent the post-graduate activities and employment of master's degree graduates: Enrolled in a post-doctoral residency/fellowship (n/a), employed in independent practice (n/a), total from the above (master's) (0).

Doctoral Degree Graduates: Of those who graduated in the academic year 2003–2004, the following categories and numbers represent the post-graduate activities and employment of doctoral degree graduates: Enrolled in a psychology doctoral program (n/a), employed in other positions at a higher education institution (1), employed in business or industry (research/consulting) (2), total from the above (doctoral) (3).

Additional Information:

Orientation, Objectives, and Emphasis of Department: Graduate training in Biological Psychology offers opportunities to: (1) study biobehavioral processes with special emphasis on neuroscience and health-related conditions; (2) focus on basic mechanisms, consequences, and treatment of substance abuse; and (3) develop a multi-level, cross-disciplinary approach to conducting basic and applied research.

Personal Behavior Statement: Confidentiality Agreement: www.ouhsc.edu.

Special Facilities or Resources: The University of Oklahoma Health Sciences Center is located in a large complex that includes University Hospital, Children's Memorial Hospital, Veterans Administration Hospital, Presbyterian Hospital, Integris Medical Center, and the Oklahoma Medical Research Foundation. Research areas: Behavioral Sciences Laboratory, Cognitive Studies Laboratory, Psychobiology Laboratory, Neuropsychopharmacology Laboratory, Women's Health Laboratory, Sleep and G.I. Diseases Laboratory.

Information for Students With Physical Disabilities: See the following Web site for more information: www.ouhsc.edu.

Application Information:

Send to: Chair, Admissions Committee, Biological Psychology Program, University of Oklahoma HSC, P.O. Box 26901, ORI 332, Oklahoma City, OK 73190-3000. Students are admitted in the Fall, application deadline March 1. Program admits every other year (next admission: Fall, 2005). *Fee:* $75.

Tulsa, University of
Department of Psychology
600 South College Avenue
Tulsa, OK 74104-3189
Telephone: (918) 631-2248
Fax: (918) 631-2833
E-mail: *sandra-barney@utulsa.edu*
Web: *http://www.cas.utulsa.edu/psych/*

Department Information:

1926. Chairperson: Dr. Kurt Kraiger. Number of Faculty: total–full-time 15, part-time 5; women–full-time 5, part-time 3.

Programs and Degrees Offered:

Listed in the following order: Program area, degree type (T if terminal Master's), number awarded 7/03–6/04. Industrial/Organizational PhD (Doctor of Philosophy) 1, Industrial/Organizational MA/MS (Master of Arts/Science) (T) 6, Clinical Psychology MA/MS (Master of Arts/Science) (T) 7, Clinical Psychology PhD (Doctor of Philosophy) 6, Clinical MA/JD (Master of Arts/Science–Juris Doctor) (T) 0, Clinical Psychology Respecialization Diploma 0, Industrial/Organizational MA/JD Other 0.

APA Accreditation: Clinical PhD (Doctor of Philosophy).

Student Applications/Admissions:

Student Applications

Industrial/Organizational PhD (Doctor of Philosophy)—Applications 2004–2005, 28. Total applicants accepted 2004–2005, 3. Number enrolled (new admits only) 2004–2005 full-time, 3. Number enrolled (new admits only) 2004–2005 part-time, 0. Openings 2005–2006, 4. The Median number of years required for completion of a degree are 6. The number of students enrolled full and part-time who were dismissed or voluntarily withdrew from this program area were 0. *Industrial/Organizational MA/MS (Master of Arts/Science)*—Applications 2004–2005, 26. Total applicants accepted 2004–2005, 16. Number enrolled (new admits only) 2004–2005 full-time, 5. Number enrolled (new admits only) 2004–2005 part-time, 0. Total enrolled 2004–2005 full-time, 14, part-time, 1. Openings 2005–2006, 8. The Median number of years required for completion of a degree are 2. The number of students enrolled full and part-time who were dismissed or voluntarily withdrew from this program area were 0. *Clinical Psychology MA/MS (Master of Arts/Science)*—Applications 2004–2005, 11. Total applicants accepted 2004–2005, 7. Number enrolled (new admits only) 2004–2005 full-time, 4. Openings 2005–2006, 5. The Median number of years required for completion of a degree are 2. The number of students enrolled full and part-time who were dismissed or voluntarily withdrew from this program area were 1. *Clinical Psychology PhD (Doctor of Philosophy)*—Applications 2004–2005, 45. Total applicants accepted 2004–2005, 18. Number enrolled (new admits only) 2004–2005 full-time, 11. Number enrolled (new admits only) 2004–2005 part-time, 0. Openings 2005–2006, 5. The Median number of years required for completion of a degree are 6. The number of students enrolled full and part-time who were dismissed or voluntarily withdrew from this program area were 1. *Clinical MA/JD (Master of Arts/Science–Juris Doctor)*—Applications 2004–2005, 3. Total applicants accepted 2004–2005, 1. Openings 2005–2006, 2. The Median number of years required for completion of a degree are 5. The number of students enrolled full and part-time who were dismissed or voluntarily withdrew from this program area were 0. *Clinical Psychology Respecialization Diploma*—Applications 2004–2005, 2. Total applicants accepted 2004–2005, 0. Number enrolled (new admits only) 2004–2005 full-time, 0. Number enrolled (new admits only) 2004–2005 part-time, 0. Openings 2005–2006, 1. The Median number of years required for completion of a degree are 3. The number of students enrolled full and part-time who were dismissed or voluntarily withdrew from this program area were 0. *Industrial/Organizational MA/JD Other*—Applications 2004–2005, 0. Total applicants accepted 2004–2005, 0. Number enrolled (new admits only) 2004–2005 full-time, 0. Number enrolled (new admits only) 2004–2005 part-time, 0. Openings 2005–2006, 1. The Median number of years required for completion of a degree are 5. The number of

students enrolled full and part-time who were dismissed or voluntarily withdrew from this program area were 0.

Admissions Requirements:

Scores: Entries appear in this order: required test or GPA, minimum score (if required), median score of students entering in 2003–2004. Master's Programs: GRE-V no minimum stated, 570; GRE-Q no minimum stated, 590; GRE-V+Q no minimum stated; overall undergraduate GPA 3.00, 3.44. Minimum undergraduate GPA of 3.0 required for admission. No minimum GRE scores. Acceptable GRE scores in comparison to current applicant pool. Medians are reported for clinical. Admissions are based on total scores and other factors. Doctoral Programs: GRE-V no minimum stated, 500; GRE-Q no minimum stated, 620; overall undergraduate GPA 3.00, 3.83. Minimum undergraduate GPA of 3.0 required for admission. GRE scores are assessed in comparison to current applicant pool. Admissions are based on total scores and other factors.

Other Criteria: (importance of criteria rated low, medium, or high): GRE/MAT scores high, research experience high, work experience low, extracurricular activity low, clinically related public service medium, GPA high, letters of recommendation high, interview high, statement of goals and objectives high, quality of undergraduate institution medium. Interview for clinical only. For additional information on admission requirements, go to: www.cas.utulsa.edu/psych.

Student Characteristics: The following represents characteristics of students in 2004–2005 in all graduate psychology programs in the department: Female–full-time 55, part-time 0; Male–full-time 28, part-time 2; African American/Black–full-time 2, part-time 0; Hispanic/Latino(a)–full-time 3, part-time 0; Asian/Pacific Islander–full-time 8, part-time 0; American Indian/Alaska Native–full-time 4, part-time 0; Caucasian–full-time 66, part-time 2; Multi-ethnic–full-time 0, part-time 0; students subject to the Americans With Disabilities Act–full-time 0, part-time 0.

Financial Information/Assistance:

Tuition for Full-Time Study: *Master's:* State residents: $674 per credit hour; Nonstate residents: $674 per credit hour. *Doctoral:* State residents: $674 per credit hour; Nonstate residents: $674 per credit hour. Tuition is subject to change. See the following Web site for updates and changes in tuition costs: http://www.utulsa.edu/graduate/Files/Expenses/costest.htm.

Financial Assistance:

First Year Students: Teaching assistantships available for first-year. Average amount paid per academic year: $10,000. Average number of hours worked per week: 20. Apply by February 1. Tuition remission given: full. Research assistantships available for first-year. Average amount paid per academic year: $10,000. Average number of hours worked per week: 20. Apply by February 1. Tuition remission given: full. Fellowships and scholarships available for first-year. Average number of hours worked per week: 20. Apply by varies. Tuition remission given: full and partial.

Advanced Students: Teaching assistantships available for advanced students. Average amount paid per academic year: $11,000. Average number of hours worked per week: 20. Apply by February 1. Tuition remission given: full. Research assistantships available for advanced students. Average amount paid per academic year: $11,000. Average number of hours worked per week: 20. Apply by February 1. Tuition remission given: full. Fellowships and scholarships available for advanced students. Average number of hours worked per week: 20. Apply by varies. Tuition remission given: full and partial.

Contact Information: Of all students currently enrolled full-time, 50% benefitted from one or more of the listed financial assistance programs. Application and information available online at: http://www.utulsa.edu/Financial/Aid.html.

Internships/Practica: Supervised applied training begins early in the program. Practicum experiences occur primarily in community settings, utilizing the wide variety of agencies with which the department has relationships and allowing the student to interact with various mental health professionals. Placements include the university health center, community mental health centers, hospitals, community service agencies, and private practice groups. Attempts are made to allow students to choose practicum activities that are most consistent with their professional goals, although it is recognized that a diversity of experiences can provide a strong foundation for professional development. Practicum activities are supervised by an on-site professional, and the practicum experience is organized and monitored by the Coordinator of Practicum Training in conjunction with the Clinical Program Committee. For those doctoral students for whom a professional internship is required prior to graduation, 2 applied in 2003–2004. Of those who applied, 2 were placed in internships listed by the Association of Psychology Postdoctoral and Internship Programs (APPIC); 2 were placed in APA accredited internships.

Housing and Day Care: On-campus housing is available. See the following Web site for more information: http://www.utulsa.edu/housing/index.html. On-campus day care facilities are available. The University of Tulsa Child Development Center offers on-campus child care for the children of TU students, staff, and faculty, and the public. The center, which opened in January 1994, is operated by Children's World Learning Center. The facility features 7,900 square feet of interior space with a capacity for 148 children between the ages of 6 weeks and 12 years, and offers all day care, before and after school programs, and transportation to and from nearby Tulsa schools.

Employment of Department Graduates:

Master's Degree Graduates: Of those who graduated in the academic year 2003–2004, the following categories and numbers represent the post-graduate activities and employment of master's degree graduates: Enrolled in a psychology doctoral program (4), enrolled in a post-doctoral residency/fellowship (n/a), employed in independent practice (n/a), employed in business or industry (research/consulting) (2), employed in business or industry (management) (3), employed in a community mental health/counseling center (1), other employment position (1), do not know (2), total from the above (master's) (13).

Doctoral Degree Graduates: Of those who graduated in the academic year 2003–2004, the following categories and numbers represent the post-graduate activities and employment of doctoral degree graduates: Enrolled in a psychology doctoral program (n/a), enrolled in a post-doctoral residency/fellowship (2), employed in business or industry (research/consulting) (2), employed in a community mental health/counseling center (2), employed in a hospital/medical center (1), total from the above (doctoral) (7).

Additional Information:

Orientation, Objectives, and Emphasis of Department: Our graduate programs in applied psychology are central to the departmental mission, which is to generate new psychological knowledge to help individuals, organizations, and communities make decisions and solve problems; to offer a future-oriented, intellectually challenging, and socially relevant curriculum; and to equip students to make a difference through their work by providing them with an extensive knowledge base as well as the analytical and practical skills needed to apply knowledge wisely. Our programs train students to do what applied psychologists actually do in today's society. The programs in I/O psychology emphasize personnel psychology and organizational development, theory and behavior, with a special focus on individual assessment. The doctoral program in clinical psychology develops scientist–practitioners by using the following training components. First, coursework is distributed across clinical core, general psychology, methodology core, and elective offerings. Second, research mentoring is experienced in the precandidacy and dissertation projects. Third, procedural knowledge is developed in clinical practicum and internship training. Fourth, declarative knowledge is developed through comprehensive written and oral examinations covering general psychological knowledge and methods and clinical psychology.

Special Facilities or Resources: The Department of Psychology is located in Lorton Hall, a building located near the center of the TU campus. The building contains faculty offices, classrooms, offices for graduate students on assistantships, research space, and clinical training space. McFarlin Library, a two-minute walk from Lorton Hall, contains more than three million items and more than 6,000 periodical subscriptions. The library's catalogue is computerized and is accessible from terminals across campus. Computer searches of the major information databases in psychology are available to students at no charge. Students in psychology are strongly encouraged to become computer literate. Major computer application suites and statistical packages (e.g., SPSS) are available for word processing, data analyses, test interpretation, and other tasks. The university has several computer labs with a variety of hardware configurations and software packages for student use. Visiting scholars and professionals often join the graduate faculty in presenting special courses, workshops, and seminars. Each year, a number of colloquium speakers offer opinions, ideas, and research on topics of current interest in psychology.

Information for Students With Physical Disabilities: See the following Web site for more information: http://www.utulsa.edu/academicsupport/DisabilityServices.htm.

Application Information:
Send to: Graduate School, University of Tulsa, 600 S. College, Tulsa, OK 74104. Application available online. URL of online application: http://www.utulsa.edu/graduate/. Students are admitted in the Fall, application deadline December 1. Applications are reviewed once a year for a Fall entering semester. The application due date for the Fall 2006 entering semester is December 1, 2005. *Fee:* $30.

George Fox University

Graduate Department of Clinical Psychology
School of Behavioral and Health Sciences
414 North Meridian Street
Newberg, OR 97132-2697
Telephone: (503) 554-2761
Fax: (503) 537-3898
E-mail: *amcconau@georgefox.edu*
Web: *http://psyd.georgefox.edu*

Department Information:

1981. Chairperson: Wayne Adams. Number of Faculty: total–full-time 7, part-time 5; women–full-time 3, part-time 3; minority–part-time 1.

Programs and Degrees Offered:

Listed in the following order: Program area, degree type (T if terminal Master's), number awarded 7/03–6/04. Clinical Psychology PsyD (Doctor of Psychology) 17.

APA Accreditation: Clinical PsyD (Doctor of Psychology).

Student Applications/Admissions:

Student Applications

Clinical Psychology PsyD (Doctor of Psychology)—Applications 2004–2005, 105. Total applicants accepted 2004–2005, 29. Number enrolled (new admits only) 2004–2005 full-time, 21. Number enrolled (new admits only) 2004–2005 part-time, 0. Openings 2005–2006, 20. The Median number of years required for completion of a degree are 5. The number of students enrolled full and part-time who were dismissed or voluntarily withdrew from this program area were 1.

Admissions Requirements:

Scores: Entries appear in this order: required test or GPA, minimum score (if required), median score of students entering in 2003–2004. Master's Programs: A master's degree is awarded within the PsyD program. However, application and acceptance is made only to the PsyD program. Doctoral Programs: GRE-V+Q 1050, 1190; GRE-Subject(Psych) none, 490; overall undergraduate GPA 3.0, 3.54; last 2 years GPA no minimum stated; psychology GPA no minimum stated, 3.71. No rigid acceptance formula is used but each application is evaluated based upon overall individual strengths, and the potential to benefit from and contribute to the program as well as become a licensed psychologist. However, evidence must exist to document strong likelihood of academic and clinical success.
Other Criteria: (importance of criteria rated low, medium, or high): GRE/MAT scores medium, research experience low, work experience medium, extracurricular activity low, clinically related public service medium, GPA high, letters of recommendation high, interview high, statement of goals and objectives high, Christian worldview medium. For additional information on admission requirements, go to: http://psyd.georgefox.edu.

Student Characteristics: The following represents characteristics of students in 2004–2005 in all graduate psychology programs in the department: Female–full-time 48, part-time 0; Male–full-time 41, part-time 0; African American/Black–full-time 1, part-time 0; Hispanic/Latino(a)–full-time 3, part-time 0; Asian/Pacific Islander–full-time 5, part-time 0; American Indian/Alaska Native–full-time 2, part-time 0; Caucasian–full-time 77, part-time 0; Multi-ethnic–full-time 1, part-time 0; students subject to the Americans With Disabilities Act–full-time 1, part-time 0.

Financial Information/Assistance:

Tuition for Full-Time Study: *Doctoral:* State residents: $619 per credit hour; Nonstate residents: $619 per credit hour. Tuition is subject to change.

Financial Assistance:

First Year Students: Fellowships and scholarships available for first-year. Average amount paid per academic year: $4,000. Average number of hours worked per week: 0. Apply by March 30. Tuition remission given: partial.

Advanced Students: Teaching assistantships available for advanced students. Average amount paid per academic year: $3,000. Average number of hours worked per week: 6. Apply by variable. Research assistantships available for advanced students. Average amount paid per academic year: $2,100. Average number of hours worked per week: 5. Apply by variable. Fellowships and scholarships available for advanced students. Average amount paid per academic year: $4,000. Average number of hours worked per week: 0. Apply by March 30.

Contact Information: Of all students currently enrolled full-time, 50% benefitted from one or more of the listed financial assistance programs. Application and information available online at: http://psyd.georgefox.edu.

Internships/Practica: Students are required to complete four years of practicum (minimum of 1500 hours) in a variety of settings in the greater Portland metropolitan area. Practicum settings include hospitals, community mental health agencies, drug and alcohol programs, behavioral medicine clinics, schools, and prisons. In-patient and out-patient experiences are available. All practicum experience is gained under the careful supervision of licensed psychologists at the practicum sites. Additionally, students receive weekly oversight on campus by core faculty. Students apply for internships within the system developed by the Association of Psychology Postdoctoral and Internship Centers (APPIC). Students complete a one-year full-time internship (2000 hours) at an approved internship site during their fifth year in the program. For those doctoral students for whom a professional internship is required prior to graduation, 14 applied in 2003–2004. Of those who applied, 13 were placed in internships listed by the Association of Psychology Postdoctoral and Internship Programs (AP-PIC); 11 were placed in APA accredited internships.

Housing and Day Care: No on-campus housing is available. No on-campus day care facilities are available.

Employment of Department Graduates:

Master's Degree Graduates: Of those who graduated in the academic year 2003–2004, the following categories and numbers

represent the post-graduate activities and employment of master's degree graduates: Enrolled in another graduate/professional program (0), enrolled in a post-doctoral residency/fellowship (n/a), employed in independent practice (n/a), still seeking employment (0), total from the above (master's) (0).

Doctoral Degree Graduates: Of those who graduated in the academic year 2003–2004, the following categories and numbers represent the post-graduate activities and employment of doctoral degree graduates: Enrolled in a psychology doctoral program (n/a), enrolled in another graduate/professional program (0), enrolled in a post-doctoral residency/fellowship (15), employed in independent practice (0), employed in an academic position at a university (0), employed in an academic position at a 2-year/4-year college (1), employed in other positions at a higher education institution (0), employed in a professional position in a school system (1), employed in business or industry (research/consulting) (0), employed in business or industry (management) (0), employed in a government agency (research) (0), employed in a government agency (professional services) (2), employed in a community mental health/counseling center (4), employed in a hospital/medical center (2), still seeking employment (0), other employment position (1), total from the above (doctoral) (26).

Additional Information:

Orientation, Objectives, and Emphasis of Department: The goal of the Graduate Department of Clinical Psychology (GDCP) is to prepare professional psychologists who are competent to provide psychological services in a wide variety of clinical settings, who are knowledgeable in critical evaluation and application of psychological research, and who are committed to the highest standards of professional ethics. The central distinctive feature of the program is the integration of a Christian worldview and the science of psychology at philosophical, practical and personal levels. Graduates are trained broadly but also as specialists in meeting the unique psychological needs of the Christian community. Other distinctives of the program include close mentoring using clinical and research team models, and an option for training emphases in Assessment, Rural and Health Psychology. Graduates are prepared for licensure as clinical psychologists. Alumni of the GDCP are licensed in numerous states throughout the U.S. They engage in practice in a variety of settings, including independent and group practice, hospitals, community mental health clinics, government, corrections, public health agencies, and church and para-church organizations. Graduates also teach in a variety of settings, including colleges and seminaries.

Personal Behavior Statement: The statement appears both on the University's Web site as well as in the application for admission.

Special Facilities or Resources: High-speed microcomputers, laser printers, and complete statistical (SPSS PC+) and graphics software are provided in a computer lab on campus. The Murdock Learning Resource Center provides library support for the psychology program. The library has excellent access to materials important to contemporary clinical and empirical work in most areas of clinical psychology. In addition, the library receives more than 140 periodicals in psychology and related disciplines. Students also have online access to major computerized databases through library services, including PsycInfo, DIALOG, ERIC, and many others. In addition to full-text access to many psychology journals, George Fox University maintains cooperative arrangements with other local educational institutions providing psychology students with a full range of user services, including interlibrary loans and direct borrowing privileges. A full range of traditional campus facilities are also available such as athletic, arts outlets, student lounge and meal service.

Information for Students With Physical Disabilities: See the following Web site for more information: http://psyd.georgefox.edu.

Application Information:
Send to: Adina McConaughey, Graduate Admission Officer, Graduate School of Clinical Psychology, George Fox University, Box 6089, 414 North Meridian Street, Newberg, OR 97132, Phone: (503) 554-2263. Application available online. Students are admitted in the Winter, application deadline January 15. Special circumstances for delayed or late applications will be considered. *Fee:* $40.

Lewis & Clark College
Counseling Psychology Department
Graduate School of Education and Counseling
0615 SW Palatine Hill Road, Box 86
Portland, OR 97219-7899
Telephone: (503) 768-6060
Fax: (503) 768-6065
E-mail: *cpsy@lclark.edu*
Web: *http://education.lclark.edu/dept/cpsy/*

Department Information:
1972. Department Chair: Tod Sloan, PhD Number of Faculty: total–full-time 10, part-time 27; women–full-time 5, part-time 16; minority–full-time 1, part-time 3.

Programs and Degrees Offered:
Listed in the following order: Program area, degree type (T if terminal Master's), number awarded 7/03–6/04. School Psychology EdS (Education Specialist) 7, Addictions Treatment MA/MS (Master of Arts/Science) (T) 17, Community Counseling MA/MS (Master of Arts/Science) (T) 63, Marriage and Family Therapy MA/MS (Master of Arts/Science) (T) 0, Psychological and Cultural Studies MA/MS (Master of Arts/Science) (T) 1.

Student Applications/Admissions:
Student Applications
School Psychology EdS (Education Specialist)—Applications 2004–2005, 34. Total applicants accepted 2004–2005, 30. Number enrolled (new admits only) 2004–2005 full-time, 23. Total enrolled 2004–2005 full-time, 59. Openings 2005–2006, 20. The Median number of years required for completion of a degree are 3. The number of students enrolled full and part-time who were dismissed or voluntarily withdrew from this program area were 0. *Addictions Treatment MA/MS (Master of Arts/Science)*—Applications 2004–2005, 6. Total applicants

accepted 2004–2005, 6. Number enrolled (new admits only) 2004–2005 full-time, 5. Total enrolled 2004–2005 full-time, 30. Openings 2005–2006, 13. The Median number of years required for completion of a degree are 3. The number of students enrolled full and part-time who were dismissed or voluntarily withdrew from this program area were 1. *Community Counseling MA/MS (Master of Arts/Science)*—Applications 2004–2005, 74. Total applicants accepted 2004–2005, 70. Number enrolled (new admits only) 2004–2005 full-time, 48. Total enrolled 2004–2005 full-time, 143. Openings 2005–2006, 60. The Median number of years required for completion of a degree are 2. The number of students enrolled full and part-time who were dismissed or voluntarily withdrew from this program area were 1. *Marriage and Family Therapy MA/MS (Master of Arts/Science)*—Applications 2004–2005, 21. Total applicants accepted 2004–2005, 18. Number enrolled (new admits only) 2004–2005 full-time, 9. Total enrolled 2004–2005 full-time, 27. Openings 2005–2006, 10. The Median number of years required for completion of a degree are 3. The number of students enrolled full and part-time who were dismissed or voluntarily withdrew from this program area were 1. *Psychological and Cultural Studies MA/MS (Master of Arts/Science)*—Applications 2004–2005, 2. Total applicants accepted 2004–2005, 1. Number enrolled (new admits only) 2004–2005 full-time, 1. Total enrolled 2004–2005 full-time, 1. The Median number of years required for completion of a degree are 2.

Admissions Requirements:

Scores: Entries appear in this order: required test or GPA, minimum score (if required), median score of students entering in 2003–2004. Master's Programs: overall undergraduate GPA 2.75, 3.3. No minimum is required for GRE V + Q + Analytical.

Other Criteria: (importance of criteria rated low, medium, or high): GRE/MAT scores medium, research experience low, work experience low, extracurricular activity low, clinically related public service low, GPA medium, letters of recommendation high, statement of goals and objectives high, The Marriage and Family Therapy application requires an interview. For additional information on admission requirements, go to: http://education.lclark.edu/dept/gseadmit/.

Student Characteristics: The following represents characteristics of students in 2004–2005 in all graduate psychology programs in the department: Female–full-time 207, part-time 0; Male–full-time 53, part-time 0; African American/Black–full-time 2, part-time 0; Hispanic/Latino(a)–full-time 3, part-time 0; Asian/Pacific Islander–full-time 5, part-time 0; American Indian/Alaska Native–full-time 1, part-time 0; Caucasian–full-time 247, part-time 0; Multi-ethnic–full-time 2, part-time 0; students subject to the Americans With Disabilities Act–full-time 2, part-time 0.

Financial Information/Assistance:

Tuition for Full-Time Study: *Master's:* State residents: $590 per credit hour; Nonstate residents: $590 per credit hour. Tuition is subject to change.

Financial Assistance:

First Year Students: No information provided.
Advanced Students: No information provided.

Contact Information: Application and information available online at: http://www.lclark.edu/dept/cpsy/.

Internships/Practica: Internship and practicum placements in community agencies and schools provide students with opportunities for supervised professional practice. As part of each placement, students receive supervision from qualified professionals in their community or school setting. Students also receive weekly instruction and supervision from on-campus instructors throughout their internship and practicum placements. Required hours, supervision, and activities meet standards set by licensing bodies for students in their respective specialty areas. This ensures that students will be qualified to pursue licensing after completing their degree program. Internships in marriage and family therapy, community counseling, and addictions counseling involve part-time placements. Internships in school psychology are full-time for one academic year and usually involve a stipend to the student.

Housing and Day Care: On-campus housing is available. The undergraduate campus has housing, but most graduate students find apartment and houses in the immediate area. No on-campus day care facilities are available.

Employment of Department Graduates:

Master's Degree Graduates: Of those who graduated in the academic year 2003–2004, the following categories and numbers represent the post-graduate activities and employment of master's degree graduates: Enrolled in a post-doctoral residency/fellowship (n/a), employed in independent practice (n/a), total from the above (master's) (0).

Doctoral Degree Graduates: Of those who graduated in the academic year 2003–2004, the following categories and numbers represent the post-graduate activities and employment of doctoral degree graduates: Enrolled in a psychology doctoral program (n/a), total from the above (doctoral) (0).

Additional Information:

Orientation, Objectives, and Emphasis of Department: Lewis & Clark College's Department of Counseling Psychology prepares professional counselors, therapists, and school psychologists to lead, serve, and work for social justice in community and school settings. Faculty and students are committed to disseminating and expanding the knowledge base relevant to this mission, promoting the use of evidence-based treatment and prevention procedures, and adhering to the highest ethical standards as practitioners and researchers. The programs in counseling psychology prepare highly qualified mental health professionals for employment in public agencies, community-based programs, and schools. Curricular options also exist for those who would like to concentrate on research and establish a foundation in pursuit of doctoral training. We are especially interested in preparing students for multicultural competence and social justice advocacy.

Personal Behavior Statement: http://www.lclark.edu/dept/cpsy/objects/EthicalGuidelines.pdf.

Special Facilities or Resources: The program has established collaborative relationships with community schools and agencies which provide students opportunities to participate in ongoing research and program evaluation. These opportunities are open to students planning to complete a thesis and also to students who wish to secure increased training and experience without doing a full thesis.

Information for Students With Physical Disabilities: See the following Web site for more information: http://www.lclark.edu/~access.

Application Information:
Send to: Counseling Psychology Department, Lewis & Clark College, 0615 SW Palatine Hill Road, Box 86, Portland, OR 97219-7899. Application available online. URL of online application: http://www.lclark.edu/dept/gseadmit/. Programs have rolling admissions. Fall deadlines: March 1 and June 1, Spring deadlines: November 1, Summer deadlines: March 1. Special Students (not fully admitted to a program who may take 9 semester hours within one year) should consult admissions office for application deadlines. *Fee:* $50. Fee waived for online application.

Oregon, University of
Counseling Psychology
College of Education
5251 University of Oregon
Eugene, OR 97403-5251
Telephone: (541) 346-5501
Fax: (541) 346-6778
E-mail: *jodik@uoregon.edu*
Web: *http://counpsych.uoregon.edu*

Department Information:
1954. Area Head: Linda Forrest. Number of Faculty: total–full-time 4, part-time 2; women–full-time 3, part-time 2; minority–full-time 1.

Programs and Degrees Offered:
Listed in the following order: Program area, degree type (T if terminal Master's), number awarded 7/03–6/04. Counseling Psychology PhD (Doctor of Philosophy) 6.

APA Accreditation: Counseling PhD (Doctor of Philosophy).

Student Applications/Admissions:
Student Applications
Counseling Psychology PhD (Doctor of Philosophy)—Applications 2004–2005, 130. Total applicants accepted 2004–2005, 8. Number enrolled (new admits only) 2004–2005 full-time, 8. Number enrolled (new admits only) 2004–2005 part-time, 0. Total enrolled 2004–2005 full-time, 33, part-time, 6. Openings 2005–2006, 8. The Median number of years required for completion of a degree are 5. The number of students enrolled full and part-time who were dismissed or voluntarily withdrew from this program area were 0.

Admissions Requirements:
Scores: Entries appear in this order: required test or GPA, minimum score (if required), median score of students entering in 2003–2004. Doctoral Programs: GRE-V+Q 1100.
Other Criteria: (importance of criteria rated low, medium, or high): GRE/MAT scores medium, research experience high,

work experience medium, extracurricular activity medium, clinically related public service medium, GPA high, letters of recommendation high, interview high, statement of goals and objectives high. For additional information on admission requirements, go to: http://counpsych.uoregon.edu.

Student Characteristics: The following represents characteristics of students in 2004–2005 in all graduate psychology programs in the department: Female–full-time 26, part-time 4; Male–full-time 7, part-time 2; African American/Black–full-time 3, part-time 1; Hispanic/Latino(a)–full-time 6, part-time 0; Asian/Pacific Islander–full-time 5, part-time 3; American Indian/Alaska Native–full-time 0, part-time 0; Caucasian–full-time 13, part-time 2; Multi-ethnic–full-time 2, part-time 0; students subject to the Americans With Disabilities Act–full-time 0, part-time 0.

Financial Information/Assistance:
Tuition for Full-Time Study: *Doctoral:* State residents: per academic year $9,918; Nonstate residents: per academic year $15,903. Tuition is subject to change. See the following Web site for updates and changes in tuition costs: http://gradschool.uoregon.edu/grad-tuition.html. Note: There are additional fees and a surcharge.

Financial Assistance:
First Year Students: Teaching assistantships available for first-year. Average amount paid per academic year: $0. Average number of hours worked per week: 20. Tuition remission given: full. Fellowships and scholarships available for first-year. Average amount paid per academic year: $0. Average number of hours worked per week: 20. Tuition remission given: full.

Advanced Students: Teaching assistantships available for advanced students. Average amount paid per academic year: $0. Average number of hours worked per week: 20. Tuition remission given: full. Research assistantships available for advanced students. Average amount paid per academic year: $0. Average number of hours worked per week: 20. Tuition remission given: full. Fellowships and scholarships available for advanced students. Average amount paid per academic year: $0. Average number of hours worked per week: 20. Tuition remission given: full.

Contact Information: Of all students currently enrolled full-time, 100% benefitted from one or more of the listed financial assistance programs. Application and information available online at: http://financialaid.uoregon.edu/.

Internships/Practica: All students are required to participate in adult and child and family practica. For those doctoral students for whom a professional internship is required prior to graduation, 3 applied in 2003–2004. Of those who applied, 3 were placed in internships listed by the Association of Psychology Postdoctoral and Internship Programs (APPIC); 2 were placed in APA accredited internships.

Housing and Day Care: On-campus housing is available. See the following Web site for more information: http://housing.uoregon.edu/. On-campus day care facilities are available.

Employment of Department Graduates:
Master's Degree Graduates: Of those who graduated in the academic year 2003–2004, the following categories and numbers represent the post-graduate activities and employment of master's degree graduates: Enrolled in a psychology doctoral program (0),

enrolled in another graduate/professional program (0), enrolled in a post-doctoral residency/fellowship (n/a), employed in independent practice (n/a), employed in an academic position at a university (0), employed in an academic position at a 2-year/4-year college (0), employed in other positions at a higher education institution (0), employed in a professional position in a school system (0), employed in business or industry (research/consulting) (0), employed in business or industry (management) (0), employed in a government agency (research) (0), employed in a government agency (professional services) (0), employed in a community mental health/counseling center (0), employed in a hospital/medical center (0), still seeking employment (0), other employment position (0), total from the above (master's) (0).

Doctoral Degree Graduates: Of those who graduated in the academic year 2003–2004, the following categories and numbers represent the post-graduate activities and employment of doctoral degree graduates: Enrolled in a psychology doctoral program (n/a), enrolled in a post-doctoral residency/fellowship (1), employed in independent practice (0), employed in an academic position at a university (2), employed in an academic position at a 2-year/4-year college (0), employed in other positions at a higher education institution (1), employed in a professional position in a school system (0), employed in business or industry (research/consulting) (0), employed in business or industry (management) (0), employed in a government agency (research) (0), employed in a government agency (professional services) (0), employed in a community mental health/counseling center (2), employed in a hospital/medical center (1), still seeking employment (0), other employment position (0), do not know (2), total from the above (doctoral) (9).

Additional Information:

Orientation, Objectives, and Emphasis of Department: Accredited by the American Psychological Association (APA) since 1955, the UO doctoral program in Counseling Psychology emphasizes an ecological model of training, research, and practice. Students' focus is on research and training in prevention and treatment relevant to work with children, adolescents, families, and adults. The ecological model holds that human behavior occurs within a context of unique social, historical, political, and cultural factors. Behaviors, cognitions, and emotions are understood within these contextual influences. Students in the CPSY program are trained to view assessment, intervention, and research within the contexts of these factors.

Special Facilities or Resources: Students work cooperatively in research areas at Oregon Social Learning Center and Oregon Research Institute.

Information for Students With Physical Disabilities: See the following Web site for more information: http://ds.uoregon.edu/.

Application Information:

Send to: Academic Secretary, Counseling Psychology, 5251 University of Oregon, Eugene, OR, 97403-5251. Application available online. URL of online application: http://counpsych.uoregon.edu/admissions. htm. Students are admitted in the Fall, application deadline January 15. *Fee:* $50. Contact UO Admissions regarding conditions for waiver or deferral of fee.

Oregon, University of
Department of Psychology
College of Arts and Sciences
1227 University of Oregon
Eugene, OR 97403-1227
Telephone: (541) 346-5060
Fax: (541) 346-4911
E-mail: *gradsec@psych.uoregon.edu*
Web: *http://psychweb.uoregon.edu*

Department Information:
1895. Department Head: Marjorie Taylor, PhD. Number of Faculty: total–full-time 27, part-time 2; women–full-time 9, part-time 1; minority–full-time 4.

Programs and Degrees Offered:
Listed in the following order: Program area, degree type (T if terminal Master's), number awarded 7/03–6/04. Clinical PhD (Doctor of Philosophy) 3, Cognitive/Neuroscience PhD (Doctor of Philosophy) 3, Developmental PhD (Doctor of Philosophy) 0, Individualized Master's MA/MS (Master of Arts/Science) (T) 13, Social/ Personality PhD (Doctor of Philosophy) 1.

APA Accreditation: Clinical PhD (Doctor of Philosophy).

Student Applications/Admissions:
Student Applications

Clinical PhD (Doctor of Philosophy)—Applications 2004–2005, 200. Total applicants accepted 2004–2005, 4. Number enrolled (new admits only) 2004–2005 full-time, 4. Total enrolled 2004–2005 full-time, 24. Openings 2005–2006, 4. The Median number of years required for completion of a degree are 5. *Cognitive/Neuroscience PhD (Doctor of Philosophy)*—Applications 2004–2005, 56. Total applicants accepted 2004–2005, 4. Number enrolled (new admits only) 2004–2005 full-time, 4. Total enrolled 2004–2005 full-time, 15. Openings 2005–2006, 2. The Median number of years required for completion of a degree are 6. *Developmental PhD (Doctor of Philosophy)*—Applications 2004–2005, 36. Total applicants accepted 2004–2005, 0. Number enrolled (new admits only) 2004–2005 full-time, 0. Total enrolled 2004–2005 full-time, 9. Openings 2005–2006, 2. *Individualized Master's MA/MS (Master of Arts/Science)*—Applications 2004–2005, 22. Total applicants accepted 2004–2005, 13. Number enrolled (new admits only) 2004–2005 full-time, 13. Total enrolled 2004–2005 full-time, 26. Openings 2005–2006, 10. *Social/Personality PhD (Doctor of Philosophy)*—Applications 2004–2005, 60. Total applicants accepted 2004–2005, 3. Number enrolled (new admits only) 2004–2005 full-time, 3. Total enrolled 2004–2005 full-time, 15. Openings 2005–2006, 2. The Median number of years required for completion of a degree are 5.

Admissions Requirements:
Scores: Entries appear in this order: required test or GPA, minimum score (if required), median score of students entering in 2003–2004. Master's Programs: overall undergraduate GPA no minimum stated, 3.44. The GRE is recommended (not required) for admission to the Individualized Masters Program. Doctoral Programs: GRE-V no minimum stated, 625; GRE-Q no minimum stated, 692; GRE-Analytical no minimum

stated, 707; overall undergraduate GPA no minimum stated, 3.65.

Other Criteria: (importance of criteria rated low, medium, or high): GRE/MAT scores high, research experience high, work experience low, extracurricular activity low, clinically related public service medium, GPA high, letters of recommendation high, interview medium, statement of goals and objectives high. Please check with department regarding interviews. For additional information on admission requirements, go to: http://psychweb.uoregon.edu.

Student Characteristics: The following represents characteristics of students in 2004–2005 in all graduate psychology programs in the department: Female–full-time 58, part-time 0; Male–full-time 31, part-time 0; African American/Black–full-time 0, part-time 0; Hispanic/Latino(a)–full-time 3, part-time 0; Asian/Pacific Islander–full-time 15, part-time 0; American Indian/Alaska Native–full-time 0, part-time 0; Caucasian–full-time 66, part-time 0; Multi-ethnic–full-time 5, part-time 0; students subject to the Americans With Disabilities Act–full-time 0, part-time 0.

Financial Information/Assistance:
Financial Assistance:

    First Year Students: Teaching assistantships available for first-year. Tuition remission given: full. Research assistantships available for first-year. Tuition remission given: full.

    Advanced Students: Teaching assistantships available for advanced students. Tuition remission given: full. Research assistantships available for advanced students. Tuition remission given: full.

    Contact Information: Of all students currently enrolled full-time, 95% benefitted from one or more of the listed financial assistance programs.

Internships/Practica: For those doctoral students for whom a professional internship is required prior to graduation, 2 applied in 2003–2004. Of those who applied, 1 was placed in internships listed by the Association of Psychology Postdoctoral and Internship Programs (APPIC); 1 was placed in APA accredited internships.

Housing and Day Care: On-campus housing is available. See the following Web site for more information: http://housing.uoregon.edu. On-campus day care facilities are available. See the following Web site for more information: http://housing.uoregon.edu/FHA/child.html.

Employment of Department Graduates:

Master's Degree Graduates: Of those who graduated in the academic year 2003–2004, the following categories and numbers represent the post-graduate activities and employment of master's degree graduates: Enrolled in a post-doctoral residency/fellowship (n/a), employed in independent practice (n/a), total from the above (master's) (0).

Doctoral Degree Graduates: Of those who graduated in the academic year 2003–2004, the following categories and numbers represent the post-graduate activities and employment of doctoral degree graduates: Enrolled in a psychology doctoral program (n/a), total from the above (doctoral) (0).

Additional Information:

Orientation, Objectives, and Emphasis of Department: The course of study is tailored largely to the student's particular needs.

There are minimal formal requirements for the doctorate, which include three course sequences (contemporary issues in psychology, statistics, and a first-year research practicum); a supporting area requirement, consisting of at least two graduate-level, graded courses, and a major project, such as a paper or teaching an original course; a major preliminary examination; and, of course, the doctoral dissertation. Clinical students engage in several practica beginning in the first year. All programs require and are organized to facilitate student research from the first year.

Special Facilities or Resources: Straub Hall houses the psychology clinic, equipment for psychophysiological research, specialized facilities for research in child and social psychology, and experimental laboratories for human research. Numerous microcomputers are available for research and teaching. A short distance from the main psychology building are well-equipped animal labs for research in physiological psychology. Graduate students and faculty participate in interdisciplinary programs in cognitive science, neuroscience, and emotions research. Local nonprofit research groups, including Oregon Research Institute, Oregon Social Learning Center and Decision Research, provide unusual auspices and opportunities for students.

Information for Students With Physical Disabilities: See the following Web site for more information: http://ds.uoregon.edu/.

Application Information:
Send to: Graduate Admissions, Department of Psychology, 1227 University of Oregon, Eugene, OR 97403-1227. Application available online. URL of online application: http://psychweb.uoregon.edu. Students are admitted in the Fall, application deadline December 15. Individualized master's deadline for fall admission is May 15. *Fee:* $50.

Pacific University
School of Professional Psychology
2004 Pacific Avenue
Forest Grove, OR 97116
Telephone: (503) 352-2240
Fax: (503) 352-2134
E-mail: *spp@pacificu.edu*
Web: *http://www.pacificu.edu*

Department Information:
    1979. Dean: Michel Hersen. Number of Faculty: total–full-time 18, part-time 22; women–full-time 11, part-time 11; minority–full-time 2, part-time 3; faculty subject to the Americans With Disabilities Act 1.

Programs and Degrees Offered:
    Listed in the following order: Program area, degree type (T if terminal Master's), number awarded 7/03–6/04. Clinical PsyD (Doctor of Psychology) 22, Counseling MA/MS (Master of Arts/Science) (T) 24.

APA Accreditation: Clinical PsyD (Doctor of Psychology).

Student Applications/Admissions:
Student Applications
    Clinical PsyD (Doctor of Psychology)—Applications 2004–2005, 184. Total applicants accepted 2004–2005, 86. Number

enrolled (new admits only) 2004–2005 full-time, 45. Number enrolled (new admits only) 2004–2005 part-time, 3. Total enrolled 2004–2005 full-time, 165, part-time, 44. Openings 2005–2006, 48. The Median number of years required for completion of a degree are 5. The number of students enrolled full and part-time who were dismissed or voluntarily withdrew from this program area were 1. *Counseling MA/MS (Master of Arts/Science)*—Applications 2004–2005, 86. Total applicants accepted 2004–2005, 32. Number enrolled (new admits only) 2004–2005 full-time, 28. Number enrolled (new admits only) 2004–2005 part-time, 2. Total enrolled 2004–2005 full-time, 55, part-time, 4. Openings 2005–2006, 28. The Median number of years required for completion of a degree are 2. The number of students enrolled full and part-time who were dismissed or voluntarily withdrew from this program area were 2.

Admissions Requirements:

Scores: Entries appear in this order: required test or GPA, minimum score (if required), median score of students entering in 2003–2004. Master's Programs: overall undergraduate GPA no minimum stated, 3.0. Doctoral Programs: GRE-V no minimum stated; GRE-Q no minimum stated; GRE-V+Q no minimum stated, 1100; GRE-Analytical no minimum stated; last 2 years GPA no minimum stated, 3.1. Master's GPA is required for advanced standing applicants.

Other Criteria: (importance of criteria rated low, medium, or high): GRE/MAT scores medium, research experience medium, work experience medium, extracurricular activity low, clinically related public service low, GPA medium, letters of recommendation high, interview high, statement of goals and objectives medium, GRE scores required for PsyD program only. For additional information on admission requirements, go to: www.pacificu.edu.

Student Characteristics: The following represents characteristics of students in 2004–2005 in all graduate psychology programs in the department: Female–full-time 168, part-time 34; Male–full-time 60, part-time 6; African American/Black–full-time 1, part-time 0; Hispanic/Latino(a)–full-time 4, part-time 0; Asian/Pacific Islander–full-time 9, part-time 9; American Indian/Alaska Native–full-time 3, part-time 2; Caucasian–full-time 200, part-time 35; Multi-ethnic–full-time 4, part-time 1; students subject to the Americans With Disabilities Act–part-time 2.

Financial Information/Assistance:

Tuition for Full-Time Study: *Master's:* State residents: per academic year $14,859, $568 per credit hour; Nonstate residents: per academic year $14,859, $568 per credit hour. *Doctoral:* State residents: per academic year $19,950, $568 per credit hour; Nonstate residents: per academic year $19,950, $568 per credit hour. Tuition for 2004-2005 11-month academic year.

Financial Assistance:

First Year Students: Research assistantships available for first-year. Average amount paid per academic year: $3,000. Average number of hours worked per week: 7. Fellowships and scholarships available for first-year. Average amount paid per academic year: $3,000. Apply by January 10.

Advanced Students: Teaching assistantships available for advanced students. Average amount paid per academic year: $3,600. Average number of hours worked per week: 7. Apply by April 1. Research assistantships available for advanced students. Average amount paid per academic year: $3,000. Average number of hours worked per week: 7. Apply by April 1. Fellowships and scholarships available for advanced students. Average amount paid per academic year: $3,000. Apply by April 1.

Contact Information: Of all students currently enrolled full-time, 25% benefitted from one or more of the listed financial assistance programs.

Internships/Practica: Each PsyD student is required to complete 6 terms (24 credits, two years) of practica. The practicum experience includes a minimum of 500 training hours per year, approximately one third to one half of which are in direct service, one fourth in supervisory and training activities, and the remainder in administrative/clerical duties related to the above. Training entails the integration of theoretical knowledge through its application in clinical practice. The experience shall include supervised practice in the application of professional psychological competencies with a range of client populations, age groups, problems and service settings. The initial year of practicum is typically served at the Psychological Service Center. Later experiences are usually taken at community placements. Upon successful completion of practicum training, required coursework, and Candidacy Examination, the student is ready to begin an internship. Internship requires one calendar year of full-time experience, or two years half time, at an approved site. Internships are available at the school's Psychological Service Center. MA Counseling Psychology students complete 15 credits (3 terms) of practicum in their second year. For those doctoral students for whom a professional internship is required prior to graduation, 23 applied in 2003–2004. Of those who applied, 12 were placed in internships listed by the Association of Psychology Postdoctoral and Internship Programs (APPIC); 10 were placed in APA accredited internships.

Housing and Day Care: No on-campus housing is available. No on-campus day care facilities are available.

Employment of Department Graduates:

Master's Degree Graduates: Of those who graduated in the academic year 2003–2004, the following categories and numbers represent the post-graduate activities and employment of master's degree graduates: Enrolled in a psychology doctoral program (5), enrolled in a post-doctoral residency/fellowship (n/a), employed in independent practice (n/a), employed in other positions at a higher education institution (2), employed in a government agency (research) (2), employed in a community mental health/counseling center (14), total from the above (master's) (23).

Doctoral Degree Graduates: Of those who graduated in the academic year 2003–2004, the following categories and numbers represent the post-graduate activities and employment of doctoral degree graduates: Enrolled in a psychology doctoral program (n/a), enrolled in a post-doctoral residency/fellowship (7), employed in independent practice (8), employed in an academic position at a university (1), employed in other positions at a higher education institution (10), employed in business or industry (research/consulting) (1), employed in a government agency (professional services) (7), employed in a community mental health/counseling center (7), employed in a hospital/medical center (1), not seeking employment (1), do not know (3), total from the above (doctoral) (46).

Additional Information:

Orientation, Objectives, and Emphasis of Department: The Pacific University School of Professional Psychology follows a practitioner-scholar model of professional education, with coursework reflecting the latest empirical findings in the field. We emphasize the integration of a broad range of theoretical perspectives and foster development of the full range of professional psychological competencies in assessment, intervention, research/evaluation, consultation/education, and management supervision. We promote provision of services to diverse populations at the individual, family, group, and community levels. We strive to create a facilitative academic community based in collaborative inquiry. Faculty and students work together in multiple roles in program development and governance. We affirm the principles of promoting humanity, integrity, and self-awareness and of honoring diversity.

Special Facilities or Resources: The Psychological Service Center of the Pacific University School of Professional Psychology provides a full range of quality outpatient psychological services to residents of the Portland Metropolitan area while providing intensive training for doctoral level clinical psychology students and providing a setting for on-going clinical research. The full range of psychodiagnostic and treatment services is provided to a variety of client populations, including intellectual, personality, and neuropsychological assessment, individual therapy, family therapy, group therapy, and consultation.

Information for Students With Physical Disabilities: See the following Web site for more information: http://www.pacificu.edu/studentlife/lss.html.

Application Information:

Send to: Office of Admissions, Pacific University, 2043 College Way, Forest Grove, OR 97116. E-mail: admissions@pacificu.edu. Phone: (503) 352-2900; (877) 722-8648 ext 2900. Students are admitted in the Fall, application deadline January 10. MA Counseling Psychology—March 5. *Fee:* $40.

Portland State University

Psychology Department
College of Liberal Arts & Sciences
P.O. Box 751
Portland, OR 97207-0751
Telephone: (503) 725-3923
Fax: (503) 725-3904
E-mail: *mankowskie@pdx.edu*
Web: *http://www.psy.pdx.edu/*

Department Information:

1955. Chairperson: Keith L. Kaufman. Number of Faculty: total–full-time 17; women–full-time 9, part-time 1; minority–full-time 2.

Programs and Degrees Offered:

Listed in the following order: Program area, degree type (T if terminal Master's), number awarded 7/03–6/04. Applied developmental PhD (Doctor of Philosophy) 2, applied social & community PhD (Doctor of Philosophy) 2, industrial/organizational PhD (Doctor of Philosophy) 4.

Student Applications/Admissions:

Student Applications

Applied developmental PhD (Doctor of Philosophy)—Applications 2004–2005, 13. Total applicants accepted 2004–2005, 6. Number enrolled (new admits only) 2004–2005 full-time, 6. Openings 2005–2006, 4. The Median number of years required for completion of a degree are 6. The number of students enrolled full and part-time who were dismissed or voluntarily withdrew from this program area were 0. *Applied social & community PhD (Doctor of Philosophy)*—Applications 2004–2005, 30. Total applicants accepted 2004–2005, 4. Number enrolled (new admits only) 2004–2005 full-time, 4. Number enrolled (new admits only) 2004–2005 part-time, 0. Openings 2005–2006, 5. The Median number of years required for completion of a degree are 6. The number of students enrolled full and part-time who were dismissed or voluntarily withdrew from this program area were 0. *Industrial/Organizational PhD (Doctor of Philosophy)*—Applications 2004–2005, 80. Total applicants accepted 2004–2005, 4. Number enrolled (new admits only) 2004–2005 full-time, 4. Number enrolled (new admits only) 2004–2005 part-time, 0. Openings 2005–2006, 5. The Median number of years required for completion of a degree are 6. The number of students enrolled full and part-time who were dismissed or voluntarily withdrew from this program area were 0.

Admissions Requirements:

Scores: Entries appear in this order: required test or GPA, minimum score (if required), median score of students entering in 2003–2004. Master's Programs: GRE-V no minimum stated; GRE-Q no minimum stated; GRE-V+Q no minimum stated; GRE-Analytical no minimum stated; overall undergraduate GPA 3.00; last 2 years GPA no minimum stated; psychology GPA no minimum stated. Doctoral Programs: GRE-V no minimum stated; GRE-Q no minimum stated; GRE-V+Q 1100; GRE-Analytical no minimum stated; overall undergraduate GPA 3.00; last 2 years GPA no minimum stated; psychology GPA no minimum stated. Verbal + (quantitative or analytic) score must be at least 1100.

Other Criteria: (importance of criteria rated low, medium, or high): GRE/MAT scores high, research experience high, work experience medium, extracurricular activity medium, clinically related public service low, GPA high, letters of recommendation high, statement of goals and objectives high.

Student Characteristics: The following represents characteristics of students in 2004–2005 in all graduate psychology programs in the department: Female–full-time 47, part-time 0; Male–full-time 19, part-time 0; African American/Black–part-time 0; Hispanic/Latino(a)–part-time 0; Asian/Pacific Islander–part-time 0; American Indian/Alaska Native–part-time 0; Caucasian–full-time 0, part-time 0.

Financial Information/Assistance:

Tuition for Full-Time Study: *Master's:* State residents: per academic year $2,404; Nonstate residents: per academic year $4,078. *Doctoral:* State residents: per academic year $2,404; Nonstate residents: per academic year $4,078. Tuition is subject to change. See the following Web site for updates and changes in tuition costs: www.ess.pdx.edu/adm/sched/200301/Files/Tuition.pdf.

Financial Assistance:

First Year Students: Teaching assistantships available for first-year. Average amount paid per academic year: $5,100. Average number of hours worked per week: 12. Tuition remission given: full. Research assistantships available for first-year. Average amount paid per academic year: $5,100. Average number of hours worked per week: 12. Tuition remission given: full. Fellowships and scholarships available for first-year. Average amount paid per academic year: $5,100. Average number of hours worked per week: 12. Tuition remission given: full.

Advanced Students: Teaching assistantships available for advanced students. Average amount paid per academic year: $5,100. Average number of hours worked per week: 12. Tuition remission given: full. Research assistantships available for advanced students. Average amount paid per academic year: $5,100. Average number of hours worked per week: 12. Tuition remission given: full. Fellowships and scholarships available for advanced students. Average amount paid per academic year: $5,100. Average number of hours worked per week: 12. Tuition remission given: full.

Contact Information: Of all students currently enrolled full-time, 100% benefitted from one or more of the listed financial assistance programs.

Internships/Practica: The university is located in downtown Portland, the major metropolitan area in the state of Oregon. Consequently internships are readily available in a variety of applied settings. Placements are also available through the ongoing research activities of the faculty. The program is structured to provide everyone with (1) training in the basics of applied psychology and research methods, and (2) expertise in the psychological theories and research methods in their area of specialty. The basic training is provided by three advanced applied courses in the three areas we consider central to the understanding of social issues: social and group processes (referred to as Applied Social); organizational and institutional processes (referred to as Industrial-Organizational); and process of change (referred to as Applied Developmental). Training in research methods is provided via a sequence of Quantitative Methods courses, two of which are required. The Department offers a number of additional quantitative offerings which include: Factor Analysis, Structural Equation Modeling and Psychometrics and Scale Construction. Since the program emphasizes applied psychology, students receive training in their area of specialty not only through close work with faculty but also through structured participation in community organizations. Graduate students work in close collaboration with their faculty advisors and other members of the faculty who serve in a mentor role. Student experiences include seminars on special topics, individual reading and conference arrangements, research practica, and collaboration on joint projects. The primary vehicles for interactions with community organizations are practica and internships. To ensure relevant learning, these are supervised by departmental faculty. The program culminates for students in their own independent research (i.e., thesis and/or dissertation). For further information, see www.psy.pdx.edu/community/community.htm.

Housing and Day Care: On-campus housing is available. See the following Web site for more information: http://www.chnw.org/. On-campus day care facilities are available. See the following Web site for more information: http://www.hgcdc.pdx.edu/info/Parent%20Handbook04-05.pdf.

Employment of Department Graduates:

Master's Degree Graduates: Of those who graduated in the academic year 2003–2004, the following categories and numbers represent the post-graduate activities and employment of master's degree graduates: Enrolled in a post-doctoral residency/fellowship (n/a), employed in independent practice (n/a), total from the above (master's) (0).

Doctoral Degree Graduates: Of those who graduated in the academic year 2003–2004, the following categories and numbers represent the post-graduate activities and employment of doctoral degree graduates: Enrolled in a psychology doctoral program (n/a), total from the above (doctoral) (0).

Additional Information:

Orientation, Objectives, and Emphasis of Department: The department accepts applicants to both the MA/MS (initiated fall 1969) and PhD (initiated fall 1986) programs. The master's program is fully integrated into the doctoral program. Those who are admitted to the master's program may later apply for admission to the doctoral program, conditional upon demonstrated competence at the master's level. The PhD, but not the master's, program requires coursework and preliminary examinations in systems science. The aim of the program is to prepare graduates for a university career and/or a research/service career in a variety of settings, such as governmental agencies, manufacturing and service industries, health organizations and labor organizations. Students are given a broad background in applied psychology. Doctoral students major in one of the following three specialty areas and select a minor in a second. Applied Developmental focuses on family studies, providing training in two areas: a) family development, i.e., the processes of change that families as systems of member relationships experience, and b) family and work, i.e., the interactive relationships between the two domains of family and work life. Industrial-Organizational covers areas of theory, research methods, and social issues relevant to organizational and occupational life. Areas of study include leadership, work motivation, job stress, organizational development, etc. Applied Social/Community deals with how social-psychological research methods, findings, and theories are applied to: a) social issues (e.g., prejudice, violence, AIDS, and energy conservation); b) professions and institutions (e.g., health and law); and c) the design and evaluation of social interventions.

Special Facilities or Resources: The Department of Psychology's location in the heart of downtown Portland offers unique academic and research opportunities in the service of the Department's applied mission. Strong collaborative relationships with local industry, organizations, and community agencies offer venues for course related projects, faculty research initiatives, practicum placements, and required student research. A number of University-based resources also enhance our students' skills and experiences. For example, the University's writing center allows faculty and students to hone technical writing skills. The Instructional Development Center provides training in computer and media-based applications to foster improved teaching and more sophisticated research approaches.

Information for Students With Physical Disabilities: See the following Web site for more information: http://www.ess.pdx.edu/iasc/DSS/.

Application Information:
Send to: Portland State University, Department of Psychology, P.O. Box 751, Portland, OR 97207. Application available online. URL of online application: http://www.psy.pdx.edu/graduate/index.html. Students are admitted in the Fall, application deadline January 15. Application deadline previously February 1. *Fee:* $50.

Arcadia University

Department of Psychology
450 South Easton Road
Glenside, PA 19038-3295
Telephone: (267) 620-4130
Fax: (215) 881-8758
E-mail: *marshj@arcadia.edu*
Web: *http://www.arcadia.edu*

Department Information:
1986. Judith Marsh, PhD, Director, MAC: Barbara Nodine, Dept. Chair. Number of Faculty: total–full-time 6, part-time 13; women–full-time 3, part-time 7; minority–full-time 2, part-time 2.

Programs and Degrees Offered:
Listed in the following order: Program area, degree type (T if terminal Master's), number awarded 7/03–6/04. Community Counseling MA/MS (Master of Arts/Science) (T) 6, Elementary School Counseling MA/MS (Master of Arts/Science) (T) 4, Secondary School Counseling MA/MS (Master of Arts/Science) (T) 7.

Student Applications/Admissions:
Student Applications
Community Counseling MA/MS (Master of Arts/Science)—Applications 2004–2005, 21. Total applicants accepted 2004–2005, 19. Total enrolled 2004–2005 full-time, 13, part-time, 18. The Median number of years required for completion of a degree are 3. The number of students enrolled full and part-time who were dismissed or voluntarily withdrew from this program area were 2. *Elementary School Counseling MA/MS (Master of Arts/Science)*—Applications 2004–2005, 7. Total applicants accepted 2004–2005, 4. Total enrolled 2004–2005 full-time, 2, part-time, 5. The Median number of years required for completion of a degree are 4. The number of students enrolled full and part-time who were dismissed or voluntarily withdrew from this program area were 0. *Secondary School Counseling MA/MS (Master of Arts/Science)*—Applications 2004–2005, 10. Total applicants accepted 2004–2005, 8. Total enrolled 2004–2005 full-time, 4, part-time, 10. The Median number of years required for completion of a degree are 4. The number of students enrolled full and part-time who were dismissed or voluntarily withdrew from this program area were 0.

Admissions Requirements:
Scores: Entries appear in this order: required test or GPA, minimum score (if required), median score of students entering in 2003–2004. Master's Programs: GRE-V 280, 430; GRE-Q 340, 540; GRE-V+Q 690, 970; MAT 21, 42; overall undergraduate GPA 2.5, 3.3; psychology GPA 2.5, 3.33. Either GRE or MAT is required.
Other Criteria: (importance of criteria rated low, medium, or high): GRE/MAT scores medium, research experience medium, work experience medium, extracurricular activity medium, clinically related public service medium, GPA high,

letters of recommendation high, interview high, statement of goals and objectives high.

Student Characteristics: The following represents characteristics of students in 2004–2005 in all graduate psychology programs in the department: Female–full-time 19, part-time 26; Male–full-time 1, part-time 6; African American/Black–full-time 1, part-time 2; Hispanic/Latino(a)–full-time 1, part-time 2; Asian/Pacific Islander–full-time 0, part-time 0; American Indian/Alaska Native–full-time 0, part-time 0; Caucasian–full-time 18, part-time 28; Multi-ethnic–full-time 0, part-time 0; students subject to the Americans With Disabilities Act–full-time 1, part-time 1.

Financial Information/Assistance:
Tuition for Full-Time Study: *Master's:* State residents: $495 per credit hour; Nonstate residents: $495 per credit hour.

Financial Assistance:
First Year Students: No information provided.
Advanced Students: No information provided.
Contact Information: No information provided.

Internships/Practica: Pre-practicum and practicum required. Practica are arranged in the local community.

Housing and Day Care: No on-campus housing is available. No on-campus day care facilities are available.

Employment of Department Graduates:
Master's Degree Graduates: Of those who graduated in the academic year 2003–2004, the following categories and numbers represent the post-graduate activities and employment of master's degree graduates: Enrolled in a psychology doctoral program (0), enrolled in another graduate/professional program (0), enrolled in a post-doctoral residency/fellowship (n/a), employed in independent practice (n/a), employed in an academic position at a university (0), employed in an academic position at a 2-year/4-year college (0), employed in other positions at a higher education institution (0), employed in a professional position in a school system (6), employed in business or industry (research/consulting) (1), employed in business or industry (management) (0), employed in a government agency (research) (0), employed in a government agency (professional services) (0), employed in a community mental health/counseling center (6), employed in a hospital/medical center (0), still seeking employment (0), other employment position (4), total from the above (master's) (17).
Doctoral Degree Graduates: Of those who graduated in the academic year 2003–2004, the following categories and numbers represent the post-graduate activities and employment of doctoral degree graduates: Enrolled in a psychology doctoral program (n/a), total from the above (doctoral) (0).

Additional Information:
Orientation, Objectives, and Emphasis of Department: The MA in counseling prepares master's level psychologists for professional positions in schools, social service, rehabilitation, industrial, health, and mental health settings. Graduates will be able to work as community mental health specialists, mental health counselors,

crisis counselors, drug and alcohol counselors, illness and wellness counselors, geriatric counselors, employee-assistance counselors, school counselors, and staff developers or trainers. The program is designed to be completed on a part-time basis for the working professional. The orientation of the program is eclectic, although an emphasis is put upon behavioral-cognitive approaches. Pennsylvania now licenses master's level counselors as Professional Licensed Counselors (LPC). Arcadia University's Master of Arts in Counseling provides the academic background to apply for licensure once 3,600 hours of mandated experience are acquired.

Application Information:

Send to: Office of Enrollment Management, Arcadia University, Glenside, PA 19038-3295. Application available online. Students are admitted in the Fall, application deadline rolling; Winter, application deadline rolling; Spring, application deadline rolling; Summer, application deadline rolling; Programs have rolling admissions. *Fee:* $40. The application fee is waived for applications submitted during Graduate Open House programs organized by the Office of Graduate and Professional Studies. Online application fee $20.

Bryn Mawr College
Department of Psychology
101 North Merion Avenue
Bryn Mawr, PA 19010-2899
Telephone: (610) 526-5010
Fax: (610) 526-7476
E-mail: *lrescorl@brynmawr.edu*
Web: *http://www.brynmawr.edu*

Department Information:

1890. Chairperson: Kimberly Cassidy. Number of Faculty: total–full-time 7, part-time 5; women–full-time 3, part-time 5; minority–full-time 1.

Programs and Degrees Offered:

Listed in the following order: Program area, degree type (T if terminal Master's), number awarded 7/03–6/04. Clinical Developmental PhD (Doctor of Philosophy) 2.

Student Applications/Admissions:

Student Applications

Clinical Developmental PhD (Doctor of Philosophy)—Applications 2004–2005, 56. Total applicants accepted 2004–2005, 10. Number enrolled (new admits only) 2004–2005 full-time, 5. Total enrolled 2004–2005 full-time, 17, part-time, 21. Openings 2005–2006, 5. The Median number of years required for completion of a degree are 7. The number of students enrolled full and part-time who were dismissed or voluntarily withdrew from this program area were 1.

Admissions Requirements:

Scores: Entries appear in this order: required test or GPA, minimum score (if required), median score of students entering in 2003–2004. Doctoral Programs: GRE-V 490, 640; GRE-Q 500, 650; GRE-Analytical 400, 450; overall undergraduate GPA 3.3, 3.8.

Other Criteria: (importance of criteria rated low, medium, or high): GRE/MAT scores medium, research experience high,

work experience high, extracurricular activity low, clinically related public service medium, GPA high, letters of recommendation high, interview high, statement of goals and objectives high, quality of undergraduate institution high.

Student Characteristics: The following represents characteristics of students in 2004–2005 in all graduate psychology programs in the department: Female–full-time 17, part-time 19; Male–full-time 0, part-time 2; African American/Black–full-time 0, part-time 0; Hispanic/Latino(a)–full-time 0, part-time 0; Asian/Pacific Islander–full-time 0, part-time 1; American Indian/Alaska Native–full-time 0, part-time 0; Caucasian–full-time 16, part-time 20.

Financial Information/Assistance:

Tuition for Full-Time Study: *Doctoral:* Nonstate residents: per academic year $26,540.

Financial Assistance:

First Year Students: Teaching assistantships available for first-year. Average amount paid per academic year: $10,000. Average number of hours worked per week: 17. Research assistantships available for first-year. Average amount paid per academic year: $10,000. Average number of hours worked per week: 17.

Advanced Students: Teaching assistantships available for advanced students. Average amount paid per academic year: $13,000. Average number of hours worked per week: 17. Research assistantships available for advanced students. Average amount paid per academic year: $13,000. Average number of hours worked per week: 17.

Contact Information: Of all students currently enrolled full-time, 25% benefitted from one or more of the listed financial assistance programs.

Internships/Practica: one-half time assessment practicum (3rd year); one-half time therapy practicum (4th year); full-time internship (6th year; required). For those doctoral students for whom a professional internship is required prior to graduation, 7 applied in 2003–2004. Of those who applied, 6 were placed in internships listed by the Association of Psychology Postdoctoral and Internship Programs (APPIC); 6 were placed in APA accredited internships.

Housing and Day Care: No on-campus housing is available. No on-campus day care facilities are available.

Employment of Department Graduates:

Master's Degree Graduates: Of those who graduated in the academic year 2003–2004, the following categories and numbers represent the post-graduate activities and employment of master's degree graduates: Enrolled in a post-doctoral residency/fellowship (n/a), employed in independent practice (n/a), total from the above (master's) (0).

Doctoral Degree Graduates: Of those who graduated in the academic year 2003–2004, the following categories and numbers represent the post-graduate activities and employment of doctoral degree graduates: Enrolled in a psychology doctoral program (n/a), enrolled in a post-doctoral residency/fellowship (1), employed in an academic position at a university (1), total from the above (doctoral) (2).

Additional Information:

Orientation, Objectives, and Emphasis of Department: The department offers a broad program of graduate coursework integrated around a conception of the developing individual in changing family, school, and societal contexts. Students enrolled in the clinical developmental psychology doctoral program obtain an understanding of basic human psychological processes in their development across the life-span and acquire the requisite skills to conduct effective research on these processes. The clinical developmental psychology program adheres to the scientist-practitioner model and offers a life-span developmental context. The focus of the program is on children and families within the larger social contexts of school and community. Students typically also obtain certification in school psychology by their fourth year in the program.

Special Facilities or Resources: The greater Philadelphia area features a very large and diverse community of psychologists, as well as many medical schools, teaching hospitals, mental health facilities, and research settings. The Child Study Institute (CSI) is the clinical training facility of the Department of Psychology. Staffed by licensed psychologists (including members of the department faculty), reading and math specialists, and pre-doctoral trainees in the clinical developmental program, CSI offers diagnostic assessment, school admission testing, individual, family, group psychotherapy, and reading, math, and study skills tutoring. Each year, two or three doctoral students have placements at CSI. All students in the program receive some family therapy training with live supervision at CSI. The Phebe Anna Thorne School is a nursery school and preschool research laboratory for the Department of Psychology and includes programs for both normally developing children and language-delayed preschoolers. Two first-year doctoral students in the Department of Psychology serve as teaching assistants in the Thorne School each year.

Application Information:
Send to: Department of Psychology, Bryn Mawr College, 101 North Merion Avenue, Bryn Mawr, PA 19010. Students are admitted in the Fall, application deadline January 15. *Fee:* $30.

Bucknell University

Department of Psychology
O'Leary Center for Psychology and Geology
Lewisburg, PA 17837
Telephone: (570) 577-1200
Fax: (570) 577-7007
E-mail: *dwevans@bucknell.edu*
Web: *http://www.bucknell.edu*

Department Information:
1927. Chairperson: Dr. T. Joel Wade. Number of Faculty: total–full-time 11; women–full-time 3; minority–full-time 1.

Programs and Degrees Offered:
Listed in the following order: Program area, degree type (T if terminal Master's), number awarded 7/03–6/04. General Experimental Psychology MA/MS (Master of Arts/Science) (T) 3.

Student Applications/Admissions:
Student Applications
General Experimental Psychology MA/MS (*Master of Arts/Science*)—Applications 2004–2005, 15. Total applicants accepted 2004–2005, 3. Number enrolled (new admits only) 2004–2005 full-time, 3. Total enrolled 2004–2005 full-time, 6. Openings 2005–2006, 3. The Median number of years required for completion of a degree are 2. The number of students enrolled full and part-time who were dismissed or voluntarily withdrew from this program area were 0.

Admissions Requirements:
Scores: Entries appear in this order: required test or GPA, minimum score (if required), median score of students entering in 2003–2004. Master's Programs: GRE-V 550, 557; GRE-Q 550, 670; GRE-V+Q 1100, 1228; GRE-Analytical no minimum stated; GRE-Subject(Psych) no minimum stated, 697.
Other Criteria: (importance of criteria rated low, medium, or high): GRE/MAT scores medium, research experience medium, work experience low, extracurricular activity low, clinically related public service low, GPA medium, letters of recommendation high, statement of goals and objectives high, match with program high. The primary criteria are that there be a strong match between the research/academic interests of the prospective student and at least one faculty member who would serve as the advisor/mentor to that student. While interviews are not required, they are strongly recommended.

Student Characteristics: The following represents characteristics of students in 2004–2005 in all graduate psychology programs in the department: Female–full-time 5, part-time 0; Male–full-time 1, part-time 0; African American/Black–full-time 0, part-time 0; Hispanic/Latino(a)–full-time 0, part-time 0; Asian/Pacific Islander full-time 0, part-time 0; American Indian/Alaska Native full-time 0, part-time 0; Caucasian–full-time 6, part-time 0.

Financial Information/Assistance:
Tuition for Full-Time Study: *Master's:* State residents: $3,290 per credit hour; Nonstate residents: $3,290 per credit hour.

Financial Assistance:
First Year Students: Teaching assistantships available for first-year. Average amount paid per academic year: $8,200. Average number of hours worked per week: 20. Apply by March 1. Tuition remission given: full.
Advanced Students: Teaching assistantships available for advanced students. Average amount paid per academic year: $8,200. Average number of hours worked per week: 20. Apply by April 1. Tuition remission given: full.
Contact Information: Of all students currently enrolled full-time, 100% benefitted from one or more of the listed financial assistance programs.

Internships/Practica: While we offer no formal internship placements, there is ample opportunity for students to gain practical experience during their graduate studies at Bucknell. Bucknell University is located near Geisinger Medical Center and Danville State Psychiatric Hospital. These settings afford some potential research and training opportunities for students outside of the classroom. Occasionally, the University Psychological Services and Counseling Center offers a graduate assistantship that gives students training in counseling, mainly with undergraduates. Our laboratory course in child developments offers opportunities to observe children at the university day care center. Field work opportunities also exist for students interested in animal behavior and comparative psychology. Recently, we have had students initiate field opportunities leading to research on chimpanzees in Uganda and macaques in Indonesia.

Housing and Day Care: No on-campus housing is available. On-campus day care facilities are available.

Employment of Department Graduates:

Master's Degree Graduates: Of those who graduated in the academic year 2003–2004, the following categories and numbers represent the post-graduate activities and employment of master's degree graduates: Enrolled in a psychology doctoral program (2), enrolled in a post-doctoral residency/fellowship (n/a), employed in independent practice (n/a), total from the above (master's) (2). *Doctoral Degree Graduates:* Of those who graduated in the academic year 2003–2004, the following categories and numbers represent the post-graduate activities and employment of doctoral degree graduates: Enrolled in a psychology doctoral program (n/a), total from the above (doctoral) (0).

Additional Information:

Orientation, Objectives, and Emphasis of Department: The department is committed to providing training to students in general experimental psychology. The Master's Program is a full-time two year program that leads to either the MA or MS. The program is small, with an average of four or five students in psychology. The small size means that students work closely with faculty. Students typically take two seminars per semester, as well as a monthly proseminar led by faculty. The main focus of the program, however, is on conducting high-quality empirical research under the supervision of a faculty mentor. These research experiences typically form the basis for the master's thesis, which is a requirement of the program. The great majority of our students intend to continue on to PhD programs, and thus our goal is to give the kind of background and experience that will prepare the students for more advanced study. All of our graduate students become heavily involved in research in one of several well-equipped laboratories in comparative, physiological, learning, social, abnormal, developmental psychopathology, personality or developmental psychology. We do not offer a program in clinical psychology and do not provide clinical training as such, although our program provides an excellent background in research and coursework for students who hope to continue in doctoral programs in clinical psychology. We have had great success in recent years in placing students in PhD programs in psychology and related fields.

Special Facilities or Resources: In the autumn of 2002 the Psychology Department opened its doors to a new, state-of-the-art psychology building, The O'Leary Center. The O'Leary Center completes Bucknell's science quadrangle and is adjacent to the Biology and Chemistry buildings. The O'Leary Center offers abundant laboratory space that allows faculty to involve their students in research. These labs are equipped with computer facilities and cutting-edge research equipment used for training graduates and undergraduates in the latest research methods. Some examples of our lab facilities include several observation rooms complete with two-way mirrors and video-monitoring equipment; child observation and testing rooms for behavioral and neuropsychological assessment of children; psychophysiological feedback of heart-rate, blood pressure and skin response for research on emotions and social interaction; eye-tracking, color vision and sensory adaptation equipment; research tools for studying human cognition and memory; resources for studying nonhuman learning as well as stereotaxic equipment for studying brain-behavior associations. The department's primate facility includes four species of semi-naturally housed primates: Hamadryas baboons, Capuchin and squirrel monkeys, and lion-tailed macaques. These extraordinary facilities distinguish Bucknell's Psychology department from other universities of its kind.

Application Information:
Send to: Graduate Admissions Office, Bucknell University, Lewisburg, PA 17837. Fall admission only, deadline for admission and financial aid applications, March 1. Applications may still be considered after March 1 if spaces remain available. Prospective applicants are encouraged to contact the department in advance of March 1 for advice. *Fee:* $25.

Carnegie Mellon University
Department of Psychology
Baker Hall 342E
Pittsburgh, PA 15213
Telephone: (412) 268-5690
Fax: (412) 268-2798
E-mail: *Erin Dohahoe <donahoe@andrew.cmu.edu>*
Web: *http://www.psy.cmu.edu/*

Department Information:
1948. Head: Michael Scheier. Number of Faculty: total–full-time 25, part-time 6; women–full-time 9, part-time 4; minority–full-time 1.

Programs and Degrees Offered:
Listed in the following order: Program area, degree type (T if terminal Master's), number awarded 7/03–6/04. Cognitive PhD (Doctor of Philosophy) 3, Cognitive Neuroscience PhD (Doctor of Philosophy) 3, Developmental PhD (Doctor of Philosophy) 1, Social PhD (Doctor of Philosophy) 0, Psychology and Behavioral Decision Research PhD (Doctor of Philosophy) 0.

Student Applications/Admissions:
Student Applications

Cognitive PhD (Doctor of Philosophy)—Openings 2005–2006, 3. The number of students enrolled full and part-time who were dismissed or voluntarily withdrew from this program area were 0. *Cognitive Neuroscience PhD (Doctor of Philosophy)*—Openings 2005–2006, 3. The number of students enrolled full and part-time who were dismissed or voluntarily withdrew from this program area were 0. *Developmental PhD (Doctor of Philosophy)*—Openings 2005–2006, 2. The number of students enrolled full and part-time who were dismissed or voluntarily withdrew from this program area were 0. *Social PhD (Doctor of Philosophy)*—Openings 2005–2006, 3. The number of students enrolled full and part-time who were dismissed or voluntarily withdrew from this program area were 1. *Psychology and Behavioral Decision Research PhD (Doctor of Philosophy)*—Total enrolled 2004–2005 full-time, 3. Openings 2005–2006, 2. The number of students enrolled full and part-time who were dismissed or voluntarily withdrew from this program area were 0.

Admissions Requirements:

Scores: Entries appear in this order: required test or GPA, minimum score (if required), median score of students entering in 2003–2004. Doctoral Programs: GRE-V no minimum stated; GRE-Q no minimum stated; GRE-Analytical no minimum stated; overall undergraduate GPA no minimum stated. No specific scores—nothing weighted more than other requirements.

Other Criteria: (importance of criteria rated low, medium, or high): GRE/MAT scores high, research experience high, work experience low, GPA high, letters of recommendation high, statement of goals and objectives high.

Student Characteristics: The following represents characteristics of students in 2004–2005 in all graduate psychology programs in the department: Female–full-time 19, part-time 0; Male–full-time 16, part-time 0; African American/Black–full-time 1, part-time 0; Hispanic/Latino(a)–full-time 1, part-time 0; Asian/Pacific Islander–full-time 4, part-time 0; American Indian/Alaska Native–full-time 0, part-time 0; Caucasian–full-time 29, part-time 0; Multi-ethnic–full-time 0, part-time 0; students subject to the Americans With Disabilities Act–full-time 0, part-time 0.

Financial Information/Assistance:
Financial Assistance:

First Year Students: No information provided.

Advanced Students: No information provided.

Contact Information: Of all students currently enrolled full-time, 100% benefitted from one or more of the listed financial assistance programs.

Internships/Practica: No information provided.

Housing and Day Care: On-campus housing is available. Limited. No on-campus day care facilities are available.

Employment of Department Graduates:

Master's Degree Graduates: Of those who graduated in the academic year 2003–2004, the following categories and numbers represent the post-graduate activities and employment of master's degree graduates: Enrolled in a post-doctoral residency/fellowship (n/a), employed in independent practice (n/a), total from the above (master's) (0).

Doctoral Degree Graduates: Of those who graduated in the academic year 2003–2004, the following categories and numbers represent the post-graduate activities and employment of doctoral degree graduates: Enrolled in a psychology doctoral program (n/a), total from the above (doctoral) (0).

Additional Information:

Orientation, Objectives, and Emphasis of Department: The department offers doctoral programs in the areas of cognitive psychology, cognitive neuroscience, social-personality psychology, and developmental psychology. Because the graduate program is small, the student's course of study can be tailored to meet individual needs and interests. Further, students have many opportunities to work closely with faculty members on research projects of mutual interest. Carnegie Mellon University has a strong tradition of interdisciplinary research, and it is easy for students to interact with faculty and students from other graduate programs on campus. Many of our students take courses or engage in research with people from the Departments of Computer Science, Statistics, Social Science, English, Philosophy, and the Graduate School of Industrial Administration.

Special Facilities or Resources: Please see Web site (www.psy.cmu.edu).

Application Information:
Send to: Graduate Program Coordinator, Department of Psychology, Carnegie Mellon University, Pittsburgh, PA 15213. Application available online. Students are admitted in the Fall, application deadline December 15. *Fee:* $45. Financial hardship.

Carnegie Mellon University
Tepper School of Business at Carnegie Mellon
Schenley Park
Pittsburgh, PA 15213
Telephone: (412) 268-2301
Fax: (412) 268-7064
E-mail: *pg14+@andrew.cmu.edu*
Web: *http://wpweb2k.tepper.cmu.edu/obt/index.html*

Department Information:
PhD Coordinator: Paul S. Goodman. Number of Faculty: total–full-time 8; women–full-time 3.

Programs and Degrees Offered:
Listed in the following order: Program area, degree type (T if terminal Master's), number awarded 7/03–6/04. Organizational PhD (Doctor of Philosophy) 2.

Student Applications/Admissions:
Student Applications

Organizational PhD (Doctor of Philosophy)—Total applicants accepted 2004–2005, 4. Total enrolled 2004–2005 full-time, 9. Openings 2005–2006, 3.

Admissions Requirements:
Scores: Entries appear in this order: required test or GPA, minimum score (if required), median score of students entering in 2003–2004. Doctoral Programs: GRE-V no minimum stated; GRE-Q no minimum stated; GRE-V+Q no minimum stated; GRE-Analytical no minimum stated; overall undergraduate GPA no minimum stated.

Other Criteria: (importance of criteria rated low, medium, or high): GRE/MAT scores high, GPA high, letters of recommendation high, statement of goals and objectives high.

Student Characteristics: The following represents characteristics of students in 2004–2005 in all graduate psychology programs in the department: Female–full-time 5, part-time 0; Male–full-time 0, part-time 0; African American/Black–full-time 0, part-time 0; Hispanic/Latino(a)–full-time 0, part-time 0; Asian/Pacific Islander–full-time 4, part-time 0; American Indian/Alaska Native–full-time 0, part-time 0; Caucasian–full-time 0, part-time 0.

Financial Information/Assistance:

Financial Assistance:

    First Year Students: Fellowships and scholarships available for first-year. Apply by February 1. Tuition remission given: full.

    Advanced Students: Fellowships and scholarships available for advanced students. Apply by February 1. Tuition remission given: full.

    Contact Information: Of all students currently enrolled full-time, 100% benefitted from one or more of the listed financial assistance programs.

Internships/Practica: No information provided.

Housing and Day Care: No on-campus housing is available. No on-campus day care facilities are available.

Employment of Department Graduates:

Master's Degree Graduates: Of those who graduated in the academic year 2003–2004, the following categories and numbers represent the post-graduate activities and employment of master's degree graduates: Enrolled in a post-doctoral residency/fellowship (n/a), employed in independent practice (n/a), total from the above (master's) (0).

Doctoral Degree Graduates: Of those who graduated in the academic year 2003–2004, the following categories and numbers represent the post-graduate activities and employment of doctoral degree graduates: Enrolled in a psychology doctoral program (n/a), total from the above (doctoral) (0).

Additional Information:

Orientation, Objectives, and Emphasis of Department: The goal of the doctoral program in organizational psychology and theory at the Graduate School of Industrial Administration is to produce scientists who will make significant research contributions to our understanding of the structure and functioning of organizations. To achieve this goal the student is placed in a learning environment where a unique set of quantitative and discipline-based skills can be acquired. The opportunities for interdisciplinary work at GSIA provide new avenues for approaching organizational problems. The program attempts to combine structure and flexibility. Structure is achieved by identifying a set of core areas in which the student should become competent. These are quantitative methods, design and measurement, organization theory, and a selected specialty area. Flexibility in the program is achieved by having students and their advisers work out a combination of learning activities consistent with the students' interests and needs. Courses, participation in research projects, summer papers, and special tutorials with individual faculty are some of these learning activities. We have a new multiple-year NSF Traineeship Program in Groups and Technology. It draws on the CMU faculty on groups and CMU expertise in technology.

Application Information:
Send to: Tepper School of Business at Carnegie Mellon, PhD Program, Carnegie Mellon University, Pittsburgh, PA 15213. Application available online. URL of online application: http://web.gsia.cmu.edu/default.aspx?id=141049. Students are admitted in the Fall, application deadline February 1. *Fee:* $50.

Chatham College
Counseling Psychology
Woodland Road
Pittsburgh, PA 15232
Telephone: (412) 365-1704
Fax: (412) 365-1505
E-mail: *gnouel@chatham.edu*

Department Information:
1998. Director: Gloria E. Nouel PhD Number of Faculty: total–full-time 6, part-time 12; women–full-time 7, part-time 5; minority–full-time 1, part-time 1.

Programs and Degrees Offered:
Listed in the following order: Program area, degree type (T if terminal Master's), number awarded 7/03–6/04. Counseling MA/MS (Master of Arts/Science) (T) 35, Community/Organizational Psychology MA/MS (Master of Arts/Science) (T) 0.

Student Applications/Admissions:
Student Applications

    Counseling MA/MS (Master of Arts/Science)—Applications 2004–2005, 80. Total applicants accepted 2004–2005, 70. Number enrolled (new admits only) 2004–2005 full-time, 30. Number enrolled (new admits only) 2004–2005 part-time, 35. Total enrolled 2004–2005 full-time, 40, part-time, 108. Openings 2005–2006, 50. The Median number of years required for completion of a degree are 2. The number of students enrolled full and part-time who were dismissed or voluntarily withdrew from this program area were 4. *Community/Organizational Psychology MA/MS (Master of Arts/Science)*—Applications 2004–2005, 8. Total applicants accepted 2004–2005, 8. Number enrolled (new admits only) 2004–2005 full-time, 1. Number enrolled (new admits only) 2004–2005 part-time, 7. Total enrolled 2004–2005 full-time, 1, part-time, 7. Openings 2005–2006, 20. The number of students enrolled full and part-time who were dismissed or voluntarily withdrew from this program area were 0.

Admissions Requirements:
Scores: Entries appear in this order: required test or GPA, minimum score (if required), median score of students entering in 2003–2004. Master's Programs: overall undergraduate GPA 3.0. Students with undergraduate GPAs less than 3.0 may gain admission to the program with approval from the Program Director.

Other Criteria: (importance of criteria rated low, medium, or high): research experience low, work experience medium, extracurricular activity medium, clinically related public service medium, GPA medium, letters of recommendation medium, statement of goals and objectives medium. For additional information on admission requirements, go to: http://www. chatham.edu/graduate/counpsych/applicdescription.htm.

Student Characteristics: The following represents characteristics of students in 2004–2005 in all graduate psychology programs in the department: Female–full-time 40, part-time 100; Male–full-time 3, part-time 12; African American/Black–full-time 4, part-time 8; Hispanic/Latino(a)–full-time 2, part-time 1; Asian/Pacific Islander–part-time 0; American Indian/Alaska Native–full-time 0, part-time 0; Caucasian–full-time 25, part-time 99; Multi-ethnic–part-time 1; students subject to the Americans With Disabilities Act–full-time 0, part-time 3.

Financial Information/Assistance:

Tuition for Full-Time Study: *Master's:* State residents: $535 per credit hour; Nonstate residents: $535 per credit hour.

Financial Assistance:

First Year Students: No information provided.
Advanced Students: No information provided.
Contact Information: No information provided.

Internships/Practica: The program requires the completion of 48 credit hours. In addition to 15 courses (42 credit hours) of classroom instruction, students complete two field experiences: a 100 hour supervised practicum and a 2 600 hour supervised internship. Through these field experiences, students have the opportunity to apply the skills learned in the classroom directly to work with clients and within organizations, all under the supervision of appropriately trained professionals. Students completing the practicum and internship receive at least one (1) hour of individual supervision and 1.5 hours of group supervision per week. Individual supervision focuses on acquisition of skills, addressing issues related to the site or client, and provision of ideas to promote the growth of the client and student. Group supervision addresses a variety of topics related to the professional practice of counseling skills, including case conceptualization, ethical issues, and counselor self-care. Field placements are available at local hospitals, outpatient clinics, schools, and counseling centers. Specific experiences are available with children and adults with a variety of problems including substance abuse, mental health issues of all kinds, everyday adjustment problems, children's difficulties with school or peers, and medical problems. Paid field placement opportunities are available.

Housing and Day Care: On-campus housing is available. See the following Web site for more information: www.chatham.edu. No on-campus day care facilities are available.

Employment of Department Graduates:

Master's Degree Graduates: Of those who graduated in the academic year 2003–2004, the following categories and numbers represent the post-graduate activities and employment of master's degree graduates: Enrolled in a post-doctoral residency/fellowship (n/a), employed in independent practice (n/a), total from the above (master's) (0).
Doctoral Degree Graduates: Of those who graduated in the academic year 2003–2004, the following categories and numbers represent the post-graduate activities and employment of doctoral degree graduates: Enrolled in a psychology doctoral program (n/a), total from the above (doctoral) (0).

Additional Information:

Orientation, Objectives, and Emphasis of Department: The Master of Counseling Psychology Program prepares students for master-level positions in professions promoting optimal development of individuals, families, groups, organizations, and environmental systems. Master level trained psychology practitioners are employed in agencies and organizations providing mental health, health and social services. Both full-time and part-time students may attend day, evening, or weekend classes. Students are able to complete the program in four (4) consecutive semesters. They also have the opportunity to participate in one of the ongoing research projects. The curriculum integrates theory, research, and experiential approaches with practice. The program provides a strong theoretical foundation from a variety of perspectives as well as individual and group therapeutic and assessment skills. Through academic study and extensive supervised internships, students develop an understanding of issues concerning individual and socio-cultural diversity and learn to assess persons with psychological difficulties, design strategies for change, and evaluate the effectiveness of those interventions. Faculty span a range of theoretical ideologies, including Humanistic, Feminist, Existential-Phenomenological, Family Systems, and Cognitive Behavioral. The department encourages the student to explore which theoretical orientation most closely relates to her/his own goal, interests, and philosophy. In addition, a diverse range of clinical and research interests amongst the faculty enables students to participate in a wide variety of experiences.

Special Facilities or Resources: Chatham College is located in a park-like setting in Pittsburgh with ready access to dynamic research and educational opportunities throughout the city. There are nine other local colleges and universities in close proximity to Chatham College. This creates a vibrant academic atmosphere in which to learn, live, and conduct quality research. The city of Pittsburgh is home to 25,000 scientists and 170 research facilities. These include some of the best hospitals in the nation, often ranked among the top research hospitals in the country. Chatham College and the department of psychology have arrangements with many of these top quality facilities for students to engage in collaborative research and grant writing. In this manner, students can integrate their classroom experiences with clinical field work and research studies. Faculty support students' participation in ongoing research studies and in development of their own research ideas. Students receive encouragement to present their research at local and national conventions and to publish their research in professional journals. Faculty serve as mentors in these research endeavors and assist in development of community contacts. Supervisors at community agencies often offer ideas for research as well. Current grant funding enables students to engage in paid research activities.

Application Information:

Send to: Dr. Gloria E. Nouel. Application available online. URL of online application: www.chatham.edu. Students are admitted in the Fall, Spring, and Summer. Students can enter the program full-time in the fall or spring and part-time in the summer. While there is a rolling admission process, students are encouraged to submit their applications early. *Fee:* $35.

Chestnut Hill College
Department of Professional Psychology
9601 Germantown Avenue
Philadelphia, PA 19118-2693
Telephone: (215) 248-7077
Fax: (215) 248-7155
E-mail: *profpsyc@chc.edu*
Web: *http://www.chc.edu*

Department Information:
1987. Interim Chair: Scott W. Browning, PhD Number of Faculty: total–full-time 8, part-time 30; women–full-time 2, part-time 13; minority–full-time 1, part-time 2.

Programs and Degrees Offered:
Listed in the following order: Program area, degree type (T if terminal Master's), number awarded 7/03–6/04. Clinical Psychology PsyD (Doctor of Psychology) 8, Clinical and Counseling Psychology MA/MS (Master of Arts/Science) 62.

Student Applications/Admissions:
Student Applications

Clinical Psychology PsyD (Doctor of Psychology)—Number enrolled (new admits only) 2004–2005 part-time, 19. Total enrolled 2004–2005 full-time, 9, part-time, 74. Openings 2005–2006, 18. The Median number of years required for completion of a degree are 6. *Clinical and Counseling Psychology MA/MS (Master of Arts/Science)*—Total enrolled 2004–2005 full-time, 52, part-time, 149.

Admissions Requirements:

Scores: Entries appear in this order: required test or GPA, minimum score (if required), median score of students entering in 2003–2004. Master's Programs: Master's programs require either the Miller Analogies Test (MAT) or the GRE (General Test; subject test not required). Minimum scores are not specified. All factors are weighted in considering applications. Doctoral Programs: The PsyD and MS/PsyD programs require either the Miller Analogies Test (MAT) or the GRE (General Test; subject test not required). Minimum scores are not specified. All factors are weighted in considering applications.
Other Criteria: (importance of criteria rated low, medium, or high): GRE/MAT scores high, research experience low, work experience medium, extracurricular activity low, clinically related public service low, GPA high, letters of recommendation high, interview high, statement of goals and objectives high, writing ability high. Master's and Doctoral Programs require personal interviews prior to acceptance. The only program that uses cutoff scores is the MS/PsyD. All programs require either the MAT or the GRE. Writing ability is considered at the doctoral level. For additional information on admission requirements, go to: http://www.chc.edu/page_template.asp?section=3&file=353_admissions_process.

Student Characteristics: The following represents characteristics of students in 2004–2005 in all graduate psychology programs in the department: Female–full-time 49, part-time 187; Male–full-time 12, part-time 36; Caucasian–full-time 0, part-time 0.

Financial Information/Assistance:
Tuition for Full-Time Study: *Master's:* State residents: $435 per credit hour; Nonstate residents: $435 per credit hour. *Doctoral:* State residents: $650 per credit hour; Nonstate residents: $650 per credit hour. Tuition is subject to change.

Financial Assistance:
First Year Students: No information provided.
Advanced Students: No information provided.
Contact Information: No information provided.

Internships/Practica: Every student who attends either the master's program or the doctoral program at Chestnut Hill College in the Department of Professional Psychology must complete a practicum and internship. We have a faculty member dedicated to assisting students in securing the most appropriate site for their experiential training. At the present time the College has 45 mental health facilities which have been approved as sites for doctoral practica or internships. Doctoral students complete an assessment practicum as well as a clinical practicum. Students have the option of completing an APA, APPIC or non-APA/APPIC Internship. Students are encouraged to apply for APA/APPIC internships. For those doctoral students for whom a professional internship is required prior to graduation, 18 applied in 2003–2004. Of those who applied, 1 was placed in an internship listed by the Association of Psychology Postdoctoral and Internship Programs (APPIC); 3 were placed in APA accredited internships.

Housing and Day Care: No on-campus housing is available. No on-campus day care facilities are available.

Employment of Department Graduates:
Master's Degree Graduates: Of those who graduated in the academic year 2003–2004, the following categories and numbers represent the post-graduate activities and employment of master's degree graduates: Enrolled in a post-doctoral residency/fellowship (n/a), employed in independent practice (n/a), total from the above (master's) (0).
Doctoral Degree Graduates: Of those who graduated in the academic year 2003–2004, the following categories and numbers represent the post-graduate activities and employment of doctoral degree graduates: Enrolled in a psychology doctoral program (n/a), total from the above (doctoral) (0).

Additional Information:
Orientation, Objectives, and Emphasis of Department: The theoretical base of the Department of Professional Psychology at Chestnut Hill College is a complementary blend of psychodynamic and systems theories. The insights of psychodynamic theory, including modern object relations theory, serve as a method for understanding the individual. Likewise, the perspective of systems theory addresses ways individuals, families and communities influence one another. This synergistic blend of psychodynamic and systems theories stimulates discussion, research, and learning among faculty and students as we all move to an increasingly holistic understanding of human behavior within the family and social contexts that help define us. Additionally, the scholarly pursuits of faculty and students address issues related to empirical support for the varied theories and therapeutic interventions that make up the study and practice of psychology.

Special Facilities or Resources: Chestnut Hill College is located in Philadelphia, Pennsylvania. Due to our location we have numerous contacts with local academic and research facilities. We are part of a library consortium that increases the available lending privileges offered to each student.

Application Information:

Send to: Director of Graduate Admissions (Master's) or Director of PsyD Admissions (PsyD), Chestnut Hill College, 9601 Germantown Avenue, Philadelphia, PA 19118-2693. Students are admitted in the Fall, Spring, and Summer. Programs have rolling admissions. The PsyD and combined MS/PsyD programs admit students beginning only in the fall semester. Early application to PsyD encouraged. *Fee:* $50. PsyD and combined MS/PsyD application fee is $75. Master's application fee is $50.

Drexel University
Department of Psychology
College of Arts and Sciences
MS 626, 245 N. 15th Street
Philadelphia, PA 19102
Telephone: (215) 762-7249
Fax: (215) 762-8625
E-mail: *kirk.heilbrun@drexel.edu*
Web: *http://www.psychology.drexel.edu*

Department Information:

2002. Chairperson: Kirk Heilbrun. Number of Faculty: total–full-time 19, part-time 21; women–full-time 8, part-time 7; minority–full-time 1.

Programs and Degrees Offered:

Listed in the following order: Program area, degree type (T if terminal Master's), number awarded 7/03–6/04. Clinical PhD (Doctor of Philosophy) 12, Law and Psychology PsyD (Doctor of Psychology) 4, MS in Psychology (Non-Clinical) MA/MS (Master of Arts/Science) (T) 0.

APA Accreditation: Clinical PhD (Doctor of Philosophy).

Student Applications/Admissions:

Student Applications

Clinical PhD (Doctor of Philosophy)—Applications 2004–2005, 260. Total applicants accepted 2004–2005, 20. Number enrolled (new admits only) 2004–2005 full-time, 11. Openings 2005–2006, 10. The Median number of years required for completion of a degree are 5. The number of students enrolled full and part-time who were dismissed or voluntarily withdrew from this program area were 1. *Law and Psychology PsyD (Doctor of Psychology)*—Applications 2004–2005, 25. Total applicants accepted 2004–2005, 6. Number enrolled (new admits only) 2004–2005 full-time, 2. Openings 2005–2006, 2. The Median number of years required for completion of a degree are 7. The number of students enrolled full and part-time who were dismissed or voluntarily withdrew from this program area were 1. *MS in Psychology (Non-Clinical) MA/MS (Master of Arts/Science)*—Applications 2004–2005, 18. Total applicants accepted 2004–2005, 10. Number enrolled (new admits only) 2004–2005 full-time, 9. Total enrolled 2004–2005 full-time,

9. Openings 2005–2006, 12. The Median number of years required for completion of a degree are 2. The number of students enrolled full and part-time who were dismissed or voluntarily withdrew from this program area was 1.

Admissions Requirements:

Scores: Entries appear in this order: required test or GPA, minimum score (if required), median score of students entering in 2003–2004. Master's Programs: GRE-V no minimum stated, 510; GRE-Q no minimum stated, 540; GRE-V+Q no minimum stated, 1050; overall undergraduate GPA no minimum stated, 3.3. Doctoral Programs: GRE-V no minimum stated, 610; GRE-Q no minimum stated, 640; GRE-V+Q no minimum stated, 1250; GRE-Subject(Psych) no minimum stated, 630; overall undergraduate GPA no minimum stated, 3.6. Higher scores and GPA are expected for applicants to the doctoral programs.

Other Criteria: (importance of criteria rated low, medium, or high): GRE/MAT scores medium, research experience high, work experience medium, extracurricular activity low, clinically related public service medium, GPA medium, letters of recommendation medium, interview high, statement of goals and objectives high, fit with faculty mentor high.

Student Characteristics: The following represents characteristics of students in 2004–2005 in all graduate psychology programs in the department: Female–full-time 71, part-time 0; Male–full-time 10, part-time 0; African American/Black–full-time 4, part-time 0; Hispanic/Latino(a)–full-time 3, part-time 0; Asian/Pacific Islander–full-time 2, part-time 0; American Indian/Alaska Native–full-time 0, part-time 0; Caucasian–full-time 72, part-time 0; Multi-ethnic–full-time 0, part-time 0; students subject to the Americans With Disabilities Act–full-time 4, part-time 0.

Financial Information/Assistance:

Tuition for Full-Time Study: *Master's:* State residents: $730 per credit hour; Nonstate residents: $730 per credit hour. *Doctoral:* State residents: $730 per credit hour; Nonstate residents: $730 per credit hour. Tuition is subject to change.

Financial Assistance:

First Year Students: Teaching assistantships available for first-year. Average amount paid per academic year: $7,000. Average number of hours worked per week: 15. Tuition remission given: full. Research assistantships available for first-year.

Advanced Students: Research assistantships available for advanced students. Average amount paid per academic year: $7,000. Average number of hours worked per week: 10. Tuition remission given: full. Traineeships available for advanced students. Tuition remission given: full.

Contact Information: Of all students currently enrolled full-time, 90% benefitted from one or more of the listed financial assistance programs.

Internships/Practica: On-campus practicum sites include the Student Counseling and Development Center, the Forensic Clinic, Projects Social Fear, STOP and Challenge, and the Heart Failure/Cardiac Transplant Center. Off-campus practicum sites include a variety of in-/outpatient psychiatric units, Children's Hospital of Philadelphia and approximately sixty other practicum sites. For those doctoral students for whom a professional internship is required prior to graduation, 17 applied in 2003–2004. Of those who applied, 16 were placed in internships listed by the Association of Psychology Postdoctoral and Internship Programs (APPIC); 16 were placed in APA accredited internships.

Housing and Day Care: On-campus housing is available. Center City Campus on Campus Housing: Stiles Alumni Hall houses up to 315 undergraduate and graduate students from the Center City Campus and Queen Lane campuses. The Hall contains one, two, and three bedroom unfurnished apartments. Each student is given their own bedroom, but will share a kitchen, bathroom and living space. The bedrooms are carpeted and each room has temperature control, cable, local phone service, and internet access. Main Campus: Drexel main campus has seven residence halls and is home to approximately 2,600 residents. Graduate students, upperclassmen and some transfer students are assigned to Van Rensselaer and North Hall. No on-campus day care facilities are available.

Employment of Department Graduates:

Master's Degree Graduates: Of those who graduated in the academic year 2003–2004, the following categories and numbers represent the post-graduate activities and employment of master's degree graduates: Enrolled in a post-doctoral residency/fellowship (n/a), employed in independent practice (n/a), total from the above (master's) (0).

Doctoral Degree Graduates: Of those who graduated in the academic year 2003–2004, the following categories and numbers represent the post-graduate activities and employment of doctoral degree graduates: Enrolled in a psychology doctoral program (n/a), enrolled in a post-doctoral residency/fellowship (4), employed in an academic position at a university (1), employed in an academic position at a 2-year/4-year college (1), employed in other positions at a higher education institution (1), employed in a government agency (research) (1), employed in a government agency (professional services) (2), employed in a community mental health/counseling center (1), employed in a hospital/medical center (4), other employment position (1), total from the above (doctoral) (16).

Additional Information:

Orientation, Objectives, and Emphasis of Department: The Drexel University Department of Psychology combines the former MCP Hahnemann Department of Clinical and Health Psychology and the Drexel psychology faculty and Neuropsychology Program from the former Department of Psychology, Sociology, and Anthropology, and has operated as a single department since 7-1-02. The doctoral programs are based heavily upon a scientist-practitioner model of training in clinical psychology and has been designed to place equal emphasis on both components. The theoretical orientation is based largely on Social Learning Theory, in which students gain proficiency in the theory and practice of broad-spectrum behavioral approaches to assessment and intervention. The PhD program offers concentrations in health psychology, neuropsychology, and forensic psychology. The Law and Psychology program has three major goals: (a) to develop scientist practitioners who will produce legally-sophisticated social science research to help the legal system make better empirically-based decisions, (b) to educate highly trained clinicians who can contribute to the advancement of forensic psychology, and (c) to produce lawyer-psychologists who can participate in the development of more data-based mental health policy in the legislature and the courts. Students can earn the PhD in clinical psychology from Drexel University and the JD degree from Villanova Law School. The MS program (non-clinical) is designed to provide students with research skills in preparation for application for doctoral training, or employment with researchers in academia, industry, or public sector settings.

Special Facilities or Resources: The graduate psychology programs at Drexel University have space on both the Drexel Main Campus in West Philadelphia and the Hahnemann campus in center city. Drexel has a major tertiary care medical center that provides exceptional opportunities in health related areas for psychology. In addition, a Division of Behavioral Neurobiology and the University Neurobiology program, as well as the University Neurosciences program, provide opportunities for learning and collaboration on research at neuropharmacologic and neurophysiologic levels to complement our neuropsychological training. In addition, in conjunction with the Villanova University School of Law, we offer the only formal JD/PhD program in the country in which the academic psychological component represents a degree in clinical psychology.

Application Information:

Send to: Graduate Admission, Drexel University, 3141 Chestnut Street, Suite 212, Philadelphia, PA 19104. Telephone: (215) 895-2000. www.drexel.edu. Application available online. URL of online application: http://psychology.drexel.edu. Students are admitted in the Fall, application deadline January 1. JD/PhD February 1. *Fee:* $50.

Duquesne University

Department of Counseling, Psychology and Special Education,
   School Psychology Program
School of Education
102C Canevin Hall
Pittsburgh, PA 15282
Telephone: (412) 396-1058
Fax: (412) 396-1340
E-mail: *morocco@duq.edu*
Web: *www.schoolpsych.duq.edu*

Department Information:
1969. Program Coordinator: Jeffrey A. Miller, PhD. Number of Faculty: total–full-time 6, part-time 3; women–full-time 4, part-time 1.

Programs and Degrees Offered:
Listed in the following order: Program area, degree type (T if terminal Master's), number awarded 7/03–6/04. Child Psychology MA/MS (Master of Arts/Science) (T) 21, Certificate of Advanced Graduate Study- School Other 11, School Psychology PhD (Doctor of Philosophy) 0.

Student Applications/Admissions:
Student Applications
   Child Psychology MA/MS (Master of Arts/Science)—Applications 2004–2005, 14. Total applicants accepted 2004–2005, 12. Number enrolled (new admits only) 2004–2005 full-time, 10. Number enrolled (new admits only) 2004–2005 part-time, 2. Total enrolled 2004–2005 full-time, 15, part-time, 8. Openings 2005–2006, 15. The Median number of years required for completion of a degree are 2. The number of students enrolled

full and part-time who were dismissed or voluntarily withdrew from this program area were 0. *Certificate of Advanced Graduate Study- School Other*—Applications 2004–2005, 30. Total applicants accepted 2004–2005, 12. Number enrolled (new admits only) 2004–2005 full-time, 12. Number enrolled (new admits only) 2004–2005 part-time, 0. Openings 2005–2006, 12. The Median number of years required for completion of a degree are 3. The number of students enrolled full and part-time who were dismissed or voluntarily withdrew from this program area were 2. *School Psychology PhD (Doctor of Philosophy)*—Applications 2004–2005, 22. Total applicants accepted 2004–2005, 6. Number enrolled (new admits only) 2004–2005 full-time, 6. Number enrolled (new admits only) 2004–2005 part-time, 0. Openings 2005–2006, 5. The Median number of years required for completion of a degree are 5. The number of students enrolled full and part-time who were dismissed or voluntarily withdrew from this program area were 1.

Admissions Requirements:

Scores: Entries appear in this order: required test or GPA, minimum score (if required), median score of students entering in 2003–2004. Master's Programs: GRE-V no minimum stated; GRE-Q no minimum stated; GRE-V+Q no minimum stated; GRE-Analytical no minimum stated; overall undergraduate GPA no minimum stated; last 2 years GPA 3.0. Doctoral Programs: GRE-V no minimum stated; GRE-Q no minimum stated; GRE-V+Q no minimum stated; GRE-Analytical no minimum stated; overall undergraduate GPA no minimum stated; last 2 years GPA 3.0.

Other Criteria: (importance of criteria rated low, medium, or high): GRE/MAT scores high, research experience medium, work experience low, extracurricular activity low, clinically related public service low, GPA high, letters of recommendation medium, interview high, statement of goals and objectives high. For additional information on admission requirements, go to: www.schoolpsych.duq.edu.

Student Characteristics: The following represents characteristics of students in 2004–2005 in all graduate psychology programs in the department: Female–full-time 50, part-time 5; Male–full-time 32, part-time 3; African American/Black–full-time 1, part-time 1; Hispanic/Latino(a)–full-time 0, part-time 0; Asian/Pacific Islander–full-time 1, part-time 0; American Indian/Alaska Native–full-time 0, part-time 0; Caucasian–full-time 79, part-time 7; Multi-ethnic–full-time 1, part-time 0; students subject to the Americans With Disabilities Act–full-time 0, part-time 0.

Financial Information/Assistance:

Tuition for Full-Time Study: *Master's:* State residents: per academic year $8,652, $721 per credit hour; Nonstate residents: per academic year $8,652, $721 per credit hour. *Doctoral:* State residents: per academic year $17,304, $721 per credit hour; Nonstate residents: per academic year $17,304, $721 per credit hour. Tuition is subject to change. Tuition costs vary by program.

Financial Assistance:

First Year Students: No information provided.

Advanced Students: Research assistantships available for advanced students. Average amount paid per academic year: $6,175. Average number of hours worked per week: 20. Apply by March 1. Tuition remission given: full and partial.

Contact Information: Of all students currently enrolled full-time, 5% benefitted from one or more of the listed financial assistance programs. Application and information available online at: www.schoolpsych.duq.edu.

Internships/Practica: For those doctoral students for whom a professional internship is required prior to graduation, 3 applied in 2003–2004. Of those who applied, 2 were placed in internships listed by the Association of Psychology Postdoctoral and Internship Programs (APPIC).

Housing and Day Care: On-campus housing is available. See the following Web site for more information: www.residencelife.duq.edu. On-campus day care facilities are available. See the following Web site for more information: www.hr.duq.edu/employment/universityprograms.

Employment of Department Graduates:

Master's Degree Graduates: Of those who graduated in the academic year 2003–2004, the following categories and numbers represent the post-graduate activities and employment of master's degree graduates: Enrolled in a psychology doctoral program (5), enrolled in another graduate/professional program (7), enrolled in a post-doctoral residency/fellowship (n/a), employed in independent practice (n/a), total from the above (master's) (12).

Doctoral Degree Graduates: Of those who graduated in the academic year 2003–2004, the following categories and numbers represent the post-graduate activities and employment of doctoral degree graduates: Enrolled in a psychology doctoral program (n/a), total from the above (doctoral) (0).

Additional Information:

Orientation, Objectives, and Emphasis of Department: The Duquesne University School Psychology Program, guided by the belief that all children can learn, is dedicated to providing both breadth and depth of professional training in a theoretically-integrated, research-based learning environment. The Program prepares ethical practitioners, scientists and scholars who are lifelong learners committed to enhancing the well-being of youth, their families, and the systems that serve them. The Program achieves this by engaging in scholarly activities that advance the field of school psychology, maintaining a modern curriculum that employs aspects of multiculturalism and diversity, examining emerging trends in the profession, conducting continuous outcome assessment for program improvement, and providing support to our graduates.

Special Facilities or Resources: The program has a library of current psychological and educational tests for training and research purposes.

Application Information:

Send to: Dr. Jeffrey A. Miller, School Psychology Program, 102C Canevin Hall, Pittsburgh, PA 15282. Students are admitted in the Fall, application deadline February 1. Master's in School Psychology has rolling admissions. *Fee:* $50.

Duquesne University
Department of Psychology
McAnulty College and Graduate School of Liberal Arts
600 Forbes Avenue
Pittsburgh, PA 15282
Telephone: (412) 396-6520
Fax: (412) 396-5197
E-mail: *psychology@duq.edu*
Web: *http://www.gradpsych.duq.edu/*

Department Information:
1959. Chairperson: Russell Walsh, PhD. Number of Faculty: total–full-time 14, part-time 5; women–full-time 4, part-time 3; minority–full-time 2.

Programs and Degrees Offered:
Listed in the following order: Program area, degree type (T if terminal Master's), number awarded 7/03–6/04. Clinical PhD (Doctor of Philosophy) 8, Developmental PhD (Doctor of Philosophy) 0.

APA Accreditation: Clinical PhD (Doctor of Philosophy).

Student Applications/Admissions:
Student Applications
Clinical PhD (Doctor of Philosophy)—Applications 2004–2005, 81. Total applicants accepted 2004–2005, 7. Number enrolled (new admits only) 2004–2005 full-time, 7. Total enrolled 2004–2005 full-time, 72. Openings 2005–2006, 7. The Median number of years required for completion of a degree are 9. The number of students enrolled full and part-time who were dismissed or voluntarily withdrew from this program area were 3. *Developmental PhD (Doctor of Philosophy)*—Applications 2004–2005, 0. Total applicants accepted 2004–2005, 0. Total enrolled 2004–2005 full-time, 4. The number of students enrolled full and part-time, who were dismissed or voluntarily withdrew from this program area were 0.

Admissions Requirements:
Scores: Entries appear in this order: required test or GPA, minimum score (if required), median score of students entering in 2003–2004. Master's Programs: MA no longer offered. Doctoral Programs: GRE-V no minimum stated; GRE-Q no minimum stated; GRE-Analytical no minimum stated; overall undergraduate GPA no minimum stated.
Other Criteria: (importance of criteria rated low, medium, or high): GRE/MAT scores medium, research experience medium, work experience medium, extracurricular activity medium, clinically related public service medium, GPA medium, letters of recommendation high, interview high, statement of goals and objectives high.

Student Characteristics: The following represents characteristics of students in 2004–2005 in all graduate psychology programs in the department: Female–full-time 41, part-time 0; Male–full-time 35, part-time 0; African American/Black–full-time 4, part-time 0; Hispanic/Latino(a)–full-time 4, part-time 0; Asian/Pacific Islander–full-time 3, part-time 0; American Indian/Alaska Native–full-time 1, part-time 0; Caucasian–full-time 61, part-time 0; Multi-ethnic–full-time 3, part-time 0; students subject to the Americans With Disabilities Act–full-time 1, part-time 0.

Financial Information/Assistance:
Financial Assistance:
First Year Students: Research assistantships available for first-year. Average amount paid per academic year: $12,000. Average number of hours worked per week: 15. Apply by December 15. Tuition remission given: full.
Advanced Students: Teaching assistantships available for advanced students. Average amount paid per academic year: $12,000. Average number of hours worked per week: 15. Apply by December 15. Tuition remission given: full. Research assistantships available for advanced students. Average amount paid per academic year: $12,000. Average number of hours worked per week: 15. Apply by December 15. Tuition remission given: full.
Contact Information: Of all students currently enrolled full-time, 100% benefitted from one or more of the listed financial assistance programs. Application and information available online at: www.gradpsych.duq.edu.

Internships/Practica: For those doctoral students for whom a professional internship is required prior to graduation, 9 applied in 2003–2004. Of those who applied, 6 were placed in internships listed by the Association of Psychology Postdoctoral and Internship Programs (APPIC); 6 were placed in APA accredited internships.

Housing and Day Care: On-campus housing is available. See the following Web site for more information: http://www.duq.edu. On-campus day care facilities are available. See the following Web site for more information: http://www.duq.edu.

Employment of Department Graduates:
Master's Degree Graduates: Of those who graduated in the academic year 2003–2004, the following categories and numbers represent the post-graduate activities and employment of master's degree graduates: Enrolled in a post-doctoral residency/fellowship (n/a), employed in independent practice (n/a), total from the above (master's) (0).
Doctoral Degree Graduates: Of those who graduated in the academic year 2003–2004, the following categories and numbers represent the post-graduate activities and employment of doctoral degree graduates: Enrolled in a psychology doctoral program (n/a), total from the above (doctoral) (0).

Additional Information:
Orientation, Objectives, and Emphasis of Department: Internationally recognized for over three decades, the Psychology Department at Duquesne University engages in the systematic and rigorous articulation of psychology as a human science. The department understands psychology as a positive response to the challenges of the 21st century—one which includes existentialism, phenomenology, hermeneutics, psychoanalylsis and depth

psychology, feminism, critical theory, post-structuralism, and a sensitivity to the diverse cultural contexts within which this response may find expression. Psychology as a human science pursues collaborative, qualitative research methods that pay special attention to what is particular to human beings and their worlds. Accordingly, the department educates psychologists who are sensitive to the multiple meanings of human life and who work toward the liberation and well-being of persons individually as well as in the community.

Special Facilities or Resources: The psychology clinic provides the opportunity for supervised training in personal counseling and for research in the field of counseling and psychotherapy. Field placements are available in clinical. The Silverman Center is a research center containing a comprehensive collection of world literature in phenomenology.

Application Information:

Send to: Department Chair. Students are admitted in the Fall, application deadline December 15. January 15 is absolute deadline for all supporting materials. *Fee:* $50.

Edinboro University of Pennsylvania

Department of Psychology
Liberal Arts
106 Compton Hall
Edinboro, PA 16444
Telephone: (814) 732-2774; (814) 732-2000
Fax: (814) 732-2005
E-mail: *Davis@Edinboro.edu*
Web: *http://www.edinboro.edu*

Department Information:

1963. Chairperson: Jack Culbertson. Number of Faculty: total–full-time 15; women–full-time 5; faculty subject to the Americans With Disabilities Act 1.

Programs and Degrees Offered:

Listed in the following order: Program area, degree type (T if terminal Master's), number awarded 7/03–6/04. Clinical MA/MS (Master of Arts/Science) (T) 12.

Student Applications/Admissions:

Student Applications

Clinical MA/MS (Master of Arts/Science)—Applications 2004–2005, 40. Total applicants accepted 2004–2005, 18. Number enrolled (new admits only) 2004–2005 full-time, 17. Number enrolled (new admits only) 2004–2005 part-time, 1. Total enrolled 2004–2005 full-time, 27, part-time, 3. Openings 2005–2006, 15. The Median number of years required for completion of a degree are 2. The number of students enrolled full and part-time who were dismissed or voluntarily withdrew from this program area were 1.

Admissions Requirements:

Scores: Entries appear in this order: required test or GPA, minimum score (if required), median score of students entering in 2003–2004. Master's Programs: GRE-V no minimum stated,

410; GRE-Q no minimum stated, 450; GRE-V+Q no minimum stated, 860; MAT no minimum stated, 48; overall undergraduate GPA 3.0, 3.73. Either GRE or MAT scores are required; both are not. Doctoral Programs: GRE-V no minimum stated, 410; GRE-Q no minimum stated, 450; GRE-V+Q no minimum stated, 860; MAT no minimum stated, 48; overall undergraduate GPA 3.0, 3.73. Either GRE or MAT scores are required. Both scores are not required.

Other Criteria: (importance of criteria rated low, medium, or high): GRE/MAT scores medium, research experience low, work experience low, extracurricular activity low, clinically related public service low, GPA high, letters of recommendation medium, statement of goals and objectives medium.

Student Characteristics: The following represents characteristics of students in 2004–2005 in all graduate psychology programs in the department: Female–full-time 20, part-time 3; Male–full-time 7, part-time 0; African American/Black–full-time 1, part-time 0; Hispanic/Latino(a)–full-time 0, part-time 0; Asian/Pacific Islander–full-time 1, part-time 0; American Indian/Alaska Native–full-time 0, part-time 0; Caucasian–full-time 25, part-time 3; Multi-ethnic–full-time 0, part-time 0; students subject to the Americans With Disabilities Act–full-time 1, part-time 0.

Financial Information/Assistance:

Tuition for Full-Time Study: *Master's:* State residents: per academic year $5,254, $292 per credit hour; Nonstate residents: per academic year $8,408, $467 per credit hour. Tuition is subject to change. See the following Web site for updates and changes in tuition costs: www.edinboro.edu.

Financial Assistance:

First Year Students: Research assistantships available for first-year. Average amount paid per academic year: $4,200. Average number of hours worked per week: 20. Apply by February 15. Tuition remission given: full and partial.

Advanced Students: Research assistantships available for advanced students. Average amount paid per academic year: $4,200. Average number of hours worked per week: 20. Apply by February 15. Tuition remission given: full and partial.

Contact Information: Of all students currently enrolled full-time, 42% benefitted from one or more of the listed financial assistance programs. Application and information available online at: edinboro.edu.

Internships/Practica: All students are required to take a semester-long, full-time clinical internship. During the internship, students are expected to receive the following: (1) experience in individual and group psychotherapy; (2) assessment experience; and (3) supervision by a licensed psychologist. Internship sites may provide ongoing didactic instruction as well. Students have performed internships in a variety of sites, including the following: community mental health centers, state psychiatric hospitals, residential facilities for children and adolescents, VA outpatient facilities, local hospitals, correctional institutions, and counseling centers. Efforts are made to help each student to find an internship site which closely matches his/her interests. There is an optional summer practicum experience available for those seeking the professional counselor license in PA.

Housing and Day Care: On-campus housing is available. See the following Web site for more information: www.Edinboro.edu or contact Residence Life and Housing (814) 732-2818. On-campus day care facilities are available. See the following Web site for more information: www.Edinboro.edu.

Employment of Department Graduates:
Master's Degree Graduates: Of those who graduated in the academic year 2003–2004, the following categories and numbers represent the post-graduate activities and employment of master's degree graduates: Enrolled in a psychology doctoral program (0), enrolled in another graduate/professional program (0), enrolled in a post-doctoral residency/fellowship (n/a), employed in independent practice (n/a), employed in an academic position at a university (0), employed in an academic position at a 2-year/4-year college (0), employed in other positions at a higher education institution (0), employed in a professional position in a school system (0), employed in business or industry (research/consulting) (0), employed in business or industry (management) (0), employed in a government agency (research) (0), employed in a government agency (professional services) (2), employed in a community mental health/counseling center (6), employed in a hospital/medical center (2), still seeking employment (0), other employment position (0), do not know (2), total from the above (master's) (12).
Doctoral Degree Graduates: Of those who graduated in the academic year 2003–2004, the following categories and numbers represent the post-graduate activities and employment of doctoral degree graduates: Enrolled in a psychology doctoral program (n/a), total from the above (doctoral) (0).

Additional Information:
Orientation, Objectives, and Emphasis of Department: The purpose of the master of arts degree program in clinical psychology is to provide training for qualified college graduates in the findings and principles of the science of psychology, and the knowledge which will enable them to function on a professional level in a variety of settings where psychological principles and skills are used to aid in the solution of specific human problems and in the general promotion of human welfare. The graduate training of this program is in the area of "clinical psychology" and is designed to prepare the graduates of the program to perform clinical services in accordance with the ethical principles of psychologists at the professional level in a wide variety of human service organizations and agencies. The orientation of the faculty is eclectic, and students get a well-rounded education in psychological assessment, therapy, psychopathology, neuropsychology, psychopharmacology, ethics, and research.

Special Facilities or Resources: Part-time study is available. All courses (except the internship) can be taken in the evening for part-time study.

Information for Students With Physical Disabilities: See the following Web site for more information: www.Edinboro.edu.

Application Information:
Send to: Graduate Studies Office, Edinboro University, Edinboro, PA 16444. Students are admitted in the Fall, application deadline February 15. Application deadline recommended; will consider application submitted after this date. However, the deadline for applying for graduate assistantships is February 15. *Fee:* $25.

Gannon University
Counseling Psychology
College of Humanities, Business and Education
109 University Square
Erie, PA 16541-0001
Telephone: (814) 871-7538
Fax: (814) 871-5511
E-mail: *fleming@gannon.edu*
Web: *http://www.gannon.edu*

Department Information:
1998. Director of Training: Linda M. Fleming. Number of Faculty: total–full-time 4, part-time 4; women–full-time 2, part-time 2.

Programs and Degrees Offered:
Listed in the following order: Program area, degree type (T if terminal Master's), number awarded 7/03–6/04. Counseling Psychology PhD (Doctor of Philosophy) 2.

Student Applications/Admissions:
Student Applications
Counseling Psychology PhD (Doctor of Philosophy)—Applications 2004–2005, 11. Total applicants accepted 2004–2005, 6. Number enrolled (new admits only) 2004–2005 full-time, 6. Number enrolled (new admits only) 2004–2005 part-time, 0. Total enrolled 2004–2005 full-time, 11, part-time, 20. Openings 2005–2006, 6. The Median number of years required for completion of a degree are 5. The number of students enrolled full and part-time who were dismissed or voluntarily withdrew from this program area were 1.

Admissions Requirements:
Scores: Entries appear in this order: required test or GPA, minimum score (if required), median score of students entering in 2003–2004. Master's Programs: GRE-V no minimum stated; GRE-Q no minimum stated; GRE-V+Q no minimum stated; GRE-Analytical no minimum stated.
Other Criteria: (importance of criteria rated low, medium, or high): GRE/MAT scores medium, research experience low, work experience high, extracurricular activity medium, clinically related public service high, GPA high, letters of recommendation high, interview high, statement of goals and objectives high. For additional information on admission requirements, go to: www.gannon.edu.

Student Characteristics: The following represents characteristics of students in 2004–2005 in all graduate psychology programs in the department: Female–full-time 10, part-time 14; Male–full-time 1, part-time 6; African American/Black–full-time 0, part-time 1; Hispanic/Latino(a)–full-time 0, part-time 0; Asian/Pacific Islander–full-time 0, part-time 1; American Indian/Alaska Native–full-time 0, part-time 0; Caucasian–full-time 11, part-time 18; Multi-ethnic–full-time 0, part-time 0; students subject to the Americans With Disabilities Act–full-time 0, part-time 0.

Financial Information/Assistance:
Tuition for Full-Time Study: *Doctoral:* State residents: per academic year $15,300, $675 per credit hour; Nonstate residents: per academic year $15,300, $675 per credit hour. Tuition is subject to change.

Financial Assistance:

First Year Students: Teaching assistantships available for first-year. Apply by May 1. Tuition remission given: partial. Research assistantships available for first-year. Apply by May 1. Tuition remission given: partial.

Advanced Students: Teaching assistantships available for advanced students. Apply by May 1. Tuition remission given: partial. Research assistantships available for advanced students. Apply by May 1. Tuition remission given: partial.

Contact Information: Of all students currently enrolled full-time, 50% benefitted from one or more of the listed financial assistance programs.

Internships/Practica: Four practica are offered in the curriculum plus a year-long, 2000 hour internship — Introductory Individual Practicum; Advanced Individual Practicum— Marriage and Family Practicum; Group Facilitation Practicum—Internship in Counseling Psychology (year-long, 2000 hours). For those doctoral students for whom a professional internship is required prior to graduation, 5 applied in 2003–2004. Of those who applied, 3 were placed in internships listed by the Association of Psychology Postdoctoral and Internship Programs (APPIC); 3 were placed in APA accredited internships.

Housing and Day Care: No on-campus housing is available. No on-campus day care facilities are available.

Employment of Department Graduates:

Master's Degree Graduates: Of those who graduated in the academic year 2003–2004, the following categories and numbers represent the post-graduate activities and employment of master's degree graduates: Enrolled in a post-doctoral residency/fellowship (n/a), employed in independent practice (n/a), total from the above (master's) (0).

Doctoral Degree Graduates: Of those who graduated in the academic year 2003–2004, the following categories and numbers represent the post-graduate activities and employment of doctoral degree graduates: Enrolled in a psychology doctoral program (n/a), employed in an academic position at a 2-year/4-year college (1), employed in other positions at a higher education institution (1), employed in a community mental health/counseling center (1), employed in a hospital/medical center (1), total from the above (doctoral) (4).

Additional Information:

Orientation, Objectives, and Emphasis of Department: The PhD degree in Counseling Psychology at Gannon University seeks to contribute to and improve quality of life by educating and training psychology practitioners who deliver high quality human services. The program seeks to prepare practitioners who are sensitive to and provide psychological services to diverse populations. The PhD degree is committed to education and training which prepares practitioners within a framework which acknowledges and respects diversity in culture, gender, and life-style.

Special Facilities or Resources: The department provides a counseling laboratory in which clients may be seen. This laboratory includes three individual counseling rooms, two marriage and family and group rooms equipped with video cameras, sound recording, VCRs and monitors in a secure observation area. Observation is direct and feedback is provided following each session.

The department Psychological Services Clinic is a separate facility with four counseling offices and video recording capabilities.

Information for Students With Physical Disabilities: fleming@gannon.edu.

Application Information:
Send to: Center for Adult Learning, Office of Graduate Studies, Gannon University, 109 University Square, Erie, PA 16541-0001. Students are admitted in the Fall, application deadline February 20. *Fee:* $50.

Geneva College
Counseling
Graduate Studies in Counseling, 3200 College Avenue
Beaver Falls, PA 15010
Telephone: (724) 847-6697
Fax: (724) 847-6101
E-mail: *counseling@geneva.edu*
Web: *http://www.geneva.edu*

Department Information:
1987. Chairperson: Carol Luce, PhD Number of Faculty: total–full-time 6, part-time 2; women–full-time 3; minority–full-time 2; faculty subject to the Americans With Disabilities Act 1.

Programs and Degrees Offered:
Listed in the following order: Program area, degree type (T if terminal Master's), number awarded 7/03–6/04. Counseling MA/MS (Master of Arts/Science) (T) 10.

Student Applications/Admissions:
Student Applications
Counseling MA/MS (*Master of Arts/Science*)—Applications 2004–2005, 26. Total applicants accepted 2004–2005, 12. Total enrolled 2004–2005 full-time, 21, part-time, 21. Openings 2005–2006, 20. The Median number of years required for completion of a degree are 3.

Admissions Requirements:
Scores: Entries appear in this order: required test or GPA, minimum score (if required), median score of students entering in 2003–2004. Master's Programs: GRE-V no minimum stated; GRE-Q no minimum stated; GRE-V+Q no minimum stated; GRE-Analytical no minimum stated; MAT no minimum stated; overall undergraduate GPA no minimum stated. GRE General Test or MAT required but not both. Scores need to be in the fiftieth percentile for acceptance.
Other Criteria: (importance of criteria rated low, medium, or high): GRE/MAT scores medium, research experience low, work experience medium, extracurricular activity medium, clinically related public service medium, GPA medium, letters of recommendation high, interview medium, statement of goals and objectives high.

Student Characteristics: The following represents characteristics of students in 2004–2005 in all graduate psychology programs in the department: Female–full-time 27, part-time 10; Male–full-time 12, part-time 4; African American/Black–full-time 2, part-time 3; Hispanic/Latino(a)–full-time 1, part-time 0; Asian/Pacific Islander–full-time 0, part-time 0; American Indian/Alaska Native–full-time 0, part-time 0; Caucasian–full-time 36, part-time 18; students subject to the Americans With Disabilities Act–full-time 5, part-time 2.

Financial Information/Assistance:
Tuition for Full-Time Study: *Master's:* State residents: $465 per credit hour; Nonstate residents: $465 per credit hour. Tuition is subject to change.

Financial Assistance:
First Year Students: Teaching assistantships available for first-year. Average amount paid per academic year: $1,500. Average number of hours worked per week: 8. Apply by July 1.
Advanced Students: Teaching assistantships available for advanced students. Average amount paid per academic year: $1,500. Average number of hours worked per week: 8. Apply by March 1.
Contact Information: Of all students currently enrolled full-time, 22% benefitted from one or more of the listed financial assistance programs.

Internships/Practica: A practicum and internship program is in place. This practicum and internship experience is in line with the CACREP standards for master's level counseling programs. Details are as follows: practica are 100 hours in length with individual and group supervision and direct client contact; marriage and family internships are 600 hours in length with 300 hours being direct client contact hours; mental health internships are 900 hours in length with 450 hours being direct client contact hours; all internships will involve site placements typically in the Beaver County and Pittsburgh area, supervision via qualified master's and/or doctoral prepared practitioners, and onsite as well as college supervision.

Housing and Day Care: No on-campus housing is available. No on-campus day care facilities are available.

Employment of Department Graduates:
Master's Degree Graduates: Of those who graduated in the academic year 2003–2004, the following categories and numbers represent the post-graduate activities and employment of master's degree graduates: Enrolled in a post-doctoral residency/fellowship (n/a), employed in independent practice (n/a), total from the above (master's) (0).
Doctoral Degree Graduates: Of those who graduated in the academic year 2003–2004, the following categories and numbers represent the post-graduate activities and employment of doctoral degree graduates: Enrolled in a psychology doctoral program (n/a), total from the above (doctoral) (0).

Additional Information:
Orientation, Objectives, and Emphasis of Department: The philosophies of counseling in the MA in Counseling Program at Geneva College are embedded in a Christian view of human nature and God's created world. A growing body of research literature affirms that Christian faith establishes a basis for healthy personality development, interpersonal relations, and mental health. A multidimensional holistic view of persons examines the interweaving of physical, emotional, social, cognitive, behavioral, and spiritual aspects of life. Integrative psychotherapeutic conceptualizations based on this multidimensionality promote healing and change. Counseling students and faculty engage in Christian spiritual growth, thus modeling adherence to the faith and values they profess and facilitating academic learning, counseling, effectiveness, and ability to consult in the larger church community and beyond. The MA in Counseling Program at Geneva College provides academic training in the development of knowledge, skills, and personal awareness pertinent to the counseling profession, and encourages students to integrate Christian faith and Biblical knowledge with the training and practice of counseling. The program is designed so that post-baccalaureate students who complete this degree and acquire the required postgraduate supervised experience in the practice of counseling will be eligible to become Licensed Professional Counselors.

Personal Behavior Statement: Adherence to APA and AACC Ethical Guidelines are expected.

Special Facilities or Resources: Department facilities include an animal lab, a computer lab, and a modern clinical counseling facility. The computer lab is equipped with WordPerfect for Windows, SPSS for Windows, and various experimental and clinical software resources. The lab is also connected to Internet and Netscape on the World Wide Web.

Application Information:
Send to: Mrs. Bridget Snebold, Director of Graduate Student Services, Geneva College, 3200 College Avenue, Beaver Falls, PA 15010. Students are admitted in the Fall, application deadline open; Spring, application deadline November 1; Summer, application deadline June 1. *Fee:* $50. Application fee can be waived for applicants with financial hardship.

Immaculata University
Department of Graduate Psychology
College of Graduate Studies
Box 500, Loyola Hall
Immaculata, PA 19345-0500
Telephone: (215) 647-4400 Exts. 3211, 3212, 3213
Fax: (610) 993-8550
E-mail: *jyalof@immaculata.edu*
Web: *www.immaculata.edu*

Department Information:
1983. Chairperson: Jed Yalof. Number of Faculty: total–full-time 9, part-time 19; women–full-time 6, part-time 11; minority–full-time 1, part-time 1.

Programs and Degrees Offered:
Listed in the following order: Program area, degree type (T if terminal Master's), number awarded 7/03–6/04. Clinical PsyD (Doctor of Psychology) 17, Counseling MA/MS (Master of Arts/Science) (T) 34, Elementary School Other, School Certification MA/MS (Master of Arts/Science), School Secondary Counseling Other, School Psychology PsyD (Doctor of Psychology) 0.

APA Accreditation: Clinical PsyD (Doctor of Psychology).

Student Applications/Admissions:

Student Applications

Clinical PsyD (Doctor of Psychology)—Applications 2004–2005, 49. Total applicants accepted 2004–2005, 18. Number enrolled (new admits only) 2004–2005 full-time, 14. Number enrolled (new admits only) 2004–2005 part-time, 13. Total enrolled 2004–2005 full-time, 36, part-time, 57. Openings 2005–2006, 20. Counseling MA/MS (Master of Arts/Science)—Applications 2004–2005, 102. Total applicants accepted 2004–2005, 86. Total enrolled 2004–2005 full-time, 25, part-time, 148. Elementary School Other—School Certification MA/MS (Master of Arts/Science)—Total enrolled 2004–2005 part-time, 17. School Secondary Counseling Other—Total enrolled 2004–2005 full-time, 1, part-time, 4. School Psychology PsyD (Doctor of Psychology)—Applications 2004–2005, 2. Total applicants accepted 2004–2005, 2. Total enrolled 2004–2005 full-time, 2, part-time, 14.

Admissions Requirements:

Scores: Entries appear in this order: required test or GPA, minimum score (if required), median score of students entering in 2003–2004. Master's Programs: MAT no minimum stated; overall undergraduate GPA 3.0. Doctoral Programs: MAT no minimum stated; overall undergraduate GPA no minimum stated. Applicants applying to the PsyD program with B.A. only- 3.3 minimum GPA required.

Other Criteria: (importance of criteria rated low, medium, or high): GRE/MAT scores medium, research experience medium, work experience high, extracurricular activity medium, clinically related public service medium, GPA high, letters of recommendation high, interview high, statement of goals and objectives high. PsyD Clinical Psychology accepts BA, MA or equivalency in psychology or MA in another field; PsyD School Psychology accepts only students already certified in school psychology. Admissions criteria differ for applicants to MA Counseling vs. PsyD Clinical and School programs.

Student Characteristics: The following represents characteristics of students in 2004–2005 in all graduate psychology programs in the department: African American/Black–full-time 2, part-time 15; Hispanic/Latino(a)–full-time 1, part-time 1; Asian/Pacific Islander–full-time 1, part-time 2; American Indian/Alaska Native–full-time 0, part-time 0; Caucasian–full-time 0, part-time 0; Multi-ethnic–part-time 1.

Financial Information/Assistance:

Tuition for Full-Time Study: Master's: State residents: $440 per credit hour. Doctoral: State residents: $675 per credit hour.

Financial Assistance:

First Year Students: No information provided.
Advanced Students: No information provided.
Contact Information: No information provided.

Internships/Practica: Students work with either the master's field site coordinator or doctoral field site and pre-doctoral internship coordinator to identify prospective field placements for their different programs of study. The Graduate Psychology Department places counseling psychology, school psychology, and clinical psychology students at sites throughout the Chester and Montgomery County areas and with supervisors with qualifications specific to student and program requirements. Clinical doctoral students complete diagnostic and therapy placements prior to internship. Elective field placements are available and encouraged for clinical psychology doctoral students. Students entering the PsyD program with BA or equivalent are required to complete a field placement early in their program of study as one of their electives. School doctoral students complete a practicum prior to internship.

Housing and Day Care: On-campus housing is available. See the following Web site for more information: graduate@immaculata.edu. No on-campus day care facilities are available.

Employment of Department Graduates:

Master's Degree Graduates: Of those who graduated in the academic year 2003–2004, the following categories and numbers represent the post-graduate activities and employment of master's degree graduates: Enrolled in a post-doctoral residency/fellowship (n/a), employed in independent practice (n/a), total from the above (master's) (0).

Doctoral Degree Graduates: Of those who graduated in the academic year 2003–2004, the following categories and numbers represent the post-graduate activities and employment of doctoral degree graduates: Enrolled in a psychology doctoral program (n/a), total from the above (doctoral) (0).

Additional Information:

Orientation, Objectives, and Emphasis of Department: The department's orientation is the professional preparation of the master's counselor in relation to counselor licensure in PA. The department also prepares students for elementary school counseling, secondary school counseling, and school psychology certification. In all cases, training emphasizes knowledge, skill and competency through classroom, practicum and internship. The department's orientation is the preparation of doctoral-level clinical-psychologists within the practitioner-scholar model of professional psychology. This preparation entails a generalist curriculum emphasizing theory, therapy, diagnostics and clinical training, with doctoral dissertation research aligned with a practitioner model. The department's preparation of doctoral-level school psychologists is practitioner-oriented, focusing on advanced assessment and intervention, human diversity, biological bases, school-neuropsychological application, research and consultation within the context of school settings.

Special Facilities or Resources: The college has a comprehensive center for academic computing and modern technology available for student computer needs and utilization. The Gabrielle Library was opened in 1993 and houses journals and texts and has online search available to students.

Information for Students With Physical Disabilities: See the following Web site for more information: www.immaculata.edu.

Application Information:

Send to: Director of Graduate Admission, Immaculata University, King Road, Box 500, Immaculata, PA 19345. Students are admitted in the Fall, application deadline rolling; Winter, application deadline rolling; Spring, application deadline rolling; Summer, application deadline rolling. PsyD: January 15 application deadline for May admissions; March 1 for Fall. Application fee is $25 for master's, $50 for doctoral programs.

Indiana University of Pennsylvania

Department of Psychology
Natural Sciences and Mathematics
201 Uhler Hall
Indiana, PA 15705
Telephone: (724) 357-4519
Fax: (724) 357-4087
E-mail: *goodwin@iup.edu*
Web: *http://www.iup.edu*

Department Information:
1984. Chairperson: Mary Lou Zanich, PhD. Number of Faculty: total–full-time 21, part-time 5; women–full-time 11, part-time 2; minority–full-time 2.

Programs and Degrees Offered:
Listed in the following order: Program area, degree type (T if terminal Master's), number awarded 7/03–6/04. Clinical Psychology PsyD (Doctor of Psychology) 4.

APA Accreditation: Clinical PsyD (Doctor of Psychology).

Student Applications/Admissions:
Student Applications
Clinical Psychology PsyD (Doctor of Psychology)—Applications 2004–2005, 125. Total applicants accepted 2004–2005, 13. Openings 2005–2006, 15. The Median number of years required for completion of a degree are 5. The number of students enrolled full and part-time who were dismissed or voluntarily withdrew from this program area were 1.

Admissions Requirements:
Scores: Entries appear in this order: required test or GPA, minimum score (if required), median score of students entering in 2003–2004. Doctoral Programs: GRE-V 500, 570; GRE-Q 500, 630; GRE-Analytical 500, 690; GRE-Subject(Psych) 500, 630; overall undergraduate GPA 3.0.
Other Criteria: (importance of criteria rated low, medium, or high): GRE/MAT scores high, research experience medium, work experience medium, clinically related public service high, GPA high, letters of recommendation medium, interview high, statement of goals and objectives medium. For additional information on admission requirements, go to: www.iup.edu/psychology.

Student Characteristics: The following represents characteristics of students in 2004–2005 in all graduate psychology programs in the department: Female–full-time 37, part-time 0; Male–full-time 10, part-time 0; African American/Black–full-time 1, part-time 0; Hispanic/Latino(a)–full-time 1, part-time 0; Asian/Pacific Islander–full-time 2, part-time 0; American Indian/Alaska Native–full-time 1, part-time 0; Caucasian–full-time 42, part-time 0; Multi-ethnic–full-time 0, part-time 0; students subject to the Americans With Disabilities Act–full-time 0, part-time 0.

Financial Information/Assistance:
Tuition for Full-Time Study: *Doctoral:* State residents: per academic year $5,772, $321 per credit hour; Nonstate residents: per academic year $9,236, $513 per credit hour. Tuition is subject to change.

Financial Assistance:
First Year Students: Research assistantships available for first-year. Average amount paid per academic year: $2,915. Average number of hours worked per week: 10. Apply by March 15. Tuition remission given: partial. Fellowships and scholarships available for first-year. Average amount paid per academic year: $5,000. Average number of hours worked per week: 0. Apply by March 15.
Advanced Students: Teaching assistantships available for advanced students. Average amount paid per academic year: $11,558. Average number of hours worked per week: 12. Apply by March 15. Research assistantships available for advanced students. Average amount paid per academic year: $2,915. Average number of hours worked per week: 10. Apply by March 15. Tuition remission given: partial.
Contact Information: Of all students currently enrolled full-time, 100% benefitted from one or more of the listed financial assistance programs.

Internships/Practica: Students begin clinical experiences in the first year through course-based practica. During the second and later years, students enroll in the department sponsored Center for Applied Psychology (CAP) training clinics. These clinics employ a live supervision model. Training in the CAP clinics is supplemented with required external practica, currently available in approximately 18 different sites. For those doctoral students for whom a professional internship is required prior to graduation, 7 applied in 2003–2004. Of those who applied, 7 were placed in internships listed by the Association of Psychology Postdoctoral and Internship Programs (APPIC); 7 were placed in APA accredited internships.

Housing and Day Care: No on-campus housing is available. No on-campus day care facilities are available.

Employment of Department Graduates:
Master's Degree Graduates: Of those who graduated in the academic year 2003–2004, the following categories and numbers represent the post-graduate activities and employment of master's degree graduates: Enrolled in a post-doctoral residency/fellowship (n/a), employed in independent practice (n/a), total from the above (master's) (0).
Doctoral Degree Graduates: Of those who graduated in the academic year 2003–2004, the following categories and numbers represent the post-graduate activities and employment of doctoral degree graduates: Enrolled in a psychology doctoral program (n/a), employed in other positions at a higher education institution (2), employed in a community mental health/counseling center (2), total from the above (doctoral) (4).

Additional Information:
Orientation, Objectives, and Emphasis of Department: The Psychology Department offers a Doctor of Psychology degree in Clinical Psychology (PsyD) that places emphasis upon professional applications of psychology based on a solid grounding in the scientific knowledge base of psychology. Training follows a generalist model with opportunities to develop advanced competencies during the last two years through courses and special practica. The core curriculum consists of seven areas including elective

coursework. Heavy emphasis is placed on integrating psychological knowledge with treatment, evaluation, consultation and service delivery program design. The program is designed to meet the academic requirements of licensure and provide the background to assume responsibilities in appropriate professional settings.

Special Facilities or Resources: The Department of Psychology includes two 16-computer laboratories, individual research space with audio/video capabilities, seminar rooms and a graduate student lounge. Each graduate student office is provided with computer access to the department server and the Internet. The facilities for the CAP include 12 treatment rooms as well as one seminar room, all connected with a master video system. The CAP also houses computer facilities for test administration and scoring.

Application Information:
Send to: Graduate School Admissions, Indiana University of Pennsylvania, Stright Hall, Indiana, PA 15705. Students are admitted in the Fall, application deadline January 10; Summer, application deadline January 10. *Fee:* $30.

LaSalle University
Clinical-Counseling Program
1900 W. Olney Avenue
Philadelphia, PA 19141
Telephone: (215) 951-1767
Fax: (215) 951-5140
E-mail: *psyma@lasalle.edu*
Web: *http://www.lasalle.edu*

Department Information:
1948. Director: John J. Rooney, PhD Number of Faculty: total–full-time 14, part-time 24; women–full-time 8, part-time 11; minority–part-time 2.

Programs and Degrees Offered:
Listed in the following order: Program area, degree type (T if terminal Master's), number awarded 7/03–6/04. Master's in Clinical Counseling Psychology MA/MS (Master of Arts/Science) 50.

Student Applications/Admissions:
Student Applications
Master's in Clinical Counseling Psychology MA/MS (Master of Arts/Science)—Applications 2004–2005, 341. Total applicants accepted 2004–2005, 180. Number enrolled (new admits only) 2004–2005 full-time, 46. Number enrolled (new admits only) 2004–2005 part-time, 134. Total enrolled 2004–2005 full-time, 79, part-time, 219. Openings 2005–2006, 200. The Median number of years required for completion of a degree are 3. The number of students enrolled full and part-time who were dismissed or voluntarily withdrew from this program area were 5.

Admissions Requirements:
Scores: Entries appear in this order: required test or GPA, minimum score (if required), median score of students entering in 2003–2004. Master's Programs: MAT 50; overall undergraduate GPA 3.0; psychology GPA 3.3.

Other Criteria: (importance of criteria rated low, medium, or high): GRE/MAT scores medium, research experience medium, work experience medium, extracurricular activity medium, clinically related public service medium, GPA high, letters of recommendation high.

Student Characteristics: The following represents characteristics of students in 2004–2005 in all graduate psychology programs in the department: Female–full-time 59, part-time 163; Male–full-time 20, part-time 56; African American/Black–full-time 12, part-time 50; Hispanic/Latino(a)–full-time 1, part-time 6; Asian/Pacific Islander–full-time 1, part-time 4; American Indian/Alaska Native–full-time 0, part-time 0; Caucasian–full-time 63, part-time 134; Multi-ethnic–full-time 2, part-time 25; students subject to the Americans With Disabilities Act–full-time 0, part-time 0.

Financial Information/Assistance:
Tuition for Full-Time Study: *Master's:* State residents: $510 per credit hour; Nonstate residents: $510 per credit hour.

Financial Assistance:
First Year Students: Fellowships and scholarships available for first-year. Average amount paid per academic year: $1,250. Apply by July/November.
Advanced Students: Teaching assistantships available for advanced students. Average amount paid per academic year: $4,500. Average number of hours worked per week: 10. Apply by July/December. Research assistantships available for advanced students. Average amount paid per academic year: $4,500. Average number of hours worked per week: 10. Apply by July/December. Traineeships available for advanced students. Fellowships and scholarships available for advanced students. Average amount paid per academic year: $2,500. Apply by July/November.
Contact Information: Of all students currently enrolled full-time, 25% benefitted from one or more of the listed financial assistance programs. Application and information available online at: www.lasalle.edu.

Internships/Practica: Internships/practica available in on-campus clinic or counseling center, as well as a wide variety of off-campus sites.

Housing and Day Care: On-campus housing is available. On-campus day care facilities are available. Contact Building Blocks Child Development Center.

Employment of Department Graduates:
Master's Degree Graduates: Of those who graduated in the academic year 2003–2004, the following categories and numbers represent the post-graduate activities and employment of master's degree graduates: Enrolled in a post-doctoral residency/fellowship (n/a), employed in independent practice (n/a), total from the above (master's) (0).
Doctoral Degree Graduates: Of those who graduated in the academic year 2003–2004, the following categories and numbers represent the post-graduate activities and employment of doctoral degree graduates: Enrolled in a psychology doctoral program (n/a), total from the above (doctoral) (0).

Additional Information:

Orientation, Objectives, and Emphasis of Department: Four areas of concentration are available within the program: psychological counseling, marriage and family therapy, addictions counseling and industrial organizational psychology. The program stresses skills training and clinical preparation for these concentrations, including preparation for Licensed Professional Counselor or Licensed Marriage and Family Therapist. It also prepares students for doctoral studies. The program is based on a holistic view of the person, which stresses the integration of the psychological, systemic, cultural, and spiritual dimensions of experience.

Special Facilities or Resources: Counselor training facilities include room and equipment for videotaping counseling sessions with individuals and families. A clinic for supervised training of students was opened in 1985. It has all the resources, equipment, and staff needed in such a facility.

Application Information:

Send to: Dr. John Rooney, La Salle University, MA Clinical Counseling Psychology, Box 268, 1900 West Olney Avenue, Philadelphia, PA 19141. Application available online. URL of online application: www.lasalle.edu. Students are admitted in the Fall. Programs have rolling admissions. Although there are no formal application deadlines, we recommend that all information necessary be received by August 1, December 1, and April 1, for the Fall, Spring, and Summer terms, respectively. International student applications should be complete at least two months prior to the dates listed above. *Fee:* $35. Fee waived for online application.

Lehigh University
Department of Education and Human Services
Education
Mountain Top Campus
111 Research Drive
Bethlehem, PA 18015
Telephone: (610) 758-3241
Fax: (610) 758-6223
E-mail: *nil3@lehigh.edu*
Web: *http://www.lehigh.edu/collegeofeducation/flashpage*

Department Information:

1995. Chairperson: Nicholas Ladany. Number of Faculty: total–full-time 31, part-time 12; women–full-time 12, part-time 7; minority–full-time 4.

Programs and Degrees Offered:

Listed in the following order: Program area, degree type (T if terminal Master's), number awarded 7/03–6/04. Counseling Psychology PhD (Doctor of Philosophy) 4, Counseling and Human Services Other 9, Elementary School Counseling Other 7, School (Doctoral) PhD (Doctor of Philosophy) 6, Secondary School Counseling Other 5, School (Education Specialist) EdS (Education Specialist) 3.

APA Accreditation: Counseling PhD (Doctor of Philosophy). School PhD (Doctor of Philosophy).

Student Applications/Admissions:

Student Applications

Counseling Psychology PhD (Doctor of Philosophy)—Applications 2004–2005, 96. Total applicants accepted 2004–2005, 9. Number enrolled (new admits only) 2004–2005 full-time, 5. Number enrolled (new admits only) 2004–2005 part-time, 0. Total enrolled 2004–2005 full-time, 26, part-time, 8. Openings 2005–2006, 5. The Median number of years required for completion of a degree are 6. The number of students enrolled full and part-time who were dismissed or voluntarily withdrew from this program area were 0. *Counseling and Human Services Other*—Applications 2004–2005, 81. Total applicants accepted 2004–2005, 31. Total enrolled 2004–2005 full-time, 26, part-time, 8. Openings 2005–2006, 35. The Median number of years required for completion of a degree are 2. The number of students enrolled full and part-time who were dismissed or voluntarily withdrew from this program area were 1. *Elementary School Counseling Other*—Applications 2004–2005, 10. Total applicants accepted 2004–2005, 4. Total enrolled 2004–2005 full-time, 11, part-time, 7. Openings 2005–2006, 7. The Median number of years required for completion of a degree are 2. The number of students enrolled full and part-time who were dismissed or voluntarily withdrew from this program area were 1. *School (Doctoral) PhD (Doctor of Philosophy)*—Applications 2004–2005, 56. Total applicants accepted 2004–2005, 9. Total enrolled 2004–2005 full-time, 26, part-time, 8. Openings 2005–2006, 7. The Median number of years required for completion of a degree are 6. The number of students enrolled full and part-time who were dismissed or voluntarily withdrew from this program area were 2. *Secondary School Counseling Other*—Applications 2004–2005, 21. Total applicants accepted 2004–2005, 9. Total enrolled 2004–2005 full-time, 8, part-time, 4. Openings 2005–2006, 10. The Median number of years required for completion of a degree are 2. The number of students enrolled full and part-time who were dismissed or voluntarily withdrew from this program area were 1. *School (Education Specialist) EdS (Education Specialist)*—Applications 2004–2005, 50. Total applicants accepted 2004–2005, 10. Total enrolled 2004–2005 full-time, 18, part-time, 2. Openings 2005–2006, 8. The Median number of years required for completion of a degree are 3. The number of students enrolled full and part-time who were dismissed or voluntarily withdrew from this program area was 1.

Admissions Requirements:

Scores: Entries appear in this order: required test or GPA, minimum score (if required), median score of students entering in 2003–2004. Master's Programs: GRE-V no minimum stated; GRE-Q no minimum stated; GRE-V+Q no minimum stated; overall undergraduate GPA 3.00; last 2 years GPA no minimum stated; psychology GPA no minimum stated. No minimums are set by the programs. Writing subtest of GRE also required if taken in past two years. Doctoral Programs: GRE-V no minimum stated; GRE-Q no minimum stated; GRE-V+Q no minimum stated; overall undergraduate GPA 3.00. Varies per program.

Other Criteria: (importance of criteria rated low, medium, or high): GRE/MAT scores medium, research experience high, work experience medium, extracurricular activity medium, clinically related public service medium, GPA high, letters of recommendation medium, interview medium, statement of goals and objectives high. Criteria vary by program.

Student Characteristics: The following represents characteristics of students in 2004–2005 in all graduate psychology programs in the department: Female–full-time 100, part-time 29; Male–full-time 15, part-time 8; African American/Black–full-time 7, part-time 3; Hispanic/Latino(a)–full-time 3, part-time 4; Asian/Pacific Islander–full-time 3, part-time 1; American Indian/Alaska Native–full-time 0, part-time 0; Caucasian–full-time 101, part-time 29; Multi-ethnic–full-time 1, part-time 0; students subject to the Americans With Disabilities Act–full-time 2, part-time 0.

Financial Information/Assistance:

Tuition for Full-Time Study: *Master's:* State residents: $490 per credit hour; Nonstate residents: $490 per credit hour. *Doctoral:* State residents: $490 per credit hour; Nonstate residents: $490 per credit hour.

Financial Assistance:

First Year Students: Research assistantships available for first-year. Average amount paid per academic year: $12,000. Average number of hours worked per week: 20. Apply by January 1. Tuition remission given: full and partial. Traineeships available for first-year. Average amount paid per academic year: $12,000. Average number of hours worked per week: 20. Apply by January 1. Tuition remission given: full and partial. Fellowships and scholarships available for first-year. Average amount paid per academic year: $12,000. Average number of hours worked per week: 20. Apply by January 1. Tuition remission given: full and partial.

Advanced Students: Research assistantships available for advanced students. Average amount paid per academic year: $12,000. Average number of hours worked per week: 20. Tuition remission given: full and partial. Traineeships available for advanced students. Average amount paid per academic year: $12,000. Average number of hours worked per week: 20. Tuition remission given: full and partial. Fellowships and scholarships available for advanced students. Average amount paid per academic year: $12,000. Average number of hours worked per week: 20. Tuition remission given: full and partial.

Contact Information: Of all students currently enrolled full-time, 80% benefitted from one or more of the listed financial assistance programs.

Internships/Practica: The Counseling Psychology Program maintains contracts with a variety of practicum settings. Training in individual, group, couples, and family counseling is readily available. Students receive at least two hours of individual and two hours group supervision per week. Many sites provide additional training on specific issues in counseling. The Counseling Psychology programs have established a partnership with a local urban school district to provide enhanced in-school psychological services in elementary and middle schools. The School Psychology program, in cooperation with Centennial School, the University affiliated school for students with emotional/behavioral disorders, supports a pre-doctoral internship opportunity in school psychology. For those doctoral students for whom a professional internship is required prior to graduation, 10 applied in 2003–2004. Of those who applied, 6 were placed in internships listed by the Association of Psychology Postdoctoral and Internship Programs (APPIC); 6 were placed in APA accredited internships.

Housing and Day Care: On-campus housing is available. See the following Web site for more information: http://www3.lehigh.edu/studentlife/slgraduatetransfer.asp. On-campus day care facilities are available. See the following Web site for more information: http://www.lehigh.edu/~inluccc/cc.html.

Employment of Department Graduates:

Master's Degree Graduates: Of those who graduated in the academic year 2003–2004, the following categories and numbers represent the post-graduate activities and employment of master's degree graduates: Enrolled in a post-doctoral residency/fellowship (n/a), employed in independent practice (n/a), total from the above (master's) (0).

Doctoral Degree Graduates: Of those who graduated in the academic year 2003–2004, the following categories and numbers represent the post-graduate activities and employment of doctoral degree graduates: Enrolled in a psychology doctoral program (n/a), total from the above (doctoral) (0).

Additional Information:

Orientation, Objectives, and Emphasis of Department: The College of Education offers degree programs in counseling and school psychology. The program in school psychology offers training at both educational specialist (NASP approved) and doctoral (PhD) levels (NASP approved and APA accredited). Within the PhD program, subspecializations in Health/Pediatric School Psychology and in Counseling Psychology/Special Education are offered. The program at all levels is behaviorally oriented, emphasizing problem-solving-based research, consultation, behavioral assessment and intervention in the implementation of school psychology services. The program in counseling psychology emphasizes a scientist-practitioner model and trains professional psychologists for employment in educational, industrial, and community settings. The counseling psychology program also offers training at the master's level.

Special Facilities or Resources: The school psychology program has a number of research and training projects that are focused on students with behavior and cognitive disabilities. The department has recently established the Center for Promoting Research to Practice, a unit that houses several major research grants involved in bringing known research findings into school and community settings. The department also has university-affiliated training and research programs that provide living arrangements and day treatment programs for adults with developmental disabilities. The department also operates a laboratory school for children and adolescents with emotional disturbance. All facilities are integrated into the training of students primarily in the school psychology programs. The counseling psychology program has a lab for videotaping and editing. Both programs have established partnerships with urban school districts. School psychology has recently established a national internship in the University laboratory school for students with emotional/behavior disorders.

Application Information:

Send to: Ms. Donna Johnson, College of Education, Lehigh University, 111 Research Drive, Bethlehem, PA 18015. Students are admitted in the Fall, application deadline January 1. Counseling Psychology Master's—March 1. Fall admission for Counseling Psychology and School Psychology. *Fee:* $50.

Lehigh University

Department of Psychology
Arts and Sciences
17 Memorial Drive East
Bethlehem, PA 18015
Telephone: (610) 758-3630
Fax: (610) 758-6277
E-mail: *hcd.gprog@lehigh.edu*
Web: *http://www.lehigh.edu/~inpsy/gradprogram.html*

Department Information:
1931. Chairperson: Barbara C. Malt. Number of Faculty: total–full-time 10, part-time 3; women–full-time 6, part-time 1.

Programs and Degrees Offered:
Listed in the following order: Program area, degree type (T if terminal Master's), number awarded 7/03–6/04. Human Cognition and Development PhD (Doctor of Philosophy) 2.

Student Applications/Admissions:
Student Applications
Human Cognition and Development PhD (Doctor of Philosophy)—Applications 2004–2005, 39. Total applicants accepted 2004–2005, 4. Number enrolled (new admits only) 2004–2005 full-time, 4. Number enrolled (new admits only) 2004–2005 part-time, 0. Openings 2005–2006, 7. The Median number of years required for completion of a degree are 6. The number of students enrolled full and part-time who were dismissed or voluntarily withdrew from this program area were 1.

Admissions Requirements:
Scores: Entries appear in this order: required test or GPA, minimum score (if required), median score of students entering in 2003–2004. Doctoral Programs: GRE-V no minimum stated, 625; GRE-Q no minimum stated, 630; overall undergraduate GPA no minimum stated, 3.7.
Other Criteria: (importance of criteria rated low, medium, or high): GRE/MAT scores medium, research experience high, work experience low, GPA medium, letters of recommendation high, interview medium, statement of goals and objectives high. For additional information on admission requirements, go to: http://www.lehigh.edu/~inpsy/requirements.html.

Student Characteristics: The following represents characteristics of students in 2004–2005 in all graduate psychology programs in the department: Female–full-time 5, part-time 0; Male–full-time 5, part-time 0; African American/Black–full-time 0, part-time 0; Hispanic/Latino(a)–full-time 0, part-time 0; Asian/Pacific Islander–full-time 0, part-time 0; American Indian/Alaska Native–full-time 0, part-time 0; Caucasian–full-time 9, part-time 0; Multi-ethnic–full-time 1, part-time 0; students subject to the Americans With Disabilities Act–full-time 0, part-time 0.

Financial Information/Assistance:
Tuition for Full-Time Study: *Master's:* State residents: $950 per credit hour. *Doctoral:* State residents: $950 per credit hour. Tuition is subject to change. See the following Web site for updates and changes in tuition costs: http://www3.lehigh.edu/arts-sciences/casgfaqs.asp.

Financial Assistance:
First Year Students: Teaching assistantships available for first-year. Average amount paid per academic year: $13,720. Average number of hours worked per week: 15. Apply by January 15. Tuition remission given: full. Research assistantships available for first-year. Average amount paid per academic year: $13,720. Average number of hours worked per week: 15. Apply by January 15. Tuition remission given: full. Fellowships and scholarships available for first-year. Average amount paid per academic year: $16,000. Average number of hours worked per week: 0. Apply by January 15. Tuition remission given: full.
Advanced Students: Teaching assistantships available for advanced students. Average amount paid per academic year: $13,720. Average number of hours worked per week: 15. Apply by n/a. Tuition remission given: full. Research assistantships available for advanced students. Average amount paid per academic year: $13,720. Average number of hours worked per week: 15. Apply by n/a. Tuition remission given: full. Fellowships and scholarships available for advanced students. Average amount paid per academic year: $20,000. Average number of hours worked per week: 0. Apply by n/a. Tuition remission given: full.
Contact Information: Of all students currently enrolled full-time, 70% benefitted from one or more of the listed financial assistance programs.

Internships/Practica: No information provided.

Housing and Day Care: On-campus housing is available. See the following Web site for more information: http://www3.lehigh.edu/studentlife/slgraduatetransfer.asp. On-campus day care facilities are available. See the following Web site for more information: http://www.lehigh.edu/~inluccc/genop.html.

Employment of Department Graduates:
Master's Degree Graduates: Of those who graduated in the academic year 2003–2004, the following categories and numbers represent the post-graduate activities and employment of master's degree graduates: Enrolled in a psychology doctoral program (1), enrolled in another graduate/professional program (2), enrolled in a post-doctoral residency/fellowship (n/a), employed in independent practice (n/a), total from the above (master's) (3).
Doctoral Degree Graduates: Of those who graduated in the academic year 2003–2004, the following categories and numbers represent the post-graduate activities and employment of doctoral degree graduates: Enrolled in a psychology doctoral program (n/a), employed in an academic position at a 2-year/4-year college (1), total from the above (doctoral) (1).

Additional Information:
Orientation, Objectives, and Emphasis of Department: The Doctoral Program in Psychology is a research intensive program that combines focus with flexibility. Focus is provided by the program emphasis on Human Cognition and Development and by a core curriculum. Flexibility is provided by the ability to tailor a research specialization in an area of Cognition and Language, Developmental Psychology, or Social Cognition and Personality. Graduate students define an area of specialization through their selection of graduate seminars and through their research experiences. All students are actively engaged in research throughout their residence in the program, and they work in collaboration with faculty members and student colleagues. Departmental faculty conduct research on basic cognitive, linguistic, and social-

cognitive processes, and the development of these processes across the life span. See Web pages to obtain a more detailed sense of the range of our current research activity. In addition to research within the psychology department, the psychology faculty and students partake in interdisciplinary endeavors with researchers from other university departments and programs, including the Cognitive Science Program.

Special Facilities or Resources: The department's well-equipped laboratories provide an excellent setting for research. The department has extensive facilities available for graduate student research, including a child study center, and cognitive, developmental, and social laboratories. Lehigh has a sophisticated network system that connects all campus computers and servers together and provides easy access to the Internet and the World Wide Web.

Information for Students With Physical Disabilities: See the following Web site for more information: http://www.lehigh.edu/~indost/missionandpurpose.htm.

Application Information:

Send to: Graduate Programs Office, Lehigh University, 9 West Packer Avenue, Bethlehem, PA 18015-3075. Application available online. URL of online application: http://www.lehigh.edu/~inpsy/applying.html. Students are admitted in the Fall, application deadline January 15. *Fee:* $60.

Marywood University
Department of Psychology and Counseling
McGowan Center for Graduate and Professional Studies
Scranton, PA 18509
Telephone: (570) 348-6226
Fax: (570) 340-6040
E-mail: *OBrien@ES.Marywood.Edu*
Web: *http://www.Marywood.Edu*

Department Information:

1940. Chairperson: Edward J. O'Brien. Number of Faculty: total–full-time 13, part-time 30; women–full-time 4, part-time 16; minority–full-time 1.

Programs and Degrees Offered:

Listed in the following order: Program area, degree type (T if terminal Master's), number awarded 7/03–6/04. Counseling for Elementary School MA/MS (Master of Arts/Science) (T) 3, Counseling for Mental Health MA/MS (Master of Arts/Science) (T) 6, Counseling for Secondary School MA/MS (Master of Arts/Science) (T) 7, General Theoretical MA/MS (Master of Arts/Science) (T) 12, School Psychology Certificate EdS (Education Specialist) 5, Clinical Psychology PsyD (Doctor of Psychology) 0, Clinical Services MA/MS (Master of Arts/Science) (T) 4, Child Clinical Services MA/MS (Master of Arts/Science) 3.

Student Applications/Admissions:

Student Applications

Counseling for Elementary School MA/MS (Master of Arts/Science)—Applications 2004–2005, 9. Total applicants accepted 2004–2005, 6. Number enrolled (new admits only) 2004–2005 full-time, 1. Number enrolled (new admits only) 2004–2005 part-time, 3. Total enrolled 2004–2005 full-time, 3, part-time, 6. Openings 2005–2006, 10. The Median number of years required for completion of a degree are 3. The number of students enrolled full and part-time who were dismissed or voluntarily withdrew from this program area were 0. *Counseling for Mental Health MA/MS (Master of Arts/Science)*—Applications 2004–2005, 20. Total applicants accepted 2004–2005, 14. Number enrolled (new admits only) 2004–2005 full-time, 3. Number enrolled (new admits only) 2004–2005 part-time, 5. Total enrolled 2004–2005 full-time, 11, part-time, 12. Openings 2005–2006, 10. The Median number of years required for completion of a degree are 3. The number of students enrolled full and part-time who were dismissed or voluntarily withdrew from this program area were 0. *Counseling for Secondary School MA/MS (Master of Arts/Science)*—Applications 2004–2005, 26. Total applicants accepted 2004–2005, 20. Number enrolled (new admits only) 2004–2005 full-time, 3. Number enrolled (new admits only) 2004–2005 part-time, 5. Total enrolled 2004–2005 full-time, 12, part-time, 13. Openings 2005–2006, 10. The Median number of years required for completion of a degree are 3. The number of students enrolled full and part-time who were dismissed or voluntarily withdrew from this program area were 0. *General Theoretical MA/MS (Master of Arts/Science)*—Applications 2004–2005, 35. Total applicants accepted 2004–2005, 24. Number enrolled (new admits only) 2004–2005 full-time, 6. Number enrolled (new admits only) 2004–2005 part-time, 8. Total enrolled 2004–2005 full-time, 14, part-time, 17. Openings 2005–2006, 15. The Median number of years required for completion of a degree are 2.5. The number of students enrolled full and part-time who were dismissed or voluntarily withdrew from this program area were 1. *School Psychology Certificate EdS (Education Specialist)*—Applications 2004–2005, 12. Total applicants accepted 2004–2005, 8. Number enrolled (new admits only) 2004–2005 full-time, 2. Number enrolled (new admits only) 2004–2005 part-time, 3. Total enrolled 2004–2005 full-time, 3, part-time, 12. Openings 2005–2006, 10. The Median number of years required for completion of a degree are 3. The number of students enrolled full and part-time who were dismissed or voluntarily withdrew from this program area were 0. *Clinical Psychology PsyD (Doctor of Psychology)*—Applications 2004–2005, 31. Total applicants accepted 2004–2005, 8. Number enrolled (new admits only) 2004–2005 full-time, 8. Total enrolled 2004–2005 full-time, 26. Openings 2005–2006, 8. The Median number of years required for completion of a degree are 5. The number of students enrolled full and part-time who were dismissed or voluntarily withdrew from this program area were 1. *Clinical Services MA/MS (Master of Arts/Science)*—Applications 2004–2005, 10. Total applicants accepted 2004–2005, 7. Number enrolled (new admits only) 2004–2005 full-time, 1. Number enrolled (new admits only) 2004–2005 part-time, 3. Total enrolled 2004–2005 full-time, 5, part-time, 6. Openings 2005–2006, 10. The Median number of years required for completion of a degree are 3.5. The number of students enrolled full and part-time who were dismissed or voluntarily withdrew from this program area were 1. *Child Clinical Services MA/MS (Master of Arts/Science)*—Applications 2004–2005, 15. Total applicants accepted 2004–2005, 9. Number enrolled (new admits only) 2004–2005 full-time, 1. Number enrolled (new admits only) 2004–2005 part-time, 3.

Total enrolled 2004–2005 full-time, 4, part-time, 8. Openings 2005–2006, 8. The Median number of years required for completion of a degree are 3.5. The number of students enrolled full and part-time who were dismissed or voluntarily withdrew from this program area were 2.

Admissions Requirements:

Scores: Entries appear in this order: required test or GPA, minimum score (if required), median score of students entering in 2003–2004. Master's Programs: GRE-V 500; GRE-Q 500; GRE-V+Q 1000; MAT 50; overall undergraduate GPA 3.0, 3.20; psychology GPA 3.0, 3.20. Students applying for master's programs may take either the GRE or the MAT. Scores listed above are preferred. Individuals with scores lower than preferred will be considered. Doctoral Programs: GRE-V 500; GRE-Q 500; GRE-V+Q 1000; GRE-Analytical 520; GRE-Subject(Psych) 500; overall undergraduate GPA 3.3; psychology GPA 3.3.

Other Criteria: (importance of criteria rated low, medium, or high): GRE/MAT scores medium, research experience medium, work experience medium, extracurricular activity low, clinically related public service medium, GPA high, letters of recommendation high, interview low, statement of goals and objectives medium. PsyD program requires an interview.

Student Characteristics: The following represents characteristics of students in 2004–2005 in all graduate psychology programs in the department: Female–full-time 53, part-time 56; Male–full-time 25, part-time 18; African American/Black–full-time 0, part-time 0; Hispanic/Latino(a)–full-time 2, part-time 1; Asian/Pacific Islander–full-time 2, part-time 1; American Indian/Alaska Native–full-time 1, part-time 0; Caucasian–full-time 73, part-time 72; Multi-ethnic–full-time 0, part-time 0; students subject to the Americans With Disabilities Act–full-time 0, part-time 1.

Financial Information/Assistance:

Tuition for Full-Time Study: *Master's:* State residents: $617 per credit hour; Nonstate residents: $617 per credit hour. *Doctoral:* State residents: $652 per credit hour; Nonstate residents: $652 per credit hour. See the following Web site for updates and changes in tuition costs: www.marywood.edu/grad_finaid/financialfacts0506.pdf.

Financial Assistance:

First Year Students: Research assistantships available for first-year. Average amount paid per academic year: $4,300. Average number of hours worked per week: 20. Apply by February 15. Tuition remission given: full. Fellowships and scholarships available for first-year. Average amount paid per academic year: $3,837. Average number of hours worked per week: 0. Apply by February 15.

Advanced Students: Research assistantships available for advanced students. Average amount paid per academic year: $4,300. Average number of hours worked per week: 20. Apply by February 15. Tuition remission given: full. Fellowships and scholarships available for advanced students. Average amount paid per academic year: $3,837. Average number of hours worked per week: 0. Apply by February 15.

Contact Information: Of all students currently enrolled full-time, 56% benefitted from one or more of the listed financial assistance programs. Application and information available online at: http://www.marywood.edu/fin_aid/index.stm.

Internships/Practica: Students in recent years have had access to many schools, psychiatric hospitals, rehabilitation programs, community mental health programs, and prisons in the region of Northeastern Pennsylvania. The long history and size of our programs has provided us with the opportunity to develop close working relationships with most schools, social services, and mental health agencies in the region. The PsyD program (initiated in 2001) is planning for both internal and external practicum sites and regional/national placements in internship sites.

Housing and Day Care: No on-campus housing is available. On-campus day care facilities are available. Contact Graduate Admissions Office for details.

Employment of Department Graduates:

Master's Degree Graduates: Of those who graduated in the academic year 2003–2004, the following categories and numbers represent the post-graduate activities and employment of master's degree graduates: Enrolled in a post-doctoral residency/fellowship (n/a), employed in independent practice (n/a), total from the above (master's) (0).

Doctoral Degree Graduates: Of those who graduated in the academic year 2003–2004, the following categories and numbers represent the post-graduate activities and employment of doctoral degree graduates: Enrolled in a psychology doctoral program (n/a), total from the above (doctoral) (0).

Additional Information:

Orientation, Objectives, and Emphasis of Department: The department provides students with a variety of coherent training experiences that lead to diverse career paths in school counseling, agency mental health work, school psychology, and doctoral-level training in clinical psychology. The psychology and counseling programs in the department work collaboratively to optimize student training. Master's students can take electives in either the psychology or counseling programs. While the two program tracks collaborate, there are significant differences in the training approaches of these programs. The psychology programs emphasize scientific core knowledge in psychology, theory, and professional skill development, while the counseling programs emphasize theory, professional practice, and experiential aspects of training. Collaboration between psychology and counseling programs allows for more effective development of training resources. Faculty routinely teach in both programs. Effective collaboration between psychology and counseling faculty helps students appreciate interdisciplinary issues in the field. Ethical and professional practice issues are considered extensively. Professional guidelines are emphasized that increase students' awareness of their developing expertise and the limits of this expertise. Professional standards for practice, certification, and licensing guidelines are integrated into courses and advisement. Licensing of master's graduates in Counseling and Psychology in Pennsylvania is a new possibility with the implementation of the Professional Counseling Act. The Counseling Programs are accredited by the Council for the Accreditation of Counseling and Related Educational Programs (CACREP). The PsyD program follows the Vail model, training students to be scholar-practitioners and is a designee of the Association of State and Provincial Psychology Boards (ASPPB). The PsyD program includes both foundation courses in psychology and applied training. The use of empirically-supported assessments and intervention techniques is emphasized along with a focus on outcome assessment. There are opportunities for work with children, adolescents, and adults. The PsyD program primarily is cognitive-behavioral in focus, with additional training provided in interpersonal and other approaches to psychotherapy.

Special Facilities or Resources: The department moved into a new building, the McGowan Center for Graduate and Professional Studies, in the Fall, 1998 semester. The new building more than doubled the research and clinical training facilities available to students and faculty in the department. Research facilities include three state-of-the-art computer laboratories that provide for group and individual instruction, computer-equipped research cubicles that provide for online data collection, psychophysiological monitoring equipment, videotaping and editing facilities, digital video and CD-ROM/DVD creation capabilities, and an extensive testing laboratory. The department operates a clinic, the Psychological Services Center, that provides treatment and observation rooms for practicum training, individual therapy, play therapy, family, and group therapy.

Information for Students With Physical Disabilities: See the following Web site for more information: http://www.marywood. edu/disabilities/disabilities.stm.

Application Information:

Send to: Graduate Admissions Office, Marywood University. Application available online. URL of online application: www.marywood. edu/admissions/graduate/apply.stm. Students are admitted in the Fall, application deadline April 15; Spring, application deadline November 15; Summer, application deadline April 15. Applications for the PsyD program are due January 15. *Fee:* $30.

Millersville University
Department of Psychology
Byerly Hall
Millersville, PA 17551
Telephone: (717) 872-3093
Fax: (717) 871-2480
E-mail: *claudia.haferkamp@millersville.edu*
Web: *http://www.millersville.edu*

Department Information:

1967. Claudia Haferkamp, Graduate Program Coordinator: Helena Tuleya-Payne. Number of Faculty: total–full-time 20, part-time 6; women–full-time 15, part-time 4; minority–full-time 4.

Programs and Degrees Offered:

Listed in the following order: Program area, degree type (T if terminal Master's), number awarded 7/03–6/04. Clinical Psychology MA/MS (Master of Arts/Science) (T) 21, School Counseling Other 10, School Psychology MA/MS (Master of Arts/Science) 19, Supervision of School Guidance MA/MS (Master of Arts/Science) 5, Supervision of School Psychology MA/MS (Master of Arts/Science) 0.

Student Applications/Admissions:

Student Applications

Clinical Psychology MA/MS (Master of Arts/Science)—Applications 2004–2005, 40. Total applicants accepted 2004–2005,

20. Total enrolled 2004–2005 full-time, 11, part-time, 37. Openings 2005–2006, 25. *School Counseling Other*—Applications 2004–2005, 48. Total applicants accepted 2004–2005, 24. Total enrolled 2004–2005 full-time, 11, part-time, 44. Openings 2005–2006, 20. *School Psychology MA/MS (Master of Arts/Science)*—Applications 2004–2005, 64. Total applicants accepted 2004–2005, 28. Total enrolled 2004–2005 full-time, 32, part-time, 12. Openings 2005–2006, 20. *Supervision of School Guidance MA/MS (Master of Arts/Science)*—Applications 2004–2005, 4. Total applicants accepted 2004–2005, 4. Openings 2005–2006, 5. *Supervision of School Psychology MA/ MS (Master of Arts/Science)*—Applications 2004–2005, 19. Total applicants accepted 2004–2005, 17. Total enrolled 2004–2005 full-time, 5, part-time, 20. Openings 2005–2006, 5.

Admissions Requirements:

Scores: Entries appear in this order: required test or GPA, minimum score (if required), median score of students entering in 2003–2004. Master's Programs: GRE-V 450; GRE-Q 450; GRE-Analytical 450; overall undergraduate GPA 2.75. The scoring of the Analytical Writing Section of the GRE General Test was changed from the 200-800 scale previously used for the General Test to a 0 to 6 scale. Millersville has established a score of 3.5 on the Analytical Writing Section of the GRE General Test as equivalent to a score of 450 in the other sections.

Other Criteria: (importance of criteria rated low, medium, or high): GRE/MAT scores medium, research experience low, work experience high, extracurricular activity low, clinically related public service high, GPA medium, letters of recommendation high, interview high, statement of goals and objectives medium, All psychology graduate programs seek to prepare practitioners for work in either school or mental health settings. Therefore, practical experience outside the classroom setting is highly valued and may include undergraduate practica/internships or special directed projects, volunteer work experiences, and a wide range of pre and post-B.A. level jobs in schools and/or mental health settings. See specific program descriptions for further details.

Student Characteristics: The following represents characteristics of students in 2004–2005 in all graduate psychology programs in the department: Female–full-time 53, part-time 97; Male–full-time 6, part-time 26; African American/Black–full-time 7, part-time 8; Caucasian–full-time 47, part-time 106; Multi-ethnic–full-time 5, part-time 8.

Financial Information/Assistance:

Tuition for Full-Time Study: *Master's:* State residents: per academic year $2,759; Nonstate residents: per academic year $4,415. Tuition is subject to change. See the following Web site for updates and changes in tuition costs: Full-time tuition costs are based on 9-15 credit hours, plus $307 for every credit over 15 hours.

Financial Assistance:

First Year Students: No information provided.

Advanced Students: No information provided.

Contact Information: Application and information available online at: Graduate assistantships offer $4000 stipend and tuition waiver. Applications are encouraged.

Internships/Practica: Practica are required of all students in the clinical, school counseling, and school psychology programs. In addition, students in the Certification Program in School Psychology are required to engage in an internship experience that occurs on a full-time basis over a period of one academic year (minimum of 1200 hours) or on a half-time basis over a period of two consecutive academic years.

Housing and Day Care: No on-campus housing is available. No on-campus day care facilities are available.

Employment of Department Graduates:

Master's Degree Graduates: Of those who graduated in the academic year 2003–2004, the following categories and numbers represent the post-graduate activities and employment of master's degree graduates: Enrolled in a post-doctoral residency/fellowship (n/a), employed in independent practice (n/a), total from the above (master's) (0).

Doctoral Degree Graduates: Of those who graduated in the academic year 2003–2004, the following categories and numbers represent the post-graduate activities and employment of doctoral degree graduates: Enrolled in a psychology doctoral program (n/a), total from the above (doctoral) (0).

Additional Information:

Orientation, Objectives, and Emphasis of Department: All programs emphasize four components: academic training in relevant theory and knowledge, research skills and an ability to evaluate research critically, practical experience that can be directly useful in subsequent professional employment, and the development in each student a high degree of self-awareness and interpersonal relationship skills. The MS program in Clinical Psychology prepares clinicians with strong skills in psychological assessment and diagnosis, and an eclectic/cognitive-behavioral repertoire of skills in individual, group and family therapies. Graduates may obtain PA licensure as "professional counselors" and work in a wide range of inpatient and outpatient mental health and human service settings with children and adults. The Certification Program in School Psychology is approved by the National Association of School Psychologists and prepares students for entry level positions as school psychologists who work with students in school settings. Knowledge about the educational process, psychological and emotional growth, and data-based decision-making are central to the training program and enable students as problem-solvers to promote effective learning in children. The MEd and Certification in School Counseling programs prepare students for the profession of school counseling for grades K-12. Operating under a prevention/intervention model, students develop into professionals who are responsive to the needs of the school setting.

Special Facilities or Resources: A microcomputer lab and terminal access to the university's mainframe computer are available in the department. There is a psychoeducational clinic with one-way observation capability and videotape facilities. Ganser Library houses approximately a half million books and provides access to nearly 3500 periodical titles. Electronic resources available via the World Wide Web, as well as the Millersville University library catalog, are accessible from the University home page. The research and information needs of faculty, staff, and students, are met by subject specialists who provide extensive reference service within the library, at off-site locations, and electronically. Scholarly research is further supported by a comprehensive and well-

developed library collection that is continuously being augmented by the most current and up-to-date resources available, both in print and electronic format. The Library belongs to several statewide and regional library consortia. These consortia allow for resource sharing, reciprocal borrowing, and collaborative purchasing of resources.

Information for Students With Physical Disabilities: See the following Web site for more information: www.millersville.edu.

Application Information:
Send to: Graduate Studies Office, Millersville University, P.O. Box 1002, Millersville, PA 17551-0302. Students are admitted in the Fall, application deadline October 1; Winter, application deadline October 1; Spring, application deadline March 1; Summer, application deadline March 1. Applicants whose graduate applications are not fully complete by the deadline may apply for "nondegree status" from Graduate Studies. Nondegree status will permit the student enroll in a graduate class with permission from the Assistant Chair. When/if the nondegree applicant is accepted into a graduate program, her/his nondegree credits may be applied to the graduate program. There is a limit of 12 nondegree credits. *Fee:* $25.

Mount Aloysius College
Office of Graduate Admissions
Liberal Arts, Sciences, and Professional Studies
7373 Admiral Peary Highway
Cresson, PA 16630
Telephone: (814) 886-6383, (888) 823-2220
Fax: (814) 886-6441
E-mail: *admissions@mtaloy.edu*
Web: *www.mtaloy.edu*

Department Information:
2002. Chairperson: Dr. Brad Hastings. Number of Faculty: total–full-time 5; women–full-time 2.

Programs and Degrees Offered:
Listed in the following order: Program area, degree type (T if terminal Master's), number awarded 7/03–6/04. Master of Arts in Psychology MA/MS (Master of Arts/Science).

Student Applications/Admissions:
Student Applications
Master of Arts in Psychology MA/MS (Master of Arts/Science)—

Admissions Requirements:
Scores: Entries appear in this order: required test or GPA, minimum score (if required), median score of students entering in 2003–2004. Master's Programs: overall undergraduate GPA 3.2.
Other Criteria: (importance of criteria rated low, medium, or high): GRE/MAT scores medium, research experience low, work experience low, extracurricular activity medium, GPA high, letters of recommendation high, interview high, statement of goals and objectives high.

Student Characteristics: The following represents characteristics of students in 2004–2005 in all graduate psychology programs in the department: Caucasian–full-time 0, part-time 0.

Financial Information/Assistance:

Tuition for Full-Time Study: *Master's:* State residents: $450 per credit hour. Tuition is subject to change. See the following Web site for updates and changes in tuition costs: www.mtaloy.edu.

Financial Assistance:

First Year Students: No information provided.
Advanced Students: No information provided.
Contact Information: Application and information available online at: www.mtaloy.edu.

Internships/Practica: No information provided.

Housing and Day Care: On-campus housing is available. On-campus day care facilities are available.

Employment of Department Graduates:

Master's Degree Graduates: Of those who graduated in the academic year 2003–2004, the following categories and numbers represent the post-graduate activities and employment of master's degree graduates: Enrolled in a post-doctoral residency/fellowship (n/a), employed in independent practice (n/a), total from the above (master's) (0).

Doctoral Degree Graduates: Of those who graduated in the academic year 2003–2004, the following categories and numbers represent the post-graduate activities and employment of doctoral degree graduates: Enrolled in a psychology doctoral program (n/a), total from the above (doctoral) (0).

Application Information:

Send to: Office of Undergraduate and Graduate Admissions, 7373 Admiral Peary Highway Cresson, PA 16630, Phone: (814) 886-6383 or (888) 823-2220 (toll free), www.mtaloy.edu (to apply online). Application available online. Students are admitted in the Fall, application deadline August 1; Spring, application deadline December 1; Summer, application deadline May 1. Programs have rolling admissions. *Fee:* $30.

Penn State Harrisburg (2004 data)
Psychology Program
777 W. Harrisburg Pike
Middletown, PA 17057-4898
Telephone: (717) 948-6059
Fax: (717) 948-6519
E-mail: *dzx@psu.edu*
Web: *http://www.hbg.psu.edu*

Department Information:

1992. Coordinator: Michael A. Becker. Number of Faculty: total–full-time 11, part-time 6; women–full-time 8, part-time 3; minority–full-time 1.

Programs and Degrees Offered:

Listed in the following order: Program area, degree type (T if terminal Master's), number awarded 7/03–6/04. Applied Clinical Psychology MA/MS (Master of Arts/Science) (T) 0, Applied Psychological Research MA/MS (Master of Arts/Science) (T) 1.

Student Applications/Admissions:

Student Applications

Applied Clinical Psychology MA/MS (Master of Arts/Science)—Applications 2004–2005, 31. Total applicants accepted 2004–2005, 22. Total enrolled 2004–2005 full-time, 11, part-time, 23. Openings 2005–2006, 15. The number of students enrolled full and part-time who were dismissed or voluntarily withdrew from this program area were 1. *Applied Psychological Research MA/MS (Master of Arts/Science)*—Applications 2004–2005, 6. Total applicants accepted 2004–2005, 5. Total enrolled 2004–2005 full-time, 4, part-time, 6. Openings 2005–2006, 15. The Median number of years required for completion of a degree are 2. The number of students enrolled full and part-time who were dismissed or voluntarily withdrew from this program area were 1.

Admissions Requirements:

Scores: Entries appear in this order: required test or GPA, minimum score (if required), median score of students entering in 2003–2004. Master's Programs: GRE-V no minimum stated, 470; GRE-Q no minimum stated, 530; GRE-Analytical no minimum stated, 5.0; last 2 years GPA 3.0, 3.5.

Other Criteria: (importance of criteria rated low, medium, or high): GRE/MAT scores high, research experience medium, work experience low, clinically related public service low, GPA high, letters of recommendation high, interview high, statement of goals and objectives high.

Student Characteristics: The following represents characteristics of students in 2004–2005 in all graduate psychology programs in the department: Female–full-time 11, part-time 23; Male–full-time 4, part-time 6; African American/Black–part-time 2; Hispanic/Latino(a)–full-time 1, part-time 1; Caucasian–full-time 0, part-time 0; students subject to the Americans With Disabilities Act–part-time 1.

Financial Information/Assistance:

Tuition for Full-Time Study: *Master's:* State residents: per academic year $10,010, $417 per credit hour; Nonstate residents: per academic year $16,512, $688 per credit hour. Tuition is subject to change.

Financial Assistance:

First Year Students: Research assistantships available for first-year. Average amount paid per academic year: $12,915. Average number of hours worked per week: 20. Apply by March 1. Tuition remission given: full. Fellowships and scholarships available for first-year. Average amount paid per academic year: $14,900. Average number of hours worked per week: 20. Apply by March. Tuition remission given: full.

Advanced Students: Fellowships and scholarships available for advanced students. Apply by varies. Tuition remission given: full.

Contact Information: Of all students currently enrolled full-time, 10% benefitted from one or more of the listed financial assistance programs. Application and information available online at: http://www.hbg.psu.edu.

Internships/Practica: Students in the Applied Clinical Psychology program are required to complete 9 credits of supervised clinical internships. Students in the Applied Psychological Research program are required to complete 6 credits of research in collaboration with the program faculty.

Housing and Day Care: On-campus housing is available. See the following Web site for more information: www.hbg.psu.edu. On-campus day care facilities are available.

Employment of Department Graduates:

Master's Degree Graduates: Of those who graduated in the academic year 2003–2004, the following categories and numbers represent the post-graduate activities and employment of master's degree graduates: Enrolled in a post-doctoral residency/fellowship (n/a), employed in independent practice (n/a), employed in a hospital/medical center (1), total from the above (master's) (1). *Doctoral Degree Graduates:* Of those who graduated in the academic year 2003–2004, the following categories and numbers represent the post-graduate activities and employment of doctoral degree graduates: Enrolled in a psychology doctoral program (n/a), total from the above (doctoral) (0).

Additional Information:

Orientation, Objectives, and Emphasis of Department: The Applied Clinical Psychology program prepares students to work as mental health professionals in a variety of settings and is intended to provide the academic training necessary for graduates to apply for master's-level licensing for mental health professionals in the Commonwealth of Pennsylvania. The overall model emphasizes the scientific bases of behavior, including biological, social, and individual difference factors. The training model is health-oriented rather than pathology-oriented and emphasizes the development of helping skills, including both assessment and intervention. Students can choose a concentration in General Clinical, Forensic Psychology, or Health Psychology. The Applied Psychological Research program focuses on the development of research skills within the context of scientific training in psychology. The program is designed to meet the needs of students who plan careers in research or administration within human services or similar organizations, who plan to conduct research in other settings, or who plan to pursue doctoral study. Students can select electives and research experiences to reflect their individual interests in consultation with their advisor.

Special Facilities or Resources: The Psychology program maintains an on-site clinic for the assessment of specific learning disorders in college students. This clinic provides advanced Applied Clinical Psychology students the opportunity to assist with psychological testing, report writing, diagnosis, and treatment recommendations under the supervision of the program faculty.

Information for Students With Physical Disabilities: Contact Lynne Davies, Disability Services Coordinator: (717) 948-6025.

Application Information:
Send to: Graduate Admissions, Penn State Harrisburg, 777 W. Harrisburg Pike, Middletown, PA 17057-4898. Application available online. Students are admitted in the Fall, application deadline May 1; Spring, application deadline November 1. January 10 application deadline for University fellowships and assistantships. *Fee:* $45 fee is for online application; fee for mail-in application is $65.

Pennsylvania State University
Counseling Psychology Program
Education
327 Cedar Building
University Park, PA 16802
Telephone: (814) 865-8304
Fax: (814) 863-7750
E-mail: *jxh34@psu.edu*
Web: *http://www.ed.psu.edu/cnpsy/index.asp*

Department Information:
1982. Head of Department: Robert B. Slaney. Number of Faculty: total–full-time 4; women–full-time 2.

Programs and Degrees Offered:
Listed in the following order: Program area, degree type (T if terminal Master's), number awarded 7/03–6/04. Counseling Psychology PhD (Doctor of Philosophy) 4.

APA Accreditation: Counseling PhD (Doctor of Philosophy).

Student Applications/Admissions:
Student Applications
Counseling Psychology PhD (Doctor of Philosophy)—Applications 2004–2005, 67. Total applicants accepted 2004–2005, 6. Number enrolled (new admits only) 2004–2005 full-time, 6. Openings 2005–2006, 7. The Median number of years required for completion of a degree are 6. The number of students enrolled full and part-time who were dismissed or voluntarily withdrew from this program area were 0.

Admissions Requirements:
Scores: Entries appear in this order: required test or GPA, minimum score (if required), median score of students entering in 2003–2004. Doctoral Programs: GRE-V 550; GRE-Q 550; GRE-V+Q 1100; GRE-Analytical no minimum stated. The numbers in the minimum score column are the preferred scores. *Other Criteria:* (importance of criteria rated low, medium, or high): GRE/MAT scores high, research experience high, work experience medium, extracurricular activity low, clinically related public service medium, GPA high, letters of recommendation high, interview high, statement of goals and objectives high.

Student Characteristics: The following represents characteristics of students in 2004–2005 in all graduate psychology programs in the department: Female–full-time 25, part-time 0; Male–full-time 10, part-time 0; African American/Black–full-time 6, part-time 0; Hispanic/Latino(a)–full-time 4, part-time 0; Asian/Pacific Islander–full-time 5, part-time 0; American Indian/Alaska Native–full-time 0, part-time 0; Caucasian–full-time 20, part-time 0; students subject to the Americans With Disabilities Act–full-time 1, part-time 0.

Financial Information/Assistance:
Tuition for Full-Time Study: *Doctoral:* State residents: per academic year $11,348, $473 per credit hour; Nonstate residents: per

academic year $21,498, $896 per credit hour. Tuition is subject to change. See the following Web site for updates and changes in tuition costs: http://www.tuition.psu.edu.

Financial Assistance:

First Year Students: Teaching assistantships available for first-year. Average amount paid per academic year: $11,790. Average number of hours worked per week: 20. Tuition remission given: full. Research assistantships available for first-year. Average amount paid per academic year: $11,790. Average number of hours worked per week: 20. Tuition remission given: full. Fellowships and scholarships available for first-year. Average amount paid per academic year: $15,200. Tuition remission given: full.

Advanced Students: Teaching assistantships available for advanced students. Average amount paid per academic year: $11,790. Average number of hours worked per week: 20. Tuition remission given: full. Research assistantships available for advanced students. Average amount paid per academic year: $11,790. Average number of hours worked per week: 20. Tuition remission given: full.

Contact Information: Of all students currently enrolled full-time, 100% benefitted from one or more of the listed financial assistance programs.

Internships/Practica: Students are placed in practicum in the College of Education Counseling Service in their first semester. Supervision consists of 1.5 hours of individual supervision and a two-hour seminar. The same supervision and seminar arrangements are provided for the second practicum at Penn State's Career Services. A counseling psychology faculty member conducts the seminar and coordinates the interaction of students with the staff at Career Services. Although the program does not require students to be on campus during the summer, most students continue their practicum work at Penn State's Counseling and Psychological Services (CAPS) during the summer of their first year and for all of their second year. At CAPS, in addition to a two-hour seminar for case discussion and presentation, individual supervision is provided by the members of the CAPS staff and interns from their APA-approved Internship Program. Students may also take an additional practicum in their third year at either an on-campus agency or an agency in the community. Students typically apply for internships in their third year and go on internship in their fourth year. The program specifies that students apply to and accept only APA-approved internship positions. For those doctoral students for whom a professional internship is required prior to graduation, 5 applied in 2003–2004. Of those who applied, 5 were placed in internships listed by the Association of Psychology Postdoctoral and Internship Programs (APPIC); 5 were placed in APA accredited internships.

Housing and Day Care: On-campus housing is available. See the following Web site for more information: http://www.hfs.psu.edu/universitypark/. On-campus day care facilities are available http://www.ohr.psu.edu/worklife/subsidies.htm.

Employment of Department Graduates:

Master's Degree Graduates: Of those who graduated in the academic year 2003–2004, the following categories and numbers represent the post-graduate activities and employment of master's degree graduates: Enrolled in a post-doctoral residency/fellowship (n/a), employed in independent practice (n/a), total from the above (master's) (0).

Doctoral Degree Graduates: Of those who graduated in the academic year 2003–2004, the following categories and numbers represent the post-graduate activities and employment of doctoral degree graduates: Enrolled in a psychology doctoral program (n/a), employed in an academic position at a university (1), employed in other positions at a higher education institution (1), other employment position (1), do not know (1), total from the above (doctoral) (4).

Additional Information:

Orientation, Objectives, and Emphasis of Department: The Counseling Psychology Program at The Pennsylvania State University endorses the scientist-practitioner model of training. Psychological training is provided within this model with equal emphasis and value placed on both scholarly and clinical work as well as their integration. A primary goal of the program is the preparation of counseling psychologists for professional roles as academics, researchers, or practitioners who are concerned with interventions involving individual behavior and institutional settings which are focused on relational, multicultural, career, and psychosocial issues. More specifically, the primary objective of Penn State's Counseling Psychology Program is to train carefully selected and promising graduate students to function as thoughtful, ethical, caring, and competent professional psychologists. Whereas the Counseling Psychology Program is fully accredited by the American Psychological Association, our faculty and students strive to exceed the standards required for accreditation. One particular area in which we attempt to do so is in engendering a multicultural perspective in our students. At Penn State, we do not merely recognize the diversity represented in our faculty, students, and clients, we actively affirm the richness of our cultures and we embrace the continual challenge of examining ourselves to determine how to more effectively serve a pluralistic society.

Special Facilities or Resources: The department maintains a Resource Center that includes many of the professional journals, reference, and testing materials pertinent to the curriculum. Doctoral students are provided offices, when available, with access to personal computers. The university provides each student with an e-mail account. The College of Education Counseling Service is located in the building and provides practicum experiences for graduate students. The Service is coordinated by a licensed psychologist and serves clients from the campus, providing personal, academic, and vocational counseling. The Service has individual counseling rooms equipped for video recording and live observation through one-way mirrors.

Information for Students With Physical Disabilities: See the following Web site for more information: http://www.lions.psu.edu/ODS/.

Application Information:

Send to: Counseling Psychology, 327 Cedar Building, Penn State, University Park, PA 16802. Application available online. Students are admitted in the Fall, application deadline December 15. *Fee:* $45.

Pennsylvania State University

Department of Human Development and Family Studies,
   Graduate Program in Human Development and Family
   Studies
College of Health and Human Development
S-110 Henderson Building
University Park, PA 16802
Telephone: (814) 863-8000
Fax: (814) 863-7963
E-mail: *cse1@psu.edu*
Web: *http://www.hhdev.psu.edu/hdfs/grad/index.html*

Department Information:

1974. Professor in Charge of Graduate Program: Craig Edelbrock. Number of Faculty: total–full-time 33; women–full-time 17; minority–full-time 5.

Programs and Degrees Offered:

Listed in the following order: Program area, degree type (T if terminal Master's), number awarded 7/03–6/04. Human Development & Family Studies PhD (Doctor of Philosophy) 15.

Student Applications/Admissions:

Student Applications

Human Development & Family Studies PhD (Doctor of Philosophy)—Applications 2004–2005, 83. Total applicants accepted 2004–2005, 29. Openings 2005–2006, 18. The Median number of years required for completion of a degree are 5. The number of students enrolled full and part-time who were dismissed or voluntarily withdrew from this program area were 0.

Admissions Requirements:

Scores: Entries appear in this order: required test or GPA, minimum score (if required), median score of students entering in 2003–2004. Doctoral Programs: GRE-V no minimum stated; GRE-Q no minimum stated; GRE-V+Q no minimum stated, 1190; GRE-Analytical no minimum stated; overall undergraduate GPA, 3.79.

Other Criteria: (importance of criteria rated low, medium, or high): GRE/MAT scores high, research experience high, work experience low, extracurricular activity low, GPA high, letters of recommendation high, interview low, statement of goals and objectives high, writing sample medium.

Student Characteristics: The following represents characteristics of students in 2004–2005 in all graduate psychology programs in the department: Female–full-time 76, part-time 0; Male–full-time 8, part-time 0; African American/Black–full-time 5, part-time 0; Hispanic/Latino(a)–full-time 3, part-time 0; Asian/Pacific Islander–full-time 8, part-time 0; American Indian/Alaska Native–full-time 0, part-time 0; Caucasian–full-time 0, part-time 0; Multiethnic–full-time 0, part-time 0; students subject to the Americans With Disabilities Act–full-time 0, part-time 0.

Financial Information/Assistance:

Tuition for Full-Time Study: *Doctoral:* State residents: per academic year $10,861; Nonstate residents: per academic year $21,722.

Financial Assistance:

First Year Students: Teaching assistantships available for first-year. Average amount paid per academic year: $14,175. Average number of hours worked per week: 20. Apply by January 5. Tuition remission given: full. Research assistantships available for first-year. Average amount paid per academic year: $14,175. Average number of hours worked per week: 20. Apply by January 5. Tuition remission given: full. Fellowships and scholarships available for first-year. Average amount paid per academic year: $15,100. Average number of hours worked per week: 10. Apply by January 5. Tuition remission given: full.

Advanced Students: Teaching assistantships available for advanced students. Average amount paid per academic year: $14,775. Average number of hours worked per week: 20. Apply by September. Tuition remission given: full. Research assistantships available for advanced students. Average amount paid per academic year: $14,775. Average number of hours worked per week: 20. Apply by September. Tuition remission given: full.

Contact Information: Of all students currently enrolled full-time, 100% benefitted from one or more of the listed financial assistance programs.

Internships/Practica: No information provided.

Housing and Day Care: On-campus housing is available. See the following Web site for more information: www.personal.psu.edu/HDFS_CDL/. On-campus day care facilities are available.

Employment of Department Graduates:

Master's Degree Graduates: Of those who graduated in the academic year 2003–2004, the following categories and numbers represent the post-graduate activities and employment of master's degree graduates: Enrolled in a post-doctoral residency/fellowship (n/a), employed in independent practice (n/a), total from the above (master's) (0).

Doctoral Degree Graduates: Of those who graduated in the academic year 2003–2004, the following categories and numbers represent the post-graduate activities and employment of doctoral degree graduates: Enrolled in a psychology doctoral program (n/a), enrolled in a post-doctoral residency/fellowship (4), employed in independent practice (0), employed in an academic position at a university (6), employed in business or industry (research/consulting) (5), total from the above (doctoral) (15).

Additional Information:

Orientation, Objectives, and Emphasis of Department: The basic objectives of the Human Development and Family Studies (HDFS) program are the following: to expand knowledge about the development and functioning of individuals, small groups, and families; to improve methods for studying processes of human development and change; and to create and disseminate improved techniques and strategies for enhancing individual and family functioning, helping people learn to cope more effectively with problems of living, and preventing normal life problems from becoming serious difficulties. The program takes a life-span perspective, recognizing that the most important aspects of development and types of life tasks and situations vary from infancy and childhood through maturity and old age, as well as through the life cycle of the family, and that each phase of development is a precursor to the next. There is a firm commitment to an interdisciplinary and multiprofessional approach to these objectives and to the development of competence in applying rigorous methods of empirical inquiry. All students are expected to acquire a broad interdisciplinary base of knowledge and to develop competence in depth in one of four primary program areas: family development, individual development, human development intervention, or methodology.

Special Facilities or Resources: Several additional facilities are associated with the College of Health and Human Development: Child development-child services laboratories are operated by the department as part of the teaching and research program. Current programs include nursery school classes and infant and preschool day care. Each unit has observational facilities, and there are adjoining rooms for study of individual and group behavior of children and adults. The "Working Collection" sponsored by the department and the Gerontology Center provides resource material for students and faculty. The collection, serving as an in-house library, includes a selection of journals, books, and conference proceedings pertinent to the study of individuals and families, particularly those focusing on adulthood and aging. The collection also includes a copy of all theses and dissertations submitted by HDFS graduates. The Individual and Family Consultation Center provides facilities for the development and operation of programs that enhance individual and family functioning through competency-building programs and the use of paraprofessionals in community mental health. The Human Development Data Laboratory provides 10 public-use terminals for accessing the IBM 370-3088 processor, the main computer on campus. In addition, the laboratory has standard statistical packages available, such as SAS and SPSS, and the laboratory staff provides consulting and programming support to students. The laboratory also provides microcomputer training and consulting.

Application Information:
Send to: Graduate Admissions, c/o Mary Jo Spicer, Penn State University, Department of Human Development and Family Studies, S110 Henderson Building, University Park, PA 16802. Students are admitted in the Winter, application deadline January 5. Must take GRE Exams no later than November to be considered for admission. *Fee:* $45 online application fee and $60 fee for paper application.

Pennsylvania State University
Department of Psychology
417 Bruce V. Moore Building
University Park, PA 16802-3104
Telephone: (814) 863-1721
Fax: (814) 863-7002
E-mail: *bjc2@psu.edu*
Web: *http://psych.la.psu.edu*

Department Information:
1933. Head, Department of Psychology: Kevin R. Murphy. Number of Faculty: total–full-time 45; women–full-time 17; minority–full-time 4.

Programs and Degrees Offered:
Listed in the following order: Program area, degree type (T if terminal Master's), number awarded 7/03–6/04. Clinical PhD (Doctor of Philosophy) 5, Clinical-Child PhD (Doctor of Philosophy) 7, Cognitive PhD (Doctor of Philosophy) 2, Developmental PhD (Doctor of Philosophy) 4, Industrial/Organizational PhD (Doctor of Philosophy) 3, Social PhD (Doctor of Philosophy) 1.

APA Accreditation: Clinical PhD (Doctor of Philosophy).

Student Applications/Admissions:
Student Applications
Clinical PhD (Doctor of Philosophy)—Applications 2004–2005, 133. Total applicants accepted 2004–2005, 7. Number enrolled (new admits only) 2004–2005 full-time, 5. Total enrolled 2004–2005 full-time, 37, part-time, 1. Openings 2005–2006, 6. The number of students enrolled full and part-time who were dismissed or voluntarily withdrew from this program area were 2. *Clinical-Child PhD (Doctor of Philosophy)*—Applications 2004–2005, 206. Total applicants accepted 2004–2005, 8. Number enrolled (new admits only) 2004–2005 full-time, 6. Total enrolled 2004–2005 full-time, 22, part-time, 2. Openings 2005–2006, 5. The number of students enrolled full and part-time who were dismissed or voluntarily withdrew from this program area were 3. *Cognitive PhD (Doctor of Philosophy)*—Applications 2004–2005, 39. Total applicants accepted 2004–2005, 13. Number enrolled (new admits only) 2004–2005 full-time, 4. Total enrolled 2004–2005 full-time, 13, part-time, 1. Openings 2005–2006, 4. The number of students enrolled full and part-time who were dismissed or voluntarily withdrew from this program area were 0. *Developmental PhD (Doctor of Philosophy)*—Applications 2004–2005, 36. Total applicants accepted 2004–2005, 11. Number enrolled (new admits only) 2004–2005 full-time, 4. Total enrolled 2004–2005 full-time, 10, part-time, 1. Openings 2005–2006, 3. The number of students enrolled full and part-time who were dismissed or voluntarily withdrew from this program area were 1. *Industrial/Organizational PhD (Doctor of Philosophy)*—Applications 2004–2005, 11. Total applicants accepted 2004–2005, 7. Number enrolled (new admits only) 2004–2005 full-time, 6. Total enrolled 2004–2005 full-time, 22, part-time, 4. Openings 2005–2006, 5. The number of students enrolled full and part-time who were dismissed or voluntarily withdrew from this program area were 1. *Social PhD (Doctor of Philosophy)*—Applications 2004–2005, 77. Total applicants accepted 2004–2005, 9. Number enrolled (new admits only) 2004–2005 full-time, 5. Total enrolled 2004–2005 full-time, 14, part-time, 2. Openings 2005–2006, 4. The number of students enrolled full and part-time who were dismissed or voluntarily withdrew from this program area were 1.

Admissions Requirements:
Scores: Entries appear in this order: required test or GPA, minimum score (if required), median score of students entering in 2003–2004. Doctoral Programs: GRE-V no minimum stated; GRE-Q no minimum stated; GRE-V+Q no minimum stated, 1272; GRE-Analytical no minimum stated, 683; last 2 years GPA no minimum stated, 3.84. We do not have a formal cut-off score. GRE Subject exam not required.
Other Criteria: (importance of criteria rated low, medium, or high): GRE/MAT scores high, research experience high, work experience medium, extracurricular activity low, clinically related public service medium, GPA high, letters of recommendation high, interview medium, statement of goals and objectives high. Clinical weighs work, clinical experience, and interviews heavily; other areas do not weight these factors

strongly. For additional information on admission requirements, go to: http://psych.la.psu.edu.

Student Characteristics: The following represents characteristics of students in 2004–2005 in all graduate psychology programs in the department: Female–full-time 88, part-time 10; Male–full-time 30, part-time 1; African American/Black–full-time 3, part-time 1; Hispanic/Latino(a)–full-time 6, part-time 0; Asian/Pacific Islander–full-time 5, part-time 2; American Indian/Alaska Native–full-time 0, part-time 0; Caucasian–full-time 104, part-time 8; students subject to the Americans With Disabilities Act–full-time 1, part-time 0.

Financial Information/Assistance:

Tuition for Full-Time Study: *Doctoral:* State residents: per academic year $11,348, $473 per credit hour; Nonstate residents: per academic year $21,498, $896 per credit hour. Tuition is subject to change. See the following Web site for updates and changes in tuition costs: www.psu.edu.

Financial Assistance:

First Year Students: Teaching assistantships available for first-year. Average amount paid per academic year: $14,200. Average number of hours worked per week: 20. Apply by December 1. Tuition remission given: full. Research assistantships available for first-year. Average amount paid per academic year: $14,200. Average number of hours worked per week: 20. Apply by December 1. Tuition remission given: full. Fellowships and scholarships available for first-year. Average amount paid per academic year: $18,000. Average number of hours worked per week: 0. Apply by December 1. Tuition remission given: full.

Advanced Students: Teaching assistantships available for advanced students. Average amount paid per academic year: $14,200. Average number of hours worked per week: 20. Apply by None. Tuition remission given: full. Research assistantships available for advanced students. Average amount paid per academic year: $14,200. Average number of hours worked per week: 20. Apply by None. Tuition remission given: full. Fellowships and scholarships available for advanced students. Average amount paid per academic year: $18,000. Average number of hours worked per week: 0. Apply by None. Tuition remission given: full.

Contact Information: Of all students currently enrolled full-time, 85% benefitted from one or more of the listed financial assistance programs.

Internships/Practica: No information is provided. For those doctoral students for whom a professional internship is required prior to graduation, 8 applied in 2003–2004. Of those who applied, 8 were placed in APA accredited internships.

Housing and Day Care: On-campus housing is available. See the following Web site for more information: www.psu.edu. On-campus day care facilities are available.

Employment of Department Graduates:

Master's Degree Graduates: Of those who graduated in the academic year 2003–2004, the following categories and numbers represent the post-graduate activities and employment of master's degree graduates: Enrolled in a post-doctoral residency/fellowship (n/a), employed in independent practice (n/a), total from the above (master's) (0).

Doctoral Degree Graduates: Of those who graduated in the academic year 2003–2004, the following categories and numbers represent the post-graduate activities and employment of doctoral degree graduates: Enrolled in a psychology doctoral program (n/a), enrolled in a post-doctoral residency/fellowship (8), employed in an academic position at a university (4), employed in an academic position at a 2-year/4-year college (1), employed in other positions at a higher education institution (1), employed in business or industry (research/consulting) (5), employed in a community mental health/counseling center (1), employed in a hospital/medical center (1), still seeking employment (1), total from the above (doctoral) (22).

Additional Information:

Orientation, Objectives, and Emphasis of Department: Graduate study in psychology at Penn State is characterized by highly flexible, individualized programs leading to the PhD in Psychology. Each student is associated with one of the five program areas offered in the department: clinical (including child clinical); cognitive; developmental; industrial/organizational; and social. (Specialization in behavioral neuroscience is possible in any program area). Students in any program area may combine their program of study with a specialization in behavioral neuroscience by choosing appropriate courses and seminars. Students choosing this specialization may pursue the integration of neuroscience methods and theories by applying these approaches to research topics within their program areas. Within each area, certain courses are usually suggested for all students. The details of a student's program, however, are worked out on an individual basis with a faculty advisor. A major specialization and breadth outside the major are required. The major is selected from among the six specialty areas of the department listed above; breadth requirements are flexible and individualized to career goals. Depending upon the individual student's particular program of study, graduates may be employed in academic departments, research institutes, industry, governmental agencies, or various service delivery settings.

Special Facilities or Resources: The department has clinical, learning-cognition, perception, physiological, psychophysiology, developmental and social laboratories; microcomputer laboratories; access to the University's mainframe and electronic communication system (e-mail and Internet) and computer laboratories; clinical practica in local mental health centers and hospitals in addition to the department's Psychological Clinic, which functions as a mental health center for the catchment area of central Pennsylvania; industrial/organizational practica in industrial and government organizations; developmental practica and research opportunities in day care and preschool settings. A number of centers or institutes are housed within, or affiliated with the department, including a new Child Study Center.

Application Information:

Send to: Graduate Admissions, Department of Psychology, Penn State University, 350 Moore Building, University Park, PA 16802. Application available online. URL of online application: http://psych.la.psu.edu. Students are admitted in the Fall. December 1 is the deadline for Clinical, I/O and Social areas; deadline for Cognitive and Developmental areas is January 15. *Fee:* $45.

Pennsylvania State University

Educational Psychology
Education
227 Cedar Building
University Park, PA 16802
Telephone: (814) 863-2286
Fax: (814) 863-1002
E-mail: rjs15@psu.edu
Web: http://espse.ed.psu.edu/edpsy2/edpsyhome.html

Department Information:

1968. Professor-in-Charge: Peggy N. Van Meter. Number of Faculty: total–full-time 8, part-time 1; women–full-time 6; minority–full-time 2.

Programs and Degrees Offered:

Listed in the following order: Program area, degree type (T if terminal Master's), number awarded 7/03–6/04. Educational PhD (Doctor of Philosophy) 5.

Student Applications/Admissions:

Student Applications

Educational PhD (Doctor of Philosophy)—Applications 2004–2005, 31. Total applicants accepted 2004–2005, 7. Total enrolled 2004–2005 full-time, 31. Openings 2005–2006, 5. The Median number of years required for completion of a degree are 6. The number of students enrolled full and part-time who were dismissed or voluntarily withdrew from this program area were 2.

Admissions Requirements:

Scores: Entries appear in this order: required test or GPA, minimum score (if required), median score of students entering in 2003–2004. Master's Programs: GRE-V no minimum stated, 550; GRE-Q no minimum stated, 600; GRE-Analytical no minimum stated, 550; last 2 years GPA no minimum stated, 3.50. Doctoral Programs: GRE-V no minimum stated, 550; GRE-Q no minimum stated, 600; GRE-Analytical no minimum stated, 550.

Other Criteria: (importance of criteria rated low, medium, or high): GRE/MAT scores medium, research experience medium, work experience medium, extracurricular activity low, GPA medium, letters of recommendation high, statement of goals and objectives high. Interview optional.

Student Characteristics: The following represents characteristics of students in 2004–2005 in all graduate psychology programs in the department: Female–full-time 17, part-time 0; Male–full-time 14, part-time 0; African American/Black–full-time 0, part-time 0; Hispanic/Latino(a)–full-time 0, part-time 0; Asian/Pacific Islander–full-time 6, part-time 0; American Indian/Alaska Native–full-time 0, part-time 0; Caucasian–full-time 0, part-time 0; students subject to the Americans With Disabilities Act–full-time 0, part-time 0.

Financial Information/Assistance:

Financial Assistance:

First Year Students: Teaching assistantships available for first-year. Average amount paid per academic year: $11,790. Average number of hours worked per week: 20. Apply by January 15.

Tuition remission given: full. Research assistantships available for first-year. Average amount paid per academic year: $13,185. Average number of hours worked per week: 20. Apply by January 15. Tuition remission given: full. Fellowships and scholarships available for first-year. Average amount paid per academic year: $14,900. Average number of hours worked per week: 20. Apply by January 15. Tuition remission given: full.

Advanced Students: Teaching assistantships available for advanced students. Average amount paid per academic year: $11,790. Average number of hours worked per week: 20. Tuition remission given: full. Research assistantships available for advanced students. Average amount paid per academic year: $13,185. Average number of hours worked per week: 20. Tuition remission given: full.

Contact Information: Of all students currently enrolled full-time, 75% benefitted from one or more of the listed financial assistance programs. Application and information available online at: espse.ed.psu.edu/edpsy2/edpsyhome.html.

Internships/Practica: No information provided.

Housing and Day Care: On-campus housing is available. On-campus day care facilities are available.

Employment of Department Graduates:

Master's Degree Graduates: Of those who graduated in the academic year 2003–2004, the following categories and numbers represent the post-graduate activities and employment of master's degree graduates: Enrolled in a psychology doctoral program (5), enrolled in another graduate/professional program (0), enrolled in a post-doctoral residency/fellowship (n/a), employed in independent practice (n/a), total from the above (master's) (5).

Doctoral Degree Graduates: Of those who graduated in the academic year 2003–2004, the following categories and numbers represent the post-graduate activities and employment of doctoral degree graduates: Enrolled in a psychology doctoral program (n/a), employed in an academic position at a university (4), employed in business or industry (research/consulting) (1), total from the above (doctoral) (5).

Additional Information:

Orientation, Objectives, and Emphasis of Department: Students may specialize and do research in one of the following areas: human learning and memory as applied to instruction, or education and educational and psychological measurement as applied to the evaluation of educational programs. There are two options in the master's program. A thesis option is available in either of the two areas. The learning faculty primarily focus on research related to learning to read and learning from reading text across the life span. There is also some emphasis on instruction for students who are at-risk. The measurement faculty focus on applied measurement issues, particularly validity and generalizabilty theory.

Special Facilities or Resources: Facilities include a research design laboratory, rooms for conducting research projects, a closed-circuit television studio for research and instruction, computer system facilities, access to the University mainframe computer, and a division resource center. The program has excellent computer resources with computers in labs and in most student offices. All computers are hard-wired to the University mainframe. Students have ready access to a variety of statistical packages and other relevant educational and research software.

Application Information:
Send to: Admissions Committee, Educational Psychology Program, 227 Cedar Building, Penn State University, University Park, PA 16802. Application available online. URL of online application: espse.ed. psu.edu/edpsy2/edpsyhome.html. Students are admitted in the Fall. Programs have rolling admissions. Fall admission open but application must be received by to January 15 for Fellowship consideration. Financial aid decisions made starting January 15. *Fee:* $45. None.

Pennsylvania State University
Program in School Psychology
College of Education
125 Cedar Building
University Park, PA 16802
Telephone: (814) 865-1881
Fax: (814) 863-1002
E-mail: *s_psy@psu.edu*
Web: *http://espse.ed.psu.edu/spsy/SPSY.ssi*

Department Information:
1965. Professor-in-Charge: Marley W. Watkins. Number of Faculty: total–full-time 5, part-time 6; women–full-time 2, part-time 4; minority–full-time 1.

Programs and Degrees Offered:
Listed in the following order: Program area, degree type (T if terminal Master's), number awarded 7/03–6/04. School PhD (Doctor of Philosophy) 3.

APA Accreditation: School PhD (Doctor of Philosophy).

Student Applications/Admissions:
Student Applications
School PhD (Doctor of Philosophy)—Applications 2004–2005, 72. Total applicants accepted 2004–2005, 7. Number enrolled (new admits only) 2004–2005 full-time, 7. Number enrolled (new admits only) 2004–2005 part-time, 0. Openings 2005–2006, 6. The Median number of years required for completion of a degree are 8. The number of students enrolled full and part-time who were dismissed or voluntarily withdrew from this program area were 1.

Admissions Requirements:
Scores: Entries appear in this order: required test or GPA, minimum score (if required), median score of students entering in 2003–2004. Doctoral Programs: GRE-V 490, 570; GRE-Q 470, 594; last 2 years GPA 3.10, 3.76.
Other Criteria: (importance of criteria rated low, medium, or high): GRE/MAT scores medium, research experience medium, work experience medium, clinically related public service low, GPA medium, letters of recommendation high, interview high, statement of goals and objectives high.

Student Characteristics: The following represents characteristics of students in 2004–2005 in all graduate psychology programs in the department: Female–full-time 21, part-time 0; Male–full-time 1, part-time 0; African American/Black–full-time 1, part-time 0; Hispanic/Latino(a)–full-time 0, part-time 0; Asian/Pacific Islander–full-time 0, part-time 0; American Indian/Alaska Native–full-time 0, part-time 0; Caucasian–full-time 21, part-time 0; Multi-ethnic–full-time 0, part-time 0; students subject to the Americans With Disabilities Act–full-time 0, part-time 0.

Financial Information/Assistance:
Tuition for Full-Time Study: *Doctoral:* State residents: per academic year $11,348; Nonstate residents: per academic year $21,498. Tuition is subject to change. See the following Web site for updates and changes in tuition costs: http://www.bursar. psu.edu/.

Financial Assistance:
First Year Students: Teaching assistantships available for first-year. Average amount paid per academic year: $12,500. Average number of hours worked per week: 20. Apply by January 1. Tuition remission given: full. Research assistantships available for first-year. Average amount paid per academic year: $12,500. Average number of hours worked per week: 20. Apply by January 1. Tuition remission given: full. Fellowships and scholarships available for first-year. Average amount paid per academic year: $14,900. Average number of hours worked per week: 0. Apply by January 1. Tuition remission given: full.

Advanced Students: Teaching assistantships available for advanced students. Average amount paid per academic year: $12,500. Average number of hours worked per week: 20. Tuition remission given: full. Research assistantships available for advanced students. Average amount paid per academic year: $12,500. Average number of hours worked per week: 20. Tuition remission given: full.

Contact Information: Of all students currently enrolled full-time, 100% benefitted from one or more of the listed financial assistance programs. Application and information available online at: http://www.gradsch.psu.edu/.

Internships/Practica: is required prior to graduation, 5 applied in 2003–2004.

Housing and Day Care: On-campus housing is available. See the following Web site for more information: http://www.gradsch.psu. edu/. On-campus day care facilities are available.

Employment of Department Graduates:
Master's Degree Graduates: Of those who graduated in the academic year 2003–2004, the following categories and numbers represent the post-graduate activities and employment of master's degree graduates: Enrolled in a psychology doctoral program (0), enrolled in another graduate/professional program (0), enrolled in a post-doctoral residency/fellowship (n/a), employed in independent practice (n/a), employed in an academic position at a university (0), employed in an academic position at a 2-year/4-year college (0), employed in other positions at a higher education institution (0), employed in a professional position in a school system (3), employed in business or industry (research/consulting) (0), employed in business or industry (management) (0), employed in a government agency (research) (0), employed in a government agency (professional services) (0), employed in a community mental health/counseling center (0), employed in a hospital/medical center (0), still seeking employment (0), not

seeking employment (0), other employment position (0), do not know (0), total from the above (master's) (3).

Doctoral Degree Graduates: Of those who graduated in the academic year 2003–2004, the following categories and numbers represent the post-graduate activities and employment of doctoral degree graduates: Enrolled in a psychology doctoral program (n/a), enrolled in another graduate/professional program (0), enrolled in a post-doctoral residency/fellowship (0), employed in independent practice (0), employed in an academic position at a university (0), employed in an academic position at a 2-year/4-year college (0), employed in other positions at a higher education institution (0), employed in a professional position in a school system (6), employed in business or industry (research/consulting) (0), employed in business or industry (management) (0), employed in a government agency (research) (0), employed in a government agency (professional services) (0), employed in a community mental health/counseling center (0), employed in a hospital/medical center (0), still seeking employment (0), other employment position (0), do not know (0), total from the above (doctoral) (6).

Additional Information:

Orientation, Objectives, and Emphasis of Department: School psychologists from Penn State are exemplary scientist/practitioners, firmly grounded in both psychology and education. Our graduates are professional school psychologists who provide solutions for the many problems facing children. They contribute to the practice and knowledge base of psychology as it relates to education. Penn State school psychologists become leaders in the field as well as in academia. In conjunction with providing psychological services, school psychologists will be life-long learners who sustain an interest in maintaining and developing sound practices, which derive from up-to-date, research-based information. Psychologists will thoughtfully and critically evaluate their practices and remain informed consumers of available literature, assessment tools, and intervention strategies. School psychologists will help to provide a bridge to integrate research with professional practice along with other educators, systems, and institutions.

Special Facilities or Resources: The School Psychology Program operates the CEDAR School Psychology Clinic. The CEDAR Clinic contains well appointed clinic rooms with direct observation facilities and a closed-circuit video system, which facilitate practicum supervision. Computers are available to students within the program, department, and university. Access to e-mail and the Internet are provided to all students and use of technology is encouraged by faculty. The Pattee and Paterno Libraries house an impressive array of scholarly resources. As a major research university, Penn State sponsors a number of research institutes and centers in education, psychology, and human development.

Information for Students With Physical Disabilities: See the following Web site for more information: http://www.lions.psu.edu/ODS/.

Application Information:

Send to: Graduate Programs in School Psychology, Admissions Committee, 125 Cedar Building, Pennsylvania State University, University Park, PA 16802. Application available online. URL of online application: http://espse.ed.psu.edu/spsy/ApplicantInfo.ssi. Students are admitted in the Fall, application deadline February 1. January 1 for consideration for assistantship/fellowship. *Fee:* $60.

Pennsylvania, University of
Department of Psychology
3720 Walnut Street
Philadelphia, PA 19104
Telephone: (215) 898-7300
Fax: (215) 898-7301
E-mail: *re@psych.upenn.edu*
Web: *http://www.psych.upenn.edu/grad.html*

Department Information:

1887. Graduate Group Chair: John Sabini. Number of Faculty: total–full-time 30; women–full-time 10.

Programs and Degrees Offered:

Listed in the following order: Program area, degree type (T if terminal Master's), number awarded 7/03–6/04. Psychology PhD (Doctor of Philosophy) 6, Clinical Psychology PhD (Doctor of Philosophy) 4.

APA Accreditation: Clinical PhD (Doctor of Philosophy).

Student Applications/Admissions:

Student Applications

Psychology PhD (Doctor of Philosophy)—Applications 2004–2005, 193. Total applicants accepted 2004–2005, 15. Number enrolled (new admits only) 2004–2005 full-time, 5. Total enrolled 2004–2005 full-time, 26. Openings 2005–2006, 6. The Median number of years required for completion of a degree are 5. The number of students enrolled full and part-time who were dismissed or voluntarily withdrew from this program area were 2. *Clinical Psychology PhD (Doctor of Philosophy)*—Applications 2004–2005, 292. Total applicants accepted 2004–2005, 10. Number enrolled (new admits only) 2004–2005 full-time, 5. Total enrolled 2004–2005 full-time, 19. Openings 2005–2006, 4. The Median number of years required for completion of a degree are 6. The number of students enrolled full and part-time who were dismissed or voluntarily withdrew from this program area were 0.

Admissions Requirements:

Scores: Entries appear in this order: required test or GPA, minimum score (if required), median score of students entering in 2003–2004. Doctoral Programs: GRE-V no minimum stated, 680; GRE-Q no minimum stated, 740; GRE-Analytical no minimum stated, 700; overall undergraduate GPA no minimum stated, 3.8.

Other Criteria: (importance of criteria rated low, medium, or high): GRE/MAT scores medium, research experience high, work experience low, clinically related public service low, GPA medium, letters of recommendation medium, interview low, statement of goals and objectives high. For additional information on admission requirements, go to: http://www.psych.upenn.edu.

Student Characteristics: The following represents characteristics of students in 2004–2005 in all graduate psychology programs in the department: Female–full-time 24, part-time 0; Male–full-time 21, part-time 0; African American/Black–full-time 0, part-time 0; Hispanic/Latino(a)–full-time 0, part-time 0; Asian/Pacific Islander–part-time 0; American Indian/Alaska Native–full-time 0, part-time 0; Caucasian–full-time 0, part-time 0.

Financial Information/Assistance:

Financial Assistance:

First Year Students: Traineeships available for first-year. Average amount paid per academic year: $20,000. Average number of hours worked per week: 12. Apply by December 15. Tuition remission given: full. Fellowships and scholarships available for first-year. Average amount paid per academic year: $20,000. Average number of hours worked per week: 12. Apply by December 15. Tuition remission given: full.

Advanced Students: Teaching assistantships available for advanced students. Average amount paid per academic year: $20,000. Average number of hours worked per week: 12. Apply by December 15. Tuition remission given: full. Research assistantships available for advanced students. Average amount paid per academic year: $20,000. Average number of hours worked per week: 12. Apply by December 15. Tuition remission given: full. Traineeships available for advanced students. Average amount paid per academic year: $20,000. Average number of hours worked per week: 12. Apply by December 15. Tuition remission given: full. Fellowships and scholarships available for advanced students. Average amount paid per academic year: $20,000. Average number of hours worked per week: 12. Apply by December 15. Tuition remission given: full.

Contact Information: Of all students currently enrolled full-time, 100% benefitted from one or more of the listed financial assistance programs.

Internships/Practica:

Because of the wealth of opportunities for clinical training in the Philadelphia area, Penn does not run an in-house psychological services clinic. Rather, Penn's clinical students have the opportunity to participate in practica at local hospitals, clinics and research facilities staffed and run by world-renowned clinical scientists. The Associate Director of Clinical Training helps students decide which practicum experiences best suit the student's needs and interests, and arranges for placements at the appropriate sites. For more information, see: http://www.psych.upenn.edu/grad/clinprog.htm#five. For those doctoral students for whom a professional internship is required prior to graduation, 3 applied in 2003–2004. Of those who applied, 3 were placed in internships listed by the Association of Psychology Postdoctoral and Internship Programs (APPIC); 3 were placed in APA accredited internships.

Housing and Day Care:

On-campus housing is available. See the following Web site for more information: http://www.upenn.edu/campus/housing.php. No on-campus day care facilities are available.

Employment of Department Graduates:

Master's Degree Graduates: Of those who graduated in the academic year 2003–2004, the following categories and numbers represent the post-graduate activities and employment of master's degree graduates: Enrolled in a post-doctoral residency/fellowship (n/a), employed in independent practice (n/a), total from the above (master's) (0).

Doctoral Degree Graduates: Of those who graduated in the academic year 2003–2004, the following categories and numbers represent the post-graduate activities and employment of doctoral degree graduates: Enrolled in a psychology doctoral program (n/a), total from the above (doctoral) (0).

Additional Information:

Orientation, Objectives, and Emphasis of Department: The Department of Psychology at the University of Pennsylvania offers curricular and research opportunities for the study of sensation, perception, cognition, cognitive neuroscience, decision-making, language, learning, motivation, emotion, motor control, psychopathology, and social processes. Biological, cultural, developmental, comparative, experimental, and mathematical approaches to these areas are used in ongoing teaching and research. The department has an APA-accredited clinical program that is designed to prepare students for research careers in inteventions, psychopathology and personality. The interests of the faculty and students in the department cover the entire field of research-oriented psychology. Still, the Department of Psychology at Pennsylvania functions as a single unit whose guiding principle is scientific excellence. Students are admitted to the department. The primary determinant of acceptance is academic promise rather than specific area of interest. Faculty join together from different subdisciplines for teaching and research purposes so that students become conversant with issues in a number of different areas. Most graduate students and faculty attend the weekly departmental colloquia. A high level of interaction among department members (students and faculty), within and across disciplines, helps generate both a shared set of interests in the theoretical, historical, and philosophical foundations of psychology and active collaboration in research projects. This level of intellectual interaction is made possible, in part, by the small size of the department; there are 23 full-time faculty members and approximately 40 graduate students in residence. The first-year program is divided between courses that introduce various areas of psychology and a focused research experience. A deep involvement in research continues throughout the graduate program, and is supplemented by participation in seminars, the weekly departmental colloquium, teaching, and general intellectual give and take.

Special Facilities or Resources: The department has a fully equipped wood, metal, and electronics shop. In addition, the department has a well-equipped laboratory building, a microvax connected to Internet (used extensively), and many accessible microcomputers. Also readily available for research in the near environs of the department are four major university-affiliated hospitals, urban public and private schools, and the Philadelphia Zoo, ten minutes from campus.

Information for Students With Physical Disabilities: See the following Web site for more information: http://www.vpul.upenn.edu/lrc/sds/index.html.

Application Information:

Send to: Graduate School of Arts and Sciences, Suite 322A, 3401 Walnut Street, Philadelphia, PA 19104. Application available online. URL of online application: https://galaxy.isc-seo.upenn.edu:7778/pls/gaadmin/gapk0101.bf00?P_SRS_DIV=GAS&P_SRS_MAJOR=PSYC. Students are admitted in the Fall, application deadline December 15. *Fee:* $65.

Pennsylvania, University of
Division of Applied Psychology and Human Development
Graduate School of Education
3700 Walnut Street
Philadelphia, PA 19104-6216
Telephone: (215) 898-4176
Fax: (215) 573-2115
E-mail: *jordane@gse.upenn.edu*
Web: *http://www.upenn.edu/gse/*

Department Information:
1975. Chair, Division of Applied Psychology and Human Development: Douglas Frye. Number of Faculty: total–full-time 5, part-time 6; women–full-time 2, part-time 3; minority–full-time 2, part-time 1.

Programs and Degrees Offered:
Listed in the following order: Program area, degree type (T if terminal Master's), number awarded 7/03–6/04. Psychological Services Other 32, Interdisciplinary Studies in Human Development Other 4, Interdisciplinary Studies in Human Development PhD (Doctor of Philosophy) 1, Professional Counseling and Psychology Other 0.

Student Applications/Admissions:
Student Applications
Psychological Services Other—Applications 2004–2005, 95. Total applicants accepted 2004–2005, 43. Number enrolled (new admits only) 2004–2005 full-time, 23. Number enrolled (new admits only) 2004–2005 part-time, 0. Total enrolled 2004–2005 full-time, 23, part-time, 1. Openings 2005–2006, 35. The Median number of years required for completion of a degree is 1. The number of students enrolled full and part-time who were dismissed or voluntarily withdrew from this program area were 0. *Interdisciplinary Studies in Human Development Other*—Applications 2004–2005, 32. Total applicants accepted 2004–2005, 15. Total enrolled 2004–2005 full-time, 3, part-time, 3. Openings 2005–2006, 20. The Median number of years required for completion of a degree is 1. *Interdisciplinary Studies in Human Development PhD (Doctor of Philosophy)*—Applications 2004–2005, 36. Total applicants accepted 2004–2005, 5. Total enrolled 2004–2005 full-time, 12, part-time, 2. Openings 2005–2006, 3. The Median number of years required for completion of a degree are 5. *Professional Counseling and Psychology Other*—Applications 2004–2005, 0. Total applicants accepted 2004–2005, 0. Number enrolled (new admits only) 2004–2005 full-time, 0. Number enrolled (new admits only) 2004–2005 part-time, 0. Openings 2005–2006, 10. The number of students enrolled full and part-time who were dismissed or voluntarily withdrew from this program area were 0.

Admissions Requirements:
Scores: Entries appear in this order: required test or GPA, minimum score (if required), median score of students entering in 2003–2004. Master's Programs: GRE-V no minimum stated; GRE-Q no minimum stated; GRE-V+Q no minimum stated; overall undergraduate GPA no minimum stated; psychology GPA no minimum stated. Doctoral Programs: GRE-V no minimum stated; GRE-Q no minimum stated; GRE-V+Q 1200, mum stated; GRE-Q no minimum stated; GRE-V+Q 1200, 1255; GRE-Analytical no minimum stated; overall undergraduate GPA 3.25, 3.41.
Other Criteria: (importance of criteria rated low, medium, or high): GRE/MAT scores high, research experience medium, work experience medium, extracurricular activity low, clinically related public service medium, GPA high, letters of recommendation high, interview high, statement of goals and objectives high.

Student Characteristics: The following represents characteristics of students in 2004–2005 in all graduate psychology programs in the department: Female–full-time 63, part-time 2; Male–full-time 3, part-time 0; African American/Black–full-time 6, part-time 0; Hispanic/Latino(a)–full-time 1, part-time 0; Asian/Pacific Islander–full-time 5, part-time 1; American Indian/Alaska Native–full-time 0, part-time 0; Caucasian–full-time 51, part-time 1; Multi-ethnic–full-time 2, part-time 0; students subject to the Americans With Disabilities Act–full-time 0, part-time 0.

Financial Information/Assistance:
Financial Assistance:
First Year Students: Teaching assistantships available for first-year. Average number of hours worked per week: 20. Apply by December 15. Tuition remission given: full. Research assistantships available for first-year. Average number of hours worked per week: 20. Apply by December 15. Tuition remission given: full. Fellowships and scholarships available for first-year. Average number of hours worked per week: 20. Apply by December 15. Tuition remission given: full.
Advanced Students: Teaching assistantships available for advanced students. Average number of hours worked per week: 20. Apply by ongoing. Research assistantships available for advanced students. Average number of hours worked per week: 20. Apply by ongoing. Fellowships and scholarships available for advanced students. Average number of hours worked per week: 20. Apply by ongoing.
Contact Information: Of all students currently enrolled full-time, 60% benefitted from one or more of the listed financial assistance programs.

Internships/Practica:
MSEd students engage in supervised practica for 8 hours a week for two semesters. Placements include schools, community colleges, clinics, and community agencies. MPhil students will be required to complete a supervised two-semester, 20-hour per week internship.

Housing and Day Care:
On-campus housing is available. See the following Web site for more information: http://www.business-services.upenn.edu/housing/. On-campus day care facilities are available. See the following Web site for more information: http://www.business-services.upenn.edu/childcare/.

Employment of Department Graduates:
Master's Degree Graduates: Of those who graduated in the academic year 2003–2004, the following categories and numbers represent the post-graduate activities and employment of master's degree graduates: Enrolled in a post-doctoral residency/fellowship (n/a), employed in independent practice (n/a), total from the above (master's) (0).
Doctoral Degree Graduates: Of those who graduated in the academic year 2003–2004, the following categories and numbers represent the post-graduate activities and employment of doctoral

degree graduates: Enrolled in a psychology doctoral program (n/a), total from the above (doctoral) (0).

Additional Information:

Orientation, Objectives, and Emphasis of Department: The Division of Applied Psychology and Human Development at Penn Graduate School of Education provides students with a foundation in the core concepts of psychology: intervention, prevention, assessment, learning and development, and field practice or research. Students engage in the challenge of framing major psychological, educational, and social questions, of identifying and developing evidence bearing on those questions, and of working productively at the level of the individual, the community, the nation, and the world. Our orientation in psychological practice and research is toward discovery of what works best, and why, advancing our understanding of ways to characterize and resolve psychological and social problems, and promoting the use of that knowledge in professional practice and in educational and public policy contexts. Students are prepared for careers in teaching, research, and practice in schools and universities, in clinical settings and mental health agencies, in government and the corporate world. Our objectives are to provide students with the richest possible opportunities to develop productive careers. The MSEd in Psychological Services prepares students for practice in diverse community agencies; graduates also may obtain certification in guidance counseling. Our new MPhil program in Professional Counseling and Psychology is for students who have already earned a master's degree in clinical or counseling psychology (or related mental health field) and wish to pursue licensure as a professional counselor (LPC).

Special Facilities or Resources: The Division houses the Center for Health Achievement, Neighborhood Growth and Ethnic Studies (CHANGES), providing students with research mentorship and opportunities. The Division maintains ongoing research programs on early numeracy development, examination of the protective roles of racial identity and racial socialization for African American youth in schools, and understanding the role of various risk and protective factors on the health and well-being of youth. Our building was recently renovated and houses state-of-the-art computer labs and renovated classrooms, as well as wireless access.

Information for Students With Physical Disabilities: See the following Web site for more information: http://www.vpul.upenn.edu/lrc/sds/index.html.

Application Information:
Send to: Admissions Office, Graduate School of Education, University of Pennsylvania, 3700 Walnut Street, Philadelphia, PA 19104-6216. Application available online. URL of online application: www.gse.upenn.edu. Students are admitted in the Fall, application deadline January 1. This deadline is for applications to the PhD program in Interdisciplinary Studies in Human Development only. Applications may be accepted the next business day. Applications for all MSEd and MPhil. programs are accepted on a rolling admissions basis. *Fee:* $65. Fee is usually waived upon request.

Philadelphia College of Osteopathic Medicine
Psychology Department
4190 City Avenue
Philadelphia, PA 19131-1693
Telephone: (215) 871-6442
Fax: (215) 871-6458
E-mail: *psyd@pcom.edu*
Web: *http://www.pcom.edu*

Department Information:
1995. Chairperson: Robert A. DiTomasso, PhD, ABPP. Number of Faculty: total–full-time 16, part-time 44; women–full-time 8, part-time 21; minority–full-time 1, part-time 3; faculty subject to the Americans With Disabilities Act 1.

Programs and Degrees Offered:
Listed in the following order: Program area, degree type (T if terminal Master's), number awarded 7/03–6/04. Certificate of Advanced Graduate Study (CAGS) Other 5, Counseling & Clinical Health Psychology MA/MS (Master of Arts/Science) (T) 8, Clinical Psychology Respecialization Diploma 0, Clinical Psychology PsyD (Doctor of Psychology) 36, Organizational Development and Leadership MA/MS (Master of Arts/Science) (T) 10, School Psychology PsyD (Doctor of Psychology) 0, School Psychology MA/MS (Master of Arts/Science) (T) 0, School Psychology EdS (Education Specialist) 0.

APA Accreditation: Clinical PsyD (Doctor of Psychology).

Student Applications/Admissions:
Student Applications
Certificate of Advanced Graduate Study (CAGS) Other—Applications 2004–2005, 10. Total applicants accepted 2004–2005, 5. Number enrolled (new admits only) 2004–2005 part-time, 5. Openings 2005–2006, 5. The Median number of years required for completion of a degree is 1. The number of students enrolled full and part-time who were dismissed or voluntarily withdrew from this program area were 0. *MS in Counseling & Clinical Health Psychology MA/MS (Master of Arts/Science)*—Applications 2004–2005, 60. Total applicants accepted 2004–2005, 27. Number enrolled (new admits only) 2004–2005 full-time, 24. Number enrolled (new admits only) 2004–2005 part-time, 3. Total enrolled 2004–2005 full-time, 48, part-time, 9. Openings 2005–2006, 30. The Median number of years required for completion of a degree are 2. The number of students enrolled full and part-time who were dismissed or voluntarily withdrew from this program area were 2. *Clinical Psychology Respecialization Diploma*—Applications 2004–2005, 0. Total applicants accepted 2004–2005, 0. Number enrolled (new admits only) 2004–2005 full-time, 0. Number enrolled (new admits only) 2004–2005 part-time, 0. Openings 2005–2006, 2. The number of students enrolled full and part-time who were dismissed or voluntarily withdrew from this program area were 0. *Clinical Psychology PsyD (Doctor of Psychology)*—Applications 2004–2005, 86. Total applicants accepted 2004–2005, 28. Number enrolled (new admits only) 2004–2005 full-time, 26. Number enrolled (new admits only) 2004–2005 part-time, 0. Openings 2005–2006, 26. The Median number of years required for completion of a degree are 6. The number of students enrolled full and part-time who were dismissed or

voluntarily withdrew from this program area were 3. *Organizational Development and Leadership (ODL) MA/MS (Master of Arts/Science)*—Applications 2004–2005, 35. Total applicants accepted 2004–2005, 30. Number enrolled (new admits only) 2004–2005 full-time, 8. Number enrolled (new admits only) 2004–2005 part-time, 22. Total enrolled 2004–2005 full-time, 9, part-time, 50. Openings 2005–2006, 30. The Median number of years required for completion of a degree are 2.5. The number of students enrolled full and part-time, who were dismissed or voluntarily withdrew from this program area were 3. *School Psychology PsyD (Doctor of Psychology)*—Applications 2004–2005, 35. Total applicants accepted 2004–2005, 17. Number enrolled (new admits only) 2004–2005 full-time, 17. Openings 2005–2006, 14. The Median number of years required for completion of a degree are 4. The number of students enrolled full and part-time who were dismissed or voluntarily withdrew from this program area were 2. *School Psychology MA/MS (Master of Arts/Science)*—Applications 2004–2005, 30. Total applicants accepted 2004–2005, 18. Number enrolled (new admits only) 2004–2005 full-time, 18. Openings 2005–2006, 14. The Median number of years required for completion of a degree is 1. The number of students enrolled full and part-time who were dismissed or voluntarily withdrew from this program area were 0. *Specialist in School Psychology EdS (Education Specialist)*—Applications 2004–2005, 30. Total applicants accepted 2004–2005, 17. Number enrolled (new admits only) 2004–2005 full-time, 17. Total enrolled 2004–2005 full-time, 17. Openings 2005–2006, 25. The Median number of years required for completion of a degree are 3. The number of students enrolled full and part-time who were dismissed or voluntarily withdrew from this program area were 1.

Admissions Requirements:

Scores: Entries appear in this order: required test or GPA, minimum score (if required), median score of students entering in 2003–2004. Master's Programs: MAT no minimum stated; overall undergraduate GPA 3.0, 3.4. The EdS program requires the subject area psychology and Praxis exam. Doctoral Programs: overall undergraduate GPA 3.0, 3.5.

Other Criteria: (importance of criteria rated low, medium, or high): GRE/MAT scores medium, research experience low, work experience high, extracurricular activity medium, clinically related public service high, GPA high, letters of recommendation high, interview high, statement of goals and objectives medium. Work experience is weighted medium as admission criteria for the MS in School Psychology, MS in Counseling & Clinical Health Psychology, and CAGS programs. Work experience is weighted high as admission criteria for the MS in ODL, EdS and PsyD programs. In addition, the EdS is an admissions requirement for the PsyD in School Psychology program. For additional information on admission requirements, go to: www.pcom.edu.

Student Characteristics: The following represents characteristics of students in 2004–2005 in all graduate psychology programs in the department: Female–full-time 222, part-time 45; Male–full-time 112, part-time 21; African American/Black–full-time 59, part-time 22; Hispanic/Latino(a)–full-time 11, part-time 0; Asian/Pacific Islander–full-time 10, part-time 0; American Indian/Alaska Native–full-time 1, part-time 0; Caucasian–full-time 252, part-time 44; Multi-ethnic–full-time 1, part-time 0; students sub-

ject to the Americans With Disabilities Act–full-time 4, part-time 0.

Financial Information/Assistance:

Tuition for Full-Time Study: *Master's:* State residents: $560 per credit hour; Nonstate residents: $560 per credit hour. *Doctoral:* State residents: $774 per credit hour; Nonstate residents: $774 per credit hour. Tuition is subject to change. See the following Web site for updates and changes in tuition costs: http://www.pcom.edu/Admissions/adm_tution_fees/adm_tution_fees.html.

Financial Assistance:

First Year Students: Research assistantships available for first-year. Average amount paid per academic year: $6,000. Average number of hours worked per week: 12. Apply by late summer.

Advanced Students: Research assistantships available for advanced students. Average amount paid per academic year: $7,200. Average number of hours worked per week: 12. Apply by late summer.

Contact Information: Of all students currently enrolled full-time, 1% benefitted from one or more of the listed financial assistance programs. Application and information available online at: http://www.pcom.edu.

Internships/Practica: Practica are nine-month fieldwork experiences completed by master's level and doctoral students that require a minimum of 8 hours per week at a Philadelphia College of Osteopathic Medicine (PCOM) approved clinical training site. Practicum sites are committed to excellence in the training of professionals and provide extensive supervision and formative clinical experiences. They offer a wide range of training, including the use of empirically supported interventions, brief treatment models, cognitive behavioral therapy, and treatment of psychological/medical problems. Students engage in evaluation, psychological testing (PsyD only), psychotherapy, and professional clinical work. Practica include seminars taught by faculty that provide a place for students to discuss their experiences and help them integrate coursework with on-site training. Students participate in pratica at the Psychology Department's Center for Brief Therapy, a multi-faceted clinical training center, as well as sites including community agencies, hospitals, university counseling centers, prisons, and specialized treatment centers. The department has a broad network of practicum sites in Pennsylvania, New Jersey, Maryland, and Delaware. Students apply for internships through the APPIC matching program. For those doctoral students for whom a professional internship is required prior to graduation, 8 applied in 2003–2004. Of those who applied, 4 were placed in internships listed by the Association of Psychology Postdoctoral and Internship Programs (APPIC); 3 were placed in APA accredited internships.

Housing and Day Care: No on-campus housing is available. No on-campus day care facilities are available.

Employment of Department Graduates:

Master's Degree Graduates: Of those who graduated in the academic year 2003–2004, the following categories and numbers represent the post-graduate activities and employment of master's degree graduates: Enrolled in a psychology doctoral program (2), enrolled in a post-doctoral residency/fellowship (n/a), employed in independent practice (n/a), employed in a professional position in a school system (1), employed in a community mental health/

counseling center (4), employed in a hospital/medical center (1), other employment position (10), total from the above (master's) (18).

Doctoral Degree Graduates: Of those who graduated in the academic year 2003–2004, the following categories and numbers represent the post-graduate activities and employment of doctoral degree graduates: Enrolled in a psychology doctoral program (n/a), enrolled in a post-doctoral residency/fellowship (1), employed in independent practice (5), employed in an academic position at a university (1), employed in other positions at a higher education institution (2), employed in a professional position in a school system (4), employed in business or industry (management) (1), employed in a government agency (professional services) (3), employed in a community mental health/counseling center (9), employed in a hospital/medical center (3), other employment position (4), do not know (3), total from the above (doctoral) (36).

Additional Information:

Orientation, Objectives, and Emphasis of Department: The mission of the Department of Psychology at PCOM is to prepare highly skilled, compassionate doctoral level psychologists and master's level psychological specialists to provide empirically based, active, focused, and collaborative assessments and treatments with sensitivity to cultural and ethnic diversity and the underserved. Grounded in the cognitive behavioral tradition, the graduate programs in psychology train practitioner-scholars to offer assessment, therapeutic interventions, consultation, and follow-up services, and to engage in scholarly activities in the fields of clinical and school psychology. The PCOM Department of Psychology offers graduate programs in psychology at several levels to suit a variety of professional needs and interests. The PsyD program in Clinical Psychology accepts students to its sites in Philadelphia and Harrisburg, PA.

Special Facilities or Resources: The academic facilities in Philadelphia include state-of-the-art amphitheaters and classroom facilities, a computer laboratory with extensive software including PsycLIT and SPSS, a recently renovated library that includes sophisticated online resources, and the HealthNet teleconferencing system. The Center for Brief Therapy, a mental health clinic housed in the Department of Psychology, provides multi-faceted clinical training and research opportunities for students. PCOM also has three neighborhood health centers in Philadelphia and one in LaPorte, Pennsylvania. The Doctor of Psychology program in Clinical Psychology has 3 program sites: Philadelphia, Harrisburg, and East Stroudsburg (the program is no longer accepting applications to the East Stroudsburg site). Each site is equipped with videoconferencing technology.

Application Information:
Send to: Philadelphia College of Osteopathic Medicine, Department of Admissions, 4170 City Avenue, Philadelphia, PA 19131. Application available online. URL of online application: http://www.pcom.edu/Admissions/Admissions.html. The PsyD in Clinical Psychology, PsyD in School Psychology, EdS in School Psychology, and MS in Counseling & Clinical Health Psychology programs admit students in the fall term only. MS in School Psychology admits students in the summer term only. MS in ODL and CAGS admit during all terms. *Fee:* $50. Attendance at any PCOM Open House will qualify applicant for fee waiver.

Pittsburgh, University of
Department of Psychology in Education
School of Education
5930 Posvar Hall
Pittsburgh, PA 15260
Telephone: (412) 624-7230
Fax: (412) 624-7231
E-mail: *psyed@pitt.edu*
Web: *http://www.education.pitt.edu*

Department Information:
1986. Chairman: Carl Johnson. Number of Faculty: total–full-time 12, part-time 6; women–full-time 7, part-time 5; minority–full-time 4.

Programs and Degrees Offered:
Listed in the following order: Program area, degree type (T if terminal Master's), number awarded 7/03–6/04. Research Methodology PhD (Doctor of Philosophy) 8, Applied Developmental Psychology MA/MS (Master of Arts/Science) 25, Applied Developmental Psycholology PhD (Doctor of Philosophy) 12, Research Methodolgy MA/MEd (Master of Arts/Education) 8.

Student Applications/Admissions:
Student Applications
Research Methodology PhD (Doctor of Philosophy)—Applications 2004–2005, 15. Total applicants accepted 2004–2005, 10. Number enrolled (new admits only) 2004–2005 full-time, 10. Total enrolled 2004–2005 full-time, 19, part-time, 10. Openings 2005–2006, 10. The Median number of years required for completion of a degree are 5. *Applied Developmental Psychology MA/MS (Master of Arts/Science)*—Applications 2004–2005, 68. Total applicants accepted 2004–2005, 58. Number enrolled (new admits only) 2004–2005 full-time, 58. Total enrolled 2004–2005 full-time, 98. Openings 2005–2006, 65. The Median number of years required for completion of a degree are 2. *Applied Developmental Psycholology PhD (Doctor of Philosophy)*—Applications 2004–2005, 20. Total applicants accepted 2004–2005, 15. Number enrolled (new admits only) 2004–2005 full-time, 15. Total enrolled 2004–2005 full-time, 8, part-time, 20. *Research Methodolgy MA/MEd (Master of Arts/Education)*—Applications 2004–2005, 5. Total applicants accepted 2004–2005, 5. Number enrolled (new admits only) 2004–2005 full-time, 5. Total enrolled 2004–2005 full-time, 10, part-time, 9. The Median number of years required for completion of a degree are 2.

Admissions Requirements:
Scores: Entries appear in this order: required test or GPA, minimum score (if required), median score of students entering in 2003–2004. Master's Programs: GRE-Analytical no minimum stated; overall undergraduate GPA no minimum stated, 3.00. GRE is not required for any of the master's programs. International students are not required to take GRE, but must

take TOEFL. Doctoral Programs: GRE-V no minimum stated; GRE-Q no minimum stated; GRE-V+Q no minimum stated; GRE-Analytical no minimum stated; overall undergraduate GPA 3.00. International students are not required to take GRE, but must take TOEFL.

Other Criteria: (importance of criteria rated low, medium, or high): GRE/MAT scores medium, research experience medium, work experience medium, extracurricular activity low, clinically related public service medium, GPA medium, letters of recommendation medium, statement of goals and objectives high. For additional information on admission requirements, go to: http://www.education.pitt.edu/.

Student Characteristics: The following represents characteristics of students in 2004–2005 in all graduate psychology programs in the department: Female–full-time 75, part-time 0; Male–full-time 13, part-time 0; African American/Black–full-time 0, part-time 0; Hispanic/Latino(a)–full-time 0, part-time 0; Asian/Pacific Islander–full-time 0, part-time 0; American Indian/Alaska Native–full-time 0, part-time 0; Caucasian–full-time 0, part-time 0.

Financial Information/Assistance:

Tuition for Full-Time Study: *Master's:* State residents: per academic year $12,448, $507 per credit hour; Nonstate residents: per academic year $24,284, $997 per credit hour. *Doctoral:* State residents: per academic year $12,448, $507 per credit hour; Nonstate residents: per academic year $24,284, $997 per credit hour. See the following Web site for updates and changes in tuition costs: www.education.pitt.edu/.

Financial Assistance:

First Year Students: Research assistantships available for first-year. Average amount paid per academic year: $10,745. Average number of hours worked per week: 20. Tuition remission given: full.

Advanced Students: Teaching assistantships available for advanced students. Average amount paid per academic year: $6,845. Average number of hours worked per week: 10. Tuition remission given: partial. Research assistantships available for advanced students. Average amount paid per academic year: $10,745. Average number of hours worked per week: 20. Tuition remission given: full.

Contact Information: Of all students currently enrolled full-time, 20% benefitted from one or more of the listed financial assistance programs. Application and information available online at: http://www.education.pitt.edu/.

Internships/Practica: Field placements are available working with research program development and developmental practice through the University's Learning Research and Development Center, Western Psychiatric Institute and Clinic, Children's Hospital of Pittsburgh, the University Office of Child Development, and many community agencies.

Housing and Day Care: No on-campus housing is available. On-campus day care facilities are available. Contact University Child Development Center, 635 Clyde Street (412) 383-2100.

Employment of Department Graduates:

Master's Degree Graduates: Of those who graduated in the academic year 2003–2004, the following categories and numbers represent the post-graduate activities and employment of master's degree graduates: Enrolled in a post-doctoral residency/fellowship (n/a), employed in independent practice (n/a), total from the above (master's) (0).

Doctoral Degree Graduates: Of those who graduated in the academic year 2003–2004, the following categories and numbers represent the post-graduate activities and employment of doctoral degree graduates: Enrolled in a psychology doctoral program (n/a), total from the above (doctoral) (0).

Additional Information:

Orientation, Objectives, and Emphasis of Department: The department offers graduate programs in two areas: Applied Developmental Psychology and Research Methodology.

Special Facilities or Resources: Research facilities are available at various locations including the Learning, Research, and Development Center (LRDC); the Pittsburgh Board of Education; and the Western Psychiatric Institute and Clinic and the Office of Child Development (OCD). These facilities are located on the university campus. Faculty in the Department have research projects on which students work.

Information for Students With Physical Disabilities: See the following Web site for more information: http://www.drs.pitt.edu/.

Application Information:

Send to: Admissions Coordinator (state the program name), Department of Psychology in Education, 5930 Posvar Hall, University of Pittsburgh, Pittsburgh, PA 15260. Application available online. URL of online application: http://www.education.pitt.edu/. Students are admitted in the Fall, application deadline February 1; Spring, application deadline November 1; Summer, application deadline February 1. Programs have rolling admissions. Applications after the deadlines are seriously considered if all the places are not filled. *Fee:* $40.

Pittsburgh, University of
Psychology
Arts and Sciences
3129 Sennott Square
210 S. Bouquet Street
Pittsburgh, PA 15260
Telephone: (412) 624-4502
Fax: (412) 624-4428
E-mail: *psygrad@pitt.edu*
Web: *http://www.pitt.edu/~psych/*

Department Information:

1904. Chairperson: Anthony R. Caggiula. Number of Faculty: total–full-time 38, part-time 4; women–full-time 15, part-time 3; minority–full-time 2.

Programs and Degrees Offered:

Listed in the following order: Program area, degree type (T if terminal Master's), number awarded 7/03–6/04. Clinical PhD (Doctor of Philosophy) 3, Cognitive PhD (Doctor of Philosophy) 1, Developmental PhD (Doctor of Philosophy) 0, Biological and Health PhD (Doctor of Philosophy) 0, Individualized PhD (Doctor of Philosophy) 0, Social PhD (Doctor of Philosophy) 2.

APA Accreditation: Clinical PhD (Doctor of Philosophy).

Student Applications/Admissions:

Student Applications

Clinical PhD (Doctor of Philosophy)—Applications 2004–2005, 290. Total applicants accepted 2004–2005, 15. Number enrolled (new admits only) 2004–2005 full-time, 5. Openings 2005–2006, 6. The Median number of years required for completion of a degree are 7. The number of students enrolled full and part-time who were dismissed or voluntarily withdrew from this program area were 1. *Cognitive PhD (Doctor of Philosophy)*—Applications 2004–2005, 70. Total applicants accepted 2004–2005, 6. Number enrolled (new admits only) 2004–2005 full-time, 4. Openings 2005–2006, 4. The Median number of years required for completion of a degree are 5. The number of students enrolled full and part-time who were dismissed or voluntarily withdrew from this program area were 3. *Developmental PhD (Doctor of Philosophy)*—Applications 2004–2005, 29. Total applicants accepted 2004–2005, 2. Number enrolled (new admits only) 2004–2005 full-time, 0. Openings 2005–2006, 4. The Median number of years required for completion of a degree are 6. The number of students enrolled full and part-time who were dismissed or voluntarily withdrew from this program area were 3. *Biological and Health PhD (Doctor of Philosophy)*—Applications 2004–2005, 29. Total applicants accepted 2004–2005, 2. Number enrolled (new admits only) 2004–2005 full-time, 2. Openings 2005–2006, 4. The Median number of years required for completion of a degree are 6. The number of students enrolled full and part-time who were dismissed or voluntarily withdrew from this program area were 0. *Individualized PhD (Doctor of Philosophy)*—Applications 2004–2005, 10. Total applicants accepted 2004–2005, 1. Number enrolled (new admits only) 2004–2005 full-time, 1. Openings 2005–2006, 1. The number of students enrolled full and part-time who were dismissed or voluntarily withdrew from this program area were 1. *Social PhD (Doctor of Philosophy)*—Applications 2004–2005, 41. Total applicants accepted 2004–2005, 3. Number enrolled (new admits only) 2004–2005 full-time, 1. Openings 2005–2006, 3. The number of students enrolled full and part-time, who were dismissed or voluntarily withdrew from this program area were 0.

Admissions Requirements:

Scores: Entries appear in this order: required test or GPA, minimum score (if required), median score of students entering in 2003–2004. Doctoral Programs: GRE-V no minimum stated, 600; GRE-Q no minimum stated, 676; GRE-Analytical no minimum stated, 676; overall undergraduate GPA no minimum stated, 3.62. GRE Psychology subject test is required for applicants to Clinical programs.

Other Criteria: (importance of criteria rated low, medium, or high): GRE/MAT scores high, research experience high, work experience medium, extracurricular activity low, clinically related public service low, GPA high, letters of recommendation high, interview high, statement of goals and objectives medium. For additional information on admission requirements, go to: http://www.pitt.edu/~psych/.

Student Characteristics: The following represents characteristics of students in 2004–2005 in all graduate psychology programs in the department: Female–full-time 65, part-time 0; Male–full-time 31, part-time 0; African American/Black–full-time 7, part-time 0; Hispanic/Latino(a)–full-time 0, part-time 0; Asian/Pacific Islander–full-time 5, part-time 0; American Indian/Alaska Native–full-time 0, part-time 0; Caucasian–full-time 84, part-time 0.

Financial Information/Assistance:

Tuition for Full-Time Study: *Doctoral:* State residents: per academic year $12,448, $507 per credit hour; Nonstate residents: per academic year $24,284, $997 per credit hour. Tuition is subject to change. See the following Web site for updates and changes in tuition costs: http://www.bc.pitt.edu/students/tuition.html.

Financial Assistance:

First Year Students: Teaching assistantships available for first-year. Average amount paid per academic year: $13,160. Average number of hours worked per week: 20. Apply by December 15. Tuition remission given: full. Research assistantships available for first-year. Average amount paid per academic year: $11,800. Average number of hours worked per week: 20. Apply by December 15. Tuition remission given: full. Traineeships available for first-year. Average amount paid per academic year: $20,000. Apply by December 15. Tuition remission given: full. Fellowships and scholarships available for first-year. Average amount paid per academic year: $15,212. Average number of hours worked per week: 0. Apply by December 15. Tuition remission given: full.

Advanced Students: Teaching assistantships available for advanced students. Average amount paid per academic year: $13,690. Average number of hours worked per week: 20. Tuition remission given: full. Research assistantships available for advanced students. Average amount paid per academic year: $12,360. Average number of hours worked per week: 20. Tuition remission given: full. Traineeships available for advanced students. Average amount paid per academic year: $20,000. Tuition remission given: full. Fellowships and scholarships available for advanced students. Average amount paid per academic year: $16,000. Average number of hours worked per week: 0. Tuition remission given: full.

Contact Information: Of all students currently enrolled full-time, 100% benefitted from one or more of the listed financial assistance programs. Application and information available online at: http://www.pitt.edu/~psych/.

Internships/Practica: For those doctoral students for whom a professional internship is required prior to graduation, 8 applied in 2003–2004. Of those who applied, 7 were placed in internships listed by the Association of Psychology Postdoctoral and Internship Programs (APPIC); 7 were placed in APA accredited internships.

Housing and Day Care: No on-campus housing is available. On-campus day care facilities are available. See the following Web site for more information: http://www.hr.pitt.edu/ucdc/.

Employment of Department Graduates:

Master's Degree Graduates: Of those who graduated in the academic year 2003–2004, the following categories and numbers represent the post-graduate activities and employment of master's degree graduates: Enrolled in a post-doctoral residency/fellowship (n/a), employed in independent practice (n/a), total from the above (master's) (0).

Doctoral Degree Graduates: Of those who graduated in the academic year 2003–2004, the following categories and numbers represent the post-graduate activities and employment of doctoral degree graduates: Enrolled in a psychology doctoral program (n/a), enrolled in a post-doctoral residency/fellowship (4), employed in an academic position at a 2-year/4-year college (1), employed in a government agency (research) (1), total from the above (doctoral) (6).

Additional Information:

Orientation, Objectives, and Emphasis of Department: Basic research training is emphasized, and most projects carry out research with important practical implications. The graduate programs include Clinical Psychology, Cognitive Psychology and Cognitive Neuroscience, Developmental Psychology, Biological and Health Psychology, Social Psychology, and joint programs in Clinical-Developmental and Clinical-Health Psychology. Some examples of training opportunities are projects on infant socialization, cognitive, language and social development of children, psychological stress on the cardiovascular and immune systems, nicotine and alcohol use, decision making in groups, stereotyping, reading processes, school and non-school learning, and brain models of attention and reading. Seminars are small (5-12 students), and close working relationships are encouraged with faculty, especially the student's advisor. Excellent relationships with other departments and schools offer unusually flexible opportunities to carry out interdisciplinary work and gain access to scholars in the Pittsburgh community. All students are expected to teach at least one course, and carry out an original research dissertation. Financial support is available for students through teaching, research, and fellowships.

Special Facilities or Resources: The facilities of the department include experimental laboratories, extensive computer facilities, a small-groups laboratory, the Clinical Psychology Center, and the laboratories of the Learning Research and Development Center. These services offer the advanced graduate student opportunities for supervised practica and research experiences. The department also maintains cooperative arrangements with many organizations in Pittsburgh engaged in various kinds of psychological work. These include Children's Hospital, Pittsburgh Cancer Institute, the Western Psychiatric Institute and Clinic, and several local agencies of the Veterans Administration Medical Centers. Collaboration with these organizations consists of part-time instruction by the staffs of these agencies, the sharing of laboratory and clinical facilities, and the appointment in those organizations of graduate students in psychology as clinical assistants, research assistants, or as part-time employees.

Information for Students With Physical Disabilities: See the following Web site for more information: http://www.drs.pitt.edu/.

Application Information:
Send to: Graduate Secretary, Department of Psychology, University of Pittsburgh, 3129 Sennott Square, 210 S. Bouquet Street, Pittsburgh, PA 15260. Application available online. URL of online application: www.pitt.edu/~psych. Students are admitted in the Fall, application deadline December 15. *Fee:* $40. Fees deferred for McNair Scholars.

Saint Joseph's University
Department of Psychology
5600 City Avenue
Philadelphia, PA 19131-1395
Telephone: (610) 660-1800
Fax: (610) 660-1819
E-mail: *jmindell@sju.edu*
Web: *http://psychology.sju.edu*

Department Information:
1960. Director, Graduate Psychology Program: Jodi A. Mindell, PhD Number of Faculty: total–full-time 10, part-time 1; women–full-time 5, part-time 1.

Programs and Degrees Offered:
Listed in the following order: Program area, degree type (T if terminal Master's), number awarded 7/03–6/04. Experimental MA/MS (Master of Arts/Science) (T) 16.

Student Applications/Admissions:
Student Applications
Experimental MA/MS *(Master of Arts/Science)*—Applications 2004–2005, 43. Total applicants accepted 2004–2005, 20. Openings 2005–2006, 20. The Median number of years required for completion of a degree are 2. The number of students enrolled full and part-time who were dismissed or voluntarily withdrew from this program area were 2.

Admissions Requirements:
Scores: Entries appear in this order: required test or GPA, minimum score (if required), median score of students entering in 2003–2004. Master's Programs: GRE-V 500, 520; GRE-Q 500, 560; GRE-Subject(Psych) 500, 560; overall undergraduate GPA 3.2, 3.5; last 2 years GPA 3.2, 3.6; psychology GPA 3.2, 3.65.
Other Criteria: (importance of criteria rated low, medium, or high): GRE/MAT scores medium, research experience high, work experience low, extracurricular activity medium, clinically related public service low, GPA high, letters of recommendation high, interview medium, statement of goals and objectives medium.

Student Characteristics: The following represents characteristics of students in 2004–2005 in all graduate psychology programs in the department: Female–full-time 24, part-time 0; Male–full-time 8, part-time 0; African American/Black–full-time 1, part-time 0; Hispanic/Latino(a)–full-time 0, part-time 0; Asian/Pacific Islander–full-time 0, part-time 0; American Indian/Alaska Native–full-time 0, part-time 0; Caucasian–full-time 31, part-time 0; students subject to the Americans With Disabilities Act–full-time 0, part-time 0.

Financial Information/Assistance:
Tuition for Full-Time Study: *Master's:* State residents: $645 per credit hour; Nonstate residents: $645 per credit hour.

Financial Assistance:
First Year Students: No information provided.
Advanced Students: Teaching assistantships available for advanced students. Average amount paid per academic year:

$7,200. Average number of hours worked per week: 20. Tuition remission given: full. Research assistantships available for advanced students. Average amount paid per academic year: $7,200. Average number of hours worked per week: 20. Tuition remission given: full.

Contact Information: Of all students currently enrolled full-time, 33% benefitted from one or more of the listed financial assistance programs.

Internships/Practica: No information provided.

Housing and Day Care: No on-campus housing is available. On-campus day care facilities are available. See the following Web site for more information: www.stjohnlm.org/address.html.

Employment of Department Graduates:

Master's Degree Graduates: Of those who graduated in the academic year 2003–2004, the following categories and numbers represent the post-graduate activities and employment of master's degree graduates: Enrolled in a post-doctoral residency/fellowship (n/a), employed in independent practice (n/a), total from the above (master's) (0).

Doctoral Degree Graduates: Of those who graduated in the academic year 2003–2004, the following categories and numbers represent the post-graduate activities and employment of doctoral degree graduates: Enrolled in a psychology doctoral program (n/a), total from the above (doctoral) (0).

Additional Information:

Orientation, Objectives, and Emphasis of Department: The Saint Joseph's University graduate program in Experimental Psychology is designed to provide students with a solid grounding in the scientific study of psychology. Students may concentrate studies in the fields of behavioral neuroscience, developmental psychology, health psychology, cognitive psychology, neuropsychology, or social psychology. Regardless of the particular concentration chosen, graduates of the program will have a firm foundation in the scientific method and the skills with which to pursue the scientific study of psychological questions. The program offers a traditional and academically oriented 36-credit curriculum, which requires a qualifying comprehensive examination and an empirical thesis project. The program is designed for successful completion over two academic years. Additionally, a five-year combined Bachelor/Master of Science degree in psychology is offered. The Saint Joseph's University psychology graduate program has been constructed to complement the strengths and interests of the present psychology faculty and facilities and to reflect the current state of the discipline of psychology. The curriculum is composed of three major components: a 12-credit common core required of all students; 20 credits of content based courses; and a 16-credit research component in which students complete the comprehensive examination and research thesis.

Special Facilities or Resources: All psychology faculty have equipped and active research laboratories in which graduate students pursue independent research projects for completion of their thesis requirement. Support facilities for graduate-level research and education are impressive. A vivarium, certifiable by the United

States Public Health Service, for the housing of animal subjects is in operation and is fully staffed. For research involving human subjects, the department coordinates a subject pool consisting of approximately 300 subjects per semester. Additionally, the Psychology Department at Saint Joseph's operates PsyNet, a state-of-the-art Macintosh-AppleShare local area network which is attached to a campus-wide computer network through an EtherNet connection. PsyNet consists of 35 Macintosh computers and peripherals for all faculty and staff plus fileservers and laser printers. Two student computer classrooms/laboratories which include an additional 20 computers are also available within the department. PsyNet software includes various word processing, statistical, spreadsheet, database, graphics, and simulation packages.

Application Information:
Send to: Graduate Admissions Office, Saint Joseph's University, 5600 City Avenue, Philadelphia, PA 19131-1395. Students are admitted in the Fall, application deadline February 1st. *Fee:* $35.

Shippensburg University
Department of Psychology
Arts and Sciences
114 Franklin Science Center
Shippensburg, PA 17257
Telephone: (717) 477-1657
Fax: (717) 477-4057
E-mail: *gradsch@ship.edu*
Web: *www.ship.edu/gradschool/deptpsy.html*

Department Information:
1970. Chair Graduate Program in Psychology: Robert L. Hale, PhD Number of Faculty: total–full-time 17, part-time 1; women–full-time 4, part-time 1; minority–full-time 2, part-time 1.

Programs and Degrees Offered:
Listed in the following order: Program area, degree type (T if terminal Master's), number awarded 7/03–6/04. General MA/MS (Master of Arts/Science) (T) 8.

Student Applications/Admissions:

Student Applications

General MA/MS (Master of Arts/Science)—Applications 2004–2005, 47. Total applicants accepted 2004–2005, 41. Number enrolled (new admits only) 2004–2005 full-time, 9. Number enrolled (new admits only) 2004–2005 part-time, 5. Total enrolled 2004–2005 full-time, 17, part-time, 5. Openings 2005–2006, 18. The Median number of years required for completion of a degree are 2. The number of students enrolled full and part-time who were dismissed or voluntarily withdrew from this program area were 0.

Admissions Requirements:

Scores: Entries appear in this order: required test or GPA, minimum score (if required), median score of students entering in 2003–2004. Master's Programs: overall undergraduate GPA 2.75, 3.13.

Other Criteria: (importance of criteria rated low, medium, or high): research experience medium, work experience low, extracurricular activity low, GPA medium, letters of recommendation medium, statement of goals and objectives medium.

Student Characteristics: The following represents characteristics of students in 2004–2005 in all graduate psychology programs in the department: Female–full-time 15, part-time 5; Male–full-time 2, part-time 0; African American/Black–full-time 1, part-time 0; Hispanic/Latino(a)–full-time 0, part-time 0; Asian/Pacific Islander–full-time 0, part-time 0; American Indian/Alaska Native–full-time 0, part-time 0; Caucasian–full-time 16, part-time 5; Multi-ethnic–full-time 0, part-time 0; students subject to the Americans With Disabilities Act–full-time 0, part-time 0.

Financial Information/Assistance:

Tuition for Full-Time Study: *Master's:* State residents: per academic year $3,213, $307 per credit hour; Nonstate residents: per academic year $4,869, $491 per credit hour. Tuition is subject to change. See the following Web site for updates and changes in tuition costs: www.ship.edu.

Financial Assistance:

First Year Students: Research assistantships available for first-year. Average amount paid per academic year: $2,163. Average number of hours worked per week: 14. Apply by April 1. Tuition remission given: full.

Advanced Students: Research assistantships available for advanced students. Average amount paid per academic year: $2,163. Average number of hours worked per week: 14. Apply by April 1. Tuition remission given: full.

Contact Information: Of all students currently enrolled full-time, 20% benefitted from one or more of the listed financial assistance programs. Application and information available online at: http://www.ship.edu.

Internships/Practica: No internships are available at the MS level.

Housing and Day Care: No on-campus housing is available. No on-campus day care facilities are available.

Employment of Department Graduates:

Master's Degree Graduates: Of those who graduated in the academic year 2003–2004, the following categories and numbers represent the post-graduate activities and employment of master's degree graduates: Enrolled in a post-doctoral residency/fellowship (n/a), employed in independent practice (n/a), total from the above (master's) (0).

Doctoral Degree Graduates: Of those who graduated in the academic year 2003–2004, the following categories and numbers represent the post-graduate activities and employment of doctoral degree graduates: Enrolled in a psychology doctoral program (n/a), total from the above (doctoral) (0).

Additional Information:

Orientation, Objectives, and Emphasis of Department: The MS program in psychology is designed to provide advanced general knowledge of the field and the opportunity to develop more specific research skills. In conference with faculty advisors, each candidate develops a personal program designed to meet his or her own specific needs and interests. This program serves as an effective stepping stone program for those desiring further graduate

training at the doctoral level. No training is provided in applied areas of psychology.

Special Facilities or Resources: The Psychology Department at Shippensburg University is housed in Franklin Science Center. Animal colonies and research facilities (wet labs and testing rooms) are located in this building, as are human research facilities, a microcomputer laboratory, research cubicles, videotaping equipment, and two-way mirrored rooms.

Information for Students With Physical Disabilities: Franklin Science Center is wheelchair accessible.

Application Information:

Send to: Office of Graduate Admissions, Shippensburg University, 1871 Old Main Drive, Shippensburg, PA 17257. Application available online. URL of online application: www.ship.edu. Students are admitted in the Fall, application deadline April 1; Spring, application deadline November 1; Summer, application deadline April 1. *Fee:* $30.

Temple University
Department of Psychological Studies in Education
Education
Ritter Hall Annex, 2nd Floor
1301 Cecil B. Moore Avenue
Philadelphia, PA 19122
Telephone: (215) 204-6009
Fax: (215) 204-6013
E-mail: *jrosenfe@temple.edu*
Web: *http://www.temple.edu*

Department Information:

1984. Chairperson, Psychological Studies in Education: Joseph G. Rosenfeld. Number of Faculty: total–full-time 21, part-time 30; women–full-time 7, part-time 12; minority–full-time 3, part-time 5.

Programs and Degrees Offered:

Listed in the following order: Program area, degree type (T if terminal Master's), number awarded 7/03–6/04. School Psychology PhD (Doctor of Philosophy) 8, Counseling Psychology PhD (Doctor of Philosophy) 14, Educational Psychology PhD (Doctor of Philosophy) 9, Educational Psychology - Instructional Learning Technology MA/MS (Master of Arts/Science) (T) 20, Adult & Organizational Development MA/MS (Master of Arts/Science) (T) 10, Counseling Psychology MA/MS (Master of Arts/Science) (T) 28, School Psychology, Master's + Certification MA/MS (Master of Arts/Science) 3.

APA Accreditation: School PhD (Doctor of Philosophy). Counseling PhD (Doctor of Philosophy).

Student Applications/Admissions:

Student Applications

School Psychology PhD (Doctor of Philosophy)—Applications 2004–2005, 33. Total applicants accepted 2004–2005, 17. Number enrolled (new admits only) 2004–2005 full-time, 11. Total enrolled 2004–2005 full-time, 74, part-time, 3. Openings

2005–2006, 4. The Median number of years required for completion of a degree are 7. The number of students enrolled full and part-time who were dismissed or voluntarily withdrew from this program area were 2. *Counseling Psychology PhD (Doctor of Philosophy)*—Applications 2004–2005, 0. Total applicants accepted 2004–2005, 0. Number enrolled (new admits only) 2004–2005 full-time, 0. Number enrolled (new admits only) 2004–2005 part-time, 0. The Median number of years required for completion of a degree are 5. *Educational Psychology PhD (Doctor of Philosophy)*—Applications 2004–2005, 23. Total applicants accepted 2004–2005, 12. Number enrolled (new admits only) 2004–2005 full-time, 3. Number enrolled (new admits only) 2004–2005 part-time, 5. Total enrolled 2004–2005 full-time, 32, part-time, 24. Openings 2005–2006, 8. The Median number of years required for completion of a degree are 7. The number of students enrolled full and part-time who were dismissed or voluntarily withdrew from this program area were 3. *Educational Psychology - Instructional Learning Technology MA/MS (Master of Arts/Science)*—Applications 2004–2005, 39. Total applicants accepted 2004–2005, 23. Number enrolled (new admits only) 2004–2005 full-time, 0. Number enrolled (new admits only) 2004–2005 part-time, 13. Total enrolled 2004–2005 full-time, 3, part-time, 41. Openings 2005–2006, 10. The Median number of years required for completion of a degree are 3. The number of students enrolled full and part-time who were dismissed or voluntarily withdrew from this program area were 2. *Adult & Organizational Development MA/MS (Master of Arts/Science)*—Applications 2004–2005, 30. Total applicants accepted 2004–2005, 20. Number enrolled (new admits only) 2004–2005 full-time, 10. Number enrolled (new admits only) 2004–2005 part-time, 10. Total enrolled 2004–2005 full-time, 20, part-time, 20. Openings 2005–2006, 15. The Median number of years required for completion of a degree are 2. The number of students enrolled full and part-time who were dismissed or voluntarily withdrew from this program area were 1. *Counseling Psychology MA/MS (Master of Arts/Science)*—Applications 2004–2005, 70. Total applicants accepted 2004–2005, 40. Number enrolled (new admits only) 2004–2005 full-time, 20. Number enrolled (new admits only) 2004–2005 part-time, 10. Total enrolled 2004–2005 full-time, 40, part-time, 20. Openings 2005–2006, 25. The Median number of years required for completion of a degree are 2.5. The number of students enrolled full and part-time who were dismissed or voluntarily withdrew from this program area were 3. *School Psychology, Master's + Certification MA/MS (Master of Arts/Science)*—Applications 2004–2005, 36. Total applicants accepted 2004–2005, 8. Number enrolled (new admits only) 2004–2005 full-time, 5. Total enrolled 2004–2005 full-time, 10. Openings 2005–2006, 12. The Median number of years required for completion of a degree are 3. The number of students enrolled full and part-time who were dismissed or voluntarily withdrew from this program area were 0.

Admissions Requirements:

Scores: Entries appear in this order: required test or GPA, minimum score (if required), median score of students entering in 2003–2004. Master's Programs: overall undergraduate GPA 3.0, 3.3. Different scores are required by different programs. The Graduate School requires a minimum GPA of 3.0 or admission test (GRE or MAT depending on the program) at the 65th percentile. The Psychology GRE is required for cer-

tain programs. Doctoral Programs: Different scores and GPAs are required for different programs. Contact the program. Most programs require a GPA of 3.25 in both graduate and undergraduate courses and GRE V+Q of 1100. For the programs that require a Psychology GRE, the score should be at least 500. **Other Criteria:** (importance of criteria rated low, medium, or high): GRE/MAT scores medium, research experience medium, work experience medium, extracurricular activity medium, clinically related public service low, GPA high, letters of recommendation high, interview high, statement of goals and objectives high.

Student Characteristics: The following represents characteristics of students in 2004–2005 in all graduate psychology programs in the department: Female–full-time 150, part-time 75; Male–full-time 69, part-time 33; American Indian/Alaska Native–part-time 0; Caucasian–full-time 0, part-time 0; students subject to the Americans With Disabilities Act–full-time 3, part-time 2.

Financial Information/Assistance:

Tuition for Full-Time Study: *Master's:* State residents: $405 per credit hour; Nonstate residents: $534 per credit hour. *Doctoral:* State residents: $405 per credit hour; Nonstate residents: $534 per credit hour. Tuition is subject to change. See the following Web site for updates and changes in tuition costs: www.temple.edu.

Financial Assistance:

First Year Students: Fellowships and scholarships available for first-year. Average amount paid per academic year: $14,000. Average number of hours worked per week: 0. Apply by January 2. Tuition remission given: full.

Advanced Students: Teaching assistantships available for advanced students. Average amount paid per academic year: $14,000. Average number of hours worked per week: 20. Apply by March 15. Tuition remission given: full. Research assistantships available for advanced students. Average amount paid per academic year: $14,000. Average number of hours worked per week: 20. Apply by March 15. Tuition remission given: full. Fellowships and scholarships available for advanced students. Average amount paid per academic year: $14,000. Average number of hours worked per week: 0. Apply by January 2. Tuition remission given: full.

Contact Information: Of all students currently enrolled full-time, 30% benefitted from one or more of the listed financial assistance programs.

Internships/Practica: For a master's degree and certification as a school psychologist, students are placed in an internship for one academic year. The average renumeration is $12,000. Practicum sites include public, private, and parochial schools and community mental health centers. Internships are supervised by department faculty and doctoral level school psychologists. For the doctoral program, one-year internships are available. Remuneration is highly variable: $8,750 to $22,000. Counseling internships are also paid. Practica experiences are part of coursework and are not paid. For those doctoral students for whom a professional internship is required prior to graduation, 18 applied in 2003–2004. Of those who applied, 6 were placed in internships listed by the Association of Psychology Postdoctoral and Internship Programs (APPIC); 6 were placed in APA accredited internships.

Housing and Day Care: On-campus housing is available. Child care is available in the community. Contact the University Housing Office, (215) 204-7184.

Employment of Department Graduates:

Master's Degree Graduates: Of those who graduated in the academic year 2003–2004, the following categories and numbers represent the post-graduate activities and employment of master's degree graduates: Enrolled in a psychology doctoral program (8), enrolled in a post-doctoral residency/fellowship (n/a), employed in independent practice (n/a), employed in a professional position in a school system (11), employed in a community mental health/counseling center (20), employed in a hospital/medical center (4), do not know (15), total from the above (master's) (58).

Doctoral Degree Graduates: Of those who graduated in the academic year 2003–2004, the following categories and numbers represent the post-graduate activities and employment of doctoral degree graduates: Enrolled in a psychology doctoral program (n/a), employed in an academic position at a university (4), employed in an academic position at a 2-year/4-year college (2), employed in other positions at a higher education institution (1), employed in a professional position in a school system (9), employed in a government agency (professional services) (3), employed in a community mental health/counseling center (11), do not know (3), total from the above (doctoral) (33).

Additional Information:

Orientation, Objectives, and Emphasis of Department: Psychological Studies in Education is a graduate level department offering master's and doctoral programs in four areas: Adult and Organizational Development (AOD), Counseling Psychology, Educational Psychology and Educational Psychology-Instructional Learning Technology, and School Psychology. Certification is also offered in School Psychology and Counseling Psychology. Counseling Psychology and the School Psychology doctoral programs are APA accredited. The AOD program offers only the Master's Degree at this time. There are a variety of objectives and emphases. The student should write to the separate program within the Department.

Special Facilities or Resources: The department conducts a psychoeducational clinic with observation and recording facilities. The National Center for the Study of Corporal Punishment and Alternatives in the Schools is an integral part of the department. Counseling Psychology runs clinics in Family and Community Counseling and Vocational and Educational Guidance.

Information for Students With Physical Disabilities: See the following Web site for more information: Disabilities Resources and Services, (215) 204-1280 (www.temple.edu).

Application Information:
Send to: Office of Student Services (R-A 238), 1301 Cecil B. Moore, Philadelphia, PA 19122. URL of online application: www.temple.edu. Students are admitted in the Fall, application deadline January 2; Spring, application deadline October 2. Counseling Pychology and School Psychology: January 2. AOD and Educational Psychology have rolling admissions and will admit for each session. *Fee:* $40.

Temple University (2004 data)
Department of Psychology
College of Liberal Arts
1701 North 13th Street, Rm 668
Philadelphia, PA 19122-6085
Telephone: (215) 204-7321
Fax: (215) 204-5539
E-mail: *overton@temple.edu*
Web: *http://www.temple.edu/psychology*

Department Information:
1924. Chairperson: Willis F. Overton. Number of Faculty: total–full-time 34, part-time 6; women–full-time 8, part-time 3; minority–full-time 1.

Programs and Degrees Offered:
Listed in the following order: Program area, degree type (T if terminal Master's), number awarded 7/03–6/04. Clinical PhD (Doctor of Philosophy) 7, Developmental PhD (Doctor of Philosophy) 3, Brain, Behavior and Cognition PhD (Doctor of Philosophy) 5, Social PhD (Doctor of Philosophy) 3, Developmental Psychopathology PhD (Doctor of Philosophy) 0.

APA Accreditation: Clinical PhD (Doctor of Philosophy).

Student Applications/Admissions:

Student Applications

Clinical PhD (Doctor of Philosophy)—Applications 2004–2005, 222. Total applicants accepted 2004–2005, 11. Openings 2005–2006, 11. The Median number of years required for completion of a degree are 6. *Developmental PhD (Doctor of Philosophy)*—Applications 2004–2005, 32. Total applicants accepted 2004–2005, 4. Openings 2005–2006, 5. The Median number of years required for completion of a degree are 5. The number of students enrolled full and part-time who were dismissed or voluntarily withdrew from this program area were 0. *Brain, Behavior and Cognition PhD (Doctor of Philosophy)*—Applications 2004–2005, 55. Total applicants accepted 2004–2005, 5. Openings 2005–2006, 5. The Median number of years required for completion of a degree are 5. *Social PhD (Doctor of Philosophy)*—Applications 2004–2005, 47. Total applicants accepted 2004–2005, 2. Openings 2005–2006, 3. The Median number of years required for completion of a degree are 5. The number of students enrolled full and part-time who were dismissed or voluntarily withdrew from this program area were 0. *Developmental Psychopathology PhD (Doctor of Philosophy)*—Applications 2004–2005, 30. Total applicants accepted 2004–2005, 2. Openings 2005–2006, 3.

Admissions Requirements:

Scores: Entries appear in this order: required test or GPA, minimum score (if required), median score of students entering in 2003–2004. Master's Programs: overall undergraduate GPA no minimum stated. Doctoral Programs: GRE-V 550, 630; GRE-Q 550, 670; GRE-V+Q 1150, 1300; GRE-Analytical no minimum stated; overall undergraduate GPA 3.5, 3.65.

Other Criteria: (importance of criteria rated low, medium, or high): GRE/MAT scores high, research experience high, work experience low, extracurricular activity low, clinically related public service low, GPA high, letters of recommendation high, interview high, statement of goals and objectives high.

Student Characteristics: The following represents characteristics of students in 2004–2005 in all graduate psychology programs in the department: Female–full-time 56, part-time 0; Male–full-time 33, part-time 0; African American/Black–full-time 5, part-time 0; Hispanic/Latino(a)–full-time 0, part-time 0; Asian/Pacific Islander–full-time 5, part-time 0; American Indian/Alaska Native–full-time 0, part-time 0; Caucasian–full-time 0, part-time 0.

Financial Information/Assistance:

Tuition for Full-Time Study: *Doctoral:* State residents: $256 per credit hour; Nonstate residents: $532 per credit hour. Tuition is subject to change. See the following Web site for updates and changes in tuition costs: www.temple.edu/psychology.

Financial Assistance:

First Year Students: Teaching assistantships available for first-year. Average amount paid per academic year: $14,167. Average number of hours worked per week: 20. Tuition remission given: full. Research assistantships available for first-year. Average amount paid per academic year: $14,167. Average number of hours worked per week: 20. Tuition remission given: full. Fellowships and scholarships available for first-year. Average amount paid per academic year: $20,000. Average number of hours worked per week: 0. Tuition remission given: full.

Advanced Students: No information provided.

Contact Information: Of all students currently enrolled full-time, 100% benefitted from one or more of the listed financial assistance programs. Application and information available online at: http://www.temple.edu/psychology.

Internships/Practica: Clinical students complete a 2,000-hour predoctoral internship at an agency or hospital typically in the Philadelphia metropolitan area. For those doctoral students for whom a professional internship is required prior to graduation, 8 applied in 2003–2004. Of those who applied, 8 were placed in APA accredited internships.

Housing and Day Care: On-campus housing is available. See the following Web site for more information: www.temple.edu. No on-campus day care facilities are available.

Employment of Department Graduates:

Master's Degree Graduates: Of those who graduated in the academic year 2003–2004, the following categories and numbers represent the post-graduate activities and employment of master's degree graduates: Enrolled in a post-doctoral residency/fellowship (n/a), employed in independent practice (n/a), total from the above (master's) (0).

Doctoral Degree Graduates: Of those who graduated in the academic year 2003–2004, the following categories and numbers represent the post-graduate activities and employment of doctoral degree graduates: Enrolled in a psychology doctoral program (n/a), total from the above (doctoral) (0).

Additional Information:

Orientation, Objectives, and Emphasis of Department: The psychology department offers graduate training in: brain, behavior and cognition; clinical; developmental; developmental psychopathology; and social and organizational. All doctoral programs are designed to prepare students for teaching in universities and colleges, conducting research in field and laboratory settings, and providing consultation in applied settings. The clinical program trains scientist–practitioners and provides students with research and clinical experience.

Special Facilities or Resources: The psychology department occupies eight floors of a high-rise building. The physical resources housed in the building include the Psychological Services Center (an in-house mental health facility where clinical students obtain practicum experience in psychotherapy), extensive laboratory space for human and animal research, a human electrophysiology lab, an infant behavior lab, numerous observation rooms with one-way mirrors, audiovisual equipment (including mobile video equipment), and excellent computer facilities, including numerous micro- and minicomputers.

Information for Students With Physical Disabilities: See the following Web site for more information: www.temple.edu.

Application Information:
Send to: Graduate Admissions Secretary. Students are admitted in the Fall, application deadline December 15. *Fee:* $40.

Villanova University
Department of Psychology
800 Lancaster Avenue
Villanova, PA 19085
Telephone: (610) 519-4720
Fax: (610) 519-4269
E-mail: *psychologyinformation@villanova.edu*
Web: *http://www.psychology.villanova.edu*

Department Information:
1962. Chairperson: Thomas Toppino. Number of Faculty: total–full-time 16, part-time 13; women–full-time 3, part-time 6; minority–part-time 1.

Programs and Degrees Offered:
Listed in the following order: Program area, degree type (T if terminal Master's), number awarded 7/03–6/04. General MA/MS (Master of Arts/Science) (T) 16.

Student Applications/Admissions:

Student Applications

General MA/MS (Master of Arts/Science)—Applications 2004–2005, 90. Total applicants accepted 2004–2005, 43. Number enrolled (new admits only) 2004–2005 full-time, 21. Openings 2005–2006, 22. The Median number of years required for completion of a degree are 2. The number of students enrolled full and part-time who were dismissed or voluntarily withdrew from this program area were 1.

Admissions Requirements:

Scores: Entries appear in this order: required test or GPA, minimum score (if required), median score of students entering in 2003–2004. Master's Programs: GRE-V no minimum stated, 530; GRE-Q no minimum stated, 630; overall undergraduate GPA no minimum stated, 3.5; psychology GPA no minimum stated, 3.8. Medians are for students entering the program during the most recent admissions cycle.

Other Criteria: (importance of criteria rated low, medium, or high): GRE/MAT scores high, research experience medium, work experience low, extracurricular activity low, clinically related public service low, GPA high, letters of recommendation high, interview medium, statement of goals and objectives medium. For additional information on admission requirements, go to: http://psychology.villanova.edu/ms.htm.

Student Characteristics: The following represents characteristics of students in 2004–2005 in all graduate psychology programs in the department: Female–full-time 28, part-time 0; Male–full-time 11, part-time 0; African American/Black–full-time 1, part-time 0; Hispanic/Latino(a)–full-time 1, part-time 0; Asian/Pacific Islander–full-time 0, part-time 0; American Indian/Alaska Native–full-time 0, part-time 0; Caucasian–full-time 37, part-time 0; Multi-ethnic–full-time 0, part-time 0; students subject to the Americans With Disabilities Act–full-time 0, part-time 0.

Financial Information/Assistance:

Tuition for Full-Time Study: *Master's:* State residents: $510 per credit hour; Nonstate residents: $510 per credit hour. Tuition is subject to change. See the following Web site for updates and changes in tuition costs: http://www.gradartsci.villanova.edu/.

Financial Assistance:

First Year Students: Research assistantships available for first-year. Average amount paid per academic year: $11,350. Average number of hours worked per week: 20. Apply by March 15. Tuition remission given: full. Traineeships available for first-year. Average amount paid per academic year: $5,675. Average number of hours worked per week: 14. Apply by March 15. Tuition remission given: full. Fellowships and scholarships available for first-year. Average amount paid per academic year: $0. Average number of hours worked per week: 7. Apply by March 15. Tuition remission given: full.

Advanced Students: Research assistantships available for advanced students. Average amount paid per academic year: $11,350. Average number of hours worked per week: 20. Apply by March 15. Tuition remission given: full. Traineeships available for advanced students. Average amount paid per academic year: $5,675. Average number of hours worked per week: 14. Apply by March 15. Tuition remission given: full. Fellowships and scholarships available for advanced students. Average amount paid per academic year: $0. Average number of hours worked per week: 7. Apply by March 15. Tuition remission given: full.

Contact Information: Of all students currently enrolled full-time, 57% benefitted from one or more of the listed financial assistance programs. Application and information available online at: http://www.gradartsci.villanova.edu/.

Internships/Practica: No information provided.

Housing and Day Care: No on-campus housing is available. No on-campus day care facilities are available.

Employment of Department Graduates:

Master's Degree Graduates: Of those who graduated in the academic year 2003–2004, the following categories and numbers represent the post-graduate activities and employment of master's degree graduates: Enrolled in a psychology doctoral program (7), enrolled in another graduate/professional program (2), enrolled in a post-doctoral residency/fellowship (n/a), employed in independent practice (n/a), employed in business or industry (research/consulting) (2), employed in a community mental health/counseling center (1), still seeking employment (3), total from the above (master's) (15).

Doctoral Degree Graduates: Of those who graduated in the academic year 2003–2004, the following categories and numbers represent the post-graduate activities and employment of doctoral degree graduates: Enrolled in a psychology doctoral program (n/a), total from the above (doctoral) (0).

Additional Information:

Orientation, Objectives, and Emphasis of Department: The department offers a program of study leading to the Master of Science in psychology. Individually tailored to meet each student's career interests and needs, the program provides a solid foundation in psychology with special emphasis on preparation for doctoral work. All incoming students are required to take a seminar in the foundations of research and a statistics course. All students also take laboratory courses in Cognition & Learning and Physiological Psychology. Depending upon the student's interest, he or she selects four elective courses from a reasonably broad range of course offerings such as psychopathology, psychological testing, developmental psychology, social psychology, personality, theories of psychotherapy, behavior modification, special topics, and individual research. During the second year, student efforts are concentrated on the thesis project, which is an intensive empirically-based project, done under the supervision of a faculty mentor. The student/faculty ratio approaches 2:1, allowing close interaction, careful advisement, and individual attention. The department has an active, research-oriented faculty.

Special Facilities or Resources: In addition to office space for faculty and all graduate assistants, the department has approximately 5800-square feet available for research. Equipment of particular interest to the graduate student includes: electronic and computer-controlled tachistoscopes; animal conditioning chambers; cognitive/computer labs; complete facilities for surgery and histology, including stereotaxic equipment for brain implantation; environmental chambers and rooms equipped for observation and automated recording of animal behavior; radial mazes; well-equipped vision labs; one-way vision rooms; audio/video recording and playback facilities; facilities for the design and development of experiments; and computer-based teaching labs. University computing facilities are all networked, with hundreds of remote terminals available.

Application Information:
Send to: Dean, Graduate School, Villanova University, 800 Lancaster Avenue, Villanova, PA 19085. Application available online. URL of online application: http://www.gradartsci.villanova.edu/. Students are admitted in the Fall. Programs have rolling admissions. Strong applications received by March 15 have a better chance of acceptance. Com-

pleted applications must be received by March 15 to ensure full consideration for financial aid. *Fee:* $50.

West Chester University of Pennsylvania
Department of Psychology
West Chester, PA 19383
Telephone: (610) 436-2945
Fax: (610) 436-2846
E-mail: *psych@wcupa.edu*
Web: *http://www.wcupa.edu/_academics/sch_cas.psy/*

Department Information:
1967. Chairperson: Sandra Kerr. Number of Faculty: total–full-time 19, part-time 9; women–full-time 10, part-time 6; minority–full-time 2, part-time 1.

Programs and Degrees Offered:
Listed in the following order: Program area, degree type (T if terminal Master's), number awarded 7/03–6/04. Clinical MA/MS (Master of Arts/Science) (T) 20, General MA/MS (Master of Arts/Science) (T) 2, Industrial/ Organizational MA/MS (Master of Arts/Science) (T) 12.

Student Applications/Admissions:

Student Applications
Clinical MA/MS (Master of Arts/Science)—Applications 2004–2005, 60. Total applicants accepted 2004–2005, 40. Total enrolled 2004–2005 full-time, 20, part-time, 20. Openings 2005–2006, 20. *General MA/MS (Master of Arts/Science)*—Applications 2004–2005, 6. Total applicants accepted 2004–2005, 3. Total enrolled 2004–2005 full-time, 3, part-time, 1. Openings 2005–2006, 4. *Industrial/Organizational MA/MS (Master of Arts/Science)*—Applications 2004–2005, 45. Total applicants accepted 2004–2005, 20. Total enrolled 2004–2005 full-time, 20, part-time, 10. Openings 2005–2006, 12.

Admissions Requirements:
Scores: Entries appear in this order: required test or GPA, minimum score (if required), median score of students entering in 2003–2004. Master's Programs: GRE-V 500, 500; GRE-Q 500, 555; GRE-V+Q 1000, 1060; GRE-Analytical no minimum stated; overall undergraduate GPA 3.00, 3.3; psychology GPA 3.20, 3.4.
Other Criteria: (importance of criteria rated low, medium, or high): GRE/MAT scores high, research experience medium, work experience medium, extracurricular activity medium, clinically related public service medium, GPA high, letters of recommendation high, statement of goals and objectives high.

Student Characteristics: The following represents characteristics of students in 2004–2005 in all graduate psychology programs in the department: Female–full-time 33, part-time 21; Male–full-time 10, part-time 10; African American/Black–full-time 2, part-time 3; Hispanic/Latino(a)–full-time 0, part-time 0; Asian/Pacific Islander–full-time 0, part-time 0; American Indian/Alaska Native–full-time 0, part-time 0; Caucasian–full-time 0, part-time 0;

students subject to the Americans With Disabilities Act–part-time 2.

Financial Information/Assistance:
Tuition for Full-Time Study: *Master's:* State residents: per academic year $2,759, $307 per credit hour; Nonstate residents: per academic year $4,415, $491 per credit hour. Tuition is subject to change.

Financial Assistance:
First Year Students: Research assistantships available for first-year. Average amount paid per academic year: $2,500. Average number of hours worked per week: 10. Apply by March 1. Tuition remission given: partial.
Advanced Students: Research assistantships available for advanced students. Average amount paid per academic year: $2,500. Average number of hours worked per week: 10. Apply by March 1. Tuition remission given: partial.
Contact Information: Of all students currently enrolled full-time, 40% benefitted from one or more of the listed financial assistance programs.

Internships/Practica: Clinical students are required to complete 6 credit hours of practicum and internship in a mental health setting. I/O students are required to complete a 3 credit hour internship in business or industry.

Housing and Day Care: On-campus housing is available. No on-campus day care facilities are available.

Employment of Department Graduates:
Master's Degree Graduates: Of those who graduated in the academic year 2003–2004, the following categories and numbers represent the post-graduate activities and employment of master's degree graduates: Enrolled in a post-doctoral residency/fellowship (n/a), employed in independent practice (n/a), total from the above (master's) (0).
Doctoral Degree Graduates: Of those who graduated in the academic year 2003–2004, the following categories and numbers represent the post-graduate activities and employment of doctoral degree graduates: Enrolled in a psychology doctoral program (n/a), total from the above (doctoral) (0).

Additional Information:
Orientation, Objectives, and Emphasis of Department: The concentration in clinical psychology is designed for students who wish to work in applied settings such as community mental health facilities, hospitals, counseling centers, and other social and rehabilitation agencies, or who wish to continue their education at the doctoral level. Students with the latter goal in mind are strongly encouraged to engage in research in the course of their master's degree training by participating in faculty members' ongoing research programs or conducting their own research under faculty supervision for research report or thesis credit. The industrial/organizational concentration is appropriate for students interested in employment in business or industry, or for those who wish to continue their education at the doctoral level in a related area. A 3-credit internship and 3- to 6-credit research report or thesis are required. With careful selection of electives, internship placement, and research focus, students are able to develop specialization in human factors, personnel evaluation and placement, or group and organizational processes. The concentration in gen-

eral psychology, in addition to exposing students to the major traditional subject matter of psychology, also provides the opportunity to explore particular areas of psychology in depth through the appropriate selection of elective coursework and research. The general concentration is appropriate for students interested in continuing their education at the doctoral level, as well as those interested in employment, particularly in research positions, upon the receipt of their master's degree.

Special Facilities or Resources: The department has laboratory space and equipment to support a variety of animal and human research.

Application Information:

Send to: Office of Graduate Studies and Sponsored Research, West Chester University, West Chester, PA 19383. Application available online. URL of online application: http://www.wcupa.edu/_ADMIS SIONS/SCH_DGR/application.html. Students are admitted in the Fall, application deadline March 1. Late applications will be reviewed if space remains in the program. *Fee:* $25.

Widener University
Institute for Graduate Clinical Psychology
One University Place
Chester, PA 19013
Telephone: (610) 499-1206
Fax: (610) 499-4625
E-mail: *graduate.psychology@widener.edu*
Web: *http://www.widener.edu*

Department Information:

1970. Associate Dean and Director: Virginia Brabender. Number of Faculty: total–full-time 13, part-time 45; women–full-time 6, part-time 25; minority–full-time 1, part-time 5.

Programs and Degrees Offered:

Listed in the following order: Program area, degree type (T if terminal Master's), number awarded 7/03–6/04. Clinical Psychology PsyD (Doctor of Psychology) 29, Law-Psychology Other 3.

APA Accreditation: Clinical PsyD (Doctor of Psychology).

Student Applications/Admissions:
Student Applications

Clinical Psychology PsyD (Doctor of Psychology)—Applications 2004–2005, 280. Total applicants accepted 2004–2005, 69. Number enrolled (new admits only) 2004–2005 full-time, 36. Number enrolled (new admits only) 2004–2005 part-time, 0. Openings 2005–2006, 33. The Median number of years required for completion of a degree are 5. The number of students enrolled full and part-time who were dismissed or voluntarily withdrew from this program area were 0. *Law-Psychology Other*—Applications 2004–2005, 25. Total applicants accepted 2004–2005, 5. Number enrolled (new admits only) 2004–2005 full-time, 4. Number enrolled (new admits only)

2004–2005 part-time, 0. Openings 2005–2006, 3. The Median number of years required for completion of a degree are 6. The number of students enrolled full and part-time who were dismissed or voluntarily withdrew from this program area were 0.

Admissions Requirements:
Scores: Entries appear in this order: required test or GPA, minimum score (if required), median score of students entering in 2003–2004. Doctoral Programs: GRE-V 600, 604; GRE-Q 600, 626; GRE-V+Q 1200; overall undergraduate GPA 3.20, 3.43. GRE-V, GRE-Q are required; GRE Psychology subject scores are highly recommended. MAT scores are not required. A minimum GPA of 3.0 for the highest degreee earned is strongly recommended. LSAT scores are required for the JD/PsyD program.
Other Criteria: (importance of criteria rated low, medium, or high): GRE/MAT scores high, work experience medium, extracurricular activity medium, clinically related public service medium, GPA high, letters of recommendation high, interview high, statement of goals and objectives high, An undergraduate major is not required. We encourage applications from individuals from various disciplines and with a wide range of experiences.

Student Characteristics: The following represents characteristics of students in 2004–2005 in all graduate psychology programs in the department: Female–full-time 134, part-time 0; Male–full-time 29, part-time 0; African American/Black–full-time 13, part-time 0; Hispanic/Latino(a)–full-time 6, part-time 0; Asian/Pacific Islander–full-time 15, part-time 0; American Indian/Alaska Native–full-time 2, part-time 0; Caucasian–full-time 123, part-time 0; Multi-ethnic–full-time 4, part-time 0; students subject to the Americans With Disabilities Act–full-time 3, part-time 0.

Financial Information/Assistance:
Tuition for Full-Time Study: *Doctoral:* State residents: per academic year $18,600; Nonstate residents: per academic year $18,600. Tuition is subject to change.

Financial Assistance:
First Year Students: Fellowships and scholarships available for first-year. Apply by December 31. Tuition remission given: partial.
Advanced Students: Fellowships and scholarships available for advanced students. Apply by December 31. Tuition remission given: partial.
Contact Information: Of all students currently enrolled full-time, 28% benefitted from one or more of the listed financial assistance programs.

Internships/Practica: The program has an exclusively affiliated internship that is half-time over a two-year period. The APA-accredited internship is housed at Widener University, but placements are within a 40-mile radius of the campus. 100% of fourth- and fifth-year students are placed. For those doctoral students for whom a professional internship is required prior to graduation, 65 applied in 2003–2004. Of those who applied, 65 were placed in APA accredited internships.

Housing and Day Care: No on-campus housing is available. No on-campus day care facilities are available.

Employment of Department Graduates:

Master's Degree Graduates: Of those who graduated in the academic year 2003–2004, the following categories and numbers represent the post-graduate activities and employment of master's degree graduates: Enrolled in a post-doctoral residency/fellowship (n/a), employed in independent practice (n/a), total from the above (master's) (0).

Doctoral Degree Graduates: Of those who graduated in the academic year 2003–2004, the following categories and numbers represent the post-graduate activities and employment of doctoral degree graduates: Enrolled in a psychology doctoral program (n/a), total from the above (doctoral) (0).

Additional Information:

Orientation, Objectives, and Emphasis of Department: The PsyD program retains the basic skills and knowledge traditional to clinical psychology, such as psychodiagnostic testing and psychotherapy, while simultaneously exposing the individual to new ideas and practices in the field. The law–psychology (JD/PsyD) program presumes that every law and court decision is in part based upon psychological assumptions about how people act and how their actions can be controlled. It is designed to train lawyer-clinical psychologists to identify and evaluate these assumptions and apply their psychological knowledge to improve the law, legal process, and legal system. Students earn a law degree from the Widener University School of Law, and a doctorate in psychology from Widener's Institute for Graduate Clinical Psychology. The PsyD/MBA program is based on the premise that health care organizations as well as the mental health and health care fields at large are in need of well-trained leaders and advocates who integrate psychological and business-organizational knowledge.

Special Facilities or Resources: One of the hallmarks of our program is the variety of internship and practica opportunities available to students, all of which are within driving distance of the university. A corollary resource is the availability of practicing clinicians to teach in the program, a factor that provides breadth, relevance, and enrichment to the curriculum. Widener University is situated near Philadelphia and in the middle of the Eastern corridor between New York and Washington, DC. As a result, our students enjoy a rich diversity of educational resources, field experiences, and employment opportunities. Here is a place where you can enjoy big cities or the beauty of the countryside, a vast array of cultural events and historical opportunities, and all forms of sports, arts, and entertainment. It is a wonderful place to live, learn and work.

Information for Students With Physical Disabilities: See the following Web site for more information: http://www.widener.edu/sss/sssmain.html.

Application Information:
Send to: Director of Admissions, The Institute for Graduate Clinical Psychology, Widener University, One University Place, Chester, PA 19013. Application available online. URL of online application: www.widener.edu. Students are admitted in the Fall, application deadline December 31. *Fee:* $75.

Widener University
Law–Psychology (JD-PsyD) Graduate Training Program
Institute for Graduate Clinical Psychology & School of Law
One University Place
Chester, PA 19013-5792
Telephone: (610) 499-1206
Fax: (610) 499-4625
E-mail: *graduate.psychology@widener.edu*
Web: *http://www.widener.edu (search for "law-psychology")*

Department Information:
1989. Director: Amiram Elwork, PhD. Number of Faculty: total–full-time 14, part-time 23; women–full-time 6, part-time 13; minority–full-time 2, part-time 3.

Programs and Degrees Offered:
Listed in the following order: Program area, degree type (T if terminal Master's), number awarded 7/03–6/04. Law–Psychology (JD/ PsyD) Other 3.

Student Applications/Admissions:
Student Applications

Law–Psychology (JD/PsyD) Other—Applications 2004–2005, 22. Total applicants accepted 2004–2005, 7. Number enrolled (new admits only) 2004–2005 full-time, 4. Openings 2005–2006, 3. The Median number of years required for completion of a degree are 6. The number of students enrolled full and part-time who were dismissed or voluntarily withdrew from this program area were 0.

Admissions Requirements:

Scores: Entries appear in this order: required test or GPA, minimum score (if required), median score of students entering in 2003–2004. Doctoral Programs: GRE-V no minimum stated, 560; GRE-Q no minimum stated, 680; GRE-V+Q no minimum stated, 1240; GRE-Analytical no minimum stated, 5.5; GRE-Subject(Psych) no minimum stated, 640; overall undergraduate GPA no minimum stated, 3.5. LSAT- Required - Median Score= 158.

Other Criteria: (importance of criteria rated low, medium, or high): GRE/MAT scores high, research experience low, work experience medium, extracurricular activity low, clinically related public service medium, GPA high, letters of recommendation medium, interview high, statement of goals and objectives high, high LSAT.

Student Characteristics: The following represents characteristics of students in 2004–2005 in all graduate psychology programs in the department: Female–full-time 14, part-time 0; Male–full-time 3, part-time 0; Asian/Pacific Islander–full-time 1, part-time 0; Caucasian–full-time 16, part-time 0.

Financial Information/Assistance:
Tuition for Full-Time Study: Doctoral: State residents: per academic year $22,500, $750 per credit hour; Nonstate residents: per academic year $22,500, $750 per credit hour. Tuition is subject to change.

Financial Assistance:
First Year Students: Fellowships and scholarships available for first-year. Average amount paid per academic year: $0. Average

number of hours worked per week: 0. Tuition remission given: partial.

Advanced Students: Traineeships available for advanced students. Average amount paid per academic year: $13,500. Average number of hours worked per week: 24. Tuition remission given: partial. Fellowships and scholarships available for advanced students. Average amount paid per academic year: $0. Average number of hours worked per week: 0. Tuition remission given: partial.

Contact Information: Of all students currently enrolled full-time, 80% benefitted from one or more of the listed financial assistance programs.

Internships/Practica: Students are in field placements during five of the 6 years of training. During two of the first three years, students are assigned to clinical psychology practica. These are introductory experiences designed to acquaint the students with a variety of settings in which they can develop fundamental psychological skills in testing/assessment and psychotherapy/intervention. Fourth year field experiences are in a legal setting (law firm, court, legal agency), where they are given an opportunity to practice their legal skills. Fifth and sixth year experiences are internship rotations that allow students the opportunity to sharpen their clinical and forensic psychology skills. Widener's APA accredited integrated clinical internship with its various rotations (including forensic rotations) is highly unusual. In most programs, students participate in internships that are independent of their graduate programs. Our internship is embedded in the program. While continuing to take their coursework, students complete their internship rotations over a 2-year period at various clinical sites affiliated with Widener. This allows for better integration between coursework and practical experience and relieves the student of the inconveniences associated with finding a separate internship and/or relocating. For those doctoral students for whom a professional internship is required prior to graduation, 4 applied in 2003–2004. Of those who applied, 4 were placed in internships listed by the Association of Psychology Postdoctoral and Internship Programs (APPIC); 4 were placed in APA accredited internships.

Housing and Day Care: On-campus housing is available. See the following Web site for more information: http://www.widener. edu. On-campus day care facilities are available.

Employment of Department Graduates:

Master's Degree Graduates: Of those who graduated in the academic year 2003–2004, the following categories and numbers represent the post-graduate activities and employment of master's degree graduates: Enrolled in a psychology doctoral program (0), enrolled in another graduate/professional program (0), enrolled in a post-doctoral residency/fellowship (n/a), employed in independent practice (n/a), employed in an academic position at a university (0), employed in an academic position at a 2-year/4-year college (0), employed in other positions at a higher education institution (0), employed in a professional position in a school system (0), employed in business or industry (research/consulting) (0), employed in business or industry (management) (0), employed in a government agency (research) (0), employed in a government agency (professional services) (0), employed in a community mental health/counseling center (0), employed in a hospital/medical center (0), still seeking employment (0), other employment position (0), total from the above (master's) (0).

Doctoral Degree Graduates: Of those who graduated in the academic year 2003–2004, the following categories and numbers represent the post-graduate activities and employment of doctoral degree graduates: Enrolled in a psychology doctoral program (n/a), enrolled in a post-doctoral residency/fellowship (0), employed in independent practice (0), employed in an academic position at a university (0), employed in an academic position at a 2-year/4-year college (0), employed in other positions at a higher education institution (0), employed in a professional position in a school system (0), employed in business or industry (research/consulting) (0), employed in business or industry (management) (0), employed in a government agency (research) (0), employed in a government agency (professional services) (0), employed in a community mental health/counseling center (2), employed in a hospital/medical center (0), still seeking employment (0), other employment position (1), total from the above (doctoral) (3).

Additional Information:

Orientation, Objectives, and Emphasis of Department: Widener University's Law-Psychology Graduate Program is based on the idea that many legal issues involve underlying psychological questions. It trains graduates to combine their knowledge of psychology and law and bring fresh insights to the process of understanding, evaluating and correcting important psycholegal problems. While a large portion of the curriculum is similar to that required of all students in the PsyD and JD programs, it includes a number of courses and requirements (e.g., dissertation) designed specifically to help students acquire an integration of psychology and law and to develop specialized skills. In addition, students are given opportunities to put their integrated skills into practice within their field placements. Students develop special expertise on many issues at the interface of law and clinical psychology and are prepared to play diverse roles in society, including: lawyer, forensic psychologist, professor, consultant, administrator, policy maker, judge, legislator, etc. This 6-year program offers several benefits: (1) It allows students to pursue clinical psychology and law simultaneously. (2) It saves students the equivalent of two years of tuition and time. (3) It trains graduates to integrate the two fields conceptually and offers them a significant way of differentiating themselves in the job market.

Special Facilities or Resources: Widener University is situated near Philadelphia and in the middle of the eastern corridor between New York and Washington, DC. As a result, our students enjoy a rich diversity of educational resources, field experiences, and employment opportunities. Whether you enjoy big cities or beautiful scenery, cultural events and history, all forms of entertainment and sports, our location is an ideal place to live, learn and work.

Information for Students With Physical Disabilities: See the following Web site for more information: http://www.widener. edu/sss/sssenable.html.

Application Information:
Send to: Law–Psychology Graduate Program—Admissions, Institute for Graduate Clinical Psychology, One University Place, Chester, PA 19013-5792. Application available online. URL of online application: https://www.applyweb.com/apply/widener/indexa.html. Students are admitted in the Fall, application deadline February 1. *Fee:* $60.

Carlos Albizu University

PsyD/PhD (clinical)
San Juan Campus
Box 9023711
Old San Juan, PR 00902-3711
Telephone: (787) 725-6500
Fax: (787) 721-7187
E-mail: *lgarcia@prip.edu*
Web: *www.albizu.edu*

Department Information:

1972. Chancellor: Lourdes R. Garcia. Number of Faculty: total–full-time 13, part-time 31; women–full-time 6, part-time 16; minority–full-time 13, part-time 30.

Programs and Degrees Offered:

Listed in the following order: Program area, degree type (T if terminal Master's), number awarded 7/03–6/04. Clinical PhD (Doctor of Philosophy) 22.

APA Accreditation: Clinical PhD (Doctor of Philosophy).

Student Applications/Admissions:

Student Applications

Clinical PhD (Doctor of Philosophy)—Applications 2004–2005, 30. Total applicants accepted 2004–2005, 20. Openings 2005–2006, 20. The Median number of years required for completion of a degree are 6. The number of students enrolled full and part-time who were dismissed or voluntarily withdrew from this program area were 8.

Admissions Requirements:

Scores: Entries appear in this order: required test or GPA, minimum score (if required), median score of students entering in 2003–2004. Master's Programs: overall undergraduate GPA no minimum stated. P.A.E.G. (Prueba de Admisión para Estudios Graduados). Doctoral Programs: overall undergraduate GPA no minimum stated. P.A.E.G. (Prueba de Admisión para Estudios Guaduados).

Other Criteria: (importance of criteria rated low, medium, or high): research experience medium, work experience medium, extracurricular activity medium, clinically related public service medium, GPA high, letters of recommendation high, interview high, statement of goals and objectives high, P.A.E.G. scores high. Clinically related service, professional license and a minimum of three years of experience in the student's concentration are requirements for admission to PhD program in General Psychology.

Student Characteristics: The following represents characteristics of students in 2004–2005 in all graduate psychology programs in the department: Female–full-time 91, part-time 0; Male–full-time 15, part-time 0; African American/Black–full-time 0, part-time 0; Hispanic/Latino(a)–full-time 99, part-time 0; Asian/Pacific Islander–full-time 0, part-time 0; American Indian/Alaska Native–full-time 0, part-time 0; Caucasian–full-time 0, part-time 0.

Financial Information/Assistance:

Financial Assistance:

First Year Students: No information provided.
Advanced Students: No information provided.
Contact Information: Of all students currently enrolled full-time, 66% benefitted from one or more of the listed financial assistance programs.

Internships/Practica: For masters students: Residency requirements: Full-time residency of two years. Clinical Practicums: Complete 780 hours at the Community Mental Clinic and/or designated agency. For doctoral students: Residency requirement: Full-time residency of three years is required of all doctoral students. Clinical Practicums: All students in a clinical degree program are required to complete the clinical practicum at the Mental Health Services Clinic and/or designated agency. Industrial/Organizational Practicum: Students are required to enroll in the industrial/organizational practicum. General Psychology Practicum: PhD students are required to enroll in the PSG6801 and 6802 General Psychology Practice and RP674-675 Research Practicums for a total of four hundred (400) hours consisting of 80 hours of teaching, 256 hours of research and 64 hours of consultation. For those doctoral students for whom a professional internship is required prior to graduation, 39 applied in 2003–2004. Of those who applied, 2 were placed in internships listed by the Association of Psychology Postdoctoral and Internship Programs (APPIC); 2 were placed in APA accredited internships.

Housing and Day Care: No on-campus housing is available. No on-campus day care facilities are available.

Employment of Department Graduates:

Master's Degree Graduates: Of those who graduated in the academic year 2003–2004, the following categories and numbers represent the post-graduate activities and employment of master's degree graduates: Enrolled in a post-doctoral residency/fellowship (n/a), employed in independent practice (n/a), total from the above (master's) (0).

Doctoral Degree Graduates: Of those who graduated in the academic year 2003–2004, the following categories and numbers represent the post-graduate activities and employment of doctoral degree graduates: Enrolled in a psychology doctoral program (n/a), total from the above (doctoral) (0).

Additional Information:

Orientation, Objectives, and Emphasis of Department: The educational objective of Carlos Albizu University is to train health, mental health, occupational health and professionals in other related fields to provide services in a manner that is sensitive and responsive to cultural and ethnic issues. Academic programs are directed towards five target areas of professional formation: 1. Development of clinical and/or organizational intervention skills with due regard for the behavioral norms, values and belief system of the client. 2. Development of appropriate assessment skills, taking into consideration multi-cultural variables, the special needs and qualities of groups, and the integration of research findings in the assessment process. 3. Awareness and understanding of the psychological and health needs and behaviors of different ethnic groups within their sociocultural context. 4. Development of clinical and/or organizational skills through supervised experiences. 5. Development of research skills through supervised research experiences.

Special Facilities or Resources: Community Mental Health Clinic—The purpose of the Community Mental Health Clinic (CMHC) of the San Juan Campus is to offer mental health services to the Puerto Rican community. Service offerings are designed for the specific needs of target populations and address the psychological needs that can be attended in a community clinic center. The Community Mental Health Clinic offers students a unique opportunity to receive high quality multicultural-multilingual professional training in the areas of psychotherapy, clinical assessment, community consultation and preventive mental health. The Carlos Albizu University is able to offer a sliding fee scale to those clients who qualify. The Carlos Albizu University serves the mental health needs of children, adolescents, adults, elderly, and families and offers specialized services to victims of sexual abuse under the Sexual Abuse Program. Continuing Education Program—The Continuing Education Program of the PRIP is a significant resource for the fulfillment of Continuing Education requirements for psychologists and other mental health professionals and health service providers. The program has been accredited by the American Psychological Association since 1984. The Continuing Education Program is a qualified provider of Continuing Education Credits as recognized by the Puerto Rico Licensing Boards for Psychologists, Occupational and Physical Therapists, Physicians, Nurses and Mental Health Educators. Scientific Research Institute—The Scientific Research Institute (SRI) is a specialized research center established for the purpose of advancing the role of science in the understanding of human behavior and society. SRI is designed to provide training experiences for students, foment faculty involvement in research, develop data banks for present and future projects, and provide specialized services to the academic community and community at large. Depending upon availability of funds, scholarships are offered for students to work in research projects sponsored by SRI. SRI is committed to multidisciplinary studies and to collaborative efforts with Puerto Rican, United States and International research centers.

Application Information:
Send to: Student Affairs Office, Box 9023711, Old San Juan, San Juan, PR 00902-3711. Students are admitted in the Fall, application deadline July 30; Spring, application deadline November 30; Summer, application deadline April 30. *Fee:* $75.

Brown University

Psychology
Graduate School
89 Waterman Street
Providence, RI 02912
Telephone: (401) 863-2727
Fax: (401) 863-1300
E-mail: Rebecca_Burwell@brown.edu
Web: http://www.brown.edu/Departments/Psychology/

Department Information:

1892. Chairperson: Eric Suuberg. Number of Faculty: total–full-time 12, part-time 1; women–full-time 5, part-time 1; minority–full-time 1.

Programs and Degrees Offered:

Listed in the following order: Program area, degree type (T if terminal Master's), number awarded 7/03–6/04. Experimental Psychology PhD (Doctor of Philosophy) 3.

Student Applications/Admissions:

Student Applications

Experimental Psychology PhD (Doctor of Philosophy)—Applications 2004–2005, 68. Total applicants accepted 2004–2005, 8. Number enrolled (new admits only) 2004–2005 full-time, 2. Number enrolled (new admits only) 2004–2005 part-time, 0. Openings 2005–2006, 5. The Median number of years required for completion of a degree are 5. The number of students enrolled full and part-time who were dismissed or voluntarily withdrew from this program area were 1.

Admissions Requirements:

Scores: Entries appear in this order: required test or GPA, minimum score (if required), median score of students entering in 2003–2004. Doctoral Programs: GRE-V no minimum stated; GRE-Q no minimum stated; GRE-Analytical no minimum stated; overall undergraduate GPA no minimum stated; last 2 years GPA no minimum stated; psychology GPA no minimum stated.

Other Criteria: (importance of criteria rated low, medium, or high): GRE/MAT scores high, research experience high, extracurricular activity low, GPA high, letters of recommendation high, interview high, statement of goals and objectives high. For additional information on admission requirements, go to: http://www.brown.edu/Departments/Psychology/.

Student Characteristics: The following represents characteristics of students in 2004–2005 in all graduate psychology programs in the department: Female–full-time 15, part-time 0; Male–full-time 7, part-time 0; African American/Black–full-time 0, part-time 0; Hispanic/Latino(a)–full-time 2, part-time 0; Asian/Pacific Islander–full-time 4, part-time 0; American Indian/Alaska Native–full-time 1, part-time 0; Caucasian–full-time 15, part-time 0; Multi-ethnic–full-time 0, part-time 0; students subject to the Americans With Disabilities Act–full-time 0, part-time 0.

Financial Information/Assistance:

Tuition for Full-Time Study: *Doctoral:* State residents: per academic year $30,672; Nonstate residents: per academic year $30,672. Tuition is subject to change.

Financial Assistance:

First Year Students: Teaching assistantships available for first-year. Average amount paid per academic year: $20,500. Apply by January 15. Tuition remission given: full. Research assistantships available for first-year. Average amount paid per academic year: $20,500. Apply by January 15. Fellowships and scholarships available for first-year. Average amount paid per academic year: $20,500. Apply by January 15. Tuition remission given: full.

Advanced Students: Teaching assistantships available for advanced students. Average amount paid per academic year: $20,500. Apply by January 15. Tuition remission given: full. Research assistantships available for advanced students. Average amount paid per academic year: $20,500. Apply by January 15. Tuition remission given: full. Fellowships and scholarships available for advanced students. Average amount paid per academic year: $20,500. Apply by January 15. Tuition remission given: full.

Contact Information: Of all students currently enrolled full-time, 100% benefitted from one or more of the listed financial assistance programs. Application and information included in graduate application form.

Internships/Practica: No information provided.

Housing and Day Care: On-campus housing is available. See the following Web site for more information: http://www.brown.edu/Administration/ResLife/. On-campus day care facilities are available. See the following Web site for more information: http://www.brown.edu/Administration/George_Street_Journal/vol24/24GSJ05f.html.

Employment of Department Graduates:

Master's Degree Graduates: Of those who graduated in the academic year 2003–2004, the following categories and numbers represent the post-graduate activities and employment of master's degree graduates: Enrolled in a post-doctoral residency/fellowship (n/a), employed in independent practice (n/a), total from the above (master's) (0).

Doctoral Degree Graduates: Of those who graduated in the academic year 2003–2004, the following categories and numbers represent the post-graduate activities and employment of doctoral degree graduates: Enrolled in a psychology doctoral program (n/a), total from the above (doctoral) (0).

Additional Information:

Orientation, Objectives, and Emphasis of Department: The graduate program in the Department of Psychology is designed to educate and train scientists and scholars who will make contributions to society through their research and teaching. PhDs in Psychology from Brown are prepared for a range of scientific careers in both academic and applied settings. The Graduate Program in Psychology is designed for candidates seeking the PhD degree. Some students also elect to take a Master's degree as a step toward the PhD, but students are not accepted for Master's level work only. Graduate training in Psychology is part of a close, collaborative relationship between the student, the faculty advisor, and the student's graduate committee. Decisions about specific coursework, research training, and teaching responsibilities are based more on the student's research interests and goals than on rigid, pre-defined programs of study. In this way, students can develop interdisciplinary curricula that take advantage of the collective strengths of Brown in the study of brain, mind, and behavior. Although students have considerable flexibility in designing their program of study, students should be aware of the major substantive areas within the Department. Degrees in Psychology are currently offered with specializations in Behavioral Neuroscience; Sensation and Perception; Cognitive Processes; and Social, Personality, and Developmental.

Special Facilities or Resources: Brown University has a number of academic and research resources that benefit students in Psychology. For example, our Brain Science Program (BSP) is a unique interdisciplinary program formed to promote collaborative theoretical and experimental study of the brain from the molecular to the behavioral and cognitive level. It unites faculty in multiple departments who study the fundamental mechanisms of nervous system function and brain-behavior relationships. The faculty are also committed to translating fundamental knowledge for the diagnosis and treatment of the devastating effects of disease and trauma of the nervous system. As a part of the BSP initiative, the Magnetic Resonance Imaging Research Facility (MRF) was created in 2000 to facilitate research and educational activities using magnetic resonance imaging technology. The MRF fosters training and research activities with MRI technology for graduate students and faculty with departmental appointments in the basic and clinical sciences. The MRF has access to installed Siemens 1.5T and 3T MRI systems at Memorial Hospital of Rhode Island, and users can acquire information about brain anatomy and function for research and education purposes. In 2006, a new Life Sciences building on the univesity campus will house biological imaging facilities including a 3T fMRI system.

Information for Students With Physical Disabilities: See the following Web site for more information: http://www.brown.edu/Student_Services/Office_of_Student_Life/dss/.

Application Information:
Preferred method of application is online. If not possible, applications can be sent to: Brown University Graduate School, 47 George Street, Box 1867, Providence, RI 02912 (401) 863-2600. Application available online. URL of online application: http://www.brown.edu/Divisions/Graduate_School/admissions/. Students are admitted in the Winter, application deadline January 16. *Fee:* $70.

Rhode Island College
Psychology
Rhode Island College
600 Mt. Pleasant Avenue
Providence, RI 02908
Telephone: (401) 456-8015
Fax: (401) 456-8751
E-mail: blounsbury@ric.edu
Web: www.ric.edu

Department Information:
Chairperson: Joan Rollins, PhD Number of Faculty: total–full-time 17, part-time 8; women–full-time 9, part-time 6; minority–full-time 1; faculty subject to the Americans With Disabilities Act 2.

Programs and Degrees Offered:
Listed in the following order: Program area, degree type (T if terminal Master's), number awarded 7/03–6/04. Psychology MA/MS (Master of Arts/Science) (T) 3.

Student Applications/Admissions:
Student Applications
Psychology MA/MS (Master of Arts/Science)—Applications 2004–2005, 5. Total applicants accepted 2004–2005, 5. Number enrolled (new admits only) 2004–2005 full-time, 2. Number enrolled (new admits only) 2004–2005 part-time, 1. Total enrolled 2004–2005 full-time, 2, part-time, 22. The Median number of years required for completion of a degree are 3. The number of students enrolled full and part-time who were dismissed or voluntarily withdrew from this program area were 2.

Admissions Requirements:
Scores: Entries appear in this order: required test or GPA, minimum score (if required), median score of students entering in 2003–2004. Master's Programs: GRE-V+Q no minimum stated; MAT no minimum stated; overall undergraduate GPA no minimum stated; psychology GPA no minimum stated. We require either the GRE or the MAT. We specify no minimum scores.

Student Characteristics: The following represents characteristics of students in 2004–2005 in all graduate psychology programs in the department: Female–full-time 1, part-time 15; Male–full-time 1, part-time 5; Caucasian–full-time 0, part-time 0.

Financial Information/Assistance:
Tuition for Full-Time Study: *Master's:* State residents: $194 per credit hour; Nonstate residents: $410 per credit hour.

Financial Assistance:
First Year Students: Research assistantships available for first-year. Average amount paid per academic year: $3,500. Apply by April 1. Tuition remission given: full. Fellowships and scholarships available for first-year.
Advanced Students: Research assistantships available for advanced students. Average amount paid per academic year: $3,500. Apply by April 1. Tuition remission given: full. Fellowships and scholarships available for advanced students.

Contact Information: No information provided.

Internships/Practica: No information provided.

Housing and Day Care: No on-campus housing is available. On-campus day care facilities are available.

Employment of Department Graduates:

Master's Degree Graduates: Of those who graduated in the academic year 2003–2004, the following categories and numbers represent the post-graduate activities and employment of master's degree graduates: Enrolled in a post-doctoral residency/fellowship (n/a), employed in independent practice (n/a), total from the above (master's) (0).

Doctoral Degree Graduates: Of those who graduated in the academic year 2003–2004, the following categories and numbers represent the post-graduate activities and employment of doctoral degree graduates: Enrolled in a psychology doctoral program (n/a), total from the above (doctoral) (0).

Additional Information:

Orientation, Objectives, and Emphasis of Department: The MA program in psychology at Rhode Island College provides a basic graduate education in psychology, with a core curriculum in personality, cognitive, developmental and social psychology, as well as quantitative and research methods. The MA in psychology has application in a wide variety of careers in human services, business and education, and provides preparation for further graduate study.

Application Information:

Send to: Dr. Barbara Anderson Lounsbury, Director Graduate Program in Psychology, Horace Mann 308, Rhode Island College, 600 Mt. Pleasant Avenue, Providence, RI 02908. Students are admitted in the Fall. Programs have rolling admissions. *Fee:* $35.

Rhode Island, University of, Chafee Social Sciences Center

Department of Psychology
Arts and Sciences
10 Chafee Road
Room 313 Chafee Building
Kingston, RI 02881
Telephone: (401) 874-2193
Fax: (401) 874-2157
E-mail: *psyadmin@etal.uri.edu*
Web: *http://www.uri.edu/artsci/psy*

Department Information:

1961. Chairperson: Dominic Valentino. Number of Faculty: total–full-time 29, part-time 1; women–full-time 9; minority–full-time 4.

Programs and Degrees Offered:

Listed in the following order: Program area, degree type (T if terminal Master's), number awarded 7/03–6/04. School Psychology MA/MS (Master of Arts/Science) (T) 4, Clinical Psychology PhD (Doctor of Philosophy) 6, School Psychology PhD (Doctor of Philosophy) 1, Experimental PhD (Doctor of Philosophy) 5.

APA Accreditation: Clinical PhD (Doctor of Philosophy). School PhD (Doctor of Philosophy).

Student Applications/Admissions:

Student Applications

School Psychology MA/MS (*Master of Arts/Science*)—Applications 2004–2005, 31. Total applicants accepted 2004–2005, 10. Number enrolled (new admits only) 2004–2005 full-time, 3. Number enrolled (new admits only) 2004–2005 part-time, 0. Openings 2005–2006, 5. The Median number of years required for completion of a degree are 3. The number of students enrolled full and part-time who were dismissed or voluntarily withdrew from this program area were 2. *Clinical Psychology PhD (Doctor of Philosophy)*—Applications 2004–2005, 167. Total applicants accepted 2004–2005, 8. Number enrolled (new admits only) 2004–2005 full-time, 5. Number enrolled (new admits only) 2004–2005 part-time, 0. Openings 2005–2006, 8. The Median number of years required for completion of a degree are 5. The number of students enrolled full and part-time who were dismissed or voluntarily withdrew from this program area were 0. *School Psychology PhD (Doctor of Philosophy)*—Applications 2004–2005, 48. Total applicants accepted 2004–2005, 8. Number enrolled (new admits only) 2004–2005 full-time, 4. Number enrolled (new admits only) 2004–2005 part-time, 0. Openings 2005–2006, 5. The Median number of years required for completion of a degree are 5. The number of students enrolled full and part-time who were dismissed or voluntarily withdrew from this program area were 2. *Experimental PhD (Doctor of Philosophy)*—Applications 2004–2005, 24. Total applicants accepted 2004–2005, 7. Number enrolled (new admits only) 2004–2005 full-time, 6. Number enrolled (new admits only) 2004–2005 part-time, 0. Openings 2005–2006, 6. The Median number of years required for completion of a degree are 5. The number of students enrolled full and part-time who were dismissed or voluntarily withdrew from this program area were 1.

Admissions Requirements:

Scores: Entries appear in this order: required test or GPA, minimum score (if required), median score of students entering in 2003–2004. Master's Programs: School Area: We recommend a minimum of 1100(MS) and 1200(PhD) for two best GRE scores. Doctoral Programs: GRE-V no minimum stated; GRE-Q no minimum stated; GRE-V+Q 1200. Experimental Program: We recommend a minimum V+Q of 1100. Clinical Program: For GRE we look at V and Q scores only and there is no minimum. There is no required minimum GPA. School Program: Academic aptitude(GRE+ GPA); quality of personal statement; research and applied experience; letters of recommendation; fit between applicant goals and program offerings. *Other Criteria:* (importance of criteria rated low, medium, or high): GRE/MAT scores medium, research experience medium, work experience medium, extracurricular activity low, clinically related public service medium, GPA medium, letters of recommendation high, interview high, statement of goals and objectives high. Importance of criteria varies per program. Experimental: High emphasis on research interest and experience; no required interview; we also look at GPA, GRE, focus and quality of personal statement, teaching experience, multicultural contribution, reference letters, and program-applicant fit. Clinical: Factors we look at are GRE, GPA, program/applicant match, research experience, clinical experience, life experience, letters of recommendation, and overall evaluation. For additional information on admission requirements, go to: www.uri.edu/artsci/psy.

Student Characteristics: The following represents characteristics of students in 2004–2005 in all graduate psychology programs in the department: Female–full-time 89, part-time 0; Male–full-time 25, part-time 0; African American/Black–full-time 5, part-time 0; Hispanic/Latino(a)–full-time 5, part-time 0; Asian/Pacific Islander–full-time 2, part-time 0; American Indian/Alaska Native–full-time 1, part-time 0; Caucasian–full-time 100, part-time 0; Multi-ethnic–full-time 1, part-time 0; students subject to the Americans With Disabilities Act–full-time 1, part-time 0.

Financial Information/Assistance:

Tuition for Full-Time Study: *Master's:* State residents: per academic year $4,338, $225 per credit hour; Nonstate residents: per academic year $12,438, $646 per credit hour. *Doctoral:* State residents: per academic year $4,338, $225 per credit hour; Nonstate residents: per academic year $12,438, $646 per credit hour. Tuition is subject to change. See the following Web site for updates and changes in tuition costs: http://www.uri.edu/es/acadinfo/acadyear/tuition.html.

Financial Assistance:

First Year Students: Teaching assistantships available for first-year. Average amount paid per academic year: $10,614. Average number of hours worked per week: 20. Apply by March 22. Tuition remission given: full. Research assistantships available for first-year. Average amount paid per academic year: $10,614. Average number of hours worked per week: 20. Apply by varies. Tuition remission given: full. Fellowships and scholarships available for first-year. Average amount paid per academic year: $10,614. Average number of hours worked per week: 0. Apply by February 21. Tuition remission given: full.

Advanced Students: Teaching assistantships available for advanced students. Average amount paid per academic year: $11,525. Average number of hours worked per week: 20. Apply by March 22. Tuition remission given: full. Research assistantships available for advanced students. Average amount paid per academic year: $11,525. Average number of hours worked per week: 20. Apply by varies. Tuition remission given: full. Fellowships and scholarships available for advanced students. Average amount paid per academic year: $11,525. Average number of hours worked per week: 0. Apply by February 21. Tuition remission given: full.

Contact Information: Of all students currently enrolled full-time, 60% benefitted from one or more of the listed financial assistance programs.

Internships/Practica: The Department has an excellent record of placing Clinical and School students in high quality approved internships for the later stages of doctoral training. Many graduates are invited to postdoctoral positions. The department's rich network of contacts in southern New England also provides placement opportunities for externship practicum experience earlier in a student's program. For those doctoral students for whom a professional internship is required prior to graduation, 7 applied in 2003–2004. Of those who applied, 7 were placed in internships listed by the Association of Psychology Postdoctoral and Internship Programs (APPIC); 7 were placed in APA accredited internships.

Housing and Day Care: On-campus housing for graduate students is available at the Graduate Student Village, an apartment complex adjacent to the campus. Contact (401) 874-5390 or (401) 874-2232 or the University Web site: www.uri.edu (see link for housing). On-campus day care facilities are available. Child care is available through a cooperative day care in the complex or in the University Child Development Center (space is limited). Please call (401) 874-2758 or via the University Web site at www.uri.edu.

Employment of Department Graduates:

Master's Degree Graduates: Of those who graduated in the academic year 2003–2004, the following categories and numbers represent the post-graduate activities and employment of master's degree graduates: Enrolled in a post-doctoral residency/fellowship (n/a), employed in independent practice (n/a), employed in a professional position in a school system (7), employed in a government agency (professional services) (1), total from the above (master's) (8).

Doctoral Degree Graduates: Of those who graduated in the academic year 2003–2004, the following categories and numbers represent the post-graduate activities and employment of doctoral degree graduates: Enrolled in a psychology doctoral program (n/a), enrolled in a post-doctoral residency/fellowship (2), employed in an academic position at a university (3), employed in a professional position in a school system (3), employed in business or industry (research/consulting) (1), employed in a government agency (professional services) (1), employed in a community mental health/counseling center (1), employed in a hospital/medical center (1), do not know (7), total from the above (doctoral) (19).

Additional Information:

Orientation, Objectives, and Emphasis of Department: The URI Psychology Department has a strong scientist-practitioner orientation in its Clinical and School Psychology programs, and an applied quantitative emphasis in its Experimental Psychology program. There is a lively interaction among the programs, which is an especially attractive feature of the department. The research and professional interests of the faculty fall into these seven interest areas: (1) health psychology; (2) gender, diversity, and multicultural research; (3) neuropsychology; (4) research methodology; (5) family, child, and community research; (6) clinical psychology practice; and (7) child and school psychology practice. Graduates of our programs have developed diverse careers in academia, government service, private industry, the nonprofit sector, and private consulting and practice.

Special Facilities or Resources: The Department operates an on-campus training facility, the Psychological Consultation Center, where students train under direct faculty supervision for professional practice service roles with individual clients, families, and children. The department is closely allied with the Cancer Prevention Research Center, one of the nation's leading centers for behavioral health promotion and disease prevention. Students also participate in research and training activities with the Department's Community Research and Services Team, the URI Family Resource Partnership, as well as with several training partnerships with medical centers and community mental health service agencies.

Information for Students With Physical Disabilities: See the following Web site for more information: www.uri.edu/disability/services/.

Application Information:
Send to: Admissions/Clinical, Admissions/School, or Admissions/Experimental, Department of Psychology, 10 Chafee Road, 313 Chafee Building, Kingston, RI 02881. Application available online. See program requirements first: www.uri.edu/artsci/psy. Students are admitted in the Fall. Deadlines: Clinical—December 15; School—January 15; Experimental—January 20. Fee: $30 instate, $45 out-of-state.

Roger Williams University
Department of Psychology
Arts and Sciences
One Old Ferry Road
Bristol, RI 02809-2921
Telephone: (401) 254-3509
Fax: (401) 254-3286
E-mail: *dwhitworth@rwu.edu*
Web: *www.rwu.edu*

Department Information:
1969. Chairperson: Don Whitworth, PhD Number of Faculty: total–full-time 11, part-time 12; women–full-time 4, part-time 9; minority–full-time 2, part-time 1.

Programs and Degrees Offered:
Listed in the following order: Program area, degree type (T if terminal Master's), number awarded 7/03–6/04. Forensic Psychology MA/MS (Master of Arts/Science) (T).

Student Applications/Admissions:
Student Applications
Forensic Psychology MA/MS (Master of Arts/Science)—Openings 2005–2006, 20.

Admissions Requirements:
Scores: Entries appear in this order: required test or GPA, minimum score (if required), median score of students entering in 2003–2004. Master's Programs: GRE-V 500; GRE-Q 500; GRE-V+Q 1000; GRE-Analytical no minimum stated; overall undergraduate GPA 3.0; last 2 years GPA 3.2; psychology GPA 3.0.
Other Criteria: (importance of criteria rated low, medium, or high): GRE/MAT scores medium, research experience high, work experience medium, extracurricular activity low, clinically related public service medium, GPA high, letters of recommendation high, statement of goals and objectives high.

Student Characteristics: The following represents characteristics of students in 2004–2005 in all graduate psychology programs in the department: Caucasian–full-time 0, part-time 0.

Financial Information/Assistance:
Financial Assistance:
First Year Students: No information provided.
Advanced Students: No information provided.
Contact Information: Application and information available online at: www.rwu.edu.

Internships/Practica: Internships and practica are available at a variety of forensic sites. Experiences include the areas of group psychotherapy, sex offender treatment, individual psychotherapy, psychological testing, and specialized assessment techniques. Research-based internships are also available. Interested students may also train in court clinic settings.

Housing and Day Care: On-campus housing is available. Housing for graduate students is limited and awarded on a first come, first served basis. No on-campus day care facilities are available.

Employment of Department Graduates:
Master's Degree Graduates: Of those who graduated in the academic year 2003–2004, the following categories and numbers represent the post-graduate activities and employment of master's degree graduates: Enrolled in a post-doctoral residency/fellowship (n/a), employed in independent practice (n/a), total from the above (master's) (0).
Doctoral Degree Graduates: Of those who graduated in the academic year 2003–2004, the following categories and numbers represent the post-graduate activities and employment of doctoral degree graduates: Enrolled in a psychology doctoral program (n/a), total from the above (doctoral) (0).

Additional Information:
Orientation, Objectives, and Emphasis of Department: The Psychology Department strives to provide assessment and treatment skills for students interested in employment in a forensic setting or further training at the doctoral level. Faculty members work closely with students to help them develop an understanding and appreciation of the role of psychologists in legal proceedings and the law. Students are prepared to apply these skills to the problems of the community and the larger society. The department stresses tolerance for the views of others and an appreciation of the value of diversity. Other departmental objectives include preparing students to evaluate published research and think critically about their own ideas and the ideas of others.

Information for Students With Physical Disabilities: See the following Web site for more information: www.rwu.edu.

Application Information:
Send to: Mr. Matthew F. McDonough, Director of Graduate Admissions, Office of Graduate Admissions, One Old Ferry Road, Bristol, RI 02809. Application available online. URL of online application: http://www.rwu.edu/Admission/For+Graduate+Students/. Students are admitted in the Fall, application deadline March 15. *Fee:* $50.

Citadel, The
Department of Psychology
171 Moultrie Street
Charleston, SC 29409
Telephone: (843) 953-5320
Fax: (843) 953-6797
E-mail: *cgps@citadel.edu*
Web: *http://www.citadel.edu*

Department Information:
1976. Department Head: Steve A. Nida. Number of Faculty: total–full-time 11, part-time 10; women–full-time 4, part-time 6; minority–full-time 1.

Programs and Degrees Offered:
Listed in the following order: Program area, degree type (T if terminal Master's), number awarded 7/03–6/04. School Psychology EdS (Education Specialist) 10, Clinical Counseling MA/MS (Master of Arts/Science) (T) 11.

Student Applications/Admissions:
Student Applications
School Psychology EdS (Education Specialist)—Applications 2004–2005, 44. Total applicants accepted 2004–2005, 24. Number enrolled (new admits only) 2004–2005 full-time, 20. Number enrolled (new admits only) 2004–2005 part-time, 4. Total enrolled 2004–2005 full-time, 48, part-time, 10. Openings 2005–2006, 25. The Median number of years required for completion of a degree are 3. The number of students enrolled full and part-time who were dismissed or voluntarily withdrew from this program area were 1. *Clinical Counseling MA/MS (Master of Arts/Science)*—Applications 2004–2005, 63. Total applicants accepted 2004–2005, 40. Number enrolled (new admits only) 2004–2005 full-time, 3. Number enrolled (new admits only) 2004–2005 part-time, 18. Total enrolled 2004–2005 full-time, 16, part-time, 69. Openings 2005–2006, 20. The Median number of years required for completion of a degree are 3. The number of students enrolled full and part-time who were dismissed or voluntarily withdrew from this program area were 11.

Admissions Requirements:
Scores: Entries appear in this order: required test or GPA, minimum score (if required), median score of students entering in 2003–2004. Master's Programs: Applicants must submit a score for either the GRE or the MAT.
Other Criteria: (importance of criteria rated low, medium, or high): GRE/MAT scores high, research experience medium, work experience medium, extracurricular activity low, clinically related public service medium, GPA high, letters of recommendation medium, statement of goals and objectives high.

Student Characteristics: The following represents characteristics of students in 2004–2005 in all graduate psychology programs in the department: Female–full-time 55, part-time 63; Male–full-time 9, part-time 16; African American/Black–full-time 4, part-time 7; Hispanic/Latino(a)–full-time 1, part-time 1; Asian/Pacific Islander–full-time 0, part-time 0; American Indian/Alaska Native–full-time 1, part-time 0; Caucasian–full-time 58, part-time 71; Multi-ethnic–full-time 0, part-time 0; students subject to the Americans With Disabilities Act–full-time 1, part-time 1.

Financial Information/Assistance:
Tuition for Full-Time Study: *Master's:* State residents: $216 per credit hour; Nonstate residents: $383 per credit hour.

Financial Assistance:
First Year Students: Teaching assistantships available for first-year. Average amount paid per academic year: $7,000. Average number of hours worked per week: 20. Research assistantships available for first-year. Average amount paid per academic year: $7,000. Average number of hours worked per week: 20.
Advanced Students: Teaching assistantships available for advanced students. Average amount paid per academic year: $7,000. Average number of hours worked per week: 20. Research assistantships available for advanced students. Average amount paid per academic year: $7,000. Average number of hours worked per week: 20.
Contact Information: Of all students currently enrolled full-time, 40% benefitted from one or more of the listed financial assistance programs. Application and information available online at: http://citadel.edu/cgps.

Internships/Practica: EdS in School Psychology: two practica courses where students provide services in the public school systems (40 and 125 hours, respectively); 1200-hour internship (paid), at least 600 of which involve direct services within the public school system. MA in Psychology: Clinical Counseling: one practicum (150 hours) and one internship (600 hours) where students provide clinical/counseling services in public mental health/substance abuse treatment facilities. These are unpaid field experiences.

Housing and Day Care: No on-campus housing is available. No on-campus day care facilities are available.

Employment of Department Graduates:
Master's Degree Graduates: Of those who graduated in the academic year 2003–2004, the following categories and numbers represent the post-graduate activities and employment of master's degree graduates: Enrolled in a psychology doctoral program (0), enrolled in another graduate/professional program (0), enrolled in a post-doctoral residency/fellowship (n/a), employed in independent practice (n/a), employed in an academic position at a university (0), employed in an academic position at a 2-year/4-year college (0), employed in other positions at a higher education institution (0), employed in a professional position in a school system (7), employed in business or industry (research/consulting) (0), employed in business or industry (management) (0), employed in a government agency (research) (0), employed in a government agency (professional services) (0), employed in a community mental health/counseling center (6), employed in a hospital/medical center (0), still seeking employment (3), other

employment position (1), do not know (4), total from the above (master's) (21).

Doctoral Degree Graduates: Of those who graduated in the academic year 2003–2004, the following categories and numbers represent the post-graduate activities and employment of doctoral degree graduates: Enrolled in a psychology doctoral program (n/a), total from the above (doctoral) (0).

Additional Information:

Orientation, Objectives, and Emphasis of Department: The School Psychology Program is based on the scientist-practitioner model and emphasizes the school psychologist as a data-based problem-solver who applies psychological principles, knowledge and skill to processes and problems of education and schooling. Students are trained to provide a range of psychological assessment, consultation, intervention, prevention, program development and evaluation services, with the goal of maximizing student learning and development. The School Psychology Program has been accredited by the National Association of School Psychologists (NASP) since 1988. Students in the Master of Arts in Psychology: Clinical Counseling Program are prepared to become scholarly practitioners of psychosocial counseling in community agencies, including college counseling centers, hospitals, mental health centers, and social services agencies. The program's model blends didactic and experience-based training to facilitate students' ability to utilize an empirical approach to assessment, goal development, intervention, and evaluation of services for a wide range of individuals and families experiencing a variety of psychosocial difficulties. The program is accredited by the Master's in Psychology Accreditation Council and is a member of The Council of Applied Master's Programs in Psychology.

Special Facilities or Resources: The Citadel's Department of Psychology enjoys a strong working relationship with the area school districts and agencies which provide mental health/substance abuse services. In addition, the nearby Medical University of South Carolina provides internship opportunities.

Information for Students With Physical Disabilities: See the following Web site for more information: http://www.citadel.edu/academics/psyc.

Application Information:

Send to: College of Graduate and Professional Studies, The Citadel, 171 Moultrie Street, Charleston, SC 29409. Students are admitted in the Fall, application deadline March 15. *Fee:* $25.

Clemson University
Department of Psychology
418 Brackett Hall
Clemson, SC 29634-1355
Telephone: (864) 656-3210
Fax: (864) 656-0358
E-mail: *cpagano@clemson.edu*
Web: *http://www.clemson.edu/psych*

Department Information:

1976. Graduate Program Coordinator: Chris Pagano. Number of Faculty: total–full-time 22, part-time 2; women–full-time 6, part-time 2; minority–full-time 2.

Programs and Degrees Offered:

Listed in the following order: Program area, degree type (T if terminal Master's), number awarded 7/03–6/04. Human Factors PhD (Doctor of Philosophy) 5, Industrial Organizational PhD (Doctor of Philosophy) 5.

Student Applications/Admissions:

Student Applications

Human Factors PhD (Doctor of Philosophy)—Applications 2004–2005, 30. Total applicants accepted 2004–2005, 6. Number enrolled (new admits only) 2004–2005 full-time, 6. Number enrolled (new admits only) 2004–2005 part-time, 0. Openings 2005–2006, 7. The Median number of years required for completion of a degree are 4. The number of students enrolled full and part-time who were dismissed or voluntarily withdrew from this program area were 1. *Industrial/Organizational PhD (Doctor of Philosophy)*—Applications 2004–2005, 150. Total applicants accepted 2004–2005, 8. Number enrolled (new admits only) 2004–2005 full-time, 5. Total enrolled 2004–2005 full-time, 20, part-time, 5. Openings 2005–2006, 7. The Median number of years required for completion of a degree are 4. The number of students enrolled full and part-time who were dismissed or voluntarily withdrew from this program area were 1.

Admissions Requirements:

Scores: Entries appear in this order: required test or GPA, minimum score (if required), median score of students entering in 2003–2004. Master's Programs: GRE-V no minimum stated, 520; GRE-Q no minimum stated, 630; GRE-Analytical no minimum stated, 650; overall undergraduate GPA no minimum stated, 3.40. Doctoral Programs: GRE-V no minimum stated, 570; GRE-Q no minimum stated, 650; GRE-Analytical no minimum stated, 690; overall undergraduate GPA no minimum stated, 3.60.

Other Criteria: (importance of criteria rated low, medium, or high): GRE/MAT scores high, research experience high, work experience medium, extracurricular activity low, GPA high, letters of recommendation high, interview medium, statement of goals and objectives high. For additional information on admission requirements, go to: http://www.clemson.edu/psych/grad.html.

Student Characteristics: The following represents characteristics of students in 2004–2005 in all graduate psychology programs in the department: Female–full-time 20, part-time 2; Male–full-time 9, part-time 3; African American/Black–full-time 1, part-time 0; Hispanic/Latino(a)–full-time 2, part-time 0; Asian/Pacific Islander–full-time 0, part-time 0; American Indian/Alaska Native–full-time 0, part-time 0; Caucasian–full-time 26, part-time 5; Multi-ethnic–full-time 0, part-time 0; students subject to the Americans With Disabilities Act–full-time 0, part-time 0.

Financial Information/Assistance:

Tuition for Full-Time Study: *Master's:* State residents: per academic year $2,018; Nonstate residents: per academic year $2,018. *Doctoral:* State residents: per academic year $2,018; Nonstate residents: per academic year $2,018. Tuition is subject to change.

Financial Assistance:

First Year Students: Teaching assistantships available for first-year. Average amount paid per academic year: $9,200. Average number of hours worked per week: 20. Apply by January 31. Tuition remission given: partial. Research assistantships available for first-year. Average amount paid per academic year: $10,000. Average number of hours worked per week: 20. Apply by January 31. Tuition remission given: partial. Fellowships and scholarships available for first-year. Average amount paid per academic year: $10,000. Average number of hours worked per week: 0. Apply by January 31.

Advanced Students: Teaching assistantships available for advanced students. Average amount paid per academic year: $10,500. Average number of hours worked per week: 20. Apply by January 31. Tuition remission given: partial. Research assistantships available for advanced students. Average amount paid per academic year: $10,500. Average number of hours worked per week: 20. Apply by January 31. Tuition remission given: partial. Fellowships and scholarships available for advanced students. Average amount paid per academic year: $10,000. Average number of hours worked per week: 0. Apply by January 31.

Contact Information: Of all students currently enrolled full-time, 100% benefitted from one or more of the listed financial assistance programs. Application and information available online at: cpagano@clemson.edu.

Internships/Practica: Students complete a summer internship as part of the requirements for the MS degree.

Housing and Day Care: On-campus housing is available. See the following Web site for more information: http://www.housing.clemson.edu/. No on-campus day care facilities are available.

Employment of Department Graduates:
Master's Degree Graduates: Of those who graduated in the academic year 2003–2004, the following categories and numbers represent the post-graduate activities and employment of master's degree graduates: Enrolled in a psychology doctoral program (3), enrolled in a post-doctoral residency/fellowship (n/a), employed in independent practice (n/a), employed in business or industry (research/consulting) (5), employed in business or industry (management) (2), employed in a government agency (research) (2), total from the above (master's) (12).
Doctoral Degree Graduates: Of those who graduated in the academic year 2003–2004, the following categories and numbers represent the post-graduate activities and employment of doctoral degree graduates: Enrolled in a psychology doctoral program (n/a), employed in an academic position at a university (1), employed in an academic position at a 2-year/4-year college (1), employed in business or industry (research/consulting) (2), total from the above (doctoral) (4).

Additional Information:
Orientation, Objectives, and Emphasis of Department: The faculty of the Psychology Department are committed to excellence in teaching and research. The primary goals of the Master of Science degree program are to provide students with an essential core of knowledge in applied psychology and to develop applied research skills. The program is specifically designed to provide the student with the requisite theoretical foundations, skills in quantitative techniques and experimental design, and the practical problem-solving skills necessary to address real world problems in industry, business, and government. The emphasis is on the direct application of acquired training upon completion of the program. Our graduate programs have a heavy out of the classroom

research component with a required empirical thesis. The PhD program prepares the student to generate and use knowledge in accordance with the scientist-practitioner model. In addition to the traditional areas of study in Industrial-Organizational Psychology and Human Factors (Engineering) Psychology, a new emphasis area in Occupational Health Psychology has been added to both the MS and PhD degree programs.

Special Facilities or Resources: The Psychology Department is housed on four floors of Brackett Hall. Students have access to several laboratories, including a Process Control Simulator Lab, Task Performance Lab, Psychophysiology Research Lab, Sleep Research Lab, Perception & Action Lab, Motion Sciences Lab, Uncoupled Motion Simulation Lab, Human Memory and Perception Lab, Visual Performance Lab, Driving Simulator Lab, Usability Testing Lab, Advanced Reading Technologies Lab, Personnel Selection and Performance Appraisal Lab, Workplace Training Research Lab, I/O Research Lab, Social Psychology Lab, Cognitive Aging Lab, Residential Research Lab, as well as Virtual Reality and Robotics and Teleoperation facilities.

Information for Students With Physical Disabilities: See the following Web site for more information: http://stuaff.clemson.edu/redfern/sds/.

Application Information:
Send to: Clemson University Graduate Admissions, 101 Sikes Hall, Clemson, SC 29634-5124. Online application: http://www.grad.clemson.edu/p_applyus.html; All applicants should contact cpagano@clemson.edu for more information. Application available online. URL of online application: http://www.grad.clemson.edu/p_applyus.html. Students are admitted in the Fall, application deadline January 15. *Fee:* $50.

Francis Marion University
Master's of Science in Applied Psychology
P.O. Box 100547
Florence, SC 29501-0547
Telephone: (843) 661-1641
Fax: (843) 661-1628
E-mail: *jhester@fmarion.edu*
Web: *http://www.fmarion.edu/academics/psychology*

Department Information:
1970. Chair: John R. Hester, PhD. Number of Faculty: total–full-time 10, part-time 4; women–full-time 4, part-time 2.

Programs and Degrees Offered:
Listed in the following order: Program area, degree type (T if terminal Master's), number awarded 7/03–6/04. Clinical/ Counseling MA/MS (Master of Arts/Science) (T) 4, School MA/MS (Master of Arts/Science) (T) 8.

Student Applications/Admissions:
Student Applications
Clinical/ Counseling MA/MS (Master of Arts/Science)—Applications 2004–2005, 28. Total applicants accepted 2004–2005, 17. Number enrolled (new admits only) 2004–2005 full-time,

2. Number enrolled (new admits only) 2004–2005 part-time, 4. Total enrolled 2004–2005 full-time, 5, part-time, 13. Openings 2005–2006, 10. The Median number of years required for completion of a degree are 3. The number of students enrolled full and part-time who were dismissed or voluntarily withdrew from this program area were 1. *School MA/MS (Master of Arts/Science)*—Applications 2004–2005, 30. Total applicants accepted 2004–2005, 17. Number enrolled (new admits only) 2004–2005 full-time, 5. Number enrolled (new admits only) 2004–2005 part-time, 4. Total enrolled 2004–2005 full-time, 11, part-time, 13. Openings 2005–2006, 10. The Median number of years required for completion of a degree are 3. The number of students enrolled full and part-time who were dismissed or voluntarily withdrew from this program area were 2.

Admissions Requirements:

Scores: Entries appear in this order: required test or GPA, minimum score (if required), median score of students entering in 2003–2004. Master's Programs: GRE-V 400, 490; GRE-Q 400, 580; GRE-V+Q 800, 1070; overall undergraduate GPA 3.00, 3.44; psychology GPA 3.00, 3.40.

Other Criteria: (importance of criteria rated low, medium, or high): GRE/MAT scores high, research experience medium, work experience medium, extracurricular activity low, clinically related public service medium, GPA high, letters of recommendation high, statement of goals and objectives medium.

Student Characteristics: The following represents characteristics of students in 2004–2005 in all graduate psychology programs in the department: Female–full-time 16, part-time 25; Male–full-time 0, part-time 1; African American/Black–full-time 0, part-time 2; Hispanic/Latino(a)–full-time 0, part-time 0; Asian/Pacific Islander–full-time 0, part-time 0; American Indian/Alaska Native–full-time 0, part-time 0; Caucasian–full-time 16, part-time 24; Multi-ethnic–full-time 0, part-time 0; students subject to the Americans With Disabilities Act–full-time 1, part-time 1.

Financial Information/Assistance:

Tuition for Full-Time Study: *Master's:* State residents: per academic year $5,146, $257 per credit hour; Nonstate residents: per academic year $10,294, $514 per credit hour. Tuition is subject to change.

Financial Assistance:

First Year Students: Fellowships and scholarships available for first-year. Average amount paid per academic year: $6,000. Average number of hours worked per week: 20.

Advanced Students: Fellowships and scholarships available for advanced students. Average amount paid per academic year: $6,000. Average number of hours worked per week: 20.

Contact Information: Of all students currently enrolled full-time, 14% benefitted from one or more of the listed financial assistance programs.

Internships/Practica: Internships occur in a variety of community settings. Typically Clinical/Counseling students complete a full-time 6 month internship in a state human service agency. The School Psychology Internship is a full-time experience as a school psychologist during a Fall and Spring semester. All interns develop a broad array of skills under supervision.

Housing and Day Care: On-campus housing is available. Contact Housing & Residence Life at (843) 661-1330. No on-campus day care facilities are available.

Employment of Department Graduates:

Master's Degree Graduates: Of those who graduated in the academic year 2003–2004, the following categories and numbers represent the post-graduate activities and employment of master's degree graduates: Enrolled in a post-doctoral residency/fellowship (n/a), employed in independent practice (n/a), total from the above (master's) (0).

Doctoral Degree Graduates: Of those who graduated in the academic year 2003–2004, the following categories and numbers represent the post-graduate activities and employment of doctoral degree graduates: Enrolled in a psychology doctoral program (n/a), total from the above (doctoral) (0).

Additional Information:

Orientation, Objectives, and Emphasis of Department: The primary purpose of the program is to prepare professionals for employment in human services agencies, schools, or similar settings. The program also provides for the continuing education of those individuals currently employed in the helping professions and prepares students for further graduate study. Students are primarily part-time, with courses taken mainly at night.

Special Facilities or Resources: The department has excellent laboratory facilities on campus, including a computer laboratory. Regional human services facilities, community agencies, and school districts are accessible off campus.

Information for Students With Physical Disabilities: See the following Web site for more information: www.fmarion.edu/students.

Application Information:
Send to: Graduate Office, FMU, P.O. Box 100547, Florence, SC 29501-0547. Students are admitted in the Fall, application deadline April 15; Spring, application deadline October 15; Programs have rolling admissions. *Fee:* $30.

South Carolina, University of
Department of Psychology
College of Arts and Sciences
1512 Pendleton Street
Columbia, SC 29208
Telephone: (803) 777-2137
Fax: (803) 777-9558
E-mail: *richards-john@sc.edu*
Web: *www.psych.sc.edu*

Department Information:
1912. Interim Department Chair: John E. Richards. Number of Faculty: total–full-time 36; women–full-time 11; minority–full-time 3.

Programs and Degrees Offered:
Listed in the following order: Program area, degree type (T if terminal Master's), number awarded 7/03–6/04. Clinical-Commu-

nity PhD (Doctor of Philosophy) 9, Experimental PhD (Doctor of Philosophy) 2, School Psychology PhD (Doctor of Philosophy) 8.

APA Accreditation: Clinical PhD (Doctor of Philosophy). School PhD (Doctor of Philosophy).

Student Applications/Admissions:

Student Applications

Clinical-Community PhD (Doctor of Philosophy)—Applications 2004–2005, 169. Total applicants accepted 2004–2005, 14. Openings 2005–2006, 8. The Median number of years required for completion of a degree are 6. The number of students enrolled full and part-time who were dismissed or voluntarily withdrew from this program area were 1. *Experimental PhD (Doctor of Philosophy)*—Applications 2004–2005, 32. Total applicants accepted 2004–2005, 9. Openings 2005–2006, 5. The Median number of years required for completion of a degree are 5. The number of students enrolled full and part-time who were dismissed or voluntarily withdrew from this program area were 1. *School Psychology PhD (Doctor of Philosophy)*—Applications 2004–2005, 38. Total applicants accepted 2004–2005, 11. Openings 2005–2006, 6. The Median number of years required for completion of a degree are 5. The number of students enrolled full and part-time who were dismissed or voluntarily withdrew from this program area were 0.

Admissions Requirements:

Scores: Entries appear in this order: required test or GPA, minimum score (if required), median score of students entering in 2003–2004. Master's Programs: GRE-V no minimum stated; GRE-Q no minimum stated; GRE-Analytical no minimum stated; GRE-Subject(Psych) no minimum stated; overall undergraduate GPA no minimum stated. Doctoral Programs: GRE-V no minimum stated, 550; GRE-Q no minimum stated, 630; GRE-Analytical no minimum stated, 620; GRE-Subject(Psych) no minimum stated, 600; overall undergraduate GPA no minimum stated, 3.4; last 2 years GPA no minimum stated, 3.8; psychology GPA no minimum stated, 3.65. Median scores vary for different programs.

Other Criteria: (importance of criteria rated low, medium, or high): GRE/MAT scores medium, research experience high, work experience medium, extracurricular activity medium, clinically related public service medium, GPA high, letters of recommendation high, interview medium, statement of goals and objectives high, Criteria vary for different programs.

Student Characteristics: The following represents characteristics of students in 2004–2005 in all graduate psychology programs in the department: Female–full-time 83, part-time 0; Male–full-time 31, part-time 0; African American/Black–full-time 18, part-time 0; Hispanic/Latino(a)–full-time 2, part-time 0; Asian/Pacific Islander–full-time 1, part-time 0; American Indian/Alaska Native–full-time 0, part-time 0; Caucasian–full-time 0, part-time 0; students subject to the Americans With Disabilities Act–full-time 0, part-time 0.

Financial Information/Assistance:

Tuition for Full-Time Study: *Doctoral:* State residents: per academic year $6,210, $305 per credit hour; Nonstate residents: per academic year $6,210. Tuition is subject to change.

Financial Assistance:

First Year Students: Teaching assistantships available for first-year. Average amount paid per academic year: $12,000. Average number of hours worked per week: 15. Tuition remission given: full. Research assistantships available for first-year. Average amount paid per academic year: $12,000. Average number of hours worked per week: 15. Tuition remission given: full.

Advanced Students: Teaching assistantships available for advanced students. Average amount paid per academic year: $12,000. Average number of hours worked per week: 15. Tuition remission given: full. Research assistantships available for advanced students. Average amount paid per academic year: $12,000. Average number of hours worked per week: 15. Tuition remission given: full.

Contact Information: Of all students currently enrolled full-time, 100% benefitted from one or more of the listed financial assistance programs. Application and information available online at: All students offered admission are considered for financial assistance by the admissions committee.

Internships/Practica: Students in school psychology and clinical-community psychology complete at least one year of half-time placement in a community service agency expanding their experience with a diverse client population and multidisciplinary service providers. For those doctoral students for whom a professional internship is required prior to graduation, 10 applied in 2003–2004. Of those who applied, 10 were placed in internships listed by the Association of Psychology Postdoctoral and Internship Programs (APPIC); 10 were placed in APA accredited internships.

Housing and Day Care: On-campus housing is available. See the following Web site for more information: www.sc.edu. On-campus day care facilities are available.

Employment of Department Graduates:

Master's Degree Graduates: Of those who graduated in the academic year 2003–2004, the following categories and numbers represent the post-graduate activities and employment of master's degree graduates: Enrolled in a psychology doctoral program (7), enrolled in a post-doctoral residency/fellowship (n/a), employed in independent practice (n/a), total from the above (master's) (7).

Doctoral Degree Graduates: Of those who graduated in the academic year 2003–2004, the following categories and numbers represent the post-graduate activities and employment of doctoral degree graduates: Enrolled in a psychology doctoral program (n/a), enrolled in a post-doctoral residency/fellowship (6), employed in other positions at a higher education institution (1), employed in a professional position in a school system (5), employed in business or industry (research/consulting) (1), employed in a community mental health/counseling center (6), employed in a hospital/medical center (1), total from the above (doctoral) (20).

Additional Information:

Orientation, Objectives, and Emphasis of Department: The department has interdisciplinary research emphases in developmental cognitive neuroscience/neurodevelopmental disorders, prevention science, reading and language, and ethnic minority health and mental health. The experimental program offers concentrations in cognitive, developmental, and behavioral neuroscience, built on broad scientific training in experimental psychology. The school psychology program includes emphasis in child assessment, individual and group consultation, educational research, and professional roles. In clinical-community, there is a wide latitude of choices: assessment, psychotherapy and behavioral interventions; community psychology; and consultation. Regular clinical-community training includes both adults and children, with an option of special emphasis on children or community settings.

Special Facilities or Resources: The special facilities and resources of the department include the university-directed psychological service center, the medical school, the VA hospital, the department-directed outpatient psychological services center, mental health centers and other educational and mental health service settings. Other laboratories include Behavioral Pharmacology Lab; Behavioral Neuroscience Lab with high density EEG and MRI; Developmental Sensory Neuroscience Lab; Experimental and Cognitive Processes Lab; Infant Attention Lab; Judgment and Decision Making Lab; and Attention and Perception Lab. We are actively involved in community agencies, the psychiatric training institution, and the psychopharmacology laboratory.

Application Information:
Send to: Graduate Records Secretary, Department of Psychology, University of South Carolina, Columbia, SC 29208. Application available online. URL of online application: http://www.gradschool.sc.edu/login. Students are admitted in the Fall. Application deadline for Fall admission in clinical–community psychology is December 1, experimental psychology and school psychology, January 1. Applications for admissions should be submitted electronically. These materials are available at http://www.gradschool.sc.edu/login. *Fee:* $40.

Winthrop University
Department of Psychology
Arts and Sciences
135 Kinard
Rock Hill, SC 29733
Telephone: (803) 323-2117
Fax: (803) 323-2371
E-mail: *prusj@winthrop.edu*
Web: *http://www.winthrop.edu*

Department Information:
1923. Chairperson: Dr. Joe Prus. Number of Faculty: total–full-time 14, part-time 4; women–full-time 7, part-time 3; minority–full-time 1.

Programs and Degrees Offered:
Listed in the following order: Program area, degree type (T if terminal Master's), number awarded 7/03–6/04. School Psychology Other 9.

Student Applications/Admissions:
Student Applications
School Psychology Other—Applications 2004–2005, 70. Total applicants accepted 2004–2005, 10. Number enrolled (new admits only) 2004–2005 full-time, 10. Number enrolled (new admits only) 2004–2005 part-time, 0. Openings 2005–2006, 10. The Median number of years required for completion of a degree are 3. The number of students enrolled full and part-

time who were dismissed or voluntarily withdrew from this program area were 0.

Admissions Requirements:
Scores: Entries appear in this order: required test or GPA, minimum score (if required), median score of students entering in 2003–2004. Master's Programs: GRE-V no minimum stated; GRE-Q no minimum stated; GRE-V+Q no minimum stated, 1040; overall undergraduate GPA no minimum stated, 3.60; last 2 years GPA no minimum stated, 3.70; psychology GPA no minimum stated, 3.60.
Other Criteria: (importance of criteria rated low, medium, or high): GRE/MAT scores low, research experience low, work experience medium, extracurricular activity low, clinically related public service medium, GPA high, letters of recommendation high, interview high, statement of goals and objectives medium, experience with children high. For additional information on admission requirements, go to: www.winthrop.edu.

Student Characteristics: The following represents characteristics of students in 2004–2005 in all graduate psychology programs in the department: Female–full-time 21, part-time 0; Male–full-time 6, part-time 0; African American/Black–full-time 4, part-time 0; Hispanic/Latino(a)–full-time 0, part-time 0; Asian/Pacific Islander–full-time 0, part-time 0; American Indian/Alaska Native–full-time 0, part-time 0; Caucasian–full-time 23, part-time 0.

Financial Information/Assistance:
Tuition for Full-Time Study: *Master's:* State residents: per academic year $7,528, $315 per credit hour; Nonstate residents: per academic year $10,854, $452 per credit hour. Tuition is subject to change. See the following Web site for updates and changes in tuition costs: www.winthrop.edu.

Financial Assistance:
First Year Students: Teaching assistantships available for first-year. Average amount paid per academic year: $3,000. Average number of hours worked per week: 20. Apply by April 15. Tuition remission given: partial. Research assistantships available for first-year. Average amount paid per academic year: $3,000. Average number of hours worked per week: 20. Apply by April 15. Tuition remission given: partial. Traineeships available for first-year. Fellowships and scholarships available for first-year. Average amount paid per academic year: $2,000. Apply by April 15. Tuition remission given: partial.
Advanced Students: Traineeships available for advanced students. Average amount paid per academic year: $6,750. Average number of hours worked per week: 30. Apply by n/a. Tuition remission given: full and partial.
Contact Information: Of all students currently enrolled full-time, 93% benefitted from one or more of the listed financial assistance programs.

Internships/Practica: The program provides paid traineeships during the second year and internships during the third year in area school districts and agencies. Rural, suburban, and urban field settings include diverse student/client populations. Some non-school internship placements are available for up to 600 clock hours of the 1,200 hour internship. The internship includes a full range of school psychological services. Each intern receives weekly supervision from both a faculty and field-based credentialed supervisor.

Housing and Day Care: On-campus housing is available. See the following Web site for more information: www.winthrop.edu. On-campus day care facilities are available.

Employment of Department Graduates:

Master's Degree Graduates: Of those who graduated in the academic year 2003–2004, the following categories and numbers represent the post-graduate activities and employment of master's degree graduates: Enrolled in a post-doctoral residency/fellowship (n/a), employed in independent practice (n/a), employed in a professional position in a school system (8), not seeking employment (1).

Doctoral Degree Graduates: Of those who graduated in the academic year 2003–2004, the following categories and numbers represent the post-graduate activities and employment of doctoral degree graduates: Enrolled in a psychology doctoral program (n/a).

Additional Information:

Orientation, Objectives, and Emphasis of Department: The Winthrop School Psychology Program is designed to prepare practitioners who are competent to provide a full range of school psychological services, including consultation, behavioral intervention, psychoeducational assessment, research and evaluation, and counseling. The three-year, full-time program leading to both MS and Specialist in School Psychology degrees qualifies graduates for state and national certification as school psychologists pending attainment of a passing score on the Praxis II specialty exam in school psychology. Program emphasis is placed on psychological and psychoeducational methods whose effectiveness has been demonstrated through behavioral research. Students are trained to work with diverse clients from birth to adulthood, including those with low-incidence disabilities, and with families, teachers, and others in the schools and community. The program provides an applied, competency-based approach to training that progresses sequentially from foundations and practica courses to a 450 hour traineeship to a 1200-hour internship, and affords maximum individualized supervision. Comprehensive assessment of student learning and development, from entry into the program to acquisition of professional positions or admissions into doctoral programs, is conducted through multiple methods. Program faculty represent considerable ethnic and experiential diversity. All have advanced degrees in school psychology, are active in the profession at local, state, and national levels, and view teaching and supervision as their primary roles. A collaborative approach to learning, and cooperation among students, are emphasized in the program.

Special Facilities or Resources: Winthrop University is a state-supported institution of about 6,500 students which provides students with access to an academic computer center, health center, university library with nearly 500,000 volumes and 4,000 periodicals and serials, and a variety of other resources. Access to such department resources as a computer workroom and school psychology mini-library and assessment resource center are available. Winthrop's 418-acre campus is located in the greater Charlotte, NC area, which includes a great variety of school districts, human service agencies, libraries, and other resources which may be of personal or professional interest to graduate students in school psychology.

Information for Students With Physical Disabilities: See the following Web site for more information: www.winthrop.edu.

Application Information:
Send to: Office of Graduate Studies, Winthrop University, Rock Hill, SC 29733. Application available online. URL of online application: www.winthrop.edu/graduate_studies. Students are admitted in the Fall, application deadline February 15. *Fee:* $50. Application fee may be waived by program director in cases of financial hardship.

South Dakota, University of

Department of Psychology
414 E. Clark Street
Vermillion, SD 57069
Telephone: (605) 677-5351
Fax: (605) 677-3195
E-mail: *rquevill@usd.edu*
Web: *http://www.usd.edu/psyc*

Department Information:

1926. Chairperson: Randal Quevillon. Number of Faculty: total–full-time 18; women–full-time 6; minority–full-time 5.

Programs and Degrees Offered:

Listed in the following order: Program area, degree type (T if terminal Master's), number awarded 7/03–6/04. Clinical PhD (Doctor of Philosophy) 7, Human Factors PhD (Doctor of Philosophy) 1.

APA Accreditation: Clinical PhD (Doctor of Philosophy).

Student Applications/Admissions:

Student Applications

Clinical PhD (Doctor of Philosophy)—Applications 2004–2005, 62. Total applicants accepted 2004–2005, 15. Number enrolled (new admits only) 2004–2005 full-time, 9. Openings 2005–2006, 9. The Median number of years required for completion of a degree are 5. The number of students enrolled full and part-time who were dismissed or voluntarily withdrew from this program area were 0. *Human Factors PhD (Doctor of Philosophy)*—Applications 2004–2005, 6. Total applicants accepted 2004–2005, 4. Number enrolled (new admits only) 2004–2005 full-time, 1. Openings 2005–2006, 3. The Median number of years required for completion of a degree are 5. The number of students enrolled full and part-time who were dismissed or voluntarily withdrew from this program area were 0.

Admissions Requirements:

Scores: Entries appear in this order: required test or GPA, minimum score (if required), median score of students entering in 2003–2004. Doctoral Programs: GRE-V no minimum stated; GRE-Q no minimum stated; GRE-V+Q 1000, 1090; GRE-Analytical no minimum stated; GRE-Subject(Psych) no minimum stated; overall undergraduate GPA 3.00, 3.45.

Other Criteria: (importance of criteria rated low, medium, or high): GRE/MAT scores medium, research experience high, work experience medium, extracurricular activity medium, clinically related public service medium, GPA medium, letters of recommendation high, statement of goals and objectives medium, GRE and GPA weightings vary by program, as do service, extracurricular and goals/objectives criteria. Applicant's responses to the Supplemental Application questions are highly weighted in the Clinical Program admissions process. For additional information on admission requirements, go to: http://www.usd.edu/ctp/ctpassup.cfm.

Student Characteristics: The following represents characteristics of students in 2004–2005 in all graduate psychology programs in the department: Female–full-time 33, part-time 0; Male–full-time 25, part-time 0; African American/Black–full-time 2, part-time 0; Hispanic/Latino(a)–full-time 2, part-time 0; Asian/Pacific Islander–full-time 3, part-time 0; American Indian/Alaska Native–full-time 4, part-time 0; Caucasian–full-time 47, part-time 0; Multi-ethnic–full-time 0, part-time 0; students subject to the Americans With Disabilities Act–full-time 1, part-time 0.

Financial Information/Assistance:

Tuition for Full-Time Study: *Doctoral:* State residents: $112 per credit hour; Nonstate residents: $331 per credit hour. See the following Web site for updates and changes in tuition costs: http://www.usd.edu/gradsch/financialinfo.cfm.

Financial Assistance:

First Year Students: Teaching assistantships available for first-year. Average amount paid per academic year: $5,500. Average number of hours worked per week: 10. Tuition remission given: partial. Research assistantships available for first-year. Average amount paid per academic year: $5,500. Average number of hours worked per week: 10. Tuition remission given: partial. Fellowships and scholarships available for first-year. Average amount paid per academic year: $9,000. Average number of hours worked per week: 16. Tuition remission given: partial.

Advanced Students: Teaching assistantships available for advanced students. Average amount paid per academic year: $6,000. Average number of hours worked per week: 16. Tuition remission given: partial. Research assistantships available for advanced students. Average amount paid per academic year: $10,000. Average number of hours worked per week: 16. Tuition remission given: partial. Traineeships available for advanced students. Average amount paid per academic year: $10,000. Average number of hours worked per week: 16. Tuition remission given: partial. Fellowships and scholarships available for advanced students. Average amount paid per academic year: $10,000. Average number of hours worked per week: 16. Tuition remission given: partial.

Contact Information: Of all students currently enrolled full-time, 100% benefitted from one or more of the listed financial assistance programs.

Internships/Practica: Several internships are available in Human Factors: placements with IBM, Lockheed, Hewlett-Packard, and Intel have been recent examples. In Clinical, a twelve month internship is required in the final year, and we are proud of the record our students have achieved in obtaining top placements. We also have available a series of paid clinical placements (see community resources). In addition, many graduate courses include practicum components, and clinical students are placed on practicum teams through the Psychological Services Center each semester. For those doctoral students for whom a professional internship is required prior to graduation, 5 applied in 2003–2004. Of those who applied, 5 were placed in internships listed by the Association of Psychology Postdoctoral and Internship Programs (APPIC); 5 were placed in APA accredited internships.

Housing and Day Care: On-campus housing is available. See the following Web site for more information: http://www.usd.edu/reslife/ also available on the student services menu at http://www.usd.edu/studentserv/. On-campus day care facilities are available. See the following Web site for more information: http://www.usd.edu/childcare/. Information is also available on the student services menu at http://www.usd.edu/studentserv/.

Employment of Department Graduates:

Master's Degree Graduates: Of those who graduated in the academic year 2003–2004, the following categories and numbers represent the post-graduate activities and employment of master's degree graduates: Enrolled in a psychology doctoral program (7), enrolled in a post-doctoral residency/fellowship (n/a), employed in independent practice (n/a), total from the above (master's) (7).

Doctoral Degree Graduates: Of those who graduated in the academic year 2003–2004, the following categories and numbers represent the post-graduate activities and employment of doctoral degree graduates: Enrolled in a psychology doctoral program (n/a), employed in independent practice (2), employed in an academic position at a 2-year/4-year college (1), employed in business or industry (research/consulting) (1), employed in a government agency (professional services) (1), employed in a community mental health/counseling center (3), employed in a hospital/medical center (1), total from the above (doctoral) (9).

Additional Information:

Orientation, Objectives, and Emphasis of Department: The department seeks to develop scholars who can contribute to the expansion of psychological information. The major goals of the theoretically eclectic program in clinical psychology are to increase students' knowledge of and identification with psychology as a method of inquiry about human behavior and to provide students with the theory, skills, and experience to function in a professional, research, or academic capacity. Training is provided in traditional areas as well as rural community psychology, cross-cultural issues (particularly work with American Indian populations), program evaluation, neuropsychology, family therapy, and women's issues. The experience thus provided serves to broaden professional competencies and increase the versatility of the program's graduates. The overall mission of Human Factors psychology is to improve living and working through knowledge of the abilities and limitations of the person part of human-machine or socio-technical systems. The program's goal is to train doctoral-level professionals qualified to do research in industry, government, and universities. As an element of their training, all graduate students conduct empirical investigations. In recent years, the Human Factors Laboratory has supported studies of information processing, human-computer interfaces, motor performance, program evaluation and testing, traffic safety, transportation systems, and the effects of chemical agents and stress on human efficiency.

Special Facilities or Resources: Available to all psychology graduate students are computer lab facilities including word processing and statistical analysis software. Microcomputers are also easily accessible within the department for personal computing and research purposes. Much general purpose, highly adaptable research equipment is available to both Clinical and Human Factors students. The Human Factors Laboratory is particularly well-equipped for experimentation within the specialty areas of current interest to associated faculty. The Department houses the Disaster Mental Health Institute, a South Dakota Board of Regents Center of Excellence, which provides unique research and service opportunities for graduate students as well as specialized coursework and assistantships. The Psychological Services Center, which supplies clinical services for both University students and the general public, accepts referrals from physicians, schools, and other community and state agencies. The Center has offices equipped for a variety of diagnostic and therapeutic activities, including neuropsychological work. Next door to the department, the University Affiliated Program affords our students opportunities to collaborate with members of other professions. The Department's students take full advantage of training and experience available at local, state, and regional mental health centers for treatment of chemical dependency and control of pain.

Information for Students With Physical Disabilities: See the following Web site for more information: http://www.usd.edu/disabrs/.

Application Information:
Send to: Dean, Graduate School, University of South Dakota, 414 E. Clark Street, Vermilion, SD 57069-2390. Application available online. Students are admitted in the Fall, application deadline February 1. Clinical Program due February 1, Human Factors Program due February 15. *Fee:* $35.

Austin Peay State University

Department of Psychology
601 College Street
Clarksville, TN 37044
Telephone: (931) 221-7233
Fax: (931) 221-6267
E-mail: *dentond@apsu.edu*
Web: *http://www.apsu.edu/psychology*

Department Information:

1968. Chairperson: David W. Denton. Number of Faculty: total–full-time 11, part-time 5; women–full-time 4, part-time 4; minority–full-time 2, part-time 1; faculty subject to the Americans With Disabilities Act 1.

Programs and Degrees Offered:

Listed in the following order: Program area, degree type (T if terminal Master's), number awarded 7/03–6/04. Community Counseling MA/MS (Master of Arts/Science) (T) 3, I/O psychology MA/MS (Master of Arts/Science) (T) 4, School Counseling MA/MS (Master of Arts/Science) (T) 3, School Counseling EdS (Education Specialist) 1.

Student Applications/Admissions:

Student Applications

Community Counseling MA/MS (Master of Arts/Science)—Applications 2004–2005, 5. Total applicants accepted 2004–2005, 4. Number enrolled (new admits only) 2004–2005 full-time, 5. Number enrolled (new admits only) 2004–2005 part-time, 1. Total enrolled 2004–2005 full-time, 14. Openings 2005–2006, 10. The Median number of years required for completion of a degree are 2.5. *I/O Psychology MA/MS (Master of Arts/Science)*—Applications 2004–2005, 14. Total applicants accepted 2004–2005, 8. Number enrolled (new admits only) 2004–2005 full-time, 4. Total enrolled 2004–2005 full-time, 7. Openings 2005–2006, 15. The Median number of years required for completion of a degree are 2. The number of students enrolled full and part-time who were dismissed or voluntarily withdrew from this program area were 0. *School Counseling MA/MS (Master of Arts/Science)*—Applications 2004–2005, 15. Total applicants accepted 2004–2005, 8. Number enrolled (new admits only) 2004–2005 full-time, 8. Number enrolled (new admits only) 2004–2005 part-time, 3. Total enrolled 2004–2005 full-time, 16. Openings 2005–2006, 10. The Median number of years required for completion of a degree are 2.5. *School Counseling EdS (Education Specialist)*—Applications 2004–2005, 3. Total applicants accepted 2004–2005, 3. Number enrolled (new admits only) 2004–2005 full-time, 0. Number enrolled (new admits only) 2004–2005 part-time, 3. Openings 2005–2006, 5. The Median number of years required for completion of a degree are 1.5.

Admissions Requirements:

Scores: Entries appear in this order: required test or GPA, minimum score (if required), median score of students entering in 2003–2004. Master's Programs: GRE-V 400, 455; GRE-Q 400, 470; overall undergraduate GPA 3.0, 3.22. We employ a compensatory admissions model such that weakness in one area may be compensated for by strength in another.

Other Criteria: (importance of criteria rated low, medium, or high): GRE/MAT scores high, research experience low, GPA high, letters of recommendation medium.

Student Characteristics: The following represents characteristics of students in 2004–2005 in all graduate psychology programs in the department: Female–full-time 28, part-time 0; Male–full-time 9, part-time 0; African American/Black–full-time 4, part-time 0; Hispanic/Latino(a)–full-time 2, part-time 0; Asian/Pacific Islander–full-time 0, part-time 0; American Indian/Alaska Native–full-time 1, part-time 0; Caucasian–full-time 30, part-time 0; students subject to the Americans With Disabilities Act–full-time 0, part-time 0.

Financial Information/Assistance:

Tuition for Full-Time Study: *Master's:* State residents: per academic year $5,285, $315 per credit hour; Nonstate residents: per academic year $12,645, $683 per credit hour. Tuition is subject to change. See the following Web site for updates and changes in tuition costs: http://www.apsu.edu/businessoffice/acctrec/tuition_fees.htm.

Financial Assistance:

First Year Students: Teaching assistantships available for first-year. Average amount paid per academic year: $7,000. Average number of hours worked per week: 20. Apply by March 1. Tuition remission given: partial.

Advanced Students: Teaching assistantships available for advanced students. Average amount paid per academic year: $7,000. Average number of hours worked per week: 20. Tuition remission given: partial.

Contact Information: Of all students currently enrolled full-time, 15% benefitted from one or more of the listed financial assistance programs. Application and information available online at: www.apsu.edu/cogs.

Internships/Practica: There are some paid internships available at the present. A variety of unpaid internships are available in mental health agencies, schools, or community agencies.

Housing and Day Care: On-campus housing is available. See the following Web site for more information: Housing: www.apsu.edu/housing. On-campus day care facilities are available. See the following Web site for more information: Child care: www.apsu.edu/clc.

Employment of Department Graduates:

Master's Degree Graduates: Of those who graduated in the academic year 2003–2004, the following categories and numbers represent the post-graduate activities and employment of master's degree graduates: Enrolled in a post-doctoral residency/fellowship

(n/a), employed in independent practice (n/a), total from the above (master's) (0).

Doctoral Degree Graduates: Of those who graduated in the academic year 2003–2004, the following categories and numbers represent the post-graduate activities and employment of doctoral degree graduates: Enrolled in a psychology doctoral program (n/a), total from the above (doctoral) (0).

Additional Information:

Orientation, Objectives, and Emphasis of Department: The programs in the department are based on the concept that both a strong foundation in theoretical principles and the development of skills in the application of these principles and techniques is necessary in the training of psychologists or counselors. The Master of Arts with a major in psychology offers three options. The industrial/organizational program educates students to design, develop, implement, and evaluate psychologically-based human resources interventions in organizations. The school counseling program is designed to meet the competencies required by the state of Tennessee and to provide students with the necessary knowledge and skills to perform efficiently in the elementary and secondary school settings. The objective of the community counseling program is to meet the needs of employment, human services, or other agency counselors requiring a master's degree related to their particular vocational needs.

Special Facilities or Resources: The department of psychology has a variety of facilities to provide learning and research opportunities. Rooms equipped with one-way observation windows, video and other monitoring equipment are available for counseling, testing and human research. The department has arranged for intern and practicum experiences with a variety of community agencies. Laboratories for vision, infant development, animal learning, and behavioral physiology are available for faculty and student research. The department has numerous microcomputers connected to the University's high-speed fiber-optic network for data collection, analysis, and the preparation of manuscripts.

Application Information:
Send to: Office of Graduate Studies, Austin Peay State University, Clarksville, TN 37044. Students are admitted in the Fall, application deadline March 1; Spring, application deadline November 1. We begin to review applications beginning March 1, but continue to accept applications and admit students until program capacity is reached. *Fee:* $25.

East Tennessee State University
Department of Psychology
College of Arts & Sciences
Box 70649 (Psychology)
Johnson City, TN 37614-0649
Telephone: (423) 439-4424
Fax: (423) 439-5695
E-mail: *dixonw@mail.etsu.edu*
Web: *http://www.etsu.edu/psychology/*

Department Information:
1966. Chairperson: Wallace E. Dixon Jr. Number of Faculty: total–full-time 10, part-time 4; women–full-time 1.

Programs and Degrees Offered:
Listed in the following order: Program area, degree type (T if terminal Master's), number awarded 7/03–6/04. Clinical Psychology MA/MS (Master of Arts/Science) (T) 2, General Psychology MA/MS (Master of Arts/Science) (T) 3.

Student Applications/Admissions:
Student Applications
Clinical Psychology MA/MS (Master of Arts/Science)—Applications 2004–2005, 30. Total applicants accepted 2004–2005, 12. Openings 2005–2006, 8. The Median number of years required for completion of a degree are 2. The number of students enrolled full and part-time who were dismissed or voluntarily withdrew from this program area were 0. *General Psychology MA/MS (Master of Arts/Science)*—Applications 2004–2005, 10. Total applicants accepted 2004–2005, 4. Openings 2005–2006, 6. The Median number of years required for completion of a degree are 2. The number of students enrolled full and part-time who were dismissed or voluntarily withdrew from this program area were 0.

Admissions Requirements:
Scores: Entries appear in this order: required test or GPA, minimum score (if required), median score of students entering in 2003–2004. Master's Programs: GRE-V 400, 511; GRE-Q 400, 560; GRE-V+Q 1000, 1000; GRE-Analytical 400, 600; GRE-Subject(Psych) 500, 500; overall undergraduate GPA 3.00, 3.40; last 2 years GPA 3.50; psychology GPA 3.3, 3.4. *Other Criteria:* (importance of criteria rated low, medium, or high): GRE/MAT scores high, research experience high, work experience high, extracurricular activity medium, clinically related public service high, GPA high, letters of recommendation high, interview medium, statement of goals and objectives high, clinically related public service medium, extracurricular activities high for General Psychology; letters of recommendation medium and interview none for Clinical Psychology.

Student Characteristics: The following represents characteristics of students in 2004–2005 in all graduate psychology programs in the department: Female–full-time 6, part-time 0; Male–full-time 7, part-time 0; African American/Black–full-time 1, part-time 0; Hispanic/Latino(a)–full-time 0, part-time 0; Asian/Pacific Islander–full-time 0, part-time 0; American Indian/Alaska Native–full-time 0, part-time 0; Caucasian–full-time 12, part-time 0.

Financial Information/Assistance:
Tuition for Full-Time Study: *Master's:* State residents: per academic year $2,183, $229 per credit hour; Nonstate residents: per academic year $3,966, $344 per credit hour. Tuition is subject to change. See the following Web site for updates and changes in tuition costs: www.etsu.edu/reg/.

Financial Assistance:
First Year Students: Teaching assistantships available for first-year. Tuition remission given: full and partial.
Advanced Students: Teaching assistantships available for advanced students. Tuition remission given: full and partial.

Contact Information: Of all students currently enrolled full-time, 90% benefitted from one or more of the listed financial assistance programs. Application and information available online at: http://www.etsu.edu/finaid/financial.htm.

Internships/Practica: Internships and practica in assessment and therapy are available to students enrolled in the clinical psychology option. They are conducted in the area mental health facilities under the joint supervision of departmental faculty and adjunct faculty located in the mental health facilities.

Housing and Day Care: On-campus housing is available. See the following Web site for more information: http://www.etsu.edu/students/housing/housing.htm. On-campus day care facilities are available. See the following Web site for more information: http://www.etsu.edu/students/caps/Childcare.htm.

Employment of Department Graduates:

Master's Degree Graduates: Of those who graduated in the academic year 2003–2004, the following categories and numbers represent the post-graduate activities and employment of master's degree graduates: Enrolled in a post-doctoral residency/fellowship (n/a), employed in independent practice (n/a), total from the above (master's) (0).

Doctoral Degree Graduates: Of those who graduated in the academic year 2003–2004, the following categories and numbers represent the post-graduate activities and employment of doctoral degree graduates: Enrolled in a psychology doctoral program (n/a), total from the above (doctoral) (0).

Additional Information:

Orientation, Objectives, and Emphasis of Department: The Department of Psychology, College of Arts and Sciences, offers a Master's of Arts Degree with options in general psychology and clinical psychology. The general psychology option prepares students for various endeavors, such as teaching at the community college level and doctoral study in psychology. The clinical psychology option provides students with training in clinical psychology leading to careers in mental health centers and other human services agencies.

Special Facilities or Resources: The psychology department maintains general experimental psychology, physiological psychology, and clinical psychology laboratory facilities. All laboratories are used for undergraduate and graduate instructional research and for student and faculty research. Assistantships/employment are available outside of the department, including the medical school.

Application Information:

Send to: School of Graduate Studies, East Tennessee State University, P.O. Box 70720, Johnson City, TN 37614-1710. Application available online. Students are admitted in the Fall, application deadline March 1. Applications submitted after March 1 may have their Financial Aid opportunities reduced. Students are normally admitted only in the Fall term, although exceptions for students in the General Option can sometimes be made. All applications are reviewed by a departmental admissions committee, and a telephone interview may be conducted. *Fee:* $25.

Memphis, University of
Department of Counseling, Educational Psychology and
  Research, Program in Counseling Psychology
Education
100 Ball Building
Memphis, TN 38152
Telephone: (901) 678-2841
Fax: (901) 678-5114
E-mail: *slease@memphis.edu*
Web: *http://cpsy.memphis.edu*

Department Information:
1972. Chairperson: Douglas Strohmer. Number of Faculty: total–full-time 23, part-time 2; women–full-time 12, part-time 2; minority–full-time 7, part-time 2; faculty subject to the Americans With Disabilities Act 1.

Programs and Degrees Offered:
Listed in the following order: Program area, degree type (T if terminal Master's), number awarded 7/03–6/04. Counseling Psychology PhD (Doctor of Philosophy) 10.

APA Accreditation: Counseling PhD (Doctor of Philosophy).

Student Applications/Admissions:
Student Applications
Counseling Psychology PhD (Doctor of Philosophy)—Applications 2004–2005, 51. Total applicants accepted 2004–2005, 15. Number enrolled (new admits only) 2004–2005 full-time, 11. Number enrolled (new admits only) 2004–2005 part-time, 0. Total enrolled 2004–2005 full-time, 36, part-time, 4. Openings 2005–2006, 8. The Median number of years required for completion of a degree are 4. The number of students enrolled full and part-time who were dismissed or voluntarily withdrew from this program area were 0.

Admissions Requirements:
Scores: Entries appear in this order: required test or GPA, minimum score (if required), median score of students entering in 2003–2004. Doctoral Programs: GRE-V no minimum stated, 550; GRE-Q no minimum stated, 560; GRE-V+Q 1000, 1123. GRE score information is for PhD in Counseling Psychology only.

Other Criteria: (importance of criteria rated low, medium, or high): GRE/MAT scores high, research experience medium, work experience medium, clinically related public service low, GPA high, letters of recommendation high, interview medium, statement of goals and objectives high, fit with program philosophy high. Criteria are for PhD in Counseling Psychology only. For additional information on admission requirements, go to: http://cpsy.memphis.edu.

Student Characteristics: The following represents characteristics of students in 2004–2005 in all graduate psychology programs in the department: Female–full-time 23, part-time 4; Male–full-time 13, part-time 0; African American/Black–full-time 2, part-time 1; Hispanic/Latino(a)–full-time 0, part-time 0; Asian/Pacific Islander–full-time 5, part-time 1; American Indian/Alaska Native–full-time 0, part-time 0; Caucasian–full-time 29, part-time 2; students subject to the Americans With Disabilities Act–full-time 0, part-time 0.

Financial Information/Assistance:

Tuition for Full-Time Study: *Master's:* State residents: per academic year $8,066, $297 per credit hour; Nonstate residents: per academic year $20,066, $661 per credit hour. *Doctoral:* State residents: per academic year $8,066, $297 per credit hour; Nonstate residents: per academic year $20,066, $661 per credit hour. Tuition is subject to change. See the following Web site for updates and changes in tuition costs: http://bf.memphis.edu/finance/bursar/fee.php.

Financial Assistance:

First Year Students: Teaching assistantships available for first-year. Average amount paid per academic year: $6,500. Average number of hours worked per week: 20. Apply by April 1. Tuition remission given: full. Research assistantships available for first-year. Average amount paid per academic year: $6,500. Average number of hours worked per week: 20. Apply by April 1. Tuition remission given: full. Fellowships and scholarships available for first-year. Apply by varies.

Advanced Students: Teaching assistantships available for advanced students. Average amount paid per academic year: $6,500. Average number of hours worked per week: 20. Apply by April 1. Tuition remission given: full. Research assistantships available for advanced students. Average amount paid per academic year: $6,500. Average number of hours worked per week: 20. Apply by April 1. Tuition remission given: full. Traineeships available for advanced students. Average amount paid per academic year: $14,000. Average number of hours worked per week: 20. Apply by varies. Tuition remission given: partial. Fellowships and scholarships available for advanced students. Apply by varies.

Contact Information: Of all students currently enrolled full-time, 97% benefitted from one or more of the listed financial assistance programs. Application and information available online at: http://academics.memphis.edu/gradschool/applicant.html.

Internships/Practica: The department has no doctoral internships. Students are expected to complete a 2000 hour predoctoral internship upon completion of their doctoral coursework. Doctoral students complete a minimum of two practica during their three years of coursework; many students complete up to four practica. The department has an extensive network of relationships with community agencies for providing practicum placements for students. These placements include: university and college counseling centers, hospitals, community mental health centers, private practice, and correctional services. For those doctoral students for whom a professional internship is required prior to graduation, 9 applied in 2003–2004. Of those who applied, 7 were placed in internships listed by the Association of Psychology Postdoctoral and Internship Programs (APPIC); 7 were placed in APA accredited internships.

Housing and Day Care: On-campus housing is available. See the following Web site for more information: http://www.people.memphis.edu/~reslife/. No on-campus day care facilities are available.

Employment of Department Graduates:

Master's Degree Graduates: Of those who graduated in the academic year 2003–2004, the following categories and numbers represent the post-graduate activities and employment of master's degree graduates: Enrolled in a post-doctoral residency/fellowship (n/a), employed in independent practice (n/a), total from the above (master's) (0).

Doctoral Degree Graduates: Of those who graduated in the academic year 2003–2004, the following categories and numbers represent the post-graduate activities and employment of doctoral degree graduates: Enrolled in a psychology doctoral program (n/a), employed in independent practice (0), employed in an academic position at a university (1), employed in a community mental health/counseling center (6), employed in a hospital/medical center (1), other employment position (1), do not know (1), total from the above (doctoral) (10).

Additional Information:

Orientation, Objectives, and Emphasis of Department: The PhD in Counseling Psychology at The University of Memphis is designed to train psychologists who promote human development in the areas of mental health, career development, emotional and social learning, and decision-making in a rapidly changing environment. Training is organized around the scientist-practitioner model of critical thinking and emphasizes responsibility and commitment to human welfare. Didactic and experiential activities are designed to anchor persons firmly within the discipline of psychology. The program emphasizes research, development, prevention, and remediation as vehicles for helping individuals, families, and groups achieve competence and a sense of well-being. The department has a strong commitment to training professionals to work with diverse populations in urban settings. Within the context of the University mission, students are expected to develop the critical thinking skills necessary for lifelong learning and to contribute to the global community. Students are expected to acquire: (1) an identity as a counseling psychologist; (2) a knowledge foundation in psychology, research, counseling, psychological evaluation, and professional standards; and (3) skills in research, practice, and teaching. The program is individualized to meet the student's goals. Graduates are prepared for positions in various settings, including counseling centers, mental health centers, hospitals, private practice, or teaching and research.

Special Facilities or Resources: Department faculty have research teams that provide opportunities for faculty and students to collaborate on research and consultation products. Faculty and students also work closely with the Center for Rehabilitation and Employment Research where there are numerous options for gaining clinical and research experiences. The center provides opportunities for faculty and students to collaborate with educational and community leaders. Students are frequently involved in grant-funded research through assistantships at the Center for Rehabilitation and Employment Research and the Memphis Community Prevention Center.

Information for Students With Physical Disabilities: See the following Web site for more information: http://www.people.memphis.edu/~sds/.

Application Information:

Send to: Suzanne Lease/Thomas Sayger, Counseling Psychology Admissions, 100 Ball Building, The University of Memphis, Memphis, TN 38152. Application available online. URL of online application: http://www.people.memphis.edu/~coe_cepr/CPSYapp.pdf. Students are admitted in the Fall, application deadline January 15. The application for the Counseling Psychology program can be obtained online from the program Web page. Applications for programs other than Counseling Psychology go to the Admissions Secretary, department office address. *Fee:* $35. This is the Graduate School application fee. Application to the Graduate School may be made at: http://academics.memphis.edu/gradschool/elecapplic.html.

Memphis, University of
Department of Psychology
College of Arts and Sciences
202 Psychology Building
Memphis, TN 38152-3230
Telephone: (901) 678-2145
Fax: (901) 678-2579
E-mail: *a-graesser@memphis.edu*
Web: *http://www.psyc.memphis.edu/*

Department Information:
1957. Chairperson: Arthur C. Graesser. Number of Faculty: total–full-time 31, part-time 5; women–full-time 8, part-time 2; minority–full-time 4, part-time 1; faculty subject to the Americans With Disabilities Act 1.

Programs and Degrees Offered:
Listed in the following order: Program area, degree type (T if terminal Master's), number awarded 7/03–6/04. Clinical Psychology PhD (Doctor of Philosophy) 15, School MA/EdS MA/MS (Master of Arts/Science) (T) 1, General Psychology MA/MS (Master of Arts/Science) (T) 2, School Psychology PhD (Doctor of Philosophy) 0, Experimental Psychology PhD (Doctor of Philosophy) 6.

APA Accreditation: Clinical PhD (Doctor of Philosophy).

Student Applications/Admissions:
Student Applications

Clinical Psychology PhD (Doctor of Philosophy)—Applications 2004–2005, 119. Total applicants accepted 2004–2005, 13. Number enrolled (new admits only) 2004–2005 full-time, 7. Total enrolled 2004–2005 full-time, 31, part-time, 6. Openings 2005–2006, 8. The Median number of years required for completion of a degree are 5. The number of students enrolled full and part-time who were dismissed or voluntarily withdrew from this program area were 2. *School MA/EdS MA/MS (Master of Arts/Science)*—Applications 2004–2005, 32. Total applicants accepted 2004–2005, 16. Number enrolled (new admits only) 2004–2005 full-time, 9. Number enrolled (new admits only) 2004–2005 part-time, 2. Total enrolled 2004–2005 full-time, 18, part-time, 8. Openings 2005–2006, 12. The Median number of years required for completion of a degree are 3. The number of students enrolled full and part-time who were dismissed or voluntarily withdrew from this program area were 1. *General Psychology MA/MS (Master of Arts/Science)*—Applications 2004–2005, 32. Total applicants accepted 2004–2005, 21. Number enrolled (new admits only) 2004–2005 full-time, 12. Number enrolled (new admits only) 2004–2005 part-time, 6. Total enrolled 2004–2005 full-time, 19, part-time, 13. Openings 2005–2006, 12. The Median number of years required for completion of a degree are 3. The number of students

enrolled full and part-time who were dismissed or voluntarily withdrew from this program area were 4. *School Psychology PhD (Doctor of Philosophy)*—Applications 2004–2005, 6. Total applicants accepted 2004–2005, 1. Number enrolled (new admits only) 2004–2005 full-time, 0. Number enrolled (new admits only) 2004–2005 part-time, 0. Total enrolled 2004–2005 full-time, 8, part-time, 1. Openings 2005–2006, 2. The Median number of years required for completion of a degree are 5. The number of students enrolled full and part-time who were dismissed or voluntarily withdrew from this program area were 0. *Experimental Psychology PhD (Doctor of Philosophy)*—Applications 2004–2005, 34. Total applicants accepted 2004–2005, 13. Number enrolled (new admits only) 2004–2005 full-time, 5. Total enrolled 2004–2005 full-time, 29, part-time, 2. Openings 2005–2006, 5. The Median number of years required for completion of a degree are 5. The number of students enrolled full and part-time who were dismissed or voluntarily withdrew from this program area were 0.

Admissions Requirements:
Scores: Entries appear in this order: required test or GPA, minimum score (if required), median score of students entering in 2003–2004. Master's Programs: GRE-V 400, 510; GRE-Q 400, 590; overall undergraduate GPA 2.5, 3.5. The minimum undergraduate GPA required for the MA/EdS is 3.0/4.0. For the MS in General Psychology, there is not a required minimum verbal or quantitative GRE-score, but a combined score of 900 is required. Doctoral Programs: GRE-V no minimum stated, 530; GRE-Q no minimum stated, 610; GRE-V+Q 1100, 1210; overall undergraduate GPA 2.75, 3.7.

Other Criteria: (importance of criteria rated low, medium, or high): GRE/MAT scores high, research experience high, work experience medium, extracurricular activity low, clinically related public service low, GPA high, letters of recommendation high, interview medium, statement of goals and objectives high.

Student Characteristics: The following represents characteristics of students in 2004–2005 in all graduate psychology programs in the department: Female–full-time 70, part-time 20; Male–full-time 35, part-time 10; African American/Black–full-time 9, part-time 2; Hispanic/Latino(a)–full-time 2, part-time 2; Asian/Pacific Islander–full-time 6, part-time 3; American Indian/Alaska Native–full-time 0, part-time 0; Caucasian–full-time 88, part-time 23; Multi-ethnic–full-time 0, part-time 0; students subject to the Americans With Disabilities Act–full-time 0, part-time 0.

Financial Information/Assistance:
Tuition for Full-Time Study: *Master's:* State residents: per academic year $7,128, $297 per credit hour; Nonstate residents: per academic year $16,584, $691 per credit hour. *Doctoral:* State residents: per academic year $7,128, $297 per credit hour; Nonstate residents: per academic year $16,584, $691 per credit hour. Tuition is subject to change. See the following Web site for updates and changes in tuition costs: http://www.psyc.memphis.edu/.

Financial Assistance:
First Year Students: Teaching assistantships available for first-year. Average amount paid per academic year: $11,000. Average number of hours worked per week: 20. Apply by February 1. Tuition remission given: full. Research assistantships available

for first-year. Average amount paid per academic year: $11,000. Average number of hours worked per week: 20. Apply by February 1. Tuition remission given: full.

Advanced Students: Teaching assistantships available for advanced students. Average amount paid per academic year: $12,000. Average number of hours worked per week: 20. Apply by February 1. Tuition remission given: full. Research assistantships available for advanced students. Average amount paid per academic year: $12,000. Average number of hours worked per week: 20. Apply by February 1. Tuition remission given: full.

Contact Information: Of all students currently enrolled full-time, 65% benefitted from one or more of the listed financial assistance programs. Application and information available online at: http://www.psyc.memphis.edu/.

Internships/Practica: The department has an extensive network of relationships with local agencies for providing practicum experiences for students. PhD clinical students work 20 hours per week at several of these practicum sites for a minimum of one year. All students can use these sites for other forms of practicum experience and research as the need arises. The department has no in-house internships. Students complete internships during the fourth or fifth year at sites nationwide. For those doctoral students for whom a professional internship is required prior to graduation, 6 applied in 2003–2004. Of those who applied, 6 were placed in internships listed by the Association of Psychology Postdoctoral and Internship Programs (APPIC); 6 were placed in APA accredited internships.

Housing and Day Care: On-campus housing is available. See the following Web site for more information: Housing: www.people.memphis.edu/~reslife/. On-campus day care facilities are available. See the following Web site for more information: Child care: https://umdrive.memphis.edu/d-reslife/childcareweb/.

Employment of Department Graduates:
Master's Degree Graduates: Of those who graduated in the academic year 2003–2004, the following categories and numbers represent the post-graduate activities and employment of master's degree graduates: Enrolled in a psychology doctoral program (2), enrolled in another graduate/professional program (0), enrolled in a post-doctoral residency/fellowship (n/a), employed in independent practice (n/a), employed in an academic position at a university (0), employed in an academic position at a 2-year/4-year college (0), employed in other positions at a higher education institution (0), employed in a professional position in a school system (0), employed in business or industry (research/consulting) (0), employed in business or industry (management) (0), employed in a government agency (research) (0), employed in a government agency (professional services) (0), employed in a community mental health/counseling center (0), employed in a hospital/medical center (0), still seeking employment (0), other employment position (0), total from the above (master's) (2).
Doctoral Degree Graduates: Of those who graduated in the academic year 2003–2004, the following categories and numbers represent the post-graduate activities and employment of doctoral degree graduates: Enrolled in a psychology doctoral program (n/a), enrolled in a post-doctoral residency/fellowship (13), employed in independent practice (0), employed in an academic position at a university (10), employed in an academic position at a 2-year/4-year college (0), employed in other positions at a higher education institution (0), employed in a professional position in

a school system (0), employed in business or industry (research/consulting) (4), employed in business or industry (management) (0), employed in a government agency (research) (2), employed in a government agency (professional services) (1), employed in a community mental health/counseling center (1), employed in a hospital/medical center (0), still seeking employment (0), other employment position (0), total from the above (doctoral) (31).

Additional Information:
Orientation, Objectives, and Emphasis of Department: The department philosophy emphasizes the training of experimentally sophisticated research scientists and practitioners. All programs have a strong research emphasis. Professional training is based upon a research foundation and students are exposed to a broad range of theoretical perspectives. Diversity of professional training activities and collaborative research activities is emphasized. Students are afforded maximum freedom to pursue their own interests and tailor programs to their needs. All PhD and master's programs are serviced by six research areas within the department: Behavioral Medicine, Behavioral Neuroscience, Child and Family Studies, Cognitive and Social Processes, Industrial/Organizational and Applied Psychology, and Psychopathology/Psychotherapy.

Special Facilities or Resources: The department as a whole has a strong research orientation, and an NSF study published in 2003 found the Psychology Department at The University of Memphis to rank sixth among psychology departments across the nation in total research and development expenditures. The department is housed in a modern, well-equipped barrier-free building, providing offices and laboratory space for all students. The department includes the Center for Applied Psychological Research (CAPR), the Institute for Intelligent Systems (IIS), the Universities Prevention Center, and the Psychological Services Center (PSC). The CAPR is the state-sponsored center of excellence that has provided the department with approximately $1 million per year for the past 20 years. The IIS is an interdisciplinary enterprise composed of researchers and students from the fields of cognitive psychology, computer science, mathematics, physics, neuroscience, education, linguistics, philosophy, anthropology, engineering, and business. The Prevention Center is a joint venture of The University of Memphis and the University of Tennessee, Memphis. Researchers and staff are dedicated to developing ways of preventing cancer and cardiovascular diseases. The Psychological Services Center is a fee-for-service outpatient mental health clinic located in the psychology building. In this clinic doctoral students receive intensive supervision as they learn to provide a wide range of assessment and intervention services. In addition, the PSC provides an invaluable resource for the conduct of a variety of research projects. The clients are referred from the greater Memphis area.

Information for Students With Physical Disabilities: See the following Web site for more information: www.people.memphis.edu/~sds/.

Application Information:
Send to: There are two applications (see Web site for directions). One is sent to the Graduate School of the University of Memphis at the following address: The University of Memphis, Graduate School, Admissions Office, Wilder Tower 101, Memphis, TN 38152. The other is sent to the Department of Psychology at the following address: Admissions Secretary, Department of Psychology, 202 Psychology

Building, University of Memphis, Memphis, TN 38152. Application available online. URL of online application: www.psyc.memphis.edu/application/. Students are admitted in the Fall. The application deadline for all PhD programs is January 15. The application deadline for the master's program in General Psychology is May 15. The application deadline for the MA/EdS in School Psychology is June 15. *Fee:* $50. The application fee for the graduate school is $35 for domestic students and $60 for international students. There is an additional fee of $15 for the Department of Psychology application.

Middle Tennessee State University
Department of Psychology
Education and Behavioral Science
Box 87
Murfreesboro, TN 37132
Telephone: (615) 898-2706
Fax: (615) 898-5027
E-mail: *alittlep@mtsu.edu*
Web: *http://www.mtsu.edu/~psych*

Department Information:
1967. Chairperson: Dennis Papini. Number of Faculty: total–full-time 45, part-time 13; women–full-time 17, part-time 9; minority–full-time 2, part-time 1.

Programs and Degrees Offered:
Listed in the following order: Program area, degree type (T if terminal Master's), number awarded 7/03–6/04. Clinical MA/MS (Master of Arts/Science) (T) 12, Experimental MA/MS (Master of Arts/Science) (T) 2, Industrial/ Organizational MA/MS (Master of Arts/Science) (T) 13, Quantitative MA/MS (Master of Arts/Science) (T) 4, School Psychology MA/MS (Master of Arts/Science) 17, School Psychology EdS (Education Specialist) 12, Professional Counseling MA/MS (Master of Arts/Science) 15.

Student Applications/Admissions:
Student Applications
Clinical MA/MS (Master of Arts/Science)—Applications 2004–2005, 38. Total applicants accepted 2004–2005, 29. Number enrolled (new admits only) 2004–2005 full-time, 11. Number enrolled (new admits only) 2004–2005 part-time, 1. Total enrolled 2004–2005 full-time, 20, part-time, 12. Openings 2005–2006, 20. The Median number of years required for completion of a degree are 3. The number of students enrolled full and part-time who were dismissed or voluntarily withdrew from this program area were 4. *Experimental MA/MS (Master of Arts/Science)*—Applications 2004–2005, 6. Total applicants accepted 2004–2005, 6. Openings 2005–2006, 20. The number of students enrolled full and part-time who were dismissed or voluntarily withdrew from this program area were 4. *Industrial/ Organizational MA/MS (Master of Arts/Science)*—Applications 2004–2005, 65. Total applicants accepted 2004–2005, 17. Number enrolled (new admits only) 2004–2005 full-time, 12. Total enrolled 2004–2005 full-time, 24, part-time, 2. Openings 2005–2006, 12. The Median number of years required for completion of a degree are 2. *Quantitative MA/MS (Master of Arts/Science)*—Applications 2004–2005, 7. Total applicants accepted 2004–2005, 7. Total enrolled 2004–2005 full-time, 9, part-time, 1. Openings 2005–2006, 6. The Median number

of years required for completion of a degree are 2. The number of students enrolled full and part-time who were dismissed or voluntarily withdrew from this program area were 0. *School Psychology MA/MS (Master of Arts/Science)*—Applications 2004–2005, 30. Total applicants accepted 2004–2005, 19. Number enrolled (new admits only) 2004–2005 full-time, 11. Number enrolled (new admits only) 2004–2005 part-time, 0. Openings 2005–2006, 10. The Median number of years required for completion of a degree are 2. The number of students enrolled full and part-time who were dismissed or voluntarily withdrew from this program area were 1. *School Psychology EdS (Education Specialist)*—Applications 2004–2005, 13. Total applicants accepted 2004–2005, 13. Number enrolled (new admits only) 2004–2005 full-time, 1. Number enrolled (new admits only) 2004–2005 part-time, 13. Total enrolled 2004–2005 full-time, 1, part-time, 13. The Median number of years required for completion of a degree is 1. *Professional Counseling MA/MS (Master of Arts/Science)*—Applications 2004–2005, 26. Total applicants accepted 2004–2005, 17. Number enrolled (new admits only) 2004–2005 full-time, 13. Number enrolled (new admits only) 2004–2005 part-time, 2. Total enrolled 2004–2005 full-time, 29, part-time, 8. Openings 2005–2006, 30. The Median number of years required for completion of a degree are 3. The number of students enrolled full and part-time who were dismissed or voluntarily withdrew from this program area were 1.

Admissions Requirements:
Scores: Entries appear in this order: required test or GPA, minimum score (if required), median score of students entering in 2003–2004. Master's Programs: GRE-V no minimum stated; GRE-Q 450; GRE-V+Q 900; GRE-Analytical no minimum stated; GRE-Subject(Psych) no minimum stated; overall undergraduate GPA 3.00. I/O only: GRE-Q+V+A (subject not required), Clinical only: GRE-Subject =no minimum; School Counseling V+Q=900
Other Criteria: (importance of criteria rated low, medium, or high): GRE/MAT scores high, research experience high, work experience low, extracurricular activity low, clinically related public service medium, GPA high, letters of recommendation high, interview high, statement of goals and objectives high, Interview: School Counseling only. Statement of goals and objectives for Experimental and School Psychology only.

Student Characteristics: The following represents characteristics of students in 2004–2005 in all graduate psychology programs in the department: Female–full-time 129, part-time 0; Male–full-time 38, part-time 0; African American/Black–full-time 12, part-time 0; Hispanic/Latino(a)–full-time 1, part-time 0; Asian/Pacific Islander–full-time 5, part-time 0; American Indian/Alaska Native–full-time 1, part-time 0; Caucasian–full-time 0, part-time 0.

Financial Information/Assistance:
Tuition for Full-Time Study: *Master's:* State residents: per academic year $1,716, $181 per credit hour; Nonstate residents: per academic year $4,952, $461 per credit hour. See the following Web site for updates and changes in tuition costs: www.mtsu.edu/~bursarmt.

Financial Assistance:
First Year Students: Research assistantships available for first-year. Average amount paid per academic year: $4,550. Aver-

age number of hours worked per week: 20. Apply by October 1. Tuition remission given: full and partial.

Advanced Students: No information provided.

Contact Information: Of all students currently enrolled full-time, 50% benefitted from one or more of the listed financial assistance programs.

Internships/Practica: Field placements are available in a variety of mental health facilities, inpatient facilities, the VA hospital, drug abuse facilities, K-12 school settings, and industrial sites.

Housing and Day Care: On-campus housing is available. See the following Web site for more information: http://www.mtsu.edu/~housing/; http://www.mtsu.edu/info/dcl.html. On-campus day care facilities are available.

Employment of Department Graduates:

Master's Degree Graduates: Of those who graduated in the academic year 2003–2004, the following categories and numbers represent the post-graduate activities and employment of master's degree graduates: Enrolled in a post-doctoral residency/fellowship (n/a), employed in independent practice (n/a), total from the above (master's) (0).

Doctoral Degree Graduates: Of those who graduated in the academic year 2003–2004, the following categories and numbers represent the post-graduate activities and employment of doctoral degree graduates: Enrolled in a psychology doctoral program (n/a), total from the above (doctoral) (0).

Additional Information:

Orientation, Objectives, and Emphasis of Department: We have an applied department with research and service priorities. A strong academic program is available for students seeking to improve their backgrounds in core areas of psychology for admission to doctoral programs. Applied programs lead to certification and/or licensure in school psychology, school counseling, and clinical (www.mtsu.edu/~psych). Industrial/Organizational program nationally acclaimed (for more about the I/O program, see www.mtsu.edu/~iopsych).

Special Facilities or Resources: On-campus facilities include a counseling laboratory for practica, an animal learning laboratory and a physiology laboratory.

Application Information:
Send to: Office of Graduate Studies, Cope Administration Building, 114 Middle, Tennessee State University, Murfreesboro, TN 37132. Application available online. URL of online application: http://www.applyweb.com/aw?mtsu. Students are admitted in the Fall, application deadline October 1; Spring, application deadline March 1. Applicants to the clinical program must submit a supplemental clinical application and three letters of recommendation on supplied forms. The supplemental application and recommendation forms can be obtained from the Department of Psychology or online through the psychology department Web site. *Fee:* $30.

Tennessee State University
Department of Psychology
Education
3500 John Merritt Boulevard
Nashville, TN 37209
Telephone: (615) 963-5141
Fax: (615) 963-5140
E-mail: rojones@tnstate.edu
Web: http://www.tnstate.edu

Department Information:
1940. Interim Department Head: Roger W. Jones, PhD Number of Faculty: total–full-time 22, part-time 17; women–full-time 12, part-time 13; minority–full-time 4, part-time 7; faculty subject to the Americans With Disabilities Act 1.

Programs and Degrees Offered:
Listed in the following order: Program area, degree type (T if terminal Master's), number awarded 7/03–6/04. School Psychology MA/MS (Master of Arts/Science) 2, School Psychology PhD (Doctor of Philosophy) 3, Counseling Psychology PhD (Doctor of Philosophy) 7, Guidance and Counseling MA/MS (Master of Arts/Science) (T) 18, Counseling Psychology PhD (Doctor of Philosophy) 6, School Psychology EdS (Education Specialist).

APA Accreditation: Counseling PhD (Doctor of Philosophy).

Student Applications/Admissions:
Student Applications
School Psychology MA/MS (Master of Arts/Science)—Applications 2004–2005, 3. Total applicants accepted 2004–2005, 3. Openings 2005–2006, 5. The Median number of years required for completion of a degree are 5. The number of students enrolled full and part-time who were dismissed or voluntarily withdrew from this program area were 0. School Psychology PhD (Doctor of Philosophy)—Applications 2004–2005, 4. Total applicants accepted 2004–2005, 3. Total enrolled 2004–2005 full-time, 3. Openings 2005–2006, 3. The Median number of years required for completion of a degree are 3. Counseling Psychology PhD (Doctor of Philosophy)—Applications 2004–2005, 22. Total applicants accepted 2004–2005, 8. Total enrolled 2004–2005 full-time, 29, part-time, 3. Openings 2005–2006, 10. The Median number of years required for completion of a degree are 5. The number of students enrolled full and part-time who were dismissed or voluntarily withdrew from this program area were 0. Guidance and Counseling MA/MS (Master of Arts/Science)—Applications 2004–2005, 42. Total applicants accepted 2004–2005, 38. Openings 2005–2006, 30. The Median number of years required for completion of a degree are 2. Counseling Psychology PhD (Doctor of Philosophy)—Applications 2004–2005, 32. Total applicants accepted 2004–2005, 11. Number enrolled (new admits only) 2004–2005 full-time, 6. Number enrolled (new admits only) 2004–2005 part-time, 1. Total enrolled 2004–2005 full-time, 28, part-time, 6. Openings 2005–2006, 8. The Median number of years required for completion of a degree are 6. The number of students enrolled full and part-time who were dismissed or voluntarily withdrew from this program area were 3. School Psychology EdS (Education Specialist)—Applications 2004–2005, 10. Total applicants accepted 2004–2005, 5. Openings

2005–2006, 10. The Median number of years required for completion of a degree are 3.

Admissions Requirements:

Scores: Entries appear in this order: required test or GPA, minimum score (if required), median score of students entering in 2003–2004. Master's Programs: GRE-V no minimum stated; GRE-Q no minimum stated; GRE-V+Q 870, 900; MAT 25, 35; overall undergraduate GPA 2.5, 3.0. A GPA of 2.5 is required for both the Pre K-12 school counseling and school psychology masters programs. Doctoral Programs: GRE-V+Q 900, 1100; MAT 44, 50. GRE is preferred over MAT.

Other Criteria: (importance of criteria rated low, medium, or high): GRE/MAT scores high, research experience high, work experience high, extracurricular activity low, clinically related public service medium, GPA medium, letters of recommendation high, interview high, statement of goals and objectives high. For additional information on admission requirements, go to: www.tnstate.edu.

Student Characteristics: The following represents characteristics of students in 2004–2005 in all graduate psychology programs in the department: Female–full-time 46, part-time 101; Male–full-time 17, part-time 29; African American/Black–full-time 41, part-time 6; Hispanic/Latino(a)–full-time 1, part-time 0; Asian/Pacific Islander–full-time 1, part-time 1; American Indian/Alaska Native–full-time 0, part-time 0; Caucasian–full-time 0, part-time 0; Multi-ethnic–full-time 3, part-time 0; students subject to the Americans With Disabilities Act–full-time 2, part-time 0.

Financial Information/Assistance:

Tuition for Full-Time Study: *Master's:* State residents: per academic year $3,884, $209 per credit hour; Nonstate residents: per academic year $10,356, $479 per credit hour. *Doctoral:* State residents: per academic year $3,884, $209 per credit hour; Nonstate residents: per academic year $10,356, $479 per credit hour. Tuition is subject to change.

Financial Assistance:

First Year Students: Teaching assistantships available for first-year. Average amount paid per academic year: $10,000. Average number of hours worked per week: 20. Tuition remission given: full. Research assistantships available for first-year. Average amount paid per academic year: $10,000. Average number of hours worked per week: 20. Tuition remission given: full.

Advanced Students: Teaching assistantships available for advanced students. Average amount paid per academic year: $10,000. Average number of hours worked per week: 20. Research assistantships available for advanced students. Average amount paid per academic year: $10,000. Average number of hours worked per week: 20.

Contact Information: No information provided.

Internships/Practica: Practica and internships are available in school psychological services in metropolitan Nashville public schools. Practica and internships in counseling psychology are available for master's students in local community mental health centers in middle Tennessee; in community agencies; in family counseling services; in correctional facilities; in state hospital settings; and in school systems throughout middle Tennessee. Counseling Psychology doctoral students complete practica in a range of sites in Middle Tennessee and obtain matches across the nation for APA approved internships. For those doctoral students for whom a professional internship is required prior to graduation, 7 applied in 2003–2004. Of those who applied, 7 were placed in internships listed by the Association of Psychology Postdoctoral and Internship Programs (APPIC); 6 were placed in APA accredited internships.

Housing and Day Care: On-campus housing is available. See the following Web site for more information: www.tnstate.edu. On-campus day care facilities are available.

Employment of Department Graduates:

Master's Degree Graduates: Of those who graduated in the academic year 2003–2004, the following categories and numbers represent the post-graduate activities and employment of master's degree graduates: Enrolled in a post-doctoral residency/fellowship (n/a), employed in independent practice (n/a), total from the above (master's) (0).

Doctoral Degree Graduates: Of those who graduated in the academic year 2003–2004, the following categories and numbers represent the post-graduate activities and employment of doctoral degree graduates: Enrolled in a psychology doctoral program (n/a), enrolled in another graduate/professional program (1), enrolled in a post-doctoral residency/fellowship (1), employed in independent practice (2), employed in an academic position at a university (0), employed in an academic position at a 2-year/4-year college (0), employed in other positions at a higher education institution (1), employed in a professional position in a school system (0), employed in business or industry (research/consulting) (0), employed in business or industry (management) (0), employed in a government agency (research) (0), employed in a government agency (professional services) (0), employed in a community mental health/counseling center (1), employed in a hospital/medical center (1), still seeking employment (0), not seeking employment (0), other employment position (0), do not know (0), total from the above (doctoral) (7).

Additional Information:

Orientation, Objectives, and Emphasis of Department: The philosophy of the Department of Psychology at Tennessee State University is embodied in the concept that psychology is a discipline that contributes to the understanding of human behavior and experience. A graduate of the Department of Psychology is expected to be both a professional person with a code of ethics and one who is committed to a scientific orientation. The doctoral program in psychology offers two concentrations: counseling and school psychology. The Counseling concentration is APA approved, while the doctoral degree as a whole is a designated doctoral program in psychology by the national designation system sponsored by the American Association of State Psychology Boards and Register for Health Services Providers in Psychology. The Master's Degree in Psychology is designed for students seeking preparation for a professional career in psychology, either for a doctoral program or for professional training at the master's level. The Guidance and Counseling master's program is designed for students preparing for careers in school counseling.

Special Facilities or Resources: Specialized facilities are available in department laboratories: 1) Counseling Laboratory consisting of videotaping equipment, observation room and a two-way communication system; 2) computer laboratory—PCs and associated software for word-processing, statistics, and tutorials; 3) Testing

Equipment- psychological test kit and assessment files for intelligence, personality and psychoeducational assessment. In addition, faculty have specialized research laboratories providing opportunities for student research involvement (e.g., biofeedback/psychophysiology laboratory, group counseling laboratory).

Information for Students With Physical Disabilities: See the following Web site for more information: www.tnstate.edu.

Application Information:
Send to: Dean of Graduate School, Tennessee State University, 3500 John A. Merritt Boulevard, Nashville, TN 37209. Application available online. Students are admitted in the Fall, application deadline July 1. July 1 deadline applies only to master's and EdS programs; deadline for admission to PhD program is December 1. *Fee:* $25.

Tennessee, University of, Chattanooga
Department of Psychology
350 Holt Hall
Chattanooga, TN 37403
Telephone: (423) 425-4262
Fax: (423) 425-4284
E-mail: *michael-biderman@utc.edu*
Web: *http://www.utc.edu/ioprog*

Department Information:
1969. Head: Paul J. Watson. Number of Faculty: total–full-time 13, part-time 4; women–full-time 4, part-time 3; minority–part-time 1.

Programs and Degrees Offered:
Listed in the following order: Program area, degree type (T if terminal Master's), number awarded 7/03–6/04. Industrial/ Organizational MA/MS (Master of Arts/Science) (T) 15, Research MA/MS (Master of Arts/Science) (T) 2.

Student Applications/Admissions:
Student Applications
Industrial/Organizational MA/MS (Master of Arts/Science)—Applications 2004–2005, 35. Total applicants accepted 2004–2005, 29. Number enrolled (new admits only) 2004–2005 full-time, 14. Openings 2005–2006, 20. The Median number of years required for completion of a degree are 2. The number of students enrolled full and part-time who were dismissed or voluntarily withdrew from this program area were 1. *Research MA/MS (Master of Arts/Science)*—Applications 2004–2005, 8. Total applicants accepted 2004–2005, 8. Number enrolled (new admits only) 2004–2005 full-time, 8. Openings 2005–2006, 8. The Median number of years required for completion of a degree are 2. The number of students enrolled full and part-time who were dismissed or voluntarily withdrew from this program area were 1.

Admissions Requirements:
Scores: Entries appear in this order: required test or GPA, minimum score (if required), median score of students entering in 2003–2004. Master's Programs: GRE-V no minimum stated, 460; GRE-Q no minimum stated, 530; overall undergraduate

GPA no minimum stated, 3.40. We use a formula: 200 x UGPA + (GREV+GREQ)/2. We generally admit those whose formula score exceeds 1150. We take letters or reference and a personal statement into account.
Other Criteria: (importance of criteria rated low, medium, or high): GRE/MAT scores high, research experience medium, work experience medium, extracurricular activity low, clinically related public service low, GPA high, letters of recommendation medium, interview low, statement of goals and objectives medium. Admission to the Research program requires sponsorship of a faculty member. For additional information on admission requirements, go to: www.utc.edu/ioprog.

Student Characteristics: The following represents characteristics of students in 2004–2005 in all graduate psychology programs in the department: Female–full-time 30, part-time 0; Male–full-time 9, part-time 0; African American/Black–full-time 1, part-time 0; Hispanic/Latino(a)–full-time 0, part-time 0; Asian/Pacific Islander–full-time 0, part-time 0; American Indian/Alaska Native–full-time 0, part-time 0; Caucasian–full-time 37, part-time 0; Multi-ethnic–full-time 1, part-time 0; students subject to the Americans With Disabilities Act–full-time 1, part-time 0.

Financial Information/Assistance:
Tuition for Full-Time Study: *Master's:* State residents: per academic year $2,372; Nonstate residents: per academic year $6,500. Tuition is subject to change. See the following Web site for updates and changes in tuition costs: www.utc.edu.

Financial Assistance:
First Year Students: Teaching assistantships available for first-year. Average amount paid per academic year: $1,000. Average number of hours worked per week: 5. Apply by August 20. Research assistantships available for first-year. Average amount paid per academic year: $2,750. Average number of hours worked per week: 10. Apply by July 1. Tuition remission given: partial.
Advanced Students: Teaching assistantships available for advanced students. Average amount paid per academic year: $1,000. Average number of hours worked per week: 5. Apply by August 20. Research assistantships available for advanced students. Average amount paid per academic year: $2,750. Average number of hours worked per week: 10. Apply by July 1. Tuition remission given: partial.
Contact Information: Of all students currently enrolled full-time, 60% benefitted from one or more of the listed financial assistance programs. Application and information available online at: www.utc.edu/gradstudies.

Internships/Practica: The integration of coursework and practice throughout the students' graduate academic program is essential to prepare I/O students for applied professional careers. To achieve this end, I/O students become involved in a variety of real life work organization activities through completion of a practicum program. They are encouraged to start this practicum after their second semester of academic work. Six semester hours of practicum credit are required (involving at least 300 hours of actual work time), and an additional three semester hours may be taken as a part of the elective portion of the program. The practicum is carried out in private and public work organizations in which the students engage in a wide variety of projects under the guidance of field supervisors, coordinated by the I/O faculty.

Housing and Day Care: On-campus housing is available. See the following Web site for more information: www.utc.edu. On-campus day care facilities are available.

Employment of Department Graduates:

Master's Degree Graduates: Of those who graduated in the academic year 2003–2004, the following categories and numbers represent the post-graduate activities and employment of master's degree graduates: Enrolled in a psychology doctoral program (4), enrolled in a post-doctoral residency/fellowship (n/a), employed in independent practice (n/a), employed in business or industry (management) (12), still seeking employment (1), total from the above (master's) (17).

Doctoral Degree Graduates: Of those who graduated in the academic year 2003–2004, the following categories and numbers represent the post-graduate activities and employment of doctoral degree graduates: Enrolled in a psychology doctoral program (n/a), total from the above (doctoral) (0).

Additional Information:

Orientation, Objectives, and Emphasis of Department: The goal of the I/O program is to provide students with the training necessary to pursue a variety of I/O related fields. These include, but are not limited to, positions in human resources, industrial/organizational consulting, training, and organization development. The I/O program can be used as a preparation for the pursuit of doctoral training in I/O related fields of study. The curriculum is organized around specific core knowledge domains particular to I/O psychology. The industrial domain includes content such as job analysis, selection, and training. The organizational domain includes content such as work motivation, attitudes, leadership, organizational development, and group processes. The third domain, research methodology, includes experimental design and univariate and multivariate statistical analysis. The research program is designed primarily to prepare students to pursue doctoral level training. Students work in an apprenticeship model with faculty to develop strong design and analysis skills.

Special Facilities or Resources: Center for Applied Social Research conducts surveys and other applied research in the community. We have a close relationship with SHRM Chattanooga, the local SHRM branch.

Information for Students With Physical Disabilities: See the following Web site for more information: www.utc.edu/Units/OfficeForStudentsWithDisabilities.

Application Information:
Send to: Graduate School, 5305 University of Tennessee, Chattanooga, Chattanooga, TN 37403. Application available online. URL of online application: http://www.utc.edu/Administration/Graduate School/GraduateForms.htm. Students are admitted in the Fall, application deadline March 15; Winter, application deadline March 15. Programs have rolling admissions. Students may be admitted after the March deadline if space permits. Programs are designed to begin in the fall semester. Spring and summer admissions are possible, though they may require longer than typical residence in a program. *Fee:* $25.

Tennessee, University of, Knoxville (2004 data)
Department of Educational Psychology and Counseling
Education, Health, and Human Sciences
A525 Claxton Complex
Knoxville, TN 37996-3452
Telephone: (865) 974-8145
Fax: (865) 974-0135
E-mail: *mccallum@utk.edu*
Web: *http://www.coe.utk.edu/programs/graduate.html*

Department Information:
1956. Head: R. Steve McCallum. Number of Faculty: total–full-time 20, part-time 10; women–full-time 7, part-time 4; minority–full-time 1, part-time 1; faculty subject to the Americans With Disabilities Act 2.

Programs and Degrees Offered:
Listed in the following order: Program area, degree type (T if terminal Master's), number awarded 7/03–6/04. School Psychology PhD (Doctor of Philosophy) 8, Educational Psychology PhD (Doctor of Philosophy) 4.

APA Accreditation: School PhD (Doctor of Philosophy).

Student Applications/Admissions:
Student Applications

School Psychology PhD (Doctor of Philosophy)—Applications 2004–2005, 42. Total applicants accepted 2004–2005, 7. Openings 2005–2006, 7. The Median number of years required for completion of a degree are 5. The number of students enrolled full and part-time who were dismissed or voluntarily withdrew from this program area were 1. *Educational Psychology PhD (Doctor of Philosophy)*—Applications 2004–2005, 28. Total applicants accepted 2004–2005, 10. Total enrolled 2004–2005 full-time, 33, part-time, 9. Openings 2005–2006, 1. The Median number of years required for completion of a degree are 4. The number of students enrolled full and part-time who were dismissed or voluntarily withdrew from this program area were 1.

Admissions Requirements:
Scores: Entries appear in this order: required test or GPA, minimum score (if required), median score of students entering in 2003–2004. Master's Programs: overall undergraduate GPA 3.0, 3.6. Doctoral Programs: GRE-V no minimum stated; GRE-Q no minimum stated; GRE-V+Q no minimum stated; GRE-Analytical no minimum stated; overall undergraduate GPA 3.0, 3.65. At least 50th percentile on V and 40th percentile on other scale for a total of 1070 this year, plus a 4 on the Analytic Writing scale. Foreign students must take the TOFLE for Ed Psych.
Other Criteria: (importance of criteria rated low, medium, or high): GRE/MAT scores medium, research experience low, work experience low, extracurricular activity medium, clinically related public service medium, GPA high, letters of recommendation medium, interview low, statement of goals and objectives medium.

Student Characteristics: The following represents characteristics of students in 2004–2005 in all graduate psychology programs in

the department: Female–full-time 82, part-time 5; Male–full-time 70, part-time 9; African American/Black–full-time 6, part-time 0; Hispanic/Latino(a)–full-time 0, part-time 0; Asian/Pacific Islander–full-time 2, part-time 0; American Indian/Alaska Native–full-time 0, part-time 0; Caucasian–full-time 0, part-time 0; Multi-ethnic–full-time 2, part-time 0; students subject to the Americans With Disabilities Act–full-time 2, part-time 0.

Financial Information/Assistance:

Tuition for Full-Time Study: *Master's:* State residents: per academic year $5,032, $272 per credit hour; Nonstate residents: per academic year $14,114, $777 per credit hour. *Doctoral:* State residents: per academic year $5,032, $272 per credit hour; Nonstate residents: per academic year $14,114, $777 per credit hour.

Financial Assistance:

First Year Students: Teaching assistantships available for first-year. Average amount paid per academic year: $5,000. Average number of hours worked per week: 10. Apply by January 31. Tuition remission given: full. Research assistantships available for first-year. Average amount paid per academic year: $4,000. Average number of hours worked per week: 10. Apply by January 31. Tuition remission given: full.

Advanced Students: Teaching assistantships available for advanced students. Average amount paid per academic year: $6,000. Average number of hours worked per week: 10. Apply by January 31. Tuition remission given: full. Research assistantships available for advanced students. Average amount paid per academic year: $5,000. Average number of hours worked per week: 10. Apply by January 31. Tuition remission given: full.

Contact Information: Of all students currently enrolled full-time, 25% benefitted from one or more of the listed financial assistance programs.

Internships/Practica: Assessment, counseling, and consultation practica are required of all school psychology/counseling students. In addition, a 1,500-hour internship is required for EdS students and a 2000-hour internship is required for PhD students. The Department is a member of an APPIC-listed internship consortium. For those doctoral students for whom a professional internship is required prior to graduation, 7 applied in 2003–2004. Of those who applied, 5 were placed in internships listed by the Association of Psychology Postdoctoral and Internship Programs (APPIC); 3 were placed in APA accredited internships.

Housing and Day Care: On-campus housing is available. On-campus day care facilities are available.

Employment of Department Graduates:

Master's Degree Graduates: Of those who graduated in the academic year 2003–2004, the following categories and numbers represent the post-graduate activities and employment of master's degree graduates: Enrolled in a psychology doctoral program (11), enrolled in another graduate/professional program (10), enrolled in a post-doctoral residency/fellowship (n/a), employed in independent practice (n/a), employed in an academic position at a university (3), employed in an academic position at a 2-year/4-year college (1), employed in other positions at a higher education institution (2), employed in a professional position in a school system (6), employed in business or industry (research/consulting) (5), total from the above (master's) (38).

Doctoral Degree Graduates: Of those who graduated in the academic year 2003–2004, the following categories and numbers represent the post-graduate activities and employment of doctoral degree graduates: Enrolled in a psychology doctoral program (n/a), enrolled in a post-doctoral residency/fellowship (0), employed in independent practice (4), total from the above (doctoral) (4).

Additional Information:

Orientation, Objectives, and Emphasis of Department: Members of the Educational Psychology and Counseling Department envision playing an instrumental role in the creation of contextually linked learning environments that promote and enhance success for all learners. We expect these environments to exemplify a spirit of collaboration and cooperation, respect for diversity, concern for mental and physical health, positive attitudes toward constructive and meaningful change, and a commitment to lifelong learning. Faculty and students in the Psychoeducational Studies Unit are expected to model the behaviors and reflect the values that are necessary to achieve this vision. The Psychoeducational Studies Unit will provide national leadership in creating learning environments that (1) foster psychological health, (2) address authentic educational needs, and (3) promote lifelong learning. Unit faculty and students will draw upon a growing body of knowledge about the psychology, biology, and social/cultural contexts of learning in promoting systematic change that leads to the enhancement of the learner. Specifically, the Unit will seek opportunities in a diversity of contexts for learners to apply information-based problem solving, engage in critical thinking, provide counseling services, and implement the structures and processes necessary for effective collaboration.

Application Information:

Send to: Graduate Admissions, College of Education, 214 Claxton Education Building Addition, The University of Tennessee, Knoxville, TN 37996-3400. Application available online. Students are admitted in the Winter. January 15 deadline for PhD and EdS in School Psychology and for EdD in Educational Psychology. No deadlines for MS in Educational Psychology. *Fee:* $35.

Tennessee, University of, Knoxville (2004 data)
Department of Psychology
Arts & Sciences
312 Austin Peay Building
Knoxville, TN 37996-0900
Telephone: (865) 974-3328
Fax: (865) 974-3330
E-mail: *cjogle@utk.edu*
Web: *http://web.utk.edu/~jlawler/newpage/admissions*

Department Information:
1957. Department Head: James E. Lawler. Number of Faculty: total–full-time 29, part-time 19; women–full-time 10, part-time 8; minority–full-time 2.

Programs and Degrees Offered:
Listed in the following order: Program area, degree type (T if terminal Master's), number awarded 7/03–6/04. Clinical PhD (Doctor of Philosophy) 9, Experimental MA/MS (Master of Arts/

Science) (T) 10, Counseling PhD (Doctor of Philosophy), Experimental PhD (Doctor of Philosophy) 2.

APA Accreditation: Clinical PhD (Doctor of Philosophy). Counseling PhD (Doctor of Philosophy).

Student Applications/Admissions:
Student Applications
Clinical PhD (Doctor of Philosophy)—Applications 2004–2005, 95. Total applicants accepted 2004–2005, 8. Openings 2005–2006, 7. *Experimental MA/MS (Master of Arts/Science)*—Applications 2004–2005, 9. Total applicants accepted 2004–2005, 4. Openings 2005–2006, 4. *Counseling PhD (Doctor of Philosophy)*—Applications 2004–2005, 40. Total applicants accepted 2004–2005, 4. Openings 2005–2006, 6. *Experimental PhD (Doctor of Philosophy)*—Applications 2004–2005, 22. Total applicants accepted 2004–2005, 6. Total enrolled 2004–2005 full-time, 34. Openings 2005–2006, 7.

Admissions Requirements:
Scores: Entries appear in this order: required test or GPA, minimum score (if required), median score of students entering in 2003–2004. Master's Programs: GRE-V+Q no minimum stated, 1172; GRE-Subject(Psych) no minimum stated, 600; overall undergraduate GPA no minimum stated, 3.51. Doctoral Programs: GRE-V+Q no minimum stated, 1200; GRE-Subject(Psych) no minimum stated, 670; overall undergraduate GPA 3.0, 3.84.
Other Criteria: (importance of criteria rated low, medium, or high): GRE/MAT scores high, research experience high, work experience low, extracurricular activity low, clinically related public service low, GPA high, letters of recommendation high, interview high, statement of goals and objectives high.

Student Characteristics: The following represents characteristics of students in 2004–2005 in all graduate psychology programs in the department: Female–full-time 60, part-time 0; Male–full-time 39, part-time 0; African American/Black–full-time 9, part-time 0; Hispanic/Latino(a)–full-time 1, part-time 0; Asian/Pacific Islander–full-time 4, part-time 0; American Indian/Alaska Native–full-time 0, part-time 0; Caucasian–full-time 0, part-time 0; Multiethnic–full-time 1, part-time 0.

Financial Information/Assistance:
Tuition for Full-Time Study: *Master's:* State residents: per academic year $6,885, $223 per credit hour; Nonstate residents: per academic year $19,413, $674 per credit hour. *Doctoral:* State residents: per academic year $6,885, $223 per credit hour; Nonstate residents: per academic year $19,413, $674 per credit hour. Tuition is subject to change. See the following Web site for updates and changes in tuition costs: http://web.utk.edu/~bursar/volxfees.html.

Financial Assistance:
First Year Students: Research assistantships available for first-year. Tuition remission given: full.
Advanced Students: Teaching assistantships available for advanced students. Research assistantships available for advanced students.
Contact Information: Of all students currently enrolled full-time, 0% benefitted from one or more of the listed financial assistance programs.

Internships/Practica: All Clinical students are required to participate in two 12-month practica, one in our Departmental Psychological Clinic and the other in a community mental health facility. Both practica are supervised by doctoral degreed clinical psychologists, and the clientele are children, adolescents, and adults who seek help for their emotional and behavioral problems. In addition, Clinical students are required to serve a one-year internship. Counseling students are also required to serve a one-year internship. Additional data on Counseling internships is not available at the time of this entry. For those doctoral students for whom a professional internship is required prior to graduation, 5 applied in 2003–2004. Of those who applied, 5 were placed in internships listed by the Association of Psychology Postdoctoral and Internship Programs (APPIC); 5 were placed in APA accredited internships.

Housing and Day Care: On-campus housing is available. See the following Web site for more information: http://uthousing.utk.edu. On-campus day care facilities are available. See the following Web site for more information: http://web.utk.edu/~utkchl.

Employment of Department Graduates:
Master's Degree Graduates: Of those who graduated in the academic year 2003–2004, the following categories and numbers represent the post-graduate activities and employment of master's degree graduates: Enrolled in a psychology doctoral program (7), enrolled in another graduate/professional program (2), enrolled in a post-doctoral residency/fellowship (n/a), employed in independent practice (n/a), total from the above (master's) (9).
Doctoral Degree Graduates: Of those who graduated in the academic year 2003–2004, the following categories and numbers represent the post-graduate activities and employment of doctoral degree graduates: Enrolled in a psychology doctoral program (n/a), enrolled in a post-doctoral residency/fellowship (2), employed in independent practice (1), employed in an academic position at a university (2), employed in an academic position at a 2-year/4-year college (1), employed in business or industry (research/consulting) (1), employed in a community mental health/counseling center (2), total from the above (doctoral) (9).

Additional Information:
Orientation, Objectives, and Emphasis of Department: The graduate faculty maintain active research programs in cognition, developmental, ethology, gender, health, organizational, personality, phenomenology, psychobiology, psychometrics, sensation/perception, and social psychology. The MA program is appropriate for students wanting a master's degree as part of progress toward a doctorate, or for those who wish to complement a degree in a different field. The Experimental PhD program prepares students for academic/research careers and for careers involving the application of psychological principles as practitioners in industrial, forensic, organizational, and community settings. Areas of concentration include applied psychology, child development, cognition and consciousness, health psychology, phenomenology, and social/personality. The Clinical PhD program combines psychodynamic and research components, requiring exposure to a wide range of theoretical views and technical practices. Minors available are child development, health psychology, and social psychology. In order to foster appropriate breadth and interdisciplinary training, some cognate work outside the department of psychology is required of all doctoral students. The Counseling Program is designed to enable students to become behavioral scientists,

skilled in psychological research and its application. Students are trained to provide services to a wide variety of clients in numerous settings. Program objectives are to train doctoral-level counseling psychologists who have knowledge of, and competence in, (a) the foundation and discipline of psychology, (b) social science research and methodology, and (c) specific therapeutic and intervention skills related to being a counseling psychologist.

Special Facilities or Resources: Facilities include computer support in equipment and staff, human and animal laboratories, a psychology clinic for training and research, and a new university library with expanded serials holdings.

Information for Students With Physical Disabilities: See the following Web site for more information: http://ods.utk.edu/.

Application Information:
Send to: Ms. Connie J. Ogle, 312D Austin Peay Building, University of Tennessee, Knoxville, TN 37996-0900. Students are admitted in the Fall. The application deadline for both Clinical and Counseling PhD programs is January 15. The application deadline for the Experimental PhD is February 15. The application deadline for the master's program is March 15. *Fee:* $35. Applicants must submit two separate applications: (1) the Graduate School application together with the $35 application fee, and (2) the Psychology Department application. These forms are to be submitted to the offices indicated on the Psychology Department application. All application materials must be received by the respective program deadlines.

Tennessee, University of, Knoxville (2004 data)
Industrial and Organizational Psychology Program
Business Administration
408 Stokely Management Center
Knoxville, TN 37996-0545
Telephone: (865) 974-4843
Fax: (865) 974-3163
E-mail: *tladd@utk.edu*
Web: *http://bus.utk.edu/iopsyc/*

Department Information:
1964. Director: David J. Woehr. Number of Faculty: total–full-time 5; women–full-time 1.

Programs and Degrees Offered:
Listed in the following order: Program area, degree type (T if terminal Master's), number awarded 7/03–6/04. Industrial/Organizational PhD (Doctor of Philosophy) 4.

Student Applications/Admissions:
Student Applications
Industrial/Organizational PhD (Doctor of Philosophy)—Applications 2004–2005, 62. Total applicants accepted 2004–2005, 9. Openings 2005–2006, 3. The Median number of years required for completion of a degree are 5. The number of students enrolled full and part-time who were dismissed or voluntarily withdrew from this program area were 1.

Admissions Requirements:
Scores: Entries appear in this order: required test or GPA, minimum score (if required), median score of students entering

in 2003–2004. Doctoral Programs: GRE-V no minimum stated, 520; GRE-Q no minimum stated, 680; GRE-V+Q 1100, 1200; overall undergraduate GPA 3.5, 3.73; last 2 years GPA no minimum stated, 3.8; psychology GPA no minimum stated. *Other Criteria:* (importance of criteria rated low, medium, or high): GRE/MAT scores high, research experience medium, work experience low, extracurricular activity low, clinically related public service low, GPA high, letters of recommendation high, statement of goals and objectives high.

Student Characteristics: The following represents characteristics of students in 2004–2005 in all graduate psychology programs in the department: Female–full-time 17, part-time 0; Male–full-time 13, part-time 0; African American/Black–full-time 1, part-time 0; Hispanic/Latino(a)–full-time 0, part-time 0; Asian/Pacific Islander–full-time 1, part-time 0; American Indian/Alaska Native–full-time 0, part-time 0; Caucasian–full-time 0, part-time 0; Multi-ethnic–full-time 0, part-time 0; students subject to the Americans With Disabilities Act–full-time 0, part-time 0.

Financial Information/Assistance:
Tuition for Full-Time Study: *Doctoral:* State residents: per academic year $3,730; Nonstate residents: per academic year $11,266. Tuition is subject to change.

Financial Assistance:
First Year Students: Research assistantships available for first-year. Average amount paid per academic year: $10,260. Average number of hours worked per week: 15. Tuition remission given: full. Fellowships and scholarships available for first-year.
Advanced Students: Teaching assistantships available for advanced students. Average amount paid per academic year: $10,260. Average number of hours worked per week: 15. Tuition remission given: full. Research assistantships available for advanced students. Average amount paid per academic year: $10,260. Average number of hours worked per week: 15. Tuition remission given: full. Traineeships available for advanced students. Fellowships and scholarships available for advanced students. Tuition remission given: full.
Contact Information: Of all students currently enrolled full-time, 100% benefitted from one or more of the listed financial assistance programs.

Internships/Practica: An internship or practicum is required but these vary considerably.

Housing and Day Care: No on-campus housing is available. No on-campus day care facilities are available.

Employment of Department Graduates:
Master's Degree Graduates: Of those who graduated in the academic year 2003–2004, the following categories and numbers represent the post-graduate activities and employment of master's degree graduates: Enrolled in a post-doctoral residency/fellowship (n/a), employed in independent practice (n/a), total from the above (master's) (0).
Doctoral Degree Graduates: Of those who graduated in the academic year 2003–2004, the following categories and numbers represent the post-graduate activities and employment of doctoral degree graduates: Enrolled in a psychology doctoral program (n/a), employed in an academic position at a university (1), employed

in business or industry (research/consulting) (3), total from the above (doctoral) (4).

Additional Information:

Orientation, Objectives, and Emphasis of Department: The industrial/organizational program is designed to prepare students for personnel, managerial, and organizational research; for university teaching; and for consulting relationships with industry. The program emphasizes a scientist-practitioner model in applying and conducting research based on accepted theory found in classical and modern organization theory, organizational behavior, psychology, management, and statistics.

Special Facilities or Resources: Computing and Academic Services (CAS) provides computing facilities, services, and support for the university's teaching, research, public service, and administrative activities. Individual UNIX and Lotus Notes accounts are provided for students, faculty and staff for the duration of their affiliation with UTK at no charge. CAS maintains six staffed computing labs, 15 unstaffed labs, and supports computing installations in all residence halls. Training and documentation are also available through CAS. Statistical and mathematical consulting is available to all students, faculty, and staff. CAS operates the core mainframe and large-scale servers; equipment includes multiple systems from SUN, SGI, and IBM systems. In addition to university computing services and facilities, the Department of Management and the College of Business Administration provide students with microcomputers in student offices, which are networked to departmental printers and the Internet. The University Libraries own approximately 2 million volumes and subscribe to more than 11,000 periodicals and other serial titles. The Libraries' membership in the Association of Research Libraries reflects the University's emphasis on graduate instruction and research and the support of comprehensive collections of library materials on a permanent basis.

Application Information:

Send to: Department chair. Application available online. Students are admitted in the Fall, application deadline February 1. *Fee:* $35.

Vanderbilt University

Department of Psychology
111 21st Avenue South
Nashville, TN 37203-0009
Telephone: (615) 322-2874
Fax: (615) 343-8449
E-mail: *patricia.m.burns@vanderbilt.edu*
Web: *http://www.vanderbilt.edu*

Department Information:

1925. Acting Chair: Randolph Blake. Number of Faculty: total–full-time 28, part-time 3; women–full-time 7, part-time 2.

Programs and Degrees Offered:

Listed in the following order: Program area, degree type (T if terminal Master's), number awarded 7/03–6/04. Neuroscience PhD (Doctor of Philosophy) 1, Clinical Science PhD (Doctor of Philosophy) 0, Cognitive Science PhD (Doctor of Philosophy) 1.

APA Accreditation: Clinical PhD (Doctor of Philosophy).

Student Applications/Admissions:

Student Applications

Neuroscience PhD (Doctor of Philosophy)—Applications 2004–2005, 47. Total applicants accepted 2004–2005, 5. Number enrolled (new admits only) 2004–2005 full-time, 1. Openings 2005–2006, 4. The Median number of years required for completion of a degree are 6. The number of students enrolled full and part-time who were dismissed or voluntarily withdrew from this program area were 0. *Clinical Science PhD (Doctor of Philosophy)*—Applications 2004–2005, 105. Total applicants accepted 2004–2005, 6. Number enrolled (new admits only) 2004–2005 full-time, 1. Openings 2005–2006, 4. The number of students enrolled full and part-time who were dismissed or voluntarily withdrew from this program area were 0. *Cognitive Science PhD (Doctor of Philosophy)*—Applications 2004–2005, 39. Total applicants accepted 2004–2005, 9. Number enrolled (new admits only) 2004–2005 full-time, 2. Openings 2005–2006, 4. The Median number of years required for completion of a degree are 9. The number of students enrolled full and part-time who were dismissed or voluntarily withdrew from this program area were 0.

Admissions Requirements:

Scores: Entries appear in this order: required test or GPA, minimum score (if required), median score of students entering in 2003–2004. Master's Programs: Not applicable. Doctoral Programs: GRE-V 550, 605; GRE-Q 550, 695; GRE-V+Q 1100, 1300; GRE-Analytical 550, 685. All requirements are the same for all program areas.

Other Criteria: (importance of criteria rated low, medium, or high): GRE/MAT scores high, research experience high, work experience low, extracurricular activity low, clinically related public service low, GPA high, letters of recommendation high, interview high, statement of goals and objectives high. For additional information on admission requirements, go to: www.vanderbilt.edu.

Student Characteristics: The following represents characteristics of students in 2004–2005 in all graduate psychology programs in the department: Female–full-time 21, part-time 0; Male–full-time 18, part-time 0; African American/Black–full-time 1, part-time 0; Hispanic/Latino(a)–full-time 0, part-time 0; Asian/Pacific Islander–full-time 12, part-time 0; American Indian/Alaska Native–full-time 0, part-time 0; Caucasian–full-time 26, part-time 0; Multi-ethnic–full-time 0, part-time 0; students subject to the Americans With Disabilities Act–full-time 0, part-time 0.

Financial Information/Assistance:

Tuition for Full-Time Study: *Doctoral:* State residents: per academic year $29,112, $1,213 per credit hour; Nonstate residents: per academic year $29,112, $1,213 per credit hour. Tuition is subject to change.

Financial Assistance:

First Year Students: Teaching assistantships available for first-year. Average amount paid per academic year: $15,000. Average number of hours worked per week: 15. Apply by December 15. Tuition remission given: full. Research assistantships available for first-year. Average amount paid per academic year: $15,000. Average number of hours worked per week: 15. Apply by December 15. Tuition remission given: full. Traineeships available for first-year. Average amount paid per academic year: $20,772. Average number of hours worked per week: 15. Apply by December 15. Tuition remission given: full. Fellowships and scholarships available for first-year. Average amount paid per academic year: $15,000. Average number of hours worked per week: 15. Apply by December 31. Tuition remission given: full.

Advanced Students: Teaching assistantships available for advanced students. Average amount paid per academic year: $15,000. Average number of hours worked per week: 15. Apply by December 15. Tuition remission given: full. Research assistantships available for advanced students. Average amount paid per academic year: $15,000. Average number of hours worked per week: 15. Apply by December 15. Tuition remission given: full. Traineeships available for advanced students. Average amount paid per academic year: $15,000. Average number of hours worked per week: 15. Apply by December 15. Tuition remission given: full. Fellowships and scholarships available for advanced students. Average amount paid per academic year: $15,000. Average number of hours worked per week: 15. Apply by December 15. Tuition remission given: full.

Contact Information: Of all students currently enrolled full-time, 80% benefitted from one or more of the listed financial assistance programs. Application and information available online at: https://graduateapplications.vanderbilt.edu/admin_logon.asp.

Internships/Practica: We offer 18 different placements for students to do their practica. These include two VA Medical Centers; VU Child and Adolescent Psychiatric Hospital; VU Diabetes Center, VU Psychological and Counseling Center; Mobile Crisis Response Service; Public School System; State Prison; and Mental Health facilities for both children and adults. For those doctoral students for whom a professional internship is required prior to graduation, 1 applied in 2003–2004. Of those who applied, 1 was placed in internships listed by the Association of Psychology Postdoctoral and Internship Programs (APPIC); 1 was placed in APA accredited internships.

Housing and Day Care: On-campus housing is available. See the following Web site for more information: http://www.vanderbilt.edu/ResEd/4d_fam.html. On-campus day care facilities are available.

Employment of Department Graduates:

Master's Degree Graduates: Of those who graduated in the academic year 2003–2004, the following categories and numbers represent the post-graduate activities and employment of master's degree graduates: Enrolled in a post-doctoral residency/fellowship (n/a), employed in independent practice (n/a), total from the above (master's) (0).

Doctoral Degree Graduates: Of those who graduated in the academic year 2003–2004, the following categories and numbers represent the post-graduate activities and employment of doctoral degree graduates: Enrolled in a psychology doctoral program (n/a), enrolled in a post-doctoral residency/fellowship (1), employed in a hospital/medical center (1), total from the above (doctoral) (2).

Additional Information:

Orientation, Objectives, and Emphasis of Department: The department emphasizes the basic science of psychology. The faculty are particularly concerned with research on cognitive abilities, the lifetime development of cognitive and neural function pathologies (especially depression and emotional disorders), and the development, organization and the function of the nervous system as it relates to these abilities and maladies. A major goal of the department is the placement of its graduates in academic settings. The program leads to the PhD in the three general areas of clinical science, cognitive science, and neuroscience. In addition to formal training, students receive extensive research experience by working intensively with individual faculty members. This experience is felt to be one of the more vital aspects of the student's training. Vanderbilt offers doctoral training designed to familiarize students with current problems in psychology and to prepare them for a variety of careers in psychological science.

Special Facilities or Resources: The psychology building includes facilities for computer-based research and teaching, as well as extensive space and equipment for modern neuroscience research. Collaborative research programs are operative with the Vanderbilt School of Medicine, the School of Engineering, the Department of Electrical and Biomedical Engineering, and the Department of Psychology and Human Development (Peabody). The general library provides a large collection of books and journals in all areas of psychology.

Information for Students With Physical Disabilities: See the following Web site for more information: http://www.vanderbilt.edu/odc/.

Application Information:
Send to: Graduate School Office, Vanderbilt University, 411 Kirkland Hall, Nashville, TN 37240. Application available online. Students are admitted in the Fall, application deadline December 31. *Fee:* $0. Applications for fall 2005 were done online and no application fee was necessary. We plan to continue this.

Vanderbilt University
Human & Organizational Development/Community Research & Action
Peabody College of Education & Human Development
Box 90, Peabody Station, 230 Appleton Place
Nashville, TN 37203
Telephone: (615) 322-8484
Fax: (615) 343-2661
E-mail: *isaac.prilleltensky@vanderbilt.edu*
Web: *http://peabody.vanderbilt.edu/depts/hod/*

Department Information:
1999. Chairperson: Joseph Cunningham, EdD. Number of Faculty: total–full-time 14, part-time 9; women–full-time 6, part-time 7; minority–full-time 4; faculty subject to the Americans With Disabilities Act 1.

Programs and Degrees Offered:
Listed in the following order: Program area, degree type (T if terminal Master's), number awarded 7/03–6/04. Human Development Counseling Other 18, Community Research & Action PhD (Doctor of Philosophy) 0, Human, Organizational, & Community Devel Other 6.

Student Applications/Admissions:
Student Applications
Human Development Counseling (HDC) Other—Applications 2004–2005, 126. Total applicants accepted 2004–2005, 24.

Number enrolled (new admits only) 2004–2005 full-time, 18. Number enrolled (new admits only) 2004–2005 part-time, 0. Openings 2005–2006, 24. The Median number of years required for completion of a degree is 1. The number of students enrolled full and part-time who were dismissed or voluntarily withdrew from this program area were 3. *Community Research & Action (CRA) PhD (Doctor of Philosophy)*—Applications 2004–2005, 68. Total applicants accepted 2004–2005, 11. Number enrolled (new admits only) 2004–2005 full-time, 7. Number enrolled (new admits only) 2004–2005 part-time, 0. Openings 2005–2006, 9. The Median number of years required for completion of a degree are 3. The number of students enrolled full and part-time who were dismissed or voluntarily withdrew from this program area were 2. *Human, Organizational, & Community Devel (HOCD) Other*—Applications 2004–2005, 60. Total applicants accepted 2004–2005, 8. Number enrolled (new admits only) 2004–2005 full-time, 6. Number enrolled (new admits only) 2004–2005 part-time, 0. Openings 2005–2006, 10. The Median number of years required for completion of a degree is 1.

Admissions Requirements:

Scores: Entries appear in this order: required test or GPA, minimum score (if required), median score of students entering in 2003–2004. Master's Programs: GRE-V 500, 600; GRE-Q 500, 600; GRE-V+Q 1000, 1200; GRE-Analytical 500, 550; MAT 410, 500; overall undergraduate GPA 3.0, 3.5; last 2 years GPA 3.2, 3.6. The MEd in HDC will take either the MAT or GRE scores. A GPA of 3.0 is essential. Doctoral Programs: GRE-V 600, 700; GRE-Q 600, 600; GRE-V+Q 1200, 1300; GRE-Analytical 500, 600; overall undergraduate GPA 3.0, 3.6; last 2 years GPA 3.3, 3.7. There is now a change in the GRE requirement and the student who has never taken the GRE before should take the standard test along with a writing assessment. Anywhere from 3.5-6 scored on the test is an acceptable score. Scores are good for 5 years back from the date taken.

Other Criteria: (importance of criteria rated low, medium, or high): GRE/MAT scores high, research experience medium, work experience low, clinically related public service low, GPA high, letters of recommendation high, interview medium, statement of goals and objectives high. Research experience and GRE less important for Master's programs than for PhD. Clinically related service helpful for counseling program; not relevant to community master's and PhD. For additional information on admission requirements, go to: peabody.vanderbilt.edu.

Student Characteristics: The following represents characteristics of students in 2004–2005 in all graduate psychology programs in the department: Female–full-time 67, part-time 0; Male–full-time 15, part-time 0; African American/Black–full-time 7, part-time 0; Hispanic/Latino(a)–full-time 1, part-time 0; Asian/Pacific Islander–full-time 5, part-time 0; American Indian/Alaska Native–full-time 0, part-time 0; Caucasian–full-time 69, part-time 0; Multi-ethnic–full-time 0, part-time 0; students subject to the Americans With Disabilities Act–full-time 1, part-time 0.

Financial Information/Assistance:

Tuition for Full-Time Study: *Master's:* State residents: per academic year $15,570, $865 per credit hour; Nonstate residents: per academic year $15,570, $865 per credit hour. *Doctoral:* State residents: per academic year $21,834, $1,213 per credit hour; Nonstate residents: per academic year $21,834, $1,213 per credit hour. Tuition is subject to change. See the following Web site for updates and changes in tuition costs: www.vanderbilt.edu/catalogs.

Financial Assistance:

First Year Students: Teaching assistantships available for first-year. Average amount paid per academic year: $12,600. Average number of hours worked per week: 20. Apply by February 1. Tuition remission given: full. Research assistantships available for first-year. Average amount paid per academic year: $12,600. Average number of hours worked per week: 20. Apply by February 1. Tuition remission given: full. Traineeships available for first-year. Average amount paid per academic year: $20,772. Average number of hours worked per week: 20. Apply by February 1. Tuition remission given: full. Fellowships and scholarships available for first-year. Average amount paid per academic year: $20,000. Average number of hours worked per week: 20. Apply by February 1. Tuition remission given: full.

Advanced Students: Teaching assistantships available for advanced students. Average amount paid per academic year: $13,500. Average number of hours worked per week: 20. Apply by February 1. Tuition remission given: full. Research assistantships available for advanced students. Average amount paid per academic year: $13,500. Average number of hours worked per week: 20. Apply by February 1. Tuition remission given: full. Traineeships available for advanced students. Average amount paid per academic year: $20,772. Average number of hours worked per week: 20. Apply by February 1. Tuition remission given: full. Fellowships and scholarships available for advanced students. Average amount paid per academic year: $20,000. Average number of hours worked per week: 20. Apply by February 1. Tuition remission given: full.

Contact Information: Of all students currently enrolled full-time, 100% benefitted from one or more of the listed financial assistance programs. Application and information available online at: http://peabody.vanderbilt.edu/admissions/financial_aid/index.htm.

Internships/Practica: The HOCD and CRA programs require an 8-to-15-week internship. Possible sites: Mayor's Office/Metro Council/Planning Commission, local or international community development organization, regional planning or civic design center, youth development center, health care corporation, neighborhood health clinic, alcohol and drug treatment center, welfare or housing agency, state health and human service agencies, Vanderbilt Institute for Public Policy Studies (Centers for Mental Health Policy, Evaluation Research and Methodology, Child and Family Policy, Crime and Justice Policy, Environmental Management Studies, Health Policy, Psychotherapy Research and Policy, State and Local Policy). The HDC Program requires a one-year internship that provides opportunities to apply knowledge and skills primarily in the areas of Social Service Agencies, Mental Health Centers, Schools (K-12), Employee Assistance Programs, Other Human Services Delivery Programs.

Housing and Day Care: On-campus housing is available. See the following Web site for more information: http://www.vanderbilt.edu/ResEd/. On-campus day care facilities are available. See the following Web site for more information: http://www.vanderbilt.edu/HRS/wellness/childcare.htm.

Employment of Department Graduates:

Master's Degree Graduates: Of those who graduated in the academic year 2003–2004, the following categories and numbers represent the post-graduate activities and employment of master's degree graduates: Enrolled in a psychology doctoral program (0), enrolled in another graduate/professional program (0), enrolled in a post-doctoral residency/fellowship (n/a), employed in independent practice (n/a), employed in an academic position at a university (0), employed in an academic position at a 2-year/4-year college (0), employed in other positions at a higher education institution (0), employed in a professional position in a school system (12), employed in business or industry (research/consulting) (2), employed in business or industry (management) (0), employed in a government agency (research) (0), employed in a government agency (professional services) (0), employed in a community mental health/counseling center (10), employed in a hospital/medical center (0), still seeking employment (0), other employment position (0), total from the above (master's) (24).

Doctoral Degree Graduates: Of those who graduated in the academic year 2003–2004, the following categories and numbers represent the post-graduate activities and employment of doctoral degree graduates: Enrolled in a psychology doctoral program (n/a), total from the above (doctoral) (0).

Additional Information:

Orientation, Objectives, and Emphasis of Department: Although the vast majority of faculty in the department are psychologists, our orientation is interdisciplinary. There are three graduate programs, all oriented to helping diverse communities and individuals identify and develop their strengths: a long-standing Master's in Human Development Counseling (HDC), a Master's in Human, Organizational, and Community Development (HOCD), and a PhD in Community Research and Action (CRA). The latter two started in 2001. The HDC Program prepares students to meet the psychological needs of the normally developing population, who sometimes require professional help. Through a humanistic training model and a two-year curriculum, students develop a strong theoretical grounding in life-span human development, and school or community counseling. The HOCD program is for those who desire training for program administration/evaluation work in either public or private, international or domestic, community service, planning, or development organizations. The Doctoral Degree in Community Research and Action is designed to train action-researchers for academic or program/policy-related careers in applied community studies: i.e., community psychology, community development, prevention, community health/mental health, organizational change, and ethics. Coursework in qualitative and quantitative methods and evaluation research is required. The program builds on the one in Community Psychology previously in the Department of Psychology and Human Development and reflects the move in the field to become interdisciplinary.

Special Facilities or Resources: Peabody College has its own library, several computer centers, and nationally known research centers, including the Learning Sciences Institute and the Kennedy Center for Research on Human Development, mental retardation and other disabilities. Also on the beautiful and historic Peabody campus is the Vanderbilt Institute for Public Policy Studies (Centers for Mental Health Policy, Evaluation Research and Methodology, Child and Family Policy, Crime and Justice Policy, Environmental Management Studies, Health Policy, Psy-

chotherapy Research and Policy, State and Local Policy). Located in Nashville, the Tennessee state capital, opportunities abound for research and internships in state and local health and human service agencies and schools.

Information for Students With Physical Disabilities: See the following Web site for more information: http://www.vanderbilt.edu/odc/.

Application Information:

For PhD and MEd programs: Office of Graduate Admissions, Peabody College of Vanderbilt University, 230 Appleton Place, MSC 327, Peabody Station, Nashville, TN 37203, Phone: (615) 322-8410, E-mail: peabody.admissions@vanderbilt.edu, Web site: http://peabody.vanderbilt.edu/admin/studentsvc/forprosp.html. For further information on application procedures, write, call or email: Graduate Secretary Department of Human and Organizational Development, Peabody College of Vanderbilt University, Box 90, Peabody Station, 230 Appleton Place, Nashville, TN 37203, Phone: (615) 322-8484, Fax (615) 343-2661. E-mail: sherrie.lane@vanderbilt.edu. Application available online. URL of online application: http://peabody.vanderbilt.edu/admissions/apply_online.htm. Students are admitted in the Fall, application deadline December 31. *Fee:* $40. Application fee is waived when applying online.

Vanderbilt University, Peabody College
Department of Psychology and Human Development
Peabody #512
230 Appleton Place
Nashville, TN 37203-5701
Telephone: (615) 322-8141
Fax: (615) 343-9494
E-mail: *sharone.k.hall@vanderbilt.edu*
Web: *http://peabody.vanderbilt.edu/psychology*

Department Information:

1915. Chairperson: Kathleen V. Hoover-Dempsey. Number of Faculty: total–full-time 27, part-time 2; women–full-time 14, part-time 1.

Programs and Degrees Offered:

Listed in the following order: Program area, degree type (T if terminal Master's), number awarded 7/03–6/04. Clinical PhD (Doctor of Philosophy) 1, Cognitive PhD (Doctor of Philosophy) 1, Developmental PhD (Doctor of Philosophy) 1, Quantitative Methods PhD (Doctor of Philosophy) 0, Community PhD (Doctor of Philosophy) 0.

APA Accreditation: Clinical PhD (Doctor of Philosophy).

Student Applications/Admissions:
Student Applications
Clinical PhD (Doctor of Philosophy)—Applications 2004–2005, 289. Total applicants accepted 2004–2005, 12. Number enrolled (new admits only) 2004–2005 full-time, 6. Number enrolled (new admits only) 2004–2005 part-time, 0. Openings 2005–2006, 6. The Median number of years required for completion of a degree are 8.5. The number of students enrolled

full and part-time who were dismissed or voluntarily withdrew from this program area were 1. *Cognitive PhD (Doctor of Philosophy)*—Applications 2004–2005, 73. Total applicants accepted 2004–2005, 4. Number enrolled (new admits only) 2004–2005 full-time, 2. Number enrolled (new admits only) 2004–2005 part-time, 0. Openings 2005–2006, 2. The Median number of years required for completion of a degree are 8.5. The number of students enrolled full and part-time who were dismissed or voluntarily withdrew from this program area were 1. *Developmental PhD (Doctor of Philosophy)*—Applications 2004–2005, 72. Total applicants accepted 2004–2005, 2. Number enrolled (new admits only) 2004–2005 full-time, 0. Number enrolled (new admits only) 2004–2005 part-time, 0. Openings 2005–2006, 7. The Median number of years required for completion of a degree are 8.5. The number of students enrolled full and part-time who were dismissed or voluntarily withdrew from this program area were 2. *Quantitative Methods PhD (Doctor of Philosophy)*—Applications 2004–2005, 29. Total applicants accepted 2004–2005, 1. Number enrolled (new admits only) 2004–2005 full-time, 1. Number enrolled (new admits only) 2004–2005 part-time, 0. Openings 2005–2006, 3. The number of students enrolled full and part-time who were dismissed or voluntarily withdrew from this program area were 1. *Community PhD (Doctor of Philosophy)*—Applications 2004–2005, 0. Total applicants accepted 2004–2005, 0. The number of students enrolled full and part-time, who were dismissed or voluntarily withdrew from this program area were 0.

Admissions Requirements:

Scores: Entries appear in this order: required test or GPA, minimum score (if required), median score of students entering in 2003–2004. Doctoral Programs: GRE-V no minimum stated, 650; GRE-Q no minimum stated, 750; GRE-V+Q no minimum stated, 1390; overall undergraduate GPA no minimum stated, 3.7.

Other Criteria: (importance of criteria rated low, medium, or high): research experience high, work experience low, extracurricular activity low, clinically related public service low, letters of recommendation high, interview medium, statement of goals and objectives high. Interview is required by clinical only.

Student Characteristics: The following represents characteristics of students in 2004–2005 in all graduate psychology programs in the department: Female–full-time 41, part-time 0; Male–full-time 16, part-time 0; African American/Black–full-time 7, part-time 0; Hispanic/Latino(a)–full-time 1, part-time 0; Asian/Pacific Islander–full-time 4, part-time 0; American Indian/Alaska Native–full-time 0, part-time 0; Caucasian–full-time 39, part-time 0; Multi-ethnic–full-time 0, part-time 0; students subject to the Americans With Disabilities Act–full-time 0, part-time 0.

Financial Information/Assistance:

Financial Assistance:

First Year Students: Research assistantships available for first-year. Apply by December 15. Traineeships available for first-year. Apply by December 15. Fellowships and scholarships available for first-year. Apply by December 15.

Advanced Students: Teaching assistantships available for advanced students. Apply by December 15. Research assistantships available for advanced students. Apply by December 15. Traineeships available for advanced students. Apply by De-

cember 15. Fellowships and scholarships available for advanced students. Apply by December 15.

Contact Information: Of all students currently enrolled full-time, 85% benefitted from one or more of the listed financial assistance programs. Application and information available online at: https://graduateapplications.vanderbilt.edu/.

Internships/Practica: For those doctoral students for whom a professional internship is required prior to graduation, 3 applied in 2003–2004. Of those who applied, 3 were placed in internships listed by the Association of Psychology Postdoctoral and Internship Programs (APPIC); 3 were placed in APA accredited internships.

Housing and Day Care: No on-campus housing is available. No on-campus day care facilities are available.

Employment of Department Graduates:

Master's Degree Graduates: Of those who graduated in the academic year 2003–2004, the following categories and numbers represent the post-graduate activities and employment of master's degree graduates: Enrolled in a post-doctoral residency/fellowship (n/a), employed in independent practice (n/a), total from the above (master's) (0).

Doctoral Degree Graduates: Of those who graduated in the academic year 2003–2004, the following categories and numbers represent the post-graduate activities and employment of doctoral degree graduates: Enrolled in a psychology doctoral program (n/a), enrolled in a post-doctoral residency/fellowship (2), do not know (1), total from the above (doctoral) (3).

Additional Information:

Orientation, Objectives, and Emphasis of Department: The Department of Psychology and Human Development offers a rigorous program of academic and research training. Students become involved immediately in scholarly inquiry under the mentorship of a faculty advisor. The department has a clear focus on child and adolescent development, and on the persons and social systems (particularly families and schools) that influence this development. Major areas of inquiry concentrate in the following: cognitive and social development, including information processing, language development, problem solving, motivation, memory development, social referencing, motor skill development, and perceptual and spatial development in both mentally retarded and non-retarded children; developmental psychopathology, including such issues as social-cognitive factors in childhood depression and antisocial behavior in children and adolescents; and behavioral pediatrics, one major focus of which is on coping with chronic childhood illness. Another major research focus is on basic and applied social psychology, including program evaluation, victimization, health psychology, and the relationships between individuals and organizations. Other areas of interest include the philosophical foundations of psychology and mental health policy, with particular interest in the ethical dimensions of intervention. Clearly, all of these research areas are integrated among clinical, developmental, cognitive, and social domains, and we attempt to recruit students who will take advantage of the unique resources available here. There is extensive scholarly collaboration between the Peabody program and the program in Vanderbilt's College of Arts and Science. Students may work with faculty and take courses in both departments.

Special Facilities or Resources: There are exceptional resources available in the Peabody/Vanderbilt community. Members of the faculty are housed in two modern buildings with laboratory and computer facilities. The University has a state-of-the-art VAX 8800 mainframe, available to students. The library system contains over 1.7 million volumes, with particular strength in education- and psychology-related publications. In addition, most members of the department's faculty are also research scholars in the John F. Kennedy Center for Research on Education and Human Development, a major national behavioral research center located on the Peabody campus. Facilities within the Kennedy Center include the Family and Child Study Center and the Susan Gray School, which serves developmentally delayed and at-risk children. There are opportunities for research collaboration with the Vanderbilt Institute for Public Policy Studies (particularly its Center for the Study of Children and Families and its Health Policy Center), as well as with such Medical Center departments as adolescent medicine, child and adolescent psychiatry, and the comprehensive developmental evaluation center. There is a university counseling center and an ample array of community agencies available for practicum experiences.

Application Information:
Send to: Psychology and Human Development, c/o The Graduate School, 411 Kirkland Hall, Vanderbilt University, Nashville, TN 37240. Application available online. URL of online application: https://graduateapplications.vanderbilt.edu/. Students are admitted in the Fall, application deadline December 15. *Fee:* $40. Apply online at zero ($0) cost.

Abilene Christian University

Department of Psychology
College of Arts & Sciences
ACU Box 28011
Abilene, TX 79699
Telephone: (325) 674-2310
Fax: (325) 674-6968
E-mail: *robert.mckelvain@psyc.acu.edu*
Web: *http://www.acu.edu/psychology*

Department Information:

1968. Chair: Robert McKelvain. Number of Faculty: total–full-time 9, part-time 3; women–full-time 1, part-time 2; minority–full-time 1.

Programs and Degrees Offered:

Listed in the following order: Program area, degree type (T if terminal Master's), number awarded 7/03–6/04. School Psychology MA/MS (Master of Arts/Science) (T) 3, Clinical Psychology MA/MS (Master of Arts/Science) (T) 9, Counseling Psychology MA/MS (Master of Arts/Science) (T) 5.

Student Applications/Admissions:

Student Applications

School Psychology MA/MS (Master of Arts/Science)—Applications 2004–2005, 8. Total applicants accepted 2004–2005, 7. Openings 2005–2006, 10. The Median number of years required for completion of a degree are 3. The number of students enrolled full and part-time who were dismissed or voluntarily withdrew from this program area were 0. *Clinical Psychology MA/MS (Master of Arts/Science)*—Applications 2004–2005, 24. Total applicants accepted 2004–2005, 21. Openings 2005–2006, 15. The Median number of years required for completion of a degree are 2. The number of students enrolled full and part-time who were dismissed or voluntarily withdrew from this program area were 0. *Counseling Psychology MA/MS (Master of Arts/Science)*—Applications 2004–2005, 0. Total applicants accepted 2004–2005, 0. The Median number of years required for completion of a degree are 2. The number of students enrolled full and part-time who were dismissed or voluntarily withdrew from this program area were 0.

Admissions Requirements:

Scores: Entries appear in this order: required test or GPA, minimum score (if required), median score of students entering in 2003–2004. Master's Programs: GRE-V+Q 1000; overall undergraduate GPA 3.00.

Other Criteria: (importance of criteria rated low, medium, or high): GRE/MAT scores high, research experience high, work experience medium, extracurricular activity medium, clinically related public service medium, GPA high, letters of recommendation high, statement of goals and objectives high.

Student Characteristics: The following represents characteristics of students in 2004–2005 in all graduate psychology programs in the department: Female–full-time 21, part-time 1; Male–full-time 14, part-time 1; African American/Black–full-time 0, part-time 0; Hispanic/Latino(a)–full-time 3, part-time 0; Asian/Pacific Islander–part-time 0; American Indian/Alaska Native–full-time 0, part-time 0; Caucasian–full-time 32, part-time 0; students subject to the Americans With Disabilities Act–full-time 0, part-time 0.

Financial Information/Assistance:

Tuition for Full-Time Study: *Master's:* State residents: $397 per credit hour; Nonstate residents: $397 per credit hour.

Financial Assistance:

First Year Students: Teaching assistantships available for first-year. Average amount paid per academic year: $2,500. Average number of hours worked per week: 10. Apply by April 15. Tuition remission given: partial. Research assistantships available for first-year. Average amount paid per academic year: $2,500. Average number of hours worked per week: 10. Apply by April 15. Tuition remission given: partial. Fellowships and scholarships available for first-year. Average amount paid per academic year: $1,000. Average number of hours worked per week: 0.

Advanced Students: Teaching assistantships available for advanced students. Average amount paid per academic year: $2,500. Average number of hours worked per week: 10. Apply by April 15. Tuition remission given: partial. Research assistantships available for advanced students. Average amount paid per academic year: $2,500. Average number of hours worked per week: 10. Apply by April 15. Tuition remission given: partial.

Contact Information: Of all students currently enrolled full-time, 80% benefitted from one or more of the listed financial assistance programs.

Internships/Practica: Full-time paid internships are available for students in the MS in School Psychology. Students in the counseling and clinical programs do practica in a variety of community agencies, health care, and school settings.

Housing and Day Care: On-campus housing is available. No on-campus day care facilities are available.

Employment of Department Graduates:

Master's Degree Graduates: Of those who graduated in the academic year 2003–2004, the following categories and numbers represent the post-graduate activities and employment of master's degree graduates: Enrolled in a post-doctoral residency/fellowship (n/a), employed in independent practice (n/a), total from the above (master's) (0).

Doctoral Degree Graduates: Of those who graduated in the academic year 2003–2004, the following categories and numbers represent the post-graduate activities and employment of doctoral degree graduates: Enrolled in a psychology doctoral program (n/a), total from the above (doctoral) (0).

Additional Information:

Orientation, Objectives, and Emphasis of Department: The MS in School Psychology is approved by the National Association of School Psychologists. The department has two objectives for its graduate programs: 1) prepare capable students for doctoral study in psychology; 2) prepare students to be effective in psychological assessment and intervention. Programs emphasize short-term cognitive-behavioral strategies with sound empirical support and thorough training in both cognitive and personality assessment. Students may focus on either adult or child and adolescent clients. Within the master's degree students may also pursue a Graduate Certificate in Conflict Resolution. Faculty share and challenge students to explore the implications and application of a Christian worldview.

Special Facilities or Resources: An explicit goal of the program is to prepare students with research tools and experience for the pursuit of doctoral study in psychology through research classes and the master's thesis. On-going collaboration with the University Counseling Center provides clinical and counseling research opportunities.

Application Information:
Send to: ACU Graduate School, ACU Box 29140, Abilene, TX 79699. Students are admitted in the Fall, application deadline April 15; Spring, application deadline November 1; Summer, application deadline March 1. *Fee:* $50.

Angelo State University
Department of Psychology and Sociology
2601 West Avenue North
San Angelo, TX 76909
Telephone: (325) 942-2068
Fax: (325) 942-2290
E-mail: *Bill.Davidson@angelo.edu*
Web: *http://www.angelo.edu/dept/psysoc*

Department Information:
1983. Department Head: William B. Davidson. Number of Faculty: total–full-time 11, part-time 6; women–full-time 2, part-time 4; minority–full-time 2, part-time 1.

Programs and Degrees Offered:
Listed in the following order: Program area, degree type (T if terminal Master's), number awarded 7/03–6/04. Counseling MA/MS (Master of Arts/Science) (T) 12, General MA/MS (Master of Arts/Science) (T) 2, Industrial/ Organizational MA/MS (Master of Arts/Science) (T) 3.

Student Applications/Admissions:
Student Applications
Counseling MA/MS (*Master of Arts/Science*)—Applications 2004–2005, 23. Total applicants accepted 2004–2005, 19. Number enrolled (new admits only) 2004–2005 full-time, 2. Number enrolled (new admits only) 2004–2005 part-time, 5. Total enrolled 2004–2005 full-time, 7, part-time, 16. Openings 2005–2006, 10. The Median number of years required for completion of a degree are 2. The number of students enrolled full and part-time who were dismissed or voluntarily withdrew from this program area were 0. General MA/MS (*Master of Arts/Science*)—Applications 2004–2005, 8. Total applicants accepted 2004–2005, 7. Number enrolled (new admits only) 2004–2005 full-time, 4. Number enrolled (new admits only) 2004–2005 part-time, 1. Total enrolled 2004–2005 full-time, 6, part-time, 1. Openings 2005–2006, 5. The Median number

of years required for completion of a degree are 2. The number of students enrolled full and part-time who were dismissed or voluntarily withdrew from this program area were 0. *Industrial/ Organizational MA/MS (Master of Arts/Science)*—Applications 2004–2005, 10. Total applicants accepted 2004–2005, 10. Number enrolled (new admits only) 2004–2005 full-time, 5. Number enrolled (new admits only) 2004–2005 part-time, 3. Total enrolled 2004–2005 full-time, 12, part-time, 5. Openings 2005–2006, 10. The Median number of years required for completion of a degree are 2. The number of students enrolled full and part-time who were dismissed or voluntarily withdrew from this program area were 0.

Admissions Requirements:
Scores: Entries appear in this order: required test or GPA, minimum score (if required), median score of students entering in 2003–2004. Master's Programs: GRE-V 450; GRE-Q 450; GRE-Analytical 450; overall undergraduate GPA 2.75.
Other Criteria: (importance of criteria rated low, medium, or high): GRE/MAT scores high, research experience low, work experience low, GPA high, statement of goals and objectives medium.

Student Characteristics: The following represents characteristics of students in 2004–2005 in all graduate psychology programs in the department: Female–full-time 17, part-time 18; Male–full-time 8, part-time 4; African American/Black–full-time 1, part-time 0; Hispanic/Latino(a)–full-time 1, part-time 2; Asian/Pacific Islander–full-time 0, part-time 0; American Indian/Alaska Native–full-time 0, part-time 0; Caucasian–full-time 23, part-time 20; Multi-ethnic–full-time 0, part-time 0; students subject to the Americans With Disabilities Act–full-time 0, part-time 0.

Financial Information/Assistance:
Financial Assistance:
First Year Students: Research assistantships available for first-year. Average amount paid per academic year: $5,255. Average number of hours worked per week: 17. Apply by April 15. Fellowships and scholarships available for first-year. Average amount paid per academic year: $2,300. Apply by February 1.
Advanced Students: Teaching assistantships available for advanced students. Average amount paid per academic year: $9,856. Average number of hours worked per week: 20. Apply by April 15. Fellowships and scholarships available for advanced students. Average amount paid per academic year: $2,300. Apply by February 1.
Contact Information: Of all students currently enrolled full-time, 36% benefitted from one or more of the listed financial assistance programs. Application and information available online at: http://www.angelo.edu/forms/pdf/applgradasstTA.pdf.

Internships/Practica: Practicum opportunities are available in many local public and private mental health facilities and also in local corporate entities.

Housing and Day Care: On-campus housing is available. See the following Web site for more information: www.angelo.edu. No on-campus day care facilities are available.

Employment of Department Graduates:
Master's Degree Graduates: Of those who graduated in the academic year 2003–2004, the following categories and numbers

represent the post-graduate activities and employment of master's degree graduates: Enrolled in a post-doctoral residency/fellowship (n/a), employed in independent practice (n/a), total from the above (master's) (0).

Doctoral Degree Graduates: Of those who graduated in the academic year 2003–2004, the following categories and numbers represent the post-graduate activities and employment of doctoral degree graduates: Enrolled in a psychology doctoral program (n/a), total from the above (doctoral) (0).

Additional Information:

Orientation, Objectives, and Emphasis of Department: The department emphasizes personalized training, small class sizes, and a balance between research skills and practitioner skills.

Special Facilities or Resources: The department is equipped with a state-of-the-art psychology laboratory and a microcomputer laboratory.

Application Information:
Send to: Office of the Graduate Dean, P.O. Box 11025, ASU. Students are admitted in the Fall, application deadline July 15; Spring, application deadline November 15; Summer, application deadline April 15. *Fee:* $25.

Argosy University/Dallas
Clinical Psychology
8080 Park Lane, Suite 400A
Dallas, TX 75231
Telephone: (214) 890-9900
Fax: (214) 696-3900
E-mail: *vramos@argosyu.edu*
Web: *http://www.argosyu.edu (see campuses)*

Department Information:
2002. Chairperson: Vincent Ramos, PhD Number of Faculty: total–full-time 9; women–full-time 4; minority–full-time 3; faculty subject to the Americans With Disabilities Act 1.

Programs and Degrees Offered:
Listed in the following order: Program area, degree type (T if terminal Master's), number awarded 7/03–6/04. Clinical Psychology PsyD (Doctor of Psychology), Clinical Psychology MA/MS (Master of Arts/Science) (T), Professional Counseling MA/MS (Master of Arts/Science) (T).

Student Applications/Admissions:

Student Applications
Clinical Psychology PsyD (Doctor of Psychology)—Applications 2004–2005, 109. Total applicants accepted 2004–2005, 78. Number enrolled (new admits only) 2004–2005 full-time, 50. Number enrolled (new admits only) 2004–2005 part-time, 16. Total enrolled 2004–2005 full-time, 119, part-time, 40. Openings 2005–2006, 70. The number of students enrolled full and part-time who were dismissed or voluntarily withdrew from this program area were 4. *Clinical Psychology MA/MS (Master of Arts/Science)*—Applications 2004–2005, 5. Total applicants accepted 2004–2005, 1. Number enrolled (new admits only) 2004–2005 full-time, 5. Number enrolled (new admits only) 2004–2005 part-time, 2. Total enrolled 2004–2005 full-time, 9, part-time, 6. Openings 2005–2006, 10. The number of students enrolled full and part-time who were dismissed or voluntarily withdrew from this program area were 0. *Professional Counseling MA/MS (Master of Arts/Science)*—Applications 2004–2005, 97. Total applicants accepted 2004–2005, 65. Number enrolled (new admits only) 2004–2005 full-time, 15. Number enrolled (new admits only) 2004–2005 part-time, 24. Total enrolled 2004–2005 full-time, 103, part-time, 58. Openings 2005–2006, 60. The number of students enrolled full and part-time who were dismissed or voluntarily withdrew from this program area were 10.

Admissions Requirements:
Scores: Entries appear in this order: required test or GPA, minimum score (if required), median score of students entering in 2003–2004. Master's Programs: last 2 years GPA 3.0; psychology GPA 3.0. Doctoral Programs: last 2 years GPA 3.25; psychology GPA 3.25.
Other Criteria: (importance of criteria rated low, medium, or high): research experience medium, work experience medium, extracurricular activity medium, clinically related public service medium, GPA high, letters of recommendation high, interview high, statement of goals and objectives high.

Student Characteristics: The following represents characteristics of students in 2004–2005 in all graduate psychology programs in the department: Female–full-time 195, part-time 86; Male–full-time 36, part-time 18; African American/Black–full-time 71, part-time 48; Hispanic/Latino(a)–full-time 44, part-time 12; Asian/Pacific Islander–full-time 5, part-time 4; American Indian/Alaska Native–full-time 1, part-time 3; Caucasian–full-time 110, part-time 37; Multi-ethnic–full-time 0, part-time 0; students subject to the Americans With Disabilities Act–full-time 1, part-time 0.

Financial Information/Assistance:
Tuition for Full-Time Study: *Master's:* State residents: $475 per credit hour; Nonstate residents: $475 per credit hour. *Doctoral:* State residents: $750 per credit hour; Nonstate residents: $750 per credit hour. Tuition is subject to change. Tuition costs vary by program. See the following Web site for updates and changes in tuition costs: http://www.argosyu.edu.

Financial Assistance:
First Year Students: Fellowships and scholarships available for first-year. Average amount paid per academic year: $500. Apply by March 15.
Advanced Students: Fellowships and scholarships available for advanced students. Average amount paid per academic year: $500. Apply by March 15.
Contact Information: Of all students currently enrolled full-time, 14% benefitted from one or more of the listed financial assistance programs. Application and information available online at: http://www.argosyu.edu.

Internships/Practica: No information provided.

Housing and Day Care: No on-campus housing is available. No on-campus day care facilities are available.

Employment of Department Graduates:

Master's Degree Graduates: Of those who graduated in the academic year 2003–2004, the following categories and numbers represent the post-graduate activities and employment of master's degree graduates: Enrolled in a post-doctoral residency/fellowship (n/a), employed in independent practice (n/a), total from the above (master's) (0).

Doctoral Degree Graduates: Of those who graduated in the academic year 2003–2004, the following categories and numbers represent the post-graduate activities and employment of doctoral degree graduates: Enrolled in a psychology doctoral program (n/a), total from the above (doctoral) (0).

Additional Information:

Orientation, Objectives, and Emphasis of Department: Current emphasis in all our graduate programs is a practitioner-scholar model with diversity integrated within all coursework and practical experience. Most teaching faculty have 10+ years of teaching, those with fewer years of teaching experience have notable clinical experiences to draw upon. All faculty have doctoral level education, with specialities in diversity, testing and assessment, psychodynamic psychotherapy, health psychology, art therapy, exceptional children, substance abuse, and forensics. Theoretical orientations range from faith-based and client-centered to psychoanalytic and cognitive-behavioral.

Information for Students With Physical Disabilities: See the following Web site for more information: www.argosyu.edu select Dallas campus.

Application Information:

Send to: Admissions Office, Argosy University, Dallas, 8080 Park Lane, Suite 400A, Dallas, TX 75231. Application available online. Students are admitted in the Fall, Winter, Spring, and Summer. Programs have rolling admissions. *Fee:* $50.

Baylor University

Department of Psychology and Neuroscience, PhD Program in Neuroscience
Arts and Sciences
One Bear Place
Waco, TX 76798-7334
Telephone: (254) 710-2961
Fax: (254) 710-3033
E-mail: *M-Rudd@baylor.edu*
Web: *http://www.baylor.edu/~Psychology*

Department Information:

1950. Chairperson: David Rudd, PhD, ABPP. Number of Faculty: total–full-time 15, part-time 9; women–full-time 3, part-time 8; minority–full-time 2, part-time 1.

Programs and Degrees Offered:

Listed in the following order: Program area, degree type (T if terminal Master's), number awarded 7/03–6/04. Clinical Psychology PsyD (Doctor of Psychology) 10, Neuroscience PhD (Doctor of Philosophy) 1.

APA Accreditation: Clinical PsyD (Doctor of Psychology).

Student Applications/Admissions:

Student Applications

Clinical Psychology PsyD (Doctor of Psychology)—Applications 2004–2005, 139. Total applicants accepted 2004–2005, 11. Openings 2005–2006, 6. The Median number of years required for completion of a degree are 4. The number of students enrolled full and part-time who were dismissed or voluntarily withdrew from this program area were 1. *Neuroscience PhD (Doctor of Philosophy)*—Applications 2004–2005, 10. Total applicants accepted 2004–2005, 4. Number enrolled (new admits only) 2004–2005 full-time, 9. Openings 2005–2006, 5. The Median number of years required for completion of a degree are 5. The number of students enrolled full and part-time who were dismissed or voluntarily withdrew from this program area were 1.

Admissions Requirements:

Scores: Entries appear in this order: required test or GPA, minimum score (if required), median score of students entering in 2003–2004. Doctoral Programs: GRE-V no minimum stated; GRE-Q no minimum stated; GRE-V+Q no minimum stated; GRE-Analytical no minimum stated; overall undergraduate GPA 2.80.

Other Criteria: (importance of criteria rated low, medium, or high): GRE/MAT scores high, research experience high, work experience medium, extracurricular activity medium, clinically related public service medium, GPA high, letters of recommendation high, interview high, statement of goals and objectives medium.

Student Characteristics: The following represents characteristics of students in 2004–2005 in all graduate psychology programs in the department: Female–full-time 36, part-time 0; Male–full-time 16, part-time 0; African American/Black–full-time 2, part-time 0; Hispanic/Latino(a)–full-time 4, part-time 0; Asian/Pacific Islander–full-time 1, part-time 0; American Indian/Alaska Native–full-time 0, part-time 0; Caucasian–full-time 0, part-time 0; students subject to the Americans With Disabilities Act–full-time 0, part-time 0.

Financial Information/Assistance:

Tuition for Full-Time Study: *Doctoral:* State residents: $794 per credit hour; Nonstate residents: $794 per credit hour. Tuition is subject to change.

Financial Assistance:

First Year Students: Teaching assistantships available for first-year. Average amount paid per academic year: $15,000. Average number of hours worked per week: 20. Apply by January 15. Tuition remission given: partial. Research assistantships available for first-year. Average amount paid per academic year: $15,000. Average number of hours worked per week: 20. Apply by January 15. Tuition remission given: partial. Traineeships available for first-year. Average amount paid per academic year: $15,000. Average number of hours worked per week: 20. Apply by January 15. Tuition remission given: partial. Fellowships and scholarships available for first-year. Tuition remission given: partial.

Advanced Students: Teaching assistantships available for advanced students. Average amount paid per academic year: $15,000. Average number of hours worked per week: 20. Apply by January 15. Tuition remission given: partial. Research assistantships available for advanced students. Average amount paid per academic year: $15,000. Average number of hours worked per week: 20. Apply by January 15. Tuition remission given: partial. Traineeships available for advanced students. Average amount paid per academic year: $15,000. Average number of hours worked per week: 20. Apply by January 15. Tuition remission given: partial. Fellowships and scholarships available for advanced students. Tuition remission given: partial.

Contact Information: Of all students currently enrolled full-time, 100% benefitted from one or more of the listed financial assistance programs.

Internships/Practica: The PsyD Program incorporates an extensive practicum program with placements available in 16 community agencies and treatment facilities. Of our graduates over the last 11 years, 105 of 107 have obtained APA-accredited internships. For those doctoral students for whom a professional internship is required prior to graduation, 12 applied in 2003–2004. Of those who applied, 12 were placed in internships listed by the Association of Psychology Postdoctoral and Internship Programs (APPIC); 12 were placed in APA accredited internships.

Housing and Day Care: No on-campus housing is available. On-campus day care facilities are available: Piper Child Development Center, 315 Washington Avenue, Waco, TX 76701.

Employment of Department Graduates:
Master's Degree Graduates: Of those who graduated in the academic year 2003–2004, the following categories and numbers represent the post-graduate activities and employment of master's degree graduates: Enrolled in a post-doctoral residency/fellowship (n/a), employed in independent practice (n/a), total from the above (master's) (0).
Doctoral Degree Graduates: Of those who graduated in the academic year 2003–2004, the following categories and numbers represent the post-graduate activities and employment of doctoral degree graduates: Enrolled in a psychology doctoral program (n/a), enrolled in a post-doctoral residency/fellowship (2), employed in independent practice (6), employed in an academic position at a university (0), employed in a community mental health/counseling center (2), employed in a hospital/medical center (2), still seeking employment (0), total from the above (doctoral) (12).

Additional Information:
Orientation, Objectives, and Emphasis of Department: The department offers a broad range of courses in the areas of clinical psychology and behavioral and molecular clinical neuroscience. The Doctor of Psychology (PsyD) program has the longest history of accreditation by the American Psychological Association. The PsyD program emphasizes the development of professional competencies based on current research and scholarship in clinical psychology. The program's emphasis on professional practice is reflected in the fact that extensive practicum experience intergrated with concurrent coursework is required of all students. A formal research dissertation is not required. The goal of Baylor's PsyD Program is to develop professional psychologists with the conceptual and clinical competencies necessary to deliver psychological services in a manner that is effective and responsive to individual and societal needs both now and in the future. Extensive training is provided in laboratory research and design for neuroscience students. PhD (neuroscience) students are expected to acquire sufficient knowledge and expertise to permit them to work as

independent scholars at the frontier of their field upon graduation, with most graduates pursuing academically oriented careers.

Special Facilities or Resources: The department has a number of well-equipped research laboratories. PhD program: Computer-controlled programmable laboratory in memory and cognition; complete facilities for research on animal learning and behavior (including animal colony); developmental psychobiology laboratory, with facilities for behavioral and pharmacological research, including teratological studies; inhalation chambers for administration of ethanol (and other substances). Single-subject brain-recording (EEG) and electron microscopy facilities are available. The Department also houses a community clinic that facilitates the clinical training and related research activities for PsyD students.

Application Information:
Send to: Graduate Coordinator, Department of Psychology, Baylor University, P.O. Box 97334, Waco, TX 76798-7334. Students are admitted in the Fall, application deadline January 15. Neuroscience January 15, Clinical Psychology January 15. *Fee:* $25.

Houston Baptist University
Psychology Department
College of Education and Behavioral Sciences
7502 Fondren Road
Houston, TX 77074
Telephone: (281) 649-3000 2436
Fax: (281) 649-3361
E-mail: *aowen@hbu.edu*

Department Information:
1985. Chair, Department of Behavioral Sciences: Ann Owen, PhD. Number of Faculty: total–full-time 6, part-time 6; women–full-time 4, part-time 5; minority–full-time 1, part-time 2.

Programs and Degrees Offered:
Listed in the following order: Program area, degree type (T if terminal Master's), number awarded 7/03–6/04. Master of Arts in Psychology MA/MS (Master of Arts/Science) (T) 18, Christian Counseling MA/MS (Master of Arts/Science) (T) 0, Master of Education - Counseling Other 0.

Student Applications/Admissions:
Student Applications
Psychology MA/MS (Master of Arts/Science)—Applications 2004–2005, 48. Total applicants accepted 2004–2005, 38. Number enrolled (new admits only) 2004–2005 full-time, 28. Number enrolled (new admits only) 2004–2005 part-time, 5. Total enrolled 2004–2005 full-time, 73, part-time, 35. Openings 2005–2006, 45. The Median number of years required for completion of a degree are 2. The number of students enrolled full and part-time who were dismissed or voluntarily withdrew from this program area were 1. *Christian Counseling MA/MS (Master of Arts/Science) (MACC)*—Applications 2004–2005, 33. Total applicants accepted 2004–2005, 9. Number enrolled (new admits only) 2004–2005 full-time, 3. Number enrolled (new admits only) 2004–2005 part-time, 1. Total enrolled 2004–2005 full-time, 15, part-time, 7. Openings 2005–2006,

30. The Median number of years required for completion of a degree are 2. The number of students enrolled full and part-time who were dismissed or voluntarily withdrew from this program area were 0. *Master of Education - Counseling Other*—Applications 2004–2005, 3. Total applicants accepted 2004–2005, 1. Number enrolled (new admits only) 2004–2005 full-time, 1. Number enrolled (new admits only) 2004–2005 part-time, 0. Openings 2005–2006, 10. The Median number of years required for completion of a degree are 2. The number of students enrolled full and part-time who were dismissed or voluntarily withdrew from this program area were 0.

Admissions Requirements:
Scores: Entries appear in this order: required test or GPA, minimum score (if required), median score of students entering in 2003–2004. Master's Programs: GRE-V 400; GRE-Q no minimum stated; GRE-V+Q 850, 900; overall undergraduate GPA 2.8.
Other Criteria: (importance of criteria rated low, medium, or high): GRE/MAT scores high, GPA high, letters of recommendation medium, statement of goals and objectives medium.

Student Characteristics: The following represents characteristics of students in 2004–2005 in all graduate psychology programs in the department: Female–full-time 30, part-time 15; Male–full-time 61, part-time 27; African American/Black–full-time 0, part-time 0; Hispanic/Latino(a)–full-time 0, part-time 0; Asian/Pacific Islander–full-time 0, part-time 0; American Indian/Alaska Native–full-time 0, part-time 0; Caucasian–full-time 0, part-time 0.

Financial Information/Assistance:
Tuition for Full-Time Study: *Master's:* State residents: $1,200 per credit hour; Nonstate residents: $1,200 per credit hour. Tuition is subject to change.

Financial Assistance:
First Year Students: No information provided.
Advanced Students: No information provided.
Contact Information: Of all students currently enrolled full-time, 0% benefitted from one or more of the listed financial assistance programs.

Internships/Practica: Students complete their practicum requirements (450 clock hours supervised by a licensed psychologist) in area hospitals, social service agencies, schools and counseling centers. MACC students complete their practica in church or Christian counseling centers. LSSP students complete a 12-hour internship in a school setting.

Housing and Day Care: On-campus housing is available. Husky Village, (281) 649-3100. No on-campus day care facilities are available.

Employment of Department Graduates:
Master's Degree Graduates: Of those who graduated in the academic year 2003–2004, the following categories and numbers represent the post-graduate activities and employment of master's degree graduates: Enrolled in a post-doctoral residency/fellowship (n/a), employed in independent practice (n/a), total from the above (master's) (0).
Doctoral Degree Graduates: Of those who graduated in the academic year 2003–2004, the following categories and numbers

represent the post-graduate activities and employment of doctoral degree graduates: Enrolled in a psychology doctoral program (n/a), total from the above (doctoral) (0).

Additional Information:
Orientation, Objectives, and Emphasis of Department: The master's program follows the scientist-practitioner model of training. Some students become psychological associates, some seek doctoral training, and a large number add the 12 hours required to become licensed specialists in school psychology. The majority pursue licensure as professional counselors.

Special Facilities or Resources: The department has a full time faculty of dedicated, teaching professionals. All graduate faculty hold terminal degrees. Two are licensed clinical psychologists, one is an LPC-S, one is an LPA, and two are social psychologists. All adjuncts have terminal degrees and many are practicing clinicians. Computer facilities are available for use in research and statistical analyses.

Application Information:
Send to: Master of Arts in Psychology, Houston Baptist University, 7502 Fondren, Houston, TX 77074. Master of Arts in Christian Counseling, Houston Baptist University, 7502 Fondren, Houston, TX 77074. Students are admitted in the Fall, application deadline August 1; Winter, application deadline November 1; Spring, application deadline February 1; Summer, application deadline May 1. Deadlines are flexible. *Fee:* $25.

Houston, University of
Department of Psychology
College of Liberal Arts and Social Sciences
126 Heyne Building
Houston, TX 77204-5022
Telephone: (713) 743-8508
Fax: (713) 743-8588
E-mail: *ptolar@uh.edu*
Web: *http://www.psychology.uh.edu*

Department Information:
1939. Chairperson: David J. Francis. Number of Faculty: total–full-time 25, part-time 4; women–full-time 10; minority–full-time 1.

Programs and Degrees Offered:
Listed in the following order: Program area, degree type (T if terminal Master's), number awarded 7/03–6/04. Clinical PhD (Doctor of Philosophy) 13, Industrial/ Organizational PhD (Doctor of Philosophy) 2, Social PhD (Doctor of Philosophy) 4, Developmental PhD (Doctor of Philosophy) 0.

APA Accreditation: Clinical PhD (Doctor of Philosophy).

Student Applications/Admissions:
Student Applications
Clinical PhD (Doctor of Philosophy)—Applications 2004–2005, 200. Total applicants accepted 2004–2005, 19. Number enrolled (new admits only) 2004–2005 full-time, 13. Number

enrolled (new admits only) 2004–2005 part-time, 0. Openings 2005–2006, 12. The Median number of years required for completion of a degree are 6.3. The number of students enrolled full and part-time who were dismissed or voluntarily withdrew from this program area were 0. *Industrial/Organizational PhD (Doctor of Philosophy)*—Applications 2004–2005, 75. Total applicants accepted 2004–2005, 10. Number enrolled (new admits only) 2004–2005 full-time, 5. Number enrolled (new admits only) 2004–2005 part-time, 0. Openings 2005–2006, 6. The Median number of years required for completion of a degree are 7. The number of students enrolled full and part-time who were dismissed or voluntarily withdrew from this program area were 0. *Social PhD (Doctor of Philosophy)*—Applications 2004–2005, 28. Total applicants accepted 2004–2005, 8. Number enrolled (new admits only) 2004–2005 full-time, 5. Number enrolled (new admits only) 2004–2005 part-time, 0. Openings 2005–2006, 4. The Median number of years required for completion of a degree are 4.75. The number of students enrolled full and part-time who were dismissed or voluntarily withdrew from this program area were 1. *Developmental PhD (Doctor of Philosophy)*—Applications 2004–2005, 0. Total applicants accepted 2004–2005, 0. Number enrolled (new admits only) 2004–2005 full-time, 0. Total enrolled 2004–2005 full-time, 3. Openings 2005–2006, 4. The number of students enrolled full and part-time who were dismissed or voluntarily withdrew from this program area were 0.

Admissions Requirements:
Scores: Entries appear in this order: required test or GPA, minimum score (if required), median score of students entering in 2003–2004. Doctoral Programs: overall undergraduate GPA no minimum stated. Specific minimums are not required.
Other Criteria: (importance of criteria rated low, medium, or high): GRE/MAT scores medium, research experience high, work experience medium, extracurricular activity medium, clinically related public service medium, GPA medium, letters of recommendation high, interview high, statement of goals and objectives high. The clinical program requires an interview. For additional information on admission requirements, go to: http://www.psych.uh.edu/GraduatePrograms/.

Student Characteristics: The following represents characteristics of students in 2004–2005 in all graduate psychology programs in the department: Female–full-time 93, part-time 0; Male–full-time 31, part-time 0; African American/Black–full-time 3, part-time 0; Hispanic/Latino(a)–full-time 8, part-time 0; Asian/Pacific Islander–full-time 5, part-time 0; American Indian/Alaska Native–full-time 0, part-time 0; Caucasian–full-time 108, part-time 0; Multi-ethnic–full-time 0, part-time 0; students subject to the Americans With Disabilities Act–full-time 1, part-time 0.

Financial Information/Assistance:
Tuition for Full-Time Study: *Doctoral:* State residents: per academic year $5,130, $171 per credit hour; Nonstate residents: per academic year $12,870, $429 per credit hour. Tuition is subject to change. See the following Web site for updates and changes in tuition costs: http://www.uh.edu/sfs/.

Financial Assistance:
First Year Students: Teaching assistantships available for first-year. Average amount paid per academic year: $11,448. Average number of hours worked per week: 20. Apply by appointment.

Tuition remission given: partial. Research assistantships available for first-year. Average amount paid per academic year: $11,448. Average number of hours worked per week: 20. Apply by appointment. Tuition remission given: partial. Fellowships and scholarships available for first-year. Average amount paid per academic year: $3,000. Apply by appointment. Tuition remission given: partial.

Advanced Students: Teaching assistantships available for advanced students. Average amount paid per academic year: $13,032. Average number of hours worked per week: 20. Apply by appointment. Tuition remission given: partial. Research assistantships available for advanced students. Average amount paid per academic year: $14,400. Average number of hours worked per week: 20. Apply by appointment. Tuition remission given: partial. Fellowships and scholarships available for advanced students. Average amount paid per academic year: $3,000. Apply by appointment. Tuition remission given: partial.

Contact Information: Of all students currently enrolled full-time, 85% benefitted from one or more of the listed financial assistance programs.

Internships/Practica: Internships are available for advanced students at a number of sites that include private industry, medical centers, state hospitals, and private practices. For those doctoral students for whom a professional internship is required prior to graduation, 10 applied in 2003–2004. Of those who applied, 10 were placed in internships listed by the Association of Psychology Postdoctoral and Internship Programs (APPIC); 10 were placed in APA accredited internships.

Housing and Day Care: On-campus housing is available. See the following Web site for more information: http://www.uh.edu/housing/. On-campus day care facilities are available. See the following Web site for more information: http://www.uh.edu/admin/ccce/.

Employment of Department Graduates:
Master's Degree Graduates: Of those who graduated in the academic year 2003–2004, the following categories and numbers represent the post-graduate activities and employment of master's degree graduates: Enrolled in a post-doctoral residency/fellowship (n/a), employed in independent practice (n/a), total from the above (master's) (0).
Doctoral Degree Graduates: Of those who graduated in the academic year 2003–2004, the following categories and numbers represent the post-graduate activities and employment of doctoral degree graduates: Enrolled in a psychology doctoral program (n/a), total from the above (doctoral) (0).

Additional Information:
Orientation, Objectives, and Emphasis of Department: Clinical offers APA-approved training in research, assessment, intervention, and consultation related to complex human problems, including behavioral problems having a neurological basis. Industrial/organizational offers broad training in industrial/organizational psychology with options for specialization in either the personnel or organizational subfields. Social emphasizes research careers in behavioral and preventive medicine, and interpersonal interaction processes, with an emphasis on close relationships and motivation. Developmental focuses on experimental research in developmental cognitive neuroscience, including perception, speech, language, reading, attention, decision-making, memory, and emotion, using

imaging, electrophysiological, and neurochemical techniques in human and animal models.

Special Facilities or Resources: The facilities of the department are comparable to those of any major department in any large university. A variety of community settings are available for applied research in all areas of specialization. Specialized laboratories have modern equipment for research in family and couple interaction, biofeedback, personnel interviewing, and electrophysiology. We have recording, transcribing, and duplication equipment. Several research and clinical practica are available within the community and at several hospitals (the Texas Medical Center is one of the largest in the world). The department has over 150 computer work stations.

Information for Students With Physical Disabilities: See the following Web site for more information: http://www.uh.edu/csd/.

Application Information:
Send to: Academic Affairs Office, Department of Psychology, 126 Heyne Building, University of Houston, Houston, TX 77204-5022. Application available online. URL of online application: http://www.uh.edu/enroll/admis/graduate/grad_applications.htm. Students are admitted in the Fall. Deadline for Clinical is December 15. Deadline for Developmental, I/O, and Social is January 15. If students apply online, please also send hard copy of application to Academic Affairs Office listed above. *Fee:* $40. In cases of financial hardship, a waiver of the application fee may be requested by writing to: Dr. Roy Lachman, Director of Graduate Education, University of Houston, Department of Psychology, 126 Heyne Building, Houston, TX 77204-5022.

Houston, University of, College of Education
Department of Educational Psychology
College of Education
491 Farish Hall
Houston, TX 77204-5029
Telephone: (713) 743-5019
Fax: (713) 743-4996
E-mail: *jhawkins@uh.edu*
Web: *http://www.coe.uh.edu*

Department Information:
1980. Chairperson: Jacqueline Hawkins. Number of Faculty: total–full-time 21, part-time 11; women–full-time 11, part-time 5; minority–full-time 3, part-time 1.

Programs and Degrees Offered:
Listed in the following order: Program area, degree type (T if terminal Master's), number awarded 7/03–6/04. Counseling Psychology PhD (Doctor of Philosophy) 4, Educational Psychology & Individual Differences PhD (Doctor of Philosophy) 6, Counseling—MEd Other 30, Educational Psychology—MEd Other 5, Special Education—MEd Other 17.

APA Accreditation: Counseling PhD (Doctor of Philosophy).

Student Applications/Admissions:
Student Applications
Counseling Psychology PhD (Doctor of Philosophy)—Applications 2004–2005, 58. Total applicants accepted 2004–2005,

11. Number enrolled (new admits only) 2004–2005 full-time, 9. Total enrolled 2004–2005 full-time, 58. Openings 2005–2006, 9. The Median number of years required for completion of a degree are 8. The number of students enrolled full and part-time who were dismissed or voluntarily withdrew from this program area were 1. *Educational Psychology & Individual Differences PhD (Doctor of Philosophy)*—Applications 2004–2005, 19. Total applicants accepted 2004–2005, 9. Number enrolled (new admits only) 2004–2005 full-time, 4. Number enrolled (new admits only) 2004–2005 part-time, 5. Total enrolled 2004–2005 full-time, 30, part-time, 21. Openings 2005–2006, 7. The Median number of years required for completion of a degree are 6. The number of students enrolled full and part-time who were dismissed or voluntarily withdrew from this program area were 4. *Counseling—MEd Other*—Applications 2004–2005, 70. Total applicants accepted 2004–2005, 42. Number enrolled (new admits only) 2004–2005 full-time, 15. Number enrolled (new admits only) 2004–2005 part-time, 27. Total enrolled 2004–2005 full-time, 30, part-time, 50. Openings 2005–2006, 35. The Median number of years required for completion of a degree are 3. The number of students enrolled full and part-time who were dismissed or voluntarily withdrew from this program area were 0. *Educational Psychology—MEd Other*—Applications 2004–2005, 10. Total applicants accepted 2004–2005, 5. Number enrolled (new admits only) 2004–2005 full-time, 5. Total enrolled 2004–2005 full-time, 5, part-time, 10. Openings 2005–2006, 8. The Median number of years required for completion of a degree are 3. The number of students enrolled full and part-time who were dismissed or voluntarily withdrew from this program area were 3. *Special Education—MEd Other*—Applications 2004–2005, 24. Total applicants accepted 2004–2005, 11. Total enrolled 2004–2005 full-time, 5, part-time, 18.

Admissions Requirements:
Scores: Entries appear in this order: required test or GPA, minimum score (if required), median score of students entering in 2003–2004. Master's Programs: GRE-V 30%; GRE-Q 30%; GRE-Analytical 30%; MAT 35; last 2 years GPA 3.0. May take either MAT or GRE Doctoral Programs: GRE-V 35%; GRE-Q 35%; GRE-Analytical 35%; last 2 years GPA 3.0.
Other Criteria: (importance of criteria rated low, medium, or high): GRE/MAT scores high, research experience high, work experience high, extracurricular activity high, clinically related public service high, GPA high, letters of recommendation high, interview high, statement of goals and objectives high. PhD programs emphasize research experience and research interests more than do the master's programs. For additional information on admission requirements, go to: www.coe.uh.edu/departments/epsy5.cfm.

Student Characteristics: The following represents characteristics of students in 2004–2005 in all graduate psychology programs in the department: Female–full-time 103, part-time 84; Male–full-time 25, part-time 15; African American/Black–full-time 7, part-time 2; Hispanic/Latino(a)–full-time 12, part-time 6; Asian/Pacific Islander–full-time 10, part-time 5; American Indian/Alaska Native–full-time 0, part-time 0; Caucasian–full-time 97, part-time 84; Multi-ethnic–full-time 2, part-time 2; students subject to the Americans With Disabilities Act–full-time 0, part-time 0.

Financial Information/Assistance:

Tuition for Full-Time Study: *Master's:* State residents: per academic year $3,078, $171 per credit hour; Nonstate residents: per academic year $7,722, $429 per credit hour. *Doctoral:* State residents: per academic year $3,078, $171 per credit hour; Nonstate residents: per academic year $7,722, $429 per credit hour. Tuition is subject to change. See the following Web site for updates and changes in tuition costs: http://www.uh.edu/sfs/Fee%20Schedule/FeeSchedule.htm.

Financial Assistance:

First Year Students: Teaching assistantships available for first-year. Average amount paid per academic year: $12,360. Average number of hours worked per week: 20. Tuition remission given: full. Research assistantships available for first-year. Average amount paid per academic year: $12,360. Average number of hours worked per week: 20. Tuition remission given: full. Fellowships and scholarships available for first-year. Tuition remission given: full and partial.

Advanced Students: Teaching assistantships available for advanced students. Average amount paid per academic year: $13,560. Average number of hours worked per week: 20. Tuition remission given: full. Research assistantships available for advanced students. Average amount paid per academic year: $13,560. Average number of hours worked per week: 20. Tuition remission given: full. Fellowships and scholarships available for advanced students. Tuition remission given: full and partial.

Contact Information: Of all students currently enrolled full-time, 30% benefitted from one or more of the listed financial assistance programs. Application and information available online at: http://www.coe.uh.edu/scholarships.cfm.

Internships/Practica: All counseling psychology doctoral students and counseling master's students participate in supervised practica at numerous sites throughout the Houston area. Examples of the types of sites at which students have completed practica include veteran's and children's hospitals, counseling centers and school districts. In addition, doctoral counseling psychology students are required to complete a one-year full-time internship approved by the faculty. These sites range widely in orientation, focus and geographic location. For those doctoral students for whom a professional internship is required prior to graduation, 12 applied in 2003–2004. Of those who applied, 10 were placed in internships listed by the Association of Psychology Postdoctoral and Internship Programs (APPIC); 10 were placed in APA accredited internships.

Housing and Day Care: On-campus housing is available. See the following Web site for more information: http://www.uh.edu/housing/. On-campus day care facilities are available. See the following Web site for more information: http://www.uh.edu/ccc/.

Employment of Department Graduates:

Master's Degree Graduates: Of those who graduated in the academic year 2003–2004, the following categories and numbers represent the post-graduate activities and employment of master's degree graduates: Enrolled in a post-doctoral residency/fellowship (n/a), employed in independent practice (n/a), total from the above (master's) (0).

Doctoral Degree Graduates: Of those who graduated in the academic year 2003–2004, the following categories and numbers represent the post-graduate activities and employment of doctoral degree graduates: Enrolled in a psychology doctoral program (n/a), employed in other positions at a higher education institution (1), employed in a professional position in a school system (1), employed in a hospital/medical center (1), do not know (1), total from the above (doctoral) (4).

Additional Information:

Orientation, Objectives, and Emphasis of Department: The primary intent of the doctoral program in counseling psychology is to prepare highly skilled psychologists in the scientist-practitioner model of counseling. Counseling psychologists may assume several roles in a variety of settings in the professional community. These may include supervision and training of counselors and other "helping" personnel; providing personal, educational and career counseling services; college and university teaching; research; and consultation to public systems, schools and other community organizations concerned with psychological and interpersonal development. The goals of the Educational Psychology and Individual Differences program area are threefold. First, the program is dedicated to the advancement and application of knowledge relevant to human learning, development, and psychological functioning and to the meaningful application of such knowledge, especially within academic contexts. To achieve this goal, the program produces high quality, innovative research and scholarship designed to advance the knowledge and understanding within these areas. The Master's of Education (MEd) Degree Program in Counseling is offered through the Department of Educational Psychology. The major objective of this Program is to prepare counselors to assume positions in education and mental health settings, such as public schools, junior colleges, university counseling and advisement centers, and community mental health agencies. The major objective of the Masters of Education (MEd) Degree Program in Educational Psychology is to offer students preparation in: 1) Psychological theories and their application (i.e., human learning, development, the individual differences that exist within these areas, and their application to teaching and learning in school and other educational settings) and 2) Research, measurement, and evaluation. The Masters of Education (MEd) Degree Program in Special Education is offered through the Department of Educational Psychology. The Masters Degree in Special Education provides students the option of meeting Texas Education Agency requirements for certification in one of three areas: Generic Special Education, Educational Diagnostician or Severely Handicapped Education.

Special Facilities or Resources: The facilities of the department are comparable to those of any major department in any large university. An extensive array of resources for data analysis and computer applications is available within the college. The Micro-Computing Center contains computer terminals that are linked to the University's mainframe running the Conversational Monitoring System (CMS). The center also includes a number of computers and multimedia laboratory which includes modern instructional media. Three graduate assistants staff the computer lab, which also functions as a teaching laboratory for courses in statistics, methodology, and data management.

Information for Students With Physical Disabilities: See the following Web site for more information: www.uh.edu/csd/.

Application Information:

Send to: Ms. Mary Bess Kelley, University of Houston, Room 160, Farish Hall, Houston, TX 77204-5871. Application available online.

URL of online application: http://www.coe.uh.edu/departments/epsy5. cfm. Students are admitted in the Fall, application deadline varies; Spring, application deadline varies. Our programs' application deadlines are on different dates during the year: Counseling Psychology PhD: January 2; Counseling MEd: January 10; Educational Psychology and Individual Differences PhD: March 15; Educational Psychology MEd and Special Education MEd: June 15 (fall), October 15 (spring). *Fee:* $45.

Lamar University—Beaumont (2004 data)
Department of Psychology
Arts & Sciences
P.O. Box 10036
Beaumont, TX 77710
Telephone: (409) 880-8285
Fax: (409) 880-1779
E-mail: *fitzpatrod@hal.lamar.edu*
Web: *http://www.Lamar.edu*

Department Information:
1964. Chairperson: Oney D. Fitzpatrick Jr. Number of Faculty: total–full-time 8, part-time 4; women–full-time 5; minority–full-time 1.

Programs and Degrees Offered:
Listed in the following order: Program area, degree type (T if terminal Master's), number awarded 7/03–6/04. Community–Clinical MA/MS (Master of Arts/Science) (T) 3, Industrial–Organizational MA/MS (Master of Arts/Science) (T) 3.

Student Applications/Admissions:
Student Applications

Community–Clinical MA/MS (Master of Arts/Science)—Applications 2004–2005, 6. Total applicants accepted 2004–2005, 4. Total enrolled 2004–2005 full-time, 3, part-time, 1. Openings 2005–2006, 6. The Median number of years required for completion of a degree are 2. The number of students enrolled full and part-time who were dismissed or voluntarily withdrew from this program area were 0. *Industrial–Organizational MA/MS (Master of Arts/Science)*—Applications 2004–2005, 8. Total applicants accepted 2004–2005, 4. Openings 2005–2006, 6. The Median number of years required for completion of a degree are 2. The number of students enrolled full and part-time who were dismissed or voluntarily withdrew from this program area were 0.

Admissions Requirements:

Scores: Entries appear in this order: required test or GPA, minimum score (if required), median score of students entering in 2003–2004. Master's Programs: GRE-V 450, 500; GRE-Q 450, 535; GRE-V+Q 900, 1035; overall undergraduate GPA 2.75, 3.05; last 2 years GPA 2.75, 3.30.

Other Criteria: (importance of criteria rated low, medium, or high): GRE/MAT scores medium, research experience medium, work experience medium, extracurricular activity low, clinically related public service low, GPA medium, letters of recommendation medium, statement of goals and objectives low.

Student Characteristics: The following represents characteristics of students in 2004–2005 in all graduate psychology programs in the department: Female–full-time 9, part-time 2; Male–full-time 4, part-time 0; African American/Black–full-time 0, part-time 0; Hispanic/Latino(a)–full-time 0, part-time 0; Asian/Pacific Islander–full-time 0, part-time 0; American Indian/Alaska Native–full-time 0, part-time 0; Caucasian–full-time 0, part-time 0.

Financial Information/Assistance:
Tuition for Full-Time Study: *Master's:* State residents: per academic year $2,024, $146 per credit hour; Nonstate residents: per academic year $7,208, $287 per credit hour.

Financial Assistance:
First Year Students: Teaching assistantships available for first-year. Average amount paid per academic year: $4,500. Average number of hours worked per week: 20. Tuition remission given: partial. Fellowships and scholarships available for first-year. Average amount paid per academic year: $1,000. Tuition remission given: partial.

Advanced Students: Teaching assistantships available for advanced students. Average amount paid per academic year: $4,500. Average number of hours worked per week: 20. Tuition remission given: partial. Fellowships and scholarships available for advanced students. Average amount paid per academic year: $1,000. Tuition remission given: partial.

Contact Information: Of all students currently enrolled full-time, 90% benefitted from one or more of the listed financial assistance programs.

Internships/Practica: A variety of community health settings provide useful practicum experiences for Community-Clinical students in child, adolescent and adult counseling and assessment. Practicum experiences for the Industrial/Organizational students place them in a variety of organizational and industrial work environments.

Housing and Day Care: On-campus housing is available. Lamar University, Office of Residence Life, Box 10041, Beaumont, TX 77710. On-campus day care facilities are available.

Employment of Department Graduates:
Master's Degree Graduates: Of those who graduated in the academic year 2003–2004, the following categories and numbers represent the post-graduate activities and employment of master's degree graduates: Enrolled in a psychology doctoral program (3), enrolled in a post-doctoral residency/fellowship (n/a), employed in independent practice (n/a), employed in an academic position at a 2-year/4-year college (4), employed in business or industry (research/consulting) (2), employed in business or industry (management) (4), employed in a government agency (professional services) (1), employed in a community mental health/counseling center (2), still seeking employment (1), total from the above (master's) (17).

Doctoral Degree Graduates: Of those who graduated in the academic year 2003–2004, the following categories and numbers represent the post-graduate activities and employment of doctoral degree graduates: Enrolled in a psychology doctoral program (n/a), total from the above (doctoral) (0).

Additional Information:
Orientation, Objectives, and Emphasis of Department: The Department of Psychology offers a program of study leading to the

Master of Science degree in applied psychology. It is designed to prepare professional personnel for employment in business, industry, or community mental health agencies. The MS in Community-Clinical Psychology includes training in therapy techniques for individuals, groups and families. The MS in Industrial/Organizational Psychology integrates the traditional areas of industrial psychology with the more contemporary areas of organizational development and analysis.

Application Information:
Send to: Graduate Admissions, Lamar University, Box 10078, Beaumont, TX 77710. Students are admitted in the Fall, application deadline March 15. *Fee:* $0.

Midwestern State University
Department of Psychology
College of Liberal Arts
3410 Taft Boulevard
Wichita Falls, TX 76308
Telephone: (940) 397-4340
Fax: (940) 397-4682
E-mail: *george.diekhoff@mwsu.edu*
Web: *http://libarts.mwsu.edu/psychology/index.asp*

Department Information:
1975. Chairperson: George M. Diekhoff. Number of Faculty: total–full-time 5, part-time 3; women–full-time 1; minority–full-time 1.

Programs and Degrees Offered:
Listed in the following order: Program area, degree type (T if terminal Master's), number awarded 7/03–6/04. Clinical and Counseling Psychology MA/MS (Master of Arts/Science) (T) 8.

Student Applications/Admissions:
Student Applications
Clinical and Counseling Psychology MA/MS (Master of Arts/Science)—Applications 2004–2005, 27. Total applicants accepted 2004–2005, 9. Number enrolled (new admits only) 2004–2005 full-time, 8. Openings 2005–2006, 15. The Median number of years required for completion of a degree are 2. The number of students enrolled full and part-time who were dismissed or voluntarily withdrew from this program area were 0.

Admissions Requirements:
Scores: Entries appear in this order: required test or GPA, minimum score (if required), median score of students entering in 2003–2004. Master's Programs: GRE-V 450, 520; GRE-Q 450, 560; overall undergraduate GPA 3.0, 3.3.
Other Criteria: (importance of criteria rated low, medium, or high): GRE/MAT scores high, research experience low, work experience low, extracurricular activity low, clinically related public service low, GPA high, letters of recommendation medium, statement of goals and objectives medium.

Student Characteristics: The following represents characteristics of students in 2004–2005 in all graduate psychology programs in

the department: Female–full-time 15, part-time 0; Male–full-time 3, part-time 0; African American/Black–full-time 2, part-time 0; Hispanic/Latino(a)–full-time 2, part-time 0; Asian/Pacific Islander–full-time 0, part-time 0; American Indian/Alaska Native–full-time 0, part-time 0; Caucasian–full-time 14, part-time 0; Multi-ethnic–full-time 0, part-time 0; students subject to the Americans With Disabilities Act–full-time 0, part-time 0.

Financial Information/Assistance:
Tuition for Full-Time Study: Master's: State residents: per academic year $3,016, $126 per credit hour; Nonstate residents: per academic year $9,208, $384 per credit hour. Tuition is subject to change. See the following Web site for updates and changes in tuition costs: www.mwsu.edu.

Financial Assistance:
First Year Students: Research assistantships available for first-year. Average amount paid per academic year: $4,250. Average number of hours worked per week: 5. Apply by July 1. Fellowships and scholarships available for first-year. Average amount paid per academic year: $1,000. Average number of hours worked per week: 0. Apply by July 1. Tuition remission given: partial.
Advanced Students: Teaching assistantships available for advanced students. Average amount paid per academic year: $4,250. Average number of hours worked per week: 5. Apply by July 1. Tuition remission given: partial. Research assistantships available for advanced students. Average amount paid per academic year: $4,250. Average number of hours worked per week: 5. Apply by July 1. Tuition remission given: partial. Fellowships and scholarships available for advanced students. Average amount paid per academic year: $1,000. Average number of hours worked per week: 0. Apply by July 1. Tuition remission given: partial.
Contact Information: Of all students currently enrolled full-time, 100% benefitted from one or more of the listed financial assistance programs.

Internships/Practica: Students completing the clinical/counseling program complete 9 credit hours of practicum for a total of between 450 clock-hours of work and study in an applied clinical/counseling setting.

Housing and Day Care: On-campus housing is available. See the following Web site for more information: www.mwsu.edu. No on-campus day care facilities are available.

Employment of Department Graduates:
Master's Degree Graduates: Of those who graduated in the academic year 2003–2004, the following categories and numbers represent the post-graduate activities and employment of master's degree graduates: Enrolled in a post-doctoral residency/fellowship (n/a), employed in independent practice (n/a), total from the above (master's) (0).
Doctoral Degree Graduates: Of those who graduated in the academic year 2003–2004, the following categories and numbers represent the post-graduate activities and employment of doctoral degree graduates: Enrolled in a psychology doctoral program (n/a), total from the above (doctoral) (0).

Additional Information:
Orientation, Objectives, and Emphasis of Department: The clinical/counseling psychology graduate program is available in either a 50-hour or 60-hour curriculum and is designed to lead to certifi-

cation as a Licensed Professional Counselor (LPC) or Licensed Psychological Associate (LPA). Students may pursue thesis or nonthesis options. Although our emphasis is on training the master's level practitioner, we actively encourage our students to pursue doctoral training, and we see the training we provide as a first step toward that goal.

Special Facilities or Resources: Midwestern State University is located near two state hospitals, a regional community mental health and mental retardation center, and two private psychiatric hospitals. A newly remodeled clinic and computer lab are available for student use, and Graduate Research and Teaching Assistants are provided with office space. Financial assistance to Texas nonresidents includes waiver of the nonresident tuition differential.

Information for Students With Physical Disabilities: See the following Web site for more information: www.mwsu.edu.

Application Information:

Send to: George M. Diekhoff, Chair, Department of Psychology, Midwestern State University, 3410 Taft, Wichita Falls, TX 76308. Students are admitted in the Fall, application deadline July 1; Spring, application deadline November 15. *Fee:* $25.

North Texas, University of
Department of Psychology
College of Arts & Sciences
P.O. Box 311280
Denton, TX 76203-1280
Telephone: (940) 565-2671
Fax: (940) 565-4682
E-mail: *amyg@unt.edu*
Web: *http://www.psyc.unt.edu*

Department Information:

1968. Chairperson: Linda L. Marshall. Number of Faculty: total—full-time 31, part-time 5; women—full-time 7, part-time 4; minority—full-time 4; faculty subject to the Americans With Disabilities Act 1.

Programs and Degrees Offered:

Listed in the following order: Program area, degree type (T if terminal Master's), number awarded 7/03–6/04. Clinical Psychology: Health & Behavioral Medicine PhD (Doctor of Philosophy) 8, School Psychology MA/MS (Master of Arts/Science) (T) 3, Experimental Psychology PhD (Doctor of Philosophy) 1, Counseling Psychology PhD (Doctor of Philosophy) 6, Industrial-Organizational Psychology PhD (Doctor of Philosophy) 0, Clinical Psychology PhD (Doctor of Philosophy) 9.

APA Accreditation: Clinical PhD (Doctor of Philosophy). Counseling PhD (Doctor of Philosophy). Clinical PhD (Doctor of Philosophy).

Student Applications/Admissions:
Student Applications
Clinical Psychology: Health & Behavioral Medicine PhD (Doctor of Philosophy)—Applications 2004–2005, 31. Total applicants

accepted 2004–2005, 18. Total enrolled 2004–2005 full-time, 34, part-time, 18. Openings 2005–2006, 10. The Median number of years required for completion of a degree are 6. The number of students enrolled full and part-time who were dismissed or voluntarily withdrew from this program area were 3. *School Psychology MA/MS (Master of Arts/Science)*—Applications 2004–2005, 20. Total applicants accepted 2004–2005, 4. Openings 2005–2006, 5. The Median number of years required for completion of a degree are 4. The number of students enrolled full and part-time who were dismissed or voluntarily withdrew from this program area were 0. *Experimental Psychology PhD (Doctor of Philosophy)*—Applications 2004–2005, 3. Total applicants accepted 2004–2005, 2. Openings 2005–2006, 5. The Median number of years required for completion of a degree are 6. The number of students enrolled full and part-time who were dismissed or voluntarily withdrew from this program area were 1. *Counseling Psychology PhD (Doctor of Philosophy)*—Applications 2004–2005, 92. Total applicants accepted 2004–2005, 12. Total enrolled 2004–2005 full-time, 43, part-time, 12. Openings 2005–2006, 10. The Median number of years required for completion of a degree are 5. The number of students enrolled full and part-time who were dismissed or voluntarily withdrew from this program area were 3. *Industrial-Organizational Psychology PhD (Doctor of Philosophy)*—Applications 2004–2005, 54. Total applicants accepted 2004–2005, 12. Openings 2005–2006, 7. The Median number of years required for completion of a degree are 5. The number of students enrolled full and part-time who were dismissed or voluntarily withdrew from this program area were 0. *Clinical Psychology PhD (Doctor of Philosophy)*—Applications 2004–2005, 115. Total applicants accepted 2004–2005, 14. Openings 2005–2006, 10. The Median number of years required for completion of a degree are 6. The number of students enrolled full and part-time who were dismissed or voluntarily withdrew from this program area were 2.

Admissions Requirements:

Scores: Entries appear in this order: required test or GPA, minimum score (if required), median score of students entering in 2003–2004. Master's Programs: GRE-V no minimum stated, 460; GRE-Q no minimum stated, 560; GRE-Analytical no minimum stated, 570; overall undergraduate GPA no minimum stated, 3.42; last 2 years GPA no minimum stated, 3.62; psychology GPA no minimum stated, 3.39. 1. Twenty-four hours in psychology (12 hours of advanced course work) including experimental psychology or research design and elementary statistics; 2. Send a resume, a statement of purpose, GRE V and Q scores, 3 letters of recommendation; 3. Meet any four of the following seven requirements: a. GRE-V: 500+ (500 on the TOEFL); b. GRE-Q: 500+; c. GRE-Analytical: 500+, or GRE-Psychology: 700+, or GRE-Technical Writing: 4+; d. undergraduate GPA: 2.8, or undergraduate GPA (last 60 hours): 3.0+; e. psychology GPA: 3.0+; f. A master's degree in another field; g. First or second author on an article in a peer reviewed major scientific or professional journal. Doctoral Programs: GRE-V no minimum stated, 520; GRE-Q no minimum stated, 610; GRE-Analytical no minimum stated, 640; overall undergraduate GPA no minimum stated, 3.60; last 2 years GPA no minimum stated, 3.70; psychology GPA no minimum stated, 3.83. 1. Twenty-four hours in psychology including statistics and three of the following psychology courses: experimental psychology (or research methods), cognition, learning, perception (sensory processes), motivation, physiological psychology (biological psychology), psychological measurement, or research thesis; 2. Send a resume, statement of purpose, GRE V and Q scores, 3 letters of recommendation; 3. Meet four of the following seven requirements: a. GRE-V: 500+ (500 on the TOEFL); b. GRE-Q: 500+; c. GRE-Analytic: 500+, or GRE-Psychology: 700+, or GRE-Technical Writing: 4+; d. undergraduate GPA: 3.0+, or undergraduate GPA(last 60 hours): 3.5+, or master's degree GPA: 3.5+ exclusive of practicum and thesis; e. psychology GPA: 3.5+; f. A doctoral degree in another field; g. First or second author on an article in a peer reviewed major scientific or professional journal.

Other Criteria: (importance of criteria rated low, medium, or high): GRE/MAT scores medium, research experience medium, work experience medium, extracurricular activity medium, clinically related public service medium, GPA medium, letters of recommendation medium, interview medium, statement of goals and objectives medium.

Student Characteristics: The following represents characteristics of students in 2004–2005 in all graduate psychology programs in the department: Female–full-time 139, part-time 24; Male–full-time 54, part-time 9; African American/Black–full-time 5, part-time 0; Hispanic/Latino(a)–full-time 1, part-time 0; Asian/Pacific Islander–full-time 3, part-time 0; American Indian/Alaska Native–full-time 1, part-time 0; Caucasian–full-time 0, part-time 0; students subject to the Americans With Disabilities Act–full-time 4, part-time 0.

Financial Information/Assistance:
Tuition for Full-Time Study: *Master's:* State residents: per academic year $5,548, $397 per credit hour; Nonstate residents: per academic year $11,740, $655 per credit hour. *Doctoral:* State residents: per academic year $5,548, $397 per credit hour; Nonstate residents: per academic year $11,740, $655 per credit hour. Tuition is subject to change. See the following Web site for updates and changes in tuition costs: www.essc.unt.edu/saucs/tuition.

Financial Assistance:
First Year Students: Teaching assistantships available for first-year. Average amount paid per academic year: $6,500. Average number of hours worked per week: 20. Apply by April 15. Tuition remission given: partial. Research assistantships available for first-year. Average amount paid per academic year: $6,800. Average number of hours worked per week: 20. Tuition remission given: partial. Traineeships available for first-year. Average amount paid per academic year: $5,000. Average number of hours worked per week: 10. Fellowships and scholarships available for first-year. Average amount paid per academic year: $1,000. Apply by April 15. Tuition remission given: partial.
Advanced Students: Teaching assistantships available for advanced students. Average amount paid per academic year: $7,200. Average number of hours worked per week: 20. Apply by April 15. Tuition remission given: partial. Research assistantships available for advanced students. Average amount paid per academic year: $6,800. Average number of hours worked per week: 20. Tuition remission given: partial. Traineeships available for advanced students. Average amount paid per academic year: $12,000. Average number of hours worked per week: 20. Tuition remission given: partial. Fellowships and scholarships available

for advanced students. Average amount paid per academic year: $12,000. Apply by January 15. Tuition remission given: partial.
Contact Information: Of all students currently enrolled full-time, 73% benefitted from one or more of the listed financial assistance programs. Application and information available online at: http://www.essc.unt.edu.

Internships/Practica: For those doctoral students for whom a professional internship is required prior to graduation, 17 applied in 2003–2004. Of those who applied, 14 were placed in internships listed by the Association of Psychology Postdoctoral and Internship Programs (APPIC); 9 were placed in APA accredited internships.

Housing and Day Care: On-campus housing is available. See the following Web site for more information: www.unt.edu/housing/. No on-campus day care facilities are available.

Employment of Department Graduates:
Master's Degree Graduates: Of those who graduated in the academic year 2003–2004, the following categories and numbers represent the post-graduate activities and employment of master's degree graduates: Enrolled in a psychology doctoral program (3), enrolled in a post-doctoral residency/fellowship (n/a), employed in independent practice (n/a), employed in a community mental health/counseling center (1), total from the above (master's) (4).
Doctoral Degree Graduates: Of those who graduated in the academic year 2003–2004, the following categories and numbers represent the post-graduate activities and employment of doctoral degree graduates: Enrolled in a psychology doctoral program (n/a), enrolled in a post-doctoral residency/fellowship (4), employed in independent practice (2), employed in an academic position at a university (2), employed in business or industry (research/consulting) (1), employed in a government agency (research) (1), employed in a government agency (professional services) (3), employed in a community mental health/counseling center (2), employed in a hospital/medical center (6), other employment position (1), total from the above (doctoral) (22).

Additional Information:
Orientation, Objectives, and Emphasis of Department: Our department adopts the scientist-practitioner model, fostering an appreciation of psychology as a science and as a profession. We embrace a multiplicity of theoretical viewpoints and research interests. Students are involved in graded research and/or clinical practicum experiences by integrating experiential with didactic instruction. Experimental psychology provides a highly individualized program for the student interested in study and research in one of several specialized areas. Clinical and counseling psychology programs support the development of a well-rounded professional psychologist. These purposes include a thorough grounding in scientific methodology and an orientation to the profession, development of competency in psychological assessment and evaluation, and training in various psychotherapeutic and counseling techniques and skills. I/O psychology prepares students for careers in business, government and higher education with the capability of helping organizations solve problems related to personnel selection and training, employee motivation and satisfaction, leadership, performance measurement, team building, and organizational development. Clinical psychology: health and behavioral medicine involves a joint program with UNT Health Science Center, which emphasizes mind/body interaction as stu-

dents focus on the matrix of biopsychosocial and environmental processes in understanding etiological and diagnostic factors of illness, prevention, and recovery in order to meet the holistic needs of the individual.

Special Facilities or Resources: Centers: Center for Sport Psychology and Performance Excellence. The center was developed to provide comprehensive and interdisciplinary research, service and training in the areas of sport and exercise psychology. Interdisciplinary Center for the Study of Work Teams. The Center for the Study of Work Teams provides learning partnerships with industry for the purposes of generating, archiving and disseminating information about work teams. The center serves as a research and education entity for organizations using team-based structures and, in conjunction with its industry partners, provides those organizations with the highest quality products and services concerning team issues. The center harnesses strengths of business and academia in a joint effort to master the challenges of designing and implementing work teams. Psychology Clinic. As part of the department's Applied Training Unit, the Psychology Clinic is a training site for graduate students. Psychological services are offered to the metroplex community. Services available to the community include psychotherapy, vocational counseling, psychological assessment and biofeedback. University of North Texas Health Science Center. Practicum and research experiences available through departments of pediatrics, family medicine, internal medicine, gerontology, and rehabilitation medicine. Labs: Brain-Mapping Facility, Applied Psychophysiology and Biofeedback Lab, Neurofeedback Lab, Psychoneuroimmunology Lab, Computer/Statistics Lab, Neuropsychology Lab,.

Information for Students With Physical Disabilities: See the following Web site for more information: www.unt.edu/oda/.

Application Information:
Send to: Psychology Department, Graduate Admissions, University of North Texas, Box 311280, Denton, TX 76203-1280. Application available online. URL of online application: http://www.psyc.unt.edu/forms/App_Form05.pdf. Students are admitted in the Fall, application deadline January 2. Counseling and Clinical Psychology: January 2 application deadline; Behavioral Medicine, Industrial/Organizational Psychology and Experimental Psychology deadline February 1.

Our Lady of the Lake University
Psychology
College of Professional Studies
411 SW 24th Street
San Antonio, TX 78207
Telephone: (210) 431-3914
Fax: (210) 431-3927
E-mail: *bievj@lake.ollusa.edu*
Web: *http://www.ollusa.edu*

Department Information:
1983. Chairperson: Joan Biever. Number of Faculty: total–full-time 12, part-time 20; women–full-time 9, part-time 12; minority–full-time 5, part-time 10.

Programs and Degrees Offered:
Listed in the following order: Program area, degree type (T if terminal Master's), number awarded 7/03–6/04. Counseling Psychology PsyD (Doctor of Psychology) 1, School MA/MS (Master of Arts/Science) (T) 6, Marriage and Family Therapy MA/MS (Master of Arts/Science) (T) 27, Counseling Psychology MA/MS (Master of Arts/Science) (T) 10.

APA Accreditation: Counseling PsyD (Doctor of Psychology).

Student Applications/Admissions:
Student Applications
Counseling Psychology PsyD (Doctor of Psychology)—Applications 2004–2005, 35. Total applicants accepted 2004–2005, 7. Number enrolled (new admits only) 2004–2005 full-time, 0. Number enrolled (new admits only) 2004–2005 part-time, 0. Total enrolled 2004–2005 full-time, 8, part-time, 20. Openings 2005–2006, 10. The Median number of years required for completion of a degree are 6. The number of students enrolled full and part-time who were dismissed or voluntarily withdrew from this program area were 0. *School MA/MS (Master of Arts/Science)*—Applications 2004–2005, 33. Total applicants accepted 2004–2005, 10. Number enrolled (new admits only) 2004–2005 full-time, 0. Number enrolled (new admits only) 2004–2005 part-time, 0. Openings 2005–2006, 10. The Median number of years required for completion of a degree are 2. The number of students enrolled full and part-time who were dismissed or voluntarily withdrew from this program area were 1. *Marriage and Family Therapy MA/MS (Master of Arts/Science)*—Applications 2004–2005, 47. Total applicants accepted 2004–2005, 32. Openings 2005–2006, 10. The Median number of years required for completion of a degree are 2. The number of students enrolled full and part-time who were dismissed or voluntarily withdrew from this program area were 1. *Counseling Psychology MA/MS (Master of Arts/Science)*—Applications 2004–2005, 68. Total applicants accepted 2004–2005, 53. Number enrolled (new admits only) 2004–2005 full-time, 34. Number enrolled (new admits only) 2004–2005 part-time, 19. Total enrolled 2004–2005 full-time, 72, part-time, 78. Openings 2005–2006, 12. The Median number of years required for completion of a degree are 2. The number of students enrolled full and part-time who were dismissed or voluntarily withdrew from this program area were 2.

Admissions Requirements:
Scores: Entries appear in this order: required test or GPA, minimum score (if required), median score of students entering in 2003–2004. Master's Programs: overall undergraduate GPA 2.5; last 2 years GPA 3.0, 3.22. May take either the GRE or the MAT with no minimum score required. Doctoral Programs: GRE-V none, 500; GRE-Q none, 520; GRE-V+Q no minimum stated; GRE-Subject(Psych) 520; overall undergraduate GPA no minimum stated. Doctoral applicants must take the GRE psychoy subject exam in addition to the standard GRE. *Other Criteria:* (importance of criteria rated low, medium, or high): GRE/MAT scores medium, research experience low, work experience high, extracurricular activity low, clinically related public service medium, GPA high, letters of recommendation high, interview high, statement of goals and objectives high.

Student Characteristics: The following represents characteristics of students in 2004–2005 in all graduate psychology programs in

the department: Female–full-time 66, part-time 82; Male–full-time 14, part-time 16; African American/Black–full-time 4, part-time 14; Hispanic/Latino(a)–full-time 30, part-time 33; Asian/Pacific Islander–full-time 0, part-time 0; American Indian/Alaska Native–full-time 0, part-time 0; Caucasian–full-time 18, part-time 32; Multi-ethnic–full-time 28, part-time 19; students subject to the Americans With Disabilities Act–full-time 3, part-time 0.

Financial Information/Assistance:

Tuition for Full-Time Study: *Master's:* State residents: $586 per credit hour; Nonstate residents: $586 per credit hour. *Doctoral:* State residents: $698 per credit hour; Nonstate residents: $698 per credit hour. Tuition is subject to change.

Financial Assistance:

First Year Students: Teaching assistantships available for first-year. Average amount paid per academic year: $7,000. Average number of hours worked per week: 12. Apply by not specific. Research assistantships available for first-year. Average amount paid per academic year: $7,000. Average number of hours worked per week: 12. Apply by not specific. Fellowships and scholarships available for first-year. Average amount paid per academic year: $11,000. Average number of hours worked per week: 0. Apply by after admiss.

Advanced Students: Teaching assistantships available for advanced students. Average amount paid per academic year: $7,000. Average number of hours worked per week: 12. Research assistantships available for advanced students. Average amount paid per academic year: $7,000. Average number of hours worked per week: 12. Fellowships and scholarships available for advanced students. Average amount paid per academic year: $11,000.

Contact Information: Of all students currently enrolled full-time, 20% benefitted from one or more of the listed financial assistance programs.

Internships/Practica: The psychology department operates a training clinic, the Community Counseling Service (CCS), which serves as the initial practical site for all master's and doctoral students. At the CCS, practica students work in teams of up to six students under the live supervision of psychology faculty. The CCS is located in and serves a low-income, predominantly Mexican-American community. Supervision of Spanish-language psychotherapy is available. A variety of off-campus sites are available to students in their second and subsequent semesters of practica. Students are placed at off-campus sites according to their career interests and training needs. Available practica sites include public and private schools, hospitals, and community agencies. For those doctoral students for whom a professional internship is required prior to graduation, 4 applied in 2003–2004. Of those who applied, 3 were placed in internships listed by the Association of Psychology Postdoctoral and Internship Programs (APPIC); 3 were placed in APA accredited internships.

Housing and Day Care: On-campus housing is available. On-campus day care facilities are available. There is a Child Development Center on campus for small children. There is also an elementary school on campus. Both services charge a fee.

Employment of Department Graduates:

Master's Degree Graduates: Of those who graduated in the academic year 2003–2004, the following categories and numbers represent the post-graduate activities and employment of master's

degree graduates: Enrolled in a post-doctoral residency/fellowship (n/a), employed in independent practice (n/a), total from the above (master's) (0).

Doctoral Degree Graduates: Of those who graduated in the academic year 2003–2004, the following categories and numbers represent the post-graduate activities and employment of doctoral degree graduates: Enrolled in a psychology doctoral program (n/a), total from the above (doctoral) (0).

Additional Information:

Orientation, Objectives, and Emphasis of Department: Graduate psychology programs at OLLU adhere to the practitioner-scholar model of training and emphasize brief, systemic approaches to psychotherapy. Postmodern and multicultural perspectives are infused throughout the curriculum, including practica. A subspecialty in psychological services for Spanish-speaking populations is available.

Special Facilities or Resources: The department's training clinic serves as both a training and research facility. Research facilities are also available in the building which houses the psychology department.

Application Information:

Send to: Graduate Admissions Office, Our Lady of the Lake University, 411 SW 24th Street, San Antonio, TX 78207. Application available online. URL of online application: https://palmtree.ollusa.edu/my publishedsite/gradapp.asp. Students are admitted in the Fall, application deadline January 15 for PsyD program, Fall Admission; March 1 for MS programs, Fall Admission; early decision July 1 for MS, Fall Admission, extended deadline. *Fee:* $25. If accepted, the fee is applied to the first semester's tuition.

Rice University
Department of Psychology
6100 Main Street
Houston, TX 77005-1892
Telephone: (713) 348-4856
Fax: (713) 348-5221
E-mail: *psyc@rice.edu*
Web: *http://ruf.rice.edu/~psyc/*

Department Information:

1966. Chairperson: Randi C. Martin. Number of Faculty: total–full-time 16; women–full-time 6.

Programs and Degrees Offered:

Listed in the following order: Program area, degree type (T if terminal Master's), number awarded 7/03–6/04. Industrial/ Organizational PhD (Doctor of Philosophy) 6, Cognitive PhD (Doctor of Philosophy) 9, Human-Computer Interaction PhD (Doctor of Philosophy) 5.

Student Applications/Admissions:

Student Applications

Industrial/ Organizational PhD (Doctor of Philosophy)—Applications 2004–2005, 110. Total applicants accepted 2004–2005, 3. Number enrolled (new admits only) 2004–2005 full-time,

2. Total enrolled 2004–2005 full-time, 10. Openings 2005–2006, 3. The Median number of years required for completion of a degree are 5. The number of students enrolled full and part-time who were dismissed or voluntarily withdrew from this program area were 0. *Cognitive PhD (Doctor of Philosophy)*—Applications 2004–2005, 47. Total applicants accepted 2004–2005, 9. Number enrolled (new admits only) 2004–2005 full-time, 6. Total enrolled 2004–2005 full-time, 19. Openings 2005–2006, 3. The Median number of years required for completion of a degree are 5. The number of students enrolled full and part-time who were dismissed or voluntarily withdrew from this program area were 1. *Human-Computer Interaction PhD (Doctor of Philosophy)*—Applications 2004–2005, 14. Total applicants accepted 2004–2005, 0. Number enrolled (new admits only) 2004–2005 full-time, 0. Total enrolled 2004–2005 full-time, 8. Openings 2005–2006, 1. The Median number of years required for completion of a degree are 5. The number of students enrolled full and part-time who were dismissed or voluntarily withdrew from this program area were 0.

Admissions Requirements:

Scores: Entries appear in this order: required test or GPA, minimum score (if required), median score of students entering in 2003–2004. Master's Programs: GRE-V no minimum stated; GRE-Q no minimum stated; GRE-V+Q no minimum stated; GRE-Analytical no minimum stated; overall undergraduate GPA no minimum stated. Doctoral Programs: GRE-V no minimum stated, 579; GRE-Q no minimum stated, 687; GRE-V+Q no minimum stated, 1267; GRE-Analytical no minimum stated, 696; overall undergraduate GPA 3.0, 3.67. There is no specific score requirement for test scores.

Other Criteria: (importance of criteria rated low, medium, or high): GRE/MAT scores high, research experience high, work experience low, extracurricular activity low, clinically related public service low, GPA high, letters of recommendation high, statement of goals and objectives high. For additional information on admission requirements, go to: http://www.ruf.rice.edu/~psyc.

Student Characteristics: The following represents characteristics of students in 2004–2005 in all graduate psychology programs in the department: Female–full-time 23, part-time 0; Male–full-time 14, part-time 0; African American/Black–full-time 2, part-time 0; Hispanic/Latino(a)–full-time 3, part-time 0; Asian/Pacific Islander–full-time 5, part-time 0; American Indian/Alaska Native–full-time 0, part-time 0; Caucasian–full-time 26, part-time 0; Multi-ethnic–full-time 1, part-time 0; students subject to the Americans With Disabilities Act–full-time 0, part-time 0.

Financial Information/Assistance:

Tuition for Full-Time Study: *Doctoral:* State residents: per academic year $22,700; Nonstate residents: per academic year $22,700. Tuition is subject to change.

Financial Assistance:

First Year Students: Fellowships and scholarships available for first-year. Average amount paid per academic year: $12,500. Apply by January 15. Tuition remission given: full.

Advanced Students: Teaching assistantships available for advanced students. Average amount paid per academic year: $12,500. Apply by January 15. Tuition remission given: full. Research assistantships available for advanced students. Average

amount paid per academic year: $12,500. Apply by January 15. Tuition remission given: full. Fellowships and scholarships available for advanced students. Average amount paid per academic year: $12,500. Apply by January 15. Tuition remission given: full.

Contact Information: Of all students currently enrolled full-time, 97% benefitted from one or more of the listed financial assistance programs.

Internships/Practica: Graduate students beyond their third year have the opportunity to work in internships in the Houston area. Although not required, many of our students work part-time in local organizations including NASA, the Texas Medical Center, Hewlett Packard, and a variety of consulting firms.

Housing and Day Care: On-campus housing is available. See the following Web site for more information: University Graduate Apartments, http://riceinfo.rice.edu/maps/space/gra/. No on-campus day care facilities are available.

Employment of Department Graduates:

Master's Degree Graduates: Of those who graduated in the academic year 2003–2004, the following categories and numbers represent the post-graduate activities and employment of master's degree graduates: Enrolled in a psychology doctoral program (15), enrolled in a post-doctoral residency/fellowship (n/a), employed in independent practice (n/a), total from the above (master's) (15).

Doctoral Degree Graduates: Of those who graduated in the academic year 2003–2004, the following categories and numbers represent the post-graduate activities and employment of doctoral degree graduates: Enrolled in a psychology doctoral program (n/a), employed in an academic position at a university (2), employed in other positions at a higher education institution (0), employed in a hospital/medical center (1), do not know (1), total from the above (doctoral) (4).

Additional Information:

Orientation, Objectives, and Emphasis of Department: The Rice program emphasizes training in basic and applied research and in the skills necessary to conduct research. The content areas to which this emphasis is applied are cognitive psychology (including cognitive neuroscience), industrial/organizational, and human-computer interaction. We believe that training in research and research skills generalizes very broadly to the kinds of tasks that professional psychologists will be asked to perform both in the university laboratory and in addressing such diverse applied questions as organizational management, system design, or program evaluation. Students in the cognitive neuroscience program are encouraged to participate in courses and research opportunities available from our joint program in Neuroscience with Baylor College of Medicine. Students in the other areas are encouraged to develop research interests that combine content areas across the department. Industrial/organizational and human factors psychologists, for example, might collaborate on research dealing with organizational communication via electronic mail. Cognitive and industrial/organizational psychologists might, for instance, investigate cognitive processes underlying performance appraisal; and human factors and cognitive psychologists might collaborate on studies of risk perception and the perceptual and attentional properties of computer displays. Although some of our students prefer to devote their energies to laboratory research in preparation for academic positions in basic areas, many students take advantage of the opportunities we provide for "real world" experience. The department arranges internships or practica in a wide variety of settings for interested advanced students.

Special Facilities or Resources: Graduate students in the Rice Psychology programs benefit from their access to a large and vital Houston business community, NASA, and over 40 teaching and research centers in the Texas Medical Center. Within the department, graduate students in all programs have ready access to a variety of powerful Macintosh (G-4 and iMac) and Windows-based computers that more than meet the needs of students for data collection, simulation, instruction, word processing, and computation. The department contains facilities for the study of dyadic and small group interaction, social judgment, decision making, and computer-interface design. In addition to the facilities physisially located in the Psychology Department, Rice University has a state-of-the-art computer laboratory for research in the social sciences that has been constructed with support from the National Science Foundation. The cognitive neuroscience area has benefitted from the recent acquisition of a transcranial magnetic stimulation (TMS) device for investigating brain function, two eye tracking devices, a Silicon Graphics workstation for neuroimaging data analysis and 3D rendering of brains from MRI scans, and a dense-sensor array (128 channel) event-related potential (ERP) recording system that allows the detailed description of neural systems. Collaborations with institutions in the nearby Texas Medical Center provide access to functional neuroimaging facilties, which include the new Houston Neuroimaging Laboratory at Baylor College of Medicine that has two 3T research-dedicated scanners.

Information for Students With Physical Disabilities: See the following Web site for more information: http://dss.rice.edu/primary.cfm?doc_id=1267.

Application Information:

Send to: Department Chair, Psychology Department, Rice University, 6100 Main Street, Houston, TX 77005. Application available online. URL of online application: http://www.ruf.rice.edu/~psyc/graduate/. Students are admitted in the Fall, application deadline January 15. *Fee:* $35. Conditions for waiver of fee: Hardship.

Sam Houston State University

Department of Psychology
Humanities and Social Sciences
Box 2447
Huntsville, TX 77341-2447
Telephone: (936) 294-1210
Fax: (936) 294-3798
E-mail: *awoodworth@shsu.edu*
Web: *http://www.shsu.edu/~psy_www/phd.htm*

Department Information:

1972. Chairperson: Donna Desforges. Number of Faculty: total–full-time 15; women–full-time 5; minority–full-time 1; faculty subject to the Americans With Disabilities Act 1.

Programs and Degrees Offered:

Listed in the following order: Program area, degree type (T if terminal Master's), number awarded 7/03–6/04. Clinical MA/MS (Master of Arts/Science) (T) 5, General MA/MS (Master of Arts/Science) (T) 2, School MA/MS (Master of Arts/Science) (T) 4, Clinical (Forensic Emphasis) PhD (Doctor of Philosophy) 4.

Student Applications/Admissions:

Student Applications

Clinical MA/MS (Master of Arts/Science)—Applications 2004–2005, 37. Total applicants accepted 2004–2005, 13. Number enrolled (new admits only) 2004–2005 full-time, 13. Openings 2005–2006, 15. The Median number of years required for completion of a degree are 2. The number of students enrolled full and part-time who were dismissed or voluntarily withdrew from this program area were 2. *General MA/MS (Master of Arts/Science)*—Applications 2004–2005, 9. Total applicants accepted 2004–2005, 5. Number enrolled (new admits only) 2004–2005 full-time, 5. Openings 2005–2006, 10. The Median number of years required for completion of a degree are 2. The number of students enrolled full and part-time who were dismissed or voluntarily withdrew from this program area were 0. *School MA/MS (Master of Arts/Science)*—Applications 2004–2005, 25. Total applicants accepted 2004–2005, 9. Number enrolled (new admits only) 2004–2005 full-time, 9. Number enrolled (new admits only) 2004–2005 part-time, 0. Total enrolled 2004–2005 full-time, 15, part-time, 1. Openings 2005–2006, 10. The Median number of years required for completion of a degree are 3. The number of students enrolled full and part-time who were dismissed or voluntarily withdrew from this program area were 0. *Clinical (Forensic Emphasis) PhD (Doctor of Philosophy)*—Applications 2004–2005, 103. Total applicants accepted 2004–2005, 7. Number enrolled (new admits only) 2004–2005 full-time, 7. Number enrolled (new admits only) 2004–2005 part-time, 0. Openings 2005–2006, 10. The Median number of years required for completion of a degree are 4. The number of students enrolled full and part-time who were dismissed or voluntarily withdrew from this program area were 1.

Admissions Requirements:

Scores: Entries appear in this order: required test or GPA, minimum score (if required), median score of students entering in 2003–2004. Master's Programs: GRE-V no minimum stated; GRE-Q no minimum stated; GRE-V+Q no minimum stated, 1105; MAT 50; overall undergraduate GPA no minimum stated, 3.5. Doctoral Programs: GRE-V no minimum stated, 588; GRE-Q no minimum stated, 636; GRE-V+Q no minimum stated, 1224; GRE-Subject(Psych) no minimum stated; overall undergraduate GPA no minimum stated, 3.62.

Other Criteria: (importance of criteria rated low, medium, or high): GRE/MAT scores high, research experience high, work experience low, extracurricular activity low, clinically related public service medium, GPA high, letters of recommendation high, interview high, statement of goals and objectives high. No interview is required for admission to our Master's program. For additional information on admission requirements, go to: http://www.shsu.edu/~psy_www/phd.htm.

Student Characteristics: The following represents characteristics of students in 2004–2005 in all graduate psychology programs in the department: Female–full-time 86, part-time 1; Male–full-time 8, part-time 0; African American/Black–full-time 3, part-time 0; Hispanic/Latino(a)–full-time 6, part-time 0; Asian/Pacific Islander–full-time 2, part-time 0; American Indian/Alaska Native–

full-time 0, part-time 0; Caucasian–full-time 82, part-time 1; Multi-ethnic–full-time 1, part-time 0; students subject to the Americans With Disabilities Act–full-time 1, part-time 0.

Financial Information/Assistance:

Tuition for Full-Time Study: *Master's:* State residents: per academic year $9,727, $390 per credit hour; Nonstate residents: per academic year $11,274, $699 per credit hour. *Doctoral:* State residents: per academic year $9,727, $390 per credit hour; Nonstate residents: per academic year $11,274, $699 per credit hour. Tuition is subject to change. See the following Web site for updates and changes in tuition costs: http://www.shsu.edu/schedule/.

Financial Assistance:

First Year Students: Teaching assistantships available for first-year. Research assistantships available for first-year. Average amount paid per academic year: $10,000. Average number of hours worked per week: 20. Fellowships and scholarships available for first-year. Average amount paid per academic year: $10,000.

Advanced Students: Teaching assistantships available for advanced students. Average amount paid per academic year: $10,000. Average number of hours worked per week: 20. Research assistantships available for advanced students. Average amount paid per academic year: $10,000. Average number of hours worked per week: 20. Traineeships available for advanced students. Average amount paid per academic year: $10,000. Average number of hours worked per week: 20. Fellowships and scholarships available for advanced students. Average amount paid per academic year: $10,000.

Contact Information: Of all students currently enrolled full-time, 75% benefitted from one or more of the listed financial assistance programs.

Internships/Practica: We offer a variety of internships and practica for each of the applied tracks. Students in the School psychology program complete a one-year internship in schools. There are a variety of placements for students in the Clinical psychology master's program, including the University Counseling Center, area community mental health centers, and the psychological services centers of the Texas Department of Criminal Justice (TDCJ). Students in the clinical doctoral program may be assigned to any of the aforementioned clinical sites, as well as to a variety of other practica, including the Harris County Psychiatric Center, ADAPT Counseling, the Houston Child Assessment Center, and the Institute for Rehabilitation and Research (neuropsychology). These students also work at our on-campus Psychological Services Center, which provides both general mental health services (e.g., individual psychotherapy, couples counseling, psychological assessment), and forensic services (e.g., risk assessments, competency and sanity evaluations). For those doctoral students for whom a professional internship is required prior to graduation, 5 applied in 2003–2004. Of those who applied, 5 were placed in internships listed by the Association of Psychology Postdoctoral and Internship Programs (APPIC); 5 were placed in APA accredited internships.

Housing and Day Care: On-campus housing is available. See the following Web site for more information: http://www.shsu.edu/~hou_www/. No on-campus day care facilities are available.

Employment of Department Graduates:

Master's Degree Graduates: Of those who graduated in the academic year 2003–2004, the following categories and numbers represent the post-graduate activities and employment of master's degree graduates: Enrolled in a psychology doctoral program (1), enrolled in a post-doctoral residency/fellowship (n/a), employed in independent practice (n/a), employed in a professional position in a school system (4), employed in a community mental health/counseling center (2), total from the above (master's) (7).

Doctoral Degree Graduates: Of those who graduated in the academic year 2003–2004, the following categories and numbers represent the post-graduate activities and employment of doctoral degree graduates: Enrolled in a psychology doctoral program (n/a), enrolled in a post-doctoral residency/fellowship (1), employed in a community mental health/counseling center (3), total from the above (doctoral) (4).

Additional Information:

Orientation, Objectives, and Emphasis of Department: The Clinical and School Master's programs are applied training programs that develop effective Master's-level practitioners. Students in those programs receive extensive and eclectic training in both psychotherapy and psychometrics and conclude their training with extensive supervised practicum experience. Graduates can seek licensure as psychological associates or as professional counselors in Texas, and graduates of the School program can seek national certification from National Association of School Psychologists, licensure as specialists in school psychology in Texas, and licensure as professional counselors in Texas. The General track involves broader exposure to psychology's core disciplines and allows the student more elective flexibility to craft an individual specialty. Graduates of all three programs often progress to doctoral training elsewhere. Our clinical doctoral program (with an emphasis in forensic clinical psychology) is a scientist-practitioner program that provides broad and general training in clinical psychology (e.g., psychotherapy, psychopathology, assessment). Students also take courses in such areas as forensic assessment and mental health law and have the opportunity to engage in clinical forensic research, studying topics such as psychopathy and risk assessment.

Special Facilities or Resources: The department enjoys ample testing and observation space, including a live animal facility. The university's computing facilities are superb, offering extensive access to personal computers loaded with the latest software. The town of Huntsville (population 32,000) is a lovely environment surrounded on three sides by national forest, with the Houston metropolis one hour away.

Information for Students With Physical Disabilities: See the following Web site for more information: http://www.shsu.edu/~counsel/sswd.html.

Application Information:

Send to: Master's applications: Rowland Miller; Applications to PhD program: David Marcus. Department of Psychology, Sam Houston State University, Huntsville, TX 77341-2447. Application available online. Students are admitted in the Fall, application deadline July 1; Spring, application deadline November 1; Summer, application deadline April 1. These deadlines are for our Master's programs, but we encourage early applications; all three Master's have rolling admissions, and admission into those programs becomes more competitive as the deadlines approach. January 20 is the deadline for the doctoral program; that program admits students only in the fall. The fee for the Master's program is $20, $40 is the application fee for the doctoral program.

Southern Methodist University

Department of Psychology
Dedman College
6424 Hilltop Lane
Dallas, TX 75275-0442
Telephone: (214) 768-4924
Fax: (214) 768-3910
E-mail: *aconner@smu.edu*
Web: *http://www.smu.edu/psychology/*

Department Information:

1925. Chairperson: Ernest Jouriles, PhD. Number of Faculty: total–full-time 15, part-time 12; women–full-time 4, part-time 9; minority–full-time 1, part-time 1.

Programs and Degrees Offered:

Listed in the following order: Program area, degree type (T if terminal Master's), number awarded 7/03–6/04. Clinical/Counseling MA/MS (Master of Arts/Science) (T) 12, Clinical psychology PhD (Doctor of Philosophy) 0.

Student Applications/Admissions:

Student Applications

Clinical/Counseling MA/MS (Master of Arts/Science)—Applications 2004–2005, 60. Total applicants accepted 2004–2005, 15. Number enrolled (new admits only) 2004–2005 full-time, 10. Total enrolled 2004–2005 full-time, 18. Openings 2005–2006, 5. The Median number of years required for completion of a degree are 2. The number of students enrolled full and part-time who were dismissed or voluntarily withdrew from this program area were 2. *Clinical psychology PhD (Doctor of Philosophy)*—Applications 2004–2005, 15. Total applicants accepted 2004–2005, 4. Number enrolled (new admits only) 2004–2005 full-time, 4. Total enrolled 2004–2005 full-time, 8. Openings 2005–2006, 4. The number of students enrolled full and part-time who were dismissed or voluntarily withdrew from this program area were 1.

Admissions Requirements:

Scores: Entries appear in this order: required test or GPA, minimum score (if required), median score of students entering in 2003–2004. Master's Programs: GRE-V 500; GRE-Q 500; overall undergraduate GPA 3.0. Doctoral Programs: GRE-V no minimum stated, 520; GRE-Q no minimum stated, 600; GRE-V+Q no minimum stated; overall undergraduate GPA 3.0.

Other Criteria: (importance of criteria rated low, medium, or high): GRE/MAT scores high, research experience high, work experience low, extracurricular activity low, clinically related public service low, GPA high, letters of recommendation high, interview medium, statement of goals and objectives high, research interests high. Match of research interests with those of faculty important for graduate programs.

Student Characteristics: The following represents characteristics of students in 2004–2005 in all graduate psychology programs in the department: Female–full-time 22, part-time 0; Male–full-time 4, part-time 0; African American/Black–part-time 0; Hispanic/Latino(a)–full-time 3, part-time 0; Asian/Pacific Islander–full-time 2, part-time 0; American Indian/Alaska Native–full-time 0, part-time 0; Caucasian–full-time 21, part-time 0; Multi-ethnic–full-time 0, part-time 0; students subject to the Americans With Disabilities Act–full-time 0, part-time 0.

Financial Information/Assistance:

Tuition for Full-Time Study: *Master's:* State residents: per academic year $16,920, $940 per credit hour; Nonstate residents: per academic year $16,920, $940 per credit hour. *Doctoral:* State residents: per academic year $16,920, $940 per credit hour; Nonstate residents: per academic year $16,920, $940 per credit hour.

Financial Assistance:

First Year Students: Research assistantships available for first-year. Average amount paid per academic year: $12,000. Average number of hours worked per week: 20. Apply by January 1. Tuition remission given: full.

Advanced Students: Research assistantships available for advanced students. Average amount paid per academic year: $12,000. Average number of hours worked per week: 20. Apply by January 1. Tuition remission given: full.

Contact Information: Of all students currently enrolled full-time, 40% benefitted from one or more of the listed financial assistance programs. Application and information available online at: http://www.smu.edu/psychology/gradprograms.htm.

Internships/Practica: Practicum placements are available for students in both the MA program and the clinical PhD program.

Housing and Day Care: On-campus housing is available. See the following Web site for more information: www.smu.edu/housing. On-campus day care facilities are available. See the following Web site for more information: www.smu.edu/catalogs/graduate/services.asp.

Employment of Department Graduates:

Master's Degree Graduates: Of those who graduated in the academic year 2003–2004, the following categories and numbers represent the post-graduate activities and employment of master's degree graduates: Enrolled in a psychology doctoral program (2), enrolled in a post-doctoral residency/fellowship (n/a), employed in independent practice (n/a), do not know (23), total from the above (master's) (25).

Doctoral Degree Graduates: Of those who graduated in the academic year 2003–2004, the following categories and numbers represent the post-graduate activities and employment of doctoral degree graduates: Enrolled in a psychology doctoral program (n/a), total from the above (doctoral) (0).

Additional Information:

Orientation, Objectives, and Emphasis of Department: The mission of SMU's 70 hour doctoral program in clinical psychology is to train psychologists whose professional activities are based on scientific knowledge and methods. The program integrates rigorous research training with state-of the-art, evidence-based clinical training. Thus, our program emphasizes the development of conceptual and research skills as well as scientifically-based clinical practice skills. The overarching goal is for our graduates to use empirical methods to advance psychological knowledge and to approach clinical phenomena in a way consistent with scientific evidence. Our 48-hour MA in clinical/counseling program includes coursework consistent with certification for a Licensed Professional Counselor in the state of Texas. The goal of this program is to train students in the delivery of psychological services. A thesis is not required as part of this program.

Special Facilities or Resources: The department houses a Family Research Center and has a number of well-equipped laboratories for research on various topics in clinical psychology.

Information for Students With Physical Disabilities: See the following Web site for more information: www.smu.edu/studentlife/OSSD_Facts.asp.

Application Information:

Send to: The Office of Graduate Studies , Southern Methodist University, P.O. Box 750240, Dallas, TX 75275-0240. Application available online. Students are admitted in the Fall, application deadline January 1 for PhD students, February 1 for MA students. *Fee:* $60.

Street Mary's University
Department of Psychology
One Camino Santa Maria
San Antonio, TX 78228-8573
Telephone: (210) 436-3314
Fax: (210) 431-4301
E-mail: *aberndt@stmarytx.edu*
Web: *http://www.stmarytx.edu*

Department Information:

1965. Chairperson: Patricia Owen. Number of Faculty: total–full-time 5, part-time 6; women–full-time 3, part-time 2; minority–part-time 1.

Programs and Degrees Offered:

Listed in the following order: Program area, degree type (T if terminal Master's), number awarded 7/03–6/04. Clinical MA/MS (Master of Arts/Science) (T) 7, Industrial/ Organizational MA/MS (Master of Arts/Science) (T) 7.

Student Applications/Admissions:

Student Applications

Clinical MA/MS (Master of Arts/Science)—Applications 2004–2005, 48. Total applicants accepted 2004–2005, 22. Number enrolled (new admits only) 2004–2005 full-time, 13. Number enrolled (new admits only) 2004–2005 part-time, 4. Total enrolled 2004–2005 full-time, 33, part-time, 8. Openings 2005–2006, 20. The Median number of years required for completion of a degree are 2. The number of students enrolled full and part-time who were dismissed or voluntarily withdrew from this program area were 2. *Industrial/ Organizational MA/ MS (Master of Arts/Science)*—Applications 2004–2005, 35. Total applicants accepted 2004–2005, 15. Number enrolled (new admits only) 2004–2005 full-time, 9. Number enrolled (new admits only) 2004–2005 part-time, 3. Total enrolled

2004–2005 full-time, 30, part-time, 11. Openings 2005–2006, 20. The Median number of years required for completion of a degree are 2. The number of students enrolled full and part-time who were dismissed or voluntarily withdrew from this program area were 0.

Admissions Requirements:

Scores: Entries appear in this order: required test or GPA, minimum score (if required), median score of students entering in 2003–2004. Master's Programs: GRE-V no minimum stated, 500; GRE-Q no minimum stated, 500; GRE-V+Q 950, 1000; overall undergraduate GPA no minimum stated, 3.0; last 2 years GPA no minimum stated, 3.2; psychology GPA 3.0, 3.0. Regular enrollment status is recommended for students who have a combined verbal and quantitative GRE score of 1000 (each section is at least 400), an undergraduate cumulative and psychology grade point average of 3.0 or greater, and final course grades of B or better in Research Methods and Statistics. *Other Criteria:* (importance of criteria rated low, medium, or high): GRE/MAT scores high, research experience high, work experience medium, extracurricular activity medium, clinically related public service medium, GPA high, letters of recommendation medium, interview low, statement of goals and objectives high, Clinically Related Public Service for Clinical MA/ MS Work Related Experience for Industrial-Organizational MA/MS.

Student Characteristics: The following represents characteristics of students in 2004–2005 in all graduate psychology programs in the department: Female–full-time 57, part-time 15; Male–full-time 6, part-time 4; African American/Black–full-time 2, part-time 0; Hispanic/Latino(a)–full-time 24, part-time 5; Asian/Pacific Islander–full-time 5, part-time 0; American Indian/Alaska Native–full-time 0, part-time 0; Caucasian–full-time 32, part-time 13; Multi-ethnic–full-time 0, part-time 1; students subject to the Americans With Disabilities Act–full-time 0, part-time 0.

Financial Information/Assistance:

Tuition for Full-Time Study: *Master's:* State residents: per academic year $10,530, $568 per credit hour; Nonstate residents: per academic year $10,530, $568 per credit hour. Tuition is subject to change. See the following Web site for updates and changes in tuition costs: http://www.stmarytx.edu/businessoffice/?go=tuit_05.

Financial Assistance:

First Year Students: Teaching assistantships available for first-year. Average amount paid per academic year: $4,000. Average number of hours worked per week: 15. Apply by March 1. Fellowships and scholarships available for first-year. Average amount paid per academic year: $4,000. Average number of hours worked per week: 15. Apply by March 15.

Advanced Students: Teaching assistantships available for advanced students. Average amount paid per academic year: $4,000. Average number of hours worked per week: 15. Apply by March 1. Fellowships and scholarships available for advanced students. Average amount paid per academic year: $4,000. Average number of hours worked per week: 15. Apply by March 15.

Contact Information: Of all students currently enrolled full-time, 1% benefitted from one or more of the listed financial assistance programs.

Internships/Practica: Clinical students are required to complete two practica under the supervision of a psychologist licensed in the state of Texas (450 total hours). Industrial/Organizational students are required to complete one practicum (225 total hours).

Housing and Day Care: On-campus housing is available. See the following Web site for more information: http://www.stmarytx.edu/reslife/. No on-campus day care facilities are available.

Employment of Department Graduates:

Master's Degree Graduates: Of those who graduated in the academic year 2003–2004, the following categories and numbers represent the post-graduate activities and employment of master's degree graduates: Enrolled in a psychology doctoral program (0), enrolled in another graduate/professional program (2), enrolled in a post-doctoral residency/fellowship (n/a), employed in independent practice (n/a), employed in an academic position at a university (0), employed in an academic position at a 2-year/4-year college (0), employed in other positions at a higher education institution (0), employed in a professional position in a school system (0), employed in business or industry (research/consulting) (1), employed in business or industry (management) (3), employed in a government agency (research) (3), employed in a government agency (professional services) (0), employed in a community mental health/counseling center (2), employed in a hospital/medical center (1), still seeking employment (2), other employment position (0), do not know (0), total from the above (master's) (14).

Doctoral Degree Graduates: Of those who graduated in the academic year 2003–2004, the following categories and numbers represent the post-graduate activities and employment of doctoral degree graduates: Enrolled in a psychology doctoral program (n/a), total from the above (doctoral) (0).

Additional Information:

Orientation, Objectives, and Emphasis of Department: Clinical Psychology graduates are trained to be proficient in assessment, diagnosis, and intervention. Their education prepares them for entry to a PhD or PsyD program in Clinical Psychology and positions in a variety of clinical settings ranging from school districts to psychiatric hospitals to university counseling centers. Industrial-Organizational Psychology graduates are trained to be proficient in job analysis, performance appraisal, personnel selection, survey development, and training, and other related areas in the field. Their education prepares them for entry to a PhD prgram in Industrial/Organizational psychology or a career in business and industry. Those interested in a career in business and industry are prepared for job opportunities in positions emphasizing the quantification of human behavior.

Special Facilities or Resources: Students have access to university services such as the Service Learning Center, the Center for Legal and Social Justice, and the 21st Century Leadership Center. Graduate students may choose to study abroad in Innsbruck, Austria for summer courses. Annual activities include the President's Peace Commission, the Lin Great Speaker Series, Oysterbake, and the Annual Research Exhibition.

Information for Students With Physical Disabilities: See the following Web site for more information: http://www.stmarytx.edu/disability/.

Application Information:
Send to: Graduate Admissions, Street Mary's University, One Camino Santa Maria, San Antonio, TX 78228. Application available online. URL of online application: http://www.stmarytx.edu/grad/graduate_application/main_menu.php. Students are admitted in the Fall, application deadline June; Spring, application deadline December 1; Summer, application deadline March. Programs have rolling admissions. The deadline for students who wish to be considered for Fall Assistantships is March 1. *Fee:* $35.

Stephen F. Austin State University
Department of Psychology
Liberal Arts
Box 13046, SFASU
Nacogdoches, TX 75962
Telephone: (936) 468-4402
Fax: (936) 468-4015
E-mail: *kstahl@sfasu.edu*
Web: *http://www.sfasu.edu/sfapsych/front.html*

Department Information:
1962. Chairperson: Dr. Kandy Stahl. Number of Faculty: total–full-time 12, part-time 5; women–full-time 6, part-time 2; minority–full-time 1.

Programs and Degrees Offered:
Listed in the following order: Program area, degree type (T if terminal Master's), number awarded 7/03–6/04. Clinical Psychology MA/MS (Master of Arts/Science) (T), Industrial / Organizational Psychology MA/MS (Master of Arts/Science) (T), Experimental Psychology MA/MS (Master of Arts/Science), Teaching of Psychology (Development) MA/MS (Master of Arts/Science).

Student Applications/Admissions:

Student Applications

Clinical Psychology MA/MS (Master of Arts/Science)—Industrial/Organizational Psychology MA/MS (Master of Arts/Science)—Experimental Psychology MA/MS (Master of Arts/Science)—Teaching of Psychology (Development) MA/MS (Master of Arts/Science)—No information provided.

Admissions Requirements:

Scores: Entries appear in this order: required test or GPA, minimum score (if required), median score of students entering in 2003–2004. Master's Programs: GRE-V no minimum stated; GRE-Q no minimum stated; GRE-V+Q no minimum stated; overall undergraduate GPA 3.00; last 2 years GPA 3.00; psychology GPA 3.00.

Other Criteria: (importance of criteria rated low, medium, or high): GRE/MAT scores medium, research experience medium, work experience low, extracurricular activity low, clinically related public service low, GPA high, letters of recommendation medium, statement of goals and objectives medium.

Student Characteristics: The following represents characteristics of students in 2004–2005 in all graduate psychology programs in

the department: Female–full-time 32, part-time 3; Male–full-time 13, part-time 2; African American/Black–full-time 0, part-time 1; Hispanic/Latino(a)–full-time 2, part-time 1; Asian/Pacific Islander–full-time 1, part-time 0; American Indian/Alaska Native–full-time 0, part-time 0; Caucasian–full-time 42, part-time 3; Multi-ethnic–full-time 0, part-time 0; students subject to the Americans With Disabilities Act–part-time 1.

Financial Information/Assistance:

Tuition for Full-Time Study: *Master's:* State residents: per academic year $1,324, $48 per credit hour; Nonstate residents: per academic year $5,333, $282 per credit hour. Tuition is subject to change. See the following Web site for updates and changes in tuition costs: Louisiana residents: $2377.00 tuition per academic year. All tuitions based on 9-hr load.

Financial Assistance:

First Year Students: Teaching assistantships available for first-year. Average amount paid per academic year: $8,100. Average number of hours worked per week: 20. Apply by April 15. Research assistantships available for first-year. Average amount paid per academic year: $8,100. Average number of hours worked per week: 20. Apply by April 15.

Advanced Students: Teaching assistantships available for advanced students. Average amount paid per academic year: $8,100. Average number of hours worked per week: 20. Research assistantships available for advanced students. Average amount paid per academic year: $8,100. Average number of hours worked per week: 20.

Contact Information: Of all students currently enrolled full-time, 85% benefitted from one or more of the listed financial assistance programs.

Internships/Practica: Praticum is an elective if chosen; the first practicum is completed on campus in the department's Psychology Clinic. Subsequently, students may elect to take further practica either in the Clinic or in a community agency approved by the faculty.

Housing and Day Care: On-campus housing is available. See the following Web site for more information: http://www.sfasu.edu/housing/. On-campus day care facilities are available. See the following Web site for more information: http://www.education.sfasu.edu/ele/centers/eclab.htm.

Employment of Department Graduates:

Master's Degree Graduates: Of those who graduated in the academic year 2003–2004, the following categories and numbers represent the post-graduate activities and employment of master's degree graduates: Enrolled in a post-doctoral residency/fellowship (n/a), employed in independent practice (n/a), total from the above (master's) (0).

Doctoral Degree Graduates: Of those who graduated in the academic year 2003–2004, the following categories and numbers represent the post-graduate activities and employment of doctoral degree graduates: Enrolled in a psychology doctoral program (n/a), total from the above (doctoral) (0).

Additional Information:

Orientation, Objectives, and Emphasis of Department: The primary goal of the MA program is to prepare students for admission to doctoral training programs in psychology, or to obtain meaningful employment opportunities if in the I/O or the Teaching of Psychology tracks. The Clinical degree track is based on the scientist-practitioner training model, with training in methodology, research, and theory supplemented by application of clinical skills. Clinical training involves formal lab courses in intellectual assessment and personality assessment. Students can then elect to complete a psychotherapy interviewing and skills course, followed by a supervised clinical practicum in the Psychology Clinic. The I/O program, which was designed to meet the standards established by the Society for Industrial and Organizational Psychology (SIOP), emphasizes research methodology and statistics, supplemented with applied independent research and an I/O practicum, with either a personnel or organizational emphasis. A 9-hour graduate minor in Management is also an option for our I/O students. The General Experimental track is intended for students interested in preparing for doctoral study in the major areas of experimental psychology. The goal of the Teaching Emphasis track is to train individuals to be competent instructors, qualified to teach at the community college level. Availability of the program depends upon number of applicants interested.

Special Facilities or Resources: The department's facilities occupy more than 20,000 square feet. The newly renovated Psychology Clinic provides space for individual, group, family, and child therapy, as well as psychological assessment. The department's Research Suite and other research spaces permit data collection either with individual participants or groups. The spaces include 50 PC microcomputers, for various programs in the department. There are also laboratories for human research in sensory psychophysics, learning, cognition, social, developmental, personality, and industrial/organizational psychology. Supplemental technical assistance from facilities in other departments on campus is available. The department is gradually equipping all classrooms with multimedia equipment. At the present time 75% of them have been equipped. The department has an instructional computing laboratory consisting of 21 networked PC microcomputers and extensive supporting hardware and software for computing across the psychology curriculum. Most laboratory areas, classrooms, and graduate assistant offices contain both PC and Macintosh microcomputers, many of which are networked and support research and instruction.

Information for Students With Physical Disabilities: See the following Web site for more information: http://www.sfasu.edu/disabilityservices/index.htm.

Application Information:

Send general graduate school application, GRE scores, official transcripts to: Graduate School of SFASU, Box 13024, Nacogdoches, TX 75962. Send all other materials (see forms on department graduate program website) and letters of recommendation to: Dr. Lauren Scharff, Graduate Program Coordinator, SFASU, Box 13046, Nacogdoches, TX 75962. Application available online. Students are admitted in the Fall, application deadline April 15; Spring, application deadline

September 15. The earlier the submission, the greater the likelihood of receiving an assistantship. We recommend applications be received by September 15 and April 15, although we will accept them later. *Fee:* $25.

Texas A&M International University

Department of Behavioral, Applied Sciences & Criminal Justice
College of Arts and Sciences
5201 University Boulevard
Laredo, TX 78041-1900
Telephone: (956) 326-2475
Fax: (956) 326-2474
E-mail: *brudolph@tamiu.edu*
Web: *http://www.tamiu.edu/coas/psy*

Department Information:
1994. Director of Master's Program in Counseling Psychology: Bonnie A. Rudolph, PhD. Number of Faculty: total–full-time 13, part-time 9; women–full-time 10, part-time 5; minority–full-time 6, part-time 6.

Programs and Degrees Offered:
Listed in the following order: Program area, degree type (T if terminal Master's), number awarded 7/03–6/04. Counseling Psychology MA/MS (Master of Arts/Science) (T) 7.

Student Applications/Admissions:
Student Applications
Counseling Psychology MA/MS (Master of Arts/Science)—Applications 2004–2005, 12. Total applicants accepted 2004–2005, 12. Total enrolled 2004–2005 full-time, 6, part-time, 24. Openings 2005–2006, 15. The Median number of years required for completion of a degree are 3. The number of students enrolled full and part-time who were dismissed or voluntarily withdrew from this program area were 0.

Admissions Requirements:
Scores: Entries appear in this order: required test or GPA, minimum score (if required), median score of students entering in 2003–2004. Master's Programs: GRE-V+Q no minimum stated; last 2 years GPA no minimum stated; psychology GPA no minimum stated.
Other Criteria: (importance of criteria rated low, medium, or high): GRE/MAT scores medium, research experience low, work experience medium, extracurricular activity medium, clinically related public service high, GPA medium, letters of recommendation medium, interview medium, statement of goals and objectives medium.

Student Characteristics: The following represents characteristics of students in 2004–2005 in all graduate psychology programs in the department: Female–full-time 5, part-time 20; Male–full-time 1, part-time 4; African American/Black–full-time 0, part-time 0; Hispanic/Latino(a)–full-time 4, part-time 23; Asian/Pacific Islander–full-time 0, part-time 0; American Indian/Alaska Native–full-time 0, part-time 0; Caucasian–full-time 1, part-time 0; Multi-ethnic–full-time 0, part-time 1; students subject to the Americans With Disabilities Act–part-time 0.

Financial Information/Assistance:
Tuition for Full-Time Study: *Master's:* State residents: per academic year $1,430, $192 per credit hour; Nonstate residents: per academic year $5,094, $450 per credit hour.

Financial Assistance:
First Year Students: Fellowships and scholarships available for first-year. Average amount paid per academic year: $1,500. Average number of hours worked per week: 0. Apply by June 1.
Advanced Students: Teaching assistantships available for advanced students. Average amount paid per academic year: $9,000. Average number of hours worked per week: 15. Apply by June 1. Research assistantships available for advanced students. Average amount paid per academic year: $9,000. Average number of hours worked per week: 15. Apply by June 1.
Contact Information: Of all students currently enrolled full-time, 15% benefitted from one or more of the listed financial assistance programs.

Internships/Practica: The practicum and internships offer unique training opportunities to prepare excellent counselors. Excellence exercises include alliance and outcome measurement as well as session process analyses, in addition to more conventional training in documentation and treatment planning. Practicum and internships consist of working at settings such as college counseling centers, forensic settings, drug and alcohol counseling/prevention agencies, domestic violence/battered women shelters, child advocacy centers, and professional counseling clinics. On-site supervisors provide thirty-minute supervision sessions. Psychologists on campus provide an additional 2.5 hours of supervision in individual, triadic, and group formats. Peer feedback and group cohesiveness are also vital parts of training. All graduates complete Practicum and Counseling Internship I. Students who choose the non-thesis (clinical) track also complete Internship II. The clinical track provides a total of 3 semesters of practical experience in counseling (600 hours), a minimum of which is 240 hours of face-to-face counseling activities.

Housing and Day Care: On-campus housing is available. See the following Web site for more information: http://www.tamiu.edu. On-campus day care facilities are available.

Employment of Department Graduates:
Master's Degree Graduates: Of those who graduated in the academic year 2003–2004, the following categories and numbers represent the post-graduate activities and employment of master's degree graduates: Enrolled in a psychology doctoral program (1), enrolled in a post-doctoral residency/fellowship (n/a), employed in independent practice (n/a), employed in an academic position at a university (2), employed in a government agency (research) (1), total from the above (master's) (4).
Doctoral Degree Graduates: Of those who graduated in the academic year 2003–2004, the following categories and numbers represent the post-graduate activities and employment of doctoral degree graduates: Enrolled in a psychology doctoral program (n/a), total from the above (doctoral) (0).

Additional Information:

Orientation, Objectives, and Emphasis of Department: The Master of Arts in Counseling Psychology provides progressive training for counselors with strong foundations in eclectic, humanistic, multicultural and community perspectives. Students in our international campus and community are self-reflective active learners. The excellent student-faculty ratio (average class=8) provides extra attention for its students to identify and achieve their own innovative goals. There is an advisory board composed of student and faculty representatives as well as community leaders, which strives to expand the counseling program to improve the quality of life in South Texas. Students complete courses in counseling theories, techniques, and attitudes, multicultural counseling, human development, psychopathology, ethical and legal issues, group counseling, career counseling, assessment, and statistical research design. Electives include coursework in crisis counseling, brief collaborative therapy, community interventions, play therapy, elderly mental health, Latino mental health, alcohol and drug counseling, and bilingualism. Faculty are specialists in brief collaborative therapy, crisis intervention, psycholinguistics, memory, multicultural counseling, psychotherapy research, counselor professional development, adolescent identity development. Graduates are eligible to sit for the Licensed Professional Counselor (LPC-Texas) Examination. Students can select a thesis track if they are interested in research and further study at the doctoral level. Unlike the vast majority of American counseling programs, our program meets every recommendation of the Multicultural Competency Checklist.

Special Facilities or Resources: The international flavor of the University and South Texas community provide a rich milieu for multicultural and community counseling exploration and education. This is one of the program's greatest resources. Additionally, Texas A&M International is one of the fastest growing communities in the United States, not only in terms of population, but also in culture and development. New buildings are continually being built on campus. Additionally, an off-campus community-counseling center, The Texas A&M International University Community Stress Center, offers free counseling and psychoeducational services. At this center student-counselors may complete practicums and internships in progressive direct and indirect community and client interventions with on-site faculty supervision. The Master's of Arts in Counseling Psychology (MACP) Program works closely with Career Services, Student Counseling, and Academic Support and Enrichment to provide training and employment opportunities for student-counselors. A departmental computer lab exists that is currently used for cognitive and language research. It is equipped for detailed analysis of research in memory, cognition, psycholinguistics, bilingualism, as well as other research. Audio-visual equipment is available for use in recording counseling sessions.

Application Information:

Send to: Texas A&M International University, College of Arts & Sciences, Department of Behavioral, Applied Sciences & Criminal Justice, 5201 University Boulevard, Laredo, TX 78041-1900. Application available online. URL of online application: tamiu.edu. Students are admitted in the Fall, application deadline April 1; Winter, application deadline November 1; Summer, application deadline March 1. *Fee:* $25. If TAMIU graduate, fee is waived.

Texas A&M University (2004 data)
Department of Psychology
Liberal Arts
Psychology Department
College Station, TX 77843-4235
Telephone: (979) 458-1710
Fax: (979) 845-4727
E-mail: *gradadv@psyc.tamu.edu*
Web: *http://www.psychology.tamu.edu*

Department Information:

1968. Department Head: Steve Rholes. Number of Faculty: total–full-time 31, part-time 4; women–full-time 13, part-time 2; minority–full-time 5.

Programs and Degrees Offered:

Listed in the following order: Program area, degree type (T if terminal Master's), number awarded 7/03–6/04. Developmental PhD (Doctor of Philosophy) 0, Industrial/Organizational PhD (Doctor of Philosophy) 2, Social PhD (Doctor of Philosophy) 1, Behavioral and Cellular Neuroscience PhD (Doctor of Philosophy) 1, Clinical PhD (Doctor of Philosophy) 5, Cognitive PhD (Doctor of Philosophy) 1.

APA Accreditation: Clinical PhD (Doctor of Philosophy).

Student Applications/Admissions:
Student Applications

Developmental PhD (Doctor of Philosophy)—Applications 2004–2005, 6. Total applicants accepted 2004–2005, 0. Total enrolled 2004–2005 full-time, 2, part-time, 2. Openings 2005–2006, 1. The number of students enrolled full and part-time who were dismissed or voluntarily withdrew from this program area were 0. *Industrial/Organizational PhD (Doctor of Philosophy)*—Applications 2004–2005, 74. Total applicants accepted 2004–2005, 6. Total enrolled 2004–2005 full-time, 19, part-time, 5. Openings 2005–2006, 4. The Median number of years required for completion of a degree are 6. The number of students enrolled full and part-time who were dismissed or voluntarily withdrew from this program area were 0. *Social PhD (Doctor of Philosophy)*—Applications 2004–2005, 35. Total applicants accepted 2004–2005, 8. Openings 2005–2006, 4. The Median number of years required for completion of a degree are 7. The number of students enrolled full and part-time who were dismissed or voluntarily withdrew from this program area were 0. *Behavioral and Cellular Neuroscience PhD (Doctor of Philosophy)*—Applications 2004–2005, 11. Total applicants accepted 2004–2005, 3. Total enrolled 2004–2005 full-time, 9, part-time, 2. Openings 2005–2006, 4. The Median number of years required for completion of a degree are 4. The number of students enrolled full and part-time who were dismissed or voluntarily withdrew from this program area were 1. *Clinical PhD (Doctor of Philosophy)*—Applications 2004–2005, 152. Total applicants accepted 2004–2005, 9. Total enrolled 2004–2005 full-time, 27, part-time, 9. Openings 2005–2006, 5. The Median number of years required for completion of a degree are 5. The number of students enrolled full and part-time who were dismissed or voluntarily withdrew from this program area were 0. *Cognitive PhD (Doctor of Philosophy)*—Applications 2004–2005, 20. Total applicants accepted

2004–2005, 10. Openings 2005–2006, 3. The Median number of years required for completion of a degree are 5. The number of students enrolled full and part-time who were dismissed or voluntarily withdrew from this program area were 0.

Admissions Requirements:

Scores: Entries appear in this order: required test or GPA, minimum score (if required), median score of students entering in 2003–2004. Doctoral Programs: GRE-V no minimum stated; GRE-Q no minimum stated; GRE-V+Q no minimum stated, 1167; GRE-Analytical no minimum stated; overall undergraduate GPA no minimum stated; last 2 years GPA 3.0, 3.72.

Other Criteria: (importance of criteria rated low, medium, or high): GRE/MAT scores high, research experience high, work experience high, extracurricular activity high, clinically related public service high, GPA high, letters of recommendation high, interview high, statement of goals and objectives high.

Student Characteristics: The following represents characteristics of students in 2004–2005 in all graduate psychology programs in the department: Female–full-time 41, part-time 13; Male–full-time 29, part-time 5; African American/Black–full-time 1, part-time 1; Hispanic/Latino(a)–full-time 10, part-time 2; Asian/Pacific Islander–full-time 11, part-time 1; American Indian/Alaska Native–full-time 1, part-time 0; Caucasian–full-time 47, part-time 14; Multi-ethnic–full-time 0, part-time 0; students subject to the Americans With Disabilities Act–full-time 0, part-time 0.

Financial Information/Assistance:

Tuition for Full-Time Study: *Doctoral:* State residents: $138 per credit hour; Nonstate residents: $374 per credit hour.

Financial Assistance:

First Year Students: Teaching assistantships available for first-year. Average amount paid per academic year: $10,354. Average number of hours worked per week: 20. Apply by January 5. Tuition remission given: partial. Research assistantships available for first-year. Average amount paid per academic year: $10,354. Average number of hours worked per week: 20. Apply by January 5. Tuition remission given: partial. Fellowships and scholarships available for first-year. Average amount paid per academic year: $23,000. Apply by January 5. Tuition remission given: full and partial.

Advanced Students: Teaching assistantships available for advanced students. Average amount paid per academic year: $10,354. Average number of hours worked per week: 20. Tuition remission given: partial. Research assistantships available for advanced students. Average amount paid per academic year: $10,354. Average number of hours worked per week: 20. Tuition remission given: partial.

Contact Information: Of all students currently enrolled full-time, 95% benefitted from one or more of the listed financial assistance programs. Application and information available online at: tamu.edu/admissions and/or psychology.tamu.edu.

Internships/Practica: For those doctoral students for whom a professional internship is required prior to graduation, 6 applied in 2003–2004. Of those who applied, 6 were placed in internships listed by the Association of Psychology Postdoctoral and Internship Programs (APPIC); 6 were placed in APA accredited internships.

Housing and Day Care: On-campus housing is available. On-campus day care facilities are available.

Employment of Department Graduates:

Master's Degree Graduates: Of those who graduated in the academic year 2003–2004, the following categories and numbers represent the post-graduate activities and employment of master's degree graduates: Enrolled in a post-doctoral residency/fellowship (n/a), employed in independent practice (n/a), total from the above (master's) (0).

Doctoral Degree Graduates: Of those who graduated in the academic year 2003–2004, the following categories and numbers represent the post-graduate activities and employment of doctoral degree graduates: Enrolled in a psychology doctoral program (n/a), enrolled in a post-doctoral residency/fellowship (2), employed in an academic position at a university (2), employed in other positions at a higher education institution (1), employed in business or industry (research/consulting) (2), employed in a hospital/medical center (2), do not know (1), total from the above (doctoral) (10).

Additional Information:

Orientation, Objectives, and Emphasis of Department: The goals of the PhD program in Psychology are: 1) to prepare students for careers as researchers and teachers at colleges and universities, and 2) to prepare students for careers as scientist–practitioners in clinical psychology and industrial/organizational psychology. The Department offers a PhD in six areas of specialization: Behavioral Neuroscience, Clinical (accredited by the APA), Cognitive, Developmental, Social, Industrial/Organizational Psychology. The Department enrolls approximately 100 graduate students and offers numerous opportunities for student collaboration with faculty. The student-faculty ratio is approximately 3:1, which allows individualized attention to develop research and/or professional skills. Over the last decade, all graduates have obtained full-time employment as researchers, teachers, or practitioners. Faculty members are heavily involved in the placement of graduate students.

Special Facilities or Resources: The Department is housed in an attractive four-story building that contains faculty and graduate student offices, research laboratories, administrative offices, and classrooms. Laboratory facilities are excellent, including labs designated for faculty and student research in behavioral neuroscience, cognitive, developmental, industrial/organizational, and social psychology. The Department also maintains a Psychology Clinic in which Clinical students are trained to provide a range of psychological services and conduct applied research under supervision from the Clinical faculty.

Information for Students With Physical Disabilities: studentlife.tamu.edu/ssd.

Application Information:

Send to: Texas A&M University, Graduate Adm. Supv., Department of Psychology, College Station, TX 77843-4235. Application available online. Students are admitted in the Fall, application deadline January 5. *Fee:* $50.

Texas A&M University—Commerce
Department of Psychology and Special Education
College of Education and Human Services
Henderson Hall
Commerce, TX 75429
Telephone: (903) 886-5594
Fax: (903) 886-5510
E-mail: *raymond_green@tamu-commerce.edu*
Web: *http://www7.tamu-commerce.edu/psychology2003/*

Department Information:
1962. Department Head: Dr. Tracy Henley. Number of Faculty: total–full-time 15, part-time 5; women–full-time 7, part-time 2; minority–full-time 2.

Programs and Degrees Offered:
Listed in the following order: Program area, degree type (T if terminal Master's), number awarded 7/03–6/04. Educational Psychology PhD (Doctor of Philosophy) 1, School MA/MS (Master of Arts/Science) (T) 8, Applied MA/MS (Master of Arts/Science) (T) 6.

Student Applications/Admissions:
Student Applications
Educational Psychology PhD (Doctor of Philosophy)—Applications 2004–2005, 34. Total applicants accepted 2004–2005, 15. Number enrolled (new admits only) 2004–2005 full-time, 8. Number enrolled (new admits only) 2004–2005 part-time, 4. Total enrolled 2004–2005 full-time, 45, part-time, 28. Openings 2005–2006, 10. The Median number of years required for completion of a degree are 6. The number of students enrolled full and part-time who were dismissed or voluntarily withdrew from this program area were 6. *School MA/MS (Master of Arts/Science)*—Applications 2004–2005, 20. Total applicants accepted 2004–2005, 17. Number enrolled (new admits only) 2004–2005 full-time, 6. Number enrolled (new admits only) 2004–2005 part-time, 7. Total enrolled 2004–2005 full-time, 50, part-time, 10. Openings 2005–2006, 10. The Median number of years required for completion of a degree are 2. The number of students enrolled full and part-time who were dismissed or voluntarily withdrew from this program area were 1. *Applied MA/MS (Master of Arts/Science)*—Applications 2004–2005, 6. Total applicants accepted 2004–2005, 4. Number enrolled (new admits only) 2004–2005 full-time, 4. Total enrolled 2004–2005 full-time, 6, part-time, 2. Openings 2005–2006, 10. The Median number of years required for completion of a degree are 2. The number of students enrolled full and part-time who were dismissed or voluntarily withdrew from this program area were 0.

Admissions Requirements:
Scores: Entries appear in this order: required test or GPA, minimum score (if required), median score of students entering in 2003–2004. Master's Programs: GRE-V no minimum stated, 450; GRE-Q no minimum stated, 450; GRE-V+Q no minimum stated, 900; overall undergraduate GPA 2.75, 3.0; last 2 years GPA 3.0, 3.2. Doctoral Programs: GRE-V no minimum stated, 500; GRE-Q no minimum stated, 540; GRE-V+Q no minimum stated, 1040; overall undergraduate GPA 3.0, 3.0; last 2 years GPA 3.00, 3.4; psychology GPA 3.00, 3.5.

Other Criteria: (importance of criteria rated low, medium, or high): GRE/MAT scores medium, research experience medium, work experience medium, GPA high, letters of recommendation medium, statement of goals and objectives high. Greater importance would be assigned to prior research experience, graduate education, and publications/scholarly activity for the doctoral program. For additional information on admission requirements, go to: http://www7.tamu-commerce.edu/psychology2003/doctoral.htm.

Student Characteristics: The following represents characteristics of students in 2004–2005 in all graduate psychology programs in the department: Female–full-time 68, part-time 29; Male–full-time 33, part-time 11; African American/Black–full-time 7, part-time 1; Hispanic/Latino(a)–full-time 3, part-time 0; Asian/Pacific Islander–full-time 9, part-time 4; American Indian/Alaska Native–full-time 0, part-time 0; Caucasian–full-time 82, part-time 35; students subject to the Americans With Disabilities Act–full-time 0, part-time 0.

Financial Information/Assistance:
Tuition for Full-Time Study: *Master's:* State residents: $227 per credit hour; Nonstate residents: $485 per credit hour. *Doctoral:* State residents: $227 per credit hour; Nonstate residents: $485 per credit hour. Tuition is subject to change. See the following Web site for updates and changes in tuition costs: http://www.tamu-commerce.edu/fiscal/PaymentInfo/Tuition_Fees/studentfees2005.html.

Financial Assistance:
First Year Students: Teaching assistantships available for first-year. Average amount paid per academic year: $10,000. Average number of hours worked per week: 20. Apply by Fall/Spring. Tuition remission given: partial. Research assistantships available for first-year. Average amount paid per academic year: $10,000. Average number of hours worked per week: 20. Apply by Fall/Spring. Tuition remission given: partial. Fellowships and scholarships available for first-year. Average amount paid per academic year: $1,000. Apply by Fall. Tuition remission given: partial.

Advanced Students: Teaching assistantships available for advanced students. Average amount paid per academic year: $11,800. Average number of hours worked per week: 20. Apply by Fall/Spring. Tuition remission given: partial. Research assistantships available for advanced students. Average amount paid per academic year: $11,800. Average number of hours worked per week: 20. Apply by Fall/Spring. Tuition remission given: partial. Fellowships and scholarships available for advanced students. Average amount paid per academic year: $1,000. Apply by Fall. Tuition remission given: partial.

Contact Information: Of all students currently enrolled full-time, 10% benefitted from one or more of the listed financial assistance programs. Application and information available online at: http://www7.tamu-commerce.edu/psychology2003/doctoral.htm.

Internships/Practica: There are on-site university clinic practica for school and applied programs. The school psychology program requires a 1200-hour internship.

Housing and Day Care: On-campus housing is available. See the following Web site for more information: http://www7.tamu-commerce.edu/housing/. On-campus day care facilities are available.

Employment of Department Graduates:

Master's Degree Graduates: Of those who graduated in the academic year 2003–2004, the following categories and numbers represent the post-graduate activities and employment of master's degree graduates: Enrolled in a psychology doctoral program (3), enrolled in another graduate/professional program (1), enrolled in a post-doctoral residency/fellowship (n/a), employed in independent practice (n/a), employed in an academic position at a university (0), employed in an academic position at a 2-year/4-year college (0), employed in other positions at a higher education institution (0), employed in a professional position in a school system (12), employed in business or industry (research/consulting) (0), employed in business or industry (management) (0), employed in a government agency (research) (0), employed in a government agency (professional services) (0), employed in a community mental health/counseling center (2), employed in a hospital/medical center (0), still seeking employment (0), other employment position (0), total from the above (master's) (18).

Doctoral Degree Graduates: Of those who graduated in the academic year 2003–2004, the following categories and numbers represent the post-graduate activities and employment of doctoral degree graduates: Enrolled in a psychology doctoral program (n/a), enrolled in a post-doctoral residency/fellowship (0), employed in independent practice (0), employed in an academic position at a university (1), employed in an academic position at a 2-year/4-year college (0), employed in other positions at a higher education institution (0), employed in a professional position in a school system (0), employed in business or industry (research/consulting) (1), employed in business or industry (management) (1), employed in a government agency (research) (0), employed in a government agency (professional services) (1), employed in a community mental health/counseling center (0), employed in a hospital/medical center (0), still seeking employment (0), other employment position (0), total from the above (doctoral) (4).

Additional Information:

Orientation, Objectives, and Emphasis of Department: The focus of the educational psychology program is human cognition and instruction. Students will acquire an in-depth knowledge of human learning and cognition, instructional strategies, and research and evaluation. This emphasis will prepare students to integrate knowledge of human cognition and instructional practice across a variety of occupational, educational and content matter domains, with emphasis on applications of learning technologies. The applied master's program is fully accredited by the Inter-organizational Board of Accreditation for Master's in Psychology Programs (IBAMPP). The applied master's program is designed to prepare students to meet the requirements for certification as an associate psychologist in the State of Texas. Associate psychologists are employed in a variety of governmental and private organizations, such as mental health centers, clinics, and hospitals. The school psychology program is structured on the basis of the NASP requirements for an extended Master's degree which includes coursework in psychological foundations, educational foundations, assessment, interventions (direct and indirect), statistics and research design, professional school psychology, practica and internship.

Special Facilities or Resources: Multimedia instructional lab, multimedia classrooms, on-site integrated university clinic, research partnerships with business industry, center for excellence-learning technologies, support for online learning.

Information for Students With Physical Disabilities: See the following Web site for more information: http://www7.tamu-commerce.edu/administration/president/procedures/A1301.htm.

Application Information:
Send to: Graduate School, P.O. Box 3011, Texas A&M—Commerce, Commerce, TX 75429-3011. Application available online. URL of online application: http://www7.tamu-commerce.edu/gradschool/. Students are admitted in the Fall, application deadline May; Spring, application deadline December. Programs have rolling admissions. *Fee:* $35.

Texas A&M University—Kingsville
Department of Psychology
Arts and Sciences
700 University Boulevard
Kingsville, TX 78363-8202
Telephone: (361) 593-4181
Fax: (361) 593-2707
E-mail: *kfjmp00@tamuk.edu*
Web: *www.tamuk.edu/psycsoci*

Department Information:
Chairperson: James M Puckett. Number of Faculty: total–full-time 6; women–full-time 1.

Programs and Degrees Offered:
Listed in the following order: Program area, degree type (T if terminal Master's), number awarded 7/03–6/04. Psychology MA/MS (Master of Arts/Science) (T) 8.

Student Applications/Admissions:

Student Applications
Psychology MA/MS (*Master of Arts/Science*)—Total enrolled 2004–2005 full-time, 24, part-time, 20.

Admissions Requirements:
Scores: Entries appear in this order: required test or GPA, minimum score (if required), median score of students entering in 2003–2004. Master's Programs: GRE-V+Q no minimum stated; overall undergraduate GPA no minimum stated.
Other Criteria: (importance of criteria rated low, medium, or high): GRE/MAT scores low, GPA high. For additional information on admission requirements, go to: http://www.tamuk.edu/grad/.

Student Characteristics: The following represents characteristics of students in 2004–2005 in all graduate psychology programs in the department: Female–full-time 15, part-time 16; Male–full-time 3, part-time 4; African American/Black–full-time 1, part-time 1; Hispanic/Latino(a)–full-time 12, part-time 14; Asian/Pacific Islander–full-time 1, part-time 1; American Indian/Alaska Native–full-time 1, part-time 0; Caucasian–full-time 3, part-time 4.

Financial Information/Assistance:
Financial Assistance:
First Year Students: No information provided.

Advanced Students: No information provided.

Contact Information: Of all students currently enrolled full-time, 0% benefitted from one or more of the listed financial assistance programs. Application and information available online at: http://www.tamuk.edu/finaid/.

Internships/Practica: A number of placement sites are available for masters students enrolled in the practicum course.

Housing and Day Care: On-campus housing is available. See the following Web site for more information: http://www.tamuk.edu/intpro/Housing.htm. On-campus day care facilities are available. See the following Web site for more information: http://www.tamuk.edu/aghs/departments/cyc/main.html.

Employment of Department Graduates:
Master's Degree Graduates: Of those who graduated in the academic year 2003–2004, the following categories and numbers represent the post-graduate activities and employment of master's degree graduates: Enrolled in a post-doctoral residency/fellowship (n/a), employed in independent practice (n/a), total from the above (master's) (0).
Doctoral Degree Graduates: Of those who graduated in the academic year 2003–2004, the following categories and numbers represent the post-graduate activities and employment of doctoral degree graduates: Enrolled in a psychology doctoral program (n/a), total from the above (doctoral) (0).

Additional Information:

Information for Students With Physical Disabilities: See the following Web site for more information: http://www.tamuk.edu/sass/LifeServices/ssd_main.htm.

Application Information:
Send to: Dean, College of Graduate Studies, Texas A&M University—Kingsville, MSC 118, Kingsville, TX 78363. Students are admitted in the Fall, Spring, and Summer. Programs have rolling admissions. Applications received and decisions made on a rolling basis.

Texas Christian University
Department of Psychology
College of Science and Engineering
TCU Box 298920
Fort Worth, TX 76129
Telephone: (817) 257-7410
Fax: (817) 257-7681
E-mail: *m.eudaly@tcu.edu*
Web: *http://www.psy.tcu.edu/*

Department Information:
1959. Chairperson: Timothy Barth. Number of Faculty: total–full-time 12, part-time 2; women–full-time 2, part-time 2; minority–full-time 3.

Programs and Degrees Offered:
Listed in the following order: Program area, degree type (T if terminal Master's), number awarded 7/03–6/04. Experimental PhD (Doctor of Philosophy) 5.

Student Applications/Admissions:
Student Applications
Experimental PhD (Doctor of Philosophy)—Applications 2004–2005, 17. Total applicants accepted 2004–2005, 13. Number enrolled (new admits only) 2004–2005 full-time, 9. Number enrolled (new admits only) 2004–2005 part-time, 0. Openings 2005–2006, 9. The Median number of years required for completion of a degree are 5. The number of students enrolled full and part-time who were dismissed or voluntarily withdrew from this program area were 1.

Admissions Requirements:
Scores: Entries appear in this order: required test or GPA, minimum score (if required), median score of students entering in 2003–2004. Doctoral Programs: GRE-V no minimum stated, 550; GRE-Q no minimum stated, 620; GRE-V+Q 1000, 1180; overall undergraduate GPA 3.2, 3.47; last 2 years GPA 3.2, 3.82; psychology GPA 3.2, 3.69.
Other Criteria: (importance of criteria rated low, medium, or high): GRE/MAT scores low, research experience high, GPA medium, letters of recommendation high, statement of goals and objectives high.

Student Characteristics: The following represents characteristics of students in 2004–2005 in all graduate psychology programs in the department: Female–full-time 21, part-time 0; Male–full-time 10, part-time 0; African American/Black–full-time 1, part-time 0; Hispanic/Latino(a)–full-time 3, part-time 0; Asian/Pacific Islander–full-time 0, part-time 0; American Indian/Alaska Native–full-time 0, part-time 0; Caucasian–full-time 27, part-time 0; Multi-ethnic–full-time 0, part-time 0; students subject to the Americans With Disabilities Act–full-time 0, part-time 0.

Financial Information/Assistance:
Tuition for Full-Time Study: *Master's:* State residents: $690 per credit hour; Nonstate residents: $690 per credit hour. *Doctoral:* State residents: $690 per credit hour; Nonstate residents: $690 per credit hour. See the following Web site for updates and changes in tuition costs: www.tcu.edu.

Financial Assistance:
First Year Students: Fellowships and scholarships available for first-year. Average amount paid per academic year: $17,000. Average number of hours worked per week: 0. Apply by none. Tuition remission given: full.
Advanced Students: Teaching assistantships available for advanced students. Average amount paid per academic year: $13,500. Average number of hours worked per week: 10. Apply by February 15. Tuition remission given: full.
Contact Information: Of all students currently enrolled full-time, 83% benefitted from one or more of the listed financial assistance programs.

Internships/Practica: No information provided.

Housing and Day Care: On-campus housing is available. See the following Web site for more information: http://www.rlh.tcu.edu/gsa.htm. No on-campus day care facilities are available.

Employment of Department Graduates:
Master's Degree Graduates: Of those who graduated in the academic year 2003–2004, the following categories and numbers

represent the post-graduate activities and employment of master's degree graduates: Enrolled in a psychology doctoral program (0), enrolled in another graduate/professional program (0), enrolled in a post-doctoral residency/fellowship (n/a), employed in independent practice (n/a), employed in an academic position at a university (0), employed in an academic position at a 2-year/4-year college (0), employed in other positions at a higher education institution (0), employed in a professional position in a school system (0), employed in business or industry (research/consulting) (0), employed in business or industry (management) (0), employed in a government agency (research) (0), employed in a government agency (professional services) (0), employed in a community mental health/counseling center (0), employed in a hospital/medical center (0), still seeking employment (0), other employment position (0), total from the above (master's) (0).

Doctoral Degree Graduates: Of those who graduated in the academic year 2003–2004, the following categories and numbers represent the post-graduate activities and employment of doctoral degree graduates: Enrolled in a psychology doctoral program (n/a), enrolled in another graduate/professional program (0), enrolled in a post-doctoral residency/fellowship (1), employed in independent practice (0), employed in an academic position at a university (1), employed in an academic position at a 2-year/4-year college (0), employed in other positions at a higher education institution (1), employed in a professional position in a school system (0), employed in business or industry (research/consulting) (2), employed in business or industry (management) (0), employed in a government agency (research) (0), employed in a government agency (professional services) (0), employed in a community mental health/counseling center (0), employed in a hospital/medical center (0), still seeking employment (0), other employment position (0), total from the above (doctoral) (5).

Additional Information:

Orientation, Objectives, and Emphasis of Department: The psychology graduate program at Texas Christian University leads to a predoctoral master's in experimental psychology and a PhD in general experimental psychology. The PhD is awarded in general experimental psychology. The program is not limited to traditional experimental psychology, nor is it committed solely to laboratory-based methods. The department has long held that a measure of specialized knowledge—built upon a firm but broad base of psychological principles and methods—constitutes the best plan for most of its students. Within this plan the student may study diverse areas of interest with emphasis possible in the following: learning-comparative, perception-cognition, social, personality, applied quantitative methods, and behavioral neuroscience. All graduate students receive training in both teaching and research. The environment is stimulating, informal, and conducive to close student-faculty relations.

Special Facilities or Resources: Assuming that physical proximity is conducive to more interdisciplinary work of substance, TCU has located all its science-related activities in or near the Science Research Center, dedicated in 1971. The Department of Psychology occupies two floors of the center's Winton-Scott Hall. The university library, containing over one million volumes, is located next to the science facilities. About 140 periodicals of psychological interest are available. Full-time personnel skilled in electronics, glass blowing, woodworking, and metal working aid in construction and maintenance of special equipment or instruments. TCU has 10 open computer labs equipped with Windows-based

PCs and Macintosh computers (over 100 Windows-based machines and 39 Mac-based machines). All of the labs provide full Internet access and laser printing. Additionally, some of the labs have scanners, zip drives, CD burners, and web cams. The Psychology department also has a computer lab with 6 Windows-based PCs, all of which are connected to the Internet, and a networked laser printer. Additionally, all of the research laboratories in the department have networked computers. From the various labs, students have access to a variety of software including SPSS, SAS, SYSTAT, and Microsoft Office. Also, the University provides e-mail accounts and storage space on the University server.

Information for Students With Physical Disabilities: See the following Web site for more information: www.acs.tcu.edu/disability.htm.

Application Information:
Send to: Charles G. Lord, Coordinator of Graduate Studies, TCU Box 298920, Fort Worth, TX 76129. Application available online. URL of online application: http://www.psy.tcu.edu. Students are admitted in the Fall. No deadline for admission; however, February 15 is recommended to be considered for funding. *Fee:* $50. Fees can be waived for exceptional or needy applicants. Contact the Graduate Director.

Texas of the Permian Basin, The University of
Department of Behavioral Science: Psychology Area
College of Arts and Sciences
4901 East University Boulevard
Odessa, TX 79762
Telephone: (432) 552-2325
Fax: (432) 552-3325
E-mail: *thompson_s@utpb.edu*
Web: *http://www.utpb.edu*

Department Information:
1973. Coordinator: Spencer Thompson. Number of Faculty: total–full-time 7, part-time 3; women–full-time 3, part-time 1.

Programs and Degrees Offered:
Listed in the following order: Program area, degree type (T if terminal Master's), number awarded 7/03–6/04. Clinical Psychology MA/MS (Master of Arts/Science) 4, Applied Research and Human Development MA/MS (Master of Arts/Science) 3.

Student Applications/Admissions:
Student Applications
Clinical Psychology MA/MS (Master of Arts/Science)—Applications 2004–2005, 20. Total applicants accepted 2004–2005, 15. Number enrolled (new admits only) 2004–2005 full-time, 10. Total enrolled 2004–2005 full-time, 20, part-time, 20. Openings 2005–2006, 15. The Median number of years required for completion of a degree are 5. The number of students enrolled full and part-time who were dismissed or voluntarily withdrew from this program area were 4. *Applied Research and Human Development MA/MS (Master of Arts/Science)*—Applications 2004–2005, 10. Total applicants accepted 2004–2005, 10. Number enrolled (new admits only) 2004–2005 full-time, 5. Total enrolled 2004–2005 full-time, 15, part-time, 5. Openings 2005–2006, 10. The Median number of years re-

quired for completion of a degree are 4. The number of students enrolled full and part-time who were dismissed or voluntarily withdrew from this program area were 4.

Admissions Requirements:

Scores: Entries appear in this order: required test or GPA, minimum score (if required), median score of students entering in 2003–2004. Master's Programs: GRE-V 500; GRE-Q 500; GRE-V+Q 1000; GRE-Analytical 500; overall undergraduate GPA 3.0; last 2 years GPA 3.0; psychology GPA 3.0. GRE scores are informational and not limits. Current formulas for regular status: Add (GPA for last 60 undergraduate hours times 200) + (Total GRE). This must equal 1600 to qualify for admission with regular status. Students are evaluated on a case by case basis and may be admitted at a provisional status.

Other Criteria: (importance of criteria rated low, medium, or high): GRE/MAT scores high, research experience low, work experience low, extracurricular activity low, clinically related public service low, GPA high, letters of recommendation high, statement of goals and objectives high.

Student Characteristics: The following represents characteristics of students in 2004–2005 in all graduate psychology programs in the department: Female–full-time 20, part-time 15; Male–full-time 15, part-time 10; African American/Black–full-time 0, part-time 0; Hispanic/Latino(a)–full-time 10, part-time 0; Asian/Pacific Islander–full-time 0, part-time 0; American Indian/Alaska Native–full-time 0, part-time 0; Caucasian–full-time 0, part-time 0; students subject to the Americans With Disabilities Act–full-time 1, part-time 0.

Financial Information/Assistance:

Tuition for Full-Time Study: *Master's:* State residents: per academic year $2,200, $122 per credit hour; Nonstate residents: per academic year $6,200, $342 per credit hour. Tuition is subject to change.

Financial Assistance:

First Year Students: Research assistantships available for first-year. Average amount paid per academic year: $8,000. Average number of hours worked per week: 19. Apply by April 15. Fellowships and scholarships available for first-year. Average amount paid per academic year: $500. Apply by July 15.

Advanced Students: Teaching assistantships available for advanced students. Average amount paid per academic year: $9,000. Apply by April 15. Fellowships and scholarships available for advanced students. Average amount paid per academic year: $500.

Contact Information: Of all students currently enrolled full-time, 5% benefitted from one or more of the listed financial assistance programs. Application and information available online at: www.utpb.edu.

Internships/Practica: The University Counseling Center has opportunities for a supervised clinical practicum. Other practicums are available in the community. Most students accumulate hours leading to Licensed Professional Counselor (LPC) certification in the State of Texas. Students also qualify for certification as Psychology Associates in the State of Texas.

Housing and Day Care: On-campus housing is available. See the following Web site for more information: www.utpb.edu. No on-campus day care facilities are available.

Employment of Department Graduates:

Master's Degree Graduates: Of those who graduated in the academic year 2003–2004, the following categories and numbers represent the post-graduate activities and employment of master's degree graduates: Enrolled in a post-doctoral residency/fellowship (n/a), employed in independent practice (n/a), employed in business or industry (management) (1), employed in a community mental health/counseling center (3), employed in a hospital/medical center (1), total from the above (master's) (5).

Doctoral Degree Graduates: Of those who graduated in the academic year 2003–2004, the following categories and numbers represent the post-graduate activities and employment of doctoral degree graduates: Enrolled in a psychology doctoral program (n/a), total from the above (doctoral) (0).

Additional Information:

Orientation, Objectives, and Emphasis of Department: The Master of Arts program in Psychology offers concentrations in both Clinical and Applied Research. The program offers students the opportunity to prepare themselves to work in mental health centers, juvenile detention centers, child service agencies, specialized school services, residential treatment facilities, family counseling agencies, to teach in community colleges, or to study at the doctoral level (PhD). The Clinical Psychology concentration is aimed at training students in the assessment and treatment of mental disorders, through individual, family, and group therapies. The program offers instruction in child, adolescent, and adult disorders. Successful completion of the Clinical Psychology concentration is designed to provide students with the opportunity to become eligible to take the state examinations for certification as a Psychological Associate (45 hours) or Licensed Professional Counselor (51 hours). The Licensed Professional Counselor certification requires an additional 2,000 supervised hours after the MA degree. The Applied Research concentration focuses on advanced psychological theory (i.e., developmental, personality, social, etc.), research methods, statistics, and manuscript preparation. The Applied Research concentration offers students the opportunity to prepare themselves to serve in government or a community college or to pursue additional graduate study at the doctoral level. All students in the Applied Research concentration are expected to be involved in research activities throughout their graduate program.

Special Facilities or Resources: We have a newly remodeled on-campus center that has a counseling area for clinical practicums and research space for applied research and thesis projects. In addition cooperative arrangements are made with community health centers, schools, governmental agencies, and mental health practitioners for research and practicum opportunities.

Information for Students With Physical Disabilities: castro_e @utpb.edu.

Application Information:
Send to: Graduate Studies, The University of Texas of the Permian Basin, 4901 E. University, Odessa, TX 79762. Application available online. URL of online application: http://www.utpb.edu/utpb_adm/academicaffairs/graduatestudiesresearch/studentinfo/graduateapplications.htm. Students are admitted in the Fall, application deadline July 15; Spring, application deadline November 15; Summer, application deadline April 15. *Fee:* $0.

Texas Southwestern Medical Center at Dallas, University of

Division of Psychology, Graduate Program in Clinical
Psychology
5323 Harry Hines Boulevard
Dallas, TX 75390-9044
Telephone: (214) 648-5277
Fax: (214) 648-5297
E-mail: *melissa.stewart@utsouthwestern.edu*
Web: *http://www.utsouthwestern.edu/utsw/home/education/
psychology/index.html*

Department Information:
1956. Chairperson: C. Munro Cullum, PhD Number of Faculty:
total–full-time 19, part-time 32; women–full-time 7, part-time 15;
minority–full-time 3, part-time 3; faculty subject to the Americans
With Disabilities Act 6.

Programs and Degrees Offered:
Listed in the following order: Program area, degree type (T if
terminal Master's), number awarded 7/03–6/04. Clinical PhD
(Doctor of Philosophy) 11.

APA Accreditation: Combination PhD (Doctor of Philosophy).

Student Applications/Admissions:
Student Applications
Clinical PhD *(Doctor of Philosophy)*—Applications 2004–2005,
149. Total applicants accepted 2004–2005, 10. Number enrolled (new admits only) 2004–2005 full-time, 9. Openings
2005–2006, 10. The Median number of years required for
completion of a degree are 5. The number of students enrolled
full and part-time who were dismissed or voluntarily withdrew
from this program area were 1.

Admissions Requirements:
Scores: Entries appear in this order: required test or GPA,
minimum score (if required), median score of students entering
in 2003–2004. Doctoral Programs: GRE-V+Q no minimum
stated, 1252; overall undergraduate GPA no minimum
stated, 3.58.
Other Criteria: (importance of criteria rated low, medium, or
high): GRE/MAT scores high, research experience medium,
work experience medium, extracurricular activity low, clinically related public service low, GPA medium, letters of
recommendation high, interview high, statement of goals and
objectives high. For additional information on admission
requirements, go to: www.utsouthwestern.edu/utsw/cda/dept
21170/files/35302.html.

Student Characteristics: The following represents characteristics
of students in 2004–2005 in all graduate psychology programs in
the department: Female–full-time 42, part-time 0; Male–full-time
12, part-time 0; African American/Black–full-time 1, part-time
0; Hispanic/Latino(a)–full-time 6, part-time 0; Asian/Pacific Islander–full-time 2, part-time 0; American Indian/Alaska Native–
full-time 0, part-time 0; Caucasian–full-time 44, part-time 0;

Multi-ethnic–full-time 1, part-time 0; students subject to the
Americans With Disabilities Act–full-time 2, part-time 0.

Financial Information/Assistance:
Tuition for Full-Time Study: *Doctoral:* State residents: $48 per
credit hour; Nonstate residents: $306 per credit hour. Tuition is
subject to change. See the following Web site for updates and
changes in tuition costs: www.utsouthwestern.edu/utsw/cda/
dept20424/files/81518.html.

Financial Assistance:
First Year Students: No information provided.
Advanced Students: Teaching assistantships available for
advanced students. Average amount paid per academic year:
$14,472. Average number of hours worked per week: 20. Research
assistantships available for advanced students. Average amount
paid per academic year: $14,472. Average number of hours worked
per week: 20.
Contact Information: Of all students currently enrolled full-
time, 66% benefitted from one or more of the listed financial
assistance programs. Application and information available online
at: http://www.utsouthwestern.edu/utsw/home/financialaid/in-
dex.html.

Internships/Practica: The program provides the equivalent of a
year's full-time APA accredited captive internship following more
than 1000 hours of practica. These clinical experiences are closely
supervised. In order to achieve the goal of broad professional
preparation, students will have a number of different clinical
placements over the course of their practicum and internship
assignments. These assignments are carried out at UT Southwestern facilities, community agencies, regional facilities, specialized
agencies, and area schools. These clinical training sites include
the following: Parkland Memorial Hospital; UT Southwestern
Neuropsychology Service; Children's Medical Center, Cystic Fibrosis Center of Children's; UT Southwestern McDermott Pain
Management Center; UT Dallas Callier Center for Communication Disorders; Public School Districts special education departments; Federal Medical Center (a facility of the Federal Bureau
of Prisons); the student mental health services of Southern Methodist University; Parkland Community Oriented Care Clinic,
and Terrell State Hospital; Dallas County Juvenile Department;
University Rehabilitation Center at UT Southwestern; Baylor
University Medical Center; Presbyterian Hospital of Dallas; University of Texas at Arlington Counseling Center; Episcopal
School of Dallas; Ursuline Academy; Shelton School; Fairhill
School. For those doctoral students for whom a professional internship is required prior to graduation, 12 applied in 2003–
2004. Of those who applied, 12 were placed in APA accredited
internships.

Housing and Day Care: On-campus housing is available. See the
following Web site for more information: http://www.utsouthwest
ern.edu/campushousing/. On-campus day care facilities are available. See the following Web site for more information: http://
www.utsouthwestern.edu/wismac.

Employment of Department Graduates:
Master's Degree Graduates: Of those who graduated in the
academic year 2003–2004, the following categories and numbers
represent the post-graduate activities and employment of master's
degree graduates: Enrolled in a post-doctoral residency/fellowship

(n/a), employed in independent practice (n/a), total from the above (master's) (0).

Doctoral Degree Graduates: Of those who graduated in the academic year 2003–2004, the following categories and numbers represent the post-graduate activities and employment of doctoral degree graduates: Enrolled in a psychology doctoral program (n/a), enrolled in a post-doctoral residency/fellowship (4), employed in independent practice (4), employed in a professional position in a school system (1), employed in a government agency (professional services) (1), employed in a hospital/medical center (1), total from the above (doctoral) (11).

Additional Information:

Orientation, Objectives, and Emphasis of Department: The Graduate Program in Clinical Psychology is a four-year doctoral program with an affiliated predoctoral internship program in clinical psychology, which is separately accredited by the APA. The program provides a combination of experience in both clinical and research settings reflecting our basic training philosophy, which is a clinician-researcher model. Our specific objectives include offering the student the opportunity to acquire, experience, or develop the following: 1. A closely knit integration between basic psychological knowledge (both theoretical and empirical) and responsible professional services; 2. A wide variety of supervised and broadly conceived clinical and consulting experiences; 3. A sensitivity to professional responsibilities in the context of significant social needs; 4. An understanding of research principles, methodology, and skill in formulating, designing, and implementing psychological research; 5. A competence and confidence in the role of psychology in multidisciplinary settings.

Special Facilities or Resources: UT Southwestern has a number of laboratories and clinical settings investigating the brain/behavior relationship, as well as many projects focusing on the psychosocial aspects of various medical and psychiatric disorders. Disorders studied include affective illness, anxiety, schizophrenia, sleep-wake dysfunctions, and medical conditions such as Alzheimer's Disease, epilepsy, temporomandibular disorder, cystic fibrosis, and organ transplantation. Notable examples of comprehensive clinical research programs at UT Southwestern include the following: an affective disorders research program; a sleep disorders research laboratory; an Alzheimer's Disease Center; a neuropsychology laboratory; a pain management program; a schizophrenia research program that includes translational research; and research programs in basic neuroscience.

Information for Students With Physical Disabilities: See the following Web site for more information: www.utsouthwestern.edu/utsw/cda/dept26446/files/70472.html.

Application Information:
Send to: Applications accepted only through Internet address: www.utsouthwestern.edu/gradapp. Application available online. URL of online application: www.utsouthwestern.edu/gradapp. Students are admitted in the Fall, application deadline January 1. Applications accepted only through Internet address above. *Fee:* $0.

Texas State University—San Marcos
Psychology Department/Health Psychology Master's Program
College of Liberal Arts
601 University Drive
San Marcos, TX 78666-4616
Telephone: (512) 245-2526
Fax: (512) 245-3153
E-mail: *gradinfo@www.psych.txstate.edu*
Web: *http://www.psych.txstate.edu*

Department Information:
1969. Chairperson: Randall E. Osborne, PhD. Number of Faculty: total–full-time 18, part-time 14; women–full-time 14, part-time 10; minority–full-time 1, part-time 2.

Programs and Degrees Offered:
Listed in the following order: Program area, degree type (T if terminal Master's), number awarded 7/03–6/04. Health Psychology MA/MS (Master of Arts/Science) (T) 9.

Student Applications/Admissions:
Student Applications
Health Psychology MA/MS *(Master of Arts/Science)*—Applications 2004–2005, 32. Total applicants accepted 2004–2005, 12. Number enrolled (new admits only) 2004–2005 full-time, 12. Number enrolled (new admits only) 2004–2005 part-time, 0. Openings 2005–2006, 16. The Median number of years required for completion of a degree are 3. The number of students enrolled full and part-time who were dismissed or voluntarily withdrew from this program area were 4.

Admissions Requirements:
Scores: Entries appear in this order: required test or GPA, minimum score (if required), median score of students entering in 2003–2004. Master's Programs: GRE-V no minimum stated; GRE-Q no minimum stated; GRE-V+Q no minimum stated, 1000; last 2 years GPA 3.0, 3.0; psychology GPA 3.0, 3.25.
Other Criteria: (importance of criteria rated low, medium, or high): GRE/MAT scores medium, research experience high, work experience medium, extracurricular activity low, clinically related public service low, GPA medium, letters of recommendation high, interview medium, statement of goals and objectives high.

Student Characteristics: The following represents characteristics of students in 2004–2005 in all graduate psychology programs in the department: Female–full-time 22, part-time 0; Male–full-time 3, part-time 0; African American/Black–full-time 0, part-time 0; Hispanic/Latino(a)–full-time 4, part-time 0; Asian/Pacific Islander–full-time 0, part-time 0; American Indian/Alaska Native–full-time 0, part-time 0; Caucasian–full-time 6, part-time 0; Multi-ethnic–full-time 2, part-time 0.

Financial Information/Assistance:
Tuition for Full-Time Study: *Master's:* State residents: per academic year $1,584, $132 per credit hour; Nonstate residents: per academic year $4,200, $350 per credit hour. Tuition is subject to change. See the following Web site for updates and changes in tuition costs: http://www.finaid.txstate.edu/cost.shtml#graduate.

Financial Assistance:

First Year Students: Teaching assistantships available for first-year. Average amount paid per academic year: $4,900. Average number of hours worked per week: 10. Apply by March 15. Research assistantships available for first-year. Average amount paid per academic year: $4,900. Average number of hours worked per week: 10. Apply by March 15. Fellowships and scholarships available for first-year. Average amount paid per academic year: $5,000. Average number of hours worked per week: 0. Apply by variable. Tuition remission given: partial.

Advanced Students: Teaching assistantships available for advanced students. Average amount paid per academic year: $4,900. Average number of hours worked per week: 10. Apply by March 15. Research assistantships available for advanced students. Average amount paid per academic year: $4,900. Average number of hours worked per week: 10. Apply by March 15. Fellowships and scholarships available for advanced students. Average amount paid per academic year: $5,000. Average number of hours worked per week: 0. Apply by variable. Tuition remission given: partial.

Contact Information: Of all students currently enrolled full-time, 55% benefitted from one or more of the listed financial assistance programs. Application and information available online at: http://www.gradcollege.txstate.edu.

Internships/Practica: Multiple practicum sites are avaliable and students must complete two-semesters of practicum or complete a research option. Practicum sites include several hospitals, rehabilitation centers, behavioral health clinics, medical research firms, medical centers, and pain clinics.

Housing and Day Care: On-campus housing is available. See the following Web site for more information: http://www.reslife.txstate.edu. On-campus day care facilities are available. See the following Web site for more information: http://www.fcs.txstate.edu/cdc.htm.

Employment of Department Graduates:

Master's Degree Graduates: Of those who graduated in the academic year 2003–2004, the following categories and numbers represent the post-graduate activities and employment of master's degree graduates: Enrolled in a psychology doctoral program (4), enrolled in another graduate/professional program (2), enrolled in a post-doctoral residency/fellowship (n/a), employed in independent practice (n/a), employed in business or industry (research/consulting) (4), employed in a government agency (research) (4), employed in a community mental health/counseling center (2), employed in a hospital/medical center (4), still seeking employment (0), other employment position (3), total from the above (master's) (23).

Doctoral Degree Graduates: Of those who graduated in the academic year 2003–2004, the following categories and numbers represent the post-graduate activities and employment of doctoral degree graduates: Enrolled in a psychology doctoral program (n/a), total from the above (doctoral) (0).

Additional Information:

Orientation, Objectives, and Emphasis of Department: The orientation of the psychology department at Texas State University is generally geared toward developmental, personality, and social psychology, due in large part to the majority of the faculty's interests and background. There are a number of experimentally oriented as well as clinically oriented faculty as well. The main objective of the department is to provide students with a strong background in health psychology for successful entry into PhD programs and many areas of employment (business, government, health) immediately upon college graduation. Recently, the department has begun a Master's program in applied Health Psychology, and has made a concerted effort to hire appropriate faculty and develop a focused curriculum. The Master's program is intended to provide Master's level students with specific clinical skills, cognitive–behavioral intervention techniques, and research skills for entry into PhD programs and direct employment in a variety of medical and health care settings.

Special Facilities or Resources: The psychology department at Texas State University is currently developing relationships with the surrounding area's medical communities, such as San Antonio's and Austin's major medical centers. We are also in the process of developing relationships with the Texas Department of Health.

Application Information:
Send to: The Graduate College, Texas State University, 601 University Drive, San Marcos, TX 78666-4605. Students are admitted in the Fall, application deadline March 15. Note that the deadline for many scholarships (including those administered by the graduate college and Liberal Arts Graduate Scholarships) is March 1. *Fee:* $40. This is the graduate college fee, not a departmental fee.

Texas Tech University
Department of Psychology
Arts & Sciences
Box 42051
Lubbock, TX 79409-2051
Telephone: (806) 742-3711
Fax: (806) 742-0818
E-mail: *psygradapp@ttu.edu*
Web: *http://www.psychology.ttu.edu*

Department Information:
1950. Chairperson: Ruth H. Maki. Number of Faculty: total–full-time 28; women–full-time 12; minority–full-time 1; faculty subject to the Americans With Disabilities Act 1.

Programs and Degrees Offered:
Listed in the following order: Program area, degree type (T if terminal Master's), number awarded 7/03–6/04. Clinical Psychology PhD (Doctor of Philosophy) 4, Cognitive/Applied Cognitive PhD (Doctor of Philosophy), Counseling Psychology PhD (Doctor of Philosophy) 4, General Experimental PhD (Doctor of Philosophy) 0, Human Factors PhD (Doctor of Philosophy), Social Psychology PhD (Doctor of Philosophy) 0.

APA Accreditation: Clinical PhD (Doctor of Philosophy). Counseling PhD (Doctor of Philosophy).

Student Applications/Admissions:
Student Applications
Clinical Psychology PhD (Doctor of Philosophy)—Applications 2004–2005, 99. Total applicants accepted 2004–2005, 7. Num-

ber enrolled (new admits only) 2004–2005 full-time, 7. Openings 2005–2006, 6. The number of students enrolled full and part-time who were dismissed or voluntarily withdrew from this program area were 0. *Cognitive/Applied Cognitive PhD (Doctor of Philosophy)*—Applications 2004–2005, 9. Total applicants accepted 2004–2005, 3. Number enrolled (new admits only) 2004–2005 full-time, 3. Openings 2005–2006, 4. The number of students enrolled full and part-time who were dismissed or voluntarily withdrew from this program area were 1. *Counseling Psychology PhD (Doctor of Philosophy)*—Applications 2004–2005, 76. Total applicants accepted 2004–2005, 5. Number enrolled (new admits only) 2004–2005 full-time, 5. Total enrolled 2004–2005 full-time, 31. Openings 2005–2006, 6. *General Experimental PhD (Doctor of Philosophy)*—Applications 2004–2005, 0. Total applicants accepted 2004–2005, 0. Openings 2005–2006, 4. *Human Factors PhD (Doctor of Philosophy)*—Applications 2004–2005, 10. Total applicants accepted 2004–2005, 2. Number enrolled (new admits only) 2004–2005 full-time, 2. Openings 2005–2006, 4. *Social Psychology PhD (Doctor of Philosophy)*—Applications 2004–2005, 16. Total applicants accepted 2004–2005, 3. Number enrolled (new admits only) 2004–2005 full-time, 3. Openings 2005–2006, 4.

Other Criteria: (importance of criteria rated low, medium, or high): GRE/MAT scores medium, research experience high, work experience medium, extracurricular activity low, clinically related public service medium, GPA medium, letters of recommendation high, statement of goals and objectives high. Work experience for experimental-low, counseling-medium, clinical-high; extracurricular activity for experimental-low, counseling-low, clinical-medium; clinically related public service for counseling-medium, clinical-medium; interview for clinical-low, experimental-low.

Student Characteristics: The following represents characteristics of students in 2004–2005 in all graduate psychology programs in the department: Female–full-time 61, part-time 0; Male–full-time 33, part-time 0; African American/Black–full-time 4, part-time 0; Hispanic/Latino(a)–full-time 12, part-time 0; Asian/Pacific Islander–full-time 5, part-time 0; American Indian/Alaska Native–full-time 0, part-time 0; Caucasian–full-time 73, part-time 0; students subject to the Americans With Disabilities Act–full-time 1, part-time 0.

Financial Information/Assistance:

Tuition for Full-Time Study: *Master's:* State residents: per academic year $1,728, $96 per credit hour; Nonstate residents: per academic year $8,532, $474 per credit hour. *Doctoral:* State residents: per academic year $1,728, $96 per credit hour; Nonstate residents: per academic year $8,532, $474 per credit hour. Tuition is subject to change. See the following Web site for updates and changes in tuition costs: www.depts.ttu.edu/studentbusinessservices.

Financial Assistance:

First Year Students: Teaching assistantships available for first-year. Average amount paid per academic year: $10,550. Average number of hours worked per week: 20. Tuition remission given: partial. Research assistantships available for first-year. Average amount paid per academic year: $10,500. Average number of hours worked per week: 20. Tuition remission given: partial. Fellowships and scholarships available for first-year. Average amount

paid per academic year: $1,000. Average number of hours worked per week: 0. Tuition remission given: partial.

Advanced Students: Teaching assistantships available for advanced students. Average amount paid per academic year: $11,542. Average number of hours worked per week: 20. Tuition remission given: partial. Research assistantships available for advanced students. Average amount paid per academic year: $11,542. Average number of hours worked per week: 20. Tuition remission given: partial. Fellowships and scholarships available for advanced students. Average amount paid per academic year: $1,000. Average number of hours worked per week: 0. Tuition remission given: partial.

Contact Information: Of all students currently enrolled full-time, 90% benefitted from one or more of the listed financial assistance programs.

Internships/Practica: Practica in our Psychology Clinic and Texas Tech University Counseling Center. Paid practica are available in the community. Such placements include working in a psychiatric prison, the pain clinic and Neuropsychiatry Department in the TTU Health Sciences Center, the local school district, a juvenile justice center, and conducting assessments at the state school and with local psychologists. For those doctoral students for whom a professional internship is required prior to graduation, 13 applied in 2003–2004. Of those who applied, 13 were placed in internships listed by the Association of Psychology Postdoctoral and Internship Programs (APPIC); 13 were placed in APA accredited internships.

Housing and Day Care: On-campus housing is available. Graduate students can live in dormatories. See the following Web site for more information: (http://www.hous.ttu.edu/studenthousing/livingoptions.htm). Day care is available through the College of Human Development on a limited basis.

Employment of Department Graduates:

Master's Degree Graduates: Of those who graduated in the academic year 2003–2004, the following categories and numbers represent the post-graduate activities and employment of master's degree graduates: Enrolled in another graduate/professional program (0), enrolled in a post-doctoral residency/fellowship (n/a), employed in independent practice (n/a), total from the above (master's) (0).

Doctoral Degree Graduates: Of those who graduated in the academic year 2003–2004, the following categories and numbers represent the post-graduate activities and employment of doctoral degree graduates: Enrolled in a psychology doctoral program (n/a), enrolled in a post-doctoral residency/fellowship (2), employed in an academic position at a university (2), employed in other positions at a higher education institution (1), employed in a community mental health/counseling center (1), other employment position (2), total from the above (doctoral) (8).

Additional Information:

Orientation, Objectives, and Emphasis of Department: The clinical program adheres to a basic scientist-practitioner model with equal emphasis given to these components of clinical training. The program strives to develop student competencies in the following areas: psychotherapy and other major patterns of psychological treatment, clinical research, psychodiagnostic assessment, psychopathology, personality, and general psychology. The doctoral specialization in counseling psychology is also firmly committed to a concept of balanced scientist-practitioner training and is designed to foster the development of competence in basic psychology, counseling and psychotherapy, psychological assessment, psychological research, and professional ethics. Programs in experimental psychology (cognitive, applied cognitive, social, human factors) encompass a variety of research interests, both basic and applied. Students in these programs are exposed to the data, methods and theories in a wide variety of basic areas of psychology while at the same time developing a commitment to an area of special interest through research with a faculty mentor. Collaborative work across departmental programs is encouraged, and the department also collaborates with colleagues in management, industrial engineering, neuroscience, and the Health Sciences Center.

Special Facilities or Resources: The department is housed in its own four-story building, which includes a large, well-equipped psychology clinic for practicum training, numerous laboratories equipped for human research activities, and sufficient student workspace and offices. The university maintains constantly expanding computing support systems that can be accessed from computers in the psychology building. The Psychology Department has a number of microcomputers and software available for student use. The university enjoys an unusually good relationship with the local metropolitan community of over 200,000 residents. Major medical facilities, a private psychiatric hospital, a psychiatric prison and a state school for the developmentally disabled are located within the city, and APA-accredited internship training is available in the University Counseling Center. The cost of living is quite low and the climate is excellent.

Application Information:
Send to: Texas Tech University Admissions, Psychology Department, Box 42051, Lubbock, TX 79409-2051. Students are admitted in the Fall. Deadlines for application: Counseling: January 2, Clinical: January 2, Experimental: February 15. All materials must be received by February 15 for consideration into the University's prestigious Chancellor's Fellowships. Presently, this is an additional $3,000/year for 3 years. *Fee:* $50. There is one application fee required to apply to all Texas State Universities using the Texas Common Application.

Texas Tech University (2004 data)
Educational Psychology and Leadership/Educational
  Psychology
College of Education
Box 41071
Lubbock, TX 79409-1071
Telephone: (806) 742-2393
Fax: (806) 742-2179
E-mail: *psygradapp@ttu.edu*
Web: *http://www.educ.ttu.edu*

Department Information:
1963. Program Coordinator: Mary Tallent Runnels, PhD Number of Faculty: total–full-time 6, part-time 2; women–full-time 3, part-time 1; minority–full-time 3.

Programs and Degrees Offered:
Listed in the following order: Program area, degree type (T if terminal Master's), number awarded 7/03–6/04. Educational Psychology EdD (Doctor of Education) 2.

Student Applications/Admissions:
Student Applications
Educational Psychology EdD (Doctor of Education)—Applications 2004–2005, 11. Total applicants accepted 2004–2005, 9. Total enrolled 2004–2005 full-time, 14, part-time, 2. Openings 2005–2006, 15. The Median number of years required for completion of a degree are 4. The number of students enrolled full and part-time who were dismissed or voluntarily withdrew from this program area were 1.

Admissions Requirements:
Scores: Entries appear in this order: required test or GPA, minimum score (if required), median score of students entering in 2003–2004. Master's Programs: GRE-V 400, 400; GRE-Q 400, 400; GRE-V+Q 800, 800; overall undergraduate GPA 3.00, 3.00; last 2 years GPA 3.00, 3.00. We have a holistic admissions process. The scores provided above are desired scores, but students can still be admitted if other data are excellent. Doctoral Programs: GRE-V 550, 550; GRE-Q 550, 550; GRE-V+Q 1100, 1100; overall undergraduate GPA 3.25, 3.25; last 2 years GPA 3.25, 3.25. Our admission system allows us to include information from these standardized tests, but no weights are assigned since our decision is made based on a holistic method which includes a variety of other material (letters of recommendation, interviews, etc.) that the student is required to submit.
Other Criteria: (importance of criteria rated low, medium, or high): research experience medium, work experience high, extracurricular activity medium, clinically related public service low, GPA medium, letters of recommendation high, interview medium, statement of goals and objectives high.

Student Characteristics: The following represents characteristics of students in 2004–2005 in all graduate psychology programs in the department: Female–full-time 11, part-time 1; Male–full-time 3, part-time 1; African American/Black–full-time 0, part-time 0; Hispanic/Latino(a)–full-time 1, part-time 0; Asian/Pacific Islander–full-time 6, part-time 0; American Indian/Alaska Native–full-time 0, part-time 0; Caucasian–full-time 8, part-time 2; Multiethnic–full-time 0, part-time 0; students subject to the Americans With Disabilities Act–full-time 0, part-time 0.

Financial Information/Assistance:
Tuition for Full-Time Study: *Master's:* State residents: per academic year $2,976, $124 per credit hour; Nonstate residents: per academic year $9,168, $382 per credit hour. *Doctoral:* State residents: per academic year $2,976, $124 per credit hour; Nonstate residents: per academic year $9,168, $382 per credit hour.

Financial Assistance:
First Year Students: Teaching assistantships available for first-year. Average amount paid per academic year: $9,450. Average number of hours worked per week: 20. Apply by March 15. Tuition remission given: partial. Research assistantships available for first-year. Average amount paid per academic year: $9,450. Average number of hours worked per week: 20. Apply by March

15. Tuition remission given: partial. Fellowships and scholarships available for first-year. Tuition remission given: partial.

Advanced Students: Teaching assistantships available for advanced students. Average amount paid per academic year: $9,450. Average number of hours worked per week: 20. Apply by March 15. Tuition remission given: partial. Research assistantships available for advanced students. Average amount paid per academic year: $9,450. Average number of hours worked per week: 20. Apply by March 15. Tuition remission given: partial.

Contact Information: Of all students currently enrolled full-time, 80% benefitted from one or more of the listed financial assistance programs. Application and information available online at: www.educ.ttu.edu.

Internships/Practica: *Master's:* State residents: per academic year $2,976, $124 per credit hour; Nonstate residents: per academic year $9,168, $382 per credit hour. is required prior to graduation, 2 applied in 2003–2004.

Housing and Day Care: On-campus housing is available. See the following Web site for more information: http://www.hous.ttu.edu/HOC/housing_on_campus.asp. On-campus day care facilities are available. See the following Web site for more information: http://www.hs.ttu.edu/cdrc/default.htm.

Employment of Department Graduates:

Master's Degree Graduates: Of those who graduated in the academic year 2003–2004, the following categories and numbers represent the post-graduate activities and employment of master's degree graduates: Enrolled in a post-doctoral residency/fellowship (n/a), employed in independent practice (n/a), employed in an academic position at a university (0), total from the above (master's) (0).

Doctoral Degree Graduates: Of those who graduated in the academic year 2003–2004, the following categories and numbers represent the post-graduate activities and employment of doctoral degree graduates: Enrolled in a psychology doctoral program (n/a), enrolled in a post-doctoral residency/fellowship (1), employed in independent practice (1), employed in an academic position at a university (8), employed in other positions at a higher education institution (1), employed in a professional position in a school system (1), still seeking employment (2), total from the above (doctoral) (14).

Additional Information:

Orientation, Objectives, and Emphasis of Department: The objectives of the Educational Psychology program are to impart the following: (a) understanding of philosophical, historical, cultural, and psychological influences on educational theory; (b) understanding of measurement processes and their relationship to educational theory and practice; (c) understanding of research processes, including the component parts of methodology and statistics and their relationship to educational theory and practice; (d) appreciation for the importance of research in graduate study and professional life; (e) ability to conduct rigorous independent research; (f) ability to add knowledge to instructional programs; and (g) ability to be a critical and reflective thinker. The doctoral program emphasizes a broad concept of professional development that focuses on knowledge of the foundations of education (history, philosophy, cultural); research (research methodology, statistics, measurement); essential areas of knowledge in educational psychology (human development, motivation and learning, etc.);

and practice (internships in college teaching, research and program development in schools, etc., individual and collaborative research). Graduates of the doctoral program are prepared to assume roles as college teachers of educational psychology, research and development specialists in schools, service centers, measurement agencies (i.e., ACT and ETS), and other agencies and organizations where the knowledge and skills of educational psychology are required.

Special Facilities or Resources: Our college has a computer lab reserved for graduate students and faculty with laser printers, VAX terminals, MacIntosh and IBM computers, and an array of graphing, word processing, and statistical software. In addition, travel money is available for students with accepted proposals to professional meetings. All students have free access to their own computer accounts for access to library services, many other databases for research, and the Internet.

Information for Students With Physical Disabilities: See the following Web site for more information: www.ttu.edu.

Application Information:
Send to: Office of Graduate Admissions, Texas Tech University, P.O. Box 41030, Lubbock, TX 79409-1070, Phone: (806) 742-2787. Application available online. Students are admitted in the Fall, application deadline May 15; Spring, application deadline October 1. Programs have rolling admissions. Application should be complete at least three months prior to the date of intended enrollment. *Fee:* $25. Fee waived or deferred for full-time Texas Tech employees, spouses, and dependents less than 25 years old.

Texas Woman's University
Department of Psychology and Philosophy
Arts & Sciences
P.O. Box 425470
Denton, TX 76204
Telephone: (940) 898-2303
Fax: (940) 898-2301
E-mail: *dmiller@mail.twu.edu*
Web: *http://www.twu.edu/as/psyphil/*

Department Information:
1942. Chairperson: Dan Miller, PhD Number of Faculty: total–full-time 14, part-time 2; women–full-time 9; minority–full-time 2.

Programs and Degrees Offered:
Listed in the following order: Program area, degree type (T if terminal Master's), number awarded 7/03–6/04. Counseling PhD (Doctor of Philosophy) 9, School PhD (Doctor of Philosophy) 3.

APA Accreditation: Counseling PhD (Doctor of Philosophy).

Student Applications/Admissions:
Student Applications
Counseling PhD (Doctor of Philosophy)—Applications 2004–2005, 73. Total applicants accepted 2004–2005, 13. Number enrolled (new admits only) 2004–2005 full-time, 7. Number

enrolled (new admits only) 2004–2005 part-time, 0. Total enrolled 2004–2005 full-time, 49, part-time, 8. Openings 2005–2006, 9. The Median number of years required for completion of a degree are 6. The number of students enrolled full and part-time who were dismissed or voluntarily withdrew from this program area were 0. *School PhD (Doctor of Philosophy)*—Applications 2004–2005, 19. Total applicants accepted 2004–2005, 12. Number enrolled (new admits only) 2004–2005 full-time, 0. Number enrolled (new admits only) 2004–2005 part-time, 10. Total enrolled 2004–2005 full-time, 10, part-time, 20. Openings 2005–2006, 9. The Median number of years required for completion of a degree are 5. The number of students enrolled full and part-time who were dismissed or voluntarily withdrew from this program area were 0.

Admissions Requirements:

Scores: Entries appear in this order: required test or GPA, minimum score (if required), median score of students entering in 2003–2004. Master's Programs: GRE-V 500, 580; GRE-Q 500, 570; GRE-V+Q 1000, 1150; overall undergraduate GPA 3.00, 3.50; last 2 years GPA 3.50, 3.60; psychology GPA 3.50, 3.75. Doctoral Programs: GRE-V 500, 585; GRE-Q 500, 585; GRE-V+Q 1000, 1170; overall undergraduate GPA 3.0, 3.60; last 2 years GPA 3.5, 3.65; psychology GPA 3.5, 3.70.

Other Criteria: (importance of criteria rated low, medium, or high): GRE/MAT scores medium, research experience medium, work experience high, extracurricular activity low, clinically related public service medium, GPA high, letters of recommendation high, interview high, statement of goals and objectives high, writing skills.

Student Characteristics: The following represents characteristics of students in 2004–2005 in all graduate psychology programs in the department: Female–full-time 70, part-time 46; Male–full-time 8, part-time 6; African American/Black–full-time 9, part-time 2; Hispanic/Latino(a)–full-time 7, part-time 1; Asian/Pacific Islander–full-time 8, part-time 2; American Indian/Alaska Native–full-time 1, part-time 1; Caucasian–full-time 0, part-time 0; students subject to the Americans With Disabilities Act–full-time 0, part-time 1.

Financial Information/Assistance:

Tuition for Full-Time Study: *Master's:* State residents: $163 per credit hour; Nonstate residents: $439 per credit hour. *Doctoral:* State residents: $163 per credit hour; Nonstate residents: $439 per credit hour. Tuition is subject to change.

Financial Assistance:

First Year Students: Teaching assistantships available for first-year. Average amount paid per academic year: $10,314. Average number of hours worked per week: 20. Apply by April. Research assistantships available for first-year. Apply by Varies.

Advanced Students: Teaching assistantships available for advanced students. Average amount paid per academic year: $10,314. Average number of hours worked per week: 20. Apply by April. Research assistantships available for advanced students. Apply by Varies.

Contact Information: Of all students currently enrolled full-time, 12% benefitted from one or more of the listed financial assistance programs. Application and information available online at: www.twu.edu/admissions/graduate.

Internships/Practica: There are numerous placements in the Dallas - Fort Worth metropolitan area. For those doctoral students for whom a professional internship is required prior to graduation, 8 applied in 2003–2004. Of those who applied, 8 were placed in internships listed by the Association of Psychology Postdoctoral and Internship Programs (APPIC); 8 were placed in APA accredited internships.

Housing and Day Care: On-campus housing is available. University Housing, 940-898-3676. On-campus day care facilities are available: TWU Pioneer School, 940-898-2321.

Employment of Department Graduates:

Master's Degree Graduates: Of those who graduated in the academic year 2003–2004, the following categories and numbers represent the post-graduate activities and employment of master's degree graduates: Enrolled in a post-doctoral residency/fellowship (n/a), employed in independent practice (n/a), total from the above (master's) (0).

Doctoral Degree Graduates: Of those who graduated in the academic year 2003–2004, the following categories and numbers represent the post-graduate activities and employment of doctoral degree graduates: Enrolled in a psychology doctoral program (n/a), enrolled in a post-doctoral residency/fellowship (2), employed in independent practice (4), employed in an academic position at a university (1), employed in a professional position in a school system (1), employed in a community mental health/counseling center (1), total from the above (doctoral) (9).

Additional Information:

Orientation, Objectives, and Emphasis of Department: Both the APA-accredited Counseling Psychology doctoral program and the Counseling Psychology master's program prepare students in the practitioner-scientist model for counseling practice with particular emphasis on family systems, gender issues, assessment, and psychotherapeutic work with individuals and families in their contextual systems. The model provides clear training in both practice and science, but emphasizes practice, practice that is informed by science. The programs' philosophy, curricula, faculty, and students, situated within the unique context of the TWU mission, attempt to create an atmosphere that is supportive, open, and flexible. Graduate training in school psychology at the master's level provides a program emphasizing direct service to school settings. Specific competencies and areas of specialization stressed in coursework and field-based training include child development, psychopathology, theories and principles of learning, behavioral intervention and prevention strategies, diagnostic assessment, and evaluation techniques. Doctoral level training in school psychology focuses on applied preparation and training experiences in professional school psychology. This program prepares students in skills required in direct-to-client services (for example, diagnostic assessment and evaluation skills, therapeutic and intervention techniques, and competencies in the application of learning principles). This program also provides training and supervised experiences in the consultation model, emphasizing such competencies as systems and organizational analysis, supervision of programs and services, diagnostic team leadership, grant proposal writing, in-service education, and general coordination of school-based services in a consultative capacity.

Special Facilities or Resources: The University Counseling Center is an APA-approved internship site.

Information for Students With Physical Disabilities: See the following Web site for more information: http://www.twu.edu/dss/.

Application Information:

Send to: Admissions Coordinator, Department of Psychology and Philosophy, Texas Woman's University, P.O. Box 425470, Denton, TX 76204-5470. Students are admitted in the Fall, application deadline February 1. March 1 and October 15 deadlines for Fall and Spring admission to MA school psychology and March 1 for MA counseling psychology program. *Fee:* $30.

Texas, University of, Arlington

Department of Psychology
College of Science
Department of Psychology, UTA Box 19528
Arlington, TX 76019-0528
Telephone: (817) 272-2281
Fax: (817) 272-2364
E-mail: *kopp@uta.edu*
Web: *http://www.uta.edu/psychology*

Department Information:

1959. Chairperson: Robert Gatchel. Number of Faculty: total–full-time 20, part-time 9; women–full-time 4, part-time 6; minority–full-time 2, part-time 2.

Programs and Degrees Offered:

Listed in the following order: Program area, degree type (T if terminal Master's), number awarded 7/03–6/04. BA-MS Industrial-Organizational MA/MS (Master of Arts/Science) (T), Experimental- General PhD (Doctor of Philosophy) 1, General MA/MS (Master of Arts/Science) 2, Industrial-Organizational MA/MS (Master of Arts/Science) (T) 2.

Student Applications/Admissions:

Student Applications

BA-MS *Industrial-Organizational MA/MS (Master of Arts/Science)—Experimental- General PhD (Doctor of Philosophy)*—Applications 2004–2005, 4. Total applicants accepted 2004–2005, 4. Number enrolled (new admits only) 2004–2005 full-time, 2. Number enrolled (new admits only) 2004–2005 part-time, 2. Total enrolled 2004–2005 full-time, 15, part-time, 2. Openings 2005–2006, 5. The Median number of years required for completion of a degree are 6. *General MA/MS (Master of Arts/Science)*—Applications 2004–2005, 46. Total applicants accepted 2004–2005, 20. Number enrolled (new admits only) 2004–2005 full-time, 12. Openings 2005–2006, 6. The Median number of years required for completion of a degree are 4. The number of students enrolled full and part-time who were dismissed or voluntarily withdrew from this program area were 0. *Industrial-Organizational MA/MS (Master of Arts/Science)*—Applications 2004–2005, 35. Total applicants accepted 2004–2005, 7. Number enrolled (new admits only) 2004–2005 full-time, 6. Number enrolled (new admits only) 2004–2005 part-time, 0. Total enrolled 2004–2005 full-time, 16, part-time, 2. Openings 2005–2006, 5. The number of students enrolled full and part-time who were dismissed or voluntarily withdrew from this program area were 2.

Admissions Requirements:

Scores: Entries appear in this order: required test or GPA, minimum score (if required), median score of students entering in 2003–2004. Master's Programs: GRE-V no minimum stated, 500; GRE-Q no minimum stated, 553; GRE-V+Q no minimum stated, 1053; last 2 years GPA no minimum stated, 3.5. Doctoral Programs: GRE-V n/a, 550; GRE-Q n/a, 670; GRE-V+Q n/a, 1220; last 2 years GPA no minimum stated, 3.63. *Other Criteria:* (importance of criteria rated low, medium, or high): GRE/MAT scores medium, research experience high, extracurricular activity low, GPA medium, letters of recommendation medium, statement of goals and objectives medium. For additional information on admission requirements, go to: www.uta.edu/psychology.

Student Characteristics: The following represents characteristics of students in 2004–2005 in all graduate psychology programs in the department: Female–full-time 38, part-time 3; Male–full-time 15, part-time 2; African American/Black–full-time 3, part-time 0; Hispanic/Latino(a)–full-time 3, part-time 0; Asian/Pacific Islander–full-time 13, part-time 0; Caucasian–full-time 0, part-time 0; students subject to the Americans With Disabilities Act–full-time 1, part-time 0.

Financial Information/Assistance:

Tuition for Full-Time Study: *Master's:* State residents: per academic year $3,336, $296 per credit hour; Nonstate residents: per academic year $7,559, $548 per credit hour. *Doctoral:* State residents: per academic year $3,336, $296 per credit hour; Nonstate residents: per academic year $7,559, $548 per credit hour. Tuition is subject to change. See the following Web site for updates and changes in tuition costs: http://oabs.uta.edu/UtaSfs/servlet/edu.uta.utasfs.Application?cmd=regfees.

Financial Assistance:

First Year Students: Teaching assistantships available for first-year. Average amount paid per academic year: $12,000. Average number of hours worked per week: 20. Research assistantships available for first-year. Average amount paid per academic year: $12,000. Average number of hours worked per week: 20.

Advanced Students: Teaching assistantships available for advanced students. Average amount paid per academic year: $13,200. Average number of hours worked per week: 20. Research assistantships available for advanced students. Average amount paid per academic year: $13,200. Average number of hours worked per week: 20.

Contact Information: Of all students currently enrolled full-time, 77% benefitted from one or more of the listed financial assistance programs.

Internships/Practica: The Arlington-Dallas-Fort Worth area is a major center of business and industrial growth in Texas and offers diverse practica opportunities in consulting firms, corporations, and government and private agencies.

Housing and Day Care: On-campus housing is available. See the following Web site for more information: See http://www.uta.edu/housing/ for information about local housing. No on-campus day care facilities are available.

Employment of Department Graduates:

Master's Degree Graduates: Of those who graduated in the academic year 2003–2004, the following categories and numbers

represent the post-graduate activities and employment of master's degree graduates: Enrolled in a psychology doctoral program (3), enrolled in another graduate/professional program (0), enrolled in a post-doctoral residency/fellowship (n/a), employed in independent practice (n/a), total from the above (master's) (3).

Doctoral Degree Graduates: Of those who graduated in the academic year 2003–2004, the following categories and numbers represent the post-graduate activities and employment of doctoral degree graduates: Enrolled in a psychology doctoral program (n/a), enrolled in a post-doctoral residency/fellowship (0), employed in an academic position at a university (1), employed in business or industry (research/consulting) (1), still seeking employment (0), total from the above (doctoral) (2).

Additional Information:

Orientation, Objectives, and Emphasis of Department: The graduate program provides comprehensive interdisciplinary training in experimental psychology and allied fields. The general experimental program trains students to be research scientists in specialty areas that include animal behavior, animal learning, neuroscience, sensation, perception, and cognitive, developmental, personality, social, mathematical or quantitative psychology. A terminal master's program emphasizing industrial-organizational psychology is also available. All students in the graduate program are broadly trained in statistics and experimental design. The objective of graduate work in the experimental psychology program is to educate the student in the methods and basic content of the discipline and to provide an apprenticeship in the execution of creative research in laboratory and/or field settings. The Master's of Science in General Experimental Psychology is designed to form a basis for the doctoral program but is open to those seeking a terminal master's degree. The terminal Master's of Science degree program emphasizing industrial-organizational psychology combines rigorous coursework in experimental design, quantitative methods, psychology and management with practicum experience enabling students to perform effectively in the workplace. The PhD program in general experimental psychology is intended to provide students with deep knowledge of a specialty area and broad knowledge of experimental psychology.

Special Facilities or Resources: Each faculty member who is active in research has his or her own research space. The Department of Psychology is fortunate to have ample space for research, avoiding conflicts that can arise when space is tight. The department has approximately 18,000 total square feet of research space; 7,000 square feet for human subject research and 11,000 square feet for animal research. Graduate students work in faculty labs and use their research facilities. The department is able to utilize modern audiovisual technology in the classroom and is equipped with computer facilities for graduate research. Graduate students have in-office network connections as well as computer access in research laboratories and departmental computer labs. In addition to the departmental computer labs, the university academic computing services operates seven on-campus computing facilities and serves the academic and research needs of the university. The University Libraries include the Central Library, the Architecture and Fine Arts Library, and the Science and Engineering Library. Library resources include a full array of modern technological access to print and electronic information, Internet access and an extensive interlibrary loan network in addition to the 2,430,000 books, periodicals, documents, technical reports, etc., on hand.

Information for Students With Physical Disabilities: See the following Web site for more information: http://www.uta.edu/disability/.

Application Information:
Send to: Graduate Advisor, Department of Psychology, Box 19528, The University of Texas at Arlington, Arlington, TX 76019-0528. Students are admitted in the Fall, application deadline June 10; Spring, application deadline October 21; Summer, application deadline March 24. These deadlines are for U.S. student applications. International student application deadlines are in April, September, and January. See http://www.uta.edu/gradcatalog/cal0304. *Fee:* $30. Application fee for international students is $60.

Texas, University of, Austin
Department of Educational Psychology
College of Education
1 University Station, D5800
Austin, TX 78712-1296
Telephone: (512) 471-4155
Fax: (512) 471-1288
E-mail: *edpsych@teachnet.edb.utexas.edu*
Web: *http://edpsych.edb.utexas.edu*

Department Information:
1923. Chairperson: Edmund T. Emmer. Number of Faculty: total–full-time 33, part-time 10; women–full-time 15, part-time 7; minority–full-time 4.

Programs and Degrees Offered:
Listed in the following order: Program area, degree type (T if terminal Master's), number awarded 7/03–6/04. Counseling Psychology PhD (Doctor of Philosophy) 5, Counselor Education (MEd) Other 17, Human Development and Education PhD (Doctor of Philosophy) 5, Learning, Cognition, and Instruction PhD (Doctor of Philosophy) 4, Quantitative Methods PhD (Doctor of Philosophy) 4, School Psychology PhD (Doctor of Philosophy) 10, Academic Educational Psychology (MEd) Other 1, Academic Educational Psychology MA/MS (Master of Arts/Science) (T) 4.

APA Accreditation: Counseling PhD (Doctor of Philosophy). School PhD (Doctor of Philosophy).

Student Applications/Admissions:
Student Applications
Counseling Psychology PhD (Doctor of Philosophy)—Applications 2004–2005, 116. Total applicants accepted 2004–2005, 20. Number enrolled (new admits only) 2004–2005 full-time, 12. Number enrolled (new admits only) 2004–2005 part-time, 0. Total enrolled 2004–2005 full-time, 48, part-time, 19. Openings 2005–2006, 12. The Median number of years required for completion of a degree are 6. The number of students enrolled full and part-time who were dismissed or voluntarily withdrew from this program area were 0. *Counselor Education (MEd) Other*—Applications 2004–2005, 54. Total applicants accepted 2004–2005, 24. Number enrolled (new admits only) 2004–2005 full-time, 15. Number enrolled (new admits only) 2004–2005 part-time, 6. Total enrolled 2004–2005 full-time, 29, part-time, 13. Openings 2005–2006, 20. The Median num-

ber of years required for completion of a degree are 2. The number of students enrolled full and part-time who were dismissed or voluntarily withdrew from this program area were 7. *Human Development and Education PhD (Doctor of Philosophy)*—Applications 2004–2005, 20. Total applicants accepted 2004–2005, 14. Number enrolled (new admits only) 2004–2005 full-time, 6. Number enrolled (new admits only) 2004–2005 part-time, 0. Total enrolled 2004–2005 full-time, 22, part-time, 7. Openings 2005–2006, 6. The Median number of years required for completion of a degree are 6. The number of students enrolled full and part-time who were dismissed or voluntarily withdrew from this program area were 2. *Learning, Cognition, and Instruction PhD (Doctor of Philosophy)*—Applications 2004–2005, 17. Total applicants accepted 2004–2005, 13. Number enrolled (new admits only) 2004–2005 full-time, 11. Number enrolled (new admits only) 2004–2005 part-time, 0. Total enrolled 2004–2005 full-time, 40, part-time, 7. Openings 2005–2006, 6. The Median number of years required for completion of a degree are 5. The number of students enrolled full and part-time who were dismissed or voluntarily withdrew from this program area were 0. *Quantitative Methods PhD (Doctor of Philosophy)*—Applications 2004–2005, 15. Total applicants accepted 2004–2005, 14. Number enrolled (new admits only) 2004–2005 full-time, 7. Number enrolled (new admits only) 2004–2005 part-time, 0. Total enrolled 2004–2005 full-time, 21, part-time, 9. Openings 2005–2006, 6. The Median number of years required for completion of a degree are 5. The number of students enrolled full and part-time who were dismissed or voluntarily withdrew from this program area were 4. *School Psychology PhD (Doctor of Philosophy)*—Applications 2004–2005, 51. Total applicants accepted 2004–2005, 22. Number enrolled (new admits only) 2004–2005 full-time, 12. Number enrolled (new admits only) 2004–2005 part-time, 0. Total enrolled 2004–2005 full-time, 60, part-time, 12. Openings 2005–2006, 12. The Median number of years required for completion of a degree are 6. The number of students enrolled full and part-time who were dismissed or voluntarily withdrew from this program area were 0. *Academic Educational Psychology (MEd) Other*—Applications 2004–2005, 12. Total applicants accepted 2004–2005, 8. Number enrolled (new admits only) 2004–2005 full-time, 6. Number enrolled (new admits only) 2004–2005 part-time, 1. Total enrolled 2004–2005 full-time, 6, part-time, 1. Openings 2005–2006, 5. The Median number of years required for completion of a degree are 2. The number of students enrolled full and part-time who were dismissed or voluntarily withdrew from this program area were 0. *Academic Educational Psychology MA/MS (Master of Arts/Science)*—Applications 2004–2005, 28. Total applicants accepted 2004–2005, 22. Number enrolled (new admits only) 2004–2005 full-time, 7. Number enrolled (new admits only) 2004–2005 part-time, 2. Total enrolled 2004–2005 full-time, 12, part-time, 6. Openings 2005–2006, 5. The Median number of years required for completion of a degree are 2. The number of students enrolled full and part-time who were dismissed or voluntarily withdrew from this program area were 8.

Admissions Requirements:

Scores: Entries appear in this order: required test or GPA, minimum score (if required), median score of students entering in 2003–2004. Master's Programs: The median upper-division and graduate coursework GPA was 3.45. Doctoral Programs:

The median upper-division and graduate coursework GPA was 3.68.

Other Criteria: (importance of criteria rated low, medium, or high): GRE/MAT scores high, research experience medium, work experience medium, extracurricular activity medium, clinically related public service medium, GPA high, letters of recommendation high, statement of goals and objectives high. For additional information on admission requirements, go to: http://edpsych.edb.utexas.edu.

Student Characteristics: The following represents characteristics of students in 2004–2005 in all graduate psychology programs in the department: Female–full-time 173, part-time 57; Male–full-time 65, part-time 17; African American/Black–full-time 7, part-time 4; Hispanic/Latino(a)–full-time 24, part-time 5; Asian/Pacific Islander–full-time 49, part-time 18; American Indian/Alaska Native–full-time 0, part-time 1; Caucasian–full-time 158, part-time 46; Multi-ethnic–full-time 0, part-time 0; students subject to the Americans With Disabilities Act–full-time 2, part-time 1.

Financial Information/Assistance:

Financial Assistance:

First Year Students: Teaching assistantships available for first-year. Average amount paid per academic year: $11,000. Average number of hours worked per week: 20. Apply by April 1. Tuition remission given: partial. Fellowships and scholarships available for first-year. Average amount paid per academic year: $2,000. Average number of hours worked per week: 0. Apply by January 15.

Advanced Students: Teaching assistantships available for advanced students. Average amount paid per academic year: $11,000. Average number of hours worked per week: 20. Apply by April 1. Tuition remission given: partial. Research assistantships available for advanced students. Average amount paid per academic year: $12,000. Average number of hours worked per week: 20. Apply by April 1. Tuition remission given: partial. Fellowships and scholarships available for advanced students. Average amount paid per academic year: $2,000. Average number of hours worked per week: 0. Apply by February 1.

Contact Information: Of all students currently enrolled full-time, 40% benefitted from one or more of the listed financial assistance programs. Application and information available online at: http://edpsych.edb.utexas.edu/admissions.

Internships/Practica: In the Counseling Psychology Program, internships are generally available in APA-approved counseling and mental health centers, other university counseling centers, and community/hospital settings that provide in-depth supervision. In the School Psychology Program, internship sites are often in APA-approved, school systems, and hospital/community settings that have an educational component. Other programs coordinate a variety of practicum settings to provide both research and applied experiences. For those doctoral students for whom a professional internship is required prior to graduation, 13 applied in 2003–2004. Of those who applied, 13 were placed in internships listed by the Association of Psychology Postdoctoral and Internship Programs (APPIC); 13 were placed in APA accredited internships.

Housing and Day Care: On-campus housing is available. See the following Web site for more information: www.utexas.edu/student/housing. On-campus day care facilities are available. See the following Web site for more information: www.utexas.edu/services/childcare.

Employment of Department Graduates:

Master's Degree Graduates: Of those who graduated in the academic year 2003–2004, the following categories and numbers represent the post-graduate activities and employment of master's degree graduates: Enrolled in a psychology doctoral program (1), enrolled in another graduate/professional program (1), enrolled in a post-doctoral residency/fellowship (n/a), employed in independent practice (n/a), employed in an academic position at a university (0), employed in an academic position at a 2-year/4-year college (0), employed in other positions at a higher education institution (1), employed in a professional position in a school system (6), employed in business or industry (research/consulting) (1), employed in business or industry (management) (0), employed in a government agency (research) (0), employed in a government agency (professional services) (0), employed in a community mental health/counseling center (1), employed in a hospital/medical center (0), still seeking employment (2), other employment position (1), do not know (11), total from the above (master's) (25).

Doctoral Degree Graduates: Of those who graduated in the academic year 2003–2004, the following categories and numbers represent the post-graduate activities and employment of doctoral degree graduates: Enrolled in a psychology doctoral program (n/a), enrolled in another graduate/professional program (1), enrolled in a post-doctoral residency/fellowship (5), employed in independent practice (0), employed in an academic position at a university (4), employed in an academic position at a 2-year/4-year college (0), employed in other positions at a higher education institution (2), employed in a professional position in a school system (4), employed in business or industry (research/consulting) (3), employed in business or industry (management) (4), employed in a government agency (research) (0), employed in a government agency (professional services) (0), employed in a community mental health/counseling center (1), employed in a hospital/medical center (0), still seeking employment (4), other employment position (0), do not know (0), total from the above (doctoral) (28).

Additional Information:

Orientation, Objectives, and Emphasis of Department: Training in educational psychology relates human behavior to the educational process as it occurs in the home, in peer groups, in nursery school through graduate school, in business and industry, in the military, in institutions for persons with physical or mental disabilities, and in a myriad of other settings. In so doing, it includes study in the following areas: the biological bases of behavior; history and systems of psychology and of education; the psychology of learning, motivation, cognition, and instruction; developmental, social, and personality psychology; psychological and educational measurement, statistics, evaluation, and research methodology; the professional areas of school psychology and counseling psychology; and general academic educational psychology.

Special Facilities or Resources: The University of Texas at Austin has the fifth largest academic library in the United States and also provides online access to hundreds of electronic databases. Our department also has access, through our college's Learning Technology Center, to several microcomputer and multimedia laboratories, technical assistance, resource materials, and audiovisual equipment and services. Academic computing facilities are extensive, ranging from mainframes to microcomputers. Additional resources include several university-wide centers with which our faculty are associated, including UT's Counseling and Mental Health Center.

Information for Students With Physical Disabilities: See the following Web site for more information: www.utexas.edu/depts/dos/ssd.

Application Information:

Send to: Official transcripts and GRE scores: GIAC, UT—Austin, P.O. Box 7608, Austin, TX 78713-7608. Letters of recommendation and personal statement: Graduate Adviser Educational Psychology, 1 University Station, D5800, Austin, TX 78712-1296 Online application: www.utexas.edu/student/giac. Application available online. URL of online application: www.utexas.edu/student/admissions/grad. Students are admitted in the Fall, application deadline see below; Spring, application deadline October 1; Summer, application deadline March 1. These are priority deadlines. PhD applicants are admitted in the fall semester only. The priority deadline for Counseling Psychology and School Psychology is December 15. The priority deadline for other PhD areas is February 1. The priority deadlines for the master's areas are October 1 for spring and March 1 for summer and fall (applications are accepted for fall through April 15). *Fee:* $50. Fee may be waived, at the discretion of Graduate Admissions, in cases of demonstrated financial need.

Texas, University of, Austin

Department of Human Ecology, Division of Human
    Development and Family Sciences
Natural Science
Department of Human Ecology, 1 University Station A2700
Austin, TX 78712-0141
Telephone: (512) 471-0337
Fax: (512) 471-5630
E-mail: *hegrad@uts.cc.utexas.edu*
Web: *http://www.utexas.edu/depts/he*

Department Information:

1932. Chairperson: Catherine Surra, PhD Number of Faculty: total–full-time 14; women–full-time 10.

Programs and Degrees Offered:

Listed in the following order: Program area, degree type (T if terminal Master's), number awarded 7/03–6/04. Human Development & Family Sciences PhD (Doctor of Philosophy) 5.

Student Applications/Admissions:

Student Applications

Human Development & Family Sciences PhD (Doctor of Philosophy)—Applications 2004–2005, 41. Total applicants accepted 2004–2005, 13. Total enrolled 2004–2005 full-time, 40, part-time, 1. Openings 2005–2006, 8. The Median number of years required for completion of a degree are 5. The number of students enrolled full and part-time who were dismissed or voluntarily withdrew from this program area were 0.

Admissions Requirements:

Scores: Entries appear in this order: required test or GPA, minimum score (if required), median score of students entering in 2003–2004. Master's Programs: GRE-V+Q no minimum stated; last 2 years GPA no minimum stated. Doctoral Programs: GRE-V+Q no minimum stated; last 2 years GPA no minimum stated.

Other Criteria: (importance of criteria rated low, medium, or high): GRE/MAT scores medium, research experience medium, clinically related public service low, GPA high, letters of recommendation high, statement of goals and objectives high.

Student Characteristics: The following represents characteristics of students in 2004–2005 in all graduate psychology programs in the department: Female–full-time 36, part-time 0; Male–full-time 4, part-time 1; African American/Black–full-time 4, part-time 0; Hispanic/Latino(a)–full-time 0, part-time 0; Asian/Pacific Islander–full-time 5, part-time 1; American Indian/Alaska Native–full-time 0, part-time 0; Caucasian–full-time 31, part-time 0.

Financial Information/Assistance:

Tuition for Full-Time Study: *Master's:* State residents: per academic year $5,012; Nonstate residents: per academic year $10,268. *Doctoral:* State residents: per academic year $5,012; Nonstate residents: per academic year $10,268. Tuition is subject to change.

Financial Assistance:

First Year Students: Teaching assistantships available for first-year. Average amount paid per academic year: $13,924. Average number of hours worked per week: 20. Apply by January 15. Tuition remission given: partial. Research assistantships available for first-year. Average amount paid per academic year: $13,924. Average number of hours worked per week: 20. Apply by January 15. Tuition remission given: full. Fellowships and scholarships available for first-year. Average amount paid per academic year: $13,924. Apply by January 15. Tuition remission given: full.

Advanced Students: Teaching assistantships available for advanced students. Average amount paid per academic year: $15,450. Apply by January 15. Tuition remission given: partial. Research assistantships available for advanced students. Average amount paid per academic year: $15,450. Apply by January 15. Tuition remission given: full. Fellowships and scholarships available for advanced students. Average amount paid per academic year: $16,000. Apply by January 15. Tuition remission given: full.

Contact Information: Of all students currently enrolled full-time, 60% benefitted from one or more of the listed financial assistance programs.

Internships/Practica: A variety of practicum experiences may be arranged to meet students' individual needs.

Housing and Day Care: On-campus housing is available. See the following Web site for more information: http://www.utexas.edu/student/housing/. On-campus day care facilities are available. See the following Web site for more information: http://www.utexas.edu/services/childcare/.

Employment of Department Graduates:

Master's Degree Graduates: Of those who graduated in the academic year 2003–2004, the following categories and numbers represent the post-graduate activities and employment of master's degree graduates: Enrolled in a post-doctoral residency/fellowship (n/a), employed in independent practice (n/a), total from the above (master's) (0).

Doctoral Degree Graduates: Of those who graduated in the academic year 2003–2004, the following categories and numbers represent the post-graduate activities and employment of doctoral degree graduates: Enrolled in a psychology doctoral program (n/a), total from the above (doctoral) (0).

Additional Information:

Orientation, Objectives, and Emphasis of Department: The program leading to the PhD in Human Development and Family Relationships is designed to prepare individuals for research, teaching, and administrative positions in colleges and universities and for positions in research, government, and other public and private settings. The focus of the program is research concerning the interplay between individual development and family relationships. Development of the individual is considered within the context of the family, peer group, community, and culture. The family is studied as a system of relationships, with attention given to roles, communication, conflict resolution and negotiation, socialization, and family members' perceptions and emotions during interactions with one another. The program emphasizes the investigation of the family and other social processes that contribute to competence and optimal development in individuals from birth to maturity and on how such competencies, once developed, are reflected in interpersonal relationships and family interactions. The MA program in child development and family relationships is designed to deepen the student's knowledge of normal development within the context of the family, peer group, community, and culture, and to develop the student's skill in generating new knowledge in the field through basic or applied research.

Special Facilities or Resources: Students in the Human Development program may become involved in the university child and family laboratory, a laboratory preschool with about 80 three- to five-year-old children enrolled each semester. The school contains research rooms and observation facilities. Students in the program also get extensive experience using state of the art micro- and mainframe computers. Research space and equipment (such as event recorders, videotape cameras, and multi-channel audiotape recorders) for audiotaping and videotaping of interviews and interactions are readily available. In addition to the departmental resources, the multi-cultural population of Austin constitutes a rich resource for both research and practicum experiences. The library, computation center, and support services of the University of Texas at Austin are among the best in the nation. Free services available to students include the Learning Skills Center, Career Choice Information Center, and Counseling Center.

Application Information:

Send to: Tamara Hornsey, Graduate Coordinator I, Human Ecology Department, University Station 1, Seay Building - Rm 2.412, Austin, TX 78712. Application available online. Students are admitted in the Fall, application deadline January 15. *Fee:* $50.

Texas, University of, Austin

Department of Psychology
1 University Station A8000
Austin, TX 78712
Telephone: (512) 471-3785
Fax: (512) 471-5935
E-mail: *gradoffice@psy.utexas.edu*
Web: *http://www.psy.utexas.edu*

Department Information:
1910. Chairperson: Michael P. Domjan. Number of Faculty: total–full-time 50, part-time 11; women–full-time 11, part-time 3; minority–full-time 6.

Programs and Degrees Offered:
Listed in the following order: Program area, degree type (T if terminal Master's), number awarded 7/03–6/04. Behavioral Neuroscience PhD (Doctor of Philosophy) 1, Clinical PhD (Doctor of Philosophy) 3, Cognition and Perception PhD (Doctor of Philosophy) 4, Developmental PhD (Doctor of Philosophy) 1, Individual Differences and Evolutionary Psychology PhD (Doctor of Philosophy) 1, Sensory Neuroscience PhD (Doctor of Philosophy) 0, Social and Personality PhD (Doctor of Philosophy) 2.

APA Accreditation: Clinical PhD (Doctor of Philosophy).

Student Applications/Admissions:
Student Applications
Behavioral Neuroscience PhD (Doctor of Philosophy)—Applications 2004–2005, 23. Total applicants accepted 2004–2005, 3. Number enrolled (new admits only) 2004–2005 full-time, 1. Openings 2005–2006, 2. The Median number of years required for completion of a degree are 7. The number of students enrolled full and part-time who were dismissed or voluntarily withdrew from this program area were 0. *Clinical PhD (Doctor of Philosophy)*—Applications 2004–2005, 247. Total applicants accepted 2004–2005, 5. Number enrolled (new admits only) 2004–2005 full-time, 4. Openings 2005–2006, 5. The Median number of years required for completion of a degree are 8. The number of students enrolled full and part-time who were dismissed or voluntarily withdrew from this program area were 0. *Cognition and Perception PhD (Doctor of Philosophy)*—Applications 2004–2005, 35. Total applicants accepted 2004–2005, 12. Number enrolled (new admits only) 2004–2005 full-time, 8. Openings 2005–2006, 4. The Median number of years required for completion of a degree are 6. The number of students enrolled full and part-time who were dismissed or voluntarily withdrew from this program area were 1. *Developmental PhD (Doctor of Philosophy)*—Applications 2004–2005, 43. Total applicants accepted 2004–2005, 8. Number enrolled (new admits only) 2004–2005 full-time, 5. Openings 2005–2006, 3. The Median number of years required for completion of a degree are 4. The number of students enrolled full and part-time who were dismissed or voluntarily withdrew from this program area were 0. *Individual Differences and Evolutionary Psychology PhD (Doctor of Philosophy)*—Applications 2004–2005, 30. Total applicants accepted 2004–2005, 2. Number enrolled (new admits only) 2004–2005 full-time, 2. Openings 2005–2006, 2. The Median number of years required for completion of a degree are 5. The number of students enrolled

full and part-time who were dismissed or voluntarily withdrew from this program area were 0. *Sensory Neuroscience PhD (Doctor of Philosophy)*—Applications 2004–2005, 0. Total applicants accepted 2004–2005, 0. *Social and Personality PhD (Doctor of Philosophy)*—Applications 2004–2005, 98. Total applicants accepted 2004–2005, 5. Number enrolled (new admits only) 2004–2005 full-time, 4. Openings 2005–2006, 4. The Median number of years required for completion of a degree are 5.

Admissions Requirements:
Scores: Entries appear in this order: required test or GPA, minimum score (if required), median score of students entering in 2003–2004. Doctoral Programs: GRE-V no minimum stated, 660; GRE-Q no minimum stated, 720; GRE-V+Q no minimum stated, 1380.
Other Criteria: (importance of criteria rated low, medium, or high): research experience high, work experience low, clinically related public service low, letters of recommendation high, interview medium, statement of goals and objectives high. For additional information on admission requirements, go to: http://www.psy.utexas.edu/psy/GradProgram/application.html.

Student Characteristics: The following represents characteristics of students in 2004–2005 in all graduate psychology programs in the department: Female–full-time 74, part-time 0; Male–full-time 49, part-time 0; African American/Black–full-time 1, part-time 0; Hispanic/Latino(a)–full-time 6, part-time 0; Asian/Pacific Islander–full-time 10, part-time 0; American Indian/Alaska Native–full-time 3, part-time 0; Caucasian–full-time 97, part-time 0; students subject to the Americans With Disabilities Act–full-time 0, part-time 0.

Financial Information/Assistance:
Tuition for Full-Time Study: *Doctoral:* State residents: $556 per credit hour; Nonstate residents: $838 per credit hour. Tuition is subject to change.

Financial Assistance:
First Year Students: Teaching assistantships available for first-year. Average amount paid per academic year: $11,400. Average number of hours worked per week: 20. Tuition remission given: full. Research assistantships available for first-year. Average amount paid per academic year: $11,400. Average number of hours worked per week: 20. Tuition remission given: full. Fellowships and scholarships available for first-year. Average amount paid per academic year: $16,000. Tuition remission given: full.
Advanced Students: Teaching assistantships available for advanced students. Average amount paid per academic year: $12,600. Average number of hours worked per week: 20. Tuition remission given: full. Research assistantships available for advanced students. Average amount paid per academic year: $12,600. Average number of hours worked per week: 20. Tuition remission given: full. Fellowships and scholarships available for advanced students. Average amount paid per academic year: $16,000. Tuition remission given: full.
Contact Information: Of all students currently enrolled full-time, 83% benefitted from one or more of the listed financial assistance programs.

Internships/Practica: Clinical students participate in practica at agencies in the Austin area, including the Austin State Hospital, Austin Child Guidance Center, Brown Schools, and the UT

Counseling-Psychological Services Center. Most students select an internship at nationally recognized clinical settings such as the Langley Porter Neuropsychiatric Institute, or the University of California at San Diego Psychological Internship Consortium. Local settings are also available. For those doctoral students for whom a professional internship is required prior to graduation, 7 applied in 2003–2004. Of those who applied, 7 were placed in APA accredited internships.

Housing and Day Care: On-campus housing is available. See the following Web sites for more information: University Apartments http://www.utexas.edu/student/housing/prospective/apartments/eligibility_rates.php (primarily for married students). Apartments not physically located on campus: http://www.utexas.edu/student/housing/prospective/apartments/eligibility_rates.php. On-campus day care facilities are available. See the following Web site for more information: http://www.utexas.edu/services/childcare/student/index.html.

Employment of Department Graduates:

Master's Degree Graduates: Of those who graduated in the academic year 2003–2004, the following categories and numbers represent the post-graduate activities and employment of master's degree graduates: Enrolled in a post-doctoral residency/fellowship (n/a), employed in independent practice (n/a), total from the above (master's) (0).

Doctoral Degree Graduates: Of those who graduated in the academic year 2003–2004, the following categories and numbers represent the post-graduate activities and employment of doctoral degree graduates: Enrolled in a psychology doctoral program (n/a), enrolled in a post-doctoral residency/fellowship (5), employed in an academic position at a university (2), employed in other positions at a higher education institution (1), employed in business or industry (research/consulting) (2), other employment position (1), total from the above (doctoral) (11).

Additional Information:

Orientation, Objectives, and Emphasis of Department: The major goal of graduate training in the Department of Psychology is to aid in developing the competence and professional commitment that are essential to scholarly contributions in the field of psychology. All students, upon completing the program, are expected to be well informed about general psychology, well qualified to conduct independent research, and prepared to teach in their area of interest. Within certain specialized areas, they will be prepared for professional practice. The program culminates in the PhD degree, and it is designed for the person committed to psychological research and an academic career. All of the graduate study areas have a strong academic research emphasis. All of the areas also recognize the necessity of developing knowledge and skills for applied research positions and, in the clinical area, for professional competence. Specific information about the emphases of the graduate program areas may be obtained from the department. If you request this information, please indicate the program areas in which you are interested.

Special Facilities or Resources: The Department of Psychology moved into the Seay Building in May of 2002. This building houses seminar rooms, offices, and research laboratories. The research space includes small rooms for individual testing and larger rooms for group experiments. Some rooms have adjacent observation rooms. An anechoic testing chamber is available for auditory research. All of the departmental laboratories have computers associated with them. Departmental computers are available for student use. Facilities for research with children include the Children's Research Laboratory with numerous experimental suites. The facilities of the Animal Resource Center support research with animals. The support resources of the department include two well-equipped shops with full-time technicians and staff for computer assistance. The support resources of the university include the Computation Center, one of the finest academic computation facilities in the United States, and the Perry-Castaneda Library, one of the largest academic libraries in the country. Faculty members in the department of Psychology are affiliated with the Center for Perceptual Systems, the Institute for Cognitive Science, and the Institute for Neuroscience.

Information for Students With Physical Disabilities: See the following Web site for more information: http://deanofstudents.utexas.edu/ssd/.

Application Information:
Send to: University of Texas, Department of Psychology, Graduate Adviser, 1 University Station A8000, Austin, TX 78712-0187. Application available online. URL of online application: www.applytexas.org. Students are admitted in the Fall, application deadline January 15. *Fee:* $50.

Texas, University of, El Paso
Department of Psychology
El Paso, TX 79968-0553
Telephone: (915) 747-5551
Fax: (915) 747-6553
E-mail: *jdecastro@utep.edu*
Web: *http://academics.utep.edu/Default.aspx?alias=acade*

Department Information:
1965. Chairperson: John de Castro. Number of Faculty: total–full-time 17, part-time 1; women–full-time 4; minority–full-time 4, part-time 1.

Programs and Degrees Offered:
Listed in the following order: Program area, degree type (T if terminal Master's), number awarded 7/03–6/04. Psychology MA/MS (Master of Arts/Science) (T) 2, Psychology PhD (Doctor of Philosophy) 2.

Student Applications/Admissions:
Student Applications
Psychology MA/MS (*Master of Arts/Science*)—Applications 2004–2005, 31. Total applicants accepted 2004–2005, 15. Number enrolled (new admits only) 2004–2005 full-time, 9. Openings 2005–2006, 8. The Median number of years required for completion of a degree are 2. The number of students enrolled full and part-time who were dismissed or voluntarily withdrew from this program area were 0. Psychology PhD (*Doctor of Philosophy*)—Applications 2004–2005, 27. Total applicants accepted 2004–2005, 13. Number enrolled (new admits only) 2004–2005 full-time, 6. Number enrolled (new admits only) 2004–2005 part-time, 0. Openings 2005–2006, 27. The Median number of years required for completion of a degree

are 6. The number of students enrolled full and part-time who were dismissed or voluntarily withdrew from this program area were 0.

Admissions Requirements:

Scores: Entries appear in this order: required test or GPA, minimum score (if required), median score of students entering in 2003–2004. Master's Programs: GRE-V no minimum stated, 500; GRE-Q no minimum stated, 500; overall undergraduate GPA 3.0. Doctoral Programs: GRE-V 500; GRE-Q 500; overall undergraduate GPA no minimum stated, 3.50.

Other Criteria: (importance of criteria rated low, medium, or high): GRE/MAT scores high, research experience high, work experience low, extracurricular activity low, clinically related public service low, GPA high, letters of recommendation high, statement of goals and objectives high.

Student Characteristics: The following represents characteristics of students in 2004–2005 in all graduate psychology programs in the department: Female–full-time 31, part-time 0; Male–full-time 15, part-time 0; African American/Black–full-time 1, part-time 0; Hispanic/Latino(a)–full-time 20, part-time 0; Asian/Pacific Islander–full-time 1, part-time 0; American Indian/Alaska Native–full-time 1, part-time 0; Caucasian–full-time 24, part-time 0; Multi-ethnic–full-time 0, part-time 0; students subject to the Americans With Disabilities Act–full-time 0, part-time 0.

Financial Information/Assistance:

Tuition for Full-Time Study: *Master's:* State residents: per academic year $3,024, $168 per credit hour; Nonstate residents: per academic year $8,460, $470 per credit hour. *Doctoral:* State residents: per academic year $3,024, $168 per credit hour; Nonstate residents: per academic year $8,460, $470 per credit hour. Tuition is subject to change.

Financial Assistance:

First Year Students: Teaching assistantships available for first-year. Average amount paid per academic year: $11,000. Average number of hours worked per week: 20. Apply by January 15. Tuition remission given: full. Research assistantships available for first-year. Average amount paid per academic year: $11,000. Average number of hours worked per week: 20. Apply by January 15. Tuition remission given: full.

Advanced Students: Teaching assistantships available for advanced students. Average amount paid per academic year: $11,000. Average number of hours worked per week: 20. Apply by January 15. Tuition remission given: full. Research assistantships available for advanced students. Average amount paid per academic year: $11,000. Average number of hours worked per week: 20. Apply by January 15. Tuition remission given: full.

Contact Information: Of all students currently enrolled full-time, 93% benefitted from one or more of the listed financial assistance programs.

Internships/Practica: The Clinical MA program requires three hours of internship.

Housing and Day Care: On-campus housing is available. On-campus day care facilities are available.

Employment of Department Graduates:

Master's Degree Graduates: Of those who graduated in the academic year 2003–2004, the following categories and numbers represent the post-graduate activities and employment of master's degree graduates: Enrolled in a psychology doctoral program (1), enrolled in another graduate/professional program (0), enrolled in a post-doctoral residency/fellowship (n/a), employed in independent practice (n/a), employed in an academic position at a university (0), employed in an academic position at a 2-year/4-year college (0), employed in other positions at a higher education institution (1), employed in a professional position in a school system (0), employed in business or industry (research/consulting) (0), employed in business or industry (management) (0), employed in a government agency (research) (0), employed in a government agency (professional services) (0), employed in a community mental health/counseling center (0), employed in a hospital/medical center (0), still seeking employment (0), not seeking employment (0), other employment position (0), do not know (0), total from the above (master's) (2).

Doctoral Degree Graduates: Of those who graduated in the academic year 2003–2004, the following categories and numbers represent the post-graduate activities and employment of doctoral degree graduates: Enrolled in a psychology doctoral program (n/a), enrolled in a post-doctoral residency/fellowship (0), employed in independent practice (0), employed in an academic position at a university (2), employed in an academic position at a 2-year/4-year college (0), employed in other positions at a higher education institution (0), employed in a professional position in a school system (0), employed in business or industry (research/consulting) (0), employed in business or industry (management) (0), employed in a government agency (research) (0), employed in a government agency (professional services) (0), employed in a community mental health/counseling center (0), employed in a hospital/medical center (0), still seeking employment (0), not seeking employment (0), other employment position (0), do not know (0), total from the above (doctoral) (2).

Additional Information:

Orientation, Objectives, and Emphasis of Department: The PhD program is designed to train research psychologists and offers three areas of focus: (1) Health (2) Legal, and (3) Social, Cognitive, & Neuroscience. The general experimental MA program, intended for students who will pursue a PhD degree, emphasizes research methodology and experimental design, and focuses on a variety of substantive areas in psychology. The clinical MA program is designed as a terminal master's degree and emphasizes all applied skills in psychological assessment. A special focus is directed toward bilingual, bicultural research issues.

Information for Students With Physical Disabilities: See the following Web site for more information: http://www.utep.edu/prospectivestudents/.

Application Information:

Send to: UTEP Graduate School, Administration Building, Room 200, 500 West University Avenue, El Paso, TX 79968-0566. Application available online. URL of online application: http://academics.utep.edu/Default.aspx?alias=academics.utep.edu/graduate. Students are admitted in the Fall, application deadline January 15. *Fee:* $15.

Texas, University of, Pan American
Department of Psychology and Anthropology, MA in
  Psychology
CoSBS
1201 West University Drive, SBSC 358
Edinburg, TX 78539
Telephone: (956) 381-3329
Fax: (956) 381-3333
E-mail: *ecardena@utpa.edu*
Web: *www.panam.edu/dept/gsprog*

Department Information:
1972. Chairperson: Wendy Aldridge, PhD, Chair. Number of Faculty: total–full-time 18, part-time 3; women–full-time 3, part-time 2; minority–full-time 3.

Programs and Degrees Offered:
Listed in the following order: Program area, degree type (T if terminal Master's), number awarded 7/03–6/04. Clinical MA/MS (Master of Arts/Science) (T) 7, Experimental MA/MS (Master of Arts/Science) (T) 1.

Student Applications/Admissions:
Student Applications
Clinical MA/MS (Master of Arts/Science)—Applications 2004–2005, 20. Total applicants accepted 2004–2005, 12. Total enrolled 2004–2005 full-time, 15, part-time, 25. Openings 2005–2006, 15. The Median number of years required for completion of a degree are 3. The number of students enrolled full and part-time who were dismissed or voluntarily withdrew from this program area were 0. *Experimental MA/MS (Master of Arts/Science)*—Applications 2004–2005, 2. Total applicants accepted 2004–2005, 1. Total enrolled 2004–2005 part-time, 2. Openings 2005–2006, 3. The Median number of years required for completion of a degree are 3. The number of students enrolled full and part-time who were dismissed or voluntarily withdrew from this program area were 0.

Admissions Requirements:
Scores: Entries appear in this order: required test or GPA, minimum score (if required), median score of students entering in 2003–2004. Master's Programs: GRE-V 400, 500; GRE-Q 400, 500; GRE-V+Q 1000; overall undergraduate GPA 2.9, 3.2; last 2 years GPA 3.0, 3.3; psychology GPA 3.0, 3.4.
Other Criteria: (importance of criteria rated low, medium, or high): GRE/MAT scores high, research experience low, work experience medium, extracurricular activity low, clinically related public service medium, GPA high, letters of recommendation high, statement of goals and objectives high.

Student Characteristics: The following represents characteristics of students in 2004–2005 in all graduate psychology programs in the department: Female–full-time 15, part-time 10; Male–full-time 4, part-time 4; African American/Black–full-time 0, part-time 0; Hispanic/Latino(a)–full-time 15, part-time 10; Asian/Pacific Islander–full-time 0, part-time 0; American Indian/Alaska Native–full-time 0, part-time 0; Caucasian–full-time 4, part-time 4.

Financial Information/Assistance:
Tuition for Full-Time Study: *Master's:* State residents: per academic year $1,197; Nonstate residents: per academic year $3,519. Tuition is subject to change. See the following Web site for updates and changes in tuition costs: small tuition increases each year are mandated by the state legislature.

Financial Assistance:
First Year Students: Teaching assistantships available for first-year. Tuition remission given: partial. Research assistantships available for first-year. Tuition remission given: partial. Fellowships and scholarships available for first-year. Tuition remission given: partial.
Advanced Students: Teaching assistantships available for advanced students. Tuition remission given: partial. Research assistantships available for advanced students. Tuition remission given: partial. Fellowships and scholarships available for advanced students. Tuition remission given: partial.
Contact Information: Of all students currently enrolled full-time, 20% benefitted from one or more of the listed financial assistance programs.

Internships/Practica: Practica are available through the graduate psychology clinic (total of 6 Semester hours). Internships are for 480 clock hours and students are placed under licensed psychologists in private practice or through public and private mental health clinics and hospitals.

Housing and Day Care: On-campus housing is available. Housing Office, Women's Residence Hall, 1201 West University Drive, Edinburg, TX, 78539-2999, Phone: (956) 381-3439. On-campus day care facilities are available.

Employment of Department Graduates:
Master's Degree Graduates: Of those who graduated in the academic year 2003–2004, the following categories and numbers represent the post-graduate activities and employment of master's degree graduates: Enrolled in a psychology doctoral program (1), enrolled in a post-doctoral residency/fellowship (n/a), employed in independent practice (n/a), employed in an academic position at a university (1), employed in a community mental health/counseling center (4), total from the above (master's) (6).
Doctoral Degree Graduates: Of those who graduated in the academic year 2003–2004, the following categories and numbers represent the post-graduate activities and employment of doctoral degree graduates: Enrolled in a psychology doctoral program (n/a), total from the above (doctoral) (0).

Additional Information:
Orientation, Objectives, and Emphasis of Department: The Master's in Clinical Psychology is designed to provide theory, research-based assessment and intervention strategies, skills training, practical knowledge, *DSM* based diagnostic assessment skills, clinical experience, and supervision of professional practices in the field of applied psychology. Multicultural professional practices are emphasized as the community service-base is largely bilingual (English/Spanish) and of Hispanic origin. The program is designed to fulfill prerequisite and academic requirements for taking the Texas State Board of Examiners of Psychologists Exam as a Psychological Associate. Two additional graduate courses through the Educational Psychology Department fulfill the academic requirements for license as a Licensed Professional Counselor (LPC).

Special Facilities or Resources: The graduate psychology clinic has 7 consultation rooms, including monitoring equipment (A/V) for individual and group sessions and supervision. The Department also has equipment and computers to conduct research on perception, cognition, psychophysiology EEG, biofeedback, hypnosis, and other areas of faculty interest. There are also facilities through the Center on Aging and the Minority Biomedical Program for conducting research activities. There is also the possibility of conducting observational primate research through the Gladys Porter Zoo.

Information for Students With Physical Disabilities: See the following Web site for more information: www.panam.edu.

Application Information:

Send to: Director of MA Program, Department of Psychology and Anthropology, University of Texas, Pan American, 1201 West University Drive, Edinburg, TX 78539. Students are admitted in the Fall, application deadline March 1; Winter, application deadline July 1; Spring, application deadline October 1. Applications are reviewed throughout the year as well. *Fee:* $0.

Texas, University of, Tyler
Department of Psychology
3900 University Boulevard
Tyler, TX 75799
Telephone: (903) 566-7130
Fax: (903) 565-5560
E-mail: *rmcclure@mail.uttyl.edu*
Web: *http://www.uttyler.edu*

Department Information:

1973. Chairperson: Henry Schreiber. Number of Faculty: total—full-time 9, part-time 10; women—full-time 2, part-time 6.

Programs and Degrees Offered:

Listed in the following order: Program area, degree type (T if terminal Master's), number awarded 7/03–6/04. Counseling MA/MS (Master of Arts/Science) (T) 3, School Counseling MA/MS (Master of Arts/Science) (T) 10, Clinical MA/MS (Master of Arts/Science) (T) 10.

Student Applications/Admissions:
Student Applications

Counseling MA/MS (Master of Arts/Science)—Applications 2004–2005, 10. Total applicants accepted 2004–2005, 8. Total enrolled 2004–2005 full-time, 16, part-time, 20. Openings 2005–2006, 30. The Median number of years required for completion of a degree are 2. *School Counseling MA/MS (Master of Arts/Science)*—Applications 2004–2005, 12. Total applicants accepted 2004–2005, 10. Total enrolled 2004–2005 full-time, 14, part-time, 10. Openings 2005–2006, 18. The Median number of years required for completion of a degree are 2. *Clinical MA/MS (Master of Arts/Science)*—Applications 2004–2005, 25. Total applicants accepted 2004–2005, 20. Total enrolled 2004–2005 full-time, 20, part-time, 18. Openings 2005–2006, 30. The Median number of years required for completion of a degree are 2. The number of students enrolled

full and part-time who were dismissed or voluntarily withdrew from this program area were 4.

Admissions Requirements:
Scores: Entries appear in this order: required test or GPA, minimum score (if required), median score of students entering in 2003–2004. Master's Programs: GRE-V 450, 550; GRE-Q 450, 540; GRE-V+Q 900, 1090; overall undergraduate GPA 3.0, 3.3; last 2 years GPA 3.0, 3.4.

Other Criteria: (importance of criteria rated low, medium, or high): GRE/MAT scores high, research experience low, work experience low, extracurricular activity low, clinically related public service low, GPA high, letters of recommendation high, interview low, statement of goals and objectives medium.

Student Characteristics: The following represents characteristics of students in 2004–2005 in all graduate psychology programs in the department: Female–full-time 38, part-time 35; Male–full-time 12, part-time 13; African American/Black–full-time 5, part-time 0; Hispanic/Latino(a)–full-time 7, part-time 1; Asian/Pacific Islander–full-time 2, part-time 0; American Indian/Alaska Native–full-time 0, part-time 0; Caucasian–full-time 0, part-time 0.

Financial Information/Assistance:
Tuition for Full-Time Study: *Master's:* State residents: per academic year $3,352, $50 per credit hour; Nonstate residents: per academic year $8,920, $282 per credit hour.

Financial Assistance:

First Year Students: Fellowships and scholarships available for first-year. Average amount paid per academic year: $1,000. Apply by February 1. Tuition remission given: partial.

Advanced Students: Research assistantships available for advanced students. Average amount paid per academic year: $5,000. Average number of hours worked per week: 20. Apply by February 1. Tuition remission given: partial. Fellowships and scholarships available for advanced students. Average amount paid per academic year: $1,000. Apply by February 1. Tuition remission given: partial.

Contact Information: Of all students currently enrolled full-time, 25% benefitted from one or more of the listed financial assistance programs.

Internships/Practica: Practica available include nearby private psychiatric hospitals, MHMR facilities, children's therapy facilities, crisis centers and safe houses for abused women, neuropsychology rehabilitation hospitals, prisons, and schools.

Housing and Day Care: On-campus housing is available. University Pines Housing: (903) 566-7082; Internet: www.uttyler.edu. No on-campus day care facilities are available.

Employment of Department Graduates:
Master's Degree Graduates: Of those who graduated in the academic year 2003–2004, the following categories and numbers represent the post-graduate activities and employment of master's degree graduates: Enrolled in a psychology doctoral program (3), enrolled in a post-doctoral residency/fellowship (n/a), employed in independent practice (n/a), employed in an academic position at a 2-year/4-year college (1), employed in a professional position in a school system (8), employed in a community mental health/

counseling center (5), employed in a hospital/medical center (2), still seeking employment (2), total from the above (master's) (21). **Doctoral Degree Graduates:** Of those who graduated in the academic year 2003–2004, the following categories and numbers represent the post-graduate activities and employment of doctoral degree graduates: Enrolled in a psychology doctoral program (n/a), total from the above (doctoral) (0).

Additional Information:

Orientation, Objectives, and Emphasis of Department: The purpose of our program is to prepare competent, applied practitioners at the master's level. The curriculum is very practical, stressing clinical assessment and intervention, and hands-on experience in relevant areas. Our students have been very successful in finding employment in mental health settings and in gaining admission to clinical and counseling doctoral programs. Special opportunities are provided for training in clinical neuropsychological assessment and psychopharmacology, for training in marital and family counseling, school counseling or for training to become a licensed specialist in school psychology.

Information for Students With Physical Disabilities: See the following Web site for more information: www.uttyler.edu.

Application Information:

Send to: Robert F. McClure, PhD, Psychology Graduate Coordinator, Department of Psychology, University of Texas at Tyler, Tyler, TX 75799. Application available online. URL of online application: www.uttyler.edu. Students are admitted in the Fall, application deadline February 1; Spring, application deadline October 1. *Fee:* $0.

Trinity University
Department of Education
One Trinity Place
San Antonio, TX 78212
Telephone: (210) 999-7501
Fax: (210) 999-7592
E-mail: *Terry.Migliore@trinity.edu*

Department Information:

1976. Director of School Psychology Program: Terry Migliore. Number of Faculty: total–full-time 2, part-time 10; women–full-time 1, part-time 5; minority–part-time 1.

Programs and Degrees Offered:

Listed in the following order: Program area, degree type (T if terminal Master's), number awarded 7/03–6/04. School Psychology Program MA/MS (Master of Arts/Science) (T) 10.

Student Applications/Admissions:

Student Applications

School Psychology Program MA/MS (Master of Arts/Science)— Applications 2004–2005, 40. Total applicants accepted 2004–2005, 15. Number enrolled (new admits only) 2004–2005 full-time, 15. Number enrolled (new admits only) 2004–2005 part-time, 0. Openings 2005–2006, 15. The Median number of years required for completion of a degree are 2. The number of students enrolled full and part-time who were dismissed or voluntarily withdrew from this program area were 2.

Admissions Requirements:

Scores: Entries appear in this order: required test or GPA, minimum score (if required), median score of students entering in 2003–2004. Master's Programs: GRE-V+Q 1000; overall undergraduate GPA 3.0; last 2 years GPA 3.0; psychology GPA 3.0.

Other Criteria: (importance of criteria rated low, medium, or high): GRE/MAT scores medium, research experience medium, work experience medium, extracurricular activity medium, clinically related public service medium, GPA medium, letters of recommendation medium, interview medium, statement of goals and objectives medium.

Student Characteristics: The following represents characteristics of students in 2004–2005 in all graduate psychology programs in the department: Female–full-time 35, part-time 0; Male–full-time 3, part-time 0; African American/Black–full-time 3, part-time 0; Hispanic/Latino(a)–full-time 6, part-time 0; Asian/Pacific Islander–full-time 1, part-time 0; American Indian/Alaska Native–full-time 0, part-time 0; Caucasian–full-time 28, part-time 0.

Financial Information/Assistance:

Financial Assistance:

First Year Students: No information provided.
Advanced Students: No information provided.
Contact Information: No information provided.

Internships/Practica: All students have graduate assistantships in career-related work. The average award per student is $14,000 per year for the 2 years of academic work ($28,000). The required 3rd year internship is funded at $28,000 for each student, or students may apply directly to school districts, which may offer a higher salary.

Housing and Day Care: No on-campus housing is available. No on-campus day care facilities are available.

Employment of Department Graduates:

Master's Degree Graduates: Of those who graduated in the academic year 2003–2004, the following categories and numbers represent the post-graduate activities and employment of master's degree graduates: Enrolled in a post-doctoral residency/fellowship (n/a), employed in independent practice (n/a), total from the above (master's) (0).

Doctoral Degree Graduates: Of those who graduated in the academic year 2003–2004, the following categories and numbers represent the post-graduate activities and employment of doctoral degree graduates: Enrolled in a psychology doctoral program (n/a), total from the above (doctoral) (0).

Additional Information:

Orientation, Objectives, and Emphasis of Department: The Trinity University Department of Education offers the 60 semester-hour master of arts in school psychology. The purpose of this program is to prepare graduates to provide psychological services in school settings. The courses and practicum experiences offer the theory and skills necessary for assessment, consultation, and counseling functions. Specific application of assessment and consultation skills to classroom instruction is stressed in Trinity's program. All graduates will be eligible to take the examination for Licensed Specialist in School Psychology and to apply for

Nationally Certified School Psychologist. The program has full approval by the National Association of School Psychologists.

Special Facilities or Resources: Part-time faculty are either psychologists or consultants with local school districts, or work at the Psychological Corporation, a major developer of assessment instruments used in schools and clinics.

Application Information:
Send to: Dr. Terry Migliore, Trinity University, Education Department, 715 Stadium Drive, San Antonio, TX 78212. Students are admitted in the Fall, application deadline February 1. *Fee:* $30.

West Texas A&M University (2004 data)
Department of Behavioral Sciences
P.O. Box 60296
Canyon, TX 79016
Telephone: (806) 651-2590
Fax: (806) 651-2728
E-mail: *gbyrd@mail.wtamu.edu*
Web: *www.wtamu.edu*

Department Information:
1971. Chairperson: Gary R. Byrd. Number of Faculty: total–full-time 5, part-time 2; women–part-time 1.

Programs and Degrees Offered:
Listed in the following order: Program area, degree type (T if terminal Master's), number awarded 7/03–6/04. Psychology MA/MS (Master of Arts/Science) (T) 4.

Student Applications/Admissions:
Student Applications
Psychology MA/MS *(Master of Arts/Science)*—Applications 2004–2005, 8. Total applicants accepted 2004–2005, 6. Total enrolled 2004–2005 full-time, 8, part-time, 18. Openings 2005–2006, 10. The Median number of years required for completion of a degree are 3. The number of students enrolled full and part-time who were dismissed or voluntarily withdrew from this program area were 1.

Admissions Requirements:
Scores: Entries appear in this order: required test or GPA, minimum score (if required), median score of students entering in 2003–2004. Master's Programs: GRE-V 360, 480; GRE-Q 410, 490; GRE-V+Q 840, 990; overall undergraduate GPA 2.3, 3.6; psychology GPA 3.00, 3.50.
Other Criteria: (importance of criteria rated low, medium, or high): GRE/MAT scores high, research experience medium, work experience low, extracurricular activity low, clinically related public service low, GPA high, letters of recommendation high, statement of goals and objectives low.

Student Characteristics: The following represents characteristics of students in 2004–2005 in all graduate psychology programs in the department: Female–full-time 2, part-time 14; Male–full-time 6, part-time 4; African American/Black–full-time 0, part-time 0; Hispanic/Latino(a)–full-time 0, part-time 0; Asian/Pacific Is-

lander–full-time 1, part-time 0; American Indian/Alaska Native–full-time 0, part-time 0; Caucasian–full-time 7, part-time 18; Multi-ethnic–full-time 0, part-time 0; students subject to the Americans With Disabilities Act–full-time 0, part-time 0.

Financial Information/Assistance:
Tuition for Full-Time Study: *Master's:* State residents: per academic year $828, $120 per credit hour; Nonstate residents: per academic year $5,076, $282 per credit hour. Tuition is subject to change. See the following Web site for updates and changes in tuition costs: http://wtamu.edu.

Financial Assistance:
First Year Students: Fellowships and scholarships available for first-year. Average amount paid per academic year: $500. Apply by August 1. Tuition remission given: partial.
Advanced Students: Teaching assistantships available for advanced students. Average amount paid per academic year: $3,350. Average number of hours worked per week: 15. Apply by May 1. Tuition remission given: partial. Research assistantships available for advanced students. Average amount paid per academic year: $3,300. Average number of hours worked per week: 15. Apply by May 1. Tuition remission given: partial. Fellowships and scholarships available for advanced students. Average amount paid per academic year: $500. Apply by August 1. Tuition remission given: partial.
Contact Information: Of all students currently enrolled full-time, 50% benefitted from one or more of the listed financial assistance programs. Application and information available online at: http://wtamu.edu.

Internships/Practica: In addition to clinical/counseling practica, the program offers internships in program evaluation with a large public foundation.

Housing and Day Care: On-campus housing is available. See the following Web site for more information: www.wtamu.edu or Office of Student Services, WTAMU, Canyon, TX 79016, Phone: (806) 651-2050. On-campus day care facilities are available.

Employment of Department Graduates:
Master's Degree Graduates: Of those who graduated in the academic year 2003–2004, the following categories and numbers represent the post-graduate activities and employment of master's degree graduates: Enrolled in a psychology doctoral program (0), enrolled in another graduate/professional program (0), enrolled in a post-doctoral residency/fellowship (n/a), employed in independent practice (n/a), employed in an academic position at a university (0), employed in an academic position at a 2-year/4-year college (0), employed in other positions at a higher education institution (0), employed in a professional position in a school system (1), employed in business or industry (research/consulting) (0), employed in business or industry (management) (0), employed in a government agency (research) (0), employed in a government agency (professional services) (0), employed in a community mental health/counseling center (1), employed in a hospital/medical center (0), still seeking employment (0), other employment position (1), total from the above (master's) (3).
Doctoral Degree Graduates: Of those who graduated in the academic year 2003–2004, the following categories and numbers represent the post-graduate activities and employment of doctoral

degree graduates: Enrolled in a psychology doctoral program (n/a), total from the above (doctoral) (0).

Additional Information:

Orientation, Objectives, and Emphasis of Department: The primary purpose of the program is to create opportunities for students who have strong qualifications for graduate work and have a bachelor's degree in psychology but need clarification as to which specialization they should seek in their doctoral studies, have a weak dimension in their application qualifications for graduate studies and wish to enhance their potential for admission to a doctoral program, do NOT have a bachelor's degree in psychology but are promising students that now wish to become competitive for psychology doctoral programs or seek employment at the master's level of professional psychology.

Special Facilities or Resources: The department has a variety of facilities that can be viewed in five functional subdivisions. First, there are several large experimental research laboratories that contain equipment for electrophysiological measures (EEG, EMG, EOG, & hemisphereric electronic equipment) is highly versatile and can be controlled by lab computers. Second, there are facilities to record data for field studies, such as the behavior of children in their home setting or animals in their natural settings. Third, a psychometric lab provides storage and space for administering psychological tests. Fourth, a large community foundation has a partnership with the department to provide a setting for training a limited number of students in program evaluation for community grants and projects. And, finally, there are eight community mental health facilities (two are residential) that provide practicum settings for students interested in clinical or counseling training.

Application Information:

Send to: Dr. Richard Harland, Psychology Graduate Coordinator, P.O. Box 60296, WTAMU, Canyon, TX 79016. Students are admitted in the Fall, application deadline August 10; Spring, application deadline December 15; Summer, application deadline May 15. *Fee:* $0.

Brigham Young University

Department of Counseling Psychology and Special Education
David O. McKay School of Education
340 MCKB
Provo, UT 84602
Telephone: (801) 422-3857
Fax: (801) 422-0198
E-mail: *aaron_jackson@byu.edu*
Web: *http://www.byu.edu/cse*

Department Information:

1969. Department Chair: Mary Anne Prater. Number of Faculty: total–full-time 7, part-time 5; women–full-time 3, part-time 1; minority–part-time 1.

Programs and Degrees Offered:

Listed in the following order: Program area, degree type (T if terminal Master's), number awarded 7/03–6/04. School Psychology Other, Counseling Psychology PhD (Doctor of Philosophy) 6.

APA Accreditation: Counseling PhD (Doctor of Philosophy).

Student Applications/Admissions:

Student Applications

School Psychology Other—Openings 2005–2006, 12. *Counseling Psychology PhD (Doctor of Philosophy)*—Applications 2004–2005, 57. Total applicants accepted 2004–2005, 6. Number enrolled (new admits only) 2004–2005 full-time, 6. Number enrolled (new admits only) 2004–2005 part-time, 0. Total enrolled 2004–2005 full-time, 40. Openings 2005–2006, 6. The number of students enrolled full and part-time who were dismissed or voluntarily withdrew from this program area were 0.

Admissions Requirements:

Scores: Entries appear in this order: required test or GPA, minimum score (if required), median score of students entering in 2003–2004. Doctoral Programs: last 2 years GPA 3.0, 3.75. *Other Criteria:* (importance of criteria rated low, medium, or high): GRE/MAT scores medium, research experience medium, work experience medium, extracurricular activity low, clinically related public service medium, GPA high, letters of recommendation medium, interview high, statement of goals and objectives high.

Student Characteristics: The following represents characteristics of students in 2004–2005 in all graduate psychology programs in the department: Female–full-time 59, part-time 0; Male–full-time 34, part-time 0; African American/Black–full-time 0, part-time 1; Hispanic/Latino(a)–full-time 2, part-time 0; Asian/Pacific Islander–full-time 2, part-time 0; American Indian/Alaska Native–full-time 1, part-time 0; Caucasian–full-time 77, part-time 9; Multi-ethnic–full-time 11, part-time 10.

Financial Information/Assistance:

Tuition for Full-Time Study: *Master's:* State residents: per academic year $4,975, $221 per credit hour; Nonstate residents: per academic year $7,463, $332 per credit hour. *Doctoral:* State residents: per academic year $4,975, $221 per credit hour; Nonstate residents: per academic year $7,463, $332 per credit hour. Tuition is subject to change. See the following Web site for updates and changes in tuition costs: http://saas.byu.edu/tuition/.

Financial Assistance:

First Year Students: Teaching assistantships available for first-year. Average amount paid per academic year: $7,800. Average number of hours worked per week: 15. Apply by varies. Tuition remission given: partial. Research assistantships available for first-year. Average amount paid per academic year: $7,800. Average number of hours worked per week: 15. Apply by varies. Tuition remission given: partial.

Advanced Students: Teaching assistantships available for advanced students. Average amount paid per academic year: $8,600. Average number of hours worked per week: 15. Apply by varies. Tuition remission given: partial. Research assistantships available for advanced students. Average amount paid per academic year: $8,600. Average number of hours worked per week: 15. Apply by varies. Tuition remission given: partial.

Contact Information: Of all students currently enrolled full-time, 100% benefitted from one or more of the listed financial assistance programs.

Internships/Practica: Master's students complete practica for 5 hours per week during the first and second years of study and a full-time internship (5/8 of teacher pay) the third year. Doctoral students admitted at the bachelor's level complete 2 semesters of introductory practicum. All doctoral students complete 4 semesters of practicum in BYU's counseling center. They also complete 1 teaching practicum and 2 community-based practica. A full-year internship is required. Assistance is given for placements. For those doctoral students for whom a professional internship is required prior to graduation, 7 applied in 2003–2004. Of those who applied, 5 were placed in internships listed by the Association of Psychology Postdoctoral and Internship Programs (APPIC); 5 were placed in APA accredited internships.

Housing and Day Care: On-campus housing is available. See the following Web site for more information: http://www.byu.edu/housing/. No on-campus day care facilities are available.

Employment of Department Graduates:

Master's Degree Graduates: Of those who graduated in the academic year 2003–2004, the following categories and numbers represent the post-graduate activities and employment of master's degree graduates: Enrolled in a post-doctoral residency/fellowship (n/a), employed in independent practice (n/a), total from the above (master's) (0).

Doctoral Degree Graduates: Of those who graduated in the academic year 2003–2004, the following categories and numbers represent the post-graduate activities and employment of doctoral degree graduates: Enrolled in a psychology doctoral program (n/a), employed in independent practice (1), employed in an academic position at a 2-year/4-year college (1), employed in other positions at a higher education institution (4), employed in a professional position in a school system (1), employed in a community mental health/counseling center (2), total from the above (doctoral) (9).

Additional Information:

Orientation, Objectives, and Emphasis of Department: The Department of Counseling Psychology and Special Education offers master's programs in Special Education, an EdS degree in School Psychology, and a PhD program in Counseling Psychology. The School Psychology program prepares students for certification as school psychologists. The Counseling Psychology program prepares individuals for licensure as psychologists. The program is both broad-based and specific in nature; that is, one is expected to take certain courses that could be required for licensure or for certification and graduation, but the program encourages students to take coursework in varied disciplines such as marriage and family therapy, organizational behavior, and other fields allied with psychology and education. The focus of the School Psychology EdS program is to prepare graduates for K-12 school settings. The doctoral program prepares counseling psychologists to work in counseling centers, academic positions, and other mental health settings.

Personal Behavior Statement: http://campuslife.byu.edu/honorcode/index.htm.

Special Facilities or Resources: The department has a Counseling Psychology Center (clinic) with five individual counseling rooms and one large group room available for the observation and videotaping of students in counseling and assessment. These are assigned specifically to the department, while an abundance of other media-related facilities for the teaching and learning experience are available on campus as well as off campus. The department also provides spacious study and work carrels. The Counseling and Career Center has eight offices for practicum students. All of these offices have videotaping capabilities and are equipped for live supervision.

Information for Students With Physical Disabilities: See the following Web site for more information: http://campuslife.byu.edu/uac/.

Application Information:

Send to: Office of Graduate Studies, B-356 ASB, BYU, Provo, UT 84602. Online applications are preferred. Application available online. URL of online application: www.byu.edu/gradstudies. Students are admitted in the Fall, application deadline January 15. Counseling Psychology and School Psychology admit fall only. *Fee:* $50.

Brigham Young University

Department of Psychology
Family, Home & Social Sciences
1001 SWKT
Provo, UT 84602-5543
Telephone: (801) 422-4287
Fax: (801) 422-0602
E-mail: *karen_christensen@byu.edu*
Web: *http://psychology.byu.edu*

Department Information:

1921. Chairperson: M. Gawain Wells. Number of Faculty: total–full-time 31, part-time 4; women–full-time 7, part-time 1; minority–full-time 1, part-time 1.

Programs and Degrees Offered:

Listed in the following order: Program area, degree type (T if terminal Master's), number awarded 7/03–6/04. General PhD (Doctor of Philosophy) 2, Clinical PhD (Doctor of Philosophy) 9, General MS MA/MS (Master of Arts/Science) (T) 17.

APA Accreditation: Clinical PhD (Doctor of Philosophy).

Student Applications/Admissions:

Student Applications

General PhD (Doctor of Philosophy)—Applications 2004–2005, 6. Total applicants accepted 2004–2005, 4. Number enrolled (new admits only) 2004–2005 full-time, 4. Total enrolled 2004–2005 full-time, 14. Openings 2005–2006, 5. The Median number of years required for completion of a degree are 5.5. *Clinical PhD (Doctor of Philosophy)*—Applications 2004–2005, 68. Total applicants accepted 2004–2005, 15. Number enrolled (new admits only) 2004–2005 full-time, 10. Total enrolled 2004–2005 full-time, 58. Openings 2005–2006, 10. The Median number of years required for completion of a degree are 6. The number of students enrolled full and part-time who were dismissed or voluntarily withdrew from this program area were 0. *General MS MA/MS (Master of Arts/Science)*—Applications 2004–2005, 20. Total applicants accepted 2004–2005, 12. Number enrolled (new admits only) 2004–2005 full-time, 5. Total enrolled 2004–2005 full-time, 25. Openings 2005–2006, 10. The Median number of years required for completion of a degree are 3.

Admissions Requirements:

Scores: Entries appear in this order: required test or GPA, minimum score (if required), median score of students entering in 2003–2004. Master's Programs: GRE-V no minimum stated, 560; GRE-Q no minimum stated, 710; GRE-V+Q no minimum stated, 1230; GRE-Analytical no minimum stated; overall undergraduate GPA no minimum stated; last 2 years GPA 3.0, 3.80. Doctoral Programs: GRE-V 500, 570; GRE-Q 500, 670; GRE-V+Q 1000, 1135; GRE-Analytical no minimum stated; overall undergraduate GPA no minimum stated; last 2 years GPA 3.0, 3.82.

Other Criteria: (importance of criteria rated low, medium, or high): GRE/MAT scores high, research experience high, work experience medium, extracurricular activity low, clinically related public service medium, GPA high, letters of recommendation high, interview high, statement of goals and objectives high. The clinically related public service refers to Clinical PhD applicants only.

Student Characteristics: The following represents characteristics of students in 2004–2005 in all graduate psychology programs in the department: Female–full-time 42, part-time 0; Male–full-time 55, part-time 0; African American/Black–full-time 2, part-time 0; Hispanic/Latino(a)–full-time 2, part-time 0; Asian/Pacific Islander–full-time 5, part-time 0; American Indian/Alaska Native–full-time 0, part-time 0; Caucasian–full-time 86, part-time 0; Multi-ethnic–full-time 2, part-time 0; students subject to the Americans With Disabilities Act–full-time 2, part-time 0.

Financial Information/Assistance:

Tuition for Full-Time Study: *Master's:* State residents: per academic year $4,140, $230 per credit hour; Nonstate residents: per academic year $6,210, $345 per credit hour. *Doctoral:* State residents: per academic year $4,140, $230 per credit hour; Nonstate residents: per academic year $6,210, $345 per credit hour. Tuition is subject to change. See the following Web site for updates and changes in tuition costs: Resident tuition given to members of the sponsoring institution regardless of state of origin.

Financial Assistance:

First Year Students: Teaching assistantships available for first-year. Average amount paid per academic year: $8,500. Average number of hours worked per week: 13. Tuition remission given: partial. Research assistantships available for first-year. Average amount paid per academic year: $8,500. Average number of hours worked per week: 13. Tuition remission given: partial.

Advanced Students: Teaching assistantships available for advanced students. Average amount paid per academic year: $9,000. Average number of hours worked per week: 13. Tuition remission given: partial. Research assistantships available for advanced students. Average amount paid per academic year: $9,000. Average number of hours worked per week: 13. Tuition remission given: partial. Traineeships available for advanced students. Average amount paid per academic year: $15,000. Average number of hours worked per week: 20. Tuition remission given: partial.

Contact Information: Of all students currently enrolled full-time, 95% benefitted from one or more of the listed financial assistance programs.

Internships/Practica: Clinical PhD students complete three types of practica: 1) BYU Comprehensive Clinic Integrative Practicum: Students see clients from the community in their first three years under the supervision of full-time clinical faculty and adjunct faculty as needed. The clinic is a unique interdisciplinary training and research facility housing state-of-the-art audiovisual and computer resources for BYU's Clinical Psychology, Marriage and Family Therapy, Social Work, and Speech Language Pathology programs. 2) Clerkships: Students are required to complete four unpaid clerkships of 45 hours each. The clerkships allow students to work with different service agencies dealing with different focus groups: usually prison, state hospital, developmentally disabled/autistic classroom, and a self-selected site. 3) Externships: The clinical program arranges reimbursed training placements for students in over 25 community agencies where students are supervised by onsite licensed professionals, who typically hold adjunct appointments in the Psychology Department. These opportunities provide an excellent foundation for the integration of classroom experiences with practical work applications. For those doctoral

students for whom a professional internship is required prior to graduation, 4 applied in 2003–2004. Of those who applied, 3 were placed in internships listed by the Association of Psychology Postdoctoral and Internship Programs (APPIC); 2 were placed in APA accredited internships.

Housing and Day Care: On-campus housing is available. For more information on housing, visit http://www.byu.edu/housing/ or contact the BYU Campus Accommodations Office at (801) 422-2611, toll-free (877) 403-0040. No on-campus day care facilities are available.

Employment of Department Graduates:

Master's Degree Graduates: Of those who graduated in the academic year 2003–2004, the following categories and numbers represent the post-graduate activities and employment of master's degree graduates: Enrolled in a psychology doctoral program (10), enrolled in a post-doctoral residency/fellowship (n/a), employed in independent practice (n/a), employed in an academic position at a university (1), employed in an academic position at a 2-year/4-year college (1), employed in a hospital/medical center (1), not seeking employment (2), other employment position (1), do not know (1), total from the above (master's) (17).

Doctoral Degree Graduates: Of those who graduated in the academic year 2003–2004, the following categories and numbers represent the post-graduate activities and employment of doctoral degree graduates: Enrolled in a psychology doctoral program (n/a), enrolled in a post-doctoral residency/fellowship (3), employed in independent practice (2), employed in an academic position at a university (1), employed in an academic position at a 2-year/4-year college (1), employed in a community mental health/counseling center (2), employed in a hospital/medical center (2), total from the above (doctoral) (11).

Additional Information:

Orientation, Objectives, and Emphasis of Department: The mission of the Psychology Department is to discover, disseminate, and apply principles of psychology within a scholarly framework that is compatible with the values and purposes of Brigham Young University and its sponsor. Three degrees are offered: Clinical Psychology PhD, General Psychology PhD (emphasis areas in Applied Social Psychology, Behavioral Neurobiology, and Theoretical/Philosophical Psychology), and General MS. For the General PhD, students complete a common core of course work during the first three semesters. By the end of the second year students complete the requirements for an MS degree, including a master's thesis, if the degree has not been previously received. For the Clinical PhD, students do not complete a master's thesis. The philosophy of the clinical psychology program adheres to the scientist-professional model. Training focuses on academic and research competence as well as on theory and practicum experiences necessary to develop strong clinical skills. The program is eclectic in its theoretical approach, drawing from a wide range of orientations in an attempt to give broad exposure to a diversity of traditional and innovative approaches. If they wish, students may elect to complete an emphasis in 1) Child, Adolescent, and Family, 2) Clinical Neuropsychology, 3) Clinical Research.

Personal Behavior Statement: While the university is sponsored by the LDS (Mormon) Church, non-LDS students are welcome and considered without bias. The university does expect that all students, regardless of religion, maintain the behavioral standards of the university. These include high standards of honor, integrity, and morality; graciousness in personal behavior; and abstinence from tobacco, alcohol, and the nonmedical use of drugs. The text of this agreement can be viewed at http://campuslife.byu.edu/honorcode/.

Special Facilities or Resources: 1) Family, Home, and Social Sciences Computing Center: The center assists faculty and students with data processing and other computing needs on mainframe and personal computers. Technical support and consultation services for both statistics and graphics are available to students working on research projects, theses, and dissertations. Special computer facilities in the department support research in psycholinguistics, neuroimaging, neurophysiology, social psychology, and experimental analysis of human and animal behavior. 2) Psychobiology Research Laboratories: These laboratories are equipped with facilities for brain-behavior analysis. Full histology and electrophysiology laboratories, along with the necessary surgical facilities, are available. 3) Neuroimaging and Behavior Laboratory: Research and training in the area of neuroimaging and cognitive neuroscience are supported by a laboratory consisting of multiple computers, video, data storage, and printer workstations. These are supported by software that allows for the capture, processing, isolation, and imaging output of specific areas of the brain from MRI and CT images and from metabolic imaging studies. 4) Multivariate Data Visualization Laboratory: Faculty and students interested in multivariate visualization of data and large-scale data analysis are supported by a mathematical psychology laboratory consisting of a network of NT workstations and laboratories for behavior analysis. Three laboratories feature online control of experimental procedures and data recording.

Information for Students With Physical Disabilities: See the following Web site for more information: http://www.byu.edu/uac/.

Application Information:

Send to: Graduate Studies Office, B-356 ASB, Brigham Young University, Provo, UT 84602. Application available online. URL of online application: https://www.byu.edu/gradstudies/admissions/onlineapp.php. Students are admitted in the Fall, application deadline January 1. Online applications are preferred. See www.byu.edu/gradstudies. *Fee:* $50.

Utah State University
Department of Psychology
Education
2810 Old Main Hill
Logan, UT 84322-2810
Telephone: (435) 797-1460
Fax: (435) 797-1448
E-mail: *PsyDept@cc.usu.edu*
Web: *http://www.coe.usu.edu/psyc/*

Department Information:

1938. Chairperson: David M. Stein. Number of Faculty: total–full-time 22, part-time 20; women–full-time 10, part-time 9; minority–full-time 3.

Programs and Degrees Offered:

Listed in the following order: Program area, degree type (T if terminal Master's), number awarded 7/03–6/04. Combined Clinical/Counseling/School PhD (Doctor of Philosophy) 2, Research and Evaluation PhD (Doctor of Philosophy) 0, School Psychology MA/MS (Master of Arts/Science) (T) 6, School Counseling MA/MS (Master of Arts/Science) (T) 38.

APA Accreditation: Combination PhD (Doctor of Philosophy).

Student Applications/Admissions:
Student Applications

Combined Clinical/Counseling/School PhD (Doctor of Philosophy)—Applications 2004–2005, 55. Total applicants accepted 2004–2005, 8. Number enrolled (new admits only) 2004–2005 full-time, 8. Number enrolled (new admits only) 2004–2005 part-time, 0. Openings 2005–2006, 8. The Median number of years required for completion of a degree are 5. The number of students enrolled full and part-time who were dismissed or voluntarily withdrew from this program area were 0. *Research and Evaluation PhD (Doctor of Philosophy)*—Applications 2004–2005, 12. Total applicants accepted 2004–2005, 6. Total enrolled 2004–2005 full-time, 12, part-time, 2. Openings 2005–2006, 5. *School Psychology MA/MS (Master of Arts/Science)*—Applications 2004–2005, 20. Total applicants accepted 2004–2005, 6. Number enrolled (new admits only) 2004–2005 full-time, 4. Total enrolled 2004–2005 full-time, 15. Openings 2005–2006, 5. The Median number of years required for completion of a degree are 3. The number of students enrolled full and part-time who were dismissed or voluntarily withdrew from this program area were 0. *School Counseling MA/MS (Master of Arts/Science)*—Applications 2004–2005, 89. Total applicants accepted 2004–2005, 78. Total enrolled 2004–2005 full-time, 62, part-time, 6. Openings 2005–2006, 45. The Median number of years required for completion of a degree are 2.

Admissions Requirements:

Scores: Entries appear in this order: required test or GPA, minimum score (if required), median score of students entering in 2003–2004. Master's Programs: GRE-V 550, 525; GRE-Q 550, 590; GRE-V+Q 1100, 1114; last 2 years GPA 3.20, 3.58; psychology GPA 3.50. MAT is accepted in lieu of GRE for School Counseling. Doctoral Programs: GRE-V 550, 562; GRE-Q 550, 620; GRE-V+Q 1100, 1200. Median scores are for the Combined clinical/counseling/school PhD program. Scores for the REM PhD program are similar. Scores for MS programs tends to be slightly lower.

Other Criteria: (importance of criteria rated low, medium, or high): GRE/MAT scores high, research experience medium, work experience medium, extracurricular activity low, clinically related public service medium, GPA high, letters of recommendation high, interview high, statement of goals and objectives high. Some programs (Clinical/Counseling/School PhD) use the above criteria in a formula, while others (REM) rely primarily on GPA, GRE and letters. For additional information on admission requirements, go to: www.coe.usu.edu/grad.html.

Student Characteristics: The following represents characteristics of students in 2004–2005 in all graduate psychology programs in the department: Female–full-time 85, part-time 13; Male–full-time 50, part-time 6; African American/Black–full-time 1, part-time 0; Hispanic/Latino(a)–full-time 3, part-time 1; Asian/Pacific Islander–full-time 1, part-time 1; American Indian/Alaska Native–full-time 4, part-time 1; Caucasian–full-time 126, part-time 16; students subject to the Americans With Disabilities Act–full-time 1, part-time 0.

Financial Information/Assistance:
   Tuition for Full-Time Study: *Master's:* State residents: per academic year $3,600, $180 per credit hour; Nonstate residents: per academic year $11,400, $570 per credit hour. *Doctoral:* State residents: per academic year $3,600, $180 per credit hour; Nonstate residents: per academic year $11,400, $570 per credit hour. Tuition is subject to change. See the following Web site for updates and changes in tuition costs: www.usu.edu/registrar/tuition/.

Financial Assistance:
   First Year Students: Teaching assistantships available for first-year. Average amount paid per academic year: $7,000. Average number of hours worked per week: 20. Apply by January 15. Research assistantships available for first-year. Average amount paid per academic year: $11,000. Average number of hours worked per week: 20. Apply by Varies. Fellowships and scholarships available for first-year. Average amount paid per academic year: $12,000. Apply by January 15.
   Advanced Students: Teaching assistantships available for advanced students. Average amount paid per academic year: $8,000. Average number of hours worked per week: 20. Apply by February 15. Research assistantships available for advanced students. Average amount paid per academic year: $11,000. Average number of hours worked per week: 20. Apply by Varies.
   Contact Information: Of all students currently enrolled full-time, 100% benefitted from one or more of the listed financial assistance programs.

Internships/Practica: Practica are available for master's and doctoral students. Students are placed in a variety of sites including community mental health centers, the USU Counseling Center, the Center for Persons with Disabilities (a University Center for Excellence), and medical facilities in the area. Students from the Combined program accept internships across the country. Internships for students in the REM program are generally with local or regional consulting firms. For those doctoral students for whom a professional internship is required prior to graduation, 8 applied in 2003–2004. Of those who applied, 8 were placed in internships listed by the Association of Psychology Postdoctoral and Internship Programs (APPIC); 7 were placed in APA accredited internships.

Housing and Day Care: On-campus housing is available. See the following Web site for more information: http://www.usu.edu/studentresources/. On-campus day care facilities are available.

Employment of Department Graduates:
   Master's Degree Graduates: Of those who graduated in the academic year 2003–2004, the following categories and numbers represent the post-graduate activities and employment of master's degree graduates: Enrolled in a psychology doctoral program (0),

enrolled in another graduate/professional program (0), enrolled in a post-doctoral residency/fellowship (n/a), employed in independent practice (n/a), employed in an academic position at a university (0), employed in an academic position at a 2-year/4-year college (0), employed in other positions at a higher education institution (0), employed in a professional position in a school system (6), employed in business or industry (research/consulting) (0), employed in business or industry (management) (0), employed in a government agency (research) (0), employed in a government agency (professional services) (0), employed in a community mental health/counseling center (0), employed in a hospital/medical center (0), still seeking employment (0), other employment position (0), do not know (38), total from the above (master's) (44).
   Doctoral Degree Graduates: Of those who graduated in the academic year 2003–2004, the following categories and numbers represent the post-graduate activities and employment of doctoral degree graduates: Enrolled in a psychology doctoral program (n/a), enrolled in a post-doctoral residency/fellowship (2), employed in independent practice (0), employed in an academic position at a university (1), employed in an academic position at a 2-year/4-year college (0), employed in other positions at a higher education institution (0), employed in a professional position in a school system (0), employed in business or industry (management) (0), employed in a government agency (research) (0), employed in a government agency (professional services) (1), employed in a community mental health/counseling center (2), employed in a hospital/medical center (2), still seeking employment (0), other employment position (0), total from the above (doctoral) (8).

Additional Information:
   Orientation, Objectives, and Emphasis of Department: The Utah State University Department of Psychology offers two graduate PhD programs. Research and Evaluation Methodology offers training emphasizing methods and techniques for conducting research and evaluation studies in psychology or education settings. The Combined Clinical/Counseling/School Psychology offers professional and scientific training in a combination of clinical, counseling, and school psychology (accredited by the American Psychological Association since 1975) and two master's degrees in school psychology and school counseling. The two graduate PhD programs share a common core of doctoral courses intended to provide an advanced overview of several major areas of psychology. All doctoral programs offer extensive training within their specific areas; however, the common core is designed to ensure that no student will complete the PhD without being exposed to the diverse theoretical and methodological perspectives in the field of psychology. The common core also provides students the opportunity to become aware of the scholarly interests of faculty members in all programs, thus broadening students' choices of faculty advisors and dissertation chairpersons. Full tuition waivers are available to PhD students for 70 semester hours of academic credit.

   Special Facilities or Resources: Students in all graduate programs benefit from the following departmental facilities: the Basic Behavior Laboratory for nonhuman research, the Human Behavior Laboratory for analysis of human behavior, the Counseling Laboratory for research and training in counseling and clinical practice, and the Community Clinic for supervised experience in actual therapy. In addition, the department has cooperative relations with other campus and off-campus facilities that provide excellent settings for student assistantships, research, and training, including the Bear River Mental Health Center, the USU Center for Persons with Disabilities, the USU Counseling Center and the Logan Regional Hospital Behavioral Medicine Unit.

Application Information:
Send to: Utah State University, School of Graduate Studies, Logan, UT 84322-0900. Application available online. URL of online application: www.usu.edu/gradsch. Students are admitted in the Fall, application deadline January 15; Spring, application deadline March 1; Summer, application deadline June 1. Research and Evaluation Methodology PhD will accept applications if the alloted openings are not filled as of February 1. Combined Clinical/Counseling/School Psychology Program deadline is January 15, School Psychology is March 1, and School Counseling is June 1. *Fee:* $55.

Utah, University of
Department of Educational Psychology, Counseling Psychology and School Psychology Programs
College of Education
1705 E. Campus Center Drive, Rm. 327
Salt Lake City, UT 84112-9255
Telephone: (801) 581-7148
Fax: (801) 581-5566
E-mail: *bhill@ed.utah.edu*
Web: *http://www.ed.utah.edu/psych*

Department Information:
1949. Chairperson: Robert D. Hill. Number of Faculty: total–full-time 16, part-time 5; women–full-time 7, part-time 3; minority–full-time 4, part-time 1.

Programs and Degrees Offered:
Listed in the following order: Program area, degree type (T if terminal Master's), number awarded 7/03–6/04. Counseling Psychology PhD (Doctor of Philosophy) 5, School Psychology PhD (Doctor of Philosophy) 10, Learning Sciences PhD (Doctor of Philosophy) 1, Instructional Design and Educational Technology Other 14, Professional Counseling MA/MS (Master of Arts/Science) (T) 12, School Counseling Other 6.

APA Accreditation: Counseling PhD (Doctor of Philosophy). School PhD (Doctor of Philosophy).

Student Applications/Admissions:
Student Applications
Counseling Psychology PhD (Doctor of Philosophy)—Applications 2004–2005, 64. Total applicants accepted 2004–2005, 5. Number enrolled (new admits only) 2004–2005 full-time, 3. Total enrolled 2004–2005 full-time, 25, part-time, 19. Openings 2005–2006, 6. The Median number of years required for completion of a degree are 6. The number of students enrolled full and part-time who were dismissed or voluntarily withdrew from this program area were 0. *School Psychology PhD (Doctor of Philosophy)*—Applications 2004–2005, 29. Total applicants accepted 2004–2005, 10. Number enrolled (new

admits only) 2004–2005 full-time, 5. Total enrolled 2004–2005 full-time, 19, part-time, 18. Openings 2005–2006, 6. The Median number of years required for completion of a degree are 6. The number of students enrolled full and part-time who were dismissed or voluntarily withdrew from this program area were 0. *Learning Sciences PhD (Doctor of Philosophy)*—Applications 2004–2005, 9. Total applicants accepted 2004–2005, 3. Number enrolled (new admits only) 2004–2005 full-time, 2. Total enrolled 2004–2005 full-time, 5, part-time, 5. Openings 2005–2006, 3. The Median number of years required for completion of a degree are 5. The number of students enrolled full and part-time who were dismissed or voluntarily withdrew from this program area were 0. *Instructional Design and Educational Technology Other*—Applications 2004–2005, 27. Total applicants accepted 2004–2005, 23. Number enrolled (new admits only) 2004–2005 part-time, 19. Total enrolled 2004–2005 full-time, 1, part-time, 34. Openings 2005–2006, 20. The Median number of years required for completion of a degree are 2. The number of students enrolled full and part-time who were dismissed or voluntarily withdrew from this program area were 0. *Professional Counseling MA/MS (Master of Arts/Science)*—Applications 2004–2005, 30. Total applicants accepted 2004–2005, 11. Number enrolled (new admits only) 2004–2005 full-time, 9. Total enrolled 2004–2005 full-time, 14, part-time, 11. Openings 2005–2006, 11. The Median number of years required for completion of a degree are 3. The number of students enrolled full and part-time who were dismissed or voluntarily withdrew from this program area were 0. *School Counseling Other*—Applications 2004–2005, 17. Total applicants accepted 2004–2005, 11. Number enrolled (new admits only) 2004–2005 full-time, 5. Number enrolled (new admits only) 2004–2005 part-time, 3. Total enrolled 2004–2005 full-time, 5, part-time, 10. Openings 2005–2006, 11. The Median number of years required for completion of a degree are 2. The number of students enrolled full and part-time who were dismissed or voluntarily withdrew from this program area were 0.

Admissions Requirements:
Scores: Entries appear in this order: required test or GPA, minimum score (if required), median score of students entering in 2003–2004. Master's Programs: GRE-V no minimum stated, 530; GRE-Q no minimum stated, 615; GRE-V+Q no minimum stated, 1150; overall undergraduate GPA 3.00, 3.47. Doctoral Programs: GRE-V no minimum stated, 545; GRE-Q no minimum stated, 600; GRE-V+Q no minimum stated, 1115; overall undergraduate GPA no minimum stated, 3.56.
Other Criteria: (importance of criteria rated low, medium, or high): GRE/MAT scores high, research experience high, work experience high, extracurricular activity medium, clinically related public service medium, GPA high, letters of recommendation high, statement of goals and objectives high. Each program reviews and rates its own applicants.

Student Characteristics: The following represents characteristics of students in 2004–2005 in all graduate psychology programs in the department: Female–full-time 50, part-time 64; Male–full-time 19, part-time 34; African American/Black–full-time 3, part-time 1; Hispanic/Latino(a)–full-time 7, part-time 9; Asian/Pacific Islander–full-time 8, part-time 4; American Indian/Alaska Native–full-time 0, part-time 0; Caucasian–full-time 51, part-time

84; Multi-ethnic–full-time 0, part-time 0; students subject to the Americans With Disabilities Act–full-time 0, part-time 0.

Financial Information/Assistance:

Tuition for Full-Time Study: *Master's:* State residents: per academic year $3,200; Nonstate residents: per academic year $10,000. *Doctoral:* State residents: per academic year $3,200; Nonstate residents: per academic year $10,000. Tuition is subject to change. See the following Web site for updates and changes in tuition costs: http://www.ed.utah.edu.

Financial Assistance:

First Year Students: Teaching assistantships available for first-year. Average amount paid per academic year: $4,250. Average number of hours worked per week: 10. Apply by April. Tuition remission given: partial. Research assistantships available for first-year. Average amount paid per academic year: $4,250. Average number of hours worked per week: 10. Apply by flexible. Tuition remission given: partial.

Advanced Students: Teaching assistantships available for advanced students. Average amount paid per academic year: $4,250. Average number of hours worked per week: 10. Apply by April. Tuition remission given: partial. Research assistantships available for advanced students. Average amount paid per academic year: $4,250. Average number of hours worked per week: 10. Apply by flexible. Tuition remission given: partial. Traineeships available for advanced students. Apply by varies. Fellowships and scholarships available for advanced students. Average number of hours worked per week: 0. Apply by varies.

Contact Information: Of all students currently enrolled full-time, 50% benefitted from one or more of the listed financial assistance programs.

Internships/Practica: Practica for counseling psychology doctoral students vary and include such settings as U of U counseling center and other campus services, community mental health settings, hospital settings, and private practice. Predoctoral internships are typically taken nationally in university counseling centers, community mental health settings, veterans hospitals, and specialty settings. For those doctoral students for whom a professional internship is required prior to graduation, 6 applied in 2003–2004. Of those who applied, 6 were placed in internships listed by the Association of Psychology Postdoctoral and Internship Programs (APPIC); 6 were placed in APA accredited internships.

Housing and Day Care: On-campus housing is available. See the following Web site for more information: Residential Living: http://www.orl.utah.edu/. On-campus day care facilities are available. See the following Web site for more information: Child Care: http://www.childcare.utah.edu/.

Employment of Department Graduates:

Master's Degree Graduates: Of those who graduated in the academic year 2003–2004, the following categories and numbers represent the post-graduate activities and employment of master's degree graduates: Enrolled in a post-doctoral residency/fellowship (n/a), employed in independent practice (n/a), employed in an academic position at a 2-year/4-year college (0), employed in a professional position in a school system (20), employed in a community mental health/counseling center (12), employed in a hospital/medical center (0), total from the above (master's) (32).

Doctoral Degree Graduates: Of those who graduated in the academic year 2003–2004, the following categories and numbers represent the post-graduate activities and employment of doctoral degree graduates: Enrolled in a psychology doctoral program (n/a), employed in an academic position at a university (5), employed in an academic position at a 2-year/4-year college (0), employed in other positions at a higher education institution (2), employed in a professional position in a school system (2), employed in business or industry (research/consulting) (1), employed in business or industry (management) (0), employed in a government agency (research) (0), still seeking employment (0), other employment position (0), do not know (0), total from the above (doctoral) (10).

Additional Information:

Orientation, Objectives, and Emphasis of Department: The department of educational psychology at the University of Utah is characterized by an emphasis on the application of behavioral sciences to educational and psychological processes. The department is organized into 3 program areas: Counseling and Counseling Psychology (MS, MEd, PhD), School Psychology (MS, PhD), Learning Sciences with three subprograms: Learning and Cognition (PhD), a master's level program in Instructional Design and Educational Technology (IDET) (MEd), and an interdepartmental program which leads to a Master's in Statistics (MSTAT). The basic master's level programming includes one to two years of academic work (and in some cases an additional year of internship). Doctoral programs include Counseling Psychology (APA accredited since 1957), School Psychology (APA accredited since 1986), and Learning Sciences, Learning and Cognition area. The emphasis of the department is on the application of psychological principles in educational and human service settings. In addition, doctoral programs represent a scientist-practitioner model with considerable emphasis on the development of research as well as professional skills. Information describing the objectives and emphases of specific program areas within the department is available on request.

Special Facilities or Resources: A variety of research and training opportunities are available to students through relationships the department has developed with various university and community facilities. Included are the university counseling center, medical center, computer center, and the adjacent regional Veterans Administration Medical Center. Community facilities include local school districts, community mental health centers, children's hospital, general hospitals, child guidance clinics, and various state social service agencies. The department maintains its own statistics laboratory. Students have access to computer stations and use of the college computer network.

Information for Students With Physical Disabilities: See the following Web site for more information: http://www.hr.utah.edu/oeo/disab/.

Application Information:

Send to: Admission, University of Utah, Department of Educational Psychology, 1705 E. Campus Center Drive, Rm. 327, Salt Lake City, UT 84112-9255. Students are admitted in the Fall, application deadline January 15. *Fee:* $45.

Utah, University of

Department of Psychology
Social & Behavioral Science
380 S. 1530 East, Room 502
Salt Lake City, UT 84112
Telephone: (801) 581-6124
Fax: (801) 581-5841
E-mail: *nancy.seegmiller@psych.utah.edu*
Web: *http://www.psych.utah.edu*

Department Information:

1925. Chairperson: Frances J. Friedrich. Number of Faculty: total–full-time 29, part-time 7; women–full-time 13, part-time 2; minority–full-time 5.

Programs and Degrees Offered:

Listed in the following order: Program area, degree type (T if terminal Master's), number awarded 7/03–6/04. Clinical Psychology PhD (Doctor of Philosophy) 1, Cognition and Neuralscience PhD (Doctor of Philosophy) 0, Developmental Psychology PhD (Doctor of Philosophy) 1, Social Psychology PhD (Doctor of Philosophy) 0.

APA Accreditation: Clinical PhD (Doctor of Philosophy).

Student Applications/Admissions:

Student Applications

Clinical Psychology PhD (Doctor of Philosophy)—Applications 2004–2005, 142. Total applicants accepted 2004–2005, 10. Number enrolled (new admits only) 2004–2005 full-time, 7. Number enrolled (new admits only) 2004–2005 part-time, 0. Openings 2005–2006, 6. The Median number of years required for completion of a degree are 10. The number of students enrolled full and part-time who were dismissed or voluntarily withdrew from this program area were 0. *Cognition and Neuralscience PhD (Doctor of Philosophy)*—Applications 2004–2005, 23. Total applicants accepted 2004–2005, 5. Number enrolled (new admits only) 2004–2005 full-time, 3. Number enrolled (new admits only) 2004–2005 part-time, 0. Openings 2005–2006, 2. The number of students enrolled full and part-time who were dismissed or voluntarily withdrew from this program area were 0. *Developmental Psychology PhD (Doctor of Philosophy)*—Applications 2004–2005, 17. Total applicants accepted 2004–2005, 5. Number enrolled (new admits only) 2004–2005 full-time, 3. Number enrolled (new admits only) 2004–2005 part-time, 0. Openings 2005–2006, 5. The Median number of years required for completion of a degree are 5. The number of students enrolled full and part-time who were dismissed or voluntarily withdrew from this program area were 2. *Social Psychology PhD (Doctor of Philosophy)*—Applications 2004–2005, 31. Total applicants accepted 2004–2005, 4. Number enrolled (new admits only) 2004–2005 full-time, 3. Number enrolled (new admits only) 2004–2005 part-time, 0. Openings 2005–2006, 2. The number of students enrolled full and part-time who were dismissed or voluntarily withdrew from this program area were 0.

Admissions Requirements:

Scores: Entries appear in this order: required test or GPA, minimum score (if required), median score of students entering in 2003–2004. Master's Programs: GRE-V no minimum stated; GRE-Q no minimum stated; GRE-V+Q no minimum stated; GRE-Analytical no minimum stated; GRE-Subject(Psych) no minimum stated. Doctoral Programs: GRE-V no minimum stated, 556; GRE-Q no minimum stated, 666; GRE-V+Q no minimum stated, 1222; GRE-Analytical no minimum stated, 650; GRE-Subject(Psych) no minimum stated, 716; overall undergraduate GPA 3.0, 3.50.

Other Criteria: (importance of criteria rated low, medium, or high): GRE/MAT scores medium, research experience high, work experience medium, extracurricular activity medium, clinically related public service medium, GPA medium, letters of recommendation high, interview high, statement of goals and objectives high.

Student Characteristics: The following represents characteristics of students in 2004–2005 in all graduate psychology programs in the department: Female–full-time 36, part-time 0; Male–full-time 26, part-time 0; African American/Black–full-time 1, part-time 0; Hispanic/Latino(a)–full-time 2, part-time 0; Asian/Pacific Islander–full-time 3, part-time 0; American Indian/Alaska Native–full-time 0, part-time 0; Caucasian–full-time 55, part-time 0; Multi-ethnic–full-time 1, part-time 0; students subject to the Americans With Disabilities Act–full-time 0, part-time 0.

Financial Information/Assistance:

Tuition for Full-Time Study: *Master's:* State residents: per academic year $3,904, $642 per credit hour; Nonstate residents: per academic year $12,220, $1,800 per credit hour. *Doctoral:* State residents: per academic year $3,904, $642 per credit hour; Nonstate residents: per academic year $12,220, $1,800 per credit hour. Tuition is subject to change. See the following Web site for updates and changes in tuition costs: www.utah.edu.

Financial Assistance:

First Year Students: Teaching assistantships available for first-year. Average amount paid per academic year: $10,000. Average number of hours worked per week: 20. Apply by TBA. Tuition remission given: full. Research assistantships available for first-year. Average amount paid per academic year: $10,000. Average number of hours worked per week: 20. Apply by TBA. Tuition remission given: full. Fellowships and scholarships available for first-year. Average amount paid per academic year: $10,000. Apply by TBA. Tuition remission given: full.

Advanced Students: Teaching assistantships available for advanced students. Average amount paid per academic year: $11,000. Average number of hours worked per week: 20. Apply by TBA. Tuition remission given: full. Research assistantships available for advanced students. Average amount paid per academic year: $11,000. Average number of hours worked per week: 20. Apply by TBA. Tuition remission given: full. Fellowships and scholarships available for advanced students. Average amount paid per academic year: $10,000. Apply by TBA. Tuition remission given: full.

Contact Information: Of all students currently enrolled full-time, 97% benefitted from one or more of the listed financial assistance programs. Application and information available online at: www.psych.utah.edu.

Internships/Practica: Extensive clinical training experiences are available through close ties with facilities in the community. A sample of these include the Veteran's Administration Hospital,

The University Medical Center, Primary Children's Hospital, the Children's Behavioral Therapy Unit, the Juvenile Detention Center, The University Neuropsychiatric Institute, the University Counseling Center, and local community health centers. There are four APA-approved internships in the local community. For those doctoral students for whom a professional internship is required prior to graduation, 3 applied in 2003–2004. Of those who applied, 3 were placed in internships listed by the Association of Psychology Postdoctoral and Internship Programs (APPIC); 3 were placed in APA accredited internships.

Housing and Day Care: On-campus housing is available. See the following Web site for more information: www.utah.edu. On-campus day care facilities are available.

Employment of Department Graduates:

Master's Degree Graduates: Of those who graduated in the academic year 2003–2004, the following categories and numbers represent the post-graduate activities and employment of master's degree graduates: Enrolled in a post-doctoral residency/fellowship (n/a), employed in independent practice (n/a), total from the above (master's) (0).

Doctoral Degree Graduates: Of those who graduated in the academic year 2003–2004, the following categories and numbers represent the post-graduate activities and employment of doctoral degree graduates: Enrolled in a psychology doctoral program (n/a), enrolled in another graduate/professional program (0), enrolled in a post-doctoral residency/fellowship (0), employed in independent practice (0), employed in an academic position at a university (0), employed in an academic position at a 2-year/4-year college (1), employed in other positions at a higher education institution (0), employed in a professional position in a school system (0), employed in business or industry (research/consulting) (0), employed in business or industry (management) (0), employed in a government agency (research) (0), employed in a government agency (professional services) (0), employed in a community mental health/counseling center (0), employed in a hospital/medical center (0), still seeking employment (0), not seeking employment (0), other employment position (0), do not know (0), total from the above (doctoral) (1).

Additional Information:

Orientation, Objectives, and Emphasis of Department: We offer comprehensive training in psychology, including Clinical (general, child-family, health, & neuropsychology emphases), Developmental, Experimental-Physiological, and Social. Students generally receive support throughout their training. Students are selected for area programs with individual faculty advisers. They do research in their areas, and clinical students also receive applied training. Graduates accept jobs in academic departments, research centers, and applied settings.

Special Facilities or Resources: Special facilities include the Early Childhood Education Center and 3 on-campus hospitals.

Application Information:

Send to: Graduate Admissions Secretary, Psychology Department, 380 S. 1530 East, Room 502, Salt Lake City, UT 84112. Application available online. URL of online application: www.psych.utah.edu/graduate/index.html. Students are admitted in the Fall, application deadline January 15. *Fee:* $45.

Castleton State College

Psychology
Psychology Building
Castleton, VT 05735
Telephone: (802) 468-1376
Fax: (802) 468-1480
E-mail: *Brenda.Russell@castleton.edu*
Web: *http://www.castleton.edu*

Department Information:
1967. Director of Forensic Graduate Program: Brenda L. Russell. Number of Faculty: total–full-time 5, part-time 2; women–full-time 1, part-time 1.

Programs and Degrees Offered:
Listed in the following order: Program area, degree type (T if terminal Master's), number awarded 7/03–6/04. Forensic Psychology MA/MS (Master of Arts/Science) (T) 13.

Student Applications/Admissions:
Student Applications

Forensic Psychology MA/MS (Master of Arts/Science)—Applications 2004–2005, 85. Total applicants accepted 2004–2005, 22. Number enrolled (new admits only) 2004–2005 full-time, 9. Number enrolled (new admits only) 2004–2005 part-time, 0. Openings 2005–2006, 15. The Median number of years required for completion of a degree are 2. The number of students enrolled full and part-time who were dismissed or voluntarily withdrew from this program area were 0.

Admissions Requirements:

Scores: Entries appear in this order: required test or GPA, minimum score (if required), median score of students entering in 2003–2004. Master's Programs: GRE-V+Q no minimum stated, 1110; overall undergraduate GPA no minimum stated, 3.61.

Other Criteria: (importance of criteria rated low, medium, or high): GRE/MAT scores low, research experience high, work experience medium, extracurricular activity medium, GPA high, letters of recommendation high, statement of goals and objectives high.

Student Characteristics: The following represents characteristics of students in 2004–2005 in all graduate psychology programs in the department: Female–full-time 23, part-time 0; Male–full-time 4, part-time 0; African American/Black–full-time 0, part-time 0; Hispanic/Latino(a)–full-time 0, part-time 0; Asian/Pacific Islander–full-time 0, part-time 0; American Indian/Alaska Native–full-time 0, part-time 0; Caucasian–full-time 0, part-time 0; Multi-ethnic–full-time 2, part-time 0; students subject to the Americans With Disabilities Act–full-time 0, part-time 0.

Financial Information/Assistance:
Tuition for Full-Time Study: *Master's:* State residents: per academic year $3,738, $314 per credit hour; Nonstate residents: per academic year $8,075, $676 per credit hour. Tuition is subject to change.

Financial Assistance:
First Year Students: Teaching assistantships available for first-year. Research assistantships available for first-year. Fellowships and scholarships available for first-year.

Advanced Students: Teaching assistantships available for advanced students. Research assistantships available for advanced students. Fellowships and scholarships available for advanced students.

Contact Information: Of all students currently enrolled full-time, 95% benefitted from one or more of the listed financial assistance programs.

Internships/Practica: The forensic program provides research internships and practica in various local, state, and federal agencies and institutions. Practicum and internship placements are available in a wide range of forensic settings. The placements are designed to provide students with practical experience that integrates classroom research skills with real-world situations. Students are encouraged to enroll in at least one practicum or internship experience during their Master's.

Housing and Day Care: On-campus housing is available. Residence Life Campus Center, Castleton State College, Castleton, VT 05735. No on-campus day care facilities are available.

Employment of Department Graduates:
Master's Degree Graduates: Of those who graduated in the academic year 2003–2004, the following categories and numbers represent the post-graduate activities and employment of master's degree graduates: Enrolled in a psychology doctoral program (18), enrolled in a post-doctoral residency/fellowship (n/a), employed in independent practice (n/a), employed in an academic position at a 2-year/4-year college (1), employed in other positions at a higher education institution (2), employed in a professional position in a school system (1), employed in business or industry (research/consulting) (12), employed in a government agency (research) (8), employed in a government agency (professional services) (1), employed in a community mental health/counseling center (1), employed in a hospital/medical center (3), total from the above (master's) (47).

Doctoral Degree Graduates: Of those who graduated in the academic year 2003–2004, the following categories and numbers represent the post-graduate activities and employment of doctoral degree graduates: Enrolled in a psychology doctoral program (n/a), total from the above (doctoral) (0).

Additional Information:
Orientation, Objectives, and Emphasis of Department: The Master's Program in Forensic Psychology at Castleton focuses on four major areas: (1) police psychology; (2) correctional psychology; (3) psychology of crime and delinquency; and (4) psychology and law. The program is designed to provide students with: (1) a comprehensive knowledge of psychology as it applies to the criminal justice and civil justice systems; (2) the research skills to evaluate competently various issues and programs within these

systems; and (3) the communication skills necessary to express their findings effectively to diverse groups within the systems. The program is a research-based Master of Arts created to prepare students for: (1) careers in the various organizations and agencies of the criminal and civil justice systems; or (2) acceptance into doctoral programs in psychology, criminal justice, political science, or other social science disciplines. Graduates will be trained to analyze, interpret, organize, apply, and transmit existing knowledge in the field of forensic psychology. The overall mission of the program is to educate students to be highly knowledgeable about the various methodologies and statistical analyses critical to conducting well-designed research. Prospective students should realize that the program will not provide training in counseling, psychotherapy, or clinical practice.

Special Facilities or Resources: The department maintains ongoing professional contacts with over 70 state and federal law enforcement agencies, including a close working relationship with the Vermont Police Academy and the Vermont Department of Corrections. Opportunities for doing research at these agencies and facilities are considerable. The department has excellent computing facilities for the support of forensic research. The college and department libraries receive virtually every major recent periodical in criminal justice and forensic psychology written in the English language. The department is also the home of the scholarly journal *Criminal Justice and Behavior*, an international journal that publishes cutting-edge research in Forensic Psychology. Graduate students will have considerable opportunity to participate in the scholarly and editorial process of the journal.

Application Information:
Send to: Admission Office, Wright House, Castleton State College, Castleton, VT 05735. Students are admitted in the Fall, application deadline February 15. *Fee:* $30.

Goddard College
MA Psychology & Counseling Program
123 Pitkin Road
Plainfield, VT 05667
Telephone: (802) 454-8311, (800) 468-4888
Fax: (802) 454-1029
E-mail: *admissions@goddard.edu*
Web: *http://www.goddard.edu*

Department Information:
1988. Chairperson: Steven E. James, PhD Number of Faculty: total–full-time 1, part-time 6; women–part-time 4; minority–full-time 1, part-time 2.

Programs and Degrees Offered:
Listed in the following order: Program area, degree type (T if terminal Master's), number awarded 7/03–6/04. Organizational Development MA/MS (Master of Arts/Science) (T) 1, Sexual Orientation MA/MS (Master of Arts/Science) (T) 0, Counseling MA/MS (Master of Arts/Science) (T) 18, Psychology MA/MS (Master of Arts/Science) (T) 2.

Student Applications/Admissions:
Student Applications
Organizational Development MA/MS (Master of Arts/Science)—Applications 2004–2005, 2. Total applicants accepted 2004–2005, 2. Openings 2005–2006, 4. The Median number of years required for completion of a degree are 2. The number of students enrolled full and part-time who were dismissed or voluntarily withdrew from this program area were 0. *Sexual Orientation MA/MS (Master of Arts/Science)*—Applications 2004–2005, 4. Total applicants accepted 2004–2005, 3. Number enrolled (new admits only) 2004–2005 full-time, 1. Number enrolled (new admits only) 2004–2005 part-time, 0. Openings 2005–2006, 4. The Median number of years required for completion of a degree are 2. The number of students enrolled full and part-time who were dismissed or voluntarily withdrew from this program area were 1. *Counseling MA/MS (Master of Arts/Science)*—Applications 2004–2005, 30. Total applicants accepted 2004–2005, 18. Number enrolled (new admits only) 2004–2005 full-time, 22. Number enrolled (new admits only) 2004–2005 part-time, 0. Openings 2005–2006, 25. The Median number of years required for completion of a degree are 2. The number of students enrolled full and part-time who were dismissed or voluntarily withdrew from this program area were 2. *Psychology MA/MS (Master of Arts/Science)*—Applications 2004–2005, 1. Total applicants accepted 2004–2005, 1. Number enrolled (new admits only) 2004–2005 full-time, 0. Number enrolled (new admits only) 2004–2005 part-time, 0. Openings 2005–2006, 5. The number of students enrolled full and part-time who were dismissed or voluntarily withdrew from this program area were 1.

Admissions Requirements:
Scores: Entries appear in this order: required test or GPA, minimum score (if required), median score of students entering in 2003–2004. Master's Programs: overall undergraduate GPA no minimum stated; psychology GPA no minimum stated.
Other Criteria: (importance of criteria rated low, medium, or high): research experience low, work experience high, extracurricular activity medium, clinically related public service high, GPA medium, letters of recommendation high, interview low, statement of goals and objectives high. For additional information on admission requirements, go to: www.goddard.edu.

Student Characteristics: The following represents characteristics of students in 2004–2005 in all graduate psychology programs in the department: Female–full-time 39, part-time 0; Male–full-time 17, part-time 0; African American/Black–full-time 4, part-time 0; Hispanic/Latino(a)–full-time 1, part-time 0; Asian/Pacific Islander–full-time 1, part-time 0; American Indian/Alaska Native–full-time 2, part-time 0; Caucasian–full-time 46, part-time 0; Multi-ethnic–full-time 2, part-time 0; students subject to the Americans With Disabilities Act–full-time 4, part-time 0.

Financial Information/Assistance:
Tuition for Full-Time Study: *Master's:* State residents: per academic year $11,054; Nonstate residents: per academic year $11,054. See the following Web site for updates and changes in tuition costs: www.goddard.edu.

Financial Assistance:
First Year Students: Fellowships and scholarships available for first-year. Average amount paid per academic year: $1,445.

Average number of hours worked per week: 0. Apply by Rolling. Tuition remission given: partial.

Advanced Students: Fellowships and scholarships available for advanced students. Average amount paid per academic year: $1,445. Average number of hours worked per week: 0. Apply by Rolling. Tuition remission given: partial.

Contact Information: Of all students currently enrolled full-time, 0% benefitted from one or more of the listed financial assistance programs. Application and information available online at: www.goddard.edu.

Internships/Practica: Students are required to complete a minimum of 300 hours of supervised practicum during the program. This practicum takes place at a location convenient to the student that has been reviewed and evaluated by the program faculty as appropriate to the student's plan of study, providing appropriate licensed supervision and offering direct counseling experience. Students propose sites at which they would like to work to the faculty for review and approval.

Housing and Day Care: On-campus housing is available. Contact McNameeA@goddard.edu. No on-campus day care facilities are available.

Employment of Department Graduates:

Master's Degree Graduates: Of those who graduated in the academic year 2003–2004, the following categories and numbers represent the post-graduate activities and employment of master's degree graduates: Enrolled in a psychology doctoral program (5), enrolled in another graduate/professional program (1), enrolled in a post-doctoral residency/fellowship (n/a), employed in independent practice (n/a), employed in an academic position at a university (1), employed in an academic position at a 2-year/4-year college (0), employed in other positions at a higher education institution (1), employed in a professional position in a school system (0), employed in business or industry (research/consulting) (3), employed in business or industry (management) (0), employed in a government agency (research) (0), employed in a government agency (professional services) (0), employed in a community mental health/counseling center (13), employed in a hospital/medical center (1), still seeking employment (1), other employment position (2), total from the above (master's) (28).

Doctoral Degree Graduates: Of those who graduated in the academic year 2003–2004, the following categories and numbers represent the post-graduate activities and employment of doctoral degree graduates: Enrolled in a psychology doctoral program (n/a), total from the above (doctoral) (0).

Additional Information:

Orientation, Objectives, and Emphasis of Department: Graduate study in Psychology and Counseling consists of a unique combination of intensive campus residencies and directed, independent study off campus. Students design their own emphasis of study or enter into the defined concentrations in organizational development or sexual orientation studies. The primary goal of the program is to develop skills in individual, family and/or community psychology, grounded in theory and research, personal experience and self-knowledge, and relevant to current social complexities. While pursuing their own specialized interests, students gain mastery in the broad range of subjects necessary for the effective and ethical practice of counseling. Study begins each semester with a week-long residency at the college, a time of planning for the ensuing semester and attending seminars. Returning home, the student begins implementation of the detailed study plan based upon the student's particular interests and needs and mastery of relevant theory and research and completion of a supervised practicum with a minimum of 300 hours. Through appropriate design of their study plan, students may meet the educational requirements for master's level licensure or certification in their state. The program is approved by the Council of Applied Master's Programs in Psychology.

Application Information:
Send to: Admissions Office. Application available online. URL of online application: http://www.goddard.edu/admissions/applyonline.html. Students are admitted in the Fall, application deadline August 15; Spring, application deadline February 15. *Fee:* $40. Waiver by written petition.

Saint Michael's College
Psychology Department/Graduate Program in Clinical Psychology
Saint Michael's College
One Winooski Park
Colchester, VT 05439
Telephone: (802) 654-2206
Fax: (802) 654-2610
E-mail: *rmiller@smcvt.edu*
Web: *http://www.smcvt.edu/gradprograms*

Department Information:
1984. Director: Ronald B. Miller. Number of Faculty: total–full-time 5, part-time 8; women–full-time 1, part-time 6.

Programs and Degrees Offered:
Listed in the following order: Program area, degree type (T if terminal Master's), number awarded 7/03–6/04. Graduate Clinical Psychology MA/MS (Master of Arts/Science) (T) 6.

Student Applications/Admissions:
Student Applications

Graduate Clinical Psychology MA/MS (Master of Arts/Science)— Applications 2004–2005, 27. Total applicants accepted 2004–2005, 19. Number enrolled (new admits only) 2004–2005 full-time, 5. Number enrolled (new admits only) 2004–2005 part-time, 12. Total enrolled 2004–2005 full-time, 6, part-time, 40. Openings 2005–2006, 16. The Median number of years required for completion of a degree are 4.5. The number of students enrolled full and part-time who were dismissed or voluntarily withdrew from this program area were 1.

Admissions Requirements:
Scores: Entries appear in this order: required test or GPA, minimum score (if required), median score of students entering in 2003–2004. Master's Programs: GRE-V 450, 490; GRE-Q 450, 535; GRE-V+Q 950, 1025; GRE-Analytical 550, 550; GRE-Subject(Psych) 550, 600; overall undergraduate GPA 3.00, 3.35; last 2 years GPA 3.25, 3.40; psychology GPA 3.25, 3.50.

Other Criteria: (importance of criteria rated low, medium, or high): GRE/MAT scores low, research experience low, work experience high, extracurricular activity medium, clinically related public service high, GPA high, letters of recommendation medium, interview high, statement of goals and objectives medium.

Student Characteristics: The following represents characteristics of students in 2004–2005 in all graduate psychology programs in the department: Female–full-time 5, part-time 35; Male–full-time 1, part-time 5; African American/Black–full-time 0, part-time 0; Hispanic/Latino(a)–full-time 0, part-time 0; Asian/Pacific Islander–full-time 0, part-time 0; American Indian/Alaska Native–full-time 0, part-time 0; Caucasian–full-time 6, part-time 40; Multi-ethnic–full-time 0, part-time 0; students subject to the Americans With Disabilities Act–full-time 0, part-time 1.

Financial Information/Assistance:

Tuition for Full-Time Study: *Master's:* State residents: $410 per credit hour; Nonstate residents: $410 per credit hour. Tuition is subject to change. See the following Web site for updates and changes in tuition costs: smcvt.edu/gradprograms.

Financial Assistance:

First Year Students: Teaching assistantships available for first-year. Average number of hours worked per week: 20. Apply by July 1. Tuition remission given: full and partial.

Advanced Students: No information provided.

Contact Information: Of all students currently enrolled full-time, 5% benefitted from one or more of the listed financial assistance programs. Application and information available online at: http://www.smcvt.edu.

Internships/Practica: We have practice and internship sites in the following settings: schools, college counseling centers, teaching hospitals, correctional centers, Visiting Nurses Association, community mental health outpatient and residential offices, drug and alcohol treatment center, adolescent day treatment program.

Housing and Day Care: No on-campus housing is available. On-campus day care facilities are available. Information can be obtained from the following Web site, www.smcvt.edu/gradprograms.

Employment of Department Graduates:

Master's Degree Graduates: Of those who graduated in the academic year 2003–2004, the following categories and numbers represent the post-graduate activities and employment of master's degree graduates: Enrolled in a psychology doctoral program (0), enrolled in another graduate/professional program (0), enrolled in a post-doctoral residency/fellowship (n/a), employed in independent practice (n/a), employed in an academic position at a university (0), employed in an academic position at a 2-year/4-year college (0), employed in other positions at a higher education institution (0), employed in a professional position in a school system (0), employed in business or industry (research/consulting) (0), employed in business or industry (management) (0), employed in a government agency (research) (0), employed in a government agency (professional services) (1), employed in a community mental health/counseling center (2), employed in a hospital/medical center (1), still seeking employment (0), other employment position (1), do not know (1), total from the above (master's) (6).

Doctoral Degree Graduates: Of those who graduated in the academic year 2003–2004, the following categories and numbers represent the post-graduate activities and employment of doctoral degree graduates: Enrolled in a psychology doctoral program (n/a), total from the above (doctoral) (0).

Additional Information:

Orientation, Objectives, and Emphasis of Department: The focus of the MA program in clinical psychology is on the integration of theory, research, and practice in the preparation of professional psychologists. Our goal is to provide an educational milieu that respects the individual educational goals of the student, and fosters intellectual, personal, and professional development. The program is eclectic in orientation and the faculty offer a diversity of interests, orientations, and experiences within the framework of our curriculum. We see ourselves as preparing students for professional practice in community agencies, schools, hospitals, and public and private clinics. Cross-registration in the courses offered by the college's other master's degree programs in education, administration, and theology is available for those wishing an interdisciplinary emphasis. The curriculum is also designed with two further objectives in mind: (1) the preparation of students for state licensing examinations, and (2) further doctoral study in professional psychology at another institution. All classes are held in the evening, permitting full- or part-time study. The program seeks to integrate a psychodynamic understanding of the therapeutic relationship with humanistic values, and a social systems perspective.

Special Facilities or Resources: Street Michael's College offers the graduate student a faculty committed to teaching and professional training in a non-bureaucratic learning environment. All clinical courses are taught by highly experienced clinical practitioners who serve as part-time faculty. The full-time faculty teach core courses in general, developmental, and social psychology, as well as research methods. The college has excellent computing facilities for the support of social science research.

Application Information:

Send to: Department Chair (Director). Students are admitted in the Fall, application deadline August 1; Spring, application deadline December 1; Summer, application deadline May 1. Fall enrollment is recommended, and applications for Fall are encouraged by July 1, in order to be eligible for TA positions. *Fee:* $35.

Vermont, University of
Department of Psychology
Arts and Sciences
2 Colchester Avenue
Burlington, VT 05405-0134
Telephone: (802) 656-2670
Fax: (802) 656-8783
E-mail: *psychology@uvm.edu*
Web: *http://www.uvm.edu/psychology*

Department Information:

1937. Chairperson: Robert B. Lawson, PhD Number of Faculty: total–full-time 23, part-time 26; women–full-time 10, part-time

13; minority–full-time 1, part-time 1; faculty subject to the Americans With Disabilities Act 1.

Programs and Degrees Offered:
Listed in the following order: Program area, degree type (T if terminal Master's), number awarded 7/03–6/04. Experimental-General PhD (Doctor of Philosophy) 0, Clinical PhD (Doctor of Philosophy) 8.

APA Accreditation: Clinical PhD (Doctor of Philosophy).

Student Applications/Admissions:
Student Applications
Experimental-General PhD (Doctor of Philosophy)—Applications 2004–2005, 36. Total applicants accepted 2004–2005, 8. Number enrolled (new admits only) 2004–2005 full-time, 4. Number enrolled (new admits only) 2004–2005 part-time, 0. Openings 2005–2006, 6. The Median number of years required for completion of a degree are 5. The number of students enrolled full and part-time who were dismissed or voluntarily withdrew from this program area were 1. *Clinical PhD (Doctor of Philosophy)*—Applications 2004–2005, 146. Total applicants accepted 2004–2005, 12. Number enrolled (new admits only) 2004–2005 full-time, 4. Number enrolled (new admits only) 2004–2005 part-time, 0. Openings 2005–2006, 7. The Median number of years required for completion of a degree are 7. The number of students enrolled full and part-time who were dismissed or voluntarily withdrew from this program area were 0.

Admissions Requirements:
Scores: Entries appear in this order: required test or GPA, minimum score (if required), median score of students entering in 2003–2004. Doctoral Programs: GRE-V 360, 591; GRE-Q 420, 618; GRE-Analytical 720, 667; GRE-Subject(Psych) 680, 659; overall undergraduate GPA 3.25, 3.62.
Other Criteria: (importance of criteria rated low, medium, or high): GRE/MAT scores high, research experience high, work experience medium, extracurricular activity low, clinically related public service medium, GPA high, letters of recommendation high, interview medium, statement of goals and objectives high. Clinically related public service is of importance for clinical program only.

Student Characteristics: The following represents characteristics of students in 2004–2005 in all graduate psychology programs in the department: Female–full-time 40, part-time 0; Male–full-time 12, part-time 0; African American/Black–full-time 0, part-time 0; Hispanic/Latino(a)–full-time 2, part-time 0; Asian/Pacific Islander–full-time 0, part-time 0; American Indian/Alaska Native–full-time 0, part-time 0; Caucasian–full-time 50, part-time 0; Multi-ethnic–full-time 0, part-time 0; students subject to the Americans With Disabilities Act–full-time 0, part-time 0.

Financial Information/Assistance:
Tuition for Full-Time Study: *Doctoral:* State residents: $379 per credit hour; Nonstate residents: $379 per credit hour. Tuition is subject to change.

Financial Assistance:
First Year Students: Teaching assistantships available for first-year. Average amount paid per academic year: $13,200. Aver-

age number of hours worked per week: 20. Tuition remission given: full. Research assistantships available for first-year. Average amount paid per academic year: $19,000. Average number of hours worked per week: 20. Traineeships available for first-year. Average amount paid per academic year: $13,200. Average number of hours worked per week: 20.

Advanced Students: Teaching assistantships available for advanced students. Average amount paid per academic year: $13,200. Average number of hours worked per week: 20. Tuition remission given: full. Research assistantships available for advanced students. Average amount paid per academic year: $19,000. Average number of hours worked per week: 20. Traineeships available for advanced students. Average amount paid per academic year: $13,200. Average number of hours worked per week: 20.

Contact Information: Of all students currently enrolled full-time, 100% benefitted from one or more of the listed financial assistance programs. Application and information available online at: http://www.uvm.edu/psychology/.

Internships/Practica: Multiple clinical practica are available, including outpatient and inpatient adult assessment and psychotherapy, outpatient child and adolescent assessment and psychotherapy, community mental health centers, and medical center hospital. All practica are funded for 20 hours per week. For those doctoral students for whom a professional internship is required prior to graduation, 10 applied in 2003–2004. Of those who applied, 10 were placed in internships listed by the Association of Psychology Postdoctoral and Internship Programs (APPIC); 9 were placed in APA accredited internships.

Housing and Day Care: On-campus housing is available. See the following Web site for more information: http://reslife.uvm.edu/?Page=housing/graduate.htm&SM=housing/sm1.html. On-campus day care facilities are available. See the following Web site for more information: http://www.uvm.edu/~ips1/ccc/.

Employment of Department Graduates:
Master's Degree Graduates: Of those who graduated in the academic year 2003–2004, the following categories and numbers represent the post-graduate activities and employment of master's degree graduates: Enrolled in a psychology doctoral program (0), enrolled in another graduate/professional program (0), enrolled in a post-doctoral residency/fellowship (n/a), employed in independent practice (n/a), employed in an academic position at a university (0), employed in an academic position at a 2-year/4-year college (0), employed in other positions at a higher education institution (0), employed in a professional position in a school system (0), employed in business or industry (research/consulting) (0), employed in business or industry (management) (0), employed in a government agency (research) (0), employed in a government agency (professional services) (0), employed in a community mental health/counseling center (0), employed in a hospital/medical center (0), still seeking employment (0), other employment position (0), total from the above (master's) (0).
Doctoral Degree Graduates: Of those who graduated in the academic year 2003–2004, the following categories and numbers represent the post-graduate activities and employment of doctoral degree graduates: Enrolled in a psychology doctoral program (n/a), enrolled in a post-doctoral residency/fellowship (5), employed in independent practice (1), employed in an academic position at a university (0), employed in an academic position at a 2-year/4-

year college (0), employed in other positions at a higher education institution (0), employed in a professional position in a school system (0), employed in business or industry (research/consulting) (0), employed in business or industry (management) (0), employed in a government agency (research) (0), employed in a government agency (professional services) (0), employed in a community mental health/counseling center (1), employed in a hospital/medical center (0), still seeking employment (0), other employment position (0), total from the above (doctoral) (7).

Additional Information:
Orientation, Objectives, and Emphasis of Department: The clinical psychology program is based upon a scientist-practitioner model and is designed to develop competent professional psychologists who can function in applied academic or research positions. Training stresses early placement in a variety of nearby clinical facilities and simultaneous research training relevant to clinical problems. Clinical orientations are primarily cognitive-behavioral, but also include psychodynamic, family and systemic, community, and prevention. The general/experimental program admits students in three broad specialty areas: (1) basic and applied developmental and social psychology that includes research on ways in which people simultaneously influence and are influenced by social situations and cultural contexts; (2) biobehavioral psychology that focuses on behavioral and neurobiological approaches to learning, memory, emotion, and drug abuse; (3) human behavioral pharmacology and substance abuse treatment. Students must fulfill general/experimental program requirements as well as requirements for the specialty area in which they are accepted. Applicants should be as specific as possible about their program interest areas.

Special Facilities or Resources: The department has excellent laboratories in behavioral neuroscience, group dynamics, developmental, human psychophysiology, and general human testing. Excellent computer facilities, and an in-house psychology clinic with clinical research equipment are available.

Information for Students With Physical Disabilities: See the following Web site for more information: www.uvm.edu/~dosa/sss/.

Application Information:
Send to: Graduate College, Admissions Office, Waterman Building, University of Vermont, Burlington, VT 05405. Application available online. URL of online application: www.uvm.edu/psychology/programs/graduate/application.html. Students are admitted in the Fall, application deadline January 1. *Fee:* $25. Possibility of waiver for minority applicants.

Argosy University/Washington, DC
Clinical Psychology
American School of Professional Psychology
1550 Wilson Boulevard, Suite 600
Arlington, VA 22209
Telephone: (703) 526-5800
Fax: (703) 243-8973
E-mail: dcadmissions@argosyu.edu
Web: http://www.argosyu.edu

Department Information:
1994. Chair, Clinical Psychology Programs: Robert F. Barrett, PhD. Number of Faculty: total–full-time 12, part-time 6; women–full-time 7, part-time 5; minority–full-time 5, part-time 1.

Programs and Degrees Offered:
Listed in the following order: Program area, degree type (T if terminal Master's), number awarded 7/03–6/04. Clinical Psychology MA/MS (Master of Arts/Science) (T) 18, Clinical Psychology PsyD (Doctor of Psychology) 35.

APA Accreditation: Clinical PsyD (Doctor of Psychology).

Student Applications/Admissions:
Student Applications
Clinical Psychology MA/MS (Master of Arts/Science)—Applications 2004–2005, 95. Total applicants accepted 2004–2005, 50. Number enrolled (new admits only) 2004–2005 full-time, 24. Total enrolled 2004–2005 full-time, 41, part-time, 10. Openings 2005–2006, 20. The Median number of years required for completion of a degree are 2. The number of students enrolled full and part-time who were dismissed or voluntarily withdrew from this program area were 4. *Clinical Psychology PsyD (Doctor of Psychology)*—Applications 2004–2005, 351. Total applicants accepted 2004–2005, 130. Number enrolled (new admits only) 2004–2005 full-time, 74. Total enrolled 2004–2005 full-time, 325, part-time, 40. Openings 2005–2006, 90. The Median number of years required for completion of a degree are 5.5. The number of students enrolled full and part-time, who were dismissed or voluntarily withdrew from this program area were 8.

Admissions Requirements:
Scores: Entries appear in this order: required test or GPA, minimum score (if required), median score of students entering in 2003–2004. Master's Programs: overall undergraduate GPA 3.0, 3.0; last 2 years GPA 3.0, 3.1; psychology GPA 3.0, 3.3. MA applicants should have minimum of 3.0 in highest degree earned. GRE scores are optional. Doctoral Programs: overall undergraduate GPA 3.25, 3.25; last 2 years GPA 3.25, 3.50; psychology GPA 3.25, 3.50. Applicants should have a minimum of 3.25 for highest degree earned. Program will review overall GPA, last 2 years GPA and psychology GPA for 3.25 GPA. GRE scores are optional.
Other Criteria: (importance of criteria rated low, medium, or high): GRE/MAT scores low, research experience low, work experience high, extracurricular activity low, clinically related public service high, GPA high, letters of recommendation high, interview high, statement of goals and objectives high. Clinical experience is less important for applicants to MA program.

Student Characteristics: The following represents characteristics of students in 2004–2005 in all graduate psychology programs in the department: Female–full-time 208, part-time 81; Male–full-time 102, part-time 24; African American/Black–full-time 55, part-time 25; Hispanic/Latino(a)–full-time 8, part-time 3; Asian/Pacific Islander–full-time 11, part-time 3; American Indian/Alaska Native–full-time 2, part-time 1; Caucasian–full-time 159, part-time 57; students subject to the Americans With Disabilities Act–full-time 6, part-time 2.

Financial Information/Assistance:
Tuition for Full-Time Study: *Master's:* State residents: per academic year $19,500, $750 per credit hour; Nonstate residents: per academic year $19,500, $750 per credit hour. *Doctoral:* State residents: per academic year $19,500, $750 per credit hour; Nonstate residents: per academic year $19,500, $750 per credit hour. Tuition is subject to change. See the following Web site for updates and changes in tuition costs: argosyu.edu.

Financial Assistance:
First Year Students: Fellowships and scholarships available for first-year. Average amount paid per academic year: $2,250. Average number of hours worked per week: 6. Apply by September 4. Tuition remission given: full and partial.
Advanced Students: Teaching assistantships available for advanced students. Average amount paid per academic year: $4,500. Average number of hours worked per week: 8. Apply by variable. Tuition remission given: full and partial. Research assistantships available for advanced students. Average amount paid per academic year: $4,500. Average number of hours worked per week: 8. Apply by variable. Tuition remission given: full and partial. Fellowships and scholarships available for advanced students. Average amount paid per academic year: $2,250. Average number of hours worked per week: 6. Apply by September 4. Tuition remission given: full and partial.
Contact Information: Of all students currently enrolled full-time, 18% benefitted from one or more of the listed financial assistance programs.

Internships/Practica: Practicum training is designed to give students the opportunity to work under supervision with a clinical population within a mental health delivery system. Students learn to apply their theoretical knowledge; implement, develop, and assess the efficacy of clinical techniques; and develop the professional attitudes important for the identity of a professional psychologist. Doctoral students complete two training practica sequences (600 hours each) focusing on assessment or psychotherapy skills or integrating the two. Master's students are required to complete one practicum (600 hours). Internship: All doctoral students are required to complete a one year (12 month) internship as a condition for graduation. This intensive and supervised contact with clients is essential for giving greater breadth and depth to the student's overall academic experience. Typically, students will begin the internship during their fourth or fifth year, depending on the student's progress through the curriculum. For those doctoral students for whom a professional internship is required prior to graduation, 52 applied in 2003–2004. Of those who applied, 27 were placed in internships listed by the Association of Psychology Postdoctoral and Internship Programs (APPIC); 25 were placed in APA accredited internships.

Housing and Day Care: No on-campus housing is available. No on-campus day care facilities are available.

Employment of Department Graduates:

Master's Degree Graduates: Of those who graduated in the academic year 2003–2004, the following categories and numbers represent the post-graduate activities and employment of master's degree graduates: Enrolled in a psychology doctoral program (14), enrolled in a post-doctoral residency/fellowship (n/a), employed in independent practice (n/a), do not know (4), total from the above (master's) (18).

Doctoral Degree Graduates: Of those who graduated in the academic year 2003–2004, the following categories and numbers represent the post-graduate activities and employment of doctoral degree graduates: Enrolled in a psychology doctoral program (n/a), enrolled in another graduate/professional program (0), enrolled in a post-doctoral residency/fellowship (4), employed in independent practice (2), employed in an academic position at a university (1), employed in an academic position at a 2-year/4-year college (0), employed in other positions at a higher education institution (0), employed in a professional position in a school system (1), employed in business or industry (research/consulting) (1), employed in business or industry (management) (0), employed in a government agency (research) (0), employed in a government agency (professional services) (0), employed in a community mental health/counseling center (2), employed in a hospital/medical center (2), still seeking employment (1), do not know (24), total from the above (doctoral) (38).

Additional Information:

Orientation, Objectives, and Emphasis of Department: Department of Clinical Psychology. The doctoral program in clinical psychology (PsyD) is designed to educate and train students to function effectively in diverse professional roles. The program emphasizes the development of attitudes, knowledge, and skills essential in the formation of professional psychologists who are committed to the ethical provision of quality services. The school offers a broad-based curriculum, providing a meaningful integration of diverse theoretical perspectives, scholarship, and practice. The program offers concentrations in forensic psychology, health and neuropsychology, child and family, and diversity. Opportunities are available for students to develop expertise in a number of specialized areas including the provision of services to specific populations such as children and families; theoretical perspectives such as cognitive-behavioral, family systems, psychodynamic, and client centered; and areas of application such as forensics and health psychology. The Master's degree (MA) clinical psychology is designed to meet the needs of both those students seeking a terminal degree for work in the mental health field and those who eventually plan to pursue a doctoral degree. The program provides a solid core of basic psychology, as well as a strong clinical orientation with an emphasis in psychological assessment.

Special Facilities or Resources: Argosy University is conveniently located minutes from downtown Washington, DC. The on-site library has developed a focused psychology collection consisting of reference titles and books, journals, diagnostic assessment instruments, and audiovisual equipment. There are two computer labs and students have full access to both computerized literature searches and electronic text of most journals. In addition, students have access to the rich library resources of the Washington, DC, area including the National Library of Medicine and the Library of Congress.

Information for Students With Physical Disabilities: ADA Contact Person: Ann Stapleton, astapleton@argosyu.edu.

Application Information:

Send to: Admissions Department, Argosy University/Washington, DC, 1550 Wilson Boulevard, Suite 600, Arlington, VA 22209. Students are admitted in the Fall, application deadline January 15; Spring, application deadline October 15. Fall application deadline—application must be completed by January 15 to qualify for the April 1 decision; Second Fall deadline is May 15, dependent on available space. *Fee:* $50.

Argosy University/Washington, DC
Department of Counseling Psychology
1550 Wilson Boulevard, Suite 600
Arlington, VA 22209
Telephone: (703) 526-5800
Fax: (703) 243-8973
E-mail: *dcadmissions@argosyu.edu*
Web: *http://www.argosyu.edu*

Department Information:

1998. Chairperson: Colleen R. Logan, PhD Number of Faculty: total–full-time 2, part-time 15; women–full-time 2, part-time 9; minority–part-time 2.

Programs and Degrees Offered:

Listed in the following order: Program area, degree type (T if terminal Master's), number awarded 7/03–6/04. Professional Counseling MA/MS (Master of Arts/Science) (T) 23, Counseling Psychology EdD (Doctor of Education) 0.

Student Applications/Admissions:

Student Applications

Professional Counseling MA/MS (Master of Arts/Science)—Applications 2004–2005, 80. Total applicants accepted 2004–2005, 70. Total enrolled 2004–2005 full-time, 129, part-time, 17. Openings 2005–2006, 40. The Median number of years required for completion of a degree are 2. The number of students enrolled full and part-time who were dismissed or voluntarily withdrew from this program area were 8. *Counseling Psychology EdD (Doctor of Education)*—Applications 2004–2005, 15. Total applicants accepted 2004–2005, 12. Number enrolled (new admits only) 2004–2005 full-time, 12. Total enrolled 2004–2005 full-time, 23. Openings 2005–2006, 12. The Median number of years required for completion of a degree are 3. The number of students enrolled full and part-time who were dismissed or voluntarily withdrew from this program area were 1.

Admissions Requirements:

Scores: Entries appear in this order: required test or GPA, minimum score (if required), median score of students entering in 2003–2004. Master's Programs: overall undergraduate GPA no minimum stated, 3.0; last 2 years GPA no minimum stated, 3.0; psychology GPA no minimum stated, 3.0.

Other Criteria: (importance of criteria rated low, medium, or high): research experience low, work experience medium, extracurricular activity medium, clinically related public service medium, GPA high, letters of recommendation high, interview low, statement of goals and objectives high. For additional information on admission requirements, go to: www.argosyu.edu.

Student Characteristics: The following represents characteristics of students in 2004–2005 in all graduate psychology programs in the department: Female–full-time 152, part-time 17; Male–full-time 20, part-time 0; African American/Black–full-time 50, part-time 0; Hispanic/Latino(a)–full-time 12, part-time 0; Asian/Pacific Islander–full-time 10, part-time 0; American Indian/Alaska Native–full-time 3, part-time 0; Caucasian–full-time 97, part-time 0; students subject to the Americans With Disabilities Act–full-time 2, part-time 0.

Financial Information/Assistance:

Tuition for Full-Time Study: *Master's:* State residents: $475 per credit hour; Nonstate residents: $475 per credit hour. *Doctoral:* State residents: $750 per credit hour; Nonstate residents: $750 per credit hour. Tuition is subject to change. See the following Web site for updates and changes in tuition costs: www.argosyu.edu.

Financial Assistance:

First Year Students: No information provided.
Advanced Students: No information provided.
Contact Information: No information provided.

Internships/Practica: The Counseling Department maintains training relationships with 40-50 local and out-of-area treatment providers and agencies. Master's level students must complete a mandatory two-semester practicum (6 credit hours) once they have completed prerequisite course work. Students apply for and secure placements in a variety of settings including Community Service Board facilities (outpatient and residential mental health, substance abuse, and psycho-social rehabilitation programs), hospital-based treatment facilities, school systems, private residential treatment facilities, non-profit social services and mental health agencies, and correctional institutions. Students are expected to work 16-20 hours per week at the training site in order to complete a 600-hour practicum that includes 250 hours of direct client contact. Students perform individual and group counseling and psychoeducational services under supervision by licensed mental health treatment providers as required by local jurisdictional regulations. The practicum aims to provide a training experience that replicates the professional environment in which students will eventually be employed. The emphasis is on professional development of the counselor trainee in core therapeutic skill areas, as well as in use of supervision, case reporting, record keeping, and development of collegial relationships with other mental health practitioners.

Housing and Day Care: No on-campus housing is available. No on-campus day care facilities are available.

Employment of Department Graduates:

Master's Degree Graduates: Of those who graduated in the academic year 2003–2004, the following categories and numbers represent the post-graduate activities and employment of master's degree graduates: Enrolled in a post-doctoral residency/fellowship (n/a), employed in independent practice (n/a), total from the above (master's) (0).

Doctoral Degree Graduates: Of those who graduated in the academic year 2003–2004, the following categories and numbers represent the post-graduate activities and employment of doctoral degree graduates: Enrolled in a psychology doctoral program (n/a), total from the above (doctoral) (0).

Additional Information:

Orientation, Objectives, and Emphasis of Department: These Master's degree programs are intended for the professional development of persons who wish to be trained to function or are currently functioning in a variety of counseling or forensic psychology roles. Each provides its students with an educational program that includes the necessary theoretical and practical elements that will allow them to become effective members of a mental health team. The counseling field continues to experience tremendous growth with available employment in a variety of settings including mental health centers, private practice, addiction services, hospitals, youth and family services, victim assistance programs, probation and parole offices, courts, police departments, and intelligence industries.

Application Information:

Send to: Admissions Department, AU/Washington, DC, 1550 Wilson Boulevard, Suite 600, Arlington, VA 22209. Application available online. Students are admitted in the Fall, application deadline June 15; Spring, application deadline November 15; Summer, application deadline March 1. *Fee:* $50.

Argosy University/Washington, DC
Forensic Psychology
American School of Professional Psychology
1550 Wilson Boulevard, Suite 600
Arlington, VA 22209
Telephone: (703) 526-5800
Fax: (703) 243-8973
E-mail: *D.C.admissions@argosyu.edu*
Web: *www.argosyu.edu*

Department Information:

2002. Program Chair: William S. Brown, PsyD. Number of Faculty: total–full-time 1, part-time 2; women–part-time 2.

Programs and Degrees Offered:

Listed in the following order: Program area, degree type (T if terminal Master's), number awarded 7/03–6/04. Forensic Psychology MA/MS (Master of Arts/Science) (T) 13.

Student Applications/Admissions:

Student Applications

Forensic Psychology MA/MS (Master of Arts/Science)—Total applicants accepted 2004–2005, 102. Total enrolled 2004–2005 full-time, 153. Openings 2005–2006, 120. The Median number of years required for completion of a degree are 2. The number of students enrolled full and part-time who were dismissed or voluntarily withdrew from this program area were 2.

Admissions Requirements:

Scores: Entries appear in this order: required test or GPA, minimum score (if required), median score of students entering in 2003–2004. Master's Programs: overall undergraduate GPA 3.0; psychology GPA 3.0.

Other Criteria: (importance of criteria rated low, medium, or high): research experience low, work experience medium, extracurricular activity low, clinically related public service low, GPA high, letters of recommendation high, interview medium, statement of goals and objectives high.

Student Characteristics: The following represents characteristics of students in 2004–2005 in all graduate psychology programs in the department: Female–full-time 115, part-time 0; Male–full-time 38, part-time 0; African American/Black–full-time 37, part-time 0; Hispanic/Latino(a)–full-time 14, part-time 0; Asian/Pacific Islander–full-time 2, part-time 0; Caucasian–full-time 95, part-time 0.

Financial Information/Assistance:

Tuition for Full-Time Study: *Master's:* State residents: $475 per credit hour; Nonstate residents: $475 per credit hour. Tuition is subject to change.

Financial Assistance:

First Year Students: No information provided.
Advanced Students: No information provided.
Contact Information: No information provided.

Internships/Practica: The field placement option of the Forensic Psychology Seminar is a supervised out-of-class experience in a forensic setting designed for students to gain experience and exposure to forensic practice within professional settings. The training provides students with the opportunity to apply theoretical knowledge and the principles of research, and to develop the professional and personal attitudes important to their professional identity.

Housing and Day Care: No on-campus housing is available. No on-campus day care facilities are available.

Employment of Department Graduates:

Master's Degree Graduates: Of those who graduated in the academic year 2003–2004, the following categories and numbers represent the post-graduate activities and employment of master's degree graduates: Enrolled in a psychology doctoral program (1), enrolled in a post-doctoral residency/fellowship (n/a), employed in independent practice (n/a), employed in a government agency (professional services) (3), other employment position (2), do not know (7), total from the above (master's) (13).

Doctoral Degree Graduates: Of those who graduated in the academic year 2003–2004, the following categories and numbers represent the post-graduate activities and employment of doctoral

degree graduates: Enrolled in a psychology doctoral program (n/a), total from the above (doctoral) (0).

Additional Information:

Orientation, Objectives, and Emphasis of Department: The master's program in Forensic Psychology at Argosy University, Washington, DC is designed to educate and train individuals who are currently employed or wish to be trained to work in fields that utilize the study and practice of forensic psychology. The curriculum provides for an understanding of theory, training, and practice of forensic psychology. The program emphasizes the development of students who are committed to the ethical provision of quality services to diverse clients and organizations. The program maintains policies and delivery formats suitable for working adults.

Special Facilities or Resources: The field placement is designed to provide the student with practical experience integrating coursework with experience. Students will have the opportunity to work with staff and/or court-mandated clients, law enforcement, or other legal systems. Examples of field placement sites include: juvenile, adult, and domestic relations court programs; court-assigned mentoring or advocacy programs; probation and parole departments; correctional facilities; police departments; and victim or offender treatment programs.

Application Information:
Send to: Admissions Department, 1550 Wilson Boulevard, Suite 600, Arlington, VA 22209. Application available online. URL of online application: www.argosyu.edu. Students are admitted in the Fall, application deadline May 15; Spring, application deadline October 15; Summer, application deadline April 1. Programs have rolling admissions. *Fee:* $50.

Christopher Newport University
Department of Psychology/ MS in Applied Industrial/ Organizational Psychology
1 University Place
Newport News, VA 23606
Telephone: (757) 594-7094
Fax: (757) 594-7342
E-mail: *gradstdy@cnu.edu*
Web: *www.cnu.edu/gradstudies*

Department Information:
Chairperson: Dr. Timothy Marshall. Number of Faculty: total–full-time 15, part-time 5; women–full-time 6, part-time 3; minority–full-time 1, part-time 1; faculty subject to the Americans With Disabilities Act 1.

Student Applications/Admissions:

Admissions Requirements:

Scores: Entries appear in this order: required test or GPA, minimum score (if required), median score of students entering in 2003–2004. Master's Programs: GRE-V+Q 950, 1050; overall undergraduate GPA 3.00, 3.1.

Other Criteria: (importance of criteria rated low, medium, or high): GRE/MAT scores high, research experience low, GPA high, letters of recommendation low, statement of goals and objectives low. For additional information on admission requirements, go to: http://www.cnu.edu/psych/grad.htm.

Student Characteristics: The following represents characteristics of students in 2004–2005 in all graduate psychology programs in the department: Female–full-time 12, part-time 5; Male–full-time 8, part-time 5; African American/Black–full-time 3, part-time 0; Asian/Pacific Islander–full-time 1, part-time 0; Caucasian–full-time 0, part-time 0.

Financial Information/Assistance:

Tuition for Full-Time Study: *Master's:* State residents: $213 per credit hour; Nonstate residents: $524 per credit hour.

Financial Assistance:

First Year Students: Research assistantships available for first-year. Average amount paid per academic year: $3,000. Average number of hours worked per week: 10. Tuition remission given: full and partial.

Advanced Students: Research assistantships available for advanced students. Average amount paid per academic year: $3,000. Average number of hours worked per week: 10. Tuition remission given: full and partial.

Contact Information: Of all students currently enrolled full-time, 10% benefitted from one or more of the listed financial assistance programs.

Internships/Practica: No information provided.

Housing and Day Care: On-campus housing is available. See the following Web site for more information: http://www.cnu.edu/aboutcnu/tour/cnuapartments.html. No on-campus day care facilities are available.

Employment of Department Graduates:

Master's Degree Graduates: Of those who graduated in the academic year 2003–2004, the following categories and numbers represent the post-graduate activities and employment of master's degree graduates: Enrolled in a psychology doctoral program (0), enrolled in another graduate/professional program (0), enrolled in a post-doctoral residency/fellowship (n/a), employed in independent practice (n/a), employed in a professional position in a school system (1), employed in business or industry (management) (2), do not know (1), total from the above (master's) (4).

Doctoral Degree Graduates: Of those who graduated in the academic year 2003–2004, the following categories and numbers represent the post-graduate activities and employment of doctoral degree graduates: Enrolled in a psychology doctoral program (n/a), total from the above (doctoral) (0).

Application Information:

Send to: Christopher Newport University, Admissions Office, 1 University Place, Newport News, VA 23606. Students are admitted in the Fall, application deadline May 1; Spring, application deadline November 1. *Fee:* $40.

George Mason University
Department of Psychology
Arts and Sciences
4400 University Drive, MSN 3F5
Fairfax, VA 22030-4444
Telephone: (703) 993-1342
Fax: (703) 993-1359
E-mail: *psycgrad@gmu.edu*
Web: *http://www.gmu.edu/departments/psychology*

Department Information:

1966. Chairperson: Robert F. Smith. Number of Faculty: total–full-time 33, part-time 27; women–full-time 12, part-time 12; minority–full-time 2, part-time 1.

Programs and Degrees Offered:

Listed in the following order: Program area, degree type (T if terminal Master's), number awarded 7/03–6/04. Clinical PhD (Doctor of Philosophy) 9, Industrial/Organizational PhD (Doctor of Philosophy) 8, Human Factors/Applied Cognition PhD (Doctor of Philosophy) 3, Applied Developmental PhD (Doctor of Philosophy) 0, Biopsychology PhD (Doctor of Philosophy) 0, School/Certificate MA/MS (Master of Arts/Science) (T) 17, Industrial/Organizational MA/MS (Master of Arts/Science) (T) 12, Human Factors/Applied Cognition MA/MS (Master of Arts/Science) (T) 8, Biopsychology MA/MS (Master of Arts/Science) (T) 7, Applied Developmental MA/MS (Master of Arts/Science) (T) 4.

APA Accreditation: Clinical PhD (Doctor of Philosophy).

Student Applications/Admissions:

Student Applications

Clinical PhD (Doctor of Philosophy)—Applications 2004–2005, 177. Total applicants accepted 2004–2005, 11. Number enrolled (new admits only) 2004–2005 full-time, 8. Number enrolled (new admits only) 2004–2005 part-time, 0. Openings 2005–2006, 9. The Median number of years required for completion of a degree are 6. The number of students enrolled full and part-time who were dismissed or voluntarily withdrew from this program area were 1. *Industrial/Organizational PhD (Doctor of Philosophy)*—Applications 2004–2005, 132. Total applicants accepted 2004–2005, 12. Number enrolled (new admits only) 2004–2005 full-time, 5. Number enrolled (new admits only) 2004–2005 part-time, 3. Total enrolled 2004–2005 full-time, 22, part-time, 22. Openings 2005–2006, 5. The Median number of years required for completion of a degree are 7. The number of students enrolled full and part-time who were dismissed or voluntarily withdrew from this program area were 0. *Human Factors/Applied Cognition PhD (Doctor of Philosophy)*—Applications 2004–2005, 26. Total applicants accepted 2004–2005, 13. Number enrolled (new admits only) 2004–2005 full-time, 5. Number enrolled (new admits only) 2004–2005 part-time, 0. Total enrolled 2004–2005 full-time, 4, part-time, 3. Openings 2005–2006, 4. The Median number of years required for completion of a degree are 7. The number of students enrolled full and part-time who were dismissed or voluntarily withdrew from this program area were 0. *Applied Developmental PhD (Doctor of Philosophy)*—Applications 2004–2005, 29. Total applicants accepted 2004–2005, 7. Number enrolled (new admits only) 2004–2005 full-time, 3. Number enrolled (new admits only) 2004–2005 part-time, 3. Total enrolled 2004–2005 full-time, 13, part-time, 17. Openings 2005–2006, 4. The number of students enrolled full and part-time who were dismissed or voluntarily withdrew from this program area were 0. *Biopsychology PhD (Doctor of Philosophy)*—Applications 2004–2005, 10. Total applicants accepted 2004–2005, 6. Number enrolled (new admits only) 2004–2005 full-time, 3. Number enrolled (new admits only) 2004–2005 part-time, 1. Total enrolled 2004–2005 full-time, 3, part-time, 9. Openings 2005–2006, 4. The number of students enrolled full and part-time who were dismissed or voluntarily withdrew from this program area were 0. *School/Certificate MA/MS (Master of Arts/Science)*—Applications 2004–2005, 83. Total applicants accepted 2004–2005, 22. Number enrolled (new admits only) 2004–2005 full-time, 9. Number enrolled (new admits only) 2004–2005 part-time, 0. Openings 2005–2006, 10. The Median number of years required for completion of a degree are 3. The number of students enrolled full and part-time who were dismissed or voluntarily withdrew from this program area were 0. *Industrial/Organizational MA/MS (Master of Arts/Science)*—Applications 2004–2005, 132. Total applicants accepted 2004–2005, 27. Number enrolled (new admits only) 2004–2005 full-time, 9. Number enrolled (new admits only) 2004–2005 part-time, 5. Total enrolled 2004–2005 full-time, 20, part-time, 10. Openings 2005–2006, 15. The Median number of years required for completion of a degree are 2. The number of students enrolled full and part-time who were dismissed or voluntarily withdrew from this program area were 4. *Human Factors/Applied Cognition MA/MS (Master of Arts/Science)*—Applications 2004–2005, 26. Total applicants accepted 2004–2005, 19. Number enrolled (new admits only) 2004–2005 full-time, 5. Number enrolled (new admits only) 2004–2005 part-time, 4. Total enrolled 2004–2005 full-time, 14, part-time, 6. Openings 2005–2006, 15. The Median number of years required for completion of a degree are 2. The number of students enrolled full and part-time who were dismissed or voluntarily withdrew from this program area were 1. *Biopsychology MA/MS (Master of Arts/Science)*—Applications 2004–2005, 15. Total applicants accepted 2004–2005, 13. Number enrolled (new admits only) 2004–2005 full-time, 2. Number enrolled (new admits only) 2004–2005 part-time, 3. Total enrolled 2004–2005 full-time, 6, part-time, 11. Openings 2005–2006, 10. The Median number of years required for completion of a degree are 3. The number of students enrolled full and part-time who were dismissed or voluntarily withdrew from this program area were 0. *Applied Developmental MA/MS (Master of Arts/Science)*—Applications 2004–2005, 33. Total applicants accepted 2004–2005, 17. Number enrolled (new admits only) 2004–2005 full-time, 5. Number enrolled (new admits only) 2004–2005 part-time, 1. Total enrolled 2004–2005 full-time, 12, part-time, 6. Openings 2005–2006, 10. The Median number of years required for completion of a degree are 2. The number of students enrolled full and part-time who were dismissed or voluntarily withdrew from this program area were 0.

Admissions Requirements:

Scores: Entries appear in this order: required test or GPA, minimum score (if required), median score of students entering in 2003–2004. Master's Programs: GRE-V no minimum stated, 515; GRE-Q no minimum stated, 616; GRE-V+Q 1000, 1131; overall undergraduate GPA no minimum stated, 3.24; last 2

years GPA 3.0, 3.5; psychology GPA 3.33. Doctoral Programs: GRE-V 500, 584; GRE-Q 600, 659; GRE-V+Q no minimum stated, 1243; GRE-Analytical no minimum stated, 639; GRE-Subject(Psych) no minimum stated, 678; overall undergraduate GPA 3.0, 3.52; last 2 years GPA 3.0; psychology GPA 3.33. Clinical program has minimum V+Q GRE scores in the 50th percentile. Clinical applicants are strongly recommended to take the GRE Psychology Subject Test. Other programs prefer at least 1100 combined but will consider other applicants.

Other Criteria: (importance of criteria rated low, medium, or high): GRE/MAT scores high, research experience high, work experience high, extracurricular activity low, clinically related public service medium, GPA high, letters of recommendation high, interview high, statement of goals and objectives high, completed by deadline high. Industrial/Organizational and Human Factors/Applied Cognition do not require an interview. The Clinical, Developmental, and School programs interview a select group. For additional information on admission requirements, go to: http://www.gmu.edu/departments/psychology.

Student Characteristics: The following represents characteristics of students in 2004–2005 in all graduate psychology programs in the department: Female–full-time 138, part-time 50; Male–full-time 66, part-time 13; African American/Black–full-time 4, part-time 3; Hispanic/Latino(a)–full-time 10, part-time 4; Asian/Pacific Islander–full-time 12, part-time 6; American Indian/Alaska Native–full-time 1, part-time 0; Caucasian–full-time 138, part-time 78; Multi-ethnic–full-time 0, part-time 1; students subject to the Americans With Disabilities Act–full-time 0, part-time 0.

Financial Information/Assistance:

Tuition for Full-Time Study: *Master's:* State residents: per academic year $6,264, $261 per credit hour; Nonstate residents: per academic year $15,816, $659 per credit hour. *Doctoral:* State residents: per academic year $6,264, $261 per credit hour; Nonstate residents: per academic year $15,816, $659 per credit hour. Tuition is subject to change. See the following Web site for updates and changes in tuition costs: http://studentaccounts.gmu.edu/index.html.

Financial Assistance:

First Year Students: Teaching assistantships available for first-year. Average amount paid per academic year: $11,000. Average number of hours worked per week: 20. Apply by January 1. Tuition remission given: full. Research assistantships available for first-year. Average amount paid per academic year: $11,000. Average number of hours worked per week: 20. Apply by January 1. Tuition remission given: full. Fellowships and scholarships available for first-year. Average amount paid per academic year: $3,000. Average number of hours worked per week: 0. Apply by January 1.

Advanced Students: Teaching assistantships available for advanced students. Average amount paid per academic year: $10,500. Average number of hours worked per week: 20. Apply by February 15. Tuition remission given: partial. Research assistantships available for advanced students. Average amount paid per academic year: $11,440. Average number of hours worked per week: 20. Apply by February 15. Tuition remission given: partial.

Contact Information: Of all students currently enrolled full-time, 75% benefitted from one or more of the listed financial

assistance programs. Application and information available online at: http://www.gmu.edu/departments/psychology.

Internships/Practica: All programs either require or offer practicum placements in a wide variety of settings, including mental health treatment facilities, medical facilities, schools, government agencies, the military, and businesses and organizations. (Please see our Web site for more information.). For those doctoral students for whom a professional internship is required prior to graduation, 11 applied in 2003–2004. Of those who applied, 10 were placed in internships listed by the Association of Psychology Postdoctoral and Internship Programs (APPIC); 10 were placed in APA accredited internships.

Housing and Day Care: On-campus housing is available. See the following Web site for more information: http://www.gmu.edu/student/living/main/index.htm. On-campus day care facilities are available. See the following Web site for more information: www.gmu.edu.

Employment of Department Graduates:

Master's Degree Graduates: Of those who graduated in the academic year 2003–2004, the following categories and numbers represent the post-graduate activities and employment of master's degree graduates: Enrolled in a psychology doctoral program (6), enrolled in a post-doctoral residency/fellowship (n/a), employed in independent practice (n/a), total from the above (master's) (6). *Doctoral Degree Graduates:* Of those who graduated in the academic year 2003–2004, the following categories and numbers represent the post-graduate activities and employment of doctoral degree graduates: Enrolled in a psychology doctoral program (n/a), total from the above (doctoral) (0).

Additional Information:

Orientation, Objectives, and Emphasis of Department: All graduate programs emphasize both basic research and the application of research to solving problems in families, schools, industry, government, and health care settings.

Personal Behavior Statement: The university has an Honor Code.

Special Facilities or Resources: The Developmental research area includes individual test rooms, a family interaction room, and a number of faculty research areas; some of the test rooms are equipped with video and computers. Biopsychology includes a rodent colony, modern facilities for behavior testing [including drug self-administration], a Neurolucida system for neuroanatomical evaluation, and extensive histological capability. Biopsychology also has collaborative relationships with the Center for Biomedical Genomics and Informatics for gene microarray work, and the Krasnow Institute for Advanced Study for neuroanatomy, neurophysiology, and neural modeling work. The Human Factors/Applied Cognitive labs include numerous workstations for computer display and data collection, several eyetrackers, several simulators [including a cockpit simulator] and human electrophysiology; a Near Infrared Imaging System is planned for the very near future. Industrial/Organizational research space includes laboratory space for work on groups, teamwork, and leadership. Clinical facilities include a professional Clinic, and research/interview space in faculty labs. The Center for Cognitive Development, housed in the same building as the Clinic, works with local School

systems, and the School and Clinical programs, on issues related to child development. Some students use nearby resources for research, such as the National Institutes of Health.

Information for Students With Physical Disabilities: See the following Web site for more information: http://www.gmu.edu/student/drc/.

Application Information:

Send to: Graduate Admissions, George Mason University, 4400 University Drive, MSN 2D2, Fairfax, VA 22030-4444. Application available online. Students are admitted in the Fall, application deadline December 1; Winter, application deadline January 1; Spring, application deadline March 15. December 1 for Clinical PhD; January 1 for all other PhD programs; January 15 for School MA; February 1 for Applied Developmental MA and Biopsychology MA; March 15 for Industrial/Organizational MA and Human Factors/Applied Cognition MA. *Fee:* $60.

James Madison University
Department of Graduate Psychology
MSC 7401
Harrisonburg, VA 22807
Telephone: (540) 568-2556
Fax: (540) 568-3322
E-mail: rogerssj@jmu.edu
Web: http://www.psyc.jmu.edu

Department Information:

1967. Head, Department of Graduate Psychology: Sheena Rogers, PhD. Number of Faculty: total–full-time 28, part-time 5; women–full-time 13, part-time 5; minority–full-time 1.

Programs and Degrees Offered:

Listed in the following order: Program area, degree type (T if terminal Master's), number awarded 7/03–6/04. Psychological Sciences MA/MS (Master of Arts/Science) (T) 7, Community Counseling EdS (Education Specialist) 11, School Psychology EdS (Education Specialist) 9, School Counseling EdS (Education Specialist) 4, College Student Personnel Administration MA/MS (Master of Arts/Science) (T) 11, Combined-Integrated Clinical and School Psychology PsyD (Doctor of Psychology) 8, Assessment and Measurement PhD (Doctor of Philosophy) 2.

APA Accreditation: Combination PsyD (Doctor of Psychology).

Student Applications/Admissions:

Student Applications

Psychological Sciences MA/MS (Master of Arts/Science)—Applications 2004–2005, 50. Total applicants accepted 2004–2005, 8. Number enrolled (new admits only) 2004–2005 full-time, 8. Total enrolled 2004–2005 full-time, 21, part-time, 2. Openings 2005–2006, 10. The Median number of years required for completion of a degree are 2. The number of students enrolled full and part-time who were dismissed or voluntarily withdrew from this program area were 0. *Community Counseling EdS (Education Specialist)*—Applications 2004–2005, 51. Total applicants accepted 2004–2005, 12. Number enrolled (new admits only) 2004–2005 full-time, 10. Number enrolled (new admits only) 2004–2005 part-time, 2. Total enrolled 2004–2005 full-time, 30, part-time, 4. Openings 2005–2006, 10. The Median number of years required for completion of a degree are 3. The number of students enrolled full and part-time who were dismissed or voluntarily withdrew from this program area were 1. *School Psychology EdS (Education Specialist)*—Applications 2004–2005, 73. Total applicants accepted 2004–2005, 10. Number enrolled (new admits only) 2004–2005 full-time, 10. Total enrolled 2004–2005 full-time, 26, part-time, 2. Openings 2005–2006, 10. The Median number of years required for completion of a degree are 3. The number of students enrolled full and part-time who were dismissed or voluntarily withdrew from this program area were 0. *School Counseling EdS (Education Specialist)*—Applications 2004–2005, 29. Total applicants accepted 2004–2005, 10. Number enrolled (new admits only) 2004–2005 full-time, 10. Total enrolled 2004–2005 full-time, 22, part-time, 3. Openings 2005–2006, 10. The Median number of years required for completion of a degree are 3. The number of students enrolled full and part-time who were dismissed or voluntarily withdrew from this program area were 1. *College Student Personnel Administration MA/MS (Master of Arts/Science)*—Applications 2004–2005, 54. Total applicants accepted 2004–2005, 17. Number enrolled (new admits only) 2004–2005 full-time, 13. Number enrolled (new admits only) 2004–2005 part-time, 2. Total enrolled 2004–2005 full-time, 23, part-time, 6. Openings 2005–2006, 14. The Median number of years required for completion of a degree are 2. The number of students enrolled full and part-time who were dismissed or voluntarily withdrew from this program area were 0. *Combined-Integrated Clinical and School Psychology PsyD (Doctor of Psychology)*—Applications 2004–2005, 40. Total applicants accepted 2004–2005, 5. Number enrolled (new admits only) 2004–2005 full-time, 5. Openings 2005–2006, 6. The Median number of years required for completion of a degree are 4. The number of students enrolled full and part-time who were dismissed or voluntarily withdrew from this program area were 0. *Assessment and Measurement PhD (Doctor of Philosophy)*—Applications 2004–2005, 10. Total applicants accepted 2004–2005, 6. Number enrolled (new admits only) 2004–2005 full-time, 6. Total enrolled 2004–2005 full-time, 8, part-time, 8. Openings 2005–2006, 45. The Median number of years required for completion of a degree are 3.75. The number of students enrolled full and part-time who were dismissed or voluntarily withdrew from this program area were 0.

Admissions Requirements:

Scores: Entries appear in this order: required test or GPA, minimum score (if required), median score of students entering in 2003–2004. Master's Programs: overall undergraduate GPA no minimum stated; last 2 years GPA no minimum stated; psychology GPA no minimum stated. Psychological Sciences—GRE-V 544; GRE-Q 614; GRE-A 624; GRE-S 650; Overall GPA 3.47; Jr/Sr GPA 3.70; Psych GPA 3.84. Community Counseling—GRE-V 525; GRE-Q 473; GRE-A546; Overall GPA 328; Jr/Sr GPA 3.53; Psych GPA 3.58. School Counseling—GRE-V 525; GRE-Q 587; GRE-A 620; Overall GPA 3.08; Jr/Sr GPA 3.22; Psych GPA 3.23. School Psychology—GRE-V 471; GRE-Q 570; GRE-A 607; Overall GPA 3.24; Jr/Sr GPA 3.59; Psych GPA 3.44. College Student Personnel Administration—GRE-V 459; GRE-Q 520; GRE-A 567; Overall GPA 3.17. GRE Subject exam recommended

for Psychological Sciences Program only. Doctoral Programs: Assessment and Measurement (PhD)—GRE-V 540; GRE-Q 570; GRE-A 630. Although the Combined-Integrated Doctoral Program in Clinical and School Psychology does require GRE V, Q, A, and Subject scores, applicants are reviewed on the basis of a wide range of admission criteria (please see http:// cep.jmu.edu/clinicalpsyd for additional information).

Other Criteria: (importance of criteria rated low, medium, or high): Psychological Sciences—GRE/MAT Scores high, research experience medium, work experience low, clinically related public service medium, letters of receeommendation high. CSPA—Research experience medium, work experience high, clinically related public service medium, GPA high, letters of recommendation high. School Psychology—GRE/ MAT Scores low, research experience medium, work experience medium, extracurricular activity medium, clinically related public service high, GPA high, letters of recommendation high. Community Counseling—GRE/MAT Scores low, research experience high, work experience low, extracurricular activity high, clinically related public service medium, GPA high, letters of recommendation medium. School Counseling—GRE/MAT Scores low, research experience high, work experience low, extracurricular activity high, clinically related public service medium, GPA high, letters of recommendation medium. PhD Assessment and Management—GRE/MAT Scores medium, research experience medium, work experience low, clinically related public servicehigh, GPA high, letters of recommendation high. PsyD Clinical and School—GRE/ MAT Scores medium, research experience high, work experience high, extracurricular activity high, clinically related public service high, GPA high, letters of recommendation high.

Student Characteristics: The following represents characteristics of students in 2004–2005 in all graduate psychology programs in the department: Female–full-time 119, part-time 24; Male–full-time 32, part-time 1; African American/Black–full-time 9, part-time 0; Hispanic/Latino(a)–full-time 2, part-time 0; Asian/Pacific Islander–full-time 5, part-time 0; American Indian/Alaska Native–full-time 0, part-time 0; Caucasian–full-time 135, part-time 25; students subject to the Americans With Disabilities Act–full-time 0, part-time 0.

Financial Information/Assistance:

Tuition for Full-Time Study: *Master's:* State residents: $226 per credit hour; Nonstate residents: $660 per credit hour.

Financial Assistance:

First Year Students: Teaching assistantships available for first-year. Average amount paid per academic year: $7,551. Average number of hours worked per week: 20. Apply by Fall. Tuition remission given: full. Research assistantships available for first-year. Average amount paid per academic year: $6,434. Average number of hours worked per week: 20. Apply by Fall. Tuition remission given: full. Traineeships available for first-year. Tuition remission given: partial. Fellowships and scholarships available for first-year. Tuition remission given: partial.

Advanced Students: Teaching assistantships available for advanced students. Average amount paid per academic year: $7,551. Average number of hours worked per week: 20. Apply by Fall. Tuition remission given: full. Research assistantships available for advanced students. Average amount paid per academic year: $6,434. Average number of hours worked per week:

20. Apply by Fall. Tuition remission given: full. Traineeships available for advanced students. Tuition remission given: partial. Fellowships and scholarships available for advanced students. Tuition remission given: partial.

Contact Information: Of all students currently enrolled full-time, 90% benefitted from one or more of the listed financial assistance programs. Application and information available online at: http://www.jmu.edu/cgapp.

Internships/Practica: The department maintains a large network of internship sites for specialists for EdS and PsyD students. These sites are housed in public school settings, community mental health agencies, hospitals, and other human service facilities. In addition, the department maintains two doctoral level internships in the Human Development Center (an on-campus comprehensive mental health clinic for children and families). The department provides practicum training through the University's Human Development Center and the Counseling and Student Development Center. For those doctoral students for whom a professional internship is required prior to graduation, 3 applied in 2003–2004. Of those who applied, 3 were placed in internships listed by the Association of Psychology Postdoctoral and Internship Programs (APPIC); 3 were placed in APA accredited internships.

Housing and Day Care: No on-campus housing is available. No on-campus day care facilities are available.

Employment of Department Graduates:

Master's Degree Graduates: Of those who graduated in the academic year 2003–2004, the following categories and numbers represent the post-graduate activities and employment of master's degree graduates: Enrolled in a post-doctoral residency/fellowship (n/a), employed in independent practice (n/a), total from the above (master's) (0).

Doctoral Degree Graduates: Of those who graduated in the academic year 2003–2004, the following categories and numbers represent the post-graduate activities and employment of doctoral degree graduates: Enrolled in a psychology doctoral program (n/a), total from the above (doctoral) (0).

Additional Information:

Orientation, Objectives, and Emphasis of Department: All specialist and doctoral programs provide the necessary academic requirements in training for certification by the State Department of Education and licensure by the State Board of Psychology in Virginia. The counseling program meets the requirements for licensure as a professional counselor (LPC) in the Commonwealth of Virginia. The Psychological Sciences program prepares students for further study at the doctoral level or for employment. The program (MA) is research based; in addition to coursework, a research apprenticeship, comprehensive examination, and thesis is required. The Combined-Integrated Doctoral Program in Clinical and School Psychology prepares students for licensure as clinical psychologists. Our program is fully accredited by the American Psychological Association, and is designed for students possessing advanced graduate degrees and professional experience in applied mental health fields. Depending upon their background, students are able to complete the coursework portion of the program in either two or three years. We have an excellent track record of placing student in APA-accredited internships; our graduates assume professional positions in a range of contexts including,

but not limited to, mental health clinics, child and family agencies, public schools, administrative and leadership positions, training and supervisory roles, and private practice. Please see http://cep.jmu.edu/clinicalpsyd for additional information about our innovative program.

Special Facilities or Resources: Students have access to a state-of-the-art university computer network, microcomputers, animal laboratory, test library, and videotape equipment.

Application Information:
Send to: Department of Graduate Psychology, Graduate Admissions, MSC 7401, James Madison University, Harrisonburg, VA 22807. Application available online. URL of online application: www.psyc.jmu.edu. Students are admitted in the Fall: application deadline—Psychological Sciences, PhD in Assessment and Measurement, and College Student Personnel Administration March 1; Community Counseling, School Counseling, and School Psychology February 15; Combined-Interated Doctoral Program in Clinical, and School Psychology February 1. *Fee:* $55.

Marymount University
Department of Psychology
2807 North Glebe Road
Arlington, VA 22207
Telephone: (703) 284-1620
Fax: (703) 284-1631
E-mail: *lisa.jackson-cherry@marymount.edu*
Web: *www.marymount.edu/academic/sehs/ps/index.html*

Department Information:
1987. Chairperson: Lisa Jackson Cherry. Number of Faculty: total–full-time 13, part-time 18; women–full-time 9, part-time 12; minority–full-time 2; faculty subject to the Americans With Disabilities Act 1.

Programs and Degrees Offered:
Listed in the following order: Program area, degree type (T if terminal Master's), number awarded 7/03–6/04. Community Counseling MA/MS (Master of Arts/Science) (T) 33, School Counseling MA/MS (Master of Arts/Science) (T) 24, Forensic Psychology MA/MS (Master of Arts/Science) (T) 12, Pastoral Counseling MA/MS (Master of Arts/Science) (T) 0.

Student Applications/Admissions:
Student Applications

Community Counseling MA/MS (Master of Arts/Science)—Applications 2004–2005, 56. Total applicants accepted 2004–2005, 26. Total enrolled 2004–2005 full-time, 32, part-time, 37. Openings 2005–2006, 50. The Median number of years required for completion of a degree are 3. The number of students enrolled full and part-time who were dismissed or voluntarily withdrew from this program area were 0. *School Counseling MA/MS (Master of Arts/Science)*—Applications 2004–2005, 35. Total applicants accepted 2004–2005, 19. Total enrolled 2004–2005 full-time, 14, part-time, 17. Openings 2005–2006, 20. The Median number of years required for completion of a degree are 3. The number of students enrolled full and part-time who were dismissed or voluntarily withdrew from this program area were 0. *Forensic Psychology MA/MS (Master of Arts/Science)*—Applications 2004–2005, 111. Total applicants accepted 2004–2005, 97. Total enrolled 2004–2005 full-time, 68, part-time, 40. Openings 2005–2006, 120. The Median number of years required for completion of a degree are 3. The number of students enrolled full and part-time who were dismissed or voluntarily withdrew from this program area were 2. *Pastoral Counseling MA/MS (Master of Arts/Science)*—Applications 2004–2005, 11. Total applicants accepted 2004–2005, 11. Openings 2005–2006, 15. The Median number of years required for completion of a degree are 3. The number of students enrolled full and part-time who were dismissed or voluntarily withdrew from this program area were 0.

Admissions Requirements:

Scores: Entries appear in this order: required test or GPA, minimum score (if required), median score of students entering in 2003–2004. Master's Programs: GRE-V 350, 500; GRE-Q 350, 500; GRE-V+Q 700, 1000; GRE-Analytical 4.0; overall undergraduate GPA 2.75, 3.00. The GRE-Writing Assessment, which is now part of the GRE, is required of all students.
Other Criteria: (importance of criteria rated low, medium, or high): GRE/MAT scores medium, research experience low, work experience medium, extracurricular activity medium, clinically related public service medium, GPA high, letters of recommendation medium, interview high, statement of goals and objectives medium.

Student Characteristics: The following represents characteristics of students in 2004–2005 in all graduate psychology programs in the department: Female–full-time 99, part-time 86; Male–full-time 16, part-time 14; African American/Black–full-time 14, part-time 12; Hispanic/Latino(a)–full-time 4, part-time 3; Asian/Pacific Islander–full-time 1, part-time 1; American Indian/Alaska Native–full-time 1, part-time 1; Caucasian–full-time 95, part-time 83; Multi-ethnic–full-time 0, part-time 0.

Financial Information/Assistance:

Tuition for Full-Time Study: *Master's:* State residents: per academic year $8,476, $546 per credit hour; Nonstate residents: per academic year $8,476, $546 per credit hour. Tuition is subject to change. See the following Web site for updates and changes in tuition costs: http://www.marymount.edu/financialinfo/current.html.

Financial Assistance:

First Year Students: Research assistantships available for first-year. Average amount paid per academic year: $2,500. Average number of hours worked per week: 20. Apply by rolling. Tuition remission given: full. Fellowships and scholarships available for first-year. Average amount paid per academic year: $1,700. Apply by July 1.
Advanced Students: Research assistantships available for advanced students. Average amount paid per academic year: $2,500. Apply by rolling. Fellowships and scholarships available for advanced students. Average amount paid per academic year: $1,700. Apply by July 1.
Contact Information: Of all students currently enrolled full-time, 26% benefitted from one or more of the listed financial assistance programs. Application and information available online at: http://www.marymount.edu/financialaid/graduate.html.

Internships/Practica: MA in Counseling/Pastoral Counseling: Students complete a one-semester pre-internship practicum in an appropriate setting. They also complete an eight-month, 600-hour experience providing direct services under supervision. The internship provides students with an opportunity to apply the principles and tenets learned in class in a supervised work setting. Internships are available at a variety of counseling settings where students are provided with a clinical case-load and expected to practice the full range of skills required of entry-level counselors. The internship experience is supervised by a university faculty member and a clinical supervisor within the participating agency. The goal of the internship is to provide a transitional professional experience that assists the intern in making the transition from student to professional by engaging in practical, day-to-day work as a counselor under supervision. MA School Counseling: Students complete a pre-internship practicum in a school system to prepare them for the internship experience. The School Counseling Internship at Marymount University is a 600 hour culminating field experience in which prospective school counselors demonstrate their knowledge of subject matter, counseling skills, and child/adolescent growth and development. This important experience occurs in an existing instructional setting of a local public or accredited private school and is supervised by qualified university faculty members and cooperating counselors/on-site supervisors. The school counseling internship experience is guided by principles and strategies prescribed by current research and theory in school counselor preparation. Forensic psychology students may choose an internship in a wide variety of settings, including local and state correctional facilities, local community mental health treatment centers, victim witness programs, domestic violence programs and shelters, national and local mental health advocacy organizations, child welfare agencies, child welfare advocacy organizations, adult services agencies (serving incapacitated and incompetent adults), juvenile court services, state and local law enforcement, federal law enforcement and justice agencies, and any and all areas in which psychological expertise and psychological services (including counseling) would be applied in a legal setting (civil proceedings, criminal justice, and juvenile justice).

Housing and Day Care: No on-campus housing is available. No on-campus day care facilities are available.

Employment of Department Graduates:

Master's Degree Graduates: Of those who graduated in the academic year 2003–2004, the following categories and numbers represent the post-graduate activities and employment of master's degree graduates: Enrolled in a post-doctoral residency/fellowship (n/a), employed in independent practice (n/a), total from the above (master's) (0).
Doctoral Degree Graduates: Of those who graduated in the academic year 2003–2004, the following categories and numbers represent the post-graduate activities and employment of doctoral degree graduates: Enrolled in a psychology doctoral program (n/a), total from the above (doctoral) (0).

Additional Information:

Orientation, Objectives, and Emphasis of Department: The department offers the MA in Counseling, Pastoral Counseling, School Counseling and Forensic Psychology. The Counseling programs provide the knowledge and skills in counseling theory, principles and practice that will allow the graduate to work in applied settings where master's level training is utilized. The programs are designed to accommodate the needs of individuals already working in the field who are seeking advancement or enhanced skills, recent undergraduates wishing to further their marketability, and individuals from other fields who wish to change careers. The general goals of the program are to provide a solid background in counseling psychology theory and research methodology, integrated with practical and supervised learning experiences; a background in professional ethics and standards; knowledge of issues related to the application of counseling services to ethnically and racially diverse populations; and specific skills in specialty areas. The focus of these programs is firmly applied and culminates in an internship placement. Our Counseling and School Counseling programs are fully accredited by CA-CREP. The Master of Arts in Forensic Psychology provides graduates with the skills and knowledge they need to provide effective, high quality services in a variety of forensic settings. These include probation and parole, victim assistance, policing, law enforcement, evaluation and testimony in civil and criminal matters. To accomplish this goal, the program balances traditional psychological knowledge and skills with a specialized understanding of the criminal justice and legal system.

Special Facilities or Resources: The location of Marymount in suburban Washington provides our students with a large number of opportunities for internships and employment in the area. Additionally, the university is a member of the Washington Consortium of College and Universities, which gives the students access to the library facilities and classes of most of the major universities in the area. Marymount's geographic location also enables us to employ high quality adjunct faculty, many of whom are experts in their fields.

Application Information:
Send to: Office of Graduate Admissions, Marymount University, 2807 North Glebe Road, Arlington, VA 22207. Application available online. Students are admitted in the Fall and Spring. Programs have rolling admissions. Group admissions interview required for counseling, pastoral counseling and school counseling. Admissions interviews usually are scheduled on the first Saturday in April, June, and November. In order to participate in group interviews, applicant's paperwork must be complete at least one week prior to the interview. *Fee:* $35.

Old Dominion University
Department of Psychology
College of Sciences
Mills Godwin Building—Room 250
Norfolk, VA 23529-0267
Telephone: (757) 683-4439 or (757) 683-4440
Fax: (757) 683-5087
E-mail: *bwinstea@odu.edu*
Web: *http://www.psychology.odu.edu*

Department Information:
1954. Chairperson: Barbara A. Winstead. Number of Faculty: total–full-time 26, part-time 6; women–full-time 11, part-time 4; minority–full-time 1, part-time 1.

Programs and Degrees Offered:
Listed in the following order: Program area, degree type (T if terminal Master's), number awarded 7/03–6/04. General MA/MS (Master of Arts/Science) (T) 13, Industrial/Organizational PhD (Doctor of Philosophy) 2, Human Factors PhD (Doctor of Philosophy) 4, Applied Experimental PhD (Doctor of Philosophy) 0.

Student Applications/Admissions:
Student Applications
General MA/MS (Master of Arts/Science)—Applications 2004–2005, 33. Total applicants accepted 2004–2005, 9. Total enrolled 2004–2005 full-time, 26, part-time, 3. Openings 2005–2006, 7. The Median number of years required for completion of a degree are 2. The number of students enrolled full and part-time who were dismissed or voluntarily withdrew from this program area were 0. *Industrial/Organizational PhD (Doctor of Philosophy)*—Applications 2004–2005, 23. Total applicants accepted 2004–2005, 4. Total enrolled 2004–2005 full-time, 17, part-time, 8. Openings 2005–2006, 3. The Median number of years required for completion of a degree are 5. The number of students enrolled full and part-time who were dismissed or voluntarily withdrew from this program area were 0. *Human Factors PhD (Doctor of Philosophy)*—Applications 2004–2005, 11. Total applicants accepted 2004–2005, 6. Number enrolled (new admits only) 2004–2005 full-time, 2. Openings 2005–2006, 4. The Median number of years required for completion of a degree are 5. The number of students enrolled full and part-time who were dismissed or voluntarily withdrew from this program area were 0. *Applied Experimental PhD (Doctor of Philosophy)*—Applications 2004–2005, 5. Total applicants accepted 2004–2005, 4. Number enrolled (new admits only) 2004–2005 full-time, 4. Total enrolled 2004–2005 full-time, 4. Openings 2005–2006, 3. The Median number of years required for completion of a degree are 5. The number of students enrolled full and part-time who were dismissed or voluntarily withdrew from this program area were 0.

Admissions Requirements:
Scores: Entries appear in this order: required test or GPA, minimum score (if required), median score of students entering in 2003–2004. Master's Programs: GRE-V no minimum stated, 440; GRE-Q no minimum stated, 580; GRE-V+Q no minimum stated, 1020; GRE-Analytical no minimum stated, 5.0; GRE-Subject(Psych) no minimum stated, 480; overall undergraduate GPA no minimum stated, 3.43. Doctoral Programs: GRE-V no minimum stated, 525; GRE-Q no minimum stated, 625; GRE-V+Q no minimum stated, 1150; GRE-Analytical no minimum stated, 5.0; GRE-Subject(Psych) no minimum stated, 590; overall undergraduate GPA no minimum stated, 3.50.
Other Criteria: (importance of criteria rated low, medium, or high): GRE/MAT scores high, research experience high, work experience low, extracurricular activity low, GPA high, letters of recommendation high, interview medium, statement of goals and objectives high.

Student Characteristics: The following represents characteristics of students in 2004–2005 in all graduate psychology programs in the department: Female–full-time 41, part-time 0; Male–full-time 15, part-time 0; African American/Black–full-time 3, part-time 0; Hispanic/Latino(a)–full-time 2, part-time 0; Asian/Pacific Islander–full-time 3, part-time 0; American Indian/Alaska Native–full-time 0, part-time 0; Caucasian–full-time 48, part-time 0; Multi-ethnic–full-time 0, part-time 0; students subject to the Americans With Disabilities Act–full-time 0, part-time 0.

Financial Information/Assistance:

Tuition for Full-Time Study: *Master's:* State residents: $246 per credit hour; Nonstate residents: $631 per credit hour. *Doctoral:* State residents: $246 per credit hour; Nonstate residents: $631 per credit hour. Tuition is subject to change.

Financial Assistance:

First Year Students: Teaching assistantships available for first-year. Average amount paid per academic year: $12,000. Average number of hours worked per week: 20. Apply by January 15. Tuition remission given: full. Fellowships and scholarships available for first-year. Average amount paid per academic year: $15,000. Apply by January 15. Tuition remission given: full.

Advanced Students: Teaching assistantships available for advanced students. Average amount paid per academic year: $12,000. Average number of hours worked per week: 20. Tuition remission given: full. Research assistantships available for advanced students. Average amount paid per academic year: $12,000. Average number of hours worked per week: 20. Tuition remission given: full. Fellowships and scholarships available for advanced students. Average amount paid per academic year: $15,000. Tuition remission given: full.

Contact Information: Of all students currently enrolled full-time, 75% benefitted from one or more of the listed financial assistance programs.

Internships/Practica: Internships are highly encouraged for the Industrial/Organizational PhD program and are available at local businesses, hospitals, and military and government agencies, as well as out-of-state. Practicum and internship experiences are also available for all graduate students.

Housing and Day Care: On-campus housing is available. See the following Web site for more information: http://www.odu.edu. On-campus day care facilities are available.

Employment of Department Graduates:

Master's Degree Graduates: Of those who graduated in the academic year 2003–2004, the following categories and numbers represent the post-graduate activities and employment of master's degree graduates: Enrolled in a psychology doctoral program (3), enrolled in another graduate/professional program (1), enrolled in a post-doctoral residency/fellowship (n/a), employed in independent practice (n/a), employed in other positions at a higher education institution (1), employed in a hospital/medical center (11), total from the above (master's) (16).

Doctoral Degree Graduates: Of those who graduated in the academic year 2003–2004, the following categories and numbers represent the post-graduate activities and employment of doctoral degree graduates: Enrolled in a psychology doctoral program (n/a), employed in an academic position at a 2-year/4-year college (1), employed in business or industry (research/consulting) (4), employed in business or industry (management) (1), other employment position (1), total from the above (doctoral) (7).

Additional Information:

Orientation, Objectives, and Emphasis of Department: The department offers PhD programs in Applied Experimental, Human Factors, and Industrial/Organizational psychology. Concentrations within Applied Experimental include community, developmental, health, and psychophysiology. Concentrations within Human Factors include aviation, cognitive processes, neuroergo-nomics, and modeling and simulation. Concentrations within Industrial/Organizational include organizational and personnel. The programs are designed to provide broad, general training in all fields of psychology, in-depth training in applied experimental, human factors, or industrial/organizational psychology and specialized training in an area of concentration. A program of graduate study leading to the degree of Master of Science with a concentration in general psychology is also offered by the department. The department participates in the Virginia Consortium Program in Clinical Psychology, which, in collaboration with the College of William & Mary, Eastern Virginia Medical School, and Norfolk State University, offers the PsyD in Clinical Psychology. For information regarding the PsyD program, see Virginia Consortium.

Special Facilities or Resources: The department has a new Human Computer Interaction and Usability Analysis lab, a state-of-the art driving simulator, psychophysiological recording equipment, an animal lab, and other research facilities. A close collaboration with the Virginia Modeling, Analysis and Simulation Center provides students with opportunities to engage in command and control simulation, surgical simulators, and virtual reality research. The psychology faculty and graduate students also maintain active collaborations with NASA Langley Research Center, with Eastern Virginia Medical School, the Center for Pediatric Research, the Children's Hospital of the King's Daughters, and community and government groups, such as the Virginia Department of Motor Vehicles, Department of Public Health, and Tidewater AIDS Crisis Taskforce.

Information for Students With Physical Disabilities: See the following Web site for more information: http://www.odu.edu/webroot/orgs/stu/stuserv.nsf/pages/dswebpage.

Application Information:
Send to: Old Dominion University, Office of Graduate Admissions, 105 Rollins Hall, Norfolk, VA 23529-0050. Application available online. URL of online application: http://admissions.odu.edu/graduate/apply.html. Students are admitted in the Winter, application deadline January 15; Spring, application deadline May 15. January 15 for PhD, May 15 for MS. *Fee:* $30. The fee is waived or deferred if the applicant is an ODU graduate.

Radford University
Department of Psychology
Arts and Sciences
P.O. Box 6946
Radford, VA 24142-6946
Telephone: (540) 831-5361
Fax: (540) 831-6113
E-mail: *hlips@radford.edu*
Web: *http://www.radford.edu/~psyc-web*

Department Information:
1937. Chairperson: Hilary M. Lips. Number of Faculty: total–full-time 19, part-time 6; women–full-time 7, part-time 4; minority–part-time 1; faculty subject to the Americans With Disabilities Act 1.

Programs and Degrees Offered:

Listed in the following order: Program area, degree type (T if terminal Master's), number awarded 7/03–6/04. Counseling MA/MS (Master of Arts/Science) (T) 11, Clinical MA/MS (Master of Arts/Science) (T) 5, Experimental MA/MS (Master of Arts/Science) (T) 5, Industrial/ Organizational MA/MS (Master of Arts/Science) (T) 12, School EdS (Education Specialist) 4.

Student Applications/Admissions:

Student Applications

Counseling MA/MS (Master of Arts/Science)—Applications 2004–2005, 105. Total applicants accepted 2004–2005, 67. Number enrolled (new admits only) 2004–2005 full-time, 19. Openings 2005–2006, 15. The Median number of years required for completion of a degree are 2. The number of students enrolled full and part-time who were dismissed or voluntarily withdrew from this program area were 0. *Clinical MA/MS (Master of Arts/Science)*—Applications 2004–2005, 28. Total applicants accepted 2004–2005, 24. Number enrolled (new admits only) 2004–2005 full-time, 7. Openings 2005–2006, 10. The Median number of years required for completion of a degree are 2. The number of students enrolled full and part-time who were dismissed or voluntarily withdrew from this program area were 3. *Experimental MA/MS (Master of Arts/Science)*—Applications 2004–2005, 25. Total applicants accepted 2004–2005, 22. Number enrolled (new admits only) 2004–2005 full-time, 5. Openings 2005–2006, 10. The Median number of years required for completion of a degree are 2. The number of students enrolled full and part-time who were dismissed or voluntarily withdrew from this program area were 1. *Industrial/ Organizational MA/MS (Master of Arts/Science)*—Applications 2004–2005, 41. Total applicants accepted 2004–2005, 25. Number enrolled (new admits only) 2004–2005 full-time, 15. Openings 2005–2006, 15. The Median number of years required for completion of a degree are 2. The number of students enrolled full and part-time who were dismissed or voluntarily withdrew from this program area were 0. *School EdS (Education Specialist)*—Applications 2004–2005, 31. Total applicants accepted 2004–2005, 28. Number enrolled (new admits only) 2004–2005 full-time, 12. Openings 2005–2006, 12. The Median number of years required for completion of a degree are 3. The number of students enrolled full and part-time who were dismissed or voluntarily withdrew from this program area were 2.

Admissions Requirements:

Scores: Entries appear in this order: required test or GPA, minimum score (if required), median score of students entering in 2003–2004. Master's Programs: GRE-V 430, 500; GRE-Q 430, 549; GRE-V+Q 995, 1044; overall undergraduate GPA 3.0, 3.44; last 2 years GPA 3.00, 3.70; psychology GPA 3.0, 3.6. *Other Criteria:* (importance of criteria rated low, medium, or high): GRE/MAT scores medium, research experience high, work experience high, extracurricular activity medium, clinically related public service high, GPA high, letters of recommendation high, statement of goals and objectives medium. Interview recommended but not required. For additional information on admission requirements, go to: http://www.radford.edu/~psyc-web/.

Student Characteristics: The following represents characteristics of students in 2004–2005 in all graduate psychology programs in the department: Female–full-time 85, part-time 0; Male–full-time 21, part-time 0; African American/Black–full-time 6, part-time 0; Hispanic/Latino(a)–full-time 0, part-time 0; Asian/Pacific Islander–full-time 2, part-time 0; American Indian/Alaska Native–full-time 0, part-time 0; Caucasian–full-time 98, part-time 0; Multi-ethnic–full-time 0, part-time 0; students subject to the Americans With Disabilities Act–full-time 1, part-time 0.

Financial Information/Assistance:

Tuition for Full-Time Study: *Master's:* State residents: per academic year $5,426, $226 per credit hour; Nonstate residents: per academic year $10,008, $417 per credit hour. Tuition is subject to change.

Financial Assistance:

First Year Students: Teaching assistantships available for first-year. Average amount paid per academic year: $8,000. Average number of hours worked per week: 20. Tuition remission given: partial. Research assistantships available for first-year. Average amount paid per academic year: $4,000. Average number of hours worked per week: 10.

Advanced Students: Teaching assistantships available for advanced students. Average amount paid per academic year: $8,700. Average number of hours worked per week: 20. Tuition remission given: partial. Research assistantships available for advanced students. Average amount paid per academic year: $4,000. Average number of hours worked per week: 10.

Contact Information: Of all students currently enrolled full-time, 90% benefitted from one or more of the listed financial assistance programs.

Internships/Practica: Internships are required for all programs.

Housing and Day Care: On-campus housing is available. See the following Web site for more information: http://www.radford.edu/~res-life/. No on-campus day care facilities are available.

Employment of Department Graduates:

Master's Degree Graduates: Of those who graduated in the academic year 2003–2004, the following categories and numbers represent the post-graduate activities and employment of master's degree graduates: Enrolled in a post-doctoral residency/fellowship (n/a), employed in independent practice (n/a), employed in a professional position in a school system (4), employed in a community mental health/counseling center (3), other employment position (1), total from the above (master's) (8).

Doctoral Degree Graduates: Of those who graduated in the academic year 2003–2004, the following categories and numbers represent the post-graduate activities and employment of doctoral degree graduates: Enrolled in a psychology doctoral program (n/a), total from the above (doctoral) (0).

Additional Information:

Orientation, Objectives, and Emphasis of Department: The department aims to train psychologists who are well versed in both the theoretical and applied aspects of the discipline. The emphasis of the department is eclectic: school, clinical, experimental, industrial/organizational and counseling options are available. The School program is an EdS program that also provides preparation for certification and licensing as a school psychologist in Virginia.

Special Facilities or Resources: Our renovated facility contains computer laboratories and research space for use by graduate students. The department has established a center for gender studies and laboratory for brain research.

Information for Students With Physical Disabilities: See the following Web site for more information: http://www.radford. edu/~dro/.

Application Information:
Send to: College of Graduate and Extended Education, P.O. Box 6928, Radford University, Radford, VA 24142. Application available online. URL of online application: https://www.applyweb.com/apply/radg/menu.html. Students are admitted in the Fall, application deadline March 1. *Fee:* $40.

Regent University
Doctoral Program in Clinical Psychology
School of Psychology & Counseling
1000 Regent University Drive
Virginia Beach, VA 23464
Telephone: (757) 226-4366
Fax: (757) 226-4304
E-mail: *psyd@regent.edu*
Web: *http://www.regent.edu/acad/schcou/programs/progpsy*

Department Information:
1996. Chairperson: William L. Hathaway, PhD. Number of Faculty: total–full-time 10, part-time 11; women–full-time 6, part-time 6; minority–full-time 3, part-time 3.

Programs and Degrees Offered:
Listed in the following order: Program area, degree type (T if terminal Master's), number awarded 7/03–6/04. Clinical Psychology PsyD (Doctor of Psychology) 17.

APA Accreditation: Clinical PsyD (Doctor of Psychology).

Student Applications/Admissions:
Student Applications
Clinical Psychology PsyD (Doctor of Psychology)—Applications 2004–2005, 120. Total applicants accepted 2004–2005, 44. Number enrolled (new admits only) 2004–2005 full-time, 25. Number enrolled (new admits only) 2004–2005 part-time, 0. Total enrolled 2004–2005 full-time, 115, part-time, 11. Openings 2005–2006, 25. The Median number of years required for completion of a degree are 4. The number of students enrolled full and part-time who were dismissed or voluntarily withdrew from this program area were 2.

Admissions Requirements:
Scores: Entries appear in this order: required test or GPA, minimum score (if required), median score of students entering in 2003–2004. Doctoral Programs: GRE-V+Q 1000; overall undergraduate GPA 3.0, 3.56. The GRE Writing exam is required for all applicants. This exam is included in the GRE General Exam as of October 2002.
Other Criteria: (importance of criteria rated low, medium, or high): GRE/MAT scores high, research experience medium, work experience medium, extracurricular activity medium,

clinically related public service medium, GPA high, letters of recommendation medium, interview medium, statement of goals and objectives medium, leadership experience medium. For more information: http://www.regent.edu/acad/schcou/admission/admissions.htm.

Student Characteristics: The following represents characteristics of students in 2004–2005 in all graduate psychology programs in the department: Female–full-time 84, part-time 9; Male–full-time 31, part-time 2; African American/Black–full-time 23, part-time 2; Hispanic/Latino(a)–full-time 10, part-time 0; Asian/Pacific Islander–full-time 8, part-time 1; American Indian/Alaska Native–full-time 1, part-time 0; Caucasian–full-time 68, part-time 8; Multi-ethnic–full-time 5, part-time 0; students subject to the Americans With Disabilities Act–full-time 1, part-time 0.

Financial Information/Assistance:
Tuition for Full-Time Study: *Doctoral:* State residents: $625 per credit hour; Nonstate residents: $625 per credit hour. Tuition is subject to change.

Financial Assistance:
First Year Students: Fellowships and scholarships available for first-year. Average amount paid per academic year: $2,979. Apply by August 1. Tuition remission given: partial.
Advanced Students: Teaching assistantships available for advanced students. Average amount paid per academic year: $6,000. Average number of hours worked per week: 12. Apply by April 1. Research assistantships available for advanced students. Average amount paid per academic year: $6,000. Average number of hours worked per week: 12. Apply by April 1. Fellowships and scholarships available for advanced students. Average amount paid per academic year: $2,979. Apply by April 1. Tuition remission given: partial.
Contact Information: Of all students currently enrolled full-time, 98% benefitted from one or more of the listed financial assistance programs.

Internships/Practica: All PsyD students complete a three semester placement in the campus training clinica, the Psychological Services Center, during their second year. A three semester practica placement is completed during the third year at any of a wide variety of community practica sites such as military and VA clinics, inpatient brain injury units, psychiatric hospitals, group practices, community mental health agencies, Christian outpatient practices, or correctional settings. For those doctoral students for whom a professional internship is required prior to graduation, 12 applied in 2003–2004. Of those who applied, 12 were placed in internships listed by the Association of Psychology Postdoctoral and Internship Programs (APPIC); 10 were placed in APA accredited internships.

Housing and Day Care: On-campus housing is available. See the following Web site for more information: http://www.regent.edu/admin/admsrv/village/. No on-campus day care facilities are available.

Employment of Department Graduates:
Master's Degree Graduates: Of those who graduated in the academic year 2003–2004, the following categories and numbers represent the post-graduate activities and employment of master's degree graduates: Enrolled in a post-doctoral residency/fellowship

(n/a), employed in independent practice (n/a), total from the above (master's) (0).

Doctoral Degree Graduates: Of those who graduated in the academic year 2003–2004, the following categories and numbers represent the post-graduate activities and employment of doctoral degree graduates: Enrolled in a psychology doctoral program (n/a), enrolled in a post-doctoral residency/fellowship (2), employed in independent practice (4), employed in an academic position at a university (3), employed in a government agency (professional services) (1), employed in a community mental health/counseling center (4), employed in a hospital/medical center (1), still seeking employment (1), other employment position (5), total from the above (doctoral) (21).

Additional Information:

Orientation, Objectives, and Emphasis of Department: The Doctoral Program in Clinical Psychology adopts a practitioner-scholar model of clinical training within an educational context committed to the integration of scientific psychology and a Christian worldview. The clinical training is broad and general, however marital and family therapy, consulting psychology, clinical child psychology, and health psychology are emphases among the faculty and in the curriculum.

Personal Behavior Statement: The Community Life form is contained in the application. It may be downloaded at http://www.regent.edu/acad/schcou/admission/AdmissionAPP.pdf.

Special Facilities or Resources: Regent is located in Virginia Beach, Virginia, which is part of Tidewater, the largest urban area in Virginia. There are numerous community resources for practica. The campus also houses the Psychological Services Center, our doctoral training clinic that provides services to the campus and surrounding community. The PSC includes state of the art technology for videotaping and observation of clinical activities.

Application Information:
Send to: Central Enrollment, SC218, 1000 Regent University Drive, Virginia Beach, VA 23464; E-mail: psycoun@regent.edu. Application available online. URL of online application: www.regent.edu/psychology/apply. Students are admitted in the Fall, application deadline January 15. *Fee:* $50.

Richmond, University of
Department of Psychology
Arts and Sciences
Richmond Hall
Richmond, VA 23173
Telephone: (804) 289-8123
Fax: (804) 287-1905
E-mail: *pli@richmond.edu*
Web: *http://www.richmond.edu/~psych*

Department Information:
1913. Chairperson: Scott Allison, Professor of Psychology. Number of Faculty: total–full-time 10, part-time 3; women–full-time 4, part-time 2; minority–full-time 1, part-time 1.

Programs and Degrees Offered:
Listed in the following order: Program area, degree type (T if terminal Master's), number awarded 7/03–6/04. General MA/MS (Master of Arts/Science) (T) 4.

Student Applications/Admissions:
Student Applications
General MA/MS (Master of Arts/Science)—Applications 2004–2005, 77. Total applicants accepted 2004–2005, 4. Openings 2005–2006, 4. The Median number of years required for completion of a degree are 2. The number of students enrolled full and part-time who were dismissed or voluntarily withdrew from this program area were 0.

Admissions Requirements:
Scores: Entries appear in this order: required test or GPA, minimum score (if required), median score of students entering in 2003–2004. Master's Programs: GRE-V 600, 610; GRE-Q 600, 620; GRE-V+Q 1200, 1230; overall undergraduate GPA 3.3, 3.3; last 2 years GPA 3.0; psychology GPA 3.5, 3.5.
Other Criteria: (importance of criteria rated low, medium, or high): GRE/MAT scores high, research experience high, work experience medium, extracurricular activity medium, clinically related public service medium, GPA high, letters of recommendation high, interview medium, statement of goals and objectives high.

Student Characteristics: The following represents characteristics of students in 2004–2005 in all graduate psychology programs in the department: Female–full-time 5, part-time 0; Male–full-time 4, part-time 0; African American/Black–full-time 1, part-time 0; Hispanic/Latino(a)–full-time 0, part-time 0; Asian/Pacific Islander–full-time 0, part-time 0; American Indian/Alaska Native–full-time 0, part-time 0; Caucasian–full-time 8, part-time 0.

Financial Information/Assistance:
Tuition for Full-Time Study: *Master's:* State residents: per academic year $34,850; Nonstate residents: per academic year $34,850. See the following Web site for updates and changes in tuition costs: http://www.richmond.edu.

Financial Assistance:
First Year Students: Teaching assistantships available for first-year. Average amount paid per academic year: $34,850. Tuition remission given: full. Fellowships and scholarships available for first-year. Average amount paid per academic year: $2,000. Tuition remission given: partial.
Advanced Students: Teaching assistantships available for advanced students. Average amount paid per academic year: $34,850. Tuition remission given: full. Fellowships and scholarships available for advanced students. Average amount paid per academic year: $2,000. Tuition remission given: partial.
Contact Information: Of all students currently enrolled full-time, 100% benefitted from one or more of the listed financial assistance programs.

Internships/Practica: Our department has many solid relationships with placement sites around Richmond. For example, we regularly place students in the Medical College of Virginia; Psychological Consultants; Virginia Treatment Center; and social services centers.

Housing and Day Care: No on-campus housing is available. No on-campus day care facilities are available.

Employment of Department Graduates:

Master's Degree Graduates: Of those who graduated in the academic year 2003–2004, the following categories and numbers represent the post-graduate activities and employment of master's degree graduates: Enrolled in a psychology doctoral program (3), enrolled in another graduate/professional program (1), enrolled in a post-doctoral residency/fellowship (n/a), employed in independent practice (n/a), employed in a government agency (research) (1), total from the above (master's) (5).

Doctoral Degree Graduates: Of those who graduated in the academic year 2003–2004, the following categories and numbers represent the post-graduate activities and employment of doctoral degree graduates: Enrolled in a psychology doctoral program (n/a), total from the above (doctoral) (0).

Additional Information:

Orientation, Objectives, and Emphasis of Department: The General MA program at the University of Richmond is comprised of a rigorous, research-oriented course of study. It sets out to produce students who are both discriminating consumers and producers of research in many different areas of psychology. The program is designed to prepare students to go on for the PhD in a variety of specialties. As soon as they arrive, students work closely with mentors in fashioning a research program and then following a course of study that will complete academic and scientific pursuits, adding new strengths and shoring-up old ones. In addition to elective courses, students choose from among courses in Biological, Cognitive/Affective and Social Basis of Behavior. Throughout, the emphasis is on research and research skills, and how to critically evaluate their own and others' scholarship. The first year is a composition of rigorous course work in the aforementioned areas, culminating in a comprehensive examination, and coupled with original research project(s). The second year focuses on the thesis and associated course work. Altogether, students complete the program with a focus and the tools to equip them for advanced training in the PhD.

Special Facilities or Resources: The Department of Psychology occupies three floors of Richmond Hall on the beautiful University of Richmond campus. The hall was renovated in 1979, and again in 1990. Currently it houses state-of-the-art laboratory facilities for neuroscience research, including image analysis and computerized microscopy; excellent laboratory facilities for performing cognitive and child development research; exceptional laboratory space and equipment for performing cognitive and aging-related research in psychology; and outstanding computer resources in general, in the form of laboratories and work-stations available to students. Moreover, there is ample money available for graduate student research and research related travel to scientific conferences, and a supportive environment for hardworking students in the area of psychology.

Information for Students With Physical Disabilities: See the following Web site for more information: www.richmond.edu.

Application Information:
Send to: Graduate School, Boatwright Administrative Wing, University of Richmond, VA 23173. Application available online. URL of online application: http://asgraduate.richmond.edu/. Students are admitted in the Fall, application deadline February 10. *Fee:* $30. Financial need must be documented to receive a waiver for the application fee.

Virginia Commonwealth University
Department of Psychology
Humanities and Sciences
808 West Franklin Street, Box 842018
Richmond, VA 23284-2018
Telephone: (804) 828-1193
Fax: (804) 828-2237
E-mail: *jforsyth@vcu.edu*
Web: *http://www.has.vcu.edu/psy/*

Department Information:
1969. Chairperson: Scott Vrana. Number of Faculty: total–full-time 38; women–full-time 19; minority–full-time 7.

Programs and Degrees Offered:
Listed in the following order: Program area, degree type (T if terminal Master's), number awarded 7/03–6/04. Clinical Psychology PhD (Doctor of Philosophy) 5, Counseling Psychology PhD (Doctor of Philosophy) 9, Experimental Psychology: Social PhD (Doctor of Philosophy) 2, Experimental Psychology: Biopsychology PhD (Doctor of Philosophy) 2, Experimental Psychology: Developmental PhD (Doctor of Philosophy) 1.

APA Accreditation: Clinical PhD (Doctor of Philosophy). Counseling PhD (Doctor of Philosophy).

Student Applications/Admissions:

Student Applications

Clinical Psychology PhD (Doctor of Philosophy)—Applications 2004–2005, 185. Total applicants accepted 2004–2005, 10. Number enrolled (new admits only) 2004–2005 full-time, 10. Total enrolled 2004–2005 full-time, 43, part-time, 1. Openings 2005–2006, 10. *Counseling Psychology PhD (Doctor of Philosophy)*—Applications 2004–2005, 185. Total applicants accepted 2004–2005, 9. Number enrolled (new admits only) 2004–2005 full-time, 9. Total enrolled 2004–2005 full-time, 39, part-time, 3. Openings 2005–2006, 9. The Median number of years required for completion of a degree are 5. *Experimental Psychology: Social PhD (Doctor of Philosophy)*—Applications 2004–2005, 24. Total applicants accepted 2004–2005, 2. Number enrolled (new admits only) 2004–2005 full-time, 2. Number enrolled (new admits only) 2004–2005 part-time, 0. Openings 2005–2006, 2. The Median number of years required for completion of a degree are 5. The number of students enrolled full and part-time who were dismissed or voluntarily withdrew from this program area were 0. *Experimental Psychology: Biopsychology PhD (Doctor of Philosophy)*—Applications 2004–2005, 22. Total applicants accepted 2004–2005, 1. Number enrolled (new admits only) 2004–2005 full-time, 1. Number enrolled (new admits only) 2004–2005 part-time, 0. Total enrolled 2004–2005 full-time, 13, part-time, 1. Openings 2005–2006, 3. The Median number of years required for completion of a degree are 4. The number of students enrolled full and part-time who were dismissed or voluntarily withdrew from this program area were 0. *Experimental Psychology: Developmental PhD (Doctor of Philosophy)*—Applications 2004–2005, 15. Total applicants accepted 2004–2005, 2. Number enrolled (new admits only) 2004–2005 full-time, 2. Total enrolled 2004–2005 full-time, 9, part-time, 3. Openings 2005–2006, 3. The Median number of years required for completion of a degree are 4.

Admissions Requirements:

Scores: Entries appear in this order: required test or GPA, minimum score (if required), median score of students entering in 2003–2004. Master's Programs: GRE-V 500, 571; GRE-Q 500, 601; GRE-V+Q 1000, 1172; overall undergraduate GPA 3.0, 3.23. Students are accepted for PhD degree only. Programs vary in their emphasis on scores and their requirements. For funding, all require a minumum of 1000 on GRE V+Q. Doctoral Programs: GRE-V 500, 571; GRE-Q 500, 601; GRE-V+Q 1000, 1172; GRE-Analytical no minimum stated; overall undergraduate GPA 3.0, 3.5.

Other Criteria: (importance of criteria rated low, medium, or high): GRE/MAT scores high, research experience high, work experience high, extracurricular activity medium, clinically related public service medium, GPA high, letters of recommendation high, interview medium, statement of goals and objectives medium. The experimental programs stress research experience, GPA, letters of recommendation, and GREs more than the clinical and counseling programs. The clinical and counseling programs stress match between student interests and faculty interests. This match is important, but not as highly stressed by the experimental programs. Clinical and counseling programs stress importance of clinically related public service, interviews, and statement of goals and objectives. For additional information on admission requirements, go to: http://www.has.vcu.edu/psy/index.html.

Student Characteristics: The following represents characteristics of students in 2004–2005 in all graduate psychology programs in the department: Female–full-time 82, part-time 6; Male–full-time 34, part-time 1; African American/Black–full-time 17, part-time 1; Hispanic/Latino(a)–full-time 1, part-time 0; Asian/Pacific Islander–full-time 4, part-time 0; American Indian/Alaska Native–full-time 2, part-time 0; Caucasian–full-time 99, part-time 6; Multi-ethnic full-time 0, part-time 0; students subject to the Americans With Disabilities Act–full-time 1, part-time 0.

Financial Information/Assistance:

Tuition for Full-Time Study: *Master's:* State residents: per academic year $7,390; Nonstate residents: per academic year $17,368. *Doctoral:* State residents: per academic year $7,390; Nonstate residents: per academic year $17,368. Tuition is subject to change. See the following Web site for updates and changes in tuition costs: Costs for the entire 2004–2005 years, see http://www.pubinfo.vcu.edu/sa/taf.asp for more information.

Financial Assistance:

First Year Students: Teaching assistantships available for first-year. Average amount paid per academic year: $9,714. Average number of hours worked per week: 20. Tuition remission given: full. Research assistantships available for first-year. Average amount paid per academic year: $9,714. Average number of hours worked per week: 20. Tuition remission given: full and partial. Fellowships and scholarships available for first-year. Average amount paid per academic year: $11,500. Tuition remission given: full.

Advanced Students: Teaching assistantships available for advanced students. Average amount paid per academic year: $9,714. Average number of hours worked per week: 20. Tuition remission given: full and partial. Research assistantships available for advanced students. Average amount paid per academic year: $9,714. Average number of hours worked per week: 20. Tuition remission given: full and partial. Fellowships and scholarships available for advanced students. Average amount paid per academic year: $11,500. Tuition remission given: full.

Contact Information: Of all students currently enrolled full-time, 80% benefitted from one or more of the listed financial assistance programs.

Internships/Practica: Practicum (external) and internship required for clinical and counseling programs. Sites range from the following: VA hospitals, federal prisons, counseling centers, medical campus opportunities, Children's Hospitals, and juvenile facilities. For those doctoral students for whom a professional internship is required prior to graduation, 17 applied in 2003–2004. Of those who applied, 11 were placed in APA accredited internships.

Housing and Day Care: On-campus housing is available. See the following Web site for more information: www.students.vcu.edu/housing. On-campus day care facilities are available.

Employment of Department Graduates:

Master's Degree Graduates: Of those who graduated in the academic year 2003–2004, the following categories and numbers represent the post-graduate activities and employment of master's degree graduates: Enrolled in a post-doctoral residency/fellowship (n/a), employed in independent practice (n/a), total from the above (master's) (0).

Doctoral Degree Graduates: Of those who graduated in the academic year 2003–2004, the following categories and numbers represent the post-graduate activities and employment of doctoral degree graduates: Enrolled in a psychology doctoral program (n/a), enrolled in another graduate/professional program (0), enrolled in a post-doctoral residency/fellowship (3), employed in an academic position at a university (4), employed in business or industry (research/consulting) (3), employed in a government agency (professional services) (2), employed in a community mental health/counseling center (2), do not know (7), total from the above (doctoral) (21).

Additional Information:

Orientation, Objectives, and Emphasis of Department: The graduate programs in psychology are designed to provide a core education in the basic science of psychology and to enable students to develop skills specific to their area of interest. Students are educated first as psychologists, and are then helped to develop competence in a more specialized area relevant to their scholarly and professional objectives. In addition to formal research requirements for the thesis and dissertation, students in the graduate programs are encouraged to conduct independent research, participate in research teams, or collaborate with faculty conducting research on an ongoing basis. The clinical and counseling psychology programs strongly emphasize the scientist-practitioner model. Students in the clinical program may elect to develop specialized competency in one of several different tracks, including behavior therapy/cognitive behavior therapy, behavioral medicine, clinical child, and adult psychotherapy process. The counseling psychology program prepares students to function in a variety of research and applied settings and to work with people experiencing a broad range of emotional, social, or behavioral problems. The experimental program stresses the acquisition of experimental skills as well as advanced training in one of three specialty areas: biopsychology, developmental psychology, or social psychology.

Personal Behavior Statement: The university requires all students to sign a standard Honor code.

Special Facilities or Resources: The department maintains laboratories for research in the areas of biopsychology, developmental, social, psychophysiology, behavioral assessment, and psychotherapy process. The department also operates the Center for Psychological Services and Development, which provides mental health services for clients referred from throughout the Richmond metropolitan area. Students in the clinical and counseling programs complete practica in the Center and in a variety of off-campus practicum facilities located in the community. Cooperation with a variety of programs and departments on the University's medical campus, the Medical College of Virginia, is extensive for both research and training.

Application Information:
Send to: School of Graduate Studies, VCU Box 843051, Richmond, VA 23284; the forms needed for application are to be downloaded from http://www.vcu.edu/graduate/ps/admission.html. Students are admitted in the Fall. Deadlines are December 15 for Counseling Psychology and Clinical Psychology, and February 15 for all the Experimental Psychology programs (social, biopsychology, and developmental). Students applying to the Experimental Program should clearly indicate the division to which they are seeking admission. Some decisions pertaining to financial aid are made in January, so students interested in such support should submit their applications by January 15. *Fee:* $50.

Virginia Consortium Program in Clinical Psychology
Program in Clinical Psychology
W&M, EVMS, NSU & ODU
Virginia Beach Higher Education Center
1881 University Drive
Virginia Beach, VA 23453
Telephone: (757) 368-1820
Fax: (757) 368-1823
E-mail: *exoneill@odu.edu*
Web: *http://www.vcpcp.odu.edu/vcpcp*

Department Information:
1978. Chairperson: Robin Lewis. Number of Faculty: total–full-time 34; women–full-time 13; minority–full-time 8.

Programs and Degrees Offered:
Listed in the following order: Program area, degree type (T if terminal Master's), number awarded 7/03–6/04. Clinical Psychology PsyD (Doctor of Psychology) 8.

APA Accreditation: Clinical PsyD (Doctor of Psychology).

Student Applications/Admissions:
Student Applications
Clinical Psychology PsyD (Doctor of Psychology)—Applications 2004–2005, 168. Total applicants accepted 2004–2005, 17. Number enrolled (new admits only) 2004–2005 full-time, 10. Openings 2005–2006, 10. The Median number of years required for completion of a degree are 4. The number of students enrolled full and part-time who were dismissed or voluntarily withdrew from this program area were 0.

Admissions Requirements:
Scores: Entries appear in this order: required test or GPA, minimum score (if required), median score of students entering in 2003–2004. Doctoral Programs: GRE-V no minimum stated, 590; GRE-Q no minimum stated, 665; GRE-Analytical no minimum stated, 5.5; GRE-Subject(Psych) no minimum stated, 675; overall undergraduate GPA 3.0, 3.50; last 2 years GPA 3.0; psychology GPA 3.0.
Other Criteria: (importance of criteria rated low, medium, or high): GRE/MAT scores medium, research experience medium, work experience medium, extracurricular activity low, clinically related public service medium, GPA medium, letters of recommendation medium, interview high, statement of goals and objectives high. For additional information on admission requirements, go to: www.vcpcp.odu.edu/vcpcp at Application Info.

Student Characteristics: The following represents characteristics of students in 2004–2005 in all graduate psychology programs in the department: Female–full-time 35, part-time 0; Male–full-time 13, part-time 0; African American/Black–full-time 10, part-time 0; Hispanic/Latino(a)–full-time 2, part-time 0; Asian/Pacific Islander–full-time 2, part-time 0; American Indian/Alaska Native–full-time 0, part-time 0; Caucasian–full-time 34, part-time 0; Multi-ethnic–full-time 0, part-time 0; students subject to the Americans With Disabilities Act–full-time 0, part-time 0.

Financial Information/Assistance:
Tuition for Full-Time Study: *Doctoral:* State residents: per academic year $9,540, $265 per credit hour; Nonstate residents: per academic year $24,804, $689 per credit hour. Tuition is subject to change. See the following Web site for updates and changes in tuition costs: www.vcpcp.odu.edu/vcpcp, at Application Information, at Financial Aid.

Financial Assistance:
First Year Students: Teaching assistantships available for first-year. Average amount paid per academic year: $5,500. Average number of hours worked per week: 6. Apply by February 15. Tuition remission given: partial. Research assistantships available for first-year. Average amount paid per academic year: $5,000. Average number of hours worked per week: 8. Apply by February 15. Tuition remission given: partial.
Advanced Students: Teaching assistantships available for advanced students. Average amount paid per academic year: $6,000. Average number of hours worked per week: 6. Apply by February 15. Tuition remission given: partial. Research assistantships available for advanced students. Average amount paid per academic year: $5,500. Average number of hours worked per week: 8. Apply by February 15. Tuition remission given: partial. Traineeships available for advanced students. Average amount

paid per academic year: $7,000. Average number of hours worked per week: 20. Apply by March 15. Tuition remission given: partial.

Contact Information: Of all students currently enrolled full-time, 97% benefitted from one or more of the listed financial assistance programs. Application and information available online at: http://www.vcpcp.odu.edu/vcpcp.

Internships/Practica: Practicum training is offered in a variety of diverse settings such as mental health centers, medical hospitals, children's residential treatment facilities, public school systems, university counseling centers, social services clinics, private practices, and neuropsychology-rehabilitation. Settings include inpatient, partial hospitalization, residential, and outpatient. Populations include infants, children, adolescents, adults, and elderly from most socioeconomic levels and ethnic groups. Services include most forms of assessment; individual, group, and family intervention modalities, and consultative and other indirect services. Placements are arranged to assure that each student is exposed to several settings and populations. For those doctoral students for whom a professional internship is required prior to graduation, 10 applied in 2003–2004. Of those who applied, 10 were placed in internships listed by the Association of Psychology Postdoctoral and Internship Programs (APPIC); 10 were placed in APA accredited internships.

Housing and Day Care: On-campus housing is available. Graduate housing is available at some of the sponsoring schools. However, because the program is on a calendar year and the schools are on an academic year, students must vacate graduate housing at the end of the spring semester while still in classes. No on-campus day care facilities are available.

Employment of Department Graduates:
Master's Degree Graduates: Of those who graduated in the academic year 2003–2004, the following categories and numbers represent the post-graduate activities and employment of master's degree graduates: Enrolled in a post-doctoral residency/fellowship (n/a), employed in independent practice (n/a), total from the above (master's) (0).
Doctoral Degree Graduates: Of those who graduated in the academic year 2003–2004, the following categories and numbers represent the post-graduate activities and employment of doctoral degree graduates: Enrolled in a psychology doctoral program (n/a), employed in independent practice (1), employed in other positions at a higher education institution (1), employed in a government agency (professional services) (1), employed in a community mental health/counseling center (2), employed in a hospital/medical center (2), other employment position (1), total from the above (doctoral) (8).

Additional Information:
Orientation, Objectives, and Emphasis of Department: The Virginia Consortium is a single, unified program co-sponsored by four institutions: The College of William and Mary, Eastern Virginia Medical School, Norfolk State University, and Old Dominion University. Its mission is to produce practicing clinical psychologists who are competent in individual and cultural diversity, educated in the basic subjects and methods of psychological science, capable of critically assimilating and generating new knowledge, proficient in the delivery and evaluation of clinical services, and able to assume leadership positions in service delivery organizations. The curriculum is generalist in content and in theoretical

orientation. It includes education in the major theoretical and technical models: psychodynamic, behavioral, phenomenological, and family systems. Training is provided in intervention at the individual, group, family, and community/organizational levels. Knowledge acquired in the classroom is applied in an orderly sequence of supervised practica providing exposure to multiple settings, populations, and intervention modalities. Practicum objectives are integrated with the goals of classroom education to facilitate systematic and cumulative acquisition of clinical skills. In the third year, the student pursues individual interests by integrating individualized coursework with advanced practica and a clinical dissertation. In the fourth year, the student receives intensive training in a full-time clinical internship.

Special Facilities or Resources: Students are considered full-time in all four sponsoring schools. This permits access to: four libraries with several computerized literature search databases and 400 periodicals in psychology; four computing centers; multiple health services; and a variety of athletic facilities. Research includes a social psychology laboratory with observational capabilities and facilities; 54 laboratory rooms, and 10 research rooms with various specialized capabilities. Research may also be conducted at practicum placement facilities.

Information for Students With Physical Disabilities: See the following Web site for more information: Please visit www.vcpcp.odu.edu/vcpcp at Our Schools.

Application Information:
Send to: Virginia Consortium Program in Clinical Psychology, Virginia Beach Higher Education Center, 1881 University Drive, Virginia Beach, VA 23453. Application available online. URL of online application: www.vcpcp.odu.edu/vcpcp. Students are admitted in the Fall, application deadline January 15. January 15 is an application and credential deadline—including transcripts and GRE scores. We require the GRE subject test, but it is not offered often. Applicants should plan accordingly by scheduling to take an October or November test. *Fee:* $40. No fee waiver available.

Virginia Polytechnic Institute and State University
Department of Psychology
College of Science
109 Williams Hall
Blacksburg, VA 24061
Telephone: (540) 231-6581
Fax: (540) 231-3652
E-mail: *stephens@vt.edu*
Web: *http://www.psyc.vt.edu/*

Department Information:
1965. Chairperson: Jack W. Finney. Number of Faculty: total–full-time 22; women–full-time 6; minority–full-time 2.

Programs and Degrees Offered:
Listed in the following order: Program area, degree type (T if terminal Master's), number awarded 7/03–6/04. Clinical PhD (Doctor of Philosophy) 10, Industrial/ Organizational PhD (Doc-

tor of Philosophy) 5, Psychological Sciences PhD (Doctor of Philosophy) 0.

APA Accreditation: Clinical PhD (Doctor of Philosophy).

Student Applications/Admissions:

Student Applications

Clinical PhD (Doctor of Philosophy)—Applications 2004–2005, 148. Total applicants accepted 2004–2005, 13. Number enrolled (new admits only) 2004–2005 full-time, 8. Openings 2005–2006, 10. The Median number of years required for completion of a degree are 5. The number of students enrolled full and part-time who were dismissed or voluntarily withdrew from this program area were 0. *Industrial/Organizational PhD (Doctor of Philosophy)*—Applications 2004–2005, 80. Total applicants accepted 2004–2005, 9. Number enrolled (new admits only) 2004–2005 full-time, 5. Total enrolled 2004–2005 full-time, 17, part-time, 3. Openings 2005–2006, 3. The Median number of years required for completion of a degree are 4. The number of students enrolled full and part-time who were dismissed or voluntarily withdrew from this program area were 0. *Psychological Sciences PhD (Doctor of Philosophy)*—Applications 2004–2005, 15. Total applicants accepted 2004–2005, 8. Number enrolled (new admits only) 2004–2005 full-time, 5. Openings 2005–2006, 4. The Median number of years required for completion of a degree are 4. The number of students enrolled full and part-time who were dismissed or voluntarily withdrew from this program area were 1.

Admissions Requirements:

Scores: Entries appear in this order: required test or GPA, minimum score (if required), median score of students entering in 2003–2004. Doctoral Programs: GRE-V no minimum stated, 560; GRE-Q no minimum stated, 670; GRE-V+Q no minimum stated, 1230; overall undergraduate GPA 3.0, 3.5.

Other Criteria: (importance of criteria rated low, medium, or high): GRE/MAT scores high, research experience high, work experience low, clinically related public service medium, GPA high, letters of recommendation high, interview medium, statement of goals and objectives medium, congruence of applicant's goals with program objectives high. For additional information on admission requirements, go to: http://www.psyc.vt.edu/.

Student Characteristics: The following represents characteristics of students in 2004–2005 in all graduate psychology programs in the department: Female–full-time 35, part-time 2; Male–full-time 32, part-time 1; African American/Black–full-time 3, part-time 0; Hispanic/Latino(a)–full-time 4, part-time 0; Asian/Pacific Islander–full-time 9, part-time 0; American Indian/Alaska Native–full-time 0, part-time 0; Caucasian–full-time 51, part-time 3; Multi-ethnic–full-time 0, part-time 0; students subject to the Americans With Disabilities Act–full-time 0, part-time 0.

Financial Information/Assistance:

Tuition for Full-Time Study: *Doctoral:* State residents: per academic year $6,462; Nonstate residents: per academic year $11,682. Tuition is subject to change. See the following Web site for updates and changes in tuition costs: http://www.bursar.vt.edu/sp/tuition.shtml.

Financial Assistance:

First Year Students: Teaching assistantships available for first-year. Average amount paid per academic year: $12,483. Average number of hours worked per week: 20. Tuition remission given: full. Research assistantships available for first-year. Average amount paid per academic year: $13,239. Average number of hours worked per week: 20. Tuition remission given: full.

Advanced Students: Teaching assistantships available for advanced students. Average amount paid per academic year: $13,608. Average number of hours worked per week: 20. Tuition remission given: full. Research assistantships available for advanced students. Average amount paid per academic year: $14,373. Average number of hours worked per week: 20. Tuition remission given: full.

Contact Information: Of all students currently enrolled full-time, 100% benefitted from one or more of the listed financial assistance programs. Application and information available online at: http://www.psyc.vt.edu/.

Internships/Practica: Students in clinical psychology complete practica in a variety of local agency and hospital settings and are required to complete a predoctoral internship as part of the PhD. Students in Industrial/Organizational psychology are encouraged to pursue summer internships. For those doctoral students for whom a professional internship is required prior to graduation, 5 applied in 2003–2004. Of those who applied, 5 were placed in internships listed by the Association of Psychology Postdoctoral and Internship Programs (APPIC); 5 were placed in APA accredited internships.

Housing and Day Care: On-campus housing is available. See the following Web site for more information: http://www.rdp.vt.edu/. No on-campus day care facilities are available.

Employment of Department Graduates:

Master's Degree Graduates: Of those who graduated in the academic year 2003–2004, the following categories and numbers represent the post-graduate activities and employment of master's degree graduates: Enrolled in a post-doctoral residency/fellowship (n/a), employed in independent practice (n/a), total from the above (master's) (0).

Doctoral Degree Graduates: Of those who graduated in the academic year 2003–2004, the following categories and numbers represent the post-graduate activities and employment of doctoral degree graduates: Enrolled in a psychology doctoral program (n/a), total from the above (doctoral) (0).

Additional Information:

Orientation, Objectives, and Emphasis of Department: The graduate programs are strongly research-oriented and designed to ensure that students receive preparation in research methods and psychological theory and to provide the students with skills necessary to be successful in either academic or applied settings. The clinical psychology program is based on the scientist-professional model and emphasizes research methods and theory. Clinical concentrations include child, adult, and health psychology. The industrial/organizational psychology program prepares students both for university teaching and research and for the solution of individual, group, and organizational problems in work settings. Psychometrics, research design, and statistics are emphasized. The Psychological Sciences program trains students in experimental psychology with a focus on preparing psychologists for teaching and research settings. Students in the Psychological Sciences program choose from a neuroscience/psychophysiology or developmental psychology concentration. All doctoral programs also offer training and experience in the teaching of psychology.

Special Facilities or Resources: The Psychological Services Center and Child Study Center are located off-campus and provide the foundation for practicum and research training in Clinical Psychology. The Center for Research in Health Behavior is also located off-campus and is primarily involved in prevention research supported by the National Institutes of Health. Faculty, students, and staff benefit from Virginia Tech's state-of-the-art communications system that links every dormitory room, laboratory, office, and classroom to computing capabilities, audio and video data, and the World Wide Web. The entire campus has easy access to supercomputers across the country, worldwide libraries and data systems. Department resources also include two state-of-the-art laboratories that are dedicated to undergraduate and graduate teaching and research. The psychophysiological laboratory includes eight computer workstations, five EEG/Evoked Potential workstations (32 channel Neuroscan; Neurosearch-24), eye tracker equipment, Coulbourn physiological units, and extensive perception equipment. The other computer laboratory includes 25 computer workstations with cognitive and neurophysiological experiments, SAS and SPSS statistical packages, Bilog and Multilog programs. Graduate students also have ready access to PC and Macintosh computers for word processing and Internet access.

Information for Students With Physical Disabilities: See the following Web site for more information: www.grads.vt.edu.

Application Information:
Send to: Office of Graduate Programs, 100 Sandy Hall, Virginia Polytechnic Institute and State University, Blacksburg, VA 24061, and Graduate Admissions Coordinator, 109 Williams Hall, Department of Psychology, 0436 Virginia Tech, Blacksburg, VA 24061. Application available online. URL of online application: http://www.grads.vt.edu/homeapply.html. Students are admitted in the Fall, application deadline December 15. Application deadline for Clinical is December 15. Application deadline for I/O and Psychological Sciences is January 15. *Fee:* $45.

Virginia State University (2004 data)
Department of Psychology
School of Engineering, Science, & Technology
1 Hayden Drive, Box 9079, Harris Hall 120
Petersburg, VA 23806
Telephone: (804) 524-5969
Fax: (804) 524-5460
E-mail: *psyntst@vsu.edu or revans@vsu.edu*
Web: *http://www.vsu.edu/catalogweb/graduate*

Department Information:
1883. Chairperson: Lera Joyce Johnson, PhD Number of Faculty: total–full-time 8, part-time 11; women–full-time 6, part-time 5; minority–full-time 6, part-time 4.

Programs and Degrees Offered:
Listed in the following order: Program area, degree type (T if terminal Master's), number awarded 7/03–6/04. Psychology MA/MS (Master of Arts/Science) (T) 25.

Student Applications/Admissions:
Student Applications
Psychology MA/MS (Master of Arts/Science)—Total applicants accepted 2004–2005, 24. Total enrolled 2004–2005 full-time, 38, part-time, 10. Openings 2005–2006, 25. The number of students enrolled full and part-time who were dismissed or voluntarily withdrew from this program area were 8.

Admissions Requirements:
Scores: Entries appear in this order: required test or GPA, minimum score (if required), median score of students entering in 2003–2004. Master's Programs: GRE-V no minimum stated; GRE-Q no minimum stated; overall undergraduate GPA no minimum stated; psychology GPA no minimum stated. Requirements are currently in revision. Please check our website for updated information.

Student Characteristics: The following represents characteristics of students in 2004–2005 in all graduate psychology programs in the department: Female–full-time 32, part-time 7; Male–full-time 6, part-time 5; African American/Black–full-time 36, part-time 10; Caucasian–full-time 2, part-time 0; students subject to the Americans With Disabilities Act–full-time 0, part-time 0.

Financial Information/Assistance:
Tuition for Full-Time Study: *Master's:* State residents: per academic year $5,346; Nonstate residents: per academic year $12,142.

Financial Assistance:
First Year Students: Research assistantships available for first-year. Average number of hours worked per week: 20. Apply by March 31. Tuition remission given: full and partial. Fellowships and scholarships available for first-year. Apply by March 31. Tuition remission given: full and partial.
Advanced Students: No information provided.
Contact Information: Application and information available online at: http://www.vsu.edu/catalogweb/graduate/financial/assistance.htm.

Internships/Practica: Clinical students must complete three sections of practicum. Placements usually match the student's career goals and the characteristics of the practicum site.

Housing and Day Care: On-campus housing is available. On-campus housing is available for single students. Average cost of on-campus housing per semester is $1,732 and costs for board is $1,272 per semester. No on-campus day care facilities are available.

Employment of Department Graduates:
Master's Degree Graduates: Of those who graduated in the academic year 2003–2004, the following categories and numbers represent the post-graduate activities and employment of master's degree graduates: Enrolled in a post-doctoral residency/fellowship (n/a), employed in independent practice (n/a), total from the above (master's) (0).

Doctoral Degree Graduates: Of those who graduated in the academic year 2003–2004, the following categories and numbers represent the post-graduate activities and employment of doctoral degree graduates: Enrolled in a psychology doctoral program (n/a), total from the above (doctoral) (0).

Additional Information:

Orientation, Objectives, and Emphasis of Department: Students who select the Educational Psychology master's program usually have a goal to apply to advanced degree programs in School Psychology. Students who select the General Psychology master's program usually plan to apply to doctoral programs. Students who select the Clinical program either have aspirations to attend a doctoral program or have a goal to obtain state licensure and practice with their Master's degree in private or public agencies. Students who have been admitted to doctoral programs after completion of any concentration—General, Educational, or Clinical—of our master's program usually matriculated successfully. Students in both the Educational and Clinical Master's programs learn diagnostic and evaluation skills, but only the Clinical students are placed in practicum sites. All students must complete a thesis.

Special Facilities or Resources: The psychology department recently renovated its Clinical lab to expand its test library, add videotaping capability, and provide electronic report writing capability. The psychology experimental computer lab will be updated in Fall, 2004. Current faculty research projects include studies of cardiovascular response to stress in African Americans, STD/HIV prevention, and health care seeking behavior in African Americans.

Application Information:
Send to: School of Graduate Studies, Research and Outreach, 1 Hayden Drive, Box 9080, VSU, Petersburg, VA 23806-0001. Application available online: http://www.vsu.edu/forms2/Graduate_admission.pdf. Students are admitted in the Fall, application deadline May 1; Spring, application deadline November 1. Programs have rolling admissions. *Fee:* $25.

Virginia, University of
Curry Programs in Clinical and School Psychology
Curry School of Education
P.O. Box 400270
Charlottesville, VA 22904-4270
Telephone: (434) 924-7472
Fax: (434) 924-1433
E-mail: *clin-psych@virginia.edu*
Web: *http://curry.edschool.virginia.edu/go/clinpsych*

Department Information:
1976. Director: Ann Loper. Number of Faculty: total–full-time 7, part-time 2; women–full-time 4, part-time 2; minority–full-time 1.

Programs and Degrees Offered:
Listed in the following order: Program area, degree type (T if terminal Master's), number awarded 7/03–6/04. Clinical PhD (Doctor of Philosophy) 10.

APA Accreditation: Clinical PhD (Doctor of Philosophy).

Student Applications/Admissions:
Student Applications
Clinical PhD (Doctor of Philosophy)—Applications 2004–2005, 183. Total applicants accepted 2004–2005, 13. Number enrolled (new admits only) 2004–2005 full-time, 10. Total enrolled 2004–2005 full-time, 41. Openings 2005–2006, 7. The Median number of years required for completion of a degree are 5. The number of students enrolled full and part-time who were dismissed or voluntarily withdrew from this program area were 2.

Admissions Requirements:
Scores: Entries appear in this order: required test or GPA, minimum score (if required), median score of students entering in 2003–2004. Doctoral Programs: GRE-V none, 600; GRE-Q none, 670; GRE-V+Q none; overall undergraduate GPA none, 3.5.
Other Criteria: (importance of criteria rated low, medium, or high): GRE/MAT scores medium, research experience medium, work experience medium, extracurricular activity low, clinically related public service medium, GPA high, letters of recommendation high, interview high, statement of goals and objectives high. For additional information on admission requirements, go to: curry.edschool.virginia.edu/clinpsych/.

Student Characteristics: The following represents characteristics of students in 2004–2005 in all graduate psychology programs in the department: Female–full-time 34, part-time 0; Male–full-time 7, part-time 0; African American/Black–full-time 3, part-time 0; Hispanic/Latino(a)–full-time 2, part-time 0; Asian/Pacific Islander–full-time 2, part-time 0; American Indian/Alaska Native–full-time 0, part-time 0; Caucasian–full-time 33, part-time 0; Multi-ethnic–full-time 1, part-time 0; students subject to the Americans With Disabilities Act–full-time 0, part-time 0.

Financial Information/Assistance:
Tuition for Full-Time Study: *Doctoral:* State residents: per academic year $9,200; Nonstate residents: per academic year $20,200.

Financial Assistance:
First Year Students: Teaching assistantships available for first-year. Average amount paid per academic year: $2,000. Average number of hours worked per week: 10. Apply by March 1. Tuition remission given: partial. Research assistantships available for first-year. Average amount paid per academic year: $3,000. Average number of hours worked per week: 10. Apply by March 1. Tuition remission given: partial. Fellowships and scholarships available for first-year. Average amount paid per academic year: $3,000. Average number of hours worked per week: 10. Apply by March 1. Tuition remission given: full.

Advanced Students: Teaching assistantships available for advanced students. Average amount paid per academic year: $2,000. Average number of hours worked per week: 10. Apply by March 1. Tuition remission given: partial. Research assistantships available for advanced students. Average amount paid per academic year: $3,000. Average number of hours worked per week: 10. Tuition remission given: partial. Fellowships and scholarships available for advanced students. Average amount paid per academic year: $3,000. Average number of hours worked per week: 10. Apply by March 1. Tuition remission given: full.

Contact Information: Of all students currently enrolled full-time, 100% benefitted from one or more of the listed financial assistance programs.

Internships/Practica: Students may select external practica in area public and private schools, state mental hospitals/residential treatment centers for children or adults, a regional medically affiliated children's rehabilitation center, a family stress clinic, and other mental health settings in the university and community. For those doctoral students for whom a professional internship is required prior to graduation, 10 applied in 2003–2004. Of those who applied, 10 were placed in internships listed by the Association of Psychology Postdoctoral and Internship Programs (APPIC); 10 were placed in APA accredited internships.

Housing and Day Care: On-campus housing is available. See the following Web site for more information: http://www.virginia.edu/housing/housing.htm. On-campus day care facilities are available.

Employment of Department Graduates:

Master's Degree Graduates: Of those who graduated in the academic year 2003–2004, the following categories and numbers represent the post-graduate activities and employment of master's degree graduates: Enrolled in a post-doctoral residency/fellowship (n/a), employed in independent practice (n/a), total from the above (master's) (0).

Doctoral Degree Graduates: Of those who graduated in the academic year 2003–2004, the following categories and numbers represent the post-graduate activities and employment of doctoral degree graduates: Enrolled in a psychology doctoral program (n/a), enrolled in a post-doctoral residency/fellowship (8), employed in business or industry (research/consulting) (1), employed in a government agency (professional services) (1), total from the above (doctoral) (10).

Additional Information:

Orientation, Objectives, and Emphasis of Department: The primary goal of the training program in the Curry School of Education is to produce clinical psychologists with the potential to make outstanding contributions to the profession in a variety of roles. The majority of graduates seek careers in settings such as hospitals, mental health centers, schools, etc. A smaller percentage choose purely academic and research careers. All students complete a common core of coursework and practica in both basic science and professional skills. The students' interests and the courses they elect determine the nature of the students' programs beyond the common core. The predominant theoretical and practice orientations of the faculty are cognitive behavioral, psychodynamic, and family systems. All students are expected to develop strong clinical and research skills. Efforts are made to integrate students' clinical and research experience. The EdD program in school psychology admits experienced school psychologists who are trained for leadership in the profession, at school district or state levels, or as trainers of school psychologists.

Special Facilities or Resources: The Curry Program operates its own comprehensive psychological clinic, the Center for Clinical Psychology Services, serving families, couples, and individuals of all ages and diverse backgrounds. The Center is well equipped for live and videotaped supervision and conveniently located in Ruffner Hall along with student and faculty offices. Program students have training opportunities with the Adjustment of Incarcerated Women Project, Adolescent Parenting Stress Project, Family Assessment Project, NICHD Study of Early Child Care, National Center for Early Development and Learning, School Crisis Network, Teaching Stress Project, Virginia Youth Violence Project, Young Women Leaders Program, and others. In addition, the Program has close working relationships with numerous community agencies, schools, clinics, and hospitals that permit training and research in many different mental health and educational fields. The Curry School of Education is a national leader in instructional technology, with outstanding computing facilities and technology support, smart classrooms, and its own library. Students enjoy easy access to the extensive University of Virginia Library system, which includes a collection of nearly 5 million volumes and has state of the art electronic library resources.

Information for Students With Physical Disabilities: See the following Web site for more information: http://www.virginia.edu/eop/disability.html.

Application Information:
Send to: Admissions Office, Curry School of Education, P.O. Box 400261, University of Virginia, Charlottesville, VA 22904-4261. Application available online. URL of online application: curry.edschool.virginia.edu/admissions/. Students are admitted in the Fall, application deadline January 5. *Fee:* $40. If fee imposes economic hardship, it may be waived. Request information from Curry School Admissions office at address above.

Virginia, University of
Department of Psychology
102 Gilmer Hall, P.O. Box 400400
Charlottesville, VA 22904-4400
Telephone: (434) 982-4750
Fax: (434) 982-4766
E-mail: *psychology@virginia.edu*
Web: *http://www.virginia.edu/~psych*

Department Information:
1929. Chairperson: David L. Hill. Number of Faculty: total–full-time 35; women–full-time 12; minority–full-time 5.

Programs and Degrees Offered:
Listed in the following order: Program area, degree type (T if terminal Master's), number awarded 7/03–6/04. Clinical PhD (Doctor of Philosophy) 4, Cognitive PhD (Doctor of Philosophy) 1, Community PhD (Doctor of Philosophy) 0, Developmental PhD (Doctor of Philosophy) 2, Psychobiology PhD (Doctor of Philosophy) 0, Quantitative PhD (Doctor of Philosophy) 1, Social PhD (Doctor of Philosophy) 0.

APA Accreditation: Clinical PhD (Doctor of Philosophy).

Student Applications/Admissions:

Student Applications

Clinical PhD (Doctor of Philosophy)—Applications 2004–2005, 219. Total applicants accepted 2004–2005, 10. Number enrolled (new admits only) 2004–2005 full-time, 5. Openings 2005–2006, 5. The Median number of years required for completion of a degree are 6. The number of students enrolled full and part-time who were dismissed or voluntarily withdrew from this program area were 0. *Cognitive PhD (Doctor of Philosophy)*—Applications 2004–2005, 23. Total applicants accepted

2004–2005, 8. Number enrolled (new admits only) 2004–2005 full-time, 3. Openings 2005–2006, 3. The Median number of years required for completion of a degree are 7. The number of students enrolled full and part-time who were dismissed or voluntarily withdrew from this program area were 0. *Community PhD (Doctor of Philosophy)*—Applications 2004–2005, 24. Total applicants accepted 2004–2005, 3. Number enrolled (new admits only) 2004–2005 full-time, 0. Openings 2005–2006, 2. *Developmental PhD (Doctor of Philosophy)*—Applications 2004–2005, 42. Total applicants accepted 2004–2005, 7. Number enrolled (new admits only) 2004–2005 full-time, 2. Openings 2005–2006, 4. The Median number of years required for completion of a degree are 6. *Psychobiology PhD (Doctor of Philosophy)*—Applications 2004–2005, 10. Total applicants accepted 2004–2005, 4. Number enrolled (new admits only) 2004–2005 full-time, 3. Openings 2005–2006, 4. *Quantitative PhD (Doctor of Philosophy)*—Applications 2004–2005, 14. Total applicants accepted 2004–2005, 5. Number enrolled (new admits only) 2004–2005 full-time, 0. Openings 2005–2006, 2. The Median number of years required for completion of a degree are 4. *Social PhD (Doctor of Philosophy)*—Applications 2004–2005, 60. Total applicants accepted 2004–2005, 6. Number enrolled (new admits only) 2004–2005 full-time, 4. Openings 2005–2006, 3.

Admissions Requirements:

Scores: Entries appear in this order: required test or GPA, minimum score (if required), median score of students entering in 2003–2004. Doctoral Programs: GRE-V no minimum stated; GRE-Q no minimum stated; GRE-Analytical no minimum stated; overall undergraduate GPA no minimum stated; last 2 years GPA no minimum stated; psychology GPA no minimum stated.

Other Criteria: (importance of criteria rated low, medium, or high): GRE/MAT scores medium, research experience high, work experience medium, extracurricular activity low, clinically related public service low, GPA high, letters of recommendation high, interview medium, statement of goals and objectives high. Publications and presentations at conferences are valued as actual work experience in an area related to the degree sought.

Student Characteristics: The following represents characteristics of students in 2004–2005 in all graduate psychology programs in the department: Female–full-time 70, part-time 0; Male–full-time 29, part-time 0; African American/Black–full-time 6, part-time 0; Hispanic/Latino(a)–full-time 4, part-time 0; Asian/Pacific Islander–full-time 5, part-time 0; American Indian/Alaska Native–full-time 0, part-time 0; Caucasian–full-time 84, part-time 0; Multi-ethnic–full-time 0, part-time 0; students subject to the Americans With Disabilities Act–full-time 0, part-time 0.

Financial Information/Assistance:

Tuition for Full-Time Study: *Doctoral:* State residents: per academic year $7,866; Nonstate residents: per academic year $19,974. Tuition is subject to change.

Financial Assistance:

First Year Students: Teaching assistantships available for first-year. Tuition remission given: full. Research assistantships available for first-year. Tuition remission given: full. Fellowships and scholarships available for first-year.

Advanced Students: Teaching assistantships available for advanced students. Tuition remission given: full. Research assistantships available for advanced students. Tuition remission given: full. Fellowships and scholarships available for advanced students.

Contact Information: Of all students currently enrolled full-time, 100% benefitted from one or more of the listed financial assistance programs.

Internships/Practica: For clinical program: Multiple practica at University hospital, State Mental Hospital for children and adults, Kluge Children's Center; Community Mental Health Center; Law and Psychiatry Unit; Department Clinic and other places as connections and student interest suggest. For those doctoral students for whom a professional internship is required prior to graduation, 7 applied in 2003–2004. Of those who applied, 3 were placed in internships listed by the Association of Psychology Postdoctoral and Internship Programs (APPIC); 4 were placed in APA accredited internships.

Housing and Day Care: On-campus housing is available. See the following Web site for more information: http://www.virginia.edu/housing/. On-campus day care facilities are available. See the following Web site for more information: http://www.virginia.edu/childdevelopmentcenter/enrollment.htm.

Employment of Department Graduates:

Master's Degree Graduates: Of those who graduated in the academic year 2003–2004, the following categories and numbers represent the post-graduate activities and employment of master's degree graduates: Enrolled in a post-doctoral residency/fellowship (n/a), employed in independent practice (n/a), employed in an academic position at a university (8), total from the above (master's) (8).

Doctoral Degree Graduates: Of those who graduated in the academic year 2003–2004, the following categories and numbers represent the post-graduate activities and employment of doctoral degree graduates: Enrolled in a psychology doctoral program (n/a), total from the above (doctoral) (0).

Additional Information:

Orientation, Objectives, and Emphasis of Department: The department emphasizes research on a wide spectrum of psychological issues with clinical, developmental, social, cognitive, psychobiology, quantitative, and community specialties. In addition, new tracks are being developed, such as social ecology and development, law and psychology, family, and minority issues.

Special Facilities or Resources: The department has in excess of 50,000 square feet for offices, laboratories, seminar rooms, and classrooms. Special facilities include rooms for psychophysical investigations, a suite of rooms devoted to developmental, clinical, and social laboratories, and specialized research facilities for the study of animal behavior and psychobiology. Sound-attenuated rooms, electrically shielded rooms, numerous one-way vision rooms, surgery and vivarium rooms, and a darkroom are all available. There is also a library for psychology and biology housed in the same building. There are ample computer facilities. All labs are connected to a local area network and a university-wide local area network. This allows the labs to connect to other available University machines such as IBM RS/6000 unix machines.

Information for Students With Physical Disabilities: See the following Web site for more information: http://www.virginia. edu/studenthealth/lnec.html.

Application Information:
Send to: Dean of the Graduate School, The University of Virginia, P.O. Box 400775, 437 Cabell Hall, Charlottesville, VA 229034-4775. Application available online. URL of online application: http://www. virginia.edu/psychology/graduate/. Students are admitted in the Fall, application deadline December 1. *Fee:* $40.

William and Mary, College of
Department of Psychology/Predoctoral MA Program
P.O. Box 8795
Williamsburg, VA 23187-8795
Telephone: (757) 221-3872
Fax: (757) 221-3896
E-mail: *bbpumi@wm.edu*
Web: *http://www.wm.edu/psyc/*

Department Information:
1946. Chairperson: W. Larry Ventis. Number of Faculty: total–full-time 18, part-time 7; women–full-time 3, part-time 4.

Programs and Degrees Offered:
Listed in the following order: Program area, degree type (T if terminal Master's), number awarded 7/03–6/04. General MA/MS (Master of Arts/Science) (T) 9.

Student Applications/Admissions:
Student Applications
General MA/MS (Master of Arts/Science)—Applications 2004–2005, 84. Total applicants accepted 2004–2005, 15. Number enrolled (new admits only) 2004–2005 full-time, 7. Number enrolled (new admits only) 2004–2005 part-time, 0. Openings 2005–2006, 7. The Median number of years required for completion of a degree are 2. The number of students enrolled full and part-time who were dismissed or voluntarily withdrew from this program area were 0.

Admissions Requirements:
Scores: Entries appear in this order: required test or GPA, minimum score (if required), median score of students entering in 2003–2004. Master's Programs: GRE-V no minimum stated, 590; GRE-Q no minimum stated, 653; GRE-Analytical no minimum stated, 651; overall undergraduate GPA no minimum stated, 3.46; psychology GPA no minimum stated, 3.65. Note: No minimums required for the above.
Other Criteria: (importance of criteria rated low, medium, or high): GRE/MAT scores medium, research experience high, work experience medium, extracurricular activity low, clinically related public service low, GPA medium, letters of recommendation high, statement of goals and objectives high. For additional information on admission requirements, go to: http://web.wm.edu/psyc/ma.htm.

Student Characteristics: The following represents characteristics of students in 2004–2005 in all graduate psychology programs in the department: Female–full-time 6, part-time 0; Male–full-time 9, part-time 0; African American/Black–full-time 0, part-time 0; Hispanic/Latino(a)–full-time 0, part-time 0; Asian/Pacific Islander–full-time 1, part-time 0; American Indian/Alaska Native–full-time 0, part-time 0; Caucasian–full-time 13, part-time 0; Multi-ethnic–full-time 1, part-time 0; students subject to the Americans With Disabilities Act–full-time 0, part-time 0.

Financial Information/Assistance:
Tuition for Full-Time Study: *Master's:* State residents: per academic year $8,198, $235 per credit hour; Nonstate residents: per academic year $19,882, $650 per credit hour. Tuition is subject to change.

Financial Assistance:
First Year Students: Teaching assistantships available for first-year. Average amount paid per academic year: $9,000. Average number of hours worked per week: 20. Apply by February 15. Tuition remission given: full. Research assistantships available for first-year. Average amount paid per academic year: $9,000. Average number of hours worked per week: 20. Apply by February 15. Tuition remission given: full. Fellowships and scholarships available for first-year. Average amount paid per academic year: $9,000. Average number of hours worked per week: 20. Apply by February 15. Tuition remission given: full.
Advanced Students: Teaching assistantships available for advanced students. Average amount paid per academic year: $9,000. Average number of hours worked per week: 20. Apply by February 15. Tuition remission given: full. Research assistantships available for advanced students. Average amount paid per academic year: $9,000. Average number of hours worked per week: 20. Apply by February 15. Tuition remission given: full. Fellowships and scholarships available for advanced students. Average amount paid per academic year: $9,000. Average number of hours worked per week: 20. Apply by February 15. Tuition remission given: full.
Contact Information: Of all students currently enrolled full-time, 100% benefitted from one or more of the listed financial assistance programs. Application and information available online at: http://web.wm.edu/psyc/.

Internships/Practica: No information provided.

Housing and Day Care: On-campus housing is available. Office of Residence Life, College of William and Mary, P.O. Box 8795, Williamsburg, VA 23187-8795. On-campus day care facilities are available.

Employment of Department Graduates:
Master's Degree Graduates: Of those who graduated in the academic year 2003–2004, the following categories and numbers represent the post-graduate activities and employment of master's degree graduates: Enrolled in a psychology doctoral program (6), enrolled in another graduate/professional program (2), enrolled in a post-doctoral residency/fellowship (n/a), employed in independent practice (n/a), total from the above (master's) (8).
Doctoral Degree Graduates: Of those who graduated in the academic year 2003–2004, the following categories and numbers represent the post-graduate activities and employment of doctoral degree graduates: Enrolled in a psychology doctoral program (n/a), total from the above (doctoral) (0).

Additional Information:

Orientation, Objectives, and Emphasis of Department: The general psychology MA program is designed to prepare students for admission to PhD programs. Students are not admitted if they are not planning to further their education. There is a heavy research emphasis throughout both years of the program.

Special Facilities or Resources: There are a limited number of assistantships available to MA students at Eastern State Hospital adjacent to the campus. Computer facilities are available in the department for MA students. Subjects accessible for research include rats, college sophomores, institutionalized geriatric and brain-injured patients, and mental hospital inpatients.

Application Information:

Application, application fee, and all supporting material should be sent in one package to The Director of Graduate Admissions, Psychology Dept., The College of William and Mary, P.O. Box 8795, Williamsburg, VA 23187-8795. GRE scores are sent directly from ETS. Application available online. URL of online application: http://www.applyweb.com/apply/wmgrad/. Students are admitted in the Fall, application deadline February 15. *Fee:* $45.

Argosy University/Seattle

Clinical Psychology (MA & PsyD)/Mental Health Counseling (MA)

Washington School of Professional Psychology

1019 8th Avenue North

Seattle, WA 98109

Telephone: (206) 283-4500

Fax: (206) 283-5777

E-mail: *hsimpson@argosyu.edu*

Web: *http://www.argosyu.edu*

Department Information:

1997. Head-Clinical/Head-Mental Health Counseling: F. Jeri Carter, PhD/ Diedra L. Clay, PsyD. Number of Faculty: total–full-time 9, part-time 1; women–full-time 7, part-time 3; minority–full-time 3; faculty subject to the Americans With Disabilities Act 2.

Programs and Degrees Offered:

Listed in the following order: Program area, degree type (T if terminal Master's), number awarded 7/03–6/04. Clinical Psychology PsyD (Doctor of Psychology) 4, Mental Health Counseling MA/MS (Master of Arts/Science) (T) 13.

Student Applications/Admissions:

Student Applications

Clinical Psychology PsyD (Doctor of Psychology)—Applications 2004–2005, 69. Total applicants accepted 2004–2005, 56. Total enrolled 2004–2005 full-time, 63, part-time, 46. The Median number of years required for completion of a degree are 5. The number of students enrolled full and part-time who were dismissed or voluntarily withdrew from this program area were 7. *Mental Health Counseling MA/MS (Master of Arts/ Science)*—Applications 2004–2005, 40. Total applicants accepted 2004–2005, 34. Total enrolled 2004–2005 full-time, 64, part-time, 2. Openings 2005–2006, 35. The Median number of years required for completion of a degree are 2. The number of students enrolled full and part-time who were dismissed or voluntarily withdrew from this program area were 2.

Admissions Requirements:

Scores: Entries appear in this order: required test or GPA, minimum score (if required), median score of students entering in 2003–2004. Master's Programs: overall undergraduate GPA 3.0; last 2 years GPA 3.0; psychology GPA 3.0. Minimum GPA for MA clinical psychology program is 3.00 from an accredited undergraduate/graduate program. If you do not meet the required GPA, you may submit GRE scores. Doctoral Programs: overall undergraduate GPA 3.25; last 2 years GPA 3.25; psychology GPA 3.25. Minimum GPA for PsyD Psychology program is 3.25 from an accredited undergraduate/graduate program.

Other Criteria: (importance of criteria rated low, medium, or high): GRE/MAT scores low, research experience medium, work experience medium, extracurricular activity medium, clinically related public service high, GPA high, letters of recommendation high, interview high, statement of goals and objectives high. For the Master of Arts in Mental Health Counseling, work experience is not expected.

Student Characteristics: The following represents characteristics of students in 2004–2005 in all graduate psychology programs in the department: Female–full-time 92, part-time 41; Male–full-time 55, part-time 13; African American/Black–full-time 4, part-time 0; Hispanic/Latino(a)–full-time 6, part-time 0; Asian/Pacific Islander–full-time 8, part-time 0; American Indian/Alaska Native–full-time 2, part-time 0; Caucasian–full-time 0, part-time 0; Multi-ethnic–full-time 4, part-time 0; students subject to the Americans With Disabilities Act–full-time 4, part-time 0.

Financial Information/Assistance:

Tuition for Full-Time Study: *Master's:* State residents: $475 per credit hour. *Doctoral:* State residents: $750 per credit hour. Tuition costs vary by program. See the following Web site for updates and changes in tuition costs: www.argosyu.edu.

Financial Assistance:

First Year Students: No information provided.

Advanced Students: Teaching assistantships available for advanced students. Research assistantships available for advanced students.

Contact Information: No information provided.

Internships/Practica: WSPP's current list of approved practicum sites for master's and doctoral level students includes state and community mental health facilities, state correctional facilities from minimum to maximum security, juvenile detention centers, outpatient clinics, private psychiatric hospitals, psychiatric units and community hospitals, treatment centers for developmentally disabled and behavior disordered, and chemical dependence treatment programs. We also have practicum placements in multicultural or diverse practicum settings, including mental health agencies serving Native Americans, Asian-Americans, and African-Americans. Local internships may involve the above sites. We are in the process of developing local internship consortia.

Housing and Day Care: No on-campus housing is available. No on-campus day care facilities are available.

Employment of Department Graduates:

Master's Degree Graduates: Of those who graduated in the academic year 2003–2004, the following categories and numbers represent the post-graduate activities and employment of master's degree graduates: Enrolled in a psychology doctoral program (7), enrolled in another graduate/professional program (2), enrolled in a post-doctoral residency/fellowship (n/a), employed in independent practice (n/a), total from the above (master's) (9).

Doctoral Degree Graduates: Of those who graduated in the academic year 2003–2004, the following categories and numbers represent the post-graduate activities and employment of doctoral degree graduates: Enrolled in a psychology doctoral program (n/a), enrolled in a post-doctoral residency/fellowship (2), employed in an academic position at a university (1), employed in other positions at a higher education institution (1), total from the above (doctoral) (4).

Additional Information:
Orientation, Objectives, and Emphasis of Department: The primary purpose of the program is to educate and train students in the major aspects of clinical practice. To ensure that students are prepared adequately, the curriculum integrates theory, training, research and practice, preparing students to work with a wide range of populations in need of psychological services and in a broad range of roles.

Application Information:
Send to: Admissions Department. Students are admitted in the Fall, application deadline April 15; Spring, application deadline November 1; Summer, application deadline March 1. Rolling admissions. The above deadline dates are recommended dates. *Fee:* $50.

Central Washington University
Department of Psychology
College of the Sciences
400 E. University Way
Ellensburg, WA 98926-7575
Telephone: (509) 963-2381
Fax: (509) 963-2307
E-mail: *steins@cwu.edu*
Web: *http://www.cwu.edu/~psych/*

Department Information:
1965. Chairperson: Stephanie Stein. Number of Faculty: total–full-time 22, part-time 27; women–full-time 7, part-time 16; minority–full-time 1.

Programs and Degrees Offered:
Listed in the following order: Program area, degree type (T if terminal Master's), number awarded 7/03–6/04. Counseling MA/MS (Master of Arts/Science) (T) 3, School Counseling Other 0, Experimental MA/MS (Master of Arts/Science) (T) 4, School Psychology Other 2, Organization Development MA/MS (Master of Arts/Science) (T) 7.

Student Applications/Admissions:
Student Applications
Counseling MA/MS (Master of Arts/Science)—Applications 2004–2005, 33. Total applicants accepted 2004–2005, 17. Number enrolled (new admits only) 2004–2005 full-time, 7. Number enrolled (new admits only) 2004–2005 part-time, 0. Total enrolled 2004–2005 full-time, 19, part-time, 4. Openings 2005–2006, 8. The Median number of years required for completion of a degree are 2. The number of students enrolled full and part-time who were dismissed or voluntarily withdrew from this program area were 1. School Counseling Other—Applications 2004–2005, 13. Total applicants accepted 2004–2005, 6. Number enrolled (new admits only) 2004–2005 full-time, 4. Total enrolled 2004–2005 full-time, 11, part-time, 2. Openings

2005–2006, 4. The Median number of years required for completion of a degree are 2. The number of students enrolled full and part-time who were dismissed or voluntarily withdrew from this program area were 0. Experimental MA/MS (Master of Arts/Science)—Applications 2004–2005, 17. Total applicants accepted 2004–2005, 13. Number enrolled (new admits only) 2004–2005 full-time, 9. Number enrolled (new admits only) 2004–2005 part-time, 1. Total enrolled 2004–2005 full-time, 19, part-time, 3. Openings 2005–2006, 12. The Median number of years required for completion of a degree are 2. School Psychology Other—Applications 2004–2005, 23. Total applicants accepted 2004–2005, 16. Number enrolled (new admits only) 2004–2005 full-time, 8. Number enrolled (new admits only) 2004–2005 part-time, 0. Total enrolled 2004–2005 full-time, 17, part-time, 5. Openings 2005–2006, 8. The Median number of years required for completion of a degree are 3. The number of students enrolled full and part-time who were dismissed or voluntarily withdrew from this program area were 0. Organization Development MA/MS (Master of Arts/Science)—Applications 2004–2005, 20. Total applicants accepted 2004–2005, 13. Number enrolled (new admits only) 2004–2005 full-time, 10. Total enrolled 2004–2005 full-time, 18, part-time, 1. Openings 2005–2006, 12. The Median number of years required for completion of a degree are 2.

Admissions Requirements:
Scores: Entries appear in this order: required test or GPA, minimum score (if required), median score of students entering in 2003–2004. Master's Programs: GRE-V 450; GRE-Q 450; GRE-V+Q 950; last 2 years GPA 3.00. Students applying to the Organization Development program may submit either GRE or GMAT scores.
Other Criteria: (importance of criteria rated low, medium, or high): GRE/MAT scores high, research experience medium, work experience medium, extracurricular activity low, clinically related public service medium, GPA high, letters of recommendation high, interview low, statement of goals and objectives high. Interview for Organizational Development program only. No interviews required for other programs. For additional information on admission requirements, go to: http://www.cwu.edu/~masters/graduateStudies/index.html.

Student Characteristics: The following represents characteristics of students in 2004–2005 in all graduate psychology programs in the department: Female–full-time 64, part-time 12; Male–full-time 20, part-time 3; African American/Black–full-time 2, part-time 0; Hispanic/Latino(a)–full-time 5, part-time 0; Asian/Pacific Islander–full-time 2, part-time 0; American Indian/Alaska Native–full-time 1, part-time 0; Caucasian–full-time 72, part-time 15; Multi-ethnic–full-time 2, part-time 0; students subject to the Americans With Disabilities Act–full-time 0, part-time 0.

Financial Information/Assistance:
Tuition for Full-Time Study: *Master's:* State residents: per academic year $5,520; Nonstate residents: per academic year $11,901. Tuition is subject to change. See the following Web site for updates and changes in tuition costs: http://www.cwu.edu/~regi/Tuitionfees2004.pdf.

Financial Assistance:

First Year Students: Teaching assistantships available for first-year. Average amount paid per academic year: $7,120. Average number of hours worked per week: 20. Apply by February 1. Tuition remission given: full and partial. Research assistantships available for first-year. Average amount paid per academic year: $7,120. Average number of hours worked per week: 20. Apply by February 1. Tuition remission given: full and partial.

Advanced Students: Teaching assistantships available for advanced students. Average amount paid per academic year: $7,120. Average number of hours worked per week: 20. Apply by February 1. Tuition remission given: full and partial. Research assistantships available for advanced students. Average amount paid per academic year: $7,120. Average number of hours worked per week: 20. Apply by February 1. Tuition remission given: full and partial.

Contact Information: Of all students currently enrolled full-time, 40% benefitted from one or more of the listed financial assistance programs. Application and information available online at: http://www.cwu.edu/~masters/.

Internships/Practica: Mental Health Counseling Psychology program requires four quarters of practica and a 900 hour internship. School Counseling program requires four quarters of practica and a 400 hour internship. School Psychology program requires two quarters of practica and a one-year internship. Recent school psychology internships have been paid positions.

Housing and Day Care: On-campus housing is available. See the following Web site for more information: http://www.cwu.edu/~housing/. On-campus day care facilities are available.

Employment of Department Graduates:

Master's Degree Graduates: Of those who graduated in the academic year 2003–2004, the following categories and numbers represent the post-graduate activities and employment of master's degree graduates: Enrolled in a psychology doctoral program (2), enrolled in a post-doctoral residency/fellowship (n/a), employed in independent practice (n/a), employed in other positions at a higher education institution (2), employed in a professional position in a school system (4), employed in business or industry (research/consulting) (0), employed in business or industry (management) (1), employed in a government agency (professional services) (2), employed in a community mental health/counseling center (4), not seeking employment (1), total from the above (master's) (16).

Doctoral Degree Graduates: Of those who graduated in the academic year 2003–2004, the following categories and numbers represent the post-graduate activities and employment of doctoral degree graduates: Enrolled in a psychology doctoral program (n/a), total from the above (doctoral) (0).

Additional Information:

Orientation, Objectives, and Emphasis of Department: Central Washington University's graduate program in psychology prepares students for professional employment in a variety of settings including mental health agencies, public schools, community colleges, and business or industry. We also prepare students for successful completion of doctoral degree programs in psychology.

The programs include extensive supervision in practicum and internship settings and research partnerships with faculty mentors. School Psychology program is NASP approved.

Special Facilities or Resources: Our facilities include an on-site community psychological services center for training in counseling and testing; animal research laboratories, including a laboratory for the study of language learning in chimpanzees; a human behavior laboratory; a computer lab; and a complete mechanical and electrical instrumentation services center.

Information for Students With Physical Disabilities: See the following Web site for more information: http://www.cwu.edu/~dss/.

Application Information:
Send to: Office of Graduate Studies, Central Washington University, 400 E. University Way, Ellensburg, WA 98926-7510. Application available online. URL of online application: http://www.cwu.edu/~masters/forms/formsGraduate.html. Students are admitted in the Fall, application deadline April 1; Winter, application deadline April 1. Winter and spring admission possible for Experimental Psychology program. Admissions may close earlier depending on available space. Winter admission is unusual and is contingent upon openings. *Fee:* $35. Application fee may be waived by demonstration of financial need.

Eastern Washington University
Department of Psychology
College of Social and Behavioral Sciences
151A Martin Hall
Cheney, WA 99004-2423
Telephone: (509) 359-2478
Fax: (509) 359-6325
E-mail: *mdalley@mail.ewu.edu*
Web: *http://www.ewu.edu/csbs/depts/psyc/programs.html*

Department Information:
1934. Chairperson: Mahlon B. Dalley, PhD Number of Faculty: total–full-time 12, part-time 1; women–full-time 4.

Programs and Degrees Offered:
Listed in the following order: Program area, degree type (T if terminal Master's), number awarded 7/03–6/04. Clinical MA/MS (Master of Arts/Science) (T) 8, Experimental/general MA/MS (Master of Arts/Science) (T) 2, School Psychology MA/MS (Master of Arts/Science) (T) 8, Post-Master's School Psychology Certification Respecialization Diploma 18.

Student Applications/Admissions:
Student Applications
Clinical MA/MS (Master of Arts/Science)—Applications 2004–2005, 40. Total applicants accepted 2004–2005, 10. Openings 2005–2006, 10. The Median number of years required for completion of a degree are 2. The number of students enrolled

full and part-time who were dismissed or voluntarily withdrew from this program area were 0. *Experimental/general MA/MS (Master of Arts/Science)*—Applications 2004–2005, 4. Total applicants accepted 2004–2005, 2. Number enrolled (new admits only) 2004–2005 full-time, 2. Openings 2005–2006, 2. The Median number of years required for completion of a degree are 2. The number of students enrolled full and part-time who were dismissed or voluntarily withdrew from this program area were 0. *School Psychology MA/MS (Master of Arts/Science)*—Applications 2004–2005, 25. Total applicants accepted 2004–2005, 12. Number enrolled (new admits only) 2004–2005 full-time, 12. Openings 2005–2006, 12. The Median number of years required for completion of a degree are 3. The number of students enrolled full and part-time who were dismissed or voluntarily withdrew from this program area were 2. *Post-Master's School Psychology Certification Respecialization Diploma*—Applications 2004–2005, 25. Total applicants accepted 2004–2005, 22. Number enrolled (new admits only) 2004–2005 part-time, 22. Total enrolled 2004–2005 part-time, 18. Openings 2005–2006, 20. The Median number of years required for completion of a degree is 1. The number of students enrolled full and part-time who were dismissed or voluntarily withdrew from this program area were 2.

Admissions Requirements:

Scores: Entries appear in this order: required test or GPA, minimum score (if required), median score of students entering in 2003–2004. Master's Programs: GRE-V no minimum stated; GRE-Q no minimum stated; GRE-V+Q no minimum stated; last 2 years GPA 3.0, 3.50; psychology GPA 3.0, 3.60.

Other Criteria: (importance of criteria rated low, medium, or high): GRE/MAT scores medium, research experience medium, work experience medium, extracurricular activity medium, clinically related public service medium, GPA high, letters of recommendation high, statement of goals and objectives high. For School Psychology, less emphasis is on research experience and more on field work and extracurricular activity. For Clinical, more emphasis is on research expereience and less on work and extracurricular activity.

Student Characteristics: The following represents characteristics of students in 2004–2005 in all graduate psychology programs in the department: Female–full-time 40, part-time 0; Male–full-time 10, part-time 0; African American/Black–full-time 2, part-time 0; Hispanic/Latino(a)–full-time 1, part-time 0; Asian/Pacific Islander–full-time 1, part-time 0; American Indian/Alaska Native–full-time 1, part-time 0; Caucasian–full-time 0, part-time 0; students subject to the Americans With Disabilities Act–full-time 0, part-time 0.

Financial Information/Assistance:

Tuition for Full-Time Study: *Master's:* State residents: per academic year $5,772, $192 per credit hour; Nonstate residents: per academic year $17,085, $569 per credit hour. See the following Web site for updates and changes in tuition costs: http://www.ewu.edu/AdminGuide/StuFinServ/home.html.

Financial Assistance:

First Year Students: Research assistantships available for first-year. Average number of hours worked per week: 20. Apply by March 1. Tuition remission given: full. Fellowships and scholar-

ships available for first-year. Apply by March 1. Tuition remission given: full and partial.

Advanced Students: Research assistantships available for advanced students. Average number of hours worked per week: 20. Apply by March 1. Tuition remission given: full.

Contact Information: Of all students currently enrolled full-time, 30% benefitted from one or more of the listed financial assistance programs. Application and information available online at: http://financialaid.ewu.edu Phone: (509) 359-2314; www.ewu.edu-psychology.

Internships/Practica: Students pursuing the clinical and school psychology options have training opportunities at both on- and off-campus facilities, which include the Psychological Counseling Services, the Spokane Community Mental Health Center, Sacred Heart Hospital, Eastern State Hospital, Local School Districts, and School Districts across the state of Washington, and for School Psychology out-of-state placement have been arranged.

Housing and Day Care: On-campus housing is available. See the following Web site for more information: www.ewu.edu—Housing and Dining Services page. (509) 359-4237. On-campus day care facilities are available. See the following Web site for more information: www.ewu.edu—Childcare at the EWU Children's Center (509) 235-5035.

Employment of Department Graduates:

Master's Degree Graduates: Of those who graduated in the academic year 2003–2004, the following categories and numbers represent the post-graduate activities and employment of master's degree graduates: Enrolled in a post-doctoral residency/fellowship (n/a), employed in independent practice (n/a), total from the above (master's) (0).

Doctoral Degree Graduates: Of those who graduated in the academic year 2003–2004, the following categories and numbers represent the post-graduate activities and employment of doctoral degree graduates: Enrolled in a psychology doctoral program (n/a), total from the above (doctoral) (0).

Additional Information:

Orientation, Objectives, and Emphasis of Department: Three areas of specialization in the Department of Psychology are general-experimental, clinical and school psychology. About one-third of those receiving the master of science degree pursue doctoral work. The remainder seek careers as school psychologists, college teachers, psychological examiners, research workers, and institutional and community mental health therapists.

Special Facilities or Resources: Students pursuing the experimental psychology option receive training and research experience in one of several well-equipped laboratories on campus. Additional facilities are available for laboratory work in memory and cognition, and human psychophysiology research.

Information for Students With Physical Disabilities: Disability Support Services: Phone (509) 359-2366.

Application Information:

Send to: Chair of Admission, Eastern WA University, Department of Psychology, 151A Martin Hall, Cheney, WA 99004-2431. Students are admitted in the Fall, application deadline March 1. Fee: $35.

Gonzaga University (2004 data)
Department of Counselor Education
School of Education
East 501 Boone Avenue
Spokane, WA 99258-0025
Telephone: (509) 323-3515
Fax: (509) 323-5964
E-mail: *phastings@soe.gonzaga.edu*
Web: *http://www.gonzaga.edu*

Department Information:
1960. Chairperson: Paul Hastings. Number of Faculty: total–full-time 3, part-time 11; women–full-time 1, part-time 6; minority–part-time 2.

Programs and Degrees Offered:
Listed in the following order: Program area, degree type (T if terminal Master's), number awarded 7/03–6/04. School Counseling MA/MS (Master of Arts/Science) (T) 5, Counseling Psychology, Community MA MA/MS (Master of Arts/Science) (T) 16.

Student Applications/Admissions:
Student Applications
School Counseling MA/MS (Master of Arts/Science)—Applications 2004–2005, 8. Total applicants accepted 2004–2005, 5. Total enrolled 2004–2005 full-time, 12, part-time, 1. Openings 2005–2006, 10. The number of students enrolled full and part-time who were dismissed or voluntarily withdrew from this program area were 1. *Counseling Psychology, Community MA MA/MS (Master of Arts/Science)*—Applications 2004–2005, 40. Total applicants accepted 2004–2005, 20. Total enrolled 2004–2005 full-time, 34, part-time, 4. Openings 2005–2006, 20.

Admissions Requirements:
Scores: Entries appear in this order: required test or GPA, minimum score (if required), median score of students entering in 2003–2004. Master's Programs: MAT no minimum stated; overall undergraduate GPA 3.0. Students may submit either the GRE or MAT.
Other Criteria: (importance of criteria rated low, medium, or high): GRE/MAT scores medium, work experience medium, extracurricular activity medium, clinically related public service medium, GPA medium, letters of recommendation high, interview high, statement of goals and objectives high.

Student Characteristics: The following represents characteristics of students in 2004–2005 in all graduate psychology programs in the department: Female–full-time 37, part-time 5; Male–full-time 9, part-time 0; African American/Black–full-time 2, part-time 1; Hispanic/Latino(a)–part-time 1; Asian/Pacific Islander–full-time 2, part-time 2; American Indian/Alaska Native–full-time 1, part-time 0; Caucasian–full-time 41, part-time 0; Multi-ethnic–full-time 1, part-time 0; students subject to the Americans With Disabilities Act–full-time 1, part-time 0.

Financial Information/Assistance:
Tuition for Full-Time Study: *Master's:* State residents: $525 per credit hour; Nonstate residents: $525 per credit hour. Tuition is subject to change. See the following Web site for updates and changes in tuition costs: www.gonzaga.edu.

Financial Assistance:
First Year Students: Teaching assistantships available for first-year. Average number of hours worked per week: 2.
Advanced Students: Teaching assistantships available for advanced students. Average number of hours worked per week: 5.
Contact Information: Of all students currently enrolled full-time, 17% benefitted from one or more of the listed financial assistance programs.

Internships/Practica: Students complete a 100 hour practicum and a 600 hour internship at a site chosen by the student to meet his or her professional interests. School track students currently are placed in schools at elementary, junior high, high school, and alternative settings. Agency track students are placed at sites including but not limited to geriatric, hospital, community mental health, adolescent, marriage and family, child, community college, career, and life-skills settings. A strong reputation within our community has afforded students to select quality placements.

Housing and Day Care: On-campus housing is available. See the following Web site for more information: www.gonzaga.edu. No on-campus day care facilities are available.

Employment of Department Graduates:
Master's Degree Graduates: Of those who graduated in the academic year 2003–2004, the following categories and numbers represent the post-graduate activities and employment of master's degree graduates: Enrolled in a psychology doctoral program (1), enrolled in a post-doctoral residency/fellowship (n/a), employed in independent practice (n/a), employed in other positions at a higher education institution (1), employed in a professional position in a school system (6), employed in a community mental health/counseling center (12), other employment position (2), total from the above (master's) (22).
Doctoral Degree Graduates: Of those who graduated in the academic year 2003–2004, the following categories and numbers represent the post-graduate activities and employment of doctoral degree graduates: Enrolled in a psychology doctoral program (n/a), total from the above (doctoral) (0).

Additional Information:
Orientation, Objectives, and Emphasis of Department: The philosophical theme running throughout the university is humanism. A realistic, balanced attitude is a necessary prerequisite for assisting others professionally. Careful selection of students helps to insure the inclusion of healthy individuals with the highest potential for success, as does faculty modeling, encouragement of trust, and communication of clear expectations. Indicators of counselor success are demonstration of skills and conflict resolution, consistent interpersonal behaviors, recognition of strengths and weaknesses, a clear grasp of goals, and self-knowledge of one's impact on others, as well as a strong academic performance. Acquisition of counseling competence comes through both personal and professional growth. Immersion in an intensive course of study with a closely linked group of peers encourages open and honest processing, which, in turn, contributes to personal growth. The department believes that students must possess insight and awareness, and clarity about the boundaries between their personal issues and those of the client. Students training to become

professionals must be treated as professionals. Faculty practice collegiality with students, maintain high standards of performance, and furnish an atmosphere of professionalism. Students share cases, exchanging professional advice and input. In addition to the presentation of major theories of counseling, students must develop a personal theory of counseling and demonstrate competence in its use. Faculty are humanistic, but eclectic, disseminating information about effective techniques without imposing any one approach on the students. Students are closely observed in the classroom, practicum and internship and receive critical monitoring and evaluation from faculty, field supervisor, and peers.

Special Facilities or Resources: The Department of Counselor Education is proud to offer a modern and complete clinic training center, with two group rooms and two individual rooms. The clinic has two-way glass, and is equipped with audio-video technological equipment which can be operated in the clinic room by either the student (for taping and reviewing personal work) or by any department faculty member from faculty offices (for viewing and/or taping).

Information for Students With Physical Disabilities: See the following Web site for more information: www.gonzaga.edu.

Application Information:
Send to: Graduate Admissions, School of Education, Gonzaga University, 502 East Boone, Spokane, WA 99258-0025. Application available online. Students are admitted in the Fall, application deadline February 1. Other enrollments accepted temporarily as non-matriculation (until fall deadline). Students may also seek admission on a part-time basis. *Fee:* $40.

Puget Sound, University of
School of Education
1500 North Warner
Tacoma, WA 98416
Telephone: (253) 879-3344
Fax: (253) 879-3926
E-mail: *kirchner@ups.edu*
Web: *http://www.ups.edu*

Department Information:
Director: Grace L. Kirchner. Number of Faculty: total–full-time 2, part-time 3; women–full-time 2, part-time 1.

Programs and Degrees Offered:
Listed in the following order: Program area, degree type (T if terminal Master's), number awarded 7/03–6/04. School Counseling Other 6, Agency Counseling Other 6.

Student Applications/Admissions:
Student Applications
School Counseling Other—Applications 2004–2005, 10. Total applicants accepted 2004–2005, 8. Openings 2005–2006, 8. The Median number of years required for completion of a degree are 3. The number of students enrolled full and part-time who were dismissed or voluntarily withdrew from this program area were 2. Agency Counseling Other—Applications

2004–2005, 3. Total applicants accepted 2004–2005, 3. Openings 2005–2006, 5. The Median number of years required for completion of a degree are 3.

Admissions Requirements:
Scores: Entries appear in this order: required test or GPA, minimum score (if required), median score of students entering in 2003–2004. Master's Programs: GRE-V no minimum stated; GRE-Q no minimum stated; GRE-Analytical no minimum stated; overall undergraduate GPA no minimum stated.
Other Criteria: (importance of criteria rated low, medium, or high): GRE/MAT scores medium, work experience medium, extracurricular activity low, clinically related public service medium, GPA medium, letters of recommendation medium, interview medium, statement of goals and objectives medium.

Student Characteristics: The following represents characteristics of students in 2004–2005 in all graduate psychology programs in the department: Female–part-time 30; Male–part-time 4; Asian/Pacific Islander–part-time 3; American Indian/Alaska Native–part-time 1; Caucasian–full-time 0, part-time 30; students subject to the Americans With Disabilities Act–part-time 0.

Financial Information/Assistance:
Tuition for Full-Time Study: Master's: State residents: $365 per credit hour; Nonstate residents: $365 per credit hour. Tuition is subject to change. See the following Web site for updates and changes in tuition costs: http://www.ups.edu/financialaid/Graduate/costs_revised.shtml.

Financial Assistance:
First Year Students: No information provided.
Advanced Students: No information provided.
Contact Information: No information provided.

Internships/Practica: We require a 400-hour internship in a school or agency setting. These 400 hours are in addition to an on-campus practicum that meets once per week for the academic year.

Housing and Day Care: No on-campus housing is available. No on-campus day care facilities are available.

Employment of Department Graduates:
Master's Degree Graduates: Of those who graduated in the academic year 2003–2004, the following categories and numbers represent the post-graduate activities and employment of master's degree graduates: Enrolled in a psychology doctoral program (0), enrolled in another graduate/professional program (0), enrolled in a post-doctoral residency/fellowship (n/a), employed in independent practice (n/a), employed in an academic position at a university (0), employed in an academic position at a 2-year/4-year college (0), employed in other positions at a higher education institution (0), employed in a professional position in a school system (6), employed in business or industry (research/consulting) (0), employed in business or industry (management) (0), employed in a government agency (research) (0), employed in a government agency (professional services) (0), employed in a community mental health/counseling center (2), employed in a hospital/medical center (0), still seeking employment (1), other employment position (0), total from the above (master's) (9).
Doctoral Degree Graduates: Of those who graduated in the academic year 2003–2004, the following categories and numbers

represent the post-graduate activities and employment of doctoral degree graduates: Enrolled in a psychology doctoral program (n/a), total from the above (doctoral) (0).

Additional Information:
Orientation, Objectives, and Emphasis of Department: We are housed in the School of Education and our primary mission is to train school counselors; however, many of our graduates find employment in social service settings.

Application Information:
Send to: Office of Admission. Application available online. URL of online application: http://www.ups.edu/admission/images/educ_app 2001.pdf. Students are admitted in the Spring, application deadline March 1. *Fee:* $65. $25 if previously admitted to University.

Seattle Pacific University
Department of Graduate Psychology
School of Psychology, Family and Community
3307 Third Avenue, W.
Seattle, WA 98119
Telephone: (206) 281-2916
Fax: (206) 281-2695
E-mail: *skidmore@spu.edu*
Web: *http://www.spu.ed/depts/grad~psych*

Department Information:
1995. Chairperson: Jay R. Skidmore, PhD. Number of Faculty: total–full-time 7, part-time 6; women–full-time 3, part-time 3; minority–full-time 2, part-time 1.

Programs and Degrees Offered:
Listed in the following order: Program area, degree type (T if terminal Master's), number awarded 7/03–6/04. Clinical psychology PhD (Doctor of Philosophy) 17.

Student Applications/Admissions:
Student Applications
Clinical Psychology PhD (Doctor of Philosophy)—Applications 2004–2005, 51. Total applicants accepted 2004–2005, 15. Number enrolled (new admits only) 2004–2005 full-time, 12. Number enrolled (new admits only) 2004–2005 part-time, 0. Total enrolled 2004–2005 full-time, 77, part-time, 30. Openings 2005–2006, 15. The Median number of years required for completion of a degree are 5. The number of students enrolled full and part-time who were dismissed or voluntarily withdrew from this program area were 3.

Admissions Requirements:
Scores: Entries appear in this order: required test or GPA, minimum score (if required), median score of students entering in 2003–2004. Doctoral Programs: GRE-V+Q 1100, 1120; overall undergraduate GPA 3.00, 3.50.
Other Criteria: (importance of criteria rated low, medium, or high): GRE/MAT scores high, research experience medium, work experience low, extracurricular activity low, clinically related public service medium, GPA high, letters of recommendation high, interview high, statement of goals and objectives

high. Match with program high. For additional information on admission requirements, go to: http://www.spu.edu/depts/pfc/clinicalpsych/.

Student Characteristics: The following represents characteristics of students in 2004–2005 in all graduate psychology programs in the department: Female–full-time 65, part-time 21; Male–full-time 12, part-time 9; African American/Black–full-time 3, part-time 2; Hispanic/Latino(a)–full-time 4, part-time 1; Asian/Pacific Islander–full-time 5, part-time 1; American Indian/Alaska Native–full-time 1, part-time 0; Caucasian–full-time 64, part-time 26; Multi-ethnic–full-time 0, part-time 0; students subject to the Americans With Disabilities Act–full-time 0, part-time 0.

Financial Information/Assistance:
Tuition for Full-Time Study: *Doctoral:* State residents: $482 per credit hour; Nonstate residents: $482 per credit hour. Tuition is subject to change.

Financial Assistance:
First Year Students: No information provided.
Advanced Students: Teaching assistantships available for advanced students. Average amount paid per academic year: $8,000. Average number of hours worked per week: 15. Research assistantships available for advanced students. Average amount paid per academic year: $4,000. Average number of hours worked per week: 8. Fellowships and scholarships available for advanced students. Average amount paid per academic year: $8,000. Average number of hours worked per week: 15.
Contact Information: Of all students currently enrolled full-time, 20% benefitted from one or more of the listed financial assistance programs.

Internships/Practica: The program's clinical training requirements include two one-year practicum placements during the 3rd and 4th years of the program (part-time, averaging 16 hours/week, thereby resulting in average total practicum experience of approximately 1200 hours), as well as a full-time one-year (2000 hours) internship in professional psychology typically during the 5th year of the PhD program. With few exceptions, practicum placements are external to the university, located in a variety of mental health centers, hospitals, medical/dental clinics, and rehabilitation facilities in the greater Puget Sound area. Students apply for their internship in the APPIC Match, and each year all or most obtain placements at competitive mental health and medical centers around the country. The theoretical orientations represented among the faculty include expertise in cognitive behavioral, psychodynamic, interpersonal, family systems, and humanistic approaches. Yet we tend to view these theoretical models as reflecting stages of development in the history of clinical psychology, and we expect students to incorporate evidence-based guidelines as well as the effective use of self and personal experience in clinical work. For those doctoral students for whom a professional internship is required prior to graduation, 19 applied in 2003–2004. Of those who applied, 13 were placed in internships listed by the Association of Psychology Postdoctoral and Internship Programs (APPIC); 6 were placed in APA accredited internships.

Housing and Day Care: No on-campus housing is available. On-campus day care facilities are available at First Free Methodist Church, across the street from SPU campus.

Employment of Department Graduates:

Master's Degree Graduates: Of those who graduated in the academic year 2003–2004, the following categories and numbers represent the post-graduate activities and employment of master's degree graduates: Enrolled in a post-doctoral residency/fellowship (n/a), employed in independent practice (n/a), total from the above (master's) (0).

Doctoral Degree Graduates: Of those who graduated in the academic year 2003–2004, the following categories and numbers represent the post-graduate activities and employment of doctoral degree graduates: Enrolled in a psychology doctoral program (n/a), employed in independent practice (22), employed in an academic position at a university (4), employed in an academic position at a 2-year/4-year college (2), employed in other positions at a higher education institution (2), employed in a professional position in a school system (2), employed in a government agency (professional services) (3), employed in a community mental health/counseling center (9), employed in a hospital/medical center (4), total from the above (doctoral) (48).

Additional Information:

Orientation, Objectives, and Emphasis of Department: The Clinical Psychology PhD Program at SPU is designed to provide training in professional psychology in accordance with the Local Clinical Scientist (LCS) model of doctoral education, described in the article, "The Local Clinical Scientist: a Bridge Between Science and Practice", published in *American Psychologist* (Stricker & Trierweiler, 1995). The Local Clinical Scientist extends the scientific and professional ideals in the original Boulder Scientist-Practitioner (BSP) model of clinical psychology (Raimy, 1950). At the same time, we try to encompass broader concepts of science and more explicitly integrate the art of clinical practice. We also endorse the core competencies outlined by the National Council of Schools and Programs of Professional Psychology (NCSPP) and are committed to helping students achieve mastery of the core competencies of clinical skills. Our doctoral program typically requires four years of graduate coursework, during which clinical practicum training as well as dissertation research are also completed, followed by a one-year full-time internship (elsewhere) in the fifth year. Our PhD program follows APA Guidelines and Principles for Accreditation of Programs in Professional Psychology [although we are not currently APA accredited] and our curriculum meets the educational requirements for licensing psychologists in the State of Washington and many other states.

Special Facilities or Resources: The School maintains a fully-equipped suite of psychology research laboratories, including a psycho-physiological lab, child-developmental lab, and social psychology lab. The University's newly-opened Science Building contains a suite of wet labs and animal learning facilities as well as a psycho-physiological demonstration classroom. The Department is housed in Marston Hall, which was completely renovated for us in 2001. The University Library is a 4-story structure with conference rooms, private study rooms and group meeting rooms. The library contains approximately 10,000 volumes relevant to the field of psychology, including books, media, a test file, and over 500 journals available either in paper, microfilm, and full-text online. In addition to traditional inter-library loan services, Seattle Pacific University is a member of ORCA, a consortium of 26 public and private academic libraries in Washington and Oregon which provides access to a combined collection of over 22 million volumes of books and other materials. Students have access to several computer labs on campus, which have SPSS installed. Each student gets an SPU e-mail account and the 24/7 access to our "Blackboard", where program forms, syllabi, schedules, etc. are posted for students to download.

Application Information:

Send to: SPU Graduate Center or Program Coordinator, Graduate Psychology Department. Application available online. URL of online application: https://app.applyyourself.com/?id=spu-grad. Students are admitted in the Fall, application deadline January 15. *Fee:* $75.

Seattle University
Graduate Psychology Program
Arts and Sciences
P.B. 222000
Seattle, WA 98122-4460
Telephone: (206) 296-5400
Fax: (206) 296-2141
E-mail: *gradpsyc@seattleu.edu*
Web: *http://www.seattleu.edu*

Department Information:

1981. Director, Graduate Program: Jan Rowe, PhD. Number of Faculty: total–full-time 6, part-time 2; women–full-time 2, part-time 1.

Programs and Degrees Offered:

Listed in the following order: Program area, degree type (T if terminal Master's), number awarded 7/03–6/04. Existential-phenomenological MA/MS (Master of Arts/Science) (T) 17.

Student Applications/Admissions:

Student Applications

*Existential-Phenomenological MA/MS (Master of Arts/Science)—*Applications 2004–2005, 60. Total applicants accepted 2004–2005, 22. Number enrolled (new admits only) 2004–2005 full-time, 18. Total enrolled 2004–2005 full-time, 41, part-time, 1. Openings 2005–2006, 20. The Median number of years required for completion of a degree are 2. The number of students enrolled full and part-time who were dismissed or voluntarily withdrew from this program area were 1.

Admissions Requirements:

Scores: Entries appear in this order: required test or GPA, minimum score (if required), median score of students entering in 2003–2004. Master's Programs: overall undergraduate GPA no minimum stated. Overall undergraduate GPA 3.0

Other Criteria: (importance of criteria rated low, medium, or high): research experience low, work experience low, extracurricular activity medium, clinically related public service medium, GPA medium, letters of recommendation medium, interview medium, Bio/writing sample. Other: Some awareness of existential-phenomenological perspective.

Student Characteristics: The following represents characteristics of students in 2004–2005 in all graduate psychology programs in the department: Female–full-time 33, part-time 1; Male–full-time 8, part-time 0; African American/Black–full-time 1, part-time 0;

Hispanic/Latino(a)–part-time 0; Asian/Pacific Islander–part-time 0; American Indian/Alaska Native–part-time 0; Caucasian–full-time 0, part-time 0; students subject to the Americans With Disabilities Act–full-time 0, part-time 0.

Financial Information/Assistance:

Tuition for Full-Time Study: *Master's:* State residents: $488 per credit hour; Nonstate residents: $488 per credit hour. Tuition is subject to change.

Financial Assistance:

First Year Students: No information provided.
Advanced Students: No information provided.
Contact Information: Of all students currently enrolled full-time, 0% benefitted from one or more of the listed financial assistance programs.

Internships/Practica: Supervised internships (typically about 20 hrs/week during second year) are available in a wide variety of community agencies, hospitals, shelters, and clinics.

Housing and Day Care: On-campus housing is available. See the following Web site for more information: www.seattleu.edu/housing, or write to Seattle University, P.B. 222000, Seattle, Washington 98122, att: Housing and Residential Life. No on-campus day care facilities are available.

Employment of Department Graduates:

Master's Degree Graduates: Of those who graduated in the academic year 2003–2004, the following categories and numbers represent the post-graduate activities and employment of master's degree graduates: Enrolled in a psychology doctoral program (1), enrolled in another graduate/professional program (2), enrolled in a post-doctoral residency/fellowship (n/a), employed in independent practice (n/a), employed in an academic position at a university (0), employed in an academic position at a 2-year/4-year college (0), employed in other positions at a higher education institution (0), employed in a professional position in a school system (0), employed in business or industry (research/consulting) (0), employed in business or industry (management) (0), employed in a government agency (research) (0), employed in a government agency (professional services) (0), employed in a community mental health/counseling center (9), employed in a hospital/medical center (0), still seeking employment (2), other employment position (4), total from the above (master's) (18).
Doctoral Degree Graduates: Of those who graduated in the academic year 2003–2004, the following categories and numbers represent the post-graduate activities and employment of doctoral degree graduates: Enrolled in a psychology doctoral program (n/a), total from the above (doctoral) (0).

Additional Information:

Orientation, Objectives, and Emphasis of Department: With an emphasis on existential-phenomenological psychology, this master's degree is designed to offer an interdisciplinary program focusing on the qualitative, experiential study of psychological events in the context of life. By laying the foundations for a therapeutic attitude, the program will prepare students for entrance into the helping professions or for further study of the psychological world. It is humanistic in that it intends to deepen the appreciation for the human condition by rigorous reflection on immediate psychological experiences and on the wisdom accumulated by the long tradition of the humanities. It is phenomenological in that it develops an attitude of openness and wonder toward psychological reality without holding theoretical prejudgments. It is therapeutic in that it focuses on the psychological conditions that help people deal with the difficulties of life.

Application Information:

Send to: (1) Graduate Admissions Office, Seattle University, 900 Broadway, Seattle, WA 98122, and some material goes to (2) Graduate Psychology, Seattle University, 900 Broadway, Seattle, WA 98122. Students are admitted in the Fall, application deadline January 25. *Fee:* $55.

Walla Walla College
School of Education and Psychology
204 South College Avenue
College Place, WA 99324
Telephone: (509) 527-2211, (800) 541-8900
Fax: (509) 527-2248
E-mail: *stoule@wwc.edu*
Web: *http://www.wwc.edu/counseling*

Department Information:

1965. Dean: Mark Haynal. Number of Faculty: total–full-time 6, part-time 1; women–full-time 3, part-time 1; minority–full-time 2.

Programs and Degrees Offered:

Listed in the following order: Program area, degree type (T if terminal Master's), number awarded 7/03–6/04. Counseling Psychology MA/MS (Master of Arts/Science) (T) 3.

Student Applications/Admissions:

Student Applications

Counseling Psychology MA/MS (Master of Arts/Science)—Applications 2004–2005, 10. Total applicants accepted 2004–2005, 9. Number enrolled (new admits only) 2004–2005 full-time, 7. Number enrolled (new admits only) 2004–2005 part-time, 1. Total enrolled 2004–2005 full-time, 13, part-time, 2. Openings 2005–2006, 9. The Median number of years required for completion of a degree are 2. The number of students enrolled full and part-time who were dismissed or voluntarily withdrew from this program area were 1.

Admissions Requirements:

Scores: Entries appear in this order: required test or GPA, minimum score (if required), median score of students entering in 2003–2004. Master's Programs: GRE-V+Q no minimum stated, 970; overall undergraduate GPA 2.75, 3.2.
Other Criteria: (importance of criteria rated low, medium, or high): GRE/MAT scores low, research experience low, work experience medium, extracurricular activity low, clinically related public service medium, GPA high, letters of recommendation high, interview high, statement of goals and objectives high.

Student Characteristics: The following represents characteristics of students in 2004–2005 in all graduate psychology programs in the department: Female–full-time 13, part-time 1; Male–full-time

0, part-time 1; Hispanic/Latino(a)–full-time 1, part-time 0; Caucasian–full-time 11, part-time 2; Multi-ethnic–full-time 1, part-time 0.

Financial Information/Assistance:

Tuition for Full-Time Study: *Master's:* State residents: $462 per credit hour; Nonstate residents: $462 per credit hour. Tuition is subject to change.

Financial Assistance:

First Year Students: Fellowships and scholarships available for first-year. Average amount paid per academic year: $4,112. Average number of hours worked per week: 0.

Advanced Students: Fellowships and scholarships available for advanced students. Average amount paid per academic year: $4,112. Average number of hours worked per week: 0.

Contact Information: Of all students currently enrolled full-time, 100% benefitted from one or more of the listed financial assistance programs.

Internships/Practica: The School of Education and Psychology operates a free counseling center for the community on site. The counseling center comprises four private counseling rooms and a group room that are equipped with one-way mirrors, video-cameras, and audio-taping capabilities. During the second year of their program, students begin working in the center and have the opportunity to develop their clinical skills counseling individuals, couples, and families presenting with a variety of concerns. Program faculty provide individual and group supervision in either live or videotaped formats on a regular basis. After successfully completing the supervised practica, students complete a 400-600 hour internship at an approved site in the community. The School has developed relationships with various agencies where students will receive quality internship experiences that fit their interests.

Housing and Day Care: On-campus housing is available: Student Administration, Walla Walla College, 204 South College Avenue, College Place, WA 99324. On-campus day care facilities are available: Child Development Center, Walla Walla College, 204 South College Avenue, College Place, WA 99324.

Employment of Department Graduates:

Master's Degree Graduates: Of those who graduated in the academic year 2003–2004, the following categories and numbers represent the post-graduate activities and employment of master's degree graduates: Enrolled in a post-doctoral residency/fellowship (n/a), employed in independent practice (n/a), employed in a community mental health/counseling center (3), total from the above (master's) (3).

Doctoral Degree Graduates: Of those who graduated in the academic year 2003–2004, the following categories and numbers represent the post-graduate activities and employment of doctoral degree graduates: Enrolled in a psychology doctoral program (n/a), total from the above (doctoral) (0).

Additional Information:

Orientation, Objectives, and Emphasis of Department: The School of Education and Psychology offers thesis and non-thesis Master of Arts degrees in counseling psychology. Our program is designed to promote clinical, theoretical, academic, and personal growth through study, supervision, and service. Students are expected to attain a broad range of competence in the core areas

in counseling psychology including human development and learning, individual and group counseling, career development, assessment, ethics, research, and statistics. Faculty present varied theoretical positions so that students may make comparisons and have opportunities to develop their own positions. Students acquire a range of clinical skills they can use in working with diverse clients and learn to apply theory to practice through supervised practica and internship experiences. In a supportive, yet challenging environment, students are encouraged to build upon life experiences and personal strengths, and take advantage of the opportunities to expand their awareness of self and others. If students desire, faculty assist them in the development and application of a philosophy of Christian service. All graduates are prepared to take the National Counselor's Exam and to become licensed Mental Health Counselors, or to continue their training in doctoral programs.

Special Facilities or Resources: The School of Education and Psychology operates a free counseling center for the community where ongoing outcome research is being conducted. An enriched preschool program for children ages 3-5 is located in the on-site child development center.

Application Information:

Send to: Graduate Studies, Walla Walla College, 204 South College Avenue, College Place, WA 99324. Application available online. URL of online application: http://www.wwc.edu/academics/graduate/checklist.html. Students are admitted in the Fall. *Fee:* $50.

Washington State University
Department of Psychology
P.O. Box 644820
Pullman, WA 99164-4820
Telephone: (509) 335-2631
Fax: (509) 335-5043
E-mail: *psych@wsu.edu*
Web: *http://www.wsu.edu/psychology*

Department Information:

Chairperson: Paul Whitney. Number of Faculty: total–full-time 30, part-time 5; women–full-time 12, part-time 4; minority–full-time 4, part-time 2.

Programs and Degrees Offered:

Listed in the following order: Program area, degree type (T if terminal Master's), number awarded 7/03–6/04. Clinical PhD (Doctor of Philosophy) 5, Experimental PhD (Doctor of Philosophy) 3.

APA Accreditation: Clinical PhD (Doctor of Philosophy).

Student Applications/Admissions:

Student Applications

Clinical PhD (Doctor of Philosophy)—Applications 2004–2005, 156. Total applicants accepted 2004–2005, 8. Openings 2005–2006, 6. The Median number of years required for completion of a degree are 5. The number of students enrolled full and part-time who were dismissed or voluntarily withdrew from this

program area were 0. *Experimental PhD (Doctor of Philosophy)*—
Applications 2004–2005, 35. Total applicants accepted 2004–
2005, 7. Total enrolled 2004–2005 full-time, 21. Openings
2005–2006, 6. The Median number of years required for completion of a degree are 5. The number of students enrolled
full and part-time who were dismissed or voluntarily withdrew
from this program area were 1.

Admissions Requirements:

Scores: Entries appear in this order: required test or GPA,
minimum score (if required), median score of students entering
in 2003–2004. Doctoral Programs: GRE-V no minimum stated,
600; GRE-Q no minimum stated, 595; GRE-V+Q no minimum stated, 1195; overall undergraduate GPA no minimum
stated, 3.62; psychology GPA no minimum stated, 3.70.

Other Criteria: (importance of criteria rated low, medium, or
high): GRE/MAT scores medium, research experience high,
work experience low, extracurricular activity low, clinically
related public service high, GPA high, letters of recommendation high, interview high, statement of goals and objectives
high. Applicants to the Experimental Psychology program are
not expected to demonstrate any clinically-related public service and are not required to have an interview, but a visit is
encouraged.

Student Characteristics: The following represents characteristics
of students in 2004–2005 in all graduate psychology programs in
the department: Female–full-time 33, part-time 0; Male–full-time
20, part-time 0; African American/Black–full-time 0, part-time
0; Hispanic/Latino(a)–full-time 4, part-time 0; Asian/Pacific Islander–full-time 3, part-time 0; American Indian/Alaska Native–
full-time 2, part-time 0; Caucasian–full-time 45, part-time 0.

Financial Information/Assistance:

Financial Assistance:

First Year Students: Teaching assistantships available for
first-year. Average amount paid per academic year: $11,000. Average number of hours worked per week: 20. Apply by January 1.
Tuition remission given: full.

Advanced Students: Teaching assistantships available for
advanced students. Average amount paid per academic year:
$11,000. Average number of hours worked per week: 20. Tuition
remission given: full.

Contact Information: Of all students currently enrolled full-
time, 100% benefitted from one or more of the listed financial
assistance programs.

Internships/Practica: Psychology Clinic Practicum; Counseling
Services Practicum; Medical Psychology Practicum at University
Hospital. For those doctoral students for whom a professional
internship is required prior to graduation, 7 applied in 2003–
2004. Of those who applied, 7 were placed in APA accredited
internships.

Housing and Day Care: On-campus housing is available. See
the following Web site for more information: www.wsu.edu. On-
campus day care facilities are available.

Employment of Department Graduates:

Master's Degree Graduates: Of those who graduated in the
academic year 2003–2004, the following categories and numbers
represent the post-graduate activities and employment of master's

degree graduates: Enrolled in a post-doctoral residency/fellowship
(n/a), employed in independent practice (n/a), total from the
above (master's) (0).

Doctoral Degree Graduates: Of those who graduated in the academic year 2003–2004, the following categories and numbers
represent the post-graduate activities and employment of doctoral
degree graduates: Enrolled in a psychology doctoral program (n/a),
enrolled in a post-doctoral residency/fellowship (2), employed in
an academic position at a university (1), employed in an academic
position at a 2-year/4-year college (2), employed in a government
agency (professional services) (1), employed in a community mental health/counseling center (1), employed in a hospital/medical
center (1), total from the above (doctoral) (8).

Additional Information:

Orientation, Objectives, and Emphasis of Department: The objectives of the graduate programs are to prepare individuals to
make contributions and hold leadership positions in basic and
applied research, teaching, clinical psychology, public service, or
some combination of these areas. The clinical program is a broad,
general one requiring student commitment to both research and
clinical work. The emphases within the experimental program are
cognitive psychology, behavior analysis, physiological psychology,
sensation and perception, and applied psychology.

Special Facilities or Resources: The Department of Psychology
is located in Johnson Tower, near the center of campus. Fully
equipped laboratories and shop facilities are available for research
in social behavior, cognition, perception, human and animal
learning, the experimental and applied analysis of behavior, and
physiological and sensory psychology. The Psychology Clinic is
operated as a training facility within the department.

Application Information:
Send to: Graduate Admissions, Attn: Chair, Graduate Admissions
Committee, Psychology Department, Washington State University,
P.O. Box 644820, Pullman, WA 99164-4820. Students are admitted
in the Fall, application deadline January 1. *Fee:* $35.

Washington, University of (2004 data)
Department of Psychology
Arts & Sciences
Box 351525
Seattle, WA 98195-1525
Telephone: (206) 543-2640
Fax: (206) 685-3157
E-mail: *psygrad@u.washington.edu*
Web: *http://web.psych.washington.edu*

Department Information:
1917. Chairperson: Ana Mari Cauce, PhD. Number of Faculty:
total–full-time 43, part-time 4; women–full-time 17, part-time 4;
minority–full-time 7.

Programs and Degrees Offered:
Listed in the following order: Program area, degree type (T if
terminal Master's), number awarded 7/03–6/04. Animal Behavior
PhD (Doctor of Philosophy) 0, Clinical PhD (Doctor of Philosophy) 10, Child Clinical PhD (Doctor of Philosophy) 1, Cognition

and Perception PhD (Doctor of Philosophy) 5, Developmental PhD (Doctor of Philosophy) 0, Behavioral Neuroscience PhD (Doctor of Philosophy) 1, Social and Personality PhD (Doctor of Philosophy) 4.

APA Accreditation: Clinical PhD (Doctor of Philosophy).

Student Applications/Admissions:

Student Applications

Animal Behavior PhD (Doctor of Philosophy)—Applications 2004–2005, 33. Total applicants accepted 2004–2005, 4. Openings 2005–2006, 2. The Median number of years required for completion of a degree are 9. The number of students enrolled full and part-time who were dismissed or voluntarily withdrew from this program area were 1. *Clinical PhD (Doctor of Philosophy)*—Applications 2004–2005, 185. Total applicants accepted 2004–2005, 7. Total enrolled 2004–2005 full-time, 34, part-time, 4. Openings 2005–2006, 56. The Median number of years required for completion of a degree are 8. The number of students enrolled full and part-time who were dismissed or voluntarily withdrew from this program area were 0. *Child Clinical PhD (Doctor of Philosophy)*—Applications 2004–2005, 166. Total applicants accepted 2004–2005, 6. Total enrolled 2004–2005 full-time, 24, part-time, 3. Openings 2005–2006, 4. The Median number of years required for completion of a degree are 8. The number of students enrolled full and part-time who were dismissed or voluntarily withdrew from this program area were 0. *Cognition and Perception PhD (Doctor of Philosophy)*—Applications 2004–2005, 39. Total applicants accepted 2004–2005, 5. Total enrolled 2004–2005 full-time, 20, part-time, 2. Openings 2005–2006, 34. The Median number of years required for completion of a degree are 6. The number of students enrolled full and part-time who were dismissed or voluntarily withdrew from this program area were 1. *Developmental PhD (Doctor of Philosophy)*—Applications 2004–2005, 39. Total applicants accepted 2004–2005, 5. Total enrolled 2004–2005 full-time, 13, part-time, 1. Openings 2005–2006, 34. The Median number of years required for completion of a degree are 10. The number of students enrolled full and part-time who were dismissed or voluntarily withdrew from this program area were 1. *Behavioral Neuroscience PhD (Doctor of Philosophy)*—Applications 2004–2005, 13. Total applicants accepted 2004–2005, 4. Total enrolled 2004–2005 full-time, 17, part-time, 1. Openings 2005–2006, 2. The Median number of years required for completion of a degree are 6. The number of students enrolled full and part-time who were dismissed or voluntarily withdrew from this program area were 0. *Social and Personality PhD (Doctor of Philosophy)*—Applications 2004–2005, 50. Total applicants accepted 2004–2005, 4. Total enrolled 2004–2005 full-time, 8, part-time, 2. Openings 2005–2006, 3. The Median number of years required for completion of a degree are 8. The number of students enrolled full and part-time who were dismissed or voluntarily withdrew from this program area were 0.

Admissions Requirements:

Scores: Entries appear in this order: required test or GPA, minimum score (if required), median score of students entering in 2003–2004. Doctoral Programs: GRE-V no minimum stated, 630; GRE-Q no minimum stated, 720; GRE-V+Q 1200, 1350;

last 2 years GPA no minimum stated, 3.85. Clinical Area GPAs are generally higher. Please refer to chart on webpage for figures for most recent admissions by individual area (http://depts.washington.edu/psych) (graduate programs/online application/admission statistics).

Other Criteria: (importance of criteria rated low, medium, or high): GRE/MAT scores high, research experience high, work experience medium, extracurricular activity low, clinically related public service low, GPA medium, letters of recommendation high, interview high, statement of goals and objectives high. Individual areas evaluate applications differently, but all require a strong background in research experience and/or statistics.

Student Characteristics: The following represents characteristics of students in 2004–2005 in all graduate psychology programs in the department: Female–full-time 90, part-time 14; Male–full-time 37, part-time 0; African American/Black–full-time 1, part-time 0; Hispanic/Latino(a)–full-time 5, part-time 0; Asian/Pacific Islander–full-time 16, part-time 1; American Indian/Alaska Native–full-time 3, part-time 1; Caucasian–full-time 0, part-time 0; Multi-ethnic–full-time 2, part-time 0; students subject to the Americans With Disabilities Act–full-time 1, part-time 1.

Financial Information/Assistance:

Tuition for Full-Time Study: *Doctoral:* State residents: per academic year $6,543; Nonstate residents: per academic year $15,630. Tuition is subject to change. See the following Web site for updates and changes in tuition costs: http://www.washington.edu/students/sfs/sao/tuition/ttn_grad1.html.

Financial Assistance:

First Year Students: Teaching assistantships available for first-year. Average amount paid per academic year: $13,050. Average number of hours worked per week: 20. Tuition remission given: full. Research assistantships available for first-year. Average amount paid per academic year: $13,050. Average number of hours worked per week: 20. Tuition remission given: full. Traineeships available for first-year. Average amount paid per academic year: $13,050. Average number of hours worked per week: 20. Tuition remission given: full.

Advanced Students: Teaching assistantships available for advanced students. Average amount paid per academic year: $13,950. Average number of hours worked per week: 20. Tuition remission given: full. Research assistantships available for advanced students. Average amount paid per academic year: $13,950. Average number of hours worked per week: 20. Tuition remission given: full. Traineeships available for advanced students. Average amount paid per academic year: $13,950. Average number of hours worked per week: 20. Tuition remission given: full.

Contact Information: Of all students currently enrolled full-time, 95% benefitted from one or more of the listed financial assistance programs.

Internships/Practica: A variety of local and national predoctoral internships are available in clinical psychology. For those doctoral students for whom a professional internship is required prior to graduation, 8 applied in 2003–2004. Of those who applied, 8 were placed in internships listed by the Association of Psychology Postdoctoral and Internship Programs (APPIC); 8 were placed in APA accredited internships.

Housing and Day Care: On-campus housing is available. See the following Web site for more information: www.washington.edu/students/hfs. On-campus day care facilities are available. www.washington.edu/students/ovpsa/cc/.

Employment of Department Graduates:

Master's Degree Graduates: Of those who graduated in the academic year 2003–2004, the following categories and numbers represent the post-graduate activities and employment of master's degree graduates: Enrolled in a post-doctoral residency/fellowship (n/a), employed in independent practice (n/a), total from the above (master's) (0).

Doctoral Degree Graduates: Of those who graduated in the academic year 2003–2004, the following categories and numbers represent the post-graduate activities and employment of doctoral degree graduates: Enrolled in a psychology doctoral program (n/a), enrolled in a post-doctoral residency/fellowship (5), employed in independent practice (1), employed in an academic position at a university (2), employed in other positions at a higher education institution (1), employed in a government agency (research) (1), employed in a community mental health/counseling center (1), employed in a hospital/medical center (1), do not know (3), total from the above (doctoral) (15).

Additional Information:

Orientation, Objectives, and Emphasis of Department: The program is committed to research-oriented scientific psychology. No degree programs are available in counseling or humanistic psychology. The clinical program emphasizes both clinical and research competencies and has areas of specialization in child clinical and subspecialities in behavioral medicine and health psychology, and community-minority psychology.

Special Facilities or Resources: University and urban settings provide many resources, including the university's hospital, child development and mental retardation center, counseling center, psychological services and training center, computer center, and regional primate center; Harborview Medical Center's Alcohol and Drug Abuse Center; Children's Hospital and Medical Center; nearby Veterans Administration facilities; and Seattle Mental Health Institute.

Information for Students With Physical Disabilities: See the following Web site for more information: http://www.washington.edu/students/gencat/front/Disabled_Student.html.

Application Information:
Send to: Graduate Selections Committee, Department of Psychology, Box 351525, University of Washington, Seattle, WA 98195-1525. Students are admitted in the Fall, application deadline December 15. November 1 for international applicants to UW Graduate School (available online); December 15 for international applicants to Psychology Department (downloadable application forms online). *Fee:* $50. $45 for online application paid by credit or debit card. Fee waived or deferred if U.S. citizen or permanent resident and financial need is approved by the Graduate School.

Washington, University of
Educational Psychology Area in College of Education
312 Miller Hall, Box 353600
Seattle, WA 98195-3600
Telephone: (206) 543-1846 or (206) 543-1139
Fax: (206) 543-8439
E-mail: *abbottr@u.washington.edu*
Web: *http://depts.washington.edu/coe/programs/ep/index.html*

Department Information:
1965. Chairperson: Robert D. Abbott. Number of Faculty: total–full-time 18, part-time 2; women–full-time 10; minority–full-time 4; faculty subject to the Americans With Disabilities Act 1.

Programs and Degrees Offered:
Listed in the following order: Program area, degree type (T if terminal Master's), number awarded 7/03–6/04. School Psychology Other 5, Human Development and Cognition Other 2, Measurement, Statistics and Research Design Other 1, Cognitive Studies in Education MEd & PhD Other 0, School Psychology PhD (Doctor of Philosophy) 3, Human Development and Cognition PhD (Doctor of Philosophy) 3, Measurement, Statistics and Research Design PhD (Doctor of Philosophy) 1.

APA Accreditation: School PhD (Doctor of Philosophy).

Student Applications/Admissions:
Student Applications
School psychology Other—Applications 2004–2005, 51. Total applicants accepted 2004–2005, 8. Number enrolled (new admits only) 2004–2005 full-time, 8. Number enrolled (new admits only) 2004–2005 part-time, 0. Openings 2005–2006, 12. The Median number of years required for completion of a degree are 3. The number of students enrolled full and part-time who were dismissed or voluntarily withdrew from this program area were 0. *Human Development and Cognition Other*—Applications 2004–2005, 29. Total applicants accepted 2004–2005, 5. Total enrolled 2004–2005 full-time, 7. Openings 2005–2006, 10. The Median number of years required for completion of a degree are 3. The number of students enrolled full and part-time who were dismissed or voluntarily withdrew from this program area were 0. *Measurement, Statistics and Research Design Other*—Applications 2004–2005, 13. Total applicants accepted 2004–2005, 2. Openings 2005–2006, 6. The Median number of years required for completion of a degree are 3. The number of students enrolled full and part-time who were dismissed or voluntarily withdrew from this program area were 0. *Cognitive Studies in Education MEd and PhD Other*—Applications 2004–2005, 30. Total applicants accepted 2004–2005, 12. Total enrolled 2004–2005 full-time, 21. Openings 2005–2006, 12. The number of students enrolled full and part-time who were dismissed or voluntarily withdrew from this program area were 0. *School Psychology PhD (Doctor of Philosophy)*—Applications 2004–2005, 4. Total applicants accepted 2004–2005, 1. Number enrolled (new admits only) 2004–2005 full-time, 1. Total enrolled 2004–2005 full-time, 15. Openings 2005–2006, 5. The Median number of years required for completion of a degree are 2. The number of students enrolled full and part-time who were dismissed or voluntarily withdrew from this program area were 0. *Human*

Development and Cognition PhD (Doctor of Philosophy)—Applications 2004–2005, 8. Total applicants accepted 2004–2005, 2. Total enrolled 2004–2005 full-time, 9, part-time, 12. Openings 2005–2006, 5. The Median number of years required for completion of a degree are 7. The number of students enrolled full and part-time who were dismissed or voluntarily withdrew from this program area were 0. *Measurement, Statistics and Research Design PhD (Doctor of Philosophy)*—Applications 2004–2005, 7. Total applicants accepted 2004–2005, 4. Total enrolled 2004–2005 full-time, 5, part-time, 7. The Median number of years required for completion of a degree are 5. The number of students enrolled full and part-time who were dismissed or voluntarily withdrew from this program area were 0.

Admissions Requirements:

Scores: Entries appear in this order: required test or GPA, minimum score (if required), median score of students entering in 2003–2004. Master's Programs: GRE-V 500, 530; GRE-Q 500, 600; GRE-V+Q 1000; last 2 years GPA 3.0, 3.6. School Psychology: GRE V+Q=1000, minimum of 500 each in V+Q or 50th percentile, which ever is higher. Doctoral Programs: GRE-V 500, 590; GRE-Q 500, 620.

Other Criteria: (importance of criteria rated low, medium, or high): GRE/MAT scores high, research experience medium, work experience high, clinically related public service medium, GPA high, letters of recommendation high, interview medium, statement of goals and objectives high.

Student Characteristics: The following represents characteristics of students in 2004–2005 in all graduate psychology programs in the department: Female–full-time 23, part-time 7; Male–full-time 2, part-time 1; African American/Black–full-time 1, part-time 0; Hispanic/Latino(a)–full-time 2, part-time 0; Asian/Pacific Islander–full-time 4, part-time 0; American Indian/Alaska Native–full-time 0, part-time 0; Caucasian–full-time 0, part-time 0; Multi-ethnic–full-time 0, part-time 0; students subject to the Americans With Disabilities Act–full-time 0, part-time 0.

Financial Information/Assistance:

Tuition for Full-Time Study: *Master's:* State residents: per academic year $6,508; Nonstate residents: per academic year $15,595. *Doctoral:* State residents: per academic year $6,508; Nonstate residents: per academic year $15,595. See the following Web site for updates and changes in tuition costs: http://www.washington.edu/students/sfs/sao/tuition/ttn_grad1.html.

Financial Assistance:

First Year Students: Teaching assistantships available for first-year. Average amount paid per academic year: $11,340. Average number of hours worked per week: 20. Apply by April/filled. Tuition remission given: full. Research assistantships available for first-year. Average amount paid per academic year: $11,340. Average number of hours worked per week: 20. Apply by Open. Tuition remission given: full. Fellowships and scholarships available for first-year. Apply by Open/Spring. Tuition remission given: full and partial.

Advanced Students: Teaching assistantships available for advanced students. Average amount paid per academic year: $13,095. Average number of hours worked per week: 20. Apply by April/filled. Tuition remission given: full. Research assistantships available for advanced students. Average amount paid per academic year: $13,095. Average number of hours worked per week: 20. Apply by Open. Tuition remission given: full. Traineeships available for advanced students. Average amount paid per academic year: $25,000. Average number of hours worked per week: 40. Apply by Winter. Fellowships and scholarships available for advanced students. Apply by Open/Spring. Tuition remission given: full and partial.

Contact Information: Of all students currently enrolled full-time, 40% benefitted from one or more of the listed financial assistance programs.

Internships/Practica: During the third year, master's students complete a 1500-hour internship in the public schools which is often paid.

Housing and Day Care: On-campus housing is available. See the following Web sites for more information: http://www.washington.edu/hfs/; http://www.washington.edu/hfs/famhous.html; http://depts.washington.edu/asuwsha/. On-campus day care facilities are available. See the following Web sites for more information: Childcare Assistance Program for Students: http://www.washington.edu/students/ovpsa/cc/ and "Resources for Graduate Students" with more info on childcare: http://www.grad.washington.edu/area/area_stud.htm.

Employment of Department Graduates:

Master's Degree Graduates: Of those who graduated in the academic year 2003–2004, the following categories and numbers represent the post-graduate activities and employment of master's degree graduates: Enrolled in a post-doctoral residency/fellowship (n/a), employed in independent practice (n/a), employed in a professional position in a school system (10), total from the above (master's) (10).

Doctoral Degree Graduates: Of those who graduated in the academic year 2003–2004, the following categories and numbers represent the post-graduate activities and employment of doctoral degree graduates: Enrolled in a psychology doctoral program (n/a), enrolled in a post-doctoral residency/fellowship (2), employed in an academic position at a university (3), employed in other positions at a higher education institution (1), employed in a professional position in a school system (5), total from the above (doctoral) (11).

Additional Information:

Orientation, Objectives, and Emphasis of Department: The emphasis is on the application of psychology to educational processes. The doctoral programs require extensive research preparation and involvement in research projects during a doctoral student's entire program. The master's degree program in School Psychology leads to national Certification as a School Psychologist (NCSP). The doctoral program in School Psychology also includes internship experience and coursework necessary for licensure as a psychologist.

Special Facilities or Resources: Library and computer facilities are of high quality and accessibility. A well-staffed Clinical Training Laboratory, located in the same building as classrooms and faculty offices, provides psychological services supervised by program faculty to infants, toddlers, school-aged children, and their parents. This clinic has video and audio recording, observation rooms, and microcomputers to support clinical services and research efforts, as well as an extensive library of psychological tests. There are within the University of Washington several other departments and programs with behavioral science emphases, including a health sciences complex that offers resources for coursework, clinical experience, and supervision.

Information for Students With Physical Disabilities: See the following Web site for more information: http://www.washington.edu/admin/eoo/dso/.

Application Information:
Send to: Office of Admissions and Academic Support, College of Education, 206 Miller, Box 353600, University of Washington, Seattle, WA 98195-3600. Students are admitted in the Fall, application deadline December 15; Winter, application deadline November 1; Spring, application deadline February 1; Summer, application deadline December 15. Deadlines vary for all of our degree programs in Educational Psychology. School Psychology MEd and PhD programs have December 15 deadline only (for entry in Summer or Autumn quarters). Only Measurement, Statistics & Research Design allows for year-round applications and four-quarter entry. *Fee:* $45.

Marshall University
Department of Psychology
Liberal Arts
One John Marshall Drive
Huntington, WV 25755-2672
Telephone: (304) 696-6446
Fax: (304) 696-2784
E-mail: *psych@marshall.edu*
Web: *http://www.marshall.edu/psych*

Department Information:
Chairperson: Martin Amerikaner. Number of Faculty: total–full-time 19, part-time 15; women–full-time 7, part-time 9; minority–full-time 2; faculty subject to the Americans With Disabilities Act 1.

Programs and Degrees Offered:
Listed in the following order: Program area, degree type (T if terminal Master's), number awarded 7/03–6/04. Clinical PsyD (Doctor of Psychology), Psychology MA/MS (Master of Arts/Science) (T) 50.

Student Applications/Admissions:
Student Applications
Clinical PsyD (Doctor of Psychology)—Applications 2004–2005, 32. Total applicants accepted 2004–2005, 11. Number enrolled (new admits only) 2004–2005 full-time, 5. Number enrolled (new admits only) 2004–2005 part-time, 0. Total enrolled 2004–2005 full-time, 23, part-time, 2. Openings 2005–2006, 10. The number of students enrolled full and part-time who were dismissed or voluntarily withdrew from this program area were 0. *Psychology MA/MS (Master of Arts/Science)*—Applications 2004–2005, 35. Total applicants accepted 2004–2005, 22. Number enrolled (new admits only) 2004–2005 full-time, 10. Number enrolled (new admits only) 2004–2005 part-time, 2. Total enrolled 2004–2005 full-time, 32, part-time, 41. Openings 2005–2006, 25. The Median number of years required for completion of a degree are 3. The number of students enrolled full and part-time who were dismissed or voluntarily withdrew from this program area were 2.

Admissions Requirements:
Scores: Entries appear in this order: required test or GPA, minimum score (if required), median score of students entering in 2003–2004. Master's Programs: GRE-V 400, 475; GRE-Q 400, 490; GRE-V+Q 900, 965; overall undergraduate GPA 3.0, 3.5; psychology GPA no minimum stated, 3.5. Applicants not meeting critieria have alternative route to admission into the MA program via completing specified graduate coursework prior to admission; please see Psychology section of the Marshall University Graduate Catalog (www.marshall.edu/psych) for details. Doctoral Programs: GRE-V no minimum stated, 540; GRE-Q no minimum stated, 570; GRE-V+Q no minimum stated, 1110; overall undergraduate GPA no minimum stated, 3.75. Psy D program requires V and Q GRE, as well as transcripts showing all prievious academic grades/GPAs.

Other Criteria: (importance of criteria rated low, medium, or high): GRE/MAT scores medium, research experience medium, work experience medium, extracurricular activity medium, clinically related public service medium, GPA high, letters of recommendation medium, interview medium, statement of goals and objectives high. MA program admission is based primarily on GPA and GRE scores; PsyD program considers these plus statement of professional goals, clinical and research experience, commitment to and understanding of rural psychological service delivery, and letters of recommendation. An interview may be required of PsyD applicants. We accept PsyD students via two routes- those with masters degrees in PSY and those who are just begining their graduate education. Criteria are similar, but weightings are a bit different for each; professional experience and demonstrated experience with rural issues are weighted more heavily in our post-MA pool. For additional information on admission requirements, go to: www.marshall.edu/psych.

Student Characteristics: The following represents characteristics of students in 2004–2005 in all graduate psychology programs in the department: Female–full-time 43, part-time 31; Male–full-time 12, part-time 12; African American/Black–full-time 0, part-time 0; Hispanic/Latino(a)–full-time 0, part-time 0; Asian/Pacific Islander–full-time 1, part-time 1; American Indian/Alaska Native–full-time 1, part-time 0; Caucasian–full-time 53, part-time 42; Multi-ethnic–full-time 0, part-time 0.

Financial Information/Assistance:
Tuition for Full-Time Study: *Master's:* State residents: per academic year $4,040; Nonstate residents: per academic year $11,306. *Doctoral:* State residents: per academic year $6,178; Nonstate residents: per academic year $14,198. Tuition is subject to change. See the following Web site for updates and changes in tuition costs: www.marshall.edu. Figures above include applicable fees for 2004-05 academic year.

Financial Assistance:
First Year Students: Research assistantships available for first-year. Average amount paid per academic year: $6,000. Average number of hours worked per week: 20. Apply by ongoing. Tuition remission given: full. Traineeships available for first-year. Average amount paid per academic year: $6,000. Average number of hours worked per week: 20. Apply by ongoing. Tuition remission given: full.
Advanced Students: Teaching assistantships available for advanced students. Average amount paid per academic year: $6,000. Average number of hours worked per week: 20. Apply by April 15. Tuition remission given: full. Research assistantships available for advanced students. Average amount paid per academic year: $6,000. Average number of hours worked per week: 20. Apply by ongoing. Tuition remission given: full. Traineeships available for advanced students. Average amount paid per academic year: $6,000. Average number of hours worked per week: 20. Apply by ongoing. Tuition remission given: full.
Contact Information: Of all students currently enrolled full-time, 20% benefitted from one or more of the listed financial

assistance programs. Application and information available online at: http://www.marshall.edu/sfa/.

Internships/Practica: PsyD program: 2nd year students work in department's clinic in Huntington; 3rd year students work at variety of sites in the Huntington community, 4th year students work at rural placements. Some are in collaboration with primary medical facilites; some may require an overnight stay. For the 2005-06 year, both of our PsyD students who applied for internships via the APPIC system were accepted by an APA accredited site. Clinical MA: Practicum students work in Marshall's community clinic in Dunbar WV; master's level interns work in area mental health agencies. MA level students interested in I/O have access to a variety of business and organizational field placements.

Housing and Day Care: On-campus housing is available. See the following Web site for more information: http://www.marshall.edu/residence-services/ or contact (304) 696-6765. On-campus day care facilities are available. See the following Web site for more information: www.marshall.edu/coe/childdevelopment or contact Child Development Academy at (304) 523-5803.

Employment of Department Graduates:

Master's Degree Graduates: Of those who graduated in the academic year 2003–2004, the following categories and numbers represent the post-graduate activities and employment of master's degree graduates: Enrolled in a post-doctoral residency/fellowship (n/a), employed in independent practice (n/a), total from the above (master's) (0).

Doctoral Degree Graduates: Of those who graduated in the academic year 2003–2004, the following categories and numbers represent the post-graduate activities and employment of doctoral degree graduates: Enrolled in a psychology doctoral program (n/a), total from the above (doctoral) (0).

Additional Information:

Orientation, Objectives, and Emphasis of Department: Our PsyD program in Clinical Psychology (offered on our Huntington WV campus) accepted its first students in Fall 2002. Thus, we are not yet eligible for APA accreditation, which requires students to be at all levels of the program prior to applying; our intent is to apply for accreditation as soon as possible. The program's emphasis is on preparing scholar-practitioners for rural/underserved populations in Appalachia and other rural areas. Particular foci of the doctoral program include understanding the needs and challenges of working in rural communities, preparing doctoral level psychologists to work within these communities, and provision of services to those areas through the training program itself. A wide range of theoretical perspectives is represented on our faculty. The MA program is based in our S. Charleston, WV campus. The MA program can be individualized to address a variety of academic and professional objectives for students. There is an "area of emphasis" available in clinical psychology which prepares students for entry level clinical work at the MA level. Students can also take coursework and do research and field placements in interest areas such as I/O psychology and a variety of disciplinary areas such as developmental, cognitive, social, etc. The Psy MA program is a popular foundation program for students intending to complete Marshall's EdS program in School Psychology (contact the School Psychology Program in the Graduate College of Education and Human Services for more information).

Special Facilities or Resources: Departmental and university computer facilities are available to students for clinical work and for research projects in all programs. Online library resources are excellent. Through department clinics, clinical students are afforded the opportunity to work, under supervision, with clients from the community and university. Placements for PsyD students are available at nearby community mental health centers, state hospitals, and the VA and the Marshall University Medical School, as well as at a variety of more rural sites for advanced training. MA level students interested in I/O have access to a variety of business and organizational field placements. Faculty have a variety of active, ongoing research projects available for student collaboration.

Information for Students With Physical Disabilities: See the following Web site for more information: http://www.marshall.edu/disabled/.

Application Information:
Send to: MA Program: Admissions Office, Marshall University Graduate College, 100 Angus Peyton Drive, S. Charleston, WV 25303-1600. PsyD Program—see instructions on application materials. Application available online. URL of online application: http://www.marshall.edu/psych/psydprogram/psydprogram.htm#Access_Application_Materials. Students are admitted in the Fall: January 15 deadline for PsyD program (all new PsyD students start in subsequent Fall semester); MA program has ongoing review of applicants; new MA students can begin in any semester. *Fee:* $30. $40 for non-residents of West Virginia.

West Virginia University
Department of Counseling, Rehabilitation Counseling and
  Counseling Psychology, Counseling Psychology Program
Human Resources and Education
502 Allen Hall, P.O. Box 6122
Morgantown, WV 26506-6122
Telephone: (304) 293-3807
Fax: (304) 293-4082
E-mail: *vicki.railing@mail.wvu.edu*
Web: *http://www.hre.wvu.edu/~crc/*

Department Information:
1948. Chairperson: Margaret K. Glenn. Number of Faculty: total–full-time 10; women–full-time 5.

Programs and Degrees Offered:
Listed in the following order: Program area, degree type (T if terminal Master's), number awarded 7/03–6/04. Counseling Psychology PhD (Doctor of Philosophy) 9.

APA Accreditation: Counseling PhD (Doctor of Philosophy).

Student Applications/Admissions:
Student Applications
Counseling Psychology PhD (Doctor of Philosophy)—Applications 2004–2005, 0. Total applicants accepted 2004–2005, 0. Number enrolled (new admits only) 2004–2005 full-time, 0. Number enrolled (new admits only) 2004–2005 part-time, 0. Total enrolled 2004–2005 full-time, 22, part-time, 12. Open-

ings 2005–2006, 6. The Median number of years required for completion of a degree are 6. The number of students enrolled full and part-time who were dismissed or voluntarily withdrew from this program area were 1.

Admissions Requirements:
Scores: Entries appear in this order: required test or GPA, minimum score (if required), median score of students entering in 2003–2004. Doctoral Programs: GRE-V no minimum stated, 500; GRE-Q no minimum stated, 500; GRE-V+Q no minimum stated, 1000; GRE-Analytical no minimum stated, 500; overall undergraduate GPA no minimum stated, 2.80.
Other Criteria: (importance of criteria rated low, medium, or high): GRE/MAT scores medium, research experience medium, work experience medium, extracurricular activity medium, clinically related public service medium, GPA medium, letters of recommendation high, interview high, statement of goals and objectives high, goodness of fit high. For additional information on admission requirements, go to: http://www.hre.wvu.edu/crc/academic/phd_counseling.php.

Student Characteristics: The following represents characteristics of students in 2004–2005 in all graduate psychology programs in the department: Female–full-time 13, part-time 8; Male–full-time 9, part-time 4; African American/Black–full-time 1, part-time 3; Hispanic/Latino(a)–full-time 0, part-time 0; Asian/Pacific Islander–full-time 0, part-time 0; American Indian/Alaska Native–full-time 1, part-time 0; Caucasian–full-time 20, part-time 9; Multi-ethnic–full-time 0, part-time 0; students subject to the Americans With Disabilities Act–full-time 0, part-time 1.

Financial Information/Assistance:
Tuition for Full-Time Study: *Master's:* State residents: per academic year $4,332, $244 per credit hour; Nonstate residents: per academic year $12,442, $694 per credit hour. *Doctoral:* State residents: per academic year $4,332, $244 per credit hour; Nonstate residents: per academic year $12,442, $694 per credit hour. See the following Web site for updates and changes in tuition costs: http:/www.arc.wvu.edu/admissions/costs.html.

Financial Assistance:
First Year Students: Teaching assistantships available for first-year. Average amount paid per academic year: $7,164. Average number of hours worked per week: 20. Tuition remission given: full. Research assistantships available for first-year. Average amount paid per academic year: $7,164. Average number of hours worked per week: 20. Tuition remission given: full. Fellowships and scholarships available for first-year. Average amount paid per academic year: $15,000. Average number of hours worked per week: 0. Tuition remission given: full.
Advanced Students: Teaching assistantships available for advanced students. Average amount paid per academic year: $7,164. Average number of hours worked per week: 20. Tuition remission given: full. Research assistantships available for advanced students. Average amount paid per academic year: $7,164. Average number of hours worked per week: 20. Tuition remission given: full. Fellowships and scholarships available for advanced students. Average amount paid per academic year: $15,000. Average number of hours worked per week: 0. Tuition remission given: full.
Contact Information: Of all students currently enrolled full-time, 55% benefitted from one or more of the listed financial

assistance programs. Application and information available online at: http://www.wvu.edu/~finaid/.

Internships/Practica: The doctoral program offers a variety of opportunities for internship and practica experience. Some of the placement sites include: The federal prison system, mental health agencies, employee assistant programs, private practices, VA hospitals, local school systems, university counseling center, and others. For those doctoral students for whom a professional internship is required prior to graduation, 3 applied in 2003–2004. Of those who applied, 3 were placed in internships listed by the Association of Psychology Postdoctoral and Internship Programs (APPIC); 3 were placed in APA accredited internships.

Housing and Day Care: On-campus housing is available. See the following Web site for more information: There is on-campus housing at WVU and information can be obtained by calling (304) 293-5840 or going to www.sa.wvu.edu/housing. No on-campus day care facilities are available.

Employment of Department Graduates:
Master's Degree Graduates: Of those who graduated in the academic year 2003–2004, the following categories and numbers represent the post-graduate activities and employment of master's degree graduates: Enrolled in a post-doctoral residency/fellowship (n/a), employed in independent practice (n/a), total from the above (master's) (0).
Doctoral Degree Graduates: Of those who graduated in the academic year 2003–2004, the following categories and numbers represent the post-graduate activities and employment of doctoral degree graduates: Enrolled in a psychology doctoral program (n/a), enrolled in another graduate/professional program (0), enrolled in a post-doctoral residency/fellowship (0), employed in independent practice (2), employed in an academic position at a university (0), employed in an academic position at a 2-year/4-year college (0), employed in other positions at a higher education institution (3), employed in a professional position in a school system (0), employed in business or industry (research/consulting) (0), employed in business or industry (management) (0), employed in a government agency (research) (0), employed in a government agency (professional services) (1), employed in a community mental health/counseling center (2), employed in a hospital/medical center (0), still seeking employment (0), not seeking employment (0), other employment position (1), do not know (0), total from the above (doctoral) (9).

Additional Information:
Orientation, Objectives, and Emphasis of Department: The department represents a variety of theoretical orientations. The objective of the department is to train professionals to serve primarily clients who are relatively normal but who are experiencing difficulties related to personal adjustment, interpersonal relationships, developmental problems, crises, academic or career stress, or decisions. The employment settings for our graduates typically include college and university counseling and testing services, community mental health agencies, clinics, hospitals, schools, rehabilitation centers, correctional centers, the United States Armed Services, and private practice.

Special Facilities or Resources: Facilities include an extensive medical center, including video equipment and computer terminals; training and observation rooms; and practicum and internship sites in a variety of settings for master's and doctoral students.

Information for Students With Physical Disabilities: See the following Web site for more information: www.wvu.edu/~socjust/disability.htm.

Application Information:
Send to: Admissions Coordinator, Department of Counseling, Rehabilitation Counseling and Counseling Psychology, West Virginia University, P.O. Box 6122, Morgantown, WV 25606-6122. Application available online. URL of online application: http://www.hre.wvu.edu/crc/academic/cpsyappl.doc. Students are admitted in the Fall, application deadline December 1. Counseling Psychology doctoral program admits for Fall only. Application deadline is December 1. *Fee:* $50.

West Virginia University
Department of Psychology
Eberly College of Arts and Sciences
P.O. Box 6040
Morgantown, WV 26506-6040
Telephone: (304) 293-2001, ext. 31628
Fax: (304) 293-6606
E-mail: *Debra.Swinney@mail.wvu.edu*
Web: *http://www.as.wvu.edu/psyc*

Department Information:
1929. Chairperson: Michael Perone. Number of Faculty: total—full-time 24, part-time 1; women—full-time 9, part-time 1; minority—full-time 1.

Programs and Degrees Offered:
Listed in the following order: Program area, degree type (T if terminal Master's), number awarded 7/03–6/04. Life-Span Developmental PhD (Doctor of Philosophy) 3, Behavior Analysis PhD (Doctor of Philosophy) 5, Clinical Child PhD (Doctor of Philosophy) 30, Clinical PhD (Doctor of Philosophy) 4, Professional Master's in Clinical Psychology MA/MS (Master of Arts/Science) (T) 2.

APA Accreditation: Clinical PhD (Doctor of Philosophy).

Student Applications/Admissions:
Student Applications
Life-Span Developmental PhD (Doctor of Philosophy)—Applications 2004–2005, 14. Total applicants accepted 2004–2005, 5. Number enrolled (new admits only) 2004–2005 full-time, 5. Number enrolled (new admits only) 2004–2005 part-time, 0. Openings 2005–2006, 4. The Median number of years required for completion of a degree are 4. The number of students enrolled full and part-time who were dismissed or voluntarily withdrew from this program area were 0. Behavior Analysis PhD (Doctor of Philosophy)—Applications 2004–2005, 39. Total applicants accepted 2004–2005, 6. Number enrolled (new admits only) 2004–2005 full-time, 4. Number enrolled (new admits only) 2004–2005 part-time, 0. Openings 2005–2006, 5. The Median number of years required for completion of a degree are 4. The number of students enrolled full and part-

time who were dismissed or voluntarily withdrew from this program area were 2. Clinical Child PhD (Doctor of Philosophy)—Applications 2004–2005, 101. Total applicants accepted 2004–2005, 5. Number enrolled (new admits only) 2004–2005 full-time, 4. Number enrolled (new admits only) 2004–2005 part-time, 0. Openings 2005–2006, 5. The Median number of years required for completion of a degree are 5. The number of students enrolled full and part-time who were dismissed or voluntarily withdrew from this program area were 1. Clinical PhD (Doctor of Philosophy)—Applications 2004–2005, 71. Total applicants accepted 2004–2005, 6. Number enrolled (new admits only) 2004–2005 full-time, 5. Number enrolled (new admits only) 2004–2005 part-time, 0. Openings 2005–2006, 5. The Median number of years required for completion of a degree are 6. The number of students enrolled full and part-time who were dismissed or voluntarily withdrew from this program area were 1. Professional Master's in Clinical Psychology MA/MS (Master of Arts/Science)—Applications 2004–2005, 18. Total applicants accepted 2004–2005, 1. Number enrolled (new admits only) 2004–2005 full-time, 1. Number enrolled (new admits only) 2004–2005 part-time, 0. Openings 2005–2006, 2. The Median number of years required for completion of a degree are 2. The number of students enrolled full and part-time who were dismissed or voluntarily withdrew from this program area were 0.

Admissions Requirements:
Scores: Entries appear in this order: required test or GPA, minimum score (if required), median score of students entering in 2003–2004. Master's Programs: GRE-V no minimum stated; GRE-Q no minimum stated; GRE-V+Q 1000, 1130; GRE-Analytical no minimum stated; overall undergraduate GPA 3.00, 3.70; last 2 years GPA no minimum stated; psychology GPA no minimum stated. Doctoral Programs: GRE-V no minimum stated; GRE-Q no minimum stated; GRE-V+Q 1000, 1172; GRE-Analytical no minimum stated; GRE-Subject(Psych) no minimum stated, 650; overall undergraduate GPA 3.00, 3.73. The GRE Subject Test in Psychology is required for students applying to the Clinical or Clinical Child Psychology doctoral programs. The Subject Test is not required for students applying to the Behavior Analysis or Life-Span Developmental Psychology doctoral programs.
Other Criteria: (importance of criteria rated low, medium, or high): GRE/MAT scores high, research experience high, work experience medium, extracurricular activity medium, clinically related public service medium, GPA high, letters of recommendation high, interview high, statement of goals and objectives high. Match between faculty and student interests is of high importance. Only clinical programs give high value to clinically related public service.

Student Characteristics: The following represents characteristics of students in 2004–2005 in all graduate psychology programs in the department: Female—full-time 55, part-time 0; Male—full-time 16, part-time 0; African American/Black—full-time 1, part-time 0; Hispanic/Latino(a)—full-time 5, part-time 0; Asian/Pacific Islander—full-time 3, part-time 0; American Indian/Alaska Native—full-time 0, part-time 0; Caucasian—full-time 62, part-time 0; Multi-ethnic—full-time 0, part-time 0; students subject to the Americans With Disabilities Act—full-time 0, part-time 0.

Financial Information/Assistance:
Tuition for Full-Time Study: *Master's:* State residents: per academic year $4,332, $244 per credit hour; Nonstate residents: per academic year $12,442, $695 per credit hour. *Doctoral:* State residents: per academic year $4,332, $244 per credit hour; Nonstate residents: per academic year $12,442, $695 per credit hour. Tuition is subject to change.

Financial Assistance:
First Year Students: Teaching assistantships available for first-year. Average amount paid per academic year: $8,250. Average number of hours worked per week: 20. Apply by January 1. Tuition remission given: full. Research assistantships available for first-year. Average amount paid per academic year: $8,250. Average number of hours worked per week: 20. Apply by January 1. Tuition remission given: full. Traineeships available for first-year. Average amount paid per academic year: $8,250. Average number of hours worked per week: 20. Apply by January 1. Tuition remission given: full. Fellowships and scholarships available for first-year. Average amount paid per academic year: $17,250. Average number of hours worked per week: 0. Apply by January 1. Tuition remission given: full.

Advanced Students: Teaching assistantships available for advanced students. Average amount paid per academic year: $8,800. Average number of hours worked per week: 20. Apply by January 1. Tuition remission given: full. Research assistantships available for advanced students. Average amount paid per academic year: $8,800. Average number of hours worked per week: 20. Apply by January 1. Tuition remission given: full. Traineeships available for advanced students. Average amount paid per academic year: $8,800. Average number of hours worked per week: 20. Apply by January 1. Tuition remission given: full. Fellowships and scholarships available for advanced students. Average amount paid per academic year: $17,500. Average number of hours worked per week: 0. Apply by January 1. Tuition remission given: full.

Contact Information: Of all students currently enrolled full-time, 100% benefitted from one or more of the listed financial assistance programs.

Internships/Practica: Paid clinical placements at out-of-department sites are available for doctoral clinical students in their second year and beyond, or in their first year and beyond if entering with a master's degree and having clinical experience. These out-of-department practicum sites include WVU Carruth Counseling Center, "Kennedy" Federal Correctional Institution, Hopemont Hospital, Sharpe Hospital, a private practice, a pain rehabilitation program, various behavioral/community mental health agencies and children and youth services agencies. These sites are located in Morgantown, and across the state and region. Practica pay stipends that range from $8,250 to $12,000, require 16 hours of work per week, and last 9 to 12 months. For those doctoral students for whom a professional internship is required prior to graduation, 5 applied in 2003–2004. Of those who applied, 5 were placed in internships listed by the Association of Psychology Postdoctoral and Internship Programs (APPIC); 5 were placed in APA accredited internships.

Housing and Day Care: On-campus housing is available. See the following Web site for more information: http://www.sa.wvu.edu/housing/. No on-campus day care facilities are available.

Employment of Department Graduates:
Master's Degree Graduates: Of those who graduated in the academic year 2003–2004, the following categories and numbers represent the post-graduate activities and employment of master's degree graduates: Enrolled in a post-doctoral residency/fellowship (n/a), employed in independent practice (n/a), employed in a community mental health/counseling center (1), employed in a hospital/medical center (1), total from the above (master's) (2).
Doctoral Degree Graduates: Of those who graduated in the academic year 2003–2004, the following categories and numbers represent the post-graduate activities and employment of doctoral degree graduates: Enrolled in a psychology doctoral program (n/a), enrolled in a post-doctoral residency/fellowship (3), employed in an academic position at a university (3), employed in an academic position at a 2-year/4-year college (1), employed in other positions at a higher education institution (2), employed in a government agency (professional services) (2), employed in a community mental health/counseling center (1), employed in a hospital/medical center (1), still seeking employment (1), do not know (1), total from the above (doctoral) (15).

Additional Information:
Orientation, Objectives, and Emphasis of Department: The Psychology Department offers the Doctor of Philosophy degree in Behavior Analysis and Developmental, Clinical Child, and Clinical Psychology, and a terminal Professional Master's degree in Clinical Psychology. The Department employs a junior colleague model of training, in which graduate students participate fully in research, teaching, and service activities. The Behavior Analysis Program trains students in basic research, theory, and applications of behavioral psychology. These three areas of study are integrated in the Behavior Analysis curriculum; however, a student may emphasize either basic or applied research. The Life-Span Developmental Program emphasizes cognitive and social/personality development across the life span. It combines breadth of exposure across a variety of perspectives on the life span with depth and rigor in research training and the opportunity to specialize in an age period such as infancy, childhood, adolescence, or adulthood and old age. The Master's and PhD Clinical Programs have a behavioral orientation. The Clinical Doctoral Programs train scientist-practitioners who function effectively in academic, medical center, or clinical applied settings. Specializations in developmental psychology, behavior analysis, and health psychology are available. The Clinical Professional Master's Program is designed to train practitioners with a terminal Master's degree to work in rural areas.

Special Facilities or Resources: The Department moved into the new Life Sciences Building in July 2002. This building has modern animal research quarters for work with rats, pigeons, and other species. There are several computer-based laboratories and other laboratories for studies of learning in humans and animals, behavioral pharmacology, and neuropsychology. There are additional facilities for human research in learning, cognition, small group processes, developmental psychology, social behavior, and psychophysiology. Clinical practicum opportunities are available through the Department's Quin Curtis Center for Psychological Service, Training, and Research, as well as in numerous mental health agencies throughout the state. Videotaping and direct observation equipment and facilities are available. The West Virginia University Medical Center provides facilities for research and training in such departments and areas as behavioral medicine and psychiatry, pediatrics, neurology, and dentistry. Local preschools and public schools have been cooperative in providing access to children and facilities for child development research, local businesses and agencies offer sites for practice and research in applied behavior analysis, local senior centers and homes provide access to elderly populations, and the University's Center on Aging-Education Unit and Center for Women's Studies facilitate research related to their purviews. The University maintains an extensive network of computer facilities, and the Department provides a computer for every graduate student.

Application Information:
Send to: Departmental Admissions Committee, Department of Psychology, West Virginia University, P.O. Box 6040, Morgantown, WV 26506-6040. Application available online. URL of online application: http://www.as.wvu.edu/psyc/Prospective/Department%20Application.pdf. Students are admitted in the Fall, application deadline January 1. Professional Master's in Clinical Psychology application deadline is March 1. *Fee:* $50.

Marquette University (2004 data)
Department of Counseling and Educational Psychology
School of Education
146 Schroeder Complex
Milwaukee, WI 53201-1881
Telephone: (414) 288-5790
Fax: (414) 288-3945
E-mail: *sallie.captain@marquette.edu*
Web: *http://www.marquette.edu/coep*

Department Information:
1996. Chairperson: Timothy P. Melchert. Number of Faculty: total–full-time 6, part-time 5; women–full-time 2, part-time 2; minority–part-time 2.

Programs and Degrees Offered:
Listed in the following order: Program area, degree type (T if terminal Master's), number awarded 7/03–6/04. Counseling MA/MS (Master of Arts/Science) (T) 13, Educational Psychology MA/MS (Master of Arts/Science) (T) 1, Counseling Psychology PhD (Doctor of Philosophy) 1.

APA Accreditation: Counseling PhD (Doctor of Philosophy).

Student Applications/Admissions:
Student Applications
Counseling MA/MS (Master of Arts/Science)—Applications 2004–2005, 82. Total applicants accepted 2004–2005, 57. Total enrolled 2004–2005 full-time, 48, part-time, 24. Openings 2005–2006, 40. The Median number of years required for completion of a degree are 2. The number of students enrolled full and part-time who were dismissed or voluntarily withdrew from this program area were 2. *Educational Psychology MA/MS (Master of Arts/Science)*—Applications 2004–2005, 4. Total applicants accepted 2004–2005, 2. Openings 2005–2006, 5. The Median number of years required for completion of a degree are 3. The number of students enrolled full and part-time who were dismissed or voluntarily withdrew from this program area were 0. *Counseling Psychology PhD (Doctor of Philosophy)*—Applications 2004–2005, 43. Total applicants accepted 2004–2005, 11. Total enrolled 2004–2005 full-time, 31, part-time, 9. Openings 2005–2006, 8. The Median number of years required for completion of a degree are 7. The number of students enrolled full and part-time who were dismissed or voluntarily withdrew from this program area were 1.

Admissions Requirements:
Scores: Entries appear in this order: required test or GPA, minimum score (if required), median score of students entering in 2003–2004. Master's Programs: GRE-V no minimum stated; GRE-Q no minimum stated; GRE-V+Q 830, 1030; overall undergraduate GPA no minimum stated, 3.4. Doctoral Programs: GRE-V no minimum stated; GRE-Q no minimum stated; GRE-V+Q 760, 1160; overall undergraduate GPA no minimum stated, 3.7.

Other Criteria: (importance of criteria rated low, medium, or high): GRE/MAT scores high, research experience medium, work experience medium, extracurricular activity low, clinically related public service medium, GPA high, letters of recommendation high, interview high, statement of goals and objectives high. Applicants' goals and objectives, interviews, and letters of recommendation are important for admission into all our master's and doctoral programs. Research experience is more important for admission into our PhD program. For additional information on admission requirements, go to: www.marquette.edu/coep.

Student Characteristics: The following represents characteristics of students in 2004–2005 in all graduate psychology programs in the department: Female–full-time 64, part-time 27; Male–full-time 15, part-time 7; African American/Black–full-time 2, part-time 3; Hispanic/Latino(a)–full-time 4, part-time 0; Asian/Pacific Islander–full-time 1, part-time 1; American Indian/Alaska Native–full-time 0, part-time 1; Caucasian–full-time 55, part-time 41; Multi-ethnic–full-time 0, part-time 0; students subject to the Americans With Disabilities Act–full-time 2, part-time 1.

Financial Information/Assistance:
Tuition for Full-Time Study: *Master's:* State residents: $495 per credit hour; Nonstate residents: $495 per credit hour. *Doctoral:* State residents: $495 per credit hour; Nonstate residents: $495 per credit hour. See the following Web site for updates and changes in tuition costs: www.marquette.edu/grad.

Financial Assistance:
First Year Students: Teaching assistantships available for first-year. Average amount paid per academic year: $5,745. Average number of hours worked per week: 10. Apply by February 15. Tuition remission given: partial. Research assistantships available for first-year. Average amount paid per academic year: $5,745. Average number of hours worked per week: 10. Apply by February 15. Tuition remission given: partial. Fellowships and scholarships available for first-year. Average amount paid per academic year: $0. Average number of hours worked per week: 0. Apply by February 15. Tuition remission given: partial.

Advanced Students: Teaching assistantships available for advanced students. Average amount paid per academic year: $6,235. Average number of hours worked per week: 10. Apply by February 15. Tuition remission given: partial. Research assistantships available for advanced students. Average amount paid per academic year: $6,025. Average number of hours worked per week: 10. Apply by February 15. Tuition remission given: partial. Traineeships available for advanced students. Average amount paid per academic year: $12,050. Average number of hours worked per week: 20. Apply by February 15. Tuition remission given: full and partial. Fellowships and scholarships available for advanced students. Average amount paid per academic year: $12,050. Average number of hours worked per week: 0. Apply by varies. Tuition remission given: full and partial.

Contact Information: Of all students currently enrolled full-time, 47% benefitted from one or more of the listed financial assistance programs. Application and information available online at: www.marquette.edu/grad.

Internships/Practica: We work with a wide range of inpatient and outpatient agencies and educational institutions serving a broad range of clients from children to seniors and from relatively minor adjustment issues to serious psychopathology. We currently work with approximately 60 agencies and schools and continually try to find additional sites which offer superior clinical experience and supervision. For those doctoral students for whom a professional internship is required prior to graduation, 3 applied in 2003–2004. Of those who applied, 3 were placed in internships listed by the Association of Psychology Postdoctoral and Internship Programs (APPIC); 3 were placed in APA accredited internships.

Housing and Day Care: On-campus housing is available. See the following Web site for more information: www.marquette.edu/reslife. On-campus day care facilities are available. Child care information is available by calling (414) 288-5655.

Employment of Department Graduates:
Master's Degree Graduates: Of those who graduated in the academic year 2003–2004, the following categories and numbers represent the post-graduate activities and employment of master's degree graduates: Enrolled in a post-doctoral residency/fellowship (n/a), employed in independent practice (n/a), total from the above (master's) (0).
Doctoral Degree Graduates: Of those who graduated in the academic year 2003–2004, the following categories and numbers represent the post-graduate activities and employment of doctoral degree graduates: Enrolled in a psychology doctoral program (n/a), total from the above (doctoral) (0).

Additional Information:
Orientation, Objectives, and Emphasis of Department: Our Master's in Counseling and PhD in Counseling Psychology programs are based on a comprehensive biopsychosocial approach to understanding human behavior. We believe that a sensitivity to biological, psychological, social, multicultural, and developmental influences on behavior increases students' effectiveness both as practitioners and as researchers. We use a generalist approach that includes broad preparation in the diverse areas needed to practice competently as psychological scientists and practitioners in today's health care systems. The objectives of the Educational Psychology program are to provide knowledge and skills in the principal content areas of basic and applied psychology as required for the preparation of researchers for work in universities, research and evaluation facilities, business and industry, and schools.

Special Facilities or Resources: Our faculty, and Marquette University as a whole, are committed to offering high quality education. Our coursework, practica, research activities, and other training opportunities are all designed to provide very current and comprehensive preparation. Our student body is small, so students receive substantial individual attention. We are also committed to developing students' competencies to work with diverse multicultural groups, and we welcome applications from individuals with diverse backgrounds.

Information for Students With Physical Disabilities: See the following Web site for more information: www.marquette.edu/oses/OSESWebpage.html.

Application Information:
Send to: Graduate School, P.O. Box 1881, Milwaukee, WI 53201. Application available online. Students are admitted in the Fall, application deadline. The application deadline for the PhD program is December 1, and January 1 for the master's programs. *Fee:* $40. Fee waived for Marquette Alumni.

Marquette University
Department of Psychology
Arts and Sciences
P.O. Box 1881
Milwaukee, WI 53201-1881
Telephone: (414) 288-7218
Fax: (414) 288-5333
E-mail: *psyc.dept@mu.edu*
Web: *http://www.marquette.edu/psyc*

Department Information:
1952. Chairperson: Michael J. Wierzbicki. Number of Faculty: total–full-time 17, part-time 2; women–full-time 7, part-time 2; minority–full-time 2.

Programs and Degrees Offered:
Listed in the following order: Program area, degree type (T if terminal Master's), number awarded 7/03–6/04. Clinical Psychology MA/MS (Master of Arts/Science) (T) 1, Clinical Psychology PhD (Doctor of Philosophy) 3.

APA Accreditation: Clinical PhD (Doctor of Philosophy).

Student Applications/Admissions:
Student Applications
Clinical Psychology MA/MS (Master of Arts/Science)—Applications 2004–2005, 18. Total applicants accepted 2004–2005, 6. Number enrolled (new admits only) 2004–2005 full-time, 4. Openings 2005–2006, 5. The Median number of years required for completion of a degree are 2. The number of students enrolled full and part-time who were dismissed or voluntarily withdrew from this program area were 1. *Clinical Psychology PhD (Doctor of Philosophy)*—Applications 2004–2005, 82. Total applicants accepted 2004–2005, 8. Number enrolled (new admits only) 2004–2005 full-time, 5. Total enrolled 2004–2005 full-time, 46, part-time, 3. Openings 2005–2006, 5. The Median number of years required for completion of a degree are 7. The number of students enrolled full and part-time who were dismissed or voluntarily withdrew from this program area were 0.

Admissions Requirements:
Scores: Entries appear in this order: required test or GPA, minimum score (if required), median score of students entering in 2003–2004. Master's Programs: GRE-V 550, 500; GRE-Q 500, 570; GRE-V+Q 1050, 1000; GRE-Analytical 500, 585; GRE-Subject(Psych) 550, 570; overall undergraduate GPA 3.2, 3.25. Doctoral Programs: GRE-V 550, 550; GRE-Q 550, 670; GRE-V+Q 1100, 1220; GRE-Analytical 500, 630; GRE-Subject(Psych) 500, 650; overall undergraduate GPA 3.40, 3.66.

Other Criteria: (importance of criteria rated low, medium, or high): GRE/MAT scores high, research experience high, work experience low, extracurricular activity low, clinically related public service medium, GPA medium, letters of recommendation high, interview medium, statement of goals and objectives high. MS program places less emphasis on research experience. For additional information on admission requirements, go to: www.mu.edu/psyc.

Student Characteristics: The following represents characteristics of students in 2004–2005 in all graduate psychology programs in the department: Female–full-time 38, part-time 3; Male–full-time 13, part-time 0; African American/Black–full-time 2, part-time 0; Hispanic/Latino(a)–full-time 1, part-time 0; Asian/Pacific Islander–full-time 1, part-time 0; American Indian/Alaska Native–full-time 1, part-time 0; Caucasian–full-time 45, part-time 3; Multi-ethnic–full-time 1, part-time 0; students subject to the Americans With Disabilities Act–full-time 0, part-time 0.

Financial Information/Assistance:

Tuition for Full-Time Study: *Master's:* State residents: $660 per credit hour; Nonstate residents: $660 per credit hour. *Doctoral:* State residents: $660 per credit hour; Nonstate residents: $660 per credit hour. Tuition is subject to change. See the following Web site for updates and changes in tuition costs: www.grad.mu.edu.

Financial Assistance:

First Year Students: Teaching assistantships available for first-year. Average amount paid per academic year: $11,490. Average number of hours worked per week: 20. Apply by January 15. Tuition remission given: full. Research assistantships available for first-year. Average amount paid per academic year: $11,490. Average number of hours worked per week: 20. Apply by January 15. Tuition remission given: full. Fellowships and scholarships available for first-year. Average amount paid per academic year: $1,890. Average number of hours worked per week: 0. Apply by January 15. Tuition remission given: full and partial.

Advanced Students: Teaching assistantships available for advanced students. Average amount paid per academic year: $11,490. Average number of hours worked per week: 20. Apply by January 15. Tuition remission given: full. Research assistantships available for advanced students. Average amount paid per academic year: $11,490. Average number of hours worked per week: 20. Apply by January 15. Tuition remission given: full. Fellowships and scholarships available for advanced students. Average amount paid per academic year: $1,890. Average number of hours worked per week: 0. Apply by January 15. Tuition remission given: full and partial.

Contact Information: Of all students currently enrolled full-time, 60% benefitted from one or more of the listed financial assistance programs. Application and information available online at: http://www.grad.mu.edu.

Internships/Practica: Doctoral and terminal master's students obtain supervised clinical experience throughout their training. Practica are offered both in the Department's training clinic, the Center for Psychological Services, and in community agencies. The Department's training clinic provides assessment and intervention services to members of the general community under the supervision of licensed clinical faculty members. Students have averaged over 750 hours in the clinic, and over 2,000 hours

in pre-internship practicum experiences. Marquette University's urban location provides a wealth of training opportunities in the community. Recent practicum experiences have included placements in agencies that provided training in neuropsychological assessment, geropsychology, behavioral medicine, pediatric health, and family therapy. Doctoral students are required to complete a 2,000 hour internship. To date, students have completed APA-approved internships in settings located in the Milwaukee area as well as eight different states. For those doctoral students for whom a professional internship is required prior to graduation, 6 applied in 2003–2004. Of those who applied, 4 were placed in internships listed by the Association of Psychology Postdoctoral and Internship Programs (APPIC); 4 were placed in APA accredited internships.

Housing and Day Care: On-campus housing is available. See the following Web site for more information: www.grad.mu.edu. On-campus day care facilities are available.

Employment of Department Graduates:

Master's Degree Graduates: Of those who graduated in the academic year 2003–2004, the following categories and numbers represent the post-graduate activities and employment of master's degree graduates: Enrolled in a post-doctoral residency/fellowship (n/a), employed in independent practice (n/a), total from the above (master's) (0).

Doctoral Degree Graduates: Of those who graduated in the academic year 2003–2004, the following categories and numbers represent the post-graduate activities and employment of doctoral degree graduates: Enrolled in a psychology doctoral program (n/a), enrolled in another graduate/professional program (0), enrolled in a post-doctoral residency/fellowship (1), employed in independent practice (4), employed in an academic position at a university (2), employed in an academic position at a 2-year/4-year college (0), employed in other positions at a higher education institution (2), employed in a professional position in a school system (1), employed in business or industry (research/consulting) (0), employed in business or industry (management) (0), employed in a government agency (research) (0), employed in a government agency (professional services) (0), employed in a community mental health/counseling center (5), employed in a hospital/medical center (1), still seeking employment (0), other employment position (2), do not know (0), total from the above (doctoral) (17).

Additional Information:

Orientation, Objectives, and Emphasis of Department: The Clinical Psychology Program offers courses and training leading to the degrees of Doctor of Philosophy (PhD) and Master of Science (MS) in Clinical Psychology. All doctoral students acquire a Master of Science degree as they progress toward the doctoral degree. Students in the terminal master's program typically accept employment after completion of the program, but some go on to doctoral study. The doctoral program is approved by the American Psychological Association to train scientist-professionals. Students receive a solid foundation in scientific areas of psychology and in the historical foundations of psychology. Training in research skills such as statistics, measurement, and research methods ensures competence in conducting empirical research and in critically evaluating one's own and others' clinical and empirical work. Students become competent in professional practice skills such as assessment, interventions, and consultation. Supervised clinical experiences are planned throughout the curriculum. Graduates of the doctoral program are prepared to practice as clinical psychologists, consultants, teachers, researchers, and administrators.

Special Facilities or Resources: The department is located in completely refurbished and modern quarters that include a psychology clinic, two undergraduate teaching laboratories, and ample space for both faculty and student research. A full range of computer services is available at no charge to students. Located in a large metropolitan area, Marquette University is within easy commuting distance to a variety of hospitals and agencies in which training and research opportunities maybe available.

Information for Students With Physical Disabilities: See the following Web site for more information: www.grad.mu.edu.

Application Information:
Send to: Graduate School, 305 Holthusen Hall, Marquette University, 1324 W. Wisconsin Avenue, Milwaukee, WI 53201-1881. Application available online. URL of online application: https://app.applyyourself. com/?id=marq-grad. Students are admitted in the Fall, application deadline January 15. *Fee:* $40. Waived for Marquette University alumni. Waived for evidence of financial need.

Wisconsin School of Professional Psychology
Professional School
9120 West Hampton Avenue, Suite 212
Milwaukee, WI 53225
Telephone: (414) 464-9777
Fax: (414) 358-5590
E-mail: *admissions@wspp.edu*
Web: *http://www.wspp.edu*

Department Information:
1980. President: Kathleen M. Rusch, PhD Number of Faculty: total–full-time 1, part-time 33; women–full-time 1, part-time 13; minority–part-time 2.

Programs and Degrees Offered:
Listed in the following order: Program area, degree type (T if terminal Master's), number awarded 7/03–6/04. Clinical PsyD (Doctor of Psychology) 10.

Student Applications/Admissions:
Student Applications
Clinical PsyD (Doctor of Psychology)—Applications 2004–2005, 20. Total applicants accepted 2004–2005, 15. Number enrolled (new admits only) 2004–2005 full-time, 8. Number enrolled (new admits only) 2004–2005 part-time, 2. Total enrolled 2004–2005 full-time, 9, part-time, 48. Openings 2005–2006, 15. The Median number of years required for completion of a degree are 5. The number of students enrolled full and part-time who were dismissed or voluntarily withdrew from this program area were 4.

Admissions Requirements:
Scores: Entries appear in this order: required test or GPA, minimum score (if required), median score of students entering

in 2003–2004. Master's Programs: GRE-V+Q 1000, 1200; GRE-Subject(Psych) 500, 520; overall undergraduate GPA 3.0, 3.5; last 2 years GPA 3.2, 3.6; psychology GPA 3.2, 3.6. Doctoral Programs: GRE-V+Q 1000, 1200; GRE-Subject(Psych) 500, 550; overall undergraduate GPA 3.0, 3.5; psychology GPA 3.2, 3.6.
Other Criteria: (importance of criteria rated low, medium, or high): GRE/MAT scores medium, research experience low, work experience high, extracurricular activity medium, clinically related public service high, GPA medium, letters of recommendation high, interview high, statement of goals and objectives high, essay high.

Student Characteristics: The following represents characteristics of students in 2004–2005 in all graduate psychology programs in the department: Female–full-time 6, part-time 39; Male–full-time 3, part-time 9; African American/Black–full-time 1, part-time 5; Hispanic/Latino(a)–full-time 0, part-time 0; Asian/Pacific Islander–full-time 0, part-time 0; American Indian/Alaska Native–full-time 0, part-time 1; Caucasian–full-time 8, part-time 37; Multi-ethnic–full-time 0, part-time 0; students subject to the Americans With Disabilities Act–full-time 1, part-time 1.

Financial Information/Assistance:
Tuition for Full-Time Study: *Master's:* State residents: $625 per credit hour; Nonstate residents: $625 per credit hour. *Doctoral:* State residents: $625 per credit hour; Nonstate residents: $625 per credit hour. Tuition is subject to change.

Financial Assistance:
First Year Students: Fellowships and scholarships available for first-year. Average amount paid per academic year: $3,000. Average number of hours worked per week: 0. Apply by February 15. Tuition remission given: partial.

Advanced Students: Traineeships available for advanced students. Average number of hours worked per week: 12. Tuition remission given: partial. Fellowships and scholarships available for advanced students. Average amount paid per academic year: $1,000. Average number of hours worked per week: 0. Apply by February 15. Tuition remission given: partial.

Contact Information: Of all students currently enrolled full-time, 4% benefitted from one or more of the listed financial assistance programs. Application and information available online at: wspp.edu.

Internships/Practica: WSPP has an on-site training clinic, the Psychology Center, which is designed to serve two purposes: to provide supervised training to students and to provide quality clinical services to an inner city multicultural disadvantaged population. The Center also maintains contracts and affiliations with a number of local service agencies to provide on-site services. Regardless of whether on- or off-site, all practica are supervised by WSPP faculty to ensure quality of supervision and communication with our DCT. Some 40 supervisors, all licensed and most National Register listed, are readily available. For assessment practica, WSPP maintains a library of psychological tests available for student use free of charge. Thus, all students are guaranteed ample practicum opportunities (the program requires 2,000 hours) without having to search for sites or supervisors. This high level of clinical training has led to our 100% internship placement rate to date. For those doctoral students for whom a professional internship is required prior to graduation, 7 applied in 2003–

2004. Of those who applied, 6 were placed in internships listed by the Association of Psychology Postdoctoral and Internship Programs (APPIC); 1 was placed in APA accredited internships.

Housing and Day Care: No on-campus housing is available. No on-campus day care facilities are available.

Employment of Department Graduates:

Master's Degree Graduates: Of those who graduated in the academic year 2003–2004, the following categories and numbers represent the post-graduate activities and employment of master's degree graduates: Enrolled in a psychology doctoral program (2), enrolled in another graduate/professional program (0), enrolled in a post-doctoral residency/fellowship (n/a), employed in independent practice (n/a), employed in an academic position at a university (0), employed in an academic position at a 2-year/4-year college (0), employed in other positions at a higher education institution (0), employed in a professional position in a school system (0), employed in business or industry (research/consulting) (0), employed in business or industry (management) (0), employed in a government agency (research) (0), employed in a government agency (professional services) (0), employed in a community mental health/counseling center (0), employed in a hospital/medical center (0), still seeking employment (0), other employment position (0), total from the above (master's) (2).

Doctoral Degree Graduates: Of those who graduated in the academic year 2003–2004, the following categories and numbers represent the post-graduate activities and employment of doctoral degree graduates: Enrolled in a psychology doctoral program (n/a), enrolled in a post-doctoral residency/fellowship (0), employed in independent practice (2), employed in an academic position at a university (0), employed in an academic position at a 2-year/4-year college (0), employed in other positions at a higher education institution (0), employed in a professional position in a school system (0), employed in business or industry (research/consulting) (0), employed in business or industry (management) (0), employed in a government agency (research) (0), employed in a government agency (professional services) (1), employed in a community mental health/counseling center (0), employed in a hospital/medical center (0), still seeking employment (0), other employment position (0), total from the above (doctoral) (3).

Additional Information:

Orientation, Objectives, and Emphasis of Department: The Wisconsin School of Professional Psychology has as its goal the provision of a doctoral level education that emphasizes the acquisition of the traditional skills which defined the professional in the past, while staying open to new developments as they emerge. Our program balances theoretical and practical coursework, taking its impetus from the American Psychological Association's Vail Conference. The school's curriculum was developed in accord with APA norms and is continually evaluated to assure compliance with the requirements of that body. WSPP trains students toward competence in the following areas: self-awareness, assessment, research and evaluation, ethics and professional standards, management and supervision, relationship, intervention, respect for diversity, consultation, social responsibility and community service. In its training philosophy, the school emphasizes clarity of verbal expression in written and oral communication, the development of clinical acumen, and an appreciation of the link between scientific data and clinical practice. Our program's small

size and large faculty create abundant opportunities for mentorship with practicing psychologists in an apprentice-like setting.

Special Facilities or Resources: The Wisconsin School of Professional Psychology maintains a Training Clinic which includes facilities for research and practicum work associated with clinical courses. The Training Center houses an outpatient mental health clinic which serves a primarily inner city culturally diverse population, as well as provides opportunities for supervised experience with a wide range of clinical problems and populations. The center offers services to the community on a sliding fee basis. Supervision provided by faculty.

Application Information:
Send to: Wisconsin School of Professional Psychology, 9120 W. Hampton Avenue, Milwaukee, WI 53225. Students are admitted in the Fall, application deadline April 15; Spring, application deadline October 15. *Fee:* $75.

Wisconsin, University of, Eau Claire

Department of Psychology
Arts and Sciences
University of Wisconsin-Eau Claire
Eau Claire, WI 54702
Telephone: (715) 836-5733
Fax: (715) 836-2214
E-mail: *lozarb@uwec.edu*
Web: *http://www.psyc.uwec.edu/eds.htm*

Department Information:
1965. Chairperson: Larry Morse. Number of Faculty: total–full-time 19, part-time 4; women–full-time 9, part-time 2.

Programs and Degrees Offered:
Listed in the following order: Program area, degree type (T if terminal Master's), number awarded 7/03–6/04. School Psychology EdS (Education Specialist) 8.

Student Applications/Admissions:

Student Applications
School Psychology EdS (Education Specialist)—Applications 2004–2005, 40. Total applicants accepted 2004–2005, 14. Number enrolled (new admits only) 2004–2005 full-time, 12. Number enrolled (new admits only) 2004–2005 part-time, 0. Total enrolled 2004–2005 full-time, 25, part-time, 2. Openings 2005–2006, 8. The Median number of years required for completion of a degree are 3. The number of students enrolled full and part-time who were dismissed or voluntarily withdrew from this program area were 0.

Admissions Requirements:
Scores: Entries appear in this order: required test or GPA, minimum score (if required), median score of students entering in 2003–2004. Master's Programs: GRE-V 450, 455; GRE-Q no minimum stated; GRE-Analytical no minimum stated; overall undergraduate GPA 3.0, 3.44. Doctoral Programs: GRE-V no minimum stated; GRE-Q no minimum stated; GRE-V+Q no minimum stated; GRE-Analytical no minimum

stated; GRE-Subject(Psych) no minimum stated; MAT no minimum stated; overall undergraduate GPA no minimum stated; last 2 years GPA no minimum stated; psychology GPA no minimum stated.

Other Criteria: (importance of criteria rated low, medium, or high): GRE/MAT scores high, research experience medium, work experience medium, extracurricular activity medium, clinically related public service medium, GPA high, letters of recommendation high, interview high, statement of goals and objectives high. For additional information on admission requirements, go to: www.psyc.uwec.edu/eds.htm.

Student Characteristics: The following represents characteristics of students in 2004–2005 in all graduate psychology programs in the department: Female–full-time 19, part-time 1; Male–full-time 6, part-time 1; African American/Black–full-time 0, part-time 0; Hispanic/Latino(a)–full-time 0, part-time 0; Asian/Pacific Islander–full-time 1, part-time 0; American Indian/Alaska Native–full-time 0, part-time 0; Caucasian–full-time 24, part-time 2; students subject to the Americans With Disabilities Act–full-time 1, part-time 0.

Financial Information/Assistance:
Tuition for Full-Time Study: *Master's:* State residents: per academic year $5,922, $331 per credit hour; Nonstate residents: per academic year $16,532, $920 per credit hour. Tuition is subject to change. See the following Web site for updates and changes in tuition costs: www.uwec.edu/gradadmiss.

Financial Assistance:
First Year Students: Teaching assistantships available for first-year. Average amount paid per academic year: $4,580. Average number of hours worked per week: 10. Apply by March 1. Fellowships and scholarships available for first-year. Average amount paid per academic year: $500. Apply by March 1.

Advanced Students: Teaching assistantships available for advanced students. Average amount paid per academic year: $4,580. Average number of hours worked per week: 10. Apply by March 1. Fellowships and scholarships available for advanced students. Average amount paid per academic year: $500. Apply by March 1.

Contact Information: Of all students currently enrolled full-time, 70% benefitted from one or more of the listed financial assistance programs. Application and information available online at: www.uwec.edu/gradadmiss/.

Internships/Practica: Internships are required for the Educational Specialist degree and constitute the third year of training. Students must complete a year of full-time practice as school psychologists under the supervision of an appropriately credentialed school psychologist. Students may enroll in the internship upon completion of all requirements except the thesis. A more detailed description of the internship requirements are available at the school psychology program website: psyc.uwec.edu/eds.htm.

Housing and Day Care: No on-campus housing is available. On-campus day care facilities are available. See the following Web site for more information: www.uwec.edu/Admin/Children; e-mail: children@uwec.edu.

Employment of Department Graduates:
Master's Degree Graduates: Of those who graduated in the academic year 2003–2004, the following categories and numbers

represent the post-graduate activities and employment of master's degree graduates: Enrolled in a post-doctoral residency/fellowship (n/a), employed in independent practice (n/a), employed in a professional position in a school system (8), total from the above (master's) (8).

Doctoral Degree Graduates: Of those who graduated in the academic year 2003–2004, the following categories and numbers represent the post-graduate activities and employment of doctoral degree graduates: Enrolled in a psychology doctoral program (n/a), total from the above (doctoral) (0).

Additional Information:
Orientation, Objectives, and Emphasis of Department: The primary goals of the EdS school psychology training program focus on preparation of a broadly skilled school psychology professional, one trained to meet the many and diverse challenges of practice in a rapidly changing work setting. Training in the delivery of evaluation and intervention (counseling, consultation, training, and research) services is eclectic, drawing heavily from behavioral (social learning, operant, and cognitive), clinical, developmental, and educational (regular and special education) theoretical foundations. Professional training prepares the practitioner to work with individuals from early childhood/preschool through youth and adult ages, providing services related to exceptional educational, at risk, and/or regular education needs. Three training strands (diagnostics, research, and intervention) have been developed which make available extensive "applied training" opportunities. Twelve practicas and a third-year internship have been structured to provide extensive supervised, professional training experiences (over 2000 hours), with two practica beginning during the student's first semester of enrollment. Faculty supervisors have a training emphasis and appropriate professional license/certification in the areas of assigned supervision (for example, clinical, behavioral, school, counseling). The program has two unique features: the Human Development Center and an ongoing collaborative relationship with the Lac du Flambeau American Indian community.

Special Facilities or Resources: Extensive on-campus and field site training opportunities are available. Two interdisciplinary clinics—The Human Development Center (Psychology-School Psychology; Special Education-Learning Disabilities and Early Childhood; Communication Disorders; and Elementary Education-Reading) and the Psychological Services Center (Psychology-School Psychology and Nursing)—provide on-campus training in diagnostics and evaluation services. Areas schools, residential facilities for developmentally disabled, emotionally disturbed youth and adults, and clinics offer an extensive array of additional supervised training settings. In addition, the program has a continuing collaborative relationship with the Lac du Flambeau American Indian community which offers opportunities for short-term or semester-long practicums.

Information for Students With Physical Disabilities: See the following Web site for more information: www.uwec.edu/SSD; Email: hicksea@uwec.edu.

Application Information:
Send to: Office of Admissions, UW-Eau Claire, Eau Claire, WI 54702-4004. Application available online. URL of online application: http://apply.wisconsin.edu/graduate.eau. Students are admitted in the Fall,

application deadline March 1. *Fee:* $45. Wisconsin law does not permit exemption or waiver of the application fee.

Wisconsin, University of, Eau Claire

School Psychology, Department of Psychology
University of Wisconsin-Eau Claire
Eau Claire, WI 54702
Telephone: (715) 836-5733
Fax: (715) 836-2214
E-mail: *herstaja@uwec.edu*
Web: *http://psyc.uwec.edu/mse.htm*

Department Information:
Chairperson: Dr. Larry Morse. Number of Faculty: total–full-time 17, part-time 2; women–full-time 6, part-time 1; minority–full-time 1.

Programs and Degrees Offered:
Listed in the following order: Program area, degree type (T if terminal Master's), number awarded 7/03–6/04. School Psychology EdS (Education Specialist) 5.

Student Applications/Admissions:
Student Applications
School Psychology EdS (Education Specialist)—Applications 2004–2005, 40. Total applicants accepted 2004–2005, 10. Total enrolled 2004–2005 full-time, 22, part-time, 1. Openings 2005–2006, 8. The Median number of years required for completion of a degree are 3. The number of students enrolled full and part-time who were dismissed or voluntarily withdrew from this program area were 0.

Admissions Requirements:
Scores: Entries appear in this order: required test or GPA, minimum score (if required), median score of students entering in 2003–2004. Master's Programs: GRE-V 400, 450; overall undergraduate GPA 3.0, 3.50.
Other Criteria: (importance of criteria rated low, medium, or high): research experience medium, work experience medium, extracurricular activity medium, clinically related public service medium, GPA high, letters of recommendation medium, interview high, statement of goals and objectives medium.

Student Characteristics: The following represents characteristics of students in 2004–2005 in all graduate psychology programs in the department: Female–full-time 13, part-time 6; Male–full-time 5, part-time 2; African American/Black–full-time 0, part-time 0; Hispanic/Latino(a)–full-time 0, part-time 0; Asian/Pacific Islander–full-time 0, part-time 0; American Indian/Alaska Native– full-time 0, part-time 0; Caucasian–full-time 0, part-time 0; students subject to the Americans With Disabilities Act–full-time 1, part-time 0.

Financial Information/Assistance:
Tuition for Full-Time Study: *Master's:* State residents: per academic year $5,300; Nonstate residents: per academic year $15,434. Tuition is subject to change. See the following Web site for updates and changes in tuition costs: http://www.uwec.edu/Admin/Grad/Gradfee.htm.

Financial Assistance:
First Year Students: Teaching assistantships available for first-year. Average amount paid per academic year: $4,000. Average number of hours worked per week: 10. Apply by March 1. Fellowships and scholarships available for first-year. Apply by March 1.
Advanced Students: Teaching assistantships available for advanced students. Average amount paid per academic year: $4,000. Average number of hours worked per week: 10. Apply by March 1. Fellowships and scholarships available for advanced students. Apply by March 1.
Contact Information: Of all students currently enrolled full-time, 80% benefitted from one or more of the listed financial assistance programs. Application and information available online at: http://www.uwec.edu/Finaid/contact.htm.

Internships/Practica: Internships are only available for students completing our school psychology program. Satisfactory completion of the first two years of training (which comprise the degree and certification phases of training) and recommendation of Graduate Review and Admissions Board are necessary for advancement to the internship phase of training. The Educational Specialist degree is awarded after completion of the internship phase.

Housing and Day Care: On-campus housing is available. See the following Web site for more information: http://www.uwec.edu/housing/. On-campus day care facilities are available. See the following Web site for more information: http://www.uwec.edu/Admin/Children/.

Employment of Department Graduates:
Master's Degree Graduates: Of those who graduated in the academic year 2003–2004, the following categories and numbers represent the post-graduate activities and employment of master's degree graduates: Enrolled in a post-doctoral residency/fellowship (n/a), employed in independent practice (n/a), employed in a professional position in a school system (5), total from the above (master's) (5).
Doctoral Degree Graduates: Of those who graduated in the academic year 2003–2004, the following categories and numbers represent the post-graduate activities and employment of doctoral degree graduates: Enrolled in a psychology doctoral program (n/a), total from the above (doctoral) (0).

Additional Information:
Orientation, Objectives, and Emphasis of Department: The primary goals of the school psychology training focus on preparation of a broadly skilled school psychology professional, one trained to meet the many and diverse challenges of practice in a rapidly changing work setting. Training in the delivery of evaluation and intervention (counseling, consultation, training, and research) services is eclectic, drawing heavily from behavioral (social learning, operant, and cognitive), clinical, developmental, and education (regular and special education) theoretical foundations. Professional training prepares the practitioner to work with individuals from early childhood/preschool through youth and adult ages, providing services related to exceptional educational, at risk, and/or regular education initiative needs. Three training strands (diagnostic, research, and intervention) have been developed which make available extensive "applied training" or "hands on" learning opportunities. Twelve practica and a third-year internship have been structured to provide extensive supervised,

professional training experiences (over 2000 hours), four practica beginning during the student's first semester of enrollment. Faculty supervisors have a training emphasis and appropriate professional license/certification in the areas of assigned supervision (for example, clinical, behavioral, school, counseling).

Special Facilities or Resources: Extensive on-campus and field site training opportunities are available. Two clinics—the Human Development Center (an interdisciplinary clinic consisting of Psychology-School Psychology; Special Education-Learning Disabilities and Early Childhood; Communication Disorders; Nursing, Social Work and Elementary Education-Reading) and the Psychological Services Center—provide on-campus training in diagnostics and evaluation. Area schools, along with residential facilities for individuals with developmental disabilities and youth and adults with emotional disabilities, offer an extensive array of additional supervised training settings.

Information for Students With Physical Disabilities: See the following Web site for more information: http://www.uwec.edu/SSD/.

Application Information:
Send to: Director, School Psychology Program, Department of Psychology, University of Wisconsin-Eau Claire, Eau Claire, WI 54702-4004. Students are admitted in the Fall, application deadline March 1. *Fee:* $45.

Wisconsin, University of, La Crosse
Department of Psychology/School Psychology
College of Liberal Studies
1725 State Street, 341 Graff Main Hall
La Crosse, WI 54601
Telephone: (608) 785-8441
Fax: (608) 785-8443
E-mail: *dixon.robe@uwlax.edu*
Web: *http://www.uwlax.edu/Graduate/psychology/*

Department Information:
1967. Director: Robert J. Dixon. Number of Faculty: total–full-time 15, part-time 2; women–full-time 9, part-time 2; minority–full-time 1.

Programs and Degrees Offered:
Listed in the following order: Program area, degree type (T if terminal Master's), number awarded 7/03–6/04. School Psychology EdS (Education Specialist) 10.

Student Applications/Admissions:
Student Applications
School Psychology EdS (Education Specialist)—Applications 2004–2005, 30. Total applicants accepted 2004–2005, 17. Number enrolled (new admits only) 2004–2005 full-time, 12. Openings 2005–2006, 12. The Median number of years required for completion of a degree are 3. The number of students enrolled full and part-time who were dismissed or voluntarily withdrew from this program area were 0.

Admissions Requirements:
Scores: Entries appear in this order: required test or GPA, minimum score (if required), median score of students entering in 2003–2004. Master's Programs: GRE-V no minimum stated, 505; GRE-Q no minimum stated, 565; GRE-V+Q no minimum stated, 1070; GRE-Analytical no minimum stated, 5.0; overall undergraduate GPA 2.85, 3.68; last 2 years GPA no minimum stated, 3.75; psychology GPA no minimum stated, 3.71. The GRE Analytical score of 5.0 refers to the Analytical Writing score. The GRE Psychology Subject test in Psychology is not required but strongly recommended if your GPA for the last two years is below 3.25 or if you have graduated without majoring in psychology.
Other Criteria: (importance of criteria rated low, medium, or high): GRE/MAT scores medium, research experience medium, work experience medium, extracurricular activity medium, clinically related public service high, GPA high, letters of recommendation high, interview high, statement of goals and objectives high.

Student Characteristics: The following represents characteristics of students in 2004–2005 in all graduate psychology programs in the department: Female–full-time 18, part-time 0; Male–full-time 5, part-time 0; African American/Black–full-time 0, part-time 0; Hispanic/Latino(a)–full-time 0, part-time 0; Asian/Pacific Islander–full-time 0, part-time 0; American Indian/Alaska Native–full-time 0, part-time 0; Caucasian–full-time 23, part-time 0; Multi-ethnic–full-time 0, part-time 0; students subject to the Americans With Disabilities Act–full-time 1, part-time 0.

Financial Information/Assistance:
Tuition for Full-Time Study: *Master's:* State residents: per academic year $6,088, $336 per credit hour; Nonstate residents: per academic year $16,698, $926 per credit hour. Tuition is subject to change.

Financial Assistance:
First Year Students: Research assistantships available for first-year. Average amount paid per academic year: $6,074. Average number of hours worked per week: 14. Apply by March 1.
Advanced Students: Research assistantships available for advanced students. Average amount paid per academic year: $6,074. Average number of hours worked per week: 14. Apply by March 1.
Contact Information: Of all students currently enrolled full-time, 13% benefitted from one or more of the listed financial assistance programs.

Internships/Practica: The School Psychology program prepares graduate students for certification as School Psychologists through academic coursework, 700 hours of supervised school practica, and a one year, 1,200 hour school internship. Graduate students are placed in local schools as early and intensively as possible. During their second, third and fourth semesters, students spend two days per week working in local schools under the direct supervision of experienced school psychologists. During these school practica, students develop professional skills in assessment, consultation, intervention, counseling, and case management. Many of the core courses require projects which are completed in the schools during practica.

Housing and Day Care: On-campus housing is available. No on-campus housing for graduate students. On-campus day care facilities are available. Child Care Center: (608) 785-8813.

Employment of Department Graduates:

Master's Degree Graduates: Of those who graduated in the academic year 2003–2004, the following categories and numbers represent the post-graduate activities and employment of master's degree graduates: Enrolled in a post-doctoral residency/fellowship (n/a), employed in independent practice (n/a), employed in a professional position in a school system (12), total from the above (master's) (12).

Doctoral Degree Graduates: Of those who graduated in the academic year 2003–2004, the following categories and numbers represent the post-graduate activities and employment of doctoral degree graduates: Enrolled in a psychology doctoral program (n/a), total from the above (doctoral) (0).

Additional Information:

Orientation, Objectives, and Emphasis of Department: The emphasis of this program is to train school psychologists who are effective teacher, parent and school consultants. The program also emphasizes a pupil services model which addresses the educational and mental health needs of all children. The School Psychology knowledge base includes areas of Professional School Psychology, Educational Psychology, Psychological Foundations, Educational Foundations, and Mental Health. To provide psychological services in education, graduates of the School Psychology program must also have considerable knowledge of curriculum, special education and pupil services. Graduates of the program are employed in public schools or educational agencies which serve public schools.

Special Facilities or Resources: Extensive fieldwork in local schools is a key to professional training. Faculty work closely with field supervisors and observe student performance in the field.

Application Information:
Send to: School Psychology Admissions, 341 Graff Main Hall, University of Wisconsin-La Crosse, 1725 State Street, La Crosse, WI 54601. Application available online. URL of online application: http://www.uwlax.edu/graduate/psychology/. Students are admitted in the Spring, application deadline January 15. *Fee:* $45.

Wisconsin, University of, Madison
Department of Counseling Psychology, Counseling Psychology
    Program
School of Education
Education Building, Room 321
1000 Bascom Mall
Madison, WI 53706
Telephone: (608) 262-0461, (608) 263-2746
Fax: (608) 265-3347
E-mail: *counpsych@education.wisc.edu*
Web: *http://www.soemadison.wisc.edu/cp*

Department Information:
1964. Chairperson: Bruce Wampold. Number of Faculty: total–full-time 9, part-time 1; women–full-time 5, part-time 1; minority–full-time 4.

Programs and Degrees Offered:
Listed in the following order: Program area, degree type (T if terminal Master's), number awarded 7/03–6/04. Counseling MA/MS (Master of Arts/Science) (T) 29, counseling psychology PhD (Doctor of Philosophy) 8.

APA Accreditation: Counseling PhD (Doctor of Philosophy).

Student Applications/Admissions:
Student Applications
    Counseling MA/MS (Master of Arts/Science)—Applications 2004–2005, 153. Total applicants accepted 2004–2005, 25. Number enrolled (new admits only) 2004–2005 full-time, 23. Total enrolled 2004–2005 full-time, 55, part-time, 5. Openings 2005–2006, 21. The Median number of years required for completion of a degree are 2. The number of students enrolled full and part-time who were dismissed or voluntarily withdrew from this program area were 0. *Counseling psychology PhD (Doctor of Philosophy)*—Applications 2004–2005, 76. Total applicants accepted 2004–2005, 15. Number enrolled (new admits only) 2004–2005 full-time, 7. Total enrolled 2004–2005 full-time, 60. Openings 2005–2006, 8. The Median number of years required for completion of a degree are 7.25. The number of students enrolled full and part-time who were dismissed or voluntarily withdrew from this program area were 0.

Admissions Requirements:
    Scores: Entries appear in this order: required test or GPA, minimum score (if required), median score of students entering in 2003–2004. Master's Programs: GRE-V no minimum stated; GRE-Q no minimum stated; GRE-Analytical no minimum stated; last 2 years GPA 3.0, 3.4. Doctoral Programs: GRE-V no minimum stated, 550; GRE-Q no minimum stated, 570; GRE-Analytical no minimum stated, 620.
    Other Criteria: (importance of criteria rated low, medium, or high): GRE/MAT scores medium, research experience medium, work experience medium, extracurricular activity high, clinically related public service high, GPA medium, letters of recommendation high, interview high, statement of goals and objectives high. For master's: research low, no interview required. All other criteria are the same.

Student Characteristics: The following represents characteristics of students in 2004–2005 in all graduate psychology programs in the department: Female–full-time 78, part-time 4; Male–full-time 26, part-time 0; African American/Black–full-time 15, part-time 0; Hispanic/Latino(a)–full-time 13, part-time 0; Asian/Pacific Islander–full-time 13, part-time 0; American Indian/Alaska Native–full-time 3, part-time 0; Caucasian–full-time 71, part-time 3; Multi-ethnic–full-time 3, part-time 0.

Financial Information/Assistance:
    Tuition for Full-Time Study: *Master's:* State residents: per academic year $8,320, $522 per credit hour; Nonstate residents: per academic year $23,590, $1,476 per credit hour. *Doctoral:* State residents: per academic year $8,320, $522 per credit hour; Nonstate residents: per academic year $23,590, $1,476 per credit hour. Tuition is subject to change. See the following Web site for updates and changes in tuition costs: http://registrar.wisc.edu.

Financial Assistance:
    First Year Students: Teaching assistantships available for first-year. Average amount paid per academic year: $14,000. Aver-

age number of hours worked per week: 13. Apply by January 5. Tuition remission given: full. Research assistantships available for first-year. Average amount paid per academic year: $14,000. Average number of hours worked per week: 13. Apply by January 5. Tuition remission given: full. Fellowships and scholarships available for first-year. Average amount paid per academic year: $14,000. Average number of hours worked per week: 13. Apply by January 5. Tuition remission given: full.

Advanced Students: Teaching assistantships available for advanced students. Average amount paid per academic year: $14,000. Average number of hours worked per week: 13. Tuition remission given: full. Research assistantships available for advanced students. Average amount paid per academic year: $14,000. Average number of hours worked per week: 13. Tuition remission given: full. Fellowships and scholarships available for advanced students. Average amount paid per academic year: $14,000. Average number of hours worked per week: 13. Tuition remission given: full.

Contact Information: Of all students currently enrolled full-time, 35% benefitted from one or more of the listed financial assistance programs.

Internships/Practica: Both master's and doctoral students are required to take at least two semesters of practica. For doctoral students (and some master's students), local sites include Dane County Community Mental Health Agency, Mendota Mental Health Institute, University of Wisconsin Counseling and Consultation Services, Veteran's Administration Hospital, and Family Therapy, Inc. Master's students may pursue practica in three types of settings: public schools, student services offices and counseling centers in higher education and community mental health agencies and private clinics. The majority of practicum placements are in the Madison area, but some are placed in nearby metropolitan areas in Wisconsin such as Milwaukee and Green Bay, as well as in rural communities served by regional mental health clinics. For those doctoral students for whom a professional internship is required prior to graduation, 6 applied in 2003–2004. Of those who applied, 4 were placed in internships listed by the Association of Psychology Postdoctoral and Internship Programs (APPIC); 4 were placed in APA accredited internships.

Housing and Day Care: On-campus housing is available. See the following Web site for more information: http://www.housing.wisc.edu/. On-campus day care facilities are available.

Employment of Department Graduates:

Master's Degree Graduates: Of those who graduated in the academic year 2003–2004, the following categories and numbers represent the post-graduate activities and employment of master's degree graduates: Enrolled in a psychology doctoral program (5), enrolled in a post-doctoral residency/fellowship (n/a), employed in independent practice (n/a), total from the above (master's) (2).

Doctoral Degree Graduates: Of those who graduated in the academic year 2003–2004, the following categories and numbers represent the post-graduate activities and employment of doctoral degree graduates: Enrolled in a psychology doctoral program (n/a), enrolled in a post-doctoral residency/fellowship (1), employed in an academic position at a university (1), employed in an academic position at a 2-year/4-year college (1), employed in other positions at a higher education institution (1), employed in a professional position in a school system (1), employed in a government agency (professional services) (1), employed in a hospital/medical center (1), do not know (1), total from the above (doctoral) (8).

Additional Information:

Orientation, Objectives, and Emphasis of Department: The master's and doctoral programs are intended to provide a closely integrated didactic experimental curriculum for the preparation of counseling professionals. The master's degree strongly emphasizes service delivery, and its practica/internship components reflect that emphasis. The doctoral degree emphasizes the integration of counseling and psychological theory and practice with substantive development of research skills in the domains encompassed by counseling psychology. The PhD program in counseling psychology is APA-accredited utilizing the scientist-practitioner model. Students are prepared for academic, service-delivery, research, and administrative positions in professional psychology. The Department infuses principles of multiculturalism throughout the curriculum.

Special Facilities or Resources: The department possesses excellent computer facilities including multimedia production. Also, two counseling psychologists employed at the University Counseling Service are adjunct professors in the department and provide us with on-going linkage with that service for practica and internships. We also have very up-to-date computer software assessment resources. The department, together with the departments of Rehabilitation Psychology, Special Education, and School Psychology, utilizes an interdisciplinary training center that provides professional training practices.

Information for Students With Physical Disabilities: See the following Web site for more information: Web:http://jumpgate.acadsvcs.wisc.edu/~mcburney.

Application Information:
Send to: Counseling Psychology, Graduate Admissions, UW—Madison, 321 Education Building, 1000 Bascom Mall, Madison, WI 53706. Application available online. URL of online application: http:info.gradsch.wisc.edu/admin/admissions/appinstr.html. Students are admitted in the Fall and Summer. For the Fall, application deadline is PhD—December 15, Master's—February 15. For the Summer, application deadlines are the same. *Fee:* $45.

Wisconsin, University of, Madison
Department of Educational Psychology, School Psychology
   Program
1025 West Johnson Street
Madison, WI 53706-1796
Telephone: (608) 262-3432
Fax: (608) 262-0843
E-mail: *edpsych@wisc.edu*
Web: *http://www.education.wisc.edu/edpsych/index.html*

Department Information:
1960. Chairperson: Ronald C. Serlin. Number of Faculty: total–full-time 17, part-time 7; women–full-time 6, part-time 2; minority–part-time 1; faculty subject to the Americans With Disabilities Act 1.

Programs and Degrees Offered:
Listed in the following order: Program area, degree type (T if terminal Master's), number awarded 7/03–6/04. School Psychology PhD (Doctor of Philosophy) 4.

APA Accreditation: School PhD (Doctor of Philosophy).

Student Applications/Admissions:
Student Applications
School Psychology PhD (Doctor of Philosophy)—Applications 2004–2005, 49. Total applicants accepted 2004–2005, 11. Total enrolled 2004–2005 full-time, 28, part-time, 1. Openings 2005–2006, 8. The number of students enrolled full and part-time who were dismissed or voluntarily withdrew from this program area were 0.

Admissions Requirements:
Scores: Entries appear in this order: required test or GPA, minimum score (if required), median score of students entering in 2003–2004. Doctoral Programs: GRE-V no minimum stated, 570; GRE-Q no minimum stated, 660; GRE-V+Q 1000, 1230; overall undergraduate GPA 3.00.
Other Criteria: (importance of criteria rated low, medium, or high): GRE/MAT scores medium, research experience medium, work experience medium, extracurricular activity low, clinically related public service medium, GPA medium, letters of recommendation high, interview high, statement of goals and objectives high.

Student Characteristics: The following represents characteristics of students in 2004–2005 in all graduate psychology programs in the department: Female–full-time 23, part-time 0; Male–full-time 5, part-time 1; African American/Black–full-time 3, part-time 0; Hispanic/Latino(a)–full-time 4, part-time 0; Asian/Pacific Islander–full-time 0, part-time 0; American Indian/Alaska Native–full-time 0, part-time 0; Caucasian–full-time 0, part-time 0; students subject to the Americans With Disabilities Act–full-time 0, part-time 0.

Financial Information/Assistance:
Tuition for Full-Time Study: *Master's:* State residents: per academic year $7,592, $475 per credit hour; Nonstate residents: per academic year $22,862, $1,430 per credit hour. *Doctoral:* State residents: per academic year $7,592, $475 per credit hour; Nonstate residents: per academic year $22,862, $1,430 per credit hour. Tuition is subject to change. See the following Web site for updates and changes in tuition costs: http://www.registrar.wisc.edu/.

Financial Assistance:
First Year Students: Teaching assistantships available for first-year. Average amount paid per academic year: $11,263. Average number of hours worked per week: 14. Apply by December 1. Tuition remission given: full. Research assistantships available for first-year. Average amount paid per academic year: $14,247. Average number of hours worked per week: 20. Apply by December 1. Tuition remission given: full. Traineeships available for first-year. Apply by December 1. Tuition remission given: full. Fellowships and scholarships available for first-year. Average amount paid per academic year: $14,400. Average number of hours worked per week: 0. Apply by December 1. Tuition remission given: full.

Advanced Students: Teaching assistantships available for advanced students. Average amount paid per academic year: $11,263. Average number of hours worked per week: 14. Apply by December 1. Tuition remission given: full. Research assistantships available for advanced students. Average amount paid per academic year: $14,247. Average number of hours worked per week: 20. Apply by December 1. Tuition remission given: full. Traineeships available for advanced students. Apply by December 1. Tuition remission given: full. Fellowships and scholarships available for advanced students. Average amount paid per academic year: $14,400. Average number of hours worked per week: 0. Apply by December 1. Tuition remission given: full.
Contact Information: Of all students currently enrolled full-time, 57% benefitted from one or more of the listed financial assistance programs.

Internships/Practica: *Master's:* State residents: per academic year $7,592, $475 per credit hour; Nonstate residents: per academic year $22,862, $1,430 per credit hour. is required prior to graduation, 2 applied in 2003–2004.

Housing and Day Care: On-campus housing is available. See the following Web site for more information: UW Housing Web site at http://www.housing.wisc.edu. On-campus day care facilities are available. See the following Web site for more information: http://www.housing.wisc.edu/partners/childcare.

Employment of Department Graduates:
Master's Degree Graduates: Of those who graduated in the academic year 2003–2004, the following categories and numbers represent the post-graduate activities and employment of master's degree graduates: Enrolled in a psychology doctoral program (4), enrolled in a post-doctoral residency/fellowship (n/a), employed in independent practice (n/a), total from the above (master's) (4).
Doctoral Degree Graduates: Of those who graduated in the academic year 2003–2004, the following categories and numbers represent the post-graduate activities and employment of doctoral degree graduates: Enrolled in a psychology doctoral program (n/a), enrolled in another graduate/professional program (0), employed in other positions at a higher education institution (1), employed in a professional position in a school system (3), employed in a government agency (professional services) (0), total from the above (doctoral) (4).

Additional Information:
Orientation, Objectives, and Emphasis of Department: The School Psychology program, within the Department of Educational Psychology, prepares professional psychologists to use knowledge of the behavioral sciences in ways that enhance the learning and adjustment of both normal and exceptional children, their families, and their teachers. A balanced emphasis is placed on developing competencies necessary for functioning in both applied settings such as schools and community agencies, and in research positions in institutions of higher education. The program focus is the study of psychological and educational principles which influence the adjustment of individuals from birth to 21 years. Students are required to demonstrate competencies in the substantive content areas of psychological and educational theory and practice.

Personal Behavior Statement: For all programs leading to a certificate or license to teach or requiring field placement, e.g., student teaching practica, counseling practica and internships, and school psychology internships, applicants for admission must disclose, among other things, whether they have ever been charged with or convicted of any crime and whether licensure has ever been denied or revoked in any state for reasons other than insufficient credits or courses. The existence of a criminal record or denial of revocation does not constitute an automatic bar to admission and will be considered only as they substantially relate to the duties and responsibilities of the programs and eventual licensure. Students who are denied admission or removed from such a placement are entitled to appeal that decision. Information about the appeals process is available in department offices of the Office of Student Services, http://www.education.wisc.edu/edpsych.index.html.

Special Facilities or Resources: The Educational and Psychological Training Center serves advanced graduate students in educational psychology. It provides diagnostic and treatment services for children and adolescents experiencing a variety of learning and behavior problems. The Laboratory of Experimental Design provides assistance to students and faculty in the design and analysis of research. Members of the laboratory include graduate students and faculty in the quantitative area.

Information for Students With Physical Disabilities: See the following Web site for more information: http://www.education.wisc.edu/edpsych/index.html.

Application Information:

Send to: Graduate Admissions Coordinator, Educational Psychology, University of Wisconsin, Madison, 1025 W. Johnson Street, Madison, WI 53706-1796. Application available online. Students are admitted in the Fall, application deadline December 1. *Fee:* $45.

Wisconsin, University of, Madison
Department of Psychology
W. J. Brogden Psychology Building, 1202 West Johnson
  Street
Madison, WI 53706
Telephone: (608) 262-2079
Fax: (608) 262-4029
E-mail: *drgreenberg@wisc.edu*
Web: *http://psych.wisc.edu*

Department Information:

1888. Director of Graduate Studies: Lyn Y. Abramson. Number of Faculty: total–full-time 33; women–full-time 13; minority–full-time 3.

Programs and Degrees Offered:

Listed in the following order: Program area, degree type (T if terminal Master's), number awarded 7/03–6/04. Biology of Brain and Behavior PhD (Doctor of Philosophy) 1, Clinical PhD (Doctor of Philosophy) 1, Cognitive and Cognitive Neurosciences PhD (Doctor of Philosophy) 1, Developmental PhD (Doctor of Philosophy) 2, Social Psychology and Personality PhD (Doctor of Philosophy) 1, Individualized Graduate Major PhD (Doctor of Philosophy) 0, Perception PhD (Doctor of Philosophy) 0.

APA Accreditation: Clinical PhD (Doctor of Philosophy).

Student Applications/Admissions:
Student Applications

Biology of Brain and Behavior PhD (Doctor of Philosophy)—Applications 2004–2005, 30. Total applicants accepted 2004–2005, 4. Number enrolled (new admits only) 2004–2005 full-time, 2. The Median number of years required for completion of a degree are 5. *Clinical PhD (Doctor of Philosophy)*—Applications 2004–2005, 179. Total applicants accepted 2004–2005, 13. Number enrolled (new admits only) 2004–2005 full-time, 7. Total enrolled 2004–2005 full-time, 27, part-time, 1. The Median number of years required for completion of a degree are 9. *Cognitive and Cognitive Neurosciences PhD (Doctor of Philosophy)*—Applications 2004–2005, 40. Total applicants accepted 2004–2005, 6. Number enrolled (new admits only) 2004–2005 full-time, 4. The Median number of years required for completion of a degree are 8. *Developmental PhD (Doctor of Philosophy)*—Applications 2004–2005, 35. Total applicants accepted 2004–2005, 8. Number enrolled (new admits only) 2004–2005 full-time, 2. Total enrolled 2004–2005 full-time, 11. The Median number of years required for completion of a degree are 5.5. *Social Psychology and Personality PhD (Doctor of Philosophy)*—Applications 2004–2005, 56. Total applicants accepted 2004–2005, 6. Number enrolled (new admits only) 2004–2005 full-time, 3. The Median number of years required for completion of a degree are 7. *Individualized Graduate Major PhD (Doctor of Philosophy)*—Applications 2004–2005, 23. Total applicants accepted 2004–2005, 7. Number enrolled (new admits only) 2004–2005 full-time, 7. Total enrolled 2004–2005 full-time, 19. *Perception PhD (Doctor of Philosophy)*—Total enrolled 2004–2005 full-time, 1.

Admissions Requirements:

Scores: Entries appear in this order: required test or GPA, minimum score (if required), median score of students entering in 2003–2004. Doctoral Programs: GRE-V no minimum stated; GRE-Q no minimum stated; GRE-V+Q 1200; GRE-Analytical no minimum stated; overall undergraduate GPA 3.00. GRE Subject test is strongly recommended, but not required.

Other Criteria: (importance of criteria rated low, medium, or high): GRE/MAT scores high, research experience high, work experience low, extracurricular activity low, clinically related public service low, GPA high, letters of recommendation high, interview high, statement of goals and objectives high.

Student Characteristics: The following represents characteristics of students in 2004–2005 in all graduate psychology programs in the department: Female–full-time 63, part-time 0; Male–full-time 25, part-time 0; African American/Black–full-time 3, part-time 0; Hispanic/Latino(a)–full-time 1, part-time 0; Asian/Pacific Islander–full-time 2, part-time 0; American Indian/Alaska Native–full-time 0, part-time 0; Caucasian–full-time 0, part-time 0.

Financial Information/Assistance:

Tuition for Full-Time Study: *Doctoral:* State residents: per academic year $4,160; Nonstate residents: per academic year $11,795. Tuition is subject to change. See the following Web site for updates and changes in tuition costs: registrar.wisc.edu/students/fees_tuition/tuition.php.

Financial Assistance:

First Year Students: Teaching assistantships available for first-year. Average amount paid per academic year: $11,263. Aver-

age number of hours worked per week: 20. Apply by January 5. Tuition remission given: full. Research assistantships available for first-year. Average amount paid per academic year: $14,526. Average number of hours worked per week: 20. Apply by January 5. Tuition remission given: full. Traineeships available for first-year. Average amount paid per academic year: $15,579. Average number of hours worked per week: 20. Apply by January 5. Tuition remission given: full. Fellowships and scholarships available for first-year. Average amount paid per academic year: $14,814. Apply by January 5. Tuition remission given: full.

Advanced Students: Teaching assistantships available for advanced students. Average amount paid per academic year: $14,100. Average number of hours worked per week: 20. Tuition remission given: full. Research assistantships available for advanced students. Average amount paid per academic year: $14,814. Average number of hours worked per week: 20. Tuition remission given: full. Traineeships available for advanced students. Average amount paid per academic year: $15,579. Average number of hours worked per week: 20. Tuition remission given: full. Fellowships and scholarships available for advanced students. Average amount paid per academic year: $14,814. Tuition remission given: full.

Contact Information: Of all students currently enrolled full-time, 95% benefitted from one or more of the listed financial assistance programs. Application and information available online at: http://info.gradsch.wisc.edu/admin/admissions/appinstr.html.

Internships/Practica: Clinical psychology graduate students are required to complete a minimum of 400 hours of practicum experience, of which at least 150 hours are in direct service experience and at least 75 hours are in formally scheduled supervision. Each student will complete a 160-hour clerkship at a preapproved site which is designed to expose students to diverse clinical populations and the practice of clinical psychology in an applied setting. Also, a one-year internship is required. For those doctoral students for whom a professional internship is required prior to graduation, 2 applied in 2003–2004. Of those who applied, 2 were placed in APA accredited internships.

Housing and Day Care: On-campus housing is available. See the following Web site for more information: www.housing.wisc.edu. On-campus day care facilities are available. See the following Web site for more information: www.housing.wisc.edu/partners/child care.

Employment of Department Graduates:
Master's Degree Graduates: Of those who graduated in the academic year 2003–2004, the following categories and numbers represent the post-graduate activities and employment of master's degree graduates: Enrolled in a post-doctoral residency/fellowship (n/a), employed in independent practice (n/a), total from the above (master's) (0).
Doctoral Degree Graduates: Of those who graduated in the academic year 2003–2004, the following categories and numbers represent the post-graduate activities and employment of doctoral degree graduates: Enrolled in a psychology doctoral program (n/a), enrolled in a post-doctoral residency/fellowship (4), employed in an academic position at a university (1), total from the above (doctoral) (5).

Additional Information:
Orientation, Objectives, and Emphasis of Department: The psychology PhD program is characterized by the following goals:

emphasis both on extensive academic training in general psychology and on intensive research training in the student's particular area of concentration, a wide offering of content courses and seminars permitting the student considerable freedom in working out a program of study in collaboration with the major professor, and early and continuing commitment to research. Students are expected to become competent scholars and creative scientists in their own areas of concentration.

Special Facilities or Resources: The department has an extraordinary array of research facilities. Virtually all laboratories are fully computer controlled, and the department's general-purpose facilities are freely available to all graduate students. The Brogden and the Harlow Primate Laboratory have special facilities for housing animals, as well as for behavioral, pharmacological, anatomical, immunological, and physiological studies. We are well-equipped for studies of visual, auditory, and language perception and other areas of cognitive psychology. In addition, the Psychology Department Research and Training Clinic is housed in the Brogden Building. Many of the faculty and graduate students are affiliated with the Institute of Aging, the Waisman Center on Mental Retardation and Human Development, the Wisconsin Regional Primate Research Center, the Health Emotions Center, the Neuroscience Training Program, the Keck Neuroimaging Center, the Hearing Training Program, the Institute for Research on Poverty, the NSF National Consortium on Violence Research, and the Women's Studies Research Center. There are strong ties to the departments of Anatomy, Anthropology, Communicative Disorders, Educational Psychology, Entomology, Immunology, Industrial Engineering, Ophthalmology, Psychiatry, Sociology, Wildlife Ecology, Zoology, the Mass Communication Research Center, the Institute for Research on Poverty, and the Survey Research Laboratory.

Information for Students With Physical Disabilities: See the following Web site for more information: www.dcs.wisc.edu./mcb/.

Application Information:
Supplementary materials should be sent to: Admissions Office, Department of Psychology, University of Wisconsin, 1202 W. Johnson Street, Madison, WI 53706. Application available online. URL of online application: http://info.gradsch.wisc.edu/admin/admissions/appinstr.html. Students are admitted in the Fall, application deadline January 5. Contact the Graduate School, 500 Lincoln Drive, 228 Bascom Hall, Madison WI 53706 or www.wisc.edu/grad. *Fee:* $45.

Wisconsin, University of, Madison
Human Development & Family Studies
School of Human Ecology
1430 Linden Drive
Madison, WI 53706
Telephone: (608) 263-2381
Fax: (608) 265-1172
E-mail: *hdfs@mail.sohe.wisc.edu*
Web: *http://www.sohe.wisc.edu/departments/hdfs*

Department Information:
1903. Chairperson: Karen Bogenschneider. Number of Faculty: total–full-time 12; women–full-time 7; minority–full-time 3.

Programs and Degrees Offered:
Listed in the following order: Program area, degree type (T if terminal Master's), number awarded 7/03–6/04. Human Ecology: Human Development & Family Studies PhD (Doctor of Philosophy) 5, Human Ecology: Human Development & Family Studies MA/MS (Master of Arts/Science) 4.

Student Applications/Admissions:

Student Applications

Human Ecology: Human Development & Family Studies PhD (Doctor of Philosophy)—Applications 2004–2005, 18. Total applicants accepted 2004–2005, 6. Number enrolled (new admits only) 2004–2005 full-time, 5. Number enrolled (new admits only) 2004–2005 part-time, 0. Total enrolled 2004–2005 full-time, 25, part-time, 6. Openings 2005–2006, 4. The Median number of years required for completion of a degree are 6. The number of students enrolled full and part-time who were dismissed or voluntarily withdrew from this program area were 0. *Human Ecology: Human Development & Family Studies MA/MS (Master of Arts/Science)*—Applications 2004–2005, 27. Total applicants accepted 2004–2005, 10. Number enrolled (new admits only) 2004–2005 full-time, 3. Number enrolled (new admits only) 2004–2005 part-time, 0. Total enrolled 2004–2005 full-time, 9, part-time, 5. Openings 2005–2006, 4. The Median number of years required for completion of a degree are 3. The number of students enrolled full and part-time who were dismissed or voluntarily withdrew from this program area were 0.

Admissions Requirements:

Scores: Entries appear in this order: required test or GPA, minimum score (if required), median score of students entering in 2003–2004. Master's Programs: GRE-V no minimum stated, 524; GRE-Q no minimum stated, 600; GRE-Analytical no minimum stated, 4.9; overall undergraduate GPA 3.0, 3.53. Doctoral Programs: GRE-V no minimum stated, 600; GRE-Q no minimum stated, 727; GRE-Analytical no minimum stated, 657; overall undergraduate GPA 3.0, 3.34.

Other Criteria: (importance of criteria rated low, medium, or high): GRE/MAT scores medium, research experience medium, work experience low, GPA high, letters of recommendation high, statement of goals and objectives high, fit with faculty interest high. For additional information on admission requirements, go to: http://info.gradsch.wisc.edu/admin/admissions/index.html or http://www.sohe.wisc.edu/departments/hdf.

Student Characteristics: The following represents characteristics of students in 2004–2005 in all graduate psychology programs in the department: Female–full-time 30, part-time 10; Male–full-time 4, part-time 1; African American/Black–full-time 0, part-time 0; Hispanic/Latino(a)–full-time 2, part-time 3; Asian/Pacific Islander–full-time 4, part-time 1; American Indian/Alaska Native–full-time 0, part-time 0; Caucasian–full-time 17, part-time 7; Multi-ethnic–full-time 0, part-time 0.

Financial Information/Assistance:
Tuition for Full-Time Study: *Master's:* State residents: $521 per credit hour; Nonstate residents: $1,476 per credit hour. *Doctoral:* State residents: $521 per credit hour; Nonstate residents: $1,476 per credit hour. Tuition is subject to change. See the following

Web site for updates and changes in tuition costs: http://registrar.wisc.edu/students/fees_tuition/tuition.php.

Financial Assistance:

First Year Students: Teaching assistantships available for first-year. Average amount paid per academic year: $10,475. Average number of hours worked per week: 20. Apply by January 10. Tuition remission given: full. Research assistantships available for first-year. Average amount paid per academic year: $11,101. Average number of hours worked per week: 20. Apply by varies. Tuition remission given: full. Fellowships and scholarships available for first-year. Average amount paid per academic year: Average number of hours worked per week: 0. Apply by January 10.

Advanced Students: Teaching assistantships available for advanced students. Average amount paid per academic year: $11,831. Average number of hours worked per week: 20. Apply by January 10. Tuition remission given: full. Research assistantships available for advanced students. Average amount paid per academic year: $11,101. Average number of hours worked per week: 20. Apply by varies. Tuition remission given: full. Fellowships and scholarships available for advanced students. Average amount paid per academic year: $2,372. Apply by January 10.

Contact Information: Of all students currently enrolled full-time, 80% benefitted from one or more of the listed financial assistance programs. Application and information available online at: http://whyuwmadison.gradsch.wisc.edu/academic/academics.html.

Internships/Practica: No information provided.

Housing and Day Care: On-campus housing is available. See the following Web site for more information: http://whyuwmadison.gradsch.wisc.edu/life/housing.html. On-campus day care facilities are available. See the following Web site for more information: http://www.housing.wisc.edu/partners/childcare/ University provides a childcare assistance subsidy.

Employment of Department Graduates:

Master's Degree Graduates: Of those who graduated in the academic year 2003–2004, the following categories and numbers represent the post-graduate activities and employment of master's degree graduates: Enrolled in another graduate/professional program (3), enrolled in a post-doctoral residency/fellowship (n/a), employed in independent practice (n/a), employed in a community mental health/counseling center (1), total from the above (master's) (4).

Doctoral Degree Graduates: Of those who graduated in the academic year 2003–2004, the following categories and numbers represent the post-graduate activities and employment of doctoral degree graduates: Enrolled in a psychology doctoral program (n/a), employed in independent practice (1), employed in an academic position at a university (3), employed in an academic position at a 2-year/4-year college (1), total from the above (doctoral) (5).

Additional Information:

Orientation, Objectives, and Emphasis of Department: The UW Human Development and Family Studies Graduate Program provides opportunities for advanced study and research on human development and families across the life span. Two assumptions are basic to the philosophy and organization of the program. First, we can only understand individual development within its social context, and families are an essential component of this context. Second, we can only understand families within their larger social context—historical change, social class, ethnicity, and public policy. The program offers courses on development in infancy, childhood, adolescence, adulthood, and old age. Other courses focus on family relationships, process, and diversity. The faculty bring the perspectives of many different disciplines and methodologies to their work. Faculty and students never lose sight, however, of the connections among human development, family life, and the broader sociohistorical context.

Special Facilities or Resources: Because the department has joint faculty in UW-Extension, students often work in the community doing community based research and outreach projects. Departmental faculty have affiliated appointments with research centers and other programs on campus, which students have access to. The Family Interaction Lab in the department provides a naturalistic home-like setting for unobtrusive videotaping of interactions. A control room is located adjacent to the interaction room for camera control, taping, editing, dubbing and coding of videotapes. The UW Preschool Laboratory is adjacent to the department.

Information for Students With Physical Disabilities: See the following Web site for more information: http://www.mcburney. wisc.edu/services.

Application Information:
Send to: Graduate Admissions, Human Development & Family Studies, Graduate Program, University of Wisconsin—Madison, 1430 Linden Drive, Madison, WI 53706. Application available online. URL of online application: https://www.gradsch.wisc.edu/eapp/eapp.pl. Students are admitted in the Fall, application deadline January 10. *Fee:* $45.

Wisconsin, University of, Milwaukee
Department of Psychology
College of Letters & Science
P.O. Box 413
Milwaukee, WI 53201-0413
Telephone: (414) 229-4747
Fax: (414) 229-5219
E-mail: *suelima@uwm.edu*
Web: *http://www.uwm.edu/Dept/Psychology*

Department Information:
1956. Chairperson: Rodney Swain. Number of Faculty: total–full-time 20; women–full-time 5.

Programs and Degrees Offered:
Listed in the following order: Program area, degree type (T if terminal Master's), number awarded 7/03–6/04. Experimental Behavior Analysis MA/MS (Master of Arts/Science) (T) 1, Experimental Health Psychology MA/MS (Master of Arts/Science) (T) 3, Experimental PhD (Doctor of Philosophy) 1, Clinical PhD (Doctor of Philosophy) 4.

APA Accreditation: Clinical PhD (Doctor of Philosophy).

Student Applications/Admissions:
Student Applications
Experimental Behavior Analysis MA/MS (Master of Arts/Science)—Applications 2004–2005, 5. Total applicants accepted

2004–2005, 2. Number enrolled (new admits only) 2004–2005 full-time, 1. Number enrolled (new admits only) 2004–2005 part-time, 0. Openings 2005–2006, 6. The Median number of years required for completion of a degree are 4. The number of students enrolled full and part-time who were dismissed or voluntarily withdrew from this program area were 0. *Experimental Health Psychology MA/MS (Master of Arts/Science)*—Applications 2004–2005, 8. Total applicants accepted 2004–2005, 5. Number enrolled (new admits only) 2004–2005 full-time, 1. Number enrolled (new admits only) 2004–2005 part-time, 0. Openings 2005–2006, 6. The Median number of years required for completion of a degree are 3. The number of students enrolled full and part-time who were dismissed or voluntarily withdrew from this program area were 0. *Experimental PhD (Doctor of Philosophy)*—Applications 2004–2005, 17. Total applicants accepted 2004–2005, 9. Number enrolled (new admits only) 2004–2005 full-time, 7. Number enrolled (new admits only) 2004–2005 part-time, 0. Openings 2005–2006, 5. The Median number of years required for completion of a degree are 8. The number of students enrolled full and part-time who were dismissed or voluntarily withdrew from this program area were 0. *Clinical PhD (Doctor of Philosophy)*—Applications 2004–2005, 70. Total applicants accepted 2004–2005, 10. Number enrolled (new admits only) 2004–2005 full-time, 5. Number enrolled (new admits only) 2004–2005 part-time, 0. Openings 2005–2006, 5. The Median number of years required for completion of a degree are 8. The number of students enrolled full and part-time who were dismissed or voluntarily withdrew from this program area were 0.

Admissions Requirements:
Scores: Entries appear in this order: required test or GPA, minimum score (if required), median score of students entering in 2003–2004. Master's Programs: GRE-V no minimum stated, 450; GRE-Q no minimum stated, 600; GRE-Analytical no minimum stated, 540; GRE-Subject(Psych) no minimum stated, 550; overall undergraduate GPA 3.0, 3.67; last 2 years GPA no minimum stated, 3.44; psychology GPA no minimum stated, 3.55. Doctoral Programs: GRE-V no minimum stated, 539; GRE-Q no minimum stated, 620; GRE-Analytical no minimum stated, 668; GRE-Subject(Psych) no minimum stated, 628; overall undergraduate GPA 3.00, 3.65. For the Experimental Doctoral Program: GRE V+Q minimum is 800.
Other Criteria: (importance of criteria rated low, medium, or high): GRE/MAT scores high, research experience medium, work experience low, extracurricular activity low, clinically related public service low, GPA high, letters of recommendation medium, interview high, statement of goals and objectives high. No interview is required for admission to the Doctoral Program in Experimental Psychology, but an interview is required for admission to the Doctoral Program in Clinical Psychology. For additional information on admission requirements, go to: http://www.uwm.edu/Dept/Psychology/gradapp. html.

Student Characteristics: The following represents characteristics of students in 2004–2005 in all graduate psychology programs in the department: Female–full-time 51, part-time 0; Male–full-time 26, part-time 0; African American/Black–full-time 2, part-time 0; Hispanic/Latino(a)–full-time 6, part-time 0; Asian/Pacific Islander–full-time 3, part-time 0; American Indian/Alaska Native–full-time 0, part-time 0; Caucasian–full-time 66, part-time 0;

Multi-ethnic–full-time 0, part-time 0; students subject to the Americans With Disabilities Act–full-time 0, part-time 0.

Financial Information/Assistance:

Tuition for Full-Time Study: *Master's:* State residents: per academic year $8,131, $686 per credit hour; Nonstate residents: per academic year $22,497, $1,584 per credit hour. *Doctoral:* State residents: per academic year $8,131, $686 per credit hour; Nonstate residents: per academic year $22,497, $1,584 per credit hour. Tuition is subject to change. See the following Web site for updates and changes in tuition costs: www.uwm.edu/Dept/DES.

Financial Assistance:

First Year Students: Teaching assistantships available for first-year. Average amount paid per academic year: $10,079. Average number of hours worked per week: 20. Apply by December 31. Tuition remission given: full. Research assistantships available for first-year. Average amount paid per academic year: $17,210. Average number of hours worked per week: 20. Apply by December 31. Tuition remission given: partial. Fellowships and scholarships available for first-year. Average amount paid per academic year: $9,000. Average number of hours worked per week: 20. Apply by December 31. Tuition remission given: full.

Advanced Students: Teaching assistantships available for advanced students. Average amount paid per academic year: $10,919. Average number of hours worked per week: 20. Apply by December 31. Tuition remission given: full. Research assistantships available for advanced students. Average amount paid per academic year: $17,210. Average number of hours worked per week: 20. Apply by December 31. Tuition remission given: partial. Fellowships and scholarships available for advanced students. Average amount paid per academic year: $14,000. Average number of hours worked per week: 20. Apply by December 31. Tuition remission given: full.

Contact Information: Of all students currently enrolled full-time, 85% benefitted from one or more of the listed financial assistance programs. Application and information available online at: http://www.uwm.edu/Dept/Psychology/gradapp.html.

Internships/Practica: Numerous training sites in the greater Milwaukee area are used for clinical training practica, providing students with excellent training in clinical psychology, including neuropsychology and health psychology. These training experiences equip clinical doctoral students to compete for nationally recognized pre-doctoral internships. For those doctoral students for whom a professional internship is required prior to graduation, 5 applied in 2003–2004. Of those who applied, 5 were placed in internships listed by the Association of Psychology Postdoctoral and Internship Programs (APPIC); 5 were placed in APA accredited internships.

Housing and Day Care: On-campus housing is available. See the following Web site for more information: http://www.uwm.edu/UWM/Student/S_housing.html. On-campus day care facilities are available. See the following Web site for more information: www.uwm.edu/Dept/CCC.

Employment of Department Graduates:

Master's Degree Graduates: Of those who graduated in the academic year 2003–2004, the following categories and numbers represent the post-graduate activities and employment of master's degree graduates: Enrolled in a psychology doctoral program (2), enrolled in another graduate/professional program (1), enrolled in a post-doctoral residency/fellowship (n/a), employed in independent practice (n/a), employed in other positions at a higher education institution (1), employed in a community mental health/counseling center (1), total from the above (master's) (5).

Doctoral Degree Graduates: Of those who graduated in the academic year 2003–2004, the following categories and numbers represent the post-graduate activities and employment of doctoral degree graduates: Enrolled in a psychology doctoral program (n/a), enrolled in a post-doctoral residency/fellowship (3), employed in independent practice (1), total from the above (doctoral) (4).

Additional Information:

Orientation, Objectives, and Emphasis of Department: The department has a PhD program in clinical psychology, a PhD program in experimental psychology, and terminal master's-level specializations in health psychology and behavior analysis. The experimental PhD program offers specialization in behavior analysis, cognition and perception, developmental psychology, health and social psychology, and neuroscience. Regardless of the specialty area, the goal of the program is to provide the students with an understanding of psychology as a scientific discipline and to prepare them for careers in research and teaching. The clinical program follows the Boulder model, in which students are trained as both scientists and practitioners through integration of research, practical experience, and coursework in personality theory, psychopathology, assessment, and psychotherapy. A predoctoral internship is required. Although a clinical student may emphasize either the basic or applied aspect of psychology, the goal of the program is excellence in both areas. Students in the clinical as well as the experimental program are directly involved in research under the direction of their major professor, during each semester in the department.

Special Facilities or Resources: The department moved to a completely remodeled building in September 1985, which contains a separate research laboratory for each member of the faculty and specifically designed quarters for teaching advanced laboratory courses in research methods, cognitive psychology, physiological psychology, and learning. Faculty have microcomputers in their offices, as well as in their laboratories, and these are also connected to the mainframe and to the World Wide Web. Special construction, air conditioning, and ventilation were included in the teaching and research laboratories to accommodate work with animal and human subjects. There is also a mechanical and woodworking shop and an excellent electronics shop, supervised by a full-time technician. The department training clinic is housed in a separate wing of the building with its own offices, clerical staff, research space, clinic rooms, and full-time director.

Information for Students With Physical Disabilities: See the following Web site for more information: www.uwm.edu/Dept/DSAD/SAC/sac.html.

Application Information:

Send to: Chairperson, Graduate Admissions Committee, Department of Psychology, P.O. Box 413, Milwaukee, WI 53201-0413. Application available online. URL of online application: http://www.uwm.edu/Dept/Psychology/gradapp.html and http://www.uwm.edu/Dept/Grad_Sch/Prospective/. Students are admitted in the Fall, application deadline December 31. Note that two separate applications are required: one to the psychology department and one to the Graduate School.

Deadline for master's in behavior analysis and master's in health psychology applications is July 1 (for entry in September of that same year). *Fee:* $45. Application fee for foreign students is $75. Under rare circumstances, one-half of foreign application fee will be waived. International applicants should consult the following Web site: www.uwm.edu/Dept/CIE.

Wisconsin, University of, Milwaukee
Educational Psychology
Education
2400 E. Hartford IP0413
Milwaukee, WI 53211
Telephone: (414) 229-4767
Fax: (414) 229-4939
E-mail: *psmith@uwm.edu*
Web: *http://www.uwm.edu/Dept/EdPsych*

Department Information:
1965. Chairperson: Philip L. Smith. Number of Faculty: total—full-time 23, part-time 16; women—full-time 11, part-time 12; minority—full-time 5, part-time 4.

Programs and Degrees Offered:
Listed in the following order: Program area, degree type (T if terminal Master's), number awarded 7/03–6/04. Counseling MA/MS (Master of Arts/Science) 83, School EdS (Education Specialist) 9, Educational Psychology MA/MS (Master of Arts/Science) 2.

Student Applications/Admissions:
Student Applications
Counseling MA/MS (Master of Arts/Science)—Applications 2004–2005, 205. Total applicants accepted 2004–2005, 89. Number enrolled (new admits only) 2004–2005 full-time, 12. Number enrolled (new admits only) 2004–2005 part-time, 51. Total enrolled 2004–2005 full-time, 67, part-time, 141. Openings 2005–2006, 75. The Median number of years required for completion of a degree are 4. *School EdS (Education Specialist)*—Applications 2004–2005, 32. Total applicants accepted 2004–2005, 12. Number enrolled (new admits only) 2004–2005 full-time, 11. Number enrolled (new admits only) 2004–2005 part-time, 1. Total enrolled 2004–2005 full-time, 23, part-time, 27. Openings 2005–2006, 14. The Median number of years required for completion of a degree are 4. *Educational Psychology MA/MS (Master of Arts/Science)*—Applications 2004–2005, 9. Total applicants accepted 2004–2005, 7. Number enrolled (new admits only) 2004–2005 full-time, 4. Number enrolled (new admits only) 2004–2005 part-time, 2. Total enrolled 2004–2005 full-time, 12, part-time, 15. Openings 2005–2006, 12. The Median number of years required for completion of a degree are 3. The number of students enrolled full and part-time who were dismissed or voluntarily withdrew from this program area were 0.

Admissions Requirements:
Scores: Entries appear in this order: required test or GPA, minimum score (if required), median score of students entering

in 2003–2004. Master's Programs: overall undergraduate GPA 2.75, 3.45. Doctoral Programs: GRE-V+Q 1050; overall undergraduate GPA 3.00. 40th percentile GRE-V, 30th percentile GRE-M.
Other Criteria: (importance of criteria rated low, medium, or high): GRE/MAT scores medium, research experience medium, work experience low, clinically related public service medium, GPA high, letters of recommendation medium, interview medium, statement of goals and objectives medium.

Student Characteristics: The following represents characteristics of students in 2004–2005 in all graduate psychology programs in the department: Caucasian—full-time 0, part-time 0.

Financial Information/Assistance:
Tuition for Full-Time Study: *Master's:* State residents: per academic year $7,402, $475 per credit hour; Nonstate residents: per academic year $21,700, $1,300 per credit hour. *Doctoral:* State residents: per academic year $7,402, $475 per credit hour; Nonstate residents: per academic year $21,700, $1,300 per credit hour. Tuition is subject to change. See the following Web site for updates and changes in tuition costs: www.uwm.edu.

Financial Assistance:
First Year Students: Teaching assistantships available for first-year. Average amount paid per academic year: $8,500. Average number of hours worked per week: 20. Apply by rolling. Tuition remission given: full. Research assistantships available for first-year. Average amount paid per academic year: $9,500. Average number of hours worked per week: 20. Apply by rolling. Tuition remission given: full. Fellowships and scholarships available for first-year. Average amount paid per academic year: $8,000. Average number of hours worked per week: 20. Apply by rolling. Tuition remission given: full.
Advanced Students: Teaching assistantships available for advanced students. Average amount paid per academic year: $9,000. Average number of hours worked per week: 20. Apply by rolling. Tuition remission given: full. Research assistantships available for advanced students. Average amount paid per academic year: $10,000. Average number of hours worked per week: 20. Apply by rolling. Tuition remission given: full. Fellowships and scholarships available for advanced students. Average amount paid per academic year: $10,000. Average number of hours worked per week: 20. Apply by rolling. Tuition remission given: full.
Contact Information: Of all students currently enrolled full-time, 65% benefitted from one or more of the listed financial assistance programs.

Internships/Practica: Students are placed in a variety of educational, business, and community settings as part of their graduate training. For those doctoral students for whom a professional internship is required prior to graduation, 7 applied in 2003–2004. Of those who applied, 7 were placed in internships listed by the Association of Psychology Postdoctoral and Internship Programs (APPIC); 6 were placed in APA accredited internships.

Housing and Day Care: On-campus housing is available. See the following Web site for more information: www.uwm.edu/Dept/Sanburg. On-campus day care facilities are available. See the following Web site for more information: www.uwm.edu/Dept/CCC.

Employment of Department Graduates:

Master's Degree Graduates: Of those who graduated in the academic year 2003–2004, the following categories and numbers represent the post-graduate activities and employment of master's degree graduates: Enrolled in a post-doctoral residency/fellowship (n/a), employed in independent practice (n/a), total from the above (master's) (0).

Doctoral Degree Graduates: Of those who graduated in the academic year 2003–2004, the following categories and numbers represent the post-graduate activities and employment of doctoral degree graduates: Enrolled in a psychology doctoral program (n/a), total from the above (doctoral) (0).

Additional Information:

Orientation, Objectives, and Emphasis of Department: The department has one MS program with majors in Community Counseling, Rehabilitation Counseling, School Counseling, School Psychology (also EdS), Quantitative Methods and Learning and Development. PhD program (through our Urban Education major) has emphases in Educational Psychology (includes Quantitative Methods and Learning & Development), School Psychology and Counseling Psychology. The PhD programs in School Psychology and Counseling Psychology follow the model of training outlined by the American Psychological Association. The programs are based on the scientist-practitioner model, in which students are trained as psychological scientists with specializations in school or counseling psychology. A strong, multicultural perspective undergirds the programs, with an emphasis on the contextual factors in students' work. The programs are housed under the umbrella of the Urban Education Doctoral Program, providing unique training in the psychological, social, and educational needs of multiethnic populations within an urban psychosocial context. Students gain the knowledge, skills, and attitudes to work in a heterogeneous environment. Students are prepared to work in academic, service delivery, research and administrative positions.

Special Facilities or Resources: The department possesses excellent computer facilities. The department enjoys a strong collaborative relationship with the Department of Psychology, working together in an on-campus psychology clinic. We also have strong linkages to urban community and school partners, which provide students with a diverse set of research and practice opportunities.

Information for Students With Physical Disabilities: See the following Web site for more information: www.uwm.edu/DSAD/SAC.

Application Information:

Send to: MS, EdS: Department of Educational Psychology, UW—Milwaukee, P.O. Box 413, Milwaukee, WI 53201. PhD: Director, Urban Education Doctoral Program, School of Education, UW—Milwaukee, P.O. Box 413, Milwaukee, WI 53201. Application available online. URL of online application: http://www.uwm.edu/Dept/Grad_Sch/Prospective/. Students are admitted in the Fall, application deadline January 15. Admission once per academic year for Counseling and School Psychology programs. Quantitative program and Learning & Development program have rolling admissions and will consider applications at anytime. *Fee:* $45.

Wisconsin, University of, Oshkosh
Department of Psychology
College of Letters and Science
800 Algoma Boulevard
Oshkosh, WI 54901
Telephone: (414) 424-2300
Fax: (414) 424-1204
E-mail: *mcfadden@uwosh.edu*
Web: *http://www.uwosh.edu/departments/psychology/*

Department Information:
1959. Chairperson: Susan H. McFadden. Number of Faculty: total–full-time 11, part-time 5; women–full-time 4, part-time 4; minority–full-time 2.

Programs and Degrees Offered:
Listed in the following order: Program area, degree type (T if terminal Master's), number awarded 7/03–6/04. Experimental Psychology MA/MS (Master of Arts/Science) (T) 3, Industrial/Organizational Psychology MA/MS (Master of Arts/Science) (T) 5.

Student Applications/Admissions:
Student Applications

Experimental Psychology MA/MS (Master of Arts/Science)—Applications 2004–2005, 7. Total applicants accepted 2004–2005, 7. Total enrolled 2004–2005 full-time, 10, part-time, 2. Openings 2005–2006, 10. The Median number of years required for completion of a degree are 2. The number of students enrolled full and part-time who were dismissed or voluntarily withdrew from this program area were 0. *Industrial/Organizational Psychology MA/MS (Master of Arts/Science)*—Applications 2004–2005, 25. Total applicants accepted 2004–2005, 15. Number enrolled (new admits only) 2004–2005 full-time, 8. Number enrolled (new admits only) 2004–2005 part-time, 0. Total enrolled 2004–2005 full-time, 17, part-time, 1. Openings 2005–2006, 9. The Median number of years required for completion of a degree are 2.

Admissions Requirements:

Scores: Entries appear in this order: required test or GPA, minimum score (if required), median score of students entering in 2003–2004. Master's Programs: GRE-V no minimum stated; GRE-Q no minimum stated; GRE-V+Q no minimum stated; GRE-Analytical no minimum stated; overall undergraduate GPA no minimum stated; last 2 years GPA no minimum stated.

Other Criteria: (importance of criteria rated low, medium, or high): GRE/MAT scores medium, research experience medium, work experience low, extracurricular activity low, GPA medium, letters of recommendation medium, statement of goals and objectives medium. Students in the Industrial/Organizational emphasis are required to submit a 2-3 page personal statement covering the origins of their interest in working in Industrial/Organizational Psychology, relevant experience (work or volunteer) in this field, and any other relevant personal information. Students in the Experimental emphasis are required to submit a personal statement at least a page or two in length. This statement should include reasons for wanting to come to UW Oshkosh and areas of research interest. The admissions committee is particularly interested in details about research experience, including class projects, assistantships, presentations, or other research experiences. If there were any extenuating circumstances leading to low performance in any aspect as an undergraduate or on GRE exams, it would be appropriate to comment on these in the personal statement.

Student Characteristics: The following represents characteristics of students in 2004–2005 in all graduate psychology programs in the department: Female–full-time 17, part-time 2; Male–full-time 7, part-time 1; African American/Black–full-time 1, part-time 0; Hispanic/Latino(a)–full-time 1, part-time 0; Asian/Pacific Islander–full-time 0, part-time 0; American Indian/Alaska Native–full-time 0, part-time 0; Caucasian–full-time 0, part-time 0; Multi-ethnic–full-time 0, part-time 0; students subject to the Americans With Disabilities Act–full-time 0, part-time 0.

Financial Information/Assistance:

Tuition for Full-Time Study: *Master's:* State residents: per academic year $5,848, $327 per credit hour; Nonstate residents: per academic year $16,458, $916 per credit hour.

Financial Assistance:

First Year Students: Research assistantships available for first-year. Average number of hours worked per week: 13. Fellowships and scholarships available for first-year.

Advanced Students: Research assistantships available for advanced students. Average number of hours worked per week: 13. Fellowships and scholarships available for advanced students.

Contact Information: Of all students currently enrolled full-time, 48% benefitted from one or more of the listed financial assistance programs.

Internships/Practica: Industrial/Organizational students participate in practica in year two. Some students also have the opportunity to do internships.

Housing and Day Care: On-campus housing is available. Contact the Residence Life office: (920) 424-3212. On-campus day care facilities are available. Contact the Children's Learning & Care Center, the on-campus child care facility, at (920) 424-0260 for more information.

Employment of Department Graduates:

Master's Degree Graduates: Of those who graduated in the academic year 2003–2004, the following categories and numbers represent the post-graduate activities and employment of master's degree graduates: Enrolled in a psychology doctoral program (2), enrolled in another graduate/professional program (0), enrolled in a post-doctoral residency/fellowship (n/a), employed in independent practice (n/a), employed in an academic position at a university (0), employed in an academic position at a 2-year/4-year college (0), employed in other positions at a higher education institution (1), employed in a professional position in a school system (0), employed in business or industry (research/consulting) (2), employed in business or industry (management) (1), employed in a government agency (research) (0), employed in a government agency (professional services) (0), employed in a community mental health/counseling center (0), employed in a hospital/medical center (0), still seeking employment (0), not seeking employment (0), other employment position (1), do not know (0), total from the above (master's) (7).

Doctoral Degree Graduates: Of those who graduated in the academic year 2003–2004, the following categories and numbers represent the post-graduate activities and employment of doctoral degree graduates: Enrolled in a psychology doctoral program (n/a), total from the above (doctoral) (0).

Additional Information:

Orientation, Objectives, and Emphasis of Department: The program offers a master's degree in psychology with emphases in industrial/organizational and general experimental psychology. Students are required to take core courses dealing with psychological methods and statistical analysis. Classes are small. Students in the I/O emphasis take two semesters of a practicum course that involves exeprience working with organizations in the local area. Students in the experimental emphasis conduct research in collaboration with faculty.

Special Facilities or Resources: Practicum placements are available for research in local agencies and industries. Animal and human laboratories are also available.

Information for Students With Physical Disabilities: See the following Web site for more information: http://www.tts.uwosh.edu/dean/disabilities.htm.

Application Information:

Send to: Graduate School and Research, University of Wisconsin, Oshkosh, 800 Algoma Boulevard, Oshkosh, WI 54901. Students are admitted in the Spring, application deadline March 15. Application deadline is for I/O program. The Experimental program has rolling admissions. *Fee:* $45.

Wisconsin, University of, Stout
Psychology Department / Applied Psychology
College of Human Development
Human Services 317
Menomonie, WI 54751-0790
Telephone: (715) 232-2478
Fax: (715) 232-5303
E-mail: *milanesil@uwstout.edu*
Web: *http://www.uwstout.edu*

Department Information:

1982. Program Director: Louis C. Milanesi. Number of Faculty: total–full-time 16, part-time 4; women–full-time 5, part-time 3; minority–full-time 4.

Programs and Degrees Offered:

Listed in the following order: Program area, degree type (T if terminal Master's), number awarded 7/03–6/04. Applied MA/MS (Master of Arts/Science) (T) 50.

Student Applications/Admissions:

Student Applications

Applied MA/MS (Master of Arts/Science)—Applications 2004–2005, 27. Total applicants accepted 2004–2005, 20. Total enrolled 2004–2005 full-time, 29, part-time, 2. Openings 2005–2006, 27. The Median number of years required for completion of a degree are 2.

Admissions Requirements:

Scores: Entries appear in this order: required test or GPA, minimum score (if required), median score of students entering in 2003–2004. Master's Programs: overall undergraduate GPA 3.0, 3.5.

Other Criteria: (importance of criteria rated low, medium, or high): research experience high, work experience high, extracurricular activity medium, clinically related public service low, GPA high, letters of recommendation high, statement of goals and objectives high, applied experience high. For additional information on admission requirements, go to: http://www.uwstout.edu/programs/msap/.

Student Characteristics: The following represents characteristics of students in 2004–2005 in all graduate psychology programs in the department: Female–full-time 29, part-time 3; Male–full-time 8, part-time 0; African American/Black–full-time 0, part-time 0; Hispanic/Latino(a)–full-time 1, part-time 0; Asian/Pacific Islander–full-time 1, part-time 0; American Indian/Alaska Native–full-time 0, part-time 0; Caucasian–full-time 0, part-time 0.

Financial Information/Assistance:

Tuition for Full-Time Study: *Master's:* State residents: per academic year $4,194; Nonstate residents: per academic year $12,552.

Financial Assistance:

First Year Students: Teaching assistantships available for first-year. Average amount paid per academic year: $5,000. Average number of hours worked per week: 13. Apply by none. Research assistantships available for first-year. Average amount paid per academic year: $4,000. Average number of hours worked per week: 10. Apply by none.

Advanced Students: Teaching assistantships available for advanced students. Average amount paid per academic year: $5,000. Average number of hours worked per week: 13. Apply by none. Research assistantships available for advanced students. Average amount paid per academic year: $4,000. Average number of hours worked per week: 10. Apply by none.

Contact Information: Of all students currently enrolled full-time, 50% benefitted from one or more of the listed financial assistance programs.

Internships/Practica: *Master's:* State residents: per academic year $4,194; Nonstate residents: per academic year $12,552. is required prior to graduation, 12 applied in 2003–2004.

Housing and Day Care: On-campus housing is available. Housing (715) 232-1121. On-campus day care facilities are available. Child Care (715) 232-1478.

Employment of Department Graduates:

Master's Degree Graduates: Of those who graduated in the academic year 2003–2004, the following categories and numbers represent the post-graduate activities and employment of master's degree graduates: Enrolled in a psychology doctoral program (5), enrolled in another graduate/professional program (0), enrolled in a post-doctoral residency/fellowship (n/a), employed in independent practice (n/a), employed in an academic position at a 2-year/4-year college (2), employed in other positions at a higher education institution (3), employed in business or industry (research/consulting) (45), total from the above (master's) (55).

Doctoral Degree Graduates: Of those who graduated in the academic year 2003–2004, the following categories and numbers represent the post-graduate activities and employment of doctoral degree graduates: Enrolled in a psychology doctoral program (n/a), total from the above (doctoral) (0).

Additional Information:

Orientation, Objectives, and Emphasis of Department: The MS in applied psychology is a two-year program designed around a core of appropriate psychological theories and principles, with three applied concentration areas of industrial/organizational psychology, program evaluation, and health psychology. It is designed to provide students with the knowledge, experience, skills, and abilities to apply the theories and methods of psychology to the identification and solution of a variety of real-world problems. What distinguishes the applied psychologist are the competencies in accessing the vast resources of psychological theories, research methods, and research findings as a base for developing new and more effective approaches to the solution of these problems. The goal of the applied psychology program is to produce competent professionals with broad knowledge of the field of psychology. They will have the skills to apply this knowledge to the complex people problems of the 1990s and the 21st century, and to act as role models in the domains of organizational development, problem-solving, interpersonal interaction, personal growth, and evaluation. Business, health, and community service and other settings in which the applied psychologist will work have a critical need for educated and responsible professionals who can participate in the solution of complex individual and organizational problems.

Special Facilities or Resources: The university has recently opened a new computer facility that is used for instruction and individual research. Several facilities/labs within the College of Human Development and the Department of Psychology will receive or will have received lab modernization funds. These labs will utilize the latest multi-media hardware and software. The experimental psychology lab is currently undergoing a major renovation.

Application Information:

Send to: Program Director, MSAP and Graduate College. Application available online. Students are admitted in the Fall, application deadline February 1; Spring, application deadline October 1; Programs have rolling admissions. All students applying to the MSAP program must be accepted by the graduate college. *Fee:* $45.

Wyoming, University of
Department of Psychology
Arts and Sciences
Dept. 3415, 1000 E. University Avenue
Laramie, WY 82071
Telephone: (307) 766-6303
Fax: (307) 766-2926
E-mail: *psyc.uw@uwyo.edu*
Web: *http://www.uwyo.edu/psychology*

Department Information:
1909. Chairperson: Narina Nunez. Number of Faculty: total–full-time 13, part-time 2; women–full-time 4, part-time 1; minority–full-time 1.

Programs and Degrees Offered:
Listed in the following order: Program area, degree type (T if terminal Master's), number awarded 7/03–6/04. Clinical PhD (Doctor of Philosophy) 3, Developmental PhD (Doctor of Philosophy) 0, General PhD (Doctor of Philosophy) 0.

APA Accreditation: Clinical PhD (Doctor of Philosophy).

Student Applications/Admissions:
Student Applications
Clinical PhD (Doctor of Philosophy)—Applications 2004–2005, 63. Total applicants accepted 2004–2005, 8. Number enrolled (new admits only) 2004–2005 full-time, 7. Openings 2005–2006, 5. The Median number of years required for completion of a degree are 6. The number of students enrolled full and part-time who were dismissed or voluntarily withdrew from this program area were 3. *Developmental PhD (Doctor of Philosophy)*—Applications 2004–2005, 6. Total applicants accepted 2004–2005, 2. Number enrolled (new admits only) 2004–2005 full-time, 0. Openings 2005–2006, 2. The number of students enrolled full and part-time who were dismissed or voluntarily withdrew from this program area were 0. *General PhD (Doctor of Philosophy)*—Applications 2004–2005, 10. Total applicants accepted 2004–2005, 2. Number enrolled (new admits only) 2004–2005 full-time, 2. Openings 2005–2006, 2. The number of students enrolled full and part-time who were dismissed or voluntarily withdrew from this program area were 0.

Admissions Requirements:
Scores: Entries appear in this order: required test or GPA, minimum score (if required), median score of students entering in 2003–2004. Doctoral Programs: GRE-V 500, 570; GRE-Q 550, 680; GRE-V+Q 1050, 1250; GRE-Subject(Psych) 550, 670; overall undergraduate GPA 3.00, 3.62.
Other Criteria: (importance of criteria rated low, medium, or high): GRE/MAT scores high, research experience high, work experience low, extracurricular activity low, clinically related public service medium, GPA medium, letters of recommendation high, interview high, statement of goals and objectives high. Public service is relevant to the Clinical program only.

Student Characteristics: The following represents characteristics of students in 2004–2005 in all graduate psychology programs in the department: Female–full-time 36, part-time 0; Male–full-time 16, part-time 0; African American/Black–full-time 0, part-time 0; Hispanic/Latino(a)–full-time 1, part-time 0; Asian/Pacific Islander–full-time 1, part-time 0; American Indian/Alaska Native–full-time 0, part-time 0; Caucasian–full-time 50, part-time 0; Multi-ethnic–full-time 0, part-time 0; students subject to the Americans With Disabilities Act–full-time 0, part-time 0.

Financial Information/Assistance:
Tuition for Full-Time Study: *Master's:* State residents: per academic year $3,528, $147 per credit hour; Nonstate residents: per academic year $10,104, $421 per credit hour. *Doctoral:* State residents: per academic year $3,528, $147 per credit hour; Nonstate residents: per academic year $10,104, $421 per credit hour. See the following Web site for updates and changes in tuition costs: www.uwyo.edu/sfa.

Financial Assistance:
First Year Students: Teaching assistantships available for first-year. Average amount paid per academic year: $10,100. Average number of hours worked per week: 20. Tuition remission given: full. Research assistantships available for first-year. Average amount paid per academic year: $10,100. Average number of hours worked per week: 20. Tuition remission given: full. Fellowships and scholarships available for first-year. Average amount paid per academic year: $2,000. Average number of hours worked per week: 0.

Advanced Students: Teaching assistantships available for advanced students. Average amount paid per academic year: $14,000. Average number of hours worked per week: 20. Tuition remission given: full. Research assistantships available for advanced students. Average amount paid per academic year: $14,000. Average number of hours worked per week: 20. Tuition remission given: full.

Contact Information: Of all students currently enrolled full-time, 100% benefitted from one or more of the listed financial assistance programs.

Internships/Practica: Given Wyoming's large geographic area (approximately 100,000 square miles) and small population (approximately 500,000), we arrange practica and clerkships for Clinical students in various settings throughout the state. Clerkships are typically conducted in the summer for extended periods of time. Practica and clerkships include a variety of clinical populations such as children, adolescents, adults, and elderly people. They occur in a range of placements including outpatient mental health centers, inpatient hospitals, VA Medical Centers and residential programs. Specialty experiences include forensic evaluation, substance abuse training, and parent training. For those doctoral students for whom a professional internship is required prior to graduation, 4 applied in 2003–2004. Of those who applied, 4 were placed in internships listed by the Association of Psychology Postdoctoral and Internship Programs (APPIC); 4 were placed in APA accredited internships.

Housing and Day Care: On-campus housing is available. See the following Web site for more information: http://uwadmnweb.

uwyo.edu/reslife-dining/. On-campus day care facilities are available. See the following Web sites for more information: http://www.uwyo.edu/Family/Child_Care/C_Care_Center.htm and http://www.uwyo.edu/Family/Child_Care/cdcnewpg.htm. The university is also building a large child care center and it will open in 2006. Other quality child care centers are available in the local community.

Employment of Department Graduates:

Master's Degree Graduates: Of those who graduated in the academic year 2003–2004, the following categories and numbers represent the post-graduate activities and employment of master's degree graduates: Enrolled in a post-doctoral residency/fellowship (n/a), employed in independent practice (n/a), total from the above (master's) (0).

Doctoral Degree Graduates: Of those who graduated in the academic year 2003–2004, the following categories and numbers represent the post-graduate activities and employment of doctoral degree graduates: Enrolled in a psychology doctoral program (n/a), enrolled in a post-doctoral residency/fellowship (1), employed in independent practice (1), employed in a community mental health/counseling center (1), total from the above (doctoral) (3).

Additional Information:

Orientation, Objectives, and Emphasis of Department: The University of Wyoming is the only four-year university in the state of Wyoming. The psychology department has a broad undergraduate teaching mission and has one of the largest number of majors in the College of Arts and Sciences. The graduate curriculum provides breadth of training in psychology and permits specialization in various content areas. The Clinical Psychology PhD program is based on the scientist-practitioner model, with an emphasis on training in integrated behavioral health care. Some clinical students may also pursue a concentration in developmental psychology, psychology and law, or social-personality with experimental graduate program faculty. The goal of the clinical program is to provide students with the knowledge base and broad conceptual skills necessary for professional practice and/or research in a variety of settings. The PhD program in Experimental Psychology provides students with broad training that can be used in a variety of academic and applied settings. Students may concentrate in Developmental Psychology or they may complete their concentration in Social Psychology. Students in any of the programs may pursue a Psychology and Law concentration. All programs contain opportunities for both applied and basic research training.

Special Facilities or Resources: The department has approximately 24,000 square feet of laboratory, office, and clinic space in a science complex with direct access to the university's science library; and various computer labs. Faculty laboratories range from wet laboratories designed for the biological aspects of human behavior to labs designed to assess mock jurors and jury decision-making. The Psychology Clinic has ample space for individual or small group assessment and treatment. These facilities also have observation mirrors and video tape-recording capability.

Information for Students With Physical Disabilities: See the following Web site for more information: www.uwyo.edu/seo.

Application Information:
Send to: Graduate Admissions Committee, Department of Psychology, University of Wyoming, Dept. 3415, 1000 E. University Avenue, Laramie, WY 82071. Application available online. URL of online application: http://www.uwyo.edu/psychology. Students are admitted in the Fall, application deadline January 15. *Fee:* $50. There is no fee for applying to the program. Only students who are accepted into and are officially entering the program are charged the fee.

Acadia University
Department of Psychology
Wolfville, NS B4P 2R6
Telephone: (902) 585-1301
Fax: (902) 585-1078
E-mail: *peter.horvath@acadiau.ca*
Web: *http://ace.acadiau.ca/science/psyc/GRAD/Home.htm*

Department Information:
1926. Head: Dr. Doug Symons. Number of Faculty: total–full-time 12, part-time 4; women–full-time 7, part-time 4.

Programs and Degrees Offered:
Listed in the following order: Program area, degree type (T if terminal Master's), number awarded 7/03–6/04. Clinical MA/MS (Master of Arts/Science) (T) 5.

Student Applications/Admissions:
Student Applications
Clinical MA/MS *(Master of Arts/Science)*—Applications 2004–2005, 40. Total applicants accepted 2004–2005, 6. Total enrolled 2004–2005 full-time, 9, part-time, 1. Openings 2005–2006, 5. The Median number of years required for completion of a degree are 2. The number of students enrolled full and part-time who were dismissed or voluntarily withdrew from this program area were 0.

Admissions Requirements:
Scores: Entries appear in this order: required test or GPA, minimum score (if required), median score of students entering in 2003–2004. Master's Programs: GRE-V 500, 580; GRE-Q 500, 610; GRE-Analytical 500, 650; overall undergraduate GPA 3.50, 3.60; psychology GPA 3.50.
Other Criteria: (importance of criteria rated low, medium, or high): GRE/MAT scores high, research experience high, work experience medium, extracurricular activity medium, clinically related public service medium, GPA high, letters of recommendation high, interview high, statement of goals and objectives high.

Student Characteristics: The following represents characteristics of students in 2004–2005 in all graduate psychology programs in the department: Female–full-time 8, part-time 1; Male–full-time 1, part-time 0; African American/Black–full-time 0, part-time 0; Hispanic/Latino(a)–full-time 0, part-time 0; Asian/Pacific Islander–full-time 0, part-time 0; American Indian/Alaska Native–full-time 0, part-time 0; Caucasian–full-time 0, part-time 0.

Financial Information/Assistance:
Tuition for Full-Time Study: *Master's:* State residents: per academic year $5,611. Tuition is subject to change.

Financial Assistance:
First Year Students: Teaching assistantships available for first-year. Average amount paid per academic year: $8,000. Average number of hours worked per week: 10. Apply by February 1.
Advanced Students: Teaching assistantships available for advanced students. Average amount paid per academic year: $8,000. Average number of hours worked per week: 10.
Contact Information: Of all students currently enrolled full-time, 60% benefitted from one or more of the listed financial assistance programs.

Internships/Practica: Two 150-hour internships are mandatory in intervention and assessment. Internship in community psychology is available.

Housing and Day Care: On-campus housing is available: ask.acadia@acadiau.ca. No on-campus day care facilities are available.

Employment of Department Graduates:
Master's Degree Graduates: Of those who graduated in the academic year 2003–2004, the following categories and numbers represent the post-graduate activities and employment of master's degree graduates: Enrolled in a psychology doctoral program (1), enrolled in a post-doctoral residency/fellowship (n/a), employed in independent practice (n/a), employed in other positions at a higher education institution (1), employed in a community mental health/counseling center (1), employed in a hospital/medical center (2), total from the above (master's) (5).
Doctoral Degree Graduates: Of those who graduated in the academic year 2003–2004, the following categories and numbers represent the post-graduate activities and employment of doctoral degree graduates: Enrolled in a psychology doctoral program (n/a), total from the above (doctoral) (0).

Additional Information:
Orientation, Objectives, and Emphasis of Department: The department's principal objective is to train MSc students in clinical psychology. The department's orientation is eclectic, although there is an emphasis on cognitive approaches to problems in psychology. Master's-level registration as a psychologist is available in all Maritime Provinces in Canada. Our curriculum is also highly respected, and graduates going on to doctoral programs elsewhere have had full recognition of coursework in all instances. We are registered with CAMPP.

Special Facilities or Resources: The department is part of the cooperative clinical PhD program of Dalhousie University.

Application Information:
Send to: Admissions Office, Acadia University, Wolfville, NS, B4P 2R6. Students are admitted in the Fall, application deadline February 1. *Fee:* $50. Applied against fellowship. Note: All dollar amounts specified in this entry are Canadian dollars.

Alberta, University of
Department of Psychology
Biological Sciences Building
Edmonton, AB T6G 2E9
Telephone: (708) 492-5216
Fax: (708) 492-1768
E-mail: *douglas.grant@ualberta.ca*
Web: *http://www.psych.ualberta.ca*

Department Information:
1961. Chair: Douglas S. Grant. Number of Faculty: total–full-time 30; women–full-time 9.

Programs and Degrees Offered:
Listed in the following order: Program area, degree type (T if terminal Master's), number awarded 7/03–6/04. Masters Program MA/MS (Master of Arts/Science) 1, Doctoral Program PhD (Doctor of Philosophy) 5.

Student Applications/Admissions:
Student Applications
Masters Program MA/MS (Master of Arts/Science)—Applications 2004–2005, 55. Total applicants accepted 2004–2005, 12. Number enrolled (new admits only) 2004–2005 full-time, 7. Total enrolled 2004–2005 full-time, 16. The Median number of years required for completion of a degree are 2. The number of students enrolled full and part-time who were dismissed or voluntarily withdrew from this program area were 2. *Doctoral Program PhD (Doctor of Philosophy)*—Applications 2004–2005, 29. Total applicants accepted 2004–2005, 12. Number enrolled (new admits only) 2004–2005 full-time, 6. Total enrolled 2004–2005 full-time, 31. The Median number of years required for completion of a degree are 6. The number of students enrolled full and part-time who were dismissed or voluntarily withdrew from this program area were 0.

Admissions Requirements:
Scores: Entries appear in this order: required test or GPA, minimum score (if required), median score of students entering in 2003–2004. Master's Programs: GRE-V+Q+Analytical no minimum stated; last 2 years GPA 3.0. Doctoral Programs: GRE-V+Q+Analytical no minimum stated; last 2 years GPA 3.0.
Other Criteria: (importance of criteria rated low, medium, or high): GRE/MAT scores high, research experience high, work experience low, extracurricular activity low, clinically related public service low, GPA high, letters of recommendation high, statement of goals and objectives high. For additional information on admission requirements, go to: http://www.psych.ualberta.ca/graduate/studentinfo.html.

Student Characteristics: The following represents characteristics of students in 2004–2005 in all graduate psychology programs in the department: Female–full-time 33, part-time 0; Male–full-time 14, part-time 0; African American/Black–full-time 0, part-time 0; Hispanic/Latino(a)–full-time 0, part-time 0; Asian/Pacific Islander–full-time 8, part-time 0; American Indian/Alaska Native–full-time 1, part-time 0; Caucasian–full-time 38, part-time 0.

Financial Information/Assistance:
Tuition for Full-Time Study: *Master's:* State residents: per academic year $3,765; Nonstate residents: per academic year $7,114. *Doctoral:* State residents: per academic year $3,765; Nonstate residents: per academic year $7,114. Tuition is subject to change. See the following Web site for updates and changes in tuition costs: http://gradfile.fgsro.ualberta.ca/current/fguides.html.

Financial Assistance:
First Year Students: Teaching assistantships available for first-year. Average amount paid per academic year: $19,563. Average number of hours worked per week: 12. Apply by January 15. Research assistantships available for first-year. Average amount paid per academic year: $19,563. Average number of hours worked per week: 12. Apply by January 15. Fellowships and scholarships available for first-year. Average number of hours worked per week: 12. Apply by January 15. Tuition remission given: full and partial.
Advanced Students: Teaching assistantships available for advanced students. Average amount paid per academic year: $20,500. Average number of hours worked per week: 12. Apply by January 15. Research assistantships available for advanced students. Average amount paid per academic year: $20,500. Average number of hours worked per week: 12. Apply by January 15. Fellowships and scholarships available for advanced students. Average number of hours worked per week: 12. Apply by January 15. Tuition remission given: full and partial.
Contact Information: Of all students currently enrolled full-time, 95% benefitted from one or more of the listed financial assistance programs. Application and information available online at: http://www.psych.ualberta.ca/graduate/studentinfo.html.

Internships/Practica: No information provided.

Housing and Day Care: On-campus housing is available. See the following Web site for more information: Housing and Food Services, (780) 492-4281, (800) 615-4807, housing@ualberta.ca, http://www.hfs.ualberta.ca/student/studenthousing.html. On-campus day care facilities are available. There are a number of child care agencies. Please ask the psychology graduate assistant for current telephone numbers for child care on campus.

Employment of Department Graduates:
Master's Degree Graduates: Of those who graduated in the academic year 2003–2004, the following categories and numbers represent the post-graduate activities and employment of master's degree graduates: Enrolled in another graduate/professional program (1), enrolled in a post-doctoral residency/fellowship (n/a), employed in independent practice (n/a), total from the above (master's) (1).
Doctoral Degree Graduates: Of those who graduated in the academic year 2003–2004, the following categories and numbers represent the post-graduate activities and employment of doctoral degree graduates: Enrolled in a psychology doctoral program (n/a), employed in an academic position at a university (2), employed in an academic position at a 2-year/4-year college (1), employed in business or industry (research/consulting) (1), do not know (1), total from the above (doctoral) (5).

Additional Information:
Orientation, Objectives, and Emphasis of Department: The goal of the graduate program is to train competent and independent researchers who will make significant contributions to the disci-

pline of psychology. The program entails early and sustained involvement in research and ensures that students attain expertise in focal and related domains. The program offers training that leads to degrees in a range of research areas, including Applied Developmental Science; Brain, Behaviour, and Cognitive Science; and Social and Cultural Psychology. Recent PhD graduates from the Department have successfully found positions in universities and colleges, branches of government, and industry. A reasonably close match between the research interests of prospective students and faculty members is essential because the program involves apprenticeship-style training. Although many faculty members conduct research on problems that have practical and social significance, we do not have programs in clinical, counseling, or industrial/organizational psychology.

Information for Students With Physical Disabilities: See the following Web site for more information: http://www.ualberta.ca/ssds.

Application Information:

Send to: Graduate Program Assistant, Department of Psychology, P-217D Biological Sciences, University of Alberta, Edmonton, AB Canada T6G 2E9. Application available online. URL of online application: http://www.psych.ualberta.ca/graduate/AppInfo.html. Students are admitted in the Fall, application deadline January 15. The Department admits approximately ten graduate students per year. Students holding an undergraduate degree are admitted either to the Master's Program or directly to the PhD program; upon successful completion of the Master's degree, they normally continue in the PhD Program. Students holding a qualifying Master's Degree are admitted directly to the PhD Program. *Fee:* $100. Note: All dollar amounts specified in this entry are Canadian dollars.

British Columbia, University of

Department of Psychology
2136 West Mall, Kenny Psychology Building
Vancouver, BC V6T 1Z4
Telephone: (604) 822-2755
Fax: (604) 822-6923
E-mail: *askus@psych.ubc.ca*
Web: *http://www.psych.ubc.ca*

Department Information:

1951. Head: Eric Eich. Number of Faculty: total–full-time 48, part-time 19; women–full-time 16, part-time 19.

Programs and Degrees Offered:

Listed in the following order: Program area, degree type (T if terminal Master's), number awarded 7/03–6/04. Behavioral Neuroscience PhD (Doctor of Philosophy) 0, Clinical PhD (Doctor of Philosophy) 1, Forensic PhD (Doctor of Philosophy) 1, Developmental PhD (Doctor of Philosophy) 1, Cognitive Science PhD (Doctor of Philosophy) 3, Social/ Personality PhD (Doctor of Philosophy) 2, Psychometrics PhD (Doctor of Philosophy) 1.

APA Accreditation: Clinical PhD (Doctor of Philosophy).

Student Applications/Admissions:

Student Applications

Behavioral Neuroscience PhD (Doctor of Philosophy)—Applications 2004–2005, 13. Total applicants accepted 2004–2005, 4. Number enrolled (new admits only) 2004–2005 full-time, 3. Number enrolled (new admits only) 2004–2005 part-time, 0. Openings 2005–2006, 5. The number of students enrolled full and part-time who were dismissed or voluntarily withdrew from this program area were 0. *Clinical PhD (Doctor of Philosophy)*—Applications 2004–2005, 129. Total applicants accepted 2004–2005, 7. Number enrolled (new admits only) 2004–2005 full-time, 6. Number enrolled (new admits only) 2004–2005 part-time, 0. Openings 2005–2006, 8. The Median number of years required for completion of a degree are 5. The number of students enrolled full and part-time who were dismissed or voluntarily withdrew from this program area were 0. *Forensic PhD (Doctor of Philosophy)*—Applications 2004–2005, 42. Total applicants accepted 2004–2005, 0. Number enrolled (new admits only) 2004–2005 full-time, 0. Number enrolled (new admits only) 2004–2005 part-time, 0. The Median number of years required for completion of a degree are 7. The number of students enrolled full and part-time who were dismissed or voluntarily withdrew from this program area were 0. *Developmental PhD (Doctor of Philosophy)*—Applications 2004–2005, 12. Total applicants accepted 2004–2005, 4. Number enrolled (new admits only) 2004–2005 full-time, 3. Number enrolled (new admits only) 2004–2005 part-time, 0. Openings 2005–2006, 5. The Median number of years required for completion of a degree are 6. The number of students enrolled full and part-time who were dismissed or voluntarily withdrew from this program area were 0. *Cognitive Science PhD (Doctor of Philosophy)*—Applications 2004–2005, 20. Total applicants accepted 2004–2005, 4. Number enrolled (new admits only) 2004–2005 full-time, 2. Number enrolled (new admits only) 2004–2005 part-time, 0. Openings 2005–2006, 6. The Median number of years required for completion of a degree are 6. The number of students enrolled full and part-time who were dismissed or voluntarily withdrew from this program area were 1. *Social/ Personality PhD (Doctor of Philosophy)*—Applications 2004–2005, 47. Total applicants accepted 2004–2005, 4. Number enrolled (new admits only) 2004–2005 full-time, 3. Number enrolled (new admits only) 2004–2005 part-time, 0. Openings 2005–2006, 8. The Median number of years required for completion of a degree are 6. The number of students enrolled full and part-time who were dismissed or voluntarily withdrew from this program area were 0. *Psychometrics PhD (Doctor of Philosophy)*—Applications 2004–2005, 12. Total applicants accepted 2004–2005, 1. Number enrolled (new admits only) 2004–2005 full-time, 0. Number enrolled (new admits only) 2004–2005 part-time, 0. Openings 2005–2006, 2. The Median number of years required for completion of a degree are 7. The number of students enrolled full and part-time who were dismissed or voluntarily withdrew from this program area were 0.

Admissions Requirements:

Scores: Entries appear in this order: required test or GPA, minimum score (if required), median score of students entering in 2003–2004. Master's Programs: GRE-V+Q+Analytical 2000; GRE-Subject(Psych) 660; last 2 years GPA B+. Doctoral Programs: GRE-V+Q+Analytical 2000; GRE-Subject(Psych) 660.

Other Criteria: (importance of criteria rated low, medium, or high): GRE/MAT scores medium, research experience high, clinically related public service low, GPA high, letters of recommendation high, statement of goals and objectives high. For additional information on admission requirements, go to: www.psych.ubc.ca/graduate.htm.

Student Characteristics: The following represents characteristics of students in 2004–2005 in all graduate psychology programs in the department: Female–full-time 66, part-time 0; Male–full-time 36, part-time 0; Caucasian–full-time 0, part-time 0.

Financial Information/Assistance:

Tuition for Full-Time Study: *Master's:* State residents: per academic year $3,712; Nonstate residents: per academic year $7,200. *Doctoral:* State residents: per academic year $0; Nonstate residents: per academic year $0. Tuition is subject to change. See the following Web site for updates and changes in tuition costs: students.ubc.ca/.

Financial Assistance:

First Year Students: Teaching assistantships available for first-year. Average amount paid per academic year: $10,000. Average number of hours worked per week: 12. Apply by January 15. Research assistantships available for first-year. Average amount paid per academic year: $5,000. Apply by January 15. Fellowships and scholarships available for first-year. Average amount paid per academic year: $17,500. Apply by January 15.

Advanced Students: Teaching assistantships available for advanced students. Average amount paid per academic year: $10,000. Average number of hours worked per week: 12. Apply by January 15. Tuition remission given: full. Research assistantships available for advanced students. Average amount paid per academic year: $4,000. Apply by January 15. Tuition remission given: full. Fellowships and scholarships available for advanced students. Average amount paid per academic year: $17,500. Apply by January 15. Tuition remission given: full.

Contact Information: Of all students currently enrolled full-time, 100% benefitted from one or more of the listed financial assistance programs. Application and information available online at: www.psych.ubc.ca/graduate.htm.

Internships/Practica: A 4-month practicum in an approved agency is required of clinical students during the summer after the second or third year of the program or during the third year. A 1-year internship at a mental health agency accredited by CPA or APA is required for the PhD in clinical psychology. For those doctoral students for whom a professional internship is required prior to graduation, 8 applied in 2003–2004. Of those who applied, 8 were placed in internships listed by the Association of Psychology Postdoctoral and Internship Programs (APPIC); 8 were placed in APA accredited internships.

Housing and Day Care: On-campus housing is available. See the following Web site for more information: www.housing.ubc.ca. On-campus day care facilities are available. See the following Web site for more information: www.childcare.ubc.ca.

Employment of Department Graduates:

Master's Degree Graduates: Of those who graduated in the academic year 2003–2004, the following categories and numbers represent the post-graduate activities and employment of master's degree graduates: Enrolled in a psychology doctoral program (15), enrolled in another graduate/professional program (0), enrolled in a post-doctoral residency/fellowship (n/a), employed in independent practice (n/a), total from the above (master's) (15).

Doctoral Degree Graduates: Of those who graduated in the academic year 2003–2004, the following categories and numbers represent the post-graduate activities and employment of doctoral degree graduates: Enrolled in a psychology doctoral program (n/a), enrolled in a post-doctoral residency/fellowship (2), employed in an academic position at a university (5), employed in business or industry (research/consulting) (1), still seeking employment (1), total from the above (doctoral) (9).

Additional Information:

Orientation, Objectives, and Emphasis of Department: The department is organized into seven subject content areas with which faculty and graduate students are affiliated. Graduate training emphasizes a high degree of research competence and, from the beginning of the program, students are involved in increasingly independent research activities.

Special Facilities or Resources: The department is housed in an attractive building of about 90,000 square feet, designed for psychological research. The department has well-equipped research facilities including a psychology clinic, observational galleries, and animal, psychophysiological, perceptual, cognitive, and social/personality laboratories.

Information for Students With Physical Disabilities: See the following Web site for more information: http://students.ubc.ca/access/drc.cfm.

Application Information:
Send to: Graduate Secretary, Department of Psychology, University of British Columbia, Vancouver, BC V6T 1Z4. Application available online. URL of online application: http://www.grad.ubc.ca/apply/online/. Students are admitted in the Fall, application deadline January 15. *Fee:* $90. The application fee for international applicants is $150. The application fee is waived for international applicants whose correspondence address is located in the following countries: Bangladesh, Bhutan, Burkina Faso, Burundi, Chad, Ethiopia, Guinea-Bissou, Lao PDR, Madagascar, Malawi, Mali, Mozambique, Nepal, Niger, Rwanda, Sierra Leona, Tanzania, and Uganda. Note: All dollar amounts specified in this entry are Canadian dollars.

Calgary, University of
Department of Psychology
2500 University Drive, N.W.
Calgary, AB T2N 1N4
Telephone: (403) 220-5561
Fax: (403) 282-8249
E-mail: *bhbland@ucalgary.ca*
Web: *http://www.psych.ucalgary.ca*

Department Information:
1964. Chairperson: Dr. Brian H. Bland. Number of Faculty: total–full-time 31; women–full-time 8; minority–full-time 1.

Programs and Degrees Offered:

Listed in the following order: Program area, degree type (T if terminal Master's), number awarded 7/03–6/04. Psychology PhD (Doctor of Philosophy) 7, Clinical Psychology PhD (Doctor of Philosophy) 4.

Student Applications/Admissions:

Student Applications

Psychology PhD (Doctor of Philosophy)—Applications 2004–2005, 56. Total applicants accepted 2004–2005, 8. Number enrolled (new admits only) 2004–2005 full-time, 8. Openings 2005–2006, 12. The Median number of years required for completion of a degree are 3. The number of students enrolled full and part-time who were dismissed or voluntarily withdrew from this program area were 0. *Clinical Psychology PhD (Doctor of Philosophy)*—Applications 2004–2005, 76. Total applicants accepted 2004–2005, 5. Number enrolled (new admits only) 2004–2005 full-time, 5. Openings 2005–2006, 8. The Median number of years required for completion of a degree are 3. The number of students enrolled full and part-time who were dismissed or voluntarily withdrew from this program area were 0.

Admissions Requirements:

Scores: Entries appear in this order: required test or GPA, minimum score (if required), median score of students entering in 2003–2004. Master's Programs: GRE-V no minimum stated; GRE-Q no minimum stated; GRE-Analytical no minimum stated; last 2 years GPA no minimum stated. Clinical Psychology, GPA of 3.7 (A-) over the last two years of study. Psychology, GPA of 3.4 (B+) over the last two years of study. Doctoral Programs: GRE-V no minimum stated; GRE-Q no minimum stated; GRE-Analytical no minimum stated; last 2 years GPA no minimum stated.

Other Criteria: (importance of criteria rated low, medium, or high): GRE/MAT scores medium, research experience high, work experience medium, extracurricular activity low, clinically related public service medium, GPA high, letters of recommendation high, interview medium, statement of goals and objectives high, research proposal high.

Student Characteristics: The following represents characteristics of students in 2004–2005 in all graduate psychology programs in the department: Female–full-time 55, part-time 0; Male–full-time 18, part-time 0; African American/Black–full-time 0, part-time 0; Hispanic/Latino(a)–full-time 0, part-time 0; Asian/Pacific Islander–full-time 4, part-time 0; American Indian/Alaska Native–full-time 0, part-time 0; Caucasian–full-time 69, part-time 0; students subject to the Americans With Disabilities Act–full-time 0, part-time 0.

Financial Information/Assistance:

Tuition for Full-Time Study: *Master's:* State residents: per academic year $5,249; Nonstate residents: per academic year $9,796. *Doctoral:* State residents: per academic year $5,249; Nonstate residents: per academic year $9,796. Tuition is subject to change. See the following Web site for updates and changes in tuition costs: www.grad.ucalgary.ca.

Financial Assistance:

First Year Students: Teaching assistantships available for first-year. Average amount paid per academic year: $13,000. Aver-age number of hours worked per week: 12. Research assistantships available for first-year. Average amount paid per academic year: $4,100. Fellowships and scholarships available for first-year. Average amount paid per academic year: $15,000. Apply by January 15.

Advanced Students: Teaching assistantships available for advanced students. Average amount paid per academic year: $13,000. Average number of hours worked per week: 12. Research assistantships available for advanced students. Average amount paid per academic year: $4,100. Fellowships and scholarships available for advanced students. Average amount paid per academic year: $15,000. Apply by January 15.

Contact Information: Of all students currently enrolled full-time, 100% benefitted from one or more of the listed financial assistance programs. Application and information available online at: www.grad.ucalgary.ca/Funding/.

Internships/Practica: Internships are available at several settings, including Foothills Hospital and Children's Hospital. For those doctoral students for whom a professional internship is required prior to graduation, 5 applied in 2003–2004. Of those who applied, 5 were placed in internships listed by the Association of Psychology Postdoctoral and Internship Programs (APPIC).

Housing and Day Care: On-campus housing is available. See the following Web site for more information: www.ucalgary.ca/residence/. On-campus day care facilities are available.

Employment of Department Graduates:

Master's Degree Graduates: Of those who graduated in the academic year 2003–2004, the following categories and numbers represent the post-graduate activities and employment of master's degree graduates: Enrolled in a psychology doctoral program (10), enrolled in another graduate/professional program (1), enrolled in a post-doctoral residency/fellowship (n/a), employed in independent practice (n/a), total from the above (master's) (11).

Doctoral Degree Graduates: Of those who graduated in the academic year 2003–2004, the following categories and numbers represent the post-graduate activities and employment of doctoral degree graduates: Enrolled in a psychology doctoral program (n/a), employed in independent practice (2), employed in an academic position at a university (3), employed in other positions at a higher education institution (1), employed in business or industry (research/consulting) (3), employed in a community mental health/counseling center (1), employed in a hospital/medical center (4), total from the above (doctoral) (14).

Additional Information:

Orientation, Objectives, and Emphasis of Department: This is a research-oriented department with a strong focus on applied problems. We offer both a clinical psychology and a psychology program. Specific research programs in psychology include: behavioural neuroscience, cognition and cognitive development (CCD), industrial/organizational psychology (I/O), social psychology, perception aging and cognitive ergonomics (PACE), and theoretical psychology.

Application Information:

Send to: Graduate Programs Administrator, Department of Psychology, 2500 University Drive NW, University of Calgary, Calgary, AB T2N1N4 Canada. Application available online. Students are admitted in the Fall, application deadline January 15; Winter, application deadline October 15; Spring, application deadline January 15. The Clinical and Industrial Organizational Psychology Programs only accept students for a start date in September. The application deadline for these programs is January 15 only. *Fee:* $60. Note: All dollar amounts specified in this entry are Canadian dollars.

Carleton University

Department of Psychology
Faculty of Arts and Social Sciences
1125 Colonel By Drive
Ottawa, ON K1S 5B6
Telephone: (613) 520-4017
Fax: (613) 520-3667
E-mail: *mary_gick@carleton.ca*
Web: *http://www.carleton.ca/psychology/*

Department Information:
1952. Chairperson: Mary Gick. Number of Faculty: total–full-time 43, part-time 3; women–full-time 16, part-time 3.

Programs and Degrees Offered:
Listed in the following order: Program area, degree type (T if terminal Master's), number awarded 7/03–6/04. MA/MS (Master of Arts/Science) 24, Neuroscience MA/MS (Master of Arts/Science) 6, PhD (Doctor of Philosophy) 10.

Student Applications/Admissions:
Student Applications
MA/MS *(Master of Arts/Science)*—Applications 2004–2005, 149. Total applicants accepted 2004–2005, 52. Number enrolled (new admits only) 2004–2005 full-time, 27. Number enrolled (new admits only) 2004–2005 part-time, 1. Total enrolled 2004–2005 full-time, 57, part-time, 18. The number of students enrolled full and part-time who were dismissed or voluntarily withdrew from this program area were 1. *Neuroscience MA/MS (Master of Arts/Science)*—Applications 2004–2005, 21. Total applicants accepted 2004–2005, 14. Number enrolled (new admits only) 2004–2005 full-time, 9. Number enrolled (new admits only) 2004–2005 part-time, 1. Total enrolled 2004–2005 full-time, 13, part-time, 5. Openings 2005–2006, 13. The number of students enrolled full and part-time who were dismissed or voluntarily withdrew from this program area were 1. *PhD (Doctor of Philosophy)*—Applications 2004–2005, 39. Total applicants accepted 2004–2005, 20. Number enrolled (new admits only) 2004–2005 full-time, 13. Number enrolled (new admits only) 2004–2005 part-time, 4. Total enrolled 2004–2005 full-time, 44, part-time, 17. The number of students enrolled full and part-time who were dismissed or voluntarily withdrew from this program area were 1.

Admissions Requirements:
Scores: Entries appear in this order: required test or GPA, minimum score (if required), median score of students entering in 2003–2004. Master's Programs: last 2 years GPA 9, 10.7; psychology GPA 9.
Other Criteria: (importance of criteria rated low, medium, or high): research experience high, work experience low, extracurricular activity low, clinically related public service low, GPA high, letters of recommendation high, statement of goals and objectives high. For additional information on admission

requirements, go to: http://www.carleton.ca/psychology/graduate/ma_admission.html.

Student Characteristics: The following represents characteristics of students in 2004–2005 in all graduate psychology programs in the department: Female–full-time 82, part-time 30; Male–full-time 32, part-time 10; , part-time 0; , part-time 0; , part-time 0; Caucasian–full-time 103, part-time 40; students subject to the Americans With Disabilities Act–full-time 0, part-time 0.

Financial Information/Assistance:
Tuition for Full-Time Study: *Master's:* State residents: per academic year $4,256; Nonstate residents: per academic year $9,293. *Doctoral:* State residents: per academic year $4,256; Nonstate residents: per academic year $9,293. Tuition is subject to change. See the following Web site for updates and changes in tuition costs: www.carleton.ca/fees.

Financial Assistance:
First Year Students: Teaching assistantships available for first-year. Average amount paid per academic year: $8,562. Average number of hours worked per week: 10. Apply by February 1. Research assistantships available for first-year. Average amount paid per academic year: $2,500. Apply by February 1. Fellowships and scholarships available for first-year.
Advanced Students: Teaching assistantships available for advanced students. Average amount paid per academic year: $8,562. Average number of hours worked per week: 10. Research assistantships available for advanced students. Average amount paid per academic year: $3,500. Fellowships and scholarships available for advanced students. Average amount paid per academic year: $6,000.
Contact Information: Of all students currently enrolled full-time, 45% benefitted from one or more of the listed financial assistance programs. Application and information available online at: http://www.carleton.ca/psychology/graduate/ma_finance.html.

Internships/Practica: N/A.

Housing and Day Care: On-campus housing is available. See the following Web site for more information: http://www.carleton.ca/housing/. On-campus day care facilities are available. E-mail cbccc@ncf.ca or call (613) 520-2715.

Employment of Department Graduates:
Master's Degree Graduates: Of those who graduated in the academic year 2003–2004, the following categories and numbers represent the post-graduate activities and employment of master's degree graduates: Enrolled in a psychology doctoral program (13), enrolled in another graduate/professional program (2), enrolled in a post-doctoral residency/fellowship (n/a), employed in independent practice (n/a), employed in an academic position at a university (4), employed in business or industry (research/consulting) (3), employed in a government agency (professional services) (3), employed in a hospital/medical center (1), do not know (4), total from the above (master's) (30).
Doctoral Degree Graduates: Of those who graduated in the academic year 2003–2004, the following categories and numbers represent the post-graduate activities and employment of doctoral degree graduates: Enrolled in a psychology doctoral program (n/a), employed in an academic position at a university (2), employed in business or industry (research/consulting) (3), employed in

business or industry (management) (2), employed in a government agency (research) (1), employed in a hospital/medical center (1), do not know (1), total from the above (doctoral) (10).

Additional Information:

Orientation, Objectives, and Emphasis of Department: The program is strongly research-oriented, although practical courses such as quantitative methods, testing and behaviour modification are available. This degree, however, does not offer training in applied areas (e.g., clinical, educational, counseling psychology etc.).

Information for Students With Physical Disabilities: See the following Web site for more information: http://www.carleton.ca/paulmenton/.

Application Information:

Send to: Graduate Studies Administrator, B-555 Loeb Building. Application available online. Students are admitted in the Fall, application deadline February 1; Winter, application deadline November 1. *Fee:* $60. Note: All dollar amounts specified in this entry are Canadian dollars.

Concordia University

Department of Psychology
7141 Sherbrooke Street West
Montreal, QC H4B 1R6
Telephone: (514)848-2424, (2205)
Fax: (514) 848-4523
E-mail: *black@vax2.concordia.ca*
Web: *http://www-psychology.concordia.ca*

Department Information:

1963. Chairperson: William Bukowski. Number of Faculty: total–full-time 45, part-time 16; women–full-time 18, part-time 16; minority–full-time 1, part-time 1.

Programs and Degrees Offered:

Listed in the following order: Program area, degree type (T if terminal Master's), number awarded 7/03–6/04. Clinical Profile PhD (Doctor of Philosophy) 5, General Profile PhD (Doctor of Philosophy) 4.

APA Accreditation: Clinical PhD (Doctor of Philosophy).

Student Applications/Admissions:

Student Applications

Clinical Profile PhD (Doctor of Philosophy)—Applications 2004–2005, 152. Total applicants accepted 2004–2005, 14. Number enrolled (new admits only) 2004–2005 full-time, 10. Number enrolled (new admits only) 2004–2005 part-time, 0. Openings 2005–2006, 10. The Median number of years required for completion of a degree are 7. The number of students enrolled full and part-time who were dismissed or voluntarily withdrew from this program area were 0. *General Profile PhD (Doctor of Philosophy)*—Applications 2004–2005, 48. Total applicants accepted 2004–2005, 16. Number enrolled (new admits only) 2004–2005 full-time, 11. Number enrolled (new admits only) 2004–2005 part-time, 0. Openings 2005–2006, 12. The Me-

dian number of years required for completion of a degree are 7. The number of students enrolled full and part-time who were dismissed or voluntarily withdrew from this program area were 1.

Admissions Requirements:

Scores: Entries appear in this order: required test or GPA, minimum score (if required), median score of students entering in 2003–2004. Master's Programs: overall undergraduate GPA 3.00, 3.95. GRE not required but highly recommended. Concordia = 4.30 grading scale. Minimum: 3.00 = B Median: 3.95 = A- Doctoral Programs: overall undergraduate GPA 3.00, 3.30. Most students are admitted at the MA level. Not required, but highly recommended GRE. Concordia = 4.30 grading scale.

Other Criteria: (importance of criteria rated low, medium, or high): GRE/MAT scores low, research experience high, work experience medium, extracurricular activity low, clinically related public service medium, GPA medium, letters of recommendation high, interview medium, statement of goals and objectives high. General Profile does not require clinically related service.

Student Characteristics: The following represents characteristics of students in 2004–2005 in all graduate psychology programs in the department: Female–full-time 93, part-time 0; Male–full-time 24, part-time 0; African American/Black–full-time 2, part-time 0; Hispanic/Latino(a)–full-time 6, part-time 0; Asian/Pacific Islander–full-time 2, part-time 0; American Indian/Alaska Native–full-time 1, part-time 0; Caucasian–full-time 103, part-time 0; Multi-ethnic–full-time 3, part-time 0; students subject to the Americans With Disabilities Act–full-time 0, part-time 0.

Financial Information/Assistance:

Tuition for Full-Time Study: Master's: State residents: per academic year $2,986; Nonstate residents: per academic year $9,763. *Doctoral:* State residents: per academic year $2,986; Nonstate residents: per academic year $9,043. Tuition is subject to change. Tuition costs vary by program. See the following Web site for updates and changes in tuition costs: http://tuitionandfees.concordia.ca.

Financial Assistance:

First Year Students: Teaching assistantships available for first-year. Average amount paid per academic year: $3,750. Average number of hours worked per week: 10. Apply by August 1. Research assistantships available for first-year. Average amount paid per academic year: $10,250. Average number of hours worked per week: 10. Fellowships and scholarships available for first-year. Average amount paid per academic year: $16,200. Apply by October.

Advanced Students: Teaching assistantships available for advanced students. Average amount paid per academic year: $7,500. Average number of hours worked per week: 10. Apply by August 1. Research assistantships available for advanced students. Average amount paid per academic year: $7,500. Average number of hours worked per week: 10. Fellowships and scholarships available for advanced students. Average amount paid per academic year: $21,200. Apply by October.

Contact Information: Of all students currently enrolled full-time, 77% benefitted from one or more of the listed financial

assistance programs. Application and information available online at: http://graduatestudies.concordia.ca/awards.

Internships/Practica: Clinical students complete a variety of practica and internships while in program residence. All clinical students receive extensive practicum experience in psychotherapy and assessment in our on-campus training clinic, the Applied Psychology Center (APC). APC clients are seen by graduate students under the supervision of clinical faculty. The types of services offered by the APC reflect the interests of clinical supervisors and students, and may include individual, family, or marital psychotherapy, behavior therapy for sexual or phobic difficulties, and treatment of child disorders. During the summer of their second year, students also complete a full-time practicum at a mental health facility in the Montreal area. During their final year in the program, students complete their full-time, predoctoral clinical internships. Recent students have undertaken predoctoral internships at a variety of mental health facilities across Canada and the United States. All students are encouraged to seek internship positions in settings accredited by either the Canadian or American Psychological Associations. For those doctoral students for whom a professional internship is required prior to graduation, 9 applied in 2003–2004. Of those who applied, 5 were placed in internships listed by the Association of Psychology Postdoctoral and Internship Programs (APPIC); 4 were placed in APA accredited internships.

Housing and Day Care: No on-campus housing is available. On-campus day care facilities are available. See the following Web site for more information: Day care: Sir George campus (514) 848-2424, ext. 8789; Loyola campus: (514) 848-2424, ext. 7788; http://advocacy.concordia.ca/daycare/.

Employment of Department Graduates:

Master's Degree Graduates: Of those who graduated in the academic year 2003–2004, the following categories and numbers represent the post-graduate activities and employment of master's degree graduates: Enrolled in a post-doctoral residency/fellowship (n/a), employed in independent practice (n/a), total from the above (master's) (0).

Doctoral Degree Graduates: Of those who graduated in the academic year 2003–2004, the following categories and numbers represent the post-graduate activities and employment of doctoral degree graduates: Enrolled in a psychology doctoral program (n/a), enrolled in a post-doctoral residency/fellowship (3), employed in independent practice (2), employed in a hospital/medical center (3), do not know (1), total from the above (doctoral) (9).

Additional Information:

Orientation, Objectives, and Emphasis of Department: Graduate education in both experimental and clinical psychology is strongly research oriented and intended for students who are planning to complete the PhD degree. The research program for all students is based on an apprentice-type model. An outstanding feature of graduate education at Concordia is that students pursuing only research studies and students pursuing research and clinical studies may conduct their research in the laboratory of any faculty member. A wide variety of contemporary research areas are available, ranging from basic infrahuman investigation to applied interventions with humans. Research findings from numerous areas are integrated in an effort to solve problems associated with appetitive motivation and drug dependence, memory and aging, human cognitive development, developmental psychobiology, adult and child psychopathology, sensory deficits, and sexual dysfunctions, to name several examples. Clinical training is based on the scientist-practitioner model. That is, clinical students meet the same research requirements as other students, and receive extensive professional training in the delivery of psychological services. Students may choose to specialize their clinical training with children or adults.

Special Facilities or Resources: The department has extensive animal and human research facilities that are supported by provincial, federal, and U.S. granting agencies as well as various internal and private sector funds. Most research laboratories are well equipped, and have microcomputers and/or local terminals to support faculty and student research. In addition to those in research laboratories, there are several microcomputers and terminals within the department specifically designated for student use; the university also has excellent computer facilities that run modern statistical packages. The department also contains 2 research centers that are jointly funded by the Government of Quebec and the University, the Center for Studies in Behavioral Neurobiology, and the Center for Research in Human Development. Both centers coordinate multidisciplinary research programs, provide state-of-the-art laboratory equipment, and sponsor colloquia by specialists from other universities in North America and abroad. All graduate students benefit from activities supported by the research centers.

Information for Students With Physical Disabilities: See the following Web site for more information: http://advocacy.concordia.ca/disabled/disabled.html.

Application Information:
Send to: Graduate Admissions Application Centre, P.O. Box 2002, Station H, Montréal, Québec H3G 2V4 Canada, Phone: (514) 848-2424, ext. 2668; Fax: (514) 848-2621. Application available online. URL of online application: www.concordia.ca then "Apply2Concordia." Students are admitted in the Fall, application deadline January 3. Psychology graduate program information and research interests are available online at http://www-psychology.concordia.ca; then choose "Graduate Programmes (MA and PhD)". *Fee:* $50. Note: All dollar amounts specified in this entry are Canadian dollars.

Dalhousie University
Department of Psychology
Life Sciences Centre
Halifax, NS B3H 4J1
Telephone: (902) 494-3839
Fax: (902) 494-6585
E-mail: *psychology@dal.ca*
Web: *http://www.dal.ca/psychology*

Department Information:
1863. Chair: Richard Brown. Number of Faculty: total–full-time 29, part-time 3; women–full-time 10, part-time 3.

Programs and Degrees Offered:
Listed in the following order: Program area, degree type (T if terminal Master's), number awarded 7/03–6/04. Clinical PhD

(Doctor of Philosophy) 4, Experimental-Animal PhD (Doctor of Philosophy) 2, Experimental—Human PhD (Doctor of Philosophy) 3, MSc Neuroscience MA/MS (Master of Arts/Science) 2, MSc Experimental—Animal MA/MS (Master of Arts/Science) 0, Neuroscience PhD (Doctor of Philosophy) 2, MSc Experimental—Human MA/MS (Master of Arts/Science) 1.

APA Accreditation: Clinical PhD (Doctor of Philosophy).

Student Applications/Admissions:

Student Applications

Clinical PhD (Doctor of Philosophy)—Applications 2004–2005, 100. Total applicants accepted 2004–2005, 7. Number enrolled (new admits only) 2004–2005 full-time, 7. Number enrolled (new admits only) 2004–2005 part-time, 0. Openings 2005–2006, 5. The Median number of years required for completion of a degree are 5. The number of students enrolled full and part-time who were dismissed or voluntarily withdrew from this program area were 1. *Experimental-Animal PhD (Doctor of Philosophy)*—Total applicants accepted 2004–2005, 0. Number enrolled (new admits only) 2004–2005 full-time, 0. The Median number of years required for completion of a degree are 5. The number of students enrolled full and part-time who were dismissed or voluntarily withdrew from this program area were 0. *Experimental—Human PhD (Doctor of Philosophy)*—Applications 2004–2005, 4. Total applicants accepted 2004–2005, 0. Number enrolled (new admits only) 2004–2005 full-time, 0. Number enrolled (new admits only) 2004–2005 part-time, 0. The Median number of years required for completion of a degree are 4. The number of students enrolled full and part-time who were dismissed or voluntarily withdrew from this program area were 0. *MSc Neuroscience MA/MS (Master of Arts/Science)*—Applications 2004–2005, 20. Total applicants accepted 2004–2005, 2. Number enrolled (new admits only) 2004–2005 full-time, 2. The Median number of years required for completion of a degree are 2. The number of students enrolled full and part-time who were dismissed or voluntarily withdrew from this program area were 0. *MSc Experimental—Animal MA/MS (Master of Arts/Science)*—Applications 2004–2005, 10. Total applicants accepted 2004–2005, 0. Number enrolled (new admits only) 2004–2005 full-time, 0. Total enrolled 2004–2005 full-time, 1. The Median number of years required for completion of a degree are 2. The number of students enrolled full and part-time who were dismissed or voluntarily withdrew from this program area were 0. *Neuroscience PhD (Doctor of Philosophy)*—Applications 2004–2005, 8. Total applicants accepted 2004–2005, 2. Number enrolled (new admits only) 2004–2005 full-time, 2. Total enrolled 2004–2005 full-time, 2. The Median number of years required for completion of a degree are 5. The number of students enrolled full and part-time who were dismissed or voluntarily withdrew from this program area were 0. *MSc Experimental—Human MA/MS (Master of Arts/Science)*—Applications 2004–2005, 12. Total applicants accepted 2004–2005, 8. Number enrolled (new admits only) 2004–2005 full-time, 6. Total enrolled 2004–2005 full-time, 7. The Median number of years required for completion of a degree are 2. The number of students enrolled full and part-time who were dismissed or voluntarily withdrew from this program area were 0.

Admissions Requirements:

Scores: Entries appear in this order: required test or GPA, minimum score (if required), median score of students entering

in 2003–2004. Master's Programs: GRE-V 600; GRE-Q 600; GRE-Analytical 600. Doctoral Programs: GRE-V 600; GRE-Q 600; GRE-Analytical 600; overall undergraduate GPA 3.70. *Other Criteria:* (importance of criteria rated low, medium, or high): research experience high, work experience low, extracurricular activity low, clinically related public service low, GPA high, letters of recommendation high, interview low, statement of goals and objectives high. Clinically related public service is high for clinical program.

Student Characteristics: The following represents characteristics of students in 2004–2005 in all graduate psychology programs in the department: Female–full-time 48, part-time 0; Male–full-time 10, part-time 0; African American/Black–full-time 1, part-time 0; Hispanic/Latino(a)–full-time 0, part-time 0; Asian/Pacific Islander–full-time 2, part-time 0; American Indian/Alaska Native–full-time 1, part-time 0; Caucasian–full-time 0, part-time 0; students subject to the Americans With Disabilities Act–full-time 0, part-time 0.

Financial Information/Assistance:

Tuition for Full-Time Study: *Master's:* State residents: per academic year $6,270. *Doctoral:* State residents: per academic year $6,552. Tuition is subject to change. See the following Web site for updates and changes in tuition costs: www.dal.ca/studentaccounts.

Financial Assistance:

First Year Students: Teaching assistantships available for first-year. Average amount paid per academic year: $2,284. Average number of hours worked per week: 10. Fellowships and scholarships available for first-year.

Advanced Students: Fellowships and scholarships available for advanced students.

Contact Information: Of all students currently enrolled full-time, 100% benefitted from one or more of the listed financial assistance programs. Application and information available online at: www.dal.ca/Psychology.

Internships/Practica: *Master's:* State residents: per academic year $6,270 is required prior to graduation, 5 applied in 2003–2004.

Housing and Day Care: On-campus housing is available. See the following Web site for information: housing@dal.ca. On-campus day care facilities are available.

Employment of Department Graduates:

Master's Degree Graduates: Of those who graduated in the academic year 2003–2004, the following categories and numbers represent the post-graduate activities and employment of master's degree graduates: Enrolled in a psychology doctoral program (1), enrolled in another graduate/professional program (1), enrolled in a post-doctoral residency/fellowship (n/a), employed in independent practice (n/a), employed in an academic position at a university (0), employed in an academic position at a 2-year/4-year college (0), employed in other positions at a higher education institution (0), employed in a professional position in a school system (0), employed in business or industry (research/consulting) (0), employed in business or industry (management) (0), employed in a government agency (research) (0), employed in a government agency (professional services) (0), employed in a community mental health/counseling center (0), employed in a hospital/medical center (0), still seeking employment (0), other employment position (0), do not know (0), total from the above (master's) (2).

Doctoral Degree Graduates: Of those who graduated in the academic year 2003–2004, the following categories and numbers represent the post-graduate activities and employment of doctoral degree graduates: Enrolled in a psychology doctoral program (n/a), enrolled in another graduate/professional program (0), enrolled in a post-doctoral residency/fellowship (3), employed in independent practice (0), employed in an academic position at a university (0), employed in an academic position at a 2-year/4-year college (0), employed in other positions at a higher education institution (0), employed in a professional position in a school system (0), employed in business or industry (research/consulting) (0), employed in business or industry (management) (0), employed in a government agency (research) (0), employed in a government agency (professional services) (0), employed in a community mental health/counseling center (0), employed in a hospital/medical center (2), still seeking employment (0), other employment position (1), do not know (4), total from the above (doctoral) (10).

Additional Information:

Orientation, Objectives, and Emphasis of Department: The Department of Psychology offers graduate training leading to MSc and PhD degrees in psychology and in psychology/neuroscience, and to a PhD in clinical psychology. Our graduate programs emphasize training for research. They are best described as "apprenticeship" programs in which students work closely with a faculty member who has agreed to supervise the student's research. Compared with many other graduate programs, we place less emphasis on coursework and greater emphasis on research, scholarship, and independent thinking. The graduate programs in psychology/neuroscience are coordinated by the Psychology Department and an interdisciplinary Neuroscience Program Committee with representation from the Departments of Anatomy, Biochemistry, Pharmacology, Physiology and Biophysics, and Psychology. Master's level students in psychology and psychology/neuroscience are expected to advance into the corresponding PhD programs. We do not have a "terminal" Master's program. The PhD program in clinical psychology is cooperatively administered by the Psychology Department and the Clinical Program Committee with representation from Acadia University, Dalhousie University, Mount Saint Vincent University, Saint Mary's University, and professional psychologists from the teaching hospitals. It is a structured five-year program which follows the "scientist-practitioner" model. The department does not offer a Master's degree in clinical psychology. During the first four years of the clinical psychology program, students complete required courses, conduct supervised and thesis research, and gain clinical experience through field placements. In the fifth year, students are placed in a full-year clinical internship.

Special Facilities or Resources: The department of psychology is located in the Life Sciences Centre, which also contains the departments of biology, earth sciences, and oceanography. The psychology building contains very extensive laboratory areas, some with circulating sea-water aquaria, and is designed for research with a range of animal groups (humans, cats, birds, fish, invertebrates) using a range of research techniques in behavior, electrophysiology, neuroanatomy, immunocytochemistry, neurogenetics, and so forth. The department also houses an electronics and woodworking shop, an animal care facility, a surgical facility, a computer lab for word processing, communications, and access to a mainframe; specific neuroscience facilities are in close proximity to hospitals.

Application Information:

Send to: Graduate Program Secretary, Psychology Department, Dalhousie University, Halifax, NS B3H 4J1. Students are admitted in the Fall, application deadline January 1. *Fee:* $70. Note: All dollar amounts specified in this entry are Canadian dollars.

Guelph, University of
Department of Psychology
College of Social and Applied Human Sciences
5th Floor MacKinnon
Guelph, ON N1G 2W1
Telephone: (519) 824-4120 ext. 53508
Fax: (519) 837-8629
E-mail: *marmurek@psy.uoguelph.ca*
Web: *http://www.psychology.uoguelph.ca*

Department Information:

1966. Chairperson: Harvey H. C. Marmurek. Number of Faculty: total–full-time 30; women–full-time 11; minority–full-time 2.

Programs and Degrees Offered:

Listed in the following order: Program area, degree type (T if terminal Master's), number awarded 7/03–6/04. Applied Cognitive Science PhD (Doctor of Philosophy) 0, Industrial/Organizational PhD (Doctor of Philosophy) 2, Applied Social PhD (Doctor of Philosophy) 3, Clinical Psychology: Applied Developmental Emphasis PhD (Doctor of Philosophy) 2, Applied Cognitive Science MA/MS (Master of Arts/Science) 0, Applied Social MA/MS (Master of Arts/Science) 1, Clinical Psychology: Applied Developmental Emphasis MA/MS (Master of Arts/Science) 5, Industrial/Organizational MA/MS (Master of Arts/Science) 2.

Student Applications/Admissions:

Student Applications

Applied Cognitive Sciene PhD (Doctor of Philosophy)—Applications 2004–2005, 2. Total applicants accepted 2004–2005, 0. Number enrolled (new admits only) 2004–2005 full-time, 0. Number enrolled (new admits only) 2004–2005 part-time, 0. Openings 2005–2006, 4. The Median number of years required for completion of a degree are 4. *Industrial/Organizational PhD (Doctor of Philosophy)*—Applications 2004–2005, 3. Total applicants accepted 2004–2005, 1. Number enrolled (new admits only) 2004–2005 full-time, 1. Number enrolled (new admits only) 2004–2005 part-time, 0. The Median number of years required for completion of a degree are 4. *Applied Social PhD (Doctor of Philosophy)*—Applications 2004–2005, 3. Total applicants accepted 2004–2005, 1. Number enrolled (new admits only) 2004–2005 full-time, 1. Number enrolled (new admits only) 2004–2005 part-time, 0. The Median number of years required for completion of a degree are 4. *Clinical Psychology: Applied Developmental Emphasi PhD (Doctor of Philosophy)*—Applications 2004–2005, 12. Total applicants accepted 2004–2005, 5. Number enrolled (new admits only) 2004–2005 full-time, 5. Number enrolled (new admits only) 2004–2005 part-time, 0. Total enrolled 2004–2005 full-time, 21, part-time, 1. The Median number of years required for completion of a degree are 4. *Applied Cognitive Science MA/MS (Master of Arts/Science)*—Applications 2004–2005, 10. Total applicants accepted 2004–2005, 2. Number enrolled (new admits only) 2004–2005 full-time, 2. Number enrolled (new admits only) 2004–2005 part-time, 0. The Median number of years required for completion of a degree are 2. *Applied Social MA/MS (Master of Arts/Science)*—Applications 2004–2005, 27. Total applicants accepted 2004–2005, 2. Number enrolled (new admits only) 2004–2005 full-time, 2. Number enrolled (new admits only) 2004–2005 part-time, 0. The Median number of years required for completion of a degree are 2. *Clinical Psychology: Applied Develpmental Emphasis MA/MS (Master of Arts/Science)*—Applications 2004–2005, 44. Total applicants accepted 2004–2005, 5. Number enrolled (new admits only) 2004–2005 full-time, 5. Number enrolled (new admits only) 2004–2005 part-time, 0. The Median number of years required for completion of a degree are 2. *Industrial/Organizational MA/MS (Master of Arts/Science)*—Applications 2004–2005, 27. Total applicants accepted 2004–2005, 3. Number enrolled (new admits only) 2004–2005 full-time, 3. Number enrolled (new admits only) 2004–2005 part-time, 0. The Median number of years required for completion of a degree are 2.

Admissions Requirements:

Scores: Entries appear in this order: required test or GPA, minimum score (if required), median score of students entering in 2003–2004. Master's Programs: GRE-V no minimum stated, 580; GRE-Q no minimum stated, 625; GRE-Analytical no minimum stated, 640; GRE-Subject(Psych) no minimum stated, 670; last 2 years GPA no minimum stated, 3.75; psychology GPA no minimum stated, 3.80. Doctoral Programs: GRE-V no minimum stated, 620; GRE-Q no minimum stated, 590; GRE-Analytical no minimum stated, 640; GRE-Subject(Psych) no minimum stated, 660.

Other Criteria: (importance of criteria rated low, medium, or high): GRE/MAT scores high, research experience high, work experience medium, extracurricular activity low, clinically related public service low, GPA high, letters of recommendation high, interview high, statement of goals and objectives high.

Student Characteristics: The following represents characteristics of students in 2004–2005 in all graduate psychology programs in the department: Female–full-time 60, part-time 1; Male–full-time 11, part-time 0; African American/Black–full-time 2, part-time 0; Hispanic/Latino(a)–full-time 0, part-time 0; Asian/Pacific Islander–full-time 4, part-time 0; American Indian/Alaska Native–full-time 1, part-time 0; Caucasian–full-time 64, part-time 1; Multi-ethnic–full-time 0, part-time 0; students subject to the Americans With Disabilities Act–full-time 0, part-time 0.

Financial Information/Assistance:

Tuition for Full-Time Study: *Master's:* State residents: per academic year $5,160; Nonstate residents: per academic year $8,148. *Doctoral:* State residents: per academic year $5,160; Nonstate residents: per academic year $8,148. Tuition is subject to change. See the following Web site for updates and changes in tuition costs: http://www.uoguelph.ca/graduatestudies/feetable.pdf.

Financial Assistance:

First Year Students: Teaching assistantships available for first-year. Average amount paid per academic year: $11,515. Average number of hours worked per week: 12. Apply by January

15. Fellowships and scholarships available for first-year. Average amount paid per academic year: $3,720. Apply by January 15.

Advanced Students: Teaching assistantships available for advanced students. Average amount paid per academic year: $11,515. Average number of hours worked per week: 12. Apply by January 15. Fellowships and scholarships available for advanced students. Average amount paid per academic year: $3,720. Apply by January 15.

Contact Information: Of all students currently enrolled full-time, 95% benefitted from one or more of the listed financial assistance programs. Application and information available online at: http://www.psychology.uoguelph.ca.

Internships/Practica: For Clinical Psychology: Applied Developmental Emphasis students work two days per week with the psychological services staff at local public school boards. During a later semester, they are placed four days a week in a service facility for atypical children. Five students have been selected for accredited internship placements, and application for accreditation by the Canadian Psychological Association in clinical psychology is in the final stage. For the Applied Social Psychology, students select practica in settings that include community health facilities, correctional and medical treatment settings, and private consulting firms. Industrial/Organizational and Applied Cognitive Science practica take place in industrial, governmental, and military settings. For those doctoral students for whom a professional internship is required prior to graduation, 1 applied in 2003–2004. Of those who applied, 1 was placed in internships listed by the Association of Psychology Postdoctoral and Internship Programs (APPIC); 1 was placed in APA accredited internships.

Housing and Day Care: On-campus housing is available. See the following Web site for more information: http://www2.uoguelph.ca/housing/website/home.cfm. On-campus day care facilities are available. See the following Web site for more information: http://www2.uoguelph.ca/studentaffairs/childcare/.

Employment of Department Graduates:

Master's Degree Graduates: Of those who graduated in the academic year 2003–2004, the following categories and numbers represent the post-graduate activities and employment of master's degree graduates: Enrolled in a psychology doctoral program (7), enrolled in a post-doctoral residency/fellowship (n/a), employed in independent practice (n/a), employed in business or industry (research/consulting) (1), employed in a government agency (research) (1), still seeking employment (1), not seeking employment (1), do not know (2), total from the above (master's) (13).

Doctoral Degree Graduates: Of those who graduated in the academic year 2003–2004, the following categories and numbers represent the post-graduate activities and employment of doctoral degree graduates: Enrolled in a psychology doctoral program (n/a), employed in an academic position at a university (3), employed in a government agency (research) (2), employed in a community mental health/counseling center (1), employed in a hospital/medical center (1), total from the above (doctoral) (7).

Additional Information:

Orientation, Objectives, and Emphasis of Department: The Department of Psychology offers graduate programs leading to a Master of Arts and a Doctor of Philosophy in four fields: Applied Cognitve Science, Applied Social Psychology, Clinical Psychology: Applied Developmental Emphasis, and Industrial/Organizational Psychology. The four fields follow a scientist-practitioner model and provide training in both research and professional skills, as well as a firm grounding in theory and research in relevant content areas. See http://www.psychology.uoguelph.ca for more information.

Special Facilities or Resources: Faculty offices and laboratories are located mainly in the MacKinnon Building and Blackwood Hall. Graduate students have office space in Blackwood Hall. The department is well supported with computer facilities. These include a microcomputer laboratory and extensive microcomputer support for research, teaching, data analysis, and word processing. Facilities for animal research include a fully equipped surgery room and physiological recording equipment. For research with human subjects, the department possesses portable video-recording equipment, observation rooms and experimental chambers. All of these facilities are supplemented by excellent workshop and technical support. The Centre for Psychological Services is a non-profit organization associated with the Department of Psychology at the University of Guelph. The Centre provides high quality psychological services at a reasonable cost, working with families and the community. The Centre is involved in training students in Clinical Psychology: Applied Developmental Emphasis and offers workshops and presentations to professionals in the community. G-CORI is a non-profit consulting and research organization that hires students in Applied Social and Industrial/Organizational Psychology, allowing them to utilize the knowledge gained in their courses. A new building for faculty offices is currently under construction.

Information for Students With Physical Disabilities: See the following Web site for more information: http://www.psychology.uoguelph.ca.

Application Information:
Send to: Graduate Secretary, Department of Psychology, University of Guelph, Guelph, Ontario N1G 2W1, Canada. Telephone: (519) 824-4120, ext. 53508. Application available online. URL of online application: http://www.uoguelph.ca/graduatestudies/. Students are admitted in the Fall, application deadline January 15. All applications are reviewed in February. *Fee:* $75. Note: All dollar amounts specified in this entry are Canadian dollars.

Laval (Université Laval)
Ecole de Psychologie
Pavillon Félix-Antoine-Savard
Québec, QC G1K 7P4
Telephone: (418) 656-5383
Fax: (418) 656-3646
E-mail: *psy@psy.ulaval.ca*
Web: *http://www.psy.ulaval.ca*

Department Information:
1961. Chairperson: François Y. Doré. Number of Faculty: total–full-time 42; women–full-time 19.

Programs and Degrees Offered:
Listed in the following order: Program area, degree type (T if terminal Master's), number awarded 7/03–6/04. Research PhD

(Doctor of Philosophy) 4, PsyD (Doctor of Psychology) 0, Research & Intervention PhD (Doctor of Philosophy) 5.

Student Applications/Admissions:
Student Applications
Research PhD *(Doctor of Philosophy)*—Applications 2004–2005, 28. Total applicants accepted 2004–2005, 13. Number enrolled (new admits only) 2004–2005 full-time, 13. Openings 2005–2006, 15. The Median number of years required for completion of a degree are 5. The number of students enrolled full and part-time who were dismissed or voluntarily withdrew from this program area were 1. PsyD *(Doctor of Psychology)*—Applications 2004–2005, 76. Total applicants accepted 2004–2005, 14. Number enrolled (new admits only) 2004–2005 full-time, 14. Openings 2005–2006, 15. The number of students enrolled full and part-time who were dismissed or voluntarily withdrew from this program area were 0. *Research & Intervention PhD (Doctor of Philosophy)*—Applications 2004–2005, 155. Total applicants accepted 2004–2005, 19. Number enrolled (new admits only) 2004–2005 full-time, 19. Openings 2005–2006, 25. The Median number of years required for completion of a degree are 5. The number of students enrolled full and part-time who were dismissed or voluntarily withdrew from this program area were 2.

Admissions Requirements:
Scores: Entries appear in this order: required test or GPA, minimum score (if required), median score of students entering in 2003–2004. Doctoral Programs: overall undergraduate GPA 3.50.
Other Criteria: (importance of criteria rated low, medium, or high): research experience high, work experience medium, extracurricular activity medium, clinically related public service medium, GPA high, letters of recommendation high, statement of goals and objectives high.

Student Characteristics: The following represents characteristics of students in 2004–2005 in all graduate psychology programs in the department: Female–full-time 100, part-time 0; Male–full-time 66, part-time 0; African American/Black–full-time 2, part-time 0; Hispanic/Latino(a)–full-time 3, part-time 0; Asian/Pacific Islander–full-time 1, part-time 0; American Indian/Alaska Native–part-time 0; Caucasian–full-time 160, part-time 0; Multiethnic–full-time 0, part-time 0; students subject to the Americans With Disabilities Act–full-time 1, part-time 0.

Financial Information/Assistance:
Tuition for Full-Time Study: *Doctoral:* State residents: per academic year $1,500, $56 per credit hour; Nonstate residents: per academic year $13,000, $480 per credit hour.

Financial Assistance:
First Year Students: Teaching assistantships available for first-year. Average amount paid per academic year: $2,000. Average number of hours worked per week: 17. Research assistantships available for first-year. Average amount paid per academic year: $2,600. Average number of hours worked per week: 17. Fellowships and scholarships available for first-year. Average amount paid per academic year: $2,000.
Advanced Students: Teaching assistantships available for advanced students. Average amount paid per academic year: $2,000. Average number of hours worked per week: 17. Research

assistantships available for advanced students. Average amount paid per academic year: $2,600. Average number of hours worked per week: 17. Fellowships and scholarships available for advanced students. Average amount paid per academic year: $2,000.

Contact Information: Of all students currently enrolled full-time, 100% benefitted from one or more of the listed financial assistance programs. Application and information available online at: http://www.ulaval.ca/fes/aide.html.

Internships/Practica: At the PhD level, a full year of internship is required from those who are enrolled in the PhD in research and intervention (clinical, clinical neuropsychology, and community psychology) as well as those enrolled in the PsyD program. For those doctoral students for whom a professional internship is required prior to graduation, 7 applied in 2003–2004. Of those who applied, 3 were placed in internships listed by the Association of Psychology Postdoctoral and Internship Programs (APPIC); 3 were placed in APA accredited internships.

Housing and Day Care: On-campus housing is available. See the following Web site for more information: www.ulaval.ca/sres. On-campus day care facilities are available. See the following Web site for more information: www.baee.ulaval.ca.

Employment of Department Graduates:
  Master's Degree Graduates: Of those who graduated in the academic year 2003–2004, the following categories and numbers represent the post-graduate activities and employment of master's degree graduates: Enrolled in a post-doctoral residency/fellowship (n/a), employed in independent practice (n/a), total from the above (master's) (0).
  Doctoral Degree Graduates: Of those who graduated in the academic year 2003–2004, the following categories and numbers represent the post-graduate activities and employment of doctoral degree graduates: Enrolled in a psychology doctoral program (n/a), total from the above (doctoral) (0).

Additional Information:
  Orientation, Objectives, and Emphasis of Department: Beginning in 2003-2004, new admissions were accepted only at the doctoral level. Three doctoral programs are offered: a research-oriented PhD (social psychology, developmental psychology, and cognitive sciences-behavioral neuroscience); a PhD in research and intervention which includes a clinical orientation with a specialization either in clinical psychology or clinical neuropsychology as well as a specialization in community psychology; and a new PsyD with a specialization either in clinical psychology or clinical neuropsychology.

  Special Facilities or Resources: The department possesses sophisticated audiovisual and data processing equipment for teaching, research, and professional training purposes. Modern laboratory facilities are available in the department on campus as well as in a number of off-campus research centers to which the researchers and graduate students of the department are affiliated. The department also possesses clinical training facilities where clinical services are provided to the general population, and it is affiliated with a number of hospitals and government agencies where the graduate students can be involved in initial professional training as well as internships.

  Information for Students With Physical Disabilities: See the following Web site for more information: www.aiphe.ulaval.ca.

Application Information:
Send to: Bureau du Registraire, 2400 Pavillon Jean-Charles-Bonenfant, Universite Laval, Sainte Foy (Quebec), G1K 7P4, reg@reg.ulaval.ca. Students are admitted in the Fall, application deadline February 1. *Fee:* $30. Note: All dollar amounts specified in this entry are Canadian dollars.

Manitoba, University of
Psychology Graduate Office
P514 Duff Roblin Building
Winnipeg, MB R3T 2N2
Telephone: (204) 474-6377
Fax: (204) 474-7917
E-mail: *inglislf@ms.umanitoba.ca*
Web: *http://www.umanitoba.ca/faculties/arts/psychology*

Department Information:
  1947. Head: Gerry N. Sande. Number of Faculty: total–full-time 39, part-time 1; women–full-time 12, part-time 1.

Programs and Degrees Offered:
  Listed in the following order: Program area, degree type (T if terminal Master's), number awarded 7/03–6/04. Applied Behavioral Analysis PhD (Doctor of Philosophy) 1, Behavioral Neuroscience PhD (Doctor of Philosophy) 2, Clinical PhD (Doctor of Philosophy) 6, Cognitive PhD (Doctor of Philosophy) 1, Developmental PhD (Doctor of Philosophy) 1, Experimental PhD (Doctor of Philosophy) 1, General PhD (Doctor of Philosophy) 0, Social/Personality PhD (Doctor of Philosophy) 2, School Psychology MA/MS (Master of Arts/Science) (T) 0.

APA Accreditation: Clinical PhD (Doctor of Philosophy).

Student Applications/Admissions:
  Student Applications
  Applied Behavioral Analysis PhD (Doctor of Philosophy)—Applications 2004–2005, 13. Total applicants accepted 2004–2005, 3. Number enrolled (new admits only) 2004–2005 full-time, 3. Total enrolled 2004–2005 full-time, 8. Openings 2005–2006, 2. The number of students enrolled full and part-time who were dismissed or voluntarily withdrew from this program area were 0. *Behavioral Neuroscience PhD (Doctor of Philosophy)*—Applications 2004–2005, 4. Total applicants accepted 2004–2005, 1. Number enrolled (new admits only) 2004–2005 full-time, 1. Total enrolled 2004–2005 full-time, 4. Openings 2005–2006, 3. The Median number of years required for completion of a degree are 3.5. The number of students enrolled full and part-time who were dismissed or voluntarily withdrew from this program area were 0. *Clinical PhD (Doctor of Philosophy)*—Applications 2004–2005, 57. Total applicants accepted 2004–2005, 8. Number enrolled (new admits only) 2004–2005 full-time, 8. Total enrolled 2004–2005 full-time, 53. Openings 2005–2006, 5. The Median number of years required for completion of a degree are 8. The number of students enrolled full and part-time who were dismissed or voluntarily withdrew from this program area were 0. *Cognitive PhD (Doctor of Philosophy)*—Applications 2004–2005, 4. Total applicants accepted 2004–2005, 2. Number enrolled (new admits only) 2004–2005 full-time, 2. Total enrolled 2004–2005 full-time, 11. Openings

2005–2006, 3. The number of students enrolled full and part-time who were dismissed or voluntarily withdrew from this program area were 0. *Developmental PhD (Doctor of Philosophy)*—Applications 2004–2005, 3. Total applicants accepted 2004–2005, 1. Number enrolled (new admits only) 2004–2005 full-time, 1. Total enrolled 2004–2005 full-time, 2, part-time, 1. Openings 2005–2006, 4. The number of students enrolled full and part-time who were dismissed or voluntarily withdrew from this program area were 1. *Experimental PhD (Doctor of Philosophy)*—Applications 2004–2005, 1. Total applicants accepted 2004–2005, 1. Number enrolled (new admits only) 2004–2005 full-time, 1. Total enrolled 2004–2005 full-time, 8. Openings 2005–2006, 3. The number of students enrolled full and part-time who were dismissed or voluntarily withdrew from this program area were 0. *General PhD (Doctor of Philosophy)*—Applications 2004–2005, 0. Total applicants accepted 2004–2005, 0. Number enrolled (new admits only) 2004–2005 full-time, 0. Total enrolled 2004–2005 full-time, 3. Openings 2005–2006, 1. The number of students enrolled full and part-time who were dismissed or voluntarily withdrew from this program area were 0. *Social/Personality PhD (Doctor of Philosophy)*—Applications 2004–2005, 19. Total applicants accepted 2004–2005, 1. Number enrolled (new admits only) 2004–2005 full-time, 1. Total enrolled 2004–2005 full-time, 14. Openings 2005–2006, 4. The Median number of years required for completion of a degree are 5.5. The number of students enrolled full and part-time who were dismissed or voluntarily withdrew from this program area were 0. *School Psychology MA/MS (Master of Arts/Science)*—Applications 2004–2005, 0. Total applicants accepted 2004–2005, 0. Number enrolled (new admits only) 2004–2005 full-time, 0. Number enrolled (new admits only) 2004–2005 part-time, 0.

Admissions Requirements:

Scores: Entries appear in this order: required test or GPA, minimum score (if required), median score of students entering in 2003–2004. Master's Programs: GRE-V no minimum stated, 557; GRE-Q no minimum stated, 625; GRE-Analytical no minimum stated; GRE-Subject(Psych) no minimum stated, 695; last 2 years GPA 3.0, 4.06. GRE-Subject (either Biology, Psychology, or Zoology) Doctoral Programs: GRE-V no minimum stated, 557; GRE-Q no minimum stated, 625; GRE-Analytical no minimum stated; GRE-Subject(Psych) no minimum stated, 695.

Other Criteria: (importance of criteria rated low, medium, or high): GRE/MAT scores high, research experience high, work experience medium, extracurricular activity low, clinically related public service medium, GPA high, letters of recommendation medium, interview low, statement of goals and objectives low.

Student Characteristics: The following represents characteristics of students in 2004–2005 in all graduate psychology programs in the department: Female–full-time 72, part-time 1; Male–full-time 31, part-time 0; Caucasian–full-time 0, part-time 0.

Financial Information/Assistance:

Tuition for Full-Time Study: *Master's:* State residents: per academic year $4,177. *Doctoral:* State residents: per academic year $4,177. Tuition is subject to change. See the following Web site for updates and changes in tuition costs: including international student fees (www.umanitoba.ca/graduate_studies).

Financial Assistance:

First Year Students: No information provided.

Advanced Students: No information provided.

Contact Information: Of all students currently enrolled full-time, 60% benefitted from one or more of the listed financial assistance programs. Application and information available online at: http://www.umanitoba.ca/faculties/arts/psychology.

Internships/Practica: Clinical students have access to practica at our Psychological Service Center. A limited number of practica within the community are available for senior graduate students. However, the department does not offer an internship program. For those doctoral students for whom a professional internship is required prior to graduation, 9 applied in 2003–2004. Of those who applied, 4 were placed in internships listed by the Association of Psychology Postdoctoral and Internship Programs (APPIC); 9 were placed in APA accredited internships.

Housing and Day Care: On-campus housing is available. See the following Web site for more information: www.umanitoba.ca/student/housing. On-campus day care facilities are available. See the following Web site for more information: www.umanitoba.ca/student/resource/playcare.

Employment of Department Graduates:

Master's Degree Graduates: Of those who graduated in the academic year 2003–2004, the following categories and numbers represent the post-graduate activities and employment of master's degree graduates: Enrolled in a psychology doctoral program (2), enrolled in a post-doctoral residency/fellowship (n/a), employed in independent practice (n/a), total from the above (master's) (2).

Doctoral Degree Graduates: Of those who graduated in the academic year 2003–2004, the following categories and numbers represent the post-graduate activities and employment of doctoral degree graduates: Enrolled in a psychology doctoral program (n/a), employed in an academic position at a university (1), employed in a government agency (professional services) (2), employed in a hospital/medical center (1), total from the above (doctoral) (4).

Additional Information:

Orientation, Objectives, and Emphasis of Department: The primary purpose of our program is to provide training in several specialized areas of psychology for individuals desiring to advance their level of knowledge, their research skills, and their applied capabilities. The MA program is designed to provide a broad foundation, as well as specialized skills, in the scientific approach to psychology. The PhD program provides a higher degree of specialization coupled with more intensive training in research and application. Specialized areas of training within the department include applied behavioral analysis, behavioral neuroscience, clinical, cognitive, developmental, experimental, general, school, and social/personality.

Special Facilities or Resources: Special facilities or resources of the department are as follows: animal research laboratories; avian laboratories; psychophysiology and psychobiology laboratories; sleep laboratories; electronics, computer, multimedia, and woodworking shops; a local area network devoted to research and teaching; and the Psychological Service Center and Elizabeth Hill Counseling Centre.

Information for Students With Physical Disabilities: See the following Web site for more information: www.umanitoba.ca.

Application Information:
Send to: Linda Inglis, Graduate Programs Coordinator, Psychology Graduate Office, P514 Duff Roblin Building, University of Manitoba, Winnipeg, MB R3T 2N2. URL of online application: http://www.umanitoba.ca/faculties/graduate_studies/prospective/admissions/newapp.pdf. Students are admitted in the Winter, application deadline January 15. *Fee:* $50. Note: All dollar amounts specified in this entry are Canadian dollars.

McGill University

Department of Educational and Counselling Psychology
Faculty of Education
3700 McTavish Street
Montreal, QC H3A 1Y2
Telephone: (514) 398-4260
Fax: (514) 398-6968
E-mail: *selma.abumerhy@mcgill.ca*
Web: *http://www.education.mcgill.ca/ecp*

Department Information:
1965. Chair: Susanne P. Lajoie. Number of Faculty: total–full-time 31, part-time 42; women–full-time 15, part-time 42.

Programs and Degrees Offered:
Listed in the following order: Program area, degree type (T if terminal Master's), number awarded 7/03–6/04. Counseling PhD (Doctor of Philosophy) 2, Educational PhD (Doctor of Philosophy) 3, School/ Applied Child PhD (Doctor of Philosophy) 6.

APA Accreditation: Counseling PhD (Doctor of Philosophy). School PhD (Doctor of Philosophy).

Student Applications/Admissions:
Student Applications
Counseling PhD (Doctor of Philosophy)—Applications 2004–2005, 6. Total applicants accepted 2004–2005, 1. Number enrolled (new admits only) 2004–2005 full-time, 1. Openings 2005–2006, 5. The Median number of years required for completion of a degree are 7. The number of students enrolled full and part-time who were dismissed or voluntarily withdrew from this program area were 0. *Educational PhD (Doctor of Philosophy)*—Applications 2004–2005, 17. Total applicants accepted 2004–2005, 14. Number enrolled (new admits only) 2004–2005 full-time, 12. Total enrolled 2004–2005 full-time, 49. Openings 2005–2006, 13. The Median number of years required for completion of a degree are 7. The number of students enrolled full and part-time who were dismissed or voluntarily withdrew from this program area were 2. *School/ Applied Child PhD (Doctor of Philosophy)*—Applications 2004–2005, 12. Total applicants accepted 2004–2005, 10. Number enrolled (new admits only) 2004–2005 full-time, 9. Number enrolled (new admits only) 2004–2005 part-time, 0. Openings 2005–2006, 10. The Median number of years required for completion of a degree are 7. The number of students enrolled full and part-time who were dismissed or voluntarily withdrew from this program area were 0.

Admissions Requirements:
Scores: Entries appear in this order: required test or GPA, minimum score (if required), median score of students entering

in 2003–2004. Master's Programs: GRE-V 500, 600; GRE-Q 500, 600; GRE-Subject(Psych) 500, 600; overall undergraduate GPA 3.0, 3.5; last 2 years GPA 3.0, 3.3; psychology GPA 3.0, 3.3. GREs are required only in School/Applied Child, Applied Developmental Psychology and Counselling Psychology—there is no minimum cut-off. Doctoral Programs: GRE-V no minimum stated; GRE-Q no minimum stated; GRE-Subject(Psych) no minimum stated; overall undergraduate GPA 3.0. As for master's, no minimums.

Other Criteria: (importance of criteria rated low, medium, or high): research experience medium, work experience medium, extracurricular activity medium, clinically related public service medium, GPA high, letters of recommendation high, interview medium, statement of goals and objectives high. Relative weight of these criteria varies across program areas.

Student Characteristics: The following represents characteristics of students in 2004–2005 in all graduate psychology programs in the department: Female–full-time 83, part-time 0; Male–full-time 15, part-time 0; Caucasian–full-time 0, part-time 0.

Financial Information/Assistance:
Tuition for Full-Time Study: *Master's:* State residents: per academic year $2,945, $120 per credit hour; Nonstate residents: per academic year $10,862, $428 per credit hour. *Doctoral:* State residents: per academic year $2,945, $120 per credit hour; Nonstate residents: per academic year $9,902, $391 per credit hour. Tuition is subject to change. Tuition costs vary by program. See the following Web site for updates and changes in tuition costs: http://www.mcgill.ca/fgsr.

Financial Assistance:
First Year Students: Teaching assistantships available for first-year. Average amount paid per academic year: $2,096. Average number of hours worked per week: 3. Apply by September 1. Research assistantships available for first-year. Average amount paid per academic year: $4,000. Average number of hours worked per week: 5.

Advanced Students: Teaching assistantships available for advanced students. Average amount paid per academic year: $4,192. Average number of hours worked per week: 6. Apply by September 1. Research assistantships available for advanced students. Average amount paid per academic year: $8,000. Average number of hours worked per week: 10. Fellowships and scholarships available for advanced students.

Contact Information: Of all students currently enrolled full-time, 10% benefitted from one or more of the listed financial assistance programs.

Internships/Practica: All students in the professional psychology programs—the MA (non-thesis) and PhD in Counseling Psychology, the MEd, MA in Educational Psychology (Special Education and Gifted Education option), and the MA (School/Applied Child Psychology option) and PhD in School/Applied Child Psychology—are required to complete internships. According to the program option, these may be in mental health facilities, community social service agencies, schools, psychoeducational clinics, etc. In some internships, more than one setting is advised or required. New internship opportunities are regularly added, and students are welcome to seek out those which may especially suit their needs, subject to program approval. For those doctoral students for whom a professional internship is required prior to graduation, 5 applied in 2003–2004. Of those who applied, 4 were placed in internships listed by the Association of Psychology Postdoctoral and Internship Programs (APPIC); 4 were placed in APA accredited internships.

Housing and Day Care: No on-campus housing is available. No on-campus day care facilities are available.

Employment of Department Graduates:

Master's Degree Graduates: Of those who graduated in the academic year 2003–2004, the following categories and numbers represent the post-graduate activities and employment of master's degree graduates: Enrolled in a psychology doctoral program (11), enrolled in another graduate/professional program (1), enrolled in a post-doctoral residency/fellowship (n/a), employed in independent practice (n/a), other employment position (1), total from the above (master's) (13).

Doctoral Degree Graduates: Of those who graduated in the academic year 2003–2004, the following categories and numbers represent the post-graduate activities and employment of doctoral degree graduates: Enrolled in a psychology doctoral program (n/a), employed in independent practice (15), employed in an academic position at a university (6), employed in other positions at a higher education institution (5), employed in a professional position in a school system (1), employed in business or industry (research/consulting) (0), employed in a government agency (professional services) (2), employed in a community mental health/counseling center (1), employed in a hospital/medical center (1), still seeking employment (1), total from the above (doctoral) (32).

Additional Information:

Orientation, Objectives, and Emphasis of Department: There are six broad areas of major graduate-level specialization: Counseling Psychology, Applied Developmental Psychology, Instructional Psychology, Applied Cognitive Psychology, Health Professions Education, Special Populations, and School/Applied Child Psychology. Minors are available in most of these; in topics which bridge the majors (e.g., computer applications, special/integrated education, gifted education, adult/professional, higher education or psychology of gender) or topics proposed by students and approved by the department. A substantial base in research methods and statistics is provided and adjusted to students' entering competence. Graduate students in professional school psychology normally enter the Master's and are considered for transfer to the PhD (if that is their goal) after 3 semesters for a further 3 years of training. Graduate studies directed toward research, academic, and leadership careers follow a similar enrollment pattern, except that the program normally requires one year less at the doctoral level. Students are welcome to take selected courses in other departments and at other Quebec universities.

Special Facilities or Resources: The Department has the Laboratory for Applied Cognitive Science, Summer Program in Gifted Education, Teaching and Learning Services, International Centre for Youth Gambling Problems and High Risk Behaviour, Neuroscience Lab for Research and Education in Developmental Disorders, Psychoeducational and Counselling Clinic, Psychoeducational Assessment Library, Educational Computer labs, and the Educational Media Centre.

Information for Students With Physical Disabilities: See the following Web site for more information: www.mcgill.ca/stuserv.

Application Information:

Send to: Diane Bernier, Program Coordinator, Professional Psychology Graduate Programs; Geri Norton, Program Coordinator, Professional Educational Psychology Graduate Programs. Application available online. URL of online application: www.mcgill.ca/applying/graduate. Students are admitted in the Fall, application deadline January 10; February 1; Spring, application deadline February 1; Summer, application deadline February 1. School/Applied Child Psychology Deadline—January 10; Counselling Psychology—February 1 Special circumstances may be examined on an individual basis. *Fee:* $60. Note: All dollar amounts specified in this entry are Canadian dollars.

McGill University
Department of Psychology
1205 Avenue Docteur Penfield
Montreal, QC H3A 1B1
Telephone: (514) 398-6124
Fax: (514) 398-4896
E-mail: *giovanna@hebb.psych.mcgill.ca*
Web: *http://www.psych.mcgill.ca*

Department Information:
1922. Chairperson: Keith Franklin. Number of Faculty: total–full-time 39, part-time 9; women–full-time 10, part-time 9.

Programs and Degrees Offered:
Listed in the following order: Program area, degree type (T if terminal Master's), number awarded 7/03–6/04. Clinical PhD (Doctor of Philosophy) 6, Experimental PhD (Doctor of Philosophy) 6.

APA Accreditation: Clinical PhD (Doctor of Philosophy).

Student Applications/Admissions:
Student Applications

Clinical PhD (Doctor of Philosophy)—Applications 2004–2005, 180. Total applicants accepted 2004–2005, 10. Number enrolled (new admits only) 2004–2005 full-time, 9. Openings 2005–2006, 8. The Median number of years required for completion of a degree are 6. The number of students enrolled full and part-time who were dismissed or voluntarily withdrew from this program area were 0. *Experimental PhD (Doctor of Philosophy)*—Applications 2004–2005, 105. Total applicants accepted 2004–2005, 25. Number enrolled (new admits only) 2004–2005 full-time, 15. Openings 2005–2006, 15. The Median number of years required for completion of a degree are 5.

Admissions Requirements:

Scores: Entries appear in this order: required test or GPA, minimum score (if required), median score of students entering in 2003–2004. Master's Programs: GRE-V+Q+Analytical no minimum stated; GRE-Subject(Psych) no minimum stated; overall undergraduate GPA no minimum stated; last 2 years GPA no minimum stated; psychology GPA no minimum stated. Refer to our Graduate Program Brochure on our Web site: www.psych.mcgill.ca. Doctoral Programs: GRE-V+Q+Analytical no minimum stated; GRE-Subject(Psych) no minimum stated; overall undergraduate GPA no minimum stated; last 2 years GPA no minimum stated; psychology GPA no minimum stated. Refer to our Graduate Program Brochure on our Web site: www.psych.mcgill.ca.

Other Criteria: (importance of criteria rated low, medium, or high): GRE/MAT scores high, research experience high, work experience medium, extracurricular activity low, clinically related public service medium, GPA high, letters of recommendation high, interview medium, statement of goals and objectives high.

Student Characteristics: The following represents characteristics of students in 2004–2005 in all graduate psychology programs in the department: Female–full-time 70, part-time 0; Male–full-time 44, part-time 0; Caucasian–full-time 0, part-time 0.

Financial Information/Assistance:

Tuition for Full-Time Study: *Master's:* State residents: per academic year $3,400; Nonstate residents: per academic year $11,000. *Doctoral:* State residents: per academic year $3,400; Nonstate residents: per academic year $10,100. Tuition is subject to change. See the following Web site for updates and changes in tuition costs: www.psych.mcgill.ca. Note: Non-Quebec Canadians for Master's $5,900.

Financial Assistance:

First Year Students: Teaching assistantships available for first-year. Apply by n/a.

Advanced Students: Teaching assistantships available for advanced students. Apply by n/a.

Contact Information: Application and information available online at: http://ww2.mcgill.ca/StuServ/.

Internships/Practica: The majority of students in our clinical program complete their internships within Montreal, especially at McGill-affiliated hospitals. These include three large and two small general hospitals, a large psychiatric hospital, and a large children's hospital, where a wide range of assessment and treatment skills can be acquired. Specialized, advanced training is provided at other institutions in the areas of neuropsychology, hearing impairments, orthopedic disabilities, and rehabilitation. One advantage of having a local internship is that it facilitates the integration of the student's clinical and research activities. In addition, the department is able to monitor the quality of the training at the placements. All placements have active, ongoing commitments to research. Students have also completed internships at a wide variety of settings in other parts of Canada, the United States, and Europe. Settings outside Montreal must meet with staff approval. For those doctoral students for whom a professional internship is required prior to graduation, 10 applied in 2003–2004. Of those who applied, 4 were placed in internships listed by the Association of Psychology Postdoctoral and Internship Programs (APPIC); 10 were placed in APA accredited internships.

Housing and Day Care: On-campus housing is available. See the following Web sites for more information: McGill Residences and Student Housing: http://www.mcgill.ca/residences/ (on-campus housing) http://www.mcgill.ca/offcampus/ (off-campus housing). On-campus day care facilities are available. See the following Web site for more information: McGill Child Care Centre http://www.mcgill.ca/ http://www.mcgill.ca/index/administrative/?Unit=913.

Employment of Department Graduates:

Master's Degree Graduates: Of those who graduated in the academic year 2003–2004, the following categories and numbers represent the post-graduate activities and employment of master's degree graduates: Enrolled in a post-doctoral residency/fellowship (n/a), employed in independent practice (n/a), total from the above (master's) (0).

Doctoral Degree Graduates: Of those who graduated in the academic year 2003–2004, the following categories and numbers represent the post-graduate activities and employment of doctoral degree graduates: Enrolled in a psychology doctoral program (n/a), enrolled in a post-doctoral residency/fellowship (7), employed in independent practice (1), employed in an academic position at a university (1), total from the above (doctoral) (9).

Additional Information:

Orientation, Objectives, and Emphasis of Department: McGill University's Department of Psychology offers graduate work leading to the PhD degree. The program in experimental psychology includes the areas of cognitive science (perception, learning, and language), developmental, social, personality, quantitative, and behavioral neuroscience. A program in clinical psychology (accredited by APA) is also offered. The basic purpose of the graduate program is to provide the student with an environment in which he or she is free to develop skills and expertise that will serve during a professional career in teaching, research, or clinical service as a psychologist. Individually conceived and conducted research in the student's area of interest is the single most important activity of all graduate students in the department.

Application Information:
Send to: Giovanna LoCascio, Graduate Program Coordinator, Department of Psychology, 1205 Docteur Penfield Avenue, Montreal, Quebec H3A 1B1. Application available online. Students are admitted in the Fall, application deadline December 15. Note: Students are required to apply online. All supporting documents must be submitted by the deadline; December 15. *Fee:* $60. Note: All dollar amounts specified in this entry are Canadian dollars.

Montreal, University of
Department of Psychology
P.O. Box 6128, Succ. Centre-Ville
Montreal, QC H3C 3J7
Telephone: (514) 343-6503
Fax: (514) 343-2285
E-mail: *michel.sabourin@umontreal.ca*
Web: *http://www.psy.umontreal.ca/*

Department Information:
1942. Chairperson: Dr.Michel Sabourin. Number of Faculty: total–full-time 55, part-time 1; women–full-time 23, part-time 1.

Programs and Degrees Offered:
Listed in the following order: Program area, degree type (T if terminal Master's), number awarded 7/03–6/04. Clinical PhD (Doctor of Philosophy) 13, Experimental PhD (Doctor of Philosophy) 15, Industrial PhD (Doctor of Philosophy) 2, Clinical Neuro-Psychology PhD (Doctor of Philosophy) 8.

Student Applications/Admissions:

Student Applications

Clinical PhD (Doctor of Philosophy)—Applications 2004–2005, 150. Total applicants accepted 2004–2005, 16. Number enrolled (new admits only) 2004–2005 full-time, 16. Total enrolled 2004–2005 full-time, 89. Openings 2005–2006, 16. The Median number of years required for completion of a degree are 4. The number of students enrolled full and part-time who were dismissed or voluntarily withdrew from this program area were 3. *Experimental PhD (Doctor of Philosophy)*—Applications 2004–2005, 30. Total applicants accepted 2004–2005, 8. Number enrolled (new admits only) 2004–2005 full-time, 8. Openings 2005–2006, 20. The Median number of years required for completion of a degree are 4. *Industrial PhD (Doctor of Philosophy)*—Applications 2004–2005, 23. Total applicants accepted 2004–2005, 5. Number enrolled (new admits only) 2004–2005 full-time, 5. Total enrolled 2004–2005 full-time, 21. Openings 2005–2006, 5. The Median number of years required for completion of a degree are 4. *Clinical Neuropsychology PhD (Doctor of Philosophy)*—Applications 2004–2005, 40. Total applicants accepted 2004–2005, 9. Number enrolled (new admits only) 2004–2005 full-time, 9. Total enrolled 2004–2005 full-time, 51. Openings 2005–2006, 10. The Median number of years required for completion of a degree are 4.

Admissions Requirements:

Scores: Entries appear in this order: required test or GPA, minimum score (if required), median score of students entering in 2003–2004. Master's Programs: psychology GPA no minimum stated, 3.8.

Other Criteria: (importance of criteria rated low, medium, or high): research experience high, extracurricular activity low, clinically related public service low, GPA high, letters of recommendation low, interview low, statement of goals and objectives medium.

Student Characteristics: The following represents characteristics of students in 2004–2005 in all graduate psychology programs in the department: Female–full-time 189, part-time 0; Male–full-time 59, part-time 0; African American/Black–full-time 2, part-time 0; Hispanic/Latino(a)–full-time 4, part-time 0; Asian/Pacific Islander–full-time 0, part-time 0; American Indian/Alaska Native–full-time 0, part-time 0; Caucasian–full-time 0, part-time 0.

Financial Information/Assistance:

Tuition for Full-Time Study: *Master's:* State residents: per academic year $2,758; Nonstate residents: per academic year $10,800. *Doctoral:* State residents: per academic year $2,758; Nonstate residents: per academic year $10,800.

Financial Assistance:

First Year Students: Teaching assistantships available for first-year. Average amount paid per academic year: $2,000. Apply by variable. Research assistantships available for first-year. Average amount paid per academic year: $2,000. Apply by variable. Fellowships and scholarships available for first-year. Average amount paid per academic year: $5,000. Apply by December.

Advanced Students: Teaching assistantships available for advanced students. Average amount paid per academic year: $5,000. Apply by variable. Research assistantships available for advanced students. Average amount paid per academic year: $5,000. Apply by variable. Fellowships and scholarships available for advanced students. Average amount paid per academic year: $8,000. Apply by December.

Contact Information: Of all students currently enrolled full-time, 68% benefitted from one or more of the listed financial assistance programs.

Internships/Practica: The PhD programs offer internships in clinical, neuropsychology and industrial/organizational psychology, in collaboration with general and psychiatric hospitals, correctional facilities, schools, industry, and governmental agencies. For those doctoral students for whom a professional internship is required prior to graduation, 15 applied in 2003–2004. Of those who applied, 2 were placed in internships listed by the Association of Psychology Postdoctoral and Internship Programs (APPIC); 2 were placed in APA accredited internships.

Housing and Day Care: On-campus housing is available. See the following Web site for more information: www.logement.umontreal.ca. On-campus day care facilities are available.

Employment of Department Graduates:

Master's Degree Graduates: Of those who graduated in the academic year 2003–2004, the following categories and numbers represent the post-graduate activities and employment of master's degree graduates: Enrolled in a post-doctoral residency/fellowship (n/a), employed in independent practice (n/a), total from the above (master's) (0).

Doctoral Degree Graduates: Of those who graduated in the academic year 2003–2004, the following categories and numbers represent the post-graduate activities and employment of doctoral degree graduates: Enrolled in a psychology doctoral program (n/a), total from the above (doctoral) (0).

Additional Information:

Orientation, Objectives, and Emphasis of Department: In several subfields, the department offers a complete graduate curriculum that is oriented either toward scientific research (MSc and PhD programs), at both the human and animal levels, or toward professional training (PhD, clinical, neuropsychology and industrial) programs. Because of its large faculty, the department presents most current theoretical perspectives and methodological approaches. The emphasis is placed on the development of the student's capacity for critical judgment, scientific analysis, and conceptual organization. With regard to professional training, the emphasis is placed on the integration of theory and practice, in both diagnosis and intervention.

Special Facilities or Resources: Because of the academic background of its faculty, our department provides the students with the opportunity of contact with both the North American and European scientific and professional traditions. The department has also organized clinical services for the general community; in this service several PhD students receive part of their professional training. Finally, the department lists on its Web site the current research of the faculty.

Information for Students With Physical Disabilities: See the following Web site for more information: www.umontreal.ca.

Application Information:

Send to: Department Chair. Students are admitted in the Fall, application deadline February 1; Winter, application deadline October 15;

Summer, application deadline February 1. *Fee:* $30. Note: All dollar amounts specified in this entry are Canadian dollars.

New Brunswick, University of
Department of Psychology
Bag Service #45444
Fredericton, NB E3B 6E4
Telephone: (506) 453-4707
Fax: (506) 447-3063
E-mail: *psychair@unb.ca*
Web: *http://www.unb.ca/psychology*

Department Information:
1966. Chairperson: Sandra Byers. Number of Faculty: total–full-time 14; women–full-time 6.

Programs and Degrees Offered:
Listed in the following order: Program area, degree type (T if terminal Master's), number awarded 7/03–6/04. Clinical PhD (Doctor of Philosophy) 2, Experimental and Applied PhD (Doctor of Philosophy) 0.

APA Accreditation: Clinical PhD (Doctor of Philosophy).

Student Applications/Admissions:
Student Applications
Clinical PhD (Doctor of Philosophy)—Applications 2004–2005, 51. Total applicants accepted 2004–2005, 9. Number enrolled (new admits only) 2004–2005 full-time, 4. Number enrolled (new admits only) 2004–2005 part-time, 0. Total enrolled 2004–2005 full-time, 31, part-time, 1. Openings 2005–2006, 6. The Median number of years required for completion of a degree are 7. The number of students enrolled full and part-time who were dismissed or voluntarily withdrew from this program area were 0. *Experimental and Applied PhD (Doctor of Philosophy)*—Applications 2004–2005, 18. Total applicants accepted 2004–2005, 8. Number enrolled (new admits only) 2004–2005 full-time, 3. Number enrolled (new admits only) 2004–2005 part-time, 1. Total enrolled 2004–2005 full-time, 14, part-time, 3. Openings 2005–2006, 5. The number of students enrolled full and part-time, who were dismissed or voluntarily withdrew from this program area were 0.

Admissions Requirements:
Scores: Entries appear in this order: required test or GPA, minimum score (if required), median score of students entering in 2003–2004. Doctoral Programs: GRE-V no minimum stated, 600; GRE-Q no minimum stated, 600; GRE-Analytical no minimum stated, 600; GRE-Subject(Psych) no minimum stated, 600; overall undergraduate GPA 3.7, 3.7. Admission to the Clinical program requires a minimum CGPA of 3.7 (equivalent to A- average). The minimum CGPA for admission to the Experimental and Applied program is 3.5 (on 4.3 scale).
Other Criteria: (importance of criteria rated low, medium, or high): GRE/MAT scores medium, research experience high, work experience medium, extracurricular activity low, clinically related public service low, GPA high, letters of recommendation high, interview high, statement of goals and objec-

tives high, More emphasis is placed on research experience for students admitted to the Experimental and Applied program. Telephone interview is required for the Clinical program. For additional information on admission requirements, go to: www. unbf.ca/arts/psychology/.

Student Characteristics: The following represents characteristics of students in 2004–2005 in all graduate psychology programs in the department: Female–full-time 38, part-time 3; Male–full-time 7, part-time 1; African American/Black–full-time 1, part-time 0; Hispanic/Latino(a)–full-time 0, part-time 0; Asian/Pacific Islander–full-time 1, part-time 0; American Indian/Alaska Native–full-time 0, part-time 0; Caucasian–full-time 42, part-time 4; Multi-ethnic–full-time 1, part-time 0; students subject to the Americans With Disabilities Act–full-time 0, part-time 0.

Financial Information/Assistance:
Tuition for Full-Time Study: *Doctoral:* State residents: per academic year $5,031; Nonstate residents: per academic year $9,355. Tuition is subject to change.

Financial Assistance:
First Year Students: Teaching assistantships available for first-year. Average amount paid per academic year: $4,000. Average number of hours worked per week: 8. Apply by January 15. Fellowships and scholarships available for first-year. Average amount paid per academic year: $8,000. Apply by January 15.
Advanced Students: Teaching assistantships available for advanced students. Average amount paid per academic year: $4,400. Average number of hours worked per week: 8. Apply by January 15. Fellowships and scholarships available for advanced students. Average amount paid per academic year: $8,800. Apply by January 15.
Contact Information: Of all students currently enrolled full-time, 31% benefitted from one or more of the listed financial assistance programs.

Internships/Practica: Students in the Clinical program have completed internships in the following types of local agencies: mental health clinic, general hospital, university counseling services, psychiatric hospital, or school system. For those doctoral students for whom a professional internship is required prior to graduation, 6 applied in 2003–2004. Of those who applied, 6 were placed in internships listed by the Association of Psychology Postdoctoral and Internship Programs (APPIC); 4 were placed in APA accredited internships.

Housing and Day Care: On-campus housing is available. See the following Web site for more information: www.unb.ca/residence/reslife.html. On-campus day care facilities are available.

Employment of Department Graduates:
Master's Degree Graduates: Of those who graduated in the academic year 2003–2004, the following categories and numbers represent the post-graduate activities and employment of master's degree graduates: Enrolled in a post-doctoral residency/fellowship (n/a), employed in independent practice (n/a), total from the above (master's) (0).
Doctoral Degree Graduates: Of those who graduated in the academic year 2003–2004, the following categories and numbers represent the post-graduate activities and employment of doctoral degree graduates: Enrolled in a psychology doctoral program (n/a),

enrolled in another graduate/professional program (0), enrolled in a post-doctoral residency/fellowship (0), employed in independent practice (0), employed in an academic position at a university (1), employed in an academic position at a 2-year/4-year college (0), employed in other positions at a higher education institution (0), employed in a professional position in a school system (0), employed in business or industry (research/consulting) (0), employed in business or industry (management) (0), employed in a government agency (research) (0), employed in a government agency (professional services) (0), employed in a community mental health/counseling center (0), employed in a hospital/medical center (1), still seeking employment (0), other employment position (0), do not know (0), total from the above (doctoral) (2).

Additional Information:

Orientation, Objectives, and Emphasis of Department: The Department of Psychology offers an integrated MA/PhD degree designed to provide extensive specialized study in either Clinical Psychology or Experimental and Applied Psychology. The Clinical Program provides graduates both with sufficient skills in assessment, treatment, and outcome evaluation to initiate careers in service settings under appropriate supervision, and with the knowledge and training needed for an academic career. The Experimental and Applied Program emphasizes individual training and the development of skills to equally prepare the student for a research oriented career in applied and academic settings.

Special Facilities or Resources: The department occupies Keirstead Hall, which is well supplied with research equipment. The facilities include laboratories for research in human learning, cognition and perception, and development, as well as physiological psychology and neuropsychology; a direct line to the computer center; space for research and teaching in clinical, community, behavior therapy, biofeedback, and other areas of applied or clinical psychology.

Application Information:

Send to: School of Graduate Studies, University of New Brunswick, P.O. Box 4400, Fredericton, New Brunswick, Canada E3B 5A3. Application available online. Students are admitted in the Fall, application deadline January 15. *Fee:* $50. The School of Graduate Studies offers "fee waivers" to selected applicants on the basis of academic merit. Note: All dollar amounts specified in this entry are in Canadian dollars.

Ottawa, University of (2004 data)
School of Psychology
Lamoureux Hall, 145 Jean-Jacques Lussier
Ottawa, ON K1N 6N5
Telephone: (613) 562-5801
Fax: (613) 562-5186
E-mail: *jdpaquet@uottawa.ca*
Web: *http://www.grad.uottawa.ca/programs/doctorates/psy*

Department Information:
1941. Director and Associate Dean: Pierre Mercier. Number of Faculty: total–full-time 42, part-time 74; women–full-time 17, part-time 74.

Programs and Degrees Offered:
Listed in the following order: Program area, degree type (T if terminal Master's), number awarded 7/03–6/04. Clinical PhD (Doctor of Philosophy) 8, Experimental PhD (Doctor of Philosophy) 8.

APA Accreditation: Clinical PhD (Doctor of Philosophy).

Student Applications/Admissions:
Student Applications

Clinical PhD (Doctor of Philosophy)—Applications 2004–2005, 116. Total applicants accepted 2004–2005, 13. Openings 2005–2006, 12. The Median number of years required for completion of a degree are 6. The number of students enrolled full and part-time who were dismissed or voluntarily withdrew from this program area were 0. *Experimental PhD (Doctor of Philosophy)*—Applications 2004–2005, 39. Total applicants accepted 2004–2005, 10. Total enrolled 2004–2005 full-time, 42, part-time, 3. Openings 2005–2006, 11. The Median number of years required for completion of a degree are 4. The number of students enrolled full and part-time who were dismissed or voluntarily withdrew from this program area were 0.

Admissions Requirements:

Scores: Entries appear in this order: required test or GPA, minimum score (if required), median score of students entering in 2003–2004. Doctoral Programs: overall undergraduate GPA 3.5.

Other Criteria: (importance of criteria rated low, medium, or high): research experience high, work experience low, extracurricular activity low, clinically related public service medium, GPA high, letters of recommendation high, interview medium, statement of goals and objectives high.

Student Characteristics: The following represents characteristics of students in 2004–2005 in all graduate psychology programs in the department: Female–full-time 91, part-time 3; Male–full-time 18, part-time 0; African American/Black–full-time 0, part-time 0; Hispanic/Latino(a)–full-time 0, part-time 0; Asian/Pacific Islander–full-time 0, part-time 0; American Indian/Alaska Native–full-time 0, part-time 0; Caucasian–full-time 0, part-time 0; Multiethnic–full-time 0, part-time 0; students subject to the Americans With Disabilities Act–full-time 0, part-time 0.

Financial Information/Assistance:
Tuition for Full-Time Study: *Doctoral:* State residents: per academic year $5,626, $321 per credit hour; Nonstate residents: per academic year $12,646, $466 per credit hour. See the following Web site for updates and changes in tuition costs: http://www.uottawa.ca/academic/info/regist/fees/fees2002_en.htm.

Financial Assistance:
First Year Students: Teaching assistantships available for first-year. Average amount paid per academic year: $8,122. Average number of hours worked per week: 10. Apply by June. Research assistantships available for first-year. Average amount paid per academic year: $8,122. Average number of hours worked per week: 10. Apply by June. Fellowships and scholarships available for first-year. Average amount paid per academic year: $6,500. Apply by March.

Advanced Students: Teaching assistantships available for advanced students. Average amount paid per academic year:

$8,122. Average number of hours worked per week: 10. Apply by June. Research assistantships available for advanced students. Average amount paid per academic year: $8,122. Average number of hours worked per week: 10. Apply by June. Traineeships available for advanced students. Average amount paid per academic year: $25,000. Average number of hours worked per week: 30. Apply by October. Fellowships and scholarships available for advanced students. Average amount paid per academic year: $6,500. Apply by October.

Contact Information: Of all students currently enrolled full-time, 95% benefitted from one or more of the listed financial assistance programs.

Internships/Practica: Internships, required of all clinical program students, take place in accredited external settings in Canada and the USA, as well as in local, approved training units. There are two units in the university: the Centre for Psychological Services, and the Career and Counseling Services. There are fifteen external units: Children's Hospital of Eastern Ontario, Ottawa General Hospital, Brockville Psychiatric Hospital, Centre Hospitalier Pierre Janet, Montfort Hospital, Ottawa-Carleton Detention Centre, Rideau Correctional and Treatment Centre, Conseil des Ecoles Catholiques de Langue Francaise, Sister of Charity of Ottawa Health Service, Center for Treatment of Sexual Abuse and Childhood Trauma, Crossroads Children's Centre, Centre Roberts/Smart, Royal Ottawa Hospital, The Rehabilitation Centre, The Children's Aid Society of Ottawa-Carleton. Internships for the Experimental Program within the University of Ottawa take place in the departments of Sociology, Physiotherapy, Epidemiology, Faculties of Education, and Administration. External internships for the Experimental Program are Royal Ottawa Hospital, Ottawa General Hospital, Children's Hospital of Eastern Ontario, Department of Psychology at Carleton University, Communications Research Center of Canada, Federal Government of Canada (Animal Care), Canadian Armed Forces, ENAP, Ministry of Health, and NORTEL. For those doctoral students for whom a professional internship is required prior to graduation, 7 applied in 2003–2004. Of those who applied, 7 were placed in internships listed by the Association of Psychology Postdoctoral and Internship Programs (APPIC); 7 were placed in APA accredited internships.

Housing and Day Care: On-campus housing is available. See the following Web site for more information: http://www.uottawa.ca/whychoose/housing/index.html. On-campus day care facilities are available. See the following Web site for more information: http://www.uottawa.ca/students/community/q&a/.

Employment of Department Graduates:
Master's Degree Graduates: Of those who graduated in the academic year 2003–2004, the following categories and numbers represent the post-graduate activities and employment of master's degree graduates: Enrolled in a post-doctoral residency/fellowship (n/a), employed in independent practice (n/a), total from the above (master's) (0).
Doctoral Degree Graduates: Of those who graduated in the academic year 2003–2004, the following categories and numbers represent the post-graduate activities and employment of doctoral degree graduates: Enrolled in a psychology doctoral program (n/a), enrolled in a post-doctoral residency/fellowship (2), employed in independent practice (3), employed in an academic position at a university (2), employed in a professional position in a school system (1), employed in a government agency (research) (1), employed in a government agency (professional services) (2), employed in a hospital/medical center (2), other employment position (1), do not know (2), total from the above (doctoral) (16).

Additional Information:
Orientation, Objectives, and Emphasis of Department: The objective of this program is to train researchers in experimental psychology with emphasis on one of the following areas: behavioral neurophysiology, psychopharmacology, psychophysiology, human and animal cognition, learning, language, sleep and dreams, social, cognitive and emotional development, personality, intergroup relations, motivation, and the social psychology of health and work. Training in behavioral neuroscience may also be provided through the Behavioural Neurosciences Specialization Program, which is a collaborative program coordinated by the University of Ottawa and Carleton University. The purpose of the clinical psychology program is to provide doctoral training in the area of clinical psychology and prepare students to work with adults and children. Professional training includes exposure to cognitive-behavioral, experiential, systemic/interpersonal, and community consultation approaches. Thesis supervisors within the clinical program have special expertise in areas such as social development of children, behavior problems in children, social skills training, depression, psychotherapy, marital therapy, family psychology, correctional psychology, community psychology and program evaluation. Training in behavioural neuroscience may also be provided through the Behavioural Neuroscience Specialization Program, which is a collaborative program coordinated by the University of Ottawa and Carleton University. Students may also elect to choose a thesis supervisor from the Experimental program.

Special Facilities or Resources: The physical facilities available at the School of Psychology take the form of integrated units serving specific purposes. These include: animal care facilities for housing rats, mice, pigeons, and bees (5,000 sq. ft.); surgery-necropsy facilities for neuroscience research; facilities for animal behavior research; individual units for testing human participants in experiments on psychophysiological, perceptual, cognitive, developmental, or social processes; Community Services Research Unit, for research related to evaluating and improving community agency programs; a sleep lab with 2 bedrooms; technical workshop facilities for building customized equipment, and computer maintenance with 2 electronic technicians, 1 programmer and 1 microcomputer specialist; local area networks (LANs); and more than 50 PCs and mainframe computer facilities for access to e-mail, library search software, scientific graphics, computer language, compilers, mathematical software library, and so on. Faculty members and graduate students have access to rich library collections of books and periodicals in English and in French. One library also houses a collection of tests and evaluation instruments in these two languages. Because Ottawa is Canada's capital and has two full-service universities, this geographical area provides access to excellent libraries (e.g., the National Library, the library of the Canada Institute for Scientific and Technical Information), research and clinical training facilities in hospitals, academic settings, and government departments.

Information for Students With Physical Disabilities: See the following Web site for more information: http://web.sass.uottawa.ca/classroom/access/.

Application Information:

Send to: Graduate Program Administrator, School of Psychology, University of Ottawa, Lamoureux Hall, 145 Jean-Jacques Lussier Street, Ottawa, K1N 6N5, Canada. Application available online. Students are admitted in the Fall, application deadline January 15. Fee: $60. Note: All dollar amounts specified in this entry are Canadian dollars.

Quebec at Montreal, University of
Department of Psychology
C.P. 8888, Succ. Centre-Ville
Montreal, QC H3C 3P8
Telephone: (514) 987-4804
Fax: (514) 987-7953
E-mail: *psycho@uqam.ca*
Web: *http://www.psycho.uqam.ca/*

Department Information:

1969. Chairperson: Louis Brunet. Number of Faculty: total–full-time 55, part-time 1; women–full-time 19, part-time 1; minority full-time 1.

Programs and Degrees Offered:

Listed in the following order: Program area, degree type (T if terminal Master's), number awarded 7/03–6/04. Community PhD (Doctor of Philosophy) 2, Development PhD (Doctor of Philosophy) 9, Education PhD (Doctor of Philosophy) 8, I/O PhD (Doctor of Philosophy) 2, Neuropsychology PhD (Doctor of Philosophy) 3, Psychodynamic PhD (Doctor of Philosophy) 7, Social PhD (Doctor of Philosophy) 4, Behavioral PhD (Doctor of Philosophy) 6.

Student Applications/Admissions:
Student Applications

Community PhD (Doctor of Philosophy)—Applications 2004–2005, 15. Total applicants accepted 2004–2005, 4. The Median number of years required for completion of a degree are 6. The number of students enrolled full and part-time who were dismissed or voluntarily withdrew from this program area were 2. *Development PhD (Doctor of Philosophy)*—Applications 2004–2005, 32. Total applicants accepted 2004–2005, 18. The Median number of years required for completion of a degree are 6. The number of students enrolled full and part-time who were dismissed or voluntarily withdrew from this program area were 2. *Education PhD (Doctor of Philosophy)*—Applications 2004–2005, 20. Total applicants accepted 2004–2005, 12. The Median number of years required for completion of a degree are 6. The number of students enrolled full and part-time who were dismissed or voluntarily withdrew from this program area

were 1. *I/O PhD (Doctor of Philosophy)*—Applications 2004–2005, 18. Total applicants accepted 2004–2005, 5. The Median number of years required for completion of a degree are 6. The number of students enrolled full and part-time who were dismissed or voluntarily withdrew from this program area were 0. *Neuropsychology PhD (Doctor of Philosophy)*—Applications 2004–2005, 23. Total applicants accepted 2004–2005, 10. The Median number of years required for completion of a degree are 6. The number of students enrolled full and part-time who were dismissed or voluntarily withdrew from this program area were 0. *Psychodynamic PhD (Doctor of Philosophy)*—Applications 2004–2005, 46. Total applicants accepted 2004–2005, 16. The Median number of years required for completion of a degree are 6. The number of students enrolled full and part-time who were dismissed or voluntarily withdrew from this program area were 5. *Social PhD (Doctor of Philosophy)*—Applications 2004–2005, 12. Total applicants accepted 2004–2005, 5. The Median number of years required for completion of a degree are 6. The number of students enrolled full and part-time who were dismissed or voluntarily withdrew from this program area were 0. *Behavioral PhD (Doctor of Philosophy)*—Applications 2004–2005, 30. Total applicants accepted 2004–2005, 12. The Median number of years required for completion of a degree are 6. The number of students enrolled full and part-time who were dismissed or voluntarily withdrew from this program area were 3.

Admissions Requirements:

Scores: Entries appear in this order: required test or GPA, minimum score (if required), median score of students entering in 2003–2004. Master's Programs: n/a Doctoral Programs: overall undergraduate GPA 76%; psychology GPA no minimum stated. Minimum score required is 3.2 / 4.3.

Other Criteria: (importance of criteria rated low, medium, or high): research experience low, work experience low, extracurricular activity low, clinically related public service low, GPA high, letters of recommendation high, interview low, statement of goals and objectives high.

Student Characteristics: The following represents characteristics of students in 2004–2005 in all graduate psychology programs in the department: Female–full-time 316, part-time 0; Male–full-time 94, part-time 0; African American/Black–full-time 1, part-time 0; Hispanic/Latino(a)–full-time 2, part-time 0; Asian/Pacific Islander–full-time 1, part-time 0; American Indian/Alaska Native–full-time 0, part-time 0; Caucasian–full-time 0, part-time 0.

Financial Information/Assistance:
Financial Assistance:

First Year Students: No information provided.
Advanced Students: No information provided.
Contact Information: Of all students currently enrolled full-time, 20% benefitted from one or more of the listed financial assistance programs.

Internships/Practica: Internship settings include about 12 Montreal general and psychiatric hospitals, 7 community settings, 6 Montreal school boards, 4 university study centers as well as a number of private centers or clinics. Internships typically cover about 1600-2000 hours of supervised clinical work, including assessment procedures, multidisciplinary seminars, and various types of therapy with various orientations. Some settings also provide training in clinical observation and research.

Housing and Day Care: On-campus housing is available. Telephone: (514) 987-6669; Fax: (514) 987-0344. On-campus day care facilities are available.

Employment of Department Graduates:

Master's Degree Graduates: Of those who graduated in the academic year 2003–2004, the following categories and numbers represent the post-graduate activities and employment of master's degree graduates: Enrolled in a post-doctoral residency/fellowship (n/a), employed in independent practice (n/a), total from the above (master's) (0).

Doctoral Degree Graduates: Of those who graduated in the academic year 2003–2004, the following categories and numbers represent the post-graduate activities and employment of doctoral degree graduates: Enrolled in a psychology doctoral program (n/a), total from the above (doctoral) (0).

Additional Information:

Special Facilities or Resources: Our department offers the following technical support to staff and graduate students: a consultant statistician, a consultant computer programmer, and a resident visual artist who designs and creates professional quality visual stimuli for research. He also prepares graphics for articles, posters, and the thesis. All labs are equipped with personal computers. Students have access to these computers and the mainframe university computer. The university offers support services for handicapped students. Please note that the teaching language in our university is French, though the majority of the literature in psychology is English. Some professors may require the students to write papers in French. Students must obtain permission to write the thesis in English. Courses in French conversation and composition are offered by the university.

Information for Students With Physical Disabilities: Intégration des personnes handicapées: (514) 987-3148.

Application Information:

Send to: Registrariat Service de l'Admission, Université du Québec à Montréal, Case postale 8888, Succursale Centre-ville, Montréal (Québec), Canada, H3C 3P8. Application available online. Students are admitted in the Fall, application deadline February 15. *Fee:* $55. Note: All dollar amounts specified in this entry are Canadian dollars.

Queen's University
Department of Psychology
Humphrey Hall, 62 Arch Street
Kingston, ON K7L 3N6
Telephone: (613) 533-6004
Fax: (613) 533-2499
E-mail: *psycgrad@post.queensu.ca*
Web: *http://psyc.queensu.ca*

Department Information:
1949. Head: V.L. Quinsey. Number of Faculty: total–full-time 32; women–full-time 17; minority–full-time 2.

Programs and Degrees Offered:
Listed in the following order: Program area, degree type (T if terminal Master's), number awarded 7/03–6/04. Brain, Behavior, and Cognitive PhD (Doctor of Philosophy) 4, Clinical PhD (Doctor of Philosophy) 3, Social-Personality PhD (Doctor of Philosophy) 0, Developmental PhD (Doctor of Philosophy) 2.

APA Accreditation: Clinical PhD (Doctor of Philosophy).

Student Applications/Admissions:
Student Applications

Brain, Behavior, and Cognitive PhD (Doctor of Philosophy)—Applications 2004–2005, 28. Total applicants accepted 2004–2005, 13. Number enrolled (new admits only) 2004–2005 full-time, 4. Number enrolled (new admits only) 2004–2005 part-time, 0. Openings 2005–2006, 8. The Median number of years required for completion of a degree are 5.5. The number of students enrolled full and part-time who were dismissed or voluntarily withdrew from this program area were 1. *Clinical PhD (Doctor of Philosophy)*—Applications 2004–2005, 126. Total applicants accepted 2004–2005, 15. Number enrolled (new admits only) 2004–2005 full-time, 7. Number enrolled (new admits only) 2004–2005 part-time, 0. Total enrolled 2004–2005 full-time, 35, part-time, 2. Openings 2005–2006, 6. The Median number of years required for completion of a degree are 6.5. The number of students enrolled full and part-time who were dismissed or voluntarily withdrew from this program area were 1. *Social-Personality PhD (Doctor of Philosophy)*—Applications 2004–2005, 48. Total applicants accepted 2004–2005, 13. Number enrolled (new admits only) 2004–2005 full-time, 11. Total enrolled 2004–2005 full-time, 23, part-time, 1. Openings 2005–2006, 5. The number of students enrolled full and part-time who were dismissed or voluntarily withdrew from this program area were 0. *Developmental PhD (Doctor of Philosophy)*—Applications 2004–2005, 14. Total applicants accepted 2004–2005, 5. Number enrolled (new admits only) 2004–2005 full-time, 1. Number enrolled (new admits only) 2004–2005 part-time, 0. Openings 2005–2006, 4. The Median number of years required for completion of a degree are 4. The number of students enrolled full and part-time who were dismissed or voluntarily withdrew from this program area were 0.

Admissions Requirements:

Scores: Entries appear in this order: required test or GPA, minimum score (if required), median score of students entering in 2003–2004. Master's Programs: GRE-V no minimum stated, 600; GRE-Q no minimum stated, 690; GRE-Analytical no minimum stated, 5.5; overall undergraduate GPA no minimum stated; last 2 years GPA no minimum stated; psychology GPA no minimum stated. Upper second class honours degree is required. Doctoral Programs: GRE-V no minimum stated, 600; GRE-Q no minimum stated, 695; GRE-Analytical no minimum stated, 650; overall undergraduate GPA no minimum stated; last 2 years GPA no minimum stated; psychology GPA no minimum stated.

Other Criteria: (importance of criteria rated low, medium, or high): GRE/MAT scores high, research experience medium, work experience low, extracurricular activity low, clinically related public service low, GPA high, letters of recommendation high, statement of goals and objectives high, supervisor availability high. For additional information on admission requirements, go to: http://psyc.queensu.ca/gradbeta1/prostu forms.html.

Student Characteristics: The following represents characteristics of students in 2004–2005 in all graduate psychology programs in the department: Female–full-time 60, part-time 3; Male–full-time 25, part-time 0; Caucasian–full-time 0, part-time 0.

Financial Information/Assistance:

Tuition for Full-Time Study: *Master's:* State residents: per academic year $5,933; Nonstate residents: per academic year $11,374. *Doctoral:* State residents: per academic year $5,933; Nonstate residents: per academic year $11,374. Tuition is subject to change. See the following Web site for updates and changes in tuition costs: http://www.queensu.ca/registrar/fees/.

Financial Assistance:

First Year Students: Teaching assistantships available for first-year. Average amount paid per academic year: $8,450. Average number of hours worked per week: 10. Apply by n/a. Fellowships and scholarships available for first-year. Average amount paid per academic year: $10,000. Average number of hours worked per week: 0. Apply by October.

Advanced Students: Teaching assistantships available for advanced students. Average amount paid per academic year: $8,450. Average number of hours worked per week: 10. Apply by n/a. Fellowships and scholarships available for advanced students. Average amount paid per academic year: $10,000. Average number of hours worked per week: 0. Apply by October.

Contact Information: Of all students currently enrolled full-time, 85% benefitted from one or more of the listed financial assistance programs.

Internships/Practica: Clinical program students must complete a pre-doctoral internship in an approved setting under the primary supervision of a registered psychologist. Students are expected to seek placement in a CPA/APA approved site. For those doctoral students for whom a professional internship is required prior to graduation, 4 applied in 2003–2004. Of those who applied, 3 were placed in internships listed by the Association of Psychology Postdoctoral and Internship Programs (APPIC); 2 were placed in APA accredited internships.

Housing and Day Care: On-campus housing is available. See the following Web site for more information: http://www.queensu.ca/dsao/housing/ah1.htm. On-campus day care facilities are available. See the following Web site for more information: http://www.queensu.ca/dsao/daycare/centre/fac2.htm.

Employment of Department Graduates:

Master's Degree Graduates: Of those who graduated in the academic year 2003–2004, the following categories and numbers represent the post-graduate activities and employment of master's degree graduates: Enrolled in a psychology doctoral program (9), enrolled in another graduate/professional program (0), enrolled in a post-doctoral residency/fellowship (n/a), employed in independent practice (n/a), employed in an academic position at a university (0), employed in an academic position at a 2-year/4-year college (0), employed in other positions at a higher education institution (0), employed in a professional position in a school system (0), employed in business or industry (research/consulting) (0), employed in business or industry (management) (0), em-

ployed in a government agency (research) (0), employed in a government agency (professional services) (0), employed in a community mental health/counseling center (0), employed in a hospital/medical center (0), still seeking employment (0), other employment position (1), do not know (1), total from the above (master's) (11).

Doctoral Degree Graduates: Of those who graduated in the academic year 2003–2004, the following categories and numbers represent the post-graduate activities and employment of doctoral degree graduates: Enrolled in a psychology doctoral program (n/a), enrolled in a post-doctoral residency/fellowship (3), employed in independent practice (0), employed in an academic position at a university (3), employed in an academic position at a 2-year/4-year college (0), employed in other positions at a higher education institution (0), employed in a professional position in a school system (0), employed in business or industry (research/consulting) (0), employed in business or industry (management) (0), employed in a government agency (research) (0), employed in a government agency (professional services) (0), employed in a community mental health/counseling center (0), employed in a hospital/medical center (2), still seeking employment (0), other employment position (0), do not know (1), total from the above (doctoral) (9).

Additional Information:

Orientation, Objectives, and Emphasis of Department: All programs stress empirical research. The Brain, Behavior, and Cognitive Science program, the Developmental program, and the Social-Personality Program emphasize research skills and scholarship, preparing students for either academic positions or for research positions in government, industry, and the like. The Clinical Program is based on a scientist-practitioner model of training that emphasizes the integration of research and clinical skills in the understanding, assessment, treatment, and prevention of psychological problems.

Special Facilities or Resources: Extensive computer and laboratory facilities are available to graduate students for research and clinical experience. Financial assistance is available in the form of federal, provincial, and university fellowships, scholarships and bursaries. For 2004-05, incoming Master's students received a minimum of $15,000, PhD students received a minimum of $17,000. A portion of this guaranteed minimum is in the form of a teaching assistantship.

Information for Students With Physical Disabilities: See the following Web site for more information: http://www.queensu.ca/dsao/resource.htm.

Application Information:

Send to: The Registrar, School of Graduate Studies and Research, Queen's University, Kingston, ON Canada K7L 3N6. Application available online. URL of online application: http://www.queensu.ca/sgsr/prospective/approcedures.php. Students are admitted in the Fall, application deadline January 15. *Fee:* $70. Not applicable. Note: All dollar amounts specified in this entry are Canadian dollars.

Regina, University of
Psychology
Department of Psychology, University of Regina
Regina, SK S4S 0A2
Telephone: (306) 585-4157
Fax: (306) 585-5429
E-mail: *william.smythe@uregina.ca*
Web: *http://www.uregina.ca*

Department Information:
1965. Department Head: William Smythe. Number of Faculty: total–full-time 20; women–full-time 8; minority–full-time 2.

Programs and Degrees Offered:
Listed in the following order: Program area, degree type (T if terminal Master's), number awarded 7/03–6/04. Clinical MA/MS (Master of Arts/Science) (T) 8, Clinical PhD (Doctor of Philosophy) 0, Experimental and Applied Psychology MA/MS (Master of Arts/Science) (T) 0, Experimental and Applied Psychology PhD (Doctor of Philosophy) 0.

Student Applications/Admissions:
Student Applications
Clinical MA/MS (Master of Arts/Science)—Applications 2004–2005, 22. Total applicants accepted 2004–2005, 6. Number enrolled (new admits only) 2004–2005 full-time, 4. Openings 2005–2006, 6. The Median number of years required for completion of a degree are 2. The number of students enrolled full and part-time who were dismissed or voluntarily withdrew from this program area were 1. *Clinical PhD (Doctor of Philosophy)*—Applications 2004–2005, 15. Total applicants accepted 2004–2005, 5. Number enrolled (new admits only) 2004–2005 full-time, 4. Number enrolled (new admits only) 2004–2005 part-time, 0. Total enrolled 2004–2005 full-time, 18, part-time, 1. Openings 2005–2006, 6. The Median number of years required for completion of a degree are 5. The number of students enrolled full and part-time who were dismissed or voluntarily withdrew from this program area were 1. *Experimental and Applied Psychology MA/MS (Master of Arts/Science)*—Applications 2004–2005, 11. Total applicants accepted 2004–2005, 5. Number enrolled (new admits only) 2004–2005 full-time, 3. Number enrolled (new admits only) 2004–2005 part-time, 0. Total enrolled 2004–2005 full-time, 3, part-time, 1. Openings 2005–2006, 5. The Median number of years required for completion of a degree are 2. The number of students enrolled full and part-time who were dismissed or voluntarily withdrew from this program area were 3. *Experimental and Applied Psychology PhD (Doctor of Philosophy)*—Applications 2004–2005, 3. Total applicants accepted 2004–2005, 1. Number enrolled (new admits only) 2004–2005 full-time, 0. Number enrolled (new admits only) 2004–2005 part-time, 0. Total enrolled 2004–2005 full-time, 1, part-time, 1. Openings 2005–2006, 3. The Median number of years required for completion of a degree are 4. The number of students enrolled full and part-time who were dismissed or voluntarily withdrew from this program area were 1.

Admissions Requirements:
Scores: Entries appear in this order: required test or GPA, minimum score (if required), median score of students entering in 2003–2004. Master's Programs: GRE-V no minimum stated; GRE-Q no minimum stated; GRE-V+Q no minimum stated; GRE-Analytical no minimum stated; GRE-V+Q+Analytical no minimum stated; GRE-Subject(Psych) no minimum stated; overall undergraduate GPA no minimum stated; psychology GPA no minimum stated. Doctoral Programs: GRE-V no minimum stated; GRE-Q no minimum stated; GRE-V+Q no minimum stated; GRE-Analytical no minimum stated; GRE-V+Q+Analytical no minimum stated; GRE-Subject(Psych) no minimum stated; overall undergraduate GPA no minimum stated; psychology GPA no minimum stated. Submission of GRE scores is optional for applicants who hold a Master's degree from a Canadian University.

Other Criteria: (importance of criteria rated low, medium, or high): GRE/MAT scores medium, research experience medium, work experience low, clinically related public service medium, GPA high, letters of recommendation high, statement of goals and objectives high.

Student Characteristics: The following represents characteristics of students in 2004–2005 in all graduate psychology programs in the department: Female–full-time 32, part-time 3; Male–full-time 5, part-time 0; African American/Black–full-time 2, part-time 0; Hispanic/Latino(a)–full-time 0, part-time 0; Asian/Pacific Islander–full-time 0, part-time 0; American Indian/Alaska Native–full-time 2, part-time 0; Caucasian–full-time 33, part-time 0; Multi-ethnic–full-time 3, part-time 0; students subject to the Americans With Disabilities Act–full-time 0, part-time 0.

Financial Information/Assistance:
Tuition for Full-Time Study: *Master's:* State residents: $227 per credit hour; Nonstate residents: $363 per credit hour. *Doctoral:* State residents: $227 per credit hour; Nonstate residents: $363 per credit hour.

Financial Assistance:
First Year Students: Teaching assistantships available for first-year. Average amount paid per academic year: $0. Average number of hours worked per week: 0. Apply by June 15. Research assistantships available for first-year. Average amount paid per academic year: $0. Average number of hours worked per week: 0. Apply by February 28. Fellowships and scholarships available for first-year. Average amount paid per academic year: $0. Average number of hours worked per week: 0. Apply by June 15.

Advanced Students: Teaching assistantships available for advanced students. Average amount paid per academic year: $5,089. Average number of hours worked per week: 10. Apply by June 15. Research assistantships available for advanced students. Average amount paid per academic year: $4,250. Apply by February 28. Fellowships and scholarships available for advanced students. Average amount paid per academic year: $4,750. Apply by June 15.

Contact Information: Of all students currently enrolled full-time, 20% benefitted from one or more of the listed financial assistance programs.

Internships/Practica: A wide array of community resources is available and well utilized in providing practicum and internship training. The department cannot guarantee placement in these facilities, but our record of supplying these has been perfect in the past. For those doctoral students for whom a professional internship is required prior to graduation, 5 applied in 2003–

2004. Of those who applied, 3 were placed in internships listed by the Association of Psychology Postdoctoral and Internship Programs (APPIC); 3 were placed in APA accredited internships.

Housing and Day Care: On-campus housing is available. See the following Web site for more information: www.uregina.ca. The University of Regina Web site breaks down into different sections, one of which relates to student services. On-campus day care facilities are available.

Employment of Department Graduates:

Master's Degree Graduates: Of those who graduated in the academic year 2003–2004, the following categories and numbers represent the post-graduate activities and employment of master's degree graduates: Enrolled in a psychology doctoral program (7), enrolled in a post-doctoral residency/fellowship (n/a), employed in independent practice (n/a), total from the above (master's) (7).

Doctoral Degree Graduates: Of those who graduated in the academic year 2003–2004, the following categories and numbers represent the post-graduate activities and employment of doctoral degree graduates: Enrolled in a psychology doctoral program (n/a), total from the above (doctoral) (0).

Additional Information:

Orientation, Objectives, and Emphasis of Department: Teaching and research are oriented toward clinical, social, and applied approaches. The majority of graduate students are in clinical psychology. Faculty orientation is eclectic. Cognitive behavioral and humanistic approaches are represented. Neuropsychology is also well represented.

Special Facilities or Resources: The department has clinical/counseling rooms for research purposes, a small testing library, permanent space for faculty research, and observation rooms and computer labs.

Information for Students With Physical Disabilities: Contact: Dianne.Mader@uregina.ca.

Application Information:

Send to: Dean, Faculty of Graduate Studies and Research, University of Regina, Regina, SK S4S 0A2. Application available online. URL of online application: uregina.ca/gradstudies/main/admissions/shtml. Students are admitted in the Fall, application deadline February 15. *Fee:* $60. Note: All dollar amounts specified in this entry are Canadian dollars.

Saint Mary's University
Department of Psychology
923 Robie Street
Halifax, NS B3H 3C3
Telephone: (902) 420-5846
Fax: (902) 496-8287
E-mail: *vic.catano@smu.ca*
Web: *http://www.smu.ca/academic/science/psych/*

Department Information:

1966. Chairperson: Victor Catano. Number of Faculty: total–full-time 16, part-time 17; women–full-time 7, part-time 17; minority–part-time 2.

Programs and Degrees Offered:

Listed in the following order: Program area, degree type (T if terminal Master's), number awarded 7/03–6/04. Masters in Applied I/O Psychology MA/MS (Master of Arts/Science) (T) 7, PhD in Industrial/Organizational Psychology PhD (Doctor of Philosophy).

Student Applications/Admissions:
Student Applications

Masters in Applied I/O Psychology MA/MS (Master of Arts/Science)—Applications 2004–2005, 31. Total applicants accepted 2004–2005, 9. Number enrolled (new admits only) 2004–2005 full-time, 4. Number enrolled (new admits only) 2004–2005 part-time, 1. Total enrolled 2004–2005 full-time, 20, part-time, 1. Openings 2005–2006, 8. The Median number of years required for completion of a degree are 2. The number of students enrolled full and part-time who were dismissed or voluntarily withdrew from this program area were 0. *PhD in Industrial/Organizational Psychology PhD (Doctor of Philosophy)*—Openings 2005–2006, 3.

Admissions Requirements:

Scores: Entries appear in this order: required test or GPA, minimum score (if required), median score of students entering in 2003–2004. Master's Programs: GRE-V+Q+Analytical 500, 610; GRE-Subject(Psych) 500, 640; overall undergraduate GPA 3.00, 3.33. Doctoral Programs: GRE-V+Q+Analytical no minimum stated; GRE-Subject(Psych) no minimum stated; overall undergraduate GPA no minimum stated.

Other Criteria: (importance of criteria rated low, medium, or high): GRE/MAT scores high, research experience high, work experience low, extracurricular activity low, GPA high, letters of recommendation high, statement of goals and objectives high.

Student Characteristics: The following represents characteristics of students in 2004–2005 in all graduate psychology programs in the department: Female–full-time 11, part-time 1; Male–full-time 9, part-time 0; African American/Black–full-time 0, part-time 0; Hispanic/Latino(a)–full-time 0, part-time 0; Asian/Pacific Islander–full-time 2, part-time 0; American Indian/Alaska Native–full-time 0, part-time 0; Caucasian–full-time 18, part-time 1; Multi-ethnic–full-time 0, part-time 0; students subject to the Americans With Disabilities Act–full-time 0, part-time 0.

Financial Information/Assistance:

Tuition for Full-Time Study: *Master's:* State residents: per academic year $3,087; Nonstate residents: per academic year $5,898. Tuition is subject to change. See the following Web site for updates and changes in tuition costs: http://www.stmarys.ca.

Financial Assistance:

First Year Students: Teaching assistantships available for first-year. Average amount paid per academic year: $4,830. Average number of hours worked per week: 12. Apply by February 1. Research assistantships available for first-year. Average amount paid per academic year: $7,500. Average number of hours worked per week: 10. Apply by no deadline. Fellowships and scholarships available for first-year. Average amount paid per academic year: $7,200. Average number of hours worked per week: 0. Apply by February 1.

Advanced Students: Teaching assistantships available for advanced students. Average amount paid per academic year: $4,830. Average number of hours worked per week: 12. Apply by June 1. Research assistantships available for advanced students. Average amount paid per academic year: $7,500. Average number of hours worked per week: 10. Traineeships available for advanced students. Average amount paid per academic year: $8,000. Average number of hours worked per week: 35. Apply by no deadline. Fellowships and scholarships available for advanced students. Average amount paid per academic year: $7,200. Average number of hours worked per week: 0. Apply by June 1.

Contact Information: Of all students currently enrolled full-time, 100% benefitted from one or more of the listed financial assistance programs.

Internships/Practica: Students are required to complete a supervised full-time, paid internship (minimum of 500 hours) in the summer following their first year or part-time during their second year. Placements are available in a variety of government agencies, human resource departments, research agencies, and private consulting firms. Salaries range from $6000 to $13,000 for the four months.

Housing and Day Care: On-campus housing is available. See the following Web site for more information: http://www.stmarys.ca. On-campus day care facilities are available.

Employment of Department Graduates:

Master's Degree Graduates: Of those who graduated in the academic year 2003–2004, the following categories and numbers represent the post-graduate activities and employment of master's degree graduates: Enrolled in a psychology doctoral program (1), enrolled in another graduate/professional program (0), enrolled in a post-doctoral residency/fellowship (n/a), employed in independent practice (n/a), employed in an academic position at a university (0), employed in an academic position at a 2-year/4-year college (1), employed in other positions at a higher education institution (0), employed in a professional position in a school system (0), employed in business or industry (research/consulting) (1), employed in business or industry (management) (0), employed in a government agency (research) (2), employed in a government agency (professional services) (1), employed in a community mental health/counseling center (0), employed in a hospital/medical center (0), still seeking employment (0), other employment position (0), do not know (0), total from the above (master's) (6).

Doctoral Degree Graduates: Of those who graduated in the academic year 2003–2004, the following categories and numbers represent the post-graduate activities and employment of doctoral degree graduates: Enrolled in a psychology doctoral program (n/a), total from the above (doctoral) (0).

Additional Information:

Orientation, Objectives, and Emphasis of Department: Students are expected to acquire a background in theory and research that is consistent with the scientist-practitioner model, keeping in mind the goal of preparing themselves for employment at the master's level of continued graduate education. Full-time students normally require two years to complete the program. Part-time students may take two to four years longer. All students are provided with financial support for two years.

Special Facilities or Resources: General experimental laboratories, gradute computer lab, small-group research space, observation rooms, graduate student offices, and an extensive tests and measurements library that includes psychological test batteries are available. Support systems include audiovisual equipment, computer facilities, and a technical workshop. Students may be involved in the CN Centre for Occupational Health & Safety, as well as the Centre for Leadership Excellence.

Application Information:
Send to: Faculty of Graduate Studies & Research, Saint Mary's University, Halifax, NS, Canada B3H 3C3. Application available online. URL of online application: http://fgsr.smu.ca/GraduateStudies/Admissions/Science.aspx. Students are admitted in the Fall, application deadline February 1. *Fee:* $70. Note: All dollar amounts specified in this entry are Canadian dollars.

Saskatchewan, University of
Department of Psychology
Arts and Science
9 Campus Drive
Saskatoon, SK S7N 5A5
Telephone: (306) 966-6657
Fax: (306) 966-6630
E-mail: *carolynn.drabble@usask.ca*
Web: *http://www.usask.ca/psychology/*

Department Information:
1946. Head: Linda McMullen. Number of Faculty: total–full-time 30, part-time 11; women–full-time 13, part-time 11.

Programs and Degrees Offered:
Listed in the following order: Program area, degree type (T if terminal Master's), number awarded 7/03–6/04. Applied Social MA/MS (Master of Arts/Science) (T) 2, Basic Behavioural Science PhD (Doctor of Philosophy) 0, Clinical PhD (Doctor of Philosophy) 9, Applied Social PhD (Doctor of Philosophy) 0, Basic Behavioural Science MA/MS (Master of Arts/Science) (T) 3.

APA Accreditation: Clinical PhD (Doctor of Philosophy).

Student Applications/Admissions:
Student Applications
Applied Social MA/MS (Master of Arts/Science)—Applications 2004–2005, 20. Total applicants accepted 2004–2005, 5. Number enrolled (new admits only) 2004–2005 full-time, 5. Total enrolled 2004–2005 full-time, 8, part-time, 2. Openings 2005–2006, 3. The Median number of years required for completion of a degree are 3. The number of students enrolled full and part-time who were dismissed or voluntarily withdrew from

this program area were 0. *Basic Behavioural Science PhD (Doctor of Philosophy)*—Applications 2004–2005, 9. Total applicants accepted 2004–2005, 1. Number enrolled (new admits only) 2004–2005 full-time, 1. Total enrolled 2004–2005 full-time, 6, part-time, 3. Openings 2005–2006, 7. The number of students enrolled full and part-time who were dismissed or voluntarily withdrew from this program area were 0. *Clinical PhD (Doctor of Philosophy)*—Applications 2004–2005, 55. Total applicants accepted 2004–2005, 7. Number enrolled (new admits only) 2004–2005 full-time, 7. Total enrolled 2004–2005 full-time, 32, part-time, 9. Openings 2005–2006, 5. The Median number of years required for completion of a degree are 6. The number of students enrolled full and part-time who were dismissed or voluntarily withdrew from this program area were 0. *Applied Social PhD (Doctor of Philosophy)*—Applications 2004–2005, 2. Total applicants accepted 2004–2005, 0. Total enrolled 2004–2005 full-time, 2, part-time, 1. The number of students enrolled full and part-time who were dismissed or voluntarily withdrew from this program area were 0. *Basic Behavioural Science MA/MS (Master of Arts/Science)*—Applications 2004–2005, 11. Total applicants accepted 2004–2005, 1. Number enrolled (new admits only) 2004–2005 full-time, 1. Total enrolled 2004–2005 full-time, 1. The Median number of years required for completion of a degree are 3. The number of students enrolled full and part-time who were dismissed or voluntarily withdrew from this program area were 0.

Admissions Requirements:

Scores: Entries appear in this order: required test or GPA, minimum score (if required), median score of students entering in 2003–2004. Master's Programs: GRE-V no minimum stated, 533; GRE-Q no minimum stated, 563; GRE-Analytical no minimum stated; GRE-Subject(Psych) no minimum stated, 645; last 2 years GPA no minimum stated; psychology GPA no minimum stated. GRE median scores are those for the Applied Social program only. Doctoral Programs: GRE-V no minimum stated, 593; GRE-Q no minimum stated, 590; GRE-Analytical no minimum stated; GRE-Subject(Psych) no minimum stated, 713; last 2 years GPA no minimum stated; psychology GPA no minimum stated. GRE Median Scores are for Clinical admission only. Students applying for admission to the Applied Social PhD program require Master's GPA. Students applying for admission to a Basic Behavioural Science (BBS) program do not require GRE scores.

Other Criteria: (importance of criteria rated low, medium, or high): GRE/MAT scores medium, research experience high, work experience medium, extracurricular activity low, clinically related public service low, GPA high, letters of recommendation high, interview high, statement of goals and objectives high, GRE scores are not required for the Basic Behavioural Science (BBS) application. For additional information on admission requirements, go to: http://www.usask. ca/psychology/.

Student Characteristics: The following represents characteristics of students in 2004–2005 in all graduate psychology programs in the department: Female–full-time 38, part-time 13; Male–full-time 11, part-time 2; African American/Black–full-time 0, part-time 0; Hispanic/Latino(a)–full-time 0, part-time 0; Asian/Pacific Islander–full-time 0, part-time 0; American Indian/Alaska Native–full-time 0, part-time 0; Caucasian–full-time 0, part-time 0; Multi-ethnic–full-time 0, part-time 0.

Financial Information/Assistance:

Tuition for Full-Time Study: *Master's:* State residents: per academic year $3,540; Nonstate residents: per academic year $3,540. *Doctoral:* State residents: per academic year $3,540; Nonstate residents: per academic year $3,540. Tuition is subject to change. See the following Web site for updates and changes in tuition costs: http://www.usask.ca/registrar/pdf/fees/gradfees.pdf.

Financial Assistance:

First Year Students: Fellowships and scholarships available for first-year. Average amount paid per academic year: $16,000.

Advanced Students: Fellowships and scholarships available for advanced students. Average amount paid per academic year: $16,000.

Contact Information: Of all students currently enrolled full-time, 80% benefitted from one or more of the listed financial assistance programs. Application and information available online at: http://www.usask.ca/psychology/.

Internships/Practica: Full-time internships and practicum training concurrent with coursework are required at the MA and PhD levels in both clinical and applied social programs. In the clinical program, four-month MA internship placements are available at a number of hospital and outpatient clinics throughout the province. At the PhD level, 12-month internships have been arranged in larger clinical settings with diversified client populations in Canada and the United States. The applied social program requires four-month applied research internships at both the MA and PhD levels. Practicum and internship placements are arranged in a wide variety of government, institutional, and business settings. 3 Internship placements were in APA, APPIC, CPA and CCPPP accredited settings; 1 was in an APPIC, CPA and CCPPP accredited setting. For those doctoral students for whom a professional internship is required prior to graduation, 5 applied in 2003–2004. Of those who applied, 5 were placed in internships listed by the Association of Psychology Postdoctoral and Internship Programs (APPIC); 3 were placed in APA accredited internships.

Housing and Day Care: On-campus housing is available. See the following Web site for more information: http://adminsrv.usask. ca/csd/ResWeb/residence.htm. On-campus day care facilities are available. See the following Web site for more information: http:// www.usask.ca/calendar/general/services/daycare/.

Employment of Department Graduates:

Master's Degree Graduates: Of those who graduated in the academic year 2003–2004, the following categories and numbers represent the post-graduate activities and employment of master's degree graduates: Enrolled in a psychology doctoral program (3), enrolled in a post-doctoral residency/fellowship (n/a), employed in independent practice (n/a), other employment position (1), do not know (1), total from the above (master's) (5).

Doctoral Degree Graduates: Of those who graduated in the academic year 2003–2004, the following categories and numbers represent the post-graduate activities and employment of doctoral

degree graduates: Enrolled in a psychology doctoral program (n/a), employed in an academic position at a university (2), employed in a government agency (professional services) (2), employed in a hospital/medical center (5), total from the above (doctoral) (9).

Additional Information:
Orientation, Objectives, and Emphasis of Department: All graduate programs are small and highly selective. The clinical program focuses on PhD training, based on a scientist-practitioner model with an eclectic theoretical perspective. The goal is to train people who will be able to function in a wide variety of community, agency, academic, and research settings. The applied social program attempts to train people at the MA and PhD levels for researcher consultant positions in applied (MA) or academic (PhD) settings. Areas of concentration include program development and evaluation, group processes, and organizational development. The basic behavioural science programs are individually structured, admitting a few students to work with active research supervisors, most frequently in physiological, neuropsychology, cognitive psychology or culture and development.

Special Facilities or Resources: The Department has a Psychological Services Centre, an animal lab, a cognitive science lab with access to fMRI facilities. There are also numerous microcomputers, excellent mainframe computer facilities, and a good research library. The Women's Studies Research Unit promotes scholarly research by, for, and about women, providing a source of support for all women studying, teaching, researching, and working on campus.

Information for Students With Physical Disabilities: See the following Web site for more information: http://www.usask.ca/services/communities/disabilities/index.html.

Application Information:
Send to: Graduate Chair, University of Saskatchewan, Department of Psychology, 9 Campus Drive, Saskatoon, SK Canada S7N 5A5. Application available online. URL of online application: www.usask.ca/psychology/. Students are admitted in the Fall, application deadline January 15. *Fee:* $50. Note: All dollar amounts specified in this entry are Canadian dollars.

Sherbrooke, University of
Department of Psychology
2500 Boulevard de l'Universite
Sherbrooke, QC J1K 2R1
Telephone: (819) 821-7222
Fax: (819) 821-7925
E-mail: *Monique.Bacon@USherbrooke.ca*
Web: *http://www.usherb.ca*

Department Information:
1967. Chairperson: Claude Charbonneau. Number of Faculty: total–full-time 18; women–full-time 10.

Programs and Degrees Offered:
Listed in the following order: Program area, degree type (T if terminal Master's), number awarded 7/03–6/04. Human Relations MA/MS (Master of Arts/Science) (T) 51, PsyD (Psychology) PsyD (Doctor of Psychology) 0.

Student Applications/Admissions:
Student Applications
Human Relations MA/MS (Master of Arts/Science)—Applications 2004–2005, 0. Total applicants accepted 2004–2005, 0. The Median number of years required for completion of a degree are 3. The number of students enrolled full and part-time who were dismissed or voluntarily withdrew from this program area were 0. *PsyD (Psychology) PsyD (Doctor of Psychology)*—Applications 2004–2005, 103. Total applicants accepted 2004–2005, 40. Number enrolled (new admits only) 2004–2005 full-time, 24. Number enrolled (new admits only) 2004–2005 part-time, 0. Openings 2005–2006, 20. The Median number of years required for completion of a degree are 4. The number of students enrolled full and part-time who were dismissed or voluntarily withdrew from this program area were 4.

Admissions Requirements:
Scores: Entries appear in this order: required test or GPA, minimum score (if required), median score of students entering in 2003–2004. Doctoral Programs: overall undergraduate GPA 3.2, 3.8.
Other Criteria: (importance of criteria rated low, medium, or high): work experience medium, extracurricular activity medium, GPA high, letters of recommendation low, interview high, statement of goals and objectives high.

Student Characteristics: The following represents characteristics of students in 2004–2005 in all graduate psychology programs in the department: Female–full-time 55, part-time 0; Male–full-time 15, part-time 0; African American/Black–full-time 2, part-time 0; Hispanic/Latino(a)–full-time 0, part-time 0; Asian/Pacific Islander–full-time 0, part-time 0; American Indian/Alaska Native–full-time 0, part-time 0; Caucasian–full-time 68, part-time 0; Multi-ethnic–full-time 0, part-time 0; students subject to the Americans With Disabilities Act–full-time 0, part-time 0.

Financial Information/Assistance:
Tuition for Full-Time Study: *Doctoral:* State residents: $1,914 per credit hour; Nonstate residents: $8,784 per credit hour. See the following Web site for updates and changes in tuition costs: www.usherb.ca.

Financial Assistance:
First Year Students: Teaching assistantships available for first-year. Average amount paid per academic year: $1,350. Average number of hours worked per week: 3.
Advanced Students: Teaching assistantships available for advanced students. Average amount paid per academic year: $1,350. Average number of hours worked per week: 3. Research assistantships available for advanced students. Average amount paid per academic year: $5,000. Average number of hours worked per week: 7. Fellowships and scholarships available for advanced students. Average amount paid per academic year: $1,300.
Contact Information: Of all students currently enrolled full-time, 75% benefitted from one or more of the listed financial assistance programs. Application and information available online at: http://www.usherb.ca.

Internships/Practica: All internships or practica are limited to students enrolled in our graduate program.

Housing and Day Care: On-campus housing is available. See the following Web site for more information: www.usherb.ca. On-campus day care facilities are available.

Employment of Department Graduates:

Master's Degree Graduates: Of those who graduated in the academic year 2003–2004, the following categories and numbers represent the post-graduate activities and employment of master's degree graduates: Enrolled in a post-doctoral residency/fellowship (n/a), employed in independent practice (n/a), do not know (51), total from the above (master's) (18).

Doctoral Degree Graduates: Of those who graduated in the academic year 2003–2004, the following categories and numbers represent the post-graduate activities and employment of doctoral degree graduates: Enrolled in a psychology doctoral program (n/a), total from the above (doctoral) (0).

Additional Information:

Orientation, Objectives, and Emphasis of Department: Our department presents itself as a professional school of psychology. It offers an undergraduate program in general psychology and a four year graduate program (PsyD) in counselling or organizational psychology. The determinants of the program are the need to develop, as a practician, competencies in the following areas: evaluation, intervention, consultation, interpersonal relations, ethics, management, and supervision. Students who choose to develop their competencies in psychotherapy have the opportunity to explore their values, interests, and skills in relation to three approaches : humanist-positive, psychodynamic, cognitive-behavioural. Those who wish to intervene in organizational psychology develop a systems approach and focus on cooperative relationships, based on the belief in human potential and the need to involve an organization's human resources in change processes that affect them. Professional skills are developed in practicum situations and finally in a full year internship. Applied research is integrated into the program and the curriculum requires the production of a thesis.

Special Facilities or Resources: Our department is a small one with 18 faculty teachers. The professorial resources are directly available to students, and the training and supervision are highly personalized. The department offers a community service of individual counseling through its intervention center, which is also the ground for research. We are affiliated with the local center for health and social services as well as the geriatric institution where colleagues from the department cooperate in research programs and where one of our teachers has a well-structured laboratory for research on sleeping patterns.

Information for Students With Physical Disabilities: See the following Web site for more information: www.usherbrooke.ca.

Application Information:
Send to: Bureau du Registraire, Universite de Sherbrooke, Sherbrooke (Quebec) J1K 2R1. Application available online. URL of online application: www.usherbrooke.ca. Students are admitted in the Fall, application deadline February 1. *Fee:* $50. Note: All dollar amounts specified in this entry are Canadian dollars.

Simon Fraser University
Department of Psychology
8888 University Drive
Burnaby, BC V5A 1S6
Telephone: (604) 291-3354
Fax: (604) 291-3427
E-mail: *kumpula@sfu.ca*
Web: *http://www.psyc.sfu.ca/*

Department Information:
1965. Chair, Department of Psychology: Daniel Weeks. Number of Faculty: total–full-time 39, part-time 1; women–full-time 11, part-time 1.

Programs and Degrees Offered:
Listed in the following order: Program area, degree type (T if terminal Master's), number awarded 7/03–6/04. Experimental Psychology-5 areas PhD (Doctor of Philosophy) 2, Clinical Psychology-3 specialty streams PhD (Doctor of Philosophy) 7.

APA Accreditation: Clinical PhD (Doctor of Philosophy).

Student Applications/Admissions:
Student Applications
Experimental Psychology-5 areas PhD (Doctor of Philosophy)—Applications 2004–2005, 49. Total applicants accepted 2004–2005, 5. Number enrolled (new admits only) 2004–2005 full-time, 5. Total enrolled 2004–2005 full-time, 37. Openings 2005–2006, 5. The Median number of years required for completion of a degree are 6. The number of students enrolled full and part-time who were dismissed or voluntarily withdrew from this program area were 0. *Clinical Psychology-3 specialty streams PhD (Doctor of Philosophy)*—Applications 2004–2005, 112. Total applicants accepted 2004–2005, 7. Number enrolled (new admits only) 2004–2005 full-time, 7. Total enrolled 2004–2005 full-time, 50. Openings 2005–2006, 7. The Median number of years required for completion of a degree are 7. The number of students enrolled full and part-time who were dismissed or voluntarily withdrew from this program area were 1.

Admissions Requirements:
Scores: Entries appear in this order: required test or GPA, minimum score (if required), median score of students entering in 2003–2004. Master's Programs: GRE-V no minimum stated, 635; GRE-Q no minimum stated, 700; GRE-Analytical no minimum stated, 5.5; GRE-Subject(Psych) no minimum stated, 715; overall undergraduate GPA no minimum stated, 3.71; psychology GPA no minimum stated, 3.80. GRE-subject (Psychology) required for clinical applicants only. Applicants must have a minimum cgpa of 3.5/4.00. Doctoral Programs: GRE-V no minimum stated, 630; GRE-Q no minimum stated, 680; GRE-Analytical no minimum stated, 745; GRE-Subject(Psych) no minimum stated, 720; overall undergraduate GPA no minimum stated, 3.61; last 2 years GPA no minimum stated; psychology GPA no minimum stated, 3.79. GRE-subject (Psychology) required for clinical applicants only. Applicants must have minimum CGPA of 3.5/4.00.
Other Criteria: (importance of criteria rated low, medium, or high): GRE/MAT scores high, research experience high, work

experience low, extracurricular activity low, clinically related public service low, GPA high, letters of recommendation high, interview high, statement of goals and objectives high. Interview is more relevant to admission to clinical program. For additional information on admission requirements, go to: www.psyc.sfu.ca.

Student Characteristics: The following represents characteristics of students in 2004–2005 in all graduate psychology programs in the department: Female–full-time 65, part-time 0; Male–full-time 22, part-time 0; African American/Black–part-time 0; Hispanic/Latino(a)–part-time 0; Asian/Pacific Islander–part-time 0; American Indian/Alaska Native–part-time 0; Caucasian–full-time 0, part-time 0.

Financial Information/Assistance:

Tuition for Full-Time Study: *Master's:* State residents: per academic year $3,201; Nonstate residents: per academic year $3,201. *Doctoral:* State residents: per academic year $3,201; Nonstate residents: per academic year $3,201. Tuition is subject to change. See the following Web site for updates and changes in tuition costs: www.sfu.ca/dean-gradstudies.

Financial Assistance:

First Year Students: Teaching assistantships available for first-year. Average amount paid per academic year: $14,907. Average number of hours worked per week: 13. Research assistantships available for first-year. Fellowships and scholarships available for first-year. Average amount paid per academic year: $6,000. Apply by March 15.

Advanced Students: Teaching assistantships available for advanced students. Average amount paid per academic year: $17,592. Average number of hours worked per week: 13. Research assistantships available for advanced students. Fellowships and scholarships available for advanced students. Average amount paid per academic year: $6,000. Apply by March 15.

Contact Information: Of all students currently enrolled full-time, 100% benefitted from one or more of the listed financial assistance programs. Application and information available online at: www.psyc.sfu.ca.

Internships/Practica: Students in the Clinical program are required to complete an MA practicum and a PhD internship. The practica take place in mostly local multi-disciplinary community settings under the overall supervision of the Director of Clinical Training. Internships are all external to the program. For those doctoral students for whom a professional internship is required prior to graduation, 8 applied in 2003–2004. Of those who applied, 6 were placed in internships listed by the Association of Psychology Postdoctoral and Internship Programs (APPIC); 6 were placed in APA accredited internships.

Housing and Day Care: On-campus housing is available. See the following Web site for more information: http://students.sfu.ca/residences/. On-campus day care facilities are available. See the following Web site for more information: http://www.sfu.ca/childcare-society/programs.html.

Employment of Department Graduates:

Master's Degree Graduates: Of those who graduated in the academic year 2003–2004, the following categories and numbers represent the post-graduate activities and employment of master's degree graduates: Enrolled in a psychology doctoral program (5), enrolled in a post-doctoral residency/fellowship (n/a), employed in independent practice (n/a), employed in a hospital/medical center (1), total from the above (master's) (6).

Doctoral Degree Graduates: Of those who graduated in the academic year 2003–2004, the following categories and numbers represent the post-graduate activities and employment of doctoral degree graduates: Enrolled in a psychology doctoral program (n/a), enrolled in another graduate/professional program (0), enrolled in a post-doctoral residency/fellowship (0), employed in an academic position at a university (1), employed in an academic position at a 2-year/4-year college (1), employed in other positions at a higher education institution (0), employed in a professional position in a school system (0), employed in business or industry (research/consulting) (1), employed in business or industry (management) (0), employed in a community mental health/counseling center (1), employed in a hospital/medical center (1), total from the above (doctoral) (5).

Additional Information:

Orientation, Objectives, and Emphasis of Department: The department has a mainstream, empirical orientation. The objectives of our undergraduate program are to produce majors who have a broad exposure to the various fields of psychology, and to produce honors students who, in addition, have received higher-level training in research methods and have completed an honors research project. The department offers graduate work leading to master's and doctoral degrees in clinical or experimental psychology. We subscribe to the scientist-practitioner model of clinical training. Within the clinical and experimental programs, all graduate students work on topics from one of the following general research areas: cognitive and biological psychology, developmental psychology, law and forensic psychology, social psychology, and theory and methods. The clinical program offers specializations in child clinical psychology, clinical forensic psychology, and clinical neuropsychology. In conjunction with the University of British Columbia, a co-ordinated LLB/PhD program in Law and Forensic Psychology is also offered.

Special Facilities or Resources: The Psychology Department Microcomputer Lab houses 21 PIII 933Mhz computers running Windows 2000 with printing support for students. The department also provides licensed statistical software packages (SPSS, BMDP, Systat, Minitab, Lisrel and Mathcad), word processing, data processing, and graphic packages. Electronic mail, file transfer, file and disk utilities are also provided. Neuroscience labs for animal studies are equipped for physiological and behavioral research, as well as advanced microscopy and image analysis. Students normally receive office space in the research laboratories of their supervisors. Most faculty labs have computers for faculty and graduate students. Projectors are available for PowerPoint and slide presentations. Facilities are available for telephone and video conferences. The department is richly supplied with technical staff to help with software and hardware. The Clinical Program operates a training clinic with a full-time Director and Office Coordinator, staffed by clinical students, supported by an extensive test library, audio and video recording, and presentation projection facilities. The Mental Health Law and Policy Institute has extra research space. The Library has excellent resources including online databases in psychology; inter-library loans of books and journals are readily accessible.

Information for Students With Physical Disabilities: See the following Web site for more information: http://www.sfu.ca/csd/.

Application Information:
Send to: Lynn Kumpula, Graduate Program Assistant, Psychology Department, Simon Fraser University, 8888 University Drive, Burnaby, BC V5A 1S6. Application available online. URL of online application: http://www.sfu.ca/dean-gradstudies/. Students are admitted in the Fall, application deadline January 4. The application materials should be sent in one complete package. *Fee:* $75. Note: All dollar amounts specified in this entry are Canadian dollars.

Toronto, University of
Department of Psychology
100 Street George Street
Toronto, ON M5S 3G3
Telephone: (416) 978-3404
Fax: (416) 976-4811
E-mail: *grad@psych.utoronto.ca*
Web: *http://www.psych.utoronto.ca*

Department Information:
1891. Chairperson: Lynn Hasher. Number of Faculty: total–full-time 75, part-time 37; women–full-time 22, part-time 37.

Programs and Degrees Offered:
Listed in the following order: Program area, degree type (T if terminal Master's), number awarded 7/03–6/04. Behavioral Neuroscience MA/MS (Master of Arts/Science) 6, Behavioral Neuroscience PhD (Doctor of Philosophy) 9, Cognition/Perception MA/MS (Master of Arts/Science) 4, Cognition/Perception PhD (Doctor of Philosophy) 2, Developmental MA/MS (Master of Arts/Science) 1, Social/Personality/Abnormal MA/MS (Master of Arts/Science) 3, Developmental PhD (Doctor of Philosophy) 2, Social/Personality/Abnormal PhD (Doctor of Philosophy) 6.

Student Applications/Admissions:
Student Applications
Behavioral Neuroscience MA/MS (Master of Arts/Science)—Applications 2004–2005, 26. Total applicants accepted 2004–2005, 6. Number enrolled (new admits only) 2004–2005 full-time, 3. Total enrolled 2004–2005 full-time, 3. Openings 2005–2006, 10. The Median number of years required for completion of a degree is 1. The number of students enrolled full and part-time who were dismissed or voluntarily withdrew from this program area were 0. *Behavioral Neuroscience PhD (Doctor of Philosophy)*—Total enrolled 2004–2005 full-time, 32. Openings 2005–2006, 10. The Median number of years required for completion of a degree are 6. *Cognition/Perception MA/MS (Master of Arts/Science)*—Applications 2004–2005, 53. Total applicants accepted 2004–2005, 21. Number enrolled (new admits only) 2004–2005 full-time, 12. Total enrolled 2004–2005 full-time, 12. Openings 2005–2006, 10. The Median number of years required for completion of a degree is 1. *Cognition/Perception PhD (Doctor of Philosophy)*—Applications 2004–2005, 10. Total applicants accepted 2004–2005, 1. Number enrolled (new admits only) 2004–2005 full-time, 1. Total enrolled 2004–2005 full-time, 21. Openings 2005–2006, 10. The Median number of years required for completion of a

degree are 6. *Developmental MA/MS (Master of Arts/Science)*—Applications 2004–2005, 2. Total applicants accepted 2004–2005, 1. Openings 2005–2006, 3. The Median number of years required for completion of a degree is 1. *Social/Personality/Abnormal MA/MS (Master of Arts/Science)*—Applications 2004–2005, 94. Total applicants accepted 2004–2005, 8. Number enrolled (new admits only) 2004–2005 full-time, 5. Total enrolled 2004–2005 full-time, 5. Openings 2005–2006, 10. The Median number of years required for completion of a degree is 1. *Developmental PhD (Doctor of Philosophy)*—Applications 2004–2005, 2. Total applicants accepted 2004–2005, 0. Total enrolled 2004–2005 full-time, 6. Openings 2005–2006, 10. The Median number of years required for completion of a degree are 6. *Social/Personality/Abnormal PhD (Doctor of Philosophy)*—Applications 2004–2005, 8. Total applicants accepted 2004–2005, 0. Total enrolled 2004–2005 full-time, 15. Openings 2005–2006, 10. The Median number of years required for completion of a degree are 5.

Admissions Requirements:
Scores: Entries appear in this order: required test or GPA, minimum score (if required), median score of students entering in 2003–2004. Master's Programs: GRE-V 600, 625; GRE-Q 600, 740; GRE-Analytical 600, 710; last 2 years GPA 3.7, 4. Doctoral Programs: GRE-V 600, 650; GRE-Q 600, 710; GRE-Analytical 600, 680; last 2 years GPA 3.7, 4.
Other Criteria: (importance of criteria rated low, medium, or high): GRE/MAT scores high, research experience high, work experience low, extracurricular activity low, GPA high, letters of recommendation high, interview medium, statement of goals and objectives high.

Student Characteristics: The following represents characteristics of students in 2004–2005 in all graduate psychology programs in the department: Female–full-time 63, part-time 0; part-time 0; part-time 0; Caucasian–full-time 0, part-time 0; part-time 0; students subject to the Americans With Disabilities Act–full-time 1, part-time 0.

Financial Information/Assistance:
Tuition for Full-Time Study: *Master's:* State residents: per academic year $6,176; Nonstate residents: per academic year $10,971. *Doctoral:* State residents: per academic year $6,176; Nonstate residents: per academic year $10,971. Tuition is subject to change. See the following Web site for updates and changes in tuition costs: http://www.sgs.utoronto.ca/current/fees/index.asp.

Financial Assistance:
First Year Students: Teaching assistantships available for first-year. Average amount paid per academic year: $6,000. Average number of hours worked per week: 10. Apply by June 1. Traineeships available for first-year. Average amount paid per academic year: $6,000. Apply by January 15. Fellowships and scholarships available for first-year. Average amount paid per academic year: $10,176. Apply by January 15.
Advanced Students: Teaching assistantships available for advanced students. Average amount paid per academic year: $6,000. Average number of hours worked per week: 10. Apply by June 1. Traineeships available for advanced students. Average amount paid per academic year: $6,000. Apply by January 15. Fellowships and scholarships available for advanced students. Av-

erage amount paid per academic year: $10,176. Apply by January 15.

Contact Information: Of all students currently enrolled full-time, 100% benefitted from one or more of the listed financial assistance programs. Application and information available online at: www.psych.utoronto.ca.

Internships/Practica: No information provided.

Housing and Day Care: On-campus housing is available. See the following Web site for more information: http://www.sgs.utoronto.ca/prospective/housing/index.asp. On-campus day care facilities are available.

Employment of Department Graduates:

Master's Degree Graduates: Of those who graduated in the academic year 2003–2004, the following categories and numbers represent the post-graduate activities and employment of master's degree graduates: Enrolled in a psychology doctoral program (14), enrolled in a post-doctoral residency/fellowship (n/a), employed in independent practice (n/a), total from the above (master's) (14). *Doctoral Degree Graduates:* Of those who graduated in the academic year 2003–2004, the following categories and numbers represent the post-graduate activities and employment of doctoral degree graduates: Enrolled in a psychology doctoral program (n/a), enrolled in a post-doctoral residency/fellowship (12), employed in an academic position at a university (2), employed in a hospital/medical center (3), do not know (2), total from the above (doctoral) (19).

Additional Information:

Orientation, Objectives, and Emphasis of Department: The purpose of graduate training at the University of Toronto is to prepare students for careers in teaching and research. Teaching and research apprenticeships, therefore, constitute a large portion of such training. Research training is supplemented by courses and seminars. In some cases the courses are designed to provide up-to-date fundamental background information in psychology. The bulk of instruction, however, takes place in informal seminars; these provide an opportunity for the discussion of theoretical issues, the formulation of research problems, and the review of current developments in specific research areas. In the past, most of our graduates have entered academic careers. More recently, graduates have also taken research and managerial positions in research institutes, hospitals, government agencies, and industrial corporations.

Special Facilities or Resources: The department has modern laboratories at the Street George, Erindale, and Scarborough campuses, as well as a fully equipped electronic workshop. Students have access to an extensive computer system including the university's central computer, the department's Sun computer, and many advanced microcomputers. The department has close ties to several medical hospitals, as well as the Clarke Psychiatric Hospital, Baycrest Center, and the Rotman Research Institute at the Center and the Addiction Research Foundation.

Information for Students With Physical Disabilities: See the following Web site for more information: http://www.sa.utoronto.ca/area.php?waid=5.

Application Information:
Send to: Graduate Studies, Department of Psychology, University of Toronto, 100 Street George Street, Toronto, ON, Canada M5S 3G3. Students are admitted in the Fall, application deadline January 15. *Fee:* $90. Note: All dollar amounts specified in this entry are Canadian dollars.

Victoria, University of
Department of Psychology
P.O. Box 3050 STN CSC
Victoria, BC V8W 3P5
Telephone: (250) 721-7525
Fax: (250) 721-8929
E-mail: *psyc@uvic.ca*
Web: *http://web.uvic.ca/psyc/*

Department Information:
1963. Chair: Catherine A. Mateer. Number of Faculty: total–full-time 27; women–full-time 13; minority–full-time 3.

Programs and Degrees Offered:
Listed in the following order: Program area, degree type (T if terminal Master's), number awarded 7/03–6/04. Clinical Neuropsychology PhD (Doctor of Philosophy) 2, Cognitive PhD (Doctor of Philosophy) 2, Experimental Neuropsychology PhD (Doctor of Philosophy) 0, Social PhD (Doctor of Philosophy) 1, Cognitive Neuroscience PhD (Doctor of Philosophy) 0, Clinical Lifespan PhD (Doctor of Philosophy) 1, Lifespan Development and Aging PhD (Doctor of Philosophy) 1.

APA Accreditation: Clinical PhD (Doctor of Philosophy).

Student Applications/Admissions:
Student Applications
Clinical Neuropsychology PhD (Doctor of Philosophy)—Applications 2004–2005, 39. Total applicants accepted 2004–2005, 4. Openings 2005–2006, 4. The Median number of years required for completion of a degree are 7. The number of students enrolled full and part-time who were dismissed or voluntarily withdrew from this program area were 0. *Cognitive PhD (Doctor of Philosophy)*—Applications 2004–2005, 11. Total applicants accepted 2004–2005, 1. Openings 2005–2006, 2. The Median number of years required for completion of a degree are 5. The number of students enrolled full and part-time who were dismissed or voluntarily withdrew from this program area were 0. *Experimental Neuropsychology PhD (Doctor of Philosophy)*—Applications 2004–2005, 9. Total applicants accepted 2004–2005, 2. Openings 2005–2006, 2. The number of students enrolled full and part-time who were dismissed or voluntarily withdrew from this program area were 0. *Social PhD (Doctor of Philosophy)*—Applications 2004–2005, 37. Total applicants accepted 2004–2005, 2. Openings 2005–2006, 3. The Median number of years required for completion of a degree are 6. The number of students enrolled full and part-time who were dismissed or voluntarily withdrew from this program area were 0. *Cognitive Neuroscience PhD (Doctor of Philosophy)*—Applications 2004–2005, 9. Total applicants accepted 2004–2005, 2. Total enrolled 2004–2005 full-time, 2. Openings 2005–2006, 2. The number of students enrolled full and part-time who

were dismissed or voluntarily withdrew from this program area were 0. *Clinical Lifespan PhD (Doctor of Philosophy)*—Applications 2004–2005, 87. Total applicants accepted 2004–2005, 6. Total enrolled 2004–2005 full-time, 6. Openings 2005–2006, 6. The Median number of years required for completion of a degree are 6.5. The number of students enrolled full and part-time who were dismissed or voluntarily withdrew from this program area were 0. *Lifespan Development and Aging PhD (Doctor of Philosophy)*—Applications 2004–2005, 27. Total applicants accepted 2004–2005, 2. Total enrolled 2004–2005 full-time, 2. Openings 2005–2006, 4. The Median number of years required for completion of a degree are 6. The number of students enrolled full and part-time who were dismissed or voluntarily withdrew from this program area were 0.

Admissions Requirements:

Scores: Entries appear in this order: required test or GPA, minimum score (if required), median score of students entering in 2003–2004. Master's Programs: GRE-V no minimum stated; GRE-Q no minimum stated; GRE-Analytical no minimum stated; last 2 years GPA no minimum stated, 7.75. Doctoral Programs: GRE-V no minimum stated, 560; GRE-Q no minimum stated, 609; GRE-Analytical no minimum stated, 589. *Other Criteria:* (importance of criteria rated low, medium, or high): GRE/MAT scores high, research experience high, work experience medium, extracurricular activity medium, clinically related public service medium, GPA high, letters of recommendation high, interview high, statement of goals and objectives high. Group interview required for Clinical Programs only.

Student Characteristics: The following represents characteristics of students in 2004–2005 in all graduate psychology programs in the department: Female–full-time 63, part-time 0; Male–full-time 19, part-time 0; African American/Black–full-time 1, part-time 0; Hispanic/Latino(a)–full-time 0, part-time 0; Asian/Pacific Islander–full-time 11, part-time 0; American Indian/Alaska Native–full-time 1, part-time 0; Caucasian–full-time 47, part-time 0; Multi-ethnic–full-time 12, part-time 0.

Financial Information/Assistance:

Tuition for Full-Time Study: *Master's:* State residents: per academic year $4,116; Nonstate residents: per academic year $4,899. *Doctoral:* State residents: per academic year $4,116; Nonstate residents: per academic year $4,889. See the following Web site for updates and changes in tuition costs: http://web.uvic.ca/grar/website/continuing/fees03.html.

Financial Assistance:

First Year Students: Teaching assistantships available for first-year. Average amount paid per academic year: $3,500. Research assistantships available for first-year. Average amount paid per academic year: $3,500. Fellowships and scholarships available for first-year. Average amount paid per academic year: $15,000.

Advanced Students: Teaching assistantships available for advanced students. Average amount paid per academic year: $3,500. Research assistantships available for advanced students. Average amount paid per academic year: $3,500. Fellowships and scholarships available for advanced students. Average amount paid per academic year: $15,000.

Contact Information: Of all students currently enrolled full-time, 95% benefitted from one or more of the listed financial assistance programs.

Internships/Practica: Internships and practica for students in the clinical program are arranged through the clinical program. For those doctoral students for whom a professional internship is required prior to graduation, 7 applied in 2003–2004. Of those who applied, 7 were placed in internships listed by the Association of Psychology Postdoctoral and Internship Programs (APPIC); 7 were placed in APA accredited internships.

Housing and Day Care: On-campus housing is available. See the following Web site for more information: On- and off-campus housing: http://www.hfcs.uvic.ca/ Day care: http://www.stas.uvic.ca/dayc/. On-campus day care facilities are available.

Employment of Department Graduates:

Master's Degree Graduates: Of those who graduated in the academic year 2003–2004, the following categories and numbers represent the post-graduate activities and employment of master's degree graduates: Enrolled in a psychology doctoral program (9), enrolled in another graduate/professional program (0), enrolled in a post-doctoral residency/fellowship (n/a), employed in independent practice (n/a), total from the above (master's) (9).

Doctoral Degree Graduates: Of those who graduated in the academic year 2003–2004, the following categories and numbers represent the post-graduate activities and employment of doctoral degree graduates: Enrolled in a psychology doctoral program (n/a), enrolled in another graduate/professional program (0), enrolled in a post-doctoral residency/fellowship (3), employed in independent practice (6), employed in an academic position at a university (4), employed in a community mental health/counseling center (5), employed in a hospital/medical center (6), total from the above (doctoral) (24).

Additional Information:

Orientation, Objectives, and Emphasis of Department: The graduate program in psychology emphasizes the training of research competence, and, in the case of neuropsychology and lifespan, the acquisition of clinical skills. The department's orientation is strongly empirical, and students are expected to develop mastery of appropriate methods and design as well as of specific content areas of psychology. The program is directed toward the PhD degree, although students must obtain a master's degree as part of the normal requirements. Formal programs of study, involving a coordinated sequence of courses, are offered for both experimental and clinical neuropsychology (up to but not including a clinical internship), life span development and aging, and clinical life span development. Individual programs of study may be designed according to the interests of individual students and faculty members in such areas as social psychology, environmental psychology, experimental and applied behavior analysis, psychopathology, cognition, and human psychophysiology.

Special Facilities or Resources: Fully equipped facilities are available, including the Psychology Clinic, providing community based assessment and intervention; a Human Interaction Laboratory; an electrophysiological facility (Brain and Cognitive Laboratory); and specialized facilities for the study of perception. The department also offers training and research opportunities within several on-campus research centres (Centre on Aging, Centre for Youth and Society, Centre for Addictions Research BC, Centre for Human Movement Analysis).

Information for Students With Physical Disabilities: See the following Web site for more information: http://www.stas.uvic.ca/osd/.

Application Information:

Send to: Graduate Admissions, Faculty of Graduate Studies, University of Victoria, P.O. Box 3025, Victoria BC, V8W 3P2, Canada. Application available online. Students are admitted in the Fall, application deadline January 1. *Fee:* $65. Non-Canadian applicant fees are $100 Canadian dollars. Note: All dollar amounts specified in this entry are Canadian dollars.

Waterloo, University of
Department of Psychology
200 University Avenue West
Waterloo, ON N2L 3G1
Telephone: (519) 888-4567
Fax: (519) 746-8631
E-mail: *gradinfo.psych@uwaterloo.ca*
Web: *http://www.psychology.uwaterloo.ca/*

Department Information:

1963. Chairperson: J. Allan Cheyne. Number of Faculty: total–full-time 32, part-time 19; women–full-time 10, part-time 19; minority–full-time 1.

Programs and Degrees Offered:

Listed in the following order: Program area, degree type (T if terminal Master's), number awarded 7/03–6/04. Industrial/ Organizational PhD (Doctor of Philosophy) 0, Social PhD (Doctor of Philosophy) 2, Cognitive PhD (Doctor of Philosophy) 6, Behavioral Neuroscience PhD (Doctor of Philosophy) 10, Clinical PhD (Doctor of Philosophy) 6, Developmental PhD (Doctor of Philosophy) 1, Industrial/ Organizational MA/MS (Master of Arts/Science) (T) 2.

APA Accreditation: Clinical PhD (Doctor of Philosophy).

Student Applications/Admissions:

Student Applications

Industrial/ Organizational PhD (Doctor of Philosophy)—Applications 2004–2005, 19. Total applicants accepted 2004–2005, 5. Number enrolled (new admits only) 2004–2005 full-time, 3. Total enrolled 2004–2005 full-time, 6, part-time, 2. Openings 2005–2006, 2. *Social PhD (Doctor of Philosophy)*—Applications 2004–2005, 29. Total applicants accepted 2004–2005, 6. Number enrolled (new admits only) 2004–2005 full-time, 3. Openings 2005–2006, 5. *Cognitive PhD (Doctor of Philosophy)*—Applications 2004–2005, 7. Total applicants accepted 2004–2005, 4. Number enrolled (new admits only) 2004–2005 full-time, 2. Total enrolled 2004–2005 full-time, 10. Openings 2005–2006, 5. *Behavioral Neuroscience PhD (Doctor of Philosophy)*—Applications 2004–2005, 12. Total applicants accepted 2004–2005, 10. Number enrolled (new admits only) 2004–2005 full-time, 2. Total enrolled 2004–2005 full-time, 8, part-time, 3. Openings 2005–2006, 6. *Clinical PhD (Doctor of Philosophy)*—Applications 2004–2005, 101. Total applicants accepted 2004–2005, 7. Number enrolled (new admits only) 2004–2005 full-time, 4. Total enrolled 2004–2005 full-time,

13, part-time, 4. Openings 2005–2006, 5. *Developmental PhD (Doctor of Philosophy)*—Applications 2004–2005, 9. Total applicants accepted 2004–2005, 5. Number enrolled (new admits only) 2004–2005 full-time, 5. Total enrolled 2004–2005 full-time, 10, part-time, 3. Openings 2005–2006, 3. *Industrial/ Organizational MA/MS (Master of Arts/Science)*—Applications 2004–2005, 11. Total applicants accepted 2004–2005, 5. Number enrolled (new admits only) 2004–2005 full-time 3. Total enrolled 2004–2005 full-time, 6. Openings 2005–2006, 4.

Admissions Requirements:

Scores: Entries appear in this order: required test or GPA, minimum score (if required), median score of students entering in 2003–2004. Master's Programs: GRE-V+Q+Analytical no minimum stated; GRE-Subject(Psych) no minimum stated; overall undergraduate GPA 3.00; last 2 years GPA 3.00. Doctoral Programs: GRE-V+Q+Analytical no minimum stated; GRE-Subject(Psych) no minimum stated; overall undergraduate GPA 3.00; last 2 years GPA 3.00.

Other Criteria: (importance of criteria rated low, medium, or high): GRE/MAT scores high, research experience medium, work experience low, clinically related public service medium, GPA high, letters of recommendation high, interview medium, statement of goals and objectives high. For additional information on admission requirements, go to: http://www.grad.uwaterloo.ca/students/applicrequirements.asp.

Student Characteristics: The following represents characteristics of students in 2004–2005 in all graduate psychology programs in the department: Female–full-time 45, part-time 11; Male–full-time 27, part-time 1; African American/Black–full-time 0, part-time 0; Hispanic/Latino(a)–full-time 0, part-time 0; Asian/Pacific Islander–full-time 0, part-time 0; American Indian/Alaska Native–full-time 0, part-time 0; Caucasian–full-time 0, part-time 0.

Financial Information/Assistance:

Tuition for Full-Time Study: *Master's:* State residents: per academic year $5,947; Nonstate residents: per academic year $14,855. *Doctoral:* State residents: per academic year $5,947; Nonstate residents: per academic year $14,855. See the following Web site for updates and changes in tuition costs: http://www.adm.uwaterloo.ca/infosp/Fin/Stdfees.htm.

Financial Assistance:

First Year Students: Teaching assistantships available for first-year. Research assistantships available for first-year. Fellowships and scholarships available for first-year.

Advanced Students: Teaching assistantships available for advanced students. Research assistantships available for advanced students. Fellowships and scholarships available for advanced students.

Contact Information: Of all students currently enrolled full-time, 100% benefitted from one or more of the listed financial assistance programs.

Internships/Practica: The Applied Master's program requires a 4-month supervised Internship. The Clinical program requires a 4-month practicum during the program of study and a 12-month Internship at the conclusion of the academic program. Most practicum placements are with local hospitals, schools or industries. For those doctoral students for whom a professional internship is required prior to graduation, 5 applied in 2003–2004. Of those who applied, 5 were placed in internships listed by the Association of Psychology Postdoctoral and Internship Programs (APPIC); 5 were placed in APA accredited internships.

Housing and Day Care: On-campus housing is available. See the following Web site for more information: www.housing.uwaterloo. ca. On-campus day care facilities are available. See the following Web site for more information: http://www.studentservices.uwat erloo.ca/childcare/.

Employment of Department Graduates:

Master's Degree Graduates: Of those who graduated in the academic year 2003–2004, the following categories and numbers represent the post-graduate activities and employment of master's degree graduates: Enrolled in a psychology doctoral program (3), enrolled in a post-doctoral residency/fellowship (n/a), employed in independent practice (n/a), employed in business or industry (management) (2), employed in a government agency (research) (1), not seeking employment (1), do not know (3), total from the above (master's) (10).

Doctoral Degree Graduates: Of those who graduated in the academic year 2003–2004, the following categories and numbers represent the post-graduate activities and employment of doctoral degree graduates: Enrolled in a psychology doctoral program (n/a), enrolled in a post-doctoral residency/fellowship (8), employed in independent practice (1), employed in an academic position at a university (4), employed in a professional position in a school system (1), employed in a community mental health/counseling center (1), employed in a hospital/medical center (1), do not know (2), total from the above (doctoral) (18).

Additional Information:

Orientation, Objectives, and Emphasis of Department: There is a strong emphasis on research in all six divisions of the PhD program, and MASc students are prepared for careers in Applied Psychology in a variety of areas. Students are involved either through participation in ongoing faculty research or through development of their own ideas; coursework is intended to provide students with general knowledge and intensive preparation in their area of concentration and for some of the programs, the blending of theory and practice is experience in internship and practicum arrangements.

Special Facilities or Resources: Within a large 4-story building, extensive laboratory facilities are available for animal and human research. Additional educational and resource centers operate in conjunction with academic and research programs; Animal Care, Preschool, two Assessment Clinics and mechanical and electronics shops. Research requiring special populations is often carried out at community institutions under the supervision of faculty members. Considerable investment has been made to technical services including excellent computer facilities and consulting personnel who are available for student research and courses.

Information for Students With Physical Disabilities: See the following Web site for more information: http://www.studentser vices.uwaterloo.ca/disabilities/.

Application Information:
Send to: Graduate Studies Office, University of Waterloo, 200 University Avenue West, Waterloo, ON N2L 3G1. Application available online. URL of online application: www.grad.uwaterloo.ca/students/

application.asp. Students are admitted in the Fall, application deadline December 15. *Fee:* $75. Note: All dollar amounts specified in this entry are Canadian dollars.

Western Ontario, The University of
Department of Psychology
Social Science Centre, 1151 Richmond Street N.
London, ON N6A 5C2
Telephone: (519) 661-2064
Fax: (519) 661-3961
E-mail: *psych-grad@uwo.ca*
Web: *http://www.ssc.uwo.ca/psychology*

Department Information:
1931. Chairperson: Klaus-Peter Ossenkopp. Number of Faculty: total–full-time 54, part-time 30; women–full-time 10, part-time 30.

Programs and Degrees Offered:
Listed in the following order: Program area, degree type (T if terminal Master's), number awarded 7/03–6/04. Clinical PhD (Doctor of Philosophy) 3, Cognition and Perception PhD (Doctor of Philosophy) 0, Developmental PhD (Doctor of Philosophy) 1, Industrial/ Organizational PhD (Doctor of Philosophy) 4, Personality and Mesurement PhD (Doctor of Philosophy) 0, Behavioural and Cognitive Neuroscience PhD (Doctor of Philosophy) 0, Social PhD (Doctor of Philosophy) 0.

APA Accreditation: Clinical PhD (Doctor of Philosophy).

Student Applications/Admissions:
Student Applications
Clinical PhD (Doctor of Philosophy)—Applications 2004–2005, 135. Total applicants accepted 2004–2005, 15. Number enrolled (new admits only) 2004–2005 full-time, 4. Number enrolled (new admits only) 2004–2005 part-time, 0. Total enrolled 2004–2005 full-time, 27, part-time, 6. Openings 2005–2006, 4. The Median number of years required for completion of a degree are 6. The number of students enrolled full and part-time who were dismissed or voluntarily withdrew from this program area were 0. *Cognition and Perception PhD (Doctor of Philosophy)*—Applications 2004–2005, 8. Total applicants accepted 2004–2005, 4. Number enrolled (new admits only) 2004–2005 full-time, 1. Number enrolled (new admits only) 2004–2005 part-time, 0. Openings 2005–2006, 3. The number of students enrolled full and part-time who were dismissed or voluntarily withdrew from this program area were 0. *Developmental PhD (Doctor of Philosophy)*—Applications 2004–2005, 16. Total applicants accepted 2004–2005, 4. Number enrolled (new admits only) 2004–2005 full-time, 0. Number enrolled (new admits only) 2004–2005 part-time, 0. Openings 2005–2006, 2. The Median number of years required for completion of a degree are 5. The number of students enrolled full and part-time who were dismissed or voluntarily withdrew from this program area were 0. *Industrial/Organizational PhD (Doctor of Philosophy)*—Applications 2004–2005, 26. Total applicants accepted 2004–2005, 14. Number enrolled (new admits only) 2004–2005 full-time, 9. Number enrolled (new admits only) 2004–2005 part-time, 0. Openings 2005–2006,

5. The Median number of years required for completion of a degree are 5. The number of students enrolled full and part-time who were dismissed or voluntarily withdrew from this program area were 1. *Personality and Measurement PhD (Doctor of Philosophy)*—Applications 2004–2005, 3. Total applicants accepted 2004–2005, 2. Number enrolled (new admits only) 2004–2005 full-time, 2. Number enrolled (new admits only) 2004–2005 part-time, 0. Openings 2005–2006, 1. The number of students enrolled full and part-time, who were dismissed or voluntarily withdrew from this program area were 0. *Behavioural and Cognitive Neuroscience PhD (Doctor of Philosophy)*—Applications 2004–2005, 22. Total applicants accepted 2004–2005, 9. Number enrolled (new admits only) 2004–2005 full-time, 6. Number enrolled (new admits only) 2004–2005 part-time, 0. Total enrolled 2004–2005 full-time, 23, part-time, 1. Openings 2005–2006, 5. The number of students enrolled full and part-time who were dismissed or voluntarily withdrew from this program area were 0. *Social PhD (Doctor of Philosophy)*—Applications 2004–2005, 30. Total applicants accepted 2004–2005, 6. Number enrolled (new admits only) 2004–2005 full-time, 3. Number enrolled (new admits only) 2004–2005 part-time, 0. Total enrolled 2004–2005 full-time, 14, part-time, 2. Openings 2005–2006, 5. The number of students enrolled full and part-time who were dismissed or voluntarily withdrew from this program area were 0.

Admissions Requirements:

Scores: Entries appear in this order: required test or GPA, minimum score (if required), median score of students entering in 2003–2004. Doctoral Programs: GRE-V 530; GRE-Q 560; GRE-Subject(Psych) no minimum stated.

Other Criteria: (importance of criteria rated low, medium, or high): GRE/MAT scores high, research experience high, work experience low, extracurricular activity low, clinically related public service low, GPA high, letters of recommendation high, interview medium, statement of goals and objectives high. For additional information on admission requirements, go to: http://www.ssc.uwo.ca/psychology/graduate.htm.

Student Characteristics: The following represents characteristics of students in 2004–2005 in all graduate psychology programs in the department: Female–full-time 72, part-time 7; Male–full-time 33, part-time 2; African American/Black–full-time 0, part-time 0; Hispanic/Latino(a)–full-time 0, part-time 0; Asian/Pacific Islander–full-time 0, part-time 0; American Indian/Alaska Native–full-time 0, part-time 0; Caucasian–full-time 0, part-time 0.

Financial Information/Assistance:

Tuition for Full-Time Study: *Doctoral:* State residents: per academic year $6,000; Nonstate residents: per academic year $12,000. Tuition is subject to change. See the following Web site for updates and changes in tuition costs: http://www.registrar.uwo.ca/.

Financial Assistance:

First Year Students: Teaching assistantships available for first-year. Average amount paid per academic year: $9,400. Average number of hours worked per week: 10. Tuition remission given: partial. Fellowships and scholarships available for first-year. Average amount paid per academic year: $6,000. Tuition remission given: partial.

Advanced Students: Teaching assistantships available for advanced students. Average amount paid per academic year: $9,400. Average number of hours worked per week: 10. Tuition remission given: partial. Fellowships and scholarships available for advanced students. Average amount paid per academic year: $12,000. Tuition remission given: partial.

Contact Information: Of all students currently enrolled full-time, 85% benefitted from one or more of the listed financial assistance programs. Application and information available online at: http://www.ssc.uwo.ca/psychology/graduate.htm.

Internships/Practica: Clinical psychology students complete a one-year internship (APA/CPA accredited) near the end of their doctoral training. Students in industrial/organizational psychology typically meet professional training requirements through a combination of practica courses and placements. For those doctoral students for whom a professional internship is required prior to graduation, 6 applied in 2003–2004. Of those who applied, 3 were placed in APA accredited internships.

Housing and Day Care: On-campus housing is available. See the following Web sites for more information: http://www.uwo.ca/hfs/. On-campus day care facilities are available. See the following Web site for more information: Flexible Child Care: http://www.usc.uwo.ca/flexcare/; Western Day Care: http://www.uwo.ca/daycare/; University Preschool: http://www.ssc.uwo.ca/psychology/preschool/.

Employment of Department Graduates:

Master's Degree Graduates: Of those who graduated in the academic year 2003–2004, the following categories and numbers represent the post-graduate activities and employment of master's degree graduates: Enrolled in a post-doctoral residency/fellowship (n/a), employed in independent practice (n/a), total from the above (master's) (0).

Doctoral Degree Graduates: Of those who graduated in the academic year 2003–2004, the following categories and numbers represent the post-graduate activities and employment of doctoral degree graduates: Enrolled in a psychology doctoral program (n/a), enrolled in a post-doctoral residency/fellowship (0), employed in independent practice (1), employed in an academic position at a university (3), employed in other positions at a higher education institution (0), employed in a professional position in a school system (1), employed in business or industry (research/consulting) (1), employed in a government agency (research) (0), employed in a government agency (professional services) (1), employed in a community mental health/counseling center (2), employed in a hospital/medical center (0), still seeking employment (0), total from the above (doctoral) (9).

Additional Information:

Orientation, Objectives, and Emphasis of Department: The department is organized into 7 subject content areas, with initial graduate selection procedures administered by area faculty and area committees. Applicants must indicate an area of interest. The department is research-intensive and is oriented toward training researchers. Graduate students are expected to be continuously involved in research as well as to complete required courses and comprehensive exams. The clinical psychology program adopts the scientist-practitioner model, where both research and professional skills are developed.

Special Facilities or Resources: Facilities for experimental research in the nine-story research wing of the Social Science

Center include animal laboratories, rooms specially designed for research with human subjects in behavioural and cognitive neuroscience, clinical, cognition and perception, developmental, industrial/organizational, personality and measurement and social psychology and, in addition, a preschool for observation and research into child development, early childhood education, curricula, materials, and teaching methods. A broad range of equipment is available, and additional special equipment necessary for a student's research may be obtained. Facilities to aid in running experiments include sophisticated general and dedicated laboratory computers. An engineering shop, an audiovisual unit, a workshop, and electronic consultants are available. The department also has easy access to the Social Science Computing Laboratory. In addition to the Student Development Centre and the Psychological Services in the University Hospital on campus, potential field settings (and sources of subjects for research) include a wide variety of schools, and a large number of psychiatric, general hospitals, and specialized centres for research and treatment with children, adolescents, and adults.

Information for Students With Physical Disabilities: See the following Web site for more information: http://www.sdc.uwo.ca/.

Application Information:
Send to: The Graduate Office, Department of Psychology, Social Science Centre, The University of Western Ontario, 1151 Richmond Street, London, ON, Canada N6A 5C2. Students are admitted in the Fall, application deadline January 15. *Fee:* $50. Note: All dollar amounts specified in this entry are Canadian dollars.

Wilfrid Laurier University
Department of Psychology
75 University Avenue, West
Waterloo, ON N2L 3C5
Telephone: (519) 884-1970
Fax: (519) 746-7605
E-mail: *rsharkey@wlu.ca*
Web: *http://www.wlu.ca/~wwwpsych*

Department Information:
1956. Chairperson: Dr. Michael Pratt. Number of Faculty: total–full-time 33, part-time 11; women–full-time 15, part-time 11.

Programs and Degrees Offered:
Listed in the following order: Program area, degree type (T if terminal Master's), number awarded 7/03–6/04. MA in Community Psychology MA/MS (Master of Arts/Science) (T) 4, PhD in Community Psychology PhD (Doctor of Philosophy) 0, MA in Social and Developmental MA/MS (Master of Arts/Science) (T) 7, PhD in Social and Developmental PhD (Doctor of Philosophy) 0, PhD in Brain and Cognition PhD (Doctor of Philosophy) 0, MSc in Brain and Cognition MA/MS (Master of Arts/Science) (T) 1.

Student Applications/Admissions:
Student Applications
MA in Community Psychology MA/MS (Master of Arts/Science)—Applications 2004–2005, 39. Total applicants accepted 2004–2005, 7. Number enrolled (new admits only) 2004–2005 full-time, 6. Number enrolled (new admits only) 2004–2005 part-time, 1. Total enrolled 2004–2005 full-time, 15, part-time, 1. Openings 2005–2006, 7. The Median number of years required for completion of a degree are 2. The number of students enrolled full and part-time who were dismissed or voluntarily withdrew from this program area were 0. *Community Psychology PhD (Doctor of Philosophy)*—Applications 2004–2005, 7. Total applicants accepted 2004–2005, 3. Number enrolled (new admits only) 2004–2005 full-time, 3. Number enrolled (new admits only) 2004–2005 part-time, 0. Openings 2005–2006, 3. The number of students enrolled full and part-time who were dismissed or voluntarily withdrew from this program area were 0. *MA in Social and Developmental MA/MS (Master of Arts/Science)*—Applications 2004–2005, 53. Total applicants accepted 2004–2005, 9. Number enrolled (new admits only) 2004–2005 full-time, 9. Openings 2005–2006, 7. The Median number of years required for completion of a degree are 2. The number of students enrolled full and part-time who were dismissed or voluntarily withdrew from this program area were 0. *PhD in Social and Developmental PhD (Doctor of Philosophy)*—Applications 2004–2005, 7. Total applicants accepted 2004–2005, 3. Number enrolled (new admits only) 2004–2005 full-time, 3. Number enrolled (new admits only) 2004–2005 part-time, 0. Openings 2005–2006, 3. The number of students enrolled full and part-time who were dismissed or voluntarily withdrew from this program area were 0. *Brain and Cognition PhD (Doctor of Philosophy)*—Applications 2004–2005, 5. Total applicants accepted 2004–2005, 3. Number enrolled (new admits only) 2004–2005 full-time, 3. Number enrolled (new admits only) 2004–2005 part-time, 0. Openings 2005–2006, 3. The number of students enrolled full and part-time, who were dismissed or voluntarily withdrew from this program area were 0. *Brain and Cognition MA/MS (Master of Arts/Science)*—Applications 2004–2005, 19. Total applicants accepted 2004–2005, 5. Number enrolled (new admits only) 2004–2005 full-time, 5. Number enrolled (new admits only) 2004–2005 part-time, 0. Openings 2005–2006, 7. The Median number of years required for completion of a degree is 1. The number of students enrolled full and part-time who were dismissed or voluntarily withdrew from this program area were 0.

Admissions Requirements:
Scores: Entries appear in this order: required test or GPA, minimum score (if required), median score of students entering in 2003–2004. Master's Programs: GRE-V+Q no minimum stated; last 2 years GPA 8.0, 10.0. GPA of 8.0 is the equivalent of a B, and 10.0 is the equivalent of an A-. GRE General Test is strongly recommended for Social/Developmental and required for Brain/Cognition. GRE General Test is not required for Community. Doctoral Programs: GRE-V+Q no minimum stated; overall undergraduate GPA 10.0. GPA of 10.0 is the equivalent of a A-. GRE General Test is strongly recommended for Social/Developmental and required for Brain/Cognition. GRE General Test is not required for Community.
Other Criteria: (importance of criteria rated low, medium, or high): research experience medium, work experience low, extracurricular activity low, clinically related public service low, letters of recommendation high, interview medium, statement of goals and objectives high.

Student Characteristics: The following represents characteristics of students in 2004–2005 in all graduate psychology programs in

the department: Female–full-time 40, part-time 0; Male–full-time 11, part-time 1; African American/Black–full-time 2, part-time 0; Hispanic/Latino(a)–full-time 0, part-time 0; Asian/Pacific Islander–full-time 2, part-time 1; American Indian/Alaska Native–full-time 0, part-time 0; Caucasian–full-time 47, part-time 0; Multi-ethnic–full-time 0, part-time 0; students subject to the Americans With Disabilities Act–full-time 0, part-time 0.

Financial Information/Assistance:
Tuition for Full-Time Study: *Master's:* State residents: per academic year $5,364; Nonstate residents: per academic year $11,820. *Doctoral:* State residents: per academic year $5,364; Nonstate residents: per academic year $11,820.

Financial Assistance:
First Year Students: No information provided.
Advanced Students: No information provided.
Contact Information: Of all students currently enrolled full-time, 0% benefitted from one or more of the listed financial assistance programs. Application and information available online at: http://www.wlu.ca/~wwwgrads.

Internships/Practica: No information provided.

Housing and Day Care: On-campus housing is available. See the following Web site for more information: On-campus housing is available see http://www.wlu.ca/~wwwhouse. On-campus day care facilities are available. Contact the Abwunza Child Care Centre at abwunzacc@kwymca.org for more information.

Employment of Department Graduates:
Master's Degree Graduates: Of those who graduated in the academic year 2003–2004, the following categories and numbers represent the post-graduate activities and employment of master's degree graduates: Enrolled in a psychology doctoral program (4), enrolled in another graduate/professional program (2), enrolled in a post-doctoral residency/fellowship (n/a), employed in independent practice (n/a), other employment position (6), total from the above (master's) (12).
Doctoral Degree Graduates: Of those who graduated in the academic year 2003–2004, the following categories and numbers represent the post-graduate activities and employment of doctoral degree graduates: Enrolled in a psychology doctoral program (n/a), total from the above (doctoral) (0).

Additional Information:
Orientation, Objectives, and Emphasis of Department: Graduate students can obtain an MA, MSc or PhD in one of the three fields of: 1) Brain and Cognition, 2) Social and Developmental Psychology, and 3) Community Psychology. The objective of the MA, MSc and PhD programs in the fields of Brain and Cognition, and Social and Developmental Psychology is to develop competence in designing, conducting, and evaluating research in the fields of Brain and Cognition, or in Social and Developmental Psychology. Five half-credit courses and a thesis constitute the degree requirements in these MA/MSc programs. The purpose of these programs is to prepare students for doctoral studies, or for employment in an environment requiring research skills. Students in good standing can be considered for admission to the PhD programs in these areas, which involve 7 half-credit courses, 2 comprehensive papers and a dissertation. In the field of Community Psychology, the objective is to train scientist–practitioners

with skills in community collaboration. Students receive training in theory, research, and practice that will enable them to analyze the implications of social change for the delivery of community services. Six half-credit courses and a thesis are required for the MA degree. Students who complete this program are prepared for either doctoral level training or for employment in community research and service. Students in good standing can be considered for admission to the PhD program in this area, which involves 6 half-credit courses, 2 comprehensive papers and a dissertation.

Special Facilities or Resources: The department has free unlimited access to the university computer, microprocessors, extensive electromechanical equipment, full-time electronics research associate, full-time field supervisor, and access to a wide variety of field settings for research and consultation.

Application Information:
Send to: Wilfrid Laurier University, Waterloo, ON N2L 3C5. Helen Paret, Coordinator of Graduate Admissions and Records, Faculty of Graduate Studies. Students are admitted in the Fall, application deadline February 1. *Fee:* $75. Note: All dollar amounts specified in this entry are Canadian dollars.

Windsor, University of
Psychology
Faculty of Arts and Social Sciences
401 Sunset Avenue
Windsor, ON N9B 3P4
Telephone: (519) 253-3000, x 2215
Fax: (519) 973-7021
E-mail: *towson@uwindsor.ca*
Web: *http://www.uwindsor.ca/psychology*

Department Information:
1944. Head: Shelagh Towson. Number of Faculty: total–full-time 32; women–full-time 16; minority–full-time 2.

Programs and Degrees Offered:
Listed in the following order: Program area, degree type (T if terminal Master's), number awarded 7/03–6/04. Applied Social PhD (Doctor of Philosophy) 3, Clinical PhD (Doctor of Philosophy) 20, Respecialization Diploma 0.

APA Accreditation: Clinical PhD (Doctor of Philosophy).

Student Applications/Admissions:
Student Applications
Applied Social PhD (Doctor of Philosophy)—Applications 2004–2005, 29. Total applicants accepted 2004–2005, 16. Number enrolled (new admits only) 2004–2005 full-time, 8. Openings 2005–2006, 5. The Median number of years required for completion of a degree are 7. The number of students enrolled full and part-time who were dismissed or voluntarily withdrew from this program area were 2. *Clinical PhD (Doctor of Philosophy)*—Applications 2004–2005, 165. Total applicants accepted 2004–2005, 22. Number enrolled (new admits only) 2004–2005 full-time, 10. Openings 2005–2006, 13. The Median number of years required for completion of a degree are

7. The number of students enrolled full and part-time who were dismissed or voluntarily withdrew from this program area were 2. *Respecialization Diploma*—Applications 2004–2005, 0. Total applicants accepted 2004–2005, 0. The number of students enrolled full and part-time who were dismissed or voluntarily withdrew from this program area were 0.

Admissions Requirements:

Scores: Entries appear in this order: required test or GPA, minimum score (if required), median score of students entering in 2003–2004. Master's Programs: Students are accepted directly into PhD Program. See Doctoral Program requirements below. Doctoral Programs: GRE-V+Q+Analytical 60, 75; GRE-Subject(Psych) 60, 90; overall undergraduate GPA 3.3. GRE numbers indicated above reflect percentile rankings not raw scores.

Other Criteria: (importance of criteria rated low, medium, or high): GRE/MAT scores high, research experience medium, work experience low, extracurricular activity low, clinically related public service medium, GPA high, letters of recommendation high, interview medium, statement of goals and objectives medium.

Student Characteristics: The following represents characteristics of students in 2004–2005 in all graduate psychology programs in the department: Female–full-time 90, part-time 0; Male–full-time 20, part-time 0; Caucasian–full-time 0, part-time 0.

Financial Information/Assistance:

Tuition for Full-Time Study: *Doctoral:* State residents: per academic year $6,000; Nonstate residents: per academic year $9,600. Tuition is subject to change. See the following Web site for updates and changes in tuition costs: U.S. Students currently pay a NAFTA tuition rate of approximately $6,700 US.

Financial Assistance:

First Year Students: Teaching assistantships available for first-year. Average amount paid per academic year: $8,227. Average number of hours worked per week: 10. Apply by January 15. Fellowships and scholarships available for first-year. Average amount paid per academic year: $6,000. Apply by January 15.

Advanced Students: Teaching assistantships available for advanced students. Average amount paid per academic year: $9,168. Average number of hours worked per week: 10. Fellowships and scholarships available for advanced students. Average amount paid per academic year: $6,000. Apply by December 15.

Contact Information: Of all students currently enrolled full-time, 75% benefitted from one or more of the listed financial assistance programs.

Internships/Practica: A wide variety of clinical practica are available in the Windsor-Detroit area, and clinical students obtain additional summer practicum positions across the country. Students are placed in predoctoral internships throughout Canada and the U.S. Applied Social students obtain practica and internships in business and industry, community and health-related agencies. For those doctoral students for whom a professional internship is required prior to graduation, 6 applied in 2003–2004. Of those who applied, 6 were placed in internships listed by the Association of Psychology Postdoctoral and Internship Programs (APPIC); 6 were placed in APA accredited internships.

Housing and Day Care: On-campus housing is available. See the following Web site for more information: www.uwindsor.ca/residence. No on-campus day care facilities are available.

Employment of Department Graduates:

Master's Degree Graduates: Of those who graduated in the academic year 2003–2004, the following categories and numbers represent the post-graduate activities and employment of master's degree graduates: Enrolled in a psychology doctoral program (10), enrolled in a post-doctoral residency/fellowship (n/a), employed in independent practice (n/a), employed in a community mental health/counseling center (2), total from the above (master's) (12).

Doctoral Degree Graduates: Of those who graduated in the academic year 2003–2004, the following categories and numbers represent the post-graduate activities and employment of doctoral degree graduates: Enrolled in a psychology doctoral program (n/a), enrolled in a post-doctoral residency/fellowship (4), employed in independent practice (3), employed in an academic position at a university (2), employed in business or industry (research/consulting) (1), employed in a government agency (professional services) (4), employed in a hospital/medical center (8), still seeking employment (1), total from the above (doctoral) (23).

Additional Information:

Orientation, Objectives, and Emphasis of Department: Graduate offerings are divided into two areas: clinical and applied social. Students applying for the clinical program apply directly into specialty areas of adult clinical, child clinical, or clinical neuropsychology. Each of the areas combines theoretical, substantive, and methodological coursework with a variety of applied training experiences.

Special Facilities or Resources: Computer facilities include a well-equipped microcomputer laboratory linked to a central computing facility. Applied training and research resources include the Psychological Services Centre, Neuropsychology Laboratory, the Child Study Centre, the Emotion/Cognition Research Laboratory, the Student Counseling Centre, the Centre for Psychological Intervention and Research, and the Psycho and Neurolinguistics Laboratory. There are faculty-student research groups in the areas of eating disorders, trauma and psychotherapy, problem gambling, feminist research, emotional competence, culture and diversity, health psychology, clinical assessment, psychodynamic processes, aging, and forgiveness.

Information for Students With Physical Disabilities: See the following Web site for more information: www.uwindsor.ca/sn (Special Needs Office).

Application Information:
Send to: Office of the Registrar, Graduate Studies Division, University of Windsor, Windsor, ON, Canada N9B 3P4. Application available online. URL of online application: www.uwindsor.ca/registrar. Students are admitted in the Fall, application deadline January 15. *Fee:* $55. U.S. equivalent for application fee: $40.00. Note: All dollar amounts specified in this entry are Canadian dollars.

York University

Graduate Program in Psychology
4700 Keele Street
Toronto, ON M3J 1P3
Telephone: (416) 736-5290
Fax: (416) 736-5814
E-mail: *schuller@yorku.ca*
Web: *http://www.yorku.ca/grads/cal/psy.htm*

Department Information:
1963. Director, Graduate Programme in Psychology: Regina A. Schuller. Number of Faculty: total–full-time 76; women–full-time 36.

Programs and Degrees Offered:
Listed in the following order: Program area, degree type (T if terminal Master's), number awarded 7/03–6/04. Brain, Behaviour and Cognitive Sciences PhD (Doctor of Philosophy) 6, Clinical PhD (Doctor of Philosophy) 14, Clinical-Developmental PhD (Doctor of Philosophy) 10, Developmental and Cognitive PhD (Doctor of Philosophy) 7, History and Theory PhD (Doctor of Philosophy) 2, Social Personality PhD (Doctor of Philosophy) 10.

APA Accreditation: Clinical PhD (Doctor of Philosophy). Clinical PhD (Doctor of Philosophy).

Student Applications/Admissions:
Student Applications
Brain, Behaviour and Cognitive Sciences PhD (Doctor of Philosophy)—Applications 2004–2005, 13. Total applicants accepted 2004–2005, 7. Number enrolled (new admits only) 2004–2005 full-time, 7. Number enrolled (new admits only) 2004–2005 part-time, 0. Openings 2005–2006, 8. The Median number of years required for completion of a degree are 6. The number of students enrolled full and part-time who were dismissed or voluntarily withdrew from this program area were 3. *Clinical PhD (Doctor of Philosophy)*—Applications 2004–2005, 144. Total applicants accepted 2004–2005, 11. Number enrolled (new admits only) 2004–2005 full-time, 11. Number enrolled (new admits only) 2004–2005 part-time, 0. Total enrolled 2004–2005 full-time, 55, part-time, 13. Openings 2005–2006, 8. The Median number of years required for completion of a degree are 6. The number of students enrolled full and part-time who were dismissed or voluntarily withdrew from this program area were 2. *Clinical-Developmental PhD (Doctor of Philosophy)*—Applications 2004–2005, 92. Total applicants accepted 2004–2005, 8. Number enrolled (new admits only) 2004–2005 full-time, 8. Number enrolled (new admits only) 2004–2005 part-time, 0. Total enrolled 2004–2005 full-time, 48, part-time, 5. Openings 2005–2006, 9. The Median number of years required for completion of a degree are 6. The number of students enrolled full and part-time who were dismissed or voluntarily withdrew from this program area were 3. *Developmental and Cognitive Processes PhD (Doctor of Philosophy)*—Applications 2004–2005, 14. Total applicants accepted 2004–2005, 7. Number enrolled (new admits only) 2004–2005 full-time, 7. Number enrolled (new admits only) 2004–2005 part-time, 0. Total enrolled 2004–2005 full-time, 26, part-time, 4. Openings 2005–2006, 9. The Median number of years required for completion of a degree are 6. The number of students

enrolled full and part-time who were dismissed or voluntarily withdrew from this program area were 2. *History and Theory PhD (Doctor of Philosophy)*—Applications 2004–2005, 2. Total applicants accepted 2004–2005, 2. Number enrolled (new admits only) 2004–2005 full-time, 1. Number enrolled (new admits only) 2004–2005 part-time, 0. Total enrolled 2004–2005 full-time, 7, part-time, 2. Openings 2005–2006, 4. The Median number of years required for completion of a degree are 6. The number of students enrolled full and part-time who were dismissed or voluntarily withdrew from this program area were 2. *Social Personality PhD (Doctor of Philosophy)*—Applications 2004–2005, 60. Total applicants accepted 2004–2005, 6. Number enrolled (new admits only) 2004–2005 full-time, 5. Number enrolled (new admits only) 2004–2005 part-time, 0. Total enrolled 2004–2005 full-time, 28, part-time, 1. Openings 2005–2006, 8. The Median number of years required for completion of a degree are 6. The number of students enrolled full and part-time who were dismissed or voluntarily withdrew from this program area were 3.

Admissions Requirements:
Scores: Entries appear in this order: required test or GPA, minimum score (if required), median score of students entering in 2003–2004. Master's Programs: GRE-V+Q+Analytical N/A, N/A; GRE-Subject(Psych) N/A, N/A; last 2 years GPA no minimum stated. Students are ranked, and GRE scores figure prominently in the rankings. The two Clinical Areas are most discriminatory in terms of GRE scores. Doctoral Programs: GREs are not required by any of the six areas in the program.
Other Criteria: (importance of criteria rated low, medium, or high): GRE/MAT scores high, research experience medium, work experience low, clinically related public service low, GPA high, letters of recommendation high, statement of goals and objectives medium. The non-clinical areas place no weight on clinically related public service. For additional information on admission requirements, go to: http://www.yorku.ca/grads/cal/psy.htm.

Student Characteristics: The following represents characteristics of students in 2004–2005 in all graduate psychology programs in the department: Female–full-time 157, part-time 22; Male–full-time 36, part-time 3; Caucasian–full-time 0, part-time 0.

Financial Information/Assistance:
Tuition for Full-Time Study: *Master's:* State residents: per academic year $5,717; Nonstate residents: per academic year $12,727. *Doctoral:* State residents: per academic year $5,717; Nonstate residents: per academic year $12,727. Tuition is subject to change. See the following Web site for updates and changes in tuition costs: http://www.yorku.ca/usfs/gradfeesmain.shtml.

Financial Assistance:
First Year Students: Teaching assistantships available for first-year. Average amount paid per academic year: $11,263. Average number of hours worked per week: 10. Research assistantships available for first-year. Average amount paid per academic year: $10,000. Average number of hours worked per week: 10. Traineeships available for first-year. Fellowships and scholarships available for first-year. Average amount paid per academic year: $4,000.
Advanced Students: Teaching assistantships available for advanced students. Average amount paid per academic year:

$16,933. Average number of hours worked per week: 10. Research assistantships available for advanced students. Average number of hours worked per week: 10. Fellowships and scholarships available for advanced students.

Contact Information: Of all students currently enrolled full-time, 100% benefitted from one or more of the listed financial assistance programs. Application and information available online at: http://www.yorku.ca/osfs/assist.shtml.

Internships/Practica: Doctoral internships are available; practicum work is done on a half-time basis during the academic year and, when possible, full-time during the summer. Research practica, and a clinical practicum as part of the Clinical Area's programme, are done on campus. Clinical internships are available in the York Counseling and Development Center and a variety of hospitals, clinics, and counseling centers in the city, and elsewhere. Descriptions of the programme and of faculty research interests are available on the Web. For those doctoral students for whom a professional internship is required prior to graduation, 17 applied in 2003–2004. Of those who applied, 9 were placed in internships listed by the Association of Psychology Postdoctoral and Internship Programs (APPIC); 9 were placed in APA accredited internships.

Housing and Day Care: On-campus housing is available. Contact (416) 736-5152. On-campus day care facilities are available: Contact 90 Atkinson Road, Room 128, M3J 2S5, Toronto, ON (416) 736-5190.

Employment of Department Graduates:

Master's Degree Graduates: Of those who graduated in the academic year 2003–2004, the following categories and numbers represent the post-graduate activities and employment of master's degree graduates: Enrolled in a psychology doctoral program (14), enrolled in another graduate/professional program (1), enrolled in a post-doctoral residency/fellowship (n/a), employed in independent practice (n/a), employed in business or industry (management) (1), do not know (4), total from the above (master's) (20).

Doctoral Degree Graduates: Of those who graduated in the academic year 2003–2004, the following categories and numbers represent the post-graduate activities and employment of doctoral degree graduates: Enrolled in a psychology doctoral program (n/a), enrolled in a post-doctoral residency/fellowship (2), employed in independent practice (0), employed in an academic position at a university (1), employed in an academic position at a 2-year/4-year college (0), employed in other positions at a higher education institution (0), employed in a professional position in a school system (0), employed in business or industry (research/consulting) (4), employed in business or industry (management) (0), employed in a government agency (research) (0), employed in a government agency (professional services) (0), employed in a community mental health/counseling center (1), employed in a hospital/medical center (0), still seeking employment (0), other employment position (0), do not know (3), total from the above (doctoral) (11).

Additional Information:

Orientation, Objectives, and Emphasis of Department: Strength and depth are emphasized in the areas of brain, behaviour and cognitive science (learning, perception, physiological, psychometrics), clinical, clinical-development, developmental cognitive processes, history and theory, and social-personality. The department attempts to prepare students as researchers and practitioners in a given area. Most students admitted to the MA are accepted on the assumption that they will continue into PhD studies.

Special Facilities or Resources: The department has a vivarium; wet laboratories; shop facilities for woodwork, electronics, metalwork, and photography; substantial computing facilities audiovisual equipment including VCRs; and observational laboratories with two-way mirrors.

Information for Students With Physical Disabilities: See the following Web site for more information: opd@yorku.ca or visit www.studentsaffairs.yorku.ca/opd.

Application Information:
Send to: Admissions Office, York University, 150 Atkinson, 4700 Keele Street, Toronto, ON M3J 1P3. Application available online. URL of online application: www.yorku.ca/admissions. Students are admitted in the Fall, application deadline January 15. *Fee:* $80. Foreign students' tuition fees are usually subsidized by the Faculty of Graduate Studies, to bring the fee is line with the domestic tuition fee. This subsidization is often maintained as the student continues in the Programme beyond the first year, as well. Note: All dollar amounts specified in this entry are Canadian dollars.

INDEX OF PROGRAMS BY AREA OF STUDY OFFERED

A

Adolescence and youth
Boston College (MA/MS—terminal)
Cornell University (PhD)
Michigan, University of (PhD)
Ohio State University (PhD)

Adult development
Akron, University of (PhD)
Southern California, University of (PhD)
Washington University in St. Louis (PhD)

Aging
Adler School of Professional Psychology (MA/MS—terminal)
Benedictine University (MA/MS—terminal)
Colorado, University of, at Colorado Springs (PhD)
Georgia Institute of Technology (PhD)
North Texas, University of (PhD)
Southern California, University of (PhD)
Syracuse University (PhD)

Applied
Argosy University/Hawaii (MA/MS—terminal)
Argosy University/Seattle (PsyD, MA/MS—terminal)
Arkansas, University of, Little Rock (MA/MS—terminal)
Auburn University (MA/MS—terminal)
Auburn University at Montgomery (MA/MS—terminal)
Augusta State University (MA/MS—terminal)
Baltimore, University of (MA/MS—terminal)
Catholic University of America, The (PhD)
Duquesne University (MA/MS—terminal)
Fordham University (MA/MS—terminal)
Institute of Transpersonal Psychology (PhD)
Jacksonville State University (MA/MS—terminal)
Kansas State University (PhD)
Manitoba, University of (PhD)
Millersville University (MA/MS—terminal)
Penn State Harrisburg (MA/MS—terminal)
Regina, University of (MA/MS—terminal, PhD)
Saint Mary's University (MA/MS—terminal)
Teachers College, Columbia University (MA/MS—terminal)
Texas A&M University—Commerce (MA/MS—terminal)
Texas of the Permian Basin, The University of (MA/MS)
Wayne State University (MA/MS)
West Virginia University (PhD)
William Paterson University (MA/MS—terminal)

Wisconsin, University of, Stout (MA/MS—terminal)
Yeshiva University (MA/MS—terminal)

Applied developmental
Alberta, University of (MA/MS, PhD)
Claremont Graduate University (MA/MS—terminal, PhD)
George Mason University (PhD, MA/MS—terminal)
Illinois, University of, Urbana–Champaign (PhD)
Maryland, University of, Baltimore County (PhD)
Miami, University of (PhD)
Nebraska, University of, Lincoln (PhD)
New Orleans, University of (PhD)
Pittsburgh, University of (MA/MS, PhD)
Portland State University (PhD)
Tufts University (MA/MS, PhD, Other)
Wayne State University (MA/MS—terminal)

Applied social
Brigham Young University (PhD)
Claremont Graduate University (MA/MS—terminal, PhD)
Colorado State University (PhD)
Loyola University of Chicago (MA/MS)
Nebraska, University of, Lincoln (PhD)
Portland State University (PhD)
Saskatchewan, University of (MA/MS, PhD)
Southern California, University of, School of Medicine (PhD)
Southern Illinois University, at Carbondale (PhD)
Windsor, University of (PhD)

Art therapy
Adler School of Professional Psychology (MA/MS—terminal)
Emporia State University (MA/MS—terminal)
Sonoma State University (MA/MS—terminal)

B

Behavior therapy
American University (PhD)
Eastern Michigan University (MA/MS—terminal)
Lehigh University (PhD, EdS)
Nebraska, University of, Lincoln (PhD)
Nevada, University of, Reno (PhD)
Quebec at Montreal, University of (PhD)
Rutgers—The State University of New Jersey (PsyD)
Western Michigan University (PhD)

Behavioral analysis
Auburn University (PhD)
Chicago School of Professional Psychology (MA/MS—terminal, PsyD)
City University of New York: Graduate Center (PhD)
Florida Institute of Technology (MA/MS—terminal)
Florida State University (MA/MS—terminal)
Florida, University of (PhD)
Long Island University (Other)
Maryland, University of, Baltimore County (MA/MS—terminal)
Mississippi State University (PhD)
Nevada, University of, Reno (PhD)
North Carolina, University of, Wilmington (MA/MS—terminal)
Northeastern University (MA/MS—terminal)
Northern Colorado, University of (MA/MS—terminal, MA/MS—terminal)
Pacific University (MA/MS—terminal)
Pacific, University of the (MA/MS—terminal)
Purdue University (PhD)
Western Michigan University (MA/MS, PhD)
Wisconsin, University of, Milwaukee (MA/MS—terminal)

Behavioral genetics
City University of New York: Graduate School and University Center (PhD)
Colorado, University of, Boulder (PhD)

Behavioral medicine
Appalachian State University (MA/MS—terminal)
Cincinnati, University of (PhD)
Iowa, University of (PhD)
North Texas, University of (PhD)
Rosalind Franklin University of Medicine and Science (PhD)
San Diego State University/University of California, San Diego Joint Doctoral Program in Clinical Psychology (PhD)

Behavioral neuroscience
Alabama, University of, at Birmingham (PhD)
American University (PhD)
Arizona, University of (PhD)
Binghamton University (PhD)
British Columbia, University of (PhD)
Brown University (PhD)
Calgary, University of (PhD)
California, University of, Berkeley (PhD)
California, University of, Los Angeles (PhD)
Carleton University (MA/MS, PhD)
Chicago, University of (PhD)
Colorado, University of, Boulder (PhD)

Fuller Theological Seminary (PhD, PsyD)
Gallaudet University (PhD)
George Fox University (PsyD)
George Mason University (PhD)
George Washington University (PsyD)
Georgia Southern University (MA/MS—terminal)
Georgia State University (PhD)
Georgia, University of (PhD)
Guelph, University of (PhD, MA/MS)
Hartford, University of (PsyD, MA/MS—terminal)
Harvard University (PhD)
Hawaii, University of, Manoa (PhD)
Hofstra University (PhD)
Houston, University of (PhD)
Howard University (PhD)
Idaho State University (PhD)
Illinois Institute of Technology (PhD)
Illinois, University of, Urbana–Champaign (PhD)
Immaculata University (PsyD)
Indiana State University (PsyD)
Indiana University (PhD)
Indiana University of Pennsylvania (PsyD)
Indiana University–Purdue University Indianapolis (PhD)
Indianapolis, University of (MA/MS)
Institute of Transpersonal Psychology (PhD, MA/MS—terminal)
Iowa, University of (PhD)
Jackson State University (PhD)
James Madison University (PsyD)
Kansas, University of (PhD)
Kent State University (PhD)
Kentucky, University of (PhD)
Laval (Université Laval) (PsyD, PhD)
Lesley University (Other)
Loma Linda University (PhD, PsyD)
Long Island University (PhD, PsyD)
Louisiana State University (PhD)
Louisville, University of (PhD)
Loyola College (MA/MS—terminal, PsyD)
Maine, University of (PhD)
Manitoba, University of (PhD)
Marquette University (PhD)
Marshall University (PsyD)
Maryland, University of (PhD)
Maryland, University of, Baltimore County (PhD)
Marywood University (PsyD)
Massachusetts School of Professional Psychology (PsyD)
Massachusetts, University of (PhD)
Massachusetts, University of, at Dartmouth (MA/MS—terminal)
Massachusetts, University of, Boston (PhD)
McGill University (PhD)
Memphis, University of (PhD)
Miami University (Ohio) (PhD)
Miami, University of (PhD)
Middle Tennessee State University (MA/MS—terminal)
Midwestern State University (MA/MS—terminal)
Midwestern University (PsyD, MA/MS)
Minnesota State University—Mankato (MA/MS)

Minnesota, University of (PhD)
Mississippi State University (MA/MS—terminal)
Mississippi, University of (PhD)
Missouri, University of, Columbia (PhD)
Missouri, University of, Kansas City (PhD)
Monmouth University (MA/MS, Other)
Montana, The University of (PhD)
Montreal, University of (PhD)
Morehead State University (Kentucky) (MA/MS—terminal)
Murray State University (MA/MS—terminal)
Nevada, University of, Las Vegas (PhD)
New Brunswick, University of (PhD)
New Mexico, The University of (PhD)
New School University (PhD)
North Carolina, University of, at Greensboro (PhD)
North Carolina, University of, Chapel Hill (PhD)
North Dakota State University (MA/MS—terminal)
North Dakota, University of (PhD)
Northern Illinois University (PhD)
Northwestern University (PhD)
Northwestern University, Feinberg School of Medicine (PhD)
Ohio State University (PhD)
Ohio University (PhD)
Oregon, University of (PhD)
Ottawa, University of (PhD)
Pacific Graduate School of Psychology (PhD, PsyD)
Pacific Graduate School of Psychology & Stanford University School of Medicine, Department of Psychiatry and Behavioral Sciences (PsyD)
Pacific University (PsyD)
Penn State Harrisburg (MA/MS—terminal)
Pennsylvania State University (PhD)
Pennsylvania, University of (PhD, Other)
Pepperdine University (MA/MS—terminal, PsyD)
Philadelphia College of Osteopathic Medicine (Other, MA/MS—terminal, PsyD)
Phillips Graduate Institute (PsyD)
Pittsburg State University (MA/MS—terminal)
Pittsburgh, University of (PhD)
Queen's University (PhD)
Radford University (MA/MS—terminal)
Regina, University of (MA/MS—terminal, PhD)
Rhode Island, University of, Chafee Social Sciences Center (PhD)
Rochester, University of (PhD)
Roosevelt University (MA/MS—terminal, PsyD)
Rutgers University—New Brunswick (PhD)
Saint Louis University (PhD)
Sam Houston State University (MA/MS—terminal, PhD)
San Francisco State University (MA/MS—terminal)
San Jose State University (MA/MS—terminal)

Saskatchewan, University of (PhD)
Saybrook Graduate School and Research Center (MA/MS, PhD)
Seattle Pacific University (PhD)
South Alabama, University of (MA/MS—terminal)
South Carolina, University of (PhD)
South Dakota, University of (PhD)
South Florida, University of (PhD)
Southern Illinois University Edwardsville (MA/MS—terminal)
Southern Illinois University, at Carbondale (PhD)
Southern Methodist University (MA/MS—terminal, PhD)
Southwest Missouri State University (MA/MS—terminal)
Spalding University (PsyD)
St. John's University (PhD)
St. Mary's University (MA/MS—terminal)
State University of New York at Buffalo (PhD)
State University of New York at Stony Brook (PhD)
State University of New York, College at Brockport (MA/MS—terminal)
Stephen F. Austin State University (MA/MS—terminal, MA/MS)
Suffolk University (PhD)
Syracuse University (PhD)
Tennessee, University of, Knoxville (PhD)
Texas A&M University (PhD)
Texas of the Permian Basin, The University of (MA/MS)
Texas Southwestern Medical Center at Dallas, University of (PhD)
Texas Tech University (PhD)
Texas, University of, Austin (PhD)
Texas, University of, Pan American (MA/MS—terminal)
Toledo, University of (PhD)
Towson University (MA/MS—terminal)
Tulsa, University of (MA/MS—terminal, PhD, Respecialization Diploma)
Uniformed Services University of the Health Sciences (PhD)
University of Missouri—St. Louis (PhD)
Vanderbilt University (PhD)
Vanderbilt University, Peabody College (PhD)
Vanguard University of Southern California (MA/MS—terminal)
Vermont, University of (PhD)
Victoria, University of (PhD)
Virginia Consortium Program in Clinical Psychology (PsyD)
Virginia Polytechnic Institute and State University (PhD)
Virginia State University (MA/MS—terminal)
Virginia, University of (PhD)
Walden University (PhD)
Washburn University (MA/MS—terminal)
Washington University in St. Louis (PhD)
Washington, University of (PhD)
Waterloo, University of (PhD)
West Chester University of Pennsylvania (MA/MS—terminal)

West Virginia University (MA/MS—
terminal)
Western Carolina University (MA/MS—
terminal)
Western Kentucky University (MA/MS—
terminal)
Western Ontario, The University of (PhD)
Wheaton College (MA/MS—terminal,
PsyD)
Widener University (PsyD)
Windsor, University of (PhD,
Respecialization Diploma)
Wisconsin, University of, Madison (PhD)
Wright Institute (PsyD)
Wright State University (PsyD)
Wyoming, University of (PhD)
Xavier University (PsyD)
Yeshiva University (PsyD)
York University (PhD)

Clinical assessment
Chicago School of Professional Psychology
(PsyD)
Seattle University (MA/MS—terminal)
Wisconsin School of Professional
Psychology (PsyD)
Wisconsin, University of, Milwaukee (PhD)

Clinical neuropsychology
Ball State University (PhD)
Cincinnati, University of (PhD)
Drexel University (PhD)
Michigan State University (PhD)
North Texas, University of (PhD)
Nova Southeastern University (PhD, PsyD)
Victoria, University of (PhD)

Clinical respecialization
Alliant International University: San
Francisco Bay (Respecialization Diploma)
Argosy University/Hawaii (Respecialization
Diploma)
Argosy University/Illinois School of
Professional Psychology, Chicago Campus
(Respecialization Diploma)
Fielding Graduate University
(Respecialization Diploma)
Massachusetts School of Professional
Psychology (PsyD)
Philadelphia College of Osteopathic
Medicine (Respecialization Diploma)
Suffolk University (Respecialization
Diploma)

Clinical—child
Bowling Green State University (PhD)
Bryn Mawr College (PhD)
Denver, University of (PhD)
Detroit–Mercy, University of (MA/MS—
terminal)
Florida, University of (PhD)
Indianapolis, University of (PsyD)
Kansas, University of (PhD)
Loyola University of Chicago (PhD)
Marywood University (MA/MS—terminal)
Miami, University of (PhD)
Missouri, University of, Columbia (PhD)
Oklahoma State University (PhD)

Pennsylvania State University (PhD)
Southern Illinois University Edwardsville
(MA/MS—terminal)
State University of New York at Albany
(PhD)
Teachers College, Columbia University
(PhD)
Virginia Commonwealth University (PhD)
Virginia, University of (PhD)
Washington State University (PhD)
York University (PhD)

Clinical—community
Arizona State University (PhD)
Auburn University (PhD)
Delaware, University of (PhD)
Eastern Illinois University (MA/MS—
terminal)
George Washington University (PhD)
Humboldt State University (MA/MS—
terminal)
Illinois, University of, Chicago (PhD)
La Verne, University of (PsyD)
Lesley University (Other, Respecialization
Diploma)
Marist College (MA/MS—terminal)
Marywood University (MA/MS—terminal)
West Texas A&M University (MA/MS—
terminal)
Western Illinois University (MA/MS—
terminal)

Clinical—school
Andrews University (EdS)
Texas, University of, Tyler (MA/MS—
terminal)
Utah State University (PhD)
Yeshiva University (PsyD)

Cognitive
Akron, University of (PhD, MA/MS—
terminal)
Arizona State University (PhD)
Ball State University (MA/MS—terminal)
Binghamton University (PhD)
Boston College (PhD)
Bowling Green State University (PhD)
Brandeis University (PhD)
British Columbia, University of (PhD)
California, University of, Davis (PhD)
California, University of, Irvine (PhD)
California, University of, Los Angeles
(PhD)
California, University of, Santa Barbara
(PhD)
California, University of, Santa Cruz (PhD)
Carnegie Mellon University (PhD)
Case Western Reserve University (PhD)
Chicago, University of (PhD)
City University of New York: Brooklyn
College (PhD)
City University of New York: Graduate
School and University Center (PhD)
Claremont Graduate University (MA/MS—
terminal, PhD)
Colorado, University of, Boulder (PhD)
Columbia University (PhD, Other)
Concordia University (PhD)

Cornell University (PhD)
Dalhousie University (PhD, MA/MS)
Delaware, University of (PhD)
Emory University (PhD)
Florida State University (PhD)
Florida, University of (PhD)
George Washington University (PhD)
Georgia, University of (PhD)
Harvard University (PhD)
Hawaii, University of, Manoa (PhD)
Houston, University of (PhD)
Illinois State University (MA/MS—
terminal)
Illinois, University of, Chicago (PhD)
Illinois, University of, Urbana–Champaign
(PhD)
Indiana University (PhD)
Iowa State University (PhD)
Johns Hopkins University (PhD)
Kansas State University (PhD)
Kansas, University of (PhD)
Kent State University (PhD)
Lehigh University (PhD)
Louisiana State University (PhD)
Louisville, University of (PhD)
Maine, University of (MA/MS)
Manitoba, University of (PhD)
Maryland, University of (PhD)
Massachusetts, University of (PhD)
Miami University (Ohio) (PhD)
Michigan State University (PhD)
Middle Tennessee State University
(MA/MS—terminal)
Mississippi State University (PhD)
Missouri, University of, Columbia (PhD)
Nebraska, University of, Lincoln (PhD)
Nebraska, University of, Omaha (MA/MS)
Nevada, University of, Reno (PhD)
New Hampshire, University of (PhD)
New Mexico State University (MA/MS—
terminal, PhD)
New Mexico, The University of (PhD)
New School University (PhD)
New York University, Graduate School of
Arts and Science (PhD)
North Carolina, University of, at
Greensboro (PhD)
North Carolina, University of, Chapel Hill
(PhD)
North Dakota State University (PhD)
North Texas, University of (PhD)
Northeastern University (PhD)
Northern Illinois University (PhD)
Northwestern University (PhD)
Notre Dame, University of (PhD)
Ohio State University (PhD)
Ohio University (PhD)
Oklahoma, University of (PhD)
Oregon, University of (PhD)
Pennsylvania State University (PhD)
Pittsburgh, University of (PhD)
Princeton University (PhD)
Queen's University (PhD)
Rice University (PhD)
South Florida, University of (PhD)
Southern California, University of (PhD)
Stanford University (PhD)

State University of New York at Albany
(PhD)
State University of New York at Buffalo
(PhD)
Texas A&M University (PhD)
Texas Christian University (PhD)
Texas Tech University (PhD)
Texas, University of, Austin (PhD)
Toronto, University of (MA/MS, PhD)
Tufts University (PhD)
Utah, University of (PhD)
Vanderbilt University (PhD)
Vanderbilt University, Peabody College
(PhD)
Victoria, University of (PhD)
Washington State University (PhD)
Washington University in St. Louis (PhD)
Washington, University of (PhD, Other)
Waterloo, University of (PhD)
Wayne State University (PhD)
Western Ontario, The University of (PhD)
Wilfrid Laurier University (PhD, MA/MS—
terminal)
Wisconsin, University of, Madison (PhD)
Yale University (PhD)
York University (PhD)

College counseling
Andrews University (PhD)
Northern Arizona University (MA/MS—
terminal)

College counseling and administration
James Madison University (MA/MS—
terminal)
Northeastern University (MA/MS—
terminal)

College teaching
East Tennessee State University (MA/MS—
terminal)

Community
Alaska, University of, Fairbanks (MA/MS—
terminal)
Appalachian State University (MA/MS—
terminal)
Central Connecticut State University
(MA/MS—terminal)
Chatham College (MA/MS—terminal)
Denver, University of (MA/MS—terminal)
DePaul University (PhD)
Georgia State University (PhD)
Hawaii, University of, Manoa (PhD)
Illinois, University of, Chicago (PhD)
Lewis & Clark College (MA/MS—terminal)
Massachusetts, University of, Lowell
(MA/MS—terminal)
Metropolitan State University (MA/MS—
terminal)
New York University, Graduate School of
Arts and Science (PhD)
North Carolina State University (PhD)
North Dakota, University of (MA/MS—
terminal)
Northern Colorado, University of
(MA/MS—terminal)
Oklahoma, University of (Other)

Quebec at Montreal, University of (PhD)
Sage Colleges, The (MA/MS—terminal)
Saint Bonaventure University (Other)
Vanderbilt University (PhD, Other)
Vanderbilt University, Peabody College
(PhD)
Wichita State University (PhD)
Wilfrid Laurier University (MA/MS—
terminal, PhD)

Community rehabilitation counseling
State University of New York at Albany
(MA/MS—terminal)
State University of New York at Buffalo
(MA/MS—terminal)
Wisconsin, University of, Milwaukee
(MA/MS)

Community—clinical
Lamar University—Beaumont (MA/MS—
terminal)
Loyola University of Chicago (MA/MS—
terminal)
North Carolina, University of, Charlotte
(MA/MS—terminal)

Community—school
Francis Marion University (MA/MS—
terminal)
Minnesota, University of (PhD, MA/MS)
San Diego State University (MA/MS—
terminal)
St. Cloud State University (MA/MS—
terminal)

Comparative
Arizona, University of (PhD)
California, University of, Davis (PhD)

Computer applications
Temple University (MA/MS—terminal)

Conditioning
Eastern Michigan University (MA/MS—
terminal)
Purdue University (PhD)

Consulting psychology
Alliant International University: San
Diego/Irvine (PhD)
Arizona State University (PhD)
North Texas, University of (PhD)
Saint Michael's College (MA/MS—
terminal)

Consumer
Cleveland State University (MA/MS—
terminal)

Counseling
Adler School of Professional Psychology
(MA/MS—terminal)
Andrews University (MA/MS—terminal,
MA/MS—terminal)
Arcadia University (MA/MS—terminal)
Argosy University/Dallas (MA/MS—
terminal)

Argosy University/Hawaii (MA/MS—
terminal)
Argosy University/Phoenix, Arizona
Professional School of Psychology
(MA/MS—terminal)
Argosy University/Washington, DC (EdD)
Arizona State University (MA/MS—
terminal)
Auburn University (PhD)
Austin Peay State University (MA/MS—
terminal)
Boston College (MA/MS—terminal)
California State University, San Bernardino
(MA/MS—terminal)
California, University of, Santa Barbara
(PhD)
Connecticut, University of (MA/MS)
Denver, University of (MA/MS—terminal)
Fayetteville State University (MA/MS—
terminal)
Geneva College (MA/MS—terminal)
Georgia, University of (MA/MS)
Governors State University (MA/MS—
terminal)
Houston, University of, College of
Education (Other)
Illinois State University (MA/MS—
terminal)
Immaculata University (MA/MS—terminal)
Iowa, University of (PhD)
James Madison University (EdS)
Kentucky, University of (MA/MS, PhD)
Lesley University (MA/MS)
Lewis & Clark College (MA/MS—terminal)
Louisiana, University of, Lafayette
(MA/MS—terminal)
Loyola University of Chicago (Other)
Marquette University (MA/MS—terminal)
Marymount University (MA/MS—terminal)
Marywood University (MA/MS—terminal)
Minnesota, University of (MA/MS—
terminal, PhD)
Northeastern University (PhD)
Northern Arizona University (MA/MS—
terminal)
Nova Southeastern University (MA/MS—
terminal)
Pittsburg State University (MA/MS—
terminal)
Puget Sound, University of (Other)
Radford University (MA/MS—terminal)
Sage Colleges, The (MA/MS—terminal)
Saint Francis, University of (MA/MS—
terminal)
Saint Mary's University of Minnesota
(MA/MS—terminal, MA/MS, Other)
Sherbrooke, University of (PsyD)
Springfield College (MA/MS—terminal)
Temple University (MA/MS—terminal)
Texas, University of, Tyler (MA/MS—
terminal)
Towson University (MA/MS—terminal)
Utah State University (MA/MS—terminal)
Utah, University of (MA/MS—terminal)
Valdosta State University (MA/MS—
terminal)
Walden University (PhD)

Counseling and guidance

Wisconsin, University of, Madison (MA/MS—terminal)

Arizona State University (Other)
Auburn University (EdS)
Austin Peay State University (MA/MS—terminal, EdS)
Houston Baptist University (Other)
Lehigh University (Other, Other)
Lesley University (MA/MS—terminal)
Lewis University (MA/MS—terminal)
Louisiana Tech University (MA/MS—terminal)
Middle Tennessee State University (MA/MS)
Missouri, University of, Kansas City (MA/MS—terminal, EdS)
New Mexico State University (MA/MS—terminal)
New York University (MA/MS—terminal)
Northeastern University (MA/MS—terminal)
Northern Colorado, University of (MA/MS—terminal)
Nova Southeastern University (MA/MS—terminal)
Oklahoma, University of (Other)
Puget Sound, University of (Other)
Saint Bonaventure University (Other)
San Diego State University (MA/MS—terminal)
Springfield College (Other)
State University of New York at Albany (Other)
State University of New York at Buffalo (Other)
Valdosta State University (EdS, Other)
Vanderbilt University (Other)
West Georgia, University of (EdS)

Counseling psychology

Abilene Christian University (MA/MS—terminal)
Akron, University of (PhD)
Alaska Pacific University (MA/MS—terminal)
Angelo State University (MA/MS—terminal)
Argosy University/Illinois School of Professional Psychology, Chicago Campus (MA/MS)
Argosy University/Orange County (EdD)
Argosy University/San Francisco Bay Area (MA/MS)
Assumption College (MA/MS—terminal)
Auburn University (PhD)
Avila University (MA/MS—terminal)
Ball State University (PhD)
Boston College (PhD)
California Institute of Integral Studies (MA/MS—terminal)
Central Arkansas, University of (MA/MS)
Central Oklahoma, University of (MA/MS—terminal, MA/MS)
Central Washington University (MA/MS—terminal)
Chatham College (MA/MS—terminal)

Connecticut, University of (PhD)
Denver, University of (PhD)
Fairleigh Dickinson University, Madison (MA/MS—terminal)
Florida State University (PhD)
Florida, University of (PhD)
Frostburg State University (MA/MS—terminal)
Gannon University (PhD)
Georgian Court University (MA/MS—terminal)
Goddard College (MA/MS—terminal)
Houston Baptist University (MA/MS—terminal)
Houston, University of, College of Education (PhD)
Illinois, University of, Urbana–Champaign (PhD)
Indiana State University (PhD)
Indiana University (PhD)
Iowa State University (PhD)
John F. Kennedy University (MA/MS—terminal)
Kansas, University of (MA/MS—terminal, PhD)
Louisiana State University in Shreveport (MA/MS—terminal)
Louisiana Tech University (PhD)
Loyola College (MA/MS—terminal)
Loyola University of Chicago (PhD)
Marquette University (PhD)
Maryland, University of (PhD)
Massachusetts, University of, Boston (Other)
McGill University (PhD)
Memphis, University of (PhD)
Miami, University of (PhD)
Minnesota, University of (PhD)
Missouri, University of, Columbia (MA/MS—terminal, EdS, PhD)
Missouri, University of, Kansas City (PhD)
Morehead State University (Kentucky) (MA/MS—terminal)
Nebraska, University of, Lincoln (PhD)
New Mexico State University (PhD)
New York University (PhD)
North Dakota, University of (PhD)
North Florida, University of (MA/MS—terminal)
Northcentral University (PhD, MA/MS)
Northeastern University (MA/MS—terminal)
Northern Arizona University (PhD)
Northern Colorado, University of (PsyD)
Northwest Missouri State University (MA/MS—terminal)
Notre Dame, University of (PhD)
Ohio State University (PhD)
Oklahoma State University (PhD)
Oklahoma, University of (PhD)
Oregon, University of (PhD)
Our Lady of the Lake University (PsyD, MA/MS—terminal)
Pennsylvania State University (PhD)
Pennsylvania, University of (Other)
Roosevelt University (MA/MS)
Rowan University (MA/MS—terminal)

Rutgers—The State University of New Jersey, New Brunswick (EdD, Other)
Saint Leo University (MA/MS—terminal)
Santa Clara University (MA/MS—terminal, MA/MS)
Seton Hall University (PhD)
Southern Illinois University, at Carbondale (PhD)
Southern Mississippi, The University of (MA/MS—terminal)
St. Thomas, University of (MA/MS—terminal, PsyD)
State University of New York at Albany (PhD)
State University of New York at Buffalo (PhD)
Teachers College, Columbia University (PhD, Other)
Temple University (PhD)
Tennessee State University (PhD)
Texas A&M International University (MA/MS—terminal)
Texas A&M University—Kingsville (MA/MS—terminal)
Texas Woman's University (PhD)
Texas, University of, Austin (PhD)
Utah, University of (PhD)
Walla Walla College (MA/MS—terminal)
West Florida, The University of (MA/MS—terminal)
West Virginia University (PhD)
Western Michigan University (MA/MS, PhD)
Wisconsin, University of, Madison (PhD)

Counseling—colleges and universities

Southern Mississippi, The University of (PhD)
Texas, University of, Austin (Other)

Counseling—elementary school

Arcadia University (MA/MS—terminal)
Auburn University (MA/MS—terminal)
Boston College (MA/MS—terminal)
Central Washington University (Other)
Gonzaga University (MA/MS—terminal)
Houston Baptist University (MA/MS—terminal)
Immaculata University (Other)
Marymount University (MA/MS—terminal)
Marywood University (MA/MS—terminal)
Millersville University (Other, MA/MS)
Northwest Missouri State University (MA/MS)
Pittsburg State University (MA/MS—terminal)
Sonoma State University (MA/MS—terminal)
Tennessee State University (MA/MS—terminal)
Texas, University of, Tyler (MA/MS—terminal)

Counseling—marriage and family

Adler School of Professional Psychology (MA/MS—terminal)
California Polytechnic State University (MA/MS—terminal)

California State University, Chico
(MA/MS—terminal)
California State University, Sacramento
(MA/MS—terminal)
Gonzaga University (MA/MS—terminal)
Lehigh University (Other)
Sonoma State University (MA/MS—
terminal)

Counseling—secondary school
Arcadia University (MA/MS—terminal)
Immaculata University (Other, PsyD)
Marywood University (MA/MS—terminal)

Curriculum and instruction
Illinois, University of, Urbana–Champaign
(PhD, Other)

D

Developmental
Alabama, University of, at Birmingham
(PhD)
Arizona State University (PhD)
Ball State University (PhD)
Boston College (PhD)
Boston University (PhD, MA/MS—
terminal)
British Columbia, University of (PhD)
California, University of, Los Angeles
(PhD)
California, University of, Santa Barbara
(PhD)
California, University of, Santa Cruz (PhD)
Carleton University (MA/MS)
Carnegie Mellon University (PhD)
Chicago, University of (PhD)
City University of New York: Brooklyn
College (MA/MS—terminal)
City University of New York: Graduate
School and University Center (PhD)
Clark University (PhD)
Connecticut, University of (PhD)
Denver, University of (PhD)
Duke University (PhD)
Florida State University (PhD)
Florida, University of (PhD)
Fordham University (PhD)
Georgetown University (PhD)
Georgia State University (PhD)
Georgia, University of (PhD)
Harvard University (PhD)
Hawaii, University of (PhD)
Hawaii, University of, Manoa (PhD)
Howard University (PhD)
Illinois State University (MA/MS—
terminal)
Illinois, University of, Urbana–Champaign
(PhD)
Indiana University (PhD)
Iowa, University of (PhD)
Johns Hopkins University (PhD)
Laval (Université Laval) (PhD)
Loyola University of Chicago (PhD)
Manitoba, University of (PhD)
Maryland, University of (PhD, MA/MS)
Massachusetts, University of (PhD)

Miami University (Ohio) (PhD)
Missouri, University of, Columbia (PhD)
Montana, The University of (PhD)
Nebraska, University of, Omaha (MA/MS,
PhD)
New Hampshire, University of (PhD)
New Mexico, The University of (PhD)
North Carolina State University (PhD)
North Carolina, University of, at
Greensboro (PhD)
North Carolina, University of, Chapel Hill
(PhD)
Notre Dame, University of (PhD)
Oklahoma, University of (PhD)
Oregon, University of (PhD)
Pennsylvania State University (PhD)
Pittsburgh, University of (PhD)
Purdue University (PhD)
Quebec at Montreal, University of (PhD)
Queen's University (PhD)
Rochester, University of (PhD)
Rutgers University—New Brunswick (PhD)
Rutgers—The State University of New
Jersey, New Brunswick (PhD)
Saint Louis University (PhD)
San Francisco State University (MA/MS—
terminal)
Simon Fraser University (PhD)
Texas A&M University (PhD)
Texas, University of, Austin (PhD)
Toronto, University of (MA/MS, PhD)
Tulane University (PhD)
Vanderbilt University, Peabody College
(PhD)
Virginia Polytechnic Institute and State
University (PhD)
Virginia, University of (PhD)
Washington, University of (PhD)
Waterloo, University of (PhD)
West Florida, The University of (MA/MS—
terminal)
West Virginia University (PhD)
Western Ontario, The University of (PhD)
Wilfrid Laurier University (MA/MS—
terminal, PhD)
Wyoming, University of (PhD)
Yeshiva University (PhD)
York University (PhD)

Developmental—comparative
Manitoba, University of (PhD)

E

Ecological
Michigan State University (PhD)
Northern Colorado, University of (EdS,
PhD)

Educational
Alliant International University: Irvine
(PsyD)
Alliant International University: Los
Angeles (PsyD)
Alliant International University: San Diego
(PsyD)

American International College (MA/MS,
EdD)
Arizona State University (Other, PhD)
Colorado, University of, Boulder (MA/MS,
PhD)
Denver, University of (PhD)
Houston, University of, College of
Education (Other)
Iowa, University of (PhD)
Kansas, University of (PhD, Other)
Kean University (MA/MS)
Kentucky, University of (MA/MS, PhD)
Louisiana Tech University (MA/MS—
terminal)
Marist College (MA/MS—terminal)
McGill University (PhD)
Michigan, University of (PhD)
Missouri, University of, Columbia
(MA/MS—terminal, EdS, PhD)
New York University (MA/MS—terminal)
Northern Arizona University (PhD)
Oklahoma State University (EdS, PhD)
Oklahoma, University of (Other, PhD)
Quebec at Montreal, University of (PhD)
Rutgers—The State University of New
Jersey, New Brunswick (Other, EdD)
Tennessee, University of, Knoxville (PhD)
Texas A&M University—Commerce (PhD)
Texas Tech University (EdD)
Texas, University of, Austin (Other,
MA/MS—terminal)
Tufts University (Other)
Utah, University of (PhD, Other)
Wayne State University (PhD)

Educational measurement
Illinois, University of, Urbana–Champaign
(PhD)
Iowa, University of (MA/MS, PhD)
Northern Colorado, University of (PhD)
Pittsburgh, University of (PhD)
State University of New York at Albany
(Other)
State University of New York at Buffalo
(PhD, MA/MS—terminal)

Educational research and evaluation
Ball State University (MA/MS—terminal)
Houston, University of, College of
Education (PhD)
James Madison University (PhD)
Manitoba, University of (PhD)
Marquette University (MA/MS—terminal)
State University of New York at Albany
(MA/MS, PhD)
Syracuse University (PhD)
Utah State University (PhD)

Engineering
Georgia Institute of Technology (PhD)
New Mexico State University (MA/MS—
terminal, PhD)

Environmental
City University of New York: Graduate
School and University Center (PhD)
Utah, University of (PhD)

George Mason University (PhD, MA/MS—terminal)
Georgia Institute of Technology (PhD)
Georgia, University of (PhD)
Hofstra University (MA/MS—terminal)
Houston, University of (PhD)
Idaho, University of (MA/MS—terminal)
Illinois Institute of Technology (PhD)
Illinois State University (MA/MS—terminal)
Illinois, University of, Urbana–Champaign (MA/MS—terminal)
Indiana University–Purdue University Indianapolis (MA/MS—terminal)
Iona College (MA/MS—terminal)
Kansas State University (PhD)
Lamar University—Beaumont (MA/MS—terminal)
Louisiana State University (PhD)
Louisiana Tech University (MA/MS—terminal)
Maryland, University of (PhD)
Michigan State University (PhD)
Middle Tennessee State University (MA/MS—terminal)
Minnesota State University—Mankato (MA/MS—terminal)
Minnesota, University of (PhD)
Montana State University (MA/MS—terminal)
Montreal, University of (PhD)
Nebraska, University of, Omaha (MA/MS, MA/MS—terminal, PhD)
New York University, Graduate School of Arts and Science (MA/MS—terminal)
North Carolina State University (PhD)
North Carolina, University of, Charlotte (MA/MS—terminal)
Northern Illinois University (PhD)
Northern Iowa, University of (MA/MS—terminal)
Ohio State University (PhD)
Ohio University (PhD)
Oklahoma, University of (MA/MS—terminal, PhD)
Old Dominion University (PhD)
Pennsylvania State University (PhD)
Philadelphia College of Osteopathic Medicine (MA/MS—terminal)
Portland State University (PhD)
Purdue University (PhD)
Quebec at Montreal, University of (PhD)
Radford University (MA/MS—terminal)
Rice University (PhD)
Roosevelt University (MA/MS—terminal)
Saint Mary's University (PhD)
San Diego State University (MA/MS—terminal)
San Francisco State University (MA/MS—terminal)
San Jose State University (MA/MS—terminal)
South Florida, University of (PhD)
Southern Illinois University Edwardsville (MA/MS—terminal)
Southwest Missouri State University (MA/MS—terminal)
Springfield College (MA/MS—terminal)

St. Cloud State University (MA/MS—terminal)
St. Mary's University (MA/MS—terminal)
State University of New York at Albany (PhD)
Tennessee, University of, Chattanooga (MA/MS—terminal)
Tennessee, University of, Knoxville (PhD)
Texas A&M University (PhD)
Texas, University of, Arlington (MA/MS—terminal)
Tulane University (PhD)
Tulsa, University of (PhD, MA/MS—terminal)
University of Missouri-St. Louis (PhD)
Valdosta State University (MA/MS—terminal)
Virginia Polytechnic Institute and State University (PhD)
Waterloo, University of (PhD, MA/MS—terminal)
Wayne State University (PhD)
West Chester University of Pennsylvania (MA/MS—terminal)
West Florida, The University of (MA/MS—terminal)
Western Kentucky University (MA/MS—terminal)
Western Ontario, The University of (PhD)
Wisconsin, University of, Oshkosh (MA/MS—terminal)
Wright State University (PhD)
Xavier University (MA/MS—terminal)

L

Law and psychology
Arizona, University of (PhD)
Catholic University of America, The (MA/MS—terminal)
Denver, University of (MA/MS—terminal)
Drexel University (PsyD)
Nebraska, University of, Lincoln (PhD)
Pacific Graduate School of Psychology (Other)
Texas Tech University (PhD)
Tulsa, University of (MA/MS—terminal, Other)
Valparaiso University (Other)
Virginia, University of (PhD)
Widener University (Other)

Learning
Arizona State University (PhD)
California, University of, Los Angeles (PhD)
City University of New York: Graduate School and University Center (PhD)
Indiana University (MA/MS)
Montana, The University of (PhD)
Nebraska, University of, Lincoln (PhD)
Yale University (PhD)

Learning—animal
Massachusetts, University of (PhD)

Learning—human
California, University of, Riverside (PhD)
Mississippi State University (PhD)

Pennsylvania State University (PhD)
Texas, University of, Austin (PhD)

Life-span development
Boston College (PhD)
California, University of, Davis (PhD)
Oklahoma State University (PhD)
Victoria, University of (PhD)
Wisconsin, University of, Madison (PhD, MA/MS)

M

Marriage and family
Kean University (Other)
Seton Hall University (MA/MS—terminal)

Marriage and family therapy
Alliant International University: Irvine (MA/MS—terminal, PsyD)
Alliant International University: San Diego (MA/MS—terminal, PsyD)
Argosy University/Orange County (MA/MS—terminal)
Argosy University/Twin Cities (MA/MS—terminal)
California Lutheran University (MA/MS—terminal)
California State University, Bakersfield (MA/MS—terminal)
LaSalle University (MA/MS)
Lewis & Clark College (MA/MS—terminal)
Miami, University of (MA/MS—terminal)
Mount St. Mary's College (MA/MS—terminal)
Northern Colorado, University of (MA/MS)
Our Lady of the Lake University (MA/MS—terminal)
Regent University (PsyD)
San Diego State University (MA/MS—terminal)
Saybrook Graduate School and Research Center (MA/MS)
Seton Hall University (EdS)
Springfield College (MA/MS—terminal)

Mental health
Argosy University/Atlanta (PsyD)
Auburn University (MA/MS—terminal)
Florida State University (EdS)
Iona College (MA/MS—terminal)
Kean University (MA/MS—terminal)
Lesley University (MA/MS—terminal)
Lewis University (MA/MS)
Massachusetts, University of, Boston (Other)
Miami, University of (MA/MS—terminal)
Minnesota, University of (PhD)
Seton Hall University (EdS)
State University of New York at Albany (MA/MS—terminal)
State University of New York at Buffalo (MA/MS—terminal)
Valparaiso University (MA/MS—terminal)

Minnesota, University of (PhD)
Oklahoma, University of (PhD)
Texas, University of, Austin (PhD)

Psychopharmacology
Alliant International University: San Francisco Bay (MA/MS—terminal)
Argosy University/Hawaii (Other)
California, University of, Santa Barbara (PhD)
Fairleigh Dickinson University, Metropolitan Campus (MA/MS—terminal)
Hartford, University of (MA/MS—terminal)
Nova Southeastern University (MA/MS—terminal)
Oklahoma, University of, Health Sciences Center (PhD)

Psychotherapy and psychoanalysis
Georgia, University of (PhD)
Quebec at Montreal, University of (PhD)

Public policy
Pacific Graduate School of Psychology (Other)

Q

Quantitative (including measurement)
California, University of, Davis (PhD)
Illinois State University (MA/MS—terminal)
Illinois, University of, Urbana–Champaign (MA/MS—terminal)
Middle Tennessee State University (MA/MS—terminal)
Minnesota, University of (PhD)
Missouri, University of, Columbia (PhD)
Nebraska, University of, Lincoln (PhD)
Notre Dame, University of (PhD)
Purdue University (PhD)
Tulane University (PhD)
Virginia, University of (PhD)
Washington, University of (Other, PhD)
Wisconsin, University of, Milwaukee (MA/MS)

Quantitative methods
Arizona State University (PhD)
Cleveland State University (MA/MS—terminal)
North Carolina, University of, Chapel Hill (PhD)
Ohio State University (PhD)
Pittsburgh, University of (MA/MS)
Southern California, University of (PhD)
Vanderbilt University, Peabody College (PhD)

R

Reading
Washington, University of (Other, PhD)

Rehabilitation
Ball State University (MA/MS—terminal)
Illinois Institute of Technology (PhD, MA/MS—terminal)

St. Cloud State University (MA/MS—terminal)

Research methodology
Drexel University (MA/MS—terminal)
Xavier University (MA/MS—terminal)

S

School
Abilene Christian University (MA/MS—terminal)
Alfred University (EdS, PsyD)
Alliant International University: Irvine (MA/MS—terminal)
Alliant International University: Los Angeles (MA/MS—terminal)
Alliant International University: San Diego (MA/MS—terminal)
Alliant International University: San Francisco Bay (MA/MS—terminal, PsyD)
Appalachian State University (MA/MS)
Argosy University/Hawaii (PsyD, MA/MS—terminal)
Argosy University/Phoenix, Arizona Professional School of Psychology (PsyD, MA/MS—terminal)
Arizona State University (PhD)
Arizona, University of (PhD, EdS)
Auburn University (PhD, MA/MS—terminal)
Ball State University (EdS)
Barry University (Other, MA/MS)
California State University, Chico (MA/MS—terminal)
California, University of, Berkeley (PhD)
California, University of, Santa Barbara (Other)
Central Arkansas, University of (PhD, MA/MS)
Central Michigan University (PhD)
Central Washington University (Other)
Cincinnati, University of (PhD, EdS)
Citadel, The (EdS)
City University of New York: Brooklyn College (MA/MS)
City University of New York: Graduate School and University Center (PhD)
Cleveland State University (Other)
Connecticut, University of (PhD, EdS)
Denver, University of (PhD)
Detroit–Mercy, University of (Other)
Duquesne University (Other, PhD)
East Carolina University (MA/MS—terminal)
Eastern Illinois University (Other)
Eastern Kentucky University (EdS)
Eastern Washington University (MA/MS—terminal, Respecialization Diploma)
Emporia State University (EdS)
Fairleigh Dickinson University, Metropolitan Campus (PsyD, MA/MS—terminal)
Fort Hays State University (EdS)
Gallaudet University (Other)
George Mason University (MA/MS—terminal)

Georgia, University of (PhD)
Georgian Court University (MA/MS)
Governors State University (MA/MS—terminal)
Hartford, University of (MA/MS)
Hofstra University (PsyD)
Illinois State University (PhD, EdS)
Immaculata University (MA/MS)
Indiana State University (PhD, Other, EdS)
Indiana University (PhD, EdS)
Iona College (MA/MS—terminal)
Iowa, University of (PhD)
James Madison University (EdS)
Kansas, University of (PhD, EdS)
Kean University (MA/MS—terminal)
Kent State University (PhD, EdS)
Kentucky, University of (MA/MS, PhD)
Lewis & Clark College (EdS)
Louisiana State University (PhD)
Louisiana State University in Shreveport (Other)
Louisiana, University of, Monroe (EdS)
Manitoba, University of (MA/MS—terminal)
Marist College (MA/MS—terminal)
Maryland, University of (PhD)
Marywood University (EdS)
McGill University (PhD)
Memphis, University of (MA/MS—terminal, PhD)
Middle Tennessee State University (MA/MS, EdS)
Millersville University (MA/MS, MA/MS)
Minnesota State University Moorhead (EdS)
Minnesota, University of (PhD)
Minot State University (EdS)
Missouri, University of, Columbia (MA/MS, EdS, PhD)
Montana, The University of (MA/MS—terminal)
Nebraska, University of, Lincoln (PhD)
Nebraska, University of, Omaha (MA/MS, EdS)
New Mexico State University (EdS)
New York University (PhD)
North Carolina State University (PhD)
North Texas, University of (MA/MS—terminal)
Northeastern University (MA/MS)
Northern Arizona University (MA/MS—terminal, Other, EdD)
Nova Southeastern University (Other)
Ohio State University (MA/MS—terminal, PhD)
Oklahoma State University (PhD)
Our Lady of the Lake University (MA/MS—terminal)
Pace University (PsyD)
Pennsylvania State University (PhD)
Philadelphia College of Osteopathic Medicine (PsyD, MA/MS—terminal, EdS)
Pittsburg State University (EdS)
Radford University (EdS)
Rensselaer Polytechnic Institute (PhD)
Rhode Island, University of, Chafee Social Sciences Center (PhD)

Rutgers—The State University of New Jersey, Graduate School of Applied and Professional Psychology (PsyD)
Sam Houston State University (MA/MS—terminal)
San Diego State University (EdS)
San Francisco State University (MA/MS—terminal)
Seton Hall University (EdS)
South Carolina, University of (PhD)
South Florida, University of (PhD, EdS)
Southern Illinois University Edwardsville (EdS)
Southern Mississippi, The University of (PhD)
St. John's University (MA/MS—terminal, PsyD)
State University of New York at Albany (PsyD, Other)
State University of New York at Buffalo (MA/MS—terminal)
State University of New York, College at Plattsburgh (MA/MS—terminal)
Temple University (PhD, MA/MS)
Tennessee State University (MA/MS, PhD, EdS)
Tennessee, University of, Knoxville (PhD)
Texas A&M University—Commerce (MA/MS—terminal)
Texas Woman's University (PhD)
Texas, University of, Austin (PhD)
Towson University (MA/MS)
Trinity University (MA/MS—terminal)
Tufts University (MA/MS)
Tulane University (PhD)
Utah State University (MA/MS—terminal)
Utah, University of (PhD, Other)
Valdosta State University (EdS)
Valparaiso University (EdS)
Washington, University of (Other, PhD)
Wayne State University (MA/MS)
West Georgia, University of (Other)
Western Carolina University (MA/MS—terminal)
Western Illinois University (Other)
Western Kentucky University (EdS)
Winthrop University (Other)
Wisconsin, University of, Eau Claire (EdS)
Wisconsin, University of, La Crosse (EdS)
Wisconsin, University of, Madison (PhD)
Wisconsin, University of, Milwaukee (EdS)
Yeshiva University (PsyD)

School psychometry
Ball State University (MA/MS)

Sensation and perception
California, University of, Davis (PhD)
Chicago, University of (PhD)
Iowa, University of (PhD)
Maryland, University of (PhD)
New Hampshire, University of (PhD)
Northeastern University (PhD)
Texas, University of, Austin (PhD)
Virginia, University of (PhD)
Yale University (PhD)

Social
Arizona State University (PhD)
Arizona, University of (PhD)
Arkansas, University of (PhD)
Ball State University (MA/MS—terminal)
Boston College (PhD)
Brandeis University (PhD)
California, University of, Davis (PhD)
California, University of, Los Angeles (PhD)
California, University of, Riverside (PhD)
California, University of, Santa Barbara (PhD)
California, University of, Santa Cruz (PhD)
Carnegie Mellon University (PhD)
Chicago, University of (PhD)
City University of New York: Graduate School and University Center (PhD)
Clark University (PhD)
Colorado, University of, Boulder (PhD)
Connecticut, University of (PhD)
Delaware, University of (PhD)
Denver, University of (PhD)
Duke University (PhD)
Florida State University (PhD)
Florida, University of (PhD)
George Washington University (PhD)
Georgia State University (PhD)
Georgia, University of (PhD)
Harvard University (PhD)
Hawaii, University of, Manoa (PhD)
Houston, University of (PhD)
Howard University (PhD)
Illinois, University of, Chicago (PhD)
Indiana University (PhD)
Iowa State University (PhD)
Iowa, University of (PhD)
Kansas, University of (PhD)
Loyola University of Chicago (PhD)
Maine, University of (PhD)
Maryland, University of (PhD)
Massachusetts, University of (PhD)
Minnesota, University of (PhD)
Missouri, University of, Columbia (PhD)
New Hampshire, University of (PhD)
New Mexico State University (MA/MS—terminal, PhD)
New Mexico, The University of (PhD)
New York University, Graduate School of Arts and Science (MA/MS—terminal, PhD)
North Carolina, University of, at Greensboro (PhD)
North Carolina, University of, Chapel Hill (PhD)
Northern Iowa, University of (MA/MS—terminal)
Northwestern University (PhD)
Ohio State University (PhD)
Oklahoma, University of (PhD)
Oregon, University of (PhD)
Pennsylvania State University (PhD)
Pittsburgh, University of (PhD)
Princeton University (PhD)
Purdue University (PhD)
Quebec at Montreal, University of (PhD)
Queen's University (PhD)
Rochester, University of (PhD)

Saint Louis University (PhD)
San Francisco State University (MA/MS—terminal)
State University of New York at Albany (PhD)
State University of New York at Buffalo (PhD, MA/MS—terminal)
State University of New York at Stony Brook (PhD)
Temple University (PhD)
Texas A&M University (PhD)
Texas Tech University (PhD)
Texas, University of, Austin (PhD)
Tulane University (PhD)
Victoria, University of (PhD)
Virginia Commonwealth University (PhD)
Virginia, University of (PhD)
Washington University in St. Louis (PhD)
Washington, University of (PhD)
Waterloo, University of (PhD)
Western Ontario, The University of (PhD)
Wisconsin, University of, Madison (PhD)
Wyoming, University of (PhD)
York University (PhD)

Sociocultural perspectives
Boston College (PhD)

Special education
Houston, University of, College of Education (Other)
Oklahoma, University of (Other, PhD)
Rutgers—The State University of New Jersey, New Brunswick (Other, EdD)

Sports
Argosy University/Phoenix, Arizona Professional School of Psychology (MA/MS—terminal)
John F. Kennedy University (MA/MS—terminal)
Springfield College (MA/MS—terminal)

Statistics
Rutgers—The State University of New Jersey, New Brunswick (Other, EdD)

Substance abuse
Adler School of Professional Psychology (Other)
Lewis & Clark College (MA/MS—terminal)
New School University (MA/MS—terminal)
North Carolina, University of, Wilmington (MA/MS—terminal)
Purdue University (PhD)

Supervision
Northern Colorado, University of (PhD)
State University of New York at Buffalo (PhD)

ALPHABETICAL INDEX OF INSTITUTIONS

NOTES

NOTES

NOTES

NOTES

NOTES

NOTES

NOTES

NOTES

NOTES

NOTES

NOTES

NOTES

NOTES

NOTES

NOTES

NOTES

NOTES

NOTES

NOTES

NOTES

NOTES

NOTES